Table of Contents

Sections

Model Index

USING THIS INFORMATION

Organization

To find where a particular model section or procedure is located, look in the Table of Contents. Main topics are listed with the page number on which they may be found. Following the main topics is an alphabetical listing of all of the procedures within the section and their page numbers.

Manufacturer and Model Coverage

This product covers 2010–2011 General Motors models that are produced in sufficient quantities to warrant coverage, and which have technical content available from the vehicle manufacturers before our publication date. Although this information is as complete as possible at the time of publication, some manufacturers may make changes which cannot be included here. While striving for total accuracy, the publisher cannot assume responsibility for any errors, changes, or omissions that may occur in the compilation of this data.

Part Numbers and Special Tools

Part numbers and special tools are recommended by the publisher and vehicle manufacturer to perform specific jobs. Before substituting any part or tool for the one recommended, you must be completely satisfied that neither your personal safety, nor the performance of the vehicle will be endangered.

ACKNOWLEDGEMENT

Portions of materials contained herein have been reprinted under license from General Motors Company, Service and Parts Operations License Agreement #1110757.

PRECAUTIONS

Before servicing any vehicle, please be sure to read all of the following precautions, which deal with personal safety, prevention of component damage, and important points to take into consideration when servicing a motor vehicle:

- Always wear safety glasses or goggles when drilling, cutting, grinding or prying.
- Steel-toed work shoes should be worn when working with heavy parts. Pockets should not be used for carrying tools. A slip or fall can drive a screwdriver into your body.
- Work surfaces, including tools and the floor should be kept clean of grease, oil or other slippery material.
- When working around moving parts, don't wear loose clothing. Long hair should be tied back under a hat or cap, or in a hair net.
- Always use tools only for the purpose for which they were designed. Never pry with a screwdriver.
- Keep a fire extinguisher and first aid kit handy.
- Always properly support the vehicle with approved stands or lift.
- Always have adequate ventilation when working with chemicals or hazardous material.
- Carbon monoxide is colorless, odorless and dangerous. If it is necessary to operate the engine with vehicle in a closed area such as a garage, always use an exhaust collector to vent the exhaust gases outside the closed area.
- When draining coolant, keep in mind that small children and some pets are attracted by ethylene glycol antifreeze, and are quite likely to drink any left in an open container, or in puddles on the ground. This will prove fatal in sufficient quantity. Always drain the coolant into a sealable container.
- To avoid personal injury, do not remove the coolant pressure relief cap while the engine is operating or hot. The cooling system is under pressure; steam and hot liquid can come out forcefully when the cap is loosened slightly. Failure to follow these instructions may result in personal injury. The coolant must be recovered in a suitable, clean container for reuse. If the coolant is contaminated it must be recycled or disposed of correctly.
- When carrying out maintenance on the starting system be aware that heavy gauge leads are connected directly to the battery. Make sure the protective caps are in place when maintenance is completed. Failure to follow these instructions may result in personal injury.
- Do not remove any part of the engine emission control system. Operating the engine without the engine emission control system will reduce fuel economy and engine ventilation. This will weaken engine performance and shorten engine life. It is also a violation of Federal law.
- Due to environmental concerns, when the air conditioning system is drained, the refrigerant must be collected using refrigerant recovery/recycling equipment. Federal law requires that refrigerant be recovered into appropriate recovery equipment and the process be conducted by qualified technicians who have been certified by an approved organization, such as MACS, ASI, etc. Use of a recovery machine dedicated to the appropriate refrigerant is necessary to reduce the possibility of oil and refrigerant incompatibility concerns. Refer to the instructions provided by the equipment manufacturer when removing refrigerant from or charging the air conditioning system.
- Always disconnect the battery ground when working on or around the electrical system.
- Batteries contain sulfuric acid. Avoid contact with skin, eyes, or clothing. Also, shield your eyes when working near batteries to protect against possible splashing of the acid solution. In case of acid contact with skin or eyes, flush immediately with water for a minimum of 15 minutes and get prompt medical attention. If acid is swallowed, call a physician immediately. Failure to follow these instructions may result in personal injury.
- Batteries normally produce explosive gases. Therefore, do not allow flames, sparks or lighted substances to come near the battery. When charging or working near a battery, always shield your face and protect your eyes. Always provide ventilation. Failure to follow these instructions may result in personal injury.
- When lifting a battery, excessive pressure on the end walls could cause acid to spew through the vent caps, resulting in personal injury, damage to the vehicle or battery. Lift with a battery carrier or with your hands on opposite corners. Failure to follow

these instructions may result in personal injury.

• Observe all applicable safety precautions when working around fuel. Whenever servicing the fuel system, always work in a well-ventilated area. Do not allow fuel spray or vapors to come in contact with a spark, open flame, or excessive heat (a hot drop light, for example). Keep a dry chemical fire extinguisher near the work area. Always keep fuel in a container specifically designed for fuel storage; also, always properly seal fuel containers to avoid the possibility of fire or explosion. Do not smoke or carry lighted tobacco or open flame of any type when working on or near any fuel-related components.

• Fuel injection systems often remain pressurized, even after the engine has been turned OFF. The fuel system pressure must be relieved before disconnecting any fuel lines. Failure to do so may result in fire and/or personal injury.

• The evaporative emissions system contains fuel vapor and condensed fuel vapor. Although not present in large quantities, it still presents the danger of explosion or fire. Disconnect the battery ground cable from the battery to minimize the possibility of an electrical spark occurring, possibly causing a fire or explosion if fuel vapor or liquid fuel is present in the area. Failure to follow these instructions can result in personal injury.

• The EPA warns that prolonged contact with used engine oil may cause a number of skin disorders, including cancer! You should make every effort to minimize your exposure to used engine oil. Protective gloves should be worn when changing oil. Wash your hands and any other exposed skin areas as soon as possible after exposure to used engine oil. Soap and water, or waterless hand cleaner should be used.

• Some vehicles are equipped with an air bag system, often referred to as a Supplemental Restraint System (SRS) or Supplemental Inflatable Restraint (SIR) system. The system must be disabled before performing service on or around system components, steering column, instrument panel components, wiring and sensors. Failure to follow safety and disabling procedures could result in accidental air bag deployment, possible personal injury and unnecessary system repairs.

• Always wear safety goggles when working with, or around, the air bag system. When carrying a non-deployed air bag, be sure the bag and trim cover are pointed away from your body. When placing a non-deployed air bag on a work surface, always face the bag and trim cover upward, away from the surface. This will reduce the motion of the module if it is accidentally deployed.

• Electronic modules are sensitive to electrical charges. The ABS module can be damaged if exposed to these charges.

• Brake pads and shoes may contain asbestos, which has been determined to be a cancer-causing agent. Never clean brake surfaces with compressed air. Avoid inhaling brake dust. Clean all brake surfaces with a commercially available brake cleaning fluid.

• When replacing brake pads, shoes, discs or drums, replace them as complete axle sets.

• When servicing drum brakes, disassemble and assemble one side at a time, leaving the remaining side intact for reference.

• Brake fluid often contains polyglycol ethers and polyglycols. Avoid contact with the eyes and wash your hands thoroughly after handling brake fluid. If you do get brake fluid in your eyes, flush your eyes with clean, running water for 15 minutes. If eye irritation persists, or if you have taken brake fluid internally, immediately seek medical assistance.

• Clean, high quality brake fluid from a sealed container is essential to the safe and proper operation of the brake system. You should always buy the correct type of brake fluid for your vehicle. If the brake fluid becomes contaminated, completely flush the system with new fluid. Never reuse any brake fluid. Any brake fluid that is removed from the system should be discarded. Also, do not allow any brake fluid to come in contact with a painted or plastic surface; it will damage the paint.

• Never operate the engine without the proper amount and type of engine oil; doing so will result in severe engine damage.

• Timing belt maintenance is extremely important! Many models utilize an interference-type, non-freewheeling engine. If the timing belt breaks, the valves in the cylinder head may strike the pistons, causing potentially serious (also time-consuming and expensive) engine damage.

• Disconnecting the negative battery cable on some vehicles may interfere with the functions of the on-board computer system (s) and may require the computer to undergo a relearning process once the negative battery cable is reconnected.

• Steering and suspension fasteners are critical parts because they affect performance of vital components and systems and their failure can result in major service expense. They must be replaced with the same grade or part number or an equivalent part if replacement is necessary. Do not use a replacement part of lesser quality or substitute design. Torque values must be used as specified during reassembly.

SPECIFICATIONS AND MAINTENANCE CHARTS

ENGINE AND VEHICLE IDENTIFICATION

	Engine						Model Year	
Code ①	Liters	Cu. In.	Cyl.	Fuel Sys.	Engine Type	Eng. Mfg.	Code ②	Year
B/5	2.4	146	4	MFI	DOHC	GM	A	2010
7	3.6	217	6	MFI	DOHC	GM	B	2011

① 8th position of VIN

② 10th position of VIN

25742_MALI_C0001

GENERAL ENGINE SPECIFICATIONS

All measurements are given in inches.

Year	Model	Engine Displacement Liters	Engine ID/VIN	Fuel System Type	Net Horsepower @ rpm	Net Torque @ rpm (ft. lbs.)	Bore x Stroke (in.)	Com- pression Ratio	Oil Pressure @ rpm
2010	Malibu	2.4	B/5	SFI	169@6400	160@4500	①	10:01	30-70@1000
		3.6	7	SFI	252@6300	251@3200	②	11.4:1	20@2000
2011	Malibu	2.4	B/5	SFI	169@6400	160@4500	①	10:01	30-70@1000
		3.6	7	SFI	252@6300	251@3200	②	11.4:1	20@2000

① 3.4668-3.4675x3.861

② 3.7008x3.37

25742_MALI_C0002

ENGINE TUNE-UP SPECIFICATIONS

Year	Engine Displacement Liters	Engine ID/VIN	Spark Plug Gap (in.)	Ignition Timing (deg.) MT	Ignition Timing (deg.) AT	Fuel Pump (psi)	Idle Speed (rpm) MT	Idle Speed (rpm) AT	Valve Clearance Intake	Valve Clearance Exhaust
2010	2.4	B/5	NA	①	②	NA	②	②	HYD	HYD
	3.6	7	0.0433	①	②	NA	②	②	HYD	HYD
2011	2.4	B/5	NA	①	②	NA	②	②	HYD	HYD
	3.6	7	0.0433	①	②	NA	②	②	HYD	HYD

① Ignition timing is preset and cannot be adjusted.

② Idle speed is maintained by the ECM

25742_MALI_C0003

CAPACITIES

Year	Model	Engine Displacement Liters	Engine ID/VIN	Engine Oil with Filter	Transaxle (pts.) Auto.	Transaxle (pts.) Manual	Drive Axle (pts.) Front	Drive Axle (pts.) Rear	Transfer Case (pts.)	Fuel Tank (gal.)	Cooling System (qts.)
2010	Malibu	2.4	B/5	5	①	NA	NA	NA	NA	16.3	7.5
		3.6	7	5.5	①	NA	NA	NA	NA	16.3	5.5
2011	Malibu	2.4	B/5	5	①	NA	NA	NA	NA	16.3	7.5
		3.6	7	5.5	①	NA	NA	NA	NA	16.3	5.5

NOTE: All capacities are approximate. Add fluid gradually and ensure a proper fluid level is obtained.

① Bottom pan removal: 14
  Overhaul: 19

25742_MALI_C0004

FLUID SPECIFICATIONS

Year	Model	Engine Displacement Liters	Engine ID/VIN	Engine Oil	Auto. Trans.	Power Steering Fluid	Brake Master Cylinder	Cooling System
2010	Malibu	2.4	B/5	5W-30	Dexron® VI	GM PS Fluid	DOT 3	DEX-COOL®
		3.6	7	5W-30	Dexron® VI	GM PS Fluid	DOT 3	DEX-COOL®
2011	Malibu	2.4	B/5	5W-30	Dexron® VI	GM PS Fluid	DOT 3	DEX-COOL®
		3.6	7	5W-30	Dexron® VI	GM PS Fluid	DOT 3	DEX-COOL®

DOT: Department Of Transpotation

25742_MALI_C0005

VALVE SPECIFICATIONS

Year	Engine Displacement Liters	Engine ID/VIN	Seat Angle (deg.)	Face Angle (deg.)	Spring Test Pressure (lbs. @ in.)	Spring Free-Length (in.)	Spring Installed Height (in.)	Stem-to-Guide Clearance (in.) Intake	Stem-to-Guide Clearance (in.) Exhaust	Stem Diameter (in.) Intake	Stem Diameter (in.) Exhaust
2010	2.4	B/5	NA	45	①	②	1.280	0.0012-0.0022	0.0020-0.0026	0.2344-0.2355	0.2337-0.2343
	3.6	7	45	44.25	NA	1.673-1.791	1.378	0.0010-0.0026	0.0014-0.0030	0.2344-0.2352	0.2341-0.2348
2011	2.4	B/5	NA	45	①	②	1.280	0.0012-0.0022	0.0020-0.0026	0.2344-0.2355	0.2337-0.2343
	3.6	7	45	44.25	NA	1.673-1.791	1.378	0.0010-0.0026	0.0014-0.0030	0.2344-0.2352	0.2341-0.2348

① 118-129@0.89
② 1.629-1.742

25742_MALI_C0006

CAMSHAFT SPECIFICATIONS

All measurements in inches unless noted

Year	Engine Displacement Liters	Engine Code/VIN	Journal Diameter	Brg. Oil Clearance	Shaft End-play	Runout	Journal Bore	Lobe Height Intake	Lobe Height Exhaust
2010	2.4	B/5	1.0604-1.0614	NA	0.0016-0.0057	NA	NA	NA	NA
	3.6	7	①	NA	0.0018-0.0085	②	0.0016-0.0033	1.6687-1.6805	1.6703-1.6821
2011	2.4	B/5	1.0604-1.0614	NA	0.0016-0.0057	NA	NA	NA	NA
	3.6	7	①	NA	0.0018-0.0085	②	0.0016-0.0033	1.6687-1.6805	1.6703-1.6821

① Front No. 1: 1.3754-1.3764
  Middle and Rear No. 2-4: 1.0605-1.0614
② Front and Rear No. 1 and 4: 0.0010
  Middle 2 and 3: 0.0020

25742_MALI_C0007

CRANKSHAFT AND CONNECTING ROD SPECIFICATIONS

All measurements are given in inches.

Year	Engine Displacement Liters	Engine ID/VIN	Crankshaft Main Brg. Journal Dia.	Crankshaft Main Brg. Oil Clearance	Crankshaft Shaft End-play	Thrust on No.	Connecting Rod Journal Diameter	Connecting Rod Oil Clearance	Connecting Rod Side Clearance
2010	2.4	B/5	2.2045-2.2050	0.0012-0.0026	0.0012-0.1500	NA	1.9291-1.9297	NA	NA
	3.6	7	2.6768-2.6775	0.0004-0.0024	0.0039-0.0130	NA	2.2044-2.2050	0.0002	NA
2011	2.4	B/5	2.2045-2.2050	0.0012-0.0026	0.0012-0.1500	NA	1.9291-1.9297	NA	NA
	3.6	7	2.6768-2.6775	0.0004-0.0024	0.0039-0.0130	NA	2.2044-2.2050	0.0002	NA

25742_MALI_C0008

PISTON AND RING SPECIFICATIONS

All measurements are given in inches.

Year	Engine Displacement Liters	Engine ID/VIN	Piston Clearance	Ring Gap Top Compression	Ring Gap Bottom Compression	Ring Gap Oil Control	Ring Side Clearance Top Compression	Ring Side Clearance Bottom Compression	Ring Side Clearance Oil Control
2010	2.4	B/5	0.0002-0.0005	0.006-0.0120	0.008-0.0180	0.009-0.0260	0.0015-0.0031	0.0012-0.0030	0.0023-0.0081
	3.6	7	0.0002-0.0005	0.0059-0.0118	0.0110-0.1890	0.0059-0.0236	0.0012-0.0026	0.0006-0.0024	0.0012-0.0067
2011	2.4	B/5	0.0002-0.0005	0.006-0.0120	0.008-0.0180	0.009-0.0260	0.0015-0.0031	0.0012-0.0030	0.0023-0.0081
	3.6	7	0.0002-0.0005	0.0059-0.0118	0.0110-0.1890	0.0059-0.0236	0.0012-0.0026	0.0006-0.0024	0.0012-0.0067

25742_MALI_C0009

TORQUE SPECIFICATIONS
All readings in ft. lbs.

Year	Engine Disp. Liters	Engine ID/VIN	Cylinder Head Bolts	Main Bearing Bolts	Rod Bearing Bolts	Crankshaft Damper Bolts	Flywheel Bolts	Manifold Intake	Manifold Exhaust	Spark Plugs	Oil Pan Drain Plug
2010	2.4	B/5	①	②	③	④	⑤	⑥	⑦	15	18
	3.6	7	⑧	⑨	⑩	⑪	⑫	⑬	15	13	18
2011	2.4	B/5	①	②	③	④	⑤	⑥	⑦	15	18
	3.6	7	⑧	⑨	⑩	⑪	⑫	⑬	15	13	18

① Step 1: 22 ft. lbs.
Step 2: Plus 155 degrees
② Step 1: 15 ft. lbs.
Step 2: Plus 70 degrees
③ Step 1: 18 ft. lbs.
Step 2: Plus 100 degrees
④ Step 1: 74 ft. lbs.
Step 2: Plus 125 degrees
⑤ Step 1: 39 ft. lbs.
Step 2: Plus 25 degrees
⑥ Intake manifold to head nut/bolt: 89 inch lbs.
Intake manifold to head stud: 53 inch lbs.
⑦ Exhaust manifold to head nut: 124 inch lbs.
Exhaust manifold to head stud: 89 inch lbs.

⑧ M8 bolt Step 1: 11 ft. lbs.
Step 2: 75 degrees
M11 bolt Step 1: 22 ft. lbs.
Step 2: 150 degrees
⑨ Inner Step 1: 15 ft. lbs.
Step 2: 80 degrees
Outer Step 1: 10 ft. lbs.
Step 2: 110 degrees
Side Step 1:22 ft. lbs
Step 2: 60 degrees
⑩ Step 1: 22 ft. lbs.
Step 2: back off to zero
Step 3: 18 ft. lbs
Step 4: 110 degrees

⑪ 74 ft. lbs. Plus 150 degrees
⑫ Flywheel specification: 22 ft. lbs. Plus 45 degrees
⑬ Upper manifold: 17 ft. lbs.
Tuning valve bolt: 89 inch lbs.

25742_MALI_C0010

WHEEL ALIGNMENT

Year	Model		Caster Range (+/-Deg.)	Caster Preferred Setting (Deg.)	Camber Range (+/-Deg.)	Camber Preferred Setting (Deg.)	Toe-in (in.)
2010	Malibu with FE4	FR	2.90 +/- 0.75	0.75	- 1.00 +/- 0.75	- 0.30 +/- 0.75	NA
		FL	2.90 +/- 0.75	0.75	- 0.70 +/- 0.75	- 0.30 +/- 0.75	NA
	Malibu without FE4	FR	2.65 +/- 0.75	0.75	- 0.75 +/- 0.75	-0.30 +/- 0.75	NA
		FL	2.65 +/- 0.75	0.75	0.45 +/- 0.75	-0.30 +/- 0.75	NA
	Malibu	RR	NA	NA	-0.80 +/- 0.60	NA	NA
		RL	NA	NA	-0.80 +/- 0.60	NA	NA
2011	Malibu with FE4	FR	2.90 +/- 0.75	0.75	- 1.00 +/- 0.75	- 0.30 +/- 0.75	NA
		FL	2.90 +/- 0.75	0.75	- 0.70 +/- 0.75	- 0.30 +/- 0.75	NA
	Malibu without FE4	FR	2.65 +/- 0.75	0.75	- 0.75 +/- 0.75	-0.30 +/- 0.75	NA
		FL	2.65 +/- 0.75	0.75	0.45 +/- 0.75	-0.30 +/- 0.75	NA
	Malibu	RR	NA	NA	-0.80 +/- 0.60	NA	NA
		RL	NA	NA	-0.80 +/- 0.60	NA	NA

25742_MALI_C0011

TIRE, WHEEL AND BALL JOINT SPECIFICATIONS

| Year | Model | OEM Tires | | Tire Pressures (psi) | | Wheel Size | Ball Joint Inspection | Lug Nut (ft. lbs.) |
		Standard	Optional	Front	Rear			
2010	Malibu	P215/55R17	NA	①	①	17	NA	100
2011	Malibu	P215/55R17	NA	①	①	17	NA	100

OEM: Original Equipment Manufacturer

PSI: Pounds Per Square Inch

NA: Information not available

① Refer to placard on the vehicle for proper inflation pressure

25742_MALI_C0012

BRAKE SPECIFICATIONS

All measurements in inches unless noted

| Year | Model | | Brake Disc | | | Brake Drum Diameter | | | Minimum Pad/Lining Thickness | | Brake Caliper | |
			Original Thickness	Minimum Thickness	Max. Runout	Original Inside Diameter	Max. Wear Limit	Maximum Machine Diamter	Front	Rear	Bracket Bolts (ft. lbs.)	Mounting Bolts (ft. lbs.)
2010	Malibu	F	1.023	0.906	0.0020	NA	NA	NA	NA	NA	96	26
		R	0.551	0.472	0.0020	NA	NA	NA	NA	NA	96	26
2011	Malibu	F	1.023	0.906	0.0020	NA	NA	NA	NA	NA	96	26
		R	0.551	0.472	0.0020	NA	NA	NA	NA	NA	96	26

F: Front

R: Rear

NA: Information not available

25742_MALI_C0013

MAINTENANCE I AND II SERVICE SCHEDULES
MALIBU

When the CHANGE ENGINE OIL light appears, certain services and inspections are required.

Required services are described as Maintenance I and Maintenance II.

The first service of a vehicle should be Maintenance I, and the second service should be Maintenance II.

Alternate between the 2 services thereafter. However, in some cases, Maintenance II may be required more often.

Maintenance I: Use Maintenance I if the CHANGE ENGINE OIL light comes on within 10 months since the vehicle was purchased or, if Maintenance II was performed.

Maintenance II: Use Maintenance II if the previous service performed was Maintenance I. Always use Maintenance II whenever the CHANGE ENGINE OIL light comes on 10 months or more since the last service, or, if the CHANGE ENGINE OIL light has not come on at all for one year.

Service Item	Maintenance I	Maintenance II
Change the engine oil and filter.	✓	✓
Reset the oil life system.	✓	✓
Visually inspect the vehicle for leaks or damage. A fluid loss in the vehicle system could indicate a problem. Inspect, repair and add fluid to the system if necessary.	✓	✓
Inspect the engine air cleaner filter. If necessary, replace the filter.	✓	✓
Rotate the tires. Inspect the tire inflation pressures and the tire wear.	✓	✓
Visually inspect the brake lines and hoses for proper hook-up, binding, leaks, cracks, chafing, etc. Inspect the disc brake pads for wear and the rotors for surface condition. Inspect the drum brake linings for wear or cracks. Inspect other brake parts, including drums, wheel cylinders, calipers, parking brake, etc. Inspect the parking brake adjustment.	✓	✓
Inspect the engine coolant and the windshield washer fluid levels. Add fluid as needed.	✓	✓
Inspect the suspension and steering components. Inspect the front and rear suspension and the steering system for damaged, loose or missing parts, or signs of wear. Inspect the power steering lines and the hoses for proper hook-up, binding, leaks, cracks,	—	✓
Visually inspect the coolant hoses and replace the hoses if they are cracked, swollen or deteriorated. Inspect all pipes, fittings and clamps; replace with GM parts as needed. To help ensure proper operation, a pressure test of the cooling system and pressure cap and cleaning the outside of the radiator and air conditioning condenser is recommended at least once a year.	—	✓
Body hinges and latches, key lock cylinders, folding seat hardware, and rear compartment hinges lubrication. Applying silicone grease on weatherstrips with a clean cloth makes them last longer, seal better, and not stick or squeak.	✓	✓
Inspect the throttle system for interference or binding and for damaged or missing parts. Replace the parts as needed. Replace any components that have high effort or excessive wear. Do not lubricate the accelerator or the cruise control cables.	—	✓
Replace the passenger compartment air filter.	—	✓
Exhaust system and nearby heat shields inspection for loose or damaged components.	✓	✓
Inspect restraint system.	✓	✓

To reset the CHANGE ENGINE OIL light:

1. Turn the ignition key to the ON/RUN position with the engine OFF.
2. Press and release the stem in the lower center of the instrument cluster until the OIL LIFE message is displayed.
3. Once the alternating OIL LIFE and RESET messages appear, press and hold the stem until several beeps sound.
   This confirms that the oil life system has been reset to 100 percent.
4. Turn the ignition key to the OFF position.
   If the CHANGE ENGINE OIL message comes back on when the vehicle is started, the engine oil life system has not been reset. Repeat the procedure.

25742_MALI_C0014

ADDITIONAL MAINTENANCE SERVICES - NORMAL
MALIBU

TO BE SERVICED	TYPE OF SERVICE	VEHICLE MILEAGE INTERVAL (x1000)					
		25	50	75	100	125	150
Automatic transaxle fluid & filter	Replace				✓		
Spark plugs	Replace				✓		
Air cleaner filter	Replace		✓		✓		✓
Engine coolant	Replace						✓
Exhaust system & heat shields	Service/ Inspect	✓	✓	✓	✓	✓	✓
Evaporative control system	Inspect	✓	✓	✓	✓	✓	✓
Accessory drive belts	Replace						✓
Accessory drive belts	Inspect	✓	✓	✓	✓	✓	✓

25742_MALI_C0015

ADDITIONAL MAINTENANCE SERVICES - SEVERE
MALIBU

TO BE SERVICED	TYPE OF SERVICE	VEHICLE MILEAGE INTERVAL (x1000)					
		25	50	75	100	125	150
Automatic transaxle fluid & filter	Replace		✓		✓		✓
Spark plugs	Replace				✓		
Air cleaner filter	Replace	✓	✓	✓	✓	✓	✓
Engine coolant	Replace						✓
Exhaust system & heat shields	Inspect	✓	✓	✓	✓	✓	✓
Cooling system hoses and clamps	Inspect	✓	✓	✓	✓	✓	✓
Evaporative control system	Inspect	✓	✓	✓	✓	✓	✓
Accessory drive belts	Replace						✓
Accessory drive belts	Inspect	✓	✓	✓	✓	✓	✓

25742_MALI_C0016

PRECAUTIONS

Before servicing any vehicle, please be sure to read all of the following precautions, which deal with personal safety, prevention of component damage, and important points to take into consideration when servicing a motor vehicle:

• Never open, service or drain the radiator or cooling system when the engine is hot; serious burns can occur from the steam and hot coolant.

• Observe all applicable safety precautions when working around fuel. Whenever servicing the fuel system, always work in a well-ventilated area. Do not allow fuel spray or vapors to come in contact with a spark, open flame, or excessive heat (a hot drop light, for example). Keep a dry chemical fire extinguisher near the work area. Always keep fuel in a container specifically designed for fuel storage; also, always properly seal fuel containers to avoid the possibility of fire or explosion. Refer to the additional fuel system precautions later in this section.

• Fuel injection systems often remain pressurized, even after the engine has been turned **OFF**. The fuel system pressure must be relieved before disconnecting any fuel lines. Failure to do so may result in fire and/or personal injury.

• Brake fluid often contains polyglycol ethers and polyglycols. Avoid contact with the eyes and wash your hands thoroughly after handling brake fluid. If you do get brake fluid in your eyes, flush your eyes with clean, running water for 15 minutes. If eye irritation persists, or if you have taken brake fluid internally, IMMEDIATELY seek medical assistance.

• The EPA warns that prolonged contact with used engine oil may cause a number of skin disorders, including cancer. You should make every effort to minimize your exposure to used engine oil. Protective gloves should be worn when changing oil. Wash your hands and any other exposed skin areas as soon as possible after exposure to used engine oil. Soap and water, or waterless hand cleaner should be used.

• All new vehicles are now equipped with an air bag system, often referred to as a Supplemental Restraint System (SRS) or Supplemental Inflatable Restraint (SIR) system. The system must be disabled before performing service on or around system components, steering column, instrument panel components, wiring and sensors. Failure to follow safety and disabling procedures could result in accidental air bag deployment, possible personal injury and unnecessary system repairs.

• Always wear safety goggles when working with, or around, the air bag system. When carrying a non-deployed air bag, be sure the bag and trim cover are pointed away from your body. When placing a non-deployed air bag on a work surface, always face the bag and trim cover upward, away from the surface. This will reduce the motion of the module if it is accidentally deployed. Refer to the additional air bag system precautions later in this section.

• Clean, high quality brake fluid from a sealed container is essential to the safe and proper operation of the brake system. You should always buy the correct type of brake fluid for your vehicle. If the brake fluid becomes contaminated, completely flush the system with new fluid. Never reuse any brake fluid. Any brake fluid that is removed from the system should be discarded. Also, do not allow any brake fluid to come in contact with a painted surface; it will damage the paint.

• Never operate the engine without the proper amount and type of engine oil; doing so WILL result in severe engine damage.

• Timing belt maintenance is extremely important. Many models utilize an interference-type, non-freewheeling engine. If the timing belt breaks, the valves in the cylinder head may strike the pistons, causing potentially serious (also time-consuming and expensive) engine damage. Refer to the maintenance interval charts for the recommended replacement interval for the timing belt, and to the timing belt section for belt replacement and inspection.

• Disconnecting the negative battery cable on some vehicles may interfere with the functions of the on-board computer system(s) and may require the computer to undergo a relearning process once the negative battery cable is reconnected.

• When servicing drum brakes, only disassemble and assemble one side at a time, leaving the remaining side intact for reference.

• Only an MVAC-trained, EPA-certified automotive technician should service the air conditioning system or its components.

BRAKES

ANTI-LOCK BRAKE SYSTEM (ABS)

GENERAL INFORMATION

PRECAUTIONS

• Certain components within the ABS system are not intended to be serviced or repaired individually.

• Do not use rubber hoses or other parts not specifically specified for and ABS system. When using repair kits, replace all parts included in the kit. Partial or incorrect repair may lead to functional problems and require the replacement of components.

• Lubricate rubber parts with clean, fresh brake fluid to ease assembly. Do not use shop air to clean parts; damage to rubber components may result.

• Use only DOT 3 brake fluid from an unopened container.

• If any hydraulic component or line is removed or replaced, it may be necessary to bleed the entire system.

• A clean repair area is essential. Always clean the reservoir and cap thoroughly before removing the cap. The slightest amount of dirt in the fluid may plug an orifice and impair the system function. Perform repairs after components have been thoroughly cleaned; use only denatured alcohol to clean components. Do not allow ABS components to come into contact with any substance containing mineral oil; this includes used shop rags.

• The Anti-Lock control unit is a microprocessor similar to other computer units in the vehicle. Ensure that the ignition switch is **OFF** before removing or installing controller harnesses. Avoid static electricity discharge at or near the controller.

• If any arc welding is to be done on the vehicle, the control unit should be unplugged before welding operations begin.

BRAKES   **BLEEDING THE BRAKE SYSTEM**

BLEEDING PROCEDURE

BLEEDING PROCEDURE

Manual Bleeding

1. Place a clean shop cloth beneath the brake master cylinder to prevent brake fluid spills.

2. With the ignition OFF and the brakes cool, apply the brakes 3-5 times, or until the brake pedal effort increases significantly, in order to deplete the brake booster power reserve.

3. If you have performed a brake master cylinder bench bleeding on this vehicle, or if you disconnected the brake pipes from the master cylinder, you must perform the following steps:

   a. Ensure that the brake master cylinder reservoir is full to the maximum-fill level. If necessary, add GM approved brake fluid from a clean, sealed brake fluid container. If removal of the reservoir cap and diaphragm is necessary, clean the outside of the reservoir on and around the cap prior to removal.

   b. With the rear brake pipe installed securely to the master cylinder, loosen and separate the front brake pipe from the front port of the brake master cylinder.

   c. Allow a small amount of brake fluid to gravity bleed from the open port of the master cylinder.

   d. Reconnect the brake pipe to the master cylinder port and tighten securely.

   e. Have an assistant slowly depress the brake pedal fully and maintain steady pressure on the pedal.

   f. Loosen the same brake pipe to purge air from the open port of the master cylinder.

   g. Tighten the brake pipe, then have the assistant slowly release the brake pedal.

   h. Wait 15 seconds, then repeat the previous 4 steps until all air is purged from the same port of the master cylinder.

   i. With the front brake pipe installed securely to the master cylinder, after all air has been purged from the front port of the master cylinder, loosen and separate the rear brake pipe from the master cylinder, then repeat the previous 5 steps.

   j. After completing the final master cylinder port bleeding procedure, ensure that both of the brake pipe-to-master cylinder fittings are properly tightened.

4. Fill the brake master cylinder reservoir with GM approved brake fluid from a clean, sealed brake fluid container. Ensure that the brake master cylinder reservoir remains at least half-full during this bleeding procedure. Add fluid as needed to maintain the proper level.

5. Clean the outside of the reservoir on and around the reservoir cap prior to removing the cap and diaphragm.

6. Install a proper box-end wrench onto the RIGHT REAR wheel hydraulic circuit bleeder valve.

7. Install a transparent hose over the end of the bleeder valve.

8. Submerge the open end of the transparent hose into a transparent container partially filled with GM approved brake fluid from a clean, sealed brake fluid container.

9. Have an assistant slowly depress the brake pedal fully and maintain steady pressure on the pedal.

10. Loosen the bleeder valve to purge air from the wheel hydraulic circuit.

11. Tighten the bleeder valve, then have the assistant slowly release the brake pedal.

12. Wait 15 seconds, then repeat the previous 2 steps until all air is purged from the same wheel hydraulic circuit.

13. With the right rear wheel hydraulic circuit bleeder valve tightened securely, after all air has been purged from the right rear hydraulic circuit, install a proper box-end wrench onto the LEFT FRONT wheel hydraulic circuit bleeder valve.

14. Install a transparent hose over the end of the bleeder valve, then repeat steps 7-11.

15. With the left front wheel hydraulic circuit bleeder valve tightened securely, after all air has been purged from the left front hydraulic circuit, install a proper box-end wrench onto the LEFT REAR wheel hydraulic circuit bleeder valve.

16. Install a transparent hose over the end of the bleeder valve, then repeat steps 7-11.

17. With the left rear wheel hydraulic circuit bleeder valve tightened securely, after all air has been purged from the left rear hydraulic circuit, install a proper box-end wrench onto the RIGHT FRONT wheel hydraulic circuit bleeder valve.

18. Install a transparent hose over the end of the bleeder valve, then repeat steps 7-11.

19. After completing the final wheel hydraulic circuit bleeding procedure, ensure that each of the 4 wheel hydraulic circuit bleeder valves are properly tightened.

20. Fill the brake master cylinder reservoir to the maximum-fill level with GM approved brake fluid from a clean, sealed brake fluid container.

21. Slowly depress and release the brake pedal. Observe the feel of the brake pedal.

➡ **If it is determined that air was inducted into the system upstream of the ABS modulator prior to servicing, the Antilock Brake System Automated Bleed must be performed.**

22. If the brake pedal feels spongy, repeat the bleeding procedure again. If the brake pedal still feels spongy after repeating the bleeding procedure, perform the following steps:

   a. Inspect the brake system for external leaks.

   b. Pressure bleed the hydraulic brake system in order to purge any air that may still be trapped in the system.

23. Turn the ignition key ON, with the engine OFF. Check to see if the brake system warning lamp remains illuminated.

➡ **DO NOT allow the vehicle to be driven until it is diagnosed and repaired.**

24. If the brake system warning lamp remains illuminated, troubleshoot the hydraulic brake system.

Pressure

1. Place a clean shop cloth beneath the brake master cylinder to prevent brake fluid spills.

2. With the ignition OFF and the brakes cool, apply the brakes 3-5 times, or until the brake pedal effort increases significantly, in order to deplete the brake booster power reserve.

3. If you have performed a brake master cylinder bench bleeding on this vehicle, or if you disconnected the brake pipes from the master cylinder, you must perform the following steps:

   a. Ensure that the brake master cylinder reservoir is full to the maximum-fill level. If necessary, add GM approved brake fluid from a clean, sealed brake fluid container. If removal of the reservoir cap and diaphragm is necessary, clean the outside of the reservoir on and around the cap prior to removal.

   b. With the rear brake pipe installed securely to the master cylinder, loosen and separate the front brake pipe from the front port of the brake master cylinder.

c. Allow a small amount of brake fluid to gravity bleed from the open port of the master cylinder.

d. Reconnect the brake pipe to the master cylinder port and tighten securely.

e. Have an assistant slowly depress the brake pedal fully and maintain steady pressure on the pedal.

f. Loosen the same brake pipe to purge air from the open port of the master cylinder.

g. Tighten the brake pipe, then have the assistant slowly release the brake pedal.

h. Wait 15 seconds, then repeat the previous 4 steps until all air is purged from the same port of the master cylinder.

i. With the front brake pipe installed securely to the master cylinder, after all air has been purged from the front port of the master cylinder, loosen and separate the rear brake pipe from the master cylinder, then repeat the previous 5 steps.

j. After completing the final master cylinder port bleeding procedure, ensure that both of the brake pipe-to-master cylinder fittings are properly tightened.

4. Fill the brake master cylinder reservoir to the maximum-fill level with GM approved brake fluid from a clean, sealed brake fluid container.

5. Clean the outside of the reservoir on and around the reservoir cap prior to removing the cap and diaphragm.

6. Install the Master Cylinder Bleeder Adapter to the brake master cylinder reservoir.

7. Check the brake fluid level in the Diaphragm Type Brake Pressure Bleeder, or equivalent . Add GM approved brake fluid from a clean, sealed brake fluid container as necessary to bring the level to approximately the half-full point.

8. Connect the Diaphragm Type Brake Pressure Bleeder, or equivalent , to the Master Cylinder Bleeder Adapter.

9. Charge the Diaphragm Type Brake Pressure Bleeder, or equivalent, air tank to 25—30 psi (175—205 kPa).

10. Open the Diaphragm Type Brake Pressure Bleeder, or equivalent, fluid tank valve to allow pressurized brake fluid to enter the brake system.

11. Wait approximately 30 seconds, then inspect the entire hydraulic brake system in order to ensure that there are no existing external brake fluid leaks.

12. Any brake fluid leaks identified require repair prior to completing this procedure.

13. Install a proper box-end wrench onto the RIGHT REAR wheel hydraulic circuit bleeder valve.

14. Install a transparent hose over the end of the bleeder valve.

15. Submerge the open end of the transparent hose into a transparent container partially filled with GM approved brake fluid from a clean, sealed brake fluid container.

16. Loosen the bleeder valve to purge air from the wheel hydraulic circuit. Allow fluid to flow until air bubbles stop flowing from the bleeder, then tighten the bleeder valve.

17. With the right rear wheel hydraulic circuit bleeder valve tightened securely, after all air has been purged from the right rear hydraulic circuit, install a proper box-end wrench onto the LEFT FRONT wheel hydraulic circuit bleeder valve.

18. Install a transparent hose over the end of the bleeder valve, then repeat steps 13-14.

19. With the left front wheel hydraulic circuit bleeder valve tightened securely, after all air has been purged from the left front hydraulic circuit, install a proper box-end wrench onto the LEFT REAR wheel hydraulic circuit bleeder valve.

20. Install a transparent hose over the end of the bleeder valve, then repeat steps 13-14.

21. With the left rear wheel hydraulic circuit bleeder valve tightened securely, after all air has been purged from the left rear hydraulic circuit, install a proper box-end wrench onto the RIGHT FRONT wheel hydraulic circuit bleeder valve.

22. Install a transparent hose over the end of the bleeder valve, then repeat steps 13-14.

23. After completing the final wheel hydraulic circuit bleeding procedure, ensure that each of the 4 wheel hydraulic circuit bleeder valves are properly tightened.

24. Close the Diaphragm Type Brake Pressure Bleeder, or equivalent , fluid tank valve, then disconnect the Diaphragm Type Brake Pressure Bleeder, or equivalent , from the Master Cylinder Bleeder Adapter .

25. Remove the Master Cylinder Bleeder Adapter from the brake master cylinder reservoir.

26. Fill the brake master cylinder reservoir to the maximum-fill level with GM approved brake fluid from a clean, sealed brake fluid container.

27. Slowly depress and release the brake pedal. Observe the feel of the brake pedal.

➡ **If it is determined that air was inducted into the system upstream of the ABS modulator prior to servicing,** the Antilock Brake System Automated Bleed must be performed.

28. If the brake pedal feels spongy, perform the following steps:

a. Inspect the brake system for external leaks.

b. Using a scan tool, perform the antilock brake system automated bleeding procedure to rcmove any air that may have been trapped in the brake pressure modulator valve (BPMV). Refer to Antilock Brake System Automated Bleed.

c. Turn the ignition key ON, with the engine OFF. Check to see if the brake system warning lamp remains illuminated.

➡ **DO NOT allow the vehicle to be driven until it is diagnosed and repaired.**

d. If the brake system warning lamp remains illuminated, troubleshoot the hydraulic brake system.

BLEEDING THE ABS SYSTEM

➡ **Before performing the ABS Automated Bleed Procedure, first perform a manual or pressure bleed of the base hydraulic brake system.**

➡ **The automated bleed procedure must be performed when a new brake pressure modulator valve (BPMV) is installed, because the secondary circuits of the new BPMV are not prefilled with brake fluid.**

➡ **The automated bleed procedure is recommended when one of the following conditions exist:**

- Base brake system bleeding does not achieve the desired pedal height or feel
- Extreme loss of brake fluid has occurred
- Air ingestion is suspected in the secondary circuits of the brake modulator assembly

The ABS Automated Bleed Procedure uses a scan tool to cycle the system solenoid valves and run the pump in order to purge any air from the secondary circuits. These circuits are normally closed off, and are only opened during system initialization at vehicle start up and during ABS operation. The automated bleed procedure opens these secondary circuits and allows any air trapped in these circuits to flow out away from the brake modulator assembly, which is then forced out at the brake corners by the pressure bleeder.

※ CAUTION

The Auto Bleed Procedure may be terminated at any time during the process by pressing the EXIT button. No further Scan Tool prompts pertaining to the Auto Bleed procedure will be given. After exiting the bleed procedure, relieve bleed pressure and disconnect bleed equipment per manufacturer's instructions. Failure to properly relieve pressure may result in spilled brake fluid causing damage to components and painted surfaces.

1. Raise and support the vehicle.
2. Remove the tire and wheel assemblies.
3. Inspect the brake system for leaks and visual damage.
4. Lower the vehicle.
5. Prepare the brake bleeding equipment and the vehicle for a pressure bleed of the base hydraulic brake system.

6. Inspect the battery state of charge.
7. Install a scan tool.
8. Turn the ignition ON, with the engine OFF.
9. With the scan tool, perform the following steps:
   a. Select diagnostics
   b. Select the appropriate vehicle information.
   c. Select chassis
   d. Select Electronic Brake Control Module (EBCM)
   e. Select special functions
   f. Select Automated Bleed
10. With an assistant ready, raise and support the vehicle.

➡ **Apply the brake pedal when instructed, using moderate effort.**

➡ **Ensure the pedal remains applied until instructed to release by the scan tool.**

➡ **Do not exceed the time period allowed by the scan tool for having the bleeder valves open.**

➡ **The bleed sequence for each corner is as follows:**

- Left front
- Right front
- Right rear
- Left rear

11. Perform the automated bleed procedure as instructed by the scan tool.
12. If the automated bleed procedure is aborted, a malfunction exists. If a DTC is detected, refer to Diagnostic Trouble Code (DTC) List to diagnose the DTC.
13. After completion of the automated bleed procedure, press and hold the brake pedal to inspect for pedal firmness.
14. If the brake pedal feels spongy, repeat the bleed procedure completely.
15. Remove the scan tool.
16. Install the tire and wheel assemblies.
17. Lower the vehicle.
18. Adjust the brake fluid level.
19. Road test the vehicle while confirming the brake pedal remains high and firm.

BRAKES
FRONT DISC BRAKES

※ CAUTION

Dust and dirt accumulating on brake parts during normal use may contain asbestos fibers from production or aftermarket brake linings. Breathing excessive concentrations of asbestos fibers can cause serious bodily harm. Exercise care when servicing brake parts. Do not sand or grind brake lining unless equipment used is designed to contain the dust residue. Do not clean brake parts with compressed air or by dry brushing. Cleaning should be done by dampening the brake components with a fine mist of water, then wiping the brake components clean with a dampened cloth. Dispose of cloth and all residue containing asbestos fibers in an impermeable container with the appropriate label. Follow practices prescribed by the Occupational Safety and Health Administration (OSHA) and the Environmental Protection Agency (EPA) for the handling, processing, and disposing of dust or debris that may contain asbestos fibers.

BRAKE CALIPER

REMOVAL & INSTALLATION

See Figures 1 through 3.

1. Inspect the fluid level in the brake master cylinder reservoir.
2. If the brake fluid level is midway between the maximum-full point and the minimum allowable level, no brake fluid needs to be removed from the reservoir before proceeding.

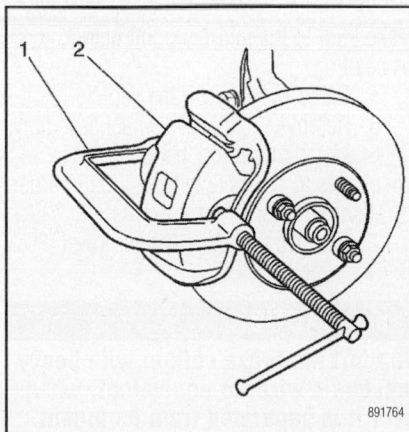

891764

Fig. 1 Installing the C-clamp (1) over the brake caliper (2)

3. If the brake fluid level is higher than midway between the maximum-full point and the minimum allowable level, remove brake fluid to the midway point before proceeding.
4. Raise and support the vehicle.
5. Remove the tire and wheel assembly.
6. Install and firmly hand tighten 2 wheel nuts to opposite wheel studs in order to retain the rotor to the hub.
7. Install a large C-clamp over the body of the brake caliper with the C-clamp ends against the rear of the caliper body and against the outer brake pad.
8. Tighten the C-clamp until the caliper piston is compressed into the caliper bore enough to allow the caliper to slide past the brake rotor.
9. Remove the C-clamp from the caliper.
10. Remove the brake hose-to-caliper bolt from the brake caliper.
11. Remove the brake hose from the brake caliper.
12. Remove and discard the 2 copper brake hose gaskets. These gaskets may be stuck to the brake caliper and/or the brake hose end.
13. Cap or plug the opening in the brake caliper and the brake hose to prevent fluid loss and contamination.

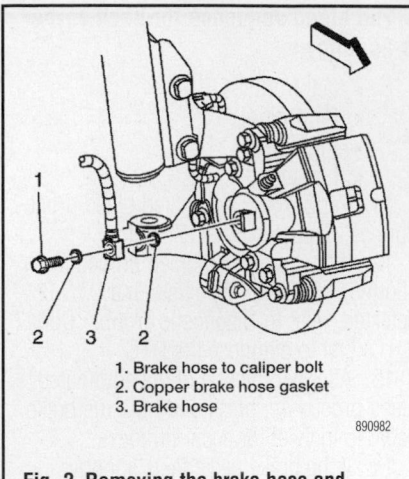

1. Brake hose to caliper bolt
2. Copper brake hose gasket
3. Brake hose

890982

Fig. 2 Removing the brake hose and gaskets

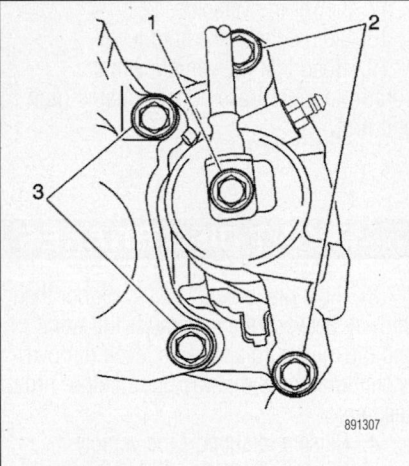

891307

Fig. 3 Removing the brake caliper guide pin bolt (2)

14. Remove the brake caliper guide pin bolts.

15. Remove the brake caliper from the caliper bracket.

16. Inspect the brake caliper guide pins for freedom of movement, and inspect the condition of the guide pin boots. Move the guide pins inboard and outboard within the bracket bores, without disengaging the slides from the boots, and observe for the following:

- Restricted caliper guide pin movement
- Looseness in the brake caliper mounting bracket
- Seized or binding caliper guide pins
- Split or torn boots

17. If any of the conditions listed are found, the brake caliper guide pins and/or boots require replacement.

To install:

18. Install the brake caliper to the brake caliper bracket.

19. Install the brake caliper guide pin bolts and tighten to 26 ft. lbs. (35 Nm).

20. Remove the caps or plugs from the brake caliper opening and the brake hose.

➡ **Do not reuse the copper brake hose gaskets.**

21. Install NEW copper brake hose gaskets to the brake hose-to-caliper bolt and to the brake hose.

22. Install the brake hose and the brake hose-to-brake caliper bolt to the brake caliper and tighten the bolt to 37 ft. lbs. (50 Nm).

23. Bleed the hydraulic brake system.

24. Remove the wheel nuts retaining the brake rotor to the wheel hub.

25. Install the tire and wheel assembly.

26. Lower the vehicle.

27. With the engine OFF, gradually apply the brake pedal to approximately ⅔ of its travel distance.

28. Slowly release the brake pedal.

29. Wait 15 seconds, then repeat steps 10 and 11 until a firm brake pedal is obtained. This will properly seat the brake caliper piston and brake pads.

DISC BRAKE PADS

REMOVAL & INSTALLATION

See Figures 4 and 5.

1. Inspect the fluid level in the brake master cylinder reservoir.

2. If the brake fluid level is midway between the maximum-full point and the minimum allowable level, no brake fluid needs to be removed from the reservoir before proceeding.

3. If the brake fluid level is higher than midway between the maximum-full point and the minimum allowable level, remove brake fluid to the midway point before proceeding.

4. Raise and support the vehicle.

5. Remove the tire and wheel assembly.

6. Install and firmly hand tighten 2 wheel nuts to opposite wheel studs in order to retain the rotor to the hub.

7. Remove the brake caliper lower guide pin bolt.

❋❋ CAUTION

Support the brake caliper with heavy mechanic wire, or equivalent, whenever it is separated from its mount and the hydraulic flexible brake hose is still connected. Failure to support the caliper in this manner will cause the flexible brake hose to bear the weight of the caliper, which may

cause damage to the brake hose and in turn may cause a brake fluid leak.

8. Without disconnecting the hydraulic brake flexible hose, pivot the caliper upward and secure the caliper with heavy mechanics wire, or equivalent.

9. Remove the brake pads from the caliper mounting bracket.

10. Push the disc brake caliper piston into the caliper bore using an old inner disc brake pad and a disc brake piston installation tool.

11. Remove the brake pad retainers from the caliper bracket.

12. Thoroughly clean the brake pad hardware mating surfaces of the caliper bracket, of any debris and corrosion.

13. Inspect the brake caliper guide pins for freedom of movement, and inspect the condition of the guide pin boots. Move the guide pins inboard and outboard within the bracket bores, without disengaging the

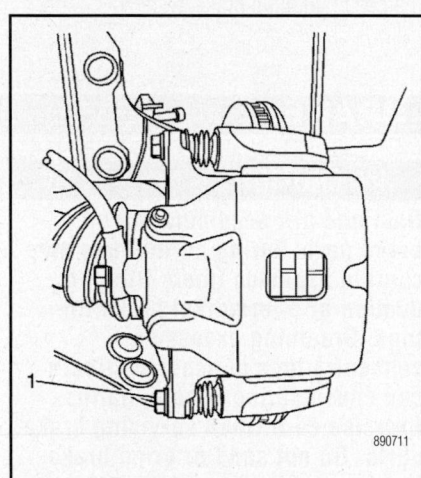

890711

Fig. 4 Removing the brake caliper lower guide pin bolt (1)

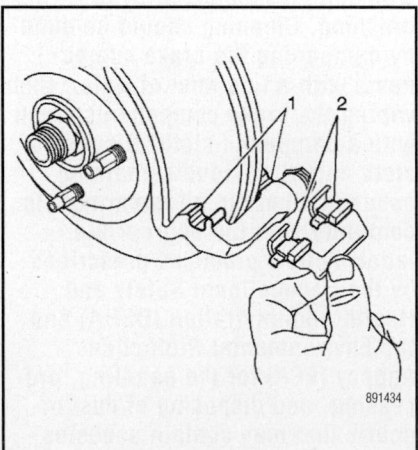

891434

Fig. 5 Removing the brake pad retainers (2) from the caliper bracket (1)

slides from the boots, and observe for the following:

- Restricted caliper guide pin movement
- Looseness in the brake caliper mounting bracket
- Seized or binding caliper guide pins
- Split or torn boots

14. If any of the conditions listed are found, the brake caliper guide pins and/or boots require replacement.

To install:

15. Ensure the brake pad hardware mating surfaces are clean.

16. Install the brake pad retainers to the brake caliper bracket.

➡The wear sensor equipped disc brake pad must be mounted inboard of the rotor with the leading edge of the sensor facing the brake rotor during forward wheel rotation, or at the top of the pad when installed in vehicle position.

17. Install the brake pads to the caliper bracket.

18. Remove the support, and rotate the brake caliper into position over the disc brake pads and to the caliper mounting bracket.

19. Install the lower brake caliper guide pin bolt and tighten to 26 ft. lbs. (35 Nm).

20. Remove the wheel nuts retaining the brake rotor to the hub.

21. Install the tire and wheel assembly.

22. Lower the vehicle.

23. With the engine OFF, gradually apply the brake pedal approximately ⅔ of its travel distance.

24. Slowly release the brake pedal.

25. Wait 15 seconds, then gradually apply the brake pedal approximately 2/3 of its travel distance again until a firm brake pedal apply is obtained. This will properly seat the brake caliper pistons and brake pads.

26. Fill the master cylinder auxiliary reservoir to the proper level.

27. Burnish the pads and rotors.

BRAKES

⚹⚹ CAUTION

Dust and dirt accumulating on brake parts during normal use may contain asbestos fibers from production or aftermarket brake linings. Breathing excessive concentrations of asbestos fibers can cause serious bodily harm. Exercise care when servicing brake parts. Do not sand or grind brake lining unless equipment used is designed to contain the dust residue. Do not clean brake parts with compressed air or by dry brushing. Cleaning should be done by dampening the brake components with a fine mist of water, then wiping the brake components clean with a dampened cloth. Dispose of cloth and all residue containing asbestos fibers in an impermeable container with the appropriate label. Follow practices prescribed by the Occupational Safety and Health Administration (OSHA) and the Environmental Protection Agency (EPA) for the handling, processing, and disposing of dust or debris that may contain asbestos fibers.

BRAKE CALIPER

REMOVAL & INSTALLATION

See Figures 6 through 8.

1. Inspect the fluid level in the brake master cylinder reservoir.

2. If the brake fluid level is midway between the maximum-full point and the minimum allowable level, no brake fluid needs to be removed from the reservoir before proceeding.

3. If the brake fluid level is higher than midway between the maximum-full point and the minimum allowable level, remove brake fluid to the midway point before proceeding.

4. Raise and suitably support the vehicle.

5. Remove the tire and wheel assembly.

6. Install a large C clamp over the body of the brake caliper with the C-clamp ends against the rear of the caliper body and against the outer brake pad.

⚹⚹ CAUTION

When using a large C-clamp to compress a caliper piston into a caliper bore of a caliper equipped with an integral park brake mechanism, do not exceed more than 0.039 inch (1 mm) of piston travel. Exceeding this amount of piston travel will cause damage to the internal adjusting mechanism and/or the integral park brake mechanism.

7. Tighten the C-clamp until the caliper piston is compressed into the caliper bore enough to allow the caliper to slide past the brake rotor. Do not exceed 1 mm (0.039 in) of caliper piston travel.

8. Remove the C-clamp from the caliper.

9. Remove the brake hose to caliper bolt from the brake caliper.

10. Remove the brake hose from the brake caliper.

11. Remove and discard the 2 copper brake hose gaskets. These gaskets may be stuck to the brake caliper and/or the brake hose end.

12. Cap or plug the opening in the brake caliper and the brake hose to prevent fluid loss and contamination.

REAR DISC BRAKES

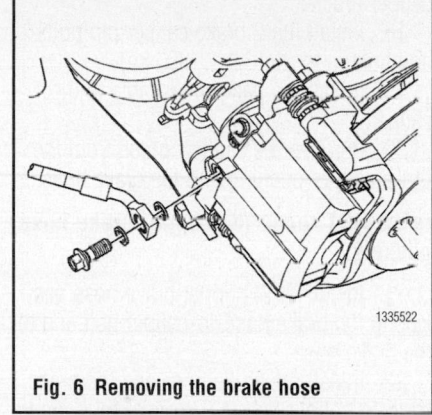

Fig. 6 Removing the brake hose

13. Remove the 2 brake caliper pin bolts.

14. Remove the park brake cable from the caliper.

15. Remove the brake caliper from the brake caliper bracket.

To Install:

16. Inspect the caliper slide boots for cuts, tears, or deterioration. If damaged, replace the slides and boots.

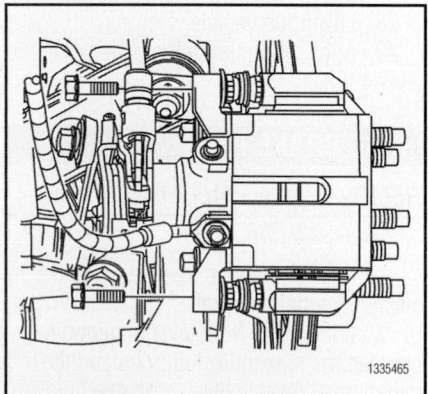

Fig. 7 Removing the brake caliper pin bolts

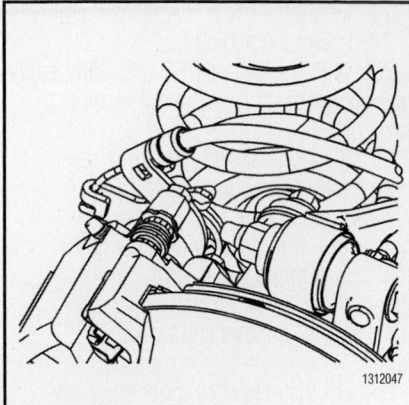

Fig. 8 Removing the parking brake cable from the caliper and the caliper from the bracket

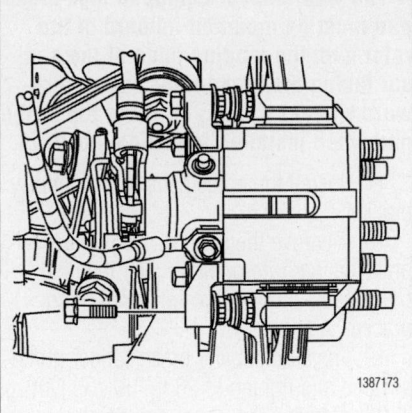

Fig. 9 Removing the lower brake caliper guide pin bolt

17. Install the brake caliper to the brake caliper bracket.

18. Install the 2 brake caliper pin bolts and tighten to 26 ft. lbs. (35 Nm).

19. Install the park brake cable to the caliper.

20. Remove the caps or plugs from the brake caliper opening and the brake hose.

➡**DO NOT reuse the copper brake hose gaskets.**

21. Install NEW copper brake hose gaskets to the brake hose-to-caliper bolt and to the brake hose.

22. Install the brake hose and the brake hose-to-caliper bolt to the brake caliper and tighten the bolt to 37 ft. lbs. (50 Nm).

23. Bleed the hydraulic brake system.

24. With the engine OFF, gradually apply the brake pedal to approximately ⅔ of its travel distance.

25. Slowly release the brake pedal.

26. Wait 15 seconds, then repeat steps 9 and 10 until a firm brake pedal is obtained. This will properly seat the brake caliper pistons and brake pads.

27. Install the tire and wheel assembly.

28. Lower the vehicle.

29. Apply and release the park brake lever 4 times.

DISC BRAKE PADS

REMOVAL & INSTALLATION

See Figures 9 through 11.

1. Inspect the fluid level in the brake master cylinder reservoir.

2. If the brake fluid level is midway between the maximum-full point and the minimum allowable level, no brake fluid needs to be removed from the reservoir before proceeding.

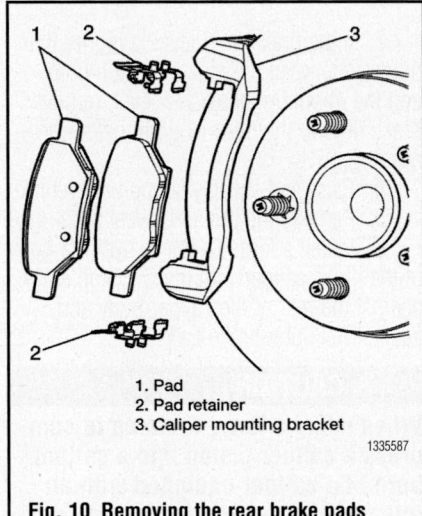

1. Pad
2. Pad retainer
3. Caliper mounting bracket

Fig. 10 Removing the rear brake pads

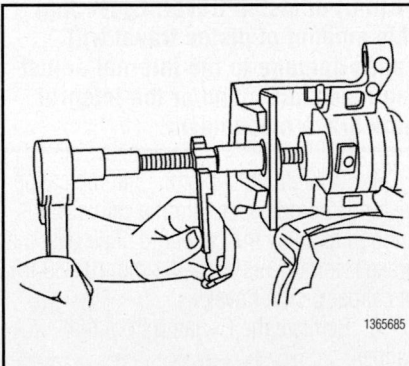

Fig. 11 Using a piston installation tool

3. Raise and suitably support the vehicle.

4. Remove the tire and wheel assembly.

5. Remove the lower brake caliper guide pin bolt.

✳✳ **CAUTION**

Support the brake caliper with heavy mechanic wire, or equivalent, when-

ever it is separated from its mount and the hydraulic flexible brake hose is still connected. Failure to support the caliper in this manner will cause the flexible brake hose to bear the weight of the caliper, which may cause damage to the brake hose and in turn may cause a brake fluid leak.

6. Pivot the brake caliper upward from the caliper bracket and support the caliper out of the way with heavy mechanic's wire or equivalent; ensure that there is no tension on the hydraulic brake flexible hose. Do NOT disconnect the hydraulic brake flexible hose from the caliper.

7. Remove the brake pads from the brake caliper mounting bracket.

8. Remove and the brake pad retainers from the brake caliper mounting bracket.

9. Inspect the following brake components for damage and corrosion:
- Brake caliper guide pin bolts
- Brake caliper guide pins
- Brake caliper guide pin bushing
- Brake caliper bracket boots
- Brake caliper bracket

10. Do not attempt to clean away any corrosion. If damaged or corroded replace the necessary components.

11. Inspect the brake caliper piston boot for deterioration, replace if damaged.

12. Use a piston installation tool in order to twist the brake caliper piston into the brake caliper bore.

To install:

13. Install the brake pad retainers to the brake caliper mounting bracket.

14. Install the brake pads to the brake caliper mounting bracket.

15. Pivot the brake caliper downward, over the brake pads and into the caliper bracket.

16. Install the brake caliper guide pin bolt to the brake caliper guide pin and tighten the bolt to 26 ft. lbs. (35 Nm).

17. Install the tire and wheel assembly.

18. Lower the vehicle.

19. With the engine OFF, gradually apply the brake pedal to approximately ⅔ of its travel distance.

20. Slowly release the brake pedal.

21. Wait 15 seconds, then repeat steps 11 and 12 until a firm brake pedal apply is obtained; this will properly seat the brake caliper pistons and brake pads.

22. Fill the brake master cylinder reservoir to the proper level.

23. Apply and release the park brake lever 4 times.

24. Burnish the pads and rotors.

CHASSIS ELECTRICAL — AIR BAG (SUPPLEMENTAL RESTRAINT SYSTEM)

GENERAL INFORMATION

> **✳✳ CAUTION**
>
> **These vehicles are equipped with an air bag system. The system must be disarmed before performing service on, or around, system components, the steering column, instrument panel components, wiring and sensors. Failure to follow the safety precautions and the disarming procedure could result in accidental air bag deployment, possible injury and unnecessary system repairs.**

SERVICE PRECAUTIONS

Disconnect and isolate the battery negative cable before beginning any airbag system component diagnosis, testing, removal, or installation procedures. Allow system capacitor to discharge for two minutes before beginning any component service. This will disable the airbag system. Failure to disable the airbag system may result in accidental airbag deployment, personal injury, or death.

Do not place an intact undeployed airbag face down on a solid surface. The airbag will propel into the air if accidentally deployed and may result in personal injury or death.

When carrying or handling an undeployed airbag, the trim side (face) of the airbag should be pointing towards the body to minimize possibility of injury if accidental deployment occurs. Failure to do this may result in personal injury or death.

Replace airbag system components with OEM replacement parts. Substitute parts may appear interchangeable, but internal differences may result in inferior occupant protection. Failure to do so may result in occupant personal injury or death.

Wear safety glasses, rubber gloves, and long sleeved clothing when cleaning powder residue from vehicle after an airbag deployment. Powder residue emitted from a deployed airbag can cause skin irritation. Flush affected area with cool water if irritation is experienced. If nasal or throat irritation is experienced, exit the vehicle for fresh air until the irritation ceases. If irritation continues, see a physician.

Do not use a replacement airbag that is not in the original packaging. This may result in improper deployment, personal injury, or death.

The factory installed fasteners, screws and bolts used to fasten airbag components have a special coating and are specifically designed for the airbag system. Do not use substitute fasteners. Use only original equipment fasteners listed in the parts catalog when fastener replacement is required.

During, and following, any child restraint anchor service, due to impact event or vehicle repair, carefully inspect all mounting hardware, tether straps, and anchors for proper installation, operation, or damage. If a child restraint anchor is found damaged in any way, the anchor must be replaced. Failure to do this may result in personal injury or death.

Deployed and non-deployed airbags may or may not have live pyrotechnic material within the airbag inflator.

Do not dispose of driver/passenger/curtain airbags or seat belt tensioners unless you are sure of complete deployment. Refer to the Hazardous Substance Control System for proper disposal.

Dispose of deployed airbags and tensioners consistent with state, provincial, local, and federal regulations.

After any airbag component testing or service, do not connect the battery negative cable. Personal injury or death may result if the system test is not performed first.

If the vehicle is equipped with the Occupant Classification System (OCS), do not connect the battery negative cable before performing the OCS Verification Test using the scan tool and the appropriate diagnostic information. Personal injury or death may result if the system test is not performed properly.

Never replace both the Occupant Restraint Controller (ORC) and the Occupant Classification Module (OCM) at the same time. If both require replacement, replace one, then perform the Airbag System test before replacing the other.

Both the ORC and the OCM store Occupant Classification System (OCS) calibration data, which they transfer to one another when one of them is replaced. If both are replaced at the same time, an irreversible fault will be set in both modules and the OCS may malfunction and cause personal injury or death.

If equipped with OCS, the Seat Weight Sensor is a sensitive, calibrated unit and must be handled carefully. Do not drop or handle roughly. If dropped or damaged, replace with another sensor. Failure to do so may result in occupant injury or death.

If equipped with OCS, the front passenger seat must be handled carefully as well.

When removing the seat, be careful when setting on floor not to drop. If dropped, the sensor may be inoperative, could result in occupant injury, or possibly death.

If equipped with OCS, when the passenger front seat is on the floor, no one should sit in the front passenger seat. This uneven force may damage the sensing ability of the seat weight sensors. If sat on and damaged, the sensor may be inoperative, could result in occupant injury, or possibly death.

CLOCKSPRING CENTERING

See Figures 12 and 13.

> **✳✳ CAUTION**
>
> **The new SIR coil assembly will be centered. Improper alignment of the SIR coil assembly may damage the unit, causing an inflatable restraint malfunction.**

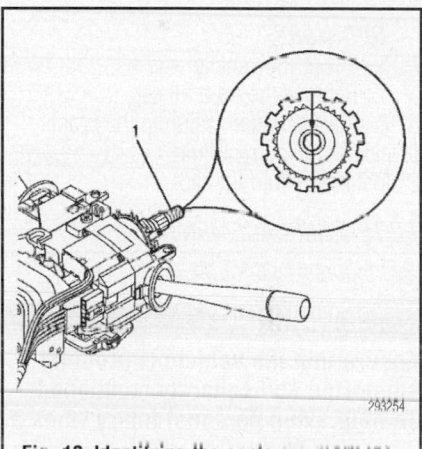

Fig. 12 Identifying the centering mark (1)

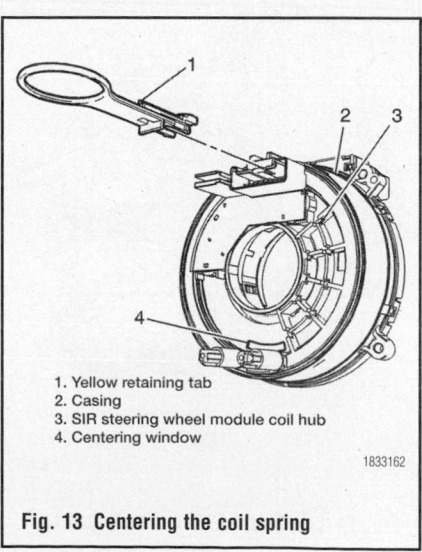

1. Yellow retaining tab
2. Casing
3. SIR steering wheel module coil hub
4. Centering window

Fig. 13 Centering the coil spring

1. Verify the following conditions before centering the supplemental inflatable restraint (SIR) steering wheel module coil:

   a. The wheels on the vehicle are straight ahead.

   b. The block tooth and the centering mark of the steering shaft is in the 12 o'clock position.

2. If available, remove the yellow retaining tab from the SIR steering wheel module coil and save the tab for reassembly.

3. Hold the SIR steering wheel module coil face up by the casing.

   a. Slowly turn the SIR steering wheel module coil hub clockwise until the coil ribbon stops.

   b. Slowly rotate the SIR steering wheel module coil hub counterclockwise 2.5 revolutions until the centering window turns yellow. This indicates the CENTER position.

➡ **If the retaining tab is not available, the use of tape to secure the SIR steering wheel module coil is recommended for installation to the steering column.**

4. Install the yellow retaining tab to the SIR steering wheel module coil.

5. Slide the centered SIR steering wheel module coil onto the steering shaft.

DRIVE TRAIN

AUTOMATIC TRANSMISSION FLUID

DRAIN AND REFILL

See Figure 14.

1. Raise and support the vehicle.
2. Remove the fluid drain plug.
3. Drain transmission fluid into a suitable container.
4. Install the fluid drain plug and tighten to 9 ft. lbs. (12 Nm).

To install:

5. Lower the vehicle.
6. Remove the fluid fill cap.
7. Fill the transmission to the proper level with the correct fluid.

Install the fluid fill cap.

FILTER REPLACEMENT

See Figures 15 through 17.

✳✳ WARNING

Ensure that the vehicle is properly supported and squarely positioned. To help avoid personal injury when a vehicle is on a hoist, provide additional support for the vehicle on the opposite end from which the components are being removed.

1. Position the vehicle on a hoist and raise the vehicle.
2. Place a drain pan under the transaxle oil pan.
3. Remove the oil pan bolts from the front and sides only.
4. Loosen the rear oil pan bolts approximately 4 times.

✳✳ CAUTION

Pry the oil pan carefully in order to prevent damage to the transaxle case or the oil pan sealing surfaces.

5. Lightly tap the oil pan with a rubber mallet or carefully pry in order to allow the oil to drain.
6. Remove the AIR.
7. Inspect the fluid color.
8. Remove the remaining oil pan bolts and the oil pan.
9. Remove the oil pan gasket.
10. Remove the oil level control valve.

11. Remove the oil filter and oil filter O-ring seal. The seal may stay in case when filter is removed.

➡ **Do not score or damage the transaxle case when removing the filter neck seal.**

12. Using a chisel, indent the top of the filter neck seal to relax the press fit.
13. Remove the filter neck seal from the transaxle case and discard.
14. Remove all traces of the old gasket material.
15. Clean the transaxle case and oil pan gasket surfaces with solvent, and allow to air dry.

To install:

✳✳ CAUTION

Use petroleum jelly when lubricating the components. Greases other than petroleum jelly will change the transaxle fluid characteristics and will cause undesirable shift conditions or filter clogging.

16. Install a new filter neck seal. A large

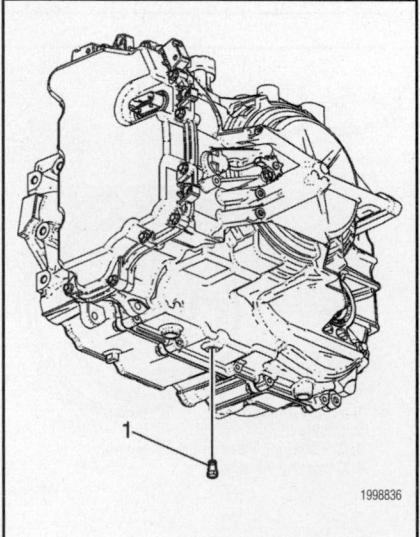

1998836

Fig. 14 Locating the fluid drain plug (1)

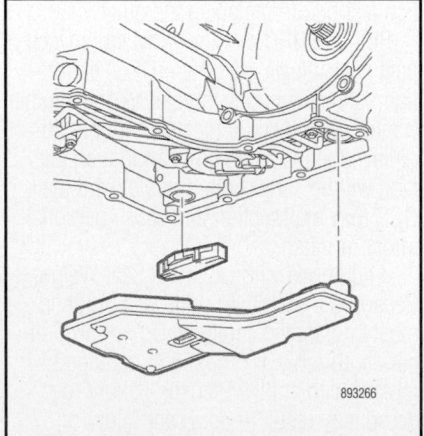

893266

Fig. 15 Removing the oil level control valve, oil filter and oil filter o-ring seal

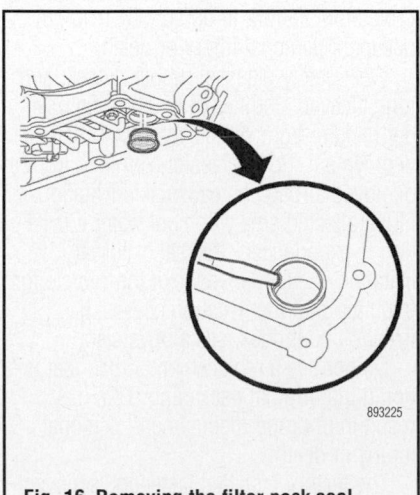

893225

Fig. 16 Removing the filter neck seal

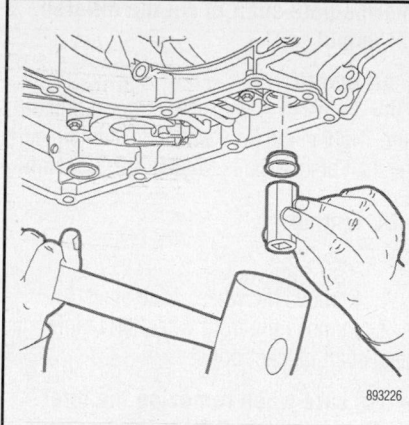

Fig. 17 Using a large socket to aid in installation of filter neck seal

socket can be used as an installation tool. Two mallets can be used as well.

17. Coat the new filter O-ring seal with a small amount of petroleum jelly, and install the filter into the case.

✳✳ CAUTION

Push straight down on the center of the oil level control valve in order to prevent damage to the case bore.

18. Install the oil level control valve.
19. Install the oil pan gasket, the oil pan, and hand start the oil pan bolts. Tighten the oil pan bolts to 9 ft. lbs. (12 Nm).
20. Lower the vehicle.
21. Refill transaxle using DEXRON® VI to the specified refill capacity.

Specification
• Bottom pan removal capacity: approximately 6.9 qt (6.5 L)
• Complete overhaul capacity: approximately 9.5 qt (9 L)
• Dry capacity: approximately 12.9 qt (12.2 L)

22. Start the engine. Warm up the transaxle and check for leaks.
23. Check for proper fluid level.

FRONT DRIVESHAFT

REMOVAL & INSTALLATION
See Figures 18 through 21.

✳✳ WARNING

To prevent personal injury and/or component damage, do not allow the weight of the vehicle to load the front wheels, or attempt to operate the vehicle, when the wheel drive shaft(s) or wheel drive shaft nut(s) are removed. To do so may cause the inner bearing race to separate, resulting in damage

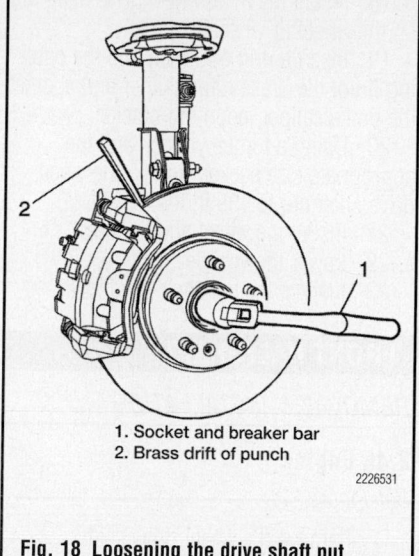

1. Socket and breaker bar
2. Brass drift of punch

Fig. 18 Loosening the drive shaft nut

to brake and suspension components and loss of vehicle control.

✳✳ CAUTION

Wheel drive shaft boots, seals and clamps should be protected from sharp objects any time service is performed on or near the wheel drive shaft(s). Damage to the boot(s), the seal(s) or the clamp(s) may cause lubricant to leak from the joint and lead to increased noise and possible failure of the wheel drive shaft.

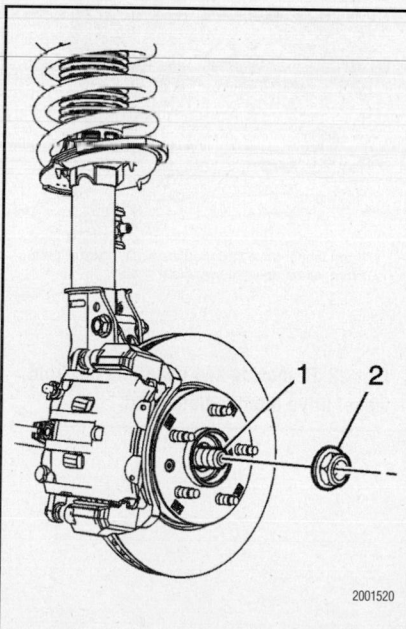

Fig. 19 Removing the wheel drive shaft nut (2) from the wheel drive shaft (1)

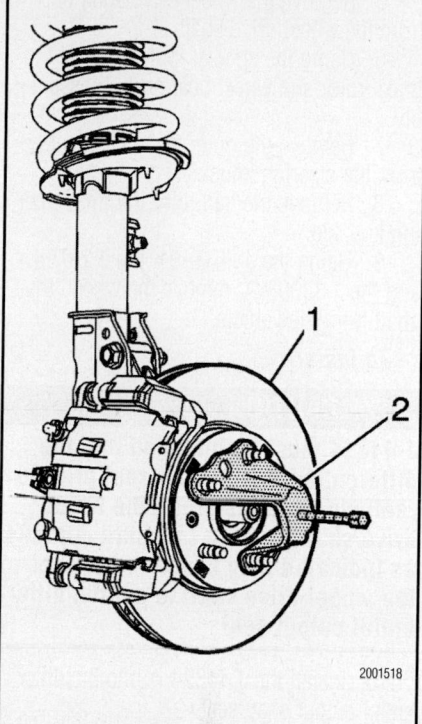

Fig. 20 Using the special tool (2) to separate the brake rotor and wheel bearing/hub assembly

1. Raise and suitably support the vehicle.
2. Remove the wheel and the tire.
3. Insert a brass drift or punch (2) in the brake rotor cooling fins rotate the brake rotor until it rest against and the brake caliper mounting bracket.
4. Using the appropriate size socket and breaker bar (1), loosen the wheel drive shaft nut.

➡**DO NOT re-use the wheel drive shaft nut. Discard the nut and replace with NEW.**

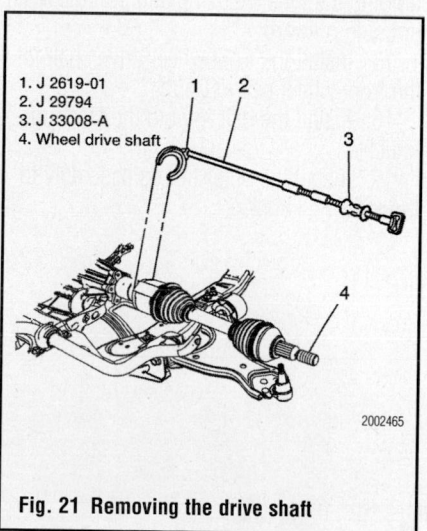

1. J 2619-01
2. J 29794
3. J 33008-A
4. Wheel drive shaft

Fig. 21 Removing the drive shaft

5. Remove the wheel drive shaft nut from the wheel drive shaft.

6. Using the special tool, separate the brake rotor and wheel bearing/hub assembly.

7. Remove the outer tie rod assembly from the steering knuckle.

8. Remove the ball joint from the steering knuckle.

9. Using the J 2619-01, the J 29794, and the J 33008-A, remove the wheel drive shaft from the vehicle.

To install:

❈❈ CAUTION

J-44394 must be installed into the differential output shaft seal prior to removing and installing the wheel drive shaft. Failure to install J-44394 as indicated may cause the splines of the wheel drive shaft to cut the differential output seal.

10. Install the J 44394-A into the differential output shaft seal.

➡**In order to prevent lubricant leaks, use care when installing the wheel drive shaft to the differential. Do not damage the oil seal. Replace the oil seal if it becomes nicked, distorted, or otherwise damaged.**

11. Carefully install the wheel drive shaft into the differential until the splines are past the J 44394-A.

12. Remove the special tool from the differential output shaft seal.

13. Installing the wheel drive shaft into the differential until the retaining ring is fully seated.

14. Confirm that the front wheel drive shaft retaining ring is properly seated by holding the inner housing and pull the inner housing outward

15. Install the front wheel drive shaft into the front wheel bearing/hub.

16. Install the ball joint to the steering knuckle.

17. Install the outer tie rod assembly to the steering knuckle.

18. Install the NEW wheel drive shaft nut on the wheel drive shaft.

19. Insert a drift or punch into the cooling fin of the brake rotor caliper and against the brake caliper mounting bracket.

20. Using a torque wrench and the appropriate size socket, tighten the wheel drive shaft nut to 159 ft. lbs. (215 Nm).

21. Install the wheel and the tire.

22. Lower the vehicle.

23. Inspect the transaxle fluid level.

FRONT HALFSHAFT

REMOVAL & INSTALLATION

2.4L Engine

See Figure 22.

1. Remove the wheel drive shaft.

2. Remove the front wheel drive intermediate shaft bracket bolts.

➡**Use care when removing the intermediate drive shaft from the transmission as not to damage the seal.**

3. Remove the front wheel drive intermediate shaft.

➡**The J 44394-A must be installed into the differential output shaft seal prior to removing and installing the intermediate shaft. Failure to install the J 44394-A may cause splines of the intermediate shaft to cut the differential output seal.**

To install:

4. To install, reverse the removal procedure. Tighten the front wheel drive intermediate shaft bracket bolts to 37 ft. lbs. (50 Nm).

3.6L Engine

See Figure 23.

1. Remove the wheel drive shaft.

2. Remove the front wheel drive intermediate shaft bracket bolts.

➡**Use care when removing the intermediate drive shaft from the transmission as not to damage the seal.**

3. Remove the front wheel drive intermediate shaft.

➡**The J 44394-A must be installed into the differential output shaft seal prior to removing and installing the intermediate shaft. Failure to install the J 44394-A may cause splines of the intermediate shaft to cut the differential output seal.**

To install:

4. To install, reverse the removal procedure. Tighten the intermediate drive shaft bracket bolts to 44 ft. lbs. (60 Nm).

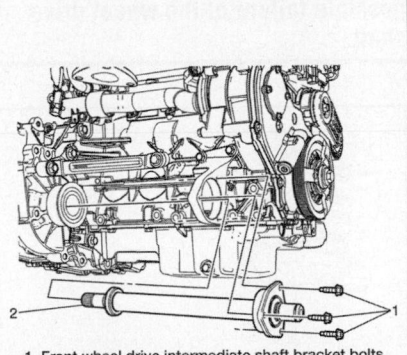

1. Front wheel drive intermediate shaft bolts
2. Front wheel drive intermediate shaft

2096644

Fig. 22 Removing and installing the front wheel drive intermediate shaft

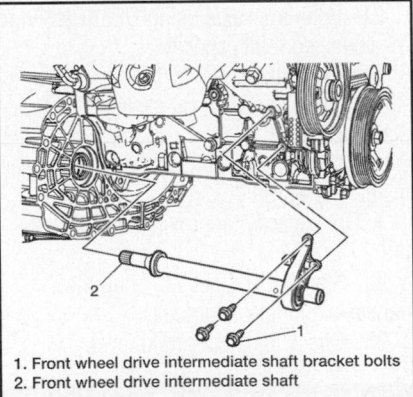

1. Front wheel drive intermediate shaft bracket bolts
2. Front wheel drive intermediate shaft

2096764

Fig. 23 Removing and installing the front wheel drive intermediate shaft

ENGINE COOLING

ENGINE COOLANT

DRAIN & REFILL PROCEDURE

V N Fill Coolant Refill Tool

See Figures 24 through 30.

1. Unscrew the surge tank cap to remove vacuum when draining the coolant.

2. Raise and support the vehicle.

3. Place a container under the radiator drain.

4. Unscrew the radiator drain plug until coolant flows out the radiator drain.

5. If a complete block drain is required, remove the drain plugs.

6. Follow the appropriate procedure based on the condition of the coolant.

   a. Normal in appearance—follow the filling procedure.

   b. Discolored—follow the flush procedure. Refer to Flushing.

Fill Procedure

➡**To prevent boiling of the coolant/water mixture in the vehicles cooling system, do not apply vacuum to a cooling system above 120°F (49°C). The tool will not operate properly when the coolant is boiling.**

7. If a complete engine block drain was required, install the engine block drain plugs.

8. Install J-42401-2 into the surge tank fill neck.

9. Install J-42401-3 to the surge tank fill neck.

10. Attach the Vac N Fill cap to the J-42401-3.

11. Attach the Vac N Fill cap to the vehicles coolant fill port.

12. Attach the vacuum gage assembly to the Vac N Fill cap.

13. Attach the fill hose to the barb fitting on the vacuum gage assembly.

14. Ensure the valve is closed.

➡**Use a 50/50 mixture of DEX-COOL® antifreeze and clean, drinkable water. Always use more coolant than necessary. This will eliminate air from being drawn into the cooling system.**

15. Pour the coolant mixture into the graduated reservoir.

16. Place the fill hose in the graduated reservoir.

➡**Prior to installing the vacuum tank onto the graduated reservoir, ensure the drain valve located on the bottom of the tank is closed.**

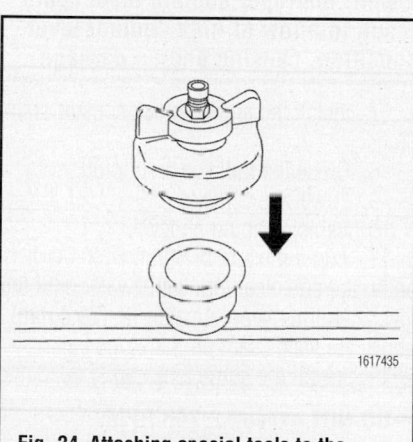

Fig. 24 Attaching special tools to the surge tank fill neck and port

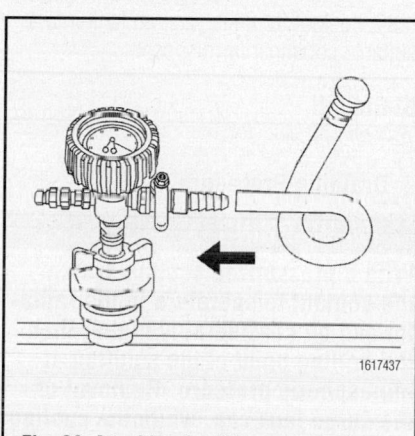

Fig. 26 Attaching the fill hose to the barb fitting on the vacuum gage assembly

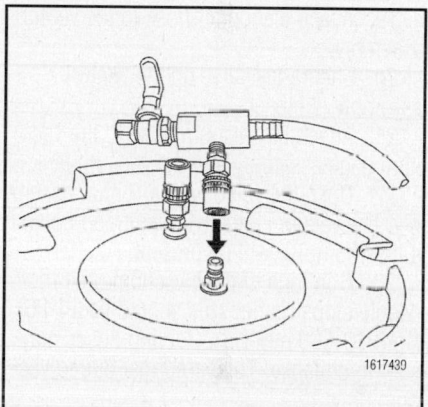

Fig. 28 Attaching the venturi assembly to the vacuum tank

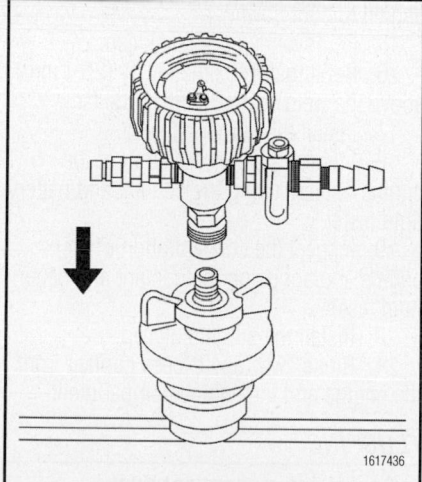

Fig. 25 Attaching the vacuum gage assembly to the Vac N Fill cap

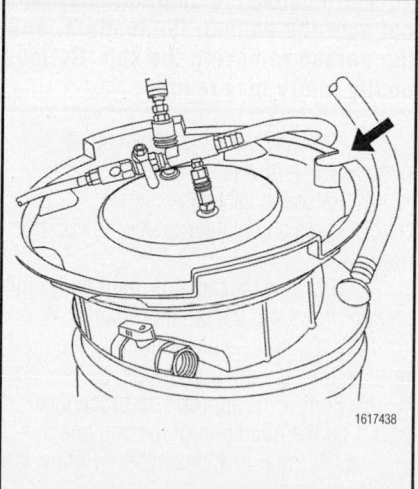

Fig. 27 Installing the vacuum tank on the graduated reservoir

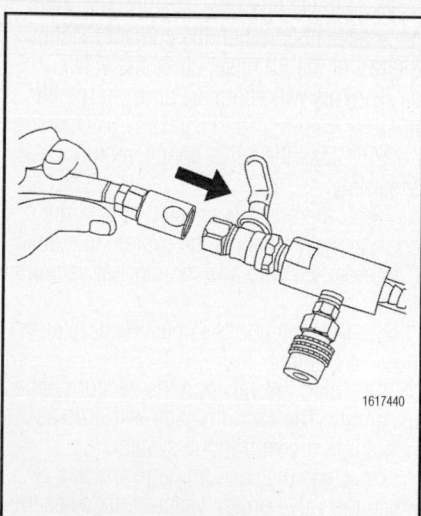

Fig. 29 Attaching a shop air hose to the venturi assembly

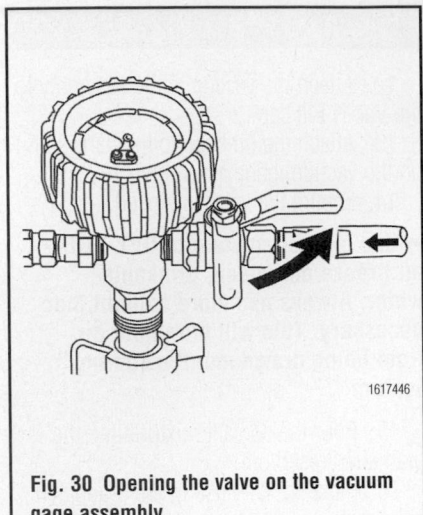

Fig. 30 Opening the valve on the vacuum gage assembly

17. Install the vacuum tank on the graduated reservoir with the fill hose routed through the cut-out area in the vacuum tank.

18. Attach the venturi assembly to the vacuum tank.

19. Attach a shop air hose to the venturi assembly.

20. Ensure the valve on the venturi assembly is closed.

21. Attach the vacuum hose to the vacuum gage assembly and the vacuum tank.

22. Open the valve on the venturi assembly. The vacuum gage will begin to rise and a hissing noise will be present.

23. Continue to draw vacuum until the needle stops rising. This should be 24-26 Hg (610-660 mm Hg). Cooling hoses may start to collapse. This is normal due to vacuum draw.

24. To aid in the fill process, position the graduated reservoir above the coolant fill port.

25. Slowly open the valve on the vacuum gage assembly. When the coolant reaches the top of the fill hose, close the valve.

26. This will eliminate air from the fill hose.

27. Close the valve on the venturi assembly.

28. If there is a suspected leak in the cooling system, allow the system to stabilize under vacuum and monitor for vacuum loss.

29. If vacuum loss is observed, refer to Loss of Coolant.

30. Open the valve on the vacuum gage assembly. The vacuum gage will drop as coolant is drawn into the system.

31. Once the vacuum gage reaches zero, close the valve on the vacuum gage assembly and repeat steps 11-17.

32. Remove the J-42401-3 from the surge tank fill neck.

33. Remove J-42401-2 from the surge tank fill neck.

34. Detach the Vac N Fill cap from the vehicles coolant fill port.

35. Add coolant to the system as necessary.

36. Inspect the concentration of the coolant mixture using J 26568.

➡ **After filling the cooling system, the extraction hose can be used to remove excess coolant to achieve the proper coolant level.**

37. Detach the vacuum hose from the vacuum gage assembly.

38. Attach the extraction hose to the vacuum hose.

39. Open the valve on the venturi assembly to start a vacuum draw.

40. Use the extraction hose to draw out coolant to the proper level.

41. Install the surge tank cap.

42. The vacuum tank has a drain valve on the bottom of the tank. Open the valve to drain coolant from the vacuum tank into a suitable container for disposal.

Static Fill
See Figure 31.

Draining Procedure

❊❊ WARNING

With a pressurized cooling system, the coolant temperature in the radiator can be considerably higher than the boiling point of the solution at atmospheric pressure. Removal of the surge tank cap, while the cooling system is hot and under high pressure, causes the solution to boil instantaneously with explosive force. This will cause the solution to spew out over the engine, the fenders, and the person removing the cap. Serious bodily injury may result.

1. Unscrew the surge tank cap to remove vacuum when draining coolant.

2. Raise the vehicle.

3. Place a container under the radiator drain.

4. Unscrew the radiator drain plug until coolant flows out the radiator drain.

5. If a complete block drain is required, remove the coolant drain plugs.

6. Follow the appropriate procedure based on the condition of the coolant:

    a. Normal in appearance—Follow the filling procedure.

    b. Discolored—Follow the flush procedure. Refer to Flushing.

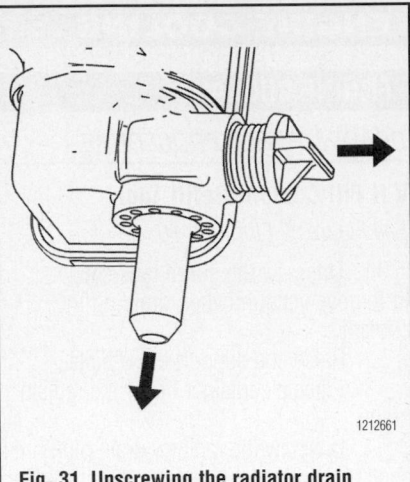

Fig. 31 Unscrewing the radiator drain plug

Fill Procedure

❊❊ CAUTION

The procedure below must be followed. Improper coolant level could result in a low or high coolant level condition, causing engine damage.

7. Install the engine block coolant drain plugs.

8. Close the radiator drain plug.

9. Lower the vehicle.

10. Vehicle should be level.

11. Add a mixture of 50/50 DEX-COOL® antifreeze and clean drinkable water until the level stabilizes approximately 1" (25.4 mm) above the weld seam on the surge tank.

12. Install the surge tank cap.

➡ **DO NOT exceed 2,200 RPM.**

13. Start the engine and run at 2,000 RPM until the engine cooling fans turn ON.

14. Turn the engine OFF and allow the engine to cool down.

15. Remove the surge tank cap.

16. Refill to approximately 1" (25.4 mm) above the weld seam on the surge tank.

17. Install the surge tank cap.

18. Inspect the concentration of the engine coolant using the coolant and battery fluid tester.

19. Inspect the concentration of the engine coolant using the coolant and battery fluid tester.

20. Install the surge tank cap.

21. Rinse away any excess coolant from the engine and the engine compartment.

FLUSHING

➡ **Do not use a chemical flush.**

Store used coolant in the proper manner, such as in a used engine coolant holding tank. Do not pour used coolant down a drain. Ethylene glycol antifreeze is a very toxic chemical. Do not dispose of coolant into the sewer system or ground water. This is illegal and ecologically unsound. Various methods and equipment can be used to flush the cooling system. If special equipment is used, such as a back flusher, follow the manufactures instruction. However, always remove the thermostat before back flushing the system.

1. Apply the park brake.
2. Drain the coolant.
3. Fill the coolant system with clean drinkable water.
4. Start the engine and run at 2,000 RPM until the thermostat opens.
5. Turn OFF the engine.
6. Drain the coolant system.
7. Repeat the above procedure until the water from the coolant system is colorless.
8. Drain the coolant system.
9. Add 1 gallon (3.8 liters) of concentrated antifreeze since there will be some water in the system.
10. Add a mixture of 50/50 DEX-COOL® antifreeze and clean drinkable water until the level stabilizes at the weld seam on the surge tank.

ENGINE FAN

REMOVAL & INSTALLATION

See Figures 32 through 37.

1. Drain the cooling system.
2. Remove the air cleaner air duct.
3. Remove the upper radiator air deflector.
4. Remove the transmission oil cooler pipes from the radiator.
5. Loop a rope around each of the upper 2 tabs of the condenser and tie a rope around the upper tie bar.

6. Remove the upper radiator support bracket bolts.
7. Remove the upper radiator support brackets.
8. Pry upward on the fan shroud tabs at the radiator clips to release the fan shroud from the radiator.
9. Remove the lower radiator air deflector.
10. Lower the vehicle.
11. Remove the radiator inlet hose from the radiator.
12. Remove the radiator outlet hose from the radiator.
13. Disconnect the cooling fan wire harness connectors.
14. Remove the A/C compressor and condenser hose assembly.
15. Raise the vehicle.
16. Remove the lower radiator support bracket bolts.
17. Remove the lower radiator support brackets.

18. Remove the transmission oil cooler pipe clip from the fan shroud.
19. Remove the fan shroud assembly.

To install:
20. Install the fan shroud assembly.
21. Install the transmission oil cooler pipes to the radiator.
22. Install the transmission oil cooler pipe clip to the fan shroud.
23. Install the lower radiator support brackets.
24. Install the lower radiator support bracket bolts and tighten to 44 ft. lbs. (60 Nm).
25. Install the cooling fan wire harness connectors.
26. Install the radiator outlet hose to the radiator.
27. Install the lower radiator air deflector.
28. Lower the vehicle.
29. Snap fan shroud tabs into the radiator clips.
30. Remove the rope attached to the condenser and upper tie bar.
31. Install the upper radiator support brackets.

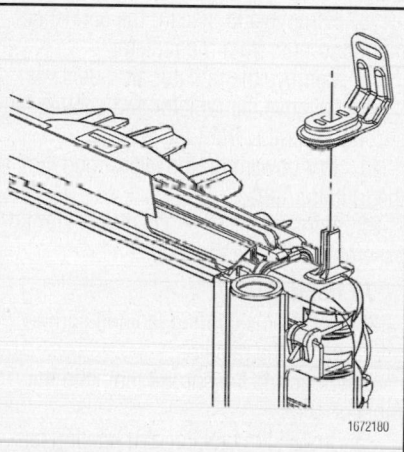

Fig. 33 Removing the upper radiator support brackets

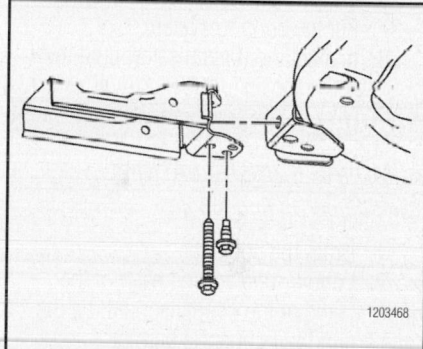

Fig. 35 Removing the lower radiator support brackets

Fig. 32 Removing the upper radiator support bracket bolts

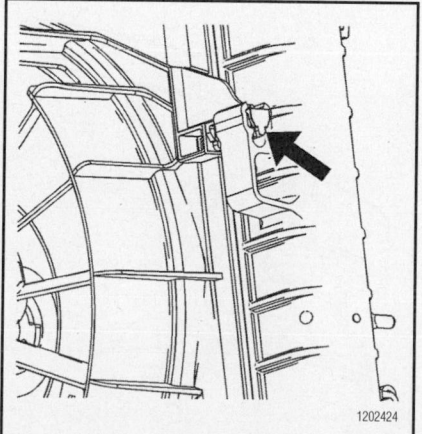

Fig. 34 Releasing the fan shroud from the radiator

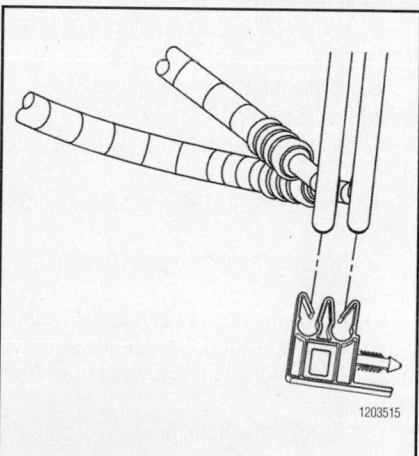

Fig. 36 Removing the transmission oil cooler pipe clip from the fan shroud

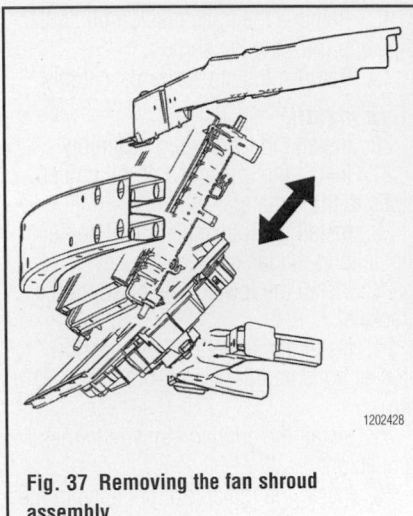

Fig. 37 Removing the fan shroud assembly

32. Install the upper radiator support bracket bolts and tighten to 89 inch lbs. (10 Nm).

33. Install the radiator inlet hose to the radiator.

34. Install the A/C compressor and condenser hose assembly.

35. Install the upper radiator air deflector.

36. Install the air cleaner air duct.

37. Fill the cooling system.

38. Inspect the transmission fluid level.

RADIATOR

REMOVAL & INSTALLATION

See Figures 38 through 40.

1. Drain the coolant.

2. Loop a rope around each of the upper 2 tabs of the condenser and tie the rope around the upper tie bar.

3. Remove the upper radiator support brackets.

4. Reposition the radiator inlet hose clamp at the radiator using the pliers.

5. Remove the radiator inlet hose from the radiator.

6. Remove the right engine splash shield retainers.

7. Remove the right engine splash shield.

8. Remove the left engine splash shield retainers.

9. Remove the left engine splash shield.

10. Reposition the radiator outlet hose clamp at the radiator using the pliers.

11. Remove the radiator outlet hose from the radiator.

12. Remove the transmission oil cooler pipes from the radiator.

13. Remove the lower radiator support bracket bolts.

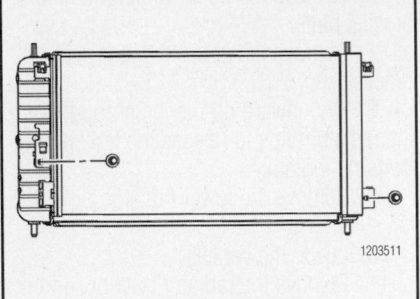

Fig. 38 Removing the condenser mounting bolts from the radiator

14. Remove the lower radiator support brackets.

15. Remove the radiator lower mounts.

16. Remove and discard the condenser mounting bolts from the radiator.

17. Push upward on the radiator and downward on the condenser to unsnap the condenser mounting tabs from the radiator clips.

18. Remove and discard the condenser mounting nuts from the radiator.

19. Remove the radiator air side seals.

20. Remove the radiator and cooling fan shroud assembly from the vehicle.

21. Pry upward on the fan shroud tabs at the radiator clips.

22. Remove the cooling fan and shroud assembly from the radiator.

To install:

23. Install the cooling fan and shroud assembly to the radiator.

24. Snap the fan shroud tabs into the radiator clips.

25. Install the radiator and cooling fan shroud assembly to the vehicle.

26. Install the radiator air side seals onto the condenser mounting tabs on the radiator.

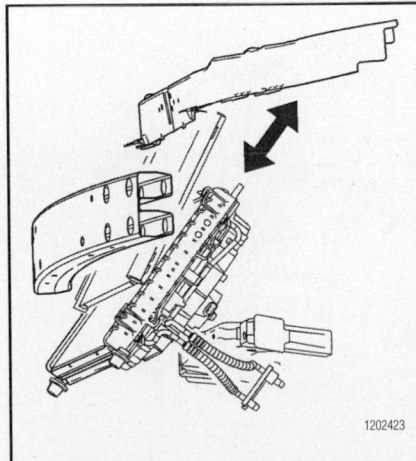

Fig. 39 Removing the radiator and cooling fan shroud assembly

✷✷ CAUTION

The bolt retaining the condenser to the radiator end tank is a special length and should be the ONLY bolt used upon reinstallation. The use of a longer bolt will damage the radiator end tank.

➡ Replace the condenser mounting bolts and nuts.

27. Install the condenser mounting nuts to the radiator.

28. Insert the condenser mounting tabs into the radiator clips.

29. Install the condenser to the radiator bolts and tighten to 53 inch lbs. (6 Nm).

30. Bend the radiator air side seals and insert the seals into the channel of the intake air splash shields.

31. The radiator air side seals must be in the proper position for proper air flow.

➡ Replace the radiator lower mounts as a pair or vibration may result.

32. Install the radiator lower mounts.

33. Install the lower radiator support brackets.

34. Install the lower radiator support bracket bolts and tighten to 44 ft. lbs. (60 Nm).

35. Install the transmission oil cooler pipes to the radiator.

36. Install the radiator outlet hose to the radiator.

37. Reposition the radiator outlet hose clamp at the radiator using the pliers.

➡ Engine splash shields must be properly installed or reduced A/C and engine cooling system performance could occur.

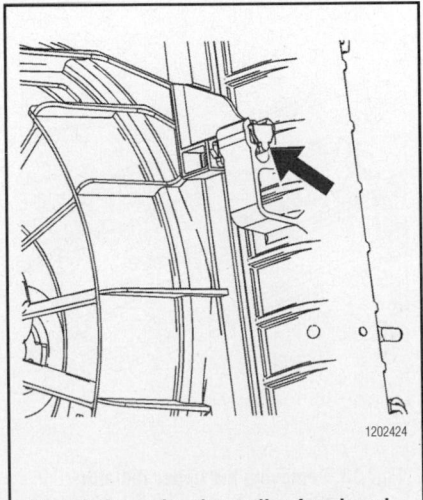

Fig. 40 Removing the cooling fan shroud

38. Install the left engine splash shield.
39. Install the left engine splash shield retainers.
40. Install the right engine splash shield.
41. Install the right engine splash shield retainers.
42. Lower the vehicle.
43. Install the radiator inlet hose to the radiator.
44. Reposition the radiator inlet hose clamp at the radiator using the pliers.
45. Remove the rope attached to the condenser and upper tie bar.
46. Install the upper radiator support brackets.
47. Fill the coolant.
48. Inspect the transmission fluid level.

THERMOSTAT

REMOVAL & INSTALLATION

2.4L Engine

See Figure 41.

1. Drain the cooling system.
2. Reposition the radiator outlet hose clamp at the thermostat cover.
3. Remove the radiator outlet hose from the thermostat cover.
4. Remove the thermostat cover bolts and cover.
5. Remove the thermostat.
6. Remove and discard the thermostat cover O-ring seal.

To install:

7. Install a NEW thermostat cover O-ring seal.
8. Install the thermostat.
9. Install the thermostat cover bolts and tighten to 89 inch lbs. (10 Nm).
10. Install the radiator outlet hose to the thermostat cover.

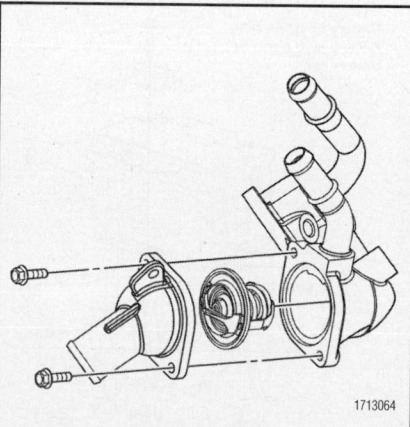

Fig. 41 Removing and installing the thermostat

11. Position the radiator outlet hose clamp at the thermostat cover.
12. Fill the cooling system.

3.6L Engine

See Figure 42.

1. Partially drain the cooling system.
2. Remove the radiator outlet hose from the thermostat housing.
3. Remove the heater inlet and outlet hoses.
4. Remove the surge tank outlet hose.
5. Remove the thermostat housing bolts.
6. Remove the housing.
7. Remove the thermostat and discard the thermostat gasket.

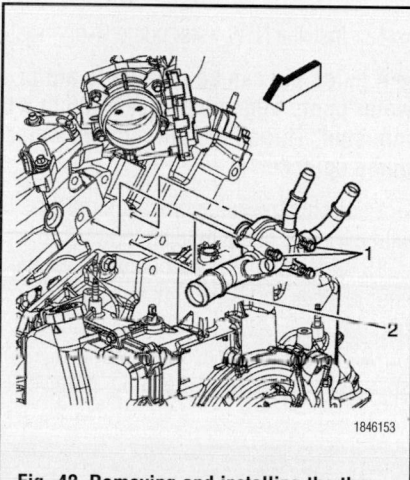

Fig. 42 Removing and installing the thermostat bolts (1) and thermostat (2)

To install:

8. Install the thermostat with a NEW thermostat gasket.
9. Install the thermostat housing bolts and tighten to 89 inch lbs. (10 Nm).
10. Install the surge tank outlet hose.
11. Install the heater inlet and outlet hoses.
12. Install the radiator outlet hose to the thermostat housing.
13. Fill the cooling system.

WATER PUMP

REMOVAL & INSTALLATION

2.4L Engine

See Figures 43 through 46.

1. Remove the thermostat housing.
2. Remove the engine splash shield.
3. Remove the water pump access plate from the front cover.

➡A drain plug has been provided at the bottom of the water pump assembly

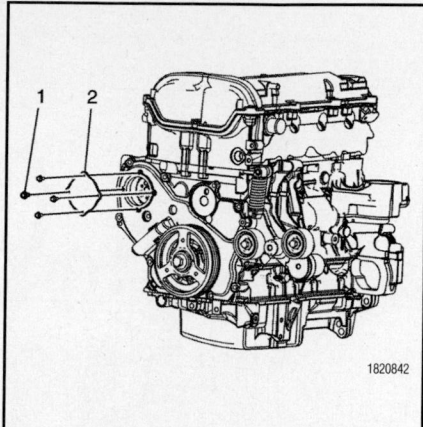

Fig. 43 Removing the water pump access plate from the front cover

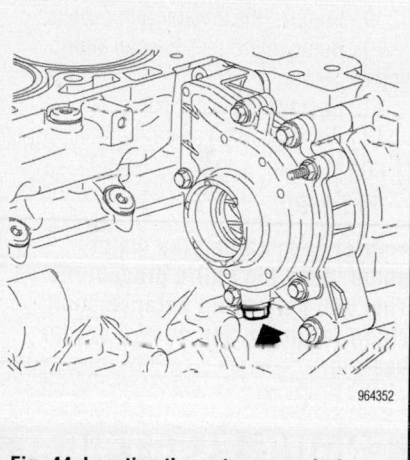

Fig. 44 Locating the water pump drain plug

for additional coolant drainage from the engine block and water pump.

4. Drain the coolant from the water pump using the plug at the bottom of the pump.

➡The water pump holding tool supports the sprocket and chain during water pump service. The tool must be used or the balance shaft must be re-timed.

5. Install the water pump holding tool into position.
6. Tighten the bolts on the water pump holding tool into the threads on the water pump sprocket.
7. Install the access cover bolts that were removed earlier to secure the water pump holding tool to the front cover assembly.
8. Remove the 3 inner water pump sprocket to water pump bolts.

➡Be sure to remove both water pump bolts from the front of the engine block.

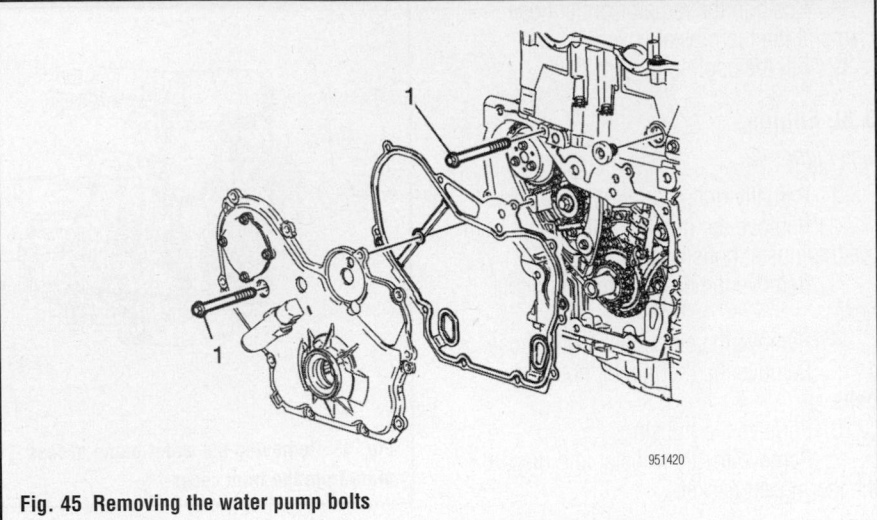

Fig. 45 Removing the water pump bolts

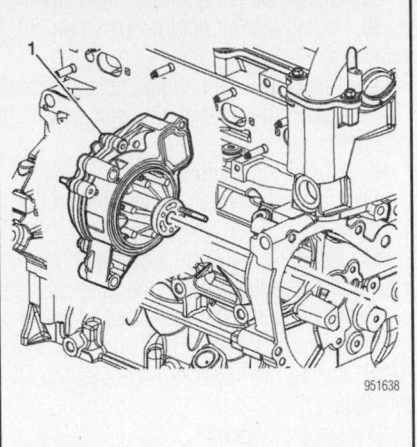

Fig. 46 Removing and installing the water pump

9. Remove the 2 water pump bolts.
10. Remove the rear 2 water pump bolts.
11. Remove the water pump.
12. Remove and discard the water pump O-ring seal.

To install:

➡**Prior to installing the water pump, read the entire procedure. This will help avoid balance shaft chain re-timing and ensure proper sealing.**

13. Install a NEW water pump O-ring seal.

➡**A guide pin can be created to aid in water pump alignment. Use a M6 m x 6 mm stud. Thread the pin into the water pump sprocket.**

14. Using the guide pin, align the pin with the water pump holding tool.
15. Position the water pump against the engine block and hand tighten the water pump bolts.
16. Install the inner water pump sprocket bolts. After 2 are snug, remove

the guide pin and install the 3rd bolt. Tighten the water pump bolts to 18 ft. lbs. (25 Nm).
17. Tighten the water pump sprocket bolts last to 89 inch lbs. (10 Nm).
18. Remove the water pump holding tool.
19. Install the water pump access plate and bolts. Tighten the bolts to 89 inch lbs. (10 Nm).
20. Install the engine splash shield.
21. Install the thermostat housing.

ENGINE ELECTRICAL

BATTERY

REMOVAL & INSTALLATION

2.4L Engine

✳✳ WARNING

Do not tip the battery over a 45 degree angle or acid could spill causing serious personal injury.

1. Disconnect the negative battery cable.
   a. Turn on the radio and record all of the radio station presets.
   b. Ensure that all lamps and accessories are turned off.
   c. Turn the ignition OFF and remove the ignition key.
   d. Open the hood.
   e. Remove the generator battery control module cover.
   f. Loosen the negative battery cable nut.
   g. Remove the negative battery cable from the battery.
   h. Disengage the two side retaining

tabs on the positive battery cable cover, and open the cover.
   i. Loosen the positive battery cable nut.
   j. Remove the positive battery cable from the battery.
   k. Reposition the positive battery cable out of the way.
2. Remove the battery hold down retainer bolt and retainer.
3. Remove the battery from the vehicle.

To install:

✳✳ WARNING

Do not tip the battery over a 45 degree angle or acid could spill causing serious personal injury.

4. Install the battery to the vehicle.
5. Install the battery hold down retainer and bolt. Tighten the bolt to 11 ft. lbs. (15 Nm).
6. Position the positive battery cable to the battery.
7. Install the positive battery cable to the battery.
8. Tighten the positive battery cable nut to 89 inch lbs. (10 Nm).

BATTERY SYSTEM

9. Close the positive battery cable cover.
10. Connect the negative battery cable.

3.6L Engine

See Figure 48.

1. Remove the battery box cover.

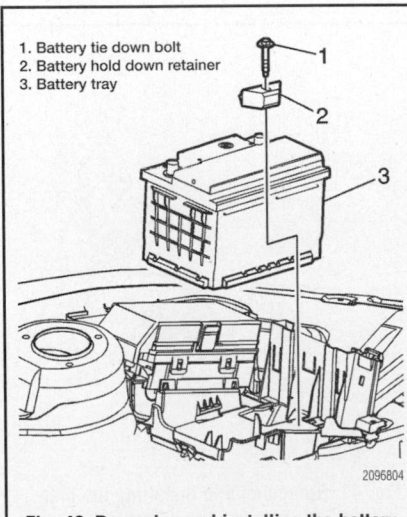

1. Battery tie down bolt
2. Battery hold down retainer
3. Battery tray

Fig. 48 Removing and installing the battery

2. Disconnect the negative battery cable.

 a. Record all of the vehicle preset radio stations.

 b. Turn OFF all the lamps and the accessories.

 c. Make sure the ignition switch is in the OFF position.

3. Disconnect the positive battery cable.

4. Remove the battery tie down bolt.

5. Remove the battery hold down retainer.

6. Remove the battery from the battery tray.

To install:

7. Position the battery in the battery tray.

8. Install the battery hold down retainer.

9. Install the battery hold down retainer bolt and tighten to 11 ft. lbs. (15 Nm).

10. Install the positive battery cable and tighten to 89 inch lbs. (10 Nm).

11. Install the negative battery cable and tighten the bolt to 89 inch lbs. (10 Nm).

12. Install the battery box cover.

BATTERY RECONNECT/RELEARN PROCEDURE

Power Window Reinitialization

1. Close the door for the window being reinitialized.

2. Turn ON the ignition, with the engine OFF.

3. Hold the window switch up for two seconds after the window is closed, release the switch, then hold the switch up again for two seconds.

4. Lower the window all the way down and hold the switch down for two seconds.

ENGINE ELECTRICAL

CHARGING SYSTEM

ALTERNATOR

REMOVAL & INSTALLATION

2.4L Engine

See Figures 49 and 50.

1. Disconnect negative battery cable.
2. Remove the drive belt.
3. Disconnect the generator electrical connector.
4. Reposition the rubber boot.
5. Remove the engine harness terminal lead to generator nut.
6. Remove the engine harness terminal from the generator stud.
7. Remove the generator fasteners (1,3 and 4).
8. Remove the generator.

To install:

9. Position the generator to the engine block.

10. Install the generator fasteners loosely.

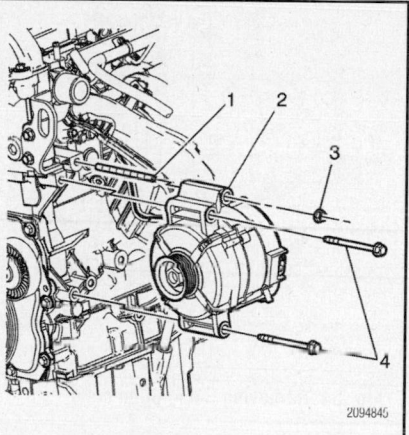

Fig. 50 Removing the generator fasteners (1, 3 and 4) and generator

11. Install the fastener (1) and tighten to 89 inch lbs. (10 Nm).

12. Install the fastener (3) and tighten to 16 ft. lbs. (22 Nm).

13. Tighten the fasteners (4) to 16 ft. lbs. (22 Nm).

14. Install the engine harness terminal to the generator stud.

15. Install the engine harness terminal lead to generator nut and tighten to 15 ft. lbs. (20 Nm).

16. Position the rubber boot over the stud.

17. Connect the generator electrical connector.

18. Install the drive belt.

19. Connect negative battery cable.

3.6L Engine

See Figures 51 and 52.

1. Disconnect the negative battery cable.

2. Remove air cleaner outlet duct.

3. Reposition the positive battery cable boot at the generator terminal.

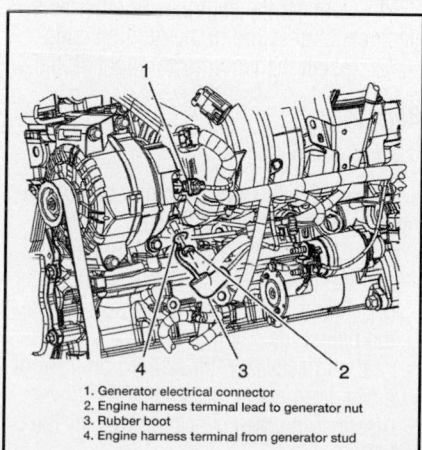

1. Generator electrical connector
2. Engine harness terminal lead to generator nut
3. Rubber boot
4. Engine harness terminal from generator stud

Fig. 49 Disconnecting the generator

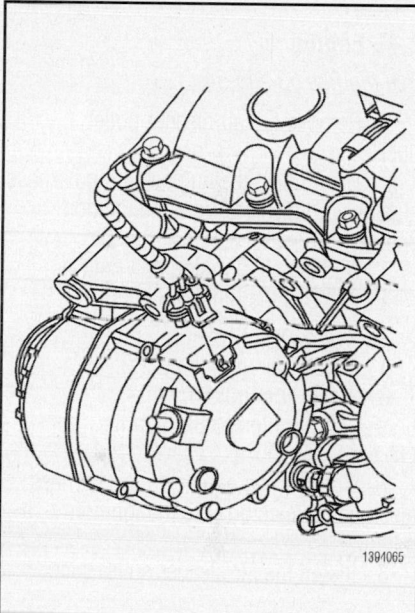

Fig. 51 Disconnecting the engine harness electrical connector from the generator

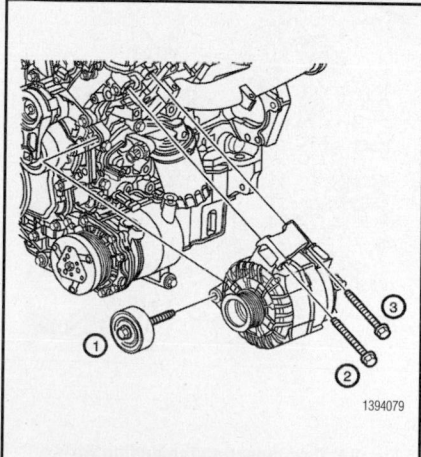

Fig. 52 Generator bolt removal and installation sequence

4. Remove the positive battery cable nut at the generator.

5. Remove the positive battery cable terminal from the generator.

6. Disconnect the engine harness electrical connector from the generator.

7. Remove the drive belt.

8. Remove the idler pulley.

9. Remove the generator bolts.

➡ **When removing the generator from the vehicle, it may be necessary to** maneuver the generator to remove it from the vehicle.

10. Remove the generator.

To install:

11. Position the generator to the engine.

12. Loosely install the generator bolts.

13. Install the idler pulley.

14. Tighten the generator bolts in the sequence shown to 37 ft. lbs. (50 Nm).

15. Install the drive belt.

16. Connect the engine harness electrical connector to the generator.

17. Install the positive battery cable terminal to the generator.

18. Install the positive battery cable nut at the generator and tighten to 15 ft. lbs. (20 Nm).

19. Position the positive battery cable boot at the generator terminal.

20. Connect the negative battery cable.

ENGINE ELECTRICAL   IGNITION SYSTEM

IGNITION COIL

REMOVAL & INSTALLATION

2.4L Engine

See Figures 53 and 54.

1. Remove the air cleaner outlet duct.

2. Disconnect the engine wiring harness electrical connectors from the ignition coil(s).

3. Remove the ignition coil bolt(s).

4. Remove the ignition coil(s).

To install:

5. Install the ignition coil(s).

6. Install the ignition coil bolt(s) and tighten to 89 inch lbs. (10 Nm).

7. Connect the engine wiring harness electrical connector(s) to the ignition coil(s).

8. Install the air cleaner outlet duct.

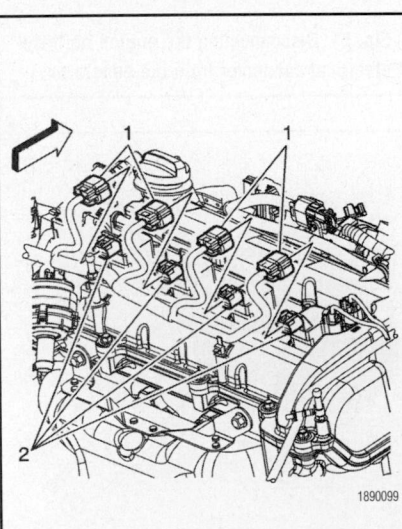

Fig. 53 Disconnecting the engine wiring harness electrical connectors (1) from the ignition coils (2)

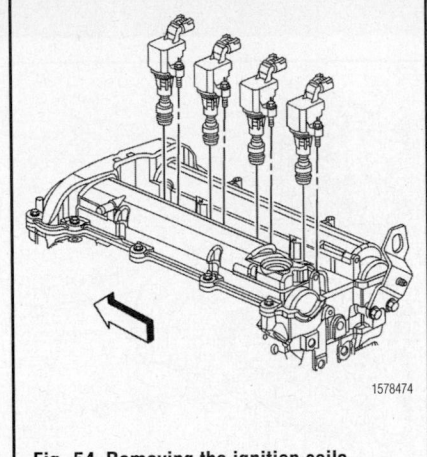

Fig. 54 Removing the ignition coils

3.6L Engine

Bank 1

See Figure 55.

1. Remove the fuel injector sight shield.

   a. Remove the oil fill cap.

   b. Grasp the cover by the upper left and the lower right corners and lift up,

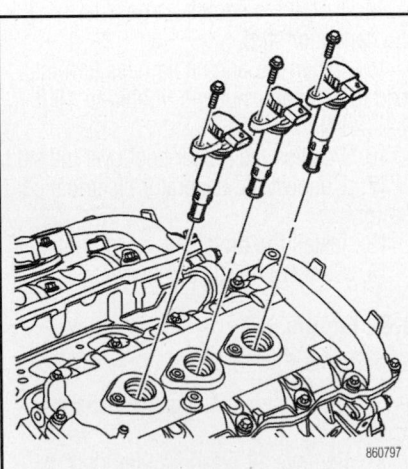

Fig. 55 Removing the ignition coils

disengaging the cover grommets from the ball studs.

   c. If necessary, lift upward on front of cover, then reach under center of cover disengaging the cover grommet for the ball stud.

2. Disconnect the engine wiring harness electrical connectors from the ignition coils.

3. If removing the number 5 cylinder ignition coil, remove the evaporative emission (EVAP) canister purge tube.

4. If removing the number one ignition coil, remove the canister purge solenoid.

5. Remove the ignition coil bolts.

6. Remove the ignition coils.

To install:

7. Install the ignition coils.

8. Install the ignition coil bolts and tighten to 89 inch lbs. (10 Nm).

9. If the number 5 cylinder ignition coil was removed, install the EVAP canister purge tube.

10. If the number one ignition coil was removed, install the canister purge solenoid.

11. Connect the engine wiring harness electrical connectors to the ignition coils.

12. Install the fuel injector sight shield.

Bank 2

See Figure 56.

1. Remove the fuel injector sight shield.

   a. Remove the oil fill cap.

   b. Grasp the cover by the upper left and the lower right corners and lift up, disengaging the cover grommets from the ball studs.

   c. If necessary, lift upward on front of cover, then reach under center of cover disengaging the cover grommet for the ball stud.

2. Disconnect the engine wiring harness electrical connector(s) from the ignition coils.

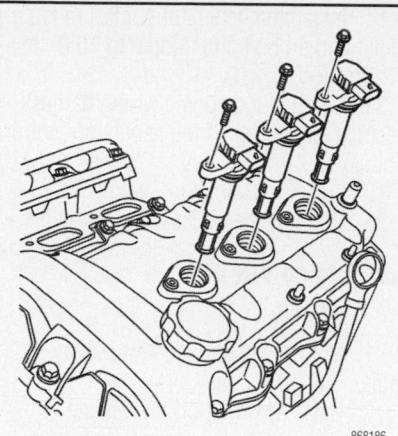

Fig. 56 Removing and installing the ignition coils

3. Remove the ignition coil bolts.
4. Remove the ignition coils.

To install:

5. Install the ignition coils.
6. Install the ignition coil bolts and tighten to 89 inch lbs. (10 Nm).
7. Connect the engine wiring harness electrical connectors to the ignition coils.
8. Install the fuel injector sight shield.

SPARK PLUGS

REMOVAL & INSTALLATION

2.4L Engine

⁜ CAUTION

This engine has aluminum cylinder heads. Do not remove the spark plugs from a hot engine, allow it to cool first. Removing the spark plugs from a hot engine may cause spark plug thread damage or cylinder head damage.

1. Remove the ignition coil(s).

➡Make sure that any water and/or debris is blown out of the spark plug holes prior to removing the spark plugs.

2. Remove the spark plugs using a ⅝ inch spark plug socket.

To install:

⁜ CAUTION

Do not coat spark plug threads with anti-seize compound. If anti-seize compound is used and spark plugs are over-torqued, damage to the cylinder head threads may result.

3. Install the spark plugs and tighten the plugs to 15 ft. lbs. (20 Nm).

➡The spark plug gap is 0.040 inch (1.0 mm).

4. Install the ignition coil(s).

3.6L Engine

1. Remove the ignition coil(s).

➡Clean the spark plug recess area before removing the spark plug. Failure to do so could result in engine damage because of dirt or foreign material entering the cylinder head, or by the contamination of the cylinder head threads. The contaminated threads may prevent the proper sealing of the new plug. Use a thread chaser to clean the threads of any contamination.

2. Use compressed air in order to remove debris from the spark plug cavity.

➡Allow the engine to cool before removing the spark plugs. Attempting to remove the spark plugs from a hot engine may cause the plug threads to seize, causing damage to cylinder head threads.

3. Remove the spark plug.

To install:

➡Use only the spark plugs specified for use in the vehicle. Do not install spark plugs that are either hotter or colder than those specified for the vehicle. Installing spark plugs of another type can severely damage the engine.

➡Check the gap of all new and reconditioned spark plugs before installation. The pre-set gaps may have changed during handling. Use a round feeler gage to ensure an accurate check. Installing the spark plugs with the wrong gap can cause poor engine performance and may even damage the engine.

4. Ensure that the spark plug gap is equivalent to the spark plug gap specification.

➡Be sure that the spark plug threads smoothly into the cylinder head and the spark plug is fully seated. Use a thread chaser, if necessary, to clean threads in the cylinder head. Cross-threading or failing to fully seat the spark plug can cause overheating of the plug, exhaust blow-by, or thread damage.

5. Install the spark plug. Tighten the spark plug to 15 ft. lbs. (20 Nm).
6. Install the ignition coil(s).

ENGINE ELECTRICAL

STARTER

REMOVAL & INSTALLATION

2.4L Engine VIN 5

See Figures 57 through 62.

1. Disconnect the negative battery cable.
2. Raise and support the vehicle.
3. Disconnect the engine wiring harness electrical connector from the generator control module coolant pump.
4. Remove the generator control module coolant pump bolt.

5. Remove the generator control module coolant pump, with the hoses attached, from the oil pan.
6. Reposition and secure the generator control module coolant pump, with the hoses attached, out of the way.
7. Disconnect the engine wiring harness electrical connector from the starter.
8. Remove the positive battery cable to starter motor nut.
9. Remove the positive battery cable lead from the starter motor.
10. Remove the starter motor bolts and starter.

STARTING SYSTEM

To install:

11. Install the starter motor and bolts and tighten to 39 ft. lbs. (53 Nm).
12. Install the positive battery cable lead to the starter motor.
13. Install the positive battery cable to starter motor nut and tighten to 89 inch lbs. (10 Nm).
14. Connect the engine wiring harness electrical connector to the starter.
15. Unsecure the generator control module coolant pump.
16. Position the generator control module coolant pump, with the hoses attached, to the oil pan. Ensure that the anti-rotation tab is inserted into the hole in the oil pan.

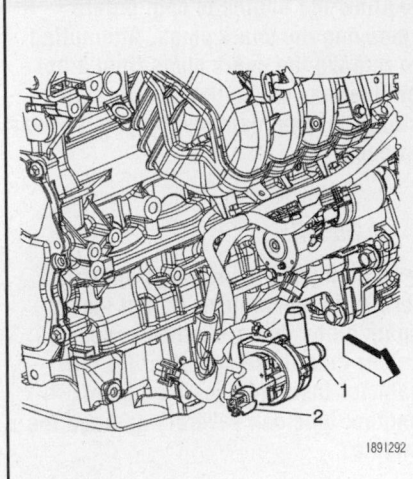

Fig. 57 Disconnecting the wiring harness electrical connector (2) from the generator control module coolant pump (1)

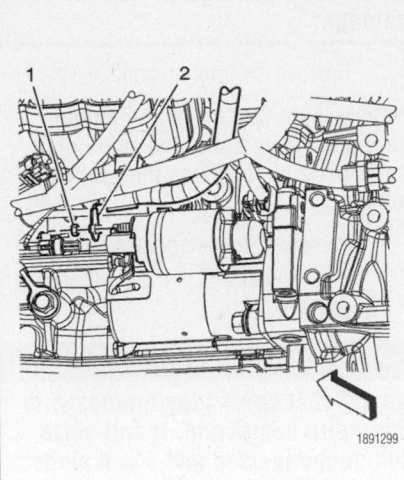

Fig. 60 Removing the positive battery cable from the starter motor

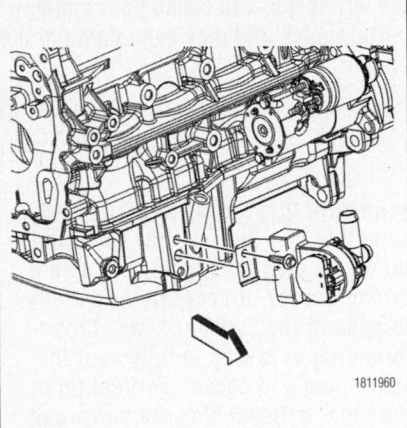

Fig. 58 Removing the generator control module coolant pump

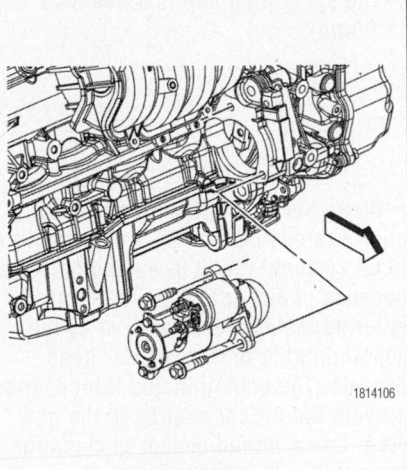

Fig. 61 Removing the starter

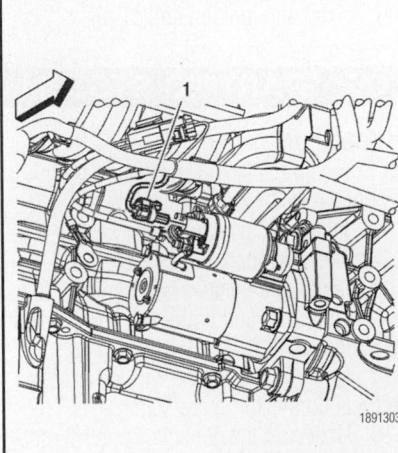

Fig. 59 Disconnecting the engine wiring harness electrical connector from the starter

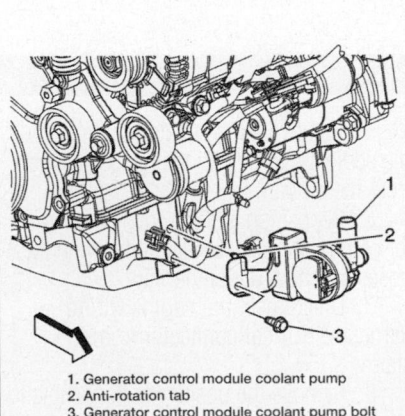

1. Generator control module coolant pump
2. Anti-rotation tab
3. Generator control module coolant pump bolt

Fig. 62 Installing the generator control module coolant pump

17. Install the generator control module coolant pump bolt and tighten to 16 ft. lbs. (22 Nm).

18. Connect the engine wiring harness electrical connector to the generator control module coolant pump.

19. Lower the vehicle.

20. Connect the negative battery cable.

2.4L Engine VIN B

See Figure 63.

1. Disconnect the negative battery cable.

2. Raise and support the vehicle.

3. Remove the S terminal connector from the starter solenoid.

4. Remove the engine harness lead from the starter.

5. Remove the positive battery cable nut from the starter solenoid.

6. Remove the positive battery cable and engine harness terminal from the starter solenoid.

7. Remove the starter motor bolts.

8. Remove the starter motor.

To install:

9. Install the starter motor.

10. Install the starter motor bolts and tighten to 30 ft. lbs. (40 Nm).

11. Install the engine harness terminal and positive battery cable to the starter solenoid.

12. Install the positive battery cable nut to the starter solenoid and tighten to 89 inch lbs. (10 Nm).

13. Install the engine harness lead to the starter.

14. Install the S terminal connector to the starter solenoid.

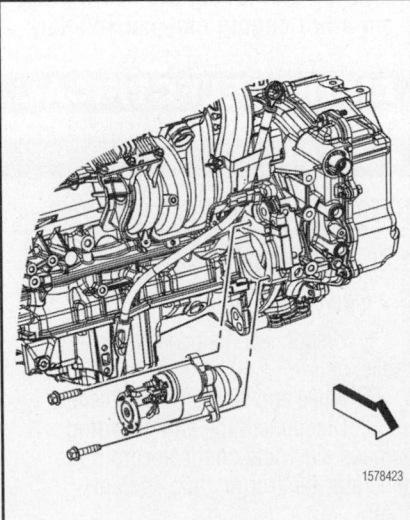

Fig. 63 Removing the starter motor

15. Lower the vehicle.

16. Connect the negative battery cable

3.6L Engine

See Figures 64 and 65.

1. Disconnect the negative battery cable.

2. Raise and support the vehicle.

3. Remove the starter solenoid BAT terminal nut.

4. Disconnect the engine harness electrical connector.

5. Unclip battery positive cable from starter bracket.

6. Disconnect the starter motor bolts and the starter.

To install:

7. Position the starter motor to the engine block.

8. Install the starter bolts and tighten to 37 ft. lbs. (50 Nm).

9. Connect the electrical connector to the starter.

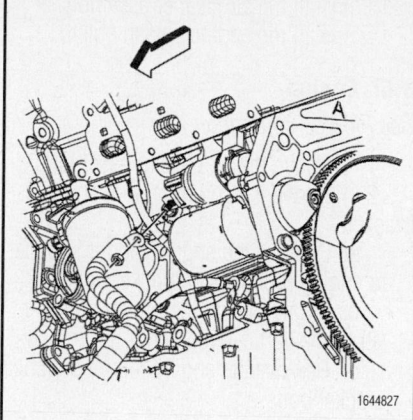

Fig. 64 Removing the starter solenoid BAT terminal nut

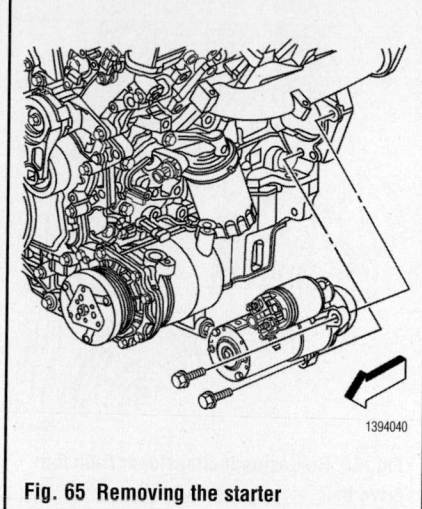

Fig. 65 Removing the starter

10. Install the starter solenoid BAT terminal nut and tighten to 9.5 ft. lbs. (13 Nm).

11. Install the knock sensor bank 2.

12. Install the left catalytic converter.

13. Lower the vehicle.

14. Connect the negative battery cable.

ENGINE MECHANICAL

➡Disconnecting the negative battery cable may interfere with the functions of the on board computer systems and may require the computer to undergo a relearning process, once the negative battery cable is reconnected.

ACCESSORY DRIVE BELTS

REMOVAL & INSTALLATION

2.4L Engine VIN 5

See Figures 66 and 67.

1. Remove the air cleaner assembly.

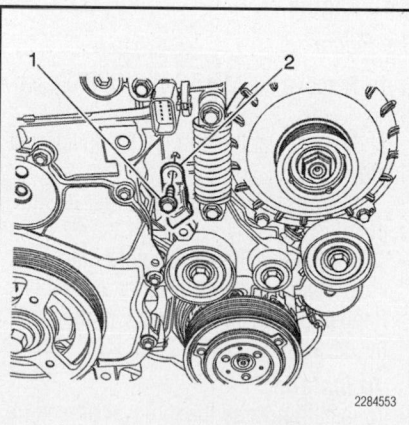

Fig. 66 Removing the tensioner stop fastener (1) and stop (2)

➡the tensioner stop is critical and must be removed prior to compressing the drive belt tensioner spring.

2. If equipped, remove the tensioner stop fastener and stop.

3. Install the Hydraulic Belt Tensioner Compressor to the drive belt tensioner spring.

4. Compress the drive belt tensioner spring fully using the Hydraulic Belt Tensioner Compressor.

5. Reposition the idler pulley to release tension off the drive belt.

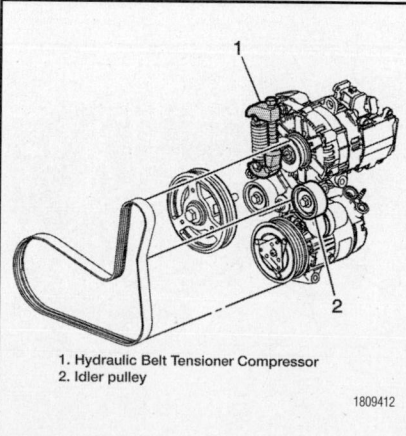

1. Hydraulic Belt Tensioner Compressor
2. Idler pulley

Fig. 67 Compressing the drive belt tensioner spring

6. Remove the drive belt from under the middle idler pulley.

7. Remove the drive belt from the vehicle.

To install:

8. Install and position the drive belt around all of the pulleys except for the middle idler pulley.

9. Install the drive belt under the middle idler pulley.

10. Reposition the idler pulley to install the drive belt.

11. Install the drive belt under the middle idler pulley.

12. Ensure the drive belt tensioner idler pulley is fully seated against the drive belt.

13. Loosen the forcing bolt on the Hydraulic Belt Tensioner Compressor and remove from the drive belt tensioner spring.

14. Ensure that the drive belt tensioner idler is fully seated against the drive belt.

15. If equipped, install the tension stop and fastener, then tighten to 89 inch lbs. (10 Nm).

16. Install the air cleaner assembly.

2.4L Engine VIN B

See Figures 68 and 69.

1. Remove the engine splash shield.

2. Remove the air cleaner assembly.

3. Install the Accessory Belt Tensioner Unloader to the drive belt tensioner.

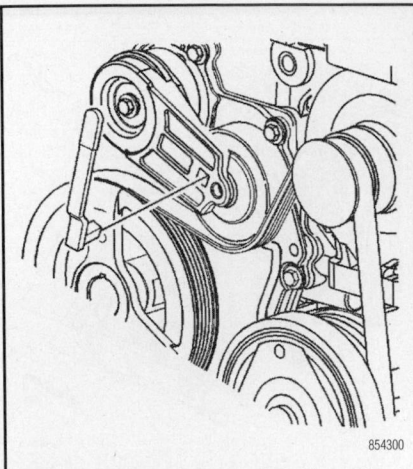

Fig. 68 Releasing the tensioner from the drive belt

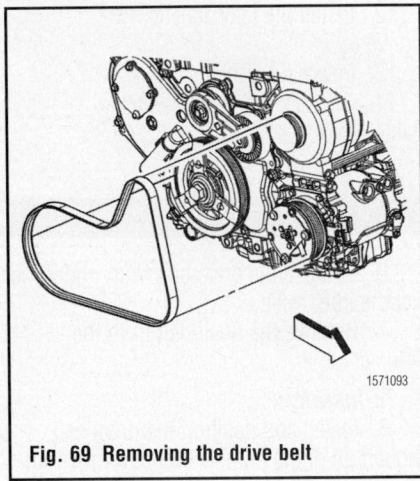

Fig. 69 Removing the drive belt

4. Using the Accessory Belt Tensioner Unloader, rotate the tensioner counterclockwise in order to release the tensioner from the drive belt.

5. Remove the drive belt.

6. Slowly rotate the Accessory Belt Tensioner Unloader and the tensioner clockwise in order to allow the tensioner to rest.

7. Remove the Accessory Belt Tensioner Unloader from the drive belt tensioner.

To install:

8. Install and position the drive belt around all of the pulleys except for the drive belt tensioner.

9. Install the Accessory Belt Tensioner Unloader to the drive belt tensioner.

10. Using the Accessory Belt Tensioner Unloader, rotate the tensioner counterclockwise.

11. Position the drive belt under the tensioner pulley.

12. Using the Accessory Belt Tensioner Unloader, rotate the tensioner clockwise in order to seat the tensioner pulley onto the drive belt.

13. Install the air cleaner assembly.

14. Install the engine splash shield.

3.6L Engine

See Figures 70 through 72.

1. Remove the air cleaner assembly.

2. Remove the engine mount snubber bracket.

　a. Remove the engine mount snubber to engine mount strut bracket bolts.

　b. Rotate the engine mount snubber (2) to the vertical position.

　c. Remove the engine mount snubber bracket bolts.

　d. Remove the engine mount snubber bracket.

3. Rotate the drive belt tensioner clockwise to release the drive belt tension.

4. Slide the drive belt off of the belt idler pulley.

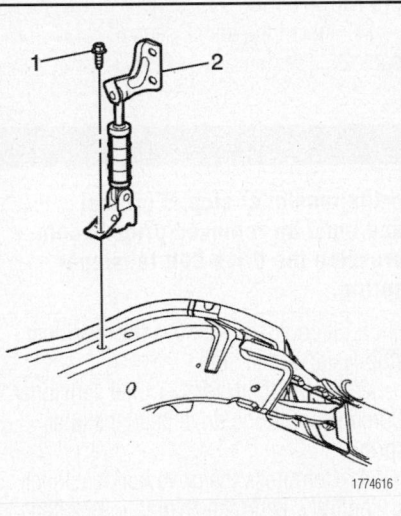

Fig. 70 Removing the engine mount snubber to engine mount strut bracket bolts (1) and rotating the snubber (2) to the vertical position

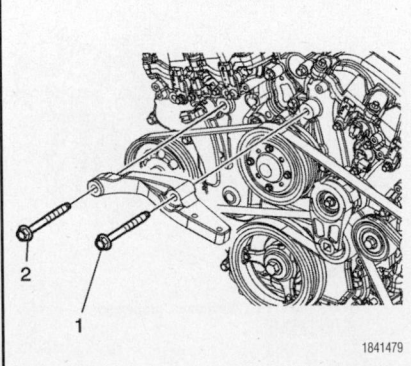

Fig. 71 Removing the engine mount snubber bracket bolts (1, 2)

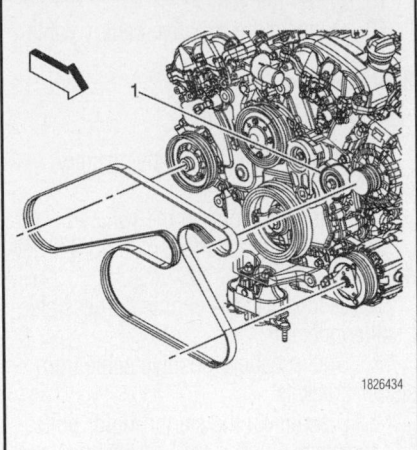

Fig. 72 Removing the drive belt off the belt idler pulley (1)

5. Slowly release the drive belt tensioner.

6. Remove the drive belt from the accessory drive pulleys.

To install:

7. Install the drive belt to the crankshaft pulley, the tensioner and the generator.

8. Rotate the drive belt tensioner clockwise.

9. Install the drive belt to the idler pulley.

➡**Ensure the drive belt is properly aligned and seated into the grooves of the accessory drive pulleys.**

10. Slowly release the drive belt tensioner.

11. Install the engine mount snubber.

12. Install the air cleaner assembly.

AIR CLEANER

REMOVAL & INSTALLATION

2.4L Engine

See Figure 73.

1. Remove the Mass Airflow (MAF) sensor.

2. Disconnect the air cleaner outlet duct clamp.

　a. Loosen the clamp in order to slide the duct off.

　b. Remove the air cleaner bolt.

　c. Remove the air cleaner assembly. Reposition the air conditioning pipe as necessary.

To install:

To install, reverse the removal procedure. Tighten the air cleaner bolt to 89 inch lbs. (10 Nm). Tighten the air cleaner outlet duct clamp to 35 inch lbs. (4 Nm).

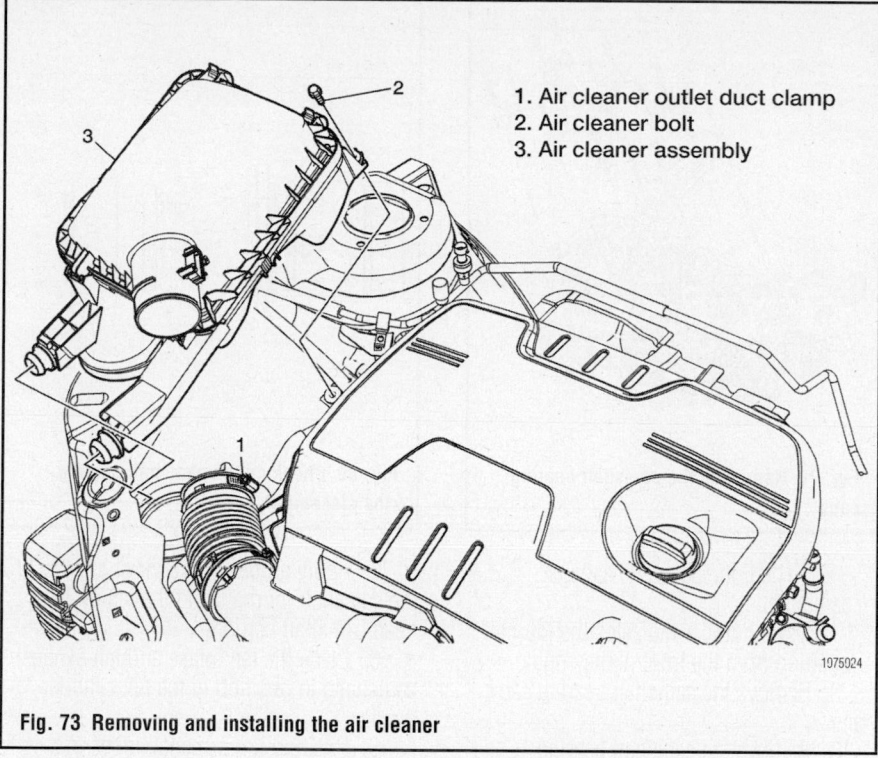

1. Air cleaner outlet duct clamp
2. Air cleaner bolt
3. Air cleaner assembly

Fig. 73 Removing and installing the air cleaner

3.6L Engine

See Figures 74 and 75.

1. Remove the air cleaner outlet duct.
2. Disconnect the engine wiring harness electrical connector from the mass airflow (MAF)/intake air temperature (IAT) sensor.
3. Remove the air cleaner housing rear bolt.
4. Reposition the air conditioning (A/C) condenser and evaporator tube clamp as required.

5. Remove the air cleaner assembly from the upper tie bar.

To Install:
6. Install the air cleaner assembly to the upper tie bar.
7. Position the A/C condenser and evaporator tube clamp as required.
8. Install the air cleaner housing rear bolt and tighten to 89 inch lbs. (10 Nm).
9. Connect the engine wiring harness electrical connector to the MAF/IAT sensor.
10. Install the air cleaner outlet duct.

FILTER/ELEMENT REPLACEMENT

2.4L Engine

See Figure 76.

1. Disconnect the engine wiring harness electrical connector (1) from the mass airflow (MAF)/intake air temperature (IAT) sensor.
2. Loosen the air cleaner outlet duct clamp at the air cleaner assembly.
3. Remove the air cleaner outlet duct from the air cleaner assembly.
4. Disengage the air cleaner cover latches.
5. Open the air cleaner cover.
6. Remove and discard the air filter assembly.

To install:
7. Install a NEW air filter assembly.
8. Close the air cleaner cover.
9. Engage the air cleaner cover latches.
10. Connect the engine wiring harness electrical connector to the MAF/IAT sensor.
11. Install the air cleaner outlet duct to the air cleaner assembly.
12. Tighten the air cleaner outlet duct clamp at the air cleaner assembly to 35 inch lbs. (4 Nm).

3.6L Engine

1. Disengage the air cleaner cover latches.
2. Open the air cleaner cover.
3. Remove and discard the air filter assembly.

To install:
4. Install a NEW air filter assembly.
5. Engage the air cleaner cover retainers to the lower air cleaner housing, and close the cover.

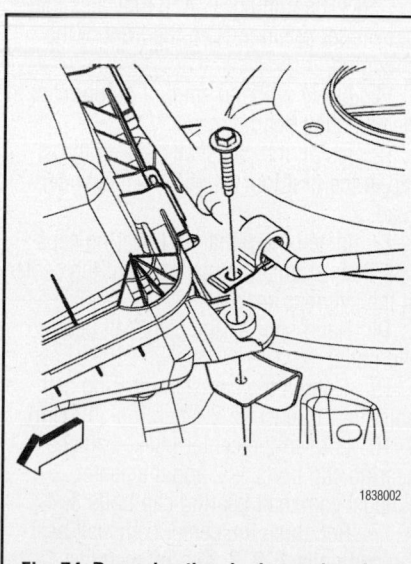

Fig. 74 Removing the air cleaner housing rear bolt

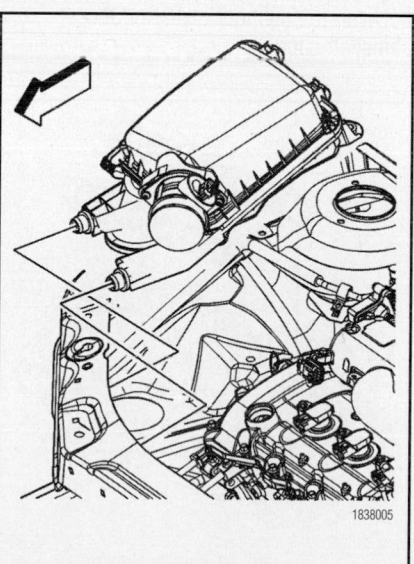

Fig. 75 Removing the air cleaner assembly

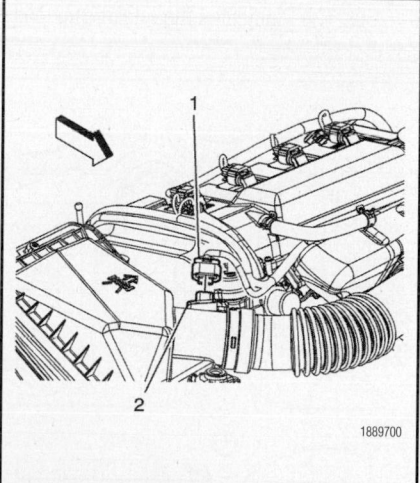

Fig. 76 Disconnecting the engine wiring harness electrical connector (1) from the MAF/IAT sensor

6. Engage the air cleaner cover latches.

7. Ensure that the air cleaner cover is secured to the lower air cleaner housing.

CAMSHAFT AND VALVE LIFTERS

INSPECTION

2.4L Engine

1. Inspect the camshaft journals and lobes for wear or scoring.

2. Inspect the camshaft sprocket alignment notch for damage.

3. Inspect the camshaft cover for damage or loose oil control baffles.

4. Clean the camshaft cover.

5. Wash the camshaft in solvent.

6. Oil the camshaft.

7. Inspect the camshaft cover for cracks or other signs of damage.

3.6L Engine

1. Clean the camshaft in solvent.

2. Dry the camshaft with compressed air.

REMOVAL & INSTALLATION

3.6L Engine

See Figures 77 through 80.

➡**Procedure is for the left side, right side similar.**

1. Observe the markings on the bearing caps. Each bearing cap is marked in order to identify its location. The markings have the following meanings:

a. The raised feature must always be oriented toward the center of the cylinder head.

b. The I indicates the intake camshaft.

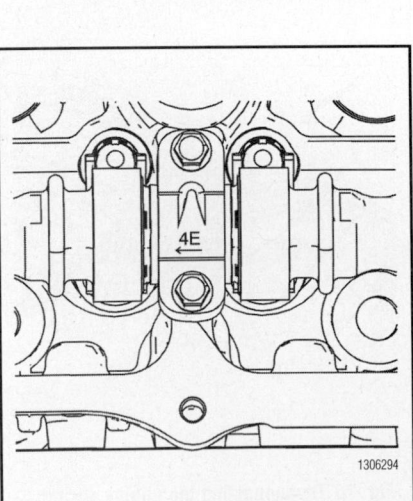

Fig. 77 Identifying the camshaft markings

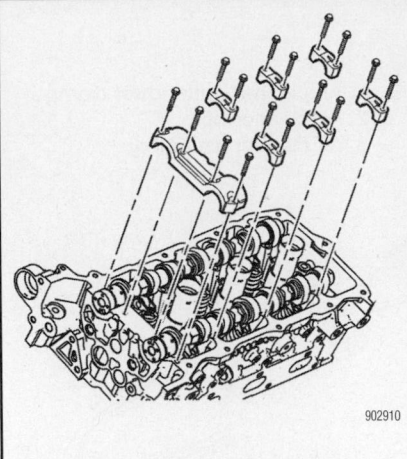

Fig. 78 Removing the camshaft bearing caps

c. The E indicates the exhaust camshaft.

d. The number indicates the journal position from the front of the engine.

2. Remove the camshaft bearing cap bolts.

3. Remove the camshaft bearing caps.

➡**Mark the camshafts upon removal to ensure installation is in the correct position.**

4. Remove the camshafts.

5. Replace the camshaft bearing caps and bolts.

To install:

6. Ensure that the camshaft sealing rings are in place in the camshaft grooves. Camshaft sealing rings must be in place below the surface of the camshaft journal in order to avoid being pinched between the cylinder head and the camshaft caps.

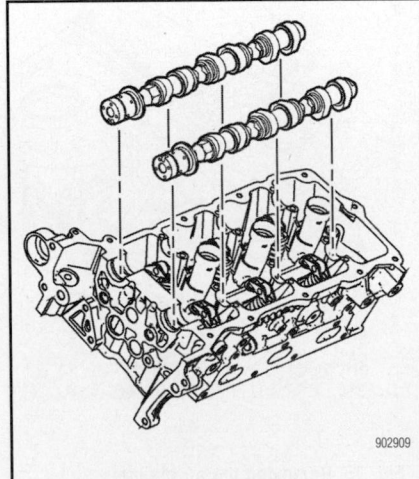

Fig. 79 Removing the camshafts

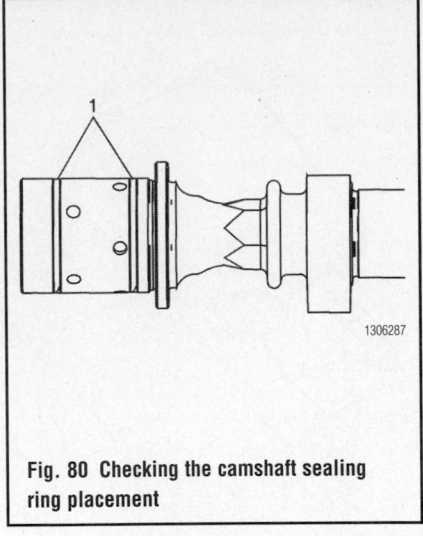

Fig. 80 Checking the camshaft sealing ring placement

7. Apply a liberal amount of lubricant to the camshaft journals and the left cylinder head camshaft carriers.

8. Place the left intake and left exhaust camshafts in position in the left cylinder head.

9. Position the camshaft lobes in a neutral position with the flats on the back of the camshafts up and parallel with the left cylinder head camshaft cover rail.

10. Observe the markings on the left cylinder head camshaft bearing caps. Each bearing cap is marked in order to identify its location. The markings have the following meanings:

a. The raised feature must always be oriented toward the center of the cylinder head.

b. The I indicates the intake camshaft.

c. The E indicates the exhaust camshaft.

d. The number 2, 4, 6 indicates the cylinder position from the front of the engine.

11. Apply a liberal amount of lubricant to the camshaft bearing caps.

12. Install the camshaft bearing thrust cap in the first journal of the left cylinder head.

13. Install the remaining bearing caps with their orientation mark toward the center of the cylinder head.

14. Hand start all the camshaft bearing cap bolts.

15. Tighten the camshaft bearing cap bolts in sequence to 89 inch lbs. (10 Nm).

16. Loosen the center intake camshaft bearing cap bolts 1, 2 and the center exhaust camshaft bearing cap bolts 3, 4.

17. Retighten the center camshaft bearing cap bolts 1, 2, 3, 4 to 89 inch lbs. (10 Nm).

CATALYTIC CONVERTER

REMOVAL & INSTALLATION

2.4L Engine

4 Speed Transmission

See Figure 81.

1. Remove the heated oxygen sensor.
2. Remove the catalytic converter to exhaust manifold nuts.
3. Remove the catalytic converter to muffler nuts.
4. Separate the exhaust pipe from the catalytic converter studs.
5. Position and support the exhaust pipe out of the way.
6. Remove the catalytic converter and gasket.

To install:

7. Install the catalytic converter along with a NEW gasket to the exhaust manifold.
8. Position and join the exhaust pipe to the catalytic converter studs.
9. Install the catalytic converter to muffler nuts and tighten to 18 ft. lbs. (25 Nm).
10. Install the catalytic converter to exhaust manifold nuts and tighten to 33 ft. lbs. (45 Nm).
11. Install the heated oxygen sensor.

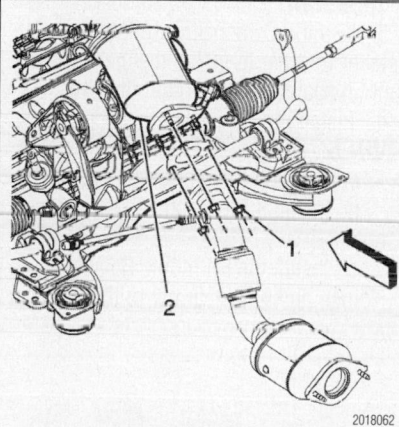

Fig. 81 Removing the catalytic converter to muffler nuts (1) and catalytic converter (2)

6 Speed Transmission

See Figure 82.

1. Raise and support the vehicle.
2. Remove the heated oxygen sensor.
3. Remove the catalytic converter to muffler nuts.
4. Separate the exhaust flexible pipe from the catalytic converter studs.
5. Position and support the exhaust pipe out of the way.

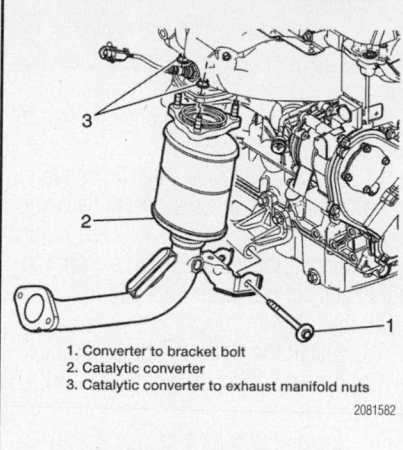

1. Converter to bracket bolt
2. Catalytic converter
3. Catalytic converter to exhaust manifold nuts

Fig. 82 Removing and installing the catalytic converter

6. Remove the converter to bracket bolt.
7. Remove the catalytic converter to exhaust manifold nuts.
8. Remove the catalytic converter and gasket. Discard the Catalytic converter gaskets.

To install:

9. Install a NEW gasket to the catalytic converter.
10. Position the catalytic converter to the exhaust manifold and converter bracket.
11. Loosely install the converter to manifold nuts and converter bracket bolt.
12. Tighten the converter to manifold nuts to 33 ft. lbs. (45 Nm).
13. Tighten the converter to bracket bolt to 42 ft. lbs. (58 Nm).
14. Install a NEW gasket between the converter and exhaust pipe.
15. Connect the exhaust flexible pipe to the converter and tighten the nuts to 18 ft. lbs. (25 Nm).
16. Install the heated oxygen sensor.
17. Lower the vehicle

3.6L Engine

Left Side

See Figures 83 and 84.

1. Remove the exhaust manifold heat shield.
2. Remove the left catalytic converter to exhaust manifold nuts.
3. Raise and support the vehicle.
4. Disconnect the bank 2 sensor 2 heated oxygen sensor (HO2S) electrical connector from the engine wiring harness electrical connector.
5. Remove the left catalytic converter to right catalytic converter nuts.
6. Remove the left catalytic converter from the vehicle.

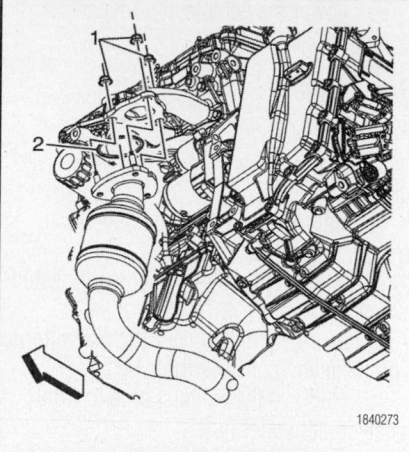

Fig. 83 Removing the left catalytic converter to exhaust manifold nuts

7. Discard the catalytic converter to exhaust manifold gasket.
8. Discard the left catalytic converter to right catalytic converter gasket.

To install:

9. Install a NEW catalytic converter seal onto the catalytic converter.
10. Install the catalytic converter to the vehicle.
11. Install a NEW left catalytic converter to right catalytic converter gasket.
12. Install the left catalytic converter to right catalytic converter nuts and tighten to 16 ft. lbs. (22 Nm).
13. Connect the bank 2 sensor 2 HO2S electrical connector to the engine wiring harness electrical connector.
14. Install the left catalytic converter to exhaust manifold nuts and tighten to 33 ft. lbs. (45 Nm).
15. Install the exhaust manifold heat shield.

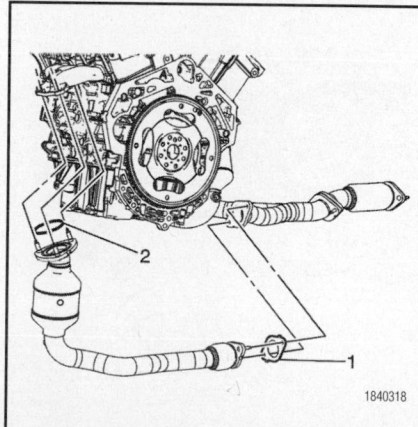

Fig. 84 Removing the catalytic converter to exhaust manifold gasket (2) and right catalytic converter gasket (1)

16. Lower the vehicle and inspect for exhaust leaks.

Right Side

See Figures 85 and 86.

1. Remove the exhaust manifold heat shield.
2. Remove the catalytic converter to exhaust manifold nuts.
3. Remove the bank 1 sensor 2 heated oxygen sensor (HO2S).
4. Remove the left catalytic converter to right catalytic converter nuts.
5. Remove the exhaust pipe to right catalytic converter nuts.
6. Remove the catalytic converter from the vehicle.
7. Remove and discard the catalytic converter to exhaust manifold gasket.
8. Remove and discard the left catalytic converter to right catalytic converter gasket.

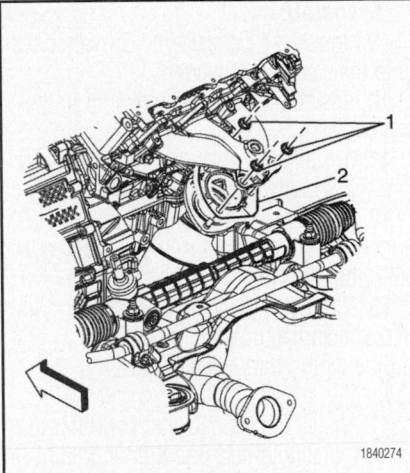

Fig. 85 Removing the catalytic converter to exhaust manifold nuts (1)

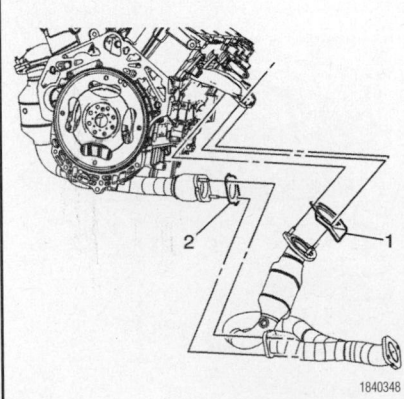

Fig. 86 Removing the catalytic converter to exhaust manifold gasket (1) and the left to right catalytic converter gasket (2)

To install:

9. Install a NEW catalytic converter to exhaust manifold gasket onto the catalytic converter.
10. Install the catalytic converter to the vehicle.
11. Install a NEW left catalytic converter to right catalytic converter gasket between the converters.
12. Install the left catalytic converter to right catalytic converter nuts and tighten to 16 ft. lbs. (22 Nm).
13. Install the exhaust pipe to right catalytic converter nuts and tighten to 18 ft. lbs. (25 Nm).
14. Install the bank 1 sensor 2 HO2S.
15. Install the catalytic converter to exhaust manifold nuts and tighten to 33 ft. lbs. (45 Nm).
16. Install the exhaust manifold heat shield.

CRANKSHAFT FRONT SEAL

REMOVAL & INSTALLATION

2.4L Engine

See Figures 87 through 89.

1. Remove the crankshaft balancer.
   VIN 5
   a. Remove the drive belt.
   b. Install the Harmonic Balancer Holder, and a breaker bar to the balancer in order to prevent the balancer from rotating when loosening the balancer bolt.
   c. Remove the Harmonic Balancer Holder and breaker bar.
   d. Remove and discard the crankshaft balancer bolt.
   e. Remove the crankshaft balancer.

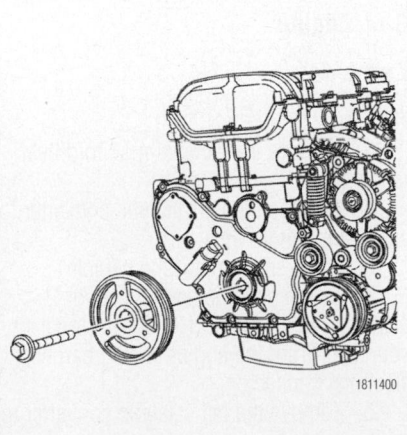

Fig. 87 Removing the crankshaft balancer

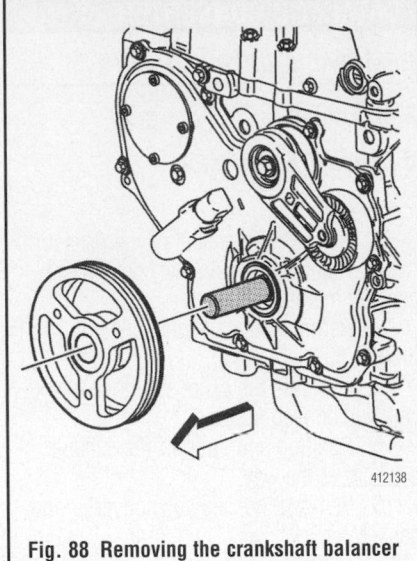

Fig. 88 Removing the crankshaft balancer

VIN B
   a. Remove the drive belt.
   b. Use Harmonic Balancer Holder to prevent the crankshaft from rotating while loosening the crankshaft balancer bolt.
   c. Remove and discard the crankshaft balancer bolt.
   d. Remove the crankshaft balancer.
2. Use a flat-bladed tool to remove the seal from the front cover.

To install:

3. Use the Camshaft/Front Main Seal Installer in order to install the crankshaft front oil seal to the engine front cover.
4. Install the crankshaft balancer.
   VIN 5
   a. Position the crankshaft balancer.
   b. Install a NEW crankshaft balancer bolt.
   c. Install the Harmonic Balancer Holder, and a breaker bar to the balancer

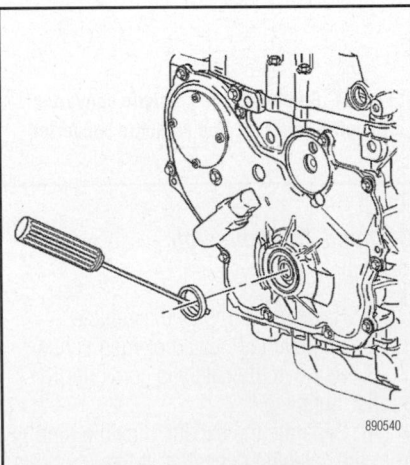

Fig. 89 Removing the crankshaft from seal

in order to prevent the balancer from rotating while tightening the bolt.

d. Tighten the crankshaft balancer bolt to 74 ft. lbs. (100 Nm) plus an additional 125 degrees using the Angle Meter.

e. Install the drive belt.

VIN B

a. Position the crankshaft balancer.

b. Install a NEW crankshaft balancer bolt.

5. Use the Angle Meter to hold the crankshaft balancer in order to prevent the balancer from rotating while tightening the bolt.

a. Tighten the crankshaft balancer bolt to 74 ft. lbs. (100 Nm) plus an additional 125 degrees using the Harmonic Balancer Holder.

6. Install the drive belt.

3.6L Engine

See Figures 90 and 91.

1. Remove the crankshaft balancer.

a. Remove the drive belt.

b. Install the engine support fixture.

c. Remove the right side engine mount.

d. Remove the starter.

e. Install the Flywheel Holding Tool through the starter mounting hole.

f. Using engine support fixture, lower engine approximately two inches.

g. Remove the crankshaft balancer bolt. Discard the bolt.

h. Install the Crankshaft Button in the nose of the crankshaft.

i. Install the Crankshaft Balancer remover in order to remove the crankshaft balancer.

j. Tighten the center bolt of the Crankshaft Balancer remover in order to pull the crankshaft balancer off of the crankshaft.

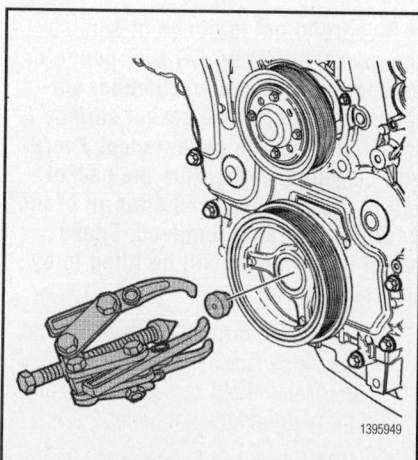

Fig. 90 Removing the crankshaft balancer

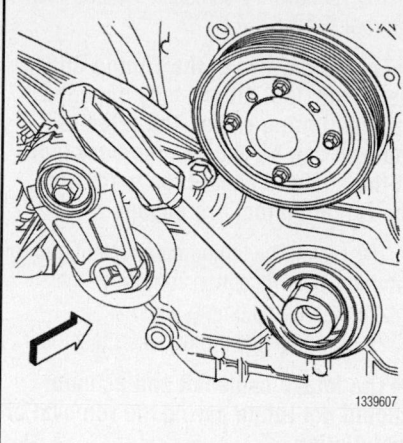

Fig. 91 Removing the crankshaft front oil seal

k. Remove the Crankshaft Balancer remover from the crankshaft balancer.

2. Use a flat-bladed tool in order to remove the crankshaft oil seal. Use care not to damage the engine front cover or the crankshaft.

To install:

➡**Do not lubricate the crankshaft front oil seal or the crankshaft balancer sealing surfaces.**

3. Use the Oil Seal Installer or equivalent to install the crankshaft front oil seal.

4. Install the crankshaft balancer

a. The Flywheel Holding tool must be installed onto the flywheel.

b. Use the Crankshaft Balancer installer, nut, bearing and washer to install the crankshaft balancer.

➡**Do not lubricate the crankshaft front oil seal or crankshaft balancer sealing surfaces. The crankshaft balancer is installed into a dry seal.**

c. Apply lubricant to the inside of the crankshaft balancer hub bore.

d. Place the crankshaft balancer in position on the crankshaft.

e. Thread the Crankshaft Balancer installer in the crankshaft. Ensure you engage at least 10 threads of the Crankshaft Balancer installer before pressing the crankshaft balancer in place.

f. Push the crankshaft balancer into position by tightening the nut on the Crankshaft Balancer installer until the large washer bottoms out on the crankshaft end.

g. Remove the Crankshaft Balancer installer.

➡**Always install a new crankshaft balancer retaining bolt and washer.**

h. Install the NEW crankshaft balancer bolt.

i. Tighten the crankshaft balancer bolt to 74 ft. lbs. (100 Nm) and an additional 150 degrees using the Angle meter.

j. Remove the Flywheel Holding tool.

k. Install the starter.

l. Using engine support fixture, raise the engine into position.

m. Install the engine mount.

n. Install the drive belt.

CYLINDER HEAD

REMOVAL & INSTALLATION

2.4L Engine

See Figures 92 through 97.

1. Drain the cooling system.

2. Remove the exhaust manifold.

3. Remove the intake manifold.

4. Reposition the radiator surge tank air bleed hose clamp.

5. Remove the radiator surge tank air bleed hose from the cylinder head.

6. Reposition the radiator inlet hose clamp using the Hose Clamp Pliers.

7. Remove the radiator inlet hose from the cylinder head.

8. Disconnect all electrical connectors as necessary.

9. Remove the spark plugs.

10. Remove the camshaft cover.

➡**If the intake camshaft actuator is moving independently of the camshaft, this means the camshaft is not locked to the actuator. Rotate the camshaft counter-clockwise while the holding tool is installed and this will lock the camshaft to the actuator.**

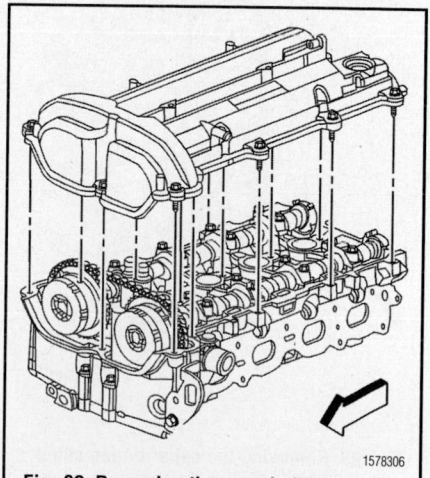

Fig. 92 Removing the camshaft cover

a. Remove the air cleaner outlet duct.

b. Remove the battery box cover, VIN 5 only.

c. Disconnect the engine wiring harness electrical connectors from the intake and exhaust camshaft position actuator solenoid valves.

d. Remove the ignition coils.

e. Remove the engine harness clips from the cover.

f. Reposition the engine wiring harness out of the way.

g. Remove the fuel feed line retainers from the engine brackets.

h. Remove the camshaft cover bolts.

i. Remove the camshaft cover.

11. Rotate the crankshaft clockwise to install the camshaft actuator locking tool Cooler Pressure Tester Adapter Set.

12. Install the Camshaft Actuator Locking Tool.

13. Install the camshaft actuator tool and bolts tighten to 89 inch lbs. (10 Nm).

14. Remove the upper timing chain guide bolts and guide.

15. Clean the timing chain and gears with solvent.

➡**Ensure the timing chain and the camshaft position actuators are marked for proper assembly.**

16. Mark the timing gear sprockets and the timing chain. It is recommended that the paint marks are located in the 12 o'clock position.

17. Loosen, but do not remove the intake and exhaust camshaft actuator bolts.

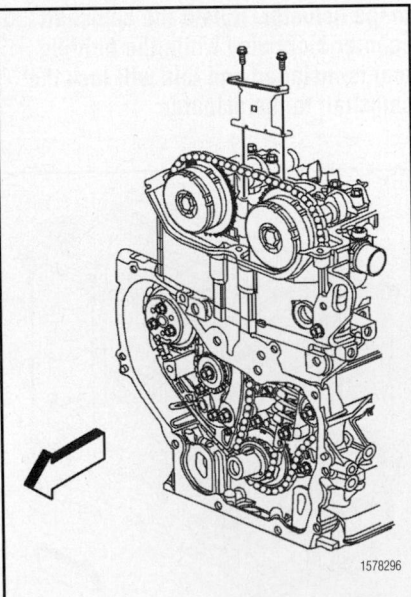

Fig. 93 Removing the upper timing chain guide

18. Remove the camshaft actuator locking tool.

➡**Ensure the tips of the Timing Chain Retention Tool Kit are fully engaged into the timing chain. The retention tool rod can be used on the back side of the chain to ensure the teeth from the retention tool are engaged.**

19. Install the timing chain retention tool Timing Chain Retention Tool Kit to the intake side of the timing chain.

20. Remove the timing chain tensioner.

➡**The Intake camshaft and actuator should not rotate during the removal or installation.**

21. Install the timing chain retention tool to the exhaust side of the timing chain.

22. Remove and discard the exhaust camshaft actuator bolt.

23. Remove the exhaust cam actuator from the exhaust camshaft while also removing the actuator from the chain.

24. Remove and discard the intake camshaft actuator bolt.

25. Remove the intake camshaft actuator from the camshaft while also removing the actuator from the timing chain.

26. Mark the cylinder head in relationship to the camshaft actuator notch is on the camshaft.

27. Remove the fixed timing chain guide access plug.

28. Remove the upper fixed timing chain guide bolt.

➡**The threaded rod from the timing chain retention tool can be used to help feed the rubber band around the chain guides.**

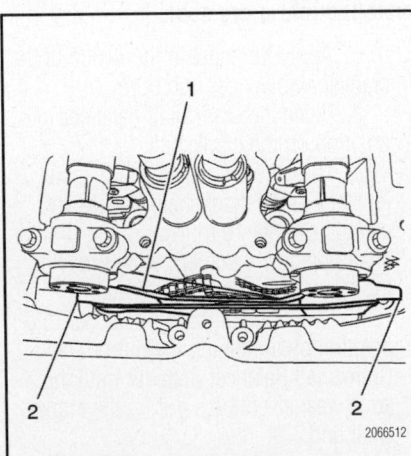

Fig. 94 Installing a rubber band (1) around the top of the upper timing chain guides (2)

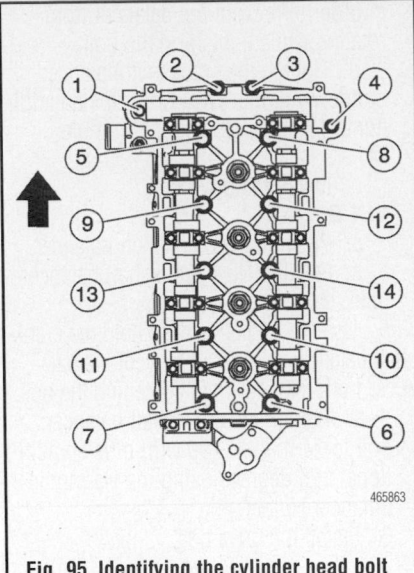

Fig. 95 Identifying the cylinder head bolt removal sequence

29. Install a rubber band around the top of the upper timing chain guides in order to pull the guides together.

30. Remove the cylinder head bolts in sequence. Discard the bolts.

31. Remove the cylinder head.

32. Remove the cylinder head gasket.

33. Clean all of the gasket surfaces.

34. Use the following steps when cleaning the cylinder head and cylinder block surfaces:

a. Use a razor blade gasket scraper to clean the cylinder head and cylinder block gasket surfaces. Do not scratch or gouge either surface.

➡**DO NOT use any other method or technique to clean these gasket surfaces.**

b. Use a NEW razor blade on the cylinder head and a NEW blade on the cylinder block.

➡**Be careful not to gouge or scratch the gasket surfaces. DO NOT gouge or scrape the combustion chamber surfaces. The feel of the gasket surface is important, not the appearance. There will be indentations from the gasket left in the cylinder head after all of the gasket material is removed. These small indentations will be filled in by the NEW gasket.**

c. Hold the razor blade as parallel to the gasket surface as possible.

d. Clean the old sealer/lube and any dirt from around the bolt holes.

➡**DO NOT use a tap to clean the cylinder head bolt holes.**

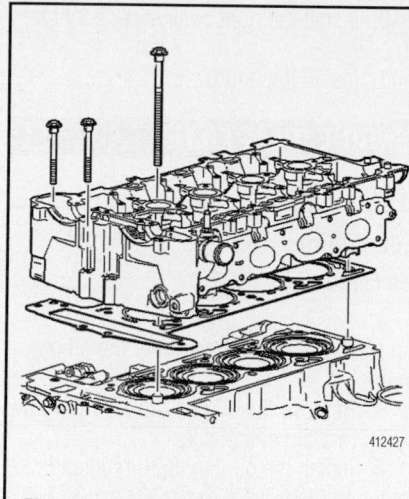

Fig. 96 Removing the cylinder head

e. Clean the bolts holes with a nylon bristle brush.

f. When cleaning the cylinder head bolt holes use suitable commercial spray liquid solvent and compressed air from an extended-tip blow gun in order to reach the bottom of the holes.

35. If replacing the cylinder head, transfer all parts as necessary.

To install:

➡**DO NOT use any sealing material.**

36. Install the cylinder head gasket.
37. Install the cylinder head.
38. Install NEW cylinder head bolts.
39. Install and tighten the cylinder head bolts in the sequence shown to 22 ft. lbs. (30 Nm) plus an additional 155 degrees using the Hose Clamp Pliers.
40. Install the NEW front cylinder head bolts and tighten the bolts to 26 ft. lbs. (35 Nm).

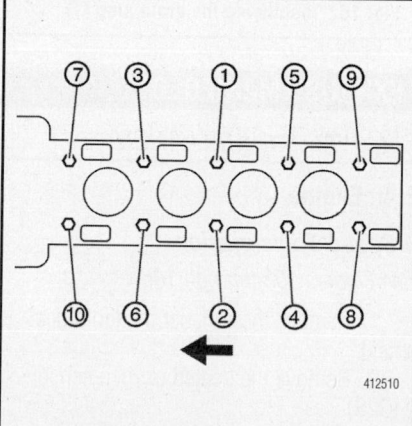

Fig. 97 Identifying the cylinder head bolt tightening sequence

41. Ensure the cylinder head and the camshaft are correctly aligned.
42. Remove the rubber band from around the top of the upper timing chain guides.
43. Install the fixed guide bolt into the cylinder head and tighten to 106 inch lbs. (12 Nm).
44. Apply sealant compound to thread and install the timing chain guide bolt access hole plug.
45. Install the fixed timing chain guide access plug and tighten the plug to 59 ft. lbs. (90 Nm).

➡**Ensure that the alignment mark made previously on the intake camshaft actuator is still aligned properly with the mark on the timing chain. If the mark made previously on the intake camshaft actuator is not aligned properly, refer to Camshaft Timing Chain, Sprocket, and Tensioner Replacement.**

46. Install the timing chain onto the intake camshaft actuator.
47. Align the intake camshaft actuator alignment mark made previously with the timing chain mark and install the actuator onto the camshaft.
48. Install a NEW intake camshaft actuator bolt until snug.
49. Remove the timing chain retention tool from the intake side of the timing chain.

➡**Ensure that the alignment mark made previously on the exhaust camshaft actuator is still aligned properly with the mark on the timing chain. The exhaust cam may have to be rotated clockwise to install the exhaust actuator.**

50. Install the timing chain onto the exhaust camshaft actuator.
51. Align the exhaust camshaft actuator alignment mark made previously with the timing chain mark and install the actuator onto the camshaft.
52. Install a NEW exhaust camshaft actuator bolt until snug.
53. Remove the timing chain retention tool from the exhaust side of the timing chain.

➡**Failure to reset the chain tensioner will put excess tension on the chain, limiting the chains life.**

54. Reset and install the timing chain tensioner.
55. Install the timing chain retention tool to the actuators.
56. Install the camshaft actuator locking

tool bolts and tighten to 89 inch lbs. (10 Nm).

57. Tighten the NEW camshaft actuator bolt to 22 ft. lbs. (30 Nm), plus an additional 100 degrees using the Hose Clamp Pliers.
58. Release the tensioner by applying a counterclockwise rotational torque of 33 ft. lbs. (45 Nm) to the harmonic balancer bolt.
59. Remove the camshaft actuator locking tool.
60. Install the upper timing chain guide bolts and guide. Tighten the bolts to 89 inch lbs. (10 Nm).
61. Install the camshaft cover.
62. Install the spark plugs.
63. Connect all electrical connectors as necessary.
64. Install the radiator inlet hose to the cylinder head.
65. Position the radiator inlet hose clamp using the Hose Clamp Pliers.
66. Install the radiator surge tank air bleed hose to the cylinder head.
67. Position the radiator surge tank air bleed hose clamp.
68. Install the exhaust manifold.
69. Install the intake manifold.
70. Fill the cooling system.

3.6L Engine

Left Side

See Figures 98 and 99.

1. Remove the left bank secondary timing chain.
2. Remove the oil level indicator.
3. Disconnect the coolant temperature sensor electrical connector.
4. Remove the wiring harness ground from the cylinder head.
5. Remove the catalytic converter.

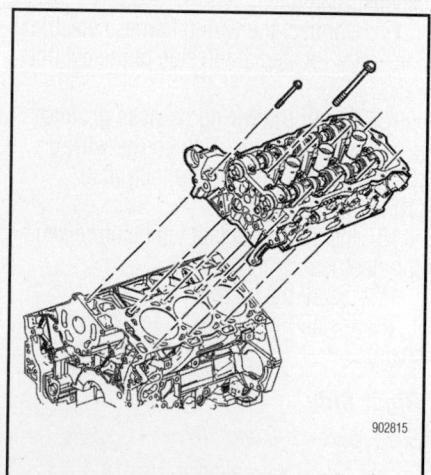

Fig. 98 Removing the cylinder head with the exhaust manifold

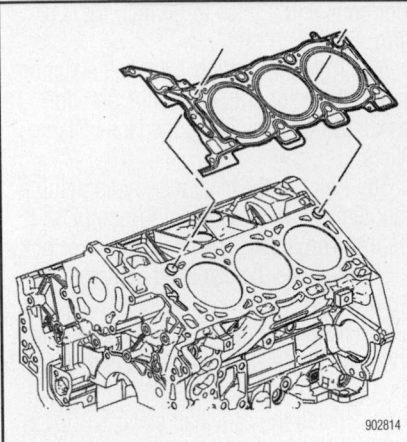

Fig. 99 Removing the cylinder head gasket

6. Remove the cylinder head with the exhaust manifold.

7. Remove and discard the cylinder head gasket.

8. Clean and inspect the cylinder head and the engine block sealing surfaces.

9. If necessary, perform the following steps:

  a. Remove the exhaust manifold from the cylinder head.

  b. Remove the camshaft.

  c. Disassemble the cylinder head.

To install:

10. If necessary, perform the following steps:

  a. Assemble the cylinder head.

  b. Install the camshaft.

  c. Install the exhaust manifold to the cylinder head.

11. Install a NEW cylinder head gasket.

12. Carefully install the cylinder head with the exhaust manifold to the engine.

13. Install the catalytic converter to the exhaust manifold.

14. Connect the wiring harness electrical connector located at the side of the cylinder head.

15. Install the wiring harness ground to the cylinder head. Tighten the wiring harness ground bolt to 89 inch lbs. (10 Nm).

16. Install the coolant temperature sensor electrical connector.

17. Install the oil level indicator.

18. Install the left bank secondary timing chain.

Right Side

See Figures 100 and 101.

1. Remove the hood.

2. Remove the right bank secondary timing chain.

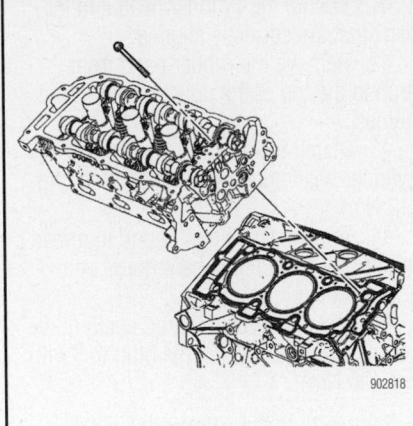

Fig. 100 Removing the cylinder head with the exhaust manifold

3. With the aid of an assistant, remove the cylinder head with the exhaust manifold.

4. Remove and discard the cylinder head gasket.

5. Clean and inspect the cylinder head and the engine block sealing surfaces.

6. If necessary, perform the following steps:

  a. Remove the exhaust manifold from the cylinder head.

  b. Remove the camshaft.

  c. Disassemble the cylinder head.

To install:

7. If necessary, perform the following steps:

  a. Assemble the cylinder head.

  b. Install the camshaft.

  c. Install the exhaust manifold to the cylinder head.

8. Install a NEW cylinder head gasket.

9. With the aid of an assistant, carefully install the cylinder head with the exhaust manifold to the engine.

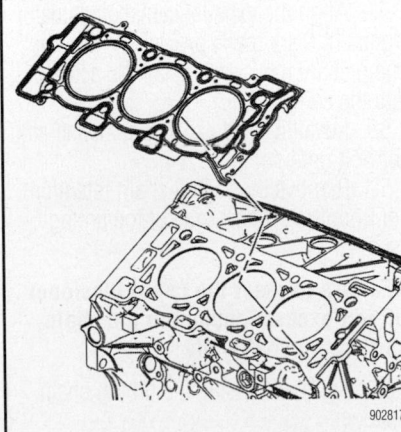

Fig. 101 Removing the cylinder head gasket

10. Install the right bank secondary timing chain.

11. Install the hood.

ENGINE OIL & FILTER

REPLACEMENT

3.6L Engine

See Figure 102.

1. Raise and support the vehicle.

2. Place a drain pan under the oil pan drain plug.

3. Remove the oil pan drain plug. Allow the oil to drain completely.

4. Install the oil pan drain plug and tighten to 15 ft. lbs. (20 Nm).

5. Place the drain pan under the oil filter.

6. Remove the oil filter. Allow the oil to drain completely.

To install:

7. Lubricate the NEW oil filter gasket with clean engine oil.

8. Tighten the oil filter to 22 ft. lbs. (30 Nm).

9. Lower the vehicle.

10. Refill the engine oil.

11. Start the engine and inspect for leaks.

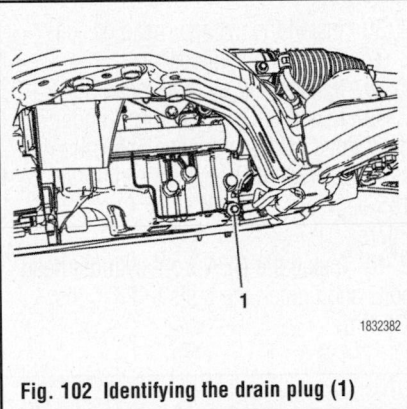

Fig. 102 Identifying the drain plug (1)

EXHAUST MANIFOLD

REMOVAL & INSTALLATION

2.4L Engine

4 Speed Transmission

See Figures 103 through 105.

1. Remove the exhaust manifold heat shield.

2. Remove the heated oxygen sensor (HO2S).

3. Remove the exhaust manifold pipe, VIN 5 only.

4. Remove the catalytic converter, VIN B only.

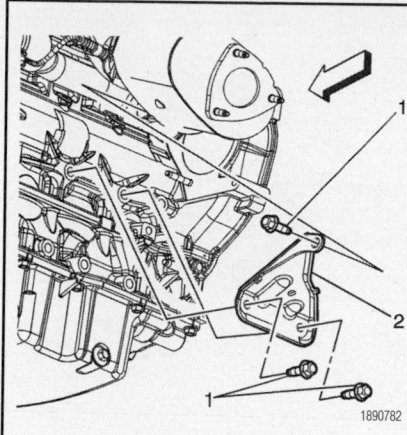

Fig. 103 Removing the upper exhaust manifold brace (2) bolts (1)

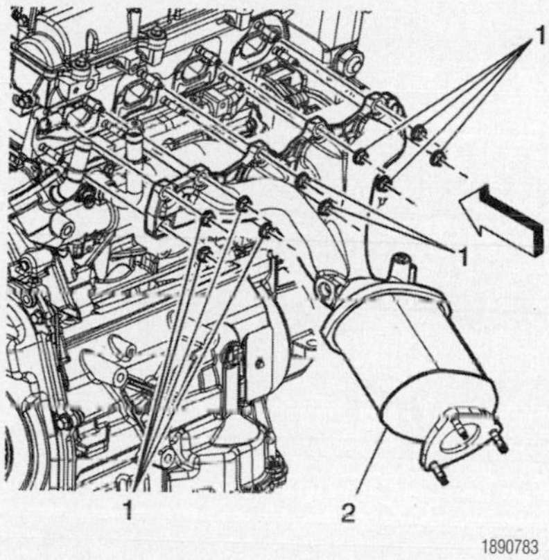

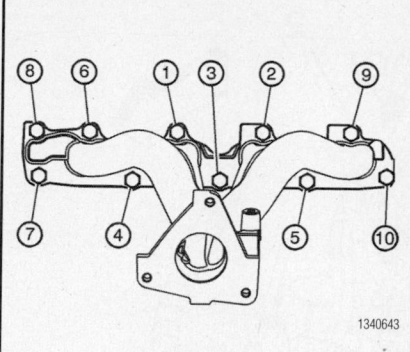

Fig. 105 Identifying the exhaust manifold nut tightening sequence

INTAKE MANIFOLD

REMOVAL & INSTALLATION

2.4L Engine

VIN 5

See Figures 107 through 111.

1. Remove the air cleaner outlet duct.
2. Remove the radiator inlet hose.
3. Disconnect the engine wiring harness electrical connector from the throttle actuator control (TAC).
4. Disconnect the engine wiring harness electrical connector from the generator starter.
5. Disconnect the engine wiring harness electrical connector from the generator starter.
6. Remove the fuel injector wiring harness electrical connector retainer from the generator starter.
7. Disconnect the fuel injector wiring harness electrical connector from the engine wiring harness electrical connector.
8. Remove the engine wiring harness clips from the intake manifold.
9. Reposition the vacuum brake booster hose clamp at the intake manifold.
10. Remove the vacuum brake booster hose from the intake manifold.
11. Remove the throttle body.
12. Disconnect the engine wiring harness electrical connector from the manifold absolute pressure (MAP) sensor.
13. Disconnect the evaporative emission (EVAP) canister purge tube from the intake manifold and the EVAP solenoid.
14. Remove the oil level indicator tube.
15. Remove the fuel rail.
16. Remove the 3-phase voltage cable bracket bolt at the oil level indicator tube.
17. Remove the generator starter bolts.
18. Reposition and secure the generator starter out of the way.
19. Remove the intake manifold lower bolts.
20. Remove the intake manifold upper bolt and nuts.
21. Remove the intake manifold.

➡ **The intake manifold gasket is reusable, only replace the gasket if damage has occurred.**

22. Remove and inspect the intake manifold gasket.

To install:

23. Install a NEW intake manifold gasket if necessary, otherwise install the old gasket.
24. Install the intake manifold.
25. Install the intake manifold upper bolt and nuts.

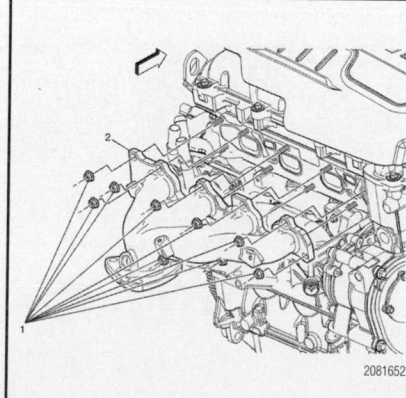

Fig. 104 Removing the exhaust manifold nuts (1) and manifold/catalytic converter assembly (2)

5. Lower the vehicle.
6. Remove the upper exhaust manifold brace bolt.
7. Remove and discard the exhaust manifold nuts.
8. Remove the exhaust manifold/catalytic converter assembly.
9. Remove and discard the exhaust manifold gasket.

To install:

10. Install a NEW exhaust manifold gasket onto the manifold studs.
11. Install the exhaust manifold/catalytic converter assembly.
12. Install the NEW exhaust manifold nuts finger tight.
13. Install the upper exhaust manifold brace bolt and tighten to 43 ft. lbs. (58 Nm).
14. Tighten the exhaust manifold nuts in the sequence shown to 10 ft. lbs. (14 Nm).
15. Raise and suitably support the vehicle.

16. Install the exhaust manifold pipe, VIN B only.
17. Install the catalytic converter, VIN 5 only.
18. Install the HO2S.
19. Install the exhaust manifold heat shield.

6 Speed Transmission

See Figure 106.

1. Remove the exhaust manifold heat shield.
2. Remove the exhaust extension pipe.
3. Remove and discard the exhaust manifold gasket.
4. Clean any exhaust manifold gasket debris from the cylinder head and exhaust manifold.

To install:

To install, reverse the removal procedure. Tighten the manifold nuts working from the center out to 124 inch lbs. (14 Nm).

Fig. 106 Removing and installing the exhaust manifold

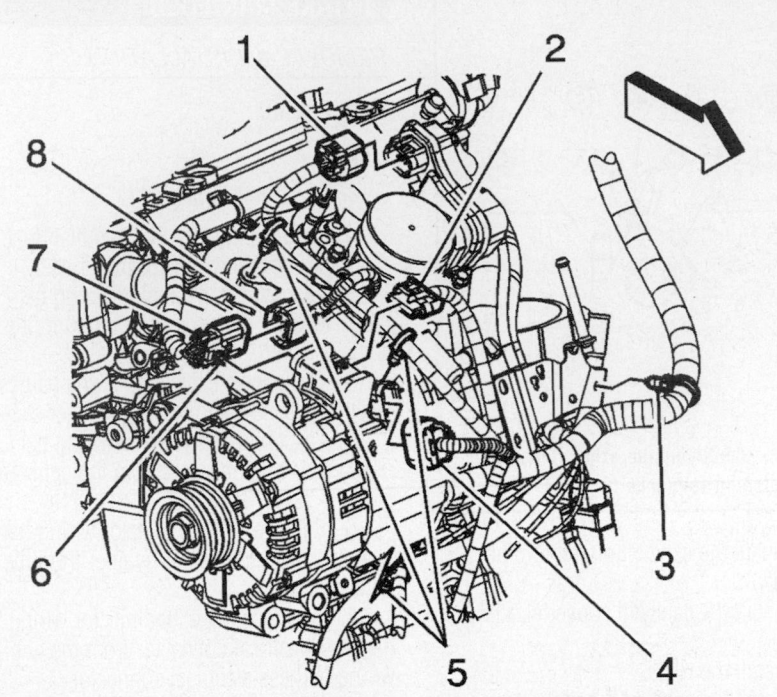

1. Engine wiring harness electrical connector from the TAC
2. Engine wiring harness electrical connector from the generator starter
3. –
4. Engine wiring harness electrical connector from the generator starter
5. Engine wiring harness clips
6. Fuel injector wiring harness electrical connector retainer
7. Fuel injector wiring harness electrical connector
8. Engine wiring harness electrical connector

1810743

Fig. 107 Disconnecting the wiring harnesses from the intake manifold

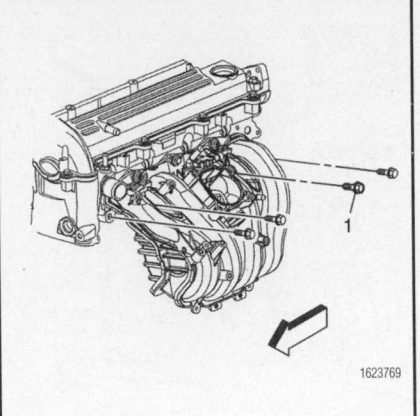

1623769

Fig. 110 Removing the intake manifold lower bolts

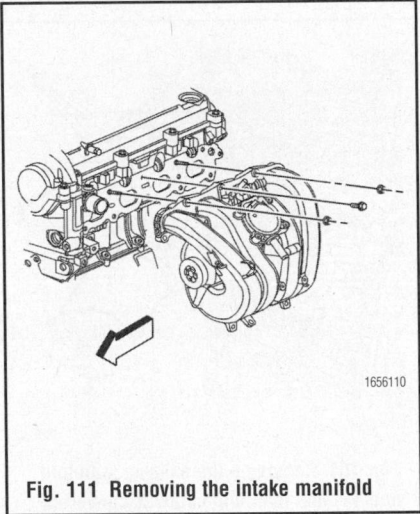

1656110

Fig. 111 Removing the intake manifold

26. Install the intake manifold lower bolts. Tighten the bolts/nuts to 89 inch lbs. (10 Nm).

27. Position the starter/generator to the bracket.

28. Install the starter/generator bolts until snug.

29. Tighten the starter generator bolts in the following sequence:
- Front

- Bottom
  a. Tighten the bolts to 43 ft. lbs. (58 Nm).

30. Install the 3-phase voltage cable bracket to the tie bar.

31. Install the 3-phase voltage cable bracket bolt at the oil level indicator tube. Tighten the bolt to 89 inch lbs. (10 Nm).

32. Install the fuel rail.

33. Install the oil level indicator tube.

34. Connect the EVAP canister purge tube to the intake manifold and the EVAP solenoid.

35. Connect the engine wiring harness electrical connector to the MAP sensor.

36. Install the throttle body.

37. Install the vacuum brake booster hose to the intake manifold.

38. Position the vacuum brake booster hose clamp at the intake manifold.

39. Install the engine wiring harness clips to the intake manifold.

40. Connect the fuel injector wiring harness electrical connector to the engine wiring harness electrical connector.

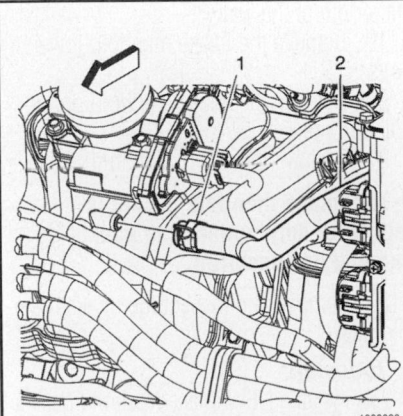

1999023

Fig. 108 Repositioning the vacuum brake booster hose clamp (1) and removing the brake booster hose (2)

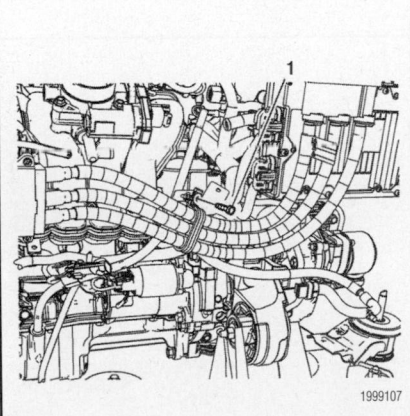

1999107

Fig. 109 Removing the 3-phase voltage cable bracket bolt

41. Install the fuel injector wiring harness electrical connector retainer to the generator starter.

42. Connect the engine wiring harness electrical connector to the generator starter.

43. Connect the engine wiring harness electrical connector to the generator starter.

44. Connect the engine wiring harness electrical connector to the TAC.

45. Install the radiator inlet hose.

46. Install the air cleaner outlet duct.

VIN B

See Figures 112 through 114.

1. Remove the throttle body.

2. Remove the fuel rail.

3. Remove the evaporative emission (EVAP) canister purge solenoid valve tube.

4. Reposition the brake booster vacuum hose clamp at the intake manifold.

5. Remove the brake booster hose from the intake manifold.

6. Remove the oil level indicator tube bolt.

7. Disconnect the engine harness electrical connector from the fuel injector inline electrical connector.

8. Remove the fuel injector inline connector clip from the intake manifold.

9. Disconnect the engine harness electrical connector from the knock sensor harness.

10. Remove the knock sensor connector clip from the oil level indicator tube.

11. Remove the intake manifold bolts and nuts.

12. Remove the intake manifold.

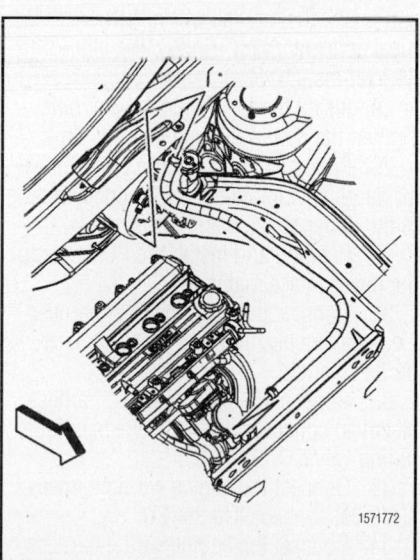

Fig. 112 Removing the brake booster hose from the intake manifold

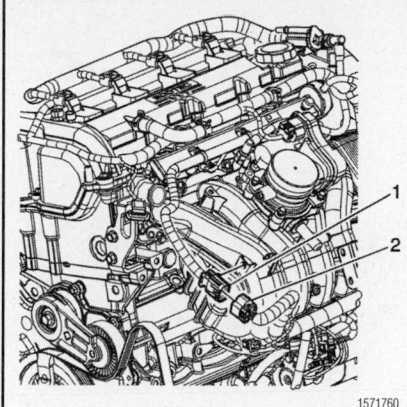

Fig. 113 Disconnecting the engine harness electrical connector (1) from the fuel injector inline electrical connector (2)

➡ **The intake manifold gasket is reusable. Only replace the gasket if damage has occurred.**

13. Remove the intake manifold gasket, if necessary.

To install:

14. Install the intake manifold gasket, if necessary.

15. Install the intake manifold.

16. Install the intake manifold bolts and nuts and tighten to 89 inch lbs. (10 Nm).

17. Connect the engine harness electrical connector to the knock sensor harness.

18. Install the knock sensor connector clip to the oil level indicator tube.

19. Connect the engine harness electrical connector to the fuel injector inline electrical connector.

20. Install the fuel injector inline connector clip to the intake manifold.

21. Install the oil level indicator tube bolt and tighten to 89 inch lbs. (10 Nm).

22. Install the brake booster hose to the intake manifold.

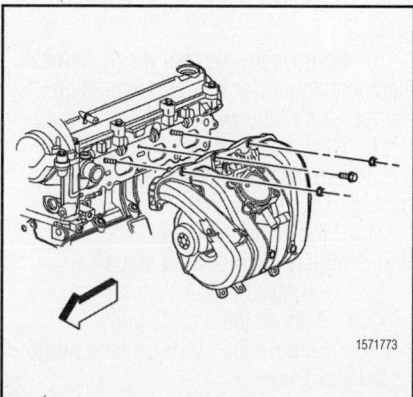

Fig. 114 Removing the intake manifold

23. Position the brake booster vacuum hose clamp at the intake manifold.

24. Install the EVAP canister purge solenoid valve tube.

25. Install the fuel rail.

26. Install the throttle body.

3.6L Engine

Lower

See Figure 115.

1. Remove the fuel injectors and fuel rail.

2. Remove the lower intake manifold bolts.

3. Remove the lower intake manifold and gasket. Discard the gasket.

4. Clean and inspect the intake manifold and sealing surfaces.

To install:

5. Place a NEW lower intake manifold gasket onto the cylinder heads.

6. Place the lower intake manifold onto the cylinder heads.

7. Install the lower intake manifold bolts. Tighten the bolts to 17 ft. lbs. (23 Nm).

8. Install the fuel injectors and fuel rail.

Fig. 115 Removing and installing the lower intake manifold

Upper

See Figures 116 through 120.

1. Remove the fuel injector sight shield.

2. Remove the air cleaner outlet duct.

3. Disconnect the fuel feed line quick connect fitting from the fuel rail.

4. Remove the fuel feed pipe line nut and remove the fuel feed line clip from the stud.

5. Reposition the fuel feed line out of the way.

6. Remove the coolant air bleed hose/pipe clip bolt from the upper intake manifold.

7. Reposition the coolant air bleed hose clamp at the water outlet.

Fig. 116 Repositioning the brake booster vacuum hose clamp (1) and removing the hose (2) from the upper intake manifold

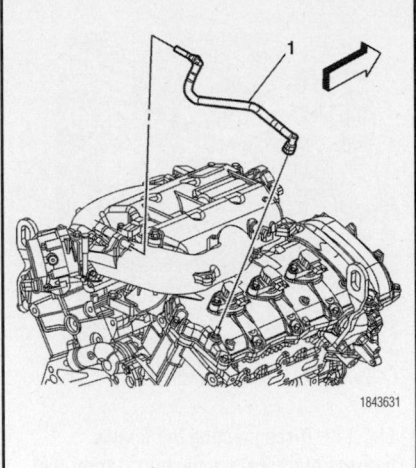

Fig. 118 Disconnecting the PCV tube

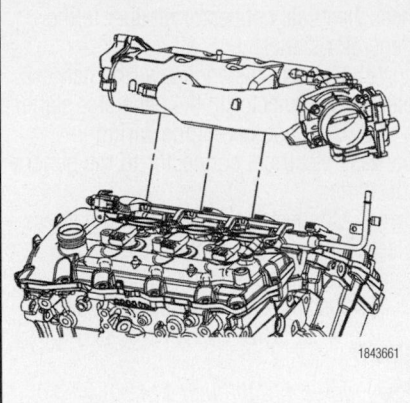

Fig. 120 Removing the upper intake manifold and gaskets

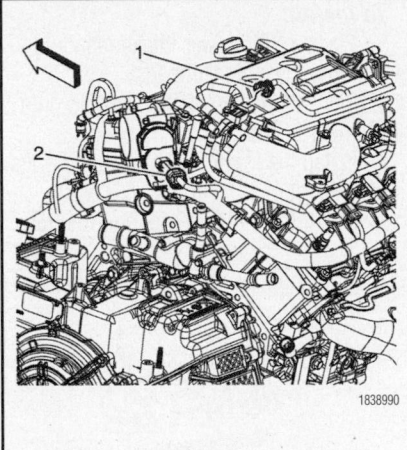

Fig. 117 Disconnecting the MAP and ETC electrical connectors

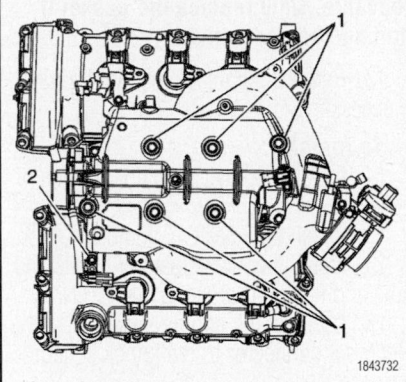

Fig. 119 Removing the fuel rail wiring harness electrical connector bolt (2) and the upper intake bolts (1)

8. Remove the coolant air bleed hose from the water outlet.

9. Remove the coolant air bleed hose/pipe clip from the upper intake manifold stud and reposition out of the way.

10. Reposition the brake booster vacuum hose clamp at the upper intake manifold.

11. Remove the brake booster vacuum hose from the upper intake manifold.

12. Disconnect the engine wiring harness electrical connector from the manifold absolute pressure (MAP) sensor.

13. Disconnect the engine wiring harness electrical connector from the electronic throttle control (ETC).

14. Disconnect the engine wiring harness electrical connector from the intake manifold tuning valve.

15. Disconnect the engine wiring harness electrical connector from the evaporative emission (EVAP) canister purge solenoid.

16. Disconnect the positive crankcase ventilation (PCV) tube from the upper intake manifold and reposition aside.

17. Disconnect the EVAP canister purge solenoid tube quick connect fitting at the upper intake manifold and reposition aside.

18. Remove the fuel rail to bracket bolt.

19. Remove the fuel rail wiring harness electrical connector bolt and reposition the harness out of the way.

20. Remove the upper intake bolts. Remove the upper intake manifold and gaskets. Discard gaskets.

21. If replacing the upper intake manifold complete the following steps:

  a. Remove the MAP sensor.

  b. Remove the throttle body.

  c. Remove the EVAP canister purge solenoid valve.

  d. Remove the intake manifold tuning valve.

To install:

22. If the upper intake manifold was replaced complete the following steps:

  a. Install the MAP sensor.

  b. Install the throttle body.

  c. Install the EVAP canister purge solenoid valve.

  d. Install the intake manifold tuning valve.

23. Place NEW upper intake manifold gaskets onto the lower intake manifold.

24. Place the upper intake manifold onto the lower intake manifold.

25. Install the upper intake bolts.

➥**Tighten the intake manifold bolts in an X pattern starting with the inside bolts and moving outward.**

26. Tighten the bolts to 18 ft. lbs. (25 Nm).

27. Position the fuel rail wiring harness and install the fuel rail wiring harness electrical connector bolt. Tighten the bolt to 89 inch lbs. (10 Nm).

28. Install the fuel rail to bracket bolt. Tighten the bolt to 89 inch lbs. (10 Nm).

29. Position and install the EVAP canister purge solenoid tube quick connect fitting to the upper intake manifold.

30. Position and install the PCV tube to the upper intake manifold.

31. Connect the engine wiring harness electrical connector to the EVAP canister purge solenoid.

32. Connect the engine wiring harness electrical connector to the intake manifold tuning valve.

33. Connect the engine wiring harness electrical connector to the ETC.

34. Connect the engine wiring harness electrical connector to the MAP sensor.

35. Install the brake booster vacuum hose to the upper intake manifold.

36. Position the brake booster vacuum hose clamp at the upper intake manifold.

37. Position and install the coolant air bleed hose/pipe clip to the upper intake manifold stud.

38. Install the coolant air bleed hose to the water outlet.

39. Position the coolant air bleed hose clamp at the water outlet.

40. Install the coolant air bleed hose/pipe clip bolt to the upper intake manifold. Tighten the bolt to 89 inch lbs. (10 Nm).

41. Position the fuel feed line and install the fuel feed line clip to the stud.

42. Install the fuel feed line nut. Tighten the nut to 89 inch lbs. (10 Nm).

43. Connect the fuel feed line quick connect fitting to the fuel rail.

44. Install the air cleaner outlet duct.

45. Install the fuel injector sight shield.

OIL PAN

REMOVAL & INSTALLATION

2.4L Engine

See Figures 121 through 125

1. Remove the drive belt.
2. Remove the oil level indicator tube.

→**The support fixture bar must be installed to provide enough access to remove and properly tighten the oil pan bolts.**

3. Install the engine support fixture.
4. Remove engine mount.
5. Using the engine support fixture, raise the engine approximately 3 inches (76 mm).
6. Raise and support the vehicle.
7. Loosen the upper air conditioning (A/C) compressor bolts.
8. Remove the lower A/C compressor bolt.
9. Place a suitable drain pan under the oil pan drain plug.

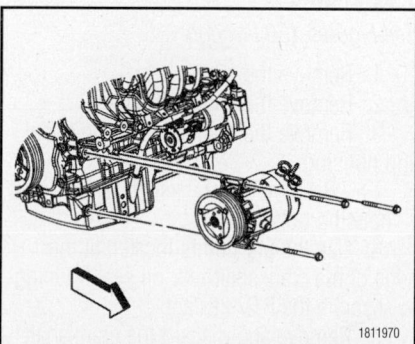

Fig. 121 Loosening the upper air conditioning compressor bolt and removing the lower bolt

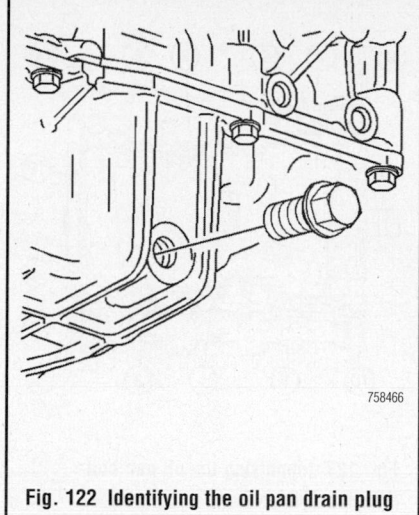

Fig. 122 Identifying the oil pan drain plug

10. Remove the oil pan drain plug.
11. Drain the engine oil.
12. Reinstall the oil pan drain plug until snug.

VIN 5 only:

13. Disconnect the engine wiring harness electrical connector from the generator control module coolant pump.

14. Remove the generator control module coolant pump bolt.

15. Remove the generator control module coolant pump from the oil pan.

All Vehicles:

16. Remove the 4 oil pan to transaxle bolts.

17. Remove the oil pan bolts.

18. Remove the oil pan

19. Remove any old oil pan sealant (1).

To install:

20. Ensure that the oil pan and the sealing surface on the lower crankcase are free of all oil and debris.

21. Apply a 2 mm bead of sealant

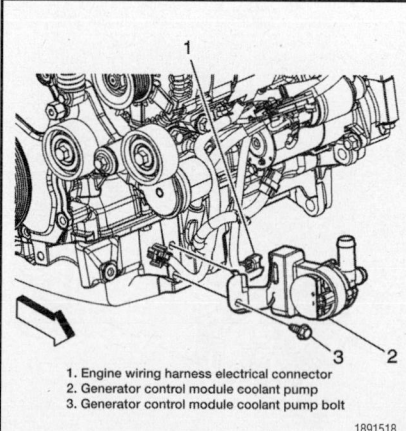

1. Engine wiring harness electrical connector
2. Generator control module coolant pump
3. Generator control module coolant pump bolt

Fig. 123 Removing the generator control module coolant pump

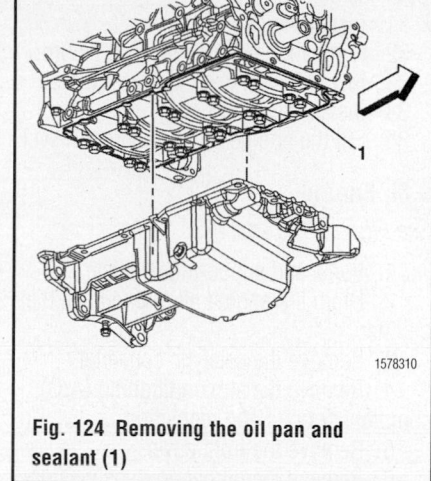

Fig. 124 Removing the oil pan and sealant (1)

around the perimeter of the oil pan and the oil suction port opening. DO NOT over apply the sealant. More than a 2 mm bead is not required.

22. Install the oil pan.

23. Install the oil pan bolts.

24. Install the 4 oil pan to transaxle bolts and tighten to 55 ft. lbs. (75 Nm).

25. Tighten the oil pan bolts in the sequence shown to 18 ft. lbs. (25 Nm).

VIN 5 only:

26. Install the generator control module coolant pump to the oil pan. Ensure that the anti-rotation tab is inserted into the hole in the oil pan.

27. Install the generator control module coolant pump bolt and tighten to 18 ft. lbs. (25 Nm).

28. Connect the engine wiring harness electrical connector to the generator control module coolant pump

All vehicles:

29. Lower the vehicle.

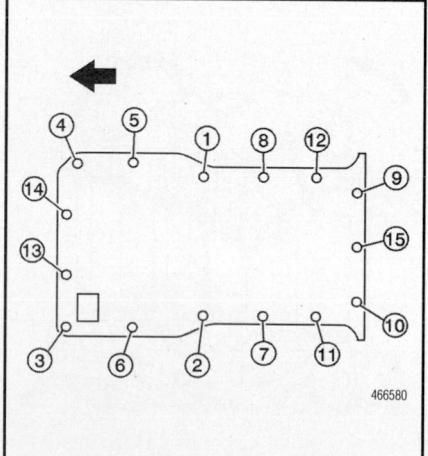

Fig. 125 Identifying the oil pan bolt tightening sequence

30. Using the engine support fixture, lower the engine.
31. Install the engine mount.
32. Remove the engine support fixture.
33. Install the oil level indicator tube.
34. Install the drive belt.
35. Fill the engine oil to the proper level.

3.6L Engine

See Figures 126 and 127.

1. Raise and support the vehicle.
2. Drain the engine oil and remove the oil filter.
3. Remove the catalytic converter.
4. Remove the air conditioning (A/C) compressor bolts and reposition.
5. Remove the front cover.
6. Remove the oil pan to transmission bolts.
7. Remove the oil pan bolts.
8. Remove the oil pan.
9. Clean the oil pan and the engine block gasket surface.

To install:

10. Install the 0.315 inch (8 mm) guides from the EN-46109 set into the center oil pan rail bolt hole on each side of the engine block.
11. Place a 0.118 inch (3 mm) bead of RTV sealant , on the block pan rail and the crankshaft rear oil seal housing.
12. Position the oil pan onto the block.
13. Remove the Guide Pin set 0.315 inch (8 mm) guides from the engine block.
14. Loosely install the oil pan bolts.
15. Tighten the oil pan bolts in sequence.
    a. The 8 mm bolts (1-11) to 17 ft. lbs. (23 Nm).
    b. The 6 mm bolts (12, 13) to 89 inch lbs. (10 Nm).

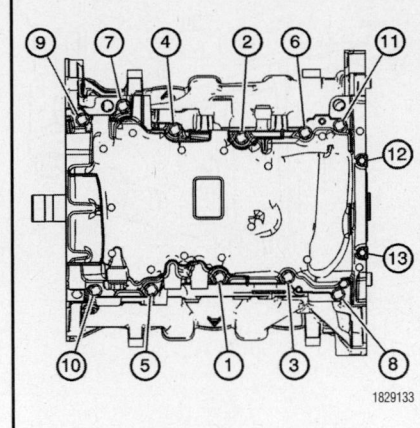

Fig. 127 Identifying the oil pan bolt tightening sequence

16. Install engine front cover.
17. Install the air conditioning (A/C) compressor.
18. Install the catalytic converter.
19. Lower the vehicle.
20. Refill the engine oil.

OIL PUMP

REMOVAL & INSTALLATION

3.6L Engine

See Figure 128.

➡**Do not remove the left bank idler sprocket.**

1. Remove the primary timing chain.
2. Remove the oil pump bolts and the oil pump.

To install:

3. Install the oil pump.
    a. Align the oil pump drive gear with the crankshaft flats and install

the oil pump to the engine block.
    b. Align the pump body with the mounting holes in the cylinder block.
    c. Install the oil pump bolts and tighten to 18 ft. lbs. (25 Nm).
4. Install the primary timing chain.

REAR MAIN SEAL

REMOVAL & INSTALLATION

2.4L Engine

See Figure 129.

1. Remove the flywheel.

➡**Do not damage the outside diameter of the crankshaft or chamber with any tool.**

2. Pry out the crankshaft rear oil seal using a flat-bladed tool.

To install:

3. Using the rear main seal installer, install a NEW crankshaft real oil seal.
4. Install the flywheel.

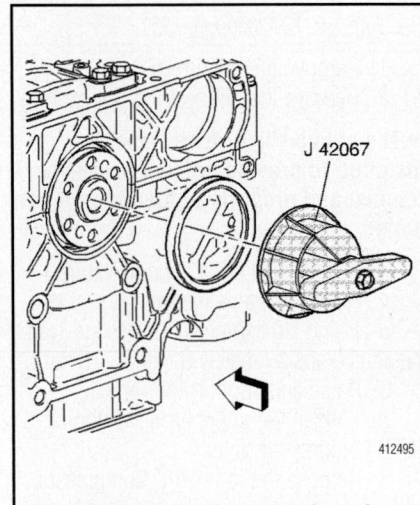

Fig. 129 Removing the rear main seal

3.6L Engine

See Figures 130 through 135.

1. Remove the oil pan.
2. Remove the engine flywheel.
3. Remove the crankshaft rear oil seal and housing.
    a. Remove the crankshaft rear oil seal housing bolts.
4. Use the pry points located at the edge of the crankshaft rear oil seal housing to separate the RTV sealant.
5. Remove and discard the crankshaft rear oil seal housing.

To install:

6. Install the crankshaft rear oil seal and housing.

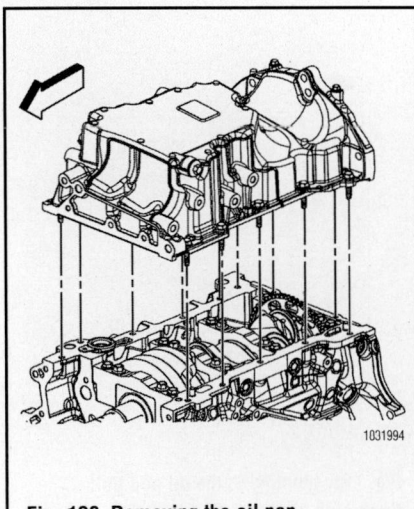

Fig. 126 Removing the oil pan

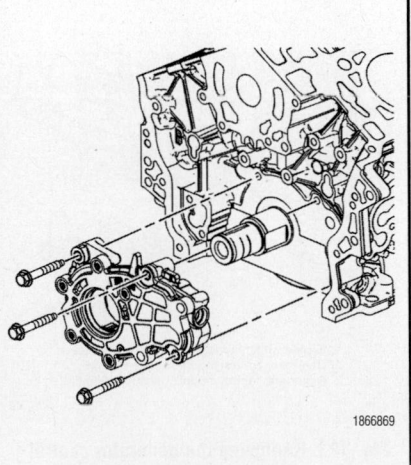

Fig. 128 Removing the oil pump

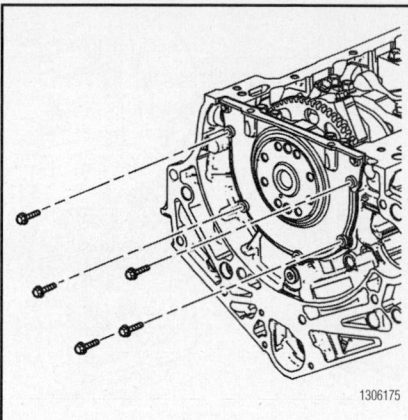

Fig. 130 Removing the crankshaft rear oil seal housing bolts

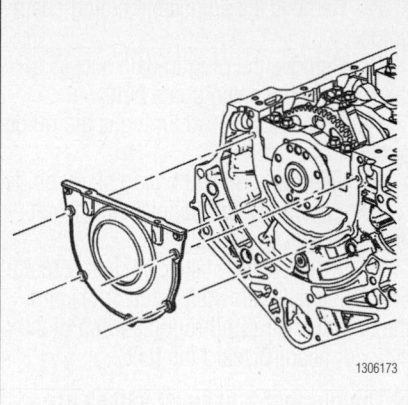

Fig. 132 Removing the crankshaft rear oil seal housing

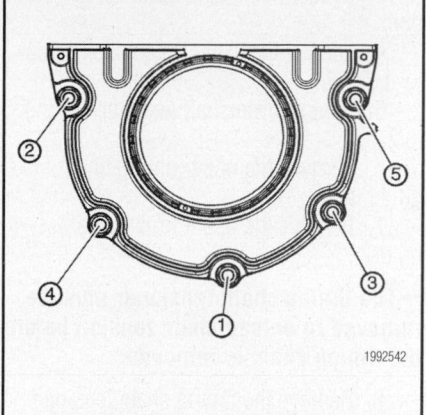

Fig. 135 Identifying the crankshaft rear oil seal housing bolt tightening sequence

a. Install the 0.236 inch (6 mm) guides from the Guide Pin set into the 2 crankshaft rear oil seal housing corner bolt holes of the engine block.

7. Install the Crankshaft Rear Oil Seal Installation tool with the handle onto the rear of the crankshaft flange.

➡**There are first design and second design crankshaft rear oil seal housings. Second design oil seal housings include additional grooves for RTV sealant near the oil seal housing to oil pan interface.**

8. Place a 0.118 inch (3 mm) bead of RTV sealant to the NEW crankshaft rear oil seal housing.

➡**Do not allow any engine oil on the area where the crankshaft rear oil seal housing is to be installed.**

9. Install the crankshaft rear oil seal housing to the engine block.

10. Remove the Guide pin set 0.236 inch (6 mm) guides from the engine block.

11. Install the crankshaft rear oil seal housing bolts.

12. Tighten the crankshaft rear oil seal housing bolts in sequence and tighten to 89 inch lbs. (10 Nm).

13. Remove the Crankshaft Rear Oil Seal Installation tool and handle from the crankshaft flange.

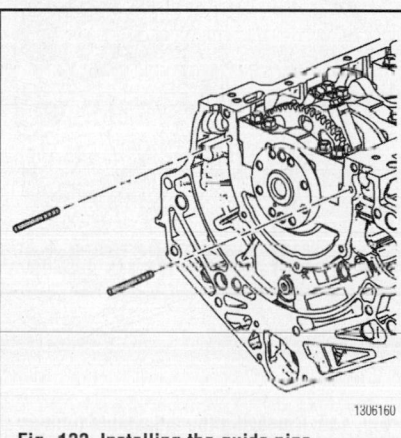

Fig. 133 Installing the guide pins

14. Install the engine flywheel.
15. Install the oil pan.

TIMING CHAIN & SPROCKETS

REMOVAL & INSTALLATION

2.4L Engine

See Figures 136 through 145.

1. Rotate the crankshaft to install Camshaft Actuator locking tool.

➡**Marking the chain and actuators is crucial to procedures operation. The camshaft actuator and timing chain must have oil removed from the surface prior to marking both actuators and chain.**

2. Install Camshaft Actuator locking tool onto the cylinder head and tighten to 89 inch lbs. (10 Nm). If the intake camshaft actuator is moving independent of cam and is not locked, rotate the intake camshaft counterclockwise and the tool will hold the actuator, locking the actuator to the cam.

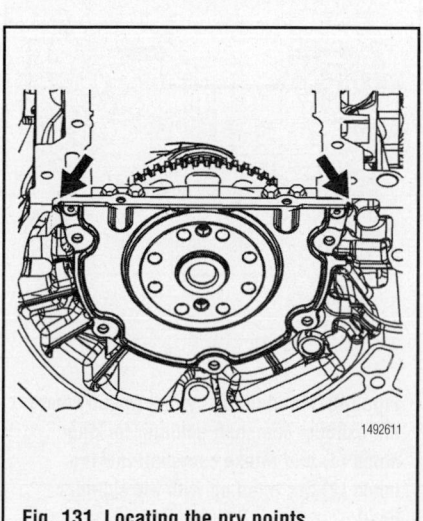

Fig. 131 Locating the pry points

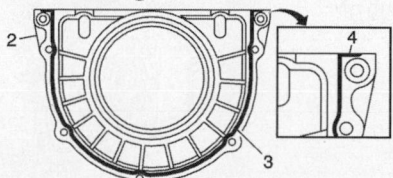

Fig. 134 Identifying the 1st and 2nd design crankshaft rear oil seal and sealant location

Fig. 136 Removing the upper timing chain guide (1)

3. Loosen the intake camshaft actuator bolt.

4. Loosen the exhaust camshaft actuator bolt.

5. Remove Camshaft Actuator locking tool.

6. Remove the upper timing chain guide bolts.

7. Remove the upper timing chain guide.

➡ **The timing chain tensioner must be removed to unload chain tension before the timing chain is removed.**

8. Remove the timing chain tensioner plunger.

9. Locate hex on the exhaust camshaft and hold with a wrench.

10. Remove the exhaust camshaft bolt and the exhaust camshaft actuator. Discard the bolt.

11. Remove the adjustable timing chain guide bolt.

12. Remove the adjustable timing chain guide.

13. Remove the plug to gain access to the fixed timing chain guide bolt.

14. Remove the fixed timing chain guide bolts.

15. Remove the fixed timing chain guide.

16. Locate hex on the intake camshaft and hold with a wrench.

17. Remove the intake camshaft actuator bolt, the intake camshaft actuator (1) and the timing chain (2) through the top of the cylinder head. Discard the bolt.

➡ **The number 3 exhaust valves are open.**

➡ **Note the position and direction of the camshafts before removal. Mark the cylinder head in relation to the locking notches before component removal.**

18. Mark the cylinder head where the exhaust camshaft actuator locking notch (1)

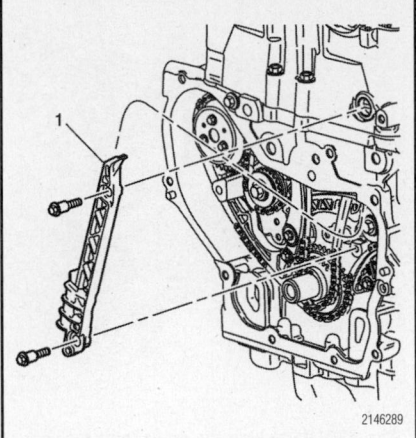
Fig. 141 Removing the fixed timing chain guide (1)

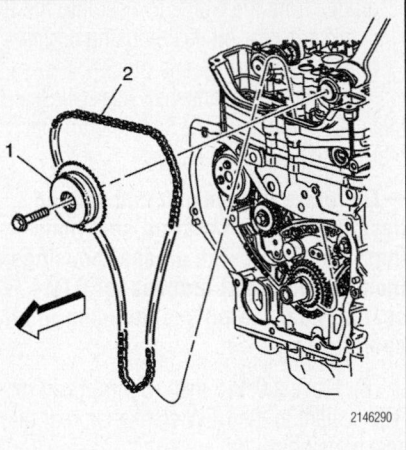
Fig. 142 Removing the intake camshaft actuator (1) and the timing chain (2)

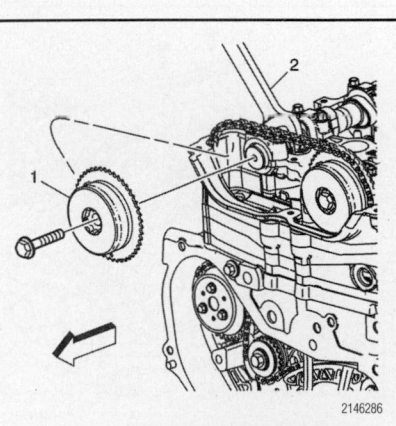
Fig. 137 Removing the timing chain tensioner plunger (1)

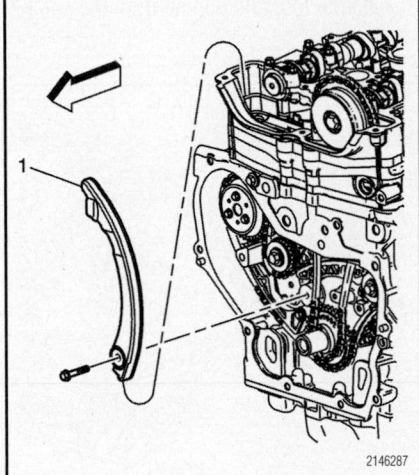
Fig. 139 Removing the adjustable timing chain guide

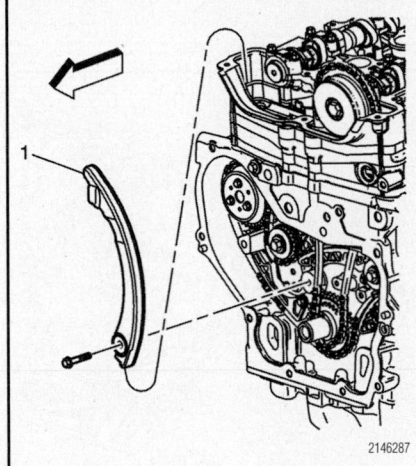
Fig. 138 Holding the exhaust camshaft with a wrench (2) and removing the exhaust camshaft actuator (1)

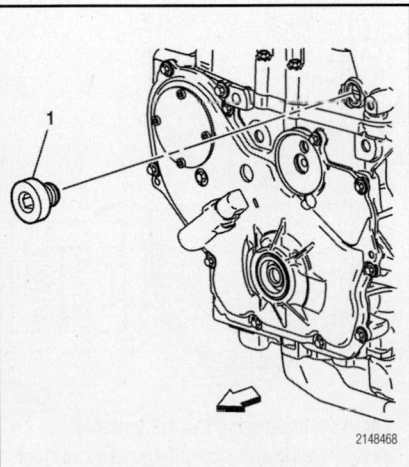
Fig. 140 Locating the plug (1)

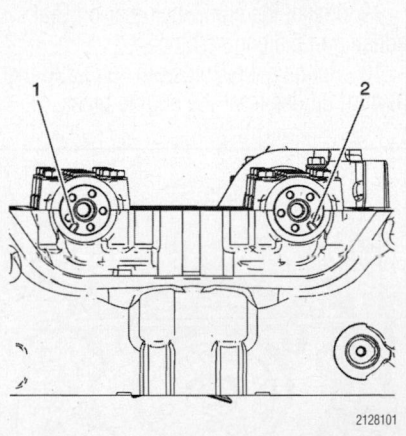
Fig. 143 Marking the cylinder head where the exhaust camshaft actuator locking notch (1) and intake camshaft locking notch (2) are lined up with the cylinder head

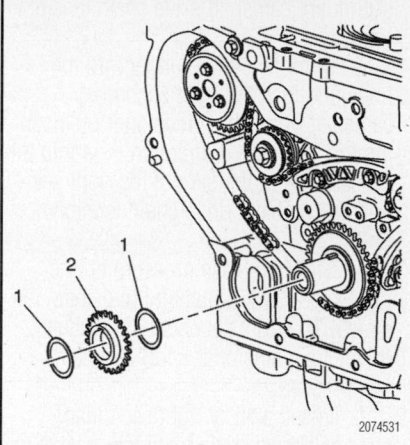

Fig. 144 Removing the crankshaft sprocket (2) and friction washers (1)

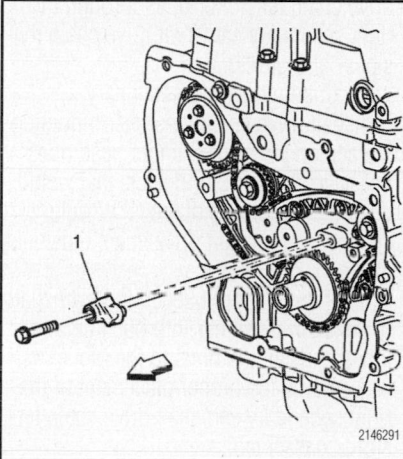

Fig. 145 Removing the timing chain oil nozzle (1)

and intake camshaft locking notch (2) are lined up with the cylinder head.

19. Remove the crankshaft sprocket (2) and friction washers (1), if equipped.

20. Remove the timing chain oil nozzle bolt.

21. Remove the timing chain oil nozzle (1).

To install:

To install, reverse the removal procedure.

3.6L Engine

See Figures 146 through 150.

1. Remove the spark plugs in order to ease crankshaft/engine rotation.

2. Remove the engine front cover.

3. Remove the right bank secondary camshaft drive chain tensioner.

　　a. Remove the right secondary camshaft drive chain tensioner bolts.

　　b. Remove the right secondary camshaft drive chain tensioner.

Fig. 146 Removing the right secondary camshaft drive chain tensioner

　　c. Remove and discard the right secondary camshaft drive chain tensioner gasket.

　　d. Inspect the right secondary camshaft drive chain tensioner mounting surface on the right cylinder head for burrs or any defects that would degrade the sealing of the NEW right secondary camshaft drive chain tensioner gasket.

4. Remove the right bank secondary camshaft drive chain shoe.

　　a. Remove the right secondary camshaft drive chain shoe bolt.

　　b. Remove the right secondary camshaft drive chain shoe.

5. Remove the right bank secondary camshaft drive chain guide.

➡ **Some models use a second design inverted tooth timing drive**

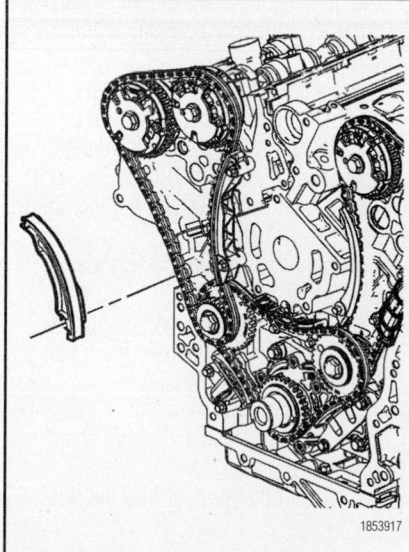

Fig. 147 Removing the right secondary camshaft drive chain shoe

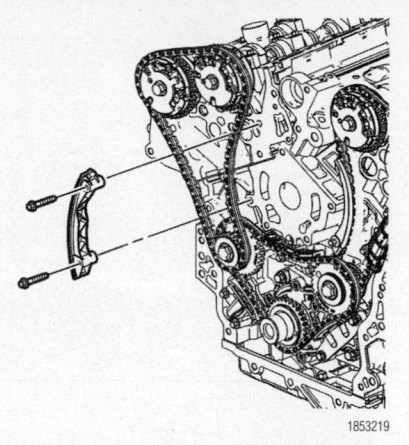

Fig. 148 Removing the right secondary camshaft drive chain guide

system on the secondary drive components.

　　a. Remove the right secondary camshaft drive chain guide bolts.

　　b. Remove the right secondary camshaft drive chain guide.

6. Remove the right bank secondary camshaft drive chain.

　　a. Remove the right secondary camshaft drive chain from the right camshaft position actuators and the right camshaft intermediate drive chain idler sprocket.

7. Remove the primary camshaft drive chain tensioner.

8. Remove the primary upper camshaft drive chain guide.

9. Remove the primary camshaft drive chain.

10. Remove the right bank camshaft intermediate drive chain idler.

11. If you are servicing the left bank camshaft intermediate drive chain idler, perform the following steps:

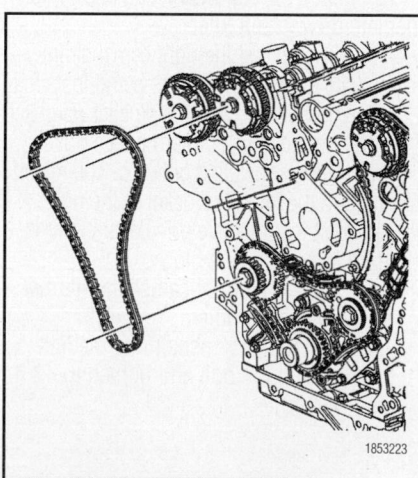

Fig. 149 Removing the right bank secondary camshaft drive chain

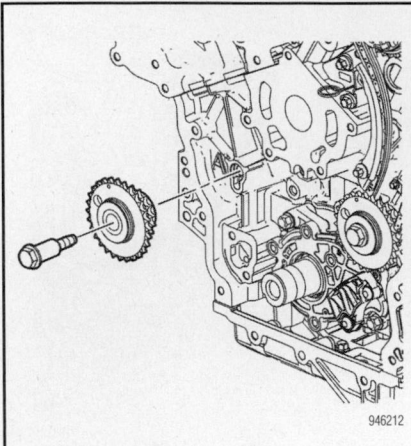

Fig. 150 Removing the left bank camshaft intermediate drive chain idler

   a. Remove the left bank secondary camshaft drive chain tensioner.

   b. Remove the left bank secondary camshaft drive chain shoe.

   c. Remove the left bank secondary camshaft drive chain guide.

   d. Remove the left bank secondary camshaft drive chain.

   e. Remove the left bank camshaft intermediate drive chain idler.

To install:

12. If you are servicing the left bank idler sprocket, perform the following steps:

   a. Install the left bank camshaft intermediate drive chain idler.

   b. Install the left bank secondary camshaft drive chain.

   c. Install the left bank secondary camshaft drive chain guide.

   d. Install the left bank secondary camshaft drive chain shoe.

   e. Install the left bank secondary camshaft drive chain tensioner.

13. Install the right bank camshaft intermediate drive chain idler.

   a. Ensure that the right camshaft intermediate drive chain idler is being installed. The recessed hub and the smaller sprocket of the right camshaft intermediate drive chain idler is installed outward. The raised hub and the larger sprocket of the right camshaft intermediate drive chain idler is installed towards the block.

   b. Install the right camshaft intermediate drive chain idler.

   c. Install the camshaft intermediate drive chain idler bolt and tighten to 43 ft. lbs. (58 Nm).

14. Install the primary camshaft drive chain.

15. Install the primary upper camshaft drive chain guide.

   a. Ensure the upper primary camshaft drive chain guide is being installed.

16. Install the upper primary camshaft drive chain guides.

17. Install the upper primary camshaft drive chain guide bolts and tighten to 18 ft. lbs. (25 Nm).

18. Install the primary camshaft drive chain tensioner.

   a. Ensure the upper primary camshaft drive chain guide is being installed.

   b. Install the upper primary camshaft drive chain guides.

   c. Install the upper primary camshaft drive chain guide bolts and tighten to 18 ft. lbs. (25 Nm).

19. Install the right bank secondary camshaft drive chain.

20. Install the right bank secondary camshaft drive chain guide.

➡ **Some models use a second design inverted tooth timing drive system on the secondary drive components.**

   a. Ensure that the right secondary camshaft drive chain guide is being installed.

   b. Position the right secondary camshaft drive chain guide.

   c. Install the secondary camshaft drive chain guide bolts. Tighten the secondary camshaft drive chain guide bolts to 17 ft. lbs. (23 Nm).

21. Install the right bank secondary camshaft drive chain shoe.

   a. Ensure that the right secondary camshaft drive chain shoe is being installed.

   b. Position the right secondary camshaft drive chain shoe.

   c. Install the secondary camshaft drive chain shoe bolt. Tighten the secondary camshaft drive chain shoe bolt to 17 ft. lbs. (23 Nm).

22. Install the right bank secondary camshaft drive chain tensioner.

   a. Ensure that the right secondary camshaft drive chain tensioner is being installed.

   b. Using the Tensioner Tool, reset the right secondary camshaft drive chain tensioner plunger.

   c. Install the plunger into the right secondary camshaft drive chain tensioner body.

   d. Compress the plunger into the body and lock the right secondary camshaft drive chain tensioner by inserting the Tensioner Retraction Pins into the access hole in the side of the right secondary camshaft drive chain tensioner body.

   e. Slowly release pressure on the right secondary camshaft drive chain tensioner. The right secondary camshaft drive chain tensioner should remain compressed.

   f. Install a NEW right secondary camshaft drive chain tensioner gasket to the right secondary camshaft drive chain tensioner.

   g. Install the right secondary camshaft drive chain tensioner bolts through the right secondary camshaft drive chain tensioner and gasket.

   h. Ensure the right secondary camshaft drive chain tensioner mounting surface on the right cylinder head does not have any burrs or defects that would degrade the sealing of the NEW right secondary camshaft drive chain tensioner gasket.

   i. Place the right secondary camshaft drive chain tensioner into position and loosely install the bolts to the block.

   j. Verify the proper placement of the right secondary camshaft drive chain tensioner gasket tab.

   k. First Pass, tighten the right secondary camshaft drive chain tensioner bolts to 44 inch lbs. (5 Nm).

   l. Final Pass, tighten the right secondary camshaft drive chain tensioner bolts to 17 ft. lbs. (23 Nm).

   m. Release the right camshaft drive chain tensioner by pulling out the Tensioner Retraction Pins and unlocking the tensioner plunger.

➡ **Ensure that all timing chain tensioners are completely released. A timing chain tensioner that is not properly released can lead to serious engine damage.**

   n. Verify all primary and secondary camshaft drive chain timing mark alignments.

   o. Remove Camshaft Retaining tools from both sets of camshafts.

23. Install the spark plugs.

24. Install the engine front cover.

ENGINE PERFORMANCE & EMISSION CONTROLS

CAMSHAFT POSITION (CMP) SENSOR

REMOVAL & INSTALLATION

2.4L Engine

Exhaust

See Figure 151.

1. Remove the air cleaner outlet duct.
2. Disconnect the engine wiring harness electrical connector from the exhaust camshaft position (CMP) sensor.
3. Remove the CMP sensor bolt.
4. Remove the CMP sensor.

To Install:

➡**Inspect the CMP sensor for damage, replace as necessary.**

5. Lubricate the CMP sensor O-ring seal with clean engine oil.
6. Install the CMP sensor.
7. Install the CMP sensor bolt and tighten to 89 inch lbs. (10 Nm).
8. Connect engine wiring harness electrical connector to the exhaust CMP sensor.
9. Install the air cleaner outlet duct.

Intake

See Figure 151.

1. Remove the air cleaner outlet duct.
2. Disconnect the engine wiring harness electrical connector from the intake camshaft position (CMP) sensor.
3. Remove the CMP sensor bolt.
4. Remove the CMP sensor.

To install:

➡**Inspect the CMP sensor for damage, replace as necessary.**

5. Lubricate the CMP sensor O-ring seal with clean engine oil.
6. Install the CMP sensor.
7. Install the CMP sensor bolt and tighten to 89 inch lbs. (10 Nm).
8. Connect the engine wiring harness electrical connector to the intake CMP sensor.
9. Install the air cleaner outlet duct.

3.6L Engine

Bank 1 Exhaust

See Figure 152.

1. Remove the air cleaner assembly.
2. Disconnect the engine wiring harness electrical connector from the bank 1 exhaust camshaft position (CMP) sensor.
3. Remove the CMP sensor bolt.
4. Remove the CMP sensor.

To install:

5. Install the CMP sensor.
6. Install the CMP sensor bolt and tighten to 89 inch lbs. (10 Nm).
7. Connect the engine wiring harness electrical connector to the bank 1 exhaust CMP sensor.
8. Install the air cleaner assembly.

Bank 1 Intake

See Figure 153.

1. Remove the air cleaner assembly.
2. Disconnect the engine wiring harness electrical connector from the

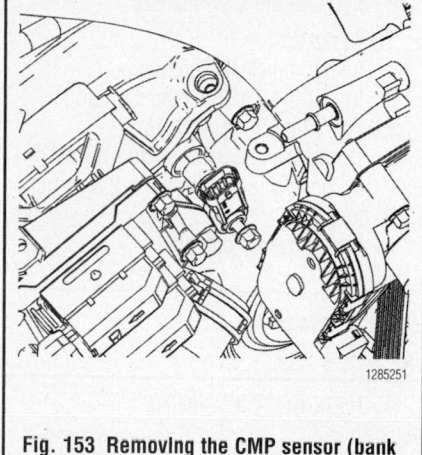

Fig. 153 Removing the CMP sensor (bank 1 intake)

bank 1 intake camshaft position (CMP) sensor.
3. Remove the CMP sensor bolt.
4. Remove the CMP sensor.

To install:

5. Install the CMP sensor.
6. Install the CMP sensor bolt and tighten to 89 inch lbs. (10 Nm).
7. Connect the engine wiring harness electrical connector to the bank 1 intake CMP sensor.
8. Install the air cleaner assembly.

Bank 2 Exhaust

See Figure 154.

1. Remove the air cleaner assembly.
2. Disconnect the engine wiring harness electrical connector from the

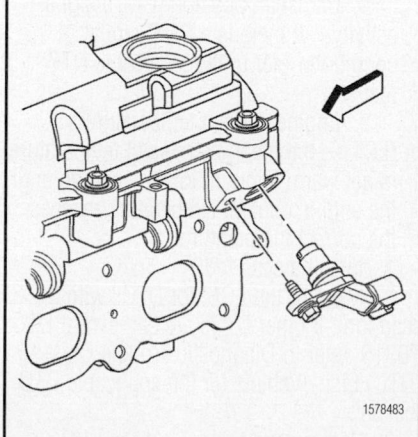

Fig. 151 Removing the CMP sensor (Intake CMP shown, exhaust CMP similar)

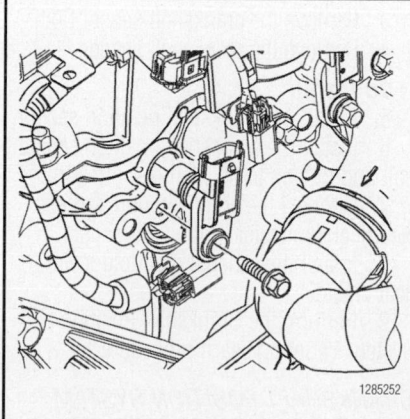

Fig. 152 Removing the CMP sensor (bank 1 exhaust)

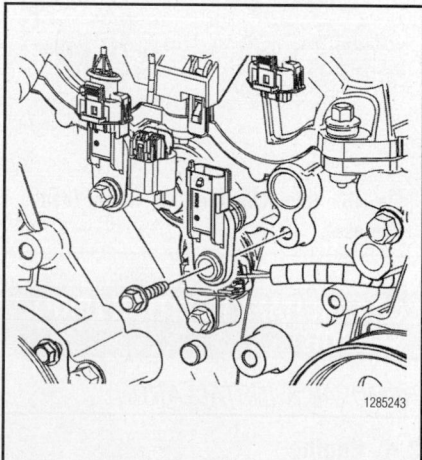

Fig. 154 Removing the CMP sensor (bank 2 exhaust)

bank 2 exhaust camshaft position (CMP) sensor.

3. Remove the CMP sensor bolt.

4. Remove the CMP sensor.

To install:

5. Install the CMP sensor.

6. Install the CMP sensor bolt and tighten to 89 inch lbs. (10 Nm).

7. Connect the engine wiring harness electrical connector to the bank 2 exhaust CMP sensor.

8. Install the air cleaner assembly.

Bank 2 Intake

See Figure 155.

1. Remove the air cleaner assembly.

2. Disconnect the engine wiring harness electrical connector from the bank 2 intake camshaft position (CMP) sensor.

3. Remove the CMP sensor bolt.

4. Remove the CMP sensor.

To install:

5. Install the CMP sensor.

6. Install the CMP sensor bolt and tighten to 89 inch lbs. (10 Nm).

7. Connect the engine wiring harness electrical connector to the bank 2 intake CMP sensor.

8. Install the air cleaner assembly.

Fig. 155 Removing the CMP sensor (bank 2 intake)

CRANKSHAFT POSITION (CKP) SENSOR

REMOVAL & INSTALLATION

2.4L Engine

See Figure 156.

1. Remove the starter.

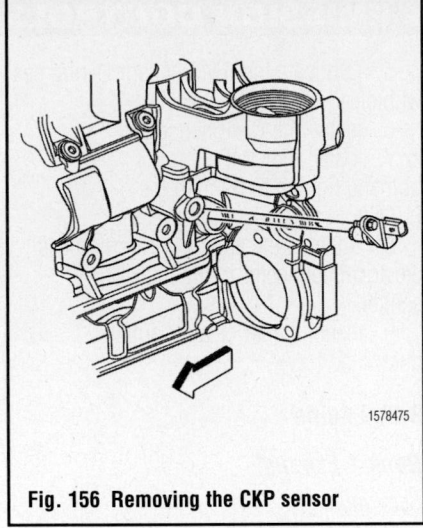

Fig. 156 Removing the CKP sensor

2. Disconnect the engine wiring harness electrical connector from the crankshaft position (CKP) sensor.

3. Remove the CKP sensor bolt.

4. Remove the CKP sensor.

To install:

5. Lubricate the CKP sensor O-ring seal with clean engine oil.

6. Install the CKP sensor.

7. Install the CKP sensor bolt and tighten to 89 inch lbs. (10 Nm).

8. Connect the engine wiring harness electrical connector to the CKP sensor.

9. Install the starter.

10. Perform the crankshaft position system variation learn procedure.

3.6L Engine

See Figure 157.

1. Remove the exhaust manifold lower heat shield.

2. Disconnect the engine wiring harness electrical connector from the crankshaft position (CKP) sensor.

3. Remove the crankshaft sensor bolt.

4. Remove the crankshaft sensor.

To install:

5. Install the crankshaft position sensor.

6. Install the crankshaft position sensor bolt and tighten to 89 inch lbs. (10 Nm).

7. Connect the engine wiring harness electrical connector to the CKP sensor.

8. Install the exhaust manifold lower heat shield.

9. Perform the Crankshaft Position System Variation Learn procedure.

CRANKSHAFT POSITION SYSTEM VARIATION LEARN PROCEDURE

➡The crankshaft position (CKP) system variation learn procedure is required

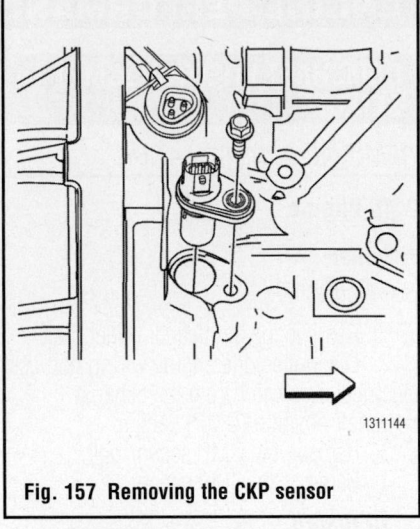

Fig. 157 Removing the CKP sensor

when the following service procedures have been performed, regardless of whether DTC P0315 is set:

- Engine replacement
- Engine control module (ECM) replacement
- Crankshaft damper replacement
- Crankshaft replacement
- CKP sensor replacement
- Any engine repairs which disturb the crankshaft to CKP sensor relationship

➡The scan tool monitors certain component signals to determine if all the conditions are met to continue with the CKP system variation learn procedure. The scan tool only displays the condition that inhibits the procedure. The scan tool monitors the following components:

a. CKP sensor activity—If there is a CKP sensor condition, refer to the applicable DTC that set.

b. Camshaft position (CMP) signal activity—If there is a CMP signal condition, refer to the applicable DTC that set.

c. Engine coolant temperature (ECT)—If the engine coolant temperature is not warm enough, idle the engine until the engine coolant temperature reaches the correct temperature.

1. Install a scan tool.

2. Monitor the ECM for DTCs with a scan tool. If other DTCs are set, except DTC P0315, refer to Diagnostic Trouble Code (DTC) List - Vehicle for the applicable DTC that set.

3. With a scan tool, select the CKP system variation learn procedure and perform the following:

a. Observe the fuel cut-off for the applicable engine.

b. Block the drive wheels.

c. Set the parking brake.

d. Place the vehicle's transmission in Park or Neutral.

e. Turn the air conditioning (A/C) OFF.

f. Cycle the ignition from OFF to ON.

g. Apply and hold the brake pedal for the duration of the procedure.

h. Start and idle the engine.

i. Accelerate to wide open throttle (WOT). The engine should not accelerate beyond the calibrated fuel cut-off RPM value noted. Release the throttle immediately if the value is exceeded.

➡ **While the learn procedure is in progress, release the throttle immediately when the engine starts to decelerate. The engine control is returned to the operator and the engine responds to throttle position after the learn procedure is complete.**

j. Release the throttle when fuel cut-off occurs.

4. The scan tool displays Learn Status: Learned this Ignition. If the scan tool indicates that DTC P0315 ran and passed, the CKP variation learn procedure is complete. If the scan tool indicates DTC P0315 failed or did not run, refer to DTC P0315. If any other DTCs set, refer to Diagnostic Trouble Code (DTC) List   Vehicle for the applicable DTC that set.

5. Turn OFF the ignition for 30 seconds after the learn procedure is completed successfully.

ENGINE COOLANT TEMPERATURE (ECT) SENSOR

REMOVAL & INSTALLATION

2.4L Engine

See Figure 158.

✳✳ CAUTION

Use care when handling the coolant sensor. Damage to the coolant sensor will affect the operation of the fuel control system.

1. Drain the cooling system.

2. Disconnect the engine wiring harness electrical connector from the engine coolant temperature (ECT) sensor.

3. Remove the ECT sensor from the thermostat housing.

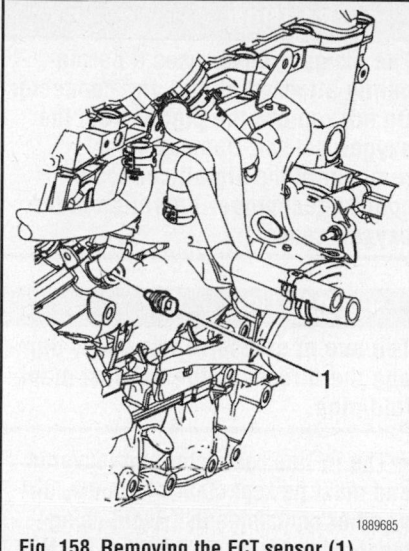

Fig. 158 Removing the ECT sensor (1)

To install:

✳✳ CAUTION

Replacement components must be the correct part number for the application. Components requiring the use of the thread locking compound, lubricants, corrosion inhibitors, or sealants are identified in the service procedure. Some replacement components may come with these coatings already applied. Do not use these coatings on components unless specified. These coatings can affect the final torque, which may affect the operation of the component. Use the correct torque specification when installing components in order to avoid damage.

✳✳ CAUTION

Use care when handling the coolant sensor. Damage to the coolant sensor will affect the operation of the fuel control system.

4. If reinstalling the original sensor, or if installing a NEW sensor without a sealer, coat the threads with sealant.

5. Install the ECT sensor to the thermostat housing and tighten the sensor to 15 ft. lbs. (20 Nm).

6. Connect the engine wiring harness electrical connector to the ECT sensor.

7. Fill the cooling system.

3.6L Engine

See Figure 159.

1. Disconnect the engine wiring harness electrical connector from the engine coolant temperature (ECT) sensor.

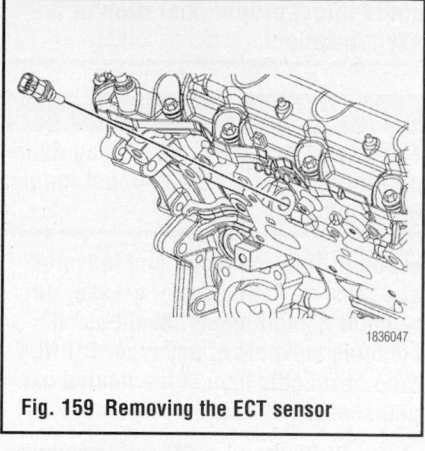

Fig. 159 Removing the ECT sensor

2. Remove the ECT sensor.

To install:

3. Install the ECT sensor and tighten to 16 ft. lbs. (22 Nm).

4. Connect the engine wiring harness electrical connector to the ECT sensor.

HEATED OXYGEN (HO2S) SENSOR

REMOVAL & INSTALLATION

2.4L Engine

Sensor 1

See Figure 160.

✳✳ CAUTION

The oxygen sensor uses a permanently attached pigtail and connector. Do not remove the pigtail from the oxygen sensor. Damage to or removal of the pigtail connector

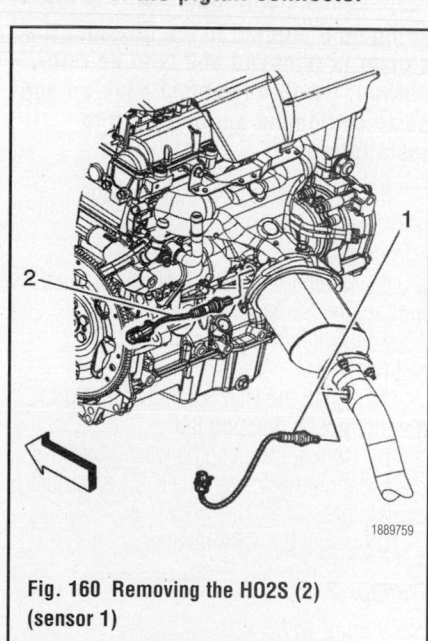

Fig. 160 Removing the HO2S (2) (sensor 1)

could affect proper operation of the oxygen sensor.

> ✳✳ **CAUTION**
>
> The use of excessive force may damage the threads in the exhaust manifold/pipe.

➡ The in-line connector and louvered end must be kept clear of grease, dirt or other contaminants. Avoid using cleaning solvents of any type. DO NOT drop or roughly handle the heated oxygen sensor (HO2S).

➡ The HO2S may be difficult to remove when the engine temperature is less than 120°F (48°C).

1. Remove the connector position assurance (CPA) retainer.
2. Disconnect the engine wiring harness electrical connector from the HO2S electrical connector.
3. Remove the HO2S connector clip from the thermostat housing tab.
4. Remove the HO2S, if necessary use the Oxygen Sensor Wrench.

To install:

➡ A special anti-seize compound is used on the heated oxygen sensor threads. The compound consists of a liquid graphite and glass beads. The graphite will burn away, but the glass beads will remain, making the sensor easier to remove. New or service replacement sensors will have the compound applied to the threads. If a sensor is removed and is to be reinstalled, the threads must have an anti-seize compound applied prior to installation.

5. If necessary, coat the threads of the HO2S with anti-seize compound.
6. Install the HO2S, if necessary use the Oxygen Sensor Wrench.
7. Tighten the sensor to 31 ft. lbs. (42 Nm).
8. Install the HO2S connector clip to the thermostat housing tab.
9. Connect the engine wiring harness electrical connector to the HO2S electrical connector.
10. Install the CPA retainer.

Sensor 2

See Figure 161.

> ✳✳ **CAUTION**
>
> The oxygen sensor uses a permanently attached pigtail and connector. Do not remove the pigtail from the oxygen sensor. Damage to or removal of the pigtail connector could affect proper operation of the oxygen sensor.

> ✳✳ **CAUTION**
>
> The use of excessive force may damage the threads in the exhaust manifold/pipe.

➡ The in-line connector and louvered end must be kept clear of grease, dirt or other contaminants. Avoid using cleaning solvents of any type. DO NOT drop or roughly handle the heated oxygen sensor (HO2S).

➡ The HO2S may be difficult to remove when the engine temperature is less than 120°F (48°C).

1. Raise and suitably support the vehicle.
2. Remove the connector position assurance (CPA) retainer.
3. Disconnect the HO2S electrical connector from the engine wiring harness electrical connector.
4. Remove the HO2S, if necessary use the Oxygen Sensor Wrench.

To install:

➡ A special anti-seize compound is used on the heated oxygen sensor threads. The compound consists of a liquid graphite and glass beads. The graphite will burn away, but the glass

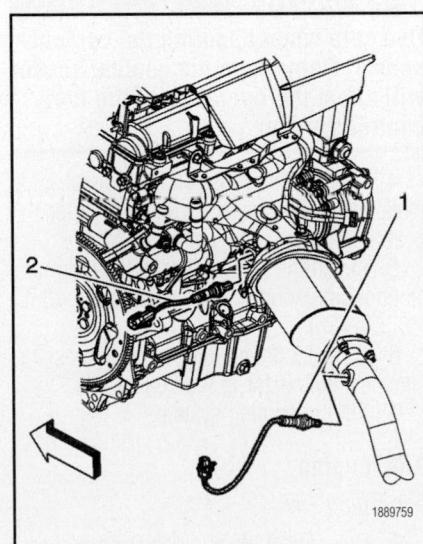

Fig. 161 Removing the HO2S (1) (sensor 2)

beads will remain, making the sensor easier to remove. New or service replacement sensors will have the compound applied to the threads. If a sensor is removed and is to be reinstalled, the threads must have an anti-seize compound applied prior to installation.

5. If necessary, coat the threads of the HO2S with anti-seize compound.
6. Install the HO2S, if necessary use the Oxygen Sensor Wrench.
7. Tighten the sensor to 31 ft. lbs. (42 Nm).
8. Connect the HO2S electrical connector to the engine wiring harness electrical connector.
9. Install the CPA retainer.
10. Lower the vehicle.

3.6L Engine

Bank 1 Senor 1

See Figure 162.

1. Raise and support the vehicle.
2. Remove the engine wiring harness heated oxygen sensor (HO2S) electrical connector clip from the engine harness.
3. Remove the connector position assurance (CPA) retainer from the HO2S electrical connection.
4. Disconnect the engine wiring harness electrical connector from the HO2S electrical connector.
5. Raise and support the vehicle to an appropriate height to reach the HO2S.
6. Remove the HO2S from the exhaust manifold.

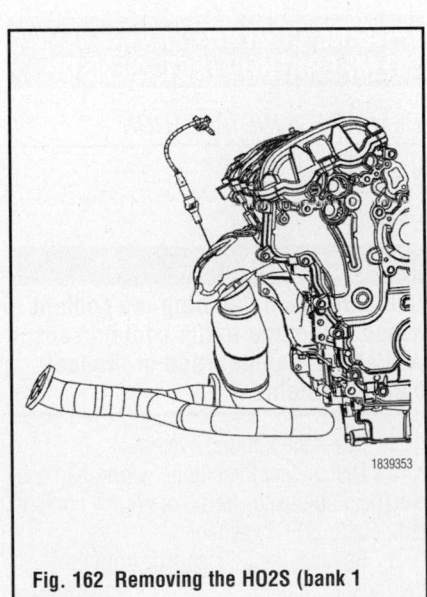

Fig. 162 Removing the HO2S (bank 1 sensor 1)

To install:

➡A special anti-seize compound is used in the HO2S threads. The compound consists of liquid graphite and glass beads. The graphite tends to burn away, but the glass beads remain, making the sensor easier to remove. New, or service replacement sensors already have the compound applied to the threads. If the sensor is removed from an exhaust component and if for any reason the sensor is to reinstalled, the threads must have anti-seize compound applied before the reinstallation.

7. If reinstalling the old sensor, coat the threads with anti-seize compound.

8. Install the HO2S to the exhaust manifold and tighten the sensor to 31 ft. lbs. (42 Nm).

9. Lower the vehicle.

10. Connect the engine wiring harness electrical connector to the HO2S electrical connector.

11. Install the engine wiring harness HO2S electrical connector clip to the engine harness.

12. Install the CPA retainer to the HO2S electrical connection.

Bank 1 Senor 2

See Figure 163.

1. Raise and support the vehicle.

2. Remove the connector position assurance (CPA) retainer from the HO2S electrical connection.

3. Disconnect the heated oxygen sensor (HO2S) electrical connector from the engine wiring harness electrical connector.

4. Remove the bank 1 sensor 2 HO2S from the catalytic converter.

To install:

➡A special anti-seize compound is used in the HO2S threads. The compound consists of liquid graphite and glass beads. The graphite tends to burn away, but the glass beads remain, making the sensor easier to remove. New, or service replacement sensors already have the compound applied to the threads. If the sensor is removed from an exhaust component and if for any reason the sensor is to reinstalled, the threads must have anti-seize compound applied before the reinstallation.

5. If reinstalling the old sensor, coat the threads with anti-seize compound.

6. Install the bank 1 sensor 2 HO2S to the catalytic converter and tighten the sensor to 31 ft. lbs. (42 Nm).

7. Connect the HO2S electrical connector to the engine wiring harness electrical connector.

8. Install the CPA retainer to the HO2S electrical connection.

9. Lower the vehicle.

Bank 2 Senor 1

See Figure 164.

1. Remove the fuel injector sight shield.

2. Remove the air cleaner outlet duct.

3. Remove the connector position assurance (CPA) retainer from the HO2S electrical connection.

4. Disconnect the engine wiring harness electrical connector from the heated oxygen sensor (HO2S) electrical connector.

5. Remove the HO2S electrical connector clip from the engine wiring harness tab.

6. Remove the HO2S from the exhaust manifold.

To install:

➡A special anti-seize compound is used in the HO2S threads. The compound consists of liquid graphite and glass beads. The graphite tends to burn away, but the glass beads remain, making the sensor easier to remove. New, or service replacement sensors already have the compound applied to the threads. If the sensor is removed from an exhaust component and if for any reason the sensor is to reinstalled, the threads must have anti-seize compound applied before the reinstallation.

7. If reinstalling the old sensor, coat the threads with anti-seize compound.

8. Install the HO2S to the exhaust manifold and tighten the sensor to 31 ft. lbs. (42 Nm).

9. Connect the engine wiring harness electrical connector to the HO2S electrical connector.

10. Install the HO2S electrical connector clip to the engine wiring harness tab.

11. Install the CPA retainer to the HO2S electrical connection.

12. Install the air cleaner outlet duct.

13. Install the fuel injector sight shield.

Bank 2 Senor 2

See Figure 165.

1. Raise and support the vehicle.

2. Remove the connector position assurance (CPA) retainer from the HO2S electrical connection.

3. Disconnect the heated oxygen sensor (HO2S) electrical connector from the engine wiring harness electrical connector.

4. Remove the bank 2 sensor 2 HO2S (1) from the catalytic converter.

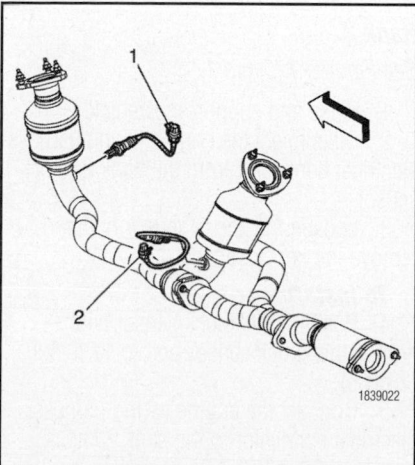

Fig. 163 Removing the bank 1 sensor 2 HO2S (2)

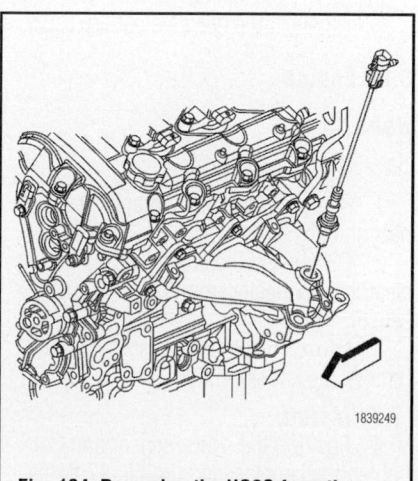

Fig. 164 Removing the HO2S from the exhaust manifold

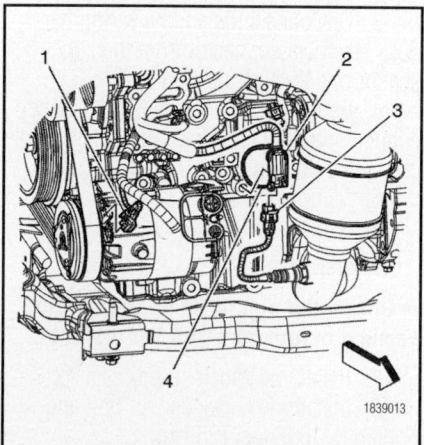

Fig. 165 Removing the HO2S (1) (bank 2 sensor 2)

To install:

➡A special anti-seize compound is used in the HO2S threads. The compound consists of liquid graphite and glass beads. The graphite tends to burn away, but the glass beads remain, making the sensor easier to remove. New, or service replacement sensors already have the compound applied to the threads. If the sensor is removed from an exhaust component and if for any reason the sensor is to reinstalled, the threads must have anti-seize compound applied before the reinstallation.

5. If reinstalling the old sensor, coat the threads with anti-seize compound.

6. Install the bank 2 sensor 2 HO2S to the catalytic converter and tighten the sensor to 31 ft. lbs. (42 Nm).

7. Connect the HO2S electrical connector to the engine wiring harness electrical connector.

8. Install the CPA retainer to the HO2S electrical connection.

9. Lower the vehicle.

INTAKE AIR TEMPERATURE (IAT) SENSOR

REMOVAL & INSTALLATION

Refer to Mass Airflow Sensor.

KNOCK SENSOR (KS)

REMOVAL & INSTALLATION

2.4L Engine

See Figures 166 and 167.

1. Disconnect the negative battery cable.

2. Raise and support the vehicle.

3. Disconnect the engine wiring harness electrical connector from the knock sensor pigtail electrical connector.

4. Remove the knock sensor electrical connector pigtail clip from the oil level indicator tube bracket.

5. Remove the knock sensor bolt.

6. Remove the knock sensor.

To install:

➡Rotate the pigtail 90 degrees from vertical before securing the fastener.

7. Install the knock sensor.

8. Install the knock sensor bolt and tighten to 18 ft. lbs. (25 Nm).

9. Install the knock sensor electrical connector pigtail clip to the oil level indicator tube bracket.

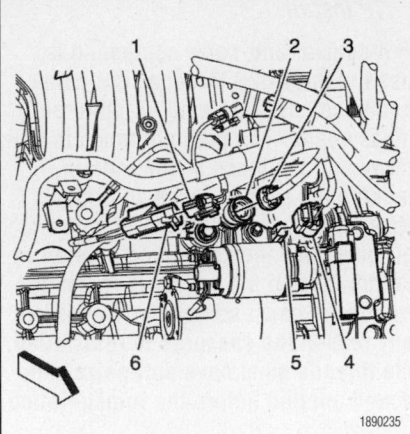

Fig. 166 Disconnecting the engine wiring harness electrical connector (1) from the knock sensor pigtail electrical connector (6)

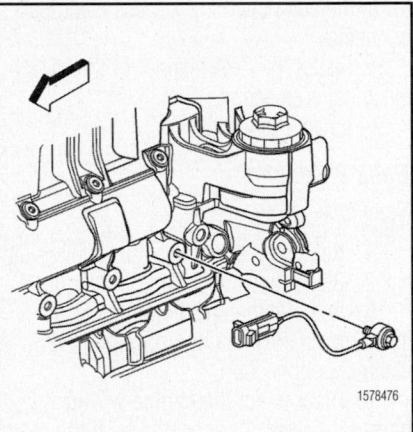

Fig. 167 Removing and installing the knock sensor

10. Connect the engine wiring harness electrical connector to the knock sensor pigtail electrical connector.

11. Lower the vehicle.

12. Connect the negative battery cable.

3.6L Engine

Bank 1

See Figures 168 and 169.

1. Remove the exhaust manifold lower heat shield.

2. Disconnect the engine wiring harness electrical connector from the bank 1 knock sensor.

3. Loosen the knock sensor bolt and remove the knock sensor.

To install:

4. Position the knock sensor and tighten the knock sensor bolt to 17 ft. lbs. (23 Nm).

5. Connect the engine wiring harness

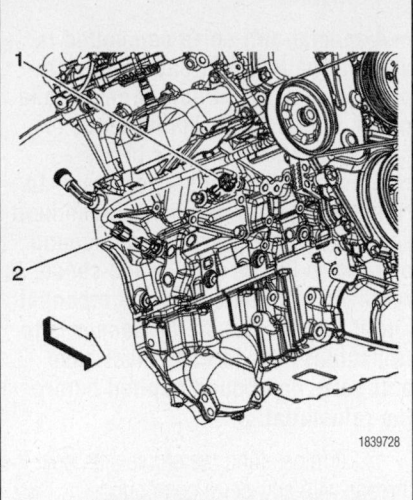

Fig. 168 Disconnecting the knock sensor bank 1 (1) electrical connector

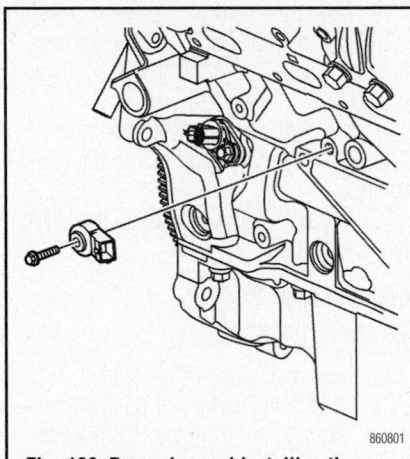

Fig. 169 Removing and installing the knock sensor bank 1

electrical connector to the bank 1 knock sensor.

6. Install the exhaust manifold lower heat shield.

Bank 2

See Figures 170 and 171.

1. Raise and support the vehicle.

2. Disconnect the engine wiring harness electrical connector from the bank 2 knock sensor.

3. Loosen the knock sensor bolt and remove the knock sensor.

To install:

4. Position the knock sensor and tighten the knock sensor bolt to 17 ft. lbs. (23 Nm).

5. Connect the engine wiring harness electrical connector to the bank 2 knock sensor.

6. Lower the vehicle.

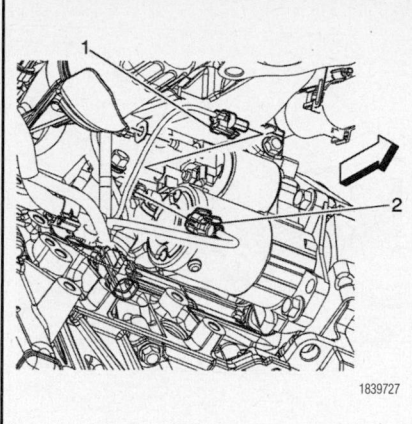

Fig. 170 Disconnecting the knock sensor bank 2 (2)

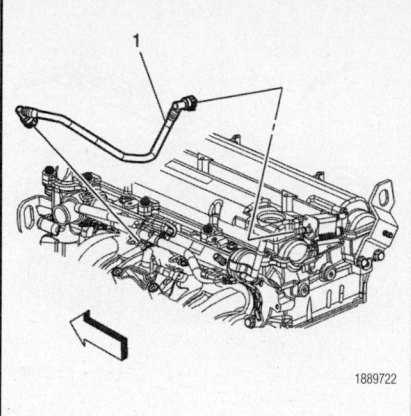

Fig. 172 Repositioning the EVAP canister purge tube

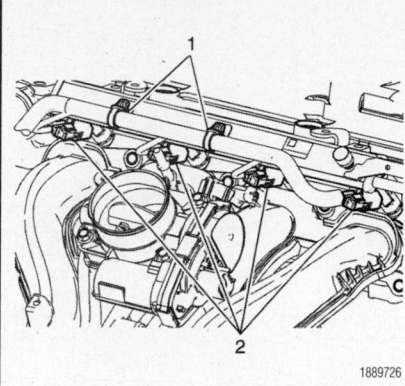

Fig. 174 Removing the fuel injector wiring clips (1) and disconnecting the fuel injector wiring harness electrical connector (2)

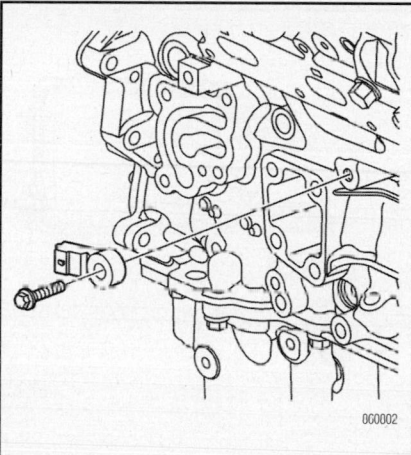

Fig. 171 Removing the knock sensor bank 2

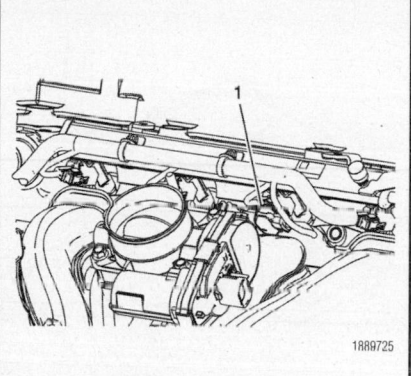

Fig. 173 Disconnecting the fuel injector wiring harness electrical connector from the MAP sensor

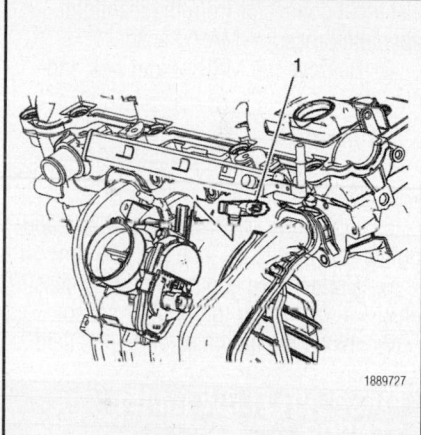

Fig. 175 Removing and installing the MAP sensor

MANIFOLD ABSOLUTE PRESSURE (MAP) SENSOR

REMOVAL & INSTALLATION

2.4L Engine

See Figures 172 through 175.

1. Remove the air cleaner outlet duct.
2. Disconnect the evaporative emission (EVAP) canister purge tube from the intake manifold.
3. Reposition the EVAP canister purge tube out of the way.
4. Disconnect the fuel injector wiring harness electrical connector from the manifold absolute pressure (MAP) sensor.
5. Remove the fuel injector wiring harness clips from the fuel rail tabs.
6. Disconnect the fuel injector wiring harness electrical connector from the number 3 fuel injector.
7. Squeeze tabs and slide the MAP sensor upward.

To install:

8. Lubricate the NEW MAP sensor seal with clean engine oil.
9. Install the MAP sensor into the intake manifold.
10. Connect the fuel injector wiring harness electrical connector to the number 3 fuel injector.
11. Install the fuel injector wiring harness clips to the fuel rail tabs.
12. Connect the fuel injector wiring harness electrical connector to the MAP sensor.
13. Position the EVAP canister purge tube out of the way.
14. Connect the EVAP canister purge tube to the intake manifold.
15. Install the air cleaner outlet duct.

3.6L Engine

See Figures 176 and 177.

1. Remove the fuel injector sight shield.
2. Disconnect the engine wiring harness

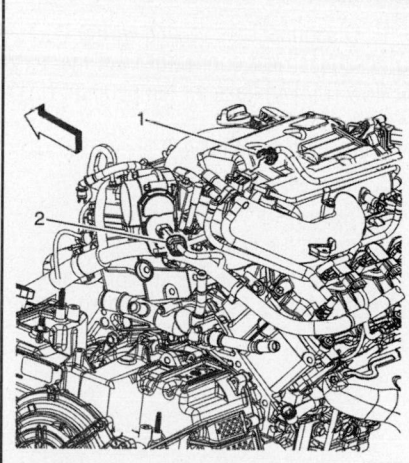

Fig. 176 Disconnecting the MAP sensor (1) electrical connector

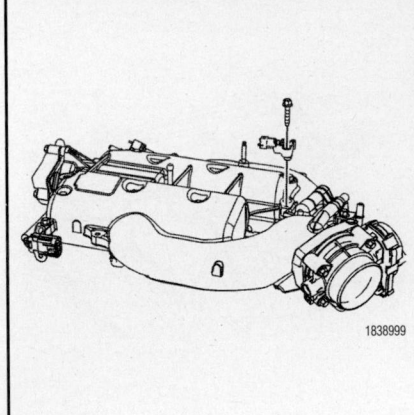

Fig. 177 Removing and installing the MAP sensor

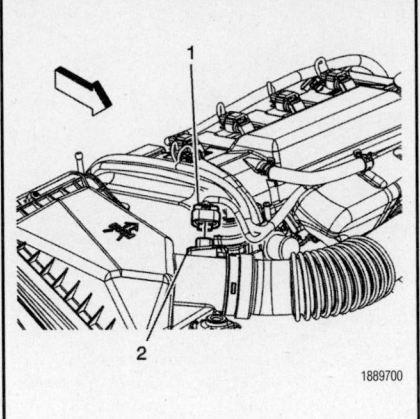

Fig. 178 Disconnecting the MAF/IAT sensor (2) electrical connector (1)

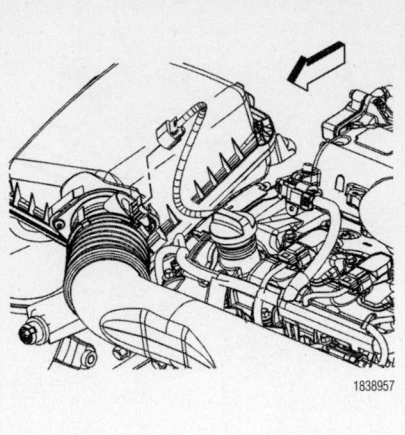

Fig. 180 Disconnecting the MAF/IAT sensor

electrical connector from the manifold absolute pressure (MAP) sensor.

3. Remove the MAP sensor bolt and sensor.

To install:

4. Lubricate the MAP sensor O-ring seal with clean engine oil.

5. Install the MAP sensor and bolt and tighten the bolt to 89 inch lbs. (10 Nm).

6. Connect the engine wiring harness electrical connector to the MAP sensor.

7. Install the fuel injector sight shield.

MASS AIR FLOW (MAF) SENSOR

REMOVAL & INSTALLATION

2.4L Engine

See Figures 178 and 179

1. Disconnect the engine wiring harness electrical connector from the mass air flow (MAF)/intake air temperature (IAT) sensor.

2. Remove the MAF/IAT sensor screws.

3. Remove the MAF/IAT sensor.

To install:

4. Install the MAF/IAT sensor.

5. Install the MAF/IAT sensor screws and tighten to 22 inch lbs. (2.5 Nm).

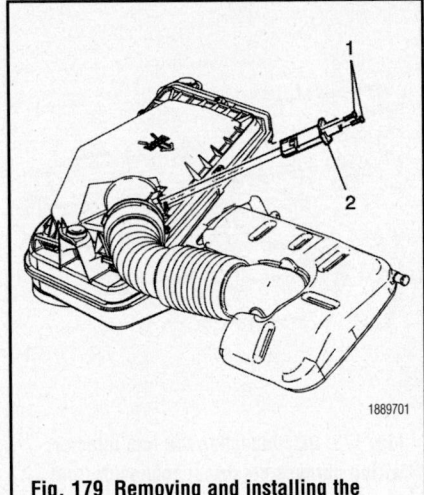

Fig. 179 Removing and installing the MAF/IAT sensor

6. Connect the engine wiring harness electrical connector to the MAF/IAT sensor.

3.6L Engine

See Figures 180 and 181.

1. Remove the air cleaner outlet duct.

2. Disconnect the engine wiring harness electrical connector from the mass airflow (MAF)/intake air temperature (IAT) sensor.

3. Remove the MAF/IAT sensor screws.

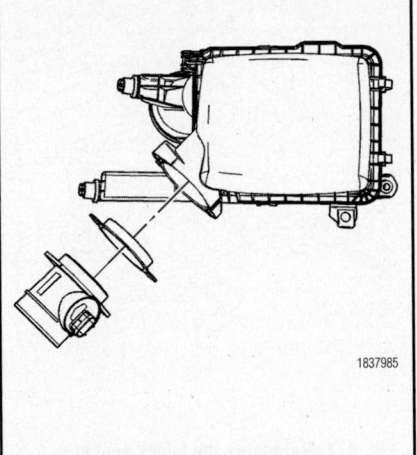

Fig. 181 Removing and installing the MAF/IAT sensor

4. Remove the MAF/IAT sensor.

5. Remove and discard the MAF/IAT sensor seal.

To install:

6. Install a NEW MAF/IAT sensor seal.

7. Install the MAF/IAT sensor.

8. Install the MAF/IAT sensor screws and tighten to 35 inch lbs. (4 Nm).

9. Connect the engine wiring harness electrical connector to the MAF/IAT sensor.

10. Install the air cleaner outlet duct.

FUEL | **GASOLINE FUEL INJECTION SYSTEM**

FUEL SYSTEM SERVICE PRECAUTIONS

Safety is the most important factor when performing not only fuel system maintenance but any type of maintenance. Failure to conduct maintenance and repairs in a safe manner may result in serious personal injury or death. Maintenance and testing of the vehicle's fuel system components can be accomplished safely and effectively by adhering to the following rules and guidelines.

• To avoid the possibility of fire and personal injury, always disconnect the negative battery cable unless the repair or test procedure requires that battery voltage be applied.

• Always relieve the fuel system pressure prior to disconnecting any fuel system component (injector, fuel rail, pressure regulator, etc.), fitting or fuel line connection. Exercise extreme caution whenever relieving fuel system pressure to avoid exposing skin, face and eyes to fuel spray. Please be advised that fuel under pressure may penetrate the skin or any part of the body that it contacts.

• Always place a shop towel or cloth around the fitting or connection prior to loosening to absorb any excess fuel due to spillage. Ensure that all fuel spillage (should it occur) is quickly removed from engine surfaces. Ensure that all fuel soaked cloths or towels are deposited into a suitable waste container.

• Always keep a dry chemical (Class B) fire extinguisher near the work area.

• Do not allow fuel spray or fuel vapors to come into contact with a spark or open flame.

• Always use a back-up wrench when loosening and tightening fuel line connection fittings. This will prevent unnecessary stress and torsion to fuel line piping.

• Always replace worn fuel fitting O-rings with new Do not substitute fuel hose or equivalent where fuel pipe is installed.

Before servicing the vehicle, make sure to also refer to the precautions in the beginning of this section as well.

RELIEVING FUEL SYSTEM PRESSURE

See Figure 182.

✳✳ WARNING

Remove the fuel tank cap and relieve the fuel system pressure before ser- vicing the fuel system in order to reduce the risk of personal injury. After you relieve the fuel system pressure, a small amount of fuel may be released when servicing the fuel lines, the fuel injection pump, or the connections. In order to reduce the risk of personal injury, cover the fuel system components with a shop towel before disconnection. This will catch any fuel that may leak out. Place the towel in an approved container when the disconnection is complete.

Digital Pressure Gauge

1. Remove the engine cover, if required.
2. Loosen the fuel fill cap in order to relieve the fuel tank vapor pressure.
3. Remove the fuel rail service port cap.

✳✳ WARNING

Wrap a shop towel around the fuel pressure connection in order to reduce the risk of fire and personal injury. The towel will absorb any fuel leakage that occurs during the connection of the fuel pressure gauge. Place the towel in an approved container when the connection of the fuel pressure gauge is complete.

4. Wrap a shop towel around the fuel rail service port.
5. Connect the CH-48027-3 (3) to the fuel rail service port.
6. Connect the CH-48027-2 (2) to the CH-48027-3 (3).
7. Place the hose on the CH-48027-2 (2) into an approved gasoline container.

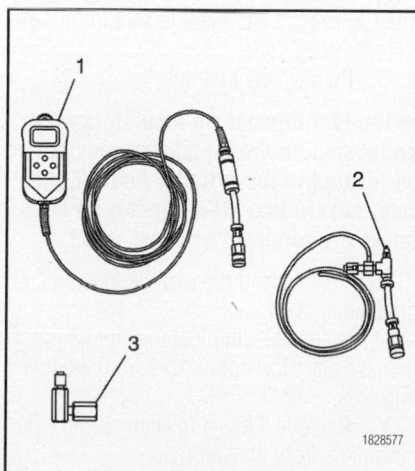

Fig. 182 Identifying the Digital Pressure Gauge (CH-48027) components

8. Open the valve on the CH-48027-2 (2) in order to bleed any fuel from the fuel rail.
9. Close the valve on the CH-48027-2 (2).
10. Remove the hose on the CH-48027-2 (2) from the approved gasoline container.

✳✳ CAUTION

Clean all of the following areas before performing any disconnections in order to avoid possible contamination in the system:

• Fuel pipe connections
• Hose connections
• Areas surrounding the connections

➡**If relieving the fuel pressure for the fuel pressure gauge installation and removal, it is NOT necessary to proceed with the following steps.**

11. Disconnect the CH-48027-2 (2) from the CH-48027-3 (3).
12. Disconnect the CH-48027-3 (3) from the fuel rail service port.
13. Remove the shop towel from around the fuel rail service port, and place in an approved gasoline container.
14. Install the fuel rail service port cap.
15. Install the engine cover, if required.
16. Tighten the fuel fill cap.

Without the Digital Pressure Gauge

✳✳ WARNING

Remove the fuel tank cap and relieve the fuel system pressure before servicing the fuel system in order to reduce the risk of personal injury. After you relieve the fuel system pressure, a small amount of fuel may be released when servicing the fuel lines, the fuel injection pump, or the connections. In order to reduce the risk of personal injury, cover the fuel system components with a shop towel before disconnection. This will catch any fuel that may leak out. Place the towel in an approved container when the disconnection is complete.

17. Loosen the fuel fill cap in order to relieve the fuel tank vapor pressure.
18. Remove the engine cover, if required.
19. Remove the fuel rail service port cap.
20. Wrap a shop towel around the fuel rail service port and using a small flat bladed tool, depress (open) the fuel rail test port valve.

21. Remove the shop towel from around the fuel rail service port, and place in an approved gasoline container.
22. Install the fuel rail service port cap.
23. Install the engine cover, if required.
24. Tighten the fuel fill cap.

FUEL INJECTORS

REMOVAL & INSTALLATION

2.4L Engine

See Figures 183 through 187.

✳ CAUTION

Use care in removing the fuel injectors in order to prevent damage to the fuel injector electrical connector pins or the fuel injector nozzles. Do not immerse the fuel injector in any type of cleaner. The fuel injector is an electrical component and may be damaged by this cleaning method.

➡If the fuel injectors are found to be leaking, the engine oil may be contaminated with fuel.

1. Relieve the fuel system pressure.
2. Remove the air cleaner outlet duct.
3. Disconnect the fuel feed line quick connect fitting from the fuel rail.
4. Disconnect the engine wiring harness electrical connector from the fuel injector wiring harness electrical connector.
5. Disconnect the fuel injector wiring harness electrical from the manifold absolute pressure (MAP) sensor.
6. Remove the engine wiring harness clips from the fuel rail tabs.
7. Remove the fuel rail bolts.

Fig. 183 Disconnecting the engine wiring harness electrical connector (3) from the fuel injector wiring harness electrical connector (4)

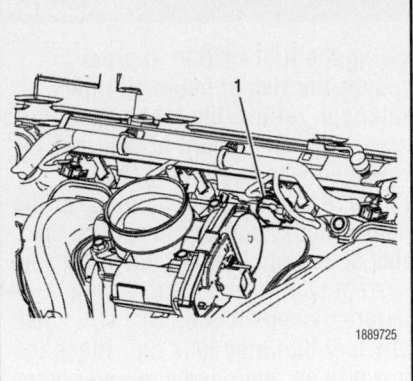

Fig. 184 Disconnecting the fuel injector wiring harness electrical connector from the MAP sensor

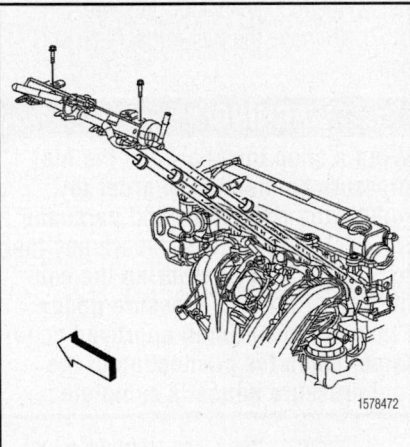

Fig. 185 Removing the fuel rail bolts and fuel rail

➡Use care when removing the fuel rail assembly in order to prevent damage to the fuel injector spray tips.

8. Pull the fuel rail back and upward in order to release the fuel injectors from the cylinder head ports.
9. Remove the fuel rail.

➡The fuel injector tip insulators may be located on the injector or may still be located in the cylinder head. Either way, ensure that all 4 injector tip insulators are removed and discarded.

10. Remove and discard the fuel injector tip insulators.
11. Disconnect the fuel injector wiring harness electrical connectors from the fuel injectors.
12. Remove the fuel injector wiring harness clips from the fuel rail.
13. Remove the fuel injector wiring harness from the fuel rail.
14. Remove the fuel injector retainer (1).

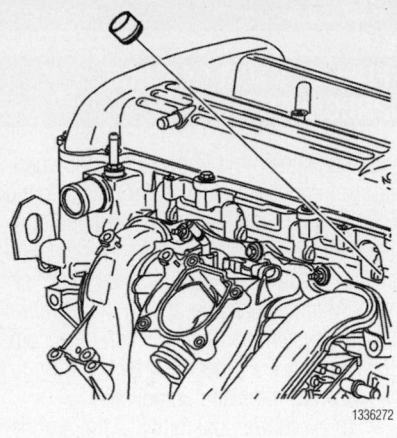

Fig. 186 Removing the fuel injector tip insulators

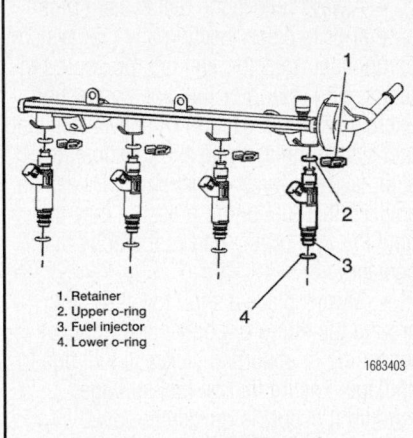

1. Retainer
2. Upper o-ring
3. Fuel injector
4. Lower o-ring

Fig. 187 Removing and installing the fuel injectors

15. Remove the fuel injector (3) from the fuel rail.
16. Remove the fuel injector upper O-ring (2).
17. Remove the fuel injector lower O-ring (4).

To install:

➡The fuel injector assembly is stamped with a part number identification. Be sure to use the correct part number when ordering replacement fuel injectors.

18. Lubricate the NEW fuel injector O-rings with clean engine oil.
19. Install the NEW fuel injector upper O-ring.
20. Install the NEW fuel injector lower O-ring.
21. Install the fuel injector to the fuel rail.
22. Install the fuel injector retainer.

➡Install only NEW lower O-rings if the fuel rail and injectors were removed and re-installed. If the fuel rail was replaced, then install NEW upper and lower O-rings. Install the fuel injector wiring harness clips to the fuel rail.

23. Connect the fuel injector wiring harness electrical connectors to the fuel injectors.

24. Lubricate the NEW fuel injector tip insulators with clean engine oil.

25. Install the NEW fuel injector tip insulators to the cylinder head.

26. Lubricate the fuel injector O-rings with clean engine oil.

27. With the fuel injectors positioned downward, lower the fuel injectors into the cylinder head ports.

28. Carefully push down on the fuel rail in order to insert the injectors into the cylinder head ports.

29. Install the fuel rail bolts and tighten to 89 inch lbs. (10 Nm).

30. Install the engine wiring harness clips to the fuel rail tabs.

31. Connect the fuel injector wiring harness electrical to the MAP sensor.

32. Connect the engine wiring harness electrical connector to the fuel injector wiring harness electrical connector.

33. Connect the fuel feed line quick connect fitting to the fuel rail.

34. Install the air cleaner outlet duct.

35. Connect the negative battery cable.

36. Inspect for fuel leaks using the following procedure:

a. Turn ON the ignition, with the engine OFF for 2 seconds.

b. Turn OFF the ignition for 10 seconds.

c. Turn ON the ignition.

d. Inspect for fuel leaks.

3.6L Engine

See Figures 188 through 191.

1. Remove the fuel injector sight shield.

2. Disconnect the engine wiring harness electrical connector from the fuel injector wiring harness electrical connector.

3. Disconnect the fuel feed pipe quick connect fitting from the fuel rail.

4. Remove the upper intake manifold.

❊❊ **WARNING**

Use Safety Glasses when using Compressed Air.

5. Use compressed air in order to remove any debris from the around the area where the fuel injectors enter the lower intake manifold.

6. Remove the fuel rail bolts.

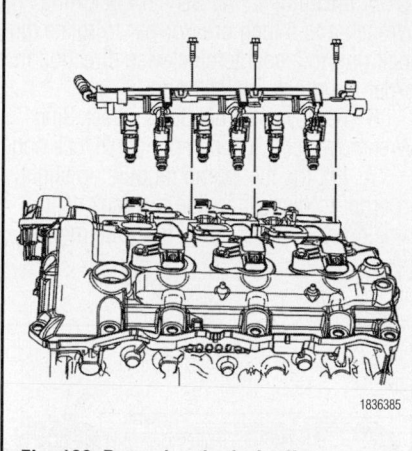

Fig. 188 Removing the fuel rail

❊❊ **CAUTION**

Remove the fuel rail assembly carefully in order to prevent damage to the injector electrical connector terminals and the injector spray tips. Support the fuel rail after the fuel rail is removed in order to avoid damaging the fuel rail components.

❊❊ **CAUTION**

Cap the fittings and plug the holes when servicing the fuel system in order to prevent dirt and other contaminants from entering open pipes and passages.

7. Remove the fuel rail with fuel injectors from the lower intake manifold.

8. Lift up the fuel injector electrical connector retainer.

9. Push in the fuel injector electrical connector tab in order to disconnect the connector from the injector.

10. Remove the fuel injector retainer clip.

11. Remove the fuel injector.

12. Remove and discard the fuel injector seals.

To install:

13. Install NEW fuel injector seals.

14. Install the fuel injector.

15. Install the fuel injector retainer clip.

16. Install the fuel injector electrical connector.

17. Push down on the fuel injector electrical connector retainer, securing the electrical connector.

18. Install the fuel rail with fuel injectors to the lower intake manifold.

19. Install the fuel rail bolts and tighten to 89 inch lbs. (10 Nm).

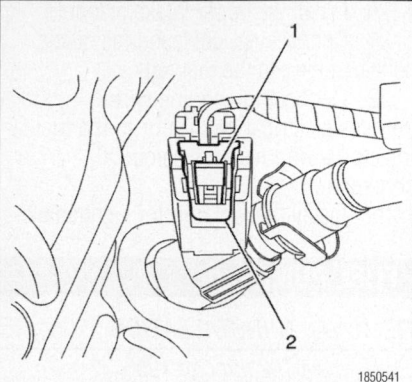

Fig. 189 Lifting the retainer (2) and pushing the tab (1) to disconnect the connector from the injector

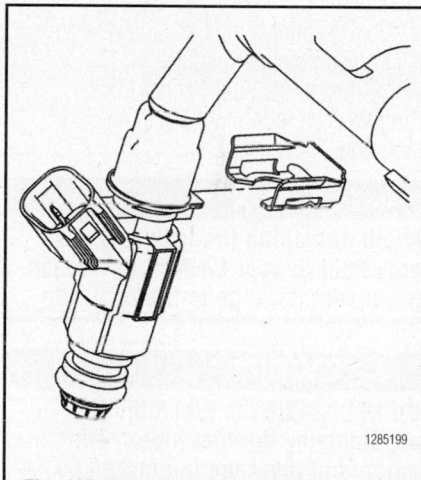

Fig. 190 Removing the retainer clip

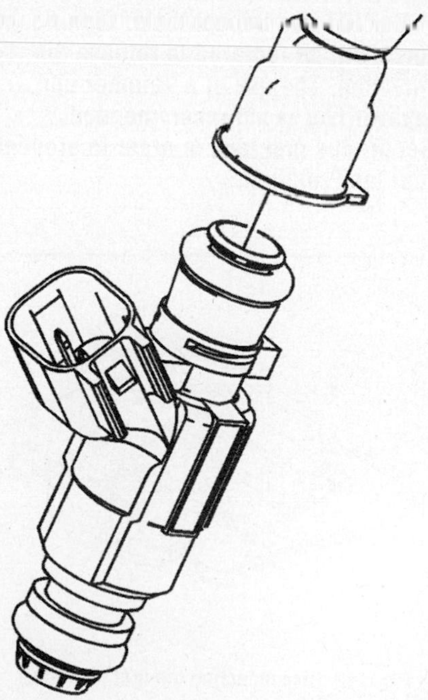

Fig. 191 Removing the injector

20. Install the upper intake manifold.

21. Connect the fuel feed pipe quick connect fitting to the fuel rail.

22. Connect the engine wiring harness electrical connector to the fuel injector wiring harness electrical connector.

23. Install the fuel injector sight shield.

FUEL PUMP

REMOVAL & INSTALLATION

See Figures 192 through 196.

1. Remove the fuel tank.

2. Disconnect the fuel tank fuel pump module wiring harness electrical connectors from the fuel pressure sensor and the module.

3. Disconnect the fuel tank vent and feed pipes from the module.

4. Install the Fuel Sender Lock Ring Wrench to the fuel pump module lock ring.

✳✳ CAUTION

Avoid damaging the lock ring. Use only Fuel Sender Lock Ring Wrench to prevent damage to the lock ring.

✳✳ CAUTION

Do Not handle the fuel sender assembly by the fuel pipes. The amount of leverage generated by handling the fuel pipes could damage the joints.

➡ Do NOT use impact tools. Significant force will be required to release the lock ring. The use of a hammer and screwdriver is not recommended. Secure the fuel tank in order to prevent fuel tank rotation.

5. Install the Fuel Sender Lock Ring Wrench and a long breaker-bar to rotate the lock ring in a counterclockwise direction in order to unlock the lock ring.

6. Remove the Fuel Sender Lock Ring Wrench from the fuel pump module lock ring.

7. Lift the fuel pump module up slightly in order to disconnect the fuel tank vent pipe quick connect fitting from the module cover.

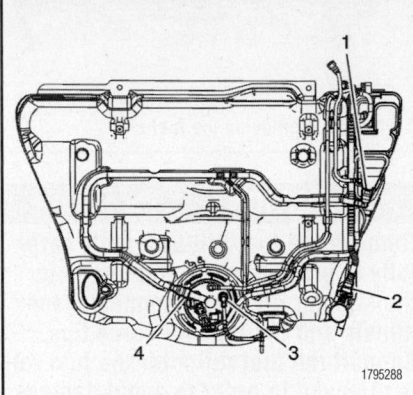

Fig. 193 Disconnecting the fuel tank vent and feed pipes (3, 4)

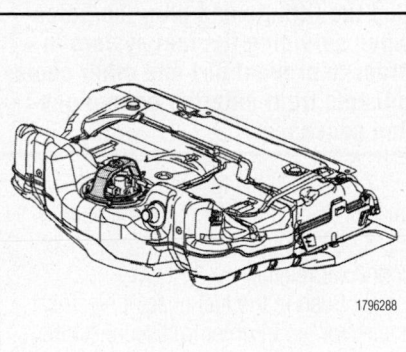

Fig. 194 Installing the lock ring wrench

8. Raise the fuel pump module up from the fuel tank. Tilt the module in order to allow the fuel level sensor arm and float to clear the module opening.

9. Remove the fuel pump module.

10. Remove and discard the fuel pump module seal.

11. Clean the fuel pump module sealing surfaces.

To install:

✳✳ WARNING

Drain the fuel from the fuel sender assembly into an approved container in order to reduce the risk of fire and personal injury. Never store the fuel in an open container

➡ Some lock rings were manufactured with "DO NOT REUSE" stamped into them. These lock rings may be reused if they are not damaged or warped.

➡ Inspect the lock ring for damage due to improper removal or installation procedures. If damage is found, install a NEW fuel pump module.

➡ Inspect the lock ring for flatness as best as possible. If the lock ring is warped, replace the fuel pump module.

12. Clean any contamination from the male pipe ends of the fuel pump module.

13. Place a NEW fuel tank module seal onto the fuel tank.

14. Insert the fuel pump module into the fuel tank allowing the sensor arm and float to clear the module opening.

15. Lower the module down into the fuel tank until the fuel tank vent pipe quick connect fitting can be connected.

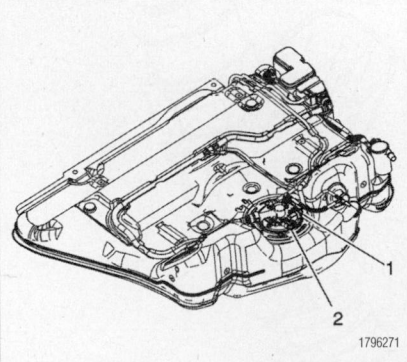

Fig. 192 Disconnecting the fuel tank fuel pump module wiring harness electrical connectors (1, 2)

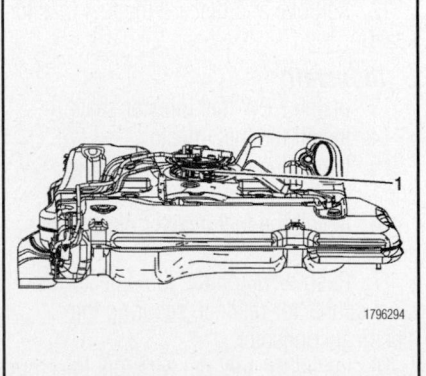

Fig. 195 Disconnecting the fuel tank vent pipe quick connect fitting

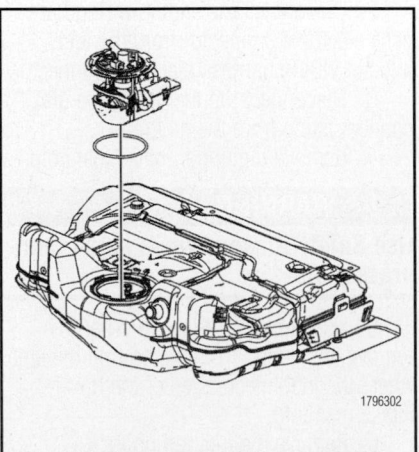

Fig. 196 Removing the fuel pump module

16. Connect the fuel tank vent pipe quick connect fitting at the module cover.

17. Press the fuel tank module downward.

18. Install the Fuel Sender Lock Ring Wrench to the fuel pump module lock ring.

➡**Ensure that the lock ring is installed with the correct side facing upward. A correctly installed lock ring will only turn in a clockwise direction.**

19. Install the Fuel Sender Lock Ring Wrench and a long breaker-bar, and rotate the lock ring in a clockwise direction in order to tighten the lock ring.

20. Remove the Fuel Sender Lock Ring Wrench from the fuel pump module lock ring.

21. Connect the fuel tank vent and fuel feed pipes to the module.

22. Connect the fuel tank fuel pump module wiring harness electrical connectors to the fuel pressure sensor and the module.

23. Install the fuel tank.

FUEL TANK

DRAINING

See Figure 197.

✳✳ WARNING

Never drain or store fuel in an open container. Always use an approved fuel storage container in order to reduce the chance of fire or explosion.

✳✳ WARNING

Place a dry chemical (Class B) fire extinguisher nearby before performing any on-vehicle service procedures. Failure to follow these precautions may result in personal injury.

1. Remove the fuel fill cap.

2. Raise and suitably support the vehicle.

3. Loosen the fuel fill pipe hose clamp at the fuel tank.

4. Separate the fuel fill pipe hose from the fuel tank.

5. Insert the Fuel Tank Drain Hose into the fuel tank until the hose reaches the bottom of the fuel tank.

6. Use an hand or air operated pump device in order to drain as much fuel as possible.

REMOVAL & INSTALLATION

See Figures 198 through 202.

➡**Clean the fuel and evaporative emission (EVAP) connections and surrounding areas prior to disconnecting the lines in order to avoid possible system contamination.**

1. Relieve the fuel system pressure.

2. Drain the fuel tank.

3. Raise and support the vehicle.

4. Disconnect the fuel tank fuel pump module wiring harness electrical connector from body wiring harness electrical connector.

5. If equipped, disconnect the fuel pressure sensor electrical connector.

6. Remove the body wiring harness electrical connector clip from the EVAP canister.

7. Disconnect the body wiring harness electrical connector from the rear antilock brake system (ABS) wiring harness electrical connector.

8. Remove the rear ABS wiring harness electrical connector clip from the EVAP canister.

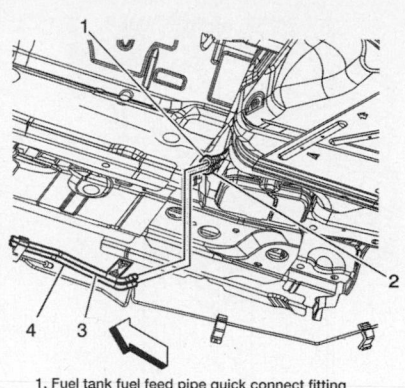

1. Fuel tank fuel feed pipe quick connect fitting
2. Fuel tank EVAP pipe quick connect fitting
3. Chassis fuel feed pipe
4. Chassis EVAP pipe

1789402

Fig. 199 Disconnecting the fuel pipe quick connect fittings

9. Disconnect the fuel tank fuel feed pipe quick connect fitting from the chassis fuel feed pipe.

10. Disconnect the fuel tank EVAP pipe quick connect fitting from the chassis EVAP pipe.

11. Cap the chassis fuel and EVAP pipes in order to prevent possible fuel and/or EVAP system contamination.

12. Disconnect the fuel tank fill EVAP emission pipe quick connect fitting from the fuel tank vent pipe.

13. Place a jackstand under the muffler assembly.

14. With the aid of an assistant, separate the muffler insulators from the underbody hangers.

15. Slowly lower the muffler assembly allowing it to rest on the jackstand. If this is not possible, remove the muffler assembly.

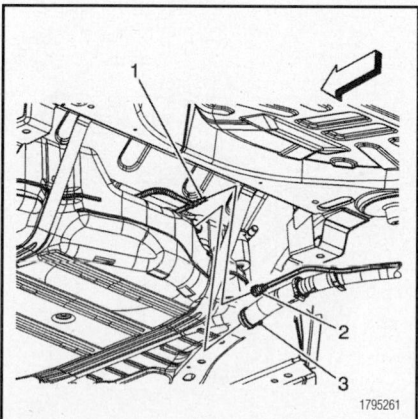

1795261

Fig. 197 Loosening the fuel fill pipe hose clamp (3)

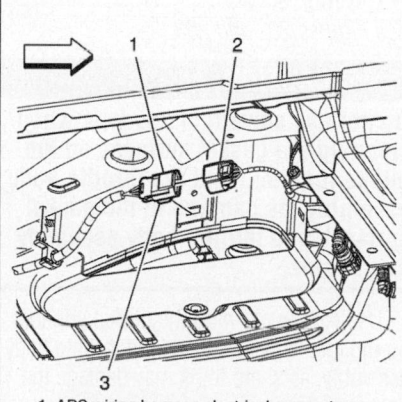

3
1. ABS wiring harness electrical connector
2. Body wiring harness
3. ABS wiring harness electrical connector clip

1795267

Fig. 198 Disconnecting the ABS electrical connectors

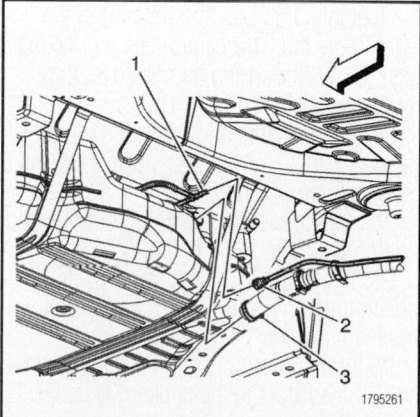

1795261

Fig. 200 Disconnecting the fuel tank fill EVAP emission pipe quick connect fitting (2) from the fuel tank vent pipe (1)

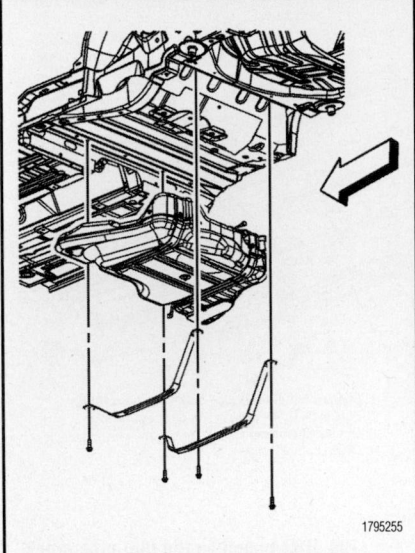

Fig. 201 Removing and installing the fuel tank

16. Have assistants support either side of the fuel tank.

17. Place a suitable adjustable jack under the fuel tank.

18. Remove fuel tank strap bolts and straps.

19. Have the assistants rest the fuel tank on the adjustable jack.

20. If applicable, in order to clear the muffler assembly, slowly lower the right side of the fuel tank.

21. Once the tank is clear of the right frame rail, lower the fuel tank down and remove forward toward the right side of the vehicle.

To install:

22. Have assistants support either side of the fuel tank.

23. If applicable, begin to install the right side of the fuel tank over the muffler assembly.

24. If applicable, raise the right side of the fuel tank into position inboard of the right frame rail. Use care in feeding the fuel feed, EVAP line wiring harness over the muffler assembly.

25. If applicable and the muffler assembly was removed, have assistants raise the fuel tank into position.

26. Install fuel tank straps and bolts and tighten the bolts to 15 ft. lbs. (20 Nm).

27. Raise the muffler assembly into position if applicable, otherwise install the muffler assembly.

28. With the aid of an assistant, install the muffler insulators to the underbody hangers.

29. Remove the jackstand from under the muffler assembly.

30. Install the fuel fill pipe hose to the fuel tank.

31. Connect the fuel tank fill EVAP emission pipe quick connect fitting to the fuel tank vent pipe.

32. Tighten the fuel fill pipe hose clamp at the fuel tank and tighten the clamp to 35 inch lbs. (4 Nm).

33. Remove the caps from the fuel and EVAP pipes.

34. Connect the fuel tank EVAP pipe quick connect fitting to the chassis EVAP pipe.

35. Connect the fuel tank fuel feed pipe quick connect fitting to the chassis fuel feed pipe.

36. Install the rear ABS wiring harness electrical connector clip to the EVAP canister.

37. Connect the body wiring harness electrical connector to the rear ABS wiring harness electrical connector.

38. Install the body wiring harness electrical connector clip to the underbody.

39. Connect the fuel pressure sensor connector if equipped.

40. Connect the fuel tank fuel pump module wiring harness electrical connector to the body wiring harness electrical connector.

41. Lower the vehicle.

42. Refill the fuel tank.

43. Tighten the fuel fill cap.

44. Inspect for leaks.

   a. Turn ON the ignition, with the engine OFF for 10 seconds.

   b. Turn OFF the ignition for 10 seconds.

   c. Turn ON the ignition, with the engine OFF.

   d. Inspect for fuel leaks.

THROTTLE BODY

REMOVAL & INSTALLATION

2.4L Engine

See Figures 202 and 203.

> ✳✳ **CAUTION**
>
> **Do not use solvent of any type when cleaning the gasket surfaces on the intake manifold and the throttle body assembly, as damage to the gasket surfaces and throttle body assembly may result.**

Use care in cleaning the gasket surfaces on the intake manifold and the throttle body assembly, as sharp tools may damage the gasket surfaces.

> ✳✳ **CAUTION**
>
> **Do not use any solvent that contains Methyl Ethyl Ketone (MEK). This solvent may damage fuel system components.**

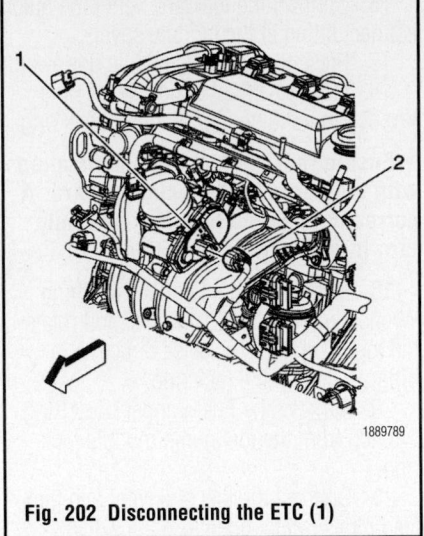

Fig. 202 Disconnecting the ETC (1)

➡**DO NOT prop open the throttle blade with the ignition key in the ON position as it may set a diagnostic trouble code (DTC).**

1. Remove the air cleaner outlet duct.

2. Disconnect the engine wiring harness electrical connector from the electronic throttle control (ETC).

3. Remove the throttle body bolts.

4. Remove the throttle body.

5. Inspect the throttle body gasket, and replace if necessary.

To install:

6. Install the throttle body.

7. Install the throttle body bolts and tighten to 89 inch lbs. (10 Nm).

8. Connect the engine wiring harness electrical connector to the ETC.

9. Install the air cleaner outlet duct.

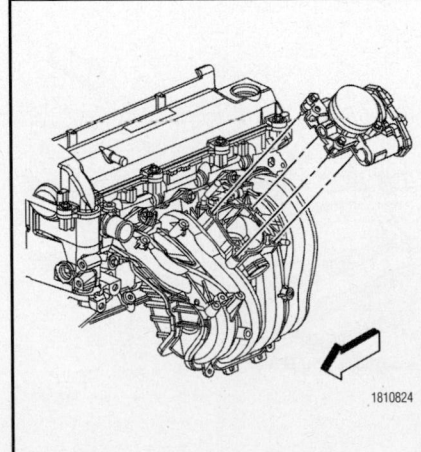

Fig. 203 Removing and installing the throttle body

10. Perform the Throttle Learn procedure.

3.6L Engine

See Figure 204.

1. Remove the air cleaner outlet duct.
2. Disconnect the engine wiring harness electrical connector from the electronic throttle control (ETC).
3. Remove the throttle body bolts.
4. Remove the throttle body and gasket. Discard the gasket.

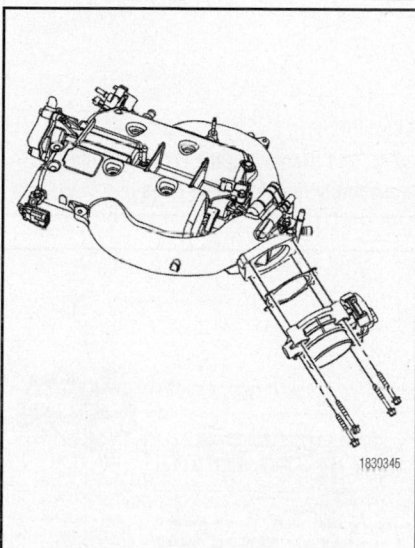

Fig. 204 Removing and installing the throttle body

To install:

5. Position a NEW throttle body gasket to the upper intake manifold.
6. Position the throttle body to the upper intake manifold.
7. Install the throttle body bolts and tighten to 89 inch lbs. (10 Nm).
8. Connect the engine wiring harness electrical connector to the ETC.
9. Install the air cleaner outlet duct.
10. Perform the Throttle Learn Procedure.

THROTTLE/IDLE LEARN PROCEDURE

2.4L Engine

3.6L Engine

After Throttle Body is Cleaned or Replaced

1. Ignition ON, engine OFF, perform the Idle Learn Reset in Module Setup with a scan tool.
2. Start the engine and monitor the TB Idle Airflow Compensation parameter. The TB Idle Airflow Compensation value should equal 0 percent and the engine should be idling at a normal idle speed.
3. Clear the DTCs and return to the diagnostic that referred you here.

After the ECM is Flashed or Replaced

➡ Do NOT perform this procedure if DTCs are set.

1. Start and idle the engine for 3 minutes.
2. With a scan tool, monitor the Desired Idle Speed and the actual Engine Speed.
3. The ECM will start to learn the new idle cells and Desired Idle Speed should start to decrease.
4. Ignition OFF for 60 seconds.
5. Start and idle the engine for 3 minutes.
6. After the 3 minute run time the engine should be idling normal.

➡ During the drive cycle the check engine light may come on with idle speed DTCs. If idle speed codes are set, clear codes so the ECM can continue to learn.

7. If the engine idle speed has not been learned the vehicle will need to be driven at speeds above 70 km/h (44 mph) with several decelerations and extended idles.
   a. After the drive cycle, the engine should be idling normally.
8. If the engine idle speed has not been learned, turn OFF the ignition for 60 seconds and repeat step 6.
   a. Once the engine speed has returned to normal, clear DTCs and return to the diagnostic that referred you here.

HEATING & AIR CONDITIONING SYSTEM

BLOWER MOTOR

REMOVAL & INSTALLATION

See Figures 205 through 208.

1. Remove the right closeout panel.
   a. Grasp the insulator panel and pull downward disengaging the retainer clips securing the insulator to the instrument panel.
   b. When replacing the instrument panel insulator assembly, transfer all necessary components.
2. Remove the blower motor wire harness connector.

➡ Cut through the case as straight as possible because the motor cup must be reused. In order to prevent damage to the component, do not cut any deeper than necessary to remove the motor cup.

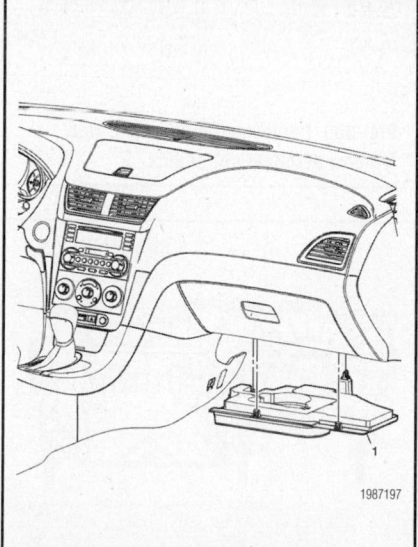

Fig. 205 Removing the right closeout panel

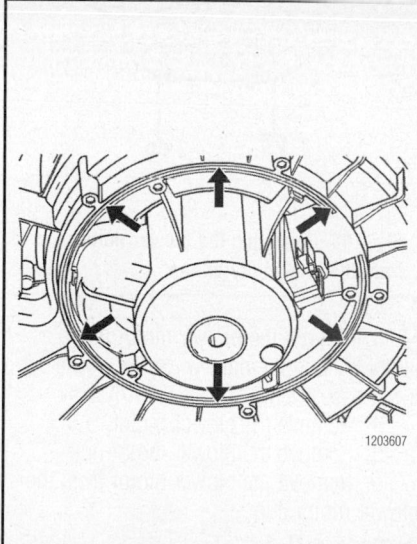

Fig. 206 Identifying the lower case narrow groove

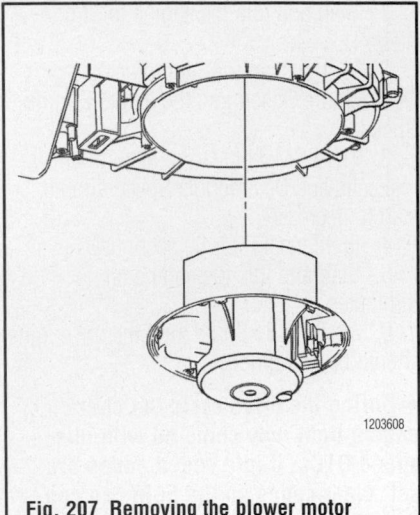

Fig. 207 Removing the blower motor

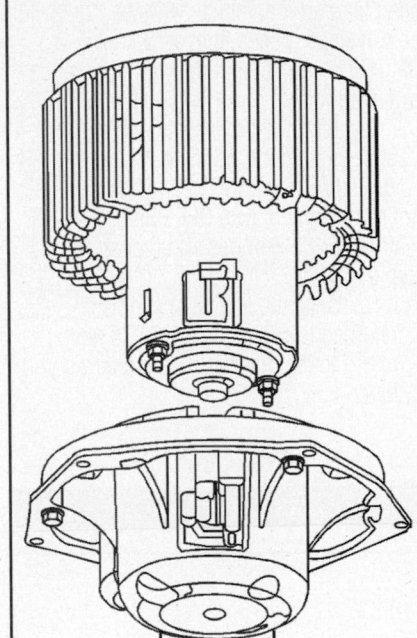

Fig. 208 Removing the blower motor from the blower motor cup

3. Cut out the blower motor using a utility knife in the narrow groove of the lower case.

4. Remove the blower motor.

5. Remove the blower motor nuts.

6. Remove the blower motor from the blower motor cup.

To install:

7. Install the new blower motor to the blower motor cup.

8. Install the blower motor nuts and tighten to 21 inch lbs. (2.4 Nm).

9. Install the motor blower seal to the blower motor service ring.

10. Install the blower motor.

11. Install the blower motor attachment ring.

12. Install the blower motor screws and tighten to 13 inch lbs. (1.5 Nm).

13. Install the blower motor wire harness connector.

14. Install the right closeout panel.

HEATER CORE

REMOVAL & INSTALLATION

See Figures 209 through 215.

1. Remove the HVAC module assembly.

a. Remove the air conditioner (A/C) lines from the thermal expansion valve.

b. Remove the heater hose from the heater core.

c. Remove the instrument panel (I/P) assembly.

d. Remove the recirculation actuator wire harness connector.

e. Remove the air temperature actuator wire harness connector.

f. Remove the mode actuator wire harness connector.

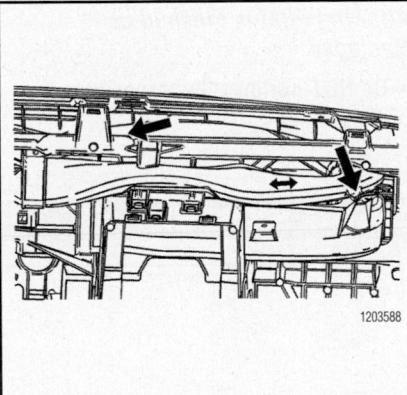

Fig. 209 Removing the left hand side window defogger outlet duct

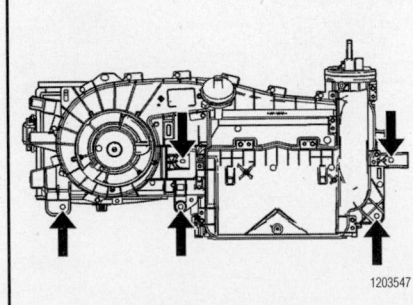

Fig. 210 Removing the HVAC module assembly mounting bolts from the instrument panel reinforcement

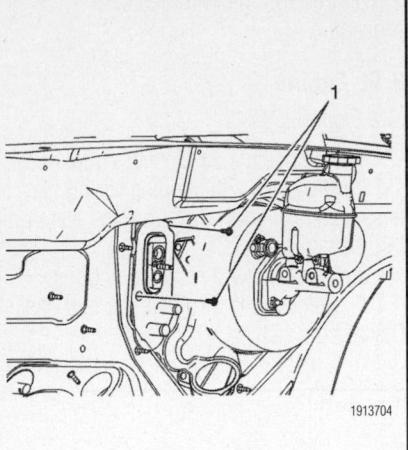

Fig. 211 Removing the HVAC module assembly to dash panel bolts

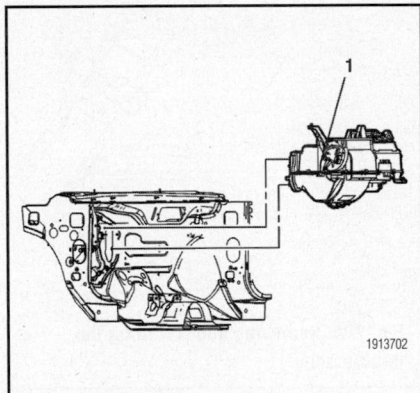

Fig. 212 Removing the HVAC module assembly

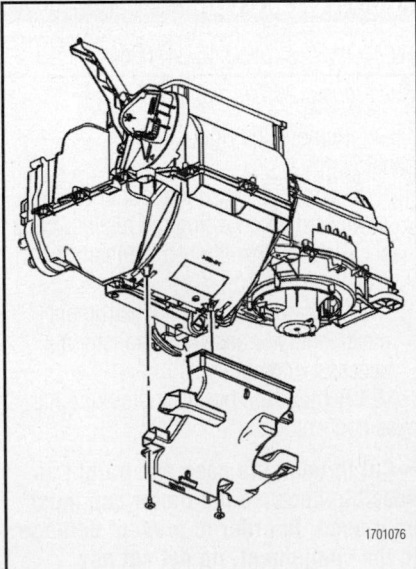

Fig. 213 Removing the center floor air outlet duct

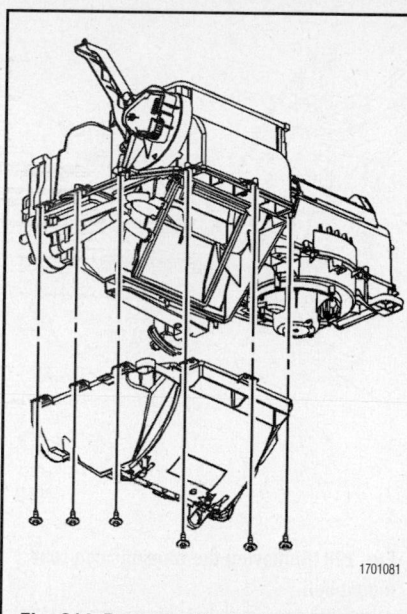

Fig. 214 Removing the heater core cover

   b. Remove the HVAC module assembly.

   3. Remove the center floor air outlet duct screws.

   4. Remove the center floor air outlet duct.

   5. Drill out the heater core cover heat stakes.

   6. Remove the heater core cover screws.

   7. Remove the heater core cover.

   8. Remove the heater core.

To install:

   9. Install the heater core.

   10. Install the heater core cover.

   11. Install the heater core cover screws and tighten to 13 inch lbs. (1.5 Nm).

   12. Install the center floor air outlet duct.

   13. Install the upper floor air outlet duct screws and tighten to 13 inch lbs. (1.5 Nm).

   14. Install the HVAC module assembly.

   a. Install the HVAC module assembly.

   b. Install the HVAC module assembly to dash panel bolts and tighten to 88 inch lbs. (10 Nm).

   c. Install the HVAC module assembly mounting bolts to the instrument panel reinforcement and tighten the bolts to 44 inch lbs. (5 Nm).

   d. Install the left hand side window defogger outlet duct.

   e. Install the blower motor resistor wire harness connector.

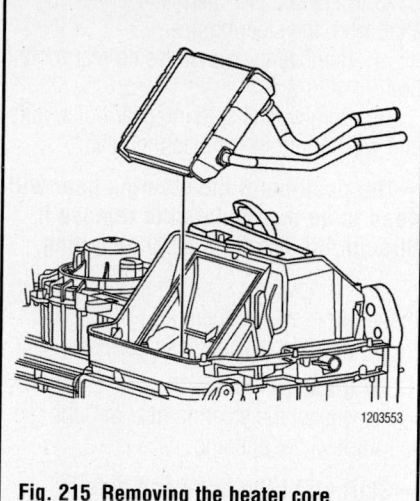

Fig. 215 Removing the heater core

   f. Install the blower motor wire harness connector.

   g. Install the mode actuator wire harness connector.

   h. Install the air temperature actuator wire harness connector.

   i. Install the recirculation actuator wire harness connector.

   j. Install the I/P assembly.

   k. Install the heater hoses to the heater core.

   l. Install the A/C lines to the thermal expansion valve.

   g. Remove the blower motor wire harness connector.

   h. Remove the blower motor resistor wire harness connector

   i. Remove the left hand side window defogger outlet duct.

   2. Remove the HVAC module assembly mounting bolts from the instrument panel reinforcement.

   a. Remove the HVAC module assembly to dash panel bolts.

STEERING

POWER STEERING GEAR

REMOVAL & INSTALLATION

Electronic Power Steering

See Figures 216 and 217.

✳✳ CAUTION

With wheels of the vehicle facing straight ahead, secure the steering wheel utilizing steering column anti-rotation pin, steering column lock, or a strap to prevent rotation. Locking of the steering column will prevent damage and a possible malfunction of the SIR system. The steering wheel must be secured in position before disconnecting the following components:

- Steering column
- Intermediate shaft(s)
- Steering gear

After disconnecting these components, do not rotate the steering

wheel or move the front tires and wheels. Failure to follow this procedure may cause the SIR coil assembly to become un-centered and cause possible damage to the SIR coil. If you think the SIR coil has become un-centered, refer to

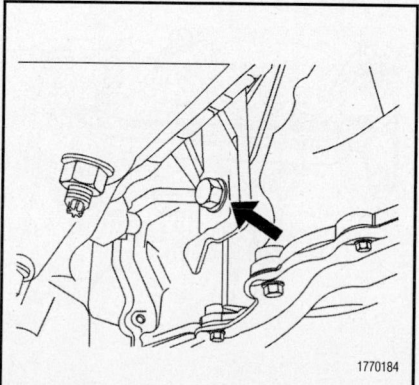

Fig. 216 Removing the transmission rear mount bolt

your specific SIR coil's centering procedure to re-center SIR Coil.

   1. Turn the front wheels to the straight forward position and secure the steering wheel from moving.

   2. Disengage the rack and pinion outer tie rod ends from the steering knuckles.

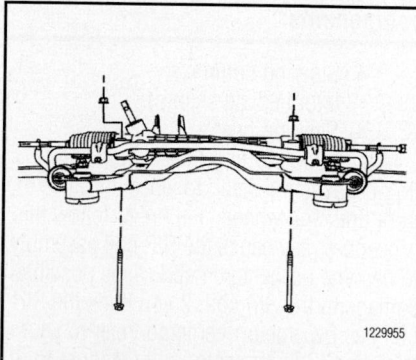

Fig. 217 Removing the steering gear bolts, nuts, and washers from the steering gear

3. Separate the intermediate steering shaft from the steering gear.

4. Remove the transmission rear mount bolt.

5. Remove the steering gear bolts, nuts, and washers from the steering gear.

➡ **The position of the steering gear will need to be manipulated to remove it through the left front wheel opening.**

6. Remove the steering gear through the left front wheel opening.

7. Transfer any parts as needed.

To install:

8. Install the steering gear through the left front wheel opening.

➡ **Start all of the bolts and nuts by hand before finalizing any torques.**

9. Install the steering gear bolts, nuts, and washers to the steering gear.

10. Tighten the bolts to 52 ft. lbs. (70 Nm) plus an additional 90°.

11. Install the transmission rear mount bolt and tighten to 66 ft. lbs. (90 Nm).

12. Install the intermediate steering shaft to the steering gear.

13. Install the rack and pinion outer tie rod ends to the steering knuckles.

14. Adjust the front toe.

Hydraulic Power Steering

See Figures 218 through 224.

✲✲ CAUTION

With wheels of the vehicle facing straight ahead, secure the steering wheel utilizing steering column anti-rotation pin, steering column lock, or a strap to prevent rotation. Locking of the steering column will prevent damage and a possible malfunction of the SIR system. The steering wheel must be secured in position before disconnecting the following components:

- Steering column
- Intermediate shaft(s)
- Steering gear

After disconnecting these components, do not rotate the steering wheel or move the front tires and wheels. Failure to follow this procedure may cause the SIR coil assembly to become un-centered and cause possible damage to the SIR coil. If you think the SIR coil has became un-centered, refer to your specific SIR coil's centering procedure to re-center SIR Coil.

1. Turn the front wheels to the straight forward position and secure the steering wheel from moving.

2. Remove as much power steering fluid from the remote power steering fluid reservoir as possible.

3. Place drain pans under the vehicle as needed.

4. Disengage the rack and pinion outer tie rod ends from the steering knuckles.

5. Separate the intermediate steering shaft from the steering gear.

6. Remove the steering gear heat shield from the steering gear.

7. Remove the transmission brace bolt.

8. Remove the transmission rear mount bolt and position the transmission brace aside.

9. Loosen the rear transmission mount bracket bolt.

10. Remove the 2 remaining transmission rear mount bolts.

11. Remove the 3 rear transmission mount bracket nuts and bolts.

12. Position the transmission rear mount and bracket aside.

13. Remove the power steering gear inlet hose bolt and disconnect the power steering gear inlet hose and the power steering gear outlet hose from the steering gear.

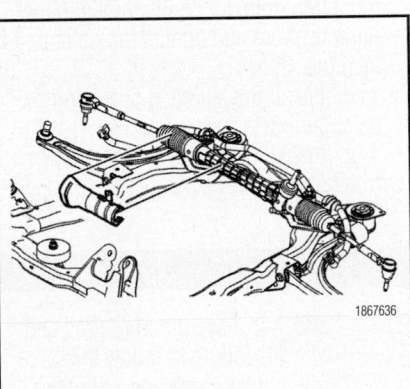

Fig. 218 Removing the steering gear heat shield from the steering gear

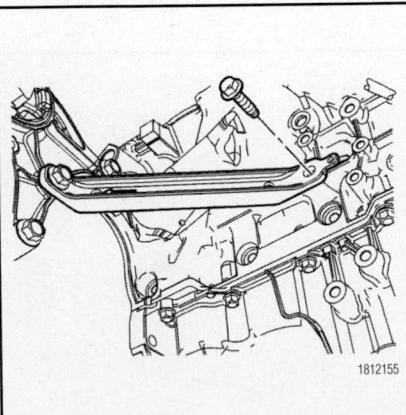

Fig. 219 Removing the transmission brace bolt

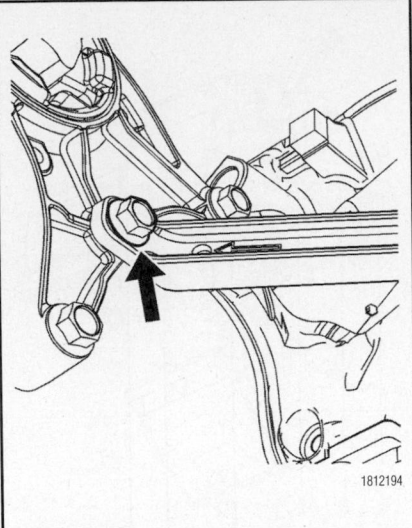

Fig. 220 Removing the transmission rear mount bolt

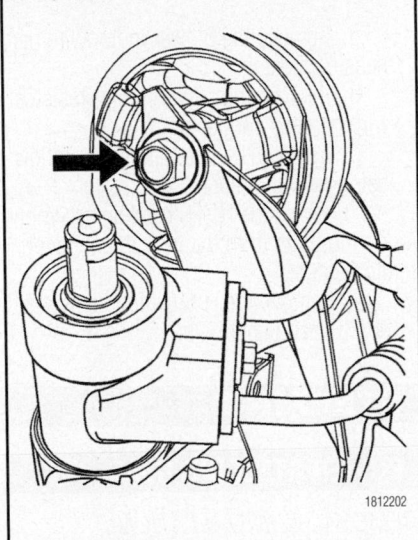

Fig. 221 Loosening the rear transmission mount bracket bolt

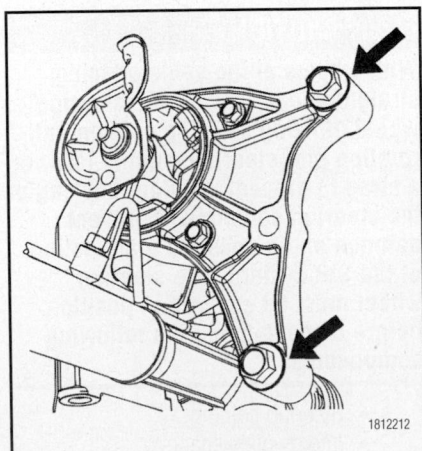

Fig. 222 Removing the 2 remaining transmission rear mount bolts

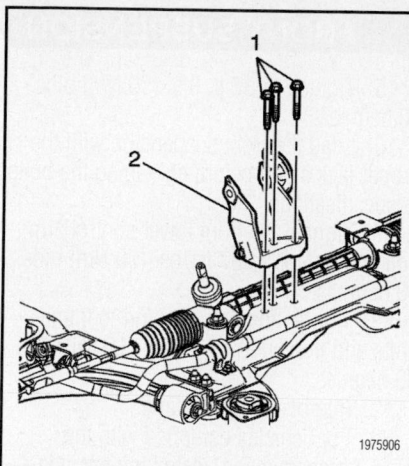

Fig. 223 Removing the 3 rear transmission mount bracket nuts and bolts (1)

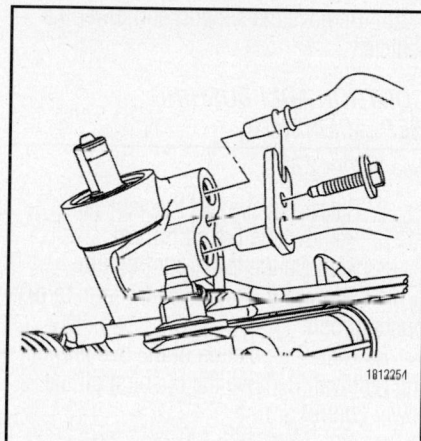

Fig. 224 Removing the power steering gear

14. Remove the steering gear bolts, nuts, and washers from the steering gear.

➡**The position of the steering gear will need to be manipulated to remove it through the left front wheel opening.**

15. Remove the steering gear through the left front wheel opening.

16. Transfer any parts as needed.

To install:

17. Install the steering gear through the left front wheel opening.

➡**Start all of the bolts and nuts by hand before finalizing any torques.**

18. Install the steering gear bolts, nuts, and washers to the steering gear.

19. Tighten the bolts and nuts to 81 ft. lbs. (110 Nm).

20. Connect the power steering gear inlet hose and the power steering gear outlet hose to the steering gear and install the power steering gear inlet hose bolt and tighten to 20 ft. lbs. (27 Nm).

21. Position the transmission rear mount and bracket in place.

22. Install the 3 rear transmission mount bracket bolts and nuts and tighten to 37 ft. lbs. (50 Nm).

23. Install the 2 remaining transmission rear mount bolts.

24. Place the transmission brace in the proper position. Install the bolt in order to secure the transmission brace to the transmission rear mount. Tighten the 3 transmission rear mount bolts to 37 ft. lbs. (50 Nm).

25. Install the transmission brace bolt and tighten to 37 ft. lbs. (50 Nm).

26. Tighten the rear transmission mount bracket bolt and tighten to 37 ft. lbs. (50 Nm).

27. Install the steering gear heat shield to the steering gear.

28. Clean any excess power steering fluid from the vehicle and remove the drain pans.

29. Install the intermediate steering shaft to the steering gear.

30. Install the rack and pinion outer tie rod ends to the steering knuckles.

31. Fill and bleed the power steering system.

32. Adjust the front toe.

POWER STEERING PUMP

REMOVAL & INSTALLATION

3.6L Engine

See Figure 225.

1. Remove the drive belt.
2. Remove the right front tire and wheel assembly.

3. Remove as much power steering fluid from the remote power steering fluid reservoir as possible.

4. Place drain pans under the vehicle as needed.

5. Disconnect the power steering fluid reservoir outlet hose clamp and hose.

6. Remove the power steering gear inlet hose.

  a. Discard the o-ring and install a new power steering gear inlet hose o-ring prior to installation of the hose.

7. Remove the engine mount adapter bolt.

8. Remove the power steering pump bolt.

9. Remove the power steering pump.

  a. Remove the power steering pump pulley.

  b. Remove the engine mount adapter bracket bolts.

  c. Remove the engine mount adapter bracket.

To install:

➡**Clean any excess power steering fluid from the vehicle.**

To install, reverse the removal procedure. Tighten the power steering pump engine mount adapter bracket bolts to 80 inch lbs. (9 Nm). Tighten the power steering pump bolt to 37 ft. lbs. (50 Nm). Tighten the engine mount adapter to 43 ft. lbs. (58 Nm). Tighten the power steering gear inlet hose to 20 ft. lbs. (27 Nm). Tighten the power Fill and bleed the power steering system.

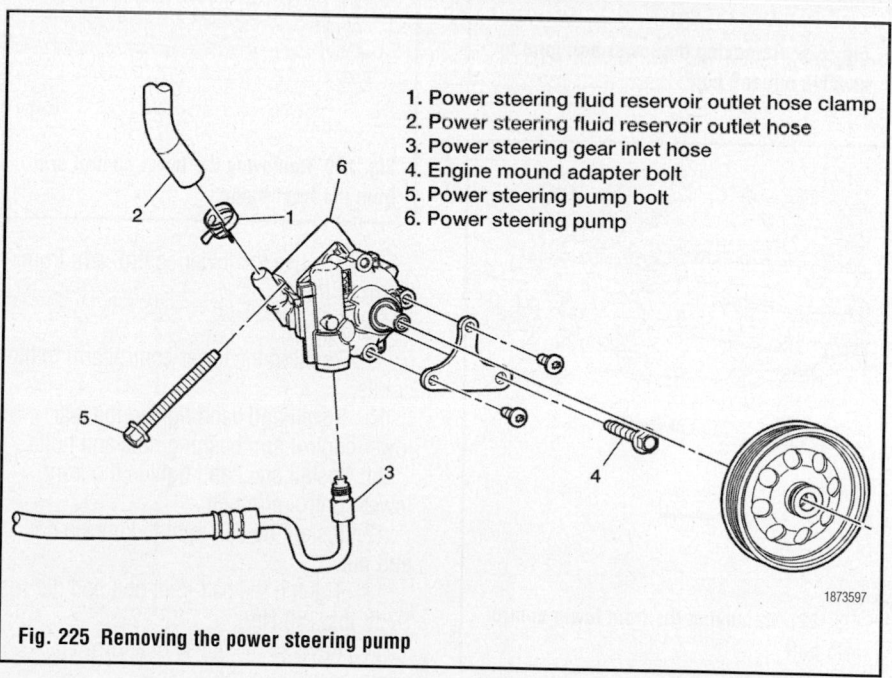

1. Power steering fluid reservoir outlet hose clamp
2. Power steering fluid reservoir outlet hose
3. Power steering gear inlet hose
4. Engine mound adapter bolt
5. Power steering pump bolt
6. Power steering pump

Fig. 225 Removing the power steering pump

LOWER CONTROL ARM

REMOVAL & INSTALLATION

See Figures 226 through 229.

1. Raise and support the vehicle.
2. Remove the tire and wheel.

➡ **DO NOT re-use the lower ball joint bolt. Discard and use NEW only.**

3. Remove the lower ball joint to knuckle nut and bolt.
4. Separate the lower control arm from the knuckle.
5. If removing the left lower control arm and the vehicle is equipped with the 4T45-E transmission, remove the left side transmission mount.
6. Remove the front lower control arm bolt.
7. Remove the rear lower control arm bushing nuts and bolts.

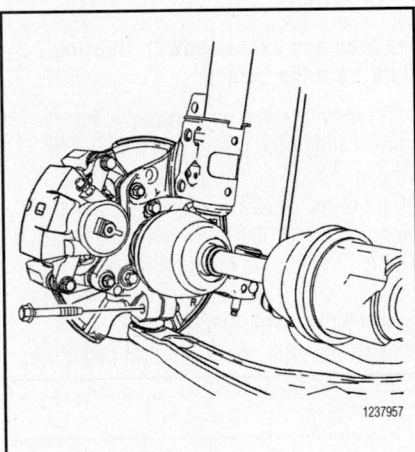

Fig. 226 Removing the lower ball joint to knuckle nut and bolt

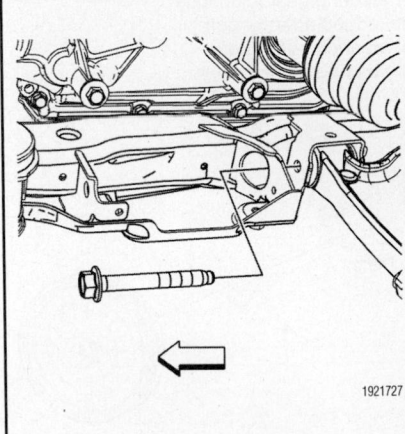

Fig. 227 Removing the front lower control arm bolt

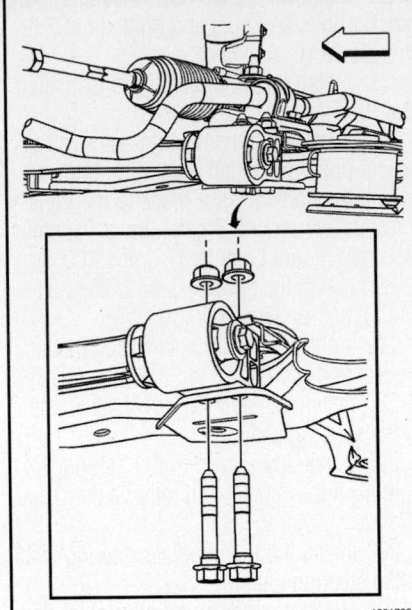

Fig. 228 Removing the rear lower control arm bushing nuts and bolts

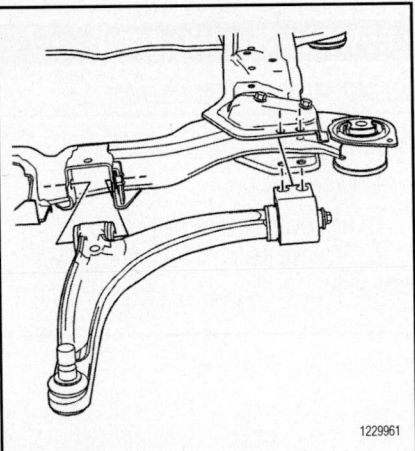

Fig. 229 Removing the lower control arm from the front frame

8. Remove the lower control arm from the front frame.

To install:

9. Position the lower control arm in the cradle.
10. Install and hand tighten the rear lower control arm bushing nuts and bolts.
11. Install and hand tighten the front lower control arm bolt.
12. Install the ball joint to knuckle bolt and nut.
13. Tighten the ball joint bolt and nut to 37 ft. lbs. (50 Nm).
14. Reverse the nut ¾ of a turn.

15. Tighten to 37 ft. lbs. (50 Nm) plus 30 degrees.
16. Load the front suspension with the proper jack stand before tightening the bolts to specifications.
17. Tighten the front lower control arm bolt and tighten to 37 ft. lbs. (50 Nm) plus 90 degrees.
18. Tighten the rear bushing to frame bolts and tighten to 37 ft. lbs. (50 Nm) plus 90 degrees.
19. Remove the jack stand.
20. For vehicles equipped with the 4T45-E transmission, install the left side transmission mount.
21. Install the tire and wheel.
22. Verify wheel alignment.
23. Remove the support and lower the vehicle.

CONTROL ARM BUSHING REPLACEMENT

See Figure 230.

1. Raise and support the vehicle.
2. Remove the tire and wheel.
3. Remove the lower control arm.
4. Remove the lower control arm to rear bushing bolt.
5. Note the position of the bushing during removal. Remove the bushing off the lower control arm.

To install:

6. Install the bushing on the lower control arm as previously noted.
7. Using LOCTITE® 234 or equivalent on the bolt threads, install the lower control arm to bushing bolt.
8. Hold the rear bushing inner sleeve when tightening the rear bushings to control arm bolt and tighten to 32 ft. lbs. (44 Nm).

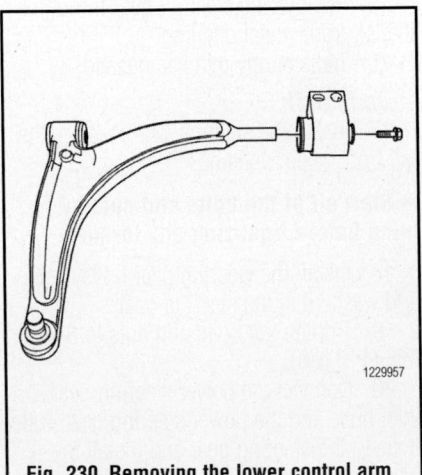

Fig. 230 Removing the lower control arm to rear bushing bolt and bushing

9. Install the lower control arm.
10. Install the tire and wheel.
11. Lower the vehicle.

STABILIZER BAR

REMOVAL & INSTALLATION

See Figures 231 and 232.

1. Raise and support the vehicle.
2. Remove the front tire and wheel assemblies.
3. Disconnect the stabilizer links from the stabilizer shaft.
4. For vehicles equipped with the 3.6L LY7, remove the exhaust pipe.
5. Using a suitable jack stand, support the rear of the frame assembly.
6. Remove the frame to body bolts.
7. Lower the rear of the frame in order to gain clearance to the stabilizer shaft.
8. Remove the stabilizer shaft clamp bolts.
9. Remove the stabilizer shaft clamps and insulators.

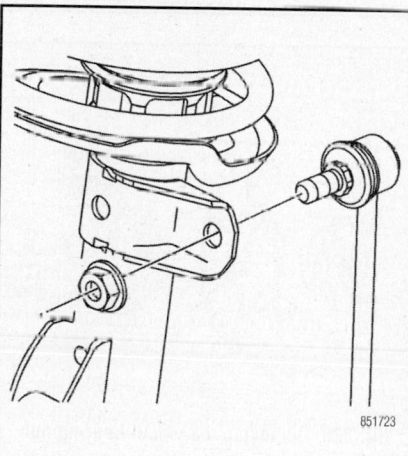

Fig. 231 Disconnecting the stabilizer links from the stabilizer shaft

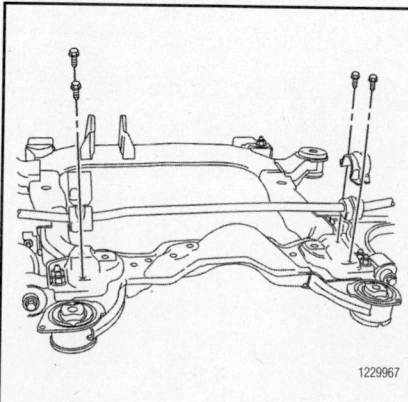

Fig. 232 Removing the stabilizer shaft

10. Remove the stabilizer shaft from the frame.

To install:

➡**Install the insulators so that the slit in the insulator is facing the rear of the vehicle.**

11. Install the insulators on the stabilizer shaft.
12. Position the stabilizer shaft to the frame.
13. Install the stabilizer bar clamps.
14. Install the stabilizer shaft clamp bolts and tighten to 18 ft. lbs. (25 Nm).
15. Raise the rear of the cradle and install the cradle bolts.
16. Remove the jack stand.
17. Connect the stabilizer link to the stabilizer bar.
18. For vehicles equipped with the 3.6L LY7, install the exhaust pipe.
19. Install the front tire and wheel assemblies.
20. Remove the support and lower the vehicle.

STEERING KNUCKLE

REMOVAL & INSTALLATION

See Figure 233.

1. Raise and support the vehicle.
2. Remove the wheel bearing/hub.
3. Separate the outer tie rod end from the knuckle.
4. Remove the nuts and bolts from the strut to the knuckle.
5. Separate the lower ball joint from the knuckle.

To install:

To install, reverse the removal procedure. Verify the front end alignment.

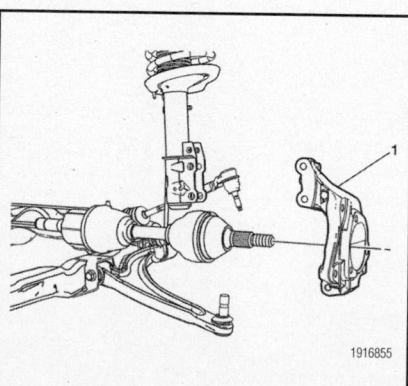

Fig. 233 Removing and installing the steering knuckle

STRUT & SPRING ASSEMBLY

REMOVAL & INSTALLATION

See Figures 234 and 235.

1. Raise and support the vehicle.
2. Remove the tire and wheel assembly.
3. Support the lower control arm with a suitable jack stand.
4. Disconnect the wheel speed sensor electrical connector at the wheel speed sensor bracket, if equipped.
5. Remove the stabilizer shaft link from the front strut.
6. Remove the front strut nuts from the bolts.

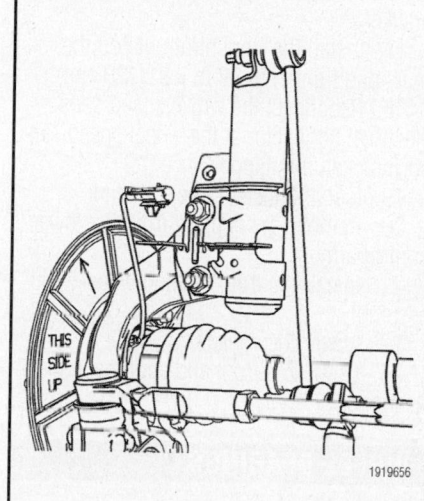

Fig. 234 Disconnecting the speed sensor electrical connector

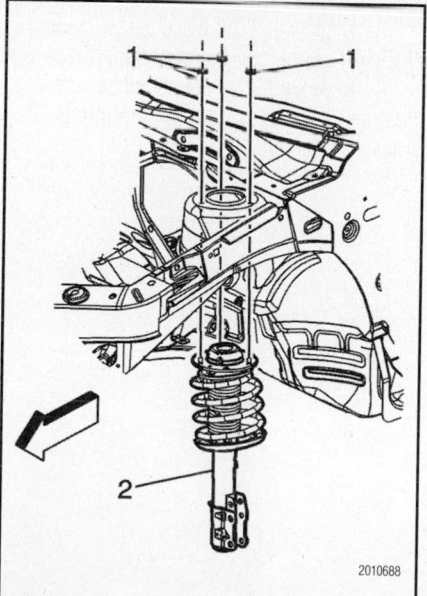

Fig. 235 Removing the strut nuts (1) and strut (2)

7. Remove the wheel speed sensor bracket from the strut.

8. Remove the strut bolts from the front strut.

9. Separate the front strut from the knuckle.

10. Remove the upper strut nuts from the strut.

11. Remove the front strut assembly from the vehicle.

To install:

12. Install the front strut assembly.

13. Install the upper strut nuts and tighten to 18 ft. lbs. (25 Nm).

14. Insert the front strut in the knuckle.

15. Install the strut bolts.

16. Install the wheel speed sensor bracket.

17. Install the front strut nuts on the bolts and tighten to 89 ft. lbs. (120 Nm).

18. Reconnect the wheel speed sensor electrical connector at the wheel speed sensor bracket, if equipped.

19. Install the stabilizer shaft link.

20. Remove the support from the lower control arm.

21. Install the front tire and wheel assembly.

22. Lower the vehicle.

23. Check the front end alignment specifications.

WHEEL BEARINGS

REMOVAL & INSTALLATION

See Figures 236 through 238.

1. Raise and support the vehicle.
2. Remove the brake rotor.
3. Disconnect the wheel speed sensor electrical connector, if equipped.
4. Remove the wheel speed sensor electrical connector from the mounting bracket, if needed.

Fig. 236 Disconnecting the wheel speed sensor electrical connector

5. Loosen the wheel drive shaft from the wheel bearing/hub.

6. Remove the wheel bearing/hub mounting bolts.

7. Remove the wheel bearing/hub and backing plate from the steering knuckle.

To install:

8. Position the backing plate and wheel bearing/hub assembly in the steering knuckle.

9. Install the wheel bearing/hub mounting bolts and tighten to 85 ft. lbs. (115 Nm).

10. Reconnect the wheel speed senor electrical connector, if needed.

11. Install the wheel speed sensor electrical connector on the retaining bracket, if needed.

12. Install the brake rotor.

13. Install the wheel drive shaft retaining nut and washer.

14. Remove the support and lower the vehicle.

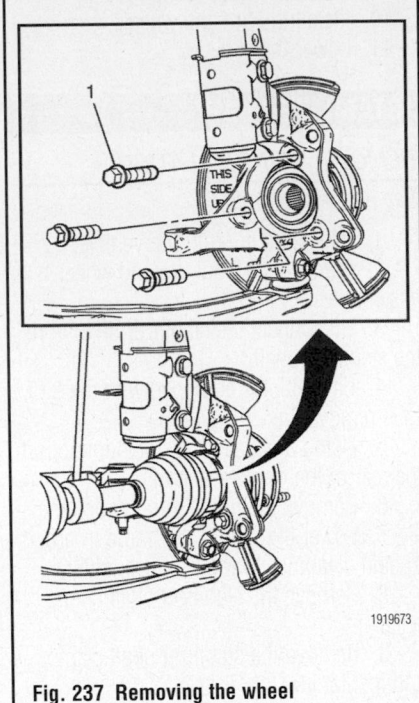

Fig. 237 Removing the wheel bearing/hub mounting bolts

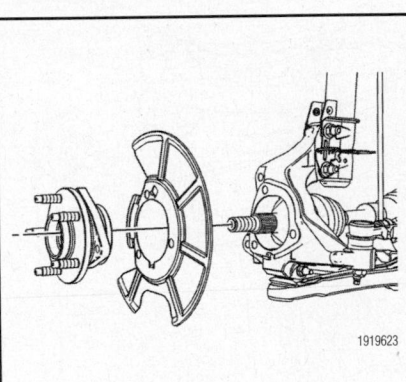

Fig. 238 Removing the wheel bearing/hub and backing plate from the steering knuckle

COIL SPRING

REMOVAL & INSTALLATION

See Figure 239.

1. Raise and support the vehicle.
2. Remove the rear tire and wheel assembly.
3. Using a suitable jack stand, support the knuckle.
4. Remove the lower control arm to knuckle bolt and nut.

✳✳ WARNING

To prevent personal injury and/or component damage, use the proper tools to support the lower control arm when removing the coil spring. The coil spring is under extreme pressure and can become a projectile should the spring separate from the lower control arm before all of the tension is relieved.

5. Using a adjustable jack stand, slowly lower control arm downward.
6. Remove the coil spring (1) from the lower control arm.
7. If needed, remove the rear spring upper insulator (2) or the lower spring insulator (3).

To install:

8. If needed, replace the upper or the lower spring insulator.

➡When installing the rear spring, ensure that the spring is positioned so that bolt for the rear stabilizer shaft can be serviced and that the rear spring is properly seated in the upper and lower insulators.

9. Position the rear spring on the lower control arm.
10. Using an adjustable jack stand, raise the lower control arm.
11. Install the lower control arm to knuckle bolt and nut.
12. Remove the jack stands from the knuckle vehicle and the lower control arm.
13. Install the rear tire and wheel assembly.
14. Lower the vehicle.
15. Check the rear wheel alignment.

LOWER CONTROL ARM

REMOVAL & INSTALLATION

See Figure 240.

1. Raise and suitably support the vehicle.
2. Remove the rear tire and wheel assembly.
3. Remove the coil spring.
4. Remove the lower control arm to support bolt/nut.
5. Remove the lower control arm.

To install:

To install, reverse the removal procedure. Tighten the lower control arm to support bolt/nut 81 ft. lbs. (110 Nm). After installation, check the rear alignment.

SHOCK ABSORBER

REMOVAL & INSTALLATION

See Figures 241 through 243.

1. Raise and support the vehicle.
2. Remove the tire and wheel.
3. Using a suitable jack stand, support the knuckle.

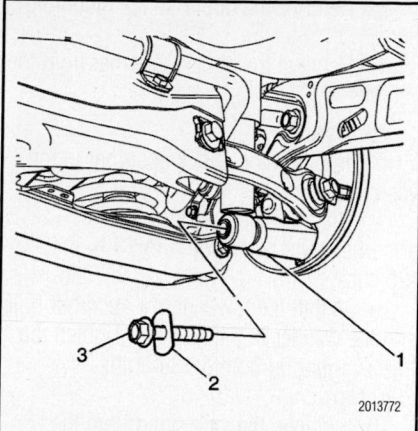

Fig. 241 Removing the lower shock absorber bolt (1) and the washer (2) from the knuckle (1)

Fig. 242 Removing the upper shock mounting nuts

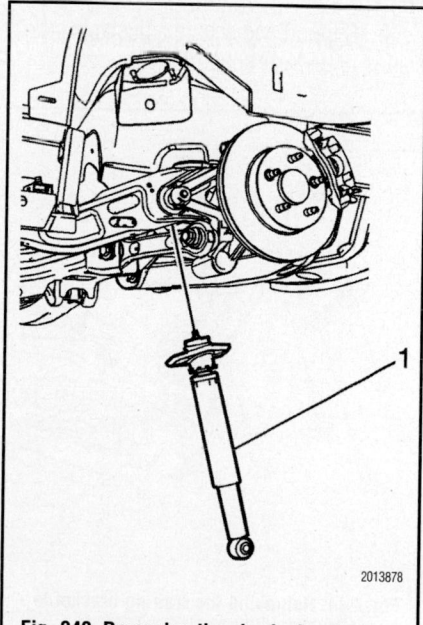

Fig. 243 Removing the shock absorber

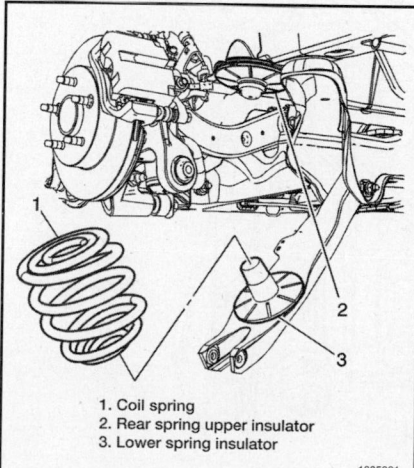

1. Coil spring
2. Rear spring upper insulator
3. Lower spring insulator

Fig. 239 Removing the coil spring

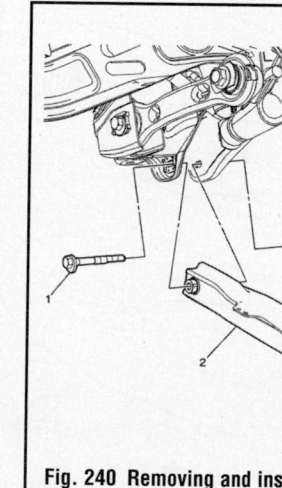

Fig. 240 Removing and installing the lower control arm

4. Remove the lower shock absorber bolt and the washer from the knuckle.

5. Remove the upper shock mounting nuts.

6. Remove the shock absorber from the vehicle.

To install:

7. Position the shock absorber in the vehicle.

8. Install the upper shock absorber nuts and tighten to 18 ft. lbs. (25 Nm).

9. Install the lower shock absorber bolt and the washer in the knuckle. Tighten the lower mounting bolt to 133 ft. lbs. (180 Nm).

10. Remove the jack stand from the knuckle.

11. Install the tire and wheel assembly.

12. Lower the vehicle.

STABILIZER BAR

REMOVAL & INSTALLATION

See Figures 244 through 247.

1. Raise and support the vehicle.

2. Remove the tire and wheel assemblies.

3. Remove the rear muffler assembly.

4. Remove the bolts from the trailing brackets to the frame.

5. Remover the rear coil springs.

6. Remove the park brake cables from the trailing arms.

7. Remove the rear brake calipers from the knuckles.

8. Remove the upper shock absorber bolts.

9. Support and secure adjustable jack stands to the rear support.

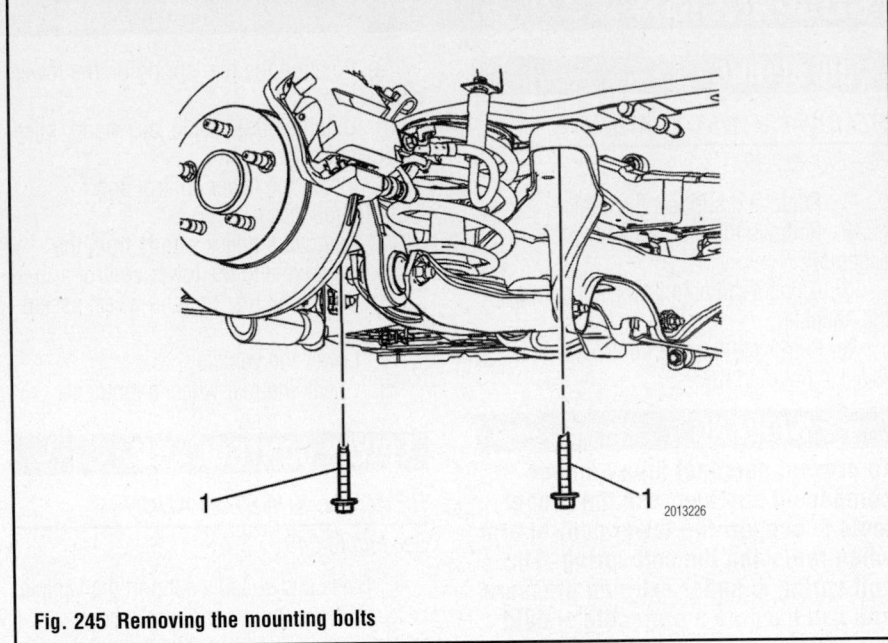
Fig. 245 Removing the mounting bolts

10. Remove the mounting bolts for the support.

11. Lower the support enough to gain access to the rear stabilizer shaft insulator clamps mounting bolts.

12. Remove the stabilizer shaft to knuckle bolts.

13. Remove the stabilizer shaft assembly from the support.

14. Remove the stabilizer shaft clamps, bolts and the insulator.

To install:

15. Install the insulators, the clamps, on the stabilizer shaft.

16. Install the stabilizer shaft on the support.

17. Install the clamp bolts and tighten to 26 ft. lbs. (35 Nm).

18. Install the stabilizer shaft to knuckle bolts and tighten the bolts to 41 ft. lbs. (55 Nm).

➡**When lifting the rear support back into position, guide the rear shock**

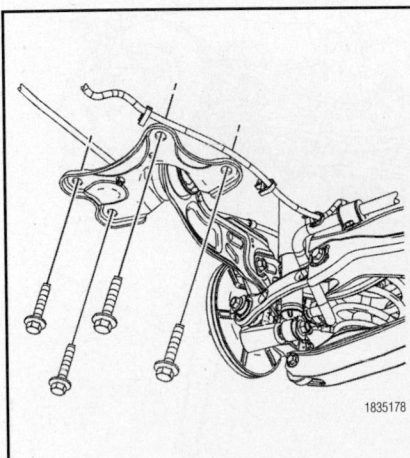
Fig. 244 Removing the trailing bracket to frame bolts

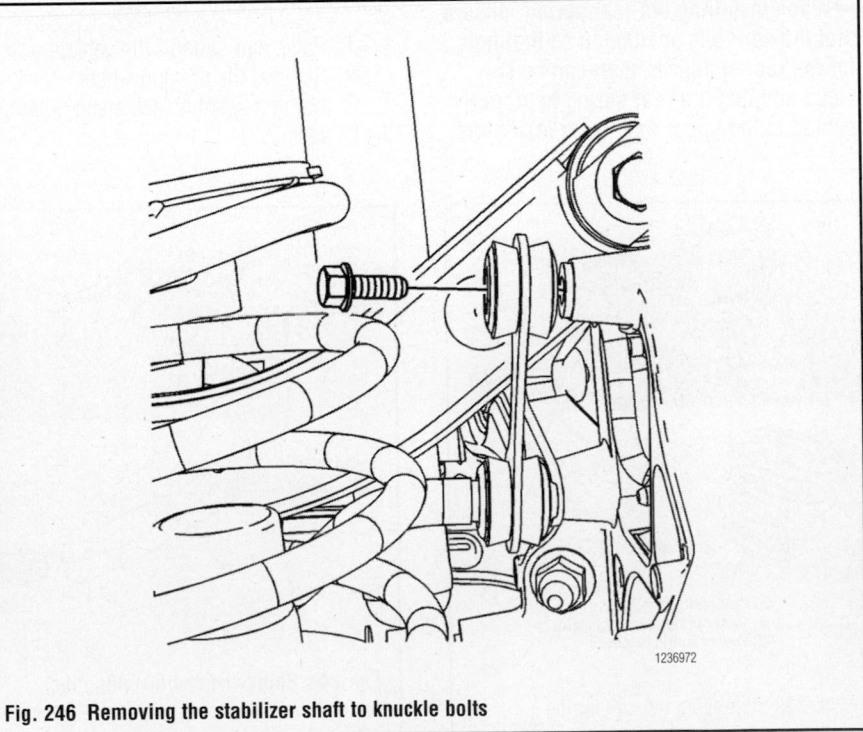
Fig. 246 Removing the stabilizer shaft to knuckle bolts

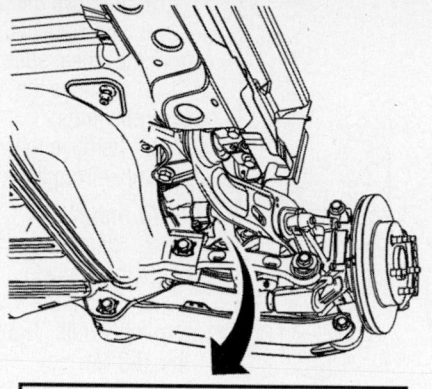

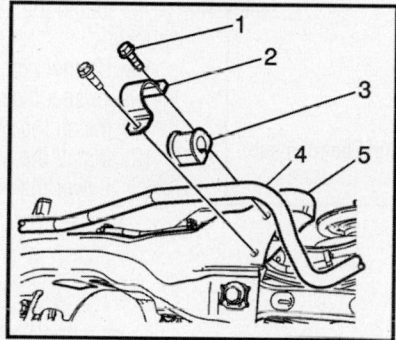

1. Bolts
2. Stabilizer shaft clamps
3. Insulator
4. Stabilizer shaft assembly
5. Support

Fig. 247 Removing the stabilizer shaft

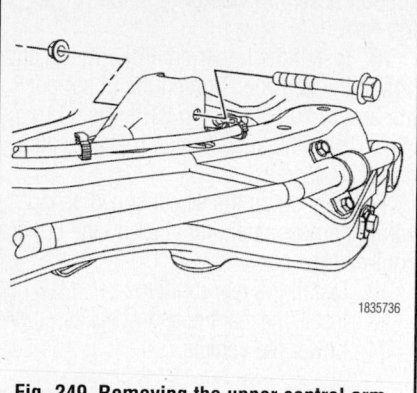

Fig. 249 Removing the upper control arm assembly nut and bolt

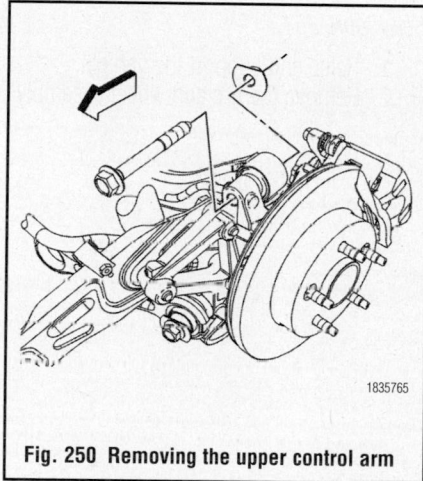

Fig. 250 Removing the upper control arm

absorbers into the proper mounting position.

19. Raise the rear support back into position.
20. Install the rear support bolts.
21. Install the upper shock absorber mounting bolts.
22. Install the trailing arm bracket bolts.
23. Install the rear coil springs.
24. Remove the adjustable jack stands from the rear support.
25. Install the rear brake calipers on the knuckles.
26. Install the park brake cables on the trailing arms.
27. Install the rear muffler assembly.
28. Install the tire and wheel assemblies.

UPPER CONTROL ARM

REMOVAL & INSTALLATION

See Figures 248 through 250.

1. Raise and support the vehicle.
2. Remove the rear tire and wheel assembly.
3. Disconnect the wheel speed sensor wiring harness retaining clips and relocate to the side.
4. Remove the rear muffler from the hangers and lower the muffler to gain

access to the upper control arm nut and bolt.

➡**Note the that the head of the bolt is facing the front of the vehicle and must be install in the same position.**

5. Remove the upper control arm assembly nut and bolt from the rear support.
6. Remove the upper control arm nut and bolt from the knuckle.

7. Remove the upper control arm from the vehicle through the wheelhouse opening.

To install:

8. Install the upper control arm in the support.
9. Install the upper control arm nut and bolt. Tighten the upper control arm to

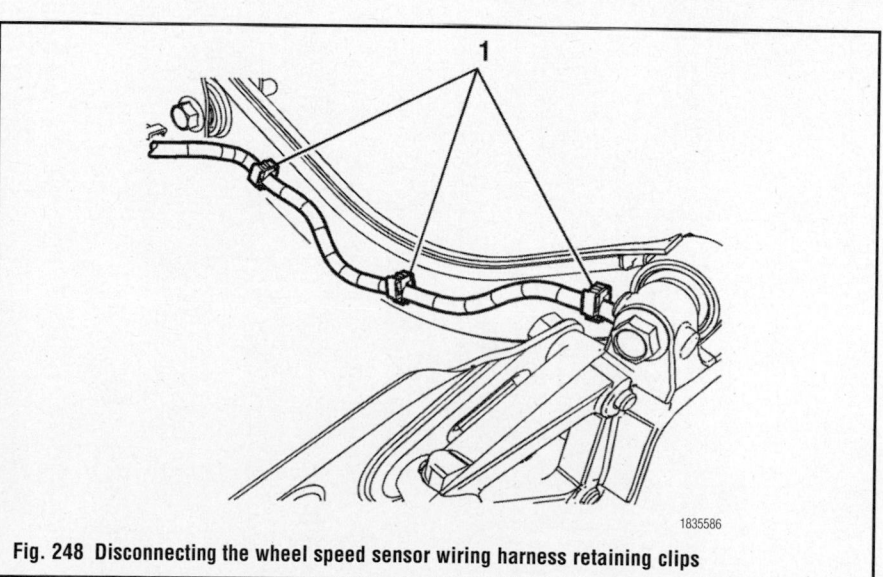

Fig. 248 Disconnecting the wheel speed sensor wiring harness retaining clips

support assembly nut to 44 ft. lbs. (60 Nm).

10. Install the upper control arm nut and bolt in the knuckle. Tighten the upper control arm to knuckle nut to 81 ft. lbs. (110 Nm). Using the angle meter, rotate an additional 70 degrees.

11. Reposition the wheel speed sensor wiring harness retaining clips on the upper control arm.

12. Install the rear muffler.

13. Install the rear tire and wheel assembly.

14. Lower the vehicle.

WHEEL BEARINGS

REMOVAL & INSTALLATION

See Figure 251.

1. Raise and support the vehicle.
2. Remove the tire and wheel assembly.

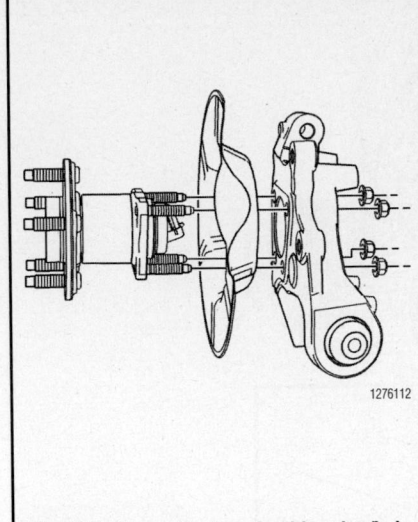

1276112

Fig. 251 Removing the wheel bearing/hub assembly

3. Remove the brake rotor.

4. Disconnect the electrical connector from the wheel speed sensor.

5. Remove the 4 wheel bearing/hub assembly nuts.

6. Remove the wheel bearing/hub assembly from the knuckle.

To install:

7. Install the wheel bearing/hub assembly to the knuckle.

8. Install the 4 wheel bearing/hub assembly nuts. Tighten the nuts to 47 ft. lbs. (63 Nm).

9. Install the stabilizer link bolt at the knuckle.

10. Connect the electrical connector to the wheel speed sensor.

11. Install the brake rotor.

12. Install the tire and wheel assembly.

13. Lower the vehicle.

BUICK

Regal

19

SPECIFICATIONS AND MAINTENANCE CHARTS

ENGINE AND VEHICLE IDENTIFICATION

Engine							Model Year	
Code ①	Liters (cc)	Cu. In.	Cyl.	Fuel Sys.	Engine Type	Eng. Mfg.	Code ②	Year
V	2.0	122	4	SIDI	DOHC	GM	B	2011
C	2.4	146	4	SIDI	DOHC	GM		

① 8th position of VIN

② 10th position of VIN

25742_REGA_C0001

GENERAL ENGINE SPECIFICATIONS

All measurements are given in inches.

Year	Model	Engine Displacement Liters	Engine ID/VIN	Fuel System Type	Net Horsepower @ rpm	Net Torque @ rpm (ft. lbs.)	Bore x Stroke (in.)	Com-pression Ratio	Oil Pressure @ rpm
2011	Regal	2.0	V	SIDI	220 @ 5300	258 @ 2000	3.39x3.39	9.2:1	30-70
		2.4	C	SIDI	182 @ 6700	172 @ 4900	3.46x3.85	11.2:1	30-70

25742_REGA_C0002

ENGINE TUNE-UP SPECIFICATIONS

Year	Engine Displacement Liters	Engine ID/VIN	Spark Plug Gap (in.)	Ignition Timing (deg.)		Fuel Pump (psi)	Idle Speed (rpm)		Valve Clearance	
				MT	AT		MT	AT	Intake	Exhaust
2011	2.0	V	0.035	NA	NA	NA	NA	NA	NA	NA
	2.4	C	0.035	NA	NA	NA	NA	NA	NA	NA

NA: Not Available

25742_REGA_C0003

CAPACITIES

Year	Model	Engine Displacement Liters	Engine ID/VIN	Engine Oil with Filter	Transaxle (pts.) Auto.	Transaxle (pts.) Manual	Drive Axle (pts.) Front	Drive Axle (pts.) Rear	Transfer Case (pts.)	Fuel Tank (gal.)	Cooling System (qts.)
2011	Regal	2.0	V	6	NA	NA	NA	NA	1.36	19.5	8.2
		2.4	C	5	18	NA	NA	NA	1.36	18.5	7.5

NOTE: All capacities are approximate. Add fluid gradually and ensure a proper fluid level is obtained.

NA: Not Available

25742_REGA_C0004

FLUID SPECIFICATIONS

Year	Model	Engine Disp. Liters	Engine Oil	Manual Trans.	Automatic Trans.	Transfer Case	Power Steering Fluid	Brake Master Cylinder	Cooling System
2011	Regal	2.0	5W-30	BOT 0402	AW-1	NA	DEXRON®-VI	DOT 3	DEX-COOL
		2.4	5W-30	BOT 0402	DEXRON®-VI	NA	DEXRON®-VI	DOT 3	DEX-COOL

DOT: Department Of Transpotation

NA: Not Available

25742_REGA_C0005

VALVE SPECIFICATIONS

Year	Engine Displacement Liters	Engine ID/VIN	Seat Angle (deg.)	Face Angle (deg.)	Spring Test Pressure (lbs. @ in.)	Spring Free-Length (in.)	Spring Installed Height (in.)	Stem-to-Guide Clearance (in.) Intake	Stem-to-Guide Clearance (in.) Exhaust	Stem Diameter (in.) Intake	Stem Diameter (in.) Exhaust
2011	2.0	V	45	45	NA	1.6299-1.7402	①	0.0012-0.0022	0.030-0.057	0.2344-0.2355	0.2337-0.2343
	2.4	C	45	45	NA	1.6299-1.7402	①	0.0012-0.0022	0.0020-0.0026	0.2344-0.2355	0.2337-0.2343

NA: Not Available

① : Closed 1.2795 inches
   Open: 0.8858 inches

25742_REGA_C0006

CAMSHAFT SPECIFICATIONS

All measurements in inches unless noted

Year	Engine Displacement Liters	Engine Code/VIN	Journal Diameter	Brg. Oil Clearance	Shaft End-play	Runout	Journal Bore	Lobe Height Intake	Lobe Height Exhaust
2011	2.0	V	1.0604-1.0614	NA	0.0016-0.0121	NA	NA	NA	NA
	2.4	C	1.0604-1.0614	NA	0.0016-0.0057	NA	NA	NA	NA

NA: Not Available

25742_REGA_C0007

CRANKSHAFT AND CONNECTING ROD SPECIFICATIONS

All measurements are given in inches.

Year	Engine Displacement Liters	Engine ID/VIN	Crankshaft Main Brg. Journal Dia.	Crankshaft Main Brg. Oil Clearance	Crankshaft Shaft End-play	Crankshaft Thrust on No.	Connecting Rod Journal Diameter	Connecting Rod Oil Clearance	Connecting Rod Side Clearance
2011	2.0	V	2.2045-2.205	0.0012-0.0026	0.0012-0.015	NA	1.9291-1.9297	NA	NA
	2.4	C	2.2045-2.205	0.0012-0.0026	0.0012-0.015	NA	1.9291-1.9297	NA	NA

NA: Not Available

25742_REGA_C0008

PISTON AND RING SPECIFICATIONS

All measurements are given in inches.

Year	Engine Displacement Liters	Engine ID/VIN	Piston Clearance	Ring Gap Top Compression	Ring Gap Bottom Compression	Ring Gap Oil Control	Ring Side Clearance Top Compression	Ring Side Clearance Bottom Compression	Ring Side Clearance Oil Control
2011	2.0	V	0.0004-0.0016	0.0078-0.0138	0.014-0.022	0.010-0.03	0.0016-0.0031	0.0001-0.0027	0.0009-0.007
	2.4	C	0.0004-0.0016	0.006-0.012	0.008-0.018	0.006-0.03	0.0015-0.0031	0.0012-0.003	0.0023-0.008

25742_REGA_C0009

TORQUE SPECIFICATIONS
All readings in ft. lbs.

Year	Engine Disp. Liters	Engine ID/VIN	Cylinder Head Bolts	Main Bearing Bolts	Rod Bearing Bolts	Crankshaft Damper Bolts	Flywheel Bolts	Manifold		Spark Plugs	Oil Pan Drain Plug
								Intake	Exhaust		
2011	2.0	V	①	②	③	④	⑤	18	15	15	18
	2.4	C	①	NA	③	④	⑤	⑥	10	15	18

NA: Not Available

① First pass: 22 ft. lbs.

Final pass: 155 degrees

② First pass: 15 ft. lbs.

Final pass: 70 degrees

③ First pass: 18 ft. lbs.

Final pass: 100 degrees

④ First pass: 74 ft. lbs.

Final pass: 125 degrees

⑤ First pass: 39 ft. lbs.

Final pass: 25 degrees

⑥ 53 INCH lbs.

25742_REGA_C0010

WHEEL ALIGNMENT

Year	Model		Caster		Camber		Toe-in (in.)
			Range (+/-Deg.)	Preferred Setting (Deg.)	Range (+/-Deg.)	Preferred Setting (Deg.)	
2011	Regal	F	0.00 ±0.75	3.8 ±0.75	0.00 ±0.75	-0.40 ±0.75	0.20 ± 0.2
		R	NA	NA	NA	①	0.10 ± 0.20

NA: Not Available

① Left camber: -0.90 ±0.75

Right camber: -0.90 ±0.75

25742_REGA_C0011

TIRE, WHEEL AND BALL JOINT SPECIFICATIONS

Year	Model	OEM Tires		Tire Pressures (psi)		Wheel Size	Ball Joint Inspection	Lug Nut (ft. lbs.)
		Standard	Optional	Front	Rear			
2011	Regal	NA	NA	35	35	16	NA	110

OEM: Original Equipment Manufacturer

PSI: Pounds Per Square Inch

NA: Information not available

25742_REGA_C0012

BRAKE SPECIFICATIONS

All measurements in inches unless noted

Year	Model		Brake Disc			Brake Drum Diameter			Minimum Pad/Lining Thickness		Brake Caliper	
			Original Thickness	Minimum Thickness	Max. Runout	Original Inside Diameter	Max. Wear Limit	Maximum Machine Diamter	Front	Rear	Bracket Bolts (ft. lbs.)	Mounting Bolts (ft. lbs.)
2011	Regal	F	1.180	1.070	0.0020	NA	NA	NA	NA	NA	③	NA
		R	①	②	0.0020	NA	NA	NA	NA	NA	④	NA

F: Front

R: Rear

NA: Information not available

① J60: 0.472 inches

   J61: 0.905 inches

② J60: 0.395

   J61: 0.827

③ 110 ft. lbs.

   Plus 45 degrees

   Plus 15 degrees

④ 74 ft. lbs. plus 60 degrees

25742_REGA_C0013

MAINTENANCE I AND II SERVICE SCHEDULES
REGAL

When the CHANGE ENGINE OIL light appears, certain services and inspections are required.

Required services are described as Maintenance I and Maintenance II.

The first service of a vehicle should be Maintenance I, and the second service should be Maintenance II.

Alternate between the 2 services thereafter. However, in some cases, Maintenance II may be required more often.

Maintenance I: Use Maintenance I if the CHANGE ENGINE OIL light comes on within 10 months since the vehicle was purchased or, if Maintenance II was performed.

Maintenance II: Use Maintenance II if the previous service performed was Maintenance I. Always use Maintenance II whenever the CHANGE ENGINE OIL light comes on 10 months or more since the last service, or, if the CHANGE ENGINE OIL light has not come on at all for one year.

Service Item	Maintenance I	Maintenance II
Change the engine oil and filter.	✓	✓
Reset the oil life system.	✓	✓
Visually inspect the vehicle for leaks or damage. A fluid loss in the vehicle system could indicate a problem. Inspect, repair and add fluid to the system if necessary.	✓	✓
Inspect the engine air cleaner filter. If necessary, replace the filter.	✓	✓
Rotate the tires. Inspect the tire inflation pressures and the tire wear.	✓	✓
Visually inspect the brake lines and hoses for proper hook-up, binding, leaks, cracks, chafing, etc. Inspect the disc brake pads for wear and the rotors for surface condition. Inspect the drum brake linings for wear or cracks. Inspect other brake parts, including drums, wheel cylinders, calipers, parking brake, etc. Inspect the parking brake adjustment.	✓	✓
Inspect the engine coolant and the windshield washer fluid levels. Add fluid as needed.	✓	✓
Inspect the suspension and steering components. Inspect the front and rear suspension and the steering system for damaged, loose or missing parts, or signs of wear. Inspect the power steering lines and the hoses for proper hook-up, binding, leaks, cracks, chafing, etc.	—	✓
Visually inspect the coolant hoses and replace the hoses if they are cracked, swollen or deteriorated. Inspect all pipes, fittings and clamps; replace with GM parts as needed. To help ensure proper operation, a pressure test of the cooling system and pressure cap and cleaning the outside of the radiator and air conditioning condenser is recommended at least once a year.	—	✓
Ensure the safety belt reminder light and all the belts, buckles, latch plates, retractors and anchorages are working properly. Look for any other loose or damaged safety belt system parts. If you see anything that might keep a safety belt system from working correctly, repair or replaced the damaged part. Replace torn or frayed safety belts, refer to Operational and Functional Checks in Seat Belts. Inspect for any opened or broken air bag coverings, and repair or replace as needed. The air bag system does require regular maintenance.	—	✓
Lubricate the body components.	—	✓
Lubricate all key lock cylinders, hood latch assemblies, secondary latches, pivots, spring anchor and release pawl, hood and door hinges, rear folding seats and liftgate hinges. Frequent lubrication may be required when exposed to a corrosive environment, refer to Fluid and Lubricant Recommendations . Applying dielectric silicone grease GM P/N 12345579 (Canadian P/N 1974984) or equivalent on the weatherstrips with a clean cloth.	—	✓
Inspect the transaxle fluid level and add fluid as needed.	—	✓
Inspect the wiper blades and replace as necessary	✓	✓
Inspect the throttle system.	—	✓
Replace the passenger compartment air filter.	—	✓

To reset the CHANGE ENGINE OIL light:

1. Turn the ignition key to the ON/RUN position with the engine OFF.
2. Press and release the stem in the lower center of the instrument cluster until the OIL LIFE message is displayed.
3. Once the alternating OIL LIFE and RESET messages appear, press and hold the stem until several beeps sound. This confirms that the oil life system has been reset to 100 percent.
4. Turn the ignition key to the OFF position. If the CHANGE ENGINE OIL message comes back on when the vehicle is started, the engine oil life system has not been reset. Repeat the procedure.

25742_REGA_C0014

ADDITIONAL MAINTENANCE SERVICES - NORMAL
REGAL

TO BE SERVICED	TYPE OF SERVICE	VEHICLE MILEAGE INTERVAL (x1000)					
		25	50	75	100	125	150
Engine coolant	Replace						✓
Air cleaner filter	Replace		✓		✓		✓
Automatic transaxle fluid	Replace				✓		
Spark plugs	Replace				✓		
Exhaust system & heat shields	Service/ Inspect	✓	✓	✓	✓	✓	✓
Fuel system	Inspect	✓	✓	✓	✓	✓	✓
Accessory drive belt	Replace						✓
Evaporative control system	Inspect		✓		✓		✓

25742_REGA_C0015

ADDITIONAL MAINTENANCE SERVICES - SEVERE
REGAL

TO BE SERVICED	TYPE OF SERVICE	VEHICLE MILEAGE INTERVAL (x1000)					
		25	50	75	100	125	150
Engine coolant	Replace						✓
Air cleaner filter	Replace	✓	✓	✓	✓	✓	✓
Automatic transaxle fluid & filter	Replace		✓		✓		✓
Spark plugs	Replace				✓		
Exhaust system & heat shields	Service/ Inspect	✓	✓	✓	✓	✓	✓
Fuel system	Inspect	✓	✓	✓	✓	✓	✓
Accessory drive belt	Inspect						✓
Evaporative control system	Inspect		✓		✓		✓

25742_REGA_C0016

PRECAUTIONS

Before servicing any vehicle, please be sure to read all of the following precautions, which deal with personal safety, prevention of component damage, and important points to take into consideration when servicing a motor vehicle:

• Never open, service or drain the radiator or cooling system when the engine is hot; serious burns can occur from the steam and hot coolant.

• Observe all applicable safety precautions when working around fuel. Whenever servicing the fuel system, always work in a well-ventilated area. Do not allow fuel spray or vapors to come in contact with a spark, open flame, or excessive heat (a hot drop light, for example). Keep a dry chemical fire extinguisher near the work area. Always keep fuel in a container specifically designed for fuel storage; also, always properly seal fuel containers to avoid the possibility of fire or explosion. Refer to the additional fuel system precautions later in this section.

• Fuel injection systems often remain pressurized, even after the engine has been turned **OFF**. The fuel system pressure must be relieved before disconnecting any fuel lines. Failure to do so may result in fire and/or personal injury.

• Brake fluid often contains polyglycol ethers and polyglycols. Avoid contact with the eyes and wash your hands thoroughly after handling brake fluid. If you do get brake fluid in your eyes, flush your eyes with clean, running water for 15 minutes. If eye irritation persists, or if you have taken brake fluid internally, IMMEDIATELY seek medical assistance.

• The EPA warns that prolonged contact with used engine oil may cause a number of skin disorders, including cancer. You should make every effort to minimize your exposure to used engine oil. Protective gloves should be worn when changing oil. Wash your hands and any other exposed skin areas as soon as possible after exposure to used engine oil. Soap and water, or waterless hand cleaner should be used.

• All new vehicles are now equipped with an air bag system, often referred to as a Supplemental Restraint System (SRS) or Supplemental Inflatable Restraint (SIR) system. The system must be disabled before performing service on or around system components, steering column, instrument panel components, wiring and sensors. Failure to follow safety and disabling procedures could result in accidental air bag deployment, possible personal injury and unnecessary system repairs.

• Always wear safety goggles when working with, or around, the air bag system. When carrying a non-deployed air bag, be sure the bag and trim cover are pointed away from your body. When placing a non-deployed air bag on a work surface, always face the bag and trim cover upward, away from the surface. This will reduce the motion of the module if it is accidentally deployed. Refer to the additional air bag system precautions later in this section.

• Clean, high quality brake fluid from a sealed container is essential to the safe and proper operation of the brake system. You should always buy the correct type of brake fluid for your vehicle. If the brake fluid becomes contaminated, completely flush the system with new fluid. Never reuse any brake fluid. Any brake fluid that is removed from the system should be discarded. Also, do not allow any brake fluid to come in contact with a painted surface; it will damage the paint.

• Never operate the engine without the proper amount and type of engine oil; doing so WILL result in severe engine damage.

• Timing belt maintenance is extremely important. Many models utilize an interference-type, non-freewheeling engine. If the timing belt breaks, the valves in the cylinder head may strike the pistons, causing potentially serious (also time-consuming and expensive) engine damage. Refer to the maintenance interval charts for the recommended replacement interval for the timing belt, and to the timing belt section for belt replacement and inspection.

• Disconnecting the negative battery cable on some vehicles may interfere with the functions of the on-board computer system(s) and may require the computer to undergo a relearning process once the negative battery cable is reconnected.

• When servicing drum brakes, only disassemble and assemble one side at a time, leaving the remaining side intact for reference.

• Only an MVAC-trained, EPA-certified automotive technician should service the air conditioning system or its components.

BRAKES

GENERAL INFORMATION

PRECAUTIONS

• Certain components within the ABS system are not intended to be serviced or repaired individually.

• Do not use rubber hoses or other parts not specifically specified for and ABS system. When using repair kits, replace all parts included in the kit. Partial or incorrect repair may lead to functional problems and require the replacement of components.

• Lubricate rubber parts with clean, fresh brake fluid to ease assembly. Do not use shop air to clean parts; damage to rubber components may result.

• Use only DOT 3 brake fluid from an unopened container.

• If any hydraulic component or line is removed or replaced, it may be necessary to bleed the entire system.

• A clean repair area is essential. Always clean the reservoir and cap thoroughly before removing the cap. The slightest amount of dirt in the fluid may plug an orifice and impair the system function. Perform repairs after components have been thoroughly cleaned; use only denatured alcohol to clean components. Do not allow ABS components to come into contact with any substance containing mineral oil; this includes used shop rags.

• The Anti-Lock control unit is a microprocessor similar to other computer units in the vehicle. Ensure that the ignition switch is **OFF** before removing or installing controller harnesses. Avoid static

ANTI-LOCK BRAKE SYSTEM (ABS)

electricity discharge at or near the controller.

• If any arc welding is to be done on the vehicle, the control unit should be unplugged before welding operations begin.

SPEED SENSORS

REMOVAL & INSTALLATION

Front

Without F45
See Figure 1.

1. Raise and support the vehicle.
2. Remove the tire and wheel assembly.
3. Clean the wheel speed sensor mounting area on the steering knuckle of any accumulated dirt and debris.

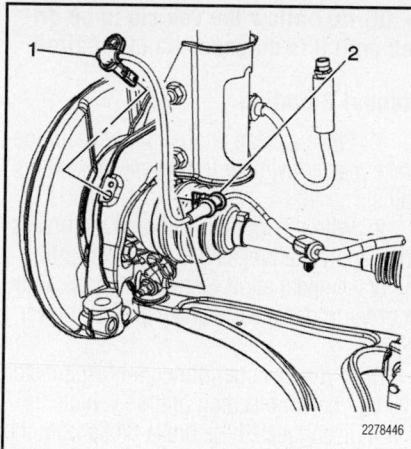

Fig. 1 Remove the wheel speed sensor (1) and release the harness clip (2)

4. Disconnect the wheel speed sensor electrical connector and release the connector from the frame.

5. Release the harness clip from the frame.

6. Release the harness clips from the lower control arm.

7. Remove any accumulated dirt and debris from the surrounding the wheel speed sensor.

8. Remove the wheel speed sensor bolt.

9. Remove the wheel speed sensor from the steering knuckle.

10. Release the harness clip from the steering knuckle and remove the wheel speed sensor.

11. To install, reverse the removal procedure.

With F45
See Figure 2.

1. Raise and support the vehicle.
2. Remove the tire and wheel assembly.
3. Clean the wheel speed sensor mounting area on the steering knuckle of any accumulated dirt and debris.
4. Disconnect the wheel speed sensor electrical connector.
5. Remove the wheel speed sensor bolt.

➡ **The wheel speed sensor wire harness routes over the steering knuckle, between the front suspension strut and the front brake shield.**

6. Using a slight twisting motion, carefully remove the wheel speed sensor assembly.
7. To install, reverse the removal procedure.

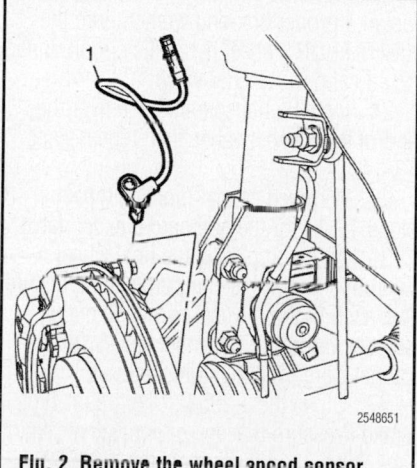

Fig. 2 Remove the wheel speed sensor assembly (1)

Rear
See Figure 3.

1. Raise and support the vehicle.
2. Remove the rear tire and wheel assembly.
3. Remove the rear wheelhouse panel liner.
4. Clean the wheel speed sensor mounting area on the suspension knuckle of any accumulated dirt and debris.
5. Disconnect the shock absorber electrical connector, if equipped.
6. Release the wheel speed sensor harness clips from the rear suspension bracket.
7. Disconnect the wheel speed sensor harness electrical connector.
8. Remove the wheel speed sensor bolt.
9. Remove the wheel speed sensor from the rear suspension knuckle.

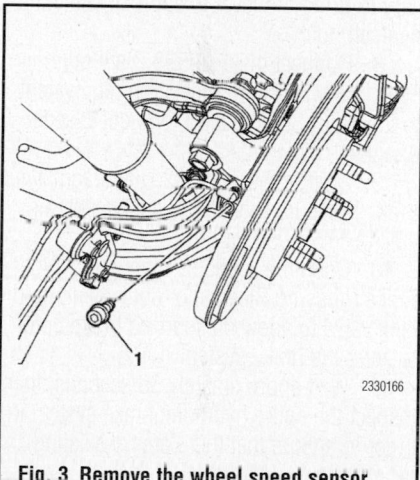

Fig. 3 Remove the wheel speed sensor bolt

BRAKES

BLEEDING THE BRAKE SYSTEM

BLEEDING PROCEDURE

BLEEDING PROCEDURE

Pressure Bleeding

1. Place a clean shop cloth beneath the brake master cylinder to prevent brake fluid spills.

2. With the ignition OFF and the brakes cool, apply the brakes 3-5 times, or until the brake pedal effort increases significantly, in order to deplete the brake booster power reserve.

3. If you have performed a brake master cylinder bench bleeding on this vehicle, or if you disconnected the brake pipes from the master cylinder, you must perform the following steps:

a. Ensure that the brake master cylinder reservoir is full to the maximum-fill level. If necessary, add GM approved brake fluid from a clean, sealed brake fluid container.

➡ **If removal of the reservoir cap and diaphragm is necessary, clean the outside of the reservoir on and around the cap prior to removal.**

b. With the rear brake pipe installed securely to the master cylinder, loosen and separate the front brake pipe from the front port of the brake master cylinder.

c. Allow a small amount of brake fluid to gravity bleed from the open port of the master cylinder.

d. Reconnect the brake pipe to the master cylinder port and tighten securely.

e. Have an assistant slowly depress the brake pedal fully and maintain steady pressure on the pedal.

f. Loosen the same brake pipe to purge air from the open port of the master cylinder.

g. Tighten the brake pipe, then have the assistant slowly release the brake pedal.

h. Wait 15 seconds, then repeat steps 3–7 until all air is purged from the same port of the master cylinder.

i. With the front brake pipe installed securely to the master cylinder, after all air has been purged from the front port of the master cylinder, loosen and separate the rear brake pipe from the master cylinder, then repeat steps 3—8

j. After completing the final master cylinder port bleeding procedure, ensure that both of the brake pipe-to-master cylinder fittings are properly tightened.

4. Fill the brake master cylinder reservoir to the maximum-fill level with GM approved brake fluid from a clean, sealed brake fluid container.

5. Clean the outside of the reservoir on and around the reservoir cap prior to removing the cap and diaphragm.

Install the J-35589-A Master Cylinder Bleeder Adapter to the brake master cylinder reservoir.

6. Check the brake fluid level in the J-29532 Diaphragm Type Brake Pressure Bleeder, or equivalent.

7.Add GM approved brake fluid from a clean, sealed brake fluid container as necessary to bring the level to approximately the half-full point.

8. Connect the J-29532 Diaphragm Type Brake Pressure Bleeder, or equivalent, to the J-35589-A Master Cylinder Bleeder Adapter .

9. Charge the J-29532 Diaphragm Type Brake Pressure Bleeder, or equivalent, air tank to 175-205 kPa (25-30 psi).

10. Open the J-29532 Diaphragm Type Brake Pressure Bleeder, or equivalent, fluid tank valve to allow pressurized brake fluid to enter the brake system.

11. Wait approximately 30 seconds, then inspect the entire hydraulic brake system in order to ensure that there are no existing external brake fluid leaks.

12. Any brake fluid leaks identified require repair prior to completing this procedure.

13. Install a proper box-end wrench onto the RIGHT REAR wheel hydraulic circuit, inboard (fixed caliper), bleeder valve.

14. Install a transparent hose over the end of the bleeder valve.

15. Submerge the open end of the transparent hose into a transparent container partially filled with GM approved brake fluid from a clean, sealed brake fluid container.

16. Loosen the bleeder valve to purge air from the wheel hydraulic circuit. Allow fluid to flow until air bubbles stop flowing from the bleeder, then tighten the bleeder valve.

17. For fixed caliper models, repeat steps 11-14 for the outboard bleeder valve.

18. With the right rear wheel hydraulic circuit bleeder valve, or valves (fixed caliper), tightened securely, after all air has been purged from the right rear hydraulic circuit, install a proper box-end wrench

onto the LEFT FRONT wheel hydraulic circuit, inboard (fixed caliper), bleeder valve.

Install a transparent hose over the end of the bleeder valve, then repeat steps 13-14.

19. For fixed caliper models, repeat steps 11-14 for the outboard bleeder valve.

20. With the left front wheel hydraulic circuit bleeder valve, or valves (fixed caliper), tightened securely, after all air has been purged from the left front hydraulic circuit, install a proper box-end wrench onto the LEFT REAR wheel hydraulic circuit, inner (fixed caliper), bleeder valve.

21. Install a transparent hose over the end of the bleeder valve, then repeat steps 13-14.

22. For fixed caliper models, repeat steps 11-14 for the outboard bleeder valve.

23. With the left rear wheel hydraulic circuit bleeder valve, or valves (fixed caliper), tightened securely, after all air has been purged from the left rear hydraulic circuit, install a proper box-end wrench onto the RIGHT FRONT wheel hydraulic circuit, inner (fixed caliper), bleeder valve.

24. Install a transparent hose over the end of the bleeder valve, then repeat steps 13-14.

25. For fixed caliper models, repeat steps 11-14 for the outboard bleeder valve.

26. After completing the final wheel hydraulic circuit bleeding procedure, ensure that each of the 4 wheel hydraulic circuit bleeder valves, or 8 bleeder valves (fixed caliper), are properly tightened.

27. Close the J-29532 Diaphragm Type Brake Pressure Bleeder, or equivalent , fluid tank valve, then disconnect the J-29532 Diaphragm Type Brake Pressure Bleeder, or equivalent , from the J-35589-A Master Cylinder Bleeder Adapter .

28. Remove the J-35589-A Master Cylinder Bleeder Adapter from the brake master cylinder reservoir.

29. Fill the brake master cylinder reservoir to the maximum-fill level with GM approved brake fluid from a clean, sealed brake fluid container.

30. Slowly depress and release the brake pedal. Observe the feel of the brake pedal.

31. If the brake pedal feels spongy perform the following steps:

a. Inspect the brake system for external leaks.

b. Using a scan tool, perform the antilock brake system automated bleeding procedure to remove any air that may have been trapped in the BPMV.

32. Turn the ignition key ON, with the engine OFF. Check to see if the brake system warning lamp remains illuminated.

➡ **DO NOT allow the vehicle to be driven until it is diagnosed and repaired.**

Manual Bleeding

1. Place a clean shop cloth beneath the brake master cylinder to prevent brake fluid spills.

2. With the ignition OFF and the brakes cool, apply the brakes 3-5 times, or until the brake pedal effort increases significantly, in order to deplete the brake booster power reserve.

3. If you have performed a brake master cylinder bench bleeding on this vehicle, or if you disconnected the brake pipes from the master cylinder, you must perform the following steps:

a. Ensure that the brake master cylinder reservoir is full to the maximum-fill level. If necessary, add GM approved brake fluid from a clean, sealed brake fluid container.

➡**If removal of the reservoir cap and diaphragm is necessary, clean the outside of the reservoir on and around the cap prior to removal.**

b. With the rear brake pipe installed securely to the master cylinder, loosen and separate the front brake pipe from the front port of the brake master cylinder.

c. Allow a small amount of brake fluid to gravity bleed from the open port of the master cylinder.

d. Reconnect the brake pipe to the master cylinder port and tighten securely.

e. Have an assistant slowly depress the brake pedal fully and maintain steady pressure on the pedal.

f. Loosen the same brake pipe to purge air from the open port of the master cylinder.

g. Tighten the brake pipe, then have the assistant slowly release the brake pedal.

h. Wait 15 seconds, then repeat steps 3.3-3.7 until all air is purged from the same port of the master cylinder.

i. With the front brake pipe installed securely to the master cylinder, after all air has been purged from the front port of the master cylinder, loosen and separate the rear brake pipe from the master cylinder, then repeat steps 3—8.

4. Fill the brake master cylinder reservoir with GM approved brake fluid from a clean, sealed brake fluid container. Ensure that the brake master cylinder reservoir remains at least half-full during this bleeding procedure. Add fluid as needed to maintain the proper level.

5. Clean the outside of the reservoir on and around the reservoir cap prior to removing the cap and diaphragm.

6. Install a proper box-end wrench onto the RIGHT REAR wheel hydraulic circuit, inboard (fixed caliper), bleeder valve.

7. Install a transparent hose over the end of the bleeder valve.

8. Submerge the open end of the transparent hose into a transparent container partially filled with GM approved brake fluid from a clean, sealed brake fluid container.

9. Have an assistant slowly depress the brake pedal fully and maintain steady pressure on the pedal.

10. Loosen the bleeder valve to purge air from the wheel hydraulic circuit.

11. Tighten the bleeder valve, then have the assistant slowly release the brake pedal.

12. Wait 15 seconds, then repeat steps 8-10 until all air is purged from the same wheel hydraulic circuit.

13. For fixed caliper models, repeat steps 5-11 for the outboard bleeder valve.

14. With the right rear wheel hydraulic circuit bleeder valve, or valves (fixed caliper), tightened securely - after all air has been purged from the right rear hydraulic circuit - install a proper box-end wrench onto the LEFT FRONT wheel hydraulic circuit, inner (fixed caliper), bleeder valve.

15. Install a transparent hose over the end of the bleeder valve, then repeat steps 7-11.

16. For fixed caliper models, repeat steps 5-11 for the outboard bleeder valve.

With the left front wheel hydraulic circuit bleeder valve, or valves (fixed caliper), tightened securely, after all air has been purged from the left front hydraulic circuit, install a proper box-end wrench onto the LEFT REAR wheel hydraulic circuit, inner (fixed caliper), bleeder valve.

17. Install a transparent hose over the end of the bleeder valve, then repeat steps 7-11.

18. For fixed caliper models, repeat steps 5-11 for the outboard bleeder valve.

19. With the left rear wheel hydraulic circuit bleeder valve, or valves (fixed caliper), tightened securely, after all air has been purged from the left rear hydraulic circuit,

install a proper box-end wrench onto the RIGHT FRONT wheel hydraulic circuit, inner (fixed caliper), bleeder valve.

20. Install a transparent hose over the end of the bleeder valve, then repeat steps 7-11.

21. For fixed caliper models, repeat steps 5-11 for the outboard bleeder valve.

22. After completing the final wheel hydraulic circuit bleeding procedure, ensure that each of the 4 wheel hydraulic circuit bleeder valves, or 8 bleeder valves (fixed caliper), are properly tightened.

23. Fill the brake master cylinder reservoir to the maximum-fill level with GM approved brake fluid from a clean, sealed brake fluid container.

24. Slowly depress and release the brake pedal. Observe the feel of the brake pedal.

If the brake pedal feels spongy, repeat the bleeding procedure again. If the brake pedal still feels spongy after repeating the bleeding procedure, perform the following steps:

a. Inspect the brake system for external leaks.

b. Pressure bleed the hydraulic brake system in order to purge any air that may still be trapped in the system.

25. Turn the ignition key ON, with the engine OFF. Check to see if the brake system warning lamp remains illuminated.

➡ **DO NOT allow the vehicle to be driven until it is diagnosed and repaired.**

BLEEDING THE ABS SYSTEM

✳✳ WARNING

Do not use any fluid other than clean brake fluid meeting manufacturer's specification. Additionally, do not use brake fluid that has been previously drained. Following these instructions will help prevent system contamination, brake component damage and the risk of serious personal injury.

✳✳ CAUTION

Brake fluid contains polyglycol ethers and polyglycols. Avoid contact with

the eyes and wash your hands thoroughly after handling brake fluid. If you do get brake fluid in your eyes, flush your eyes with clean, running water for 15 minutes. If eye irritation persists, or if you have taken brake fluid internally, IMMEDIATELY seek medical assistance.**

➡ **Follow the Pressure Bleeding or Manual Bleeding procedure steps to bleed the system.**

1. If equipped with a fire suppression system, depower the system, disconnect the negative battery cable and wait one minute.

2. Connect the scan tool and follow the ABS Service Bleed instructions.

3. Repeat the Pressure Bleeding or Manual Bleeding procedure steps to bleed the system.

4. If equipped with a fire suppression system, repower the system. Connect the negative battery cable.

FLUID FILL PROCEDURE

1. Visually inspect the brake fluid level through the brake master cylinder reservoir.

2. If the brake fluid level is at or below the half-full point during routine fluid checks, the brake system should be inspected for wear and possible brake fluid leaks.

3. If the brake fluid level is at or below the half-full point during routine fluid checks, and an inspection of the brake system did not reveal wear or brake fluid leaks, the brake fluid may be topped-off up to the maximum-fill level.

4. If brake system service was just completed, the brake fluid may be topped-off up to the maximum-fill level.

5. If the brake fluid level is above the half-full point, adding brake fluid is not recommended under normal conditions.

6. If brake fluid is to be added to the master cylinder reservoir, clean the outside of the reservoir on and around the reservoir cap prior to removing the cap and diaphragm. Use only GM approved brake fluid from a clean, sealed brake fluid container.

BRAKES

FRONT DISC BRAKES

✳✳ CAUTION

Dust and dirt accumulating on brake parts during normal use may contain asbestos fibers from production or aftermarket brake linings. Breathing excessive concentrations of asbestos fibers can cause serious bodily harm. Exercise care when servicing brake parts. Do not sand or grind brake lining unless equipment used is designed to contain the dust residue. Do not clean brake parts with compressed air or by dry brushing. Cleaning should be done by dampening the brake components with a fine mist of water, then wiping the brake components clean with a dampened cloth. Dispose of cloth and all residue containing asbestos fibers in an impermeable container with the appropriate label. Follow practices prescribed by the Occupational Safety and Health Administration (OSHA) and the Environmental Protection Agency (EPA) for the handling, processing, and disposing of dust or debris that may contain asbestos fibers.

BRAKE CALIPER

REMOVAL & INSTALLATION

See Figure 4.

1. Raise and support the vehicle.
2. Remove the tire and wheel assembly.
3. Remove the brake hose fitting bolt.

➡ **Do not reuse the brake hose fitting gaskets.**

4. Remove and discard the brake hose fitting gaskets from the brake hose fitting.
5. Cap the brake hose fitting to prevent brake fluid loss and contamination.

➡ **DO NOT use any air tools to remove or install the guide pin bolts. Use hand tools ONLY. Install an open end wrench to hold the caliper guide pin in line with the brake caliper while removing or installing the caliper guide pin bolt. DO NOT allow the open end wrench to come in contact with the brake caliper. Allowing the open end wrench to come in contact with the brake caliper will cause a pulsation when the brakes are applied.**

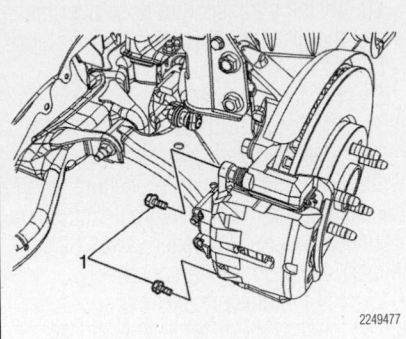

Fig. 4 Remove the brake caliper guide pin bolts

6. Using a backup wrench to hold the brake caliper guide pin stationary, remove the brake caliper guide pin bolts.
7. Remove the brake caliper.

To install:

8. Install the brake caliper.
9. Hold the brake caliper guide pin stationary and install the brake caliper guide pin bolts and tighten to 20 ft. lbs. (27 Nm).

➡ **Install new brake hose fitting gaskets.**

10. Assemble the brake hose fitting bolt and the 2 new brake hose fitting gaskets to the front brake hose fitting.
11. Install the brake hose assembly and tighten the brake hose fitting bolt to 30 ft. lbs. (40 Nm).
12. Bleed the hydraulic brake system.
13. Install the tire and wheel assembly.

DISC BRAKE PADS

REMOVAL & INSTALLATION

See Figure 5.

1. Inspect the fluid level in the brake master cylinder reservoir.
2. If the brake fluid level is midway between the maximum-full point and the minimum allowable level, no brake fluid needs to be removed before proceeding.
3. If the brake fluid level is higher than midway between the maximum-full point and the minimum allowable level, remove brake fluid to the midway point before proceeding.
4. Raise and support the vehicle.
5. Remove the tire and wheel assembly.
6. Place a large C-clamp over the brake caliper body and against the outer brake pad.

7. Using the C-clamp, compress the brake caliper piston fully into the brake caliper bore.

➡ **DO NOT use any air tools to remove or install the guide pin bolts. Use hand tools ONLY. Install an open end wrench to hold the caliper guide pin in line with the brake caliper while removing or installing the caliper guide pin bolt. DO NOT allow the open end wrench to come in contact with the brake caliper. Allowing the open end wrench to come in contact with the brake caliper will cause a pulsation when the brakes are applied.**

8. Using a backup wrench to hold the brake caliper guide pin stationary, remove the lower brake caliper guide pin bolt.

✳✳ CAUTION

Support the brake caliper with heavy mechanic wire, or equivalent, whenever it is separated from its mount and the hydraulic flexible brake hose is still connected. Failure to support the caliper in this manner will cause the flexible brake hose to bear the weight of the caliper, which may cause damage to the brake hose and in turn may cause a brake fluid leak.

9. Pivot the brake caliper upward and support with heavy mechanics wire or equivalent.

➡ **Note the location of the brake pad wear sensor for correct installation.**

10. Remove the inner brake pad and the outer brake pad.
11. Remove the upper and lower brake pad springs.

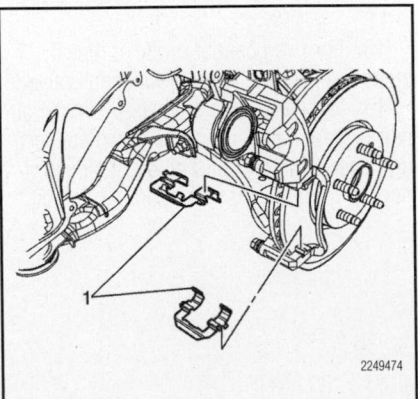

Fig. 5 Remove the upper and lower brake pad springs (1)

12. If installing new brake pads, discard the springs.

To install:

➡ **If installing new brake pads, install new springs.**

13. Install the upper and lower brake pad springs.

➡ **Note the location of the brake pad wear sensor for correct installation.**

BRAKES

BRAKE CALIPER

REMOVAL & INSTALLATION

See Figure 6.

1. Raise and support the vehicle.
2. Remove the tire and wheel assembly.
3. Remove the rear disc brake pads.

➡ **Do not reuse the brake caliper bracket bolts.**

4. Remove and discard the brake caliper bracket bolts.
5. Remove the brake caliper bracket.

To install:

6. Install the brake caliper bracket.
7. Prepare the brake caliper bracket bolts and the bracket threaded holes for assembly:

  a. Thoroughly clean the residue from the bolt threads with denatured alcohol or equivalent and allow to dry
  b. Thoroughly clean the residue from the threaded holes with denatured alcohol or equivalent and allow to dry.
  c. Apply threadlocker to 2/3 of the threaded length of the caliper bracket bolts.

  d. Ensure there are no gaps in the threadlocker along the length of the filled area of the bolts.
  e. Allow the threadlocker to cure approximately 10 minutes before installation

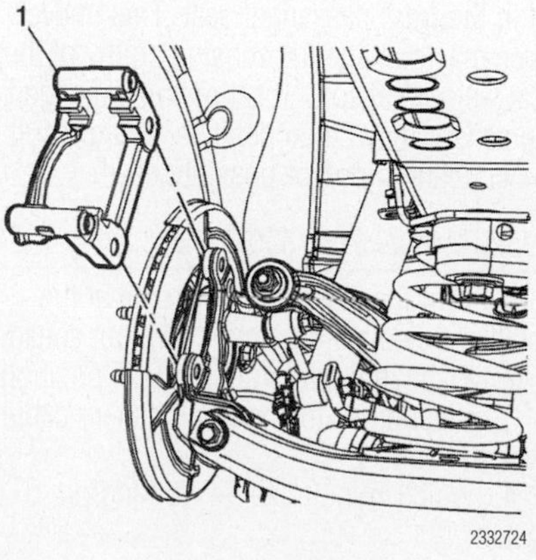

➡ **Do not reuse the brake caliper bracket bolts.**

8. Install new brake caliper bracket bolts and tighten to 74 ft. lbs. (100 Nm) + 60 degrees.
9. Install the rear disc brake pads.
10. Install the tire and wheel assembly.

DISC BRAKE PADS

REMOVAL & INSTALLATION

See Figure 7.

1. Inspect the fluid level in the brake master cylinder reservoir.
2. If the brake fluid level is midway between the maximum-full point and the minimum allowable level, no brake fluid needs to be removed before proceeding.
3. If the brake fluid level is higher than midway between the maximum-full point and the minimum allowable level, remove brake fluid to the midway point before proceeding.
4. Raise and support the vehicle.
5. Remove the tire and wheel assembly.

➡ **DO NOT use any air tools to remove or install the guide pin bolts. Use hand tools ONLY. Install an open end wrench to hold the caliper guide pin in line with the brake caliper while removing or installing the caliper guide pin bolt. DO NOT allow the open end wrench to come in contact with the brake caliper. Allowing the open end wrench to come in contact with the brake caliper will cause a pulsation when the brakes are applied.**

6. Using a backup wrench to hold the brake caliper guide pin stationary, remove the brake caliper guide pin bolts.

14. Install the inner brake pad and the outer brake pad.
15. Pivot the brake caliper to the installed position.
16. Using a backup wrench to hold the brake caliper guide pin stationary, install the lower brake caliper guide pin bolt and tighten to 20 ft. lbs. (27 Nm).
17. Install the tire and wheel assembly.

18. With the engine OFF, gradually apply the brake pedal to approximately 2/3 of its travel distance.
19. Slowly release the brake pedal.
20. Wait 15 seconds, then repeat steps 6-7 until a firm brake pedal is obtained. This will properly seat the brake caliper piston and brake pads.
21. Fill the master cylinder reservoir.
22. Burnish the brake pads and rotors.

REAR DISC BRAKES

✹ CAUTION

Support the brake caliper with heavy mechanic wire, or equivalent, whenever it is separated from its mount and the hydraulic flexible brake hose is still connected. Failure to support the caliper in this manner will cause the flexible brake hose to bear the weight of the caliper, which may cause damage to the brake hose and in turn may cause a brake fluid leak.

7. Remove the brake caliper from the brake caliper bracket and support with heavy mechanics wire or equivalent.
8. Remove the brake caliper bracket bolts.
9. Remove the brake caliper bracket assembly.
10. Remove the outer brake pad.

➡ **The inner brake pad is equipped with the wear sensor.**

11. Remove the inner brake pad.
12. Remove the upper and lower brake pad springs.
13. If installing new brake pads, discard the springs.

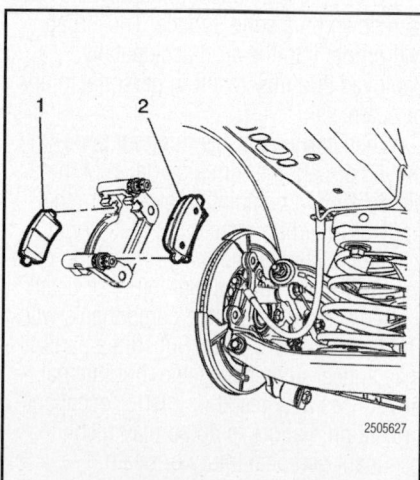

Fig. 7 Removing the outer (1) and outer (2) brake pads

Fig. 6 Remove the brake caliper bracket (1)

To install:

➡ **If installing new brake pads, install new springs.**

14. Install new brake pad springs.

15. Install the outer brake pad.

➡ **The inner brake pad is equipped with the wear sensor.**

16. Install the inner brake pad.

17. Prepare the brake caliper bracket bolts and the bracket threaded holes for assembly:

   a. Thoroughly clean the residue from the bolt threads with denatured alcohol or equivalent and allow to dry.

   b. Thoroughly clean the residue from the threaded holes with denatured alcohol or equivalent and allow to dry.

18. Install the caliper.

19. Install the tire and wheel assembly.

20. With the engine OFF, gradually apply the brake pedal to approximately 2/3 of its travel distance.

21. Slowly release the brake pedal.

22. Wait 15 seconds, then repeat steps 10-11 until a firm brake pedal is obtained. This will properly seat the brake caliper piston and brake pads.

23. Fill the master cylinder reservoir.

24. Burnish the brake pads and rotors.

CHASSIS ELECTRICAL   AIR BAG (SUPPLEMENTAL RESTRAINT SYSTEM)

GENERAL INFORMATION

✳ CAUTION

These vehicles are equipped with an air bag system. The system must be disarmed before performing service on, or around, system components, the steering column, instrument panel components, wiring and sensors. Failure to follow the safety precautions and the disarming procedure could result in accidental air bag deployment, possible injury and unnecessary system repairs.

SERVICE PRECAUTIONS

Disconnect and isolate the battery negative cable before beginning any airbag system component diagnosis, testing, removal, or installation procedures. Allow system capacitor to discharge for two minutes before beginning any component service. This will disable the airbag system. Failure to disable the airbag system may result in accidental airbag deployment, personal injury, or death.

Do not place an intact undeployed airbag face down on a solid surface. The airbag will propel into the air if accidentally deployed and may result in personal injury or death.

When carrying or handling an undeployed airbag, the trim side (face) of the airbag should be pointing away from the body to minimize possibility of injury if accidental deployment occurs. Failure to do this may result in personal injury or death.

Replace airbag system components with OEM replacement parts. Substitute parts may appear interchangeable, but internal differences may result in inferior occupant protection. Failure to do so may result in occupant personal injury or death.

Wear safety glasses, rubber gloves, and long sleeved clothing when cleaning powder residue from vehicle after an airbag

deployment. Powder residue emitted from a deployed airbag can cause skin irritation. Flush affected area with cool water if irritation is experienced. If nasal or throat irritation is experienced, exit the vehicle for fresh air until the irritation ceases. If irritation continues, see a physician.

Do not use a replacement airbag that is not in the original packaging. This may result in improper deployment, personal injury, or death.

The factory installed fasteners, screws and bolts used to fasten airbag components have a special coating and are specifically designed for the airbag system. Do not use substitute fasteners. Use only original equipment fasteners listed in the parts catalog when fastener replacement is required.

During, and following, any child restraint anchor service, due to impact event or vehicle repair, carefully inspect all mounting hardware, tether straps, and anchors for proper installation, operation, or damage. If a child restraint anchor is found damaged in any way, the anchor must be replaced. Failure to do this may result in personal injury or death.

Deployed and non-deployed airbags may or may not have live pyrotechnic material within the airbag inflator.

Do not dispose of driver/passenger/curtain airbags or seat belt tensioners unless you are sure of complete deployment. Refer to the Hazardous Substance Control System for proper disposal.

Dispose of deployed airbags and tensioners consistent with state, provincial, local, and federal regulations.

After any airbag component testing or service, do not connect the battery negative cable. Personal injury or death may result if the system test is not performed first.

If the vehicle is equipped with the Occupant Classification System (OCS), do not connect the battery negative cable before performing the OCS Verification Test using the scan tool and the appropriate diagnostic information. Personal injury or death may

result if the system test is not performed properly.

Never replace both the Occupant Restraint Controller (ORC) and the Occupant Classification Module (OCM) at the same time. If both require replacement, replace one, then perform the Airbag System test before replacing the other.

Both the ORC and the OCM store Occupant Classification System (OCS) calibration data, which they transfer to one another when one of them is replaced. If both are replaced at the same time, an irreversible fault will be set in both modules and the OCS may malfunction and cause personal injury or death.

If equipped with OCS, the Seat Weight Sensor is a sensitive, calibrated unit and must be handled carefully. Do not drop or handle roughly. If dropped or damaged, replace with another sensor. Failure to do so may result in occupant injury or death.

If equipped with OCS, the front passenger seat must be handled carefully as well. When removing the seat, be careful when setting on floor not to drop. If dropped, the sensor may be inoperative, could result in occupant injury, or possibly death.

If equipped with OCS, when the passenger front seat is on the floor, no one should sit in the front passenger seat. This uneven force may damage the sensing ability of the seat weight sensors. If sat on and damaged, the sensor may be inoperative, could result in occupant injury, or possibly death.

DISARMING THE SYSTEM

1. Turn the steering wheel so that the vehicles wheels are pointing straight ahead.

2. Place the ignition in the OFF position.

3. Disconnect the negative battery cable from the battery.

4. Wait 1 minute before working on system.

ARMING THE SYSTEM

1. Place the ignition in the OFF position.

2. Connect the negative battery cable to the battery.

3. Turn the ignition switch to the ON position. The AIR BAG indicator will flash then turn OFF.

4. Using a scan tool, perform the Diagnostic System Check - Vehicle if the AIR BAG warning indicator does not operate as described.

CLOCKSPRING CENTERING

➡**The Regal utilizes a Steering Angle Sensor.**

The steering angle sensor does not require a centering often. Centering of the steering angle sensor might be required after certain service procedures are performed. Some of these procedures are as follows:

   a. Electronic brake control module (EBCM) replacement

   b. Steering angle sensor replacement.

   c. Steering gear replacement.

   d. Steering column replacement.

   e. Collision or other physical damage.

1. The steering angle sensor centering procedure can be completed with a scan tool using the following steps:

2. Using the steering wheel, align the front wheels forward.

3. Apply the parking brake, or set the transmission in the P position.

4. Install the scan tool to the data link connector.

5. Ignition ON, engine OFF

6. Select Steering Wheel Angle Sensor Reset in the Steering Wheel Angle Sensor Module Configuration/Reset Functions list.

7. Follow the scan tool directions to complete the reset procedure.

8. Select Steering Wheel Angle Sensor Learn in the Steering Wheel Angle Sensor Module Configuration/Reset Functions list.

9. Follow the scan tool directions to complete the learn procedure.

10. Clear any DTCs that may be set.

DRIVE TRAIN

MANUAL TRANSMISSION ASSEMBLY

REMOVAL & INSTALLATION

See Figures 8 through 10.

1. Remove the intake manifold cover.

2. Remove the battery tray. Refer to Battery in Engine Electrical.

3. Remove the shift lever cables from the selector on the transmission.

4. Remove the clutch actuator cylinder hose.

5. Disconnect the connector from the reverse light switch.

6. Remove the upper transmission fasteners.

7. Install the engine support fixture.

8. Remove the exhaust front pipe.

9. Remove the drivetrain and front suspension frame.

10. Remove the transmission front mount.

11. Remove the transmission rear mount bracket.

12. Remove the intermediate shaft.

13. Remove the left driveshaft from the transmission.

14. Lower the vehicle.

15. Remove the fasteners to the transmission bracket left side.

16. Lower the engine enough to access the transmission.

17. Raise the vehicle.

18. Secure the transmission to a suitable transmission jack.

19. Remove the lower transmission fasteners.

20. Separate the transmission from the engine.

To install:

21. Lubricate the input shaft splines and the two guiding sleeves.

22. Position the transmission to the engine.

23. Install the lower transmission fasteners and tighten to 44 ft. lbs. (60 Nm).

24. Install the lower transmission fasteners and tighten to 44 ft. lbs. (60 Nm).

25. Remove the transmission jack.

26. Lower the vehicle.

27. Raise the engine to the correct level with the engine support fixture.

28. Install the fasteners to the transmission bracket left side.

29. Remove the engine support fixture.

30. Install the upper transmission fasteners and tighten to 60 Nm (44 lb ft).

31. Raise the vehicle.

32. Install the rear transmission mount bracket.

33. Install the transmission front mount.

34. Install the intermediate shaft and the right driveshaft.

35. Install the left driveshaft to the transmission.

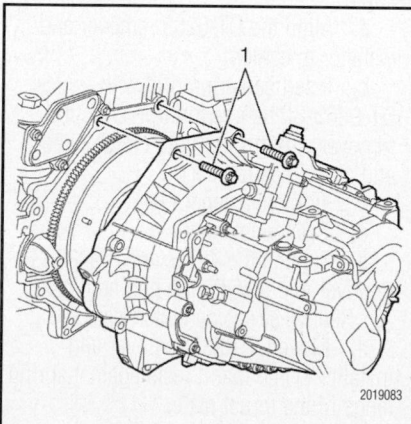

Fig. 8 Removing the upper transmission fasteners (1)

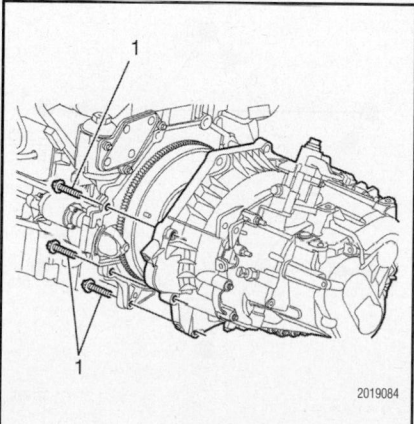

Fig. 9 Removing the lower transmission fasteners (1)—1 of 2

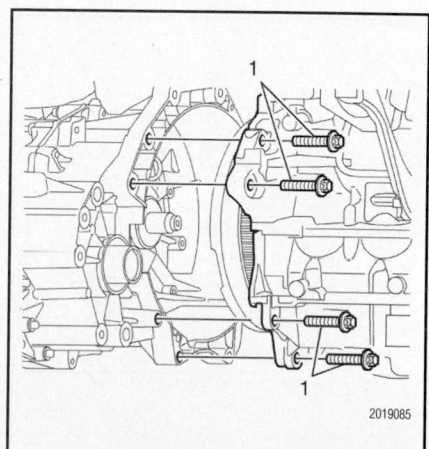

Fig. 10 Removing the lower transmission fasteners (1)—2 of 2

36. Install the drivetrain and front suspension frame.

37. Install the exhaust front pipe.

38. Lower the vehicle.

39. Install the clutch actuator cylinder hose.

40. Install the shift lever cables to the selector on the transmission.

41. Connect the connector to the reverse light switch.

42. Install the battery tray.

43. Install the intake manifold cover.

MANUAL TRANSMISSION FLUID

DRAIN AND REFILL

See Figure 11.

✳✳ WARNING

When the transmission is at operating temperatures, take necessary precautions when removing the check/fill plug, to avoid being burned by draining fluid.

1. Remove the battery tray.

2. Remove the filler plug.

3. Place pan under transmission to collect fluid.

4. Remove the drain plug

5. Allow the transmission fluid to completely drain out.

6. Tighten the drain plug to 22 ft. lbs. (30 Nm).

7. Fill the transmission with 1.7 quarts of transmission fluid.

8. If a new transmission is being installed, the new transmission must be filled with 1.7 quarts of transmission fluid.

9. Tighten the filler plug to 22 ft. lbs. (30 Nm).

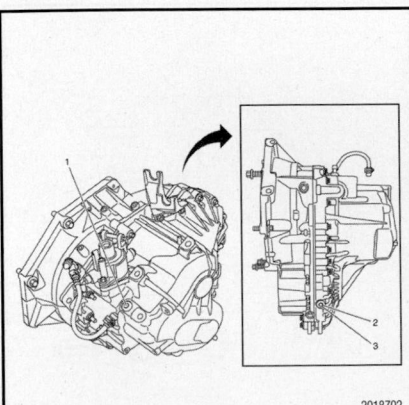

2018702

Fig. 11 Locating the filler plug (1), drain plug (2) and fluid hole (3)

CLUTCH

REMOVAL & INSTALLATION

Without DT–6263

See Figure 12.

1. Remove the transmission.

➡ **Discard the bolts.**

2. Remove the 6 clutch pressure plate bolts.

3. Remove the clutch pressure plate and driven plate.

➡ **Clutch pressure plate and driven plates contaminated by foreign bodies (oil, cleaning agent etc.) have to be replaced. Check clutch driven plate for damage and friction rust in the hub profile and replace if necessary. Do not clean clutch pressure plate and driven plate with a high pressure cleaner or component washing machine.**

4. Inspect the clutch pressure plate and driven plate and replace if necessary. Inspect for the following conditions:
   • Excessive wear
   • Burned friction surface
   • Oil on friction surface
   • Damaged spline hub
   • Damaged springs

➡ **The clutch driven plate has to be replaced if the lining projection is less than 0.020 inches.**

5. Inspect projection of lining at the clutch lining rivets.

6. Slide the clutch driven plate onto the transmission input shaft and check for easy movement.

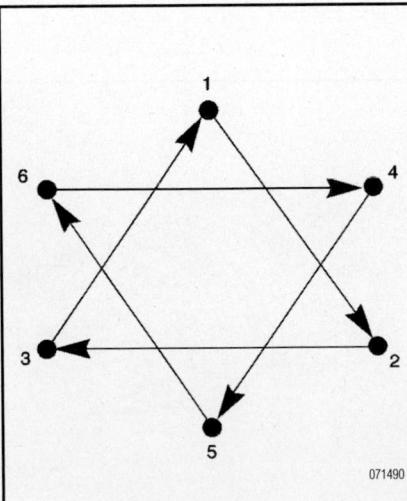

071490

Fig. 12 Tighten the clutch pressure plate bolts in sequence

To install:

7. Clean 6 threads in flywheel for fastening clutch pressure plate.

➡ **Clutch driven plate must be installed so that the lettering on the hub faces the transmission.**

8. Install the driven plate and clutch pressure plate.

9. Hand start 6 NEW clutch pressure plate bolts, leaving the clutch pressure plate lose enough to reposition for alignment

10. Using DT-50194 Clutch Disc Alignment Tool or equivalent, align the clutch driven plate to the clutch pilot bearing.

11. Tighten the clutch pressure plate bolts in sequence to 21 ft. lbs. (28Nm).

12. Install the transmission.

With DT

See Figure 13.

1. Remove the transmission.

➡**To prevent damage to the spring tangs of the thrust plate use DT-6263 remover and installer to remove and install the thrust plate.**

2. Note the different lengths of the brackets for attaching DT-6263 remover and installer to lower engine block. Thrust plate and clutch disc for vehicles with self-adjusting clutch (SAC) are only available in as a set.

➡ **DT-6263 remover and installer may only be attached to the engine block and not to the oil pan, do not tighten bolts yet.**

3. Attach the DT-6263 remover and installer to engine block.

4. Attach the DT-6263-30 handle to centering drift.

5. Fasten the DT-6263 remover and installer:
   a. Align the DT-6263 remover and installer in center.
   b. Insert centering drift with DT-6263-30 handle through DT-6263 remover and installer into clutch plate and crankshaft (center).
   c. Tighten fastener (1).
   d. Tighten fastener (3).
   e. Tighten the 4x fastener DT-6263 remover and installer on engine block.

6. Relieve stress on clutch disc.
   a. Move DT-6263 remover and installer (1) so that it rests against spring tangs of the thrust plate.
   b. Turn DT-6263 remover and installer clockwise to the stop.

7. Remove thrust plate from flywheel. Remove 6 fasteners.

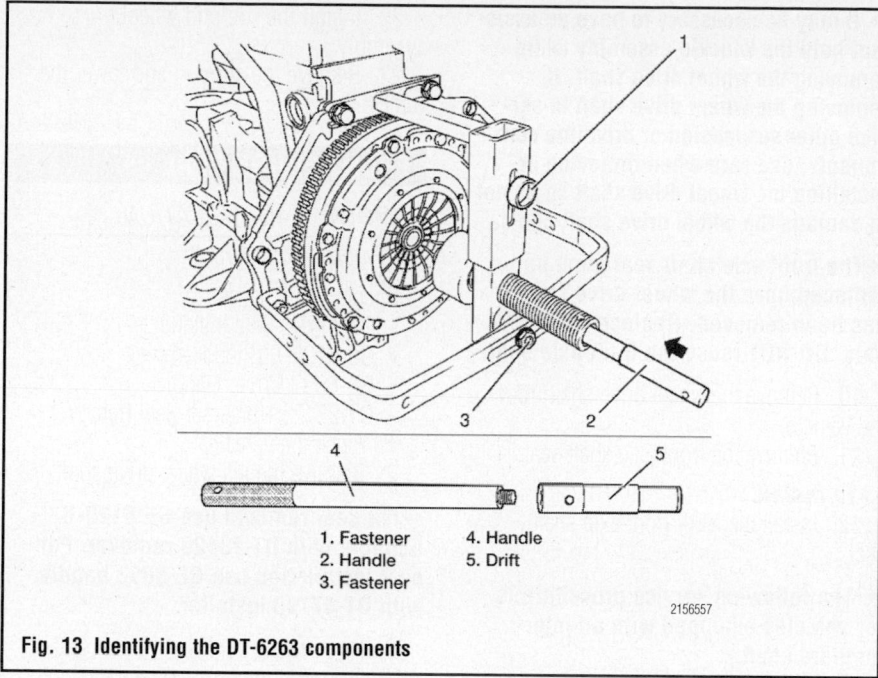

1. Fastener
2. Handle
3. Fastener
4. Handle
5. Drift

2156557

Fig. 13 Identifying the DT-6263 components

8. Detach thrust plate and clutch plate.
   a. Turn DT-6263 remover and installer (1) anticlockwise to the stop.
   b. Pull out centering drift with DT-6263-30 handle (2).

➡ **Clutch plates contaminated by foreign bodies (oil, cleaning agent etc.) must be replaced as a matter of principle. Check clutch disc for damage and friction rust in the hub profile and replace if necessary. Do not clean thrust plate and clutch disc with a high pressure cleaner or component washing machine.**

9. Check clutch plate for wear: Check the projection of the lining at the clutch lining rivets. The clutch plate must be replaced if the lining projection is less than 0.5 mm. Also, press the clutch plate onto the transmission input shaft and check for ease of movement.

To install:

➡ **Lettering "transmission side" faces the transmission. Do not tighten bolts yet. For a clearer representation, illustration 2156562 shows clutch without centering drift with DT-6263-30 handle**

10. Attach clutch disc and thrust plate to flywheel.
11. Center thrust plate and clutch plate with centering drift and DT-6263-30 handle.

➡ **Tighten fastener crosswise.**

12. Attach thrust plate to flywheel and turn DT-6263 remover and installer clockwise to the stop.
    a. Tighten the trust plate fastener M7 to 11 ft. lbs. (15 Nm).
    b. Tighten the trust plate fastener M8 to 16 ft. lbs. (22 Nm).
13. Detach DT-6263 remover and installer (1) from engine block.
    a. Turn DT-6263 remover and installer (3) anticlockwise to the stop.
    b. Detach centering drift and DT-6263-30 handle (2).
    c. Remove the 4x fastener DT-6263 remover and installer on engine block.
14. Install the transmission.

FRONT DRIVESHAFT

REMOVAL & INSTALLATION

See Figure 14.

1. Remove the right front halfshaft.
2. Drain the transmission fluid.
3. Remove the 3 shaft flange fasteners.

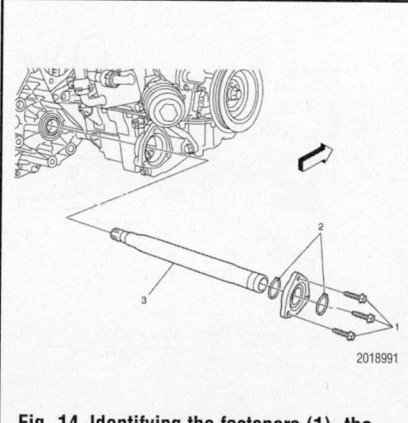

2018991

Fig. 14 Identifying the fasteners (1), the retaining rings (2) and shaft (3)

4. Remove the 2 retaining rings.
5. Remove the shaft.
6. To install, reverse the removal procedure.
7. Insert shaft into the gearbox until 20 mm is left. Use protective collar to protect the sealing.
8. Tighten the shaft flange fasteners to 16 ft. lbs. (22 Nm).

FRONT HALFSHAFT

REMOVAL & INSTALLATION

Left Side

See Figure 15.

1. Raise and support the vehicle.
2. Remove the tire and wheel assembly.
3. Insert a drift or punch in the cooling fins of the brake rotor.
4. Rotate the brake rotor until the drift or punch contacts the brake caliper mounting bracket.
5. Using a breaker bar, loosen the wheel drive shaft nut.
6. Using the appropriate tool, separate the wheel drive shaft from the knuckle.
7. Remove the wheel drive shaft nut.
8. Remove the lower control arm from the knuckle. Refer to Lower Control Arm in Front Suspension.
9. Remove the outer tie rod end from the knuckle.

➡ **It may be necessary to have an assistant hold the knuckle assembly while removing the wheel drive shaft. If removing the wheel drive shaft to service other suspension or driveline components, use care when removing or installing the wheel drive shaft so as not to damage the wheel drive shaft boots.**

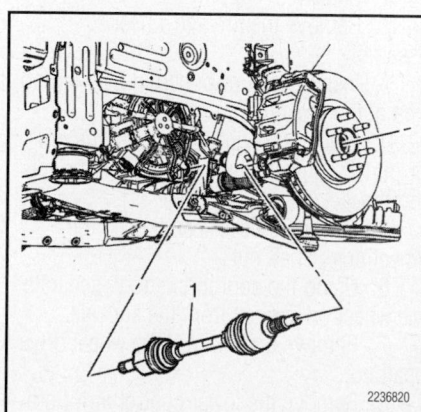

2236820

Fig. 15 Remove the left half shaft (1) from the vehicle

➡The front axle shaft seal must be replaced once the wheel drive shaft has been removed. Replace with NEW only. DO NOT reuse the front axle seal.

10. Remove the half shaft from the vehicle.

➡ If there is no washer on the wheel drive shaft, install a NEW washer.

11. Remove and discard the washer from the wheel drive shaft. DO NOT re-use the washer, replace with NEW only.

12. Remove the front axle shaft pinion seal. Refer to Front Pinion Seal.

To install:

13. Install the NEW front axle shaft seal.

14. Install the NEW washer on the wheel drive shaft.

15. Position the wheel drive shaft in the vehicle.

16. Insert the wheel drive shaft in the knuckle.

17. Install the lower control arm in the knuckle.

18. Install the outer tie rod end in the knuckle.

19. Install the wheel drive shaft nut.

20. Insert a drift or punch in the cooling fins of the brake rotor.

21. Rotate the brake rotor until the drift or punch contacts the brake caliper mounting bracket.

22. Using a torque wrench, tighten the wheel drive shaft nut to 111 ft. lbs. (150 Nm). Then back off 45°, re-torque to 184 ft. lbs. (250 Nm).

23. Install the tire and wheel assembly.

24. Remove the support and lower the vehicle.

Right Side

See Figure 16.

1. Raise and support the vehicle.

2. Remove the tire and wheel assembly.

3. Insert a drift or punch in the cooling fins of the brake rotor.

4. Rotate the brake rotor until the drift or punch contacts the brake caliper mounting bracket.

5. Using a breaker bar, loosen the wheel drive shaft nut.

6. Using the appropriate tool, separate the wheel drive shaft from the knuckle.

7. Remove and discard the wheel drive shaft nut.

8. Remove the lower control arm from the knuckle. Refer to Lower Control Arm.

9. Remove the outer tie rod end from the knuckle.

➡ It may be necessary to have an assistant hold the knuckle assembly while removing the wheel drive shaft. If removing the wheel drive shaft to service other suspension or driveline components, use care when removing or installing the wheel drive shaft so as not to damage the wheel drive shaft boots.

➡The front axle shaft seal must be replaced once the wheel drive shaft has been removed. Replace with NEW only. DO NOT reuse the front axle seal.

10. Remove the wheel drive shaft from the vehicle.

11. Remove the front axle shaft seal.

To install:

12. Install the NEW front axle shaft seal.

➡ The following service procedure is for vehicles equipped with an intermediate shaft.

13. For the right wheel drive shaft, apply a very small amount of grease to the splines of the wheel drive shaft inner joint.

14. Position the wheel drive shaft in the vehicle.

15. Insert the wheel drive shaft in the knuckle.

16. Install the lower control arm in the knuckle.

17. Install the outer tie rod end in the knuckle.

18. Install the wheel drive shaft nut.

19. Insert a drift or punch in the cooling fins of the brake rotor.

20. Rotate the brake rotor until the drift or punch contacts the brake caliper mounting bracket.

21. Using a torque wrench, tighten the wheel drive shaft nut to 111 ft. lbs. (150 Nm). Then back off 45°, re-torque to 184 ft. lbs. (250 Nm).

22. Install the tire and wheel assembly.

23. Remove the support and lower the vehicle.

FRONT PINION SEAL

REMOVAL & INSTALLATION

See Figures 17 and 18.

Special tools necessary:
- DT-47790 Seal Installer
- GE-6125-B Slide Hammer
- GE-8092 Driver Handle
- DT-23129 Universal Seal Remover

1. Raise the vehicle.
2. Remove the left wheel drive shaft.

➡For seal removal use GE-6125-B hammer with DT-23129 remover. For seal installation use GE-8092 handle with DT-47790 installer.

3. Remove the left Front pinion seal.
4. To install, reverse the removal procedure.

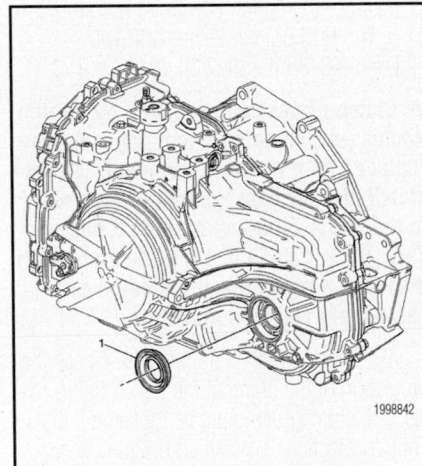

Fig. 17 Removing the left front pinion seal

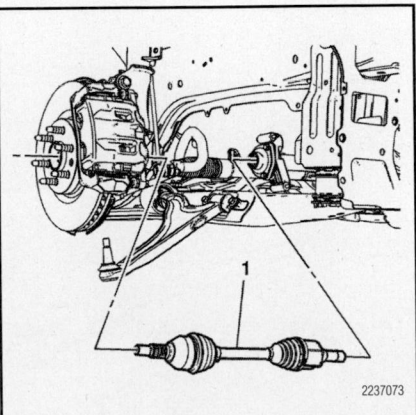

Fig. 16 Remove the right half shaft (1) from the vehicle

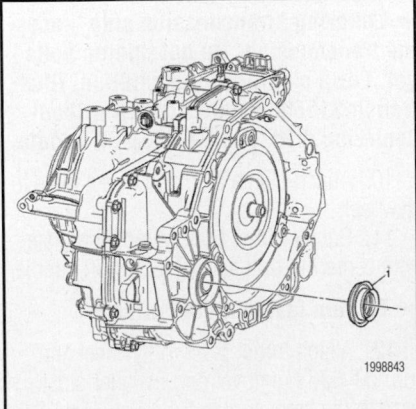

Fig. 18 Removing the right front pinion seal

ENGINE COOLING

ENGINE COOLANT

DRAIN & REFILL PROCEDURE

Draining

> ### ❊❊ WARNING
>
> **To avoid being burned, do not remove the radiator cap or surge tank cap while the engine is hot. The cooling system will release scalding fluid and steam under pressure if radiator cap or surge tank cap is removed while the engine and radiator are still hot.**

1. Remove the coolant pressure cap from the radiator surge tank.
2. Raise and support the vehicle.
3. Place a drain pan under the drain cock.
4. Loosen the radiator drain cock.
5. Drain the cooling system.
6. Lower the vehicle.
7. Inspect the coolant.
8. Follow the appropriate procedure based on the condition of the coolant.

   a. Normal in appearance: Follow the filling procedure

   b. Discolored: Follow the flush procedure. Refer to Flushing

Filling

> ### ❊❊ CAUTION
>
> **The procedure below must be followed. Improper coolant level could result in a low or high coolant level condition, causing engine damage.**

1. Raise and support the vehicle.
2. Tighten the radiator drain cock.
3. Lower the vehicle.

➡ **Use a 50/50 mixture of DEX-COOL antifreeze and clean drinkable water.**

4. Slowly fill the radiator with a 50/50 coolant mixture until the coolant level reaches the base of the radiator surge tank.
5. Allow 30 seconds for the coolant level to stabilize and continue to fill the coolant filler neck until the level stabilizes for at least 2 minutes.
6. Start the engine and allow to the engine to idle in PARK or NEUTRAL with the parking brake engaged.
7. Slowly fill the coolant mixture until the level stabilizes at the base of the radiator surge tank.
8. Install the coolant pressure cap.

9. Raise the engine RPM to 2500 rpm for 30-40 seconds.
10. Shut the engine OFF.
11. Allow the engine to cool, remove coolant fill cap and repeat steps 4-10 until the coolant level has completely stabilized within the radiator surge tank.
12. Inspect the concentration of the engine coolant using the J 26568 Coolant and Battery Fluid Tester
13. Inspect and if necessary, fill the coolant reservoir bottle as necessary.
14. Rinse away any excess coolant from the engine and the engine compartment
15. Inspect the cooling system for leaks.
16. Top off the radiator surge tank if necessary.

FLUSHING

➡ **Do not use a chemical flush.**

➡ **Store used coolant in the proper manner, such as in a used engine coolant holding tank. Do not pour used coolant down a drain. Ethylene glycol antifreeze is a very toxic chemical. Do not dispose of coolant into the sewer system or ground water. This is illegal and ecologically unsound.**

➡ **Various methods and equipment can be used to flush the cooling system. If special equipment is used, such as a back flusher, follow the manufacturer's instruction. Always remove the thermostat before flushing the cooling system.**

When the cooling system becomes contaminated, the cooling system should be flushed thoroughly to remove the contaminants before the engine is seriously damaged.

1. Drain the cooling system.
2. Remove the coolant recovery reservoir.
3. Clean and flush the coolant recovery reservoir with clean, drinkable water.
4. Install the coolant recovery reservoir.
5. Follow the drain and fill procedure using only clean, drinkable water.
6. Run the engine for 20 minutes.
7. Stop the engine.
8. Drain the cooling system.
9. Repeat the procedure if necessary, until the fluid is nearly colorless.
10. Fill the cooling system.

ENGINE FAN

REMOVAL & INSTALLATION
See Figure 19.

1. Reposition power steering reservoir without disconnecting hoses.

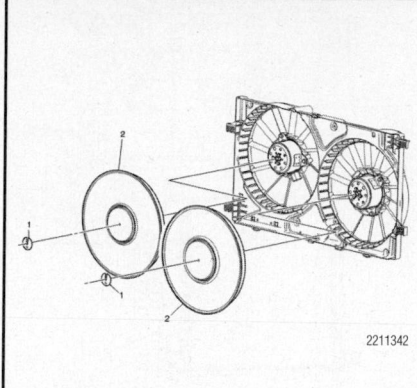

Fig. 19 Removing the Engine Coolant Fan Retainer (1) and fan (2)

2. Remove the radiator outlet hose.
3. Remove the transmission fluid cooler hoses.
4. Disconnect the engine coolant fan motor electrical connectors.
5. Unclip all wiring harness that are connected to the shroud.
6. Release the 2 tabs at the lower retainers allowing the shroud to slide upward.
7. Reposition the A/C condenser and compressor hose without discharging the system.
8. Remove the Engine Coolant Fan Retainer.
9. Remove the Engine Coolant Fan.
10. To install, reverse the removal procedure.

RADIATOR

REMOVAL & INSTALLATION
See Figure 20.

1. Drain the cooling system.
2. Remove the radiator inlet hose.
3. Remove the radiator outlet hose.
4. Remove transmission oil cooler lines.
5. Reposition and secure the A/C condenser to the impact bar without disconnecting the lines.
6. Disconnect the engine coolant fan harness electrical connectors.
7. Remove the radiator support brackets.

   a. Remove the front bumper fascia.

   b. Support the radiator.

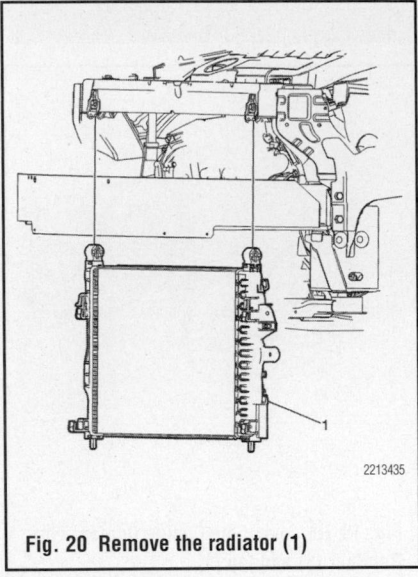

Fig. 20 Remove the radiator (1)

c. Remove the radiator support bracket.

8. Release the 2 condenser assembly retainers.

9. Remove the engine coolant fan shroud from the radiator.

10. Remove the radiator.

11. To install, reverse the removal procedure.

THERMOSTAT

REMOVAL & INSTALLATION

2.0L Engine

See Figure 21.

1. Drain the cooling system.
2. Raise the vehicle by its full height.
3. Remove the turbocharger coolant return pipe. Refer to Turbocharger in Engine Mechanical.

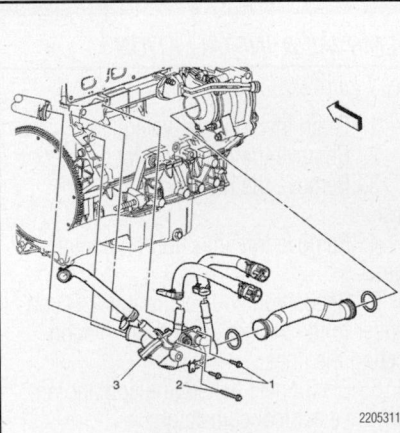

Fig. 21 Exploded view of the thermostat housing bolts (1, 2) and thermostat housing (3)

4. Disconnect the engine coolant temperature sensor.

5. Disconnect the radiator outlet hose, heater inlet hose, heater outlet hose and the radiator surge tank outlet hose, from the thermostat housing.

6. Remove the outlet and inlet hoses.

7. Remove the thermostat bolts and housing.

8. To install, reverse the removal procedure.

9. Tighten the thermostat housing bolts to 88 inch lbs. (10 Nm).

2.4L Engine

See Figure 22.

1. Drain the cooling system.
2. Raise the vehicle by its full height.
3. Disconnect the radiator outlet hose from the water inlet housing.
4. Remove the thermostat bolts and housing.
5. To install, reverse the removal procedure.
6. Tighten the thermostat housing bolts to 88 inch lbs. (10 Nm).

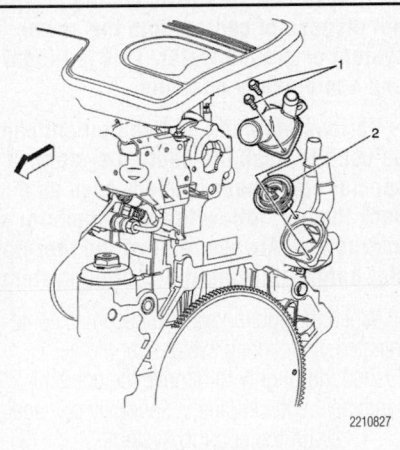

Fig. 22 Removing the thermostat bolt (1) and thermostat (2)

WATER PUMP

REMOVAL & INSTALLATION

2.0L Engine

See Figure 23.

1. Remove the air cleaner assembly.
2. Remove the intake manifold cover.
3. If equipped, remove the coolant heater.
4. Remove the catalytic converter. Refer to Catalytic Converter in Engine Mechanical.
5. Remove the engine coolant thermostat housing.

6. Remove the water pump cover, fasteners and gasket from the engine front cover.

➡A drain plug has been provided at the bottom of the water pump assembly for additional coolant drainage from the engine block and water pump.

7. Drain the coolant from the water pump using the plug at the bottom of the pump. Install the plug when finished.

➡The water pump holding tool supports the sprocket and chain during water pump service. The tool must be used or the balance shaft must be retimed.

8. Align the EN-43651 water pump holding tool with the threads on the water pump sprocket. Tighten the water pump holding tool fasteners.

9. Secure the water pump holding tool with the previously removed water pump cover fasteners into the engine front cover.

10. Remove the water pump sprocket to water pump fasteners.

➡Be sure to remove both water pump bolts from the front of the engine block.

11. Remove the front water pump fasteners.

12. Remove the rear water pump fasteners.

13. Remove the water pump.

14. If replacing the water pump cover remove the water pump rear cover fasteners.

15. Separate the water pump cover from the water pump.

16. Remove and discard the water pump O-ring seal.

Fig. 23 Align the EN-43651 water pump holding tool

To install:

17. If replacing the water pump cover, install a new O-ring to the water pump and tighten the fasteners to 18 ft. lbs. (25 Nm).

➡ **A guide pin can be created to aid in water pump alignment. Use a M 6 m x 6 mm x 50.8 mm stud (2 in). Thread the pin into the water pump sprocket.**

18. Using a guide pin, align the pin with the water pump holding tool.

19. Position the water pump against the engine block and hand tighten the water pump fasteners.

20. Install 2 water pump sprocket to water pump fasteners . After the fasteners are snug, remove the guide pin and install the third fastener and tighten to 89 inch lbs. (10 Nm).

21. Install the water pump fasteners at the front of the engine. Hand tighten at this time.

22. Tighten the water pump fasteners at the front and rear of the water pump to 18 ft. lbs. (25 Nm).

23. Remove the water pump cover fasteners from the engine front cover and water pump holding tool.

24. Remove the EN-43651 water pump holding tool from the water pump sprocket.

25. Install the water pump access plate gasket and fasteners and tighten to 89 inch lbs. (10 Nm).

26. If equipped, install the coolant heater.

27. Install the engine coolant thermostat housing.

28. Install the catalytic converter.

29. Install the intake manifold cover.

30. Install the air cleaner assembly.

31. Refill the coolant system.

ENGINE ELECTRICAL

BATTERY

REMOVAL & INSTALLATION
See Figures 24 and 25.

✳✳ WARNING

Batteries contain sulfuric acid and produce explosive gases. Work in a well-ventilated area. Do not allow the battery to come in contact with flames, sparks or burning substances. Avoid contact with skin, eyes or clothing. Shield eyes when working near the battery to protect against possible splashing of acid solution. In case of acid contact with skin or eyes, flush immediately with water for a minimum of 15 minutes, then get prompt medical attention. If acid is swallowed, call a physician immediately. Failure to follow these instructions may result in serious personal injury.

✳✳ WARNING

Always deplete the backup power supply before repairing or installing

BATTERY SYSTEM

any new front or side air bag supplemental restraint system (SRS) component and before servicing, removing, installing, adjusting or striking components near the front or side impact sensors or the restraints control module (RCM). Nearby components include doors, instrument panel, console, door latches, strikers, seats and hood latches.

➡ To deplete the backup power supply energy, disconnect the battery ground cable and wait at least 1 minute. Be sure to disconnect auxiliary batteries and power supplies (if equipped).

✳✳ WARNING

Failure to follow these instructions may result in serious personal injury or death in the event of an accidental deployment.

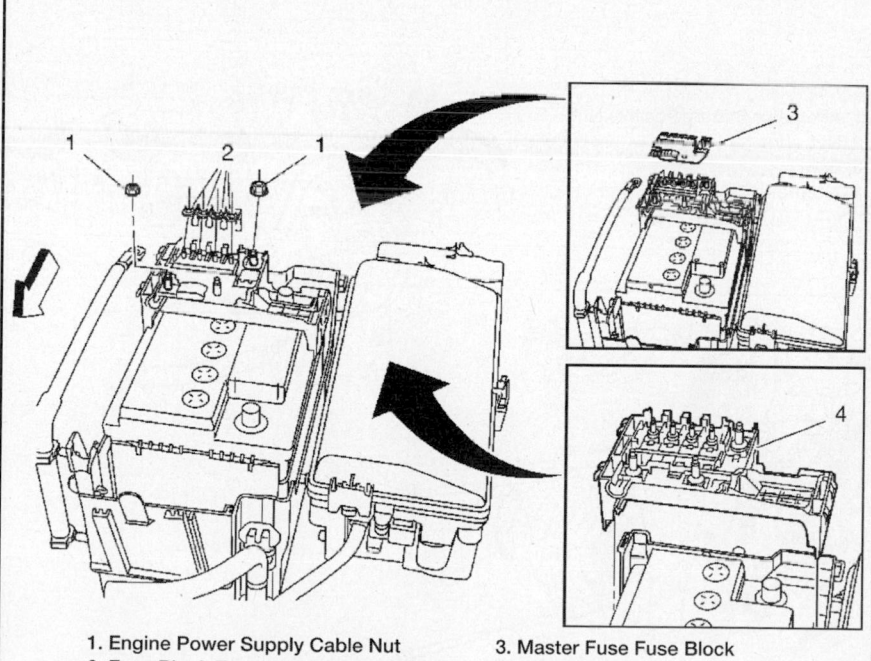

1. Engine Power Supply Cable Nut
2. Fuse Block Terminal Wiring Harness
3. Master Fuse Fuse Block
4. Fuse Block

2194351

Fig. 24 Removing the fuse block

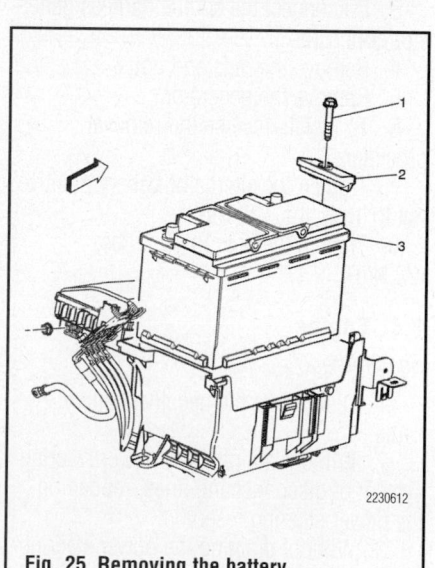

2230612

Fig. 25 Removing the battery

1. Remove the battery cover.
2. Disconnect the negative battery cable and then positive cable.
3. Remove the fuse block.
   a. Remove the front compartment fuse block positive cable and engine power supply cable nuts.
   b. Remove the fuse block terminal wiring harness.
   c. Remove the master fuse from the battery positive splitter.
   d. Unclip and remove the battery positive splitter housing from the battery.
   e. Remove the fuse block.
4. Remove the retainer fastener.
5. Remove the retainer bracket.
6. Remove the battery.
7. To install, reverse the removal procedure.

BATTERY RECONNECT/RELEARN PROCEDURE

✳✳ WARNING

Batteries contain sulfuric acid and produce explosive gases. Work in a well-ventilated area. Do not allow the battery to come in contact with flames, sparks or burning substances. Avoid contact with skin, eyes or clothing. Shield eyes when working near the battery to protect against possible splashing of acid solution. In case of acid contact with skin or eyes, flush immediately with water for a minimum of 15 minutes, then get prompt medical attention. If acid is swallowed, call a physician immediately. Failure to follow these instructions may result in serious personal injury.

✳✳ WARNING

Always deplete the backup power supply before repairing or installing any new front or side air bag supplemental restraint system (SRS) component and before servicing, removing, installing, adjusting or striking components near the front or side impact sensors or the restraints control module (RCM). Nearby components include doors, instrument panel, console, door latches, strikers, seats and hood latches.

To deplete the backup power supply energy, disconnect the battery ground cable and wait at least 1 minute. Be sure to disconnect auxiliary batteries and power supplies (if equipped). Failure to follow these instructions may result in serious personal injury or death in the event of an accidental deployment.

✳✳ WARNING

Always lift a plastic-cased battery with a battery carrier or with hands on opposite corners. Excessive pressure on the battery end walls may cause acid to flow through the vent caps, resulting in personal injury and/or damage to the vehicle or battery.

➥When the battery (or PCM) is disconnected and connected, some abnormal drive symptoms may occur while the vehicle relearns its adaptive strategy. The charging system setpoint may also vary. The vehicle may need to be driven to relearn its strategy.

ENGINE ELECTRICAL

CHARGING SYSTEM

ALTERNATOR

REMOVAL & INSTALLATION

2.0L Engine

See Figure 26.

1. Disconnect the negative battery cable.
2. Remove the accessory drive belt.
3. Disconnect the engine harness generator connector.
4. Remove the nuts and bolts.
5. Remove the generator.
6. To install, reverse the removal procedure.
7. Tighten the alternator battery positive nut to 15 ft. lbs. (20 Nm).
8. Tighten the nuts to 16 ft. lbs. (22 Nm).

2.4L Engine

See Figure 27.

1. Disconnect the negative battery cable.
2. Without draining the power steering system of disconnecting lines, reposition the power steering reservoir.
3. Without draining the power steering system of disconnecting lines, reposition

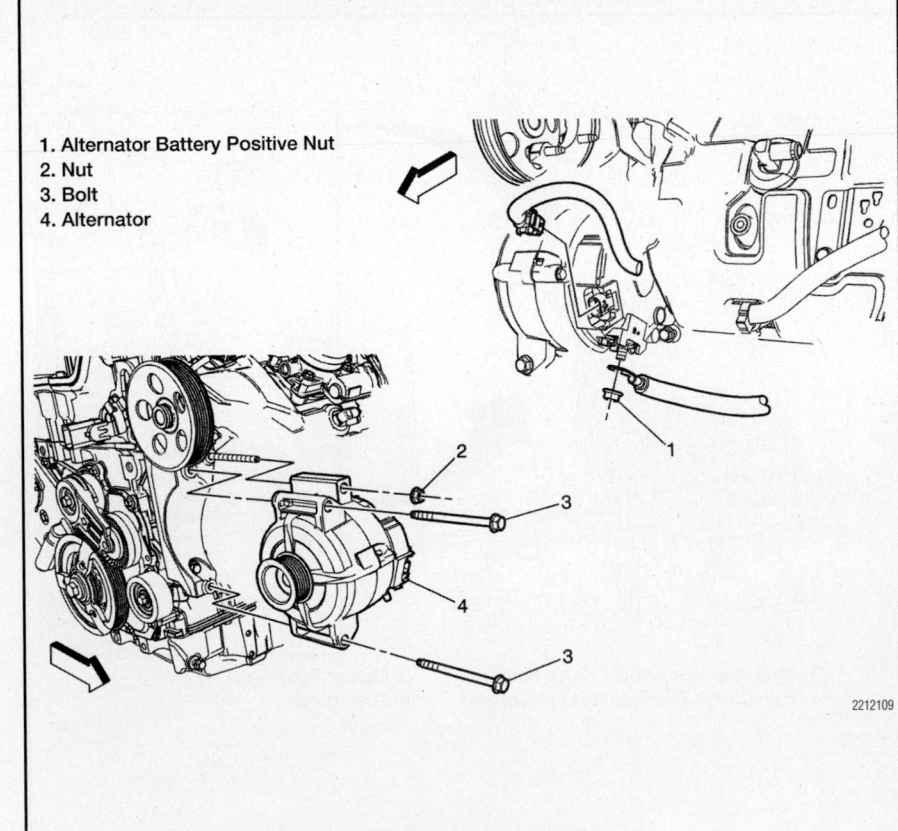

1. Alternator Battery Positive Nut
2. Nut
3. Bolt
4. Alternator

Fig. 26 Exploded view of the alternator assembly—2.0L Engine

2212109

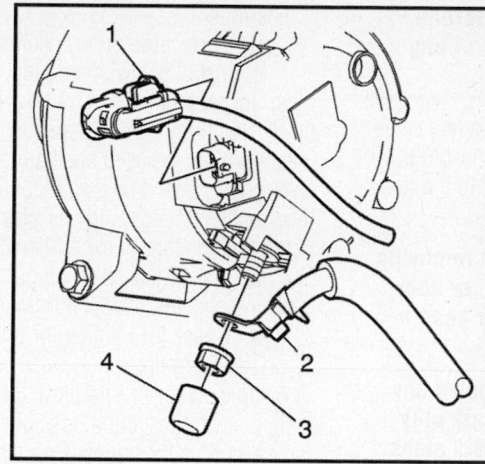
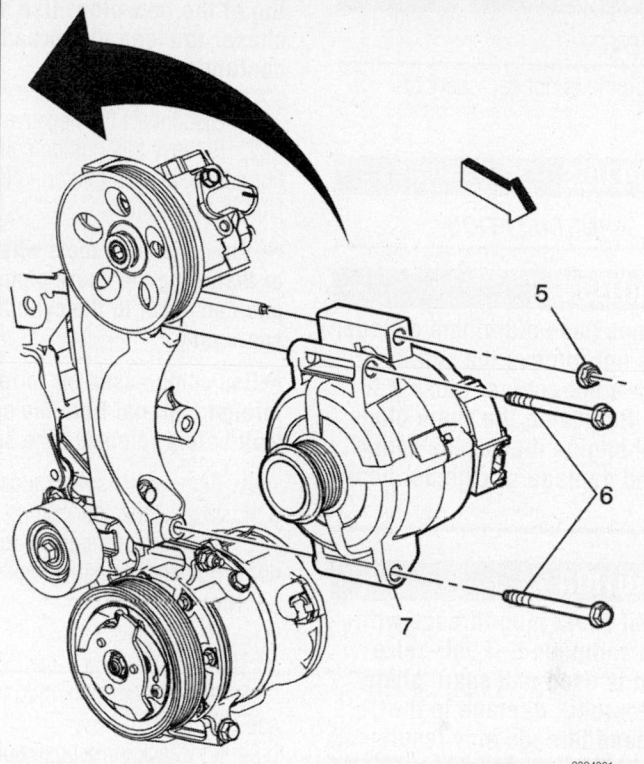

1. Engine Harness Alternator Connector
2. Alternator Nut Protective Cap
3. Alternator Nut
4. Battery Positive Cable Terminal
5. Alternator Mounting Nut
6. Alternator Mounting Bolt
7. Alternator

2324361

Fig. 27 Exploded view of the alternator assembly—2.4L Engine

the power steering pump to the right side of the vehicle. Refer to Power Steering Pump.

4. Disconnect the engine harness generator connector.

5. Remove the alternator nut protective cap.

6. Remove the alternator nut.

7. Remove the battery positive cable terminal.

8. Remove the alternator bolts and nuts

9. Remove the generator.

10. To install, reverse the removal procedure.

11. Tighten the alternator mounting bolt to 16 ft. lbs. (22 Nm).

12. Tighten the alternator mounting nut to 16 ft. lbs. (22 Nm).

13. Tighten the generator nut to 9 ft. lbs. (12 Nm).

ENGINE ELECTRICAL

FIRING ORDER

2.0L and 2.4L engine: 1-2-3-4.

IGNITION COIL

REMOVAL & INSTALLATION

See Figures 28 and 29.

1. Disconnect the negative battery cable.

2. Remove the intake manifold.

3. Disconnect the electrical connector.

4. Remove the ignition coil fasteners.

5. Remove the ignition coil.

6. To install, reverse the removal procedure.

IGNITION SYSTEM

2020561

Fig. 28 Removing the bolt (1) and ignition coil (2)—2.0L Engine

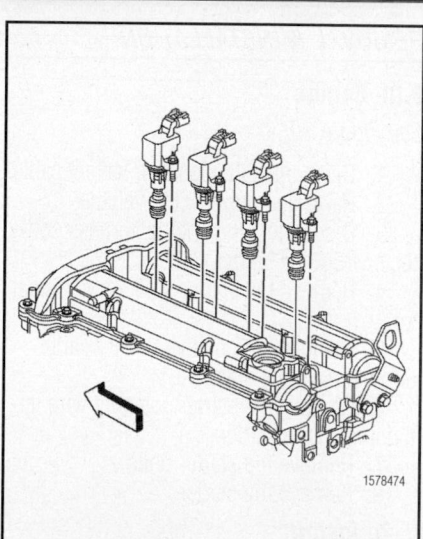

1578474

Fig. 29 Removing the bolt and ignition coil—2.4L Engine

IGNITION TIMING

ADJUSTMENT

Ignition timing is not necessary or possible.

SPARK PLUGS

REMOVAL & INSTALLATION

✳✳ CAUTION

2.4L engines have aluminum cylinder heads. Do not remove the spark plugs from a hot engine, allow it to cool first. Removing the spark plugs from a hot engine may cause spark plug thread damage or cylinder head damage.

✳✳ CAUTION

Do not coat spark plug threads with anti-seize compound. If anti-seize compound is used and spark plugs are over-torqued, damage to the cylinder head threads may result.

✳✳ CAUTION

Clean the spark plug recess area before removing the spark plug. Failure to do so could result in engine damage because of dirt or foreign material entering the cylinder head, or by the contamination of the cylinder head threads. The contaminated threads may prevent the proper seating of the new plug. Use a thread chaser to clean the threads of any contamination.

1. Disconnect the negative battery cable.
2. Remove the ignition coil-on-plugs. For additional information, refer to Ignition Coil in this section.

➡ **Only use hand tools when removing or installing the spark plugs, or damage can occur to the cylinder head or spark plug.**

➡**Use compressed air to remove any foreign material from the spark plug well before removing the spark plugs.**

3. Remove the spark plugs.
4. Inspect the spark plugs.
5. To install, reverse the removal procedure. Tighten the spark plugs to 15 ft. lbs. (20 Nm).

INSPECTION

1. Inspect the spark plug for a bridged gap.
   a. Check for deposit build-up closing the gap between the electrodes. Deposits are caused by oil or carbon fouling.
   b. Install a new spark plug.
2. Check for oil fouling.
   a. Check for wet, black deposits on the insulator shell bore electrodes, caused by excessive oil entering the combustion chamber through worn rings and pistons, excessive valve-to-guide clearance or worn or loose bearings.
   b. Correct the oil leak concern.
   c. Install a new spark plug.
3. Inspect for carbon fouling. Look for black, dry, fluffy carbon deposits on the insulator tips, exposed shell surfaces and electrodes, caused by a spark plug with an incorrect heat range, dirty air cleaner, too rich a fuel mixture or excessive idling.
   a. Install new spark plugs.
4. Inspect for normal burning.
   a. Check for light tan or gray deposits on the firing tip.
5. Inspect for pre-ignition, identified by melted electrodes and a possibly damaged insulator. Metallic deposits on the insulator indicate engine damage. This may be caused by incorrect ignition timing, wrong type of fuel or the unauthorized installation of a heli-coil insert in place of the spark plug threads.
   a. Install a new spark plug.
6. Inspect for overheating, identified by white or light gray spots and a bluish-burnt appearance of electrodes. This is caused by engine overheating, wrong type of fuel, loose spark plugs, spark plugs with an incorrect heat range, low fuel pump pressure or incorrect ignition timing.
   a. Install a new spark plug.
7. Inspect for fused deposits, identified by melted or spotty deposits resembling bubbles or blisters. These are caused by sudden acceleration.
   a. Install new spark plugs.

ENGINE ELECTRICAL

STARTING SYSTEM

STARTER

REMOVAL & INSTALLATION

2.0L Engine

See Figure 30.

1. Disconnect the negative battery cable.
2. Raise and support the vehicle.
3. Disconnect the engine harness connector from the starter.
4. Remove the starter solenoid terminal nut.
5. Remove the positive battery cable terminal from the starter.
6. Remove the starter solenoid wire terminal from the starter.
7. Remove the starter bolts.
8. Remove the starter.

To install:

9. Position the starter to the engine.
10. Install the starter bolts and tighten to 30 ft. lbs. (40 Nm).

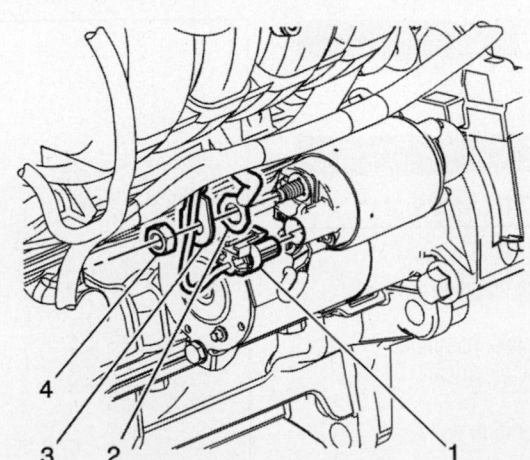

1. Engine harness connector
2. Starter solenoid wire terminal
3. Positive battery cable terminal
4. Starter solenoid terminal nut

2102329

Fig. 30 Removing the starter components

11. Install the starter solenoid wire terminal to the starter.

12. Install the positive battery cable terminal to the starter Ensure that the anti-rotational tab is correctly located into the indexing slot.

13. Install the starter solenoid terminal nut and tighten to 8 ft. lbs. (11 Nm).

14. Connect the engine harness connector to the starter.

15. Lower the vehicle.

16. Connect the negative battery cable.

2.4L Engine

See Figure 31.

1. Disconnect the negative battery cable.

2. Raise and support the vehicle.

3. Disconnect the engine harness connector.

4. Remove the starter solenoid nut.

5. Remove the battery positive cable terminal.

6. Remove the battery negative cable terminal.

7. Remove the battery negative cable ground nut.

8. Remove the starter mounting bolt.

9. Remove the starter mounting stud/nut.

10. Remove the starter.

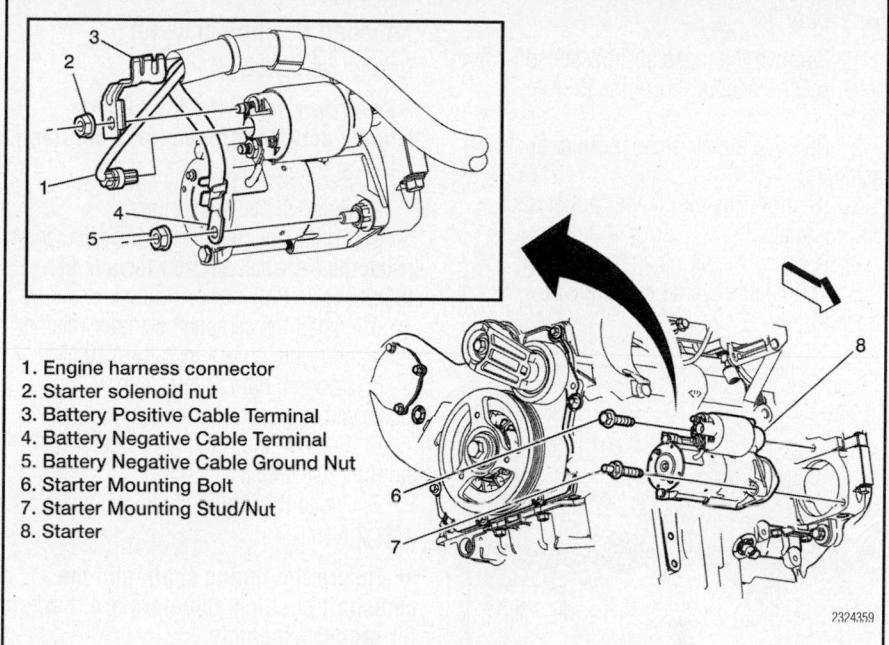

1. Engine harness connector
2. Starter solenoid nut
3. Battery Positive Cable Terminal
4. Battery Negative Cable Terminal
5. Battery Negative Cable Ground Nut
6. Starter Mounting Bolt
7. Starter Mounting Stud/Nut
8. Starter

Fig. 31 Exploded view of the starter and components

11. To install, reverse the removal procedure.

12. Tighten the Starter Mounting Stud/Nut to 43 ft. lbs. (58 Nm).

13. Tighten the starter mounting bolt to 43 ft. lbs. (58 Nm).

14. Tighten the Battery Negative Cable Ground Nut to 16 ft. lbs. (22 Nm).

15. Tighten the starter solenoid nut to 9 ft. lbs. (12 Nm).

ENGINE MECHANICAL

➡**Disconnecting the negative battery cable may interfere with the functions of the on board computer systems and may require the computer to undergo a relearning process, once the negative battery cable is reconnected.**

ACCESSORY DRIVE BELTS

ACCESSORY BELT ROUTING

See Figure 32.

INSPECTION

Inspect for glazing, cracking, splitting, delaminating and shredding. Replace as necessary.

ADJUSTMENT

Adjustment is not possible or necessary.

REMOVAL & INSTALLATION

1. Rotate the tensioner clockwise and remove the accessory drive belt.

2. To install, reverse the removal procedure.

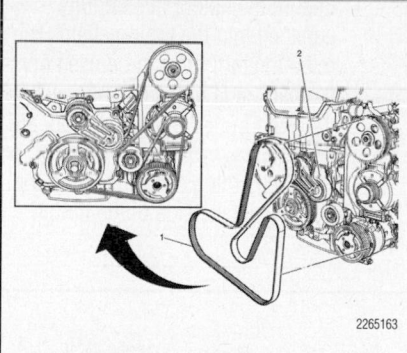

Fig. 32 2.0L and 2.4L drive belt (1) and tensioner (2) routing

3. Clean and inspect the drive belt surfaces of all the pulleys.

4. Inspect the drive belt for correct alignment.

AIR CLEANER

REMOVAL & INSTALLATION

2.0L Engine

See Figure 33.

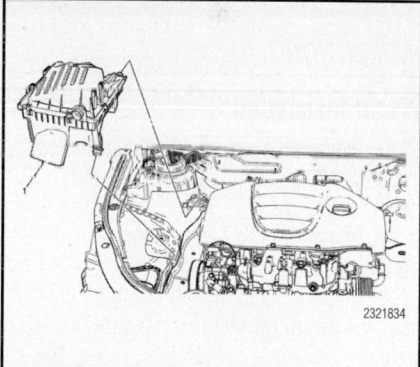

Fig. 33 Removing the air cleaner assembly (1)

1. Disconnect the negative battery cable.

2. Disconnect the PCV connector.

3. Remove the air cleaner outlet duct.

4. Lift upwards to dislodge the rubber grommet and remove he air cleaner assembly.

5. To install, reverse the removal procedure.

2.4L Engine

See Figure 34.

1. Remove the mass air flow sensor. Refer to MAF sensor in Engine Performance.

2. Remove the air cleaner outlet duct fasteners.

3. Remove the air cleaner outlet duct with resonator.

4. Remove the air cleaner assembly.

5. To install, reverse the removal procedure.

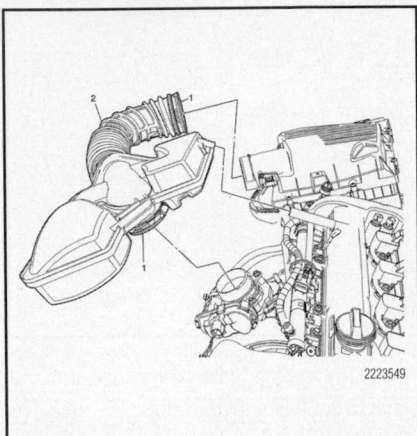

Fig. 34 Removing the air cleaner outlet duct with resonator

CAMSHAFT AND VALVE LIFTERS

INSPECTION

Visual Inspection

1. Inspect the camshaft oil feed holes to the camshaft position actuator for dirt, debris or blockage.

2. Inspect the threaded hole for damage.

3. Inspect the camshaft position actuator locating notch for damage or wear.

4. Inspect the camshaft sealing grooves for damage.

5. Inspect the camshaft thrust surface for damage.

6. Inspect the camshaft lobes and journals for the following conditions:
   a. Excessive scoring or pitting.
   b. Discoloration from overheating.
   c. Deformation from excessive wear, especially the camshaft lobes.

7. If any of the above conditions exist on the camshaft, replace the camshaft.

REMOVAL & INSTALLATION

Camshaft position actuator

See Figures 35 and 36.

➡ **Procedure is for the intake side, exhaust actuator procedure is similar.**

1. Remove the valve cover.

2. Remove the spark plugs.

3. Rotate the crankshaft clockwise and install the camshaft actuator retainer EN-48953 (1).

4. Install the camshaft actuator retainer bolts and tighten to 89 inch lbs. (10 Nm).

5. Loosen, but DO NOT remove the intake camshaft actuator bolt.

6. Remove the camshaft actuator locking tool, EN-48953.

7. Clean the timing chain and gears with solvent.

➡ **Ensure the timing chain and the camshaft position actuators are marked for proper assembly.**

8. Mark the intake and exhaust camshaft actuators and the respective locations on the timing chain.

9. Remove the upper timing chain guide bolts and guide.

10. Remove the timing chain tensioner.

➡**Note the following:**

- The intake camshaft actuator should not rotate during the removal or installation.

- Ensure the tips of the are fully engaged into the timing chain. The retention tool rod can be used on the back side of the chain to ensure the teeth from the retention tool are engaged.

11. Install the timing chain retention tool EN-48749 to the intake side of the timing chain.

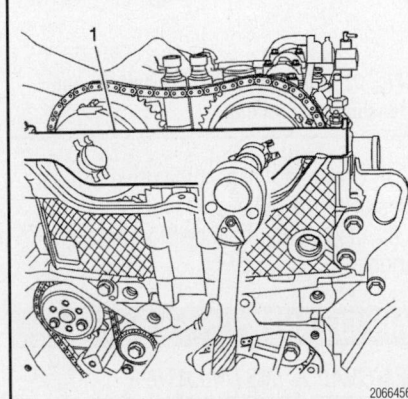

Fig. 35 Install the camshaft actuator retainer EN-48953 (1)

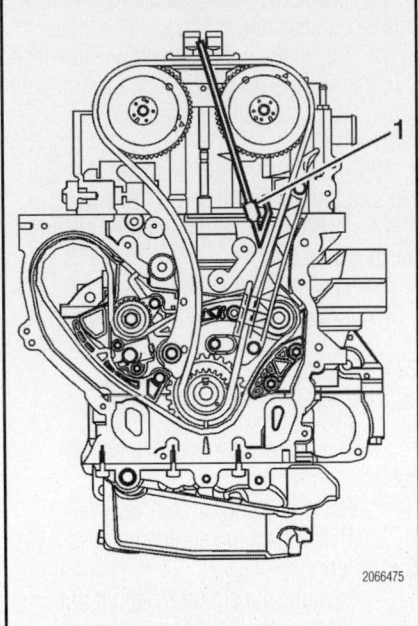

Fig. 36 Install the timing chain retention tool EN-48749 (1)

12. Install the timing chain retention tool EN-48749 to the exhaust side of the timing chain.

13. Remove and discard the intake camshaft actuator bolt.

14. Rotate the exhaust camshaft clockwise slightly to take the tension off of the timing chain on the intake actuator.

15. Remove the intake camshaft actuator from the camshaft while also removing the actuator from the timing chain.

To install:

16. Ensure that the alignment mark made previously on the intake camshaft actuator is still aligned properly with the mark on the timing chain.

17. Install the timing chain onto the intake camshaft actuator.

18. Align the intake camshaft actuator alignment mark made previously with the timing chain mark and install the actuator onto the camshaft rotating the exhaust camshaft clockwise, if required.

19. Install a NEW intake camshaft actuator bolt until snug.

20. Remove the timing chain retention tool from the intake side of the timing chain.

➡ **Ensure that the alignment mark previously on the intake camshaft actuator is still aligned properly with the timing chain. If the mark made previously on the intake camshaft actuator is not aligned properly, refer to Camshaft Timing Chain, Sprocket, and Tensioner.**

21. Remove the timing chain retention tool from the exhaust side of the timing chain.

➡ **Failure to reset the tensioner will allow the tensioner to over extend. limiting the timing chain life.**

22. Reset and install the timing chain tensioner. Refer to Timing Chain Tensioner.

23. Install the camshaft actuator retainer EN-48953 Camshaft Actuator Locking Tool.

24. Install the camshaft actuator retainer bolts and tighten to 89 inch lbs. (10 Nm).

25. Tighten the NEW camshaft actuator bolt to 22 ft. lbs. (30 Nm) plus an additional 100 degrees using the EN-45059 Angle Meter .

➡ **You must have the EN-48953 installed to perform this procedure.**

26. To release the tensioner apply a counterclockwise rotational torque to the crankshaft balancer bolt of 33 ft. lbs. (45 Nm).

27. Remove the camshaft actuator retainer EN-48953.

28. Install the upper timing chain guide and bolts and tighten to 89 inch lbs. (10 Nm).

29. Install the spark plugs. Refer to Spark Plugs.

30. Install the valve cover.

Camshaft and Valve lifter

See Figure 37.

➡ **Procedure is for the intake side, exhaust actuator procedure is similar.**

1. Remove the camshaft position intake actuator.

➡ **Remove each bolt on each cap one turn at a time until there is no spring tension pushing on the camshaft.**

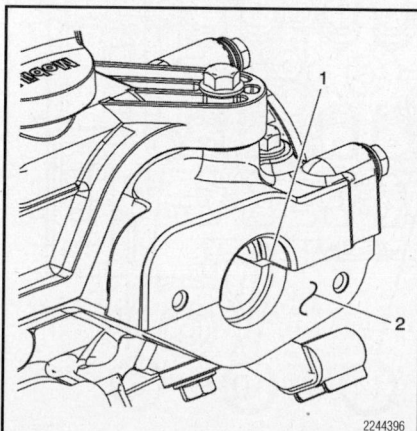

Fig. 37 Remove all excess sealing material from the fuel pump roller lifter orifice (1)

2. Mark the bearing caps to ensure they are installed in the original position.
3. Remove the bearing cap bolts.
4. Remove the bearing caps.
5. Remove the intake camshaft.

➡ **Keep all of the roller followers and hydraulic adjusters in order so that they can be reinstalled in their respective locations.**

6. Remove the camshaft roller followers.
7. Remove the hydraulic element lash adjusters.

To install:

8. Install the hydraulic element lash adjusters into their bores in the cylinder head. Install the camshaft caps and hand start the camshaft cap bolts.
9. Lubricate the valve tips.
10. Install the camshaft caps.
11. Tighten the camshaft cap bolts in increments of 3 turns until they are seated. Tighten the camshaft caps to 89 inch lbs (10 Nm).

➡ **Note the following:**

- It is critical during installation to ensure the bearing rear cap and cylinder head alignment is correct and the mating surfaces are flush.
- Ensure that all sealing material has been removed from the components, and the sealing surfaces are

clean and free of contamination prior to applying the sealer.
- Install and align the rear cap within 20 minutes of applying the sealer.
- Apply the sealer to all locations centrally locating the bead on the rail.

12. Apply a 3.5 mm bead of sealer to the cylinder head at the number 6 intake camshaft rear cap mating surface.

13. Install the number 6 intake camshaft rear cap.
  a. Tighten the cap bolts evenly to 44 inch lbs. (5 Nm).
  b. Tighten the cap bolts evenly a final pass to 89 inch lbs. (10 Nm).

14. Remove all excess sealing material from the fuel pump roller lifter orifice, and ensure the orifice is free of debris.

15. Remove all excess sealing material from the sealing surfaces.

16. Install the rear cylinder head opening plate and bolts and tighten to 10 Nm (89 lb in).

17. Install the camshaft position intake actuator.

REMOVAL & INSTALLATION

See Figures 38 and 39.

1. Remove the catalytic converter heat shield if equipped.

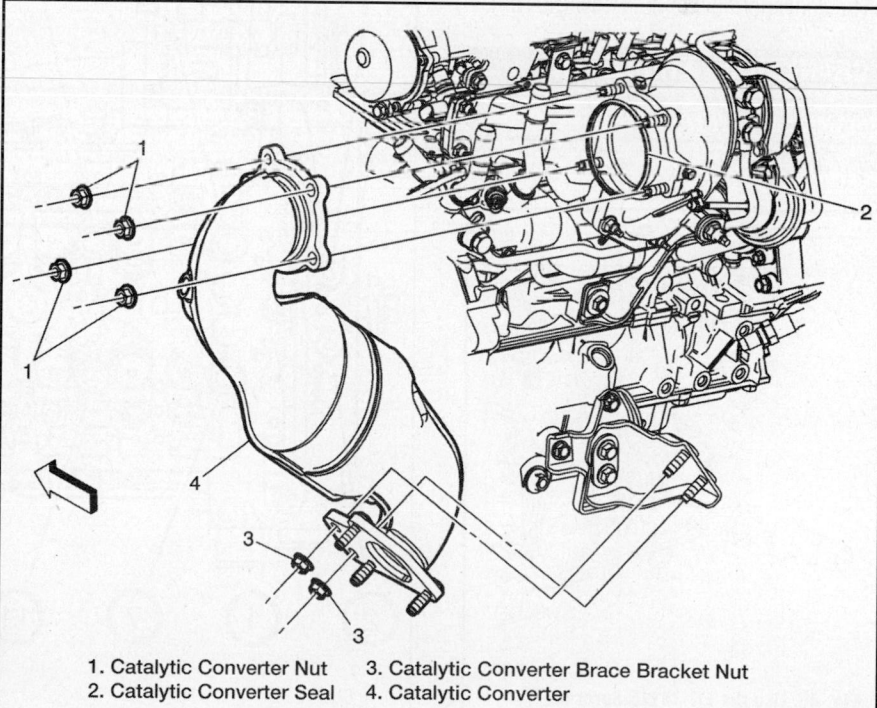

1. Catalytic Converter Nut
2. Catalytic Converter Seal
3. Catalytic Converter Brace Bracket Nut
4. Catalytic Converter

Fig. 38 Exploded view of the catalytic converter assembly—2.0L engines

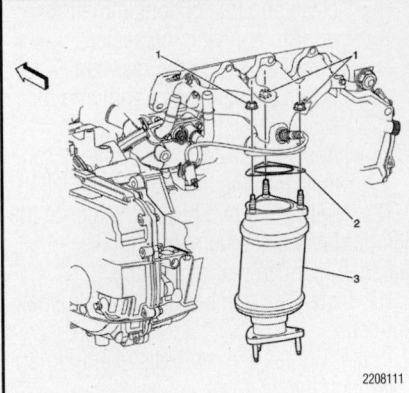

Fig. 39 Removing the catalytic converter nuts (1), gasket (2) and catalytic converter (3)—2.4L Engine

2. Raise and support the vehicle.

3. Remove the front exhaust pipe.

4. For 2.0L engines, remove the 4 catalytic converter nuts.

5. For 2.4L engines, remove the 3 catalytic converter nuts.

6. For 2.0L engines, remove the catalytic converter brace bracket nut.

7. Remove the gasket and catalytic converter.

8. To install, reverse the removal procedure.

9. For 2.0L engines, tighten the catalytic converter nuts to 26 ft. lbs. (35 Nm).

10. For 2.4L engines, tighten the catalytic converter nuts to 36 ft. lbs. (50 Nm).

CRANKSHAFT FRONT SEAL

REMOVAL & INSTALLATION

See Figure 40.

1. Remove crankshaft balancer. Refer to Timing Chain and Sprockets.

2. Use a flat-bladed tool in order to remove the crankshaft oil seal.

3. To install:

   a. Use the EN-34115 Sprocket Bearing Installer in order to install the oil seal to the front cover.

   b. Install the crankshaft balancer.

CYLINDER HEAD

REMOVAL & INSTALLATION

See Figures 41 and 42.

1. Disconnect the negative battery cable.

2. Drain the cooling system.

3. Remove the valve cover. Refer to Valve Cover.

4. Remove the intake manifold. Refer to Intake Manifold.

5. Remove the exhaust manifold. Refer to Exhaust Manifold.

6. Remove the camshaft timing chain. Refer to Timing Chain and Sprockets.

7. Remove the cylinder head in sequence.

8. Remove the cylinder head and the cylinder head gasket from the block.

9. Clean all of the gasket surfaces.

To install:

➡ **Do not use any sealing material.**

10. Install the cylinder head gasket to the cylinder block. On right side pay attention to the cylinder head lock pin.

11. Ensure the number 1 cylinder is at top dead center (TDC).

12. Setting up the crankshaft balancer mark (to the oil pump housing mark.

➡ **Always use NEW cylinder head fasteners.**

13. Install the cylinder head.

14. Install NEW cylinder head fasteners.

   a. Tighten the fastener in sequence to 22 ft. lbs. (30 Nm).

   b. Tighten the fastener in additional 155 degrees in sequence using the EN-45059 angle meter

15. Install the front cylinder head fastener and tighten to 26 ft. lbs. (35 Nm).

16. To complete installation, reverse the removal procedure.

Fig. 40 Use the EN-34115 Sprocket Bearing Installer to install the crankshaft front oil seal

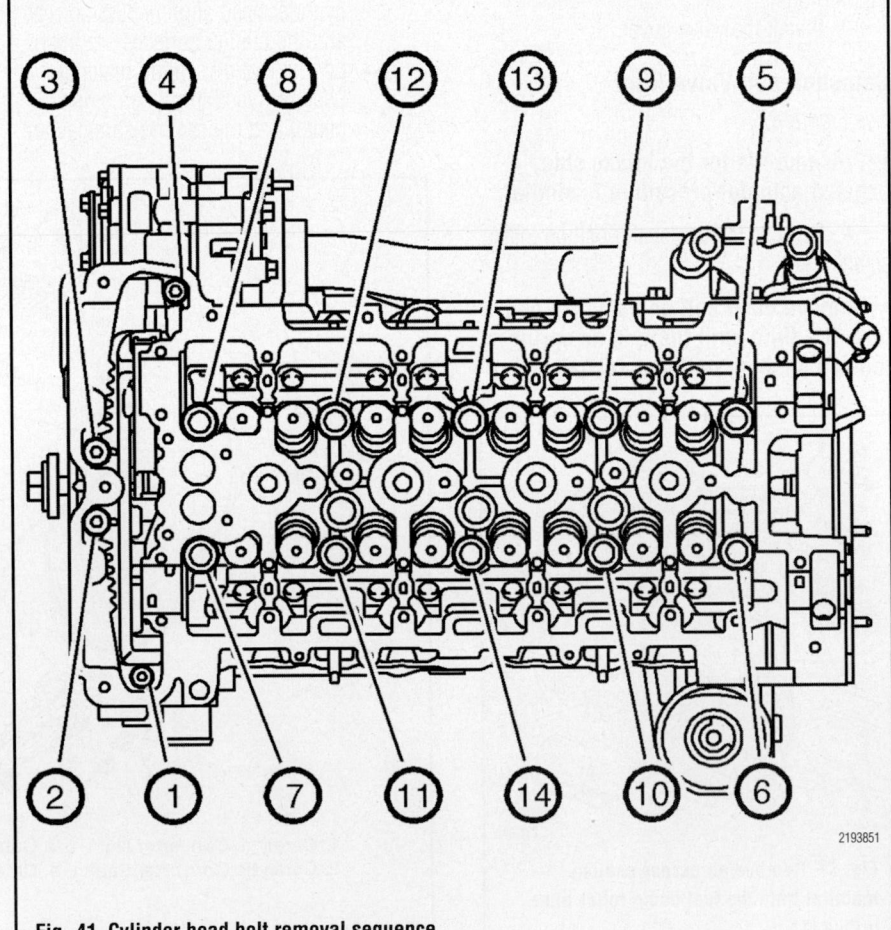

Fig. 41 Cylinder head bolt removal sequence

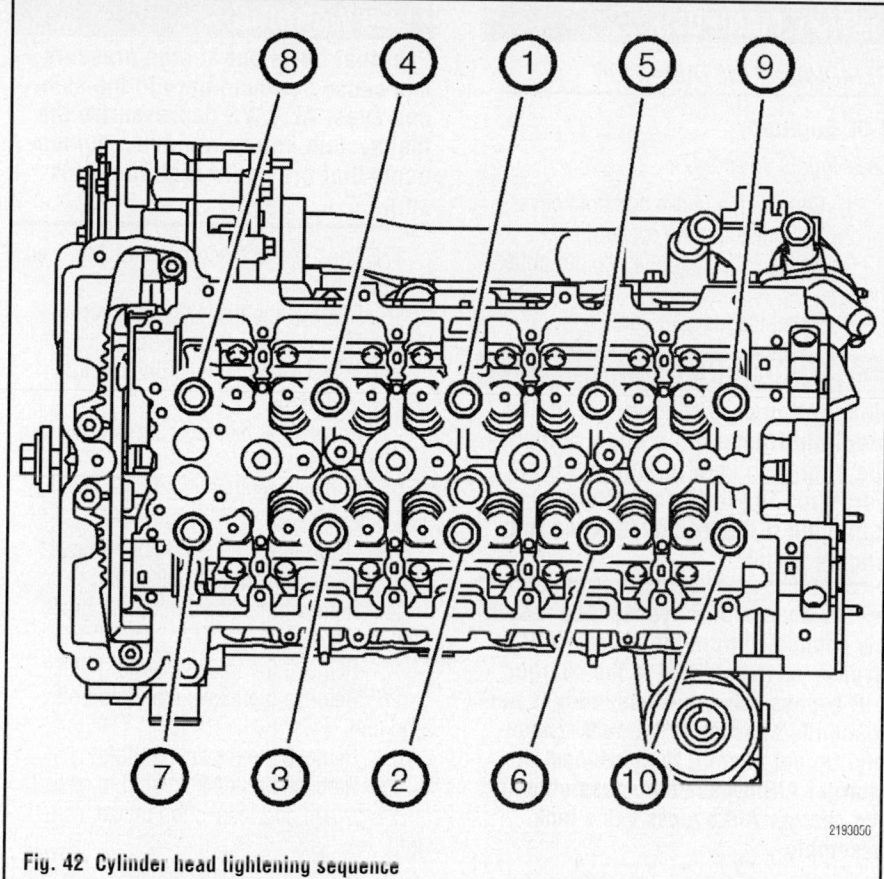

Fig. 42 Cylinder head tightening sequence

➡ DO NOT use an open end wrench on the hex on top of the oil filter cap.

8. Use EN-44887 wrench to remove the oil filter cap.

9. Remove the oil filter from the cap and discard.

10. Clean the oil filter housing in the engine block.

To install:

11. Install a new oil filter on the oil filter cap.

12. Lubricate the oil filter cap O-ring with engine oil.

❋❋ CAUTION

Over torquing the oil filter cap may cause damage to the oil filter cap resulting in an oil leak.

➡ DO NOT use an open end wrench on the hex on top of the oil filter cap.

13. Use the EN-44887 wrench to install the oil filter and cap. Tighten the oil filter cap until fully seated. DO NOT exceed 16 ft. lbs. (22 Nm).

EXHAUST MANIFOLD

REMOVAL & INSTALLATION

2.0L Engine

See Figure 44.

1. Remove the turbocharger. Refer to Turbocharger.

17. Fill the cooling system.
18. Connect the negative battery cable.

ENGINE OIL & FILTER

REPLACEMENT

See Figure 13.

1. Remove the intake manifold cover.
2. Raise and support the vehicle.
3. Place a drain pan under the oil drain plug.
4. Remove the oil pan drain plug.

5. Allow the oil to drain completely.
6. Install the oil pan drain plug and tighten to 18 ft. lbs. (25 Nm).
7. Lower the vehicle.

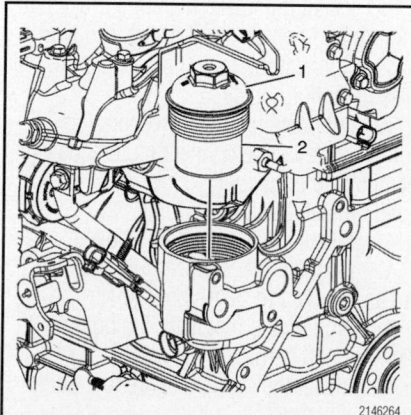

Fig. 43 Remove the oil filter cap (1) and oil filter (2)

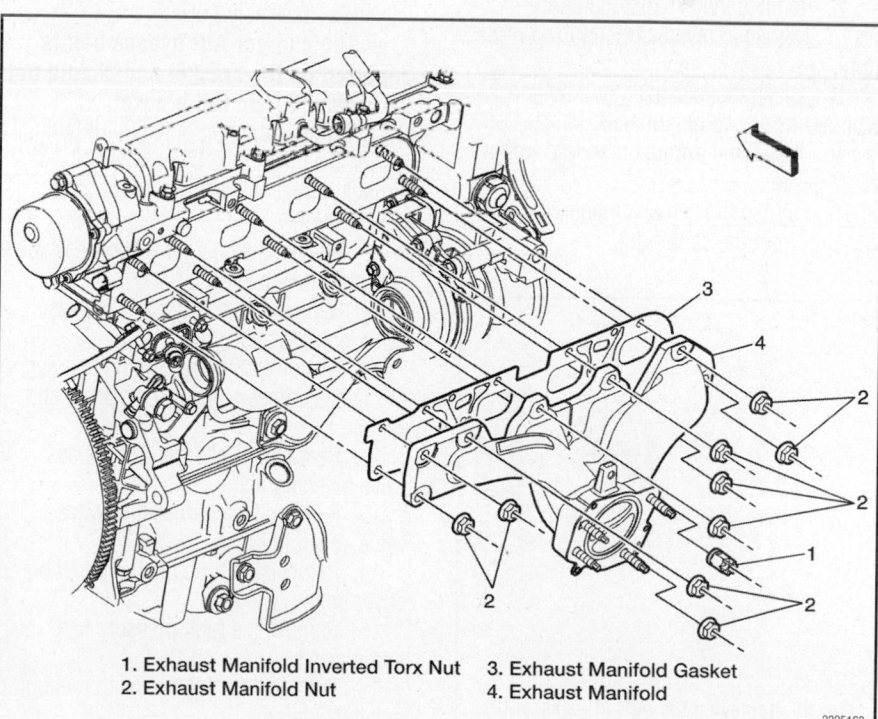

1. Exhaust Manifold Inverted Torx Nut
2. Exhaust Manifold Nut
3. Exhaust Manifold Gasket
4. Exhaust Manifold

Fig. 44 Removing the exhaust manifold assembly—2.0L engine

2. Remove the exhaust manifold heat shield.

3. Remove the exhaust manifold inverted Torx® nut.

➡Replace copper inverted Torx® nut with a NEW one.

4. Remove the exhaust manifold nuts.
5. Remove the gasket and discard.
6. Remove the exhaust manifold.
7. To install, reverse the removal procedure.
8. Clean the exhaust manifold and cylinder head mating surfaces.
9. Install the exhaust manifold with a NEW gasket.
10. Working from the inside out, tighten the exhaust manifold nuts to
   a. First Pass: 10 ft. lbs. (14 Nm).
   b. Second Pass: 10 ft. lbs. (14 Nm).
11. Tighten copper inverted Torx® nut to 10 ft. lbs. (14 Nm).

2.4L Engine

See Figure 45.

1. Remove the exhaust front pipe.
2. Remove the exhaust manifold heat shield.
3. Remove the exhaust manifold heated oxygen sensor. Refer to Engine Performance.
4. Remove the exhaust manifold nuts.
5. Remove the gasket.
6. Remove the exhaust manifold.
7. To install, reverse the removal procedure.
8. Clean the exhaust manifold and cylinder head mating surfaces.
9. Install the exhaust manifold with a NEW gasket.
10. Tighten the exhaust manifold nuts working from the center out.

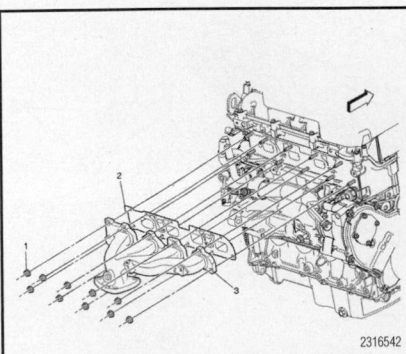

2316542

Fig. 45 Removing the nuts (1), gasket (2) and manifold (3)

INTAKE MANIFOLD

REMOVAL & INSTALLATION

2.0L Engine

See Figures 46 and 47.

1. Remove the intake manifold cover.
2. Drain the cooling system.
3. Release the charge air cooler outlet pipe.
4. Relief the fuel pressure.

✳✳ CAUTION

Never attempt to remove the intake manifold from a hot engine, allow the engine to cool to ambient temperature. The intake manifold can be damaged if it is removed when the engine is hot.

➡ **The charger AIR bypass tube assembly connected from the charger AIR bypass valve solenoid to the charger AIR bypass valve tank assembly is permanently attached to the tank assembly. Do not attempt to disconnect the charger AIR bypass tube assembly at the charger AIR bypass valve tank assembly.**

5. Disconnect the charger AIR bypass tube assembly from the intake manifold.
6. Disconnect the charger AIR bypass tube with the retaining clip from the charger AIR bypass valve solenoid.
7. Remove the charger AIR bypass valve tank assembly nut.

➡ **The charger AIR bypass bolt is captured on the bracket and should not be removed from the bracket.**

8. Loosen the bolt only until it is no longer attached to the block when removing the charger AIR bypass valve tank assembly.
9. Loosen the charger AIR bypass valve tank assembly bolt.
10. Remove the charger AIR bypass valve tank assembly.
11. Disconnect the remaining charger AIR bypass tubes at the turbocharger and vehicle.
12. Remove the charger AIR bypass valve solenoid bolts.
13. Remove the charger AIR bypass valve solenoid.
14. Remove the high pressure fuel pump cover bolts.
15. Remove the high pressure fuel pump cover.
16. Remove the high pressure fuel pump noise insulator.

✳✳ WARNING

Fuel that flows out at high pressure can cause serious injury to the skin and eyes. ALWAYS depressurize the fuel system before removing components that are under high fuel pressure.

17. Loosen and disconnect the fuel feed line tube nut.
18. Remove the fuel feed line bolts.
19. Remove the fuel feed line.
20. Inspect the fuel feed line nut for damaged threads.
21. Inspect the fuel feed line sealing bail for damage or debris.
22. Replace the fuel feed line if any damage is found.
23. Disconnect the rear knock sensor from the intake manifold brace.
24. Remove the intake manifold brace bolt and nut.
25. Remove the intake manifold brace.
26. Remove the intake manifold bolts and nuts .
27. Remove the intake manifold.
28. Remove the intake manifold gasket.
29. Clean and Inspection intake manifold.
30. Transfer parts as needed.
31. Disconnect electrical connectors as needed.

To install:

32. Install a NEW intake manifold gasket.
33. Install the intake manifold.
34. Install the intake manifold bolts and nuts finger tight.
35. Tighten the intake manifold bolts and nuts in sequence:
   a. Tighten the intake manifold bolts to 18 ft. lbs. (25 Nm).
   b. Tighten the intake manifold nuts to 16 ft. lbs. (22 Nm).
36. Install the intake manifold brace.
37. Install the intake manifold brace bolt and nut and tighten to 18 ft. lbs. (25 Nm).
38. Connect the rear knock sensor to the intake manifold brace.
39. Lubricate the high pressure fuel pump fuel feed line connection threads with clean 5W30 engine oil.
40. Install the fuel feed line.
41. Install the fuel feed line bolts.
42. Connect the low pressure fuel line nut and tighten to 22 ft. lbs. (30 Nm).
43. Tighten the fuel feed line bolts to 89 inch lbs. (10 Nm).
44. Install the high pressure fuel pump noise insulator.
45. Install the high pressure fuel pump cover.

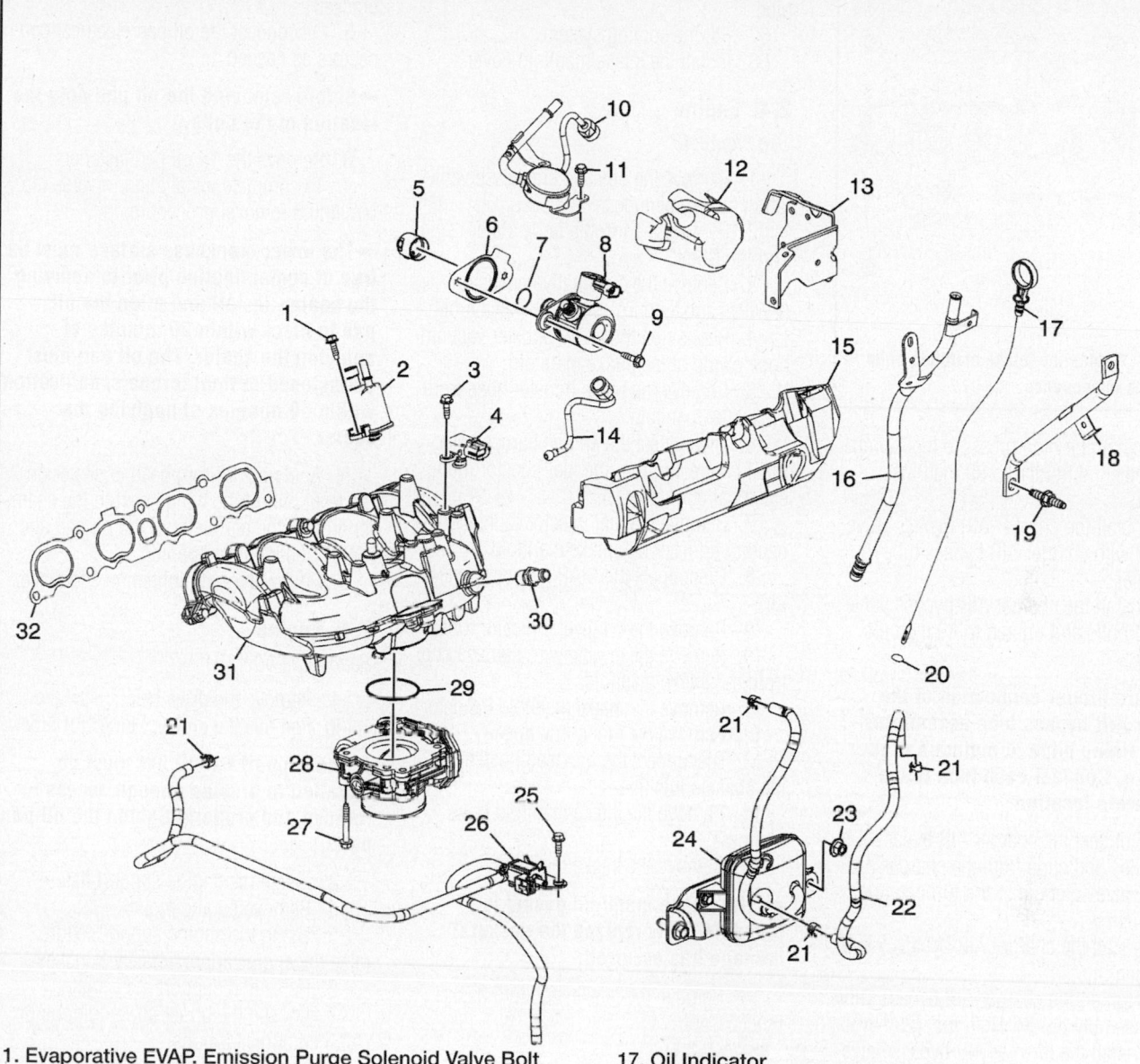

1. Evaporative EVAP. Emission Purge Solenoid Valve Bolt
2. EVAP Purge Solenoid Valve
3. Manifold Absolute Pressure MAP. Sensor Bolt
4. MAP Sensor
5. Fuel Pump Lifter
6. High Pressure Fuel Pump Gasket
7. High Pressure Fuel Pump O-Ring
8. High Pressure Fuel Pump
9. High Pressure Fuel Pump Bolt
10. Fuel Feed Line
11. Fuel Feed Line Bolt
12. High Pressure Fuel Pump Insulator
13. High Pressure Fuel Pump Cover
14. High Pressure Fuel Line
15. Fuel Injector Insulator
16. Oil Indicator Tube

17. Oil Indicator
18. Intake Manifold Brace
19. Intake Manifold Brace Stud
20. Oil Indicator O-Ring
21. Charger AIR Bypass Tube Clamp
22. Charger AIR Bypass Tube Assembly
23. Charger AIR Bypass Valve Tank Assembly Nut
24. Charger AIR Bypass Valve Tank Assembly, Some Models
25. Charger AIR Bypass Valve Solenoid Bolt
26. Charger AIR Bypass Valve Solenoid
27. Throttle Body Bolt
28. Throttle Body
29. Throttle Body Seal
30. Power Brake Booster Fitting
31. Intake Manifold
32. Intake Manifold Gasket

2063479

Fig. 46 Exploded view of the intake manifold assembly and components—2.0L Engine

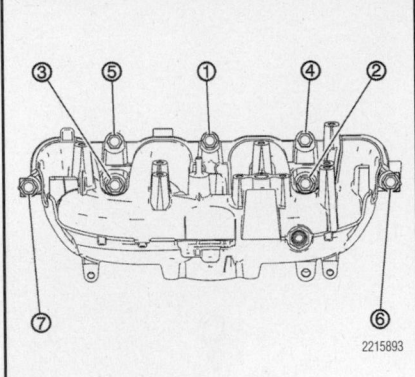

Fig. 47 Tighten the intake manifold bolts and nuts in sequence

46. Install the high pressure fuel pump cover bolts and tighten to 89 inch lbs. (10 Nm).

47. Install the charger AIR bypass valve solenoid with charger AIR bypass tube assemblies.

48. Install the charger AIR bypass valve solenoid bolts and tighten to 89 inch lbs. (10 Nm).

➡ **Ensure proper connection of the charger AIR bypass tube assemblies and retaining clips to maintain proper pressure. Connect each tube to the appropriate location.**

49. Connect the charger AIR bypass tube assemblies and clips from the charger AIR bypass valve solenoid to the turbocharger and vehicle.

50. Install the charger AIR bypass valve tank assembly.

51. Tighten the charger AIR bypass valve tanks assembly bolt to 18 ft. lbs. (25 Nm).

52. Install the charger AIR bypass valve tank assembly nut and tighten to 18 ft. lbs. (25 Nm).

➡ **Ensure proper connection of the charger AIR bypass tube assemblies and retaining clips to maintain proper pressure. Connect each tube to the appropriate location. The tube with retaining clamp located on the charger AIR bypass valve tank assembly left side connects to the charger AIR bypass valve solenoid.**

53. The right side, permanently attached tube connects to the intake manifold.

54. Connect the appropriate charger AIR bypass tube assembly to the intake manifold.

55. Connect the final charger AIR Bypass tube assembly from the charger AIR bypass valve tank assembly to the charger AIR bypass valve solenoid.

56. Install the charge air cooler outlet pipe.

57. Fill the cooling system.

58. Install the intake manifold cover.

2.4L Engine

See Figure 48.

1. Remove the positive crankcase ventilation hose/pipe/tube.

2. Remove the throttle body. Refer to Throttle Body.

3. Remove the evaporative emission (EVAP) canister purge solenoid valve tube.

4. Reposition the brake booster vacuum hose clamp at the intake manifold.

5. Remove the brake booster hose from the intake manifold.

6. Disconnect the engine harness electrical connector from the fuel injector inline electrical connector.

7. Remove the fuel injector inline connector clip from the intake manifold.

8. Disconnect the MAP sensor connector.

9. Remove the oil level indicator tube.

10. Remove the engine wire harness clip from the intake manifold.

11. Remove the intake manifold insulator.

12. Remove the fuel pump cover.

13. Disconnect the fuel feed hose from the chassis fuel line.

14. Remove the intake manifold bolts and nuts.

15. Remove the intake manifold.

➡ **The intake manifold gasket is reusable. Only replace the gasket if damage has occurred.**

16. Remove the intake manifold gasket, if necessary.

To install:

17. Install the intake manifold gasket, if necessary.

18. Install the intake manifold.

19. Install the intake manifold bolts and nuts and tighten to 89 inch lbs. (10 Nm).

20. Install the intake manifold insulator.

21. To complete installation, reverse the remaining removal procedure.

OIL PAN

REMOVAL & INSTALLATION

2.0L Engine

See Figure 49.

1. Drain the oil.

2. Remove the oil level indicator Tube.

3. Remove the air conditioning compressor bracket.

4. Remove the catalytic converter bracket.

5. Disconnect the oil pan electrical connectors as needed.

➡ **Before removing the oil pan note the location of the bolts.**

6. Remove the 15 oil pan fasteners.

7. To complete installation, reverse the remaining removal procedure.

➡ **The lower crankcase surface must be free of contamination prior to applying the sealer. Install and align the oil pan to block within 20 minutes of applying the sealer. The oil pan must be fastened to final torque specification within 60 minutes of applying the sealer.**

8. Apply a 2.25 mm bead of sealer on the level part of the flange next to the chamfer around the perimeter of the oil pan and the oil suction port opening.

9. Follow the bolt tightening sequence.

2.4L Engine

See Figure 50.

1. Remove the drive belt.

2. Remove the oil level indicator tube.

➡ **The support fixture bar must be installed to provide enough access to remove and properly tighten the oil pan bolts.**

3. Install the engine support fixture.

4. Remove engine mount.

5. Using the engine support fixture, raise the engine approximately 3 inches.

6. Raise and support the vehicle.

7. Loosen the upper air conditioning (A/C) compressor bolts.

8. Remove the lower A/C compressor bolt.

9. Place a suitable drain pan under the oil pan drain plug.

10. Remove the oil pan drain plug.

11. Drain the engine oil.

12. Reinstall the oil pan drain plug until snug.

13. Remove the 4 oil pan to transaxle bolts.

14. Remove the oil pan bolts.

15. Remove the oil pan

16. Remove any old oil pan sealant .

To install:

17. Ensure that the oil pan and the sealing surface on the lower crankcase are free of all oil and debris.

18. Apply a 2 mm bead of sealant around the perimeter of the oil pan and the oil suction port opening.

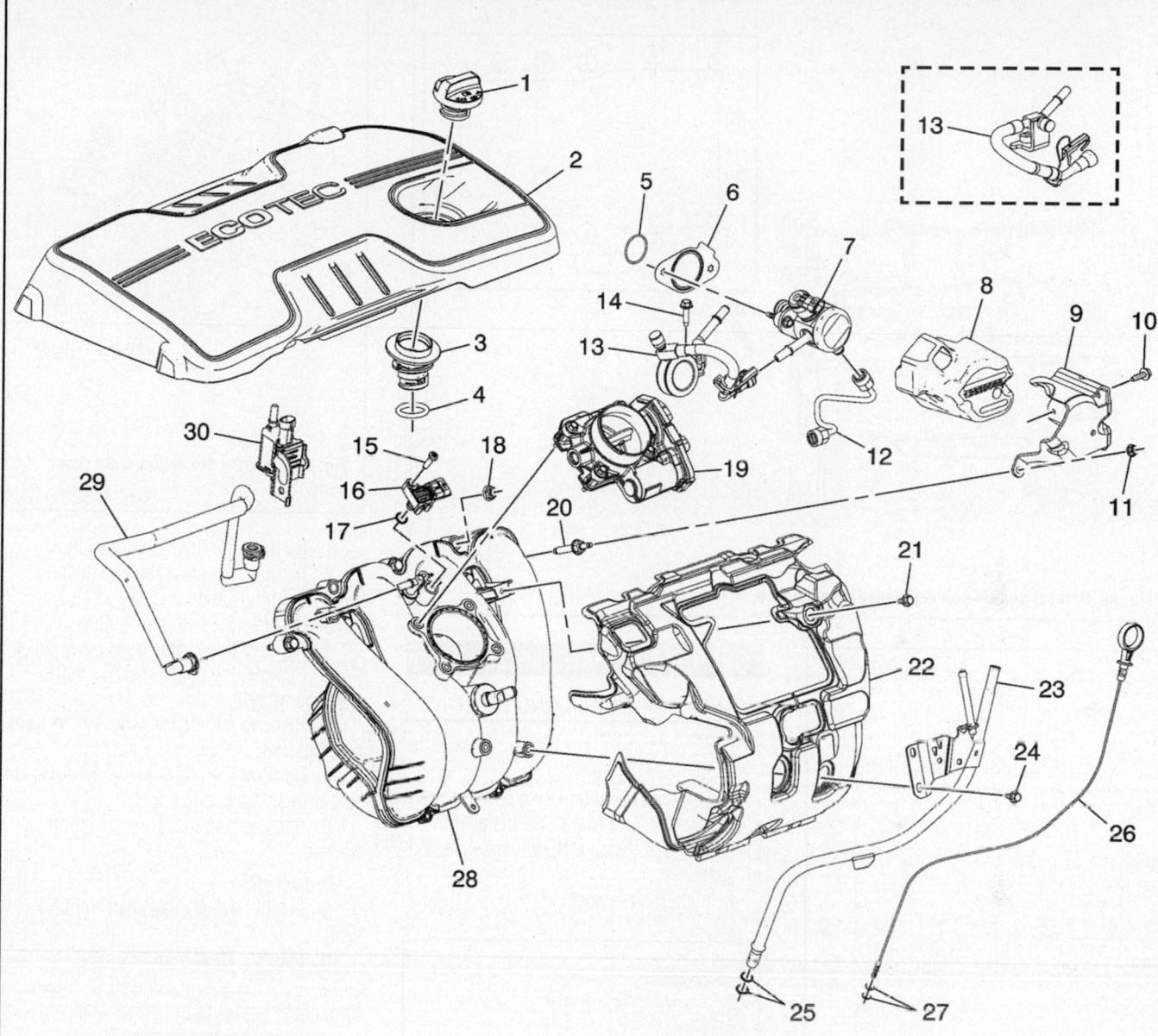

1. Oil Fill Cap
2. Intake Manifold Cover
3. Oil Fill Tube Assembly
4. Oil Fill Cap O-Ring
5. Fuel Pump Housing Seal
6. Fuel Pump Gasket
7. Fuel Pump Assembly
8. Fuel Pump Insulator
9. Fuel Pump Cover
10. Fuel Pump Cover Bolt
11. Fuel Pump Cover Nut
12. Fuel Feed Intermediate Pipe
13. Low Pressure Fuel Pipe Assembly,
   model dependent
14. Low Pressure Fuel Pipe Assembly Bolt
15. Manifold Absolute Pressure (MAP) Sensor Bolt

16. MAP Sensor
17. MAP Sensor O-Ring
18. Intake Manifold Nut
19. Throttle Body
20. Intake Manifold Stud
21. Intake Manifold Insulator Bolt
22. Intake Manifold Insulator
23. Oil Indicator Tube
24. Oil Indicator Tube Bolt
25. Oil Indicator Tube O-Ring
26. Oil Indicator
27. Oil Indicator O-Ring
28. Intake Manifold
29. Evaporative (EVAP) Emission
   Canister Purge Tube Assembly
30. EVAP Emission Canister Purge Solenoid Valve

2470755

Fig. 48 Exploded view of the intake manifold assembly and components—2.4L Engine

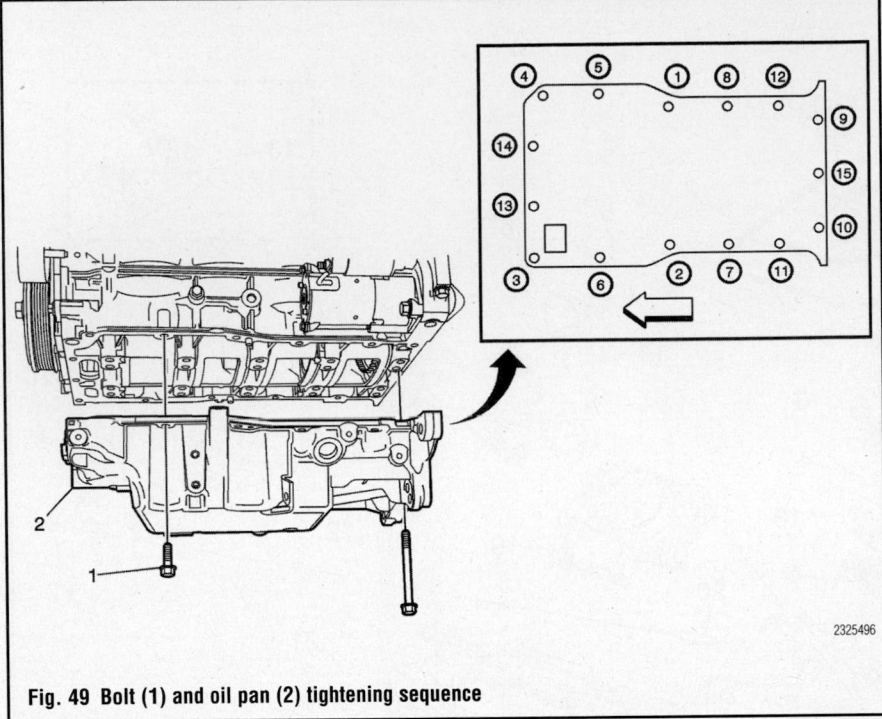

Fig. 49 Bolt (1) and oil pan (2) tightening sequence

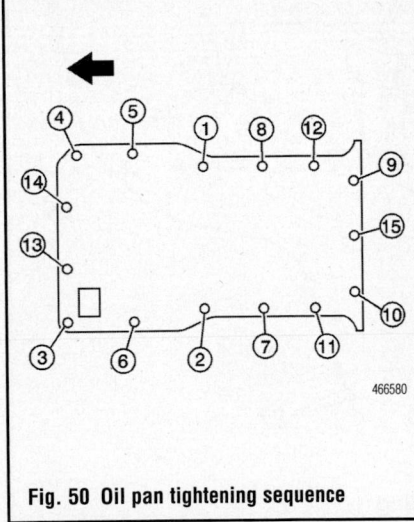

Fig. 50 Oil pan tightening sequence

➡**DO NOT over apply the sealant. More than a 2 mm bead is not required.**

19. Install the oil pan.
20. Install the oil pan bolts.
21. Install the 4 oil pan to transaxle bolts and tighten to 55 ft. lbs. (75 Nm).
22. Tighten the oil pan bolts in the sequence shown to 18 ft. lbs. (25 Nm).
23. Lower the vehicle.
24. Using the engine support fixture, lower the engine.
25. Install the engine mount.
26. Remove the engine support fixture.
27. Install the oil level indicator tube.
28. Install the drive belt.
29. Fill the engine oil to the proper level.

REAR MAIN SEAL

REMOVAL & INSTALLATION

See Figure 51.

1. Remove the flywheel.
2. Use flat-bladed tool to remove the seal.
3. Use the Rear Main Seal Installer EN-42027 and install a NEW crankshaft real oil seal.
4. Install the flywheel.

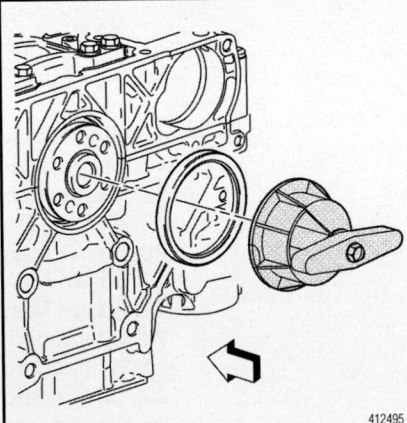

Fig. 51 Using the Rear Main Seal Installer EN-42027

TIMING CHAIN FRONT COVER

REMOVAL & INSTALLATION

See Figure 52.

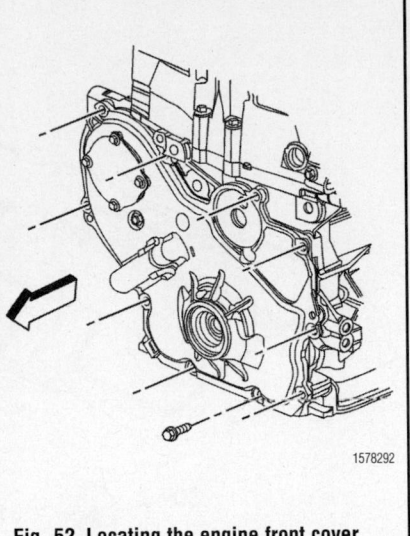

Fig. 52 Locating the engine front cover bolts

1. Remove the drive belt tensioner.
2. Remove the crankshaft balancer. Refer to Timing Chain and Sprockets.
3. Remove the belt idler pulley.
4. Remove the engine front cover bolts.
5. Remove the engine front cover to water pump bolt.
6. Remove and discard the engine front cover gasket.
7. Remove the crankshaft front cover oil seal with an appropriate tool.
8. Remove and discard the friction washer.

To install:

9. Install a NEW crankshaft front oil seal.
10. Install a NEW friction washer.
11. Position and install a NEW engine front cover gasket to the dowel pins.
12. Install the engine front cover bolts
13. Install the long water pump bolt. Tighten the bolt to 18 ft. lbs. (25 Nm).
14. Install the crankshaft balancer.
15. Install the belt idler pulley.
16. Install the drive belt tensioner.

TIMING CHAIN & SPROCKETS

REMOVAL & INSTALLATION

Crankshaft Balancer

See Figure 53.

1. Remove the engine drive belt.
2. Raise and suitably support the vehicle.
3. Use the EN-47981 Harmonic Balancer Holder to prevent the crankshaft from rotating while loosening the crankshaft balancer bolt.

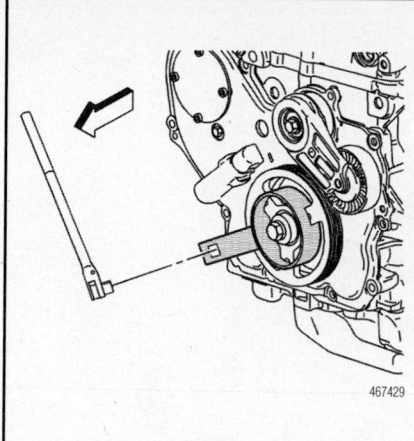

Fig. 53 Using the EN-47981 Harmonic Balancer Holder

4. Remove the crankshaft balancer bolt. Discard the bolt.

5. Remove the balancer using a universal removal tool.

To install:

※※ CAUTION

Ensure both components are aligned correctly or serious engine damage will occur.

6. Install the crankshaft balancer onto the crankshaft indexing keyway. Use care to properly align the keyway and the flats on the balancer with the oil pump drive.

7. Install the crankshaft balancer using a universal balancer installer.

➡ **Always install a NEW crankshaft balancer bolt and washer.**

8. Install a NEW crankshaft balancer bolt. Use the EN-47981 Harmonic Balancer Holder to prevent the crankshaft from rotating when tightening the bolt.

9. Tighten the bolt to 74 ft. lbs. (100 Nm) plus an additional 125 degrees using the EN-45059 Angle Meter .

10. Lower the vehicle.

11. Install the engine drive belt.

Camshaft Timing Chain, Sprocket and Tensioner

See Figures 54 and 55.

1. Remove the number 1 cylinder spark plug.

2. Rotate the crankshaft in the engine rotational direction clockwise, until the number 1 piston is at top dead center (TDC) on the exhaust stroke.

3. Remove the camshaft cover.

4. Remove the engine front cover.

5. Remove the upper timing chain guide bolts and guide.

➡ **The timing chain tensioner must be removed to unload chain tension before the timing chain is removed. If it is not, the timing chain will become cocked and it will be difficult to remove.**

6. Remove the timing chain tensioner.

7. Install a 24 mm wrench on the hex on the exhaust camshaft in order to hold the camshaft.

8. Remove and discard the exhaust camshaft actuator bolt.

9. Remove the exhaust camshaft actuator (1, 3) from the camshaft and timing chain.

10. Remove the timing chain tensioner guide bolt and guide.

11. Remove the fixed timing chain guide access plug.

12. Remove the fixed timing chain guide bolts and guide.

13. Install a 24 mm wrench on the hex on the intake camshaft in order to hold the camshaft.

14. Remove and discard the intake camshaft actuator bolt.

15. Remove the intake camshaft actuator, and the timing chain through the top of the cylinder head.

16. Remove the timing chain crankshaft sprocket.

17. If replacing the balance shaft timing chain and sprocket, perform the following steps, if not proceed to step 10 in the installation procedure.

18. Remove the balance shaft drive chain tensioner bolts and tensioner.

19. Remove the adjustable balance shaft chain guide bolt and guide.

20. Remove the small balance shaft drive chain guide bolts and guide.

21. Remove the upper balance shaft drive chain guide bolts and guide.

➡ **It may ease removal of the balance shaft drive chain to get all the slack in the chain between the crankshaft and water pump sprockets.**

22. Remove the balance shaft drive chain.

23. Remove the balance shaft drive sprocket.

To install:

24. If replacing the balance shaft timing chain, perform the following steps, if not proceed to step 10. Install the balance shaft drive sprocket.

➡ **If the balance shafts are not properly timed to the engine, the engine may vibrate or make noise.**

Install the balance shaft drive chain with the colored link lined up with the marks on the balance shaft sprockets and the balance shaft drive sprocket. There are 3 colored links on the chain. Two are chrome and 1 is copper. Use the following steps in order to line up the links with the sprockets.

a. Place the copper link so that it lines up with the timing mark on the intake side balance shaft sprocket.

b. Working clockwise around the chain, place the chrome link in line with the timing mark on the balance shaft drive sprocket. (approximately 6 o'clock position on the sprocket).

c. Place the chain on the water pump drive sprocket. The alignment is not critical.

d. Align the last chrome link with the timing mark on the exhaust side balance shaft drive

25. Install the upper balance shaft drive chain guide and bolts and tighten to 11 ft. lbs. (15 Nm).

26. Install the small balance shaft drive chain guide and bolts and tighten to 11 ft. lbs. (15 Nm).

27. Install the adjustable balance shaft chain guide and bolt and tighten to 10 Nm (89 lb in).

28. Reset the timing chain tensioner by performing the following steps:

a. Rotate the tensioner plunger 90 degrees in its bore and compress the plunger.

b. Rotate the tensioner back to the original 12 o'clock position and insert a paper clip through the hole in the plunger body and into the hose in the tensioner plunger.

29. Install the balance shaft drive chain tensioner and bolts and tighten to 89 inch lbs. (10 Nm).

30. Remove the paper clip from the balance shaft drive chain tensioner.

31. On 2.4L engines, ensure the intake camshaft notch is in the 5 o'clock position and the exhaust camshaft notch is in the 7 o'clock position. The number 1 piston should be at TDC, crankshaft key at 12 o'clock.

32. Install the timing chain drive sprocket to the crankshaft with the timing mark in the 5 o'clock position and the front of the sprocket facing out.

➡ **There are 3 colored links on the timing chain. Two links are of matching color, and 1 link is of a unique color. Use the following procedure to line up the links with the actuators. Orient the**

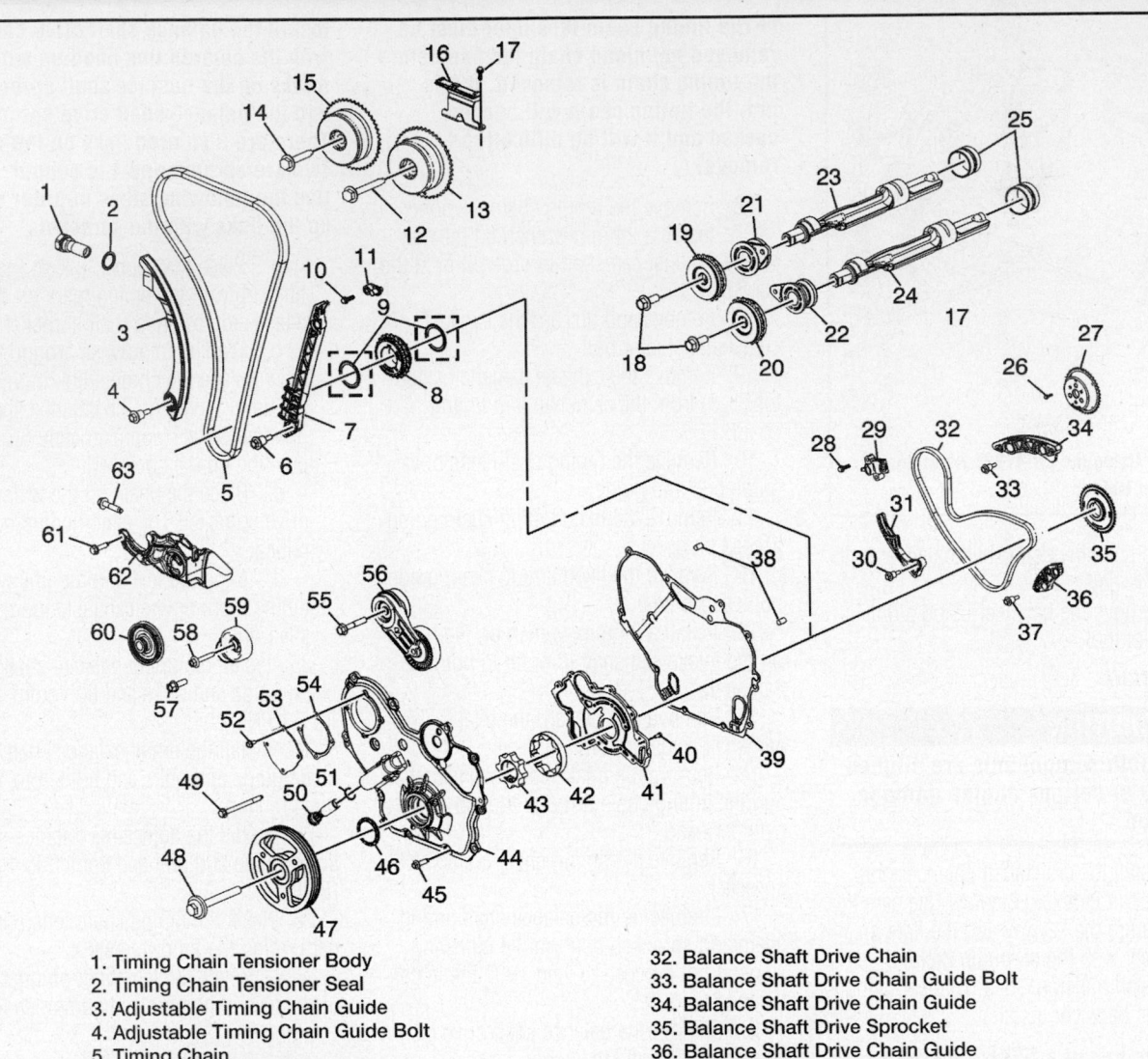

1. Timing Chain Tensioner Body
2. Timing Chain Tensioner Seal
3. Adjustable Timing Chain Guide
4. Adjustable Timing Chain Guide Bolt
5. Timing Chain
6. Fixed Timing Chain Guide Bolt
7. Fixed Timing Chain Guide
8. Timing Chain Drive Sprocket
9. Friction Washers, if equipped
10. Timing Chain Oil Nozzle Bolt
11. Timing Chain Oil Nozzle
12. Camshaft Position Actuator Bolt
13. Intake Camshaft Position Actuator
14. Camshaft Position Actuator Bolt
15. Exhaust Camshaft Position Actuator
16. Upper Timing Chain Guide
17. Upper Timing Chain Guide Bolt
18. Balance Shaft Drive Sprocket Bolts
19. Exhaust Balance Shaft Drive Sprocket
20. Intake Balance Shaft Drive Sprocket
21. Exhaust Balance Shaft Bearing Carrier
22. Intake Balance Shaft Bearing Carrier
23. Exhaust Balance Shaft
24. Intake Balance Shaft
25. Balance Shaft Rear Bearing
26. Water Pump Drive Sprocket Bolt
27. Water Pump Drive Sprocket
28. Balance Shaft Drive Chain Tensioner Assembly Bolt
29. Balance Shaft Drive Chain Tensioner Assembly
30. Adjustable Balance Shaft Drive Chain Guide Bolt
31. Adjustable Balance Shaft Drive Chain Guide

32. Balance Shaft Drive Chain
33. Balance Shaft Drive Chain Guide Bolt
34. Balance Shaft Drive Chain Guide
35. Balance Shaft Drive Sprocket
36. Balance Shaft Drive Chain Guide
37. Balance Shaft Drive Chain Guide Bolt
38. Engine Front Cover Alignment Pins
39. Engine Front Cover Gasket
40. Oil Pump Cover Bolt
41. Oil Pump Cover
42. Oil Pump Gear
43. Oil Pump Inner Rotor
44. Engine Front Cover
45. Engine Front Cover Bolt
46. Crankshaft Front Oil Seal
47. Crankshaft Balancer
48. Crankshaft Balancer Bolt
49. Engine Front Cover Bolt
50. Oil Pressure Relief Valve
51. Oil Pressure Relief Valve O-Ring
52. Water Pump Sprocket Access Cover Bolt
53. Water Pump Sprocket Access Cover
54. Water Pump Sprocket Access Cover Gasket
55. Belt Tensioner Bolt
56. Belt Tensioner
57. Belt Tensioner Bolt
58. Belt Tensioner Pulley Bolt
59. Belt Tensioner
60. Power Steering Pump Pulley
61. Power Steering Pump Bolt
62. Power Steering Pump Bracket
63. Power Steering Pump Bracket Bolt

2141355

Fig. 54 Exploded view of the timing chain and components

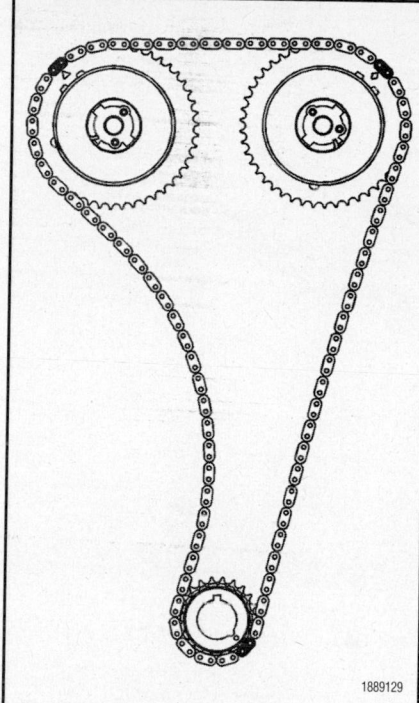

Fig. 55 Verifying all of the colored links and the appropriate timing marks are still aligned

chain so that the colored links are visible. Always use new actuator bolts.

33. Assemble the intake camshaft actuator into the timing chain with the timing mark lined up with the uniquely colored link.

34. Lower the timing chain through the opening in the cylinder head. Use care to ensure that the chain goes around both sides of the cylinder block bosses (1, 2).

35. Install the intake camshaft actuator onto the intake camshaft while aligning the dowel pin into the camshaft slot.

36. Hand tighten the new intake camshaft actuator bolt.

37. Route the timing chain around the crankshaft sprocket and line up the first matching colored link with the timing mark on the crankshaft sprocket, in approximately the 5 o'clock position.

38. Rotate the crankshaft clockwise to remove all chain slack. Do not rotate the intake camshaft. Install the adjustable timing chain guide down through the opening in the cylinder head and install the adjustable timing chain bolt. Tighten the adjustable timing chain guide bolt to 10 Nm (89 lb in).

➡ **Always install NEW actuator bolts.**

39. Install the exhaust camshaft actuator into the timing chain with the timing mark lined up with the second matching colored link.

40. Install the exhaust camshaft actuator onto the exhaust camshaft, aligning the dowel pin into the camshaft slot.

41. Using a 23 mm open end wrench, rotate the exhaust camshaft approximately 45 degrees until the dowel pin in the camshaft actuator goes into the camshaft slot.

42. When the actuator seats on the cam, tighten the new exhaust camshaft actuator bolt hand tight.

43. Verify that all of the colored links and the appropriate timing marks are still aligned. If they are not aligned, repeat the portion of the procedure necessary to align the timing marks.

44. Install the fixed timing chain guide and bolts. Tighten the fixed timing chain guide bolts to 89 inch lbs. (10 Nm).

45. Install the upper timing chain guide and bolts. Tighten the upper timing chain guide bolts to 89 inch lbs. (10 Nm).

46. Reset the timing chain tensioner by performing the following steps:
 a. Remove the snap ring.
 b. Remove the piston assembly from the body of the timing chain tensioner
 c. Install the EN-45027-2 into a vise
 d. Install the notch end of the piston assembly into the J-45027-2.
 e. Using the EN-45027-1, turn the ratchet cylinder into the piston
 f. Reinstall the piston assembly into the body of the tensioner.
 g. Install the snap ring.

47. Inspect the timing chain tensioner seal for damage. If damaged, replace the seal.

48. Inspect to ensure all dirt and debris is removed from the timing chain tensioner threaded hole in the cylinder head.

➡ **Ensure the timing chain tensioner seal is centered throughout the torque procedure to eliminate the possibility of an oil leak.**

49. Install the timing chain tensioner assembly. Tighten the timing chain tensioner to 55 ft. lbs. (75 Nm).

50. The timing chain tensioner is released by compressing it 2 mm (0.079 in), which will release the locking mechanism in the ratchet. To release the timing chain tensioner, use a suitable tool with a rubber tip on the end. Feed the tool down through the cam drive chest to rest on the cam chain. Then give a sharp jolt diagonally downwards to release the tensioner.

51. Using a 23 mm wrench, engage the hex on the intake camshaft, and using a torque wrench, tighten the camshaft actuator bolt. Tighten the intake camshaft position actuator bolt to 22 ft. lbs. (30 Nm) plus 100 degrees using the EN-45059 meter .

52. Using a 23 mm wrench, engage the hex on the exhaust camshaft, and using a torque wrench, tighten the camshaft actuator bolt. Tighten the exhaust camshaft position actuator bolt to 22 ft. lbs. (30 Nm) plus 100 degrees using the EN-45059 meter.

53. Install the timing chain oiling nozzle. Tighten the timing chain oiling nozzle bolt to 89 inch lbs. (10 Nm).

54. Apply sealant compound to the thread of the timing chain guide bolt access hole plug.

55. Install the timing chain guide bolt access hole plug. Tighten the access hole plug to 66 ft. lbs. (90 Nm).

56. Install the engine front cover.

57. Install the camshaft cover.

58. Install the number 1 cylinder spark plug.

TURBOCHARGER

REMOVAL & INSTALLATION

2.0L Engine
See Figure 56.

✳ CAUTION

If a turbocharger has failed, clean any turbocharger debris or excessive oil from the charge air cooler system before installing the new turbocharger. Failure to clean debris from the charge air cooler system will cause severe turbocharger and engine damage upon startup. Failure to clean excessive oil from the charge air cooler system may cause an engine runaway condition on startup, resulting in severe engine damage.

1. Drain the cooling system.
2. Remove the intake manifold cover.
3. Remove the air cleaner outlet duct.
4. Remove the catalytic converter.

➡ **Do not twist the turbocharger oil feed pipe. Twisting of the feed pipe will result in the collapse and deformation of the plastic pipe, restricting oil flow and causing turbocharger damage. During turbocharger replacement, gently push the oil feed pipe towards the**

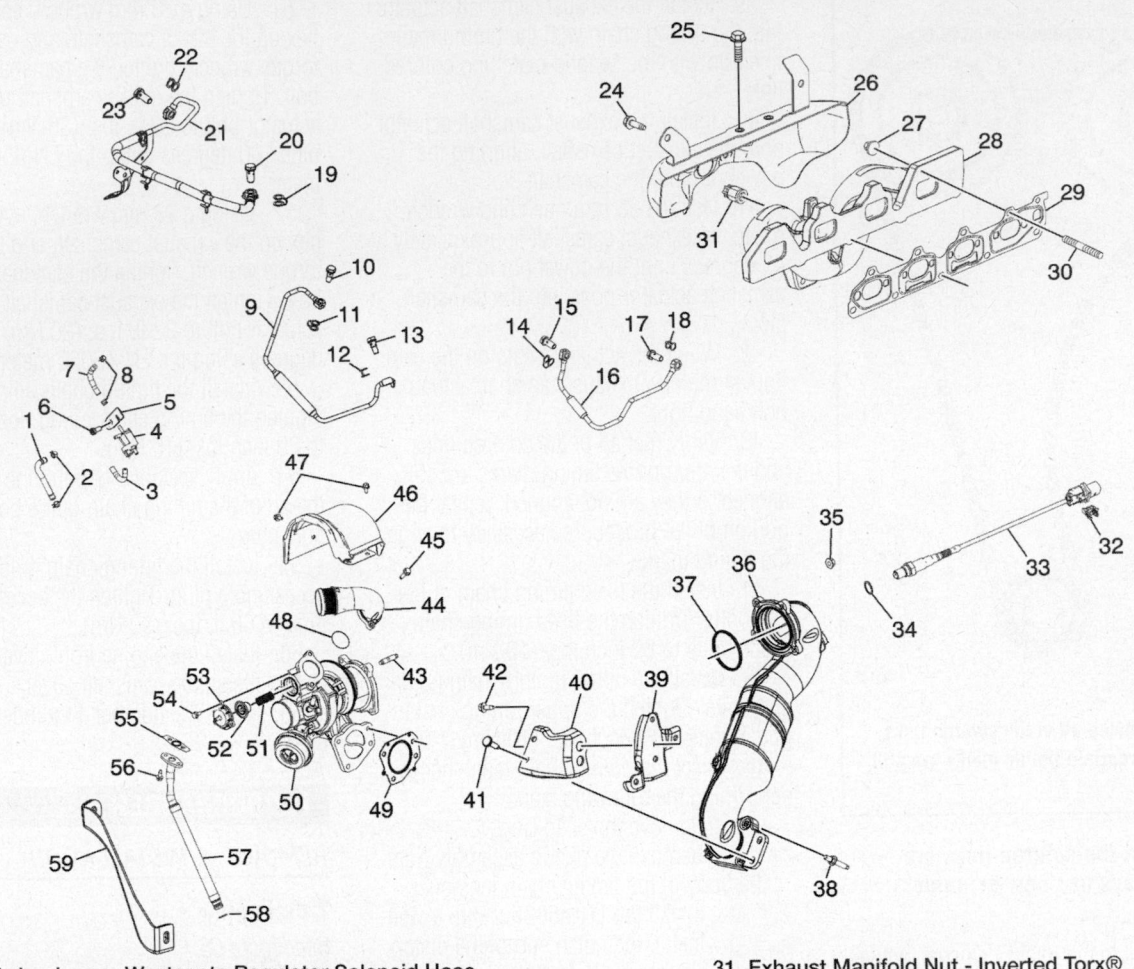

1. Turbocharger Wastegate Regulator Solenoid Hose
2. Turbocharger Wastegate Regulator Solenoid Hose Clamp
3. Turbocharger Wastegate Regulator Solenoid Hose
4. Turbocharger Wastegate Regulator Solenoid Valve Assembly
5. Turbocharger Wastegate Regulator Solenoid Valve Bracket
6. Turbocharger Wastegate Regulator Solenoid Valve Bracket Bolt/Screw
7. Turbocharger Wastegate Regulator Solenoid Hose
8. Turbocharger Wastegate Regulator Solenoid Hose Clamp
9. Turbocharger Oil Feed Pipe
10. Turbocharger Oil Feed Pipe Bolt
11. Turbocharger Oil Feed Pipe Gasket
12. Turbocharger Oil Feed Pipe Gasket
13. Turbocharger Oil Feed Pipe Bolt
14. Turbocharger Coolant Return Pipe Gasket
15. Turbocharger Coolant Return Pipe Bolt
16. Turbocharger Coolant Return Pipe
17. Turbocharger Coolant Return Pipe Bolt
18. Turbocharger Coolant Return Pipe Gasket
19. Turbocharger Coolant Feed Pipe Gasket
20. Turbocharger Coolant Feed Pipe Bolt
21. Turbocharger Coolant Feed Pipe
22. Turbocharger Coolant Feed Pipe Gasket
23. Turbocharger Coolant Feed Pipe Bolt
24. Exhaust Manifold Heat Shield Bolt
25. Exhaust Manifold Heat Shield Bolt
26. Exhaust Manifold Heat Shield
27. Exhaust Manifold Nut
28. Exhaust Manifold
29. Exhaust Manifold Gasket
30. Exhaust Manifold Stud
31. Exhaust Manifold Nut - Inverted Torx®
32. Oxygen Sensor Fastener
33. Oxygen Sensor
34. Oxygen Sensor Gasket
35. Catalytic Converter Nut
36. Catalytic Converter
37. Catalytic Converter Seal
38. Catalytic Converter Stud
39. Catalytic Converter Bracket
40. Catalytic Converter L-Bracket
41. Catalytic Converter Bolt
42. Catalytic Converter Bracket Bolt
43. Catalytic Converter Stud
44. Turbocharger Air Cooler Outlet Pipe
45. Turbocharger Air Cooler Outlet Pipe Bolt
46. Turbocharger Heat Shield
47. Turbocharger Heat Shield Bolts
48. Turbocharger Air Cooler Outlet Pipe Seal
49. Turbocharger Gasket
50. Turbocharger
51. Turbocharger Air Bypass Valve Spring
52. Turbocharger Air Bypass Diaphragm Assembly
53. Turbocharger Air Bypass Valve Cover
54. Turbocharger Air Bypass Valve Cover Bolt
55. Turbocharger Oil Return Pipe Gasket
56. Turbocharger Oil Return Pipe Bolt
57. Turbocharger Oil Return Pipe
58. Turbocharger Oil Return Pipe O-Ring
59. Turbocharger Brace

2074503

Fig. 56 Exploded view of the turbocharger and related components—2.0L engine

front of the engine to clear the turbocharger. **Assistance may be required to keep the pipes clear of the turbocharger during removal or installation.**

5. Remove the turbocharger oil feed pipe bolts.

6. Remove the turbocharger oil feed pipe gaskets.

7. Remove the turbocharger oil feed pipe.

8. Remove the turbocharger coolant return pipe bolts.

9. Remove the turbocharger coolant return pipe gaskets.

10. Remove the turbocharger coolant return pipe.

11. Remove the turbocharger air cooler outlet pipe.

12. Remove the turbocharger coolant feed pipe bolts.

13. Remove the turbocharger coolant feed pipe gaskets.

14. Remove the turbocharger coolant feed pipe.

15. Remove the turbocharger brace nuts.

16. Remove the turbocharger brace.

➡ **The PCV hose should not be disconnected from the camshaft cover. The PCV hose and the camshaft cover cannot be serviced individually.**

17. Remove the PCV hose fitting bolt at the turbocharger.

18. Remove the PCV hose fitting from the turbocharger.

19. Remove the turbocharger nuts.

20. Remove the turbocharger and the oil return pipe.

21. Remove the turbocharger gasket.

22. Remove the turbocharger oil return pipe bolts.

23. Remove the turbocharger oil return pipe from the turbocharger.

24. Remove and discard the turbocharger oil return pipe gasket.

25. Disconnect vacuum hose as needed.

26. Disconnect coolant hoses as needed.

27. Disconnect electrical connectors as needed.

To install:

28. Install a new turbocharger oil return pipe gasket.

29. Install the turbocharger oil return pipe on the turbocharger.

30. Install the turbocharger oil return pipe bolts and tighten to 89 inch lbs. (10 Nm).

31. Attach the positive crankcase ventilation (PCV) hose and fitting with O-ring from the camshaft cover to the turbocharger.

32. Install the PCV hose fitting bolt and tighten to 89 inch lbs. (10 Nm).

33. Lubricate the O-ring on the turbocharger oil return pipe with clean engine oil.

34. Install a new turbocharger gasket.

35. Install the turbocharger with the oil return pipe.

36. Install the turbocharger nuts.

a. Tighten the turbocharger nuts to 22 ft. lbs. (30 Nm).

b. Tighten the turbocharger nuts a second time to 26 ft. lbs. (35 Nm).

37. Install the turbocharger brace.

38. Install the turbocharger brace nuts and tighten to 37 ft. lbs. (50 Nm).

39. Install the catalytic converter. Refer to Catalytic Converter.

40. Install the turbocharger coolant feed pipe.

41. Install the turbocharger coolant feed pipe gaskets.

42. Install the turbocharger coolant feed pipe bolts.

a. Tighten the turbocharger coolant feed pipe bolts to 26 ft. lbs. (35 Nm).

b. Tighten the turbocharger coolant feed pipe mounting bolt to 89 inch lbs. (10 Nm).

43. Connect the PCV and hose assembly.

44. Install the air cleaner outlet duct.

❋❋ **CAUTION**

Do not twist the turbocharger oil feed pipe. Twisting of the feed pipe will result in the collapse and deformation of the plastic pipe, restricting oil flow and causing turbocharger damage. During turbocharger replacement, gently push the oil feed pipe towards the front of the engine to clear the turbocharger.

➡ **Assistance may be required to keep the pipes clear of the turbocharger during removal or installation.**

➡ **The engine block end of the oil feed pipe fitting has an anti-rotation feature. Ensure that the fitting is fully seated against the block when installing the bolt.**

45. Install the turbocharger oil feed pipe on the engine block side.

46. Install the turbocharger oil feed pipe gasket on the engine block side.

47. Install the bolt and tighten to 30 ft. lbs. (40 Nm).

48. Install the turbocharger coolant return pipe.

49. Install the turbocharger coolant return pipe gaskets.

50. Install the turbocharger coolant return pipe bolts and tighten to 26 ft. lbs. (35 Nm).

❋❋ **CAUTION**

Do not twist the turbocharger oil feed pipe. Twisting of the feed pipe will result in the collapse and deformation of the plastic pipe, restricting oil flow and causing turbocharger damage. During turbocharger replacement, gently push the oil feed pipe towards the front of the engine to clear the turbocharger.

51. Assistance may be required to keep the pipes clear of the turbocharger during removal or installation.

52. Install the turbocharger oil feed pipe onto the turbocharger.

53. Install the turbocharger oil feed pipe gasket for the turbocharger side.

54. Install the turbocharger oil feed pipe bolt and tighten to 30 ft. lbs. (40 Nm).

55. Install the catalytic converter.

56. Install the intake manifold cover.

57. Replace the oil filter and fill the engine oil system.

VALVE COVERS

REMOVAL & INSTALLATION

See Figure 57.

1. Remove the intake manifold cover.

2. Remove the ignition coil. Refer to Engine Electrical.

3. For 2.0L engines, remove the Charge air cooler inlet air tube.

4. Remove the air cleaner outlet duct.

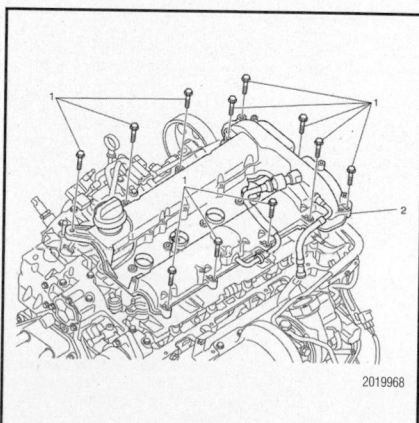

2019968

Fig. 57 Removing the bolts (1) and valve cover (2)

5. For 2.0L engines, remove the positive crankcase ventilation hose from the turbocharger.

6. Remove the camshaft position actuator sensor intake and exhaust. Refer to Camshafts.

7. For 2.0L engines, remove the Power Brake Booster Pump.

8. For 2.4L engines, remove ignition coil wiring harness clips from the camshaft cover.

9. Remove the 11 valve cover fasteners.

10. Disconnect any electrical connectors as necessary.

11. Remove the cover and discard the gasket.

➡**Use a new gasket.**

12. To install reverse the removal procedure.

13. Tighten the valve cover bolts to 89 inch lbs. (10 Nm).

ENGINE PERFORMANCE & EMISSION CONTROLS

CAMSHAFT POSITION (CMP) SENSOR

2.0L Engine

See Figures 58 and 59.

1. Disconnect the negative battery cable.

2. Disconnect the electrical connector.

3. Remove the sensor fastener and the sensor.

4. To install, reverse the removal procedure.

2.4L Engine

See Figures 60 and 61.

1. Remove the air cleaner outlet duct.

2. Remove the intake manifold cover.

3. Disconnect the engine wiring harness electrical connector from the intake camshaft position (CMP) sensor.

4. Remove the intake CMP sensor bolt.

5. Remove the intake CMP sensor.

To install:

➡**Inspect the intake CMP sensor for damage, replace as necessary.**

6. Lubricate the intake CMP sensor O-ring seal with clean engine oil.

7. Install the intake CMP sensor.

8. Install the intake CMP sensor bolt. Tighten the bolt to 89 inch lbs. (10 Nm).

9. Connect the engine wiring harness electrical connector (1) to the intake CMP sensor.

10. Install the intake manifold cover.

11. Install the air cleaner outlet duct.

CRANKSHAFT POSITION (CKP) SENSOR

REMOVAL & INSTALLATION

See Figures 62 and 63.

1. Disconnect the negative battery cable.

2. For 2.0L engines, remove the starter motor. Refer to Engine Electrical.

3. Disconnect the electrical connector.

4. Remove the sensor fastener and the sensor.

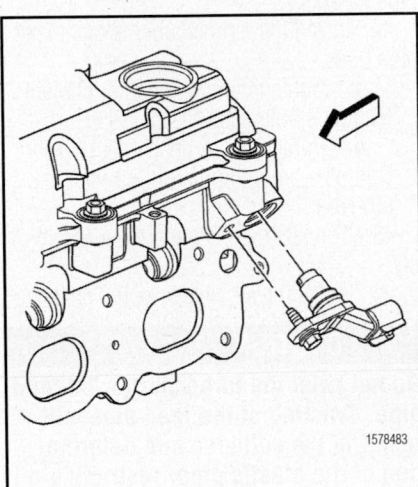

Fig. 60 Removing the intake CMP sensor

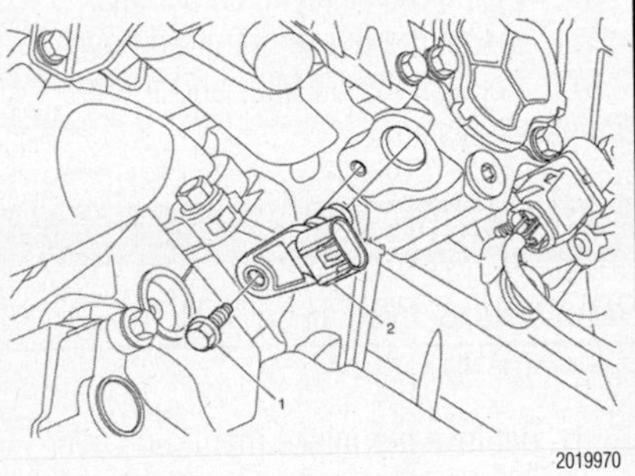

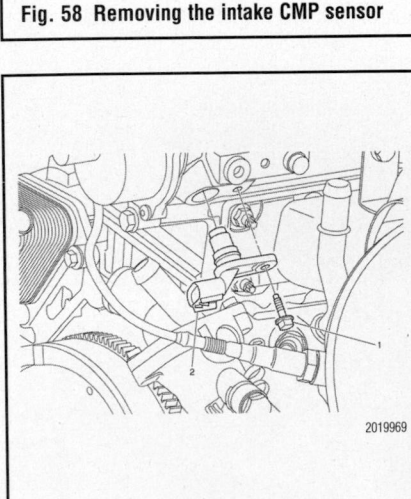

Fig. 58 Removing the intake CMP sensor

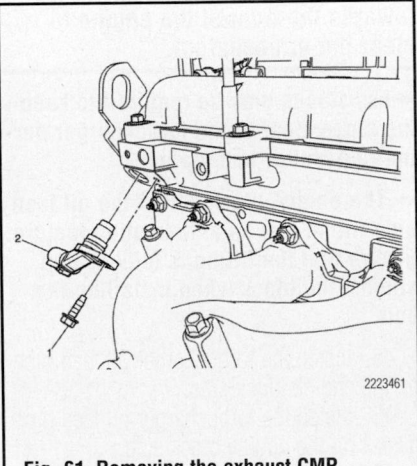

Fig. 61 Removing the exhaust CMP sensor

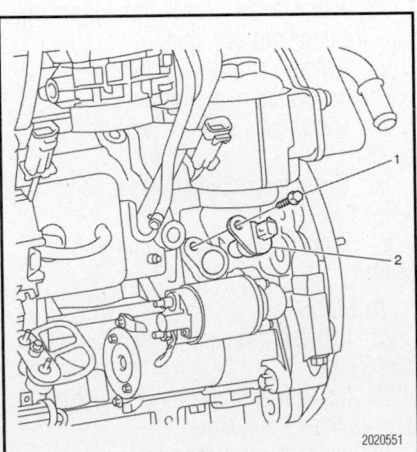

Fig. 62 Remove the CKP sensor—2.0L engine

Fig. 59 Removing the exhaust CMP sensor

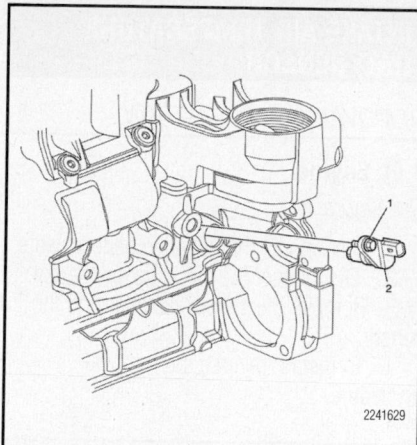

Fig. 63 Remove the CKP sensor—2.4L engine

5. To install, reverse the removal procedure.

ELECTRONIC CONTROL MODULE (ECM)

REMOVAL & INSTALLATION

See Figures 64 and 65.

1. Disconnect the negative battery cable.
2. Disconnect the electrical connector.
3. Pull up the engine control module from the battery box.
4. Open with caution both retainers at the sides and pull the engine control module outside the bracket.
5. Remove the ECM.
6. To install, reverse the removal procedure.

MODULE CONFIGURATION

ECM Replacement and Reprogramming

If the engine control module (ECM) is replaced or reprogrammed, the following procedures must be performed:

Fig. 64 Removing the retainer (1) and ECM (2)—2.0L engine

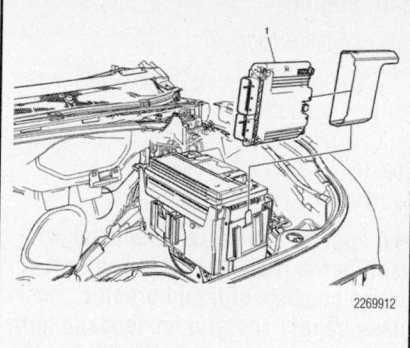

Fig. 65 Removing the ECM (1)—2.4L engine

1. ECM Reprogramming.
2. Theft Deterrent. The ECM will learn the incoming fuel continue password immediately upon receipt of a password message. Once a password message is received, and a password is learned, a learn procedure must be performed to change this password again. An ECM which has been previously installed in another vehicle will have learned the other vehicle's fuel continue password, and will require a learn procedure after programming to learn the current vehicle's password.
3. Clutch pedal position sensor learn—Refer to Clutch Pedal Position Sensor Learn.
4. Idle Learn Procedure..
5. Engine Oil Life Remaining—When available, use a scan tool to reset the Engine Oil Life Remaining back to the original percentage recorded before the module was replaced.

ENGINE COOLANT TEMPERATURE (ECT) SENSOR

LOCATION

See Figure 66.

REMOVAL & INSTALLATION

> ✳✳ **CAUTION**
>
> To avoid any vehicle damage, serious personal injury or death when major components are removed from the vehicle and the vehicle is supported by a hoist, support the vehicle with jack stands at the opposite end from which the components are being removed and strap the vehicle to the hoist.

> ✳✳ **CAUTION**
>
> Replacement components must be the correct part number for the appli-

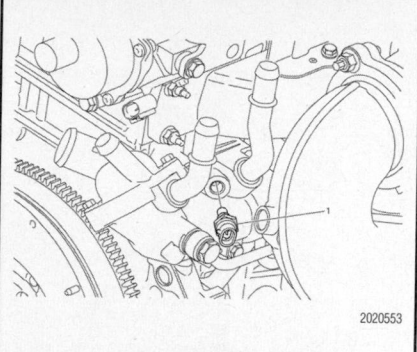

Fig. 66 ECT sensor (1) location—2.0L shown, 2.4L similar

cation. Components requiring the use of the thread locking compound, lubricants, corrosion inhibitors, or sealants are identified in the service procedure. Some replacement components may come with these coatings already applied. Do not use these coatings on components unless specified. These coatings can affect the final torque, which may affect the operation of the component. Use the correct torque specification when installing components in order to avoid damage.

> ✳✳ **CAUTION**
>
> Use care when handling the coolant sensor. Damage to the coolant sensor will affect the operation of the fuel control system.

1. Disconnect the negative battery cable.
2. Remove the intake cover.
3. Partially drain the cooling system.
4. Disconnect the electrical connector.
5. Remove the ECT sensor.
6. To install, reverse the removal procedure.
7. Use a new gasket.
8. Tighten the ECT sensor to 15 ft. lbs. (20 Nm).

HEATED OXYGEN (HO2S) SENSOR

REMOVAL & INSTALLATION

2.0L Engine

See Figures 67 and 68.

1. Disconnect the negative battery cable.
2. Disconnect the electrical connector.
3. Remove the heated oxygen sensor 1 with CH-6179 remover/installer and GE-611 wrench.

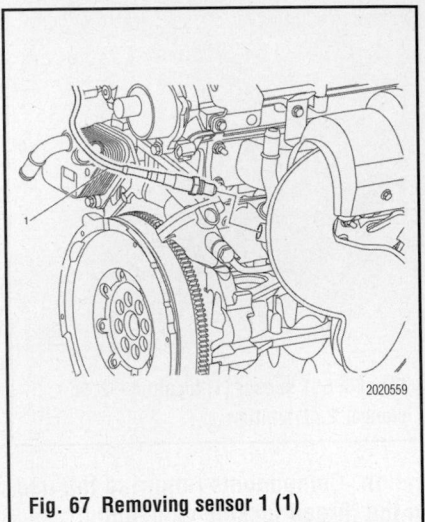

Fig. 67 Removing sensor 1 (1)

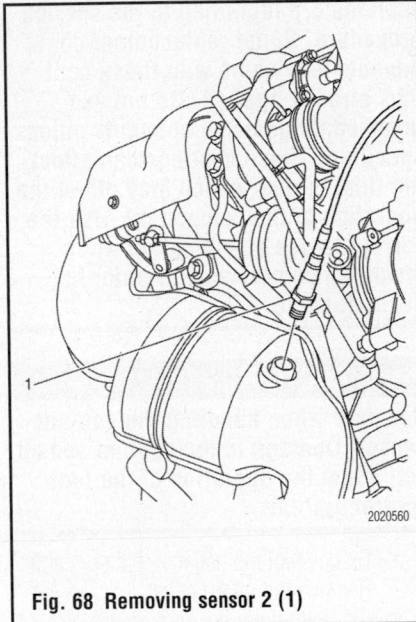

Fig. 68 Removing sensor 2 (1)

4. To install, reverse the removal procedure.

5. If reinstalling the old sensor, coat the threads with anti-seize compound.

➡A special anti-seize compound is used in the HO2S threads. The compound consists of liquid graphic and glass beads. The graphic tends to burn away, but the glass beads remain, making the sensor easier to remove. New, or service replacement sensors already have the compound applied to the threads. If the sensor is removed from an exhaust component and if for any reason the sensor is to be reinstalled, the threads must have anti-seize compound applied before reinstallation.

6. Tighten the sensor to 31 ft. lbs. (42 Nm).

2.4L Engine

See Figures 69 and 70.

1. Disconnect the heated oxygen sensor harness connector.

2. If reinstalling the old sensor, coat the threads with anti-seize compound.

➡A special anti-seize compound is used in the HO2S threads. The compound consists of liquid graphic and glass beads. The graphic tends to burn away, but the glass beads remain, making the sensor easier to remove. New or service replacement sensors already have the compound applied to the threads. If the sensor is removed from an exhaust component and if for any reason the sensor is to be reinstalled, the threads must have anti-seize compound applied before reinstallation.

3. To install, reverse the removal procedure.

4. Tighten the sensor to 31 ft. lbs. (42 Nm).

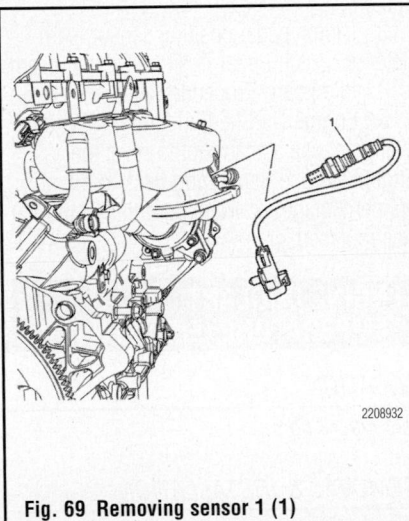

Fig. 69 Removing sensor 1 (1)

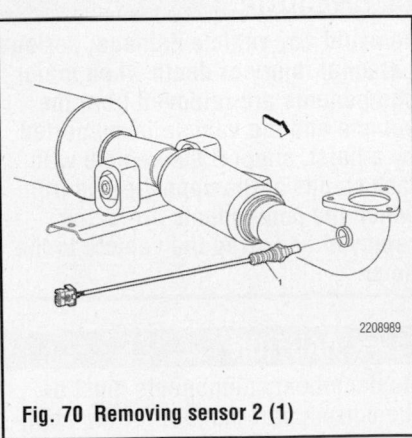

Fig. 70 Removing sensor 2 (1)

INTAKE AIR TEMPERATURE (IAT) SENSOR

REMOVAL & INSTALLATION

2.0L Engine

See Figure 71.

1. Disconnect the negative battery cable.
2. Disconnect the electrical connector.
3. Remove the sensor fastener and the sensor.
4. To install, reverse the removal procedure.

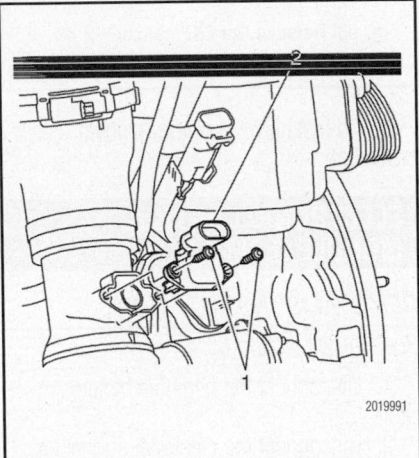

Fig. 71 Removing the IAT screws (1) and sensor (2)

KNOCK SENSOR (KS)

REMOVAL & INSTALLATION

2.0L Engine

See Figures 72 and 73.

1. Disconnect the negative battery cable.
2. Disconnect the electrical connector.

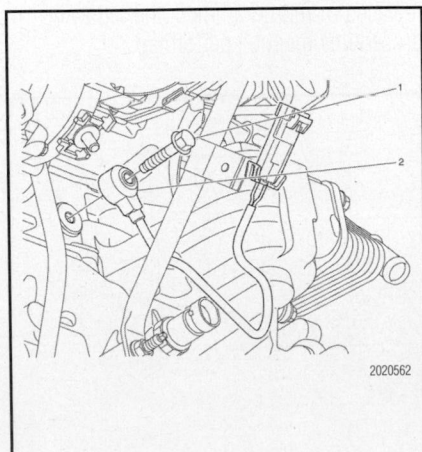

Fig. 72 Removing the left knock sensor screw (1) and sensor (2)

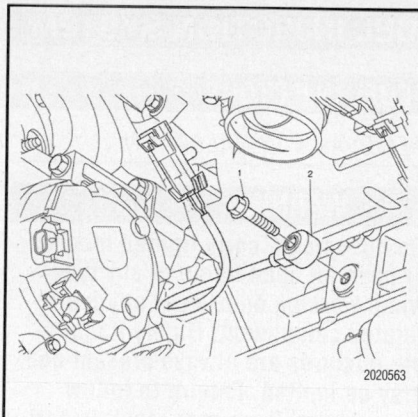

Fig. 73 Removing the right knock sensor screw (1) and sensor (2)

3. Remove the sensor fastener and the sensor.

4. To install, reverse the removal procedure.

5. Tighten the sensor to 18 ft. lbs. (25 Nm).

MANIFOLD ABSOLUTE PRESSURE (MAP) SENSOR

REMOVAL & INSTALLATION

See Figures 74 and 75.

1. Disconnect the negative battery cable.

2. Remove the engine cover

3. Disconnect the electrical connector.

4. Remove the sensor fastener and the sensor.

5. To install, reverse the removal procedure.

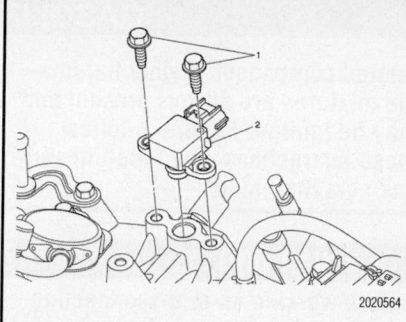

Fig. 74 Removing the MAP sensor—2.0L engine

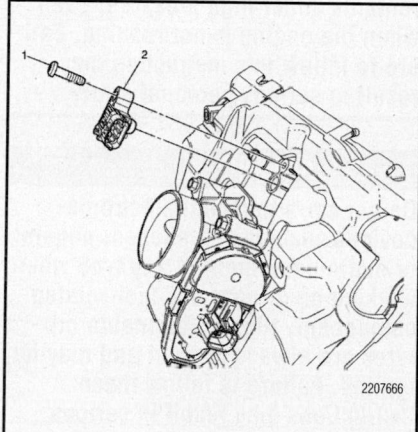

Fig. 75 Removing the MAP sensor—2.4L engine

MASS AIR FLOW (MAF) SENSOR

REMOVAL & INSTALLATION

See Figures 76 and 77.

1. Disconnect the negative battery cable.

2. Remove the engine cover

3. Disconnect the electrical connector.

4. Remove the sensor fastener and the sensor.

5. To install, reverse the removal procedure.

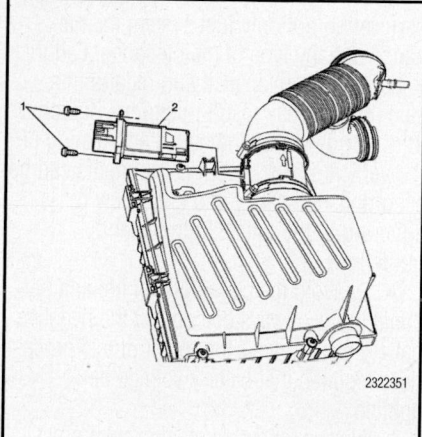

Fig. 76 Removing the MAF sensor screws (1) and sensor (2)—2.0L engines

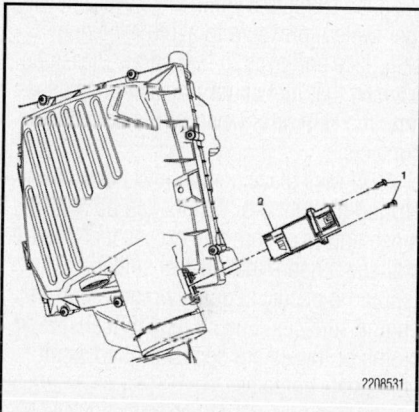

Fig. 77 Removing the MAF sensor screws (1) and sensor (2)—2.4L engines

FUEL SYSTEM SERVICE PRECAUTIONS

Safety is the most important factor when performing not only fuel system maintenance but any type of maintenance. Failure to conduct maintenance and repairs in a safe manner may result in serious personal injury or death. Maintenance and testing of the vehicle's fuel system components can be accomplished safely and effectively by adhering to the following rules and guidelines.

• To avoid the possibility of fire and personal injury, always disconnect the negative battery cable unless the repair or test procedure requires that battery voltage be applied.

• Always relieve the fuel system pressure prior to disconnecting any fuel system component (injector, fuel rail, pressure regulator, etc.), fitting or fuel line connection. Exercise extreme caution whenever relieving fuel system pressure to avoid exposing skin, face and eyes to fuel spray. Please be advised that fuel under pressure may penetrate the skin or any part of the body that it contacts.

• Always place a shop towel or cloth around the fitting or connection prior to loosening to absorb any excess fuel due to spillage. Ensure that all fuel spillage (should it occur) is quickly removed from engine surfaces. Ensure that all fuel soaked cloths or towels are deposited into a suitable waste container.

• Always keep a dry chemical (Class B) fire extinguisher near the work area.

• Do not allow fuel spray or fuel vapors to come into contact with a spark or open flame.

• Always use a back-up wrench when loosening and tightening fuel line connection fittings. This will prevent unnecessary stress and torsion to fuel line piping.

• Always replace worn fuel fitting O-rings with new Do not substitute fuel hose or equivalent where fuel pipe is installed.

Before servicing the vehicle, make sure to also refer to the precautions in the beginning of this section as well.

RELIEVING FUEL SYSTEM PRESSURE

⁑ WARNING

Do not smoke, carry lighted tobacco or have an open flame of any type when working on or near any fuel-related component. Highly flammable mixtures are always present and may be ignited. Failure to follow these instructions may result in serious personal injury.

⁑ WARNING

Before working on or disconnecting any of the fuel tubes or fuel system components, relieve the fuel system pressure to prevent accidental spraying of fuel. Fuel in the fuel system remains under high pressure, even when the engine is not running. Failure to follow this instruction may result in serious personal injury.

⁑ WARNING

Do not carry personal electronic devices such as cell phones, pagers or audio equipment of any type when working on or near any fuel-related component. Highly flammable mixtures are always present and may be ignited. Failure to follow these instructions may result in serious personal injury.

⁑ WARNING

When handling fuel, always observe fuel handling precautions and be prepared in the event of fuel spillage. Spilled fuel may be ignited by hot vehicle components or other ignition sources. Failure to follow these instructions may result in serious personal injury.

⁑ WARNING

Fuel that flows out at high pressure can cause serious injury to the skin and eyes. ALWAYS depressurize the fuel system before removing components that are under high fuel pressure.

➡ If a scan tool is not available, WAIT at LEAST 2 hours after the engine has been run, before removing the high pressure fuel line.

1. Remove the fuel pump module 20A fuse from the underhood electrical center.
2. Start the vehicle and allow the engine to idle until the engine stops. The engine will stop in approximately 20-30 seconds.
3. Turn the ignition OFF.

FUEL INJECTORS

REMOVAL & INSTALLATION

⁑ WARNING

Do not smoke, carry lighted tobacco or have an open flame of any type when working on or near any fuel-related component. Highly flammable mixtures are always present and may be ignited. Failure to follow these instructions may result in serious personal injury.

⁑ WARNING

Do not carry personal electronic devices such as cell phones, pagers or audio equipment of any type when working on or near any fuel-related component. Highly flammable mixtures are always present and may be ignited. Failure to follow these instructions may result in serious personal injury.

⁑ WARNING

Before working on or disconnecting any of the fuel tubes or fuel system components, relieve the fuel system pressure to prevent accidental spraying of fuel. Fuel in the fuel system remains under high pressure, even when the engine is not running. Failure to follow this instruction may result in serious personal injury.

⁑ WARNING

When handling fuel, always observe fuel handling precautions and be prepared in the event of fuel spillage. Spilled fuel may be ignited by hot vehicle components or other ignition sources. Failure to follow these instructions may result in serious personal injury.

⁑ WARNING

Always disconnect the battery ground cable at the battery when working on an evaporative emission (EVAP) system or fuel-related component. Highly flammable mixtures are always present and may be ignited. Failure to follow these instructions may result in serious personal injury.

✷✷ WARNING

Shut off the electrical power to the air suspension system prior to hoisting or jacking an air suspension equipped vehicle. Failure to do so may result in unexpected inflation or deflation of the air springs, which may result in shifting of the vehicle during these operations. Failure to follow this instruction may result in serious personal injury.

2.4L Engine

See Figures 78 and 79.

1. Relieve the fuel system pressure.
2. Remove the intake manifold. Refer to Engine Mechanical.
3. Disconnect the fuel rail electrical connector.
4. Remove and discard the fuel injector retainers.
5. Clean and inspect the fuel rail and injectors.

To install:

6. Install NEW fuel injector retainers.

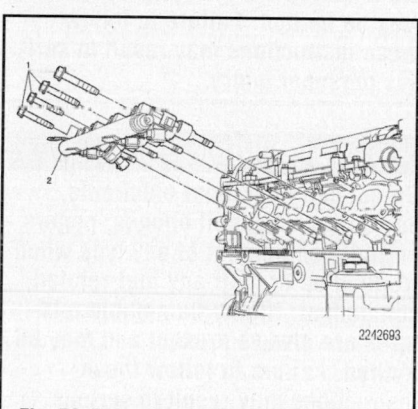

Fig. 78 Removing the fuel rail bolts (1) and fuel rail (2)

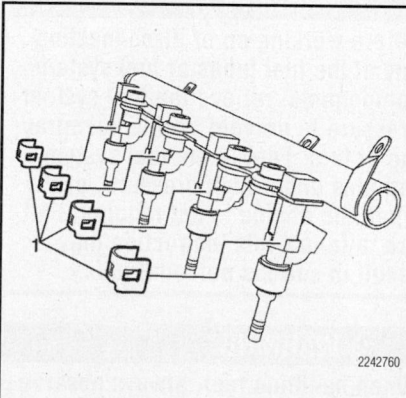

Fig. 79 Removing the fuel injector retainers (1)

➡The fuel injectors have an alignment feature and must be reinstalled as noted during removal.

7. To complete installation, reverse the remaining removal procedure.
8. Tighten the fuel injection fuel rail fasteners to 18 ft. lbs. (25 Nm).

FUEL PUMP

REMOVAL & INSTALLATION

✷✷ WARNING

Do not smoke, carry lighted tobacco or have an open flame of any type when working on or near any fuel-related component. Highly flammable mixtures are always present and may be ignited. Failure to follow these instructions may result in serious personal injury.

✷✷ WARNING

Do not carry personal electronic devices such as cell phones, pagers or audio equipment of any type when working on or near any fuel-related component. Highly flammable mixtures are always present and may be ignited. Failure to follow these instructions may result in serious personal injury.

✷✷ WARNING

Before working on or disconnecting any of the fuel tubes or fuel system components, relieve the fuel system pressure to prevent accidental spraying of fuel. Fuel in the fuel system remains under high pressure, even when the engine is not running. Failure to follow this instruction may result in serious personal injury.

✷✷ WARNING

When handling fuel, always observe fuel handling precautions and be prepared in the event of fuel spillage. Spilled fuel may be ignited by hot vehicle components or other ignition sources. Failure to follow these instructions may result in serious personal injury.

✷✷ WARNING

Always disconnect the battery ground cable at the battery when working on

an evaporative emission (EVAP) system or fuel-related component. Highly flammable mixtures are always present and may be ignited. Failure to follow these instructions may result in serious personal injury.

2.0L Engine

See Figures 80 and 81.

1. Properly relieve the fuel system pressure.
2. Remove the intake manifold cover.
3. Remove the fuel feed intermediate pipe.
4. Release the fuel feed pipe - metal.
5. Remove the fuel pump fasteners.
6. Haul the fuel pump insulator of the fuel pump module.
7. Disconnect the electrical connector.
8. To install, reverse the removal procedure.
9. Tighten the fuel pump module bolts to 11 ft. lbs. (15 Nm).
10. Tighten the fuel feed intermediate pipe fastener to 22 ft. lbs. (30 Nm).

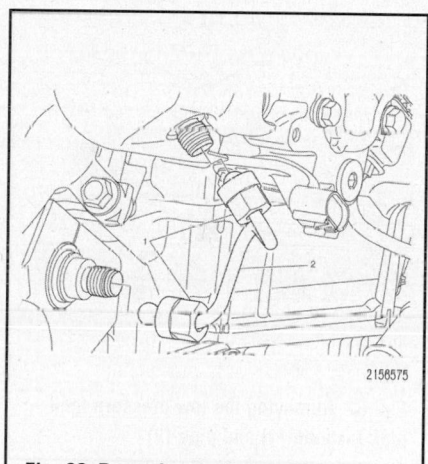

Fig. 80 Removing the fuel feed intermediate pipe

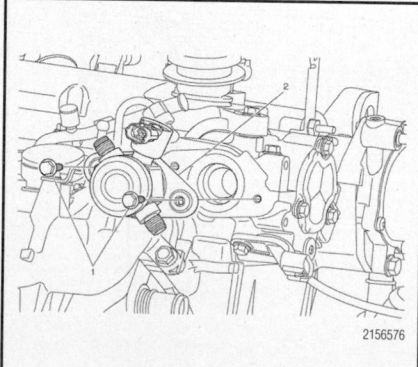

Fig. 81 Removing the fuel pump fasteners (1) and fuel pump (2)

2.4L Engine

See Figures 82 through 84.

1. Relieve the low and high side fuel system pressure.

2. Disconnect the engine wiring harness electrical connector from the high pressure fuel pump.

3. Remove the low pressure feed pipe.

4. Remove the high pressure pipe. Discard this pipe.

5. Remove and discard the high pressure fuel pump bolts.

6. Remove the high pressure fuel pump.

7. Remove and discard the high pressure fuel pump O-ring.

8. Remove and discard the high pressure fuel pump gasket.

9. Remove the high pressure fuel pump roller lifter.

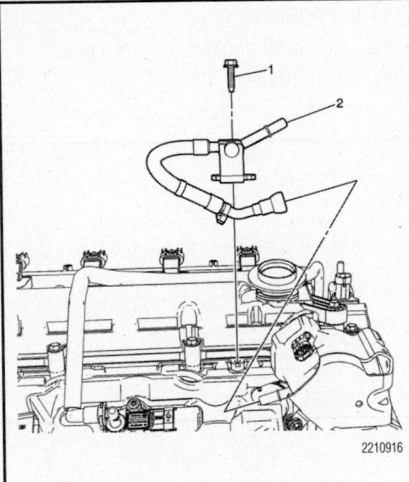

Fig. 82 Removing the low pressure feed pipe fastener (1) and pipe (2)

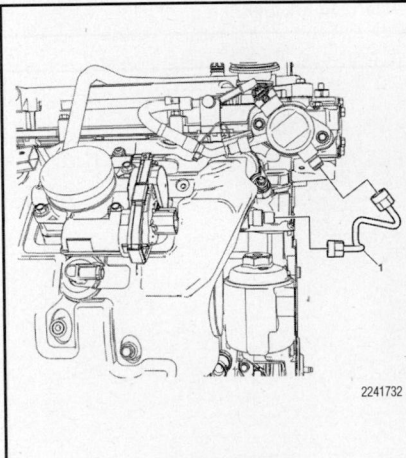

Fig. 83 Removing the fuel feed intermediate pipe (1)

To install:

➡ **The camshaft must be in the base circle position before the high pressure fuel pump is installed.**

10. Use the EN-48896 alignment gauge to ensure that the camshaft lobe is in the base circle position. At base circle the tool will be flush with the head.

11. Lubricate the high pressure fuel pump cylinder head bore and roller lifter with camshaft prelube GM P/N 12345501 (Canadian P/N 992704) or equivalent.

➡ **The high pressure fuel pump gasket has a retaining feature to hold the pump retaining bolts in place.**

12. Install the high pressure fuel pump roller lifter.

13. Install a NEW high pressure fuel pump O-ring.

14. Position the NEW high pressure fuel pump gasket and bolts to the fuel pump.

15. Install the high pressure fuel pump. Force will be required while hand tightening the bolts.

16. Tighten the high pressure fuel pump retaining bolts to 11 ft. lbs. (15 Nm).

17. Ensure the high pressure fuel pump and fuel rail fittings are clean prior to assembly.

18. Install a NEW high pressure fuel pipe.
   a. Lubricate the pipes with silicon free engine oil.
   b. Tighten to 22 ft. lbs. (30 Nm).

19. Install the fuel feed pipe to the high pressure fuel pump. Tighten the fastener to 89 inch lbs. (10 Nm).

20. Connect the high pressure fuel pump wiring harness.

21. Install the fuel tank cap.

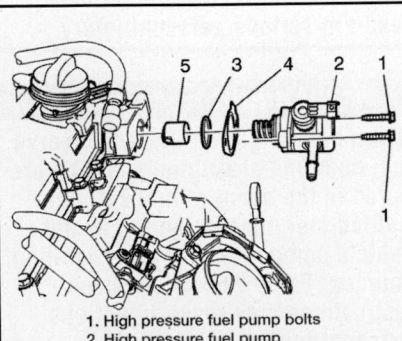

1. High pressure fuel pump bolts
2. High pressure fuel pump
3. High pressure fuel pump O-ring
4. Gasket
5. High pressure fuel pump roller lifter

Fig. 84 Removing the fuel pump assembly

➡ If a fuel leak accrues at the fuel rail, the fuel rail will need to be replaced.

22. Inspect for leaks using the following procedure:
   a. Turn ON the ignition, with the engine OFF for 2 seconds.
   b. Turn OFF the ignition, for 10 seconds
   c. Turn ON the ignition, with the engine OFF
   d. Inspect for fuel leaks

23. Install the pressure relief cap to the fuel feed pipe.

24. Install the high pressure fuel pump cover.

FUEL TANK

DRAINING

✳✳ WARNING

Do not smoke, carry lighted tobacco or have an open flame of any type when working on or near any fuel-related component. Highly flammable mixtures are always present and may be ignited. Failure to follow these instructions may result in serious personal injury.

✳✳ WARNING

Do not carry personal electronic devices such as cell phones, pagers or audio equipment of any type when working on or near any fuel-related component. Highly flammable mixtures are always present and may be ignited. Failure to follow these instructions may result in serious personal injury.

✳✳ WARNING

Before working on or disconnecting any of the fuel tubes or fuel system components, relieve the fuel system pressure to prevent accidental spraying of fuel. Fuel in the fuel system remains under high pressure, even when the engine is not running. Failure to follow this instruction may result in serious personal injury.

✳✳ WARNING

When handling fuel, always observe fuel handling precautions and be prepared in the event of fuel spillage. Spilled fuel may be ignited by hot

vehicle components or other ignition sources. Failure to follow these instructions may result in serious personal injury.

✳✳ WARNING

Always disconnect the battery ground cable at the battery when working on an evaporative emission (EVAP) system or fuel-related component. Highly flammable mixtures are always present and may be ignited. Failure to follow these instructions may result in serious personal injury.

1. Disconnect the battery ground cable.
2. Remove the fuel filler cap.

➡ **Lubricate the fuel drain hose with lubricant J 36850 or equivalent to aid in hose insertion and removal. Do not use an unapproved lubricant.**

3. Insert the fuel drain hose J 45004 into the fuel tank until the hose reaches the bottom of the fuel tank.
4. Use an air operated pump device in order to drain the fuel into an approved gasoline container.
5. Up to 7 gallons of residual fuel may remain in the secondary side of the fuel tank.
6. Simultaneously twist and pull in order to remove the J 45004 from the fuel tank.

REMOVAL & INSTALLATION

See Figure 85.

✳✳ WARNING

To avoid any vehicle damage, serious personal injury or death when major components are removed from the vehicle and the vehicle is supported by a hoist, support the vehicle with jack stands at the opposite end from which the components are being removed and strap the vehicle to the hoist.

1. Relieve the system fuel pressure.
2. Drain the fuel tank.
3. Disconnect the evaporative emission and fuel pipes.
4. Disconnect the fuel pressure sensor electrical connector.
5. Loosen the hose clamps and remove the filler tube.

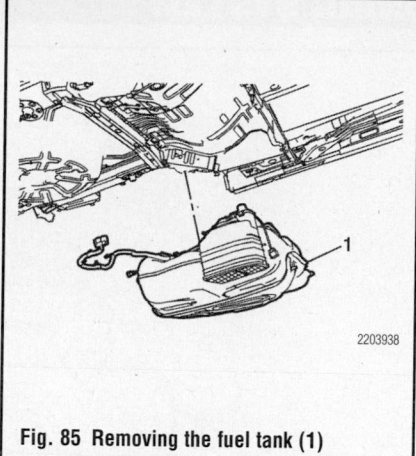

Fig. 85 Removing the fuel tank (1)

6. Disconnect the fuel tank harness electrical connector.
7. Support the fuel tank with a suitable jack.
8. Remove the fuel tank strap bolt.
9. Swing the fuel tank straps out of the way.
10. Remove the fuel tank.
11. Remove the following components if replacing just the fuel tank.
    a. Fuel tank fuel pump module.
    b. Evaporative emission carbon canister.
    c. Transfer components as necessary.

To install:

12. Use a suitable jack and install the fuel tank.
13. Reposition the fuel tank straps.
14. Install the fuel tank strap bolts and tighten to 20 ft. lbs. (27 Nm).
15. Connect the fuel tank harness electrical connector.
16. Install the filler tube and tighten the hose clamps.
17. Connect the evaporative emission line.
18. Connect the evaporative emission and fuel pipes.
19. Connect the fuel pressure sensor electrical connector.
20. Refill the fuel tank.
21. Inspect for fuel leaks.

IDLE SPEED

ADJUSTMENT

Idle speed adjustment is not necessary or possible.

THROTTLE BODY

REMOVAL & INSTALLATION

See Figures 86 and 87.

1. Disconnect the negative battery cable.
2. For 2.0L engines, release the charge air cooler outlet pipe.
3. For 2.4L engines, remove the outlet duct.
4. Disconnect the electrical connector.
5. Remove the 4 throttle body fasteners.
6. To install, reverse the removal procedure.
7. For 2.4L engines, use a NEW throttle body o-ring.
8. Tighten the throttle body fasteners to 89 inch lbs. (10 Nm).

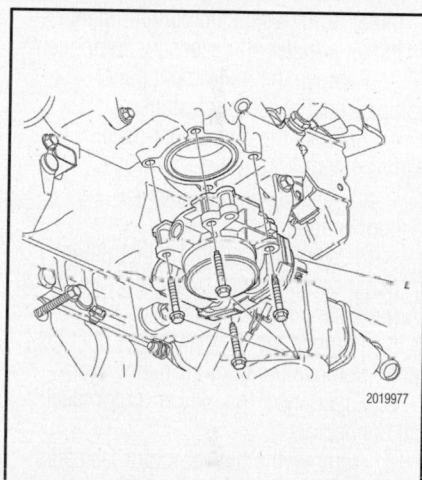

Fig. 86 Removing the throttle body fasteners (1) and throttle body (2)—2.0L engine

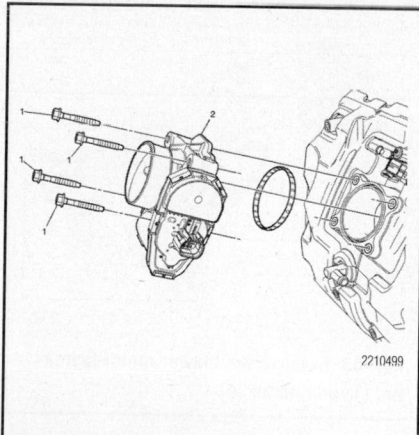

Fig. 87 Removing the throttle body fasteners (1) and throttle body (2)—2.4L engine

HEATING & AIR CONDITIONING SYSTEM

BLOWER MOTOR

REMOVAL & INSTALLATION

See Figure 88.

1. Remove the instrument panel outer trim cover.

   a. Use a flat-bladed plastic trim tool to aid in the removal of the outer trim cover.

   b. When replacing the instrument panel outer trim cover, transfer the inflatable restraint disable switch, if equipped.

2. Remove the instrument panel lower extension compartment panel retainer

   a. Disconnect electrical connections, if applicable.

   b. When replacing the instrument panel lower extension compartment panel, transfer all necessary components.

3. Remove the instrument panel compartment assembly fastener.

4. Remove the instrument panel compartment assembly:

   a. Disconnect the electrical connections.

   b. When replacing the instrument panel compartment assembly, transfer all necessary components.

5. Remove the floor air outlet duct fastener. Remove the floor air outlet duct.

6. Disconnect the blower motor electrical connector.

7. Remove the blower motor fasteners and blower motor.

8. To install, reverse the removal procedure.

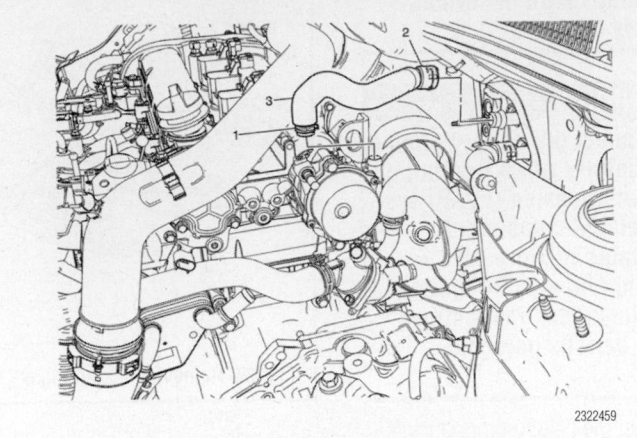

Fig. 89 Removing the clamp (1), clip (2) and inlet hose (3)—2.0L engines

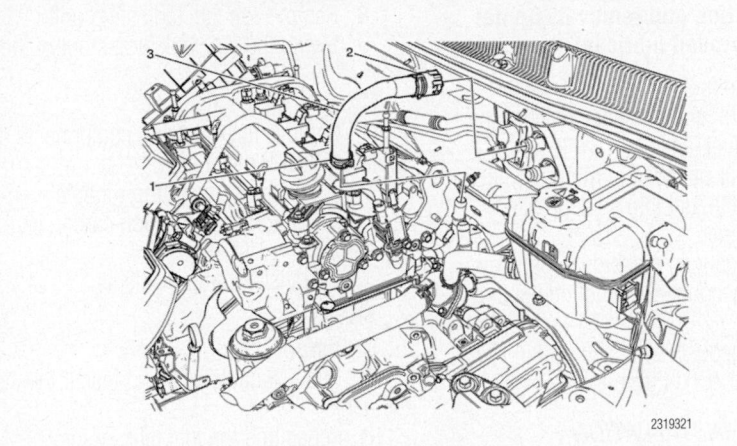

Fig. 90 Removing the clamp (1), clip (2) and inlet hose (3)—2.4L engines

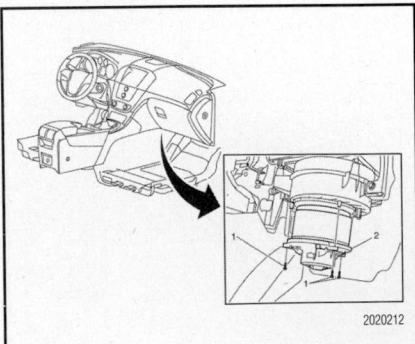

Fig. 88 Remove the blower motor fasteners (1) and motor (2)

HEATER CORE

REMOVAL & INSTALLATION

See Figures 89 through 91.

1. Drain and recycle the engine coolant.

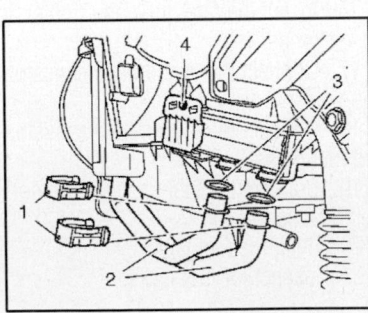
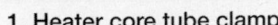
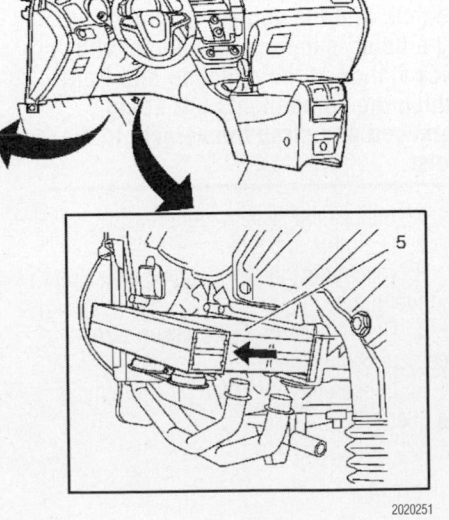

1. Heater core tube clamp
2. Heater core tube assembly
3. Heater core tube seal
4. Heater core bracket fastner
5. Heater core

Fig. 91 Removing the heater core

2. Remove the heater inlet hose from the heater core tube.

3. Remove the heater outlet hose from the heater core tube:

4. Loosen the carpet in the range of the heater core.

5. Remove the heater core tube assembly. Coolant may still be in the heater core, collect coolant or blow out heater core with compressed air.

6. Remove the 2 heater core tube seal.

7. Remove the heater core bracket fastener.

8. Pull out the heater core.

9. To install, reverse the removal procedure.

STEERING

POWER STEERING GEAR

REMOVAL & INSTALLATION

See Figure 94.

✳ CAUTION

With wheels of the vehicle facing straight ahead, secure the steering wheel utilizing steering column anti-rotation pin, steering column lock, or a strap to prevent rotation. Locking of the steering column will prevent damage and a possible malfunction of the SIR system. The steering wheel must be secured in position before disconnecting the following components:

a. The steering column
b. The intermediate shaft(s)
c. The steering gear

After disconnecting these components, do not rotate the steering wheel or move the front tires and wheels. Failure to follow this procedure may cause the SIR coil assembly to become un-centered and cause possible damage to the SIR coil. If you think the SIR coil has became un-centered, refer to your specific SIR coil's centering procedure to re center SIR Coil.

1. With the wheels of the vehicle in the straight ahead position, LOCK the steering column.

2. Disconnect the intermediate steering shaft from the steering gear.

3. Raise and support the vehicle.

4. Perform the following steps in order to lower the rear part of the frame.

a. Remove the front tire and wheel assemblies.

b. Disconnect the 2 stabilizer shaft links from the struts.

c. Remove the front exhaust pipe.

d. Support the frame with a jack.

e. Remove the transmission mount bolts.

f. Remove the rear frame-to-body bolts.

g. Lower the rear part of the frame a maximum of 50 mm (2 in) in order to gain clearance for the steering gear.

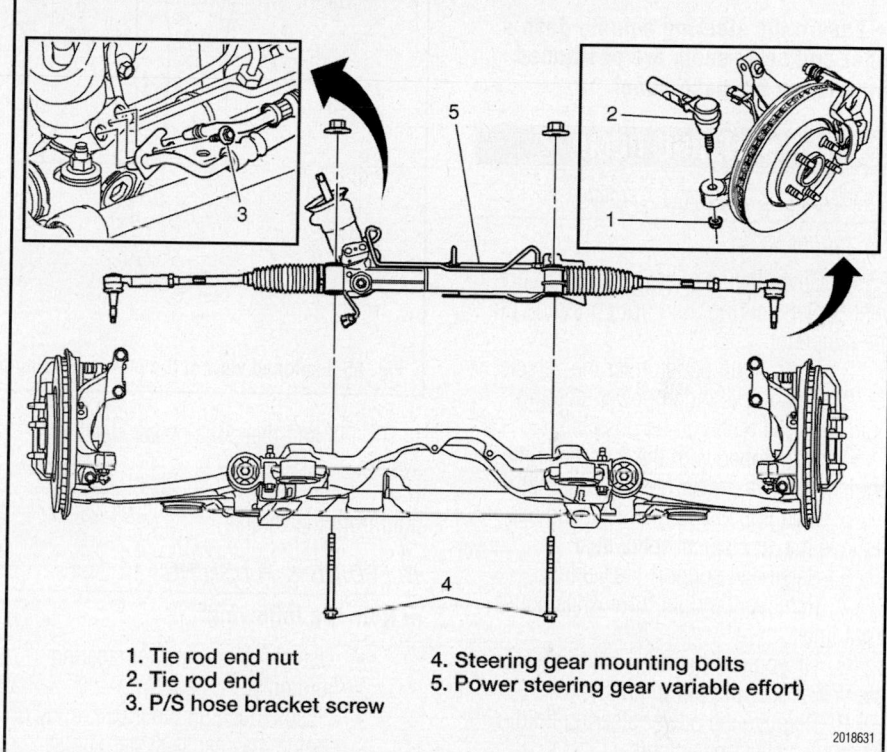

1. Tie rod end nut
2. Tie rod end
3. P/S hose bracket screw
4. Steering gear mounting bolts
5. Power steering gear variable effort)

2018631

Fig. 94 Exploded view of the power steering gear assembly

5. Steering Linkage Outer Tie Rod Nut (Qty: 2)

✳ CAUTION

This component is equipped with torque-to-yield fasteners. Install a NEW torque-to-yield fastener when installing this component. Failure to replace the torque-to-yield fastener could cause damage to the vehicle or component.

6. Remove the 2 steering linkage outer tie rod nuts.

7. Discard the nuts. Upon installation, install 2 NEW steering linkage outer tie rod nuts and tighten them to 26 ft. lbs. (30 Nm) plus 30 degrees.

8. Disconnect the 2 steering linkage outer tie rods from the steering knuckles.

9. Remove the steering gear inlet and outlet hose fastener:

10. Place drain pans under the vehicle in order to catch any power steering fluid.

11. Remove the 2 steering gear seals. Discard the seals. Upon Install 2 NEW steering gear seals.

12. Remove the 2 steering gear nuts and the 2 steering gear bolts.

13. Discard the nuts and the bolts. Upon installation, install 2 NEW steering gear nuts and 2 NEW steering gear bolts. Hold the steering gear nuts while tightening the steering gear bolts. Tighten to 81 ft. lbs. (110 Nm) plus 150 degrees.

14. Disconnect any electrical connectors as necessary.

15. Rotate the front stabilizer shaft in order to gain clearance for the steering gear. DO NOT loosen the stabilizer shaft insulator clamp bolts.

16. Remove the steering gear through the left front wheel opening.

17. Transfer components if necessary.

18. To install, reverse the removal procedure.

19. After the installation is complete, fill and bleed the power steering system.

20. Measure and adjust the front toe.

➡ **The front stabilizer shaft insulators grip the stabilizer shaft and provide resistance to rotating the stabilizer shaft.**

➡ **Ensure the steering column dash inner and outer seals are positioned properly on the dash panel.**

POWER STEERING PUMP

REMOVAL & INSTALLATION

See Figure 95.

1. Cover the alternator in order to prevent power steering fluid from dripping on the generator.

2. Place drain pans under the vehicle.

3. Remove as much power steering fluid from the reservoir as possible.

4. If equipped with the 2.0L gasoline engine, remove the air cleaner assembly.

5. If equipped with the 2.4L engine, remove the air cleaner outlet duct.

6. Raise and support the vehicle.

7. Remove the right front wheelhouse front liner.

8. Disconnect the drive belt only from the power steering pump pulley.

9. Remove the power steering fluid reservoir outlet hose clamp.

10. Disconnect the power steering fluid reservoir outlet hose from the power steering pump.

11. Remove the steering gear inlet hose fitting bolt. Upon installation, install 2 NEW power steering gear inlet hose fitting seals and tighten to 28 ft. lbs. (38 Nm).

12. Disconnect the power steering gear inlet hose from the power steering pump.

13. Remove the 3 power steering pump bolts. Upon installation, tighten the bolts to 16 ft. lbs. (22 Nm).

14. Remove the power steering pump.

➡ **Use the CH-25034-C remover in order to remove the power steering pump pulley. Use the CH-25033-C installer in order to install the power steering pump pulley.**

➡ **Ensure the power steering pump pulley is flush with the power steering pump shaft and is aligned with the other pulleys.**

15. To install, reverse the removal procedure.

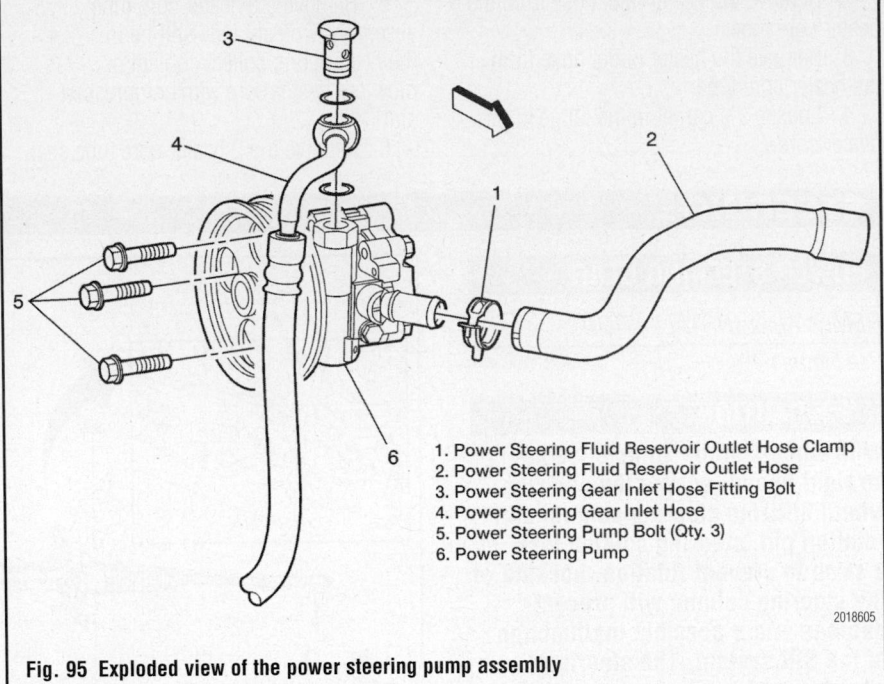

1. Power Steering Fluid Reservoir Outlet Hose Clamp
2. Power Steering Fluid Reservoir Outlet Hose
3. Power Steering Gear Inlet Hose Fitting Bolt
4. Power Steering Gear Inlet Hose
5. Power Steering Pump Bolt (Qty. 3)
6. Power Steering Pump

2018605

Fig. 95 Exploded view of the power steering pump assembly

16. Fill and bleed the power steering system.

17. Clean any excess power steering fluid from the vehicle.

BLEEDING & FLUSHING

➡**Note the following:**

- Use clean, new power steering fluid only.
- Hoses touching the frame, body or engine may cause system noise. Ensure the hoses do not touch any other part of the vehicle.
- Loose connections may not leak, but could allow air into the steering system. Ensure all hose connections are tight.
- Maintain the power steering fluid level throughout the bleeding procedure.

1. Fill the power steering fluid reservoir with fluid to the minimum system level, the FULL COLD level, or the middle of the hash mark on the cap stick fluid level indicator, as applicable.

2. Raise the vehicle until the front wheels are off the ground.

3. With the key in the ON position and with the engine OFF, turn the steering wheel from stop to stop 12 times.

4. If the vehicle is equipped with longer length power steering hoses, turn the steering wheel from stop to stop 15 to 20 times.

5. Verify the power steering fluid level.

6. Start the engine. Rotate the steering wheel from left to right. Inspect the power

steering system for signs of cavitation or fluid aeration, like pump noise or whining.

7. Verify the fluid level. Repeat the bleed procedure, if necessary.

8. Lower the vehicle.

FLUID FILL PROCEDURE

1. Run the engine until the power steering fluid reaches about 80°C (170°F).

2. Turn the engine OFF.

3. If the power steering fluid reservoir is covered by a shield or a cover, remove the shield or the cover, as applicable.

4. Clean the power steering fluid reservoir and the reservoir cap.

5. Remove the reservoir cap.

➡ **Inspect the power steering pump fluid level at regular intervals.**

6. Inspect the power steering fluid level in the reservoir or on the cap stick, as applicable. Ensure that the fluid level is at the HOT/FULL/MAX mark on the cap stick or on the reservoir, as applicable.

✳✳ CAUTION

When adding fluid or making a complete fluid change, always use the proper power steering fluid.

7. Failure to use the proper fluid will cause hose and seal damage and fluid leaks.

8. Add power steering fluid if necessary.

9. Install the reservoir cap.

10. If you removed a shield or a cover, install the shield or the cover, as applicable.

COIL SPRING

REMOVAL & INSTALLATION

See Figure 96.

✳✳ WARNING

To prevent personal injury and/or component damage, use the proper tools to support and compress the coil spring prior to removal of the strut shaft nut when removing the coil spring. The coil spring is under extreme pressure and can become a projectile should the spring separate from the strut before all of the tension is relieved.

1. Raise and support the vehicle.
2. Remove the strut assembly.
3. Using the CH 48845 compressor, compress the front strut assembly.
4. Using the CH 49375 wrench and a TORX® bit, remove the strut mount nut. Upon installation, tighten to 52 ft. lbs. (70 Nm).
5. To disassemble the strut assembly, refer to illustration.
6. To install, reverse the removal procedure.

CONTROL LINKS

REMOVAL & INSTALLATION

See Figure 97.

1. Raise and support the vehicle.
2. Remove the tire and wheels.

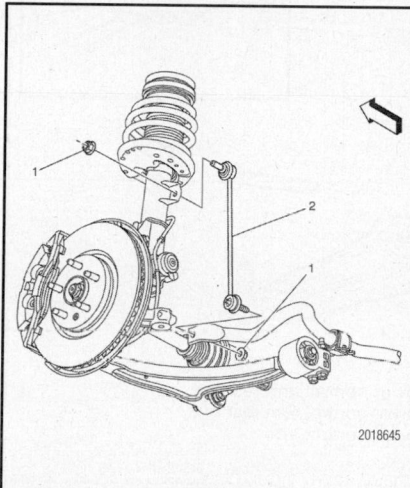

Fig. 97 Removing the control link nuts (1) and link (2) assembly

3. Use the appropriate size socket or wrench to hold the ball stud while removing the stabilizer shaft nut.
4. After the nut has been removed, discard and replace with NEW.
5. Remove the Stabilizer Shaft Link.
6. To install, reverse the removal procedure.
7. Tighten the nuts to 48 ft. lbs. (65 Nm).

LOWER CONTROL ARM

REMOVAL & INSTALLATION

See Figure 98.

1. Raise and support the vehicle.
2. Remove the tire and wheels.
3. Support the knuckle with the proper jack stand.
4. Using the Ball Joint Remover CH 43631 remover , separate the ball joint from the knuckle. Upon installation ; tighten First Pass: 37 ft. lbs. (50 Nm). Final Pass: plus 30 degrees.
5. Discard the steering knuckle bolt. DO NOT re-use, replace with NEW.
6. Remove the front lower control arm nut. Discard the nut. DO NOT re-use, replace with NEW.
7. Remove front lower control arm front bolt. Discard the bolt. DO NOT re-use, replace with NEW. Upon installation; tighten First Pass: 74 ft. lbs (100 Nm). Final Pass: plus 90 degrees.
8. Remove the 2 front lower control arm rear nuts.
9. Remove the 2 front lower control arm rear bolt.
10. Remove and discard the bolt. DO NOT re-use, replace with NEW. Upon installation, tighten First Pass: 74 ft. lbs (100 Nm). Final Pass: plus 75 degrees.
11. Remove the front lower control arm.

✳✳ CAUTION

This component is equipped with torque-to-yield fasteners. Install a NEW torque-to-yield fastener when installing this component. Failure to replace the torque-to-yield fastener could cause damage to the vehicle or component.

12. To install, reverse the removal procedure.
13. Verify the wheel alignment.

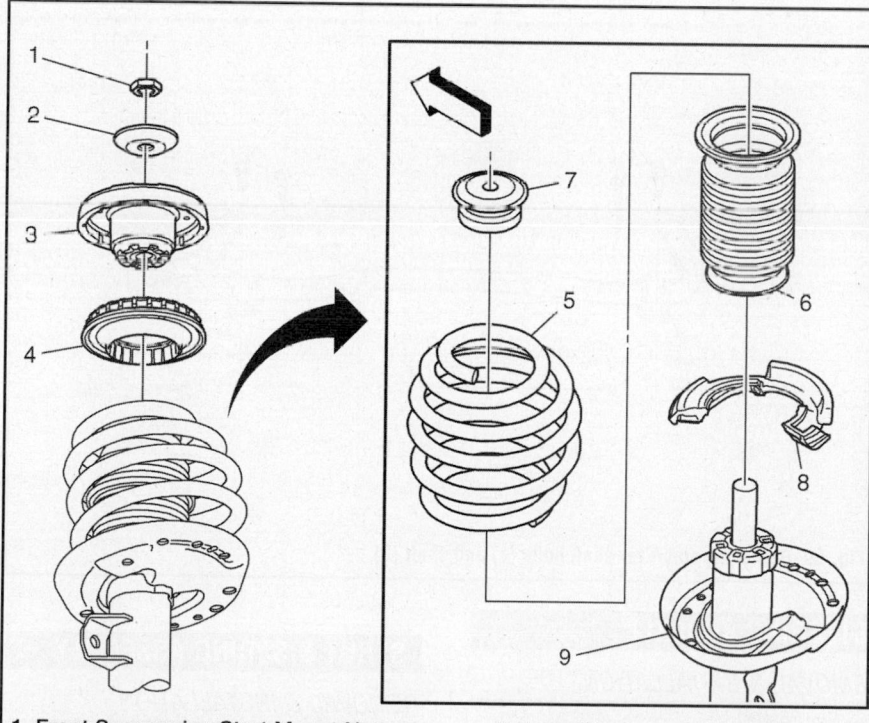

1. Front Suspension Strut Mount Nut
2. Front Suspension Strut Mount Washer
3. Front Suspension Strut Mount Insulator
4. Front Suspension Strut Mount Bearing
5. Front Spring
6. Front Shock Absorber Boot
7. Front Suspension Strut Bumper
8. Front Spring Lower Insulator
9. Front Suspension Strut

Fig. 96 Exploded view of the coil and strut assembly

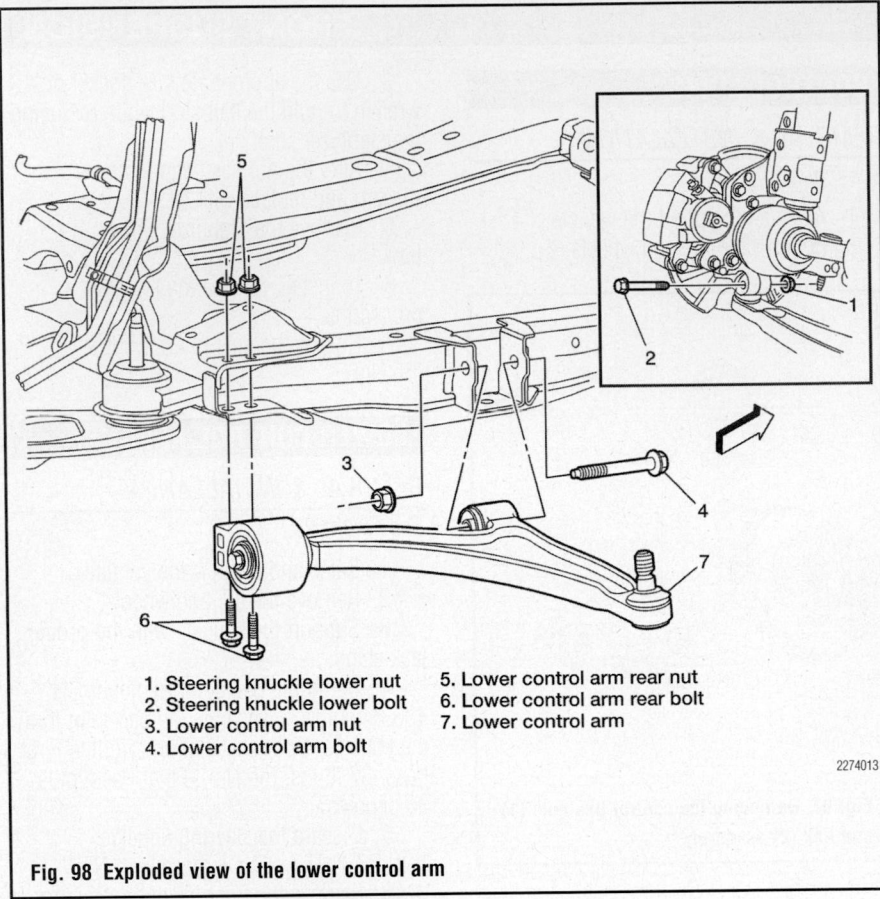

1. Steering knuckle lower nut
2. Steering knuckle lower bolt
3. Lower control arm nut
4. Lower control arm bolt
5. Lower control arm rear nut
6. Lower control arm rear bolt
7. Lower control arm

Fig. 98 Exploded view of the lower control arm

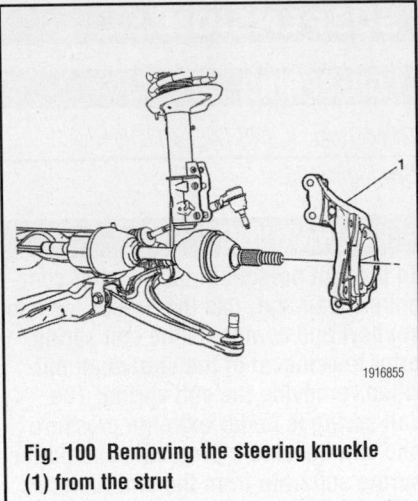

Fig. 100 Removing the steering knuckle (1) from the strut

5. Remove the strut nuts and bolts from the strut to the knuckle.

6. Separate the lower ball joint from the knuckle.

To install:

7. To complete installation, reverse the remaining removal procedure.

8. Check and adjust the front wheel alignment, if needed.

STABILIZER BAR

REMOVAL & INSTALLATION

See Figure 99.

➡The front stabilizer shaft is serviced with the insulators and clamps.

1. Raise and support the vehicle.

2. Remove the tire and wheel assembly.

3. Support the front cradle with the proper jackstands.

4. Remove the stabilizer shaft links from the stabilizer shaft.

5. Remove rear transmission bolt.

6. Lower the rear front cradle to gain enough clearance to remove the stabilizer shaft.

7. Remove and discard the bolts. DO NOT reuse, replace with NEW only.

➡Perform this procedure with the suspension in the neutral position, with the vehicle on a level surface.

8. Remove the stabilizer shaft insulators clamp nuts.

9. To install, reverse the removal procedure.

10. Tighten the clamp nuts to 16 ft. lbs. (22 Nm) plus 30 degrees.

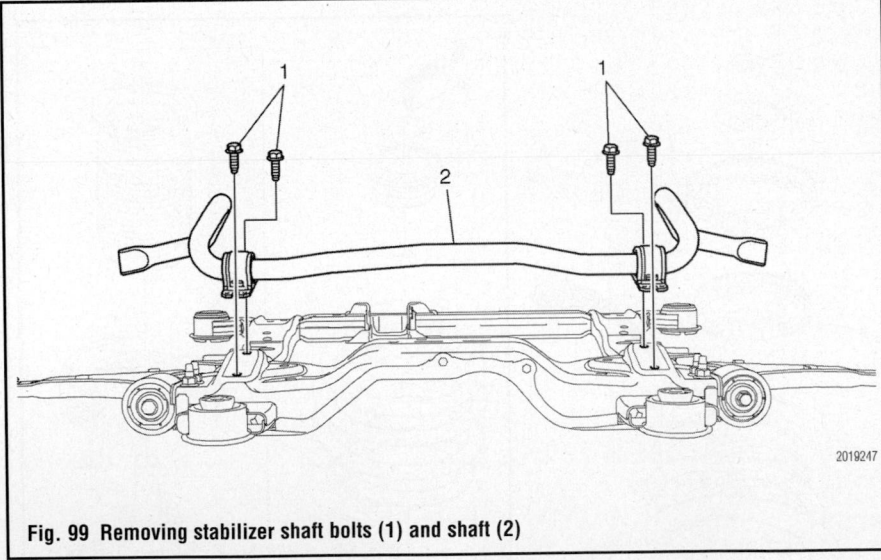

Fig. 99 Removing stabilizer shaft bolts (1) and shaft (2)

STEERING KNUCKLE

REMOVAL & INSTALLATION

See Figure 100.

1. Raise and support the vehicle.

2. Remove the tire and wheel assembly.

3. Remove the wheel bearing/hub.

4. Separate the outer tie rod end from the knuckle.

STRUT & SPRING ASSEMBLY

REMOVAL & INSTALLATION

See Figure 101.

1. Raise and support the vehicle.

2. Remove the tire and wheel assembly.

3. Remove the stabilizer shaft link from the strut.

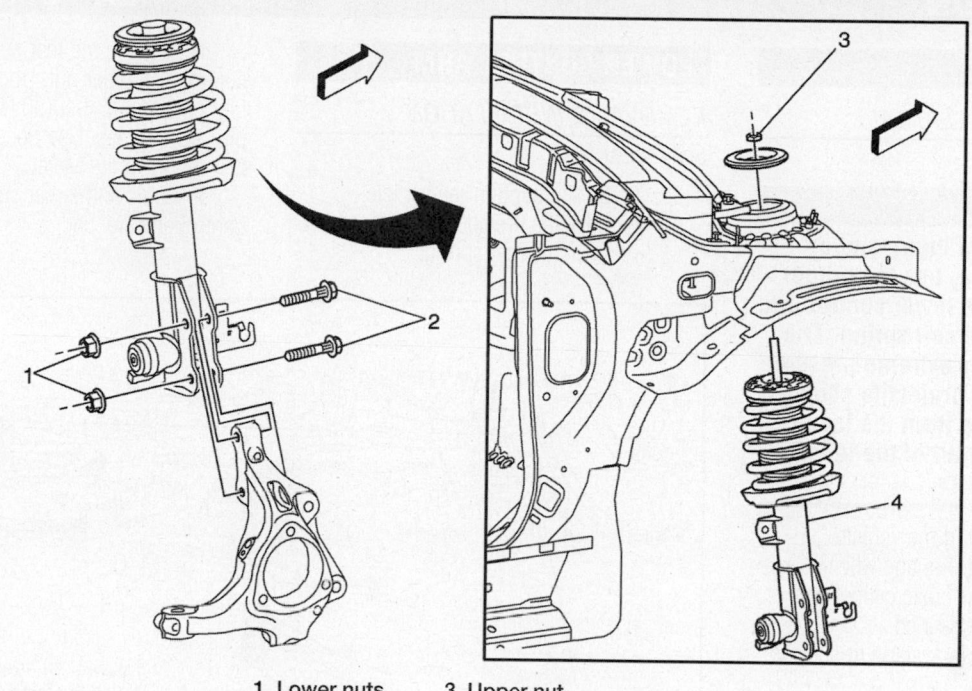

1. Lower nuts   3. Upper nut
2. Lower bolts   4. Strut and spring assembly

2304973

Fig. 101 Remove the front suspension strut from the vehicle

4. Using a suitable jack stand, support the front lower control arm.

5. Disconnect the wheel speed sensor electrical connector from the front strut, if equipped.

6. Remove brake hose, connector and clip from the strut.

7. Remove the steering knuckle to strut nuts. Upon installation; first pass: 63 ft. lbs. (85 Nm). Final pass: 60 degrees

8. Remove and discard the 2 steering knuckle bolt. Replace with NEW only.

9. Remove the Front Suspension Strut Mount Nut plastic cap, if equipped. Using the CH 49375 wrench , remove the nut. Upon installation, tighten to 40 ft. lbs. (55 Nm).

✳✳ CAUTION

This component is equipped with torque-to-yield fasteners. Install a NEW torque-to-yield fastener when installing this component. Failure to replace the torque-to-yield fastener could cause damage to the vehicle or component.

10. Remove the strut.

To install:

11. To complete installation, reverse the removal procedure.

12. Check and adjust the front wheel alignment, if needed.

WHEEL BEARINGS

REMOVAL & INSTALLATION

See Figure 102.

1. Raise and support the vehicle.
2. Remove the tire and wheel.
3. Remove the wheel speed sensor.
4. Remove the front brake rotor.

5. If needed, remove the front brake splash shield.

6. Remove the 3 bolts.

7. Use the appropriate tool to separate the wheel bearing/hub from the wheel drive shaft.

8. To install, reverse the removal procedure.

9. Tighten the wheel bearing bolts to 79 ft. lbs. (108 Nm).

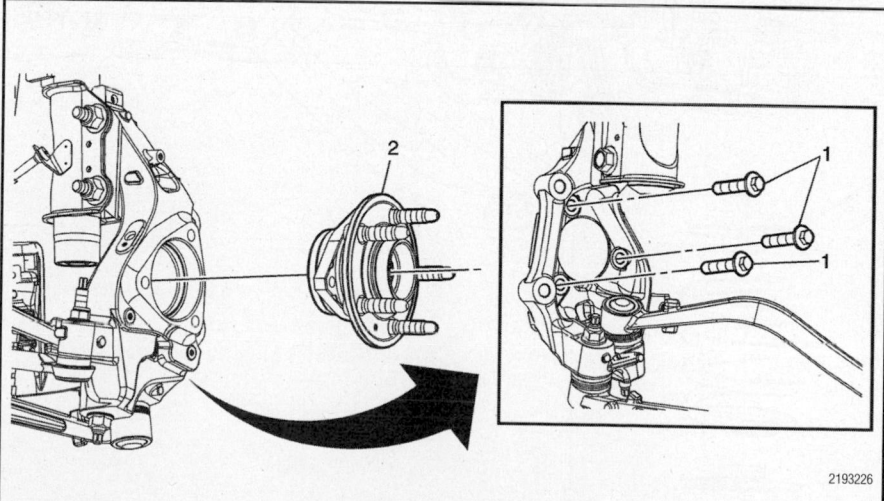

2193226

Fig. 102 View of the front wheel bearing bolts (1) and bearing/hub assembly (2)

SUSPENSION

REAR SUSPENSION

COIL SPRING

REMOVAL & INSTALLATION

See Figure 103.

✳✳ WARNING

To prevent personal injury and/or component damage, use the proper tools to support the lower control arm when removing the coil spring. The coil spring is under extreme pressure and can become a projectile should the spring separate from the lower control arm before all of the tension is relieved.

1. Raise and support the vehicle.
2. Remove the rear tire and wheel.
3. Remove the rear brake caliper and relocate to the side, if needed.
4. Use the proper jack stand to support the lower control arm.
5. Disconnect the lower control arm from the rear wheel hub bracket.
6. Remove the rear spring insulator (upper).
7. Remove the rear spring insulator (lower).
8. To install, reverse the removal procedure.

LOWER CONTROL ARM

REMOVAL & INSTALLATION

See Figure 104.

1. Raise and support the vehicle.
2. Remove the tire and wheel assembly.
3. Remove the rear spring.

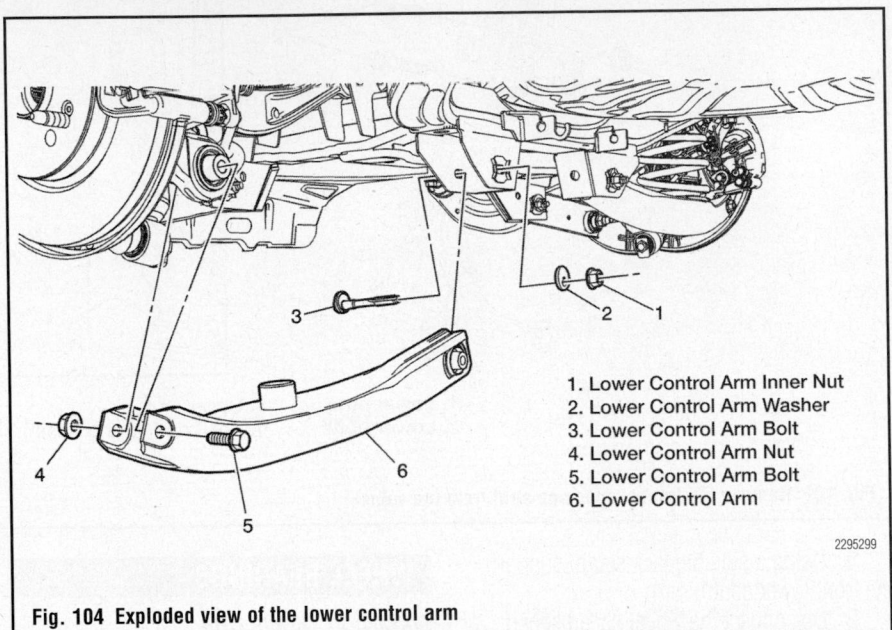

1. Lower Control Arm Inner Nut
2. Lower Control Arm Washer
3. Lower Control Arm Bolt
4. Lower Control Arm Nut
5. Lower Control Arm Bolt
6. Lower Control Arm

Fig. 104 Exploded view of the lower control arm

4. Remove the rear suspension lower control arm inner nut. Upon installation, first pass: 66 ft. lbs. (90 Nm). Final Pass: plus 60 degrees. Use Special Tool EN-45059 Angle Meter.
5. Remove the rear suspension lower control arm washer.

6. Remove the rear suspension lower control arm bolt. Remove and discard the bolt. DO NOT reuse, replace with NEW only.
7. Remove the rear suspension lower control arm nut.
8. Rear Suspension Lower Control Arm Bolt

   a. Remove and discard the bolt. DO NOT reuse, replace with NEW only.
   b. First Pass: 51 ft. lbs. (70 Nm).
   c. Final Pass: plus 90 degrees
9. Remove the rear lower control arm.

✳✳ CAUTION

This component is equipped with torque-to-yield fasteners. Install a NEW torque-to-yield fastener when installing this component. Failure to replace the torque-to-yield fastener could cause damage to the vehicle or component.

10. To install, reverse the removal procedure.
11. Check the rear alignment after installation.

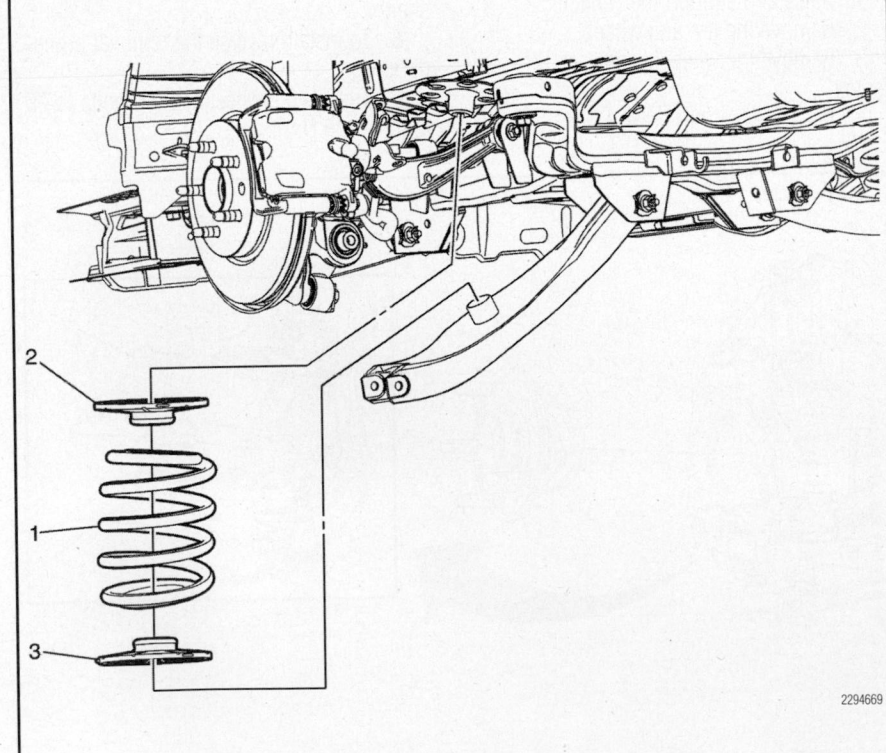

Fig. 103 Exploded view of the rear spring (1), upper (2) and lower (3) rear spring insulator

STABILIZER BAR

REMOVAL & INSTALLATION

See Figure 105.

1. Raise and support the vehicle.
2. Remove the tire and wheel assembly.
3. Remove the rear muffler assembly.
4. Remove the rear suspension control arm bolts from the body.
5. Remove the rear spring.
6. Remove the park brake cables from the trailing arms.
7. Without disconnecting the hydraulic brake hose from the caliper, remove and support the brake caliper.
8. Remove the lower shock absorber bolts.
9. Support and secure adjustable jack stands to the rear support.
10. Mark up support position to body with spray paint.
11. Remove the mounting bolts for the support.
12. Lower the support enough to gain access to the rear stabilizer shaft insulator clamps mounting bolts.
13. Remove the stabilizer shaft from the stabilizer shaft link
14. Remove the stabilizer shaft bolts.
15. Remove the stabilizer shaft assembly from the support.

To install:

16. Load the suspension with the proper jack stand before tightening the bolts to specifications.
17. Install the stabilizer shaft on the support.
18. Using a ratchet wrench and the EN-45059 meter, tighten the NEW clamp bolts to:
    a. First Pass: 16 ft. lbs. (22 Nm).

b. Final Pass: plus 30 degrees.
19. Install the stabilizer shaft to stabilizer shaft link.
20. Raise the rear support back into position.
21. To complete the installation, reverse the removal procedure.

STRUT ASSEMBLY

REMOVAL & INSTALLATION

See Figure 106.

1. Raise and support the vehicle.
2. Remove the rear tire and wheel assembly.
3. Remove the rear wheelhouse panel liner from the vehicle.
4. Rear Shock Absorber Bolts:
   a. Remove and discard the bolt. Replace with NEW only.
   b. Upon installation, tighten to 74 ft. lbs. (100 Nm).
5. Rear Shock Absorber Bolt:
   a. Remove and discard the bolt. Replace with NEW only.
   b. Upon installation, tighten: First Pass:110 ft. lbs. (150 Nm). Final Pass: plus 70 degrees. Use Special Tools EN-45059 Angle Meter .

6. Remove the shock absorber nut. Upon installation, tighten to 15 ft. lbs. (20 Nm)
7. Remove the rear shock absorber upper mount.
8. Transfer the upper mount to the new shock absorber.
9. Remove the shock absorber
10. Disconnect any electrical connectors, if equipped.
11. To complete the installation, reverse the removal procedure.

UPPER CONTROL ARM

REMOVAL & INSTALLATION

See Figure 107.

1. Raise and support the vehicle.
2. Remove the tire and wheel assembly.
3. Rear Suspension Upper Control Arm Nut
4. Remove and discard the bolt. DO NOT reuse, replace with NEW only. Upon installation, tighten: First Pass: 52 ft. lbs. (70 Nm). Final Pass: plus 60 degrees.2
5. Remove the rear suspension upper control arm.

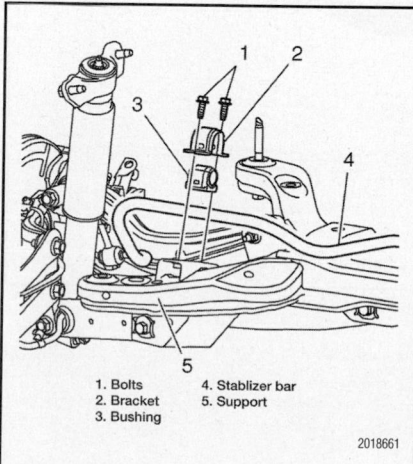

1. Bolts   4. Stablizer bar
2. Bracket
3. Bushing
5. Support

2018661

Fig. 105 Removing the stabilizer shaft assembly

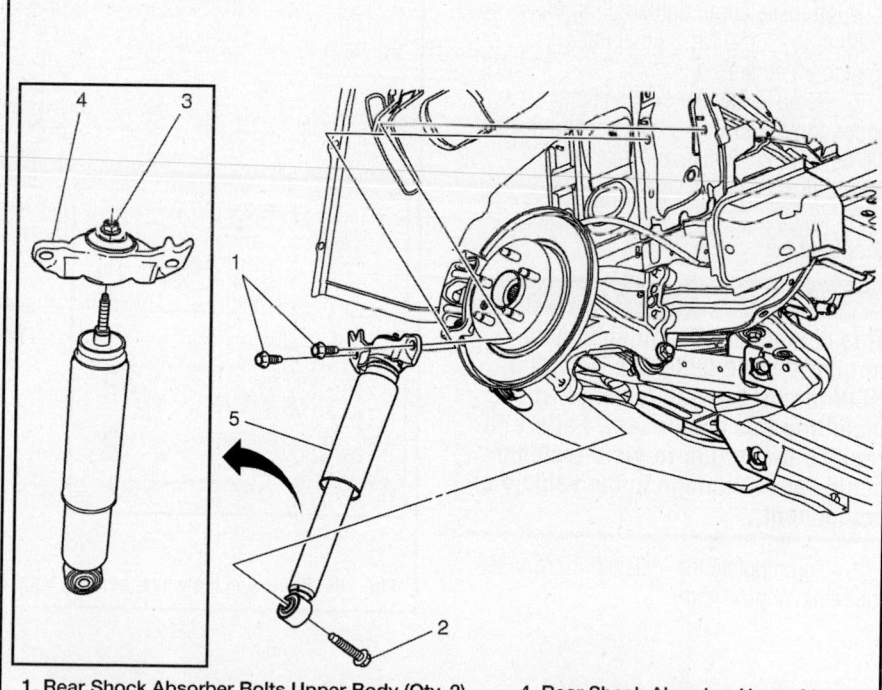

1. Rear Shock Absorber Bolts Upper Body (Qty. 2)
2. Rear Shock Absorber Bolt
3. Shock Absorber Nut
4. Rear Shock Absorber Upper Mount
5. Shock Absorber

2018669

Fig. 106 Exploded view of the shock absorber assembly

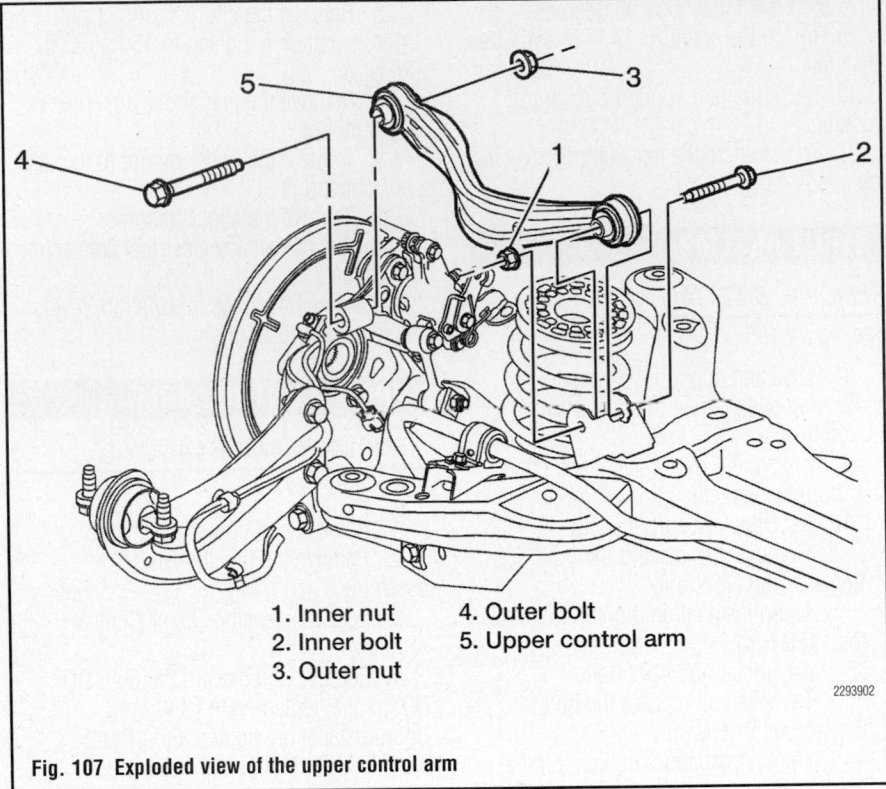

Fig. 107 Exploded view of the upper control arm

1. Inner nut
2. Inner bolt
3. Outer nut
4. Outer bolt
5. Upper control arm

6. Rear Suspension Upper Control Arm Nut

   a. Remove and discard the bolt. DO NOT reuse, replace with NEW only. Upon installation, tighten: First Pass: 85 ft. lbs. (150 Nm). Final Pass: plus 90 degrees .

7. Remove the rear suspension upper control arm bolt. Remove and discard the bolt. Do Not reuse, replace with NEW only.

8. Remove the rear suspension upper control arm.

✳✳ CAUTION

This component is equipped with torque-to-yield fasteners. Install a NEW torque-to-yield fastener when installing this component. Failure to replace the torque-to-yield fastener could cause damage to the vehicle or component.

9. To complete the installation, reverse the removal procedure.

WHEEL BEARINGS

REMOVAL & INSTALLATION

See Figure 108.

1. Remove the rear tire and wheel.
2. Remove the rear wheel speed sensor.
3. Remove the rear brake rotor.
4. Remove and discard the 5 wheel bearing bolts. DO NOT reuse, replace with NEW only.

   a. Upon installation, tighten to 66 ft. lbs. (90 Nm) +75 degrees.

5. Remove the rear wheel bearing.

✳✳ CAUTION

This component is equipped with torque-to-yield fasteners. Install a NEW torque-to-yield fastener when installing this component. Failure to replace the torque-to-yield fastener could cause damage to the vehicle or component.

6. To complete the installation, reverse the removal procedure.

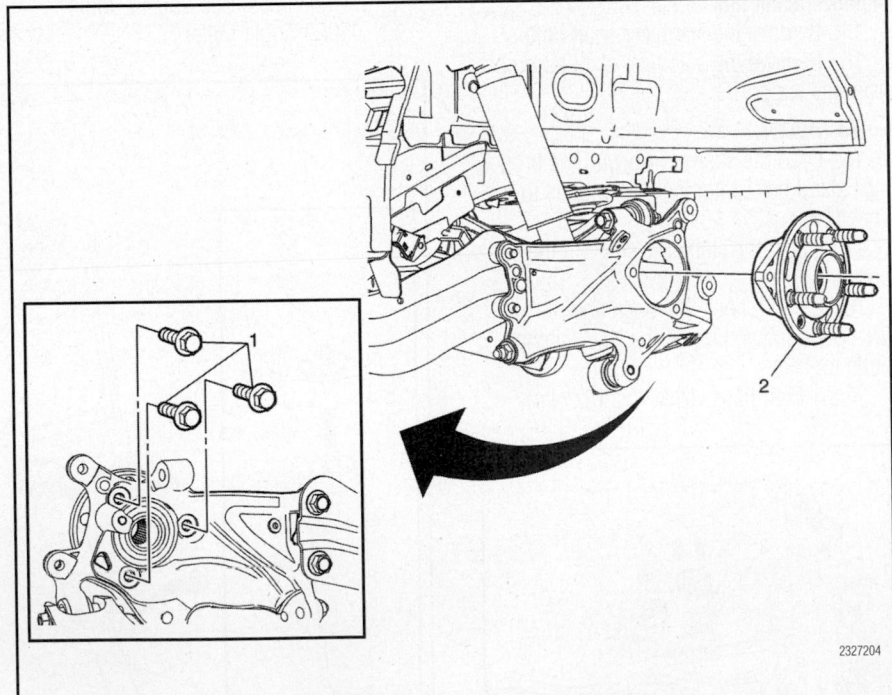

Fig. 108 Removing the wheel bearing bolts (1) and wheel bearing (2)

CHEVROLET AND GMC

20

Sierra • Sierra Hybrid • Silverado • Silverado Hybrid

SPECIFICATIONS AND MAINTENANCE CHARTS

ENGINE AND VEHICLE IDENTIFICATION

Code ①	Liters (cc)	Cu. In.	Cyl.	Fuel Sys.	Engine Type	Eng. Mfg.
X	4.3 (4297)	262	6	MFI	V6	GM
A	4.8 (4796)	293	8	SFI	V8	GM
3	5.3 (5296)	323	8	SFI	V8	GM
0	5.3 (5296)	323	8	SFI	V8	GM
K	6.0 (5995)	366	8	SFI	V8	GM
G	6.0 (5995)	366	8	SFI	V8	GM
J	6.0 (5995)	366	8	SFI	Hybrid	GM
2	6.2 (6195)	378	8	SFI	V8	GM
6	6.6 (6595)	402	8	DPI	Diesel	Isuzu/GM
8	6.6 (6595)	402	8	DPI	Diesel	Isuzu/GM
L	6.6 (6595)	402	8	DPI	Diesel	Isuzu/GM

Code ②	Year
A	2010
B	2011

① 8th position of VIN

② 10th position of VIN

25742_SIER_C0001

GENERAL ENGINE SPECIFICATIONS

All measurements are given in inches.

Year	Model	Engine Displacement Liters (cc)	Engine ID/VIN	Fuel System Type	Net Horsepower @ rpm	Net Torque @ rpm (ft. lbs.)	Bore x Stroke (in.)	Compression Ratio	Oil Pressure @ rpm
2010-2011	Sierra/Silverado	4.3 (4297)	LU3/X	MFI	NA	NA	4.01x3.48	9.2:1	24@4000
2010-2011	Sierra/Silverado	4.8 (4796)	L20/A	SFI	302@5600	305@4600	3.78x3.27	9.08:1	24@4000
2010-2011	Sierra/Silverado	5.3 (5296)	LC9/3	SFI	315@5200	335@4000	3.78x3.62	9.95:1	24@4000
2010-2011	Sierra/Silverado	5.3 (5296)	LMG/0	SFI	315@5200	335@4000	3.78x3.62	9.95:1	24@4000
2010 Only	Sierra/Silverado	6.0 (5995)	LY6/K	SFI	360@5400	380@4200	4.00x3.62	9.67:1	24@4000
2010-2011	Sierra/Silverado	6.0 (5995)	L96/G	SFI	360@5400	380@4200	4.00x3.62	9.67:1	24@4000
2010-2011	Sierra/Silverado	6.0 (5995) Hybrid	LZ1/J	SFI	NA	NA	4.00x3.62	10.7:1	45@4000
2010-2011	Sierra/Silverado	6.2 (6195)	L9H/2	SFI	NA	NA	4.07x3.62	10.5:1	24@4000
2010 Only	Sierra/Silverado	6.6 (6595) Diesel	LMM/6	DPI	300@3000	520@1600	4.06x3.90	16.8:1	28@1800
2011 Only	Sierra/Silverado	6.6 (6595) Diesel	LML/8	DPI	300@3000	520@1600	4.06x3.90	16.8:1	28@1800
2011 Only	Sierra/Silverado	6.6 (6595) Diesel	LGH/L	DPI	300@3000	520@1600	4.06x3.90	16.8:1	28@1800

NA Not Available

25742_SIER_C0002

ENGINE TUNE-UP SPECIFICATIONS

Year	Engine Displacement Liters	Engine ID/VIN	Spark Plug Gap (in.)	Ignition Timing (deg.)		Fuel Pump (psi)	Idle Speed (rpm)		Valve Clearance	
				MT	AT		MT	AT	Intake	Exhaust
2010-2011	4.3 (4297)	LU3/X	0.060	①	①	NA	NA	NA	NA	NA
2010-2011	4.8 (4796)	L20/A	0.040	①	①	NA	NA	NA	②	②
2010-2011	5.3 (5296)	LC9/3	0.040	①	①	NA	NA	NA	②	②
2010-2011	5.3 (5296)	LMG/0	0.040	①	①	NA	NA	NA	②	②
2010 Only	6.0 (5995)	LY6/K	0.040	①	①	NA	NA	NA	②	②
2010-2011	6.0 (5995)	L96/G	0.040	①	①	NA	NA	NA	②	②
2010-2011	6.0 (5995) Hybrid	LZ1/J	0.040	①	①	NA	NA	NA	②	②
2010-2011	6.2 (6195)	L9H/2	0.040	①	①	NA	NA	NA	②	②
2010 Only	6.6 (6595) Diesel	LMM/6	NA	NA	NA	NA	680	680	NA	NA
2011 Only	6.6 (6595) Diesel	LML/8	NA	NA	NA	NA	680	680	NA	NA
2011 Only	6.6 (6595) Diesel	LGH/L	NA	NA	NA	NA	680	680	NA	NA

① Ignition timing is controlled by the Engine Control Module (ECM).

② Net Lash - No adjustment

25742_SIFR_C0003

CAPACITIES

Year	Model	Engine Displacement Liters	Engine ID/VIN	Engine Oil with Filter	Transmission (pts.) Auto.	Transmission (pts.) Manual	Drive Axle (pts.) Front	Drive Axle (pts.) Rear	Transfer Case (pts.)	Fuel Tank (gal.)	Cooling System (qts.)
2010-2011	Sierra/ Silverado	4.3 (4297)	LU3/X	4.5	①	②	③	④	3.2	⑤	16.5
2010-2011	Sierra/ Silverado	4.8 (4796)	L20/A	6.0	①	②	③	④	3.2	⑤	16.9
2010-2011	Sierra/ Silverado	5.3 (5296)	LC9/3	6.0	①	②	③	④	3.2	⑤	16.9
2010-2011	Sierra/ Silverado	5.3 (5296)	LMG/0	6.0	①	②	③	④	3.2	⑤	16.9
2010 Only	Sierra/ Silverado	6.0 (5995)	LY6/K	6.0	①	②	③	④	3.2	⑤	⑥
2010-2011	Sierra/ Silverado	6.0 (5995)	L96/G	6.0	①	②	③	④	3.2	⑤	⑥
2010-2011	Sierra/ Silverado	6.0 (5995) Hybrid	LZ1/J	6.0	①	②	③	④	3.2	⑤	17.2
2010-2011	Sierra/ Silverado	6.2 (6195)	L9H/2	6.0	①	②	③	④	3.2	⑤	⑦
2010 Only	Sierra/ Silverado	6.6 (6595) Diesel	LMM/6	10.0	①	②	③	④	3.2	⑤	21.6
2011 Only	Sierra/ Silverado	6.6 (6595) Diesel	LML/8	10.0	①	②	③	④	3.2	⑤	21.6
2011 Only	Sierra/ Silverado	6.6 (6595) Diesel	LGH/L	10.0	①	②	③	④	3.2	⑤	21.6

NOTE: All capacities are approximate. Add fluid gradually and ensure a proper fluid level is obtained.

① Auto Trans Capacities: Pan removal

    2ML70: 11.5 qts.

    4L60-E/4L65-E/4L70-E: 5.0 qts.

    6L80-E: 6.0 qts.

    6L90-E: 6.3 qts.

    Allison: Initial fill: 12.7 qts.; Refill: 7.4 qts.

② Manual Trans Capacities:

    Tremec 5-speed M96: 3.7 qts.

    Tremec 5-speed TZ0: 4.6 qts.

③ Front Axle 1000 Series (8.25"): 1.51 qts

    Front Axle 2000 Series (9.25"): 1.83 qts.

④ 1000 Series with 8.6": 2.15 qts.

    1000 Series 9.5" with Light Duty Beam: 2.75 qts.

    2000 Series 9.5" with Heavy Duty Beam: 2.75 qts.

    2000 Series 10.5": 2.75 qts.

    2000 Series 11.5": 3.17 qts.

    3000 Series 11.5": 3.17 qts.

⑤ 1500 Series standard and short box: 26.0 gal.

    1500 Series long box: 34.0 gal.

    2010 2500 Series standard box: 26.0 gal.

    2011 2500 Series standard box: 36.0 gal.

    2010 2500 Series Long box: 34.0 gal.

    2011 2500 Series long box: 36.0 gal.

⑥ 1500 Series: 16.8 qts.

    2500 Series: 16.4 qts.

⑦ 2010 model: 17.6 qts.

    2011 model: 16.8 qts.

25742_SIER_C0004

FLUID SPECIFICATIONS

Year	Model	Engine Disp. Liters	Engine ID/VIN	Engine Oil	Manual Trans.	Auto. Trans.	Drive Axle Front	Drive Axle Rear	Transfer Case	Power Steering Fluid	Brake Master Cylinder	Cooling System
2010-2011	Sierra/ Silverado	4.3 (4297)	LU3/X	5W-30	①	②	③	④	②	⑤	DOT-3	⑥
2010-2011	Sierra/ Silverado	4.8 (4796)	L20/A	5W-30	①	②	③	④	②	⑤	DOT-3	⑥
2010-2011	Sierra/ Silverado	5.3 (5296)	LC9/3	5W-30	①	②	③	④	②	⑤	DOT-3	⑥
2010-2011	Sierra/ Silverado	5.3 (5296)	LMG/0	5W-30	①	②	③	④	②	⑤	DOT-3	⑥
2010 Only	Sierra/ Silverado	6.0 (5995)	LY6/K	5W-30	①	②	③	④	②	⑤	DOT-3	⑥
2010-2011	Sierra/ Silverado	6.0 (5995)	L96/G	5W-30	①	②	③	④	②	⑤	DOT-3	⑥
2010-2011	Sierra/ Silverado Hybrid	6.0 (5995)	LZ1/J	5W-30	①	②	③	④	②	⑤	DOT-3	⑥
2010-2011	Sierra/ Silverado	6.2 (6195)	L9H/2	5W-30	①	②	③	④	②	⑤	DOT-3	⑥
2010 Only	Sierra/ Silverado Diesel	6.6 (6595)	LMM/6	15W-40	①	②	③	④	②	⑤	DOT-3	⑥
2011 Only	Sierra/ Silverado Diesel	6.6 (6595)	LML/8	15W-40	①	②	③	④	②	⑤	DOT-3	⑥
2011 Only	Sierra/ Silverado Diesel	6.6 (6595)	LGH/L	15W-40	①	②	③	④	②	⑤	DOT-3	⑥

DOT Department of Transportation

① Syncromesh Transmission Fluid GM P/N 12345349

② DEXRON-VI ATF

③ 1500 Series: 80W-90 Axle Lubricant
   2500 Series: 75W-90 Synthetic Axle Lubricant

④ 75W-90 Synthetic Axle Lubricant

⑤ GM Power Steering Fluid GM P/N 89021186

⑥ 50/50 mixture of clean, drinkable water and DEX-COOL coolant

25742_SIER_C0005

VALVE SPECIFICATIONS

Year	Engine Displacement Liters	Engine ID/VIN	Seat Angle (deg.)	Face Angle (deg.)	Spring Test Pressure (lbs. @ in.)	Spring Free-Length (in.)	Spring Installed Height (in.)	Stem-to-Guide Clearance (in.) Intake	Stem-to-Guide Clearance (in.) Exhaust	Stem Diameter (in.) Intake	Stem Diameter (in.) Exhaust
2010-2011	4.3 (4297)	LU3/X	46	45	76-84@ 1.70	2.020	1.670-1.700	0.0010-0.0027	0.0010-0.0027	NA	NA
2010-2011	4.8 (4796)	L20/A	46	45	76@1.80	2.080	1.800	0.0010-0.0026	0.0010-0.0026	0.3130-0.3140	0.3130-0.3140
2010-2011	5.3 (5296)	LC9/3	46	45	76@1.80	2.080	1.800	0.0010-0.0026	0.0010-0.0026	0.3130-0.3140	0.3130-0.3140
2010-2011	5.3 (5296)	LMG/0	46	45	76@1.80	2.080	1.800	0.0010-0.0026	0.0010-0.0026	0.3130-0.3140	0.3130-0.3140
2010 Only	6.0 (5995)	LY6/K	46	45	76@1.80	2.080	1.800	0.0010-0.0026	0.0010-0.0026	0.3130-0.3140	0.3130-0.3140
2010-2011	6.0 (5995)	L96/G	46	45	76@1.80	2.080	1.800	0.0010-0.0026	0.0010-0.0026	0.3130-0.3140	0.3130-0.3140
2010-2011	6.0 (5995) Hybrid	LZ1/J	46	45	76@1.80	2.080	1.800	0.0010-0.0026	0.0010-0.0026	0.3130-0.3140	0.3130-0.3140
2010-2011	6.2 (6195)	L9H/2	46	45	76@1.80	2.080	1.800	0.0010-0.0026	0.0010-0.0026	0.3130-0.3140	0.3130-0.3140
2010 Only	6.6 (6595) Diesel	LMM/6	45	45	71-81.6@ 1.61	2.228	1.614	0.0012-0.0025	0.0015-0.0028	0.2800	0.2800
2011 Only	6.6 (6595) Diesel	LML/8	45	45	71-81.6@ 1.61	2.228	1.614	0.0012-0.0025	0.0015-0.0028	0.2800	0.2800
2011 Only	6.6 (6595) Diesel	LGH/L	45	45	71-81.6@ 1.61	2.228	1.614	0.0012-0.0025	0.0015-0.0028	0.2800	0.2800

NA Not Available

25742_SIER_C0006

CAMSHAFT SPECIFICATIONS

All measurements in inches unless noted

Year	Engine Displacement Liters	Engine Code/VIN	Journal Diameter	Brg. Oil Clearance	Shaft End-play	Runout	Journal Bore	Lobe Lift	
								Intake	Exhaust
2010-2011	4.3 (4297)	LU3/X	1.8677-1.8696	NA	0.001-0.009	0.0039	NA	0.2704	0.2793
2010-2011	4.8 (4796)	L20/A	2.164-2.166	0.0009-0.0038	0.001-0.012	0.002	①	0.2740	0.2810
2010-2011	5.3 (5296)	LC9/3	2.164-2.166	0.0009-0.0038	0.001-0.012	0.002	①	0.2740	0.2810
2010-2011	5.3 (5296)	LMG/0	2.164-2.166	0.0009-0.0038	0.001-0.012	0.002	①	0.2740	0.2810
2010 Only	6.0 (5995)	LY6/K	2.164-2.166	0.0009-0.0038	0.001-0.012	0.002	①	0.2740	0.2810
2010-2011	6.0 (5995)	L96/G	2.164-2.166	0.0009-0.0038	0.001-0.012	0.002	①	0.2740	0.2810
2010-2011	6.0 (5995) Hybrid	LZ1/J	2.165-2.166	0.0002-0.0038	0.001-0.012	0.002	①	②	③
2010-2011	6.2 (6195)	L9H/2	2.164-2.166	0.0009-0.0038	0.001-0.012	0.002	①	0.2740	0.2810
2010 Only	6.6 (6595) Diesel	LMM/6	2.399-2.400	NA	0.0079	0.002	2.4016-2.4028	0.2863	0.2326
2011 Only	6.6 (6595) Diesel	LML/8	2.399-2.400	NA	0.0079	0.002	2.4016-2.4028	0.2863	0.2326
2011 Only	6.6 (6595) Diesel	LGH/L	2.399-2.400	NA	0.0079	0.002	2.4016-2.4028	0.2863	0.2326

NA Not Available

① Bearing bore 1 & 5: 2.345-2.347 inches

   Bearing bore 2 & 4: 2.325-2.327 inches

   Bearing bore 3: 0.306-2.308 inches

② Non Active Fuel Management (AFM) cylinders: 0.279 inches

   AFM cylinders: 0.283 inches

③ Non AFM cylinders: 0.282 inches

CRANKSHAFT AND CONNECTING ROD SPECIFICATIONS

All measurements are given in inches.

Year	Engine Displacement Liters	Engine ID/VIN	Crankshaft				Connecting Rod		
			Main Brg. Journal Dia.	Main Brg. Oil Clearance	Shaft End-play	Thrust on No.	Journal Diameter	Oil Clearance	Side Clearance
2010-2011	4.3 (4297)	LU3/X	①	②	0.0020-0.0080	NA	2.2487-2.2497	0.0015-0.0031	0.0060-0.0170
2010-2011	4.8 (4796)	L20/A	①	②	0.0020-0.0080	3	2.2487-2.2497	0.0015-0.0031	0.0060-0.0170
2010-2011	5.3 (5296)	LC9/3	①	②	0.0020-0.0080	3	2.2487-2.2497	0.0015-0.0031	0.0060-0.0170
2010-2011	5.3 (5296)	LMG/0	①	②	0.0020-0.0080	3	2.2487-2.2497	0.0015-0.0031	0.0060-0.0170
2010 Only	6.0 (5995)	LY6/K	①	②	0.0020-0.0080	3	2.2487-2.2497	0.0015-0.0031	0.0060-0.0170
2010-2011	6.0 (5995)	L96/G	①	②	0.0020-0.0080	3	2.2487-2.2497	0.0015-0.0031	0.0060-0.0170
2010-2011	6.0 (5995) Hybrid	LZ1/J	2.5580-2.5590	0.0008-0.0021	0.0015-0.0078	3	2.0991-2.0999	0.0009-0.0025	0.00433-0.0200
2010-2011	6.2 (6195)	L9H/2	①	②	0.0020-0.0080	3	2.2487-2.2497	0.0015-0.0031	0.0060-0.0170
2010 Only	6.6 (6595) Diesel	LMM/6	3.1459-3.1466	0.0015-0.0028	0.0016-0.0081	NA	2.4764-2.4772	0.0014-0.0030	0.0122-0.0193
2011 Only	6.6 (6595) Diesel	LML/8	3.1459-3.1466	0.0015-0.0028	0.0016-0.0081	NA	2.4764-2.4772	0.0014-0.0030	0.0122-0.0193
2011 Only	6.6 (6595) Diesel	LGH/L	3.1459-3.1466	0.0015-0.0028	0.0016-0.0081	NA	2.4764-2.4772	0.0014-0.0030	0.0122-0.0193

NA Not available

① #1 Main: 2.4488-2.4495 inches

#2 & 3 Mains: 2.4485-2.4494 inches

#4 Main: 2.4480-2.4489 inches

② #1 Main: 0.0008-0.0020 inches

#2, 3 &4 Mains: 0.0011-0.0023 inches

PISTON AND RING SPECIFICATIONS

All measurements are given in inches.

Year	Engine Displacement Liters	Engine ID/VIN	Piston Clearance	Ring Gap			Ring Side Clearance		
				Top Compression	Bottom Compression	Oil Control	Top Compression	Bottom Compression	Oil Control
2010-2011	4.3 (4297)	LU3/X	0.0007-0.0024	0.0100-0.0160	0.0150-0.0230	0.0100-0.0290	0.0012-0.0027	0.0030-0.0110	0.0018-0.0077
2010-2011	4.8 (4796)	L20/A	-0.0014 0.0006	0.0090-0.0170	0.0170-0.0270	0.0070-0.0290	0.00157-0.00335	0.00157-0.00310	0.0005-0.0078
2010-2011	5.3 (5296)	LC9/3	-0.0014 0.0006	0.0090-0.0170	0.0170-0.0270	0.0070-0.0290	0.00157-0.00335	0.00157-0.00310	0.0005-0.0078
2010-2011	5.3 (5296)	LMG/0	-0.0014 0.0006	0.0090-0.0170	0.0170-0.0270	0.0070-0.0290	0.00157-0.00335	0.00157-0.00310	0.0005-0.0078
2010 Only	6.0 (5995)	LY6/K	-0.0014 0.0006	0.0090-0.0170	0.0170-0.0270	0.0070-0.0290	0.00157-0.00335	0.00157-0.00310	0.0005-0.0078
2010-2011	6.0 (5995)	L96/G	-0.0014 0.0006	0.0090-0.0170	0.0170-0.0270	0.0070-0.0290	0.00157-0.00335	0.00157-0.00310	0.0005-0.0078
2010-2011	6.0 (5995) Hybrid	LZ1/J	-0.0012 0.0008	0.0079-0.0161	0.0146-0.0272	0.0086-0.0311	0.0016-0.0033	0.0014-0.0031	0.0005-0.0079
2010-2011	6.2 (6195)	L9H/2	-0.0014 0.0006	0.0090-0.0170	0.0170-0.0270	0.0070-0.0290	0.00157-0.00335	0.00157-0.00310	0.0005-0.0078
2010 Only	6.6 (6595) Diesel	LMM/6	0.0035-0.0047	0.0118-0.0177	0.0197-0.0256	0.0059-0.0138	0.0030-0.0067	0.0004-0.0012	0.0004-0.0012
2011 Only	6.6 (6595) Diesel	LML/8	0.0035-0.0047	0.0118-0.0177	0.0197-0.0256	0.0059-0.0138	0.0030-0.0067	0.0004-0.0012	0.0004-0.0012
2011 Only	6.6 (6595) Diesel	LGH/L	0.0035-0.0047	0.0118-0.0177	0.0197-0.0256	0.0059-0.0138	0.0030-0.0067	0.0004-0.0012	0.0004-0.0012

25742_SIFR_C0009

TORQUE SPECIFICATIONS
All readings in ft. lbs.

Year	Engine Disp. Liters	Engine ID/VIN	Cylinder Head Bolts	Main Bearing Bolts	Rod Bearing Bolts	Crankshaft Damper Bolts	Flywheel Bolts	Manifold Intake	Manifold Exhaust	Spark Plugs	Oil Pan Drain Plug
2010-2011	4.3 (4297)	LU3/X	①	②	③	70	74	④	⑤	11	18
2010-2011	4.8 (4796)	L20/A	⑥	⑦	⑧	⑨	⑩	⑪	⑫	11	18
2010-2011	5.3 (5296)	LC9/3	⑥	⑦	⑧	⑨	⑩	⑪	⑫	11	18
2010-2011	5.3 (5296)	LMG/0	⑥	⑦	⑧	⑨	⑩	⑪	⑫	11	18
2010 Only	6.0 (5995)	LY6/K	⑥	⑦	⑧	⑨	⑩	⑪	⑫	11	18
2010-2011	6.0 (5995)	L96/G	⑥	⑦	⑧	⑨	⑩	⑪	⑫	11	18
2010-2011	6.0 (5995) Hybrid	LZ1/J	⑥	⑬	⑧	⑭	⑩	⑪	⑫	11	18
2010-2011	6.2 (6195)	L9H/2	⑥	⑦	⑧	⑨	⑩	⑪	⑫	11	18
2010 Only	6.6 (6595) Diesel	LMM/6	⑮	⑯	⑰	⑱	⑲	⑳	42	NA	18
2011 Only	6.6 (6595) Diesel	LML/8	⑮	⑯	⑰	⑱	⑲	⑳	42	NA	18
2011 Only	6.6 (6595) Diesel	LGH/L	⑮	⑯	⑰	⑱	⑲	⑳	42	NA	18

① Step 1: All bolts: 22 ft. lbs.
   Step 2: Long bolts: Adt'l 75 deg.
   Step 3: Medium bolts: Adt'l 65 deg.
   Step 4: Short bolts: Adt'l 55 deg.

② Step 1: 15 ft. lbs.
   Step 2: Adt'l 73 deg.

③ Step 1: 15 ft. lbs.
   Step 2: Adt'l 100 deg.

④ Lower Intake Manifold:
   Step 1: 27 inch lbs.
   Step 2: 106 inch lbs.
   Step 3: 11 ft. lbs.
   Upper Intake Manifold:
   Step 1: 44 inch lbs.
   Step 2: 80 inch lbs.

⑤ Step 1: 11 ft. lbs.
   Step 2: 22 ft. lbs.

⑥ Step 1: M8 bolts: 22 ft. lbs.
   Step 2: M11 bolts: 22 ft. lbs.
   Step 3: M11 bolts: Adt'l 90 deg.
   Step 4: M11 bolts: Adt'l 70 deg.

⑦ Step 1: M8 bolts (1-5): 15 ft. lbs.
   Step 2: M8 bolts (1-5): 22 ft. lbs.
   Step 3: M8 bolts (6-10): 15 ft. lbs.
   Step 4: M8 bolts (6-10): 22 ft. lbs.
   Step 5: M10 bolts: 15 ft. lbs.
   Step 6: M10 bolts: Adt'l 80 deg.
   Step 7: M10 studs: 15 ft. lbs.
   Step 8: M10 studs: Adt'l 51 deg.

⑧ Step 1: 15 ft. lbs.
   Step 2: Adt'l 85 deg.

⑨ Step 1: Used bolt: 240 ft. lbs.
   Step 2: Remove and discard used bolt
   Step 3: New bolt: 110 ft. lbs.
   Step 4: Loosen 360 deg.
   Step 5: 59 ft. lbs.
   Step 6: Adt'l 125 deg.

⑩ Flywheel: 74 ft. lbs.
   Flex Plate: 4L60-E/4L70-E/6L80: 47 ft. lbs.
   Flex Plate: 4L80-E: 44 ft. lbs.

⑪ Step 1: 44 inch lbs.
   Step 2: 89 inch lbs.

⑫ Step 1: 11 ft. lbs.
   Step 2: 15 ft. lbs.

⑬ Step 1: M8 bolts: 18 ft. lbs.
   Step 2: M10 bolts: 15 ft. lbs.
   Step 3: M10 bolts: Adt'l 80 deg.
   Step 4: M10 studs: 15 ft. lbs.
   Step 5: M10 studs: Adt'l 51 deg.

⑭ Step 1: 110 ft. lbs.
   Step 2: Loosen 360 deg.
   Step 3: 59 ft. lbs.
   Step 4: Adt'l 125 deg.

⑮ Step 1: M12 bolts: 37 ft. lbs.
   Step 2: M12 bolts: 59 ft. lbs.
   Step 3: M12 bolts: Adt'l 60 deg.
   Step 4: M12 bolts: Adt'l 60 deg.
   Step 5: M8 bolts: 24 ft. lbs.

⑯ Step 1: 72 ft. lbs.
   Step 2: 97 ft. lbs.
   Step 3: Adt'l 60 deg.
   Step 4: Bearing cap side bolts: 52 ft. lbs.

⑰ Step 1: 47 ft. lbs.
   Step 2: Adt'l 30 deg.
   Step 3: Adt'l 30 deg.

⑱ Step 1: 74 ft. lbs.
   Step 2: Adt'l 90 deg.

⑲ Step 1: 59 ft. lbs.
   Step 2: Adt'l 60 deg.
   Step 3: Adt'l 60 deg.

⑳ Lower nuts/bolts: 18 ft. lbs.
   Center nuts and bolts: 89 inch lbs.

WHEEL ALIGNMENT

Year	Model		Caster Range (+/-Deg.)	Caster Preferred Setting (Deg.)	Camber Range (+/-Deg.)	Camber Preferred Setting (Deg.)	Total Toe-in (in.)
2010-2011	①	Left	1.0	3.00	0.75	-0.10	0.10 +/-0.20
		Right	1.0	3.15	0.75	-0.10	
	②	Left	1.0	3.20	0.75	0.10	0.10 +/-0.20
		Right	1.0	3.00	0.75	0.10	
	③	Left	1.0	3.15	0.75	-0.10	0.10 +/-0.20
		Right	1.0	3.05	0.75	-0.10	
	④	Left	1.0	3.25	0.75	-0.10	0.10 +/-0.20
		Right	1.0	3.00	0.75	-0.10	
	⑤	Left	1.0	2.35	0.75	-0.10	0.10 +/-0.20
		Right	1.0	2.25	0.75	-0.10	
	⑥	Left	1.0	2.45	0.75	-0.10	0.10 +/-0.20
		Right	1.0	2.20	0.75	-0.10	
	⑦	Left	1.0	2.40	0.75	-0.10	0.10 +/-0.20
		Right	1.0	2.25	0.75	-0.10	
	⑧	Left	1.0	2.55	0.75	-0.10	0.10 +/-0.20
		Right	1.0	2.00	0.75	-0.10	
	⑨	Left	1.0	2.55	0.75	-0.10	0.10 +/-0.20
		Right	1.0	2.10	0.75	-0.10	
	⑩	Left	1.0	3.05	0.75	-0.10	0.10 +/-0.20
		Right	1.0	3.15	0.75	-0.10	
	⑪	Left	1.0	3.25	0.75	-0.10	0.10 +/-0.20
		Right	1.0	2.95	0.75	-0.10	
	⑫	Left	1.0	2.45	0.75	-0.10	0.10 +/-0.20
		Right	1.0	2.15	0.75	-0.10	
	⑬	Left	1.0	3.35	0.75	-0.10	0.10 +/-0.20
		Right	1.0	2.90	0.75	-0.10	
	⑭	Left	1.0	3.00	0.75	0.25	0.20 +/- 0.20
		Right	1.0	3.20	0.75	0.25	
	⑮	Left	1.0	3.00	0.75	0.25	0.20 +/- 0.20
		Right	1.0	2.70	0.75	0.25	
	⑯	Left	1.0	3.20	0.75	0.25	0.20 +/- 0.20
		Right	1.0	3.40	0.75	0.25	
	⑰	Left	1.0	3.10	0.75	0.25	0.20 +/- 0.20
		Right	1.0	2.80	0.75	0.25	
	⑱	Left	1.0	3.10	0.75	0.25	0.20 +/- 0.20
		Right	1.0	3.40	0.75	0.25	
	⑲	Left	1.0	3.30	0.75	0.25	0.20 +/- 0.20
		Right	1.0	3.00	0.75	0.25	

25742_SIER_C0011

WHEEL ALIGNMENT

		Caster		Camber		
Year	Model	Range (+/-Deg.)	Preferred Setting (Deg.)	Range (+/-Deg.)	Preferred Setting (Deg.)	Total Toe-in (in.)

FOOTNOTES:

① 1500 Crew Cab Short Box; Ext. Cab Standard Box with LT24570R17 tires

② 1500 Crew Cab Short Box; Ext. Cab Standard Box; Reg. Cab Long Box; Ext Cab Short box with P265/65R18 tires

③ 1500 Ext Cab Long Box with LT265/65R18 tires; Crew Cab Short Box; Ext. Cab Standard Box with P265/70R17 or P275/55R20 tires;
   Reg. Cab Long Box Ext. Cab Long Box with P275/55R20 or P265/65R18 tires; Ext Cab Long Box with P265/65R18 or P265/70R17 tires

④ 1500 Crew Cab Short Box; Ext. Cab Standard Box; Reg. Cab Long Box; Ext. Cab Short Box with P245/70R17, P245/70R17, P265/70R17 or P265/65R18 tires

⑤ 1500 Reg. Cab Standard Box with LT245/70R17, P265/65R18 or P265/70R17 tires

⑥ 1500 Reg. Cab Standard Box with P265/70R17, P275/55R20, or P265/65R18 tires

⑦ 1500 Reg. Cab Standard Box

⑧ 1500 Reg. Cab Standard Box with P275/55R20 tires

⑨ 1500 Reg. Cab Standard Box with P245/70R17 tires

⑩ 1500 Ext. Cab Long Box; Reg. Cab Long Box; Ext. Cab Short Box with P265/65R18, P265/70R17, or LT245/70R17 tires

⑪ 1500 Ext. Cab Long Box with P245/70R17 or P275/55R20 tires

⑫ 1500 Reg. Cab Standard Box with P265/R18 tires

⑬ 1500 Reg. Cab Long Box; Crew Cab Short Box; Ext. Cab Standard Box with P275/55R20 Tires

⑭ 2500 Reg. Cab Long Box, single Rear Wheel without LT265/70R17 tires

⑮ 2500 Reg. Cab Long Box, Single Rear Wheel with LT265/70R17 tires

⑯ 2500 Ext. Cab Standard Box or Long Box, Single Rear Wheel without LT265/70R17 tires

⑰ 2500 Ext. Cab Standard Box or Long Box, Single Rear Wheel with LT265/70R17 tires

⑱ 2500 Crew Cab Standard Box, Single Rear Wheel without LT265/70R17 tires

⑲ 2500 Crew Cab Standard Box, Single Rear Wheel with LT265/70R17 tires

25742_SIER_C0014

TIRE, WHEEL AND BALL JOINT SPECIFICATIONS

Year	Model	OEM Tires		Tire Pressures (psi)		Wheel Size	Ball Joint Inspection	Lug Nut (ft. lbs.)
		Standard	Optional	Front	Rear			
2010	1500	P265/70R17	①	②	②	17	NA	140
	2500	LT265/70R17	①	②	②	17	NA	140
2011	1500	P265/70R17	①	②	②	17	NA	140
	2500	LT265/70R17	①	②	②	17	NA	140

OEM: Original Equipment Manufacturer

PSI: Pounds Per Square Inch

NA: Information not available

① Numerous tire options available depending on the configuration of the vehicle. Contact GM or local tire retailer for details.

② Refer to the plate attached to the driver's door frame for tire pressure recommendations.

25742_SIER_C0012

BRAKE SPECIFICATIONS

All measurements in inches unless noted

| Year | Model | | Brake Disc | | | Brake Drum Diameter | | | Minimum Pad/Lining Thickness | | Brake Caliper | |
			Original Thickness	Minimum Thickness	Max. Runout	Original Inside Diameter	Max. Wear Limit	Maximum Runout	Front	Rear	Bracket Bolts (ft. lbs.)	Mounting Bolts (ft. lbs.)
2010	1500	F	1.181	1.100	0.002	NA	NA	NA	NA	NA	129	74
		R	0.787	0.728	0.002	NA	11.673	0.0024	NA	NA	148	38
	2500	F	1.496	1.457	0.005	NA	NA	NA	NA	NA	221	80
		R	1.151	1.102	0.005	NA	11.673	0.0024	NA	NA	148	80
2011	1500	F	1.181	1.100	0.002	NA	NA	NA	NA	NA	129	74
		R	0.787	0.728	0.002	NA	11.673	0.0024	NA	NA	148	38
	2500	F	1.496	1.457	0.005	NA	NA	NA	NA	NA	221	80
		R	1.151	1.102	0.005	NA	11.673	0.0024	NA	NA	148	80

F: Front

R: Rear

NA: Not available

25742_SIER_C0013

MAINTENANCE I AND II SERVICE SCHEDULES
SILVERADO, SIERRA

When the CHANGE ENGINE OIL light appears, certain services and inspections are required.

Required services are described as Maintenance I and Maintenance II.

The first service of a vehicle should be Maintenance I, and the second service should be Maintenance II.

Alternate between the 2 services thereafter. However, in some cases, Maintenance II may be required more often.

Maintenance I: Use Maintenance I if the CHANGE ENGINE OIL light comes on within 10 months since the vehicle was purchased or, if Maintenance II was performed.

Maintenance II: Use Maintenance II if the previous service performed was Maintenance I. Always use Maintenance II whenever the CHANGE ENGINE OIL light comes on 10 months or more since the last service, or, if the CHANGE ENGINE OIL light has not come on at all for one year.

Service Item	Maintenance I	Maintenance II
Change engine oil and filter, lubricate chassis components. Reset oil life system.	✓	✓
Lubricate the front suspension, steering linkage and parking brake cable guides. Control arm ball joints on pickup models require lubrication but should not be lubricated unless their temperature is -12°C (10°F) or higher, or they could be damaged. Vehicles used under severe commercial operating conditions require lubrication on a regular basis every 5 000 km/3,000 miles.	✓	✓
Restraint system component check.	✓	✓
Rotate the tires. Inspect the tire inflation pressures and the tire wear. Tires should be rotated every 12 000 km/7,500 miles.	✓	✓
Fluids visual leak check (or every 12 months, whichever occurs first). A leak in any system must be repaired and the fluid level checked.	✓	✓
Engine cooling system inspection. Visual inspection of Coolant, hoses, pipes, fittings, clamps and replacement, if needed.	✓	✓
Windshield washer fluid level check.	✓	✓
Engine air cleaner filter inspection.	✓	✓
Add diesel exhaust fluid. (Diesel Engines)	✓	✓
Body component lubrication. Lubricate all key lock cylinders, body door hinges, hood latch assembly, secondary latch, pivots, spring anchor, release pawl, fuel door hinge, locks, latches, and any folding or moving seat hardware. Pickup models: Lubricate tailgate hinges, tailgate linkage, tailgate handle pivot points, and latch bolt. Van models: Lubricate hood hinges and rear compartment hinges. See Recommended Fluids and Lubricants. More frequent lubrication may be required when the vehicle is exposed to a corrosive environment. Applying silicone grease on weatherstrips with a clean cloth makes them last longer, seal better, and not stick or squeak.	—	✓
Steering and suspension inspection. Visually inspect front and rear suspension and steering system for damaged, loose, or missing parts, signs of wear or lack of lubrication. Inspect power steering lines and hoses for proper hook-up, binding, leaks, cracks, chafing, etc. Pickup models: Visually check constant velocity joints, rubber boots, and axle seals for leaks	—	✓
Inspect the transmission fluid level and add fluid as needed.	✓	✓
Brake system inspection (or every 12 months, whichever occurs first).	✓	✓
Windshield wiper blade inspection for wear, cracking, or contamination and windshield and wiper blade cleaning, if contaminated.	✓	✓
Fuel system inspection for damage or leaks.	—	✓
Gas engines check all exhaust system components. Diesel engines check the DPF pressure lines, and nearby heat shields inspection for loose or damaged components. Check to be sure that mud or dirt is not caked on the exhaust system, especially in the area of the diesel particulate filter and tailpipe. Clean the area as needed.	—	✓

MAINTENANCE I AND II SERVICE SCHEDULES
SILVERADO, SIERRA

When the CHANGE ENGINE OIL light appears, certain services and inspections are required.

Required services are described as Maintenance I and Maintenance II.

The first service of a vehicle should be Maintenance I, and the second service should be Maintenance II.

Alternate between the 2 services thereafter. However, in some cases, Maintenance II may be required more often.

Maintenance I: Use Maintenance I if the CHANGE ENGINE OIL light comes on within 10 months since the vehicle was purchased or, if Maintenance II was performed.

Maintenance II: Use Maintenance II if the previous service performed was Maintenance I. Always use Maintenance II whenever the CHANGE ENGINE OIL light comes on 10 months or more since the last service, or, if the CHANGE ENGINE OIL light has not come on at all for one year.

Service Item	Maintenance I	Maintenance II
Air intake system check. Check the air intake system installation to assure that gaskets are properly sealed and that all hose connections, fasteners, and other components are tight. Also check to be sure that the air cleaner housing is properly seated and the cover fits tightly. Tighten connections and fasteners or replace damaged parts as necessary.	—	✓
Fuel filter service (Diesel Engines). This vehicle has a CHANGE FUEL FILTER message in the Driver Information Center (DIC) to tell you when to replace the fuel filter. See Fuel System Messages. Change the fuel filter a minimum of once every two years. The PERCENT FUEL FILTER LIFE REMAINING message may be used to decide if the filter should be changed during routine vehicle service.	—	✓
Inspect the throttle system.	—	✓

To reset the CHANGE ENGINE OIL light:

1. Turn the ignition key to the ON/RUN position with the engine OFF.
2. Press and release the stem in the lower center of the instrument cluster until the OIL LIFE message is displayed.
3. Once the alternating OIL LIFE and RESET messages appear, press and hold the stem until several beeps sound. This confirms that the oil life system has been reset to 100 percent.
4. Turn the ignition key to the OFF position. If the CHANGE ENGINE OIL message comes back on when the vehicle is started, the engine oil life system has not been reset. Repeat the procedure.

25742_SIER_C0016

ADDITIONAL MAINTENANCE SERVICES - NORMAL
SILVERADO, SIERRA

TO BE SERVICED	TYPE OF SERVICE	VEHICLE MILEAGE INTERVAL (x1000)					
		25	50	75	100	125	150
Engine coolant	Replace						✓
Air cleaner filter	Replace		✓		✓		✓
Automatic transmission fluid & filter	Replace				✓		
Spark plugs (Gas engines)	Replace				✓		
Exhaust system & heat shields	Service/Inspect	✓	✓	✓	✓	✓	✓
Cooling system hoses and clamps	Service/Inspect	✓	✓	✓	✓	✓	✓
Fuel system	Inspect	✓	✓	✓	✓	✓	✓
Accessory drive belt	Replace						✓
Evaporative control system	Inspect		✓		✓		✓
Transfer case fluid	Replace				✓		

25742_SIER_C0017

ADDITIONAL MAINTENANCE SERVICES - SEVERE
SILVERADO, SIERRA

TO BE SERVICED	TYPE OF SERVICE	VEHICLE MILEAGE INTERVAL (x1000)					
		25	50	75	100	125	150
Engine coolant	Replace						✓
Air cleaner filter	Replace	✓	✓	✓	✓	✓	✓
Automatic transmisison fluid & filter	Replace		✓		✓		✓
Spark plugs (Gas engines)	Replace				✓		
Exhaust system & heat shields	Service/ Inspect	✓	✓	✓	✓	✓	✓
Cooling system hoses and clamps	Service/ Inspect	✓	✓	✓	✓	✓	✓
Fuel system	Inspect	✓	✓	✓	✓	✓	✓
Accessory drive belt	Inspect						✓
Evaporative control system	Inspect		✓		✓		✓
Transfer case fluid	Replace		✓		✓		✓

25742_SIER_C0018

PRECAUTIONS

Before servicing any vehicle, please be sure to read all of the following precautions, which deal with personal safety, prevention of component damage, and important points to take into consideration when servicing a motor vehicle:

• Never open, service or drain the radiator or cooling system when the engine is hot; serious burns can occur from the steam and hot coolant.

• Observe all applicable safety precautions when working around fuel. Whenever servicing the fuel system, always work in a well-ventilated area. Do not allow fuel spray or vapors to come in contact with a spark, open flame, or excessive heat (a hot drop light, for example). Keep a dry chemical fire extinguisher near the work area. Always keep fuel in a container specifically designed for fuel storage; also, always properly seal fuel containers to avoid the possibility of fire or explosion. Refer to the additional fuel system precautions later in this section.

• Fuel injection systems often remain pressurized, even after the engine has been turned **OFF**. The fuel system pressure must be relieved before disconnecting any fuel lines. Failure to do so may result in fire and/or personal injury.

• Brake fluid often contains polyglycol ethers and polyglycols. Avoid contact with the eyes and wash your hands thoroughly after handling brake fluid. If you do get brake fluid in your eyes, flush your eyes with clean, running water for 15 minutes. If eye irritation persists, or if you have taken brake fluid internally, IMMEDIATELY seek medical assistance.

• The EPA warns that prolonged contact with used engine oil may cause a number of skin disorders, including cancer. You should make every effort to minimize your exposure to used engine oil. Protective gloves should be worn when changing oil. Wash your hands and any other exposed skin areas as soon as possible after exposure to used engine oil. Soap and water, or waterless hand cleaner should be used.

• All new vehicles are now equipped with an air bag system, often referred to as a Supplemental Restraint System (SRS) or Supplemental Inflatable Restraint (SIR) system. The system must be disabled before performing service on or around system components, steering column, instrument panel components, wiring and sensors. Failure to follow safety and disabling procedures could result in accidental air bag deployment, possible personal injury and unnecessary system repairs.

• Always wear safety goggles when working with, or around, the air bag system. When carrying a non-deployed air bag, be sure the bag and trim cover are pointed away from your body. When placing a non-deployed air bag on a work surface, always face the bag and trim cover upward, away from the surface. This will reduce the motion of the module if it is accidentally deployed. Refer to the additional air bag system precautions later in this section.

• Clean, high quality brake fluid from a sealed container is essential to the safe and proper operation of the brake system. You should always buy the correct type of brake fluid for your vehicle. If the brake fluid becomes contaminated, completely flush the system with new fluid. Never reuse any brake fluid. Any brake fluid that is removed from the system should be discarded. Also, do not allow any brake fluid to come in contact with a painted surface; it will damage the paint.

• Never operate the engine without the proper amount and type of engine oil; doing so WILL result in severe engine damage.

• Timing belt maintenance is extremely important. Many models utilize an interference-type, non-freewheeling engine. If the timing belt breaks, the valves in the cylinder head may strike the pistons, causing potentially serious (also time-consuming and expensive) engine damage. Refer to the maintenance interval charts for the recommended replacement interval for the timing belt, and to the timing belt section for belt replacement and inspection.

• Disconnecting the negative battery cable on some vehicles may interfere with the functions of the on-board computer system(s) and may require the computer to undergo a relearning process once the negative battery cable is reconnected.

• When servicing drum brakes, only disassemble and assemble one side at a time, leaving the remaining side intact for reference.

• Only an MVAC-trained, EPA-certified automotive technician should service the air conditioning system or its components.

BRAKES

GENERAL INFORMATION

PRECAUTIONS

• Certain components within the ABS system are not intended to be serviced or repaired individually.

• Do not use rubber hoses or other parts not specifically specified for and ABS system. When using repair kits, replace all parts included in the kit. Partial or incorrect repair may lead to functional problems and require the replacement of components.

• Lubricate rubber parts with clean, fresh brake fluid to ease assembly. Do not use shop air to clean parts; damage to rubber components may result.

• Use only DOT 3 brake fluid from an unopened container.

• If any hydraulic component or line is removed or replaced, it may be necessary to bleed the entire system.

• A clean repair area is essential. Always clean the reservoir and cap thoroughly before removing the cap. The slightest amount of dirt in the fluid may plug an orifice and impair the system function. Perform repairs after components have been thoroughly cleaned; use only denatured alcohol to clean components. Do not allow ABS components to come into contact with any substance containing mineral oil; this includes used shop rags.

• The Anti-Lock control unit is a microprocessor similar to other computer units in the vehicle. Ensure that the ignition switch is **OFF** before removing or installing controller harnesses. Avoid static

ANTI-LOCK BRAKE SYSTEM (ABS)

electricity discharge at or near the controller.

• If any arc welding is to be done on the vehicle, the control unit should be unplugged before welding operations begin.

SPEED SENSORS

REMOVAL & INSTALLATION

1500 and Hybrid Series

Front

See Figure 1.

1. Raise and support the vehicle.
2. Remove the tire and wheel assembly.
3. Remove the brake rotor.
4. Disconnect the electrical connector.

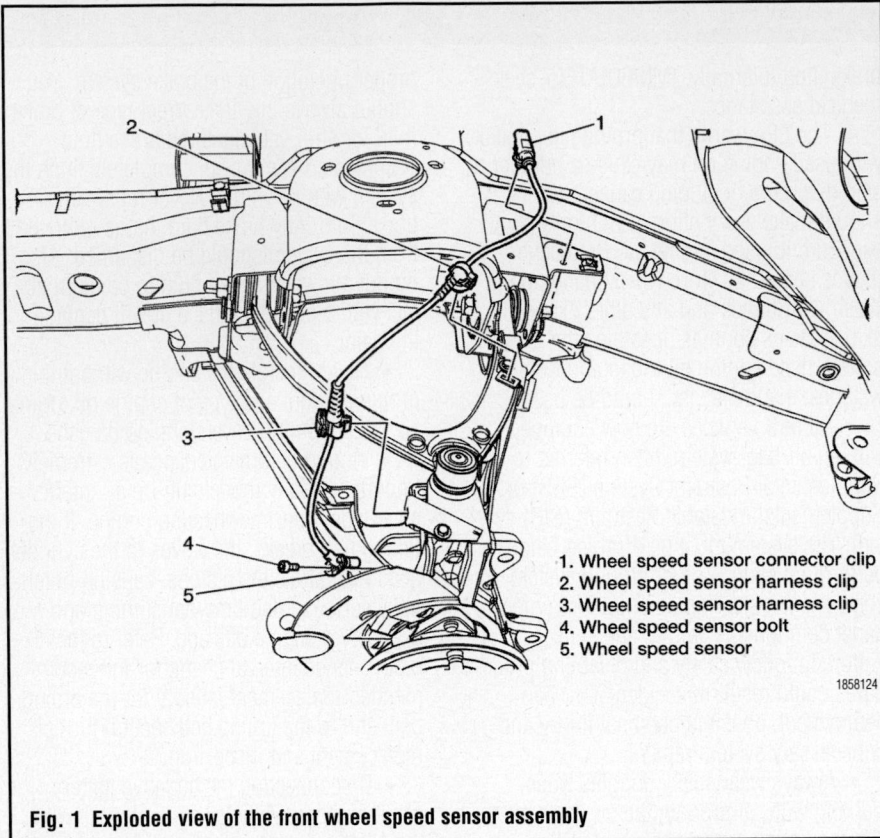

1. Wheel speed sensor connector clip
2. Wheel speed sensor harness clip
3. Wheel speed sensor harness clip
4. Wheel speed sensor bolt
5. Wheel speed sensor

1858124

Fig. 1 Exploded view of the front wheel speed sensor assembly

2500 Series

Front

See Figure 3.

1. Raise and support the vehicle.
2. Remove the tire and wheel assembly.
3. Remove the brake rotor.
4. Disconnect the electrical connector.
5. Release the wheel speed sensor electrical connector clip from the frame.
6. Release the wheel speed sensor harness clip from the frame.
7. Release the wheel speed sensor harness clip from the upper control arm.
8. Release the wheel speed sensor harness clip from the brake hose bracket.
9. Installation is the reverse of removal.
10. Tighten the wheel sensor bolt to 10 ft. lbs. (13 Nm).

Rear

See Figures 4 through 6.

1. Raise and support the vehicle.
2. Disconnect the wheel speed sensor electrical connector.

---

5. Release the wheel speed sensor electrical connector clip from the brake hose bracket.
6. Release the wheel speed sensor harness clip from the brake hose bracket.
7. Release the wheel speed sensor harness clip from the steering knuckle bracket.
8. Remove the wheel speed sensor bolt and the wheel speed sensor.
9. Installation is the reverse of removal.
10. Tighten the wheel sensor bolt to 10 ft. lbs. (13 Nm).

Rear

See Figure 2.

1. Raise and support the vehicle.
2. Remove the tire and wheel assembly.
3. Remove the brake rotor.
4. Disconnect the wheel speed sensor electrical connector.
5. Release the wheel speed sensor harness clip from the frame rail.
6. Release the wheel speed sensor harness clip from the rear axle.
7. Remove the wheel speed sensor bolt.
8. Remove the wheel speed sensor.
9. Installation is the reverse of removal.

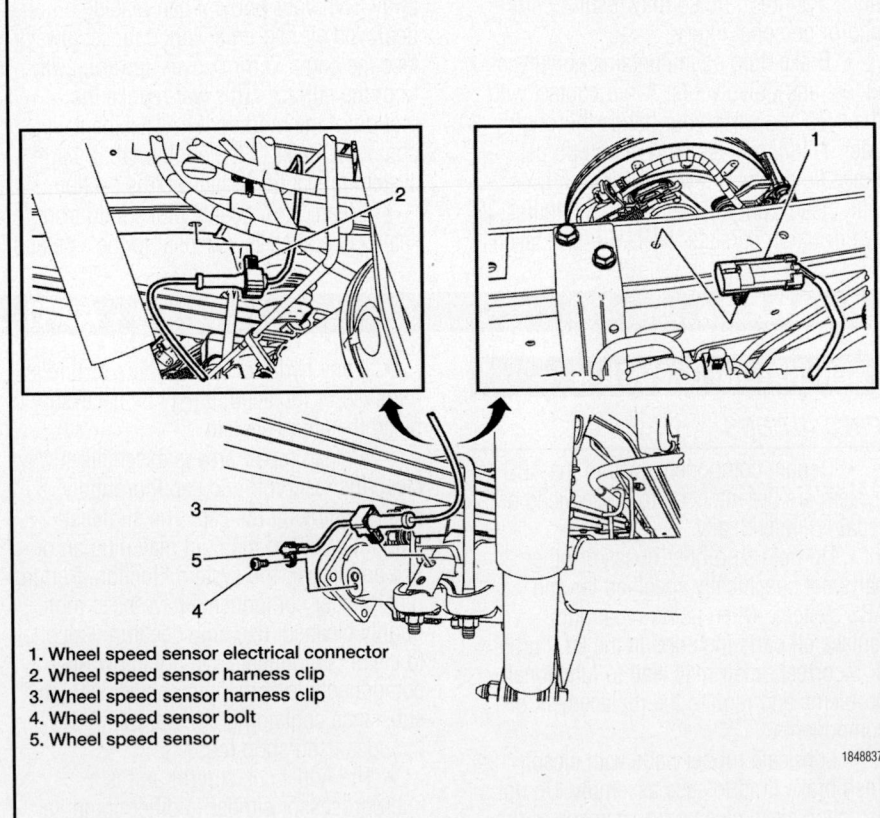

1. Wheel speed sensor electrical connector
2. Wheel speed sensor harness clip
3. Wheel speed sensor harness clip
4. Wheel speed sensor bolt
5. Wheel speed sensor

1848837

Fig. 2 Exploded view of the rear wheel speed sensor assembly

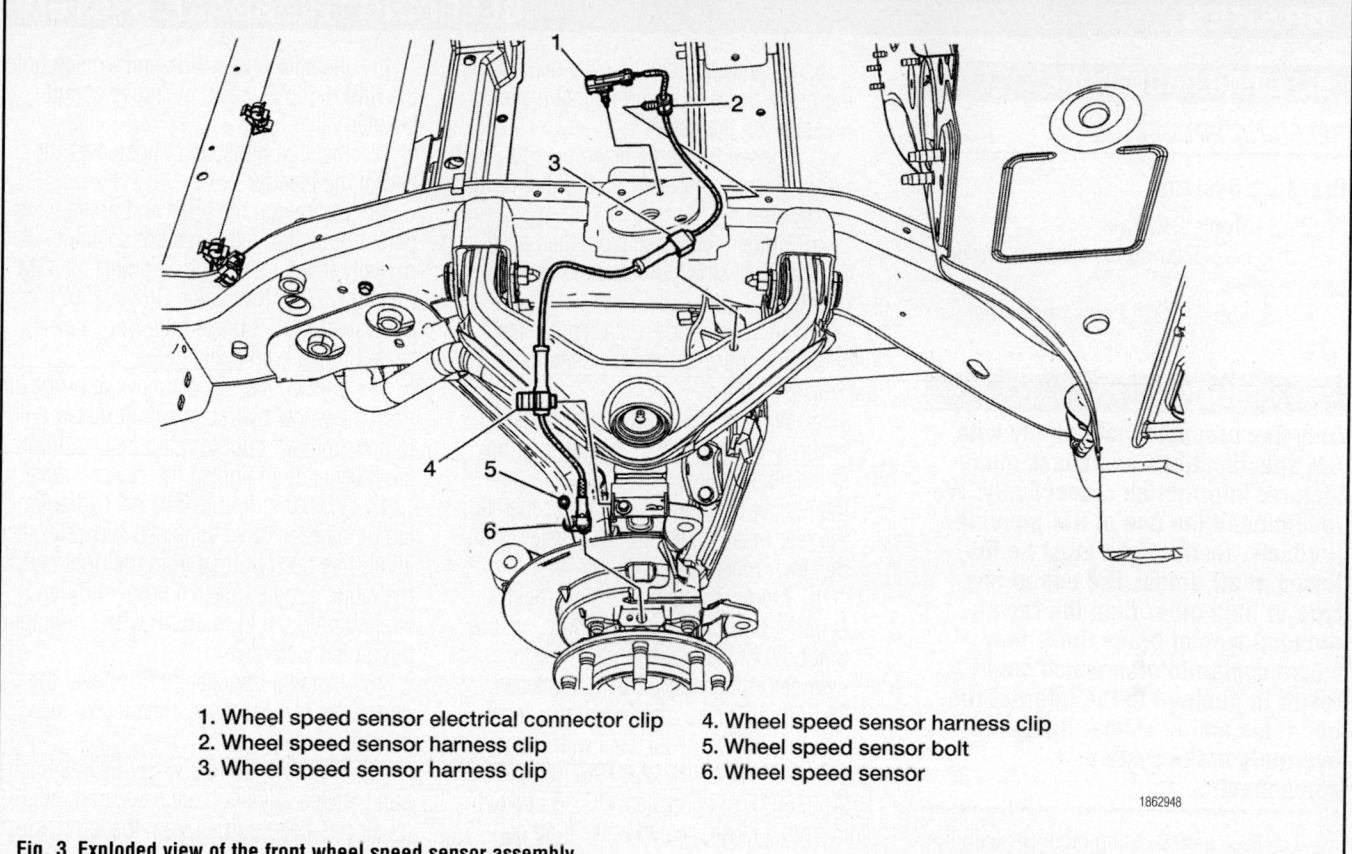

1. Wheel speed sensor electrical connector clip
2. Wheel speed sensor harness clip
3. Wheel speed sensor harness clip
4. Wheel speed sensor harness clip
5. Wheel speed sensor bolt
6. Wheel speed sensor

1862948

Fig. 3 Exploded view of the front wheel speed sensor assembly

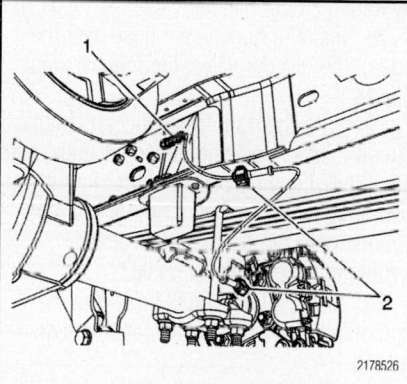

2178526

Fig. 4 Disconnect the wheel speed sensor electrical connector (1) and release the wheel speed sensor electrical connector and sensor harness clips (2) from the inboard frame rail

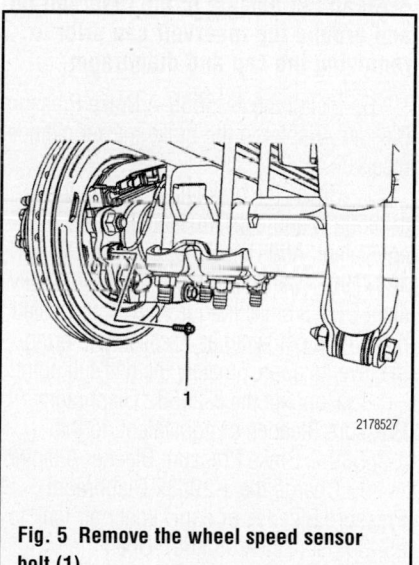

2178527

Fig. 5 Remove the wheel speed sensor bolt (1)

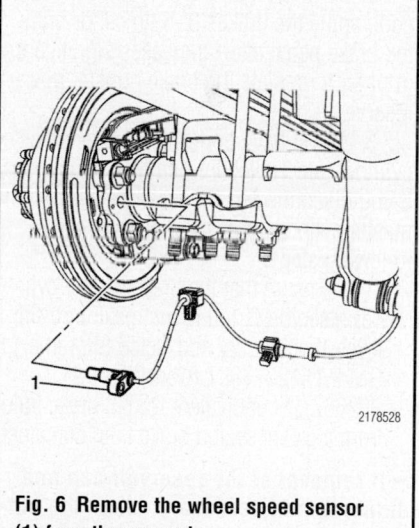

2178528

Fig. 6 Remove the wheel speed sensor (1) from the rear axle

3. Release the wheel speed sensor electrical connector and sensor harness clips from the inboard frame rail.
4. Remove the wheel speed sensor bolt.
5. Remove the wheel speed sensor from the rear axle.

To install:
6. Install the wheel speed sensor to the rear axle.
7. Install the wheel speed sensor bolt and tighten to 80 inch lbs. (9 Nm).

8. Connect the wheel speed sensor electrical connector.
9. Install the wheel speed sensor electrical connector and sensor harness clips to the inboard frame rail.

BRAKES BLEEDING THE BRAKE SYSTEM

BLEEDING PROCEDURE

BLEEDING PROCEDURE

Pressure System

Special Tools Required:
- J-29532 Diaphragm Pressure Bleeder, or equivalent
- J-35589-A Brake Pressure Bleeder Adapter

✳✳ CAUTION

Only use products that comply with GM specifications and check manufacturer information respectively. We recommend the use of GM genuine products. Instructions must be followed at all times. The use of any type of fluid other than the recommended type of brake fluid, may cause contamination which could result in damage to the internal rubber seals and/or rubber linings of hydraulic brake system components.

1. Place a clean shop cloth beneath the brake master cylinder to prevent brake fluid spills.
2. With the ignition OFF and the brakes cool, apply the brakes 3–5 times, or until the brake pedal effort increases significantly, in order to deplete the brake booster power reserve.
3. If you have performed a brake master cylinder bench bleeding on this vehicle, or if you disconnected the brake pipes from the master cylinder, you must perform the following steps:
   a. Ensure that the brake master cylinder reservoir is full to the maximum-fill level. If necessary add Delco Supreme 11, GM P/N 12377967 (Canadian P/N 992667), or equivalent DOT-3 brake fluid from a clean, sealed brake fluid container.

➡**If removal of the reservoir cap and diaphragm is necessary, clean the outside of the reservoir on and around the cap prior to removal.**

   b. With the rear brake pipe installed securely to the master cylinder, loosen and separate the front brake pipe from the front port of the brake master cylinder.
   c. Allow a small amount of brake fluid to gravity bleed from the open port of the master cylinder.
   d. Reconnect the brake pipe to the master cylinder port and tighten securely.

   e. Have an assistant slowly depress the brake pedal fully and maintain steady pressure on the pedal.
   f. Loosen the same brake pipe to purge air from the open port of the master cylinder.
   g. Tighten the brake pipe, then have the assistant slowly release the brake pedal.
4. Wait 15 seconds, then repeat steps until all air is purged from the same port of the master cylinder.
   a. With the front brake pipe installed securely to the master cylinder, after all air has been purged from the front port of the master cylinder, loosen and separate the rear brake pipe from the master cylinder, then repeat steps.
   b. After completing the final master cylinder port bleeding procedure, ensure that both of the brake pipe-to-master cylinder fittings are properly tightened.
5. Fill the brake master cylinder reservoir to the maximum-fill level with Delco Supreme 11, GM P/N 12377967 (Canadian P/N 992667), or equivalent DOT-3 brake fluid from a clean, sealed brake fluid container.

➡**Clean the outside of the reservoir on and around the reservoir cap prior to removing the cap and diaphragm.**

6. Install the J-35589-A Brake Pressure Bleeder Adapter to the brake master cylinder reservoir.
7. Check the brake fluid level in the J-29532 Diaphragm Pressure Bleeder, or equivalent. Add Delco Supreme 11, GM P/N 12377967 (Canadian P/N 992667), or equivalent DOT-3 brake fluid from a clean, sealed brake fluid container as necessary to bring the level to approximately the half-full point.
8. Connect the J-29532 Diaphragm Pressure Bleeder, or equivalent, to the J-35589-A Brake Pressure Bleeder Adapter.
9. Charge the J-29532 Diaphragm Pressure Bleeder, or equivalent , air tank to 25–30 psi (175–205 kPa). Open the J-29532 Diaphragm Pressure Bleeder, or equivalent , fluid tank valve to allow pressurized brake fluid to enter the brake system.
10. Wait approximately 30 seconds, then inspect the entire hydraulic brake system in order to ensure that there are no existing external brake fluid leaks.

➡**Any brake fluid leaks identified require repair prior to completing this procedure.**

11. Install a proper box-end wrench onto the RIGHT REAR wheel hydraulic circuit bleeder valve.
12. Install a transparent hose over the end of the bleeder valve.
13. Submerge the open end of the transparent hose into a transparent container partially filled with Delco Supreme 11, GM P/N 12377967 (Canadian P/N 992667), or equivalent DOT-3 brake fluid from a clean, sealed brake fluid container.
14. Loosen the bleeder valve to purge air from the wheel hydraulic circuit. Allow fluid to flow until air bubbles stop flowing from the bleeder, then tighten the bleeder valve.
15. With the right rear wheel hydraulic circuit bleeder valve tightened securely, after all air has been purged from the right rear hydraulic circuit, install a proper box-end wrench onto the LEFT REAR wheel hydraulic circuit bleeder valve.
16. Install a transparent hose over the end of the bleeder valve, then repeat steps 13–14.
17. With the left rear wheel hydraulic circuit bleeder valve tightened securely, after all air has been purged from the left rear hydraulic circuit, install a proper box-end wrench onto the RIGHT FRONT wheel hydraulic circuit bleeder valve.
18. Install a transparent hose over the end of the bleeder valve, then repeat steps 13–14.
19. With the right front wheel hydraulic circuit bleeder valve tightened securely, after all air has been purged from the right front hydraulic circuit, install a proper box-end wrench onto the LEFT FRONT wheel hydraulic circuit bleeder valve.
20. Install a transparent hose over the end of the bleeder valve, then repeat steps 13–14.
21. After completing the final wheel hydraulic circuit bleeding procedure, ensure that each of the 4 wheel hydraulic circuit bleeder valves are properly tightened.
22. Close the J-29532 Diaphragm Pressure Bleeder, or equivalent, fluid tank valve, then disconnect the J-29532 Diaphragm Pressure Bleeder, or equivalent, from the J-35589-A Brake Pressure Bleeder Adapter.
23. Remove the J-35589-A Brake Pressure Bleeder Adapter from the brake master cylinder reservoir.
24. Fill the brake master cylinder reservoir to the maximum-fill level with Delco Supreme 11, GM P/N 12377967 (Canadian P/N 992667), or equivalent DOT-3 brake fluid from a clean, sealed brake fluid container.

25. Slowly depress and release the brake pedal. Observe the feel of the brake pedal.

26. If the brake pedal feels spongy perform the following steps:

 a. Inspect the brake system for external leaks.

 b. Using a scan tool, perform the antilock brake system automated bleeding procedure to remove any air that may have been trapped in the Brake Pressure Modulator Valve (BPMV). Refer to the following procedures, as appropriate:

 • Antilock Brake System Automated Bleed for Two-mode Hybrid vehicles

 • Antilock Brake System Automated Bleed for non-hybrid vehicles less than 8600 lbs. (3900 kg) GVW

 • Antilock Brake System Automated Bleed for non-hybrid vehicles greater than/equal to 8600 lbs. (3900 kg) GVW

27. Turn the ignition key ON, with the engine OFF. Check to see if the brake system warning lamp remains illuminated.

➡**If the brake system warning lamp remains illuminated, DO NOT allow the vehicle to be driven until it is diagnosed and repaired.**

Manual System

1. With the ignition OFF and the brakes cool, apply the brakes 3–5 times, or until the brake pedal effort increases significantly, in order to deplete the brake booster power reserve.

2. If you have performed a brake master cylinder bench bleeding on this vehicle, or if you disconnected the brake pipes from the master cylinder, you must perform the following steps:

 a. Ensure that the brake master cylinder reservoir is full to the maximum-fill level. If necessary add GM approved brake fluid from a clean, sealed brake fluid container.

3. If removal of the reservoir cap and diaphragm is necessary, clean the outside of the reservoir on and around the cap prior to removal.

 a. With the rear brake pipe installed securely to the master cylinder, loosen and separate the front brake pipe from the front port of the brake master cylinder.

 b. Allow a small amount of brake fluid to gravity bleed from the open port of the master cylinder.

 c. Reconnect the brake pipe to the master cylinder port and tighten securely.

 d. Have an assistant slowly depress the brake pedal fully and maintain steady pressure on the pedal.

 e. Loosen the same brake pipe to purge air from the open port of the master cylinder.

 f. Tighten the brake pipe, then have the assistant slowly release the brake pedal.

 g. Wait 15 seconds, then repeat steps until all air is purged from the same port of the master cylinder.

 h. With the front brake pipe installed securely to the master cylinder, after all air has been purged from the front port of the master cylinder, loosen and separate the rear brake pipe from the master cylinder, then repeat steps.

 i. After completing the final master cylinder port bleeding procedure, ensure that both of the brake pipe-to-master cylinder fittings are properly tightened.

4. Fill the brake master cylinder reservoir with GM approved brake fluid from a clean, sealed brake fluid container. Ensure that the brake master cylinder reservoir remains at least half-full during this bleeding procedure. Add fluid as needed to maintain the proper level.

5. Clean the outside of the reservoir on and around the reservoir cap prior to removing the cap and diaphragm.

6. Install a proper box-end wrench onto the RIGHT REAR wheel hydraulic circuit bleeder valve.

7. Install a transparent hose over the end of the bleeder valve.

8. Submerge the open end of the transparent hose into a transparent container partially filled with GM approved brake fluid from a clean, sealed brake fluid container.

9. Have an assistant slowly depress the brake pedal fully and maintain steady pressure on the pedal.

10. Loosen the bleeder valve to purge air from the wheel hydraulic circuit.

11. Tighten the bleeder valve, then have the assistant slowly release the brake pedal.

12. Wait 15 seconds, then repeat steps 8-10 until all air is purged from the same wheel hydraulic circuit.

13. With the right rear wheel hydraulic circuit bleeder valve tightened securely, after all air has been purged from the right rear hydraulic circuit install a proper box-end wrench onto the LEFT REAR wheel hydraulic circuit bleeder valve.

14. Install a transparent hose over the end of the bleeder valve, then repeat steps 7–11.

15. With the left rear wheel hydraulic circuit bleeder valve tightened securely, after all air purged from the left rear hydraulic circuit, install a proper box-end wrench onto the RIGHT FRONT wheel hydraulic circuit bleeder valve.

16. Install a transparent hose over the end of the bleeder valve, then repeat steps 7–11.

17. With the right front wheel hydraulic circuit bleeder valve tightened securely, after all air has been purged from the right front hydraulic circuit, install a proper box-end wrench onto the LEFT FRONT wheel hydraulic circuit bleeder valve.

18. Install a transparent hose over the end of the bleeder valve, then repeat steps 7–11.

19. After completing the final wheel hydraulic circuit bleeding procedure, ensure that each of the 4 wheel hydraulic circuit bleeder valves are properly tightened.

20. Fill the brake master cylinder reservoir to the maximum-fill level with GM approved brake fluid from a clean, sealed brake fluid container.

21. Slowly depress and release the brake pedal. Observe the feel of the brake pedal.

22. If the brake pedal feels spongy, repeat the bleeding procedure again. If the brake pedal still feels spongy after repeating the bleeding procedure, perform the following steps:

 a. Inspect the brake system for external leaks.

 b. Pressure bleed the hydraulic brake system in order to purge any air that may still be trapped in the system.

23. Turn the ignition key ON, with the engine OFF. Check to see if the brake system warning lamp remains illuminated.

➡**If the brake system warning lamp remains illuminated, DO NOT allow the vehicle to be driven until it is diagnosed and repaired.**

Hybrid Vehicles

Special Tools Required:

 • J-29532-A Brake Pressure Bleeder , or J-29532 Diaphragm Pressure Bleeder , or equivalent

 • J-35589-A Brake Pressure Bleeder Adapter, or equivalent

✳✳ CAUTION

When adding fluid to the brake master cylinder reservoir, use only GM approved or equivalent DOT-3 brake fluid from a clean, sealed brake fluid container. The use of any type of fluid other than the recommended type of brake fluid may cause contamination which could result in damage to the internal rubber seals and/or rubber linings of hydraulic brake system components.

1. Place the transmission in the PARK position.

2. Place a clean shop cloth beneath the brake master cylinder to prevent brake fluid spills.

➡ **The ignition must be in the OFF position, without pausing at ACCESSORY, and without applying the brake pedal to ensure the brake modulator and High Pressure Accumulator (HPA) pressure relief occurs. This process will take approximately 1–3 minutes.**

3. Turn the ignition to OFF, without pausing at ACCESSORY, and without applying the brake pedal. Remove the ignition key.

4. Raise and support the vehicle.

5. Remove the tire and wheel assemblies.

6. Visually inspect the brake system for brake fluid leaks and damage. Repair or replace components as necessary.

7. Lower the vehicle to a working height to bleed the hydraulic brake system.

8. If you have performed a brake master cylinder bench bleeding on this vehicle, or if you disconnected the brake pipes from the master cylinder, or from the Brake Pressure Modulator Valve (BPMV), you must perform the following steps to bleed air at the ports of the hydraulic brake component:

　a. Ensure that the brake master cylinder reservoir is full to the maximum-fill level. If necessary add GM approved, or equivalent DOT-3 brake fluid from a clean, sealed brake fluid container.

➡ **If removal of the reservoir cap and diaphragm is necessary, clean the outside of the reservoir on and around the cap prior to removal.**

　b. Clean the outside of the master cylinder reservoir on and around the cap prior to removal.

　c. With the brake pipes installed securely to the affected hydraulic brake system component, loosen and separate one of the brake pipes from the port of the affected hydraulic brake system component.

　d. Allow a small amount of brake fluid to gravity bleed from the open port of the affected hydraulic brake system component.

9. Reconnect the brake pipe to the affected hydraulic brake system component port and tighten securely.

　a. Have an assistant slowly depress the brake pedal fully and maintain steady pressure on the pedal.

10. Loosen the same brake pipe to purge air from the open port of the affected hydraulic brake system component.

11. Tighten the brake pipe, then have the assistant slowly release the brake pedal.

12. Wait 15 seconds, then repeat steps until all air is purged from the same port of the affected hydraulic brake system component.

　a. With the brake pipe installed securely to the affected hydraulic brake system component, after all air has been purged from the first port of the affected hydraulic brake system component that was bled, loosen and separate the next brake pipe from the affected hydraulic brake system component, then repeat steps.

　b. After completing the final affected hydraulic brake system component port bleeding procedure, ensure that each of the brake pipe-to-component fittings are properly tightened.

13. Fill the brake master cylinder reservoir to the maximum-fill level with GM approved, or equivalent DOT-3 brake fluid from a clean, sealed brake fluid container.

➡ **Clean the outside of the reservoir on and around the reservoir cap prior to removing the cap and diaphragm.**

14. Install the J-35589-A Brake Pressure Bleeder Adapter, or equivalent , to the brake master cylinder reservoir.

15. Inspect the brake fluid level in the J-29532-A Brake Pressure Bleeder , or J-29532 Diaphragm Pressure Bleeder , or equivalent. Clean the outside of the J-29532-A or the J-29532 and add GM approved, or equivalent, brake fluid from a clean sealed brake fluid container, as necessary.

16. Connect the J-29532-A Brake Pressure Bleeder, or J-29532 Diaphragm Pressure Bleeder, or equivalent, to the J-35589-A Brake Pressure Bleeder Adapter, or equivalent.

17. Set the pressure regulator of the J-29532-A Brake Pressure Bleeder, or charge the air tank of the J-29532 Diaphragm Pressure Bleeder, to 30 psi (200 kPa).

Open the J-29532-A Brake Pressure Bleeder, or J-29532 Diaphragm Pressure Bleeder, or equivalent, fluid tank valve to allow pressurized brake fluid to enter the brake system. Wait approximately 30 seconds, then inspect the entire hydraulic brake system in order to ensure there are no existing external brake fluid leaks.

➡ **Any brake fluid leaks identified require repair prior to completing this procedure.**

18. Use the following sequence for bleeding the wheel hydraulic circuits:
- Right rear
- Left rear
- Right front
- Left front

19. Install a proper box-end wrench onto the appropriate wheel hydraulic circuit bleeder valve.

20. Secure a transparent bleeder hose to the bleeder valve.

21. Submerge the open end of the transparent hose into a transparent container partially filled with GM approved or equivalent DOT-3 brake fluid from a clean, sealed brake fluid container.

22. Loosen the bleeder valve to purge air from the wheel hydraulic circuit. Allow fluid to flow for 30 seconds, or until air bubbles stop flowing from the bleeder, then tighten the bleeder valve.

23. With the first wheel hydraulic circuit bleeder valve tightened securely, repeat steps 18–21 for the remaining wheel hydraulic circuits in the proper sequence.

24. After completing the final wheel hydraulic circuit bleeding procedure, ensure that each of the 4 wheel hydraulic circuit bleeder valves are properly tightened.

25. Close the J-29532-A Brake Pressure Bleeder, or J-29532 Diaphragm Pressure Bleeder, or equivalent, fluid tank valve, then disconnect the J-29532-A Brake Pressure Bleeder, or J-29532 Diaphragm Pressure Bleeder, or equivalent, from the J-35589-A Brake Pressure Bleeder Adapter, or equivalent.

26. Remove the J-35589-A Brake Pressure Bleeder Adapter, or equivalent from the brake master cylinder reservoir.

27. Fill the brake master cylinder reservoir to the maximum-fill level with GM approved, or equivalent DOT-3 brake fluid from a clean, sealed brake fluid container.

28. Slowly depress and release the brake pedal. Observe the feel of the brake pedal.

➡ **If it is determined that air was introduced into the system upstream of the ABS modulator prior to servicing, the Antilock Brake System Automated Bleed Procedure must be performed.**

29. If the brake pedal feels spongy perform the following steps:

　a. Inspect the brake system for external leaks.

　b. Using a scan tool, perform the antilock brake system automated bleeding procedure to remove any air that may have been trapped in the Brake Pressure Modulator Valve (BPMV).

30. Turn the ignition key ON, with the engine OFF. Check to see if the brake system warning lamp remains illuminated.

➡ **If the brake system warning lamp remains illuminated, DO NOT allow the vehicle to be driven until it is diagnosed and repaired.**

ABS Automated Bleed System

➡ **The base hydraulic brake system must be bled before performing this automated bleeding procedure. If you have not yet performed the base hydraulic brake system bleeding procedure, refer to Hydraulic Brake System Bleeding before proceeding.**

1. Install a scan tool to the vehicle.
2. Start the engine and allow the engine to idle.
3. Using the scan tool, begin the automated bleed procedure.
4. Follow the instructions on the scan tool to complete the automated bleed procedure. Apply the brake pedal when instructed by the scan tool.
5. Turn the ignition OFF.
6. Remove the scan tool from the vehicle.
7. Fill the brake master cylinder reservoir to the maximum-fill level with Delco Supreme 11, GM P/N 12377967 (Canadian P/N 992667), or equivalent DOT-3 brake fluid from a clean, sealed brake fluid container.
8. Bleed the hydraulic brake system.
9. With the ignition OFF, apply the brakes 3–5 times, or until the brake pedal becomes firm, in order to deplete the brake booster power reserve.
10. Slowly depress and release the brake pedal. Observe the feel of the brake pedal.
11. If the brake pedal feels spongy, repeat the automated bleeding procedure. If the brake pedal still feels spongy after repeating the automated bleeding procedure inspect the brake system for external leaks.
12. Turn the ignition key ON, with the engine OFF; check to see if the brake system warning lamp remains illuminated.
13. If the brake system warning lamp remains illuminated, DO NOT allow the vehicle to be driven until it is diagnosed and repaired.
14. Drive the vehicle to exceed 8 mph (13 km/h) to allow ABS initialization to occur. Observe brake pedal feel.

15. If the brake pedal feels spongy, repeat the automated bleeding procedure until a firm brake pedal is obtained.

MASTER CYLINDER BLEEDING

Non-Hybrid Vehicles

1. Secure the mounting flange of the brake master cylinder in a bench vise so that the rear of the primary piston is accessible.
2. Remove the master cylinder reservoir cap and diaphragm.
3. Install suitable fittings to the master cylinder ports that match the type of flare seat required and also provide for hose attachment.
4. Install transparent hoses to the fittings installed to the master cylinder ports, then route the hoses into the master cylinder reservoir.
5. Fill the master cylinder reservoir to at least the half-way point with GM approved brake fluid from a clean, sealed brake fluid container.
6. Ensure that the ends of the transparent hoses running into the master cylinder reservoir are fully submerged in the brake fluid.
7. Using a smooth, round-ended tool, depress and release the primary piston as far as it will travel, a depth of about 1 inch (25 mm), several times. Observe the flow of fluid coming from the ports.

➡ **As air is bled from the primary and secondary pistons, the effort required to depress the primary piston will increase and the amount of travel will decrease.**

8. Continue to depress and release the primary piston until fluid flows freely from the ports with no evidence of air bubbles.
9. Remove the transparent hoses from the master cylinder reservoir.
10. Install the master cylinder reservoir cap and diaphragm.
11. Remove the fittings with the transparent hoses from the master cylinder ports. Wrap the master cylinder with a clean shop cloth to prevent brake fluid spills.
12. Remove the master cylinder from the vise.

Hybrid Vehicles

➡ **The ignition must be in the OFF position, without pausing at ACCESSORY, and without applying the brake pedal to ensure the brake modulator and High Pressure Accumulator (HPA) pressure relief occurs. This process will take approximately 1 to 3 minutes.**

1. Turn the ignition to OFF, without pausing at ACCESSORY, and remove the ignition key.
2. Wait approximately 1 to 3 minutes until the brake modulator and HPA pressure relief is complete.
3. Remove the master cylinder reservoir cap and diaphragm.
4. Mark the location of the master cylinder brake pipe fittings.
5. Disconnect the master cylinder brake pipe fittings.
6. Install suitable fittings to the master cylinder ports that match the type of flare seat required and also provide for hose attachment.
7. Install transparent hoses to the fittings installed to the master cylinder ports, then route the hoses into the master cylinder reservoir.
8. Fill the master cylinder reservoir to at least the half-way point with Delco Supreme 11, GM P/N 12377967 (Canadian P/N 992667), or equivalent DOT-3 brake fluid from a clean, sealed brake fluid container.
9. Ensure that the ends of the transparent hoses running into the master cylinder reservoir are fully submerged in the brake fluid.
10. Press and release the brake pedal as far as it will travel several times. With the aid of an assistant, observe the flow of fluid coming from the ports.

➡ **As air is bled from the primary and secondary pistons, the effort required to depress the primary piston will increase and the amount of travel will decrease.**

11. Continue to press and release the brake pedal until fluid flows freely from the ports with no evidence of air bubbles.
12. Remove the transparent hoses from the master cylinder reservoir.
13. Install the master cylinder brake pipe fittings, noting their location and tighten the fittings to 22 ft. lbs. (30 Nm).
14. Fill the brake master cylinder reservoir.
15. Install the master cylinder reservoir cap and diaphragm.

BLEEDING THE ABS SYSTEM

See Bleeding Procedures in this section.

FLUID FILL PROCEDURE

Non-Hybrid Vehicles

1. Visually inspect the brake fluid level through the brake master cylinder reservoir.

2. If the brake fluid level is at or below the half-full point during routine fluid checks, the brake system should be inspected for wear and possible brake fluid leaks.

3. If the brake fluid level is at or below the half-full point during routine fluid checks, and an inspection of the brake system did not reveal wear or brake fluid leaks, the brake fluid may be topped-off up to the maximum-fill level.

4. If brake system service was just completed, the brake fluid may be topped-off up to the maximum-fill level.

5. If the brake fluid level is above the half-full point, adding brake fluid is not recommended under normal conditions.

6. If brake fluid is to be added to the master cylinder reservoir, clean the outside of the reservoir on and around the reservoir cap prior to removing the cap and diaphragm. Use only Delco Supreme 11, GM P/N 12377967 (Canadian P/N 992667), or equivalent DOT-3 brake fluid from a clean, sealed brake fluid container.

Hybrid Vehicles

➡**The ignition must be in the OFF position, without pausing at ACCESSORY, and without applying the brake pedal to ensure the brake modulator and High Pressure Accumulator (HPA) pressure**

relief occurs. This process will take approximately 1 to 3 minutes.

1. Turn the ignition to OFF, without pausing at ACCESSORY, and remove the ignition key.

➡**During the pressure relief process, the fluid level in the master cylinder reservoir will rise. Do not remove the master cylinder reservoir cap during the pressure relief process.**

2. Wait approximately 1 to 3 minutes until the brake modulator and HPA pressure relief is complete.

3. Visually inspect the brake fluid level through the brake master cylinder reservoir.

4. The brake fluid level should rise to the upper full fill level mark after the brake fluid level stabilizes.

5. If the brake fluid level is below or rises above the upper fill level mark after the brake fluid level stabilizes, the brake system should be inspected.

6. If the brake fluid level is at the upper fill level mark, do not add brake fluid to the master cylinder reservoir.

7. Start the engine.

8. As the brake modulator draws brake fluid from the master cylinder reservoir to charge the brake modulator and the HPA, the brake fluid level will decrease.

9. The brake fluid level should be at or above the midway point of the MAX and MIN level marks of the master cylinder reservoir after the brake fluid level stabilizes.

10. If the brake fluid level is at or below the midway point of the MAX and MIN level marks on the master cylinder reservoir after the brake fluid level stabilizes, the brake system should be inspected for wear and possible brake fluid leaks.

11. If the brake fluid level is at or below the midway point of the MAX and MIN level marks on the master cylinder reservoir point during routine fluid checks, and an inspection of the brake system did not reveal wear or brake fluid leaks, the brake fluid may be filled to the MAX level mark.

12. If brake system service was just completed, brake fluid should be added to bring the level in the master cylinder reservoir the MAX level mark.

13. If the brake fluid level is at the MAX level mark, adding brake fluid is not recommended under normal conditions.

14. If brake fluid is to be added to the master cylinder reservoir, clean the outside of the reservoir on and around the reservoir cap prior to removing the cap and diaphragm. Use only Delco Supreme 11, GM P/N 12377967 (Canadian P/N 992667), or equivalent DOT-3 brake fluid from a clean, sealed brake fluid container.

BRAKES

FRONT DISC BRAKES

✳✳ CAUTION

Dust and dirt accumulating on brake parts during normal use may contain asbestos fibers from production or aftermarket brake linings. Breathing excessive concentrations of asbestos fibers can cause serious bodily harm. Exercise care when servicing brake parts. Do not sand or grind brake lining unless equipment used is designed to contain the dust residue. Do not clean brake parts with compressed air or by dry brushing. Cleaning should be done by dampening the brake components with a fine mist of water, then wiping the brake components clean with a dampened cloth. Dispose of cloth and all residue containing asbestos fibers in an impermeable container with the appropriate label. Follow practices prescribed by the Occupational Safety and Health Administration (OSHA) and the Environmental Protection Agency (EPA) for the han-

dling, processing, and disposing of dust or debris that may contain asbestos fibers.

BRAKE CALIPER

REMOVAL & INSTALLATION

1500 Series

See Figure 7.

1. Raise and support the vehicle.
2. Remove the tire and wheel assembly.
3. Remove the brake hose fitting bolt.
4. Remove the brake hose fitting gaskets and discard.
5. Plug the brake hose fitting to prevent brake fluid loss and contamination.
6. Remove the brake caliper guide pin bolts.

   a. DO NOT use any air tools to remove or install the brake caliper guide pin bolts. Use hand tools ONLY.

   b. Install an open end wrench to hold the caliper guide pin in line with the brake caliper while removing or installing

the caliper guide pin bolts. DO NOT allow the open end wrench to contact the brake caliper. Allowing the open end wrench to contact the brake caliper will

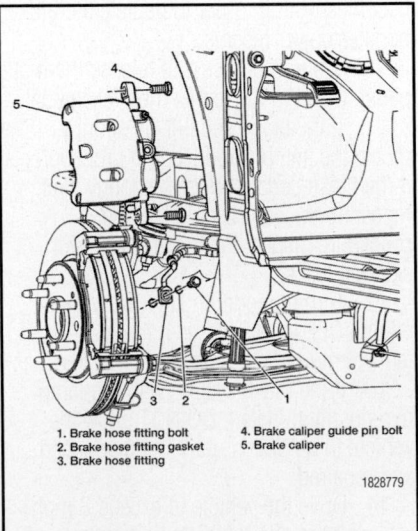

1. Brake hose fitting bolt
2. Brake hose fitting gasket
3. Brake hose fitting
4. Brake caliper guide pin bolt
5. Brake caliper

1828779

Fig. 7 Exploded view of the front brake caliper assembly

cause a pulsation when the brakes are applied.

c. Ensure the brake caliper guide pin seal is fully seated in the groove of the brake caliper guide pin and the guide pin slides freely in caliper bracket bore.

7. Remove the brake caliper.

To install:

8. Installation is the reverse of removal.

9. Ensure the brake caliper guide pin seal is fully seated in the groove of the brake caliper guide pin and the guide pin slides freely in caliper bracket bore.

10. Tighten the brake caliper guide pin bolts to 74 ft. lbs. (100 Nm).

11. Install new brake hose fitting gaskets.

12. Tighten the brake hose fitting bolt to 30 ft. lbs. (40 Nm).

13. Bleed the hydraulic brake system.

14. After the installation is complete and with the engine OFF, gradually apply the brake pedal to approximately ⅔ of its travel distance.

15. Slowly release the brake pedal.

16. Wait 15 seconds, then repeat steps until a firm brake pedal is obtained. This will properly seat the brake caliper piston and the brake pads.

17. Fill the master cylinder to the proper level.

2500 Series

See Figure 8.

1. Raise and support the vehicle.
2. Remove the tire and wheel assembly.

3. Remove the brake hose fitting bolt.

4. Remove the brake hose fitting gaskets and discard.

5. Plug the brake hose fitting to prevent brake fluid loss and contamination.

6. Remove the brake caliper guide pin bolts.

a. DO NOT use any air tools to remove or install the brake caliper guide pin bolts. Use hand tools ONLY.

b. Install an open end wrench to hold the caliper guide pin in line with the brake caliper while removing or installing the caliper guide pin bolts. DO NOT allow the open end wrench to contact the brake caliper. Allowing the open end wrench to contact the brake caliper will cause a pulsation when the brakes are applied.

c. Ensure the brake caliper guide pin seal is fully seated in the groove of the brake caliper guide pin and the guide pin slides freely in caliper bracket bore.

7. Remove the brake caliper.

To install:

8. Installation is the reverse of removal.

9. Tighten the brake caliper guide pin bolts to 80 ft. lbs. (108 Nm).

10. Install new brake hose fitting gaskets.

11. Tighten the brake hose fitting bolt to 30 ft. lbs. (40 Nm).

12. Bleed the hydraulic brake system.

13. After the installation is complete and with the engine OFF, gradually apply the brake pedal to approximately ⅔ of its travel distance.

14. Slowly release the brake pedal.

15. Wait 15 seconds, then repeat steps until a firm brake pedal is obtained. This will properly seat the brake caliper piston and the brake pads.

16. Fill the master cylinder to the proper level.

DISC BRAKE PADS

REMOVAL & INSTALLATION

1500 Series

See Figure 9.

※ CAUTION

Support the brake caliper with heavy mechanic wire, or equivalent, whenever it is separated from its mount and the hydraulic flexible brake hose is still connected. Failure to support the caliper in this manner will cause the flexible brake hose to bear the weight of the caliper, which may cause damage to the brake hose and in turn may cause a brake fluid leak.

1. Inspect the fluid level in the brake master cylinder reservoir.

2. If the brake fluid level is midway between the maximum-full point and the minimum allowable level, no brake fluid needs to be removed before proceeding.

3. If the brake fluid level is higher than midway between the maximum-full point and the minimum allowable level, remove

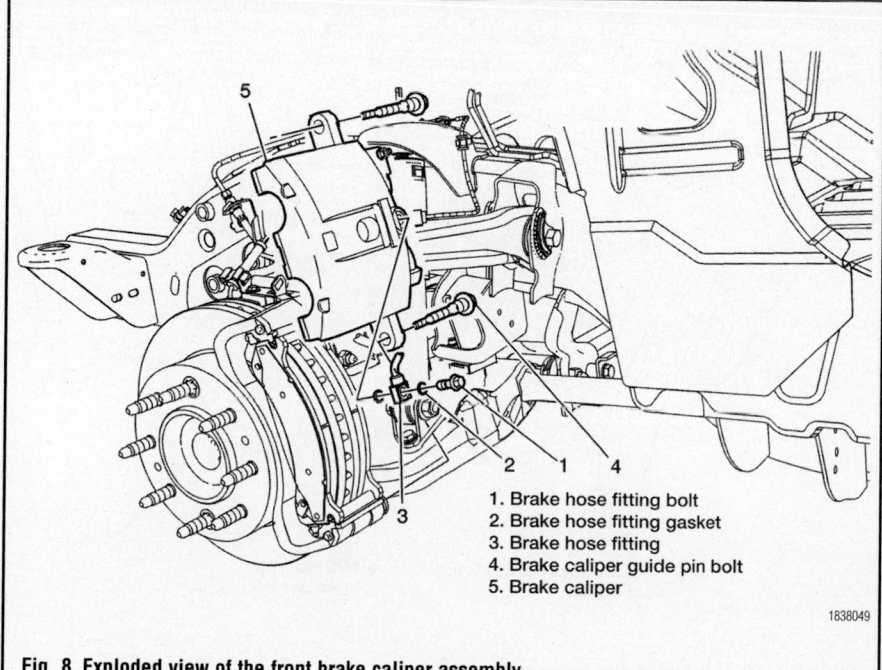

1. Brake hose fitting bolt
2. Brake hose fitting gasket
3. Brake hose fitting
4. Brake caliper guide pin bolt
5. Brake caliper

1838049

Fig. 8 Exploded view of the front brake caliper assembly

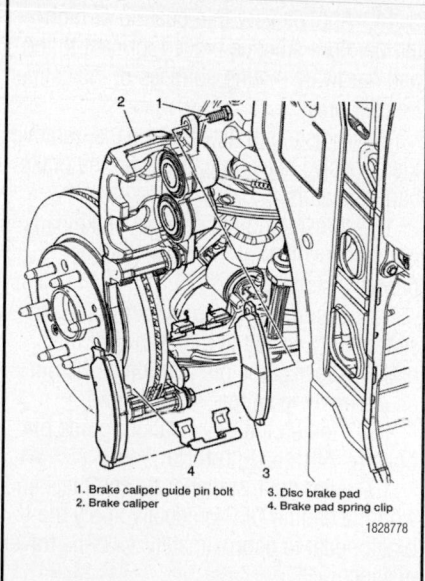

1. Brake caliper guide pin bolt
2. Brake caliper
3. Disc brake pad
4. Brake pad spring clip

1828778

Fig. 9 Exploded view of the brake pad assembly

brake fluid to the midway point before proceeding.

4. Raise and support the vehicle.
5. Remove the tire and wheel assembly.
6. Remove the caliper guide pin bolts.

a. DO NOT use any air tools to remove or install the brake caliper guide pin bolts. Use hand tools ONLY.

b. Install an open end wrench to hold the caliper guide pin in line with the brake caliper while removing or installing the caliper guide pin bolts. DO NOT allow the open end wrench to contact the brake caliper. Allowing the open end wrench to contact the brake caliper will cause a pulsation when the brakes are applied.

7. Remove the brake caliper.

a. Install 2 large C-clamps over the top of the caliper housing and against the back of the outboard brake pad.

b. Slowly and evenly tighten the C-clamps until the caliper pistons are completely retracted into the brake caliper bores.

c. Remove the C-clamps.

d. Without disconnecting the brake hose, pivot the brake caliper upward.

e. Support the brake caliper with heavy mechanics wire or equivalent.

8. Remove the disc brake pads. and spring clips.

To install:

9. Installation is the reverse of removal.

10. Thoroughly clean the brake pad hardware mating surfaces of the caliper bracket of any debris and corrosion with denatured alcohol and allow to dry.

11. Apply a very thin coating of high temperature silicone brake lubricant to the pad hardware mating surfaces of the caliper bracket only.

12. If installing new brake pads, remove the adhesive backing paper from the brake pad insulators.

13. If installing the original brake pads, note the location of the brake pads for proper installation.

14. Ensure the brake caliper guide pin seal is fully seated in the groove of the brake caliper guide pin and the guide pin slides freely in caliper bracket bore.

15. Tighten the brake caliper guide pin bolts to 74 ft. lbs. (100 Nm).

16. After the installation is complete and with the engine OFF, gradually apply the brake pedal to approximately ⅔ of its travel distance.

17. Slowly release the brake pedal.

18. Wait 15 seconds, then repeat steps until a firm brake pedal is obtained. This

will properly seat the brake caliper pistons and brake pads.

19. Fill the master cylinder to the proper level.

20. Burnish the brake pads and rotors.

2500 Series

See Figure 10.

✳✳ CAUTION

Support the brake caliper with heavy mechanic wire, or equivalent, whenever it is separated from its mount and the hydraulic flexible brake hose is still connected. Failure to support the caliper in this manner will cause the flexible brake hose to bear the weight of the caliper, which may cause damage to the brake hose and in turn may cause a brake fluid leak.

1. Inspect the fluid level in the brake master cylinder reservoir.

2. If the brake fluid level is midway between the maximum-full point and the minimum allowable level, no brake fluid needs to be removed before proceeding.

3. If the brake fluid level is higher than midway between the maximum-full point and the minimum allowable level, remove brake fluid to the midway point before proceeding.

4. Raise and support the vehicle.

5. Remove the tire and wheel assembly.

6. Remove the lower caliper guide pin bolt.

7. Remove the brake caliper.

a. Install 2 large C-clamps over the top of the caliper housing and against the back of the outboard brake pad.

b. Slowly and evenly tighten the C-clamps until the caliper pistons are completely retracted into the brake caliper bores.

c. Remove the C-clamps.

d. Without disconnecting the brake hose, pivot the brake caliper upward.

e. Support the brake caliper with heavy mechanics wire or equivalent.

8. Remove the disc brake pads.

➡Note the location of the inner and outer brake pads to aid in installation.

9. Remove and discard the brake pad shims.

To install:

10. Installation is the reverse of removal.

11. Thoroughly clean the brake pad hardware mating surfaces of the caliper bracket of any debris and corrosion.

12. Tighten the brake caliper guide pin bolts to 80 ft. lbs. (108 Nm).

13. After the installation is complete and with the engine OFF, gradually apply the brake pedal to approximately ⅔ of its travel distance.

14. Slowly release the brake pedal.

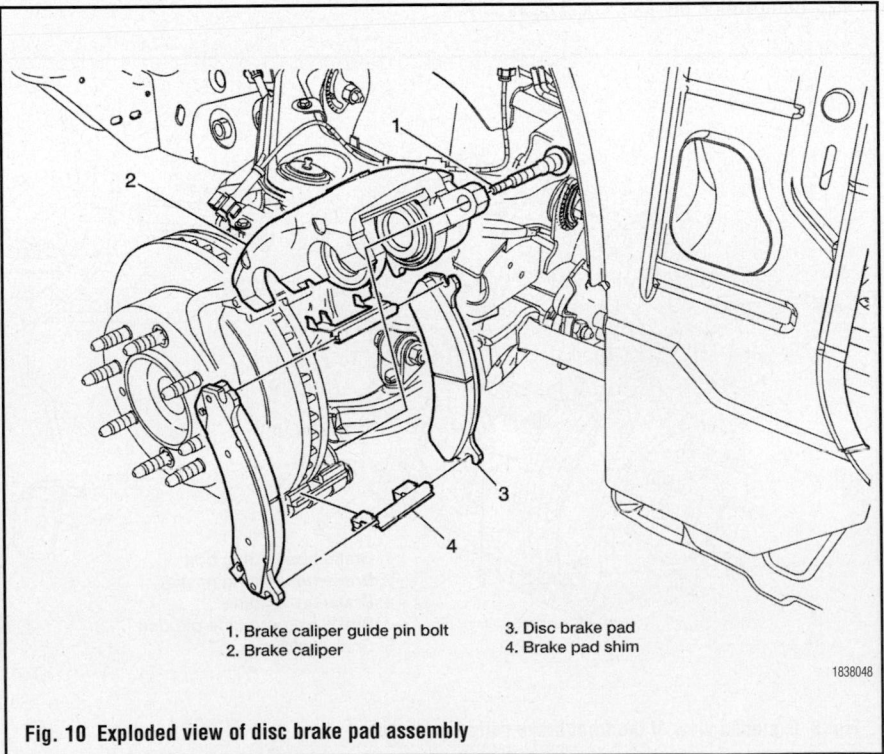

1. Brake caliper guide pin bolt
2. Brake caliper
3. Disc brake pad
4. Brake pad shim

1838048

Fig. 10 Exploded view of disc brake pad assembly

15. Wait 15 seconds, then repeat steps until a firm brake pedal is obtained. This will properly seat the brake caliper pistons and brake pads.

16. Fill the master cylinder to the proper level.

17. Burnish the brake pads and rotors.

BRAKE PAD AND ROTOR BURNISHING

> **✳✳ WARNING**
>
> Road test a vehicle under safe conditions and while obeying all traffic laws. Do not attempt any maneuvers that could jeopardize vehicle control. Failure to adhere to these precautions could lead to serious personal injury and vehicle damage.

Burnishing the brake pads and brake rotors is necessary in order to ensure that the braking surfaces are properly prepared after service has been performed on the disc brake system.

This procedure should be performed whenever the disc brake rotors have been refinished or replaced, and/or whenever the disc brake pads have been replaced.

1. Select a smooth road with little or no traffic.

2. Accelerate the vehicle to 30 mph (48 km/h).

➡**Use care to avoid overheating the brakes while performing this step.**

3. Using moderate to firm pressure, apply the brakes to bring the vehicle to a stop. Do not allow the brakes to lock.

4. Repeat steps until approximately 20 stops have been completed. Allow sufficient cooling periods between stops in order to properly burnish the brake pads and rotors.

BRAKES

> **✳✳ CAUTION**
>
> Dust and dirt accumulating on brake parts during normal use may contain asbestos fibers from production or aftermarket brake linings. Breathing excessive concentrations of asbestos fibers can cause serious bodily harm. Exercise care when servicing brake parts. Do not sand or grind brake lining unless equipment used is designed to contain the dust residue. Do not clean brake parts with compressed air or by dry brushing. Cleaning should be done by dampening the brake components with a fine mist of water, then wiping the brake components clean with a dampened cloth. Dispose of cloth and all residue containing asbestos fibers in an impermeable container with the appropriate label. Follow practices prescribed by the Occupational Safety and Health Administration (OSHA) and the Environmental Protection Agency (EPA) for the handling, processing, and disposing of dust or debris that may contain asbestos fibers.

BRAKE CALIPER

REMOVAL & INSTALLATION

1500 Series

See Figure 11.

1. Raise and support the vehicle.
2. Remove the tire and wheel assembly.
3. Remove the brake hose fitting bolt.
4. Remove the brake hose fitting gaskets.
5. Plug the brake hose fitting to prevent brake fluid loss and contamination.

6. Remove the brake caliper guide pin bolts.

   a. DO NOT use any air tools to remove or install the brake caliper guide pin bolts. Use hand tools ONLY.

   b. Install an open end wrench to hold the caliper guide pin in line with the brake caliper while removing or installing the caliper guide pin bolts. DO NOT allow the open end wrench to contact the brake caliper. Allowing the open end wrench to contact the brake caliper will cause a pulsation when the brakes are applied.

   c. Discard the brake caliper guide pin bolts.

7. Remove the brake caliper.

To install:

8. Installation is the reverse of removal.

REAR DISC BRAKES

9. Ensure the brake caliper guide pin seal is fully seated in the groove of the brake caliper guide pin and the guide pin slides freely in caliper bracket bore.

10. Tighten the brake caliper guide pin bolts to 38 ft. lbs. (52 Nm).

11. Tighten the brake hose fitting bolt to 30 ft. lbs. (40 Nm).

12. Bleed the hydraulic brake system.

13. After the installation is complete and with the engine OFF, gradually apply the brake pedal to approximately ⅔ of its travel distance.

14. Slowly release the brake pedal.

15. Wait 15 seconds, then repeat steps until a firm brake pedal is obtained. This will properly seat the brake caliper piston and the brake pads.

16. Fill the master cylinder to the proper level.

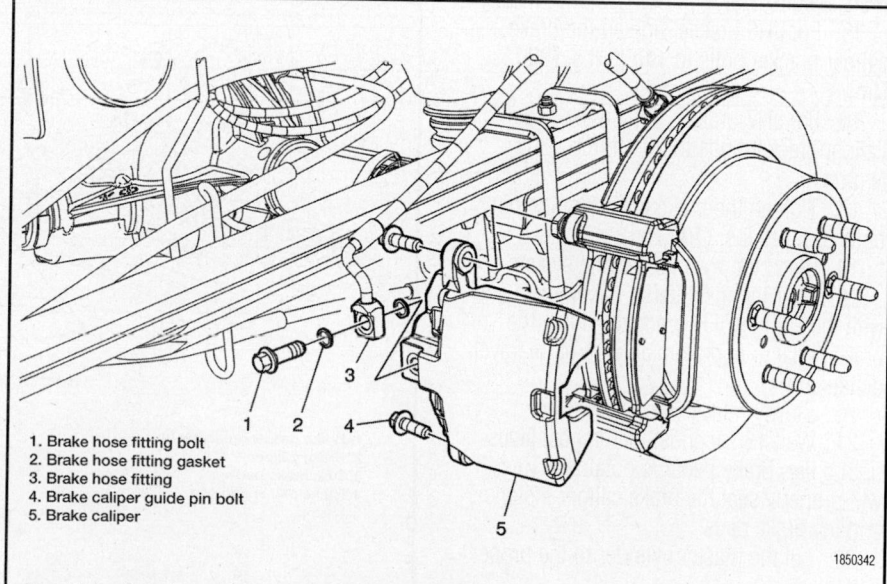

1. Brake hose fitting bolt
2. Brake hose fitting gasket
3. Brake hose fitting
4. Brake caliper guide pin bolt
5. Brake caliper

1850342

Fig. 11 Exploded view of the brake caliper assembly

2500 Series

See Figure 12.

1. Raise and support the vehicle.
2. Remove the tire and wheel assembly.
3. Remove the brake hose fitting bolt.
4. Remove and discard the brake hose fitting gaskets.
5. Plug the brake hose fitting to prevent brake fluid loss and contamination.
6. Remove the lower brake caliper guide pin bolt.

➡**The upper brake caliper guide pin bolt cannot be removed until the brake caliper and bracket assembly are removed from the rear axle.**

7. Loosen the upper brake caliper guide pin bolt.
8. Remove the brake caliper bracket.
9. Remove the upper brake caliper guide pin bolt.
10. Remove the brake caliper.

To install:

11. Installation is the reverse of removal.
12. Remove all traces of the adhesive patch on the brake caliper bracket bolts and threaded holes of the brake caliper bracket.
13. Clean the brake caliper bracket bolt threads and the threaded holes of the brake caliper bracket with denatured alcohol or equivalent and allow to dry.
14. Apply threadlocker G/M P/N 12345493 (Canadian P/N 10953488) to ⅔ of the threaded portion of the brake caliper bracket bolts.
15. For JH6 brakes, tighten the brake caliper bracket bolts to 148 ft. lbs. (200 Nm).
16. For JH7 brakes, tighten the brake caliper bracket bolts to 221 ft. lbs. (300 Nm).
17. Tighten the brake caliper guide pin bolts to 80 ft. lbs. (108 Nm).
18. Bleed the hydraulic brake system.
19. After the installation is complete and with the engine OFF, gradually apply the brake pedal to approximately ⅔ of its travel distance.
20. Slowly release the brake pedal.
21. Wait 15 seconds, then repeat steps until a firm brake pedal is obtained. This will properly seat the brake caliper pistons and the brake pads.
22. Fill the master cylinder to the proper level.

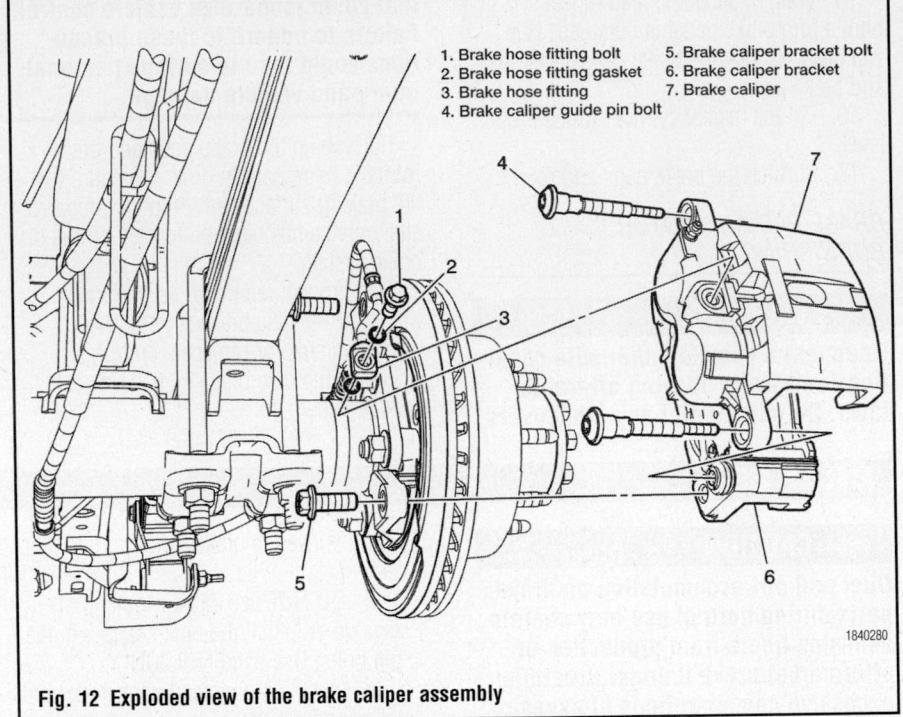

1. Brake hose fitting bolt
2. Brake hose fitting gasket
3. Brake hose fitting
4. Brake caliper guide pin bolt
5. Brake caliper bracket bolt
6. Brake caliper bracket
7. Brake caliper

Fig. 12 Exploded view of the brake caliper assembly

DISC BRAKE PADS

REMOVAL & INSTALLATION

1500 Series

See Figure 13.

> ✳✳ **CAUTION**
>
> **Support the brake caliper with heavy mechanic wire, or equivalent, whenever it is separated from its mount and the hydraulic flexible brake hose is still connected. Failure to support the caliper in this manner will cause the flexible brake hose to bear the weight of the caliper, which may cause damage to the brake hose and in turn may cause a brake fluid leak.**

1. Inspect the fluid level in the brake master cylinder reservoir.
2. If the brake fluid level is midway between the maximum-full point and the minimum allowable level, no brake fluid needs to be removed before proceeding.

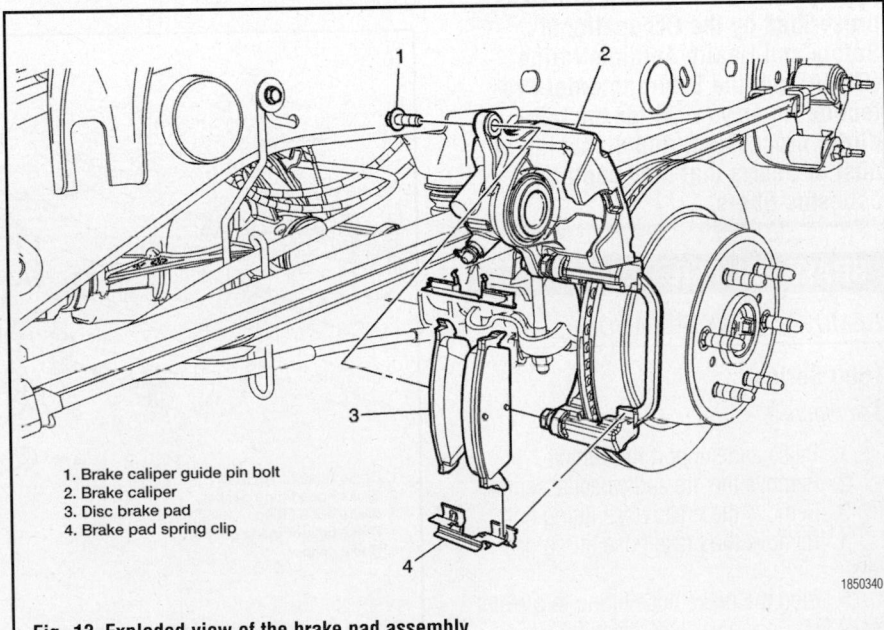

1. Brake caliper guide pin bolt
2. Brake caliper
3. Disc brake pad
4. Brake pad spring clip

Fig. 13 Exploded view of the brake pad assembly

3. If the brake fluid level is higher than midway between the maximum-full point and the minimum allowable level, remove brake fluid to the midway point before proceeding.

4. Raise and support the vehicle.

5. Remove the tire and wheel assembly.

6. Remove the caliper guide pin bolts.

a. DO NOT use any air tools to remove or install the brake caliper guide pin bolts. Use hand tools ONLY.

b. Install an open end wrench to hold the caliper guide pin in line with the brake caliper while removing or installing the caliper guide pin bolts. DO NOT allow the open end wrench to contact the brake caliper. Allowing the open end wrench to contact the brake caliper will cause a pulsation when the brakes are applied.

7. Remove the brake caliper.

a. Install a large C-clamp over the top of the caliper housing and against the back of the outboard brake pad.

b. Slowly and evenly tighten the C-clamp until the caliper pistons are completely retracted into the brake caliper bore.

c. Remove the C-clamp.

d. Without disconnecting the brake hose, pivot the brake caliper upward.

e. Support the brake caliper with heavy mechanics wire or equivalent.

8. Remove the disc brake pads. and spring clips.

To install:

9. Installation is the reverse of removal.

10. Thoroughly clean the brake pad hardware mating surfaces of the caliper bracket of any debris and corrosion with denatured alcohol and allow to dry.

11. Apply a very thin coating of high temperature silicone brake lubricant to the pad hardware mating surfaces of the caliper bracket only.

12. If installing new brake pads, remove the adhesive backing paper from the brake pad insulators.

13. If installing the original brake pads, note the location of the brake pads for proper installation.

14. Ensure the brake caliper guide pin seal is fully seated in the groove of the brake caliper guide pin and the guide pin slides freely in caliper bracket bore.

15. Tighten the brake caliper guide pin bolts to 38 ft. lbs. (52 Nm).

16. After the installation is complete and with the engine OFF, gradually apply the brake pedal to approximately ⅔ of its travel distance.

17. Slowly release the brake pedal.

18. Wait 15 seconds, then repeat steps until a firm brake pedal is obtained. This will properly seat the brake caliper pistons and brake pads.

19. Fill the master cylinder to the proper level.

20. Burnish the brake pads and rotors.

2500 Series

See Figure 14.

✳✳ CAUTION

Support the brake caliper with heavy mechanic wire, or equivalent, whenever it is separated from its mount and the hydraulic flexible brake hose is still connected. Failure to support the caliper in this manner will cause the flexible brake hose to bear the weight of the caliper, which may cause damage to the brake hose and in turn may cause a brake fluid leak.

1. Inspect the fluid level in the brake master cylinder reservoir.

2. If the brake fluid level is midway between the maximum-full point and the minimum allowable level, no brake fluid needs to be removed before proceeding.

3. If the brake fluid level is higher than midway between the maximum full point and the minimum allowable level, remove brake fluid to the midway point before proceeding.

4. Raise and support the vehicle.

5. Remove the tire and wheel assembly.

6. Compress the brake caliper pistons.

a. Install 2 large C-clamps over the top of the caliper housing and against the back of the outboard brake pad.

b. Slowly and evenly tighten the C-clamps until the caliper pistons are completely retracted into the brake caliper bores.

c. Remove the C-clamps.

7. Remove the lower caliper guide pin bolt.

8. Remove the brake caliper.

a. Without disconnecting the brake hose, pivot the brake caliper upward.

b. Support the brake caliper with heavy mechanics wire or equivalent.

9. Remove the disc brake pads.

➡ Note the location of the inner and outer brake pads to aid in installation.

10. Remove and discard the brake pad shims.

To install:

11. Installation is the reverse of removal.

12. Thoroughly clean the brake pad hardware mating surfaces of the caliper bracket of any debris and corrosion.

13. Tighten the brake caliper guide pin bolts to 80 ft. lbs. (108 Nm).

14. After the installation is complete and with the engine OFF, gradually apply the brake pedal to approximately ⅔ of its travel distance.

15. Slowly release the brake pedal.

16. Wait 15 seconds, then repeat steps until a firm brake pedal is obtained. This

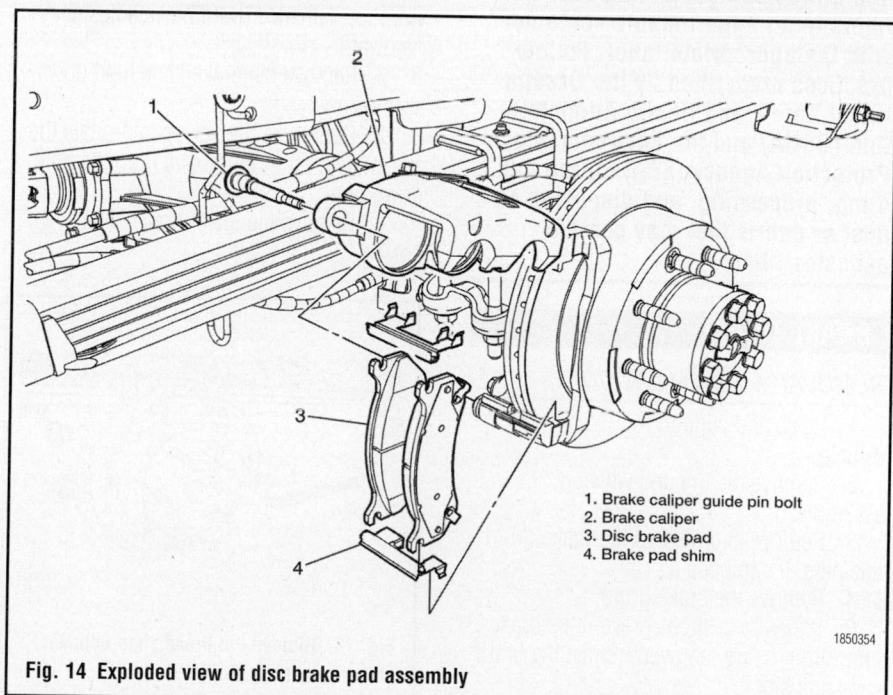

1. Brake caliper guide pin bolt
2. Brake caliper
3. Disc brake pad
4. Brake pad shim

1850354

Fig. 14 Exploded view of disc brake pad assembly

will properly seat the brake caliper pistons and brake pads.

17. Fill the master cylinder to the proper level.

18. Burnish the brake pads and rotors.

BRAKE PAD AND ROTOR BURNISHING

> **✸✸ WARNING**
>
> Road test a vehicle under safe conditions and while obeying all traffic laws. Do not attempt any maneuvers that could jeopardize vehicle control.

Failure to adhere to these precautions could lead to serious personal injury and vehicle damage.

Burnishing the brake pads and brake rotors is necessary in order to ensure that the braking surfaces are properly prepared after service has been performed on the disc brake system.

This procedure should be performed whenever the disc brake rotors have been refinished or replaced, and/or whenever the disc brake pads have been replaced.

1. Select a smooth road with little or no traffic.

2. Accelerate the vehicle to 30 mph (48 km/h).

→ Use care to avoid overheating the brakes while performing this step.

3. Using moderate to firm pressure, apply the brakes to bring the vehicle to a stop. Do not allow the brakes to lock.

4. Repeat steps until approximately 20 stops have been completed. Allow sufficient cooling periods between stops in order to properly burnish the brake pads and rotors.

BRAKES

REAR DRUM BRAKES

> **✸✸ CAUTION**
>
> Dust and dirt accumulating on brake parts during normal use may contain asbestos fibers from production or aftermarket brake linings. Breathing excessive concentrations of asbestos fibers can cause serious bodily harm. Exercise care when servicing brake parts. Do not sand or grind brake lining unless equipment used is designed to contain the dust residue. Do not clean brake parts with compressed air or by dry brushing. Cleaning should be done by dampening the brake components with a fine mist of water, then wiping the brake components clean with a dampened cloth. Dispose of cloth and all residue containing asbestos fibers in an impermeable container with the appropriate label. Follow practices prescribed by the Occupational Safety and Health Administration (OSHA) and the Environmental Protection Agency (EPA) for the handling, processing, and disposing of dust or debris that may contain asbestos fibers.

BRAKE DRUM

REMOVAL & INSTALLATION

1. Raise and support the vehicle.

2. Remove the tire and wheel assembly.

3. Remove and discard the brake drum retainers, if equipped.

4. Remove the brake drum.

5. If the brake shoes prevent the brake drum from being removed, retract the brake shoe adjuster.

To install:

6. Using the J-42450-A Wheel Hub Resurfacing Kit , remove any corrosion from the rear axle flange contact surface.

7. Install the brake drum.

8. Adjust the drum brakes.

9. Install the tire and wheel assembly.

BRAKE SHOES

REMOVAL & INSTALLATION

See Figures 15 through 22.

1. Remove the brake drum.

2. Remove the brake shoe adjuster actuator lever spring.

3. Remove the adjuster actuator lever.

4. Spread the brake shoes apart slightly and remove the brake shoe adjuster.

5. Inspect and replace any missing, worn, or damaged drum brake adjuster hardware.

6. Remove the brake shoe hold down springs and cups.

7. Compress the spring and rotate the assembly ¼ turn to remove from the hold down pins.

8. Remove the lower brake shoe spring.

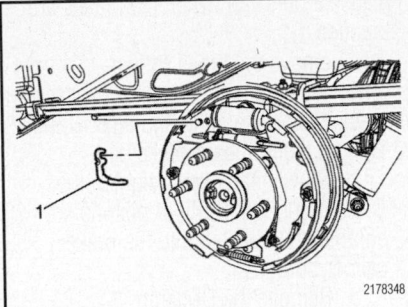

Fig. 16 Remove the adjuster actuator lever (1)

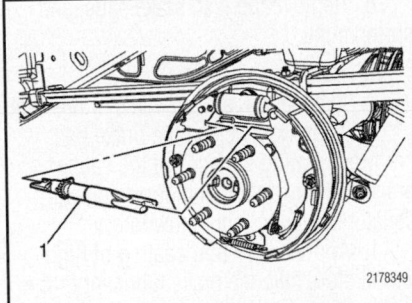

Fig. 17 Remove the brake shoe adjuster (1)

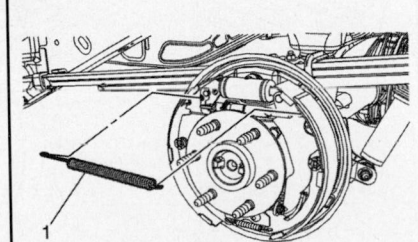

Fig. 15 Remove the brake shoe adjuster actuator lever spring (1)

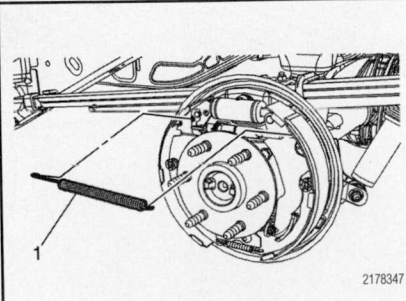

Fig. 18 Remove the brake shoe hold down springs and cups (1)

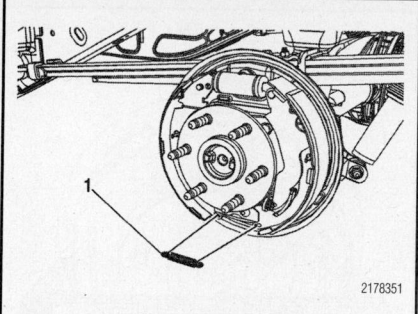

Fig. 19 Remove the lower brake shoe spring (1)

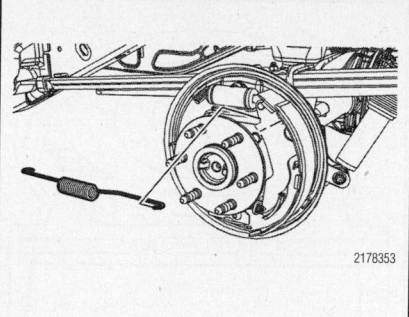

Fig. 21 Remove the brake shoe return spring

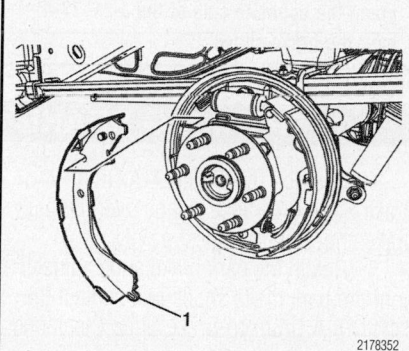

Fig. 20 Rotate the primary brake shoe (1) outward, disengage the return spring from the brake shoe web and remove the primary brake shoe

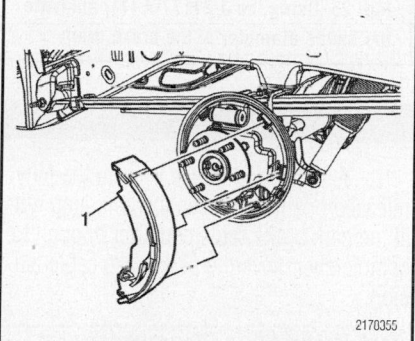

Fig. 22 Compress the park brake cable spring, disengage the park brake cable fitting end from the park brake lever and remove the secondary brake shoe (1)

9. Rotate the primary brake shoe outward, disengage the return spring from the brake shoe web and remove the primary brake shoe.

10. Remove the brake shoe return spring.

11. Compress the park brake cable spring, disengage the park brake cable fitting end from the park brake lever and remove the secondary brake shoe.

12. Clean the backing plate and apply high temperature brake lubricant to the brake shoe contact surfaces of the rear brake backing plate.

13. Inspect and replace any missing, worn, or damaged drum brake hardware.

To install:

14. Compress the park brake cable spring and insert the park brake cable fitting end to the park brake on the secondary brake shoe.

15. Position the secondary brake shoe to the rear brake backing plate.

16. Install the brake shoe return spring. Insert the hook end of the return spring to the brake shoe from behind the web.

17. Install the primary brake shoe return spring and position the primary brake shoe

to the rear brake backing plate. Insert the hook end of the return spring to the brake shoe web from the outer face.

18. Install the lower brake shoe spring.

19. Install the brake shoe hold down springs and cups.

20. Compress the spring and rotate the assembly ¼ turn to install to the hold down pins.

21. Disassemble, clean and lubricate the threads of the brake shoe adjuster with high temperature brake lubricant.

22. Assemble the brake shoe adjuster.

23. Spread the brake shoes apart slightly and install the brake shoe adjuster.

24. Install the adjuster actuator lever to the pivot pin on the primary brake shoe.

25. Install the brake shoe adjuster actuator lever spring.

26. Install the brake drum.

ADJUSTMENT

See Figures 23 through 26.

Special Tools Required:
• J-21177-A Drum to Brake Shoe Clearance Gauge
• J-42450-A Wheel Hub Resurfacing Kit

➡ This procedure must be performed after replacing the brake shoes or whenever the brake shoes have been removed.

1. Raise and support the vehicle.

2. Remove the rear tire and wheel.

3. Disable the park brake cable automatic adjuster.

4. Remove the brake shoe adjuster access plug from the backing plate.

5. Insert a thin bladed tool through the adjuster access hole in the backing plate until it contacts the adjuster lever.

6. Push the adjuster lever away from the adjuster screw.

7. Using a suitable tool, rotate the adjuster screw upward.

8. Remove the brake drum.

9. Using the J-42450-A, clean the mating surface of the rear axle flange.

10. Using the J-21177-A, measure the inside diameter of the brake drum.

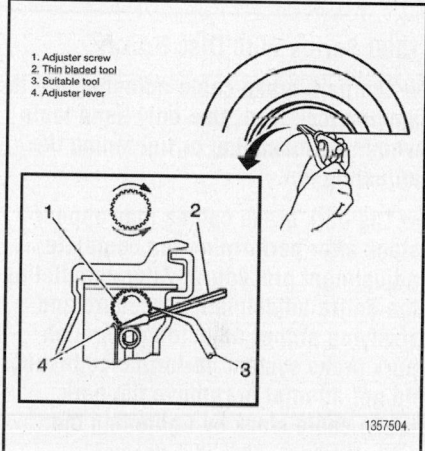

1. Adjuster screw
2. Thin bladed tool
3. Suitable tool
4. Adjuster lever

Fig. 23 Insert a thin bladed tool through the adjuster access hole in the backing plate until it contacts the adjuster lever

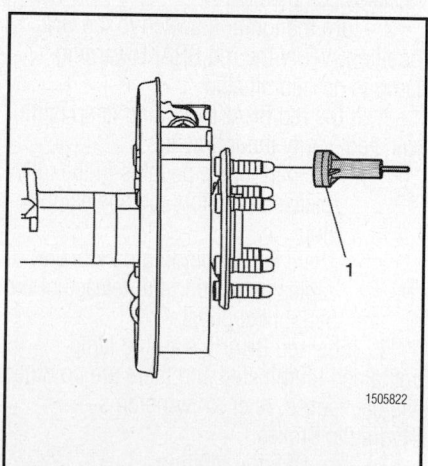

Fig. 24 Using the J-42450-A (1), clean the mating surface of the rear axle flange

11. With the set screw locked, place the opposite side of the J-21177-A over the brake shoes.

12. Rotate the brake shoe adjuster screw until the brake shoes just contact the J-21177-A.

13. Inspect the clearance between the brake shoes and the brake drum. Approximately 0.030 inches (0.76 mm).

14. Install the brake drum.

15. Enable the park brake cable automatic adjuster.

16. If necessary, adjust the park brake cable tension.

17. Install the tire and wheel.

18. Lower the vehicle.

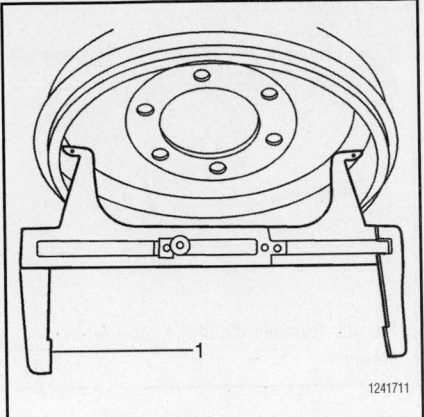

Fig. 25 Using the J-21177-A (1), measure the inside diameter of the brake drum

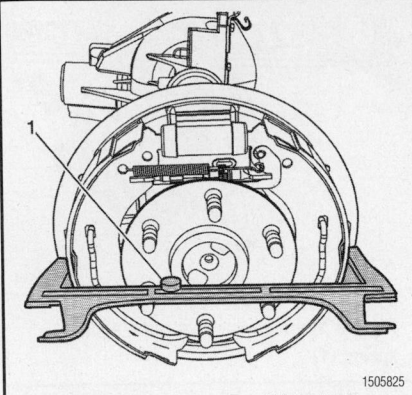

Fig. 26 With the set screw (1) locked, place the opposite side of the J-21177-A over the brake shoes

BRAKES

PARKING BRAKE

PARKING BRAKE CABLES

ADJUSTMENT

1500 Series With Disc Brakes

➡The park brake cable adjusting nut is a nylon lock type. Use only hand tools whenever loosening or tightening the adjusting nut.

➡The park brake cables may appear slack after performing the complete adjustment procedure. After completing the entire adjustment procedure and verifying proper adjustment through park brake system performance testing, do not attempt to remove the park brake cable slack by tightening the adjusting nut. This is a normal condition.

1. Apply and fully release the park brake 2–3 times. Verify that the park brake pedal releases completely.

2. Turn the ignition switch to the ON position. Verify the red BRAKE warning lamp is not illuminated.

3. If the red BRAKE warning lamp is illuminated, verify the following:

- The park brake pedal is in the fully released position and against the stop.
- There are no binding park brake cables preventing full release of the park brake pedal.

4. If the red BRAKE warning lamp remained illuminated and there are no other visible causes, refer to Symptoms—Hydraulic Brakes.

5. Turn OFF the ignition.

6. Raise and support the vehicle.

7. With the park brake lever in the fully released position, loosen the adjusting nut at the park brake cable equalizer enough to completely relieve the park brake cable tension.

Park Brake Shoe Clearance Adjustment

See Figures 27 and 28.

1. Without disconnecting the hydraulic brake hoses, remove the brake calipers and brackets as an assembly and support with heavy mechanics wire or equivalent.

2. Remove the rear brake rotors.

3. Set the J-21177-A Drum-to-Brake Shoe Clearance Gauge so that it lightly contacts the parking brake shoe friction surface of the brake rotor at its widest point.

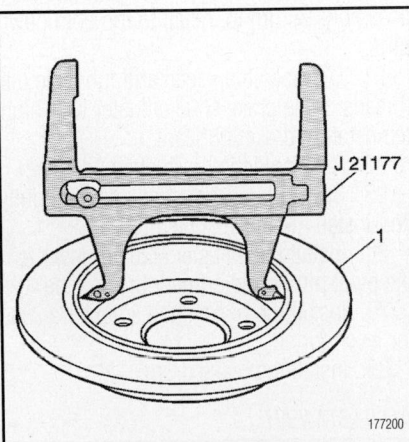

Fig. 27 Set the J-21177-A Drum-to-Brake Shoe Clearance Gauge so that it lightly contacts the parking brake shoe friction surface of the brake rotor (1) at its widest point

4. Position the J-21177-A Drum-to-Brake Shoe Clearance Gauge over the park brake shoes at the widest point.

5. Rotate the park brake shoe adjuster until the park brake shoes just contact the J-21177-A Drum-to-Brake Shoe Clearance Gauge.

6. Using a feeler gauge, set the parking brake shoe clearance to 0.026 inches (0.66 mm).

7. Repeat steps 3–6 for the opposite side.

8. Install the rear brake rotors and secure with hand tightened wheel nuts installed with the cone facing outward.

9. With all tension relieved from the park brake cables, rotate the rear brake rotors. Observe the amount of effort required for rotation, and the amount of drag, if present.

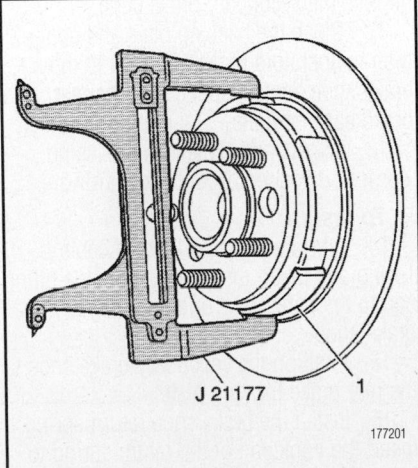

Fig. 28 Position the J-21177-A Drum-to-Brake Shoe Clearance Gauge over the park brake shoes (1) at the widest point

10. If drag is present, repeat steps 3–6.

Cable Tension Adjustment

1. Position a sheet of ordinary printer or copier paper between the park brake apply lever and the disc brake backing plate on the RH side of the vehicle.

2. Tighten the park brake cable adjusting nut until the paper inserted between the park brake apply lever and the backing plate slips out.

3. Loosen the adjustment nut 1 full turn.

Park Brake Adjustment Verification Check

1. Apply and release the park brake lever 3–5 times.

2. Install the J-28662 Brake Pedal Effort Gauge to the park brake lever pedal.

3. Observe the number of detents required to apply the park brake pedal to the amount of force specified, as indicated on the J-28662 Brake Pedal Effort Gauge.

➡ **3–5 detents required to apply the park brake pedal to 112 lbs. (500 N) of force.**

4. If the number of detents required to achieve correct force is less than the specification, then the cable tension is too high. Repeat adjustment steps as necessary.

5. If the number is detents required to achieve correct force is greater than the specification, then the cable tension is too low. Repeat adjustment steps as necessary.

6. Remove the wheel nuts.

7. Install the brake caliper and bracket assemblies.

8. Install the rear tire and wheel assemblies.

1500 Series With Drum Brake

➡ **The park brake cable adjusting nut is a nylon lock type. Use only hand tools whenever loosening or tightening the adjusting nut.**

➡ **The park brake cables may appear slack after performing the complete adjustment procedure. After completing the entire adjustment procedure and verifying proper adjustment through park brake system performance testing, do not attempt to remove the park brake cable slack by tightening the adjusting nut. This is a normal condition.**

1. Apply and fully release the park brake 2–3 times. Verify that the park brake pedal releases completely.

2. Turn the ignition switch to the ON position. Verify the red BRAKE warning lamp is not illuminated.

3. If the red BRAKE warning lamp is illuminated, verify the following:

- The park brake pedal is in the fully released position and against the stop.
- There are no binding park brake cables preventing full release of the park brake pedal.

4. If the red BRAKE warning lamp remained illuminated and there are no other visible causes, refer to Symptoms—Hydraulic Brakes.

5. Turn OFF the ignition.

6. Raise and support the vehicle.

7. With the park brake lever in the fully released position, loosen the adjusting nut at the park brake cable equalizer enough to completely relieve the park brake cable tension.

Brake Shoe Clearance Adjustment

1. Remove the rear brake drums.

2. Adjust the rear drum brakes.

3. Install the rear brake drums and secure with hand tightened wheel nuts installed with the cone facing outward.

4. With all tension relieved from the park brake cables, rotate the rear brake drums. Observe the amount of effort required for rotation, and the amount of drag, if present.

5. If drag is present, repeat steps 1–4.

Cable Tension Adjustment

1. Remove the wheel nuts and rear brake drums.

2. Position a piece of ordinary printer or copier paper between the park brake apply lever contact rest and the drum brake shoe on each side of the vehicle.

3. Tighten the park brake cable adjusting nut until the first piece of paper inserted between the park brake apply lever and the drum brake shoe on either side slips out.

4. Loosen the adjustment nut 4 full turns.

Park Brake Adjustment Verification Check

1. Install the rear brake drums and secure with hand tightened wheel nuts installed with the cone facing outward.

2. Apply and release the park brake lever 3–5 times.

3. Install the J-28662 Brake Pedal Effort Gauge to the park brake lever pedal.

4. Observe the number of detents required to apply the park brake pedal to the amount of force specified, as indicated on the J-28662 Brake Pedal Effort Gauge.

➡ **8–10 detents required to apply the park brake pedal to 112 lbs. (500 N) of force.**

5. If the number of detents required to achieve correct force is less than the specification, then the cable tension is too high. Repeat adjustment steps as necessary.

6. If the number is detents required to achieve correct force is greater than the specification, then the cable tension is too low. Repeat adjustment steps as necessary.

7. Remove the wheel nuts.

8. Install the rear tire and wheel assemblies.

2500 Series

Special Tools Required:
- J-21177-A Drum-to-Brake Shoe Clearance Gauge
- J-28662 Brake Pedal Effort Gauge

➡ **The park brake cable adjusting nut is a nylon lock type. Use only hand tools whenever loosening or tightening the adjusting nut.**

➡ **The park brake cables may appear slack after performing the complete adjustment procedure. After completing the entire adjustment procedure and verifying proper adjustment through park brake system performance testing, do not attempt to remove the park brake cable slack by tightening the adjusting nut. This is a normal condition.**

1. Identify if the vehicle is equipped with a first-design or a second-design park brake pedal assembly:

- First-design park brake pedal assemblies have the brake pedal pad positioned inboard of the pedal arm, and have no holes in the pedal arm near the pivot. The upper and lower formed edges of the pedal arm face inboard.
- Second-design park brake pedal assemblies have the brake pedal pad positioned outboard of the pedal arm, and have an 0.315 inches (8 mm) diameter hole in the pedal arm near the pivot. The upper and lower formed edges of the pedal arm face outboard.

2. Apply and fully release the park brake 2–3 times. Verify that the park brake pedal releases completely.

3. Turn the ignition switch to the ON position. Verify the red BRAKE warning lamp is not illuminated.

4. If the red BRAKE warning lamp is illuminated, verify the following:
- The park brake pedal is in the fully released position and against the stop.
- There are no binding park brake cables preventing full release of the park brake pedal.

5. If the red BRAKE warning lamp remained illuminated and there are no other visible causes, refer to Symptoms—Hydraulic Brakes.

6. Turn OFF the ignition.

7. Raise and support the vehicle.

8. With the park brake lever in the fully released position, loosen the adjusting nut at the park brake cable equalizer enough to completely relieve the park brake cable tension.

Park Brake Shoe Clearance Adjustment

See Figures 29 and 30.

1. Without disconnecting the hydraulic brake hoses, remove the brake calipers and brackets as an assembly and support with heavy mechanics wire or equivalent.

2. Remove the rear brake rotors.

3. Set the J-21177-A Drum-to-Brake Shoe Clearance Gauge so that it lightly contacts the parking brake shoe friction surface of the brake rotor at its widest point.

4. Position the J-21177-A Drum-to-Brake Shoe Clearance Gauge over the park brake shoes (1) at the widest point.

5. Rotate the park brake shoe adjuster until the park brake shoes just contact the J-21177-A Drum-to-Brake Shoe Clearance Gauge.

6. Using a feeler gauge, set the parking brake shoe clearance to 0.026 inches (0.66 mm).

7. Repeat steps 3–6 for the opposite side.

8. Install the rear brake rotors and secure with hand tightened wheel nuts installed with the cone facing outward.

9. With all tension relieved from the park brake cables, rotate the rear brake rotors. Observe the amount of effort required for rotation, and the amount of drag, if present.

10. If drag is present, repeat steps 3–6

Cable Tension Adjustment

1. Remove the wheel nuts.

2. Install the brake caliper and bracket assemblies.

3. Install the tire and wheel assemblies.

4. With the aid of an assistant, rotate both rear tire and wheel assemblies while slowly tightening the park brake cable adjustment nut.

5. Tighten the adjustment nut until both rear tire and wheel assemblies cannot be rotated.

6. Slowly loosen the park brake cable adjustment nut while simultaneously attempting to rotate the rear tire and wheel assemblies.

7. When the rear tire and wheel assemblies just begin to move, loosen the park brake cable adjustment nut the additional number of turns specified:
- 2500 series with first-design park brake pedal assembly: 20 additional turns

- 2500 series with second-design park brake pedal assembly: 12 additional turns

Park Brake Adjustment Verification Check

1. Apply and release the park brake lever 3–5 times.

2. Install the J-28662 Brake Pedal Effort Gauge to the park brake lever pedal.

3. Observe the number of detents required to apply the park brake pedal to the amount of force specified, as indicated on the J-28662 Brake Pedal Effort Gauge.

a. 2500 series with first-design park brake pedal assembly: 9–10 detents to apply the park brake pedal to 90 lbs. (400 N) of force.

b. 2500 series with second-design park brake pedal assembly: 6–8 detents to apply the park brake pedal to 67 lbs. (300 N) of force.

4. If the number of detents required to achieve correct force is less than the specification, then the cable tension is too high. Repeat adjustment steps as necessary.

5. If the number is detents required to achieve correct force is greater than the specification, then the cable tension is too low. Repeat adjustment steps as necessary.

PARKING BRAKE SHOES

REMOVAL & INSTALLATION

1500 Series

See Figure 31.

1. Raise and support the vehicle.
2. Remove the brake rotor.

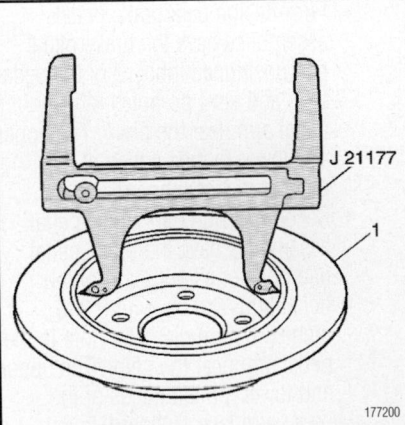

Fig. 29 Set the J-21177-A Drum-to-Brake Shoe Clearance Gauge so that it lightly contacts the parking brake shoe friction surface of the brake rotor (1) at its widest point

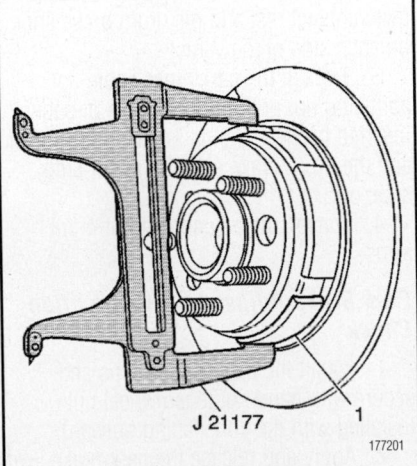

Fig. 30 Position the J-21177-A Drum-to-Brake Shoe Clearance Gauge over the park brake shoes (1) at the widest point

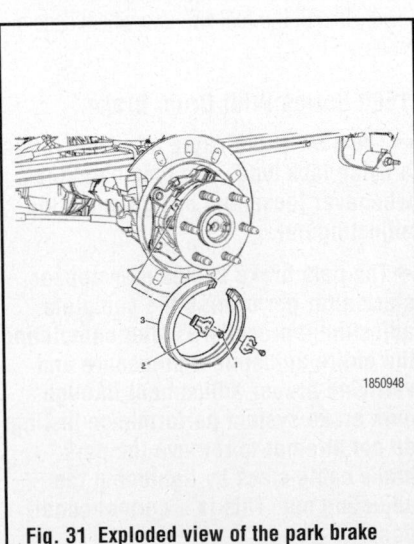

Fig. 31 Exploded view of the park brake assembly showing the shoe retaining clip bolts (1), the shoe retaining clips (2), and the park brake shoe and lining (3)

3. Disconnect the park brake cable from the actuator.

4. Remove the park brake shoe retaining clip bolts.

5. Remove the park brake shoe retaining clips.

6. Remove the park brake shoe and lining

➡**To remove and install the park brake shoe, place the open end of the park brake shoe over the axle flange and rotate it until the shoe has cleared the flange.**

To install:

7. Installation is the reverse of removal.

8. Apply a thin coat of high temperature silicone brake lubricant to the contact areas of the brake shoe and the backing plate.

9. Tighten the park brake shoe retaining clip bolts to 11 ft. lbs. (15 Nm).

10. Adjust the park brake.

2500 Series

See Figure 32.

1. Raise and support the vehicle.

2. Remove the rear tire and wheel assembly.

3. Remove the rear brake rotor.

4. Remove the park brake shoe adjuster spring.

5. Remove the park brake shoe adjuster.

6. Remove the park brake shoe hold down springs.

➡**Compress the spring and rotate ¼ turn to release.**

7. Remove the park brake shoe hold down spring pins.

8. Remove the park brake shoe return spring.

park brake shoes.

To install:

9. Installation is the reverse of removal.

10. Use denatured alcohol to clean brake

dust or grease from the park brake shoes and hardware.

11. If reinstalling the park brake shoes, note the location of the park brake shoes for installation.

12. Apply a small amount of high temperature silicone grease to the brake shoe and backing plate contact points.

13. After the installation is complete, adjust the park brake.

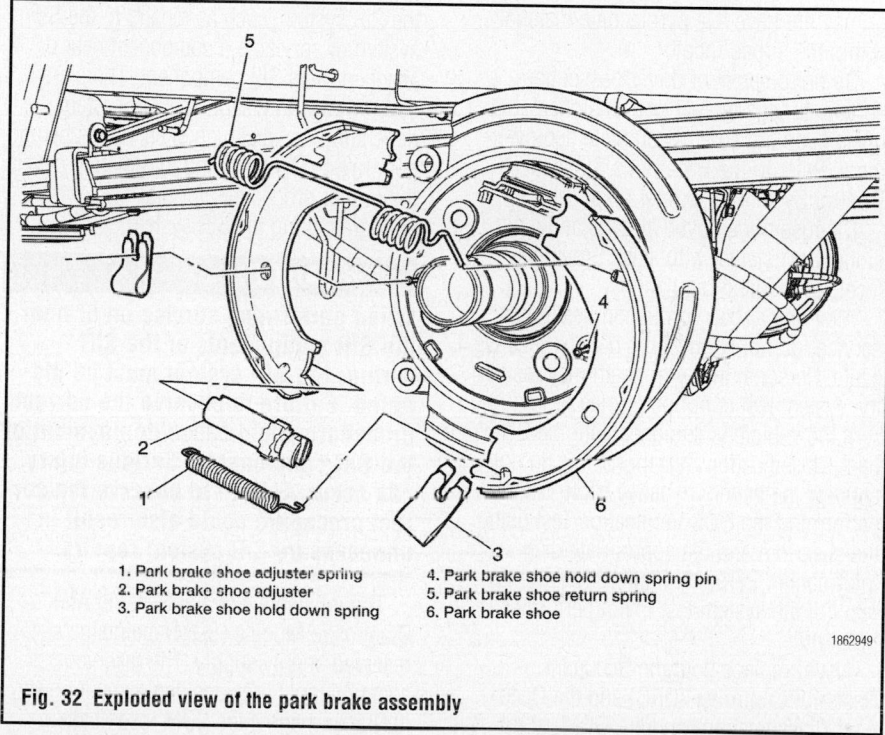

1. Park brake shoe adjuster spring
2. Park brake shoe adjuster
3. Park brake shoe hold down spring
4. Park brake shoe hold down spring pin
5. Park brake shoe return spring
6. Park brake shoe

1862949

Fig. 32 Exploded view of the park brake assembly

CHASSIS ELECTRICAL

AIR BAG (SUPPLEMENTAL RESTRAINT SYSTEM)

GENERAL INFORMATION

✳✳ CAUTION

These vehicles are equipped with an air bag system. The system must be disarmed before performing service on, or around, system components, the steering column, instrument panel components, wiring and sensors. Failure to follow the safety precautions and the disarming procedure could result in accidental air bag deployment, possible injury and unnecessary system repairs.

SERVICE PRECAUTIONS

Disconnect and isolate the battery negative cable before beginning any airbag system component diagnosis, testing, removal, or installation procedures. Allow system

capacitor to discharge for two minutes before beginning any component service. This will disable the airbag system. Failure to disable the airbag system may result in accidental airbag deployment, personal injury, or death.

Do not place an intact undeployed airbag face down on a solid surface. The airbag will propel into the air if accidentally deployed and may result in personal injury or death.

When carrying or handling an undeployed airbag, the trim side (face) of the airbag should be pointing away from the body to minimize possibility of injury if accidental deployment occurs. Failure to do this may result in personal injury or death.

Replace airbag system components with OEM replacement parts. Substitute parts may appear interchangeable, but internal differences may result in inferior occupant

protection. Failure to do so may result in occupant personal injury or death.

Wear safety glasses, rubber gloves, and long sleeved clothing when cleaning powder residue from vehicle after an airbag deployment. Powder residue emitted from a deployed airbag can cause skin irritation. Flush affected area with cool water if irritation is experienced. If nasal or throat irritation is experienced, exit the vehicle for fresh air until the irritation ceases. If irritation continues, see a physician.

Do not use a replacement airbag that is not in the original packaging. This may result in improper deployment, personal injury, or death.

The factory installed fasteners, screws and bolts used to fasten airbag components have a special coating and are specifically designed for the airbag system. Do not use substitute fasteners. Use only original equipment fasteners listed in the parts catalog when fastener replacement is required.

During, and following, any child restraint anchor service, due to impact event or vehicle repair, carefully inspect all mounting hardware, tether straps, and anchors for proper installation, operation, or damage. If a child restraint anchor is found damaged in any way, the anchor must be replaced. Failure to do this may result in personal injury or death.

Deployed and non-deployed airbags may or may not have live pyrotechnic material within the airbag inflator.

Do not dispose of driver/passenger/curtain airbags or seat belt tensioners unless you are sure of complete deployment. Refer to the Hazardous Substance Control System for proper disposal.

Dispose of deployed airbags and tensioners consistent with state, provincial, local, and federal regulations.

After any airbag component testing or service, do not connect the battery negative cable. Personal injury or death may result if the system test is not performed first.

If the vehicle is equipped with the Occupant Classification System (OCS), do not connect the battery negative cable before performing the OCS Verification Test using the scan tool and the appropriate diagnostic information. Personal injury or death may result if the system test is not performed properly.

Never replace both the Occupant Restraint Controller (ORC) and the Occupant Classification Module (OCM) at the same time. If both require replacement, replace one, then perform the Airbag System test before replacing the other.

Both the ORC and the OCM store Occupant Classification System (OCS) calibration data, which they transfer to one another when one of them is replaced. If both are replaced at the same time, an irreversible fault will be set in both modules and the OCS may malfunction and cause personal injury or death.

If equipped with OCS, the Seat Weight Sensor is a sensitive, calibrated unit and must be handled carefully. Do not drop or handle roughly. If dropped or damaged, replace with another sensor. Failure to do so may result in occupant injury or death.

If equipped with OCS, the front passenger seat must be handled carefully as well. When removing the seat, be careful when setting on floor not to drop. If dropped, the sensor may be inoperative, could result in occupant injury, or possibly death.

If equipped with OCS, when the passenger front seat is on the floor, no one should sit in the front passenger seat. This uneven force may damage the sensing ability of the seat weight sensors. If sat on and damaged, the sensor may be inoperative, could result in occupant injury, or possibly death.

DISARMING THE SYSTEM

SIR component location affects how a vehicle should be serviced. There are parts of the SIR system installed in various locations around a vehicle.

There are several reasons for disabling the SIR system, such as repairs to the SIR system or servicing a component near or attached to an SIR component. There are several ways to disable the SIR system depending on what type of service is being performed. The following information covers the proper procedures for disabling/enabling the SIR system.

✸ CAUTION

When performing service on or near the SIR components or the SIR wiring, the SIR system must be disabled. Failure to observe the correct procedure could cause deployment of the SIR components. Serious injury can occur. Failure to observe the correct procedure could also result in unnecessary SIR system repairs.

The inflatable restraint Sensing And Diagnostic Module (SDM) maintains a reserved energy supply. The reserved energy supply provides deployment power for the air bags if the SDM loses battery power during a collision. Deployment power is available for as much as 1 minute after disconnecting the vehicle power. Waiting 1 minute before working on the system after disabling the SIR system prevents deployment of the air bags from the reserved energy supply.

General Service Instructions

1. The following are general service instructions which must be followed in order to properly repair the vehicle and return it to its original integrity:

   a. Do not expose inflator modules to temperatures above 150°F (65°C).

   b. Verify the correct replacement part number. Do not substitute a component from a different vehicle.

   c. Use only original GM replacement parts available from your authorized GM dealer. Do not use salvaged parts for repairs to the SIR system.

2. Discard any of the following components if it has been dropped from a height of 3 ft. (91 cm) or greater:

- Inflatable restraint SDM
- Any Inflatable restraint air bag module
- Inflatable restraint steering wheel module coil
- Any Inflatable restraint sensor
- Inflatable restraint seat belt pretensioners
- Inflatable restraint Passenger Presence System (PPS) module or sensor

Disabling Procedure—Air Bag Fuse

1. Turn the steering wheel so that the vehicles wheels are pointing straight ahead.
2. Place the ignition in the OFF position.

➡**The SDM may have more than one fused power input. To ensure there is no unwanted SIR deployment, personal injury, or unnecessary SIR system repairs, remove all fuses supplying power to the SDM. With all SDM fuses removed and the ignition switch in the ON position, the AIR BAG warning indicator illuminates. This is normal operation, and does not indicate a SIR system malfunction.**

3. Locate and remove the fuse(s) supplying power to the SDM.
4. Wait 1 minute before working on the system.

Disabling Procedure—Negative Battery Cable

1. Turn the steering wheel so that the vehicles wheels are pointing straight ahead.
2. Place the ignition in the OFF position.
3. Disconnect the negative battery cable from the battery.
4. Wait 1 minute before working on system.

ARMING THE SYSTEM

Enabling Procedure—Air Bag Fuse

1. Place the ignition in the OFF position.
2. Install the fuse(s) supplying power to the SDM.
3. Turn the ignition switch to the ON position. The AIR BAG indicator will flash then turn OFF.
4. Perform the Diagnostic System Check—Vehicle if the AIR BAG warning indicator does not operate as described.

Enabling Procedure—Negative Battery Cable

1. Place the ignition in the OFF position.
2. Connect the negative battery cable to the battery.

3. Turn the ignition switch to the ON position. The AIR BAG indicator will flash then turn OFF.

4. Perform the Diagnostic System Check—Vehicle if the AIR BAG warning indicator does not operate as described.

CLOCKSPRING CENTERING

Inflatable Restraint Steering Wheel Module Coil Centering

See Figures 33 and 34.

✻✻ CAUTION

The new SIR coil assembly will be centered. Improper alignment of the SIR coil assembly may damage the unit, causing an inflatable restraint malfunction.

1. Verify the following conditions before centering the SIR coil:
- The front wheels of the vehicle are in the straight ahead position.
- The block tooth of the steering shaft assembly is in the 12 o'clock position.
- The ignition switch is in the LOCK position.

➡**If a double wire harness strap is installed onto the wire harness assembly and the column, you must reuse the holder for the wire straps during the installation.**

2. Remove the wire harness strap or straps where necessary.

3. Hold the SIR coil and look at the side with the letters POM.

4. Rotate the coil hub clockwise until the coil ribbon stops.

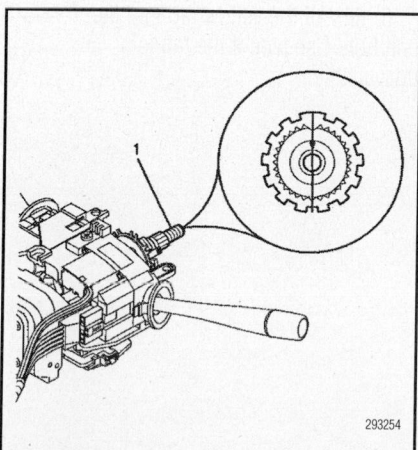

293254

Fig. 33 The block tooth (1) of the steering shaft assembly is in the 12 o'clock position

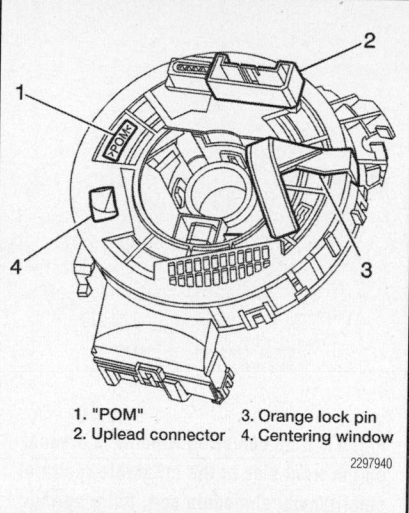

1. "POM"
2. Upload connector
3. Orange lock pin
4. Centering window

2297940

Fig. 34 Hold the SIR coil and look at the side with the letters POM

✻✻ CAUTION

Do not rotate the SIR coil more than 3 turns counterclockwise from the center position. There is no stop in the counterclockwise direction. Rotating the SIR coil more than 3 turns counterclockwise from the center position will damage the SIR coil, causing an inflatable restraint malfunction.

5. From the clockwise stop, rotate the coil hub slowly counterclockwise approximately 3.3 turns. Place the upload connector in the 12 o'clock position. Ensure the flat wire cable loop appears in the centering window. This is the CENTER position.

6. If you have the orange lock pin, use the lock pin to lock the SIR coil in the center position.

7. If you do not have the orange lock pin, hold the SIR coil in the center position.

8. Align the SIR coil with the horn tower and slide the SIR coil onto the steering shaft assembly.

9. If a double wire harness strap is installed onto the wire harness assembly and the column, you must route the wires up against the steering column. One wire harness strap will surround one lead from the coil to the steering column. The other wire harness strap will surround all other leads to the steering column.

Inflatable Restraint Steering Wheel Module Coil Centering

See Figures 33, 35 through 38.

✻✻ CAUTION

The new SIR coil assembly will be centered. Improper alignment of the

SIR coil assembly may damage the unit, causing an inflatable restraint malfunction.

1. Verify the following before centering the inflatable restraint steering wheel module coil:
- The wheels on the vehicle are straight ahead.
- The block tooth of the steering shaft assembly is in the 12 o'clock position.
- The ignition switch is in the LOCK position.

2. If the front of the inflatable restraint steering wheel module coil has a centering window, and on the back side a spring service lock, perform the following steps:

a. Hold the inflatable restraint steering wheel module coil with the face up.

b. While depressing the spring service lock, rotate the coil hub clockwise until the coil ribbon stops.

c. Rotate the coil hub slowly, counterclockwise, until the centering window appears yellow and both arrows line up.

d. Release spring service lock between the locking tab. The inflatable restraint steering wheel module coil is now centered.

e. Align the centered inflatable restraint steering wheel module coil with the horn tower and slide onto the steering shaft assembly.

3. If the front of the inflatable restraint steering wheel module coil has a centering window and no spring service lock on the back side, perform the following steps:

a. Hold the inflatable restraint steering wheel module coil with the face up.

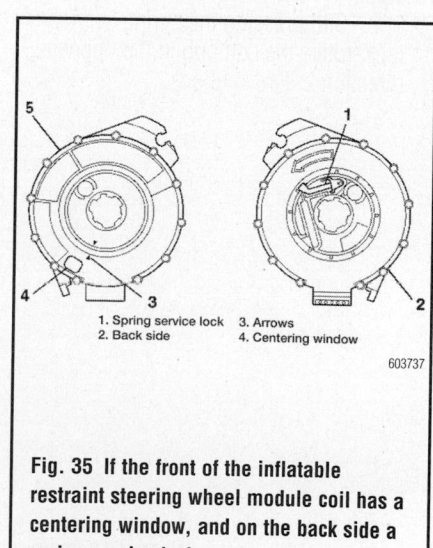

1. Spring service lock
2. Back side
3. Arrows
4. Centering window

603737

Fig. 35 If the front of the inflatable restraint steering wheel module coil has a centering window, and on the back side a spring service lock

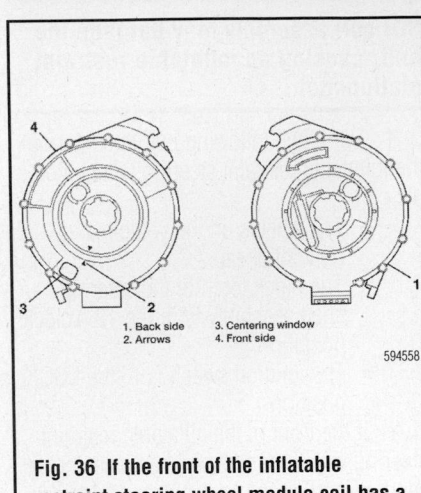

1. Back side
2. Arrows
3. Centering window
4. Front side

594558

Fig. 36 If the front of the inflatable restraint steering wheel module coil has a centering window and no spring service lock on the back side

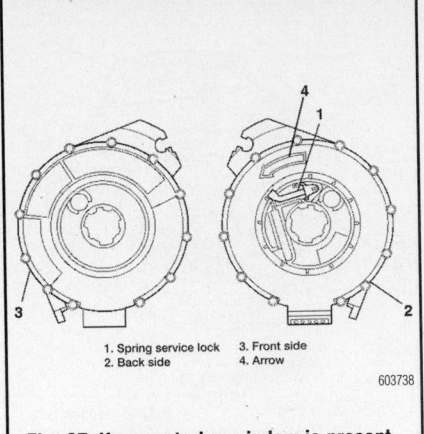

1. Spring service lock
2. Back side
3. Front side
4. Arrow

603738

Fig. 37 If no centering window is present on the front side of the inflatable restraint steering wheel module coil, but a spring service lock is on the back side

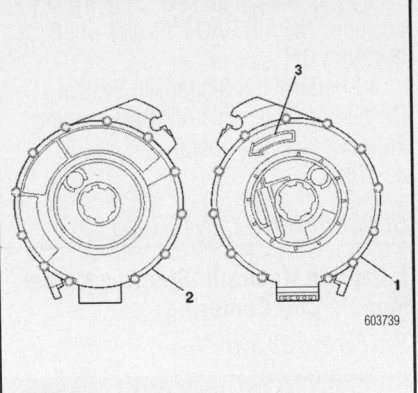

603739

Fig. 38 For no centering window on the front side (2) of the inflatable restraint steering wheel module coil and no spring service lock on the back side (1); arrow (3)

b. Rotate the coil hub clockwise until the coil ribbon stops.

c. Rotate the coil hub slowly, counter-clockwise until the centering window appears yellow and both arrows line up. This is the CENTER position.

d. While holding the coil hub in the CENTER position, align the inflatable restraint steering wheel module coil with the horn tower and slide onto the steering shaft assembly.

4. If no centering window is present on the front side of the inflatable restraint steering wheel module coil, but a spring service lock is on the back side, perform the following steps:

a. Hold the inflatable restraint steering wheel module coil with the back side up.

b. While depressing the spring service lock, rotate the coil hub in the direction of the arrow (4) until the coil ribbon stops.

c. Still pressing the spring service lock, rotate the coil hub in the opposite direction 2½ revolutions.

d. Release the spring service lock between locking tabs. The inflatable restraint steering wheel module coil is now centered.

e. Align the centered inflatable restraint steering wheel module coil with the horn tower and slide onto the steering shaft assembly.

5. For no centering window on the front side of the inflatable restraint steering wheel module coil and no spring service lock on the back side, perform the following steps:

a. Hold the inflatable restraint steering wheel module coil with the face up.

b. Rotate the coil hub in the direction of the arrow until the coil ribbon stops.

c. Rotate the coil hub, slowly, counterclockwise, for 2½ revolutions. This is the CENTER position.

d. While maintaining the coil hub in the CENTER position, align the centered inflatable restraint steering wheel module coil with the horn tower and slide onto the steering shaft assembly.

Alignment Procedure

✲✲ CAUTION

The new SIR coil assembly will be centered. Improper alignment of the SIR coil assembly may damage the unit, causing an inflatable restraint malfunction.

1. If available remove the yellow tab and save for reassembly.

2. Gently rotate the coil hub clockwise until a slight tension is present.

3. Count the number of revolutions, while gently rotating the coil hub counter clockwise until a slight tension is present.

4. Gently rotate the coil hub clockwise one half of the previously counted revolutions.

5. Rotate the coil hub as required to align the yellow tab.

6. Install the yellow tab into the coil hub. Use tape if the tab is unavailable.

DRIVE TRAIN

AUTOMATIC TRANSMISSION FLUID

DRAIN AND REFILL

4L60-E/4L65-E/4L70-E Transmission

See Figures 39 through 41.

1. Raise and suitably support the vehicle.

2. Place a drain pan under the transmission oil pan.

3. Remove the oil pan drain plug, if equipped.

4. If necessary, remove the bolts and position aside the range selector cable bracket for clearance while lowering the pan. It is not necessary to remove the cable from the lever or bracket.

5. Remove the oil pan bolts from the front and sides of the pan only.

6. Loosen the rear oil pan bolts approximately 4 turns.

7. Lightly tap the oil pan with a rubber mallet in order to loosen the pan to allow the fluid to drain.

8. Remove the remaining oil pan bolts.

9. Remove the oil pan and the gasket.

10. Grasp firmly while pulling down with a twisting motion in order to remove the filter.

11. Remove and discard the filter seal. The filter seal may be stuck in the pump; if necessary, carefully use pliers or another suitable tool to remove the seal.

12. Inspect the fluid color.

13. Inspect the filter. Pry the metal crimping away from the top of the filter and pull apart. The filter may contain the following evidence for root cause diagnosis:

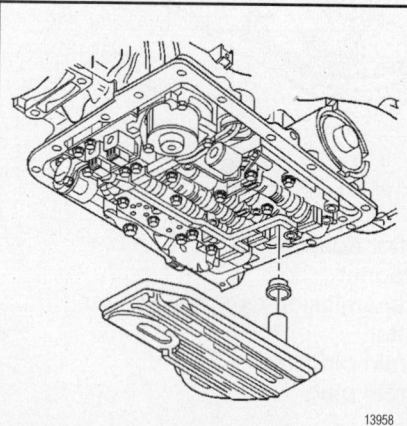

Fig. 39 Grasp firmly while pulling down with a twisting motion in order to remove the filter

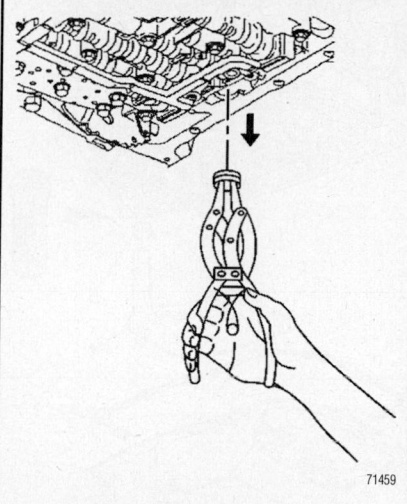

Fig. 40 The filter seal may be stuck in the pump; if necessary, carefully use pliers or another suitable tool to remove the seal

- Clutch material
- Bronze slivers indicating bushing wear
- Steel particles

14. Clean the transmission case and the oil pan gasket surfaces with solvent, and air dry. You must remove all traces of the old gasket material.

To install:

15. Coat the NEW filter seal with automatic transmission fluid.

16. Install the NEW filter seal into the transmission case. Tap the seal into place using a suitable size socket.

17. Install the NEW filter.

18. Install the oil pan and NEW gasket.

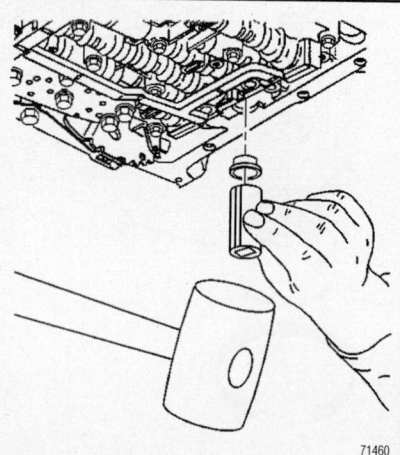

Fig. 41 Install the NEW filter seal into the transmission case

19. Install the oil pan bolts. Tighten the bolts alternately and evenly to 97 inch lbs. (11 Nm).

20. If previously removed, install the range selector cable bracket and bolts. Tighten the bolts to 18 ft. lbs. (25 Nm).

21. Apply a small amount of sealant GM P/N 12346004 (Canadian P/N 10953480), or equivalent to the threads of the oil pan drain plug, if equipped.

22. Lower the vehicle.

23. Fill the transmission to the proper level with DEXRON® VI transmission fluid.

24. Check the COLD fluid level reading for initial fill only.

25. Inspect the oil pan gasket for leaks.

6L45/6L50/6L80/6L90 Transmission

See Figure 42.

> ✳✳ **CAUTION**
>
> **Use Dexron VI transmission fluid only. Failure to use the proper fluid may result in transmission internal damage.**

1. Raise and support the vehicle.

2. Disconnect and lower the catalytic converter.

3. Place a suitable drain pan under the transmission.

4. Remove the transmission fluid pan bolts.

5. Remove the transmission fluid pan assembly.

   a. Check the condition of the draining fluid.

   b. Fill the transmission with the proper fluid.

   c. Fill the transmission with the proper amount of transmission fluid.

6. Remove the transmission fluid pan gasket.

➡ **The fluid pan gasket is reusable. Inspect the gasket to determine if it may be reused.**

7. Pull the fluid filter assembly straight out. Do not bend or twist the filter neck.

8. Remove the fluid filter seal assembly. Use a screwdriver or snap ring pliers to remove the filter seal.

> ✳✳ **CAUTION**
>
> **Do not damage the case sealing surface when removing the filter seal assembly.**

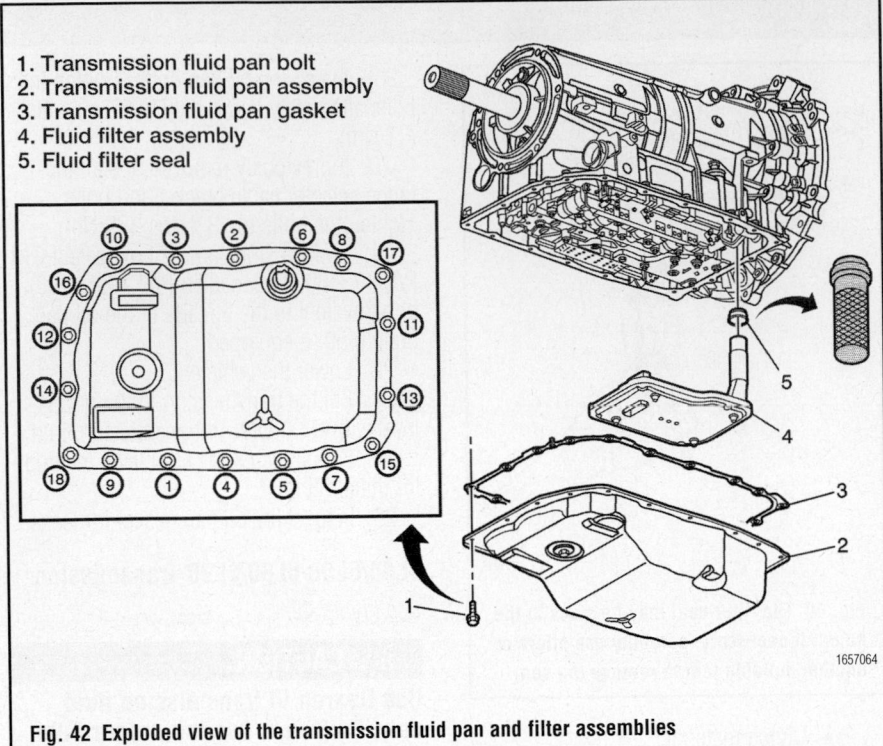

1. Transmission fluid pan bolt
2. Transmission fluid pan assembly
3. Transmission fluid pan gasket
4. Fluid filter assembly
5. Fluid filter seal

Fig. 42 Exploded view of the transmission fluid pan and filter assemblies

To install:

9. Installation is the reverse of removal.

10. Use the Seal Installer (DT 47848) and the Driver Handle (J-42183) to install the filter seal. Use new filter seals.

11. Lubricate the filter seal with transmission fluid before installing the filter.

12. Tighten the bolts in the sequence shown. Tighten the bolts to 90 inch lbs. (9 Nm).

Allison Transmission

See Figure 43.

➡**DO NOT drain the fluid if only the transmission external oil filter is being replaced.**

1. Remove the drain plug and drain plug seal. Drain the transmission fluid into a suitable container.

2. Inspect the drained fluid.

➡**Use a standard strap-type filter wrench to remove the transmission external oil filter.**

3. Remove the filter by rotating in the counterclockwise direction.

4. Remove the magnet from the filter adapter in the converter housing or from the top of the transmission external oil filter.

5. Clean any metal debris from the magnet. Presence of any metal pieces larger than dust may indicate that transmission replacement or overhaul is required.

To install:

6. Install the magnet onto the filter adapter which is in the converter housing.

7. Lubricate the gasket on the transmission external oil filter with transmission fluid.

8. Install, by hand, the transmission external oil filter until the gasket on the filter touches the converter housing.

❊❊ CAUTION

Turning the transmission external oil filter more than ONE FULL TURN after gasket contact will damage the filter and may cause fluid leakage.

9. Turn the filter ONE FULL TURN ONLY after gasket contact.

10. Install the drain plug and drain plug seal. Tighten the drain plug to 26 ft. lbs. (35 Nm).

11. Refill Transmission with DEXRON® VI Automatic Transmission Fluid.

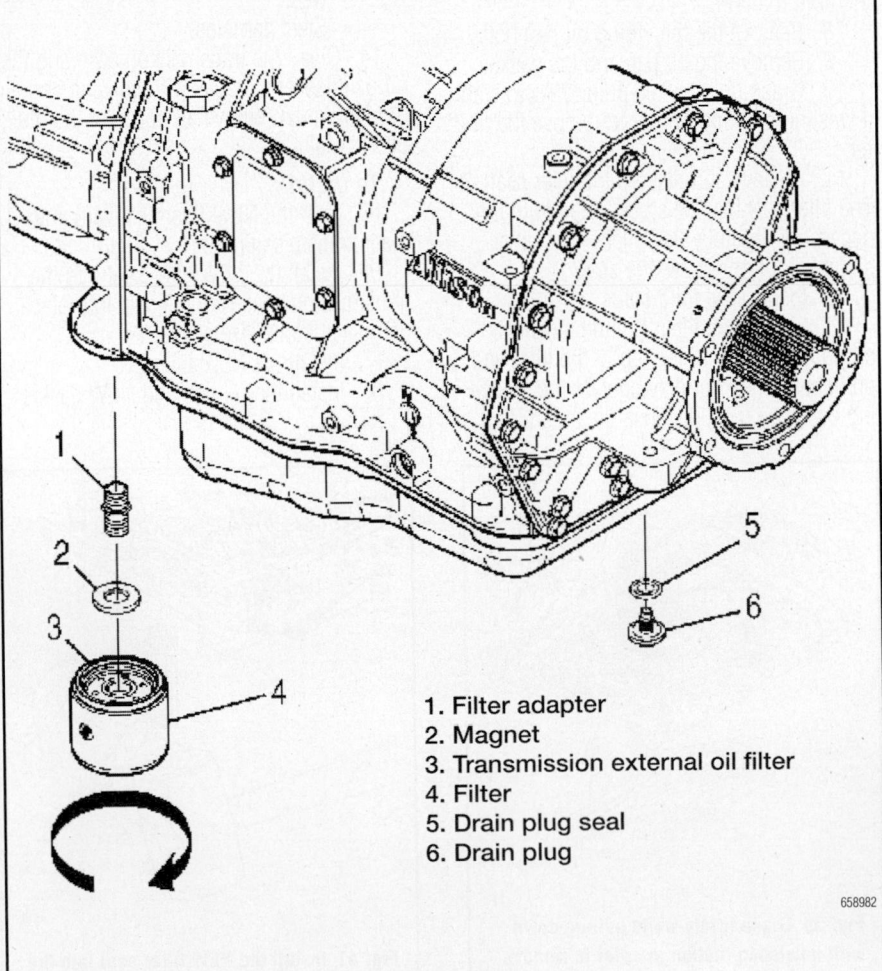

1. Filter adapter
2. Magnet
3. Transmission external oil filter
4. Filter
5. Drain plug seal
6. Drain plug

Fig. 43 Exploded view of the transmission filter assembly

➡ **DTC P0701 may often set following fluid service. Cycling the ignition clears the code and allows Drive or Reverse range to be attained.**

12. Cycle the ignition until Drive or Reverse range is attained.

➡ **Fluid remains in the external circuits and transmission cavities after draining the transmission.**

13. Check the transmission fluid level.

FILTER REPLACEMENT

2ML70 Transmission

See Figure 44.

1. Remove the transmission fluid pan.
2. Remove the fluid filter.

> ✳✳ **CAUTION**
>
> **Pull the fluid filter assembly straight out to avoid damage. Do not bend or twist the filter neck.**

3. Remove the fluid filter seal.

> ✳✳ **CAUTION**
>
> **Do not damage the case sealing surface when removing the filter seal assembly.**

4. Remove the auxiliary fluid filter.

> ✳✳ **CAUTION**
>
> **Pull the fluid filter assembly straight out to avoid damage. Do not bend or twist the filter neck.**

5. Remove the auxiliary fluid filter seals.

> ✳✳ **CAUTION**
>
> **Do not damage the case sealing surface when removing the filter seal assembly.**

6. Installation is the reverse of removal.

4L60-E/4L65-E/4L70-E Transmission

See Figures 45 through 47.

1. Raise and suitably support the vehicle.
2. Place a drain pan under the transmission oil pan.
3. Remove the oil pan drain plug, if equipped.
4. If necessary, remove the bolts and position aside the range selector cable bracket for clearance while lowering the pan. It is not necessary to remove the cable from the lever or bracket.
5. Remove the oil pan bolts from the front and sides of the pan only.
6. Loosen the rear oil pan bolts approximately 4 turns.
7. Lightly tap the oil pan with a rubber mallet in order to loosen the pan to allow the fluid to drain.
8. Remove the remaining oil pan bolts.
9. Remove the oil pan and the gasket.
10. Grasp firmly while pulling down with a twisting motion in order to remove the filter.
11. Remove and discard the filter seal. The filter seal may be stuck in the pump; if necessary, carefully use pliers or another suitable tool to remove the seal.
12. Inspect the fluid color.
13. Inspect the filter. Pry the metal crimping away from the top of the filter and pull apart. The filter may contain the following evidence for root cause diagnosis:

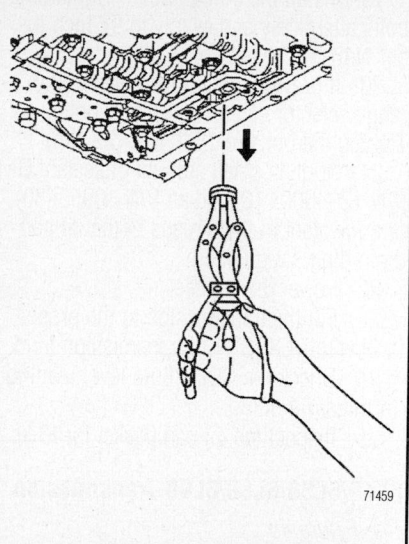

Fig. 46 The filter seal may be stuck in the pump; if necessary, carefully use pliers or another suitable tool to remove the seal

- Clutch material
- Bronze slivers indicating bushing wear
- Steel particles

14. Clean the transmission case and the oil pan gasket surfaces with solvent, and air dry. You must remove all traces of the old gasket material.

To install:

15. Coat the NEW filter seal with automatic transmission fluid.
16. Install the NEW filter seal into the transmission case. Tap the seal into place using a suitable size socket.
17. Install the NEW filter.
18. Install the oil pan and NEW gasket.

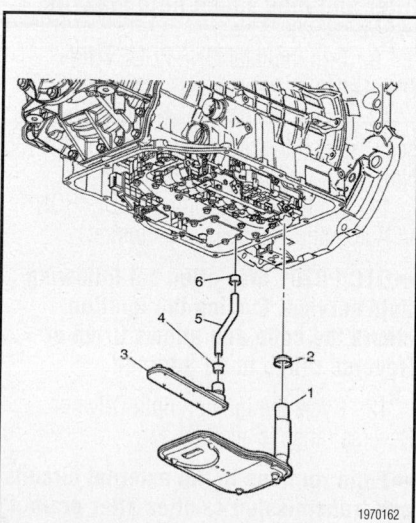

Fig. 44 Exploded view of the A/T fluid filter and auxiliary fluid pump filter assemblies

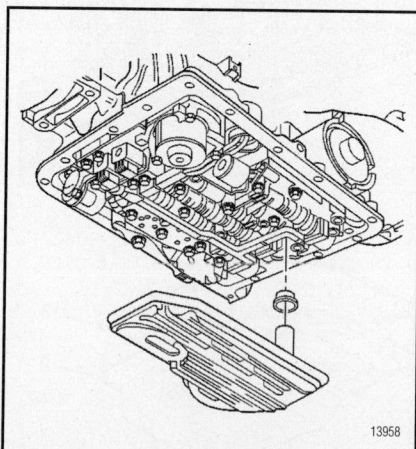

Fig. 45 Grasp firmly while pulling down with a twisting motion in order to remove the filter

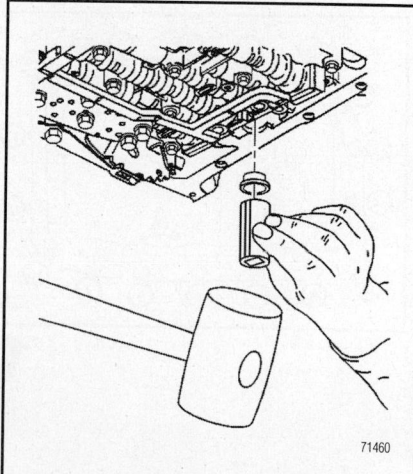

Fig. 47 Install the NEW filter seal into the transmission case

19. Install the oil pan bolts. Tighten the bolts alternately and evenly to 97 inch lbs. (11 Nm).

20. If previously removed, install the range selector cable bracket and bolts. Tighten the bolts to 18 ft. lbs. (25 Nm).

21. Apply a small amount of sealant GM P/N 12346004 (Canadian P/N 10953480), or equivalent to the threads of the oil pan drain plug, if equipped.

22. Lower the vehicle.

23. Fill the transmission to the proper level with DEXRON® VI transmission fluid.

24. Check the COLD fluid level reading for initial fill only.

25. Inspect the oil pan gasket for leaks.

6L45/6L50/6L80/6L90 Transmission

See Figure 48.

✳ CAUTION

Use Dexron VI transmission fluid only. Failure to use the proper fluid may result in transmission internal damage.

1. Raise and support the vehicle.

2. Disconnect and lower the catalytic converter.

3. Place a suitable drain pan under the transmission.

4. Remove the transmission fluid pan bolts.

5. Re move the transmission fluid pan assembly.

a. Check the condition of the draining fluid.

b. Fill the transmission with the proper fluid.

c. Fill the transmission with the proper amount of transmission fluid.

6. Remove the transmission fluid pan gasket.

➡**The fluid pan gasket is reusable. Inspect the gasket to determine if it may be reused.**

7. Pull the fluid filter assembly straight out. Do not bend or twist the filter neck.

8. Remove the fluid filter seal assembly. Use a screwdriver or snap ring pliers to remove the filter seal.

✳ CAUTION

Do not damage the case sealing surface when removing the filter seal assembly.

To install:

9. Installation is the reverse of removal.

10. Use the Seal Installer (DT 47848) and the Driver Handle (J-42183) to install the filter seal. Use new filter seals.

11. Lubricate the filter seal with transmission fluid before installing the filter.

12. Tighten the bolts in the sequence shown. Tighten the bolts to 90 inch lbs. (9 Nm).

Allison Transmission

See Figure 49.

➡**DO NOT drain the fluid if only the transmission external oil filter is being replaced.**

1. Remove the drain plug and drain plug seal. Drain the transmission fluid into a suitable container.

2. Inspect the drained fluid.

➡**Use a standard strap-type filter wrench to remove the transmission external oil filter.**

3. Remove the filter by rotating in the counterclockwise direction.

4. Remove the magnet from the filter adapter in the converter housing or from the top of the transmission external oil filter.

5. Clean any metal debris from the magnet. Presence of any metal pieces larger than dust may indicate that transmission replacement or overhaul is required.

To install:

6. Install the magnet onto the filter adapter which is in the converter housing.

7. Lubricate the gasket on the transmission external oil filter with transmission fluid.

8. Install, by hand, the transmission external oil filter until the gasket on the filter touches the converter housing.

✳ CAUTION

Turning the transmission external oil filter more than ONE FULL TURN after gasket contact will damage the filter and may cause fluid leakage.

9. Turn the filter ONE FULL TURN ONLY after gasket contact.

10. Install the drain plug and drain plug seal. Tighten the drain plug to 26 ft. lbs. (35 Nm).

11. Refill Transmission with DEXRON® VI Automatic Transmission Fluid.

➡**DTC P0701 may often set following fluid service. Cycling the ignition clears the code and allows Drive or Reverse range to be attained.**

12. Cycle the ignition until Drive or Reverse range is attained.

➡**Fluid remains in the external circuits and transmission cavities after draining the transmission.**

13. Check the transmission fluid level.

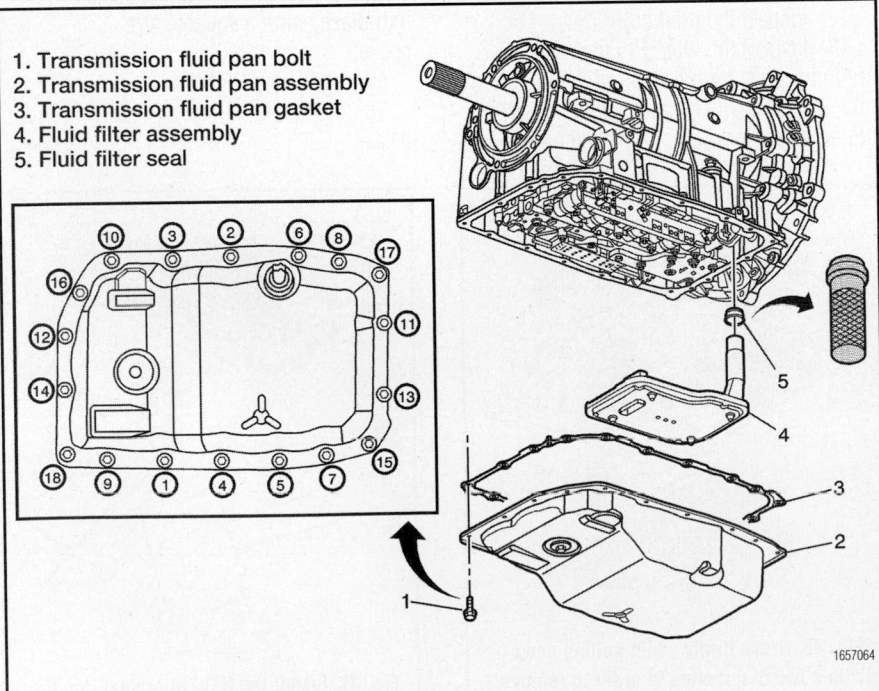

1. Transmission fluid pan bolt
2. Transmission fluid pan assembly
3. Transmission fluid pan gasket
4. Fluid filter assembly
5. Fluid filter seal

1657064

Fig. 48 Exploded view of the transmission fluid pan and filter assemblies

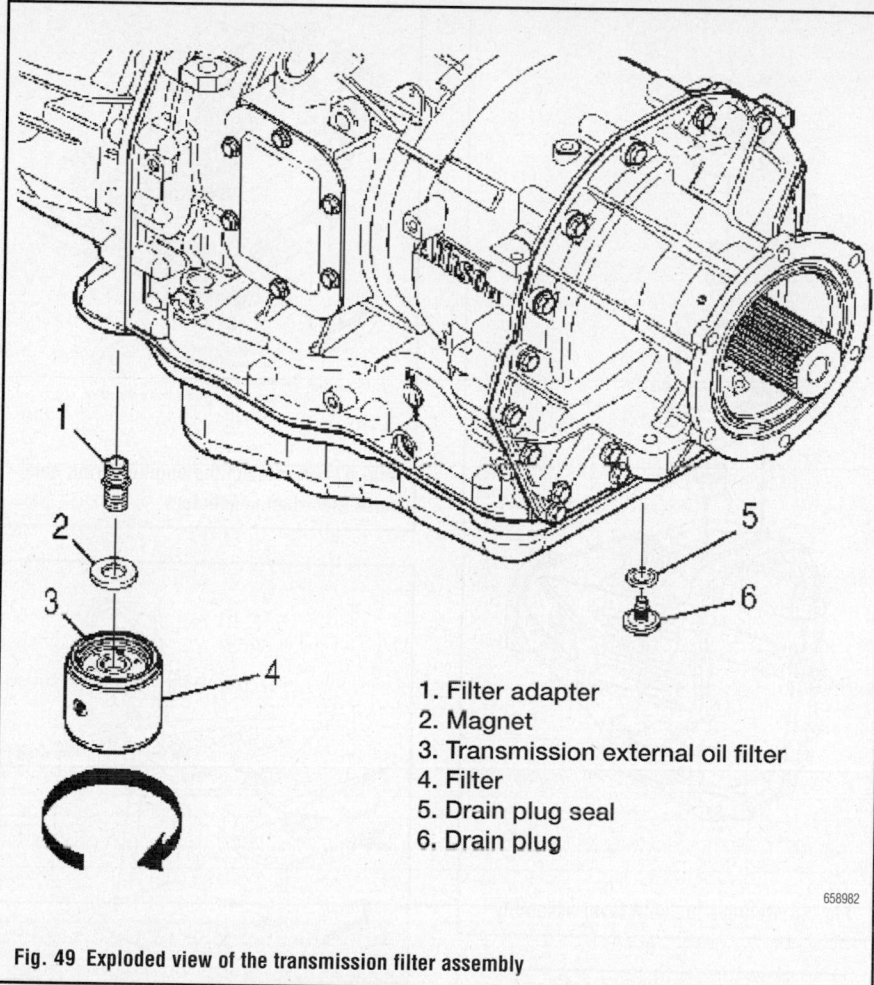

1. Filter adapter
2. Magnet
3. Transmission external oil filter
4. Filter
5. Drain plug seal
6. Drain plug

Fig. 49 Exploded view of the transmission filter assembly

MANUAL TRANSMISSION ASSEMBLY

REMOVAL & INSTALLATION

Tremec 5-Speed (M96) Transmission

See Figures 50 through 54.

1. Remove the shift lever.
2. Remove the propeller shaft.
3. Using a Hydraulic Clutch Line Separator (J-42371), push back on the sleeve on the quick connect in order to disconnect the clutch actuator cylinder to clutch master cylinder quick connect fitting.
4. Disconnect the electrical wiring harness connector from the backup lamp switch.
5. Disconnect the electrical wiring harness connector from the vehicle speed sensor.
6. Remove the engine electrical wiring harness clip from the fuel pipe bracket.
7. Remove the fuel pipes from the fuel pipe bracket.
8. Support the transmission using a suitable transmission jack.

9. Remove the transmission support crossmember.
10. Remove the transmission to clutch housing bolts.
11. Remove the transmission from the clutch housing.
12. If servicing the clutch, remove the clutch housing bolts and studs.

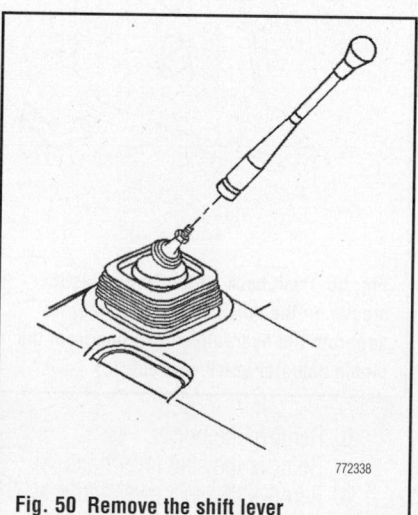

Fig. 50 Remove the shift lever

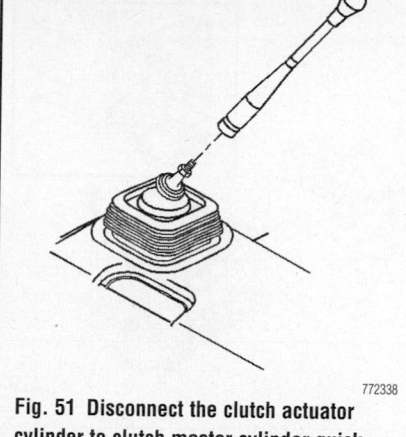

Fig. 51 Disconnect the clutch actuator cylinder to clutch master cylinder quick connect fitting

13. Remove the clutch housing.

To install:

14. Install the clutch housing if previously removed.
15. Install the clutch housing bolts and studs. Tighten the bolts and studs to 37 ft. lbs. (50 Nm).
16. Position the transmission to the clutch housing.
17. Install the transmission to clutch housing bolts. Tighten the bolts to 74 ft. lbs. (100 Nm).
18. Install the transmission support.
19. Remove the transmission jack.
20. Install the fuel pipes to the fuel pipe bracket.
21. Install the engine electrical wiring harness clip to the fuel pipe bracket.
22. Connect the electrical wiring harness connector to the backup lamp switch.
23. Connect the electrical wiring harness connector to the vehicle speed sensor.

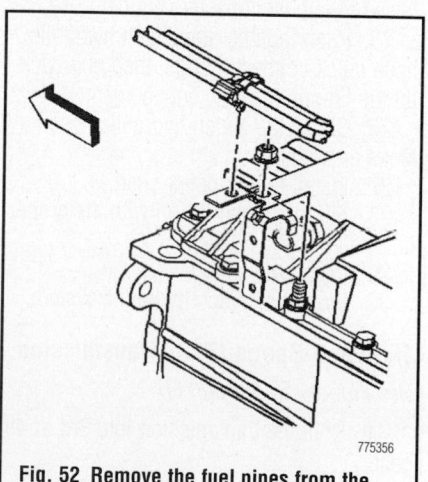

Fig. 52 Remove the fuel pipes from the fuel pipe bracket

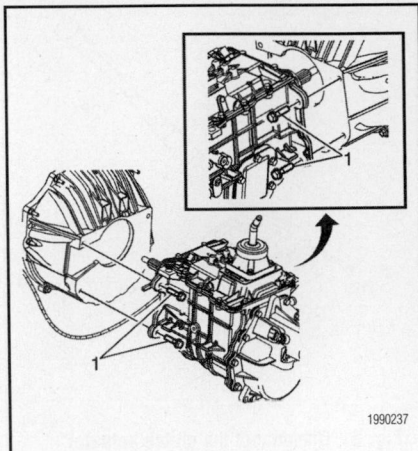

Fig. 53 Remove the transmission to clutch housing bolts (1)

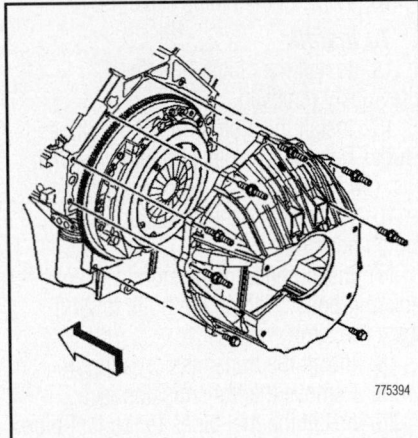

Fig. 54 If servicing the clutch, remove the clutch housing bolts and studs

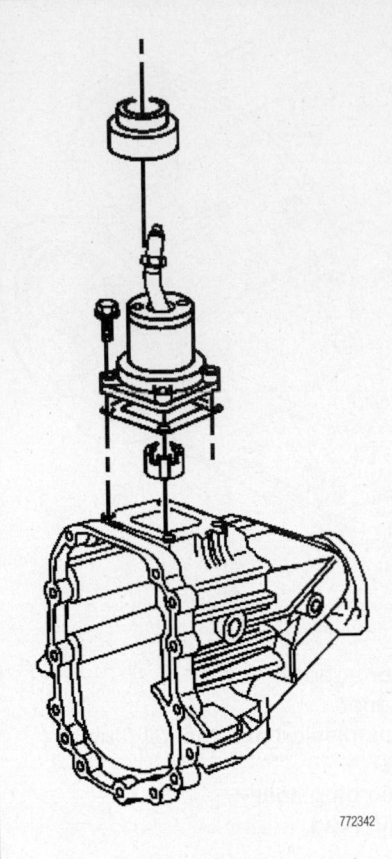

Fig. 55 Remove the shift lever assembly

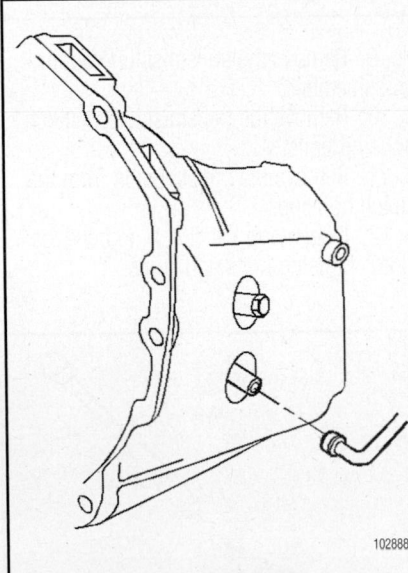

Fig. 56 Push back on the white plastic sleeve on the quick connect in order to separate the hydraulic clutch line from the clutch actuator quick connect

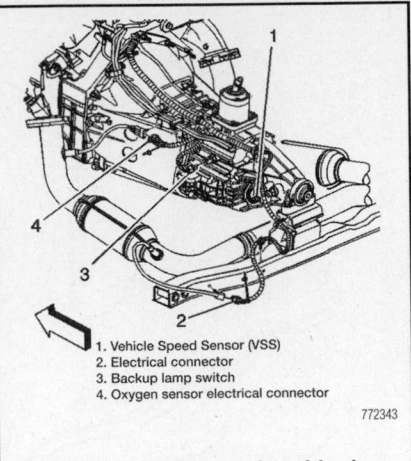

1. Vehicle Speed Sensor (VSS)
2. Electrical connector
3. Backup lamp switch
4. Oxygen sensor electrical connector

Fig. 57 Disconnect the engine wiring harness electrical connectors

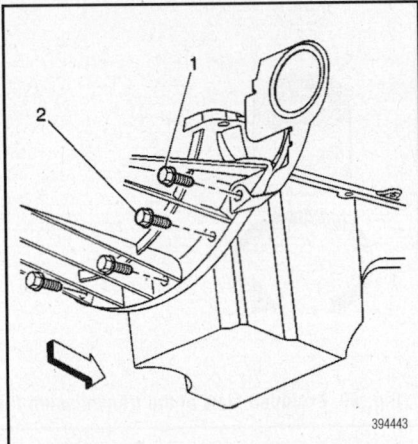

Fig. 58 Remove the bolts (1, 2) securing the bottom right side of the transmission to the engine

➡ **DO NOT rely on an audible click or a visual verification on the clutch hydraulic hose quick connect fitting connection.**

24. Connect the clutch actuator cylinder hose to the clutch master cylinder hose.

25. Push together the clutch hydraulic hose quick connect fittings, then pull back on the fittings to verify engagement.

26. Check the clutch hydraulic hose for kinks or twists.

27. Install the propeller shaft.

28. Fill the transmission with the proper fluid to the correct level.

29. Install the shift lever.

30. Bleed the clutch hydraulic system.

Tremec 5-Speed (TZO) Transmission

See Figures 55 through 60.

1. Shift the transmission into 3rd or 4th gear.

2. Remove the shift lever assembly.
   a. Remove the control lever and boot.
   b. Remove the boot.
   c. Remove the shift lever bolts.
   d. Remove the shift lever and seal.
   e. Remove the shift lever insulator.

3. Remove the propeller shaft.

4. Using a Hydraulic Clutch Line Separator (J-42371), push back on the white plastic sleeve on the quick connect in order to separate the hydraulic clutch line from the clutch actuator quick connect.

5. Disconnect the following engine wiring harness electrical connectors:
   • Vehicle Speed Sensor (VSS)
   • Backup lamp switch
   • Oxygen sensor

6. Remove the engine harness clips from the fuel feed/return line clips and transmission.

7. Remove the starter motor.

8. Support the transmission using a suitable transmission jack.

9. Remove the transmission support crossmember.

10. Remove the bolts securing the bottom right side of the transmission to the engine.

11. Remove the transmission cover.

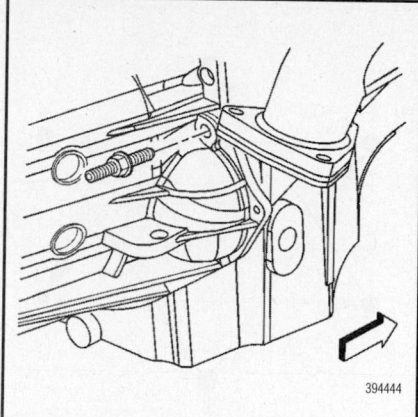

Fig. 59 Remove the stud securing the right side of the transmission to the engine

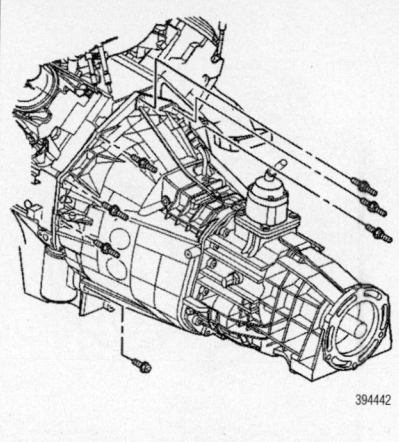

Fig. 60 Remove the bolt and studs securing the transmission to the engine

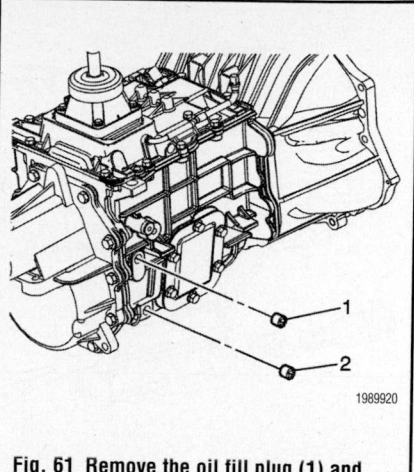

Fig. 61 Remove the oil fill plug (1) and the oil drain plug (2)

12. Remove the stud securing the right side of the transmission to the engine.

13. Remove the bolt and studs securing the transmission to the engine.

14. Pull the transmission straight back off the clutch hub splines. Do not let the transmission hang from the clutch assembly.

15. Remove the transmission from the vehicle.

To install:

16. Install the transmission to the vehicle:

   a. Ensure the transmission is positioned in the 3rd or 4th gear.

   b. Rotate the transmission clockwise onto the clutch hub splines.

   c. Install the bolt and studs securing the transmission to the engine.

   d. Tighten the bolt/studs to 37 ft. lbs. (50 Nm).

17. Install the stud securing the right side of the transmission to the engine. Tighten the stud to 37 ft. lbs. (50 Nm).

18. Install the transmission cover.

19. Install the 2 bolts securing the bottom right side of the transmission to the engine. Tighten the bolts to 37 ft. lbs. (50 Nm).

20. Install the transmission support crossmember.

21. Remove the transmission jack.

22. Install the starter motor.

23. Install the engine harness clips to the fuel feed/return line clips and transmission.

24. Connect the following engine harness electrical connectors:

• VSS
• Backup lamp switch
• Oxygen sensor

➡**DO NOT rely on an audible click or a visual verification on the clutch hydraulic hose quick connect fitting connection.**

25. Connect the clutch actuator cylinder hose to the clutch master cylinder hose.

26. Push together the clutch hydraulic hose quick connect fittings, then pull back on the fittings to verify engagement.

27. Check the clutch hydraulic hoses for kinks or twists.

28. Install the propeller shaft.

29. Fill the transmission with fluid.

30. Install the shift lever assembly.

31. Bleed the clutch hydraulic system.

MANUAL TRANSMISSION FLUID

DRAIN AND REFILL

Tremec 5-Speed (M96) Transmission

See Figure 61.

1. Raise and suitably support the vehicle.

2. Place a suitable drain pan under the transmission in order to catch the drained transmission fluid.

3. Remove the oil fill plug.

4. Remove the oil drain plug.

5. Remove any old sealant from the transmission housing.

To install:

6. Apply a thin bead of sealant GM P/N 12346004 (Canadian P/N 10953480), or equivalent to the oil drain plug threads.

7. Install the oil drain plug. Tighten the plug to 27 ft. lbs. (37 Nm).

8. Fill the transmission with the proper fluid to just below the bottom of the fill plug hole.

9. Apply a thin bead of sealant GM P/N

12346004 (Canadian P/N 10953480), or equivalent to the oil fill plug threads.

10. Install the oil fill plug. Tighten the plug to 27 ft. lbs. (37 Nm).

11. Lower the vehicle.

Tremec 5-Speed (TZ0) Transmission

See Figures 62 and 63.

1. Raise and suitably support the vehicle.

2. Using the 17 mm Oil Fill/Drain Plug Hex Bit (J-36511) remove the oil fill plug.

3. Place a suitable drain pan under the transmission in order to catch the drained transmission fluid.

4. Using J-36511 remove the oil drain plug.

5. Remove any old sealant from the transmission housing.

To install:

6. Apply sealant GM P/N 12346004 (Canadian P/N 10953480), or equivalent to the oil drain and fill plug threads.

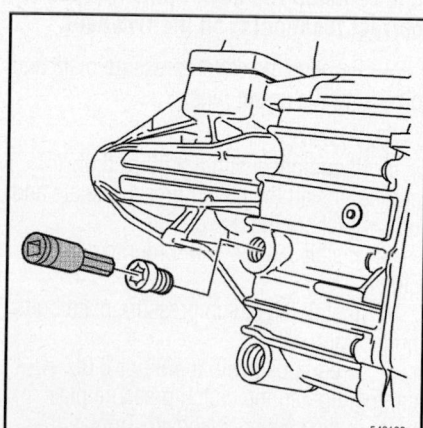

Fig. 62 Using the 17 mm Oil Fill/Drain Plug Hex Bit (J-36511) remove the oil fill plug

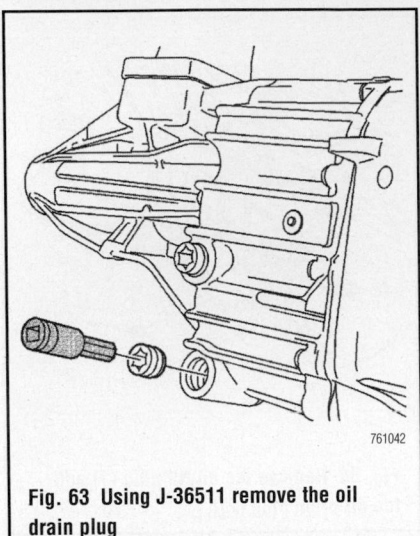

Fig. 63 Using J-36511 remove the oil drain plug

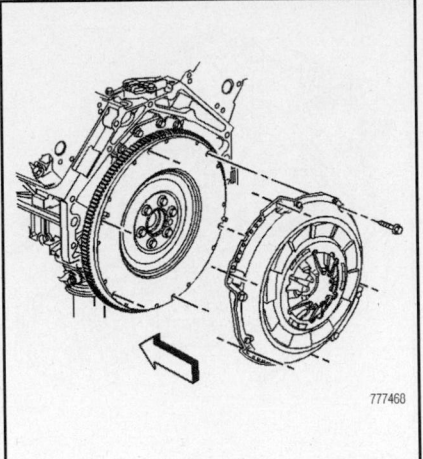

Fig. 64 Remove the clutch pressure plate bolts

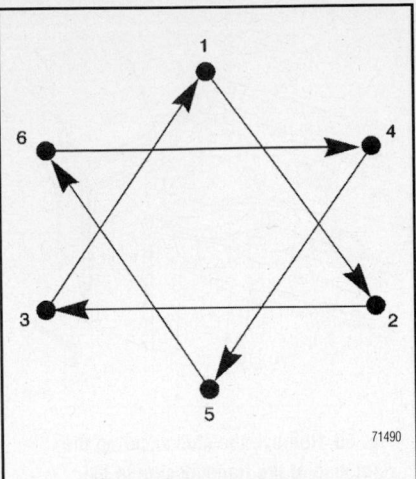

Fig. 65 Tighten the clutch pressure plate bolts in the sequence shown

7. Using J-36511 install the oil drain plug. Tighten the plug to 22 ft. lbs. (30 Nm).

8. Remove and drain the drain pan used to catch the used transmission fluid.

9. Fill the transmission to just below the bottom of the fill plug hole.

10. Using J-36511 install the oil fill plug. Tighten the plug to 22 ft. lbs. (30 Nm).

11. Lower the vehicle.

CLUTCH

REMOVAL & INSTALLATION

See Figures 64 and 65.

1. Remove the transmission.
2. Remove the clutch pressure plate bolts.

➡ **Dowel pins are used to align the flywheel and pressure plate. When removing the pressure plate check to see if the dowel pins are rusted into the pressure plate, if so remove, clean, and reinstall the dowel pins into the correct location(s) on the flywheel.**

3. Remove the clutch pressure plate and disc from the dowel pins.

To install:

4. If equipped with a 4.8L or 6.0L engine, install the clutch pressure plate and driven plate to the dowel pins.

5. Install J-5824-A in order to align the clutch.

6. Install the clutch pressure plate bolts finger tight.

7. If equipped with a 4.8L or 6.0L engine, tighten the clutch pressure plate bolts in the sequence shown. Tighten the bolts to 52 ft. lbs. (70 Nm).

8. Remove the J-5824-A.

9. Install the transmission.

BLEEDING

❊❊ CAUTION

DO NOT use fluid which has been bled from a hydraulic clutch system, in order to fill the clutch master cylinder reservoir, due to the possibility that the fluid may be aerated, have too much moisture content, or be contaminated and may cause system or vehicle damage.

1. Ensure the reservoir is filled to the fill line with new hydraulic clutch fluid. Add fluid if required. Use hydraulic clutch fluid GM P/N 12345347 (Canadian P/N 10953517).

2. Press the clutch pedal in completely to the floor panel.

3. Open the bleeder screw in order to purge the air from the system.

4. Close the bleeder and release the clutch pedal.

➡ **Ensure no air is drawn into the clutch system.**

5. Repeat the previous 3 steps until all the air is out of the clutch system.

  a. Check and refill the reservoir as needed while bleeding.

  b. After bleeding, pump the clutch pedal several times. If clutch engagement is not satisfactory, repeat the bleed procedure.

6. If the previous procedures are unsuccessful, perform the following steps.

  a. Pump the clutch pedal very fast with full strokes for 30 seconds.

  b. Stop pumping and let the air escape into the reservoir while moving the rubber pad up and down 0.5 inches (12 mm) for 30 seconds.

  c. Repeat this procedure, as necessary.

CLUTCH ACTUATOR CYLINDER

REMOVAL & INSTALLATION

Tremec 5-Speed (M96) Transmission

See Figure 66.

1. Remove the transmission.
2. Remove the clutch actuator cylinder bolts.
3. Remove the clutch actuator cylinder.
4. Installation is the reverse of removal.

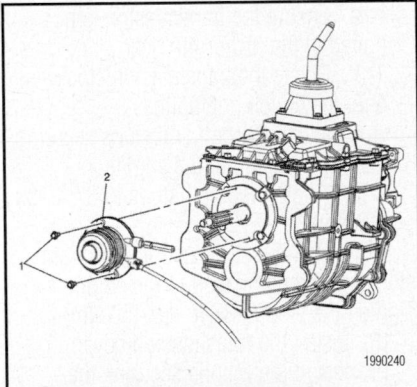

Fig. 66 Remove the clutch actuator cylinder bolts (1) and clutch actuator cylinder (2)

Tremec 5-Speed (TZ0) Transmission

See Figures 67 through 70.

1. Disconnect the clutch pedal position switch electrical connector.

2. Push the clutch pedal in and squeeze the pushrod bushing tabs in, in order to release the pushrod bushing from the clutch pedal.

3. Disconnect the clutch actuator cylinder to clutch master cylinder quick connect fitting.

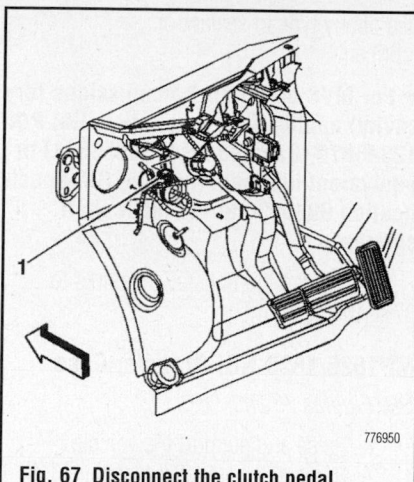

Fig. 67 Disconnect the clutch pedal position switch electrical connector (1)

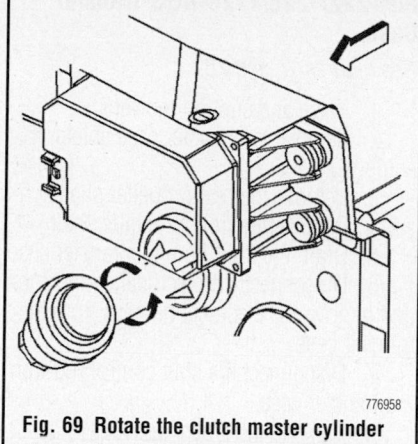

Fig. 69 Rotate the clutch master cylinder 45 degrees clockwise to the unlocked position

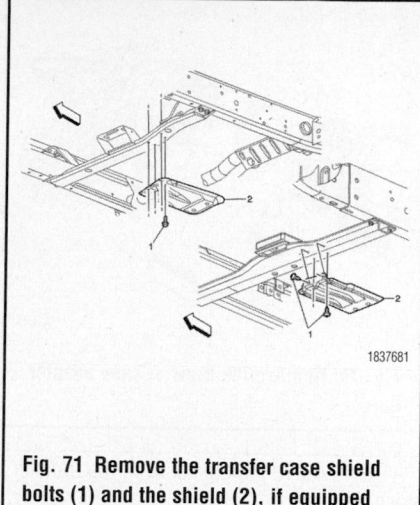

Fig. 71 Remove the transfer case shield bolts (1) and the shield (2), if equipped

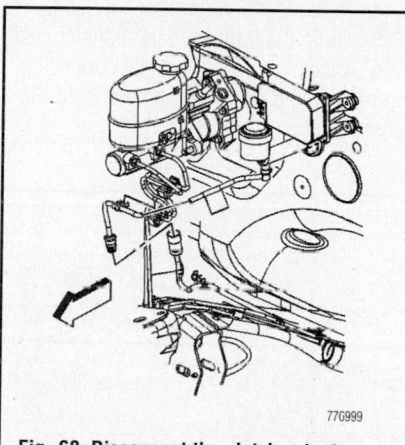

Fig. 68 Disconnect the clutch actuator cylinder to clutch master cylinder quick connect fitting

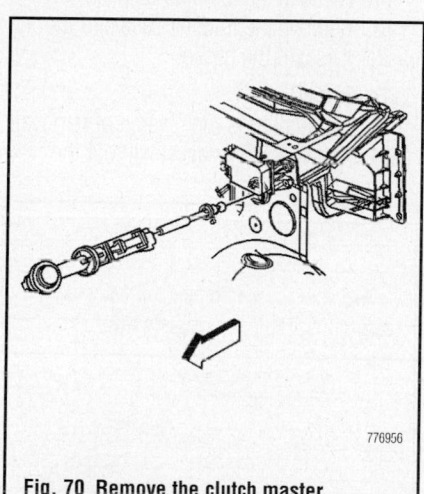

Fig. 70 Remove the clutch master cylinder

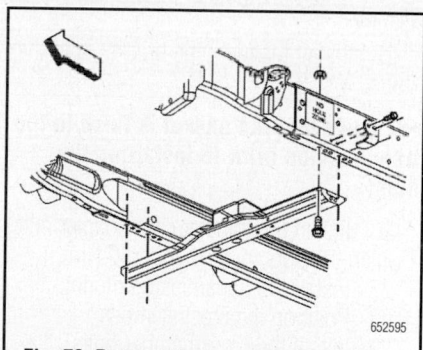

Fig. 72 Remove the transmission mount nuts and bolts

4. Remove the clutch master cylinder clip from the brake pressure module valve pipe.

5. Rotate the clutch master cylinder 45 degrees clockwise to the unlocked position.

6. Remove the clutch master cylinder.

To install:

7. Install the clutch master cylinder.

8. Push in and rotate the clutch master cylinder 45 degrees counterclockwise to the locked position.

9. Disconnect the clutch actuator cylinder to clutch master cylinder quick connect fitting.

10. Install the clutch master cylinder clip to the brake pressure module valve pipe.

11. Apply light pressure to the clutch pedal to couple the pushrod socket to the clutch pedal.

12. Connect the clutch pedal position switch electrical connector.

13. Pump the clutch pedal 3 time prior to starting the vehicle to ensure connection is complete.

TRANSFER CASE ASSEMBLY

REMOVAL & INSTALLATION

BW4485-NR3 Transfer Case

See Figures 71 through 74.

1. Raise and suitably support the vehicle.

2. Remove the transfer case shield, if equipped.

3. Remove the rear propeller shaft.

4. Remove the front propeller shaft.

5. Drain the fluid from the transfer case.

6. Support the transmission with a suitable jack stand.

7. Remove the transmission mount nuts and bolts.

8. Remove the crossmember bolts.

9. Remove the crossmember.

10. Remove the transmission mount.

11. Install a suitable transmission jack to the transfer case.

12. Remove the transfer case adapter nuts.

13. Remove the fuel pipe bracket from the studs.

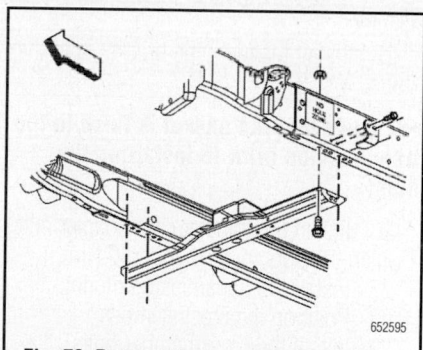

Fig. 73 Remove the crossmember bolts

➡Pull straight back on the transfer case in order to position the transfer case so that it can be rotated parallel to the transmission.

14. Remove the transfer case from the adapter.

15. Rotate the transfer case so that it is perpendicular to the torsion bar mounting bracket.

16. Lower the transfer case.

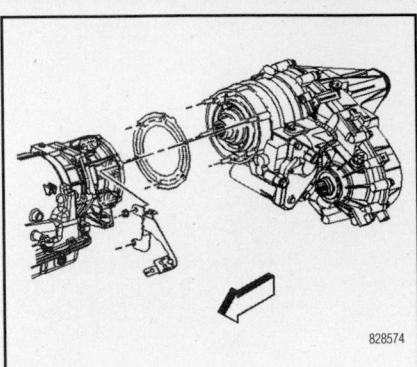

Fig. 74 Remove the transfer case adapter nuts

17. Remove the gasket from the transfer case.

18. Remove the transfer case from the transmission jack.

To install:

19. Install the transfer case onto a suitable transmission jack.

➡ **When installing a new transfer case gasket, the gasket must be installed with the tab oriented up, and the yellow printing towards to front of the vehicle. Install the gasket without the use of any type of sealant or of lubricant.**

20. Install a NEW transfer case gasket.

21. Rotate the transfer case so that it is parallel to the torsion bar mounting bracket.

22. Raise the transfer case into position.

23. Rotate the transfer case so that it is aligned with the adapter.

24. Install the transfer case to the adapter.

25. Install the fuel pipe bracket onto the studs.

➡ **Ensure that the gasket is flush to the transmission prior to installing the nuts.**

26. Install the transfer case adapter nuts. Tighten the nuts to 37 ft. lbs. (50 Nm).

27. Install the transmission mount.

28. Position the crossmember.

29. Install the crossmember bolts. Tighten the bolts to 52 ft. lbs. (70 Nm).

30. Install the transmission mount nuts and bolts. Tighten the nuts and bolts to 30 ft. lbs. (40 Nm).

31. Remove the jack stand from the transmission.

32. Install the front propeller shaft.

33. Install the rear propeller shaft.

34. Fill the transfer case with fluid.

35. Install the transfer case shield, if equipped.

36. Lower the vehicle.

MP1222/1225/1226-NQG Transfer Case

See Figures 75 and 76.

1. Raise and support the vehicle.

2. Remove the transfer case shield, if equipped.

3. Remove the rear propeller shaft.

4. Remove the front propeller shaft.

5. Drain the fluid from the transfer case.

6. Disconnect the electrical connectors and remove the electrical harness from the transfer case.

7. Disconnect the shift control rod from the transfer case.

8. Remove the crossmember.

9. Remove the transmission mount.

10. Remove the transfer case nuts.

11. Remove the fuel line bracket.

12. Remove the transfer case and the gasket. Discard the gasket.

To install:

13. Installation is the reverse of removal.

14. Install a NEW gasket without the

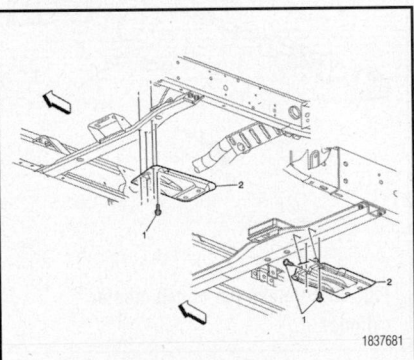

Fig. 75 Remove the transfer case shield bolts (1) and the shield (2), if equipped

use of any type of sealant or lubricant.

➡ **For MYC and MYD transmissions (dry cavity) applications only, apply GM P/N 12345879 (Canadian P/N 10953511) or equivalent lubricant meeting GM Specification 9985830 to the input shaft splines.**

15. Tighten the transfer case nuts to 37 ft. lbs. (50 Nm).

MP1625/1626-NQF Transfer Case

See Figures 75 and 77.

1. Raise and support the vehicle.

2. Remove the transfer case shield, if equipped.

3. Remove the rear propeller shaft.

4. Remove the front propeller shaft.

5. Drain the fluid from the transfer case.

6. Disconnect the electrical connectors and remove the electrical harness from the transfer case.

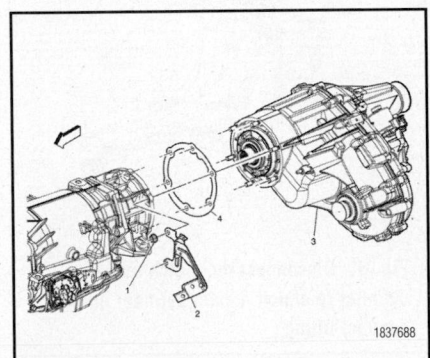

Fig. 77 Exploded view of the transfer case assembly

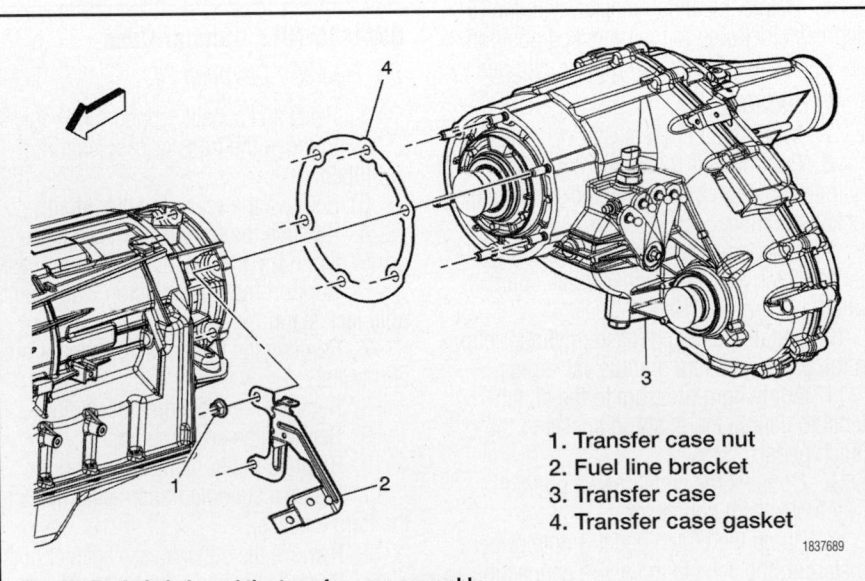

1. Transfer case nut
2. Fuel line bracket
3. Transfer case
4. Transfer case gasket

Fig. 76 Exploded view of the transfer case assembly

7. Disconnect the vent tube from the transfer case.

8. Remove the crossmember.

9. Remove the transmission mount.

10. Remove the transfer case nuts/bolts.

11. Remove the fuel line bracket.

12. Remove the transfer case and the gasket. Discard the gasket.

To install:

13. Installation is the reverse of removal.

14. Install a NEW gasket without the use of any type of sealant or lubricant.

➡For MYC and MYD transmissions (dry cavity) applications only, apply GM P/N 12345879 (Canadian P/N 10953511) or equivalent lubricant meeting GM Specification 9985830 to the input shaft splines.

15. Tighten the transfer case nuts/bolts to 37 ft. lbs. (50 Nm).

MP3023/3024-NQH Transfer Case

See Figures 75 and 78.

1. Raise and support the vehicle.

2. Remove the transfer case shield, if equipped.

3. Remove the rear propeller shaft.

4. Remove the front propeller shaft.

5. Drain the fluid from the transfer case.

6. Disconnect the electrical connectors and remove the electrical harness from the transfer case.

7. Remove the crossmember.

8. Remove the transmission mount.

9. Remove the transfer case nuts.

10. Remove the transfer case and the gasket. Discard the gasket.

To install:

11. Installation is the reverse of removal.

12. Install a NEW gasket without the use of any type of sealant or lubricant.

➡For MYC and MYD transmissions (dry cavity) applications only, apply GM P/N 12345879 (Canadian P/N 10953511) or equivalent lubricant meeting GM Specification 9985830 to the input shaft splines.

13. Tighten the transfer case nuts to 37 ft. lbs. (50 Nm).

➡If installing a new or repaired transfer case, perform the Transfer Case High/Low Clutch reset.

TRANSFER CASE HIGH/LOW CLUTCH RESET

Using a Scan Tool

Key ON, engine OFF. Go to the Special Functions heading in the scan tool.

Select Clutch Reset Procedure (Motor Learn Procedure/ATC Motor Learn).

When the Clutch Reset Procedure is initiated you should hear the motor engage, indicating a successful learn procedure.

Using The Transfer Case Shift Control Switch

➡The Learn procedure is performed with the ignition in the ACCESSORY position. The shift to transfer case NEUTRAL procedure uses this same procedure, but with the key in the RUN position.

Key OFF for at least 30 seconds.

Engage parking brake.

Place transmission in Neutral.

Turn the Transfer Case Shift Control Switch (TCSCS) to the 2WD HI position for at least 5 seconds.

Turn the TCSCS clockwise past the 4WD LO position to the neutral request position and hold for at least 30 seconds.

An audible noise from the transfer case encoder motor should occur indicating a successful learn procedure.

FRONT AXLE TUBE BEARING

REMOVAL & INSTALLATION

See Figures 79 through 86.

Special Tools Required:
• J-8092 ¾ inch Universal Driver Handle 10 inches in length
• J-2619-01 Slide Hammer
• J-29369-1 Bushing and Bearing Remover
• J-29369-2 Bushing and Bearing Remover (2–3 inch)
• J-36609 Axle Tube Bearing Installer
• J-45225 Axle Seal Installer

1. Raise the vehicle.

2. Drain the differential carrier assembly.

3. Remove the right side seal and/or bearing by performing the following steps:

   a. Remove the inner axle shaft and housing assembly from the differential carrier case assembly.

   b. Remove the clutch fork assembly components and the inner axle shaft from the inner axle shaft housing.

   c. Install the inner axle shaft housing into a vise.

➡Clamp only on the mounting flange of the inner axle shaft housing.

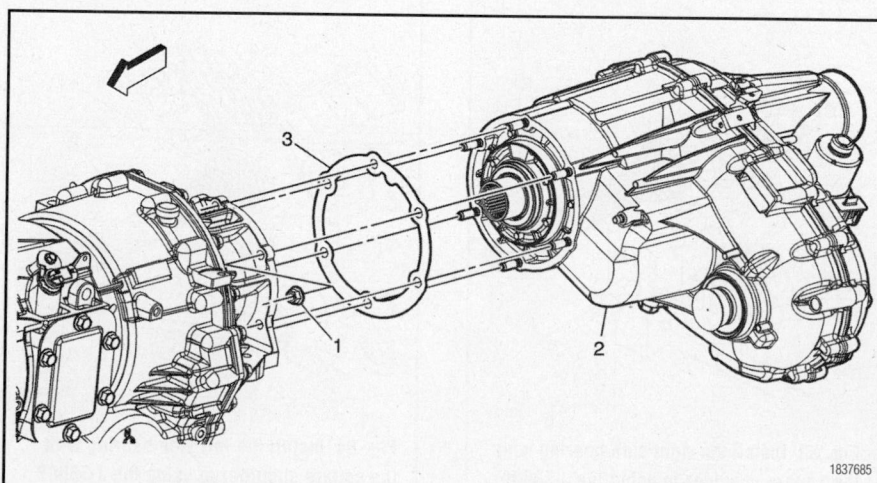

Fig. 78 Remove the transfer case nuts (1), transfer case (2), and the gasket (3)

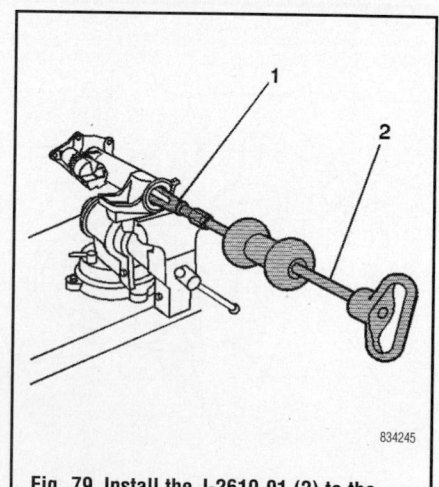

Fig. 79 Install the J-2619-01 (2) to the J-29369-1 or the J-29369-2 (1)

d. Install the J-29369-1 , 8.25 inch axle, or the J-29369-2 , 9.25 inch axle, behind the inner axle shaft seal or the inner axle shaft bearing as necessary.

e. Install the J-2619-01 to the J-29369-1 or the J-29369-2.

f. Remove the inner axle shaft seal and/or the inner axle shaft bearing using the J-2619-01.

➡ **Support the wheel drive shaft in order to not over flex the CV joint.**

4. If only replacing the left side seal, perform the following steps:

a. Place an alignment mark between the inner axle shaft and the wheel drive shaft.

b. If servicing the 8.25 inch axle, remove the shock module.

c. Disconnect the wheel drive shaft from the inner axle shaft.

d. Remove the inner axle shaft using a hammer and a brass drift.

e. Remove the inner axle shaft seal using a suitable seal remover tool.

5. If replacing both the left side seal and bearing, perform the following steps:

a. Remove the differential carrier assembly.

b. Place the differential carrier assembly into a vise.

➡ **Clamp only on the mounting flange of the differential carrier assembly case.**

c. Remove the inner axle shaft using a hammer and a brass drift.

d. Install the J-29369-1, 8.25 inch axle, or the J-29369-2, 9.25 inch axle, behind the inner axle shaft seal or the inner axle shaft bearing as necessary.

e. Install the J-2619-01 to the J-29369-1 or the J-29369-2.

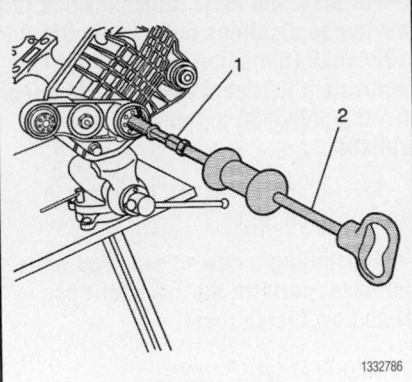

Fig. 81 Install the J-29369-1 , 8.25 inch axle, or the J-29369-2 , 9.25 inch axle (1), behind the inner axle shaft seal or the inner axle shaft bearing as necessary; install the J-2619-01 (2) to the J-29369-1 or the J-29369-2

f. Remove the inner axle shaft seal and/or the inner axle shaft bearing using the J-2619-01.

To install:

6. Install the right side bearing with the square shoulder in using the J-36609 and the J-8092.

7. Install the new axle shaft seal using the J-45225 and the J-8092.

8. Install the inner axle shaft into the inner axle shaft housing.

Carefully tap the inner axle shaft into place with a soft-faced mallet.

9. Install the inner axle shaft and clutch fork assembly components into the inner shaft housing.

10. Install the inner axle shaft and housing assembly to the differential carrier case assembly.

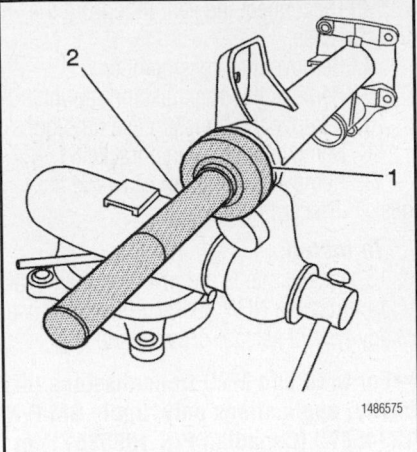

Fig. 83 Install the new axle shaft seal using the J-45225 (1) and the J-8092 (2)

11. If both the left side bearing and seal was removed, perform the following step. Install the left side bearing with the square shoulder in using the J-36609 and the J-8092.

12. If both the left side bearing and seal was removed, perform the following step. Install the new axle shaft seal using the J-45225 and the J-8092.

13. If both the left side bearing and seal was removed, perform the following step. Install the inner axle shaft into the differential case side gear using a soft-faced mallet until the retaining ring on the inner axle shaft is fully seated within the groove in the differential case side gear.

14. Pull back on the inner axle shaft to ensure that the inner axle shaft is properly retained in the differential case side gear.

15. If both the left side bearing and seal was removed, perform the following step. Install the front differential carrier assembly.

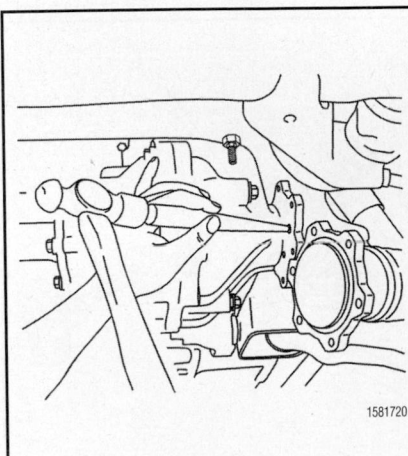

Fig. 80 Remove the inner axle shaft using a hammer and a brass drift

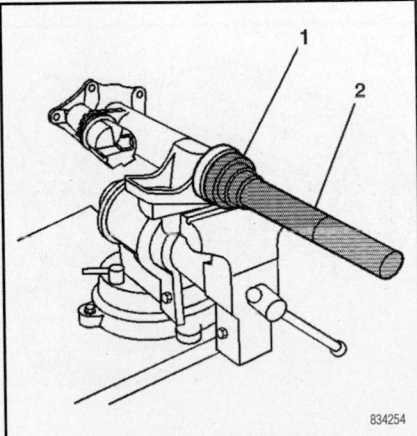

Fig. 82 Install the right side bearing with the square shoulder in using the J-36609 (1) and the J-8092 (2)

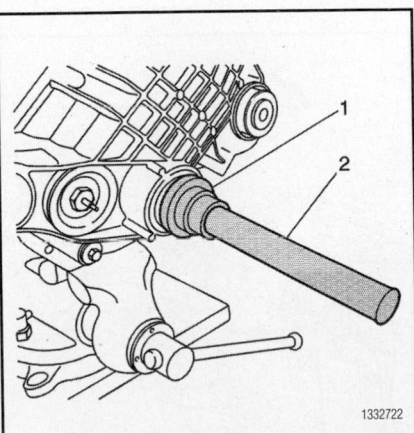

Fig. 84 Install the left side bearing with the square shoulder in using the J-36609 (1) and the J-8092 (2)

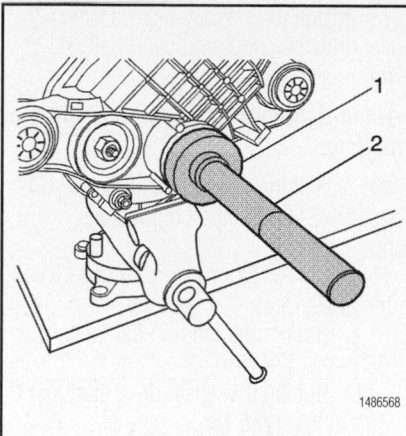

Fig. 85 Install the new axle shaft seal using the J-45225 (1) and the J-8092 (2)

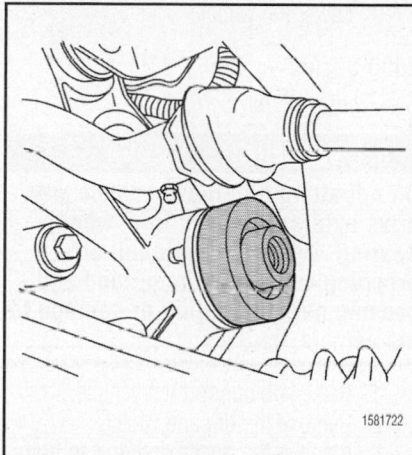

Fig. 86 Install the seal using the J-45225 and a soft-faced mallet

16. If only the left side seal was removed, perform the following step. Install the seal using the J-45225 and a soft-faced mallet.

➡**Tap only on the center portion of the J-45225 in order to drive the seal in evenly.**

17. If only the left side seal was removed, perform the following step. Install the inner axle shaft into the differential case side gear using a soft-faced mallet until the retaining ring on the inner axle shaft is fully seated within the groove in the differential case side gear.

18. Pull back on the inner axle shaft to ensure that the inner axle shaft is properly retained in the differential case side gear.

19. If servicing the 8.25 inch axle, install the shock module.

20. If only the left side seal was removed, perform the following step. Install the wheel drive shaft to the inner axle shaft.

21. If only the left side seal was

removed, perform the following step. Install the wheel drive shaft to the inner axle shaft bolts and tighten to 58 ft. lbs. (79 Nm).

22. Fill the differential carrier assembly. Use the correct fluid.

23. Lower the vehicle.

FRONT DRIVESHAFT

REMOVAL & INSTALLATION

See Figures 87 through 89.

➡**Before disassembly, observe and accurately reference mark all driveline components relative to the propeller shaft and axles. These items include the following components:**

- The propeller shafts
- The wheel drive shafts
- The pinion flanges
- The output shafts

Assemble all components in the exact relationship to each other as they were prior to removal. Observe all published specifications and torque values, and any measurements obtained prior to disassembly.

1. Raise the vehicle.

2. Remove the clamp at the transfer case by prying up the exposed end of the clamp with a flat-bladed tool.

3. Reference mark the relationship of the propeller shaft to the front axle pinion yoke.

✳✳ CAUTION

When removing the propeller shaft, do not attempt to remove the shaft by pounding on the yoke ears or using a tool between the yoke and the universal joint. If the propeller shaft is removed by using such means, the injection joints may fracture and lead to premature failure of the joint.

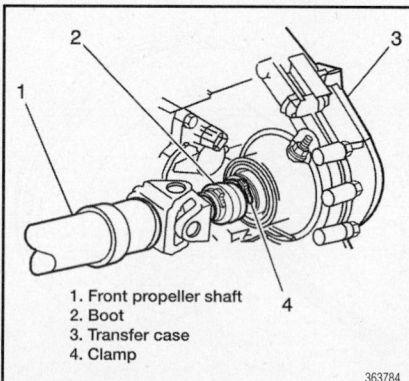

1. Front propeller shaft
2. Boot
3. Transfer case
4. Clamp

Fig. 87 Remove the clamp at the transfer case by prying up the exposed end of the clamp with a flat-bladed tool

4. Remove the bolts and the yoke retainers from the front axle pinion yoke.

➡**Do not drop the bearing cap assemblies of the yoke end.**

5. Disconnect the propeller shaft (2) from the front axle pinion yoke (1).

6. Wrap the bearing caps with tape in order to prevent the loss of bearing rollers. Use tape to secure the bearing caps.

7. Remove the boot from the groove on the transfer case output shaft.

8. Remove the propeller shaft from the transfer case output shaft by sliding the propeller shaft forward.

9. Remove the clamp from the propeller shaft boot, if needed.

10. Remove the propeller shaft boot from the propeller shaft, if needed.

To install:

11. Inspect the splines of the transfer case output shaft for a sufficient coating of lubricant. If the output shaft does not have a sufficient coating of lubricant, lubricate the shaft with grease, GM P/N 12345879

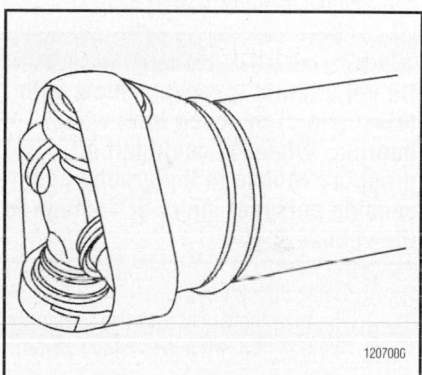

Fig. 88 Wrap the bearing caps with tape in order to prevent the loss of bearing rollers

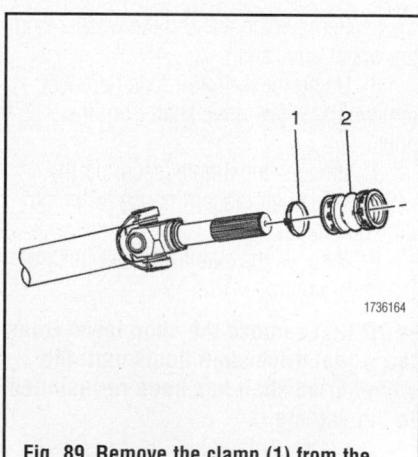

Fig. 89 Remove the clamp (1) from the propeller shaft boot (2), if needed

(Canadian P/N 10953511), or equivalent lubricant meeting GM Specification 9985830.

12. Install the propeller shaft boot.

13. Install the propeller shaft boot clamp.

14. Install the propeller shaft splines into the transfer case output shaft.

15. Install the propeller shaft to the front axle pinion yoke. Align the reference marks made during removal.

16. Install the yoke retainers and the bolts. Tighten the yoke retainer bolts to 18 ft. lbs. (25 Nm).

17. Install the boot onto the transfer case output shaft until the boot snaps into the groove on the output shaft.

18. Using the Narrow Jaw Clamp Pliers (J-43218) to crimp both clamps.

19. Lower the vehicle.

FRONT HALFSHAFT

REMOVAL & INSTALLATION

1500 Series

See Figures 90 and 91.

✱✱ WARNING

Do not attempt to move vehicle with drive axle(s) removed from wheel bearing. Wheel(s) could fall off, dropping vehicle to the ground and causing personal injury or damage to the vehicle.

1. Raise the vehicle.

2. Remove the wheel and tire assembly.

3. Remove the drive axle center cap, if equipped.

4. Insert a drift or a large screwdriver brake rotor.

➡**DO NOT reuse the wheel drive shaft nut. Discard and replace with new.**

5. Remove the nut and the washer from the wheel drive shaft.

6. Using the J-45859 Axle Remover, remove the wheel drive shaft from the hub.

7. Remove the 6 bolts securing the wheel drive shaft inboard flange to the output shaft flange.

8. Remove the stabilizer shaft link from the lower control arm.

➡**DO NOT remove the shop towel from the wheel drive shaft boots until the wheel drive shaft has been re-installed in the vehicle.**

9. Wrap shop towels around both the inner and the outer wheel drive shaft boots

in order to avoid damage to the boots during removal and installation.

10. Pull the wheel drive shaft through the lower control arm opening.

To install:

11. Wrap shop towels around both the inner and the outer wheel drive shaft boots in order to avoid damage to the boots during removal and installation.

➡**Clean the steering knuckle and the wheel drive shaft splines and threads. These areas must be dry and free of grease, dirt, and contamination.**

12. Insert the wheel drive shaft into the knuckle.

✱✱ CAUTION

Use only a genuine GM front wheel drive shaft nut. Installation of anything but an OEM front wheel drive shaft nut could cause damage to the vehicle.

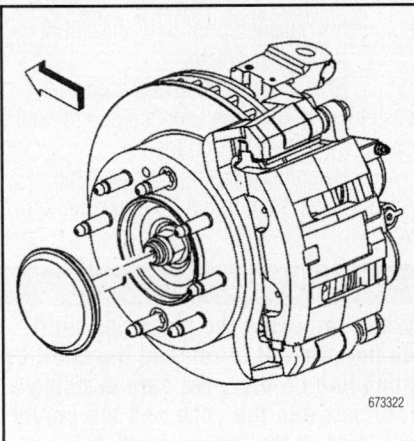

Fig. 90 Remove the drive axle center cap, if equipped

Fig. 91 Using the J-45859 Axle Remover, remove the wheel drive shaft from the hub

13. Install the washer and the NEW wheel drive shaft nut and hand tighten ONLY.

➡**Hand tighten the flange bolts ONLY at this time.**

14. Install the flange bolts from the wheel drive shaft to the output shaft flange.

15. Insert a drift or a large screwdriver 1 of the brake rotor.

   a. Tighten the inboard flange bolts to 58 ft. lbs. (79 Nm).

   b. Tighten the wheel drive shaft nut to 188 ft. lbs. (255 Nm).

16. Install the drive axle center cap, if equipped.

17. Install the stabilizer shaft link.

18. Install the wheel and tire assembly.

19. Lower the vehicle.

2500 Series

See Figures 91 through 94.

✱✱ WARNING

Do not attempt to move vehicle with drive axle(s) removed from wheel bearing. Wheel(s) could fall off, dropping vehicle to the ground and causing personal injury or damage to the vehicle.

1. Raise and support the vehicle.

2. Remove the tire and wheel.

3. Remove the front axle hub cap from the wheel bearing, if equipped.

4. Insert a drift or large screwdriver through the brake caliper into one of the brake rotor vanes in order to prevent the wheel drive shaft from turning.

➡**DO NOT reuse the wheel drive shaft nut, use a NEW nut only.**

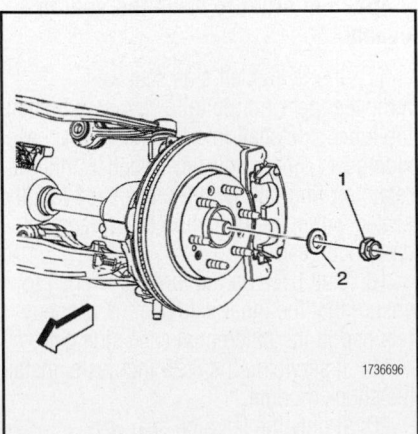

Fig. 92 Remove the nut (1) and washer (2) from the hub

5. Remove the nut and washer from the hub.

6. Using the J-45859 Axle Remover, remove the wheel drive shaft from the hub.

7. Remove the retaining bolts from the drive flange.

8. Remove the stabilizer shaft link from the lower control arm.

9. Remove the shock module.

10. Remove the wheel drive shaft through the lower control arm opening.

11. Remove all dirt and debris from the splines on the wheel hub/bearing.

To install:

12. Install the wheel drive shaft in the steering knuckle.

➡**Install the NEW nut and washer, but DO NOT tighten at this time.**

13. Install the NEW nut and washer.

14. Install the retaining bolts and finger tighten.

15. Insert a drift or large screwdriver through the brake caliper into one of the brake rotor vanes in order to prevent the wheel drive shaft from turning.

16. Tighten the wheel drive shaft retaining bolts and tighten to 58 ft. lbs. (79 Nm).

17. Tighten the wheel drive shaft retaining nut and tighten to 188 ft. lbs. (255 Nm).

18. Install the shock module.

19. Install the stabilizer shaft link from the lower control arm.

20. Install the front axle hub cap to the wheel bearing, if equipped.

21. Install the tire and wheel.

22. Lower the vehicle.

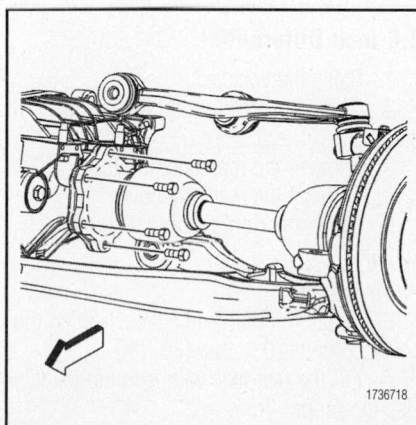

Fig. 93 Remove the retaining bolts from the drive flange

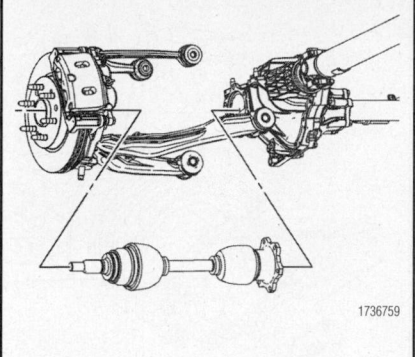

Fig. 94 Remove the wheel drive shaft through the lower control arm opening

FRONT PINION SEAL

REMOVAL & INSTALLATION

See Figures 95 through 100.

Special Tools Required:
- J-8614-01 Flange and Pulley Holding Tool
- J-36366 Pinion Oil Seal Installer

1. Raise the vehicle.
2. Drain the drive axle.
3. Remove the tire and wheel assemblies.
4. Remove the brake calipers.
5. Remove the engine shield, if equipped.
6. Reference mark the relationship of the propeller shaft to the front axle pinion yoke.
7. Remove the yoke retainer bolts and the yoke retainers from the front axle pinion yoke.

✳✳ CAUTION

When removing the propeller shaft, do not attempt to remove the shaft by pounding on the yoke ears or using a tool between the yoke and the universal joint. If the propeller shaft is removed by using such means, the injection joints may fracture and lead to premature failure of the joint.

8. Disconnect the propeller shaft universal joint from the front axle pinion yoke.

9. Wrap the bearing caps with tape in order to prevent the loss of bearing rollers.

10. Support the propeller shaft and move out of the way as necessary.

11. Measure the torque required in order to rotate the pinion. Use an inch-pound torque wrench. Record the torque value for reassembly. This will give the combined preload for the following components:
- The pinion bearings
- The pinion seal
- The carrier bearings
- The axle bearings
- The axle seals

12. Scribe an alignment line between the pinion shaft and the pinion yoke.

13. Install the J-8614-01 onto the pinion as shown.

14. Remove the pinion nut while holding the J-8614-01.

15. Install the J-8614-2 and the J-8614-3 into the J-8614-01 as shown.

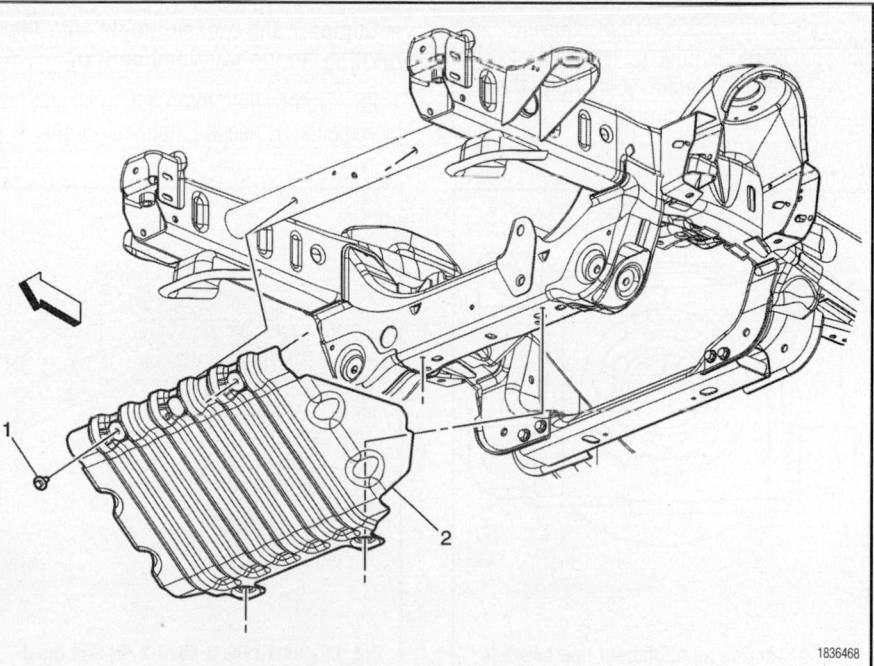

Fig. 95 Remove the engine shield bolts (1) and engine shield (2)

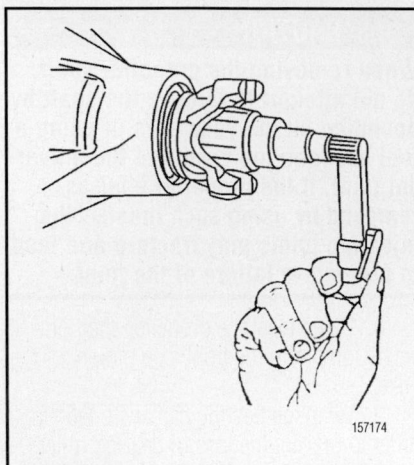

Fig. 96 Measure the torque required in order to rotate the pinion

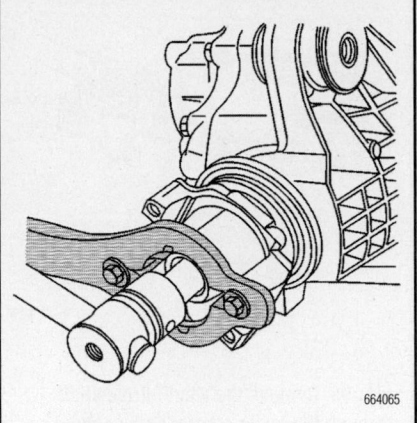

Fig. 98 Install the J-8614-01 onto the pinion as shown

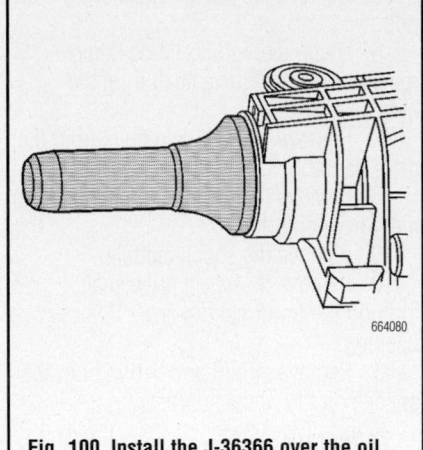

Fig. 100 Install the J-36366 over the oil seal

16. Remove the pinion yoke by turning the J-8614-3 clockwise while holding the J-8614-01.

➡**Carefully remove the oil seal from the bore. Do not distort or scratch the aluminum case.**

17. Remove the oil seal using a suitable seal removal tool.

To install:

18. Install the oil seal by doing the following:

  a. Position the oil seal over the seal bore.

  b. Install the J-36366 over the oil seal.

  c. Strike the J-36366 with a hammer until the seal flange seats on the axle housing surface.

19. Apply sealant GM P/N 12346004 (Canadian P/N 10953480) or equivalent to the splines of the drive pinion yoke.

20. Install the pinion yoke. Align the reference marks made during removal.

21. Seat the pinion yoke onto the pinion shaft by tapping it with a soft-faced hammer until a few pinion shaft threads show through the yoke.

22. Install the washer and a new pinion nut.

23. Install the J-8614-01 onto the pinion yoke.

➡**If the rotating torque is exceeded, the pinion will have to be removed and a new collapsible spacer installed.**

24. Tighten the pinion nut while holding the J-8614-01. Tighten the pinion nut until the pinion end play is just taken up. Rotate the pinion while tightening the nut to seat the bearings.

25. Measure the rotating torque of the pinion using an inch-pound torque wrench.

➡**Compare the measurement with the rotating torque recorded earlier.**

26. Tighten the pinion nut, in small increments, as needed, until the torque required in order to rotate the pinion is 3–5 inch lbs. (0.40–0.57 Nm) greater than the torque recorded during removal.

27. Once the specified torque is obtained, rotate the pinion several times to ensure the bearings have seated. Recheck the rotating torque and adjust if necessary.

28. Install the propeller shaft universal joint to the pinion yoke. Align the reference marks made during removal.

29. Install the yoke retainers and the yoke retainer bolts to the pinion yoke. Tighten the yoke retainer bolts to 18 ft. lbs. (25 Nm).

30. Inspect the axle lubricant level, and add, if necessary.

31. Install the engine shield, if equipped.

32. Install the brake calipers.

33. Fill the drive axle.

34. Install the tire and wheel assemblies.

35. Lower the vehicle.

REAR AXLE HOUSING

REMOVAL & INSTALLATION

8.6-Inch Differential

1. Raise the vehicle.

2. Clean the area around the rear axle fill plug.

3. Remove the rear axle fill plug.

4. Remove the rear axle cover.

5. Drain the lubricant into a suitable container.

To install:

6. Install the rear axle cover. Tighten the cover bolts to 20 ft. lbs. (30 Nm).

7. Fill the rear axle with axle lubricant. Use the proper fluid.

8. Install the rear axle fill plug and tighten to 24 ft. lbs. (33 Nm).

9. Lower the vehicle.

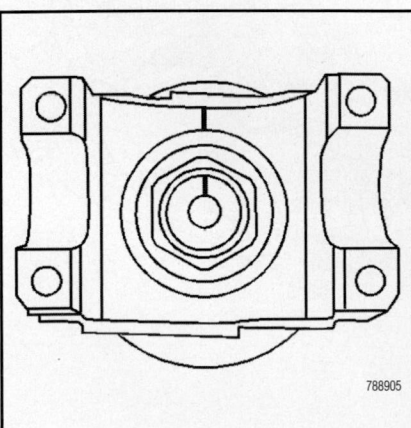

Fig. 97 Scribe an alignment line between the pinion shaft and the pinion yoke

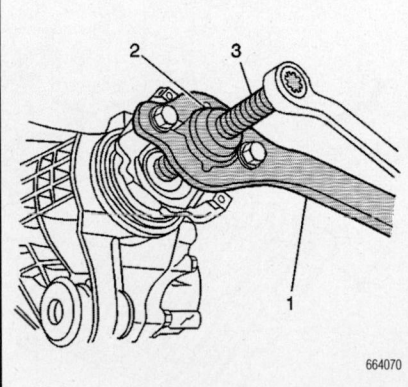

Fig. 99 Install the J-8614-2 (2) and the J-8614-3 (3) into the J-8614-01 (1) as shown

9.5-Inch Differential

1. Raise and support the vehicle.
2. Remove the drain plug.
3. Remove the fill plug.

To install:

4. Install the drain plug and tighten to 24 ft. lbs. (33 Nm).
5. Fill the rear drive axle.
6. Install the fill plug and tighten to 24 ft. lbs. (33 Nm).
7. Remove the support and lower the vehicle.

10.5-Inch Differential

1. Raise the vehicle.
2. Remove the fill plug.
3. Remove the rear axle drain plug.
4. Drain the lubricant into a suitable container.

To install:

5. Install the rear axle drain plug and tighten to 24 ft. lbs. (33 Nm).
6. Fill the rear axle with the proper fluid.
7. Install the fill plug and tighten to 24 ft. lbs. (33 Nm).
8. Remove the support and lower the vehicle.

11.5-Inch Differential

1. Raise the vehicle.
2. Remove the fill plug.
3. Remove the rear axle drain plug.
4. Drain the lubricant into a suitable container.
5. Inspect the drain plug for excessive metal particle accumulation. This accumulation is symptomatic of extreme wear.
6. Clean the drain plug.

To install:

7. Install the rear axle drain plug and tighten to 24 ft. lbs. (33 Nm).
8. Fill the rear axle. Use the proper fluid.
9. Install the fill plug and washer and tighten to 24 ft. lbs. (33 Nm).
10. Lower the vehicle.

REAR AXLE SHAFT, BEARING & SEAL

REMOVAL & INSTALLATION

See Figures 101 through 103.

Special Tools Required:
• J-2619-01 Slide Hammer W ½ x 13 Adapter
• J-8092 Universal Driver Handle ¾ x 10 inch
• J-21128 Axle Pinion Oil Seal Installer

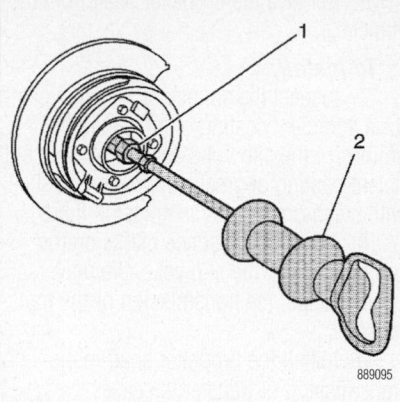

Fig. 101 Using the J-44685 remover (1) and the J-2619-01 hammer (2), remove the rear axle shaft seal

• J-23690 Axle Bearing Installer
• J-44685 Rear Axle Seal and Bearing Remover
• J-45857 VSES Wheel Bearing Remover

1. Raise and support the vehicle.
2. Remove the tire and wheel assembly.
3. Remove the rear axle housing cover.
4. Remove the axle shaft.

➡ **If the vehicle is equipped with VSES, proceed to step 5.**

5. Using the J-44685 remover and the J-2619-01 hammer, remove the rear axle shaft seal.
6. Using the J-45857 remover and the J-2619-01 hammer, remove the rear axle shaft seal, bearing and the wheel speed sensor reluctor ring, if equipped.

To install:

7. Install the rear wheel speed sensor reluctor ring, if equipped.

➡ **Ensure that the axle shaft bearing is fully seated in the rear axle shaft housing.**

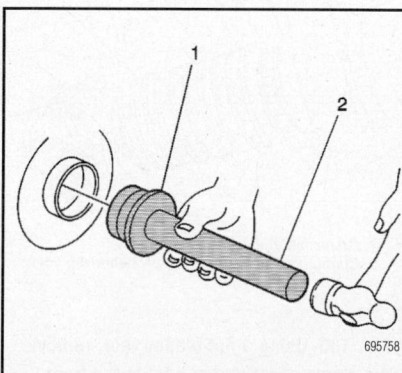

Fig. 102 Using the J-23690 installer (1) and the J-8092 driver (2), install the axle shaft bearing

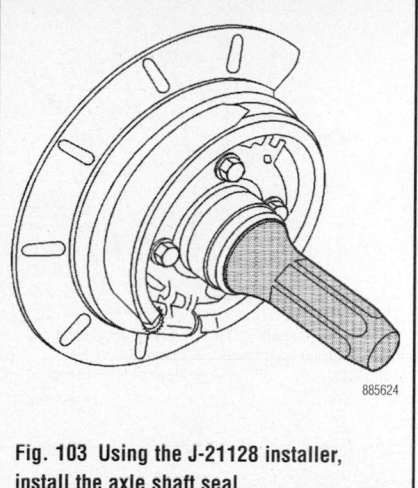

Fig. 103 Using the J-21128 installer, install the axle shaft seal

8. Using the J-23690 installer and the J-8092 driver, install the axle shaft bearing.
9. Using the J-21128 installer, install the axle shaft seal.
10. Drive the tool into the bore until the axle shaft seal bottoms flush with the tube.
11. Install the rear axle shaft.
12. Install the rear axle housing cover.
13. Install the tire and wheel assembly.
14. Fill the rear axle.
15. Remove the support and lower the vehicle.

REAR DRIVESHAFT

REMOVAL & INSTALLATION

One-Piece Propeller Shaft

See Figures 104 and 105.

➡ **Observe and accurately reference mark all driveline components relative to the propeller shaft and axles before disassembly. These components include the propeller shafts, the drive axles, the pinion flanges, the output shafts, etc. All components must be reassembled in the exact relationship to each other as they were when removed. In addition, published specifications and torque values, as well as any measurements made prior to disassembly must be followed.**

1. Raise and support the vehicle.
2. Reference mark the propeller shaft, the universal joint strap, universal bearing cap, the drive pinion yoke, and the rear axle housing.

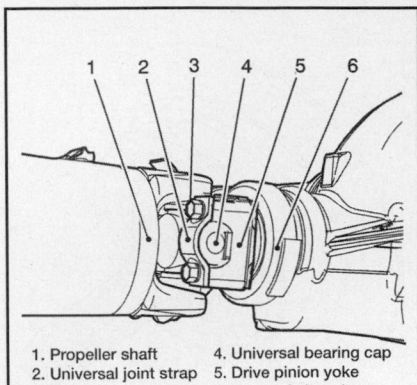

1. Propeller shaft
2. Universal joint strap
3. Bolts
4. Universal bearing cap
5. Drive pinion yoke
6. Rear axle housing

2082911

Fig. 104 Reference mark the propeller shaft, the universal joint strap, universal bearing cap, the drive pinion yoke, and the rear axle housing

➡ **DO NOT re-use the universal straps. Discard and replace with NEW only.**

3. Remove the bolts and the universal straps from the rear axle pinion yoke.

✳✳ CAUTION

When removing the propeller shaft, do not attempt to remove the shaft by pounding on the yoke ears or using a tool between the yoke and the universal joint. If the propeller shaft is removed by using such means, the injection joints may fracture and lead to premature failure of the joint.

4. Remove the propeller shaft from the rear axle pinion yoke.
5. Reference mark the transmission or the transfer case, propeller shaft flip yoke, universal joint bearing cap, and the propeller shaft.

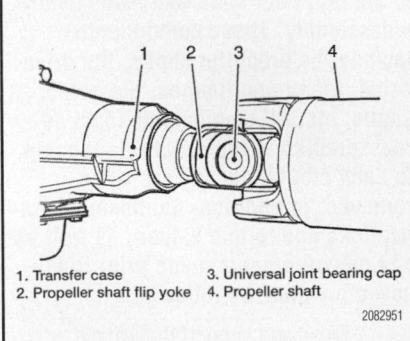

1. Transfer case
2. Propeller shaft flip yoke
3. Universal joint bearing cap
4. Propeller shaft

2082951

Fig. 105 Reference mark the transmission or the transfer case, propeller shaft flip yoke, universal joint bearing cap, and the propeller shaft

6. Remove the propeller shaft from the vehicle.

To install:

7. Inspect the splines of the slip yoke for a sufficient coating of grease. If the splines of the slip yoke does not have a sufficient coating of grease, lubricate the shaft with clean grease or transmission fluid.
8. Align the reference marks on the propeller shaft, the slip yoke, the universal bearing caps, the transmission or the transfer case.
9. Install the propeller shaft in the transmission or transfer the case.

➡ **Ensure that the reference marks are aligned before installing the propeller shaft.**

10. Align the reference marks on the propeller shaft, universal bearing cap, pinion flange, and the rear axle housing.
11. With the reference marks aligned, install the propeller shaft on the rear axle.
12. Install the rear propeller shaft bolts and the NEW strap. Tighten the yoke retainer bolts to 18 ft. lbs. (25 Nm).
13. Remove the support and lower the vehicle.

Two-Piece Propeller Shaft

See Figures 104, 106 through 111.

➡ **Observe and accurately reference mark all driveline components relative to the propeller shaft and axles before disassembly. These components include the propeller shafts, the drive axles, the pinion flanges, the output**

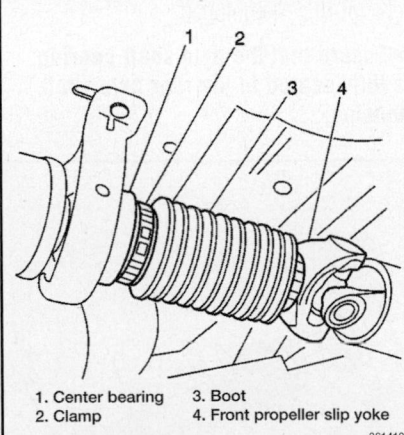

1. Center bearing
2. Clamp
3. Boot
4. Front propeller slip yoke

361410

Fig. 106 Using a flat bladed tool, remove the clamp securing the boot to the front propeller slip yoke and at the center bearing by prying up the exposed end of the clamp

shafts, etc. All components must be reassembled in the exact relationship to each other as they were when removed. In addition, published specifications and torque values, as well as any measurements made prior to disassembly must be followed.

1. Raise and support the vehicle.
2. Reference mark the propeller shaft, the universal joint strap, the universal bearing cap, the drive pinion yoke, and the rear axle housing.

➡ **DO NOT reuse the universal joint strap. Discard and replace with NEW only.**

3. Remove the rear propeller shaft bolts and the universal joint strap.
4. Using a flat bladed tool, remove the clamp securing the boot to the front propeller slip yoke and at the center bearing by prying up the exposed end of the clamp.

✳✳ CAUTION

When removing the propeller shaft, do not attempt to remove the shaft by pounding on the yoke ears or using a tool between the yoke and the universal joint. If the propeller shaft is removed by using such means, the injection joints may fracture and lead to premature failure of the joint.

5. Remove the rear propeller shaft from the rear axle and the center support bearing.

➡ **Step 6 is for those vehicles that have a slip yoke from the transmission from transfer case to the propeller shaft.**

6. Reference mark the transmission or the transfer case, propeller shaft slip yoke, universal bearing cap, and the propeller shaft.

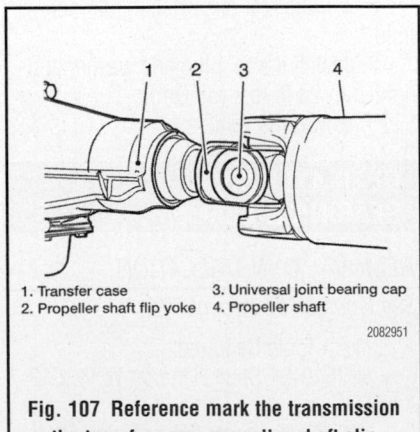

1. Transfer case
2. Propeller shaft flip yoke
3. Universal joint bearing cap
4. Propeller shaft

2082951

Fig. 107 Reference mark the transmission or the transfer case, propeller shaft slip yoke, universal bearing cap, and the propeller shaft

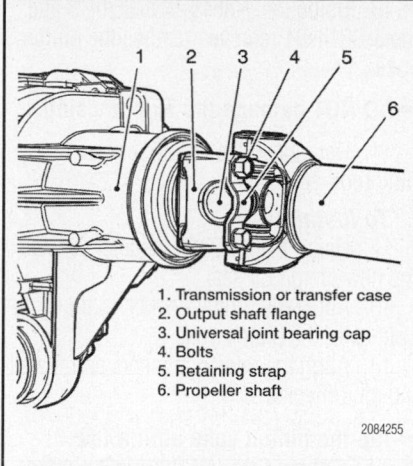

1. Transmission or transfer case
2. Output shaft flange
3. Universal joint bearing cap
4. Bolts
5. Retaining strap
6. Propeller shaft

2084255

Fig. 108 Reference mark the transmission or transfer case, output shaft flange, universal joint bearing cap, and the propeller shaft

➡**Step 7 is for those vehicles that have the yoke attached to the output shaft.**

7. Reference mark the transmission or transfer case, output shaft flange, universal joint bearing cap, and the propeller shaft.

8. Remove the center bearing support nuts.

9. Remove the center bearing support.

➡**For those vehicles equipped with the yoke attached to the output shaft, proceed to step 10. Those vehicles equipped with a slip yoke, proceed to step 12.**

10. For vehicles equipped with the yoke attached to the output shaft, use a suitable jack stand support the propeller shaft until propeller shaft is to be removed.

➡**DO NOT reuse the strap. Discard and replace with NEW only.**

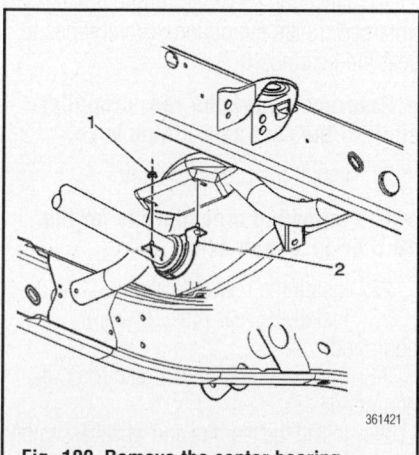

1
2

361421

Fig. 109 Remove the center bearing support nuts (1) and the center bearing support (2)

11. Remove the propeller shaft bolts, the straps, and the propeller shaft from the transmission or the transfer case.

12. Remove the propeller shaft from the transmission or the transfer case.

To install:

➡**If servicing a propeller shaft with a slip yoke, proceed to step 1. If servicing a propeller shaft with the yoke attached to the output shaft of the transmission or the transfer case, proceed to step 3.**

13. Align the reference marks on the transmission or the transfer case, slip yoke, universal bearing cap, and the propeller shaft.

14. Install the propeller shaft.

15. Align the reference marks on the transmission or the transfer case, output shaft yoke, and the propeller shaft.

➡**When installing the propeller shaft bolts, hand tighten the bolts. DO NOT tighten them to specification until the center bearing support bolts have been installed and torqued to specifications.**

16. Install the propeller shaft, the NEW straps, the propeller shaft bolts on the transmission or the transfer case.

17. Position the center support bearing on the frame.

18. Install the center bearing support nuts. Tighten the center support bearing nuts to 30 ft. lbs. (40 Nm).

19. Tighten the propeller shaft bolts to 18 ft. lbs. (25 Nm).

20. Install the boot and the new clamps onto the front propeller shaft slip yoke.

➡**Ensure that the master splines on the slip yoke and the stub shaft are aligned before installing the rear propeller shaft.**

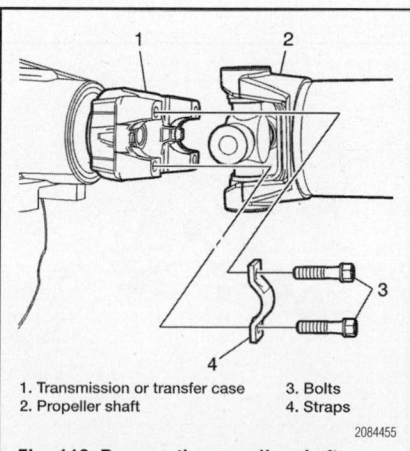

1
2

3

4

1. Transmission or transfer case   3. Bolts
2. Propeller shaft   4. Straps

2084455

Fig. 110 Remove the propeller shaft bolts, the straps, and the propeller shaft from the transmission or the transfer case

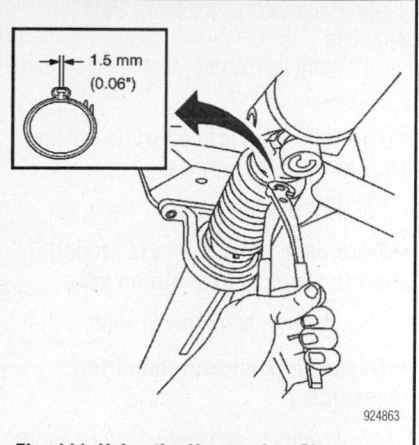

1.5 mm
(0.06")

924863

Fig. 111 Using the Narrow Jaw Clamp Pliers (J-43218), crimp the boot clamps until the dimensions shown are obtained

21. Apply a small amount of clean chassis grease to the slip yoke and the rear propeller shaft.

22. Install the rear portion of the propeller into the front portion of the propeller shaft.

23. Align the reference marks on the rear axle housing, pinion yoke, universal bearing cap, and the rear propeller shaft.

24. Install the NEW straps and the bolts. Tighten the yoke retainer bolts to 18 ft. lbs. (25 Nm).

25. Using the Narrow Jaw Clamp Pliers (J-43218), crimp the boot clamps until the dimensions shown are obtained.

26. Remove the support and lower that vehicle.

REAR PINION SEAL

REMOVAL & INSTALLATION

See Figures 112 through 116.

Special Tools Required:
• J-8614-01 Flange Holder and Remover
• J-22388 Pinion Oil Seal Installer
• J-44414 Pinion Oil Seal Installer

➡**Observe and mark the positions of all the driveline components, relative to the propeller shaft and the axles, prior to disassembly. These components include the propeller shafts, drive axles, pinion flanges, output shafts, etc. Reassemble all the components in the exact places in which you removed the parts. Follow any specifications, torque values, and any measurements made prior to disassembly.**

1. Raise and support the vehicle.
2. Remove the rear tire and wheel assembly.

3. Remove the rear brake drum, if equipped.

4. Remove the rear disc brake rotor, if equipped.

→The following procedure is for the 10.5 or 11.5 inch axles.

5. Remove the rear axle shafts.

→Reference mark the rear propeller shaft to the rear axle pinion yoke.

6. Remove the propeller shaft.

→Record this measurement for reassembly.

7. Using an inch-pound torque wrench, measure the rotational torque of the differential ring and pinion gear and related components.

8. Place an alignment mark between the pinion and the pinion yoke.

→DO NOT reuse the pinion nut, replace with NEW. For the 11.5 inch axle, use J-34826 socket.

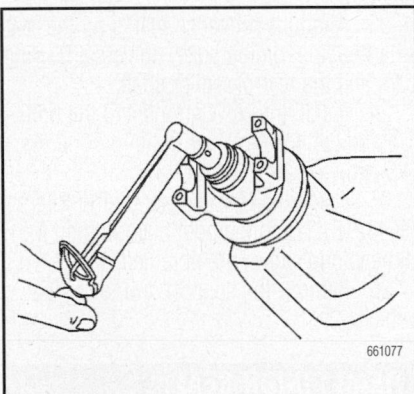

Fig. 112 Using an inch-pound torque wrench (1), measure the rotational torque of the differential ring and pinion gear and related components

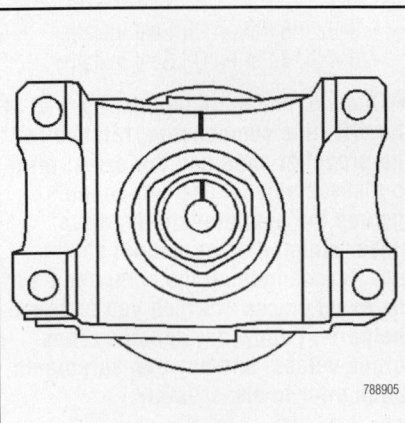

Fig. 113 Place an alignment mark between the pinion and the pinion yoke

9. Using the J-8614-01 holder and remover or the J-34826 socket, remove and discard the pinion the pinion nut.

→Remove the pinion yoke by turning the J-8614-3 clockwise.

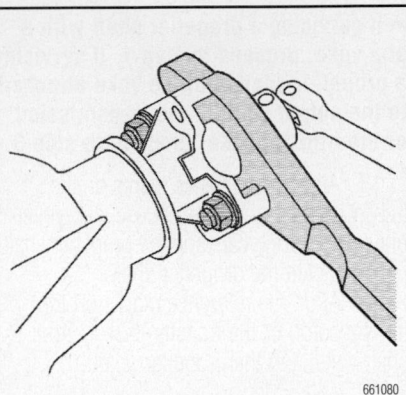

Fig. 114 Using the J-8614-01 holder and remover or the J-34826 socket, remove and discard the pinion the pinion nut

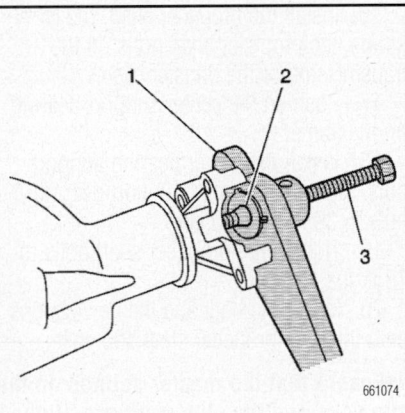

Fig. 115 Using the J-8614-2 (2), J-8614-3 (3) and the J-8614-01 remover (1), remove the pinion yoke

10. Using the J-8614-2, J-8614-3 and the J-8614-01 remover, remove the pinion yoke.

→DO NOT damage the axle housing.

11. Using a suitable tool, remove the pinion oil seal.

To install:

12. Using the J-22388 installer , install the new pinion oil seal.

13. Apply the proper sealant to the splines of the pinion yoke.

14. Align the reference marks and install the pinion yoke.

→Tap the pinion yoke until a few threads show through the pinion yoke.

15. Using a soft faced hammer, seat the pinion yoke onto the pinion shaft.

16. Install the washer and a NEW pinion nut.

→If the rotating torque is exceeded, the pinion will have to be removed and a new collapsible spacer installed. For the 11.5 inch axle, use J-34826 socket.

17. Holding the J-8614-01 holder or the J-34826 socket, tighten the pinion nut until the pinion end play is just taken up.

18. Rotate the pinion while tightening the nut to seat the bearings.

→Compare this measurement with the rotating torque recorded during removal.

19. Using an inch pound torque wrench and tightening in small increments, measure the rotating torque of the pinion until the reading is greater than 3–5 inch lbs. (0.40–0.57 Nm), the rotational torque noted at removal.

→Recheck the rotating torque and adjust if necessary.

20. Once the specified torque is obtained, rotate the pinion several times to seat the bearings.

→Reference mark the rear propeller shaft to the rear axle pinion yoke.

21. Install the propeller shaft.

→The following procedure is for the 10.5 or 11.5 inch axles.

22. Install the rear axle shafts.

23. Install the rear brake drum, if equipped.

24. Install the rear disc brake rotor, if equipped.

25. Install the rear tire and wheel assembly.

26. Inspect and add axle lubricant to the axle housing, if necessary.

27. Remove the support and lower the vehicle.

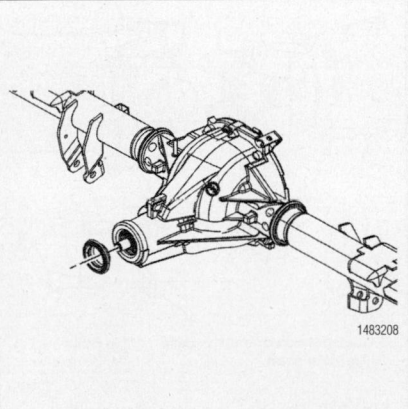

Fig. 116 Using a suitable tool, remove the pinion oil seal

ENGINE COOLING

ENGINE COOLANT

DRAIN & REFILL PROCEDURE

Static Fill

> #### �֍ WARNING
>
> **To avoid being burned, do not remove the radiator cap or surge tank cap while the engine is hot. The cooling system will release scalding fluid and steam under pressure if radiator cap or surge tank cap is removed while the engine and radiator are still hot.**

1. Follow the steps below in order to remove the surge tank fill cap:
   a. Slowly rotate the cap counterclockwise.
   b. Stop rotating and allow the hissing to stop.
   c. After all the hissing stops, continue turning counterclockwise in order to remove the cap.
2. Raise and support the vehicle.
3. Place a drain pan under the lower radiator hose and/or drain cock.
4. Using the J-38185, reposition the lower radiator hose clamp.
5. Reposition the lower radiator hose and/or drain cock from the radiator.
6. Drain the cooling system.
7. If a complete engine block drain is required, remove the left and right engine block coolant drain plugs.
8. Remove the engine block coolant heater, if equipped.
9. Inspect the coolant.
10. Follow the appropriate procedure based on the condition of the coolant:
    - Normal in appearance: Follow the filling procedure.
    - Discolored: Follow the flush procedure.

To refill:

> #### ✖✖ CAUTION
>
> **The procedure below must be followed. Improper coolant level could result in a low or high coolant level condition, causing engine damage.**

11. Install the lower radiator hose and/or drain cock to the radiator.
12. Using the J-38185, reposition the lower radiator hose clamp.
13. If the left and right engine block coolant drain plugs were removed, perform the following:

   a. Apply pipe sealer to the drain plugs.
   b. Install the drain plugs.
   c. Tighten the drain plugs to 44 ft. lbs. (60 Nm).
14. Install the engine block coolant heater, if equipped.
15. Lower the vehicle.

➡ **Use a 50/50 mixture of DEX-COOL® antifreeze and clean, drinkable water.**

16. Slowly fill the cooling system with a 50/50 coolant mixture.
17. Install the coolant pressure cap.
18. Start the engine.
19. Run the engine at 2,000–2,500 RPM until the engine reaches normal operating temperature. Engine should reach an operating temperature of 194°F (90°C) and the upper radiator hose should be HOT.
20. Allow the engine to idle for 3 minutes.
21. Shut the engine OFF.
22. Allow the engine to cool.
23. Top off the coolant as necessary.
24. Inspect the concentration of the engine coolant using the J-26568.
25. Rinse away any excess coolant from the engine and the engine compartment.

Vac-N-Fill

Special Tools Required:
- GE-47716 Vac-N-Fill Coolant Refill Tool
- J-26568 Coolant and Battery Tester
- J-42401 Radiator Cap and Surge Tank Test Adapter

Draining Procedure

> #### ✖✖ WARNING
>
> **With a pressurized cooling system, the coolant temperature in the radiator can be considerably higher than the boiling point of the solution at atmospheric pressure. Removal of the surge tank cap, while the cooling system is hot and under high pressure, causes the solution to boil instantaneously with explosive force. This will cause the solution to spew out over the engine, the fenders, and the person removing the cap. Serious bodily injury may result.**

1. Park the vehicle on a level surface.
2. Remove the coolant pressure cap.
3. Raise and support the vehicle.

4. Place a drain pan under the drain cock and/or lower radiator hose.
5. Reposition the radiator drain cock and/or lower radiator hose.
6. Drain the cooling system.
7. If a complete engine block drain is required, remove the engine block drain plug.
8. Inspect the coolant.
9. Follow the appropriate procedure based on the condition of the coolant.
   - Normal in appearance: Follow the filling procedure.
   - Discolored: Follow the flush procedure.

Vac-N-Fill Procedure

See Figures 117 through 127.

➡ **To prevent boiling of the coolant/water mixture in the vehicles cooling system, do not apply vacuum to a cooling system above 120°F (49°C). The tool will not operate properly when the coolant is boiling.**

1. Install the J-42401.
2. Attach the Vac-N-Fill cap to the vehicles coolant fill port.
3. Attach the vacuum gauge assembly to the Vac-N-Fill cap.
4. Attach the fill hose to the barb fitting on the vacuum gauge assembly. Ensure that the valve is closed.

➡ **Use a 50/50 mixture of DEX-COOL® antifreeze and clean, drinkable water. Always use more coolant than necessary. This will eliminate air from being drawn into the cooling system.**

5. Pour the coolant mixture into the graduated reservoir.

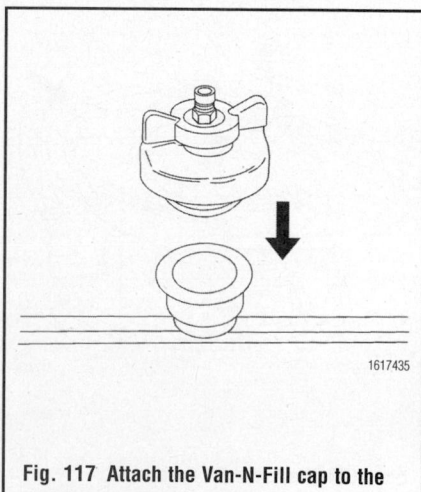

1617435

Fig. 117 Attach the Van-N-Fill cap to the vehicles coolant fill port

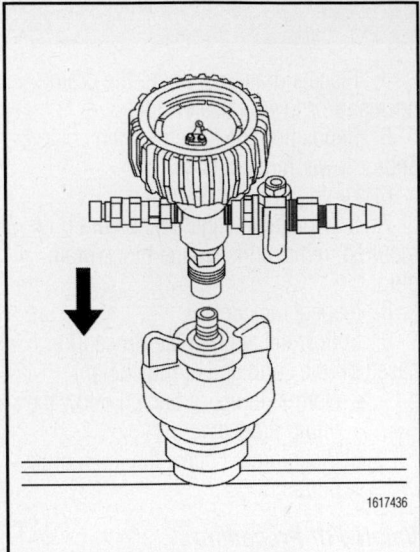

Fig. 118 Attach the vacuum gauge assembly to the Vac-N-Fill cap

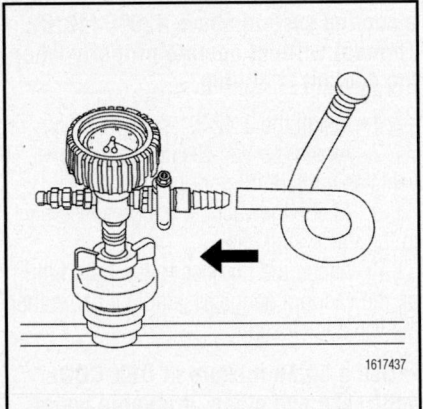

Fig. 119 Attach the fill hose to the barb fitting on the vacuum gauge assembly

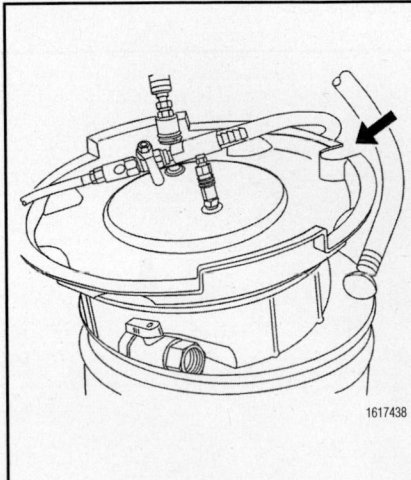

Fig. 120 Place the fill hose in the graduated reservoir

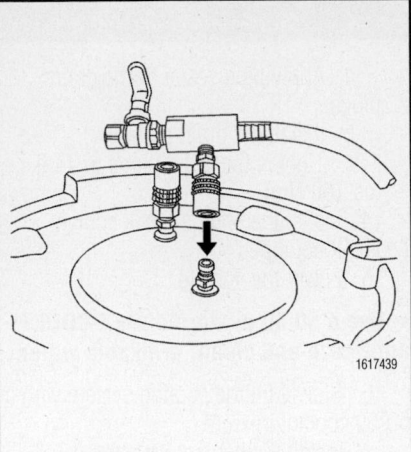

Fig. 121 Attach the venture assembly to the vacuum tank

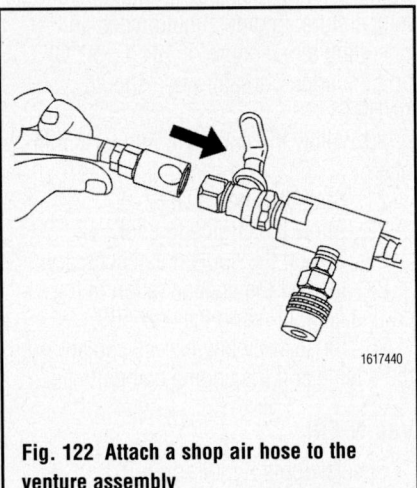

Fig. 122 Attach a shop air hose to the venture assembly

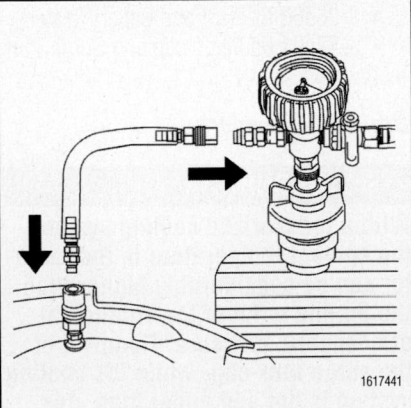

Fig. 123 Attach the vacuum hose to the vacuum gauge assembly and the vacuum tank

6. Place the fill hose in the graduated reservoir.

➡**Prior to installing the vacuum tank onto the graduated reservoir, ensure that the drain valve located on the bottom of the tank is closed.**

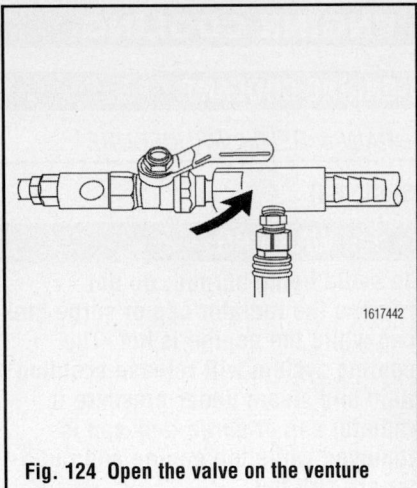

Fig. 124 Open the valve on the venture assembly

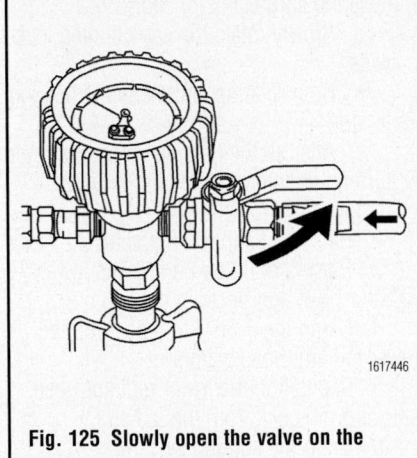

Fig. 125 Slowly open the valve on the vacuum gauge assembly

7. Install the vacuum tank on the graduated reservoir with the fill hose routed through the cut-out area in the vacuum tank.

8. Attach the venture assembly to the vacuum tank.

9. Attach a shop air hose to the venture assembly. Ensure the valve on the venture assembly is closed.

10. Attach the vacuum hose to the vacuum gauge assembly and the vacuum tank.

11. Clamp off the overflow hose.

12. Open the valve on the venture assembly. The vacuum gauge will begin to rise and a hissing noise will be present.

13. Continue to draw vacuum until the needle stops rising. This should be 24–26 in HG (610–660 mm Hg).

Cooling hoses may start to collapse. This is normal due to vacuum draw.

14. To aid in the fill process, position the graduated reservoir above the coolant fill port.

15. Slowly open the valve on the vacuum gauge assembly. When the coolant reaches

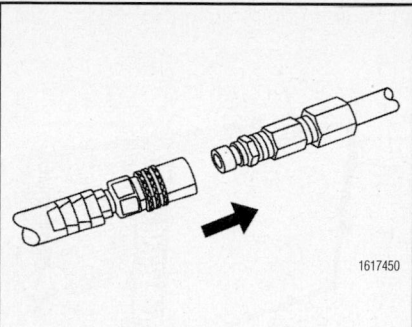

Fig. 126 Attach the extraction hose to the vacuum hose

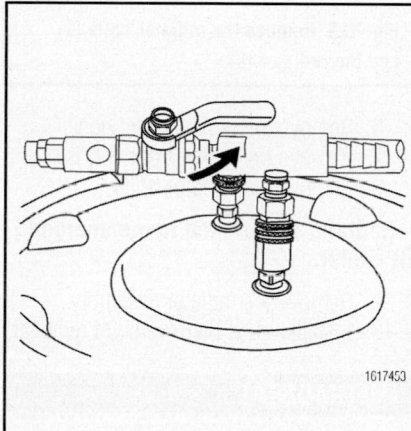

Fig. 127 Open the valve on the venture assembly to start a vacuum draw

the top of the fill hose, close the valve. This will eliminate air from the fill hose.

16. Close the valve on the venture assembly.

17. If there is a suspected leak in the cooling system, allow the system to stabilize under vacuum and monitor for vacuum loss.

18. Open the valve on the vacuum gauge assembly. The vacuum gauge will drop as coolant is drawn into the system.

19. Once the vacuum gauge reaches zero, close the valve on the vacuum gauge assembly and repeat steps 11–17.

20. Remove the J-42401.

21. Detach the Vac-N-Fill cap from the vehicles coolant fill port.

22. Add coolant to the system as necessary.

23. Inspect the concentration of the coolant mixture using J-26568.

➡**After filling the cooling system, the extraction hose can be used to remove excess coolant to achieve the proper coolant level.**

24. Detach the vacuum hose form the vacuum gauge assembly.

25. Attach the extraction hose to the vacuum hose.

26. Open the valve on the venture assembly to start a vacuum draw.

27. Use the extraction hose to draw out coolant to the proper level.

28. The vacuum tank has a drain valve on the bottom of the tank. Open the valve to drain coolant from the vacuum tank into a suitable container for disposal.

FLUSHING

Important:
• Do not use a chemical flush.
• Store used coolant in the proper manner, such as in a used engine coolant holding tank. Do not pour used coolant down a drain. Ethylene glycol antifreeze is a very toxic chemical. Do not dispose of coolant into the sewer system or ground water. This is illegal and ecologically unsound.
• Various methods and equipment can be used to flush the cooling system. If special equipment is used (such as a back flusher) follow the manufacturer's instructions. However, always remove the thermostat before back flushing the system.

1. Block the drive wheels.
2. Place the transmission in park (P) or neutral (N).
3. Engage the park brake.
4. Run the engine until the thermostat opens.
5. Stop the engine.
6. Follow the drain and fill procedure using only clean drinkable water. Repeat the procedure if necessary, until the fluid is nearly colorless.
7. Fill the coolant reservoir to the FULL HOT mark.
8. Fill the cooling system.

ENGINE FAN

REMOVAL & INSTALLATION

See Figures 128 through 131.

1. Drain the cooling system.
2. Remove air inlet duct.
3. Disconnect upper radiator hose from radiator.
4. Disengage the radiator inlet hose clip at the fan shroud.
5. If necessary, reposition the surge tank inlet hose clamp at the radiator.
6. If necessary, remove the surge tank inlet hose from the radiator.
7. Disconnect the electrical connectors from the cooling fans.

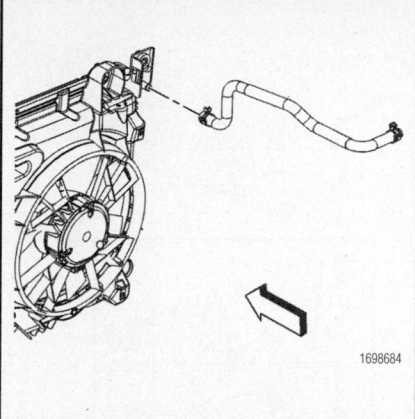

Fig. 128 If necessary, remove the surge tank inlet hose from the radiator

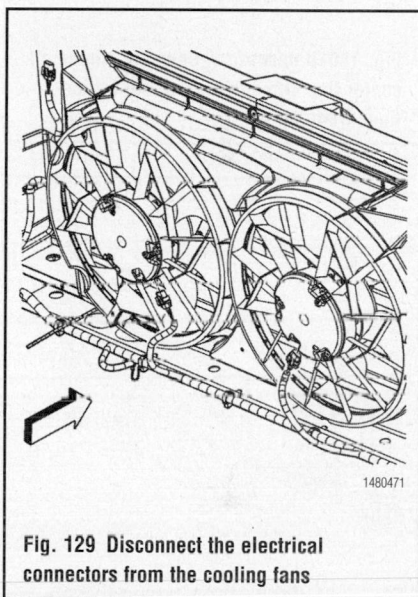

Fig. 129 Disconnect the electrical connectors from the cooling fans

8. Remove the clip attaching the wiring harness to the shroud.
9. Remove transmission cooler lines bolts from fan shroud.
10. If necessary, open the engine oil cooler line clip and remove the cooler lines from the clip.
11. Remove the cooling fan shroud bolts.
12. Remove the cooling fan and shroud.

To install:

➡**Insert the 3 lower tabs into the radiator support flange. Keeping the shroud parallel to the radiator will ensure the correct installation of the lower tabs.**

13. Install the cooling fan and shroud.
14. Install the cooling fan shroud bolts. Tighten the bolts to 80 inch lbs. (9 Nm).

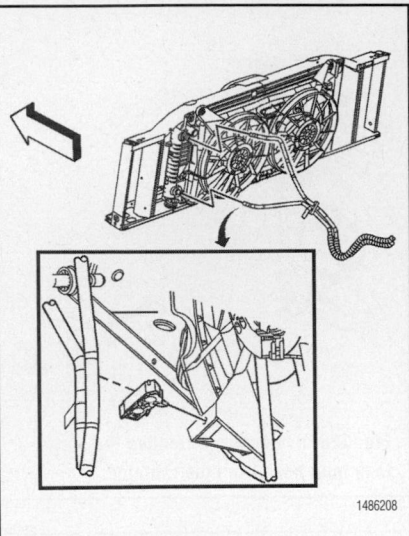

Fig. 130 If necessary, open the engine oil cooler line clip and remove the cooler lines from the clip

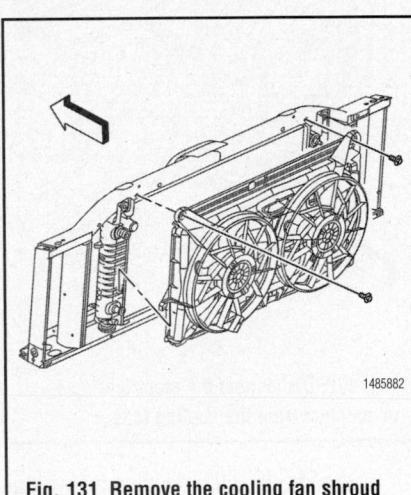

Fig. 131 Remove the cooling fan shroud bolts

15. If equipped, install the cooler lines to the clip and close the clip.

16. Connect the electrical connectors to the cooling fans.

17. Install the clip attaching the wiring harness to the shroud.

18. Install the transmission cooling line bolts to fan shroud.

19. If necessary, install the surge tank inlet hose to the radiator.

20. If necessary, reposition the surge tank inlet hose clamp at the radiator.

21. Engage the radiator inlet hose clip at the fan shroud.

22. Connect upper radiator hose from radiator.

23. Install air inlet duct.

24. Fill the cooling system.

RADIATOR

REMOVAL & INSTALLATION

Gasoline Engines

See Figure 132.

1. Remove the cooling fan and shroud.

2. Remove the radiator outlet hose for the 4.3L engine, or the 4.8L, 5.3L and 6.0L engines.

3. Disconnect the engine oil cooler lines from the radiator, if equipped.

4. Disconnect the transmission oil cooler lines from the radiator, if equipped.

5. Remove the radiator bolts.

6. Remove the radiator.

To install:

7. Install the radiator.

8. Install the radiator bolts. Tighten the bolts to 18 ft. lbs. (25 Nm).

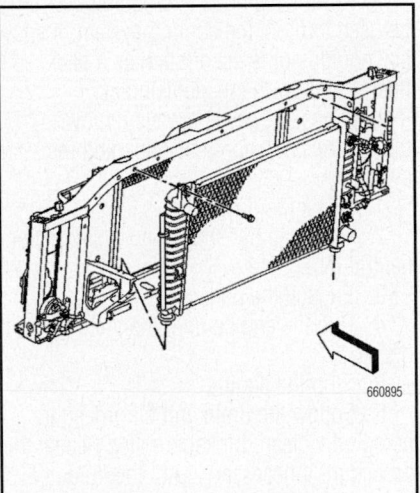

Fig. 132 Remove the radiator bolts

9. Connect the transmission oil cooler lines to the radiator, if equipped.

10. Connect the engine oil cooler lines to the radiator, if equipped.

11. Install the radiator outlet hose for the 4.3L engine, or the 4.8L, 5.3L and 6.0L engines.

12. Install the cooling fan and shroud.

Diesel Engines

See Figure 133.

1. Drain the cooling system.

2. If necessary, remove air cleaner resonator duct.

3. Remove the cooling fan.

4. Remove the surge tank inlet hose.

5. Remove the charge air cooler inlet and outlet pipes.

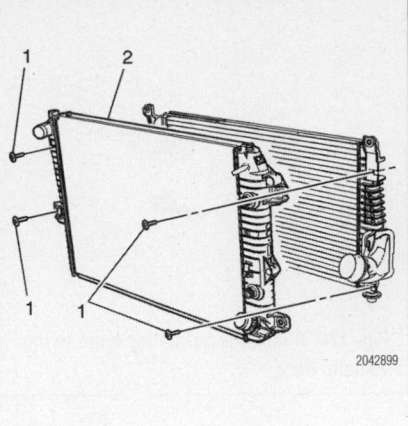

Fig. 133 Remove the radiator bolts (1) and the radiator (2)

6. Remove the radiator inlet hose.

7. Remove the radiator outlet hose.

8. Remove the radiator bolts.

➡**Radiator is mounted to the charged air cooler.**

9. Remove the radiator assembly.

10. Installation is the reverse of removal.

THERMOSTAT

REMOVAL & INSTALLATION

Gasoline Engines

See Figures 134 and 135.

1. Drain the cooling system.

2. Remove the air cleaner outlet duct.

3. Reposition the radiator outlet hose clamp at the water pump inlet.

4. Remove the radiator outlet hose from the water pump inlet.

5. Remove the water pump inlet bolts.

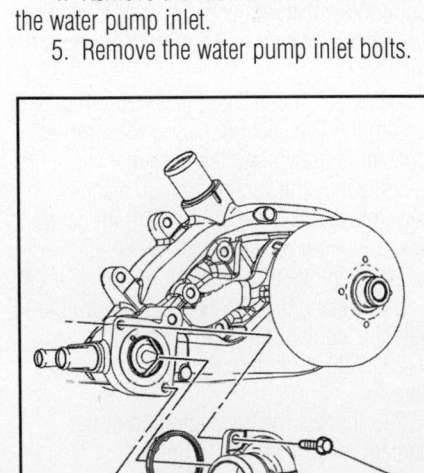

Fig. 134 Remove the water pump inlet bolts (1)

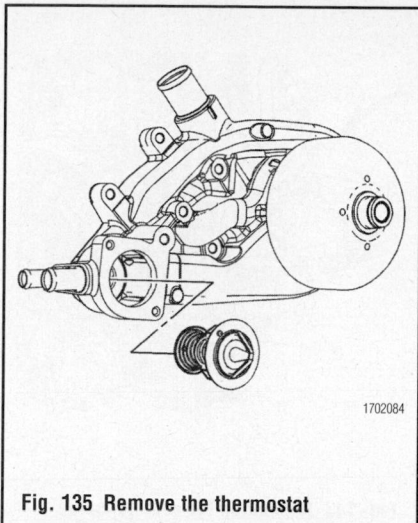

Fig. 135 Remove the thermostat

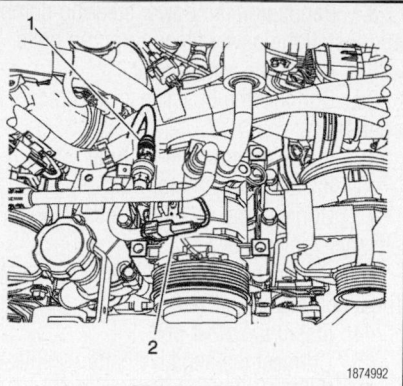

Fig. 136 Disconnect the Air Conditioning (A/C) pressure switch electrical connector (1) and the A/C compressor clutch electrical connector (2)

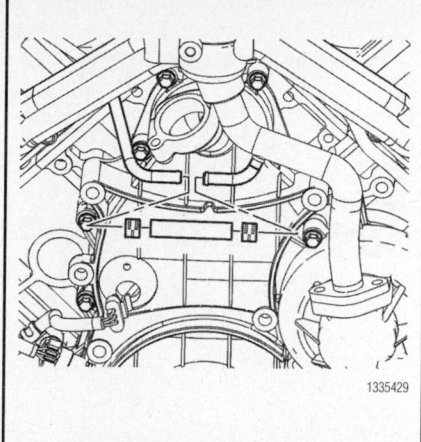

Fig. 138 Remove the turbocharger coolant return pipe hose

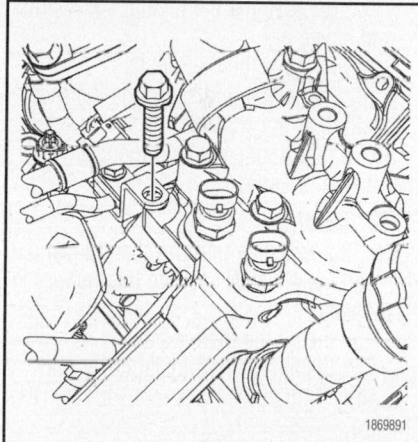

Fig. 139 Remove the fuel line bracket bolt at the thermostat housing crossover

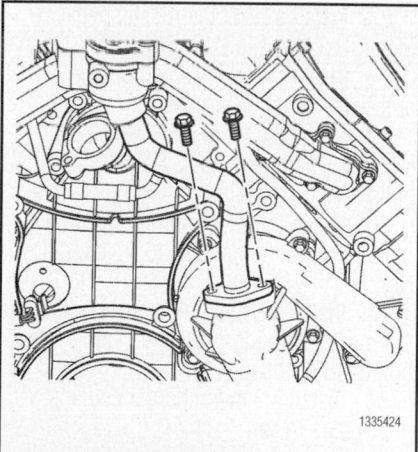

Fig. 140 Remove the water pump inlet pipe bolts

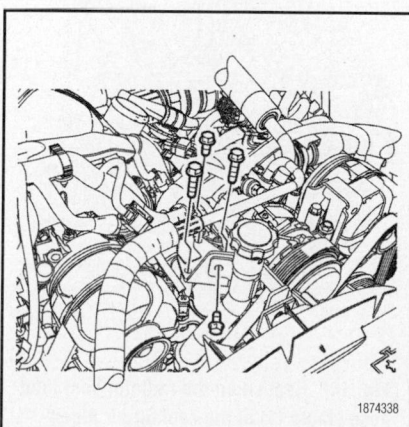

Fig. 137 Remove the bolts and wiring harness bracket at the thermostat housing

6. Remove the water pump inlet from the water pump.

7. Remove and discard the water pump inlet seal.

8. Remove the thermostat.

To install:

9. Install the thermostat.

10. Install a NEW water pump inlet seal to the water pump inlet.

11. Position the water pump inlet to the water pump.

12. Install the water pump inlet bolts and tighten to 11 ft. lbs. (15 Nm).

13. Install the radiator outlet hose to the water pump inlet.

14. Position the radiator outlet hose clamp at the water pump inlet.

15. Install the air cleaner outlet duct.

16. Fill the cooling system.

Diesel Engines

See Figures 136 through 141.

1. Remove the air cleaner.

2. Drain the cooling system.

3. Disconnect the negative battery cables.

4. Remove the drive belt.

5. Disconnect the Air Conditioning (A/C) pressure switch electrical connector.

6. Disconnect the A/C compressor clutch electrical connector.

7. Remove the alternator bracket.

8. Remove the front oil fill tube.

9. Disconnect the Engine Coolant Temperature (ECT) sensor electrical connectors.

10. Remove the water outlet.

11. Without disconnecting the power steering hoses, remove the power steering pump bolts and the power steering pump. Reposition the power steering pump and secure to the side.

12. Remove the power steering pump bracket.

13. Remove the bolts and wiring harness bracket at the thermostat housing.

14. Position the bracket and wiring harness aside.

15. Remove the cooling fan pulley.

16. Reposition the turbocharger coolant return pipe hose clamp.

17. Remove the turbocharger coolant return pipe hose.

18. Remove the fuel line bracket bolt at the thermostat housing crossover.

19. Remove the water pump inlet pipe bolts.

20. Remove the thermostat housing crossover bolts and nuts.

21. Remove the thermostat housing crossover, with the bypass pipe.

22. Remove and discard the thermostat bypass pipe to water pump O-ring seal.

23. Remove and discard the thermostat housing crossover gaskets.

24. If necessary, perform the following:

a. Remove the thermostat bypass pipe from the thermostat housing crossover.

b. Remove and discard the thermostat bypass pipe O-ring seal.

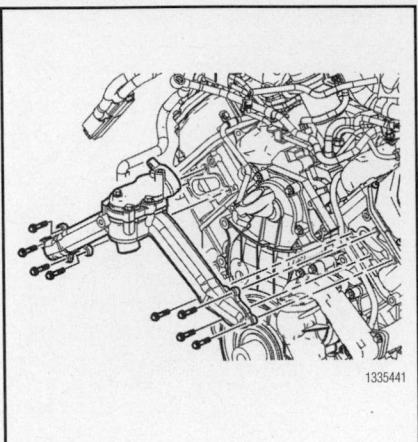

Fig. 141 Remove the thermostat housing crossover bolts and nuts

c. Remove the thermostat cover bolts and cover.

d. Remove the thermostats.

e. Remove and discard the thermostat seals.

25. If required, clean and inspect the thermostat housing.

To install:

26. If necessary, perform the following:

a. Install NEW seals to the thermostats.

b. Install the thermostats.

c. Install the thermostat cover and bolts. Tighten the bolts to 15 ft. lbs. (21 Nm).

d. Install a NEW O-ring seal to the thermostat bypass pipe.

e. Install the thermostat bypass pipe to the thermostat housing.

27. Install a NEW thermostat bypass pipe to water pump O-ring seal.

28. Install the thermostat housing crossover using NEW gaskets.

29. Install the thermostat housing crossover bolts and nuts. Tighten the bolts/nuts to 15 ft. lbs. (21 Nm).

30. Install the water pump inlet pipe bolts. Tighten the bolts to 15 ft. lbs. (21 Nm).

31. Install the fuel line bracket bolt at the thermostat housing crossover. Tighten the bolt to 15 ft. lbs. (21 Nm).

32. Install the turbocharger coolant return pipe hose.

33. Position the turbocharger coolant return pipe hose clamp.

34. Install the wiring harness bracket and bolts to the thermostat housing. Tighten the bolts to 89 inch lbs. (10 Nm).

35. Install the cooling fan pulley.

36. Install the power steering pump bracket.

37. Reposition the power steering pump and install the power steering pump bolts.

38. Install the water outlet.

39. Connect the ECT sensor electrical connectors.

40. Install the front oil fill tube.

41. Install the alternator bracket.

42. Connect the A/C compressor clutch electrical connector.

43. Connect the A/C cut out switch electrical connector.

44. Install the drive belt.

45. Connect the negative battery cables.

46. Fill the cooling system.

47. Install the air cleaner.

WATER PUMP

REMOVAL & INSTALLATION

Gasoline Engines

See Figures 142 through 145.

1. Remove the air cleaner outlet duct.

2. Drain the cooling system.

3. Reposition the radiator vent inlet hose clamp at the coolant air bleed pipe fitting.

4. Remove the radiator vent inlet hose from the coolant air bleed pipe fitting.

5. Reposition the radiator inlet hose clamp at the water pump.

6. Remove the radiator inlet hose from the water pump.

7. Reposition the radiator inlet hose and vent inlet hose out of the way.

8. Remove the accessory drive belt.

9. Reposition the radiator outlet hose clamp at the water pump.

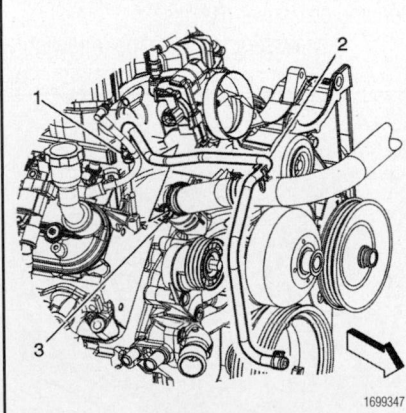

Fig. 142 Reposition the radiator vent inlet hose clamp (1) at the coolant air bleed pipe fitting and remove the radiator vent inlet hose (2); reposition the radiator inlet hose clamp (3) at the water pump

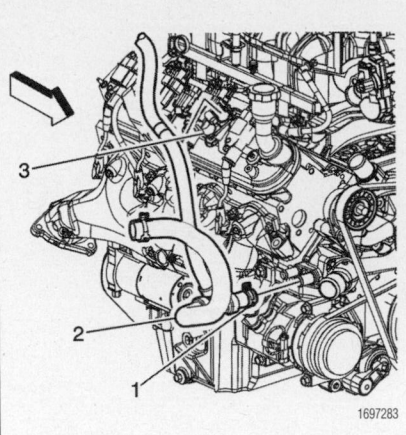

Fig. 143 Reposition the radiator surge tank outlet hose clamp at the water pump (1) and remove the radiator surge tank outlet hose (2)

10. Remove the radiator outlet hose from the water pump.

11. Reposition the outlet hose out of the way.

12. Reposition the radiator surge tank outlet hose clamp at the water pump.

13. Remove the radiator surge tank outlet hose from the water pump.

14. Reposition the outlet hose out of the way.

15. Reposition the heater inlet hose clamp at the water pump.

16. Remove the heater inlet hose from the water pump.

17. Reposition the inlet hose out of the way.

18. Remove the water pump bolts.

19. Remove the water pump and gaskets. Discard the gaskets.

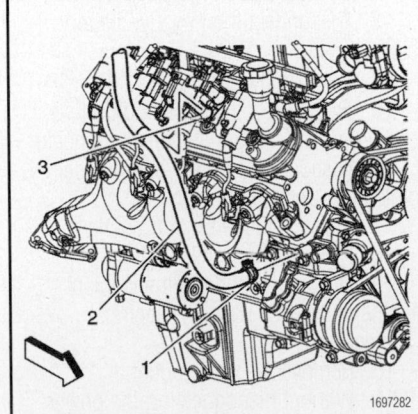

Fig. 144 Reposition the heater inlet hose clamp (1) at the water pump and remove the heater inlet hose (2)

To install:

✳✳ CAUTION

DO NOT use cooling system seal tabs, or similar compounds, unless otherwise instructed. The use of cooling system seal tabs, or similar compounds, may restrict coolant flow through the passages of the cooling system or the engine components. Restricted coolant flow may cause engine overheating and/or damage to the cooling system or the engine components/assembly.

➡**All gaskets surfaces are to be free of oil or other foreign material during assembly.**

20. Inspect the drained coolant for sand or other debris, flush the system as needed.

21. Inspect and clear the radiator vent hose fitting, if necessary.

➡**There is a small 0.080 inches (2.0 mm) orifice (vent hose fitting) in the neck of the radiator where the coolant vent hose from the engine attaches to the radiator.**

22. Position the water pump and NEW gaskets to the engine block.

23. Install the water pump bolts.
   a. Tighten the bolts a first pass to 11 ft. lbs. (15 Nm).
   b. Tighten the bolts a final pass to 22 ft. lbs. (30 Nm).

24. Position and install the heater inlet hose to the water pump.

25. Position the heater inlet hose clamp at the water pump.

26. Position and install the radiator surge tank outlet hose to the water pump.

27. Position the radiator surge tank outlet hose clamp at the water pump.

28. Position and install the radiator outlet hose to the water pump.

29. Position the radiator outlet hose clamp at the water pump.

30. Install the accessory drive belt.

31. Position the radiator inlet hose and vent inlet hose to the correct position.

32. Install the radiator inlet hose to the water pump.

33. Position the radiator inlet hose clamp at the water pump.

34. Install the radiator vent inlet hose to the coolant air bleed pipe fitting.

35. Position the radiator vent inlet hose clamp at the coolant air bleed pipe fitting.

36. Fill the cooling system.

37. Install the air cleaner outlet duct.

Diesel Engines

See Figures 146 and 147.

1. Remove the left wheelhouse inner panel.

2. Remove the thermostat housing crossover.

3. Remove the crankshaft balancer.

4. Remove the water pump to engine coolant pipe nuts.

5. Remove the engine wiring harness retainer from the inner stud.

6. Remove the water pump bolts.

➡**Note the location of the bolts. The bolts are three different lengths.**

7. Remove the water pump.

8. Remove and discard the water pump O-ring and coolant pipe gasket.

9. If required, clean and inspect the water pump.

To install:

10. Lubricate the water pump O-ring with engine oil.

11. Install the engine coolant pipe gasket and water pump O-ring.

12. Install the water pump.

13. Install the water pump bolts. Tighten the bolts to 15 ft. lbs. (21 Nm).

➡**Ensure the correct length bolt is used in the proper location.**

14. Install the engine wiring harness retainer on the water pump outlet pipe inner stud.

15. Install the water pump to engine coolant pipe nuts. Tighten the nuts to 15 ft. lbs. (21 Nm).

16. Install the thermostat housing crossover.

17. Install the crankshaft balancer.

18. Install the left wheelhouse inner panel.

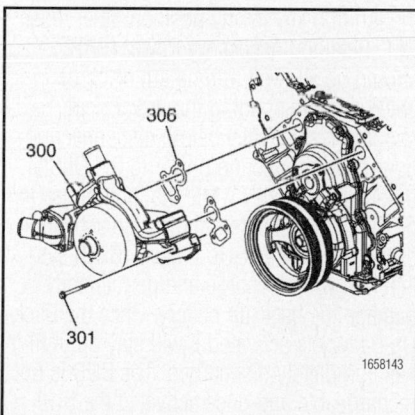

Fig. 145 Remove the water pump bolts (301), the water pump (300) and gaskets (306)

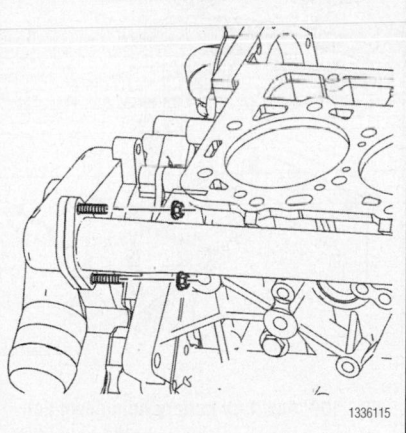

Fig. 146 Remove the water pump to engine coolant pipe nuts

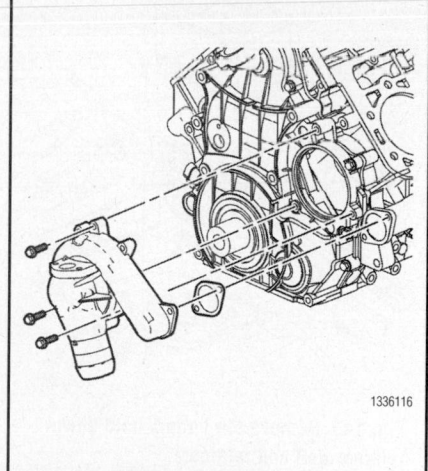

Fig. 147 Remove the water pump bolts

BATTERY

REMOVAL & INSTALLATION

See Figures 148 and 149.

1. Disconnect the negative battery cable.
2. Open the positive cable cover at the positive battery terminal.
3. Loosen the positive cable nut.
4. Remove the positive cable from the positive battery terminal.
5. Reposition the positive cable out of the way.

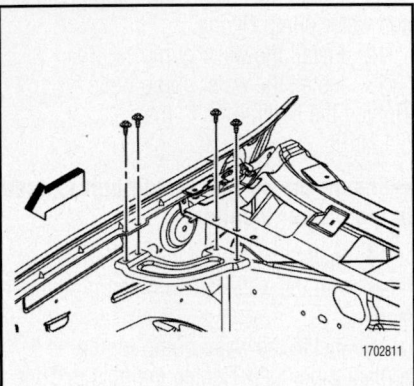

Fig. 148 Remove the front fender rear upper brace bolts and brace

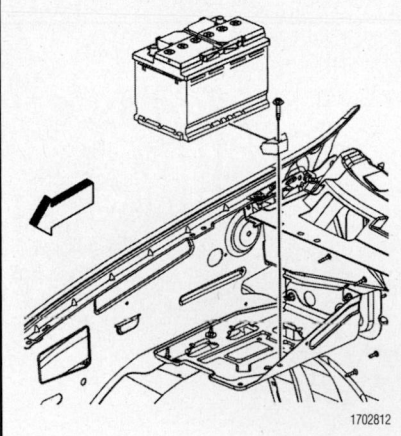

Fig. 149 Remove the battery hold down retainer bolt and retainer

6. Remove the front fender rear upper brace bolts and brace.
7. Remove the battery hold down retainer bolt and retainer.
8. Remove the battery.

To install:

9. Install the battery.
10. Install the battery hold down retainer and bolt and tighten to 18 ft. lbs. (25 Nm).
11. Install the front fender rear upper brace and bolts and tighten to 80 inch lbs. (9 Nm).
12. Position the positive cable to the battery.
13. Install the positive cable to the positive battery terminal.
14. Tighten the positive cable nut.
15. Close the positive cable cover at the positive battery terminal.
16. Connect the negative battery cable.

Auxiliary Battery

See Figure 150.

1. Disconnect the battery cables.
2. Remove the front end sheet metal diagonal brace.

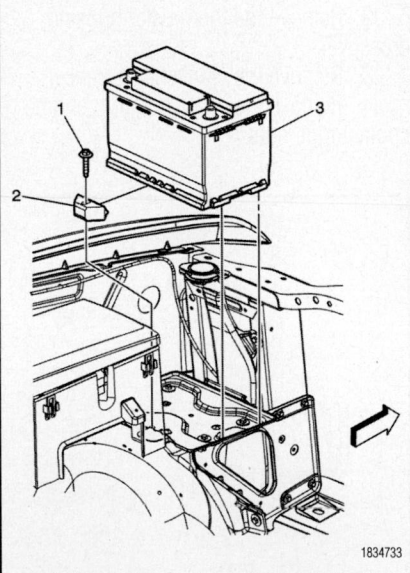

Fig. 150 Auxiliary battery hold down bolt (1), the hold down (2), and the auxiliary battery (3)

3. Remove the auxiliary battery hold down bolt.
4. Remove the auxiliary battery hold down.
5. Remove the auxiliary battery.
6. Installation is the reverse of removal.
7. Tighten the auxiliary battery hold down bolt to 18 ft. lbs. (25 Nm).

BATTERY RECONNECT/ RELEARN PROCEDURE

✳ WARNING

Unless directed otherwise, the ignition and start switch must be in the OFF or LOCK position, and all electrical loads must be OFF before servicing any electrical component. Disconnect the negative battery cable to prevent an electrical spark should a tool or equipment come in contact with an exposed electrical terminal. Failure to follow these precautions may result in personal injury and/or damage to the vehicle or its components.

For Vehicles equipped with OnStar (UE1) with Back Up Battery:

The Back Up Battery is a redundant power supply to allow limited OnStar functionality in the event of a main vehicle battery power disruption to the VCIM (OnStar module). Do not disconnect the main vehicle battery or remove the OnStar fuse with the ignition key in any position other than OFF. Retained Accessory Power (RAP) should be allowed to time out or be disabled (simply opening the driver door should disable RAP) before disconnecting power. Disconnecting power to the OnStar module in any way while the ignition is On or with RAP activated may cause activation of the OnStar Back-Up Battery (BUB) system and will discharge and permanently damage the back-up battery. Once the Back-Up Battery is activated it will stay on until it has completely discharged. The BUB is not rechargeable and once activated the BUB must be replaced.

ENGINE ELECTRICAL　　　　　　　　　　　**CHARGING SYSTEM**

ALTERNATOR

REMOVAL & INSTALLATION

V6 Engines

See Figures 151 through 154.

1. Disconnect the negative battery cable.
2. Remove the air cleaner outlet resonator.
3. Remove the drive belt.
4. Remove the engine wiring harness clip from the Air Conditioning (A/C) compressor/condenser hose bracket.
5. Remove the A/C compressor and condenser hose bracket bolt.
6. Remove the heater outlet hose clamp bolt at the alternator bracket.

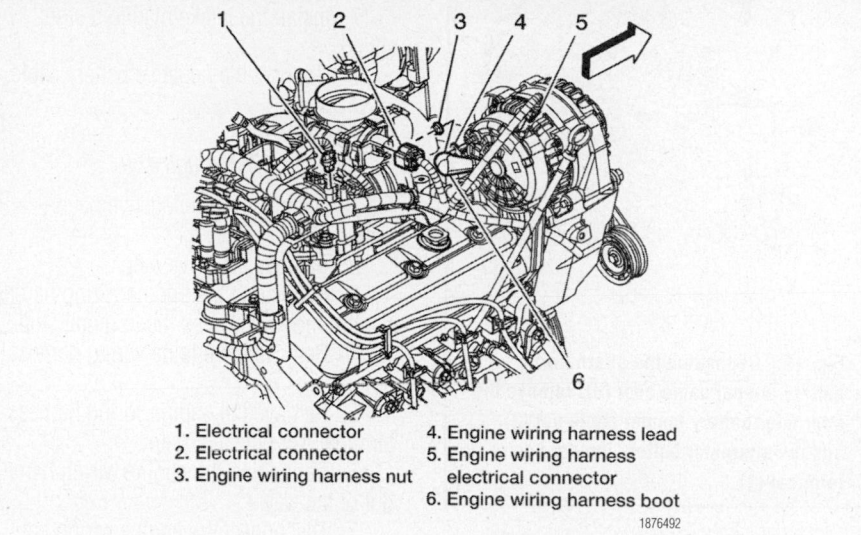

1. Electrical connector
2. Electrical connector
3. Engine wiring harness nut
4. Engine wiring harness lead
5. Engine wiring harness electrical connector
6. Engine wiring harness boot

1876492

Fig. 153 Disconnect the engine wiring harness electrical connector from the alternator

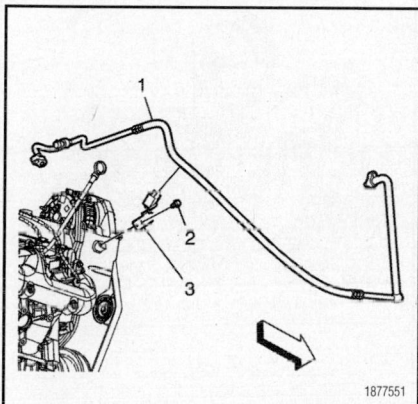

1877551

Fig. 161 Remove the A/C compressor and condenser hose bracket bolt (2) and bracket (3) for the hose (1)

7. Disconnect the engine wiring harness electrical connector from the alternator.
8. Reposition the engine wiring harness boot.
9. Remove the engine wiring harness nut from the alternator.
10. Remove the engine wiring harness lead from the alternator stud.
11. Remove the alternator bolts.
12. Reposition the heater outlet, and AC compressor/condenser hoses as necessary in order to remove the alternator.
13. Remove the alternator from the alternator bracket.

To install:

14. Install the alternator into the alternator bracket.
15. Position the heater outlet, and AC compressor/condenser hoses as necessary.
16. Install the alternator bolts. Tighten the bolts to 37 ft. lbs. (50 Nm).
17. Install the engine wiring harness lead to the alternator stud.
18. Install the engine wiring harness nut to the alternator. Tighten the nut to 80 inch lbs. (9 Nm).
19. Position the engine wiring harness boot over the alternator stud.
20. Connect the engine wiring harness electrical connector to the alternator.
21. Install the heater outlet hose clamp bolt at the alternator bracket. Tighten the bolt to 18 ft. lbs. (25 Nm).
22. Install the A/C compressor and condenser hose bracket bolt. Tighten the bolt to 18 ft. lbs. (25 Nm).
23. Install the engine wiring harness clip to the A/C compressor/condenser hose bracket.
24. Install the drive belt.
25. Install the air cleaner outlet resonator.
26. Connect the negative battery cable.

V8 Engines

See Figures 155 and 156.

1. Disconnect the negative battery cable.
2. Remove the intake manifold sight shield.
3. Remove the accessory drive belt.

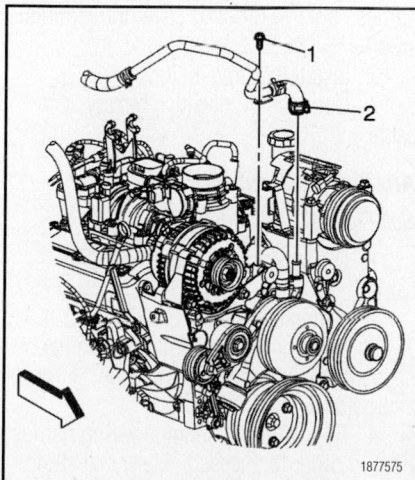

1877575

Fig. 152 Remove the heater outlet hose clamp bolt (1) at the alternator bracket; clamp (2)

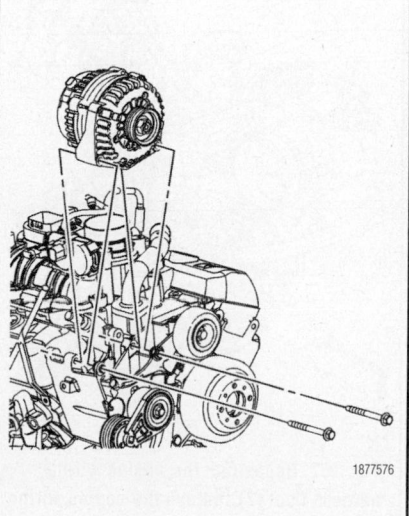

1877576

Fig. 154 Remove the alternator bolts

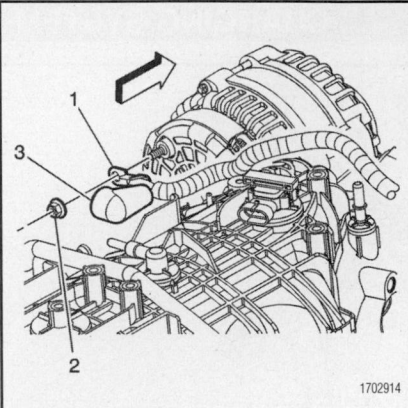

Fig. 155 Reposition the alternator battery jumper cable boot (3), remove the alternator battery jumper cable nut (2), and the alternator battery jumper cable terminal (1)

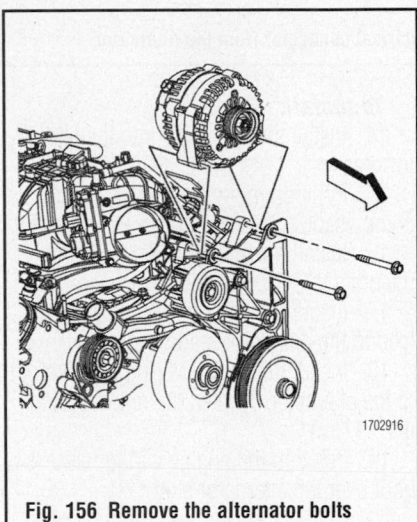

Fig. 156 Remove the alternator bolts

4. Disconnect the engine harness electrical connector from the alternator.

5. Reposition the alternator battery jumper cable boot.

6. Remove the alternator battery jumper cable nut from the alternator.

7. Remove the alternator battery jumper cable terminal from the alternator stud.

8. Remove the alternator bolts.

9. Remove the alternator.

To install:

10. Install the alternator.

11. Install the alternator bolts. Tighten the bolts to 41 ft. lbs. (55 Nm).

12. Install the alternator battery jumper cable terminal to the alternator stud.

13. Install the alternator battery jumper cable nut to the alternator. Tighten the nut to 80 inch lbs. (9 Nm).

14. Position the alternator battery jumper cable boot.

15. Connect the engine harness electrical connector to the alternator.

16. Install the accessory drive belt.

17. Install the intake manifold sight shield.

18. Connect the negative battery cable.

Diesel Engines

See Figures 157 through 159.

1. Disconnect the negative battery cable.

2. Remove the drive belt.

3. Reposition the engine wiring harness boot in order to access the terminal stud.

4. Remove the engine wiring harness nut.

5. Remove the engine wiring harness terminal from the alternator.

6. Reposition the engine wiring harness out of the way.

7. Disconnect the engine wiring harness electrical connector from the alternator.

8. Remove the alternator bolts.

9. Remove the alternator.

To install:

10. Install the alternator.

11. Install the alternator bolts. Tighten the bolts to 37 ft. lbs. (50 Nm).

12. Connect the engine wiring harness electrical connector to the alternator.

13. Install the engine wiring harness terminal to the alternator.

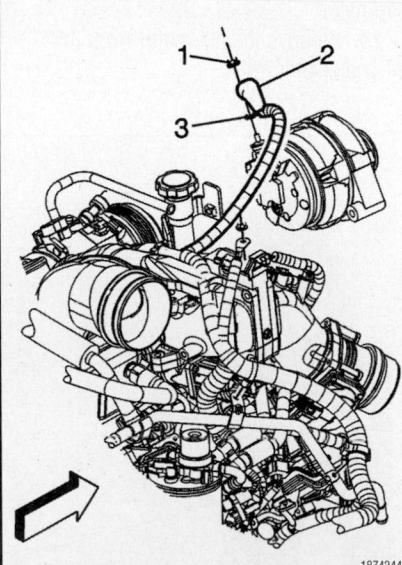

Fig. 157 Reposition the engine wiring harness boot (2), remove the engine wiring harness nut (1), and the engine wiring harness terminal (3)

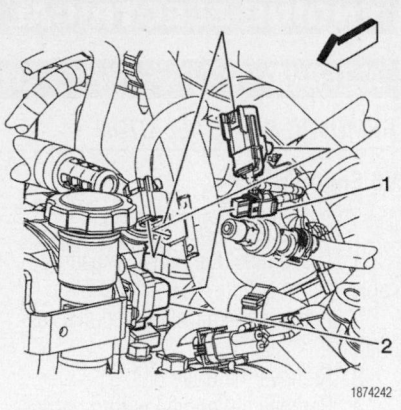

Fig. 158 Disconnect the engine wiring harness electrical connector (1) from the alternator (2)

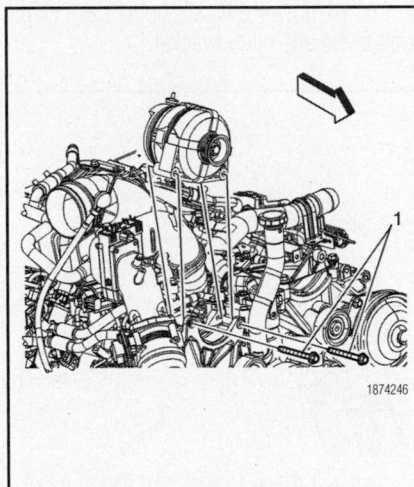

Fig. 159 Remove the alternator bolts (1)

14. Install the engine wiring harness nut. Tighten the nut to 80 inch lbs. (9 Nm).

15. Position the engine wiring harness boot in order to cover the terminal stud.

16. Install the drive belt.

17. Connect the negative battery cable.

Auxiliary Alternator

See Figures 160 and 161.

1. Disconnect the negative battery cable.

2. Remove the drive belt.

3. Disconnect the engine wiring harness electrical connector from the alternator.

4. Reposition the engine wiring harness boot in order to access the terminal stud.

5. Remove the engine wiring harness nut.

6. Remove the engine wiring harness terminal from the alternator.

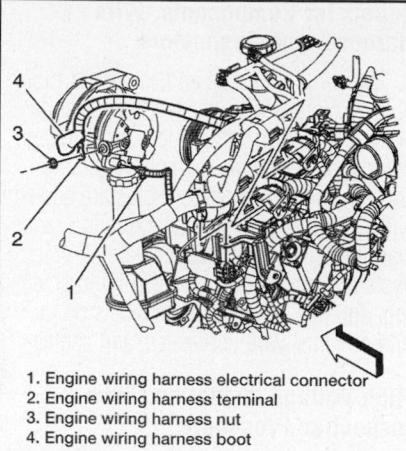

1. Engine wiring harness electrical connector
2. Engine wiring harness terminal
3. Engine wiring harness nut
4. Engine wiring harness boot

1874251

Fig. 160 Disconnect the engine wiring harness electrical connector from the alternator

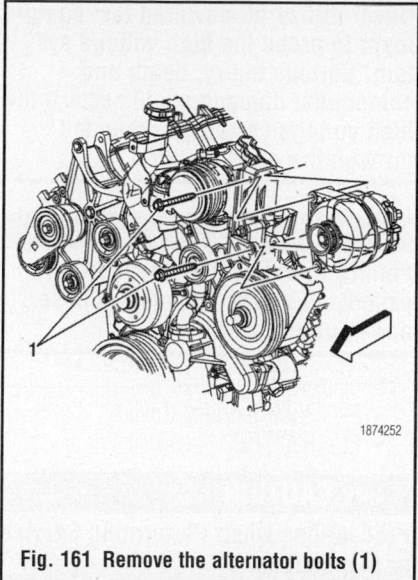

1874252

Fig. 161 Remove the alternator bolts (1)

7. Remove the alternator bolts.
8. Remove the alternator.

To install:

9. Install the alternator.
10. Install the alternator bolts. Tighten the bolts to 37 ft. lbs. (50 Nm).
11. Install the engine wiring harness terminal to the alternator.
12. Install the engine wiring harness nut. Tighten the nut to 80 inch lbs. (9 Nm).
13. Position the engine wiring harness boot in order to cover the terminal stud.
14. Connect the engine wiring harness electrical connector to the alternator.
15. Install the drive belt.
16. Connect the negative battery cable.

ENGINE ELECTRICAL

HYBRID SYSTEM

PRECAUTIONS

Before working on any part of the Hybrid high voltage system, observe the following precautions:

✳✳ CAUTION

The nominal high voltage traction battery voltage is 330 volts DC. The buffer zone must be set up and insulated rubber gloves and a face shield must be worn. Failure to follow these instructions may result in severe injury or death.

✳✳ CAUTION

The high voltage traction battery and charging system contains high voltage components and wiring. High voltage insulated safety gloves and a face shield must be worn when carrying out any diagnostics on this vehicle. Failure to follow these instructions may result in severe personal injury or death.

✳✳ CAUTION

Before carrying out any removal and installation procedures of the high voltage traction battery system, the high voltage traction battery must be Disarmed. Failure to follow these instructions may result in severe personal injury or death.

✳✳ CAUTION

The rubber insulating gloves that are to be worn while working on the high voltage system should be of the appropriate safety and protection rating for use on the high voltage system. They must be inspected before use and must always be worn in conjunction with the leather outer gloves. Any hole in the rubber insulating glove is a potential entry point for high voltage. Failure to follow these instructions may result in severe personal injury or death.

➡The high voltage insulated safety gloves must be re-certified every 6 months to remain within Occupational Safety and Health Administration (OSHA) guidelines:

• Roll the glove up from the open end until the lower portion of the glove begins to balloon from the resulting air pressure. If the glove leaks any air, it must not be used.
• The gloves should not be used if they exhibit any signs of wear and tear.
• The leather gloves must always be worn over the rubber insulating gloves in order to protect them.
• The rubber insulating gloves must be class "00" and meet all of the American Society for Testing and Materials (ASTM) standards.

✳✳ CAUTION

High voltage insulated safety gloves and a face shield must be worn when working with high voltage cables. The ignition switch must be OFF for a minimum of 5 minutes before removing high voltage cables. Failure to follow these instructions may result in severe personal injury or death.

✳✳ CAUTION

Establish a buffer zone before servicing the high voltage system. The buffer zone is required only when working with the high voltage system. See the text for buffer zone establishment. Failure to follow these instructions may result in severe personal injury or death. Do not allow any unauthorized personnel into the buffer zone during repairs involving the high voltage system. Only personnel trained for repair on the high voltage system are to be permitted in the buffer zone.

✳✳ CAUTION

Disarm the high voltage traction battery (HVTB) before working on the high voltage system. See the text for the Disarming procedure. Failure to follow these instructions may result in severe personal injury or death.

HIGH VOLTAGE SAFETY

✳✳ WARNING

Always perform the High Voltage Disabling procedure prior to servicing any High Voltage component or connection. Personal Protection Equipment (PPE) and proper procedures must be followed.

The High Voltage Disabling procedure will perform the following tasks:
• Identify how to disable high voltage.
• Identify how to test for the presence of high voltage.
• Identify condition under which high voltage is always present and Personal Protection Equipment (PPE) and proper procedures must be followed.

✳✳ WARNING

Failure to follow the procedures exactly as written may result in serious injury or death.

✳✳ WARNING

Ensure all High Voltage safety procedures are followed. Failure to follow the procedure exactly as written may result in serious injury or death.

✳✳ WARNING

Before working on any high voltage system, be sure to wear the following Personal Protection Equipment:

• Safety glasses with appropriate side shields when within 50 feet of the vehicle, either indoors or outdoors
• Certified and up-to-date Class "0" Insulation gloves rated at 1000V with leather protectors
• Visually and functionally inspect the gloves before use.
• Wear the Insulation gloves at all times when working with the high voltage battery assembly, whether the system is energized or not.

✳✳ WARNING

Failure to follow the procedure exactly as written may result in serious injury or death.

✳✳ WARNING

This vehicle is equipped with a high voltage battery that is completely isolated from the chassis ground.

Never utilize AC powered test equipment to probe the high voltage system. Serious injury, death and component damage could occur if the high voltage system is grounded through the electric utility.

✳✳ WARNING

Failure to follow the procedure exactly as written may result in serious injury or death.

Special Tools Required:
• EL-48569 Terminal Covers
• EL-48900 HEV Safety Kit

✳✳ CAUTION

Precautions when Performing Service or Inspections

• Always verify that the high voltage has been disabled before working on or around high voltage components, wires, cables, or harnesses.
• Remove all metal objects such as rings and watches.
• The EL-48900 HEV Safety Kit contains safety cones. Place the safety cones around the vehicle to alert other technicians that you are working on the High Voltage system.
• Attach the ignition key to the high voltage manual disconnect lever and put the lever and the ignition key in a secure place.
• Always wear certified and tested high voltage insulation gloves when inspecting or testing any high voltage wires and components.
• Use the "One Hand" rule:
• Work with only one hand whenever possible.
• Keep the other hand behind your back.
• DO NOT carry any metal objects such as a mechanical pencil or a measuring tape that could fall and cause a short circuit.
• After removing any high voltage wires, protect and insulate the terminal ends immediately with the EL-48569 terminal covers and UL Listed or equivalent insulation tape rated at a minimum of 600 volts.
• Always tighten the high voltage terminal fasteners to the specified torque. Insufficient or excessive torque will cause malfunctions or damage.
• After finishing work on the high voltage systems and before reinstalling the high voltage manual disconnect lever, inspect for the following:
• Verify high voltage system integrity and that all connectors are installed.
• Verify that all tools or loose components have been removed.

Labels for Components, Wire Harness, and Connectors

The wire harnesses and cables for high voltage circuits are encased in an orange colored covering. In addition, high voltage components such as the Energy Storage System and high voltage cables are affixed with "High Voltage" red danger and orange warning labels. The intermediate 42 volt system is encased in a blue colored covering, and has yellow caution labels on the components, wire harnesses, and cables.

High Voltage insulation Glove Inspection Procedure

The following procedure visually and functionally inspects the insulation gloves to be used while performing service on high voltage systems. This inspection procedure should be performed prior to any procedure that requires the use of class "0" insulation gloves rated at 1000 volts.
1. Remove glove from leather protector.
2. Inflate glove and seal opening. Pinch the opening closed tightly to prevent any air loss.
3. Press glove to increase pressure.
4. Inspect for the following conditions:
• Pin holes
• Air leaks
• Wear, tears, or abrasions
• Damp or wet material
• Certified up-to-date

✳✳ CAUTION

If any of the above conditions are met, do not use the gloves.

DRIVE MOTOR GENERATOR CONTROL MODULE

REMOVAL & INSTALLATION
See Figures 162 through 169.

✳✳ WARNING

Always perform the High Voltage Disabling procedure prior to servicing any High Voltage component or connection. Personal Protection Equipment (PPE) and proper procedures must be followed.

The High Voltage Disabling procedure will perform the following tasks:
• Identify how to disable high voltage.
• Identify how to test for the presence of high voltage.
• Identify condition under which high voltage is always present and Personal

Protection Equipment (PPE) and proper procedures must be followed.

※※ WARNING

Failure to follow the procedures exactly as written may result in serious injury or death.

1. Perform the High Voltage Disabling procedure.
2. Remove the air cleaner.
3. Disconnect the drive motor generator control module assembly connector.
4. Drain the power electronics cooling system.

※※ CAUTION

Always remove and install the High Voltage terminal fasteners with a magnet tipped socket. Never touch the exposed electronic circuit board surface or components. Dropped fasteners or physical contact may result in electronic circuit board damage.

5. Remove the drive motor generator Power Inverter Control Module (PIM) 3 phase cable terminal fasteners.

※※ CAUTION

High Voltage (HV) cables should never be removed from the mounting block. Removal of the individual HV cable from the mounting block may result in HV cable and/or component damage from improper:

- Cable sealing
- Electrical shielding
- Terminal position assurance

6. Remove the PIM 3 phase cable mounting fasteners.
7. Remove the PIM 3 phase cables from the PIM distribution box.
8. Remove and discard the seals.

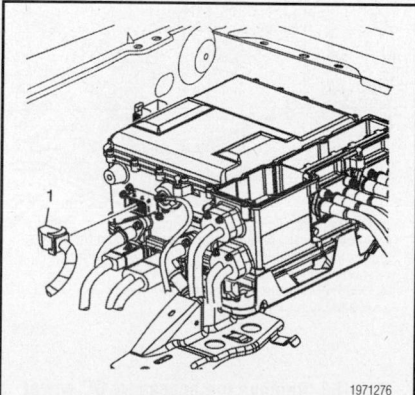

Fig. 162 Disconnect the drive motor generator control module assembly connector (1)

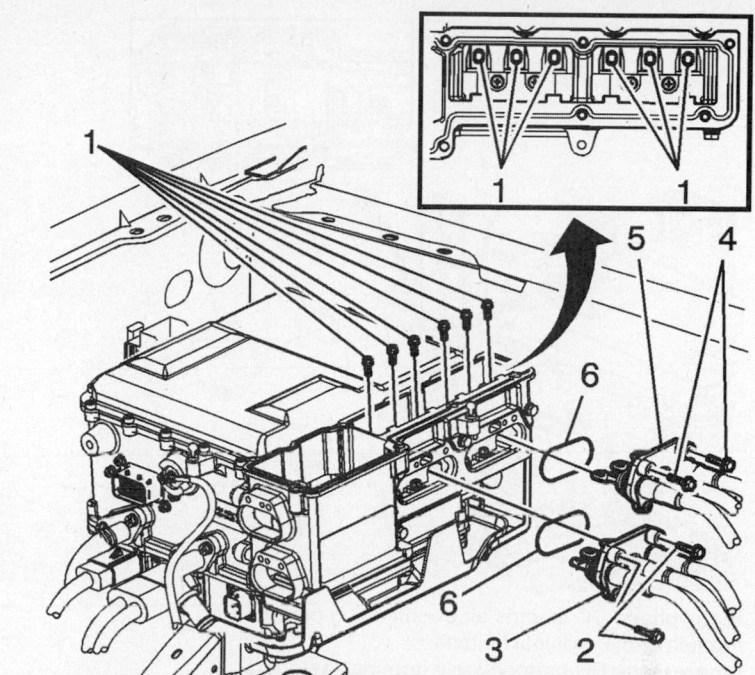

1. Drive motor generator power inverter control module 3 phase cable terminal fasteners
2. Power inverter module 3 phase cable mounting fasteners
3. Power inverter module 3 phase cables
4. Power inverter module 3 phase cable mounting fasteners
5. Power inverter module 3 phase cables
6. Seals

1971277

Fig. 163 Remove the drive motor generator power inverter control module 3 phase cable terminal fasteners

※※ CAUTION

Always remove and install the High Voltage terminal fasteners with a magnet tipped socket. Never touch the exposed electronic circuit board surface or components. Dropped fasteners or physical contact may result in electronic circuit board damage.

9. Remove the HV DC electric Air Conditioning Compressor Module (ACCM) cable terminal fasteners.
10. Remove the HV DC electric ACCM cable mounting fasteners.
11. Remove the HV DC electric ACCM cable from the PIM distribution box.
12. Remove the HV DC battery cable terminal fasteners.
13. Remove the HV DC battery cable mounting fasteners.
14. Remove the HV DC battery cable from the PIM distribution box.
15. Inspect and retain the seals.
16. Remove the drive motor generator position sensor shield circuit fastener.

17. Remove the shield circuit harness.
18. Remove the PIM cooling inlet and outlet hoses.
19. Cap the coolant pipes to prevent coolant spillage when lifting the drive motor generator control module assembly from the vehicle.

➡ The gray side tabs on the Accessory dc Power Control Module (APM) assembly connector (2) must be pressed in before rotating the lever.

20. Disconnect the APM assembly connector using the following procedure:
   a. Push the green tab.
   b. Squeeze the gray side tabs, then rotate the lever.
21. Disconnect the APM assembly connector using the following procedure:
   a. Remove the locking tab.
   b. Insert a small flat blade screwdriver into the locking tab area and raise the tab while pulling on the connector.

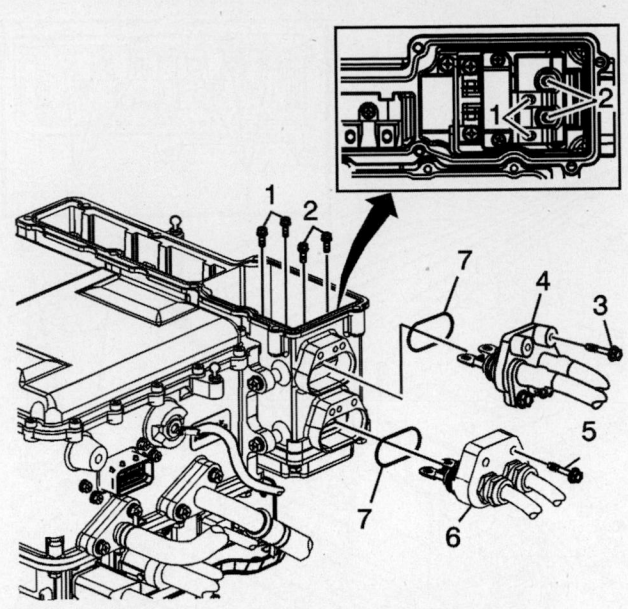

1. High voltage DC electric air conditioning compressor module cable terminal fasteners
2. High voltage DC battery cable terminal fasteners
3. High voltage DC electric air conditioning compressor module cable mounting fasteners
4. High voltage DC electric air conditioning compressor module cable
5. High voltage DC battery cable mounting fasteners
6. High voltage DC battery cable
7. Seals

1971278

Fig. 164 Exploded view of the high voltage DC electric air conditioning compressor module

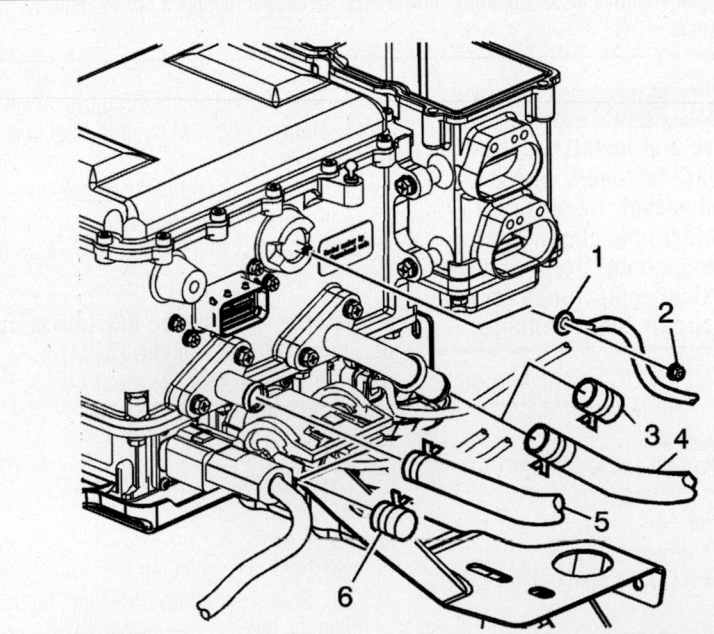

1. Shield circuit harness
2. Sensor shield circuit fastener
3. Coolant pipe
4. Power inverter module cooling inlet
5. Power inverter module cooling outlet
6. Coolant pipe

1971281

Fig. 165 Remove the drive motor generator position sensor shield circuit fastener

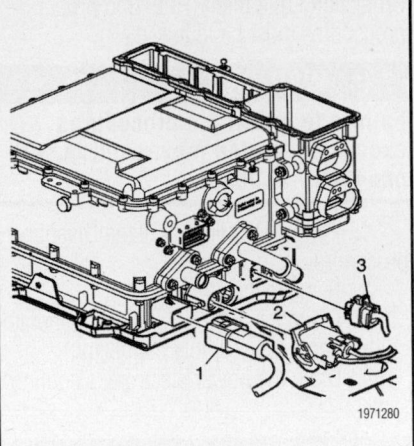

1971280

Fig. 166 Accessory DC power control module assembly connectors (1, 2, 3)

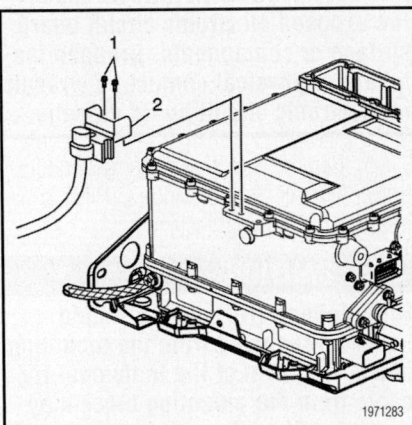

1971283

Fig. 167 Remove the sight shield circuit breaker fasteners (1) and the sight shield circuit breaker (2)

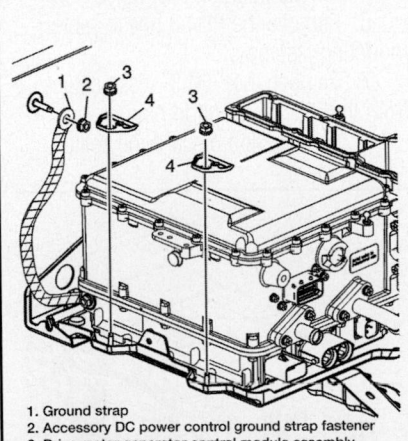

1. Ground strap
2. Accessory DC power control ground strap fastener
3. Drive motor generator control module assembly mounting fasteners
4. Drive motor generator control module assembly retainers

1971286

Fig. 168 Remove the accessory DC power control module ground strap fastener and ground strap

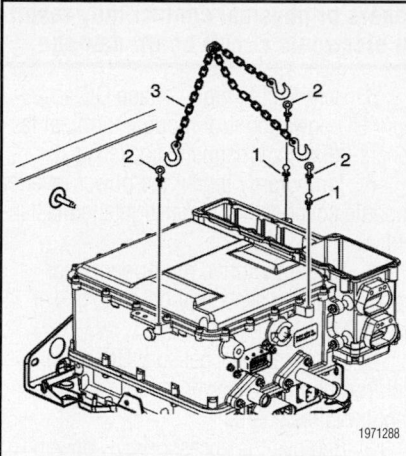

Fig. 169 Remove the ball studs (1); attach a lifting device (2, 3)

22. Disconnect the remaining APM assembly connector.

23. Remove the sight shield circuit breaker fasteners.

24. Remove the sight shield circuit breaker.

25. Remove the APM ground strap fastener and ground strap.

26. Remove the drive motor generator control module assembly mounting fasteners and retainers.

27. Remove the ball studs from the drive motor generator control module.

28. Attach a lifting device to the drive motor generator control module assembly at the three identified locations.

29. Lift the drive motor generator control module assembly from the vehicle.

30. To replace the drive motor generator Power Inverter Module (PIM) assembly, refer to Drive Motor Generator Power Inverter Module Removal and Installation. To replace the accessory DC power control module, refer to Accessory DC Power Control Module Removal and Installation.

To install:

31. Attach a lifting device to the drive motor generator control module assembly at the three identified locations.

32. Lift the drive motor generator control module assembly into the vehicle.

33. Remove the lifting device and install the ball studs. Tighten the ball studs to 89 inch lbs. (10 Nm).

34. Install the drive motor generator control module assembly retainers and mounting nuts. Tighten the mounting nuts to 80 inch lbs. (9 Nm).

35. Install the APM ground strap and APM ground strap nut. Tighten the nut to 80 inch lbs. (9 Nm).

36. Install the sight shield circuit breaker and secure with bolts.

37. Connect the APM assembly connectors and install any removed locking tabs.

38. Connect the APM assembly connector using the following procedure:

a. Push the lever up.

➡**Install the connector without disturbing the position of the lever. DO NOT use the lever to install the connector in place.**

b. Install the connector onto the terminals by pushing on the connector only.

c. Rotate the lever after the terminals are engaged.

d. Push the green tab to lock the lever.

39. Remove the caps from the drive motor generator power inverter coolant pipes.

40. Connect the drive motor generator Power Inverter Module (PIM) cooling inlet and outlet hoses.

41. Install the shield circuit harness and terminal fastener. Tighten the terminal fastener to 80 inch lbs. (9 Nm).

42. Install the PIM 3 phase cables into the PIM distribution box with new seals.

43. Install the PIM 3 phase cable mounting fasteners. Tighten the mounting fastener to 80 inch lbs. (9 Nm).

✳✳ CAUTION

Always remove and install the High Voltage terminal fasteners with a magnet tipped socket. Never touch the exposed electronic circuit board surface or components. Dropped fasteners or physical contact may result in electronic circuit board damage.

44. Install the PIM 3 phase cable terminal fasteners. Tighten the terminal fastener to 80 inch lbs. (9 Nm).

45. Install the HV DC battery cable with seal into the PIM distribution box.

46. Install the HV DC battery cable mounting fasteners. Tighten the mounting fastener to 80 inch lbs. (9 Nm).

✳✳ CAUTION

Always remove and install the High Voltage terminal fasteners with a magnet tipped socket. Never touch the exposed electronic circuit board surface or components. Dropped fasteners or physical contact may result in electronic circuit board damage.

47. Install the High Voltage (HV) dc battery cable terminal fasteners. Tighten the terminal fastener to 80 inch lbs. (9 Nm).

48. Install the HV dc electric Air Conditioning Compressor Module (ACCM) cable with seal into the PIM distribution box.

49. Install the HV dc electric ACCM cable mounting fasteners. Tighten the mounting fasteners to 80 inch lbs. (9 Nm).

✳✳ CAUTION

Always remove and install the High Voltage terminal fasteners with a magnet tipped socket. Never touch the exposed electronic circuit board surface or components. Dropped fasteners or physical contact may result in electronic circuit board damage.

50. Install the HV DC electric ACCM cable terminal fasteners. Tighten the terminal fastener to 80 inch lbs. (9 Nm).

51. Install a new seal on the PIM distribution box.

➡**DO NOT use excessively abrasive cleaning tools on the sealing surface. Hand sanding with wet 400 grit sandpaper or use of a hand scraper is recommended.**

52. Clean the sealing surface of the 3 phase cable cover as necessary.

53. Position the 3 phase cable cover onto the PIM distribution box ensuring the seal remains in place.

54. Tighten the 3 phase cable cover fasteners. Tighten the fasteners to 80 inch lbs. (9 Nm).

55. Connect the drive motor generator control module assembly connector.

56. Fill the power electronics cooling system and test for leaks at all serviced connections.

57. Install the sight shield.

58. Install the fender cross brace.

59. Perform the High Voltage Enabling procedure.

60. Install the air cleaner.

DRIVE MOTOR GENERATOR POWER INVERTER MODULE

REMOVAL & INSTALLATION

See Figures 170 through 174.

1. Remove the drive motor generator control module from the vehicle.

2. Remove the temporary coolant pipe caps.

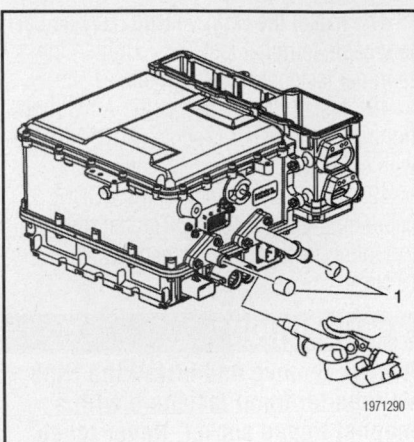

Fig. 170 Remove the temporary coolant pipe caps (1)

✳✳ CAUTION

The module must be drained of all residual coolant prior to disassembly. Failure to properly drain all residual coolant may cause electronic circuit damage to occur during disassembly.

➡Place a container under the coolant outlet pipe to capture the escaping coolant.

3. Drain the drive motor generator control module assembly of residual coolant by applying 30 psi regulated compressed air to the coolant inlet pipe until no coolant remains.

4. Remove the drive motor generator power inverter control module cover fasteners.

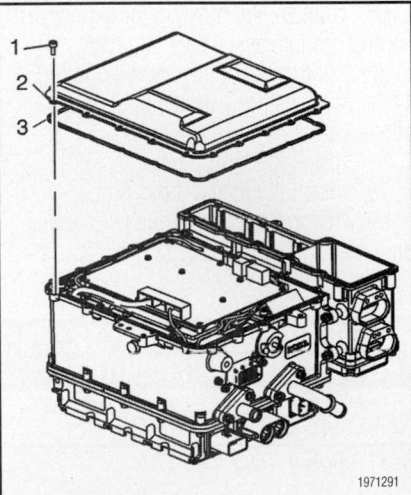

Fig. 171 Remove the drive motor generator power inverter control module cover fasteners (1), the cover (2), and the seal (3)

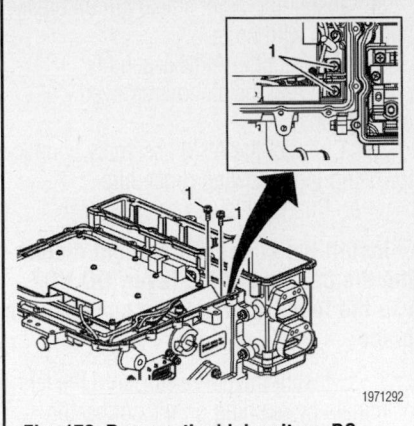

Fig. 172 Remove the high voltage DC accessory DC power control module terminal fasteners (1)

5. Remove the power inverter module cover. Discard the cover seal.

✳✳ CAUTION

Always remove and install the High Voltage terminal fasteners with a magnet tipped socket. Never touch the exposed electronic circuit board surface or components. Dropped fasteners or physical contact may result in electronic circuit board damage.

6. Remove the high voltage DC accessory DC power control module terminal fasteners utilizing a magnetic socket.

7. Temporarily install the power inverter module cover with 4 finger-tightened fasteners.

8. Rotate the drive motor generator control module assembly onto the power inverter module cover.

9. Remove the accessory DC power control module to power inverter module mounting fasteners.

10. Remove the accessory DC power control module and discard the coolant seal.

➡**A service replacement power inverter module contains pre-installed coolant pipes. The following steps are necessary for coolant pipe seal replacement only.**

11. Remove the drive motor generator power inverter coolant pipes:

   a. Remove the drive motor generator power inverter coolant pipe bolts.

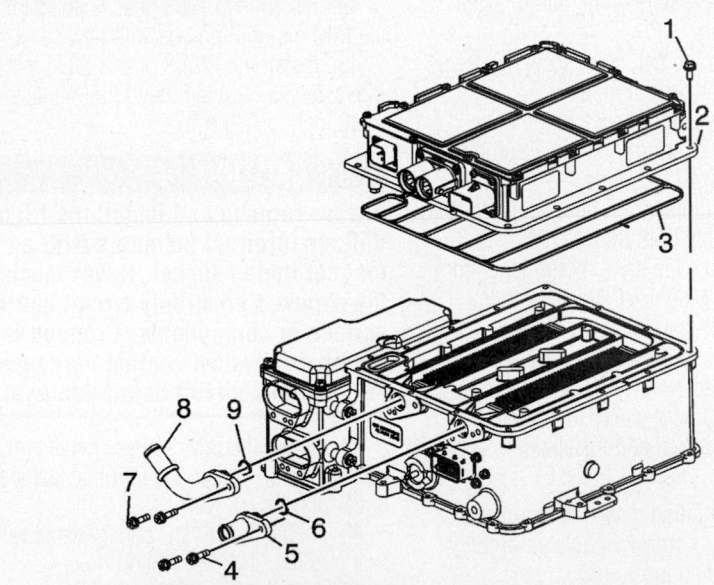

1. Accessory DC power control module to power inverter module mounting fasteners
2. Accessory DC power control module
3. Coolant seal
4. Drive motor generator power inverter coolant pipe bolts
5. Drive motor generator power inverter coolant pipe
6. Coolant seal
7. Drive motor generator power inverter coolant pipe bolts
8. Drive motor generator power inverter coolant pipe
9. Coolant seal

Fig. 173 Remove the accessory DC power control module to power inverter module mounting fasteners

b. Remove the drive motor generator power inverter coolant pipes.

c. Remove and discard coolant seals.

To install:

12. Install new accessory DC power control module coolant seal.

13. Position the accessory DC power control module onto the power inverter module ensuring the seals remain in place.

14. Install the accessory DC power control module mounting fasteners. Tighten the mounting fasteners to 89 inch lbs. (10 Nm).

➡ **Only use pre-mixed DEX-COOL® on the coolant pipe O-ring to aid in tube installation.**

15. Install the drive motor generator power inverter coolant pipes unless a service replacement power inverter module is being installed:

a. Lubricate the new seals with pre-mixed DEX-COOL.

b. Install new seals onto the drive motor generator power inverter coolant pipes.

c. Install the coolant pipes to the power inverter module assembly with bolts.

16. Rotate the drive motor generator control module assembly onto the accessory DC power control module.

17. Clamp the Power Electronics Pressure Test (GE-48494) adapter kit components to a coolant pipe.

18. Plug the remaining coolant pipe with the GE-48494 adapter kit plug and clamp.

19. Apply 20 psi (138 kPa) pressure with J-24460-01 pressure tester.

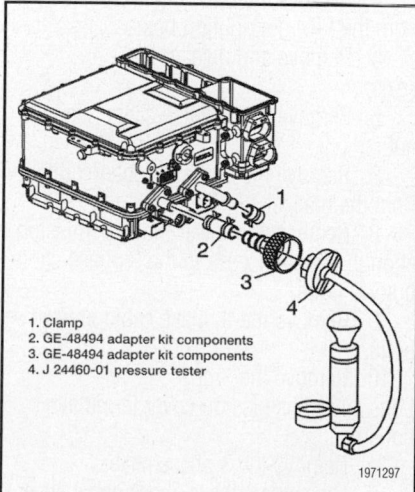

1. Clamp
2. GE-48494 adapter kit components
3. GE-48494 adapter kit components
4. J 24460-01 pressure tester

1971297

Fig. 174 Clamp the Power Electronics Pressure Test (GE-48494) adapter kit components to a coolant pipe

20. Monitor the pressure tester gauge for 5 minutes and ensure that pressure remains at the specified value.

a. If the specified pressure cannot be maintained, disassemble the drive motor generator control module assembly and replace the coolant seal.

b. If pressure remains at the specified value, proceed to the next step.

21. Remove all GE-48494 adapter kit components.

22. Remove the power inverter module cover retaining bolts.

23. Remove the power inverter module cover.

✸✸ CAUTION

Always remove and install the High Voltage terminal fasteners with a magnet tipped socket. Never touch the exposed electronic circuit board surface or components. Dropped fasteners or physical contact may result in electronic circuit board damage.

24. Install the high voltage DC accessory DC power control module terminal fasteners utilizing a magnetic socket. Tighten the terminal fasteners to 80 inch lbs. (9 Nm).

25. Install a new power inverter module cover seal.

➡ **DO NOT use excessively abrasive cleaning tools on the sealing surface. Hand sanding with wet 400 grit sandpaper or use of a hand scraper is recommended.**

26. Clean the sealing surface of the power inverter module cover as necessary.

27. Position the power inverter module cover onto the power inverter module ensuring the seal remains in place.

28. Install the power inverter module cover fasteners.

29. Install the drive motor generator control module.

DRIVE MOTOR GENERATOR CONTROL MODULE SIGHT SHIELD

REMOVAL & INSTALLATION

See Figures 175 and 176.

1. Remove the fender brace.

➡ **Removing the sight shield disengages the High Voltage Interlock Circuit (HVIC). The sight shield mounting fastener must be installed and properly tightened for the HVIC to be closed.**

Failure to properly tighten the sight shield mounting fastener may result in an open HVIC condition and DTCs.

2. Loosen the sight shield mounting fastener and lift the sight shield from the ball studs.

✸✸ WARNING

Always perform the High Voltage Disabling procedure prior to servicing any High Voltage component or connection. Personal Protection Equipment (PPE) and proper procedures must be followed.

The High Voltage Disabling procedure will perform the following tasks:

• Identify how to disable high voltage.

• Identify how to test for the presence of high voltage.

• Identify condition under which high voltage is always present and Personal Protection Equipment (PPE) and proper procedures must be followed.

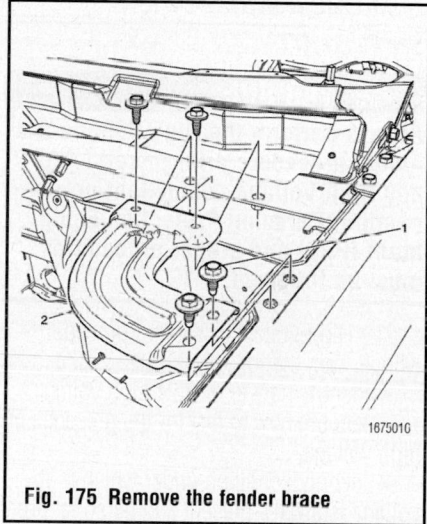

1675010

Fig. 175 Remove the fender brace

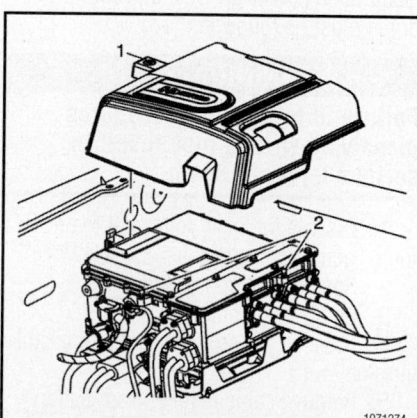

1971274

Fig. 176 Loosen the sight shield mounting fastener (1) and lift the sight shield from the ball studs (2)

3. Perform the High Voltage Disabling procedure.

To install:

➡The sight shield mounting fastener must be installed and tightened. Failure to properly tighten the sight shield mounting fastener may result in an open High Voltage Interlock Circuit (HVIC) condition and DTCs.

4. Install the sight shield onto the ball studs and tighten the sight shield mounting fastener.
5. Install the fender brace.
6. Enable high voltage.

GENERATOR BATTERY VENT FAN

REMOVAL & INSTALLATION

See Figure 177.

The High Voltage Disabling procedure will perform the following tasks:
- Identify how to disable high voltage.
- Identify how to test for the presence of high voltage.
- Identify condition under which high voltage is always present and personal protection equipment (PPE) and proper procedures must be followed.

1. Disable the high voltage at the drive motor generator battery.
2. Remove the upper cover.
3. Remove the outlet ducts.
4. Remove the drive motor battery cable terminal nut.
5. Remove cable retainer from battery fan assembly. When cable is removed, install protective cover to cable end.
6. Remove the generator battery vent fan bolt.

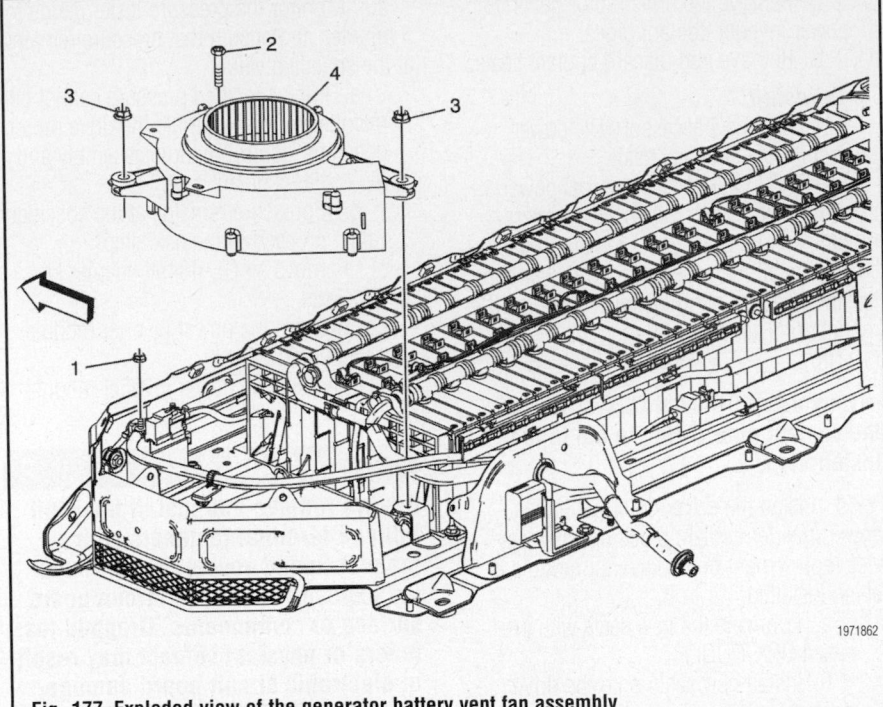

Fig. 177 Exploded view of the generator battery vent fan assembly

7. Remove the drive motor generator cooling blower nuts.
8. Remove the generator battery vent fan.
9. Installation is the reverse of removal.

GENERATOR CONTROL MODULE 3-PHASE CABLE ASSEMBLY

REMOVAL & INSTALLATION

See Figures 178 through 180.

The High Voltage Disabling procedure will perform the following tasks:
- Identify how to disable high voltage.
- Identify how to test for the presence of high voltage.
- Identify condition under which high voltage is always present and Personal Protection Equipment (PPE) and proper procedures must be followed.

1. Perform the high voltage disabling.

2. Remove the Power Inverter Module (PIM) 3 phase cable terminal fasteners.
3. Remove the PIM 3 phase cable mounting fasteners.
4. Remove the PIM 3 phase cables from the PIM distribution box.
5. Remove and discard the seals.
6. Remove the 3 phase cable retainer nut.
7. Remove the 3 phase cable retainer from the bracket.
8. Remove and lower the transmission enough to gain access to the 3 phase cable bracket bolts.
9. Remove the 3 phase cable bracket bolts.
10. Remove the 3 phase cover bolts and transmission cover terminal housing.
11. Remove the 3 phase cover.
12. Disconnect the 3 phase cable cover connector.
13. Remove the 3 phase cable bolt protective cover.

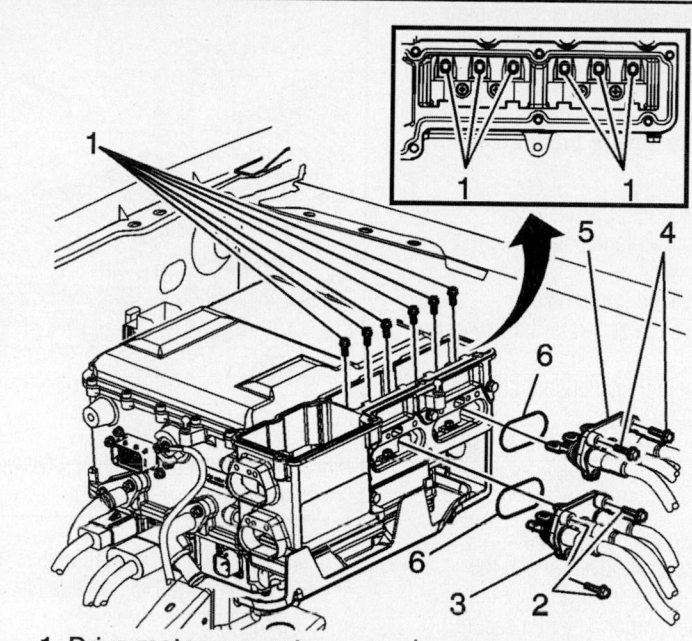

1. Drive motor generator power inverter control module 3 phase cable terminal fasteners
2. Power inverter module 3 phase cable mounting fasteners
3. Power inverter module 3 phase cables
4. Power inverter module 3 phase cable mounting fasteners
5. Power inverter module 3 phase cables
6. Seals

Fig. 178 Exploded view of the Power Inverter Module (PIM) assembly

14. Remove the 3 phase cable retaining bolts.

15. Remove the 3 phase cables and housing.

16. Finish removal of the transmission while allowing the 3 phase cables to remain in the vehicle.

17. Remove the 3 phase cables from the vehicle.

To install:

✳✳ CAUTION

To avoid high voltage 3-phase cable or vehicle damage properly attach the cables and brackets, and check for and correct any interference.

18. Position the 3 phase cables in the vehicle.

19. Begin installation of the transmission.

20. Install a new 3 phase cable housing seal.

21. Install the 3 phase cables and housing.

22. Install the 3 phase cable retaining bolts. Tighten the bolts to 106 inch lbs. (12 Nm).

23. Install the 3 phase cable bolt protective cover.

24. Install a new 3 phase cable cover seal.

25. Reconnect the 3 phase cable cover connector.

26. Install the 3 phase cable cover.

27. Install the transmission cover terminal housing.

28. Install the 3 phase cable cover bolts. Tighten the bolts to 106 inch lbs. (12 Nm).

29. Install the 3 phase cable bracket bolts. Tighten the bolts to 106 inch lbs. (12 Nm).

30. Complete the installation of the transmission.

31. Lower the vehicle.

32. Install the 3 phase cable retainer to the bracket.

33. Install the 3 phase cable retainer nut. Tighten the nut to 80 inch lbs. (9 Nm).

34. Install the PIM 3 phase cables into the PIM distribution box with new seals.

35. Install the PIM 3 phase cable mounting fasteners. Tighten the mounting fastener to 80 inch lbs. (9 Nm).

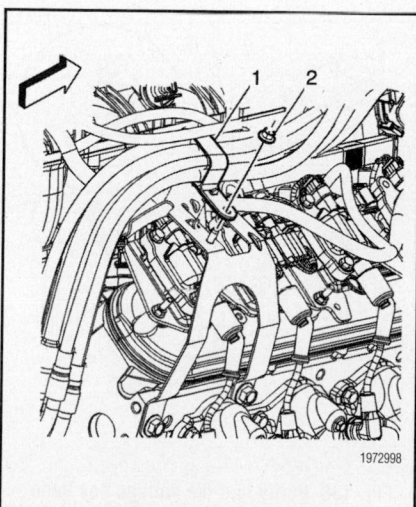

Fig. 179 Remove the 3 phase cable retainer (1) and nut (2)

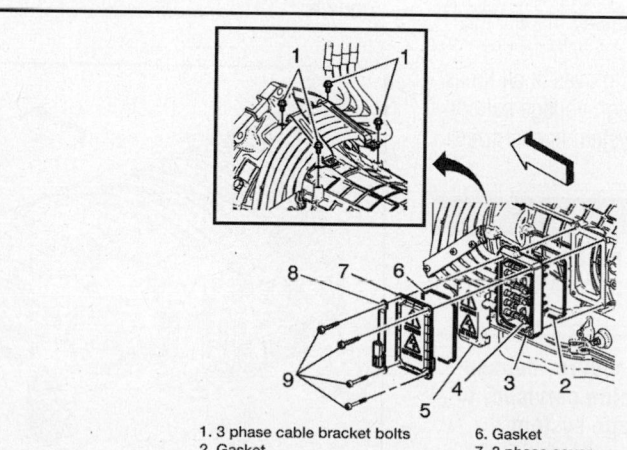

1. 3 phase cable bracket bolts
2. Gasket
3. Housing
4. 3 phase cable retaining bolts
5. 3 phase cable bolt protective cover
6. Gasket
7. 3 phase cover
8. Transmission cover terminal housing
9. 3 phase cover bolts

Fig. 180 Exploded view of the 3 phase cable assembly

✳✳ CAUTION

Always remove and install the High Voltage terminal fasteners with a magnet tipped socket. Never touch the exposed electronic circuit board surface or components. Dropped fasteners or physical contact may result in electronic circuit board damage.

36. Install the PIM 3 phase cable terminal fasteners. Tighten the terminal fastener to 80 inch lbs. (9 Nm).

37. Install a new seal on the PIM distribution box.

38. Position the terminal cover onto the PIM distribution box ensuring the seal remains in place.

39. Tighten the terminal cover fasteners to 80 inch lbs. (9 Nm).

40. Perform the high voltage enabling.

HIGH VOLTAGE DISABLING

✳✳ WARNING

Ensure all High Voltage safety procedures are followed. Failure to follow the procedure exactly as written may result in serious injury or death.

✳✳ WARNING

Before working on any high voltage system, be sure to wear the following Personal Protection Equipment:

- Safety glasses with appropriate side shields when within 50 feet of the vehicle, either indoors or outdoors
- Certified and up-to-date Class "0" Insulation gloves rated at 1000V with leather protectors
- Visually and functionally inspect the gloves before use.
- Wear the Insulation gloves at all times when working with the high voltage battery assembly, whether the system is energized or not.

✳✳ WARNING

Failure to follow the procedure exactly as written may result in serious injury or death.

➡Use the correct procedure, depending on components being serviced, to disable the High Voltage system.

When Servicing Drive Motor Generator Battery Assembly or 300 V DC Cables

See Figures 181 through 184.

1. Review the high voltage safety information prior to performing the High Voltage Disabling procedure.

➡**The 12 V battery must be disconnected to ensure proper test results.**

2. Disconnect the 12 V battery.

3. Disable the voltage sources to the 2 mode hybrid vehicle.

   a. Remove the ignition key.

   b. Remove the generator battery cover access door.

   c. Lift the rear seat cushion the full upright position.

   d. Carefully disconnect the access door clips from the generator battery cover.

   e. Remove the high voltage manual disconnect lever. Attach the ignition key to the lever and put the lever and the ignition key in a secure place.

   f. Wait 5 minutes before continuing, to allow the capacitors to discharge.

➡**Wear your High Voltage Insulation gloves until you have determined that a high voltage exposure risk is no longer present.**

4. Remove the terminal extension cover assembly.

5. To verify that the voltage has been disabled at the drive motor generator battery assembly terminals, perform the following:

   a. Set the Digital Multi Meter (DMM) to DC mode. Verify the DMM

   b. works by measuring the voltage of the 12 V battery.

   c. Using the DMM, verify the voltage measures less than 3 V at the following points:

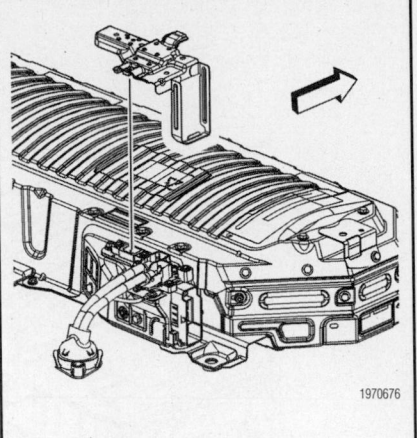

Fig. 182 Remove the terminal extension cover assembly

- High voltage DC (+) positive and high voltage DC (-) negative terminals.
- High voltage DC (+) positive to vehicle chassis ground.
- High voltage DC (-) negative to vehicle chassis ground.
- High voltage manual disconnect terminal to the high voltage DC positive and negative terminal connections.
- High voltage manual disconnect terminal to the high voltage DC positive and negative terminal connections.

   d. If the test result was greater than 3 V, there is a stuck closed contactor and a loss of isolation within the drive motor generator battery assembly.

6. Retest the DMM by measuring the 12 V battery.

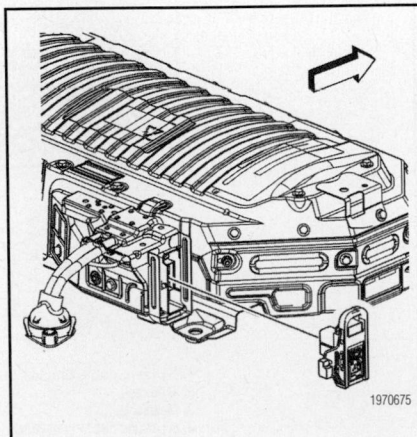

Fig. 181 Remove the high voltage manual disconnect lever

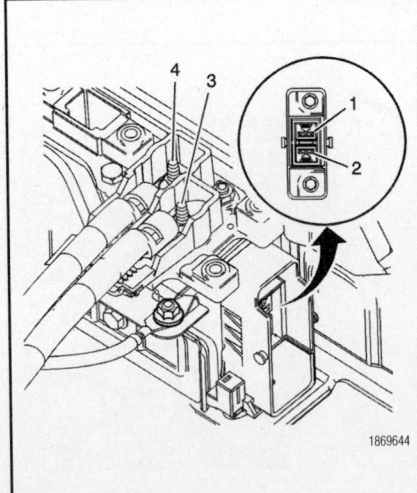

Fig. 183 Verify that the voltage has been disabled at the drive motor generator battery assembly terminals

a. If the DMM does not properly measure the 12 V battery, repair or replace the DMM and repeat all voltage measurements.

b. If all the test results were less than 3 V, the 300 V DC cables can now be removed from the drive motor generator battery assembly.

When Servicing Drive Motor Generator Control Module Assembly or Cable Connections

See Figures 184 and 185.

1. Review the high voltage safety information prior to performing the High Voltage Disabling procedure.

➡**The 12 V battery must be disconnected to ensure proper test results.**

2. Disconnect the 12 V battery.
3. Disable the voltage sources to the 2 mode hybrid vehicle.

a. Remove the ignition key.

b. Remove the Generator Battery Cover Access Door Replacement.

c. Remove the high voltage manual disconnect lever. Attach the ignition key to the lever and put the lever and the ignition key in a secure place.

d. Wait 5 minutes before continuing, to allow the capacitors to discharge.

4. Remove the drive motor generator control module sight shield.

➡**Wear your High Voltage Insulation gloves until you have determined that a high voltage exposure risk is no longer present.**

5. Remove the 3 phase cable cover.
6. To verify that no voltage is present at the high voltage connection for the drive motor generator control module, perform the following:

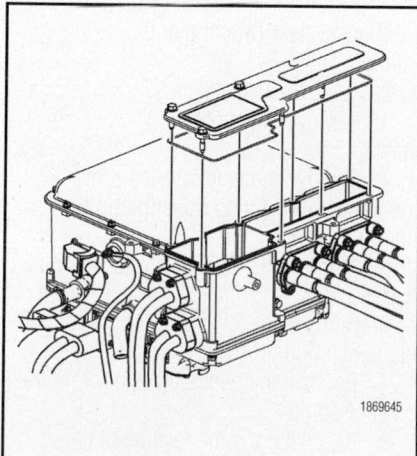

Fig. 184 Remove the 3 phase cable cover

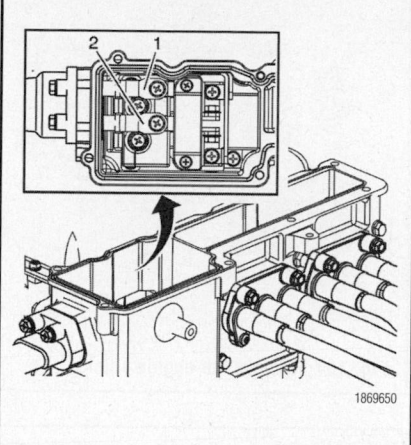

Fig. 185 High voltage DC (+) positive (1) and (-) negative terminals

a. Set the Digital Multi Meter (DMM) to DC mode. Verify the DMM works by measuring the voltage of the 12 V battery.

b. Using the DMM, verify the voltage measures less than 3 V at the following points:

- High voltage DC (+) positive and high voltage DC (-) negative terminals.
- High voltage DC (+) positive to vehicle chassis ground.
- High voltage DC (-) negative to vehicle chassis ground.

c. If the test result was greater than 3 V, there is a stuck closed contactor and a loss of isolation within the drive motor generator battery assembly.

7. Retest the DMM by measuring the 12 V battery.

a. If the DMM does not properly measure the 12 V battery, repair or replace the DMM and repeat all voltage measurements.

8. If all the test results were less than 3 V, the cables can now be removed from the drive motor generator control module assembly.

HIGH VOLTAGE ENABLING

See Figure 186.

> ✷✷ **WARNING**
>
> **Ensure all High Voltage safety procedures are followed. Failure to follow the procedure exactly as written may result in serious injury or death.**

> ✷✷ **WARNING**
>
> **Before working on any high voltage system, be sure to wear the following Personal Protection Equipment:**

- Safety glasses with appropriate side shields when within 50 feet of the vehicle, either indoors or outdoors
- Certified and up-to-date Class "0" Insulation gloves rated at 1000V with leather protectors
- Visually and functionally inspect the gloves before use.
- Wear the Insulation gloves at all times when working with the high voltage battery assembly, whether the system is energized or not.

> ✷✷ **WARNING**
>
> **Failure to follow the procedure exactly as written may result in serious injury or death.**

Review the High Voltage Safety information prior to performing the High Voltage Enabling procedure.

1. Ensure that the 12 V battery is disconnected.

> ✷✷ **CAUTION**
>
> **Always tighten the high voltage fasteners to the specified torque. Insufficient or excessive torque will cause malfunctions or damage.**

2. After finishing work on the high voltage systems and before reinstalling the high voltage manual disconnect lever, inspect for the following:

a. Verify that all tools or loose components have been removed.

b. Verify high voltage system integrity and that all connectors are installed.

c. Verify that all high voltage interlock circuit (HVIC) connectors and covers are installed.

3. Install the high voltage manual disconnect lever.

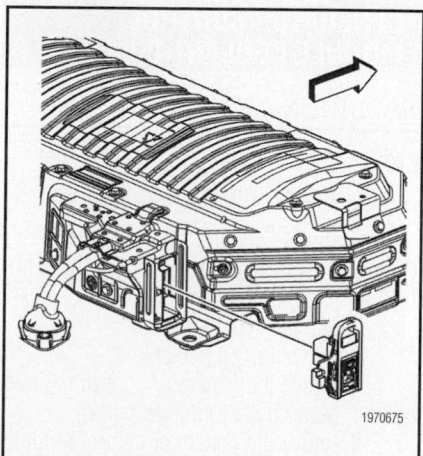

Fig. 186 Install the high voltage manual disconnect lever

4. Install the rear seat riser finish cover.

5. Connect the 12 V battery.

6. Start the engine, then turn the ignition OFF.

➡**The EBCM may set DTC C0561 71, and the DTC will not clear until the engine has been started.**

7. Ignition ON, clear all DTC Information with a scan tool.

8. Ignition OFF wait 2 minutes.

9. Ignition ON, verify with a scan tool no DTCs are set. If DTCs are set go to appropriate DTC information.

10. Verify that High Voltage has enabled by observing the HPCM 300 V Circuit voltage scan tool parameter. If High Voltage is not enabled and no DTCs are set, return to Step 6.

11. Start and idle the engine for 2 minutes.

12. Ignition OFF wait 5 minutes.

13. Ignition ON, verify with the scan tool HPCM DTC Information that the following DTCs have Ran Since Code Clear and have not set:

   a. Contactor relay DTCs P0ADC, P0AE7 and P0AE0

   b. Discharge and Pre-charge DTCs P0C76, P0C77, and P1A20

   c. Motor position sensor learn DTCs P0C17 and P0C18

   d. High voltage loss of isolation DTCs P1AE7, P1AF0 and P1AF2.

   • If the DTCs have Ran and Passed, test drive the vehicle and verify no DTCs are set.

   • If the DTCs are set, go to the appropriate DTC information.

   • If the DTCs have Not Ran Since Code Clear, review and operate the vehicle according to the applicable DTC Conditions for Running and ensure the DTCs run and pass.

GENERATOR CONTROL MODULE COOLANT PUMP

REMOVAL & INSTALLATION

Left

See Figures 187 through 190.

1. Drain the cooling system. Refer to Generator Control Module Cooling System Draining and Filling.

2. Raise the vehicle.

3. Remove the engine shield.

4. Remove the generator control module coolant pump hose (pump to pump).

5. Remove the generator control module coolant pump hose (pump to radiator).

6. Remove the 2 generator control module coolant pump bolts.

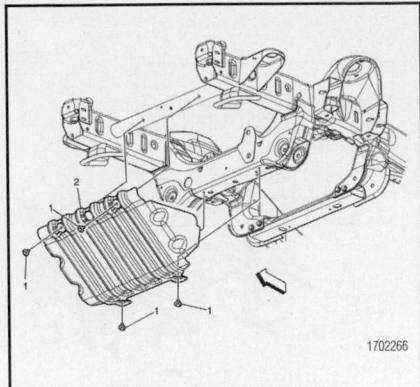

Fig. 187 Remove the engine shield

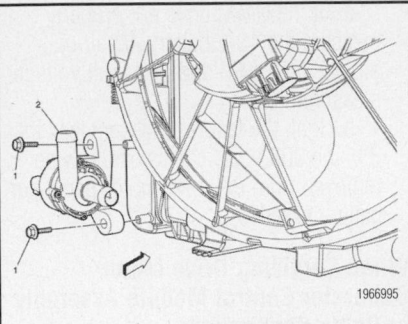

Fig. 190 Remove the 2 generator control module coolant pump bolts (1) and the generator control module coolant pump (2)

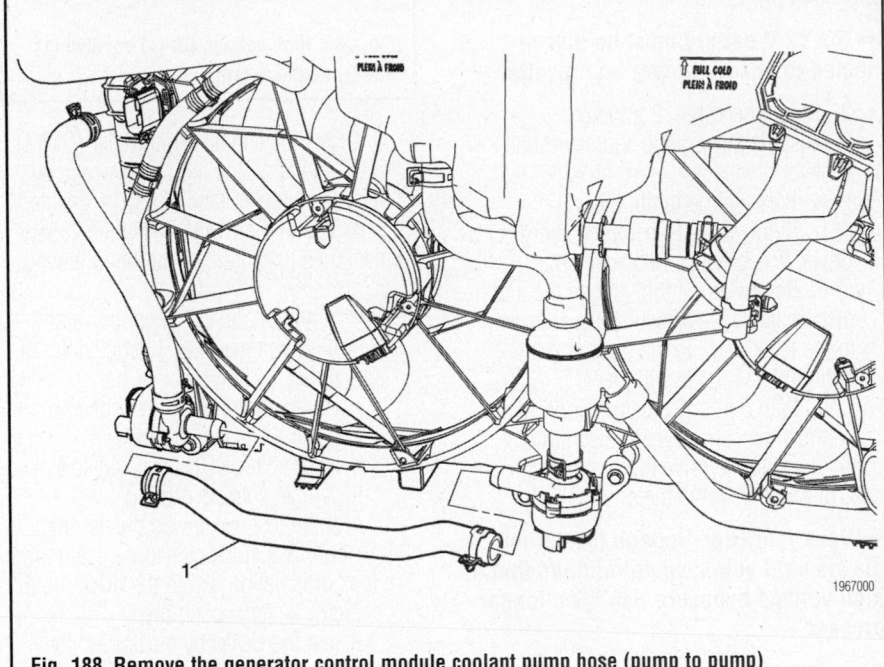

Fig. 188 Remove the generator control module coolant pump hose (pump to pump)

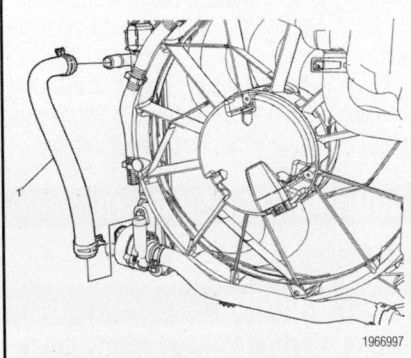

Fig. 189 Remove the generator control module coolant pump hose (pump to radiator)

7. Remove the generator control module coolant pump.

8. Installation is the reverse of the removal procedure.

Right

See Figures 187, 188 and 191.

1. Drain the cooling system. Refer to Generator Control Module Cooling System Draining and Filling.

2. Raise the vehicle.

3. Remove the engine shield.

4. Remove the generator control module coolant pump hose (pump to pump).

5. Remove the radiator surge tank outlet hose.

6. Remove the 2 generator control module coolant pump bolts.

7. Remove the generator control module coolant pump.

8. Installation is the reverse of the removal procedure.

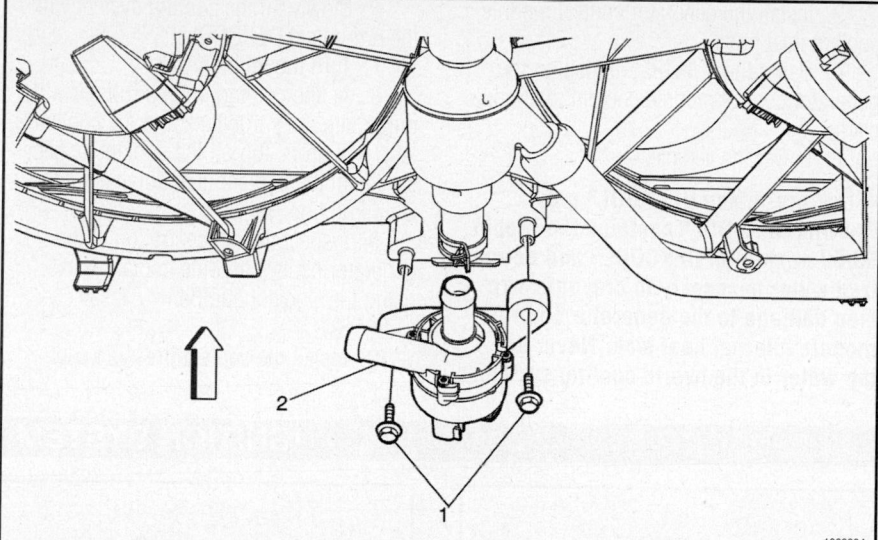

Fig. 191 Remove the 2 generator control module coolant pump bolts (1) and the generator control module coolant pump (2)

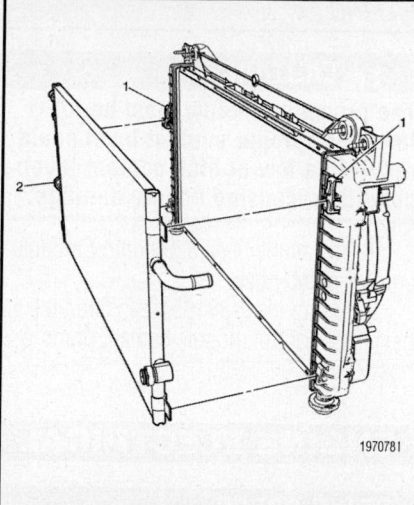

Fig. 193 Radiator tabs (1) and generator control module coolant radiator (2)

GENERATOR CONTROL MODULE COOLANT RADIATOR

REMOVAL & INSTALLATION

See Figures 189, 192 and 193.

1. Drain the cooling system. Refer to Generator Control Module Cooling System Draining and Filling.
2. Remove radiator air upper baffle and deflector.
3. Remove the condenser.
4. Remove transmission cooler pipes.

5. Remove the generator control module coolant outlet hose.
6. Remove the generator control coolant pump hose (pump to radiator).
7. Push radiator tabs in and lift up on generator control module coolant radiator.
8. Remove the generator control module coolant radiator.
9. Installation is the reverse of the removal procedure.

GENERATOR CONTROL MODULE COOLING SYSTEM DRAINING AND FILLING

DRAINING

✳✳ WARNING

To avoid being burned, do not remove the radiator cap or surge tank cap while the engine is hot. The cooling system will release scalding fluid and steam under pressure if radiator cap or surge tank cap is removed while the engine and radiator are still hot.

1. Follow the steps below in order to remove the surge tank fill cap:
   a. Slowly rotate the cap counterclockwise.
   b. Stop rotating and allow the hissing to stop.
   c. After all the hissing stops, continue turning counterclockwise in order to remove the cap.
2. Raise and support the vehicle.
3. Place a drain pan under the generator control module coolant pump hose.
4. Using the Hose Clamp Pliers (J-38185), reposition the generator control module coolant pump hose clamp.
5. Remove the generator control module coolant pump hose from the coolant pump.
6. Drain the coolant.
7. Place a drain pan under the generator control module coolant inlet hose.
8. Using the J-38185, reposition the generator control module coolant inlet hose clamp.
9. Drain the coolant.

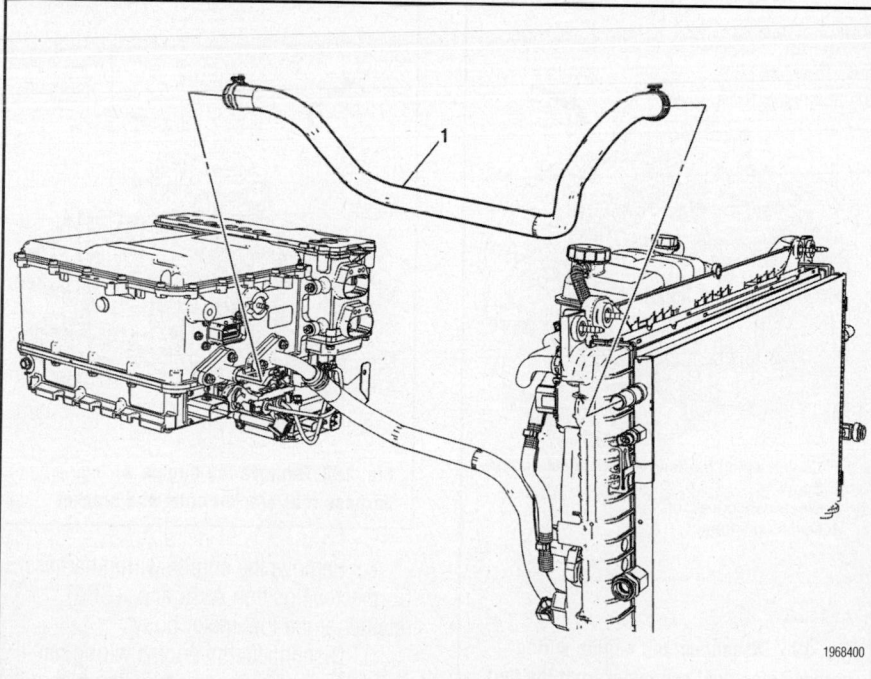

Fig. 192 Remove the generator control module coolant outlet hose (1)

FILLING

✳✳ CAUTION

The procedure below must be followed. Improper coolant level could result in a low or high coolant level condition, causing engine damage.

1. Install the generator control module coolant pump hose.
2. Using the J-38185, reposition the generator control module coolant pump hose clamp.

3. Install the generator control module coolant inlet hose.
4. Using the J-38185, reposition the generator control module coolant inlet hose clamp.
5. Lower the vehicle.

➡ **Use pre-mixed DEXCOOL® only. Pre-mix DEXCOOL® contains the proper 50/50 mixture of DEXCOOL® and de-ionized water necessary to prevent corrosion damage to the generator control module internal heat sink. Never use tap water in the hybrid cooling system.**

6. Slowly fill the cooling system with the pre-mixed DEXCOOL®.
7. Turn the ignition ON.
8. As the cooling pumps run, air will purge into the surge tank and the coolant level will drop. Top off the coolant as necessary until the coolant is maintained at the Cold Full line.
9. Inspect the concentration of the generator control module coolant using the Coolant and Battery Tester (J-26568).
10. Install the coolant pressure cap.

ENGINE ELECTRICAL   IGNITION SYSTEM

FIRING ORDER

The firing order for the V6 engine is: 1–6–5–4–3–2.
The firing order for all V8 engines is: 1–8–7–2–6–5–4–3.

IGNITION COIL

REMOVAL & INSTALLATION

V6 Engine

See Figures 194 through 200.

1. Remove the air cleaner outlet resonator.
2. Disconnect the chassis fuel feed pipe quick connect fitting from the engine fuel feed pipe.
3. Disconnect the engine wiring harness electrical connector from the Manifold Absolute Pressure (MAP) sensor.
4. Disconnect the engine wiring harness electrical connector from the Evaporative Emission (EVAP) canister purge solenoid valve.

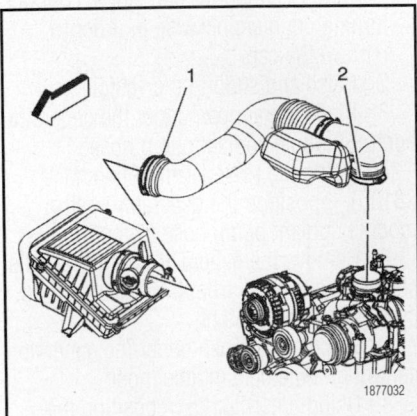

Fig. 194 Remove the air cleaner outlet resonator; clamps (1, 2)

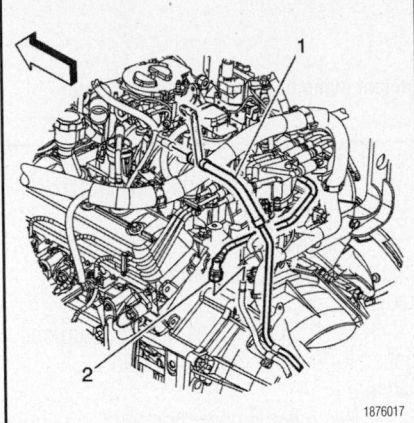

Fig. 195 Disconnect the chassis fuel feed pipe (1) quick connect fitting from the engine fuel feed pipe; quick connect (2)

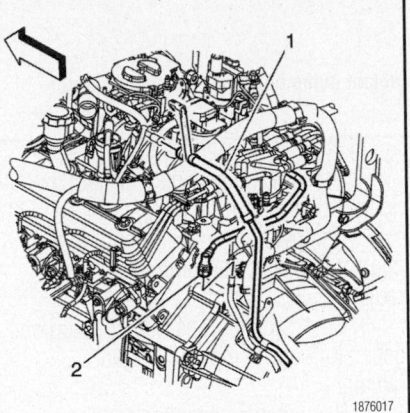

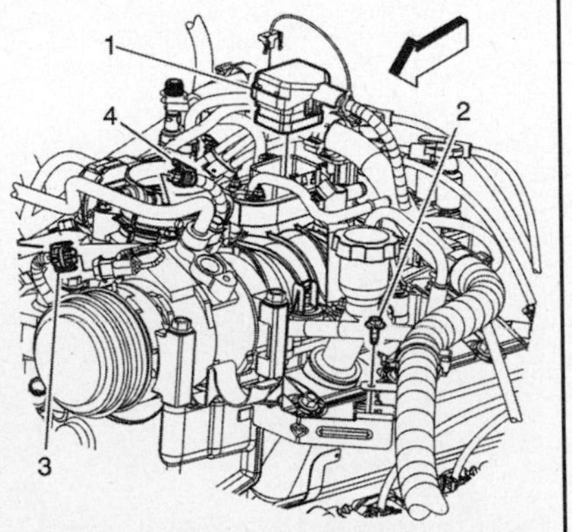

1. Engine wiring harness electrical connector
2. Screw
3. Electrical connector
4. Quick disconnect

Fig. 196 Disconnect the engine wiring harness electrical connector from the fuel meter body

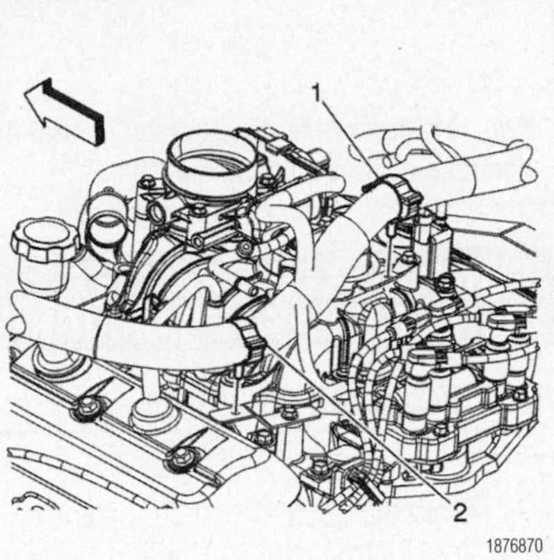

Fig. 197 Remove the engine wiring harness clips (1, 2) from the engine harness brackets

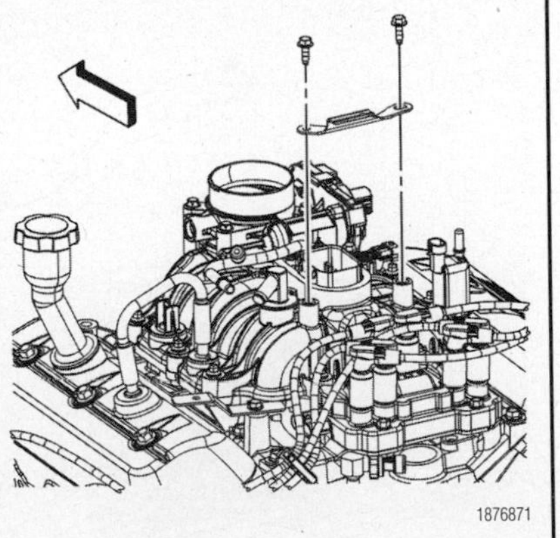

Fig. 198 Remove the engine wiring harness rear bracket bolts and bracket

5. Remove the engine wiring harness Connector Position Assurance (CPA) retainer at the fuel meter body.
6. Disconnect the engine wiring harness electrical connector from the fuel meter body.

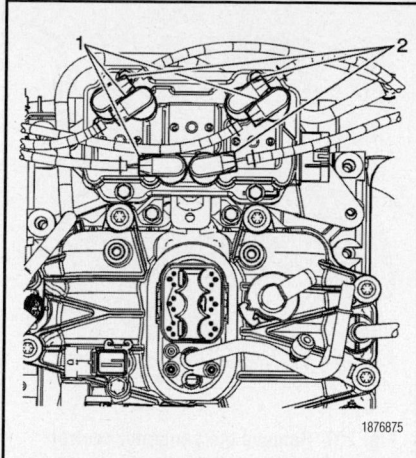

Fig. 199 Disconnect the spark plug wires (1, 2) from the ignition coil

7. Remove the engine wiring harness clips from the engine harness brackets.

8. Remove the engine wiring harness rear bracket bolts and bracket.

➡**Note the routing of the spark plug wires prior to disconnecting the wires from the ignition coil.**

9. Disconnect the spark plug wires from the ignition coil.

10. Reposition the spark plug wires out of the way.

11. Disconnect engine wiring harness electrical connector from the ignition coil.

12. Reposition the engine wiring harness branches out of the way as required.

13. Remove the ignition coil bolts and coil from the bracket.

14. If required, remove the ignition coil bracket bolts and bracket.

To install:

15. If required, position the ignition coil bracket to the lower intake manifold and install the bolts. Tighten the bolts to 106 inch lbs. (12 Nm).

16. Place the ignition coil on top of the bracket and install the bolts. Tighten the bolts to 106 inch lbs. (12 Nm).

17. Position the engine wiring harness branches as required.

18. Connect engine wiring harness electrical connector to the ignition coil.

19. Position the spark plug wires to the ignition coil.

20. Connect the spark plug wires to the ignition coil as noted during removal.

21. Place the engine wiring harness rear bracket onto the upper intake manifold and install the bolts. Tighten the bolts to 89 inch lbs. (10 Nm).

22. Install the engine wiring harness clips to the engine harness brackets.

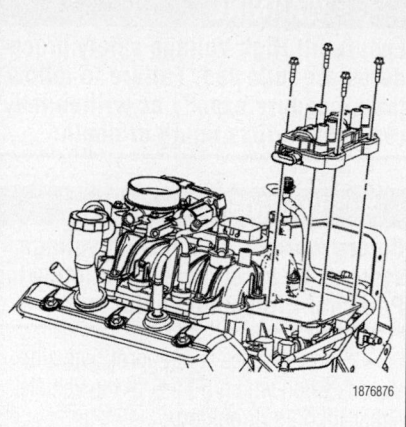

Fig. 200 Remove the ignition coil bolts and coil from the bracket

23. Connect the engine wiring harness electrical connector to the fuel meter body.

24. Install the engine wiring harness CPA retainer at the fuel meter body.

25. Connect the engine wiring harness electrical connector to the EVAP canister purge solenoid valve.

26. Connect the engine wiring harness electrical connector to the MAP sensor.

27. Connect the chassis fuel feed pipe quick connect fitting to the engine fuel feed pipe.

28. Install the air cleaner outlet resonator.

Non-Hybrid V8 Engines

See Figures 201 through 205.

1. Remove the intake manifold sight shield.

2. Disconnect the ignition coil wiring harness electrical connector from the ignition coil.

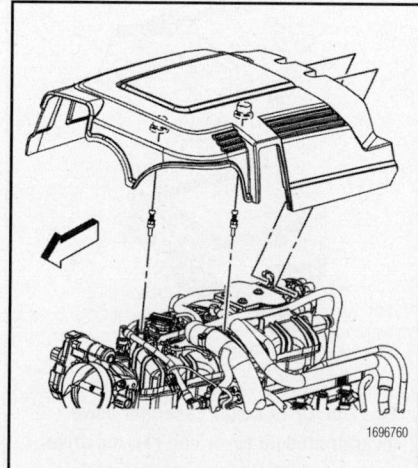

Fig. 201 Remove the intake manifold sight shield

3. Remove the spark plug wire from the ignition coil.

a. Twist the spark plug wire boot a ½ turn.

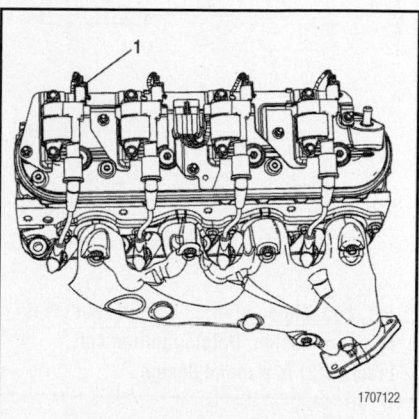

Fig. 202 Disconnect the ignition coil wiring harness electrical connector (1) from the ignition coil

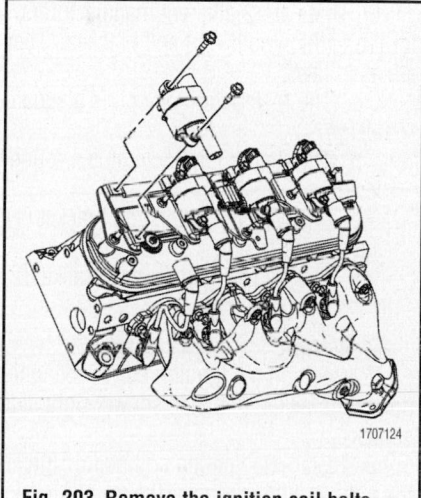

Fig. 203 Remove the ignition coil bolts

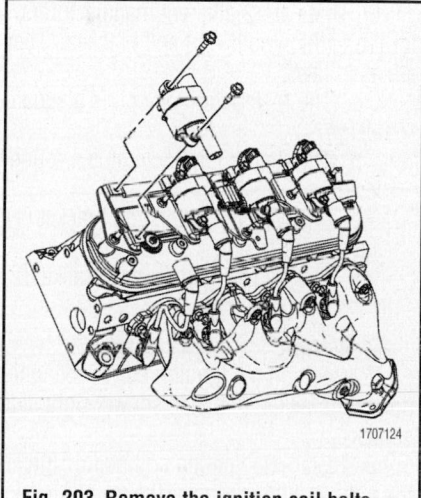

Fig. 204 Melco (1) ignition coil is a square design; Delphi (2) ignition coil is a round design

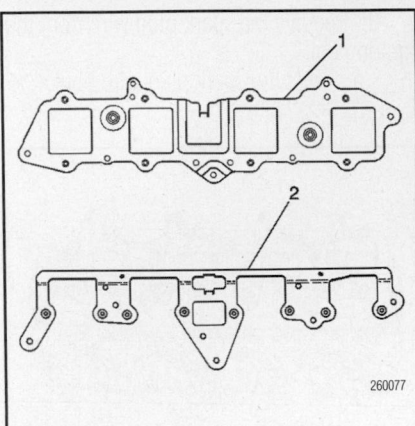

Fig. 205 Melco ignition coil bracket (1) is a square design; Delphi ignition coil bracket (2) is a round design

b. Pull only on the boot in order to remove the wire from the ignition coil.

4. Remove the ignition coil bolts.

5. Remove the ignition coil from the bracket. (left side shown, right side similar).

6. There are 2 different manufacturers for the ignition coils and coil brackets. They are as follows:

   a. The Melco ignition coil is a square design.

   b. The Delphi ignition coil is a round design.

   c. The Melco ignition coil bracket (1) is a square design.

   d. The Delphi ignition coil bracket (2) is a round design.

To install:

7. Position the ignition coil to the ignition coil bracket. (left side shown, right side similar).

8. Install the ignition coil bolts. Tighten the bolts to 89 inch lbs. (10 Nm).

9. Install the spark plug wire to the ignition coil.

10. Inspect the spark plug wire for proper installation:

   a. Push sideways on each boot in order the inspect the seating.

   b. Reinstall any loose boot.

11. Connect the ignition coil wiring harness electrical connector to the ignition coil.

12. Install the intake manifold sight shield.

Hybrid V8 Engines

See Figures 206 through 214.

1. Remove the intake manifold sight shield, as required.

2. If replacing one of the rear 2 ignitions coils on the right side perform steps 3 through 13, otherwise proceed to step 14.

> ※※ **WARNING**
>
> Ensure all High Voltage safety procedures are followed. Failure to follow the procedure exactly as written may result in serious injury or death.

> ※※ **WARNING**
>
> Before working on any high voltage system, be sure to wear the following Personal Protection Equipment:
>
> • Safety glasses with appropriate side shields when within 50 feet of the vehicle, either indoors or outdoors
> • Certified and up-to-date Class "0" Insulation gloves rated at 1000V with leather protectors

→Visually and functionally inspect the gloves before use.

> ※※ **WARNING**
>
> Wear the Insulation gloves at all times when working with the high voltage battery assembly, whether the system is energized or not.

> ※※ **WARNING**
>
> Failure to follow the procedure exactly as written may result in serious injury or death.

3. Perform the service disconnect. Refer to High Voltage Disabling.

4. Disconnect the engine wiring harness electrical connector from the drive motor generator power inverter module cover.

5. Loosen the drive motor generator power inverter module cover bolt.

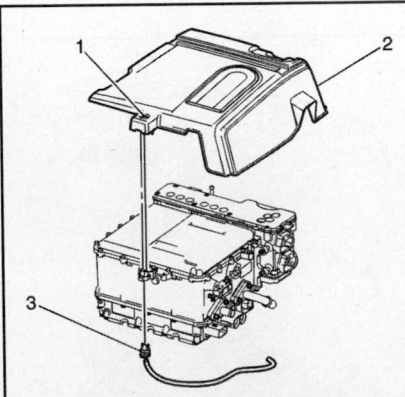

Fig. 206 Drive motor generator power inverter module cover bolt (1), the drive motor generator power inverter module cover (2); the engine wiring harness electrical connector (3)

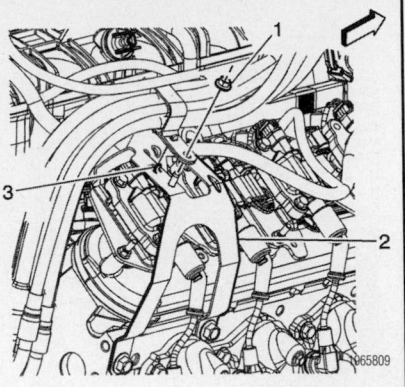

Fig. 207 Remove the generator control module 3 phase cable clip nut (1); remove the generator control module 3 phase cable clip from the engine bracket (2); NA (3)

6. Remove the drive motor generator power inverter module cover.

7. Remove the generator control module 3 phase cable clip nut.

8. Remove the generator control module 3 phase cable clip from the engine bracket.

9. Reposition the generator control module 3 phase cables out of the way.

10. Remove the right wheelhouse liner.

11. Working through the wheel opening, remove the engine bracket bolts.

12. Lower the vehicle.

13. Remove the engine bracket nut from the ignition coil bracket stud and remove the bracket.

14. Disconnect the ignition coil wiring harness electrical connector from the ignition coil.

15. Remove the spark plug wire from the ignition coil.

   a. Twist the spark plug wire boot a ½ turn.

   b. Pull only on the boot in order to remove the wire from the ignition coil.

16. Remove the ignition coil bolts.

17. Remove the ignition coil from the bracket. (left side shown, right side similar).

18. There are 2 different manufacturers for the ignition coils and coil brackets. They are as follows:

   a. The Melco ignition coil is a square design.

   b. The Delphi ignition coil is a round design.

   c. The Melco ignition coil bracket (1) is a square design.

   d. The Delphi ignition coil bracket (2) is a round design.

To install:

19. Position the ignition coil to the ignition coil bracket. (left side shown, right side similar).

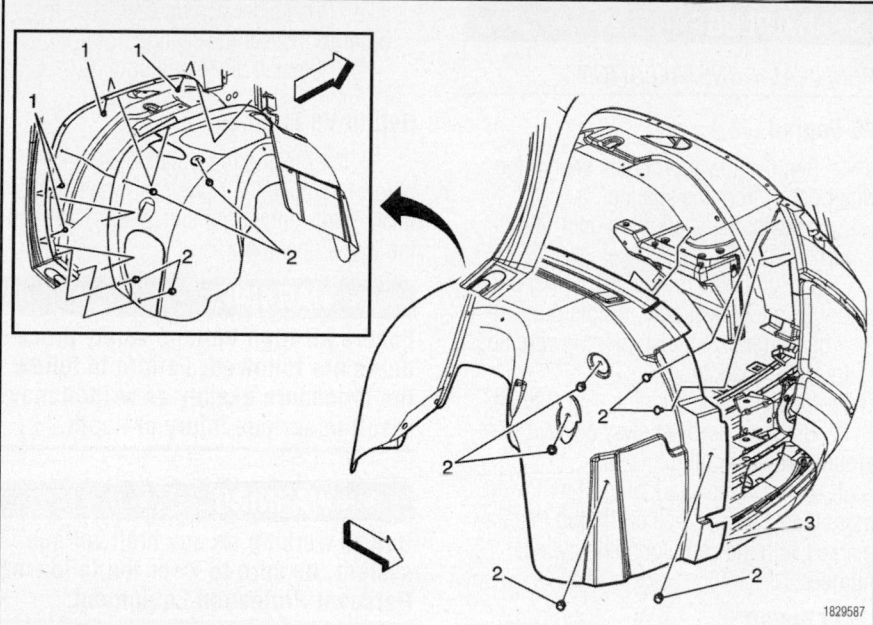

Fig. 208 For GMC, remove the right wheelhouse liner screws (1), the plastic retainers (2), and the wheelhouse liner (3)

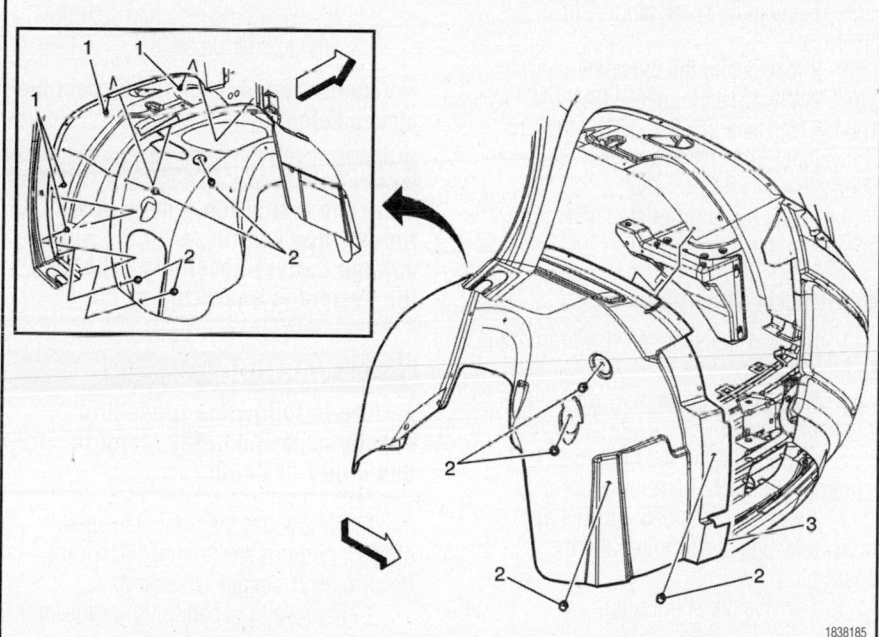

Fig. 209 For Chevrolet, remove the right wheelhouse liner screws (1), the plastic retainers (2), and the wheelhouse liner (3)

Fig. 210 Remove the engine bracket bolts (2), the engine bracket nut (1) from the ignition coil bracket stud and remove the bracket (3)

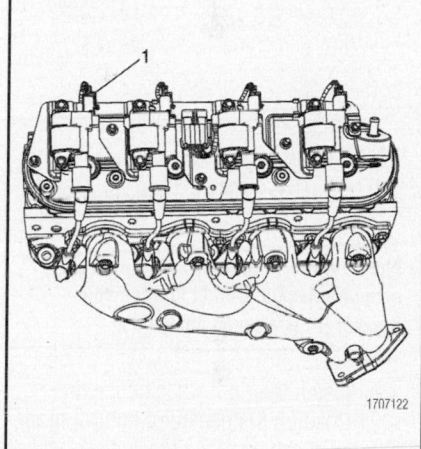

Fig. 211 Disconnect the ignition coil wiring harness electrical connector (1) from the ignition coil

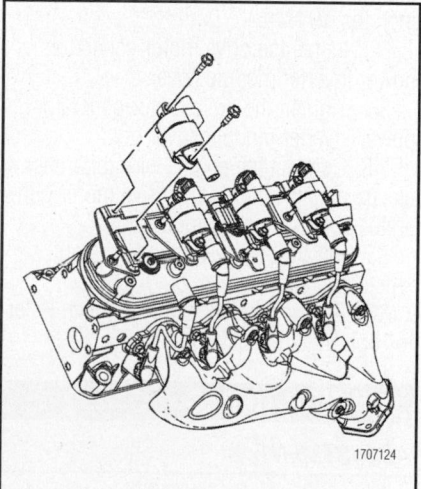

Fig. 212 Remove the ignition coil bolts

20. Install the ignition coil bolts. Tighten the bolts to 89 inch lbs. (10 Nm).

21. Install the spark plug wire to the ignition coil.

22. Inspect the spark plug wire for proper installation:

    a. Push sideways on each boot in order the inspect the seating.

    b. Reinstall any loose boot.

23. Connect the ignition coil wiring harness electrical connector to the ignition coil.

24. If replacing one of the rear 2 ignitions coils on the right side perform steps 7 through 16, otherwise proceed to step 17.

25. Install the engine bracket to the ignition coil bracket stud and install nut. Tighten the nut to 80 inch lbs. (9 Nm).

26. Raise the vehicle half way.

27. Working through the wheel opening, install the engine bracket bolts. Tighten the bolts to 37 ft. lbs. (50 Nm).

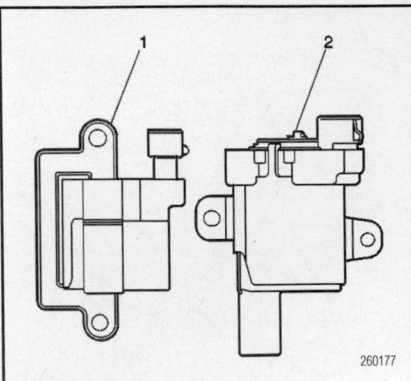

Fig. 221 Melco (1) ignition coil is a square design; Delphi (2) ignition coil is a round design

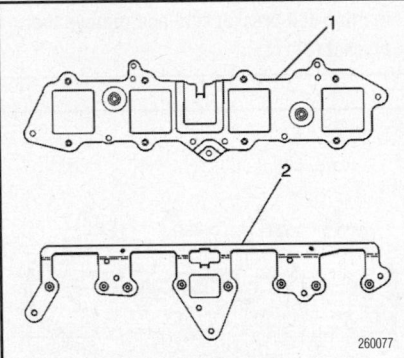

Fig. 214 Melco ignition coil bracket (1) is a square design; Delphi ignition coil bracket (2) is a round design

28. Install the right wheelhouse liner.

29. Position the generator control module 3 phase cables to the bracket channel.

30. Install the generator control module 3 phase cable clip to the tab on the engine bracket.

31. Install the generator control module 3 phase cable clip nut. Tighten the nut to 80 inch lbs. (9 Nm).

32. Install the drive motor generator power inverter module cover.

33. Tighten the drive motor generator power inverter module cover bolt.

34. Connect the engine wiring harness electrical connector to the drive motor generator power inverter module cover.

35. Install the intake manifold sight shield, as required.

36. Perform the service reconnect. Refer to High Voltage Enabling.

IGNITION TIMING

ADJUSTMENT

Ignition timing is controlled by the Engine Control Module (ECM). No adjustment is necessary or possible.

SPARK PLUGS

REMOVAL & INSTALLATION

V6 Engine

1. Remove the appropriate spark plug wire boot(s) from the spark plug.

   a. Twist the spark plug boot ½ turn.

   b. Pull ONLY on the spark plug boot or use a tool designed for this purpose in order to remove the spark plug wire boot from the spark plug.

2. Loosen the spark plug 1 or 2 turns.

3. Brush or air blast away any dirt from around the spark plug.

4. Remove the spark plug. If removing more than 1 plug, place each plug in a tray marked with the corresponding cylinder number.

To install:

5. Inspect the spark plug gap. Adjust the gap as needed.

6. Install the spark plug into the cylinder head by hand.

7. Tighten the spark plug to 11 ft. lbs. (15 Nm).

8. If reinstalling the old spark plug wires, apply dielectric grease GM P/N 12345579 (Canadian P/N 10953481), or equivalent to the inside the spark plug wire boots.

9. Install the appropriate spark plug wire boot(s) to the spark plug.

Non-Hybrid V8 Engines

1. Remove the spark plug wire from the spark plug.

   a. Twist the spark plug wire boot a ½ turn.

   b. Pull only on the boot in order to remove the wire from the spark plug.

2. Brush or using compressed air, blow away any dirt from around the spark plug.

3. Remove the spark plug.

➡If removing more than one plug, place each plug in a tray marked with the corresponding cylinder number.

To install:

4. Inspect the spark plug gap. Adjust the gap as needed.

5. Hand start the spark plug in the corresponding cylinder.

6. Tighten the spark plug to 11 ft. lbs. (15 Nm).

7. Install the spark plug wire to the spark plug.

8. Inspect the spark plug wire for proper installation:

   a. Push sideways on each boot in order to inspect the seating.

   b. Reinstall any loose boot.

Hybrid V8 Engines

1. If replacing the right side spark plug(s), remove the right front wheelhouse liner. Remove the right side plug(s) through the wheel opening.

✳✳ WARNING

Ensure all High Voltage safety procedures are followed. Failure to follow the procedure exactly as written may result in serious injury or death.

✳✳ WARNING

Before working on any high voltage system, be sure to wear the following Personal Protection Equipment:

- Safety glasses with appropriate side shields when within 50 feet of the vehicle, either indoors or outdoors
- Certified and up-to-date Class "0" Insulation gloves rated at 1000V with leather protectors

➡Visually and functionally inspect the gloves before use.

✳✳ WARNING

Wear the Insulation gloves at all times when working with the high voltage battery assembly, whether the system is energized or not.

✳✳ WARNING

Failure to follow the procedure exactly as written may result in serious injury or death.

2. If replacing the right side spark plug(s), perform the service disconnect. Refer to High Voltage Disabling.

3. Remove the spark plug wire from the spark plug.

   a. Twist the spark plug wire boot a ½ turn.

   b. Pull only on the boot in order to remove the wire from the spark plug.

4. Brush or using compressed air, blow away any dirt from around the spark plug.

5. Remove the spark plug.

➡If removing more than one plug, place each plug in a tray marked with the corresponding cylinder number.

To install:

6. Inspect the spark plug gap. Adjust the gap as needed.

7. Hand start the spark plug in the corresponding cylinder.

8. Tighten the spark plug to 11 ft. lbs. (15 Nm).

9. Install the spark plug wire to the spark plug.

10. Inspect the spark plug wire for proper installation:

   a. Push sideways on each boot in order to inspect the seating.

   b. Reinstall any loose boot.

11. If a right side spark plug(s) was replaced, install the right front wheelhouse liner.

12. If a right side spark plug(s) was replaced, perform the service reconnect. Refer to High Voltage Enabling.

ENGINE ELECTRICAL | STARTING SYSTEM

STARTER

REMOVAL & INSTALLATION

V6 Engine

See Figures 215 through 218.

1. Disconnect the negative battery cable.

2. Raise and suitably support the vehicle.

3. Remove the oil pan skid plate bolts and plate, if equipped.

4. Remove the starter solenoid cable clip bolt from the frame.

5. Remove the starter motor bolts.

6. Remove the starter solenoid cable lead nut.

7. Remove the starter solenoid cable lead from the starter.

8. Remove the engine wiring harness lead nut.

9. Remove the engine wiring harness lead from the starter.

10. Remove the starter from the vehicle.

➡**If the starter shield is damaged, replace the starter shield.**

11. If replacing the starter, remove the starter heat shield.

To install:

12. If the starter was replaced, install the starter heat shield to the starter.

13. Position the starter to the vehicle.

14. Install the engine wiring harness lead to the starter.

15. Install the engine wiring harness lead nut.

16. Install the starter solenoid cable lead to the starter.

17. Install the starter solenoid cable nut. Tighten the nut to 80 inch lbs. (9 Nm).

18. Install the starter motor bolts. Tighten the bolts to 37 ft. lbs. (50 Nm).

19. Position the starter solenoid cable clip to the frame and install the starter solenoid cable clip bolt. Tighten the bolt to 89 inch lbs. (10 Nm).

20. Position the oil pan skid plate and install the bolts, if equipped. Tighten the bolts to 21 ft. lbs. (28 Nm).

21. Lower the vehicle.

22. Connect the negative battery cable.

V8 Engines

See Figures 219 through 221.

1. Disconnect the negative battery cable.

2. Raise and support the vehicle.

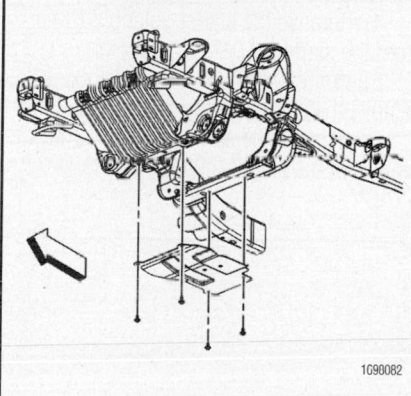

Fig. 215 Remove the oil pan skid plate bolts and plate, if equipped

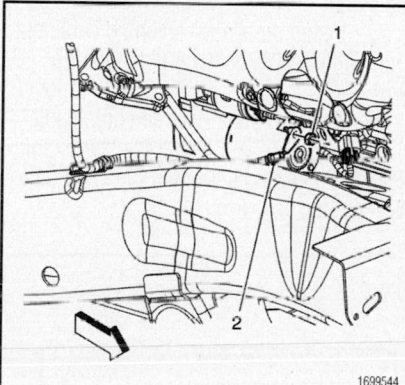

Fig. 217 Remove the starter solenoid cable lead nut (1) and the starter solenoid cable lead (2) from the starter

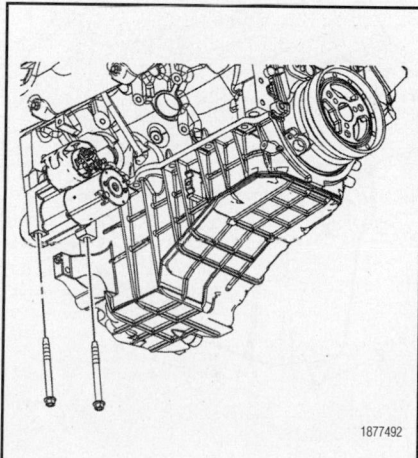

Fig. 216 Remove the starter motor bolts

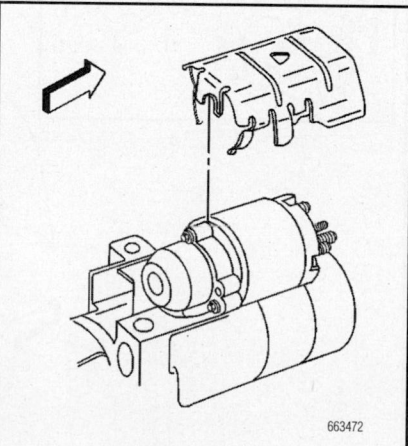

Fig. 218 If replacing the starter, remove the starter heat shield

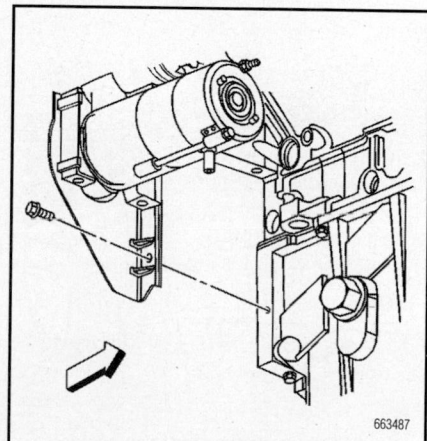

Fig. 219 Remove the transmission cover bolt

3. Remove the oil pan skid plate if equipped.

4. Remove the transmission cover bolt.

5. Remove the starter bolts.

6. Disconnect the engine wiring harness electrical connector from the oil level sensor.

✳✳ CAUTION

Avoid cable and wiring damage. DO NOT suspend the starter by the cables or wires attached to the solenoid terminals. Use a rope or mechanics wire to suspend the starter.

7. Slide the starter forward until the starter clears the transmission and properly support the starter.

8. Lower the vehicle half way.

9. Remove the right front wheel and tire.

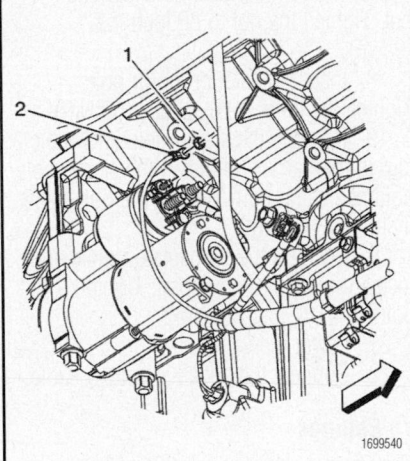

Fig. 220 Remove the engine wiring harness lead nut (1), and the engine wiring harness lead terminal (2) from the starter

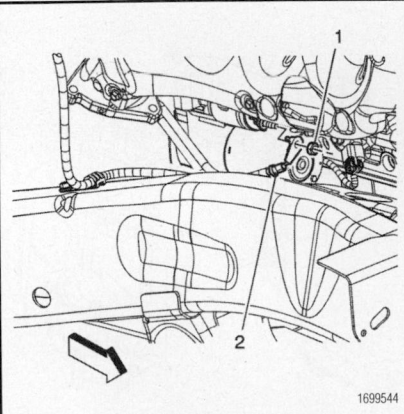

Fig. 221 Remove the starter solenoid cable nut (1) and the starter solenoid cable (2) from the starter

10. Working through the right wheel well opening, remove the engine wiring harness lead nut.

11. Remove the engine wiring harness lead terminal from the starter.

12. Remove the starter solenoid cable clip bolt from the frame.

13. Remove the starter solenoid cable nut.

14. Remove the starter solenoid cable from the starter.

15. Remove the starter through the wheel well opening.

16. If replacing the starter, unsnap the transmission cover from the starter.

17. If replacing the starter, remove the starter heat shield.

To install:

18. If the starter was replaced, install the starter heat shield.

19. If the starter was replaced, snap the transmission cover onto the starter.

20. Install the starter through the wheel well opening.

21. Install the starter solenoid cable to the starter.

22. Install the starter solenoid cable nut. Tighten the cable nut to 80 inch lbs. (9 Nm).

23. Position the starter solenoid cable clip to the frame and install the starter solenoid cable clip bolt. Tighten the clip bolt to 89 inch lbs. (10 Nm).

24. Install the engine wiring harness lead terminal to the starter.

25. Install the engine wiring harness lead nut.

26. Position the starter into place.

27. Install the starter bolts. Tighten the starter bolts to 37 ft. lbs. (50 Nm).

28. Install the right front wheel and tire.

29. Raise the vehicle.

30. Connect the engine wiring harness electrical connector to the oil level sensor.

31. Install the transmission cover bolt. Tighten the cover bolt to 80 inch lbs. (9 Nm).

32. Install the oil pan skid plate if equipped.

33. Connect the negative battery cable.

Diesel Engines

See Figures 222 through 225.

1. Disconnect the negative battery cable.

2. Remove the right wheelhouse liner.

3. Working through the wheelhouse, remove the starter solenoid cable nut from the starter.

4. Remove the starter solenoid cable from the starter.

5. Working through the wheelhouse, remove the engine wiring harness lead nut.

6. Remove the engine wiring harness lead from the starter motor.

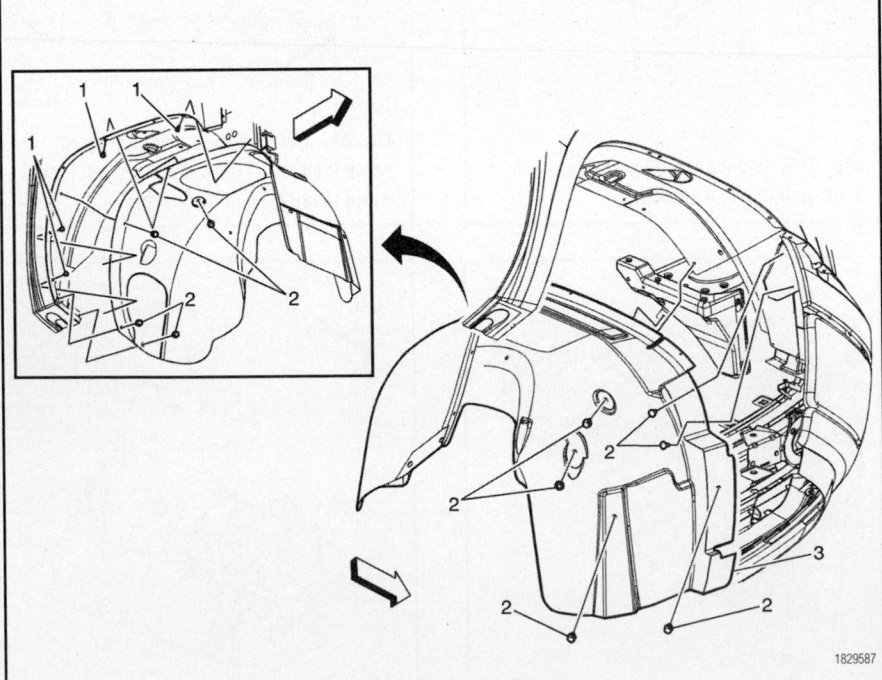

Fig. 222 For GMC, remove the right wheelhouse liner screws (1), the plastic retainers (2), and the wheelhouse liner (3)

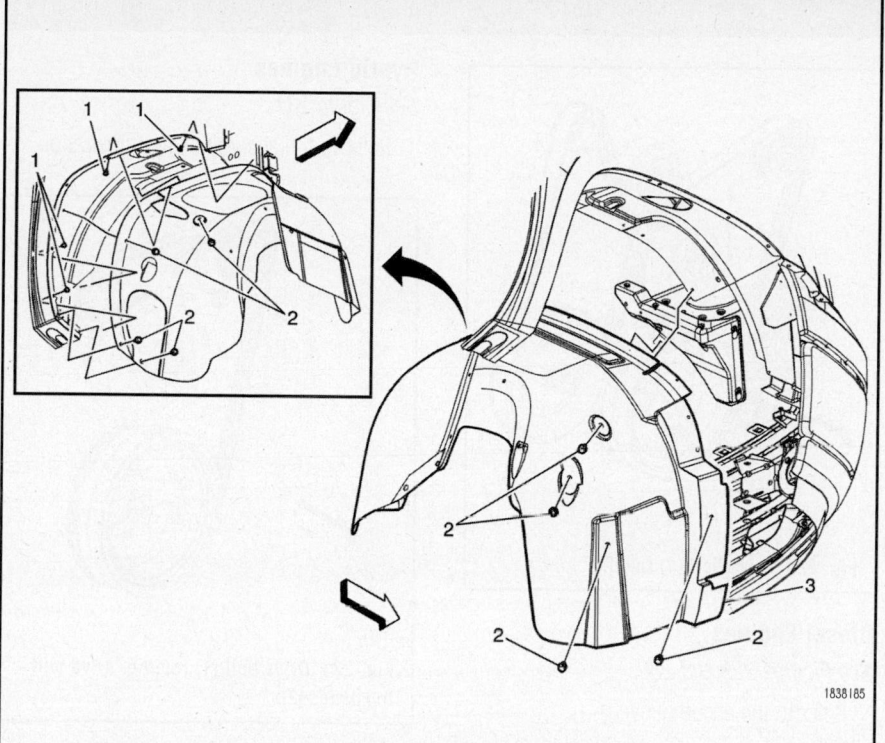

Fig. 223 For Chevrolet, remove the right wheelhouse liner screws (1), the plastic retainers (2), and the wheelhouse liner (3)

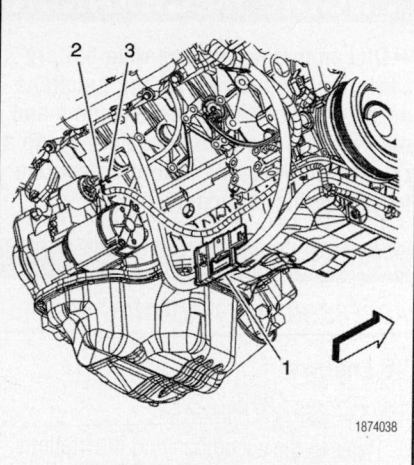

Fig. 224 Remove the engine wiring harness lead nut (3) and the engine wiring harness lead (2) from the starter motor; hose retainer (1)

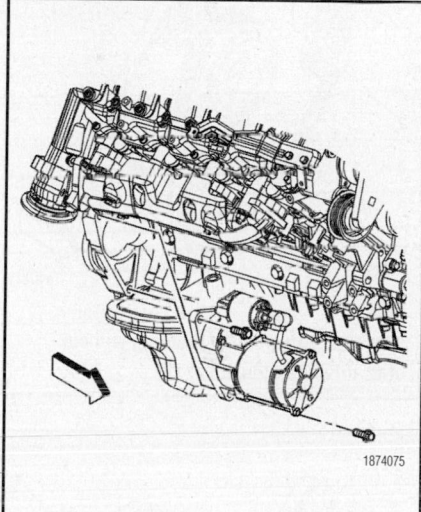

Fig. 225 From under the vehicle, remove the starter motor bolts (1)

7. Remove the exhaust manifold-to-catalytic converter pipe.

8. From under the vehicle, remove the starter motor bolts.

9. Remove the starter motor.

To install:

10. Install the starter motor.

11. Install the starter motor bolts. Tighten the bolts to 63 ft. lbs. (85 Nm).

12. Install the exhaust manifold-to-catalytic converter pipe.

13. Install the engine wiring harness lead to the starter motor.

14. Install the engine wiring harness lead nut.

15. Install the starter solenoid cable to the starter.

16. Install the starter solenoid cable nut to the starter. Tighten the nut to 80 inch lbs. (9 Nm).

17. Install the wheelhouse liner.

18. Connect the negative battery cable.

ENGINE MECHANICAL

➡ Disconnecting the negative battery cable may interfere with the functions of the on board computer systems and may require the computer to undergo a relearning process, once the negative battery cable is reconnected.

ACCESSORY DRIVE BELTS

ACCESSORY BELT ROUTING

V6 Engines

See Figures 226 and 227.

Refer to the accompanying illustrations.

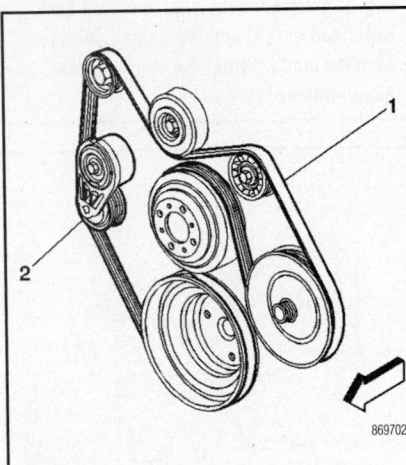

Fig. 226 Drive belt (1) routing without A/C; drive belt tensioner (2)

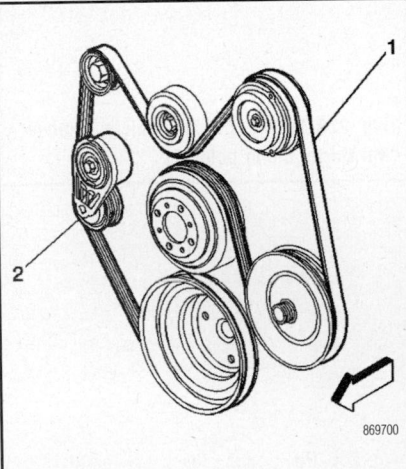

Fig. 227 Drive belt (1) routing with A/C; drive belt tensioner (2)

V8 Engines

See Figure 228.

Refer to the accompanying illustration.

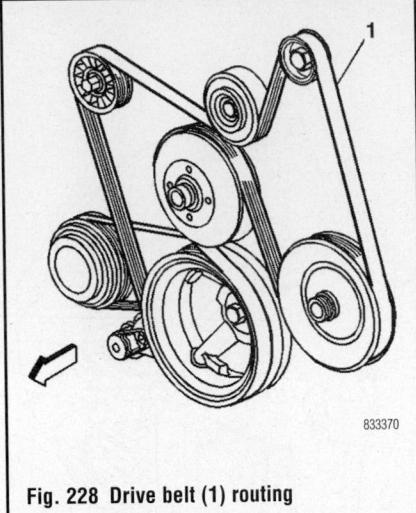

Fig. 228 Drive belt (1) routing

Diesel Engines

See Figures 229 and 230.

Refer to the accompanying illustrations.

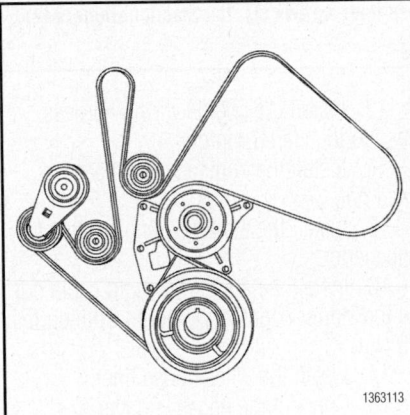

Fig. 229 Drive belt routing with single alternator

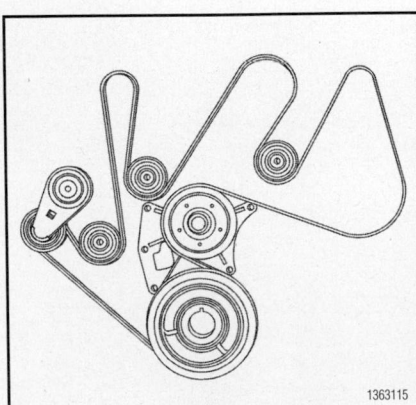

Fig. 230 Drive belt routing with dual alternators

Hybrid Engines

See Figure 231.

Refer to the accompanying illustration.

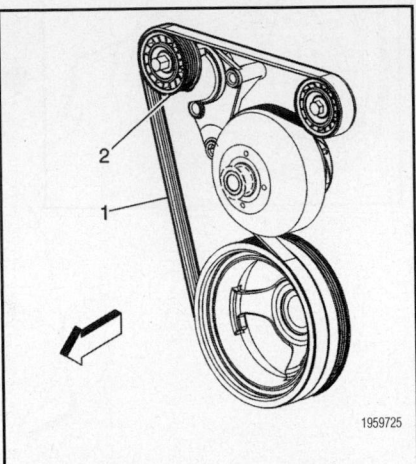

Fig. 231 Drive belt (1) routing; drive belt tensioner (2)

INSPECTION

The accessory drive belt should be inspected for the following:
- Cracks
- Tears
- Fraying
- Damaged ribs

ADJUSTMENT

The drive belt tension is maintained by the automatic drive belt tensioner. No adjustment is necessary or possible.

REMOVAL & INSTALLATION

V6 Engines

1. Install a ⅜ inch drive breaker bar to the drive belt tensioner arm.
2. Rotate the drive belt tensioner counterclockwise in order to relieve tension on the belt.
3. If equipped without Air Conditioning (A/C), remove the belt from the pulleys and the drive belt tensioner.
4. If equipped with A/C, remove the belt from the pulleys and the drive belt tensioner.
5. Slowly release the tension on the drive belt tensioner.
6. Remove the breaker bar from the drive belt tensioner.
7. Clean and inspect the belt surfaces of all the pulleys.

To install:

8. Route the belt around all the pulleys except the flat idler pulley.

9. Install a ⅜ inch drive breaker bar to the drive belt tensioner arm.

10. Rotate the belt tensioner counter-clockwise in order to relieve the tension on the tensioner.

11. If equipped with A/C, install the belt under the flat idler pulley.

12. If equipped without A/C, install the belt to the pulleys and the drive belt tensioner.

13. Slowly release the tension on the belt tensioner.

14. Remove the breaker bar from the drive belt tensioner.

15. Inspect the drive belt for proper installation and alignment.

V8 Engines

1. Open the hood.

2. Remove the air cleaner outlet duct.

3. Install a breaker bar with hex-head socket to the drive belt tensioner bolt.

4. Rotate the drive belt tensioner clockwise in order to relieve tension on the belt.

5. Remove the drive belt from the pulleys and the drive belt tensioner.

6. Slowly release the tension on the drive belt tensioner.

7. Remove the breaker bar and socket and from the drive belt tensioner bolt.

8. Clean and inspect the belt surfaces of all the pulleys.

To install:

9. Route the drive belt around all the pulleys except the idler pulley.

10. Install the breaker bar with hex-head socket to the belt tensioner bolt.

11. Rotate the belt tensioner clockwise in order to relieve the tension on the tensioner.

12. Install the drive belt under the idler pulley.

13. Slowly release the tension on the belt tensioner.

14. Remove the breaker bar and socket from the belt tensioner bolt.

15. Inspect the drive belt for proper installation and alignment.

16. Install the air cleaner outlet duct.

17. Start the vehicle and inspect the drive belt for proper operation.

18. Close the hood.

Air Conditioning Compressor Belt

See Figures 232 through 237.

1. Remove the accessory drive belt.

2. Remove the engine shield.

3. Cut the belt from Air Conditioning (A/C) and crankshaft pulleys.

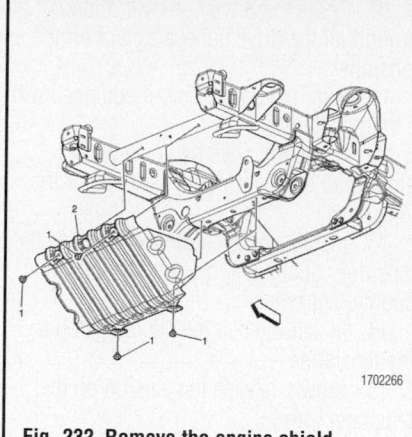

Fig. 232 Remove the engine shield

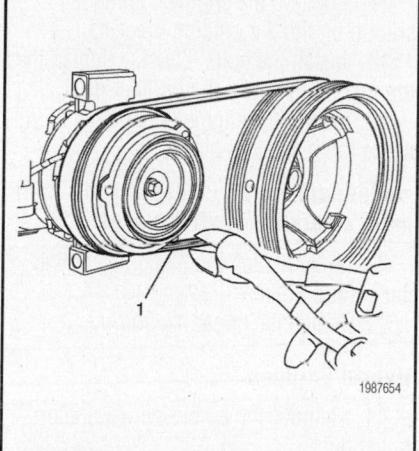

Fig. 233 Cut the belt (1) from Air Conditioning (A/C) and crankshaft pulleys

To install:

➡The OEM replacement stretchy belt is packaged with a disposable installation tool.

4. Position the belt behind the rear face of the balancer and off of the A/C pulley.

5. Install the belt installation tool onto the balancer.

6. Slide the belt installation tool upward, installing the belt onto the belt installation tool.

7. Slide the belt installation tool downward, positioning the belt onto the A/C pulley, applying light tension to the belt.

8. Position the lower portion of the belt with the ribbed area facing forward.

9. Slowly rotate the crankshaft pulley in a clockwise direction while using finger pressure to pull the belt forward. Ensure that the ribbed area of the belt remains facing forward and the belt aligns properly to the A/C pulley.

10. Remove the belt installation tool.

11. Inspect the drive belt for proper installation and alignment.

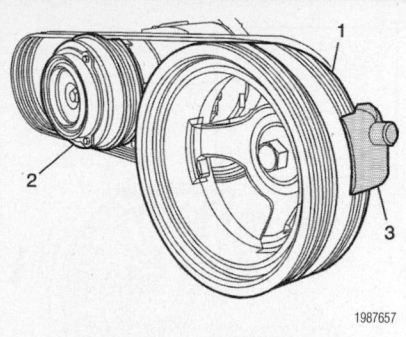

Fig. 234 Position the belt behind the rear face of the balancer (1) and off of the A/C pulley (2); install the belt installation tool (3) onto the balancer

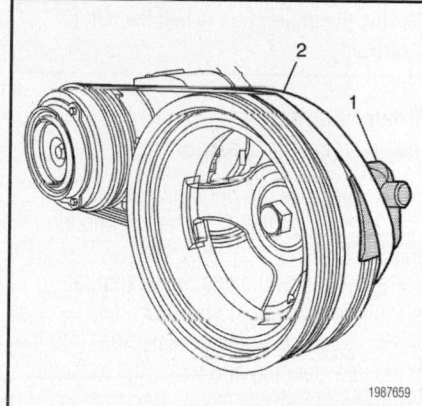

Fig. 235 Slide the belt installation tool (1) upward, installing the belt (2) onto the belt installation tool

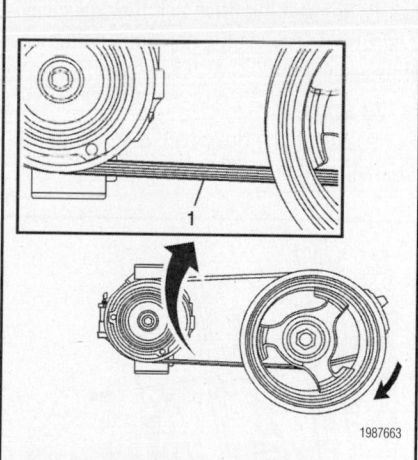

Fig. 236 Position the lower portion of the belt (1) with the ribbed area facing forward

12. Rotate the balancer and additional 360 degrees to ensure proper belt installation.

13. Install the engine shield.

14. Install the accessory drive belt.

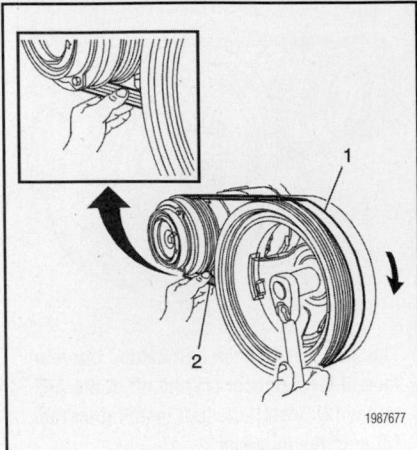

Fig. 237 Slowly rotate the crankshaft pulley (1) in a clockwise direction while using finger pressure to pull the belt (2) forward

Diesel Engines

See Figures 238 and 239.

1. Remove the upper fan shroud.
2. Remove the 3 engine cooling fan shroud bolts.
3. Position the engine cooling fan shroud forward to the radiator.
4. Install a ½ inch breaker bar into the tensioner opening and rotate the tensioner counterclockwise.
5. Remove the belt from the tensioner.
6. Slowly release the tension on the tensioner arm.
7. Remove the drive belt from the drive pulleys.
8. Inspect the drive belt for excessive cracking or any visible damage and replace if necessary.

To install:

9. Install the drive belt, if equipped with dual alternators.

10. Route the drive belt over and/or around all the drive pulleys except for the tensioner.
11. Install the drive belt, if equipped with a single alternator.
12. Route the drive belt over and/or around all the drive pulleys except for the tensioner.
13. Install a ½ inch breaker bar into the tensioner opening and rotate the tensioner counterclockwise.
14. Install the belt over and/or around the tensioner.
15. Slowly release the tension on the tensioner arm.
16. Inspect the drive belt for proper installation on and/or around all pulleys.
17. Position the engine cooling fan shroud on the 3 mounting brackets.
18. Install the bolts. Loosely tighten the top mounting bolt at the oil filler neck.
19. Center the engine cooling fan shroud to the fan blade in 3 places.

➡**Maintain a 0.25 inches (6 mm) minimum clearance at all 3 places.**

20. Fully tighten the 3 engine cooling fan shroud bolts.
21. Install the upper fan shroud.

Hybrid Engines

1. Remove the air cleaner resonator outlet duct.
2. Install a breaker bar with hex-head socket to the drive belt tensioner bolt.
3. Rotate the drive belt tensioner clockwise in order to relieve tension on the belt.
4. Remove the belt from the pulleys and the drive belt tensioner.
5. Slowly release the tension on the drive belt tensioner.

6. Remove the breaker bar and socket from the drive belt tensioner bolt.
7. Clean and inspect the belt surfaces of all the pulleys.

To install:

8. Route the drive belt around all the pulleys except the idler pulley.
9. Install the breaker bar with hex-head socket to the belt tensioner bolt.
10. Rotate the belt tensioner clockwise in order to relieve the tension on the tensioner.
11. Install the drive belt under the idler pulley.
12. Slowly release the tension on the belt tensioner.
13. Remove the breaker bar and socket from the belt tensioner bolt.
14. Inspect the drive belt for proper installation and alignment.
15. Install the air cleaner resonator outlet duct.

AIR CLEANER

REMOVAL & INSTALLATION

V6 and V8 Engines

See Figure 240.

1. If replacing, remove the mass airflow sensor.
2. Disconnect the air cleaner outlet duct from the air cleaner assembly.
3. Remove the air cleaner assembly.
4. Pull upward in a jerking manner in order to disengage the air cleaner housing from the insulators.
5. Installation is the reverse of removal.

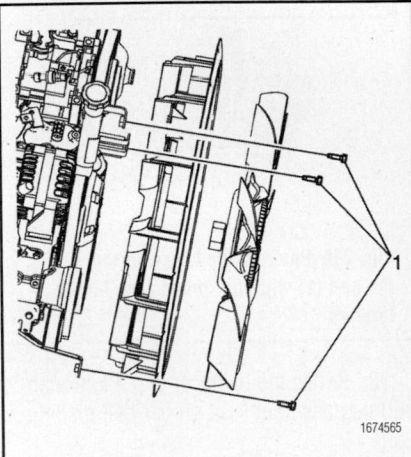

Fig. 238 Remove the 3 engine cooling fan shroud bolts (1)

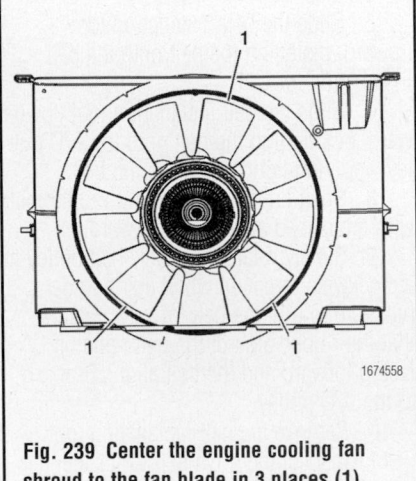

Fig. 239 Center the engine cooling fan shroud to the fan blade in 3 places (1)

Fig. 240 Remove the air cleaner assembly (1)

Diesel Engines

See Figures 241 and 242.

1. Disconnect the engine wiring harness electrical connector from the Mass Air Flow (MAF)/Intake Air Temperature (IAT) sensor.

2. Remove the air cleaner outlet duct.

3. Grasp the air cleaner assembly and pull up on the assembly in order to disengage the retaining pins from the grommets.

To install:

4. Line up the retaining pins with the grommets.

5. Install the air cleaner assembly until the air cleaner is seated fully on the mounts and is up against the fender apron.

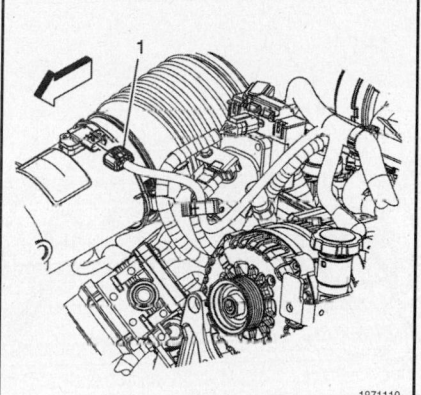

Fig. 241 Disconnect the engine wiring harness electrical connector (1) from the MAF/IAT sensor

Fig. 242 Grasp the air cleaner assembly and pull up on the assembly in order to disengage the retaining pins from the grommets

6. Install the air cleaner outlet duct.

7. Connect the engine wiring harness electrical connector to the MAF/IAT sensor.

Hybrid Engines

See Figures 243 through 245.

1. Remove the air cleaner outlet duct from the Mass Air Flow (MAF)/Intake Air Temperature (IAT) sensor.

2. Disconnect the engine wiring harness electrical connector from the MAF/IAT sensor.

3. Pull up on the front of the air cleaner assembly in order to release the retainers from the air cleaner adapter.

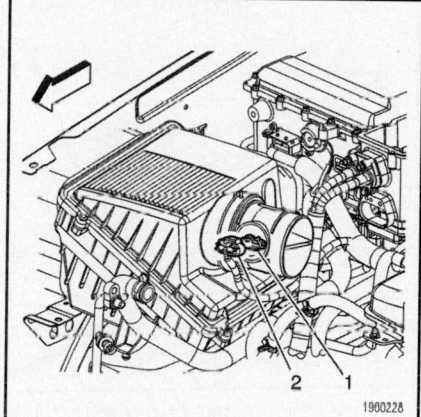

Fig. 243 Disconnect the engine wiring harness electrical connector (2) from the MAF/IAT sensor (1)

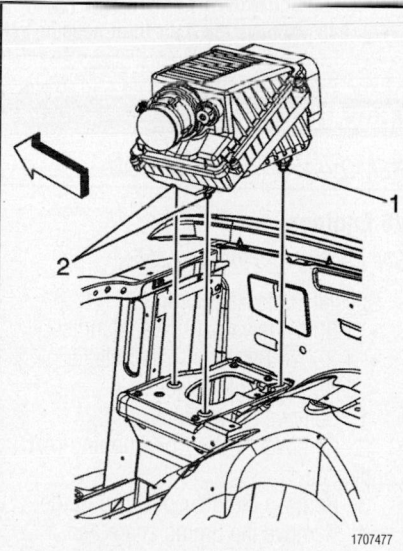

Fig. 244 Pull up on the front of the air cleaner assembly in order to release the retainers (2), slide the air cleaner assembly forward disengaging the locator (1) from the adapter

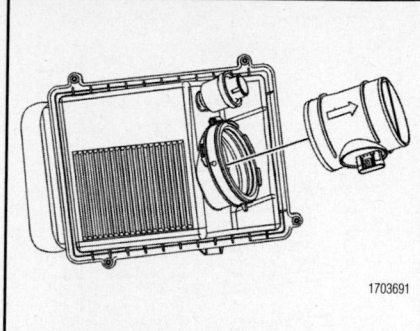

Fig. 245 The arrow must point toward the engine

4. Slide the air cleaner assembly forward disengaging the locator from the adapter.

5. Remove the air cleaner assembly.

6. If replacing the air cleaner assembly proceed to the following step otherwise proceed to step 5 in the installation procedure.

7. Loosen the MAF/IAT sensor adapter clamp.

8. Remove the MAF/IAT sensor and adapter.

To install:

➡ **If the MAF/IAT sensor is installed backwards, the fuel system goes rich. An arrow cast into the plastic portion of the sensor indicates proper air flow direction. The arrow must point toward the engine.**

9. If the air cleaner assembly was replaced proceed to the following step otherwise proceed to step 5.

10. Install the MAF/IAT sensor adapter clamp to the air cleaner assembly.

11. Install the MAF/IAT sensor

12. Tighten the MAF/IAT sensor adapter clamp.

13. Install the air cleaner assembly.

   a. Insert the locator on the right rear of the air cleaner into the inboard side of the slot in the adapter bracket.

   b. Slide the air cleaner towards the fender to engage the adapter.

   c. Push down on the air cleaner in order to install the retainers into the adapter bracket.

14. Connect the engine wiring harness electrical connector to the MAF/IAT sensor.

15. Install the air cleaner outlet duct.

FILTER/ELEMENT REPLACEMENT

V6 and V8 Gasoline Engines—Except Hybrids

See Figure 246.

1. Remove the air cleaner housing cover screws.

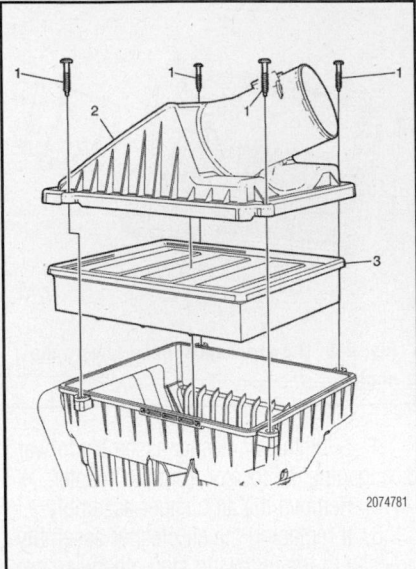

Fig. 246 Remove the cover screws (1), the air cleaner housing (2), and the air cleaner element (3)

2. Remove the air cleaner housing.
3. Remove the air cleaner element.
4. Installation is the reverse of removal.

Diesel Engines

See Figure 247.

1. Loosen the screw holding the air cleaner housing door in place.
2. Remove the air cleaner housing door.
3. Remove the air filter element.

To install:

4. Stand facing the front fender on the passenger side of the vehicle. Insert the element into the housing. Place the palm of your hand on the inboard end of the element, and press the element into position.

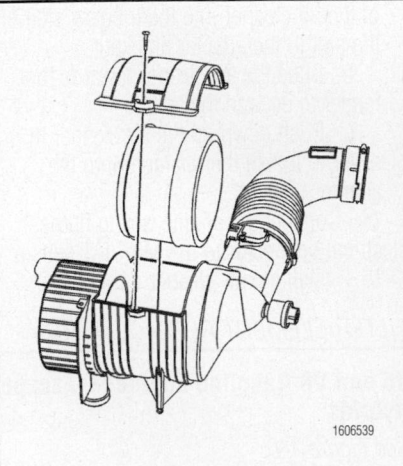

Fig. 247 Loosen the screw holding the air cleaner housing door in place

5. Press both downward and inboard until the outboard end of the element clicks into place inboard of the locating tab.
6. Install the air cleaner housing door and tighten the screw.

Hybrid Engines

See Figure 248.

1. Remove the 4 air filter housing screws.
2. Remove the air filter element.
3. Installation is the reverse of removal.

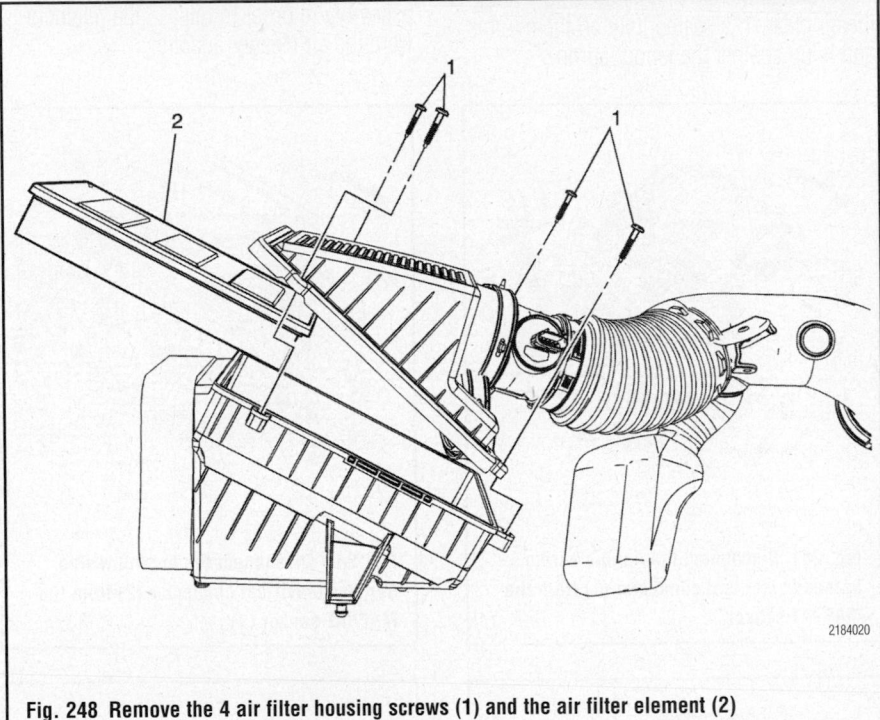

Fig. 248 Remove the 4 air filter housing screws (1) and the air filter element (2)

BALANCE SHAFT

REMOVAL & INSTALLATION

V6 Engines

See Figures 249 through 256.

Special Tools Required:
• J-8092 Universal Driver Handle
• J-36996 Balance Shaft Installer
• J-45059 Angle Meter

1. Remove the radiator.
2. Remove the Air Conditioning (A/C) condenser.
3. Remove the lifter pushrod guide.
4. Remove the timing chain and camshaft sprocket.
5. Remove the balance shaft drive gear.
6. Remove the balance shaft driven gear bolt.

   a. Use a wrench in order to secure the balance shaft. Place the wrench onto the balance shaft near to the balance shaft front bearing.

   b. Remove the balance shaft bolt.

   c. Remove the wrench from the balance shaft.

7. Remove the balance shaft driven gear.
8. Remove the balance shaft retainer bolts and retainer.

➡**The balance shaft and the balance shaft front bearing are serviced only as a package. Do not remove the balance**

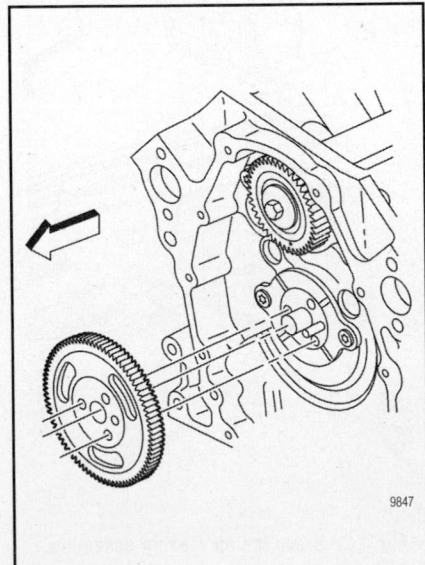

Fig. 249 Remove the balance shaft drive gear

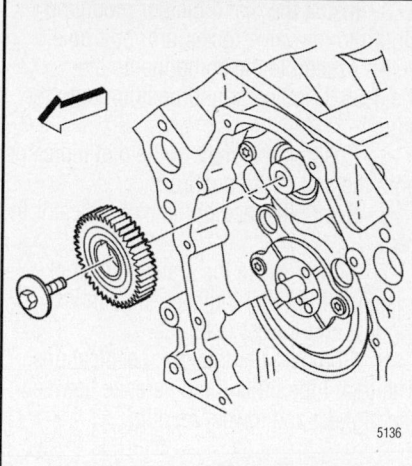

Fig. 250 Remove the balance shaft driven gear bolt

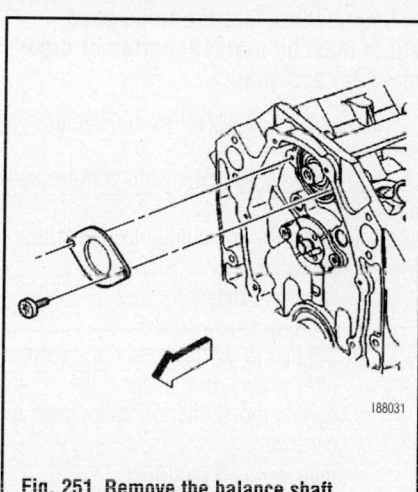

Fig. 251 Remove the balance shaft retainer bolts and retainer

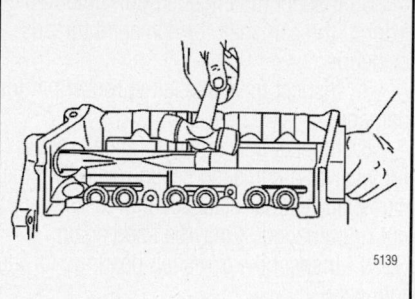

Fig. 252 Use a soft-faced hammer in order to remove the balance shaft from the engine block

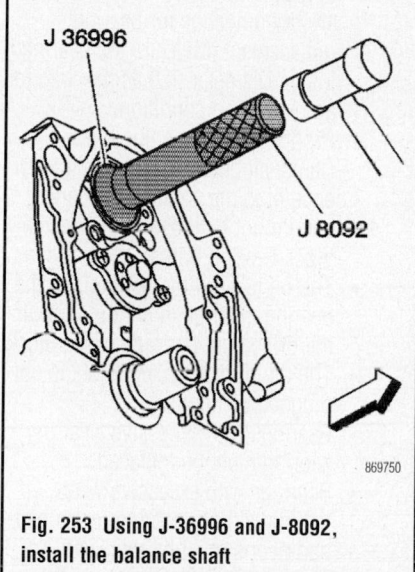

Fig. 253 Using J-36996 and J-8092, install the balance shaft

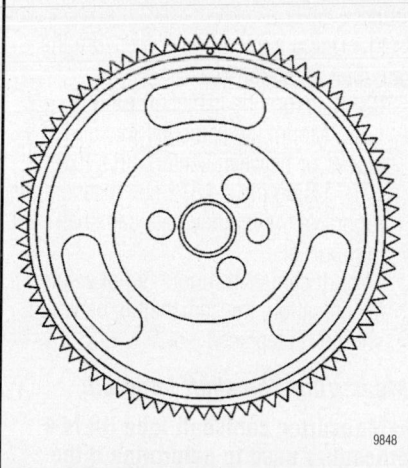

Fig. 254 Rotate the camshaft so that the timing mark on the balance shaft drive gear is in the 12 o'clock position

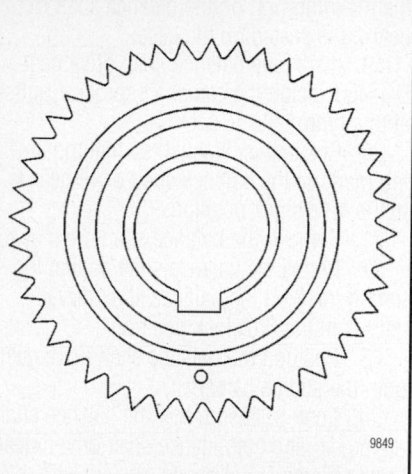

Fig. 255 Rotate the balance shaft so that the timing mark on the balance shaft driven gear is in the 6 o'clock position

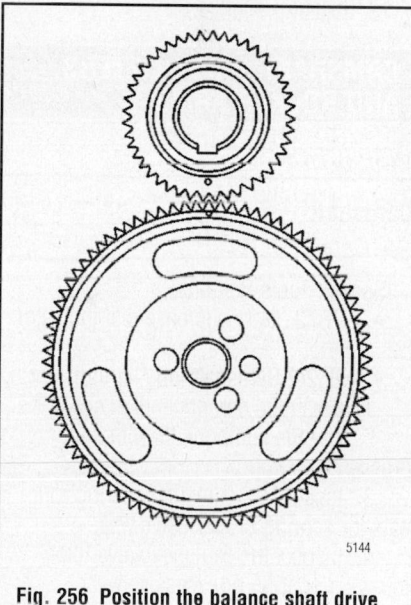

Fig. 256 Position the balance shaft drive gear onto the engine camshaft

shaft front bearing from the balance shaft.

9. Use a soft-faced hammer in order to remove the balance shaft from the engine block.

10. Clean and inspect the balance shaft, if necessary.

To install:

➡The balance shaft drive and balance shaft driven gears are serviced as a set. The set includes the balance shaft driven gear bolt.

11. Apply clean engine oil to the balance shaft front bearing.

12. Using J-36996 and J-8092, install the balance shaft.

13. Install the balance shaft retainer and bolts. Tighten the bolts to 106 inch lbs. (12 Nm).

14. Install the balance shaft driven gear.

15. If reusing the fastener, apply thread-locker to the threads of the balance shaft driven gear bolt.

16. Install the balance shaft driven gear bolt.

a. Use a wrench to secure the balance shaft. Place the wrench onto the balance shaft near to the balance shaft front bearing.

b. Install the balance shaft driven gear bolt.

c. Tighten the bolt a first pass to 15 ft. lbs. (20 Nm).

d. Tighten the bolt a final pass an additional 35 degrees using J-45059.

17. Remove the wrench from the balance shaft.

18. Rotate the balance shaft by hand in order to ensure that there is clearance between the balance shaft and the valve lifter pushrod guide. If the balance shaft does not rotate freely, check to ensure that

the retaining ring on the balance shaft front bearing is seated on the case.

19. Install the balance shaft drive gear. DO NOT install the camshaft sprocket bolts at this time.

20. Rotate the camshaft so that the timing mark on the balance shaft drive gear is in the 12 o'clock position.

21. Remove the balance shaft drive gear.

22. Rotate the balance shaft so that the timing mark on the balance shaft driven gear is in the 6 o'clock position.

23. Position the balance shaft drive gear onto the engine camshaft.

24. Look to ensure that the balance shaft drive gear and the balance shaft driven gear timing marks are aligned.

25. Install the timing chain and the camshaft sprocket.

26. Install the valve lifter pushrod guide.

27. Install the A/C condenser.

28. Install the radiator.

CAMSHAFT, VALVE LIFTERS, AND ROCKER ARMS

INSPECTION

Camshaft

See Figure 257.

Special Tools Required:
- J-7872: Magnetic base dial indicator set
- J-8520: Camshaft lobe lift indicator

1. Clean the components in solvent.

2. Dry the components with compressed air.

3. Inspect the camshaft bearing journals for scoring or excessive wear.

4. Inspect the camshaft valve lifter lobes for scoring or excessive wear.

5. Inspect the Camshaft Position (CMP) actuator oil passages for restrictions.

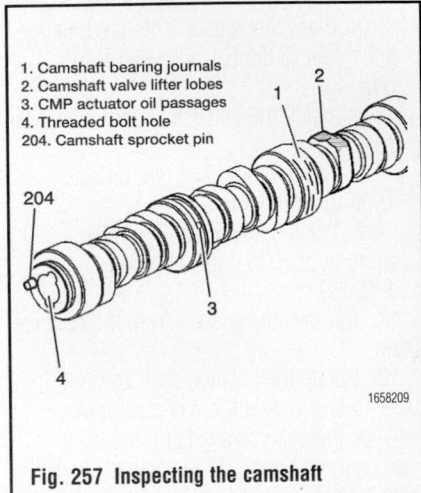

1. Camshaft bearing journals
2. Camshaft valve lifter lobes
3. CMP actuator oil passages
4. Threaded bolt hole
204. Camshaft sprocket pin

1658209

Fig. 257 Inspecting the camshaft

6. Inspect the threaded bolt hole in the front of the camshaft for damaged threads or debris.

7. Inspect the camshaft sprocket pin for damage.

8. Inspect the camshaft retainer plate for wear or a damaged sealing gasket. If the camshaft retainer plate sealing gasket is not cut or damaged, it may be used again.

9. Inspect the camshaft bearings for the following:
- Excessive wear, evidence of galling, pitting, scoring, or embedded debris. The appearance of the bearing material being different shades of gray are considered normal, and are not guideline for bearing replacement. Measure the bearing Inside Diameter (ID) as required for an over-sized condition.
- Proper fit in the engine block. Camshaft bearings have an interference fit to the engine block and should not be loose in the engine block bearing bores.
- The oil lubrication feed hole in the bearing must be in alignment with the drilled out passage in the block.
- The oil lubrication feed hole is not plugged by debris.
- Bearings with excessive wear or scoring must be replaced.
- Bearings with excessive wear, galling, pitting, scoring, or embedded debris must be replaced.

10. Using a micrometer, measure the camshaft journals for wear and out-of-round.

11. Using a micrometer, measure the camshaft lobes for wear.

12. Measure the camshaft runout.

a. Mount the camshaft in wooden V-blocks or between centers on a fixture.

b. Using the J-7872 set, measure the runout of the intermediate camshaft bearing journals.

c. If camshaft runout is not within specification, the camshaft is bent and should be replaced.

Measuring Camshaft Lobe Lift

➡️**Measuring camshaft lobe lift is a procedure used to determine if the camshaft lobes have worn. This test is to be performed prior to engine disassembly and with the camshaft and valve train components installed in the engine.**

1. Using the J-8520 indicator, measure camshaft lobe lift.

2. Remove the valve rocker arms and bolts.

3. Install the dial indicator mounting stud into the valve rocker arm bolt hole.

4. Assemble the components of the J-8520 indicator and position onto the stud.

5. Position the shaft of the dial indicator onto the end of the pushrod.

6. Rotate the face of the dial indicator to zero.

7. Slowly rotate the crankshaft clockwise, until the dial indicator obtains its highest and lowest readings.

8. Compare the total to specifications. The total lobe lift is the difference between the highest and lowest reading.

Non Active Fuel Management Valve Lifters

See Figure 258.

➡️**Components that are to be used again must be marked, sorted or organized for assembly.**

1. Clean the components in cleaning solvent.

2. Dry the components with compressed air.

3. Inspect the valve lifters for the following conditions:
- Bent or broken clip
- Worn pushrod socket
- Scuffed or worn sides: If the valve lifter shows wear, inspect the engine block lifter bores for wear or damage.
- Flat spots on the roller
- Loose or damaged pin
- Plugged oil hole
- Worn or damaged roller bearing: The roller should rotate freely with no binding or roughness.

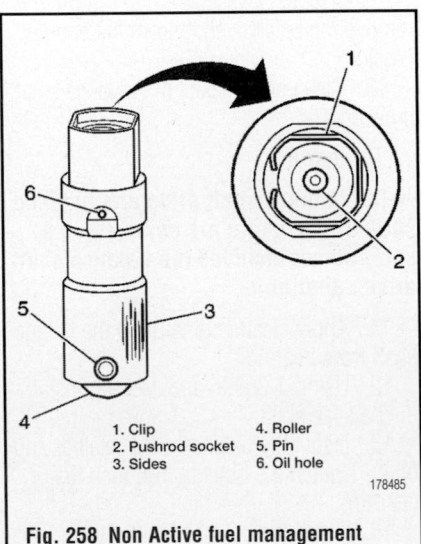

1. Clip
2. Pushrod socket
3. Sides
4. Roller
5. Pin
6. Oil hole

178485

Fig. 258 Non Active fuel management valve lifter

Active Fuel Management Valve Lifters

See Figure 259.

➡ **Components that are to be used again must be marked, sorted or organized for assembly.**

1. Clean the components in cleaning solvent.

2. Dry the components with compressed air.

3. Inspect the valve lifters for the following conditions:

- Broken or collapsed spring
- Worn pushrod socket
- Plugged lubrication hole
- Plugged lifter oil-switching hole
- Flat spots on the roller
- Worn or damaged roller bearing: The roller should rotate freely with no binding or roughness.
- Scuffed or worn sides

Valve Guides

1. Inspect the valve lifter guides for the following conditions:

- Cracks or damage
- Excessive wear in the lifter mounting bores

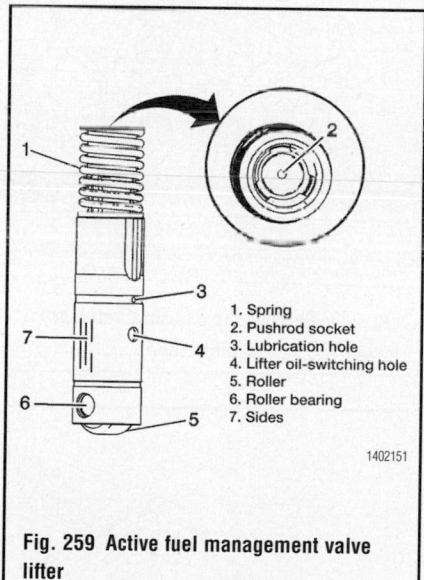

1. Spring
2. Pushrod socket
3. Lubrication hole
4. Lifter oil-switching hole
5. Roller
6. Roller bearing
7. Sides

1402151

Fig. 259 Active fuel management valve lifter

Valve Rocker Arms and Pushrods

See Figure 260.

➡ **Parts that are to be used again must be marked, sorted or organized for assembly.**

1. Mark, sort, or organize the components for assembly.

2. Clean the components with cleaning solvent.

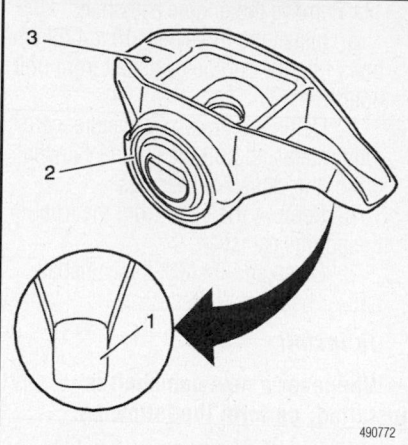

490772

Fig. 260 Rocker arm showing valve stem mating surface (1), rocker arm bearing (2), and pushrod sockets (3)

3. Dry the components with compressed air.

4. Inspect the valve rocker arms bearings for binding or roughness.

5. Inspect the valve rocker arm pushrod sockets and valve stem mating surfaces. These surfaces should be smooth with no scoring or exceptional wear.

6. Inspect the pushrods for worn or scored ends. These surfaces should be smooth with no scoring or exceptional wear.

7. Inspect the pushrods for bends. Roll the pushrod on a flat surface to determine if the pushrod is bent.

8. Inspect the pushrod oil passages for restrictions.

9. Inspect the rocker arm pivot supports for cracks, wear, or other damage.

REMOVAL & INSTALLATION

V6 Engines

See Figures 261 through 266.

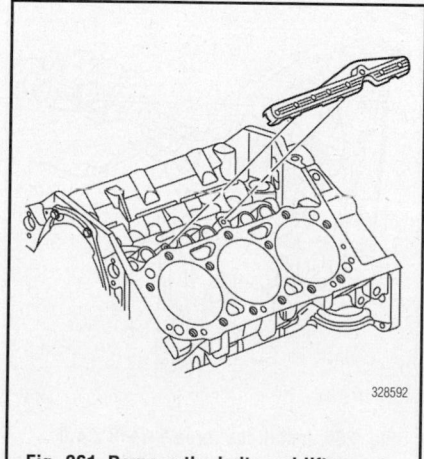

328592

Fig. 261 Remove the bolts and lifter pushrod guide

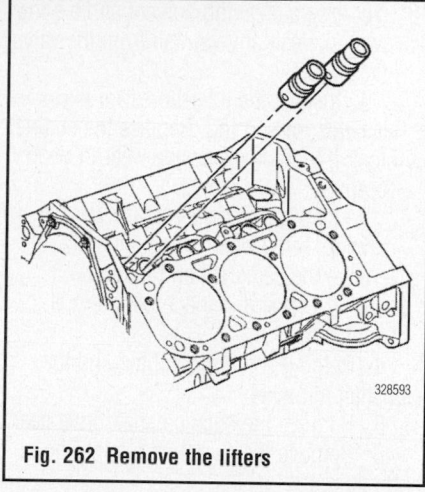

328593

Fig. 262 Remove the lifters

1. Remove the radiator.
2. Remove the Air Conditioning (A/C) condenser.
3. Remove the lifters.
   a. Remove the intake manifold.
   b. Remove the pushrods.

➡ **Place the components in a rack so that the components can be installed to their original location.**

   c. Remove the bolts and lifter pushrod guide.

➡ **Place the valve lifters in the rack in the upright position in order to maintain the oil inside the valve lifters.**

   d. Remove the lifters.

➡ **Some valve lifters may be stuck in the valve lifter bores because of gum or varnish deposits and may require the use of the Valve Lifter Remover (J-3049-A) for removal.**

   e. Use the J-3049-A in order to remove the stuck valve lifters.

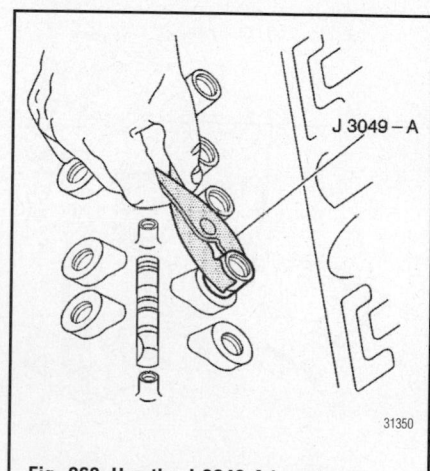

J 3049-A

31350

Fig. 263 Use the J-3049-A in order to remove the stuck valve lifters

f. Use a cleaning solvent and a shop towel to clean any varnish from the valve lifter bores.

g. Inspect the lifter bores for excessive wear or scoring. Replace the engine block if there is excessive wear or deep scoring.

h. Inspect the camshaft for wear or damage. If the wear is questionable remove the camshaft and inspect.

i. Clean and inspect the lifters, if necessary.

4. Remove the timing chain and the camshaft sprocket.

5. Remove the balance shaft drive gear.

6. Remove the camshaft retainer bolts and retainer.

> ❋❋ **CAUTION**
>
> **All camshaft journals are the same diameter, so care must be used in removing or installing the camshaft to avoid damage to the camshaft bearings.**

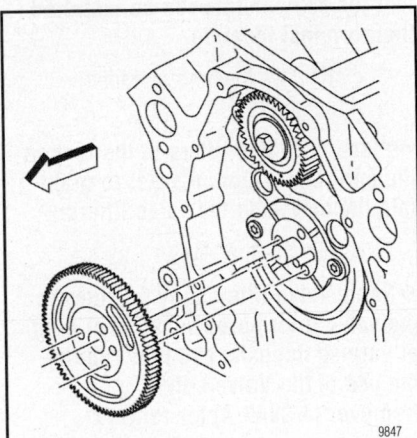

Fig. 264 Remove the timing chain and the camshaft sprocket

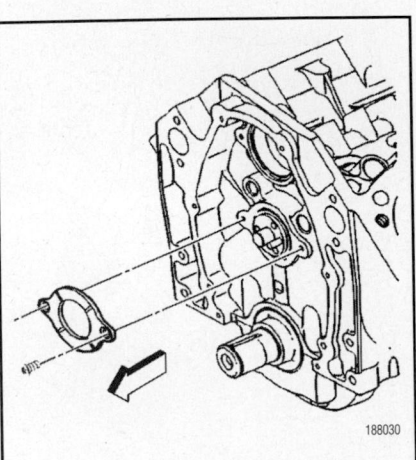

Fig. 265 Remove the camshaft retainer bolts and retainer

7. Remove the engine camshaft.

a. Install the three ⁵⁄₁₆–18 x 4.0 inch bolts into the engine camshaft front bolt holes.

b. Using the bolts as a handle, carefully rotate and pull the engine camshaft out of the camshaft bearings.

c. Remove the bolts from the front of the engine camshaft.

d. Clean and inspect the camshaft and/or bearings, if necessary.

To install:

➡ **Whenever a new camshaft is installed, perform the following:**

- Change the engine oil and filter.
- Add engine oil supplement to the engine oil.

8. Apply lubricant or engine oil supplement to the following components:

- The engine camshaft lobes
- The camshaft bearing journals
- The camshaft bearings

9. Install three ⁵⁄₁₆–18 x 4.0 inch bolts into the engine camshaft front bolt holes.

> ❋❋ **CAUTION**
>
> **All camshaft journals are the same diameter, so care must be used in removing or installing the camshaft to avoid damage to the camshaft bearings.**

10. Using the bolts as a handle, install the engine camshaft.

11. Remove the 3 bolts from the front of the engine camshaft.

12. If reusing the fasteners, apply threadlocker to the threads of the camshaft retainer bolts.

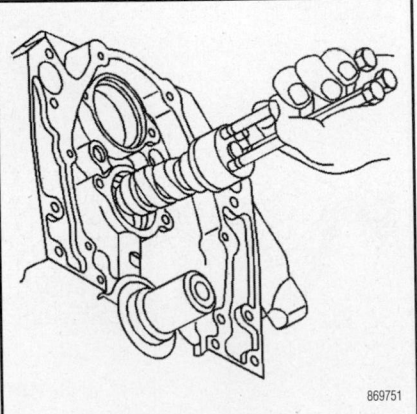

Fig. 266 Install the three ⁵⁄₁₆–18 x 4.0 inch bolts into the engine camshaft front bolt holes

13. Install the camshaft retainer and bolts. Tighten the bolts to 106 inch lbs. (12 Nm).

14. Install the balance shaft drive gear. Refer to Balance Shaft Installation, for alignment of the balance shaft drive gear and the driven gear.

15. Install the timing chain and camshaft sprocket.

16. Install the lifters.

17. Install the A/C condenser.

18. Install the radiator.

V8 Engines Including Hybrids

Camshaft

See Figures 267 and 268.

1. Remove the radiator support.

2. Remove the valve lifters.

3. Remove the Timing Chain, Camshaft Position Actuator, and Solenoid Valve.

4. Remove the camshaft retainer bolts and retainer.

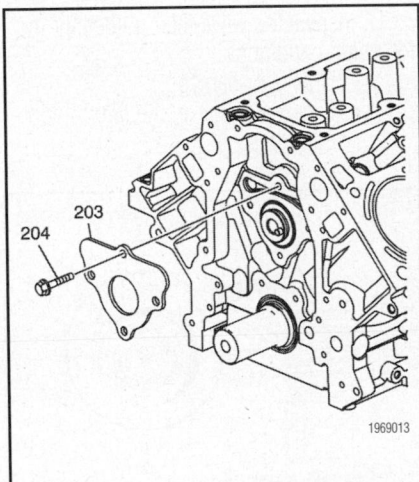

Fig. 267 Remove the camshaft retainer bolts (204) and retainer (203)

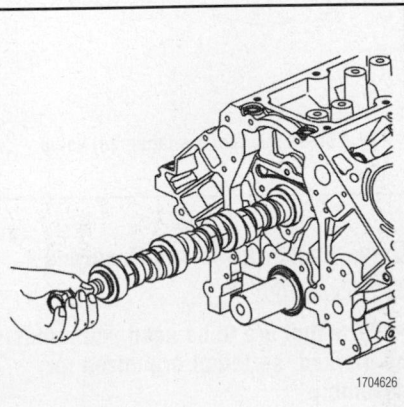

Fig. 268 Using the bolt as a handle, carefully rotate and pull the camshaft out of the engine block

> ※※ **CAUTION**
>
> **All camshaft journals are the same diameter, so care must be used in removing or installing the camshaft to avoid damage to the camshaft bearings.**

5. Install a bolt into the camshaft.

6. Using the bolt as a handle, carefully rotate and pull the camshaft out of the engine block.

7. Clean and inspect the camshaft and bearings.

To install:

➡**If camshaft replacement is required, the valve lifters must also be replaced.**

8. Lubricate the camshaft journals and the bearings with clean engine oil.

> ※※ **CAUTION**
>
> **All camshaft journals are the same diameter, so care must be used in removing or installing the camshaft to avoid damage to the camshaft bearings.**

9. Using the bolt as a handle, carefully install the camshaft into the engine block.

10. Remove the bolt from the front of the camshaft.

➡**Install the retainer with the sealing gasket facing the engine block. The gasket surface on the engine block should be clean and free of dirt and/or debris.**

11. Install the camshaft retainer (203) and bolts (204).

12. Tighten the camshaft retainer bolts.

　a. Tighten the first design hex head bolts to 18 ft. lbs. (25 Nm).

　b. Tighten the second design TORX head bolts to 11 ft. lbs. (15 Nm).

13. Install the Timing Chain, Camshaft Position Actuator, and Solenoid Valve.

14. Install the valve lifters.

15. Install the radiator support.

Valve Lifters Without Active Fuel Management (AFM)

See Figures 269 and 270.

1. Remove the cylinder head and gasket.

2. Remove the valve lifter guide bolts.

3. Remove the valve lifter guides with the lifters. Note the installed position of the guides. The notched area of the guides is to align with the locating tab on the engine block.

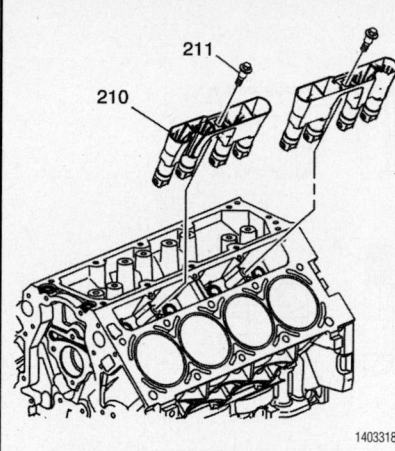

Fig. 269 Remove the valve lifter guide bolts (211) and the valve lifter guides (210) with the lifters

4. Remove the valve lifters from the guide.

5. Organize or mark the components so that they can be installed in the same location from which they were removed, if required.

6. Clean and inspect the valve lifters, if required.

To install:

➡**Note the following:**

- If camshaft replacement is required, the valve lifters must also be replaced.
- When reusing valve lifters, install the lifters to their original locations

7. Lubricate the valve lifters and engine block valve lifter bores with clean engine oil.

8. Insert the valve lifters into the lifter guides. Align the flat area on the top of the

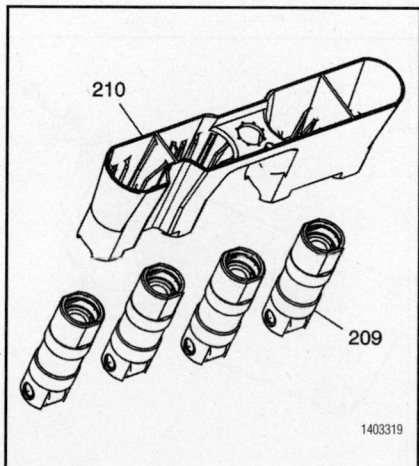

Fig. 270 Remove the valve lifters (209) from the guide (210)

lifter with the flat area in the lifter guide bore. Push the lifter completely into the guide bore.

9. Install the valve lifters and guide to the engine block.

10. Install the valve lifter guide bolts. Tighten the bolt to 106 inch lbs. (12 Nm).

11. Install the cylinder head and gasket.

Valve Lifters With Active Fuel Management (AFM)

See Figures 271 through 273.

1. Remove the cylinder head and gasket.

2. Remove the valve lifter guide bolts.

3. Remove the valve lifter guides with the lifters. Note the installed position of the guides. The notched area of the guides is to align with the locating tab on the engine block.

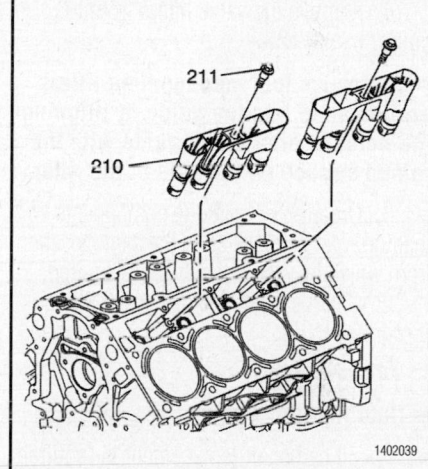

Fig. 271 Remove the valve lifter guide bolts (211) and the valve lifter guides (210) with the lifters

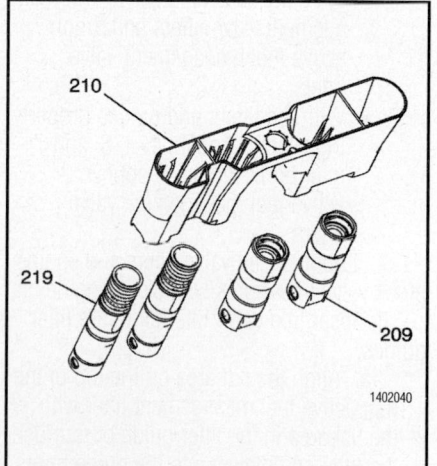

Fig. 272 Remove the valve lifters (209, 219) from the guide (210)

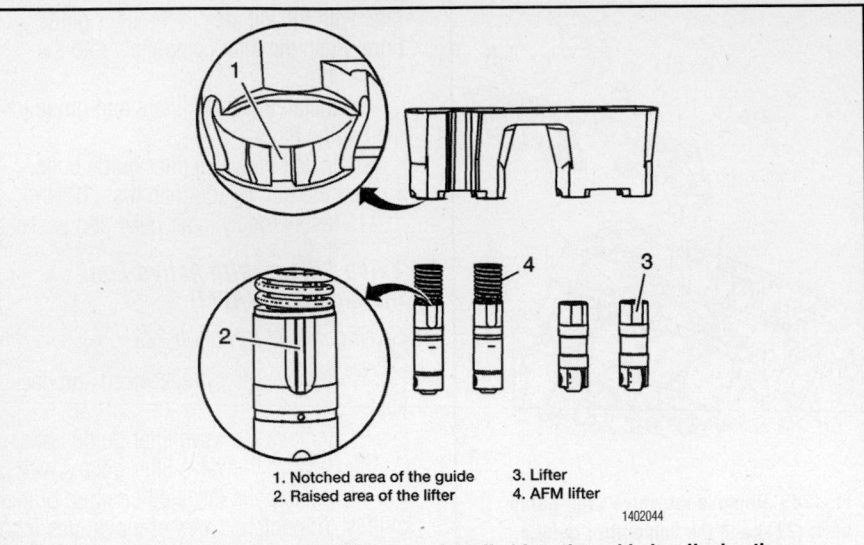

1. Notched area of the guide
2. Raised area of the lifter
3. Lifter
4. AFM lifter

1402044

Fig. 273 The active fuel management lifters are installed into the guide by aligning the notched area of the guide with the raised surface on the side of the lifter

4. Remove the valve lifters from the guide.

➡ **The active fuel management lifters are installed into the guide by aligning the notched area of the guide with the raised surface on the side of the lifter.**

5. Organize or mark the components so that they can be installed in the same location from which they were removed, if required.

6. Clean and inspect the valve lifters, if required.

To install:

➡ **Note the following:**

- If camshaft replacement is required, the valve lifters must also be replaced.
- When reusing valve lifters, install the lifters to their original locations.
- Each of the 4 valve guide assemblies will contain 2 active fuel management valve lifters and 2 non active fuel management valve lifters.
- With the lifters and guides properly installed, cylinders 1, 4, 6, and 7 lifter bores will each contain 2 active fuel management valve lifters.

7. Lubricate the valve lifters and engine block valve lifter bores with clean engine oil.

8. Insert the valve lifters into the lifter guides.

   a. Align the flat area on the top of the non active fuel management lifter with the flat area in the lifter guide bore. Push the lifter completely into the guide bore.

   b. The active fuel management lifters are to be installed into the guide, with the notch in the guide aligned with the raised area of the lifter.

9. Install the valve lifters and guide to the engine block.

10. Install the valve lifter guide bolts. Tighten the bolt to 106 inch lbs. (12 Nm).

11. Install the cylinder head and gasket.

Rocker arms and Push rods
See Figures 274 through 276.

1. Remove the rocker arm cover.

➡ **The engine firing order is 1, 8, 7, 2, 6, 5, 4, 3. Cylinders 1, 3, 5 and 7 are the left bank.**

2. Remove the number one cylinder spark plug.

➡ **Place the rocker arms, pushrods, and pivot support, in a rack so that they can be installed in the same location from which they were removed.**

3. Remove the rocker arm bolts.
4. Remove the rocker arms.
5. Remove the rocker arm pivot support.
6. Remove the pushrods.
7. Clean and inspect the rocker arms and pushrods, if required.

To install:

➡ **When reusing the valve train components, always install the components to the original location and position.**

➡ **Valve lash is net build, no valve adjustment is required.**

8. Lubricate the rocker arms and pushrods with clean engine oil.

9. Lubricate the flange of the rocker arm bolts with clean engine oil. Lubricate the flange or washer surface of the bolt that will contact the rocker arm.

10. Install the rocker arm pivot support.

➡ **Make sure that the pushrods seat properly to the valve lifter sockets.**

11. Install the pushrods.

➡ **Make sure that the pushrods seat properly to the ends of the rocker arms. DO NOT tighten the rocker arm bolts at this time.**

12. Install the rocker arms and bolts.

➡ **The engine firing order is 1, 8, 7, 2, 6, 5, 4, 3. Cylinders 1, 3, 5 and 7 are the left bank. Cylinders 2, 4, 6 and 8 are the right bank.**

13. Rotate the crankshaft until the number one piston is at top dead center (TDC) of the compression stroke. In this position, the number one cylinder rocker arms will be off lobe lift.

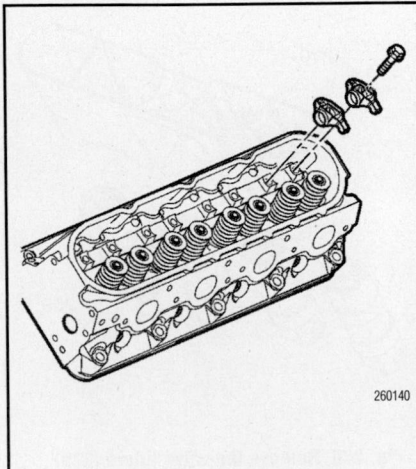

260140

Fig. 274 Remove the rocker arm bolts

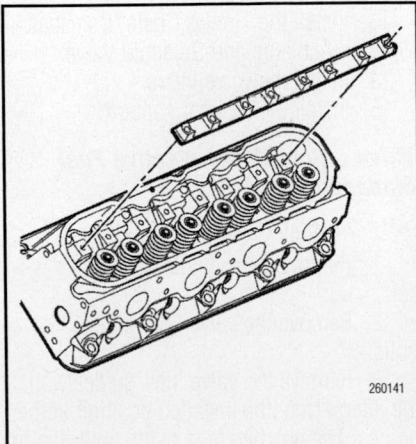

260141

Fig. 275 Remove the rocker arm pivot support

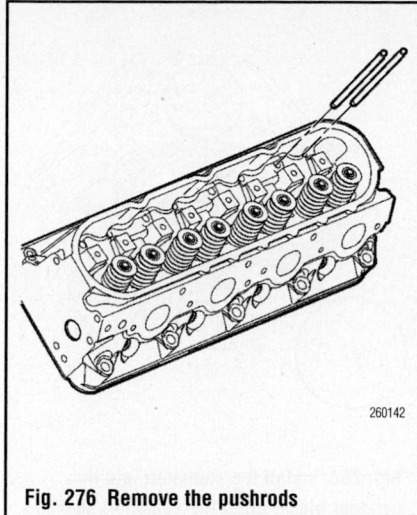

Fig. 276 Remove the pushrods

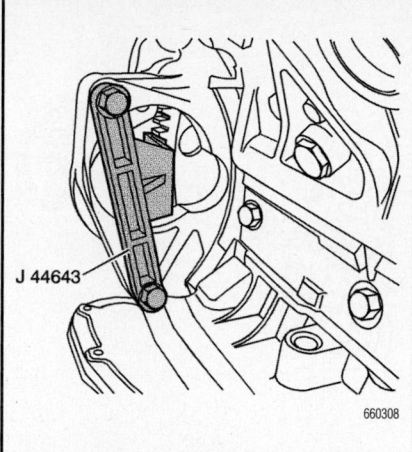

Fig. 277 Install J-44643 tool (2) flush to the flywheel (1) opening

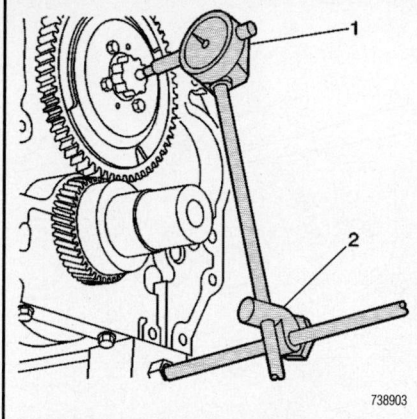

Fig. 280 Using J-26900-12 indicator (1) and J-26900-13 base (2), measure the camshaft end play

14. With the engine in the number one firing position, tighten the following rocker arm bolts:

 a. Tighten cylinders 1,2,7 and 8 exhaust valve rocker arm bolts to 22 ft. lbs. (30 Nm).

 b. Tighten cylinders 1,3,4 and 5 intake valve rocker arm bolts to 22 ft. lbs. (30 Nm).

15. Rotate the crankshaft 360 degrees.

16. Tighten the following rocker arm bolts:

 a. Tighten cylinders 3, 4, 5 and 6 exhaust valve rocker arm bolts to 22 ft. lbs. (30 Nm).

 b. Tighten cylinders 2, 6, 7 and 8 intake valve rocker arm bolts to 22 ft. lbs. (30 Nm).

17. Install the number one cylinder spark plug.

18. Install the rocker arm cover.

Diesel Engines

Camshaft

See Figures 277 through 286.

Special Tools Required:
- J-26900-12 Dial Indicator
- J-26900-13 Magnetic Base
- J-44643 Flywheel Holding Tool

1. Remove the engine assembly.

2. Remove the valve lifters.

3. Install J-44643 tool flush to the flywheel opening.

4. Remove the engine front cover.

5. Remove the oil pump driven gear nut.

6. Remove the oil pump driven gear.

➡ The crankshaft reluctor and the oil pump drive gear are timed together at the factory. Do not remove the crankshaft reluctor from the oil pump drive gear.

Fig. 278 Remove the oil pump driven gear nut

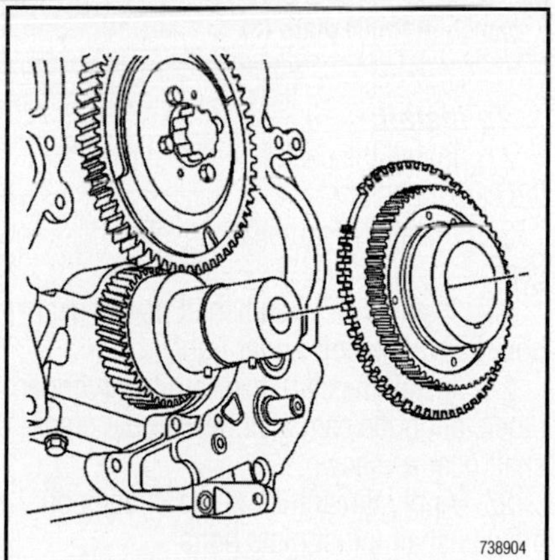

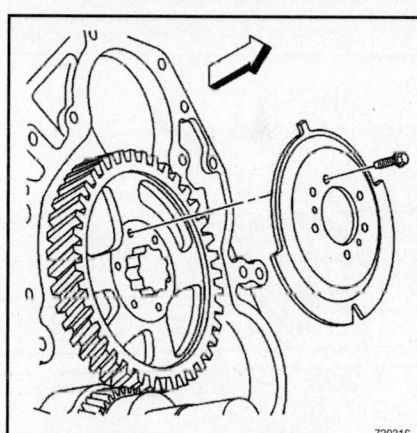

Fig. 279 Remove the oil pump drive gear and crankshaft reluctor (1)

7. Remove the oil pump drive gear and crankshaft reluctor.

 a. Do not remove the crankshaft reluctor bolts.

 b. Do not damage the reluctor teeth.

Fig. 281 Remove the camshaft reluctor screws (1) and the camshaft reluctor (2); camshaft gear (3)

8. Using J-26900-12 indicator and J-26900-13 base, measure the camshaft end play.

 a. The production value is 0.002–0.0045 inches (0.050–0.114 mm) and service limit is 0.0008 inches (0.20 mm).

 b. Replace the camshaft gear or the camshaft thrust plate if measured value exceeds the service limit.

9. Remove the camshaft reluctor screws.

10. Remove the camshaft reluctor.

✳✳ WARNING

The two piece cam gear must be bolted together to prevent the spring tension from unloading upon removal. Additionally, the two piece cam gear must remain bolted together until it is re-installed to the camshaft and fully engaged to the crankshaft gear. Failure to do so may result in personal injury.

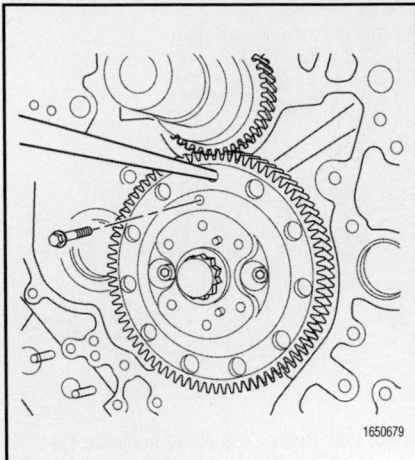

Fig. 282 Align the threaded hole with a suitable tool and install an exciter ring bolt to secure the spring tension

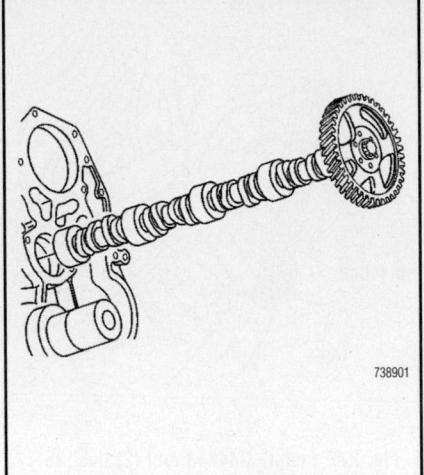

Fig. 284 Remove the camshaft (1) with the camshaft gear (2) attached

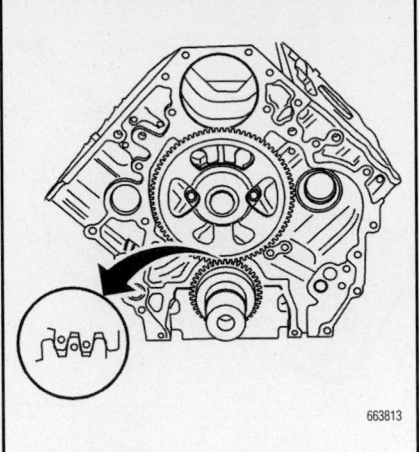

Fig. 286 Install the camshaft into the cylinder block, align the camshaft gear to the crankshaft gear as shown

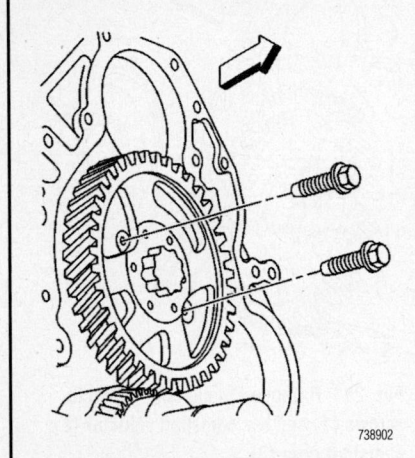

Fig. 283 Remove the camshaft thrust plate bolts (1) through the holes in the camshaft gear (2)

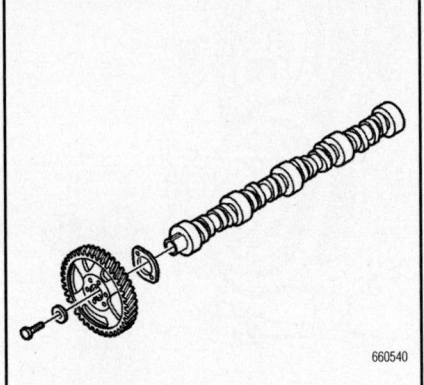

Fig. 285 Remove the camshaft gear bolt (1), the camshaft gear (2), and the camshaft thrust plate (3)

11. Remove the camshaft exciter ring.

12. Align the threaded hole with a suitable tool and install an exciter ring bolt to secure the spring tension.

13. In order to loosen the camshaft gear bolt use J-44643 tool in order to hold the engine from turning.

14. Loosen the camshaft gear bolt and leave the bolt finger tight.

15. Remove the camshaft thrust plate bolts through the holes in the camshaft gear.

16. Remove the camshaft with the camshaft gear attached.

17. Remove the camshaft gear bolt and discard.

18. Remove the camshaft gear.

19. Remove the camshaft thrust plate.

20. Clean and inspect the camshaft and bearings.

To install:

21. Install the camshaft thrust plate to the camshaft.

22. Install the camshaft driven gear.

23. Install a NEW camshaft driven gear bolt. Leave the bolt finger tight.

24. Install the camshaft into the cylinder block, align the camshaft gear to the crankshaft gear as shown.

25. Apply threadlock to the threads of the camshaft thrust plate bolts.

26. Install the camshaft thrust plate bolts and tighten to 16 ft. lbs. (22 Nm).

➡**Use a suitable tool to relieve the spring tension while removing the locking bolt.**

27. Remove the exciter ring bolt that was installed to hold the spring tension of the two piece cam gear.

28. Install the camshaft reluctor to the camshaft gear.

29. Install the camshaft reluctor bolts. Tighten the bolts in a cross-bolt pattern to 80 inch lbs. (9 Nm).

30. Reinstall J-44643 tool in the starter opening, if removed.

31. Install a NEW camshaft gear bolt and tighten to 173 ft. lbs. (234 Nm).

32. Using J-26900-12 indicator and J-26900-13 base measure the camshaft end play.

 a. The production value is 0.002–0.0045 inches (0.050–0.114 mm) and service limit is 0.0008 inches (0.20 mm).

 b. Replace the camshaft gear or the camshaft thrust plate if measured value exceeds the service limit.

➡**Do not damage the teeth on the crankshaft reluctor.**

33. Install the oil pump drive gear and reluctor to the crankshaft.

34. Install the oil pump driven gear.

35. Install the oil pump driven gear nut and tighten to 74 ft. lbs. (100 Nm).

36. Install the engine front cover.

37. Install the engine assembly.

38. Install the valve lifters.

Valve Lifters

See Figure 287.

1. Remove the cylinder head.

2. Loosen the valve lifter guide retainer bolts.

3. Remove the valve lifter guide retainers.

4. Remove the valve lifter guides.

5. Remove the valve lifters.

6. If required, clean and inspect the lifters.

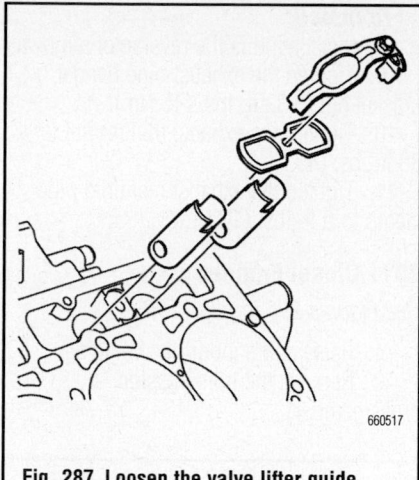

Fig. 287 Loosen the valve lifter guide retainer bolts

To install:

7. Apply clean engine oil to the roller and outside of the valve lifter.

8. Install the valve lifter.

9. Install the valve lifter guides.

10. Install the valve lifter guide retainer.

11. Install the valve lifter guide retainer bolt. Tighten the bolt to 97 inch lbs. (11 Nm).

12. Install the cylinder head.

CATALYTIC CONVERTER

REMOVAL & INSTALLATION

Catalytic Converter with Exhaust Clamp

See Figure 288.

1. Remove the engine skid plate (if equipped).

2. Remove the transmission support crossmember.

3. Disconnect the oxygen sensors.

4. Remove the left exhaust manifold nuts.

5. Remove the seal.

6. Remove the right exhaust manifold nuts.

7. Remove the seal.

8. Remove the exhaust muffler clamp nut.

➡**Replace the exhaust muffler clamp with a NEW clamp.**

9. Remove the catalytic converter.

To install:

10. Installation is the reverse of removal.

11. Tighten the exhaust muffler clamp to 21 ft. lbs. (28 Nm).

12. Tighten the right exhaust manifold nuts to 37 ft. lbs. (50 Nm).

13. Torque the left rear nut first and then

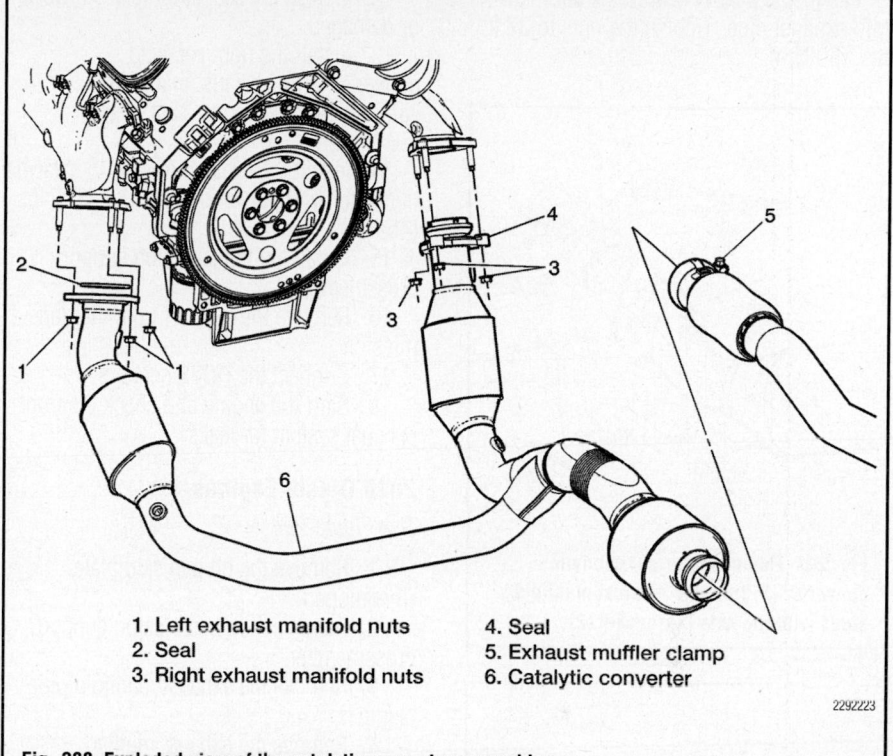

1. Left exhaust manifold nuts
2. Seal
3. Right exhaust manifold nuts
4. Seal
5. Exhaust muffler clamp
6. Catalytic converter

Fig. 288 Exploded view of the catalytic converter assembly

the remaining left catalytic converter nuts. Tighten the catalytic converter nuts to 37 ft. lbs. (50 Nm).

6.0L Engine with Fleetside Body

See Figures 289 through 293.

1. Disconnect the Heated Oxygen Sensor (HO2S).

2. Support the transmission with a suitable transmission jack.

3. Remove the transmission support crossmember.

4. Remove the exhaust muffler to exhaust manifold pipe nuts.

5. Remove the exhaust manifold pipe to exhaust manifold nuts and replace the seal with a NEW one.

6. Remove the right catalytic converter from the exhaust manifold studs with the nuts.

7. Separate the catalytic converter hanger rod from the exhaust isolator.

8. With the aid of an assistant, lower the catalytic converter from the vehicle.

9. If replacing the catalytic converter, transfer the oxygen sensors.

To install:

10. Install the catalytic converter hanger rod into the exhaust isolator.

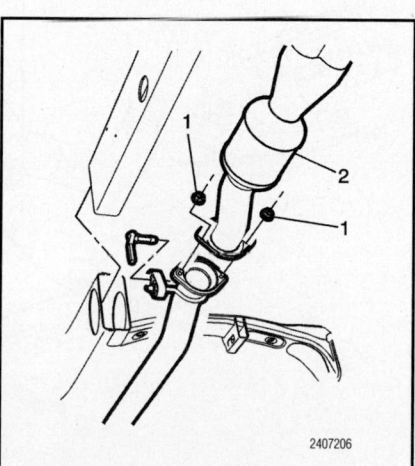

Fig. 289 Remove the exhaust muffler (2) to exhaust manifold pipe nuts (1)

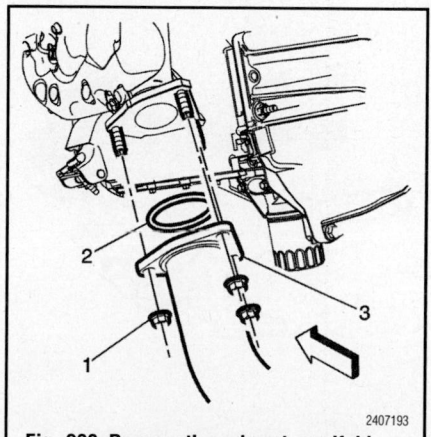

Fig. 290 Remove the exhaust manifold pipe to exhaust manifold nuts (1) and the seal (2); exhaust flange (3)

11. Install a NEW seal to the left manifold exhaust pipe. Tighten the nuts to 37 ft. lbs. (50 Nm).

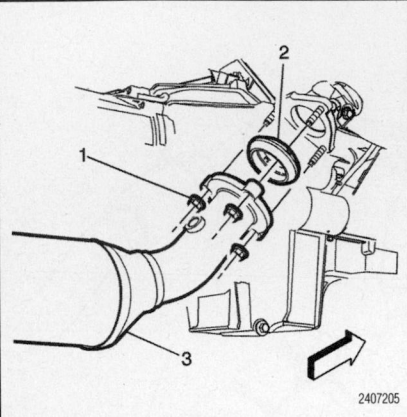

Fig. 291 Remove the right catalytic converter (3) from the exhaust manifold studs with the nuts (1); gasket (2)

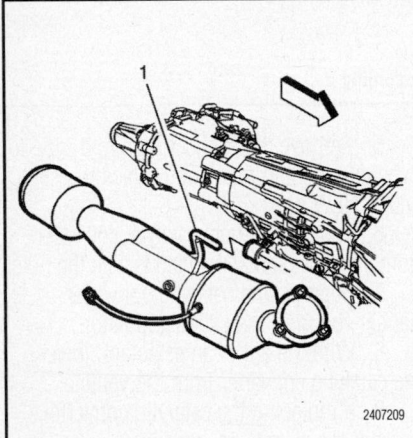

Fig. 292 Separate the catalytic converter hanger rod (1) from the exhaust isolator

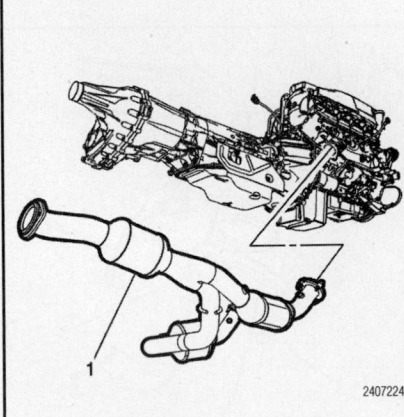

Fig. 293 With the aid of an assistant, lower the catalytic converter (1) from the vehicle

12. Inspect the seal and replace if worn or damaged.

13. Install the right catalytic converter to the exhaust manifold with nuts and tighten to 37 ft. lbs. (50 Nm).

14. Install the exhaust muffler to catalytic converter with nuts and tighten to 33 ft. lbs. (45 Nm).

15. Install the transmission support crossmember.

16. Remove the support from the transmission.

17. Connect the HO2S sensors.

18. Start the engine and check the front exhaust system for leaks

2010 Diesel Engines

See Figure 294.

1. Remove the oil pan skid plate (if equipped).

2. Remove the transmission support crossmember.

3. Remove the exhaust manifold pipe clamp.

4. Remove the exhaust muffler nut.

5. Remove the gasket.

6. Remove the exhaust pipe hanger bracket nut.

7. Remove the catalytic converter.

To install:

8. Installation is the reverse of removal.

9. Tighten the exhaust pipe hanger bracket nut to 33 ft. lbs. (45 Nm).

10. Tighten the exhaust muffler nut to 33 ft. lbs. (45 Nm).

11. Tighten the exhaust manifold pipe clamp to 9 ft. lbs. (12 Nm).

2011 Diesel Engines

See Figures 295 through 298.

1. Raise and support the vehicle.

2. Remove the transmission crossmember.

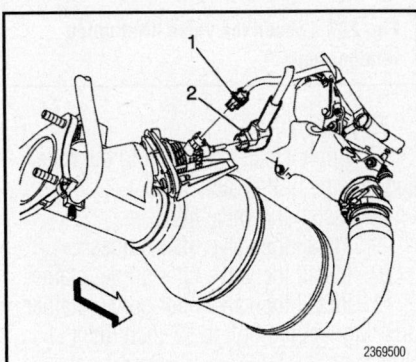

Fig. 295 Disconnect the engine harness connector (1), the emission reduction fluid injector connector (2), and the temperature sensor from the catalytic converter

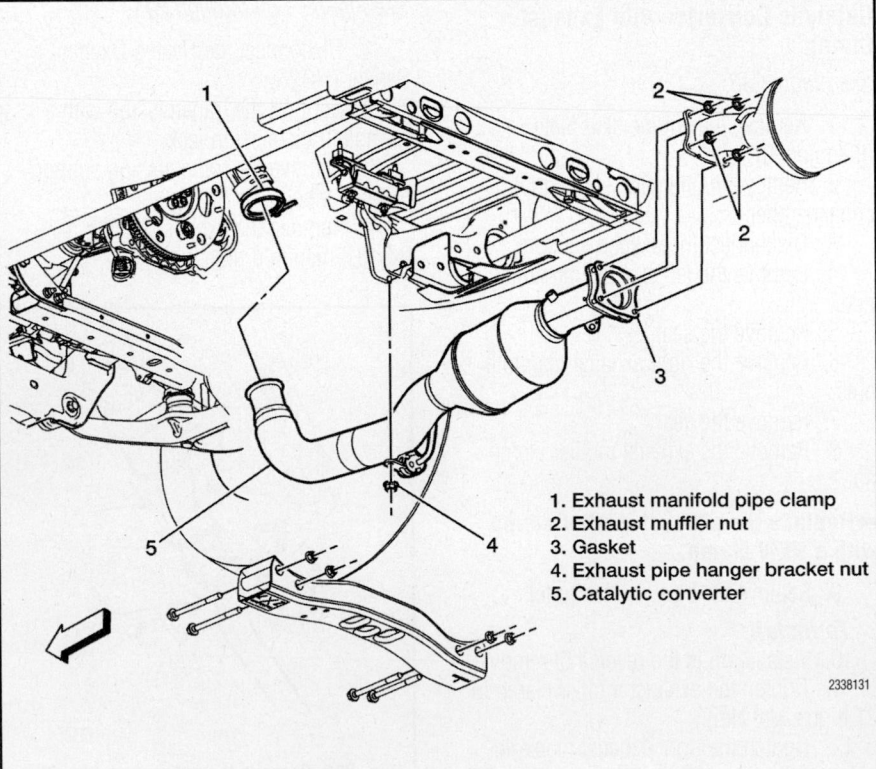

1. Exhaust manifold pipe clamp
2. Exhaust muffler nut
3. Gasket
4. Exhaust pipe hanger bracket nut
5. Catalytic converter

Fig. 294 Exploded view of the catalytic converter assembly

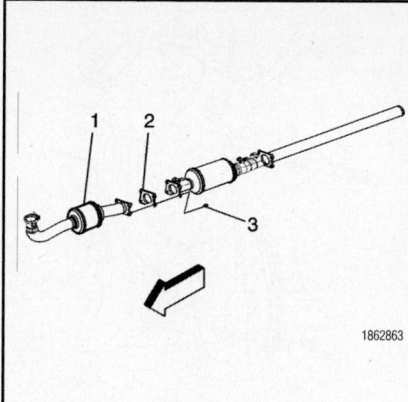

Fig. 296 Remove the catalytic converter (1) to diesel particulate filter nuts (3); gasket (2)

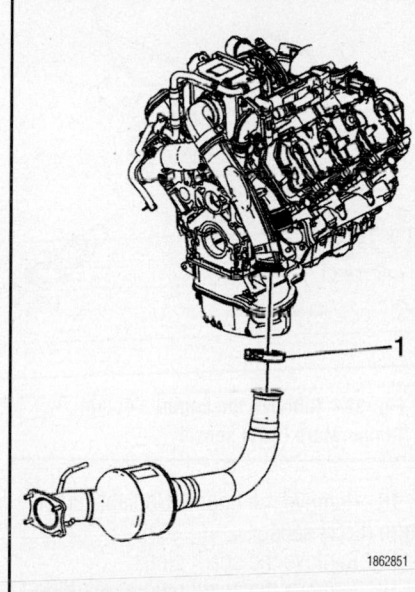

Fig. 297 Loosen the turbocharger exhaust pipe-to-catalytic converter clamp (1)

3. Disconnect the engine harness connector, the emission reduction fluid injector connector, and the temperature sensor from the catalytic converter.

4. Remove the catalytic converter to diesel particulate filter nuts.

5. Loosen the turbocharger exhaust pipe-to-catalytic converter clamp.

6. Remove the exhaust hanger bracket bolt and bracket stud.

7. With the catalytic converter exhaust isolator attached, lower the catalytic converter with the exhaust bracket.

8. If replacing catalytic converter, transfer the exhaust isolator and the exhaust temperature sensor.

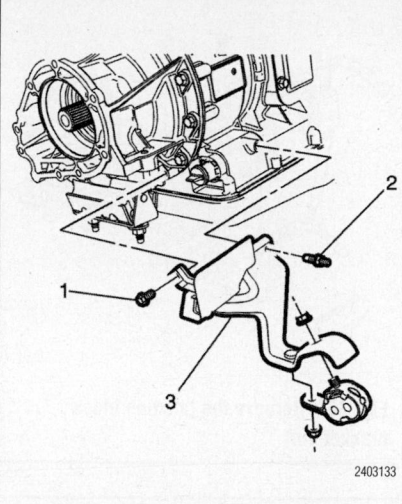

Fig. 298 Remove the exhaust hanger bracket bolt (1) and bracket stud (2); exhaust bracket (3)

To install:

9. If replacing the catalytic converter, apply water based lubricant to the exhaust isolator for ease of installation.

10. Position the catalytic converter to the turbocharger exhaust outlet pipe.

11. Position the catalytic converter with the exhaust bracket to the engine.

12. Tighten the bolt and stud to 18 ft. lbs. (25 Nm).

13. Install a NEW catalytic converter to diesel particulate filter gasket.

14. Install the catalytic converter to particulate filter nuts until snug.

➡ **Ensure that the manifold pipe is square to the exhaust pipe adapter.**

15. Slide the exhaust pipe clamp down and around the pipe connection.

16. Tighten the exhaust pipe clamp to 106 inch lbs. (12 Nm).

17. Tighten the catalytic to diesel particulate filter nuts to 33 ft. lbs. (45 Nm).

18. Connect the emission reduction fluid injector connector and the engine harness connector.

19. Install the transmission crossmember.
20. Lower the vehicle.
21. Start the engine and check for leaks.
22. Perform the scan tool Diesel Particulate Filter (DPF) Regeneration Enable.

CRANKSHAFT FRONT SEAL

REMOVAL & INSTALLATION

V6 Engines

1. Remove the crankshaft balancer.

2. Inspect the engine front cover seal bore area for damage.

3. Use a suitable seal puller, remove the crankshaft front oil seal.

To install:

4. Lubricate the exterior of the NEW seal with clean engine oil.

5. Using the Cover Aligner and Seal Installer (J-35468) and a hammer, install the crankshaft front oil seal.

6. Ensure the crankshaft front oil seal is flush and square to the engine front cover.

7. Install the crankshaft balancer.

V8 Engines Including Hybrids

1. Remove the crankshaft balancer.
2. Remove the crankshaft front oil seal from the front cover.

To install:

➡ **Do not lubricate the oil seal sealing surface. Do not reuse the crankshaft front oil seal.**

3. Lubricate the outer edge of the oil seal with clean engine oil.

4. Lubricate the front cover oil seal bore with clean engine oil.

5. Install the crankshaft front oil seal onto the J-41478 guide.

6. Install the J-41478 threaded rod (with nut, washer, guide, and oil seal) into the end of the crankshaft.

7. Use the J-41478 in order to install the oil seal into the cover bore.

   a. Use a wrench and hold the hex on the installer bolt.

   b. Use a second wrench and rotate the installer nut clockwise until the seal bottoms in the cover bore.

   c. Remove the J-41478.

   d. Inspect the oil seal for proper installation. The oil seal should be installed evenly and completely into the front cover bore.

8. Install the crankshaft balancer.

Diesel Engines

See Figures 299 and 300.

Special Tools Required:
• J-44644 Crankshaft Front Oil Seal Remover
• J-44645 Crankshaft Front Oil Seal Installer

1. Remove the crankshaft balancer.

2. Install the button of J-44644 into the crankshaft.

3. Press the jaws of J-44644 into the felt portion of the seal far enough to engage the inner lip of the seal.

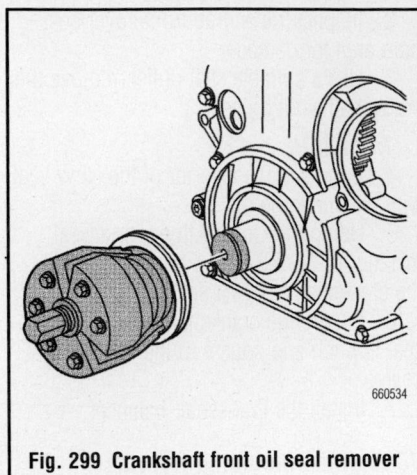

Fig. 299 Crankshaft front oil seal remover

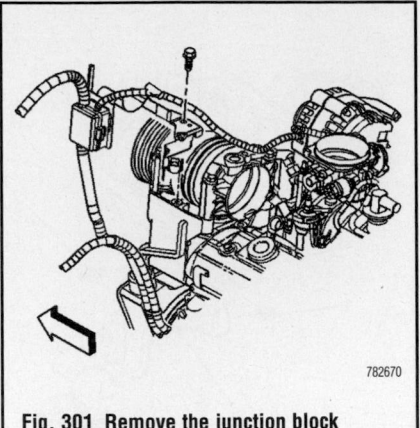

Fig. 301 Remove the junction block bracket bolt

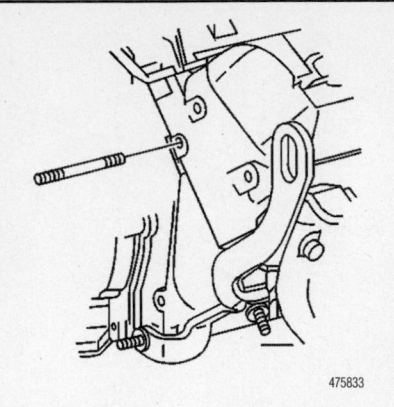

Fig. 303 Remove the P/S pump bracket stud

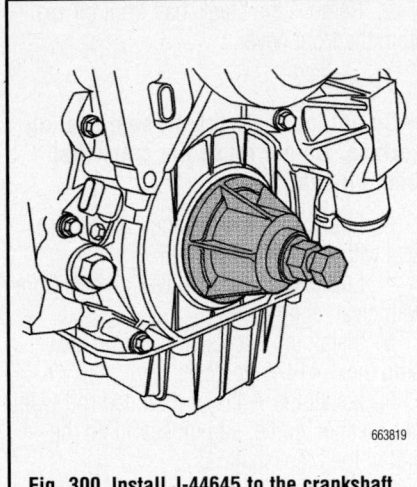

Fig. 300 Install J-44645 to the crankshaft

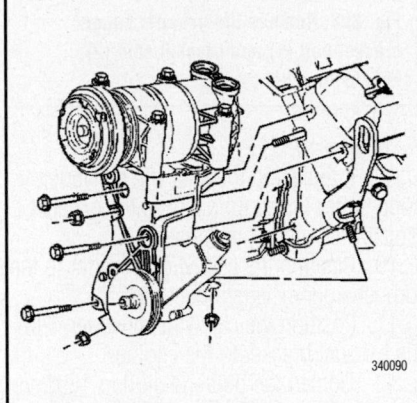

Fig. 302 Exploded view of the P/S pump and A/C compressor assemblies

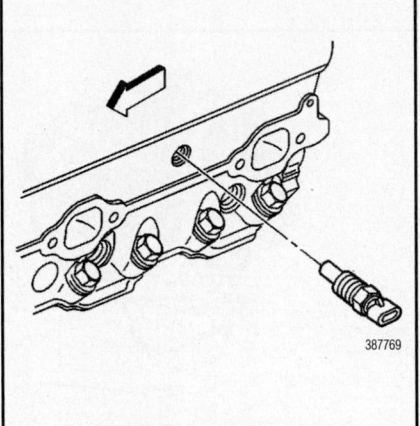

Fig. 304 Remove the Engine Coolant Temperature (ECT) sensor

4. While holding the J-44644 tightly to the seal inner sleeve, tighten the jaw bolts.

5. Using J-44644 , remove the crankshaft front oil seal.

To install:

6. Clean the front crankshaft seal bore and the crankshaft.

7. Lubricate the crankshaft sealing surface with clean engine oil.

8. Place the crankshaft front oil seal onto the crankshaft.

9. Install J-44645 to the crankshaft.

10. Press the crankshaft front oil seal onto the crankshaft using J-44645 until the tool bottoms out.

11. Remove J-44645.

12. Install the crankshaft balancer.

CYLINDER HEAD

REMOVAL & INSTALLATION

V6 Engines

Left Side

See Figures 301 through 306.

1. Drain the cooling system.
2. Remove the drive belt.
3. Remove the lower intake manifold.
4. Remove the left exhaust manifold.
5. Remove the left side pushrods.
6. Remove the junction block bracket bolt.
7. Position the bracket and wiring harness aside.
8. Loosen the Power Steering (P/S) pump rear bracket nut.
9. Remove the P/S pump rear bracket front nut.
10. Remove the bolts and nut for the P/S pump bracket.
11. Leave the Air Conditioning (A/C) compressor, if equipped, and the P/S pump on the bracket.
12. Slide the P/S pump bracket off of the stud and set aside.
13. Remove the P/S pump bracket stud.
14. Remove the harness ground bolt.
15. Position the harness ground and ground strap.

16. Remove the Engine Coolant Temperature (ECT) sensor.
17. Remove the spark plugs.
18. Remove the spark plug wire support bolts and support.
19. Remove and discard the cylinder head bolts.
20. Remove the cylinder head.
21. Remove and discard the cylinder head gasket.
22. Remove the cylinder head locator pins, if necessary.
23. Clean and inspect the cylinder head, if necessary.
24. Disassemble the cylinder head, if necessary.

To install:

25. Assemble the cylinder head, if necessary.
26. Install the cylinder head locator pins, if necessary.

➡Do not use any type of sealer on the cylinder head gasket.

27. Install a NEW cylinder head gasket.

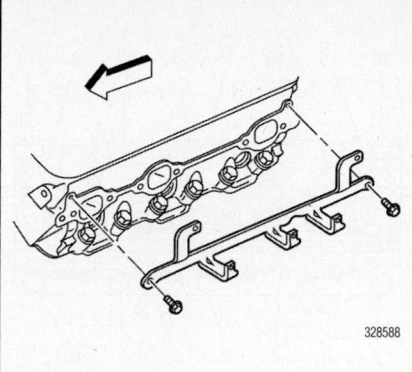

Fig. 305 Remove the spark plug wire support bolts and support

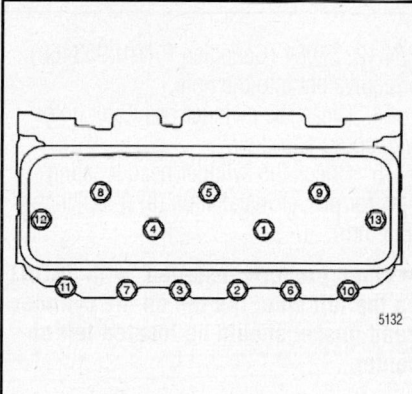

Fig. 306 Tighten the cylinder head bolts using the sequence shown

28. Install the cylinder head.
29. Apply sealant to the threads of the NEW cylinder head bolts.
30. Install the cylinder head bolts finger tight.
31. Tighten the cylinder head bolts using the sequence shown.

  a. Tighten the bolts a first pass to 22 ft. lbs. (30 Nm).

  b. Tighten the long bolts (1, 4, 5, 8, 9) a final pass to 75 degrees using J-45059.

  c. Tighten the medium bolts (12, 13) a final pass to 65 degrees using J-45059.

  d. Tighten the short bolts (2, 3, 6, 7, 10, 11) a final pass to 55 degrees using J-45059.

32. Install the spark plug wire support and bolts. Tighten the bolts to 106 inch lbs. (12 Nm).
33. Install the spark plugs.
34. If installing NEW spark plugs measure for the correct gap. Adjust the spark plug gap if necessary.

  a. Tighten the plugs in a USED cylinder head to 11 ft. lbs. (15 Nm).

  b. Tighten the plugs on the initial installation of a NEW cylinder head to 22 ft. lbs. (30 Nm).

35. Install the ECT sensor. If reusing the old sensor, apply sealant to the threads. Tighten the sensor to 15 ft. lbs. (20 Nm).
36. Position the ground strap and harness ground.
37. Install the harness ground bolt. Tighten the bolt to 12 ft. lbs. (16 Nm).
38. Install the P/S pump bracket stud. Tighten the stud to 15 ft. lbs. (20 Nm).
39. Slide the P/S pump bracket rearward.
40. Install the bolts and nuts for the P/S pump bracket.
41. Install the P/S pump rear bracket front nut.
42. Tighten the P/S pump rear bracket nut. Tighten the bolts and nuts to 30 ft. lbs. (41 Nm).
43. Position the bracket and wiring harness.
44. Install the junction block bracket bolt. Tighten the bolt to 18 ft. lbs. (25 Nm).
45. Install the left side pushrods.
46. Install the left exhaust manifold.
47. Install the lower intake manifold.
48. Install the drive belt.
49. Fill the cooling system.

Right Side

See Figures 306 through 309.

1. Drain the cooling system.
2. Remove the alternator bracket.
3. Remove the intake manifold.
4. Remove the right exhaust manifold.
5. Remove the right pushrods.
6. Remove the alternator bracket stud from the cylinder head.
7. Remove the spark plugs.
8. Remove the spark plug wire support bolts and support.

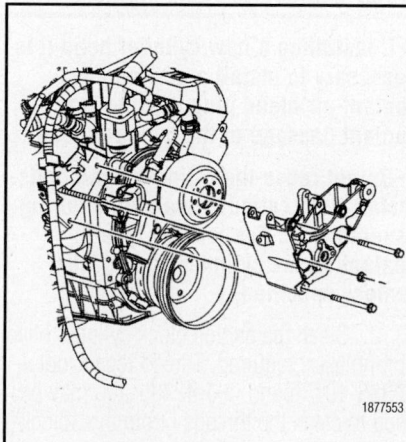

Fig. 307 Remove the alternator bracket

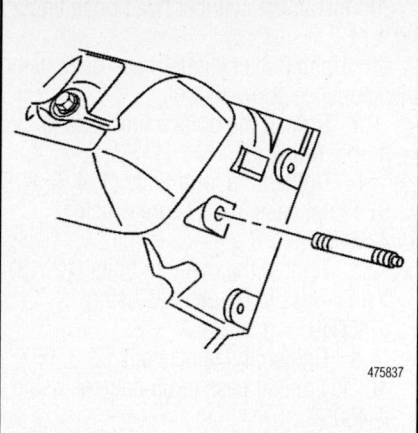

Fig. 308 Remove the alternator bracket stud from the cylinder head

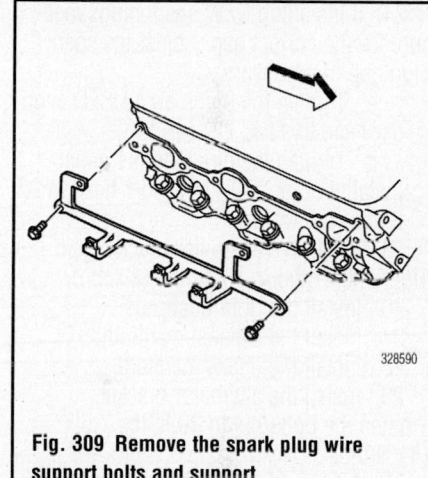

Fig. 309 Remove the spark plug wire support bolts and support

9. Remove and discard the cylinder head bolts.
10. Remove the cylinder head.
11. Remove and discard the cylinder head gasket.
12. Remove the cylinder head locator pins, if necessary.
13. Clean and inspect the cylinder head, if necessary.
14. Disassemble the cylinder head, if necessary.

To install:
15. Assemble the cylinder head, if necessary.
16. Install the cylinder head locator pins, if necessary.

➡**Do not use any type of sealer on the cylinder head gasket.**

17. Install a NEW cylinder head gasket.
18. Install the cylinder head.
19. Apply sealant to the threads of the NEW cylinder head bolts.

20. Install the cylinder head bolts finger tight.

21. Tighten the cylinder head bolts using the sequence shown.

   a. Tighten the bolts a first pass to 22 ft. lbs. (30 Nm).

   b. Tighten the long bolts (1, 4, 5, 8, 9) a final pass to 75 degrees using J-45059.

   c. Tighten the medium bolts (12, 13) a final pass to 65 degrees using J-45059.

   d. Tighten the short bolts (2, 3, 6, 7, 10, 11) a final pass to 55 degrees using J-45059.

22. Install the spark plug wire support and bolts. Tighten bolts to 106 inch lbs. (12 Nm).

23. Install the spark plugs.

24. If installing NEW spark plugs measure for the correct gap. Adjust the spark plug gap, if necessary.

   a. Tighten the plugs on a USED cylinder head to 11 ft. lbs. (15 Nm).

   b. Tighten the plugs on the initial installation of a NEW cylinder head to 22 ft. lbs. (30 Nm).

25. Install the alternator bracket stud. Tighten the stud to 15 ft. lbs. (20 Nm).

26. Install the right pushrods.

27. Install the exhaust manifold.

28. Install the intake manifold.

29. Install the alternator bracket. Tighten the bolts/nut to 30 ft. lbs. (41 Nm).

30. Fill the cooling system.

V8 Engines

Left Side

See Figures 310 and 311.

Special Tools Required:
- J-45059: Angle meter
- J-42385-200: Common thread repair kit

1. Remove the alternator bracket.
2. Remove the intake manifold.
3. Remove the coolant air bleed pipe.
4. Remove the left exhaust manifold.
5. Remove the pushrods.
6. Remove the engine ground strap bolt from the rear of the cylinder head.
7. Remove the ground strap from the cylinder head.

➡ **The cylinder head bolts are of a torque-to-yield design and are NOT to be reused.**

8. Remove and discard the cylinder head bolts.

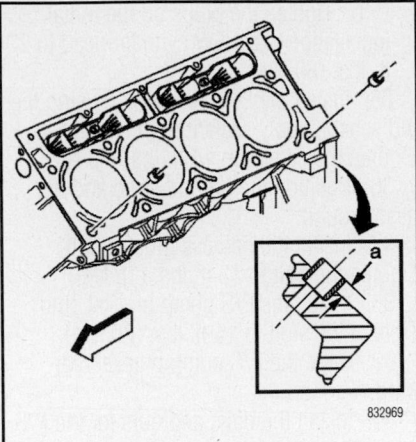

Fig. 310 Check the cylinder head locating pins for proper installation (a)

※※ CAUTION

After removal, place the cylinder head on 2 wood blocks in order to prevent damage to the sealing surfaces.

9. Remove the cylinder head.

10. Remove and discard the cylinder head gasket.

11. If required, clean and inspect the cylinder head.

To install:

※※ WARNING

Wear safety glasses in order to avoid eye damage.

※※ CAUTION

Clean all dirt, debris, and coolant from the engine block cylinder head bolt holes. Failure to remove all foreign material may result in damaged threads, improperly tightened fasteners or damage to components.

➡ **If installing a new cylinder head it is necessary to install a new engine coolant air bleed plug into the rear coolant passage of the cylinder head.**

➡ **Do not reuse the cylinder head bolts. Install NEW cylinder head bolts during assembly. Do not use any type of sealant on the cylinder head gasket (unless specified).**

12. Clean the engine block cylinder head bolt holes, if required. Thread repair tool J-42385-107, found in J-42385-200 may be used to clean the threads of old threadlocking material.

13. Spray cleaner GM P/N 12346139,

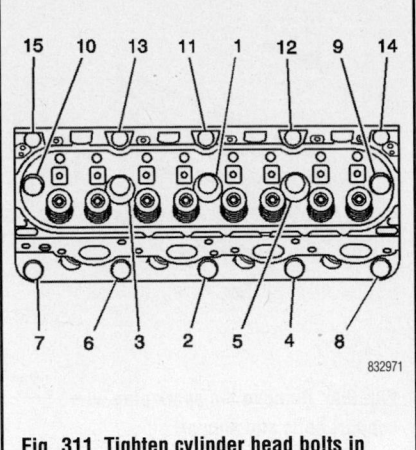

Fig. 311 Tighten cylinder head bolts in sequence

P/N 12377981 (Canadian P/N 10953463), or equivalent into the hole.

14. Clean the cylinder head bolt holes with compressed air.

15. Check the cylinder head locating pins for proper installation (a) 0.327 inches (8.3 mm).

➡ **When properly installed, with FRONT on the left side, the tab on the cylinder head gasket should be located left of center.**

16. Install the NEW cylinder head gasket onto the locating pins.

17. Install the cylinder head onto the locating pins.

18. Install the NEW cylinder head bolts.

19. Tighten the cylinder head bolts.

   a. Tighten the M11 cylinder head bolts (1–10) a first pass in sequence to 22 ft. lbs. (30 Nm).

   b. Tighten the M11 cylinder head bolts (1–10) a second pass in sequence to 90 degrees using J-45059.

   c. Tighten the M11 cylinder head bolts (1–10) a final pass to 70 degrees using J-45059.

   d. Tighten the M8 cylinder head bolts (11–15) to 22 ft. lbs. (30 Nm). Begin with the center bolt (11) and alternating side-to-side, work outward tightening all of the bolts.

20. Position the ground strap to the rear of the left cylinder head.

21. Install the engine ground strap bolt to the rear of the left cylinder head and tighten the bolt to 12 ft. lbs. (16 Nm).

22. Install the pushrods.

23. Install the left exhaust manifold.

24. Install the coolant air bleed pipe.

25. Install the intake manifold.

26. Install the alternator bracket.

Right Side

See Figures 312 through 314.

Special Tools Required:
- J-45059: Angle meter
- J-42385-200: Common thread repair kit

1. Remove the oil level indicator.
2. Remove the intake manifold.
3. Remove the coolant air bleed pipe.
4. Remove the right exhaust manifold.
5. Remove the pushrods.
6. Remove the negative battery cable stud from the front of the right cylinder head.
7. Remove the negative battery cable terminal and the engine harness terminal from the cylinder head.

➡ **The cylinder head bolts are of a torque-to-yield design and are NOT to be reused.**

8. Remove and discard the cylinder head bolts.

✳✳ CAUTION

After removal, place the cylinder head on 2 wood blocks in order to prevent damage to the sealing surfaces.

9. Remove the cylinder head.
10. Remove and discard the cylinder head gasket.
11. If required, clean and inspect the cylinder head.

To install:

✳✳ WARNING

Wear safety glasses in order to avoid eye damage.

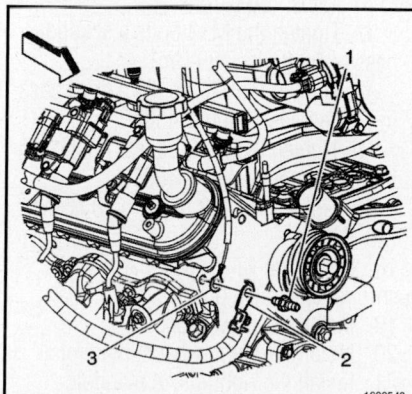

Fig. 312 Remove the negative battery cable stud (1), the negative battery cable terminal (2) and the engine harness terminal (3)

✳✳ CAUTION

Clean all dirt, debris, and coolant from the engine block cylinder head bolt holes. Failure to remove all foreign material may result in damaged threads, improperly tightened fasteners or damage to components.

➡ **If installing a new cylinder head it is necessary to install a new engine coolant air bleed plug into the rear coolant passage of the cylinder head.**

➡ **Do not reuse the cylinder head bolts. Install NEW cylinder head bolts during assembly. Do not use any type of sealant on the cylinder head gasket (unless specified).**

12. Clean the engine block cylinder head bolt holes, if required. Thread repair tool J-42385-107, found in J-42385-200 may be used to clean the threads of old threadlocking material.
13. Spray cleaner GM P/N 12346139, P/N 12377981 (Canadian P/N 10953463), or equivalent into the hole.
14. Clean the cylinder head bolt holes with compressed air.
15. Check the cylinder head locating pins for proper installation (a) 0.327 inches (8.3 mm).

➡ **When properly installed, with FRONT on the right side, the tab on the cylinder head gasket should be located right of center.**

16. Install the NEW cylinder head gasket onto the locating pins.
17. Install the cylinder head onto the locating pins.
18. Install the NEW cylinder head bolts.

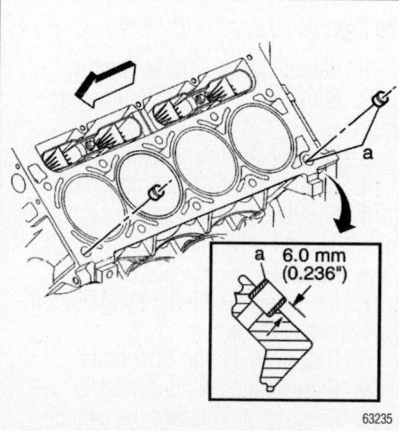

Fig. 313 Check the cylinder head locating pins for proper installation (a)

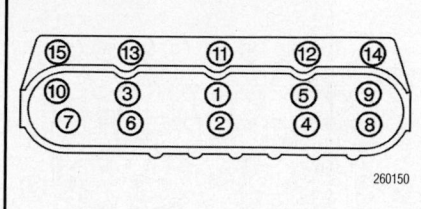

Fig. 314 Tighten the cylinder head bolts in sequence

19. Tighten the cylinder head bolts.
   a. Tighten the M11 cylinder head bolts (1–10) a first pass in sequence to 22 ft. lbs. (30 Nm).
   b. Tighten the M11 cylinder head bolts (1–10) a second pass in sequence to 90 degrees using J-45059.
   c. Tighten the M11 cylinder head bolts (1–10) a final pass to 70 degrees in sequence using J-45059.
   d. Tighten the M8 cylinder head bolts (11–15) to 22 ft. lbs. (30 Nm). Begin with the center bolt (11) and alternating side-to-side, work outward tightening all of the bolts.
20. Ensure that the engine harness terminal is positioned behind the negative battery cable terminal.
21. Position the negative battery cable terminal to the cylinder head.
22. Install the negative battery cable stud to the front of the right cylinder head and tighten the stud to 18 ft. lbs. (25 Nm).
23. Install the pushrods.
24. Install the right exhaust manifold.
25. Install the coolant air bleed pipe.
26. Install the intake manifold.
27. Install the oil level indicator.

2010 Diesel Engines

Left Side

See Figures 315 and 316.

1. Remove the engine assembly.
2. Remove the thermostat housing crossover.
3. Remove the intake manifold.
4. Remove the exhaust manifold.
5. Remove the valve rocker arm shaft, pushrods, and valve bridges.
6. Remove the glow plugs.
7. Remove the cylinder head bolts in the sequence shown.
8. Discard the large M12 bolts.
9. Remove the cylinder head.

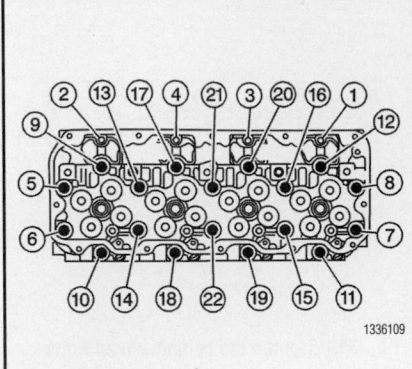

Fig. 315 Remove the cylinder head bolts in the sequence shown

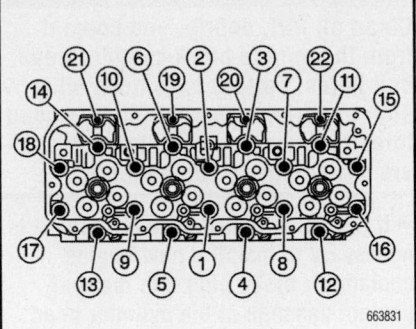

Fig. 316 Tighten the cylinder head bolts in the following steps using the sequence shown

10. Remove and discard the cylinder head gasket.

11. Clean the sealing surface of the engine block and the cylinder head.

❋❋ CAUTION

Clean all dirt, debris, and coolant from the engine block cylinder head bolt holes. Failure to remove all foreign material may result in damaged threads, improperly tightened fasteners or damage to components.

12. Clean the cylinder head bolt holes in the engine block.

To install:

❋❋ CAUTION

The left and right cylinder head gaskets are not interchangeable. Improper placement of the cylinder head gasket will block coolant and oil passages. Blocked coolant and oil passages will cause severe engine damage.

13. Install the cylinder head gasket of the correct grade.

14. Install the cylinder head.

❋❋ CAUTION

This component uses bolts with a pre-applied molybdenum disulfide coating for thread lubrication. Do not remove the coating or use any additional lubricant. Improperly lubricated threads will adversely affect the bolt torque and clamp load. Improper bolt torque and clamp load can lead to engine damage.

15. Install NEW M12 cylinder head bolts.

16. Reuse the M8 cylinder head bolts.

17. Tighten the cylinder head bolts in the following steps using the sequence shown:

   a. Tighten the M12 bolts a first pass to 37 ft. lbs. (50 Nm).

   b. Tighten the M12 bolts a second pass to 59 ft. lbs. (80 Nm)

   c. Tighten the M12 bolts a third pass to 60 degrees, using J-45059.

   d. Tighten the M12 bolts a final pass to 60 degrees, using J-45059.

   e. Tighten the M8 bolts to 18 ft. lbs. (25 Nm).

18. Install the glow plugs.

19. Install the valve rocker arm shaft, pushrods, and valve bridges.

20. Install the exhaust manifold.

21. Install the intake manifold.

22. Install the thermostat housing crossover.

23. Install the engine assembly.

24. Road test the vehicle for normal operation.

Right Side

See Figures 315 and 316.

1. Remove the engine assembly.

2. Remove the thermostat housing crossover.

3. Remove the intake manifold.

4. Remove the exhaust manifold..

5. Remove the valve rocker arm shaft, pushrods, and valve bridges.

6. Remove the glow plugs.

7. Remove the cylinder head bolts in the sequence shown.

8. Discard the large M12 bolts.

9. Remove the cylinder head.

10. Remove and discard the cylinder head gasket.

11. Clean the sealing surface of the engine block and the cylinder head.

❋❋ CAUTION

Clean all dirt, debris, and coolant from the engine block cylinder head bolt holes. Failure to remove all foreign material may result in damaged threads, improperly tightened fasteners or damage to components.

12. Clean the cylinder head bolt holes in the engine block.

To install:

❋❋ CAUTION

The left and right cylinder head gaskets are not interchangeable. Improper placement of the cylinder head gasket will block coolant and oil passages. Blocked coolant and oil passages will cause severe engine damage.

13. Install the cylinder head gasket of the correct grade.

14. Install the cylinder head.

❋❋ CAUTION

This component uses bolts with a pre-applied molybdenum disulfide coating for thread lubrication. Do not remove the coating or use any additional lubricant. Improperly lubricated threads will adversely affect the bolt torque and clamp load. Improper bolt torque and clamp load can lead to engine damage.

15. Install the NEW M12 cylinder head bolts.

16. Reuse the M8 cylinder head bolts.

17. Tighten the cylinder head bolts in the following steps using the sequence shown:

   a. Tighten the M12 bolts a first pass to 37 ft. lbs. (50 Nm).

   b. Tighten the M12 bolts a second pass to 59 ft. lbs. (80 Nm)

   c. Tighten the M12 bolts a third pass to 60 degrees, using J-45059.

   d. Tighten the M12 bolts a final pass to 60 degrees, using J-45059.

   e. Tighten the M8 bolts to 18 ft. lbs. (25 Nm).

18. Install the valve rocker arm shaft, pushrods, and valve bridges.

19. Install the glow plugs.

20. Install the right exhaust manifold.

21. Install the right intake manifold.

22. Install the thermostat housing crossover.

23. Road test the vehicle for normal operation.

24. Install the engine assembly.

2011 Diesel Engines

Left Side

See Figures 315, 317 and 318.

1. Remove the engine assembly.
2. Remove the valve rocker arm shaft, pushrods, and valve bridges.
3. Remove the intake manifold.
4. Remove the exhaust pipe.
5. Remove the exhaust manifold.
6. Remove the engine wiring harness nut(s) from the glow plug(s).
7. Remove the engine wiring harness lead(s) from the glow plug(s).
8. Remove the left lower valve rocker arm cover and cover bolts.
9. Remove and discard the valve rocker arm cover gasket, valve rocker arm cover grommets and valve rocker arm cover bolts if they are serviced with the grommet.
10. Remove the cylinder head bolts in the sequence shown.
11. Discard the large M12 bolts.
12. Remove the cylinder head and discard the cylinder head gasket.
13. Clean the sealing surface of the engine block and the cylinder head.

✳✳ CAUTION

Clean all dirt, debris, and coolant from the engine block cylinder head bolt holes. Failure to remove all foreign material may result in damaged threads, improperly tightened fasteners or damage to components.

14. Clean the cylinder head bolt holes in the engine block.

To install:

✳✳ CAUTION

The left and right cylinder head gaskets are not interchangeable. Improper placement of the cylinder head gasket will block coolant and oil passages. Blocked coolant and oil passages will cause severe engine damage.

➡The stamped letter, R or L, must face up. R is the right bank, L is the left bank.

15. The markings on the gasket are as follows:
  - Grade A
  - Grade B
  - Grade C
  - Block over-bored 0.010–0.030 inches (0.254–0.762 mm)
  - Block over-bored 0.010–0.030 inches (0.254–0.762 mm) and deck milled 0.008 inches (0.203 mm)

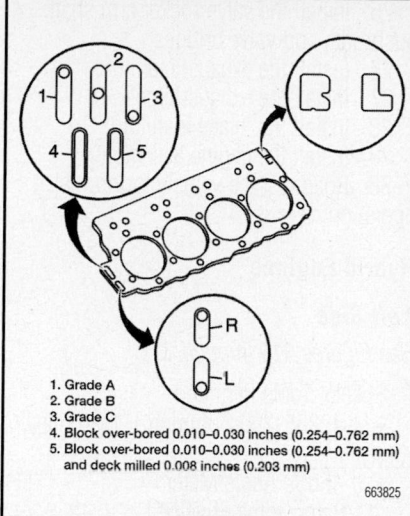

1. Grade A
2. Grade B
3. Grade C
4. Block over-bored 0.010-0.030 inches (0.254-0.762 mm)
5. Block over-bored 0.010-0.030 inches (0.254-0.762 mm) and deck milled 0.008 inches (0.203 mm)

663825

Fig. 317 The stamped letter, R or L, must face up. R is the right bank, L is the left bank

16. Install the left cylinder head gasket of the correct grade. The left and right cylinder head gaskets are not interchangeable.
17. Install the cylinder head.

✳✳ CAUTION

This component uses bolts with a pre-applied molybdenum disulfide coating for thread lubrication. Do not remove the coating or use any additional lubricant. Improperly lubricated threads will adversely affect the bolt torque and clamp load. Improper bolt torque and clamp load can lead to engine damage.

18. Install NEW M12 cylinder head bolts.
19. Tighten the M12 cylinder head bolts in sequence in four steps:
  a. 1st step: 37 ft. lbs. (50 Nm).
  b. 2nd step: 59 ft. lbs. (80 Nm).
  c. 3rd step tighten 60 degrees using J-45059 meter.
  d. Final step tighten 60 degrees using J-45059 meter.
20. Reuse the M8 bolts. Install the M8 bolts and tighten the M8 cylinder head bolts to 18 ft. lbs. (25 Nm).
21. Install the glow plug(s) to the cylinder head and tighten to 13 ft. lbs. (18 Nm).
22. Install the engine wiring harness lead(s) to the glow plug(s).
23. Install the engine wiring harness nut(s) to the glow plug(s) and tighten.
24. Install the left lower valve rocker arm cover and cover bolts.
25. Install the valve rocker arm shaft, pushrods, and valve bridges.

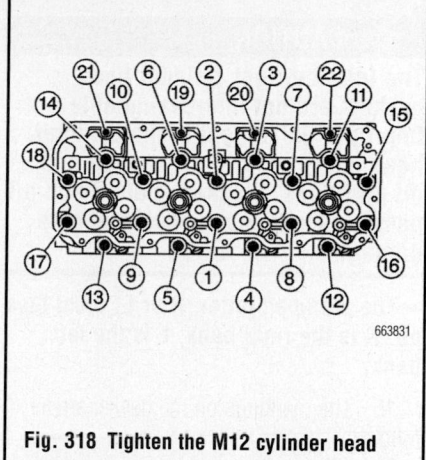

663831

Fig. 318 Tighten the M12 cylinder head bolts in sequence in four steps

26. Install the exhaust manifold.
27. Install the exhaust pipe.
28. Install the intake manifold.
29. Install the engine assembly.
30. Road test the vehicle for normal operation.

Right Side

See Figures 315, 317 and 318.

1. Remove the engine assembly.
2. Remove the valve rocker arm shaft, pushrods, and valve bridges.
3. Remove the intake manifold.
4. Remove the exhaust pipe.
5. Remove the exhaust manifold.
6. Remove the engine wiring harness nut(s) from the glow plug(s).
7. Remove the engine wiring harness lead(s) from the glow plug(s).
8. Remove the right lower valve rocker arm cover and cover bolts.
9. Remove and discard the valve rocker arm cover gasket, valve rocker arm cover grommets and valve rocker arm cover bolts if they are serviced with the grommet.
10. Remove the cylinder head bolts in the sequence shown.
11. Discard the large M12 bolts.
12. Remove the cylinder head and discard the cylinder head gasket.
13. Clean the sealing surface of the engine block and the cylinder head.

✳✳ CAUTION

Clean all dirt, debris, and coolant from the engine block cylinder head bolt holes. Failure to remove all foreign material may result in damaged threads, improperly tightened fasteners or damage to components.

14. Clean the cylinder head bolt holes in the engine block.

To install:

❊❊ CAUTION

The left and right cylinder head gaskets are not interchangeable. Improper placement of the cylinder head gasket will block coolant and oil passages. Blocked coolant and oil passages will cause severe engine damage.

➡ The stamped letter, R or L, must face up. R is the right bank, L is the left bank.

15. The markings on the gasket are as follows:
   • Grade A
   • Grade B
   • Grade C
   • Block over-bored 0.010–0.030 inches (0.254–0.762 mm)
   • Block over-bored 0.010–0.030 inches (0.254–0.762 mm) and deck milled 0.008 inches (0.203 mm)
16. Install the right cylinder head gasket of the correct grade. The left and right cylinder head gaskets are not interchangeable.
17. Install the cylinder head.

❊❊ CAUTION

This component uses bolts with a pre-applied molybdenum disulfide coating for thread lubrication. Do not remove the coating or use any additional lubricant. Improperly lubricated threads will adversely affect the bolt torque and clamp load. Improper bolt torque and clamp load can lead to engine damage.

18. Install NEW M12 cylinder head bolts. Reuse the M8 bolts.
19. Tighten the M12 cylinder head bolts in sequence in four steps:
   a. 1st step 37 ft. lbs. (50 Nm).
   b. 2nd step 59 ft. lbs. (80 Nm).
   c. 3rd step tighten 60 degrees using J-45059 meter.
   d. Final step tighten 60 degrees using J-45059 meter
20. Install the M8 bolts and tighten the M8 cylinder head bolts to 18 ft. lbs. (25 Nm).
21. Install the glow plug(s) to the cylinder head and tighten to 13 ft. lbs. (18 Nm).
22. Install the engine wiring harness lead(s) to the glow plug(s).
23. Install the engine wiring harness nut(s) to the glow plug(s).
24. Install the right lower valve rocker arm cover and cover bolts.

25. Install the valve rocker arm shaft, pushrods, and valve bridges.
26. Install the exhaust manifold.
27. Install the exhaust pipe.
28. Install the intake manifold.
29. Install the engine assembly.
30. Road test the vehicle for normal operation.

Hybrid Engines

Left Side

See Figures 319 through 321.

Special Tools Required:
• J-42385-200 Common Thread Repair Kit
• J-45059 Angle Meter

1. Remove the drive belt.
2. Remove the drive belt idler pulley bracket bolts.
3. Remove the drive belt idler pulley bracket.
4. Remove the intake manifold.
5. Remove the coolant air bleed pipe.
6. Remove the left exhaust manifold.
7. Remove the pushrods.
8. Remove the engine ground strap bolt from the rear of the cylinder head.
9. Remove the ground strap from the cylinder head.

➡ The cylinder head bolts are of a torque-to-yield design and are NOT to be reused.

10. Remove and discard the cylinder head bolts.

❊❊ CAUTION

After removal, place the cylinder head on 2 wood blocks in order to prevent damage to the sealing surfaces.

Fig. 319 Remove the drive belt idler pulley bracket bolts (1) and the drive belt idler pulley bracket (2)

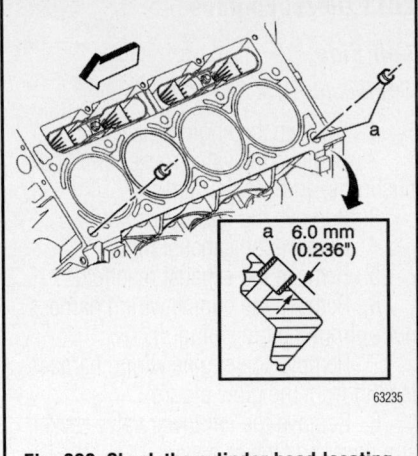

Fig. 320 Check the cylinder head locating pins for proper installation (a)

11. Remove the cylinder head.
12. Remove and discard the cylinder head gasket.
13. If required, clean and inspect the cylinder head.

To install:

❊❊ WARNING

Wear safety glasses in order to avoid eye damage.

❊❊ CAUTION

Clean all dirt, debris, and coolant from the engine block cylinder head bolt holes. Failure to remove all foreign material may result in damaged threads, improperly tightened fasteners or damage to components.

➡ If installing a new cylinder head it is necessary to install a new engine coolant air bleed plug into the rear coolant passage of the cylinder head.

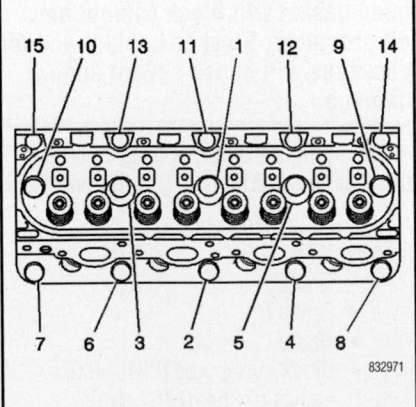

Fig. 321 Tighten the cylinder head bolts in sequence shown

➡ Do not reuse the cylinder head bolts. Install NEW cylinder head bolts during assembly.

➡ Do not use any type of sealant on the cylinder head gasket (unless specified).

14. Clean the engine block cylinder head bolt holes, if required. Thread repair tool J-42385-107, found in J-42385-200 may be used to clean the threads of old thread-locking material.

15. Spray cleaner GM P/N 12346139, P/N 12377981 (Canadian P/N 10953463), or equivalent into the hole.

16. Clean the cylinder head bolt holes with compressed air.

17. Check the cylinder head locating pins for proper installation (a) 0.327 inches (8.3 mm).

➡ When properly installed, with FRONT on the left side, the tab on the cylinder head gasket should be located left of center.

18. Install the NEW cylinder head gasket onto the locating pins.

19. Install the cylinder head onto the locating pins.

20. Install the NEW cylinder head bolts.

21. Tighten the cylinder head bolts in sequence shown.

   a. Tighten the M11 cylinder head bolts (1-10) a first pass in sequence to 22 ft. lbs. (30 Nm).

   b. Tighten the M11 cylinder head bolts (1-10) a second pass in sequence to 90 degrees using J-45059.

   c. Tighten the M11 cylinder head bolts (1-10) a final pass to 70 degrees using J-45059.

   d. Tighten the M8 cylinder head bolts (11-15) to 22 ft. lbs. (30 Nm). Begin with the center bolt (11) and alternating side-to-side, work outward tightening all of the bolts.

22. Position the ground strap to the rear of the left cylinder head.

23. Install the engine ground strap bolt to the rear of the left cylinder head and tighten the bolt to 12 ft. lbs. (16 Nm).

24. Install the pushrods.

25. Install the left exhaust manifold.

26. Install the coolant air bleed pipe.

27. Install the intake manifold.

28. Position the drive belt idler pulley bracket.

29. Install the drive belt idler pulley

bracket bolts and tighten to 37 ft. lbs. (50 Nm).

30. Remove the drive belt.

Right Side

See Figures 320 and 322.

Special Tools Required:
   • J-42385-200 Common Thread Repair Kit
   • J-45059 Angle Meter

1. Remove the drive motor generator control module.

2. Remove the oil level indicator.

3. Remove the intake manifold.

4. Remove the coolant air bleed pipe.

5. Remove the right exhaust manifold.

6. Remove the pushrods.

7. Remove the engine harness stud from the front of the right cylinder head.

8. Position the engine harness aside.

➡ The cylinder head bolts are of a torque-to-yield design and are NOT to be reused.

9. Remove and discard the cylinder head bolts.

✹✹ CAUTION

All camshaft journals are the same diameter, so care must be used in removing or installing the camshaft to avoid damage to the camshaft bearings.

10. Remove the cylinder head.

11. Remove and discard the cylinder head gasket.

12. If required, clean and inspect the cylinder head.

To install:

✹✹ WARNING

Wear safety glasses in order to avoid eye damage.

✹✹ CAUTION

Clean all dirt, debris, and coolant from the engine block cylinder head bolt holes. Failure to remove all foreign material may result in damaged threads, improperly tightened fasteners or damage to components.

➡ If installing a new cylinder head it is necessary to install a new engine coolant air bleed plug into the rear coolant passage of the cylinder head.

➡ Do not reuse the cylinder head bolts. Install NEW cylinder head bolts during assembly.

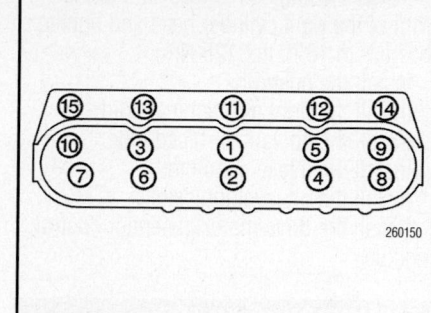

Fig. 322 Tighten the cylinder head bolts in the sequence shown

➡ Do not use any type of sealant on the cylinder head gasket, unless specified.

13. Clean the engine block cylinder head bolt holes, if required. Thread repair tool J-42385-107, found in J-42385-200 may be used to clean the threads of old threadlocking material.

14. Spray cleaner GM P/N 12346139, P/N 12377981 (Canadian P/N 10953463), or equivalent into the hole.

15. Clean the cylinder head bolt holes with compressed air.

16. Check the cylinder head locating pins for proper installation (a) 0.327 inches (8.3 mm).

➡ When properly installed, with FRONT on the right side, the tab on the cylinder head gasket should be located right of center.

17. Install the NEW cylinder head gasket onto the locating pins.

18. Install the cylinder head onto the locating pins.

19. Install the NEW cylinder head bolts.

20. Tighten the cylinder head bolts in the sequence shown.

   a. Tighten the M11 cylinder head bolts (1–10) a first pass in sequence to 22 ft. lbs. (30 Nm).

   b. Tighten the M11 cylinder head bolts (1–10) a second pass in sequence to 90 degrees using J-45059.

   c. Tighten the M11 cylinder head bolts (1–10) a final pass to 70 degrees in sequence using J-45059.

21. Tighten the M8 cylinder head bolts (11–15) to 22 ft. lbs. (30 Nm). Begin with the center bolt (11) and alternating side-to-side, work outward tightening all of the bolts.

Position the engine harness to the cylinder head.

Install the engine harness stud to the front of the right cylinder head and tighten the stud to 18 ft. lbs. (25 Nm).

Install the pushrods.

Install the right exhaust manifold.

Install the coolant air bleed pipe.

Install the intake manifold.

Install the oil level indicator.

Install the drive motor generator control module.

ENGINE OIL & FILTER

REPLACEMENT

1. Open the hood.
2. Remove the oil fill cap.
3. Raise and suitably support the vehicle.
4. Place a oil drain pan under the oil pan drain plug.
5. Remove the oil pan drain plug.
6. Allow the oil to drain completely.
7. Clean and inspect the oil pan drain plug, replace if necessary.
8. Clean and inspect the oil pan sealing surface, replace the oil pan if necessary.
9. Wipe any remaining oil from the drain plug hole and reinstall the oil pan drain plug until snug.
10. Position the drain pan under the oil filter.
11. Remove the oil filter.
12. Ensure that the oil filter gasket is still on the old filter if not, remove the oil filter gasket from the oil pan.

To install:

13. Apply clean engine oil to the NEW oil filter seal.
14. Install the NEW oil filter and tighten to 22 ft. lbs. (30 Nm).
15. Tighten the oil pan drain plug to 18 ft. lbs. (25 Nm).
16. Remove the oil drain pan from under the vehicle.
17. Lower the vehicle.
18. Fill the engine with new engine oil.
19. Start the engine.
20. Inspect for oil leaks after engine start up.
21. Turn off the engine and allow the oil a few minutes to drain back into the oil pan.
22. Remove the oil level indicator from the indicator tube.
23. Clean off the indicator end of the oil level indicator with a clean paper towel or cloth.
24. Install the oil level indicator into the oil level indicator tube until the oil level indicator handle contacts the top of the oil level indicator tube.
25. Again, remove the oil level indicator

from the oil level indicator tube keeping the tip of the oil level indicator down.

26. Check the level of the engine oil on the oil level indicator.
27. If necessary, adjust the oil level by adding or draining oil.
28. Check for oil leaks.
29. Close the hood.

EXHAUST MANIFOLD

REMOVAL & INSTALLATION

V6 Engines

Left Side

See Figures 323 through 325.

1. Raise and suitably support the vehicle.
2. Remove the catalytic converter to exhaust manifold nuts.
3. Lower the vehicle.
4. Remove the exhaust manifold heat shield bolts and shield.
5. Remove the spark plugs.
6. Reposition the spark plug wires out of the way, if necessary.
7. Remove the exhaust manifold bolts and stud.
8. Remove the exhaust manifold and gaskets. Discard the gaskets.
9. Remove the exhaust manifold to catalytic converter seal. Discard the seal.

To install:

10. Install a NEW exhaust manifold to catalytic converter seal into the relief in the catalytic converter.
11. Place the exhaust manifold into position and install the manifold studs to the catalytic converter.
12. Place the NEW exhaust manifold gaskets between the manifold and the cylinder head.

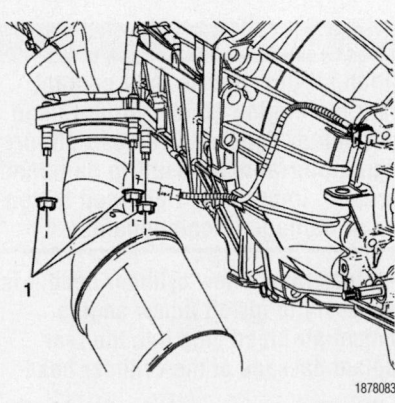

Fig. 323 Remove the catalytic converter to exhaust manifold nuts (1)

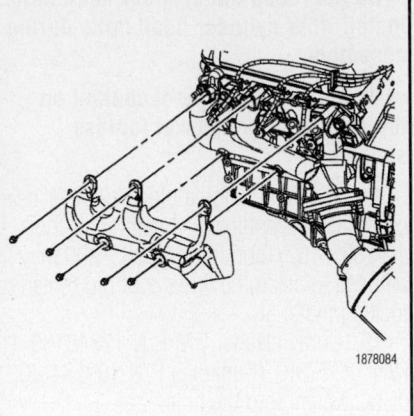

Fig. 324 Remove the exhaust manifold heat shield bolts and shield

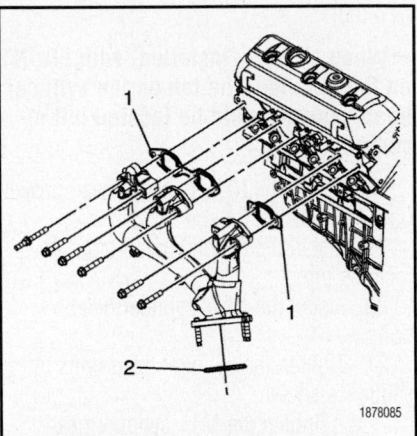

Fig. 325 Remove the exhaust manifold and gaskets (1) and the exhaust manifold to catalytic converter seal (2)

13. Install the exhaust manifold bolts and stud. Tighten the bolts/stud to 22 ft. lbs. (30 Nm).
14. Install the spark plugs.
15. Position the exhaust manifold heat shield to the manifold and install the bolts. Tighten the bolts to 80 inch lbs. (9 Nm).
16. Raise and support the vehicle.
17. Install the catalytic converter to exhaust manifold nuts. Tighten the nuts to 37 ft. lbs. (50 Nm).
18. Lower the vehicle.

Right Side

See Figures 326 through 328.

1. Remove the heated oxygen sensor (HO2S).
2. Remove the catalytic converter to exhaust manifold nuts.
3. Lower the vehicle.
4. Remove the exhaust manifold heat shield bolts and shield.
5. Remove the spark plugs.

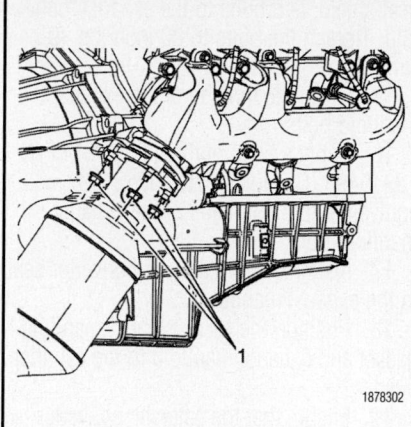

Fig. 326 Remove the catalytic converter to exhaust manifold nuts (1)

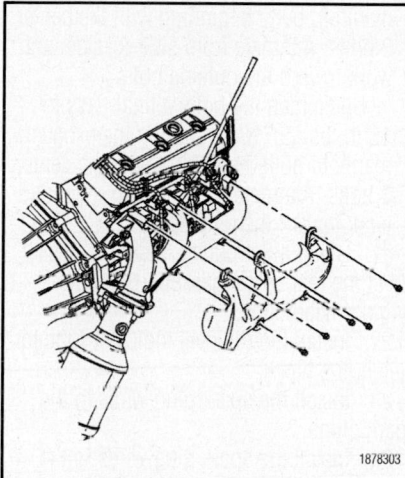

Fig. 327 Remove the exhaust manifold heat shield bolts and shield

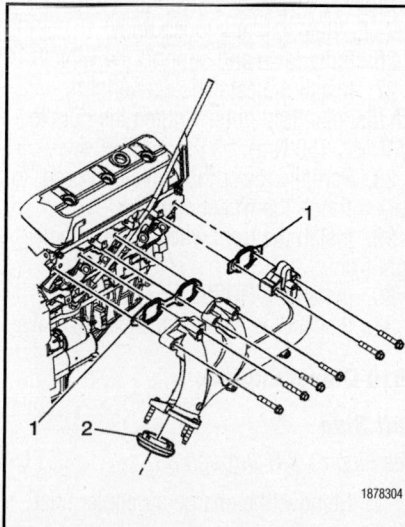

Fig. 328 Remove the exhaust manifold and gaskets (1) and the exhaust manifold to catalytic converter seal (2)

6. Reposition the spark plug wires out of the way, if necessary.

7. Remove the exhaust manifold bolts.

8. Remove the exhaust manifold and gaskets. Discard the gaskets.

9. Remove the exhaust manifold to catalytic converter seal. Discard the seal.

To install:

10. Install a NEW exhaust manifold to catalytic converter seal into the exhaust manifold.

11. Place the exhaust manifold into position and install the manifold studs to the catalytic converter.

12. Place the NEW exhaust manifold gaskets between the manifold and the cylinder head.

13. Install the exhaust manifold bolts and stud. Tighten the bolts/stud to 22 ft. lbs. (30 Nm).

14. Install the spark plugs.

15. Position the exhaust manifold heat shield to the manifold and install the bolts. Tighten the bolts to 80 inch lbs. (9 Nm).

16. Raise and support the vehicle.

17. Install the catalytic converter to exhaust manifold nuts. Tighten the nuts to 37 ft. lbs. (50 Nm).

18. Lower the vehicle.

V8 Engines

Left Side

See Figures 329 and 330.

1. Install the Steering Column Anti-Rotation Pin (J-42640) into the steering column lower access hole.

2. Remove the left wheelhouse liner.

3. Fully raise and support the vehicle.

4. Remove the catalytic converter to exhaust manifold nuts.

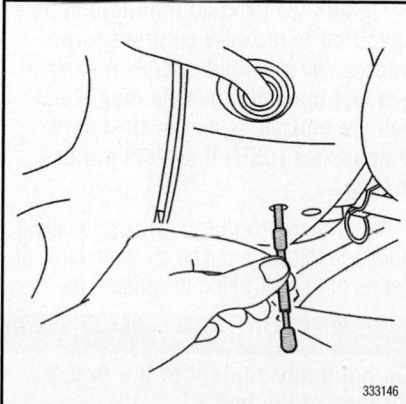

Fig. 329 Install the Steering Column Anti-Rotation Pin (J-42640) into the steering column lower access hole

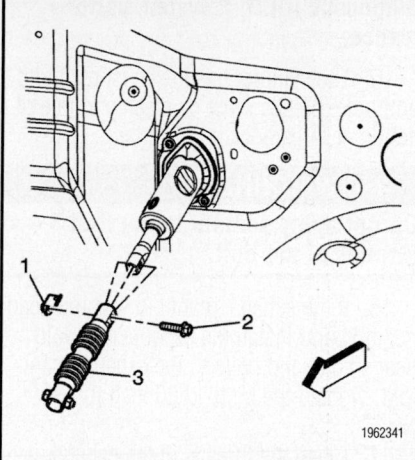

Fig. 330 Remove the steering shaft coupling bolt (2) and nut (1) from the upper intermediate steering shaft; separate the upper intermediate steering shaft (3) from the steering column

5. Lower the vehicle part way in order to work through the wheel opening.

6. Remove the spark plug wires from the spark plugs.

a. Twist the spark plug wire boot a ½ turn.

b. Pull only on the boot in order to remove the wire from the spark plug.

7. Remove the spark plug wires from the ignition coils.

a. Twist the spark plug wire boot a ½ turn.

b. Pull only on the boot in order to remove the wire from the ignition coil.

8. Mark the relationship of the upper intermediate steering shaft to the steering column.

9. Remove the steering shaft coupling bolt and nut from the upper intermediate steering shaft.

10. Separate the upper intermediate steering shaft from the steering column, position both shafts out of the way.

11. Remove the exhaust manifold bolts, and exhaust manifold.

12. Remove and discard the exhaust manifold gasket.

13. Remove and discard the catalytic converter seal.

14. If replacing the exhaust manifold, remove the exhaust manifold heat shield bolts, and shield from the exhaust manifold.

To install:

➡Tighten the exhaust manifold bolts as specified in the service procedure. Improperly installed and/or leaking exhaust manifold gaskets may affect vehicle emissions and/or On-Board

Diagnostic (OBD) II system performance.

15. The cylinder head exhaust manifold bolt hole threads must be clean and free of debris or threadlocking material.

⁂ WARNING

Do not apply sealant to the first 3 threads of the bolt.

16. If the exhaust manifold was replaced, position and install the exhaust manifold heat shield, and bolts to the exhaust manifold. Tighten the bolts to 80 inch lbs. (9 Nm).

17. Clean the threads of the exhaust manifold bolts.

18. Apply a band of threadlock GM P/N 12345493 (Canadian P/N 10953488), or equivalent to the threads of the exhaust manifold bolts.

19. Install a NEW catalytic converter seal to the catalytic converter.

20. Position the NEW exhaust manifold gasket and exhaust manifold to the cylinder head.

21. Ensure that the exhaust manifold is seated to the catalytic converter.

22. Install the exhaust manifold bolts.

   a. Tighten the bolts a first pass to 11 ft. lbs. (15 Nm). Tighten the exhaust manifold bolts beginning with the center 2 bolts. Alternate from side-to-side, and work toward the outside bolts.

   b. Tighten the bolts a final pass to 15 ft. lbs. (20 Nm). Tighten the exhaust manifold bolts beginning with the center 2 bolts. Alternate from side-to-side, and work toward the outside bolts.

23. Using a flat punch, bend the gasket tab at the rear of the gasket around the cylinder head edge.

24. Position and align the marks on the upper intermediate steering shaft and the steering column.

25. Install the upper intermediate steering shaft to the steering column.

26. Install the steering shaft coupling bolt and nut to the upper intermediate steering shaft. Tighten the bolt/nut to 37 ft. lbs. (50 Nm).

27. Install the spark plug wires to the spark plugs.

28. Install the spark plug wires to the ignition coils.

29. Inspect the spark plug wires for proper installation.

   a. Push sideways on each boot in order to inspect the seating.

   b. Reinstall any loose boot.

30. Fully raise and support the vehicle.

31. Install the catalytic converter to exhaust manifold nuts. Tighten the nuts to 37 ft. lbs. (50 Nm).

32. Partially lower the vehicle.

33. Install the left wheelhouse liner.

34. Remove the J-42640 from the steering column lower access hole.

Right Side

1. Remove the Heated Oxygen Sensor (HO2S).

2. Fully raise and suitably support the vehicle.

3. Remove the catalytic converter to exhaust manifold nuts.

4. Remove the front wheel house liner—right side.

5. Partially lower the vehicle in order to work through the wheel opening.

6. Remove the spark plug wires from the spark plugs.

   a. Twist the spark plug wire boot a ½ turn.

   b. Pull only on the boot in order to remove the wire from the spark plug.

7. Remove the spark plug wires from the ignition coils.

   a. Twist the spark plug wire boot a ½ turn.

   b. Pull only on the boot in order to remove the wire from the ignition coil.

8. Remove the oil level indicator tube from the engine block.

9. Remove the exhaust manifold bolts and exhaust manifold.

10. Remove and discard the exhaust manifold gasket.

11. Remove and discard the exhaust manifold seal.

12. If replacing the exhaust manifold, remove the exhaust manifold heat shield bolts, and shield from the exhaust manifold.

To install:

➡ Tighten the exhaust manifold bolts as specified in the service procedure. Improperly installed and/or leaking exhaust manifold gaskets may affect vehicle emissions and/or On-Board Diagnostics (OBD) II system performance.

13. The cylinder head exhaust manifold bolt hole threads must be clean and free of debris or threadlocking material.

⁂ WARNING

Do not apply sealant to the first 3 threads of the bolt.

14. If the exhaust manifold was replaced, position and install the exhaust manifold heat shield, and bolts to the exhaust manifold. Tighten the bolts to 80 inch lbs. (9 Nm).

15. Clean the threads of the exhaust manifold bolts.

16. Apply a bead of threadlock GM P/N 12345493 (Canadian P/N 10953488), or equivalent to the threads of the exhaust manifold bolts.

17. Install a NEW catalytic converter seal to the exhaust manifold.

18. Position the NEW exhaust manifold gasket and exhaust manifold to the cylinder head.

19. Ensure that the catalytic converter seal is seated to the catalytic converter.

20. Install the exhaust manifold bolts.

   a. Tighten the bolts a first pass to 11 ft. lbs. (15 Nm). Tighten the exhaust manifold bolts beginning with the center 2 bolts. Alternate from side-to-side, and work toward the outside bolts.

   b. Tighten the bolts a final pass to 15 ft. lbs. (20 Nm). Tighten the exhaust manifold bolts beginning with the center 2 bolts. Alternate from side-to-side, and work toward the outside bolts.

21. Using a flat punch, bend the gasket tab at the rear of the gasket around the cylinder head edge.

22. Install the oil level indicator tube to the engine block.

23. Install the spark plug wires to the spark plugs.

24. Install the spark plug wires to the ignition coils.

25. Inspect the spark plug wires for proper installation.

   a. Push sideways on each boot in order to inspect the seating.

   b. Reinstall any loose boot.

26. Fully raise and support the vehicle.

27. Install the catalytic converter to exhaust manifold nuts. Tighten the nuts to 37 ft. lbs. (50 Nm).

28. Partially lower the vehicle in order to work through the wheel opening.

29. Install the front wheel house liner—right front.

30. Install the HO2S.

31. Inspect the exhaust system for leaks.

2010 Diesel Engines

Left Side

See Figures 331 through 337.

1. Remove the charge air cooler inlet pipe.

2. Remove the wheelhouse liner.

➡ Perform the following steps working through the wheelhouse opening.

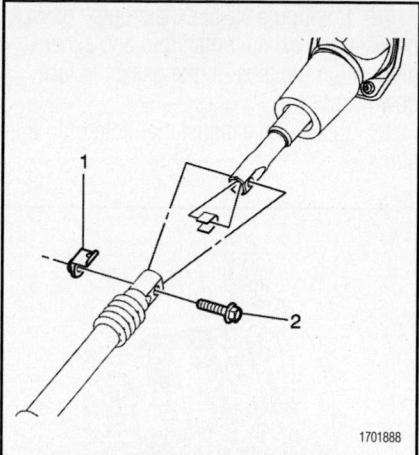

Fig. 331 Remove the steering coupling nut (1) and bolt (2) at the upper intermediate steering shaft

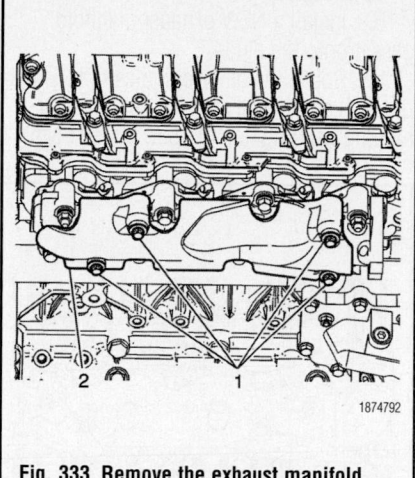

Fig. 333 Remove the exhaust manifold heat shield bolts (1) and shield (2)

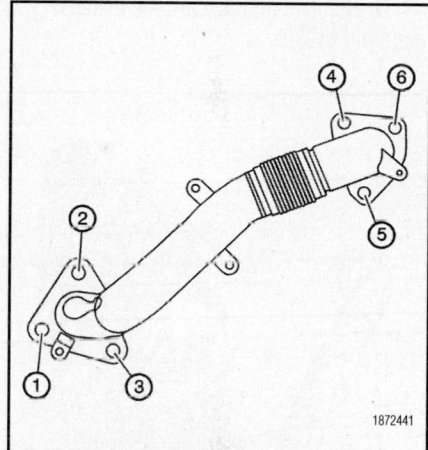

Fig. 336 Install and tighten the exhaust manifold bolts and nuts in the sequence shown

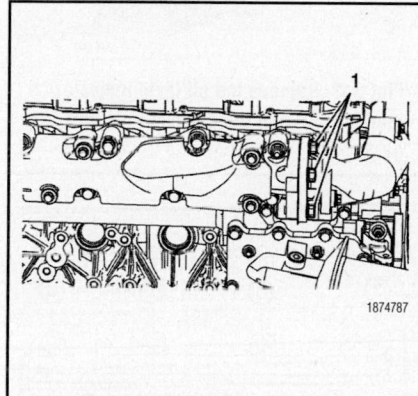

Fig. 332 Remove the exhaust pipe to exhaust manifold bolts (1)

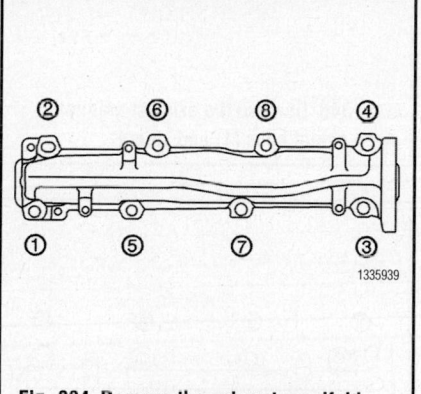

Fig. 334 Remove the exhaust manifold bolts and nuts in the sequence shown

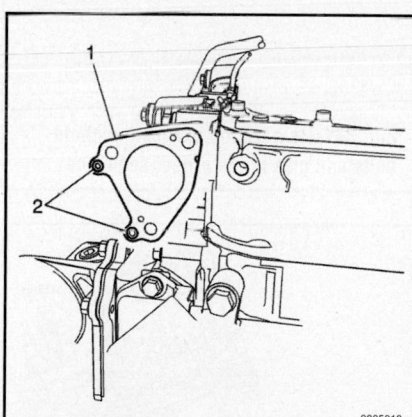

Fig. 337 Install and tighten the exhaust pipe to exhaust manifold bolts in the sequence shown

3. Remove the steering coupling nut and bolt at the upper intermediate steering shaft.

4. Separate the steering shaft coupling from the intermediate shaft.

5. Remove the exhaust pipe to exhaust manifold bolts.

6. Remove the exhaust manifold heat shield bolts and shield.

7. Remove the exhaust manifold bolts and nuts in the sequence shown.

8. Remove the exhaust manifold and gasket. Discard the gasket.

To install:

9. Install the NEW exhaust manifold gasket onto the manifold studs.

➡Position the exhaust pipe gaskets with the tabs shown. Failure to do so will cause improper alignment of the gaskets and result in exhaust leaks.

10. Position a NEW exhaust pipe gasket between the exhaust manifold and the exhaust pipe. Align the tabs on the gasket to face outward.

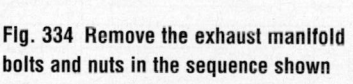

Fig. 335 Position a NEW exhaust pipe gasket (1) between the exhaust manifold and the exhaust pipe. Align the tabs (2) on the gasket to face outward

11. Install the exhaust manifold onto the studs.

12. Install and tighten the exhaust manifold bolts and nuts in the sequence shown to 42 ft. lbs. (57 Nm).

13. Tighten the 4 center bolts/nuts an additional pass to 42 ft. lbs. (57 Nm).

14. Install and tighten the exhaust pipe to exhaust manifold bolts in the sequence shown to 39 ft. lbs. (53 Nm).

15. Position the exhaust manifold heat shield to the manifold and install the bolts and tighten to 89 inch lbs. (10 Nm).

16. Install the steering shaft coupling to the intermediate shaft.

17. Install the steering shaft coupling nut and bolt at the steering shaft coupling and tighten to 37 ft. lbs. (50 Nm).

18. Install the wheelhouse liner.

19. Remove the charge air cooler inlet pipe.

20. Lower the vehicle.

Right Side

See Figures 338 through 346.

1. Remove the wheelhouse liner.
2. Perform the following steps working through the wheelhouse opening.
3. Remove the exhaust pipe to turbocharger exhaust pipe bracket bolt.
4. Remove the exhaust pipe to exhaust manifold bolts and bracket.
5. Remove the exhaust manifold heat shield bolts and shield.
6. Remove the exhaust manifold bolts and nuts in the proper sequence.
7. Remove the exhaust manifold and exhaust manifold to pipe gasket.
8. Remove the oil level indicator tube bolt and rotate the oil level indicator tube out of the way.
9. Remove and discard the exhaust manifold gasket.

To install:

10. Install a NEW exhaust manifold gasket onto the studs.
11. Rotate the oil level indicator tube into position and install the oil level indicator tube bolt and tighten to 15 ft. lbs. (21 Nm).

12. Position a NEW exhaust pipe gasket between the exhaust manifold and exhaust pipe. Align the tabs on the gasket to face downward.
13. Install the exhaust manifold onto the studs.

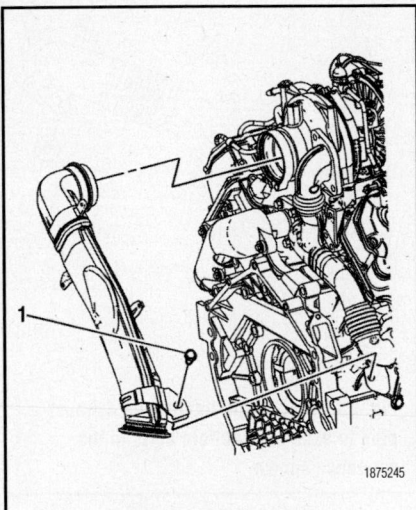

Fig. 338 Remove the exhaust pipe to turbocharger exhaust pipe bracket bolt (1)

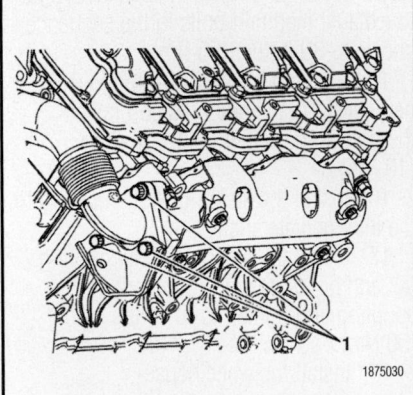

Fig. 339 Remove the exhaust pipe to exhaust manifold bolts (1) and bracket

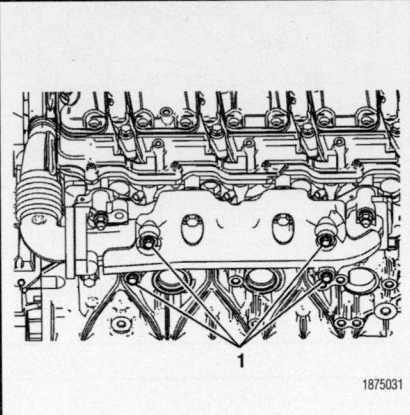

Fig. 340 Remove the exhaust manifold heat shield bolts (1) and shield

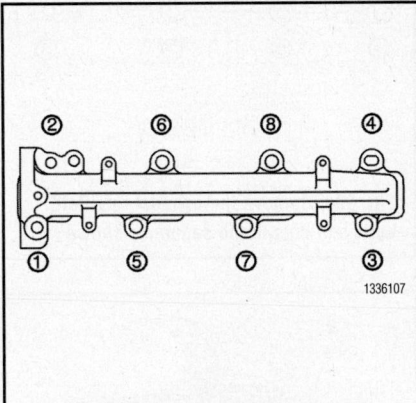

Fig. 341 Remove the exhaust manifold bolts and nuts in the proper sequence

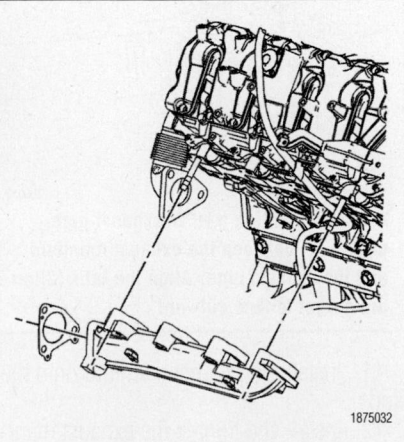

Fig. 342 Remove the exhaust manifold and exhaust manifold to pipe gasket

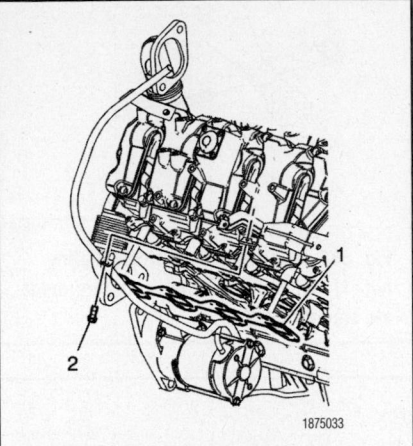

Fig. 343 Remove the oil level indicator tube bolt (2) and the exhaust manifold gasket (1)

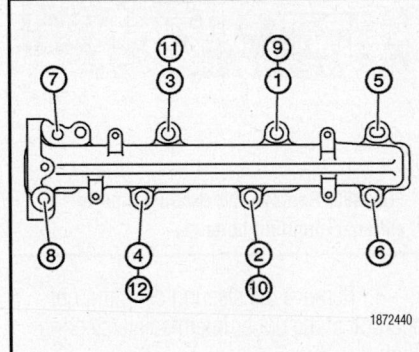

Fig. 344 Install and tighten the exhaust manifold bolts and nuts in the sequence shown

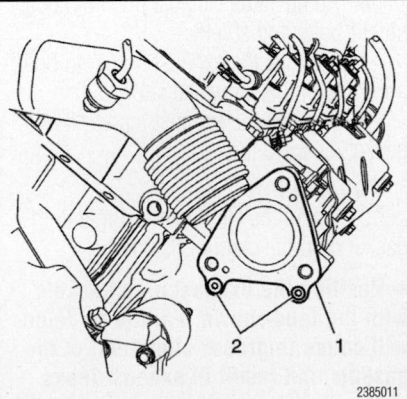

Fig. 345 Install a NEW gasket (1) to the exhaust manifold with the tabs (2) facing downward

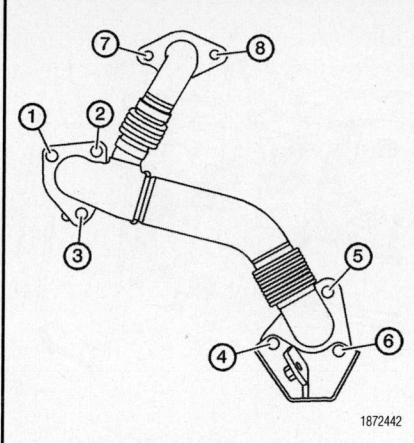

Fig. 346 Tighten the exhaust pipe to exhaust manifold bolts in the sequence shown

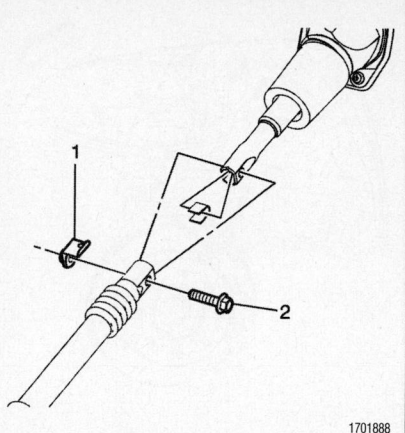

Fig. 347 Remove the steering coupling nut (1) and bolt (2) at the upper intermediate steering shaft

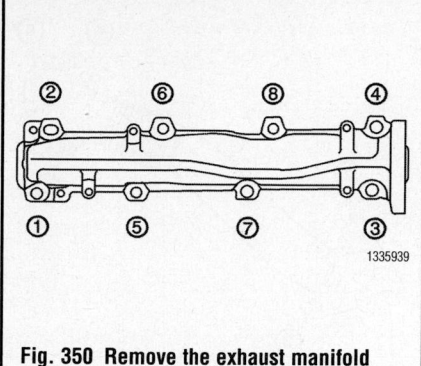

Fig. 350 Remove the exhaust manifold bolts and nuts in the sequence shown

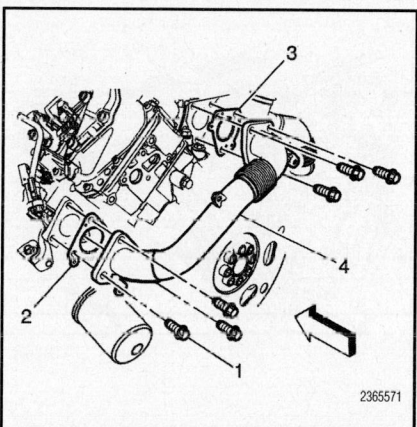

Fig. 348 Remove the left exhaust manifold outlet pipe to the exhaust manifold bolts

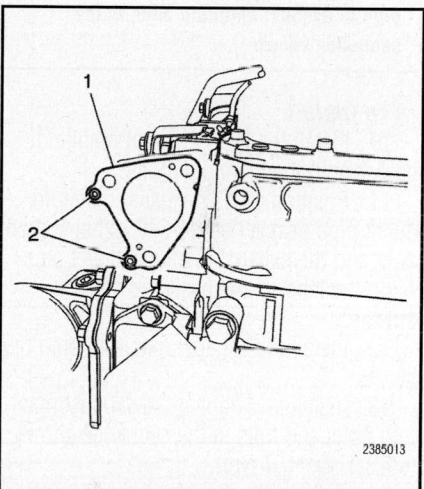

Fig. 351 Position a NEW exhaust manifold outlet pipe gasket (1) between the exhaust manifold and the exhaust manifold outlet pipe. Align the tabs (2) on the gasket to face outward

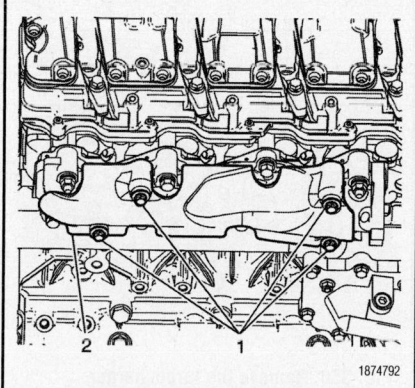

Fig. 349 Remove the exhaust manifold heat shield bolts (1) and shield (2)

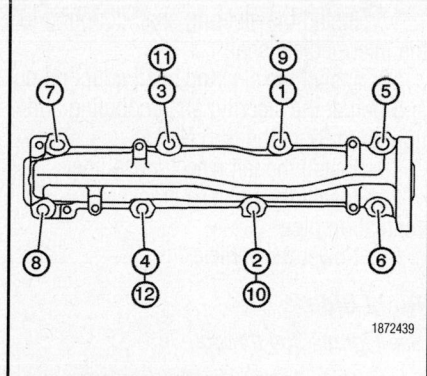

Fig. 352 Install and tighten the exhaust manifold bolts and nuts in the sequence shown

14. Install and tighten the exhaust manifold bolts and nuts in the sequence shown and tighten to 42 ft. lbs. (57 Nm).

15. Tighten the 4 center bolts/nuts an additional pass to 42 ft. lbs. (57 Nm).

16. Position the exhaust manifold heat shield to the manifold and install the exhaust manifold bolts and tighten to 89 inch lbs. (10 Nm).

➡Position the exhaust pipe gaskets with the tabs shown. Failure to do so will cause improper alignment of the gaskets and result in exhaust leaks.

17. Install a NEW gasket to the exhaust manifold with the tabs facing downward.

18. Install the exhaust pipe bracket and the exhaust pipe to exhaust manifold bolts.

19. Tighten the exhaust pipe to exhaust manifold bolts in the sequence shown to 39 ft. lbs. (53 Nm).

20. Install the exhaust pipe to turbocharger exhaust pipe bracket bolt and tighten to 25 ft. lbs. (34 Nm).

21. Install the wheelhouse liner.
22. Lower the vehicle.

2011 Diesel Engines

Left Side

See Figures 347 through 353.

1. Remove the positive crankcase ventilation pipe.

2. Remove the left wheelhouse liner.
3. Perform the following steps working through the wheelhouse opening.

4. Remove the steering coupling nut and bolt at the upper intermediate steering shaft.

5. Separate the steering shaft coupling from the intermediate shaft.

6. Remove the left exhaust manifold outlet pipe to the exhaust manifold bolts. Discard the gasket.

7. Remove the exhaust manifold heat shield bolts and shield.

8. Remove the exhaust manifold bolts and nuts in the sequence shown.

9. Remove the exhaust manifold and gasket. Discard the gasket.

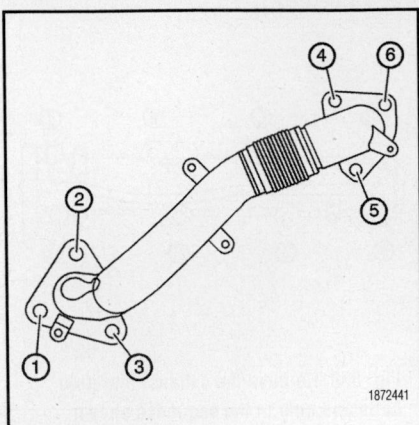

Fig. 353 Install and tighten the exhaust pipe to exhaust manifold bolts in the sequence shown

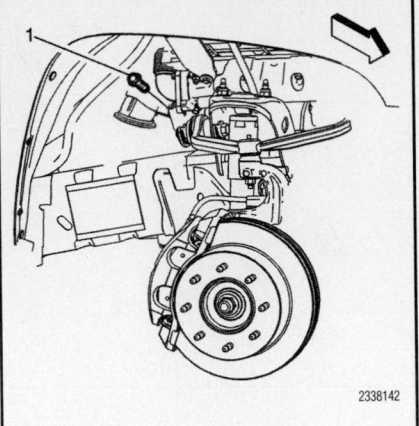

Fig. 354 Remove the exhaust pipe to turbocharger exhaust pipe bracket bolt (1)

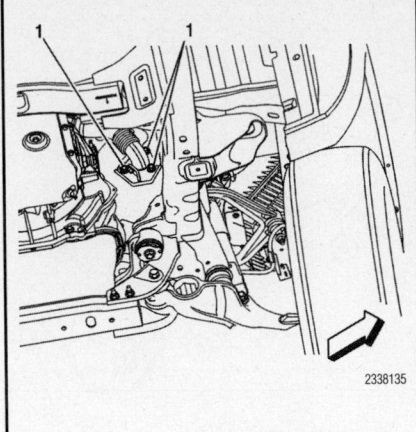

Fig. 357 Remove the exhaust manifold to turbocharger exhaust pipe bolts (1)

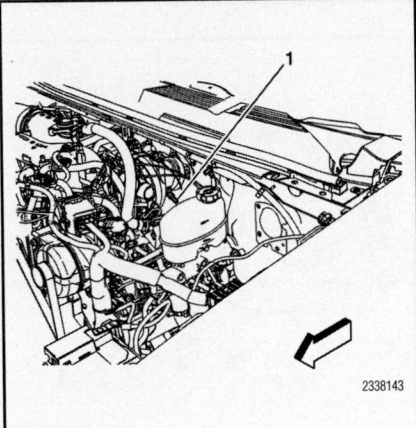

Fig. 355 Loosen the turbocharger exhaust pipe clamp nut (1)

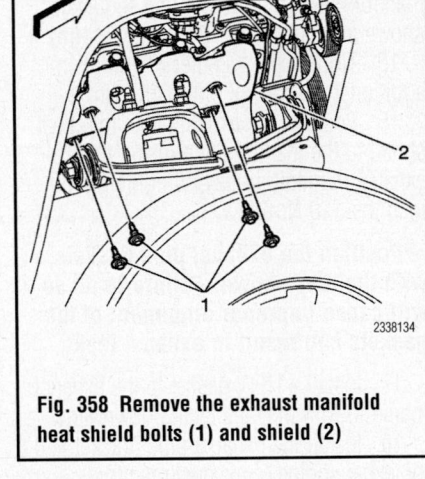

Fig. 358 Remove the exhaust manifold heat shield bolts (1) and shield (2)

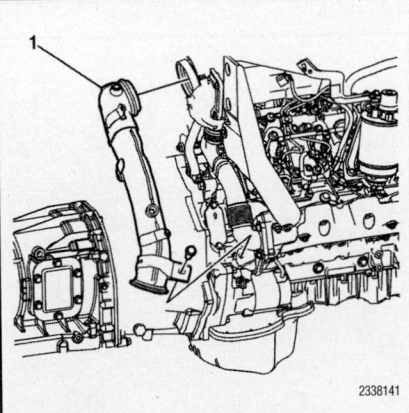

Fig. 356 Remove the turbocharger exhaust pipe (1) from the engine compartment

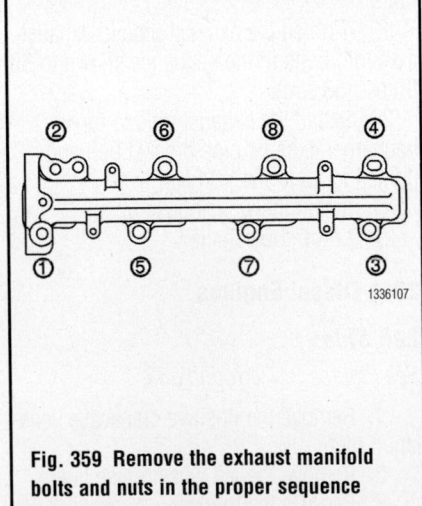

Fig. 359 Remove the exhaust manifold bolts and nuts in the proper sequence

To install:

10. Install the NEW exhaust manifold gasket onto the manifold studs.

11. Position a NEW exhaust manifold outlet pipe gasket between the exhaust manifold and the exhaust manifold outlet pipe. Align the tabs on the gasket to face outward.

12. Install the exhaust manifold onto the studs.

13. Install and tighten the exhaust manifold bolts and nuts in the sequence shown to 42 ft. lbs. (57 Nm).

14. Tighten the 4 center bolts/nuts an additional pass to 42 ft. lbs. (57 Nm).

15. Install and tighten the exhaust pipe to exhaust manifold bolts in the sequence shown to 39 ft. lbs. (53 Nm).

16. Position the exhaust manifold heat shield to the manifold and install the bolts and tighten to 89 inch lbs. (10 Nm).

17. Install the steering shaft coupling to the intermediate shaft.

18. Install the steering shaft coupling nut and bolt at the steering shaft coupling and tighten to 37 ft. lbs. (50 Nm).

19. Install the left wheelhouse liner.

20. Install the positive crankcase ventilation pipe.

21. Lower the vehicle.

Right Side

See Figures 354 through 363.

1. Remove the wheelhouse liner.
2. Disconnect the oxygen sensor.
3. Raise and support the vehicle.
4. Remove the catalytic converter.

➡**Perform the following steps working through the wheelhouse opening.**

5. Remove the exhaust pipe to turbocharger exhaust pipe bracket bolt.

6. Loosen the turbocharger exhaust pipe clamp nut.

7. Remove the turbocharger exhaust pipe from the engine compartment.

8. Remove the exhaust manifold to turbocharger exhaust pipe bolts.

9. Discard the exhaust gasket.

10. Remove the exhaust manifold heat shield bolts and shield.

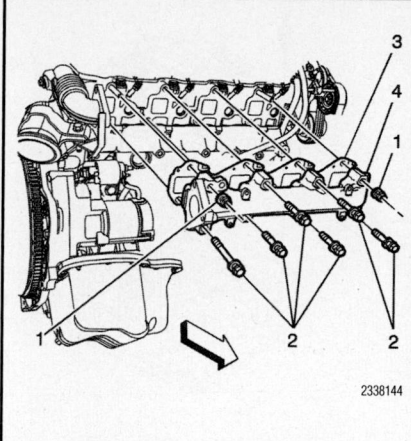

Fig. 360 Remove the exhaust manifold nuts and bolts

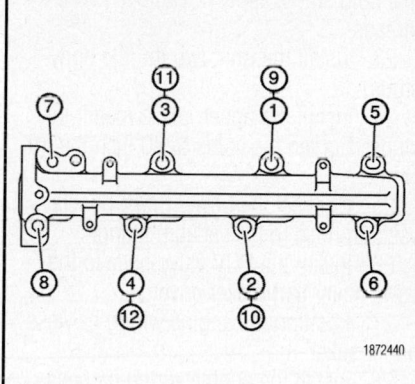

Fig. 361 Install and tighten the exhaust manifold bolts and nuts in the sequence shown

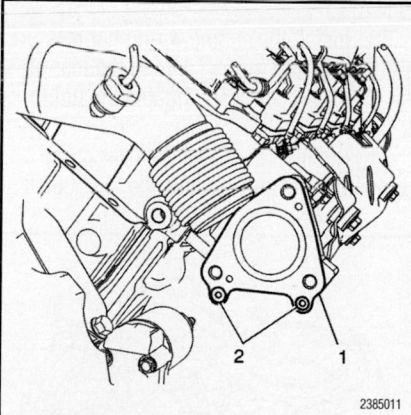

Fig. 362 Install a NEW gasket (1) to the exhaust manifold outlet pipe with the tabs (2) facing downward

11. Remove the exhaust manifold bolts and nuts in the proper sequence.

12. Remove the exhaust manifold nuts and bolts.

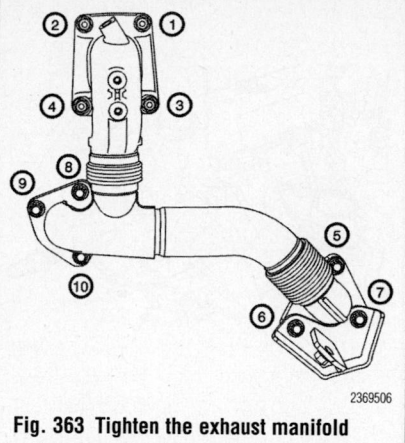

Fig. 363 Tighten the exhaust manifold outlet pipe to exhaust manifold bolts in the sequence shown

13. Remove the exhaust manifold and discard the gasket.

To install:

14. Install a NEW exhaust manifold gasket onto the studs.

15. Install the exhaust manifold onto the studs.

16. Install and tighten the exhaust manifold bolts and nuts in the sequence shown. Tighten to 42 ft. lbs. (57 Nm).

17. Tighten the 4 center bolts/nuts an additional pass to 42 ft. lbs. (57 Nm).

18. Position the exhaust manifold heat shield to the manifold and install the exhaust manifold heat shield bolts. Tighten to 89 inch lbs. (10 Nm).

19. Install a NEW gasket to the exhaust manifold outlet pipe with the tabs facing downward.

20. Tighten the exhaust manifold outlet pipe to exhaust manifold bolts in the sequence shown to 37 ft. lbs. (50 Nm).

21. Install the turbocharger exhaust pipe to the turbocharger and exhaust pipe bracket.

22. Tighten turbocharger exhaust pipe bracket bolt to 25 ft. lbs. (34 Nm).

23. Install the catalytic converter to the turbocharger exhaust pipe.

24. Install the wheelhouse liner.

25. Lower the vehicle.

INTAKE MANIFOLD

REMOVAL & INSTALLATION

V6 Engines

Upper Intake Manifold

See Figures 364 through 373.

1. Remove the fuel pipes/hoses.

2. Disconnect the following electrical connectors:

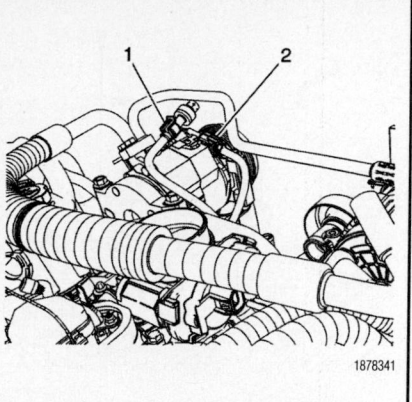

Fig. 364 Disconnect the A/C pressure switch (1); the A/C compressor clutch (2), if equipped

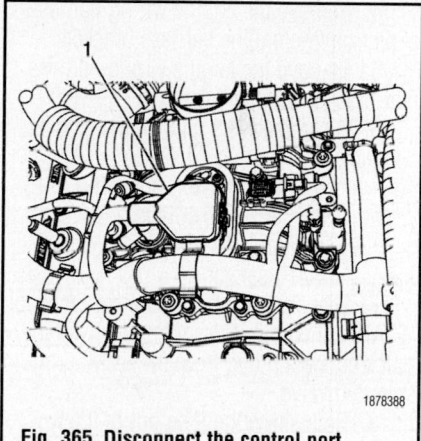

Fig. 365 Disconnect the control port injector module (1)

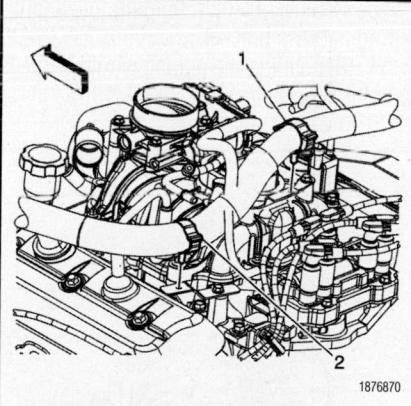

Fig. 366 Remove the engine wiring harness clips (1, 2) from the engine harness brackets

- The A/C pressure switch, if equipped
- The Air Conditioning (A/C) compressor clutch, if equipped

3. Disconnect the control port injector module.

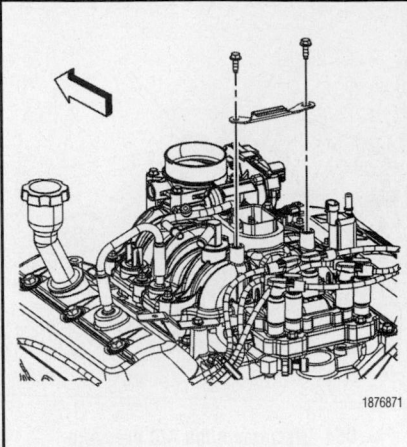

Fig. 367 Remove the engine wiring harness rear bracket bolts and bracket

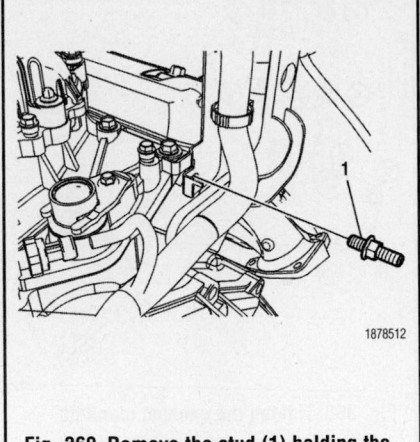

Fig. 369 Remove the stud (1) holding the engine wiring harness bracket

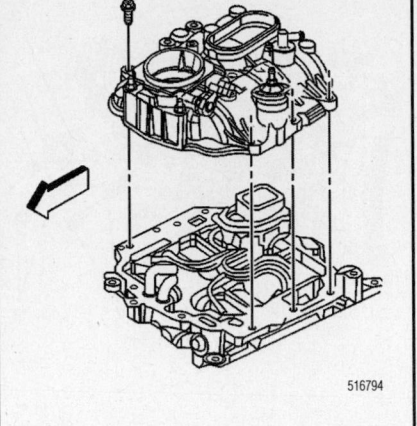

Fig. 371 Remove the upper intake manifold studs

4. Remove the engine wiring harness clips from the engine harness brackets.

5. Remove the engine wiring harness rear bracket bolts and bracket.

6. Disconnect the following electrical connectors:
- The Evaporative Emission (EVAP) canister purge solenoid valve
- The Manifold Absolute Pressure (MAP) sensor

7. Disconnect the Evaporative Emission (EVAP) canister purge solenoid valve tube quick connect fitting from the EVAP purge solenoid valve.

8. Reposition the tube out of the way.

9. Remove the engine wiring harness ground nut and ground wire from the rear of the right cylinder head.

10. Remove the stud holding the engine wiring harness bracket.

11. Reposition the engine wiring harness with the bracket aside.

12. Remove the Positive Crankcase Ventilation (PCV) valve hose from the valve and rocker cover.

13. Disconnect the power brake booster vacuum hose from the vacuum fitting.

14. Remove the upper intake manifold studs.

15. Remove the front 2 throttle body studs.

16. Remove the upper intake manifold.

17. Remove and discard the upper intake manifold gasket.

18. Remove and discard the O-ring seal from the fuel meter body.

To install:

19. Install a NEW O-ring seal to the fuel meter body.

20. Install a NEW upper intake manifold gasket.

21. Install the upper intake manifold.

22. If reusing the old throttle body/intake

manifold studs, apply threadlock to the threads.

23. Install the front two throttle body studs.

24. Install the upper intake manifold studs. Tighten the studs to 80 inch lbs. (9 Nm).

25. Connect the power brake booster vacuum hose to the vacuum fitting.

26. Install the PCV valve hose to the valve cover and rocker cover.

27. Position the engine wiring harness and bracket.

28. Install the engine wiring harness bracket stud. Tighten the stud to 18 ft. lbs. (25 Nm).

29. Install the engine wiring harness rear bracket nut at the EVAP canister purge solenoid valve. Tighten the nut to 80 inch lbs. (9 Nm).

30. Install the engine wiring harness ground nut and ground wire to the rear of the right cylinder head. Tighten the nut to 12 ft. lbs. (16 Nm).

31. Position the EVAP canister purge solenoid tube, and connect the tube quick

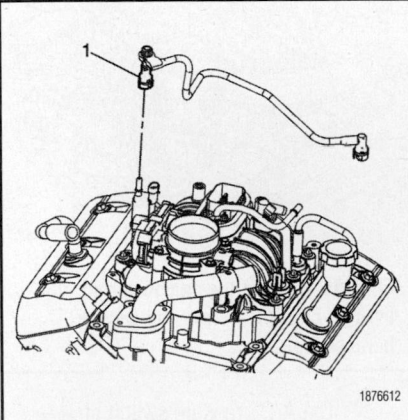

Fig. 368 Disconnect the Evaporative Emission (EVAP) canister purge solenoid valve tube quick connect fitting (1) from the EVAP purge solenoid valve

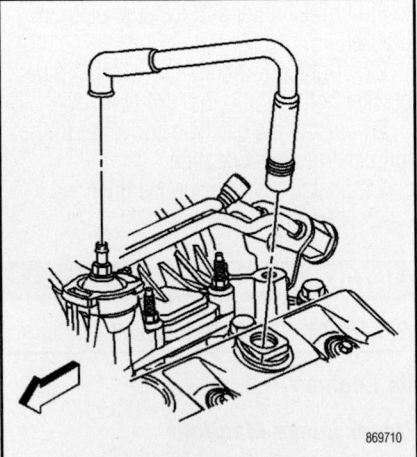

Fig. 370 Remove the Positive Crankcase Ventilation (PCV) valve hose from the valve and rocker cover

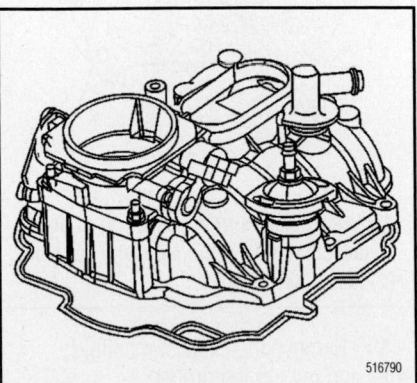

Fig. 372 Remove and discard the upper intake manifold gasket

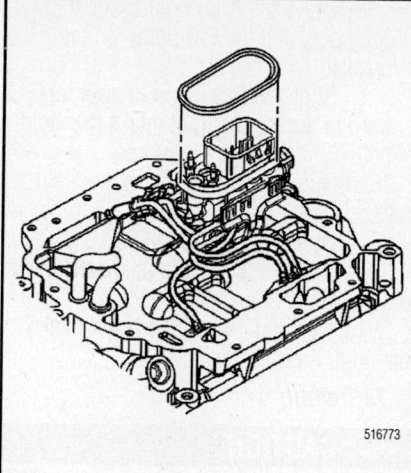

Fig. 373 Remove and discard the O-ring seal from the fuel meter body

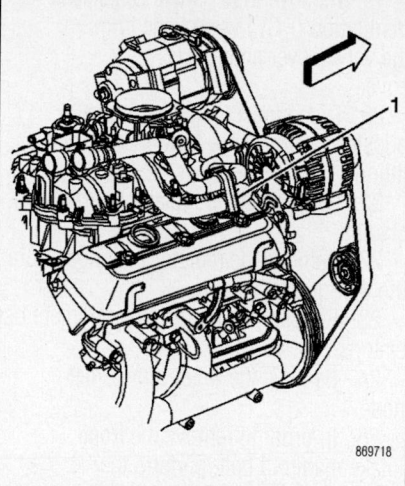

Fig. 374 Remove the heater hose clamp (1)

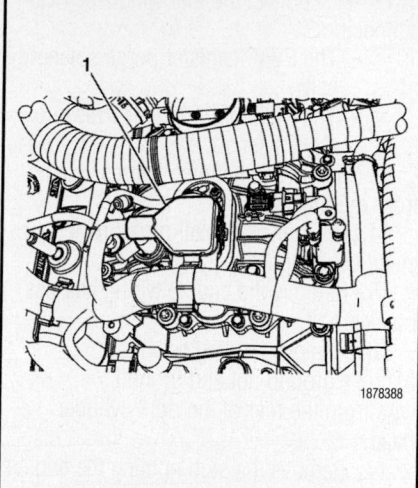

Fig. 376 Disconnect the control port injector module (1)

connect fitting to the EVAP purge solenoid valve.

32. Connect the following electrical connectors:

- The EVAP canister purge solenoid valve
- The MAP sensor

33. Place the engine wiring harness rear bracket onto the upper intake manifold and install the bolts. Tighten the bolts to 89 inch lbs. (10 Nm).

34. Install the engine wiring harness clips to the engine harness brackets.

35. Connect the control port injector module.

36. Connect the following electrical connectors:

- The A/C compressor clutch, if equipped
- The A/C pressure switch, if equipped

37. Install the fuel pipes/hoses.

Lower Intake Manifold

See Figures 374 through 384.

➡ **Note the following:**

- The intake manifold may be removed as an assembly. Do not remove the specific intake manifold components unless component service is required.
- It is not necessary to remove the upper intake manifold in order to remove the lower intake manifold.
- Do not allow dirt or debris to enter the fuel system. Ensure that the ends of the fuel system are properly sealed.
- Do not disassemble the central Sequential Fuel Injection (SFI) unit, unless service is required.

1. Drain the cooling system.
2. Remove the fuel pipes/hoses.

3. Remove the ignition coil assembly.

4. Remove the Evaporative Emission (EVAP) canister tube.

5. Remove the heater hose clamp.

6. Open the heater outlet hose clamp and remove the hose from the intake manifold.

7. Open the heater inlet hose clamp and remove the hose from the water pump.

8. Reposition the heater inlet and outlet hoses.

9. Disconnect the engine wiring harness electrical connector (2) from the throttle body.

10. Disconnect the following electrical connectors:

- The A/C pressure switch, if equipped
- The Air Conditioning (A/C) compressor clutch, if equipped

11. Disconnect the control port injector module.

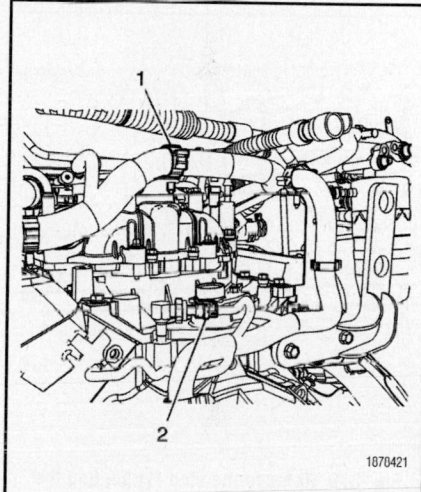

Fig. 377 Remove the engine harness clamp (1) from the bracket; disconnect the oil pressure sensor electrical connector (2)

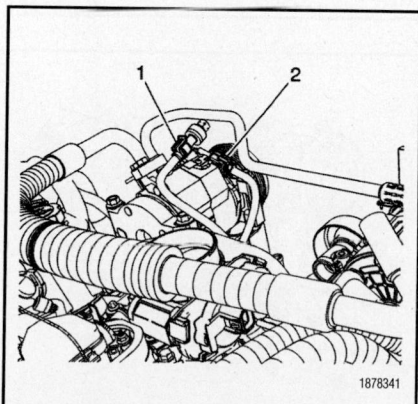

Fig. 375 Disconnect the A/C pressure switch (1); the A/C compressor clutch (2), if equipped

Fig. 378 Remove the engine wiring harness bracket bolt

12. Disconnect the following electrical connectors:
  - The EVAP canister purge solenoid valve
  - The Manifold Absolute Pressure (MAP) sensor

13. Remove the engine harness clamp from the bracket.

14. Disconnect the oil pressure sensor electrical connector.

15. Remove the engine wiring harness bracket bolt.

16. Remove the engine wiring harness ground nut and ground wire from the rear of the right cylinder head.

17. Remove the stud holding the engine wiring harness bracket.

18. Reposition the engine wiring harness with the bracket aside.

19. Remove the Positive Crankcase Ventilation (PCV) valve hose from the valve cover and rocker cover.

20. Disconnect the power brake booster vacuum hose from the vacuum fitting.

21. Reposition the radiator inlet hose clamps.

22. Remove the radiator inlet hose from the thermostat housing.

23. Reposition the water pump inlet hose clamps.

24. Remove the water pump inlet hose.

25. In order to remove the front intake manifold bolt, perform the following:
  a. Remove the drive belt.
  b. Loosen the Power Steering (P/S) pump rear bracket nut.
  c. Remove the P/S pump rear bracket front nut.
  d. Remove the bolts and the nut for the P/S pump bracket.

  e. Leave the A/C compressor, if equipped, and the P/S pump on the bracket.
  f. Slide the P/S pump bracket forward to access the front intake manifold bolt.

26. Remove the lower intake manifold bolts.

27. Remove the intake manifold.

28. Remove and discard the intake manifold gaskets.

29. Clean and inspect the lower intake manifold, if necessary.

To install:

※※ CAUTION

Apply the proper amount of the sealant when assembling this component. Excessive use of the sealant can prohibit the component from sealing properly. A component that is not sealed properly can leak leading to extensive engine damage.

30. Apply a patch of adhesive to the cylinder head side of the intake manifold gasket at each end.

➡The intake manifold gasket must be installed while the adhesive is still wet to the touch.

31. Install the intake manifold gasket onto the cylinder head. Use the gasket locating pins in order to properly seat the gasket.

➡The intake manifold must be installed and the fasteners tightened while the adhesive is still wet to the touch.

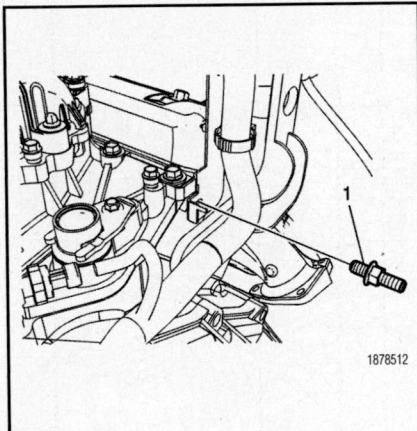

Fig. 379 Remove the stud (1) holding the engine wiring harness bracket

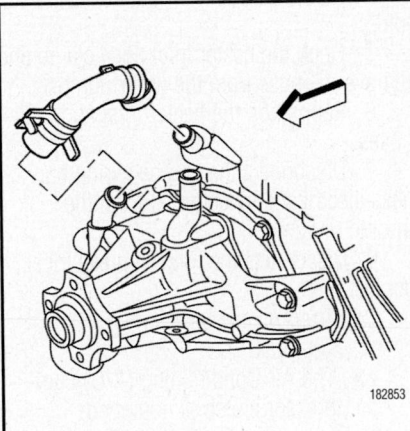

Fig. 381 Remove the water pump inlet hose

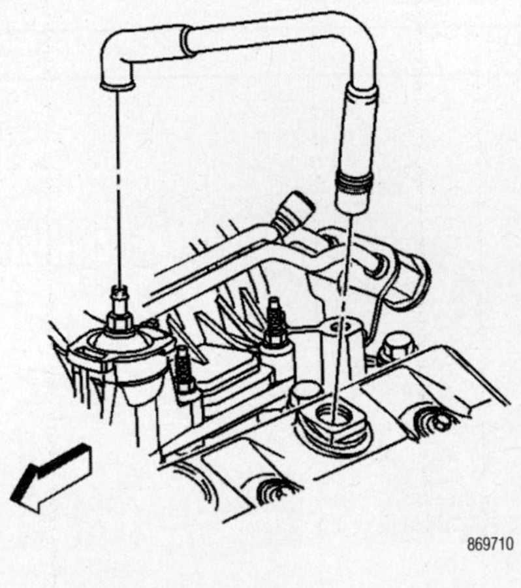

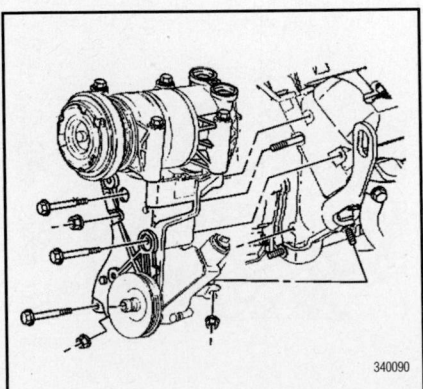

Fig. 380 Remove the Positive Crankcase Ventilation (PCV) valve hose from the valve cover and rocker cover

Fig. 382 Exploded view of the P/S assembly

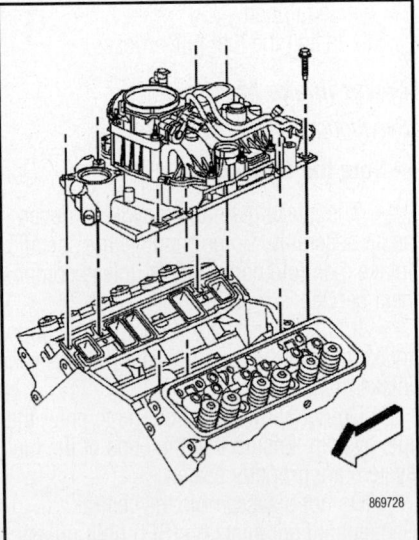

Fig. 383 Remove the lower intake manifold bolts

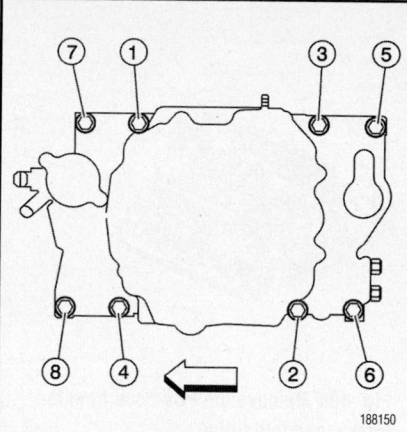

Fig. 384 Tighten the lower intake manifold bolts in the sequence shown

32. Apply a bead of adhesive to the front top of the engine block.

33. Extend the adhesive bead up onto each intake manifold gasket.

34. Apply a bead of adhesive to the rear top of the engine block.

35. Extend the adhesive bead up onto each intake manifold gasket.

36. Install the intake manifold.

37. If reusing the old fasteners, apply threadlock to the threads of the intake manifold - lower bolts.

38. Install the lower intake manifold bolts.

❄❄ CAUTION

Proper lower intake manifold fastener tightening sequence and torque is critical. Always follow the tightening sequence, and torque the intake manifold bolts using the 3 step method. Failing to do so may distort the crankshaft bearing bore alignment and cause damage to the crankshaft bearings.

39. Tighten the lower intake manifold bolts in the sequence shown.

  a. Tighten the bolts a first pass to 27 inch lbs. (3 Nm).

  b. Tighten the bolts a second pass to 106 inch lbs. (12 Nm).

  c. Tighten the bolts a final pass to 11 ft. lbs. (15 Nm).

40. Slide the P/S pump bracket rearward.

41. Install the bolts and the nut for the P/S pump bracket.

42. Install the P/S pump rear bracket front nut.

43. Tighten the P/S pump rear bracket nut. Tighten the bolts and nuts to 30 ft. lbs. (41 Nm).

44. Install the drive belt.

45. Install the water pump inlet hose.

46. Position the water pump inlet hose clamps.

47. Install the radiator inlet hose to the thermostat housing.

48. Position the radiator inlet hose clamps.

49. Connect the power brake booster vacuum hose to the vacuum fitting.

50. Install the PCV valve hose to the valve cover and rocker cover.

51. Position the engine wiring harness and bracket.

52. Install the engine wiring harness bracket stud. Tighten the stud to 18 ft. lbs. (25 Nm).

53. Install the engine wiring harness rear bracket nut at the EVAP canister purge solenoid valve. Tighten the nut to 80 inch lbs. (9 Nm).

54. Install the engine wiring harness ground nut and ground wire to the rear of the right cylinder head. Tighten the nut to 12 ft. lbs. (16 Nm).

55. Install the engine wiring harness bracket bolt. Tighten the bolt to 106 inch lbs. (12 Nm).

56. Install the EVAP canister tube.

57. Connect the oil pressure sensor electrical connector.

58. Install the engine harness clamp to the bracket.

59. Connect the following electrical connectors:
- The EVAP canister purge solenoid valve
- The MAP sensor

60. Connect the control port injector module.

61. Connect the following electrical connectors:
- The A/C compressor clutch, if equipped
- The A/C pressure switch, if equipped

62. Connect the engine wiring harness electrical connector to the throttle body.

63. Position the heater inlet and outlet hoses.

64. Open the heater inlet hose clamp and install the hose to the water pump.

65. Open the heater outlet hose clamp and install the hose to the intake manifold.

66. Install the heater hose clamp.

67. Install the fuel pipes/hoses.

68. Install the ignition coil assembly.

69. Fill the cooling system.

V8 Engines

See Figures 385 through 394.

1. Remove the air cleaner outlet duct.

2. Remove the alternator.

3. Remove the engine harness retainer nut.

4. Remove the engine harness retainer from the stud and locator pin.

5. Disconnect the engine harness electrical connector from the Evaporative Emission (EVAP) canister purge solenoid.

6. Disconnect the engine wiring harness electrical connector from the Manifold Absolute Pressure (MAP) sensor.

7. Remove the Connector Position Assurance (CPA) retainer.

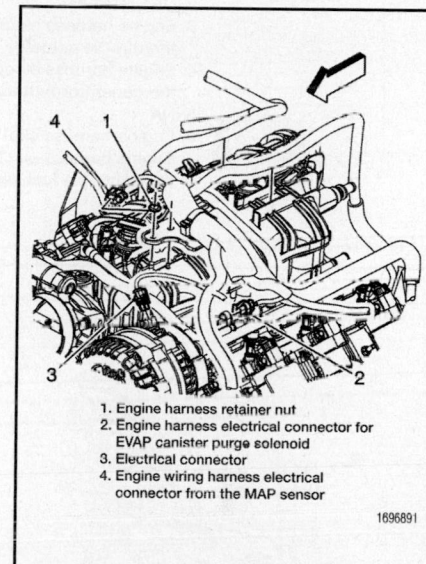

1. Engine harness retainer nut
2. Engine harness electrical connector for EVAP canister purge solenoid
3. Electrical connector
4. Engine wiring harness electrical connector from the MAP sensor

Fig. 385 Remove the engine harness retainer nut

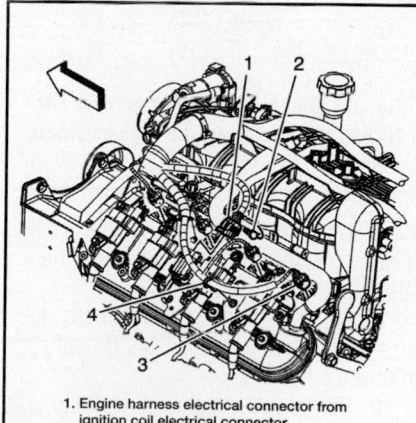

1. Engine harness electrical connector from ignition coil electrical connector
2. CPA retainer
3. Engine harness electrical connector from left side fuel injectors
4. Engine harness clip

Fig. 386 Remove the Connector Position Assurance (CPA) retainer

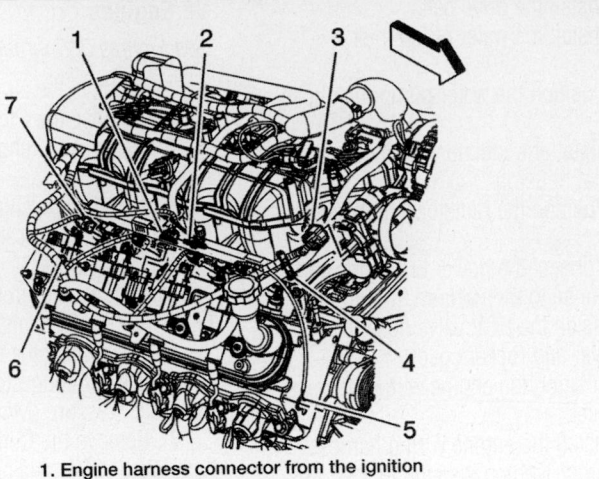

1. Engine harness connector from the ignition coil electrical connector
2. CPA retainer
3. Engine harness electrical connector from the throttle actuator
4. Engine harness electrical connector from the generator battery jumper cable
5. NA
6. Engine harness clip
7. Engine harness electrical connectors from the right side fuel injectors

Fig. 387 Remove the CPA retainer

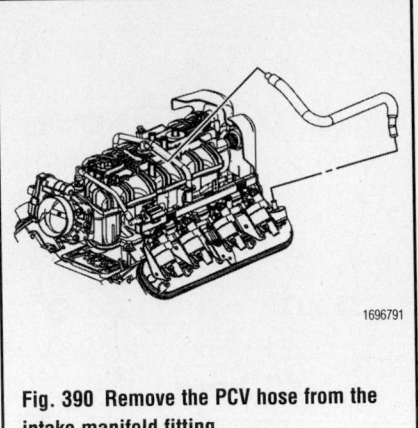

Fig. 390 Remove the PCV hose from the intake manifold fitting

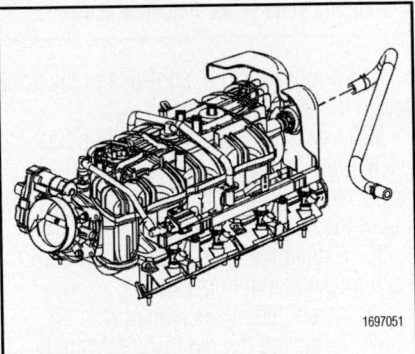

Fig. 391 Remove the brake booster vacuum hose from the intake manifold nipple

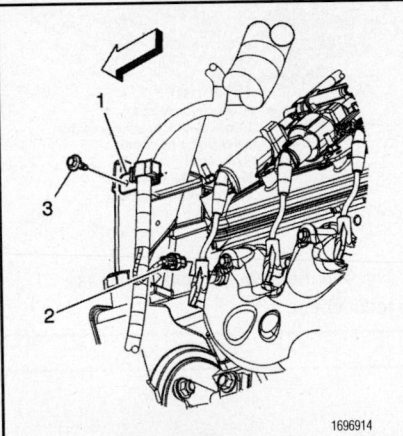

Fig. 388 Remove the engine harness clip (1) bolt (3); disconnect the engine harness electrical connector (2)

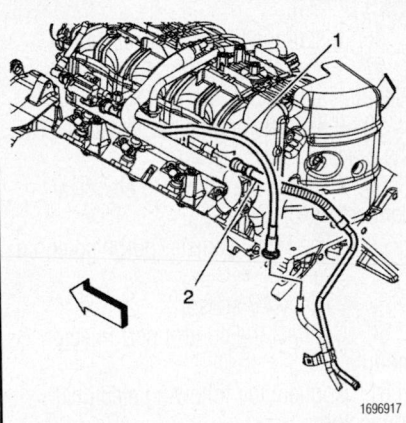

Fig. 389 Disconnect the EVAP canister purge tube (1) quick connect fitting and the fuel feed line quick connect fitting (2)

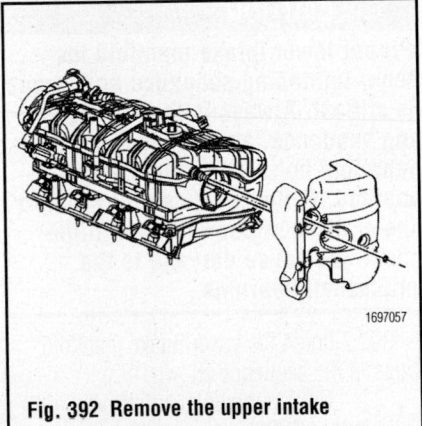

Fig. 392 Remove the upper intake manifold cover

8. Disconnect the engine harness electrical connector from the ignition coil harness electrical connector.

9. Disconnect the engine harness electrical connectors from the left side fuel injectors.

10. Remove the engine harness clip from the ignition coil bracket stud.

11. Remove the CPA retainer.

12. Disconnect the engine harness electrical connector from the ignition coil harness electrical connector.

13. Disconnect the engine harness electrical connector from the throttle actuator.

14. Remove the engine harness clip from the alternator battery jumper cable.

15. Remove the engine harness clip from the ignition coil bracket stud.

16. Disconnect the engine harness electrical connectors from the right side fuel injectors.

17. Remove the engine harness clip bolt.

18. Disconnect the engine harness electrical connector from the Engine Coolant Temperature (ECT) sensor.

19. Gather the engine harness branches and tie the harness up out of the way to the cowl panel.

20. Reposition the brake booster vacuum hose clamp at the booster.

21. Remove the brake booster vacuum hose from the booster fitting.

22. Secure the brake booster vacuum hose to the intake manifold.

23. Disconnect the EVAP canister purge tube quick connect fitting from the EVAP canister purge solenoid.

24. Disconnect the fuel feed line quick connect fitting from the fuel rail.

25. Remove the Positive Crankcase Ventilation (PCV) hose from the intake manifold fitting.

26. Position the hose out of the way.

27. Loosen the intake manifold bolts.

➡ **The aid of an assistant may be helpful in holding the engine harness up out of the way so the upper intake manifold cover does not get caught against the engine harness.**

28. Remove the intake manifold.

29. Cover the cylinder head passages in order to prevent dirt or debris from entering the passages.

30. Remove and discard the intake manifold gaskets.

31. If replacing the intake manifold, perform the following steps, otherwise proceed to step 21 of the installation procedure.

32. Place the intake manifold on a clean work surface.

33. Reposition the brake booster vacuum hose clamp at the intake manifold.

34. Remove the brake booster vacuum hose from the intake manifold nipple.

35. Remove the upper intake manifold cover nut.

36. Remove the upper intake manifold cover.

37. Remove the manifold absolute pressure (MAP) sensor retainer.

38. Remove the MAP sensor.

39. Disconnect the EVAP tube quick connect fitting at the intake manifold.

40. Disengage the retainer securing the EVAP canister purge solenoid to the fuel rail.

41. Remove the EVAP tube and purge solenoid.

42. Remove the throttle body bolts/nuts.

43. Remove the throttle body.

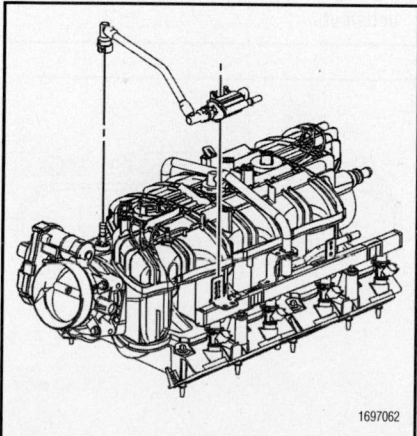

Fig. 393 Remove the EVAP tube and purge solenoid

44. Remove and discard the throttle body gasket.

45. Remove the fuel rail bolts.

➡ **Lift evenly on both sides of the fuel rail until all injectors are removed from their bores.**

46. Remove the fuel rail.

47. Remove and discard the fuel injector lower O-ring seals.

➡ **Evenly push in the RED collar in order to remove the nipple.**

48. Remove the brake booster vacuum hose nipple.

To install:

49. If the intake manifold was replaced perform the following steps, otherwise proceed to step 21.

➡ **Evenly push in the RED collar in order to install the nipple.**

50. Install the brake booster vacuum hose nipple to the NEW intake manifold.

51. Install NEW fuel injector lower O-ring seals onto the injectors.

52. Lubricate the NEW O-ring seals with clean engine oil.

➡ **Push down firmly on both sides of the rail until all the injectors have been seated into their bores.**

53. Install the fuel rail.

54. Install the fuel rail bolts and tighten to 89 inch lbs. (10 Nm).

55. Install a NEW throttle body gasket to the intake manifold.

56. Install the throttle body.

57. Install the throttle body bolts/nuts and tighten to 89 inch lbs. (10 Nm).

58. Install the EVAP tube and purge solenoid.

59. Install the EVAP canister purge solenoid to the fuel rail bracket and engage the retainer.

60. Connect the EVAP tube quick connect fitting at the intake manifold.

61. Lubricate the MAP sensor seal with clean engine oil.

62. Install the MAP sensor.

63. Install the MAP sensor retainer.

64. Install the upper intake manifold cover.

65. Install the upper intake manifold cover nut until snug

66. Install the brake booster vacuum hose to the intake manifold nipple.

67. Position the brake booster vacuum hose clamp at the intake manifold.

68. Secure the brake booster vacuum hose to the intake manifold.

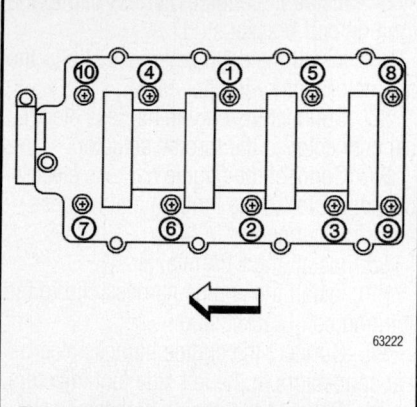

Fig. 394 Tighten the intake manifold bolts in two phases

69. Install NEW intake manifold gaskets to the intake manifold.

70. Remove the covers from the cylinder head passages.

71. Install the intake manifold.

➡ **The aid of an assistant may be helpful in holding the engine harness up out of the way so the upper intake manifold cover does not get caught against the engine harness.**

72. Tighten the intake manifold bolts until snug.

73. Tighten the intake manifold bolts in two phases.

a. Tighten the bolts a first pass in the sequence shown to 44 inch lbs. (5 Nm).

b. Tighten the bolts a final pass in the sequence shown to 89 inch lbs. (10 Nm).

74. Position and install the PCV hose to the intake manifold fitting.

75. Connect the fuel feed line quick connect fitting to the fuel rail.

76. Connect the EVAP canister purge tube quick connect fitting to the EVAP canister purge solenoid.

77. Unsecure the brake booster vacuum hose from the intake manifold.

78. Install the brake booster vacuum hose to the booster fitting.

79. Position the brake booster vacuum hose clamp at the booster.

80. Untie the engine harness branches from the cowl panel and position over the engine.

81. Connect the engine harness electrical connector to the ECT sensor.

82. Position the engine harness clip to the alternator bracket and install the bolt. Tighten the bolt to 80 inch lbs. (9 Nm).

83. Connect the engine harness electrical connectors to the right side fuel injectors.

84. Install the engine harness clip to the ignition coil bracket stud.

85. Install the engine harness clip to the alternator battery jumper cable.

86. Connect the engine harness electrical connector to the throttle actuator.

87. Connect the engine harness electrical connector to the ignition coil harness electrical connector.

88. Install the CPA retainer.

89. Install the engine harness clip to the ignition coil bracket stud.

90. Connect the engine harness electrical connectors to the left side fuel injectors.

91. Connect the engine harness electrical connector to the ignition coil harness electrical connector.

92. Install the CPA retainer.

93. Connect the engine wiring harness electrical connector to the MAP sensor.

94. Connect the engine harness electrical connector to the EVAP canister purge solenoid.

95. Install the engine harness retainer to the stud and locator pin.

96. Install the engine harness retainer nut.

97. Install the alternator.

98. Install the air cleaner outlet duct.

2010 Diesel Engines

Center Intake Manifold

See Figures 395 through 397.

1. Remove the Exhaust Gas Recirculation (EGR) valve cooler tube.

2. Remove the water outlet tube.

3. Remove the intake manifold tube.

4. Remove and discard the 2 intake manifold tube gaskets.

5. Remove the turbocharger.

6. Disconnect the Intake Air Temperature (IAT) sensor electrical connector.

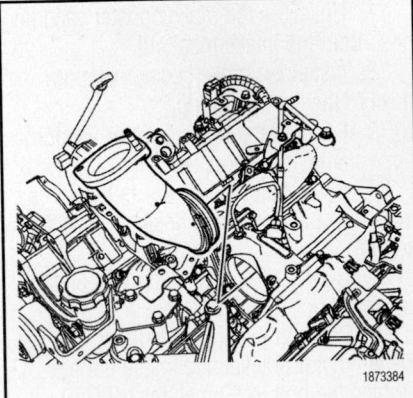

Fig. 395 Remove the intake manifold tube

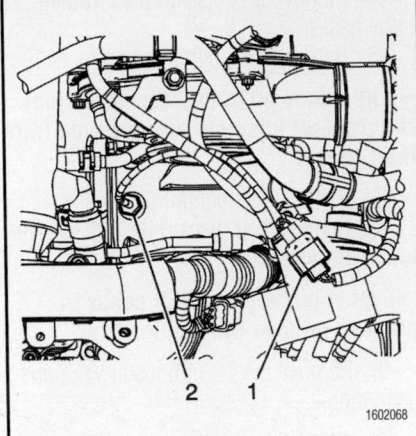

Fig. 396 Disconnect the Intake Air Temperature (IAT) sensor electrical connector (1) and remove the IAT sensor (2)

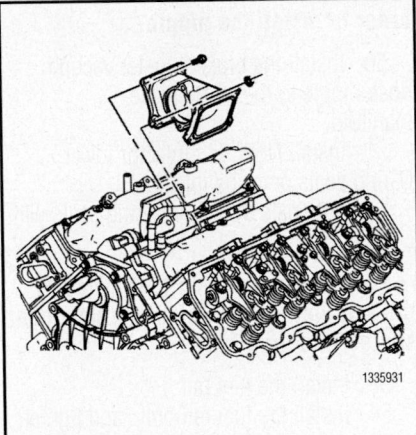

Fig. 397 Remove the center intake manifold bolts/nuts

7. Remove the IAT sensor.

8. Remove the center intake manifold bolts/nuts.

9. Pull-up the center intake manifold in order to remove.

10. Remove and discard the gaskets.

11. Clean the center intake manifold in cleaning solvent and air dry.

To install:

12. Install NEW center intake manifold gaskets.

13. Install the center intake manifold.

14. Install the center intake manifold bolts/nuts. Tighten the bolts/nuts to 89 inch lbs. (10 Nm).

15. Install the IAT sensor. Tighten the sensor to 89 inch lbs. (10 Nm).

16. Connect the IAT sensor electrical connector.

17. Install the turbocharger.

18. Install 2 NEW O-rings onto the intake manifold tube.

19. Lubricate the O-rings with clean engine oil to aid in the installation.

20. Install the intake manifold tube.

21. Install the water outlet tube.

22. Install the EGR valve cooler tube.

Left Side

See Figures 398 and 399.

1. Remove the center intake manifold.

2. Remove the glow plug module and bracket.

3. Remove the left fuel rail.

4. Remove the intake manifold bolts/nuts.

➡ **The intake manifold uses sealer. Pry at the area by the fuel rail bolt holes in order to avoid damage to the sealing surfaces.**

5. Remove the intake manifold.

6. To prevent entry of debris in the cylinder head tape the openings.

7. If required, clean and inspect the intake manifold.

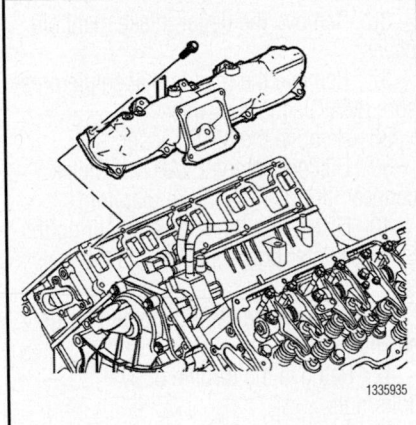

Fig. 398 Remove the intake manifold bolts/nuts

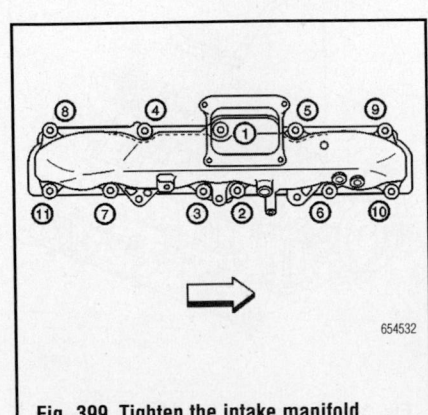

Fig. 399 Tighten the intake manifold bolts/nuts in the sequence shown

To install:

8. Apply a bead of sealant to the intake manifold.

9. Install the intake manifold.

10. Install the intake manifold bolts/nuts.

11. Tighten the intake manifold bolts/nuts in the sequence shown. Tighten the bolts/nuts to 15 ft. lbs. (21 Nm).

12. Install the left fuel rail.

13. Install the glow plug module and bracket.

14. Install the center intake manifold.

Right Side

See Figures 398 and 399.

1. Remove the center intake manifold.

2. Remove the glow plug module and bracket.

3. Remove the right fuel rail.

4. Remove the intake manifold bolts/nuts.

➡**The intake manifold uses sealer. Pry at the area by the fuel rail bolt holes in order to avoid damage to the sealing surfaces.**

5. Remove the intake manifold.

6. To prevent entry of debris in the cylinder head tape the openings.

7. If required, clean and inspect the intake manifold.

To install:

8. Apply a bead of sealant to the intake manifold.

9. Install the intake manifold.

10. Install the intake manifold bolts/nuts.

11. Tighten the intake manifold bolts/nuts in the sequence shown. Tighten the bolts/nuts to 15 ft. lbs. (21 Nm).

12. Install the right fuel rail.

13. Install the glow plug module and bracket.

14. Install the center intake manifold.

2011 Diesel Engines

Center Intake Manifold

See Figure 400.

1. Remove the front EGR cooler.

2. Remove the turbocharger air Inlet adapter.

3. Remove the center intake manifold fasteners.

4. Remove the center intake manifold.

　a. Ensure to replace the center intake manifold gasket whenever the intake is removed.

　b. Disconnect electrical connectors as needed.

　c. Transfer components as necessary.

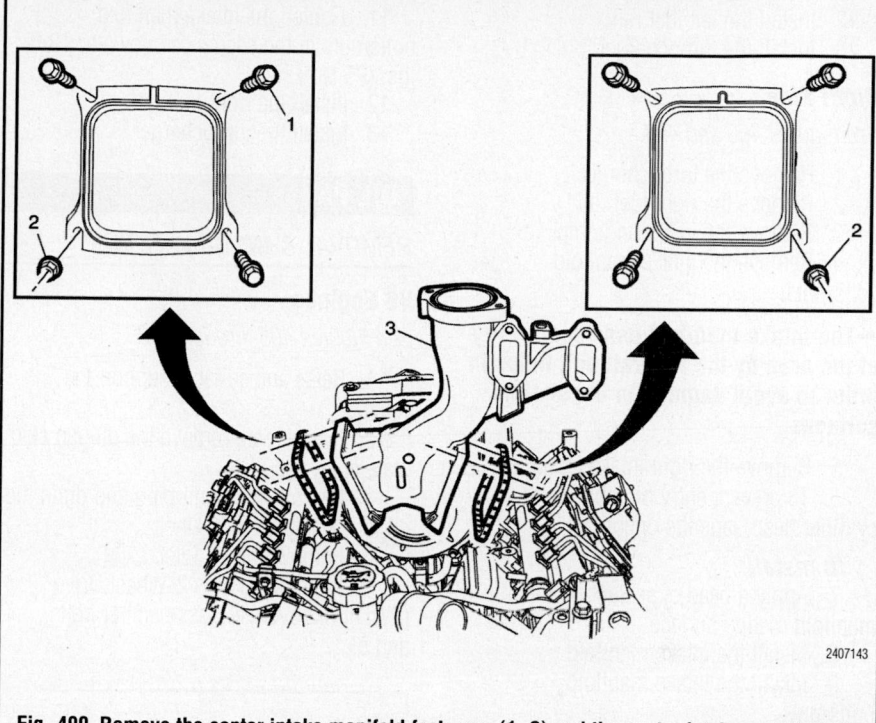

Fig. 400 Remove the center intake manifold fasteners (1, 2) and the center intake manifold (3)

5. Installation is the reverse of removal.

6. Tighten the center intake manifold fasteners 89 inch lbs. (10 Nm).

Left Side

See Figures 401 and 402.

1. Remove the turbocharger.

2. Remove the injection pump.

3. Remove the left fuel rail.

➡**The intake manifold uses sealer. Pry at the area by the fuel rail bolt holes in order to avoid damage to the sealing surface.**

4. Remove the left intake manifold bolts. Do not forget to remove the bolt inside the intake manifold tube.

5. Separate the intake manifold from the cylinder head using J-37228 cutter.

6. Remove the left intake manifold.

7. Inspect and clean.

To install:

8. Apply a bead of sealant on the intake manifold mating surface.

9. Install the intake manifold.

10. Install the intake manifold bolts and nuts and tighten in sequence to 18 ft. lbs (25 Nm).

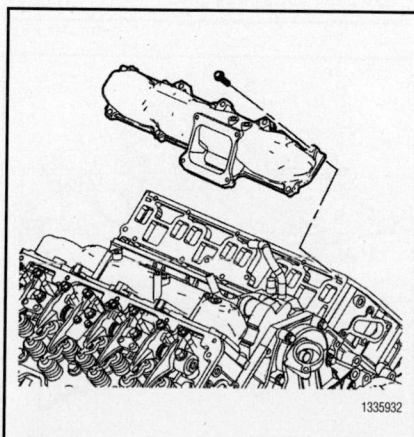

Fig. 401 Remove the left intake manifold bolts (1), separate the intake manifold (2) from the cylinder head (3)

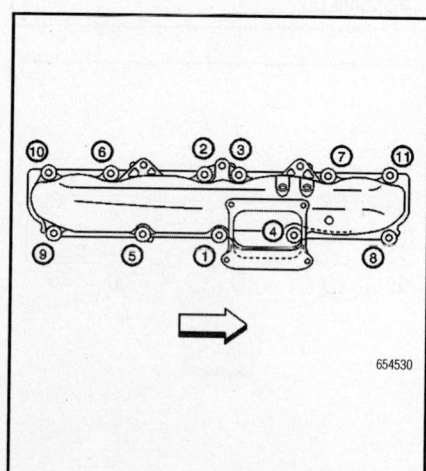

Fig. 402 Install the intake manifold bolts and nuts and tighten in sequence

11. Install the injection pump.
12. Install the left fuel rail.
13. Install the turbocharger.

Right Side

See Figures 403 and 404.

1. Remove the turbocharger.
2. Remove the right fuel rail.
3. Remove the injection pump.
4. Remove the intake manifold bolts/nuts.

➡**The intake manifold uses sealer. Pry at the area by the fuel rail bolt holes in order to avoid damage to the sealing surfaces.**

5. Remove the right intake manifold.
6. To prevent entry of debris in the cylinder head, tape the openings.

To install:

7. Apply a bead of sealant on the intake manifold mating surface.
8. Install the intake manifold.
9. Install the intake manifold bolts/nuts.

10. Install the injection pump.
11. Tighten the intake manifold bolts/nuts in the sequence shown to 18 ft. lbs. (25 Nm).
12. Install the right fuel rail.
13. Install the turbocharger.

OIL PAN

REMOVAL & INSTALLATION

V6 Engines

See Figures 405 through 413.

1. Raise and suitably support the vehicle.
2. If equipped, remove the oil pan skid plate bolts and plate.
3. Remove the drain plug and drain the oil into a suitable container.
4. Remove the oil filter.
5. If equipped with 2-Wheel Drive (2WD), remove the crossmember bolts and bar.

6. If equipped with 4-Wheel Drive (4WD), remove the crossmember bolts and bar.
7. If equipped with 4WD, remove the front differential carrier.
8. Remove the engine harness bracket bolts.
9. Remove the starter.
10. Remove the transmission cover.
11. Remove the engine harness and transmission tube bracket.
12. Remove two engine wire harness bracket bolts.
13. Remove the manual transmission bolts, if equipped.
14. Remove the automatic transmission bolts, if equipped.
15. Remove the oil pan bolts and nuts.
16. Remove the oil pan.
17. Remove and discard the oil pan gasket.
18. Clean and inspect the oil pan, if necessary.

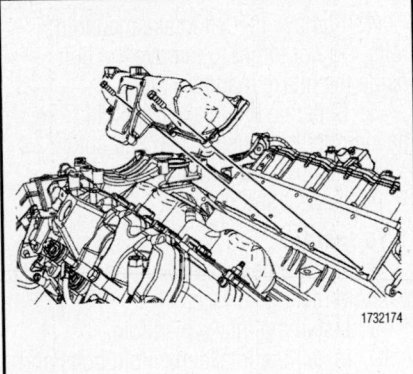

1732174

Fig. 403 Remove the intake manifold bolts/nuts (1) and the right intake manifold (2)

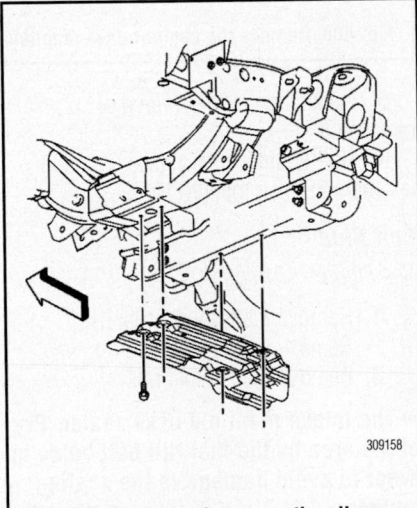

309158

Fig. 405 If equipped, remove the oil pan skid plate bolts and plate

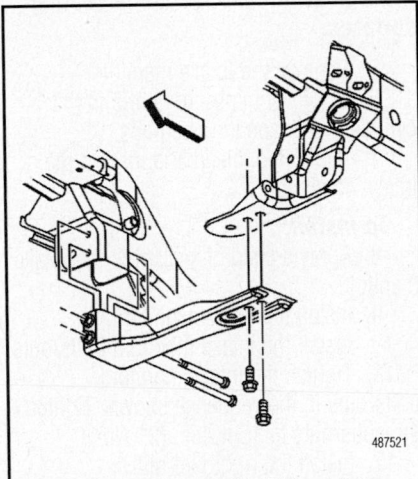

487521

Fig. 407 If equipped with 4-Wheel Drive (4WD), remove the crossmember bolts and bar

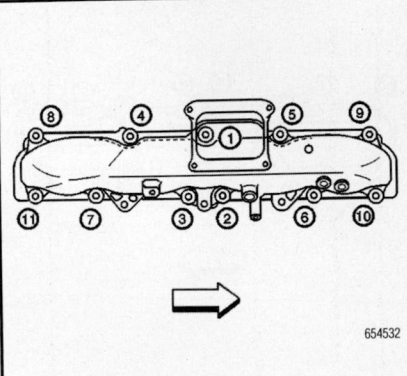

654532

Fig. 404 Tighten the intake manifold bolts/nuts in the sequence shown

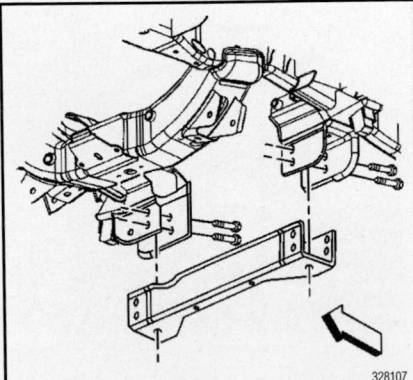

328107

Fig. 406 If equipped with 2-Wheel Drive (2WD), remove the crossmember bolts (1) and bar (2)

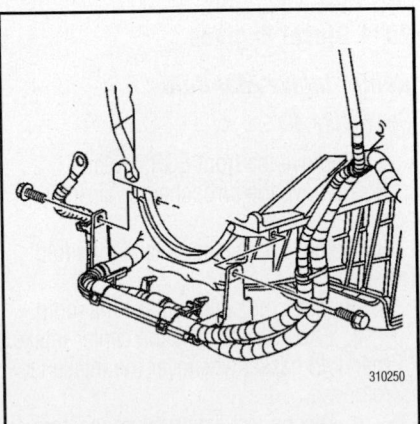

310250

Fig. 408 Remove the engine harness bracket bolts

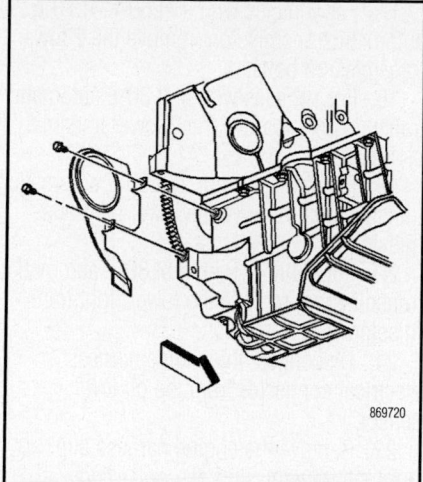

Fig. 409 Remove the transmission cover

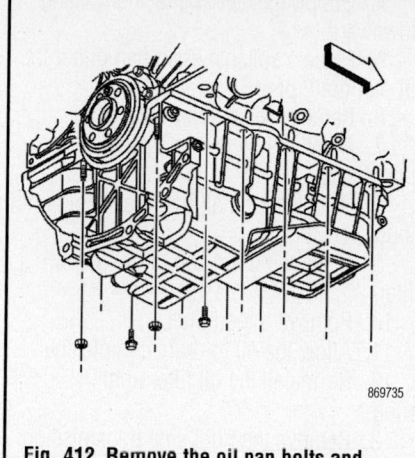

Fig. 412 Remove the oil pan bolts and nuts

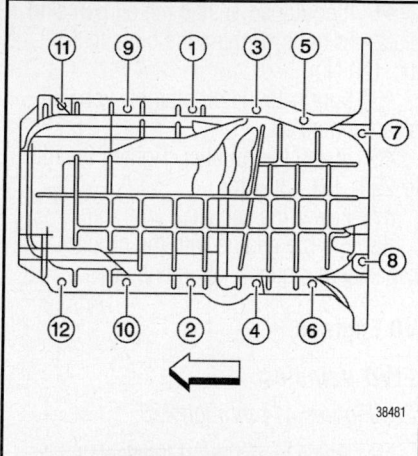

Fig. 413 Tighten the oil pan bolts and nuts in the sequence shown

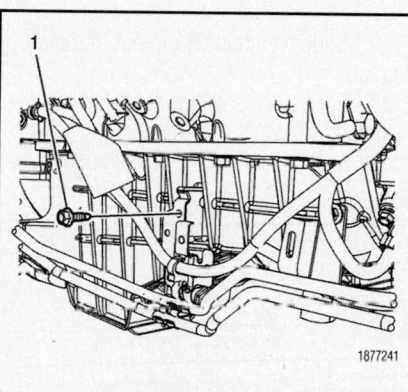

Fig. 410 Remove the engine harness and transmission tube bracket (1)

Fig. 411 Remove two engine wire harness bracket bolts (1)

To install:

⁂ CAUTION

Any time the transmission and the engine oil pan are off of the engine at the same time, install the transmission before the oil pan. This is to allow for the proper oil pan alignment. Failure to achieve the correct oil pan alignment can result in transmission failure.

19. Apply a bead of adhesive to both the right and left sides of the front cover to engine block junction at the oil pan sealing surfaces.

20. Apply a bead of adhesive to the entire length of rear oil seal housing to engine block junction at the oil pan sealing surfaces.

21.

➡Always install a NEW oil pan gasket. The oil pan gasket and oil pan must be installed and the fasteners tightened while the adhesive is still wet to the touch.

22. Install a NEW oil pan gasket into the groove in the oil pan.

➡The oil pan alignment must always be flush or forward no more than 0.011 inches (0.3 mm) from the rear face of the engine block.

23. Install the oil pan.
24. Press the oil pan gasket into the grooves of the engine front cover and crankshaft rear oil seal housing.
25. Slide the oil pan back against a suitable straight edge.
26. Install the oil pan bolts and nuts until snug.
27. Measure the oil pan-to-transmission housing clearance using a feeler gauge and a straight edge.
28. Use the feeler gauge to check the clearance at the oil pan-to-transmission housing measurement points. If the clearance exceeds 0.011 inches (0.3 mm) at any of the oil pan-to-transmission housing

measurement points, then repeat the step until the oil pan-to-transmission housing clearance is within specifications. The oil pan must always be forward of the rear face of the engine block.

29. Tighten the oil pan bolts and nuts in the sequence shown. Tighten the bolts to 18 ft. lbs. (25 Nm).
30. Measure the clearance at the oil pan-to-transmission housing measurement points in order to ensure proper alignment.
31. Install a NEW drain plug O-ring seal onto the drain plug.
32. Install the drain plug. Tighten the plug to 18 ft. lbs. (25 Nm).
33. Install the transmission cover. Tighten the bolts to 106 inch lbs. (12 Nm).
34. Install the automatic transmission bolts, if equipped.
35. Install the manual transmission bolts, if equipped. Tighten the bolts to 37 ft. lbs. (50 Nm).
36. Install two engine wire harness bracket bolts.
37. Install the engine harness and transmission tube bracket bolt. Tighten the bolt to 80 inch lbs. (9 Nm).
38. Install the starter.
39. Connect the oil level sensor electrical connector.
40. Install the engine harness bracket bolts. Tighten the bolts to 106 inch lbs. (12 Nm).
41. If equipped with 2WD, install the crossmember and bolts. Tighten the bolts to 74 ft. lbs. (100 Nm).
42. Install the front differential carrier, if equipped with 4WD.
43. If equipped with 4WD, install the crossmember and bolts. Tighten the bolts to 74 ft. lbs. (100 Nm).

44. If equipped, install the oil pan skid plate and bolts. Tighten the bolts to 15 ft. lbs. (20 Nm).

45. Lubricate the oil filter gasket with clean engine oil.

46. Install the oil filter. Tighten the filter to 22 ft. lbs. (30 Nm).

47. Lower the vehicle.

48. Fill the engine with the proper capacity and quality of engine oil.

V8 Engines

2WD Vehicles

See Figures 414 through 428.

1. Raise and support the vehicle.

2. For 1500 series vehicles, remove the oil pan skid plate bolts and skid plate, if equipped.

3. For 2500 series vehicles, loosen the 2 rear oil pan skid plate bolts, remove the 2 front oil pan skid plate bolts and skid plate, if equipped.

4. Unbolt the steering rack and hang downward.

5. Place a suitable drain pan under the oil pan drain plug.

6. Remove the oil pan drain plug.

7. Allow the oil pan to drain completely.

8. Re-install the oil pan drain plug until snug.

9. Place the drain pan under the oil filter.

10. Remove the oil filter.

11. Allow the oil to drain completely.

12. Re-install the oil filter until snug.

13. Remove the right side transmission cover bolt.

14. Remove the left side transmission cover bolt and cover.

15. For 1500 series vehicles, remove the crossbar bolts/nuts and crossbar.

16. For 2500 series vehicles, remove the crossbar bolts/nuts and crossbar.

17. For vehicles with a 4L60-E/4L70-E automatic transmission, remove the 2 lower transmission bolts.

18. For vehicles with a 4L80-E automatic transmission, remove the 2 lower transmission bolts.

19. For vehicles with a 6L80-E automatic transmission, remove the lower left transmission bolt.

20. For vehicles with a 6L80-E automatic transmission, remove the lower right transmission stud.

21. Disconnect the engine harness electrical connector from the oil level sensor.

22. Remove the engine harness clip from the transmission oil cooler line bracket.

23. Remove the battery cable channel bolt.

24. Slide the channel pin out of the oil pan tab.

25. For vehicles with a 4L60-E/4L70-E automatic transmission, remove the oil cooler lines from the clip, if equipped.

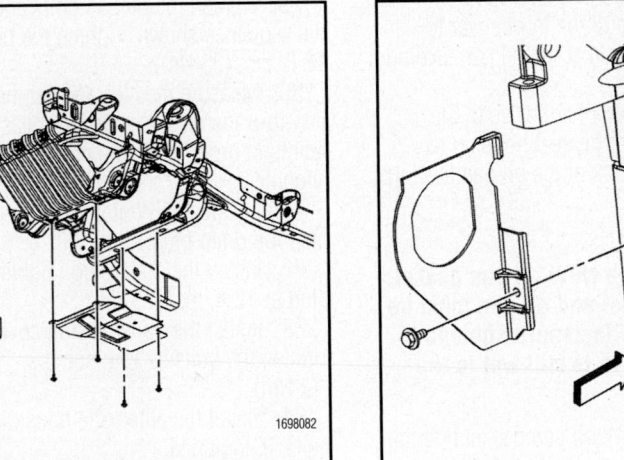

Fig. 414 For 1500 series vehicles, remove the oil pan skid plate bolts and skid plate, if equipped

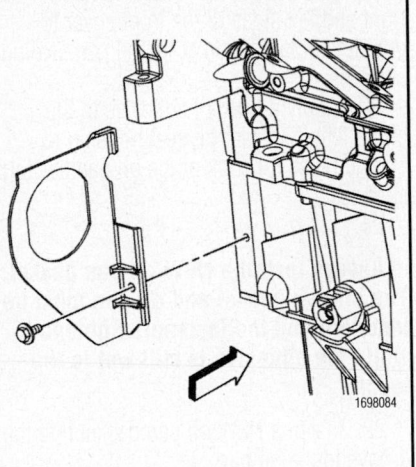

Fig. 416 Remove the right side transmission cover bolt

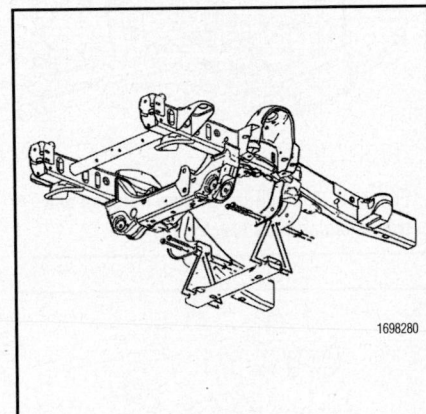

Fig. 418 For 1500 series vehicles, remove the crossbar bolts/nuts and crossbar

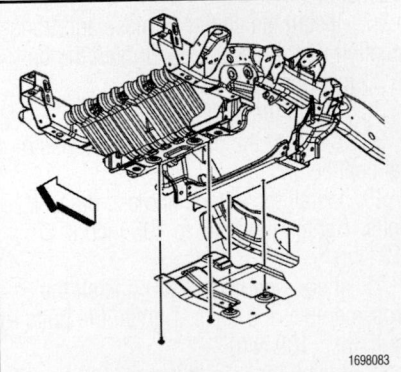

Fig. 415 For 2500 series vehicles, loosen the 2 rear oil pan skid plate bolts, remove the 2 front oil pan skid plate bolts and skid plate, if equipped

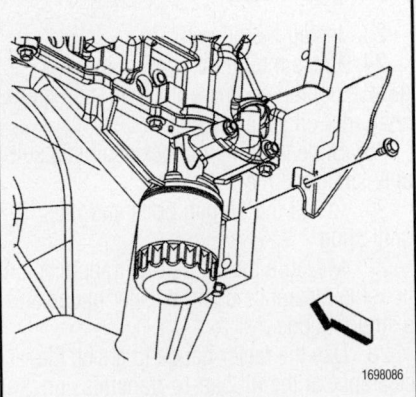

Fig. 417 Remove the left side transmission cover bolt and cover

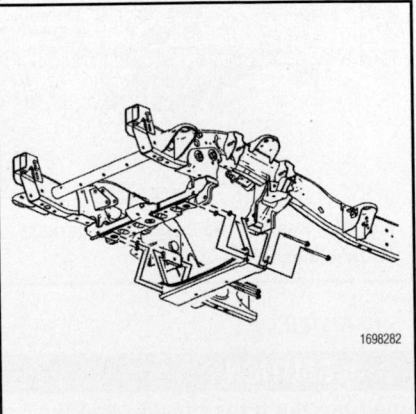

Fig. 419 For 2500 series vehicles, remove the crossbar bolts/nuts and crossbar

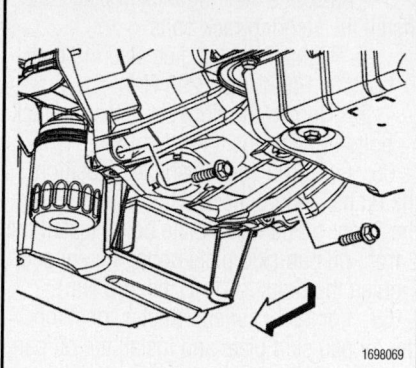

Fig. 420 For vehicles with a 4L60-E/4L70-E automatic transmission, remove the 2 lower transmission bolts

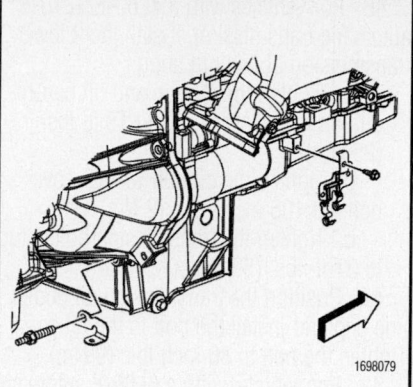

Fig. 423 For vehicles with a 6L80-E automatic transmission, remove the lower right transmission stud

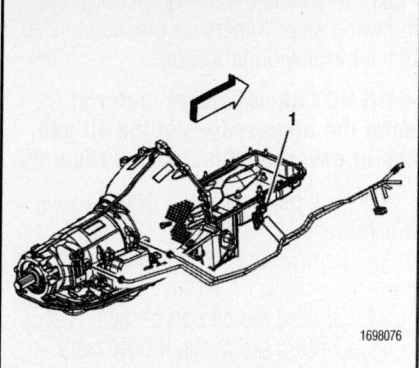

Fig. 426 For vehicles with a 4L80-E automatic transmission, remove the oil cooler lines from the clip (1), if equipped

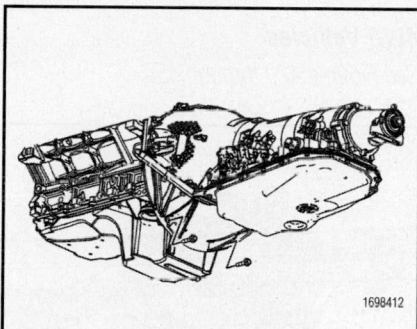

Fig. 421 For vehicles with a 4L80-E automatic transmission, remove the 2 lower transmission bolts

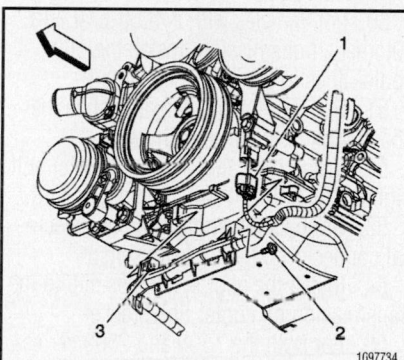

Fig. 424 Remove the battery cable channel bolt (2), slide the channel pin (3) out of the oil pan tab; electrical connector (1)

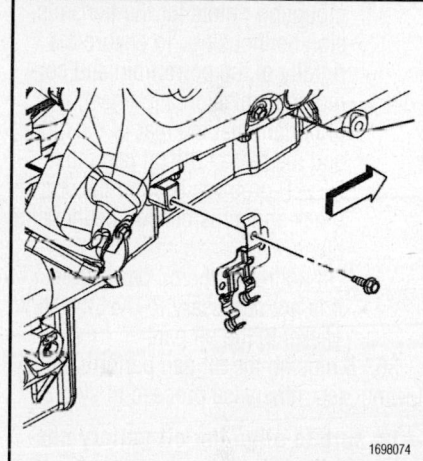

Fig. 427 Remove the transmission oil cooler line clip bolt and clip from the oil pan

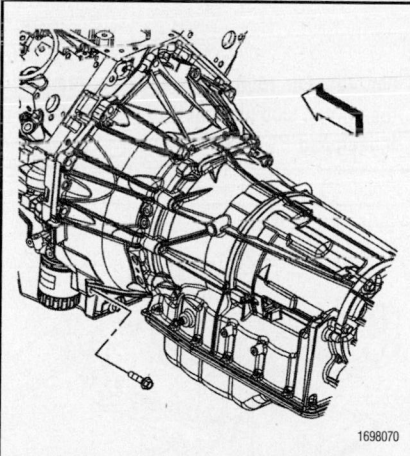

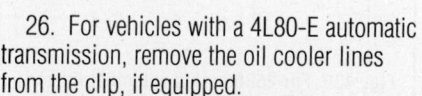

Fig. 422 For vehicles with a 6L80-E automatic transmission, remove the lower left transmission bolt

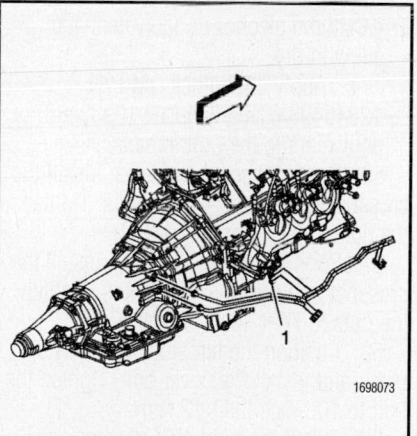

Fig. 425 For vehicles with a 4L60-E/4L70-E automatic transmission, remove the oil cooler lines from the clip (1), if equipped

26. For vehicles with a 4L80-E automatic transmission, remove the oil cooler lines from the clip, if equipped.

27. For vehicles with a 6L80-E automatic transmission, remove the oil cooler lines from the clip.

28. Remove the transmission oil cooler line clip bolt and clip from the oil pan.

29. Remove the oil pan bolts.

30. Remove the oil pan.

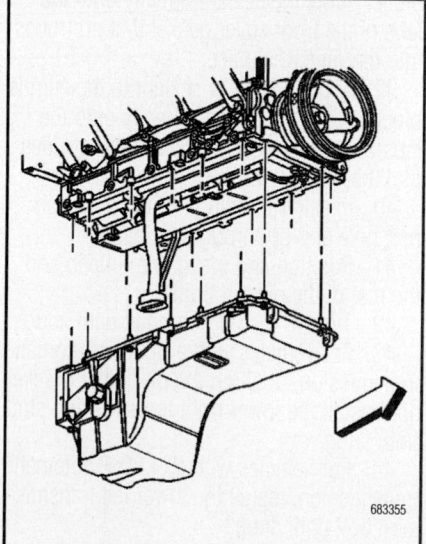

Fig. 428 Remove the oil pan bolts

31. If reusing the oil pan perform the following steps, otherwise proceed to step 3 of the installation procedure.

➡ **DO NOT allow foreign material to enter the oil passages of the oil pan, cap or cover the openings as required.**

32. Drill out the oil pan gasket rivets, if necessary.

33. Remove the oil pan gasket from the pan.

34. Discard the oil pan gasket.

35. Discard the rivets, if necessary.

To install:

➡ **Note the following:**

- The alignment of the structural oil pan is critical. The rear bolt hole locations of the oil pan provide mounting points for the transmission bellhousing. To ensure the rigidity of the powertrain and correct transmission alignment, it is important that the rear of the block and the rear of the oil pan must NEVER protrude beyond the engine block and transmission bellhousing plane.
- Do not reuse the oil pan gasket.
- It is not necessary to rivet the NEW gasket to the oil pan.

36. If reusing the oil pan perform the following step, otherwise proceed to step 3.

➡ **Be sure to align the oil gallery passages in the oil pan and engine block properly with the oil pan gasket.**

37. Place a NEW oil pan gasket onto the oil pan.

38. Apply a bead of sealant to the engine block. Apply the sealant directly onto the tabs of the front cover gasket that protrudes into the oil pan surface.

39. Apply a bead of sealant to the engine block. Apply the sealant directly onto the tabs of the rear cover gasket that protrudes into the oil pan surface.

40. Install 1 oil pan bolt into a oil pan bolt hole and up through the gasket.

41. Position and install the oil pan and the rest of the oil pan bolts.

42. Tighten the oil pan bolts until snug.

43. For vehicles with a 6L80-E automatic transmission, position the oil cooler bracket and install the lower right transmission stud until snug.

44. For vehicles with a 6L80-E automatic transmission, install the lower left transmission bolt until snug.

45. For vehicles with a 4L80-E automatic transmission, install the 2 lower transmission bolts until snug.

46. For vehicles with a 4L60-E/4L70-E automatic transmission, install the 2 lower transmission bolts until snug.

a. Tighten the oil pan and oil pan-to-oil pan front cover bolts to 18 ft. lbs. (25 Nm).

b. Tighten the oil pan-to-rear cover bolts to 106 inch lbs. (12 Nm).

c. Tighten the transmission bolts/stud to 37 ft. lbs. (50 Nm).

47. Position the transmission oil cooler line clip and install the bolt to the oil pan. Tighten the bolt to 80 inch lbs. (9 Nm).

48. For vehicles with a 6L80-E automatic transmission, install the oil cooler lines to the clip.

49. For vehicles with a 4L80-E automatic transmission, install the oil cooler lines to the clip, if equipped.

50. For vehicles with a 4L60-E/4L70-E automatic transmission, install the oil cooler lines to the clip, if equipped.

51. Position the channel and slide the channel pin into the oil pan tab.

52. Install the battery cable channel bolt. Tighten the bolt to 106 inch lbs. (12 Nm).

53. Connect the engine harness electrical connector to the oil level sensor.

54. Install the engine harness clip to the transmission oil cooler line bracket.

55. For both the 1500 and 2500 series, perform the following steps prior to installing the crossbar bolts.

a. Remove all traces of the original adhesive patch.

b. Clean the threads of the bolts with denatured alcohol or equivalent and allow to dry.

c. Apply threadlock GM P/N 12345493 (Canadian P/N 10953488) or equivalent to the bolt threads.

56. For 2500 series vehicles, install the crossbar and crossbar bolts/nuts. Tighten the nuts to 89 ft. lbs. (120 Nm).

57. For 1500 series vehicles, install the crossbar and crossbar bolts/nuts. Tighten the nuts to 74 ft. lbs. (100 Nm).

58. Position the left side transmission cover and install the cover bolt. Tighten the bolt to 106 inch lbs. (12 Nm).

59. Install the right side transmission cover bolt. Tighten the bolt to 106 inch lbs. (12 Nm).

60. If reusing the old oil pan remove the old oil filter and install a NEW oil filter.

61. Lubricate the NEW oil filter seal with clean engine oil.

62. Install the NEW oil filter. Tighten the oil filter to 22 ft. lbs. (30 Nm).

63. Ensure that the oil pan drain plug is tight. Tighten the drain plug to 18 ft. lbs. (25 Nm).

64. Raise the steering rack in place and install the steering rack bolts.

a. Tighten the left side steering rack bolts to 148 ft. lbs. (200 Nm).

b. Tighten the right side steering rack bolts to 74 ft. lbs. (100 Nm).

65. For 2500 series vehicles, position the oil pan skid plate and tighten until snug the 2 rear oil pan skid plate bolts, install the 2 front oil pan skid plate bolts, if equipped. Tighten the bolts to 21 ft. lbs. (28 Nm).

66. For 1500 series vehicles, position the oil pan skid plate and install the oil pan skid plate bolts, if equipped. Tighten the bolts to 21 ft. lbs. (28 Nm).

67. Lower the vehicle.

68. Fill the engine with NEW engine oil.

69. Start the engine and inspect for leaks.

4WD Vehicles

See Figures 429 through 454.

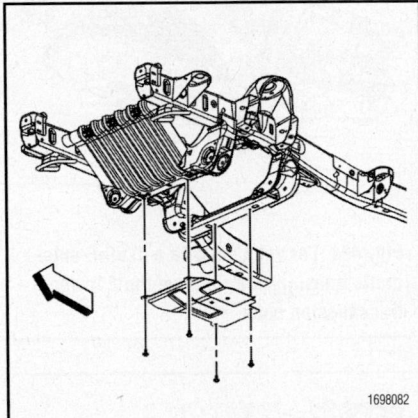

Fig. 429 For 1500 series vehicles, remove the oil pan skid plate bolts and skid plate, if equipped

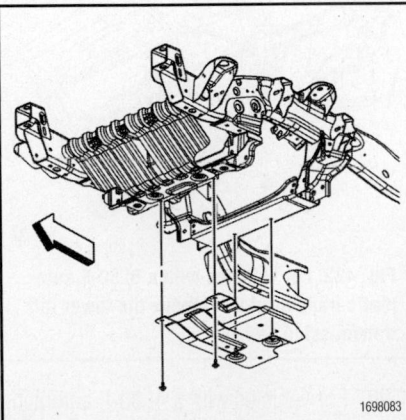

Fig. 430 For 2500 series vehicles, loosen the 2 rear oil pan skid plate bolts, remove the 2 front oil pan skid plate bolts and skid plate, if equipped

1. Raise and support the vehicle.
2. For 1500 series vehicles, remove the oil pan skid plate bolts and skid plate, if equipped.
3. For 2500 series vehicles, loosen the 2 rear oil pan skid plate bolts, remove the 2 front oil pan skid plate bolts and skid plate, if equipped.
4. For 1500 series vehicles, remove the front differential carrier.

   a. Remove the lower control arm crossmember.

➡ **If removing the differential carrier assembly to service other components, it is not necessary to drain the differential carrier.**

   b. Drain the differential carrier.
   c. Remove the wiring harness from the differential carrier, if needed.
   d. Remove the electrical connector from the actuator motor.
   e. Remove the differential carrier vent hose.

   f. Remove the wheel drive shaft mounting bolts.
   g. Remove the front propeller shaft.
   h. Support the differential carrier with a transmission jack.
   i. Remove the right differential carrier mounting nuts and washers.
   j. Remove the left differential carrier mounting bolts.
   k. With the aid of an assistant, pivot the differential carrier forward and down to remove the it from the vehicle.
   l. Remove the differential carrier assembly from the vehicle.
5. For 2500 series vehicles, remove the front differential carrier.

   a. Drain the differential carrier assembly.
   b. Disconnect the front propeller shaft from the differential carrier assembly.
   c. Remove the steering linkage.
   d. Support the differential carrier

assembly with a transmission jack or equivalent.
   e. Remove the wheel drive shaft inboard flange bolts from the inner axle shaft, both sides.

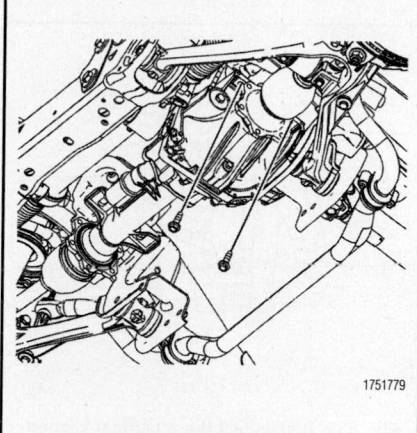

Fig. 435 Remove the left differential carrier mounting bolts

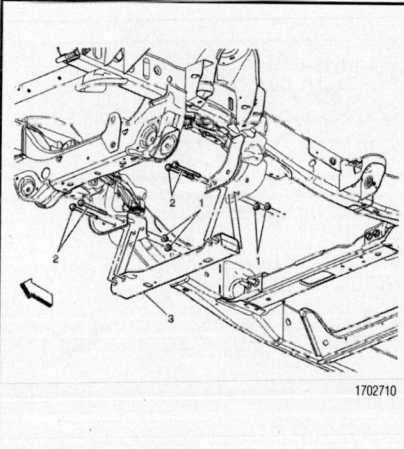

Fig. 431 Remove the nuts (1), bolts (2) and the crossmember (3)

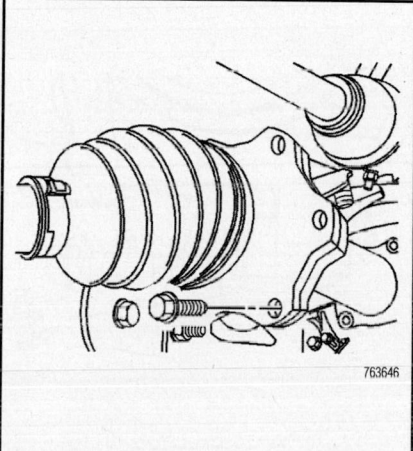

Fig. 433 Remove the wheel drive shaft mounting bolts (1)

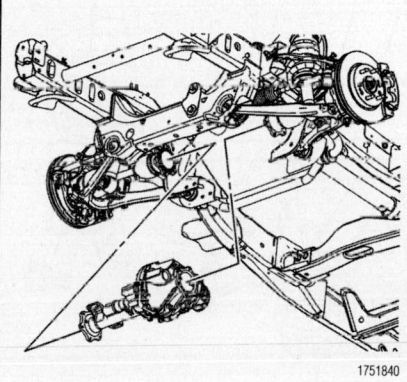

Fig. 436 With the aid of an assistant, pivot the differential carrier forward and down to remove the it from the vehicle

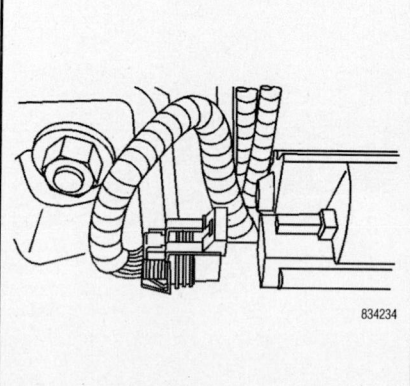

Fig. 432 Remove the electrical connector (1) from the actuator motor

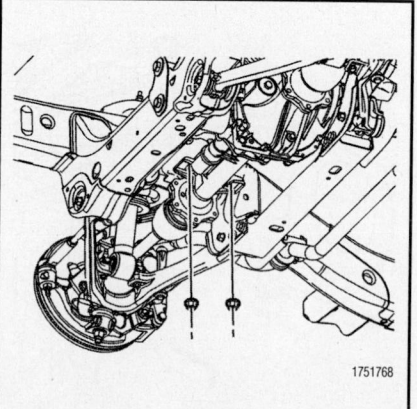

Fig. 434 Remove the right differential carrier mounting nuts and washers

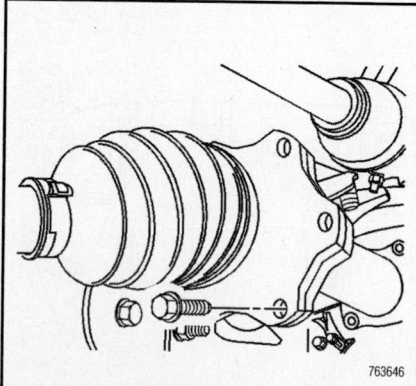

Fig. 437 Remove the wheel drive shaft inboard flange bolts (1) from the inner axle shaft, both sides

f. Disconnect the electrical connector from the front axle actuator, S4WD axle only.

g. Disconnect the wire harness from the inner axle shaft housing, S4WD axle only.

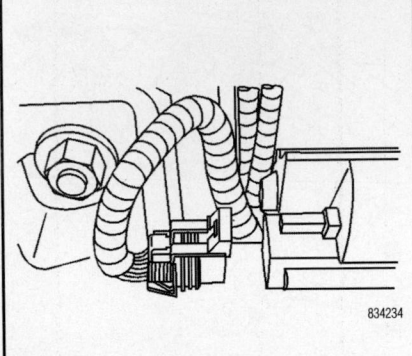

Fig. 438 Disconnect the electrical connector (1) from the front axle actuator, S4WD axle only

h. Disconnect the wire harness from the differential carrier assembly, S4WD axle only.

i. Disconnect the vent hose from the differential carrier assembly.

j. Remove the inner axle housing nuts and washers from the bracket.

k. Remove the differential carrier assembly upper mounting bolt and the nut.

l. Pivot the differential carrier assembly forward and down on the lower mount bolt while it is being supported by the transmission jack.

m. Secure the differential carrier assembly to the jack.

n. Remove the differential carrier assembly lower mounting bolt and the nut.

o. Remove the differential carrier assembly.

6. Unbolt the steering rack and hang downward.

7. Place a suitable drain pan under the oil pan drain plug.

8. Remove the oil pan drain plug.

9. Allow the oil pan to drain completely.

10. Re-install the oil pan drain plug until snug.

11. Place the drain pan under the oil filter.

12. Remove the oil filter.

13. Allow the oil to drain completely.

14. Re-install the oil filter until snug.

15. Remove the right side transmission cover bolt.

16. Remove the left side transmission cover bolt and cover.

17. For 1500 series vehicles, remove the crossbar bolts/nuts and crossbar.

18. For 2500 series vehicles, remove the crossbar bolts/nuts and crossbar.

19. For vehicles with a 4L60-E/4L70-E automatic transmission, remove the 2 lower transmission bolts.

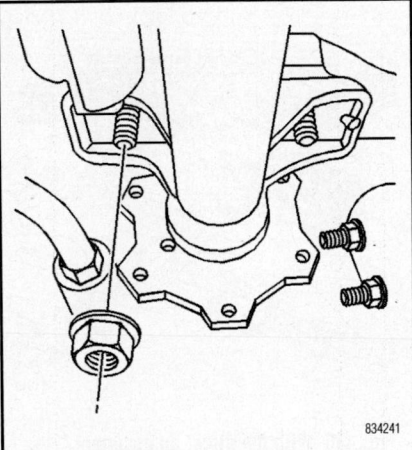

Fig. 439 Remove the inner axle housing nuts and washers from the bracket

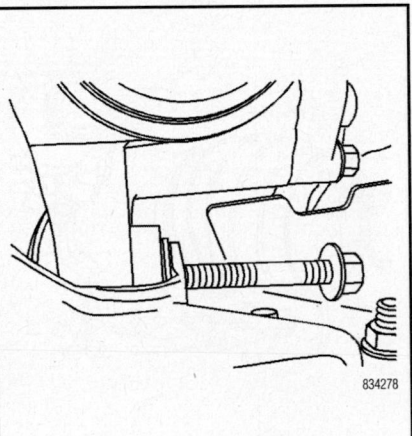

Fig. 441 Remove the differential carrier assembly lower mounting bolt and the nut

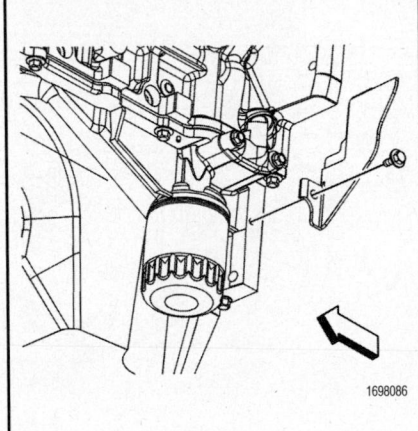

Fig. 443 Remove the left side transmission cover bolt and cover

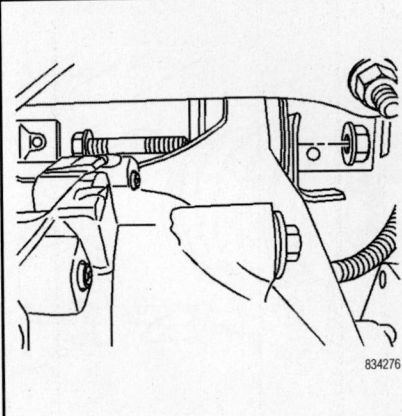

Fig. 440 Remove the differential carrier assembly upper mounting bolt and the nut

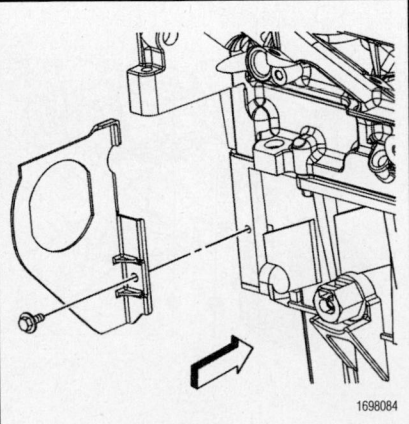

Fig. 442 Remove the right side transmission cover bolt

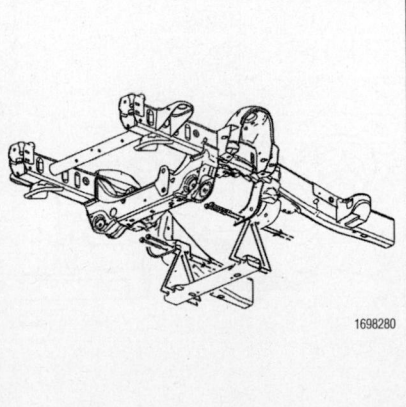

Fig. 444 For 1500 series vehicles, remove the crossbar bolts/nuts and crossbar

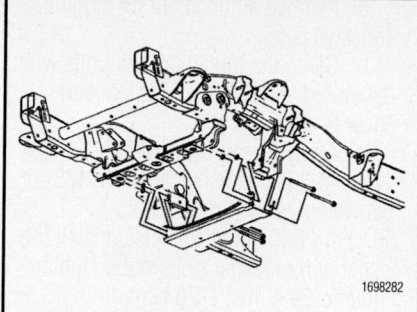

Fig. 445 For 2500 series vehicles, remove the crossbar bolts/nuts and crossbar

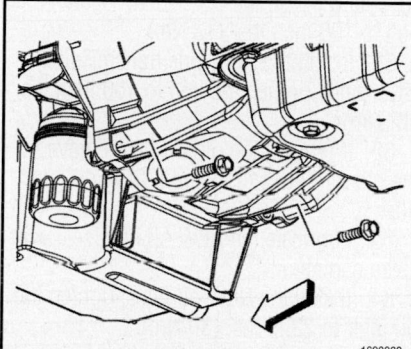

Fig. 446 For vehicles with a 4L60-E/4L70-E automatic transmission, remove the 2 lower transmission bolts

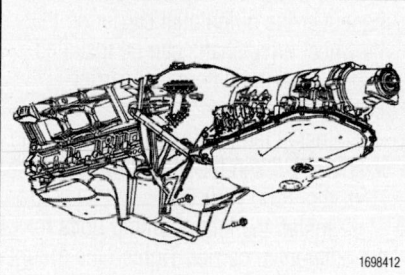

Fig. 447 For vehicles with a 4L80-E automatic transmission, remove the 2 lower transmission bolts

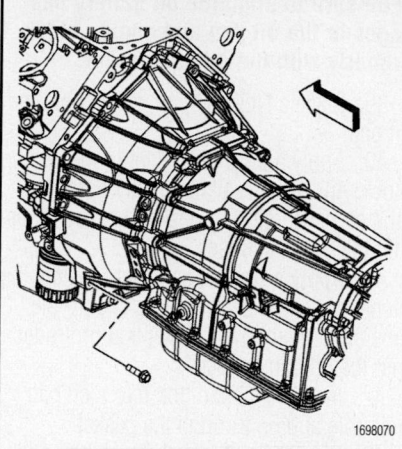

Fig. 448 For vehicles with a 6L80-E automatic transmission, remove the lower left transmission bolt

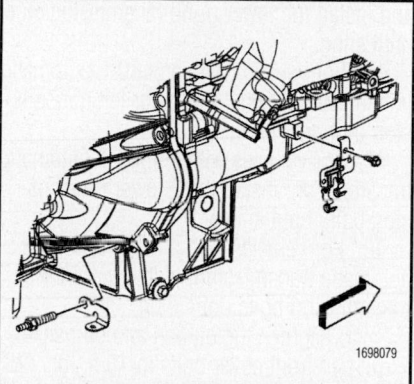

Fig. 449 For vehicles with a 6L80-E automatic transmission, remove the lower right transmission stud

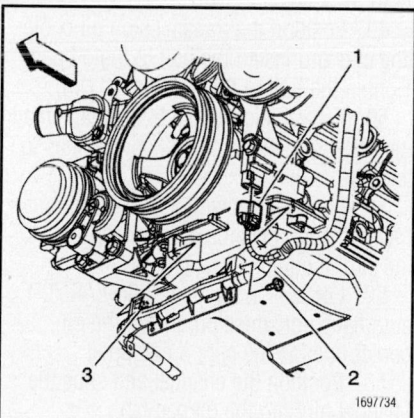

Fig. 450 Remove the battery cable channel bolt (2), slide the channel pin (3) out of the oil pan tab; electrical connector (1)

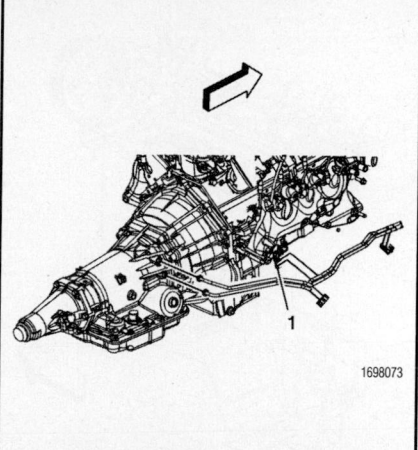

Fig. 451 For vehicles with a 4L60-E/4L70-E automatic transmission, remove the oil cooler lines from the clip (1), if equipped

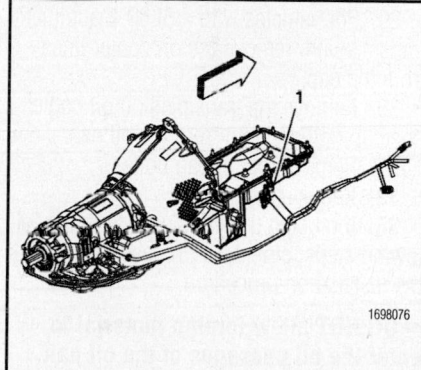

Fig. 452 For vehicles with a 4L80-E automatic transmission, remove the oil cooler lines from the clip (1), if equipped

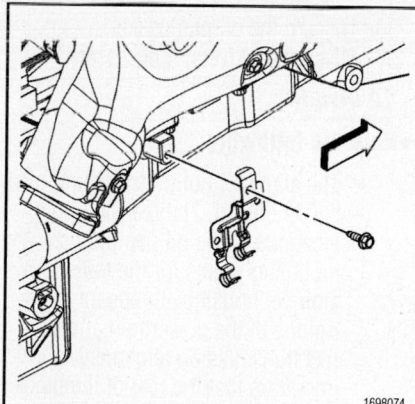

Fig. 453 Remove the transmission oil cooler line clip bolt and clip from the oil pan

20. For vehicles with a 4L80-E automatic transmission, remove the 2 lower transmission bolts.

21. For vehicles with a 6L80-E automatic transmission, remove the lower left transmission bolt.

22. For vehicles with a 6L80-E automatic transmission, remove the lower right transmission stud.

23. Disconnect the engine harness electrical connector from the oil level sensor.

24. Remove the engine harness clip from the transmission oil cooler line bracket.

25. Remove the battery cable channel bolt.

26. Slide the channel pin out of the oil pan tab.

27. For vehicles with a 4L60-E/4L70-E automatic transmission, remove the oil cooler lines from the clip, if equipped.

28. For vehicles with a 4L80-E automatic transmission, remove the oil cooler lines from the clip, if equipped.

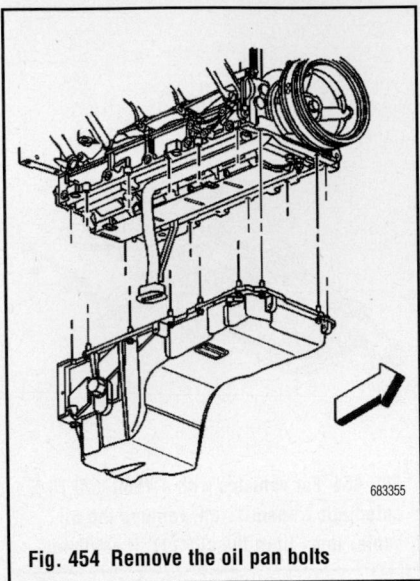

Fig. 454 Remove the oil pan bolts

29. For vehicles with a 6L80-E automatic transmission, remove the oil cooler lines from the clip.

30. Remove the transmission oil cooler line clip bolt and clip from the oil pan.

31. Remove the oil pan bolts.

32. Remove the oil pan.

33. If reusing the oil pan perform the following steps, otherwise proceed to step 3 of the installation procedure.

➡**DO NOT allow foreign material to enter the oil passages of the oil pan, cap or cover the openings as required.**

34. Drill out the oil pan gasket rivets, if necessary.

35. Remove the oil pan gasket from the pan.

36. Discard the oil pan gasket.

37. Discard the rivets, if necessary.

To install:

➡**Note the following:**

- The alignment of the structural oil pan is critical. The rear bolt hole locations of the oil pan provide mounting points for the transmission bellhousing. To ensure the rigidity of the powertrain and correct transmission alignment, it is important that the rear of the block and the rear of the oil pan must NEVER protrude beyond the engine block and transmission bellhousing plane.
- Do not reuse the oil pan gasket.
- It is not necessary to rivet the NEW gasket to the oil pan.

38. If reusing the oil pan perform the following step, otherwise proceed to step 3.

➡**Be sure to align the oil gallery passages in the oil pan and engine block properly with the oil pan gasket.**

39. Place a NEW oil pan gasket onto the oil pan.

40. Apply a bead of sealant to the engine block. Apply the sealant directly onto the tabs of the front cover gasket that protrudes into the oil pan surface.

41. Apply a bead of sealant to the engine block. Apply the sealant directly onto the tabs of the rear cover gasket that protrudes into the oil pan surface.

42. Install 1 oil pan bolt into a oil pan bolt hole and up through the gasket.

43. Position and install the oil pan and the rest of the oil pan bolts.

44. Tighten the oil pan bolts until snug.

45. For vehicles with a 6L80-E automatic transmission, position the oil cooler bracket and install the lower right transmission stud until snug.

46. For vehicles with a 6L80-E automatic transmission, install the lower left transmission bolt until snug.

47. For vehicles with a 4L80-E automatic transmission, install the 2 lower transmission bolts until snug.

48. For vehicles with a 4L60-E/4L70-E automatic transmission, install the 2 lower transmission bolts until snug.

a. Tighten the oil pan and oil pan-to-oil pan front cover bolts to 18 ft. lbs. (25 Nm).

b. Tighten the oil pan-to-rear cover bolts to 106 inch lbs. (12 Nm).

c. Tighten the transmission bolts/stud to 37 ft. lbs. (50 Nm).

49. Position the transmission oil cooler line clip and install the bolt to the oil pan. Tighten the bolt to 80 inch lbs. (9 Nm).

50. For vehicles with a 6L80-E automatic transmission, install the oil cooler lines to the clip.

51. For vehicles with a 4L80-E automatic transmission, install the oil cooler lines to the clip, if equipped.

52. For vehicles with a 4L60-E/4L70-E automatic transmission, install the oil cooler lines to the clip, if equipped.

53. Position the channel and slide the channel pin into the oil pan tab.

54. Install the battery cable channel bolt. Tighten the bolt to 106 inch lbs. (12 Nm).

55. Connect the engine harness electrical connector to the oil level sensor.

56. Install the engine harness clip to the transmission oil cooler line bracket.

57. For both the 1500 and 2500 series, perform the following steps prior to installing the crossbar bolts.

a. Remove all traces of the original adhesive patch.

b. Clean the threads of the bolts with denatured alcohol or equivalent and allow to dry.

c. Apply threadlock GM P/N 12345493 (Canadian P/N 10953488) or equivalent to the bolt threads.

58. For 2500 series vehicles, install the crossbar and crossbar bolts/nuts. Tighten the nuts to 89 ft. lbs. (120 Nm).

59. For 1500 series vehicles, install the crossbar and crossbar bolts/nuts. Tighten the nuts to 74 ft. lbs. (100 Nm).

60. Position the left side transmission cover and install the cover bolt. Tighten the bolt to 106 inch lbs. (12 Nm).

61. Install the right side transmission cover bolt. Tighten the bolt to 106 inch lbs. (12 Nm).

62. If reusing the old oil pan remove the old oil filter and install a NEW oil filter.

63. Lubricate the NEW oil filter seal with clean engine oil.

64. Install the NEW oil filter. Tighten the oil filter to 22 ft. lbs. (30 Nm).

65. Ensure that the oil pan drain plug is tight. Tighten the drain plug to 18 ft. lbs. (25 Nm).

66. For 1500 series vehicles, install the front differential carrier.

a. With the aid of an assistant, maneuver the differential carrier so that the wheel drive shafts can be installed.

b. Install the differential carrier assembly.

c. Install the right mounting nuts and washers. Tighten the mounting nuts to 75 ft. lbs. (100 Nm).

d. Install the left mounting bolts for the differential carrier. Tighten the mounting nuts to 75 ft. lbs. (100 Nm).

e. Remove the transmission jack stand.

f. Install the wiring harness on the differential carrier, if needed.

g. Install the electrical connector to the actuator motor, if needed.

h. Install the differential carrier vent hose.

i. Install the propeller shaft.

j. Install the wheel drive shaft mounting bolts. Tighten the mounting bolts to 58 ft. lbs. (79 Nm).

k. Install the lower control arm crossmember.

l. Fill the differential carrier.

67. Raise the steering rack in place and install the steering rack bolts.

a. Tighten the left side steering rack bolts to 148 ft. lbs. (200 Nm).

b. Tighten the right side steering rack bolts to 74 ft. lbs. (100 Nm).

68. For 2500 series vehicles, install the front differential carrier.

　a. Install the differential carrier assembly.

　b. Install the differential carrier assembly lower mounting bolt and the nut. Do not tighten the bolt at this time.

　c. Pivot the differential carrier assembly up and back on the lower mount bolt while it is being supported by the transmission jack.

　d. Install the differential carrier assembly upper mounting bolt and the nut.

　e. Install the inner axle housing washers and nuts to the bracket. Tighten the inner axle housing nuts to 75 ft. lbs. (100 Nm).

　f. Tighten the upper and the lower differential carrier assembly bolts to 75 ft. lbs. (100 Nm).

　g. Connect the vent hose to the differential carrier assembly.

　h. Remove the transmission jack.

　i. Connect the wire harness to the differential carrier assembly, S4WD axle only.

　j. Connect the wire harness to the inner axle shaft housing, S4WD axle only.

　k. Connect the electrical connector to the front axle actuator, S4WD axle only.

　l. Install the wheel drive shaft inboard flange to inner axle shaft bolts, both sides. Tighten the wheel drive shaft inboard flange to inner axle shaft bolts to 58 ft. lbs. (79 Nm).

　m. Install the steering linkage.

　n. Install the front propeller shaft to the differential carrier assembly.

　o. Fill the differential carrier assembly.

69. For 2500 series vehicles, position the oil pan skid plate and tighten until snug the 2 rear oil pan skid plate bolts, install the 2 front oil pan skid plate bolts, if equipped. Tighten the bolts to 21 ft. lbs. (28 Nm).

70. For 1500 series vehicles, position the oil pan skid plate and install the oil pan skid plate bolts, if equipped. Tighten the bolts to 21 ft. lbs. (28 Nm).

71. Lower the vehicle.

72. Fill the engine with NEW engine oil.

73. Start the engine and inspect for leaks.

2010 Diesel Engines

Lower Oil Pan

See Figures 455 through 460.

1. Raise and suitably support the vehicle.

2. Place a suitable container under the engine in order to drain the oil.

3. Remove the oil drain plug.

4. Drain the engine oil.

5. Remove the oil pan skid plate bolts and plate, if equipped.

6. For a 2-Wheel Drive (2WD) vehicle, remove the crossmember bolts and crossmember.

7. If equipped with a 4-Wheel Drive (4WD) vehicle, remove the crossmember bolts and crossmember.

8. Disconnect the oil level sensor electrical connector.

9. Remove the lower oil pan bolts/nuts.

➠**DO NOT** damage the sealing surfaces when separating the lower oil pan from the upper oil pan.

10. Separate the lower oil pan from the upper oil pan using Seal Cutter (J-37228).

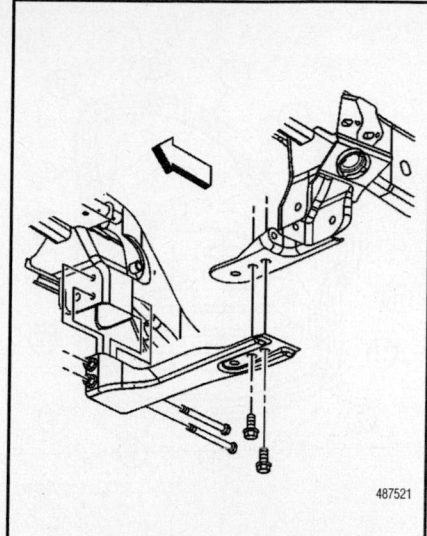

Fig. 457 **If equipped with a 4-Wheel Drive (4WD) vehicle, remove the crossmember bolts and crossmember**

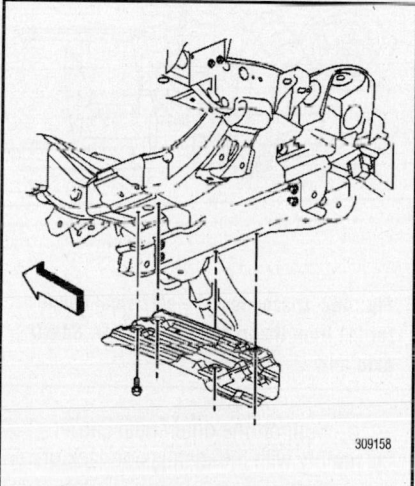

Fig. 455 **Remove the oil pan skid plate bolts and plate, if equipped**

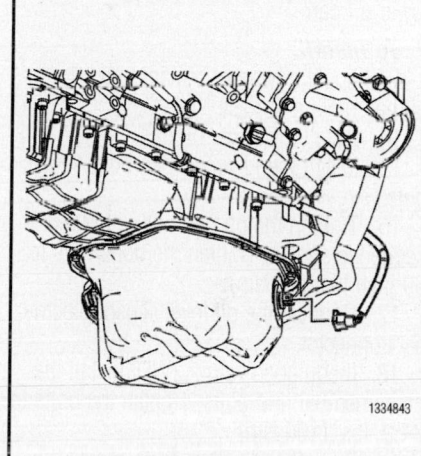

Fig. 458 **Disconnect the oil level sensor (2) electrical connector (1)**

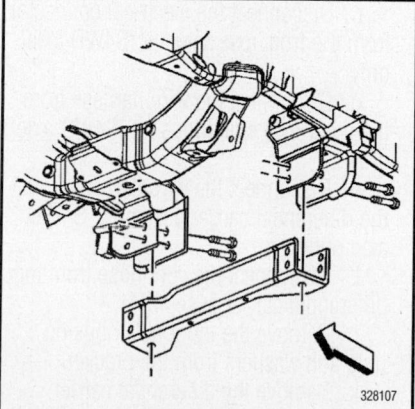

Fig. 456 **For a 2-Wheel Drive (2WD) vehicle, remove the crossmember bolts (1) and crossmember (2)**

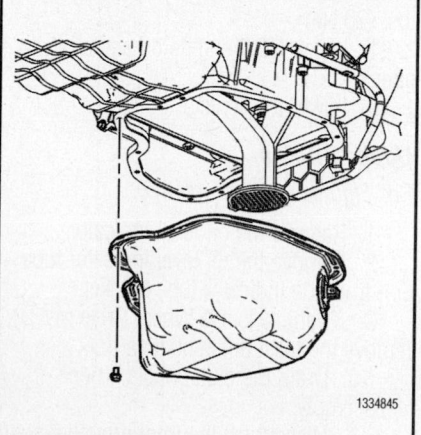

Fig. 459 **Remove the lower oil pan bolts/nuts**

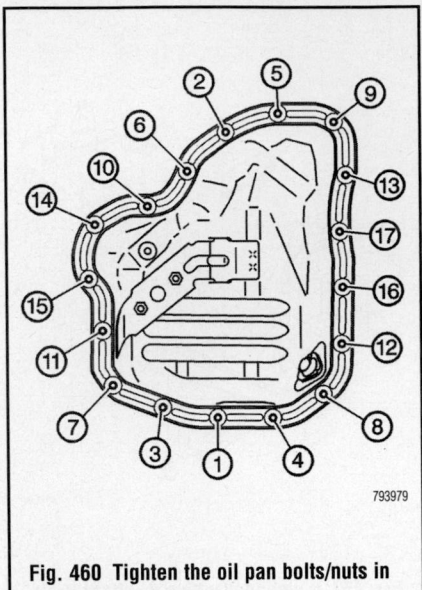

Fig. 460 Tighten the oil pan bolts/nuts in the sequence shown

11. Remove the lower oil pan.

12. If necessary, clean and inspect the lower oil pan.

To install:

13. Apply a bead of sealant to the lower oil pan mating surface.

14. Install the lower oil pan.

15. Install the lower oil pan bolts/nuts.

16. Tighten the oil pan bolts/nuts in the sequence shown. Tighten the bolts/nuts to 89 inch lbs. (10 Nm).

17. Connect the oil level sensor electrical connector.

18. If equipped with a 2WD, install the crossmember and bolts. Tighten the bolts to 74 ft. lbs. (100 Nm).

19. If equipped with a 4WD, install the crossmember and bolts. Tighten the bolts to 74 ft. lbs. (100 Nm).

20. Install the oil pan skid plate and bolts, if equipped. Tighten the bolts to 15 ft. lbs. (20 Nm).

21. Install NEW engine oil and a oil filter.

22. Lower the vehicle.

Upper Oil Pan

See Figures 461 through 470.

1. Remove the oil level indicator.

2. Remove the oil level indicator tube bolt from the indicator tube bracket.

3. If vehicle is a 4-Wheel Drive (4WD), remove the front differential carrier.

  a. Drain the differential carrier assembly.

  b. Disconnect the front propeller shaft from the differential carrier assembly.

  c. Remove the steering linkage.

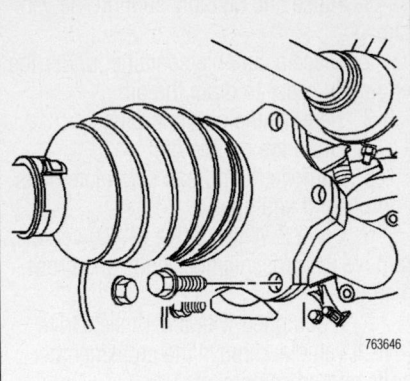

Fig. 461 Remove the wheel drive shaft inboard flange bolts (1) from the inner axle shaft, both sides

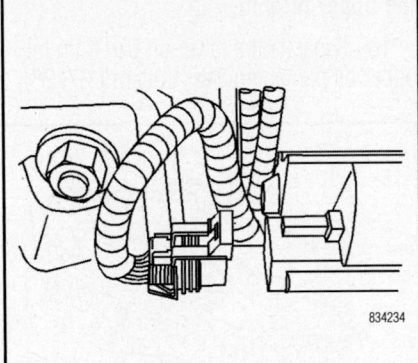

Fig. 462 Disconnect the electrical connector (1) from the front axle actuator, S4WD axle only

  d. Support the differential carrier assembly with a transmission jack or equivalent.

  e. Remove the wheel drive shaft inboard flange bolts from the inner axle shaft, both sides.

  f. Disconnect the electrical connector from the front axle actuator, S4WD axle only.

  g. Disconnect the wire harness from the inner axle shaft housing, S4WD axle only.

  h. Disconnect the wire harness from the differential carrier assembly, S4WD axle only.

  i. Disconnect the vent hose from the differential carrier assembly.

  j. Remove the inner axle housing nuts and washers from the bracket.

  k. Remove the differential carrier assembly upper mounting bolt and the nut.

  l. Pivot the differential carrier assembly forward and down on the lower

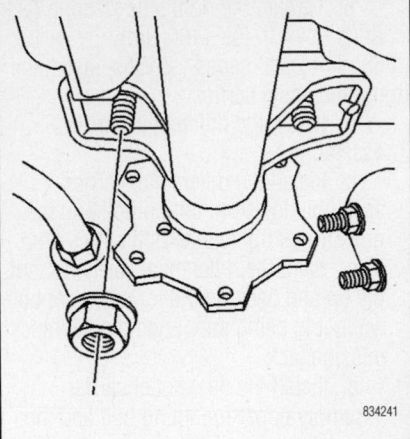

Fig. 463 Remove the inner axle housing nuts and washers from the bracket

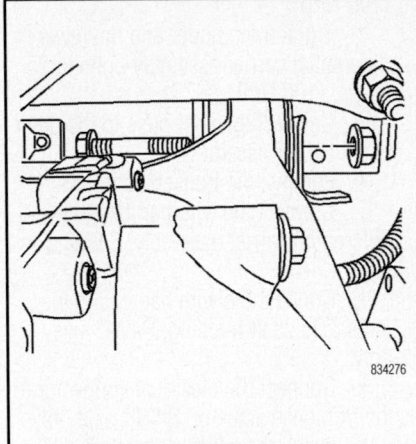

Fig. 464 Remove the differential carrier assembly upper mounting bolt and the nut

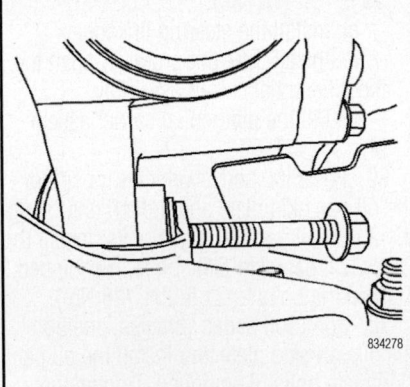

Fig. 465 Remove the differential carrier assembly lower mounting bolt and the nut

mount bolt while it is being supported by the transmission jack.

  m. Secure the differential carrier assembly to the jack.

  n. Remove the differential carrier assembly lower mounting bolt and the nut.

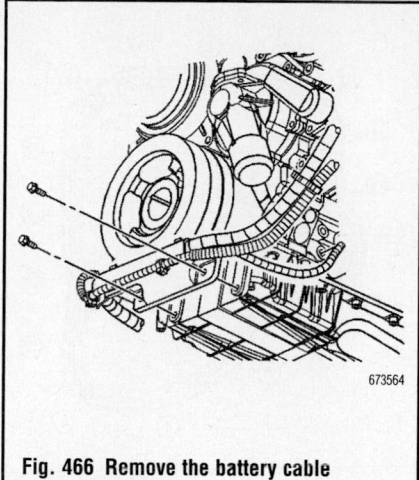

Fig. 466 Remove the battery cable bracket bolts

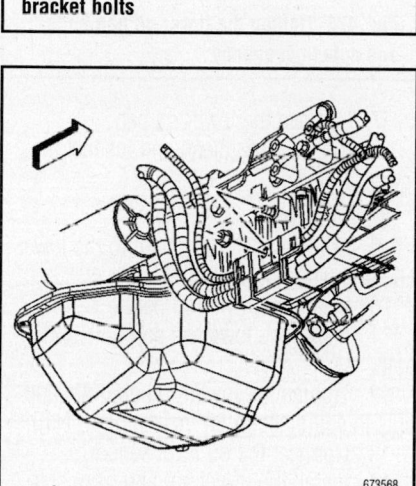

Fig. 467 Remove the battery cable bracket nut

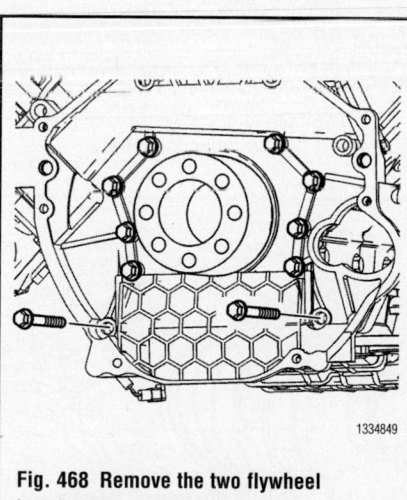

Fig. 468 Remove the two flywheel housing to upper oil pan bolts

o. Remove the differential carrier assembly.

4. If vehicle is a 2-Wheel Drive (2WD), disconnect the relay rod from the pitman arm and idler arm.

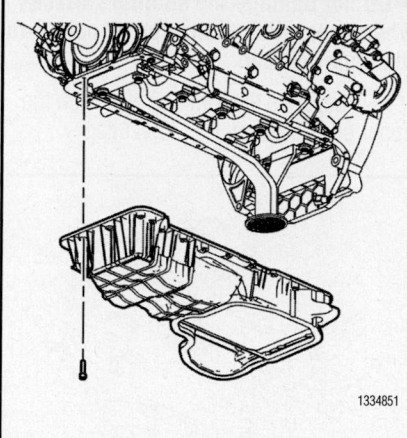

Fig. 469 Remove the upper oil pan bolts and any brackets

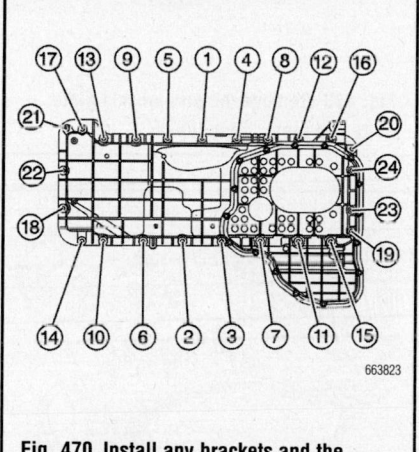

Fig. 470 Install any brackets and the upper oil pan bolts in the sequence shown

5. Remove the lower oil pan.
6. Remove the engine flywheel.
7. Remove the battery cable bracket bolts.
8. Remove the battery cable bracket nut.
9. Remove the two flywheel housing to upper oil pan bolts.
10. Remove the upper oil pan bolts and any brackets. Mark the bolt location of the bracket.
11. Separate the upper oil pan from the engine block using Seal Cutter (J-37228).
12. Remove the upper oil pan. The oil level indicator tube needs to be removed while lowering the upper oil pan.
13. If required, clean and inspect the upper oil pan.

To install:

14. Apply a bead of sealant to the upper oil pan mating surfaces.
15. Apply a bead of sealant to the flywheel housing sealing surface.

16. Install the upper oil pan to the engine block. Ensure the oil level indicator tube is installed into the upper oil pan.
17. Install any brackets and the upper oil pan bolts in the sequence shown. Tighten the bolts to 15 ft. lbs. (20 Nm).
18. Install the two flywheel housing to upper oil pan bolts. Tighten the bolts to 37 ft. lbs. (50 Nm).
19. Install the battery cable bracket bolts. Tighten the bolts to 106 inch lbs. (12 Nm).
20. Install the battery cable bracket nut.
21. Install the engine flywheel.
22. Install the lower oil pan.
23. If vehicle is a 4WD, install the front differential carrier.

  a. Install the differential carrier assembly.

  b. Install the differential carrier assembly lower mounting bolt and the nut. Do not tighten the bolt at this time.

  c. Pivot the differential carrier assembly up and back on the lower mount bolt while it is being supported by the transmission jack.

  d. Install the differential carrier assembly upper mounting bolt and the nut.

  e. Install the inner axle housing washers and nuts to the bracket. Tighten the inner axle housing nuts to 75 ft. lbs. (100 Nm).

  f. Tighten the upper and the lower differential carrier assembly bolts to 75 ft. lbs. (100 Nm).

  g. Connect the vent hose to the differential carrier assembly.

  h. Remove the transmission jack.

  i. Connect the wire harness to the differential carrier assembly, S4WD axle only.

  j. Connect the wire harness to the inner axle shaft housing, S4WD axle only.

  k. Connect the electrical connector to the front axle actuator, S4WD axle only.

  l. Install the wheel drive shaft inboard flange to inner axle shaft bolts, both sides. Tighten the wheel drive shaft inboard flange to inner axle shaft bolts to 58 ft. lbs. (79 Nm).

  m. Install the steering linkage.

  n. Install the front propeller shaft to the differential carrier assembly.

  o. Fill the differential carrier assembly.

24. If vehicle is a 2WD, Connect the relay rod to the pitman arm and idler arm.
25. Lower the vehicle.
26. Install the oil level indicator tube bolt to the indicator tube bracket. Tighten the bolt to 15 ft. lbs. (21 Nm).

27. Install the oil level indicator.
28. Fill the engine with oil.

2011 Diesel Engines

Lower Oil Pan

See Figures 471 through 476.

1. Remove the drivetrain and front suspension crossmember.

   a. For a 2-Wheel Drive (2WD) vehicle, remove the crossmember bolts and crossmember.

   b. If equipped with a 4-Wheel Drive (4WD) vehicle, remove the crossmember bolts and crossmember.

2. If equipped, remove the oil pan skid plate.

3. Drain the engine oil.

4. Disconnect the engine harness electrical connector from the oil level sensor.

5. Remove the lower oil pan bolts and nuts.

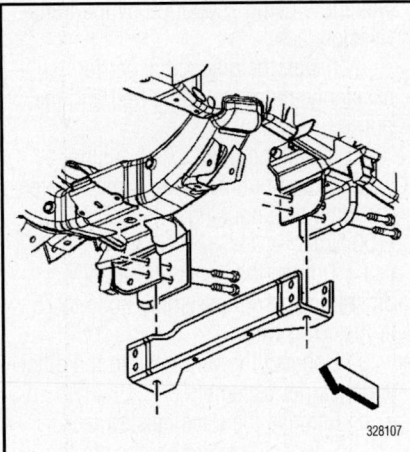

Fig. 471 For a 2-Wheel Drive (2WD) vehicle, remove the crossmember bolts (1) and crossmember (2)

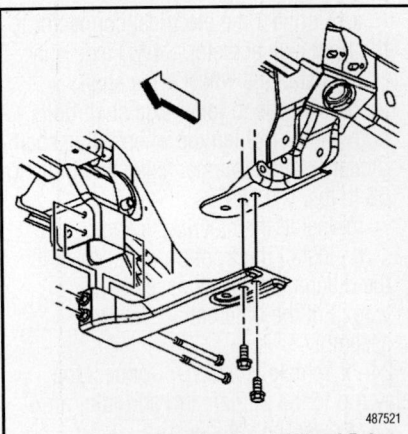

Fig. 472 If equipped with a 4-Wheel Drive (4WD) vehicle, remove the crossmember bolts and crossmember

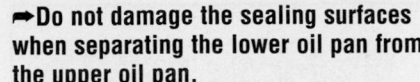

➥ **Do not damage the sealing surfaces when separating the lower oil pan from the upper oil pan.**

6. Separate the lower oil pan from the upper oil pan using J-37228 cutter.

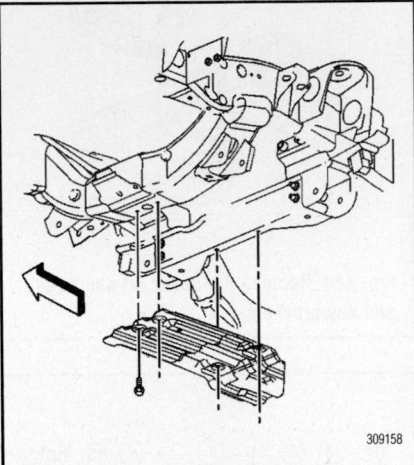

Fig. 473 Remove the oil pan skid plate bolts and plate, if equipped

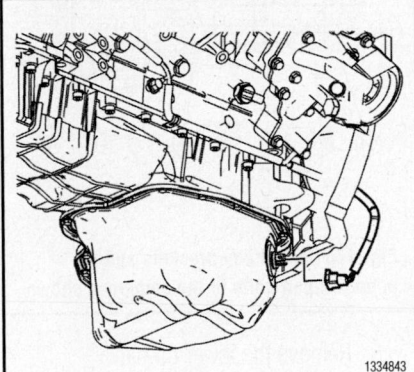

Fig. 474 Disconnect the engine harness electrical connector (1) from the oil level sensor (2)

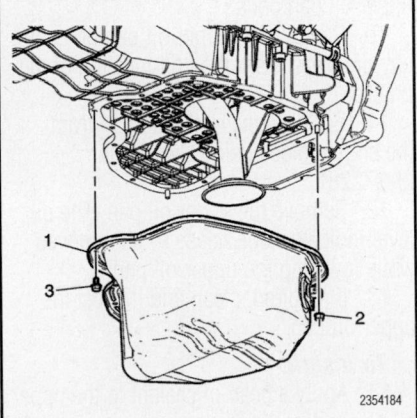

Fig. 475 Remove the lower oil pan (1) bolts (3) and nuts (2)

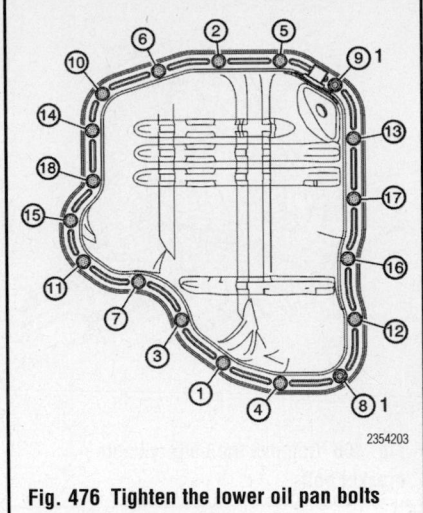

Fig. 476 Tighten the lower oil pan bolts and nuts in sequence

7. Remove the lower oil pan.

8. If necessary, clean and inspect the lower oil pan.

To install:

9. Apply a bead of sealant to the lower oil pan mating surface.

10. Install the lower oil pan.

11. Install the lower oil pan nuts and bolts.

12. Tighten the lower oil pan bolts and nuts in sequence to 89 inch lbs. (10 Nm).

13. Connect the oil level sensor.

14. Install the drivetrain and front suspension crossmember.

15. If equipped, install the oil pan skid plate.

16. Fill the engine oil.

Upper Oil Pan

See Figures 477 through 483.

1. If vehicle is a 4-Wheel Drive (4WD), remove the front differential carrier.

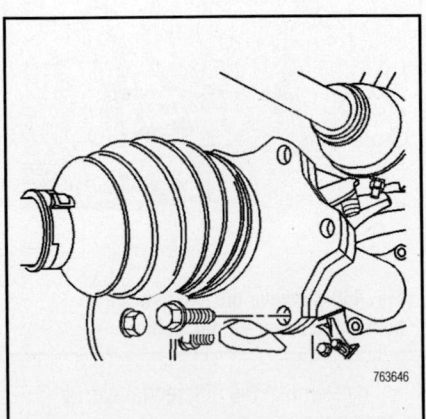

Fig. 477 Remove the wheel drive shaft inboard flange bolts (1) from the inner axle shaft, both sides

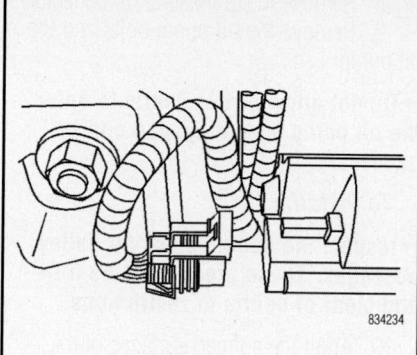

Fig. 478 Disconnect the electrical connector (1) from the front axle actuator, S4WD axle only

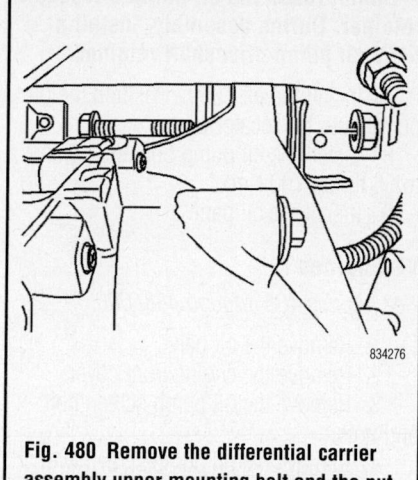

Fig. 480 Remove the differential carrier assembly upper mounting bolt and the nut

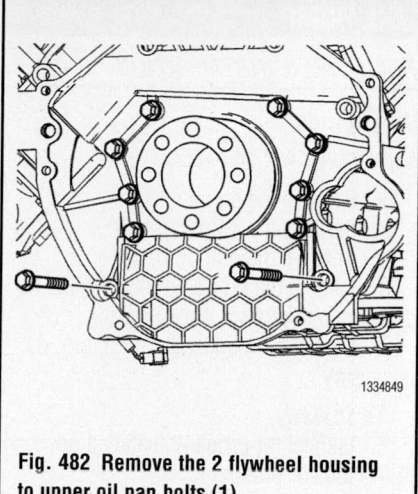

Fig. 482 Remove the 2 flywheel housing to upper oil pan bolts (1)

a. Drain the differential carrier assembly.

b. Disconnect the front propeller shaft from the differential carrier assembly.

c. Remove the steering linkage.

d. Support the differential carrier assembly with a transmission jack or equivalent.

e. Remove the wheel drive shaft inboard flange bolts from the inner axle shaft, both sides.

f. Disconnect the electrical connector from the front axle actuator, S4WD axle only.

g. Disconnect the wire harness from the inner axle shaft housing, S4WD axle only.

h. Disconnect the wire harness from the differential carrier assembly, S4WD axle only.

i. Disconnect the vent hose from the differential carrier assembly.

j. Remove the inner axle housing nuts and washers from the bracket.

k. Remove the differential carrier assembly upper mounting bolt and the nut.

l. Pivot the differential carrier assembly forward and down on the lower mount bolt while it is being supported by the transmission jack.

m. Secure the differential carrier assembly to the jack.

n. Remove the differential carrier assembly lower mounting bolt and the nut.

o. Remove the differential carrier assembly.

2. If vehicle is a 2-Wheel Drive (2WD), disconnect the relay rod from the pitman arm and idler arm.

3. Remove the lower oil pan.

4. Remove the engine flywheel.

5. Remove the 2 flywheel housing to upper oil pan bolts.

6. Remove the upper oil pan bolts.

7. Remove the wiring harness clips.

8. Separate the upper oil pan from the engine block using the J-37228 cutter.

9. Remove the upper oil pan (1).

To install:

10. Apply a bead of sealant to the upper oil pan mating surfaces.

11. Apply a bead of sealant to the flywheel housing sealing surface.

12. Install the upper oil pan to the engine block.

13. Install the wiring harness clips.

14. Install the upper oil pan bolts.

15. Tighten the upper oil pan bolts in sequence to 15 ft. lbs. (21 Nm).

16. Install the 2 flywheel housing to upper oil pan bolts and tighten to 37 ft. lbs. (50 Nm).

17. Install the engine flywheel.

18. Install the lower oil pan.

19. If vehicle is a 4WD, install the front differential carrier.

20. If vehicle is a 2WD, connect the relay rod to the pitman arm and idler arm.

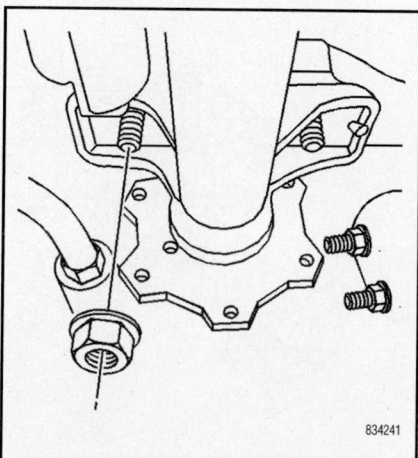

Fig. 479 Remove the inner axle housing nuts and washers from the bracket

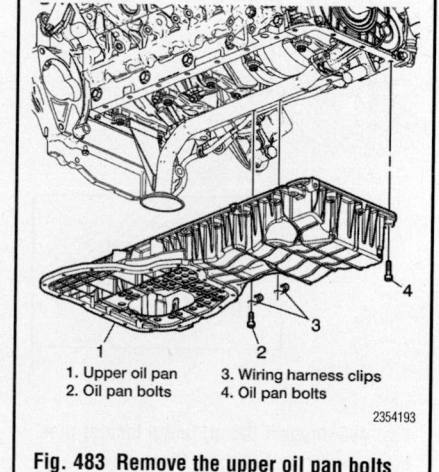

1. Upper oil pan
2. Oil pan bolts
3. Wiring harness clips
4. Oil pan bolts

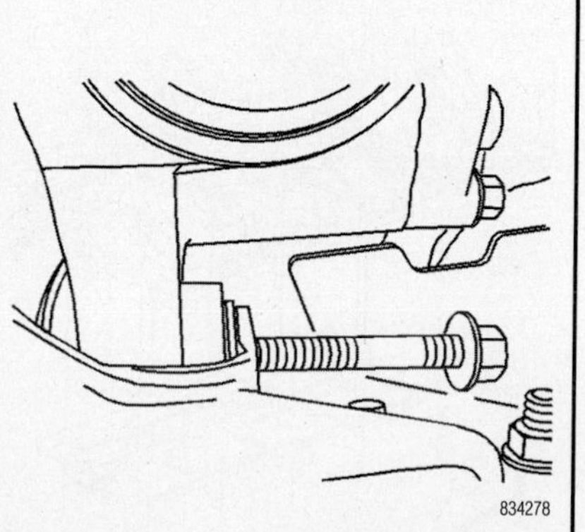

Fig. 481 Remove the differential carrier assembly lower mounting bolt and the nut

Fig. 483 Remove the upper oil pan bolts

OIL PUMP

REMOVAL & INSTALLATION

V6 Engines

See Figures 484 and 485.

1. Remove the oil pan.
2. Remove the oil pump bolt.
3. Remove the oil pump.
4. Inspect the oil pump locator pins for damage, and replace if required.
5. Clean and inspect the oil pump, if necessary.

To install:

6. Inspect for properly installed oil pump locator pins.

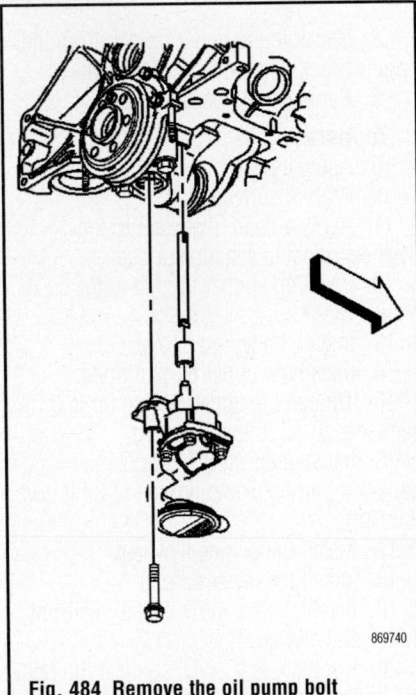

Fig. 484 Remove the oil pump bolt

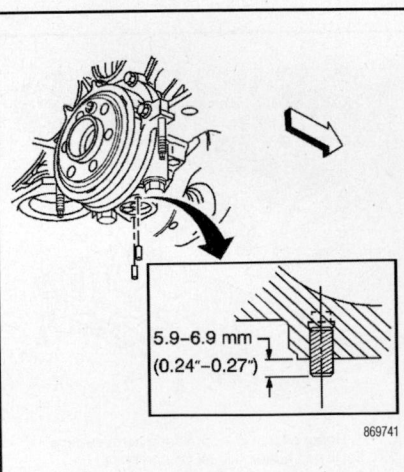

Fig. 485 Inspect the oil pump locator pins for damage, and replace if required

➡Do not reuse the oil pump driveshaft retainer. During assembly, install a NEW oil pump driveshaft retainer.

7. Install the oil pump. Position the oil pump onto the locator pins.
8. Install the oil pump bolt and tighten to 66 ft. lbs. (90 Nm).
9. Install the oil pan.

V8 Engines

See Figures 486 through 488, 000.

1. Remove the oil pan.
2. Remove the engine front cover.
3. Remove the oil pump screen bolt and nuts.
4. Remove the oil pump screen with O-ring seal.
5. Remove the O-ring seal from the pump screen.
6. Discard the O-ring seal.
7. Remove the remaining crankshaft oil deflector nuts.

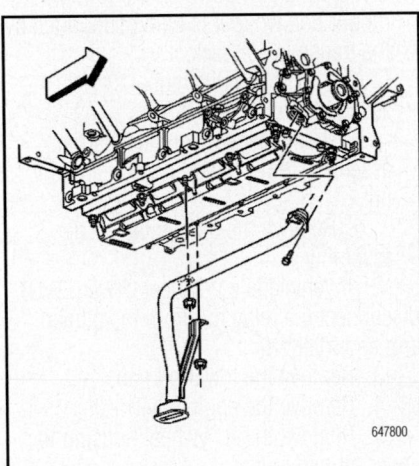

Fig. 486 Remove the oil pump screen bolt and nuts

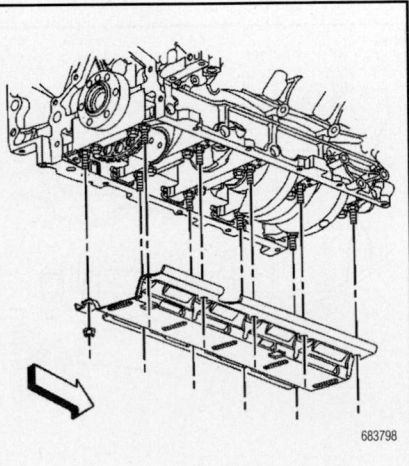

Fig. 487 Remove the remaining crankshaft oil deflector nuts

8. Remove the crankshaft oil deflector.
9. Remove the oil pump bolts and the oil pump.

➡Do not allow dirt or debris to enter the oil pump assembly, cap end as necessary.

To install:

➡Inspect the engine block oil galley passages. These areas must be free and clear of debris or restrictions.

10. Align the splined surfaces of the crankshaft sprocket and the oil pump drive gear and install the oil pump.
11. Install the oil pump onto the crankshaft sprocket until the pump housing contacts the face of the engine block.
12. Install the oil pump bolts. Tighten the bolts to 18 ft. lbs. (25 Nm).
13. Position the crankshaft oil deflector and install the nuts until snug.
14. Lubricate a NEW oil pump screen O-ring seal with clean engine oil.
15. Install the NEW O-ring seal onto the oil pump screen.

➡Push the oil pump screen tube completely into the oil pump prior to tightening the bolt. Do not allow the bolt to pull the tube into the pump.

16. Align the oil pump screen mounting brackets with the correct crankshaft bearing cap studs.
17. Install the oil pump screen.
18. Install the oil pump screen bolt and nuts.

   a. Tighten the bolt to 106 inch lbs. (12 Nm).
   b. Tighten the nuts to 18 ft. lbs. (25 Nm).

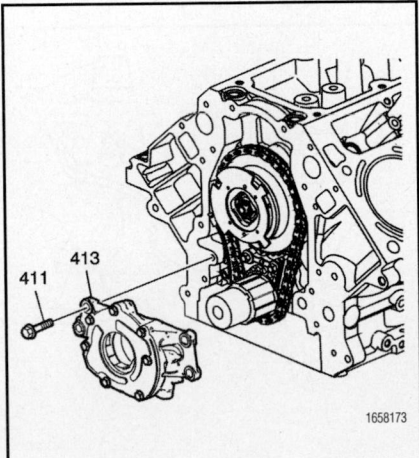

Fig. 488 Remove the oil pump bolts (411) and the oil pump (413)

19. Install the engine front cover.
20. Install the oil pan.

Diesel Engines

See Figures 489 through 494.

1. Remove the engine front cover.
2. Remove the oil pump screen bolts and nuts.
3. Remove the oil pump screen.
4. Remove and discard the oil pump screen gasket.
5. Block the crankshaft from turning with a wooden handle.

➥Look for an "L" on the end of the oil pump shaft. If there is an "L" present, the nut and shaft have left hand threads. Service the nut accordingly.

6. While holding the secondary oil pump shaft with a hex driver, remove the oil pump driven gear nut.

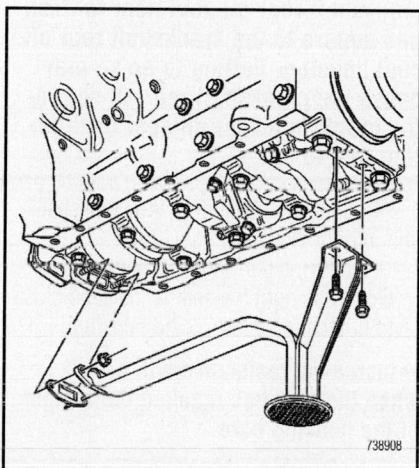

Fig. 489 Remove the oil pump screen bolts and nuts (1) and the oil pump screen (2)

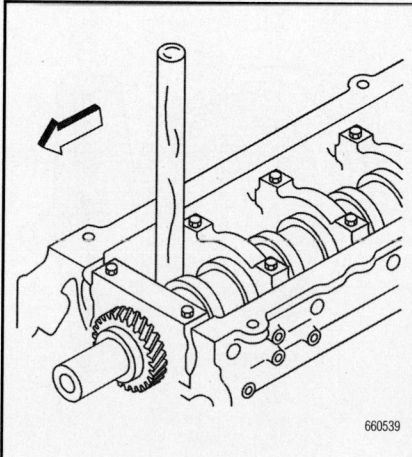

Fig. 490 Block the crankshaft (1) from turning with a wooden handle (2)

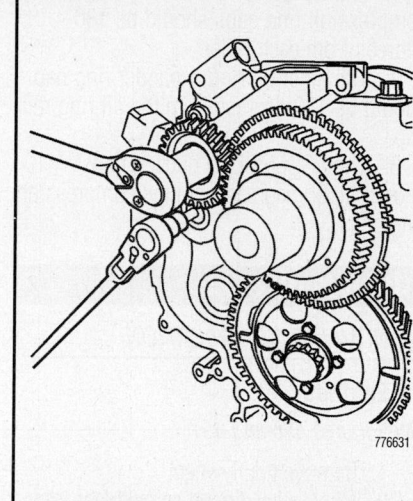

Fig. 491 While holding the secondary oil pump shaft with a hex driver (1), remove the oil pump driven gear (2) nut

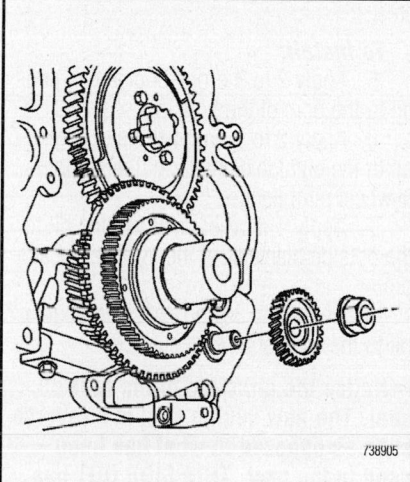

Fig. 492 Remove the oil pump driven gear (1)

Fig. 493 Remove the oil pump drive gear (1) and crankshaft reluctor

7. Remove the oil pump driven gear.

➥Do not damage the crankshaft reluctor. Do not remove the crankshaft reluctor to oil pump drive bolts.

8. Remove the oil pump drive gear and crankshaft reluctor.
   a. Use a brass drift.
   b. Tap on the back as close to the center of the reluctor.
9. Remove the hex head and the Allen head bolt in order to remove the oil pump.
10. Remove the oil pump.
11. Remove the O-ring seal for the oil pump.
12. If required, clean and inspect the oil pump.

To install:

13. Install a NEW oil pump O-ring seal.
14. Install the oil pump.
15. Install the oil pump bolts and tighten to 15 ft. lbs. (21 Nm).
16. Inspect the oil pump drive gear for wear.
17. Replace the oil pump drive gear pin if worn.
18. Install the oil pump drive gear and reluctor to the crankshaft.
19. Install the oil pump driven gear.
20. While holding the secondary oil pump shaft with a hex driver, install the oil pump driven gear nut. Tighten the nut to 74 ft. lbs. (100 Nm).
21. Install a NEW oil pump screen gasket to the oil pump.
22. Install the oil pump screen.
23. Install the oil pump screen bolts and nuts. Tighten the bolts/nuts to 18 ft. lbs. (25 Nm).
24. Install the engine front cover.

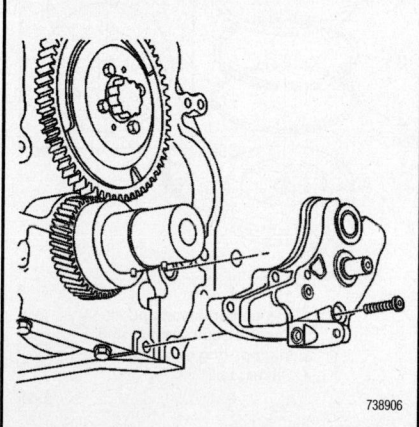

Fig. 494 Remove the hex head (1) and the Allen head bolt in order to remove the oil pump (2)

PISTON AND RING

POSITIONING

> ※※ **CAUTION**
>
> **When installing piston rings, use a ring expander pliers type tool. Do not roll the rings into the grooves of the piston. Use caution and care to expand the rings only slightly larger than the Outside Diameter (OD) of the piston.**

1. Using piston ring pliers, install the piston rings onto the piston. The cylinder contact face, outboard edge, of the top compression ring has a shinier finish than the lower compression ring. The dimple or mark on the piston ring should face the top of the piston. If no dimple or mark can be found on the top compression ring, it may be installed in either direction.

V6 Engines

1. Position the compression ring end gaps 120 degrees opposite each other.
2. Position the oil control ring end gaps 90 degrees opposite each other.

V8 Engines

1. Position the compression ring end gaps 180 degrees opposite each other.
2. Position the oil control ring end gaps 180 degrees opposite each other.

Diesel Engines

See Figure 495.

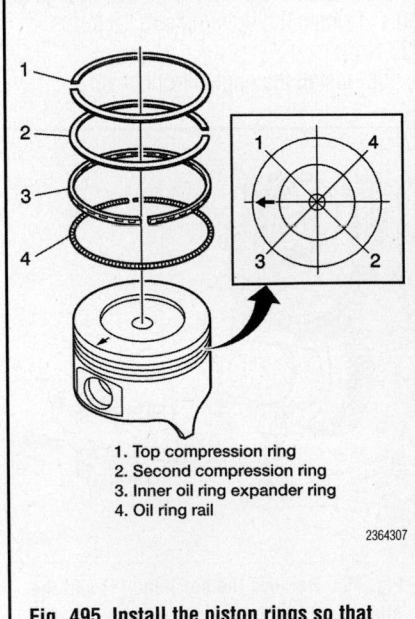

1. Top compression ring
2. Second compression ring
3. Inner oil ring expander ring
4. Oil ring rail

2364307

Fig. 495 Install the piston rings so that the gaps are orientated as shown

1. The top compression ring and second compression ring gaps should be 180 degrees from each other.
2. The inner oil ring expander ring gap should be 180 degrees from the oil ring rail gap.
3. The ASSEMBLED oil ring gaps should be 90 degrees from the compression ring gaps.

REAR MAIN SEAL

REMOVAL & INSTALLATION

V6 Engines

See Figures 496 and 497.

1. Remove the flywheel.
2. Insert a flat-tipped screwdriver into the access notches and carefully pry the seal from the housing.
3. Discard the seal.
4. Clean off any dirt or rust in the area.

To install:

5. Apply 2 to 3 drops of clean engine oil to the bore of the housing.
6. Apply 2 to 3 drops of clean engine oil to the outside diameter of the engine flywheel pilot flange.
7. Apply 1 drop of clean engine oil to the outside diameter of the flywheel locator pin.
8. Apply 2 to 3 drops of clean engine oil to the crankshaft seal surface.

➡ **Notice the direction of the rear oil seal. The new design seal is a reverse style as opposed to what has been used in the past. THIS SIDE OUT has been stamped into the seal as shown in the graphic.**

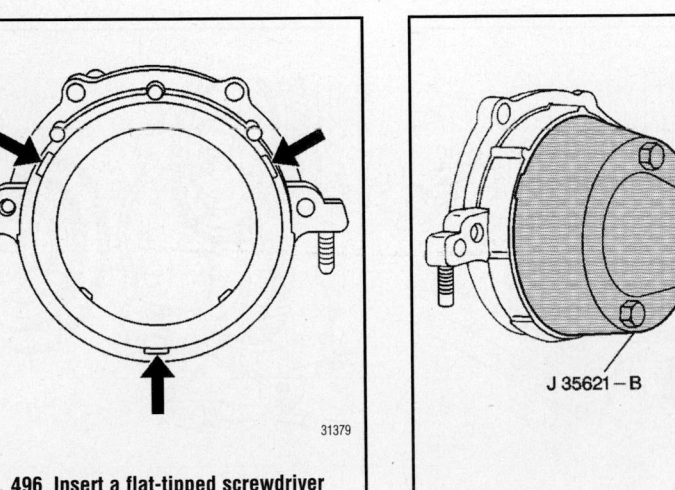

31379

Fig. 496 Insert a flat-tipped screwdriver into the access notches and carefully pry the seal from the housing

9. Inspect the Rear Main Seal Installer (J-35621-B) flange for imperfections that may damage the NEW seal. Minor imperfections may be removed with a fine grade emery cloth.

➡ **DO NOT allow oil or any other lubricants to contact the seal lip surface of the seal.**

10. Remove the sleeve from the seal.
11. Apply 2 to 3 drops of clean engine oil to the outside diameter of the seal.
12. Install the seal onto the J-35621-B.
13. Install the J-35621-B onto the rear of the crankshaft and hand tighten the tool bolts until snug.

> ※※ **CAUTION**
>
> **Proper alignment of the crankshaft rear oil seal is critical. Install the crankshaft rear oil seal near to flush and square to the crankshaft rear oil seal housing. Failing to do so may cause the crankshaft rear oil seal or the crankshaft rear oil seal installation tool to fail.**

14. Install the seal onto the crankshaft and into the housing:
   a. Turn the J-35621-B wing nut clockwise until the seal is installed close to flush and square to the housing.

➡ **Increased resistance will be felt when the seal has reached the bottom of the housing bore.**

   b. Turn the J-35621-B wing nut counterclockwise to release the J-35621-B from the seal.
15. Remove the J-35621-B.

J 35621 – B

334550

Fig. 497 Rear Main Seal Installer (J-35621-B)

16. Wipe off any excess engine oil with a clean rag.

17. Install the engine flywheel.

V8 Engines

See Figures 498 and 499.

1. Remove the automatic transmission flexplate.

2. Remove and discard the crankshaft rear oil seal.

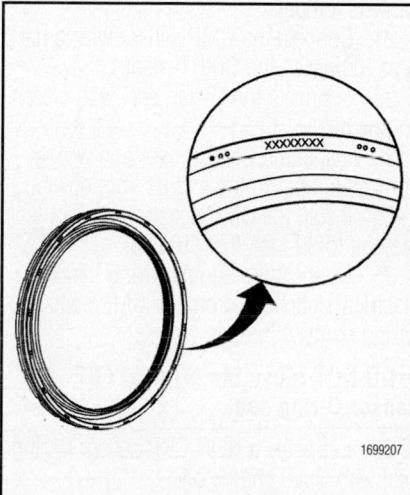

Fig. 498 The part number is applied to the outside face of the seal, as shown

To install:

➡️**For proper orientation, note the installation direction of the oil seal. The oil seal is a reverse-lip design. The part number is applied to the outside face of the seal, as shown.**

3. Inspect the seal and identify the part number markings for proper orientation.

4. Install the Crankshaft Rear Oil Seal Installer (J-41479) cone and bolts onto the rear of the crankshaft.

5. Tighten the bolts until snug. Do not overtighten.

6. Install the rear oil seal onto the tapered cone and push the seal to the rear seal bore. Install the oil seal with the part number markings facing away from the engine.

7. Thread the J-41479 threaded rod into the tapered cone until the tool contacts the oil seal.

8. Align the oil seal into the tool.

9. Rotate the handle of the tool clockwise until the seal enters the rear cover and bottoms into the cover bore.

10. Remove the J-41479.

11. Install the automatic transmission flexplate.

Diesel Engines

See Figures 500 and 501.

Special Tools Required:
• J-44641 Crankshaft Rear Oil Seal Remover
• J-44642 Crankshaft Rear Oil Seal Installer

1. Remove the engine flywheel.

2. Install the button of J-44641 into the crankshaft.

3. Press the jaws of J-44641 into the felt portion of the seal far enough to engage the inner lip of the seal.

4. While holding the jaws of J-44641 tightly to the seals inner sleeve, tighten the jaw bolts.

5. Remove the crankshaft rear oil seal using the J-44641.

To install:

6. Place the crankshaft rear oil seal onto the crankshaft.

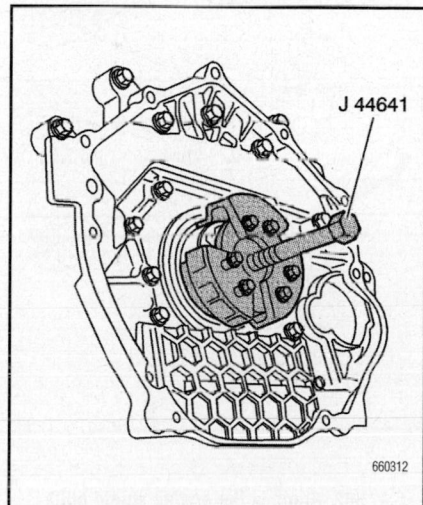

Fig. 500 Install the button of J-44641 into the crankshaft

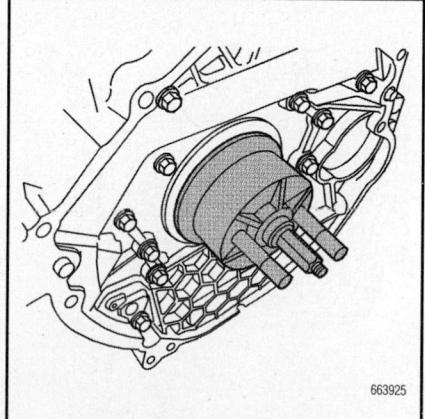

Fig. 501 The J-44642 must be fully secured to the crankshaft to ensure proper seal depth

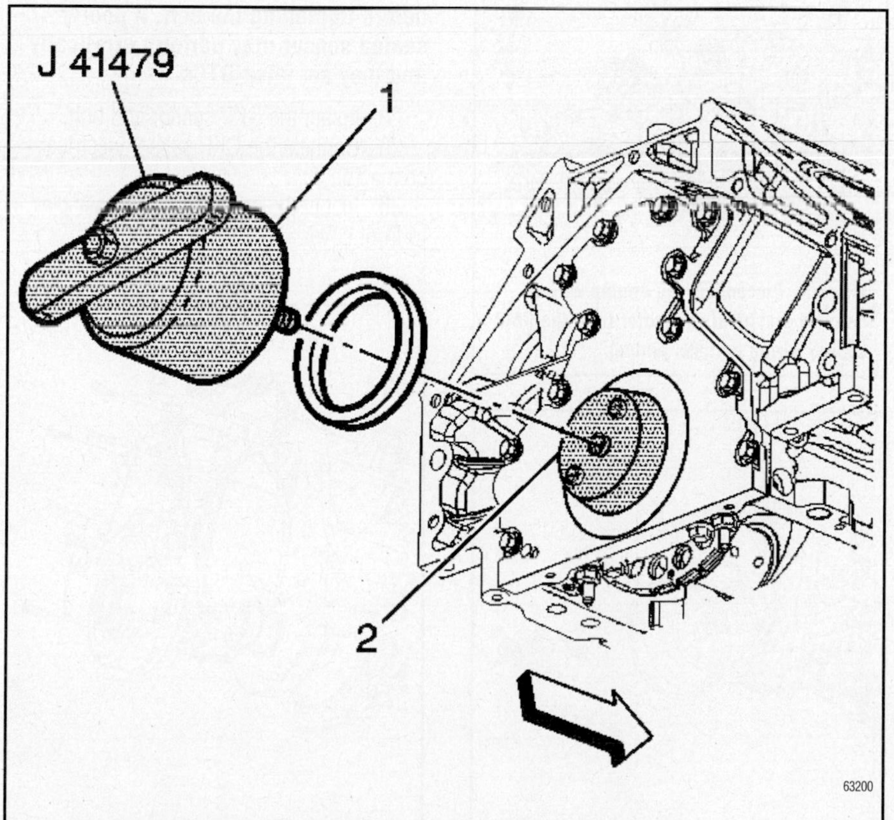

Fig. 499 Crankshaft Rear Oil Seal Installer (J-41479) cone (2) and tool (1)

➡ **The J-44642 must be fully secured to the crankshaft to ensure proper seal depth.**

7. Install the J-44642 to the crankshaft.
8. Press the crankshaft rear oil seal into position using the J-44642. The J-44642 will bottom out when the seal reaches the proper depth.
9. Remove the J-44642.
10. Install the engine flywheel.

TIMING CHAIN FRONT COVER

REMOVAL & INSTALLATION

V6 Engines

See Figures 502 through 506.

1. Remove the water pump.
2. Remove the crankshaft balancer.
3. Remove the oil pan.

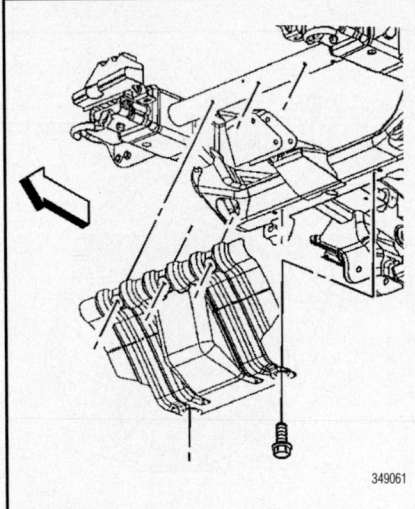

Fig. 502 Remove the engine shield bolts and shield

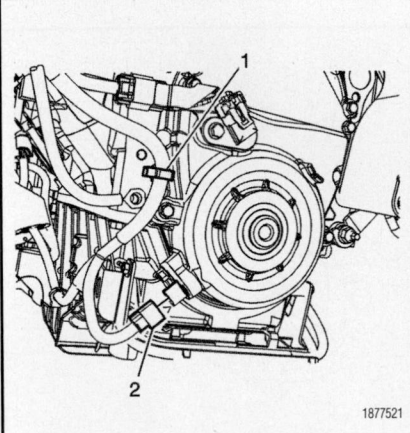

Fig. 503 Remove engine wire harness clip (1) from front cover and disconnect the CKP sensor electrical connector (2)

4. Remove the engine shield bolts and shield.
5. Remove engine wire harness clip from front cover.
6. Disconnect the Crankshaft Position (CKP) sensor electrical connector.
7. Remove the CKP sensor bolt and sensor.
8. Remove and discard the CKP sensor O-ring seal.
9. Disconnect the engine wiring harness electrical connector from the Camshaft Position (CMP) sensor wiring harness jumper.
10. Remove the CMP sensor bolt.
11. Remove the CMP sensor and wiring harness jumper from the engine front cover.
12. Disconnect the CMP sensor wiring harness jumper from the CMP sensor.
13. Remove the CMP sensor from the wiring harness jumper.
14. Remove the front cover bolts.

➡ **After the composite front cover is removed do not reinstall the front cover. Always install a NEW front cover.**

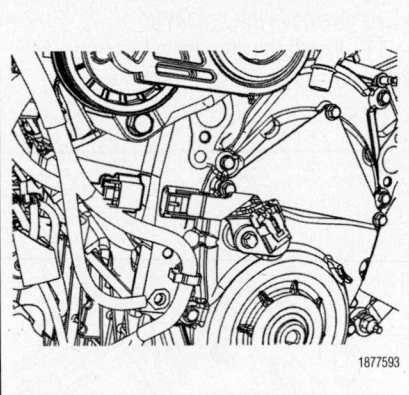

Fig. 504 Disconnect the engine wiring harness electrical connector from the CMP sensor wiring harness jumper

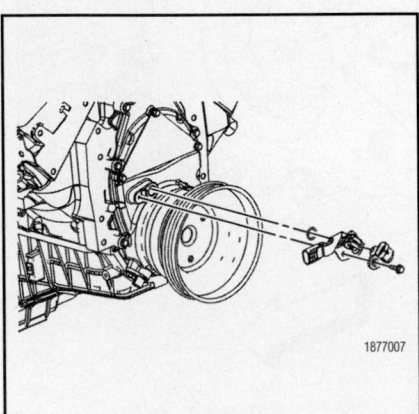

Fig. 505 Remove the CMP sensor bolt

15. Remove and discard the front cover.
16. Clean all sealing surfaces.

To install:

17. Install a NEW front cover.
18. Install the front cover bolts. Tighten the bolts to 106 inch lbs. (12 Nm).

➡ **Do not reuse the original O-ring seal.**

19. If reinstalling the old CMP sensor, install a NEW O-ring seal onto the sensor.
20. Install the CMP sensor to the wiring harness jumper.
21. Connect the CMP sensor wiring harness jumper to the CMP sensor.
22. Lubricate the O-ring seal with clean engine oil.
23. Install the CMP sensor and wiring harness jumper to the engine front cover.
24. Install the CMP sensor bolt. Tighten the bolt to 89 inch lbs. (10 Nm).
25. Connect the engine wiring harness electrical connector from the CMP sensor wiring harness jumper.

➡ **DO NOT reuse the original CKP sensor O-ring seal.**

26. Lubricate a NEW CKP sensor O-ring seal with clean engine oil.
27. Install the NEW O-ring seal onto the CKP sensor.

➡ **When installing the CKP sensor, make sure the sensor is fully seated before tightening the bolt. A poorly seated sensor may perform erratically and may set false DTCs.**

28. Install the CKP sensor and bolt.
29. Connect the CKP sensor electrical connector.
30. Install the engine wire harness clip to front cover.

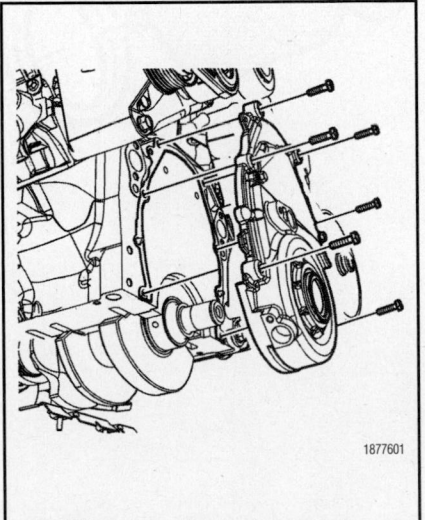

Fig. 506 Remove the front cover bolts

31. Install the engine shield and bolts. Tighten the bolts to 15 ft. lbs. (20 Nm).
32. Install the oil pan.
33. Install the crankshaft balancer.
34. Install the water pump.

V8 Engines

See Figures 507 through 510.

1. Remove the water pump.
2. Remove the crankshaft balancer.
3. Disconnect the engine harness electrical connector from the Camshaft Position (CMP) sensor wire harness electrical connector.
4. Remove the oil pan-to-front cover bolts.
5. Remove the front cover bolts.
6. Remove the front cover and gasket.
7. Discard the front cover gasket.
8. Remove the crankshaft front oil seal.

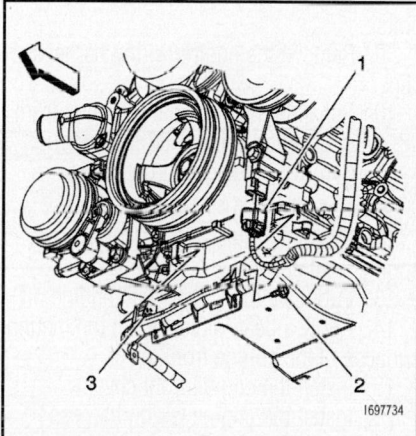

Fig. 507 Disconnect the engine harness electrical connector (1) from the Camshaft Position (CMP) sensor wire harness electrical connector; battery cable channel bolt (2); slide the channel pin (3)

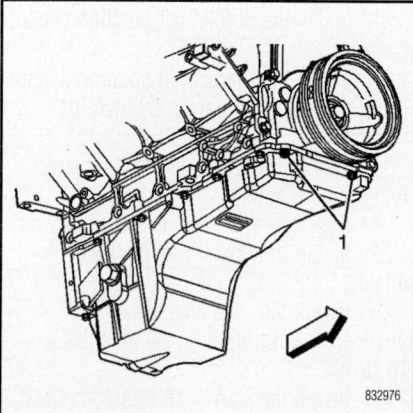

Fig. 508 Remove the oil pan-to-front cover bolts (1)

To install:

➡ **Note the following:**

- Do not reuse the crankshaft oil seal or front cover gasket.
- Do not apply any type of sealant to the front cover gasket, unless specified.
- The special tool in this procedure is used to properly center the front crankshaft front oil seal.
- All gasket surfaces should be free of oil or other foreign material during assembly.
- The crankshaft front oil seal MUST be centered in relation to the crankshaft.
- An improperly aligned front cover may cause premature front oil seal wear and/or engine oil leaks.

9. Apply a bead of sealant to the oil pan to engine block junction.
10. Position the NEW engine front cover gasket and front cover to the engine.

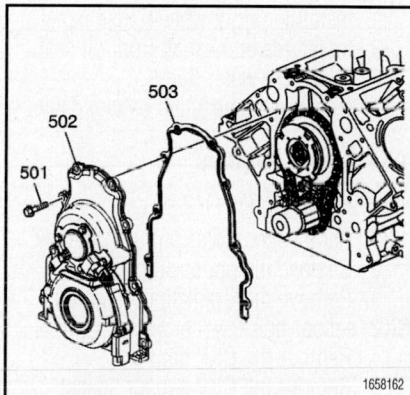

Fig. 509 Remove the front cover bolts (501), the front cover (502) and gasket (503)

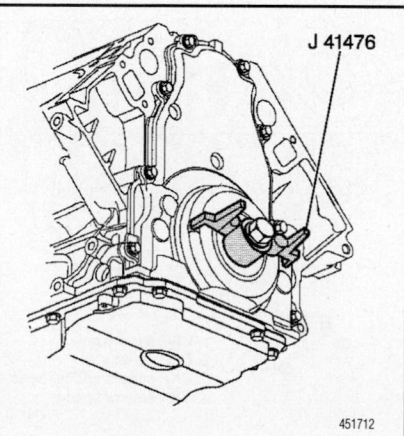

Fig. 510 Install the Front and Rear Cover Alignment Tool (J-41476) to the front cover

11. Install the front cover bolts until snug. Do not overtighten.
12. Install the oil pan-to-front cover bolts until snug. Do not over tighten.
13. Install the Front and Rear Cover Alignment Tool (J-41476) to the front cover.
14. Align the tapered legs of the J-41476 with the machined alignment surfaces on the front cover.
15. Install the crankshaft balancer bolt until snug. Do not overtighten.
  a. Tighten the oil pan to front cover bolts to 18 ft. lbs. (25 Nm).
  b. Tighten the engine front cover bolts to 18 ft. lbs. (25 Nm).
16. Remove the J-41476.
17. Connect the engine harness electrical connector to the CMP sensor wire harness electrical connector.
18. Install a NEW crankshaft front oil seal.
19. Install the water pump.

2010 Diesel Engines

See Figures 511 through 513.

1. Disconnect the negative battery cable.
2. Remove the water pump.
3. Remove the crankshaft front oil seal.
4. Remove the right wheelhouse panel.
5. Disconnect the Crankshaft Position (CKP) sensor electrical connector.
6. Remove the CKP sensor bolt and sensor.
7. Remove the CKP sensor spacer bolts and spacer.
8. Remove and discard the O-rings from the sensor and the spacer.
9. Remove the upper oil pan-to-engine front cover bolts.
10. Remove the engine front cover bolts.

Fig. 511 Disconnect the Crankshaft Position (CKP) sensor electrical connector

Fig. 512 Remove the upper oil pan-to-engine front cover bolts

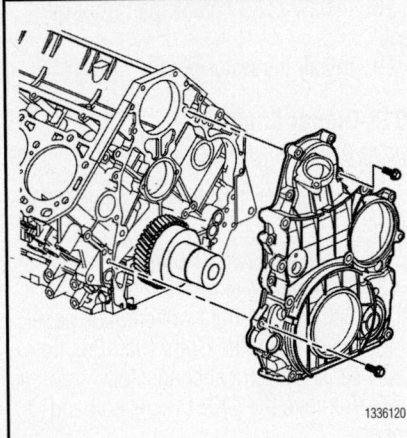

Fig. 513 Remove the engine front cover bolts

11. Separate the engine front cover from the cylinder block and upper oil pan using Seal Cutter (J-37228).

➡ **Do not bend the turbocharger coolant pipe.**

12. Remove the engine front cover.
13. If necessary, remove the pressure relief valve O-ring.
14. Clean and inspect the front cover.

To install:

15. If necessary, install a NEW pressure relief valve O-ring.
16. Lubricate the O-ring with engine oil. Tighten the valve to 29 ft. lbs. (39 Nm).
17. Apply a bead of sealant to the engine front cover sealing surface to the engine block.
18. Apply a bead of sealant to the engine front cover sealing surface to the upper oil pan.
19. Install the engine front cover.
20. Install the engine front cover bolts. Tighten the bolts to 18 ft. lbs. (25 Nm).

21. Install the upper oil pan to engine front cover bolts. Tighten the bolts to 15 ft. lbs. (21 Nm).
22. Install a NEW O-ring to the CKP sensor spacer.
23. Lubricate the O-ring with clean engine oil.

➡ **The crankshaft position sensor spacers are machined with different timing positions. However, if the crankshaft position sensor spacer requires replacement, replace with a grade "C" spacer.**

24. Install the CKP sensor spacer and bolts. Tighten the bolts to 89 inch lbs. (10 Nm).
25. Install a NEW O-ring to the CKP sensor.
26. Lubricate the O-ring with clean engine oil.
27. Install the CKP sensor and bolt. Tighten the bolt to 89 inch lbs. (10 Nm).
28. Connect the CKP sensor electrical connector.
29. Install the right wheelhouse panel.
30. Install the crankshaft front oil seal.
31. Install the water pump.
32. Connect the negative battery cable.

2011 Diesel Engines

See Figures 514 and 515.

1. Remove the water pump assembly.
2. Remove the upper oil pan.
3. Remove the Crankshaft Position (CKP) sensor bolt.
4. Remove the CKP sensor.
5. Remove the CKP sensor spacer bolts.
6. Remove the CKP position sensor spacer.

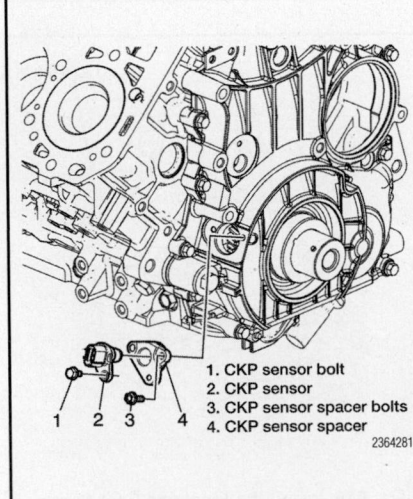

1. CKP sensor bolt
2. CKP sensor
3. CKP sensor spacer bolts
4. CKP sensor spacer

Fig. 514 Remove the CKP sensor bolt

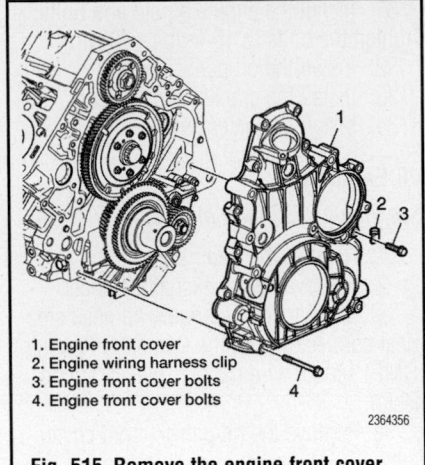

1. Engine front cover
2. Engine wiring harness clip
3. Engine front cover bolts
4. Engine front cover bolts

Fig. 515 Remove the engine front cover bolts

7. Remove the Camshaft Position (CMP) sensor.
8. Remove the engine front cover bolts.
9. Remove the engine wiring harness clip.
10. Separate the engine front cover from the cylinder block using J-37228 cutter.
11. Remove the engine front cover.

To install:

12. Install the relief valve O-ring to the engine front cover.
13. Lubricate the O-ring with engine oil.
14. Apply a bead of sealant to the mating surfaces of the engine front cover.
15. Install the engine front cover.
16. Install the engine wiring harness clip.
17. Install the engine front cover bolts.
18. Tighten the engine front cover bolts (1, 2) in sequence to 18 ft. lbs. (25 Nm).
19. Install a NEW O-ring to the crankshaft position sensor spacer.
20. Lubricate the O-ring with engine oil.
21. Install the crankshaft position sensor spacer.
22. Install the crankshaft position sensor spacer bolts and tighten to 89 inch lbs. (10 Nm).
23. Install a NEW O-ring to the crankshaft position sensor.
24. Lubricate the O-ring with engine oil.
25. Install the crankshaft position sensor.
26. Install the crankshaft position sensor bolt and tighten to 89 inch lbs. (10 Nm).
27. Install the Camshaft Position (CMP) sensor.
28. Install the upper oil pan.
29. Install the water pump assembly.

TIMING CHAIN & SPROCKETS

REMOVAL & INSTALLATION

V6 Engines

See Figures 516 through 526.

1. Remove the crankshaft position sensor reluctor ring.

2. Remove the timing chain tensioner shoe using a downward motion.

3. Remove the timing chain tensioner bracket bolt and bracket.

4. Check the camshaft timing chain free play.

    a. Rotate the camshaft sprocket counterclockwise until all slack is removed from the camshaft timing chain.

    b. Measure the free play on the slack side of the camshaft timing chain.

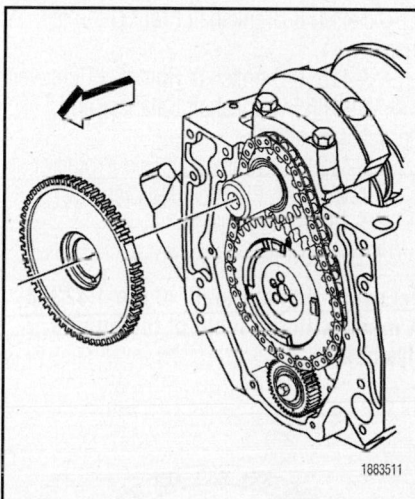

Fig. 516 Remove the crankshaft position sensor reluctor ring

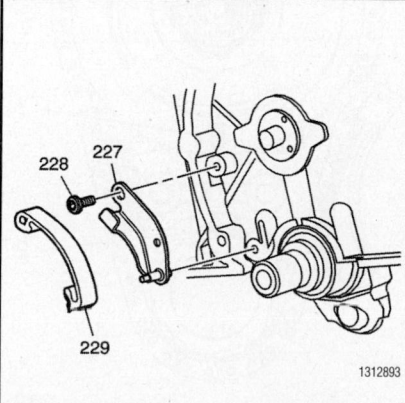

Fig. 517 Remove the timing chain tensioner shoe (229) using a downward motion and remove the timing chain tensioner bracket bolt and bracket (227, 228)

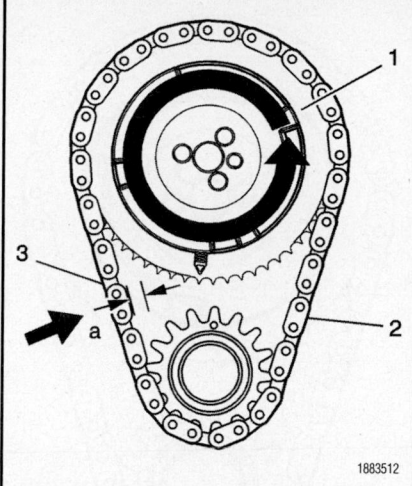

Fig. 518 Rotate the camshaft sprocket (1) counterclockwise until all slack is removed from the camshaft timing chain (2); measure the free play on the slack side (3) of the camshaft timing chain

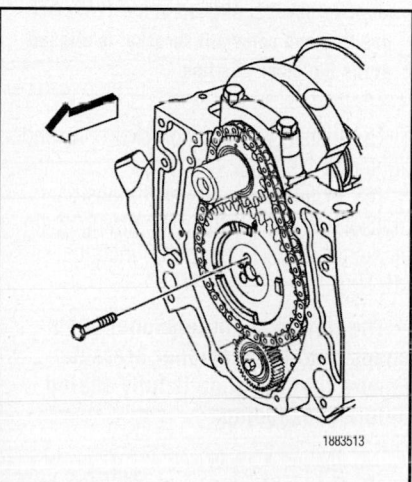

Fig. 519 Remove the camshaft sprocket bolts

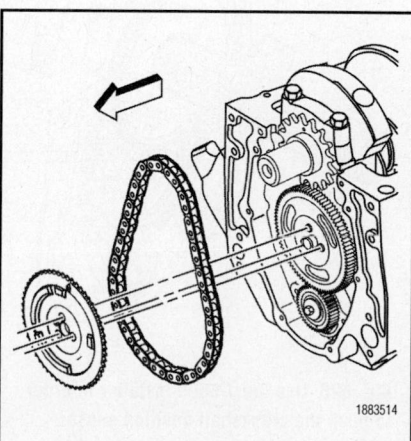

Fig. 520 Remove the camshaft sprocket and the camshaft timing chain

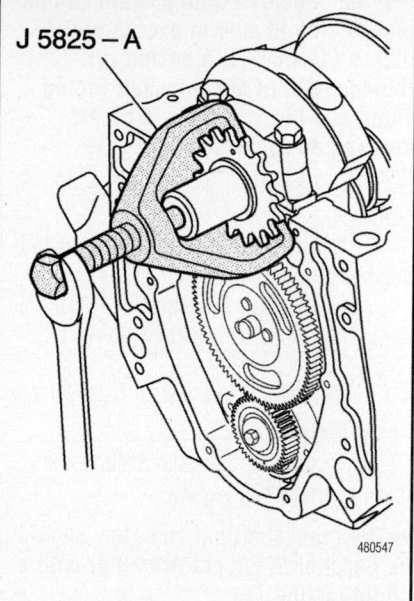

Fig. 521 Remove the crankshaft sprocket using the J-5825-A remover

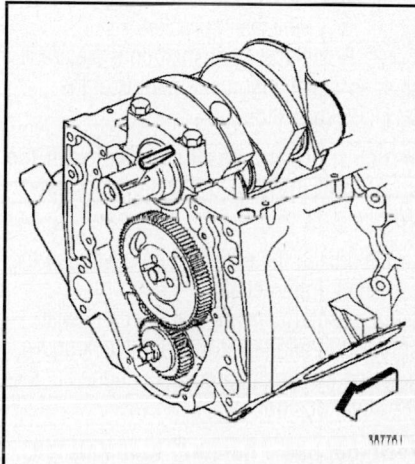

Fig. 522 Remove the crankshaft balancer key

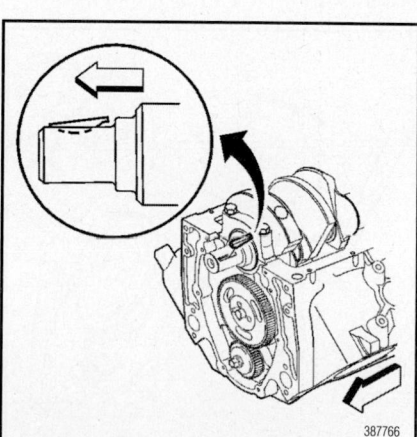

Fig. 523 The crankshaft balancer key should be parallel to the crankshaft or with a slight incline

➡If the camshaft timing chain can be moved side to side in excess of 0.43 inches (11 mm), dimension (a), replacement of the camshaft timing chain and the sprockets is recommended during assembly.

5. Remove the camshaft sprocket bolts.

6. Remove the camshaft sprocket and the camshaft timing chain.

7. Remove the crankshaft sprocket using the Crankshaft Gear Remover (J-5825-A).

8. Remove the crankshaft balancer key.

To install:

9. Install the crankshaft balancer key into the crankshaft keyway.

➡The crankshaft balancer key should be parallel to the crankshaft or with a slight incline.

10. Align the keyway of the crankshaft sprocket with the crankshaft balancer key.

11. Use the J-5590 installer in order to install the crankshaft sprocket.

12. Rotate the crankshaft until the crankshaft sprocket alignment mark is at the 12 o'clock position.

➡Install the camshaft sprocket with the alignment mark at the 6 o'clock position.

13. Install the camshaft sprocket and the camshaft timing chain.

14. Look to ensure that the crankshaft sprocket is aligned at the 12 o'clock position and camshaft sprocket is aligned at the 6 o'clock position.

➡Do not use a hammer to install the camshaft sprocket onto the camshaft. To do so may dislodge the expansion cup plug, camshaft rear bearing hole.

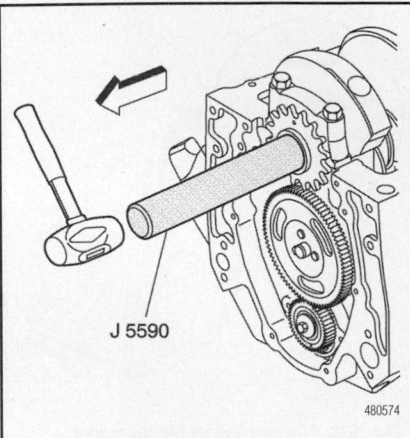

Fig. 524 Use the J-5590 installer in order to install the crankshaft sprocket

Fig. 525 Look to ensure that the crankshaft sprocket is aligned at the 12 o'clock position and camshaft sprocket is aligned at the 6 o'clock position

15. Install camshaft sprocket bolts and tighten to 18 ft. lbs. (25 Nm).

16. Install the timing chain tensioner bracket and bolt. Tighten the timing chain tensioner bracket bolt to 106 inch lbs. (12 Nm).

➡The timing chain tensioner shoe snaps onto the tensioner bracket. Ensure that the shoe is fully seated before proceeding.

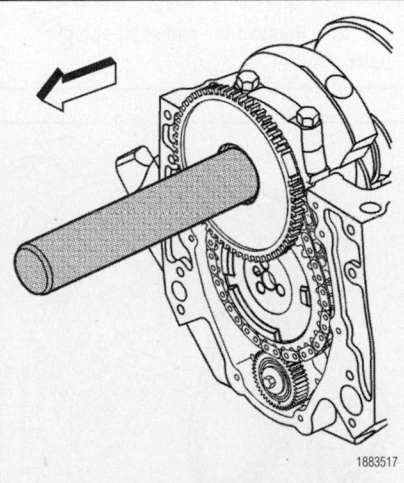

Fig. 526 Use the J-5590 installer in order to push the crankshaft position sensor reluctor ring onto the crankshaft until completely seated against the crankshaft sprocket

17. Install the timing chain tensioner shoe using an upwards motion.

18. Install the crankshaft position sensor reluctor ring.

a. Align the keyway on the crankshaft position sensor reluctor ring with the crankshaft balancer key in the crankshaft.

b. Use the J-5590 installer in order to push the crankshaft position sensor reluctor ring onto the crankshaft until completely seated against the crankshaft sprocket.

V8 and Diesel Engines

See Figures 527 and 528.

Special Tools Required:
- EN 46330 Timing Belt Tensioner Retaining Pin
- J-8433 Two Jaw Puller
- J-41478 Crankshaft Front Oil Seal Installer
- J-41558 Crankshaft Sprocket Remover
- J-41665 Crankshaft Balancer and Sprocket Installer
- J-41816-2 Crankshaft End Protector
- J-42386-A Flywheel Holding Tool
- J-45059 Angle Meter

1. Remove the oil pump.

➡Ensure that the teeth of the J-42386-A mesh with the teeth of the engine flywheel.

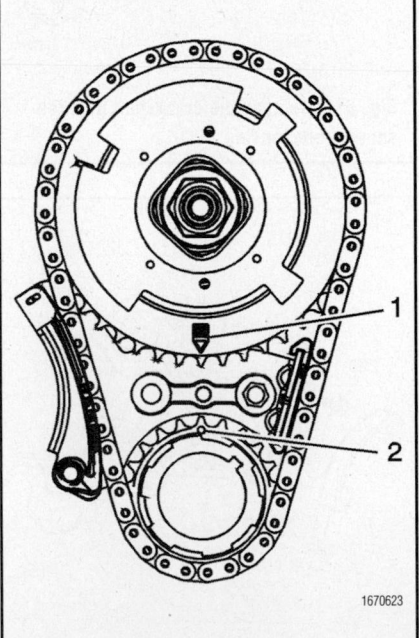

Fig. 527 Rotate the crankshaft sprocket until the Camshaft Position (CMP) actuator alignment mark (1) and the crankshaft sprocket alignment mark (2) are aligned

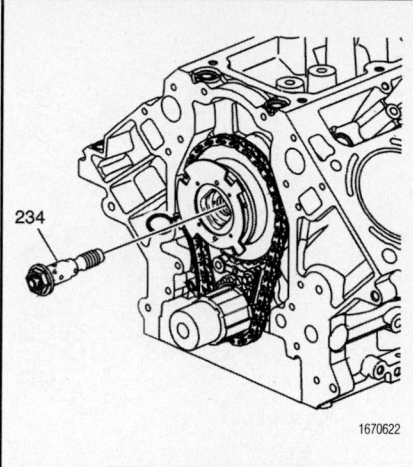

Fig. 528 Remove and discard the CMP actuator solenoid valve (234)

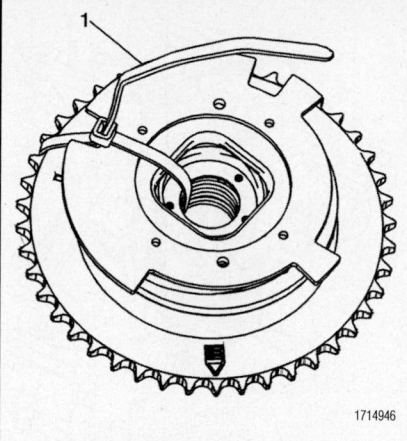

Fig. 530 Insert and secure a tie strap (1) through the center of the actuator and over the reluctor wheel

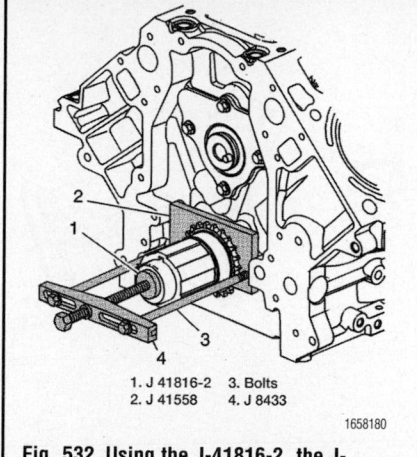

1. J 41816-2   3. Bolts
2. J 41558   4. J 8433

Fig. 532 Using the J-41816-2, the J-41558, bolts and the J-8433 in order to remove the crankshaft sprocket

2. Rotate the crankshaft sprocket until the Camshaft Position (CMP) actuator alignment mark and the crankshaft sprocket alignment mark are aligned.

3. Install the J-42386-A.

4. Tighten the J-42386-A.

5. Remove and discard the CMP actuator solenoid valve.

6. Loosen and separate the CMP actuator and timing chain from the camshaft. Position your fingers behind the actuator sprocket and pull the actuator away from the front of the camshaft. Never pull on the reluctor wheel when attempting to remove the actuator.

✳✳ CAUTION

Do not turn the crankshaft assembly after the timing chain has been removed in order to prevent damage to the piston assemblies or the valves.

7. Remove the CMP actuator and timing chain.

8. Insert and secure a tie strap through the center of the actuator and over the reluctor wheel.

9. Remove the timing chain tension bolts (231) and tensioner (232).

10. Using the J-41816-2, the J-41558, bolts and the J-8433 in order to remove the crankshaft sprocket.

11. Remove the crankshaft sprocket.

12. Remove the crankshaft sprocket key, if required.

To install:

13. Install the key into the crankshaft keyway, if previously removed.

14. Tap the key into the keyway until both ends of the key bottom onto the crankshaft.

15. Install the crankshaft sprocket onto the front of the crankshaft. Align the crankshaft key with the crankshaft sprocket keyway.

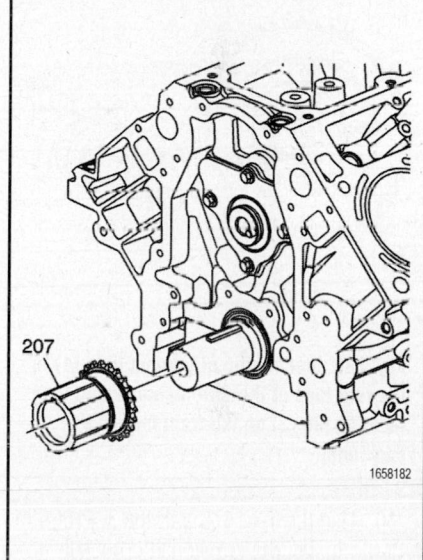

Fig. 533 Remove the crankshaft sprocket (207)

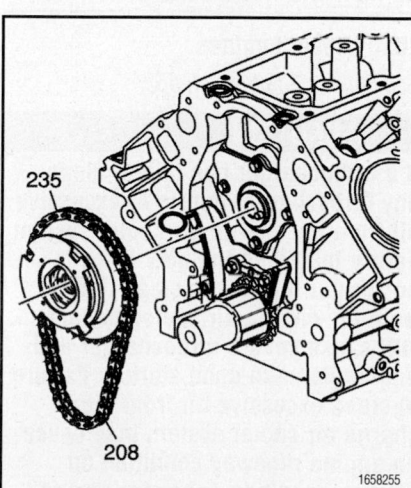

Fig. 529 Remove the CMP actuator (235) and timing chain (208)

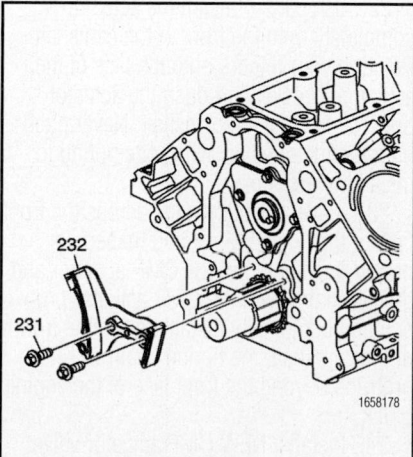

Fig. 531 Remove the timing chain tension bolts (231) and tensioner (232)

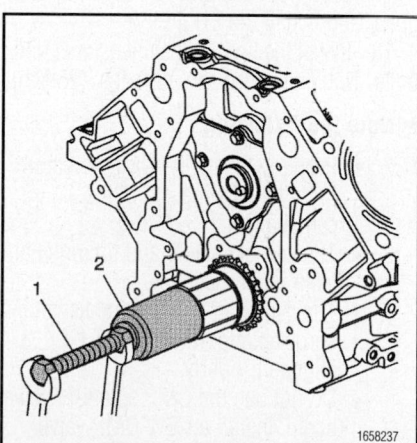

Fig. 534 Use the J-41478 (1) and the J-41665 (2) in order to install the crankshaft sprocket

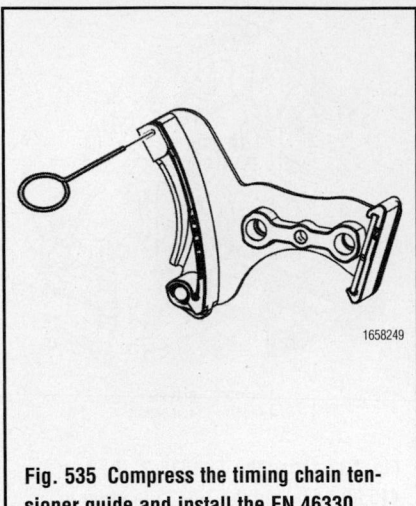

Fig. 535 Compress the timing chain tensioner guide and install the EN 46330

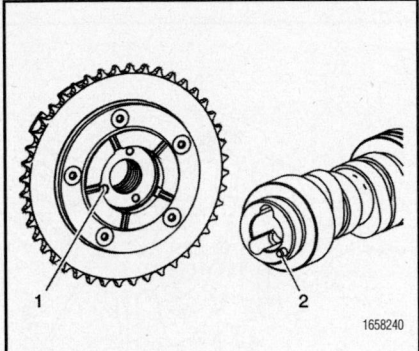

Fig. 536 Identify the alignment hole (1) in the rear face of the CMP actuator and the locating pin (2) on the front face of the camshaft

16. Use the J-41478 and the J-41665 in order to install the crankshaft sprocket. Install the sprocket onto the crankshaft until fully seated against the crankshaft flange.

17. Compress the timing chain tensioner guide and install the EN 46330.

18. Install the timing chain tensioner and bolts. Tighten the bolts to 18 ft. lbs. (25 Nm).

➡ **Note the following:**

- Properly locate the CMP actuator onto the locating pin of the camshaft.
- The sprocket teeth and timing chain teeth must mesh.
- The camshaft and the crankshaft sprocket alignment MUST be aligned properly.
- Do not use the CMP solenoid valve again. Install a NEW CMP valve during assembly.

19. Identify the alignment hole in the rear face of the CMP actuator and the locating pin on the front face of the camshaft.

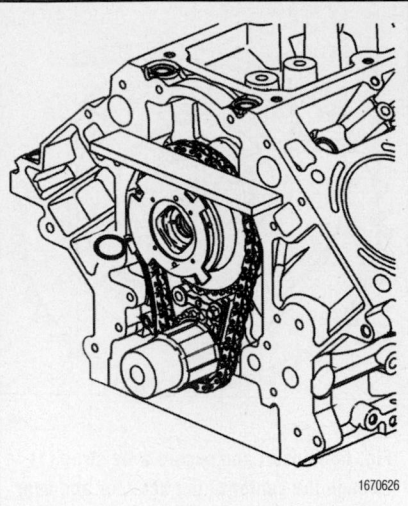

Fig. 537 Place a straight edge across the front face of the engine block and inspect for proper installation of the CMP actuator and timing chain

20. Align the CMP actuator so the timing mark is in the 6 o'clock position.

21. Install the CMP actuator and timing chain. Align the hole in the face of the CMP actuator with the locating pin on the front face of the camshaft.

✴✴ WARNING

Do not push or pull on the reluctor wheel of the Camshaft Position (CMP) actuator during removal or installation. The reluctor wheel is retained to the front of the CMP actuator by 3 roll pins. Pushing or pulling on the wheel may dislodge the wheel from the front of the actuator. The actuator return spring is under tension and may rotate the dislodged reluctor wheel, causing personal injury.

22. Use care to install the actuator completely onto the front of the camshaft. Position your fingers onto the face of the actuator sprocket and push the actuator onto the front of the camshaft. Never push on the reluctor wheel when attempting to install the actuator.

23. Place a straight edge across the front face of the engine block and inspect for proper installation of the CMP actuator and timing chain. With the CMP actuator properly and completely installed onto the front of the camshaft, the timing chain will not protrude beyond the front face of the engine block.

24. Install a NEW CMP actuator valve. With the CMP actuator properly positioned onto the camshaft, the CMP actuator solenoid valve can be threaded completely into

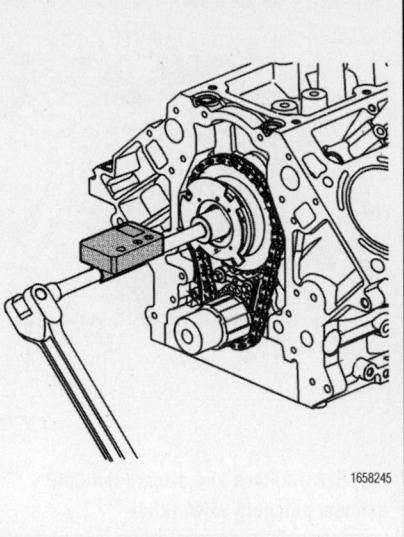

Fig. 538 Tighten the bolt a final pass an additional 90 degrees using J-45059

the camshaft using light hand pressure. Tighten by hand until snug.

25. Inspect the sprockets for proper alignment. The mark on the CMP actuator sprocket should be located in the 6 o'clock position and the mark on the crankshaft sprocket should be located in the 12 o'clock position.

26. Remove the EN 46330.

27. Tighten the CMP actuator bolt.

   a. Tighten the bolt a first pass to 48 ft. lbs. (65 Nm).

   b. Tighten the bolt a final pass an additional 90 degrees using J-45059.

28. Remove the J-42386-A.

29. Install the oil pump.

TURBOCHARGER

REMOVAL & INSTALLATION

2010 Diesel Engines
See Figures 539 through 563.

✴✴ CAUTION

If a turbocharger has failed, clean any turbocharger debris or excessive oil from the charge air cooler system before installing the new turbocharger. Failure to clean debris from the charge air cooler system will cause severe turbocharger and engine damage upon startup. Failure to clean excessive oil from the charge air cooler system may cause an engine runaway condition on startup, resulting in severe engine damage.

➡If a turbocharger failure is thought to be caused due to lack of oil, the camshaft bearing should be checked. The number 4 camshaft bearing bore feeds the turbocharger oil supply (feed) pipe. If this camshaft bearing spins in the bore, the turbocharger will be starved for oil. This will cause a failure of the turbocharger. Failure to diagnosis this condition will result in repeat turbocharger failures.

1. Remove the transmission.

2. Remove the left and right wheelhouse liners.

3. Loosen the exhaust pipe clamp. Slide the clamp onto the exhaust pipe.

4. Remove the left exhaust pipe.

a. Remove the exhaust heat shield nuts and heat shield from the dash panel.

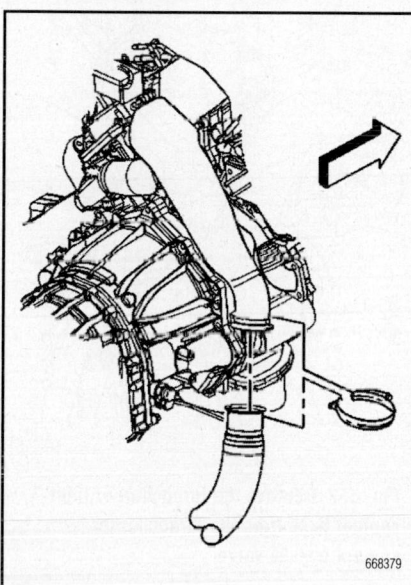

Fig. 539 Loosen the exhaust pipe clamp

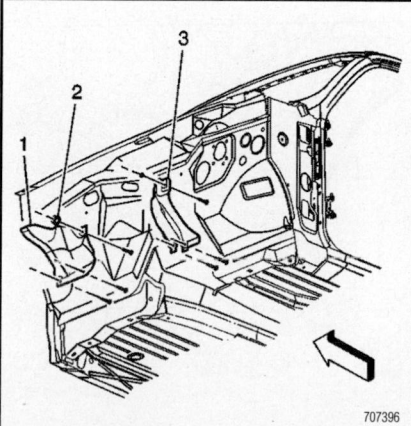

Fig. 540 Remove the exhaust heat shield nuts (2) and heat shield (3) from the dash panel (1)

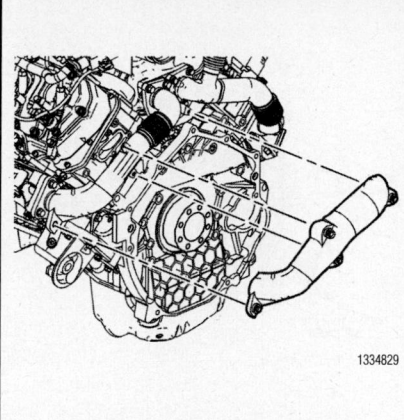

Fig. 541 Remove the exhaust pipe heat shield bolts and shield

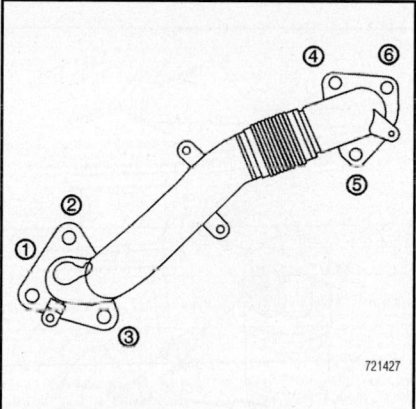

Fig. 542 Remove the exhaust pipe bolts in the sequence shown

b. Remove the exhaust pipe heat shield bolts and shield.

c. Remove the exhaust pipe bolts in the sequence shown.

d. Remove the exhaust pipe and gaskets. Discard the gaskets.

5. Remove the turbocharger exhaust pipe.

a. Remove the Exhaust Gas Recirculation (EGR) valve cooler.

b. Remove the turbocharger upper heat shield bolts and shield.

c. Loosen the turbocharger exhaust pipe to turbocharger clamp bolt.

d. Remover the catalytic converter.

e. Perform the following steps working through the wheelhouse opening.

f. Remove the transmission fluid fill tube to bellhousing nuts.

g. Position the transmission fluid fill tube to the right side of the vehicle. The tube does not require removal from the transmission.

h. Remove the turbocharger exhaust pipe heat shield bolts and shield.

i. Remove the turbocharger exhaust pipe to bracket bolt.

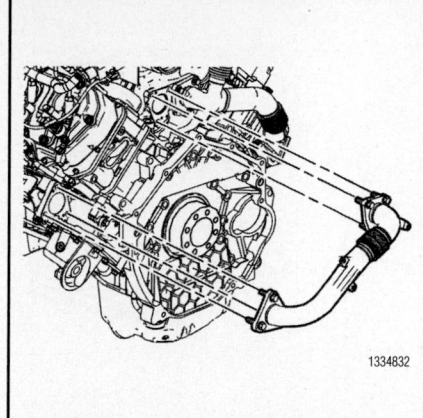

Fig. 543 Remove the exhaust pipe and gaskets

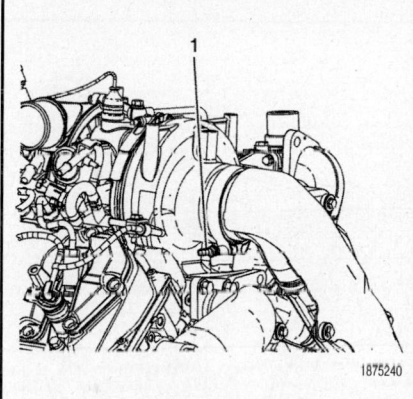

Fig. 544 Loosen the turbocharger exhaust pipe to turbocharger clamp bolt (1)

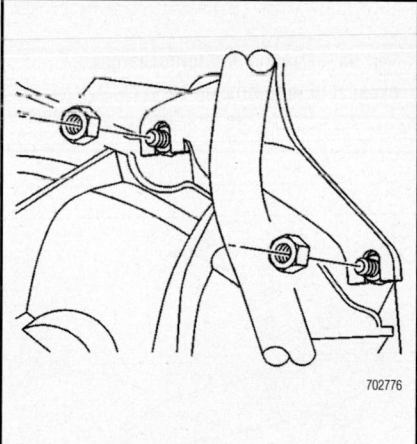

Fig. 545 Remove the transmission fluid fill tube to bellhousing nuts

j. Remove the turbocharger exhaust pipe.

6. Remove the right exhaust pipe.

a. Remove the exhaust pipe bolts in the proper sequence.

b. Remove the exhaust pipe, bracket and gaskets. Discard the gaskets.

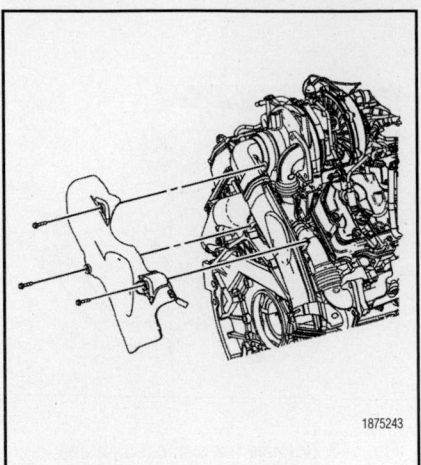

Fig. 546 Remove the turbocharger exhaust pipe heat shield bolts and shield

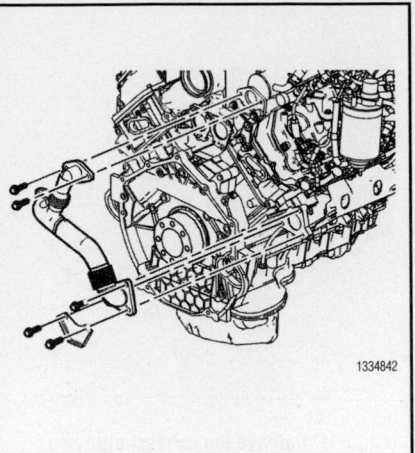

Fig. 549 Remove the exhaust pipe, bracket and gaskets

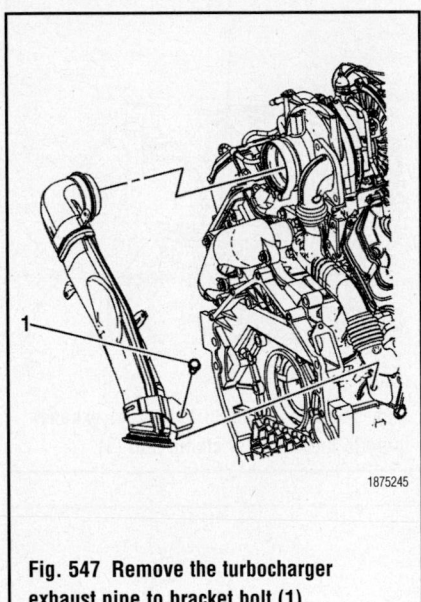

Fig. 547 Remove the turbocharger exhaust pipe to bracket bolt (1)

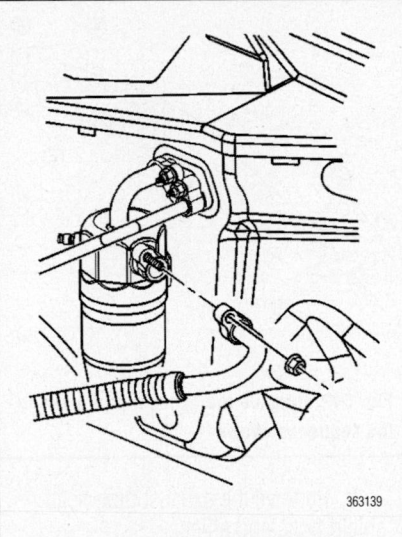

Fig. 550 Remove the Air Conditioning (A/C) suction hose

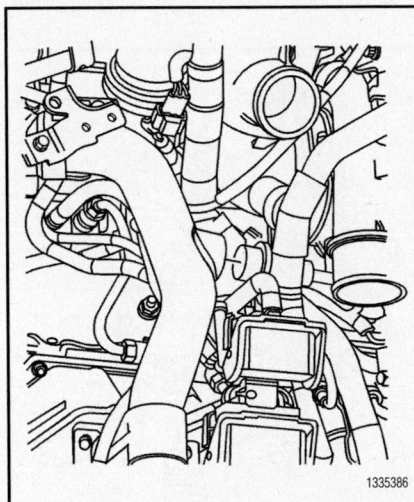

Fig. 552 Remove the turbocharger inlet coolant hose from the turbocharger coolant bypass valve

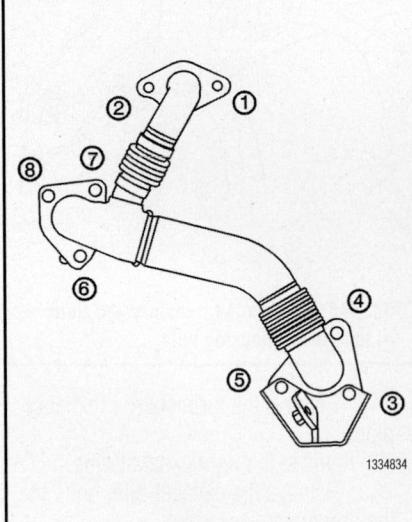

Fig. 548 Remove the exhaust pipe bolts in the proper sequence

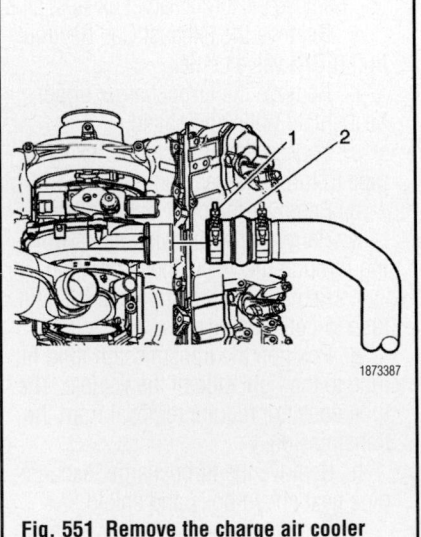

Fig. 551 Remove the charge air cooler inlet pipe (2); clamp (1)

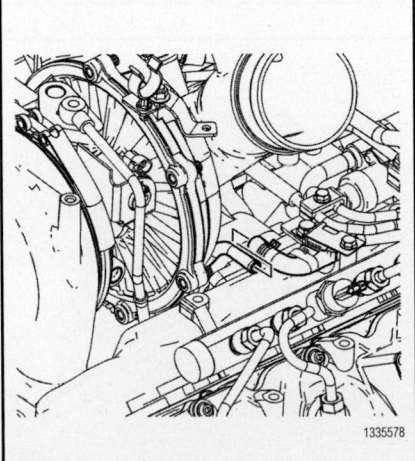

Fig. 553 Reposition the hose clamp and remove the turbocharger outlet coolant hose from the turbocharger

7. Remove the Exhaust Gas Recirculation (EGR) valve cooler.

8. Remove the Air Conditioning (A/C) suction hose.

9. Reposition the suction hose aside.

➡**After removing the charged air cooler duct, cover the turbocharger opening with tape in order to prevent entry of objects.**

10. Remove the charge air cooler inlet pipe.

11. Remove the turbocharger inlet coolant hose from the turbocharger coolant bypass valve.

➡**Use care not to damage this hose during the procedure.**

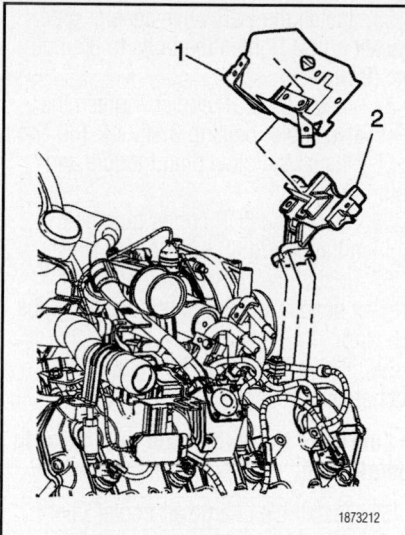

Fig. 554 Remove the glow plug module (1) and both brackets (2)

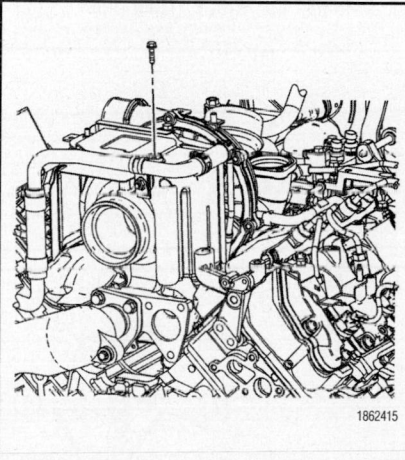

Fig. 555 Remove the EGR cooler pipe bolt

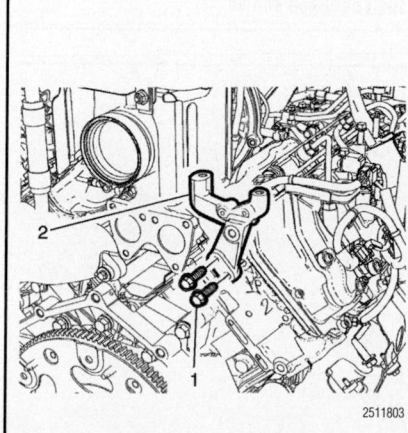

Fig. 556 Remove the EGR/engine lift hook bracket bolts (1)

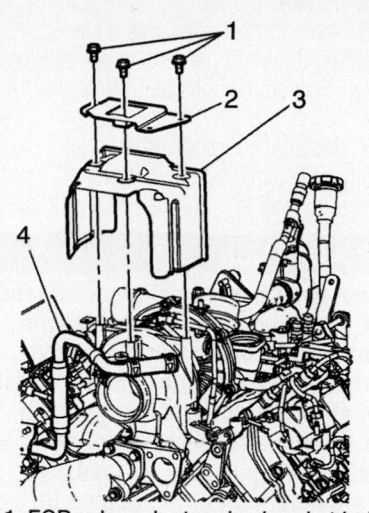

1. EGR valve adapter pipe bracket bolts
2. Bracket
3. Bracket
4. EGR cooler pipe

Fig. 557 Reposition the EGR cooler pipe out of the way

12. Reposition the hose clamp and remove the turbocharger outlet coolant hose from the turbocharger.

13. Remove the Positive Crankcase Ventilation (PCV) hose/pipe.

14. Remove the glow plug module and both brackets.

15. Remove the EGR cooler pipe bolt.

16. Remove the exhaust gas recirculation coolant hoses/pipes.

17. Remove the EGR/engine lift hook bracket bolts (1).

18. Remove the EGR/engine lift hook bracket.

19. Reposition the EGR cooler pipe out of the way.

20. Remove the EGR valve adapter pipe bracket bolts.

21. Rotate the turbocharger heat shield and remove from the right side of the engine compartment.

✺✺ CAUTION

Do not twist the turbocharger oil feed pipe. Twisting of the feed pipe will result in the collapse and deformation of the plastic pipe, restricting oil flow and causing turbocharger damage. During turbocharger replacement, gently push the oil feed pipe towards the front of the engine to clear the turbocharger. Assistance may be required to keep the pipes clear of the turbocharger during removal or installation.

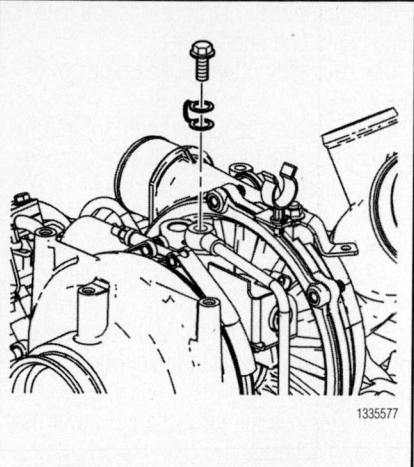

Fig. 558 Remove the turbocharger oil feed pipe banjo bolt and washer

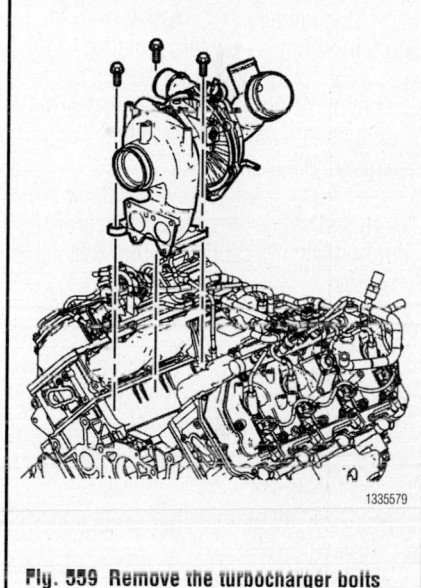

Fig. 559 Remove the turbocharger bolts

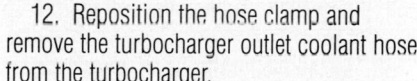

Fig. 560 Remove the oil feed pipe bolt, washer, and pipe, if necessary

22. Remove the turbocharger oil feed pipe banjo bolt and washer.

23. Reposition the oil feed pipe out of the way.

24. Remove the turbocharger oil return pipe nuts at the top of the flywheel housing.

25. Disconnect the turbocharger vane position sensor electrical connector.

26. Remove the turbocharger bolts.

27. Remove the turbocharger (with the oil return pipe).

28. Remove and discard the turbocharger oil return pipe gasket at the flywheel housing.

29. Remove the turbocharger lower heat shield, if necessary.

30. Remove the oil feed pipe bolt, washer, and pipe, if necessary.

31. If the turbocharger has failed, perform the following steps the verify the condition of the number 4 camshaft bearing before installing a new turbocharger:

   a. Visually inspect for correct alignment of the number 4 camshaft bearing oil hole through the turbocharger oil supply hole in the block.

   b. Turn the engine over by hand 1/2 turn and inspect for camshaft bearing movement, indicating a spun camshaft bearing.

   c. If the bearing is spun the engine MUST be replaced.

32. Remove the turbocharger outlet coolant pipe banjo bolt and washers.

33. If replacing the turbocharger, remove the oil return pipe bolts, pipe and gasket. Discard the gasket.

34. Clean all turbocharger to engine gasket mating surfaces.

35. If required, clean and inspect the turbocharger.

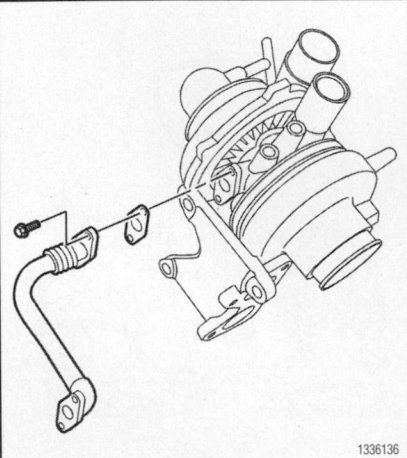

Fig. 561 If replacing the turbocharger, remove the oil return pipe bolts, pipe and gasket

To install:

36. If the turbocharger was replaced, install the oil return pipe, bolts, and a NEW gasket. Tighten the bolts to 15 ft. lbs. (21 Nm).

37. Install the turbocharger outlet coolant pipe banjo bolt and washers. Tighten the bolt to 19 ft. lbs (26 Nm).

✳✳ CAUTION

Do not twist the turbocharger oil feed pipe. Twisting of the feed pipe will result in the collapse and deformation of the plastic pipe, restricting oil flow and causing turbocharger damage. During turbocharger replacement, gently push the oil feed pipe towards the front of the engine to clear the turbocharger. Assistance may be required to keep the pipes clear of the turbocharger during removal or installation.

➡**Lubricate the washer with diesel fuel prior to installing.**

38. Install the oil feed pipe, washer, and bolt, if necessary. Tighten the bolt to 25 ft. lbs. (34 Nm).

39. Install the turbocharger lower heat shield, if necessary.

40. Install a NEW turbocharger oil return pipe gasket at the flywheel housing.

41. Install the turbocharger (with the oil return pipe).

42. Install the turbocharger bolts. Tighten the bolts to 80 ft. lbs. (108 Nm).

43. Install the turbocharger oil return pipe nuts at the top of the flywheel housing. Tighten the nuts to 18 ft. lbs. (25 Nm).

44. Connect the turbocharger vane position sensor electrical connector.

45. If installing a NEW turbocharger, add about 4–5 oz (120–150 cc) of clean engine oil in the turbocharger oil feed pipe opening while rotating the impeller.

46. Position the oil feed pipe to the turbocharger.

47. Install a NEW turbocharger oil feed pipe washer and the banjo bolt. Tighten the bolt to 25 ft. lbs. (34 Nm).

48. Install the PCV hose/pipe.

49. If the cooling outlet hose eye bolts were removed, install the cooling outlet hose eye bolts.

50. Install the turbocharger outlet coolant hose to the turbocharger and position the hose clamp.

51. Install the turbocharger inlet coolant hose to the turbocharger coolant bypass valve.

52. Install the turbocharger heat shield.

53. Install the EGR valve adapter pipe bracket bolts. Tighten the bolts to 80 inch lbs. (9 Nm).

54. Install the EGR cooler. Tighten the EGR valve cooler bolts to 37 ft. lbs. (50 Nm).

55. Install the glow plug module and both brackets.

56. Install the EGR cooler pipe bolt. Tighten the bolt to 80 inch lbs. (9 Nm).

57. Install the EGR/engine lift hook bracket bolts. Tighten the bolts to 11 ft. lbs. (16 Nm).

58. Remove the tape from the turbocharger openings.

➡**Lubricate the end of the duct prior to installation.**

59. Install the charge air cooler inlet pipe.

60. Install the A/C suction hose.

61. Install the air intake pipe.

62. Fill the cooling system.

63. Install the right exhaust pipe.

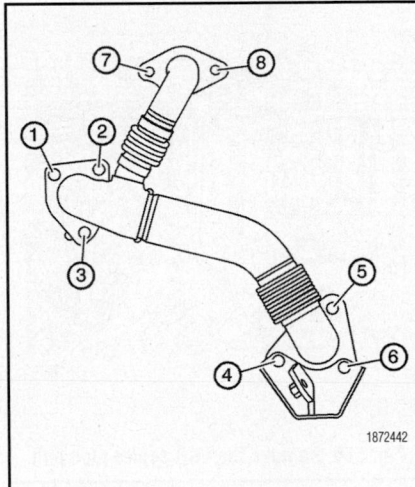

Fig. 562 Tighten the exhaust pipe bolts in the sequence shown

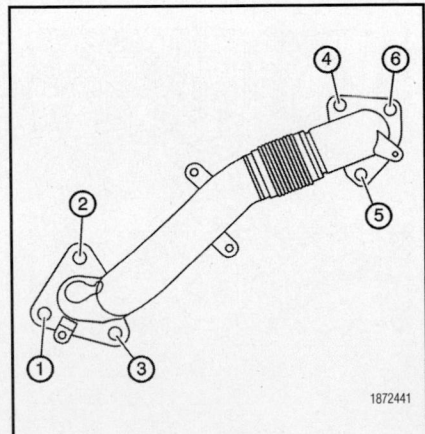

Fig. 563 Tighten the exhaust pipe bolts in the sequence shown

a. Tighten the exhaust pipe bolts in the sequence shown.

b. Tighten the exhaust pipe bolts to 39 ft. lbs. (53 Nm).

64. Install the turbocharger exhaust pipe.

65. Install the left exhaust pipe.

a. Tighten the exhaust pipe bolts in the sequence shown.

b. Tighten the bolts to 39 ft. lbs. (53 Nm).

66. Slide the clamp onto the exhaust pipe. Tighten the exhaust pipe clamp. Tighten the clamp to 30 ft. lbs. (40 Nm).

67. Install the left and right wheelhouse liners.

68. Install the transmission.

69. Install NEW engine oil and a NEW oil filter.

70. If a NEW turbocharger was installed, perform the turbocharger learn procedure.

71. Road test the vehicle for normal operation.

72. Inspect for coolant, oil, or exhaust leaks. Correct as necessary.

2011 Diesel Engines

See Figures 564 through 575.

✳ CAUTION

If a turbocharger has failed, clean any turbocharger debris or excessive oil from the charge air cooler system before installing the new turbocharger. Failure to clean debris from the charge air cooler system will cause severe turbocharger and engine damage upon startup. Failure to clean excessive oil from the charge air cooler system may cause an engine runaway condition on startup, resulting in severe engine damage.

1. Remove the turbocharger exhaust pipe.

2. Remove the exhaust gas recirculation manifold cooling feed pipe.

3. Remove the right side exhaust pipe. Remove the exhaust manifold outlet pipe bolts in the proper sequence.

4. Remove the left side exhaust pipe. Remove the exhaust manifold outlet pipe bolts in the proper sequence.

5. Remove the exhaust gas recirculation cooler assembly.

6. Remove the center intake.

7. Remove the turbocharger upper heat shield bolts.

8. Remove the turbocharger upper heat shield.

9. Remove the eye bolt and washers from the turbocharger oil feed pipe.

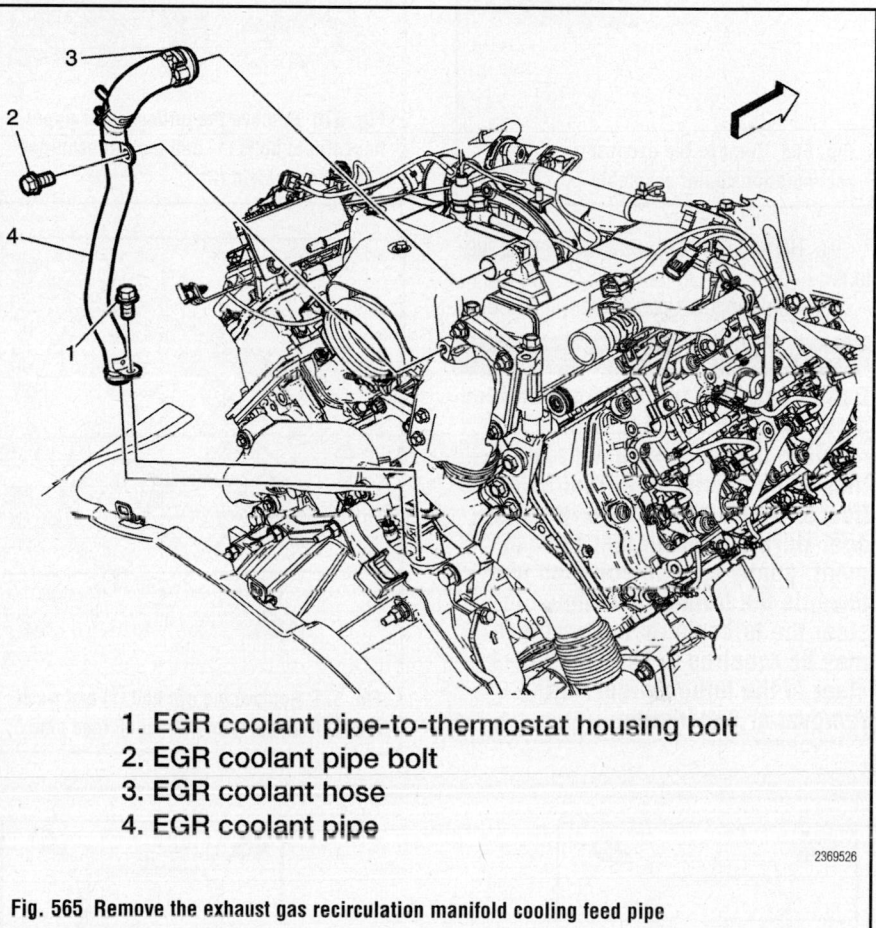

1. EGR coolant pipe-to-thermostat housing bolt
2. EGR coolant pipe bolt
3. EGR coolant hose
4. EGR coolant pipe

2369526

Fig. 565 Remove the exhaust gas recirculation manifold cooling feed pipe

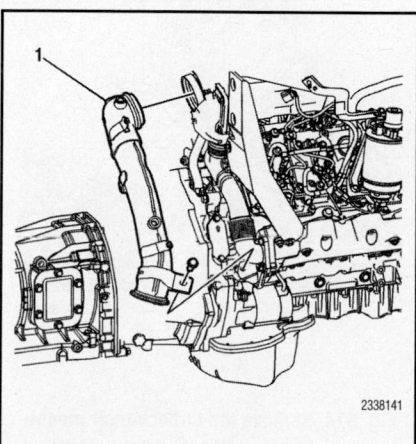

2338141

Fig. 564 Remove the turbocharger exhaust pipe (1)

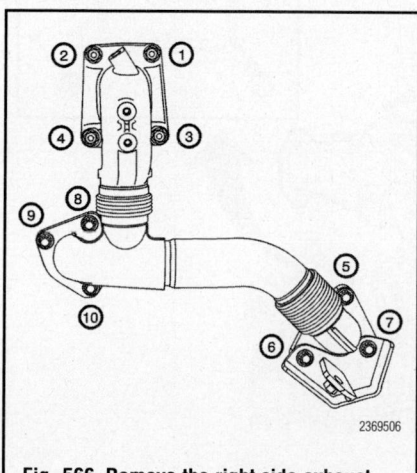

2369506

Fig. 566 Remove the right side exhaust pipe

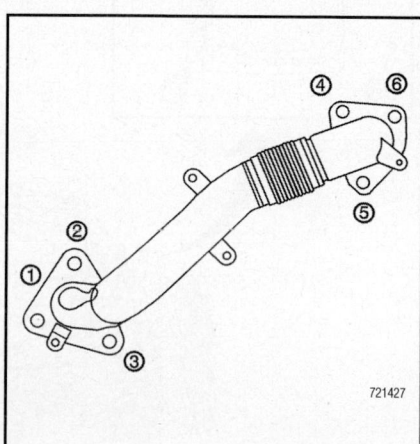

721427

Fig. 567 Remove the left side exhaust pipe

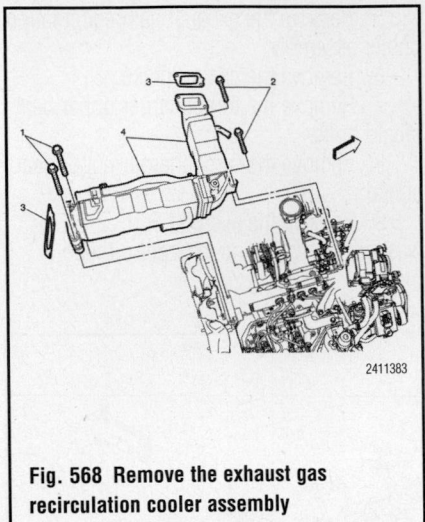

Fig. 568 Remove the exhaust gas recirculation cooler assembly

Fig. 570 Remove the turbocharger upper heat shield bolts (1) and the turbocharger upper heat shield (2)

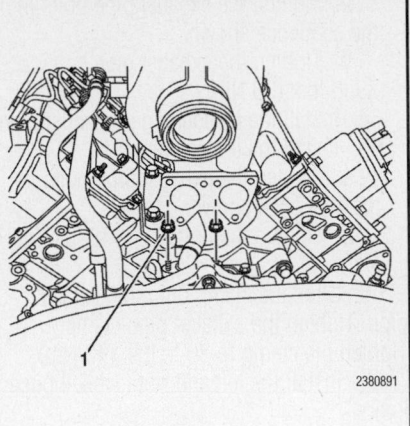

Fig. 572 Remove the turbo oil return pipe fastener (1)

10. Remove the turbo oil return pipe fastener.

11. Remove the turbo coolant feed hose.

✳✳ CAUTION

Do not twist the turbocharger oil feed pipe. Twisting of the feed pipe will result in the collapse and deformation of the plastic pipe, restricting oil flow and causing turbocharger damage. During turbocharger replacement, gently push the oil feed pipe towards the front of the engine to clear the turbocharger. Assistance may be required to keep the pipes clear of the turbocharger during removal or installation.

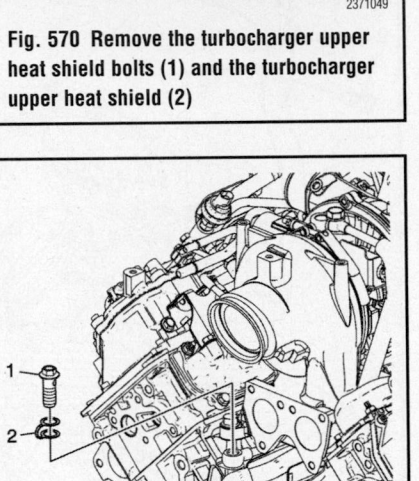

Fig. 571 Remove the eye bolt (1) and washers (2) from the turbocharger oil feed pipe

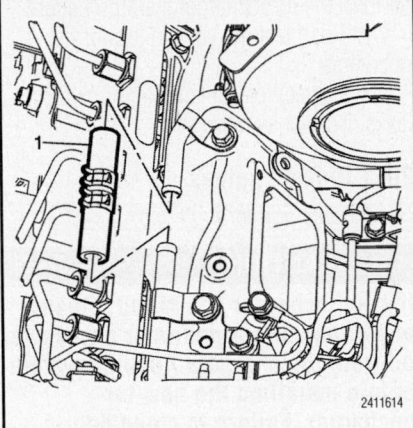

Fig. 573 Remove the turbo coolant feed hose (1)

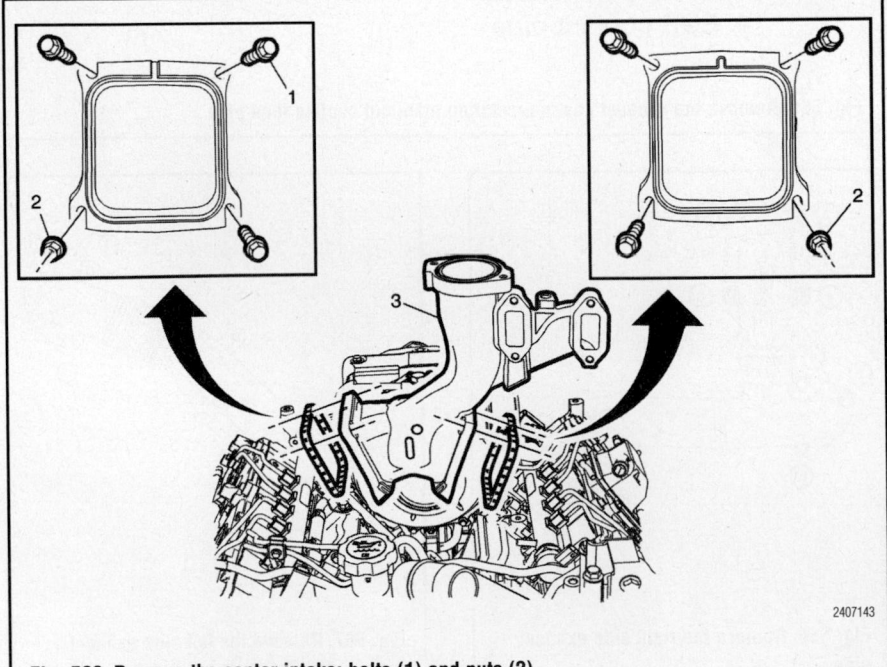

Fig. 569 Remove the center intake; bolts (1) and nuts (2)

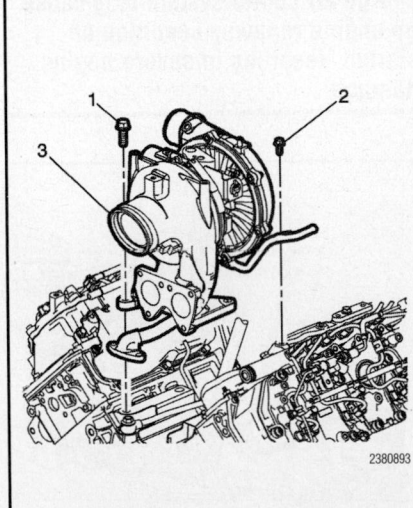

Fig. 574 Remove the turbocharger mounting bolts (1), the turbocharger cooling return pipe bolt (2), and the turbocharger assembly (3)

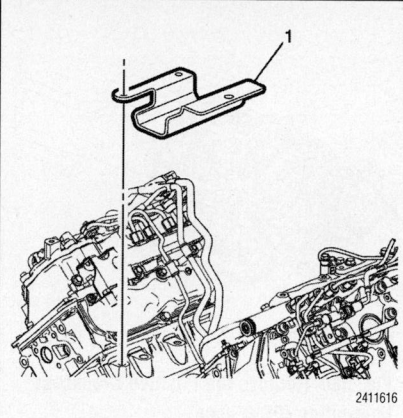

Fig. 575 Remove the turbocharger lower heat shield (1)

12. Remove the turbocharger mounting bolts.

13. Remove the turbocharger cooling return pipe bolt.

14. Remove the turbocharger assembly with the oil feed pipe, oil return pipe and cooling return pipe.

15. Remove the turbocharger lower heat shield.

16. Disconnect electrical connector as necessary.

17. Transfer parts as necessary.

18. Clean and inspect the turbocharger.

To install:

19. Install the turbocharger lower heat shield.

❄❄ CAUTION

Do not twist the turbocharger oil feed pipe. Twisting of the feed pipe will result in the collapse and deformation of the plastic pipe, restricting oil flow and causing turbocharger damage. During turbocharger replacement, gently push the oil feed pipe towards the front of the engine to clear the turbocharger. Assistance may be required to keep the pipes clear of the turbocharger during removal or installation.

20. Install the turbocharger assembly with the oil feed pipe, oil return pipe and cooling return pipe.

21. Install the turbocharger mounting bolts and tighten to 58 ft. lbs. (78 Nm).

22. Install the turbocharger cooling return pipe bolt and tighten to 18 ft. lbs. (25 Nm).

23. Install the turbo oil return pipe fastener and tighten to 18 ft. lbs. (25 Nm).

24. Install the turbo coolant feed hose.

➡️ **Lubricate the washers with diesel fuel before installing.**

25. Install the turbocharger oil feed pipe eye bolt and washers. Tighten the eye bolt to 26 ft. lbs. (35 Nm).

26. Install the turbocharger heat shield.

27. Install the turbocharger upper heat shield bolts and tighten to 89 inch lbs. (10 Nm).

28. Install the center intake. Tighten the fasteners to 89 inch lbs. (10 Nm).

29. Install the charge air cooler inlet pipe.

30. Install the exhaust gas recirculation cooler assembly. Tighten the EGR cooler bolts to 18 ft. lbs. (25 Nm).

31. Install the left side exhaust pipe.

a. Tighten the exhaust manifold outlet pipe bolts in sequence.

b. Tighten the bolts to 39 ft. lbs. (53 Nm).

32. Install the right side exhaust pipe.

a. Tighten the exhaust manifold outlet pipe bolts in sequence.

b. Tighten the bolts to 39 ft. lbs. (53 Nm).

33. Install the exhaust gas recirculation manifold cooling feed pipe.

34. Install the turbocharger exhaust pipe.

35. Relearn the turbocharger.

36. Perform the scan tool Diesel Particulate Filter (DPF) Regeneration Enable.

DIESEL PARTICULATE FILTER (DPF) REGENERATION ENABLE

➡️ **The DPF Regeneration Enable is required when specific service procedures have been performed. Do not perform a DPF Regeneration Enable unless instructed to in the Repair Instruction section of the service procedure. After the system is repair, perform the following to avoid possible damage to the DPF.**

1. Ignition ON, clear the DTCs with a scan tool.

2. Select DPF Regeneration Enable with a scan tool.

➡️ **The Engine Control Module (ECM) activates the DPF Regeneration when the engine running conditions are met.**

3. Select ON. The DPF Regeneration Reason parameter should display DLC Override.

4. Exit the Special Function menu. Remove the scan tool.

VALVE COVERS

REMOVAL & INSTALLATION

V6 Engines

Left Side

See Figures 576 and 577.

1. Remove the engine wiring harness bracket bolt.

2. Position the engine wiring harness bracket and engine harness aside.

3. Remove the engine wiring harness clip bolt.

4. Disconnect the Engine Coolant Temperature (ECT) sensor electrical connector.

5. Reposition the engine wiring harness and bracket.

6. Disconnect the power brake booster vacuum hose from the vacuum fitting.

7. Remove the Positive Crankcase Ventilation (PCV) valve hose from the valve rocker arm cover.

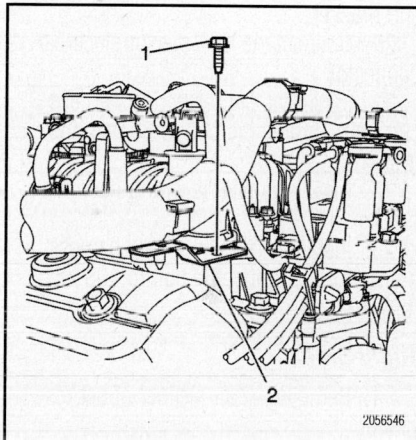

Fig. 576 Remove the engine wiring harness bracket (1) bolt (2)

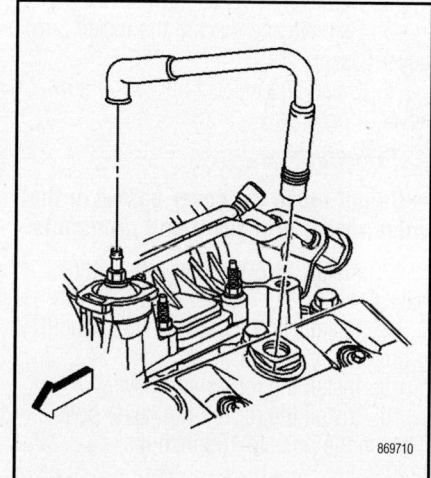

Fig. 577 Remove the PCV valve hose from the valve rocker arm cover

8. Remove the rocker arm cover bolts.

9. Remove and discard the rocker arm cover bolt grommets, if necessary.

10. Remove the rocker arm cover.

11. Remove and discard the rocker arm cover gasket.

12. Clean and inspect the rocker arm cover, if necessary.

To install:

➡**Do not reuse the rocker cover gasket or the rocker arm cover bolt grommets.**

13. Install a NEW rocker arm cover gasket to the cover.

14. Install NEW rocker arm cover bolt grommets to the cover, if necessary.

15. Install the rocker arm cover.

16. Install the rocker arm cover bolts. Tighten the bolts to 106 inch lbs. (12 Nm).

17. Install the PCV valve hose to the valve cover and rocker cover.

18. Connect the power brake booster vacuum hose to the vacuum fitting.

19. Position the engine wiring harness and bracket.

20. Connect the ECT sensor electrical connector.

21. Install the engine wiring harness clip bolt. Tighten the bolt to 80 inch lbs. (9 Nm).

22. Install the engine wiring harness bracket.

23. Install the engine wiring harness bracket bolt. Tighten the bolt to 106 inch lbs. (12 Nm).

Right Side

1. Remove the air cleaner outlet resonator.

2. Remove the rocker arm cover bolts.

3. Remove and discard the rocker arm cover bolt grommets, if necessary.

4. Remove the rocker arm cover.

5. Remove and discard the rocker arm cover gasket.

6. Clean and inspect the rocker arm cover, if necessary.

To install:

➡**Do not reuse the cover gasket or the valve rocker arm cover bolt grommets.**

7. Install a NEW rocker arm cover gasket.

8. Install NEW rocker arm cover bolt grommets, if necessary.

9. Install the rocker arm cover.

10. Install the rocker arm cover bolts. Tighten the bolts to 106 inch lbs. (12 Nm).

11. Install the air cleaner outlet resonator.

V8 Engines

Left Side

See Figures 578 through 580.

1. Remove the intake manifold cover.

2. Remove the Connector Position Assurance (CPA) retainer.

3. Disconnect the engine harness electrical connector from the ignition coil wire harness.

4. Remove the engine harness clip from the ignition coil bracket stud.

5. Reposition the engine harness, as necessary.

6. Remove the spark plug wires from the ignition coils.

   a. Twist each plug wire ½ turn.

   b. Pull only on the boot in order to remove the wire from the ignition coil.

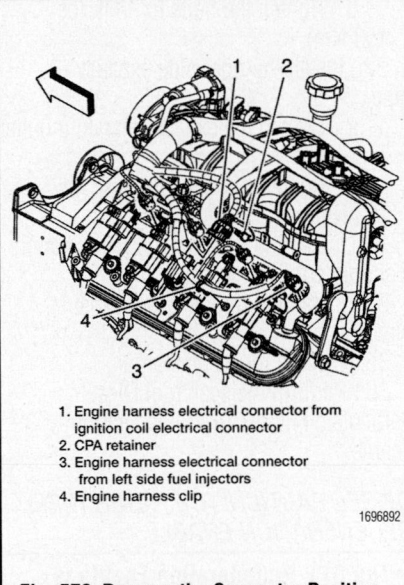

1. Engine harness electrical connector from ignition coil electrical connector
2. CPA retainer
3. Engine harness electrical connector from left side fuel injectors
4. Engine harness clip

1696892

Fig. 578 Remove the Connector Position Assurance (CPA) retainer

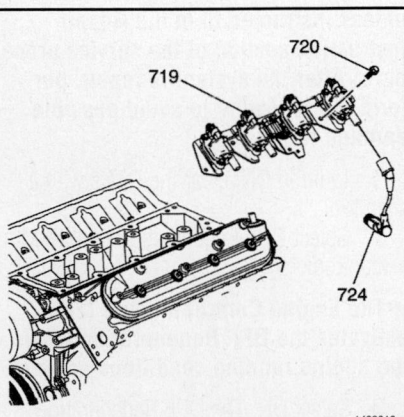

1402016

Fig. 579 Spark plug wires (724), ignition coil bracket studs (720), and ignition coil bracket (719)

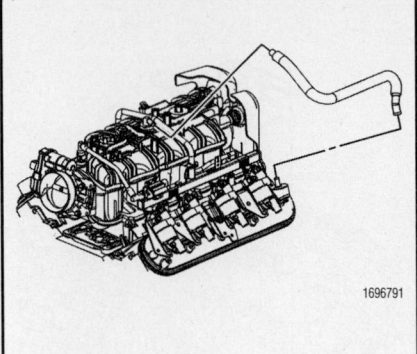

1696791

Fig. 580 Remove the Positive Crankcase Ventilation (PCV) hose

7. Remove the ignition coil bracket studs.

8. Remove the ignition coil bracket.

9. Remove the Positive Crankcase Ventilation (PCV) hose.

10. Loosen the valve rocker arm cover bolts.

11. Remove the valve rocker arm cover.

12. Remove and discard the old gasket.

To install:

➡**Note the following:**

- All gasket surfaces should be free of oil and/or other foreign material during assembly.
- DO NOT reuse the valve rocker arm cover gasket.
- If the PCV valve grommet has been removed from the rocker cover, install a NEW grommet during assembly.

13. Install a NEW rocker cover gasket.

14. Install the valve rocker arm cover.

15. Tighten the rocker arm cover bolts. Tighten the bolts to 106 inch lbs. (12 Nm).

16. Install the PCV hose.

17. Apply threadlock to the threads of the ignition coil bracket studs.

18. Position the ignition coil bracket onto the rocker cover.

19. Install the ignition coil bracket studs. Tighten the studs to 106 inch lbs. (12 Nm).

20. Install the spark plug wires to the ignition coils.

21. Position the engine harness, as necessary.

22. Install the engine harness clip to the ignition coil bracket stud.

23. Connect the engine harness electrical connector to the ignition coil wire harness.

24. Install the CPA retainer.

25. Install the intake manifold cover.

Right Side

See Figures 581 through 585.

1. Remove the intake manifold cover.
2. Remove the Connector Position Assurance (CPA) retainer.
3. Disconnect the engine harness electrical connector from the ignition coil wire harness.
4. Remove the engine wiring harness (electronic throttle control branch) clip from the ignition coil bracket stud.
5. Reposition the engine wiring harness (electronic throttle control branch) as necessary.
6. Remove the alternator battery cable clip from the ignition coil bracket stud.
7. Reposition the alternator battery cable as necessary.
8. Remove the heater inlet hose from the heater hose bracket.

Fig. 583 Remove the heater hose bracket nut and bracket

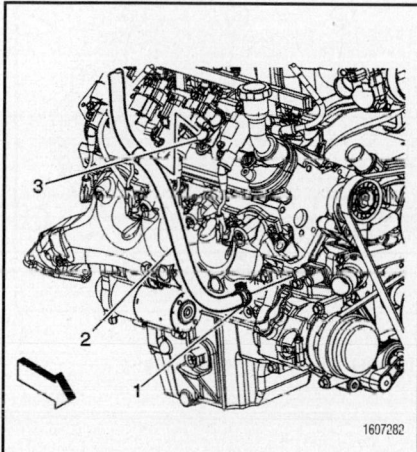

Fig. 581 Remove the heater inlet hose (2) from the heater hose bracket (3); hose clamp (1)

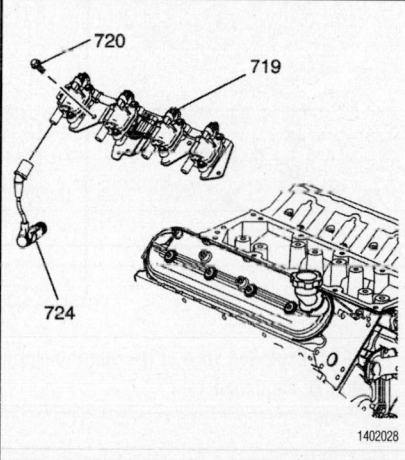

Fig. 584 Spark plug wires (724), ignition coil bracket studs (720), and ignition coil bracket (719).

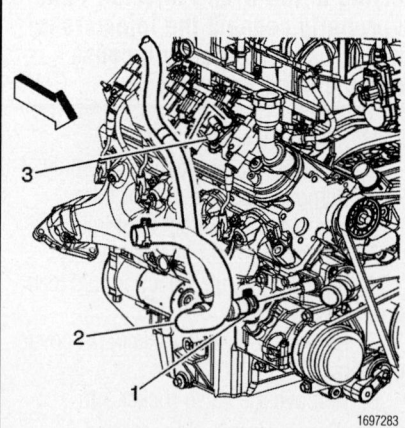

Fig. 582 Remove the surge tank outlet hose (2) from the heater hose bracket (3); hose clamp (1)

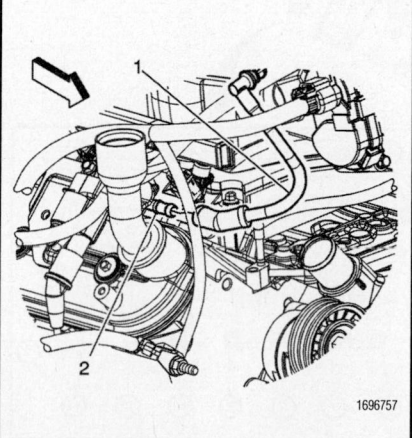

Fig. 585 Remove the Positive Crankcase Ventilation (PCV) tube (1) from the valve rocker cover (2)

9. Remove the surge tank outlet hose from the heater hose bracket.
10. Remove the heater hose bracket nut and bracket.
11. Remove the spark plug wires from the ignition coils.
   a. Twist each plug wire ½ turn.
   b. Pull only on the boot in order to remove the wire from the ignition coil.
12. Remove the ignition coil bracket studs.
13. Remove the ignition coil bracket.
14. Remove the Positive Crankcase Ventilation (PCV) tube from the valve rocker cover.
15. Loosen the valve rocker arm cover bolts.
16. Remove the valve rocker arm cover.
17. Remove and discard the old gasket.
18. Remove the oil fill cap from the oil fill tube, if necessary.
19. Remove and discard the oil fill tube, if necessary.

To install:

➡ **Note the following:**

* All gasket surfaces should be free of oil or other foreign material during assembly.
* DO NOT reuse the valve rocker arm cover gasket.
* If the oil fill tube has been removed from the rocker arm cover, install a NEW fill tube during assembly.

20. Lubricate the O-ring seal of the NEW oil fill tube with clean engine oil.
21. Insert the NEW oil fill tube into the rocker arm cover.
22. Rotate the tube clockwise until locked in the proper position.
23. Install the oil fill cap into the tube.
24. Rotate the cap clockwise until locked in the proper position.
25. Install a NEW rocker cover gasket into the valve rocker arm cover lip.
26. Install the valve rocker arm cover.
27. Tighten the rocker arm cover bolts. Tighten the bolts to 106 inch lbs. (12 Nm).
28. Install the PCV tube to the valve rocker cover.
29. Apply threadlock GM P/N 12345382 (Canadian P/N 10953489), or equivalent to the threads of the ignition coil bracket studs.
30. Position the ignition coil bracket onto the rocker cover.
31. Install the ignition coil bracket studs. Tighten the studs to 106 inch lbs. (12 Nm).
32. Install the spark plug wires to the ignition coils.
33. Install the heater hose bracket and nut. Tighten the nut to 80 inch lbs. (9 Nm).
34. Install the surge tank outlet hose to the heater hose bracket.

35. Install the heater inlet hose to the heater hose bracket.

36. Position the alternator battery cable as necessary.

37. Install the alternator battery cable clip to the ignition coil bracket stud.

38. Position the engine wiring harness (electronic throttle control branch) as necessary.

39. Install the engine wiring harness (electronic throttle control branch) clip to the ignition coil bracket stud.

40. Connect the engine harness electrical connector to the ignition coil wire harness.

41. Install the CPA retainer.

42. Install the intake manifold cover.

Diesel Engines

Left Side Upper Cover

See Figure 586.

> ✳✳ **CAUTION**
>
> **Label all the injector electrical connectors before the connectors are removed in order to prevent reconnecting to the wrong injector. Failure to properly connect the injectors in the correct sequence will cause severe engine damage.**

1. Remove the positive crankcase ventilation oil separator.

2. Remove the fuel injection fuel feed pipe left side.

3. Remove the auxiliary alternator, if equipped.

4. Remove the fuel line protective bracket.

5. Remove the valve rocker arm cover fasteners.

6. Remove the valve rocker arm cover.

  a. Disconnect the electrical connectors, as necessary.

  b. Transfer components as necessary.

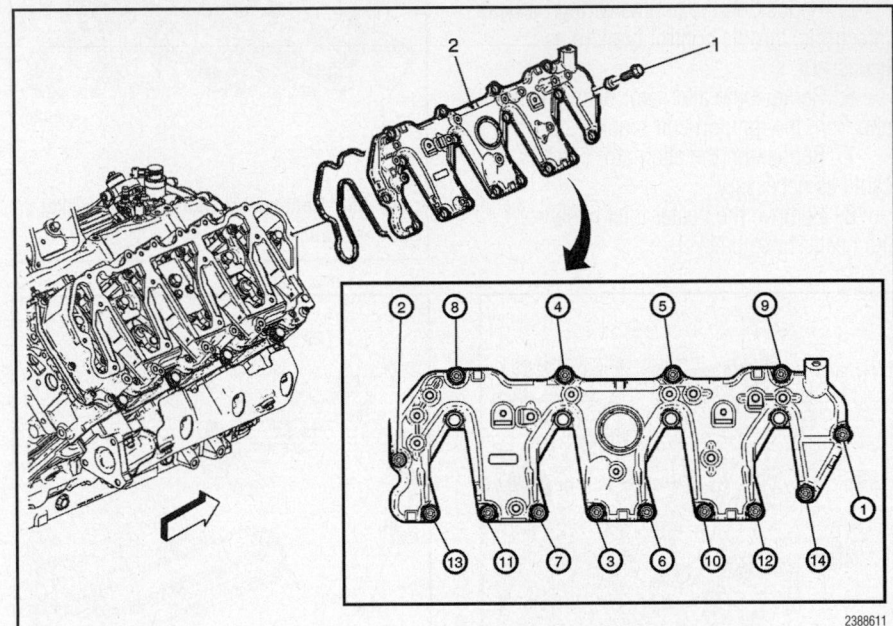

Fig. 587 Exploded view of the upper cover (2) and fastener (1) assembly showing tightening sequence

To install:

7. Installation is the reverse of removal.

8. Ensure to replace the grommets and gasket whenever the cover is removed.

9. Ensure to tighten the bolts in sequence shown.

10. Tighten the upper cover bolts to 89 inch lbs. (10 Nm).

Right Side Upper Cover

See Figure 587.

> ✳✳ **CAUTION**
>
> **Label all the injector electrical connectors before the connectors are removed in order to prevent reconnecting to the wrong injector. Failure to properly connect the injectors in the correct sequence will cause severe engine damage.**

1. Remove the alternator.

2. Remove the air cleaner assembly.

3. Remove the oil indicator tube.

4. Remove the Indirect Fuel Injector.

5. Remove the fuel filter assembly.

6. Remove the fuel injection fuel feed pipe right side.

7. Remove the valve rocker arm cover fasteners.

8. Remove the valve rocker arm cover.

9. Disconnect the electrical connectors, as necessary.

10. Transfer components as necessary.

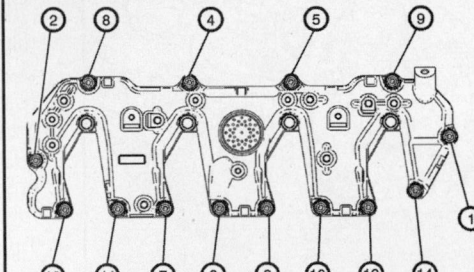

Fig. 586 Exploded view of the upper cover (2) and fastener (1) assembly showing tightening sequence

To install:

11. Installation is the reverse of removal.

12. Ensure to replace the grommets and gasket whenever the cover is removed.

13. Ensure to tighten the bolts in sequence shown.

14. Tighten the cover bolts to 89 inch lbs. (10 Nm).

Left Side Lower Cover

See Figure 588.

✳✳ CAUTION

Label all the injector electrical connectors before the connectors are removed in order to prevent reconnecting to the wrong injector. Failure to properly connect the injectors in the correct sequence will cause severe engine damage.

1. Remove the valve rocker arm cover upper left side.

2. Remove the 4 fuel injectors.

3. Remove the A/C bracket.

4. Remove the valve rocker arm cover fasteners.

➡**The gasket may be reused if it is not torn, cracked, stretched, or swollen.**

5. Remove the valve rocker arm cover.

6. Disconnect the electrical connectors, as necessary.

7. Transfer components as necessary.

To install:

8. Installation is the reverse of removal.

9. Ensure to tighten the bolts in sequence shown.

10. Tighten the cover bolts to 89 inch lbs. (10 Nm).

Right Side Lower Cover

See Figure 589.

✳✳ CAUTION

Label all the injector electrical connectors before the connectors are removed in order to prevent reconnecting to the wrong injector. Failure to properly connect the injectors in

the correct sequence will cause severe engine damage.

1. Remove the valve rocker arm cover upper right side.

2. Remove the four fuel injectors.

3. Remove the alternator bracket.

4. Remove the valve rocker arm cover fasteners.

➡**The gasket may be reused if it is not torn, cracked, stretched, or swollen.**

5. Remove the valve rocker arm cover.

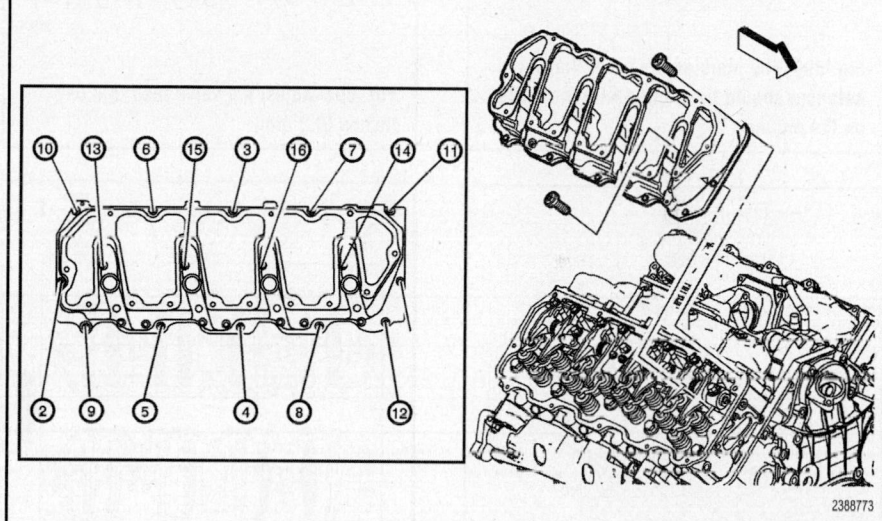

Fig. 589 Exploded view of the lower cover (2) and fastener (1) assembly showing tightening sequence

6. Disconnect the electrical connectors, as necessary.

7. Transfer components as necessary.

To install:

8. Installation is the reverse of removal.

9. Ensure to tighten the bolts in sequence shown.

10. Tighten the cover bolts to 89 inch lbs. (10 Nm)

VALVE LASH

ADJUSTMENT

Gasoline and Hybrid Engines

Valve lash is net build, no valve adjustment is required.

Diesel Engines

See Figures 590 through 593.

1. Rotate the crankshaft to bring the number 1 cylinder at the top dead center of

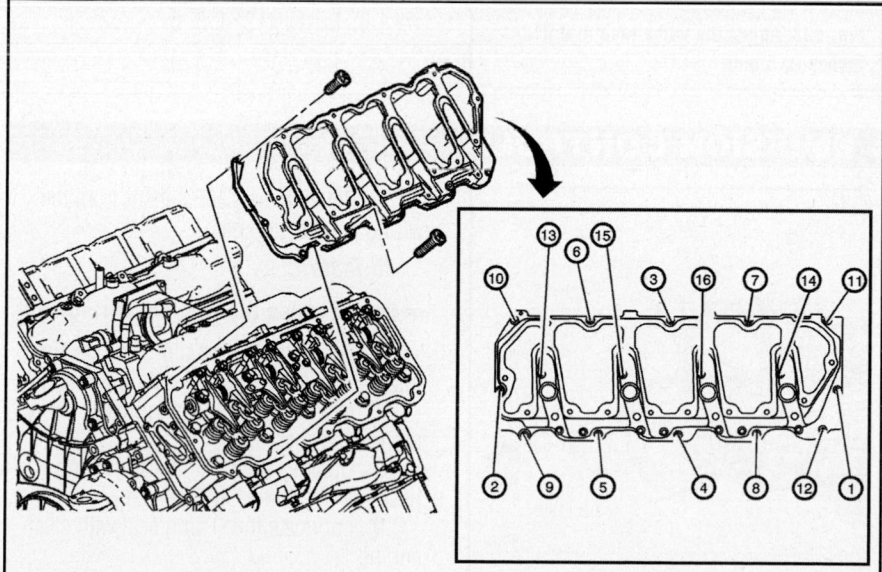

Fig. 588 Exploded view of the lower cover (2) and fastener (1) assembly showing tightening sequence

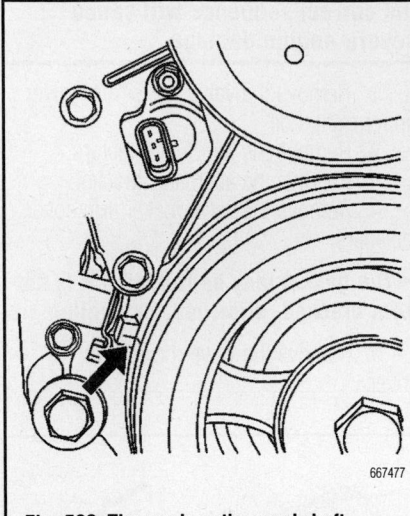

Fig. 590 The mark on the crankshaft balancer should be aligned with the mark on the engine

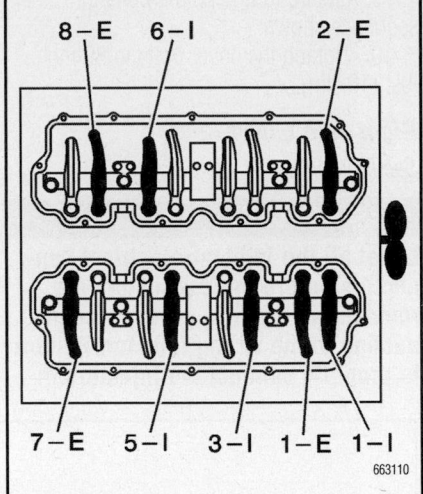

Fig. 592 Adjust the valve lash to 0.012 inches (0.3 mm)

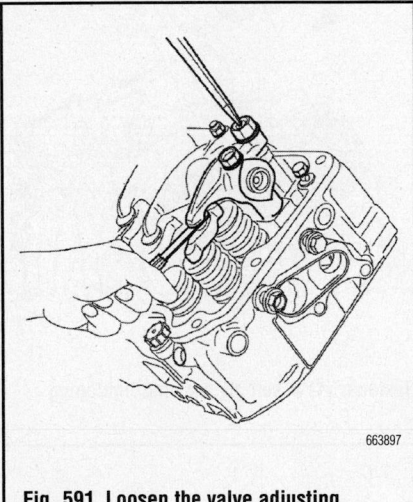

Fig. 591 Loosen the valve adjusting screws

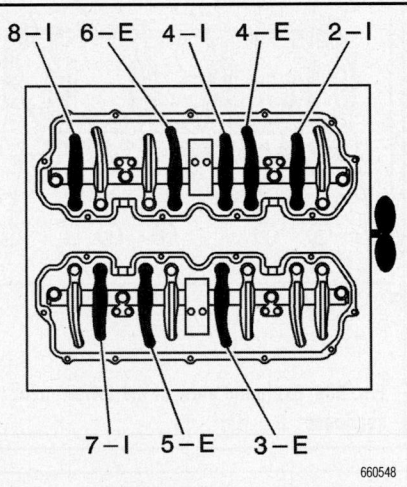

Fig. 593 Adjust the valve lash to 0.012 inches (0.3 mm)

the compression stroke. The number 1 cylinder is the front cylinder on the right bank. The mark on the crankshaft balancer should be aligned with the mark on the engine.

2. Loosen the valve adjusting screws.

3. Insert a feeler gauge between the tip of the rocker arm and the valve bridge.

4. Adjust the valve lash to 0.012 inches (0.3 mm). Refer to Valve Clearance Adjustment Specifications to determine which valves that can be adjusted when the engine is at Top Dead Center. Tighten the valve lash lock nut to 16 ft. lbs. (22 Nm).

5. Rotate the crankshaft one revolution to bring the number 1 cylinder at Top Dead Center of the exhaust stroke.

6. Adjust the valve lash to 0.012 inches (0.3 mm). Refer to Valve Clearance Adjustment Specifications to determine which valves that can be adjusted when the engine is at Top Dead Center. Tighten the valve lash lock nut to 16 ft. lbs. (22 Nm).

Valve Clearance Adjustment Specifications

Cylinders: Left Bank: 2, 4, 6, 8. Right Bank: 1, 3, 5, 7

1. Adjust at No. 1 Compression Stroke TDC:
   a. Intake: 1, 3, 5, 6
   b. Exhaust: 1, 2, 7, 8
2. Adjust at No.1 Exhaust Stroke TDC:
   a. Intake: 2, 4, 7, 8
   b. Exhaust: 3, 4, 5, 6

ENGINE PERFORMANCE & EMISSION CONTROLS

CAMSHAFT POSITION (CMP) SENSOR

LOCATION

Refer to the graphics in the Removal and Installation section for the location(s).

REMOVAL & INSTALLATION

V6 Engines

See Figure 594.

1. Remove the water pump.
2. Remove the CMP sensor bolt.
3. Remove the CMP sensor and wiring harness jumper from the engine front cover.
4. Disconnect the CMP sensor wiring harness jumper from the CMP sensor.

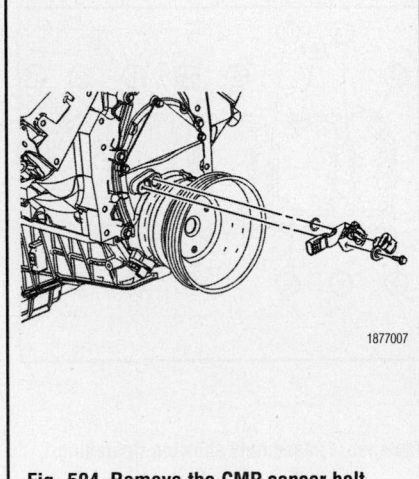

Fig. 594 Remove the CMP sensor bolt

5. Remove the CMP sensor from the wiring harness jumper.

To install:

➡ Do not reuse the original O-ring seal.

6. If reinstalling the old CMP sensor, install a NEW O-ring seal onto the sensor.

7. Install the CMP sensor to the wiring harness jumper.

8. Connect the CMP sensor wiring harness jumper to the CMP sensor.

9. Lubricate the O-ring seal with clean engine oil.

10. Install the CMP sensor and wiring harness jumper to the engine front cover.

11. Install the CMP sensor bolt. Tighten the bolt to 89 inch lbs. (10 Nm).

12. Install the water pump.

V8 Engines

See Figures 595 and 596.

➡️The manufacturer does not provide a specific Removal and Installation procedure for this component. Refer to the graphic(s) when servicing this component.

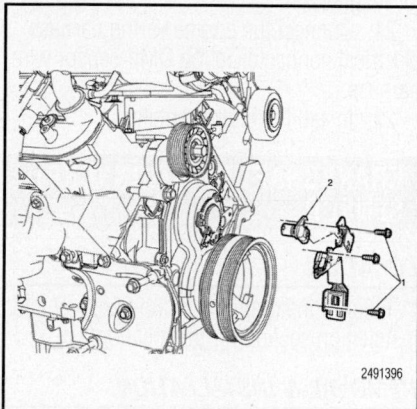

Fig. 595 Camshaft Position (CMP) sensor (2) with actuator and fasteners (1)

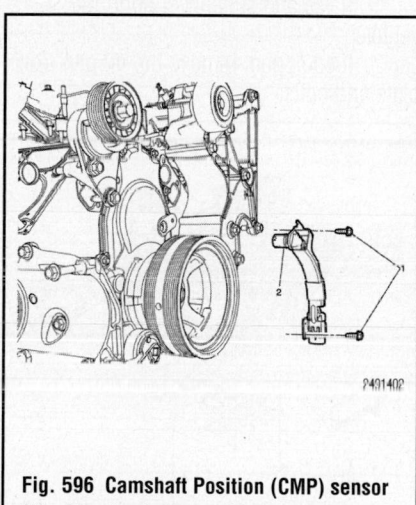

Fig. 596 Camshaft Position (CMP) sensor (2) without actuator and fasteners (1)

2010 Diesel Engines

See Figure 597.

1. Remove the cooling fan pulley.
2. Remove the Camshaft Position (CMP) sensor bolt.
3. Remove the CMP sensor.

To install:

4. Lubricate the CMP sensor O-ring with clean engine oil.
5. Install the CMP sensor.
6. Install the CMP sensor bolt. Tighten the bolt to 89 inch lbs. (10 Nm).
7. Install the cooling fan pulley.

Fig. 597 Remove the Camshaft Position (CMP) sensor bolt

2011 Diesel Engines

See Figure 598.

1. Disconnect the negative battery cable.
2. Remove the radiator fan and clutch.
3. Disconnect the Camshaft Position (CMP) sensor electrical connector.

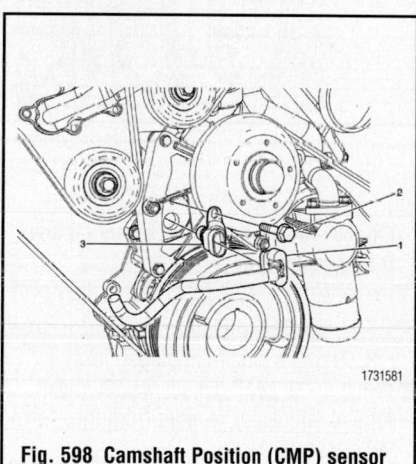

Fig. 598 Camshaft Position (CMP) sensor electrical connector (1), bolt (2) and the sensor (3)

4. Remove the Camshaft Position (CMP) sensor bolt.
5. Remove the Camshaft Position (CMP) sensor.

To install:

6. Installation is the reverse of removal.
7. Lubricate the Camshaft Position (CMP) sensor O-ring with engine oil prior to installation
8. Tighten the Camshaft Position (CMP) sensor bolt to 89 inch lbs. (10 Nm).

Hybrid Vehicles

See Figures 599 through 605.

➡️Clean the area around the Camshaft Position (CMP) sensor before removal

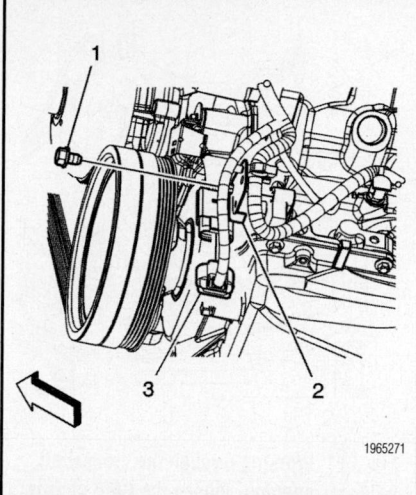

Fig. 599 Disconnect the engine wiring harness electrical connector (3) from the CMP sensor wire harness; bolt (1)

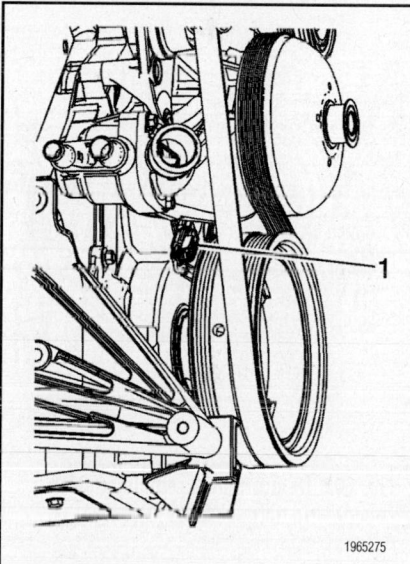

Fig. 600 Disconnect the CMP sensor wire harness electrical connector (1) from the CMP actuator magnet

in order to prevent debris from entering the engine.

1. Raise and suitably support the vehicle.
2. Remove the engine shield.
3. Disconnect the engine wiring harness electrical connector from the CMP sensor wire harness.
4. Disconnect the CMP sensor wire harness electrical connector from the CMP actuator magnet.
5. Working through the crankshaft balancer opening, loosen the CMP sensor wire harness bolt 2 turns using a box wrench.
6. Remove the 2 remaining CMP sensor wire harness bolts.

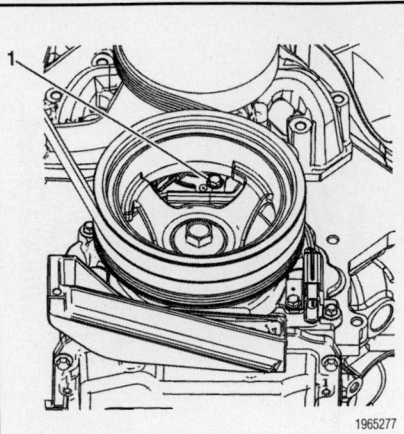

Fig. 601 Working through the crankshaft balancer opening, loosen the CMP sensor wire harness bolt (1) 2 turns using a box wrench

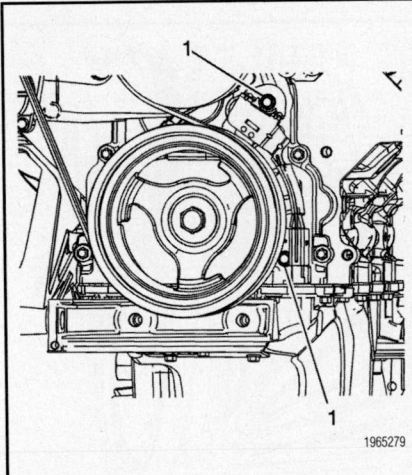

Fig. 602 Remove the 2 remaining CMP sensor wire harness bolts (1)

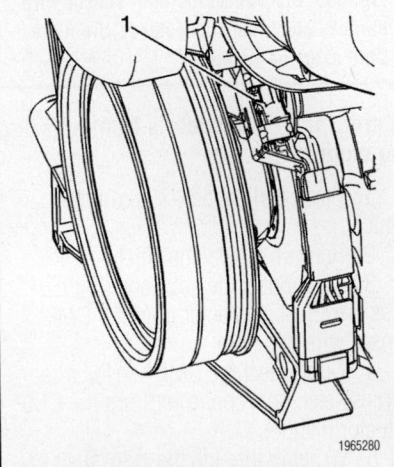

Fig. 603 Using a small flat bladed tool, disengage the CMP sensor wire harness electrical connector retainer (1) from the CMP sensor

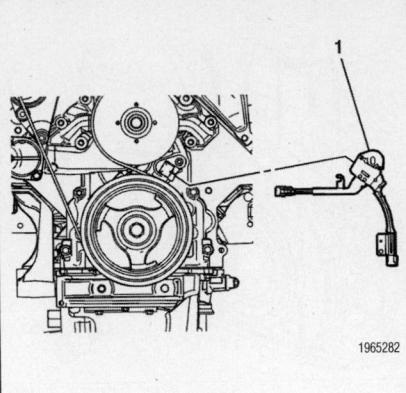

Fig. 604 Remove the CMP sensor wire harness (1)

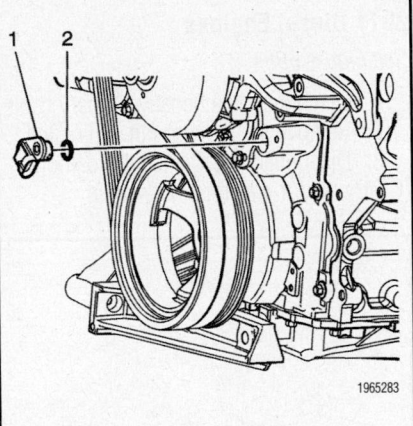

Fig. 605 Remove the CMP sensor (1) and O-ring seal (2)

7. Lower the vehicle.

8. Using a small flat bladed tool, disengage the CMP sensor wire harness electrical connector retainer from the CMP sensor.

9. Remove the CMP sensor wire harness.

10. Remove the CMP sensor and O-ring seal.

To install:

11. Inspect the CMP O-ring seal for cuts or damage. If the seal is not damaged, it may be reused.

12. Lubricate the O-ring seal with clean engine oil.

13. Install the O-ring seal onto the sensor.

14. Install the CMP sensor to the front cover.

15. Install the CMP sensor wire harness.

16. Connect the CMP sensor wire harness electrical connector, ensure that the retainer fully engages the CMP sensor.

17. Raise and suitably support the vehicle.

18. Install the 2 rear CMP sensor wire harness bolts. Tighten the bolt to 106 inch lbs. (12 Nm).

19. Working through the crankshaft balancer opening, tighten the CMP sensor wire harness bolt using a box wrench.

20. Connect the CMP sensor wire harness electrical connector to the CMP actuator magnet.

21. Connect the engine wiring harness electrical connector to the CMP sensor wire harness.

22. Install the engine shield.

CRANKSHAFT POSITION (CKP) SENSOR

LOCATION

Refer to the graphics in the Removal and Installation section for the location(s).

REMOVAL & INSTALLATION

V6 Engines

See Figures 606 and 607.

1. Raise and suitably support the vehicle.

2. If equipped, remove the oil pan skid plate and bolts.

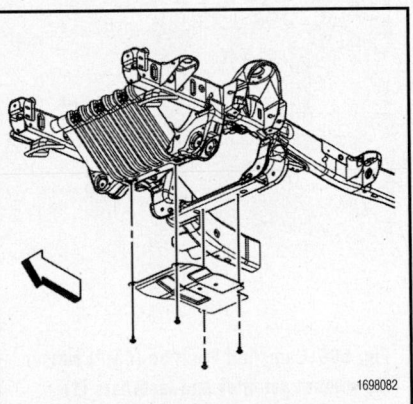

Fig. 606 If equipped, remove the oil pan skid plate and bolts

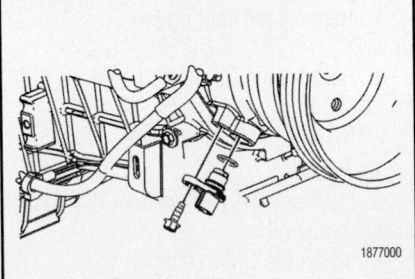

Fig. 607 Remove the CKP sensor bolt and sensor

3. Disconnect the engine wiring harness electrical connector from the Crankshaft Position (CKP) sensor.

4. Remove the CKP sensor bolt and sensor.

To install:

➡When installing the CKP sensor, make sure the sensor is fully seated before tightening the bolt. A poorly seated CKP sensor may perform erratically and may set false Diagnostic Trouble Codes (DTCs).

➡Do not reuse the original O-ring seal.

5. If reinstalling the old CKP sensor, install a NEW O-ring seal onto the sensor.

6. Lubricate the O-ring seal with clean engine oil.

7. Install the CKP sensor and bolt. Tighten the bolt to 89 inch lbs. (10 Nm).

8. Connect the engine wiring harness electrical connector to the CKP sensor.

9. If equipped, position the oil pan skid plate and install the bolts. Tighten the bolts to 21 ft. lbs. (28 Nm).

10. Lower the vehicle.

V8 Engines

See Figures 608 and 609.

➡Perform the Crankshaft Position System Variation Learn whenever the crankshaft position sensor is removed or replaced.

1. Remove the starter.

2. Working through the wheel well opening, disconnect the engine wiring harness electrical connector from the Crankshaft Position (CKP) sensor.

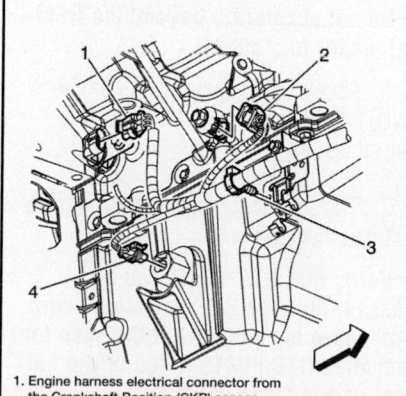

1. Engine harness electrical connector from the Crankshaft Position (CKP) sensor
2. Engine harness electrical connector from the knock sensor
3. Engine harness clip
4. Engine harness electrical connector from the oil level sensor

1698087

Fig. 608 Disconnect the engine wiring harness electrical connector from the CKP sensor

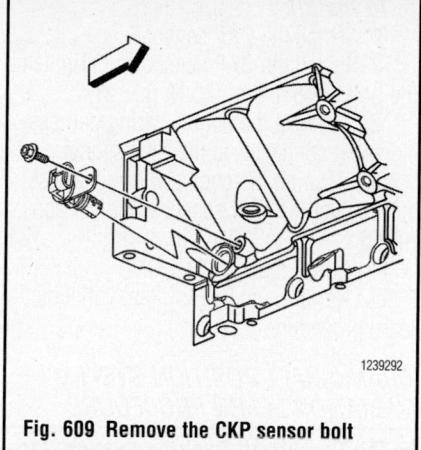

1239292

Fig. 609 Remove the CKP sensor bolt

3. Clean the area around the CKP sensor before removal in order to avoid debris from entering the engine.

4. Remove the CKP sensor bolt.

5. Remove the CKP sensor.

To install:

6. Install the CKP sensor.

7. Install the CKP sensor bolt. Tighten the bolt to 18 ft. lbs. (25 Nm).

8. Connect the engine wiring harness electrical connector to the CKP sensor.

9. Install the starter.

10. Perform the CKP system variation learn procedure.

2010 Diesel Engines

See Figures 610 and 611.

1. Disconnect the negative battery cable.

2. Remove the right wheelhouse panel.

3. Disconnect the Crankshaft Position (CKP) sensor electrical connector.

4. Remove the CKP sensor bolt.

5. Remove the CKP sensor.

1335470

Fig. 610 Disconnect the Crankshaft Position (CKP) sensor electrical connector

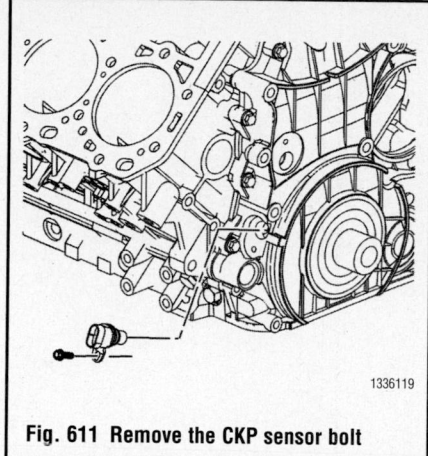

1336119

Fig. 611 Remove the CKP sensor bolt

6. If necessary, remove the CKP sensor spacer bolts.

7. If necessary, remove the CKP sensor spacer.

To install:

8. If necessary, lubricate a NEW CKP spacer O-ring with clean engine oil.

9. If necessary, install the NEW O-ring to the CKP sensor spacer.

➡The crankshaft position sensor spacers are machined with different timing positions. However, if the crankshaft position sensor spacer requires replacement, replace with a grade "C" spacer.

10. If necessary, install the CKP sensor spacer.

11. If necessary, install the CKP sensor spacer bolts. Tighten the bolts to 89 inch lbs. (10 Nm).

12. Lubricate a NEW CKP sensor O-ring with clean engine oil.

13. Install the NEW O-ring to the CKP sensor.

14. Install the CKP sensor.

15. Install the CKP sensor bolt. Tighten the bolt to 89 inch lbs. (10 Nm).

16. Connect the CKP sensor electrical connector.

17. Install the right wheelhouse panel.

18. Connect the negative battery cable.

2011 Diesel Engines

See Figure 612.

1. Raise and support the vehicle.

2. Remove the crankshaft position sensor bolt.

3. Remove the crankshaft position sensor.

4. Disconnect the electrical connector

5. Installation is the reverse of removal.

6. Tighten the CKP sensor bolt to 89 inch lbs. (10 Nm).

Fig. 612 Remove the crankshaft position sensor bolt (1) and the sensor (2)

7. Perform the crankshaft variation learn procedure.

Hybrid Engines

See Figures 613 and 614.

➡**Perform the Crankshaft Position System Variation Learn whenever the crankshaft position sensor is removed or replaced.**

1. Raise and suitably support the vehicle.
2. Reposition the engine wiring harness sleeve.
3. Disconnect the engine wiring harness electrical connector from the Crankshaft Position (CKP) sensor.
4. Clean the area around the CKP sensor before removal in order to avoid debris from entering the engine.
5. Remove the CKP sensor bolt.
6. Remove the CKP sensor.

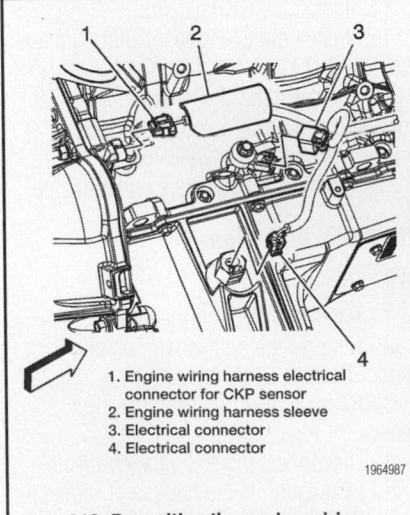

1. Engine wiring harness electrical connector for CKP sensor
2. Engine wiring harness sleeve
3. Electrical connector
4. Electrical connector

Fig. 613 Reposition the engine wiring harness sleeve

To install:

7. Install the CKP sensor.
8. Install the CKP sensor bolt. Tighten the bolt to 18 ft. lbs. (25 Nm).
9. Connect the engine wiring harness electrical connector to the CKP sensor.
10. Position the engine wiring harness sleeve over the CKP sensor electrical connection.
11. Lower the vehicle.
12. Perform the CKP system variation learn procedure.

CRANKSHAFT POSITION SYSTEM VARIATION LEARN PROCEDURE

➡**The Crankshaft Position System Variation Learn procedure is required when the following service procedures have been performed, regardless of whether DTC P0315 is set:**

- A crankshaft position sensor replacement
- An Engine Control Module (ECM) replacement
- An engine replacement
- A crankshaft balancer replacement
- A crankshaft replacement
- Any engine repairs which disturb the crankshaft to crankshaft position sensor relationship.

➡**The ECM monitors certain component signals to determine if all the conditions are met to continue with the Crankshaft Position System Variation Learn Procedure.**

1. Ignition ON, observe the DTC information with a scan tool. Verify no other DTCs are set, except DTCs P0300-P0308, or P0315.

➡**If DTCs are set, except DTCs P0300-P0308, or P0315, refer to Diagnostic Trouble Code (DTC) List—Vehicle for further diagnosis.**

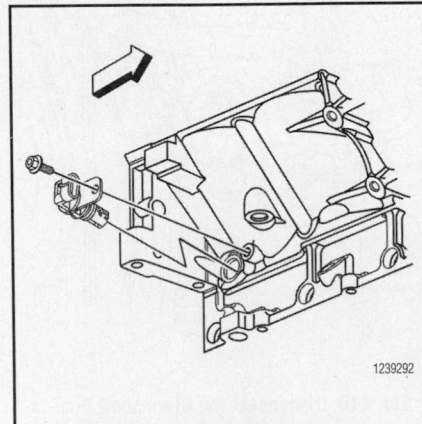

Fig. 614 Remove the CKP sensor bolt

2. Select the Crankshaft Pos. Variation Learn procedure with a scan tool.

➡**Close the hood.**

➡**Observe the appropriate RPM values for fuel cut-off.**

➡**The engine must be at operating temperature.**

3. The scan tool instructs you to perform the following:
- Block drive wheels.
- Set parking brake.
- Cycle the ignition.
- Apply and hold brake pedal.

➡**The vehicle must remain in PARK/NEUTRAL.**
- Start and idle the engine.

➡**The scan tool monitors certain component signals to determine if all the conditions are met to continue with the procedure. The scan tool only displays the conditions that inhibit the procedure. The scan tool monitors the following components:**

- CKP sensors activity—If there is a CKP sensor condition, refer to the applicable DTC that set.
- Camshaft Position (CMP) sensor activity—If there is a CMP sensor condition, refer to the applicable DTC that set.
- Engine Coolant Temperature (ECT)—If the ECT is not warm enough, idle the engine until the engine coolant reaches the correct temperature.

4. Enable the CKP System Variation Learn Procedure with a scan tool.

➡**Do not accelerate beyond the RPM values for fuel cut-off.**

5. Accelerate to Wide Open Throttle (WOT) and release the throttle when fuel cut-off occurs.
6. Test in progress.
7. The scan tool displays Learn Status: Learned this ignition.

➡**Verify that DTC P0315 ran and passed; then the CKP Variation Learn Procedure is complete. If the scan tool indicates DTC P0315 failed or did not run, or any other DTCs set.**

8. Once the Learn Procedure has successfully completed, and in order to store the crankshaft position system variation values in the ECM, turn OFF the ignition and verify all vehicle systems are OFF. This may take up to 2 minutes.

ENGINE CONTROL MODULE (ECM)

LOCATION

Refer to the graphics in the Removal and Installation section for the location(s).

REMOVAL & INSTALLATION

Gasoline Engines

See Figures 615 and 616.

❋❋ **CAUTION**

Note the following:

- Turn the ignition OFF when installing or removing the control module connectors and disconnecting or reconnecting the power to the control module (battery cable, Powertrain Control Module (PCM)/Engine Control Module (ECM)/Transmission Control Module (TCM) pigtail, control module fuse, jumper cables, etc.) in order to prevent internal control module damage.
- Control module damage may result when the metal case contacts battery voltage. DO NOT contact the control module metal case with battery voltage when servicing a control module, using battery booster cables, or when charging the vehicle battery.
- In order to prevent any possible electrostatic discharge damage to the control module, do not touch the connector pins or the soldered components on the circuit board.
- Remove any debris from around the control module connector surfaces before servicing the control module. Inspect the control module connector gaskets when diagnosing or replacing the control module. Ensure that the gaskets are installed correctly. The gaskets prevent contaminant intrusion into the control module.
- The replacement control module must be programmed.

➡**Record the current Engine Oil Life percentage, and use a scan tool to update the NEW ECM, if replacing.**

1. Record the current Engine Oil Life percentage, and use a scan tool to update the NEW ECM, if replacing.
2. Disconnect the negative battery cable.

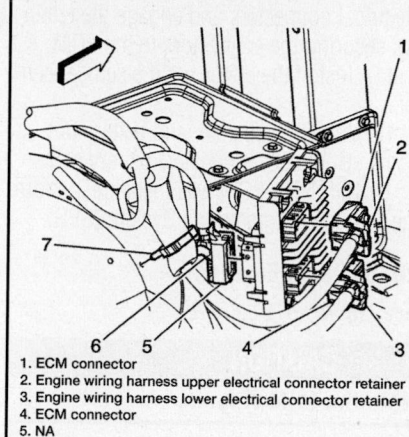

1. ECM connector
2. Engine wiring harness upper electrical connector retainer
3. Engine wiring harness lower electrical connector retainer
4. ECM connector
5. NA
6. NA
7. Tie strap

1703437

Fig. 615 Disengage the engine wiring harness upper electrical connector retainer and remove the connector from the ECM

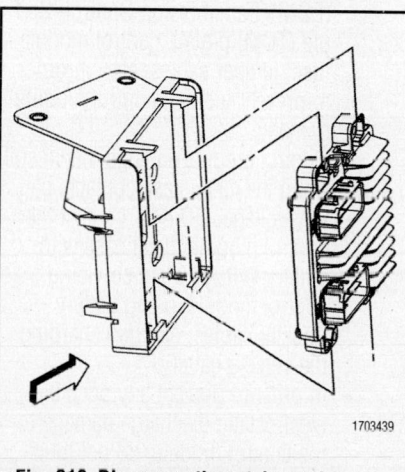

1703439

Fig. 616 Disengage the retainer tabs securing the ECM to the bracket

3. Disengage the engine wiring harness upper electrical connector retainer and remove the connector from the ECM.
4. Disengage the engine wiring harness lower electrical connector retainer and remove the connector from the ECM.
5. Disengage the retainer tabs securing the ECM to the bracket.
6. Remove the ECM.

To install:

7. Install the bottom ECM tabs into the bracket.
8. Push the ECM in securing the ECM to the bracket.
9. Position the engine wiring harness lower electrical connector and engage the retainer securing the lower connector to the ECM.

10. Position the engine wiring harness upper electrical connector and engage the retainer securing the upper connector to the ECM.
11. Connect the negative battery cable.
12. If a NEW ECM was installed, program the ECM.

Hybrid Engines

See Figures 617 and 618.

❋❋ **CAUTION**

Note the following:

- Turn the ignition OFF when installing or removing the control module connectors and disconnecting or reconnecting the power to the control module (battery cable, Powertrain Control Module (PCM)/Engine Control Module (ECM)/Transmission Control Module (TCM) pigtail, control module fuse, jumper cables, etc.) in order to prevent internal control module damage.
- Control module damage may result when the metal case contacts battery voltage. DO NOT contact the control module metal case with battery voltage when servicing a control module, using battery booster cables, or when charging the vehicle battery.
- In order to prevent any possible electrostatic discharge damage to the control module, do not touch the connector pins or the soldered components on the circuit board.
- Remove any debris from around the control module connector surfaces before servicing the control module. Inspect the control module connector gaskets when diagnosing or replacing the control module. Ensure that the gaskets are installed correctly. The gaskets prevent contaminant intrusion into the control module.
- The replacement control module must be programmed.

➡**It is necessary to record the remaining engine oil life. If the replacement module is not programmed with the remaining engine oil life, the engine oil life will default to 100 percent. If the replacement module is not programmed with the remaining engine oil life, the engine oil will need to be changed at 3,000 mi (5,000 km mi) from the last oil change.**

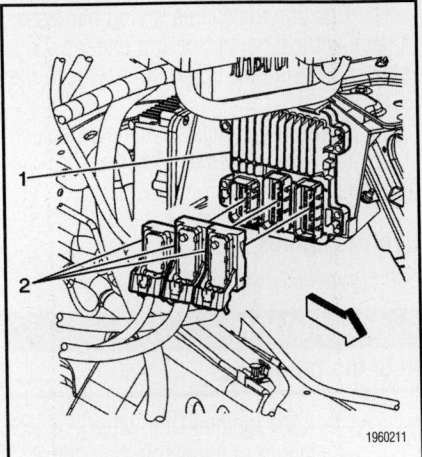

Fig. 617 Disengage the engine wiring harness electrical connector retainers and remove the connectors (2) from the ECM (1)

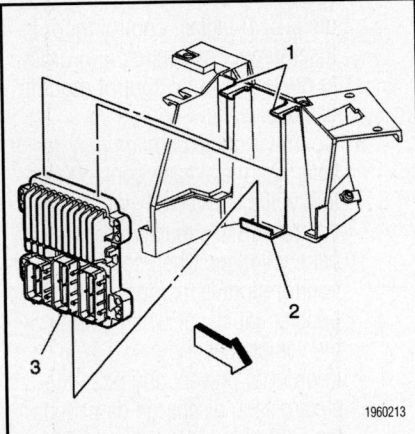

Fig. 618 Disengage the bracket retainer tabs (1) securing the ECM to the bracket, remove the ECM (3) from the bracket (2)

1. Using a scan tool, retrieve the percentage of remaining engine oil. Record the remaining engine oil life.
2. Disconnect the negative battery cable.
3. Remove the battery and battery tray.
4. Remove the under hood electrical center.
5. Disengage the engine wiring harness electrical connector retainers and remove the connectors from the ECM.
6. Disengage the bracket retainer tabs securing the ECM to the bracket.
7. Remove the ECM from the bracket.

To install:

8. Set the bottom of ECM into the ECM bracket tab.
9. Push the ECM in securing the ECM to the bracket.

10. Position the engine wiring harness electrical connectors and engage the retainers securing the connectors to the ECM.
11. Install the under hood electrical center.
12. Install the battery and battery tray.
13. Connect the negative battery cable.
14. If a NEW ECM was installed, perform the Service Programming System (SPS).

2010 Diesel Engines

See Figures 619 and 620.

※※ CAUTION

Note the following:

- Turn the ignition OFF when installing or removing the control module connectors and disconnecting or reconnecting the power to the control module (battery cable, Powertrain Control Module (PCM)/Engine Control Module (ECM)/Transmission Control Module (TCM) pigtail, control module fuse, jumper cables, etc.) in order to prevent internal control module damage.
- Control module damage may result when the metal case contacts battery voltage. DO NOT contact the control module metal case with battery voltage when servicing a control module, using battery booster cables, or when charging the vehicle battery.
- In order to prevent any possible electrostatic discharge damage to the control module, do not touch the connector pins or the soldered components on the circuit board.
- Remove any debris from around the control module connector surfaces before servicing the control module. Inspect the control module connector gaskets when diagnosing or replacing the control module. Ensure that the gaskets are installed correctly. The gaskets prevent contaminant intrusion into the control module.
- The replacement control module must be programmed.

➡ Before removing the Engine Control Module (ECM), use the scan tool to capture the ECM data. This captured data will then need to be restored into the NEW ECM.

1. Using a scan tool, capture the ECM data.

2. Disconnect the negative battery cable.
3. Disconnect the ECM electrical connectors.
4. Release the ECM upper retaining tabs.
5. Remove the ECM from the bracket.

To install:

6. Place the bottom edge of the ECM into the bracket lower retainers.
7. Push the ECM towards the bracket until the upper edge of the ECM snaps into place.
8. Connect the ECM electrical connectors.
9. Connect the negative battery cable.
10. If a NEW ECM was installed, program the ECM.

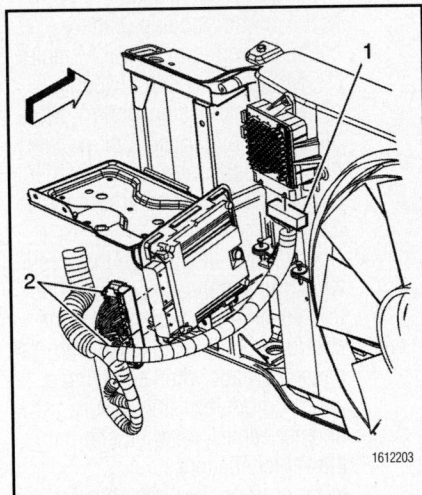

Fig. 619 Disconnect the ECM electrical connectors (1, 2)

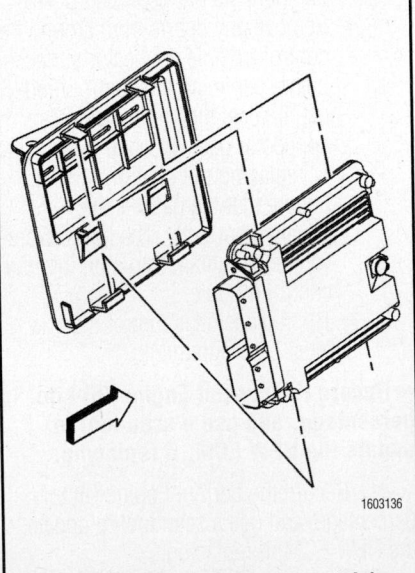

Fig. 620 Release the ECM upper retaining tabs

2011 Diesel Engines

See Figure 621.

➡**The manufacturer does not provide a specific Removal and Installation procedure for this component. Refer to the graphic(s) when servicing this component.**

ECM PROGRAMMING AND SETUP

The following service procedures require either a programming or a setup event performed for a complete repair.

ECM Replacement

If the Engine Control Module (ECM) is replaced, the following procedures must be performed:

1. The ECM Reprogramming—Refer to Service Programming System (SPS).

2. The CKP Variation Learn—Refer to Crankshaft Position System Variation Learn for the 4.8L, 5.3L, 6.0L or 6.2L and Crankshaft Position System Variation Learn for the 6.0L Hybrid.

3. The Throttle/Idle Learn procedure—Refer to the following:
- Throttle/Idle Learn for the 4.8L, 5.3L, 6.0L or 6.2L
- Throttle/Idle Learn for the 6.0L Hybrid

4. The Theft Deterrent Programming—Refer to Theft Deterrent Control Module Programming and Setup.

5. The Fuel Composition Diagnostic, as necessary—Refer to Fuel Composition Diagnosis.

6. Engine Oil Life Remaining—When available, use a scan tool to reset the Engine Oil Life Remaining back to the original percentage recorded before the module was replaced.

7. Transmission Fluid Life Remaining—When available, use a scan tool to reset the Transmission Fluid Life Remaining back to the original percentage recorded before the module was replaced.

ECM Reprogramming

➡**DO NOT reprogram a FlexFuel (E85) vehicle while the fuel composition learn function is active. If necessary, drive the vehicle until the scan tool indicates that the fuel composition learn parameter is inactive. Programming with the fuel composition learn active will result in fuel trim DTCs.**

1. If the ECM needs to be reprogrammed, refer to Service Programming System (SPS).

2. Engine Oil Life Remaining—When available, use a scan tool to reset the Engine Oil Life Remaining back to the original percentage recorded before the module was reprogrammed.

3. Transmission Fluid Life Remaining—When available, use a scan tool to reset the Transmission Fluid Life Remaining back to the original percentage recorded before the module was reprogrammed.

Setup for Component Replacement

The replacement of some components will require a setup procedure for complete repair.

1. If any of the following components are replaced, a CKP Variation Learn Procedure must be performed. Refer to Crankshaft Position System Variation Learn for the 4.8L, 5.3L, 6.0L or 6.2L and Crankshaft Position System Variation Learn for the 6.0L Hybrid.
- Engine replacement
- Any engine repair that disturbs the Crankshaft Position (CKP) sensor or its relationship with the crankshaft reluctor wheel
- CKP sensor

2. If the throttle body is replaced or a throttle body cleaning procedure is completed, the Throttle/Idle Learn Procedure must be performed. Refer to the following:
- Throttle/Idle Learn for the 4.8L, 5.3L, 6.0L or 6.2L
- Throttle/Idle Learn for the 6.0L Hybrid

ENGINE COOLANT TEMPERATURE (ECT) SENSOR

LOCATION

Refer to the graphics in the Removal and Installation section for the location(s).

REMOVAL & INSTALLATION

V6 Engines

See Figures 622 and 623.

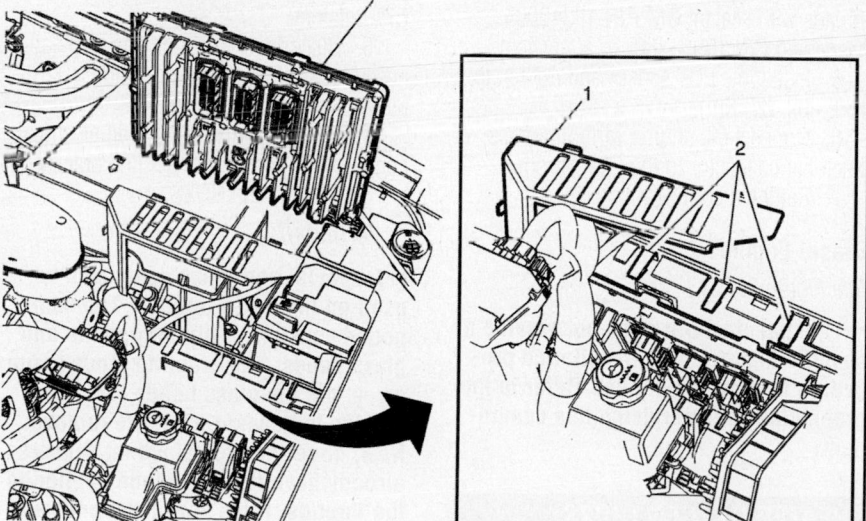

Fig. 621 Engine control module cover (1), engine control module bracket (2), and engine control module (3)

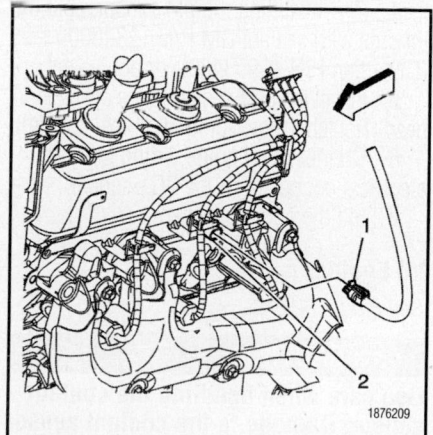

Fig. 622 Disconnect the engine wiring harness electrical connector (1) from the Engine Coolant Temperature (ECT) sensor (2)

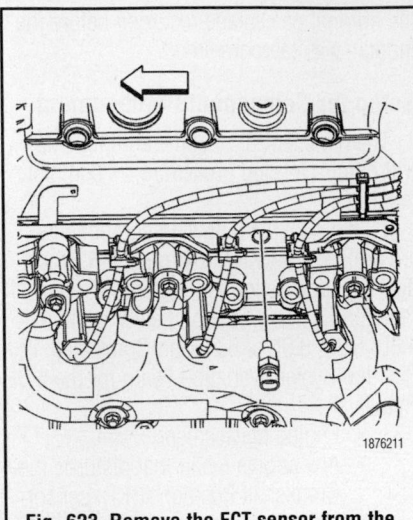

Fig. 623 Remove the ECT sensor from the cylinder head

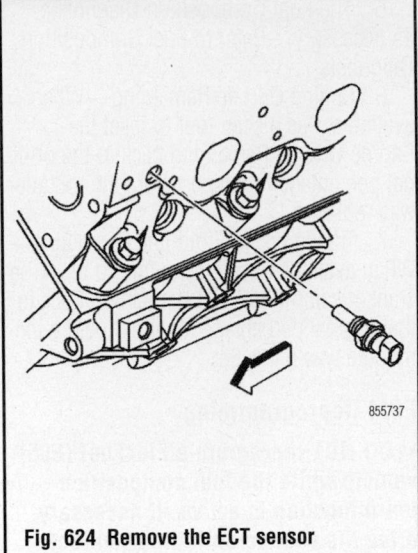

Fig. 624 Remove the ECT sensor

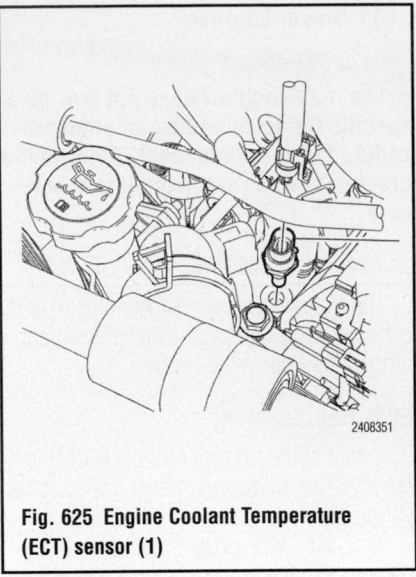

Fig. 625 Engine Coolant Temperature (ECT) sensor (1)

> ❊❊ **CAUTION**
>
> **Use care when handling the coolant sensor. Damage to the coolant sensor will affect the operation of the fuel control system.**

1. Drain the cooling system.
2. Disconnect the engine wiring harness electrical connector from the Engine Coolant Temperature (ECT) sensor.
3. Remove the ECT sensor from the cylinder head.

To install:

> ❊❊ **CAUTION**
>
> **Use care when handling the coolant sensor. Damage to the coolant sensor will affect the operation of the fuel control system.**

4. If re-installing the old sensor, coat the threads with sealant GM P/N 12346004 (Canadian P/N 10953480), or equivalent.
5. Install the ECT sensor to the cylinder head. Tighten the sensor to 15 ft. lbs. (20 Nm).
6. Connect the engine wiring harness electrical connector to the ECT sensor.
7. Fill the cooling system.

V8 Engines

See Figure 624.

> ❊❊ **CAUTION**
>
> **Use care when handling the coolant sensor. Damage to the coolant sensor will affect the operation of the fuel control system.**

1. Drain the cooling system to a level below the Engine Coolant Temperature (ECT) sensor.

2. Disconnect the engine wiring harness electrical connector from the ECT sensor.
3. Remove the ECT sensor.

To install:

> ❊❊ **CAUTION**
>
> **Do not insert any tools into the throttle body bore in order to avoid damage to the throttle valve plate.**

> ❊❊ **CAUTION**
>
> **Use care when handling the coolant sensor. Damage to the coolant sensor will affect the operation of the fuel control system.**

4. If installing the old sensor, coat the threads with sealant GM P/N 12346004 (Canadian P/N 10953480) or equivalent.
5. Install the ECT sensor and tighten to 15 ft. lbs. (20 Nm).
6. Connect the engine wiring harness electrical connector to the ECT sensor.
7. Refill the cooling.

Diesel Engines

See Figure 625.

➥The manufacturer does not provide a specific Removal and Installation procedure for this component. Refer to the graphic(s) when servicing this component.

HEATED OXYGEN (HO2S) SENSOR

LOCATION

Refer to the graphics in the Removal and Installation section for the location(s).

REMOVAL & INSTALLATION

V6 Engines

Bank 1 Sensor 1

See Figure 626.

1. Raise and suitably support the vehicle.
2. If vehicle is a 2-Wheel Drive (2WD) perform the following steps, otherwise proceed to step 5.
3. Disconnect the Connector Position Assurance (CPA) retainer.
4. Disconnect the HO2S pigtail electrical connector from the engine wiring harness electrical connector.
5. If vehicle is a 4-Wheel Drive (4WD) perform the following steps, disconnect the CPA retainer.
6. Disconnect the engine wiring harness electrical connector from the HO2S pigtail electrical connector.
7. Remove the HO2S pigtail electrical connector clip from the fuel line bracket.
8. Remove the HO2S.

To install:

➥A special anti-seize compound is used on the HO2S threads. The compound consists of liquid graphite and glass beads. The graphite tends to burn away, but the glass beads remain, making the sensor easier to remove. New, or service replacement sensors already have the compound applied to the threads. If the sensor is removed from an exhaust component and if for any reason the sensor is to be reinstalled, the threads must have anti-seize compound applied before the reinstallation.

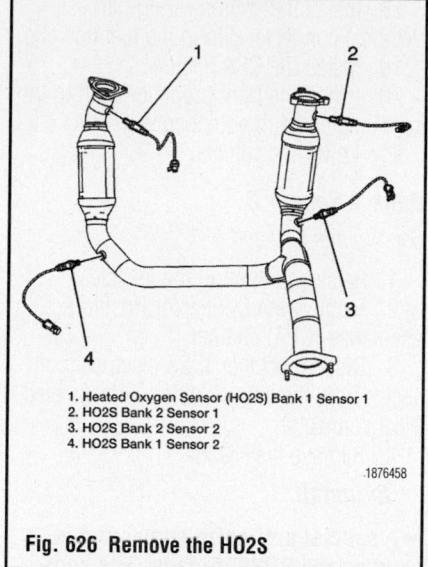

1. Heated Oxygen Sensor (HO2S) Bank 1 Sensor 1
2. HO2S Bank 2 Sensor 1
3. HO2S Bank 2 Sensor 2
4. HO2S Bank 1 Sensor 2

.1876458

Fig. 626 Remove the HO2S

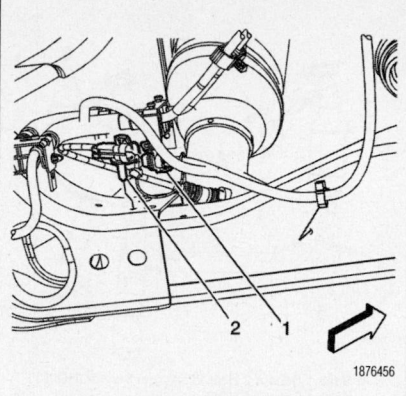

1876456

Fig. 627 Disconnect the engine wiring harness electrical connector (1) from the HO2S pigtail electrical connector; remove the HO2S pigtail electrical connector clip (2) from the frame

9. If reinstalling the old sensor, coat the threads with anti-seize compound GM P/N 12377953, or equivalent.

10. Install the HO2S. Tighten the sensor to 31 ft. lbs. (42 Nm).

11. If vehicle is a 4WD perform the following steps otherwise proceed to step 7.

12. Install the HO2S pigtail electrical connector clip to the fuel line bracket.

13. Connect the engine wiring harness electrical connector to the HO2S pigtail electrical connector.

14. Connect the CPA retainer.

15. If vehicle is a 2WD perform the following steps, connect the HO2S pigtail electrical connector to the engine wiring harness electrical connector.

16. Connect the CPA retainer.

17. Lower the vehicle.

Bank 1 Sensor 2

See Figures 626 and 627.

1. Raise and suitably support the vehicle.

2. Disconnect the Connector Position Assurance (CPA) retainer.

3. Disconnect the engine wiring harness electrical connector from the HO2S pigtail electrical connector.

4. Remove the HO2S pigtail electrical connector clip from the frame.

5. Remove the HO2S.

To install:

➡A special anti-seize compound is used on the HO2S threads. The compound consists of liquid graphite and glass beads. The graphite tends to burn away, but the glass beads remain, making the sensor easier to remove.

New, or service replacement sensors already have the compound applied to the threads. If the sensor is removed from an exhaust component and if for any reason the old sensor is to be reinstalled, the threads must have anti-seize compound applied before the reinstallation.

6. If reinstalling the old HO2S, coat the threads with anti-seize compound GM P/N 12377953, or equivalent.

7. Install the HO2S. Tighten the sensor to 31 ft. lbs. (42 Nm).

8. Install the HO2S pigtail electrical connector clip to the frame.

9. Connect the engine wiring harness electrical connector to the HO2S pigtail electrical connector.

10. Connect the CPA retainer.

11. Lower the vehicle.

Bank 2 Sensor 1

See Figure 626.

1. Raise and suitably support the vehicle.

2. Remove the Connector Position Assurance (CPA) retainer.

3. Disconnect the HO2S pigtail electrical connector from the engine wiring harness electrical connector.

4. Remove the HO2S.

To install:

➡A special anti-seize compound is used on the HO2S threads. The compound consists of liquid graphite and glass beads. The graphite tends to burn away, but the glass beads remain, making the sensor easier to remove. New, or service replacement sensors

already have the compound applied to the threads. If the sensor is removed from an exhaust component and if for any reason the old sensor is to be reinstalled, the threads must have anti-seize compound applied before the reinstallation.

5. If reinstalling the old HO2S, coat the threads with anti-seize compound GM P/N 12377953, or equivalent.

6. Install the HO2S. Tighten the sensor to 31 ft. lbs. (42 Nm).

7. Connect the HO2S pigtail electrical connector to the engine wiring harness electrical connector.

8. Install the CPA retainer.

9. Lower the vehicle.

Bank 2 Sensor 2

See Figure 626.

1. Raise and suitably support the vehicle.

2. Remove the Connector Position Assurance (CPA) retainer.

3. Disconnect the engine wiring harness electrical connector from the HO2S pigtail electrical connector.

4. Remove the HO2S pigtail electrical connector clip from the engine wiring harness clip.

5. Remove the HO2S.

To install:

➡A special anti-seize compound is used on the HO2S threads. The compound consists of liquid graphite and glass beads. The graphite tends to burn away, but the glass beads remain, making the sensor easier to remove. New, or service replacement sensors already have the compound applied to the threads. If the sensor is removed from an exhaust component and if for any reason the old sensor is to be reinstalled, the threads must have anti-seize compound applied before the reinstallation.

6. If reinstalling the old HO2S, coat the threads with anti-seize compound GM P/N 12377953, or equivalent.

7. Install the HO2S. Tighten the sensor to 31 ft. lbs. (42 Nm).

8. Install the HO2S pigtail electrical connector clip to the engine wiring harness clip.

9. Connect the engine wiring harness electrical connector to the HO2S pigtail electrical connector.

10. Install the CPA retainer.

11. Lower the vehicle.

V8 Engines

Bank 1 Sensor 1

See Figures 628 through 630.

1. Raise and support the vehicle.
2. Unbolt the front propeller shaft from the front differential, if equipped with four wheel drive (4WD).
3. For vehicles equipped with a 4L60-E/4L70-E automatic transmission perform the following steps, for vehicles equipped with a 6L80-E automatic transmission proceed to step 7.
4. Remove the Connector Position Assurance (CPA) retainer.
5. Disconnect the engine wiring harness electrical connector from the HO2S.
6. Remove the HO2S electrical connector clip from the fuel line clip.

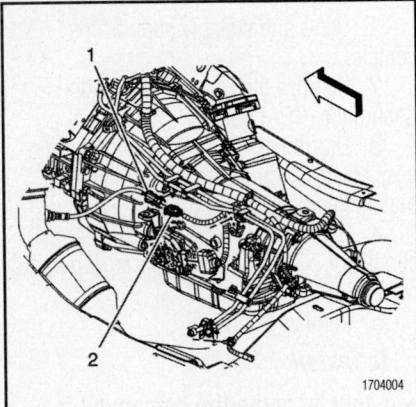

Fig. 628 Disconnect the engine wiring harness electrical connector (2) from the HO2S; remove the HO2S electrical connector clip (1) from the fuel line clip

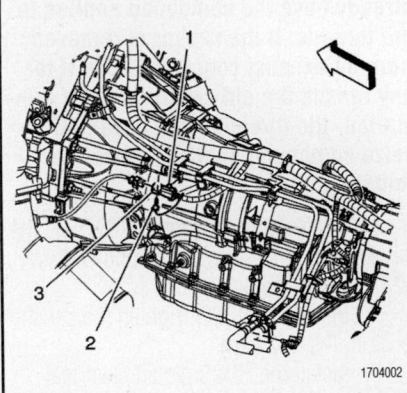

Fig. 629 Remove the CPA retainer (2); remove the engine wiring harness electrical connector clip (1) from the fuel line clip; and disconnect the engine wiring harness electrical connector (3) from the HO2S

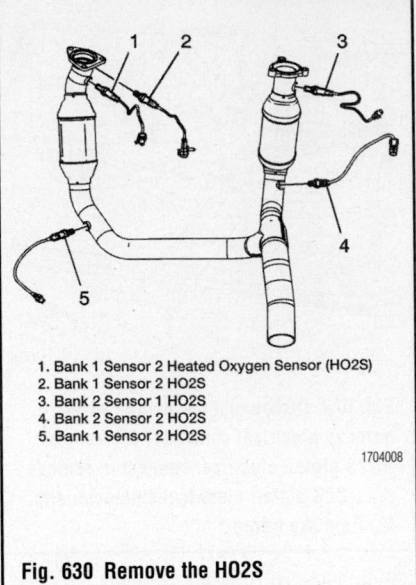

1. Bank 1 Sensor 2 Heated Oxygen Sensor (HO2S)
2. Bank 1 Sensor 2 HO2S
3. Bank 2 Sensor 1 HO2S
4. Bank 2 Sensor 2 HO2S
5. Bank 1 Sensor 2 HO2S

Fig. 630 Remove the HO2S

7. Remove the CPA retainer.
8. Remove the engine wiring harness electrical connector clip from the fuel line clip.
9. Disconnect the engine wiring harness electrical connector from the HO2S.
10. Remove the HO2S.

To install:

➡A special anti-seize compound is used on the HO2S threads. The compound consists of liquid graphite and glass beads. The graphite tends to burn away, but the glass beads remain, making the sensor easier to remove. New, or service replacement sensors already have the compound applied to the threads. If the sensor is removed from an exhaust component and if for any reason the sensor is to be reinstalled, the threads must have anti-seize compound applied before the reinstallation.

11. If reinstalling the old sensor, coat the threads with anti-seize compound GM P/N 12377953, or equivalent.
12. Install the HO2S and tighten to 31 ft. lbs. (42 Nm).
13. For vehicles equipped with a 4L60-E/4L70-E automatic transmission perform the following steps, for vehicles equipped with a 6L80-E automatic transmission proceed to step 7.
14. Install the HO2S electrical connector clip to the fuel line clip.
15. Connect the engine wiring harness electrical connector to the HO2S.
16. Install the CPA retainer.
17. Connect the engine wiring harness electrical connector to the HO2S.

18. Install the engine wiring harness electrical connector clip to the fuel line clip.
19. Install the CPA retainer.
20. Install the front propeller shaft to the front differential, if equipped with 4WD.
21. Lower the vehicle.

Bank 1 Sensor 2

See Figures 630 and 631.

1. Raise and support the vehicle.
2. Remove the Connector Position Assurance (CPA) retainer.
3. Disconnect the HO2S electrical connector from the engine wiring harness electrical connector.
4. Remove the HO2S.

To install:

➡A special anti-seize compound is used on the HO2S threads. The compound consists of liquid graphite and glass beads. The graphite tends to burn away, but the glass beads remain, making the sensor easier to remove. New, or service replacement sensors already have the compound applied to the threads. If the sensor is removed from an exhaust component and if for any reason the sensor is to be reinstalled, the threads must have anti-seize compound applied before the reinstallation.

5. If reinstalling the old sensor, coat the threads with anti-seize compound GM P/N 12377953, or equivalent.
6. Install the HO2S and tighten to 31 ft. lbs. (42 Nm).
7. Connect the HO2S electrical connector to the engine wiring harness electrical connector.

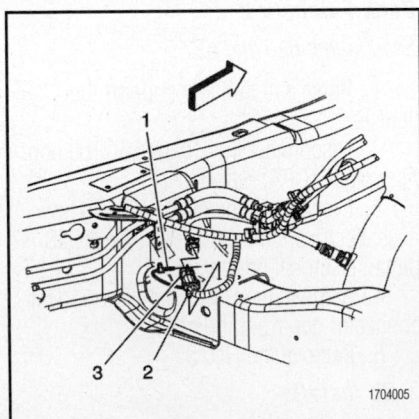

Fig. 631 Remove the Connector Position Assurance (CPA) retainer (1); disconnect the HO2S electrical connector from the engine wiring harness electrical connector (3); wiring harness retainer (2)

8. Install the CPA retainer.

9. Lower the vehicle.

Bank 2 Sensor 1

See Figures 630 and 632.

1. Remove the right wheelhouse liner.

2. Remove the Connector Position Assurance (CPA) retainer.

3. Disconnect the HO2S electrical connector from the engine wiring harness electrical connector.

4. Remove the HO2S clip from the engine wiring harness.

5. Remove the HO2S.

To install:

➡ **A special anti-seize compound is used on the HO2S threads. The compound consists of liquid graphite and glass beads. The graphite tends to burn away, but the glass beads remain, making the sensor easier to remove. New, or service replacement sensors already have the compound applied to the threads. If the sensor is removed from an exhaust component and if for any reason the sensor is to be reinstalled, the threads must have anti-seize compound applied before the reinstallation.**

6. If reinstalling the old sensor, coat the threads with anti-seize compound GM P/N 12377953, or equivalent.

7. Install the HO2S and tighten to 31 ft. lbs. (42 Nm).

8. Connect the HO2S electrical connector to the engine wiring harness electrical connector.

9. Install the CPA retainer.

10. Install the HO2S clip to the engine wiring harness.

11. Install the right wheelhouse liner.

Bank 2 Sensor 2

See Figures 630 and 632.

1. Raise and support the vehicle.

2. Remove the Connector Position Assurance (CPA) retainer.

3. Disconnect the engine wiring harness electrical connector from the HO2S electrical connector.

4. Remove the HO2S electrical connector clip from the engine harness clip.

5. Remove the HO2S.

To install:

➡ **A special anti-seize compound is used on the HO2S threads. The compound consists of liquid graphite and glass beads. The graphite tends to burn away, but the glass beads remain, making the sensor easier to remove. New, or service replacement sensors already have the compound applied to the threads. If the sensor is removed from an exhaust component and if for any reason the sensor is to be reinstalled, the threads must have anti-seize compound applied before the reinstallation.**

6. If reinstalling the old sensor, coat the threads with anti-seize compound GM P/N 12377953, or equivalent.

7. Install the HO2S and tighten to 31 ft. lbs. (42 Nm).

8. Install the HO2S electrical connector clip to the engine harness clip.

9. Connect the engine wiring harness electrical connector to the HO2S electrical connector.

10. Install the CPA retainer.

11. Lower the vehicle.

Hybrid Vehicles

Bank 1 Sensor 1

See Figures 633 and 634.

1. Raise and support the vehicle.

2. Unbolt the front propeller shaft from the front differential, if equipped with four wheel drive (4WD).

3. Remove the Connector Position Assurance (CPA) retainer.

4. Disconnect the engine wiring harness electrical connector from the HO2S.

5. Remove the HO2S electrical connector clip from the fuel line clip.

6. Remove the HO2S.

To install:

➡ **A special anti-seize compound is used on the HO2S threads. The compound consists of liquid graphite and glass beads. The graphite tends to burn away, but the glass beads remain, making the sensor easier to remove. New, or service replacement sensors already have the compound applied to the threads. If the sensor is removed from an exhaust component and if for any reason the sensor is to be reinstalled, the threads must have anti-seize compound applied before the reinstallation.**

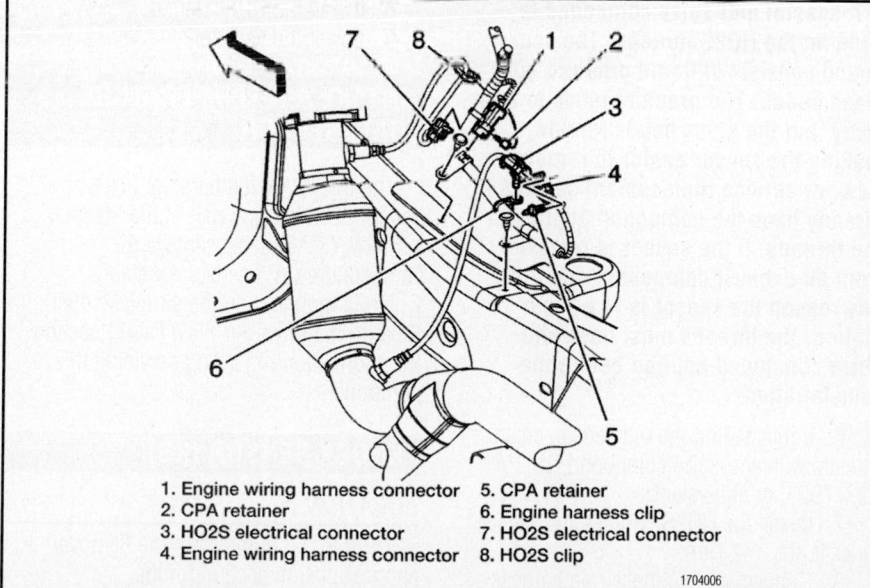

1. Engine wiring harness connector
2. CPA retainer
3. HO2S electrical connector
4. Engine wiring harness connector
5. CPA retainer
6. Engine harness clip
7. HO2S electrical connector
8. HO2S clip

1704006

Fig. 632 Remove the Connector Position Assurance (CPA) retainer

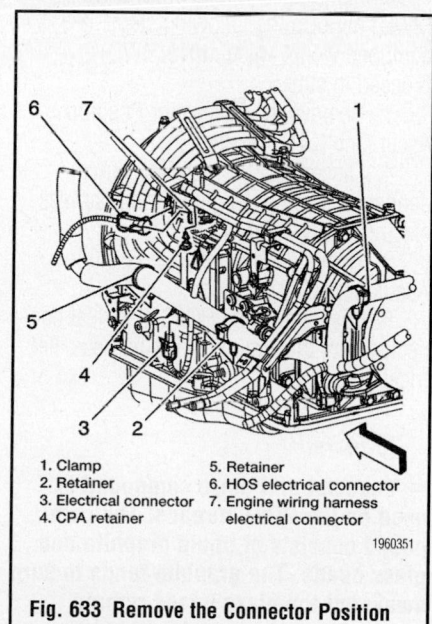

1. Clamp
2. Retainer
3. Electrical connector
4. CPA retainer
5. Retainer
6. HOS electrical connector
7. Engine wiring harness electrical connector

1960351

Fig. 633 Remove the Connector Position Assurance (CPA) retainer

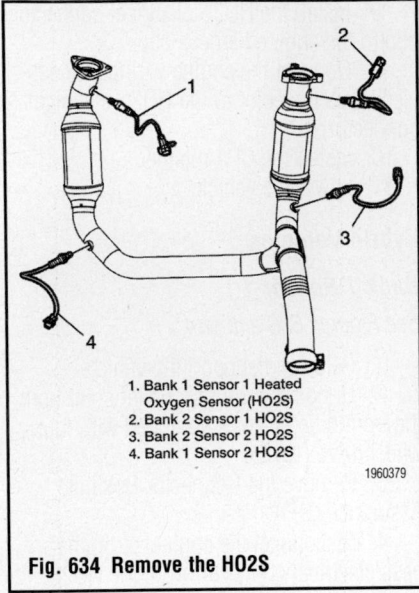

1. Bank 1 Sensor 1 Heated
   Oxygen Sensor (HO2S)
2. Bank 2 Sensor 1 HO2S
3. Bank 2 Sensor 2 HO2S
4. Bank 1 Sensor 2 HO2S

1960379

Fig. 634 Remove the HO2S

7. If reinstalling the old sensor, coat the threads with anti-seize compound GM P/N 12377953, or equivalent.

8. Install the HO2S. Tighten the sensor to 31 ft. lbs. (42 Nm).

9. Connect the engine wiring harness electrical connector to the HO2S.

10. Install the engine wiring harness electrical connector clip to the fuel line clip.

11. Install the CPA retainer.

12. Install the front propeller shaft to the front differential, if equipped with 4WD.

13. Lower the vehicle.

Bank 1 Sensor 2

See Figure 634.

1. Raise and support the vehicle.

2. If equipped with 2 wheel drive (2WD) perform the following steps, if equipped with 4 wheel drive (4WD) proceed to step 5.

3. Remove the Connector Position Assurance (CPA) retainer.

4. Disconnect the HO2S electrical connector from the engine wiring harness electrical connector.

5. Remove the Connector Position Assurance (CPA) retainer.

6. Disconnect the HO2S electrical connector from the engine wiring harness electrical connector.

7. Remove the HO2S.

To install:

➡A special anti-seize compound is used on the HO2S threads. The compound consists of liquid graphite and glass beads. The graphite tends to burn away, but the glass beads remain, making the sensor easier to remove.

New, or service replacement sensors already have the compound applied to the threads. If the sensor is removed from an exhaust component and if for any reason the sensor is to be reinstalled, the threads must have anti-seize compound applied before the reinstallation.

8. If reinstalling the old sensor, coat the threads with anti-seize compound GM P/N 12377953, or equivalent.

9. Install the HO2S. Tighten the sensor to 31 ft. lbs. (42 Nm).

10. If equipped with 4WD perform the following steps, if equipped with 2WD proceed to step 6.

11. Connect the HO2S electrical connector to the engine wiring harness electrical connector.

12. Install the CPA retainer.

13. Connect the HO2S electrical connector to the engine wiring harness electrical connector.

14. Install the CPA retainer.

15. Lower the vehicle.

Bank 2 Sensor 1

See Figure 634.

1. Raise and support the vehicle.

2. Remove the Connector Position Assurance (CPA) retainer.

3. Disconnect the engine wiring harness electrical connector from the HO2S electrical connector.

4. Remove the HO2S clip from the engine wiring harness clip.

5. Remove the HO2S.

To install:

➡A special anti-seize compound is used on the HO2S threads. The compound consists of liquid graphite and glass beads. The graphite tends to burn away, but the glass beads remain, making the sensor easier to remove. New, or service replacement sensors already have the compound applied to the threads. If the sensor is removed from an exhaust component and if for any reason the sensor is to be reinstalled, the threads must have anti-seize compound applied before the reinstallation.

6. If reinstalling the old sensor, coat the threads with anti-seize compound GM P/N 12377953, or equivalent.

7. Install the HO2S. Tighten the sensor to 31 ft. lbs. (42 Nm).

8. Connect the engine wiring harness electrical connector to the HO2S electrical connector.

9. Install the CPA retainer.

10. Install the HO2S clip to the engine wiring harness clip.

11. Lower the vehicle.

Bank 2 Sensor 2

See Figure 634.

1. Raise and support the vehicle.

2. Remove the Connector Position Assurance (CPA) retainer.

3. Disconnect the HO2S electrical connector from the engine wiring harness electrical connector.

4. Remove the HO2S.

To install:

➡A special anti-seize compound is used on the HO2S threads. The compound consists of liquid graphite and glass beads. The graphite tends to burn away, but the glass beads remain, making the sensor easier to remove. New, or service replacement sensors already have the compound applied to the threads. If the sensor is removed from an exhaust component and if for any reason the sensor is to be reinstalled, the threads must have anti-seize compound applied before the reinstallation.

5. If reinstalling the old sensor, coat the threads with anti-seize compound GM P/N 12377953, or equivalent.

6. Install the HO2S. Tighten the sensor to 31 ft. lbs. (42 Nm).

7. Connect the HO2S electrical connector to the engine wiring harness electrical connector.

8. Install the CPA retainer.

9. Lower the vehicle.

INTAKE AIR TEMPERATURE (IAT) SENSOR

The Intake Air Temperature (IAT) sensor is an integral part of the Mass Air Flow (MAF) sensor/Intake Air Temperature (IAT) sensor assembly which is mounted on the air intake duct. Refer to the Mass Air Flow (MAF) section for information regarding servicing this component.

KNOCK SENSOR (KS)

LOCATION

Refer to the graphics in the Removal and Installation section for the location(s).

REMOVAL & INSTALLATION

V6 Engines

Knock Sensor 1

See Figures 635 and 636.

1. Raise and suitably support the vehicle.
2. If equipped, remove the oil pan skid plate and bolts.
3. Remove the knock sensor heat shield bolt and shield.
4. Reposition the knock sensor sleeve down, away from the knock sensor.
5. Disconnect the engine wiring harness electrical connector from the knock sensor.
6. Remove the knock sensor bolt and sensor.

To install:

7. Position the knock sensor to the engine block and install the bolt. Tighten the bolt to 18 ft. lbs. (25 Nm).
8. Connect the engine wiring harness electrical connector to the knock sensor.
9. Position the knock sensor sleeve up and over the knock sensor.

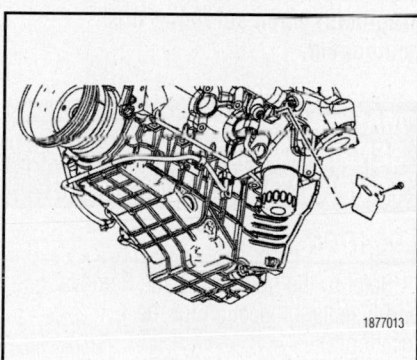

Fig. 635 Remove the knock sensor heat shield bolt and shield

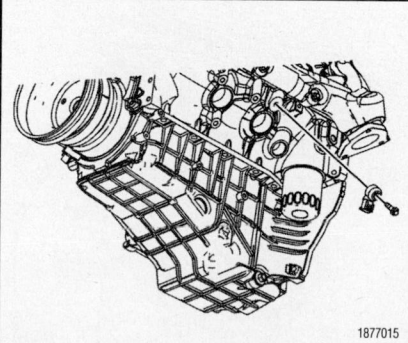

Fig. 636 Remove the knock sensor bolt and sensor

10. Position the knock sensor heat shield to the engine block and install the bolt. Tighten the bolt to 89 inch lbs. (10 Nm).
11. If equipped, position the oil pan skid plate and install the bolts. Tighten the bolts to 21 ft. lbs. (28 Nm).
12. Lower the vehicle.

Knock Sensor 2

See Figure 637.

1. Raise and suitably support the vehicle.
2. If equipped, remove the oil pan skid plate and bolts.
3. Reposition the knock sensor sleeve down, away from the knock sensor.
4. Disconnect the engine wiring harness electrical connector from the knock sensor.
5. Remove the knock sensor bolt and sensor.

To install:

6. Position the knock sensor to the engine block and install the bolt. Tighten the bolt to 18 ft. lbs. (25 Nm).
7. Connect the engine wiring harness electrical connector to the knock sensor.

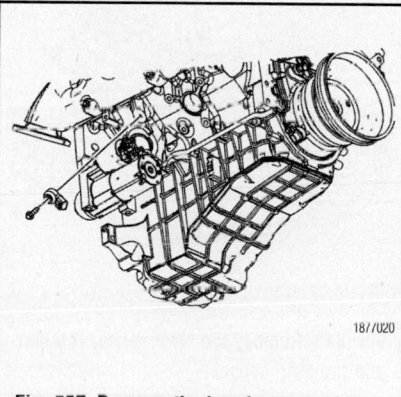

Fig. 637 Remove the knock sensor bolt and sensor

8. Position the knock sensor sleeve up and over the knock sensor.
9. Position the knock sensor heat shield to the engine block and install the bolt. Tighten the bolt to 89 inch lbs. (10 Nm).
10. If equipped, position the oil pan skid plate and install the bolts. Tighten the bolts to 21 ft. lbs. (28 Nm).
11. Lower the vehicle.

V8 Engines

Knock Sensor 1

See Figure 638.

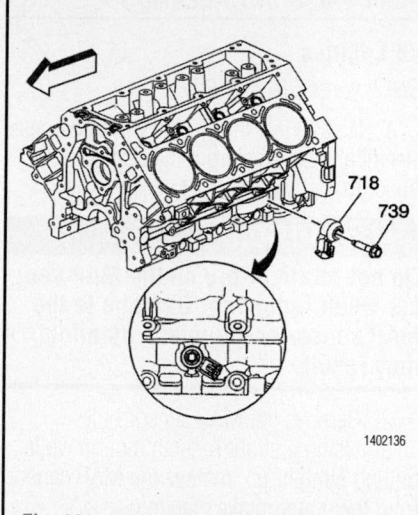

Fig. 638 Remove the knock sensor bolt (739) and knock sensor (718)

1. Lift and support the vehicle.
2. Disconnect the engine wiring harness electrical connector from knock sensor.
3. Remove the knock sensor bolt and knock sensor.

To install:

4. Position the knock sensor to the engine block and install the knock sensor bolt. Tighten the bolt to 18 ft. lbs. (25 Nm).
5. Connect the engine wiring harness electrical connector to knock sensor.

Knock Sensor 2

See Figure 638.

1. Lift and support the vehicle.
2. Disconnect the engine wiring harness electrical connector from knock sensor.
3. Remove the knock sensor bolt and knock sensor.

➡Knock sensor 1 shown, sensor 2 similar on the opposite side of engine block.

To install:

4. Position the knock sensor to the engine block and install the knock sensor bolt. Tighten the bolt to 18 ft. lbs. (25 Nm).
5. Connect the engine wiring harness electrical connector to knock sensor.

MANIFOLD ABSOLUTE PRESSURE (MAP) SENSOR

LOCATION

Refer to the graphics in the Removal and Installation section for the location(s).

REMOVAL & INSTALLATION

V6 Engines

See Figures 639 and 640.

1. Disconnect the engine wiring harness electrical connector from the Manifold Absolute Pressure (MAP) sensor.

> **❋❋ CAUTION**
>
> **Do not rotate or pry on the MAP sensor when removing. Damage to the MAP sensor or the intake manifold may result.**

2. Remove the MAP sensor bolt.
3. Using a slight rocking motion while pulling straight up, remove the MAP sensor from the upper intake manifold.
4. Inspect the MAP sensor seal for damage, replace the seal if necessary.

To install:

5. Install a NEW MAP sensor seal to the MAP sensor, if necessary.
6. Install the MAP sensor to the upper intake manifold.

7. Install the MAP sensor bolt. Tighten the bolt to 89 inch lbs. (10 Nm).
8. Connect the engine wiring harness electrical connector to the MAP sensor.

V8 Engines

See Figure 641.

1. Remove the intake manifold sight shield.
2. Disconnect the engine wiring harness electrical connector from the Manifold Absolute Pressure (MAP) sensor.
3. Remove the MAP sensor retainer.
4. Remove the MAP sensor.

To install:

➡**Lightly coat the MAP sensor seal with clean engine oil before installing the sensor.**

5. Install the MAP sensor.
6. Install the MAP sensor retainer.
7. Connect the engine harness wiring electrical connector to the MAP sensor.
8. Install the intake manifold sight shield.

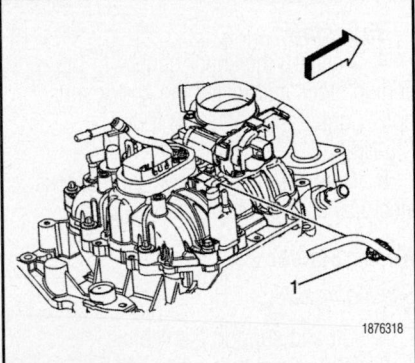

Fig. 639 Disconnect the engine wiring harness electrical connector (1) from the MAP sensor

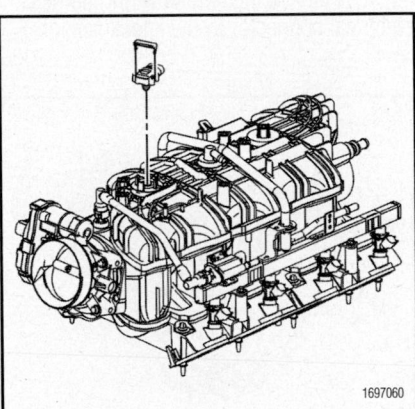

Fig. 641 Remove the MAP sensor retainer and the MAP sensor

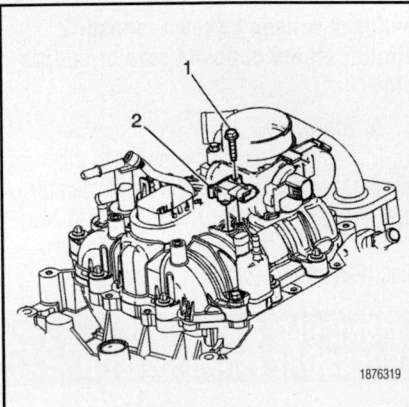

Fig. 640 Remove the MAP sensor bolt (1) and the MAP sensor (2)

2010 Diesel Engines

See Figure 642.

1. Disconnect the engine wiring harness electrical connector from the Manifold Absolute Pressure (MAP) sensor.
2. Remove the MAP sensor bolt.
3. Remove the MAP sensor bracket and sensor.

To install:

4. Install the MAP sensor and bracket.
5. Install the MAP sensor bolt. Tighten the bolt to 89 inch lbs. (10 Nm).
6. Connect the engine wiring harness electrical connector to the MAP sensor.

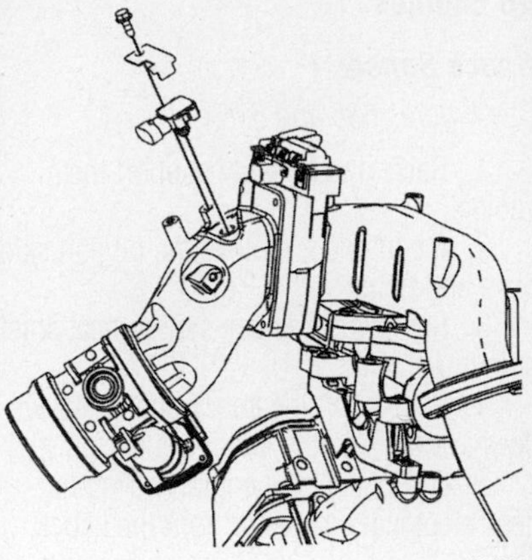

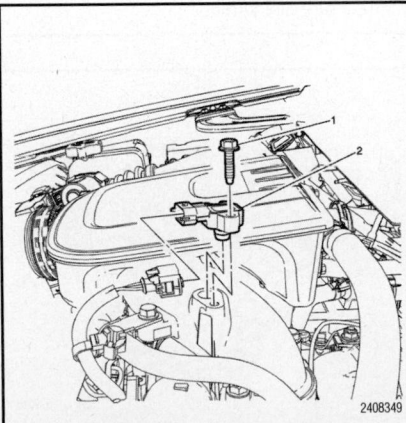

Fig. 642 Remove the MAP sensor bolt, bracket, and sensor

2011 Diesel Engines

See Figure 643.

➡**The manufacturer does not provide a specific Removal and Installation procedure for this component. Refer to the graphic(s) when servicing this component.**

MASS AIR FLOW (MAF) SENSOR/INTAKE AIR TEMPERATURE (IAT) SENSOR

LOCATION

Refer to the graphics in the Removal and Installation section for the location(s).

Fig. 643 Remove the Manifold Absolute Pressure (MAP) sensor bolt (1) and the MAP sensor (2)

REMOVAL & INSTALLATION

V6 Engines

See Figure 644.

➡The manufacturer does not provide a specific Removal and Installation procedure for this component. Refer to the graphic(s) when servicing this component.

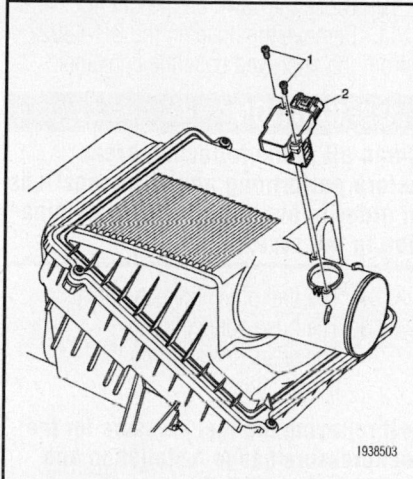

Fig. 644 Remove the Mass Air Flow (MAF) sensor screw (1) and sensor (2)

V8 Engines

See Figure 645.

➡The manufacturer does not provide a specific Removal and Installation procedure for this component. Refer to the graphic(s) when servicing this component.

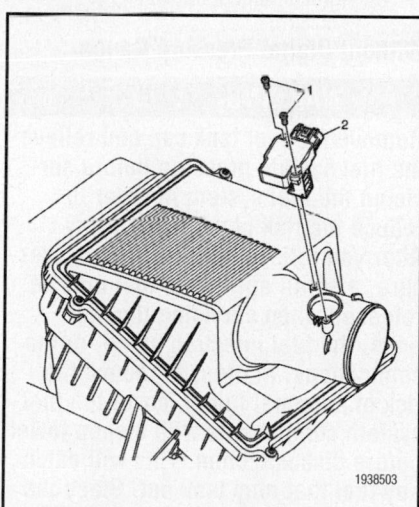

Fig. 645 Mass Airflow Sensor/Intake Air Temperature Sensor (2) and mounting screws (1)

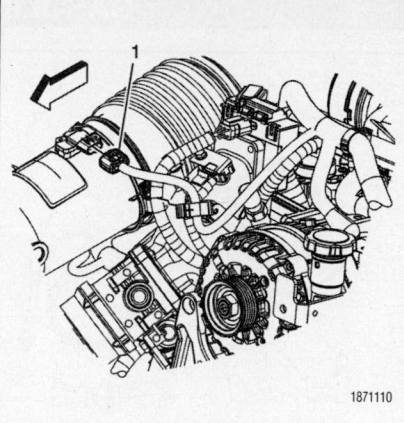

Fig. 646 Disconnect the engine wiring harness electrical connector (1) from the MAF/IAT sensor

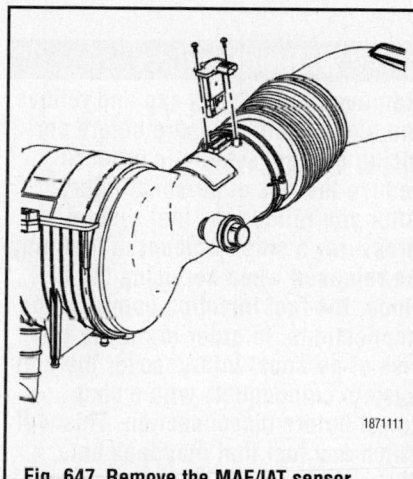

Fig. 647 Remove the MAF/IAT sensor TORX screws and the sensor

2010 Diesel Engines

See Figures 646 and 647.

1. Disconnect the engine wiring harness electrical connector from the Mass Air Flow (MAF)/Intake Air Temperature (IAT) sensor.
2. Remove the MAF/IAT sensor TORX screws.
3. Remove the MAF/IAT sensor.

To install:

4. Install the MAF/IAT sensor.
5. Install the MAF/IAT sensor TORX screws.
6. Connect the engine wiring harness electrical connector to the MAF/IAT sensor

Intake Air Temperature (IAT) Sensor 2

See Figure 648.

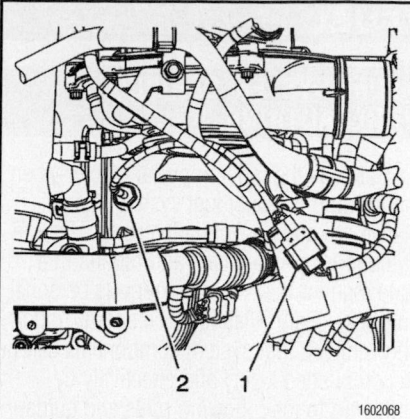

Fig. 648 Disconnect the engine wiring harness electrical connector (1) from the IAT sensor 2 pigtail, remove the IAT sensor (2)

1. Remove the air intake pipe.
2. Disconnect the engine wiring harness electrical connector from the Intake Air Temperature (IAT) sensor 2 pigtail.
3. Remove the IAT sensor from the center intake manifold.

To install:

4. Install the IAT sensor to the center intake manifold. Tighten the sensor to 18 ft. lbs. (25 Nm),
5. Connect the engine wiring harness electrical connector to the IAT sensor pigtail.
6. Install the air intake pipe.

2011 Diesel Engines

See Figure 649.

➡The manufacturer does not provide a specific Removal and Installation procedure for this component. Refer to the graphic(s) when servicing this component.

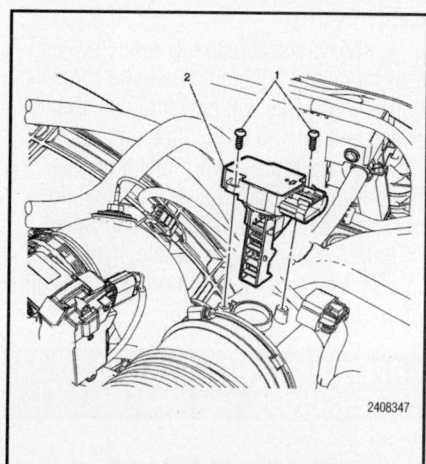

Fig. 649 Remove the Mass Air Flow (MAF) sensor screw (1) and sensor (2)

FUEL **GASOLINE FUEL INJECTION SYSTEM**

FUEL SYSTEM SERVICE PRECAUTIONS

Safety is the most important factor when performing not only fuel system maintenance but any type of maintenance. Failure to conduct maintenance and repairs in a safe manner may result in serious personal injury or death. Maintenance and testing of the vehicle's fuel system components can be accomplished safely and effectively by adhering to the following rules and guidelines.

• To avoid the possibility of fire and personal injury, always disconnect the negative battery cable unless the repair or test procedure requires that battery voltage be applied.

• Always relieve the fuel system pressure prior to disconnecting any fuel system component (injector, fuel rail, pressure regulator, etc.), fitting or fuel line connection. Exercise extreme caution whenever relieving fuel system pressure to avoid exposing skin, face and eyes to fuel spray. Please be advised that fuel under pressure may penetrate the skin or any part of the body that it contacts.

• Always place a shop towel or cloth around the fitting or connection prior to loosening to absorb any excess fuel due to spillage. Ensure that all fuel spillage (should it occur) is quickly removed from engine surfaces. Ensure that all fuel soaked cloths or towels are deposited into a suitable waste container.

• Always keep a dry chemical (Class B) fire extinguisher near the work area.

• Do not allow fuel spray or fuel vapors to come into contact with a spark or open flame.

• Always use a back-up wrench when loosening and tightening fuel line connection fittings. This will prevent unnecessary stress and torsion to fuel line piping.

• Always replace worn fuel fitting O-rings with new Do not substitute fuel hose or equivalent where fuel pipe is installed.

Before servicing the vehicle, make sure to also refer to the precautions in the beginning of this section as well.

RELIEVING FUEL SYSTEM PRESSURE

With Digital Pressure Gauge
See Figure 650.

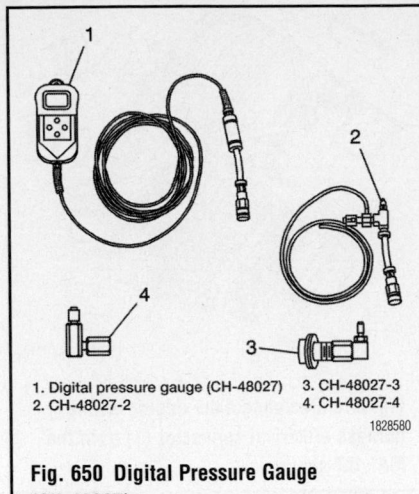

1. Digital pressure gauge (CH-48027)
2. CH-48027-2
3. CH-48027-3
4. CH-48027-4

1828580

Fig. 650 Digital Pressure Gauge (CH-48027)

✳✳ WARNING

Remove the fuel tank cap and relieve the fuel system pressure before servicing the fuel system in order to reduce the risk of personal injury. After you relieve the fuel system pressure, a small amount of fuel may be released when servicing the fuel lines, the fuel injection pump, or the connections. In order to reduce the risk of personal injury, cover the fuel system components with a shop towel before disconnection. This will catch any fuel that may leak out. Place the towel in an approved container when the disconnection is complete.

1. If the fuel system requires repair, prevent fuel spillage by removing the fuel pump fuse.
2. Remove the engine cover, if required.
3. Loosen the fuel fill cap in order to relieve the fuel tank vapor pressure.
4. Remove the fuel rail service port cap.

✳✳ WARNING

Wrap a shop towel around the fuel pressure connection in order to reduce the risk of fire and personal injury. The towel will absorb any fuel leakage that occurs during the connection of the fuel pressure gauge. Place the towel in an approved container when the connection of the fuel pressure gauge is complete.

5. Wrap a shop towel around the fuel rail service port.

6. Connect the CH-48027-3 to the fuel rail service port.
7. Connect the CH-48027-2 to the CH-48027-3.
8. Place the hose on the CH-48027-2 into an approved gasoline container.
9. Open the valve on the CH-48027-2 in order to bleed any fuel from the fuel rail.
10. Close the valve on the CH-48027-2.
11. Remove the hose on the CH-48027-2 from the approved gasoline container.

✳✳ CAUTION

Clean all of the following areas before performing any disconnections in order to avoid possible contamination in the system:

• The fuel pipe connections
• The hose connections
• The areas surrounding the connections

➡ **If relieving the fuel pressure for the fuel pressure gauge installation and removal, it is NOT necessary to proceed with the following steps.**

12. Disconnect the CH-48027-2 from the CH-48027-3.
13. Disconnect the CH-48027-3 from the fuel rail service port.
14. Remove the shop towel from around the fuel rail service port, and place in an approved gasoline container.
15. Install the fuel rail service port cap.
16. Install the engine cover, if required.
17. Tighten the fuel fill cap.

Without Digital Pressure Gauge

✳✳ WARNING

Remove the fuel tank cap and relieve the fuel system pressure before servicing the fuel system in order to reduce the risk of personal injury. After you relieve the fuel system pressure, a small amount of fuel may be released when servicing the fuel lines, the fuel injection pump, or the connections. In order to reduce the risk of personal injury, cover the fuel system components with a shop towel before disconnection. This will catch any fuel that may leak out. Place the towel in an approved container when the disconnection is complete.

1. If the fuel system requires repair, prevent fuel spillage by removing the fuel pump fuse.

2. Loosen the fuel fill cap in order to relieve the fuel tank vapor pressure.

3. Remove the engine cover, if required.

4. Remove the fuel rail service port cap.

5. Wrap a shop towel around the fuel rail service port and using a small flat-bladed tool, depress (open) the fuel rail test port valve.

6. Remove the shop towel from around the fuel rail service port, and place in an approved gasoline container.

7. Install the fuel rail service port cap.

8. Install the engine cover, if required.

9. Tighten the fuel fill cap.

FUEL FILTER

REMOVAL & INSTALLATION

The fuel filter is an integral part of the fuel tank pump module. Refer to the fuel tank pump module to service this component.

FUEL INJECTORS

REMOVAL & INSTALLATION

V6 Engines

See Figure 651.

➡The engine oil may be contaminated with fuel if the fuel injectors are leaking.

1. Remove the fuel meter body.

2. Remove the injector retainer lock nuts and retainer.

✳✳ CAUTION

Use care in removing the fuel injectors to prevent damage to the electri-

cal connector terminals. The fuel injector is serviced as a complete assembly only. Also since the injectors are electrical components, these injectors should not be immersed in any type of liquid solvent or cleaner as damage may occur. Fuel injector cleaning is not recommended.

3. While pulling the fuel injector downward, push with a small tip punch down between the injector terminals until the injector is removed.

To install:

➡When ordering new fuel injectors, be sure to order the correct injector for the application being serviced.

4. Lubricate the NEW injector O-ring seals with clean engine oil.

5. Install the fuel injector into the fuel meter body injector socket.

6. Install the injector retainer and the injector retainer lock nuts.

7. Install the fuel meter body.

V8 Engines

See Figures 652 through 660.

✳✳ CAUTION

Use care in removing the fuel injectors in order to prevent damage to the fuel injector electrical connector pins or the fuel injector nozzles. Do not immerse the fuel injector in any type of cleaner. The fuel injector is an electrical component and may be damaged by this cleaning method.

➡An 8-digit identification number is located on the fuel rail. Refer to this identification number when servicing or when part replacement is required.

➡The engine oil may be contaminated with fuel if the fuel injectors are leaking.

1. Remove the air cleaner outlet duct.

2. Relieve the fuel system pressure.

3. Remove the engine wiring harness bracket nut.

4. Disconnect the engine wiring harness electrical connector from the Evaporative Emission (EVAP) purge solenoid.

5. Disconnect the engine wiring harness electrical connector from the alternator.

6. Disconnect the engine wiring harness electrical connector from the Manifold Absolute Pressure (MAP) sensor.

7. Remove the Connector Position Assurance (CPA) retainer.

8. Disconnect the engine wiring harness electrical connector from the ignition coil main electrical connector.

9. Disconnect the engine wiring harness electrical connectors from the fuel injectors, perform the following:

   a. Mark the connectors to their corresponding injectors to ensure correct reassembly.

   b. Pull the CPA retainer on the connector up 1 click.

   c. Push the tab on the connector in.

   d. Disconnect the fuel injector electrical connector.

10. Remove the CPA retainer.

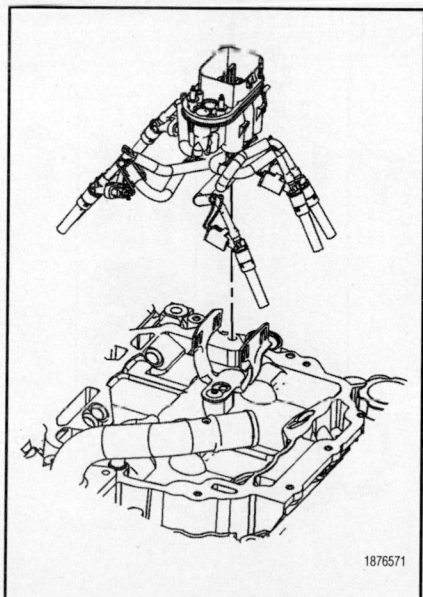

Fig. 651 Remove the fuel meter body

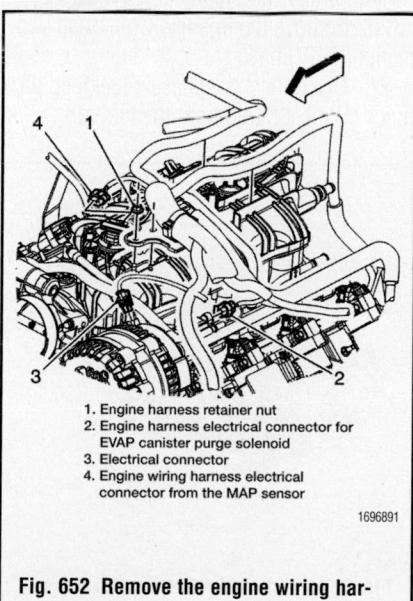

1. Engine harness retainer nut
2. Engine harness electrical connector for EVAP canister purge solenoid
3. Electrical connector
4. Engine wiring harness electrical connector from the MAP sensor

1696891

Fig. 652 Remove the engine wiring harness bracket nut

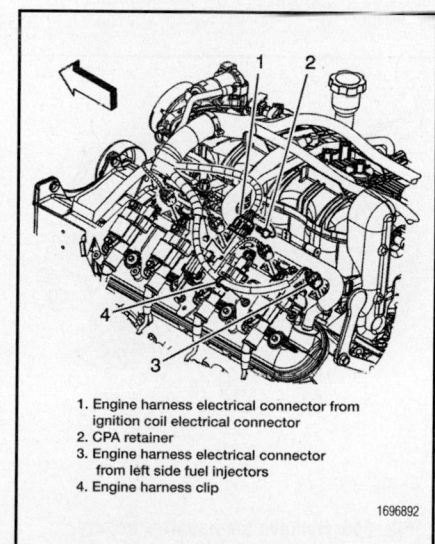

1. Engine harness electrical connector from ignition coil electrical connector
2. CPA retainer
3. Engine harness electrical connector from left side fuel injectors
4. Engine harness clip

1696892

Fig. 653 Remove the Connector Position Assurance (CPA) retainer

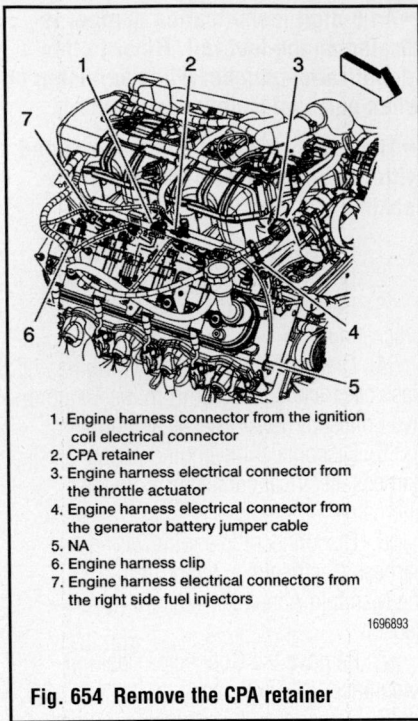

1. Engine harness connector from the ignition coil electrical connector
2. CPA retainer
3. Engine harness electrical connector from the throttle actuator
4. Engine harness electrical connector from the generator battery jumper cable
5. NA
6. Engine harness clip
7. Engine harness electrical connectors from the right side fuel injectors

Fig. 654 Remove the CPA retainer

11. Disconnect the engine wiring harness electrical connector from the ignition coil main electrical connector.

12. Disconnect the engine wiring harness electrical connector from the electronic throttle control.

13. Disconnect the engine wiring harness electrical connectors from the fuel injectors, perform the following:

    a. Mark the connectors to their corresponding injectors to ensure correct reassembly.

    b. Pull the CPA retainer on the connector up 1 click.

    c. Push the tab on the connector in.

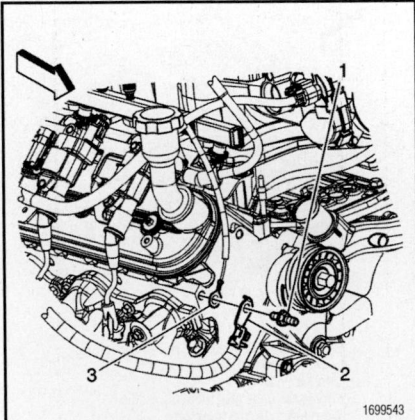

Fig. 655 Remove the negative battery cable stud (1), the negative battery cable terminal (2) and engine wiring harness ground terminal (3)

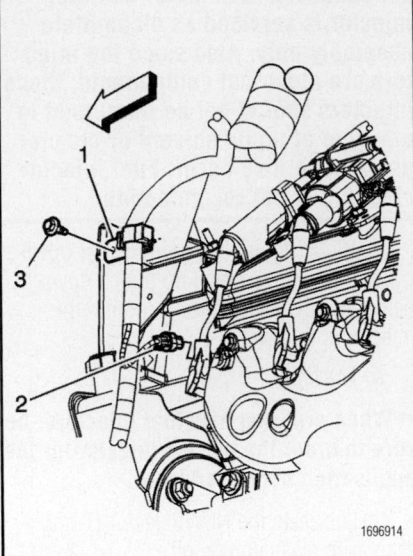

Fig. 656 Remove the engine wiring harness clip (1) bolt (3) from the alternator bracket; electrical connector (2)

    d. Disconnect the fuel injector electrical connector.

14. Remove the engine wiring harness clip from the alternator battery jumper cable.

15. Remove the engine wiring harness clip from the ignition coil bracket stud.

16. Remove the negative battery cable stud from the right cylinder head.

17. Remove the negative battery cable terminal and engine wiring harness ground terminal from the cylinder head.

18. Remove the engine wiring harness clip bolt from the alternator bracket.

19. Gather the branches of the engine wiring harness and reposition the aside.

20. Remove the Positive Crankcase Ventilation (PCV) hose.

21. Disconnect the chassis fuel feed pipe quick connect fitting from the fuel rail.

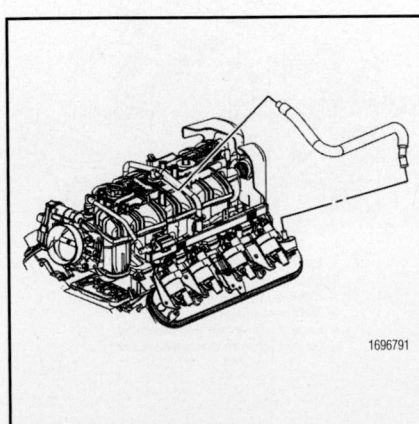

Fig. 657 Remove the Positive Crankcase Ventilation (PCV) hose

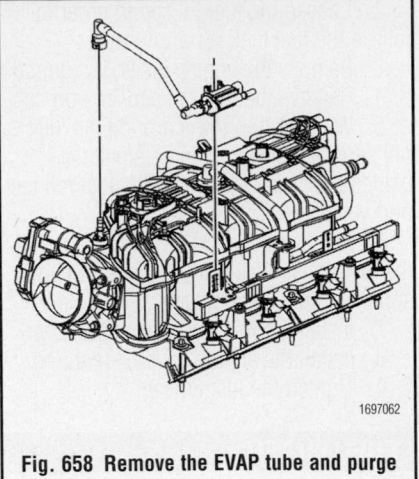

Fig. 658 Remove the EVAP tube and purge solenoid

22. Disconnect the EVAP tube quick connect fitting at the intake manifold.

23. Disconnect the chassis EVAP tube quick connect fitting at the EVAP canister purge solenoid.

24. Disengage the retainer securing the EVAP canister purge solenoid to the fuel rail.

25. Remove the EVAP tube and purge solenoid.

26. Remove the fuel rail bolts.

✳✳ CAUTION

Remove the fuel rail assembly carefully in order to prevent damage to the injector electrical connector terminals and the injector spray tips. Support the fuel rail after the fuel rail is removed in order to avoid damaging the fuel rail components.

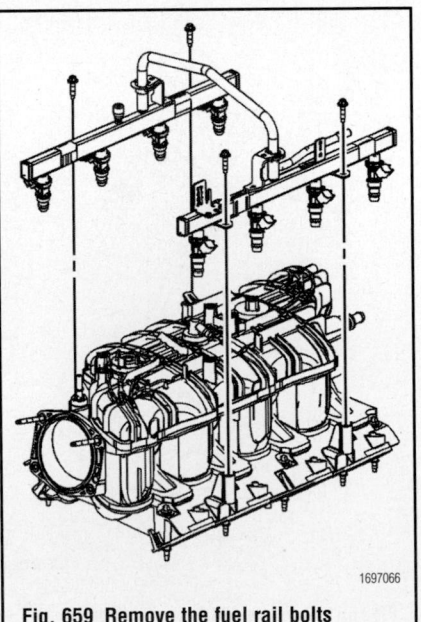

Fig. 659 Remove the fuel rail bolts

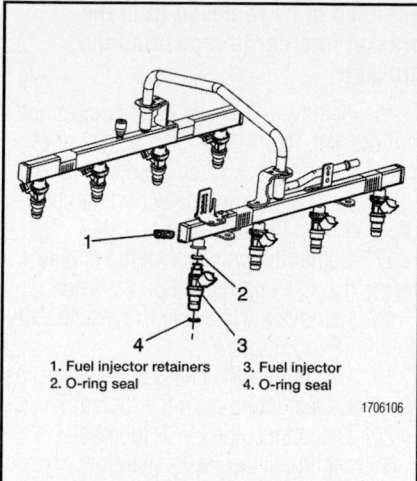

1. Fuel injector retainers   3. Fuel injector
2. O-ring seal   4. O-ring seal

1706106

Fig. 660 Remove the fuel rail assembly

✳✳ CAUTION

Cap the fittings and plug the holes when servicing the fuel system in order to prevent dirt and other contaminants from entering open pipes and passages.

➡ Before removal, clean the fuel rail with a spray type engine cleaner, such as GM X-30A or equivalent, if necessary. Follow the package instructions. Do not soak the fuel rail in liquid cleaning solvent.

➡ Lift evenly on both sides of the fuel rail until all injectors are removed from their bores.

27. Remove the fuel rail assembly.
28. Remove the fuel injector retainers.
29. Remove the fuel injectors from the fuel rail.
30. Remove and discard the fuel injector upper and lower O-ring seals.

To install:

31. Lubricate the NEW fuel injector O-ring seals with clean engine oil.
32. Install the NEW fuel injector upper and lower O-ring seals onto the injectors.
33. Install the fuel injectors into the fuel rails.
34. Install the fuel injector retainers.
35. Ensure the fuel injector lower O-ring seals are adequately lubricated, if not lubricate the fuel injector lower O-ring seals with clean engine oil.
36. Position the fuel rail onto the intake manifold.
37. Firmly push down on both the centers of the left and right fuel rails, until the rails are fully seated against the intake manifold.

➡ Push down firmly on both sides of the rail until all injectors have been seated into their bores.

38. Install the fuel rail bolts. Tighten the bolts to 89 inch lbs. (10 Nm).
39. Install the EVAP tube and purge solenoid.
40. Install the EVAP canister purge solenoid to the fuel rail bracket and engage the retainer.
41. Connect the chassis EVAP tube quick connect fitting at the EVAP canister purge solenoid.
42. Connect the EVAP tube quick connect fitting at the intake manifold.
43. Connect the chassis fuel feed pipe quick connect fitting to the fuel rail.
44. Install the PCV hose.
45. Gather the branches of the engine wiring harness and position over the top of the engine.
46. Position the engine wiring harness clip to the alternator bracket and install the clip bolt. Tighten the bolts to 80 inch lbs. (9 Nm).
47. Position the negative battery cable terminal and engine wiring harness ground terminal to the right cylinder head.
48. Install the negative battery cable stud to the cylinder head. Tighten the stud to 18 ft. lbs. (25 Nm).
49. Connect the engine wiring harness electrical connector to the ignition coil main electrical connector.
50. Install the CPA retainer.
51. Connect the engine wiring harness electrical connector to the electronic throttle control.
52. Connect the engine wiring harness electrical connectors to the fuel injectors, perform the following:
   a. Ensure that the CPA retainer is pulled out 1 click.
   b. Connect the electrical connectors to their corresponding injectors.
   c. Push the CPA retainer in 1 click.
   d. Ensure that the connector is secured.
53. Install the engine wiring harness clip to the alternator battery jumper cable.
54. Install the engine wiring harness clip to the ignition coil bracket stud.
55. Connect the engine wiring harness electrical connector to the ignition coil main electrical connector.
56. Install the CPA retainer.
57. Connect the engine wiring harness electrical connectors to the fuel injectors, perform the following:
   a. Ensure that the CPA retainer is pulled out 1 click.

   b. Connect the electrical connectors to their corresponding injectors.
   c. Push the CPA retainer in 1 click.
   d. Ensure that the connector is secured.
58. Connect the engine wiring harness electrical connector to the MAP sensor.
59. Connect the engine wiring harness electrical connector to the alternator.
60. Connect the engine wiring harness electrical connector to the EVAP purge solenoid.
61. Install the engine wiring harness bracket nut.
62. Connect the negative battery cable.
63. Use the following procedure in order to inspect for leaks:
   a. Turn the ignition ON, with the engine OFF for 2 seconds.
   b. Turn the ignition OFF for 10 seconds.
   c. Turn the ignition ON, with the engine OFF.
   d. Inspect for leaks.
64. Install the air cleaner outlet duct.

Hybrid Engines

See Figures 661 through 669.

✳✳ CAUTION

Use care in removing the fuel injectors in order to prevent damage to the fuel injector electrical connector pins or the fuel injector nozzles. Do not immerse the fuel injector in any type of cleaner. The fuel injector is an electrical component and may be damaged by this cleaning method.

➡ An 8-digit identification number is located on the fuel rail. Refer to this identification number when servicing or when part replacement is required.

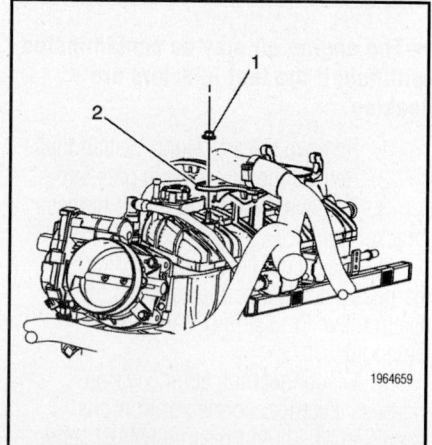

1964659

Fig. 661 Remove the engine wiring harness bracket nut (1)

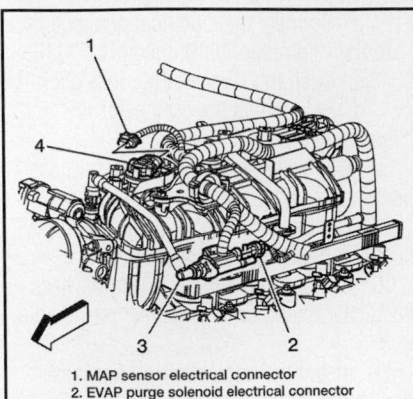

Fig. 662 Disconnect the engine wiring harness electrical connector from the Evaporative Emission (EVAP) purge solenoid

1. MAP sensor electrical connector
2. EVAP purge solenoid electrical connector
3. EVAP purge solenoid
4. MAP sensor

1960247

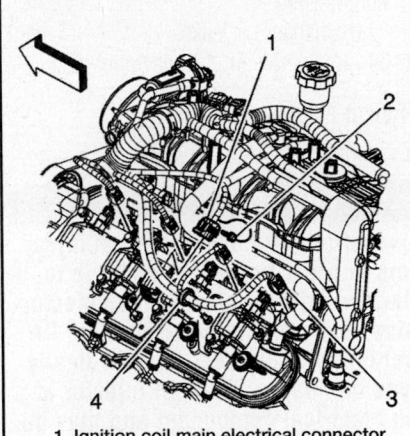

1. Ignition coil main electrical connector
2. CPA retainer
3. Fuel injector electrical connectors
4. Engine wiring harness clip

1964662

Fig. 663 Remove the Connector Position Assurance (CPA) retainer

➡The engine oil may be contaminated with fuel if the fuel injectors are leaking.

1. Remove the air cleaner outlet duct.
2. Relieve the fuel system pressure.
3. Remove the engine wiring harness bracket nut.
4. Disconnect the engine wiring harness electrical connector from the Evaporative Emission (EVAP) purge solenoid.
5. Disconnect the engine wiring harness electrical connector from the Manifold Absolute Pressure (MAP) sensor.
6. Remove the Connector Position Assurance (CPA) retainer.

7. Disconnect the engine wiring harness electrical connector from the ignition coil main electrical connector.
8. Disconnect the engine wiring harness electrical connectors from the fuel injectors, perform the following:
   a. Mark the connectors to their corresponding injectors to ensure correct reassembly.
   b. Pull the CPA retainer on the connector up 1 click.
   c. Push the tab on the connector in.
   d. Disconnect the fuel injector electrical connector.
9. Remove the engine wiring harness clip from the ignition coil bracket stud.
10. Remove the CPA retainer.
11. Disconnect the engine wiring harness electrical connector from the ignition coil main electrical connector.
12. Disconnect the engine wiring harness electrical connector from the electronic throttle control.
13. Disconnect the engine wiring harness electrical connectors from the fuel injectors, perform the following:
   a. Mark the connectors to their corresponding injectors to ensure correct reassembly.
   b. Pull the CPA retainer on the connector up 1 click.
   c. Push the tab on the connector in.
   d. Disconnect the fuel injector electrical connector.
14. Remove the engine wiring harness clip from the ignition coil bracket stud.

➡The auxiliary heater water pump hose and the surge tank outlet hose do

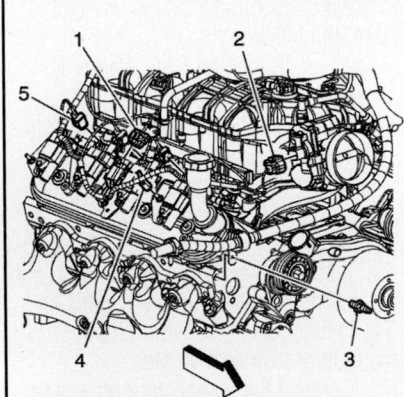

1. Ignition coil main electrical connector
2. Electronic throttle control electrical connector
3. Stud bolt
4. Engine wiring harness clip
5. Fuel injector electrical connectors

1960882

Fig. 664 Disconnect the engine wiring harness electrical connector from the ignition coil main electrical connector

not need to be removed from the bracket in order to reposition the bracket.

15. Remove the heater hose bracket nut and bracket. Reposition the bracket out of the way. Hoses shown removed for clarity.
16. Remove the engine wiring harness clip bolt from the alternator bracket.
17. Gather the branches of the engine wiring harness and reposition the aside.
18. Remove the Positive Crankcase Ventilation (PCV) hose.
19. Disconnect the chassis fuel feed pipe quick connect fitting from the fuel rail.
20. Disconnect the EVAP tube quick connect fitting at the intake manifold.
21. Disconnect the chassis EVAP tube quick connect fitting at the EVAP canister purge solenoid.
22. Disengage the retainer securing the EVAP canister purge solenoid to the fuel rail.
23. Remove the EVAP tube and purge solenoid.

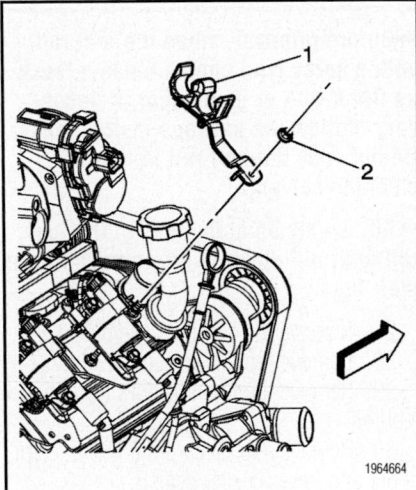

1964664

Fig. 665 Remove the heater hose bracket nut (2) and bracket (1)

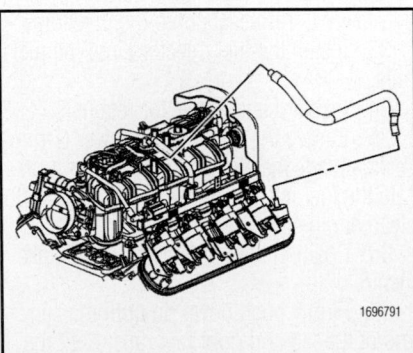

1696791

Fig. 666 Remove the Positive Crankcase Ventilation (PCV) hose

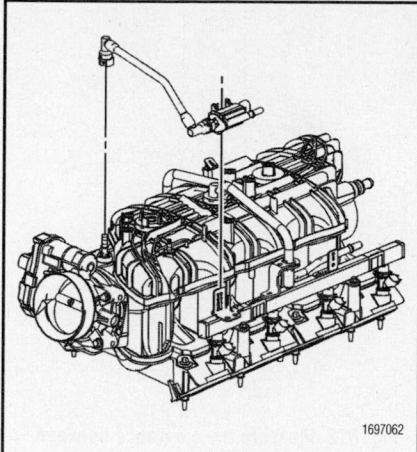

Fig. 667 Remove the EVAP tube and purge solenoid

24. Remove the fuel rail bolts.

> ☀☀ **CAUTION**
>
> **Remove the fuel rail assembly carefully in order to prevent damage to the injector electrical connector terminals and the injector spray tips. Support the fuel rail after the fuel rail is removed in order to avoid damaging the fuel rail components.**

> ☀☀ **CAUTION**
>
> **Cap the fittings and plug the holes when servicing the fuel system in order to prevent dirt and other contaminants from entering open pipes and passages.**

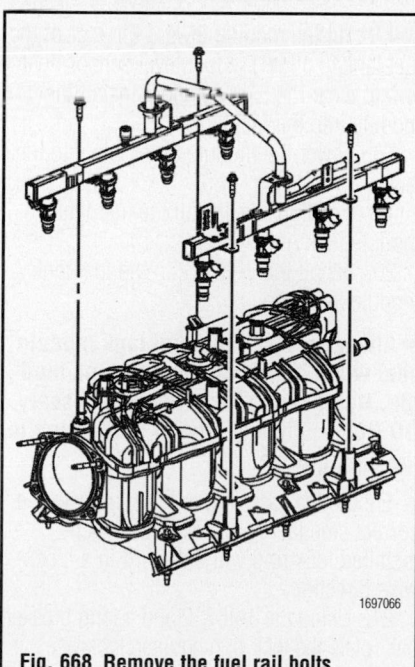

Fig. 668 Remove the fuel rail bolts

➡️**Before removal, clean the fuel rail with a spray type engine cleaner, such as GM X-30A or equivalent, if necessary. Follow the package instructions. Do not soak the fuel rail in liquid cleaning solvent.**

➡️**Lift evenly on both sides of the fuel rail until all injectors are removed from their bores.**

25. Remove the fuel rail assembly.
26. Remove the fuel injector retainers.
27. Remove the fuel injectors from the fuel rail.
28. Remove and discard the fuel injector upper and lower O-ring seals.

To install:
29. Lubricate the NEW fuel injector O-ring seals with clean engine oil.
30. Install the NEW fuel injector upper and lower O-ring seals onto the injectors.
31. Install the fuel injectors into the fuel rails.
32. Install the fuel injector retainers.
33. Ensure the fuel injector lower O-ring seals are adequately lubricated, if not lubricate the fuel injector lower O-ring seals with clean engine oil.
34. Position the fuel rail onto the intake manifold.
35. Firmly push down on both the centers of the left and right fuel rails, until the rails are fully seated against the intake manifold.

➡️**Push down firmly on both sides of the rail until all injectors have been seated into their bores.**

36. Install the fuel rail bolts. Tighten the bolts to 89 inch lbs. (10 Nm).
37. Install the EVAP tube and purge solenoid.

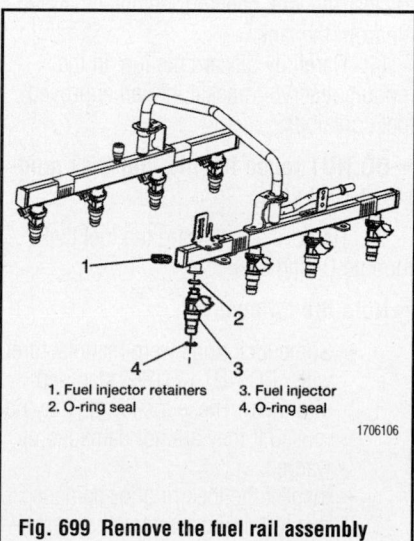

1. Fuel injector retainers
2. O-ring seal
3. Fuel injector
4. O-ring seal

Fig. 699 Remove the fuel rail assembly

38. Install the EVAP canister purge solenoid to the fuel rail bracket and engage the retainer.
39. Connect the chassis EVAP tube quick connect fitting at the EVAP canister purge solenoid.
40. Connect the EVAP tube quick connect fitting at the intake manifold.
41. Connect the chassis fuel feed pipe quick connect fitting to the fuel rail.
42. Install the PCV hose.
43. Gather the branches of the engine wiring harness and position over the top of the engine.
44. Position the engine wiring harness clip to the alternator bracket and install the clip bolt. Tighten the bolt to 80 inch lbs. (9 Nm).
45. Position and install the heater hose bracket to the ignition coil bracket stud. Hoses shown removed for clarity.
46. Install the heater hose bracket nut. Tighten the nut to 80 inch lbs. (9 Nm).
47. Connect the engine wiring harness electrical connector to the ignition coil main electrical connector.
48. Install the CPA retainer.
49. Connect the engine wiring harness electrical connector to the electronic throttle control.
50. Connect the engine wiring harness electrical connectors to the fuel injectors, perform the following:
   a. Ensure that the CPA retainer is pulled out 1 click.
   b. Connect the electrical connectors to their corresponding injectors.
   c. Push the CPA retainer in 1 click.
   d. Ensure that the connector is secured.
51. Install the engine wiring harness clip to the ignition coil bracket stud.
52. Connect the engine wiring harness electrical connector to the ignition coil main electrical connector.
53. Install the CPA retainer.
54. Connect the engine wiring harness electrical connectors to the fuel injectors, perform the following:
   a. Ensure that the CPA retainer is pulled out 1 click.
   b. Connect the electrical connectors to their corresponding injectors.
   c. Push the CPA retainer in 1 click.
   d. Ensure that the connector is secured.
55. Install the engine wiring harness clip to the ignition coil bracket stud.
56. Connect the engine wiring harness electrical connector to the MAP sensor.
57. Connect the engine wiring harness electrical connector to the EVAP purge solenoid.

58. Install the engine wiring harness bracket nut.

59. Connect the negative battery cable.

60. Use the following procedure in order to inspect for leaks:

    a. Turn the ignition ON, with the engine OFF for 2 seconds.

    b. Turn the ignition OFF for 10 seconds.

    c. Turn the ignition ON, with the engine OFF.

    d. Inspect for leaks.

61. Install the air cleaner outlet duct.

FUEL PUMP

REMOVAL & INSTALLATION

See Figures 670 through 672.

1. Remove the fuel tank.

2. Disconnect the fuel tank fuel feed pipe quick connect fitting from the fuel tank module.

3. Disconnect the fuel tank Evaporative Emission (EVAP) pipe quick connect fittings from the fuel tank module.

4. Reposition the fuel and EVAP pipes out of the way.

5. Install the Fuel Sender Lock Ring Wrench (J-45722) to the fuel tank module lock ring.

✳✳ CAUTION

Avoid damaging the lock ring. Use only J-45722 to prevent damage to the lock ring.

➡️**Do NOT use impact tools. Significant force will be required to release the lock ring. The use of a hammer and screwdriver is not recommended. Secure the fuel tank in order to prevent fuel tank rotation.**

6. Using the J-45722 and a long breaker bar, rotate the lock ring clockwise

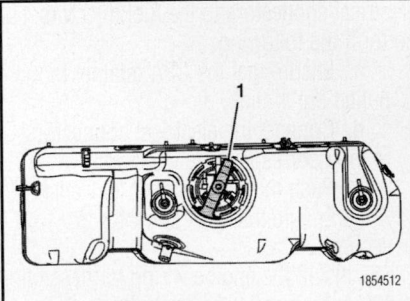

Fig. 670 Install the Fuel Sender Lock Ring Wrench (J-45722) (1) to the fuel tank module lock ring

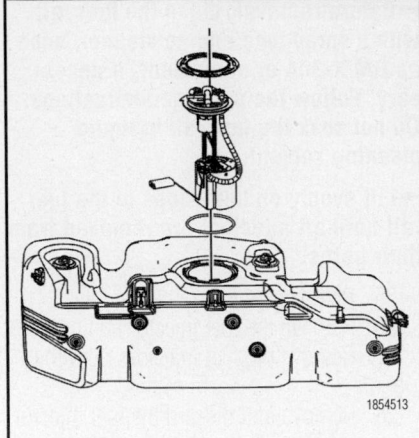

Fig. 671 Remove the fuel tank module lock ring

unlocking the fuel tank module lock ring.

7. Remove the J-45722.

8. Remove the fuel tank module lock ring.

✳✳ CAUTION

Do Not handle the fuel sender assembly by the fuel pipes. The amount of leverage generated by handling the fuel pipes could damage the joints.

9. Slowly raise the module until the fuel level sensor float arm is just visible.

➡️**When removing the module from the fuel tank, be aware that the module reservoir bucket is full of fuel. The module must be tipped slightly during removal to avoid bending the fuel level sensor float arm.**

10. Tilt the module toward the rear of the fuel tank to allow the level sensor float arm to clear the tank opening. Remove the module from the tank.

11. Carefully discard the fuel in the module reservoir bucket into an approved fuel container.

➡️**DO NOT reuse the old fuel tank module O-ring seal.**

12. Remove and discard the fuel tank module O-ring seal.

➡️**Note the following:**

- Some lock rings were manufactured with "DO NOT REUSE" stamped into them. These lock rings may be reused if they are not damaged or warped.
- Inspect the lock ring for damage due to improper removal or instal-

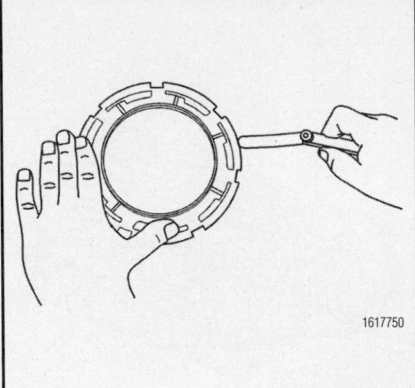

Fig. 672 Measure the clearance between the lock ring and the flat surface using a feeler gauge at 7 points

lation procedures. If damage is found, install a NEW lock ring.

- Check the lock ring for flatness.

13. Place the lock ring on a flat surface. Measure the clearance between the lock ring and the flat surface using a feeler gauge at 7 points.

14. If warpage is less than 0.016 inches (0.41 mm), the lock ring does not require replacement.

15. If warpage is greater than 0.016 inches (0.41 mm), the lock ring must be replaced.

To install:

16. Install a NEW fuel tank module O-ring seal onto the fuel tank.

➡️**The bucket must be tipped slightly during installation to avoid bending the fuel level sensor float arm.**

17. Tilt the module toward the rear of the fuel tank to allow the fuel level sensor float arm to clear the tank opening. Install the module into the fuel tank.

18. Lower the module assembly into the tank.

19. Position and install the fuel tank module lock ring.

20. Install the J-45722 to the fuel tank module lock ring.

➡️**Always replace the fuel tank module seal when installing the fuel tank module. Replace the lock ring if necessary. DO NOT apply any type of lubrication in the seal groove.**

Ensure the lock ring is installed with the correct side facing upward. A correctly installed lock ring will only turn in a clockwise direction.

21. Using the J-45722 and a long breaker bar, rotate the lock ring counterclockwise locking the fuel tank module lock ring.

22. Remove the J-45722 from the fuel tank module lock ring.
23. Position the fuel and EVAP pipes to the module.
24. Connect the fuel tank EVAP pipe quick connect fittings to the fuel tank module.
25. Connect the fuel tank fuel feed pipe quick connect fitting to the fuel tank module.
26. Install the fuel tank.

FUEL TANK

DRAINING

✳✳ WARNING

Gasoline or gasoline vapors are highly flammable. A fire could occur if an ignition source is present. Never drain or store gasoline or diesel fuel in an open container, due to the possibility of fire or explosion. Have a dry chemical (Class B) fire extinguisher nearby.

1. Remove the fuel filler cap.
2. Insert the Fuel Tank Drain Hose (J-45004) down the fuel filler tube attached to the appropriate draining devise.
3. Drain a much fuel as possible.

REMOVAL & INSTALLATION

1500 Series Regular Cab With 26 Gallon Tank

See Figures 673 through 682.

➡Clean the fuel and Evaporative Emission (EVAP) connections and surrounding areas prior to disconnecting the lines in order to avoid possible system contamination.

1. Relieve the fuel system pressure..
2. Drain the fuel tank.
3. Remove the fuel tank fill pipe.
4. Disconnect the fuel tank fuel feed and EVAP line quick connect fittings from the chassis lines.
5. Cap the fuel and EVAP lines in order to prevent possible system contamination.
6. Remove the EVAP canister vent solenoid pipe clip from the frame crossmember.
7. Disconnect the EVAP canister pipe quick connect fitting from the fuel tank EVAP pipe.
8. Disconnect the EVAP canister vent solenoid pipe quick connect fitting from the EVAP canister.
9. Disconnect the chassis wiring harness electrical connector from the EVAP canister vent solenoid.
10. Remove the chassis wiring harness clip from the fuel tank shield.

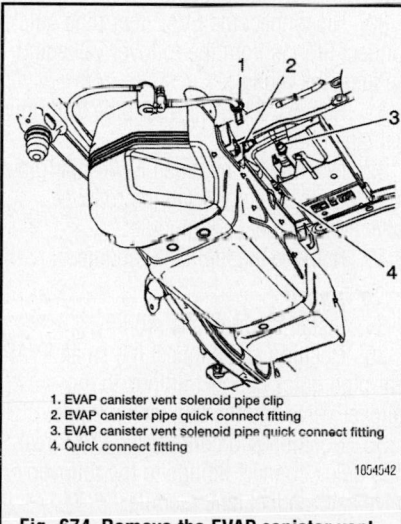

1. EVAP canister vent solenoid pipe clip
2. EVAP canister pipe quick connect fitting
3. EVAP canister vent solenoid pipe quick connect fitting
4. Quick connect fitting

1854542

Fig. 674 Remove the EVAP canister vent solenoid pipe clip from the frame crossmember

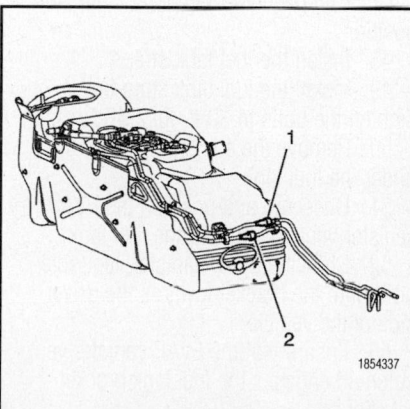

1854337

Fig. 673 Disconnect the fuel tank fuel feed (1) and EVAP (2) line quick connect fittings from the chassis lines

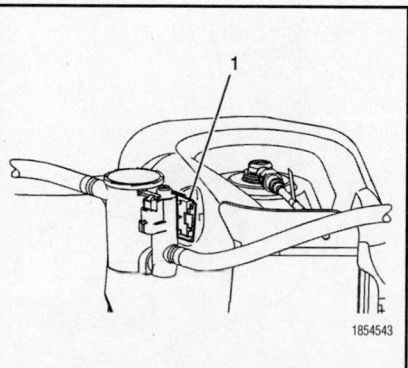

1854543

Fig. 675 Insert a small flat bladed tool between the EVAP canister vent solenoid and the fuel tank bracket, disengaging the retainer (1)

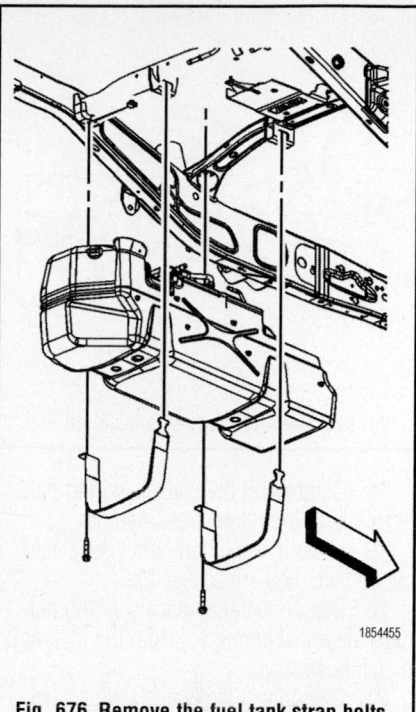

1854455

Fig. 676 Remove the fuel tank strap bolts

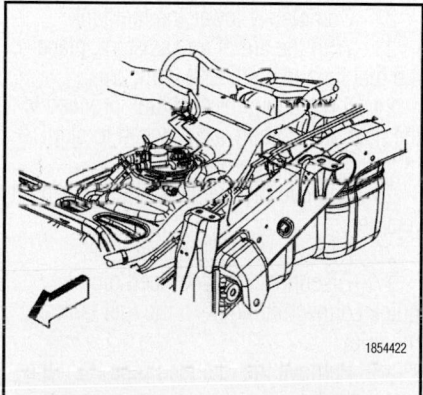

1854422

Fig. 677 Disconnect the chassis wiring harness electrical connector from the fuel tank pressure sensor

11. Insert a small flat bladed tool between the EVAP canister vent solenoid and the fuel tank bracket, disengaging the retainer.
12. Slide the EVAP canister vent solenoid off the bracket towards the passenger side of the vehicle.
13. Position and secure the EVAP canister vent solenoid out of the way.
14. Place a suitable adjustable jack under the fuel tank.
15. Remove the fuel tank strap bolts.
16. Remove the fuel tank straps.

➡When lowering the tank, ensure that the fill neck on the tank does not get hung up on the chassis wiring harness.

17. Lower the fuel tank half way.

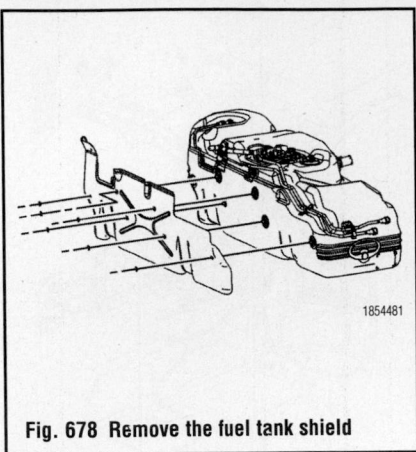

Fig. 678 Remove the fuel tank shield

18. Disconnect the chassis wiring harness clip at the frame crossmember.

19. Lower the fuel tank until the electrical connections are accessible.

20. Disconnect the chassis wiring harness electrical connector from the fuel tank pressure sensor.

21. Disconnect the chassis wiring harness electrical connector from the fuel tank module.

22. Completely lower the fuel tank.

23. With the aid of an assistant, place the fuel tank in a suitable work area.

24. If replacing the fuel tank proceed to the next step, otherwise proceed to step 10 in the installation procedure.

25. Remove the fuel tank shield push on retainers.

26. Remove the fuel tank shield.

27. Disconnect the fuel feed pipe quick connect fitting from the fuel tank module.

28. Remove the fuel feed pipe from the fuel tank clip.

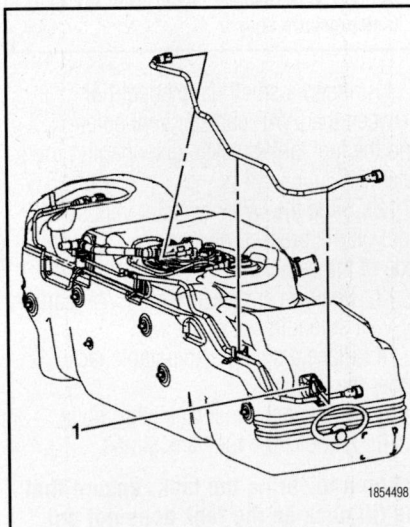

Fig. 679 Remove the fuel feed pipe from the fuel tank clip (1)

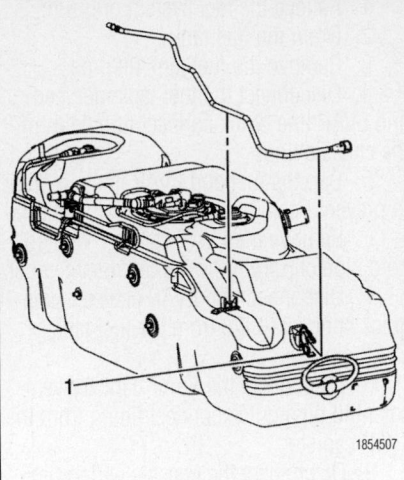

Fig. 680 Remove the EVAP canister purge pipe from the fuel tank clip (1)

29. Remove the EVAP canister purge pipe from the fuel tank clip.

30. Disconnect the EVAP rear pipe quick connect fittings from the rollover valve and the fuel tank module.

31. Remove the EVAP rear pipe from the fuel tank clips.

32. Disconnect the small EVAP rear pipe quick connect fittings from the rollover valve and the fuel tank module.

33. Remove the fuel tank module.

To install:

34. Install the fuel tank module.

35. Position and connect the small EVAP rear pipe quick connect fittings to the rollover valve and the fuel tank module.

36. Position and connect the EVAP rear pipe quick connect fittings to the rollover valve and the fuel tank module.

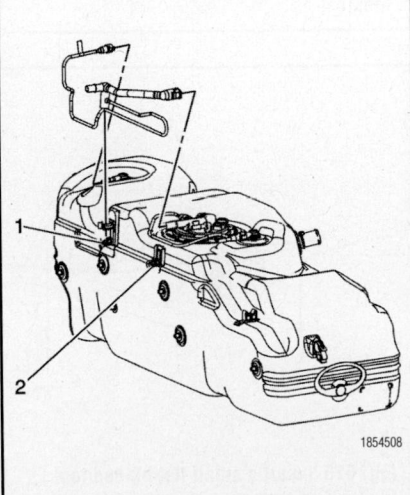

Fig. 681 Remove the EVAP rear pipe from the fuel tank clips (1, 2)

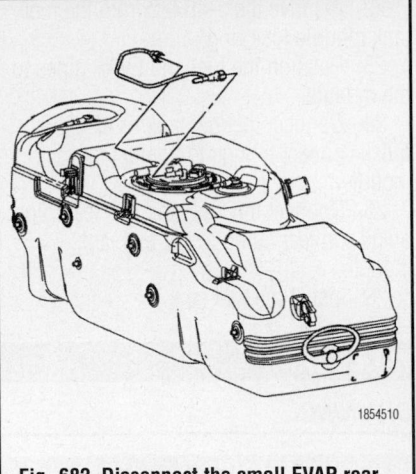

Fig. 682 Disconnect the small EVAP rear pipe quick connect fittings from the rollover valve and the fuel tank module

37. Install the EVAP rear pipe to the fuel tank clips.

38. Install the EVAP canister purge pipe to the fuel tank clip.

39. Position and connect the fuel feed pipe quick connect fitting to the fuel tank module.

40. Install the fuel feed pipe to the fuel tank clip.

41. Position and install the fuel tank shield.

42. Install the fuel tank shield push on retainers.

43. With the aid of an assistant, place the fuel tank in a the adjustable jack.

44. Raise the fuel tank until the electrical connections can be made.

45. Connect the chassis wiring harness electrical connector to the fuel tank module.

46. Connect the chassis wiring harness electrical connector from the fuel pressure sensor.

47. Completely raise the fuel tank into position.

48. Install the fuel tank straps.

49. Install the fuel tank strap bolts. Tighten the bolts to 30 ft. lbs. (40 Nm).

50. Remove the adjustable jack from under the fuel tank.

51. Unsecure and position the EVAP canister vent solenoid to the fuel tank.

52. Slide the EVAP canister vent solenoid onto the bracket towards the driver side of the vehicle.

53. Ensure that the EVAP canister vent solenoid engages the fuel tank bracket retainer.

54. Connect the EVAP canister vent solenoid pipe quick connect fitting to the EVAP canister.

55. Connect the EVAP canister pipe quick connect fitting to the fuel tank EVAP pipe.

56. Install the EVAP canister vent solenoid pipe clip to the frame crossmember.

57. Connect the chassis wiring harness electrical connector to the EVAP canister vent solenoid.

58. Install the chassis wiring harness clip to the fuel tank shield.

59. Remove the caps from the fuel and EVAP lines.

60. Connect the fuel tank fuel feed and EVAP line quick connect fittings to the chassis lines.

61. Install the fuel tank fill pipe.

62. Refill the fuel tank.

63. Install the fuel cap.

64. Connect the negative battery cable.

65. Perform the following procedure in order to inspect for leaks:

    a. Turn the ignition ON, with the engine OFF, for 2 seconds.

    b. Turn the ignition OFF for 10 seconds.

    c. Turn the ignition ON, with the engine OFF.

    d. Inspect for fuel leaks.

1500 Series Extended/Crew Cab With 26 Gallon Tank

See Figures 683 through 691.

➡**Clean the fuel and Evaporative Emission (EVAP) connections and surrounding areas prior to disconnecting the lines in order to avoid possible system contamination.**

1. Relieve the fuel system pressure.
2. Drain the fuel tank.
3. Remove the fuel tank shield bolts, if equipped.

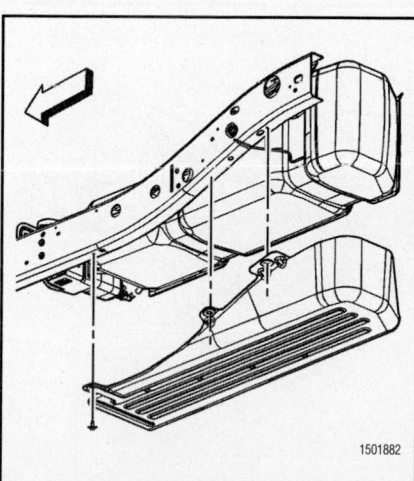

Fig. 683 Remove the fuel tank shield bolts, if equipped

4. Remove the fuel tank shield from the fuel tank shield tabs, if equipped.

5. Disconnect the fuel tank fuel feed line quick connect fitting from the chassis line.

6. Disconnect the fuel tank EVAP line quick connect fitting from the EVAP canister.

7. Cap the fuel and EVAP lines in order to prevent possible system contamination.

8. Place a suitable adjustable jack under the fuel tank.

9. Remove the fuel tank strap bolts.

10. Remove the fuel tank straps.

➡**When lowering the tank, ensure that the fill neck on the tank does not get hung up on the chassis wiring harness.**

11. Lower the fuel tank half way.

    a. Loosen the fuel fill pipe clamp at the fuel tank.

    b. Separate the fuel fill pipe from the fuel tank.

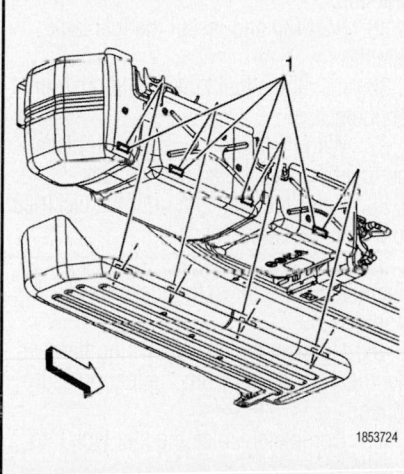

Fig. 684 Remove the fuel tank shield from the fuel tank shield tabs (1), if equipped

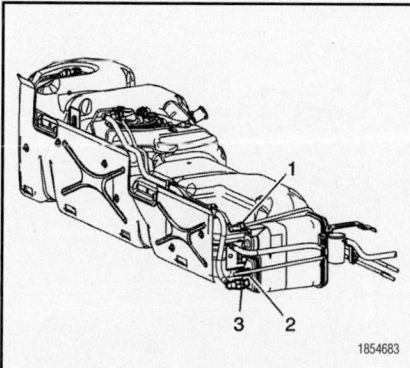

Fig. 685 Disconnect the fuel tank fuel feed line quick connect fitting (1) from the chassis line and the fuel tank EVAP line quick connect fitting (3) from the EVAP canister; pipe (2)

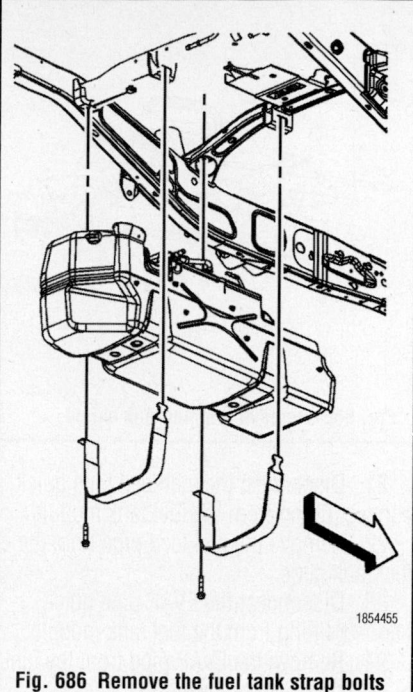

Fig. 686 Remove the fuel tank strap bolts

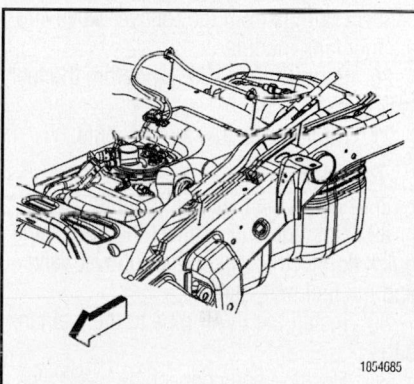

Fig. 687 Disconnect the chassis wiring harness electrical connector from the fuel tank pressure sensor

12. Disconnect the chassis wiring harness clip at the frame crossmember.

13. Lower the fuel tank until the electrical connections are accessible.

14. Disconnect the chassis wiring harness electrical connector from the fuel tank pressure sensor.

15. Disconnect the chassis wiring harness electrical connector from the fuel tank module.

16. Completely lower the fuel tank.

17. With the aid of an assistant, place the fuel tank in a suitable work area.

18. If replacing the fuel tank proceed to the next step, otherwise proceed to step 10 in the installation procedure.

19. Remove the fuel tank shield push on retainers.

20. Remove the fuel tank shield.

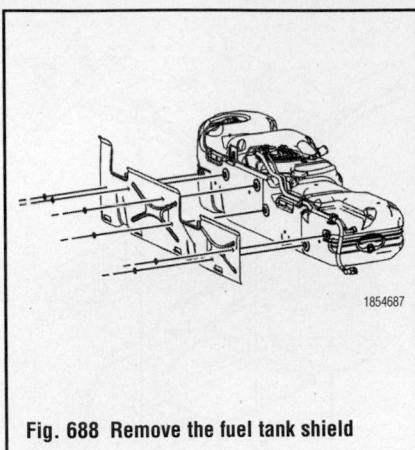

Fig. 688 Remove the fuel tank shield

21. Disconnect the fuel feed pipe quick connect fitting from the fuel tank module.

22. Remove the fuel feed pipe from the fuel tank clips.

23. Disconnect the EVAP pipe quick connect fitting from the fuel tank module.

24. Remove the EVAP pipe from the fuel tank clips.

25. Disconnect the EVAP pipe quick connect fittings from the rollover valve and the fuel tank module.

26. Remove the EVAP pipe from the fuel tank clips.

27. Remove the fuel tank module.

To install:

28. Install the fuel tank module.

29. Position and connect the EVAP pipe quick connect fittings to the rollover valve and the fuel tank module.

30. Install the EVAP pipe to the fuel tank clips.

31. Position and connect the EVAP pipe quick connect fitting to the fuel tank module.

32. Install the EVAP pipe to the fuel tank clips.

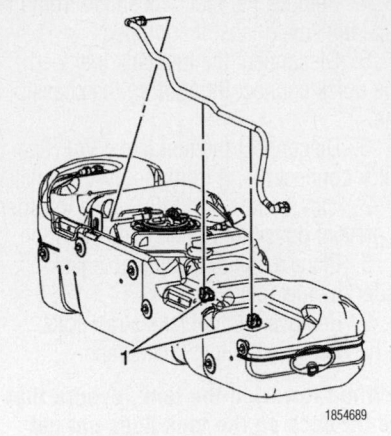

Fig. 690 Remove the EVAP pipe from the fuel tank clips (1)

33. Position and connect the fuel feed pipe quick connect fitting to the fuel tank module.

34. Install the fuel feed pipe to the fuel tank clips.

35. Position and install the fuel tank shield.

36. Install the fuel tank shield push on retainers.

37. With the aid of an assistant, place the fuel tank in a the adjustable jack.

38. Raise the fuel tank until the electrical connections can be made.

39. Connect the chassis wiring harness electrical connector to the fuel tank module.

40. Connect the chassis wiring harness electrical connector from the fuel pressure sensor.

41. Completely raise the fuel tank into position.

42. Install the fuel tank straps.

43. Install the fuel tank strap bolts. Tighten the bolts to 30 ft. lbs. (40 Nm).

44. Remove the adjustable jack from under the fuel tank.

45. Remove the caps from the fuel and EVAP lines.

46. Connect the fuel tank EVAP line quick connect fitting to the EVAP canister.

47. Connect the fuel tank fuel feed line quick connect fitting to the chassis line.

48. Position and install the fuel tank shield onto the fuel tank shield tabs, if equipped.

49. Install the fuel tank shield bolts, if equipped. Tighten the bolts to 13 ft. lbs. (18 Nm).

50. Refill the fuel tank.

51. Install the fuel cap.

52. Connect the negative battery cable.

53. Perform the following procedure in order to inspect for leaks:

a. Turn the ignition ON, with the engine OFF, for 2 seconds.

b. Turn the ignition OFF for 10 seconds.

c. Turn the ignition ON, with the engine OFF.

d. Inspect for fuel leaks.

1500 Series Regular/Extended/Crew Cab With 34 Gallon Tank

See Figures 692 through 702.

➡**Clean the fuel and Evaporative Emission (EVAP) connections and surrounding areas prior to disconnecting the lines in order to avoid possible system contamination.**

1. Relieve the fuel system pressure.
2. Drain the fuel tank.

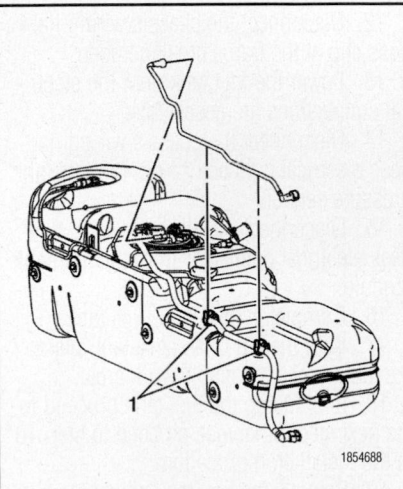

Fig. 689 Remove the fuel feed pipe from the fuel tank clips (1)

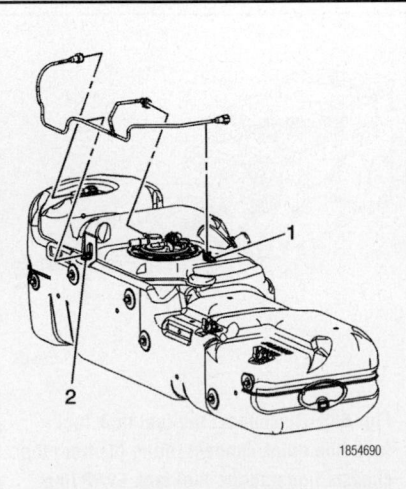

Fig. 691 Remove the EVAP pipe from the fuel tank clips (1, 2)

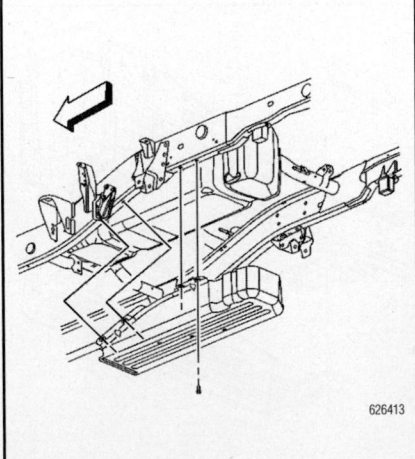

Fig. 692 Remove the fuel tank shield bolts, if equipped

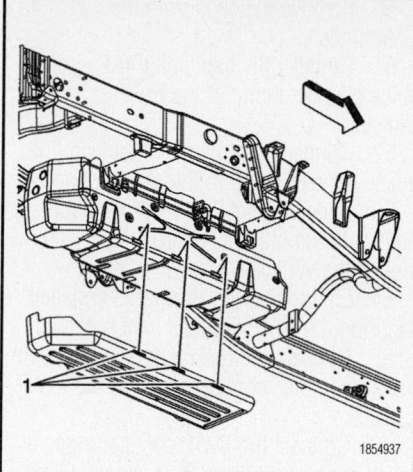

Fig. 693 Remove the fuel tank shield from the fuel tank shield tabs (1), if equipped

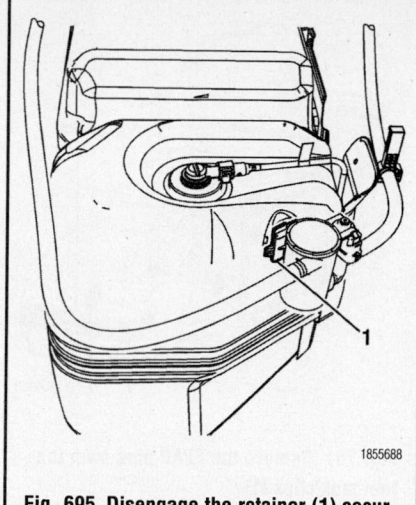

Fig. 695 Disengage the retainer (1) securing the EVAP canister vent solenoid

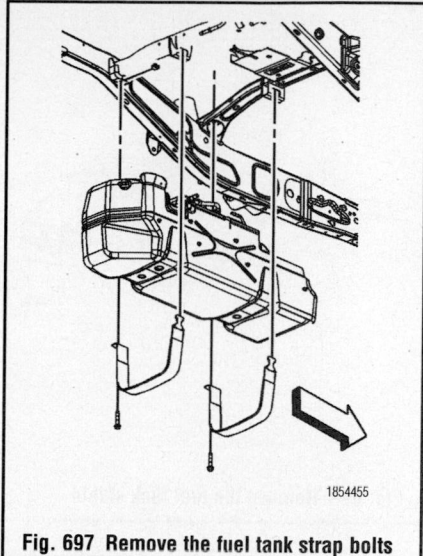

Fig. 697 Remove the fuel tank strap bolts

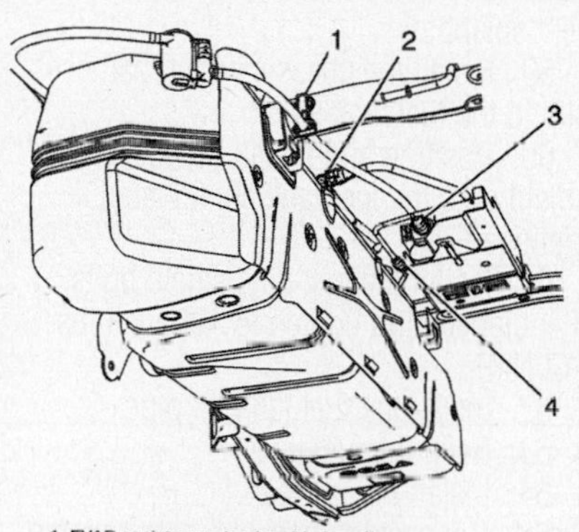

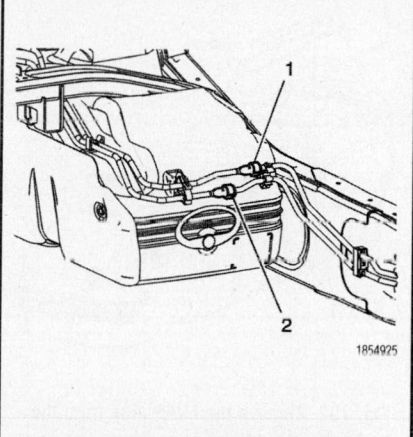

1. EVAP canister vent solenoid pipe clip
2. EVAP canister pipe quick connect fitting
3. EVAP canister vent solenoid pipe quick connect fitting
4. Quick connect fitting

Fig. 694 Remove the EVAP canister vent solenoid pipe clip from the frame crossmember

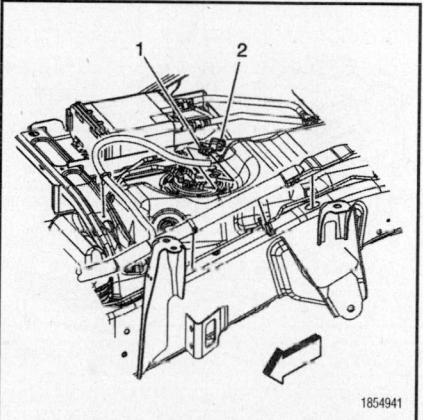

Fig. 696 Disconnect the fuel tank fuel feed line quick connect fitting (1) from the chassis line and the fuel tank EVAP line quick connect fitting (2) from the EVAP canister

Fig. 698 Disconnect the chassis wiring harness electrical connector (1) from the fuel tank pressure sensor and the chassis wiring harness electrical connector (2) from the fuel tank module

3. Remove the fuel tank fill pipe.
4. Remove the fuel tank shield bolts, if equipped.
5. Remove the fuel tank shield from the fuel tank shield tabs, if equipped.
6. Remove the EVAP canister vent solenoid pipe clip from the frame crossmember.
7. Disconnect the EVAP canister pipe quick connect fitting from the fuel tank EVAP pipe.
8. Disconnect the EVAP canister vent solenoid pipe quick connect fitting from the EVAP canister.
9. Disconnect the chassis wiring harness electrical connector from the EVAP canister vent solenoid.
10. Remove the chassis wiring harness clip from the fuel tank shield.
11. Disengage the retainer securing the EVAP canister vent solenoid.

12. Slide the EVAP canister vent solenoid off the bracket towards the passenger side of the vehicle.
13. Disconnect the fuel tank fuel feed line quick connect fitting from the chassis line.
14. Disconnect the fuel tank EVAP line quick connect fitting from the EVAP canister.
15. Cap the fuel and EVAP lines in order to prevent possible system contamination.
16. Place a suitable adjustable jack under the fuel tank.
17. Remove the fuel tank strap bolts.
18. Remove the fuel tank straps.

➡**When lowering the tank, ensure that the fill neck on the tank does not get hung up on the chassis wiring harness.**

19. Lower the fuel tank half way.

20. Disconnect the chassis wiring harness clip at the frame crossmember.
21. Lower the fuel tank until the electrical connections are accessible.
22. Disconnect the chassis wiring harness electrical connector from the fuel tank pressure sensor.
23. Disconnect the chassis wiring harness electrical connector from the fuel tank module.
24. Completely lower the fuel tank.
25. With the aid of an assistant, place the fuel tank in a suitable work area.
26. If replacing the fuel tank proceed to the next step, otherwise proceed to step 9 in the installation procedure.
27. Remove the fuel tank shield push on retainers.
28. Remove the fuel tank shield.

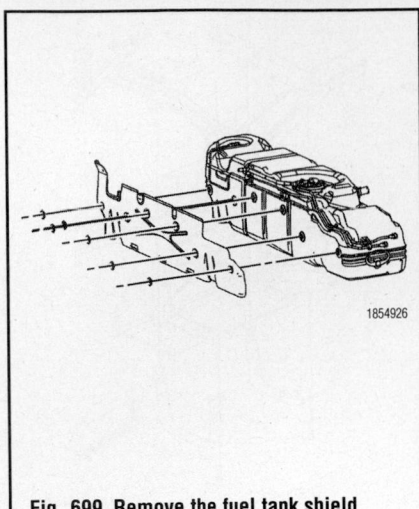

Fig. 699 Remove the fuel tank shield

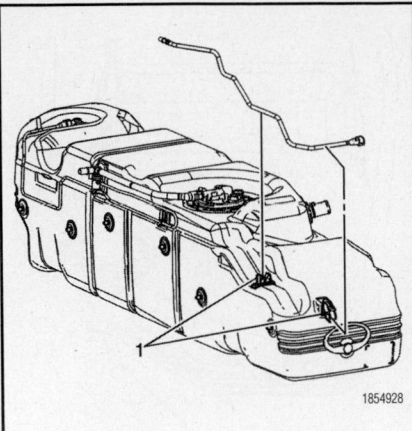

Fig. 701 Remove the EVAP pipe from the fuel tank clips (1)

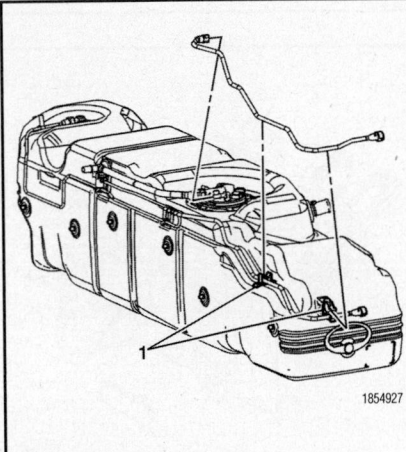

Fig. 700 Remove the fuel feed pipe from the fuel tank clips (1)

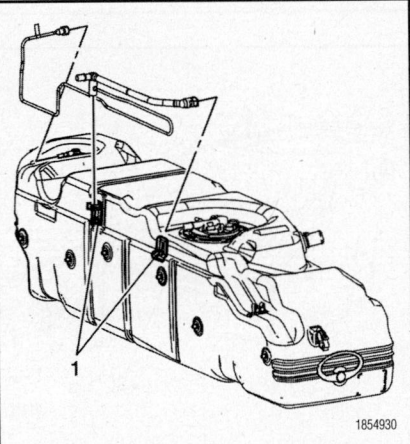

Fig. 702 Remove the EVAP pipe from the fuel tank clips (1)

29. Disconnect the fuel feed pipe quick connect fitting from the fuel tank module.

30. Remove the fuel feed pipe from the fuel tank clips.

31. Remove the EVAP pipe from the fuel tank clips.

32. Disconnect the EVAP pipe quick connect fittings from the rollover valve and the fuel tank module.

33. Remove the EVAP pipe from the fuel tank clips.

34. Remove the fuel tank module.

To install:

35. Install the fuel tank module.

36. Position and connect the EVAP pipe quick connect fittings to the rollover valve and the fuel tank module.

37. Install the EVAP pipe to the fuel tank clips.

38. Position and connect the fuel feed pipe quick connect fitting to the fuel tank module.

39. Install the fuel feed pipe to the fuel tank clips.

40. Position and install the fuel tank shield.

41. Install the fuel tank shield push on retainers.

42. With the aid of an assistant, place the fuel tank in a the adjustable jack.

43. Raise the fuel tank until the electrical connections can be made.

44. Connect the chassis wiring harness electrical connector to the fuel tank module.

45. Connect the chassis wiring harness electrical connector from the fuel pressure sensor.

46. Completely raise the fuel tank into position.

47. Install the fuel tank straps.

48. Install the fuel tank strap bolts and tighten to 30 ft. lbs. (40 Nm).

49. Remove the adjustable jack from under the fuel tank.

50. Remove the caps from the fuel and EVAP lines.

51. Connect the fuel tank EVAP line quick connect fitting to the EVAP canister.

52. Connect the fuel tank fuel feed line quick connect fitting to the chassis line.

53. Slide the EVAP canister vent solenoid onto the bracket towards the driver side of the vehicle.

54. Ensure that the retainer is engaged, securing the EVAP canister vent solenoid.

55. Connect the EVAP canister vent solenoid pipe quick connect fitting to the EVAP canister.

56. Connect the EVAP canister pipe quick connect fitting to the fuel tank EVAP pipe.

57. Install the EVAP canister vent solenoid pipe clip to the frame crossmember.

58. Connect the chassis wiring harness electrical connector to the EVAP canister vent solenoid.

59. Install the chassis wiring harness clip to the fuel tank shield.

60. Position and install the fuel tank shield onto the fuel tank shield tabs, if equipped.

61. Install the fuel tank shield bolts, if equipped, and tighten to 106 inch lbs. (12 Nm).

62. Install the fuel tank fill pipe.

63. Refill the fuel tank.

64. Install the fuel cap.

65. Connect the negative battery cable.

66. Perform the following procedure in order to inspect for leaks:

   a. Turn the ignition ON, with the engine OFF, for 2 seconds.

   b. Turn the ignition OFF for 10 seconds.

   c. Turn the ignition ON, with the engine OFF.

   d. Inspect for fuel leaks.

1500/2500 Series Regular/Extended/Crew Cab With 34 Gallon Tank

See Figures 703 through 713.

➥**Clean the fuel and Evaporative Emission (EVAP) connections and surrounding areas prior to disconnecting the lines in order to avoid possible system contamination.**

1. Relieve the fuel system pressure.

2. Drain the fuel tank.

3. Remove the fuel tank fill pipe.

4. Remove the fuel tank shield bolts, if equipped.

5. Remove the fuel tank shield from the fuel tank shield tabs, if equipped.

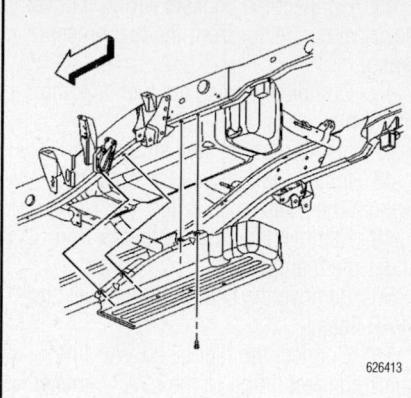

Fig. 703 Remove the fuel tank shield bolts, if equipped

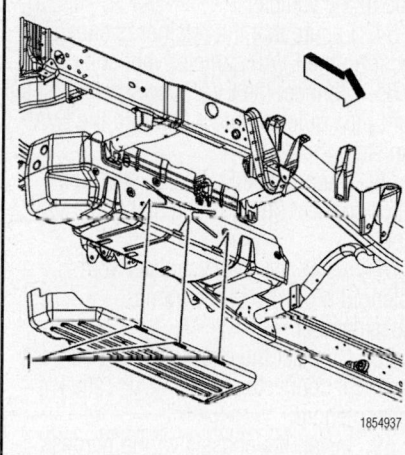

Fig. 704 Remove the fuel tank shield from the fuel tank shield tabs (1), if equipped

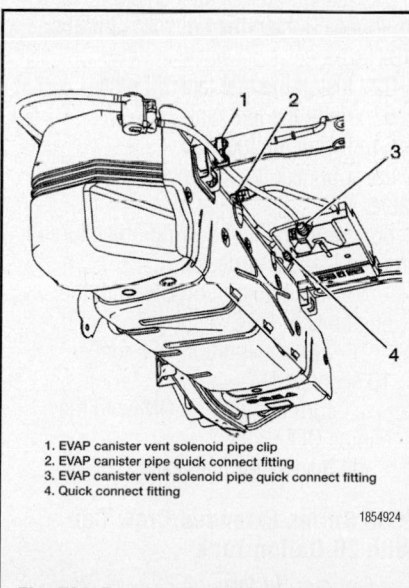

1. EVAP canister vent solenoid pipe clip
2. EVAP canister pipe quick connect fitting
3. EVAP canister vent solenoid pipe quick connect fitting
4. Quick connect fitting

Fig. 705 Remove the EVAP canister vent solenoid pipe clip from the frame crossmember

6. Remove the EVAP canister vent solenoid pipe clip from the frame crossmember.

7. Disconnect the EVAP canister pipe quick connect fitting from the fuel tank EVAP pipe.

8. Disconnect the EVAP canister vent solenoid pipe quick connect fitting from the EVAP canister.

9. Disconnect the chassis wiring harness electrical connector from the EVAP canister vent solenoid.

10. Remove the chassis wiring harness clip from the fuel tank shield.

11. Disengage the retainer securing the EVAP canister vent solenoid.

12. Slide the EVAP canister vent solenoid off the bracket towards the passenger side of the vehicle.

13. Disconnect the fuel tank fuel feed line quick connect fitting from the chassis line.

14. Disconnect the fuel tank EVAP line quick connect fitting from the EVAP canister.

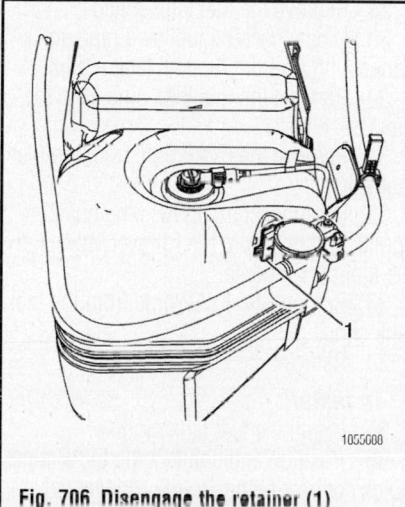

Fig. 706 Disengage the retainer (1) securing the EVAP canister vent solenoid

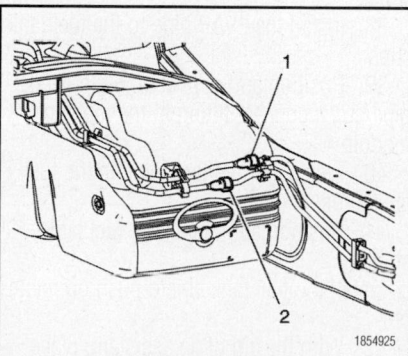

Fig. 707 Disconnect the fuel tank fuel feed line quick connect fitting (1) from the chassis line and the fuel tank EVAP line quick connect fitting (2) from the EVAP canister

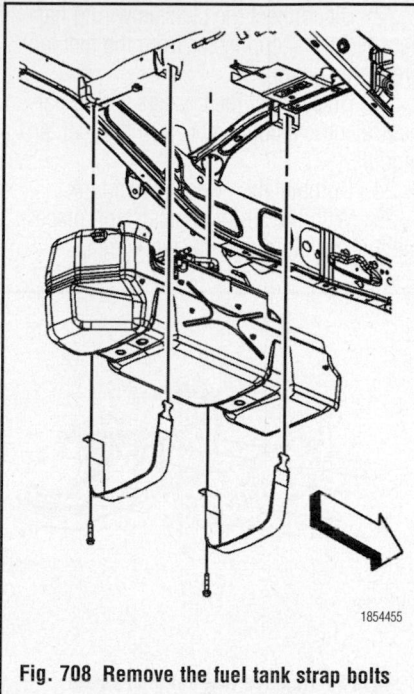

Fig. 708 Remove the fuel tank strap bolts

15. Cap the fuel and EVAP lines in order to prevent possible system contamination.

16. Place a suitable adjustable jack under the fuel tank.

17. Remove the fuel tank strap bolts.

18. Remove the fuel tank straps.

➡ **When lowering the tank, ensure that the fill neck on the tank does not get hung up on the chassis wiring harness.**

19. Lower the fuel tank half way.

20. Disconnect the chassis wiring harness clip at the frame crossmember.

21. Lower the fuel tank until the electrical connections are accessible.

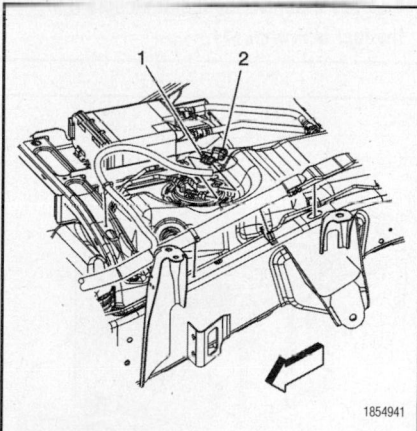

Fig. 709 Disconnect the chassis wiring harness electrical connector (1) from the fuel tank pressure sensor and the chassis wiring harness electrical connector (2) from the fuel tank module

22. Disconnect the chassis wiring harness electrical connector from the fuel tank pressure sensor.

23. Disconnect the chassis wiring harness electrical connector from the fuel tank module.

24. Completely lower the fuel tank.

25. With the aid of an assistant, place the fuel tank in a suitable work area.

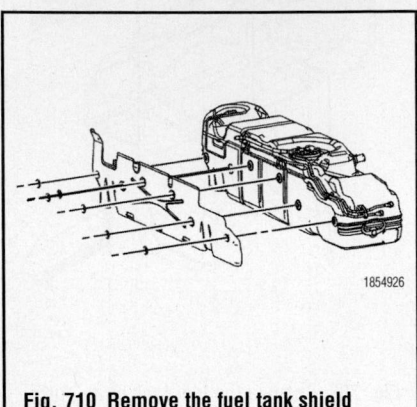

Fig. 710 Remove the fuel tank shield

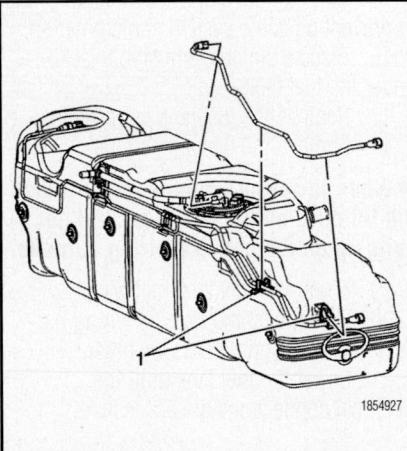

Fig. 711 Remove the fuel feed pipe from the fuel tank clips (1)

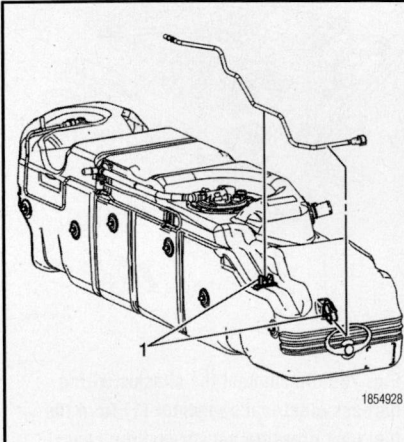

Fig. 712 Remove the EVAP pipe from the fuel tank clips (1)

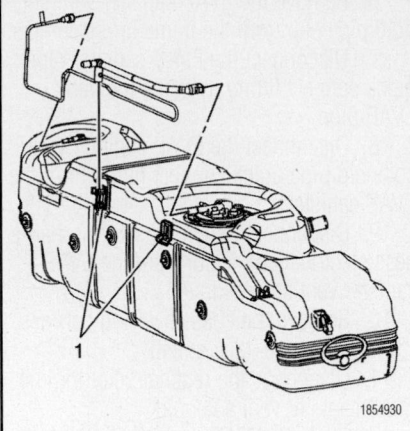

Fig. 713 Remove the EVAP pipe from the fuel tank clips (1)

26. If replacing the fuel tank proceed to the next step, otherwise proceed to step 9 in the installation procedure.

27. Remove the fuel tank shield push on retainers.

28. Remove the fuel tank shield.

29. Disconnect the fuel feed pipe quick connect fitting from the fuel tank module.

30. Remove the fuel feed pipe from the fuel tank clips.

31. Remove the EVAP pipe from the fuel tank clips.

32. Disconnect the EVAP pipe quick connect fittings from the rollover valve and the fuel tank module.

33. Remove the EVAP pipe from the fuel tank clips.

34. Remove the fuel tank module.

To install:

35. Install the fuel tank module.

36. Position and connect the EVAP pipe quick connect fittings to the rollover valve and the fuel tank module.

37. Install the EVAP pipe to the fuel tank clips.

38. Install the EVAP pipe to the fuel tank clips.

39. Position and connect the fuel feed pipe quick connect fitting to the fuel tank module.

40. Install the fuel feed pipe to the fuel tank clips.

41. Position and install the fuel tank shield.

Install the fuel tank shield push on retainers.

42. With the aid of an assistant, place the fuel tank in a the adjustable jack.

43. Raise the fuel tank until the electrical connections can be made.

44. Connect the chassis wiring harness electrical connector to the fuel tank module.

45. Connect the chassis wiring harness electrical connector from the fuel pressure sensor.

46. Completely raise the fuel tank into position.

47. Install the fuel tank straps.

48. Install the fuel tank strap bolts. Tighten the bolts to 30 ft. lbs. (40 Nm).

49. Remove the adjustable jack from under the fuel tank.

50. Remove the caps from the fuel and EVAP lines.

51. Connect the fuel tank EVAP line quick connect fitting to the EVAP canister.

52. Connect the fuel tank fuel feed line quick connect fitting to the chassis line.

53. Slide the EVAP canister vent solenoid onto the bracket towards the driver side of the vehicle.

54. Ensure that the retainer is engaged, securing the EVAP canister vent solenoid.

55. Connect the EVAP canister vent solenoid pipe quick connect fitting to the EVAP canister.

56. Connect the EVAP canister pipe quick connect fitting to the fuel tank EVAP pipe.

57. Install the EVAP canister vent solenoid pipe clip to the frame crossmember.

58. Connect the chassis wiring harness electrical connector to the EVAP canister vent solenoid.

59. Install the chassis wiring harness clip to the fuel tank shield.

60. Position and install the fuel tank shield onto the fuel tank shield tabs, if equipped.

61. Install the fuel tank shield bolts, if equipped. Tighten the bolts to 13 ft. lbs. (18 Nm).

62. Install the fuel tank fill pipe.

63. Refill the fuel tank.

64. Install the fuel cap.

65. Connect the negative battery cable.

66. Perform the following procedure in order to inspect for leaks:

   a. Turn the ignition ON, with the engine OFF, for 2 seconds.

   b. Turn the ignition OFF for 10 seconds.

   c. Turn the ignition ON, with the engine OFF.

   d. Inspect for fuel leaks.

2500 Series Extended/Crew Cab With 26 Gallon Tank

See Figures 714 through 723.

→Clean the fuel and Evaporative Emission (EVAP) connections and surround-

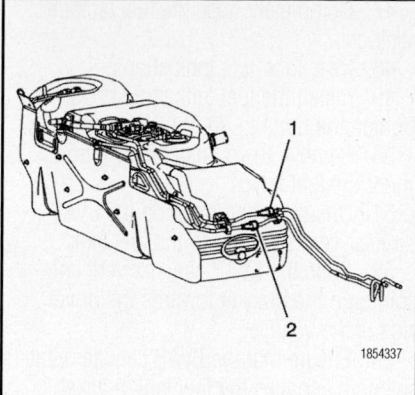

Fig. 714 Disconnect the fuel tank fuel feed (1) and EVAP (2) line quick connect fittings from the chassis lines

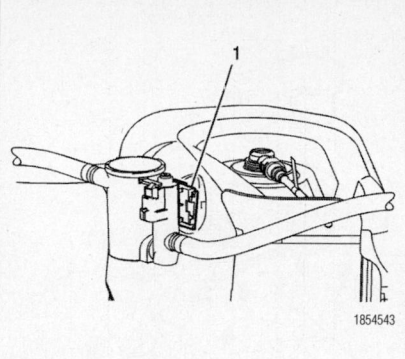

Fig. 716 Insert a small flat bladed tool between the EVAP canister vent solenoid and the fuel tank bracket, disengaging the retainer (1)

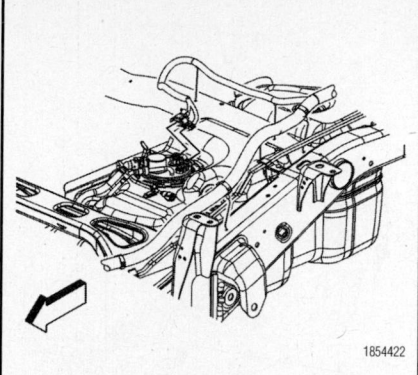

Fig. 718 Disconnect the chassis wiring harness electrical connector from the fuel tank pressure sensor

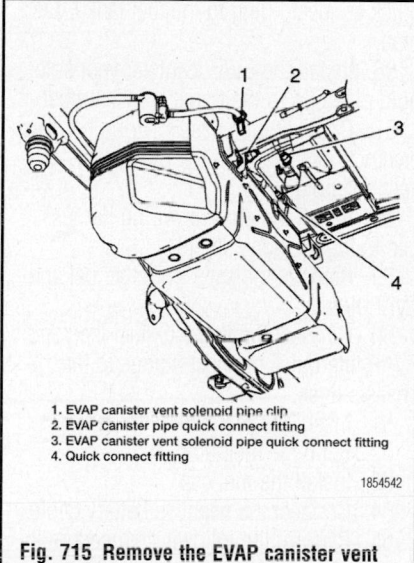

1. EVAP canister vent solenoid pipe clip
2. EVAP canister pipe quick connect fitting
3. EVAP canister vent solenoid pipe quick connect fitting
4. Quick connect fitting

Fig. 715 Remove the EVAP canister vent solenoid pipe clip from the frame cross-member

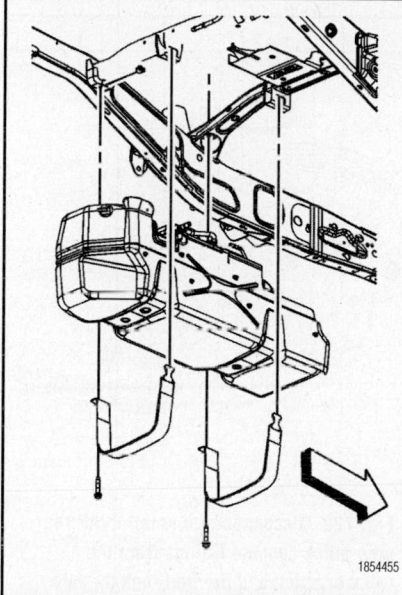

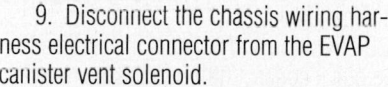

Fig. 717 Remove the fuel tank strap bolts

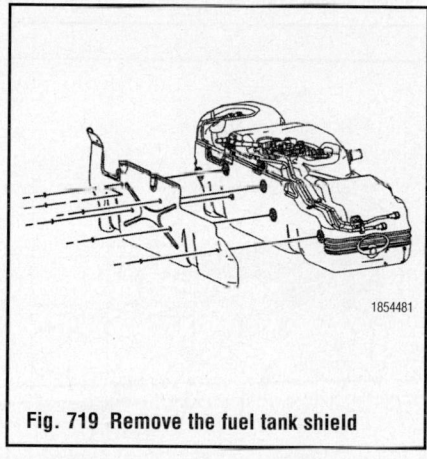

Fig. 719 Remove the fuel tank shield

ing areas prior to disconnecting the lines in order to avoid possible system contamination.

1. Relieve the fuel system pressure.
2. Drain the fuel tank.
3. Remove the fuel tank fill pipe.
4. Disconnect the fuel tank fuel feed and EVAP line quick connect fittings from the chassis lines.
5. Cap the fuel and EVAP lines in order to prevent possible system contamination.
6. Remove the EVAP canister vent solenoid pipe clip from the frame crossmember.
7. Disconnect the EVAP canister pipe quick connect fitting from the fuel tank EVAP pipe.
8. Disconnect the EVAP canister vent solenoid pipe quick connect fitting from the EVAP canister.

9. Disconnect the chassis wiring harness electrical connector from the EVAP canister vent solenoid.
10. Remove the chassis wiring harness clip from the fuel tank shield.
11. Insert a small flat bladed tool between the EVAP canister vent solenoid and the fuel tank bracket, disengaging the retainer.
12. Slide the EVAP canister vent solenoid off the bracket towards the passenger side of the vehicle.
13. Position and secure the EVAP canister vent solenoid out of the way.
14. Place a suitable adjustable jack under the fuel tank.
15. Remove the fuel tank strap bolts.
16. Remove the fuel tank straps.

➥**When lowering the tank, ensure that the fill neck on the tank does not get hung up on the chassis wiring harness.**

17. Lower the fuel tank half way.
10. Disconnect the chassis wiring harness clip at the frame crossmember.
19. Lower the fuel tank until the electrical connections are accessible.
20. Disconnect the chassis wiring harness electrical connector from the fuel tank pressure sensor.
21. Disconnect the chassis wiring harness electrical connector from the fuel tank module.
22. Completely lower the fuel tank.
23. With the aid of an assistant, place the fuel tank in a suitable work area.
24. If replacing the fuel tank proceed to the next step, otherwise proceed to step 10 in the installation procedure.
25. Remove the fuel tank shield push on retainers.
26. Remove the fuel tank shield.
27. Disconnect the fuel feed pipe quick connect fitting from the fuel tank module.
28. Remove the fuel feed pipe from the fuel tank clip.

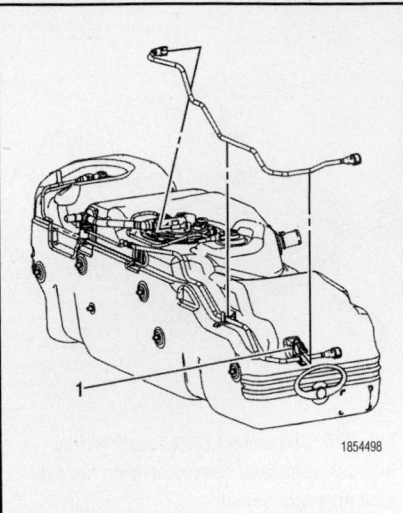

Fig. 720 Remove the fuel feed pipe from the fuel tank clip (1)

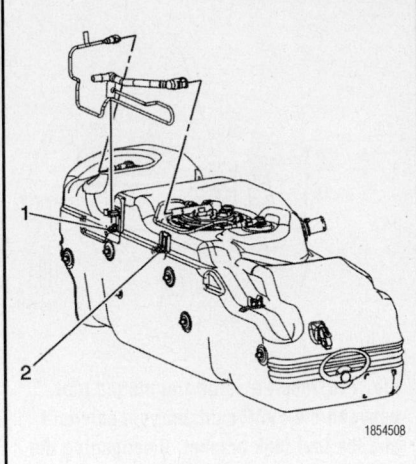

Fig. 722 Remove the EVAP rear pipe from the fuel tank clips (1, 2)

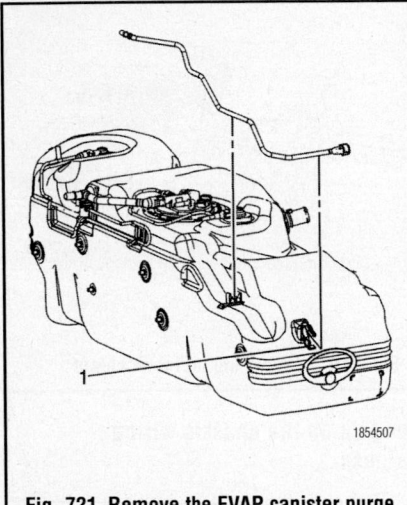

Fig. 721 Remove the EVAP canister purge pipe from the fuel tank clip (1)

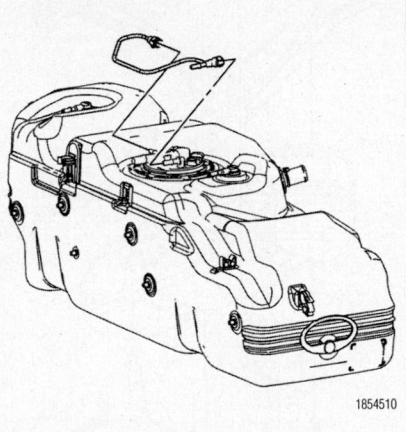

Fig. 723 Disconnect the small EVAP rear pipe quick connect fittings from the rollover valve and the fuel tank module

29. Remove the EVAP canister purge pipe from the fuel tank clip.

30. Disconnect the EVAP rear pipe quick connect fittings from the rollover valve and the fuel tank module.

31. Remove the EVAP rear pipe from the fuel tank clips.

32. Disconnect the small EVAP rear pipe quick connect fittings from the rollover valve and the fuel tank module.

33. Remove the fuel tank module.

To install:

34. Install the fuel tank module.

35. Position and connect the small EVAP rear pipe quick connect fittings to the rollover valve and the fuel tank module.

36. Position and connect the EVAP rear pipe quick connect fittings to the rollover valve and the fuel tank module.

37. Install the EVAP rear pipe to the fuel tank clips.

38. Install the EVAP canister purge pipe to the fuel tank clip.

39. Position and connect the fuel feed pipe quick connect fitting to the fuel tank module.

40. Install the fuel feed pipe to the fuel tank clip.

41. Position and install the fuel tank shield.

42. Install the fuel tank shield push on retainers.

43. With the aid of an assistant, place the fuel tank in a the adjustable jack.

44. Raise the fuel tank until the electrical connections can be made.

45. Connect the chassis wiring harness electrical connector to the fuel tank module.

46. Connect the chassis wiring harness electrical connector from the fuel pressure sensor.

47. Completely raise the fuel tank into position.

48. Install the fuel tank straps.

49. Install the fuel tank strap bolts. Tighten the bolts to 30 ft. lbs. (40 Nm).

50. Remove the adjustable jack from under the fuel tank.

51. Unsecure and position the EVAP canister vent solenoid to the fuel tank.

52. Slide the EVAP canister vent solenoid onto the bracket towards the driver side of the vehicle.

53. Ensure that the EVAP canister vent solenoid engages the fuel tank bracket retainer.

54. Connect the EVAP canister vent solenoid pipe quick connect fitting to the EVAP canister.

55. Connect the EVAP canister pipe quick connect fitting to the fuel tank EVAP pipe.

56. Install the EVAP canister vent solenoid pipe clip to the frame crossmember.

57. Connect the chassis wiring harness electrical connector to the EVAP canister vent solenoid.

58. Install the chassis wiring harness clip to the fuel tank shield.

59. Remove the caps from the fuel and EVAP lines.

60. Connect the fuel tank fuel feed and EVAP line quick connect fittings to the chassis lines.

61. Install the fuel tank fill pipe.

62. Refill the fuel tank.

63. Install the fuel cap.

64. Connect the negative battery cable.

65. Perform the following procedure in order to inspect for leaks:

   a. Turn the ignition ON, with the engine OFF, for 2 seconds.

   b. Turn the ignition OFF for 10 seconds.

   c. Turn the ignition ON, with the engine OFF.

   d. Inspect for fuel leaks.

Cab/Chassis Rear Tank

See Figures 724 through 727.

1. Relieve the fuel system pressure.

2. Raise the vehicle.

3. Drain the fuel tank.

4. Remove the fuel tank shield bolts and the fuel tank shield.

5. Loosen the fuel fill hose clamp.

6. Support the fuel tank with a suitable jack.

7. Remove the fuel tank strap fastener and the strap.

8. Lower the tank enough to access the fuel pump module.

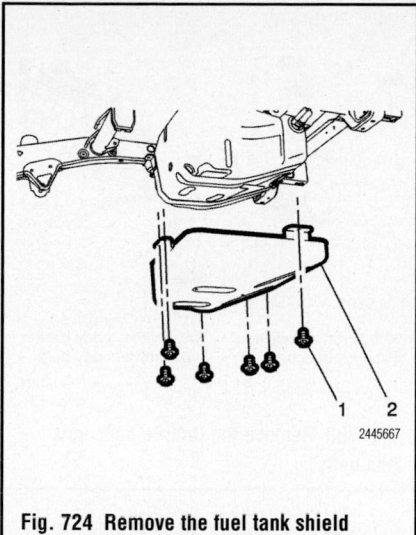

Fig. 724 Remove the fuel tank shield bolts (1) and the fuel tank shield (2)

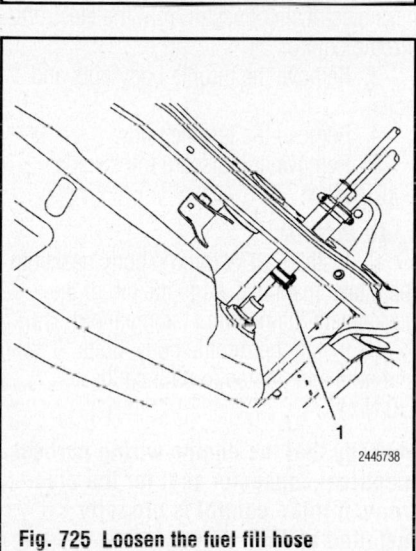

Fig. 725 Loosen the fuel fill hose clamp (1)

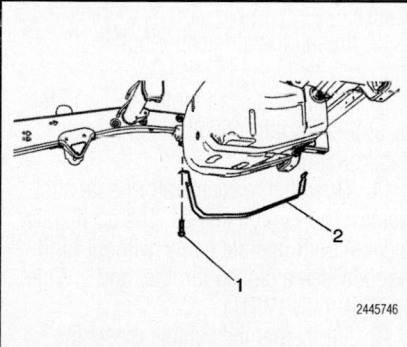

Fig. 726 Remove the fuel tank strap fastener (1) and the strap (2)

9. Disconnect the electrical connector and the evaporative emissions lines and the fuel lines.
10. Lower the fuel tank.
11. If replacing the fuel tank, remove

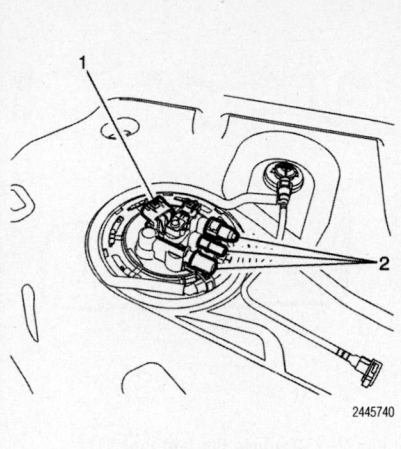

Fig. 727 Disconnect the electrical connector (1) and the evaporative emissions lines and the fuel lines (2)

the fuel pump module from the fuel tank.

12. Cap the fuel and EVAP pipes in order to prevent possible fuel system contamination.

To install:

13. If removed, install the fuel pump module.
14. Partially raise the fuel tank enough to access the fuel pump module.
15. Connect the electrical connector and fuel and evaporative emission lines.
16. Support the fuel tank with a suitable jack.
17. Install the fuel tank strap fastener and tighten to 30 ft. lbs. (40 Nm).
18. Tighten the fuel fill hose clamp.
19. Install the fuel tank shield and tighten the fuel tank shield bolts to 21 ft. lbs. (18 Nm).
20. Refill the fuel tank.
21. Install the fuel filler cap.
22. Use the following procedure in order to inspect for leaks:
  a. Turn ON the ignition, with the engine OFF, for 2 seconds.
  b. Turn OFF the ignition for 10 seconds.
  c. Turn ON the ignition, with the engine OFF.
  d. Inspect for fuel leaks.

Cab/Chassis Front Tank

See Figures 728 through 732.

1. Relieve the fuel system pressure.
2. Drain the fuel tank.
3. Remove the fuel shield fasteners and fuel shield.
4. Loosen the filler hose clamp (1) and disconnect the filler hose.

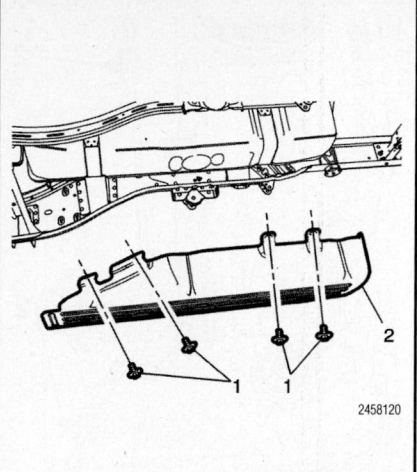

Fig. 728 Remove the fuel shield fasteners (1) and fuel shield (2)

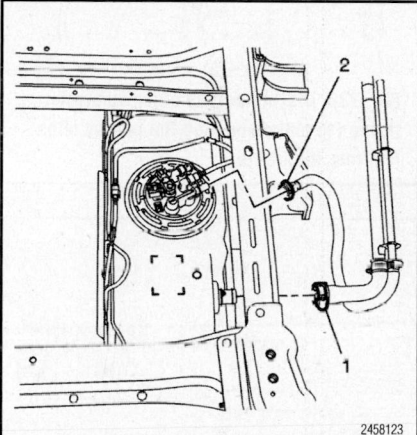

Fig. 729 Loosen the filler hose clamp (1) and disconnect the filler hose and the quick connect fitting (2)

5. Disconnect the quick connect fitting.
6. Disconnect the quick connect fitting.
7. Disengage the plastic clips from the frame.
8. Disconnect the fuel pump wiring harness connector.
9. If replacing the fuel tank proceed to the next step, otherwise proceed to step 9 in the installation procedure.
10. Support the tank with a suitable jack.
11. Remove the fuel tank strap fasteners.
12. Remove the fuel tank.
13. If replacing the tank, remove the fuel tank module.
14. Transfer components as necessary.

To install:

15. If the tank was replaced, install the fuel tank module.
16. Using a suitable jack, install the fuel tank into position.

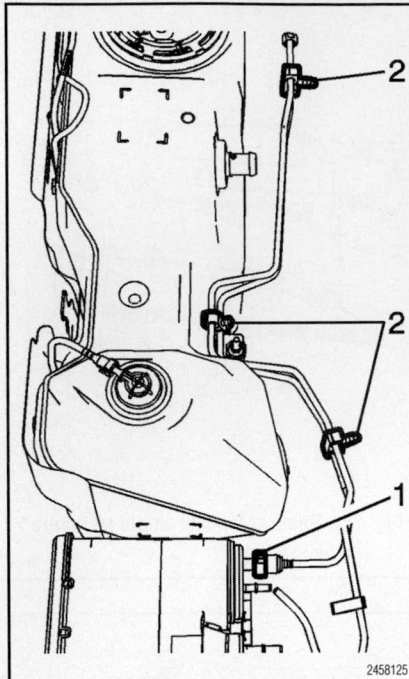

Fig. 730 Disconnect the quick connect fitting (1) and disengage the plastic clips (2) from the frame

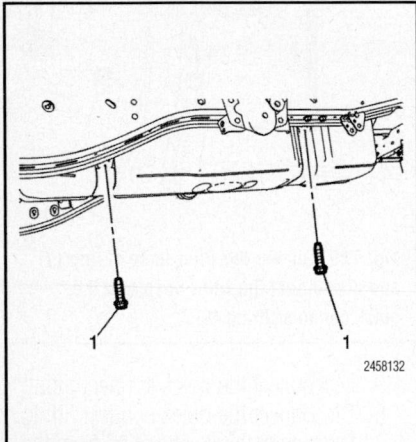

Fig. 731 Remove the fuel tank strap fasteners (1)

17. Install the fuel tank shield fasteners and tighten to 30 ft. lbs. (40 Nm).
18. Engage the plastic clips to the frame.
19. Connect the quick connect fitting.
20. Connect the fuel pump wiring harness connector.
21. Tighten the filler hose clamp.
22. Connect the quick connect fitting.
Connect the EVAP canister pipe quick connect fitting to the fuel tank EVAP pipe.
23. Install the fuel tank shield and fasteners and tighten to 13 ft. lbs. (18 Nm).

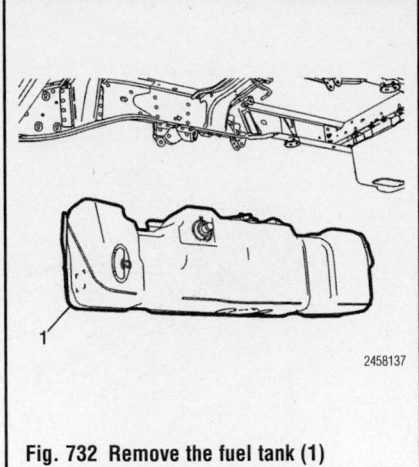

Fig. 732 Remove the fuel tank (1)

24. Refill the fuel tank.
25. Perform the following procedure in order to inspect for leaks:
   a. Turn the ignition ON, with the engine OFF, for 2 seconds.
   b. Turn the ignition OFF for 10 seconds.
   c. Turn the ignition ON, with the engine OFF.
   d. Inspect for fuel leaks.

IDLE SPEED

ADJUSTMENT

Idle speed is controlled by the Engine Control Module (ECM). No adjustment is necessary.

THROTTLE BODY

REMOVAL & INSTALLATION
See Figure 733.

✸✸ CAUTION

Handle the electronic throttle control components carefully. Use cleanliness in order to prevent damage. Do not drop the electronic throttle control components. Do not roughly handle the electronic throttle control components. Do not immerse the electronic throttle control components in cleaning solvents of any type.

✸✸ CAUTION

DO NOT for any reason, insert a screwdriver or other small hand tools into the throttle body to hold open the throttle plate, as the wedge inside the throttle body could be damaged.

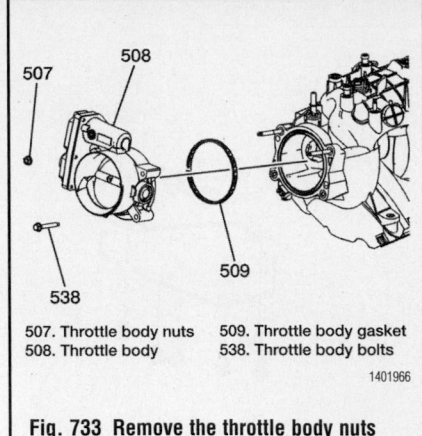

507. Throttle body nuts
508. Throttle body
509. Throttle body gasket
538. Throttle body bolts

Fig. 733 Remove the throttle body nuts and bolts

1. Remove the air cleaner outlet duct.
2. Disconnect the engine wiring harness electrical connector from the electronic throttle control.
3. Remove the throttle body nuts and bolts.
4. Remove the throttle body.
5. Remove and discard the throttle body gasket.

To install:

6. Install a NEW throttle body gasket to the intake manifold. Align the tab of the gasket with the notch in the manifold.
7. Install the throttle body, bolts, and nuts and tighten to 89 inch lbs. (10 Nm).

➡**Verify that the engine wiring harness electrical connector seal for the electronic throttle control is properly installed and not damaged.**

8. Connect the engine wiring harness electrical connector to the electronic throttle control.
9. Install the air cleaner outlet duct.
10. Connect a scan tool in order to test for proper throttle-opening and throttle-closing range.
11. Operate the accelerator pedal and monitor the throttle angles. The accelerator pedal should operate freely, without binding, between a closed throttle, and a Wide Open Throttle (WOT).
12. Verify that the vehicle meets the following conditions:
   • The vehicle is not in a reduced engine power mode.
   • The ignition is ON.
   • The engine is OFF.
13. Perform the Throttle Learn Procedure.
14. Inspect for coolant leaks.

THROTTLE LEARN PROCEDURE

Reset Procedure (Performed After The Throttle Body Is Cleaned Or Replaced)

1. Ignition ON, engine OFF, perform the Idle Learn Reset in Module Setup with a scan tool.
2. Start the engine and monitor the TB Idle Airflow Compensation parameter. The TB Idle Airflow Compensation value should equal 0 percent and the engine should be idling at a normal idle speed.
3. Clear the DTCs and return to the diagnostic that referred you here.

Learn Procedure (Performed After The ECM Is Flashed Or Replaced)

➡ **Do NOT perform this procedure if DTCs are set.**

1. Start and idle the engine for 3 minutes.
2. With a scan tool, monitor the Desired Idle Speed and the actual Engine Speed.
3. The ECM will start to learn the new idle cells and Desired Idle Speed should start to decrease.
4. Ignition OFF for 60 seconds.
5. Start and idle the engine for 3 minutes.
6. After the 3 minute run time the engine should be idling normal.

➡ **During the drive cycle the check engine light may come on with idle speed DTCs. If idle speed codes are** set, clear codes so the ECM can continue to learn.

➡ **If the engine idle speed has not been learned the vehicle will need to be driven at speeds above 44 MPH (70 km/h) with several decelerations and extended idles.**

7. After the drive cycle, the engine should be idling normally.

➡ **If the engine idle speed has not been learned, turn OFF the ignition for 60 seconds and repeat step 6.**

8. Once the engine speed has returned to normal, clear DTCs and return to the diagnostic that referred you here.

FUEL — DIESEL FUEL INJECTION SYSTEM

FUEL SYSTEM SERVICE PRECAUTIONS

Safety is the most important factor when performing not only fuel system maintenance but any type of maintenance. Failure to conduct maintenance and repairs in a safe manner may result in serious personal injury or death. Maintenance and testing of the vehicle's fuel system components can be accomplished safely and effectively by adhering to the following rules and guidelines.

- To avoid the possibility of fire and personal injury, always disconnect the negative battery cable unless the repair or test procedure requires that battery voltage be applied.
- Always relieve the fuel system pressure prior to disconnecting any fuel system component (injector, fuel rail, pressure regulator, etc.), fitting or fuel line connection. Exercise extreme caution whenever relieving fuel system pressure to avoid exposing skin, face and eyes to fuel spray. Please be advised that fuel under pressure may penetrate the skin or any part of the body that it contacts.
- Always place a shop towel or cloth around the fitting or connection prior to loosening to absorb any excess fuel due to spillage. Ensure that all fuel spillage (should it occur) is quickly removed from engine surfaces. Ensure that all fuel soaked cloths or towels are deposited into a suitable waste container.
- Always keep a dry chemical (Class B) fire extinguisher near the work area.
- Do not allow fuel spray or fuel vapors to come into contact with a spark or open flame.
- Always use a back-up wrench when loosening and tightening fuel line connection fittings. This will prevent unnecessary stress and torsion to fuel line piping.
- Always replace worn fuel fitting O-rings with new. Do not substitute fuel hose or equivalent where fuel pipe is installed.

Before servicing the vehicle, make sure to also refer to the precautions in the beginning of this section as well.

RELIEVING FUEL SYSTEM PRESSURE

See Figure 734

✳✳ WARNING

Remove the fuel tank cap and relieve the fuel system pressure before servicing the fuel system in order to reduce the risk of personal injury. After you relieve the fuel system pressure, a small amount of fuel may be released when servicing the fuel lines, the fuel injection pump, or the connections. In order to reduce the risk of personal injury, cover the fuel system components with a shop towel before disconnection. This will catch any fuel that may leak out. Place the towel in an approved container when the disconnection is complete.

1. If the fuel system requires repair, prevent fuel spillage by removing the fuel pump fuse.
2. Remove the engine cover, if required.
3. Loosen the fuel fill cap in order to relieve the fuel tank vapor pressure.

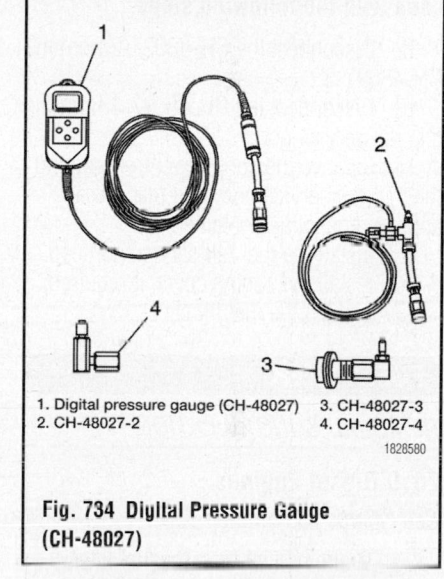

1. Digital pressure gauge (CH-48027)
2. CH-48027-2
3. CH-48027-3
4. CH-48027-4

1828580

Fig. 734 Digital Pressure Gauge (CH-48027)

4. Remove the fuel rail service port cap.

✳✳ WARNING

Wrap a shop towel around the fuel pressure connection in order to reduce the risk of fire and personal injury. The towel will absorb any fuel leakage that occurs during the connection of the fuel pressure gauge. Place the towel in an approved container when the connection of the fuel pressure gauge is complete.

5. Wrap a shop towel around the fuel rail service port.
6. Connect the CH-48027-3 to the fuel rail service port.
7. Connect the CH-48027-2 to the CH-48027-3.

8. Place the hose on the CH-48027-2 into an approved gasoline container.

9. Open the valve on the CH-48027-2 in order to bleed any fuel from the fuel rail.

10. Close the valve on the CH-48027-2.

11. Remove the hose on the CH-48027-2 from the approved gasoline container.

✳✳ CAUTION

Clean all of the following areas before performing any disconnections in order to avoid possible contamination in the system:

- The fuel pipe connections
- The hose connections
- The areas surrounding the connections

➡**If relieving the fuel pressure for the fuel pressure gauge installation and removal, it is NOT necessary to proceed with the following steps.**

12. Disconnect the CH-48027-2 from the CH-48027-3.

13. Disconnect the CH-48027-3 from the fuel rail service port.

14. Remove the shop towel from around the fuel rail service port, and place in an approved gasoline container.

15. Install the fuel rail service port cap.

16. Install the engine cover, if required.

17. Tighten the fuel fill cap.

FUEL FILTER

REMOVAL & INSTALLATION

2010 Diesel Engines

See Figures 735 through 738.

1. Drain the fuel from the fuel filter.
2. Remove the air cleaner outlet duct.

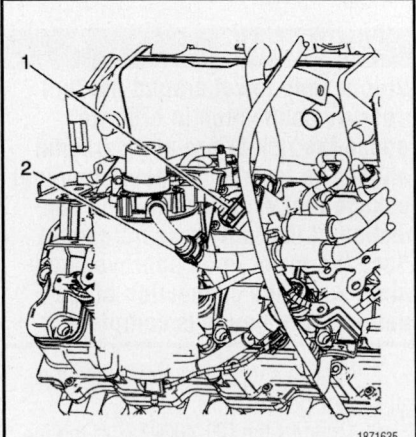

Fig. 735 Reposition the fuel filter hose clamps (1, 2)

3. Remove the heater inlet hose bracket nut from the fuel filter adapter stud.

4. Remove the heater inlet hose bracket from the stud and position the hose out of the way.

5. Reposition the fuel filter hose clamps.

6. Remove the fuel filter hoses from the fuel filter adapter.

7. Disconnect the fuel filter heater wiring pigtail from the engine wiring harness electrical connector.

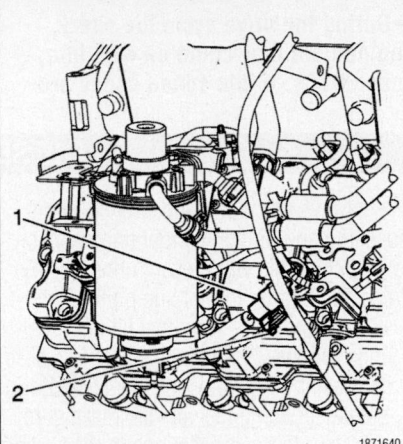

Fig. 736 Disconnect the fuel filter heater wiring pigtail (1) and the water in fuel sensor wiring pigtail (2) from the engine wiring harness electrical connector

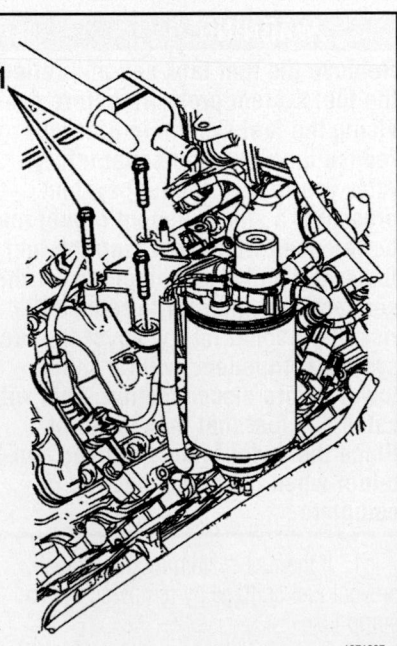

Fig. 737 Remove the fuel filter bracket bolts (1)

8. Disconnect the water in fuel sensor wiring pigtail from the engine wiring harness electrical connector.

9. Remove the fuel filter bracket bolts.

10. Remove the fuel filter and bracket assembly.

To install:

11. Position the fuel filter and bracket assembly to the upper valve rocker arm cover.

12. Install the fuel filter bracket bolts. Tighten the bolts to 15 ft. lbs. (20 Nm).

13. Connect the fuel filter heater wiring pigtail to the engine wiring harness electrical connector.

14. Connect the water in fuel sensor wiring pigtail to the engine wiring harness electrical connector.

15. Install the fuel filter hoses to the fuel filter adapter.

16. Position the fuel filter hose clamps.

17. Position the heater inlet hose and install the heater inlet hose bracket to the stud.

18. Install the heater inlet hose bracket nut to the fuel filter adapter stud. Tighten the nut to 80 inch lbs. (9 Nm).

19. Prime the fuel system.

20. Start the engine. If the engine stalls, repeat the above step.

21. Once the engine starts, inspect for fuel leaks.

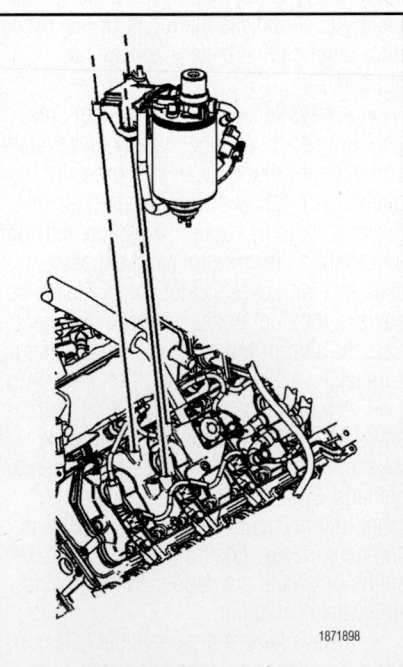

Fig. 738 Remove the fuel filter and bracket assembly

DRAINING WATER FROM THE SYSTEM

See Figures 739 through 741.

1. Attach a small piece of hose to the drain onto the water in fuel sensor.
2. Place the other end of the piece of hose into an approved fuel-resistant container.
3. Open the drain 3 or 4 turns or until the water contaminated fuel seeps from the drain.
4. Operate the priming pump until only diesel fuel is visible. Allow the pump to fully return upward between pushes.
5. Tighten the drain.
6. Remove the container and hose.

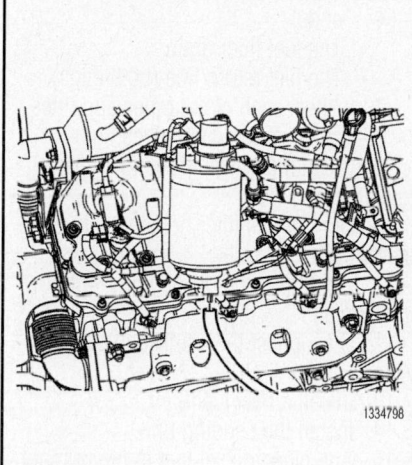

Fig. 739 Attach a small piece of hose to the drain onto the water in fuel sensor

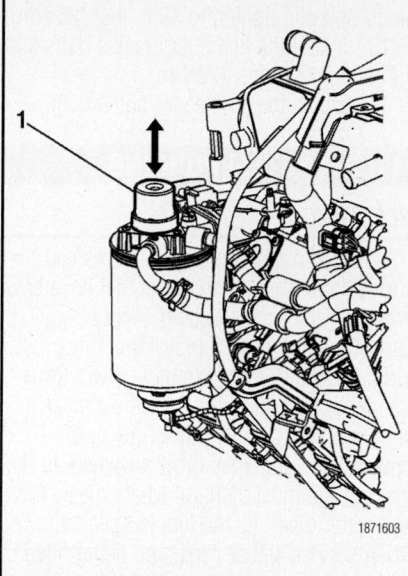

Fig. 741 Operate the priming pump (1) until only diesel fuel is visible

FUEL SYSTEM PRIMING

See Figures 742 and 743.

➡ In order for the diesel fuel system to work properly, the fuel lines must be full of fuel and contain no air. If air gets into the fuel lines, it will be necessary to prime the fuel system to eliminate the air before operating the vehicle. Air could have entered the system in one of the following ways:

- The vehicle ran out of fuel.
- The filter was removed for service or replacement.
- The fuel lines were removed or disconnected for servicing.
- The fuel filter water drain cock was opened while the engine was running.

If one or more of the above occurred, air has entered the fuel system and you will need to prime the system prior to operating the vehicle.

1. Prior to priming the fuel system, ensure that the following has been completed:
   a. There is fuel in the fuel tank.
   b. The fuel filter has been installed and properly tightened.
   c. The fuel lines are properly connected.
   d. The fuel filter is cool to the touch.
   e. Any dirt or debris has been removed from the fuel filter adapter and vent valve screw.
2. Remove the air cleaner outlet duct.
3. Open the vent valve screw by turning the screw counterclockwise several full turns.
4. Operate the priming pump by repeatedly pumping until a small amount of fuel seeps from the vent valve. Allow the pump to fully return upward between pumps. When fuel is present, the filter is full of fuel and the system is primed.
5. Close the vent valve screw.
6. Clean any fuel which accumulated on the fuel filter adapter.
7. Install the air cleaner outlet duct.
8. Start the engine and allow the engine to idle for a few minutes.
9. Check the fuel system for leaks.

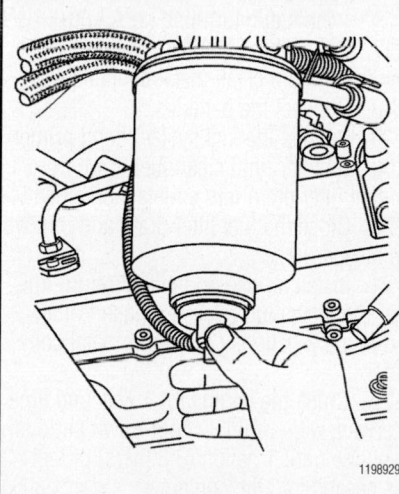

Fig. 740 Open the drain 3 or 4 turns or until the water contaminated fuel seeps from the drain

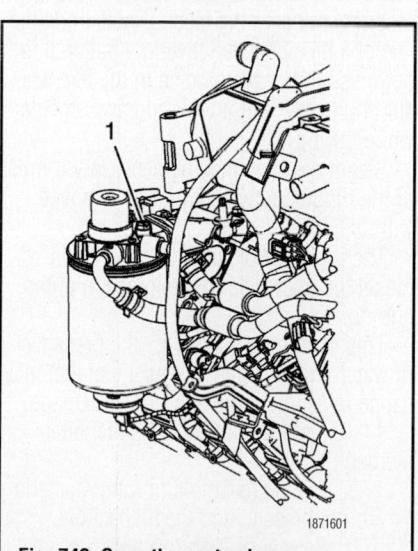

Fig. 742 Open the vent valve screw (1) by turning the screw counterclockwise several full turns

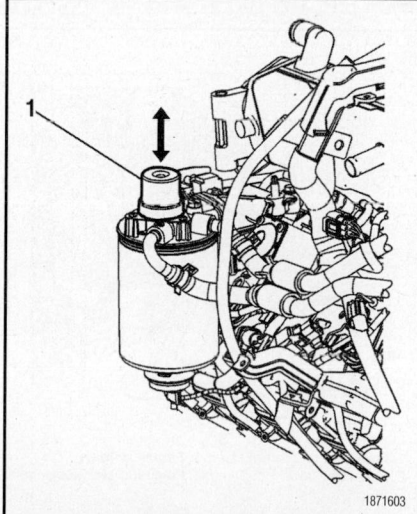

Fig. 743 Operate the priming pump (1) by repeatedly pumping until a small amount of fuel seeps from the vent valve

2011 Diesel Engines

See Figures 744 and 745.

1. Remove the air cleaner outlet duct.
2. Remove the upper intake manifold brace bolt.
3. Remove the fuel filter bracket bolts.
4. Remove the upper intake manifold brace.
5. Remove the fuel filter hoses.
6. Remove the fuel filter bracket bolts.
7. Remove the fuel filter and bracket.

To install:

8. Install the fuel filter bracket bolts and tighten to 18 ft. lbs. (25 Nm).
9. Install the fuel filter hoses.
10. Install the upper intake manifold brace.

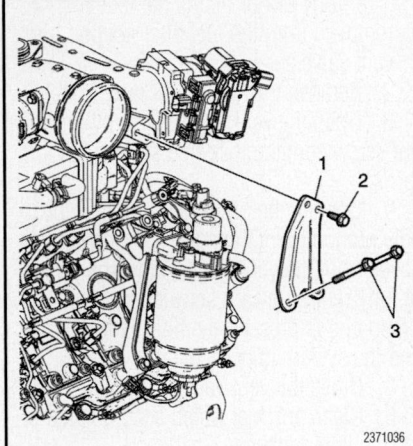

Fig. 744 Remove the upper intake manifold brace bolt (2), the fuel filter bracket bolts (3), and the upper intake manifold brace (1)

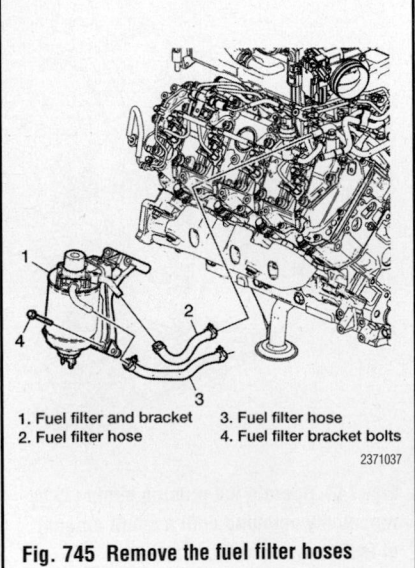

1. Fuel filter and bracket   3. Fuel filter hose
2. Fuel filter hose   4. Fuel filter bracket bolts

Fig. 745 Remove the fuel filter hoses

11. Install the upper intake manifold brace bolt and tighten to 18 ft. lbs. (25 Nm).
12. Install the fuel filter bracket bolts and tighten to 18 ft. lbs. (25 Nm).
13. Install the air cleaner outlet duct.

FUEL SYSTEM PURGING

BLEEDING

Fungi and other microorganisms can survive and multiply in diesel fuel if water is present. The fungi can be present in any part of the fuel handling system. These fungi grow into long strings and will form into large globules. The growths appear slimy and are usually black, green, or brown. The fungi may grow anywhere in the fuel but are most plentiful where diesel fuel and water meet. As the fuel is agitated, when service station tanks are being filled, fungi are distributed throughout the tank and may be pumped into a vehicle.

Fungi use the fuel as their main energy supply and need only trace amounts of water and minerals. As they grow and multiply, they change fuel into water, sludge, acids, and products of metabolism. The most common symptom is fuel filter plugging; however, various metal components including the fuel sending unit, pipes, fuel injectors, and injection pump can corrode.

✳ WARNING

Avoid physical contact with the biocides in order to avoid personal injury.

If fungi have caused fuel system contamination, use a diesel fuel biocide to sterilize the fuel system. Do not exceed the dosage recommended on the label. Discontinue the use of a biocide when towing a trailer. It is permissible to have biocide in the fuel when starting to tow, but do not add any biocide while towing.

Steam cleaning may be necessary if most of the fungus growth cannot be removed with biocides.

The presence of water or gasoline in diesel fuel may also cause injection pump and nozzle damage.

This procedure checks for the presence of water and gasoline in diesel fuel that may cause injection pump and nozzle damage.

1. Remove and inspect the fuel filter element.
   a. If water, gasoline or fungi/bacteria are not present, end the inspection.
   b. If water or fungi/bacteria are present, proceed to Cleaning Water from the Fuel System.

c. If gasoline is present, proceed to Cleaning Gasoline from the Fuel System.

Cleaning Water from the Fuel System

1. Disconnect the negative battery.
2. Remove the sending unit.
3. Inspect the fuel tank and the fuel sender for rust, fungi or bacteria. If there is rust, replace the rusted components.
4. Clean the inside of the fuel tank and the fuel sender with hot water.
5. Use compressed air in order to dry the fuel tank and the fuel sender.
6. Disconnect the ends of the following lines:
   • The fuel filter inlet line (both ends)
   • The transfer pump pressure line and suction line (if applicable)
   • The fuel filter outlet line (both ends)
   • The fuel filter drain
   • The fuel return line (both ends)
7. Inspect each of the pipes and lines.
8. Replace any rusted pipes.
9. Clean the inside of the fuel filter housing.
10. Dry the fuel filter housing with compressed air.
11. Dry the inside of each line with low pressure air.
12. Disconnect the crankshaft position sensor.
13. Install a new fuel filter.
14. Install the sending unit.
15. Add clean diesel fuel to the primary tank until the tank is ¼ full.
16. Reconnect the following lines:
   • The fuel filter inlet line
   • The fuel filter outlet line
   • The transfer pump pressure and suction (both ends) lines
   • The fuel return line (tank end)
17. Connect the fuel filter drain to a line that flows into a clean metal container.
18. Connect the batteries.
19. Operate the fuel system hand primer at the fuel filter until clean fuel flows from the fuel filter drain into a metal container.
20. Close the fuel filter drain and remove the bleeder hose.
21. Install a hose on the fuel return line near the glow plug relay, and insert other end into a 2 gallons (7.6 liters) metal container.
22. Crank the engine for 15 second time intervals, with 1 minute cool-down periods. Continue until 1 gallon (3.8 liters) of fuel has passed into the container.
23. Connect the fuel return line.
24. Reconnect the crankshaft position sensor.

25. Start and run the engine.
26. Stop the engine.
27. Clean any fuel spillage from the engine.
28. Fill the fuel tank and add a biocide, if needed.

Cleaning Gasoline from the Fuel System

1. Drain the fuel tank.
2. Fill the fuel tank to ¼ full.
3. Loosen the fuel filter drain and connect the filter to a hose that flows into a metal container.
4. Operate the fuel system hand primer at the fuel filter until clean fuel flows from the fuel filter drain into the metal container.
5. Hand tighten the fuel filter drain and disconnect the hose.
6. Install a hose on the fuel return line near the glow plug relay, and insert the other end into a 2 gallons (7.6 liters) metal container.
7. Crank the engine for 30 second time intervals, with 1 minute cool-down periods. Continue until 1 gallon (3.8 liters) of fuel has passed into the container.
8. Reconnect the fuel return line.
9. Attempt to start and run the engine for 15 minutes. If the engine does not start, operate the hand primer for 30 strokes, or until firm.
10. Stop the engine.
11. Clean any fuel spillage from the engine.
12. Clear the engine of any Diagnostic Trouble Codes (DTCs).

INJECTION TIMING

ADJUSTMENT

Circuit/System Description

The control functions for the fuel injection system are integrated in the Engine Control Module (ECM). Each injector's flow rate information and cylinder position are stored in the memory of both the Glow Plug Control Module (GPCM) and the ECM. The fuel injector flow rate programming must be done when any of the following procedures are performed:
- The ECM is replaced
- The GPCM is replaced
- Any fuel injectors are replaced

If the ECM does not communicate, the flow rate information can be retrieved from the GPCM. If both control modules fail to communicate, the fuel injector flow rate information, or Injection Quantity Adjustment (IQA) flow rate numbers, will need to be retrieved from each individual injector.

Before Programming A Control Module

➡ **DO NOT program a control module unless you are directed by a service procedure or you are directed by a General Motors service bulletin. Programming a control module at any other time will not permanently correct a customer's concern.**

1. Ensure the following conditions are met before programming a control module:
   a. Vehicle system voltage:
   - There is no charging system concern. All charging system concerns must be repaired before programming a control module.
   - Battery voltage is between 12–16 volts. The battery must be charged before programming the control module if the battery voltage is low.
   - A battery charger is NOT connected to the vehicle battery. Incorrect system voltage or voltage fluctuations from a battery charger may cause programming failure or control module damage.
   b. Turn OFF or disable any of the following systems that may put a load on the vehicle battery:
   - Twilight sentinel
   - Interior lights
   - Daytime Running Lights (DRL)— Applying the parking brake, on most vehicles, disables the DRL system.
   - HVAC systems
   - Engine cooling fans, etc.
   c. The ignition switch is in the proper position—The scan tool prompts you to turn ON the ignition, with the engine OFF. DO NOT change the position of the ignition switch during the programming procedure, unless instructed to do so.
   d. All of the following tool connections are secure:
   - The connection at the Data Link Connector (DLC)
   - The voltage supply circuits
   e. DO NOT disturb the tool harnesses while programming. If an interruption occurs during the programming procedure, programming failure or control module damage may occur.

Circuit/System Verification

Review the Display ECM & GPCM Inj. Flow Rates parameter with a scan tool. All cylinders should be programmed with a flow rate number. Both the GPCM and the ECM should be programmed with the same flow rate numbers for the corresponding cylinders.

Circuit/System Testing

➡ **If the flow rate number is not available in either control module, the numbers will need to be retrieved from each individual injector.**

Fuel Injector Identification Numbers

See Figure 775.

1. With a scan tool installed, enter the vehicle information and select the following options:
   - Engine Control Module
   - Module Setup
   - Injector Flow Rate Programming
   - Display ECM & GPCM Inj. Flow Rates
2. Record all flow rate numbers with the corresponding cylinders from the control modules.

➡ **When installing a new fuel injector, ensure that the IQA data number from the yellow IQA Data Tag, shipped with the new injector, is programmed to the correct cylinder.**

a. If any injectors are replaced, go to Reprogram Injector Flow Rates parameter and enter the flow rate number of the new injector to the corresponding cylinder.

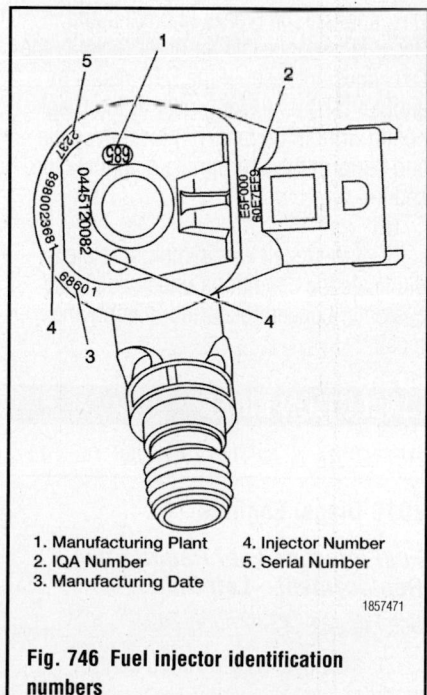

1. Manufacturing Plant
2. IQA Number
3. Manufacturing Date
4. Injector Number
5. Serial Number

1857471

Fig. 746 Fuel injector identification numbers

The flow rate numbers will automatically update both control modules.

b. If the ECM was replaced, go to Copy GPCM Inj. Flow Rates to ECM parameter and reprogram the ECM. This will update the ECM with the GPCM flow rate numbers.

c. If the GPCM was replaced or the flow rate numbers are not the same for both modules, go to Copy ECM Inj. Flow Rates to GPCM parameter and reprogram the GPCM. This will update the GPCM with the ECM flow rate numbers.

d. If both control modules were replaced, go to Reprogram Injector Flow Rates parameter and enter the previously recorded flow rate numbers or the numbers retrieved from each individual injector, to the corresponding cylinders.

Repair Instructions

➡**The ECM and the GPCM must be allowed to completely power down after programming is complete.**

1. Install any components or connectors that have been removed or replaced during diagnosis.

2. Perform any adjustment, programming or setup procedures that are required when a component or module is removed or replaced.

3. Turn ON the ignition, with the engine OFF, and clear the DTCs.

4. Disconnect the scan tool and turn OFF the ignition for 2 minutes.

5. If the repair was related to a DTC, duplicate the Conditions for Running the DTC and use the Freeze Frame/Failure Records, if applicable, in order to verify the DTC does not reset. If the DTC resets or another DTC is present, refer to the Diagnostic Trouble Code (DTC) List—Vehicle and perform the appropriate diagnostic procedure.

OR

6. If the repair was symptom related, duplicate the conditions under which the customer concern occurred to verify the repair.

INJECTION LINES

REMOVAL & INSTALLATION

2010 Diesel Engines

Fuel Injection Fuel Return Pipe Replacement—Left Side

See Figures 747 through 749.

1. Remove the glow plug control module.

Fig. 747 Remove the fuel injection fuel return pipe clips (1)

2. Remove the fuel injection fuel return pipe clips.

3. Disconnect the fuel injection fuel return pipe from the fuel injectors.

4. Cut the tie strap securing the fuel injection fuel return pipe to the engine wiring harness.

5. Disconnect the fuel injection fuel return pipe from the fuel return pipe.

➡**Note the routing of the fuel injection fuel return pipe under the engine wiring harness.**

6. Remove the fuel injection fuel return pipe from the engine.

To install:

7. Position the fuel injection fuel return pipe to the engine. Ensure to route the fuel injection fuel return pipe under the engine wiring harness.

8. Connect the fuel injection fuel return pipe to the fuel return pipe.

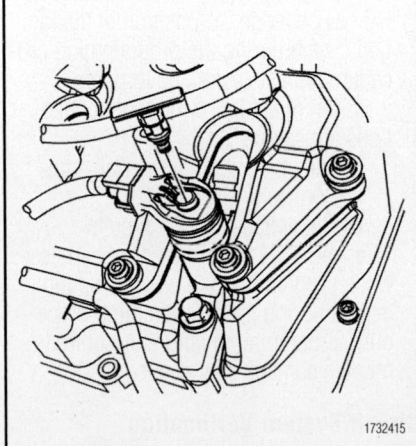

Fig. 748 Disconnect the fuel injection fuel return pipe from the fuel injectors

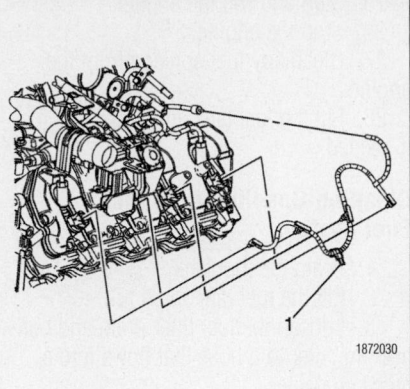

Fig. 749 Cut the tie strap (1) securing the fuel injection fuel return pipe to the engine wiring harness

9. Install a NEW tie strap securing the fuel injection fuel return pipe to the engine wiring harness in the location shown.

10. Connect the fuel injection fuel return pipe to the fuel injectors.

11. Install the fuel injection fuel return pipe clips.

12. Install the glow plug control module.

13. Prime the fuel system.

14. Start the engine. If the engine stalls, repeat the above step.

15. Once the engine starts, inspect for fuel leaks.

Fuel Injection Fuel Return Pipe Replacement—Right Side

See Figures 747, 748 and 750.

1. Remove the fuel filter and bracket.

2. Remove the intake air heater.

3. Remove the fuel injection fuel return pipe clips.

4. Disconnect the fuel injection fuel return pipe from the fuel injectors.

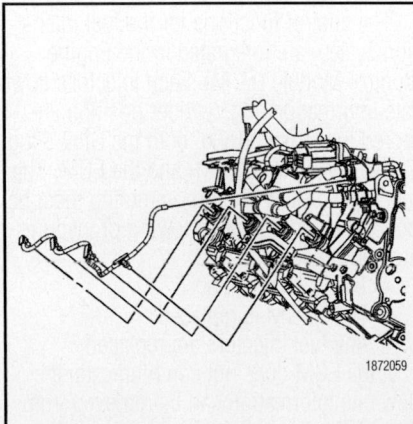

Fig. 750 Disconnect the fuel injection fuel return pipe from the fuel injection fuel feed manifold

5. Disconnect the fuel injection fuel return pipe from the fuel injection fuel feed manifold.

➡**Note the routing of the fuel injection fuel return pipe under/behind the engine wiring harness.**

6. Remove the fuel injection fuel return pipe from the engine.

To install:

7. Position the fuel injection fuel return pipe to the engine. Ensure to route the fuel injection fuel return pipe under/behind the engine wiring harness.

8. Connect the fuel injection fuel return pipe to the fuel injection fuel feed manifold.

9. Connect the fuel injection fuel return pipe to the fuel injectors.

10. Install the fuel injection fuel return pipe clips.

11. Install the intake air heater.

12. Install the fuel filter and bracket.

13. Prime the fuel system.

14. Start the engine. If the engine stalls, repeat the above step.

15. Once the engine starts, inspect for fuel leaks.

Fuel Feed Pipe

See Figures 751 through 756.

1. Remove the water outlet tube.

2. Remove the intake manifold tube.

3. Remove the alternator.

4. Disconnect the chassis fuel feed pipe quick connect fitting from the fuel feed pipe.

5. Disconnect the engine wiring harness electrical connectors from the Engine Coolant Temperature (ECT) sensors, and reposition the wiring out of the way.

6. Reposition the fuel filter hose clamp at the fuel feed pipe.

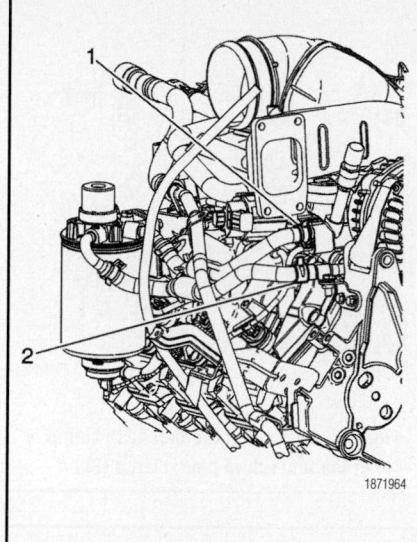

Fig. 752 Reposition the fuel filter hose clamp (2) at the fuel feed pipe

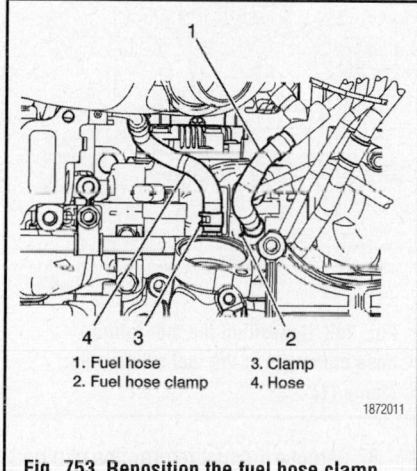
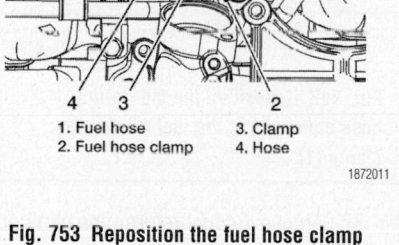

1. Fuel hose
2. Fuel hose clamp
3. Clamp
4. Hose

Fig. 753 Reposition the fuel hose clamp at the fuel injection pump

7. Remove the fuel filter hose from the fuel feed pipe.

8. Reposition the fuel hose clamp at the fuel injection pump.

9. Remove the fuel hose from the injection pump and reposition the hose out of the way.

10. Remove the fuel feed pipe clip nuts and bolt.

11. Remove the fuel pipe bracket bolt and fuel feed pipe clip.

➡**Note the routing of the fuel feed pipe under the engine wiring harness.**

12. Remove the fuel feed pipe.

To install:

➡**Ensure to route the fuel feed pipe under the engine wiring harness as noted during removal.**

13. Position and install the fuel feed pipe to the engine.

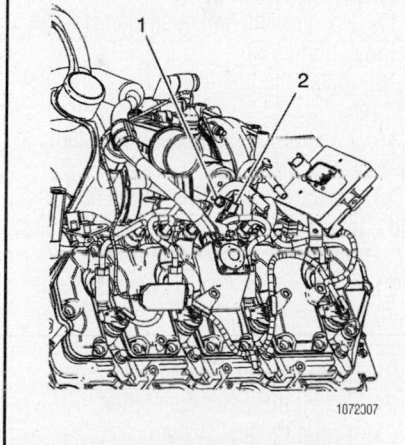

Fig. 755 Remove the fuel pipe bracket bolt (1) and fuel feed pipe clip (2)

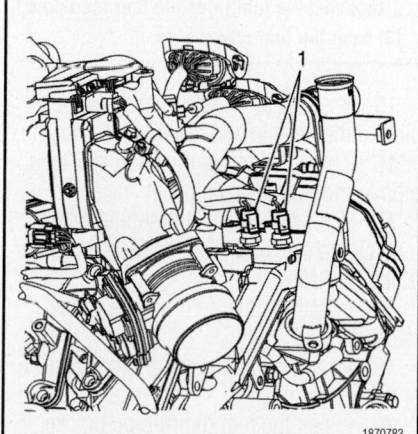

Fig. 751 Disconnect the engine wiring harness electrical connectors (1) from the ECT sensors

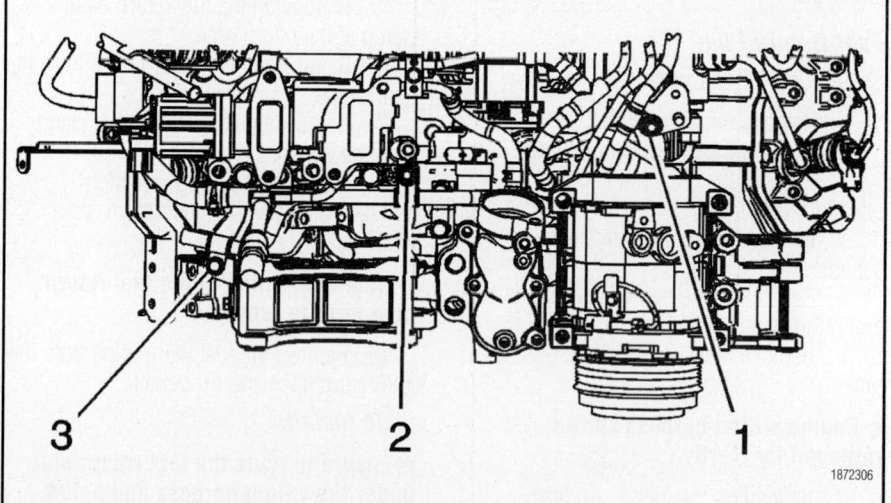

Fig. 754 Remove the fuel feed pipe clip nuts (1, 2) and bolt (3)

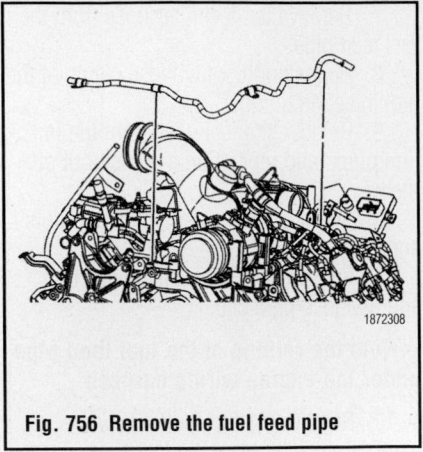

Fig. 756 Remove the fuel feed pipe

14. Position fuel feed pipe clip behind the fuel pipe bracket and install the bolt. Tighten the bolt to 18 ft. lbs. (24 Nm).

15. Install the fuel feed pipe clip nuts and bolt. Tighten the bolt/nuts to 18 ft. lbs. (24 Nm).

16. Position the fuel hose and install the hose to the injection pump.

17. Position the fuel hose clamp at the fuel injection pump.

18. Install the fuel filter hose to the fuel feed pipe.

19. Position the fuel filter hose clamp at the fuel feed pipe.

20. Position the engine wiring harness and connect the engine wiring harness electrical connectors to the ECT sensors.

21. Connect the chassis fuel feed pipe quick connect fitting to the fuel feed pipe.

22. Install the alternator.

23. Install the intake manifold tube.

24. Install the water outlet tube.

25. Prime the fuel system.

26. Start the engine. If the engine stalls, repeat the above step.

27. Once the engine starts, inspect for fuel leaks.

Fuel Return Pipe

See Figures 757 through 761.

1. Remove the water outlet.
2. Remove the intake manifold tube.
3. Remove the glow plug control module and bracket.
4. Remove the fuel temperature sensor.
5. Reposition the fuel hose clamp at the fuel return pipe.
6. Remove the fuel hose from the return pipe.

➡**Engine wiring harness shown removed for clarity.**

7. Reposition the fuel return hose clamp at the fuel return pipe.

Fig. 757 Reposition the fuel hose clamp (1) at the fuel return pipe; clamp (2)

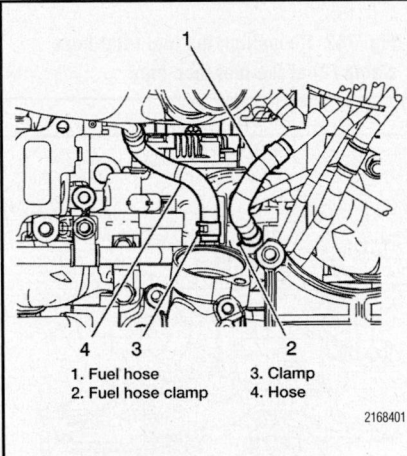

1. Fuel hose
2. Fuel hose clamp
3. Clamp
4. Hose

Fig. 758 Reposition the fuel return hose clamp (2) at the fuel return pipe; clamp (1)

8. Remove the fuel return pipe clip bolt and clip.

9. Remove the fuel return pipe clamp bolt and bracket.

10. Reposition the fuel return hose clamp at the return pipe.

11. Remove the fuel return hose from the return pipe.

12. Remove the fuel return pipe clamp bolt and clamp.

13. Disconnect the fuel injection fuel feed pipe from the fuel return pipe.

➡**Note the routing of the fuel return pipe prior to removal.**

14. Remove the fuel return pipe from the fuel return hose and the vehicle.

To install:

➡**Ensure to route the fuel return pipe under the wiring harness and noted during removal.**

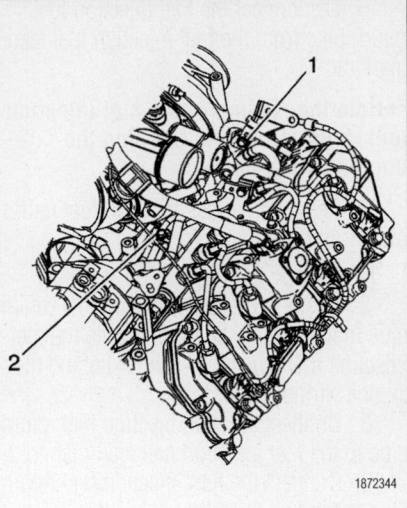

Fig. 759 Remove the fuel return pipe clip bolt (2) and clip; remove the fuel return pipe clamp bolt (1) and bracket

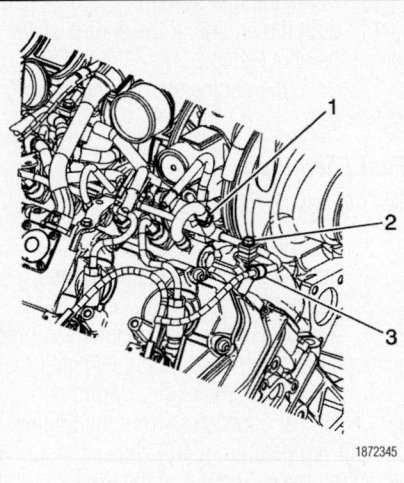

Fig. 760 Reposition the fuel return hose clamp (1) at the return pipe, remove the fuel return pipe clamp bolt (2) and clamp, disconnect the fuel injection fuel feed pipe (3) from the fuel return pipe

15. Position and install the fuel return pipe to the vehicle and the fuel return hose.

16. Connect the fuel injection fuel feed pipe to the fuel return pipe.

17. Position and install the fuel return pipe clamp and bolt. Tighten the bolt to 18 ft. lbs. (24 Nm).

18. Install the fuel return hose to the return pipe.

19. Position the fuel return hose clamp at the return pipe.

20. Install the fuel return pipe bracket, clamp, and bolt. Tighten the bolt to 18 ft. lbs. (24 Nm).

21. Install the fuel return pipe clip and bolt. Tighten the bolt to 18 ft. lbs. (24 Nm).

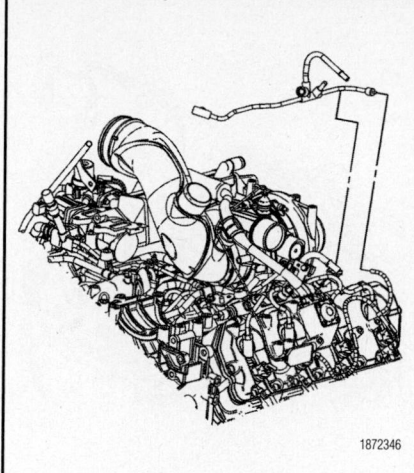

Fig. 761 Remove the fuel return pipe from the fuel return hose and the vehicle

22. Position the fuel return hose clamp at the fuel return pipe.

23. Install the fuel hose to the return pipe.

24. Position the fuel hose clamp at the fuel return pipe.

25. Install the fuel temperature sensor.

26. Install the glow plug control module and bracket.

27. Install the intake manifold tube.

28. Install the water outlet.

29. Prime the fuel system.

30. Start the engine. If the engine stalls, repeat the above step.

31. Once the engine starts, inspect for fuel leaks.

Fuel Injection Fuel Feed Front Pipe—Right Side

See Figures 762 and 763.

1. Remove the fuel feed pipe.

2. Remove the Exhaust Gas Recirculation (EGR) valve cooler.

➡ **Engine wiring harness shown removed for clarity.**

3. Remove the fuel rail fuel feed pipe clamp bolts and upper clamps.

4. Loosen the fuel rail fuel feed pipe fitting at the left fuel rail.

5. Loosen the fuel rail fuel feed pipe fitting at the right fuel rail.

6. Remove the right fuel rail fuel feed pipe.

To install:

7. Position and install the right fuel rail fuel feed pipe.

8. Install the fuel rail fuel feed pipe upper clamps and bolts. Tighten the bolts to 18 ft. lbs. (24 Nm).

9. Tighten the fuel rail fuel feed pipe fit-

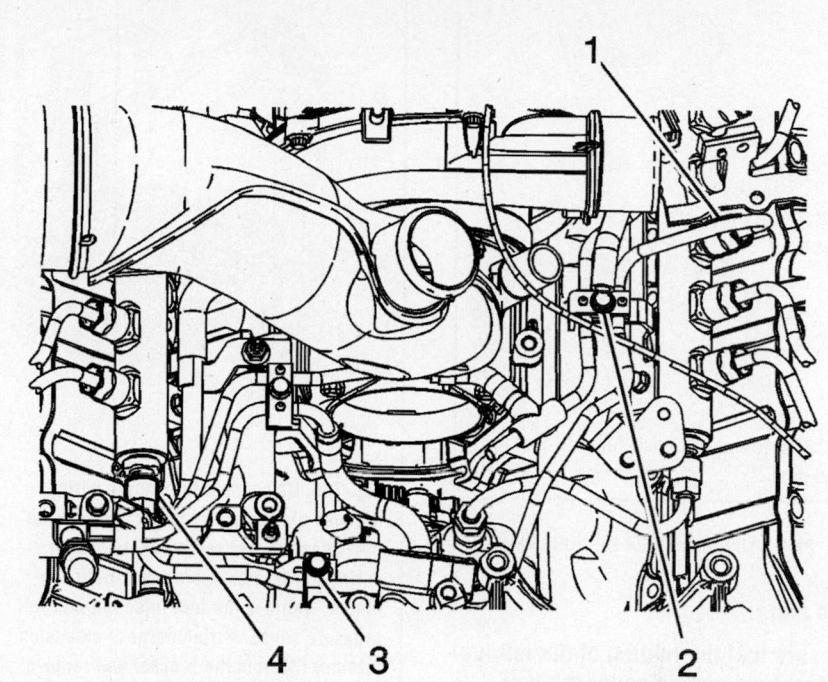

1. Fuel feed pipe fitting
2. Fuel feed pipe clamp bolts
3. Fuel feed pipe clamp bolts
4. Fuel feed pipe fitting

Fig. 762 Remove the fuel rail fuel feed pipe clamp bolts and upper clamps

ting at the right fuel rail. Tighten the fitting to 30 ft. lbs. (41 Nm).

10. Tighten the fuel rail fuel feed pipe fitting at the left fuel rail. Tighten the fitting to 30 ft. lbs. (41 Nm).

11. Install the EGR valve cooler.

12. Install the fuel feed pipe.

13. Prime the fuel system.

14. Start the engine. If the engine stalls, repeat the above step.

15. Once the engine starts, inspect for fuel leaks.

Fuel Injection Fuel Feed Front Pipe—Left Side

See Figures 764 and 765.

1. Remove the fuel return pipe to fuel injection pump fuel hose.

2. Loosen the left fuel rail fuel feed pipe fittings.

➡ **Note the routing of the left fuel rail fuel feed pipe under the fuel feed and return pipes.**

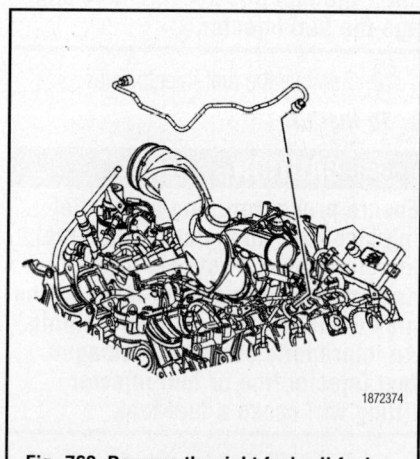

Fig. 763 Remove the right fuel rail fuel feed pipe

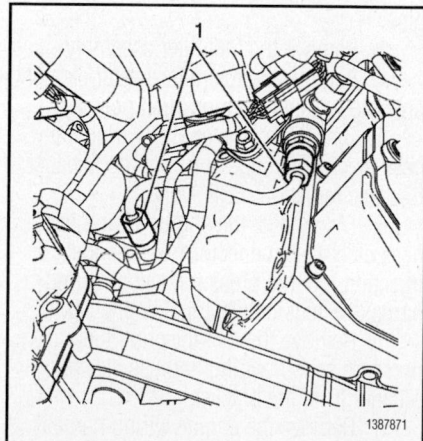

Fig. 764 Loosen the left fuel rail fuel feed pipe fittings (1)

Fig. 765 Remove the left fuel rail fuel feed pipe

3. Remove the left fuel rail fuel feed pipe.

To install:

→Ensure that the routing of the left fuel rail fuel feed pipe is under the fuel feed and return pipes.

4. Position and install the left fuel rail fuel feed pipe.

5. Tighten the left fuel rail fuel feed pipe fittings. Tighten the fittings to 30 ft. lbs. (41 Nm).

6. Install the fuel return pipe to fuel injection pump fuel hose.

7. Prime the fuel system.

8. Start the engine. If the engine stalls, repeat the above step.

9. Once the engine starts, inspect for fuel leaks.

Fuel Injector Fuel Feed Pipe—Right Side

See Figures 766 and 767.

1. Remove the air cleaner outlet duct.

2. Remove the charge air cooler outlet pipe.

3. Remove the fuel filter assembly.

4. Remove the fuel filter/heater element housing to fuel feed block fuel hoses.

5. Disconnect the engine wiring harness electrical connector from the Exhaust Gas Recirculation (EGR) valve.

6. Disconnect the engine wiring harness electrical connector from the fuel injection fuel rail pressure sensor wiring harness extension electrical connector.

7. Remove the fuel injection fuel rail pressure sensor wiring harness extension retainer from the bracket.

8. Remove the engine wiring harness bracket bolts and remove the bracket.

9. Reposition the engine wiring harness

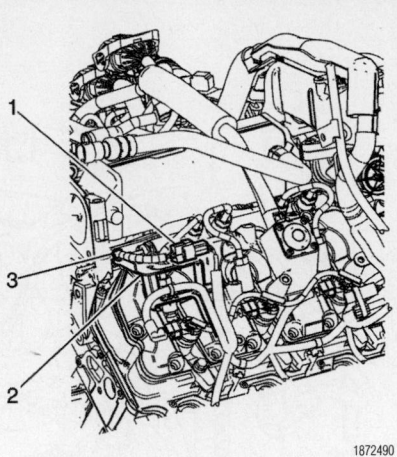

Fig. 766 Disconnect the engine wiring harness electrical connector (1) from the fuel injection fuel rail pressure sensor wiring harness extension electrical connector; Remove the fuel injection fuel rail pressure sensor wiring harness extension retainer (3) from the bracket and remove the bracket (2)

slightly in order to access the front fuel injection fuel feed pipe.

10. Prior to removing the fuel injector pipes, use compressed air to blow any debris from between the injector line and fittings. Wipe the fittings clean of debris.

11. Spray lithium grease, GM P/N 12346293 or equivalent, between the fuel injector line and fittings to assist in containing any debris during removal.

✴✴ CAUTION

DO NOT use compressed air to clean debris from the fuel injector inlet after the fuel line is removed. Using compressed air can allow debris to enter the fuel injector inlet and damage the fuel injector.

12. Remove the fuel injector pipes.

To install:

✴✴ CAUTION

Ensure proper torquing of the fuel injector line. An under-torqued fuel injector line will not seal properly and an over-torqued fuel injector line may damage the fuel injector fitting. An improperly sealed or damaged fuel injector line or fuel injector fitting will cause a fuel leak.

13. Install the fuel injector pipes. Tighten the fittings to 30 ft. lbs. (41 Nm).

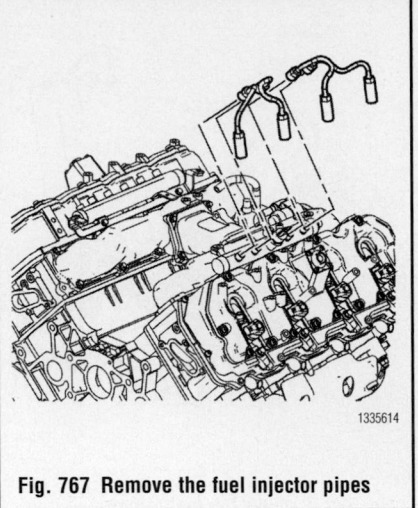

Fig. 767 Remove the fuel injector pipes

14. Reposition the engine wiring harness as necessary.

15. Position the engine wiring harness bracket to the valve rocker arm cover and install the bracket bolts. Tighten the bolts to 18 ft. lbs. (24 Nm).

16. Connect the engine wiring harness electrical connector to the fuel injection fuel rail pressure sensor wiring harness extension electrical connector.

17. Install the fuel injection fuel rail pressure sensor wiring harness extension retainer to the bracket.

18. Connect the engine wiring harness electrical connector to the EGR valve.

19. Install the fuel filter/heater element housing to fuel feed block fuel hoses.

20. Install the fuel filter assembly.

21. Install the charge air cooler outlet pipe.

22. Install the air cleaner outlet duct.

23. Prime the fuel system.

24. Start the engine. If the engine stalls, repeat the above step.

25. Once the engine starts, inspect for fuel leaks.

Fuel Injector Fuel Feed Pipe—Left Side

See Figures 768 through 770.

1. Remove the charge air cooler inlet pipe.

2. Remove the water outlet.

3. Remove the glow plug control module and bracket.

4. Disconnect the chassis fuel feed and return line quick connect fittings from the engine fuel feed and return pipes.

5. Remove the fuel line bracket nut.

6. Remove the fuel line bracket from the stud.

7. Remove the engine wiring harness clip from the fuel line bracket.

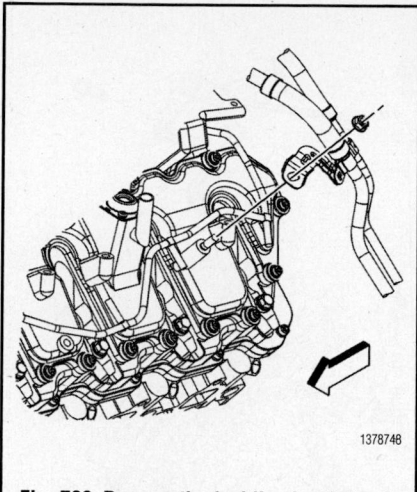

Fig. 768 Remove the fuel line bracket nut

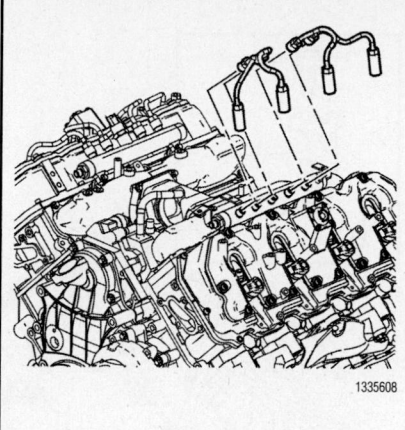

Fig. 770 Remove the left fuel injector pipes

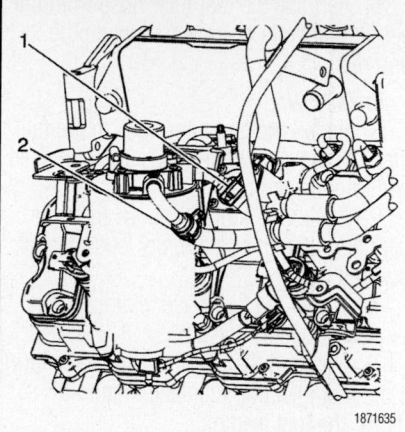

Fig. 771 Reposition the fuel filter hose clamp(s) (1, 2) at the fuel filter adapter

8. Remove the fuel line bracket bolts, clamp, and bracket.

9. Prior to removing the fuel injector pipes, use compressed air to blow any debris from between the injector line and fittings. Wipe the fittings clean of debris.

10. Spray lithium grease, GM P/N 12346293 or equivalent, between the fuel injector line and fittings to assist in containing any debris during removal.

✳✳ CAUTION

DO NOT use compressed air to clean debris from the fuel injector inlet after the fuel line is removed. Using compressed air can allow debris to enter the fuel injector inlet and damage the fuel injector.

11. Remove the left fuel injector pipes.

To install:

✳✳ CAUTION

Ensure proper torquing of the fuel injector line. An under-torqued fuel

injector line will not seal properly and an over-torqued fuel injector line may damage the fuel injector fitting. An improperly sealed or damaged fuel injector line or fuel injector fitting will cause a fuel leak.

12. Install the fuel injector pipes. Tighten the fittings to 30 ft. lbs. (41 Nm).

13. Position the fuel line bracket to the valve rocker arm cover, and install the clamp and bolts. Tighten the bolts to 18 ft. lbs. (24 Nm).

14. Install the engine wiring harness clip to the fuel line bracket.

15. Install the fuel line bracket to the stud.

16. Install the fuel line bracket nut. Tighten the nut to 15 ft. lbs. (21 Nm).

17. Connect the chassis fuel feed and return line quick connect fittings to the engine fuel feed and return pipes.

18. Install the glow plug control module and bracket.

19. Install the water outlet.
Install the charge air cooler inlet pipe.

20. Prime the fuel system.

21. Start the engine. If the engine stalls, repeat the above step.

22. Once the engine starts, inspect for fuel leaks.

2011 Diesel Engines

Fuel Filter/Heater Element Housing To Fuel Feed Block

See Figures 771 through 773.

1. Reposition the fuel filter hose clamp(s) at the fuel filter adapter.

2. Reposition the fuel filter hose clamp(s) at the fuel injection fuel feed manifold and/or the fuel feed pipe.

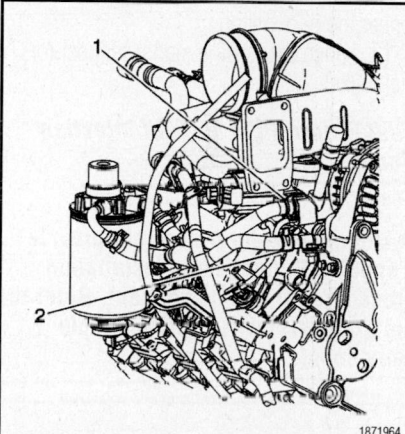

Fig. 772 Reposition the fuel filter hose clamp(s) (1, 2) at the fuel injection fuel feed manifold and/or the fuel feed pipe

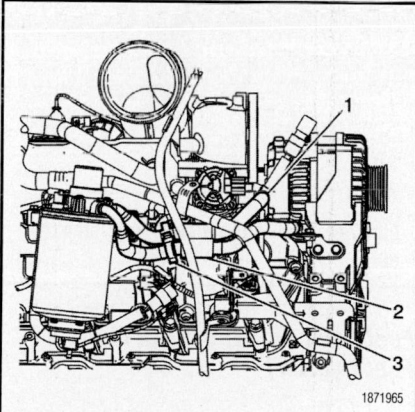

Fig. 773 Remove the fuel hose retainer (3), the fuel filter hose (1), and the fuel filter hose (2)

3. Remove the fuel hose retainer from the appropriate fuel filter hose.

4. Remove the fuel filter hose from the fuel filter adapter and the fuel injection fuel feed manifold, if required.

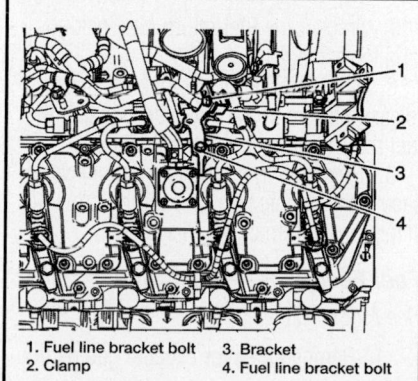

1. Fuel line bracket bolt
2. Clamp
3. Bracket
4. Fuel line bracket bolt

Fig. 769 Remove the fuel line bracket bolts, clamp, and bracket

5. Remove the fuel filter hose from the fuel filter adapter and the fuel feed pipe, if required.

To install:

6. Install the fuel filter hose to the fuel filter adapter and the fuel injection fuel feed manifold, if required.

7. Install the fuel filter hose from the fuel filter adapter and the fuel feed pipe, if required.

8. Install the fuel hose retainer to the fuel filter hose(s).

9. Position the fuel filter hose clamp(s) at the fuel injection fuel feed manifold and/or the fuel feed pipe.

10. Position the fuel filter hose clamp(s) at the fuel filter adapter.

11. Prime the fuel system.

12. Start the engine. If the engine stalls, repeat the above step.

13. Once the engine starts, inspect for fuel leaks.

Fuel Return Pipe To Fuel Injection Pump

See Figure 774.

➡The manufacturer does not provide a specific Removal and Installation procedure for this component. Refer to the graphic(s) when servicing this component.

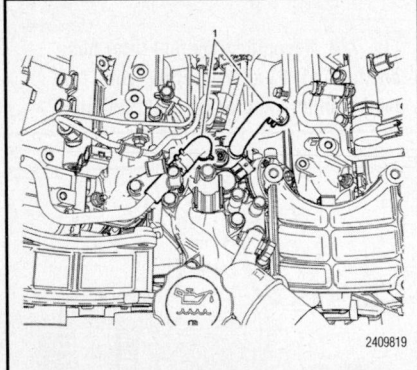

Fig. 774 Fuel return pipe to fuel injection pump (1)

Fuel Feed Pipe (Pump To Indirect Fuel Injector)

See Figure 775.

➡The manufacturer does not provide a specific Removal and Installation procedure for this component. Refer to the graphic(s) when servicing this component.

Fuel Return Hose

See Figures 776 and 777.

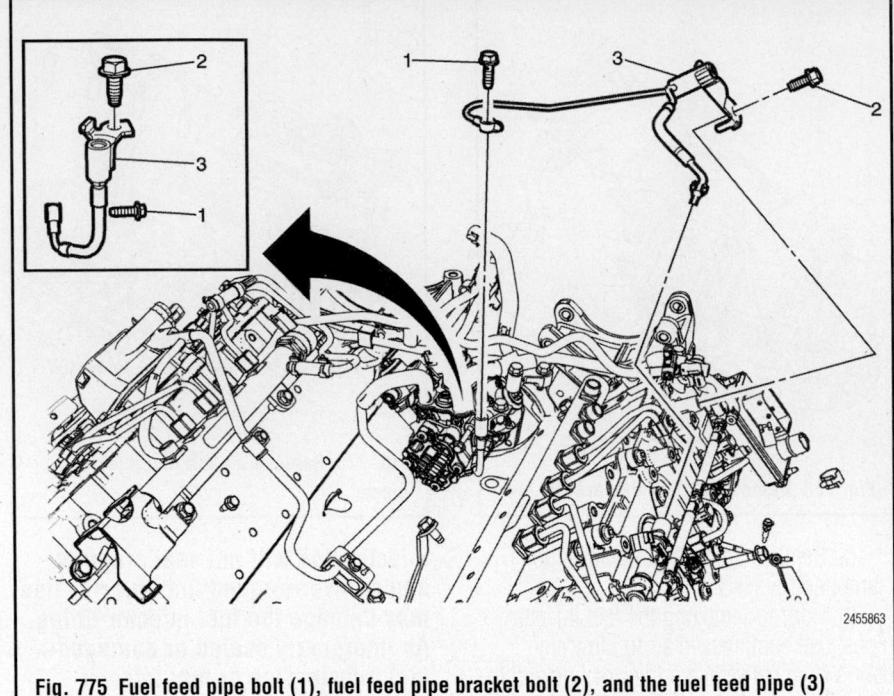

Fig. 775 Fuel feed pipe bolt (1), fuel feed pipe bracket bolt (2), and the fuel feed pipe (3)

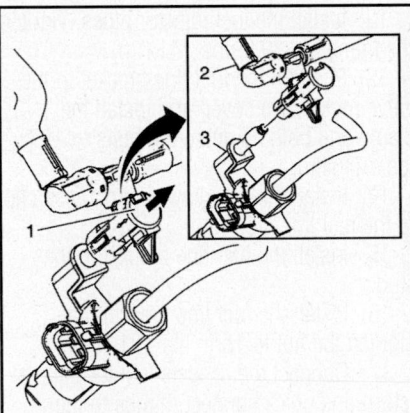

Fig. 776 Disengage the fuel return line by pulling upward on the cylindrical locking sleeve (1); remove the fuel return line (2) from the fuel injector (3)

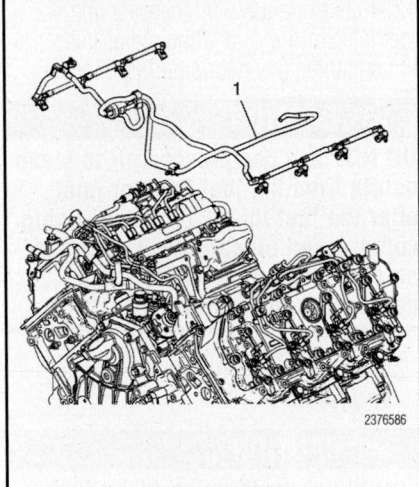

Fig. 777 Remove the fuel injector fuel return line assembly (1)

1. Disengage the fuel return line by pulling upward on the cylindrical locking sleeve.

2. Remove the fuel return line from the fuel injector.

3. Repeat the previous steps for the remaining injectors.

4. Remove the fuel injector fuel return line assembly.

To install:

5. Install the fuel injector fuel return line assembly.

6. Inspect the O-rings for damage. Replace if necessary. Replace the fuel return line assembly if necessary.

7. Inspect the fuel return line locking tabs for damage.

8. With the cylindrical locking sleeve released in the upward position, install the fuel return line to the fuel injector.

9. Press down on the locking sleeve to secure the connection. Repeat the previous steps for the remaining injectors.

Fuel Feed Pipe—Right Side

See Figure 778.

1. Remove the rear exhaust gas recirculation cooler.

2. Prior to removing the fuel injector pipes, use compressed air to blow any

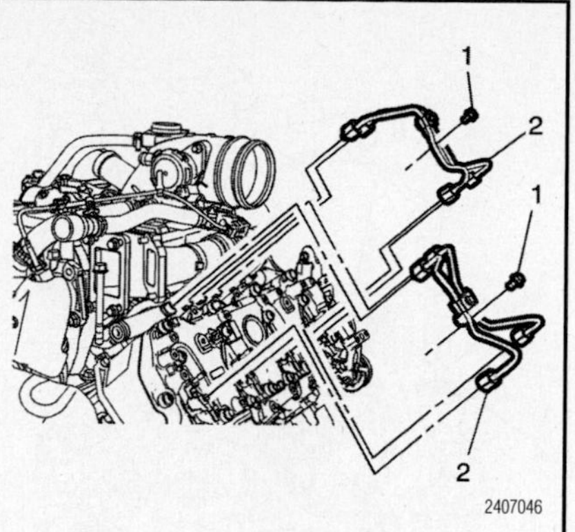

Fig. 778 Remove the fuel pipe bracket fasteners (1) and fuel injector pipes (2)

debris from between the injector line and fittings. Wipe the fittings clean of debris.

3. Spray lithium grease, GM P/N 12346293 or equivalent, between the fuel injector line and fittings to assist in containing any debris during removal.

✲✲ CAUTION

DO NOT use compressed air to clean debris from the fuel injector inlet after the fuel line is removed. Using compressed air can allow debris to enter the fuel injector inlet and damage the fuel injector.

4. Remove the fuel pipe bracket fasteners and fuel injector pipes.

To install:

✲✲ CAUTION

Ensure proper torquing of the fuel injector line. An under-torqued fuel injector line will not seal properly and an over-torqued fuel injector line may damage the fuel injector fitting. An improperly sealed or damaged fuel injector line or fuel injector fitting will cause a fuel leak.

5. Install the fuel injector pipes. Tighten the fittings to 22 ft. lbs. (30 Nm).
6. After installing the fuel injector pipes, clean the injector pipes and apply sealant GM P/N 97720043, at the fittings to prevent moisture and debris from collecting between the line and fitting.
7. Install the fuel pipe bracket fasteners and tighten to 89 inch lbs. (10 Nm).
8. Install the rear exhaust gas recirculation cooler.
9. Start the engine.
10. If the engine stalls, repeat the above step.
11. Inspect the fuel system for fuel leaks.

Fuel Feed Pipe—Left Side

See Figure 779.

1. Remove the front exhaust gas recirculation cooler.
2. Reposition the charge air cooler pipe from the turbo.
3. Remove the fuel rail pressure sensor bracket shield.
4. Prior to removing the fuel injector pipes, use compressed air to blow any debris from between the injector line and fittings. Wipe the fittings clean of debris.
5. Spray lithium grease, GM P/N 12346293 or equivalent, between the fuel injector line and fittings to assist in containing any debris during removal.

✲✲ CAUTION

DO NOT use compressed air to clean debris from the fuel injector inlet after the fuel line is removed. Using compressed air can allow debris to enter the fuel injector inlet and damage the fuel injector.

6. Remove the fuel pipe bracket fasteners and pipes.

To install:

✲✲ CAUTION

Ensure proper torquing of the fuel injector line. An under-torqued fuel injector line will not seal properly and an over-torqued fuel injector line may damage the fuel injector fitting. An improperly sealed or damaged fuel injector line or fuel injector fitting will cause a fuel leak.

7. Install the fuel injector pipes. Tighten the fittings to 22 ft. lbs. (30 Nm).
8. Install the fuel pipe bracket fasteners and tighten to 89 inch lbs. (10 Nm).

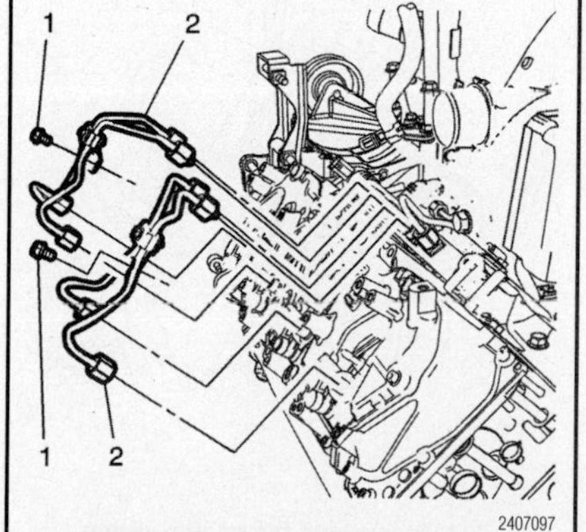

Fig. 779 Remove the fuel pipe bracket fasteners (1) and fuel injector pipes (2)

9. After installing the fuel injector pipes, clean the injector pipes and apply sealant GM P/N 97720043, at the fittings to prevent moisture and debris from collecting between the line and fitting.
10. Install the fuel rail pressure sensor bracket shield.
11. Reposition the charge air cooler pipe to the turbo.
12. Install the front exhaust gas recirculation cooler.
13. Start the engine.
14. If the engine stalls, repeat the above step.
15. Inspect the fuel system for fuel leaks.

Fuel High Pressure Pipe—Rail-To-Rail

See Figures 780 and 781.

1. Remove the high pressure fuel pipe fastener.
2. Remove the turbo charger assembly.
3. Remove the high pressure fuel pipe fasteners.
4. Remove the high pressure fuel pipe fitting.

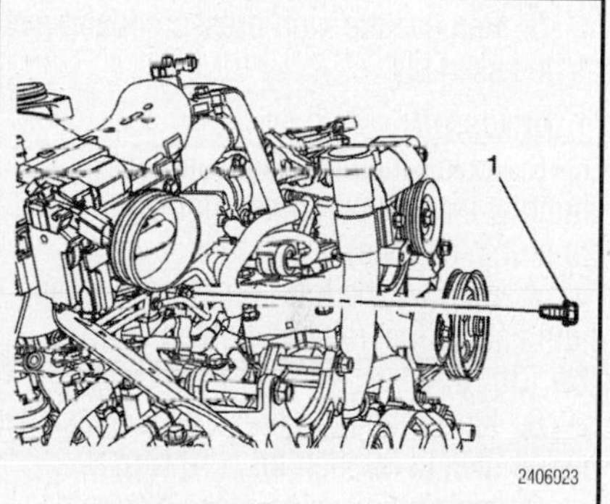

Fig. 780 Remove the high pressure fuel pipe fastener (1)

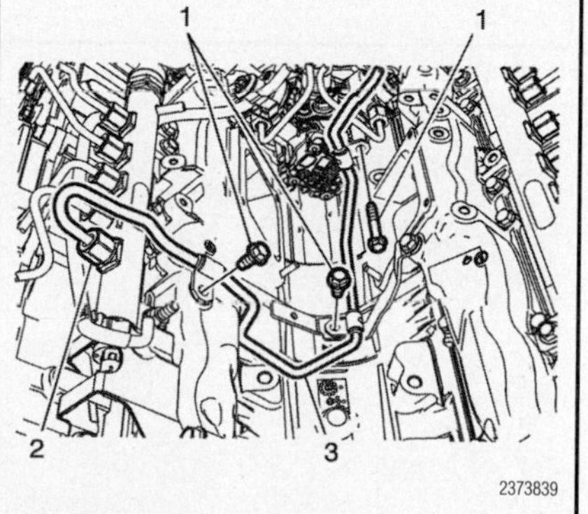

Fig. 781 Remove the high pressure fuel pipe fasteners (1), the fuel pipe fitting (2), and the fuel pipe (3)

5. Remove the high pressure fuel pipe.

To install:

6. Install the high pressure fuel pipe fitting and tighten to 22 ft. lbs. (30 Nm).

7. Install the high pressure fuel pipe fasteners and tighten to 89 inch lbs. (10 Nm).

8. Install the high pressure fuel fastener and tighten to 89 inch lbs. (10 Nm).

9. Install the turbo charger assembly.

10. Start the engine.

11. If the engine does not start, repeat the above step.

12. Inspect the fuel system for leaks.

Fuel High Pressure Pipe— Pump-To-Rail

See Figures 782 and 783.

1. Remove the high pressure fuel pipe fastener.

2. Remove the center intake manifold.

3. Remove the high pressure fuel pipe fitting at the fuel pump.

4. Remove the high pressure fuel pipe fitting at the fuel rail.

5. Remove the high pressure fuel pipes as an assembly.

To install:

6. Install the high pressure fuel pipe fitting at the fuel pump and tighten to 28 ft. lbs. (38 Nm).

7. Remove the high pressure fuel pipe fitting at the fuel rail and tighten to 22 ft. lbs. (30 Nm).

8. Install the high pressure fuel fastener and tighten to 89 inch lbs. (10 Nm)

9. Install the center intake manifold.

10. Start the engine.

11. If the engine does not start, repeat the above step.

12. Inspect the fuel system for leaks.

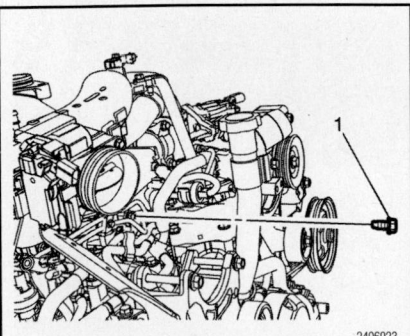

Fig. 782 Remove the high pressure fuel pipe fastener (1)

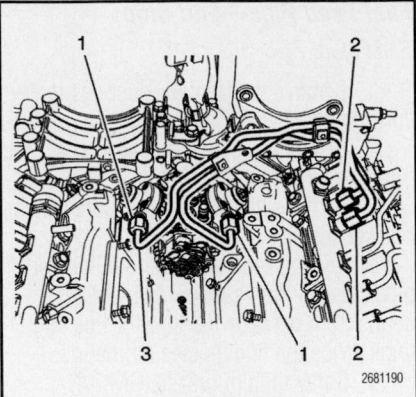

Fig. 783 Remove the high pressure fuel pipe fitting (1) at the fuel pump, the high pressure fuel pipe fitting (2) at the fuel rail, and the high pressure fuel pipes (3) as an assembly

INJECTORS

REMOVAL & INSTALLATION

2010 Diesel Engines

Right Side

See Figures 784 through 790.

1. Remove the right fuel injection fuel feed pipes.

2. Remove the right fuel injection fuel return pipe.

✳✳ CAUTION

Label all the injector electrical connectors before the connectors are removed in order to prevent reconnecting to the wrong injector. Failure to properly connect the injectors in the correct sequence will cause severe engine damage.

Fig. 784 Disconnect the engine wiring harness electrical connectors from the fuel injectors

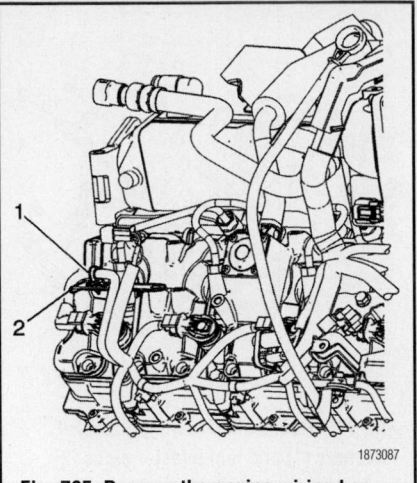

Fig. 785 Remove the engine wiring harness clip (1) from the wiring harness bracket and remove the bracket (2)

3. Disconnect the engine wiring harness electrical connectors from the fuel injectors.

4. Remove the engine wiring harness clip from the wiring harness bracket and remove the bracket.

5. Remove the engine wiring harness clips from the wiring harness bracket.

6. Remove the engine wiring harness bracket bolts and bracket.

7. Remove the engine wiring harness clip from the oil level indicator tube bracket.

8. Remove the oil level indicator tube bolt.

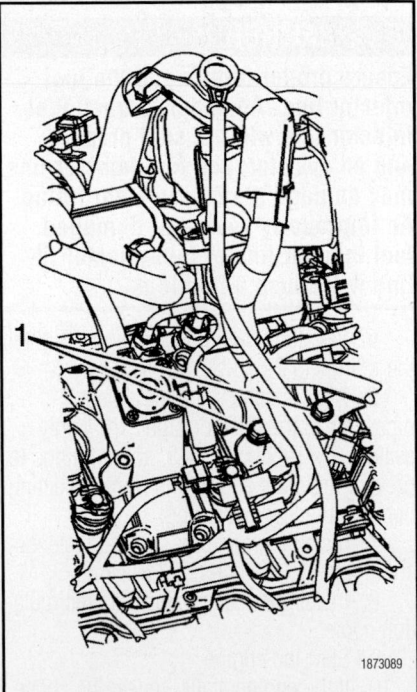

Fig. 786 Remove the engine wiring harness bracket bolts (1) and bracket

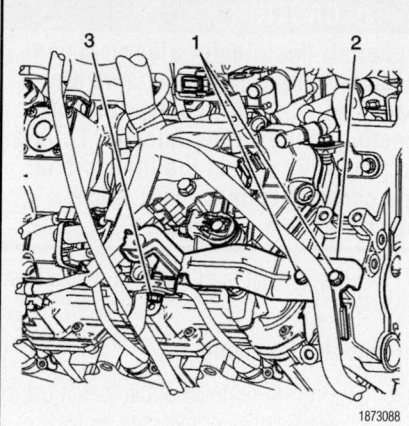

Fig. 787 Remove the engine wiring harness clip from the oil level indicator tube bracket (2), the oil level indicator tube bolt (3), and the oil level indicator tube bracket bolts (1)

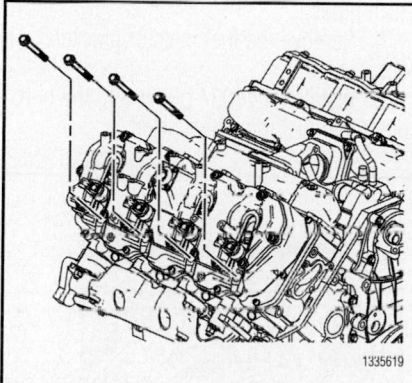

Fig. 788 Remove the fuel injector bracket bolts

9. Remove the oil level indicator tube bracket bolts.

10. Remove the oil level indicator tube bracket.

11. Remove the fuel injector bracket bolts.

12. Install the Fuel Injector Puller (J-46594) into the bolt hole in the fuel injector bracket.

13. Install a flare nut wrench onto the J-46594 and pull back away from the fuel injector, until the injector releases from its seat.

14. Remove the J-46594.

➡ The unique fuel injector flow rates are programmed into the ECM according to cylinder location. Mark the injectors for correct re-installation to the same cylinders. Failure to do so may result in a poor driveability condition.

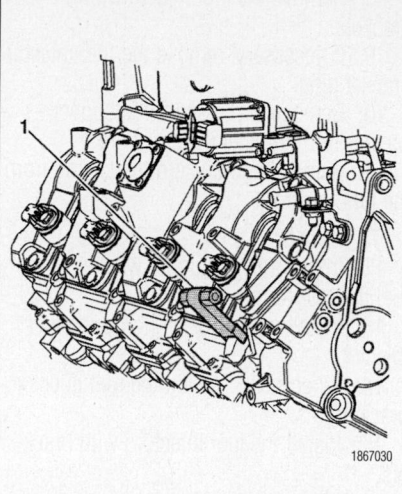

Fig. 789 Install the Fuel Injector Puller (J-46594) (1) into the bolt hole in the fuel injector bracket

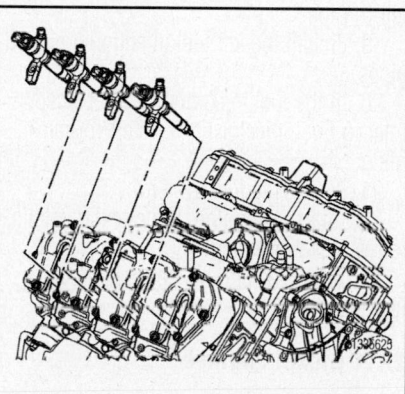

Fig. 790 Remove the fuel injectors with brackets

15. Remove the fuel injectors with brackets.

16. If necessary, remove the fuel injector bracket pins.

17. Remove and discard the copper washer from the fuel injector bore.

18. Remove and discard the O-ring from the fuel injector.

To install:

19. Install a NEW copper washer to the fuel injector bore.

20. Install a NEW O-ring onto the fuel injector.

21. If necessary, install the fuel injector bracket pins.

22. Install the fuel injectors with brackets.

23. Install the fuel injector bracket bolts. Tighten the bolts to 22 ft. lbs. (30 Nm).

24. Position the oil level indicator tube bracket to the alternator bracket.

25. Install the oil level indicator tube bracket bolts. Tighten the bolts to 15 ft. lbs. (21 Nm).

26. Install the oil level indicator tube bolt. Tighten the bolt to 15 ft. lbs. (21 Nm).

27. Install the wiring harness clip to the oil level indicator tube bracket.

28. Position the engine wiring harness bracket onto the upper valve rocker arm cover and install the bolts. Tighten the bolts to 15 ft. lbs. (21 Nm).

29. Install the engine wiring harness clips to the wiring harness bracket.

30. Position the engine wiring harness bracket onto the upper valve rocker arm cover and install the engine wiring harness clip to the wiring harness bracket.

31. Connect the engine wiring harness electrical connectors to the fuel injectors.

32. Install the right fuel injection fuel return pipe.

33. Install the right fuel injection fuel feed pipes.

34. If the fuel injectors were replaced, refer to Fuel Injector Flow Rate Programming.

35. Prime the fuel system.

36. Start the engine. If the engine stalls, repeat the above step.

37. Once the engine starts, inspect for fuel leaks.

Left Side

See Figures 784, 791 through 793.

1. Remove the left fuel injection fuel feed pipes.

2. Remove the left fuel injection fuel return pipe.

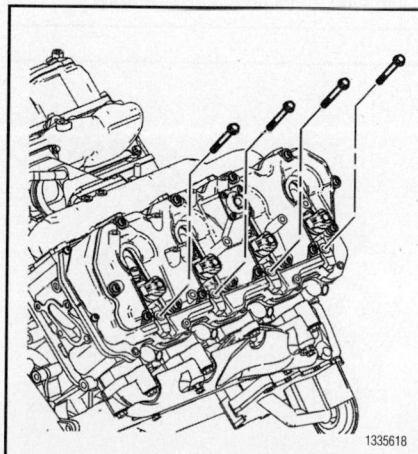

Fig. 791 Remove the fuel injector bracket bolts

❈❈ CAUTION

Label all the injector electrical connectors before the connectors are removed in order to prevent reconnecting to the wrong injector. Failure to properly connect the injectors in the correct sequence will cause severe engine damage.

3. Disconnect the engine wiring harness electrical connectors from the fuel injectors.

4. Remove the fuel injector bracket bolts.

5. Install the J-46594 into the bolt hole in the fuel injector bracket.

6. Install a flare nut wrench onto the J-46594 and pull back away from the fuel injector, until the injector releases from its seat.

7. Remove the J-46594.

➡ The unique fuel injector flow rates are programmed into the ECM according to cylinder location. Mark the injectors for correct re-installation to the same cylinders. Failure to do so may result in a poor driveability condition.

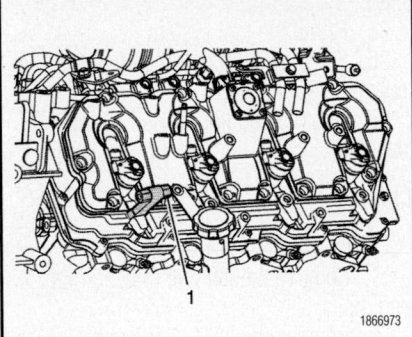

Fig. 792 Install the J-46594 (1) into the bolt hole in the fuel injector bracket

Fig. 793 Remove the fuel injectors with brackets

8. Remove the fuel injectors with brackets.

9. If necessary, remove the fuel injector bracket pins.

10. Remove and discard the copper washer from the fuel injector bore.

11. Remove and discard the O-ring from the fuel injector.

To install:

12. Install a NEW copper washer to the fuel injector bore.

13. Install a NEW O-ring onto the fuel injector.

14. If necessary, install the fuel injector bracket pins.

15. Install the fuel injectors with brackets.

16. Install the fuel injector bracket bolts. Tighten the bolts to 22 ft. lbs. (30 Nm).

17. Connect the engine wiring harness electrical connectors to the fuel injectors.

18. Install the left fuel injection fuel return pipe.

19. Install the left fuel injection fuel feed pipes.

20. If the fuel injectors were replaced, refer to Fuel Injector Flow Rate Programming.

21. Prime the fuel system.

22. Start the engine. If the engine stalls, repeat the above step.

23. Once the engine starts, inspect for fuel leaks.

2011 Diesel Engines

Left Side

See Figures 794 through 797.

1. Remove the left side fuel injection fuel feed pipes.

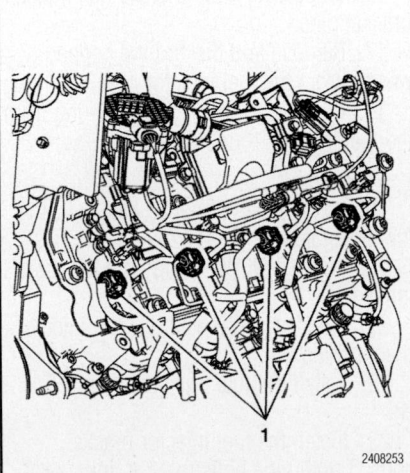

Fig. 794 Disconnect the fuel injector electrical connectors (1)

❈❈ CAUTION

Label all the injector electrical connectors before the connectors are removed in order to prevent reconnecting to the wrong injector. Failure to properly connect the injectors in the correct sequence will cause severe engine damage.

2. Disconnect the fuel injector electrical connectors.

➡ Note the following:

• Prior to removal of the fuel injector pipes, use compressed air to remove any debris from the injector line and fittings.

• Spray lithium grease, GM P/N 12346293 or equivalent, between the fuel injector line and fittings to assist with removal.

3. Disconnect and reposition the fuel return pipes.

4. Remove the fuel injector bracket bolts.

5. Install EN 46954 puller into the bolt hole in the fuel injector bracket.

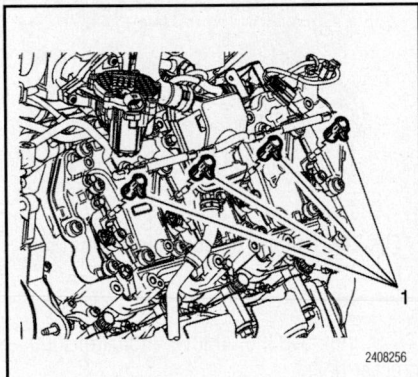

Fig. 795 Disconnect and reposition the fuel return pipes (1)

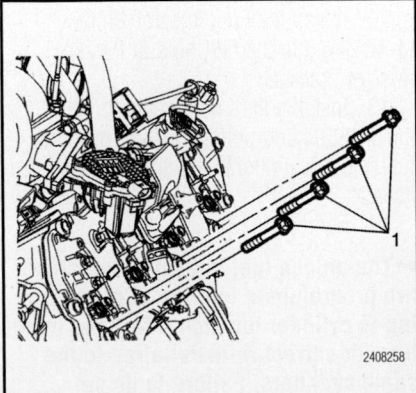

Fig. 796 Remove the fuel injector bracket bolts (1)

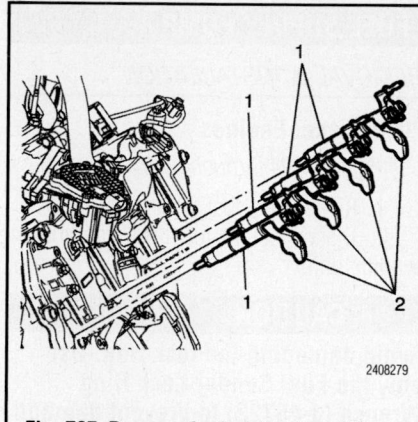

Fig. 797 Remove the fuel injectors (1) with the brackets (2)

Fig. 798 Disconnect the fuel injector electrical connectors (1)

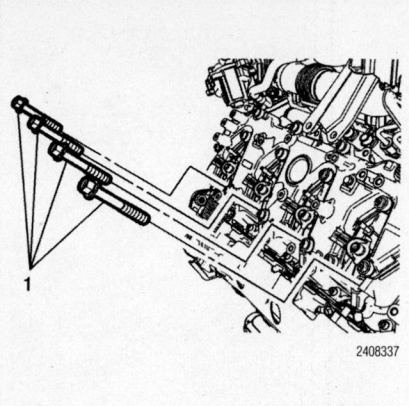

Fig. 800 Remove the fuel injector bracket bolts (1)

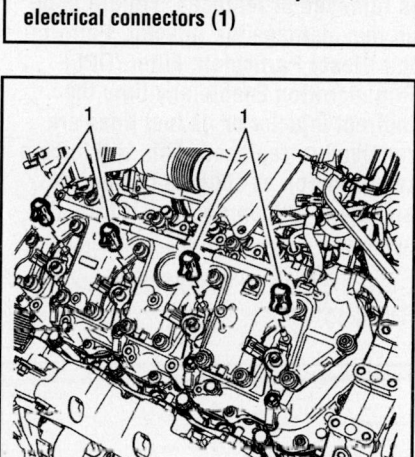

Fig. 799 Disconnect and reposition the fuel return pipes (1)

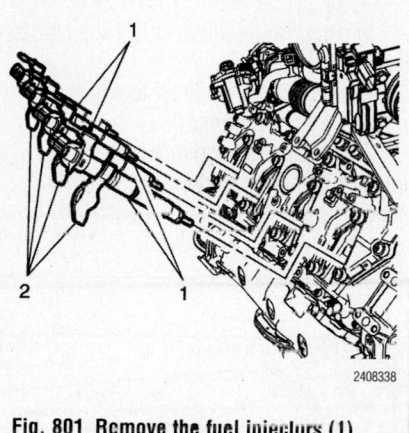

Fig. 801 Remove the fuel injectors (1) with the brackets (2)

6. Install a flare nut wrench onto EN 46954 puller , and work the tool outward until the injector releases from its seat.

7. Remove the EN 46954 puller.

8. Remove the fuel injectors with the brackets.

9. Remove and discard the copper washer from the fuel injector bore.

10. Remove and discard the fuel injector O-ring from the injector.

To install:

11. Install a NEW copper washer to the fuel injector bore.

12. Install a NEW fuel injector O-ring to the injector.

13. Install the fuel injectors with brackets.

14. Install the fuel injector bracket bolts and tighten to 22 ft. lbs. (30 Nm).

15. Reposition and connect and the fuel return pipes.

16. Connect the fuel injector electrical connectors.

17. If the fuel injectors were replaced, program the flow rate.

18. Prime the fuel system.

19. Start the engine. If the engine stalls, repeat the above step.

20. Once the engine starts, inspect for fuel leaks.

Right Side

See Figures 798 through 801.

1. Remove the fuel filter bracket.

2. Remove the right side fuel injection fuel feed pipes.

✴✴ CAUTION

Label all the injector electrical connectors before the connectors are removed in order to prevent reconnecting to the wrong injector. Failure to properly connect the injectors in the correct sequence will cause severe engine damage.

3. Disconnect the fuel injector electrical connectors.

➡ Note the following:

• Prior to removal of the fuel injector pipes, use compressed air to remove any debris from the injector line and fittings.

• Spray lithium grease, or equivalent, between the fuel injector line and fittings to assist with removal.

4. Disconnect and reposition the fuel return pipes.

5. Remove the fuel injector bracket bolts.

6. Install EN 46954 puller into the bolt hole in the fuel injector bracket.

7. Install a flare nut wrench onto EN 46954 puller , and work the tool outward until the injector releases from its seat.

8. Remove the EN 46954 puller.

9. Remove the fuel injectors with the brackets.

10. Remove and discard the copper washer from the fuel injector bore.

11. Remove and discard the fuel injector O-ring from the injector.

To install:

12. Install a NEW copper washer to the fuel injector bore.

13. Install a NEW fuel injector O-ring to the injector.

14. Install the fuel injectors with brackets.

15. Install the fuel injector bracket bolts and tighten to 22 ft. lbs. (30 Nm).

16. Reposition and connect and the fuel return pipes.

17. Connect the fuel injector electrical connectors.

18. If the fuel injectors were replaced, program the flow rate.

19. Prime the fuel system.

20. Start the engine. If the engine stalls, repeat the above step.

21. Once the engine starts, inspect for fuel leaks.

Indirect Fuel Injector

See Figures 802 and 803.

1. Remove the right side wheelhouse liner.

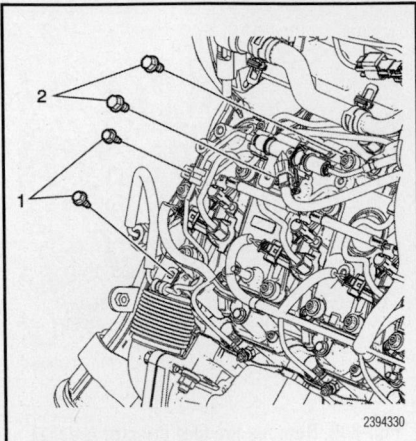

Fig. 802 Remove the indirect fuel injector fasteners (1, 2)

2. Remove the indirect fuel injector fasteners.

3. Remove the indirect fuel injector retainer from the fitting.

4. Remove the indirect fuel injector using the Hydrocarbon Injector Quick Connect Release Tool (CH-49736).

5. Remove the indirect injector fitting.

To install:

6. Install the indirect fuel injector retainer to the fitting.

7. Install the indirect fuel injector and tighten the fitting to 33 ft. lbs. (45 Nm).

8. Install the indirect fuel injector fasteners to 18 ft. lbs. (25 Nm).

9. Tighten the indirect fuel injector fitting to 33 ft. lbs. (45 Nm).

10. Install the right side wheelhouse liner.

➡The indirect fuel injector and its fuel lines must be purged of air any time it is removed or replaced. Failure to do so may damage the injector. Perform the Diesel Particulate Filter (DPF) Regeneration Enable any time the indirect injector or its fuel lines are removed or replaced. This will force a regeneration as soon as conditions allow and will purge any air from the system.

11. Perform the Diesel Particulate Filter Regeneration.

FUEL SUPPLY PUMP

REMOVAL & INSTALLATION

2010 Diesel Engines

See Figures 804 through 806.

1. Remove the fuel tank.

2. Disconnect the fuel lines from the sending unit.

✳✳ CAUTION

Avoid damaging the lock ring. Use only the Fuel Sender Lock Ring Wrench (J-45722) to prevent damage to the lock ring.

✳✳ CAUTION

Do Not handle the fuel sender assembly by the fuel pipes. The amount of leverage generated by handling the fuel pipes could damage the joints.

➡Do NOT use impact tools. Significant force will be required to release the lock ring. The use of a hammer and

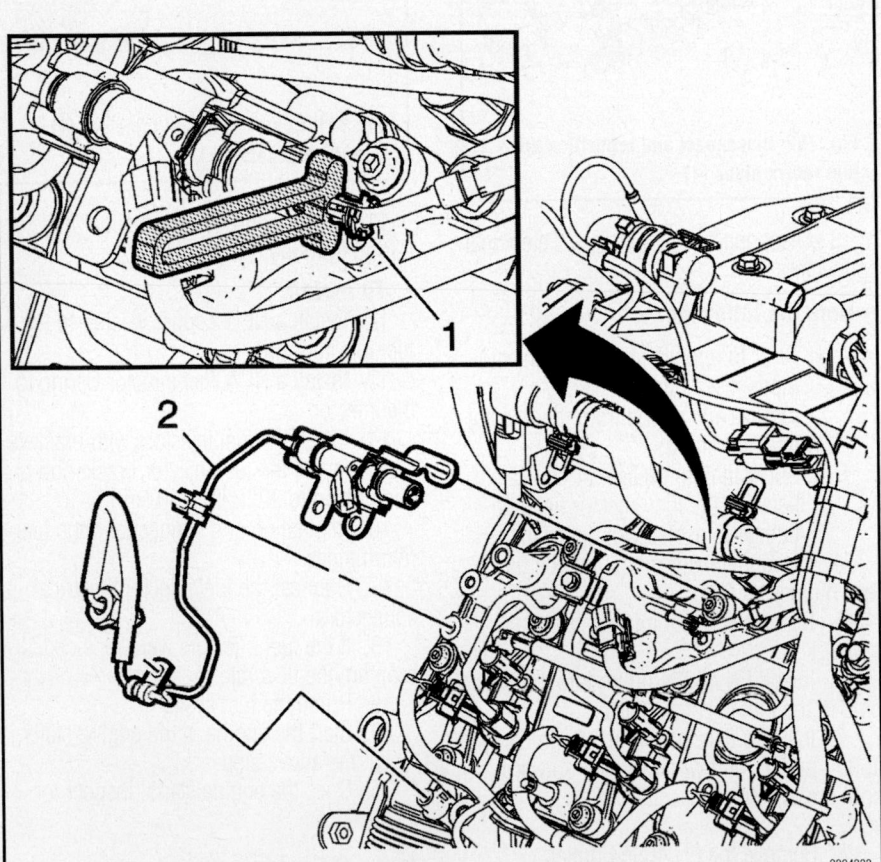

Fig. 803 Remove the chndirect fuel injector retainer (1) from the fitting; remove the indirect fuel injector (2) using the CH-49736

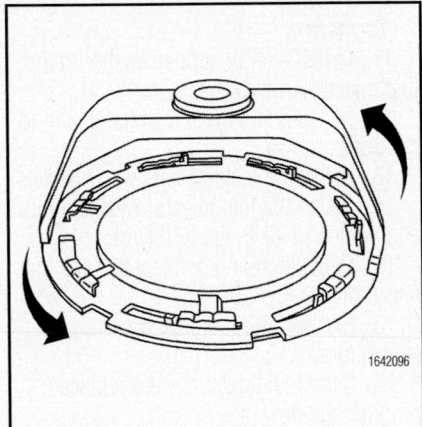

Fig. 804 Use the J-45722 and a long breaker-bar in order to unlock the fuel sender lock ring

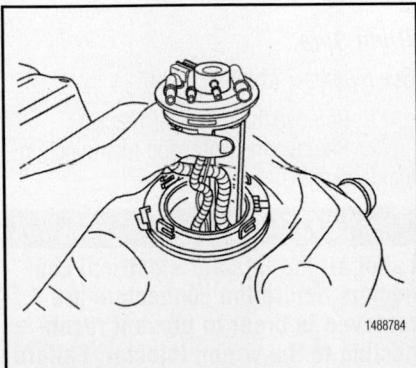

Fig. 805 Remove the sending unit and seal

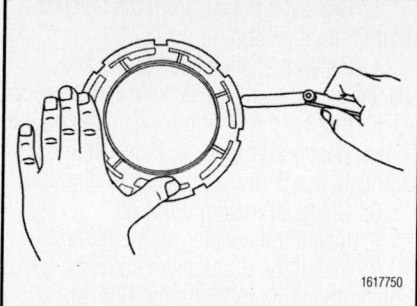

Fig. 806 Measure the clearance between the lock ring and the flat surface using a feeler gauge at 7 points

screwdriver is not recommended. Secure the fuel tank in order to prevent fuel tank rotation.

3. Use the J-45722 and a long breaker-bar in order to unlock the fuel sender lock ring.

4. Remove the sending unit and seal. Discard the seal.

5. Clean the sending unit sealing surfaces.

➡ Some lock rings were manufactured with "DO NOT REUSE" stamped into them. These lock rings may be reused if they are not damaged or warped.

➡ Inspect the lock ring for damage due to improper removal or installation procedures. If damage is found, install a NEW lock ring.

➡ Check the lock ring for flatness.

6. Place the lock ring on a flat surface. Measure the clearance between the lock ring and the flat surface using a feeler gauge at 7 points.

7. If warpage is less than 0.016 inches (0.41 mm), the lock ring does not require replacement.

8. If warpage is greater than 0.016 inches (0.41 mm), the lock ring must be replaced.

To install:
9. Install the sending unit and a NEW seal.

➡ Always replace the fuel sender seal when installing the fuel sender assembly. Replace the lock ring if necessary. DO NOT apply any type of lubrication in the seal groove. Ensure the lock ring is installed with the correct side facing upward. A correctly installed lock ring will only turn in a clockwise direction.

10. Use the J-45722 in order to install the fuel sender lock ring. Turn the fuel

sender lock ring in a clockwise direction.

11. Connect the fuel lines to the sending unit.

12. Install the fuel tank.

2011 Diesel Engines

See Figures 807 through 809.

1. Remove the fuel tank.
2. Disconnect the fuel feed and return pipes.
3. Using the Fuel Tank Sender Wrench (CH-45722), remove the cam lock ring by turning counter-clockwise.
4. Remove the fuel sender assembly and O-ring.

To install:
5. Install the fuel sender assembly and O-ring.
6. Using the Fuel Tank Sender Wrench (CH-45722), install the cam lock ring by turning clockwise.
7. Connect the fuel feed and return pipes.
8. Install the fuel tank.

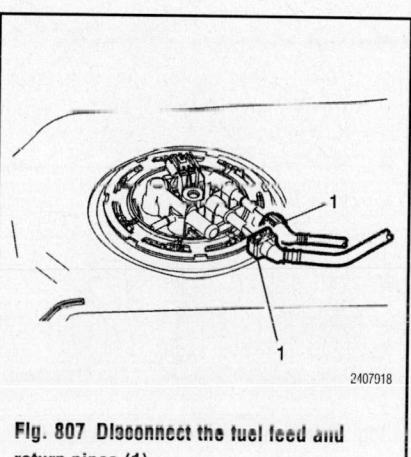

Fig. 807 Disconnect the fuel feed and return pipes (1)

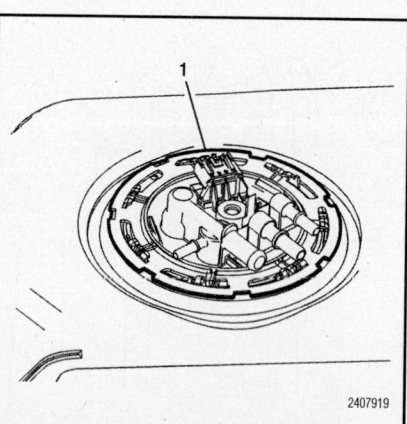

Fig. 808 Using the CH-45722, remove the cam lock ring (1) by turning counter-clockwise

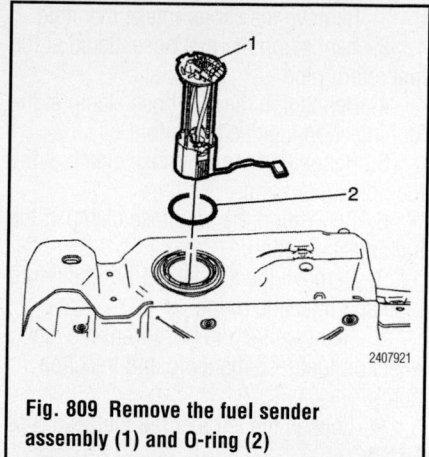

Fig. 809 Remove the fuel sender assembly (1) and O-ring (2)

INJECTION PUMP

REMOVAL & INSTALLATION

2010 Diesel Engines

See Figures 810 through 817.

1. Remove the thermostat housing crossover.

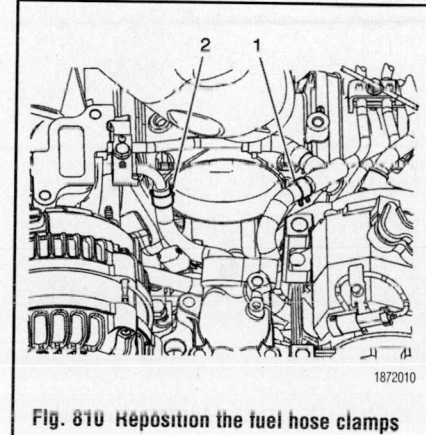

Fig. 810 Reposition the fuel hose clamps (1, 2)

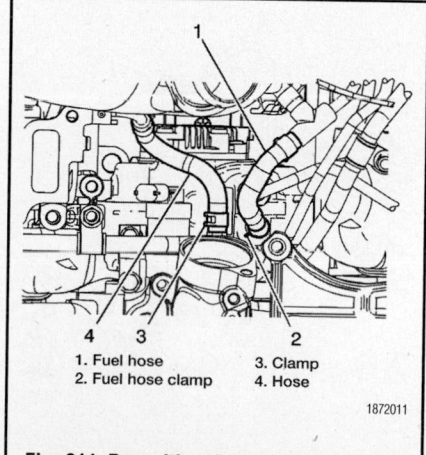

1. Fuel hose
2. Fuel hose clamp
3. Clamp
4. Hose

Fig. 811 Reposition the fuel hose clamp at the fuel injection pump

2. Remove the center intake manifold.

3. Reposition the fuel hose clamp at the fuel return pipe.

4. Reposition the fuel hose clamp at the fuel injection fuel feed manifold.

5. Reposition the fuel hose clamp at the fuel injection pump.

6. Reposition the fuel hose clamp at the fuel injection pump.

7. Remove the fuel hose from the return pipe and injection pump.

8. Remove the fuel hose from the fuel injection fuel feed manifold and injection pump.

9. Loosen the left fuel rail fuel feed pipe fittings.

10. Remove the left fuel rail fuel feed pipe.

➡**Be careful not to damage any mating surfaces.**

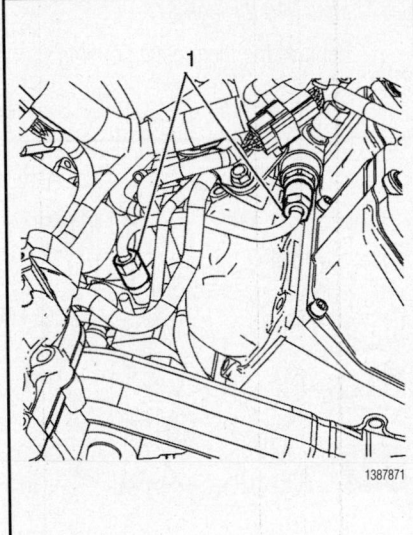

Fig. 812 Loosen the left fuel rail fuel feed pipe fittings (1)

Fig. 813 Remove the left fuel rail fuel feed pipe

11. Remove the fuel injection pump.

a. Remove the camshaft gear access hole cover bolt.

b. Remove the camshaft gear access hole cover.

c. Rotate the crankshaft until the camshaft gear tension relief hole is in line with the front cover access hole.

d. Use a suitable tool to unload the spring tension from the two piece cam gear. Apply pressure towards the right side of the engine while removing the injection pump.

e. Remove the four fuel injection pump bolts.

f. Remove the fuel injection pump.

Preparing The Fuel Injection Pump

1. Hold the fuel pump by the drive gear in a vice with copper jaw liners.

2. Loosen the gear nut until the nut is even with the end of the gear shaft.

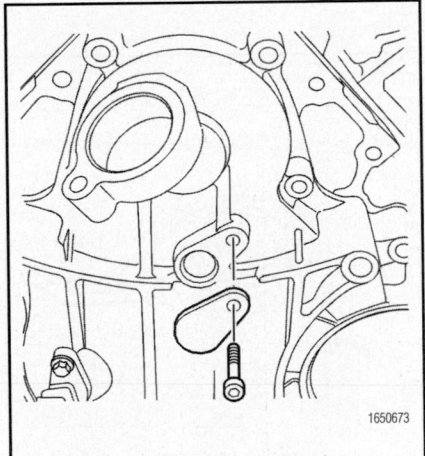

Fig. 814 Remove the camshaft gear access hole cover bolt

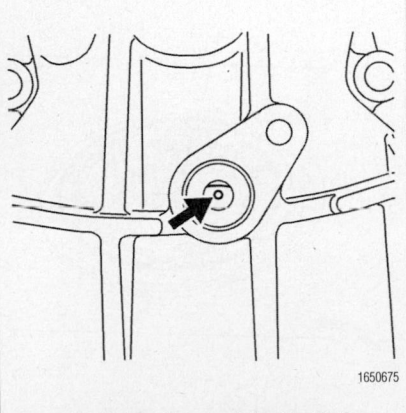

Fig. 815 Rotate the crankshaft until the camshaft gear tension relief hole is in line with the front cover access hole

3. Remove the gear from the tapered shaft of the injection pump.

4. Separate the injection pump and adapter by removing the 3 bolts and spacers.

5. Inspect the O-ring for damage on the pump adapter and replace, if necessary. Lubricate the O-ring with clean engine oil.

6. Clean all mating surfaces.

7. Install the adapter on the pump.

8. Install the 3 bolts and spacers. Tighten the bolts to 15 ft. lbs. (20 Nm).

9. Install the gear and nut. Tighten nut to 52 ft. lbs. (70 Nm).

To install:

10. Install the fuel injection pump.

a. Lubricate the O-ring on the fuel injection pump adapter with engine oil.

b. Use a suitable tool to unload the spring tension from the two piece cam gear. Apply pressure towards the right side of the engine while installing the fuel injection pump.

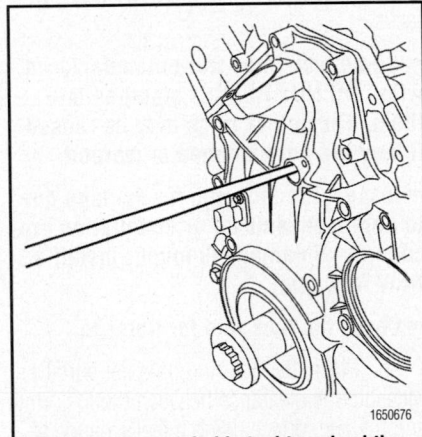

Fig. 816 Use a suitable tool to unload the spring tension from the two piece cam gear

Fig. 817 Remove the four fuel injection pump bolts

c. Install the fuel injection pump and adapter assembly.

d. Install the fuel injection pump bolts and tighten to 18 ft. lbs. (25 Nm).

11. Position the left fuel rail fuel feed pipe.

12. Tighten the left fuel rail fuel feed pipe fittings. Tighten fittings to 30 ft. lbs. (41 Nm).

13. Install the fuel hose to the fuel injection fuel feed manifold and injection pump.

14. Install the fuel hose from the return pipe and injection pump.

15. Position the fuel hose clamp at the fuel injection pump.

16. Position the fuel hose clamp at the fuel injection pump.

17. Position the fuel hose clamp at the fuel injection fuel feed manifold.

18. Position the fuel hose clamp at the fuel return pipe.

19. Install the center intake manifold.

20. Install the thermostat housing crossover.

21. Prime the fuel system.

22. Start the engine. If the engine stalls, repeat the above step.

23. Once the engine starts, inspect for fuel leaks.

2011 Diesel Engines

See Figures 818 through 820.

1. Remove the center intake manifold.

2. Remove and reposition the high pressure fuel pipes from the fuel injection pump.

3. Remove and reposition the indirect fuel injector feed pipe from the injection pump.

4. Disconnect the electrical connectors.

5. Collapse the hose clamps and remove the fuel return and fuel feed hoses.

6. Remove the engine cooling crossover housing.

7. Remove the camshaft gear access hole plug (1).

➡**The fuel pump must be correctly timed to the camshaft gear.**

8. Rotate the crankshaft until the fuel injection pump gear timing marks are aligned with camshaft gear timing marks.

9. Remove the fuel injection pump bolts.

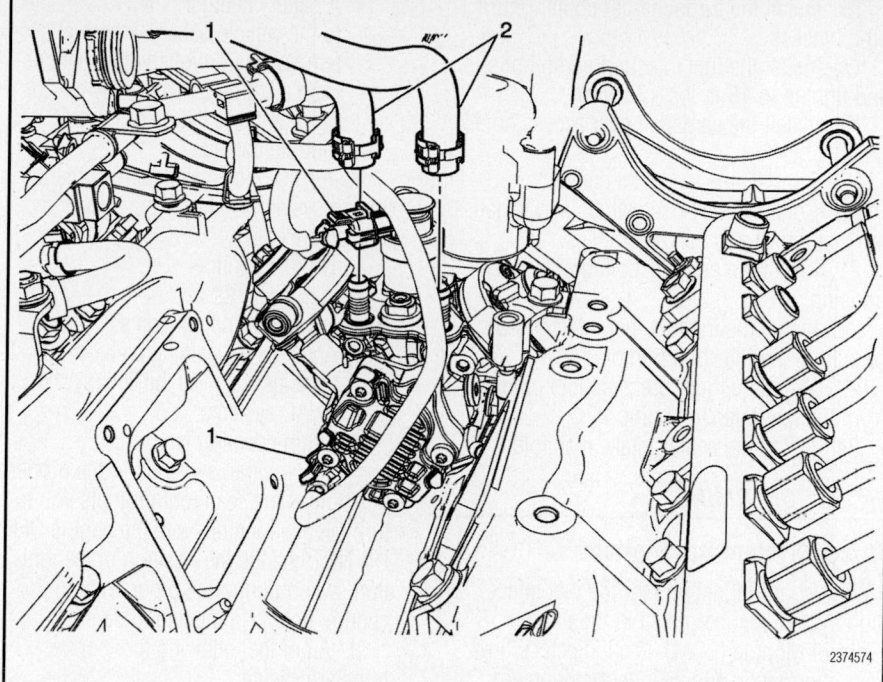

Fig. 818 Disconnect the electrical connectors (1) and remove the fuel return and fuel feed hoses (2)

10. Remove the turbocharger cooler return pipe bracket.

11. Remove the fuel injection pump.

12. Remove the fuel pressure regulator and inspect for metal debris on the end of the regulator tip.

➡**If any metal debris is found, replace the following components: fuel injection pump, fuel rails, fuel injectors, fuel return line assembly, all high pressure fuel pipes, indirect fuel injector and fuel feed pipes (pump to indirect fuel injector).**

To install:

➡**The fuel pump must be correctly timed to the camshaft gear.**

13. Rotate the crankshaft to align the camshaft gear timing marks with the center of the inspection hole

14. Lubricate the O-ring on the fuel injection pump adapter with engine oil.

15. Install the fuel injection pump and adapter assembly so that the timing mark on the fuel pump gear is aligned with the timing marks on the camshaft gear.

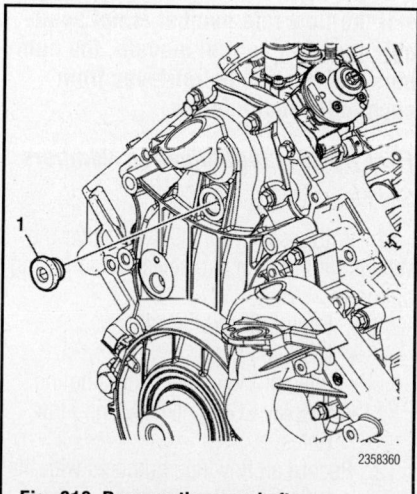

Fig. 819 Remove the camshaft gear access hole plug (1)

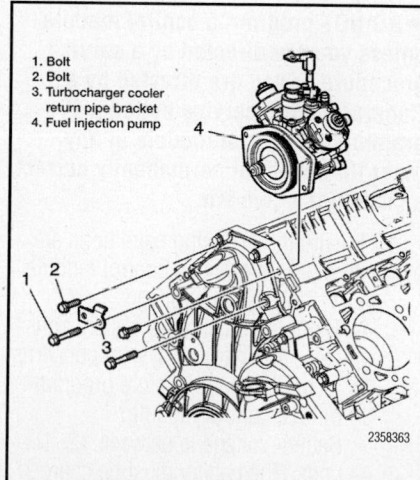

1. Bolt
2. Bolt
3. Turbocharger cooler return pipe bracket
4. Fuel injection pump

Fig. 820 Remove the fuel injection pump bolts

16. Install the turbocharger cooler return pipe bracket.

17. Install the fuel injection pump bolts and tighten to 18 ft. lbs. (25 Nm).

18. Install the camshaft gear access hole plug.

19. Connect the electrical connectors.

20. Collapse the hose clamps and install the fuel return and fuel feed hoses.

21. Install the engine cooling crossover housing.

22. Install the indirect fuel injector feed pipe from the injection pump.

23. Install the high pressure fuel pipes from the fuel injection pump.

24. Install the center intake manifold.

INJECTION TIMING

Circuit/System Description

The control functions for the fuel injection system are integrated in the Engine Control Module (ECM). Each injector's flow rate information and cylinder position are stored in the memory of both the Glow Plug Control Module (GPCM) and the ECM. The fuel injector flow rate programming must be done when any of the following procedures are performed:

- The ECM is replaced
- The GPCM is replaced
- Any fuel injectors are replaced

If the ECM does not communicate, the flow rate information can be retrieved from the GPCM. If both control modules fail to communicate, the fuel injector flow rate information, or Injection Quantity Adjustment (IQA) flow rate numbers, will need to be retrieved from each individual injector.

Before Programming A Control Module

➡**DO NOT program a control module unless you are directed by a service procedure or you are directed by a General Motors service bulletin. Programming a control module at any other time will not permanently correct a customer's concern.**

1. Ensure the following conditions are met before programming a control module:

   a. Vehicle system voltage:

- There is no charging system concern. All charging system concerns must be repaired before programming a control module.
- Battery voltage is between 12–16 volts. The battery must be charged before programming the control module if the battery voltage is low.

- A battery charger is NOT connected to the vehicle battery. Incorrect system voltage or voltage fluctuations from a battery charger may cause programming failure or control module damage.

   b. Turn OFF or disable any of the following systems that may put a load on the vehicle battery:

- Twilight sentinel
- Interior lights
- Daytime Running Lights (DRL)— Applying the parking brake, on most vehicles, disables the DRL system.
- HVAC systems
- Engine cooling fans, etc.

   c. The ignition switch is in the proper position—The scan tool prompts you to turn ON the ignition, with the engine OFF. DO NOT change the position of the ignition switch during the programming procedure, unless instructed to do so.

   d. All of the following tool connections are secure:

- The connection at the Data Link Connector (DLC)
- The voltage supply circuits

   e. DO NOT disturb the tool harnesses while programming. If an interruption occurs during the programming procedure, programming failure or control module damage may occur.

Circuit/System Verification

Review the Display ECM & GPCM Inj. Flow Rates parameter with a scan tool. All cylinders should be programmed with a flow rate number. Both the GPCM and the ECM should be programmed with the same flow rate numbers for the corresponding cylinders.

Circuit/System Testing

➡**If the flow rate number is not available in either control module, the numbers will need to be retrieved from each individual injector.**

Fuel Injector Identification Numbers

See Figure 821.

1. With a scan tool installed, enter the vehicle information and select the following options:

- Engine Control Module
- Module Setup
- Injector Flow Rate Programming
- Display ECM & GPCM Inj. Flow Rates

2. Record all flow rate numbers with the corresponding cylinders from the control modules.

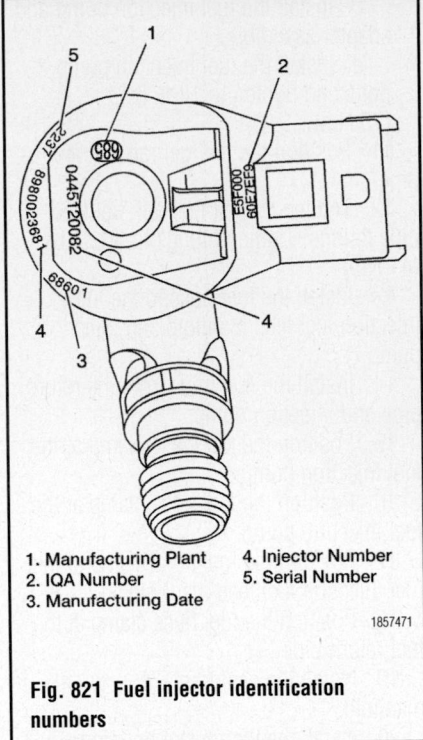

1. Manufacturing Plant
2. IQA Number
3. Manufacturing Date
4. Injector Number
5. Serial Number

1857471

Fig. 821 Fuel injector identification numbers

➡**When installing a new fuel injector, ensure that the IQA data number from the yellow IQA Data Tag, shipped with the new injector, is programmed to the correct cylinder.**

   a. If any injectors are replaced, go to Reprogram Injector Flow Rates parameter and enter the flow rate number of the new injector to the corresponding cylinder. The flow rate numbers will automatically update both control modules.

   b. If the ECM was replaced, go to Copy GPCM Inj. Flow Rates to ECM parameter and reprogram the ECM. This will update the ECM with the GPCM flow rate numbers.

   c. If the GPCM was replaced or the flow rate numbers are not the same for both modules, go to Copy ECM Inj. Flow Rates to GPCM parameter and reprogram the GPCM. This will update the GPCM with the ECM flow rate numbers.

   d. If both control modules were replaced, go to Reprogram Injector Flow Rates parameter and enter the previously recorded flow rate numbers or the numbers retrieved from each individual injector, to the corresponding cylinders.

Repair Instructions

➡**The ECM and the GPCM must be allowed to completely power down after programming is complete.**

1. Install any components or connectors that have been removed or replaced during diagnosis.

2. Perform any adjustment, programming or setup procedures that are required when a component or module is removed or replaced.

3. Turn ON the ignition, with the engine OFF, and clear the DTCs.

4. Disconnect the scan tool and turn OFF the ignition for 2 minutes.

5. If the repair was related to a DTC, duplicate the Conditions for Running the DTC and use the Freeze Frame/Failure Records, if applicable, in order to verify the DTC does not reset. If the DTC resets or another DTC is present, refer to the Diagnostic Trouble Code (DTC) List—Vehicle and perform the appropriate diagnostic procedure.

OR

6. If the repair was symptom related, duplicate the conditions under which the customer concern occurred to verify the repair.

GLOW PLUGS

REMOVAL & INSTALLATION

2010 Diesel Engines

Right Side

See Figure 822.

1. Disconnect the negative battery cable.

2. Remove the right wheelhouse panel.

3. Remove the engine wiring harness nut(s) from the glow plug(s).

4. Remove the engine wiring harness lead(s) from the glow plug(s).

➡️If a glow plug is replaced and the tip is missing or burned off, the cylinder head must be removed and all debris must be cleaned out of the cylinder.

5. Remove the glow plug(s) from the cylinder head.

To install:

6. Install the glow plug(s) to the cylinder head and tighten to 13 ft. lbs. (18 Nm).

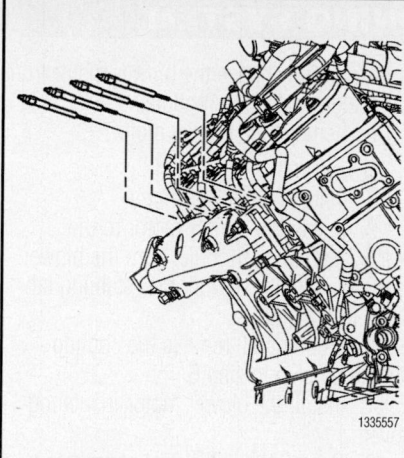

Fig. 822 Remove the glow plug(s) from the cylinder head

7. Install the engine wiring harness lead(s) to the glow plug(s).

8. Install the engine wiring harness nut(s) to the glow plug(s).

9. Install the right wheelhouse panel.

10. Connect the negative battery cable.

Left Side

See Figure 823.

1. Disconnect the negative battery cable.

2. Remove the left wheelhouse panel.

3. Remove the engine wiring harness nut(s) from the glow plug(s).

4. Remove the engine wiring harness lead(s) from the glow plug(s).

➡️If a glow plug is replaced and the tip is missing or burned off, the cylinder head must be removed and all debris must be cleaned out of the cylinder.

5. Remove the glow plug(s) from the cylinder head.

To install:

6. Install the glow plug(s) to the cylinder head and tighten to 13 ft. lbs. (18 Nm).

7. Install the engine wiring harness lead(s) to the glow plug(s).

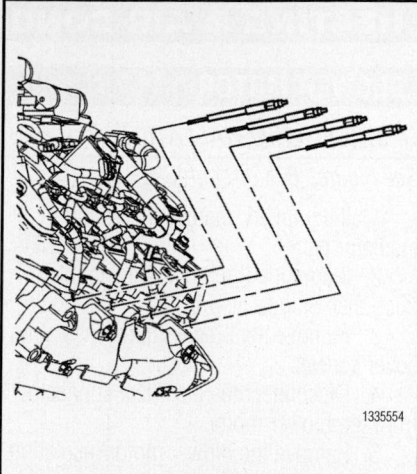

Fig. 823 Remove the glow plug(s) from the cylinder head

8. Install the engine wiring harness nut(s) to the glow plug(s).

9. Install the left wheelhouse panel.

10. Connect the negative battery cable.

2011 Diesel Engines

See Figure 824.

➡️The manufacturer does not provide a specific Removal and Installation procedure for this component. Refer to the graphic(s) when servicing this component.

➡️Right side shown, left side similar.

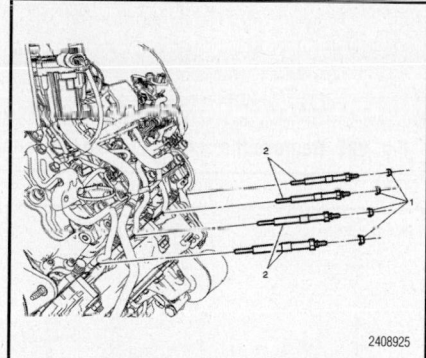

Fig. 824 Remove the glow plug fasteners (1) and the glow plugs (2)

HEATING & AIR CONDITIONING SYSTEM

BLOWER MOTOR

REMOVAL & INSTALLATION

See Figures 825 through 828.

1. If equipped, remove the sound insulator panel.
2. If equipped, remove the cooling duct, then skip to step 6.
3. Remove the blower motor insulating cover screws.
4. Disconnect the electrical connector from the blower motor.
5. Remove the blower motor insulating cover.
6. Pull the retaining tab down while turning the blower motor counterclockwise in order to disengage the blower motor from the heater/ventilation module.
7. Remove the blower motor.

To install:

8. Install the blower motor.
9. Install the blower motor to the heater/ventilation module. Turn the blower assembly clockwise until the retaining tab locks into place.
10. If equipped, remove the cooling duct, then skip to step 6.
11. Install the blower motor insulating cover.
12. Connect the electrical connector to the blower motor.
13. Install the blower motor insulating cover screws.

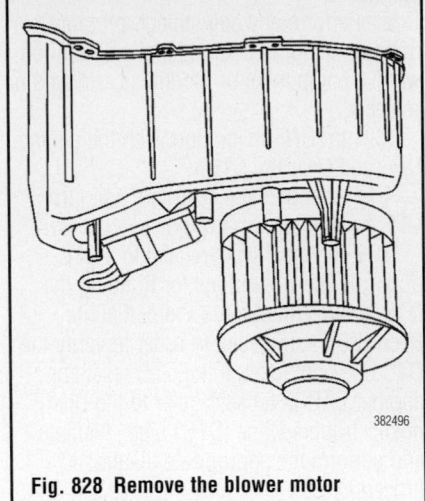

Fig. 828 Remove the blower motor

14. If equipped, install the sound insulator panel.

HEATER CORE

REMOVAL & INSTALLATION

See Figure 829.

1. Remove the HVAC module.
2. Disconnect the wiring harness retainer from the heater core cover.
3. Remove the heater core cover screw.
4. Remove the heater core cover.
5. Remove the heater core pass through seal.
6. Remove the heater core.
7. Installation is the reverse of removal.

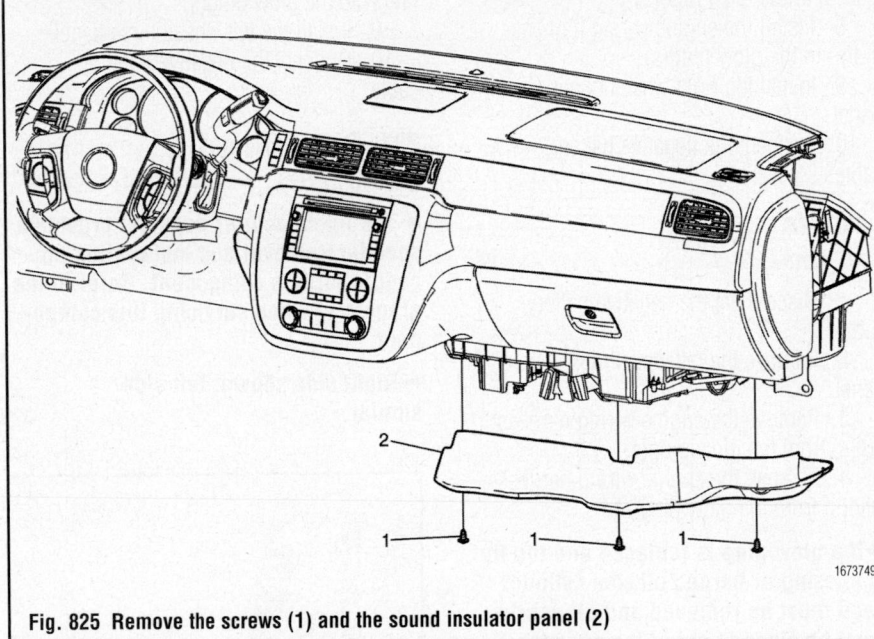

Fig. 825 Remove the screws (1) and the sound insulator panel (2)

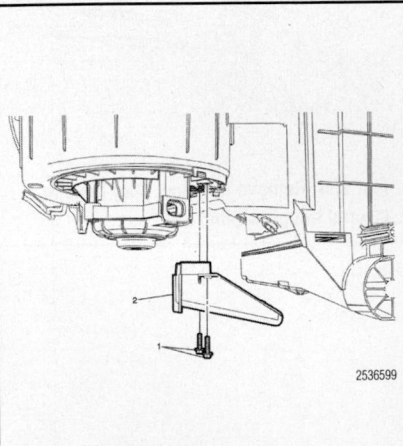

Fig. 826 Remove the screws (1) and the cooling duct (2)

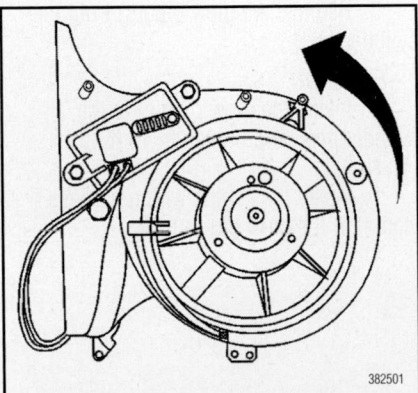

Fig. 827 Pull the retaining tab down while turning the blower motor counterclockwise in order to disengage the blower motor from the heater/ventilation module

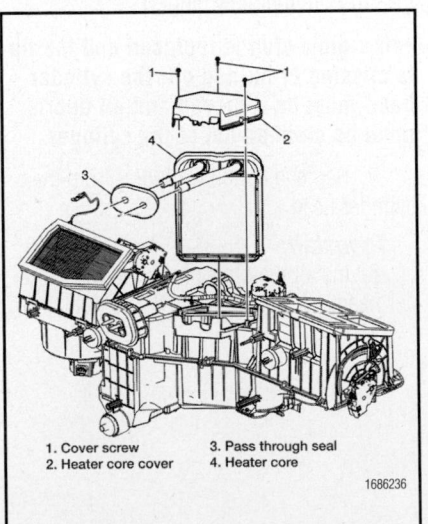

1. Cover screw
2. Heater core cover
3. Pass through seal
4. Heater core

Fig. 829 Exploded view of the heater core assembly

HVAC MODULE

REMOVAL & INSTALLATION

Except Hybrid Vehicles

See Figures 830 through 834.

1. Drain the engine coolant.
2. Using the Heater Line Quick Connect Release Tool (J-43181) disconnect the inlet heater hose from the heater core.

   a. Install the J-43181 to the heater core pipe.

   b. Close the tool around the heater core pipe.

   c. Firmly pull the tool into the quick connect end of the heater hose.

   d. Firmly grasp the heater hose. Pull the heater hose forward in order to discngage the inlet hose from the heater core.

3. Using the J-43181 disconnect the surge tank outlet hose from the heater core.

   a. Install the J-43181 to the heater core pipe.

   b. Close the tool around the heater core pipe.

   c. Firmly pull the tool into the quick connect end of the heater hose.

   d. Firmly grasp the heater hose. Pull the heater hose forward in order to disengage the surge tank outlet hose from the heater core.

4. Remove the upper intake manifold sight shield.
5. Remove the battery.
6. Remove the accumulator.
7. Remove the instrument panel to the service position.
8. Remove the nuts from the HVAC module.
9. Remove the bolts from the HVAC module.
10. Remove the HVAC module.

To install:

11. If replacing the HVAC module, transfer the components from the old HVAC module as necessary.
12. Install the HVAC module.
13. Install the nuts to the HVAC module. Tighten the nuts to 80 inch lbs. (9 Nm).

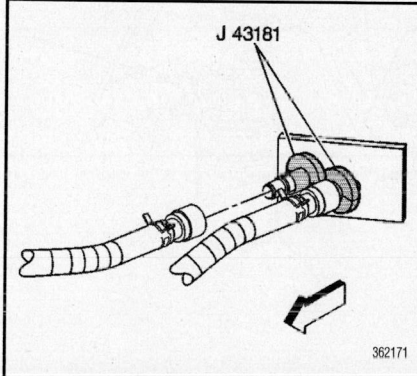

Fig. 830 Using the Heater Line Quick Connect Release Tool (J-43181) disconnect the inlet heater hose from the heater core

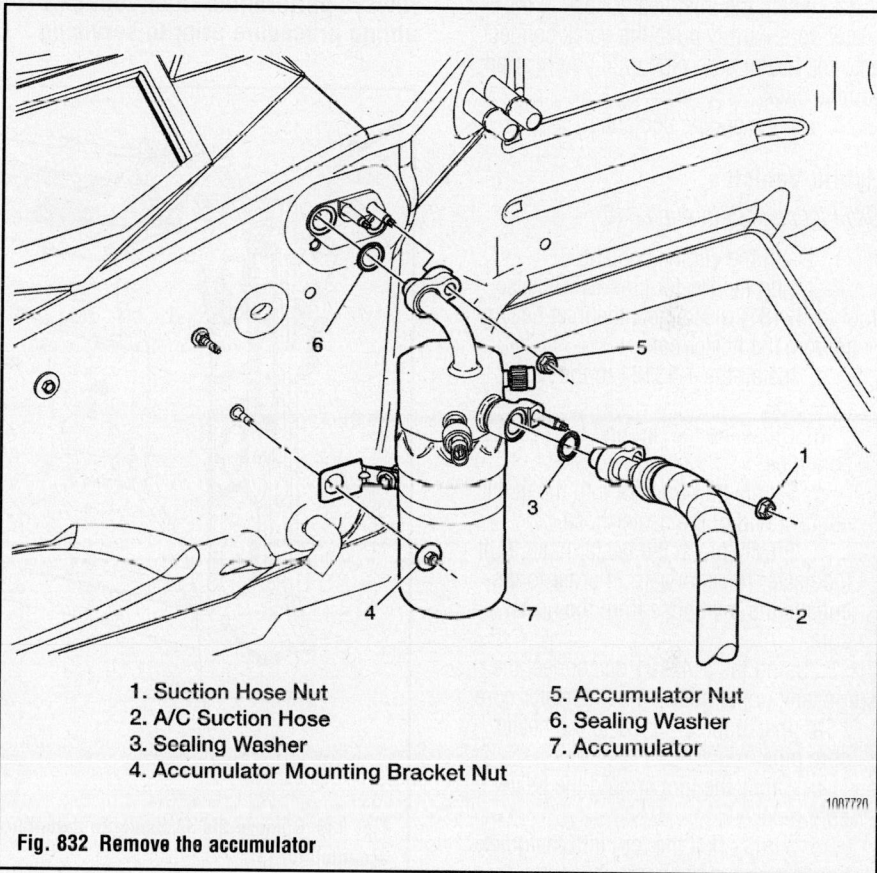

1. Suction Hose Nut
2. A/C Suction Hose
3. Sealing Washer
4. Accumulator Mounting Bracket Nut
5. Accumulator Nut
6. Sealing Washer
7. Accumulator

Fig. 832 Remove the accumulator

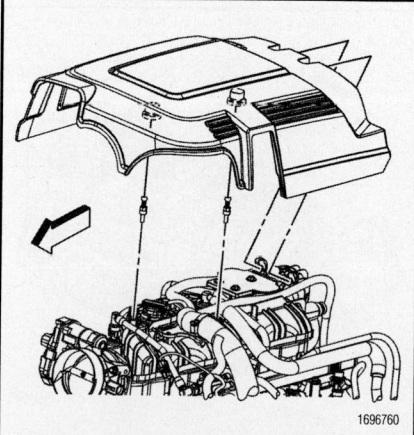

Fig. 831 Remove the upper intake manifold sight shield

Fig. 833 Remove the instrument panel (1) to the service position

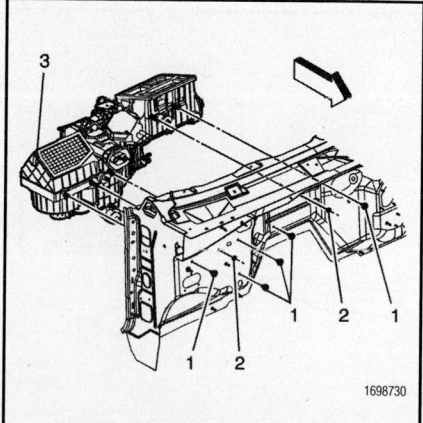

Fig. 834 Remove the bolts (1), nuts (2) and the HVAC module (3)

14. Install the bolts to the HVAC module.
15. Connect the electrical harness and the ground connections.
16. Install the HVAC module drain hose.
17. Install the instrument panel.
18. Install the upper intake manifold sight shield.
19. Install the battery.
20. Install the accumulator.
21. Install the surge tank outlet hose to the heater core. Firmly push the quick connect onto the heater core pipe until you hear an audible click.
22. Install the inlet heater hose to the heater core. Firmly push the quick connect onto the heater core pipe until you hear an audible click.
23. Fill the engine coolant.

Hybrid Vehicles

See Figures 835 through 840.

1. Drain the engine coolant.
2. Using the Heater Line QC Release Tool (J-43181) disconnect the inlet heater hose from the heater core.
   a. Install the J-43181 to the heater core pipe.
   b. Close the tool around the heater core pipe.
   c. Firmly pull the tool into the quick connect end of the heater hose.
   d. Firmly grasp the heater hose. Pull the heater hose forward in order to disengage the inlet hose from the heater core.
3. Using the J-43181 disconnect the surge tank outlet hose from the heater core.
   a. Install the J-43181 to the heater core pipe.
   b. Close the tool around the heater core pipe.
   c. Firmly pull the tool into the quick connect end of the heater hose.

d. Firmly grasp the heater hose. Pull the heater hose forward in order to disengage the surge tank outlet hose from the heater core.
4. Remove the upper intake manifold sight shield.
5. Remove the drive motor generator control module assembly. Refer to the Hybrid section.
6. Remove the battery.
7. Remove the accumulator.

✳✳ WARNING

Always perform the High Voltage Disabling procedure prior to servicing any High Voltage component or connection. Personal Protection Equipment (PPE) and proper procedures must be followed.

The High Voltage Disabling procedure will perform the following tasks:
• Identify how to disable high voltage.
• Identify how to test for the presence of high voltage.
• Identify condition under which high voltage is always present and Personal Protection Equipment (PPE) and proper procedures must be followed.

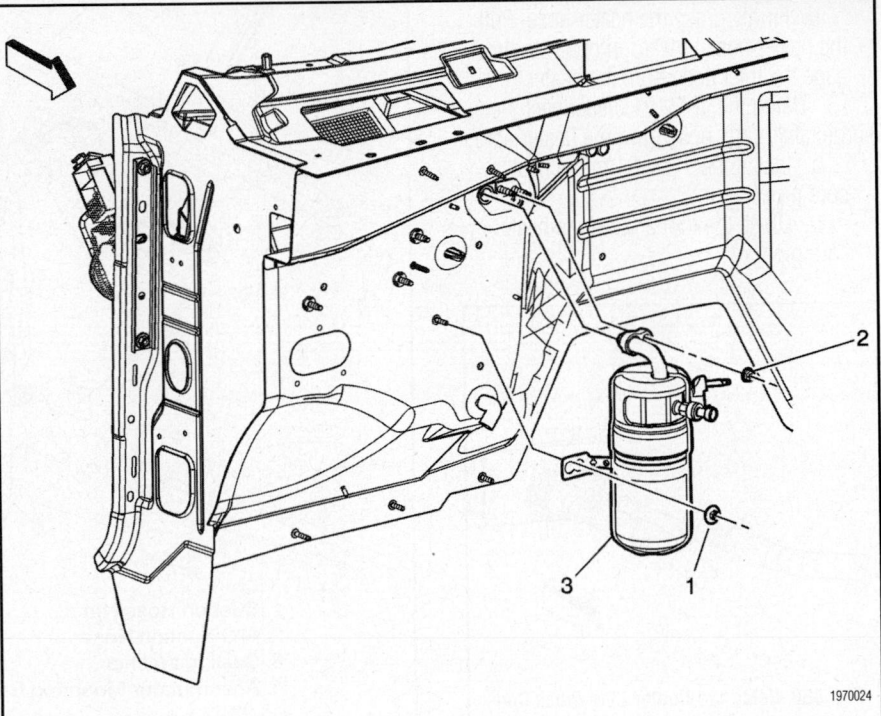

Fig. 836 Remove the accumulator mounting bracket nut (1), the accumulator nut (2), and the accumulator (3)

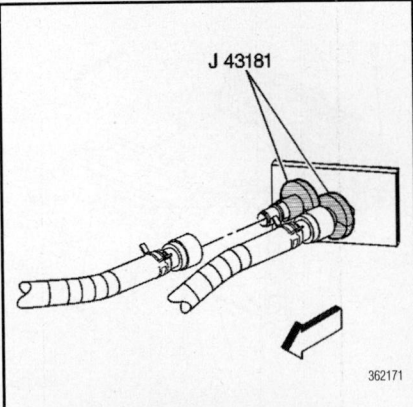

Fig. 835 Using the Heater Line QC Release Tool (J-43181) disconnect the inlet heater hose from the heater core

Fig. 837 Remove the instrument panel to the service position

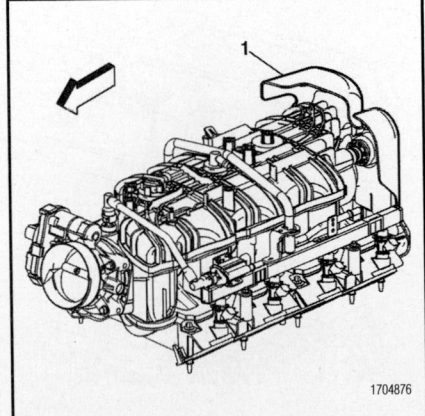

Fig. 838 Locate the rear engine cover (1) on rear of intake manifold

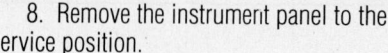

✳✳ WARNING

Failure to follow the procedures exactly as written may result in serious injury or death.

a. Recover the refrigerant.

b. Raise and support the vehicle.

c. Remove the right front wheelhouse liner.

d. Remove the air cleaner.

e. Remove air cleaner resonator outlet duct.

f. Remove the suction hose.

g. Disconnect electrical connector from A/C low pressure switch.

h. Remove the accumulator mounting bracket nut, the accumulator nut, and the accumulator.

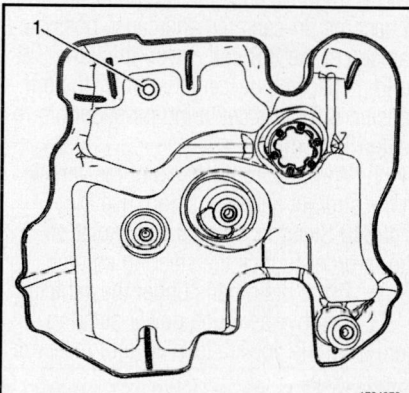

Fig. 839 Reposition the acoustic foam (if applicable) down from the access location (1)

8. Remove the instrument panel to the service position.

9. Remove the HVAC module drain hose.

10. Disconnect the electrical harnesses and the ground connections from the HVAC module.

11. Locate the rear engine cover on rear of intake manifold.

12. Reposition the acoustic foam (if applicable) down from the access location.

➡**Drill an 1 inch (25 mm) diameter hole in the rear engine cover to access the HVAC module retaining nut located behind rear engine cover.**

13. Remove the nuts from the HVAC module.

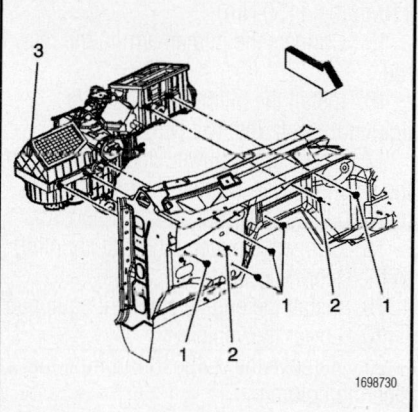

Fig. 840 Remove the nuts (2) and bolts (1) from the HVAC module (3)

14. Remove the bolts from the HVAC module.

15. Remove the HVAC module.

To install:

16. If replacing the HVAC module, transfer the components from the old HVAC module as necessary.

17. Install the HVAC module.

18. Install the nuts to the HVAC module.

19. Install the bolts to the HVAC module.

20. Reposition acoustic foam (if applicable) to original position or cover access hole with equivalent foam tape.

21. Connect the electrical harness and the ground connections.

22. Install the HVAC module drain hose.

23. Install the instrument panel.

24. Install the upper intake manifold sight shield.

25. Install the drive motor generator control module assembly.

26. Install the battery.

27. Install the accumulator.

28. Install the surge tank outlet hose to the heater core.

29. Firmly push the quick connect onto the heater core pipe until you hear an audible click.

30. Install the inlet heater hose to the heater core.

31. Firmly push the quick connect onto the heater core pipe until you hear an audible click.

32. Fill the engine coolant.

STEERING

POWER STEERING GEAR

REMOVAL & INSTALLATION

Recirculating Ball

See Figures 841 through 844.

Special Tools Required:
• J-24319-B Steering Linkage and Tie Rod Puller
• J-42640 Steering Column Anti-Rotation Pin

✳✳ CAUTION

With wheels of the vehicle facing straight ahead, secure the steering wheel utilizing steering column anti-rotation pin, steering column lock, or a strap to prevent rotation. Locking of the steering column will prevent damage and a possible malfunction of the SIR system. The steering

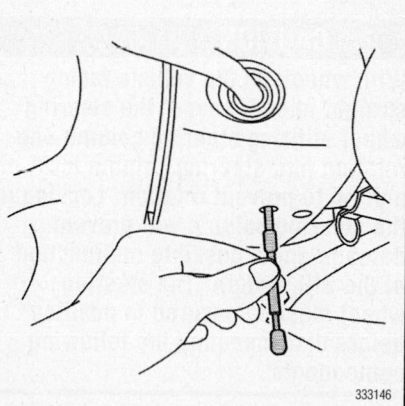

Fig. 841 With the front wheels of the vehicle in the straight ahead position, use the J-42640 Pin in order to lock the steering column

wheel must be secured in position before disconnecting the following components:

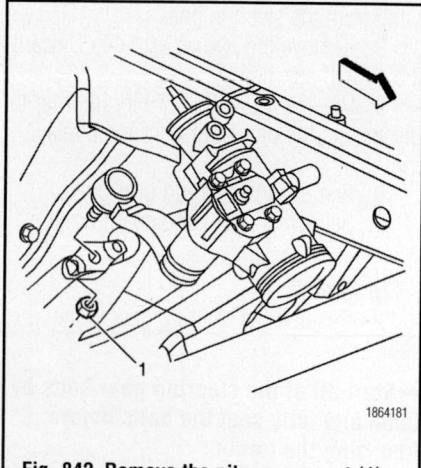

Fig. 842 Remove the pitman arm nut (1)

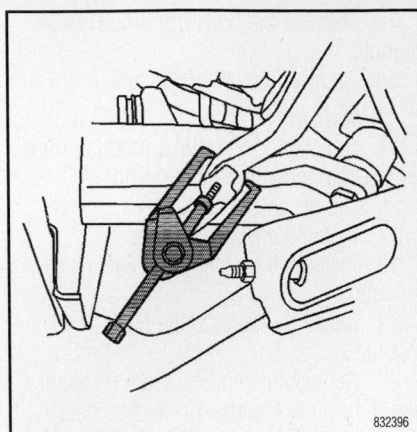

Fig. 843 Use the J-24319-B Puller in order to disconnect the pitman arm from the relay rod

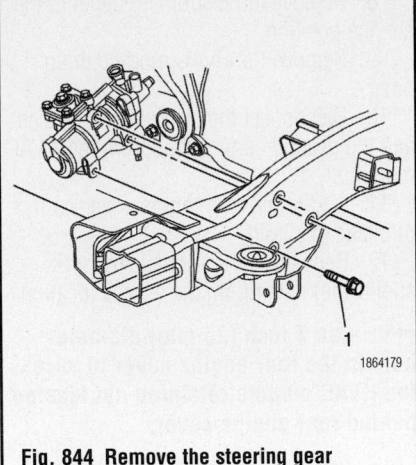

Fig. 844 Remove the steering gear bolts (1)

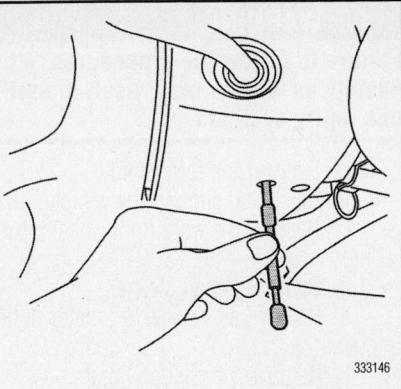

Fig. 845 With the front wheels of the vehicle in the straight ahead position, use the J-42640 Pin in order to lock the steering column

- The steering column
- The intermediate shaft(s)
- The steering gear

After disconnecting these components, do not rotate the steering wheel or move the front tires and wheels. Failure to follow this procedure may cause the SIR coil assembly to become un-centered and cause possible damage to the SIR coil. If you think the SIR coil has became un-centered, refer to your specific SIR coil's centering procedure to re-center SIR Coil.

1. With the front wheels of the vehicle in the straight ahead position, use the J-42640 Pin in order to lock the steering column.

2. Remove as much power steering fluid from the power steering fluid reservoir as possible.

3. Place drain pans under the vehicle.

4. Raise and support the vehicle.

5. Remove the engine shield, if equipped.

6. Disconnect the steering hoses from the steering gear.

7. Disconnect the steering shaft coupling from the steering gear.

8. Remove the pitman arm nut. Discard the pitman arm nut.

9. Use the J-24319-B Puller in order to disconnect the pitman arm from the relay rod.

10. Remove the steering gear bolts.

11. Remove the steering gear from the vehicle.

To install:

12. Position the steering gear in the vehicle.

➡Start all of the steering gear bolts by hand and fully seat the bolts before finalizing the torque.

13. Install the steering gear bolts.

14. Tighten the steering gear bolts to 110 ft. lbs. (150 Nm).

15. Connect the pitman arm to the relay rod.

16. Install the pitman arm nut and tighten to 46 ft. lbs. (62 Nm).

17. Connect the power steering hoses to the steering gear. Tighten the hose fittings to 24 ft. lbs. (32 Nm).

18. Connect the steering shaft coupling to the steering gear.

19. Install the engine shield, if equipped.

20. Lower the vehicle.

21. Remove the J-42640 Pin from the steering column.

22. Fill and bleed the power steering system.

23. Remove the drain pans.

24. Clean any excess fluid from the vehicle.

Hydraulic Rack and Pinion

See Figure 845.

✳ CAUTION

With wheels of the vehicle facing straight ahead, secure the steering wheel utilizing steering column anti-rotation pin, steering column lock, or a strap to prevent rotation. Locking of the steering column will prevent damage and a possible malfunction of the SIR system. The steering wheel must be secured in position before disconnecting the following components:

- The steering column
- The intermediate shaft(s)
- The steering gear

After disconnecting these components, do not rotate the steering wheel or move the front tires and wheels. Failure to follow this

procedure may cause the SIR coil assembly to become un-centered and cause possible damage to the SIR coil. If you think the SIR coil has became un-centered, refer to your specific SIR coil's centering procedure to re-center SIR Coil.

1. With the front wheels of the vehicle in the straight ahead position, use the J-42640 Steering Column Anti-Rotation Pin in order to lock the steering column.

2. Place drain pans under the vehicle.

3. Remove as much power steering fluid from the power steering fluid reservoir as possible.

4. Remove the front tire and wheel assemblies.

5. Remove the oil pan skid plate, if equipped.

6. Disconnect the steering shaft coupling from the steering gear.

7. Remove the steering linkage outer tie rod nuts.

8. Disconnect the steering linkage outer tie rods from the steering knuckles.

9. Remove the power steering gear inlet hose retaining plate bolt.

10. Disconnect the power steering gear inlet and outlet hoses from the steering gear.

11. Remove the left side steering gear bolts.

12. Remove the right side steering gear bolts.

13. Remove the steering gear.

To install:

14. Installation is the reverse of removal.

   a. Tighten the right side steering gear bolts to 74 ft. lbs. (100 Nm).

   b. Tighten the left side steering gear bolts to 148 ft. lbs. (200 Nm).

   c. Tighten the power steering gear

inlet hose retaining plate bolt to 106 inch lbs. (12 Nm).

d. Tighten the steering linkage outer tie rod nuts to 44 ft. lbs. (60 Nm).

e. Use the J-44586 remover/installer in order to replace the steering gear seals if necessary.

f. Fill and bleed the power steering system.

g. Clean any excess power steering fluid from the vehicle.

h. Measure and adjust the front toe.

Two Mode Hybrid

See Figures 846 through 849.

❋❋ WARNING

Always perform the High Voltage Disabling procedure prior to servicing any High Voltage component or connection. Personal Protection Equipment (PPE) and proper procedures must be followed.

The High Voltage Disabling procedure will perform the following tasks:
- Identify how to disable high voltage.
- Identify how to test for the presence of high voltage.
- Identify condition under which high voltage is always present and Personal Protection Equipment (PPE) and proper procedures must be followed. Failure to follow the procedures exactly as written may result in serious injury or death.

❋❋ CAUTION

With wheels of the vehicle facing straight ahead, secure the steering wheel utilizing steering column anti-rotation pin, steering column lock, or a strap to prevent rotation. Locking of the steering column will prevent damage and a possible malfunction of the SIR system. The steering wheel must be secured in position before disconnecting the following components:

- The steering column
- The intermediate shaft(s)
- The steering gear

After disconnecting these components, do not rotate the steering wheel or move the front tires and wheels. Failure to follow this procedure may cause the SIR coil assembly to become un-centered and cause possible damage to the SIR coil. If you think the SIR coil has became un-centered, refer to your specific SIR coil's centering procedure to re-center SIR Coil.

➡The steering gear harness is not repairable. Only replace the harness and never attempt to repair it. The wiring harness protective cover is intended to keep the wiring harness connectors contaminant free. Do not remove the protective cover from the power steering assist motor wiring harness connectors until the harness has been routed to the correct position.

1. Perform the high voltage disabling procedure.

2. Remove the front tire and wheel assemblies.

3. Remove the steering shaft coupling bolt at the steering gear.

4. Separate the steering shaft coupling from the steering gear.

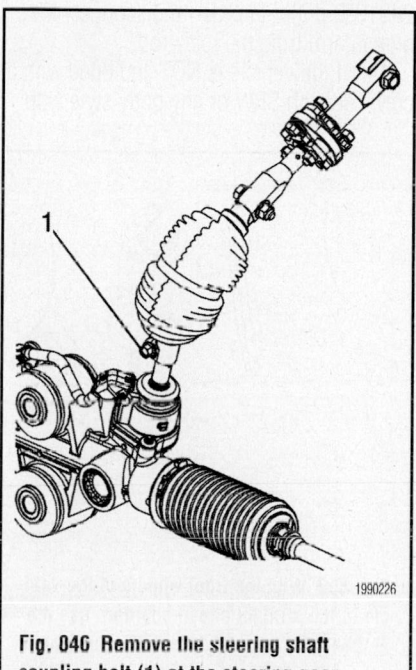

Fig. 846 Remove the steering shaft coupling bolt (1) at the steering gear

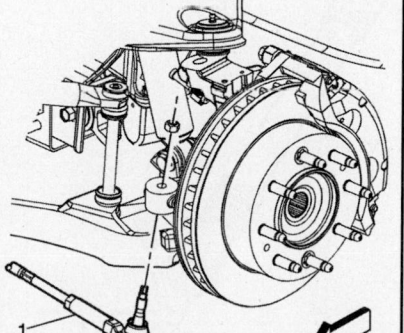

Fig. 847 Remove the steering linkage outer tie rod nuts from the steering linkage outer tie rods (1)

5. Remove the steering linkage outer tie rod nuts from the steering linkage outer tie rods and discard them.

6. Separate the steering linkage outer tie rods from the steering knuckles.

7. Support the steering gear with jackstands.

8. Remove the steering gear bolts from the left side of the steering gear.

9. Remove the steering gear bolts from the right side of the steering gear.

10. Remove the steering gear from the vehicle.

11. Transfer any parts as needed.

To install:

12. Position the steering gear in the vehicle and support it with jackstands.

➡**Start all steering gear bolts by hand before finalizing the torques.**

13. Install the steering gear bolts at the right side of the steering gear and tighten to 74 ft. lbs. (100 Nm).

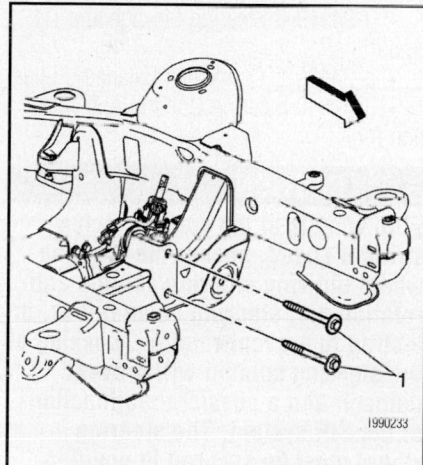

Fig. 848 Remove the steering gear bolts (1) from the left side of the steering gear

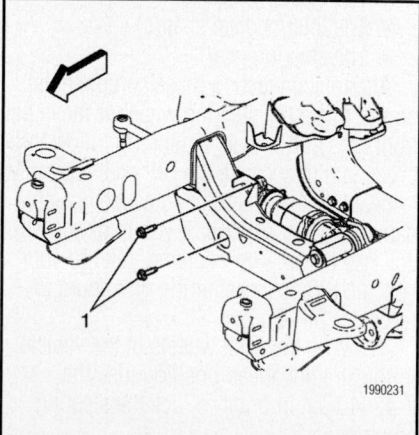

Fig. 849 Remove the steering gear bolts (1) from the right side of the steering gear

14. Install the steering gear bolts to the left side of the steering gear and tighten to 148 ft. lbs. (200 Nm).

15. Connect the steering linkage outer tie rods to the steering knuckles.

16. Install the new steering linkage outer tie rod nuts and tighten to 44 ft. lbs. (60 Nm).

17. Connect the steering shaft coupling to the steering gear.

18. Install the steering shaft coupling bolt at the steering gear and tighten to 35 ft. lbs. (47 Nm).

19. Install the front tire and wheel assemblies.

20. Perform the high voltage enabling procedure.

21. Perform the power steering control module setup procedure.

Diesel Engine Steering Gear

See Figures 850 through 854.

Special Tools Required:
- CH-49824 Steering Linkage Separator
- J-24319-B Steering Linkage and Tie Rod Puller
- J-24420-C Crankshaft Balancer Puller
- J-42640 Steering Column Anti-rotation Pin

✳✳ CAUTION

With wheels of the vehicle facing straight ahead, secure the steering wheel utilizing steering column anti-rotation pin, steering column lock, or a strap to prevent rotation. Locking of the steering column will prevent damage and a possible malfunction of the SIR system. The steering wheel must be secured in position before disconnecting the following components:

- The steering column
- The intermediate shaft(s)
- The steering gear

After disconnecting these components, do not rotate the steering wheel or move the front tires and wheels. Failure to follow this procedure may cause the SIR coil assembly to become un-centered and cause possible damage to the SIR coil. If you think the SIR coil has became un-centered, refer to your specific SIR coil's centering procedure to re-center SIR Coil.

1. With the front wheels of the vehicle in the straight ahead position, use the J-42640 pin in order to lock the steering column.

2. Place drain pans under the vehicle.

3. Remove as much power steering fluid from the reservoir as possible.

4. Raise and support the vehicle.

5. Remove the engine shield, if equipped.

6. Remove the left front wheelhouse liner.

7. Remove the charge air cooler inlet pipe.

8. Remove the front stabilizer shaft.

9. Disconnect the steering hoses from the steering gear.

10. Disconnect the steering shaft coupling from the steering gear.

11. Remove the pitman arm nut. Discard the pitman arm nut.

12. Remove the steering linkage relay rod bushing, if equipped.

13. If the vehicle is equipped with a crew cab with Single Rear Wheels (SRW) or any body style with dual rear wheels, use the J-24319-B puller in order to disconnect the pitman arm from the relay rod.

14. If the vehicle is NOT equipped with a crew cab with SRW or any body style with dual rear wheels, use the CH-49824 separator and the J-24420-C puller in order to disconnect the pitman arm from the relay rod.

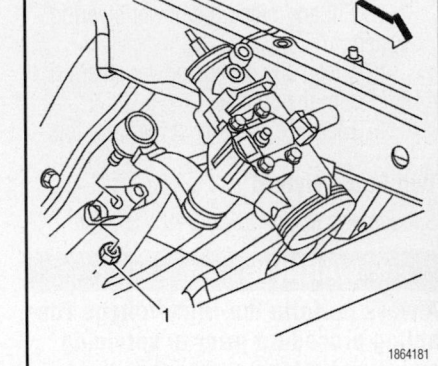

Fig. 852 Remove the pitman arm nut (1)

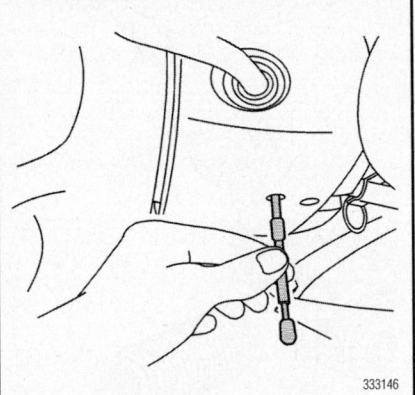

Fig. 850 With the front wheels of the vehicle in the straight ahead position, use the J-42640 Pin in order to lock the steering column

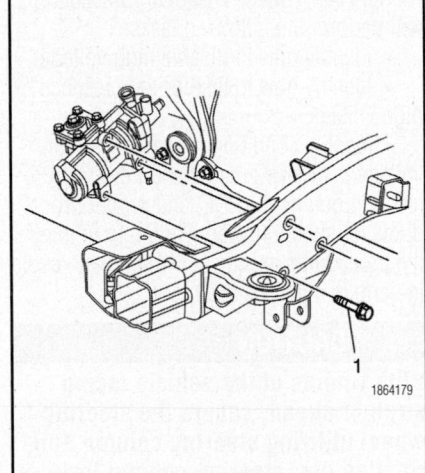

Fig. 853 Remove the steering gear bolts (1)

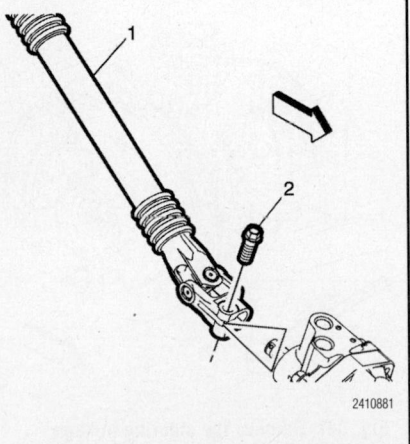

Fig. 851 Disconnect the steering shaft (1) coupling from the steering gear; bolt (2)

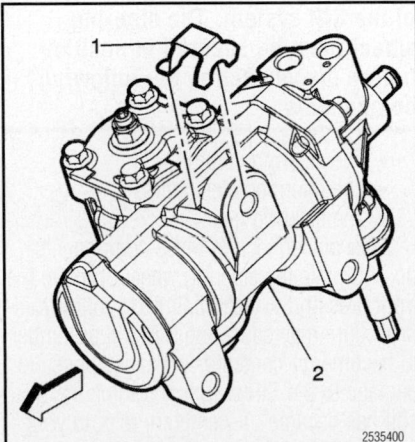

Fig. 854 If equipped with a spacer (1) on the steering gear (2), save the spacer

15. Remove the steering gear bolts.
16. Remove the steering gear from the vehicle.
17. If equipped with a spacer on the steering gear, save the spacer.
18. Transfer the pitman arm, if necessary.

To install:

19. If you removed the pitman arm, install the pitman arm.
20. If the old steering gear was equipped with a spacer, install the spacer to the new steering gear.
21. Position the steering gear in the vehicle.

➡ **Start all of the steering gear bolts by hand and fully seat the bolts before finalizing the torque.**

22. Install the steering gear bolts.
23. Tighten the steering gear bolts to 203 ft. lbs. (275 Nm).
24. Connect the pitman arm to the relay rod.
25. Install the steering linkage relay rod bushing, if equipped.
26. Install the NEW pitman arm nut and tighten to 92 ft. lbs. (125 Nm).
27. Connect the power steering hoses to the steering gear. Tighten the hose fittings to 24 ft. lbs. (33 Nm).
28. Connect the steering shaft coupling to the steering gear. Tighten the bolt to 35 ft. lbs. (47 Nm).
29. Install the front stabilizer shaft.
30. Install the charge air cooler inlet pipe.
31. Install the left front wheelhouse liner.
32. If you removed the engine shield, install the engine shield.
33. Lower the vehicle.
34. Remove the J-42640 pin from the steering column.
35. Fill and bleed the power steering system.
36. Clean any excess fluid from the vehicle.
37. Remove the drain pans.

POWER STEERING PUMP

REMOVAL & INSTALLATION

V6 Engines

See Figures 851, 855 through 859.

1. Remove the power steering pump pulley.
2. Remove as much power steering fluid from the power steering fluid reservoir as possible.

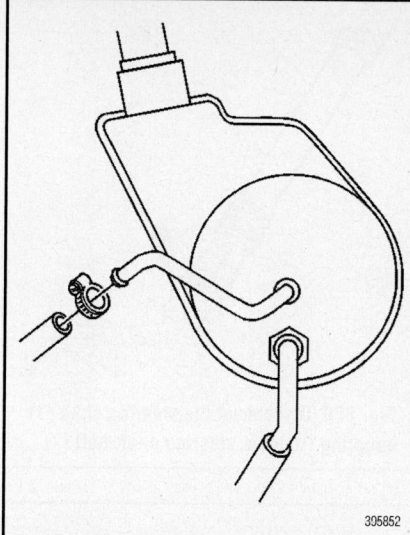

Fig. 855 Disconnect the power steering fluid cooler hose clamp and the power steering fluid cooler hose from the power steering pump assembly

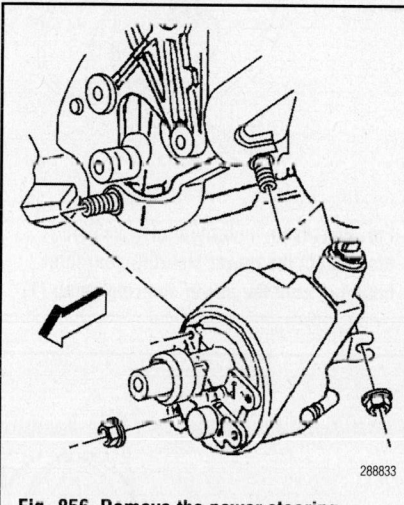

Fig. 856 Remove the power steering pump rear bracket nuts

3. Disconnect the steering shaft coupling from the steering gear.
4. Remove the engine shield.
5. Place drain pans under the vehicle as needed.
6. Disconnect the power steering fluid cooler hose clamp and the power steering fluid cooler hose from the power steering pump assembly.
7. Remove the power steering pump rear bracket nuts.
8. Remove the power steering pump bolts.
9. Remove the power steering pump bracket bolts and nut.
10. Pull the power steering pump bracket forward.

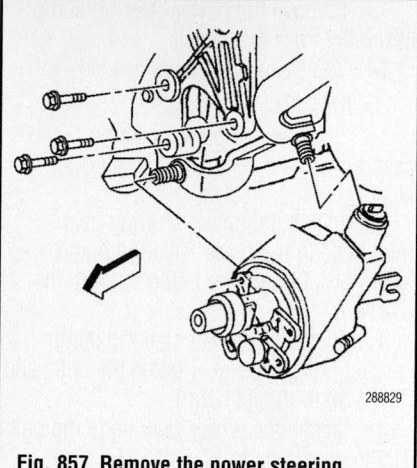

Fig. 857 Remove the power steering pump bolts

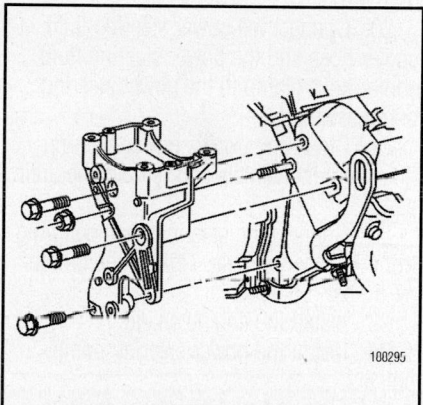

Fig. 858 Remove the power steering pump bracket bolts and nut

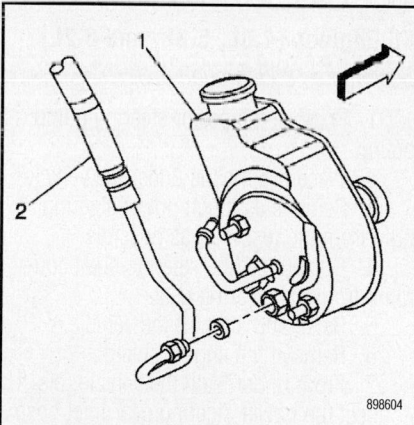

Fig. 859 Remove the power steering gear inlet hose (2) from the power steering pump assembly (1)

11. Separate the power steering pump assembly from the power steering pump bracket.
12. Remove the power steering gear inlet hose from the power steering pump assembly.

13. Remove the power steering pump assembly from the vehicle.

14. Transfer any parts as needed.

To install:

15. Position the power steering pump assembly in the vehicle with the power steering pump bracket.

16. Install the power steering gear inlet hose to the power steering pump assembly. Tighten the fitting to 24 ft. lbs. (32 Nm).

17. Install the power steering pump bracket bolts and nut. Tighten the bolts and nut to 30 ft. lbs. (41 Nm).

18. Install the power steering pump bolts. Tighten the bolts to 37 ft. lbs. (50 Nm).

19. Install the power steering pump rear bracket nuts. Tighten the nuts to 30 ft. lbs. (41 Nm).

20. Connect the power steering fluid cooler hose and the power steering fluid cooler hose clamp to the power steering pump assembly.

21. Clean any excess power steering fluid from the vehicle and remove the drain pans.

22. Connect the steering shaft coupling from the steering gear. Tighten the bolt to 37 ft. lbs. (50 Nm).

23. Install the engine shield.

24. Install the power steering pump pulley.

25. Fill and bleed the power steering system.

26. Program the power steering control module.

V8 Engines (4.8L, 5.3L, and 6.2L)

See Figures 860 through 863.

1. Remove the power steering pump pulley.

2. Place drain pans under the vehicle.

3. Remove as much power steering fluid from the reservoir as possible.

4. Disconnect the steering shaft coupling from the steering gear.

5. Raise and support the vehicle.

6. Remove the engine shield.

7. From underneath the vehicle, disconnect the power steering gear inlet hose from the power steering pump.

8. Loosen the power steering fluid cooler hose clamp and disconnect the power steering fluid cooler hose from the power steering pump.

9. If equipped with hydroboost, loosen the power brake booster outlet hose clamp and disconnect the power brake booster outlet hose from power steering pump.

10. Remove the power steering pump bracket bolt from the side of the engine.

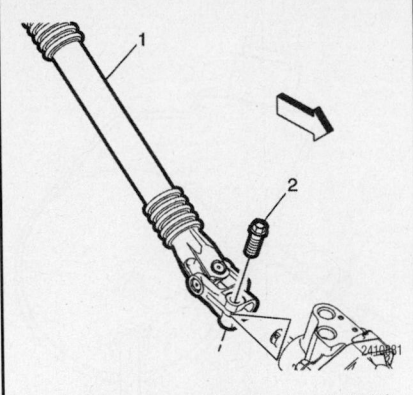

Fig. 860 Disconnect the steering shaft (1) coupling from the steering gear; bolt (2)

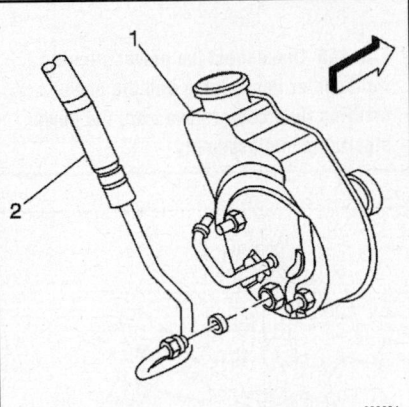

Fig. 861 From underneath the vehicle, disconnect the power steering gear inlet hose (2) from the power steering pump (1)

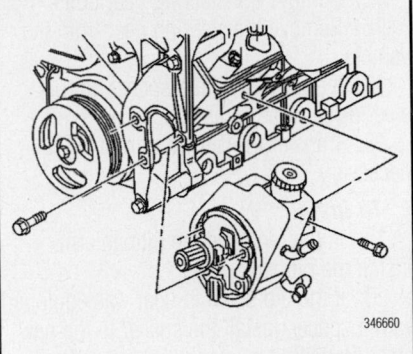

Fig. 863 Remove the power steering pump bracket bolt from the side of the engine

11. Remove the power steering pump bolts.

12. Remove the power steering pump and the reservoir as an assembly from the vehicle.

To install:

13. Install the power steering pump and the reservoir as an assembly to the vehicle.

➡ **Start all the bolts by hand before finalizing each torque.**

14. Install the power steering pump bracket bolt to the side of the engine and tighten to 37 ft. lbs. (50 Nm).

15. Install the power steering pump bolts and tighten to 37 ft. lbs. (50 Nm).

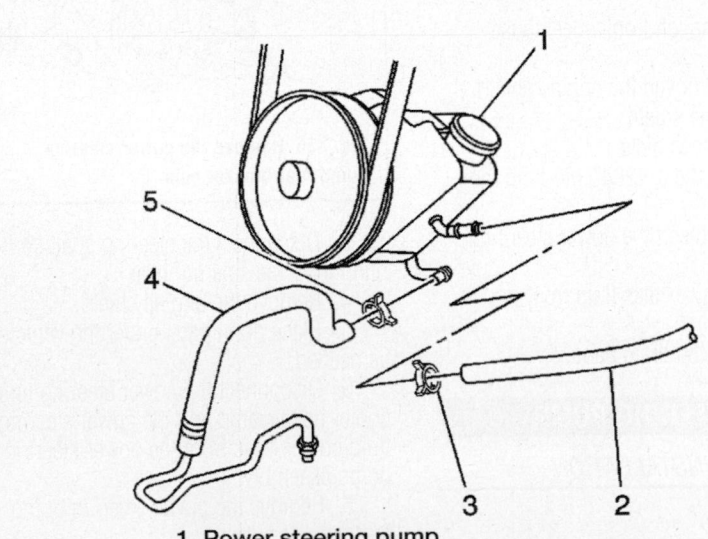

1. Power steering pump
2. Power brake booster outlet hose
3. Power brake booster outlet hose clamp
4. Power steering fluid cooler hose
5. Power steering fluid cooler hose clamp

Fig. 862 Exploded view of the power steering pump assembly

16. Connect the power steering fluid cooler hose and the power steering fluid cooler hose clamp to the power steering pump.

17. If equipped with hydroboost, connect the power brake booster outlet hose and the power brake booster outlet hose clamp to the power steering pump.

18. Connect the power steering gear inlet hose to the power steering pump. Tighten the fitting to 24 ft. lbs. (33 Nm).

19. Connect the steering shaft coupling. Tighten the bolt to 37 ft. lbs. (50 Nm).

20. Install the engine shield.

21. Install the power steering pump pulley.

22. Fill and bleed the power steering system.

23. Clean any excess fluid power steering fluid from the vehicle.

24. Remove the drain pans.

25. Lower the vehicle.

V8 Engines (6.0L)

See Figure 864.

➡The manufacturer does not provide a specific Removal and Installation procedure for this component. Refer to the graphic(s) when servicing this component. Remove the parts in numerical order.

2010 Diesel Engines

See Figures 865 through 867.

1. Remove the drive belt.

2. Place a drain pan under the vehicle.

3. Remove the bolts from the rear of the pump.

4. Remove the bolts from the front of the pump bracket.

➡Note the location of the battery cables for reinstallation.

5. Disconnect the negative battery clip from the power steering pump front bracket.

6. Remove the power steering return hoses from the power steering pump.

7. Remove the power steering pump from the accessory mounting bracket to gain access to the power brake booster inlet pipe.

8. Remove the power brake booster inlet pipe from the power steering pump.

9. Remove the power steering pump from the vehicle.

10. Remove the power steering pulley.

11. Remove the front bracket from the power steering pump.

12. Remove the rear bracket from the power steering pump.

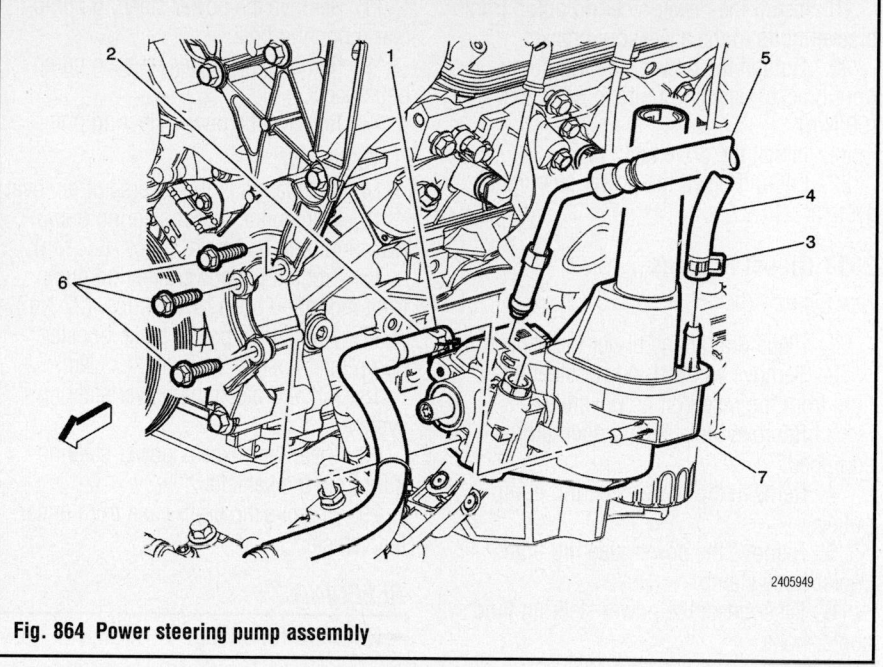

Fig. 864 Power steering pump assembly

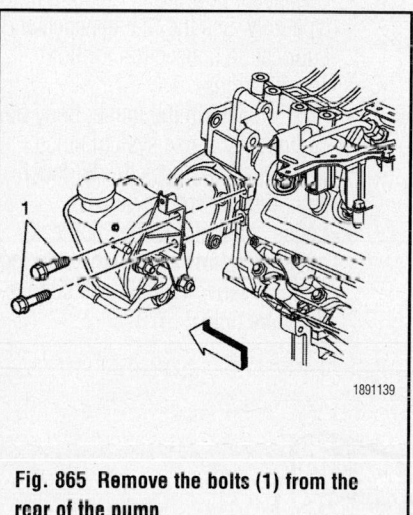

Fig. 865 Remove the bolts (1) from the rear of the pump

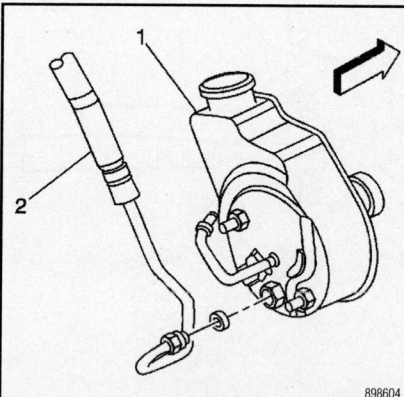

Fig. 866 Remove the power steering pump (1) from the accessory mounting bracket to gain access to the power brake booster inlet pipe (2)

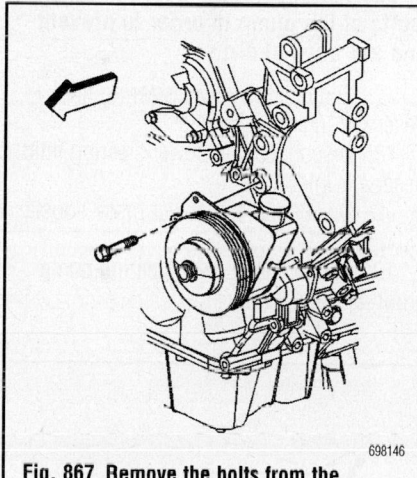

Fig. 867 Remove the bolts from the front of the pump bracket

To install:

13. Install the rear bracket to the power steering pump. Tighten the rear bracket retaining nuts to 37 ft. lbs. (50 Nm).

14. Install the front bracket to the power steering pump. Tighten the front bracket retaining nuts to 37 ft. lbs. (50 Nm).

15. Install the power steering pulley.

16. Install the power brake booster inlet pipe to the power steering pump. Tighten the fittings to 24 ft. lbs. (32 Nm).

17. Install the power steering return hoses and retaining clamps to the power steering pump.

18. Reposition the power steering pump to the accessory bracket and install the bolts to the rear of the power steering pump. Tighten the rear bolts to 37 ft. lbs. (50 Nm).

19. Install the power steering pump front bracket bolts to the accessory bracket.

20. Tighten the power steering pump front bracket retaining bolts to 37 ft. lbs. (50 Nm).

21. Install the drive belt.

22. Fill and bleed the power steering system.

2011 Diesel Engines

See Figure 868.

1. Place drain pans under the vehicle.

2. Remove as much power steering fluid from the reservoir as possible.

3. Remove the auxiliary alternator, if equipped.

4. Remove the power steering pump pulley.

5. Remove the power steering fluid cooler hose clamp.

6. Disconnect the power steering fluid cooler hose.

➡**Cap the ends of the hoses and the ports of the pump in order to prevent the entrance of dirt.**

7. Remove the power steering fluid reservoir inlet hose clamp.

8. Disconnect the power steering fluid reservoir inlet hose.

9. Disconnect the power brake booster pump inlet hose.

10. Remove the power steering pump front mounting bolts.

11. Remove the power steering pump rear mounting bolt.

12. Remove the power steering pump bolt spacer.

13. Remove the power steering pump.

To install:

14. Installation is the reverse of removal.

15. Tighten the power steering pump rear mounting bolt to 16 ft. lbs. (22 Nm).

16. Tighten the power steering pump front mounting bolts to 16 ft. lbs. (22 Nm).

17. Tighten the power brake booster pump inlet hose to 24 ft. lbs. (33 Nm).

18. Fill and bleed the power steering system.

19. Clean any excess power steering fluid from the vehicle.

20. Remove the drain pans from under the vehicle.

BLEEDING

➡**Note the following:**

- Use clean, new power steering fluid type only. See the Maintenance and Lubrication subsection for fluid specifications.
- Hoses touching the frame, body or engine may cause system noise. Verify that the hoses do not touch any other part of the vehicle.
- Loose connections may not leak, but could allow air into the steering system. Verify that all hose connections are tight.

➡**Power steering fluid level must be maintained throughout bleed procedure.**

1. Fill pump reservoir with fluid to minimum system level, FULL COLD level, or middle of hash mark on cap stick fluid level indicator.

➡**With hydro-boost only, the oil level will appear falsely high if the hydro-boost accumulator is not fully charged. Do not apply the brake pedal with the engine OFF. This will discharge the hydro-boost accumulator.**

2. If equipped with hydro-boost, fully charge the hydro-boost accumulator using the following procedure:
   a. Start the engine.
   b. Firmly apply the brake pedal 10–15 times.
   c. Turn the engine OFF.

3. Raise the vehicle until the front wheels are off the ground.

4. Key on engine OFF, turn the steering wheel from stop to stop 12 times.

➡**Vehicles equipped with hydro-boost systems or longer length power steering hoses may require turns up to 15 to 20 stop to stops.**

5. Verify power steering fluid level per operating specification.

6. Start the engine. Rotate steering wheel from left to right. Check for sign of cavitation or fluid aeration (pump noise/whining).

7. Verify the fluid level. Repeat the bleed procedure, if necessary.

FLUID FILL PROCEDURE

Without Hydroboost

> ✳✳ **CAUTION**
>
> **When adding fluid or making a complete fluid change, always use the proper power steering fluid. Failure to use the proper fluid will cause hose and seal damage and fluid leaks.**

1. Clean the area surrounding the reservoir cap.

2. Remove the reservoir cap.

3. Inspect the power steering pump fluid level at regular intervals. Use the appropriate procedure below.

4. Add fluid when required.

Fluid Is Cold

1. Remove the reservoir cap.

2. Inspect the fluid level on the capstick.

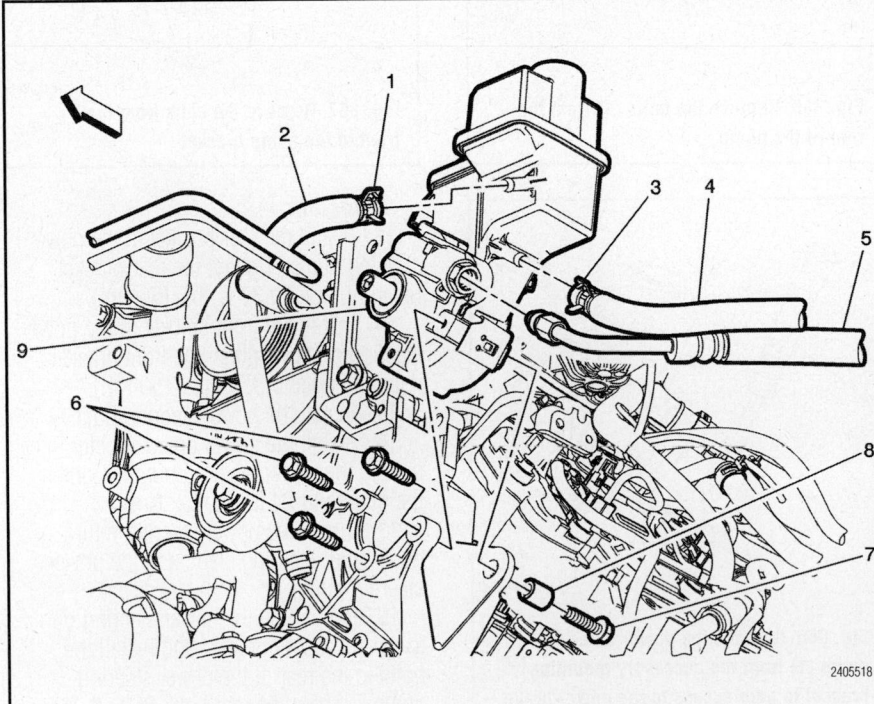

Fig. 868 Exploded view of the power steering pump assembly

2405518

3. Ensure that the fluid level is between the bottom of the COLD/FULL mark and the end of the capstick.

Fluid Is Hot

1. Run the engine until the fluid reaches about 170°F (80°C).

2. Turn the engine OFF.
3. Remove the reservoir cap.
4. Inspect the fluid level on the capstick.
5. Ensure that the fluid level is between the HOT/FULL and the COLD/FULL marks on the capstick.

6. If the fluid level is low, add power steering fluid to the proper level.
7. Install the reservoir cap.
8. When checking the fluid level after servicing the steering system, bleed the air from the system.

SUSPENSION

CONTROL LINKS

REMOVAL & INSTALLATION

Stabilizer Shaft Link—1500 Series
See Figure 869.

1. Remove the wheel and tire assembly.
2. Remove the stabilizer shaft link nut.
3. Remove the stabilizer shaft link bolt.
4. Remove the 2 washers.
5. Remover the 4 insulators.
6. Remove the stabilizer shaft link spacer.
7. Installation is the reverse of removal.
8. Tighten the stabilizer shaft link nut to 17 ft. lbs. (23 Nm).

Stabilizer Shaft Link—2500 Series
See Figure 870.

1. Raise and support the vehicle.
2. Remove the engine shield, if equipped.
3. Loosen the stabilizer shaft insulator, if needed.

4. Remove the stabilizer shaft link retaining nut.
5. Remove the front stabilizer shaft insulators.
6. Remove the front stabilizer shaft washers.
7. Remove the front stabilizer shaft spacer.

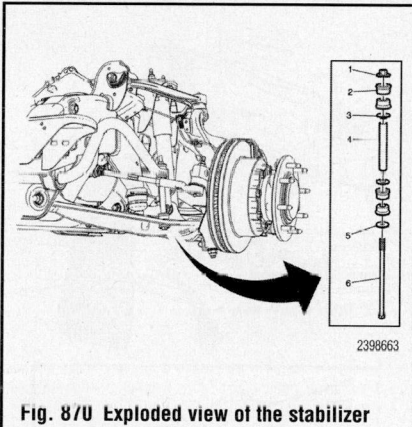

Fig. 870 Exploded view of the stabilizer shaft link assembly

FRONT SUSPENSION

8. Remove the front stabilizer shaft washer.
9. Remove the front stabilizer shaft bolt.
10. Installation is the reverse of removal.
11. Tighten the stabilizer shaft link retaining nut to 17 ft. lbs. (23 Nm).

LOWER BALL JOINT

REMOVAL & INSTALLATION

1500 Series
See Figures 871 through 875.

Special Tools Required:
• CH-49240 Ball Joint Crimper and Install Kit
• J-41805 Ball Joint Remover Install Kit

1. Raise and support the vehicle.
2. Remove the wheel drive shaft, if needed.

➡**Ensure that the knuckle is secured away from the lower control arm.**

3. Remove the steering knuckle from the vehicle.
4. Using a hammer chisel, remove the locking tabs from the ball joint body.

➡**Ensure that the upper ball joint is not being rubbed on the ratchet during the removal or installation of the lower ball joint. Rubbing on the upper ball joint**

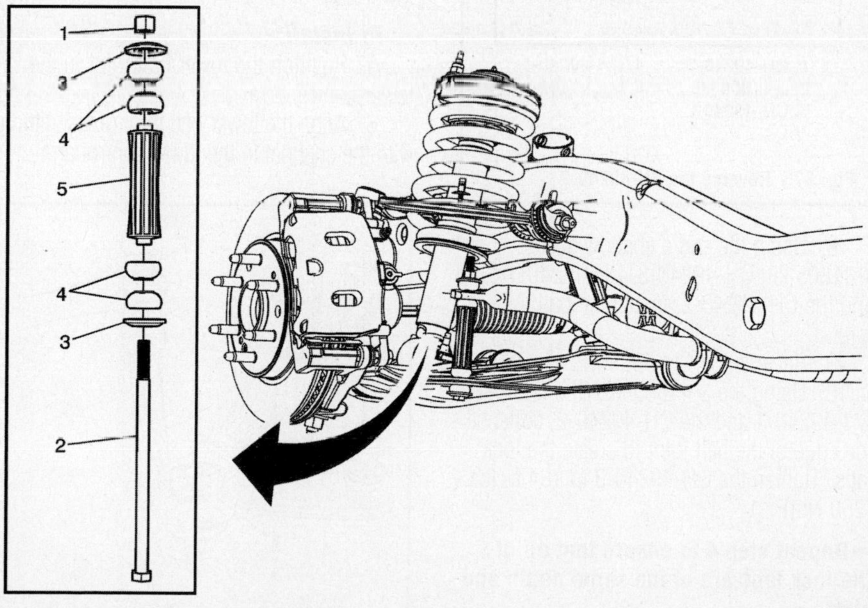

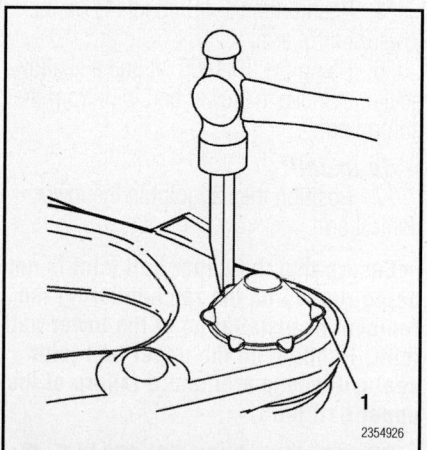

Fig. 871 Using a hammer chisel, remove the locking tabs (1) from the ball joint body

Fig. 869 Exploded view of the stabilizer shaft link assembly

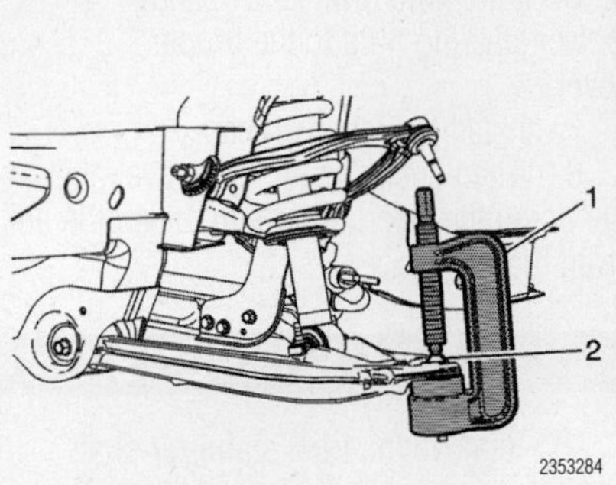

Fig. 872 Position the J-41805 kit (1) on the lower control arm; remove the lower ball joint (2) from the control arm

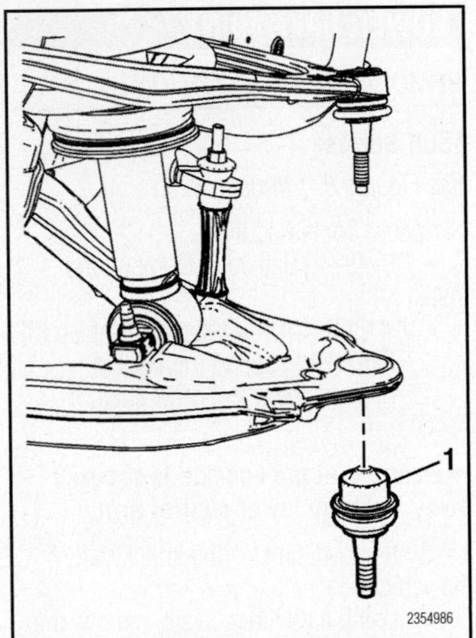

Fig. 873 Position the ball joint (1) in the lower control arm

seal will cause premature failure of the upper ball joint.

5. Position the J-41805 kit (1) on the lower control arm.
6. Using the J-41805 kit and a shallow socket, remove the lower ball joint from the control arm.

To install:

7. Position the ball joint in the lower control arm.

➡Ensure that the upper ball joint is not being rubbed on the ratchet during the removal or installation of the lower ball joint. Rubbing on the upper ball joint seal will cause premature failure of the upper ball joint.

➡When using adapter CH-49240-2, the ensure that the teeth for the lock tabs are facing upward.

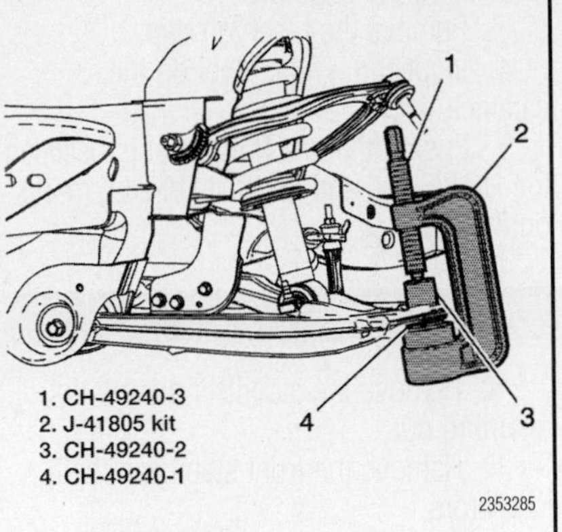

Fig. 874 Using the and a shallow socket J-41805 kit, CH-49240-3, CH-49240-1 and the CH-49240-2, install the ball joint

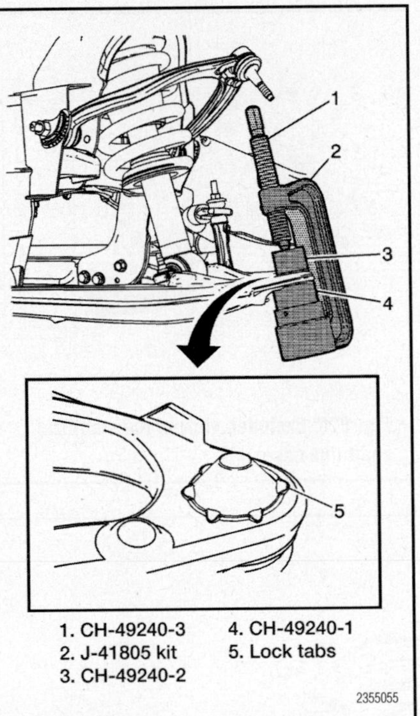

Fig. 875 Reverse the CH-49240-2

8. Using the and a shallow socket J-41805 kit, CH-49240-3, CH-49240-1 and the CH-49240-2, install the ball joint.
9. Reverse the CH-49240-2.
10. Using the J-41805 kit, CH-49240-3, CH-49240-1 and the CH-49240-2, collapse the edge of the ball joint to create the lock tabs. Tighten the CH-49240-3 to 184 ft. lbs. (250 Nm).

➡Repeat step 4 to ensure that all of the lock tabs are of the same depth and size.

11. Rotate the J-41805 kit 180 degrees and repeat the process.
12. Install the wheel drive shaft, if needed.
13. Install the steering knuckle in the vehicle.
14. Install the lower ball joint stud nut and tighten to:
    a. First Pass: 37 ft. lbs. (50 Nm)
    b. Final Pass: additional 130 degrees
15. Remove the supports and lower the vehicle.

2500 Series

See Figures 876 through 879.

Special Tools Required:

- CH-49240 Ball Joint Crimper and Install Kit
- J-41805 Ball Joint remover/Installer

1. Raise and support the vehicle.

➡When removing the knuckle, DO NOT remove any of the brake or electrical components from the knuckle. Secure the knuckle assembly to the side.

2. Remove the knuckle from the vehicle.
3. Using a hammer and a chisel, remove the lock tabs from the lower ball joint.

➡Ensure that the upper ball joint is not being rubbed on by the ratchet during the removal or installation of the lower ball joint. Rubbing on the upper ball joint seal will cause premature failure of the upper ball joint.

4. Using the J-41805 remover/installer and the appropriate adapter, remove the lower ball joint.

To install:

5. Position the lower ball joint in the lower control arm.
6. Align the lower ball joint grease fitting with the channel in the lower control arm.

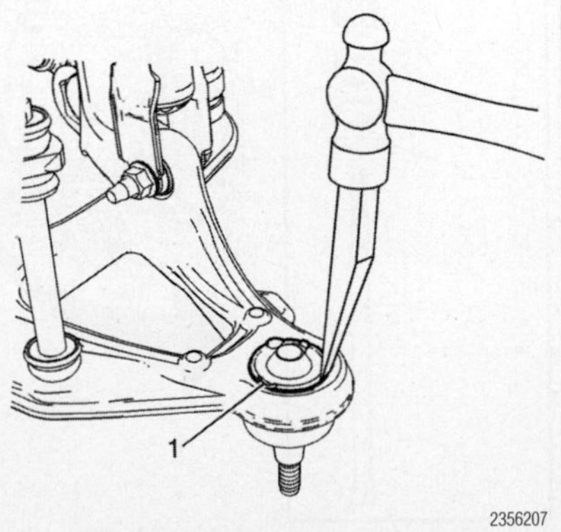

Fig. 876 Using a hammer and a chisel, remove the lock tabs (1) from the lower ball joint

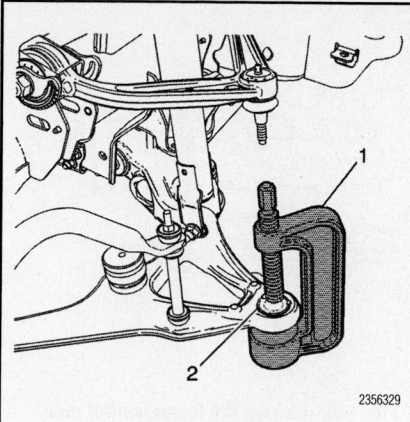

Fig. 877 Using the J-41805 remover/installer (1) and the appropriate adapter, remove the lower ball joint (2)

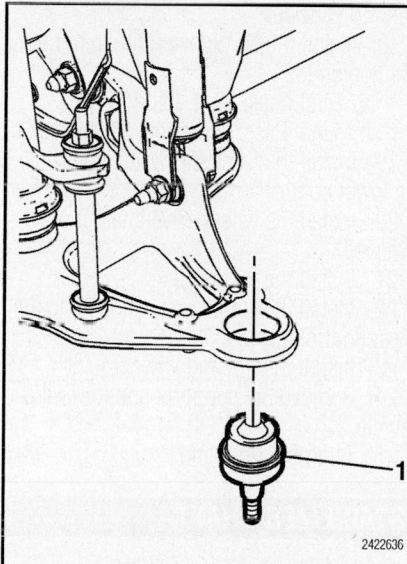

Fig. 878 Position the lower ball joint (1) in the lower control arm

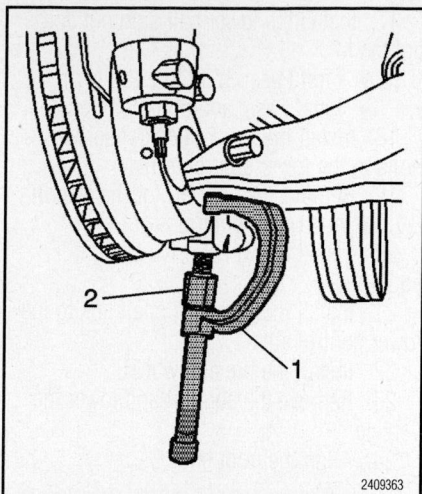

➡Ensure that the upper ball joint is not being rubbed on by the ratchet during the removal or installation of the lower ball joint. Rubbing on the upper ball joint seal will cause premature failure of the upper ball joint.

7. Using the J-41805 remover/installer, the appropriate adapter, and the CH-49240 install Kit, install the lower ball joint.

8. Ensure that the ball joint is fully seated against the lower control arm.

9. Using a hammer and a punch, create the lock tabs for the lower ball joint.

10. Install the knuckle.

11. Install the lower ball joint stud nut and tighten to:
- First Pass: 37 ft. lbs. (50 Nm)
- Final Pass: additional 95 degrees

12. Remove the support and lower the vehicle.

LOWER CONTROL ARM

REMOVAL & INSTALLATION

1500 Series

See Figures 880 through 882.

➡For vehicles equipped with the aluminum lower control arm, the ball joint is NOT service separately. If the ball joint in the aluminum lower control arm is found to have excessive wear and is damaged, replace the lower control arm as an assembly.

1. Raise and support the vehicle.
2. Remove the tire and wheel.
3. Remove the stabilizer shaft link from the lower control arm.
4. Remove the wheel drive shaft, if equipped.
5. Using mechanics wire or equivalent, support the knuckle assembly and upper control arm.

Fig. 881 Using the CH-3631 separator (1) and the J-45851 (2), remove the lower ball joint from the steering knuckle

6. Remove and discard the lower ball joint retaining nut.

7. Remove the lower shock bolts from the lower control arm.

8. Using the CH-3631 separator and the J-45851, remove the lower ball joint from the steering knuckle.

9. Remove the lower control arm nuts and washers.

10. Remove the control arm bolts.

11. Remove the control arm.

To install:

12. Install the lower control arm.

13. Install the lower control arm bolts.

14. Install the washers.

15. Install the lower control arm retaining nuts and tighten to 129 ft. lbs. (175 Nm).

16. Install the lower ball joint in the steering knuckle.

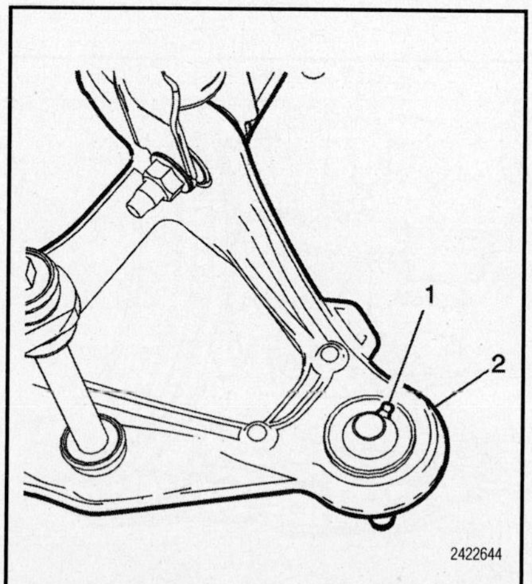

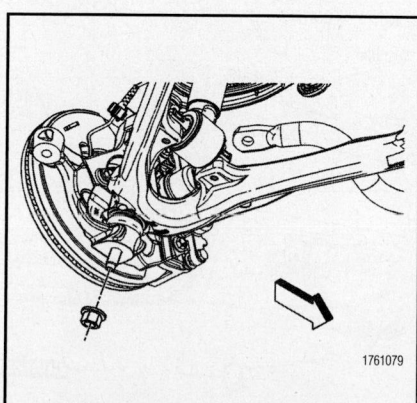

Fig. 879 Align the lower ball joint grease fitting (1) with the channel (2) in the lower control arm

Fig. 880 Remove and discard the lower ball joint retaining nut (1)

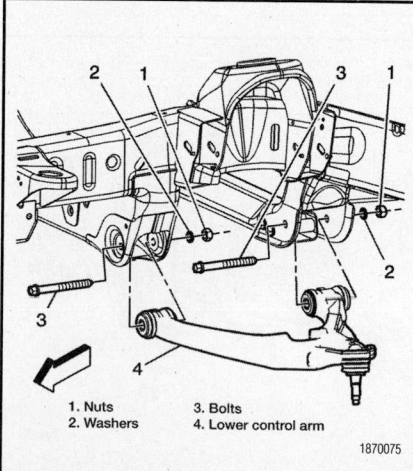

1. Nuts   3. Bolts
2. Washers   4. Lower control arm

Fig. 882 Exploded view of the lower control arm assembly

17. Install the lower ball stud nut and tighten to:
- First Pass: 37 ft. lbs. (50 Nm)
- Final Pass: additional 95 degrees

18. Install the lower shock absorber bolts to the lower control arm.

19. Remove the support for the steering knuckle and upper control arm.

20. Install the wheel drive shaft, if equipped.

21. Install the stabilizer shaft link to the lower control arm.

22. Install the tire and wheel.

23. Remove the support and lower the vehicle.

24. Align the front end.

2500 Series

See Figures 883 through 886.

Special Tools Required:
- CH-43631 Ball Joint Separator
- J-45851 Ball Joint Separator Protector Adapters

1. Raise and support the vehicle.

2. Remove the tire and wheel.

3. Remove the stabilizer shaft links from the lower control arm.

4. Remove the torsion bars.

5. Remove the front shock absorber from the lower control arm.

6. Remove the wheel drive shaft, if needed.

7. Remove and discard the lower ball joint retaining nut. Replace with NEW only.

8. Using the CH-43631 separator and the J-45851 adapters, remove the lower ball joint from the steering knuckle.

9. Remove the front lower control arm nut and bolt.

10. Remove the lower control rear nut and bolt.

11. Remove the lower control arm.

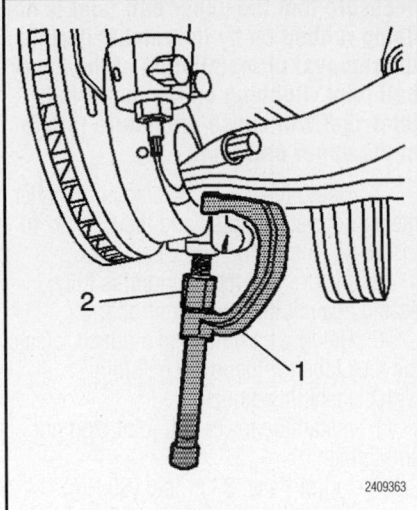

Fig. 884 Using the CH-43631 separator (1) and the J-45851 adapters (2), remove the lower ball joint from the steering knuckle

To install:

12. Position the lower control arm in the frame.

13. Install the lower control arm rear bolt and nut and hand tighten.

14. Install the lower control arm front bolt and nut and hand tighten.

15. Before tighten the lower control nuts to the specified torque, perform the following to ensure the proper trim height settings:
- a. Support the lower control arm.
- b. Using an appropriate hydraulic jack, raise the lower control arm until just contacts both jumper bumpers.

16. Tighten the front and rear lower control arm mounting nuts:
- a. First Pass: 133 ft. lbs. (180 Nm).
- b. Final Pass: additional 60 degrees.

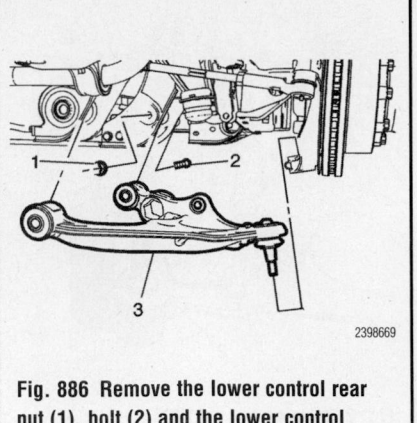

Fig. 886 Remove the lower control rear nut (1), bolt (2) and the lower control arm (3)

17. Install the lower ball joint in the steering knuckle.

18. Install the NEW lower ball joint nut and tighten to:
- a. First Pass: 37 ft. lbs. (50 Nm).
- b. Final Pass: additional 95 degrees.

19. Install the front shock absorber to the lower control arm.

20. Install the wheel drive shaft, if removed.

21. Install the torsion bars.

22. Install the stabilizer shaft links to the lower control arm.

23. Install the tire and wheel.

24. Remove the supports and lower the vehicle.

25. Align the front end.

STABILIZER SHAFT

REMOVAL & INSTALLATION

1500 Series

See Figure 887.

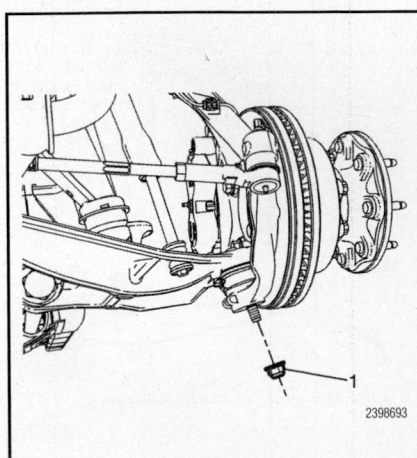

Fig. 883 Remove and discard the lower ball joint retaining nut (1)

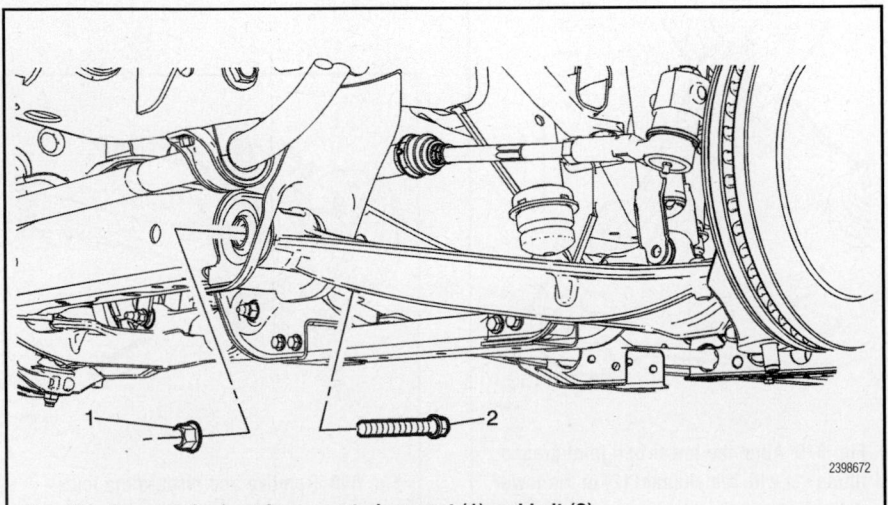

Fig. 885 Remove the front lower control arm nut (1) and bolt (2)

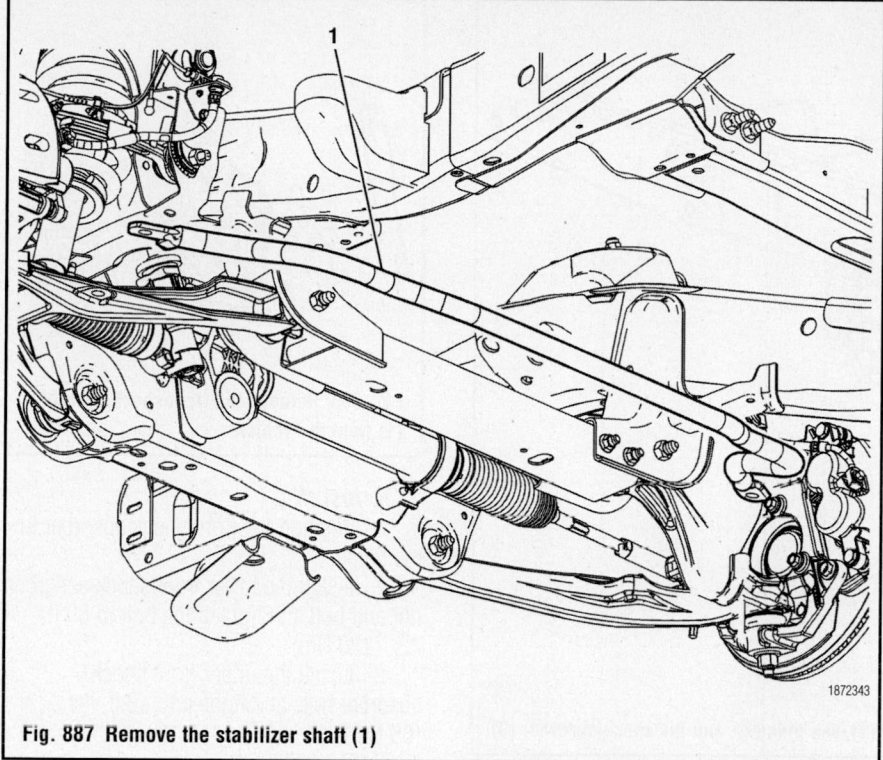

Fig. 887 Remove the stabilizer shaft (1)

1. Raise and support the vehicle.
2. Remove the front stabilizer shaft links.
3. Remove the front stabilizer shaft insulators.
4. Remove the stabilizer shaft.
5. Installation is the reverse of removal.

2500 Series

See Figure 888.

1. Raise and support the vehicle.
2. Remove the engine shield, if equipped.
3. Remove the front stabilizer shaft links.
4. Remove the front stabilizer shaft insulators.
5. Remove the stabilizer shaft.
6. Installation is the reverse of removal.

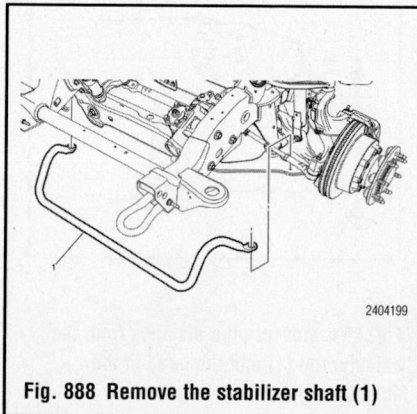

Fig. 888 Remove the stabilizer shaft (1)

STEERING KNUCKLE

REMOVAL & INSTALLATION

See Figure 889.

1. Raise and support the vehicle.
2. Remove the tire and wheel.
3. Remove the wheel bearing/hub assembly from the steering knuckle.
4. Remove the steering knuckle.
   a. Remove the outer tie rod end from the steering knuckle.
   b. Separate the upper control arm from the steering knuckle.

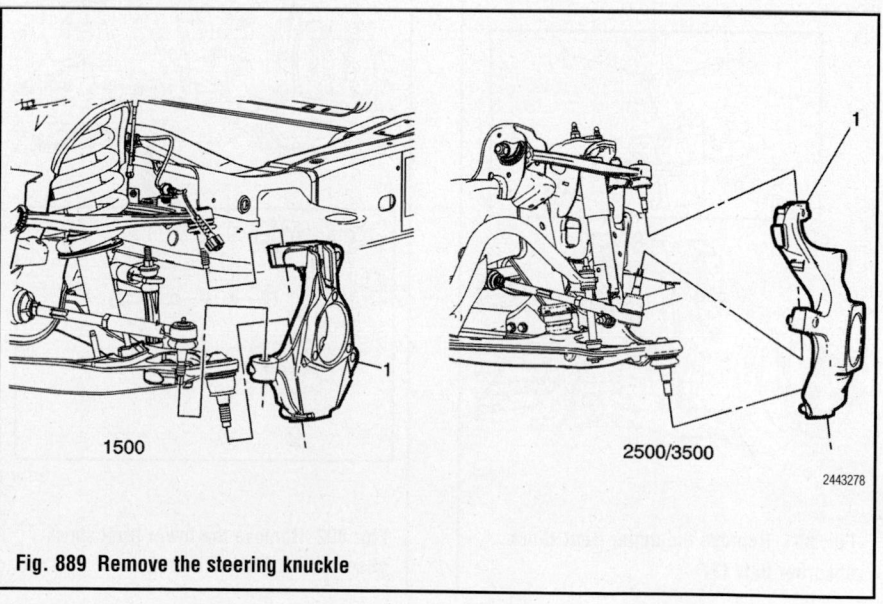

1500   2500/3500

Fig. 889 Remove the steering knuckle

   c. Separate the lower control arm from the steering knuckle.
5. Installation is the reverse of removal.
6. Verify the wheel alignment.

STRUT & SPRING ASSEMBLY

REMOVAL & INSTALLATION

1500 Series

See Figure 890.

1. Raise and support the vehicle.
2. Remove the front tire and wheel assembly.
3. Disconnect the outer tie rod from the steering knuckle.
4. Remove the shock absorber module bolts.
5. Support the lower control arm.

✴✴ CAUTION

Do not use air powered tools in order to disassemble or assemble any vehicle component. Bolt torques are vital to diagnosis. You can detect bolt torques only when using hand tools. Improper bolt torques can contribute to vehicle repair problems.

6. Remove the shock absorber module nuts.
7. Remove the shock absorber module.
8. Installation is the reverse of removal.
9. Tighten all nuts and bolts to 37 ft. lbs. (50 Nm).

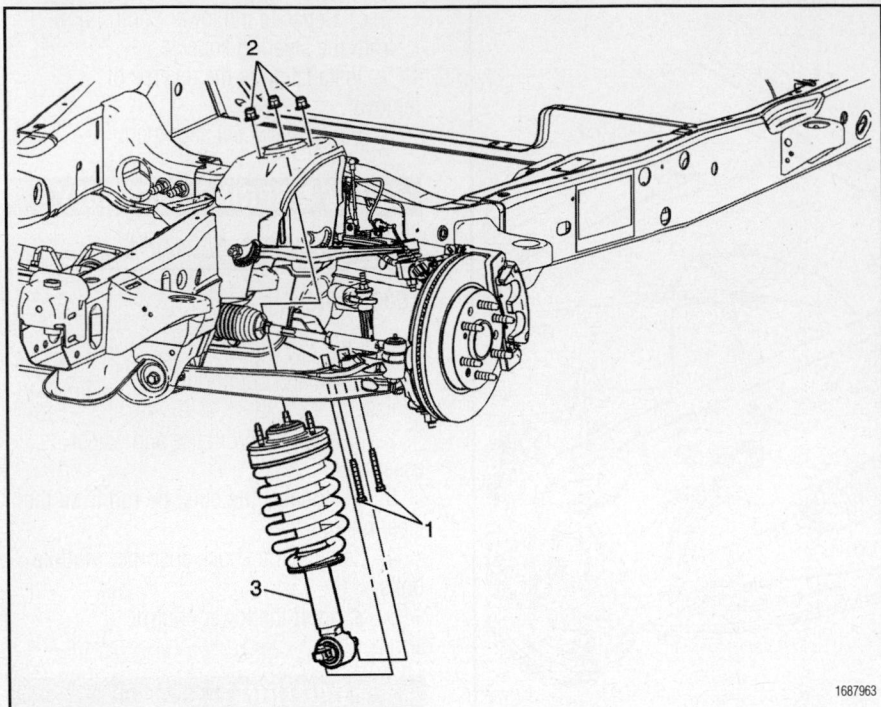

Fig. 890 Remove the shock absorber module bolts (1), the nuts (2), and the shock absorber (3)

SHOCK ABSORBER

REMOVAL & INSTALLATION

2500 Series

See Figures 891 through 893.

1. Raise the vehicle enough to place a floor jack under the lower control arm.

2. Reposition the engine splash shield between the frame and the inner wheel house to gain access to the upper shock absorber nuts.

3. Remove the upper front shock absorber nuts.

4. Remove the lower front shock absorber nut and bolt.

➡**Turn the tire and wheel assembly to gain enough clearance to remove the shock absorber.**

5. Remove the front shock absorber from the vehicle.

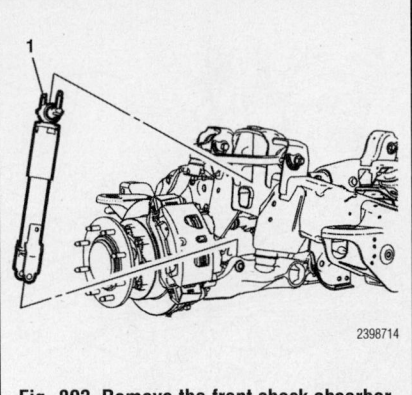

Fig. 893 Remove the front shock absorber (1) from the vehicle

To install:

6. Position the front shock absorber in the frame.

7. Install the lower front shock absorber nut and bolt and tighten the bolt to 89 ft. lbs. (120 Nm).

8. Install the upper front shock absorber nuts and tighten to 48 ft. lbs. (65 Nm).

9. Reposition the engine splash shield.

10. Remove the support from the lower control arm.

11. Lower the vehicle.

TORSION BAR

REMOVAL & INSTALLATION

2500 Series

See Figures 894 through 899.

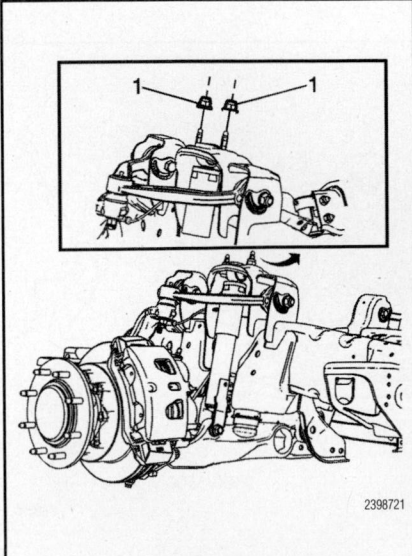

Fig. 891 Remove the upper front shock absorber nuts (1)

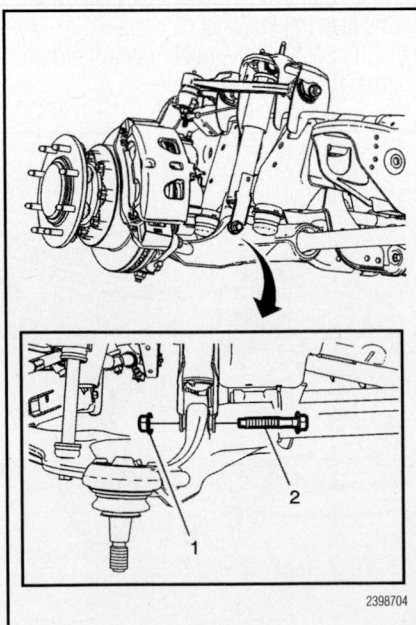

Fig. 892 Remove the lower front shock absorber nut (1) and bolt (2)

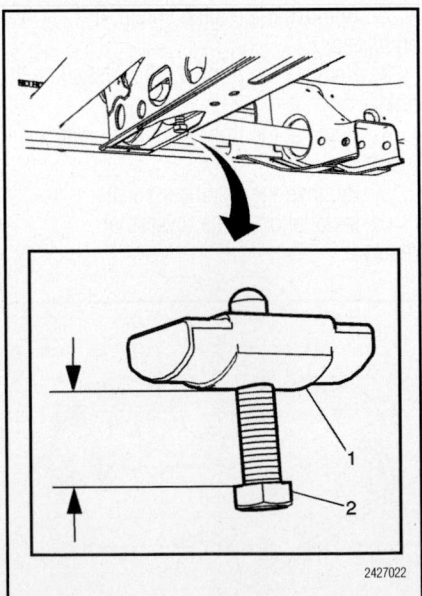

Fig. 894 Measure the distance from the adjuster nut (1) and the head of the adjuster bolt (2)

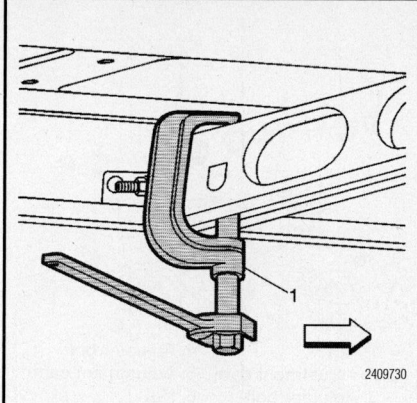

Fig. 895 Using the Torsion Bar Unloading/Loading Tool (CH-48809) (1), increase the tension on the adjustment arm until the load is removed from the adjuster nut

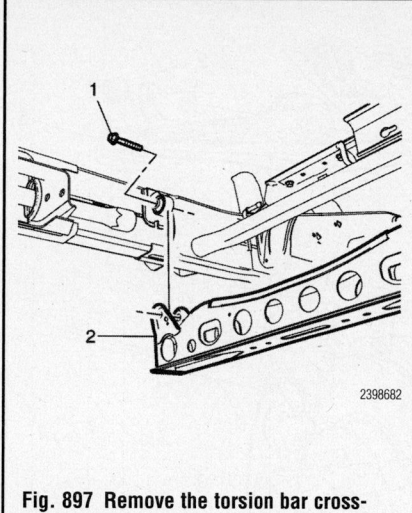

Fig. 897 Remove the torsion bar crossmember bolt (1)

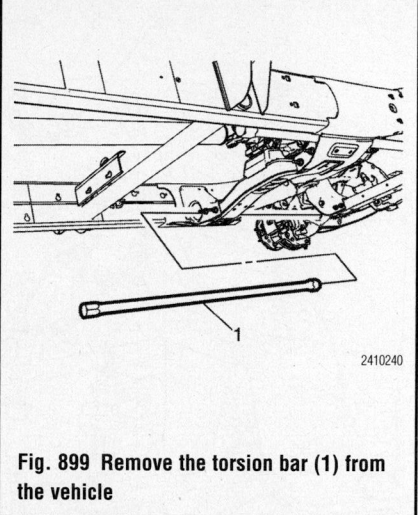

Fig. 899 Remove the torsion bar (1) from the vehicle

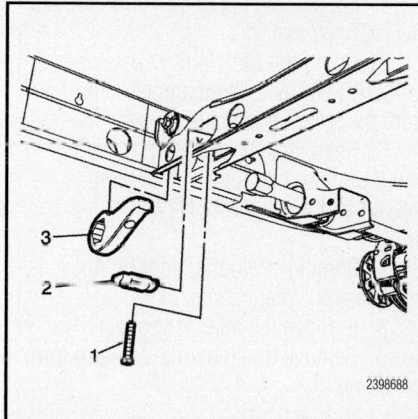

Fig. 896 Remove the adjust bolt (1) and nut (2) from the crossmember; Adjustment arm (3)

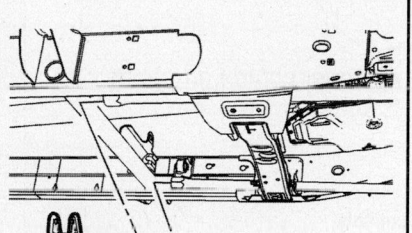

Fig. 898 Remove the torsion bar support (1) from the frame

❄ CAUTION

Use care when handling the torsion bars in order to avoid chipping or scratching the coating. Damage to the coating will result in premature failure of the torsion bars.

➡**When lifting the vehicle to service the torsion bars or related components, DO NOT lift the vehicle by the front suspension. Use the appropriate hoist to lift the vehicle by the frame.**

1. Raise and support the vehicle.

➡**This measurement step must be performed before removing the torsion bar support.**

2. Before removing the torsion bar support, measure the distance from the adjuster nut and the head of the adjuster bolt. Record the measurement.

3. Remove the torsion bar adjuster bolt from the adjuster nut and allow the adjuster arm to rest on in the crossmember.

4. Using the Torsion Bar Unloading/Loading Tool (CH-48809), increase the tension on the adjustment arm until the load is removed from the adjuster nut.

5. Remove the adjust bolt and nut from the crossmember.

6. Using the CH-48809 tool , unload the torsion bar.

7. Remove the adjustment arm by sliding the torsion bar forward.

8. Remove the torsion bar crossmember bolt.

9. Remove the torsion bar support from the frame.

➡**The left and right torsion bars are different and are not interchangeable.**

10. Remove the torsion bar from the vehicle.

To install:

11. Position the torsion bar in the lower control arm.

12. Install the torsion bar support in the frame.

13. Install the torsion bar crossmember bolt and tighten to 92 ft. lbs. (125 Nm).

14. Install the adjustment arm in the crossmember.

15. Install the torsion bar into the adjustment arm until the torsion bar is fully seated.

16. Using the CH-48809 tool (1), increase the tension on the adjustment arm to load the torsion bar.

17. Install the adjuster nut in the crossmember.

18. Unload the CH-48809 tool (1) to allow adjuster arm to rest on the adjuster and remove the CH-48809 tool (1) from the crossmember.

19. Install the adjuster bolt (2) in the adjuster nut and turn the adjuster bolt until it contacts the adjuster arm.

➡**Refer to step 2 in the removal procedure.**

20. Turn the adjuster bolt until the length of the adjuster bolt is the same distance from the adjuster bolt head to the adjuster nut prior to removing the bolt.

21. Remove the safety stands and lower the vehicle.

22. Measure the Z height.

UPPER CONTROL ARM

REMOVAL & INSTALLATION

1500 Series
See Figure 900.

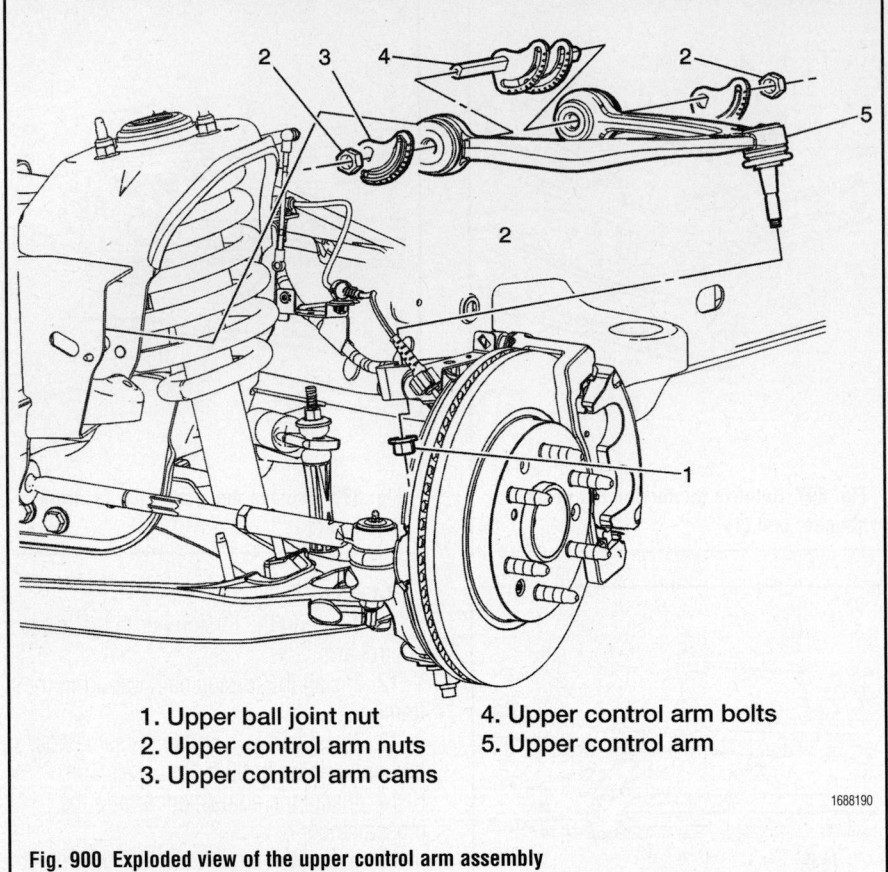

1. Upper ball joint nut
2. Upper control arm nuts
3. Upper control arm cams
4. Upper control arm bolts
5. Upper control arm

Fig. 900 Exploded view of the upper control arm assembly

1. Raise and support the vehicle.
2. Remove the front tire and wheel assembly.
3. Remove the upper ball joint nut.
   a. Disconnect the speed sensor electrical connector.
   b. Place a suitable support under the lower control arm and load the suspension.
   c. Use the J-42188-B to separate the ball joint from the steering knuckle.
   d. Remove and discard the ball joint nut. Replace with NEW only.
4. Remove the upper control arm nuts.
5. Remove the upper control arm alignment cams.
6. Remove the upper control arm bolts.
7. Remove the upper control arm.

To install:
8. Installation is the reverse of the removal procedure.
9. Tighten the upper control arm nuts to 140 ft. lbs. (190 Nm)
10. Tighten the upper ball joint nut to 37 ft. lbs. (50 Nm)
11. Verify wheel alignment.

2500 Series

See Figures 901 through 903.

1. Remove the tire and wheel.
2. Lower the vehicle and support the lower control arm.
3. Remove the front shock absorber.

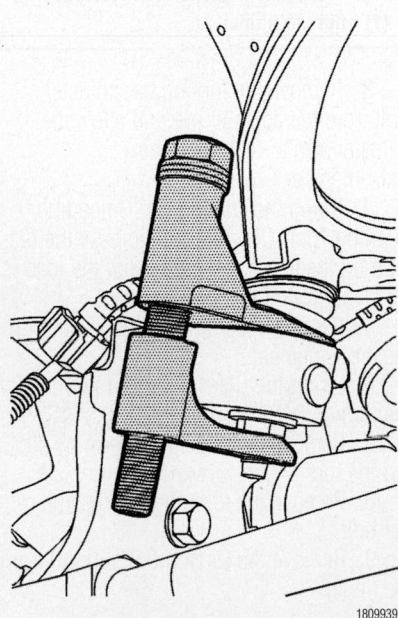

Fig. 901 Using the Ball Joint Separator (J-42188-B), remove the upper control arm from the steering knuckle

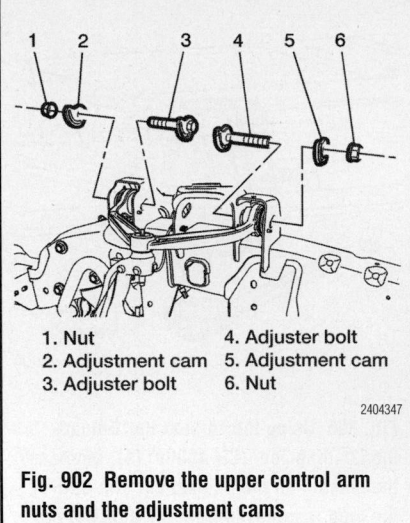

1. Nut
2. Adjustment cam
3. Adjuster bolt
4. Adjuster bolt
5. Adjustment cam
6. Nut

Fig. 902 Remove the upper control arm nuts and the adjustment cams

4. Loosen the upper ball joint nut, but DO NOT remove.
5. Using the Ball Joint Separator (J-42188-B), remove the upper control arm from the steering knuckle.
6. Remove the J-42188-B separator and the upper ball joint nut. Discard the nut and replace with NEW only.
7. Remove the upper control arm nuts and the adjustment cams.
8. Remove the adjuster bolts.
9. Remove the upper control arm from the frame.

To install:
10. Position the upper control arm in the frame.
11. Install the upper control arm bolts and the adjusters.
12. Install the upper control arm nuts and tighten to 192 ft. lbs. (260 Nm).
13. Install the upper control arm to the steering knuckle.

Fig. 903 Remove the upper control arm (1) from the frame

14. Install the NEW nut to the upper ball joint stud and tighten to 37 ft. lbs. (50 Nm).

15. Install the front shock absorber.

16. Raise the vehicle and remove the support for the lower control arm.

17. Install the tire and wheel.

18. Verify the wheel alignment.

WHEEL BEARINGS

REMOVAL & INSTALLATION

1500 Series

See Figure 904.

1. Raise and support the vehicle.
2. Remove the brake rotor.
3. Remove the speed sensor, if equipped.
4. For vehicles equipped with 4WD, remove the wheel drive shaft from the wheel bearing and hub assembly.
5. Remove the wheel bearing and hub bolts.
6. Remove the wheel hub and bearing assembly.

To install:

7. Installation is the reverse of the removal procedure.
8. Tighten the hub bolts to 133 ft. lbs. (180 Nm)

➡ **New wheel bearing comes with a wheel speed sensor installed.**

2500 Series

See Figure 905.

✳✳ CAUTION

Never place vehicle on the ground with the halfshaft removed or the halfshaft nut torqued improperly. Otherwise, bearing seals may become dislodged causing premature wear and/or damage to the hub and bearing assembly.

1. Raise and support the vehicle.
2. Remove the tire and wheel.
3. Remove the brake rotor.
4. Remove the wheel speed sensor from the wheel hub and bearing.

➡ **Steps 6 through 8 applies to those vehicles equipped with 4WD**

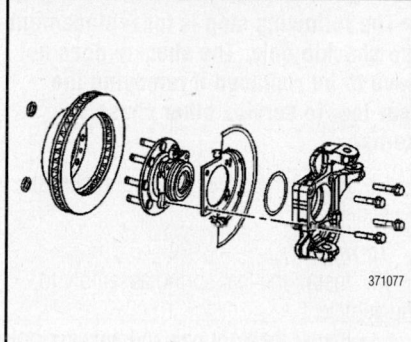

371077

Fig. 905 Remove the wheel hub and bearing mounting bolts

5. Remove the wheel driveshaft nut retaining cover.

✳✳ CAUTION

Wheel drive shaft boots, seals and clamps should be protected from sharp objects any time service is performed on or near the wheel drive shaft(s). Damage to the boot(s), the seal(s) or the clamp(s) may cause lubricant to leak from the joint and lead to increased noise and possible failure of the wheel drive shaft.

6. Wrap shop towel around the inner and outer wheel drive shaft boot.
7. Separate the wheel driveshaft assembly from the wheel hub and bearing.
8. Remove the wheel hub and bearing mounting bolts.
9. Remove the wheel hub and bearing and splash shield from the vehicle.
10. Remove the O-ring seal from the steering knuckle bore.
11. Clean and inspect the O-ring seal.
12. Replace the seal if the following conditions exist:
    • Nicks
    • Cuts
    • Dry or brittle
    • Compression set

To install:

13. Clean all corrosion or contaminates from the steering knuckle bore and the hub and bearing assembly.
14. Lubricate the steering knuckle bore with wheel bearing grease or the equivalent.
15. Install the O-ring to the steering knuckle.
16. Install the wheel speed sensor to the wheel hub and bearing.
17. Install the wheel hub and bearing and splash shield to the vehicle.
18. Install the wheel hub and bearing mounting bolts to 133 ft. lbs. (180 Nm).

➡ **The following service procedure applies to those vehicles equipped with 4WD.**

19. Install the nut and washer retaining the wheel drive shaft assembly to the wheel hub and bearing.
20. Install the brake rotor.
21. Install the tire and wheel.
22. Lower the vehicle.

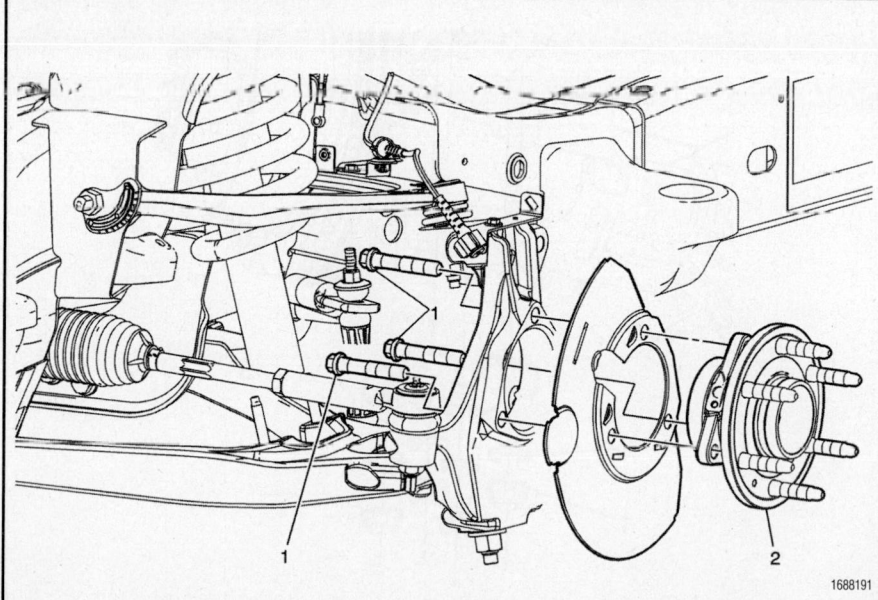

Fig. 904 Remove the wheel bearing and hub bolts (1) and the wheel bearing and hub assembly (2)

1688191

SUSPENSION

REAR SUSPENSION

LEAF SPRING

REMOVAL & INSTALLATION

1500 Series

See Figures 906 through 908.

1. Raise and support the vehicle.
2. Support the rear axle independently in order to relieve the tension on the leaf springs.
3. Remove the trailer hitch, if equipped.
4. Remove the fuel tank.
5. Remove the U-bolt nuts.
6. Remove the U-bolts.
7. Remove the spring spacer, if equipped.
8. Remove the anchor plate.
9. Remove the rear spring bracket nut and bolt.
10. Remove the front spring bracket nut and bolt.
11. Remove the leaf spring assembly from the vehicle.

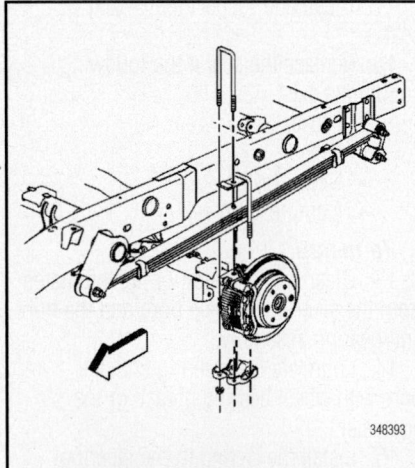

Fig. 906 Remove the U-bolt nuts

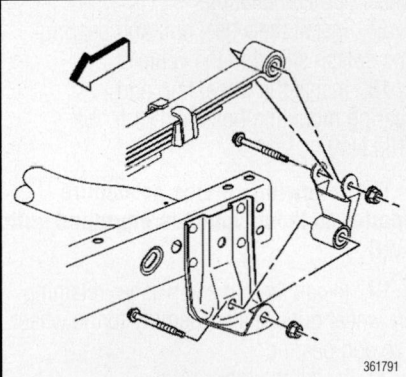

Fig. 907 Remove the rear spring bracket nut and bolt

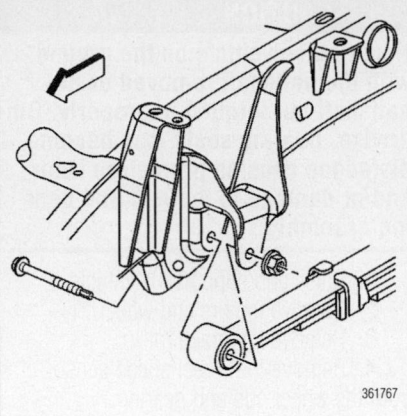

Fig. 908 Remove the front spring bracket nut and bolt

➡**The following step is for replacement the shackle only. The shackle does not have to be replaced if removing the rear leaf to service other chassis items.**

12. Remove the rear leaf spring shackle, if needed.

To install:

13. Install the leaf spring assembly to the vehicle.
14. Install the front bolt and nuts but do not tighten.
15. Install the rear leaf spring hanger to shackle nut and bolt.

16. Install the rear leaf spring front nut and tighten to 125 ft. lbs. (170 Nm) plus 48 degrees.
17. Tighten the rear leaf spring hanger nut and bolt to 70 ft. lbs. (95 Nm).

➡**Do not reuse the U-bolts.**

18. Install the spring spacer, if equipped.
19. Install the U-bolts.
20. Raise the rear axle until it touches the leaf spring and applies light compression to the leaf spring.
21. Install the anchor plate.
22. Install and tighten the U-bolts in a criss-cross sequence to 74 ft. lbs. (100 Nm).
23. Install the fuel tank.
24. Install the trailer hitch, if equipped.
25. Remove the rear axle support.
26. Remove the safety stands.
27. Lower the vehicle.

2500 Series

See Figures 909 through 913.

1. Raise and support the vehicle.

➡**Support the axle independently from the vehicle.**

2. Support the rear axle to relieve the tension on the leaf springs.
3. Remove the trailer hitch, if equipped.

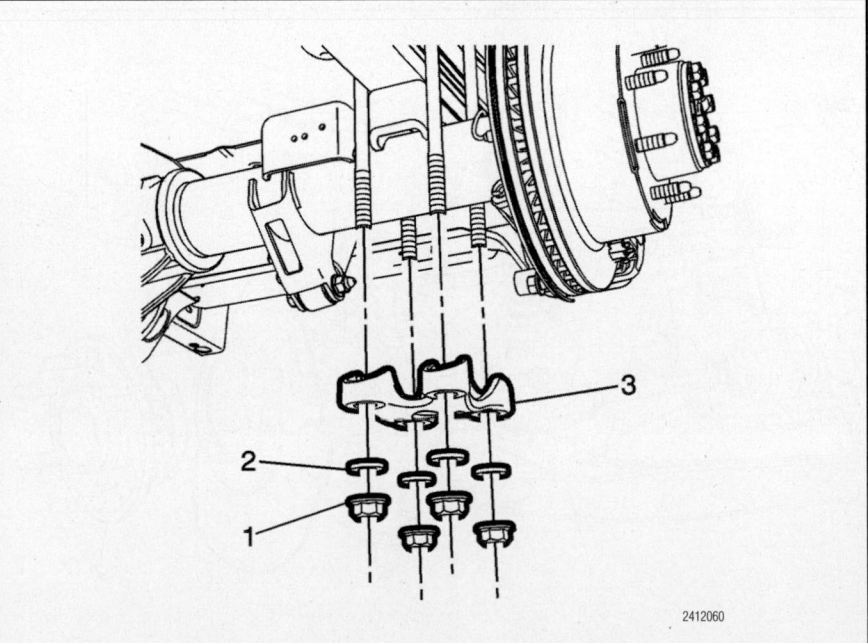

Fig. 909 Remove the rear spring U-bolt nuts (1), the washers (2), and the rear spring anchor plate (3)

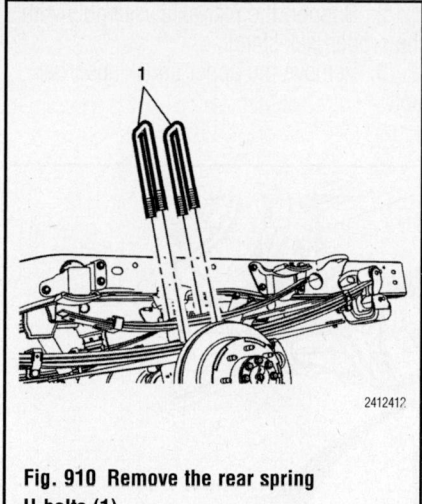

Fig. 910 Remove the rear spring U-bolts (1)

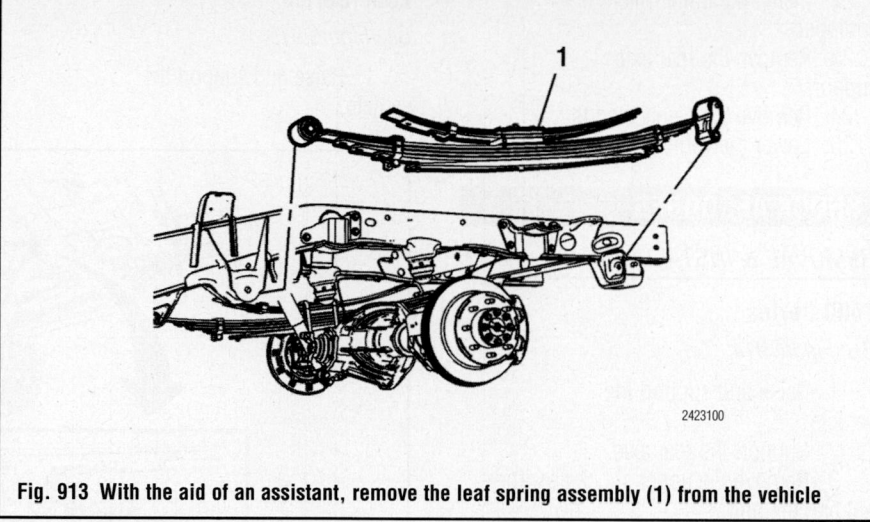

Fig. 913 With the aid of an assistant, remove the leaf spring assembly (1) from the vehicle

Fig. 911 Remove the rear spring front bolt (1)

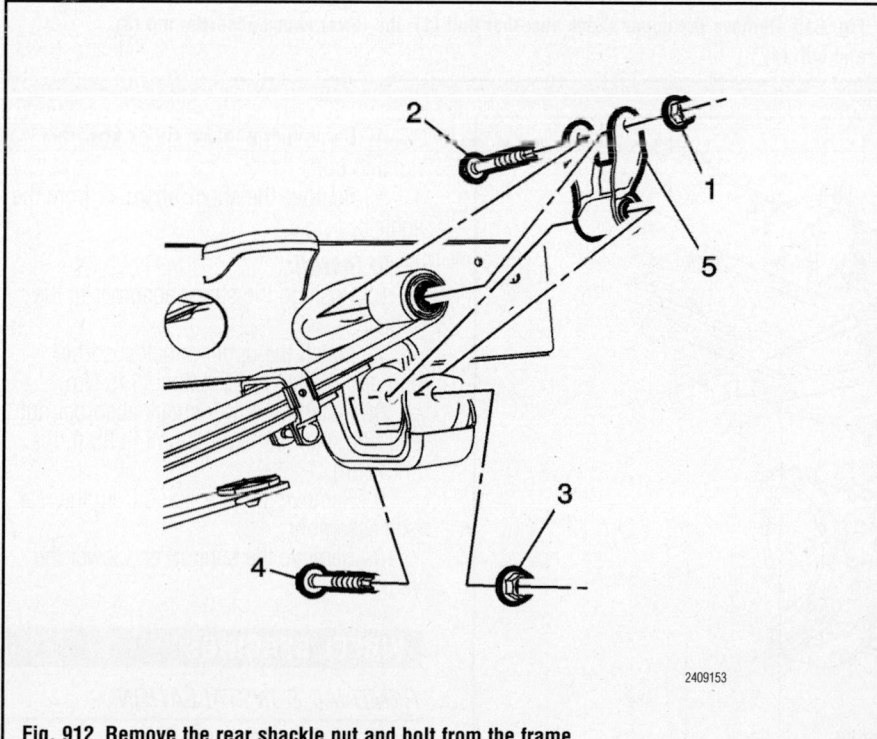

Fig. 912 Remove the rear shackle nut and bolt from the frame

4. Remove the auxiliary fuel tank assembly, if needed.

5. Remove and discard the rear spring U-bolt nuts and the washers. Replace with NEW only.

6. Remove the rear spring anchor plate.

7. Remove and discard the rear spring U-bolts. Replace with NEW only.

8. Remove the rear spring front bolt.

9. Remove the rear shackle nut and bolt from the frame.

10. With the aid of an assistant, remove the leaf spring assembly from the vehicle.

11. Remove the rear leaf spring shackle, if needed.

To install:

➡**DO NOT tighten the rear shackle to specifications, leave loose.**

12. Install the rear leaf spring shackle, if needed.

13. With the aid of an assistant, position the rear leaf spring in the vehicle.

➡**DO NOT tighten the rear spring front bolt or the rear shackle nut and bolt. Leave the bolts lose to allow the rear spring assembly to move.**

14. Install the rear spring front bolt.

15. Install the rear spring shackle to frame bolt.

16. Position the NEW U-bolts on the rear axle assembly

17. Using a hydraulic jack stand, lift the rear axle assembly until the it comes in contact with the rear spring assembly.

18. Install the rear spring anchor plate, washers and tighten the U-bolt nuts in a crisscross pattern to:
    a. First Pass: 74 ft. lbs. (100 Nm).
    b. Final Pass: additional 180 degrees.

19. Tighten the rear spring front bolt to 162 ft. lbs. (220 Nm).

20. Tighten the rear spring shackle to frame bolt.
    a. Tighten the rear spring shackle nut to 129 ft. lbs. (175 Nm).
    b. Tighten the rear shackle spring nut to 129 ft. lbs. (175 Nm).

21. Install the fuel tank assembly, if removed.

22. Install the trailer hitch, if equipped.

23. Remove the rear axle support.

24. Remove the safety stands.

25. Lower the vehicle.

SHOCK ABSORBER

REMOVAL & INSTALLATION

1500 Series

See Figure 914.

1. Raise and support the vehicle.

2. Support the rear axle.

3. Remove the upper shock absorber nut and the bolt.

4. Remove the lower shock absorber nut and the bolt.

5. Remove the shock absorber.

To install:

6. Install the shock absorber.

7. Install the upper shock absorber nut and bolt.

8. Install the lower shock absorber nut and bolt.

   a. Tighten the upper shock absorber bolts to 85 ft. lbs. (115 Nm).

   b. Tighten the lower shock absorber bolts to 85 ft. lbs. (115 Nm).

9. Remove the support from the rear axle.

10. Remove the safety stands.

11. Lower the vehicle.

2500 Series

See Figure 915.

1. Raise and support the vehicle.

2. Support the rear axle assembly with the proper jack stand.

3. Remove the upper shock absorber bolt.

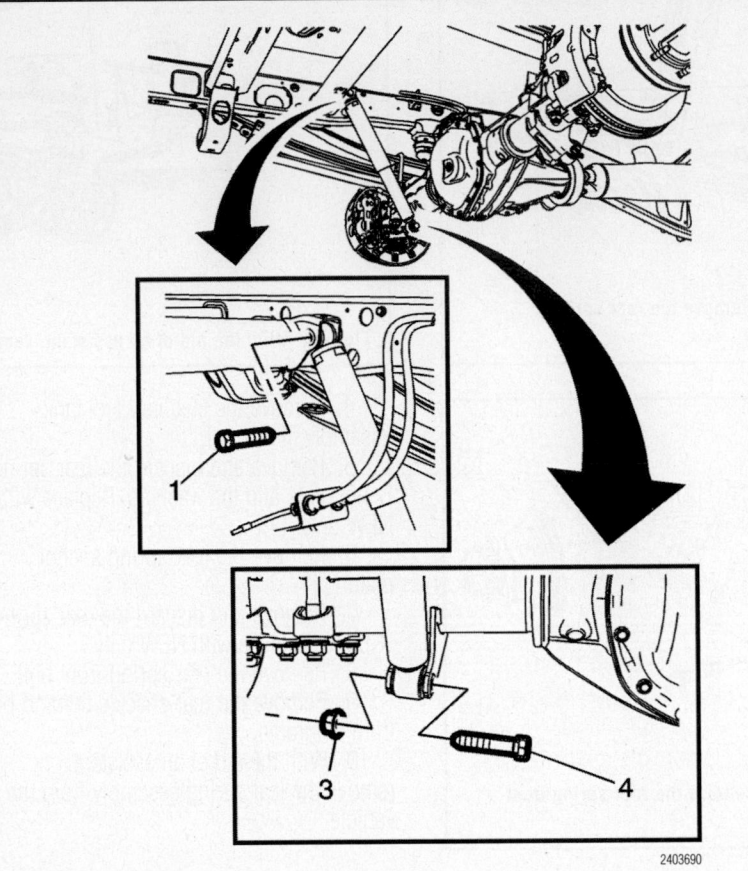

Fig. 915 Remove the upper shock absorber bolt (1), the lower shock absorber nut (3) and bolt (4)

4. Remove the lower shock absorber nut and bolt.

5. Remove the shock absorber from the vehicle.

To install:

6. Position the shock absorber in the vehicle.

7. Install the upper shock absorber bolt and tighten to 85 ft. lbs. (115 Nm).

8. Install the lower shock absorber nut and bolt, then tighten the bolt to 85 ft. lbs. (115 Nm).

9. Remove the jack stand from the rear axle assembly.

10. Remove the support and lower the vehicle.

WHEEL BEARINGS

REMOVAL & INSTALLATION

See Figures 916 through 918.

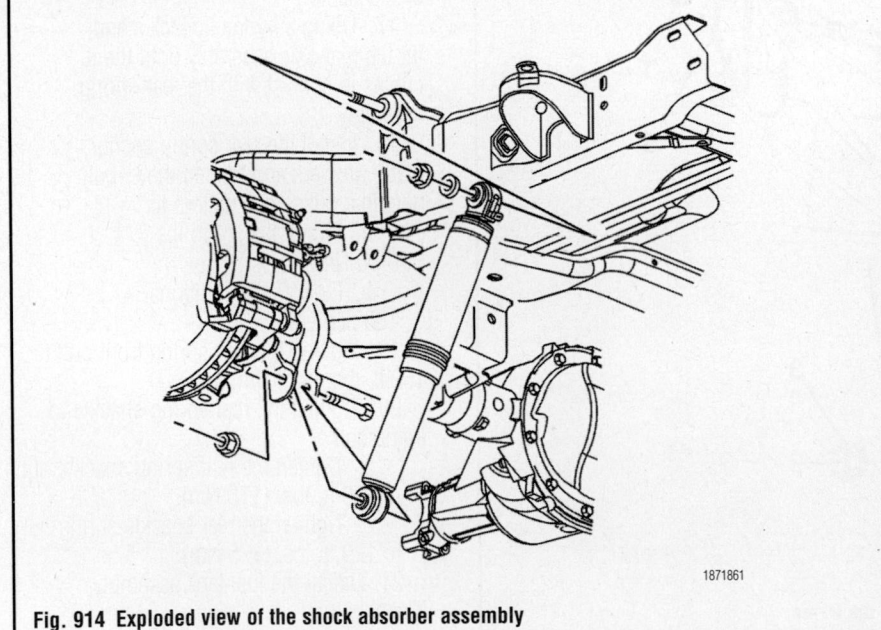

Fig. 914 Exploded view of the shock absorber assembly

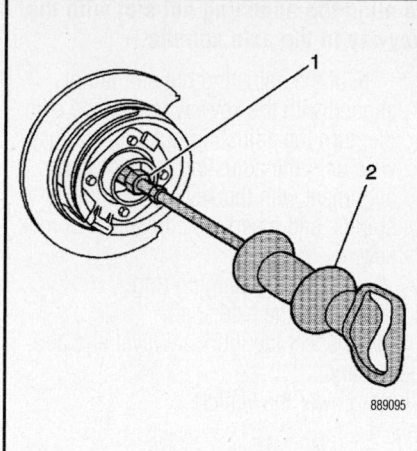

Fig. 916 Using the J-44685 remover (1) and the J-2619-01 hammer (2), remove the rear axle shaft seal

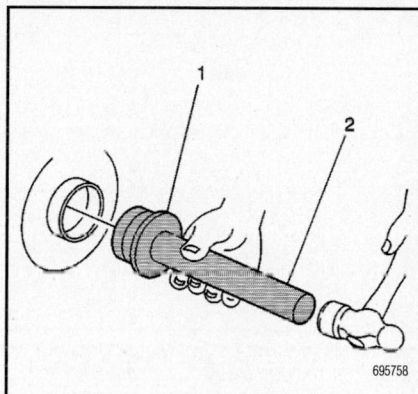

Fig. 917 Using the J-23690 installer (1) and the J-8092 driver (2), install the axle shaft bearing

Special Tools Required:
- J-2619-01 Slide Hammer W ½ x 13 Adapter
- J-8092 Universal Driver Handle ¾ x 10 inch
- J-21128 Axle Pinion Oil Seal Installer
- J-23690 Axle Bearing Installer
- J-44685 Rear Axle Seal and Bearing Remover
- J-45857 VSES Wheel Bearing Remover

1. Raise and support the vehicle.
2. Remove the tire and wheel assembly.
3. Remove the rear axle housing cover.
4. Remove the axle shaft.

➡**If the vehicle is equipped with VSES, proceed to step 5.**

5. Using the J-44685 remover and the J-2619-01 hammer, remove the rear axle shaft seal.
6. Using the J-45857 remover and the J-2619-01 hammer, remove the rear axle

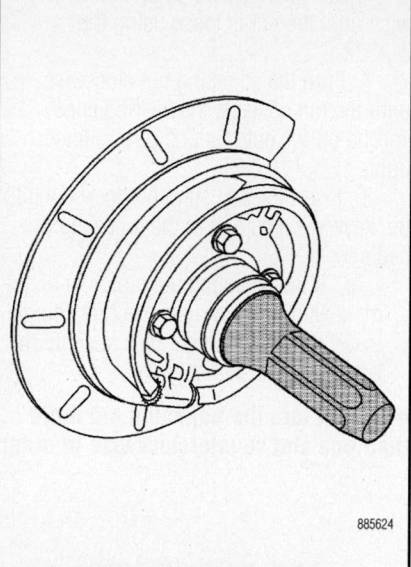

Fig. 918 Using the J-21128 installer, install the axle shaft seal

shaft seal, bearing and the wheel speed sensor reluctor ring, if equipped.

To install:

7. Install the rear wheel speed sensor reluctor ring, if equipped.

➡**Ensure that the axle shaft bearing is fully seated in the rear axle shaft housing.**

8. Using the J-23690 installer and the J-8092 driver, install the axle shaft bearing.
9. Using the J-21128 installer, install the axle shaft seal.
10. Drive the tool into the bore until the axle shaft seal bottoms flush with the tube.
11. Install the rear axle shaft.
12. Install the rear axle housing cover.
13. Install the tire and wheel assembly.
14. Fill the rear axle.
15. Remove the support and lower the vehicle.

ADJUSTMENT

➡**Ensure the brakes are fully released and do not drag.**

1. Pull or push the tire at the top back and forth in order to test the wheel bearing play.
   a. Use a pry bar under the tire as an alternative.
   b. If the wheel bearing adjustment is correct, the movement will be barely noticeable.
   c. If the movement is excessive, adjust the bearings.

Adjustment Procedure
See Figures 919 through 921.

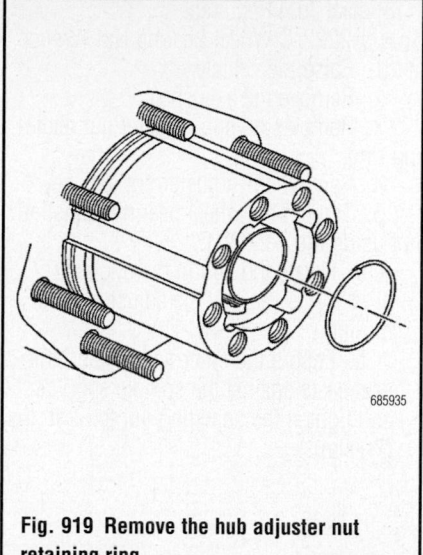

Fig. 919 Remove the hub adjuster nut retaining ring

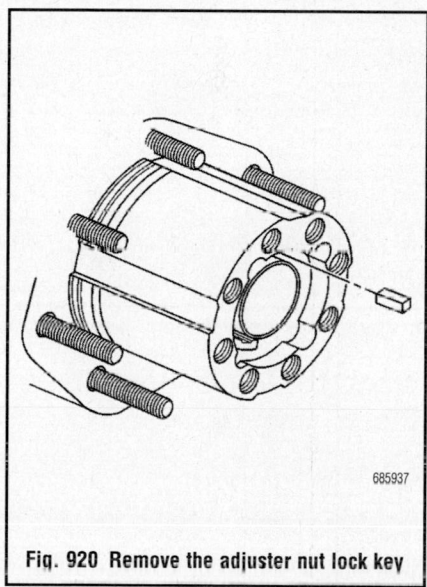

Fig. 920 Remove the adjuster nut lock key

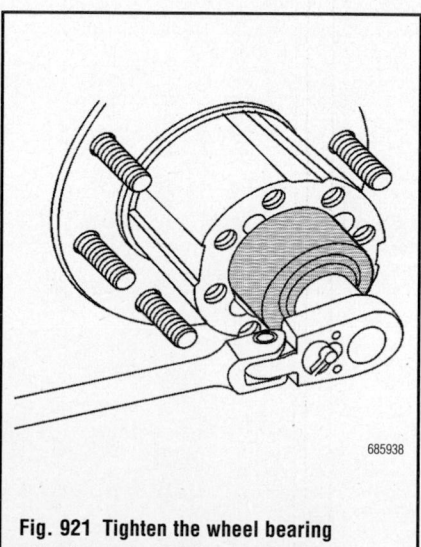

Fig. 921 Tighten the wheel bearing adjusting nut using the J-2222-C (1)

Special Tool Required:
• J-2222-C Wheel Bearing Nut Wrench

1. Raise the vehicle.
2. Remove the axle shaft.
3. Remove the hub adjuster nut retaining ring.
4. Remove the adjuster nut lock key.
5. Tighten the wheel bearing adjusting nut using the J-2222-C.

   a. Rotate the hub in the opposite direction to the way the adjuster nut is turning.

   b. Ensure the inner bearing and the seal seats against the spindle shoulder and tighten the adjusting nut to 52 ft. lbs. (70 Nm).

6. Turn the adjusting nut counterclockwise until the nut is loose using the J-2222-C.
7. Turn the adjusting nut clockwise until the nut contacts the bearing cone. Torque on the nut must be zero to finger tight.
8. Insert the adjusting nut lock key into the keyway using one of the following procedures:

   a. If the adjusting nut slot is in alignment with the keyway in the axle spindle, insert the adjusting nut lock key into the keyway in the axle spindle.

➡**Do not turn the adjusting nut more than one slot counterclockwise in order to align the adjusting nut slot with the keyway in the axle spindle.**

   b. If the adjusting nut slot is not aligned with the keyway in the axle spindle, turn the adjusting nut counterclockwise until the adjusting nut slot is in alignment with the keyway in the axle spindle and insert the adjusting nut lock key.

9. Install the retaining ring.
10. Install the axle shaft.
11. Inspect the lubricant level and add, if necessary.
12. Lower the vehicle.

SPECIFICATIONS AND MAINTENANCE CHARTS

ENGINE AND VEHICLE IDENTIFICATION

| | Engine | | | | | | Model Year | |
| | | | | | | | | |
Code ①	Liters	Cu. In.	Cyl.	Fuel Sys.	Engine Type	Eng. Mfg.	Code ②	Year
M	2.0	122	4	MFI	DOHC	GM	A	2010
B	2.4	146	4	MFI	DOHC	GM		

MFI: Multi-port Fuel Injection

DOHC: Double Overhead Camshafts

① 8th digit of VIN

② 10th digit of VIN

25742_SOLS_C0001

GENERAL ENGINE SPECIFICATIONS

Year	Model	Engine Displacement Liters	Engine VIN	Net Horsepower @ rpm	Net Torque @ rpm (ft. lbs.)	Bore x Stroke (in.)	Compression Ratio	Oil Pressure @ rpm
2010	SKY	2.0	M	260@5300	260@5250	3.388x3.388	9.2:1	50-80@1000
		2.4	B	173@5800	166@4800	3.467x3.861	10:01	50-80@1000
	Solstice	2.0	M	260@5300	260@5250	3.388x3.388	9.2:1	50-80@1000
		2.4	B	173@5800	166@4800	3.467x3.861	10:01	50-80@1000

25742_SOLS_C0002

GASOLINE ENGINE TUNE-UP SPECIFICATIONS

Year	Engine Displacement Liters	Engine VIN	Spark Plug Gap (in.)	Ignition Timing (deg.) MT	Ignition Timing (deg.) AT	Fuel Pump (psi)	Idle Speed (rpm) MT	Idle Speed (rpm) AT	Valve Clearance In.	Valve Clearance Ex.
2010	2.0	M	0.035	①	①	57-67	①	①	HYD	HYD
	2.4	B	0.040	①	①	50-60	①	①	HYD	HYD

NOTE: The Vehicle Emission Control Information label often reflects specification changes changes made during production.

The label figures must be used if they differ from those in this chart.

HYD: Hydraulic

① Electronically controlled and cannot be adjusted

25742_SOLS_C0003

CAPACITIES

Year	Model	Engine VIN	Engine Displacement Liters	Engine Oil with Filter (qts.)	Transmission (pts.) Manual	Transmission (pts.) Auto. *	Rear Axle (pts.)	Fuel Tank (gal.)	Cooling System (qts.)
2010	SKY	B	2.0	5.0	NA	14.8	2.37 ①	13.6	9.2
		M	2.4	5.0	NA	14.8	2.37 ①	13.6	8.7
	Solstice	B	2.0	5.0	5.5	NA	2.37 ①	13.6	9.5
		M	2.4	5.0	5.5	NA	2.37 ①	13.6	8.9

NA: Not Applicable

* Bottom pan removed

① Use limited slip additive 2.37oz drain and fill

25742_SOLS_C0004

FLUID SPECIFICATIONS

Year	Model	Engine Displacement Liters	Engine ID/VIN	Engine Oil	Auto. Trans.	Manual Trans.	Drive Axle	Power Steering Fluid	Brake Master Cylinder	Engine Coolant
2010	SKY	2.0	M	5W-30 ①	Dexron® VI	②	75W-90 ③	GM PS Fluid	DOT 3	Dex-Cool
		2.4	B	5W-30	Dexron® VI	②	75W-90 ③	GM PS Fluid	DOT 3	Dex-Cool
	Solstice	2.0	M	5W-30 ①	Dexron® VI	②	75W-90 ③	GM PS Fluid	DOT 3	Dex-Cool
		2.4	B	5W-30	Dexron® VI	②	75W-90 ③	GM PS Fluid	DOT 3	Dex-Cool

DOT: Department Of Transpotation

① Synthetic motor oil is recommended

② Manual transmission (GM part number 89021806)

③ Sythetic axle lubricant and limited-slip addative
   for limited-slip differentials

25742_SOLS_C0011

VALVE SPECIFICATIONS

Year	Engine Displacement Liters	Engine VIN	Seat Angle (deg.)	Face Angle (deg.)	Spring Test Pressure (lbs. @ in.)	Spring Installed Height (in.)	Stem-to-Guide Clearance (in.) Intake	Stem-to-Guide Clearance (in.) Exhaust	Stem Diameter (in.) Intake	Stem Diameter (in.) Exhaust
2010	2.0	M	NS	NS	NS	1.28	0.0012-0.0022	0.0020-0.0026	0.2344-0.2355	0.2337-0.2343
	2.4	B	NS	NS	NS	1.28	0.0012-0.0022	0.0020-0.0026	0.2344-0.2355	0.2337-0.2343

NS: Not Supplied

25742_SOLS_C0005

CAMSHAFT AND BEARING SPECIFICATIONS CHART

All measurements are given in inches.

Year	Engine Displacement Liters	Engine VIN	Journal Dia.	Brg. Oil Clearance	Shaft End-play	Runout	Journal Bore	Lobe Height Intake	Lobe Height Exhaust
2010	2.0	M	1.0604-1.0614	NS	0.0016-0.0121	NS	NS	NS	NS
	2.4	B	1.0604-1.0614	NS	0.0016-0.0057	NS	NS	NS	NS

NA: Not Supplied

25742_SOLS_C0006

CRANKSHAFT AND CONNECTING ROD SPECIFICATIONS

All measurements are given in inches.

Year	Engine Displacement Liters	Engine VIN	Crankshaft Main Brg. Journal Dia.	Crankshaft Main Brg. Oil Clearance	Crankshaft Shaft End-play	Crankshaft Thrust on No.	Connecting Rod Journal Diameter	Connecting Rod Oil Clearance	Connecting Rod Side Clearance
2010	2.0	M	2.2045-2.2050	0.0012-0.0026	0.0012-0.0150	2	1.9291-1.9297	0.0011-0.0029	0.0028-0.0146
	2.4	B	2.2045-2.2050	0.0012-0.0026	0.0012-0.0150	2	1.9291-1.9297	0.0011-0.0029	0.0028-0.0146

25742_SOLS_C0007

PISTON AND RING SPECIFICATIONS

All measurements are given in inches.

Year	Engine Displacement Liters	Engine VIN	Piston Clearance	Ring Gap Top Compression	Ring Gap Bottom Compression	Ring Gap Oil Control	Ring Side Clearance Top Compression	Ring Side Clearance Bottom Compression	Ring Side Clearance Oil Control
2010	2.0	M	0.0004-0.0016	0.0078-0.0138	0.014-0.022	0.010-0.030	0.0016-0.0031	0.0001-0.0027	0.0009-0.0069
	2.4	B	0.0004-0.0016	0.006-0.012	0.008-0.018	0.006-0.020	0.0015-0.0031	0.0012-0.0030	0.0011-0.0069

25742_SOLS_C0008

TORQUE SPECIFICATIONS
All readings in ft. lbs.

Year	Engine Displacement Liters	Engine VIN	Cylinder Head Bolts	Main Bearing Bolts	Rod Bearing Bolts	Crankshaft Damper Bolts	Flywheel Bolts	Manifold		Spark Plugs	Oil Pan Drain Plug
								Intake	Exhaust		
2010	2.0	M	①	②	③	④	⑤	⑥	10	15	18
	2.4	B	①	②	③	④	⑤	⑥	10	15	18

① Step 1: 22 ft. lbs. (30 Nm).

  Step 2: plus 155 degress

  For 2.4L front chaincase bolts: 26 ft. lbs.

② Bedplate-to-block

  Cap bolts

  Step 1: 15 ft. lbs. (20 Nm).

  Step 2: plus 77 degrees

  Perimeter bolts: 18 ft. lbs.

③ Step 1: 18 ft. lbs. (25 Nm).

  Step 2: plus 100 degrees

④ Step 1: 74 ft. lbs. (100 Nm).

  Step 2: plus 125 degrees

⑤ Step 1: 39 ft. lbs. (53 Nm).

  Step 2: plus 25 degrees

⑥ Bolts and nuts: 89 inch. lbs. (10 Nm);

  studs: 53 inch. lbs. (6 Nm).

25742_SOLS_C0009

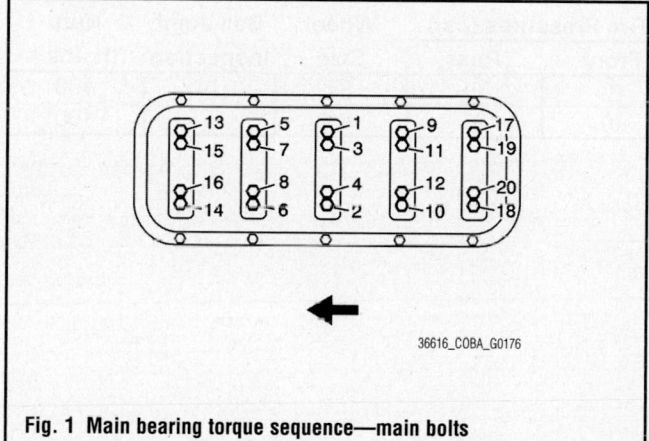

36616_COBA_G0176

Fig. 1 Main bearing torque sequence—main bolts

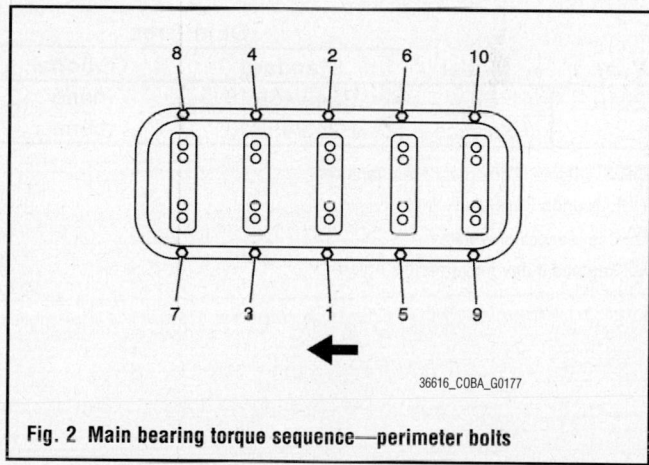

36616_COBA_G0177

Fig. 2 Main bearing torque sequence—perimeter bolts

WHEEL ALIGNMENT

Year	Model		Caster Range (+/-Deg.)	Caster Preferred Setting (Deg.)	Camber Range (+/-Deg.)	Camber Preferred Setting (Deg.)	Toe-in (in.)
2010	SKY	F	0.60	+7.50	0.60	-0.50	0.10+/-0.20
		R	0.75	-4.00	0.60	-0.50	0.10+/-0.20
	Solstice	F	0.60	+7.50	0.60	-0.50	0.10+/-0.20
		R	0.75	-4.00	0.60	-0.50	0.10+/-0.20

25742_SOLS_C0010

TIRE, WHEEL AND BALL JOINT SPECIFICATIONS

Year	Model	OEM Tires Standard	OEM Tires Optional	Tire Pressures (psi) Front	Tire Pressures (psi) Rear	Wheel Size	Ball Joint Inspection	Lug Nuts (ft. lbs.)
2010	SKY	P245/45R18	none	①	①	8J	②	100
	Solstice	P245/45R18	none	①	①	8J	②	100

OEM: Original Equipment Manufacturer

PSI: Pounds Per Square Inch

① See placard on vehicle

② Replace if any movement is noted

25742_SOLS_C0012

BRAKE SPECIFICATIONS
All measurements in inches unless noted

Year	Model		Brake Disc Original Thickness	Brake Disc Minimum Thickness	Brake Disc Maximum Run-out	Minimum Lining Thickness	Brake Caliper Bracket Bolts (ft. lbs.)	Brake Caliper Mounting Bolts (ft. lbs.)
2010	SKY	F	1.023	0.906	0.002	NS	85	25
		R	0.465	0.394	0.002	NS	85	20
	Solstice	F	1.023	0.906	0.002	NS	85	25
		R	0.465	0.394	0.002	NS	85	20

NS: Not Supplied

25742_SOLS_C0013

MAINTENANCE I AND II SERVICE SCHEDULES
Pontiac Solstice and Saturn SKY

When the CHANGE ENGINE OIL light appears, certain services and inspections are required. Services are described below. Generally, it is recommended that the first service be Maintenance I, second service be Maintenance II, and that services are then alter
Required services are described as Maintenance I and Maintenance II.
The first service of a vehicle should be Maintance I, and the second service should be Maintenance II.
Alternate between the 2 services thereafter. However, in some cases, Maintenance II may be required more
Maintenance I: Use Maintenance I if the Service Engine Oil light comes on within 10 months since the vehicle was purcahses or, if Maintenance II was performed.
Maintenance II: Use Maintenance II if the previous service performed was Maintenance I. Always used Maintenance II whenever the CHANGE ENGINE OIL light comes on 10 months or more since the last service, or, if the CHANGE ENGINE OIL light has not come on a

Service	Maintenance I	Maintenance II
Change engine oil and filter. Reset oil life system.	✓	✓
Visually check for any leaks or damage. A fluid loss in the vehicle system could indicate a problem. Inspect, repair and add fluid to the system, if necessary.	✓	✓
Inspect engine air cleaner filter. If necessary, replace filter.	—	✓
Rotate tires and check inflation pressures and wear.	✓	✓
Visually inspect brake lines and hoses for proper hook-up, binding, leaks, cracks, chafing, etc. Inspect the disc brake pads for wear and the rotors for surface condition. Inspect other brake parts, calipers, parking brake, etc.	✓	✓
Check engine coolant and windshield washer fluid levels and add fluid as needed.	✓	✓
Perform any needed additional services.	✓	✓
Inspect the suspension and steering components. Inspect the front and rear suspension systems and steering system for damaged, loose, or missing parts, or signs of wear. Inspect the power steering lines and the hoses for proper hook-up, binding, leaks, cracks, chafing, etc.	—	✓
Inspect the coolant hoses and replace the hoses if they are crackes, swollen or deteriorated. Inspect all pipes, fittings and clamps; replace with OEM parts as needed. To help ensure proper operation, a pressure test of the cooling system and pressure cap and cleaning the outside of the radiator and air conditioning condenser is recommended at least once a	—	✓
Inspect wiper blades for wear or cracking. Replace as necessary.	—	✓
Inspect restraint system components. Make sure the safety belt reminder light and safety belt assemblies are working properly. Look for any other loose or damaged safety belt system parts. If you see anything that might keep a safety belt system from doing its job, have it repaired. Have any torn or frayed safety belts replaced.	—	✓
Lubricate all key lock cylinders, latch assemblies and hinges. Lubricate all key lock cylinders. Lubricate all hinges and latches, including those for the body doors, hood, secondary latch, pivots, spring anchor, release pawl, rear compartment, glove box door, and console door. More frequent lubrication may be required when exposed to a corrosive environment. Applying silicone grease on weatherstrips with a clean cloth will make them last longer, seal better, and not stick or squeak.	—	✓

To reset the CHANGE ENGINE OIL LIGHT:
1. Turn the ignition to ON/RUN, with the engine off.
2. Press the information and reset buttons on the Driver Information Center (DIC) at the same time to enter the personalization menu.
3. Press the information button to scroll through the available personalization menu modes until the DIC display shows OIL-LIFE RESET.
4. Press and hold the reset button until the DIC display shows ACKNOWLEDGED. This will tell you the system has been reset.

ADDITIONAL MAINTENANCE SERVICES
Pontiac Solstice and Saturn SKY

TO BE SERVICED	TYPE OF SERVICE	VEHICLE MILEAGE INTERVAL (x1000)					
		25	50	75	100	125	150
Air cleaner filter	R		✓		✓		✓
Accessory drive belt ①	I						✓
Auto. Trans. Fluid ②	R		✓		✓		✓
Cooling system hoses and clamps	S/I						✓
Engine coolant	R						✓
Fuel system	I	✓	✓	✓	✓	✓	✓
Exhaust system & heat shields	S/I	✓	✓	✓	✓	✓	✓
Spark plugs	R				✓		

R: Replace

S/I: Inspect and service, if necessary

① Visually inspect belt for fraying, excessive cracks, or obvious damage. Replace belt if necessary.

② Replace if any of the following condition are met:

Heavy city traffic where the outside temperature regularly reaches 90 degrees F (32 degrees C) or higher.

Hilly or mountainous terrain

Frequent trailer towing

Taxi, police or delivery service

Otherwise, change every 100,000 miles

25742_SOLS_C0015

PRECAUTIONS

Before servicing any vehicle, please be sure to read all of the following precautions, which deal with personal safety, prevention of component damage, and important points to take into consideration when servicing a motor vehicle:

• Never open, service or drain the radiator or cooling system when the engine is hot; serious burns can occur from the steam and hot coolant.

• Observe all applicable safety precautions when working around fuel. Whenever servicing the fuel system, always work in a well-ventilated area. Do not allow fuel spray or vapors to come in contact with a spark, open flame, or excessive heat (a hot drop light, for example). Keep a dry chemical fire extinguisher near the work area. Always keep fuel in a container specifically designed for fuel storage; also, always properly seal fuel containers to avoid the possibility of fire or explosion. Refer to the additional fuel system precautions later in this section.

• Fuel injection systems often remain pressurized, even after the engine has been turned **OFF**. The fuel system pressure must be relieved before disconnecting any fuel lines. Failure to do so may result in fire and/or personal injury.

• Brake fluid often contains polyglycol ethers and polyglycols. Avoid contact with the eyes and wash your hands thoroughly after handling brake fluid. If you do get brake fluid in your eyes, flush your eyes with clean, running water for 15 minutes. If eye irritation persists, or if you have taken brake fluid internally, IMMEDIATELY seek medical assistance.

• The EPA warns that prolonged contact with used engine oil may cause a number of skin disorders, including cancer. You should make every effort to minimize your exposure to used engine oil. Protective gloves should be worn when changing oil. Wash your hands and any other exposed skin areas as soon as possible after exposure to used engine oil. Soap and water, or waterless hand cleaner should be used.

• All new vehicles are now equipped with an air bag system, often referred to as a Supplemental Restraint System (SRS) or Supplemental Inflatable Restraint (SIR) system. The system must be disabled before performing service on or around system components, steering column, instrument panel components, wiring and sensors. Failure to follow safety and disabling procedures could result in accidental air bag deployment, possible personal injury and unnecessary system repairs.

• Always wear safety goggles when working with, or around, the air bag system. When carrying a non-deployed air bag, be sure the bag and trim cover are pointed away from your body. When placing a non-deployed air bag on a work surface, always face the bag and trim cover upward, away from the surface. This will reduce the motion of the module if it is accidentally deployed. Refer to the additional air bag system precautions later in this section.

• Clean, high quality brake fluid from a sealed container is essential to the safe and proper operation of the brake system. You should always buy the correct type of brake fluid for your vehicle. If the brake fluid becomes contaminated, completely flush the system with new fluid. Never reuse any brake fluid. Any brake fluid that is removed from the system should be discarded. Also, do not allow any brake fluid to come in contact with a painted surface; it will damage the paint.

• Never operate the engine without the proper amount and type of engine oil; doing so WILL result in severe engine damage.

• Timing belt maintenance is extremely important. Many models utilize an interference-type, non-freewheeling engine. If the timing belt breaks, the valves in the cylinder head may strike the pistons, causing potentially serious (also time-consuming and expensive) engine damage. Refer to the maintenance interval charts for the recommended replacement interval for the timing belt, and to the timing belt section for belt replacement and inspection.

• Disconnecting the negative battery cable on some vehicles may interfere with the functions of the on-board computer system(s) and may require the computer to undergo a relearning process once the negative battery cable is reconnected.

• When servicing drum brakes, only disassemble and assemble one side at a time, leaving the remaining side intact for reference.

• Only an MVAC-trained, EPA-certified automotive technician should service the air conditioning system or its components.

BRAKES

GENERAL INFORMATION

PRECAUTIONS

• Certain components within the ABS system are not intended to be serviced or repaired individually.

• Do not use rubber hoses or other parts not specifically specified for and ABS system. When using repair kits, replace all parts included in the kit. Partial or incorrect repair may lead to functional problems and require the replacement of components.

• Lubricate rubber parts with clean, fresh brake fluid to ease assembly. Do not use shop air to clean parts; damage to rubber components may result.

• Use only DOT 3 brake fluid from an unopened container.

• If any hydraulic component or line is removed or replaced, it may be necessary to bleed the entire system.

• A clean repair area is essential. Always clean the reservoir and cap thoroughly before removing the cap. The slightest amount of dirt in the fluid may plug an orifice and impair the system function. Perform repairs after components have been thoroughly cleaned; use only denatured alcohol to clean components. Do not allow ABS components to come into contact with any substance containing mineral oil; this includes used shop rags.

• The Anti-Lock control unit is a microprocessor similar to other computer units in the vehicle. Ensure that the ignition switch is **OFF** before removing or

ANTI-LOCK BRAKE SYSTEM (ABS)

installing controller harnesses. Avoid static electricity discharge at or near the controller.

• If any arc welding is to be done on the vehicle, the control unit should be unplugged before welding operations begin.

WHEEL SPEED SENSORS

REMOVAL & INSTALLATION

See Figure 3.

The wheel speed sensors are part of the wheel hub and bearing assembly. Refer to Wheel Hub & Bearing Removal & Installation in the Suspension Section.

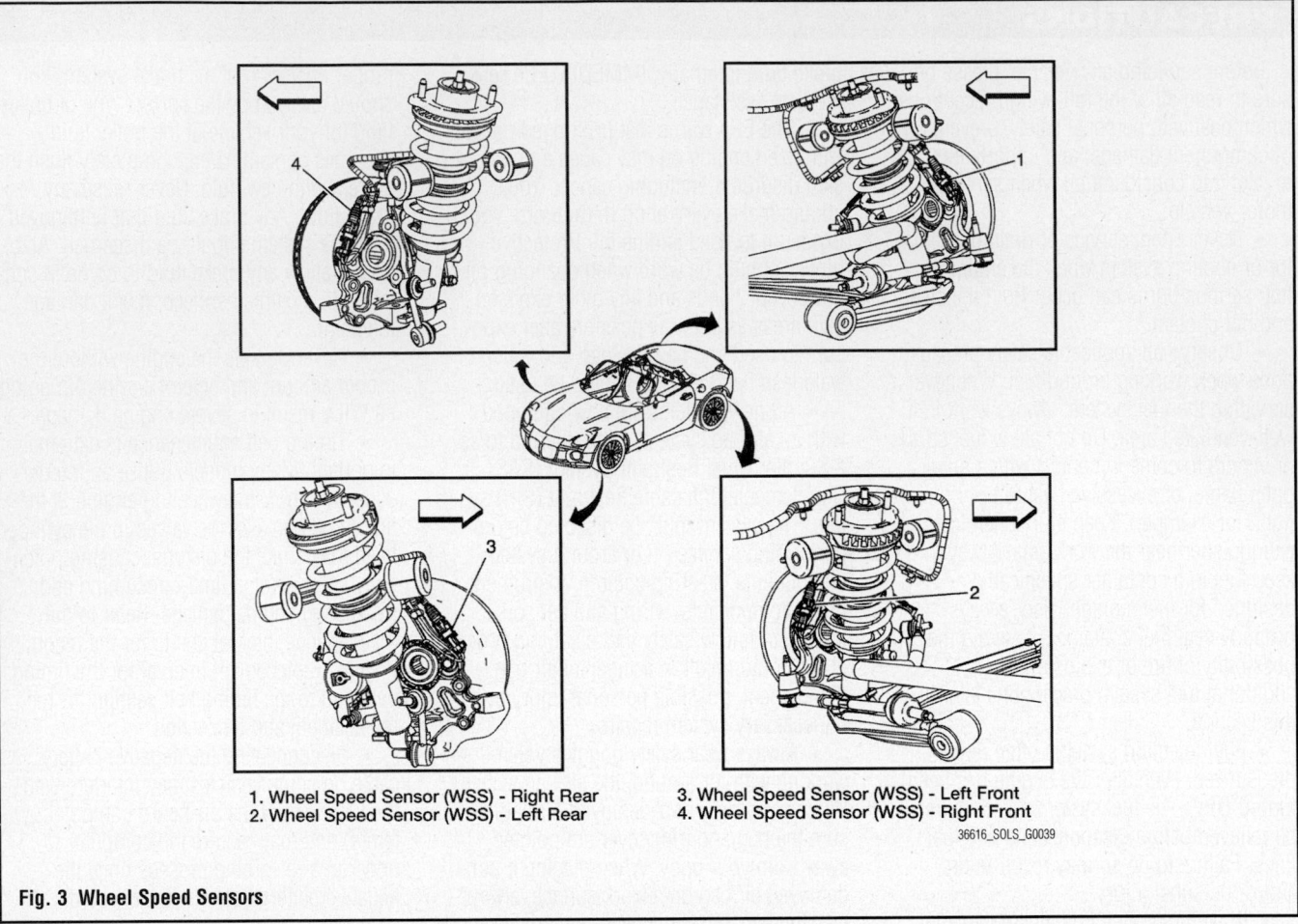

1. Wheel Speed Sensor (WSS) - Right Rear
2. Wheel Speed Sensor (WSS) - Left Rear
3. Wheel Speed Sensor (WSS) - Left Front
4. Wheel Speed Sensor (WSS) - Right Front

36616_SOLS_G0039

Fig. 3 Wheel Speed Sensors

BRAKES   **BLEEDING THE BRAKE SYSTEM**

BLEEDING PROCEDURE

1. Before servicing the vehicle, refer to the Precautions Section.

❉❉ CAUTION

When adding fluid to the brake master cylinder reservoir, use only Delco Supreme 11®, GM P/N 12377967 (Canadian P/N 992667), or equivalent DOT-3 brake fluid from a clean, sealed brake fluid container. The use of any type of fluid other than the recommended type of brake fluid, may cause contamination which could result in damage to the internal rubber seals and/or rubber linings of hydraulic brake system components.

2. Place a clean shop cloth beneath the brake master cylinder to prevent brake fluid spills.

3. With the ignition OFF and the brakes cool, apply the brakes 3–5 times, or until the brake pedal effort increases significantly, in order to deplete the brake booster power reserve.

4. If you have performed a brake master cylinder bench bleeding on this vehicle, or if you disconnected the brake pipes from the master cylinder, or disconnected the brake pipes from the proportioning valve assembly or the brake modulator assembly, you must perform the following steps to bleed air at the ports of the hydraulic component:

a. Ensure that the brake master cylinder reservoir is full to the maximum-fill level. If necessary, add GM approved, or equivalent DOT-3 brake fluid from a clean, sealed brake fluid container. If removal of the reservoir cap and diaphragm is necessary, clean the outside of the reservoir on and around the cap prior to removal.

b. With the brake pipes installed securely to the master cylinder, proportioning valve assembly, or brake modulator assembly, loosen and separate one of the brake pipes from the port of the component. For the proportioning valve assembly or the brake modulator assembly perform these steps in the sequence of system flow; begin with the fluid feed pipes from the master cylinder.

c. Allow a small amount of brake fluid to gravity bleed from the open port of the component.

d. Reconnect the brake pipe to the component port and tighten securely.

e. Have an assistant slowly depress the brake pedal fully and maintain steady pressure on the pedal.

f. Loosen the same brake pipe to purge air from the open port of the component.

g. Tighten the brake pipe, then have the assistant slowly release the brake pedal.

h. Wait 15 seconds, then repeat the previous 5 steps until all air is purged from the same port of the component.

i. With the brake pipe installed securely to the master cylinder, proportioning valve assembly, or brake modulator assembly, after all air has been purged from the first port of the component that was bled, loosen and separate the next brake pipe from the component, then repeat the previous 6 steps until each of the ports on the component have been bled.

j. After completing the final component port bleeding procedure, ensure that each of the brake pipe-to-component fittings are properly tightened.

5. Fill the brake master cylinder reservoir with GM approved, or equivalent DOT-3 brake fluid from a clean, sealed brake fluid container. Ensure that the brake master cylinder reservoir remains at least half-full during this bleeding procedure. Add fluid as needed to maintain the proper level. Clean the outside of the reservoir on and around the reservoir cap prior to removing the cap and diaphragm.

6. Install a proper box-end wrench onto the RIGHT REAR wheel hydraulic circuit bleeder valve.

7. Install a transparent hose over the end of the bleeder valve.

8. Submerge the open end of the transparent hose into a transparent container partially filled with GM approved, or equivalent DOT-3 brake fluid from a clean, sealed brake fluid container.

9. Have an assistant slowly depress the brake pedal fully and maintain steady pressure on the pedal.

10. Loosen the bleeder valve to purge air from the wheel hydraulic circuit.

11. Tighten the bleeder valve, then have the assistant slowly release the brake pedal.

12. Wait 15 seconds, then repeat steps 9–11 until all air is purged from the same wheel hydraulic circuit.

13. With the right rear wheel hydraulic circuit bleeder valve tightened securely, after all air has been purged from the right rear hydraulic circuit, install a proper box-end wrench onto the LEFT FRONT wheel hydraulic circuit bleeder valve.

14. Install a transparent hose over the end of the bleeder valve, then repeat steps 8–12.

15. With the left front wheel hydraulic circuit bleeder valve tightened securely, after all air has been purged from the left front hydraulic circuit, install a proper box-end wrench onto the LEFT REAR wheel hydraulic circuit bleeder valve.

16. Install a transparent hose over the end of the bleeder valve, then repeat steps 8–12.

17. With the left rear wheel hydraulic circuit bleeder valve tightened securely, after all air has been purged from the left rear hydraulic circuit, install a proper box-end wrench onto the RIGHT FRONT wheel hydraulic circuit bleeder valve.

18. Install a transparent hose over the end of the bleeder valve, then repeat steps 8–12.

19. After completing the final wheel hydraulic circuit bleeding procedure, ensure that each of the 4 wheel hydraulic circuit bleeder valves are properly tightened.

20. Fill the brake master cylinder reservoir to the maximum-fill level with GM approved, or equivalent DOT-3 brake fluid from a clean, sealed brake fluid container.

21. Slowly depress and release the brake pedal. Observe the feel of the brake pedal.

➡ If it is determined that air was inducted into the system upstream of the ABS modulator prior to servicing, the ABS Automated Bleed Procedure must be performed.

22. If the brake pedal feels spongy, repeat the bleeding procedure again. If the brake pedal still feels spongy after repeating the bleeding procedure, perform the following steps:

a. Inspect the brake system for external leaks.

b. Pressure bleed the hydraulic brake system in order to purge any air that may still be trapped in the system.

23. Turn the ignition key ON, with the engine OFF. Check to see if the brake system warning lamp remains illuminated.

⁕⁕ WARNING

DO NOT allow the vehicle to be driven until it is diagnosed and repaired.

BLEEDING THE ABS SYSTEM

⁕⁕ CAUTION

Brake fluid may irritate eyes and skin. In case of eye contact, rinse thoroughly with water. In case of skin contact, wash with soap and water. If ingested, consult a physician immediately.

⁕⁕ WARNING

Avoid spilling brake fluid onto painted surfaces, electrical connections, wiring, or cables. Brake fluid will damage painted surfaces and cause corrosion to electrical components. If any brake fluid comes in contact with painted surfaces, immediately flush the area with water. If any brake fluid comes in contact with electrical connections, wiring, or cables, use a clean shop cloth to wipe away the fluid.

1. Before servicing the vehicle, refer to the Precautions Section.

Before performing the ABS Automated Bleed Procedure, first perform a manual or pressure bleed of the base brake system. The automated bleed procedure is recommended when one of the following conditions exist:

• Base brake system bleeding does not achieve the desired pedal height or feel

• Extreme loss of brake fluid has occurred

• Air ingestion is suspected in the secondary circuits of the brake modulator assembly

The ABS Automated Bleed Procedure uses a scan tool to cycle the system solenoid valves and run the pump in order to purge any air from the secondary circuits. These circuits are normally closed off, and are only opened during system initialization at vehicle start up and during ABS operation. The automated bleed procedure opens these secondary circuits and allows any air trapped in these circuits to flow out toward the brake corners.

⁕⁕ WARNING

The Auto Bleed Procedure may be terminated at any time during the process by pressing the EXIT button. No further Scan Tool prompts pertaining to the Auto Bleed procedure will be given. After exiting the bleed procedure, relieve bleed pressure and disconnect bleed equipment per manufacturer's instructions. Failure to properly relieve pressure may result in spilled brake fluid causing damage to components and painted surfaces.

Perform the automated bleed procedure as follows:

2. Raise and support the vehicle.

3. Remove all four tire and wheel assemblies.

4. Inspect the brake system for leaks and visual damage.

5. Lower the vehicle.

6. Inspect the battery state of charge.

7. Install a scan tool.

8. Turn the ignition ON, with the engine OFF.

9. With the scan tool, establish communications with the ABS system. Select Special Functions. Select Automated Bleed from the Special Functions menu.

10. Raise and support the vehicle.

11. Following the directions given on the scan tool, pressure bleed the base brake system.

12. Follow the scan tool directions until the desired brake pedal height is achieved.

13. If the bleed procedure is aborted, a malfunction exists. Perform the following steps before resuming the bleed procedure:

   a. If a DTC is detected, diagnose the appropriate DTC.

b. If the brake pedal feels spongy, perform the conventional brake bleed procedure again.

14. When the desired pedal height is achieved, press the brake pedal to inspect for firmness.

15. Lower the vehicle.

16. Remove the scan tool.

17. Install the tire and wheel assemblies.

18. Inspect the brake fluid level.

19. Road test the vehicle while inspecting that the pedal remains high and firm.

BRAKES

BRAKE CALIPER

REMOVAL & INSTALLATION

See Figure 4.

1. Before servicing the vehicle, refer to the Precautions Section.

2. Raise and support the vehicle.

3. Remove the tire and wheel.

4. Remove the brake hose bolt.

5. Remove the brake hose bolt washers.

6. Remove the front brake hose.

7. Cap or plug the brake hose to prevent fluid loss and contamination

8. Remove the brake caliper bolt.

9. Remove the brake caliper.

To install:

10. Installation is the reverse of removal procedure. Note the following tightening specifications:

- Caliper mounting bolts: 25 ft. lbs. (34 Nm)
- Brake hose bolt: 30 ft. lbs. (40 Nm)

11. If any of the disc brake caliper hardware is found to have excessive wear, replace the hardware.

12. Bleed the hydraulic brake system.

13. After the installation is complete and with the engine OFF, gradually apply the brake pedal to approximately ⅔ of its travel distance.

14. Slowly release the brake pedal.

15. Wait 15 seconds, then repeat steps 4–5 until a firm brake pedal is obtained. This will properly seat the brake caliper piston and the brake pads.

16. Fill the master cylinder to the proper level.

FRONT DISC BRAKES

✳ WARNING

Do not reuse the brake hose bolt washers.

DISC BRAKE PADS

REMOVAL & INSTALLATION

See Figure 5.

1. Before servicing the vehicle, refer to the Precautions Section.

✳ WARNING

Support the brake caliper with heavy mechanic wire, or equivalent, whenever it is separated from its mount and the hydraulic flexible brake hose is still connected. Failure to support the caliper in this manner will cause the flexible brake hose to bear the weight of the caliper, which may cause damage to the brake hose and in turn may cause a brake fluid leak.

2. Inspect the fluid level in the brake master cylinder reservoir.

3. If the brake fluid level is midway between the maximum-full point and the minimum allowable level, no brake fluid needs to be removed from the reservoir before proceeding.

4. If the brake fluid level is higher than midway between the maximum-full point and the minimum allowable level, remove brake fluid to the midway point before proceeding.

5. Raise and support the vehicle.

6. Remove the tire and wheel.

7. Remove the lower brake caliper guide pin bolt.

8. Without disconnecting the brake hose, pivot the brake caliper upward and support with heavy mechanics wire or equivalent.

9. Place a block of wood or an old disc brake pad against the brake caliper piston.

10. Using a large C-clamp, slowly and evenly compress the brake caliper piston squarely into the caliper bore.

11. Remove the brake pads.

12. Remove the brake pad springs.

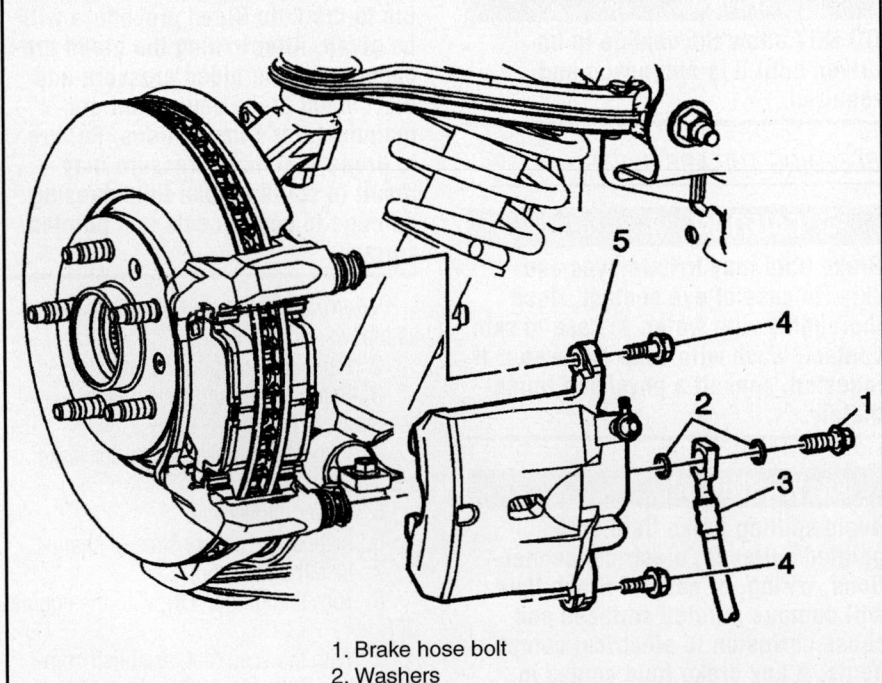

1. Brake hose bolt
2. Washers
3. Brake hose
4. Caliper bolts
5. Caliper

06025-SOLS-G101

Fig. 4 Front caliper mounting

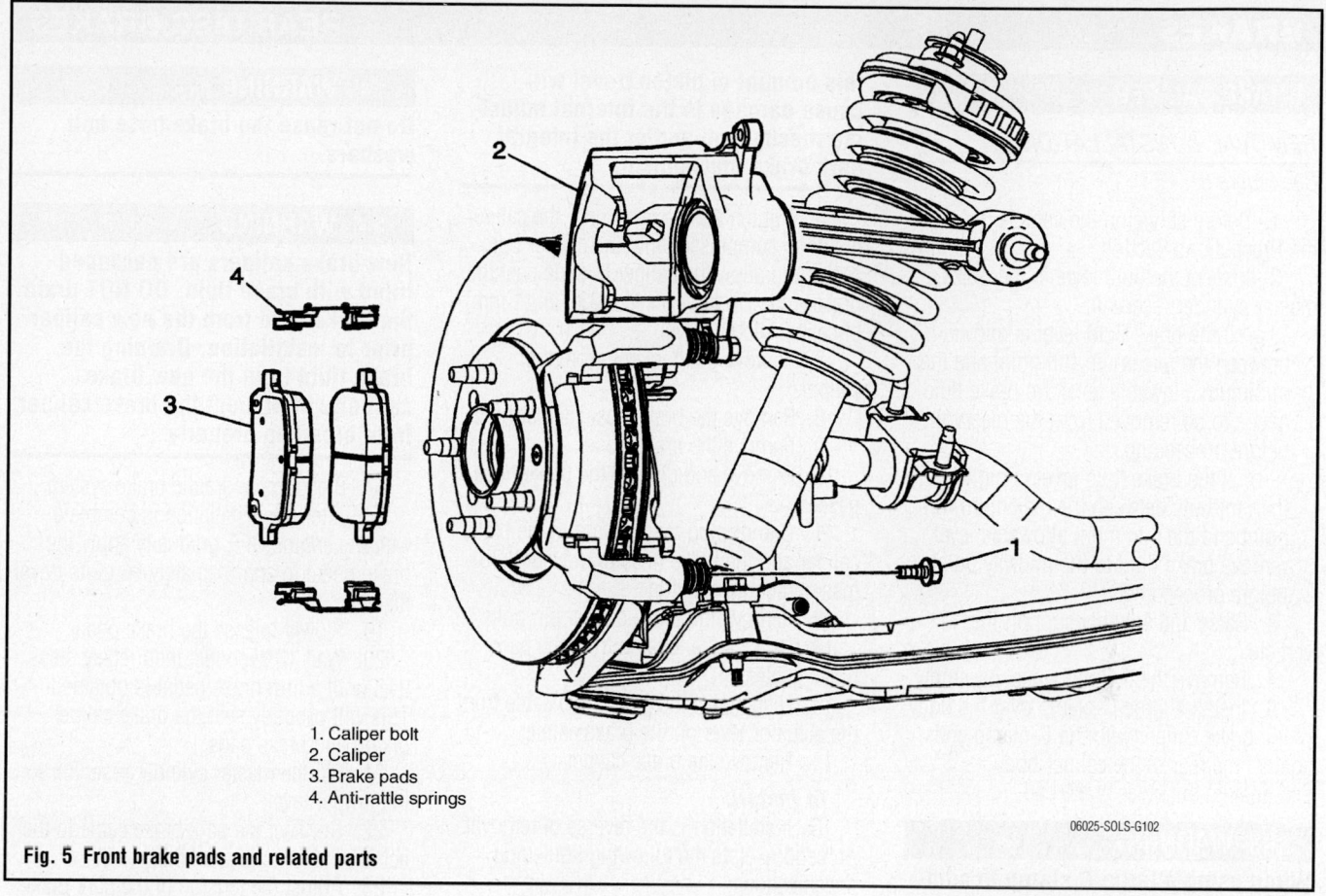

1. Caliper bolt
2. Caliper
3. Brake pads
4. Anti-rattle springs

06025-SOLS-G102

Fig. 5 Front brake pads and related parts

13. Remove about half of the fluid from the master cylinder.

14. Using an appropriate tool, force the caliper piston back into the caliper.

➡ **If replacing the brake pads, DO NOT reuse the brake pad springs. Install NEW brake pad springs.**

➡ **If reinstalling the brake pads, inspect the brake pad springs. If any of the following conditions are found, the pad springs require replacement: bent mounting tabs, excessive corrosion, looseness at the brake caliper mounting bracket, or looseness at the disc brake pads.**

To install:

15. Thoroughly clean the brake pad hardware mating surfaces of the caliper bracket of any debris and corrosion.

16. Inspect the brake caliper guide pins for freedom of movement and inspect the condition of the guide pin boots. Move the guide pins inboard and outboard within the bracket bores without disengaging the slides from the boots, and observe for the following conditions. If any of the conditions listed are found, the brake caliper guide pins and/or boots require replacement.:

- Restricted caliper guide pin movement

- Looseness in the brake caliper mounting bracket
- Seized or binding caliper guide pins
- Split or torn boots

17. Apply a very thin coating of high temperature silicone brake lubricant to the pad hardware mating surfaces of the caliper bracket only.

18. Installation is the reverse of removal. Tighten the caliper bolt to 25 ft. lbs. (34 Nm).

19. After the installation is complete, with the engine OFF, gradually apply the brake pedal to approximately ⅔ of its travel distance.

20. Slowly release the brake pedal.

21. Wait 15 seconds, then repeat steps 5–6 until a firm brake pedal is obtained. This will properly seat the brake caliper piston and brake pads.

22. Fill the master cylinder reservoir to the proper level.

23. Burnish the brake pads and rotors.

BRAKE PAD & ROTOR BURNISHING

❊❊ **CAUTION**

Road test a vehicle under safe conditions and while obeying all traffic

laws. Do not attempt any maneuvers that could jeopardize vehicle control. Failure to adhere to these precautions could lead to serious personal injury and vehicle damage.

Burnishing the brake pads and brake rotors is necessary in order to ensure that the braking surfaces are properly prepared after service has been performed on the disc brake system.

This procedure should be performed whenever the disc brake rotors have been refinished or replaced, and/or whenever the disc brake pads have been replaced.

1. Select a smooth road with little or no traffic.

2. Accelerate the vehicle to 30 mph (48 km/h).

3. Using moderate to firm pressure, apply the brakes to bring the vehicle to a stop. Do not allow the brakes to lock.

➡ **Use care to avoid overheating the brakes while performing this step.**

4. Repeat steps 2 and 3 until approximately 20 stops have been completed. Allow sufficient cooling periods between stops in order to properly burnish the brake pads and rotors

BRAKES

BRAKE CALIPER

REMOVAL & INSTALLATION
See Figure 6.

1. Before servicing the vehicle, refer to the Precautions Section.

2. Inspect the fluid level in the brake master cylinder reservoir.

  a. If the brake fluid level is midway between the maximum-full point and the minimum allowable level, no brake fluid needs to be removed from the reservoir before proceeding.

  b. If the brake fluid level is higher than midway between the maximum-full point and the minimum allowable level, remove brake fluid to the midway point before proceeding.

3. Raise and suitably support the vehicle.

4. Remove the tire and wheel assembly.

5. Install a large C-clamp over the body of the brake caliper with the C-clamp ends against the rear of the caliper body and against the outer brake pad.

> **✳✳ WARNING**
>
> **When using a large C-clamp to compress a caliper piston into a caliper bore of a caliper equipped with an integral park brake mechanism, do not exceed more than 0.039 in. (1 mm) of piston travel. Exceeding**

this amount of piston travel will cause damage to the internal adjusting mechanism and/or the integral park brake mechanism.

6. Tighten the C-clamp until the caliper piston is compressed into the caliper bore enough to allow the caliper to slide past the brake rotor. Do not exceed 0.039 in. (1 mm) of caliper piston travel.

7. Remove the C-clamp from the caliper.

8. Remove the brake hose caliper bolt.

9. Remove the brake hose.

10. Remove and discard the brake hose gaskets.

11. Cap or plug the opening in the brake caliper and the brake hose to prevent fluid loss and contamination

12. Remove the brake caliper pin bolts.

13. Release the tension from the park brake cables.

14. Disconnect the park brake cable from the actuator lever on the brake caliper.

15. Remove the brake caliper.

To install:

16. Installation is the reverse of removal procedure. Note the following tightening specifications:

- Caliper mounting bolts: 20 ft. lbs. (27 Nm)
- Brake hose bolt: 30 ft. lbs. (40 Nm)

> **✳✳ WARNING**
>
> **Do not reuse the brake hose bolt washers.**

> **✳✳ WARNING**
>
> **New brake calipers are packaged filled with brake fluid. DO NOT drain the brake fluid from the new caliper prior to installation. Draining the brake fluid from the new brake caliper will prevent the brake caliper from bleeding properly.**

17. Bleed the hydraulic brake system.

18. After the installation is complete, with the engine OFF, gradually apply the brake pedal to approximately ⅔ of its travel distance.

19. Slowly release the brake pedal.

20. Wait 15 seconds, then repeat steps 2–3 until a firm brake pedal is obtained. This will properly seat the brake caliper piston and brake pads.

21. Fill the master cylinder reservoir to the proper level.

22. Connect the park brake cable to the actuator lever on the caliper.

23. Adjust the tension of the park brake cables.

24. Burnish the brake pads and rotors. Refer to Brake Pads and Rotor Burnishing, in the Brake Pad Section.

DISC BRAKE PADS

REMOVAL & INSTALLATION
See Figure 7.

1. Before servicing the vehicle, refer to the Precautions Section.

> **✳✳ WARNING**
>
> **Support the brake caliper with heavy mechanic wire, or equivalent, whenever it is separated from its mount and the hydraulic flexible brake hose is still connected. Failure to support the caliper in this manner will cause the flexible brake hose to bear the weight of the caliper, which may cause damage to the brake hose and in turn may cause a brake fluid leak.**

2. Inspect the fluid level in the brake master cylinder reservoir.

  a. If the brake fluid level is midway between the maximum-full point and the minimum allowable level, no brake fluid

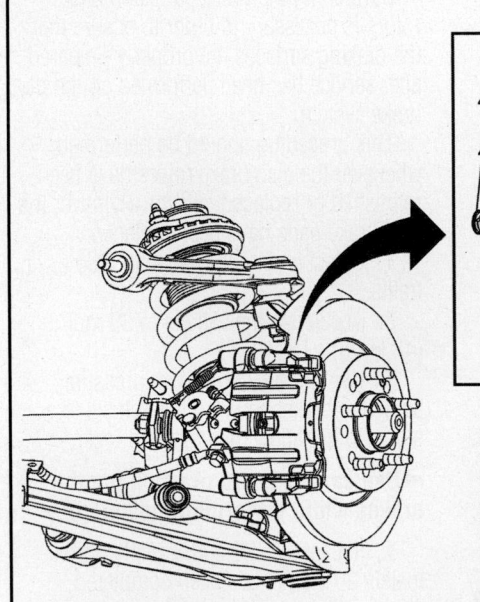
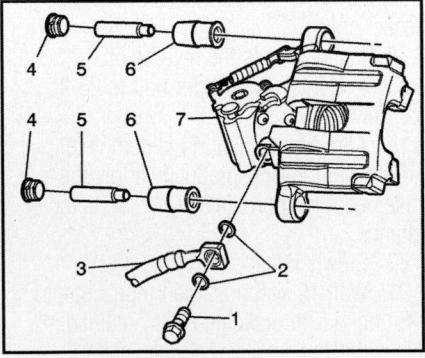

1. Brake hose caliper bolt
2. Brake hose gaskets
3. Brake hose
4. Brake caliper guide pin seals
5. Brake caliper guide pins
6. Brake caliper guide pin bushings
7. Brake caliper

36616_SOLS_G0034

Fig. 6 Rear brake caliper and related components

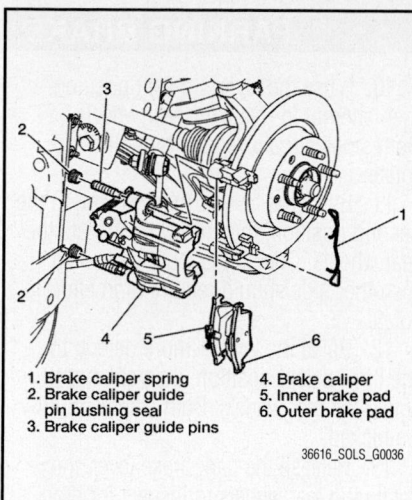

1. Brake caliper spring
2. Brake caliper guide pin bushing seal
3. Brake caliper guide pins
4. Brake caliper
5. Inner brake pad
6. Outer brake pad

36616_SOLS_G0036

Fig. 7 Rear brake pads and related components

needs to be removed from the reservoir before proceeding.

b. If the brake fluid level is higher than midway between the maximum-full point and the minimum allowable level, remove brake fluid to the midway point before proceeding.

3. Raise and suitably support the vehicle.

4. Remove the tire and wheel assembly.

5. Install a large C-clamp over the body of the brake caliper with the C-clamp ends against the rear of the caliper body and against the outer brake pad.

✲✲ WARNING

When using a large C-clamp to compress a caliper piston into a caliper bore of a caliper equipped with an integral park brake mechanism, do not exceed more than 0.039 in. (1 mm) of piston travel. Exceeding this amount of piston travel will cause damage to the internal adjusting mechanism and/or the integral park brake mechanism.

6. Tighten the C-clamp until the caliper piston is compressed into the caliper bore enough to allow the caliper to slide past the brake rotor. Do not exceed 0.039 in. (1 mm) of caliper piston travel.

7. Remove the C-clamp from the caliper.

8. Remove the lower brake caliper guide pin bolt.

9. Rotate the brake caliper up and forward until it rests on the brake caliper mounting bracket. The brake hose does not have to be removed from the brake caliper.

10. Remove the brake pads.

11. Remove the brake pad springs.

To install:

12. Thoroughly clean the brake pad hardware mating surfaces of the caliper bracket of any debris and corrosion.

13. Inspect the brake caliper guide pins for freedom of movement and inspect the condition of the guide pin bushings. Move the guide pins in and out within the bushings and observe for the following conditions. If any of the conditions listed are found, the brake caliper guide pins and/or bushings require replacement.:

- Restricted caliper guide pin movement
- Seized or binding caliper guide pins
- Split or torn bushings

14. Installation is the reverse of removal, noting the following:

a. Ensure the brake pad equipped with the spring is installed facing the inner friction surface of the brake rotor.

b. Tighten the caliper bolt to 20 ft. lbs. (27 Nm).

15. After the installation is complete, with the engine OFF, gradually apply the brake pedal to approximately ⅔ of its travel distance.

16. Slowly release the brake pedal.

17. Wait 15 seconds, then repeat steps 4–5 until a firm brake pedal is obtained. This will properly seat the brake caliper piston and brake pads.

18. Fill the master cylinder reservoir to the proper level.

19. Burnish the brake pads and rotors.

BRAKE PAD & ROTOR BURNISHING

✲✲ CAUTION

Road test a vehicle under safe conditions and while obeying all traffic laws. Do not attempt any maneuvers that could jeopardize vehicle control. Failure to adhere to these precautions could lead to serious personal injury and vehicle damage.

Burnishing the brake pads and brake rotors is necessary in order to ensure that the braking surfaces are properly prepared after service has been performed on the disc brake system.

This procedure should be performed whenever the disc brake rotors have been refinished or replaced, and/or whenever the disc brake pads have been replaced.

1. Select a smooth road with little or no traffic.

2. Accelerate the vehicle to 30 mph (48 km/h).

3. Using moderate to firm pressure, apply the brakes to bring the vehicle to a stop. Do not allow the brakes to lock.

➡**Use care to avoid overheating the brakes while performing this step.**

4. Repeat steps 2 and 3 until approximately 20 stops have been completed. Allow sufficient cooling periods between stops in order to properly burnish the brake pads and rotors

BRAKES | PARKING BRAKE

PARKING BRAKE CABLES

ADJUSTMENT

1. Remove the front floor console.
2. Cycle the park lever several times. Verify the lever releases fully.
3. Turn the ignition ON. Verify the red BRAKE warning lamp is not illuminated. If the warning lamp is illuminated, verify the following:
   a. The lever is fully released and against the stop.
   b. There is not excessive slack in the cables.
   c. If the warning lamp remained illuminated and there were no visible causes, check hydraulic system.
   d. Turn the ignition OFF.
4. Raise and support the vehicle

enough to raise the rear tire and wheel assemblies off the ground.
5. Ensure the park brake lever is fully released.
6. Loosen the cable tension adjusting nut just enough to back the nut away from the lever cam.
7. Tighten the adjusting nut just until slack in the front cable is removed and the nut rests against the lever cam.

➡**The park brake cable adjusting nut is a nylon lock type. Use ONLY HAND TOOLS whenever tightening or loosening the adjusting nut.**

8. Cycle the park brake lever several times.
9. With the lever fully released, tighten the adjusting nut just enough to remove slack in the front cable.

10. Raise the lever 1 detent position, then attempt to rotate the rear wheels. Both sides should require high effort to rotate.
11. Raise the lever 1 more detent, to the second position, then attempt to rotate the rear wheels. One side should be locked, the other side should require high effort to rotate.
12. Raise the lever 1 more detent, to the third detent position, then attempt to rotate the rear wheels. Both sides should be locked.
13. Release the park brake lever, then rotate the rear wheels to inspect for drag. There should not be any drag from the park brake system.
14. Inspect the brake caliper park brake levers to ensure that they are resting against the stops.

CHASSIS ELECTRICAL | AIR BAG (SUPPLEMENTAL RESTRAINT SYSTEM)

GENERAL INFORMATION

✳✳ CAUTION

These vehicles are equipped with an air bag system. The system must be disarmed before performing service on, or around, system components, the steering column, instrument panel components, wiring and sensors. Failure to follow the safety precautions and the disarming procedure could result in accidental air bag deployment, possible injury and unnecessary system repairs.

SERVICE PRECAUTIONS

✳✳ CAUTION

When performing service on or near the SIR components or the SIR wiring, the SIR system must be disabled. Failure to observe the correct procedure could cause deployment of the SIR components. Serious injury can occur. Failure to observe the correct procedure could also result in unnecessary SIR system repairs.

✳✳ CAUTION

The inflatable restraint Sensing and Diagnostic Module (SDM) maintains a reserved energy supply. The reserved energy supply provides

deployment power for the air bags if the SDM loses battery power during a collision. Deployment power is available for as much as 1 minute after disconnecting the vehicle power. Waiting 1 minute before working on the system after disabling the SIR system prevents deployment of the air bags from the reserved energy supply.

When carrying an undeployed inflator module:
  • Do not carry the inflator module by the wires or connector.
  • Make sure the air bag opening points away from you.

When storing an undeployed inflator module:
  • Make sure the air bag opening points away from the surface on which the inflator module rests.
  • Provide free space for the air bag to expand in case of an accidental deployment.
  • When storing a steering column, do not rest the column with the air bag opening facing down and the column vertical. Lay the column on its side.

Use caution when handling or storing a live (undeployed) inflator module. An inflator module deployment produces a rapid generation of gas. This may cause the inflator module, or an object in front of the inflator module, to project through the air in the event of an unlikely deployment.

Wear safety glasses, rubber gloves, and long sleeved clothing when cleaning powder residue from vehicle after an airbag deployment. Powder residue emitted from a deployed airbag can cause skin irritation. Flush affected area with cool water if irritation is experienced. If nasal or throat irritation is experienced, exit the vehicle for fresh air until the irritation ceases. If irritation continues, see a physician.

Do not use a replacement airbag that is not in the original packaging. This may result in improper deployment, personal injury, or death.

Discard any of the following components if it has been dropped from a height of 91 cm (3 feet) or greater:
  • Inflatable restraint Sensing and Diagnostic Module (SDM)
  • Any Inflatable restraint air bag module
  • Inflatable restraint steering wheel module coil
  • Any Inflatable restraint sensor
  • Inflatable restraint seat belt pretensioners
  • Inflatable restraint passenger presence detection module or sensor

During, and following, any child restraint anchor service, due to impact event or vehicle repair, carefully inspect all mounting hardware, tether straps, and anchors for proper installation, operation, or damage. If a child restraint anchor is found damaged in any way, the anchor must be replaced. Failure to do this may result in personal injury or death.

Deployed and non-deployed airbags may or may not have live pyrotechnic material within the airbag inflator.

After any airbag component testing or service, do not connect the battery negative cable. Personal injury or death may result if the system test is not performed first.

Do not expose inflator modules to temperatures above 150°F (65°C).

Verify the correct replacement part number. Do not substitute a component from a different vehicle.

Use only original GM replacement parts available from your authorized GM dealer. Do not use salvaged parts for repairs to the SIR system.

The factory installed fasteners, screws and bolts used to fasten airbag components have a special coating and are specifically designed for the airbag system. Do not use substitute fasteners. Use only original equipment fasteners listed in the parts catalog when fastener replacement is required.

Improper alignment of the SIR coil assembly may damage the unit, causing an inflatable restraint malfunction.

Do not dispose of an undeployed inflator module as normal shop waste. Do not dispose of driver/passenger/curtain airbags or seat belt tensioners unless you are sure of complete deployment. Undeployed inflator modules contain substances that could cause severe illness or personal injury if their sealed containers are damaged during disposal. Refer to the Hazardous Substance Control System for proper disposal. Failure to observe the proper disposal methods may be a violation of federal, state, or local laws.

Dispose of deployed airbags and tensioners consistent with state, provincial, local, and federal regulations.

If the vehicle is equipped with the Occupant Classification System (OCS) and/or Occupant Restraint Controller (ORC), observe the following precautions:

• Do not connect the battery negative cable before performing the OCS Verification Test using the scan tool and the appropriate diagnostic information. Personal injury or death may result if the system test is not performed properly.

• Never replace both the ORC and the OCM at the same time. If both require replacement, replace one, then perform the Airbag System test before replacing the other.

• Both the ORC and the OCM store Occupant Classification System (OCS) calibration data, which they transfer to one another when one of them is replaced. If both are replaced at the same time, an irre-versible fault will be set in both modules and the OCS may malfunction and cause personal injury or death.

• If equipped with OCS, the Seat Weight Sensor is a sensitive, calibrated unit and must be handled carefully. Do not drop or handle roughly. If dropped or damaged, replace with another sensor. Failure to do so may result in occupant injury or death.

• The front passenger seat must be handled carefully as well. When removing the seat, be careful when setting on floor not to drop. If dropped, the sensor may be inoperative, could result in occupant injury, or possibly death.

• When the passenger front seat is on the floor, no one should sit in the front passenger seat. This uneven force may damage the sensing ability of the seat weight sensors. If sat on and damaged, the sensor may be inoperative, could result in occupant injury, or possibly death.

DISABLING THE SYSTEM

Air Bag Fuse Disabling

1. Before servicing the vehicle, refer to the Precautions Section.
2. Turn the steering wheel so that the vehicles wheels are pointing straight ahead.
3. Place the ignition in the OFF position.

> ✳✳ **CAUTION**
>
> **The SDM may have more than one fused power input. To ensure there is no unwanted SIR deployment, personal injury, or unnecessary SIR system repairs, remove all fuses supplying power to the SDM. With all SDM fuses removed and the ignition switch in the ON position, the AIR BAG warning indicator illuminates. This is normal operation, and does not indicate an SIR system malfunction.**

4. Locate and remove the fuse(s) supplying power to the SDM. Refer to Floor Console Fuse Block in Fuses & Flashers.
5. Wait 1 minute before working on the system.

Negative Battery Cable Disabling

1. Before servicing the vehicle, refer to the Precautions Section.
2. Turn the steering wheel so that the vehicles wheels are pointing straight ahead.
3. Place the ignition in the OFF position.
4. Disconnect the negative battery cable from the battery.
5. Wait 1 minute before working on system.

ENABLING THE SYSTEM

Air Bag Fuse Enabling

1. Before servicing the vehicle, refer to the Precautions Section.
2. Place the ignition in the OFF position.
3. Install the fuse(s) supplying power to the SDM.
4. Turn the ignition switch to the ON position. The AIR BAG indicator will flash then turn OFF.
5. Perform the Diagnostic System Check if the AIR BAG warning indicator does not operate as described. Refer to Diagnostic System Check in General Information.

Negative Battery Cable Enabling

1. Before servicing the vehicle, refer to the Precautions Section.
2. Place the ignition in the OFF position.
3. Connect the negative battery cable to the battery.
4. Turn the ignition switch to the ON position. The AIR BAG indicator will flash then turn OFF.
5. Perform the Diagnostic System Check if the AIR BAG warning indicator does not operate as described. Refer to Diagnostic System Check in General Information.

CLOCKSPRING CENTERING

See Figures 8 and 9.

> ✳✳ **CAUTION**
>
> **Improper alignment of the SIR coil assembly may damage the unit, causing an inflatable restraint malfunction.**

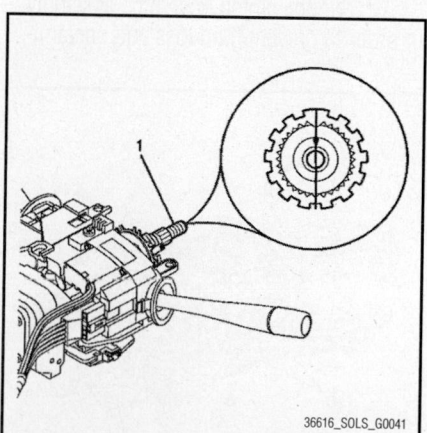

36616_SOLS_G0041

Fig. 8 Verify the block tooth and the centering mark (1) of the steering shaft is in the 12 o'clock position

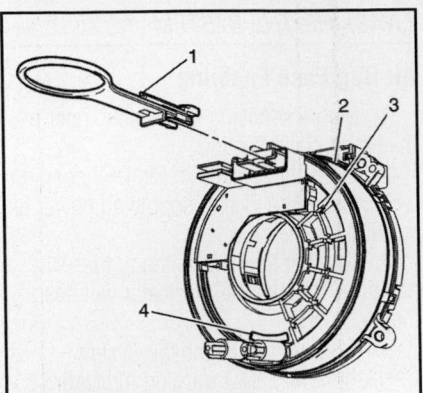

1. Yellow retaining tab
2. Steering wheel module coil
3. Steering wheel module coil hub
4. Centering window

22116_SOLS_G0063

Fig. 9 Steering wheel module coil

1. Before servicing the vehicle, refer to the Precautions Section.

2. Verify the following conditions before centering the SIR steering wheel module coil:

   a. The wheels on the vehicle are straight ahead.

   b. The block tooth and the centering mark (1) of the steering shaft is in the 12 o'clock position.

3. If available, remove the yellow retaining tab (1) from the SIR steering wheel module coil and save the tab for reassembly.

4. Hold the SIR steering wheel module coil face up by the casing (2).

   a. Slowly turn the SIR steering wheel module coil hub (3) clockwise until the coil ribbon stops.

   b. Slowly rotate the SIR steering wheel module coil hub (3) counterclockwise 2.5 revolutions until the centering window (4) turns yellow. This indicates the CENTER position.

➡ **If the retaining tab is not available, the use of tape to secure the SIR steering wheel module coil is recommended for installation to the steering column.**

5. Install the yellow retaining tab (1) to the SIR steering wheel module coil.

6. Slide the centered SIR steering wheel module coil onto the steering shaft.

DRIVE TRAIN

MANUAL TRANSMISSION ASSEMBLY

REMOVAL & INSTALLATION

With Sport Package (Z0K)

See Figures 10 through 13.

1. Before servicing the vehicle, refer to the Precautions Section.

2. Remove the control lever knob and boot assembly.

3. Remove the catalytic converter. Refer to Catalytic Converter Removal & Installation in the Engine Mechanical Section.

4. Remove the clutch hose/pipe assembly retainer clip from the clutch master cylinder.

5. Disconnect the clutch hose/pipe assembly from the clutch master cylinder.

6. Cap the clutch hose/pipe assembly in order to prevent fluid loss and contamination. It is not necessary to plug the lower hose end or slave cylinder fitting as they are equipped with check valves, only minimal fluid loss may be experienced.

7. Remove the starter. Refer to Starter Removal & Installation in the Engine Electrical Section.

8. Drain the transmission fluid if necessary.

9. Remove the propeller shaft. Refer to Propeller Shaft Removal & Installation.

10. Disconnect the electrical connector (2) from the backup lamp switch (5).

11. Disconnect the electrical connector (3) from the Vehicle Speed Sensor (VSS) (4).

12. Disconnect the wiring harness (1) from the clip bracket.

13. Disconnect the wiring harness clips (6) from the clip brackets, and position the harness aside.

14. Support the transmission using a transmission jack.

15. Remove the transmission support.

16. Remove the 5 transmission to engine mounting bolts (1).

17. Remove the 2 engine to transmission mounting bolts (2).

18. Remove the 2 remaining transmission mounting bolts (2).

✳✳ WARNING

Do not allow the transmission to hang from the clutch assembly.

19. Pull the transmission straight back off the clutch hub splines.

20. Ensure clearance is maintained between the transmission and the following:

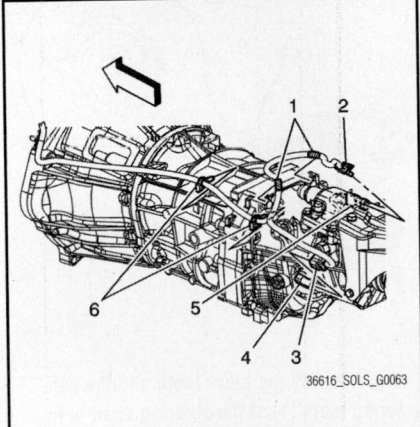

Fig. 10 Electrical connections

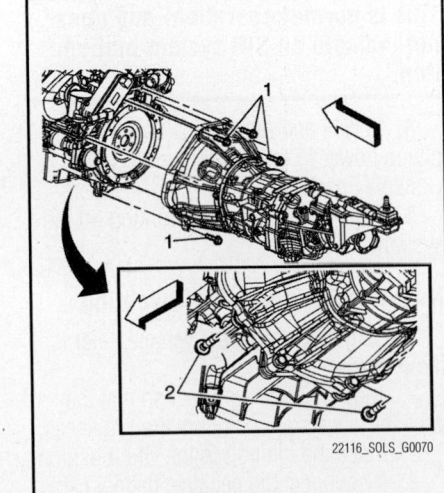

22116_SOLS_G0070

Fig. 11 Manual transmission and mounting bolts (1, 2)

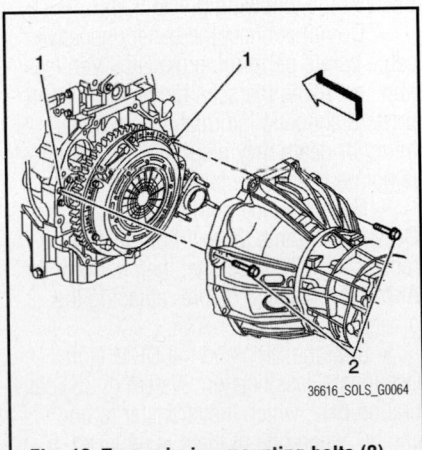

36616_SOLS_G0064

Fig. 12 Transmission mounting bolts (2)

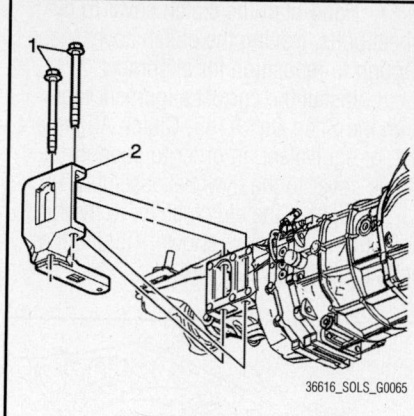

Fig. 13 Transmission mount bracket (2) and bolts (1)

- The catalytic converter
- The clutch assembly
- The engine wiring harness
- The clutch actuator pipe and hose

21. Using the transmission jack, carefully lower the transmission from the vehicle.

22. Remove the transmission mount bracket bolts (1).

23. Remove the transmission mount bracket (2).

To install:

24. Install the transmission mount bracket.

25. Install the transmission mount bracket bolts and tighten to 177 ft. lbs. (240 Nm).

26. Ensure clearance is maintained between the transmission and the following:
- The catalytic converter
- The clutch assembly
- The engine wiring harness

27. Using the transmission jack, carefully raise the transmission to the engine.

28. Align the transmission with the engine dowels

29. Install the 2 transmission mounting bolts and tighten to 37 ft. lbs. (50 Nm).

30. Install the 2 engine to transmission mounting bolts and tighten to 37 ft. lbs. (50 Nm).

31. Install the 5 transmission to engine mounting bolts and tighten to 37 ft. lbs. (50 Nm).

32. Install the transmission support.

33. Remove the transmission jack.

34. Install the starter.

35. Lay the engine wiring harness over the transmission.

36. Connect the wiring harness clips to the clip brackets.

37. Connect the wiring harness to the clip bracket.

38. Connect the electrical connector to the VSS.

39. Connect the electrical connector to the backup lamp switch.

40. Install the rear propeller shaft.

41. Fill the transmission fluid if removed.

✱✱ WARNING

Ensure the clutch hydraulic hose does not come in contact with any sharp or potentially hot surfaces.

42. Install the clutch hose/pipe assembly retainer clip to the clutch master cylinder.

43. Connect the clutch hose/pipe assembly to the clutch master cylinder.

44. Tug gently on the clutch hose/pipe assembly to ensure proper retention into the clutch master cylinder.

45. Install the catalytic converter.

46. Install the control lever knob and boot assembly.

Without Sport Package (ZOK)

See Figures 10 through 12.

1. Before servicing the vehicle, refer to the Precautions Section.

2. Remove the control lever knob and boot assembly.

3. Remove the catalytic converter. Refer to Catalytic Converter Removal & Installation in the Engine Mechanical Section.

4. Remove the clutch hose/pipe assembly retainer clip from the clutch master cylinder.

5. Disconnect the clutch hose/pipe assembly from the clutch master cylinder.

6. Cap the clutch hose/pipe assembly in order to prevent fluid loss and contamination. It is not necessary to plug the lower hose end or slave cylinder fitting as they are equipped with check valves, only minimal fluid loss may be experienced.

7. Remove the starter. Refer to Starter Removal & Installation in the Engine Electrical Section.

8. Remove the transmission support.

9. Drain the transmission fluid if necessary.

10. Disconnect the electrical connector (2) from the backup lamp switch (5).

11. Disconnect the electrical connector (3) from the Vehicle Speed Sensor (VSS) (4).

12. Disconnect the wiring harness (1) from the clip bracket.

13. Disconnect the wiring harness clips (6) from the clip brackets, and position the harness aside.

14. Support the transmission using a transmission jack.

15. Remove the propeller shaft and driveline support. Refer to Propeller Shaft Removal & Installation.

16. Remove the driveline support.

17. Remove the transmission support.

18. Remove the 5 transmission to engine mounting bolts (1).

19. Remove the 2 engine to transmission mounting bolts (2).

20. Remove the 2 remaining transmission mounting bolts (2).

✱✱ WARNING

Do not allow the transmission to hang from the clutch assembly.

21. Pull the transmission straight back off the clutch hub splines.

22. Ensure clearance is maintained between the transmission and the following:
- The catalytic converter
- The clutch assembly
- The engine wiring harness
- The clutch actuator pipe and hose

23. Using the transmission jack, carefully lower the transmission from the vehicle.

To install:

24. Ensure clearance is maintained between the transmission and the following:
- The catalytic converter
- The clutch assembly
- The engine wiring harness

25. Using the transmission jack, carefully raise the transmission to the engine.

26. Align the transmission with the engine dowels

27. Install the 2 transmission mounting bolts and tighten to 37 ft. lbs. (50 Nm).

28. Install the 2 engine to transmission mounting bolts and tighten to 37 ft. lbs. (50 Nm).

29. Install the 5 transmission to engine mounting bolts and tighten to 37 ft. lbs. (50 Nm).

30. Install the propeller shaft and driveline support.

31. Install the driveline support.

32. Install the transmission support.

33. Remove the transmission jack.

34. Lay the engine wiring harness over the transmission.

35. Connect the wiring harness clips to the clip brackets.

36. Connect the wiring harness to the clip bracket.

37. Connect the electrical connector to the VSS.

38. Connect the electrical connector to the backup lamp switch.

39. Fill the transmission fluid if removed.

40. Install the transmission support and closeout panels.

41. Install the starter.

✳✳ WARNING

Ensure the clutch hydraulic hose does not come in contact with any sharp or potentially hot surfaces.

42. Install the clutch hose/pipe assembly retainer clip to the clutch master cylinder.

43. Connect the clutch hose/pipe assembly to the clutch master cylinder.

44. Tug gently on the clutch hose/pipe assembly to ensure proper retention into the clutch master cylinder.

45. Install the catalytic converter.

46. Install the control lever knob and boot assembly.

TRANSMISSION FINAL TEST & INSPECTION

Complete the following procedure after the transmission is installed in the vehicle:

1. With the ignition OFF or disconnected and clutch pedal depressed, crank the engine several times.

2. Listen for any unusual noises or evidence that any parts are binding.

3. Place the transmission in neutral, start the engine and listen for any unusual noises or evidence that any parts are binding.

4. Turn OFF the ignition.

5. Perform a final inspection for the proper fluid level.

6. Road test the vehicle.

CLUTCH DRIVEN DISC & PRESSURE PLATE

REMOVAL & INSTALLATION

See Figures 14 through 16.

1. Before servicing the vehicle, refer to the Precautions Section.

2. Remove the transmission.

3. Remove the clutch cover bolts one turn at a time, until spring pressure is relieved.

4. Remove the clutch cover and the clutch disc.

To install:

5. Adjust the clutch pressure plate, if necessary.

6. Install the clutch disc and the clutch cover.

7. Hand-start the clutch cover to flywheel bolts, leaving the clutch cover loose enough to reposition for alignment.

8. Install the correct alignment tool from the Snap On® A145, Clutch Alignment Set, or equivalent, in order to support the clutch cover to the flywheel assembly.

9. Tighten the clutch cover to flywheel bolts in the sequence shown. Tighten the bolts to 22 ft. lbs. (30 Nm).

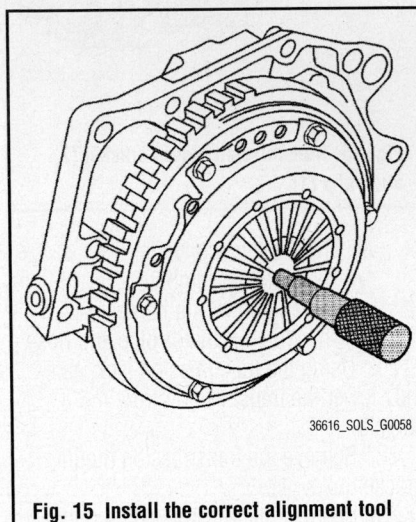

36616_SOLS_G0058

Fig. 15 Install the correct alignment tool

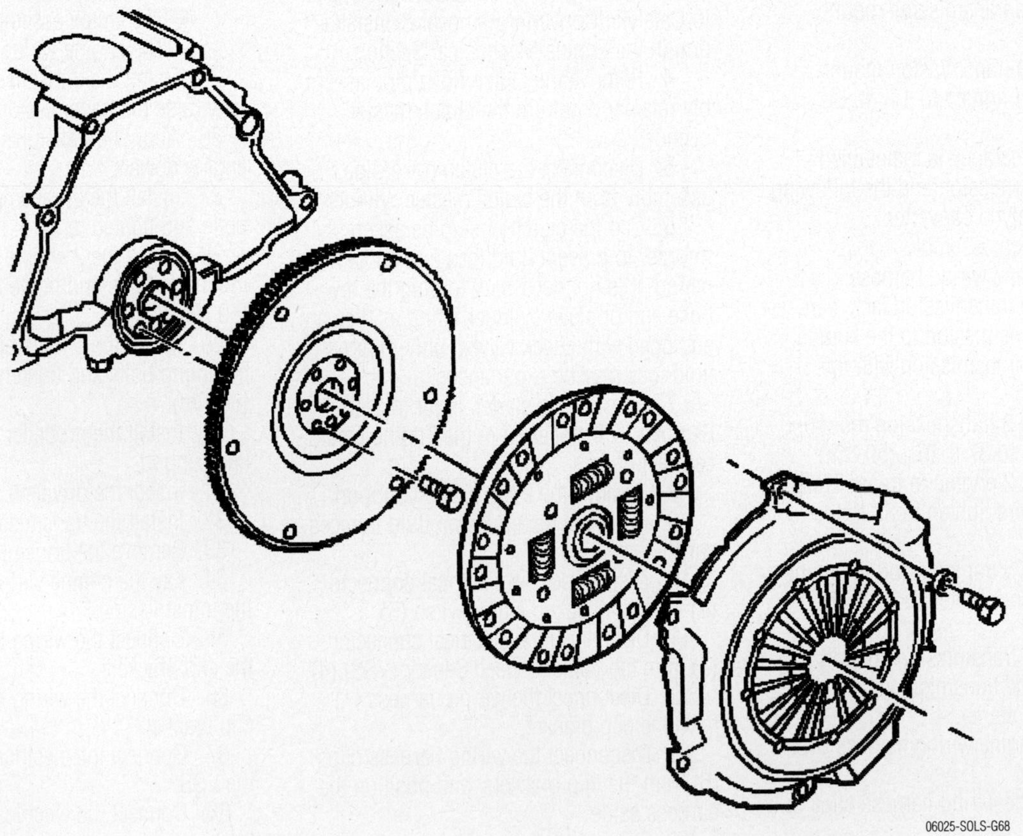

Fig. 14 Clutch components

06025-SOLS-G68

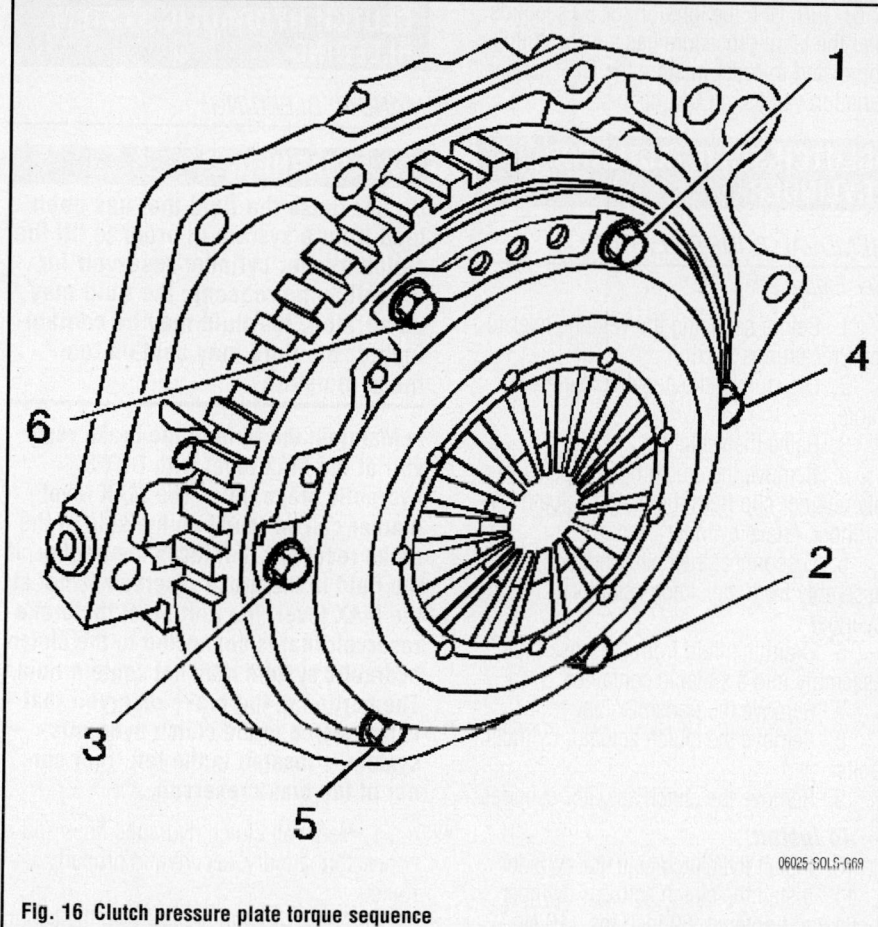

Fig. 16 Clutch pressure plate torque sequence

10. Recheck each bolt torque using the tightening sequence.

11. Remove the Snap On® A145 tool.

➡**Excessive amounts of lubricant on the input shaft splines may contaminate the clutch disc and cause clutch shudder.**

12. Lubricate the inside diameter of the bearing with Saturn P/N 21005995, or equivalent.

13. Install the transmission.

14. Bleed the hydraulic system.

15. Connect the negative battery cable.

ADJUSTMENTS

This vehicle has a self-adjusting clutch that is constantly adjusting.

CLUTCH MASTER CYLINDER

REMOVAL & INSTALLATION

See Figures 17 through 19.

1. Before servicing the vehicle, refer to the Precautions Section.

2. Remove the instrument panel left closeout/insulator panel.

3. Remove the clutch master cylinder push rod retainer (2) from the clutch pedal arm integral stud.

4. Remove the clutch master cylinder push rod (1) from the clutch pedal arm integral stud.

5. Place a shop towel under the clutch master cylinder in order to catch any fluid loss.

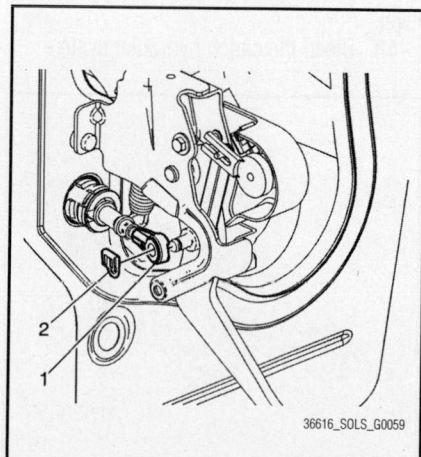

Fig. 17 Clutch master cylinder push rod (1) and retainer (2)

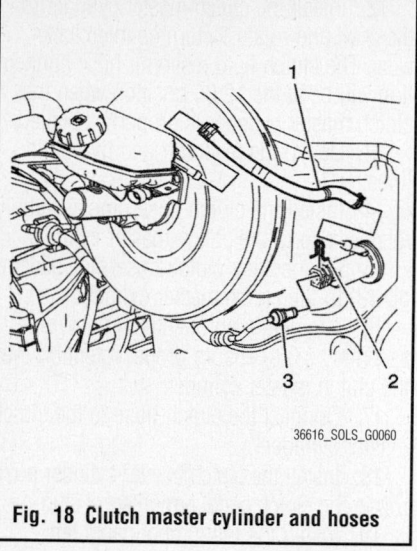

Fig. 18 Clutch master cylinder and hoses

6. Disconnect the clutch hose (1) from the clutch master cylinder and position the hose end above the brake master cylinder reservoir in order to prevent fluid loss.

7. Remove the clutch hose/pipe assembly retainer clip (2) from the clutch master cylinder.

8. Disconnect the clutch hose/pipe assembly (3) from the clutch master cylinder.

9. Cap the reservoir and clutch hoses in order to prevent fluid loss and contamination.

10. Rotate the clutch master cylinder (2) one ¼ turn clockwise and remove the cylinder from the cowl (1).

To install:

➡**While installing, ensure that the clutch master cylinder pushrod is aligned with the clutch pedal.**

11. Align the keys of the clutch master cylinder with the tabs on the cowl.

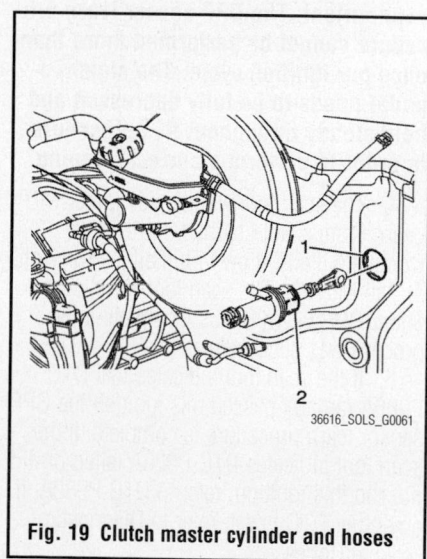

Fig. 19 Clutch master cylinder and hoses

12. Install the clutch master cylinder to the cowl and rotate ¼ turn counterclockwise. The clutch fluid reservoir hose connection will be at the 12:00 position when the clutch master cylinder is properly installed.

13. Uncap the reservoir and hydraulic lines.

14. Install the clutch hose/pipe assembly retainer clip to the clutch master cylinder.

15. Connect the clutch hose/pipe assembly (3) to the clutch master cylinder.

16. Tug gently on the clutch hose/pipe assembly (3) to ensure proper retention into the clutch master cylinder.

17. Connect the clutch hose to the clutch master cylinder.

18. Install the clutch master cylinder push rod to the clutch pedal arm integral stud.

19. Install the instrument panel left closeout/insulator panel.

20. Bleed the clutch hydraulic system.

CLUTCH PEDAL POSITION SENSOR LEARN PROCEDURE

The Clutch Pedal Position (CPP) sensor learn procedure is required when the following service procedures have been performed regardless of whether DTC P080A is set:
• An Engine Control Module (ECM) replacement
• A CPP sensor replacement
• Any repairs which affect the CPP sensor relationship

1. Install a scan tool.

2. Monitor the ECM for DTCs with a scan tool. If other DTCs are set, except DTC P080A, refer to Diagnostic Trouble Codes.

3. With a scan tool, select Clutch Pedal Position Learn under Module Setup in Manual Transmission, and perform the following instructions displayed on the scan tool screen.

➡Important: The CPP sensor learn procedure cannot be performed more than once per ignition cycle. The clutch pedal needs to be fully depressed and held steady throughout this procedure in order to perform a correct learning.

4. The scan tool will display under CPP Learn Status: Not Learned, In Process, Complete, Fail—Low Volt, Fail—High Volt, or Fail Moving. The scan tool will display under CPP Learn Status Complete if the process was successful.

5. If the scan tool indicates that DTC P080A ran and passed this ignition the CPP sensor learn procedure is complete. If the scan tool indicates DTC P080A failed or did not run this ignition, refer to DTC P080A. If any other DTC is set, refer to Diagnostic Trouble Codes.

6. Turn OFF the ignition for 30 seconds after the learn procedure has successfully completed in order to store the CPP sensor variation values in ECM history.

CLUTCH SLAVE (ACTUATOR) CYLINDER

REMOVAL & INSTALLATION

See Figure 20.

1. Before servicing the vehicle, refer to the Precautions Section.

2. Disconnect the negative battery cable.

3. Raise the vehicle.

4. Remove the clutch hose/pipe assembly retainer clip from the clutch actuator cylinder, (slave cylinder).

5. Disconnect the clutch hose/pipe assembly from the clutch actuator cylinder.

6. Drain the fluid from the hose/pipe assembly into a suitable container.

7. Remove the transmission.

8. Remove the clutch actuator cylinder bolts.

9. Remove the clutch actuator cylinder.

To install:

10. Install the clutch actuator cylinder.

11. Install the clutch actuator cylinder bolts and tighten to 89 inch lbs. (10 Nm).

12. Install the transmission.

13. Reconnect the clutch hose/pipe assembly from the clutch actuator cylinder and install retainer clip.

14. Check transmission fluid level and add as needed.

15. Lower the vehicle

16. Connect the negative battery cable.

17. Fill the brake/clutch reservoir with DOT 3 hydraulic fluid to the proper fluid level.

18. Bleed the clutch hydraulic system.

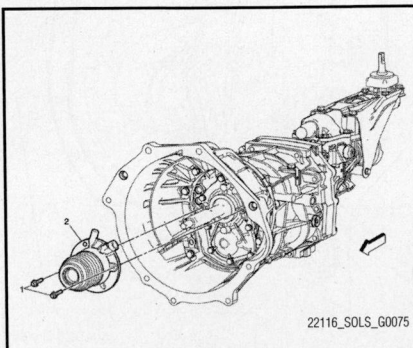

Fig. 20 Clutch actuator cylinder, (slave cylinder) and transmission

22116_SOLS_G0075

CLUTCH HYDRAULIC SYSTEM BLEEDING

MANUAL BLEEDING

✳✳ WARNING

Do not reuse the fluid that has been bled from a system in order to fill the clutch master cylinder reservoir for the following reasons: the fluid may be aerated, the fluid may be contaminated, the fluid may contain too much moisture.

➡**Maintain the fluid in the brake reservoir at the MAX level with DOT 3 hydraulic brake fluid. The MAX level marker can be found on the side of the brake reservoir that faces the engine, If the fluid in the brake reservoir is not at the MAX level, the portion of the brake reservoir that is connected to the clutch hydraulic system may not contain fluid. The portion of the brake reservoir that is connected to the clutch hydraulic system is located in the left, rear corner of the brake reservoir.**

1. Verify all clutch hydraulic lines and connectors are dry, secure and properly routed.

2. Clean dirt and grease from the cap in order to ensure that no foreign substances enter the system.

3. Remove the brake reservoir cap and fill the entire brake reservoir to the MAX level.

4. Depress the clutch pedal slowly to the full depressed position.

5. Let the clutch pedal return to the up stop position and hold for 5 seconds.

6. Check the brake reservoir to see if the portion of the brake reservoir that is connected to the clutch hydraulic system has the same fluid level as the rest of the brake reservoir. If the fluids are not the same, add DOT 3 hydraulic brake fluid until the entire brake reservoir is at the MAX level.

7. Repeat steps 3–5 until air is purged from the clutch system and the clutch pedal feels firm.

8. Replace the cap on the brake reservoir.

✳✳ CAUTION

Do not start the engine while the transmission is in gear, only while in the neutral position. This vehicle is equipped with a concentric actuator cylinder and may move if started in gear.

9. Fully apply the PARK brake.

10. Place the transmission into the neutral position, depress the clutch pedal, and start the engine.

11. Pump the clutch pedal until firm.

12. Pump the brake pedal until firm.

13. If needed, add additional DOT 3 hydraulic brake fluid to fill the brake reservoir to the MAX level.

➡The clutch and braking systems are integrated into one reservoir. The brake may be soft when first applying.

14. Road test the vehicle to ensure proper operation.

VACUUM BLEEDING

➡Check the clutch hose assembly for the correct routing. The clutch hose assembly should be routed above the rubber boot for the steering column and above the grommet for the hood release cables. If the clutch hose assembly is not routed correctly, the clutch hydraulic system will be very difficult or impossible to bleed. If the clutch hose assembly is not routed correctly, change the clutch hose assembly routing before bleeding the clutch hydraulic system.

1. Verify that all the hydraulic lines are dry, secure and correctly routed.

2. Clean dirt and grease from the brake reservoir cap in order to ensure that no foreign substances enter the system.

3. Remove the brake reservoir cap.

➡Maintain the fluid in the brake reservoir at the MAX level with DOT 3 hydraulic brake fluid. The MAX level marker can be found on the side of the brake reservoir that faces the engine. If the fluid in the brake reservoir is not at the MAX level, the portion of the brake reservoir that is connected to the clutch hydraulic system may not contain fluid. The portion of the brake reservoir that is connected to the clutch hydraulic system is located in the left, rear corner of the brake reservoir.

4. Fill the entire brake reservoir to the MAX level using DOT 3 hydraulic brake fluid.

5. Install the J 43485 power steering bleeder adapter and the J 35555 to the reservoir.

➡Make sure equipment is clean and free of contaminants.

6. Hold the J 43485 into position while applying 15–20 hg (51–68 kPa) of vacuum.

7. Remove the adapter and refill the brake reservoir to the MAX level.

8. Depress the clutch pedal slowly to the full depressed position.

9. Let the clutch pedal return to the up stop position and hold for 5 seconds.

10. Repeat steps 4—9 until all air is removed from the clutch system.

11. Replace the cap on the brake reservoir.

✳✳ CAUTION

Do not start the engine while the transmission is in gear, only while in the neutral position. This vehicle is equipped with a concentric actuator cylinder and may move if started in gear.

12. Fully apply the PARK brake.

13. Place the transmission into the neutral position, depress the clutch pedal, and start the engine.

14. Pump the clutch pedal until firm.

➡The clutch and braking systems are integrated into one reservoir. The brake may be soft when first applying.

15. Pump the brake pedal until firm.

16. If needed, add additional DOT 3 hydraulic brake fluid to fill the brake reservoir to the MAX level.

17. Road test the vehicle to ensure proper operation.

REAR AXLE HOUSING/ DIFFERENTIAL

REMOVAL & INSTALLATION

See Figures 21 through 23.

1. Before servicing the vehicle, refer to the Precautions Section.

2. Raise and support the vehicle.

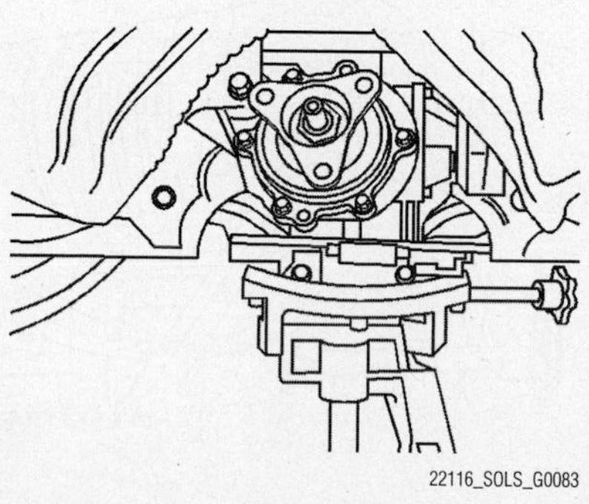

3. Remove propeller shaft. Refer to Propeller Shaft Removal & Installation.

4. Remove the rear tire and wheel assemblies.

5. Remove the right and left wheel drive axle shafts. Refer to Halfshaft Removal & Installation.

6. Position a transmission jack beneath the differential.

7. Firmly secure the differential to the transmission jack.

8. Remove the driveline support bracket from the rear differential assembly, if equipped.

9. Remove the front differential carrier bracket to frame bolt (1).

10. Remove the left (1) and right (2) differential rear mounting bolts.

11. Lower the jack slightly until the mounting ear at the front of the differential clears the support attachment point.

12. Remove the differential from the vehicle.

To install:

➡The differential is shipped with a plastic vent plug. Remove the plastic

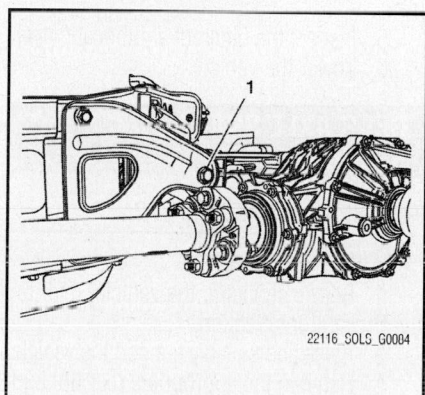

Fig. 22 Front differential carrier bracket to frame bolt (1)

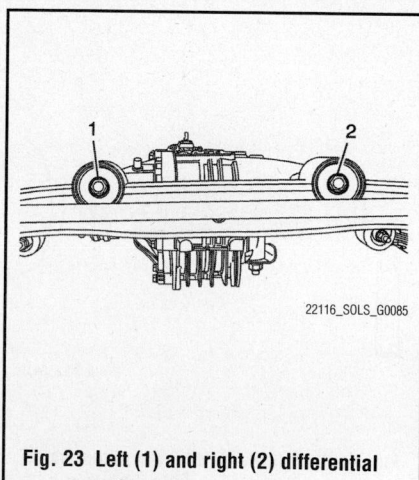

Fig. 23 Left (1) and right (2) differential rear mounting bolts

Fig. 21 Rear differential with support jack

vent plug prior to differential vent installation.

13. When replacing the differential. remove the plastic vent plug and install a new differential vent. The vent flange must be fully seated.

14. With the differential firmly attached to the jack, raise the differential to the vehicle.

15. Install the driveline support bracket to the rear differential assembly, if equipped.

16. Hand install the differential carrier bracket-to-frame bolt in order to locate the differential to the rear support.

17. With the differential firmly attached to the jack, raise the differential to the rear support.

18. Position the differential to the support.

19. Install the left and right differential rear mounting bolts. Tighten the differential mounting bolts to 129 ft. lbs. (175 Nm).

20. Tighten the differential carrier bracket to frame bolt to 129 ft. lbs. (175 Nm).

21. Remove the transmission jack.

22. Install propeller shaft.

23. Install the wheel drive shafts.

24. Install the rear tire and wheel assemblies.

25. Inspect the differential lubricant level.

26. Lower the vehicle.

REAR AXLE SHAFT, BEARING & SEAL

REMOVAL & INSTALLATION

See Figure 24.

1. Before servicing the vehicle, refer to the Precautions Section.

2. Raise and suitably support the vehicle.

3. Remove the appropriate rear tire and wheel assembly.

4. Remove the appropriate wheel drive shaft.

5. Using a flat bladed tool, remove the differential output shaft seal.

➥**Take care not to damage any sealing surfaces.**

To install:

6. Lubricate the wheel drive shaft sealing surface of the oil seal with (75W90) synthetic axle lubricant.

7. Install the differential output shaft seal (2) to the J 45017 seal driver.

8. Using the J 45017 (1), install the differential output shaft seal (2).

9. Remove J 45017 (1) from the differential output shaft seal (2).

10. Install the wheel drive shaft.

11. Inspect the fluid level.

12. Install the rear tire and wheel assembly.

13. Lower the vehicle.

REAR HALFSHAFTS

REMOVAL & INSTALLATION

See Figures 25 through 27.

1. Before servicing the vehicle, refer to the Precautions Section.

2. Raise and support the vehicle.

3. Remove the tire and wheel assembly.

4. Remove the rear brake rotor. Refer to Rear Brake Rotor Removal & Installation in the Brake Section.

✳✳ WARNING

The wheel drive shaft spindle nut must not be reused. Replace the wheel drive shaft spindle nut with a new nut whenever it is removed.

5. Remove and discard the wheel drive shaft spindle nut.

6. Using a Universal Hub Puller, disengage the wheel drive shaft from the wheel bearing/hub.

7. Remove the adjustment link.

8. Separate the upper ball joint from the rear knuckle.

9. Using a suitable tool, carefully release the wheel drive shaft from the rear differential enough to install the J 44394 seal protector.

✳✳ WARNING

J-44394 must be installed into the differential output shaft seal prior to removing and installing the wheel drive shaft. Failure to install J-44394 as indicated may cause the splines of the wheel drive shaft to cut the differential output seal.

10. Carefully install the J 44394 over the wheel drive shaft

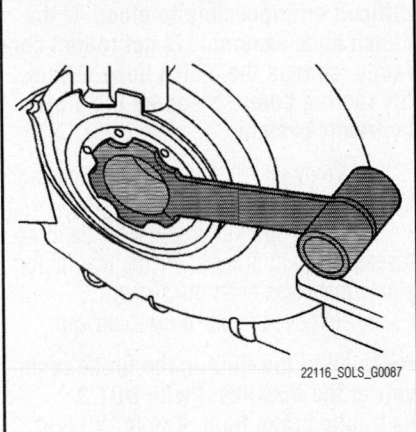

22116_SOLS_G0087

Fig. 26 J 44394 installed into the differential output shaft seal

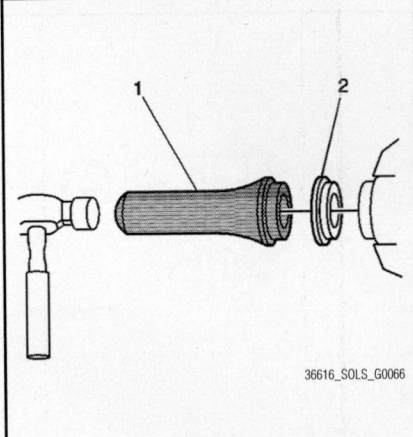

36616_SOLS_G0066

Fig. 24 Install the differential output shaft seal (2) to the J 45017 seal driver (1)

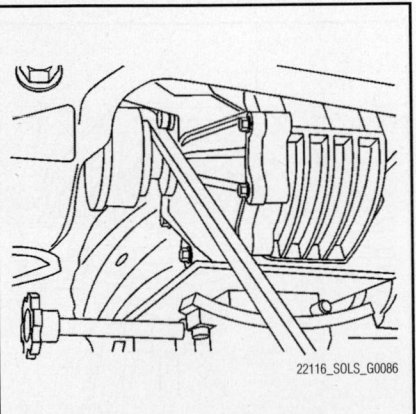

22116_SOLS_G0086

Fig. 25 Releasing the wheel drive shaft from the rear differential

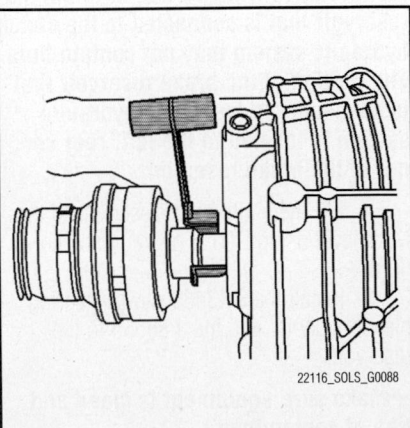

22116_SOLS_G0088

Fig. 27 J 44394 removal from the differential output shaft seal

11. Carefully slide the J 44394 into the differential output shaft seal.

12. Remove the wheel drive shaft from the vehicle.

13. If reusing the wheel drive shaft, remove and discard the wheel drive shaft retaining ring. The wheel drive shaft retaining ring is on the splined shaft of the cross groove joint.

To install:

14. Install the new wheel drive shaft retaining ring. The wheel drive shaft retaining ring is on the splined shaft of the cross groove joint.

15. If previously removed, carefully install J 44394 into the differential output shaft seal.

➡**In order to prevent lubricant leaks, use care when installing the wheel drive shaft to the differential. Do not damage the oil seal. Replace the oil seal if it becomes nicked, distorted, or is otherwise damaged.**

16. Carefully install the wheel drive shaft into the differential until the splines are past the J 44394. Ensure that the retaining ring is installed in the upright position.

17. Carefully remove the J 44394 from the differential output shaft seal.

18. Carefully remove J 44394 from the wheel drive shaft.

19. Carefully install the wheel drive shaft into the differential until the retaining ring is engaged.

20. Ensure the wheel drive shaft retaining ring is fully engaged to the differential by grasping the inner housing and pulling outward. The wheel drive shaft will stay positively engaged if properly installed to the differential.

21. Install the upper ball joint to the rear knuckle.

22. Loosely install the new wheel drive shaft spindle nut.

23. Install the adjustment link.

24. Use the new wheel drive shaft spindle nut to slowly pull the spindle to the wheel hub and bearing assembly.

25. Tighten the wheel drive shaft spindle nut to 159 ft. lbs. (215 Nm).

26. Install the rear brake rotor.

27. Install the tire and wheel assembly.

28. Inspect the differential lubricant level.

29. Lower the vehicle.

REAR PINION SEAL

REMOVAL & INSTALLATION

See Figures 28 through 30.

1. Before servicing the vehicle, refer to the Precautions Section.

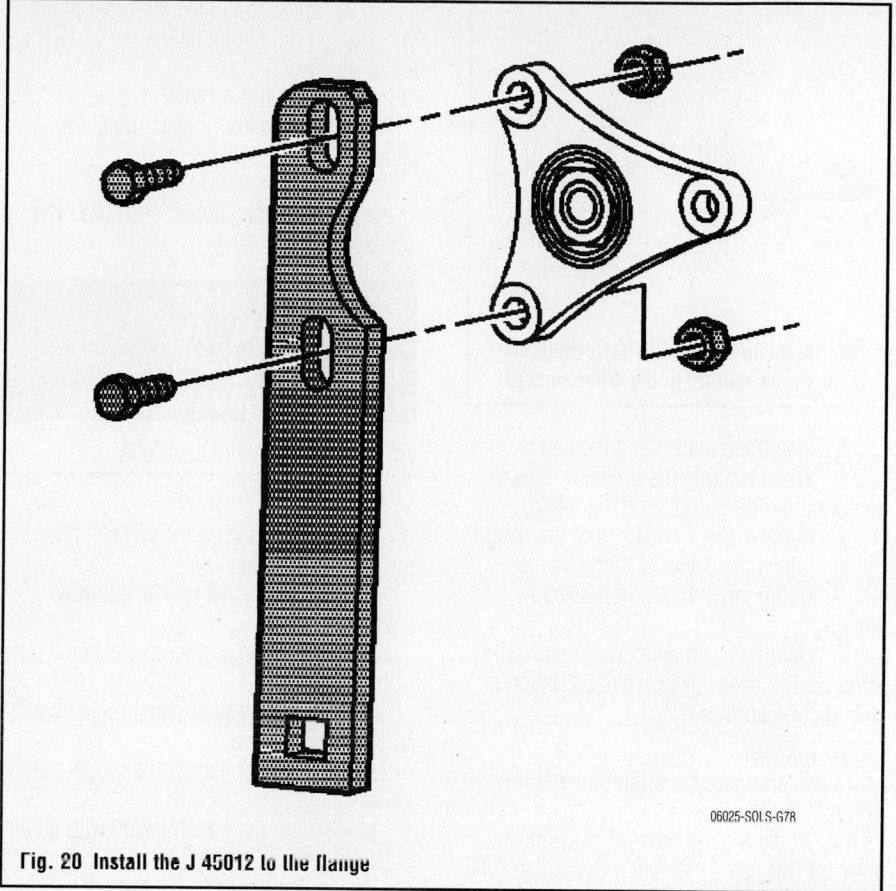

06025-SOLS-G78

Fig. 20 Install the J 45012 to the flange

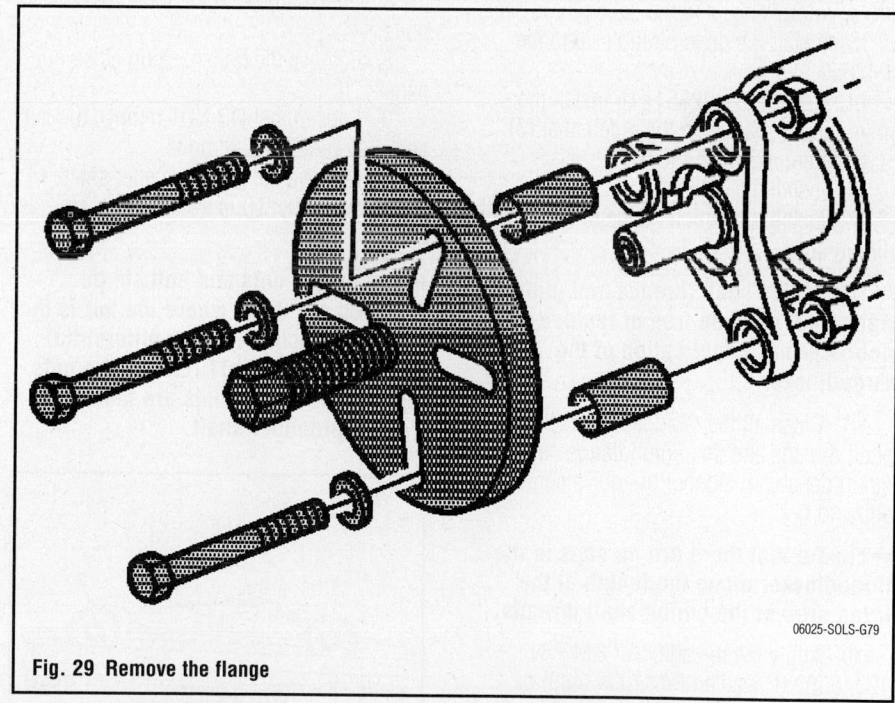

06025-SOLS-G79

Fig. 29 Remove the flange

2. Raise and support vehicle.

3. Remove the floor panel tunnel rear panel.

➡**Remove only the propeller shaft coupler to differential flange bolts. DO NOT remove the coupler from the propeller shaft.**

4. Remove the propeller shaft from the rear differential. Refer to Propeller Shaft Removal & Installation.

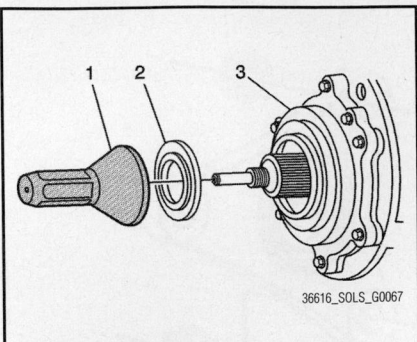

Fig. 30 Using the J 42851 (1), install the drive pinion seal (2) in the differential (3)

5. Install the J 45012 to the flange.

6. While holding the J 45012, remove the drive pinion nut using the J 34826 .

7. Remove the J 45012 from the flange.

8. Install the J 45019 to the flange.

9. Using the J 45019, remove the flange.

10. Using a flat-bladed tool, remove the drive pinion seal. Take care not to damage any sealing surfaces.

To install:

11. Ensure that the pinion bore is free of dirt and debris.

12. Apply a small amount of synthetic gear oil GM P/N 121378514 (Canadian P/N 88901045) or equivalent to the surface of the drive pinion flange and the drive pinion seal.

13. Install the drive pinion seal to the J 42851.

14. Using the J 42851 (1), install the drive pinion seal (2) in the differential (3).

15. Remove the J 45019 (1).

16. Install the J 45012.

17. Install the pinion flange to the drive pinion shaft.

➡**The pinion shaft threads and pinion flange nut must be free of residue and debris prior to application of the threadlocker.**

18. Clean all the residue from the pinion shaft threads and the pinion flange nut by using denatured alcohol or equivalent and allow to dry.

➡**Ensure that there are no gaps in the threadlocker along the length of the filled area of the pinion shaft threads.**

19. Apply the threadlocker GM P/N 12345382 (Canadian P/N 10953489) or equivalent to ⅔ of the threads length of the pinion shaft threads.

20. Allow the threadlocker to cure approximately 10 minutes before installation.

21. Install the drive pinion flange nut to the pinion shaft. While holding the J 45012,

use the J 34826 to tighten the drive pinion nut. Tighten the pinion flange nut to 181 ft. lbs. (245 Nm).

22. Remove the J 45012.

23. Install the floor panel tunnel rear panel.

24. Inspect the fluid level.

25. Remove the support and lower the vehicle.

PROPELLER SHAFT, DIFFERENTIAL, AND DRIVELINE SUPPORT (MANUAL TRANSMISSION)

REMOVAL & INSTALLATION

See Figures 31 through 35.

1. Before servicing the vehicle, refer to the Precautions Section.

2. Remove the left rear wheel drive shaft.

3. Remove the muffler and exhaust pipe from the vehicle.

4. Remove the floor panel tunnel panel front closeout panel.

5. Remove the floor panel tunnel rear panel

6. Support the transmission with a suitable jack stand.

7. Loosen but DO NOT remove the driveline support to the transmission bolts.

8. Remove the transmission close out panel.

9. Loosen, but DO NOT remove the left and right motor mount bolts.

10. Remove the front propeller shaft bolts and washer support tabs from the transmission.

➡**The proper nuts and bolts to be removed are those where the nut is the closest or facing the rear differential drive flange. DO NOT remove the nuts and bolt where the nuts are facing the front or propeller shaft.**

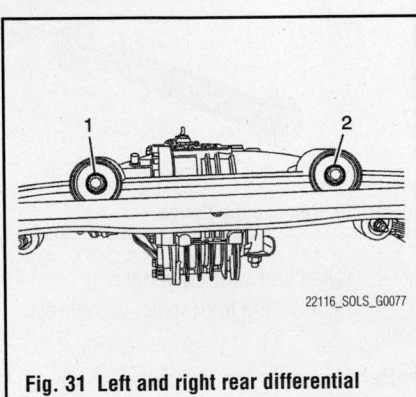

Fig. 31 Left and right rear differential mount bolts

11. Remove the propeller shaft nuts and bolts from the rear differential.

12. Support the rear differential with a transmission jack stand.

13. Remove the left and right rear differential mount bolts.

14. Lower the rear differential enough to clear the rear crossmember.

15. Using the J 44394 seal protector , move the rear differential to the left side of the vehicle, remove the right rear wheel drive shaft.

16. Remove the four differential carrier bracket bolts.

17. Separate the differential carrier from the driveline support bracket

18. Remove the propeller shaft from the vehicle.

➡**Steps 18 and 19 are for the replacing the driveline support.**

19. Remove the driveline support bolts and the washers from the transmission.

20. Remove the driveline support from the transmission and the rear differential assembly.

➡**Support the right rear wheel drive shaft with mechanics wire or equivalent.**

To install:

21. Clean the bolt holes in the differential carrier with brake cleaner or other suitable solvents to remove any adhesive.

22. If servicing the driveline support, position the driveline support (4) on the differential housing.

23. Install the bolt plate, bolts, nuts for the driveline support on the differential housing. Tighten the nuts to 177 ft. lbs. (240 Nm).

24. Position the driveline support on the transmission.

25. Install the driveline support bolts and washers. Leave the bolts loose.

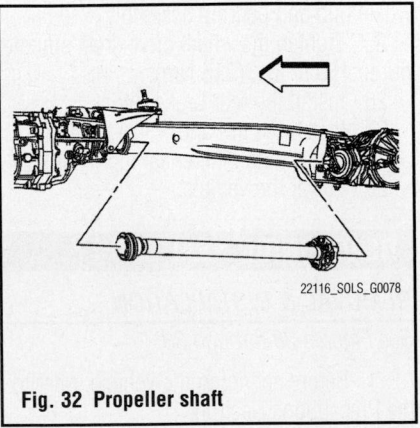

Fig. 32 Propeller shaft

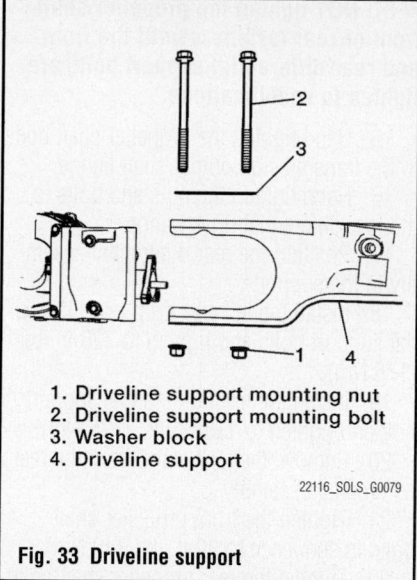

1. Driveline support mounting nut
2. Driveline support mounting bolt
3. Washer block
4. Driveline support

22116_SOLS_G0079

Fig. 33 Driveline support

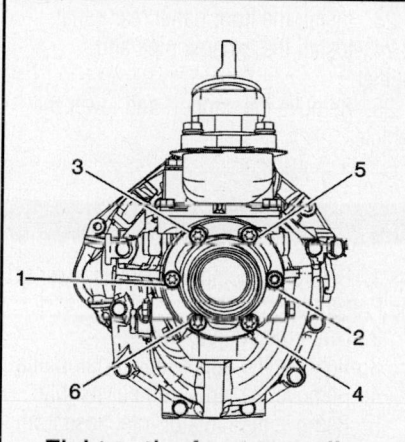

Tighten the front propeller shaft bolts in sequence (1-6).

22116_SOLS_G0080

Fig. 34 Front propeller shaft bolts tightening sequence

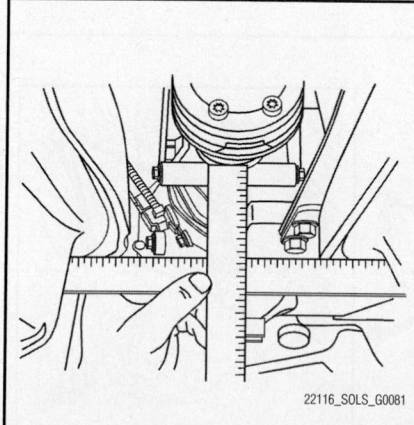

22116_SOLS_G0081

Fig. 35 Checking driveline angle measurement for (3.150 inch. (80 mm)

26. Raise the differential to just below the rear crossmember.

27. Clean the pilot shaft and the pilot hole of any dirt or debris

28. Apply a small amount of chassis lube on the pilot shaft.

29. Align the pilot shaft and the pilot hole.

30. Install the propeller shaft to the transmission and differential.

➡In steps 11 and 12, finger tighten the front and rear propeller shaft nuts and bolts only. DO NOT torque the propeller shaft nuts and bolts until the differential and driveline support have been aligned and torqued to specifications.

31. Install the propeller shaft bolts and washer support tabs in the transmission drive flange.

32. Install the propeller shaft nuts and bolts to the differential drive flange.

33. Remove the wheel drive shaft from the mechanics wire.

34. Position the J 44394 on the right wheel drive shaft.

35. Moving the differential to the right, install the wheel drive shaft.

36. Remove the J 44394 from the wheel drive shaft.

37. Align the differential carrier and the torque beam bracket.

38. Install the four new driveline support bracket bolts.

➡Use only hands tools to tighten the bolts.

39. Tighten the four new driveline support bracket bolts to 66 ft. lbs. (90 Nm).

40. Raise and position the differential in the rear support.

41. Hand install the left and right rear differential mounting bolts tighten to 129 ft. lbs. (175 Nm).

42. Tighten the rear propeller shaft bolts to 63 ft. lbs. (85 Nm).

43. Tighten the front propeller shaft bolts in sequence to 30 ft. lbs. (40 Nm).

44. Install the left rear wheel drive shaft.

✳✳ WARNING

Failing to perform the following service procedure will create the wrong driveline angle for the propeller shaft and alignment of the transmission and the rear differential.

45. Position a scale or known straight edge across the floor pan where the drive-line tunnel closeout mounts to the body.

46. Position another scale at the transmission output shaft oil seal slinger.

47. Using the jack stand, raise or lower the transmission until a measurement of 3.150 inch. (80 mm) is obtained.

48. Tighten the driveline support bolts at the transmission to 177 ft. lbs. (240 Nm).

49. Remove the jack stand from the rear differential.

50. Tighten the left and right motor mount bolts.

51. Remove the transmission jack stand.

52. Install the transmission close out panel.

53. Install the floor panel tunnel panel front closeout panel.

54. Install the floor panel tunnel rear panel.

55. Install the muffler and exhaust pipe from the vehicle.

PROPELLER SHAFT (AUTOMATIC TRANSMISSION)

REMOVAL & INSTALLATION

See Figures 36 through 38.

1. Before servicing the vehicle, refer to the Precautions Section.

2. Raise and support the vehicle.

3. Remove the exhaust pipe and muffler.

4. Remove the floor panel rear panel.

5. Support the rear differential assembly with a suitable jack stand.

6. Remove the left (1) and right (2) rear differential support bolts.

7. Remove the front differential support bolt.

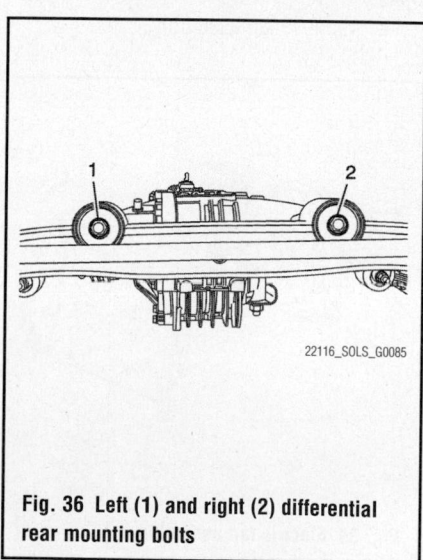

22116_SOLS_G0085

Fig. 36 Left (1) and right (2) differential rear mounting bolts

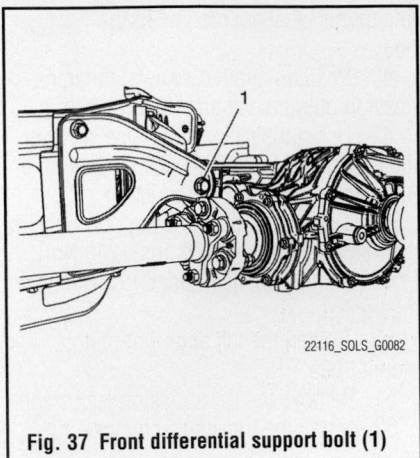

Fig. 37 Front differential support bolt (1)

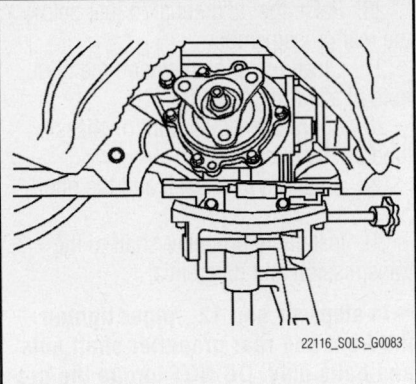

Fig. 38 Front propeller shaft bolts tightening sequence

➡ **DO NOT tighten the propeller shaft front or rear fasteners until the front and rear differential support bolts are tighten to specifications.**

8. Remove the propeller shaft bolts from the transmission output flange.

9. Remove the propeller shaft nut and bolts from the differential drive flange.

10. Lower the rear differential assembly enough to remove the propeller shaft from the vehicle.

To install:

11. Remove all debris from the pilot shaft.

12. Apply a small amount of chassis lube on the pilot shaft and pilot shaft hole in the propeller shaft.

13. Position the propeller shaft on the transmission output flange.

14. Raise the rear differential at the same time as aligning the propeller shaft pilot shaft and the propeller shaft pilot hole.

15. Hand tighten the propeller shaft bolts to the transmission output shaft flange.

16. Hand tighten the nuts and bolts to the rear differential drive flange.

17. Position the rear differential assembly in the support.

18. Install the left and right rear differential support bolts and tighten to 129 ft. lbs. (175 Nm).

19. Install the front differential support bolt and tighten to 129 ft. lbs. (175 Nm).

20. Remove the jack stand from the rear differential assembly.

21. Tighten the front propeller shaft bolts in sequence to 30 ft. lbs. (40 Nm).

22. Tighten the rear propeller shaft bolts to 63 ft. lbs. (85 Nm).

23. Install the floor panel rear panel.

24. Install the exhaust pipe and muffler.

25. Remove the support and lower the vehicle.

ENGINE COOLING

ENGINE FAN

REMOVAL & INSTALLATION

See Figure 39.

1. Before servicing the vehicle, refer to the Precautions Section.

2. Remove the air cleaner assembly.

3. Remove the air cleaner duct.

4. Disconnect the cooling fan motor electrical connector.

5. Remove fan assembly mounting bolts.

6. Remove fan assembly.

To install:

7. Install fan assembly.

8. Install fan assembly mounting bolts and tighten to 18 ft. lbs. (25 Nm).

9. Reconnect the cooling fan motor electrical connector.

10. Install the air cleaner duct.

11. Install the air cleaner assembly.

RADIATOR

REMOVAL & INSTALLATION

See Figure 40.

1. Before servicing the vehicle, refer to the Precautions Section.

2. Drain the cooling system.

3. Remove the upper radiator air baffle.

4. Remove the fan shroud assembly.

5. Remove the radiator inlet hose from the radiator.

6. Remove the radiator outlet hose from the radiator.

7. Remove the surge tank inlet hose from radiator.

8. Remove the radiator support brackets.

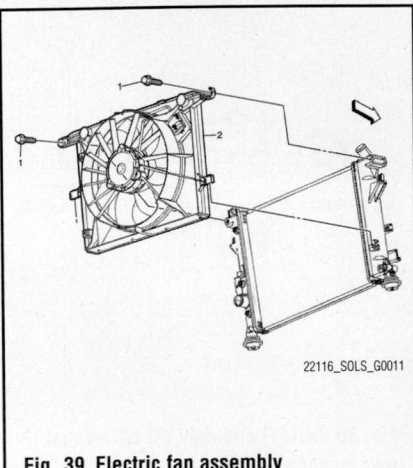

Fig. 39 Electric fan assembly

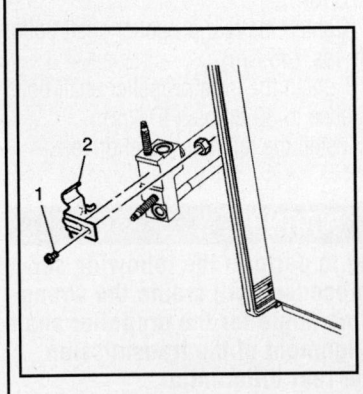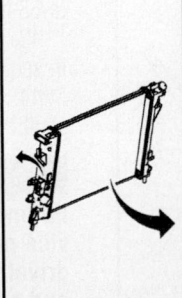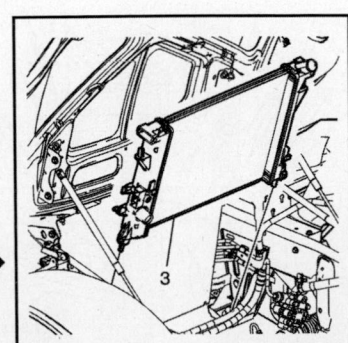

Fig. 40 Radiator assembly, (3) condenser bracket, (2) bolt, (1)

9. Remove the A/C condenser bolt and bracket.

10. Remove radiator assembly.

To install:

11. Install radiator assembly.

12. Install the A/C condenser bolt and bracket.

13. Tighten the condenser bracket bolt to 80 inch lbs. (9 Nm).

14. Install the radiator support brackets and tighten to 80 inch lbs. (9 Nm).

15. Install the surge tank inlet hose to the radiator.

16. Install the radiator outlet and inlet hoses to the radiator.

17. Install the fan shroud assembly.

18. Install the upper radiator air baffle.

19. Refill and bleed cooling system.

20. Check for leaks.

THERMOSTAT

REMOVAL & INSTALLATION

See Figure 41.

1. Before servicing the vehicle, refer to the Precautions Section.

2. Drain the cooling system.

3. Remove the air inlet grill panel.

4. Reposition the radiator outlet hose clamp at the thermostat housing.

5. Remove the radiator outlet hose from the thermostat housing.

6. For 2.4L engines, remove the radiator outlet hose clip from the outlet hose bracket.

7. Remove the thermostat housing cover bolts and cover.

8. Remove the thermostat.

9. Remove and discard the thermostat housing O ring seal.

To install:

10. Install a new thermostat housing cover O-ring seal onto the housing.

11. Install the thermostat housing cover and bolts.

12. Tighten mounting bolts to 89 inch lbs. (10 Nm).

13. Install the radiator outlet hose to the thermostat housing.

14. Reposition the radiator outlet hose clamp at the thermostat housing.

15. Install the radiator outlet hose clip to the outlet hose bracket.

16. Install the air inlet grill panel.

17. Fill and bleed the cooling system.

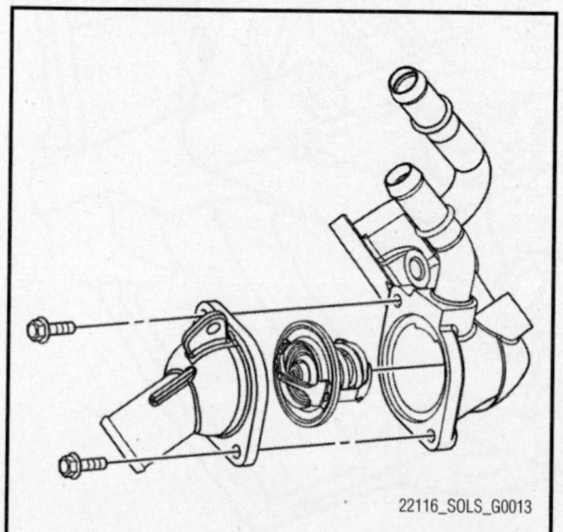

THERMOSTAT HOUSING

REMOVAL & INSTALLATION

See Figures 41 and 42.

1. Before servicing the vehicle, refer to the Precautions Section.

➡**A drain has been provided at the bottom of the water pump for engine block coolant drainage.**

2. Drain the cooling system.

3. Drain the coolant from the engine block at the water pump drain. After the coolant has drained, tighten the drain bolt. Tighten the drain plug to 15 ft. lbs. (20 Nm).

4. Lower the vehicle.

5. Remove the air inlet grill panel.

6. Disconnect the engine wiring harness electrical connector from the Engine Coolant Temperature (ECT) sensor.

7. Remove the ECT sensor, if necessary.

8. Reposition the radiator outlet hose clamp at the thermostat housing.

9. Remove the radiator outlet hose from the thermostat housing.

10. For 2.0L engines, remove the catalytic converter. Refer to Catalytic Converter Removal & Installation in the Engine Mechanical Section.

11. Remove the radiator outlet hose clip from the outlet hose bracket.

12. For 2.4L engines, remove the exhaust heat shield and bolts.

13. Reposition the heater inlet and outlet hose clamps at the thermostat housing pipes.

14. Disconnect the heater inlet and outlet hoses from the thermostat housing pipes.

15. Remove the thermostat housing bolts.

➡**Twist the water transfer pipe while pulling in order to remove it from the water pump.**

16. Remove the thermostat housing from the vehicle.

17. Remove the water transfer pipe from the thermostat housing, if necessary.

18. Remove and discard the water transfer pipe O-ring seals, if necessary.

19. Remove the thermostat housing cover bolts and cover, if necessary.

20. Remove the thermostat, if necessary.

21. Remove and discard the thermostat housing O-ring seal, if necessary.

22. Remove all debris and thread sealant from the engine coolant temperature sensor and bolt holes if the housing is being re-used.

To install:

23. Install a NEW thermostat housing cover O-ring seal into the recess groove.

24. Install the thermostat, if necessary.

25. Install the thermostat housing cover bolts, if necessary. Tighten the bolts to 89 inch lbs. (10 Nm).

26. Install a NEW thermostat housing to engine gasket onto the thermostat housing.

27. Load the thermostat housing assembly into position while the vehicle is lowered.

28. Raise and support the vehicle.

➡**The water feed pipe seals can be lightly lubricated with coolant to aid during installation.**

29. Install NEW O-ring seals onto the water feed pipe.

➡**Lubricate the O-rings with coolant ONLY.**

30. Install the water feed pipe into the thermostat housing aligning locator tab.

31. Align the water pipe to water pump.

32. Seat the water feed O-ring seal by pushing inward toward the water pump. Take care not to tear or damage the O-ring.

33. Lower the vehicle.

34. Position the thermostat housing against the engine.

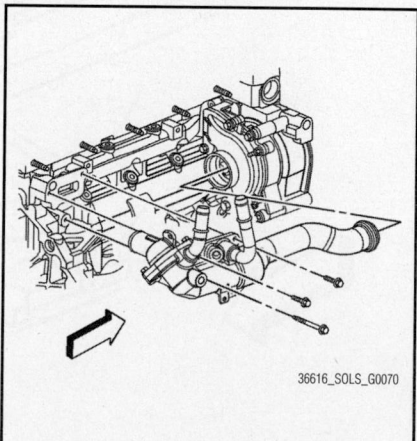

22116_SOLS_G0013

Fig. 41 Thermostat and housing assembly

36616_SOLS_G0070

Fig. 42 Thermostat housing and bolts

35. Install the thermostat housing bolts and tighten to 89 inch lbs. (10 Nm).

36. Connect the heater inlet and outlet hoses to the thermostat housing pipes.

37. Position the heater inlet and outlet hose clamps at the thermostat housing pipes.

38. For 2.0L engines, install the catalytic converter.

39. For 2.4L engines, install the exhaust heat shield and bolts and tighten the bolts to 17 ft. lbs. (23 Nm).

40. Install the radiator outlet hose to the thermostat housing.

41. Reposition the radiator outlet hose clamp at the thermostat housing.

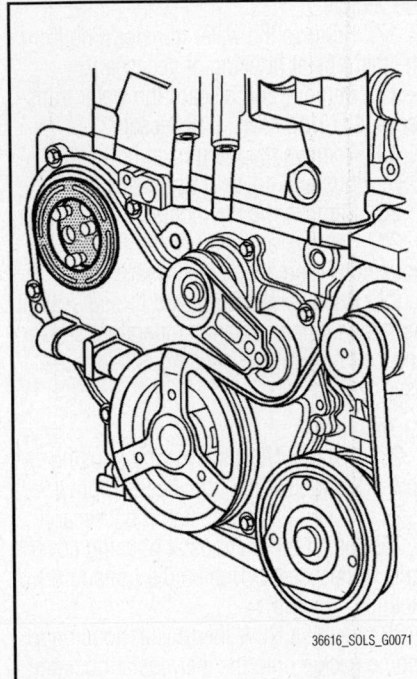

36616_SOLS_G0071

Fig. 43 Water pump holding tool—2.4L engine

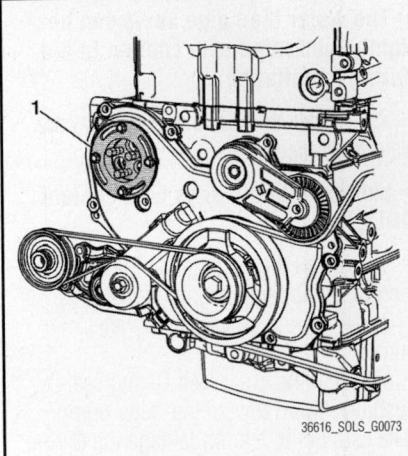

36616_SOLS_G0073

Fig. 44 Water pump holding tool—2.0L engine

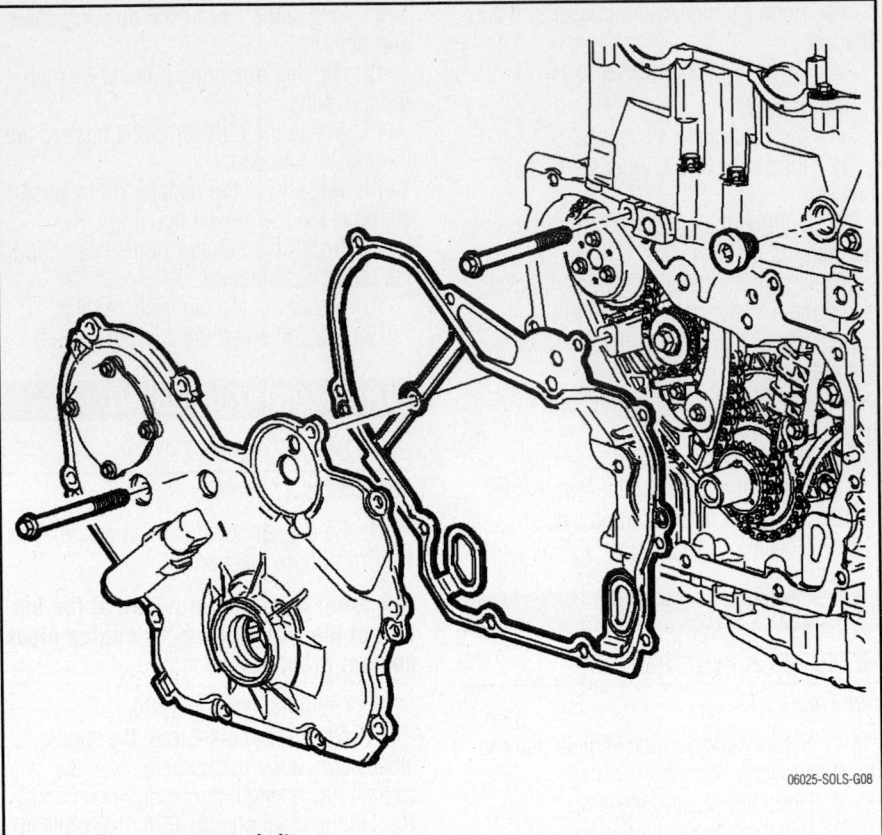

06025-SOLS-G08

Fig. 45 Front water pump bolts

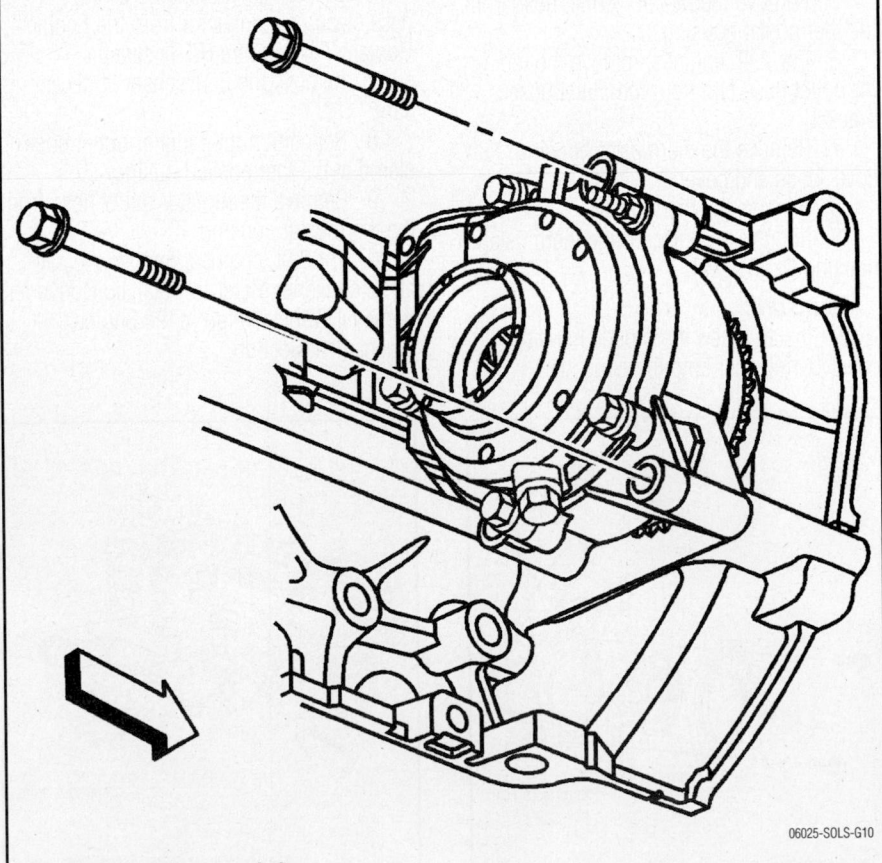

06025-SOLS-G10

Fig. 46 Rear water pump bolts

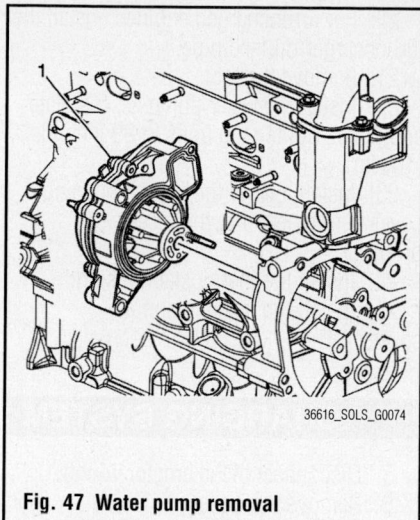

Fig. 47 Water pump removal

42. Install the radiator outlet hose clip to the outlet hose bracket.

43. If reinstalling the old sensor, coat the threads with sealant.

44. Install the ECT sensor, if necessary. Tighten the sensor to 15 ft lbs (20 Nm).

45. Connect the engine wiring harness electrical connector to the ECT sensor.

46. Install the air inlet grill panel.

➡ **The vehicle must be level when filling the cooling system.**

47. Verify the drain plugs at the radiator and water pump are tightened.

48. Fill the cooling system.

49. Lower the vehicle.

50. Inspect for any leaks.

WATER PUMP

REMOVAL & INSTALLATION

See Figures 43 through 48.

1. Before servicing the vehicle, refer to the Precautions Section.

2. Remove the intake manifold cover. Refer to Intake Manifold Removal & Installation in the Engine Mechanical Section.

3. Remove the thermostat housing. Refer to Thermostat Housing Removal & Installation.

4. Remove the water pump access plate from the front cover.

➡ **A drain plug has been provided at the bottom of the water pump assembly for additional coolant drainage from the engine block and water pump.**

5. Drain the coolant from the water pump using the plug at the bottom of the pump.

➡ **The water pump holding tool supports the sprocket and chain during water pump service. The tool must be used or the balance shaft must be re-timed.**

6. Install water pump holding tool J 43651 into position.

7. Tighten the bolts on the water pump holding tool into the threads on the water pump sprocket.

8. Install the access cover bolts that were removed earlier to secure the water pump holding tool to the front cover assembly.

9. Remove the 3 inner water pump sprocket to water pump bolts.

10. For turbocharged engines, remove the turbocharger oil feed pipe.

11. Remove the 2 water pump bolts.

➡ **Be sure to remove both water pump bolts from the front of the engine block.**

12. Remove the rear 2 water pump bolts.

13. Remove the water pump.

14. Remove and discard the water pump O-ring seal.

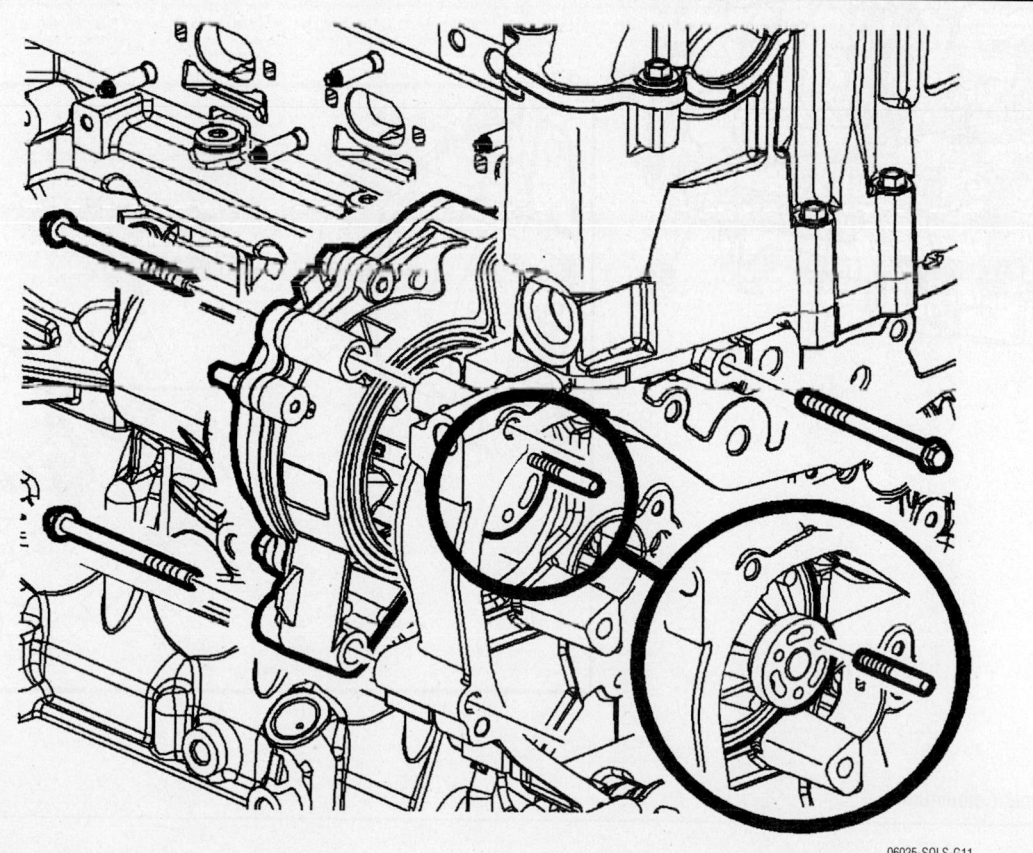

Fig. 48 Guide pin installation

To install:

➡️ **Prior to installing the water pump, read the entire procedure. This will help avoid balance shaft chain re-timing and ensure proper sealing.**

15. Install a NEW water pump O-ring seal.

➡️ **A guide pin can be created to aid in water pump alignment. Use an M 6 m x 6 mm stud. Thread the pin into the water pump sprocket.**

16. Using the guide pin, align the pin with the water pump holding tool.

17. Position the water pump against the engine block and hand tighten the water pump bolts.

18. Install the inner water pump sprocket bolts. After 2 are snug, remove the guide pin and install the 3rd bolt. Tighten the bolts to 25 Nm (18 ft. lbs.).

19. Tighten the water pump sprocket bolts last. Tighten the bolts to 89 inch lbs. (10 Nm).

20. For turbocharged engines, install the turbocharger oil feed pipe.

21. Remove the tool.

22. Install the water pump access plate and bolts. Tighten the bolts to 89 inch lbs. (10 Nm).

23. Install a NEW thermostat housing cover O-ring seal into the recess groove.

24. Install the thermostat housing.

25. Install the intake manifold cover.

ENGINE ELECTRICAL

ALTERNATOR

REMOVAL & INSTALLATION
See Figure 49.

1. Before servicing the vehicle, refer to the Precautions Section.

2. Disconnect the negative battery cable. Refer to Negative Battery Cable Disconnection & Connection.

3. Remove the air cleaner outlet duct.

4. Remove the drive belt.

CHARGING SYSTEM

5. Disconnect the alternator wiring.

6. Remove the bolts.

To install:

7. Installation is the reverse of removal. Tighten the mounting bolts to 16 ft. lbs. (22 Nm).

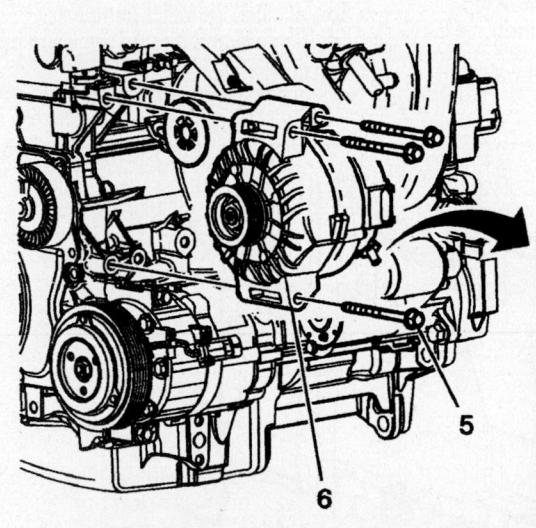

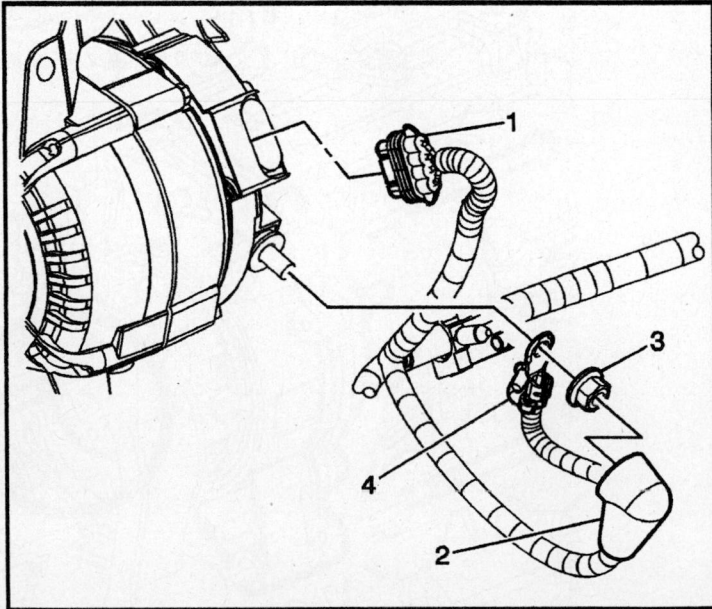

06025-SOLS-G05

Fig. 49 Alternator mounting

IGNITION COIL

REMOVAL & INSTALLATION

2.0L (LNF) Engine

See Figures 50 and 51.

1. Before servicing the vehicle, refer to the Precautions Section.
2. Remove the air cleaner assembly.
3. Disconnect the ignition coil electrical connectors.
4. Remove the ignition coil bolts.
5. Remove the ignition coils.

To install:

6. Apply dielectric compound to the spark plug boots and make sure no corrosion is present.

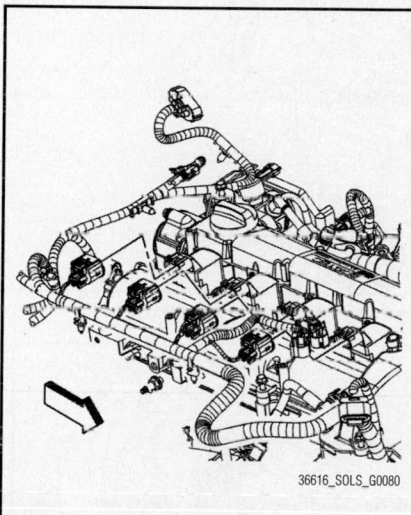

Fig. 50 Disconnect the ignition coil electrical connectors

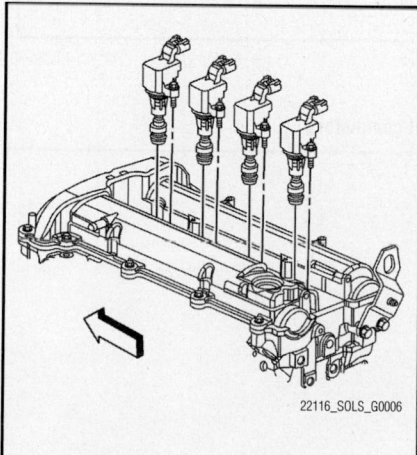

Fig. 51 Ignition coils removed

7. Install the ignition coils.
8. Install the ignition coil bolts and tighten to 89 inch lbs. (10 Nm).
9. Connect the ignition coil electrical connectors.
10. Install the air cleaner assembly.

2.4L (LE5) Engine

See Figures 51 and 52.

1. Before servicing the vehicle, refer to the Precautions Section.
2. Remove the intake manifold cover. Refer to Intake Manifold Removal & Installation in the Engine Mechanical Section.
3. Disconnect the ignition coil electrical connectors.
4. Remove the ignition coil bolts.
5. Remove the ignition coils.

To install:

6. Apply dielectric compound to the spark plug boots and make sure no corrosion is present.
7. Install the ignition coils.
8. Install the ignition coil bolts and tighten to 89 inch lbs. (10 Nm).
9. Connect the ignition coil electrical connectors.
10. Install the intake manifold cover.

IGNITION TIMING

ADJUSTMENT

The ignition timing is controlled by the Powertrain Control Module (PCM). No adjustment is necessary or possible.

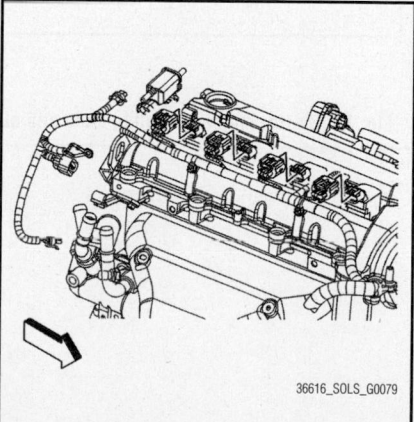

Fig. 52 Disconnect the ignition coil electrical connectors

SPARK PLUGS

REMOVAL & INSTALLATION

2.0L (LNF) Engine

See Figure 53.

> **✳ WARNING**
>
> **This engine has aluminum cylinder heads. Do not remove the spark plugs from a hot engine, allow it to cool first. Removing the spark plugs from a hot engine may cause spark plug thread damage or cylinder head damage.**

1. Before servicing the vehicle, refer to the Precautions Section.
2. Remove the ignition coils. Refer to Ignition Coil Module Removal & Installation.

> **✳ WARNING**
>
> **Make sure that any water and/or debris is blown out of the spark plug holes prior to removing the spark plugs.**

3. Remove the spark plugs using a ⅝ inch spark plug socket

To install:

➡**Do not coat spark plug threads with anti-seize compound. If anti-seize compound is used and spark plugs are over-torqued, damage to the cylinder head threads may result.**

4. Check that the spark plug gap is 0.035 inch. (0.90 mm).

Fig. 53 Spark plugs

5. Install the spark plugs.

6. Tighten the plugs to 15 ft. lbs. (20 Nm).

7. Apply dielectric compound to the spark plug boots and make sure no corrosion is present.

8. Install the ignition coils.

2.4L (LE5) Engine

See Figure 51.

1. Before servicing the vehicle, refer to the Precautions Section.

2. Remove the ignition coils. Refer to Ignition Coil Module Removal & Installation.

✳✳ WARNING

Make sure that any water and/or debris is blown out of the spark plug holes prior to removing the spark plugs.

3. Remove the spark plugs using a ⅝ inch spark plug socket.

To install:

➡**Do not coat spark plug threads with anti-seize compound. If anti-seize compound is used and spark plugs are over-torqued, damage to the cylinder head threads may result.**

4. Check that the spark plug gap is 0.040 inch. (1.0 mm).

5. Install the spark plugs.

6. Tighten the plugs to 15 ft. lbs. (20 Nm).

7. Apply dielectric compound to the spark plug boots and make sure no corrosion is present.

8. Install the ignition coils.

ENGINE ELECTRICAL

STARTING SYSTEM

STARTER

REMOVAL & INSTALLATION

See Figure 54.

1. Before servicing the vehicle, refer to the Precautions Section.

2. Disconnect the negative battery cable.

3. Remove the intake manifold. Refer to Intake Manifold Removal & Installation in the Engine Mechanical Section.

4. Disconnect the positive battery cable and nut.

5. Disconnect the starter solenoid terminal nut.

6. Disconnect the starter solenoid "S" terminal nut.

7. Remove engine harness terminals.

8. Remove starter motor bolts.

9. Remove starter motor.

To install:

10. Install starter motor and tighten mounting bolts to 30 ft. lbs. (40 Nm).

11. Install the engine harness terminals

12. Reconnect the starter solenoid "S" terminal nut. Tighten to 27 inch lbs. (3 Nm).

13. Reconnect the starter solenoid nut. Tighten to 89 inch lbs. (10 Nm).

14. Install the intake manifold.

15. Connect the negative battery cable.

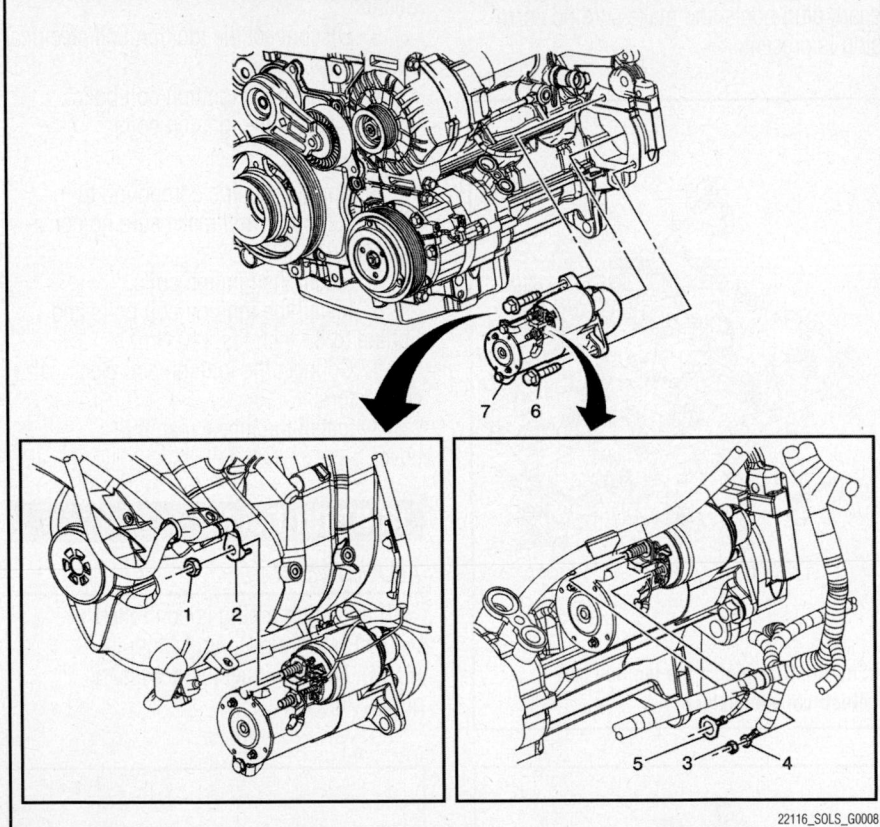

22116_SOLS_G0008

Fig. 54 Starter motor, mounting bolts and electrical connectors

ENGINE MECHANICAL

ACCESSORY DRIVE BELTS

ACCESSORY BELT ROUTING

See Figures 55 and 56.

INSPECTION

Inspect the drive belt for signs of glazing or cracking. A glazed belt will be perfectly smooth from slippage, while a good belt will have a slight texture of fabric visible. Cracks will usually start at the inner edge of the belt and run outward. All worn or damaged drive belts should be replaced immediately.

ADJUSTMENT

The drive belts for this model are equipped with automatic belt tensioners.

REMOVAL & INSTALLATION

Primary Drive Belt

See Figures 57 and 58.

1. Before servicing the vehicle, refer to the Precautions Section.
2. Remove the intake manifold cover. Refer to Intake Manifold Removal & Installation.
3. Raise the vehicle.

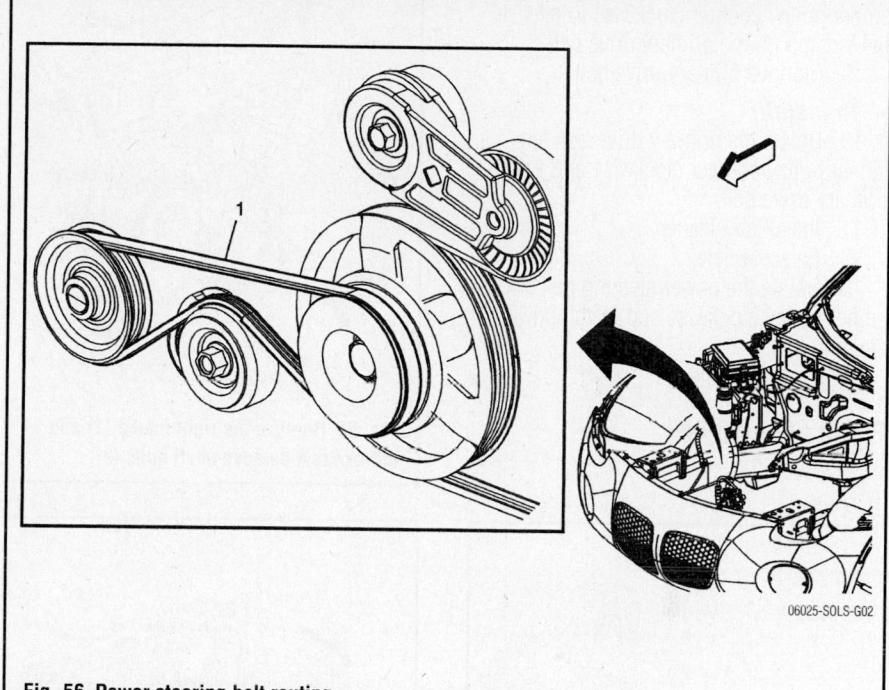

06025-SOLS-G02

Fig. 56 Power steering belt routing

4. Rotate the power steering belt tensioner pulley clockwise to release the tension on the power steering pump drive belt.
5. Remove power steering drive belt.

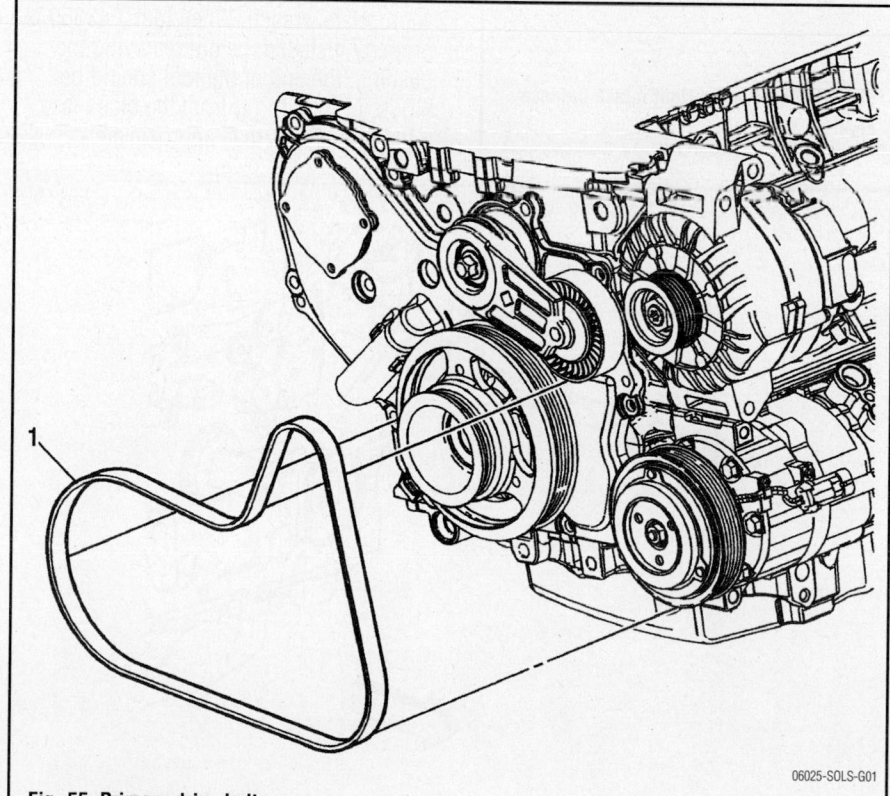

06025-SOLS-G01

Fig. 55 Primary drive belt

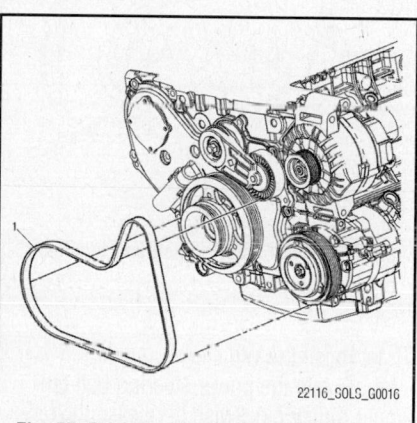

22116_SOLS_G001G

Fig. 57 Primary drive belt—with A/C shown

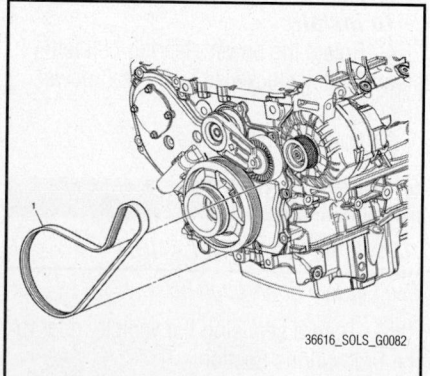

36616_SOLS_G0082

Fig. 58 Primary drive belt—without A/C shown

6. Lower vehicle.

7. Remove the air cleaner.

8. Rotate the primary drive belt tensioner pulley counter clockwise to release the tension on the primary drive belt.

9. Remove primary drive belt.

To install:

10. Rotate the primary drive belt tensioner pulley counter clockwise and install primary drive belt.

11. Install air cleaner.

12. Raise vehicle.

13. Rotate the power steering belt tensioner pulley clockwise and install power steering belt.

14. Lower vehicle.

Power Steering Belt

See Figure 59.

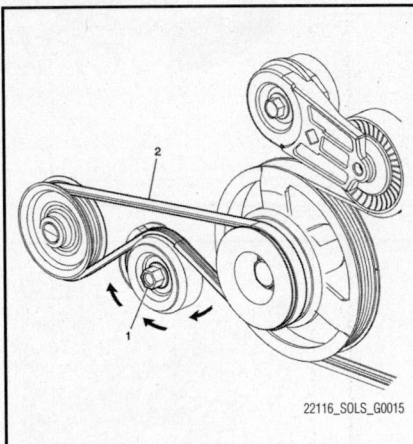

Fig. 59 Power steering belt and tensioner rotation shown

1. Raise the vehicle.

2. Rotate the power steering belt tensioner pulley clockwise to release the tension on the power steering pump drive belt.

3. Remove power steering drive belt.

To install:

4. Rotate the power steering belt tensioner pulley clockwise and install power steering belt.

5. Lower vehicle.

BALANCE SHAFT

REMOVAL & INSTALLATION

See Figures 60 through 66.

1. Before servicing the vehicle, refer to the Precautions Section.

2. Remove the radiator. Refer to Radiator Removal & Installation in the Engine Cooling Section.

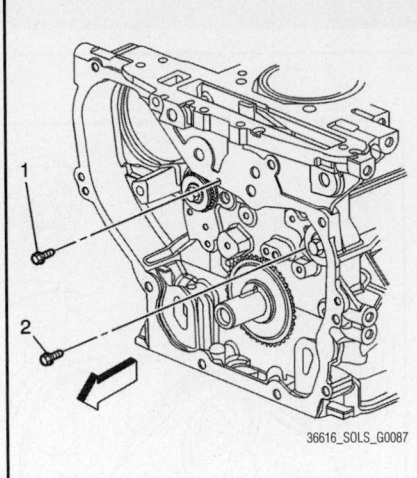

Fig. 60 Remove the right intake (1) and left exhaust balance shaft bolts (2)

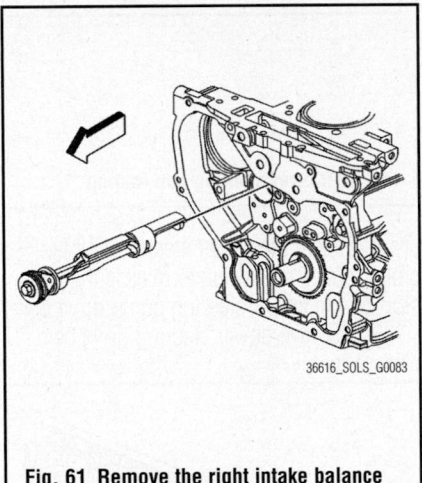

Fig. 61 Remove the right intake balance shaft

3. Remove A/C condenser.

4. Remove the timing chain, sprocket and tensioner. Refer to Timing Chain & Sprocket Removal & Installation.

5. Remove the right intake balance shaft bolt (1).

6. Remove the left exhaust balance shaft bolt (2).

➡**DO NOT remove the bolt holding the sprocket.**

7. Remove the right intake balance shaft and left exhaust balance shaft.

✳✳ WARNING

Proper centering of the tool is required on the balance shaft bushing. If the tool is not properly centered then damage to the bearing bore and block will occur.

8. Install tool J 43650 into the balance shaft holes. Insert the tool with the foot parallel to the shaft.

9. When the tool is inserted in the block, turn the tool so that the foot becomes perpendicular to the shaft.

10. Center the foot of the tool on the balance shaft bushing.

11. Once the tool is centered on the balance shaft bushing, then insert the centering guide into the front balance shaft bore and tighten the nut with an appropriate wrench. When tool J 43650 is properly installed, before removing the bushing, the end of the tool should be 4.6 in. (116 mm) (a) from the block face. If the tool is less than approximately

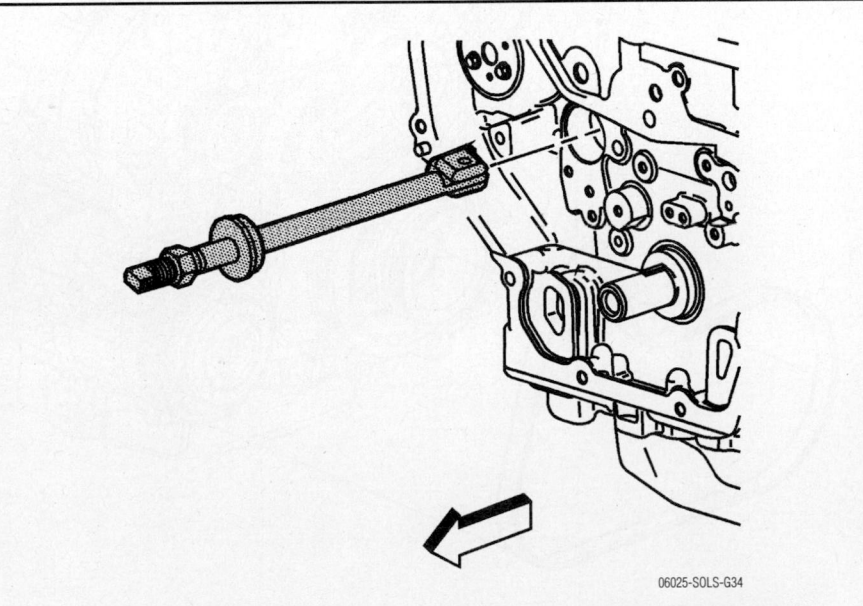

Fig. 62 Install tool J 43650 into the balance shaft hole—right side shown, left side similar

Fig. 63 The end of the tool should be 4.6 in. (116 mm) (a) from the block face

06025-SOLS-G35

Fig. 64 Remove the right intake balance shaft—right side shown, left side similar

36616_SOLS_G0084

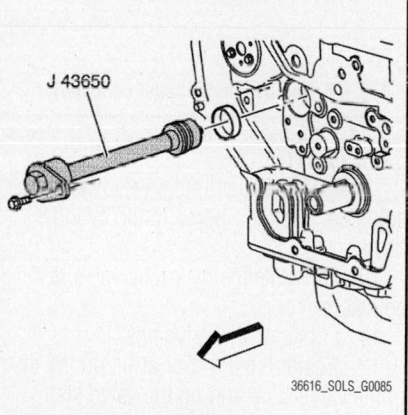

Fig. 65 Install the balance shaft bushing using tool J 43650—right side shown, left side similar

36616_SOLS_G0085

4.5 in. (114 mm) (a), recheck the tool alignment.

12. Tighten the nut on tool J 43650 until the tension releases. When the tension releases, remove the tool and the balance shaft bushing.

To install:

→Service the balance shaft as an assembly. DO NOT disassemble or assemble the balance shaft.

13. Install the balance shaft bushing using tool J 43650.

14. Seat the balance shaft bushing into the bore using tool J 43650 and a wrench.

15. When tool J 43650 is fully seated in the engine block remove it with a wrench.

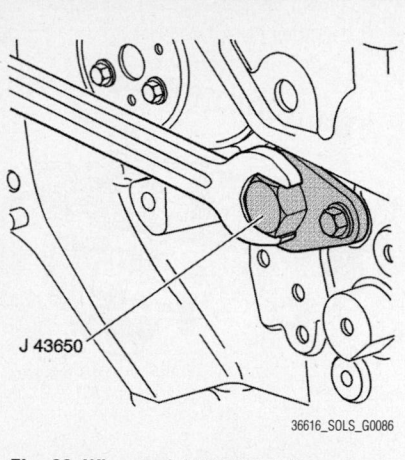

Fig. 66 When tool J 43650 is fully seated in the engine block remove it with a wrench

36616_SOLS_G0086

→If the balance shafts are not properly timed to the engine, the engine may vibrate or make noise.

16. Place the number one piston at Top Dead Center (TDC).

17. Lubricate the balance shaft lobes with engine oil.

18. Install the right intake and left exhaust balance shafts.

19. Install the right intake and left exhaust balance shaft bolts. Tighten to 89 inch lbs. (10 Nm).

20. Install the timing chain, sprocket and tensioner.

21. Install the A/C condenser.

22. Install the radiator.

CAMSHAFT & VALVE LIFTERS

REMOVAL & INSTALLATION

2.0L (LNF) Engine

Exhaust

See Figures 67 through 71.

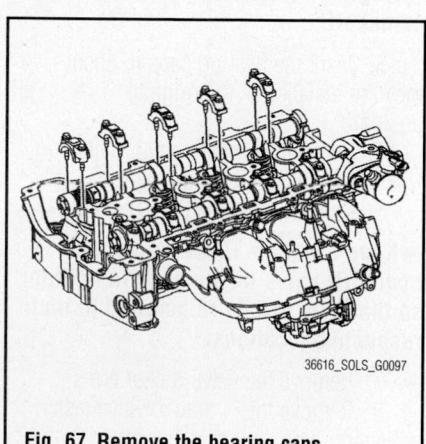

Fig. 67 Remove the bearing caps

36616_SOLS_G0097

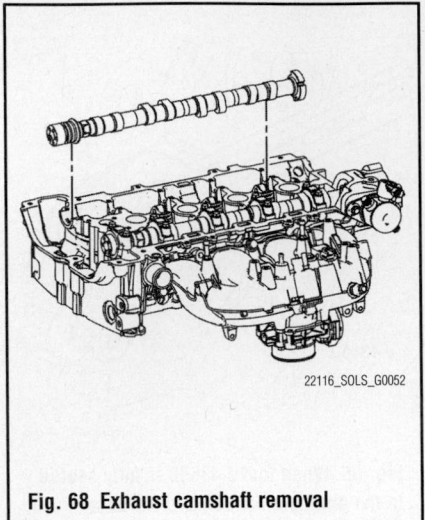

Fig. 68 Exhaust camshaft removal

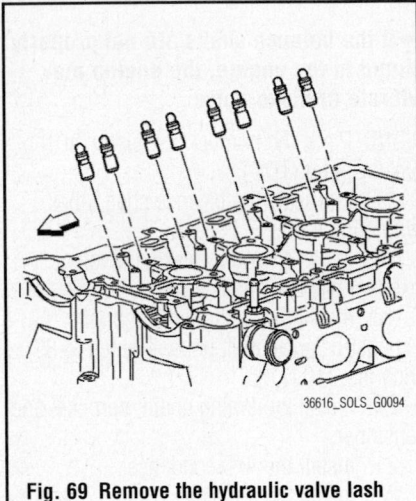

Fig. 69 Remove the hydraulic valve lash adjusters

1. Before servicing the vehicle, refer to the Precautions Section.

2. Remove the exhaust camshaft position actuator.

➡**Remove each bolt on each cap one turn at a time until there is no spring tension pushing on the camshaft.**

3. Mark the bearing caps to ensure they are installed in the original position.

4. Remove the bearing cap bolts.

5. Remove the bearing caps.

6. Remove the exhaust camshaft.

➡**Keep all of the rocker arms and hydraulic valve lash adjusters in order so that they can be reinstalled in their respective locations.**

7. Remove the valve rocker arms.

8. Remove the hydraulic valve lash adjusters.

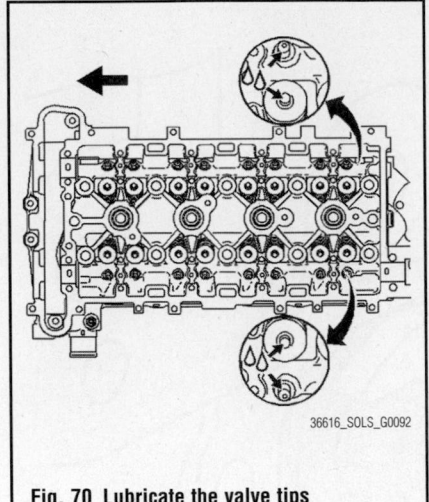

Fig. 70 Lubricate the valve tips

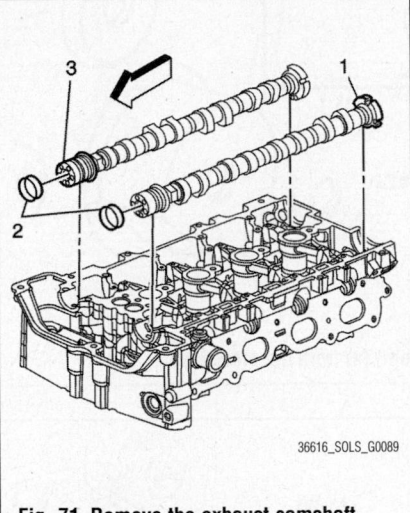

Fig. 71 Remove the exhaust camshaft

To install:

9. Install the hydraulic valve lash adjusters into their bores in the cylinder head.

10. Lubricate the hydraulic valve lash adjusters.

11. Lubricate the valve tips.

12. Position the rocker arms on the tip of the valve stem and on the valve lash adjuster. Lubricate the rocker arms.

➡**Used rocker arms MUST be returned to the original position on the camshaft. If the camshaft is being replaced, the rocker arms MUST also be replaced.**

13. Position the rocker arms on the tip of the valve stem and on the valve lash adjuster. Lubricate the rocker arms.

14. Install the exhaust camshaft. Lubricate the camshaft.

15. Position the camshaft bearing caps. Install the bearing cap bolts hand tight.

16. Tighten the bearing cap bolts in increments of 3 turns until they are seated.

17. Tighten the bolts to 89 inch lbs. (10 Nm).

18. Install the camshaft position exhaust actuator.

19. Install the camshaft cover with new gasket and tighten to 89 inch lbs. (10 Nm).

Intake

See Figures 72 through 77.

1. Before servicing the vehicle, refer to the Precautions Section.

2. Remove the intake camshaft position actuator.

➡**Remove each bolt on each cap one turn at a time until there is no spring tension pushing on the camshaft.**

3. Mark the bearing caps to ensure they are installed in the original position.

4. Remove the bearing cap bolts.

5. Remove the bearing caps.

6. Remove the intake camshaft (1).

➡**Keep all of the roller followers and hydraulic adjusters in order so that they can be reinstalled in their respective locations.**

7. Remove the camshaft roller followers.

8. Remove the hydraulic element adjusters.

To install:

9. Install the hydraulic element lash adjusters into their bores in the cylinder head. Install the camshaft caps and hand start the camshaft cap bolts.

10. Install the camshaft caps.

11. Tighten the camshaft cap bolts in increments of 3 turns until they are seated. Tighten the camshaft caps to 89 inch lbs. (10 Nm).

❈❈ WARNING

It is critical during installation to ensure the bearing rear cap and cylinder head alignment is correct and the mating surfaces are flush.

12. Ensure that all sealing material has been removed from the components, and the sealing surfaces are clean and free of contamination prior to applying the sealer.

13. Install and align the rear cap within 20 minutes of applying the sealer. Apply the

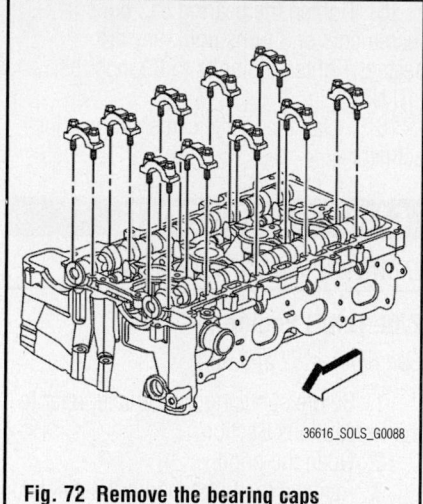

Fig. 72 Remove the bearing caps

Fig. 74 Remove the camshaft roller followers

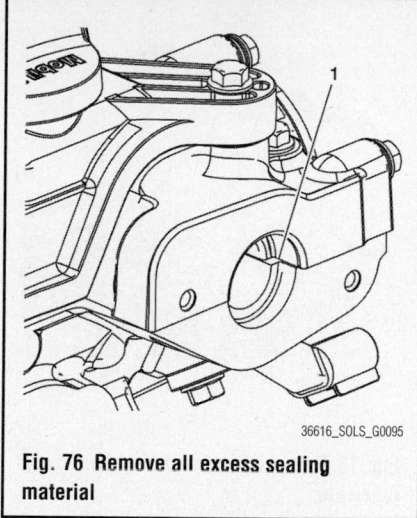

Fig. 76 Remove all excess sealing material

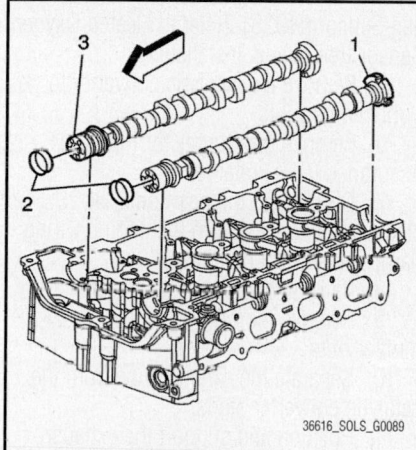

Fig. 73 Remove the intake camshaft (1) or exhaust camshaft (3), as necessary

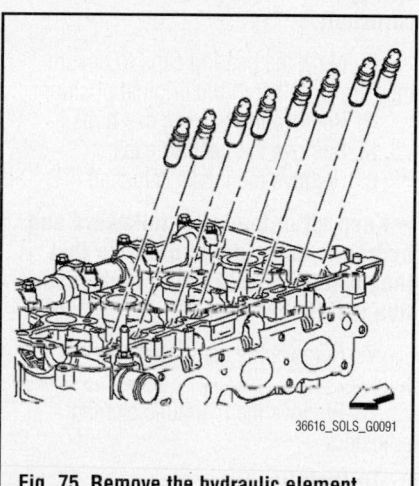

Fig. 75 Remove the hydraulic element adjusters

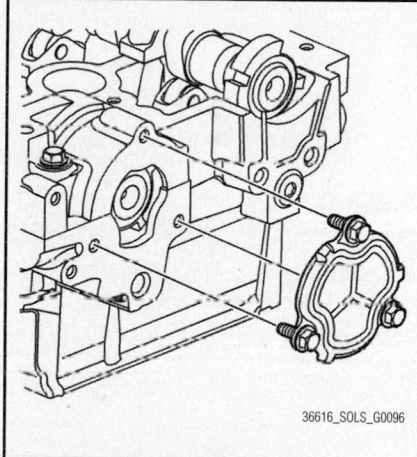

Fig. 77 Install the rear cylinder head opening plate and bolts

sealer to all locations centrally locating the head on the rail.

14. Apply a 3.5 mm bead of sealer GM P/N 12378521 (Canadian P/N 88901148) to the cylinder head at the number 6 intake camshaft rear cap mating surface.

15. Install the number 6 intake camshaft rear cap.

    a. Tighten the cap bolts evenly to 44 inch lbs. (5 Nm).

    b. Tighten the cap bolts evenly a final pass to 89 inch lbs. (10 Nm).

16. Remove all excess sealing material from the fuel pump roller lifter orifice (1), and ensure the orifice is free of debris.

17. Remove all excess sealing material from the sealing surfaces.

18. Install the rear cylinder head opening plate and bolts and tighten to 89 inch lbs. (10 Nm).

19. Install the camshaft position intake actuator.

2.4L (LE5) Engine

Exhaust

See Figures 72, 73, 78 through 80.

1. Before servicing the vehicle, refer to the Precautions Section.

2. Remove the exhaust camshaft position actuator.

➡**Remove each bolt on each cap one turn at a time until there is no spring tension pushing on the camshaft.**

3. Mark the bearing caps to ensure they are installed in the original position.

4. Remove the bearing cap bolts.

5. Remove the bearing caps.

6. Remove the exhaust camshaft (3).

➡**Keep all of the roller followers and hydraulic adjusters in order so that they can be reinstalled in their respective locations.**

7. Remove the camshaft roller followers.

8. Remove the hydraulic element adjusters.

To install:

9. Install the hydraulic element lash adjusters into their bores in the cylinder head.

10. Lubricate the hydraulic lash adjusters with GM PN 12345501 (Canadian PN 992704) or equivalent.

11. Lubricate the valve tips with GM PN 12345501 (Canadian PN 992704) or equivalent.

➡**Used roller followers MUST be returned to their original position on the camshaft. If the camshaft is being replaced, the roller followers actuated by the camshaft must also be replaced.**

12. Position the roller followers on the tip of the valve stem and on the lash

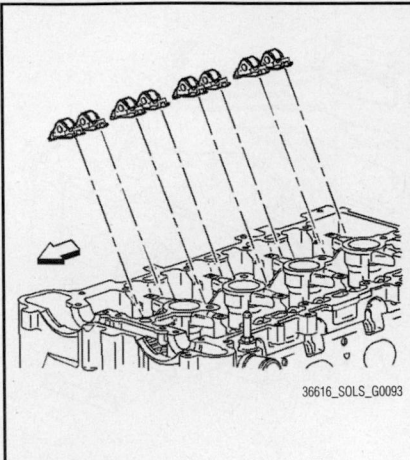

Fig. 78 Remove the camshaft roller followers

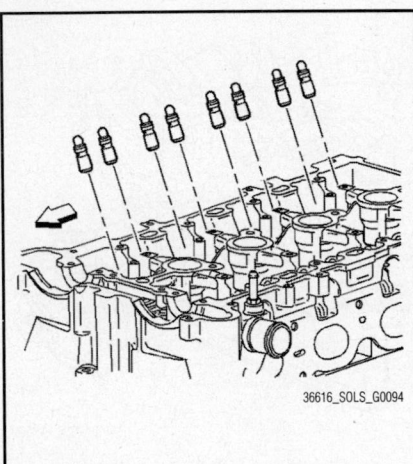

Fig. 79 Remove the hydraulic element adjusters

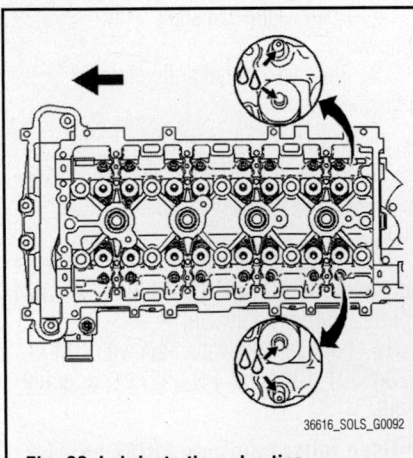

Fig. 80 Lubricate the valve tips

adjuster. Lubricate the roller followers with GM PN 12345501 (Canadian PN 992704) or equivalent.

13. Install the exhaust camshaft. Lubricate with GM PN 12345501 (Canadian PN 992704) or equivalent.

14. Install the camshaft bearing caps. Hand tighten the cap bolts.

15. Tighten the bearing cap bolts in increments of 3 turns until they are seated. Tighten the bolts to 89 inch lbs. (10 Nm).

16. Install the exhaust camshaft position actuator.

Intake

See Figures 72 through 75 and 80.

1. Before servicing the vehicle, refer to the Precautions Section.

2. Remove the intake camshaft position actuator.

➡ **Remove each bolt on each cap one turn at a time until there is no spring tension pushing on the camshaft.**

3. Mark the bearing caps to ensure they are installed in the original position.

4. Remove the bearing cap bolts.

5. Remove the bearing caps.

6. Remove the intake camshaft (1).

➡ **Keep all of the roller followers and hydraulic adjusters in order so that they can be reinstalled in their respective locations.**

7. Remove the camshaft roller followers.

8. Remove the hydraulic element adjusters.

To install:

9. Install the hydraulic element lash adjusters into their bores in the cylinder head.

10. Lubricate the hydraulic lash adjusters with GM PN 12345501 (Canadian PN 992704) or equivalent.

11. Lubricate the valve tips with GM PN 12345501 (Canadian PN 992704) or equivalent.

➡ **Used roller followers MUST be returned to their original position on the camshaft. If the camshaft is being replaced, the roller followers actuated by the camshaft must also be replaced.**

12. Position the camshaft roller followers on the tip of the valve stem and on the lash adjuster. Lubricate the roller followers with GM PN 12345501 (Canadian PN 992704) or equivalent.

13. Install the intake camshaft. Lubricate with GM PN 12345501 (Canadian PN 992704) or equivalent.

14. Install the camshaft bearing caps. Hand tighten the cap bolts.

15. Tighten the bearing cap bolts in increments of 3 turns until they are seated. Tighten the bolts to 89 inch lbs. (10 Nm).

16. Install the intake camshaft position actuator.

CATALYTIC CONVERTER

REMOVAL & INSTALLATION

2.0L (LNF) Engine

See Figures 81 and 82.

1. Before servicing the vehicle, refer to the Precautions Section.

2. Open the hood.

3. Remove the turbocharger heat shield bolts and shield.

4. Remove the position 1 Heated Oxygen Sensor (HO2S). Refer to Heated Oxygen Sensor Removal & Installation.

5. Remove the catalytic converter to turbocharger nuts.

6. Remove the Connector Position Assurance (CPA) retainer.

7. Disconnect the position 2 HO2S electrical connector from the engine wiring harness electrical connector.

8. Raise and support the vehicle.

9. Remove the catalytic converter to muffler nuts.

10. Separate the exhaust pipe from the catalytic converter studs.

11. Position and support the exhaust pipe out of the way.

12. Loosen, DO NOT REMOVE the driver side engine mount to frame lower nut.

13. Remove the passenger side engine mount to frame lower nut.

14. Place an adjustable jack and a block of wood under the oil pan. Using the adjustable jack, raise the oil pan slightly.

15. Remove the catalytic converter to catalytic converter bracket bolts.

16. Reposition the catalytic converter out of the way.

17. Remove the catalytic converter bracket bolt and nut.

18. Remove the catalytic converter bracket.

19. Rotate and remove the catalytic converter (3).

20. Remove and discard the catalytic converter gasket (2).

To install:

21. Install a NEW catalytic converter gasket onto the turbocharger studs.

22. Install, rotate, and position the catalytic converter.

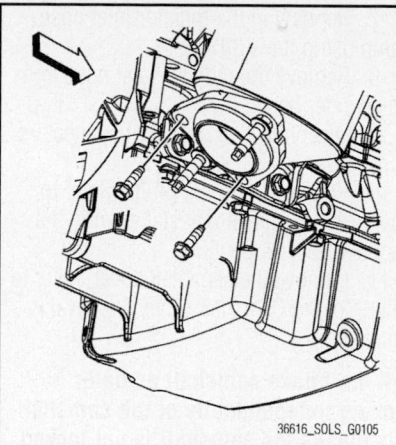

Fig. 81 Remove the catalytic converter to catalytic converter bracket bolts

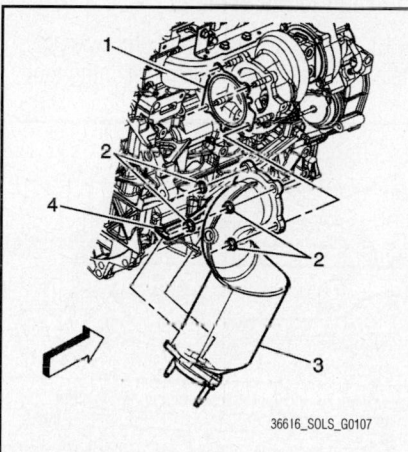

Fig. 82 Remove the catalytic converter (3) and gasket (2)

23. Position the catalytic converter bracket to the engine block.

24. Install the catalytic converter bracket bolt and nut. Tighten the bolt/nut to 43 ft. lbs. (58 Nm).

25. Install the catalytic converter onto the turbocharger studs.

26. Install the catalytic converter to catalytic converter bracket bolts. Tighten the bolts to 16 ft. lbs. (22 Nm).

27. Using the adjustable jack, lower the oil pan.

28. Install the passenger side engine mount to frame lower nut. Tighten the nut to 41 ft. lbs. (55 Nm).

29. Tighten the driver side engine mount to frame lower nut. Tighten the nut to 41 ft. lbs. (55 Nm).

30. Position and install the exhaust pipe to the catalytic converter studs.

31. Install the catalytic converter to muffler nuts. Tighten the nuts to 13 ft. lbs. (17 Nm).

32. Lower the vehicle.

33. Connect the position 2 HO2S electri-

cal connector to the engine wiring harness electrical connector.

34. Install the CPA retainer.

35. Install the catalytic converter to turbocharger nuts. Tighten the nuts to 43 ft. lbs. (58 Nm).

36. Install the position 1 HO2S.

37. Install the turbocharger heat shield and bolts. Tighten the bolts to 89 inch lbs. (10 Nm).

38. Close the hood.

2.4L (LE5) Engine

See Figures 83 and 84.

1. Before servicing the vehicle, refer to the Precautions Section.

2. Open the hood.

3. Remove the exhaust manifold heat shield bolts and shield.

4. Remove the catalytic converter to exhaust manifold nuts.

5. Remove the Connector Position Assurance (CPA) retainer.

6. Disconnect the engine wiring harness electrical connector from the position 2 Heated Oxygen Sensor (HO2S).

7. Raise and support the vehicle.

8. Remove the catalytic converter to catalytic converter brace bracket bolt.

9. Remove the catalytic converter to muffler nuts.

10. Separate the exhaust pipe from the catalytic converter studs.

11. Position and support the exhaust pipe out of the way.

12. Separate the exhaust pipe from the catalytic converter studs.

13. Position and support the exhaust pipe out of the way.

14. Remove the catalytic converter and gasket.

To install:

15. Install the catalytic converter along with a NEW gasket to the exhaust manifold.

16. Position and join the exhaust pipe to the catalytic converter studs.

17. Loosely install the catalytic converter to muffler nuts.

18. Install the catalytic converter to catalytic converter brace bracket bolt. Tighten the catalytic converter to muffler nuts to 13 ft. lbs. (17 Nm). Tighten the catalytic converter to catalytic converter brace bracket bolt to 37 ft. lbs. (50 Nm).

19. Lower the vehicle

20. Connect the engine wiring harness electrical connector to the position 2 HO2S.

21. Install the CPA retainer.

22. Install the catalytic converter to exhaust manifold nuts. Tighten the nuts to 37 ft. lbs. (50 Nm).

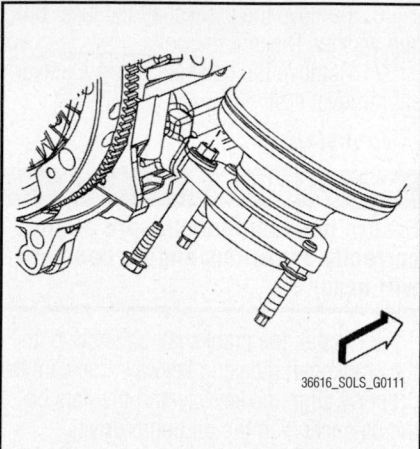

Fig. 83 Remove the catalytic converter to catalytic converter brace bracket bolt

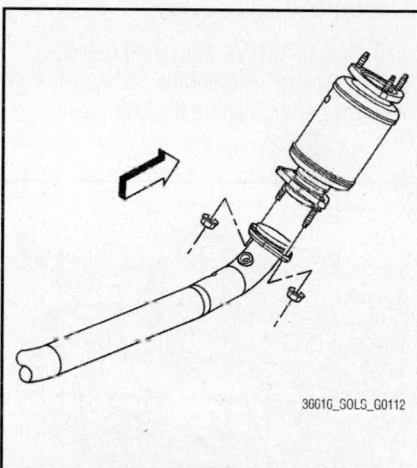

Fig. 84 Separate the exhaust pipe from the catalytic converter studs

23. Install the exhaust manifold heat shield and bolts. Tighten the bolts to 89 inch lbs. (10 Nm).

24. Close the hood.

CRANKSHAFT DAMPER (BALANCER)

REMOVAL & INSTALLATION

See Figures 85 and 86.

1. Before servicing the vehicle, refer to the Precautions Section.

2. Remove the engine drive belt. Refer to Accessory Drive Belt Removal & Installation.

3. Remove the starter motor. Refer to Starter Removal & Installation in the Engine Electrical Section.

4. Raise and suitably support the vehicle.

5. Install the J 43653 (1) to the engine block, in order to hold the flywheel.

6. Remove the crankshaft balancer bolt and washer. Discard the bolt.

7. Remove the balancer using a universal removal tool.

To install:

✳✳ WARNING

Ensure both components are aligned correctly or serious engine damage will occur.

8. Install the crankshaft balancer onto the crankshaft indexing keyway. Use care to properly align the keyway and the flats on the balancer with the oil pump drive.

9. Install the crankshaft balancer using a universal balancer installer.

➡**Always install a NEW crankshaft balancer bolt and washer.**

10. Install a NEW crankshaft balancer bolt and washer. Prevent the crankshaft from rotating when tightening the bolt.

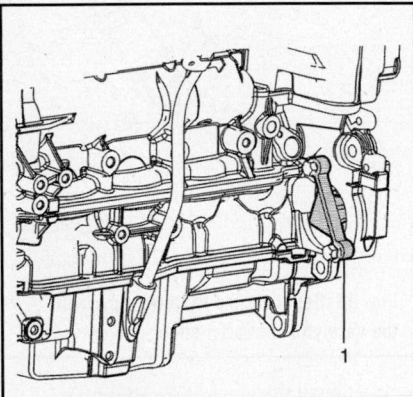

1. Special tool J 43653

22116_SOLS_G0053

Fig. 85 Special tool J 43653 installed

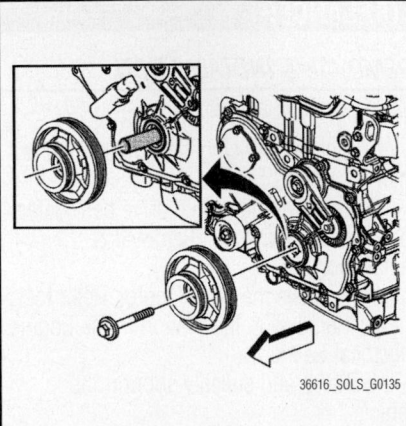

36616_SOLS_G0135

Fig. 86 Remove the balancer bolt and balancer

11. Tighten the bolt to 100 Nm (74 ft. lbs.) plus an additional 125 degrees using the J 45059.

12. Remove the J 43653 from the engine block.

13. Lower the vehicle.

14. Install the starter motor.

15. Install the engine drive belt.

CRANKSHAFT FRONT SEAL

REMOVAL & INSTALLATION

See Figure 87.

1. Before servicing the vehicle, refer to the Precautions Section.

2. Remove the crankshaft balancer.

3. Using a flat-bladed tool, remove the oil seal from the front cover.

To install:

4. Use the J 35268-A seal driver to install the oil seal in the front cover.

5. Install the crankshaft balancer.

CYLINDER HEAD

REMOVAL & INSTALLATION

See Figures 88 through 98.

1. Before servicing the vehicle, refer to the Precautions Section.

2. Drain the cooling system.

3. Remove the exhaust manifold. Refer to Exhaust Manifold Removal & Installation.

4. Remove the intake manifold. Refer to Intake Manifold Removal & Installation.

5. Reposition the radiator surge tank air bleed hose clamp.

6. Remove the radiator surge tank air bleed hose from the cylinder head.

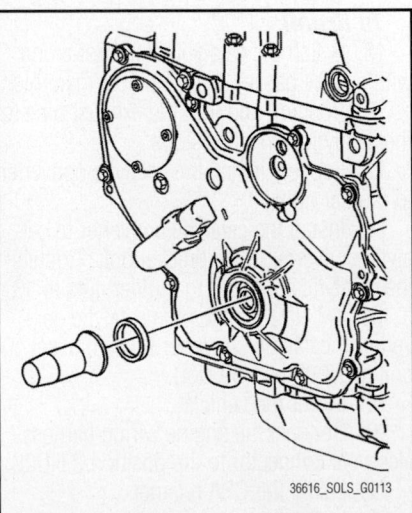

36616_SOLS_G0113

Fig. 87 Use the J 35268-A seal driver to install the oil seal in the front cover

7. Reposition the radiator inlet hose clamp using the J 38185.

8. Remove the radiator inlet hose from the cylinder head.

9. Disconnect all electrical connectors as necessary.

10. Remove the spark plugs. Refer to Spark Plug Removal & Installation in the Engine Electrical Section.

11. Remove the camshaft cover. Refer to Valve Covers/Camshaft Cover Removal & Installation.

➡**If the intake camshaft actuator is moving independently of the camshaft, this means the camshaft is not locked to the actuator. Rotate the camshaft counter-clockwise while the holding tool is installed and this will lock the camshaft to the actuator.**

12. Rotate the crankshaft clockwise to install the camshaft actuator retaining tool

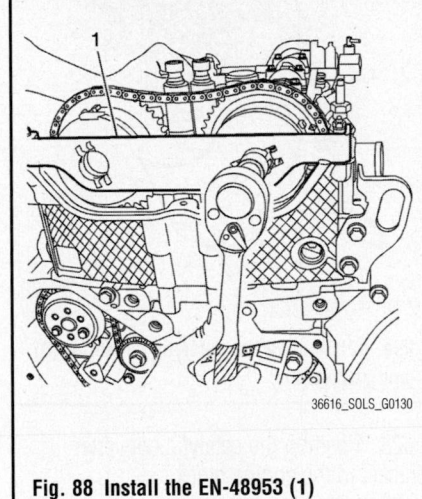

36616_SOLS_G0130

Fig. 88 Install the EN-48953 (1)

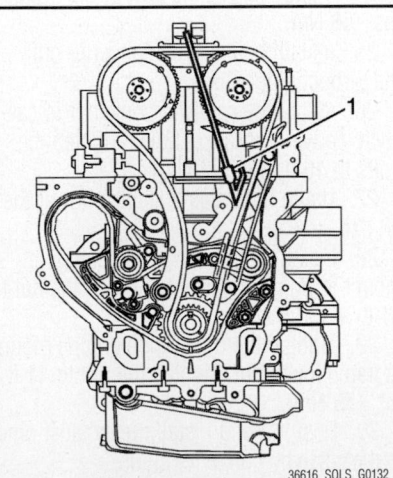

36616_SOLS_G0132

Fig. 89 Install the timing chain retention tool EN-48749 (1) to the intake side of the timing chain

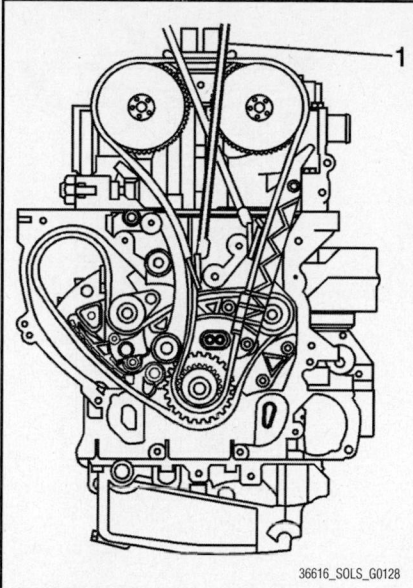

Fig. 90 Install the timing chain retention tool EN-48749 (1)

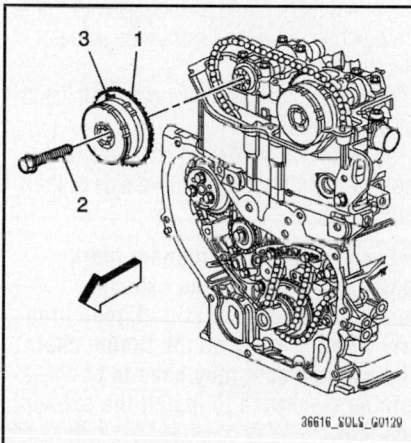

Fig. 91 Remove the exhaust camshaft actuator (3) and bolt (2)

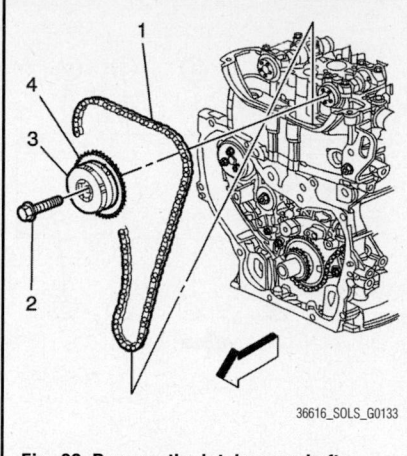

Fig. 92 Remove the intake camshaft actuator (3) and bolt (2)

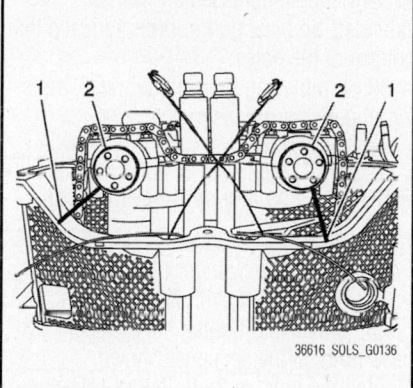

Fig. 93 Mark the cylinder head (1) in relationship to the camshaft actuator notch is on the camshaft (2)

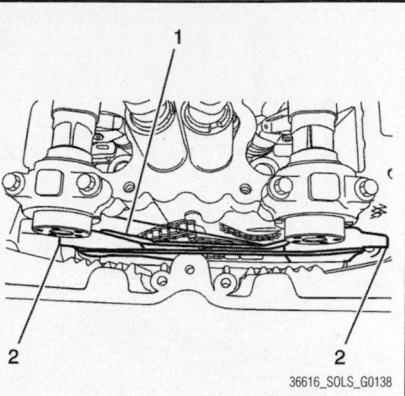

Fig. 94 Install a rubber band (1) around the top of the upper timing chain guides (2) in order to pull the guides together

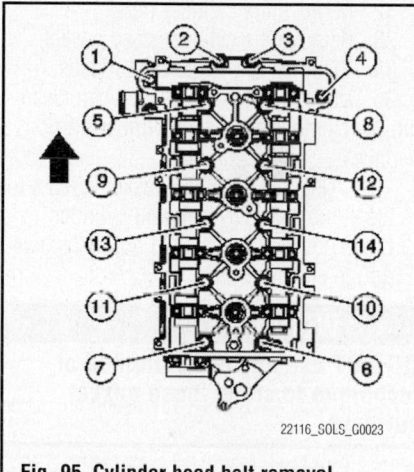

Fig. 95 Cylinder head bolt removal sequence

EN-48953, EGR Cooler Pressure Tester Adapter Set.

13. Install the EN-48953 (1).

14. Install the camshaft actuator tool and bolts and tighten to 89 inch lbs. (10 Nm).

15. Remove the upper timing chain guide bolts and guide.

16. Clean the timing chain and gears with solvent.

➡ **Ensure the timing chain and the camshaft position actuators are marked for proper assembly.**

17. Mark the timing gear sprockets and the timing chain. It is recommended that the paint marks are located in the 12 o'clock position.

18. Loosen, but do not remove the intake and exhaust camshaft actuator bolts.

19. Remove the camshaft actuator locking tool, EN-48953.

➡ **Ensure the tips of the EN-48749 are fully engaged into the timing chain. The retention tool rod can be used on the back side of the chain to ensure the teeth from the retention tool are engaged.**

20. Install the timing chain retention tool EN-48749 (1) to the intake side of the timing chain.

21. Remove the timing chain tensioner.

➡ **The intake camshaft and actuator should not rotate during the removal or installation.**

22. Install the timing chain retention tool EN-48749 (1) to the exhaust side of the timing chain.

23. Remove and discard the exhaust camshaft actuator bolt (2).

24. Remove the exhaust cam actuator (3) from the exhaust camshaft while also removing the actuator from the chain.

25. Remove and discard the intake camshaft actuator bolt (2).

26. Remove the intake camshaft actuator (3) from the camshaft while also removing the actuator from the timing chain.

27. Mark the cylinder head (1) in relationship to the camshaft actuator notch is on the camshaft (2).

28. Remove the fixed timing chain guide access plug.

29. Remove the upper fixed timing chain guide bolt.

➡ **The threaded rod from the timing chain retention tool can be used to help feed the rubber band around the chain guides.**

30. Install a rubber band (1) around the top of the upper timing chain guides (2) in order to pull the guides together.

31. Remove the cylinder head bolts in the sequence shown. Discard the bolts.

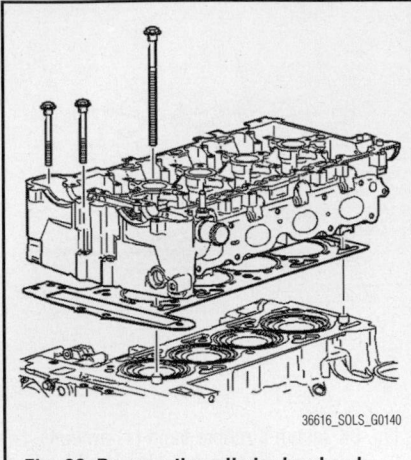

Fig. 96 Remove the cylinder head and gasket

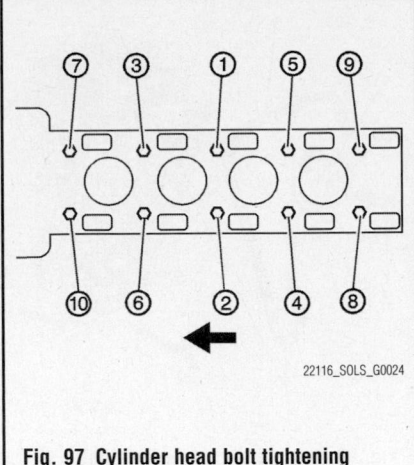

Fig. 97 Cylinder head bolt tightening sequence

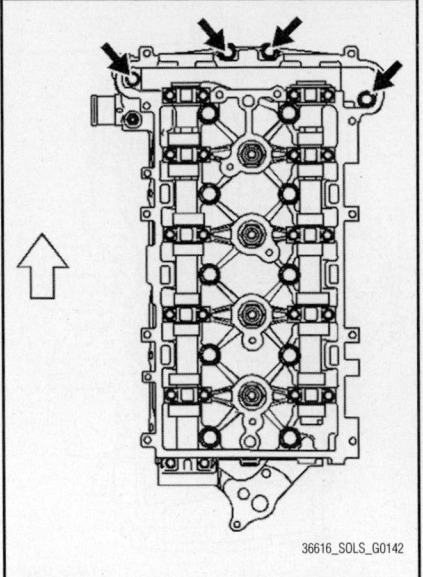

Fig. 98 Front cylinder head bolt tightening sequence

32. Remove the cylinder head.

33. Remove the cylinder head gasket.

34. Clean all of the gasket surfaces.

35. Use the following steps when cleaning the cylinder head and cylinder block surfaces:

a. Use a razor blade gasket scraper to clean the cylinder head and cylinder block gasket surfaces. Do not scratch or gouge either surface.

⁂ WARNING

DO NOT use any other method or technique to clean these gasket surfaces.

b. Use a NEW razor blade on the cylinder head and a NEW blade on the cylinder block.

⁂ WARNING

Be careful not to gouge or scratch the gasket surfaces. DO NOT gouge or scrape the combustion chamber surfaces. The feel of the gasket surface is important, not the appearance. There will be indentations from the gasket left in the cylinder head after all of the gasket material is removed. These small indentations will be filled in by the NEW gasket.

c. Hold the razor blade as parallel to the gasket surface as possible.

36. Clean the old sealer/lube and any dirt from around the bolt holes.

➡**DO NOT use a tap to clean the cylinder head bolt holes.**

37. Clean the bolts holes with a nylon bristle brush.

38. When cleaning the cylinder head bolt holes use suitable commercial spray liquid solvent and compressed air from an extended-tip blow gun in order to reach the bottom of the holes.

39. If replacing the cylinder head, transfer all parts as necessary.

To install:

➡**DO NOT use any sealing material.**

40. Install the cylinder head gasket.

41. Install the cylinder head.

42. Install NEW cylinder head bolts.

43. Install and tighten the cylinder head bolts in the sequence shown. Tighten the bolts to 22 ft. lbs. (30 Nm) plus an additional 155 degrees using the J 45059.

44. Install the NEW front cylinder head bolts and tighten to 26 ft. lbs (35 Nm).

45. Ensure the cylinder head and the camshaft are correctly aligned.

46. Remove the rubber band from around the top of the upper timing chain guides.

47. Install the fixed guide bolt into the cylinder head and tighten to 106 inch lbs. (12 Nm)

48. Apply sealant compound to thread and install the timing chain guide bolt access hole plug.

49. Install the fixed timing chain guide access plug and tighten to 59 ft. lbs (90 Nm).

➡**Ensure that the alignment mark made previously on the intake camshaft actuator is still aligned properly with the mark on the timing chain. If the mark made previously on the intake camshaft actuator is not aligned properly, refer to Timing Chain and Sprocket Removal & Installation.**

50. Install the timing chain onto the intake camshaft actuator.

51. Align the intake camshaft actuator alignment mark made previously with the timing chain mark and install the actuator onto the camshaft.

52. Install a NEW intake camshaft actuator bolt until snug.

53. Remove the timing chain retention tool EN-48749 from the intake side of the timing chain.

➡**Ensure that the alignment mark made previously on the exhaust camshaft actuator is still aligned properly with the mark on the timing chain. The exhaust cam may have to be rotated clockwise to install the exhaust actuator.**

54. Install the timing chain onto the exhaust camshaft actuator.

55. Align the exhaust camshaft actuator alignment mark made previously with the timing chain mark and install the actuator onto the camshaft.

56. Install a NEW exhaust camshaft actuator bolt until snug.

57. Remove the timing chain retention tool EN-48749 from the exhaust side of the timing chain.

⁂ WARNING

Failure to reset the chain tensioner will put excess tension on the chain, limiting the chain's life.

58. Reset and install the timing chain tensioner.

59. Install the EN-48953 to the actuators.

60. Install the camshaft actuator locking

tool bolts and tighten to 89 inch lbs.
(10 Nm).

61. Tighten the NEW camshaft actuator bolt to 22 ft. lbs. (30 Nm), plus an additional 100 degrees using the J 45059.

62. Release the tensioner by applying a counterclockwise rotational torque of 33 ft. lbs (45 Nm) to the harmonic balancer bolt.

63. Remove the camshaft actuator locking tool, EN-48953.

64. Install the upper timing chain guide bolts and guide and tighten to 89 inch lbs. (10 Nm).

65. Install the camshaft cover.

66. Install the spark plugs.

67. Connect all electrical connectors as necessary.

68. Install the radiator inlet hose to the cylinder head.

69. Position the radiator inlet hose clamp using the J 38185.

70. Install the radiator surge tank air bleed hose to the cylinder head.

71. Position the radiator surge tank air bleed hose clamp.

72. Install the exhaust manifold.

73. Install the intake manifold.

74. Fill the cooling system.

EXHAUST MANIFOLD

REMOVAL & INSTALLATION

2.0L (LNF) Engine

See Figures 99 and 100.

1. Before servicing the vehicle, refer to the Precautions Section.

2. Remove the turbocharger. Refer to Turbocharger Removal & Installation.

3. Remove the exhaust manifold heat shield bolts.

4. Remove the heat shield.

5. Remove and discard the exhaust manifold nuts.

6. Remove the exhaust manifold.

7. Remove and discard the exhaust manifold gasket.

To install:

8. Install a new exhaust manifold gasket onto the studs.

9. Install the exhaust manifold.

10. Install the new exhaust manifold nuts.

11. Tighten the exhaust manifold nuts in the sequence shown to 10 ft. lbs. (14 Nm).

12. Install the heat shield.

13. Install the exhaust manifold heat shield bolts and tighten to 18 ft. lbs. (25 Nm).

14. Install the turbocharger.

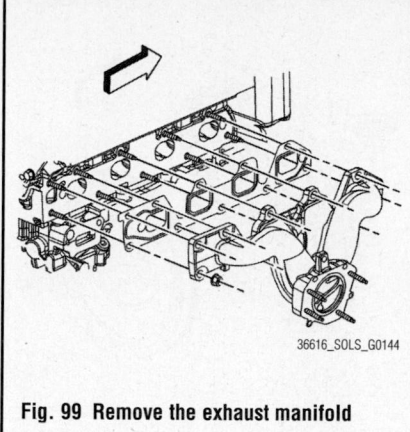

Fig. 99 Remove the exhaust manifold

36616_SOLS_G0144

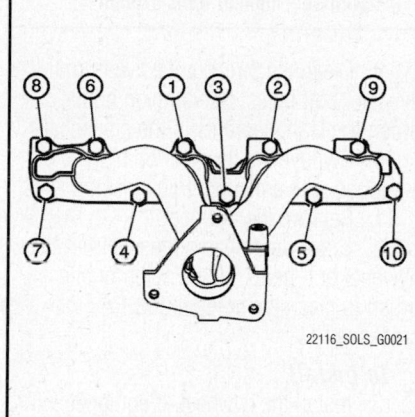

22116_SOLS_G0021

Fig. 100 Exhaust manifold tightening sequence

2.4L (LE5) Engine

See Figures 100 and 101.

1. Before servicing the vehicle, refer to the Precautions Section.

2. Remove the intake manifold cover. Refer to Intake Manifold Removal & Installation.

3. Remove the Connector Position Assurance (CPA) retainer.

4. Disconnect the Heated Oxygen Sensor (HO2S) electrical connector.

➡ **The HO2S uses a permanently attached pigtail and connector. This pigtail should not be removed from the sensor. Damage or removal of the pigtail or connector will affect proper operation of the sensor.**

5. Remove the HO2S. Refer to Heated Oxygen Sensor Removal & Installation in the Engine Performance & Emission Control Section.

6. Remove the exhaust manifold heat shield bolts.

7. Remove the heat shield.

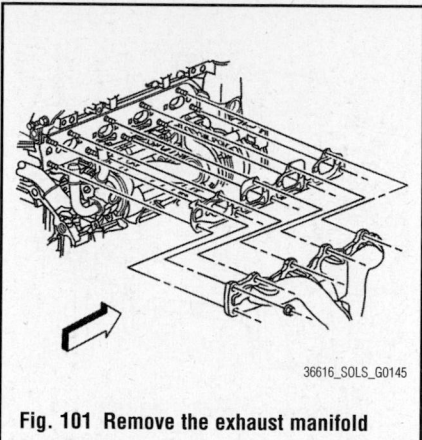

Fig. 101 Remove the exhaust manifold

36616_SOLS_G0145

8. Remove the catalytic converter to exhaust manifold nuts.

9. Remove and discard the exhaust manifold nuts.

10. Remove the exhaust manifold.

11. Remove and discard the exhaust manifold gasket.

To install:

12. Install a NEW exhaust manifold gasket onto the studs.

13. Install the exhaust manifold.

14. Install the NEW exhaust manifold nuts finger tight.

15. Install the catalytic converter to exhaust manifold nuts and tighten the bolts to 37 ft. lbs. (50 Nm).

16. Tighten the exhaust manifold nuts in the sequence shown. Tighten the nuts to 10 ft. lbs. (14 Nm).

17. Install the heat shield.

18. Install the exhaust manifold heat shield bolts and tighten to 89 inch lbs. (10 Nm).

19. Install the HO2S.

20. Connect the HO2S electrical connector.

21. Install the CPA retainer.

22. Start the vehicle and inspect for leaks.

23. Install the intake manifold cover.

FLYWHEEL

REMOVAL & INSTALLATION

2.0L (LNF) Engine

See Figures 102 through 104.

1. Before servicing the vehicle, refer to the Precautions Section.

2. Disconnect the negative battery cable.

3. Remove the automatic transmission, if equipped. Refer to Automatic Transmission Removal & Installation, in the Drive Train Section.

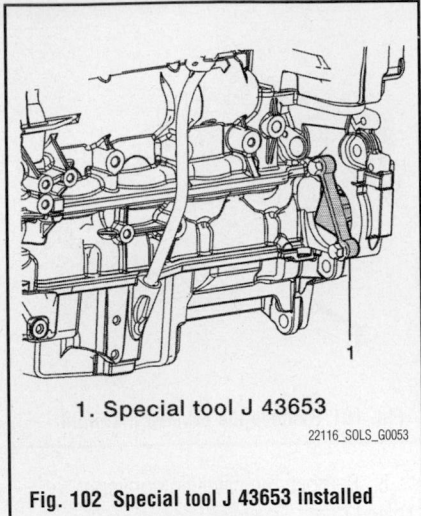

1. Special tool J 43653

22116_SOLS_G0053

Fig. 102 Special tool J 43653 installed

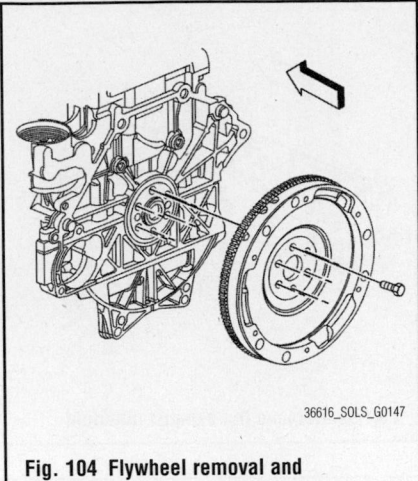

36616_SOLS_G0147

Fig. 104 Flywheel removal and installation—manual transmission

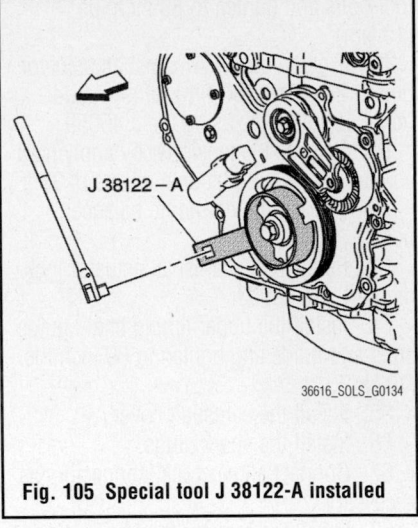

J 38122 – A

36616_SOLS_G0134

Fig. 105 Special tool J 38122-A installed

4. Remove the starter, if equipped with a manual transmission. Refer to Starter Removal & Installation, in the Engine Electrical Section.

5. Remove the clutch, if equipped. Refer to Clutch Driven Disc & Pressure Plate Removal & Installation, in the Drive Train Section.

6. Install the J 43653 or equivalent to the engine block in order to hold the flywheel.

➡ **It may be necessary to remove the chamfer (bevel) from the edge of an 18 mm socket in order to get full engagement on the thin-headed flywheel bolts.**

7. Remove the flywheel bolts, if equipped with an automatic transmission.

➡ **Do not orientate the flywheel to the crankshaft. It is balanced separately from the engine.**

8. Remove the flywheel.

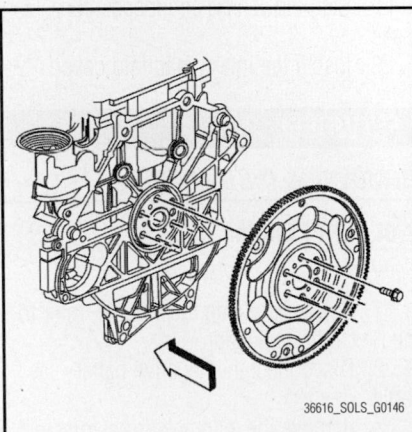

36616_SOLS_G0146

Fig. 103 Flywheel removal and installation— automatic transmission

9. Clean the thread adhesive from the flywheel bolt holes. Use a nylon bristle brush to clean the holes in the crankshaft.

10. Remove the flywheel bolts, if equipped with a manual transmission.

11. Remove the flywheel.

12. Clean the thread adhesive from the flywheel bolt holes. Use a nylon bristle brush to clean the holes in the crankshaft.

To install:

13. Install the flywheel, if equipped with a manual transmission.

14. Install the flywheel bolts.

15. Tighten the bolts in a star pattern to 39 ft. lbs. (53 Nm) plus an additional 25 degrees using a angle meter.

16. Install the flywheel if equipped with an automatic transmission.

17. Install the flywheel bolts.

18. Tighten the bolts in a star pattern to 39 ft. lbs. (53 Nm) plus an additional 25 degrees using a angle meter.

19. Remove the J 43653 tool from the engine block.

20. Install the clutch, if equipped.

21. Install the starter, if equipped with a manual transmission.

22. Install the automatic transmission, if equipped.

23. Connect the negative battery cable.

2.4L (LE5) Engine

See Figures 103 through 105.

1. Before servicing the vehicle, refer to the Precautions Section.

2. Disconnect the negative battery cable.

3. Remove the automatic transmission, if equipped. Refer to Automatic Transmission Removal & Installation, in the Drive Train Section.

4. Remove the clutch, if equipped. Refer to Clutch Driven Disc & Pressure Plate Removal & Installation, in the Drive Train Section.

5. Using the J 38122-A, hold the crankshaft balancer.

➡ **It may be necessary to remove the chamfer (bevel) from the edge of an 18 mm socket in order to get full engagement on the thin-headed flywheel bolts.**

6. Remove the flywheel bolts, if equipped with an automatic transmission.

➡ **Do not orientate the flywheel to the crankshaft. It is balanced separately from the engine.**

7. Remove the flywheel.

8. Clean the thread adhesive from the flywheel bolt holes. Use a nylon bristle brush to clean the holes in the crankshaft.

9. Remove the flywheel bolts, if equipped with a manual transmission.

10. Remove the flywheel.

11. Clean the thread adhesive from the flywheel bolt holes. Use a nylon bristle brush to clean the holes in the crankshaft.

To install:

12. Install the flywheel, if equipped with a manual transmission.

13. Install the flywheel bolts.

14. Tighten the bolts in a star pattern to 39 ft. lbs. (53 Nm) plus an additional 25 degrees using a angle meter.

15. Install the flywheel, if equipped with an automatic transmission.

16. Install the flywheel bolts.

17. Tighten the bolts in a star pattern to 39 ft. lbs. (53 Nm) plus an additional 25 degrees using a angle meter.

18. Remove the J 38122-A tool from the engine block.

19. Install the clutch, if equipped.

20. Install the automatic transmission, if equipped.

21. Connect the negative battery cable.

INTAKE MANIFOLD

REMOVAL & INSTALLATION

2.0L (LNF) Engine

See Figures 106 through 109.

❊❊ WARNING

Never attempt to remove the intake manifold from a hot engine, allow the engine to cool to ambient temperature. The intake manifold is made of a composite plastic and can be damaged if it is removed when the engine is hot.

1. Before servicing the vehicle, refer to the Precautions Section.

2. Remove the intake manifold cover, as follows:

   a. Grasp the intake manifold cover by the front right corner and pull up in order to disengage the cover from the stud.

   b. Grasp the intake manifold cover by the front left corner and pull up in order to disengage the cover from the stud.

   c. Grasp the intake manifold cover by the rear and pull up in order to disengage the cover from the stud.

   d. Remove the intake manifold cover.

3. Remove the oil level indicator tube.

4. Disconnect the fuel feed line quick connect fitting from the fuel rail.

5. Disconnect the Evaporative Emission (EVAP) line quick connect fitting from the EVAP purge solenoid.

6. Reposition the brake booster vacuum hose clamp at the intake manifold.

7. Remove the brake booster hose from the intake manifold.

8. Remove the knock sensor electrical connector clip from the intake manifold brace.

9. Remove the knock sensor electrical connector clip from the oil level indicator tube bracket.

10. Disconnect the engine wiring harness electrical connector (1) from the EVAP canister purge solenoid.

11. Disconnect the engine wiring harness electrical connector (2) from the Manifold Absolute Pressure (MAP) sensor.

12. Disconnect the engine wiring harness electrical connector from the charge air bypass vale solenoid.

13. Disconnect the engine wiring harness electrical connector (1) from the Throttle Actuator Control (TAC) module.

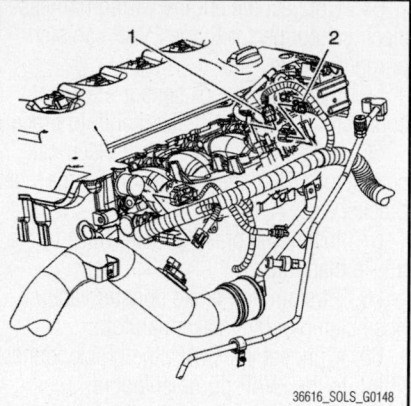

Fig. 106 Engine wiring harness electrical connectors—EVAP canister purge solenoid (1), MAP sensor (2)

36616_SOLS_G0148

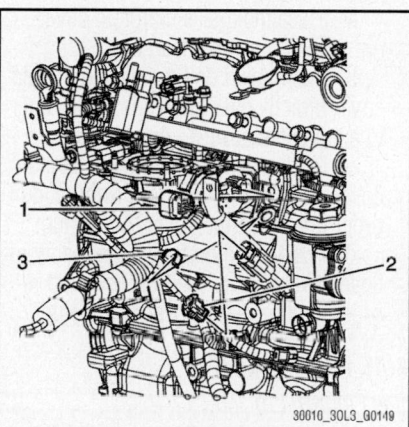

Fig. 107 TAC module (1) electrical connector, intake manifold brace engine wiring harness clip (3)

30010_3OL3_G0149

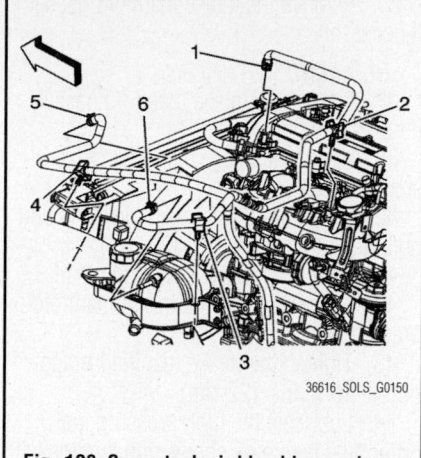

Fig. 108 Surge tank air bleed hose, clamp (1), and clip (2)

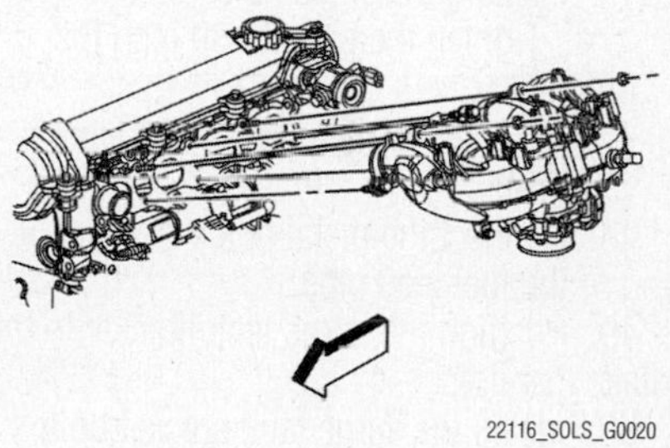

36616_SOLS_G0150

Fig. 109 Intake manifold

22116_SOLS_G0020

14. Remove the engine wiring harness clip (3) from the intake manifold brace.

15. Reposition the surge tank air bleed hose clamp at the engine.

16. Remove the surge tank air bleed hose from the engine (1).

17. Remove the surge tank air bleed hose clip (2) from the surge tank bracket.

18. Reposition the surge tank air bleed hose out of the way.

19. Reposition the charge air bypass valve vacuum hose clamp at the intake manifold.

20. Remove the charge air bypass valve vacuum hose from the intake manifold.

21. Remove the charge air bypass valve solenoid bolts.

22. Reposition the charge air bypass valve solenoid assembly out of the way.

23. Remove the surge tank bracket bolt and stud.

24. Remove the surge tank bracket.

25. Remove the surge tank hose retainer and hose from the surge tank bracket.

26. Disconnect the metal quick connect fitting from the fuel feed pipe.

27. Disconnect the fuel feed pipe fitting from the fuel pump.

28. Remove the fuel feed pipe bolts.

29. Remove the fuel feed pipe.

30. Inspect the fuel feed pipe nut for damaged threads.

31. Inspect the fuel feed pipe sealing bail for damage or debris.

32. Replace the fuel feed pipe if any damage is found.

33. Remove the intake manifold brace bolt.

34. Remove the intake manifold brace.

35. Remove the intake manifold bolts and nuts.

36. Remove the intake manifold and place on a clean work surface.

➡The intake manifold gasket is reusable. Only replace the gasket if damage has occurred.

37. Remove the intake manifold gasket, if necessary

To install:

38. Install new intake manifold gasket, if necessary.

39. Install the intake manifold to the studs.

40. Install the intake manifold bolts and nuts, tighten to 16 ft. lbs. (22 Nm).

41. Install the intake manifold brace.

42. Loosely install the intake manifold brace bolt.

43. Tighten the intake manifold brace bolt to 16 ft. lbs. (22 Nm).

44. Lubricate the high pressure fuel pump fuel feed pipe connection threads with silicon free engine oil.

45. Place the fuel feed pipe on top of the intake manifold.

46. Connect the fuel feed pipe fitting to the high pressure fuel pump.

47. Install the fuel feed pipe bolts.

   a. Tighten the bolts to 89 inch lbs. (10 Nm).

   b. Tighten the fittings to 22 ft. lbs. (30 Nm).

48. Connect the metal quick connect fitting to the fuel feed pipe.

49. Position the surge tank bracket to the intake manifold.

50. Install the surge tank bracket bolt and stud. Tighten the bolt and stud to 80 inch lbs. (9 Nm).

51. Install the surge tank hose retainer and hose to the surge tank bracket.

52. Position the charge air bypass valve solenoid assembly to the intake manifold.

53. Install the charge air bypass valve solenoid bolts and tighten to 89 inch lbs. (10 Nm).

54. Install the charge air bypass valve vacuum hose to the intake manifold.

55. Position the charge air bypass valve vacuum hose clamp at the intake manifold.

56. Position the surge tank air bleed hose to the engine.

57. Install the surge tank air bleed hose to the engine.

58. Position the surge tank air bleed hose clamp at the engine.

59. Install the surge tank air bleed hose clip to the surge tank bracket.

60. Connect the engine wiring harness electrical connector to the TAC module.

61. Install the engine wiring harness clip to the intake manifold brace.

62. Connect the engine wiring harness electrical connector to the charge air bypass vale solenoid

63. Connect the engine wiring harness electrical connector to the MAP sensor.

64. Connect the engine wiring harness electrical connector to the EVAP canister purge solenoid.

65. Install the knock sensor electrical connector clip to the intake manifold brace.

66. Install the knock sensor electrical connector clip to the oil level indicator tube bracket.

67. Install the brake booster hose to the intake manifold.

68. Position the brake booster vacuum hose clamp at the intake manifold.

69. Connect the EVAP line quick connect fitting to the EVAP purge solenoid.

70. Connect the fuel feed line quick connect fitting from the fuel rail.

71. Install the oil level indicator tube.

72. Install the intake manifold cover, as follows:

   a. Place the intake manifold cover onto the engine over the studs.

   b. Push down on the intake manifold cover directly over the rear stud in order to engage the cover to the stud.

   c. Push down on the intake manifold cover directly over the front right stud in order to engage the cover to the stud.

   d. Push down on the intake manifold cover directly over the front left stud in order to engage the cover to the stud.

2.4L (LE5) Engine
See Figures 110 and 111.

> ❄❄ **WARNING**
>
> **Never attempt to remove the intake manifold from a hot engine, allow the engine to cool to ambient temperature. The intake manifold is made of a composite plastic and can be damaged if it is removed when the engine is hot.**

1. Before servicing the vehicle, refer to the Precautions Section.

2. Remove the intake manifold cover, as follows:

   a. Grasp the intake manifold cover by the front right corner and pull up in order to disengage the cover from the stud.

   b. Grasp the intake manifold cover by the front left corner and pull up in order to disengage the cover from the stud.

   c. Grasp the intake manifold cover by the rear and pull up in order to disengage the cover from the stud.

   d. Remove the intake manifold cover.

3. Remove the throttle body.

4. Remove the fuel rail.

5. Remove the Evaporative Emission (EVAP) canister purge solenoid valve tube.

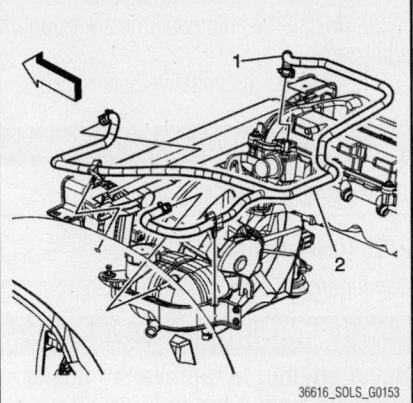

Fig. 110 Reposition the radiator surge tank air bleed hose clamp (1), and remove the air bleed hose (2) from the engine and reposition

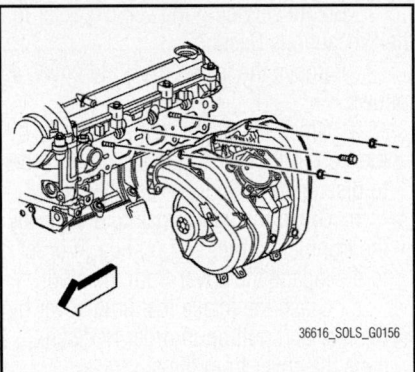

Fig. 111 Intake manifold removal and installation

6. Reposition the brake booster vacuum hose clamp at the intake manifold.

7. Remove the brake booster hose from the intake manifold.

8. Remove the oil level indicator tube bolt.

9. Disconnect the engine harness electrical connector from the fuel injector electrical connector.

10. Disconnect the electronic throttle actuator electrical connector.

11. Disconnect the windshield wiper motor electrical connector.

12. Remove the engine harness clip from the wiper motor.

13. Remove the engine harness clip from the surge tank air bleed hose.

14. Reposition the radiator surge tank air bleed hose clamp at the engine (1).

15. Remove the air bleed hose (2) from the engine and reposition.

16. Disconnect the Air Conditioning (A/C) refrigerant pressure sensor electrical connector.

17. Remove the engine harness clip from the intake manifold.

18. Disconnect the engine harness electrical connector from the knock sensor harness.

19. Remove the knock sensor connector clip from the oil level indicator tube.

20. Reposition the engine harness.

21. Remove the intake manifold bolts and nuts.

22. Remove the intake manifold.

➡**The intake manifold gasket is reusable. Only replace the gasket if damage has occurred.**

23. Remove the intake manifold gasket, if necessary.

To install:

❊❊ CAUTION

Wear safety glasses in order to avoid eye damage.

24. Install a new intake manifold gasket, if necessary.

25. Install the intake manifold.

26. Install the intake manifold bolts and nuts. Tighten the bolts and nuts to 89 inch lbs. (10 Nm).

27. Position the engine harness.

28. Install the knock sensor connector clip to the oil level indicator tube.

29. Connect the engine harness electrical connector to the knock sensor harness.

30. Install the engine harness clip to the intake manifold.

31. Connect the A/C refrigerant pressure sensor electrical connector.

32. Position and install the air bleed hose to the engine.

33. Position the radiator surge tank air bleed hose clamp at the engine.

34. Install the engine harness clip to the surge tank air bleed hose.

35. Connect the windshield wiper motor electrical connector.

36. Install the engine harness clip to the wiper motor.

37. Connect the electronic throttle actuator electrical connector.

38. Connect the engine harness electrical connector to the fuel injector electrical connector.

39. Install the oil level indicator tube bolt and tighten to 89 inch lbs. (10 Nm).

40. Install the brake booster hose to the intake manifold.

41. Position the brake booster vacuum hose clamp at the intake manifold.

42. Install the EVAP canister purge solenoid valve tube.

43. Install the fuel rail.

44. Install the throttle body. Tighten the bolts and nuts to 89 inch lbs. (10 Nm).

45. Install the intake manifold cover, as follows:

a. Place the intake manifold cover onto the engine over the studs.

b. Push down on the intake manifold cover directly over the rear stud in order to engage the cover to the stud.

c. Push down on the intake manifold cover directly over the front right stud in order to engage the cover to the stud.

d. Push down on the intake manifold cover directly over the front left stud in order to engage the cover to the stud.

OIL PAN

REMOVAL & INSTALLATION

See Figures 112 through 115.

1. Before servicing the vehicle, refer to the Precautions Section.

2. Remove the engine from vehicle.

3. Remove the oil pan bolts.

4. Remove the oil pan at pry points.

5. Clean the oil pan mating surface.

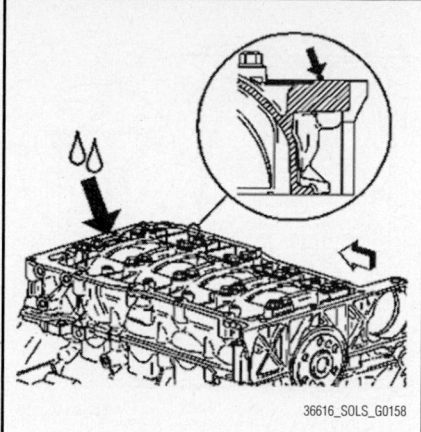

36616_SOLS_G0158

Fig. 113 Oil pan sealant application— 2.0L engines

➡**For 2.4L engines, the oil pan baffle and pickup screen are not removable from the oil pan.**

6. For 2.0L engines, remove the oil pan baffle bolts and oil pan baffle.

➡**Do not remove the pickup screen. It is press-fit into the oil pan.**

7. Clean the oil pan. Remove all the sludge and the oil deposits.

8. Inspect the threads for the engine oil drain plug.

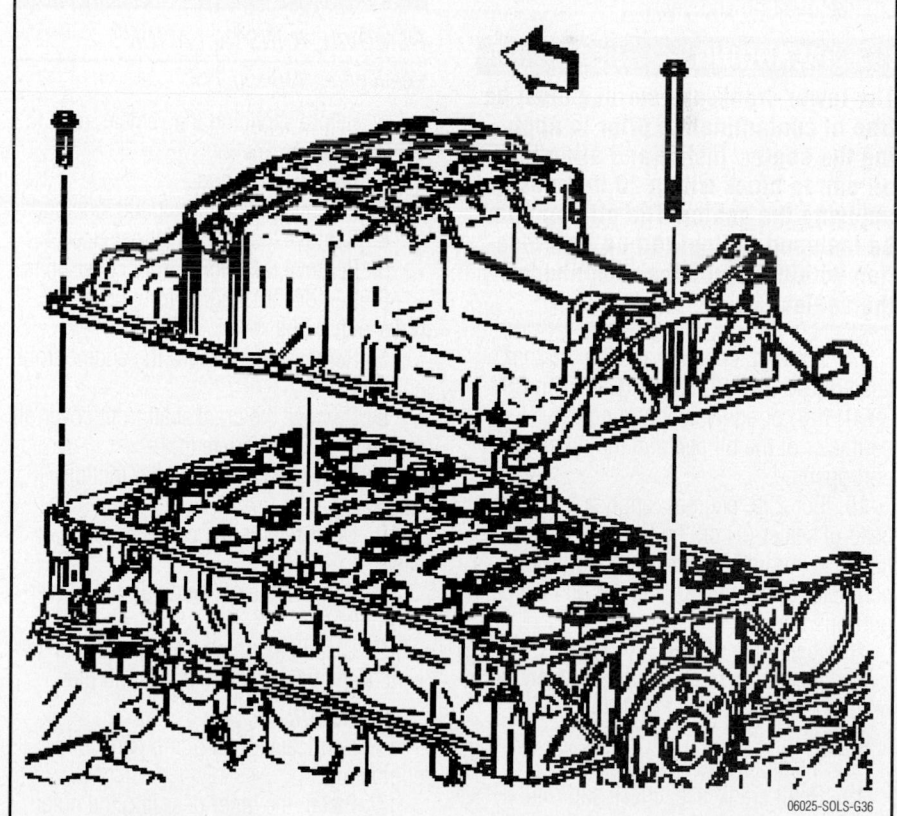

06025-SOLS-G36

Fig. 112 Oil pan pry points

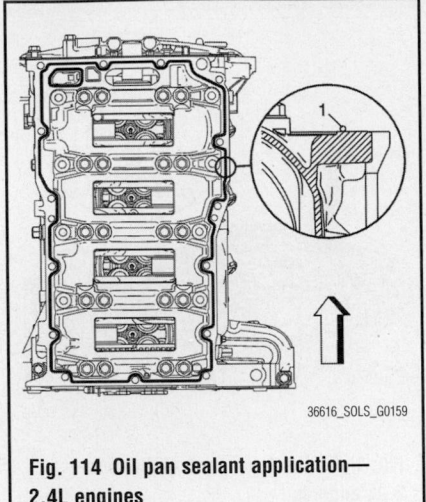

Fig. 114 Oil pan sealant application—2.4L engines

9. Inspect the oil pan for cracking near the pan rail and the transmission mounting points.

10. Inspect the oil pan for cracking resulting from impact or flying road debris.

11. Inspect the oil pan baffle and pickup screen.

12. Repair or replace the oil pan as necessary.

To install:

13. Make sure that the oil pan and mounting surface on the lower crankcase are free of all oil and debris.

✳✳ WARNING

The lower crankcase surface must be free of contamination prior to applying the sealer. Install and align the oil pan to block within 20 minutes of applying the sealer. The oil pan must be fastened to final torque specification within 60 minutes of applying the sealer.

14. For 2.0L engines, apply a 3.5 mm bead of GM P/N 12378521 (Canadian P/N 88901148) or equivalent around the perimeter of the oil pan and the oil suction port opening.

15. For 2.4L engines, apply a 2.25 mm bead of sealer (1) on the level part of the flange next to the chamfer around the perimeter of the oil pan and the oil suction port opening.

16. Install the oil pan.

17. Install the oil pan bolts. Tighten the oil pan bolts to 25 Nm (18 ft. lbs.) in sequence.

18. Install engine in vehicle.

19. Refill crankcase, check and refill fluids as needed.

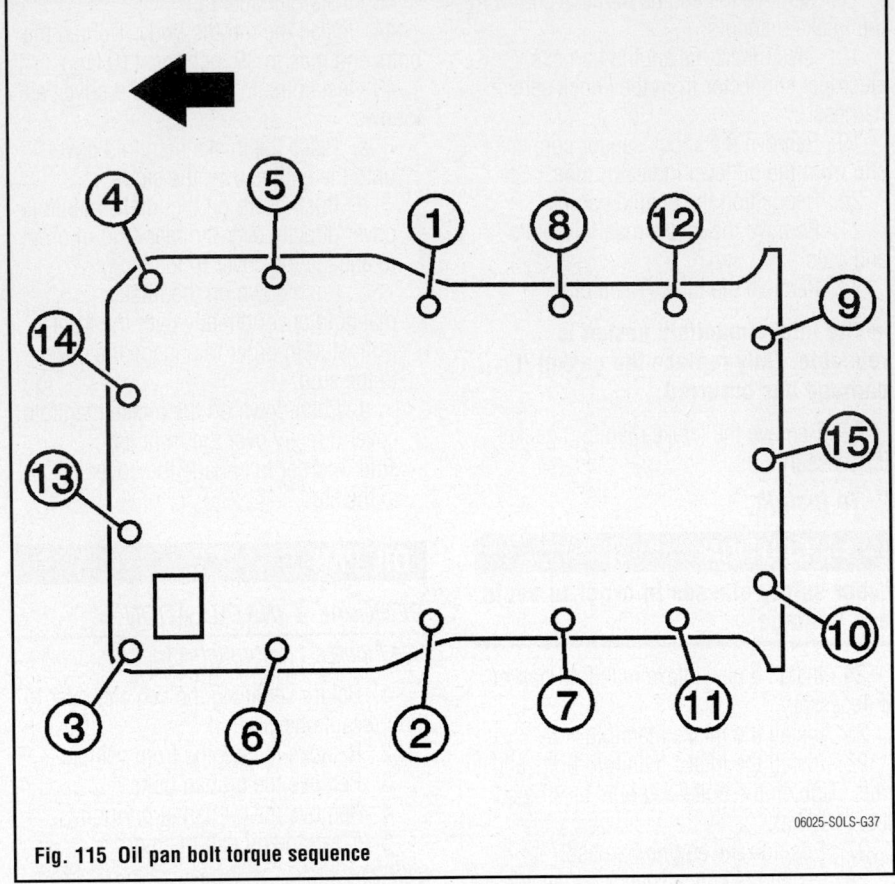

Fig. 115 Oil pan bolt torque sequence

OIL PUMP

REMOVAL & INSTALLATION

See Figures 116 and 117.

1. Before servicing the vehicle, refer to the Precautions Section.

2. Remove the hood.

3. Remove the drive belt and tensioner.

4. Remove the crankshaft balancer.

5. Remove the engine front cover bolts.

6. Remove the engine front cover to water pump bolt.

7. Remove and discard the engine front cover gasket.

8. Remove the crankshaft front cover oil seal with an appropriate tool.

9. Remove and discard the friction washer.

10. Disassemble the pressure relief valve.

11. Remove the oil pump gerotor cover and bolts.

12. Clean all of the parts in cleaning solvent. Remove varnish, sludge, and dirt.

To install:

13. Lubricate all oil pump parts with engine oil.

14. Install the inner gear into the outer gear.

➡ **If gears are improperly installed in the front cover, the gerotor cover will not bolt on.**

15. Install the gears together into the front cover with the hub of the center gear facing the front cover.

16. Install the oil pump gerotor cover and bolts.

17. Tighten the oil pump gerotor cover bolts to 53 inch lbs. (6 Nm).

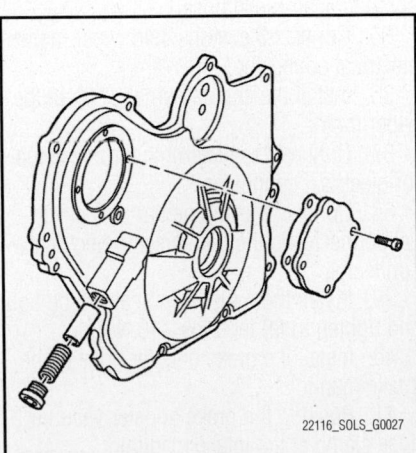

Fig. 116 Oil pressure relief valve removal shown

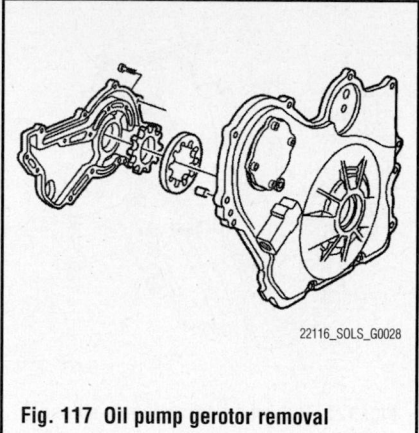

Fig. 117 Oil pump gerotor removal

18. Install the pressure relief valve piston.

19. Install the pressure relief valve spring and tighten to 30 ft. lbs. (40 Nm).

20. Install a new crankshaft front oil seal.

21. Install a new friction washer.

22. Position and install a new engine front cover gasket to the dowel pins.

23. Position and install the engine front cover.

24. Install the engine front cover to water pump bolt and tighten to 18 ft. lbs. (25 Nm).

25. Install the engine front cover bolts and tighten to 18 ft. lbs. (25 Nm).

26. Install the crankshaft balancer.

27. Install the drive belt and tensioner.

28. Install the hood.

PISTON & RING

POSITIONING

See Figure 118.

REAR MAIN SEAL

REMOVAL & INSTALLATION

See Figure 119.

1. Before servicing the vehicle, refer to the Precautions Section.

2. Remove the flywheel. Refer to Flywheel Removal & Installation.

➡**Do not damage the outside diameter of the crankshaft or chamber with any tool.**

3. Pry out the crankshaft rear oil seal using a flat-bladed tool.

To install:

4. Using a J 42067 seal driver, install a NEW crankshaft real oil seal.

5. Install the flywheel.

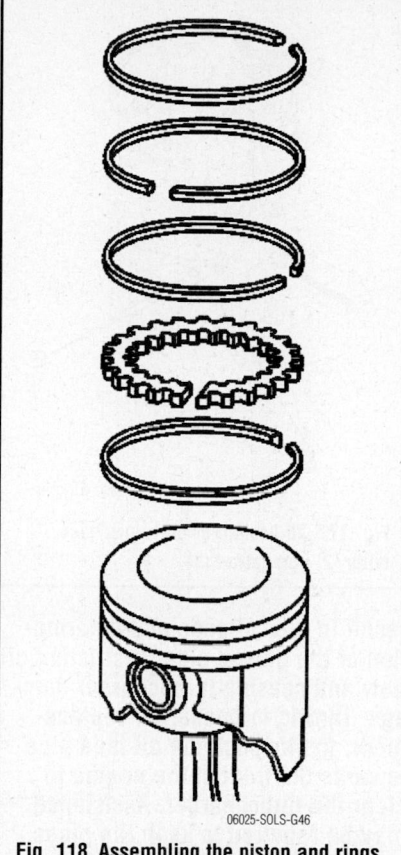

Fig. 118 Assembling the piston and rings

TURBOCHARGER

REMOVAL & INSTALLATION

2.0L (LNF) Engine

See Figures 120 through 123.

1. Before servicing the vehicle, refer to the Precautions Section.

2. Drain the cooling system.

3. Remove the charge air cooler inlet pipe.

4. Remove the charge air cooler pipe bolts at the turbocharger.

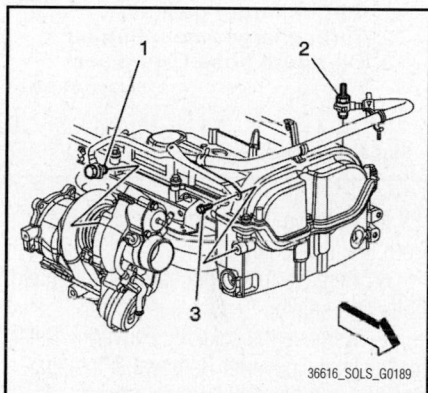

Fig. 120 Turbocharger coolant feed pipe bolts (1, 3) and gasket

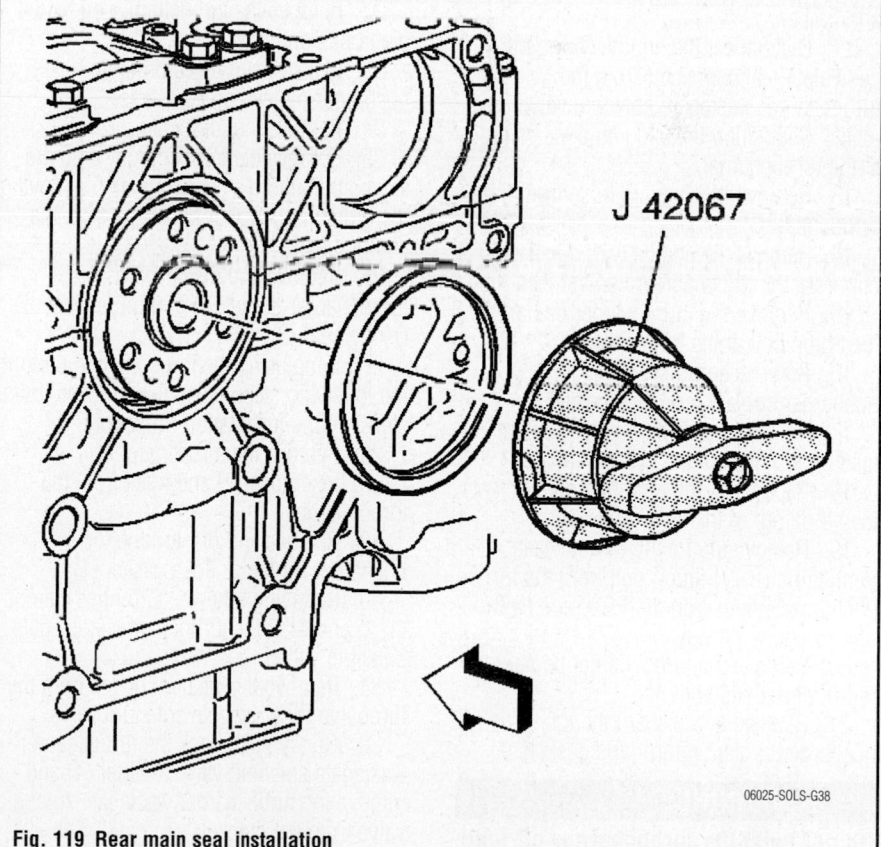

Fig. 119 Rear main seal installation

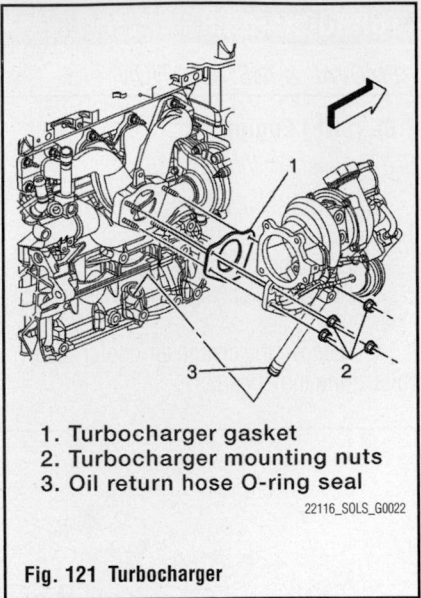

1. Turbocharger gasket
2. Turbocharger mounting nuts
3. Oil return hose O-ring seal

22116_SOLS_G0022

Fig. 121 Turbocharger

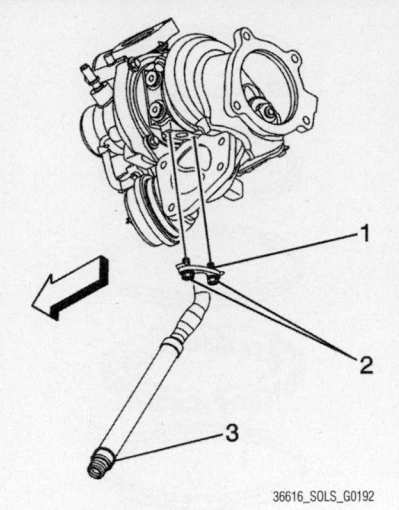

36616_SOLS_G0192

Fig. 122 Turbocharger oil return hose bolts (2) and gasket (1)

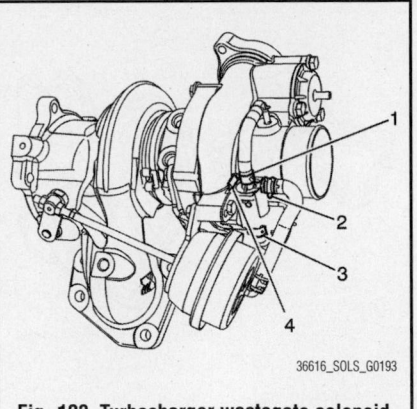

36616_SOLS_G0193

Fig. 123 Turbocharger wastegate solenoid valve and retainer (4); vacuum hose clamps (1, 2, and 3)

5. Remove the charge air cooler pipe from the turbocharger.

6. Remove the turbocharger heat shield bolts and shield.

7. Remove the catalytic converter. Refer to Catalytic Converter Removal & Installation.

8. Remove the catalytic converter bracket bolt, nut, and bracket.

9. Lower the vehicle

10. Remove the turbocharger brace nut and brace.

11. Disconnect the engine wiring harness electrical connector from the turbocharger wastegate solenoid valve.

12. Reposition the vacuum hose clamp at the turbocharger.

13. Remove the vacuum hose from the turbocharger.

14. Remove the engine wiring harness clip from the turbocharger coolant feed pipe.

15. Remove the turbocharger coolant feed pipe bolt at the turbocharger.

16. Remove and discard the turbocharger coolant feed pipe gasket.

17. Remove the turbocharger coolant feed pipe bolt from the cylinder head.

18. Reposition the turbocharger coolant feed pipe out of the way.

19. Remove the Positive Crankcase Ventilation (PCV) fitting bolt from the turbocharger. Reposition the PCV pipe (with fitting) out of the way.

20. Remove the turbocharger coolant return pipe bolts and pipe.

21. Remove and discard the turbocharger coolant return pipe gaskets.

⁂ **WARNING**

Do not twist the turbocharger oil feed pipe. Twisting of the feed pipe will

result in the collapse and deformation of the plastic pipe, restricting oil flow and causing turbocharger damage. During turbocharger replacement, gently push the oil feed pipe towards the front of the engine to clear the turbocharger. Assistance may be required to keep the pipes clear of the turbocharger during removal or installation.

22. Remove the turbocharger oil feed pipe bolts and pipe.

23. Remove and discard the turbocharger oil feed pipe gaskets.

24. Remove the turbocharger nuts (2).

25. Remove the turbocharger from the exhaust manifold studs while also removing the turbocharger oil return hose from the engine block.

26. Remove and discard the turbocharger gasket (1) and oil return hose O-ring seal (3).

27. If replacing the turbocharger, perform the following steps otherwise proceed to step 7 in the Installation Procedure.

28. Remove the turbocharger oil return hose bolts (2) and hose from the turbocharger.

29. Remove and discard the turbocharger oil return hose gasket (1).

30. Reposition the vacuum hose clamps (1, 2, and 3) at the turbocharger wastegate solenoid valve.

31. Remove the vacuum hoses from the turbocharger wastegate solenoid valve.

32. Gently push back the turbocharger wastegate solenoid valve retainer (4) and remove the turbocharger wastegate solenoid valve from the bracket.

To install:

33. If replacing the turbocharger, perform the following steps otherwise proceed to step 7.

34. Install the turbocharger wastegate solenoid valve to the bracket until the retainer clips into place.

35. Install the vacuum hoses to the turbocharger wastegate solenoid valve.

36. Position the vacuum hose clamps at the turbocharger wastegate solenoid valve.

37. Position a NEW turbocharger oil return hose gasket on the turbocharger oil return hose.

38. Install the turbocharger oil return hose and bolts and tighten to 89 inch lbs. (10 Nm).

39. Install a new turbocharger gasket onto the exhaust manifold studs.

40. Lubricate and install a new turbocharger oil return hose O-ring seal.

41. Install the turbocharger oil return hose to the engine block while also installing the turbocharger to the exhaust manifold studs.

42. Install the turbocharger nuts and tighten to 26 ft. lbs. (35 Nm).

43. Install new gaskets onto the turbocharger oil feed pipe fittings.

44. Install the turbocharger oil feed pipe and bolts. Tighten the bolts to 24 ft. lbs. (32 Nm).

45. Install new gaskets onto the turbocharger coolant return pipe fittings.

46. Install the turbocharger coolant return pipe and bolts. Tighten the bolts to 26 ft. lbs. (35 Nm).

47. Install a new O-ring seal to the PCV fitting.

48. Position the PCV pipe (with fitting) and install the PCV fitting bolt to the turbocharger. Tighten the bolt to 89 inch lbs. (10 Nm).

49. Position the turbocharger coolant feed pipe to the turbocharger.

50. Install NEW gaskets onto the turbocharger coolant feed pipe fitting.

51. Install the turbocharger coolant feed pipe bolt at the turbocharger. Tighten the bolt to 26 ft. lbs. (35 Nm).

52. Install the turbocharger coolant feed pipe bolt to the cylinder head. Tighten the bolt to 89 inch lbs. (10 Nm).

53. Install the engine wiring harness clip to the turbocharger coolant feed pipe.

54. Install the vacuum hose to the turbocharger.

55. Position the vacuum hose clamp at the turbocharger.

56. Connect the engine wiring harness electrical connector to the turbocharger wastegate solenoid valve.

57. Install the turbocharger brace bolt and nut. Tighten the nut to 43 ft. lbs. (58 Nm).

58. Raise and suitably support the vehicle.

59. Position the catalytic converter bracket to the engine.

60. Install the catalytic converter bracket bolt, and nut until snug.

61. Install the catalytic converter

62. Tighten the catalytic converter bracket bolt and nut to 43 ft. lbs. (58 Nm).

63. Lower the vehicle.

64. Install the turbocharger heat shield and bolts. Tighten the bolts to 89 inch lbs. (10 Nm).

65. Install the charge air cooler pipe and gasket to the turbocharger.

66. Install the charge air cooler pipe bolts at the turbocharger. Tighten the bolts to 16 ft. lbs. (22 Nm).

67. Install the charge air cooler inlet pipe.

68. Fill and bleed the cooling system.

TIMING CHAIN COVER & SEAL

REMOVAL & INSTALLATION

2.0L (LNF) Engine

See Figures 124 and 125.

1. Before servicing the vehicle, refer to the Precautions Section.

2. Remove the hood.

3. Remove the drive belt tensioner.

4. Remove the crankshaft balancer. Refer to Crankshaft Damper Removal & Installation.

5. Remove the engine front cover bolts.

6. Remove the engine front cover-to-water pump bolt.

7. Remove and discard the engine front cover gasket.

8. Remove the crankshaft front cover oil seal with an appropriate tool.

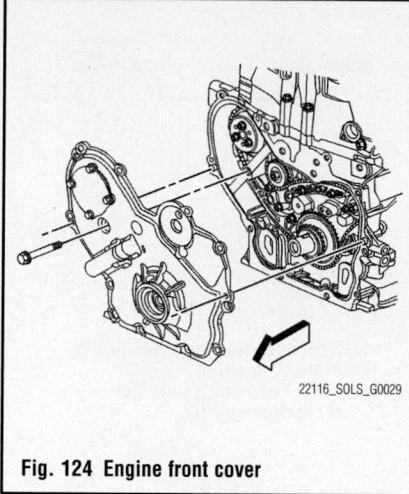

Fig. 124 Engine front cover

22116_SOLS_G0029

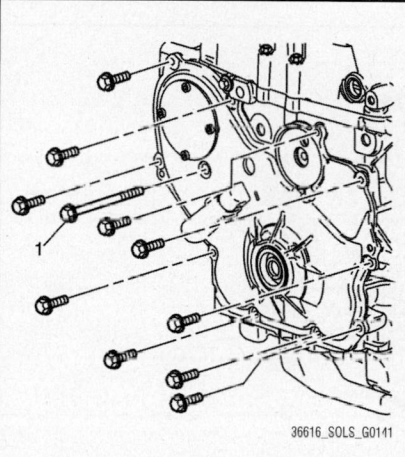

Fig. 125 Water pump bolts; install the center (1) bolt first

36616_SOLS_G0141

9. Remove and discard the friction washer.

To install:

10. Install a NEW crankshaft front oil seal.

11. Install a NEW friction washer.

12. Position and install a NEW engine front cover gasket to the dowel pins.

13. Install the engine front cover bolts.

➡The center bolt (1) should be tightened last.

14. Install the long water pump bolt (1) and tighten to 18 ft. lbs. (25 Nm).

15. Install the crankshaft balancer.

16. Install the drive belt tensioner. Torque to 33 ft. lbs. (45 Nm).

17. Install hood.

2.4L (LE5) Engine

See Figure 124.

1. Before servicing the vehicle, refer to the Precautions Section.

2. Remove the hood.

3. Remove the drive belt tensioner.

4. Remove the crankshaft balancer. Refer to Crankshaft Damper Removal & Installation.

5. Remove the engine front cover bolts.

6. Remove the engine front cover-to-water pump bolt.

7. Remove and discard the engine front cover gasket.

To install:

8. Position and install a NEW engine front cover gasket to the dowel pins.

9. Position and install the engine front cover.

10. Install the engine front cover to water pump bolt. Tighten the bolt to 18 ft. lbs. (25 Nm).

11. Install the engine front cover bolts. Tighten the bolts to 18 ft. lbs. (25 Nm).

12. Install the crankshaft balancer.

13. Install the drive belt tensioner. Tighten to 33 ft. lbs. (45 Nm).

14. Install hood.

TIMING CHAIN & SPROCKETS

REMOVAL & INSTALLATION

See Figures 126 through 135.

1. Remove the hood.

2. Remove the No. 1 cylinder spark plug.

3. Rotate the crankshaft in the engine rotational direction clockwise, until the No. 1 piston is at Top Dead Center (TDC) on the exhaust stroke.

4. Remove the camshaft cover.

5. Remove the engine front cover.

6. Remove the upper timing chain guide bolts and guide.

✳✳ WARNING

The timing chain tensioner must be removed to unload chain tension before the timing chain is removed. If it is not, the timing chain will become cocked and it will be difficult to remove.

7. Remove the timing chain tensioner.

8. Install a 24 mm wrench on the hex on the exhaust camshaft in order to hold the camshaft.

9. Remove and discard the exhaust camshaft actuator bolt.

10. Remove the exhaust camshaft actuator from the camshaft and timing chain.

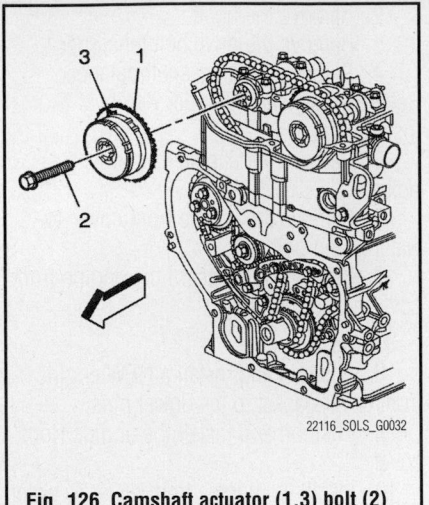

Fig. 126 Camshaft actuator (1,3) bolt (2)

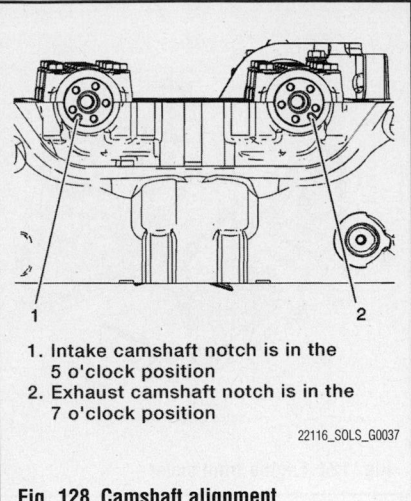

1. Intake camshaft notch is in the 5 o'clock position
2. Exhaust camshaft notch is in the 7 o'clock position

Fig. 128 Camshaft alignment

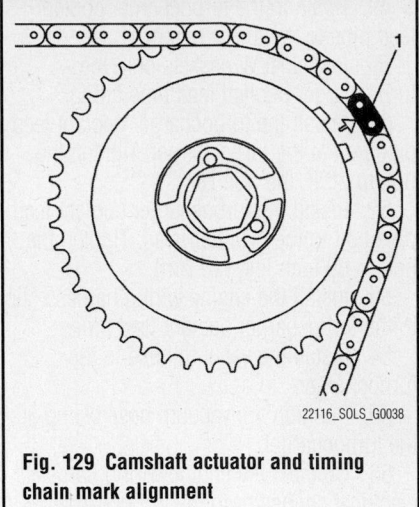

Fig. 129 Camshaft actuator and timing chain mark alignment

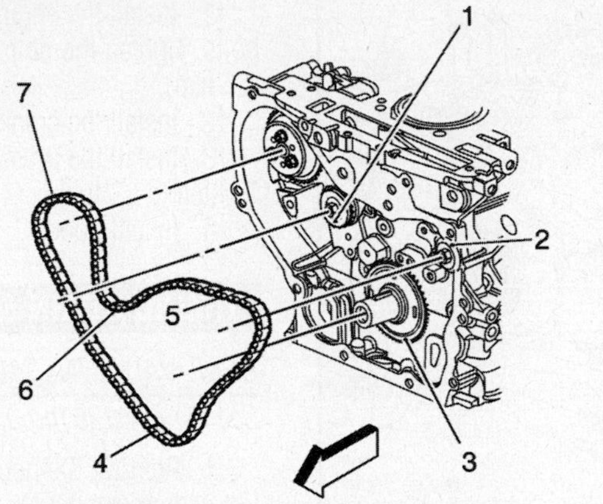

![Timing chain alignment diagram]

1. Balance shaft sprocket timing mark
2. Intake side balance shaft sprocket timing mark
3. Balance shaft drive sprocket timing mark
4. Chrome link
5. Copper link
6. Chrome link
7. Timing chain

Fig. 127 Timing chain alignment

11. Remove the timing chain tensioner guide bolt and guide.

12. Remove the fixed timing chain guide access plug.

13. Remove the fixed timing chain guide bolts and guide.

14. Install a 24 mm wrench on the hex on the intake camshaft in order to hold the camshaft.

15. Remove and discard the intake camshaft actuator bolt.

16. Remove the intake camshaft actuator, and the timing chain through the top of the cylinder head.

17. Remove the timing chain crankshaft sprocket.

18. If replacing the balance shaft timing chain and sprocket, perform the following steps. If not, proceed to step 10 in the installation procedure.

19. Remove the balance shaft drive chain tensioner bolts and tensioner.

20. Remove the adjustable balance shaft chain guide bolt and guide.

21. Remove the small balance shaft drive chain guide bolts and guide.

22. Remove the upper balance shaft drive chain guide bolts and guide.

➡ It may ease removal of the balance shaft drive chain to get all the slack in the chain between the crankshaft and water pump sprockets.

23. Remove the balance shaft drive chain.

24. Remove the balance shaft drive sprocket.

To install:

25. If replacing the balance shaft timing chain, perform the following steps. If not, proceed to step 10.

26. Install the balance shaft drive sprocket.

❄ WARNING

If the balance shafts are not properly timed to the engine, the engine may vibrate or make noise.

27. Install the balance shaft drive chain (1) with the colored link lined up with the marks on the balance shaft sprockets and the balance shaft drive sprocket. There are three colored links on the chain. Two are chrome and one is copper. Use the following steps in order to line up the links with the sprockets:

   a. Place the copper link (5) so that it lines up with the timing mark (2) on the intake side balance shaft sprocket.

   b. Working clockwise around the chain, place the chrome link (4) in line with the timing mark (3) on the balance shaft drive sprocket. (Approximately 6 o'clock position on the sprocket.)

   c. Place the chain (7) on the water pump drive sprocket. The alignment is not critical.

   d. Align the last chrome link (6) with the timing mark (1) on the exhaust side balance shaft drive sprocket.

28. Install the upper balance shaft drive chain guide and bolts. Tighten bolts to 11 ft. lbs. (15 Nm).

29. Install the small balance shaft drive chain guide and bolts. Tighten bolts to 11 ft. lbs. (15 Nm).

30. Install the adjustable balance shaft chain guide and bolt and tighten to 89 inch lbs. (10 Nm).

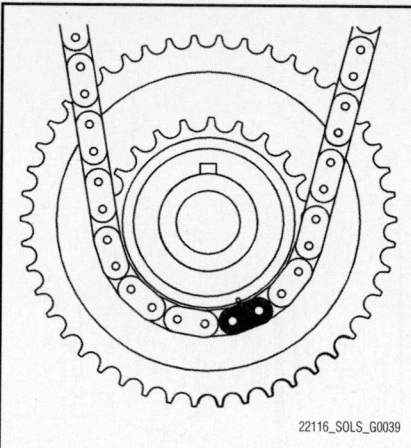

Fig. 130 Crankshaft sprocket and timing chain mark alignment

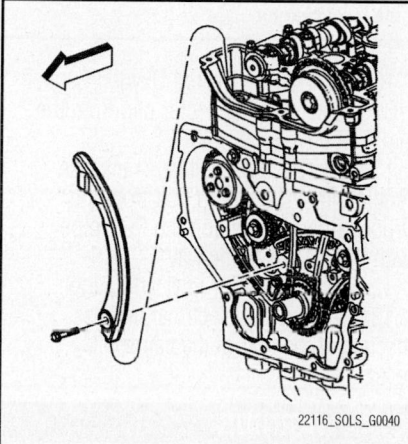

Fig. 131 Installation of the adjustable timing chain guide

31. Reset the timing chain tensioner by performing the following steps:

a. Rotate the tensioner plunger 90 degrees in its bore and compress the plunger.

b. Rotate the tensioner back to the original 12 o'clock position and insert a paper clip through the hole in the plunger body and into the hose in the tensioner plunger.

32. Install the balance shaft drive chain tensioner and bolts and tighten to 89 inch lbs. (10 Nm).

33. Remove the paper clip from the balance shaft drive chain tensioner.

34. Ensure the intake camshaft notch is in the 5 o'clock position (2) and the exhaust camshaft notch is in the 7 o'clock position (1). The number 1 piston should be at TDC, crankshaft key at 12 o'clock.

※※ WARNING

There are 3 colored links on the timing chain. 2 links are of matching

color, and 1 link is of a unique color. Use the following procedure to line up the links with the actuators. Orient the chain so that the colored links are visible. Always use new actuator bolts.

35. Install the timing chain drive sprocket to the crankshaft with the timing mark in the 5 o'clock position and the front of the sprocket facing out.

36. Assemble the intake camshaft actuator into the timing chain with the timing mark lined up with the uniquely colored link.

37. Lower the timing chain through the opening in the cylinder head. Use care to ensure that the chain goes around both sides of the cylinder block bosses.

38. Install the intake camshaft actuator onto the intake camshaft while aligning the dowel pin into the camshaft slot.

39. Hand tighten the new intake camshaft actuator bolt.

40. Route the timing chain around the crankshaft sprocket and line up the first matching colored link with the timing mark on the crankshaft sprocket, in approximately the 5 o'clock position.

41. Rotate the crankshaft clockwise to remove all chain slack. Do not rotate the intake camshaft.

42. Install the adjustable timing chain guide down through the opening in the cylinder head and install the adjustable timing chain bolt. Tighten the adjustable timing chain guide bolt to 89 inch lbs. (10 Nm).

➡**Always install new actuator bolts.**

43. Install the exhaust camshaft actuator into the timing chain with the timing mark lined up with the second matching colored link.

44. Install the exhaust camshaft actuator onto the exhaust camshaft, aligning the dowel pin into the camshaft slot.

45. Using a 23 mm open end wrench, rotate the exhaust camshaft approximately 45 degrees until the dowel pin in the camshaft actuator goes into the camshaft slot.

46. When the actuator seats on the cam, tighten the new exhaust camshaft actuator bolt hand tight.

47. Verify that all of the colored links and the appropriate timing marks are still aligned. If they are not aligned, repeat the portion of the procedure necessary to align the timing marks.

48. Install the fixed timing chain guide and bolts. Tighten the fixed timing chain guide bolts to 106 inch lbs. (12 Nm).

49. Install the upper timing chain guide and bolts, tighten to 89 inch lbs. (10 Nm).

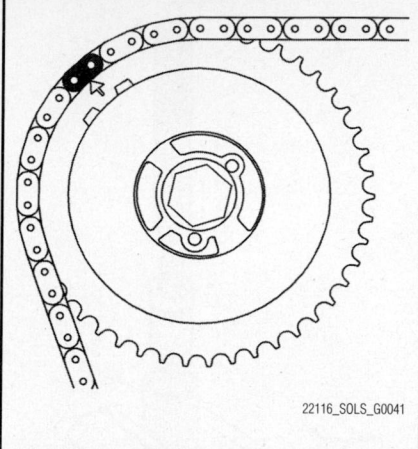

Fig. 132 Camshaft actuator and timing chain mark alignment

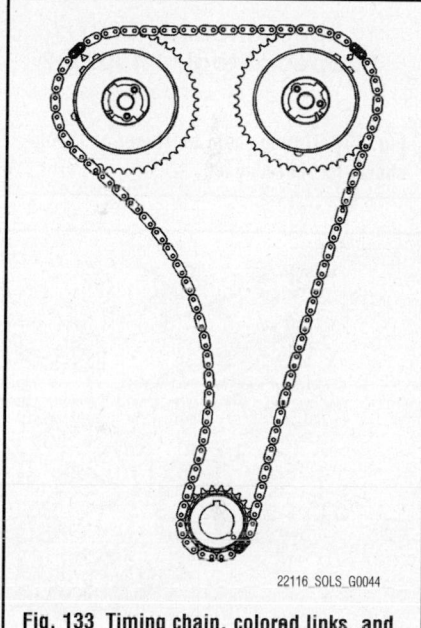

Fig. 133 Timing chain, colored links, and marks

50. Reset the timing chain tensioner by performing the following steps:

a. Remove the snap ring.

b. Remove the piston assembly from the body of the timing chain tensioner.

c. Install the J 45027-2 (2) into a vise.

d. Install the notch end of the piston assembly into the J 45027-2 (2).

e. Using the J 45027-1 (1), turn the ratchet cylinder into the piston.

f. Reinstall the piston assembly into the body of the tensioner.

g. Install the snap ring.

51. Inspect the timing chain tensioner seal for damage. If damaged, replace the seal.

52. Inspect to ensure all dirt and debris is removed from the timing chain tensioner threaded hole in the cylinder head.

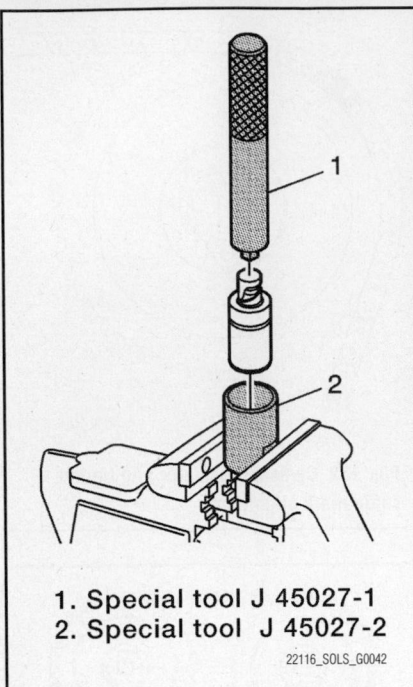

1. Special tool J 45027-1
2. Special tool J 45027-2

22116_SOLS_G0042

Fig. 134 Timing chain tensioner and tools shown for resetting

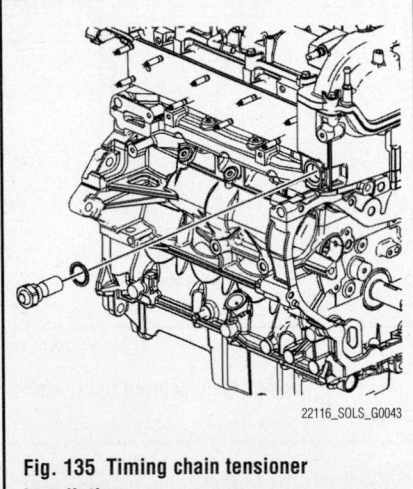

22116_SOLS_G0043

Fig. 135 Timing chain tensioner installation

☼☼ WARNING

Ensure the timing chain tensioner seal is centered throughout the torque procedure to eliminate the possibility of an oil leak.

53. Install the timing chain tensioner assembly and tighten to 55 ft. lbs. (75 Nm).

54. The timing chain tensioner is released by compressing it 0.079 inch (2 mm), which will release the locking mechanism in the ratchet. To release the timing chain tensioner, use a suitable tool with a rubber tip on the end. Feed the tool down through the cam drive chest to rest on the cam chain. Then give a sharp jolt diagonally downwards to release the tensioner.

55. Using a 23 mm wrench, engage the hex on the intake camshaft, and using a torque wrench, tighten the camshaft actuator bolt. Tighten the intake camshaft position actuator bolt to 22 ft. lbs. (30 Nm). plus an additional 100 degrees using the J 45059 angle meter.

56. Using a 23 mm wrench, engage the hex on the exhaust camshaft, and using a torque wrench, tighten the camshaft actuator bolt. Tighten the exhaust camshaft position actuator bolt to 22 ft. lbs. (30 Nm). plus an additional 100 degrees using the J 45059 angle meter.

57. Install the timing chain oiling nozzle and tighten to 89 inch lbs. (10 Nm).

58. Apply sealant compound GM P/N 12345382 (Canadian P/N 10953489) to the thread of the timing chain guide bolt access hole plug.

59. Install the timing chain guide bolt access hole plug and tighten to 66 ft. lbs. (90 Nm).

60. Install the engine front cover.

61. Install the camshaft cover.

62. Install the No. 1 cylinder spark plug.

63. Install the hood.

VALVE COVERS/CAMSHAFT COVER

REMOVAL & INSTALLATION

2.0L (LNF) Engine

See Figure 136.

1. Before servicing the vehicle, refer to the Precautions Section.

2. Remove the intake manifold cover. Refer to Intake Manifold Removal & Installation.

3. Remove the intake manifold cover studs.

4. Remove the air cleaner outlet.

5. Disconnect the engine wiring harness intake and exhaust electrical connectors from the camshaft position actuator solenoid valves.

6. Remove the engine wiring harness clip from the camshaft cover.

7. Remove the engine wiring harness clips from the camshaft cover.

8. Disconnect the engine wiring harness electrical connector from the Evaporative Emission (EVAP) canister purge solenoid valve.

9. Remove the ignition coils. Refer to Ignition Coil Module Removal & Installation.

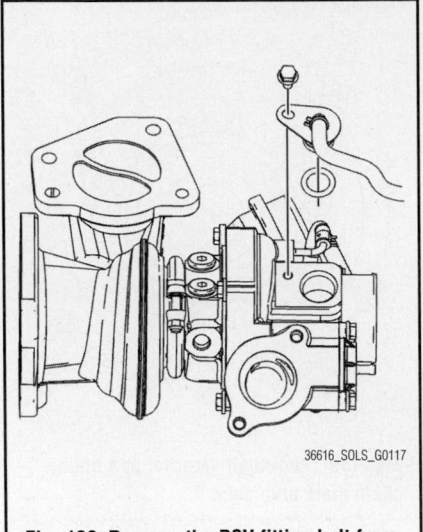

36616_SOLS_G0117

Fig. 136 Remove the PCV fitting bolt from the turbocharger

10. Remove the Heated Oxygen Sensor (HO2S) electrical connector clip from the camshaft cover.

11. Remove the Positive Crankcase Ventilation (PCV) fitting bolt from the turbocharger. Reposition the PCV pipe (with fitting) out of the way.

12. Remove the air inlet grill panel.

13. Remove the electrical harness attached at the rear of the camshaft cover.

☼☼ WARNING

The PCV hose should NOT be disconnected from the camshaft cover as damage to the hose connection will result.

14. Remove the camshaft cover bolts.

15. Remove the camshaft cover.

To install:

16. Install the camshaft cover and bolts and tighten to 89 inch lbs. (10 Nm).

17. Attach the electrical harness at the rear of the camshaft cover.

18. Install the air inlet grill panel.

19. Install a NEW O-ring seal to the PCV fitting.

20. Position the PCV pipe (with fitting), install the PCV fitting bolt to the turbocharger and tighten to 89 inch lbs. (10 Nm).

21. Install the HO2S electrical connector clip to the camshaft cover.

22. Install the ignition coils.

23. Disconnect the engine wiring harness electrical connector from the EVAP canister purge solenoid valve.

24. Install the engine harness clips to the camshaft cover.

25. Install the engine wiring harness clip to the camshaft cover.

26. Connect the engine wiring harness intake and exhaust electrical connectors to the camshaft position actuator solenoid valves.

27. Install the air cleaner outlet.

28. Install the intake manifold cover studs and tighten to 80 inch lbs. (9 Nm).

29. Install the intake manifold cover.

2.4L (LE5) Engine

See Figures 137 and 138.

1. Before servicing the vehicle, refer to the Precautions Section.

2. Remove the intake manifold cover. Refer to Intake Manifold Removal & Installation.

3. Remove the intake manifold cover studs.

4. Remove the air cleaner outlet resonator.

5. Reposition the Positive Crankcase Ventilation (PCV) hose clamp.

6. Remove the PCV hose from the cover.

7. Disconnect the intake (1) and exhaust (2) camshaft position actuator solenoid valve electrical connectors.

8. Remove the engine harness clip from the cam cover.

9. Remove the engine harness bracket (1) from the intake manifold cover stud.

10. Disconnect the Evaporative Emission (EVAP) canister purge solenoid valve electrical connector (1).

11. Remove the engine harness clip (2) from the EVAP purge solenoid bracket.

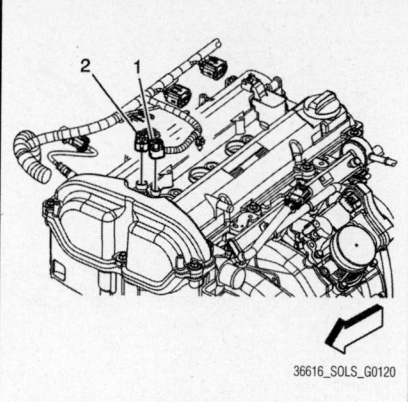

Fig. 137 Disconnect the intake (1) and exhaust (2) camshaft position actuator solenoid valve electrical connectors

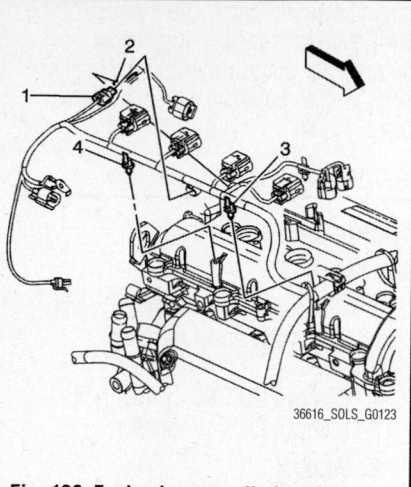

Fig. 138 Engine harness clip locations

12. Remove the engine harness clips (3, 4) from the cam cover.

13. Remove the ignition coils. Refer to Ignition Coil Module Removal & Installation.

14. Remove the camshaft cover bolts.

15. Remove the camshaft cover.

To install:

16. Install the camshaft cover and bolts. Tighten the bolts to 89 inch lbs. (10 Nm).

17. Install the ignition coils.

18. Install the engine harness clips to the cam cover.

19. Install the engine harness clip to the EVAP purge solenoid bracket.

20. Connect the EVAP canister purge solenoid valve electrical connector.

21. Install the engine harness bracket to the intake manifold cover stud.

22. Install the engine harness clip to the cam cover.

23. Connect the intake and exhaust) camshaft position actuator solenoid valve electrical connectors.

24. Install the PCV hose from the cover.

25. Position the PCV hose clamp.

26. Install the air cleaner outlet resonator.

27. Install the intake manifold cover studs. Tighten the studs to 80 inch lbs. (9 Nm).

28. Install the intake manifold cover.

VALVE LASH

ADJUSTMENT

Hydraulic lash adjusters are used on all engines and no adjustment is necessary.

ENGINE PERFORMANCE & EMISSION CONTROLS

ACCELERATOR PEDAL POSITION (APP) SENSOR

LOCATION

The Accelerator Pedal Position (APP) Sensor is located inside the vehicle. It is mounted at the top of the accelerator pedal and is part of the assembly.

REMOVAL & INSTALLATION

See Figure 139.

1. Remove the knee bolster.

2. Disconnect the Accelerator Pedal Position (APP) sensor electrical connector.

3. Remove the APP sensor nuts.

4. Remove the APP sensor from the vehicle.

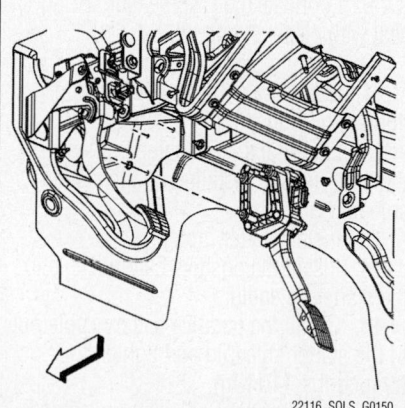

Fig. 139 Accelerator Pedal Position (APP) sensor

To Install:

5. Install the APP sensor to the vehicle.

6. Install the APP sensor nuts and tighten to 89 inch lbs. (10 Nm).

7. Connect the APP sensor electrical connector.

8. Confirm that the APP sensor connector locking clip is fully secured.

9. Verify the operation of the accelerator pedal.

10. Install the knee bolster.

CAMSHAFT POSITION (CMP) SENSOR

LOCATION

There are two Camshaft Position Sensors (CMP). They are located to the rear of the engine cylinder head. The exhaust CMP sensor is located just below the canister purge valve and the intake sensor is on opposite side of cylinder head.

REMOVAL & INSTALLATION

Engine Intake Sensor

See Figure 140.

1. Disconnect the intake Camshaft Position (CMP) sensor electrical connector.
2. Remove the CMP sensor bolt.
3. Remove the CMP sensor.

To install:

➡ **Inspect the CMP sensor for damage, replace as necessary.**

4. Lubricate the CMP sensor O-ring seal with clean engine oil.
5. Install the CMP sensor.
6. Install the CMP sensor bolt and tighten to 89 inch lbs. (10 Nm).

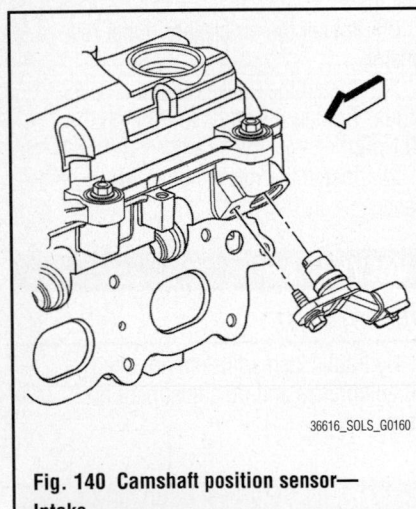

Fig. 140 Camshaft position sensor—Intake

Engine Exhaust Sensor

See Figure 141.

1. Disconnect the exhaust Camshaft Position (CMP) sensor electrical connector.
2. Remove the CMP sensor bolt.
3. Remove the CMP sensor.

To install:

➡ **Inspect the CMP sensor for damage, replace as necessary.**

4. Lubricate the CMP sensor O-ring seal with clean engine oil.
5. Install the CMP sensor.
6. Install the CMP sensor bolt and tighten to 89 inch lbs. (10 Nm).

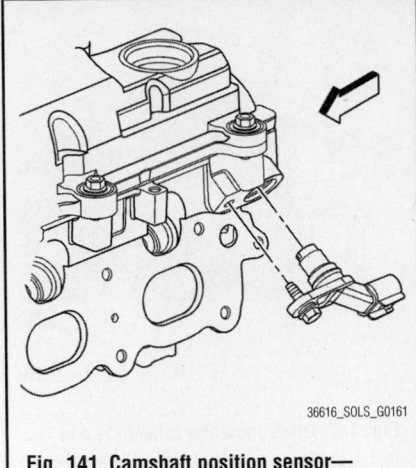

Fig. 141 Camshaft position sensor—Exhaust

CRANKSHAFT POSITION (CKP) SENSOR

LOCATION

The 2.4L (LE5) and 2.0L (LNF) engine Crankshaft Position (CKP) sensor is mounted to the rear of the engine block, and above the starter motor.

REMOVAL & INSTALLATION

See Figure 142.

1. Disconnect the negative battery cable.
2. Disconnect the Crankshaft Position (CKP) sensor electrical connector.
3. Remove the oil level indicator tube.
4. Remove the positive battery cable nut from the starter solenoid.
5. Remove the positive battery cable from the starter solenoid.
6. Remove Starter motor.
7. Remove the CKP sensor bolt.
8. Remove the CKP sensor.

To Install:

9. Lubricate the CKP sensor O-ring seal with clean engine oil.
10. Install the CKP sensor.
11. Install the CKP sensor bolt and tighten to 89 inch lbs. (10 Nm).
12. Ensure that the engine harness terminal no. is still installed on the starter solenoid.
13. Install starter motor.
14. Install the positive battery cable to the starter solenoid.
15. Install the positive battery cable nut to the starter solenoid and tighten to 89 inch lbs. (10 Nm).
16. Connect the CKP sensor electrical connector (3).
17. Install the oil level indicator tube.

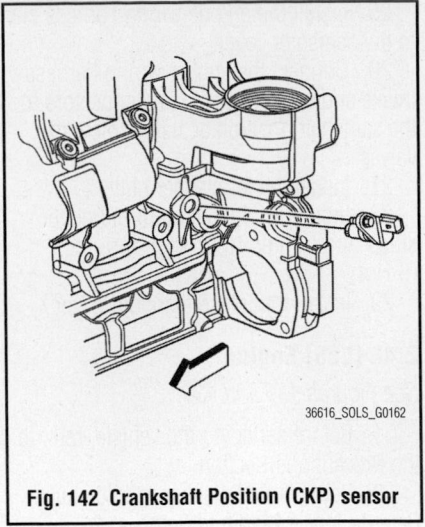

Fig. 142 Crankshaft Position (CKP) sensor

18. Connect the negative battery cable.

CRANKSHAFT POSITION SYSTEM VARIATION LEARN

The Crankshaft Position (CKP) system variation learn procedure is required when the following service procedures have been performed, regardless of whether DTC P0315 is set:

- Engine replacement
- Engine Control Module (ECM) replacement
- Crankshaft damper replacement
- Crankshaft replacement
- CKP sensor replacement
- Any engine repairs which disturb the crankshaft to CKP sensor relationship

The scan tool monitors certain component signals to determine if all the conditions are met to continue with the CKP system variation learn procedure. The scan tool only displays the condition that inhibits the procedure. The scan tool monitors the following components:

- CKP sensor activity: If there is a CKP sensor condition, refer to the applicable DTC that set.
- Camshaft Position (CMP) signal activity: If there is a CMP signal condition, refer to the applicable DTC that set.
- Engine Coolant Temperature (ECT): If the engine coolant temperature is not warm enough, idle the engine until the engine coolant temperature reaches the correct temperature.

1. Install a scan tool.
2. Monitor the ECM for DTCs with a scan tool. If other DTCs are set, except DTC P0315, refer to Diagnostic Trouble Code (DTC) List.
3. With a scan tool, select the CKP system variation learn procedure and perform the following:

a. Observe the fuel cut-off for the applicable engine.

b. Block the drive wheels.

c. Set the parking brake.

d. Place the vehicle's transmission in Park or Neutral.

e. Turn the Air Conditioning (A/C) OFF.

f. Cycle the ignition from OFF to ON.

g. Apply and hold the brake pedal for the duration of the procedure.

h. Start and idle the engine.

i. Accelerate to Wide Open Throttle (WOT). The engine should not accelerate beyond the calibrated fuel cut-off RPM value noted in step (A). Release the throttle immediately if the value is exceeded.

➡ While the learn procedure is in progress, release the throttle immediately when the engine starts to decelerate. The engine control is returned to the operator and the engine responds to throttle position after the learn procedure is complete.

j. Release the throttle when fuel cut-off occurs.

4. The scan tool displays Learn Status: Learned this Ignition. If the scan tool indicates that DTC P0315 ran and passed, the CKP variation learn procedure is complete. If the scan tool indicates DTC P0315 failed or did not run, refer to DTC P0315. If any other DTCs set, refer to Diagnostic Trouble Code (DTC).

5. Turn OFF the ignition for 30 seconds after the learn procedure is completed successfully.

ELECTRONIC CONTROL MODULE (ECM)

LOCATION

The Electronic Control Module (ECM) is located in the left front fender above windshield washer container.

REMOVAL & INSTALLATION

See Figure 143.

✳✳ WARNING

Turn the ignition OFF when installing or removing the control module connectors and disconnecting or reconnecting the power to the control module (battery cable, Powertrain Control Module (PCM) Electronic Control Module (ECM) Transaxle Control Module (TCM) pigtail, control module fuse, jumper cables, etc.) in order to

prevent internal control module damage. Control module damage may result when the metal case contacts battery voltage. DO NOT contact the control module metal case with battery voltage when servicing a control module, using battery booster cables, or when charging the vehicle battery.

✳✳ WARNING

In order to prevent any possible electrostatic discharge damage to the control module, do not touch the connector pins or the soldered components on the circuit board. Remove any debris from around the control module connector surfaces before servicing the control module. Inspect the control module connector gaskets when diagnosing or replacing the control module. Ensure that the gaskets are installed correctly. The gaskets prevent contaminant intrusion into the control module.

➡ The replacement control module must be programmed.

1. Using a scan tool, retrieve the percentage of remaining engine oil. Record the remaining engine oil life.

2. Record the preset radio stations.

3. Turn the ignition OFF.

4. Disconnect the negative battery cable.

5. Remove the left front fender.

6. Remove the windshield washer solvent container.

7. Release the Engine Control Module (ECM) bracket upper and lower retaining tabs using a small screwdriver or other suitable tool.

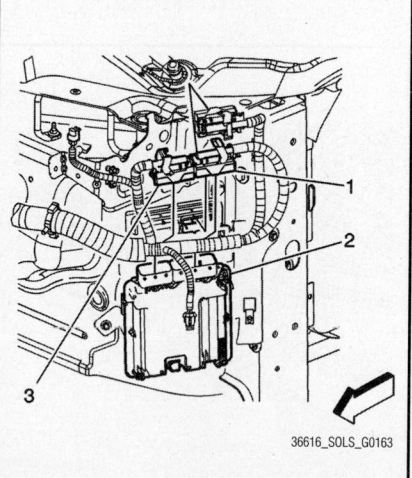

Fig. 143 Electronic Control Module location

8. Remove the ECM from the bracket by lifting upward after releasing the tabs.

9. Disconnect the engine wiring harness electrical connectors from the ECM.

To install:

10. Connect the engine wiring harness electrical connectors to the ECM.

11. Slide the ECM into the bracket.

12. Push down on the ECM until the upper and lower retaining tabs snap into place.

13. Connect the negative battery cable.

14. Install the windshield washer solvent container.

15. Install the left front fender.

16. Reset the clock and preset radio stations.

17. If a new ECM was installed, the ECM must be programmed.

RESET

Clearing diagnostic trouble codes resets ECM.

ENGINE COOLANT TEMPERATURE (ECT) SENSOR

LOCATION

2.0L (LNF) Engine

The Engine Coolant Temperature (ECT) sensor is located to the rear of engine and behind the turbocharger. It is mounted between two coolant pipes next to the thermostat housing.

2.4L (LE5) Engine

The Engine Coolant Temperature (ECT) sensor is located to the rear of engine just below the Camshaft Position (CMP) sensor.

REMOVAL & INSTALLATION

See Figure 144.

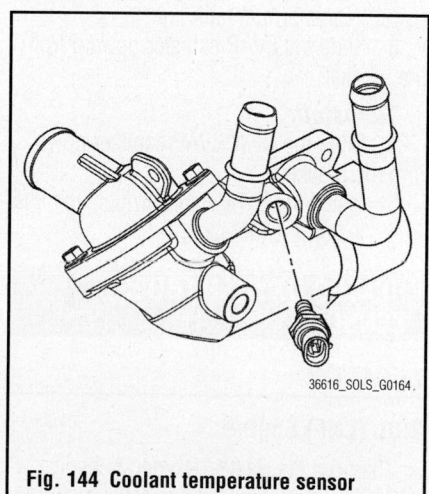

Fig. 144 Coolant temperature sensor

1. Partially drain the cooling system.
2. Disconnect the engine wiring harness electrical connector from the Engine Coolant Temperature (ECT) sensor.
3. Remove the ECT.

To install:

4. Install the ECT.
5. Tighten the ECT sensor to 15 ft. lbs. (20 Nm).
6. Connect the engine wiring harness electrical connector to the ECT sensor.
7. Fill and bleed the cooling system as needed.

EVAPORATIVE EMISSIONS (EVAP) CANISTER

LOCATION

See Figure 145.

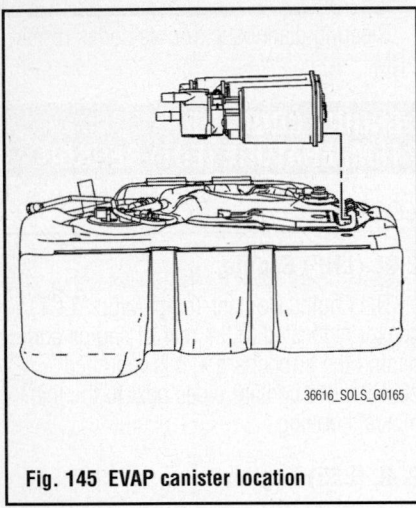

36616_SOLS_G0165

Fig. 145 EVAP canister location

REMOVAL & INSTALLATION

See Figure 145.

1. Remove the fuel tank. Refer to Fuel Tank in Fuel Systems.
2. Remove the Evaporative Emission (EVAP) canister/fuel tank line.
3. Slide the EVAP canister upward from the bracket.

To install:

4. Slide the NEW EVAP canister down into the bracket.
5. Install the EVAP canister/fuel tank line.
6. Install the fuel tank.

HEATED OXYGEN (HO2S) SENSOR

LOCATION

2.0L (LNF) Engine

The front (1) Heated Oxygen Sensor (HO2S) is mounted in the exhaust manifold after the turbocharger and before the catalytic converter.

The rear (2) Heated Oxygen Sensor (HO2S) in mounted in the front exhaust pipe and after the catalytic converter

2.4L (LE5) Engine

The front (1) Heated Oxygen Sensor (HO2S) is mounted in the exhaust manifold and before the catalytic converter.

The rear (2) Heated Oxygen Sensor (HO2S) in mounted in the front exhaust pipe and after the catalytic converter.

REMOVAL & INSTALLATION

2.4L (LE5) Engine Front (1) and Rear (2)

See Figure 146.

> **❊❊ WARNING**
>
> **The oxygen sensor uses a permanently attached pigtail and connector. Do not remove the pigtail from the oxygen sensor. Damage to or removal of the pigtail connector could affect proper operation of the oxygen sensor. The use of excessive force may damage the threads in the exhaust manifold/pipe.**

➡ The Heated Oxygen Sensors (HO2S) may be difficult to remove when the engine temperature is less than 120°F (48°C).

1. Open the hood.
2. Remove the Connector Position Assurance (CPA) retainer.
3. Disconnect the HO2S electrical connector.
4. Remove the HO2S electrical connector clip from the junction block bracket.

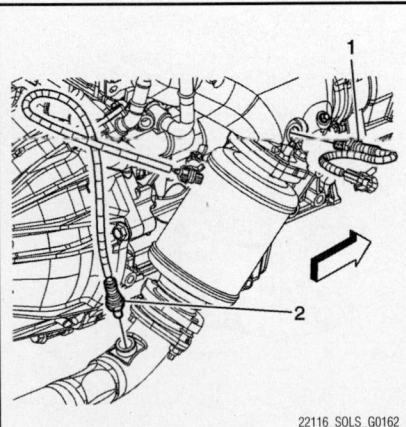

22116_SOLS_G0162

Fig. 146 Front (1) and Rear (2) Heated Oxygen Sensors

5. Raise and support the vehicle for removal of the rear HO2S only.
6. Using an approved oxygen sensor wrench, remove the HO2S.

To install:

➡ A special anti-seize compound is used on the HO2S threads. The compound consists of a liquid graphite and glass beads. The graphite will burn away, but the glass beads will remain, making the sensor easier to remove. New or service sensors will have the compound applied to the threads. If a sensor is removed and is to be reinstalled, the threads must have an anti-seize compound applied before installation.

7. If reinstalling the old HO2S, coat the threads with anti-seize compound.
8. Using an approved oxygen sensor wrench, install the HO2S.
9. Tighten the HO2S to 30 ft. lbs. (41 Nm).
10. Lower vehicle if rear HO2S was installed.
11. Connect the HO2S electrical connector.
12. Install the CPA retainer.
13. Close the hood.

2.0L (LNF) Engine Front (1) and Rear (2)

See Figures 147 and 148.

> **❊❊ WARNING**
>
> **The oxygen sensor uses a permanently attached pigtail and connector. Do not remove the pigtail from the oxygen sensor. Damage to or removal of the pigtail connector could affect proper operation of the oxygen sensor. The use of excessive force may damage the threads in the exhaust manifold/pipe.**

➡ The Heated Oxygen Sensors (HO2S) may be difficult to remove when the engine temperature is less than 120°F (48°C).

1. Open the hood.
2. Remove the Connector Position Assurance (CPA) retainer.
3. Disconnect the HO2S electrical connector from the engine wiring harness electrical connector.
4. Raise and support the vehicle for removal of the rear HO2S only.
5. Using an approved oxygen sensor wrench, remove the HO2S.

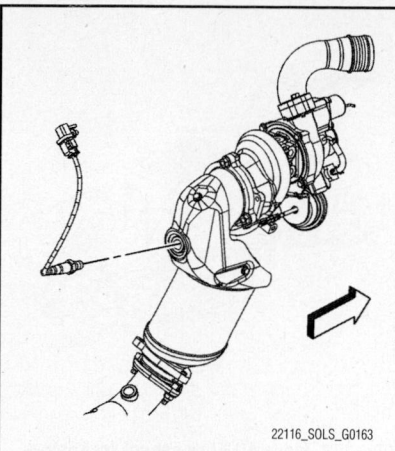

Fig. 147 Front (1) Heated Oxygen Sensors—2.0L (LNF) engine

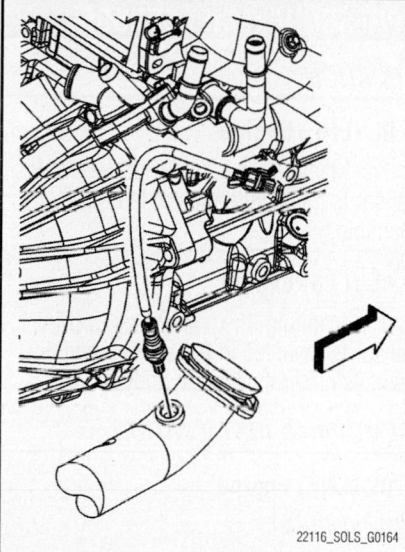

Fig. 148 Rear (2) Heated Oxygen Sensors—2.0L (LNF) engine

To install:

➡A special anti-seize compound is used on the HO2S threads. The compound consists of a liquid graphite and glass beads. The graphite will burn away, but the glass beads will remain, making the sensor easier to remove. New or service sensors will have the compound applied to the threads. If a sensor is removed and is to be reinstalled, the threads must have an anti-seize compound applied before installation.

6. If reinstalling the old HO2S, coat the threads with anti-seize compound.

7. Using an approved oxygen sensor wrench, install the HO2S.

8. Tighten the HO2S to 31 ft. lbs. (42 Nm).

9. Lower vehicle if rear HO2S was installed.

10. Connect the HO2S electrical connector.

11. Install the CPA retainer.

12. Close the hood.

INTAKE AIR TEMPERATURE (IAT) SENSOR

LOCATION

2.0L (LNF) Engine

The Intake Air Temperature (IAT) and pressure sensor is mounted to the fresh air tube before the throttle body.

REMOVAL & INSTALLATION

2.0L (LNF) Engine

See Figure 149.

1. Disconnect the engine wiring harness electrical connector from the intake air pressure and temperature sensor.

2. Remove the intake air pressure and temperature sensor bolts.

3. Remove the intake air pressure and temperature sensor.

To install:

4. Lubricate the intake air pressure and temperature sensor O-ring with clean engine oil.

5. Install the intake air pressure and temperature sensor.

6. Install the intake air pressure and temperature sensor bolts.

7. Tighten the bolts to 80 inch lbs. (9 Nm).

8. Connect the engine wiring harness electrical connector to the intake air pressure and temperature sensor.

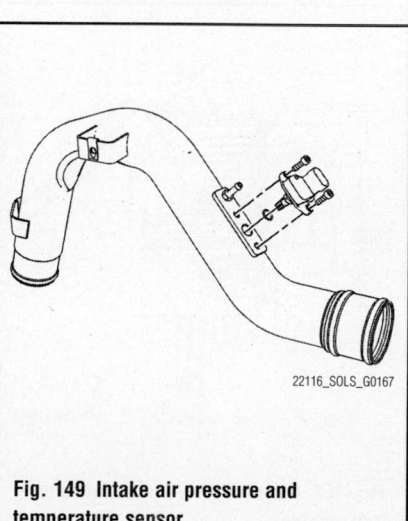

Fig. 149 Intake air pressure and temperature sensor

KNOCK SENSOR (KS)

LOCATION

2.0L (LNF) Engine

The 2.0L (LNF) engine uses two Knock Sensors (KS) that are mounted on the left side of the engine block. The sensors are mounted parallel to each other.

2.4L (LE5) Engine

The Knock Sensor (KS) is located at the left rear of the engine block and just before the oil filter housing.

REMOVAL & INSTALLATION

2.0L (LNF) Engine

See Figure 150.

1. Disconnect the engine wiring harness electrical connector from the front knock sensor, if required.

2. Disconnect the engine wiring harness electrical connector from the rear knock sensor, if required.

3. Remove the front knock sensor clip from the oil level indicator tube, if required.

4. Remove the rear knock sensor clip from the intake manifold brace, if required.

5. Loosen the appropriate knock bolt.

6. Remove the appropriate knock sensor.

To install:

➡Rotate the pigtail 90 degrees from vertical before securing the fastener.

7. Position the appropriate knock sensor to the engine block.

8. Tighten the appropriate knock sensor mounting bolt to 18 ft. lbs. (25 Nm).

9. Install the front knock sensor clip to the oil level indicator tube, if required.

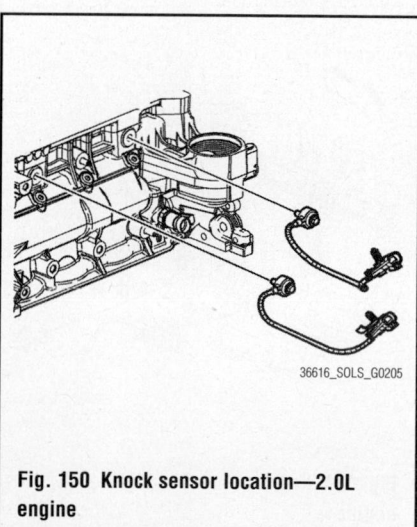

Fig. 150 Knock sensor location—2.0L engine

10. Install the rear knock sensor clip to the intake manifold brace, if required.

11. Connect the engine wiring harness electrical connector to the rear knock sensor.

12. Connect the engine wiring harness electrical connector to the front knock sensor.

2.4L (LE5) Engine

See Figure 157.

1. Disconnect the Knock Sensor (KS) electrical connector.

2. Remove the KS electrical connector clip from the oil level indicator tube bracket.

3. Remove the KS bolt.

4. Remove the KS.

To install:

➥**Rotate the pigtail 90 degrees from vertical before securing the fastener.**

5. Install the KS.

6. Install the KS bolt and tighten to 18 ft. lbs. (25 Nm).

7. Disconnect the KS electrical connector.

8. Install the KS electrical connector clip to the oil level indicator tube bracket.

MALFUNCTION INDICATOR LIGHT (MIL)

RESET PROCEDURE

The control module turns OFF the Malfunction Indicator Lamp (MIL) after 3 consecutive ignition cycles that the diagnostic system runs and does not fail

1. A current Diagnostic Trouble Code (DTC) clears when the diagnostic cycle runs and passes.

2. There may still be a history of DTCs stored in the system. These will clear after 40 consecutive warm-up cycles, if no failures are reported by any other related diagnostic system

3. Manual resetting of the MIL and any DTC stored in the system requires the use of an OBD 2 scan tool connected to the data link connector for communication with the vehicle. Follow the instructions of the scan tool for both retrieval and resetting of DTCs.

If the error symptoms causing the MIL to illuminate have been corrected, the MIL will return to normal operation. Road testing may be necessary.

MASS AIR FLOW (MAF) SENSOR

LOCATION

The Mass Air Flow (MAF) sensor is mounted on the top of the air filter housing.

REMOVAL & INSTALLATION

See Figures 152 and 153.

1. Disconnect the Mass Air Flow (MAF)/Intake Air Temperature (IAT) sensor electrical connector.

➥**For 2.0L (LNF) engines, the IAT is not part of the MAF.**

2. Remove the MAF/IAT sensor screws.

3. Remove the MAF/IAT sensor.

To install:

4. Install the MAF/IAT sensor.

5. Install the MAF/IAT sensor screws and tighten to 5 inch lbs. (0.6 Nm).

6. Connect the MAF/IAT sensor electrical connector.

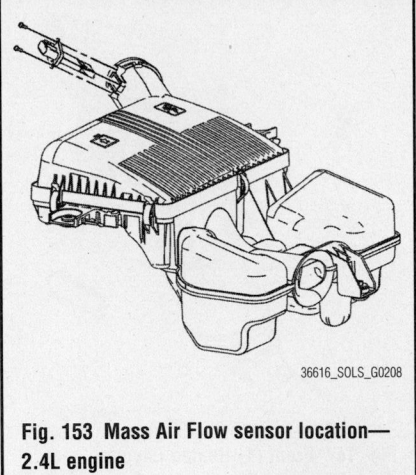

Fig. 153 Mass Air Flow sensor location—2.4L engine

MANIFOLD ABSOLUTE PRESSURE (MAP) SENSOR

LOCATION

2.0L (LNF) Engine

The Manifold Absolute Pressure (MAP) sensor is mounted on top of the intake manifold.

2.4L (LE5) Engine

The Manifold Absolute Pressure (MAP) sensor is mounted in the intake manifold and sits under the throttle body.

REMOVAL & INSTALLATION

2.0L (LNF) Engine

See Figure 154.

1. Disconnect the engine wiring harness electrical connector from the Manifold Absolute Pressure (MAP) sensor.

2. Remove the MAP sensor bolts.

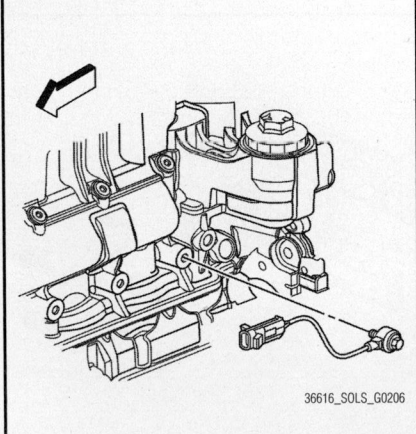

Fig. 151 Knock sensor location—2.4L engine

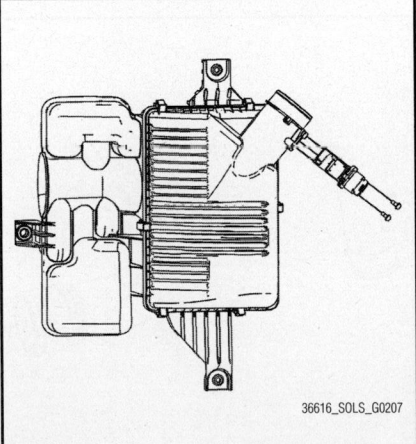

Fig. 152 Mass Air Flow sensor location—2.0L engine

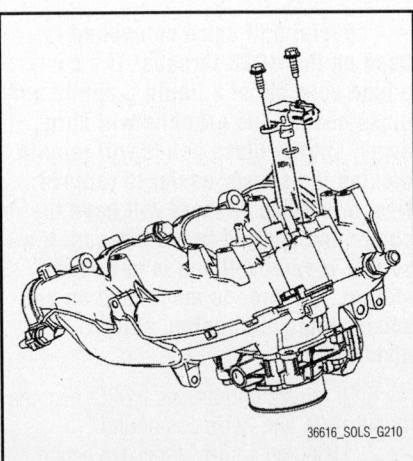

Fig. 154 Manifold absolute pressure sensor—2.0L engine

3.   Remove the MAP sensor and O-ring seal from the intake manifold.

To install:

4.   Lubricate the O-ring seal with clean engine oil.

5.   Install the MAP sensor to the intake manifold.

6.   Install the MAP sensor bolts.

7.   Tighten the bolts to 89 inch lbs. (10 Nm).

8.   Connect the engine wiring harness electrical connector to the MAP sensor.

2.4L (LE5) Engine

See Figure 155.

1.   Remove the throttle body.

2.   Disconnect the Manifold Absolute Pressure (MAP) sensor electrical connector.

3.   Remove the MAP sensor and the MAP sensor port seal if it is still retained in the intake manifold.

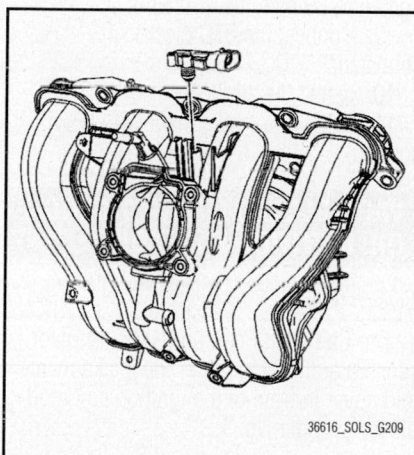

Fig. 155 Manifold absolute pressure sensor—2.4L engine

To install:

4.   Install the MAP sensor with the port seal into the intake manifold

5.   Connect the MAP sensor electrical connector.

6.   Install the throttle body.

THROTTLE CONTROL ACTUATOR (TAC)

LOCATION

See Figures 156 and 157.

REMOVAL & INSTALLATION

2.0L (LNF) Engine

See Figure 156.

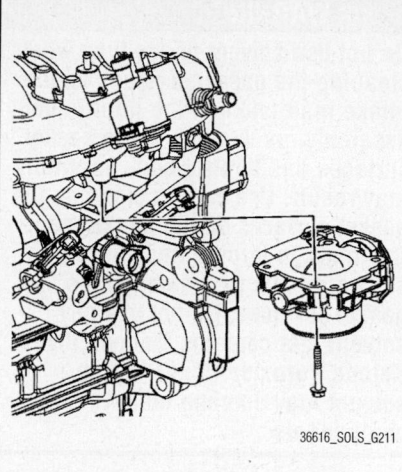

Fig. 156 Throttle actuator control and Throttle Position Sensor (TPS)—2.0L engine

> ☀ **WARNING**
>
> **Do not use solvent of any type when cleaning the gasket surfaces on the intake manifold and the throttle body assembly, as damage to the gasket surfaces and throttle body assembly may result. Use care in cleaning the gasket surfaces on the intake manifold and the throttle body assembly, as sharp tools may damage the gasket surfaces. Do not use any solvent that contains Methyl Ethyl Ketone (MEK). This solvent may damage fuel system components.**

1.   Remove the charge air cooler outlet pipe.

2.   Disconnect the engine wiring harness electrical connector from the Electronic Throttle Control (ETC).

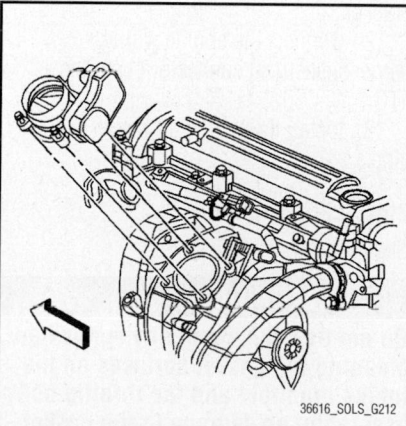

Fig. 157 Throttle actuator control and Throttle Position Sensor (TPS)—2.4L engine

3.   Disconnect the engine wiring harness electrical connector from the brake booster auxiliary pump.

4.   Remove the brake booster auxiliary pump electrical connector clip from the bracket.

5.   Remove the throttle body bolts.

6.   Remove the throttle body and seal from the intake manifold.

To install:

7.   Inspect the throttle body seal, and replace if necessary.

8.   Position the throttle body to the intake manifold.

9.   Install the throttle body bolts and tighten to 89 inch lbs. (10 Nm).

10.   Connect the engine wiring harness electrical connector to the brake booster auxiliary pump.

11.   Install the brake booster auxiliary pump electrical connector clip to the bracket.

12.   Connect the engine wiring harness electrical connector to the ETC.

13.   Install the charge air cooler outlet pipe.

2.4L (LE5) Engine

See Figure 157.

> ☀ **WARNING**
>
> **Do not use solvent of any type when cleaning the gasket surfaces on the intake manifold and the throttle body assembly, as damage to the gasket surfaces and throttle body assembly may result. Use care in cleaning the gasket surfaces on the intake manifold and the throttle body assembly, as sharp tools may damage the gasket surfaces. Do not use any solvent that contains Methyl Ethyl Ketone (MEK). This solvent may damage fuel system components.**

1.   Remove the intake manifold cover. Refer to Intake Manifold Removal & Installation in the Engine Mechanical Section.

2.   Remove the air cleaner outlet.

3.   Disconnect the Electronic Throttle Control (ETC) electrical connector.

4.   Remove the throttle body bolts.

5.   Remove the throttle body from the intake manifold.

To install:

6.   Inspect the throttle body gasket and replace if necessary.

7.   Position the throttle body to the intake manifold.

8. Install the throttle body bolts and tighten to 89 inch lbs. (10 Nm).

9. Connect the ETC electrical connector.

10. Install the air cleaner outlet.

11. Install the intake manifold cover.

12. Perform the throttle learn procedure.

THROTTLE LEARN

1. The engine speed is between 450–4,000 RPM.

2. The Manifold Absolute Pressure (MAP) is greater than 5 kPa.

3. The Mass Air Flow (MAF) is greater than 2 g/s.

4. The ignition 1 voltage is greater than 10 volts.

5. Start and idle the engine in Park for 3 minutes.

6. With a scan tool, monitor desired and actual RPM.

7. The ECM will start to learn the new idle cells and Desired RPM should start to decrease.

8. Ignition OFF for 60 seconds.

9. Start and idle the engine in Park for 3 minutes.

➡ **During the drive cycle the check engine light may come on with idle speed DTCs. If idle speed codes are set, clear codes so the ECM can continue to learn.**

10. After the 3 minute run time the engine should be idling normal.

　a. If the engine idle speed has not been learned the vehicle will need to be driven at speeds above 44 mph (70 km per hour) with several decelerations and extended idles.

11. After the drive cycle, the engine should be idling normally.

　a. If the engine idle speed has not been learned, turn OFF the ignition for 60 seconds and repeat step 6.

12. Once the engine speed has returned to normal, clear DTCs.

THROTTLE POSITION SENSOR (TPS)

LOCATION

The Throttle Position (TP) sensors 1 and 2 are located within the throttle body assembly.

REMOVAL & INSTALLATION

2.0L (LNF) Engine

See Figure 156.

✳ WARNING

Do not use solvent of any type when cleaning the gasket surfaces on the intake manifold and the throttle body assembly, as damage to the gasket surfaces and throttle body assembly may result. Use care in cleaning the gasket surfaces on the intake manifold and the throttle body assembly, as sharp tools may damage the gasket surfaces. Do not use any solvent that contains Methyl Ethyl Ketone Peroxide (MEKP). This solvent may damage fuel system components.

1. Remove the charge air cooler outlet pipe.

2. Disconnect the engine wiring harness electrical connector from the Electronic Throttle Control (ETC).

3. Disconnect the engine wiring harness electrical connector from the brake booster auxiliary pump.

4. Remove the brake booster auxiliary pump electrical connector clip from the bracket.

5. Remove the throttle body bolts.

6. Remove the throttle body and seal from the intake manifold.

To install:

7. Inspect the throttle body seal, and replace if necessary.

8. Position the throttle body to the intake manifold.

9. Install the throttle body bolts and tighten to 89 inch lbs. (10 Nm).

10. Connect the engine wiring harness electrical connector to the brake booster auxiliary pump.

11. Install the brake booster auxiliary pump electrical connector clip to the bracket.

12. Connect the engine wiring harness electrical connector (1) to the ETC.

13. Install the charge air cooler outlet pipe.

2.4L (LE5) Engine

See Figure 157.

✳ WARNING

Do not use solvent of any type when cleaning the gasket surfaces on the intake manifold and the throttle body assembly, as damage to the gasket surfaces and throttle body assembly may result. Use care in cleaning the gasket surfaces on the intake manifold and the throttle body assembly,

as sharp tools may damage the gasket surfaces. Do not use any solvent that contains Methyl Ethyl Ketone Peroxide (MEKP). This solvent may damage fuel system components.**

1. Remove the intake manifold cover. Refer to Intake Manifold Removal & Installation in the Engine Mechanical Section.

2. Remove the air cleaner outlet.

3. Disconnect the Electronic Throttle Control (ETC) electrical connector.

4. Remove the throttle body bolts.

5. Remove the throttle body from the intake manifold.

To install:

6. Inspect the throttle body gasket and replace if necessary.

7. Position the throttle body to the intake manifold.

8. Install the throttle body bolts and tighten to 89 inch lbs. (10 Nm).

9. Connect the ETC electrical connector.

10. Install the air cleaner outlet.

11. Install the intake manifold cover.

VARIABLE CAMSHAFT TIMING OIL CONTROL SOLENOID

LOCATION

The Camshaft Position (CMP) actuator sensors are located under the intake manifold cover in front of the ignition coil module for cylinder No. 1.

REMOVAL & INSTALLATION

See Figures 158 and 159.

1. Remove the air cleaner assembly, as necessary.

2. Remove the intake manifold cover, as necessary. Refer to Intake Manifold Removal & Installation in the Engine Mechanical Section.

3. Disconnect the engine wiring harness electrical connector from either the intake (2) or exhaust (1) camshaft position actuator solenoid valve, as necessary.

4. Remove the exhaust (1) camshaft position actuator solenoid valve bolt and valve, as required.

5. Remove the intake (2) Camshaft Position (CMP) actuator solenoid valve bolt and valve, as required.

6. Inspect the solenoid valve O-ring seals from damage, replace as necessary.

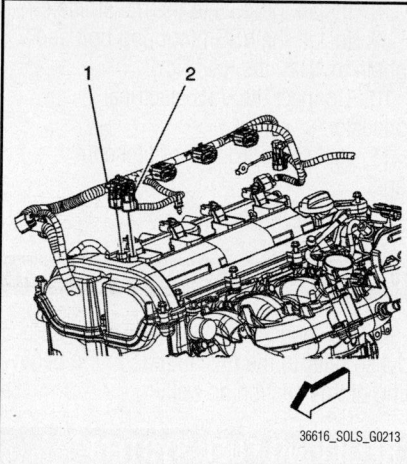

Fig. 158 Camshaft position actuator solenoid valve electrical connections

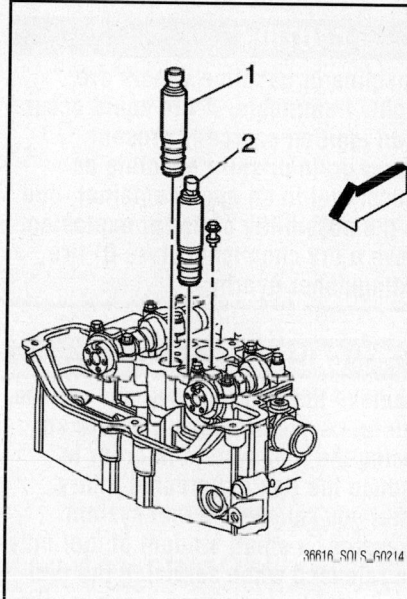

Fig. 159 Camshaft position actuator solenoid valve removal

To Install:

7. Lubricate the solenoid valve O-ring seals with clean engine oil.

8. Install the intake CMP actuator solenoid valve and bolt, as required and tighten the bolt to 89 inch lbs. (10 Nm).

9. Install the exhaust CMP actuator solenoid valve and bolt, as required and tighten the bolt to 89 inch lbs. (10 Nm).

10. Connect the intake or exhaust camshaft position actuator solenoid valve electrical connector, as necessary.

11. Install the intake manifold cover, as necessary.

12. Install air cleaner, as necessary.

VEHICLE SPEED SENSOR (VSS)/OUTPUT SHAFT SPEED SENSOR (OSS)

LOCATION

See Figures 160 and 161.

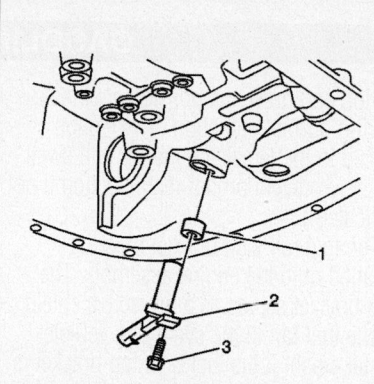

1. **Output speed sensor spacer**
2. **Output speed sensor**
3. **Mounting bolt**

Fig. 160 Output Speed Sensor (OSS)—Automatic transmission

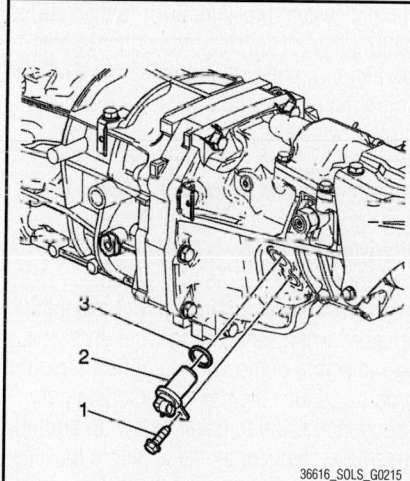

Fig. 161 Vehicle Speed Sensor location—Manual transmission

REMOVAL & INSTALLATION

Automatic Transmission 5L40—E/5L50—E Output Speed Sensor (OSS)

See Figures 160 and 162.

1. Raise and support the vehicle.

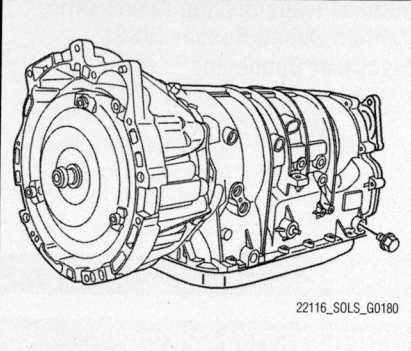

Fig. 162 Transmission fluid check plug location

2. Remove the floor panel tunnel.

3. Drain the transmission fluid.

4. Remove the transmission fluid pan and filter.

5. Disconnect the electrical wiring harness connector from the output speed sensor.

6. Remove the output speed sensor bolt.

7. Remove the output speed sensor.

8. Remove the output speed sensor spacer.

9. Inspect the output speed sensor for the following conditions:
   - Damaged or missing magnet
   - Damaged housing
   - Bent or missing electrical terminals

To install:

10. Install the output speed sensor spacer.

11. Install the output speed sensor.

12. Install the output speed sensor mounting bolt and tighten to 97 inch lbs. (11 Nm).

13. Connect the electrical wiring harness connector to the output speed sensor.

14. Install the transmission fluid pan and filter.

15. Tighten the transmission pan bolts to 97 inch lbs. (11 Nm).

16. Add DEXRON®VI automatic transmission fluid in increments of 0.5 qt (0.5 L) until the fluid drains from the hole plug.

17. Install the floor panel tunnel.

18. Lower vehicle.

19. Recheck fluid level if needed.

Manual Transmission Aisin—AR5
Vehicle Speed Sensor (VSS)
Electrical Connector

See Figure 161.

1. Raise and support the vehicle.
2. Remove the front floor closeout panel.

3. Disconnect the Vehicle Speed Sensor (VSS) electrical connector.
4. Remove the VSS bolt.
5. Remove the VSS.
6. Remove the O-ring seal from the VSS.

To install:

7. Install the O-ring seal to the VSS.

8. Install the VSS to the transmission.
9. Install the VSS mounting bolt and tighten to 13 ft. lbs. (17 Nm).
10. Connect the VSS electrical connector.
11. Install the front floor closeout panel.
12. Lower the vehicle.

FUEL

GASOLINE FUEL INJECTION SYSTEM

FUEL SYSTEM SERVICE PRECAUTIONS

Safety is the most important factor when performing not only fuel system maintenance but any type of maintenance. Failure to conduct maintenance and repairs in a safe manner may result in serious personal injury or death. Maintenance and testing of the vehicle's fuel system components can be accomplished safely and effectively by adhering to the following rules and guidelines.

Gasoline or gasoline vapors are highly flammable. A fire could occur if an ignition source is present. Never drain or store gasoline or diesel fuel in an open container, due to the possibility of fire or explosion. Have a dry chemical (Class B) fire extinguisher nearby.

Fuel Vapors can collect while servicing fuel system parts in enclosed areas such as a trunk. To reduce the risk of fire and increased exposure to vapors: Use forced air ventilation such as a fan set outside of the trunk. Plug or cap any fuel system openings in order to reduce fuel vapor formation. Clean up any spilled fuel immediately. Avoid sparks and any source of ignition. Use signs to alert others in the work area that fuel system work is in process.

In order to reduce the risk of fire and personal injury observe the following items:

• Replace all nylon fuel pipes that are nicked, scratched or damaged during installation, do not attempt to repair the sections of the nylon fuel pipes

• Do not hammer directly on the fuel harness body clips when installing new fuel pipes. Damage to the nylon pipes may result in a fuel leak.

• Always cover nylon vapor pipes with a wet towel before using a torch near them. Also, never expose the vehicle to temperatures higher than 239°F (115°C) for more than one hour, or more than 194°F (90°C) for any extended period.

• Apply a few drops of clean engine oil to the male pipe ends before connecting fuel pipe fittings. This will ensure proper recon-

nection and prevent a possible fuel leak. (During normal operation, the O-rings located in the female connector will swell and may prevent proper reconnection if not lubricated.)

The fuel rail stop bracket must be installed onto the engine assembly. The stop bracket serves as a protective shield for the fuel rail in the event of a vehicle frontal crash. If the fuel rail stop bracket is not installed and the vehicle is involved in a frontal crash, fuel could be sprayed possibly causing a fire and personal injury from burns.

To avoid the possibility of fire and personal injury, always disconnect the negative battery cable unless the repair or test procedure requires that battery voltage be applied.

Always remove the fuel tank cap relieve the fuel system pressure prior to disconnecting any fuel system component (injector, fuel rail, pressure regulator, etc.), fitting or fuel line connection. Exercise extreme caution whenever relieving fuel system pressure to avoid exposing skin, face and eyes to fuel spray. Please be advised that fuel under pressure may penetrate the skin or any part of the body that it contacts.

After you relieve the fuel system pressure, a small amount of fuel may be released when servicing the fuel lines, the fuel injection pump, or the connections. In order to reduce the risk of personal injury, use a shop towel to cover and wrap around the fuel system components before loosening or disconnection. This will catch any fuel that may leak out. Ensure that all fuel spillage (should it occur) is quickly removed from engine surfaces. Place the towel in an approved container when the disconnection is complete.

Always keep a dry chemical (Class B) fire extinguisher near the work area.

Always use a back-up wrench when loosening and tightening fuel line connection fittings. This will prevent unnecessary stress and torsion to fuel line piping.

Always replace worn fuel fitting O-rings with new. Do not substitute fuel hose or equivalent where fuel pipe is installed.

Before servicing the vehicle, make sure to also refer to the precautions in the beginning of this section as well.

RELIEVING FUEL SYSTEM PRESSURE

LOW PRESSURE SIDE WITH FUEL GAUGE

✳✳ CAUTION

Gasoline or gasoline vapors are highly flammable. A fire could occur if an ignition source is present. Never drain or store gasoline or diesel fuel in an open container, due to the possibility of fire or explosion. Have a dry chemical (Class B) fire extinguisher nearby.

✳✳ CAUTION

Remove the fuel tank cap and relieve the fuel system pressure before servicing the fuel system in order to reduce the risk of personal injury. After you relieve the fuel system pressure, a small amount of fuel may be released when servicing the fuel lines, the fuel injection pump, or the connections. In order to reduce the risk of personal injury, cover the fuel system components with a shop towel before disconnection. This will catch any fuel that may leak out. Place the towel in an approved container when the disconnection is complete.

1. Remove the engine cover, if required.
2. Loosen the fuel fill cap in order to relieve the fuel tank vapor pressure.
3. Remove the fuel rail service port cap.
4. Wrap a shop towel around the fuel rail service port.
5. Connect the adapter to the fuel rail service port.
6. Connect service port adapter to pressure tester.
7. Place the relief hose on the tester into an approved gasoline container.

8. Open the valve on the tester in order to bleed any fuel from the fuel rail.

9. Close the valve on the tester.

10. Remove the relief hose on the tester from the approved gasoline container.

11. Disconnect service port adapter and tester.

12. Install the fuel rail service port cap.

13. Install fuel cap.

LOW PRESSURE SIDE WITHOUT FUEL GAUGE

✴ CAUTION

Gasoline or gasoline vapors are highly flammable. A fire could occur if an ignition source is present. Never drain or store gasoline or diesel fuel in an open container, due to the possibility of fire or explosion. Have a dry chemical (Class B) fire extinguisher nearby.

✴ CAUTION

Remove the fuel tank cap and relieve the fuel system pressure before servicing the fuel system in order to reduce the risk of personal injury. After you relieve the fuel system pressure, a small amount of fuel may be released when servicing the fuel lines, the fuel injection pump, or the connections. In order to reduce the risk of personal injury, cover the fuel system components with a shop towel before disconnection. This will catch any fuel that may leak out. Place the towel in an approved container when the disconnection is complete.

1. Loosen the fuel fill cap in order to relieve the fuel tank vapor pressure.

2. Remove the engine cover, if required.

3. Remove the fuel rail service port cap.

4. Wrap a shop towel around the fuel rail service port and using a small flat bladed tool, depress (open) the fuel rail test port valve.

5. Remove the shop towel from around the fuel rail service port, and place in an approved gasoline container.

6. Install the fuel rail service port cap.

7. Install the engine cover, if required.

8. Install fuel cap.

HIGH PRESSURE SIDE

✴ CAUTION

Fuel that flows out at high pressure can cause serious injury to the skin and eyes. ALWAYS depressurize the fuel system before removing components that are under high fuel pressure.

✴ CAUTION

Gasoline or gasoline vapors are highly flammable. A fire could occur if an ignition source is present. Never drain or store gasoline or diesel fuel in an open container, due to the possibility of fire or explosion. Have a dry chemical (Class B) fire extinguisher nearby.

✴ CAUTION

Remove the fuel tank cap and relieve the fuel system pressure before servicing the fuel system in order to reduce the risk of personal injury. After you relieve the fuel system pressure, a small amount of fuel may be released when servicing the fuel lines, the fuel injection pump, or the connections. In order to reduce the risk of personal injury, cover the fuel system components with a shop towel before disconnection. This will catch any fuel that may leak out. Place the towel in an approved container when the disconnection is complete.

1. Install a scan tool to the vehicle and command the fuel pump relay OFF, allowing the low pressure fuel pump to shut off.

2. Start the vehicle and allow the engine to idle until the engine stops. The engine will stop in approximately 20–30 seconds.

3. Turn the ignition OFF.

4. Using the scan tool, verify that there is little to no fuel pressure, if there still is fuel pressure repeat step 2.

✴ WARNING

If a scan tool is not available, WAIT at LEAST 2 hours after the engine has been run, before removing the high pressure fuel line.

5. Remove the high pressure fuel line.

FUEL FILTER

REMOVAL & INSTALLATION

There is no routinely replaced fuel filter. A plastic mesh strainer is part of the fuel pump module located in the fuel tank.

FUEL PUMP MODULE

REMOVAL & INSTALLATION

Fuel Pump

See Figures 163 through 165.

✴ CAUTION

Gasoline or gasoline vapors are highly flammable. A fire could occur if an ignition source is present. Never drain or store gasoline or diesel fuel in an open container, due to the possibility of fire or explosion. Have a dry chemical (Class B) fire extinguisher nearby.

✴ CAUTION

Remove the fuel tank cap and relieve the fuel system pressure before servicing the fuel system in order to reduce the risk of personal injury. After you relieve the fuel system pressure, a small amount of fuel may be released when servicing the fuel lines, the fuel injection pump, or the connections. In order to reduce the risk of personal injury, cover the fuel system components with a shop towel before disconnection. This will catch any fuel that may leak out. Place the towel in an approved container when the disconnection is complete.

1. Before servicing the vehicle, refer to the Precautions Section.

✴ CAUTION

In order to reduce the risk of fire and personal injury that may result from a fuel leak, always replace the fuel sender gasket when reinstalling the fuel sender assembly.

✴ WARNING

Cap the fittings and plug the holes when servicing the fuel system in order to prevent dirt and other contaminants from entering the open pipes and passages.

2. Disconnect the negative battery cable.

3. Relieve the fuel system pressure.

4. Remove the rear compartment trim panel.

5. Remove the fuel pump module/sending unit access cover bolts.

6. Remove the access cover.

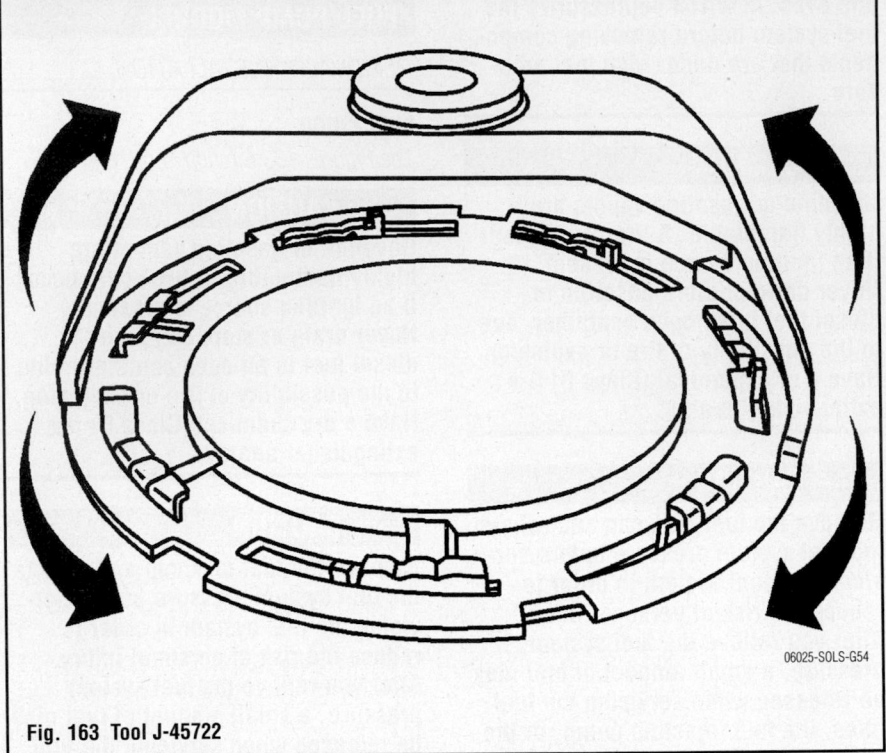

Fig. 163 Tool J-45722

06025-SOLS-G54

7. Disconnect the fuel sender electrical connector.

8. Disconnect the fuel pressure sensor electrical connector.

9. Disconnect the fuel fill pipe Evaporative Emission (EVAP) pipe quick connect fitting.

10. Disconnect the fuel feed pipe quick connect fitting.

✳✳ WARNING

Avoid damaging the lockring. Use only tool J-45722 to prevent damage to the lockring.

✳✳ WARNING

Do Not handle the fuel sender assembly by the fuel pipes. The amount of leverage generated by handling the fuel pipes could damage the joints.

➡ The fuel sender assembly may spring up from its position. When removing the fuel sender assembly from the fuel tank, be aware that the reservoir bucket is full of fuel. It must be tipped slightly during removal to avoid damage to the float. Discard the fuel sender assembly O-ring and replace it with a new one. Carefully discard the fuel in the reservoir bucket into an approved container.

➡ **Do NOT use impact tools. Significant force will be required to release the lockring. The use of a hammer and screwdriver is not recommended. Secure the fuel tank in order to prevent fuel tank rotation.**

11. Use tool J 45722 and a long breaker-bar in order to unlock the fuel sender lockring. Turn the fuel sender lockring in a counterclockwise direction.

12. Raise the fuel sender up slightly.

13. Connect the large EVAP canister quick connect fitting.

14. Remove the fuel sender assembly.

15. Remove and discard the fuel sender O-ring.

➡ **Some lockrings were manufactured with DO NOT REUSE stamped into them. These lockrings may be reused if they are not damaged or warped.**

➡ **Inspect the lockring for damage due to improper removal or installation procedures. If damage is found, install a NEW lockring.**

➡ **Check the lockring for flatness.**

16. Place the lockring on a flat surface. Measure the clearance between to lockring and the flat surface using a feeler gage at 7 points.

17. If the warpage is less than 0.016 in. (0.41 mm), the lockring does not require replacement.

18. If the warpage is greater than 0.016 in. (0.41 mm), the lockring must be replaced.

To install:

19. Install a NEW fuel sender O-ring.

20. Install the fuel sender assembly.

➡ **Always replace the fuel sender seal when installing the fuel sender assembly. Replace the lockring if necessary. Do not apply any type of lubrication in the seal groove. Ensure the lockring is installed with the correct side facing upward. A correctly installed lockring will only turn in a clockwise direction.**

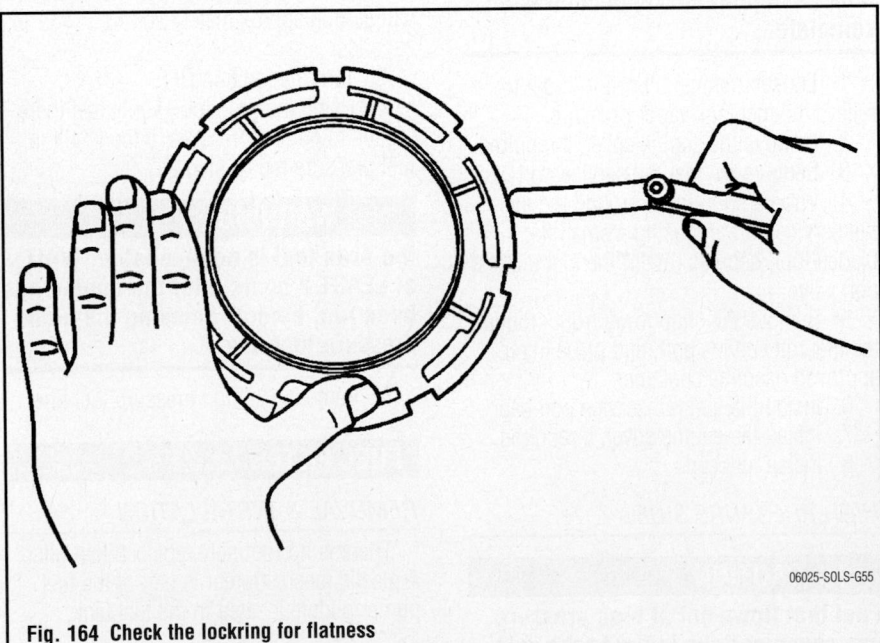

06025-SOLS-G55

Fig. 164 Check the lockring for flatness

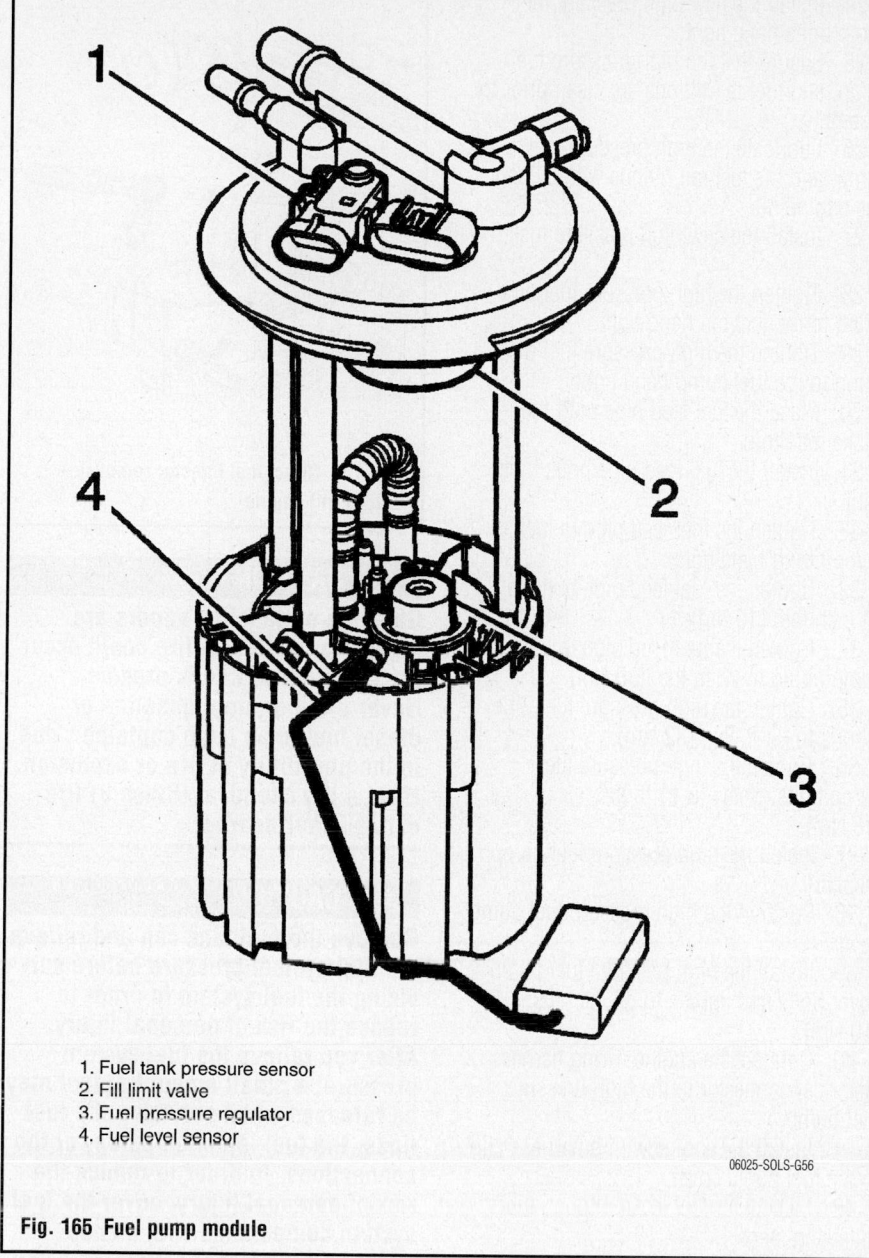

1. Fuel tank pressure sensor
2. Fill limit valve
3. Fuel pressure regulator
4. Fuel level sensor

06025-SOLS-G56

Fig. 165 Fuel pump module

⁂ **CAUTION**

Gasoline or gasoline vapors are highly flammable. A fire could occur if an ignition source is present. Never drain or store gasoline or diesel fuel in an open container, due to the possibility of fire or explosion. Have a dry chemical (Class B) fire extinguisher nearby.

⁂ **CAUTION**

Remove the fuel tank cap and relieve the fuel system pressure before servicing the fuel system in order to reduce the risk of personal injury. After you relieve the fuel system pressure, a small amount of fuel may be released when servicing the fuel lines, the fuel injection pump, or the connections. In order to reduce the risk of personal injury, cover the fuel system components with a shop towel before disconnection. This will catch any fuel that may leak out. Place the towel in an approved container when the disconnection is complete.

1. Before servicing the vehicle, refer to the Precautions Section.
2. Relieve the low and high side fuel system pressure.
3. Disconnect the engine wiring harness electrical connector from the high pressure fuel pump.
4. Remove the engine wiring harness clip from the high pressure fuel pump cover.
5. Remove the high pressure fuel pump cover bolts.
6. Remove the high pressure fuel pump cover.

21. Using the tool, rotate the fuel sender assembly lockring clockwise until the ring is locked into place on the fuel tank.
22. Connect the large EVAP canister quick connect fitting.
23. Connect the fuel feed pipe quick connect fitting.
24. Connect the fuel fill pipe EVAP pipe quick connect fitting.
25. Connect the fuel pressure sensor electrical connector.
26. Connect the fuel sender electrical connector.
27. Install the access cover.
28. Install the fuel sending unit/pump module access cover bolts.

29. Install the rear compartment trim panel.
30. Refill the tank.
31. Connect the negative battery cable.
32. Inspect for fuel leaks through the following steps:
   a. Turn the ignition to the ON position for 2 seconds.
   b. Turn the ignition to the OFF position for 10 seconds.
   c. Turn the ignition to the ON position
   d. Check for fuel leaks.

High Pressure Fuel Pump—2.0L (LNF) Engine

See Figures 166 and 167.

22116_SOLS_G0061

Fig. 166 High pressure fuel pump removal—2.0L (LNF) engine

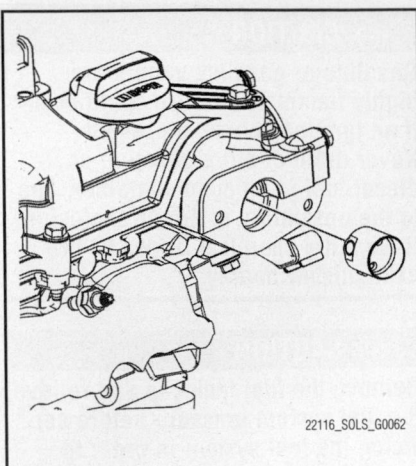

Fig. 167 High pressure fuel pump roller lifter—2.0L (LNF) engine

7. Remove the high pressure fuel pump insulator.

8. Loosen the fuel feed pipe to fuel pump fitting.

9. Remove the fuel feed pipe bolts.

10. Remove the fuel feed pipe from the intake manifold.

11. Loosen the high pressure fuel pipe fitting at the fuel pump.

12. Loosen the high pressure fuel pipe fitting at the fuel rail.

13. Remove and discard the high pressure fuel pipe.

14. Remove and discard the high pressure fuel pump bolts.

15. Remove the high pressure fuel pump.

16. Remove and discard the high pressure fuel pump gasket.

17. Remove and discard the high pressure fuel pump O-ring.

18. Remove the high pressure fuel pump roller lifter, if necessary.

To install:

19. Lubricate the high pressure fuel pump cylinder head bore and roller lifter with silicon free engine oil.

20. Install the high pressure fuel pump roller lifter, if necessary.

21. Install a new high pressure fuel pump O-ring.

22. Position the new high pressure fuel pump gasket to the cylinder head.

➡**Ensure the plastic bolt retainers are installed in the high pressure fuel pump mounting holes prior to installing.**

23. Install the high pressure fuel pump. Push the pump into the cylinder head bore by hand, applying force to the top of the pump.

24. Install the new high pressure fuel pump bolts hand tight.

25. Ensure that the high pressure fuel pump, and fuel rail fittings are clean prior to assembly.

26. Lubricate the high pressure fuel pump, and the fuel rail fittings with silicon free engine oil.

27. Install the new high pressure fuel pipe.

28. Tighten the high pressure fuel pipe fitting to the fuel rail hand tight.

29. Tighten the high pressure fuel pipe fitting to the fuel pump hand tight.

30. Place the fuel feed pipe onto the intake manifold.

31. Install the fuel feed pipe bolts hand tight.

32. Tighten the fuel feed pipe to fuel pump fitting hand tight.

33. Tighten the fuel feed pipe bolts to 89 inch lbs. (10 Nm).

34. Tighten the fuel feed pipe to fuel pump fitting to 22 ft. lbs. (30 Nm).

35. Tighten the high pressure fuel pipe fittings to 24 ft. lbs. (32 Nm).

36. Tighten the high pressure fuel pump bolts evenly to 11 ft. lbs. (15 Nm).

37. Install the high pressure fuel pump insulator.

38. Position the high pressure fuel pump cover.

39. Install the high pressure fuel pump cover bolts and tighten to 89 inch lbs. (10 Nm).

40. Connect the engine wiring harness electrical connector to the high pressure fuel pump.

41. Install the engine wiring harness clip to the fuel pump cover.

42. Inspect for fuel leaks through the following steps:

   a. Turn ON the ignition, with the engine OFF for 2 seconds.

   b. Turn the ignition to the OFF position for 10 seconds.

   c. Turn ON the ignition, with the engine OFF.

   d. Check for fuel leaks.

43. Install the low side fuel pressure service port cap.

44. Tighten the fuel fill cap.

45. Install the intake manifold cover.

FUEL RAIL & INJECTORS

REMOVAL & INSTALLATION

2.0L (LNF) Engine

See Figures 168 through 171.

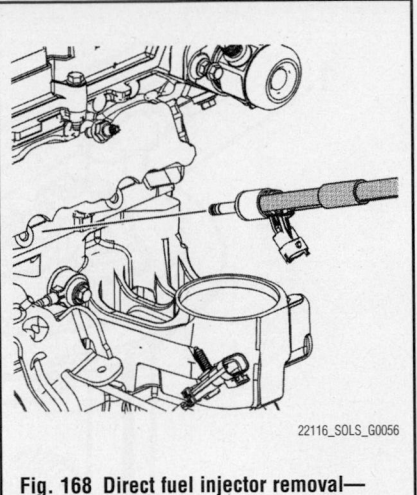

Fig. 168 Direct fuel injector removal—2.0L (LNF) engine

⁂ CAUTION

Gasoline or gasoline vapors are highly flammable. A fire could occur if an ignition source is present. Never drain or store gasoline or diesel fuel in an open container, due to the possibility of fire or explosion. Have a dry chemical (Class B) fire extinguisher nearby.

⁂ CAUTION

Remove the fuel tank cap and relieve the fuel system pressure before servicing the fuel system in order to reduce the risk of personal injury. After you relieve the fuel system pressure, a small amount of fuel may be released when servicing the fuel lines, the fuel injection pump, or the connections. In order to reduce the risk of personal injury, cover the fuel system components with a shop towel before disconnection. This will catch any fuel that may leak out. Place the towel in an approved container when the disconnection is complete.

1. Before servicing the vehicle, refer to the Precautions Section.

2. Disconnect the engine wiring harness electrical connector from the fuel injector wiring harness electrical connector.

3. Remove the air cleaner assembly.

4. Remove the fuel injector insulator.

5. Relieve the high side fuel system pressure.

6. Disconnect the engine wiring harness electrical connector from the high pressure fuel pump.

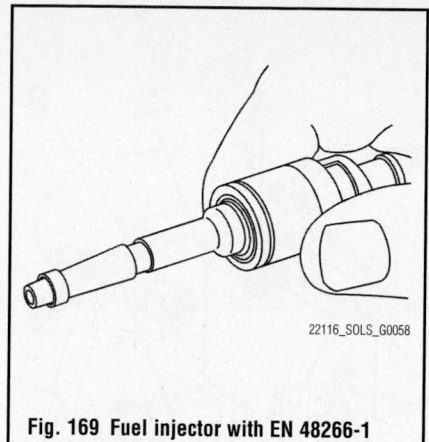

Fig. 169 Fuel injector with EN 48266-1 tool and O-ring

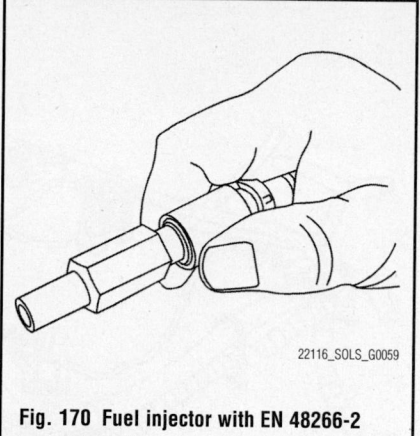

Fig. 170 Fuel injector with EN 48266-2 tool installed

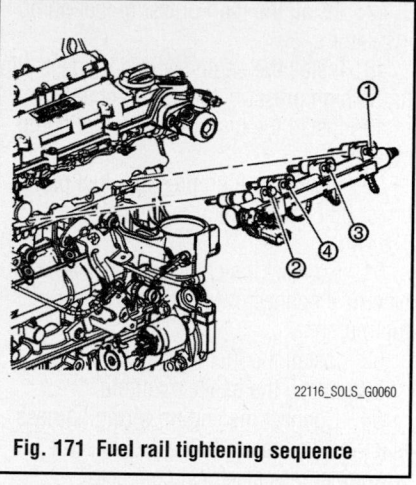

Fig. 171 Fuel rail tightening sequence

7. Remove the high pressure fuel pump cover bolts.

8. Remove the high pressure fuel pump cover.

9. Remove the engine wiring harness clip from the high pressure fuel pump cover.

10. Remove the high pressure fuel pump insulator.

11. Loosen the high pressure fuel pipe fitting at the fuel pump.

12. Loosen the high pressure fuel pipe fitting at the fuel rail.

13. Remove and discard the high pressure fuel pipe.

14. Disconnect the fuel injector wiring harness electrical connectors from the fuel injectors.

15. Remove the fuel rail bolts.

16. Carefully remove the fuel rail.

➥The fuel injectors may come out of the cylinder head with the fuel rail.

17. A fuel injector may remain stuck in the cylinder head. If this occurs, complete the following steps:

a. Remove the fuel injector hold-down clamp before removing the fuel injector.

b. Use the injector remover and slide hammer to pull the fuel injector straight out along the fuel injector axis. DO NOT tilt or twist the fuel injector during this process.

c. Use J-37281-A injector remover, and J 2619-01 hammer to remove the fuel injector.

d. Once injectors have been removed it will be necessary to clean and rebuild all the injectors.

✳✳ **WARNING**

Applying force to the plastic housing of the sensor will destroy the sensor.

To tighten or loosen, only apply force to the attached hexagon.

18. If replacing the fuel rail, remove the fuel injection fuel rail fuel pressure sensor.

19. Remove the fuel injector wiring harness.

To install:

20. Install a new plastic spacer onto the fuel injector.

21. Lubricate a new O-ring seal with silicon free engine oil.

22. Carefully install the new O-ring seal onto the fuel injector.

23. From the EN-48266, position the EN 48266-1 to the injector tip.

24. Install a new seal onto the EN 48266-1.

25. Pull the new seal by hand over the EN 48266-1 and into the groove in the injector.

26. Remove the EN 48266-1 from the injector tip.

27. From the EN-48266, install the EN 48266-2 to the injector tip.

28. Using the EN 48266-2, resize the seal. Install the EN 48266-2, until it bottoms out against the injector body, and rotate the EN 48266-2 while applying only moderate force 180 degrees in one direction and then 180 degrees back in the other direction.

29. Remove the EN 48266-2.

30. Install the direct fuel injectors to the cylinder head.

31. Install the new direct fuel injector hold down clamps.

32. If the fuel rail was replaced, lubricate the threads and sealing cone of the NEW fuel rail with silicon free engine oil GM P/N 12345610 (Canadian P/N 993193) or equivalent.

33. Lubricate the threads and sealing

cone of the sensor with silicon free engine oil GM P/N 12345610 (Canadian P/N 993193) or equivalent.

➥**Applying force to the plastic housing of the sensor will destroy the sensor. To tighten or loosen, only apply force to the attached hexagon.**

34. Install the fuel injection fuel rail fuel pressure sensor and tighten to 25 ft. lbs. (33 Nm).

35. Install the fuel injector wiring harness.

36. Place the fuel rail into position.

37. Install the fuel rail with injectors into the cylinder head evenly.

38. Install the outer fuel rail bolts first, hand tight, and install the remaining bolts, hand tight.

39. Connect the fuel injector wiring harness electrical connectors to the fuel injectors

40. Tighten the fuel rail bolts in the sequence shown to:

a. Tighten the bolts a first pass to 16 ft. lbs. (22 Nm).

b. Tighten the bolts a final pass to 16 ft. lbs. (22 Nm).

41. Ensure that the high pressure fuel pump and fuel rail fittings are clean prior to assembly.

42. Lubricate the high pressure fuel pump and the fuel rail fittings with silicon free engine oil GM P/N 12345610 (Canadian P/N 993193) or equivalent.

43. Install the new high pressure fuel pipe.

44. Tighten the new high pressure fuel pipe fitting to the fuel rail hand tight.

45. Tighten the new high pressure fuel pipe fitting to the fuel pump hand tight.

46. Tighten the fittings to 24 ft. lbs. (32 Nm).

47. Install the high pressure fuel pump insulator.

48. Install the engine wiring harness clip to the high pressure fuel pump cover.

49. Install the high pressure fuel pump cover.

50. Install the high pressure fuel pump cover bolts and tighten to 89 inch lbs. (10 Nm).

51. Connect the engine wiring harness electrical connector to the high pressure fuel pump

52. Install the fuel injector insulator.

53. Install the intake manifold.

54. Connect the engine wiring harness electrical connector to the fuel injector wiring harness electrical connector.

55. Inspect for leaks using the following procedure:

- Turn ON the ignition, with the engine OFF for 2 seconds.
- Turn OFF the ignition, for 10 seconds.
- Turn ON the ignition, with the engine OFF.
- Inspect for fuel leaks.

56. Install the low side fuel pressure service port cap.

57. Tighten the fuel fill cap.

58. Install the air cleaner assembly.

2.4L Engine

See Figures 172 and 173.

> **✳✳ CAUTION**
>
> **Gasoline or gasoline vapors are highly flammable. A fire could occur if an ignition source is present. Never drain or store gasoline or diesel fuel in an open container, due to the possibility of fire or explosion. Have a dry chemical (Class B) fire extinguisher nearby.**

> **✳✳ CAUTION**
>
> **Remove the fuel tank cap and relieve the fuel system pressure before servicing the fuel system in order to reduce the risk of personal injury. After you relieve the fuel system pressure, a small amount of fuel may be released when servicing the fuel lines, the fuel injection pump, or the connections. In order to reduce the risk of personal injury, cover the fuel system components with a shop towel before disconnection. This will catch any fuel that may leak out. Place the towel in an approved container when the disconnection is complete.**

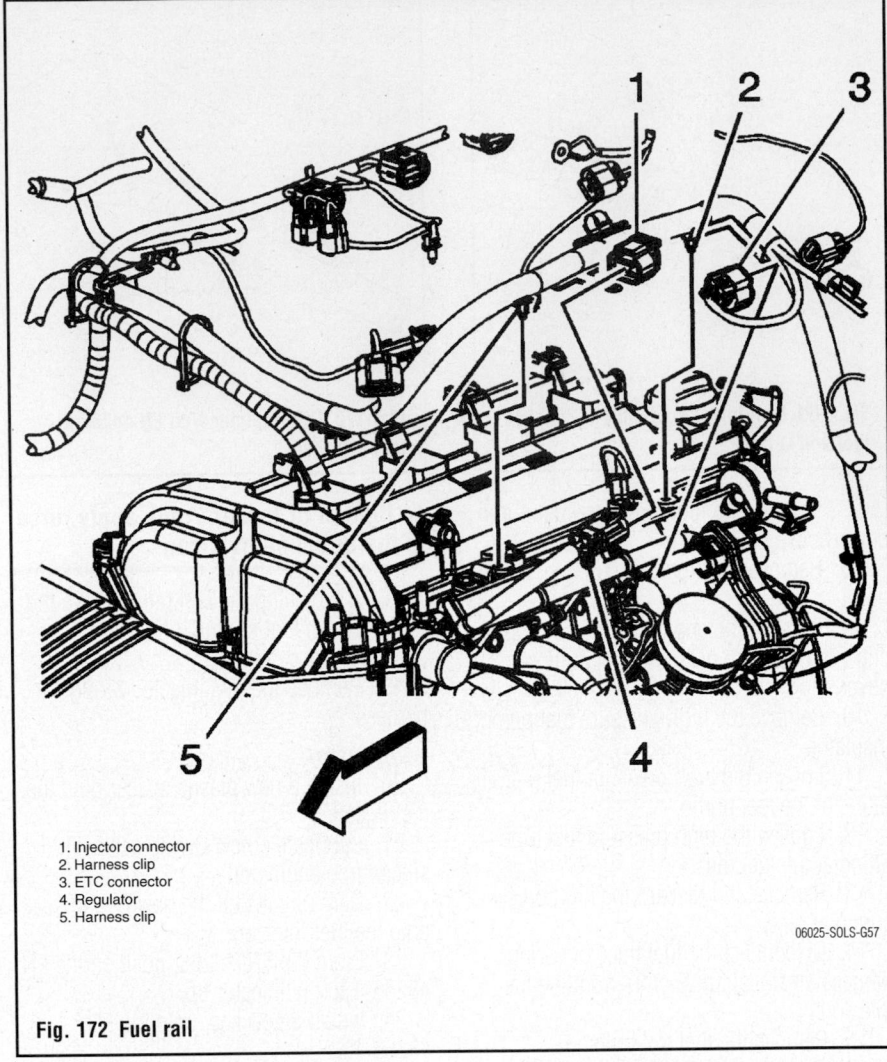

1. Injector connector
2. Harness clip
3. ETC connector
4. Regulator
5. Harness clip

06025-SOLS-G57

Fig. 172 Fuel rail

1. Before servicing the vehicle, refer to the Precautions Section.

2. Relieve the fuel system pressure.

3. Disconnect the fuel feed line quick connect fitting from the fuel rail.

4. Remove the air cleaner outlet duct.

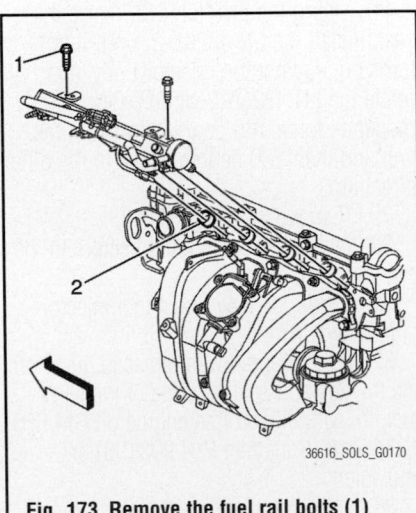

36616_SOLS_G0170

Fig. 173 Remove the fuel rail bolts (1)

5. Disconnect the fuel injector inline electrical connector.

6. Disconnect the Electronic Throttle Control (ETC) electrical connector.

7. Remove the 2 engine harness clips from the fuel rail tabs.

8. Remove the fuel rail bolts.

➡**Use care when removing the fuel rail assembly in order to prevent damage to the fuel injectors electrical connector terminals and spray tips.**

9. Pull the fuel rail back and upward in order to release the fuel injectors from the cylinder head ports.

10. Remove the fuel rail.

> **✳✳ WARNING**
>
> **Use care in removing the fuel injectors in order to prevent damage to the fuel injector electrical connector pins or the fuel injector nozzles. Do not immerse the fuel injector in any type of cleaner. The fuel injector is an electrical component and may**

be damaged by this cleaning method.

➡ If the fuel injectors are found to be leaking, the engine oil may be contaminated with fuel.

11. Remove the fuel injector retaining clip.

12. Remove the fuel injector from the fuel rail.

13. Remove the fuel injector upper O-ring.

14. Remove the fuel injector lower O-ring.

To install:

➡ Be sure to use the correct part number when ordering replacement fuel injectors.

15. The fuel injector assembly is stamped with a part number identification.

16. Lubricate the new injector O-rings with clean engine oil.

17. Install the fuel injector upper O-ring.

18. Install the fuel injector lower O-ring.

19. Install the fuel injector to the fuel rail.

20. Install the fuel injector retaining clip.

➡ Install NEW lower O-rings when reusing fuel injectors. Lubricate the lower O-rings prior to installing the injectors into the intake manifold.

21. With the fuel injectors positioned downward, lower the fuel injectors into the cylinder head ports.

22. Carefully push the fuel injectors into the cylinder head ports.

23. Install the fuel rail bolts. Tighten the bolts to 89 inch lbs. (10 Nm).

24. Install the 2 engine harness clips to the fuel rail tabs.

25. Connect the ETC electrical connector.

26. Connect the fuel injector inline electrical connector.

27. Install the air cleaner outlet duct.

28. Connect the fuel feed line quick connect fitting to the fuel rail.

29. Connect the negative battery cable.

30. Inspect for fuel leaks using the following procedure:

• Turn ON the ignition, with the engine OFF for 2 seconds.
• Turn OFF the ignition for 10 seconds.
• Turn ON the ignition.
• Inspect for fuel leaks.

FUEL TANK

REMOVAL & INSTALLATION

See Figures 174 and 175.

✳✳ CAUTION

Gasoline or gasoline vapors are highly flammable. A fire could occur if an ignition source is present. Never drain or store gasoline or diesel fuel in an open container, due to the possibility of fire or explosion. Have a dry chemical (Class B) fire extinguisher nearby.

✳✳ CAUTION

Remove the fuel tank cap and relieve the fuel system pressure before servicing the fuel system in order to reduce the risk of personal injury. After you relieve the fuel system pressure, a small amount of fuel may be released when servicing the fuel lines, the fuel injection pump, or the connections. In order to reduce the risk of personal injury, cover the fuel system components with a shop towel before disconnection. This will catch any fuel that may leak out. Place the towel in an approved container when the disconnection is complete.

1. Before servicing the vehicle, refer to the Precautions Section.

2. Relieve the fuel system pressure.

➡ Ensure that the fuel tank is completely drained because of the severe angle that the tank will need to be tipped, in order to remove the tank.

3. Disconnect the negative battery cable.

4. Drain the fuel tank.

5. Remove the rear compartment trim panel.

6. Remove the fuel pump module access cover bolts.

7. Remove the fuel pump module access cover.

8. Disconnect the fuel sending unit electrical connector (3).

9. Disconnect the fuel tank pressure sensor electrical connector (5).

10. Disconnect the Evaporative Emission (EVAP) canister vent solenoid electrical connector (2).

11. Disconnect the fuel pump fuel feed line quick connect fitting from the module.

12. Disconnect the EVAP canister purge line quick connect fitting from the module.

13. Secure the fuel feed and EVAP purge lines up out of the way.

14. Remove the fuel fill pipe.

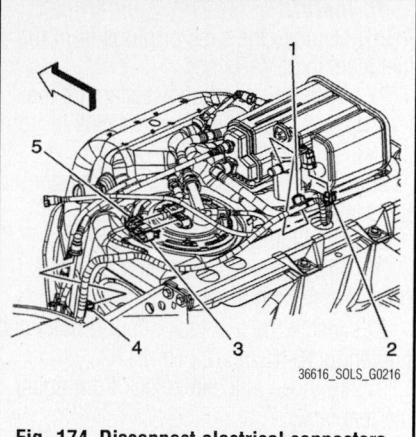

Fig. 174 Disconnect electrical connectors

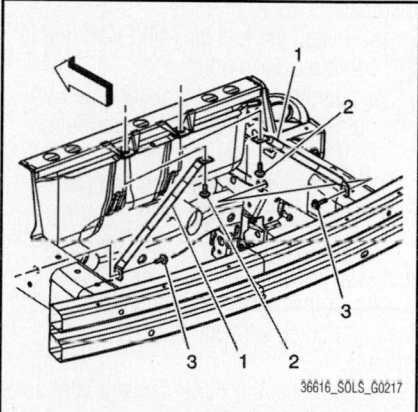

Fig. 175 Remove the fuel tank supports (1), support bolts (3), and strap/support bolts (2)

15. Disconnect the fuel tank fill pipe EVAP line quick connect fitting (1) from the module.

16. Remove the fuel tank fill EVAP line out through the access hole in order to prevent damage to the pipe when removing the tank.

17. Remove the rear suspension crossmember.

18. Remove the stabilizer shaft.

19. Position an adjustable jack under the fuel tank.

20. Remove the fuel tank strap/support bolts (2).

21. Remove the fuel tank support bolts (3).

22. Remove the fuel tank supports (1).

23. Remove the adjustable jack from under the fuel tank and with the aid of an assistant, tilt the tank down towards the left side of the vehicle and carefully remove the tank.

24. Place the fuel tank onto a suitable work surface.

25. Cap or plug the fuel feed and EVAP lines in order to prevent fuel loss and/or system contamination.

To install:

26. Remove the caps or plugs from the fuel feed and EVAP lines.

27. With the aid of an assistant tilt the tank up and carefully install the tank in from the left side of the vehicle.

28. Position an adjustable jack under the fuel tank.

29. Position the fuel tank supports.

30. Install the fuel tank strap/support bolts and tighten to 16 ft. lbs. (22 Nm).

31. Install the fuel tank support bolts and tighten to 16 ft. lbs. (22 Nm).

32. Remove adjustable jack from under the fuel tank.

33. Install the stabilizer shaft.

34. Install the rear suspension cross-member.

35. Install the fuel tank fill EVAP line in through the access hole.

36. Connect the fuel tank fill pipe EVAP line quick connect fitting to the module.

37. Install the fuel fill pipe.

38. Unsecure the fuel feed and EVAP purge lines and position to the module.

39. Connect the EVAP canister purge line quick connect fitting to the module.

40. Connect the fuel pump fuel feed line quick connect fitting to the module.

41. Connect the EVAP canister vent solenoid electrical connector.

42. Connect the fuel tank pressure sensor electrical connector.

43. Connect the fuel sending unit electrical connector.

44. Install the pump module access cover.

45. Install the fuel pump module access cover bolts and tighten to 89 inch lbs. (10 Nm).

46. Install the rear compartment trim panel.

47. Connect the negative battery cable.

48. Inspect for leaks using the following procedures:

- Turn ON the ignition, with the engine OFF for 2 seconds.
- Turn OFF the ignition for 10 seconds.
- Turn ON the ignition, with the engine OFF.
- Inspect for fuel leaks.

THROTTLE BODY

REMOVAL & INSTALLATION

2.0L (LNF) Engine

See Figure 176.

> ※※ **WARNING**
>
> Do not use solvent of any type when cleaning the gasket surfaces on the intake manifold and the throttle body assembly, as damage to the gasket surfaces and throttle body assembly may result. Use care in cleaning the gasket surfaces on the intake manifold and the throttle body assembly, as sharp tools may damage the gasket surfaces. Do not use any solvent that contains Methyl Ethyl Ketone (MEK). This solvent may damage fuel system components.

1. Before servicing the vehicle, refer to the Precautions Section.

2. Remove the charge air cooler outlet pipe.

3. Disconnect the engine wiring harness electrical connector from the Electronic Throttle Control (ETC).

4. Disconnect the engine wiring harness electrical connector from the brake booster auxiliary pump.

5. Remove the brake booster auxiliary pump electrical connector clip from the bracket.

6. Remove the throttle body bolts.

7. Remove the throttle body and seal from the intake manifold.

To install:

8. Inspect the throttle body seal, and replace if necessary.

9. Position the throttle body to the intake manifold.

10. Install the throttle body bolts and tighten to 89 inch lbs. (10 Nm).

11. Connect the engine wiring harness electrical connector to the brake booster auxiliary pump.

12. Install the brake booster auxiliary

pump electrical connector clip to the bracket.

13. Connect the engine wiring harness electrical connector to the ETC.

14. Install the charge air cooler outlet pipe.

2.4L (LE5) Engine

See Figure 177.

> ※※ **WARNING**
>
> Do not use solvent of any type when cleaning the gasket surfaces on the intake manifold and the throttle body assembly, as damage to the gasket surfaces and throttle body assembly may result. Use care in cleaning the gasket surfaces on the intake manifold and the throttle body assembly, as sharp tools may damage the gasket surfaces. Do not use any solvent that contains Methyl Ethyl Ketone (MEK). This solvent may damage fuel system components.

1. Before servicing the vehicle, refer to the Precautions Section.

2. Remove the intake manifold cover. Refer to Intake Manifold Removal & Installation in the Engine Mechanical Section.

3. Remove the air cleaner outlet.

4. Disconnect the Electronic Throttle Control (ETC) electrical connector.

5. Remove the throttle body bolts.

6. Remove the throttle body from the intake manifold.

To install:

7. Inspect the throttle body gasket and replace if necessary.

8. Position the throttle body to the intake manifold.

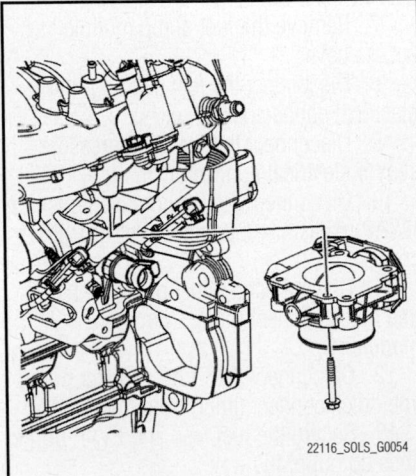

Fig. 176 Throttle body—2.0L (LNF) engine

22116_SOLS_G0054

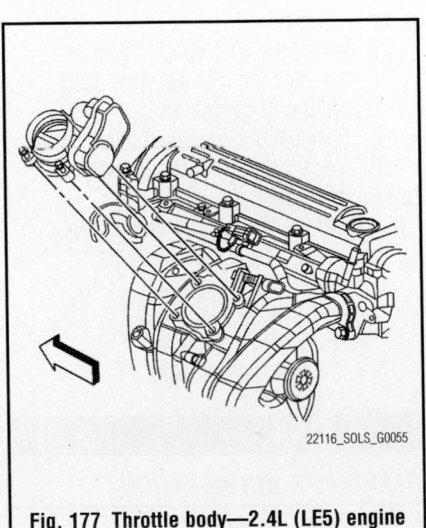

Fig. 177 Throttle body—2.4L (LE5) engine

22116_SOLS_G0055

9. Install the throttle body bolts and tighten to 89 inch lbs. (10 Nm).
10. Connect the ETC electrical connector.
11. Install the air cleaner outlet.
12. Install the intake manifold cover.

THROTTLE RELEARN PROCEDURE

1. The engine speed is between 450–4,000 RPM.
2. The Manifold Absolute Pressure (MAP) is greater than 5 kPa.
3. The Mass Air Flow (MAF) is greater than 2 g/s.
4. The ignition 1 voltage is greater than 10 volts.
5. Start and idle the engine in Park for 3 minutes.
6. With a scan tool, monitor desired and actual RPM.
7. The ECM will start to learn the new idle cells and Desired RPM should start to decrease.
8. Ignition OFF for 60 seconds.
9. Start and idle the engine in Park for 3 minutes.

➡During the drive cycle the check engine light may come on with idle speed DTCs. If idle speed codes are set, clear codes so the ECM can continue to learn.

10. After the 3 minute run time the engine should be idling normal.
    a. If the engine idle speed has not been learned the vehicle will need to be driven at speeds above 44 mph (70 km per hour) with several decelerations and extended idles.
11. After the drive cycle, the engine should be idling normally.
    a. If the engine idle speed has not been learned, turn OFF the ignition for 60 seconds and repeat step 6.

HEATING & AIR CONDITIONING SYSTEM

BLOWER MOTOR

REMOVAL & INSTALLATION

See Figure 178.

1. Before servicing the vehicle, refer to the Precautions Section.

⁂ CAUTION

This vehicle is equipped with a Supplemental Inflatable Restraint (SIR) System. Refer to the SIR Precautions in the Chassis Electrical Section. Failure to follow the correct procedure could lead to air bag deployment, which could cause personal injury or death.

2. Remove the Instrument Panel (I/P) compartment.
3. Disconnect the blower motor resistor electrical connector.
4. Remove blower motor resistor screws.
5. Remove blower motor resistor.
6. Remove blower motor screws.
7. Remove blower motor assembly.

To install:

8. Install blower motor assembly.
9. Install blower motor screws and tighten to 13 inch lbs. (1.5 Nm).
10. Install blower motor resistor.
11. Install blower motor resistor screws and tighten to 13 inch lbs. (1.5 Nm).
12. Reconnect the blower motor resistor electrical connector.
13. Install the I/P compartment.

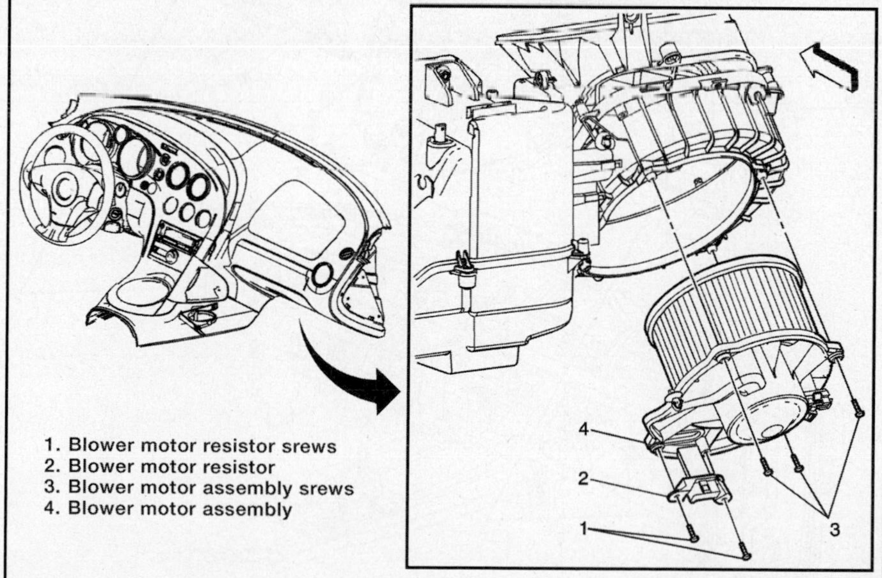
4
2
1
3
22116_SOLS_G0112

1. Blower motor resistor srews
2. Blower motor resistor
3. Blower motor assembly srews
4. Blower motor assembly

Fig. 178 Blower motor assembly and resistor

HEATER CORE

REMOVAL & INSTALLATION

See Figure 179.

1. Before servicing the vehicle, refer to the Precautions Section.

⁂ CAUTION

This vehicle is equipped with a Supplemental Inflatable Restraint (SIR) System. Refer to the SIR Precautions in the Chassis Electrical Section. Failure to follow the correct procedure could lead to air bag deployment, which could cause personal injury or death.

2. Disable the SIR system.
3. Disconnect the negative battery cable.
4. Drain the cooling system.
5. Recover the refrigerant.
6. Remove the HVAC module assembly. Refer to Heating & Air Conditioning Module Assembly Removal & Installation.
7. Disconnect the actuator electrical connectors from the air distribution case.
8. Remove the air outlet duct screw.
9. Remove the air outlet duct.
10. Remove the heater core cover screw.
11. Remove the heater core cover.
12. Remove the heater core pass-through seal.
13. Remove the air distribution case screw.
14. Remove the air distribution case.
15. Remove the heater core bracket screws.
16. Remove the heater core bracket.
17. Remove the heater core.

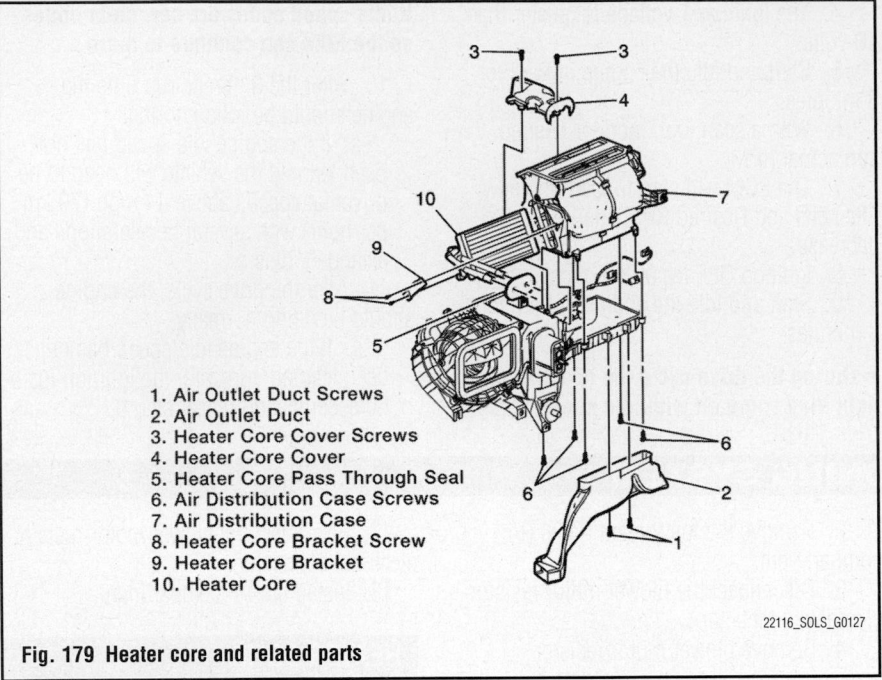

1. Air Outlet Duct Screws
2. Air Outlet Duct
3. Heater Core Cover Screws
4. Heater Core Cover
5. Heater Core Pass Through Seal
6. Air Distribution Case Screws
7. Air Distribution Case
8. Heater Core Bracket Screw
9. Heater Core Bracket
10. Heater Core

22116_SOLS_G0127

Fig. 179 Heater core and related parts

To install:

18. Installation is the reverse of removal, noting the following:

   a. Tighten the heater core bracket screws to 14 inch lbs. (1.5 Nm).

   b. Tighten the air distribution case screw to 14 inch lbs. (1.5 Nm).

   c. Tighten the heater core cover screw to 14 inch lbs. (1.5 Nm).

   d. Tighten the air outlet duct screw to 14 inch lbs. (1.5 Nm).

19. Replace all seals.

20. Evacuate and recharge A/C system.

21. Refill and bleed the cooling system.

22. Enable the SIR system.

23. Connect the negative battery cable.

HVAC MODULE

REMOVAL & INSTALLATION

See Figures 180 through 182.

1. Before servicing the vehicle, refer to the Precautions Section.

✷✷ CAUTION

This vehicle is equipped with a Supplemental Inflatable Restraint (SIR) System. Refer to the SIR Precautions in the Chassis Electrical Section. Failure to follow the correct procedure could lead to air bag deployment, which could cause personal injury or death.

2. Disable the SIR system.

3. Disconnect the negative battery cable.

4. Drain the cooling system.

5. Recover the refrigerant.

6. Remove the evaporator tube from the thermal expansion valve, as follows:

   a. Remove the A/C compressor tube assembly nut.

   b. Remove the thermal expansion valve bolts.

   c. Remove and discard the sealing washers.

   d. Remove the thermal expansion valve.

7. Remove the air inlet grill panel.

8. Remove the heater inlet and outlet hoses from the heater core.

9. Remove the Instrument Panel (I/P) tie bar, as follows:

   a. Remove the I/P carrier assembly.

   b. Note the routing of the I/P wiring harness around the I/P tie bar to aid in the reinstallation procedure.

   c. Remove the nuts securing the air distribution duct to the I/P tie bar.

   d. Remove the bolts securing the I/P tie bar to the brake pedal bracket.

   e. Remove the I/P tie bar bolts.

   f. Remove the I/P tie bar assembly.

10. Disconnect the HVAC module assembly electrical connectors.

11. Remove the HVAC module assembly nuts (1).

12. Remove the HVAC module assembly (2).

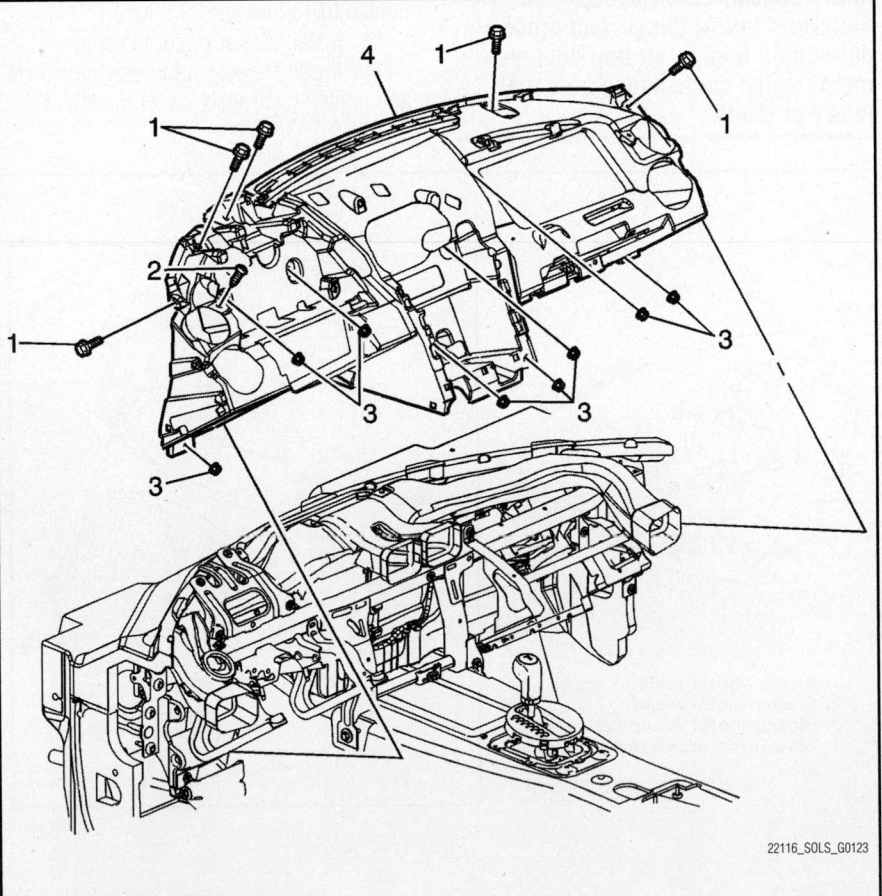

22116_SOLS_G0123

Fig. 180 Instrument panel carrier

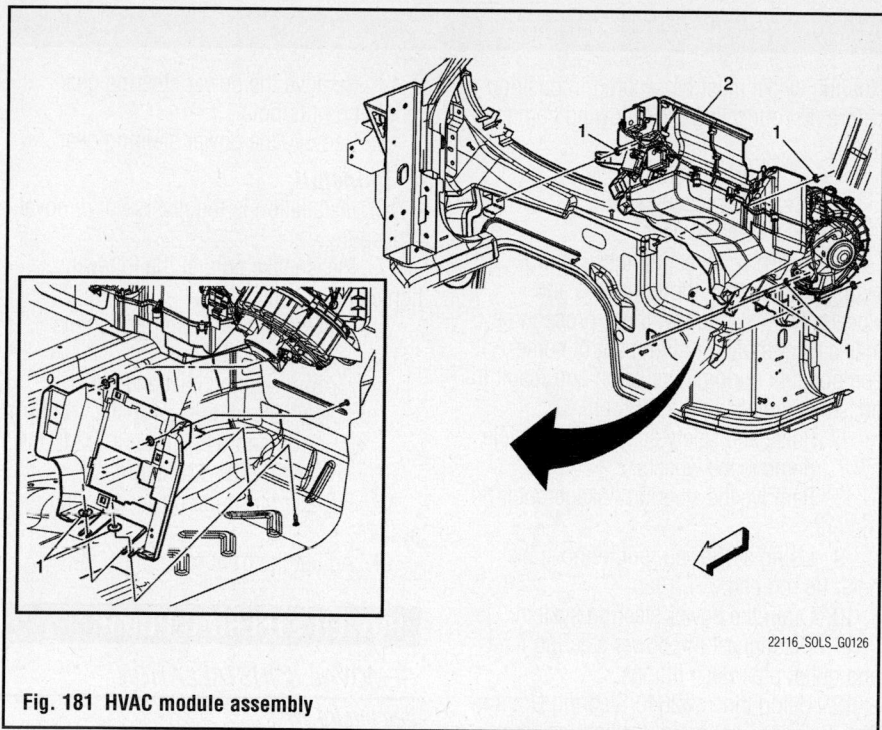

22116_SOLS_G0126

Fig. 181 HVAC module assembly

➡ **Note routing of wiring harness to ensure proper installation.**

To install:

13. Installation is the reverse of removal, noting the following tightening specifications:

    a. Tighten the HVAC module assembly nuts to 80 inch lbs. (9 Nm).

    b. Tighten the Solstice instrument panel tie bar bolts, (1) to 18 ft. lbs. (25 Nm), and (2) to 106 inch lbs. (12 Nm).

    c. Tighten the Sky instrument panel tie bar bolts, (1) to 18 ft. lbs. (25 Nm), and (2) to 34 ft. lbs. (58 Nm).

    d. Tighten the thermal expansion valve bolts to 12 ft. lbs. (16 Nm).

    e. Tighten the A/C compressor tube assembly nut to 12 ft. lbs. (16 Nm).

14. Replace all seals.

15. Evacuate and recharge A/C system.

16. Refill and bleed the cooling system.

17. Enable the SIR system.

18. Connect the negative battery cable.

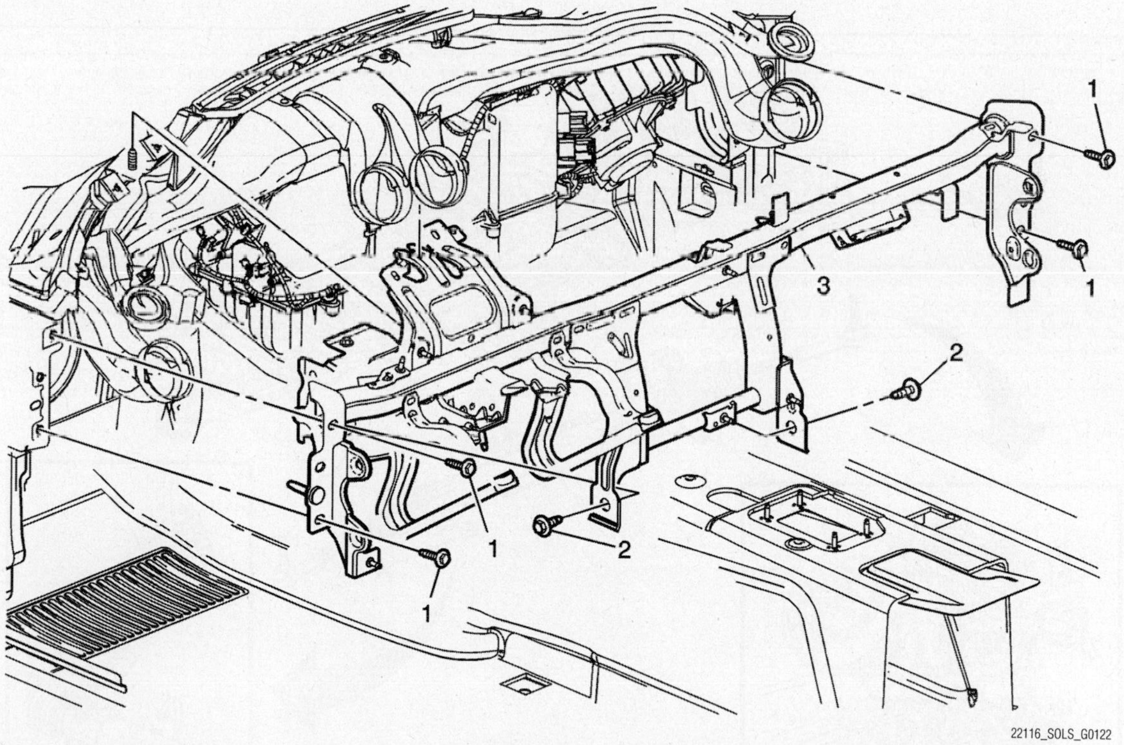

22116_SOLS_G0122

Fig. 182 Instrument panel tie bar

STEERING

POWER RACK & PINION STEERING GEAR

REMOVAL & INSTALLATION

See Figure 183.

1. Before servicing the vehicle, refer to the Precautions Section.

✳✳ CAUTION

This vehicle is equipped with a Supplemental Inflatable Restraint (SIR) System. Refer to the SIR Precautions in the Chassis Electrical Section. Failure to follow the correct procedure could lead to air bag deployment, which could cause personal injury or death.

2. Disable the Supplemental Inflatable Restraint (SIR) system and wait at least one minute.
3. Disconnect the negative battery cable.
4. Secure the steering wheel utilizing a strap to prevent rotation. Locking of the steering column will prevent damage and a possible malfunction of the SIR system. The steering wheel must be secured in position before disconnecting the following components:
    - The steering column
    - The intermediate shaft
    - The steering gear
5. After disconnecting these components, do not move the front tires and wheels. Failure to follow these procedures may cause improper alignment of some components during installation and result in possible damage to the SIR coil.
6. Raise and safely support the vehicle.
7. Remove the wheels.
8. Remove the steering linkage outer tie rod nut.
9. Using a 2-jawed tool, remove the outer tie rod end.
10. Drain the power steering system.
11. Disconnect the power steering inlet and outlet pipe/hose fittings.
12. Using tool J 42640 Steering Column Anti-Rotation Pin, or equivalent, lock the steering wheel in place.
13. Remove the intermediate shaft bolt from the steering gear. Refer to Intermediate Shaft Removal & Installation under Steering Linkage.
14. Remove the power steering gear mounting nuts/bolts.
15. Remove the power steering gear.

To install:

16. Installation is the reverse of removal procedure.
17. Please take note of the following tightening specifications:
    - Steering gear mount bolts/nuts: 44 ft. lbs. (60 Nm)
    - Power steering inlet and outlet pipe/hose fittings: 24 ft. lbs. (32 Nm)
    - Tie rod end ball stud nut: 22 ft. lbs. (30 Nm) plus 115 degrees
18. Fill and bleed the power steering system.
19. Adjust the front toe.

POWER STEERING PUMP

REMOVAL & INSTALLATION

See Figure 184.

1. Before servicing the vehicle, refer to the Precautions Section.
2. Remove the intake manifold cover. Refer to Intake Manifold Removal & Installation in the Engine Mechanical Section.

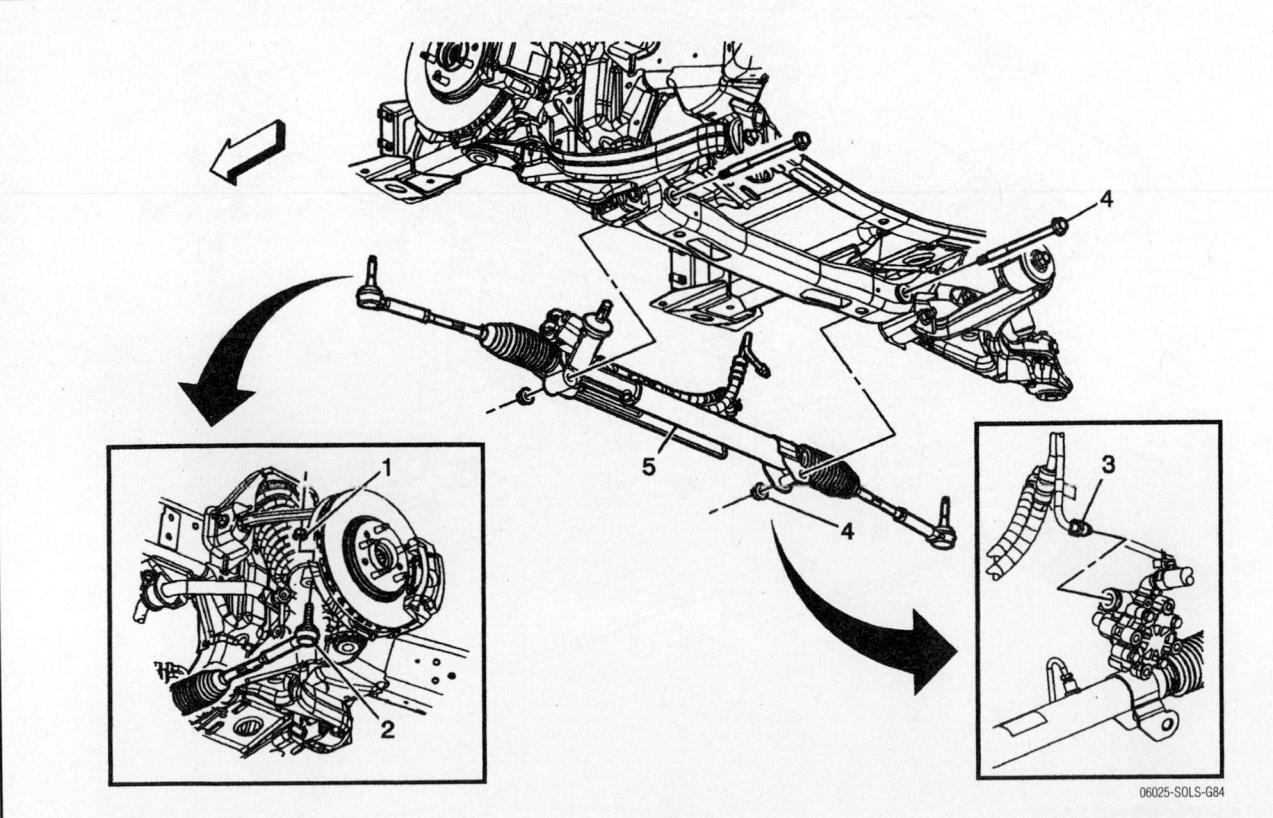

06025-SOLS-G84

Fig. 183 Power steering gear removal

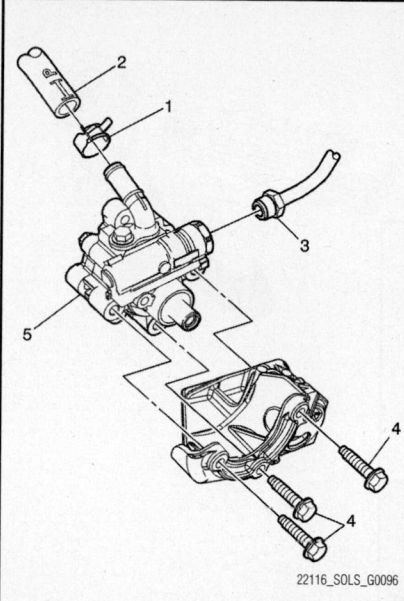

Fig. 184 Power steering pump and related parts

3. Remove the air cleaner assembly.

4. Use the remover J 25034-C to remove the power steering pump pulley.

5. Remove the power steering outlet hose clamp.

6. Remove the outlet hose.

7. Remove the power steering inlet hose fitting.

8. Remove the power steering mounting bolts.

9. Remove the steering pump.

To install:

10. Install the steering pump.

11. Install the power steering mounting bolts and tighten to 16 ft. lbs. (22 Nm).

12. Install the power steering inlet hose fitting and tighten to 24 ft. lbs. (32 Nm).

13. Install the power steering outlet hose and tighten clamp.

14. Use installer J 25033-C to install the power steering pump pulley.

15. Fill and bleed the power steering system.

BLEEDING

> ❊❊ **WARNING**
>
> Use clean, new power steering fluid type only. See the Maintenance and Lubrication subsection for fluid specifications. Hoses touching the frame, body or engine may cause system noise. Verify that the hoses do not touch any other part of the vehicle. Loose connections may not leak, but could allow air into the steering system. Verify that all hose connections are tight.

1. Fill pump reservoir with fluid to minimum system level, FULL COLD level, or middle of hash mark on cap stick fluid level indicator.

> ❊❊ **WARNING**
>
> With hydro-boost only, the oil level will appear falsely high if the hydro-boost accumulator is not fully charged. Do not apply the brake pedal with the engine OFF. This will discharge the hydro-boost accumulator.

2. If equipped with hydro-boost, fully charge the hydro-boost accumulator using the following procedure:

   a. Start the engine.

   b. Firmly apply the brake pedal 10–15 times.

   c. Turn the engine OFF.

3. Raise the vehicle until the front wheels are off the ground.

4. Key on engine OFF, turn the steering wheel from stop to stop 12 times.

5. Vehicles equipped with hydro-boost systems or longer length power steering hoses may require turns up to 15 to 20 steering stop to steering stop.

➡ **Power steering fluid level must be maintained throughout bleed procedure.**

6. Verify power steering fluid level per operating specification.

7. Start the engine. Rotate steering wheel from left to right. Check for signs of cavitation or fluid aeration (pump noise/whining).

8. Verify the fluid level. Repeat the bleed procedure, if necessary.

SUSPENSION

FRONT SUSPENSION

CONTROL LINKS

REMOVAL & INSTALLATION

See Figure 185.

1. Before servicing the vehicle, refer to the Precautions Section.

2. Raise and support the vehicle.

3. Remove the tire and wheel.

4. Remove upper and lower control link retaining nuts.

5. Remove control link.

To install:

6. Install control link.

7. Tighten upper and lower control link retaining nuts to 53 ft. lbs. (72 Nm).

8. Install the tire and wheel.

9. Lower vehicle.

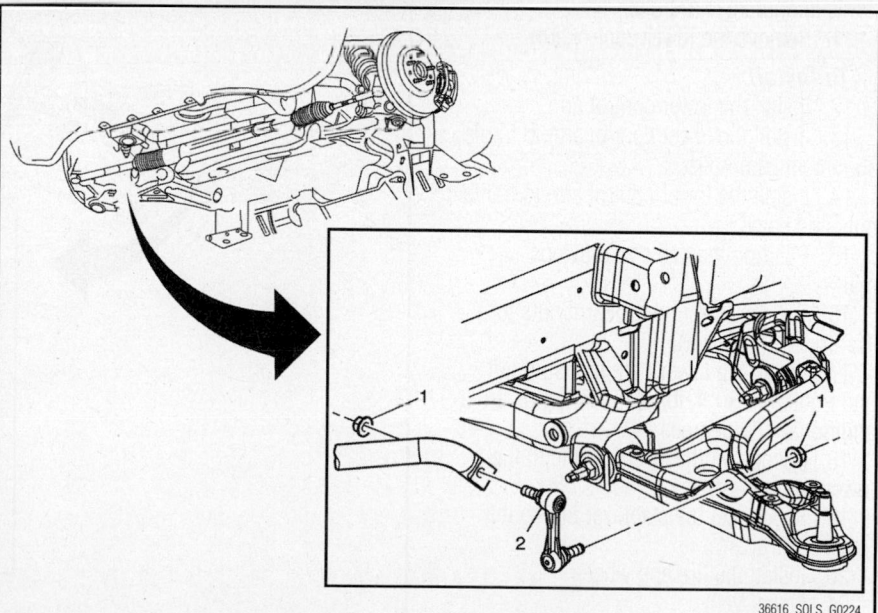

Fig. 185 Control link (2) and nuts (1)

LOWER CONTROL ARM

REMOVAL & INSTALLATION

See Figure 186.

1. Before servicing the vehicle, refer to the Precautions Section.
2. Raise and support the vehicle.
3. Remove the tire and wheel.
4. Disconnect the stabilizer link from the lower control arm.
5. Disconnect the strut module from the lower control arm.
6. Separate the outer tie rod end from the steering knuckle. DO NOT loosen the adjustment jamb nut.

➡**Loosen but DO NOT remove the nut until the ball stud has been separated from the knuckle.**

❋❋ WARNING

The ball stud must not rotate during disassembly or reassembly. Hand tools must be used to keep the ball stud from rotating. If air tools are used and the stud is allowed to rotate, damage to the ball stud and/or stud mounting hole may occur.

7. Using the J-42188-B Ball Joint Separator, separate the ball stud from the knuckle.
8. Remove the lower ball joint stud nut.

➡**Mark frame alignment cams for installation.**

9. Remove the lower control arm to frame nuts and cam.
10. Remove the lower control arm to frame alignment cam bolts.
11. Remove the lower control arm.

To install:

12. Install the lower control arm.
13. Install the lower control arm to frame alignment cam bolts.
14. Install the lower control arm to frame nuts and cams.
15. Position the cams to previous marks.
16. Tighten lower control arm nuts to 122 ft. lbs. (165 Nm).
17. Install the lower ball joint stud nut and tighten to 30 ft. lbs. (40 Nm), plus an additional 130 degrees.
18. Reconnect the strut module to the lower control arm.
19. Reconnect the stabilizer link to the lower control arm.
20. Install the tire and wheel.
21. Lower vehicle.
22. Check wheel alignment.

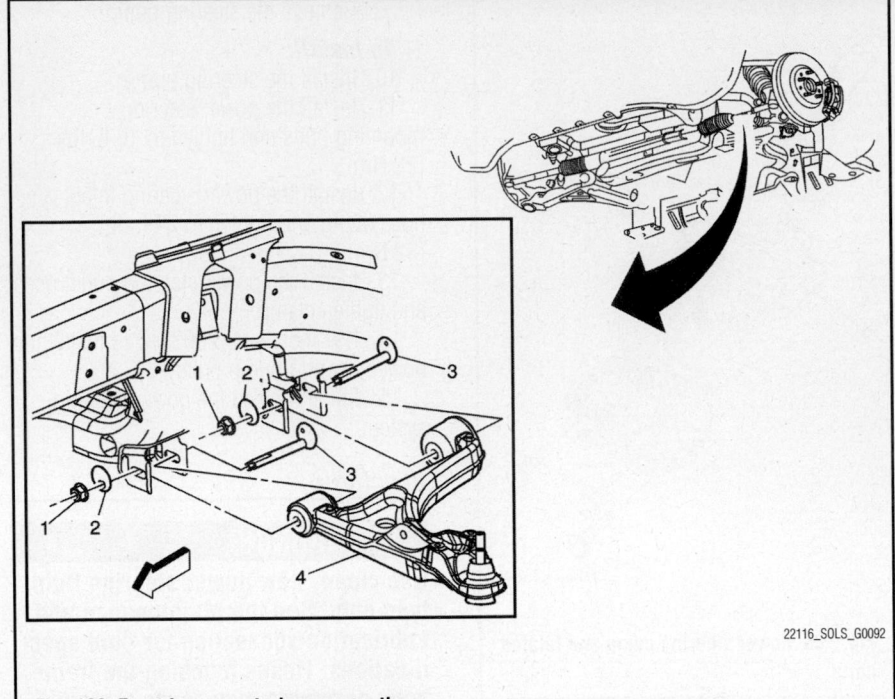

Fig. 186 Front lower control arm mounting

STABILIZER SHAFT

REMOVAL & INSTALLATION

See Figure 187.

1. Before servicing the vehicle, refer to the Precautions Section.
2. Raise and support the vehicle.
3. Remove the tire and wheel.
4. Remove the stabilizer shaft bar from the stabilizer shaft links. Refer to Control Links Removal & Installation.
5. Remove stabilizer shaft bar bolts.
6. Remove stabilizer shaft bar and brackets.
7. If replacing bar remove insulators and replace if necessary.

To install:

8. Install insulators if previously replaced.
9. Lift stabilizer shaft bar into place with brackets.

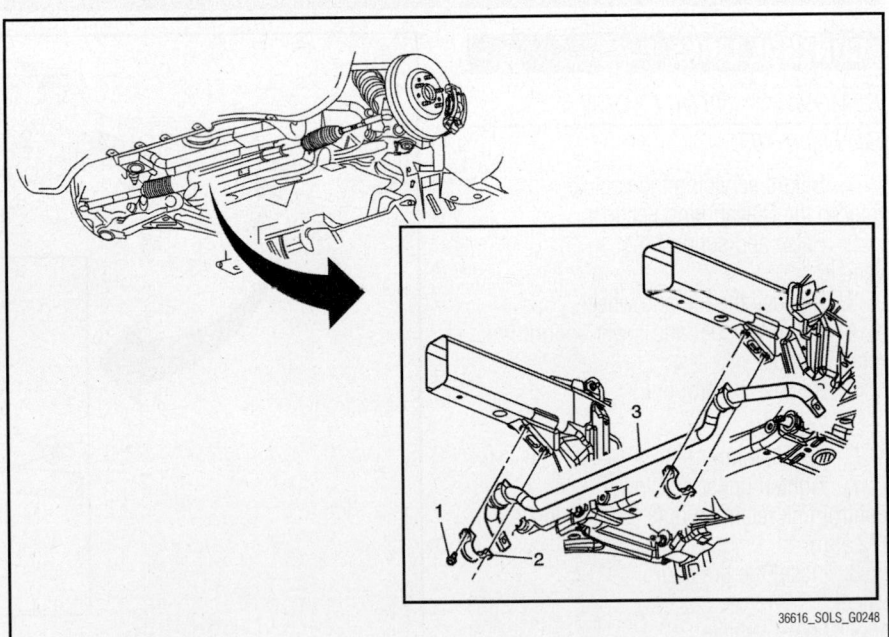

Fig. 187 Stabilizer shaft

10. Install bracket mounting bolts and tighten to 41 ft. lbs. (55 Nm).

11. Reattach the stabilizer shaft bar to the stabilizer shaft links.

12. Tighten stabilizer link retaining nuts to 53 ft. lbs. (72 Nm).

13. Install the tires and wheels.

14. Lower vehicle.

STEERING KNUCKLE

REMOVAL & INSTALLATION

See Figure 188.

1. Before servicing the vehicle, refer to the Precautions Section.

2. Raise and support the vehicle.

3. Remove the tire and wheel.

4. Remove the tie rod end nut.

5. Using the appropriate tool, remove the tie rod end from the steering knuckle.

➡**Loosen but DO NOT remove the nuts until the ball studs have been separated from the knuckle.**

6. Use the appropriate tool to remove the upper and lower ball joint from the steering knuckle.

7. Remove the upper and lower ball joint nuts.

8. Remove the steering knuckle.

To install:

9. Install the steering knuckle.

10. Install the upper and lower ball joint nuts.

11. Tighten the upper ball joint retaining nut to 22 ft. lbs. (30 Nm). plus an additional 150 degrees.

12. Tighten the lower ball joint retaining nut to 30 ft. lbs. (40 Nm). plus an additional 135 degrees.

13. Install tie rod end and retaining nut and tighten to 22 ft. lbs. (30 Nm). plus an additional 115 degrees.

14. Install the tire and wheel.

15. Lower vehicle.

16. Check wheel alignment.

STRUT

REMOVAL & INSTALLATION

See Figure 189.

1. Before servicing the vehicle, refer to the Precautions Section.

2. Raise and safely support the vehicle.

3. Remove the wheels.

4. Without disconnecting the hydraulic brake hose from the caliper, remove and support the brake caliper with bracket as an assembly.

5. Separate the lower control arm ball stud from the steering knuckle.

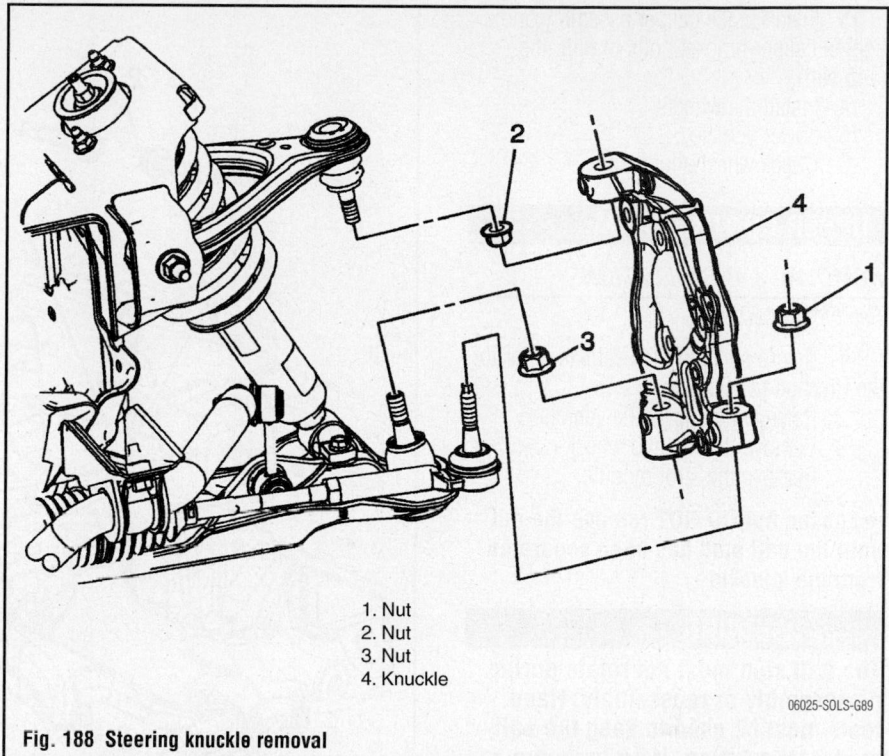

1. Nut
2. Nut
3. Nut
4. Knuckle

06025-SOLS-G89

Fig. 188 Steering knuckle removal

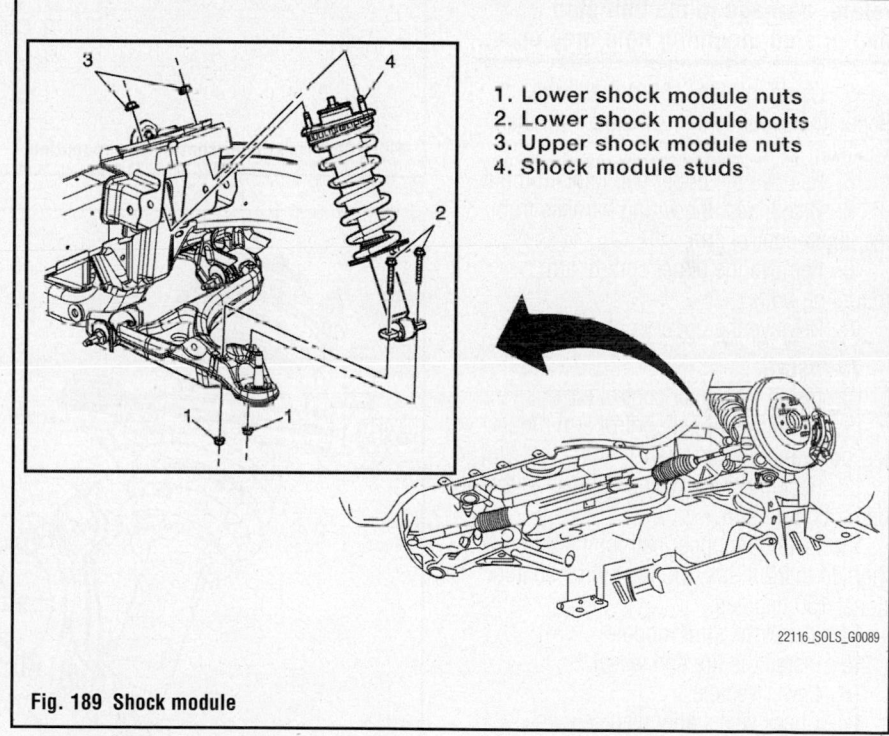

1. Lower shock module nuts
2. Lower shock module bolts
3. Upper shock module nuts
4. Shock module studs

22116_SOLS_G0089

Fig. 189 Shock module

6. Remove the lower shock mounting bolts.

7. Remove the upper shock mounting nuts.

➡**Raise the steering knuckle and upper control arm while removing the shock module toward the rear of the vehicle.**

8. Remove the shock module.

To install:

9. Install the shock module.

10. Install the upper strut nuts and tighten to 35 ft. lbs. (47 Nm)

11. Install the lower strut bolts, nuts and tighten to 21 ft. lbs. (28 Nm)

12. Reconnect the lower control arm ball stud to the steering knuckle and tighten to 30 ft. lbs. (40 Nm) plus an additional 135°

13. Install brake caliper assembly and tighten caliper bracket bolts to 85ft. lbs. (115 Nm).

14. Install the wheels.

15. Lower vehicle.

16. Check wheel alignment.

UPPER CONTROL ARM

REMOVAL & INSTALLATION

See Figure 190.

1. Before servicing the vehicle, refer to the Precautions Section.

2. Raise and support the vehicle.

3. Remove the tire and wheel.

4. Remove the strut module.

➡️**Loosen but DO NOT remove the nut until the ball stud has been separated from the knuckle.**

✱✱ WARNING

The ball stud must not rotate during disassembly or reassembly. Hand tools must be used to keep the ball stud from rotating. If air tools are used and the stud is allowed to rotate, damage to the ball stud and/or stud mounting hole may occur.

5. Using the J-42188-B Ball Joint Separator, separate the ball stud from the knuckle.

6. Remove the upper ball joint stud nut.

7. Disconnect the wiring harness from the upper control arm.

8. Remove the upper control arm mounting bolts.

9. Remove the upper control arm.

To install:

10. Install the upper control arm.

11. Install the upper control arm mounting bolts and tighten to 81 ft. lbs. (110 Nm).

12. Reconnect the wiring harness to the upper control arm.

13. Install the upper ball joint stud nut. Tighten to 22 ft. lbs. (30 Nm), plus an additional 150 degrees.

14. Install the strut module.

15. Install the tire and wheel.

16. Lower vehicle.

17. Check wheel alignment.

WHEEL HUB & BEARING

REMOVAL & INSTALLATION

See Figure 191.

1. Before servicing the vehicle, refer to the Precautions Section.

2. Raise and support the vehicle.

3. Remove the tire and wheel.

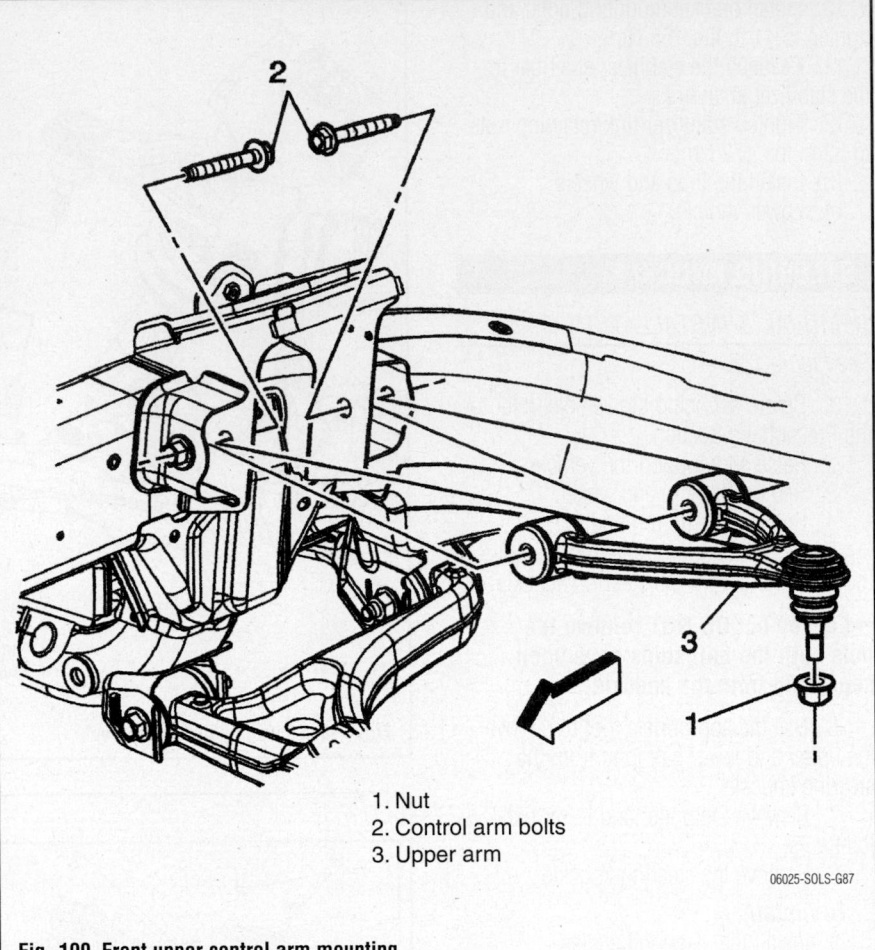

1. Nut
2. Control arm bolts
3. Upper arm

06025-SOLS-G87

Fig. 190 Front upper control arm mounting

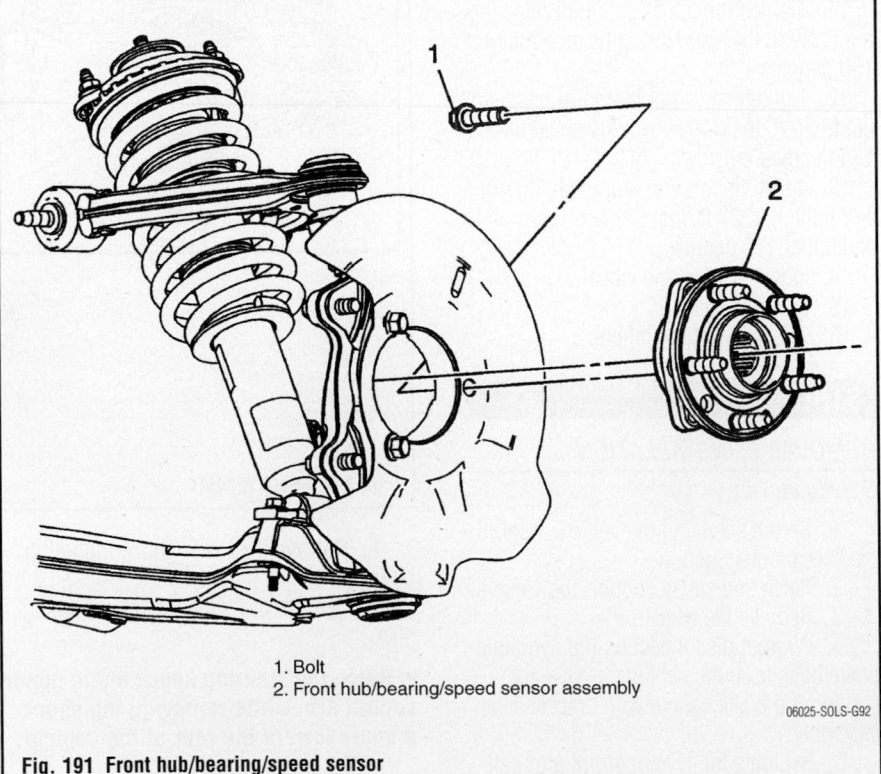

1. Bolt
2. Front hub/bearing/speed sensor assembly

06025-SOLS-G92

Fig. 191 Front hub/bearing/speed sensor

4. Remove the brake caliper with mounting bracket. Refer to Front Disc Brake Caliper Removal & Installation in the Brake Section.

5. Remove the brake rotor.

6. Disconnect the speed sensor electrical connector and the wiring harness from the retainers on the steering knuckle.

7. Remove the wheel hub mounting bolts.

8. Remove the wheel hub/bearing/speed sensor assembly.

To install:

9. Install the wheel hub and bearing/speed sensor assembly.

10. Tighten the wheel hub and bearing assembly mounting bolts to 85 ft. lbs. (115 Nm).

11. Reconnect the speed sensor electrical connector and the wiring harness to the retainers on the steering knuckle.

12. Install the brake rotor.

13. Install brake caliper assembly and

tighten bracket mounting bolts to 85 ft. lbs. (115 Nm).

14. Install the tire and wheel.

15. Lower vehicle.

ADJUSTMENT

The front wheel hub and bearing assembly is a sealed unit and does not require adjustments or repacking.

SUSPENSION
REAR SUSPENSION

ADJUST LINKS

REMOVAL & INSTALLATION

See Figure 192.

1. Before servicing the vehicle, refer to the Precautions Section.

✳✳ WARNING

The ball stud must not rotate during disassembly or reassembly. Hand tools must be used to keep the ball stud from rotating. If air tools are used and the stud is allowed to rotate, damage to the ball stud and/or stud mounting hole may occur.

2. Raise and support the vehicle.

3. Remove the tire and wheel.

4. Remove the adjust link retaining nut.

5. Use the appropriate tool to remove the toe link ball joint from the rear knuckle.

➡**If the adjustment link is being reused, DO NOT loosen the adjustment jamb nut.**

6. Clean off threads and apply a small amount of penetrating oil to the thread of the link and allow to sit for a very minutes. This will aid in the removal of the nut and not damage the threads.

7. Remove the adjust link-to-frame nut.

8. Remove the adjust link.

To install:

9. Installation is the reverse of removal procedure.

10. Please take note of the following tightening specifications:
- Adjust link retaining nut: 22 ft. lbs. (30 Nm), plus 150 degrees.
- Adjust link to frame nut: 74 ft. lbs. (100 Nm).

11. Adjust the rear toe.

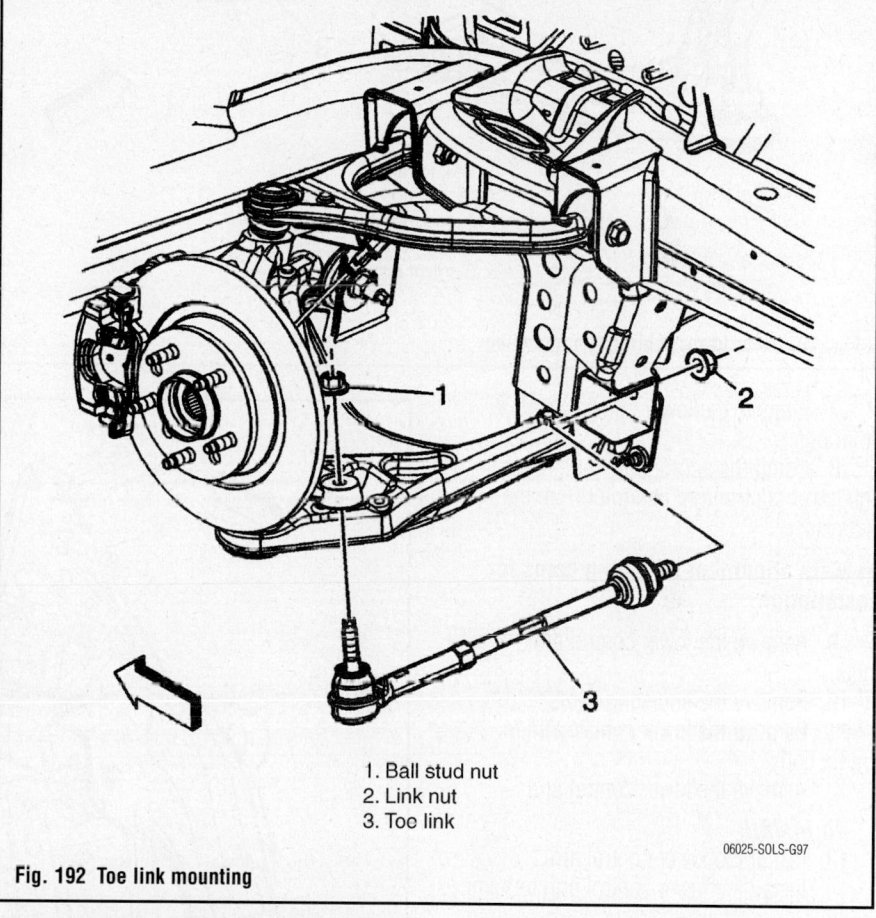

1. Ball stud nut
2. Link nut
3. Toe link

06025-SOLS-G97

Fig. 192 Toe link mounting

CONTROL ARMS/LINKS

REMOVAL & INSTALLATION

Lower Control Arm

See Figure 193.

1. Before servicing the vehicle, refer to the Precautions Section.

✳✳ WARNING

The ball stud must not rotate during disassembly or reassembly. Hand tools must be used to keep the ball stud from rotating. If air tools are

used and the stud is allowed to rotate, damage to the ball stud and/or stud mounting hole may occur.

2. Raise and support the vehicle.

3. Remove the tire and wheel.

4. Disconnect the stabilizer link from the lower control arm.

5. Disconnect the strut module from the lower control arm.

6. Separate the rear adjustment link from the suspension knuckle. DO NOT loosen the adjustment jamb nut.

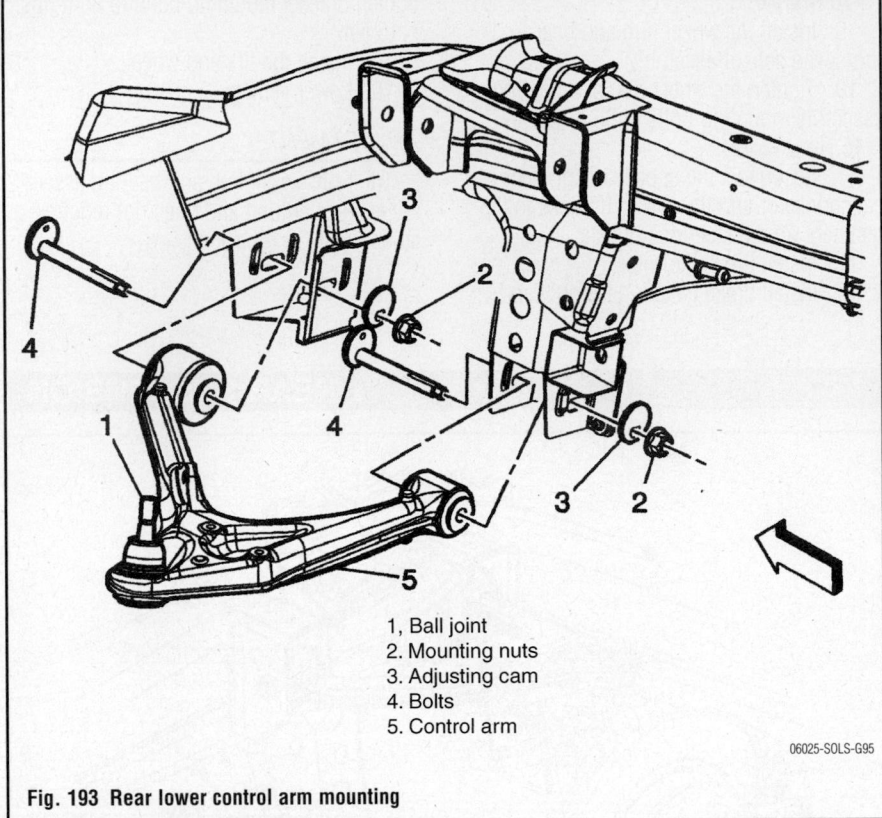

1, Ball joint
2. Mounting nuts
3. Adjusting cam
4. Bolts
5. Control arm

06025-SOLS-G95

Fig. 193 Rear lower control arm mounting

7. Remove the lower control arm ball joint nut.

8. Using the appropriate tool, separate the lower control arm ball joint from the knuckle.

➡ **Mark alignment adjusting cams for installation.**

9. Remove the lower control arm nuts.

10. Remove the adjusting cams.

11. Remove the lower control arm to frame bolts.

12. Remove the lower control arm.

To install:

13. Install the lower control arm.

14. Install the lower control arm to frame bolts.

15. Install adjusting cams and control arm nuts.

➡ **Install cams in original location previously marked.**

16. Tighten the lower control arm nuts to 122 ft. lbs. (165 Nm).

17. Install the lower control arm ball joint stud in the knuckle.

18. Install the lower control arm ball joint retaining nut to 30 ft. lbs. (40 Nm). plus an additional 135 degrees.

19. Reconnect the strut module to the lower control arm.

20. Reconnect the stabilizer link to the lower control arm.

21. Install the tire and wheel.

22. Lower vehicle.

23. Check wheel alignment.

Upper Control Arm

See Figure 194.

1. Before servicing the vehicle, refer to the Precautions Section.

> ※※ **WARNING**
>
> **The ball stud must not rotate during disassembly or reassembly. Hand tools must be used to keep the ball stud from rotating. If air tools are used and the stud is allowed to rotate, damage to the ball stud and/or stud mounting hole may occur.**

2. Raise and support the vehicle.

3. Remove the tire and wheel.

4. Remove the upper ball joint nut.

5. Using the appropriate tool, separate the upper control arm ball joint from the knuckle.

6. Remove the rear strut module.

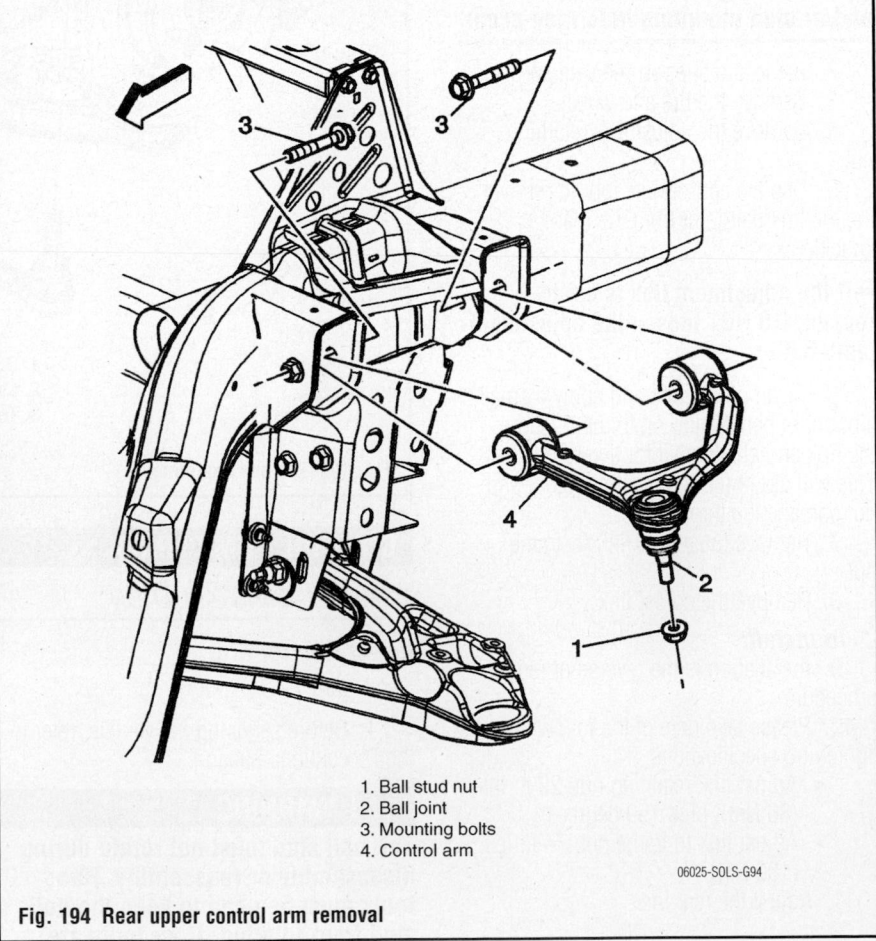

1. Ball stud nut
2. Ball joint
3. Mounting bolts
4. Control arm

06025-SOLS-G94

Fig. 194 Rear upper control arm removal

7. Remove the upper control arm mounting bolts.

8. Remove the upper control arm.

To install:

9. Install the upper control arm.

10. Install the upper control arm mounting bolts and tighten to 81 ft. lbs. (110 Nm).

11. Install the rear strut module.

12. Install ball stud into knuckle and start ball joint retaining nut.

13. Tighten ball joint retaining nut to 22 ft. lbs. (30 Nm). plus an additional 150 degrees.

14. Install the tire and wheel.

15. Lower vehicle.

KNUCKLE

REMOVAL & INSTALLATION

See Figure 195.

1. Before servicing the vehicle, refer to the Precautions Section.

✳✳ WARNING

The ball stud must not rotate during disassembly or reassembly. Hand tools must be used to keep the ball stud from rotating. If air tools are used and the stud is allowed to rotate, damage to the ball stud and/or stud mounting hole may occur.

2. Raise and support the vehicle.

3. Remove the tire and wheel.

4. Remove the wheel bearing hub assembly.

5. Using the J-42188-B Ball Joint Separator, separate the rear adjustment link from the suspension knuckle.

6. Remove the upper ball joint retaining nut.

7. Use the appropriate tool to remove the upper ball joint from the knuckle.

8. Remove the lower ball joint retaining nut.

9. Use the appropriate tool to remove the lower ball joint ball joint from the knuckle.

10. Remove the knuckle.

To install:

11. Installation is the reverse of removal procedure.

12. Please take note of the following tightening specifications:

- Rear adjustment link retaining nut: 22 ft. lbs. (30 Nm) plus an additional 150 degrees.
- Upper ball stud nut: 22 ft. lbs. (30 Nm) plus an additional 150 degrees.

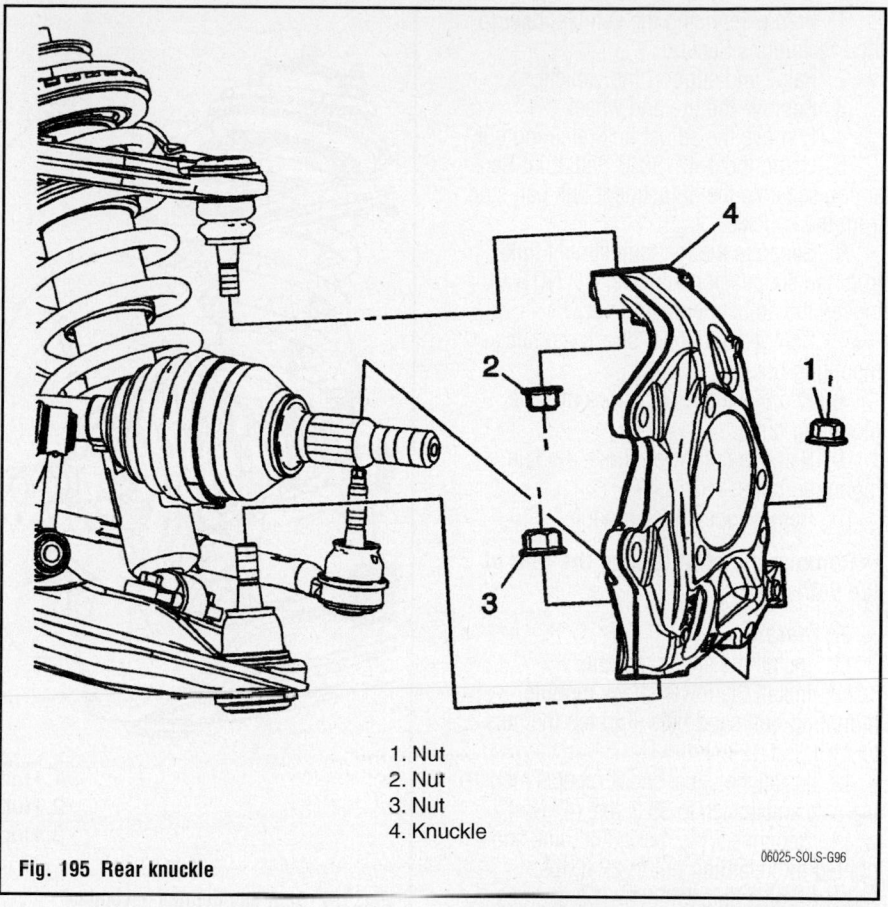

1. Nut
2. Nut
3. Nut
4. Knuckle

06025-SOLS-G96

Fig. 195 Rear knuckle

- Lower ball stud nut: 30 ft. lbs. (40 Nm) plus an additional 135 degrees.

13. Check the alignment.

STRUT

REMOVAL & INSTALLATION

See Figure 196.

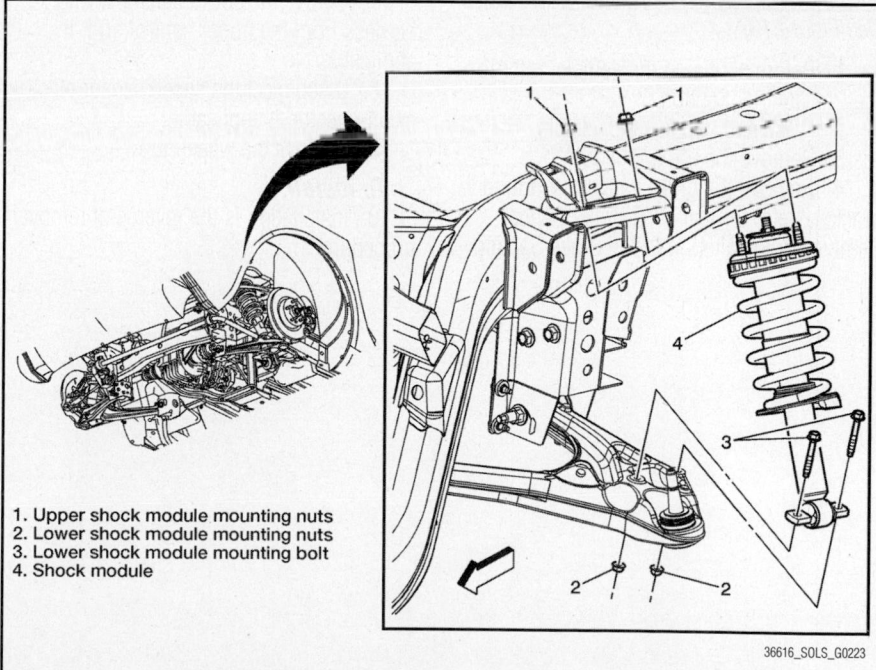

1. Upper shock module mounting nuts
2. Lower shock module mounting nuts
3. Lower shock module mounting bolt
4. Shock module

36616_SOLS_G0223

Fig. 196 Rear strut mounting

1. Before servicing the vehicle, refer to the Precautions Section.

2. Raise and support the vehicle.

3. Remove the tire and wheel.

4. Remove the adjust link retaining nut.

5. Using the J-42188-B Ball Joint Separator, separate the adjustment link ball stud from the knuckle.

6. Separate the rear adjustment link from the suspension knuckle. DO NOT loosen the adjustment jamb nut.

7. Remove the upper shock module mounting nuts.

8. Remove the lower shock module mounting nuts.

9. Remove the lower shock module mounting bolts.

10. Remove the shock module.

➡**Remove the strut toward the rear of the vehicle.**

To install:

11. Install the shock module.

12. Install the lower shock module mounting bolt sand nuts. Tighten the nuts to 21 ft. lbs. (28 Nm).

13. Install the upper shock module mounting nuts and tighten to 35 ft. lbs. (47 Nm).

14. Reconnect the rear adjust link and tighten the retaining nut to 22 ft. lbs. (30 Nm). plus an additional 150 degrees.

15. Install tire and wheel.

16. Lower vehicle.

WHEEL HUB & BEARING

REMOVAL & INSTALLATION

See Figure 197.

1. Before servicing the vehicle, refer to the Precautions Section.

2. Raise and support the vehicle.

3. Remove the tire and wheel.

4. Remove the brake caliper mounting bracket. Refer to Rear Disc Brake Caliper Removal & Installation in the Brake Section.

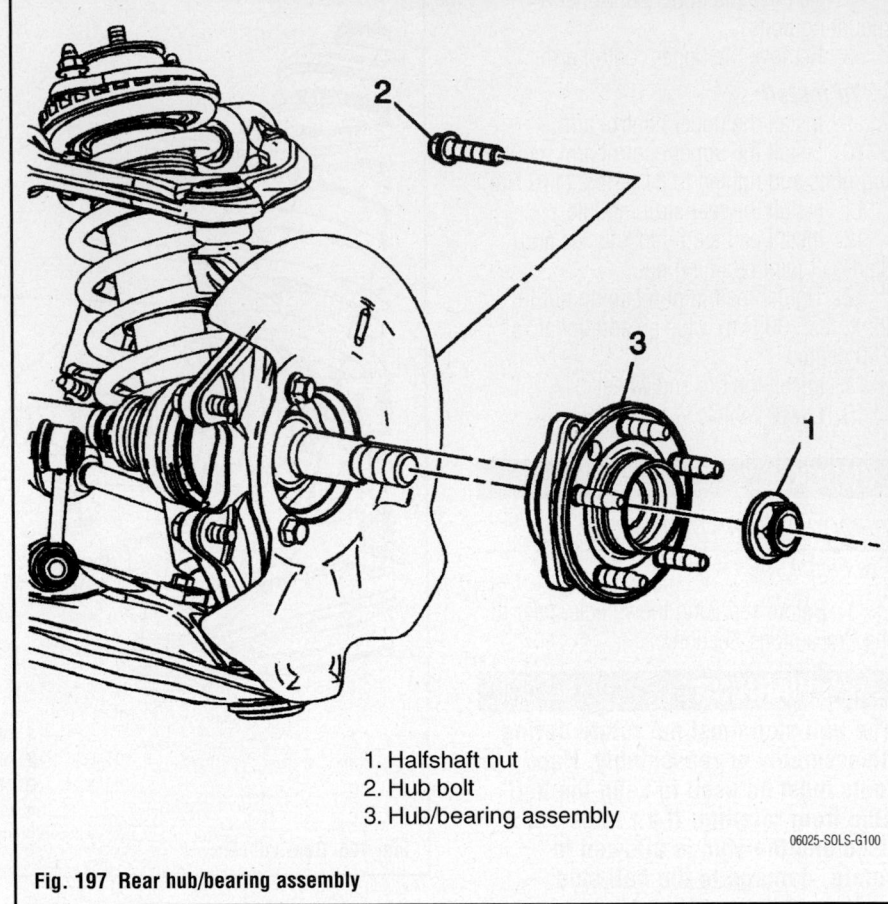

1. Halfshaft nut
2. Hub bolt
3. Hub/bearing assembly

06025-SOLS-G100

Fig. 197 Rear hub/bearing assembly

5. Remove the drive axle retaining nut.

6. Remove the wheel/hub mounting bolt.

7. Using a small flat-blade screw driver, remove the speed sensor wiring harness from the upper control arm, if applicable.

8. Disconnect the speed sensor electrical connector, if applicable.

9. Remove the wheel hub.

To install:

10. Installation is the reverse of removal procedure.

11. Please take note of the following tightening specifications:

- Tighten the new halfshaft nut to 159 ft. lbs. (215 Nm).
- Tighten wheel bearing hub assembly mounting bolts to 85 ft. lbs. (115 Nm).

ADJUSTMENT

The rear wheel hub and bearing assembly is a sealed unit and does not require adjustments or repacking.

CADILLAC

SRX

22

SPECIFICATIONS AND MAINTENANCE CHARTS

ENGINE AND VEHICLE IDENTIFICATION

			Engine					Model Year	
Code ①	Liters	Cu. In.	Cyl.	Fuel Sys.	Engine Type	Eng. Mfg.		Code ②	Year
6	2.8	170	V6	SFI	DOHC	GM		A	2010
Y	3.0	183	V6	SIDI	DOHC	GM		B	2011

① 8th position of VIN

② 10th position of VIN

25742_CSRX_C0001

GENERAL ENGINE SPECIFICATIONS

All measurements are given in inches.

Year	Model	Engine Displacement Liters	Engine ID/VIN	Fuel System Type	Net Horsepower @ rpm	Net Torque @ rpm (ft. lbs.)	Bore x Stroke (in.)	Compression Ratio	Oil Pressure @ rpm
2010	SRX	2.8	6	SFI	300@5500	295@1850	3.50x2.95	10.0:1	20@2000
		3.0	Y	SIDI	265@6950	223@5700	3.50x3.16	11.7:1	20@2000
2011	SRX	3.0	Y	SIDI	265@6950	223@5700	3.50x3.16	11.7:1	20@2000

25742_CSRX_C0002

ENGINE TUNE-UP SPECIFICATIONS

Year	Engine Displacement Liters	Engine ID/VIN	Spark Plug Gap (in.)	Ignition Timing (deg.)		Fuel Pump (psi)	Idle Speed (rpm)		Valve Clearance (in.)	
				MT	AT		MT	AT	Intake	Exhaust
2010	2.8	6	0.43	①	①	276-725 PSI	①	①	②	②
	3.0	Y	0.43	①	①	276-725 PSI	①	①	②	②
2011	3.0	Y	0.43	①	①	276-725 PSI	①	①	②	②

NS Not Supplied

NA Not Applicable

① Ignition timing and idle speed are computer controlled and not adjustable.

② Hydraulic lifters

25742_CSRX_C0003

CAPACITIES

Year	Model	Engine Displacement Liters	Engine ID/VIN	Engine Oil with Filter (qts.)	Transmission (pts.) Auto.	Transmission (pts.) Manual	Transfer Case (pts.)	Drive Axle (pts.)	Fuel Tank (gal.)	Cooling System (qts.)
2010	SRX	2.8	6	6.0	NA	NA	1.5	1.4	21.0	12.15
		3.0	Y	6.0	18.0	NA	1.5	1.4	21.0	12.3
2011	SRX	3.0	Y	6.0	18.0	NA	1.5	1.4	21.0	12.3

NOTE: All capacities are approximate. Add fluid gradually and ensure a proper fluid level is obtained.

25742_CSRX_C0004

FLUID SPECIFICATIONS

Year	Model	Engine Displacement Liters	Engine Oil	Manual Trans.	Auto. Trans.	Drive Axle Rear	Power Steering Fluid	Brake Master Cylinder	Cooling System
2010	SRX	2.8	5W-30	NA	AW-1	②	③	④	⑤
		3.0	5W-30	NA	①	②	③	④	⑤
2011	SRX	3.0	5W-30	NA	①	②	③	④	⑤

DOT: Department Of Transpotation
① Dexron IV
② GM part #88861950
③ GM Power Steering Fluid
④ DOT 3 or equivalent
⑤ Green Engine Coolant

25742_CSRX_C0005

VALVE SPECIFICATIONS

Year	Engine Displacement Liters	Engine ID/VIN	Seat Angle (deg.)	Face Angle (deg.)	Spring Test Pressure (lbs. @ in.)	Spring Installed Height (in.)	Stem-to-Guide Clearance (in.) Intake	Stem-to-Guide Clearance (in.) Exhaust	Stem Diameter (in.) Intake	Stem Diameter (in.) Exhaust
2010	2.8	6	45.0	44.25	61 lbs. @ 1.378 in.	1.378	0.0010-0.0026	0.0014-0.0030	0.2344-0.2352	0.2341-0.2348
	3.0	Y	45.0	44.25	61 lbs. @ 1.378 in.	1.3870-1.445	0.0010-0.0026	0.0014-0.0030	0.2344-0.2352	0.2341-0.2348
2011	3.0	Y	45.0	44.25	61 lbs. @ 1.378 in.	1.3870-1.445	0.0010-0.0026	0.0014-0.0030	0.2344-0.2352	0.2341-0.2348

25742_CSRX_C0006

CAMSHAFT SPECIFICATIONS
All measurements in inches unless noted

Year	Engine Displacement Liters	Engine Code/VIN	Journal Diameter	Brg. Oil Clearance	Shaft End-play	Runout	Journal Bore	Lobe Height Intake	Lobe Height Exhaust
2010	2.8	6	①	0.0016- 0.0033	0.0018- 0.0085	②	NS	1.6687- 1.6805	1.6715- 1.6833
	3.0	Y	①	0.0016- 0.0033	0.0018- 0.0085	②	NS	1.6687- 1.6805	1.6715- 1.6833
2011	3.0	Y	①	0.0016- 0.0033	0.0018- 0.0085	②	NS	1.6687- 1.6805	1.6715- 1.6833

① Journal Diameter 1st: 1.3779-1.3787, Journal Diameter Other: 1.0630-1.0638

② Runout 1st: 1.3779-1.3787, Other: 1.0630-1.0638

25742_CSRX_C0007

CRANKSHAFT AND CONNECTING ROD SPECIFICATIONS
All measurements are given in inches.

Year	Engine Displacement Liters	Engine ID/VIN	Crankshaft Main Brg. Journal Dia.	Crankshaft Main Brg. Oil Clearance	Crankshaft Shaft End-play	Crankshaft Thrust on No.	Connecting Rod Journal Diameter	Connecting Rod Oil Clearance	Connecting Rod Side Clearance
2010	2.8	6	2.6772	0.0004- 0.0024	0.0039- 0.0130	2	2.2044- 2.2050	0.0004- 0.0028	0.0037- 0.0140
	3.0	Y	2.6772	0.0004- 0.0024	0.0039- 0.0130	2	2.2044- 2.2050	0.0004- 0.0028	0.0037- 0.0140
2011	3.0	Y	2.6772	0.0004- 0.0024	0.0039- 0.0130	2	2.2044- 2.2050	0.0004- 0.0028	0.0037- 0.0140

25742_CSRX_C0008

PISTON AND RING SPECIFICATIONS
All measurements are given in inches.

Year	Engine Displacement Liters	Engine ID/VIN	Piston Clearance	Ring Gap Top Compression	Ring Gap Bottom Compression	Ring Gap Oil Control	Ring Side Clearance Top Compression	Ring Side Clearance Bottom Compression	Ring Side Clearance Oil Control
2010	2.8	6	0.0008- 0.0013	0.0059- 0.0118	0.0110- 0.0189	0.0059- 0.0236	0.0012- 0.0026	0.0006- 0.0024	0.0012- 0.0067
	3.0	Y	0.0008- 0.0013	0.0059- 0.0118	0.0110- 0.0189	0.0059- 0.0236	0.0012- 0.0026	0.0006- 0.0024	0.0012- 0.0067
2011	3.0	Y	0.0008- 0.0013	0.0059- 0.0118	0.0110- 0.0189	0.0059- 0.0236	0.0012- 0.0026	0.0006- 0.0024	0.0012- 0.0067

① Measured in cylinder bore

25742_CSRX_C0009

TORQUE SPECIFICATIONS
All readings in ft. lbs.

Year	Engine Disp. Liters	Engine ID/VIN	Cylinder Head Bolts	Main Bearing Bolts	Rod Bearing Bolts	Crankshaft Damper Bolts	Flywheel Bolts	Manifold		Spark Plugs	Oil Pan Drain Plug
								Intake	Exhaust		
2010	2.8	6	①	②	③	④	49	18	15	13	18
	3.0	Y	①	②	③	④	49	18	15	13	18
2011	3.0	Y	①	②	③	④	49	18	15	13	18

NS Not supplied

① Step 1: 22 ft. lbs.

   Step 2: Plus 150 degrees

   Step 1: M8 Bolt: 11 ft. lbs.

   Step 2: Plus 75 degrees

② Inner bolts: 15 ft. lbs. plus 80 degrees

   Outer bolts: 11 ft. lbs. plus 110 degrees

   Side bolts: 22 ft. lbs. plus 60 degrees

③ Step 1: 22 ft. lbs.

   Step 2: Zero

   Step 3: 18 ft. lbs.

   Step 4: Plus 110 degrees

④ Step 1: 74 ft. lbs.

   Step 2: plus 150 degrees

25742_CSRX_C0010

WHEEL ALIGNMENT

Year	Model		Caster		Camber		Toe-in
			Range (+/-Deg.)	Preferred Setting (Deg.)	Range (+/-Deg.)	Preferred Setting (Deg.)	(Deg.)
2010	SRX	Front	0.75	4.50	0.75	0.60	0.20+/-0.20
		Rear	—	—	0.75	-1.00	0.20+/-0.20
2011	SRX	Front	0.75	4.50	0.75	0.60	0.20+/-0.20
		Rear	—	—	0.75	-1.00	0.20+/-0.20

25742_CSRX_C0011

TIRE AND WHEEL SPECIFICATIONS

Year	Model	OEM Tires		Tire Pressures (psi)		Wheel Size	Lug Nut (ft. lbs.)
		Front	Rear	Front	Rear		
2010	SRX	P235/65R18	P235/55R20	①	①	②	100
2011	SRX	P235/65R18	P235/55R20	①	①	②	100

OEM: Original Equipment Manufacturer

PSI: Pounds Per Square Inch

① See vehicle tire placard.

② 18: standard; 20: optional

25742_CSRX_C0012

BRAKE SPECIFICATIONS

All measurements in inches unless noted

Year	Model		Brake Disc			Minimum Pad/Lining Thickness		Brake Caliper	
			Original Thickness	Minimum Thickness	Max. Runout	Front	Rear	Bracket Bolts (ft. lbs.)	Mounting Bolts (ft. lbs.)
2010	SRX	F	NS	1.060	0.002	NS	NS	81	44
		R	0.906	0.846	0.002	NS	NS	81	44
2011	SRX	F	NS	1.060	0.002	NS	NS	81	44
		R	0.906	0.846	0.002	NS	NS	81	44

F: Front

R: Rear

NS: Information not supplied

25742_CSRX_C0013

MAINTENANCE I AND II SERVICE SCHEDULES
SRX

When the CHANGE ENGINE OIL light appears, certain services and inspections are required.

Required services are described as Maintenance I and Maintenance II.

The first service of a vehicle should be Maintenance I, and the second service should be Maintenance II.

Alternate between the 2 services thereafter. However, in some cases, Maintenance II may be required more often.

Maintenance I: Use Maintenance I if the CHANGE ENGINE OIL light comes on within 10 months since the vehicle was purchased or, if Maintenance II was performed.

Maintenance II: Use Maintenance II if the previous service performed was Maintenance I. Always use Maintenance II whenever the CHANGE ENGINE OIL light comes on 10 months or more since the last service, or, if the CHANGE ENGINE OIL light has not come on at all for one year.

Service Item	Maintenance I	Maintenance II
Change the engine oil and filter.	✓	✓
Reset the oil life system.	✓	✓
Visually inspect the vehicle for leaks or damage. A fluid loss in the vehicle system could indicate a problem. Inspect, repair and add fluid to the system if necessary.	✓	✓
Inspect the engine air cleaner filter. If necessary, replace the filter.	✓	✓
Rotate the tires. Inspect the tire inflation pressures and the tire wear.	✓	✓
Visually inspect the brake lines and hoses for proper hook-up, binding, leaks, cracks, chafing, etc. Inspect the disc brake pads for wear and the rotors for surface condition. Inspect the drum brake linings for wear or cracks. Inspect other brake parts, including drums, wheel cylinders, calipers, parking brake, etc. Inspect the parking brake adjustment.	✓	✓
Inspect engine coolant and windshield washer fluid levels. Add fluid as needed.	✓	✓
Inspect the suspension and steering components. Inspect the front and rear suspension and the steering system for damaged, loose or missing parts, or signs of wear. Inspect the power steering lines and the hoses for proper hook-up, binding, leaks, cracks, chafing, etc.	—	✓
Visually inspect the coolant hoses and replace the hoses if they are cracked, swollen or deteriorated. Inspect all pipes, fittings and clamps; replace with GM parts as needed. To help ensure proper operation, a pressure test of the cooling system and pressure cap and cleaning the outside of the radiator and air conditioning condenser is recommended at least once a year.	—	✓
Ensure the safety belt reminder light and all the belts, buckles, latch plates, retractors and anchorages are working properly. Look for any other loose or damaged safety belt system parts. If you see anything that might keep a safety belt system from working correctly, repair or replaced the damaged part. Replace torn or frayed safety belts, refer to Operational and Functional Checks in Seat Belts. Inspect for any opened or broken air bag coverings, and repair or replace as needed. The air bag system does require regular maintenance.	—	✓
Lubricate the body components.	✓	✓
Lubricate all key lock cylinders, hood latch assemblies, secondary latches, pivots, spring anchor and release pawl, hood and door hinges, rear folding seats and liftgate hinges. Frequent lubrication may be required when exposed to a corrosive environment, refer to Fluid and Lubricant Recommendations . Applying dielectric silicone grease GM P/N 12345579 (Canadian P/N 1974984) or equivalent on the weatherstrips with a clean cloth.	—	✓
Inspect the wiper blades and replace as necessary.	✓	✓
Inspect the throttle and fuel system.	—	✓
Replace the passenger compartment air filter.	—	✓
Inspect exhaust system and heat shields.	✓	✓

To reset the CHANGE ENGINE OIL light:

1. Turn the ignition key to the ON/RUN position with the engine OFF.
2. Press and release the stem in the lower center of the instrument cluster until the OIL LIFE message is displayed.
3. Once the alternating OIL LIFE and RESET messages appear, press and hold the stem until several beeps sound.
    This confirms that the oil life system has been reset to 100 percent.
4. Turn the ignition key to the OFF position.
    If the CHANGE ENGINE OIL message comes back on when the vehicle is started, the engine oil life system has not been reset. Repeat the procedure.

25742_CSRX_C0014

ADDITIONAL MAINTENANCE SERVICES - NORMAL
SRX

TO BE SERVICED	TYPE OF SERVICE	VEHICLE MILEAGE INTERVAL (x1000)					
		25	50	75	100	125	150
Engine coolant	Replace						✓
Air cleaner filter	Replace		✓		✓		✓
Automatic transmisison fluid & filter	Replace				✓		
Spark plugs	Replace				✓		
Transfer case fluid	Replace				✓		
Exhaust system & heat shields	Service/Inspect	✓	✓	✓	✓	✓	✓
Cooling system hoses and clamps	Service/Inspect						✓
Fuel system	Inspect	✓	✓	✓	✓	✓	✓
Accessory drive belts	Replace						✓
Evaporative control system	Inspect		✓		✓		✓
Passenger compartment air filter	Replace	✓	✓	✓	✓	✓	✓

25742_CSRX_C0015

ADDITIONAL MAINTENANCE SERVICES - SEVERE
SRX

TO BE SERVICED	TYPE OF SERVICE	VEHICLE MILEAGE INTERVAL (x1000)					
		25	50	75	100	125	150
Engine coolant	Replace						✓
Air cleaner filter	Replace	✓	✓	✓	✓	✓	✓
Automatic transaxle fluid	Replace		✓		✓		✓
Spark plugs	Replace				✓		
Transfer case fluid	Replace		✓		✓		✓
Exhaust system & heat shields	Inspect	✓	✓	✓	✓	✓	✓
Cooling system hoses and clamps	Inspect	✓	✓	✓	✓	✓	✓
Fuel system	Inspect	✓	✓	✓	✓	✓	✓
Accessory drive belt(s)	Replace						✓
Evaporative control system	Inspect		✓		✓		✓
Passenger compartment air cleaner	Replace	✓	✓	✓	✓	✓	✓

25742_CSRX_C0016

PRECAUTIONS

Before servicing any vehicle, please be sure to read all of the following precautions, which deal with personal safety, prevention of component damage, and important points to take into consideration when servicing a motor vehicle:

• Never open, service or drain the radiator or cooling system when the engine is hot; serious burns can occur from the steam and hot coolant.

• Observe all applicable safety precautions when working around fuel. Whenever servicing the fuel system, always work in a well-ventilated area. Do not allow fuel spray or vapors to come in contact with a spark, open flame, or excessive heat (a hot drop light, for example). Keep a dry chemical fire extinguisher near the work area. Always keep fuel in a container specifically designed for fuel storage; also, always properly seal fuel containers to avoid the possibility of fire or explosion. Refer to the additional fuel system precautions later in this section.

• Fuel injection systems often remain pressurized, even after the engine has been turned **OFF**. The fuel system pressure must be relieved before disconnecting any fuel lines. Failure to do so may result in fire and/or personal injury.

• Brake fluid often contains polyglycol ethers and polyglycols. Avoid contact with the eyes and wash your hands thoroughly after handling brake fluid. If you do get brake fluid in your eyes, flush your eyes with clean, running water for 15 minutes. If eye irritation persists, or if you have taken brake fluid internally, IMMEDIATELY seek medical assistance.

• The EPA warns that prolonged contact with used engine oil may cause a number of skin disorders, including cancer. You should make every effort to minimize your exposure to used engine oil. Protective gloves should be worn when changing oil. Wash your hands and any other exposed skin areas as soon as possible after exposure to used engine oil. Soap and water, or waterless hand cleaner should be used.

• All new vehicles are now equipped with an air bag system, often referred to as a Supplemental Restraint System (SRS) or Supplemental Inflatable Restraint (SIR) system. The system must be disabled before performing service on or around system components, steering column, instrument panel components, wiring and sensors. Failure to follow safety and disabling procedures could result in accidental air bag deployment, possible personal injury and unnecessary system repairs.

• Always wear safety goggles when working with, or around, the air bag system. When carrying a non-deployed air bag, be sure the bag and trim cover are pointed away from your body. When placing a non-deployed air bag on a work surface, always face the bag and trim cover upward, away from the surface. This will reduce the motion of the module if it is accidentally deployed. Refer to the additional air bag system precautions later in this section.

• Clean, high quality brake fluid from a sealed container is essential to the safe and proper operation of the brake system. You should always buy the correct type of brake fluid for your vehicle. If the brake fluid becomes contaminated, completely flush the system with new fluid. Never reuse any brake fluid. Any brake fluid that is removed from the system should be discarded. Also, do not allow any brake fluid to come in contact with a painted surface; it will damage the paint.

• Never operate the engine without the proper amount and type of engine oil; doing so WILL result in severe engine damage.

• Timing belt maintenance is extremely important. Many models utilize an interference-type, non-freewheeling engine. If the timing belt breaks, the valves in the cylinder head may strike the pistons, causing potentially serious (also time-consuming and expensive) engine damage. Refer to the maintenance interval charts for the recommended replacement interval for the timing belt, and to the timing belt section for belt replacement and inspection.

• Disconnecting the negative battery cable on some vehicles may interfere with the functions of the on-board computer system(s) and may require the computer to undergo a relearning process once the negative battery cable is reconnected.

• When servicing drum brakes, only disassemble and assemble one side at a time, leaving the remaining side intact for reference.

• Only an MVAC-trained, EPA-certified automotive technician should service the air conditioning system or its components.

BRAKES

GENERAL INFORMATION

PRECAUTIONS

• Certain components within the ABS system are not intended to be serviced or repaired individually.

• Do not use rubber hoses or other parts not specifically specified for and ABS system. When using repair kits, replace all parts included in the kit. Partial or incorrect repair may lead to functional problems and require the replacement of components.

• Lubricate rubber parts with clean, fresh brake fluid to ease assembly. Do not use shop air to clean parts; damage to rubber components may result.

• Use only DOT 3 brake fluid from an unopened container.

• If any hydraulic component or line is removed or replaced, it may be necessary to bleed the entire system.

• A clean repair area is essential. Always clean the reservoir and cap thoroughly before removing the cap. The slightest amount of dirt in the fluid may plug an orifice and impair the system function. Perform repairs after components have been thoroughly cleaned; use only denatured alcohol to clean components. Do not allow ABS components to come into contact with any substance containing mineral oil; this includes used shop rags.

• The Anti-Lock control unit is a microprocessor similar to other computer units in the vehicle. Ensure that the ignition switch is **OFF** before removing or installing controller harnesses. Avoid static electricity discharge at or near the controller.

ANTI-LOCK BRAKE SYSTEM (ABS)

• If any arc welding is to be done on the vehicle, the control unit should be unplugged before welding operations begin.

SPEED SENSORS

REMOVAL & INSTALLATION

Front

See Figure 1.

1. Before servicing the vehicle, refer to the Precautions Section.
2. Raise and support the vehicle.
3. Remove the tire and wheel assembly.
4. Remove the wheel speed sensor bolt.
5. Clean the wheel speed sensor mounting area on the suspension knuckle of any accumulated dirt and debris.

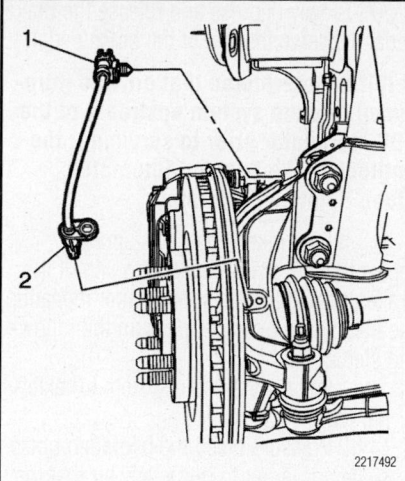

Fig. 1 Disconnect the electrical connector (1) and remove the front wheel speed sensor (2)

6. Disconnect the wheel speed sensor electrical connector and release the connector from the steering knuckle.

7. Remove the wheel speed sensor by pulling the sensor straight out of the steering knuckle.

To install:

8. Connect the wheel speed sensor electrical connector and secure the connector to the steering knuckle.

9. Install the wheel speed sensor to the steering knuckle.

10. Install the wheel speed sensor bolt and tighten to 80 inch lbs. (9 Nm).

11. Install the tire and wheel assembly.

Rear

See Figure 2.

1. Before servicing the vehicle, refer to the Precautions Section.

2. Raise and support the vehicle.

3. Remove the tire and wheel assembly.

4. Remove the rear suspension link.

5. Remove the wheel speed sensor bolt.

6. Clean the wheel speed sensor mounting area on the suspension knuckle of any accumulated dirt and debris.

7. Remove the wheel speed sensor by pulling the sensor straight out of the rear suspension knuckle.

8. Release the wheel speed sensor harness from the retainers.

9. Disconnect the wheel speed sensor electrical connector.

10. Release the wheel speed sensor electrical connector retainer and remove the wheel speed sensor.

To install:

11. Install the wheel speed sensor connector retainer to the rear suspension cradle.

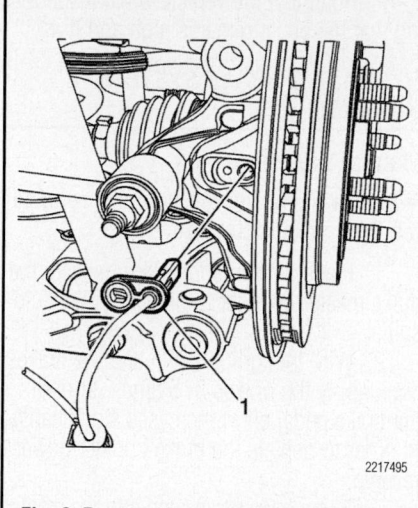

Fig. 2 Remove the rear wheel speed sensor (1)

12. Connect the wheel speed sensor electrical connector.

13. Install the wheel speed sensor harness to the retainers.

14. Install the wheel speed sensor to the rear suspension knuckle.

15. Install the wheel speed sensor bolt and tighten to 80 inch lbs. (9 Nm).

16. Install the rear suspension link.

17. Install the tire and wheel assembly.

BRAKES   BLEEDING THE BRAKE SYSTEM

BLEEDING PROCEDURE

BLEEDING THE ABS SYSTEM

1. Before servicing the vehicle, refer to the Precautions Section.

➡**Before performing the ABS Automated Bleed Procedure, first perform a pressure bleed of the base brake system. The automated bleed procedure is recommended when one of the following conditions exist: base brake system bleeding does not achieve the desired pedal height or feel, extreme loss of brake fluid has occurred, air ingestion is suspected in the secondary circuits of the brake modulator assembly.**

❋❋ WARNING

The Auto Bleed Procedure may be terminated at any time during the process by pressing the EXIT button. No further Scan Tool prompts pertaining to the Auto Bleed procedure will be given. After exiting the bleed procedure, relieve bleed pressure and disconnect bleed equipment per manufacturer's instructions. Failure to properly relieve pressure may result in spilled brake fluid causing damage to components and painted surfaces.

The ABS Automated Bleed Procedure uses a scan tool to cycle the system solenoid valves and run the pump in order to purge any air from the secondary circuits. These circuits are normally closed off, and are only opened during system initialization at vehicle start up and during ABS operation. The automated bleed procedure opens these secondary circuits and allows any air trapped in these circuits to flow out toward the brake corners.

2. Raise and support the vehicle.

3. Remove all four tire and wheel assemblies.

4. Inspect the brake system for leaks and visual damage.

5. Lower the vehicle.

6. Inspect the battery state of charge.

7. Install a scan tool.

8. Turn the ignition ON, with the engine OFF.

9. With the scan tool, establish communications with the ABS system. Select Special Functions. Select Automated Bleed from the Special Functions menu.

10. Raise and support the vehicle.

11. Following the directions given on the scan tool, pressure bleed the base brake system.

12. Follow the scan tool directions until the desired brake pedal height is achieved.

13. If the bleed procedure is aborted, a malfunction exists. Perform the following steps before resuming the bleed procedure:

   a. If a DTC is detected, refer to Diagnostic Trouble Codes (DTC) and diagnose the appropriate DTC.

   b. If the brake pedal feels spongy, perform the conventional brake bleed procedure again.

14. When the desired pedal height is achieved, press the brake pedal to inspect for firmness.

15. Lower the vehicle.

16. Remove the scan tool.

17. Install the tire and wheel assemblies.

18. Inspect the brake fluid level.

19. Road test the vehicle while inspecting that the pedal remains high and firm.

HYDRAULIC BRAKE SYSTEM BLEEDING

Manual Bleeding

➡ Before servicing the vehicle, refer to the Precautions Section.

1. Place a clean shop cloth beneath the brake master cylinder to prevent brake fluid spills.

2. With the ignition OFF and the brakes cool, apply the brakes 3–5 times, or until the brake pedal effort increases significantly, in order to deplete the brake booster power reserve.

3. If you have performed a brake master cylinder bench bleeding on this vehicle, or if you disconnected the brake pipes from the master cylinder, you must perform the following steps:

a. Ensure that the brake master cylinder reservoir is full to the maximum-fill level. If necessary, add GM approved brake fluid from a clean, sealed brake fluid container. If removal of the reservoir cap and diaphragm is necessary, clean the outside of the reservoir on and around the cap prior to removal.

b. With the rear brake pipe installed securely to the master cylinder, loosen and separate the front brake pipe from the front port of the brake master cylinder.

c. Allow a small amount of brake fluid to gravity bleed from the open port of the master cylinder.

d. Reconnect the brake pipe to the master cylinder port and tighten securely.

e. Have an assistant slowly depress the brake pedal fully and maintain steady pressure on the pedal.

f. Loosen the same brake pipe to purge air from the open port of the master cylinder.

g. Tighten the brake pipe, then have the assistant slowly release the brake pedal.

h. Wait 15 seconds, then repeat the above 5 steps until all air is purged from the same port of the master cylinder.

i. With the front brake pipe installed securely to the master cylinder, after all air has been purged from the front port of the master cylinder, loosen and separate the rear brake pipe from the master cylinder, then repeat the above 6 steps.

j. After completing the final master cylinder port bleeding procedure, ensure that both of the brake pipe-to-master cylinder fittings are properly tightened.

4. Fill the brake master cylinder reservoir with brake fluid. Ensure that the brake master cylinder reservoir remains at least half-full during this bleeding procedure. Add fluid as needed to maintain the proper level. Clean the outside of the reservoir on and around the reservoir cap prior to removing the cap and diaphragm.

5. Install a proper box-end wrench onto the RIGHT REAR wheel hydraulic circuit bleeder valve.

6. Install a transparent hose over the end of the bleeder valve.

7. Submerge the open end of the transparent hose into a transparent container partially filled with GM approved brake fluid from a clean, sealed brake fluid container.

8. Have an assistant slowly depress the brake pedal fully and maintain steady pressure on the pedal.

9. Loosen the bleeder valve to purge air from the wheel hydraulic circuit.

10. Tighten the bleeder valve, then have the assistant slowly release the brake pedal.

11. Wait 15 seconds, then repeat steps 8–10 until all air is purged from the same wheel hydraulic circuit.

12. With the right rear wheel hydraulic circuit bleeder valve tightened securely, after all air has been purged from the right rear hydraulic circuit, install a proper box-end wrench onto the LEFT FRONT wheel hydraulic circuit bleeder valve.

13. Install a transparent hose over the end of the bleeder valve, then repeat steps 7–11.

14. With the left front wheel hydraulic circuit bleeder valve tightened securely, after all air has been purged from the left front hydraulic circuit, install a proper box-end wrench onto the LEFT REAR wheel hydraulic circuit bleeder valve.

15. Install a transparent hose over the end of the bleeder valve, then repeat steps 7–11.

16. With the left rear wheel hydraulic circuit bleeder valve tightened securely, after all air has been purged from the left rear hydraulic circuit, install a proper box-end wrench onto the RIGHT FRONT wheel hydraulic circuit bleeder valve.

17. Install a transparent hose over the end of the bleeder valve, then repeat steps 7–11.

18. After completing the final wheel hydraulic circuit bleeding procedure, ensure that each of the 4 wheel hydraulic circuit bleeder valves are properly tightened.

19. Fill the brake master cylinder reservoir to the maximum-fill level with GM approved brake fluid from a clean, sealed brake fluid container.

20. Slowly depress and release the brake pedal. Observe the feel of the brake pedal.

➡ If it is determined that air was introduced into the system upstream of the ABS modulator prior to servicing, the Antilock Brake System Automated Bleed must be performed.

21. If the brake pedal feels spongy, repeat the bleeding procedure again. If the brake pedal still feels spongy after repeating the bleeding procedure, perform the following steps:

a. Inspect the brake system for external leaks.

b. Pressure bleed the hydraulic brake system in order to purge any air that may still be trapped in the system.

22. Turn the ignition key ON, with the engine OFF. Check the brake system warning lamp. If it remains illuminated, diagnose and repair.

❄❄ CAUTION

DO NOT allow the vehicle to be driven until it is diagnosed and repaired.

Pressure Bleeding

➡ Before servicing the vehicle, refer to the Precautions Section.

1. Place a clean shop cloth beneath the brake master cylinder to prevent brake fluid spills.

2. With the ignition OFF and the brakes cool, apply the brakes 3–5 times, or until the brake pedal effort increases significantly, in order to deplete the brake booster power reserve.

3. If you have performed a brake master cylinder bench bleeding on this vehicle, or if you disconnected the brake pipes from the master cylinder, you must perform the following steps:

a. Ensure that the brake master cylinder reservoir is full to the maximum-fill level. If necessary, add GM approved brake fluid from a clean, sealed brake fluid container. If removal of the reservoir cap and diaphragm is necessary, clean the outside of the reservoir on and around the cap prior to removal.

b. With the rear brake pipe installed securely to the master cylinder, loosen and separate the front brake pipe from the front port of the brake master cylinder.

c. Allow a small amount of brake fluid to gravity bleed from the open port of the master cylinder.

d. Reconnect the brake pipe to the master cylinder port and tighten securely.

e. Have an assistant slowly depress the brake pedal fully and maintain steady pressure on the pedal.

f. Loosen the same brake pipe to purge air from the open port of the master cylinder.

g. Tighten the brake pipe, then have the assistant slowly release the brake pedal.

h. Wait 15 seconds, then repeat the above 5 steps until all air is purged from the same port of the master cylinder.

i. With the front brake pipe installed securely to the master cylinder, after all air has been purged from the front port of the master cylinder, loosen and separate the rear brake pipe from the master cylinder, then repeat the above 6 steps.

j. After completing the final master cylinder port bleeding procedure, ensure that both of the brake pipe-to-master cylinder fittings are properly tightened.

4. Fill the brake master cylinder reservoir to the maximum-fill level with GM approved brake fluid from a clean, sealed brake fluid container. Clean the outside of the reservoir on and around the reservoir cap prior to removing the cap and diaphragm.

5. Install an appropriate brake pressure bleeder adapter to the brake master cylinder reservoir.

6. Check the brake fluid level in the brake pressure bleeder. Add GM approved brake fluid from a clean, sealed brake fluid container as necessary to bring the level to approximately the half-full point.

7. Connect the brake pressure bleeder to the brake pressure bleeder adapter.

8. Charge the brake pressure bleeder air tank to 25–30 psi (175–205 kPa).

9. Open the brake pressure bleeder fluid tank valve to allow pressurized brake fluid to enter the brake system.

10. Wait approximately 30 seconds, then inspect the entire hydraulic brake system in order to ensure that there are no existing external brake fluid leaks. Any brake fluid leaks identified require repair prior to completing this procedure.

11. Install a proper box-end wrench onto the RIGHT REAR wheel hydraulic circuit bleeder valve.

12. Install a transparent hose over the end of the bleeder valve.

13. Submerge the open end of the transparent hose into a transparent container partially filled with GM approved brake fluid from a clean, sealed brake fluid container.

14. Loosen the bleeder valve to purge air from the wheel hydraulic circuit. Allow fluid to flow until air bubbles stop flowing from the bleeder, then tighten the bleeder valve.

15. With the right rear wheel hydraulic circuit bleeder valve tightened securely, after all air has been purged from the right rear hydraulic circuit, install a proper box-end wrench onto the LEFT FRONT wheel hydraulic circuit bleeder valve.

16. Install a transparent hose over the end of the bleeder valve, then repeat steps 13–14.

17. With the left front wheel hydraulic circuit bleeder valve tightened securely, after all air has been purged from the left front hydraulic circuit, install a proper box-end wrench onto the LEFT REAR wheel hydraulic circuit bleeder valve.

18. Install a transparent hose over the end of the bleeder valve, then repeat steps 13–14.

19. With the left rear wheel hydraulic circuit bleeder valve tightened securely, after all air has been purged from the left rear hydraulic circuit, install a proper box-end wrench onto the RIGHT FRONT wheel hydraulic circuit bleeder valve

20. Install a transparent hose over the end of the bleeder valve, then repeat steps 13–14.

21. After completing the final wheel hydraulic circuit bleeding procedure, ensure that each of the 4 wheel hydraulic circuit bleeder valves are properly tightened.

22. Close the brake pressure bleeder fluid tank valve, then disconnect the brake pressure bleeder from the brake pressure bleeder adapter.

23. Remove the brake pressure bleeder adapter from the brake master cylinder reservoir.

24. Fill the brake master cylinder reservoir to the maximum-fill level with GM approved brake fluid from a clean, sealed brake fluid container.

25. Slowly depress and release the brake pedal. Observe the feel of the brake pedal.

➡ **If it is determined that air was introduced into the system upstream of the ABS modulator prior to servicing, the Antilock Brake System Automated Bleed must be performed.**

26. If the brake pedal feels spongy perform the following steps:

a. Inspect the brake system for external leaks.

b. Using a scan tool, perform the antilock brake system automated bleeding procedure to remove any air that may have been trapped in the BPMV.

27. Turn the ignition key ON, with the engine OFF. Check the brake system warning lamp. If it remains illuminated, diagnose and repair.

✳✳ CAUTION

DO NOT allow the vehicle to be driven until it is diagnosed and repaired.

MASTER CYLINDER BENCH BLEEDING

➡**Before servicing the vehicle, refer to the Precautions Section.**

1. Secure the mounting flange of the brake master cylinder in a bench vise so that the rear of the primary piston is accessible.

2. Remove the master cylinder reservoir cap and diaphragm.

3. Install suitable fittings to the master cylinder ports that match the type of flare seat required and also provide for hose attachment.

4. Install transparent hoses to the fittings installed to the master cylinder ports, then route the hoses into the master cylinder reservoir.

5. Fill the master cylinder reservoir to at least the half-way point with GM approved brake fluid from a clean, sealed brake fluid container.

6. Ensure that the ends of the transparent hoses running into the master cylinder reservoir are fully submerged in the brake fluid.

7. Using a smooth, round-ended tool, depress and release the primary piston as far as it will travel, a depth of about 1 in. (25 mm), several times. Observe the flow of fluid coming from the ports. As air is bled from the primary and secondary pistons, the effort required to depress the primary piston will increase and the amount of travel will decrease.

8. Continue to depress and release the primary piston until fluid flows freely from the ports with no evidence of air bubbles.

9. Remove the transparent hoses from the master cylinder reservoir.

10. Install the master cylinder reservoir cap and diaphragm.

11. Remove the fittings with the transparent hoses from the master cylinder ports. Wrap the master cylinder with a clean shop cloth to prevent brake fluid spills.

12. Remove the master cylinder from the vise.

FLUID FILL PROCEDURE

1. Visually inspect the brake fluid level through the brake master cylinder reservoir.

2. If the brake fluid level is at or below

the half-full point during routine fluid checks, the brake system should be inspected for wear and possible brake fluid leaks.

3. If the brake fluid level is at or below the half-full point during routine fluid checks, and an inspection of the brake system did not reveal wear or brake fluid leaks,

the brake fluid may be topped-off up to the maximum-fill level.

4. If brake system service was just completed, the brake fluid may be topped-off up to the maximum-fill level.

5. If the brake fluid level is above the half-full point, adding brake fluid is not recommended under normal conditions.

6. If brake fluid is to be added to the master cylinder reservoir, clean the outside of the reservoir on and around the reservoir cap prior to removing the cap and diaphragm. Use only GM approved brake fluid from a clean, sealed brake fluid container.

BRAKES

✳✳ CAUTION

Dust and dirt accumulating on brake parts during normal use may contain asbestos fibers from production or aftermarket brake linings. Breathing excessive concentrations of asbestos fibers can cause serious bodily harm. Exercise care when servicing brake parts. Do not sand or grind brake lining unless equipment used is designed to contain the dust residue. Do not clean brake parts with compressed air or by dry brushing. Cleaning should be done by dampening the brake components with a fine mist of water, then wiping the brake components clean with a dampened cloth. Dispose of cloth and all residue containing asbestos fibers in an impermeable container with the appropriate label. Follow practices prescribed by the Occupational Safety and Health Administration (OSHA) and the Environmental Protection Agency (EPA) for the handling, processing, and disposing of dust or debris that may contain asbestos fibers.

BRAKE CALIPER

REMOVAL & INSTALLATION

See Figure 3.

1. Before servicing the vehicle, refer to the Precautions Section.
2. Raise and support the vehicle.
3. Remove the tire and wheel assembly.
4. Remove the brake hose fitting bolt.
5. Remove the 2 brake hose fitting gaskets from the brake hose fitting and discard the gaskets.
6. Cap the brake hose fitting to prevent brake fluid loss and contamination.
7. Using a backup wrench to hold the brake caliper guide pins stationary, remove the brake caliper guide pin bolts.

➡**DO NOT use any air tools to remove or install the guide pin bolts. Use hand tools ONLY. Install an open end wrench**

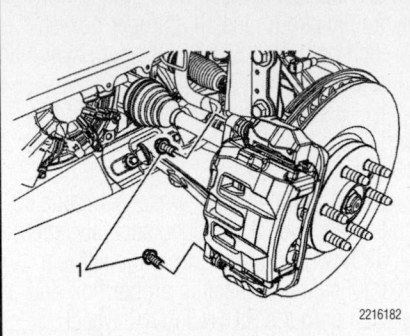

Fig. 3 Remove the brake caliper guide pin bolts (1)

to hold the caliper guide pin in line with the brake caliper while removing or installing the caliper guide pin bolt. DO NOT allow the open end wrench to come in contact with the brake caliper. Allowing the open end wrench to come in contact with the brake caliper will cause a pulsation when the brakes are applied.

8. Remove the brake caliper.

To install:

9. Install the brake caliper to the caliper bracket.
10. Using a backup wrench to hold the brake caliper guide pins stationary, install the brake caliper guide pin bolts and tighten to 44 ft. lbs. (60 Nm).
11. Assemble the brake hose fitting bolt and 2 new brake hose fitting gaskets to the brake hose fitting.
12. Install the brake hose assembly to the brake caliper and tighten the fitting bolt to 30 ft. lbs. (40 Nm).
13. Bleed the hydraulic brake system.
14. Install the tire and wheel assembly.
15. Lower vehicle.

DISC BRAKE PADS

REMOVAL & INSTALLATION

See Figure 4.

1. Before servicing the vehicle, refer to the Precautions Section.

FRONT DISC BRAKES

2. Inspect the fluid level in the brake master cylinder reservoir.

a. If the brake fluid level is midway between the maximum full point and the minimum allowable level, no brake fluid needs to be removed from the reservoir before proceeding.

b. If the brake fluid level is higher than midway between the maximum full point and the minimum allowable level, remove brake fluid to the midway point before proceeding.

3. Raise and support the vehicle.
4. Remove the tire and wheel assembly.
5. Install a C-clamp against the outer brake pad and the rear of the brake caliper body.
6. Slowly tighten the C-clamp until the brake caliper pistons are compressed into the brake caliper bores.

➡**DO NOT use any air tools to remove or install the guide pin bolts. Use hand tools ONLY. Install an open end wrench to hold the caliper guide pin in line with the brake caliper while removing or installing the caliper guide pin bolt. DO NOT allow the open end wrench to come in contact with the brake caliper. Allowing the open end wrench to come in contact with the brake caliper will**

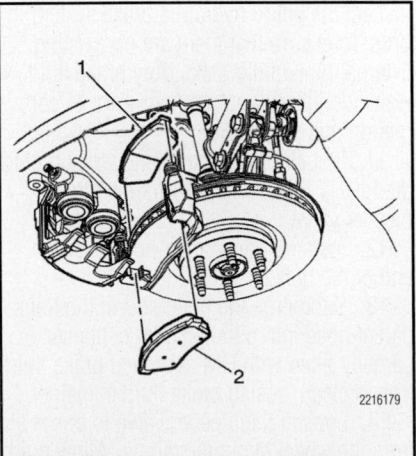

Fig. 4 Remove the inner (1) and outer brake pads (2)

cause a pulsation when the brakes are applied.

7. Using a backup wrench to hold the brake caliper guide pin stationary, remove the upper brake caliper guide pin bolt.

❉❉ WARNING

Support the brake caliper with heavy mechanic wire, or equivalent, whenever it is separated from its mount and the hydraulic flexible brake hose is still connected.

8. Pivot the brake caliper forward and support with heavy mechanics wire or equivalent.

9. Place a block of wood or an old brake pad against the brake caliper pistons.

10. Using a brake pad spreader tool or equivalent, fully seat the caliper pistons in the caliper bores.

11. Remove the inner brake pad and the outer brake pad.

12. Remove the upper and lower brake pad springs. If installing new brake pads, discard the springs.

To install:

13. Install the upper and lower brake pad springs.

14. Install the inner brake pad and the outer brake pad.

15. Rotate the brake caliper into position.

16. Using a backup wrench to hold the brake caliper guide pin stationary, install the brake caliper guide pin bolt and tighten to 44 ft. lbs. (60 Nm).

17. Install the tire and wheel assembly.

18. With the engine OFF, gradually apply the brake pedal to approximately ⅔ of its travel distance.

19. Slowly release the brake pedal.

20. Wait 15 seconds, then repeat the above 2 steps until a firm brake pedal apply is obtained; this will properly seat the brake caliper pistons and brake pads.

21. Fill the brake master cylinder reservoir to the proper level.

22. Burnish the brake pads and rotors:

a. Select a smooth road with little or no traffic.

b. Accelerate the vehicle to 30 mph (48 km/h). Use care to avoid overheating the brakes while performing this step.

c. Using moderate to firm pressure, apply the brakes to bring the vehicle to a stop. Do not allow the brakes to lock.

d. Repeat the above 2 steps until approximately 20 stops have been completed. Allow sufficient cooling periods between stops in order to properly burnish the brake pads and rotors.

BRAKES

REAR DISC BRAKES

❉❉ CAUTION

Dust and dirt accumulating on brake parts during normal use may contain asbestos fibers from production or aftermarket brake linings. Breathing excessive concentrations of asbestos fibers can cause serious bodily harm. Exercise care when servicing brake parts. Do not sand or grind brake lining unless equipment used is designed to contain the dust residue. Do not clean brake parts with compressed air or by dry brushing. Cleaning should be done by dampening the brake components with a fine mist of water, then wiping the brake components clean with a dampened cloth. Dispose of cloth and all residue containing asbestos fibers in an impermeable container with the appropriate label. Follow practices prescribed by the Occupational Safety and Health Administration (OSHA) and the Environmental Protection Agency (EPA) for the handling, processing, and disposing of dust or debris that may contain asbestos fibers.

BRAKE CALIPER

REMOVAL & INSTALLATION

See Figure 5.

1. Release the electronic parking brake cable tension.

2. Raise and support the vehicle.

3. Remove the tire and wheel assembly.

4. Remove the brake hose fitting bolt.

➡**Do not reuse the brake hose fitting gaskets.**

5. Remove the brake hose fitting gaskets and the brake hose.

6. Discard the brake hose fitting gaskets.

➡**DO NOT use any air tools to remove or install the guide pin bolts. Use hand tools ONLY. Install an open end wrench to hold the caliper guide pin in line with the brake caliper while removing or installing the caliper guide pin bolt. DO NOT allow the open end wrench to come in contact with the brake caliper. Allowing the open end wrench to come in contact with the brake caliper will cause a pulsation when the brakes are applied.**

7. Using a backup wrench to hold the brake caliper guide pins stationary, remove the brake caliper guide pin bolts.

8. Remove the brake caliper.

To install:

9. Install the brake caliper.

10. Using a backup wrench to hold the brake caliper guide pins stationary, install the brake caliper guide pin bolts and tighten to 44 ft. lbs. (60 Nm).

11. Assemble the brake hose fitting bolt and 2 new brake hose fitting gaskets to the brake hose.

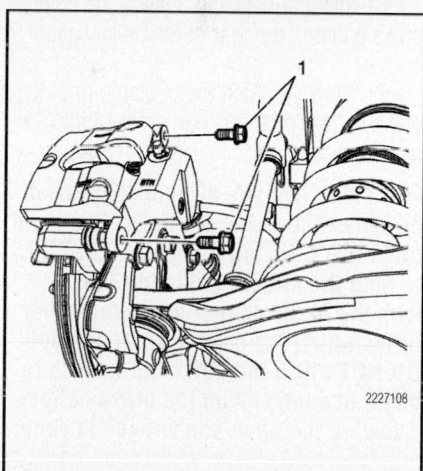

2227108

Fig. 5 Remove the brake caliper guide pin bolts

12. Install the brake hose assembly to the caliper and tighten the fitting bolt to 30 ft. lbs. (40 Nm).

13. Bleed the hydraulic brake system.

14. Install the tire and wheel assembly.

15. With the engine OFF, gradually apply the brake pedal to approximately ⅔ of its travel distance.

16. Slowly release the brake pedal.

17. Wait 15 seconds, then repeat the above 2 steps until a firm brake pedal apply is obtained. This will properly seat the brake caliper pistons and brake pads.

18. Fill the brake master cylinder reservoir to the proper level.

19. Set the electronic parking brake cable tension.

DISC BRAKE PADS

REMOVAL & INSTALLATION

See Figure 6.

1. Before servicing the vehicle, refer to the Precautions Section.

2. Inspect the fluid level in the brake master cylinder reservoir.

   a. If the brake fluid level is midway between the maximum full point and the minimum allowable level, no brake fluid needs to be removed from the reservoir before proceeding.

   b. If the brake fluid level is higher than midway between the maximum full point and the minimum allowable level, remove brake fluid to the midway point before proceeding.

3. Release the electronic parking brake cable tension, if equipped.

4. Raise and support the vehicle.

5. Remove the tire and wheel assembly.

6. Install a C-clamp against the outer brake pad and the rear of the brake caliper body.

7. Slowly tighten the C-clamp until the brake caliper piston is compressed into the brake caliper bore.

➡ **DO NOT use any air tools to remove or install the guide pin bolts. Use hand tools ONLY. Install an open end wrench to hold the caliper guide pin in line with the brake caliper while removing or installing the caliper guide pin bolt. DO NOT allow the open end wrench to come in contact with the brake caliper. Allowing the open end wrench to come**

Fig. 6 Remove the outer (1) and inner (2) brake pads

in contact with the brake caliper will cause a pulsation when the brakes are applied.

8. Using a backup wrench on the brake caliper guide pin, remove the lower brake caliper guide pin bolt.

✳✳ WARNING

Support the brake caliper with heavy mechanic wire, or equivalent, whenever it is separated from its mount and the hydraulic flexible brake hose is still connected.

9. Pivot the brake caliper forward and support with heavy mechanics wire or equivalent.

10. Remove the outer brake pad.

11. Remove the inner brake pad.

12. Remove the brake pad springs. If

installing new brake pads, discard the brake pad springs.

To install:

13. Install the brake pad springs.

14. Install the outer brake pad.

15. Install the inner brake pad.

16. Pivot the brake caliper into position.

17. Using a backup wrench to hold the brake caliper guide pin stationary, install the brake caliper guide pin bolt and tighten to 44 ft. lbs. (60 Nm).

18. Install the tire and wheel assembly.

19. With the engine OFF, gradually apply the brake pedal to approximately ⅔ of its travel distance.

20. Slowly release the brake pedal.

21. Wait 15 seconds, then repeat the above 2 steps until a firm brake pedal apply is obtained. This will properly seat the brake caliper pistons and brake pads.

22. Fill the brake master cylinder reservoir to the proper level.

23. Set the electronic parking brake cable tension, if equipped.

24. Burnish the brake pads and rotors:

   a. Select a smooth road with little or no traffic.

   b. Accelerate the vehicle to 30 mph (48 km/h). Use care to avoid overheating the brakes while performing this step.

   c. Using moderate to firm pressure, apply the brakes to bring the vehicle to a stop. Do not allow the brakes to lock.

   d. Repeat the above 2 steps until approximately 20 stops have been completed. Allow sufficient cooling periods between stops in order to properly burnish the brake pads and rotors.

BRAKES

PARKING BRAKE CABLES

ADJUSTMENT

The parking brake cable tension is controlled by the Electronic Park Brake (EPB) module.

PARKING BRAKE SHOES

REMOVAL & INSTALLATION

See Figure 7.

1. Before servicing the vehicle, refer to the Precautions Section.

2. Disable the parking brake cable adjuster.

3. Raise and support the vehicle.

4. Remove the tire and wheel assembly.

5. Remove the rear brake rotor.

6. Remove the parking brake shoe upper return spring.

7. Compress the parking brake shoe hold down springs and rotate the pins ¼ turn to remove the hold down springs.

8. Remove the parking brake shoes by grasping the shoes near the parking brake shoe actuator, spread the parking brake shoes apart and lift around the wheel hub and bearing assembly.

9. Cross the top of one of the parking brake shoes over the opposite parking brake shoe.

10. Remove the parking brake shoe lower return spring.

11. Remove the parking brake shoe adjuster.

12. Disassemble the parking brake shoe adjuster.

PARKING BRAKE

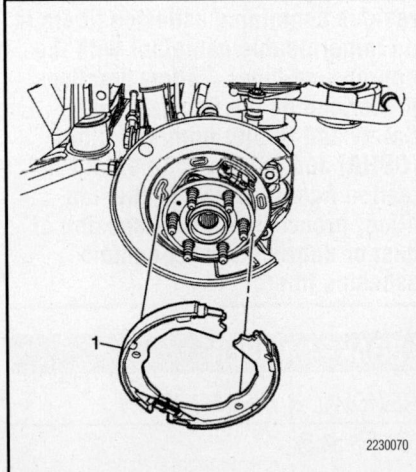

Fig. 7 Remove the parking brake shoes (1)

13. Clean the parking brake shoe adjuster components of any corrosion or debris.

14. Lubricate the parking brake shoe adjuster threads with high temperature brake lubricant.

15. Lubricate the parking brake shoe adjuster clevis with high temperature brake lubricant.

16. Assemble the parking brake shoe adjuster to the fully retracted position.

To install:

17. Install the parking brake shoe adjuster to the parking brake shoes.

18. Cross the top of one of the parking brake shoe over the opposite parking brake shoe.

19. Install the parking brake shoe return spring.

20. Clean the parking brake shoe mounting plate.

21. Apply high temperature brake lubricant to the parking brake shoe mounting plate contact points.

22. Install the parking brake shoes by grasping the shoes near the parking brake shoe actuator, spread the parking brake shoes apart and lift around the wheel hub and bearing assembly.

23. Install the hold down spring pins through the parking brake shoe mounting plate.

24. Compress the parking brake shoe hold down springs and rotate the pins ¼ turn to install the hold down springs.

25. Install the parking brake shoe upper return spring.

26. Adjust the parking brake.

27. Install the rear brake rotor.

28. Install the tire and wheel assembly.

29. Enable the parking brake cable adjuster

PARKING BRAKE ADJUSTER DISABLING

The parking brake cable tension is controlled by the Electronic Park Brake (EPB) module. Tension can be fully released from the parking brake cables to allow for service of the parking brake system. Perform one of the following three methods to fully release cable tension.

With Scan Tool—Preferred Method

1. Block the drive wheels.
2. Install a scan tool to the vehicle.

3. Turn the ignition switch to the ON/RUN position with the engine OFF.

4. Using the scan tool, perform the following:

   a. From the scan tool menu, select Diagnostics

   b. Enter the appropriate vehicle information

   c. Select Chassis

   d. Select Parking Brake Control Module

   e. Select Special Functions

   f. Select Cable Replacement

5. Follow the instructions on the scan tool to fully release the tension on the parking brake cables.

Without Scan Tool—Optional Method

6. Block the drive wheels.

7. Turn the ignition switch to the ON/RUN position with the engine OFF.

8. Place the automatic transmission in PARK or manual transmission in NEUTRAL, as equipped.

9. Apply and hold the brake pedal. The brake pedal must remain applied throughout the parking brake cable tension release process.

10. Press and hold down the EPB switch approximately 5 seconds.

11. Observe the PARK BRAKE lamp on the instrument cluster.

12. When the PARK BRAKE lamp flashes, release then immediately press and release the EPB switch. The parking brake cable tension is fully released.

13. Release the brake pedal.

Manual Parking Brake Cable Tension Release

If the other methods to release the parking brake cable tension are unsuccessful, the following procedure may be necessary to release the parking brake cable tension.

14. Raise and support the vehicle.

15. Remove the protective plug from the EPB manual release. The protective plug for the manual release is located near the electrical connector.

16. Using an appropriate square-drive tool, rotate the mechanism clockwise until the tension is fully released from the parking brake cables. Up to 50 cycles may be

required until the parking brake cable tension is fully released.

17. Install the protective plug to the EPB module.

PARKING BRAKE ADJUSTER ENABLING

The parking brake cable tension is controlled by the Electronic Park Brake (EPB) module. Cable tension needs to be set and the EPB module needs to be calibrated following the cable tension disabling procedure. Perform one of the following two methods to fully restore cable tension.

With Scan Tool—Preferred Method

1. Block the drive wheels.
2. Install a scan tool to the vehicle.

3. Turn the ignition switch to the ON/RUN position with the engine OFF.

4. Using the scan tool, perform the following:

   a. From the scan tool menu, select Diagnostics

   b. Enter the appropriate vehicle information

   c. Select Chassis

   d. Select Parking Brake Control Module

   e. Select Module Setup

   f. Select Parking Brake Calibration

5. The EPB module will be calibrated and proper tension will be applied to the parking brake cables.

Without Scan Tool—Optional Method

6. Block the drive wheels.

7. Turn the ignition switch to the ON/RUN position with the engine OFF.

8. Apply the brake pedal.

9. Place the automatic transmission in PARK or manual transmission in NEUTRAL, as equipped.

10. Momentarily lift then release the EPB switch to apply the EPB.

11. Momentarily press down then release the EPB switch to release the EPB.

12. Repeat the above two steps to cycle the EPB on then off an additional 4 times.

13. The EPB module will be calibrated and proper tension will be applied to the parking brake cables.

GENERAL INFORMATION

❋❋ CAUTION

These vehicles are equipped with an air bag system. The system must be disarmed before performing service on, or around, system components, the steering column, instrument panel components, wiring and sensors. Failure to follow the safety precautions and the disarming procedure could result in accidental air bag deployment, possible injury and unnecessary system repairs.

SERVICE PRECAUTIONS

Disconnect and isolate the battery negative cable before beginning any airbag system component diagnosis, testing, removal, or installation procedures. Allow system capacitor to discharge for two minutes before beginning any component service. This will disable the airbag system. Failure to disable the airbag system may result in accidental airbag deployment, personal injury, or death.

Do not place an intact undeployed airbag face down on a solid surface. The airbag will propel into the air if accidentally deployed and may result in personal injury or death.

When carrying or handling an undeployed airbag, the trim side (face) of the airbag should be pointing away from the body to minimize possibility of injury if accidental deployment occurs. Failure to do this may result in personal injury or death.

Replace airbag system components with OEM replacement parts. Substitute parts may appear interchangeable, but internal differences may result in inferior occupant protection. Failure to do so may result in occupant personal injury or death.

Wear safety glasses, rubber gloves, and long sleeved clothing when cleaning powder residue from vehicle after an airbag deployment. Powder residue emitted from a deployed airbag can cause skin irritation. Flush affected area with cool water if irritation is experienced. If nasal or throat irritation is experienced, exit the vehicle for fresh air until the irritation ceases. If irritation continues, see a physician.

Do not use a replacement airbag that is not in the original packaging. This may result in improper deployment, personal injury, or death.

The factory installed fasteners, screws and bolts used to fasten airbag components have a special coating and are specifically designed for the airbag system. Do not use substitute fasteners. Use only original equipment fasteners listed in the parts catalog when fastener replacement is required.

During, and following, any child restraint anchor service, due to impact event or vehicle repair, carefully inspect all mounting hardware, tether straps, and anchors for proper installation, operation, or damage. If a child restraint anchor is found damaged in any way, the anchor must be replaced. Failure to do this may result in personal injury or death.

Deployed and non-deployed airbags may or may not have live pyrotechnic material within the airbag inflator.

Do not dispose of driver/passenger/curtain airbags or seat belt tensioners unless you are sure of complete deployment. Refer to the Hazardous Substance Control System for proper disposal.

Dispose of deployed airbags and tensioners consistent with state, provincial, local, and federal regulations.

After any airbag component testing or service, do not connect the battery negative cable. Personal injury or death may result if the system test is not performed first.

If the vehicle is equipped with the Occupant Classification System (OCS), do not connect the battery negative cable before performing the OCS Verification Test using the scan tool and the appropriate diagnostic information. Personal injury or death may result if the system test is not performed properly.

Never replace both the Occupant Restraint Controller (ORC) and the Occupant Classification Module (OCM) at the same time. If both require replacement, replace one, then perform the Airbag System test before replacing the other.

Both the ORC and the OCM store Occupant Classification System (OCS) calibration data, which they transfer to one another when one of them is replaced. If both are replaced at the same time, an irreversible fault will be set in both modules and the OCS may malfunction and cause personal injury or death.

If equipped with OCS, the Seat Weight Sensor is a sensitive, calibrated unit and must be handled carefully. Do not drop or handle roughly. If dropped or damaged, replace with another sensor. Failure to do so may result in occupant injury or death.

If equipped with OCS, the front passenger seat must be handled carefully as well. When removing the seat, be careful when setting on floor not to drop. If dropped, the sensor may be inoperative, could result in occupant injury, or possibly death.

If equipped with OCS, when the passenger front seat is on the floor, no one should sit in the front passenger seat. This uneven force may damage the sensing ability of the seat weight sensors. If sat on and damaged, the sensor may be inoperative, could result in occupant injury, or possibly death.

DISARMING THE SYSTEM

Air Bag Fuse Method

1. Before servicing the vehicle, refer to the Precautions Section.
2. Turn the steering wheel so that the vehicles wheels are pointing straight ahead.
3. Place the ignition in the OFF position.

➡**The SDM may have more than one fused power input. To ensure there is no unwanted SIR deployment, personal injury, or unnecessary SIR system repairs, remove all fuses supplying power to the SDM. With all SDM fuses removed and the ignition switch in the ON position, the AIR BAG warning indicator illuminates. This is normal operation, and does not indicate a SIR system malfunction.**

4. Locate and remove the fuse(s) supplying power to the Sensing and Diagnostic Module (SDM).
5. Wait 1 minute before working on the system.

Negative Battery Cable Method

1. Before servicing the vehicle, refer to the Precautions Section.
2. Turn the steering wheel so that the vehicles wheels are pointing straight ahead.
3. Place the ignition in the OFF position.
4. Disconnect the negative battery cable from the battery.
5. Wait 1 minute before working on system.

ARMING THE SYSTEM

Air Bag Fuse Method

1. Before servicing the vehicle, refer to the Precautions Section.
2. Place the ignition in the OFF position.
3. Install the fuse(s) supplying power to the SDM.
4. Turn the ignition switch to the ON position. The AIR BAG indicator will flash then turn OFF. If the AIR BAG warning indi-

cator does not operate as described, perform the Diagnostic System Check.

Negative Battery Cable Method

1. Before servicing the vehicle, refer to the Precautions Section.
2. Place the ignition in the OFF position.
3. Connect the negative battery cable to the battery.
4. Turn the ignition switch to the ON position. The AIR BAG indicator will flash then turn OFF. If the AIR BAG warning indicator does not operate as described, perform the Diagnostic System Check.

CLOCKSPRING CENTERING

See Figure 8.

1. Before servicing the vehicle, refer to the Precautions Section.
2. Verify the following before centering the Supplemental Inflatable Restraint (SIR) coil:
   a. The wheels on the vehicle are straight ahead.
   b. The centering mark of the steering shaft assembly is in the 6 o'clock position.
3. Turn the lobe of the clock spring clockwise until the coil ribbon stops. Do not force.
4. Turn the lobe of the clock spring counterclockwise approximately 3 turns to the Neutral position.
5. Properly align until the centering window turns yellow. This indicates the CENTER position.

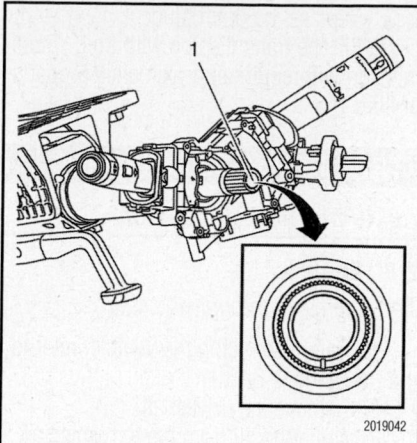

Fig. 8 Clockspring with centering mark (1) in the 6 o'clock position

DRIVE TRAIN

AUTOMATIC TRANSMISSION FLUID

CHECKING FLUID

✳✳ WARNING

Use Dexron VI transmission fluid only. Failure to use the proper fluid may result in transmission internal damage. Ensure the transmission has enough fluid in it to safely start the vehicle without damaging the transmission. With the vehicle off there must be at least enough fluid to wet the end of the dipstick bullet. This will ensure that there is enough fluid in the sump to fill the components once the vehicle is started.

➡ **Check the transmission fluid level when the Transmission Fluid Temperature (TFT) is between 180°F–200°F (82°C –93°C).**

1. Park the vehicle on a level surface, apply the parking brake and place the shift lever in PARK (P).
2. Start the engine.
3. Depress the brake pedal and move the shift lever through each gear range, pausing for about 3 seconds in each range. Then move the shift lever back to PARK (P).
4. Allow the engine to idle 500–800 rpm for at least 1 minute. Release the brake pedal.
5. Keep the engine running and observe the Transmission Fluid Temperature (TFT) using the Driver Information Center or a scan tool.

6. Remove the dipstick and wipe it with a clean rag or paper towel.
7. Inspect the fluid color. The fluid should be red or dark brown.
   a. If the fluid color is very dark or black and has a burnt odor, inspect the fluid for excessive metal particles or other debris. A small amount of "friction" material is a "normal" condition. If large pieces and/or metal particles are noted in the fluid, flush the oil cooler and cooler lines and overhaul the transmission. If there are no signs of transmission internal damage noted, replace the fluid, repair the oil cooler, and flush the cooler lines. Fluid that is cloudy or milky or appears to be contaminated with water indicates engine coolant or water contamination.
8. Install the dipstick and tighten. Wait three seconds and then remove it again.

➡ **Always check the fluid level at least twice. Consistent readings are important to maintaining proper fluid level. If inconsistent readings are noted, inspect the transmission vent assembly to ensure it is clean and unclogged.**

9. Check both sides of the dipstick and read the lower level.

➡ **It is not necessary to get the fluid level all the way up to the MAX mark. Anywhere within the crosshatch band is acceptable.**

10. Install and remove the dipstick again to verify the reading.
11. If the fluid level is not within the crosshatch band, add or drain fluid as necessary to bring the level into the crosshatch band. If the fluid level is low, add only enough fluid to bring the level into the crosshatch band.
   a. Do not add more than one pint (0.5L) at a time without rechecking the level. Once the oil is on the dipstick bullet, it will not take much more fluid to raise the fluid level into the crosshatch band. Do not overfill. Also, if the fluid level is low, inspect the transmission for leaks.
12. If the fluid level is in the acceptable range, install the dipstick.
13. If the fluid was changed, reset the transmission oil life monitor, if applicable.

FLUID REFILL

See Figure 9.

1. Place a drain pan capable of containing more than 5 quarts of fluid under the transmission.
2. Remove the drain plug and drain the fluid.

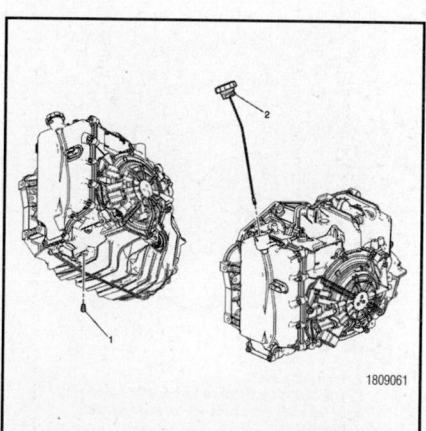

Fig. 9 Fluid fill tube plug assembly (1) hole, and oil level check plug (2) hole

3. Replace the drain plug.

4. Fill the transmission with fluid. Transmission will require approximately 5 quarts of fluid.

TRANSFER CASE ASSEMBLY

REMOVAL & INSTALLATION

2.8L Engines

See Figures 10 through 12.

1. Before servicing the vehicle, refer to the Precautions Section.

2. Remove the driveshaft.

3. Drain the oil from the transmission.

4. Remove the right halfshaft.

5. Remove the transmission rear mount bracket.

6. Remove the front catalytic converters.

7. Remove the transfer case vent hose strap, bolt, and hose.

8. Remove the transfer case bracket-to-transfer case bolts.

9. Remove the transfer case bracket-to-engine bolts.

10. Remove the brackets.

11. Support the transfer case with a suitable jack and secure with suitable straps.

12. Remove the transfer case-to-transmission bolts. The center bolt is accessed through the opening in the center of the transfer case.

13. Remove the remaining transfer case-to-transmission bolts.

14. Separate the transfer case from the transmission and remove the transfer case.

15. Remove and discard the transfer case-to-transmission O-ring.

To install:

16. Clean the contact surfaces between the transfer case and the transmission.

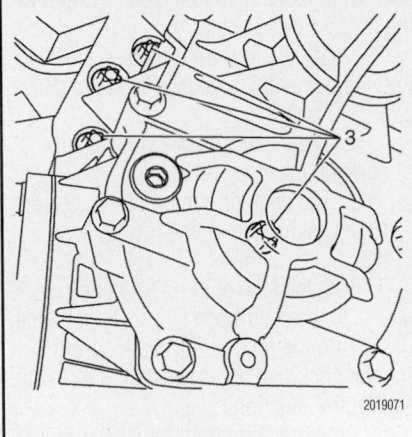

Fig. 11 Remove the transfer case-to-transmission bolts (3)

17. Install a new transfer case-to-transmission O-ring.

18. Support the transfer case with a suitable jack, and secure with suitable straps.

19. Raise and align the transfer case in the correct position in relation to the transmission.

20. Install the transfer case to the transmission.

21. Install the transfer case-to-transmission bolts. Tighten to 81 ft. lbs. (110 Nm).

22. Install the transfer case-to-transmission bolts (3). The center bolt is accessed through the opening in the center of the transfer case.

   a. Tighten the bolts a first pass to 73 ft. lbs. (100 Nm).

   b. Tighten the bolts a second pass 60 degrees.

23. Install the bracket (4).

24. Install the transfer case bracket-to-transfer case bolts (2).

25. Install the transfer case bracket-to-engine bolts (5, 6).

26. Tighten the bracket-to-transfer case bolts to 44 inch lbs. (5 Nm).

27. Tighten the bracket-to-engine bolts to 16 ft. lbs. (22 Nm).

28. Tighten the bracket-to-transfer case bolts to 42 ft. lbs. (58 Nm).

29. Install the transmission rear mount bracket.

30. Install the transfer case vent hose, strap, and bolt.

31. Tighten the transfer case vent hose bolt to 17 ft. lbs. (22 Nm).

32. Install the front catalytic converters.

33. Install the right halfshaft.

34. Install the driveshaft.

35. Fill the transmission with oil.

36. Fill with transfer case oil.

3.0L Engines

See Figures 13 and 14.

1. Before servicing the vehicle, refer to the Precautions Section.

2. Remove the driveshaft.

3. Drain the oil from the transmission.

4. Remove the right halfshaft.

5. Remove the transmission rear mount bracket.

6. Remove the front catalytic converters.

7. Remove the transfer case vent hose strap, bolt, and hose.

8. Remove the transfer case bracket-to-transfer case bolts.

9. Remove the transfer case bracket-to-engine bolts.

10. Remove the brackets.

11. Support the transfer case with a suitable jack and secure with suitable straps.

12. Remove the remaining transfer case-to-transmission bolts.

13. Separate the transfer case from the transmission and remove the transfer case.

14. Remove and discard the transfer case-to-transmission O-ring.

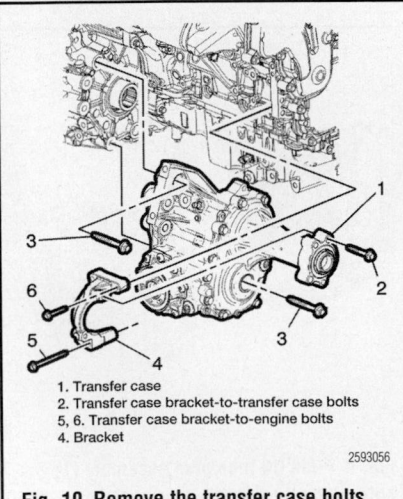

1. Transfer case
2. Transfer case bracket-to-transfer case bolts
5, 6. Transfer case bracket-to-engine bolts
4. Bracket

Fig. 10 Remove the transfer case bolts

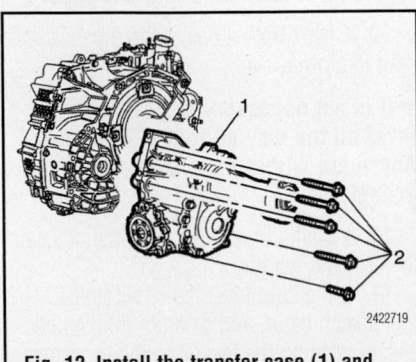

Fig. 12 Install the transfer case (1) and the transfer case-to-transmission bolts (2)

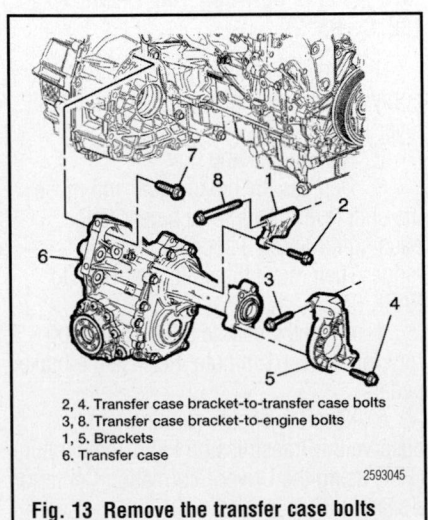

2, 4. Transfer case bracket-to-transfer case bolts
3, 8. Transfer case bracket-to-engine bolts
1, 5. Brackets
6. Transfer case

Fig. 13 Remove the transfer case bolts

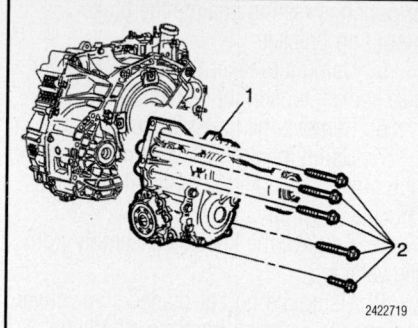

Fig. 14 Remove the remaining transfer case-to-transmission bolts (2) and separate the transfer case (1)

To install:

15. Clean the contact surfaces between the transfer case and the transmission.

16. Install a new transfer case-to-transmission O-ring.

17. Support the transfer case with a suitable jack, and secure with suitable straps.

18. Raise and align the transfer case in the correct position in relation to the transmission.

19. Install the transfer case to the transmission.

20. Install the transfer case-to-transmission bolts and tighten to 81 ft. lbs. (110 Nm).

21. Install the brackets (1, 5).

22. Install the transfer case bracket-to-transfer case bolts (2, 4).

23. Install the transfer case bracket-to-engine bolts (3, 6).

24. Tighten the bracket-to-transfer case bolts (2, 4) to 44 inch lbs. (5 Nm).

25. Tighten the bracket-to-engine bolts (3, 6) to 16 ft. lbs. (22 Nm).

26. Tighten the bracket-to-transfer case bolts (2, 4) to 42 ft. lbs. (50 Nm)

27. Install the transmission rear mount bracket.

28. Install the transfer case vent hose, strap, and bolt.

29. Tighten the transfer case vent hose bolt to 17 ft. lbs. (22 Nm).

30. Install the front catalytic converters.

31. Install the right halfshaft.

32. Install the driveshaft.

33. Fill the transmission with oil.

34. Fill with transfer case oil.

FRONT HALFSHAFT

REMOVAL & INSTALLATION

See Figure 15.

1. Before servicing the vehicle, refer to the Precautions Section.

2. Raise and safely support the vehicle.

3. Remove the tire and wheel assembly.

4. Insert a drift or punch in the cooling fins of the brake rotor.

5. Rotate the brake rotor until the drift or punch contacts the brake caliper mounting bracket.

6. Using a breaker bar, loosen the halfshaft (wheel drive shaft) nut.

7. Remove the halfshaft nut.

8. Using the J-45859 puller, separate the halfshaft from the knuckle assembly.

9. Remove the lower control arm from the knuckle.

10. Remove the outer tie rod end from the knuckle.

11. Using a large flat-bladed screwdriver, remove the halfshaft from the differential.

12. Remove the halfshaft from the vehicle.

➡ It may be necessary to have an assistant hold the knuckle assembly while removing the halfshaft. If removing the halfshaft to service other suspension or driveline components, use care when removing or installing the halfshaft so as not to damage the halfshaft boots. The front axle shaft seal must be replaced once the halfshaft has been removed. Replace with NEW only. DO NOT reuse the front shaft axle seal.

13. Remove and discard the washer from the halfshaft. DO NOT re-use the washer, replace with NEW only. If there is no washer on the halfshaft, install a NEW washer.

14. Remove the front axle shaft seal.

To install:

15. Install the NLW front axle shaft seal.

Fig. 15 Remove the halfshaft (1)

16. Install the DT-44394-A protector into the differential seal. Halfshaft seal protector must be installed into the differential output shaft seal prior to removing and installing the halfshaft.

❋❋ WARNING

Failure to install the halfshaft seal protector as indicated may cause the splines of the halfshaft to cut the differential output seal.

17. For vehicles equipped with an intermediate shaft, on the right halfshaft, apply a very small amount of grease to the splines of the halfshaft inner joint.

18. Install the halfshaft into the differential.

19. Remove the DT-44394-A protector from the halfshaft.

20. Insert the halfshaft in the knuckle.

21. Install the lower control arm in the knuckle.

22. Install the outer tie rod end in the knuckle.

23. Install the halfshaft nut.

24. Insert a drift or punch in the cooling fins of the brake rotor.

25. Rotate the brake rotor until the drift or punch contacts the brake caliper mounting bracket.

26. Using a torque wrench, tighten the halfshaft nut to 184 ft. lbs. (250 Nm).

27. Install the tire and wheel assembly.

28. Remove the support and lower the vehicle.

REAR AXLE FLUID

DRAIN & REFILL

1. Before servicing the vehicle, refer to the Precautions Section.

2. Raise and support the vehicle.

3. Ensure the vehicle is level.

4. Inspect the rear axle for leaks, repair if necessary.

5. Position a drain pan under drain plug.

6. Remove the drain plug and drain the fluid.

7. Install the drain plug and tighten to 18 ft. lbs. (25 Nm).

8. Remove the fill plug.

9. Clean the area around the rear axle fill plug.

10. Add lubricant until the level is even with the bottom edge of the fill plug opening. Use the proper fluid.

11. Install the fill plug to and tighten to 18 ft. lbs. (25 Nm).

12. Lower the vehicle.

REAR DRIVESHAFT (PROPELLER SHAFT)

REMOVAL & INSTALLATION

See Figure 16.

1. Before servicing the vehicle, refer to the Precautions Section.
2. Raise and support the vehicle.
3. Mark a reference point between the propeller shaft and the rear differential flange.
4. Using the appropriate tools, remove the rear differential drive flange bolts and retainers.
5. Pull the propeller shaft from the rear differential (use the DT 49064 puller, if necessary).
6. Lower the evaporator canister to gain access to the center bearing bolts.
7. Support the support bearings with jack stands and remove the support bearing mounting bolts.
8. Using the DT-49030 fork, remove the propeller shaft from the transfer case. It may be necessary to have the help of an assistant to remove the propeller shaft.

To install:

9. Installation is the reverse of removal, noting the following:
    a. Apply grease on the propeller shaft spline.
    b. Clean the mounting bolt threads, apply thread locker to the bolts, and tighten the bolts to 43 ft. lbs. (58 Nm).
    c. Tighten the rear differential drive flange bolts to 27 ft. lbs. (36 Nm).

REAR HALFSHAFT

REMOVAL & INSTALLATION

See Figure 17.

➡**Before servicing the vehicle, refer to the Precautions Section.**

1. Raise and safely support the vehicle.
2. Remove the tire and wheel assembly.
3. Insert a brass drift or punch in the cooling fins of the brake rotor.
4. Rotate the brake rotor until the drift or punch is resting against the brake mounting bracket.
5. Using a breaker bar and the proper size socket, loosen the halfshaft nut.
6. Remove the halfshaft nut.
7. Using the J 45859 tool or equivalent hub puller, separate the halfshaft from the knuckle assembly.
8. Remove the knuckle assembly from the vehicle.
9. Using a long flat-bladed screwdriver, remove the halfshaft from the differential
10. Remove the halfshaft from the vehicle.
11. Remove the washer from the halfshaft.

To install:

12. Install the NEW washer on the halfshaft, if needed.
13. Install the rear halfshaft in the rear differential.
14. Install the knuckle assembly.
15. Install the halfshaft nut.
16. Insert a brass drift or punch in the cooling fins of the brake rotor.
17. Rotate the brake rotor until the brass drift or punch rest against the brake caliper mounting bracket.
18. Using a torque wrench and the proper size socket, tighten the halfshaft nut to184 ft. lbs. (250 Nm).
19. Install the tire and wheel assembly.
20. Remove the support and lower the vehicle.

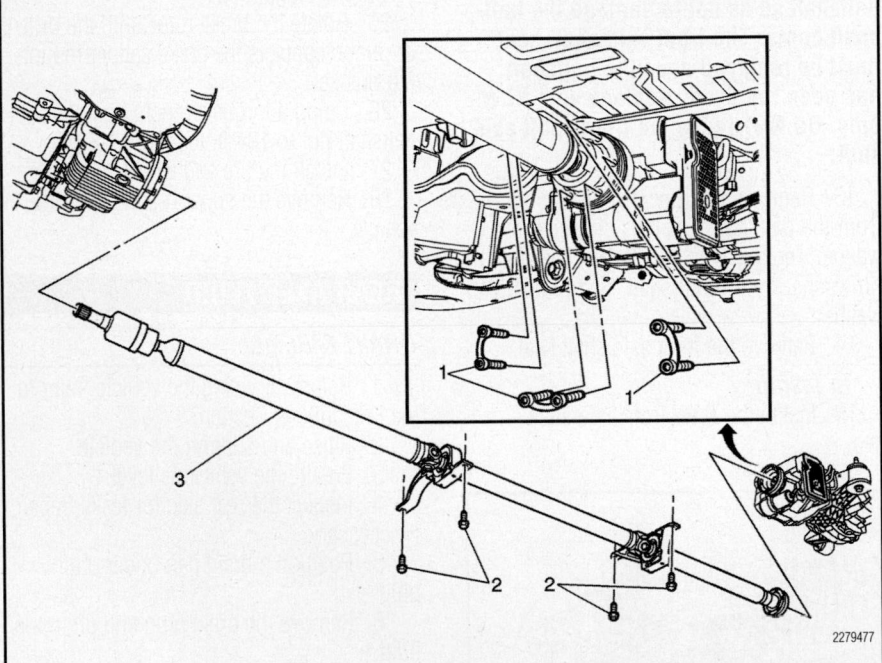

Fig. 16 Rear differential drive flange bolts and retainers (1), support bearing mounting bolts (2), and propeller shaft (3)

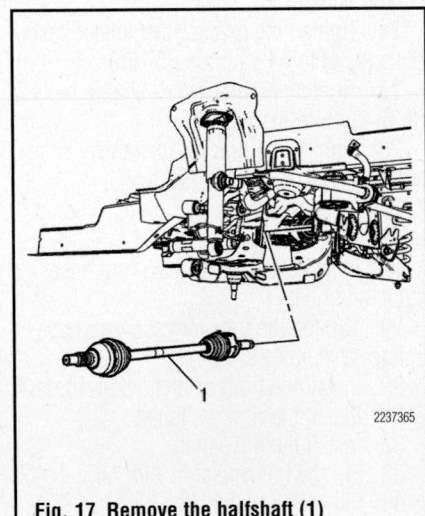

Fig. 17 Remove the halfshaft (1)

ENGINE COOLING

ENGINE COOLANT

DRAIN & REFILL PROCEDURE

✳✳ CAUTION

Do not remove the radiator cap or surge tank cap while the engine is hot. The cooling system will release scalding fluid and steam under pressure if radiator cap or surge tank cap is removed while the engine and radiator are still hot.

1. Before servicing the vehicle, refer to the Precautions Section.
2. Remove the coolant pressure cap from the radiator surge tank.
3. Raise and support the vehicle.
4. Remove the radiator air lower deflector.
5. Place a drain pan under the drain cock.
6. Loosen the radiator drain cock.
7. Drain the cooling system.
8. Lower the vehicle.
9. Inspect the coolant.
10. Follow the appropriate procedure based on the condition of the coolant:
   - Discolored appearance: Follow the flush procedure
   - Normal in appearance: Follow the fill procedure below

To install:
11. Use a coolant refill tool according the manufacturer's instructions, or, if not using a coolant refill tool, perform a static refill as directed below.

✳✳ WARNING

The fill procedure below must be followed. Improper coolant level could result in a low or high coolant level condition, causing engine damage.

12. Raise and support the vehicle.
13. Tighten the radiator drain cock to 18 inch lbs. (2 Nm).
14. Install the radiator air lower deflector.
15. Lower the vehicle.
16. Slowly fill the radiator with a mixture of 50/50 DEX-COOL antifreeze and clean drinkable water until the coolant level reaches the base of the radiator surge tank.
17. Allow 30 seconds for the coolant level to stabilize and continue to fill the coolant filler neck until the level stabilizes for at least 2 minutes.

18. Start the engine and allow to the engine to idle in PARK or NEUTRAL with the parking brake engaged.
19. Slowly fill the coolant mixture until the level stabilizes at the base of the radiator surge tank.
20. Install the coolant pressure cap.
21. Raise the engine RPM to 2500 RPM for 30–40 seconds.
22. Shut the engine OFF.
23. Allow the engine to cool, remove coolant fill cap and repeat steps 4–10 until the coolant level has completely stabilized within the radiator surge tank.
24. Inspect the concentration of the engine coolant using a tester (GE-26568 Coolant and Battery Fluid Tester, or equivalent).
25. Inspect and fill the coolant reservoir bottle as necessary.
26. Rinse away any excess coolant from the engine and the engine compartment.
27. Inspect the cooling system for leaks.
28. Top off the radiator surge tank, if necessary.

FLUSHING

✳✳ WARNING

Do not use a chemical flush.

✳✳ CAUTION

Store used coolant in the proper manner, such as in a used engine coolant holding tank. Do not pour used coolant down a drain. Ethylene glycol antifreeze is a very toxic chemical. Do not dispose of coolant into the sewer system or ground water. This is illegal and ecologically unsound.

➡ **Various methods and equipment can be used to flush the cooling system. If special equipment is used, such as a back flusher, follow the manufacturer's instruction. However, always remove the thermostat before back flushing the system.**

1. Before servicing the vehicle, refer to the Precautions Section.
2. Block the drive wheels.
3. Place the transmission in PARK (P).
4. Engage the park brake.
5. Run the engine until the thermostat opens.
6. Stop the engine.

✳✳ CAUTION

Approved safety glasses and gloves should be worn when performing this procedure to reduce the chance of personal injury.

7. Follow the drain and fill procedure using only clean drinkable water. Repeat the procedure if necessary, until the fluid is nearly colorless.
8. Fill the cooling system when flushing is complete.

ENGINE FAN

REMOVAL & INSTALLATION
See Figure 18.

✳✳ CAUTION

An electric fan under the hood can start up even when the engine is not running and can injure you. Keep hands, clothing and tools away from any under hood electric fan.

1. Before servicing the vehicle, refer to the Precautions Section.
2. Disconnect the negative battery cable.
3. Remove or reposition the components necessary to access the radiator and cooling fan.
4. Reposition the radiator forward.
5. Disconnect the cooling fan electrical connectors.
6. Remove the fan shroud bolts and the shroud.
7. Remove the cooling fan retainer bolts and remove the cooling fan from the shroud.
8. Unclip cooling fan motor wiring harness from cooling fan shroud.

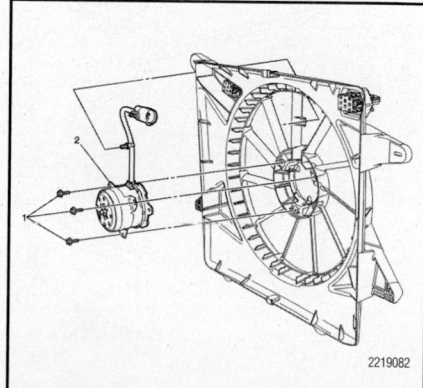

2219082

Fig. 18 Remove the cooling fan motor (2) and bolts (1)

9. Remove the mounting bolts and the motor.

To install:

10. Installation is the reverse of removal, noting the following:

   a. Tighten the motor mounting bolts to 62 inch lbs. (7 Nm).

   b. Tighten the shroud mounting bolts to 70 inch lbs. (8 Nm).

RADIATOR

REMOVAL & INSTALLATION

See Figure 19.

1. Before servicing the vehicle, refer to the Precautions Section.
2. Drain the cooling system.
3. Disconnect the negative battery cable.
4. Remove the front bumper fascia.
5. Remove the front compartment front sight shield.
6. Remove the hood primary latch bracket.
7. Remove the cooling fan and shroud.
8. Remove the radiator air upper seal.
9. Remove the radiator air lower seal.
10. Remove the radiator air side seal.
11. Remove the radiator air side baffles.
12. Remove the air conditioning condenser.
13. Remove the charge air cooler, if applicable.
14. Remove the radiator inlet and outlet hoses.
15. Remove the radiator upper support bracket bolts.
16. Remove the radiator upper support brackets.
17. Remove the radiator from the vehicle.

To install:

18. Install the radiator to the vehicle.
19. Install the radiator upper support bracket.
20. Install the radiator upper support bracket bolts and tighten to 80 inch lbs. (9 Nm).
21. Install the radiator outlet and inlet hoses.
22. Install the charge air cooler, if applicable.
23. Install the air conditioning condenser.
24. Install the radiator air side baffles.
25. Install the radiator air side seal.
26. Install the radiator air lower seal.
27. Install the radiator air upper seal.
28. Install the cooling fan and shroud.
29. Install the primary latch bracket.
30. Install the front compartment front sight shield.
31. Install the front bumper fascia.
32. Fill the cooling system.
33. Connect the negative battery cable.
34. Fill the cooling system.

THERMOSTAT

REMOVAL & INSTALLATION

3.0L Engines

See Figure 20.

1. Before servicing the vehicle, refer to the Precautions Section.
2. Drain the cooling system.

3. Disconnect the negative battery cable.
4. Remove the intake manifold cover.
5. Remove the fuel pipe shield.
6. Remove the heater outlet hose.
7. Remove the heater inlet hose.
8. Remove the surge tank hose.
9. Remove the radiator outlet hose.
10. Remove the thermostat housing.
11. Remove the thermostat and discard the gasket.

To install:

12. Clean the engine block and the thermostat gasket surfaces.
13. Install the thermostat with a new gasket.
14. Install the thermostat housing and tighten the bolts to 88 inch lbs. (10 Nm).
15. Install the hoses. Replace any worn hoses.
16. Install the fuel pipe shield.
17. Install the intake manifold cover.
18. Connect the negative battery cable.
19. Fill the cooling system.

WATER PUMP

REMOVAL & INSTALLATION

2.8L Engines

See Figure 21.

1. Before servicing the vehicle, refer to the Precautions Section.
2. Drain the cooling system.
3. Disconnect the negative battery cable.

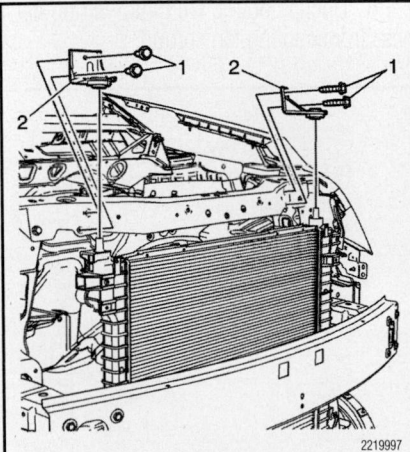

Fig. 19 Remove the radiator upper support brackets (2) and bolts (1)

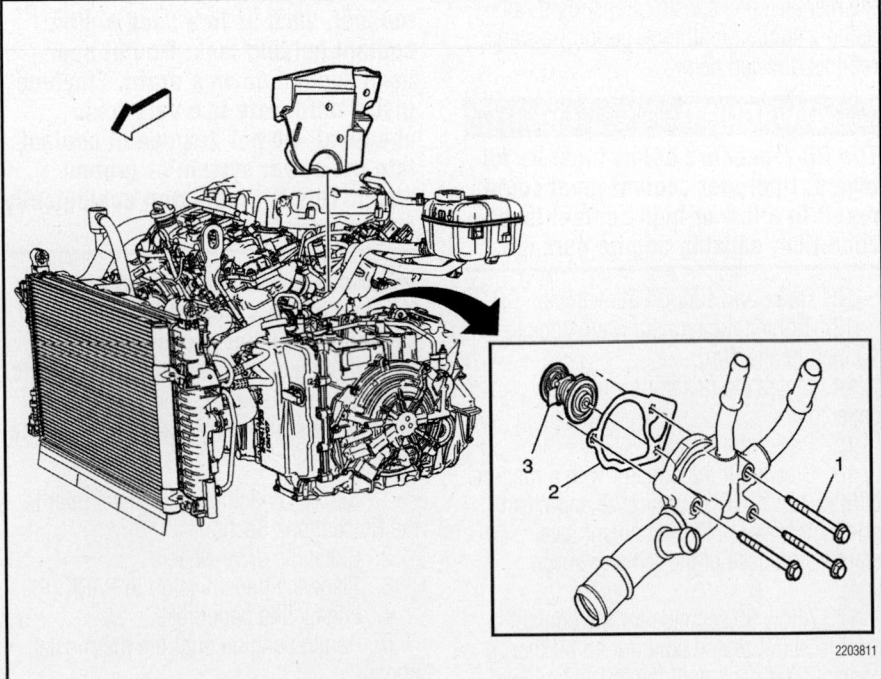

Fig. 20 Bolts (1), thermostat (3) and gasket (2)

Fig. 21 Remove the water pump

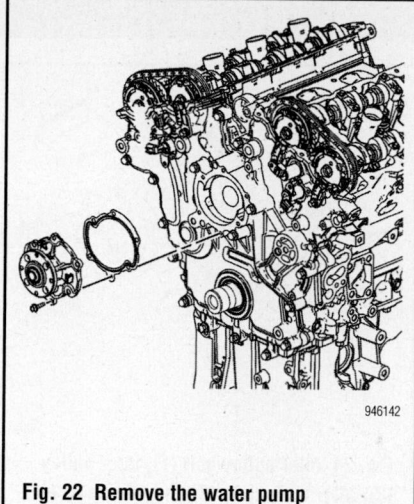

946142

Fig. 22 Remove the water pump

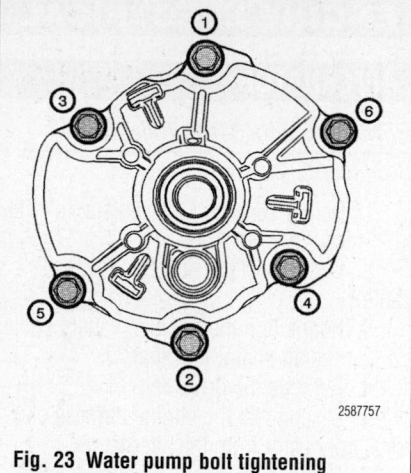

2587757

Fig. 23 Water pump bolt tightening sequence

4. Remove the drive belt.

5. Remove the water pump bolts.

6. Remove the water pump.

7. Remove and DISCARD the water pump seal.

8. Carefully clean the water pump sealing surfaces.

To install:

9. Install a NEW water pump seal.

10. Install the water pump.

11. Tighten the water pump bolts to 88 inch lbs. (10 Nm).

12. Install the drive belt.

13. Fill the cooling system.

14. Connect the negative battery cable.

3.0L Engines

See Figures 22 and 23.

1. Before servicing the vehicle, refer to the Precautions Section.

2. Drain the cooling system.

3. Disconnect the negative battery cable.

4. Remove the alternator drive belt.

5. Use the EN 46104 or equivalent holding tool to secure the water pump pulley.

6. Remove the water pump pulley bolts.

7. Remove the water pump pulley.

8. Remove the water pump bolts.

9. Remove the water pump.

10. Remove and DISCARD the water pump seal.

11. Carefully clean the water pump sealing surfaces.

To install:

12. Install a NEW water pump seal.

13. Install the water pump.

14. Hand tighten the water pump bolts.

15. Tighten the water pump bolts in sequence to 106 inch lbs. (12 Nm).

16. Tighten the water pump bolts a second pass in sequence to 106 inch lbs. (12 Nm).

17. Install the water pump pulley and the water pump pulley bolts.

18. Use the holding tool to secure the water pump pulley.

19. Tighten water pump pulley bolts to 106 inch lbs. (12 Nm).

20. Install the alternator drive belt.

21. Fill the cooling system.

22. Connect the negative battery cable.

ENGINE ELECTRICAL

BATTERY

REMOVAL & INSTALLATION

1. Before servicing the vehicle, refer to the Precautions Section.

2. Remove the battery cover/Engine Control Module (ECM).

3. Disconnect the negative battery cable.

4. Open the battery fuse block cover and remove the battery positive fuse block cable.

5. Remove the fuse block nuts, the body harness terminal nut, and the fuse block.

6. Remove the battery retainer.

7. Remove the battery.

BATTERY SYSTEM

To install:

8. Installation is the reverse of removal, noting the following:

a. Tighten the battery retainer bolt to 89 inch lbs. (10 Nm).

b. Tighten the fuse block nuts to 106 inch lbs. (12 Nm).

ENGINE ELECTRICAL — CHARGING SYSTEM

ALTERNATOR

REMOVAL & INSTALLATION

See Figure 24.

1. Before servicing the vehicle, refer to the Precautions Section.
2. Disconnect the battery negative cable.
3. Reposition the positive battery cable boot at the alternator terminal.
4. Remove the drive belt.
5. Disconnect the engine harness electrical connector from the alternator.
6. Remove the positive battery cable nut at the alternator.
7. Remove the positive battery cable terminal from the alternator.
8. Remove the idler pulley bolt and idler pulley.

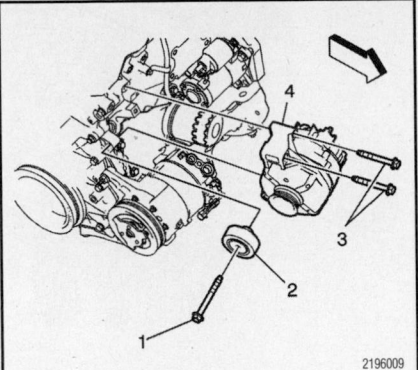

Fig. 24 Idler pulley bolt (1), idler pulley (2), alternator bolts (3) and alternator (4)

9. Remove the alternator bolts.
10. Remove the alternator.

To install:

11. Position the alternator to the engine.
12. Loosely install the alternator bolts.
13. Install the idler pulley.
14. Tighten the alternator bolts in the sequence shown to:
    - 2.8L Engines: 43 ft. lbs. (58 Nm)
    - 3.0L Engines: 37 ft. lbs. (50 Nm)
15. Install the drive belt.
16. Connect the engine harness electrical connector to the alternator.
17. Install the positive battery cable terminal to the alternator.
18. Install the positive battery cable nut at the alternator and tighten to 11 ft. lbs. (15 Nm).
19. Position the positive battery cable boot at the alternator terminal.
20. Connect the negative battery cable.

ENGINE ELECTRICAL — IGNITION SYSTEM

FIRING ORDER

2.8L and 3.0L Engines: 1–2–3–4–5–6

IGNITION COIL

REMOVAL & INSTALLATION

See Figure 25.

1. Before servicing the vehicle, refer to the Precautions Section.
2. Disconnect the negative battery cable.
3. For Bank 1 ignition coils, remove the intake manifold.
4. For Bank 2 ignition coils, remove the intake manifold cover.
5. Disconnect the engine wiring harness electrical connectors from the ignition coils.
6. Remove the ignition coil bolts.
7. Remove the ignition coils.

To install:

8. Install the ignition coils.
9. Install the ignition coil bolts and tighten to 89 inch lbs. (10 Nm).
10. Connect the engine wiring harness electrical connectors to the ignition coils.
11. For Bank 1 ignition coils, install the intake manifold.
12. For Bank 2 ignition coils, install the intake manifold cover.
    a. Press the fuel injector sight shield down firmly on the ball stud at the right front corner.
    b. Install the oil fill cap.

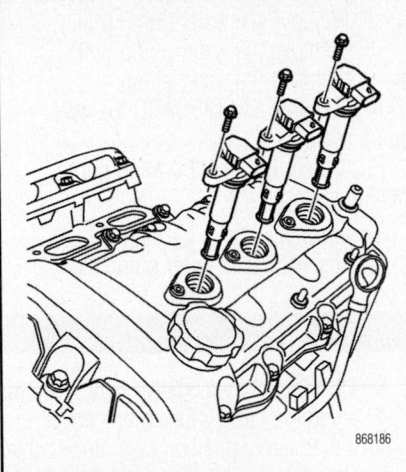

Fig. 25 Remove the ignition coils

13. Connect the negative battery cable.

IGNITION TIMING

ADJUSTMENT

The ignition timing is controlled by the Engine Control Module (ECM). No adjustment is necessary or possible.

SPARK PLUGS

REMOVAL & INSTALLATION

1. Before servicing the vehicle, refer to the Precautions Section.
2. Turn the ignition OFF.
3. Disconnect the negative battery cable.
4. Remove the ignition coils.

✳✳ WARNING

Allow the engine to cool before removing the spark plugs. Attempting to remove the spark plugs from a hot engine may cause damage to cylinder head threads. Clean the spark plug recess area before removing the spark plug. Failure to do so could result in engine damage.

5. Use compressed air in order to remove debris from the spark plug cavity.
6. Remove the spark plug.

To install:

✳✳ WARNING

Use only the spark plugs specified for use in the vehicle. Failure to do so could result in severe engine damage. Check the gap of all new and reconditioned spark plugs before installation.

7. Ensure that the spark plug gap is equivalent to the specification. Specified gap: 0.043 in. (1.1 mm).
8. Install the spark plug and tighten to 13 ft. lbs. (18 Nm). Be sure that the spark plug threads smoothly into the cylinder head and the spark plug is fully seated. Use a thread chaser, if necessary, to clean threads in the cylinder head.
9. Install the ignition coil.
10. Connect the negative battery cable.

ENGINE ELECTRICAL

STARTER

REMOVAL & INSTALLATION

2.8L Engines

See Figure 26.

1. Before servicing the vehicle, refer to the Precautions Section.
2. Turn the ignition OFF.
3. Disconnect the negative battery cable.
4. Remove the secondary air injection pump.
5. Remove the battery positive cable nut and terminal from the starter.
6. Remove the engine wiring harness nut and the engine harness terminal from the starter solenoid.

7. Remove the starter mounting bolts.
8. Remove the starter from the engine.

To install:

9. Install the starter motor.
10. Install the starter motor mounting bolts and tighten to 43 ft. lbs. (58 Nm).
11. Install the battery positive cable terminal and nut to the starter solenoid and tighten to 9 ft. lbs. (15 Nm).
12. Install the engine harness terminal and nut to the starter solenoid and tighten to 53 inch lbs. (6 Nm).
13. Reposition and install the secondary air injection pump and bracket.
14. Connect the battery negative cable.

3.0L Engines

See Figure 27.

1. Before servicing the vehicle, refer to the Precautions Section.
2. Turn the ignition OFF.
3. Disconnect the negative battery cable.
4. Remove the starter heat shield.
5. Remove the left catalytic converter head nuts and reposition catalytic converter away from cylinder head.
6. Raise and support the vehicle.
7. Disconnect the knock sensor connector.
8. Remove the battery positive nut and the engine harness connector from the starter solenoid.
9. Remove the starter motor mounting bolts.
10. Remove the starter motor.

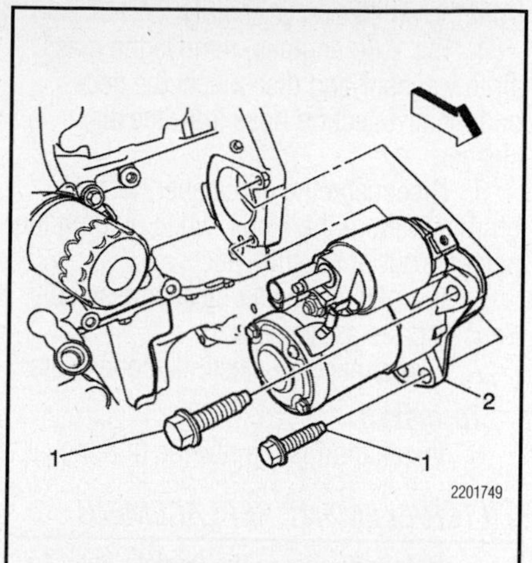

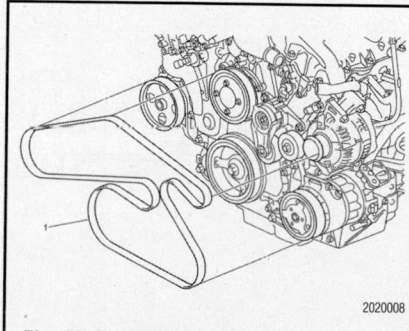

Fig. 27 Remove the mounting bolts (1) and the starter (2)

To install:

11. Install the starter motor and tighten the mounting bolts to 43 ft. lbs. (58 Nm).
12. Install the battery positive cable and engine harness connector to the starter. Tighten the battery positive cable nut to 9 ft. lbs. (15 Nm).
13. Install the engine harness connector to the starter solenoid.
14. Install the starter heat shield and tighten the bolt to 62 inch lbs. (7 Nm).
15. Connect the knock sensor connector.
16. Install the left catalytic converter to the cylinder head. Tighten:
   - First Pass: 15 ft. lbs. (20 Nm)
   - Final Pass: 34 ft. lbs. (46 Nm)
17. Connect the negative battery cable.

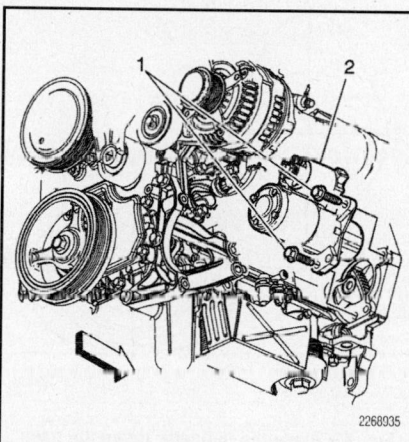

Fig. 26 Remove the mounting bolts (1) and the starter (2)

ENGINE MECHANICAL

➡**Disconnecting the negative battery cable may interfere with the functions of the on board computer systems and may require the computer to undergo a relearning process, once the negative battery cable is reconnected.**

ACCESSORY DRIVE BELTS

ACCESSORY BELT ROUTING

See Figure 28.

Refer to the accompanying illustration.

INSPECTION

Inspect the drive belt for signs of glazing or cracking. A glazed belt will be perfectly smooth from slippage, while a good belt will have a slight texture of fabric visible. Cracks will usually start at the inner edge of the belt

and run outward. All worn or damaged drive belts should be replaced immediately.

ADJUSTMENT

Tension is automatically adjusted by the belt tensioner.

Fig. 28 Drive belt routing

REMOVAL & INSTALLATION

1. Before servicing the vehicle, refer to the Precautions Section.
2. Disconnect the negative battery cable.
3. Remove the engine mount bracket.
4. Rotate the drive belt tensioner clockwise to release the drive belt tension.
5. Slide the drive belt off the belt idler pulley.
6. Slowly release the drive belt tensioner.
7. Remove the drive belt.

To install:

8. Installation is the reverse of removal.

AIR CLEANER

REMOVAL & INSTALLATION

1. Before servicing the vehicle, refer to the Precautions Section.

2. Disconnect the negative battery cable.

3. Disconnect the air cleaner outlet duct from the air cleaner assembly.

4. For 2.8L engines, remove the mass airflow sensor and disconnect the secondary air injection hose from the air cleaner.

5. Disengage the air cleaner housing grommets from the studs, while guiding the housing out of the inlet duct.

6. If replacing the air cleaner assembly, transfer parts as necessary.

7. Disconnect the electrical connectors.

To install:

8. Installation is the reverse of removal.

FILTER/ELEMENT REPLACEMENT

1. Before servicing the vehicle, refer to the Precautions Section.

2. Disconnect the negative battery cable.

3. Disconnect the air cleaner outlet duct from the air cleaner.

4. For 2.8L engines, disconnect the secondary air injection hose from the air cleaner assembly.

5. Disconnect the mass airflow sensor electrical connector.

6. For 3.0L engines, disconnect the throttle inlet absolute pressure sensor electrical connector.

7. Release the air cleaner retaining clips and remove the element.

To install:

8. Installation is the reverse of removal.

CAMSHAFT AND VALVE LIFTERS

INSPECTION

See Figures 29 through 32.

1. Inspect the camshaft oil feed holes to the camshaft position actuator for dirt, debris or blockage.

2. Inspect the threaded hole for damage.

3. Inspect the camshaft position actuator locating notch for damage or wear.

4. Inspect the camshaft sealing grooves for damage.

5. Inspect the camshaft thrust surface for damage.

6. Inspect the camshaft lobes and journals for the following conditions:
   - Excessive scoring or pitting
   - Discoloration from overheating
   - Deformation from excessive wear, especially the camshaft lobes

7. If any of the above conditions exist on the camshaft, replace the camshaft.

8. With the camshaft in a suitable fixture, measure the camshaft for wear.

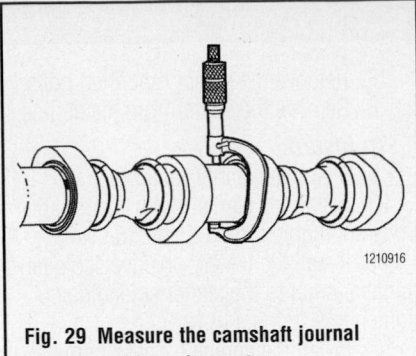

Fig. 29 Measure the camshaft journal diameter with a micrometer

9. Measure the camshaft journals for diameter and out-of-round using an outside micrometer.

   a. If the diameter is smaller than specifications, replace the camshaft.

   b. If the out-of-round exceeds specifications, replace the camshaft.

10. Measure the camshaft runout using a dial indicator (GE 7872 or equivalent tool).

11. Measure the camshaft thrust width for wear using a depth micrometer.

12. Measure the camshaft thrust wall surface for runout using a dial indicator (GE 7872 or equivalent tool). If the camshaft is damaged or worn beyond specifications, replace the camshaft. No machining of the camshaft is allowed.

13. Measure the camshaft lobes for wear using a dial indicator (GE 7872 or equivalent tool).

14. Place the dial indicator (GE 7872 or equivalent tool) with the indicator tip on the base circle of the camshaft lobe.

   a. Place the indicator tool at zero.

   b. Rotate the camshaft until the indicator tip is at the highest point on the lobe. This reading is the lift of the camshaft lobe.

   c. If the indicated measurement is significantly lower than these specifications, replace the camshaft or engine performance will be reduced.

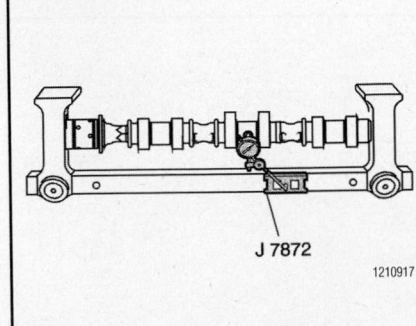

Fig. 30 Measure the camshaft runout

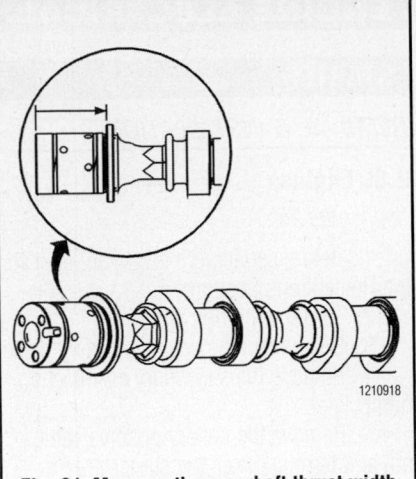

Fig. 31 Measure the camshaft thrust width

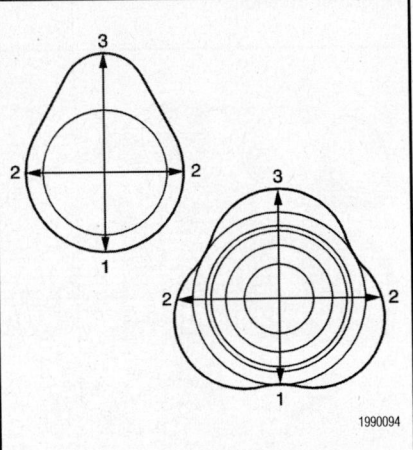

Fig. 32 Place the indicator tip on the base circle (1) of the camshaft lobe and rotate the camshaft until the indicator is at the highest point (3) on the lobe

15. Inspect the valve lifters:

   a. Inspect the Stationary Hydraulic Lash Adjuster (SHLA) in the following areas:
   - A plugged oil passage
   - A scored or worn camshaft follower pivot area
   - A damaged or broken retainer
   - A severely scuffed or worn SHLA body

   b. Replace the SHLA or as necessary.

REMOVAL & INSTALLATION

See Figures 33 through 41.

1. Before servicing the vehicle, refer to the Precautions Section.

2. Disconnect the negative battery cable.

3. Remove the intake manifold.

4. Remove the fuel pump from the cylinder head.

5. Remove the valve covers.

6. Remove the camshaft sensors.

7. Remove the camshaft position actuator solenoids.

8. Remove the camshaft position actuator.

9. Remove the crankshaft balancer.

10. Rotate the crankshaft with a crankshaft rotation socket (EN-46111 or equivalent) until the camshafts are in a neutral (low tension) position. The camshaft flats will be parallel with the camshaft cover rail.

11. Loosen the camshaft position actuator bolt. Use an open-end wrench at the camshaft hex to prevent camshaft/engine rotation. DO NOT remove the camshaft position actuator bolt at this time.

✳✳ WARNING

A wrench must be used on the hex of the camshaft when loosening or tightening in order to prevent component damage. Failure to prevent the torque reaction against the timing drive chain can lead to timing drive chain failure.

12. Install the timing chain retention tool (EN-48313 or equivalent) and secure the timing chain. Ensure that the tips of the retention tool are fully engaged into the timing chain. Firmly tighten the retention tool nuts.

13. Matchmark the timing chain and the respective locations on the camshaft position actuators.

14. Remove the camshaft position actuator bolt.

15. Remove the camshaft bearing cap bolts.

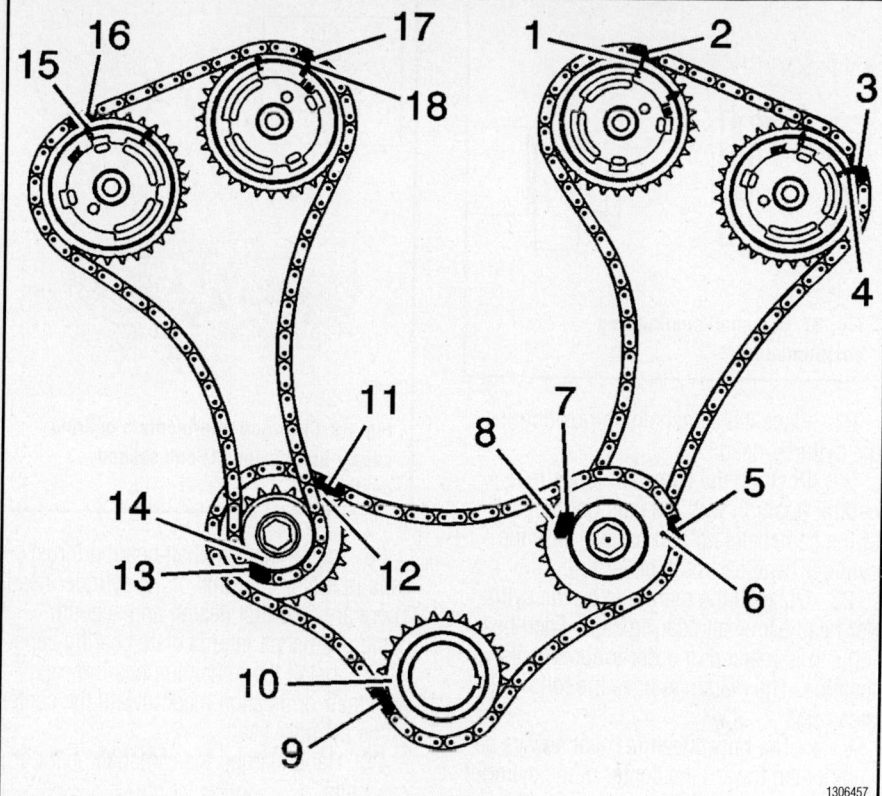

Fig. 34 Matchmark the timing chain and the respective locations on the camshaft position actuators (15–18))—right side

16. Remove the camshaft bearing caps.

17. Remove the camshafts. Matchmark the camshafts upon removal to ensure installation is in the correct position.

To install:

18. Position the camshafts to the cylinder head and assemble the camshaft actuators to the camshafts. Ensure that the marks on the camshaft position actuator and the timing chain are aligned. DO NOT tighten the camshaft position actuator bolt at this time.

19. Ensure that the camshaft sealing rings are in place in the camshaft grooves. Camshaft sealing rings must be in place below the surface of the camshaft journal in order to avoid being pinched between the cylinder head and the camshaft caps.

20. Apply a liberal amount of lubricant to the camshaft journals and the cylinder head camshaft carriers.

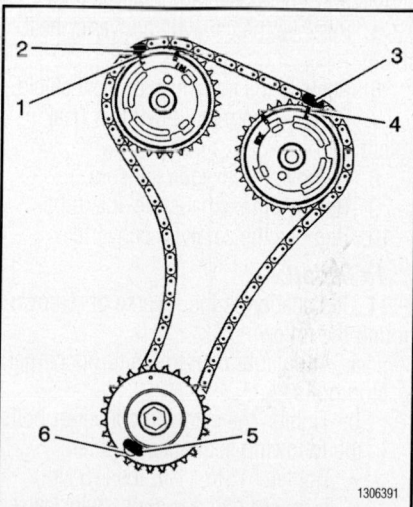

Fig. 33 Matchmark the timing chain and the respective locations on the camshaft position actuators (1–4)—left side

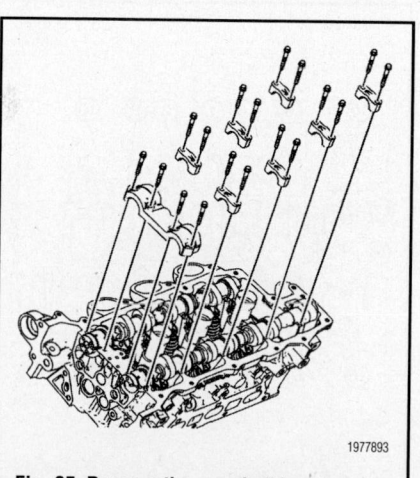

Fig. 35 Remove the camshaft bearing caps—left side shown, right side similar

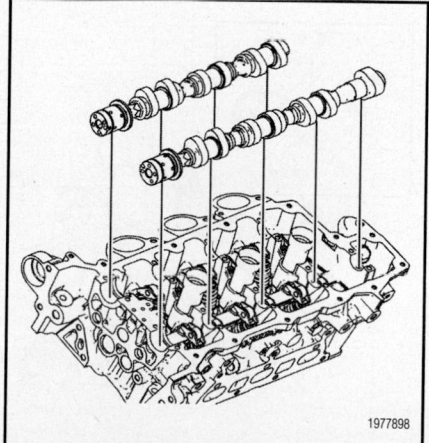

Fig. 36 Remove the camshafts—left side shown, right side similar

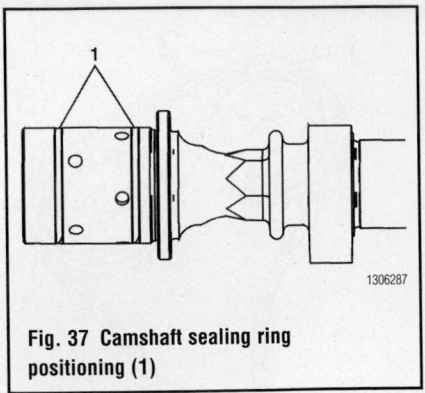

Fig. 37 Camshaft sealing ring positioning (1)

21. Place the camshafts in position in the cylinder head.

22. Position the camshaft lobes in a neutral position with the flats on the back of the camshafts up and parallel with the cylinder head camshaft cover rail.

23. Observe the markings on the cylinder head camshaft bearing caps. Each bearing cap is marked in order to identify its location. The markings have the following meanings:

  a. The raised feature must always be oriented toward the center of the cylinder head.

  b. The I indicates the intake camshaft.

  c. The E indicates the exhaust camshaft.

  d. The number indicates the cylinder position from the front of the engine.

24. Apply a liberal amount of lubricant to the camshaft bearing caps.

25. There are first design and second design camshaft front bearing caps. For vehicles that have a second design camshaft bearing cap, apply a liberal amount of lubricant to the camshaft bearing cap and camshaft thrust surface.

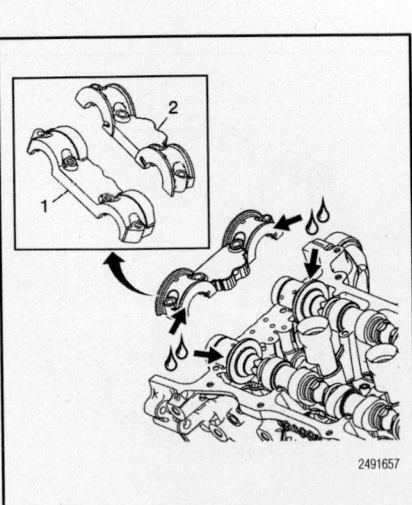

Fig. 38 Camshaft front bearing caps—first design (1) and second design (2)

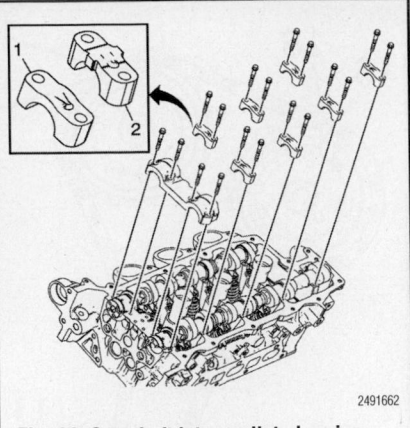

Fig. 39 Camshaft intermediate bearing caps—first design (1) and second design (2)

26. Install the camshaft bearing thrust caps in the first journal of the cylinder head. There are also first design and second design camshaft intermediate bearing caps.

27. Install the remaining bearing caps with their orientation mark toward the center of the cylinder head.

28. Hand start all the camshaft bearing cap bolts.

29. Tighten the camshaft bearing cap bolts in the sequence shown to 89 lb in. (10 Nm).

30. Loosen the center intake camshaft bearing cap bolts 1, 2 and the center exhaust camshaft bearing cap bolts 3, 4.

31. Retighten the center camshaft bearing cap bolts 1, 2, 3, 4 and retighten the camshaft bearing cap bolts to 89 lb in. (10 Nm).

32. Remove the retention tool.

33. Install and tighten the camshaft position actuators. Use an open-end wrench at the camshaft hex to prevent camshaft/ engine rotation.

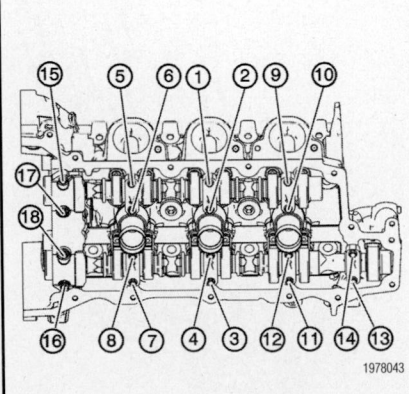

Fig. 40 Camshaft bearing cap bolt tightening sequence—left side

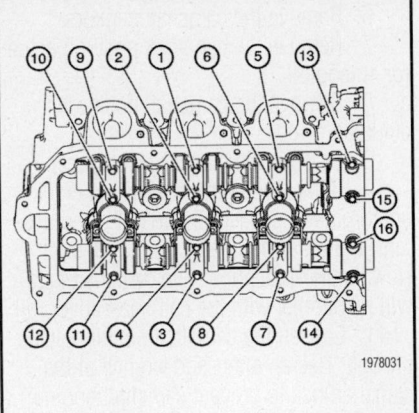

Fig. 41 Camshaft bearing cap bolt tightening sequence—right side

34. Install the intake camshaft position actuator solenoid.

35. Install the camshaft sensors.

36. Install the crankshaft balancer.

37. Install the valve cover.

38. Install the fuel pump to the cylinder head.

39. Install the intake manifold.

CATALYTIC CONVERTER/ EXHAUST MANIFOLD

REMOVAL & INSTALLATION

2.8L Engine

See Figure 42.

1. Before servicing the vehicle, refer to the Precautions Section.

2. Disconnect the negative battery cable.

3. Remove the battery tray.

4. Remove the radiator surge tank engine and inlet hoses at the surge tank.

5. Remove the catalytic converter heat shield.

6. Remove the transmission heat shield.

7. Remove the master cylinder heat shield.

8. Remove the oxygen sensors.

9. Remove the exhaust flexible pipe.

10. Remove the catalytic converter.

To install:

11. Installation is the reverse of removal, noting the following:

  a. Apply lubricant to the turbocharger stud bolts.

  b. Tighten the catalytic converter bolts in the following sequence. Tighten:

  • Tighten "1" to 11 ft. lbs (15 Nm). Turn 270 degrees counterclockwise.

  • Tighten "2" to 11 ft. lbs (15 Nm). Turn 270 degrees counterclockwise.

  • Tighten "3" to 15 ft. lbs (20 Nm).

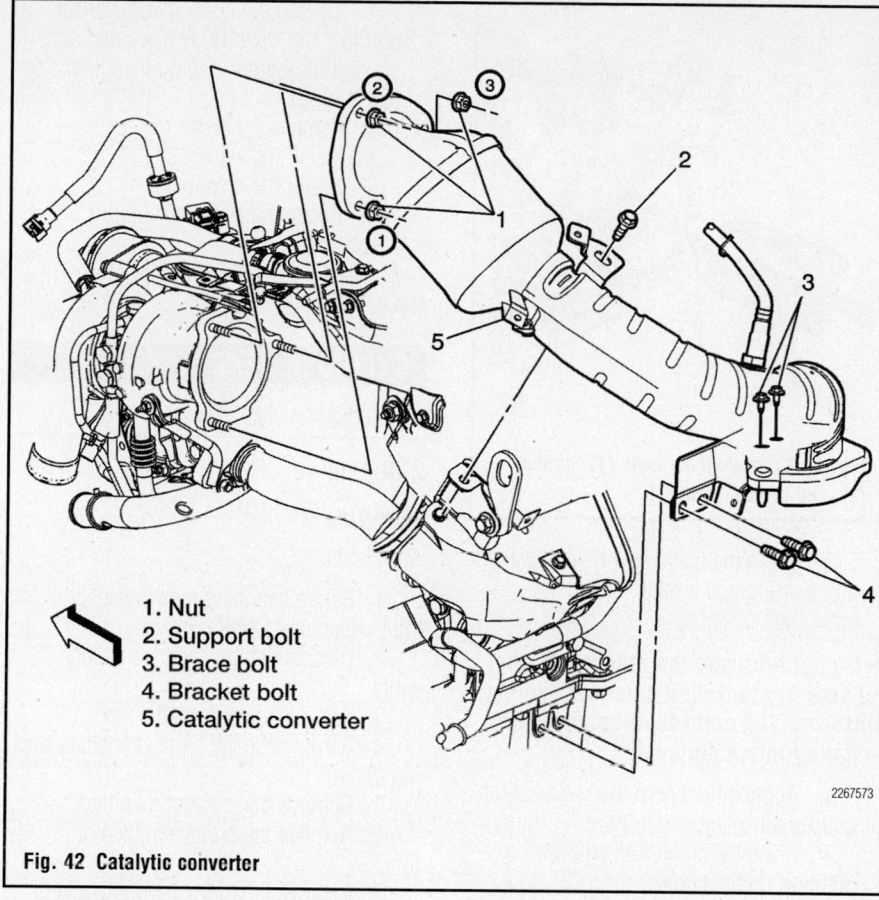

1. Nut
2. Support bolt
3. Brace bolt
4. Bracket bolt
5. Catalytic converter

2267573

Fig. 42 Catalytic converter

• Tighten "1" to 18 ft. lbs (25 Nm).
• Tighten "2" to 18 ft. lbs (25 Nm).
  c. Tighten the catalytic converter bracket bolts to 15 ft. lbs (20 Nm).
  d. Tighten the catalytic converter brace bolts to 15 ft. lbs (20 Nm).
  e. Tighten the catalytic support bolt to 16 ft. lbs (22 Nm).

3.0L Engine

Left Side

See Figure 43.

1. Before servicing the vehicle, refer to the Precautions Section.
2. Disconnect the heated oxygen sensor before and after the left catalytic converter.
3. Remove the left catalytic converter nuts to left cylinder head. Replace gasket with a new one.
4. Remove the nuts to the rear muffler assembly.
5. Remove the nuts from the right catalytic converter.

➡It may be easier to remove catalytic converter by removing the left cylinder studs.

6. Remove the exhaust bracket insulator from the hanger and lower catalytic converter.

7. Carefully lower the catalytic converter to the floor.
8. Transfer oxygen sensors if replacing catalytic converter.

To install:

❋❋ WARNING

To prevent damage to the exhaust manifold flange or stud, make sure the flange is fully seated before tightening.

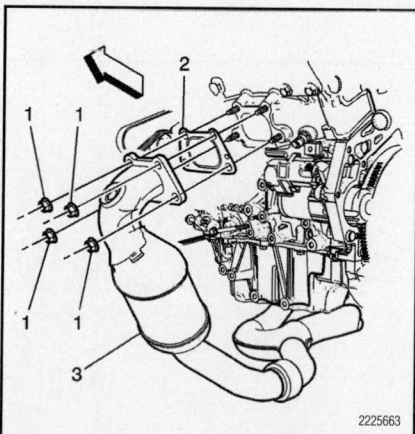

2225663

Fig. 43 Remove the left catalytic converter nuts (1) and the gasket (2)

9. Replace the left catalytic converter-to-cylinder head nuts and gaskets with new ones; tighten nuts in a criss-cross pattern. Tighten:
  • First Pass: 15 ft. lbs (20 Nm)
  • Final Pass: 34 ft. lbs (46 Nm)
10. Attach left catalytic converter to insulator hanger bracket.
11. Install the left catalytic converter nuts to the rear muffler assembly. Tighten to 34 ft. lbs (46 Nm).
12. Install the nuts to the right catalytic converter. Tighten to 34 ft. lbs (46 Nm).
13. Connect the heated oxygen sensor.

❋❋ WARNING

Improperly installed and/or leaking exhaust manifold gaskets may affect vehicle emissions and/or On-Board Diagnostics (OBD) II system performance.

14. Inspect the exhaust system for leaks.

Right Side

See Figure 44.

1. Before servicing the vehicle, refer to the Precautions Section.
2. Remove the left side catalytic converter.
3. Disconnect the heated oxygen sensors before and after the right catalytic converter.
4. Remove the right exhaust manifold nuts.
5. Remove the right exhaust manifold studs on the right cylinder head, if necessary.
6. Remove the right side catalytic converter.

To install:

7. Installation is the reverse of removal, noting the following:

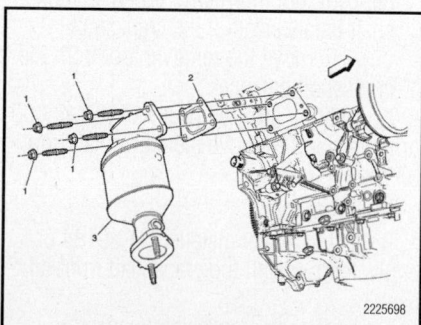

2225698

Fig. 44 Right catalytic converter (3), nuts (1), and gasket (2)

a. Clean and inspect the studs on the engine cylinder head. Replace as necessary.

b. To prevent damage to the exhaust manifold flange or stud, make sure the flange is fully seated before tightening.

c. Verify that the studs are fully seated. Stud collar should touch the surface of the engine cylinder head.

d. Replace the nuts and gasket. Tighten the nuts in a criss-cross pattern. Tighten:
- First Pass: 15 ft. lbs. (20 Nm)
- Final Pass: 34 ft. lbs. (46 Nm)

➡Improperly installed and/or leaking exhaust manifold gaskets may affect vehicle emissions and/or On-Board Diagnostics (OBD) II system performance.

CRANKSHAFT FRONT SEAL

REMOVAL & INSTALLATION

See Figures 45 and 46.

1. Before servicing the vehicle, refer to the Precautions Section.
2. Remove the crankshaft balancer:
   a. Remove the drive belt.
   b. Install the engine support fixture.
   c. Remove the starter.
   d. Install the flywheel holding tool (EN-46106 or equivalent) through the starter mounting hole.
   e. Using engine support fixture, lower engine approximately two inches.
   f. Remove the crankshaft balancer bolt. Discard the bolt.
   g. Install the crankshaft button (EN-38416-2) in the nose of the crankshaft.
   h. Install the removal tool (EN-41816 or equivalent) in order to remove the crankshaft balancer.
   i. Tighten the center bolt of the removal tool in order to pull the crankshaft balancer off of the crankshaft.
   j. Remove the removal tool from the crankshaft balancer.
3. Using a seal removal tool (EN-45000 or equivalent), remove the crankshaft front oil seal.

To install:
4. Using a seal installer (J-29184 or equivalent), install the crankshaft front oil seal.
5. Install the crankshaft balancer:
   a. The flywheel holding tool must be installed onto the flywheel.

Fig. 45 Crankshaft balancer (1), button (2), and removal tool (3)

b. Using the installer (EN-41998-B), nut, bearing and washer, install the crankshaft balancer.

➡Do not lubricate the crankshaft front oil seal or crankshaft balancer sealing surfaces. The crankshaft balancer is installed into a dry seal.

   c. Apply lubricant to the inside of the crankshaft balancer hub bore.
   d. Place the crankshaft balancer in position on the crankshaft.
   e. Thread the installer in the crankshaft. Ensure you engage at least 10 threads of the installer before pressing the crankshaft balancer in place.
   f. Push the crankshaft balancer into position by tightening the nut on the installer until the large washer bottoms out on the crankshaft end.
   g. Remove the installer.

➡Always install a new crankshaft balancer retaining bolt and washer.

   h. Install the NEW crankshaft balancer bolt.

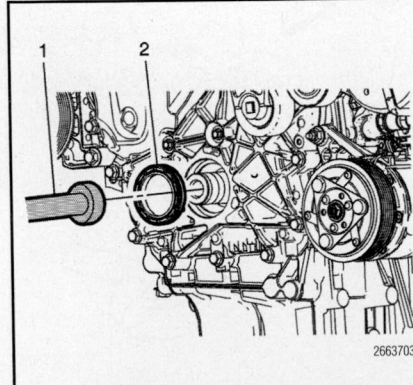

Fig. 46 Using a seal installer (1), install the crankshaft oil seal (2)

   i. Tighten the crankshaft balancer bolt to 74 ft. lbs. (100 Nm) and an additional 150 degrees using an angle meter (EN-45059).
   j. Remove the angle meter.
   k. Install the starter.
   l. Install the drive belt.
   m. Remove the engine support fixture.
6. Start the engine and check for leaks.

CYLINDER HEAD

REMOVAL & INSTALLATION

2.8L Engine

Left Side

See Figure 47.

1. Before servicing the vehicle, refer to the Precautions Section.
2. Disconnect the negative battery cable.
3. Remove the camshaft cover.
4. Remove the left bank secondary timing chain.
5. Remove the exhaust manifold.
6. Remove the oil level indicator tube.
7. Remove the turbocharger bracket.
8. Remove the 2 front M8 left cylinder head bolts.
9. Remove the left cylinder head bolts.
10. Remove the left cylinder head.
11. Remove and discard the left cylinder head gasket.
12. Clean and inspect the cylinder head and the engine block sealing surfaces.

To install:
13. Ensure the cylinder head locating pins are securely mounted in the cylinder block deck face.
14. Install a new left cylinder head gasket using the deck face locating pins for retention.
15. Align the left cylinder head with the deck face locating pins.
16. Place the left cylinder head in position on the deck face.

➡Do not allow oil on the cylinder head bolt bosses. Do not reuse the old cylinder head bolts.

17. Install new M11 cylinder head bolts:
   a. Tighten the M11 cylinder head bolts a first pass in sequence to 22 ft. lbs. (30 Nm).
   b. Tighten the M11 cylinder head bolts a second pass in sequence an addi-

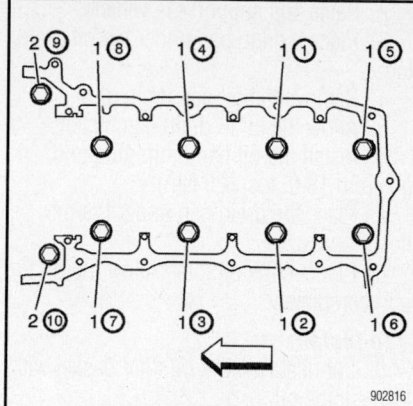

Fig. 47 M11 cylinder head bolts (1), M8 cylinder head bolts (2), and cylinder head bolt tightening sequence

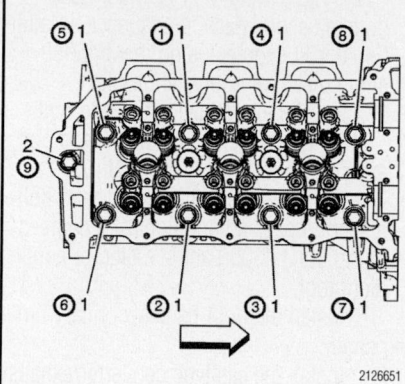

Fig. 48 M11 cylinder head bolts (1), M8 cylinder head bolts (2), and cylinder head bolt tightening sequence

tional 150 degrees using the J-45059 angle meter, or equivalent tool.

18. Install 2 new front M8 left cylinder head bolts:

a. Tighten the M8 cylinder head bolts a first pass to 11 ft. lbs. (15 Nm).

b. Tighten the M8 cylinder head bolts a second pass in sequence an additional 75 degrees using the J-45059 angle meter, or equivalent tool.

19. Install the turbocharger bracket.

20. Install the left bank secondary timing chain.

21. Install the camshaft cover.

22. Install the exhaust manifold.

23. Install the oil level indicator tube.

Right Side

See Figure 48.

1. Before servicing the vehicle, refer to the Precautions Section.

2. Disconnect the negative battery cable.

3. Remove the camshaft cover.

4. Remove the right bank secondary timing chain.

5. Remove the exhaust manifold.

6. Remove the right engine lift bracket at the rear of the right cylinder head.

7. Remove the right cylinder head bolts.

8. Remove the right cylinder head.

9. Remove and discard the cylinder head gasket.

10. Clean and inspect the cylinder head and the engine block sealing surfaces.

11. Disassemble the cylinder head if needed.

To install:

12. Ensure the cylinder head locating pins are securely mounted in the cylinder block deck face.

13. Install a new right cylinder head gasket using the deck face locating pins for retention.

14. Align the right cylinder head with the deck face locating pins.

15. Place the right cylinder head in position on the deck face.

➡ **Do not allow oil on the cylinder head bolt bosses. Do not reuse the old cylinder head bolts.**

16. Install new M11 cylinder head bolts.

a. Tighten the M11 cylinder head bolts a first pass in sequence to 22 ft. lbs. (30 Nm).

b. Tighten the M11 cylinder head bolts a second pass in sequence an additional 150 degrees using the J 45059 angle meter, or equivalent tool.

17. Install a new M0 cylinder head bolt.

a. Tighten the M8 cylinder head bolt a first pass to 11 ft. lbs. (15 Nm).

b. Tighten the M8 cylinder head bolt a second pass an additional 75 degrees using the J 45059 angle meter, or equivalent tool.

18. Install the right bank secondary timing chain.

19. Install the right engine lift bracket.

20. Install the exhaust manifold.

21. Install the camshaft cover.

3.0L Engine

Left Side

See Figure 47.

1. Before servicing the vehicle, refer to the Precautions Section.

2. Disconnect the negative battery cable.

3. Remove the camshaft cover.

4. Remove the alternator.

5. Remove the left bank secondary timing chain.

6. Remove the fuel pump.

7. Remove the catalytic converter/exhaust manifold.

8. Remove the oil level indicator tube.

9. Remove the 2 front M8 left cylinder head bolts.

10. Remove the left cylinder head bolts.

11. Remove the left cylinder head.

12. Remove the ground wire bolt and ground wire.

13. Disconnect and reposition harness as necessary.

14. Remove and discard the left cylinder head gasket.

15. Clean and inspect the cylinder head and the engine block sealing surfaces.

16. Transfer parts as needed.

To install:

17. Ensure the cylinder head locating pins are securely mounted in the cylinder block deck face.

18. Install a new left cylinder head gasket using the deck face locating pins for retention.

19. Align the left cylinder head with the deck face locating pins.

20. Place the left cylinder head in position on the deck face.

➡ **Do not allow oil on the cylinder head bolt bosses. Do not reuse the old cylinder head bolts.**

21. Install new M11 cylinder head bolts:

a. Tighten the M11 cylinder head bolts a first pass in sequence to 22 ft. lbs. (30 Nm).

b. Tighten the M11 cylinder head bolts a second pass in sequence an additional 150 degrees using the J-45059 angle meter, or equivalent tool.

22. Install 2 new front M8 left cylinder head bolts:

a. Tighten the M8 cylinder head bolts a first pass to 11 ft. lbs. (15 Nm).

b. Tighten the M8 cylinder head bolts a second pass in sequence an additional 75 degrees using the J-45059 angle meter, or equivalent tool.

23. Install the left bank secondary timing chain.

24. Install the fuel pump.

25. Install the alternator.

26. Install the catalytic converter/exhaust manifold.

27. Install the oil level indicator tube.

28. Install the camshaft cover.
29. Connect the negative battery cable.

Right Side

See Figure 49.

1. Before servicing the vehicle, refer to the Precautions Section.
2. Disconnect the negative battery cable.
3. Remove the camshaft cover.
4. Remove the right bank secondary timing chain.
5. Position the power brake booster pump aside.
6. Remove the catalytic converter/exhaust manifold.
7. Remove the right cylinder head bolts.
8. Remove the right cylinder head.
9. Remove ground wire and harness and position aside.
10. Remove and discard the cylinder head gasket.
11. Clean and inspect the cylinder head and the engine block sealing surfaces.
12. Transfer parts as needed.

To install:

13. Ensure the cylinder head locating pins are securely mounted in the cylinder block deck face.
14. Install a new right cylinder head gasket using the deck face locating pins for retention.
15. Align the right cylinder head with the deck face locating pins.
16. Place the right cylinder head in position on the deck face.

➡**Do not allow oil on the cylinder head bolt bosses. Do not reuse the old cylinder head bolts.**

17. Install new M11 cylinder head bolts.
   a. Tighten the M11 cylinder head bolts a first pass in sequence to 22 ft. lbs. (30 Nm).

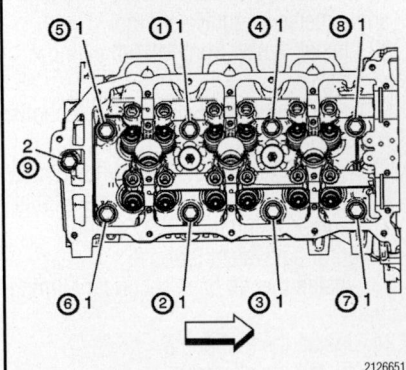

Fig. 49 M11 cylinder head bolts (1), M8 cylinder head bolts (2), and cylinder head bolt tightening sequence

   b. Tighten the M11 cylinder head bolts a second pass in sequence an additional 150 degrees using the J 45059 angle meter, or equivalent tool.
18. Install new M8 cylinder head bolt.
   a. Tighten the M8 cylinder head bolt a first pass to 11 ft. lbs. (15 Nm).
   b. Tighten the M8 cylinder head bolt a second pass an additional 75 degrees using the J 45059 angle meter, or equivalent tool.
19. Install the right bank secondary timing chain.
20. Install the catalytic converter/exhaust manifold.
21. Install the camshaft cover.
22. Connect the negative battery cable.

ENGINE OIL & FILTER

REPLACEMENT

2.8L Engine

1. Before servicing the vehicle, refer to the Precautions Section.
2. Raise and support the vehicle.
3. Place a drain pan under the oil drain plug.
4. Remove the oil pan drain plug.
5. Allow the oil to drain completely.
6. Install the oil pan drain plug and tighten to 18 ft. lbs. (25 Nm).
7. Use a 1 ¼ in. (32 mm) socket on the hex on top of the oil filter cap, or an oil filter wrench on the outside diameter of the oil filter cap. DO NOT use an open end wrench on the hex on top of the oil filter cap.
8. Remove the oil filter cap and filter.
9. Remove the filter from the cap.

To install:

10. Install the NEW oil filter to the cap.
11. Install the oil filter cap and filter.
12. Use a 1 ¼ in. (32 mm) socket on the hex on the top of the oil filter cap, or an oil filter wrench on the outside diameter of the oil filter cap. Tighten the oil filter cap until fully seated. DO NOT exceed 18 ft. lbs. (25 Nm).

✳✳ WARNING

Over tightening the oil filter cap may cause damage to the oil filter cap resulting in an oil leak.

13. Refill the engine oil.
14. Start the engine and inspect for leaks.

3.0L Engine

1. Before servicing the vehicle, refer to the Precautions Section.

2. Raise and support the vehicle.
3. Place a drain pan under the oil drain plug.
4. Remove the oil pan drain plug.
5. Allow the oil to drain completely.
6. Install the oil pan drain plug and tighten to 18 ft. lbs. (25 Nm).
7. Place the drain pan under the oil filter.
8. Remove the oil filter. Allow the oil to drain completely.

To install:

9. Lubricate a NEW oil filter gasket with clean engine oil.
10. Install the oil filter and tighten to 18 ft. lbs. (25 Nm).
11. Lower the vehicle.
12. Refill the engine oil.
13. Start the engine and inspect for leaks.

EXHAUST MANIFOLD

REMOVAL & INSTALLATION

2.8L Engine

Left Side

See Figure 50.

1. Before servicing the vehicle, refer to the Precautions Section.
2. Remove the secondary air injection pump pipe:
   a. Remove the intake manifold cover. Remove the oil cap before removing the intake manifold cover.
   b. Remove the secondary injection shutoff valve pressure sensor.
   c. Disconnect the air pump connectors.
3. Remove the secondary air injection pump hose.
4. Remove the oil level indicator tube.
5. Remove the harness bracket bolt above the exhaust manifold heat shield and reposition the engine harness.

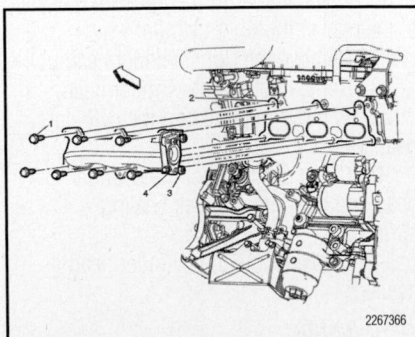

Fig. 50 Exhaust manifold (4), nuts (1), and gasket (2); exhaust turbocharger inlet pipe nuts (3)—left side

6. Remove the bolts and the left exhaust manifold heat shield.

7. Remove the secondary air injection pipe bolts from the manifold.

8. Raise and support the vehicle.

9. Remove the exhaust manifold nuts.

10. Remove the exhaust turbocharger inlet pipe nuts.

11. Remove the exhaust manifold and gasket. Discard the gasket.

12. Clean any gasket debris from the cylinder head and exhaust manifold.

To install:

13. Installation is the reverse of removal, noting the following:

  a. Tighten the exhaust manifold nuts to 15 ft. lbs. (20 Nm), working from the center out.

  b. Tighten the exhaust turbocharger inlet pipe nuts to 15 ft. lbs. (20 Nm).

  c. Tighten the exhaust manifold heat shield bolts to 84 inch lbs. (10 Nm).

Right Side

See Figure 51.

1. Before servicing the vehicle, refer to the Precautions Section.

2. Raise and support the vehicle.

3. Remove the catalytic converter.

4. Remove the right catalytic converter heat shield.

5. Disconnect the exhaust turbocharger inlet pipe, Bank 2.

6. Remove the exhaust manifold nuts.

7. Remove the exhaust manifold and gasket. Discard the gasket.

8. Clean any exhaust manifold gasket debris from the cylinder head and exhaust manifold.

To install:

9. Installation is the reverse of removal, noting the following:

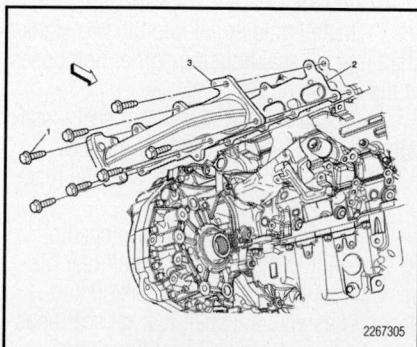

Fig. 51 Exhaust manifold (3), nuts (1), and gasket (2)—right side

  a. Tighten the exhaust manifold nuts to 15 ft. lbs. (20 Nm), working from the center out.

  b. Tighten the exhaust turbocharger inlet pipe nuts to 15 ft. lbs. (20 Nm).

  c. Tighten the exhaust manifold heat shield bolts to 84 inch lbs. (10 Nm).

3.0L Engine

See Catalytic Converter/Exhaust Manifold Removal & Installation.

INTAKE MANIFOLD

REMOVAL & INSTALLATION

See Figures 52 and 53.

1. Before servicing the vehicle, refer to the Precautions Section.

2. Remove the power steering fluid reservoir upper bracket only.

3. Remove the power brake booster vacuum check valve and hose.

4. Remove the coolant air bleed pipe.

5. Remove the intake manifold cover.

6. Disconnect and remove the Positive Crankcase Ventilation (PCV) tube (1) from the intake manifold and right camshaft cover.

7. Remove the Evaporative Emission (EVAP) hose from the intake manifold and EVAP solenoid.

8. Remove the fuel pipe shield.

9. Unclip wire harnesses as necessary.

10. Remove the intake manifold bolts.

11. Remove the intake manifold assembly.

12. Remove and discard the intake manifold gasket.

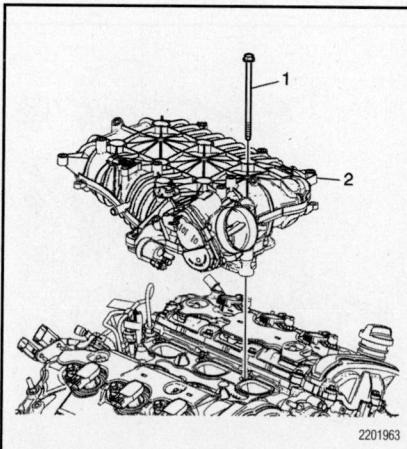

Fig. 52 Remove the intake manifold (2) and bolts (1)

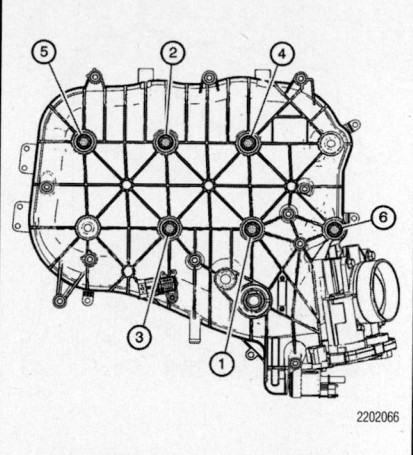

Fig. 53 Intake manifold bolt tightening sequence

To install:

13. Assemble the intake manifold if needed.

14. Install the NEW intake manifold gasket.

15. Install the intake manifold assembly.

16. Install the intake manifold bolts.

17. Tighten the intake manifold bolts in the sequence shown.

18. Tighten the intake manifold bolts in sequence to 18 ft. lbs. (25 Nm).

19. Tighten the intake manifold bolts a second pass in sequence to 18 ft. lbs. (25 Nm).

20. Remove the fuel pipe shield.

21. Connect the EVAP hose to the upper intake manifold and EVAP solenoid.

22. Connect the PCV tube assembly to the upper intake manifold and the right camshaft cover.

23. Install coolant hose.

24. Install intake manifold cover.

25. Install the coolant air bleed pipe.

26. Install the power steering fluid reservoir upper bracket.

27. Install the power brake booster vacuum check valve and hose.

OIL PAN

REMOVAL & INSTALLATION

See Figures 54 and 55.

1. Before servicing the vehicle, refer to the Precautions Section.

2. Drain the engine oil and remove the oil filter.

3. Remove the catalytic converter.

4. Remove the air conditioning (A/C) compressor bolts and reposition.

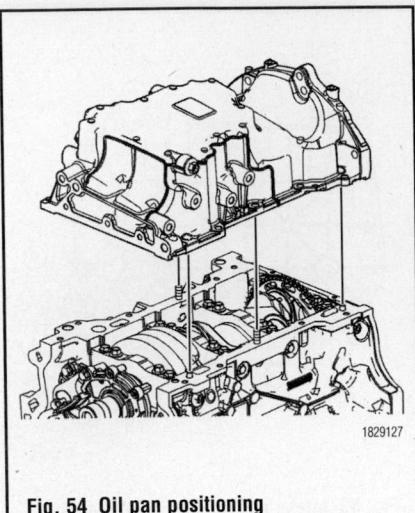

Fig. 54 Oil pan positioning

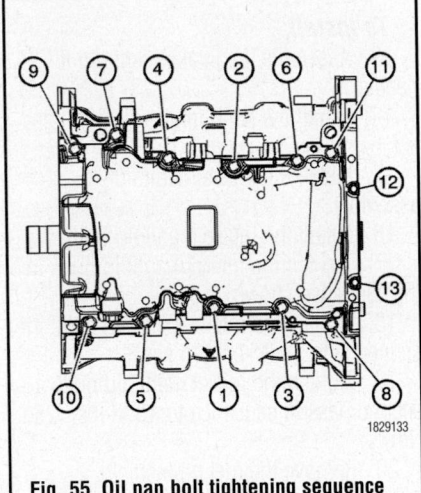

Fig. 55 Oil pan bolt tightening sequence

5. Remove the front cover.
6. Remove the oil pan to transmission bolts.
7. Remove the oil pan bolts.
8. Remove the oil pan.
9. Clean the oil pan and the engine block gasket surface.

To install:

10. Install the 8 mm guides from the EN 46109 or equivalent guide pin set into the center oil pan rail bolt hole on each side of the engine block.
11. Place a 0.118 in. (3 mm) bead of RTV sealant on the block pan rail and the crankshaft rear oil seal housing.
12. Position the oil pan onto the block.
13. Remove the guide pins from the engine block.
14. Loosely install the oil pan bolts.
15. Tighten the oil pan bolts in sequence as follows:

  a. Tighten the 8mm bolts (1–11) to 18 ft. lbs. (25 Nm).

  b. Tighten the 6mm bolts (12–13) to 89 inch lbs. (10 Nm).

16. Install the front cover.
17. Install the A/C compressor.
18. Install the catalytic converter.
19. Lower the vehicle.
20. Refill the engine oil.
21. Start the engine and check for leaks.

OIL PUMP

REMOVAL & INSTALLATION

See Figure 56.

1. Before servicing the vehicle, refer to the Precautions Section.
2. Removing the primary timing chain and crankshaft sprocket.
3. Remove the oil pump and bolts.

To install:

4. Align the oil pump drive gear with the crankshaft flats and install the oil pump to the engine block.
5. Align the pump body with the mounting holes in the cylinder block.
6. Install the oil pump mounting bolts and tighten to 18 ft. lbs. (25 Nm).
7. Install the crankshaft sprocket and timing chain.
8. Refill the engine with oil to the correct level.
9. Start the engine and check for leaks.

INSPECTION

There are no serviceable components within the oil pump. Disassemble the pump only to diagnose an oiling concern. A disassembled oil pump must be replaced. Inspect the oil pump housing, cover, relief valve components, primary camshaft drive chain lower guide, and the inner and outer drives gears for damage. If inner diameter damage

Fig. 56 Remove the oil pump and bolts

is found, ensure the crankshaft is also inspected. If debris or damage is present within the oil pump, further inspection of all of the engine components is necessary.

PISTON AND RING

POSITIONING

See Figure 57.

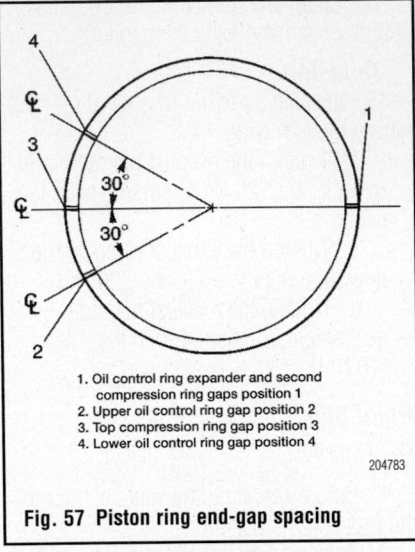

1. Oil control ring expander and second compression ring gaps position 1
2. Upper oil control ring gap position 2
3. Top compression ring gap position 3
4. Lower oil control ring gap position 4

Fig. 57 Piston ring end-gap spacing

REAR MAIN SEAL

REMOVAL & INSTALLATION

See Figures 58 through 60.

1. Before servicing the vehicle, refer to the Precautions Section.
2. Remove the flywheel.
3. Remove the oil pan, if necessary.
4. Remove the rear oil seal housing bolts.
5. Using the pry points located at the edge of the crankshaft rear main seal housing, separate the RTV sealant.
6. Remove the rear main oil seal. Discard the rear main seal housing.

To install:

7. Install guide pins into the two crankshaft rear oil seal housing corner bolt hoses of the engine block.
8. Install the crankshaft rear seal installation tool (EN-47839 tool with the EN 42183 handle, or equivalent) onto the rear of the crankshaft flange.
9. Apply a 0.118 in. (3 mm) bead of RTV sealant to the new crankshaft rear oil seal housing. There are first design and second design crankshaft rear oil seal housings. Second design oil seal housings include additional grooves for RTV sealant near the oil seal housing to oil pan interface.

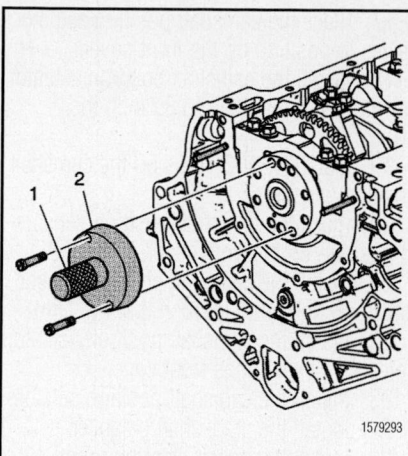

Fig. 58 Crankshaft rear seal installation tool (2) and handle (1)

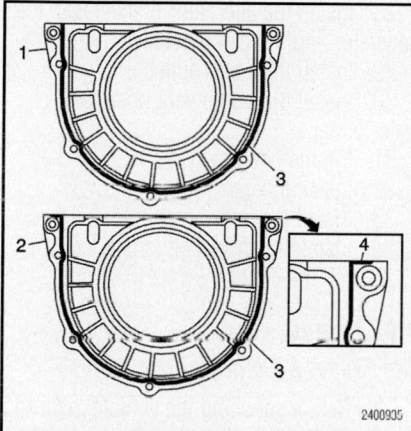

Fig. 59 First design (1) and second design (2) sealant application (3), showing additional grooves (4)

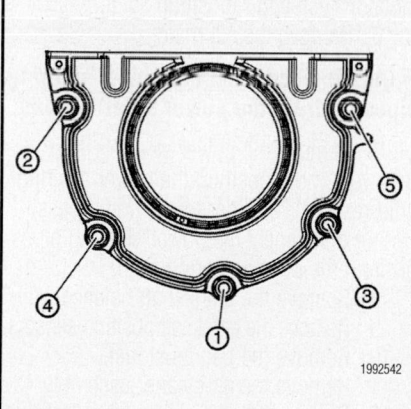

Fig. 60 Oil seal housing bolt tightening sequence

➡**Do not allow any engine oil on the area where the crankshaft rear oil seal housing is to be installed.**

10. Install the rear seal housing to the engine block.

11. Remove the guide pins and install the housing bolts. Tighten the bolts in the sequence shown to 89 inch lbs. (10 Nm).

12. Remove the rear seal installation tool from the crankshaft flange.

13. Install the oil pan, as applicable.

14. Install the flywheel.

15. Start the engine and check for leaks.

TIMING CHAIN FRONT COVER

REMOVAL & INSTALLATION

2.8L Engine

See Figures 61 through 66.

1. Before servicing the vehicle, refer to the Precautions Section.

2. Remove the intake manifold.

3. Remove the camshaft covers.

4. Drain the cooling system.

5. Remove the water outlet with the radiator hose and reposition aside.

6. Remove the alternator.

➡**Do not disconnect the power steering pipes or drain the power steering fluid.**

7. Remove the power steering fluid reservoir and reposition the power steering fluid reservoir in order to provide access. Do not disconnect the power steering pipes or drain the power steering fluid.

8. Remove the crankshaft balancer.

9. Remove the camshaft position sensors.

10. Remove the camshaft position actuator valves from the front cover.

11. Remove the engine front cover bolts that hold the engine front cover deadener into position, and remove front cover deadener.

12. Remove the remaining engine front cover bolts. There are a total of 22 M8 bolts that must be removed and 3 optional M12

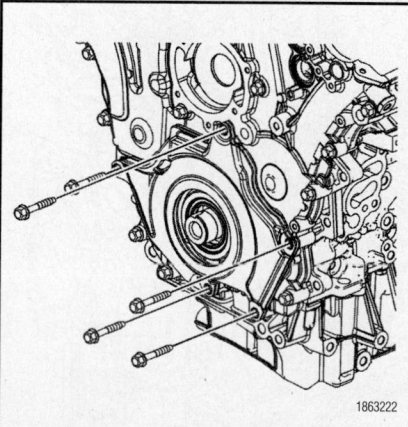

Fig. 61 Remove the engine front cover deadener bolts

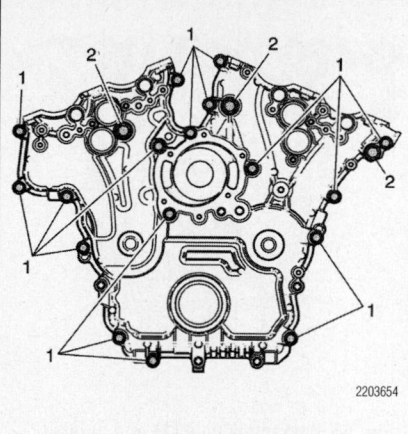

Fig. 62 Remove the remaining engine front cover bolts (1) and (2)

bolts that may need to be removed before the front cover will separate from the engine block. Engine front cover bolts in the number 2 location are model dependent and may have already been removed.

❋❋ WARNING

Do not use the jackscrew hole without first removing all engine front cover bolts. Failure to remove all engine front cover bolts before using the jackscrew hole could result in damage to components. Do not pry between the engine front cover and the camshaft position sensors or the camshaft position actuators in order to separate the RTV. Use the pry points and a bolt in the jackscrew hole in order to remove the engine front cover. Damage to the camshaft position sensors or the camshaft position actuators may occur if the camshaft position sensors or the camshaft position actuators are used to pry against in order to remove the engine front cover.

13. Loosely install a 10 x 1.5 mm bolt in the jackscrew hole.

14. Using the pry points located at the edge of the front cover and the jackscrew, separate the room temperature vulcanizing (RTV) sealant.

15. Remove the engine front cover.

To install:

16. Use the installation guide pins (EN-46109) in order to install the engine front cover:

a. Install the 0.315 in. (8 mm) guide from the installation guide pins into the cylinder block positions as shown.

b. Install the NEW engine front cover-to-cylinder block seal.

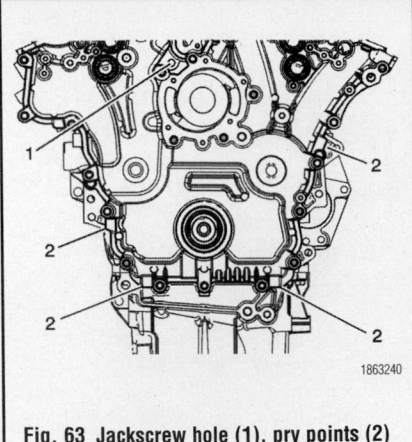

Fig. 63 Jackscrew hole (1), pry points (2)

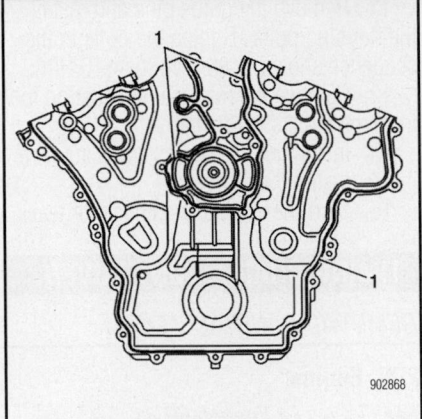

Fig. 65 Sealant application

c. Place a 0.118 in. (3 mm) bead of RTV sealant on the engine front cover as shown.

d. Place the engine front cover onto the installation guide pins and slide into position.

e. Remove the pins from the cylinder block.

f. Install the engine front cover deadener.

g. Loosely install the engine front cover bolts to hold the engine front cover deadener into position.

h. Loosely install the remaining engine front cover bolts. Engine front cover bolts in the number 23 location are model dependent and may not apply.

i. Tighten the engine front cover bolts (1–22) in sequence shown to 14 ft. lbs. (20 Nm).

j. Tighten the engine front cover bolts (1–22) a second pass in sequence an additional 60 degrees.

k. Tighten the engine front cover bolts (23) to 48 ft. lbs. (65 Nm).

17. Place the camshaft position actuator valves in position on the front cover.

18. Install the camshaft position actuator valve bolts and tighten to 89 inch lbs. (10 Nm).

19. Install NEW O-rings on the camshaft position sensor.

20. Place the camshaft position sensors in position on the front cover.

21. Install the camshaft position sensor bolts and tighten to 89 inch lbs. (10 Nm).

22. Install the camshaft position actuator solenoid valves to the front cover.

23. Install the camshaft position sensors.

24. Install the crankshaft balancer.

25. Install the power steering pump.

26. Install the power steering pump pulley.

27. Install the power steering fluid reservoir.

28. Install the alternator bracket with the generator and the belt tensioner.

29. Install the water outlet.

30. Install the purge vent hose to the water outlet.

31. Fill the cooling system.

32. Install the camshaft covers.

33. Install the intake manifold.

34. Install the drive belt tensioner.

35. Fill the cooling system.

3.0L Engine

See Figures 67 through 71.

1. Before servicing the vehicle, refer to the Precautions Section.

2. Remove the intake manifold.

3. Remove the camshaft covers.

4. Drain the cooling system.

5. Remove the water outlet with the radiator hose and reposition aside.

6. Remove the alternator.

➡ **Do not disconnect the power steering pipes or drain the power steering fluid.**

7. Remove the power steering fluid reservoir and reposition the power steering fluid reservoir in order to provide access. Do not disconnect the power steering pipes or drain the power steering fluid.

8. Remove the crankshaft balancer.

9. Remove the camshaft position sensors.

10. Remove the belt tensioner.

11. Remove the air cleaner assembly.

12. Remove the engine mounting bracket.

13. Remove the camshaft position actuator solenoid valves from the front cover.

14. Remove the engine front cover with the water pump:

a. Remove the engine front cover bolts. There are a total of 23 M8 bolts and 2 M6 bolts that must be removed, and 3 optional M12 bolts that may need

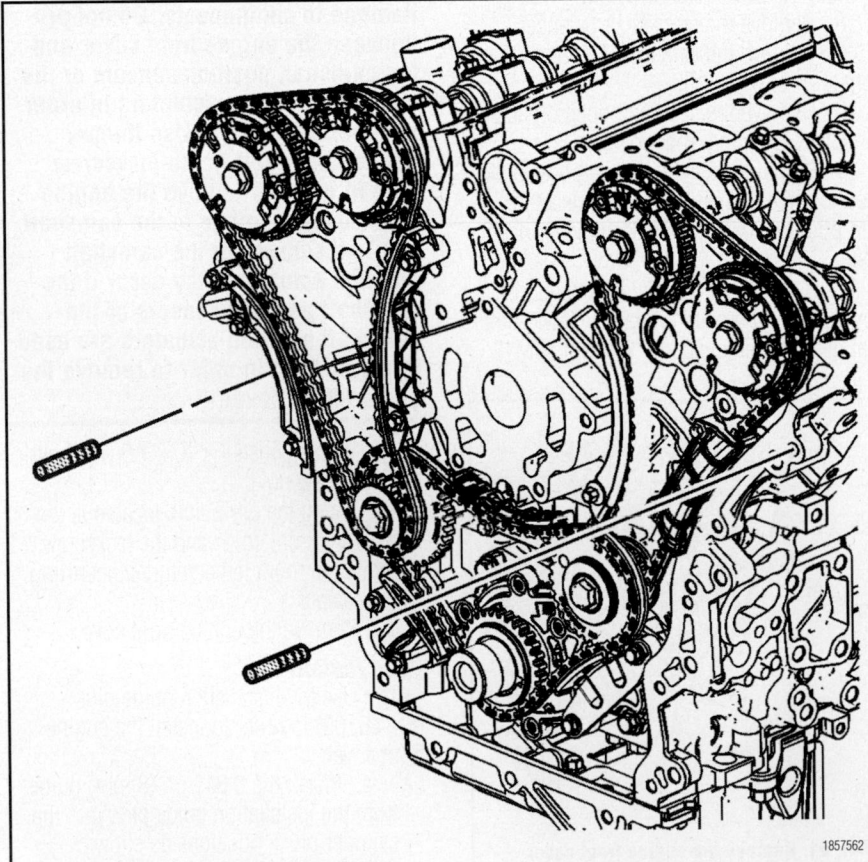

Fig. 64 Install the installation guide pins

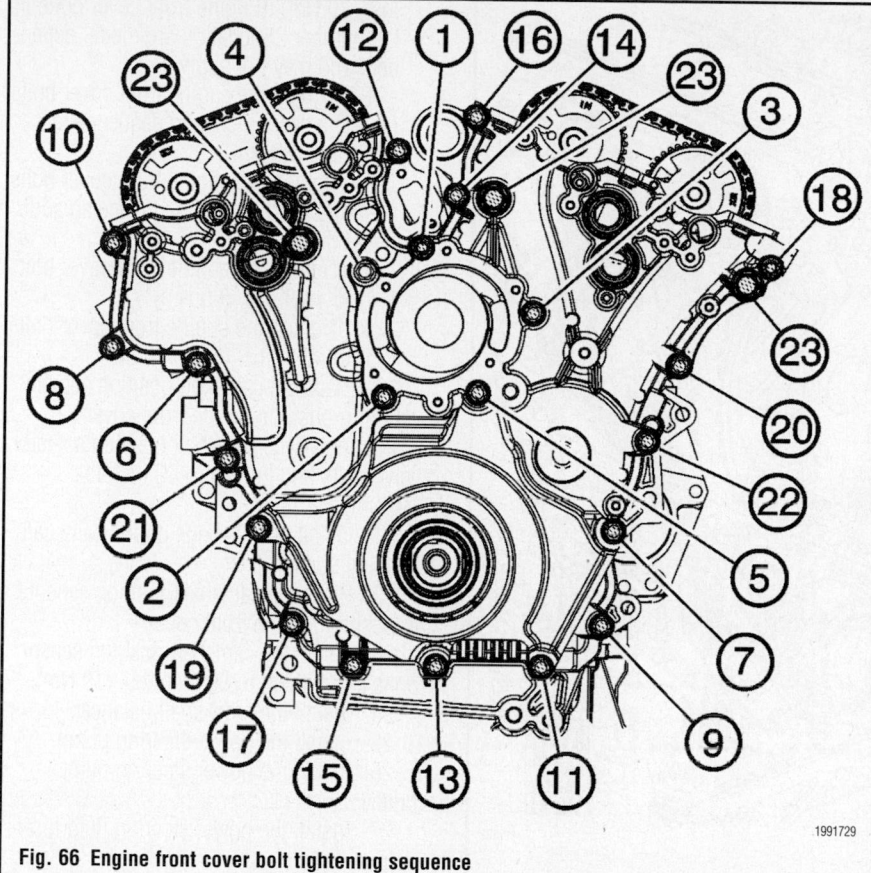

Fig. 66 Engine front cover bolt tightening sequence

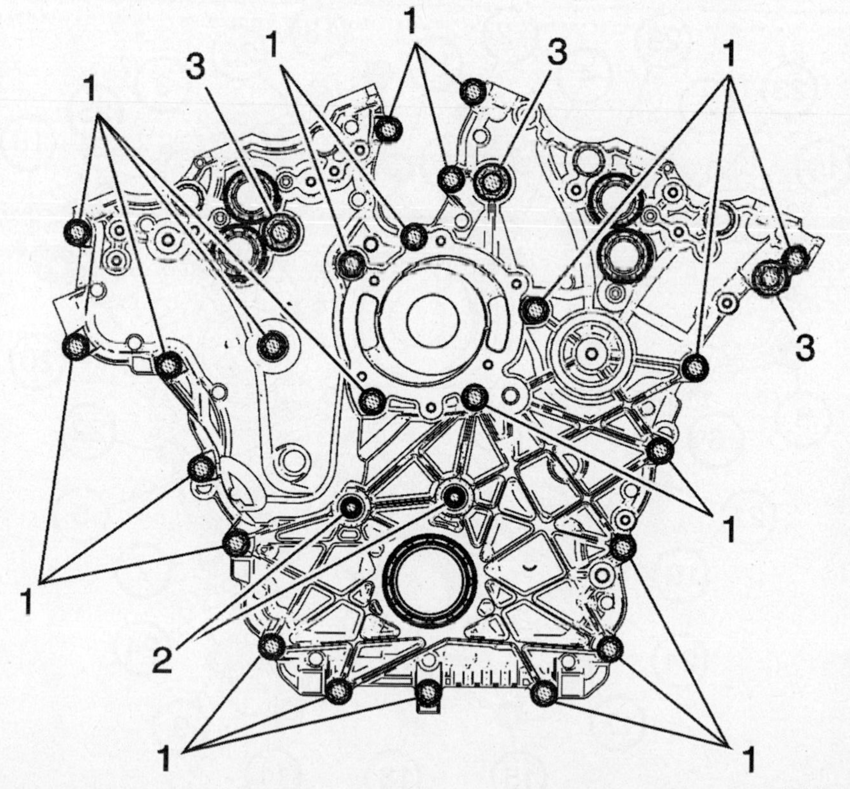

1991729

to be removed before the front cover will separate from the engine block. Engine front cover bolts in the number 3 location are model dependent and may have already been removed.

✳✳ WARNING

Do not use the jackscrew hole without first removing all engine front cover bolts. Failure to remove all engine front cover bolts before using the jackscrew hole could result in damage to components. Do not pry between the engine front cover and the camshaft position sensors or the camshaft position actuators in order to separate the RTV. Use the pry points and a bolt in the jackscrew hole in order to remove the engine front cover. Damage to the camshaft position sensors or the camshaft position actuators may occur if the camshaft position sensors or the camshaft position actuators are used to pry against in order to remove the engine front cover.

15. Loosely install a 10 x 1.5 mm bolt in the jackscrew hole.

16. Using the pry points located at the edge of the front cover and the jackscrew, separate the room temperature vulcanizing (RTV) sealant.

17. Remove the engine front cover.

To install:

18. Use the installation guide pins (EN-46109) in order to install the engine front cover:

a. Install the 0.315 in. (8 mm) guide from the installation guide pins into the cylinder block positions as shown.

Fig. 67 Engine front cover M8 bolts (1) and M6 bolts (2); M12 bolts (3) are model dependent and may have already been removed

2220323

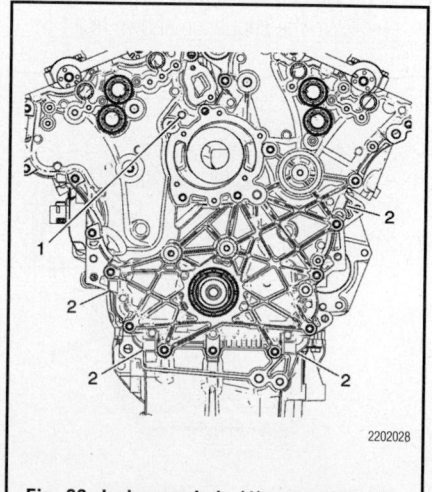

Fig. 68 Jackscrew hole (1), pry points (2)

2202028

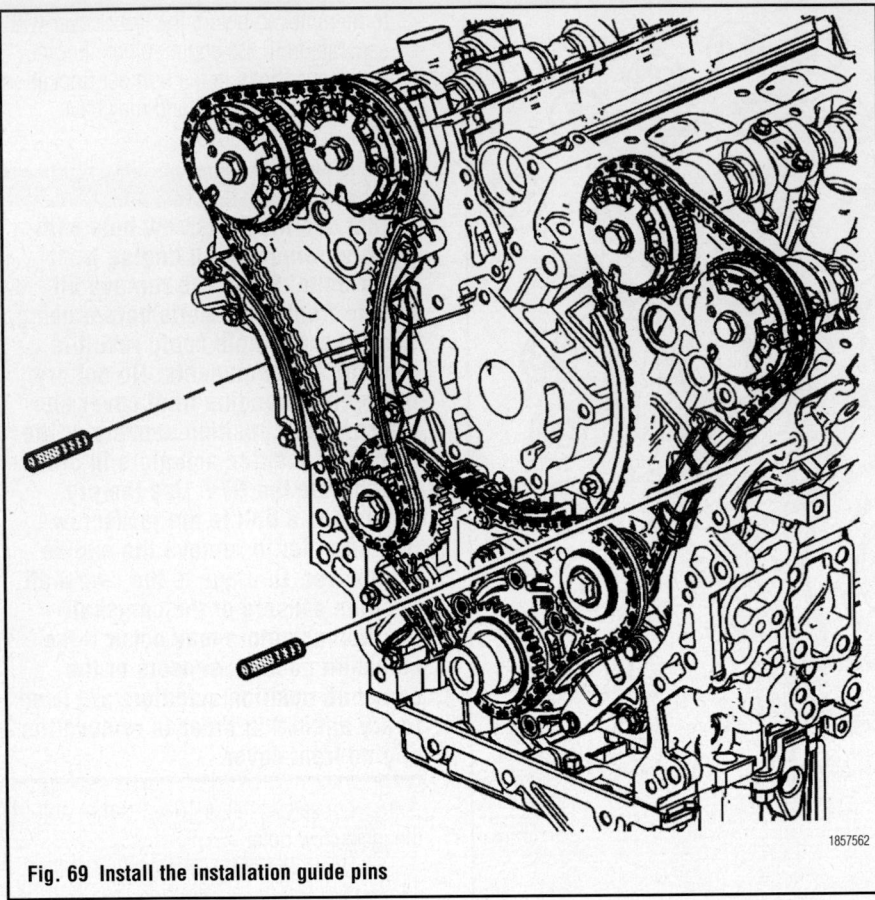

Fig. 69 Install the installation guide pins

lbs. (20 Nm). (Engine front cover bolts in the number 25 location are model dependent and may not apply.):

h. Tighten the engine front cover bolts (1–23) a second pass in sequence to 14 ft. lbs. (20 Nm).

i. Tighten the engine front cover bolts (1–23) a third pass in sequence an additional 60 degrees.

j. Tighten the engine front cover bolts (24) to 48 ft. lbs. (65 Nm).

k. Tighten the engine front cover bolts (25) to 48 ft. lbs. (65 Nm).

19. Place the camshaft position actuator valves in position on the front cover.

20. Install the camshaft position actuator valve bolts and tighten to 89 inch lbs. (10 Nm).

21. Install new O-rings on the camshaft position sensor.

22. Place the camshaft position sensors in position on the front cover.

23. Install the camshaft position sensor bolts and tighten to 89 inch lbs. (10 Nm).

24. Install the crankshaft balancer.

25. Install the power steering pump.

26. Install the power steering pump pulley.

27. Install the power steering fluid reservoir.

b. Install the NEW engine front cover-to-cylinder block seal.

c. Place a 0.118 in. (3 mm) bead of RTV sealant on the engine front cover as shown.

d. Place the engine front cover onto the installation guide pins and slide into position.

e. Remove the pins from the cylinder block.

f. Hand start all of the engine front cover bolts.

g. Tighten the engine front cover bolts (1–23) in the sequence shown to 14 ft.

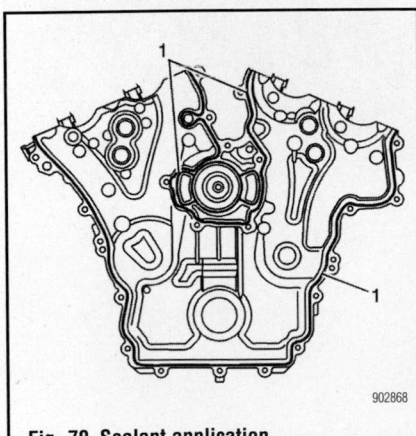

Fig. 70 Sealant application

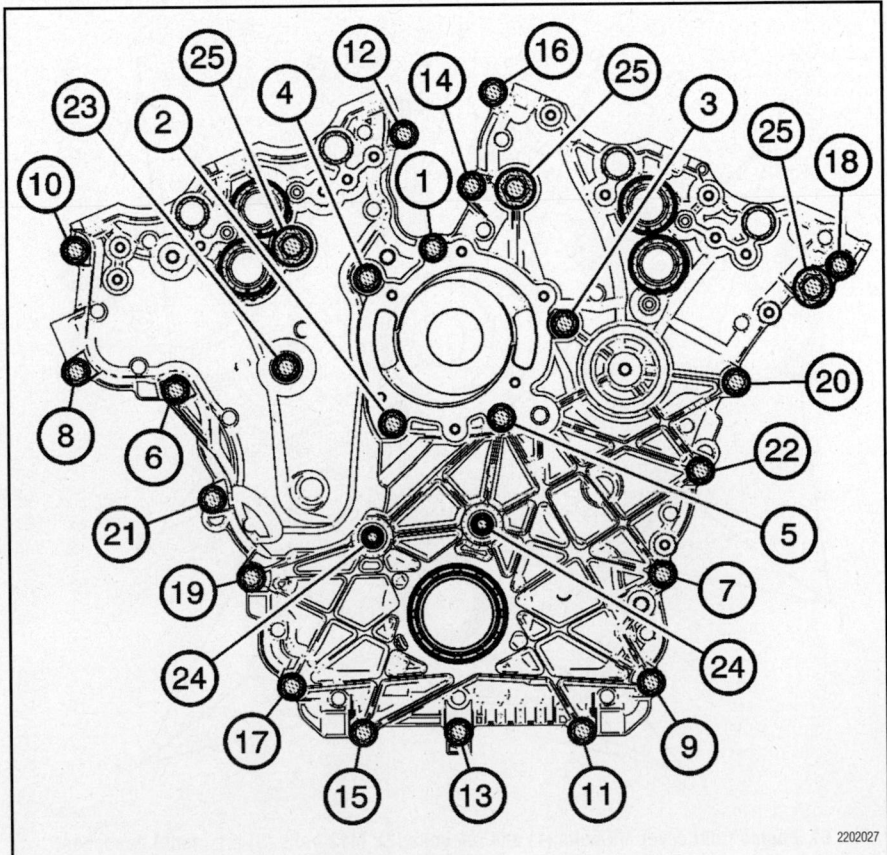

Fig. 71 Engine front cover bolt tightening sequence

28. Install the alternator bracket with the alternator and the belt tensioner.

29. Install the A/C compressor and power steering belt tensioner.

30. Install the accessory drive belts.

31. Install the water outlet.

32. Install the purge vent hose to the water outlet.

33. Refill the engine cooling system to the correct level.

34. Install the camshaft covers.

35. Install the intake manifold.

36. Install the engine cover.

37. Start the engine and check for leaks.

TIMING CHAIN & SPROCKETS

REMOVAL & INSTALLATION

See Figures 72 through 82.

1. Before servicing the vehicle, refer to the Precautions Section.

2. Remove the timing chain front cover.

3. Remove the right secondary camshaft drive chain tensioner bolts and remove the tensioner. Remove and discard the gasket.

4. Remove the right secondary camshaft drive chain shoe bolt and remove the drive chain shoe.

5. Remove the right secondary camshaft drive chain guide bolts and remove the right secondary drive chain guide.

6. Remove the right secondary camshaft drive chain from the right camshaft position actuators and the right camshaft intermediate drive chain idler sprocket.

7. Remove the primary camshaft drive chain tensioner bolts and remove the primary drive chain tensioner. Remove and discard the gasket.

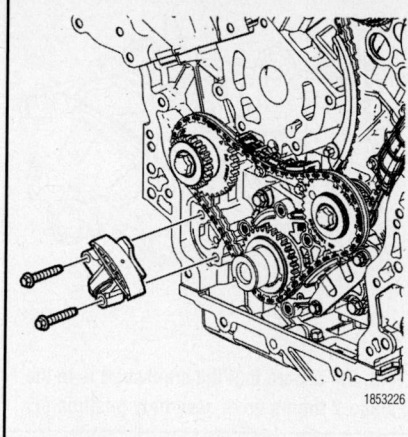

Fig. 73 Remove the primary camshaft drive chain tensioner

8. Remove the primary camshaft drive chain upper guide bolts and remove the upper guides.

9. Remove the primary camshaft timing chain.

To install:

10. Ensure that the crankshaft is in the stage one timing drive assembly position.

11. Install the primary timing chain.

a. Wrap the primary camshaft drive chain around the large sprockets of each camshaft intermediate drive chain idler and the crankshaft sprocket.

b. The left camshaft intermediate drive chain idler timing mark will align with a timing camshaft drive chain link.

c. The right camshaft intermediate drive chain idler timing mark will align with a timing camshaft drive chain link.

d. The crankshaft sprocket timing mark will align with a timing camshaft drive chain link.

e. Ensure all the timing marks are

properly aligned with the timing camshaft drive chain links.

12. Install the upper primary camshaft drive chain guides. Tighten the bolts to 18 ft. lbs. (25 Nm).

13. Install the primary camshaft drive chain tensioner as follows:

a. Use the tensioner tool (J-45027 or equivalent) to reset the primary camshaft drive chain tensioner plunger.

b. Install the plunger into the tensioner body.

c. Compress the plunger into the body and lock the tensioner by inserting the retraction pins (EN-46112 or equivalent) into the access hole in the side of the tensioner body.

d. Slowly release pressure on the tensioner. The tensioner should remain compressed.

e. Install a new gasket to the drive chain tensioner.

f. Place the primary camshaft drive chain tensioner into position and loosely install the bolts to the block.

g. Verify the proper placement of the tensioner gasket tab.

h. Tighten the tensioner bolts to 44 inch lbs. (5 Nm) and then retighten to 18 ft. lbs. (25 Nm).

i. Release the tensioner by pulling out the retraction pins and unlocking the tensioner plunger.

j. Verify the primary and left secondary camshaft drive chain timing mark alignments.

k. Remove the camshaft retaining tool (EN 48383-1 or equivalent) from the rear of the left camshafts.

l. Using the crankshaft rotation socket (EN-48589 or equivalent), rotate the crankshaft and crankshaft sprocket from

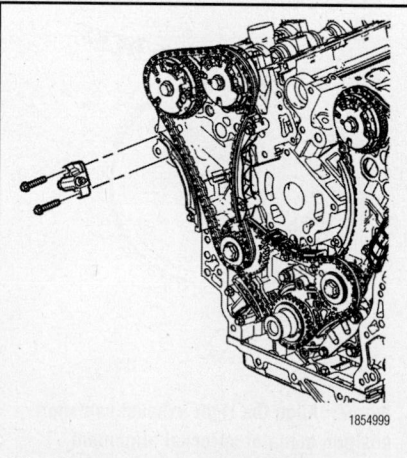

Fig. 72 Remove the right secondary camshaft drive chain tensioner

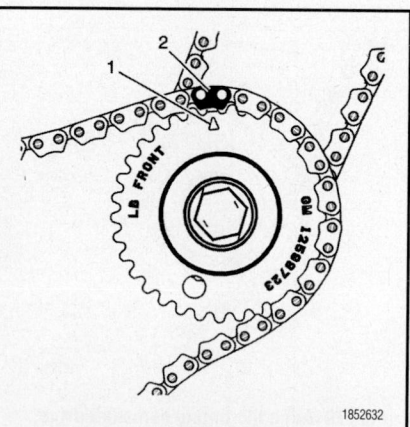

Fig. 74 The left camshaft intermediate drive chain idler timing mark (1) will align with a timing camshaft drive chain link (2)

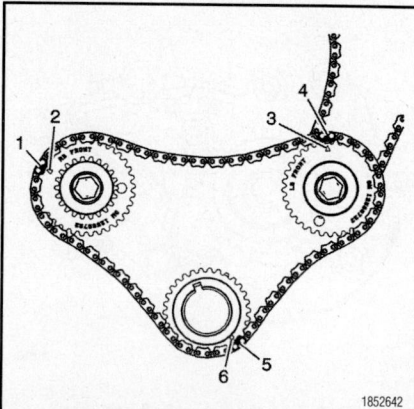

Fig. 75 Ensure all the timing marks (2, 3, and 6) are properly aligned with the timing camshaft drive chain links (1, 4, and 5)

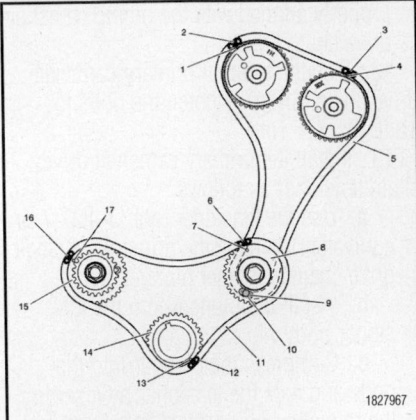

Fig. 76 Primary and left secondary camshaft drive chain timing mark alignments, stage one

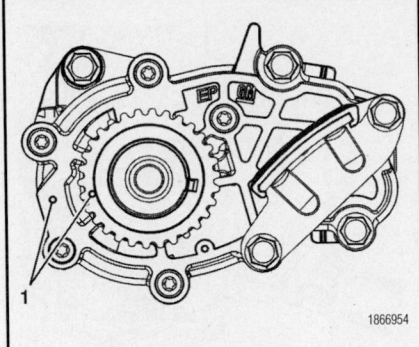

Fig. 78 Ensure that the crankshaft is in the stage 2 timing drive assembly position (1)

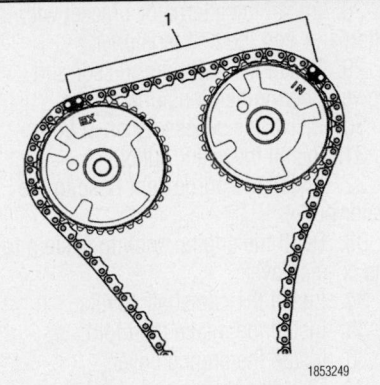

Fig. 80 Ensure there are 10 links (1) between the timing camshaft drive chain links for the camshaft position actuator sprockets

the stage 1 alignment position to the stage 2 alignment position, 115 crankshaft degrees, in order to install the right secondary camshaft drive chain components.

m. Install the camshaft retaining tool (EN 48383-2 or equivalent) onto the rear of the left camshafts.

n. Install the camshaft retaining tool (EN 48383-3 or equivalent) onto the rear of the right camshafts.

14. Ensure that the crankshaft is in the stage 2 timing drive assembly position.

15. Install the right bank secondary camshaft drive chain.

a. Place the secondary camshaft drive chain around the right camshaft intermediate drive chain idler outer sprocket, aligning the timing camshaft drive chain link with the alignment access hole made in the right camshaft intermediate drive chain idler inner sprocket.

b. Wrap the secondary camshaft drive chain around both right actuator drive sprockets.

c. Ensure there are 10 links between the timing camshaft drive chain links for the camshaft position actuator sprockets.

d. Align the right exhaust camshaft position actuator sprocket alignment triangle mark with the timing camshaft drive chain link.

e. Align the right intake camshaft position actuator sprocket alignment triangle mark with the timing camshaft drive chain link.

f. There will be 22 links between the right camshaft intermediate drive chain idler timing camshaft drive chain link and each right camshaft position actuator sprocket timing camshaft drive chain link.

16. Install the right secondary camshaft drive chain guide. Tighten the bolts to 18 ft. lbs. (25 Nm).

17. Install the right secondary camshaft drive chain shoe. Tighten the bolt to 18 ft. lbs. (25 Nm).

18. Install the right secondary camshaft drive chain tensioner as follows:

a. Use the tensioner tool (J-45027 or equivalent) to reset the primary camshaft drive chain tensioner plunger.

b. Install the plunger into the tensioner body

c. Compress the plunger into the body and lock the tensioner by inserting the retraction pins (EN-46112 or equivalent) into the access hole in the side of the tensioner body.

d. Slowly release pressure on the tensioner. The tensioner should remain compressed.

e. Install a new gasket to the drive chain tensioner.

f. Place the primary camshaft drive chain tensioner into position and loosely install the bolts to the block.

g. Verify the proper placement of the right secondary camshaft drive chain tensioner gasket tab.

h. Tighten the tensioner bolts to 44 inch lbs. (5 Nm) and then retighten to 18 ft. lbs. (25 Nm).

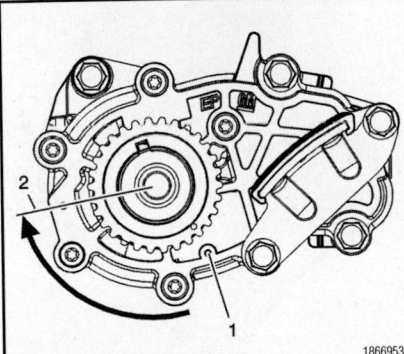

Fig. 77 Rotate the crankshaft and crankshaft sprocket from the stage 1 alignment position (1) to the stage 2 alignment position (2)

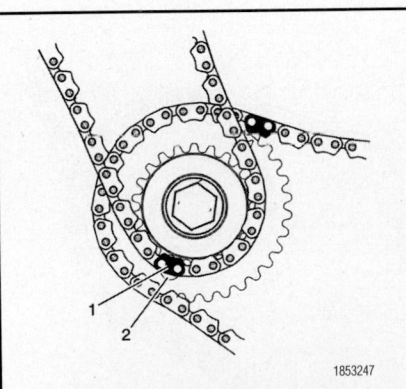

Fig. 79 Align the timing camshaft drive chain link (1) with the alignment access hole (2) made in the right camshaft intermediate drive chain idler inner sprocket

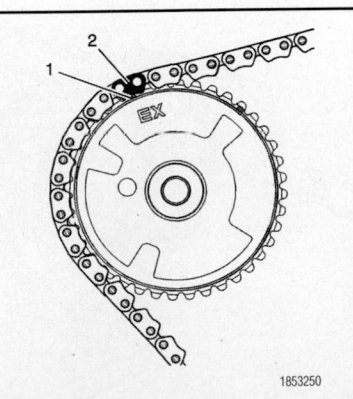

Fig. 81 Align the right exhaust camshaft position actuator sprocket alignment triangle mark (1) with the timing camshaft drive chain link (2)

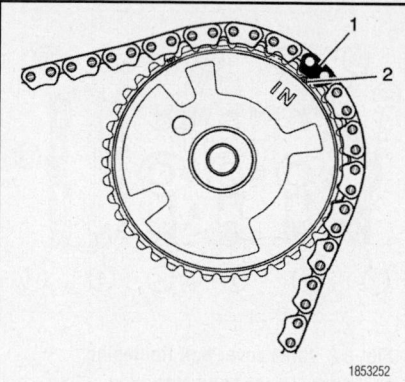

Fig. 82 Align the right intake camshaft position actuator sprocket alignment triangle mark (2) with the timing camshaft drive chain link (1)

i. Release the tensioner by pulling out the retraction pins and unlocking the tensioner plunger.

❈❈ WARNING

Ensure that all timing chain tensioners are completely released. A timing chain tensioner that is not properly released can lead to serious engine damage.

19. Install the timing chain front cover.

TURBOCHARGER

REMOVAL & INSTALLATION

2.8L Engines
See Figure 83.

❈❈ WARNING

If a turbocharger has failed, clean any turbocharger debris or excessive oil from the charge air cooler system before installing the new turbocharger. Failure to clean debris from the charge air cooler system will cause severe turbocharger and engine damage upon startup. Failure to clean excessive oil from the charge air cooler system may cause an engine runaway condition on startup, resulting in severe engine damage.

1. Before servicing the vehicle, refer to the Precautions Section.
2. Disconnect the negative battery cable.
3. Remove the air cleaner outlet duct.
4. Disconnect the turbocharger oil feed pipe at the turbo.
5. Disconnect the turbocharger coolant feed pipe at the turbo.

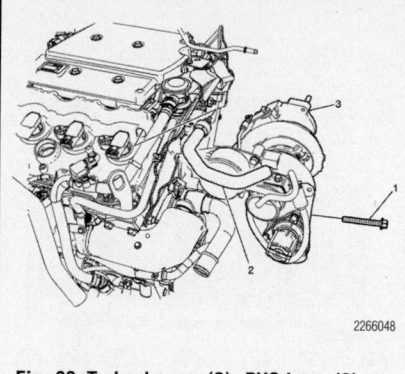

Fig. 83 Turbocharger (3), PVC hose (2), and bolt (1)

6. Disconnect the turbocharger coolant return pipe at the turbo.
7. Disconnect the turbocharger oil return pipe at the turbo.
8. Remove the radiator outlet pipe.
9. Remove the left side exhaust turbocharger inlet pipe:
   a. Remove the radiator outlet pipe.
   b. Remove the left side exhaust manifold heat shield.
10. Disconnect the right side exhaust turbocharger inlet pipe.
11. Remove the exhaust manifold/catalytic converter.
12. Disconnect PCV hose from the camshaft cover.
13. Disconnect vacuum hoses as necessary.
14. Transfer parts as necessary.

To install:

15. Installation is the reverse of removal, noting the following:
   a. Tighten the turbocharger bolt to 48 ft. lbs. (65 Nm).
   b. Tighten the left side exhaust turbocharger inlet pipe nuts to 15 ft. lbs. (20 Nm).
   c. Install NEW engine oil and a NEW oil filter.

VALVE COVERS

REMOVAL & INSTALLATION

2.8L Engine
See Figures 84 and 85.

1. Before servicing the vehicle, refer to the Precautions Section.
2. Disconnect the negative battery cable.
3. Remove the ignition coils.
4. Disconnect and remove the engine harness from the valve cover.
5. Remove the upper intake manifold.

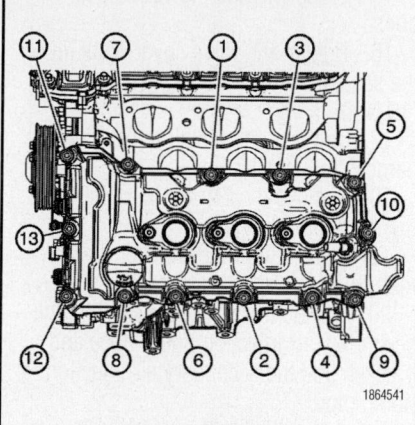

Fig. 84 Valve cover bolt tightening sequence—left-hand side

6. For the left valve cover, remove the secondary air injection pump hose and bracket; and the secondary air injection pump pipe.
7. Remove the positive crankcase ventilation tube (valve cover to turbocharger).
8. Remove the valve cover bolts.
9. Remove the valve cover from the cylinder head.
10. Clean the mating surfaces of the cylinder head and the valve cover.
11. Install the spark plug tube seal guide (EN-46101) onto the spark plug tubes.

To install:

12. Install new valve cover bolt grommets prior to installing the valve cover bolts.
13. Place a bead 0.3150 in. (8 mm) in diameter by 0.1575 in. (4 mm) in height of RTV sealant, on the engine front cover split lines.
14. Place the valve cover into position onto the cylinder head.

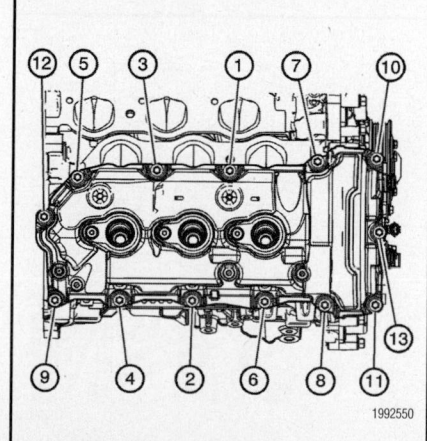

Fig. 85 Valve cover bolt tightening sequence—right-hand side

15. Loosely install the valve cover bolts.

16. Tighten the valve cover bolts in the sequence shown to 89 inch lbs. (10 Nm).

17. Connect and install the engine harness to the valve cover.

18. Remove the EN-46101 guide from the spark plug tubes.

19. Install the upper intake manifold.

20. For the left valve cover, install the secondary air injection pump hose and bracket, and the secondary air injection pump pipe.

21. Install the ignition coils.

22. Install the positive crankcase ventilation hose/pipe/tube.

3.0L Engine

See Figures 86 and 87.

1. Before servicing the vehicle, refer to the Precautions Section.

2. Disconnect the negative battery cable.

3. Remove the ignition coils.

4. Disconnect and remove the engine harness from the valve cover.

5. Remove the intake manifold.

6. Remove the valve cover bolts.

7. Remove the valve cover from the cylinder head.

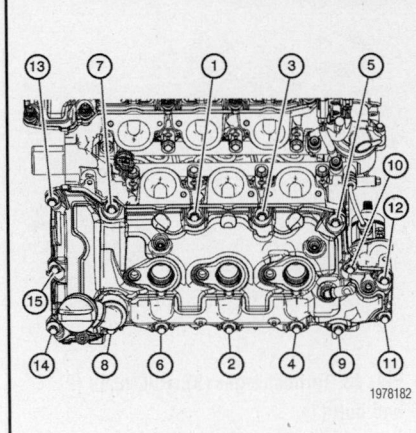

Fig. 86 Valve cover bolt tightening sequence—left-hand side

8. Clean the mating surfaces of the cylinder head and the valve cover.

9. Install the spark plug tube seal guide (EN-46101) onto the spark plug tubes.

To install:

10. Install new valve cover bolt grommets prior to installing the valve cover bolts.

11. Place a bead 0.3150 in. (8 mm) in diameter by 0.1575 in. (4 mm) in height of RTV sealant, on the engine front cover split lines.

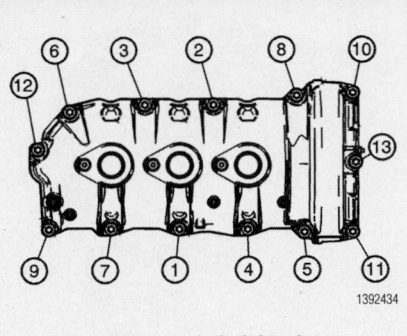

Fig. 87 Valve cover bolt tightening sequence—right-hand side

12. Place the valve cover into position onto the cylinder head.

13. Loosely install the valve cover bolts.

14. Tighten the valve cover bolts in the sequence shown to 89 inch lbs. (10 Nm).

15. Connect and install the engine harness to the valve cover.

16. Remove the EN-46101 guide from the spark plug tubes.

17. Install the ignition coils.

VALVE LASH

ADJUSTMENT

The valve lash is not adjustable.

ENGINE PERFORMANCE & EMISSION CONTROLS

CAMSHAFT POSITION (CMP) SENSOR

LOCATION

See Figures 88 through 91.

1. Refer to the accompanying illustrations.

REMOVAL & INSTALLATION

1. Disconnect the negative battery cable.

2. For Bank 1 sensors, remove the air cleaner assembly.

3. For Bank 2 sensors, remove engine mounting bracket.

4. Disconnect the electrical connector.

5. Remove the CMP sensor bolt.

6. Remove the CMP sensor.

To install:

7. Installation is the reverse of removal. Tighten the mounting bolt to 89 inch lbs. (10 Nm).

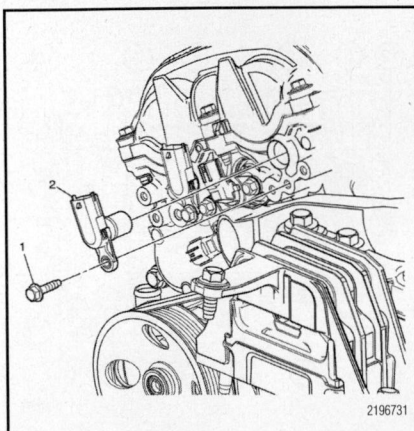

Fig. 88 Camshaft Position (CMP) Sensor—Bank 1, Intake

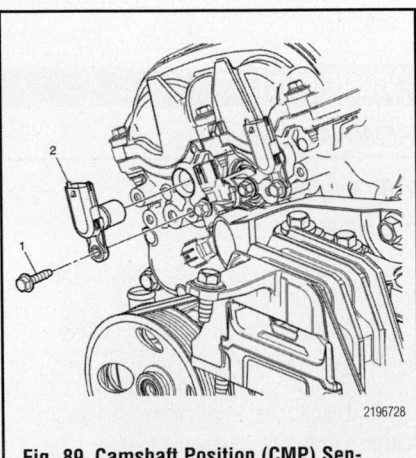

Fig. 89 Camshaft Position (CMP) Sensor—Bank 1, Exhaust

Fig. 90 Camshaft Position (CMP) Sensor—Bank 2, Intake

Fig. 91 Camshaft Position (CMP) Sensor—Bank 2, Exhaust

CRANKSHAFT POSITION (CKP) SENSOR

LOCATION

See Figure 92.

1. Refer to the accompanying illustration.

REMOVAL & INSTALLATION

1. Disconnect the negative battery cable.
2. Raise and safely support the vehicle.
3. Remove the exhaust manifold lower heat shield, as necessary.
4. Disconnect the crankshaft position (CKP) electrical connector.
5. Remove the crankshaft sensor bolt.
6. Remove the crankshaft sensor.

To install:

7. Install the Crankshaft Position (CKP)

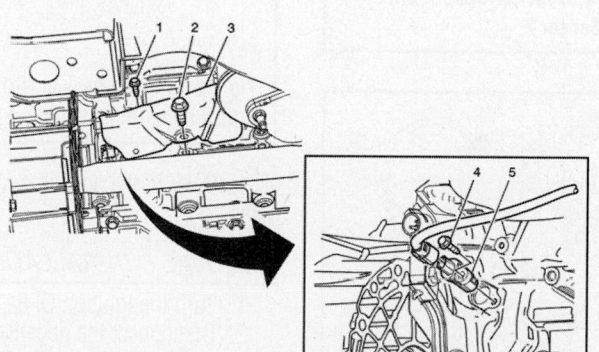

Fig. 92 Crankshaft Position (CKP) Sensor (5), bolts (1, 2, 4), and exhaust manifold lower heat shield (3)

sensor and tighten the bolt to 89 inch lbs. (10 Nm).
8. Connect the CKP electrical connector.
9. Install the exhaust manifold lower heat shield, as applicable.
10. Lower the vehicle.

ELECTRONIC CONTROL MODULE (ECM)

LOCATION

See Figure 93.

1. Refer to the accompanying illustration.

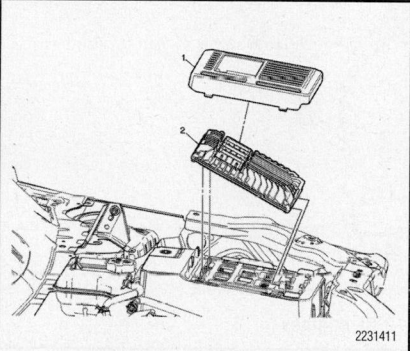

Fig. 93 Electronic Control Module (ECM) (1)

REMOVAL & INSTALLATION

1. Using a scan tool, retrieve the percentage of remaining engine oil and automatic transmission fluid life. Record the remaining engine oil and automatic transmission fluid life.
2. Turn the ignition OFF
3. Disconnect the negative battery cable.

4. Unlock and disconnect the engine wiring harness electrical connectors from the ECM.
5. Remove the ECM.

To install:

6. Install the ECM.
7. Connect the negative battery cable.
8. Using a scan tool, program the ECM, if required.
9. Turn OFF the ignition for at least 5 seconds after the programming event is complete.

ENGINE COOLANT TEMPERATURE (ECT) SENSOR

LOCATION

See Figures 94 and 95.

1. Refer to the accompanying illustrations.

REMOVAL & INSTALLATION

2.8L Engine

1. Turn the ignition to the OFF position.
2. Disconnect the negative battery cable.
3. Remove the intake manifold cover.
4. Remove the oil level indicator tube.
5. Partially drain the cooling system.
6. Disconnect the ECT sensor harness connector.
7. Remove the coolant temperature sensor.

To install:

8. Installation is the reverse order of removal. Tighten the retaining bolt to 16 ft. lbs. (22 Nm).

3.0L Engine

1. Turn the ignition to the OFF position.
2. Disconnect the negative battery cable.
3. Reposition the sensor heat shield.
4. Disconnect the ECT sensor harness connector.
5. Remove the coolant temperature sensor.

To install:

6. Installation is the reverse order of removal. Tighten the retaining bolt to 15 ft. lbs. (20 Nm).

HEATED OXYGEN SENSOR (HO2S)

LOCATION

See Figures 96 through 101.

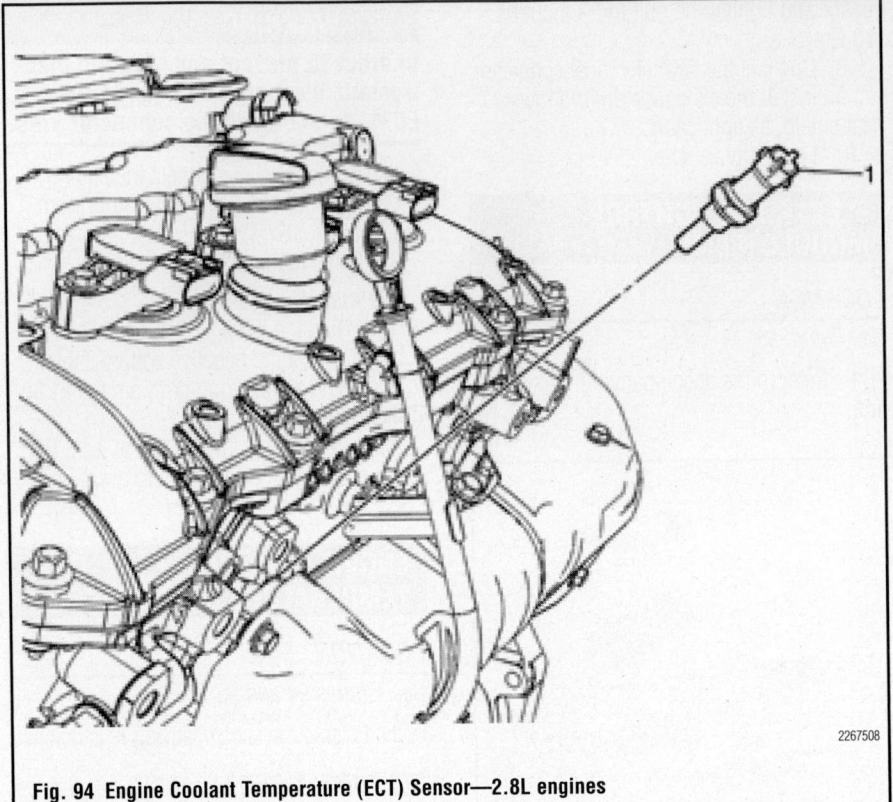

Fig. 94 Engine Coolant Temperature (ECT) Sensor—2.8L engines

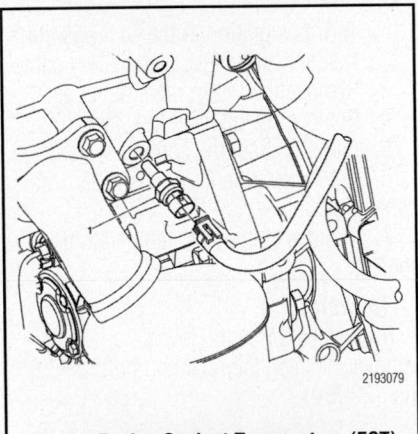

Fig. 95 Engine Coolant Temperature (ECT) Sensor—3.0L engines

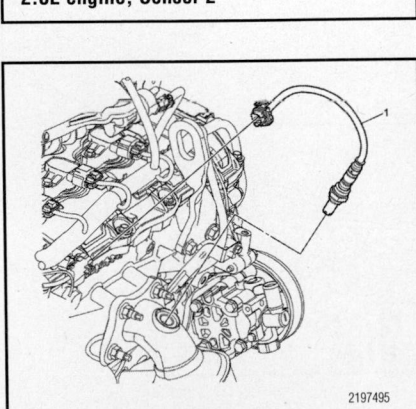

Fig. 97 Heated Oxygen (HO2S) Sensor— 2.8L engine, Sensor 2

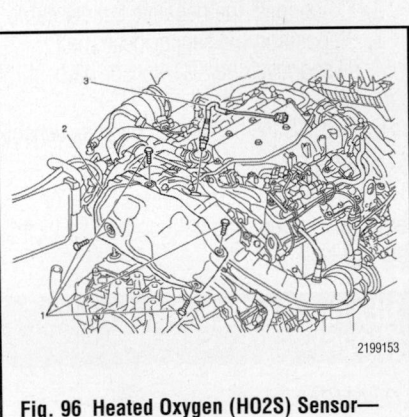

Fig. 96 Heated Oxygen (HO2S) Sensor— 2.8L engine, Sensor 1

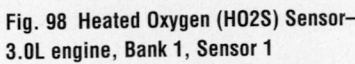

Fig. 98 Heated Oxygen (HO2S) Sensor— 3.0L engine, Bank 1, Sensor 1

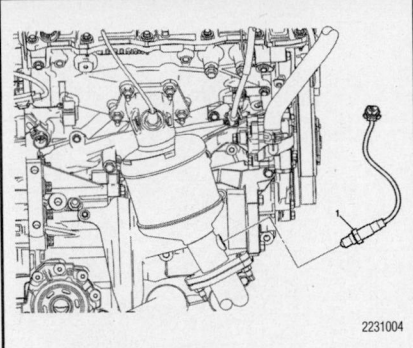

Fig. 99 Heated Oxygen (HO2S) Sensor— 3.0L engine, Bank 1, Sensor 2

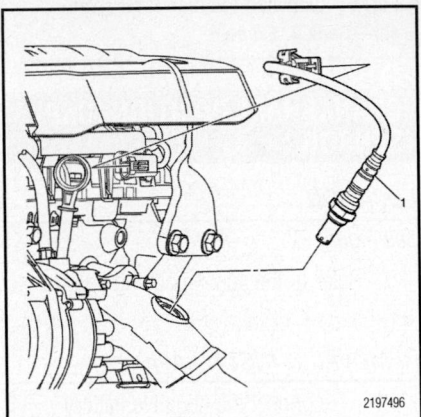

Fig. 100 Heated Oxygen (HO2S) Sensor— 3.0L engine, Bank 2, Sensor 1

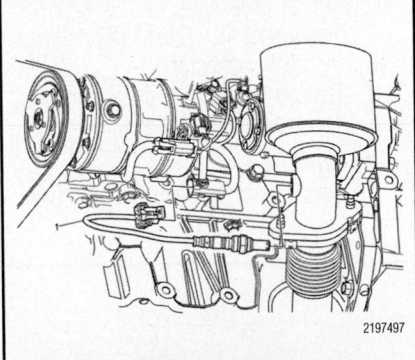

Fig. 101 Heated Oxygen (HO2S) Sensor— 3.0L engine, Bank 2, Sensor 2

1. Refer to the accompanying illustrations.

REMOVAL & INSTALLATION

1. Turn the ignition OFF.
2. Disconnect the negative battery cable.
3. For Sensor 1, remove the catalytic converter front heat shield.
4. For Sensor 2, remove the intake manifold cover.
5. Disconnect the Heated Oxygen Sensor (HO2S) electrical connector.

6. Remove any wire harness retainers and note the wire harness routing for reassembly.

7. Remove the right side catalytic converter, if necessary.

8. Remove the HO2S.

To install:

➡A special anti-seize compound is used in the HO2S threads. The compound consists of liquid graphite and glass beads. The graphite tends to burn away, but the glass beads remain, making the sensor easier to remove. New, or service replacement sensors already have the compound applied to the threads. If the sensor is removed from an exhaust component and if for any reason the sensor is to be reinstalled, the threads must have anti-seize compound applied before reinstallation

9. Installation is the reverse order of removal. If reinstalling the old sensor, coat the threads with anti-seize compound. Tighten the HO2S to 31 ft. lbs. (42 Nm).

INTAKE AIR TEMPERATURE (IAT) SENSOR

LOCATION

See Mass Air Flow (MAF) Sensor.

REMOVAL & INSTALLATION

See Mass Air Flow (MAF) Sensor.

KNOCK SENSOR (KS)

LOCATION

See Figures 102 and 103.

1. Refer to the accompanying illustrations.

REMOVAL & INSTALLATION

Bank 1

1. Before servicing the vehicle, refer to the Precautions Section.

2. Disconnect the negative battery cable.

3. If equipped with AWD, remove the right side catalytic converter.

4. Raise and safely support the vehicle.

5. Remove the exhaust manifold lower heat shield.

6. Remove the Knock Sensor (KS) electrical connector.

7. Remove the KS bolt.

8. Remove the KS.

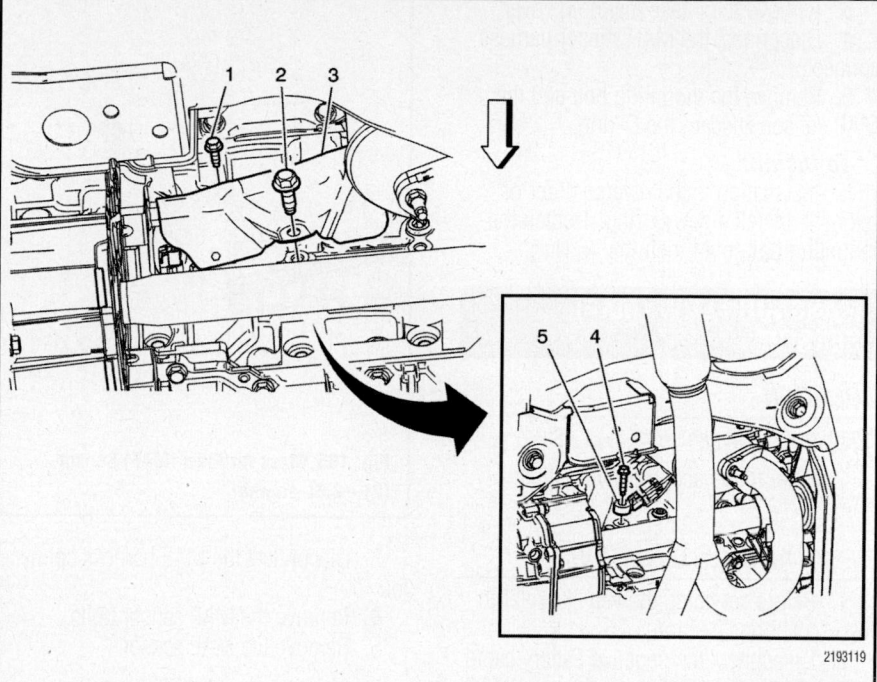

Fig. 102 Knock Sensor (5), bolts (1, 2, 4), and exhaust manifold lower heat shield (3)—Bank 1

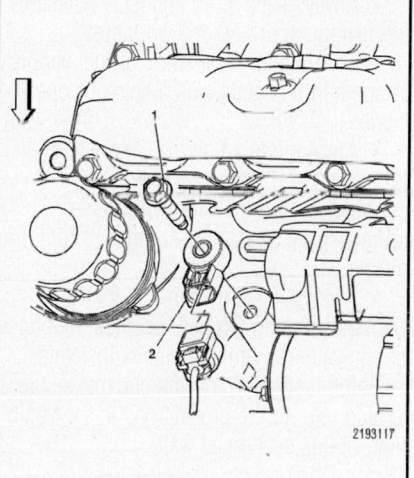

Fig. 103 Knock Sensor (KS)—Bank 2

To install:

9. Installation is the reverse order of removal. Tighten the KS bolts to 17 ft. lbs. (23 Nm).

Bank 2

1. Before servicing the vehicle, refer to the Precautions Section.

2. Disconnect the negative battery cable.

3. Remove the Knock Sensor (KS) electrical connector.

4. Remove the KS bolt.

5. Remove the KS.

To install:

6. Installation is the reverse order of removal. Tighten to 17 ft. lbs. (23 Nm).

MANIFOLD ABSOLUTE PRESSURE (MAP) SENSOR

LOCATION

See Figure 104.

1. Refer to the accompanying illustration.

REMOVAL & INSTALLATION

3.0L Engine

1. Before servicing the vehicle, refer to the Precautions Section.

2. Disconnect the negative battery cable.

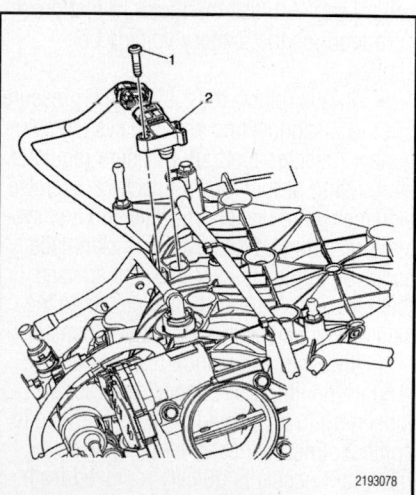

Fig. 104 Manifold Absolute Pressure (MAP) Sensor (2)—3.0L engines

3. Remove the intake manifold cover.

4. Disconnect the MAP sensor harness connector.

5. Remove the mounting bolt and the MAP sensor. Discard the O-ring.

To install:

6. Installation is the reverse order of removal. Install a new O-ring. Tighten the mounting bolt to 44 inch lbs. (5 Nm).

MASS AIR FLOW (MAF) SENSOR

LOCATION

See Figures 105 and 106.

1. Refer to the accompanying illustrations.

REMOVAL & INSTALLATION

1. Before servicing the vehicle, refer to the Precautions Section.

2. Disconnect the negative battery cable.

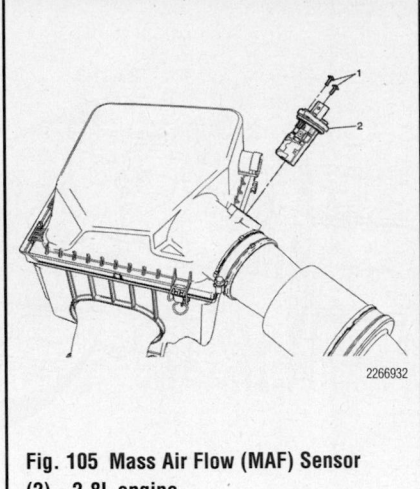

Fig. 105 Mass Air Flow (MAF) Sensor (2)—2.8L engine

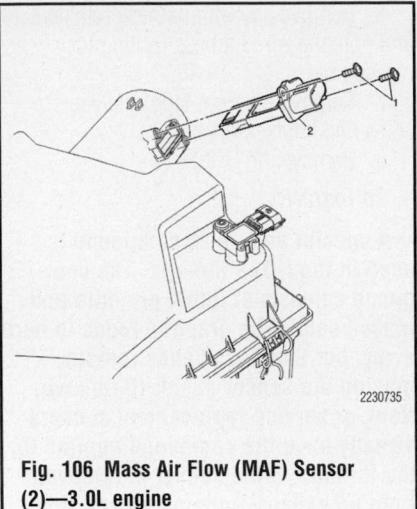

Fig. 106 Mass Air Flow (MAF) Sensor (2)—3.0L engine

3. Disconnect the MAF harness connector.

4. Remove the MAF sensor bolts.

5. Remove the MAF sensor.

To install:

6. Installation is the reverse order of removal. Tighten the mounting bolts to 27 inch lbs. (3 Nm).

FUEL   GASOLINE FUEL INJECTION SYSTEM

FUEL SYSTEM SERVICE PRECAUTIONS

Safety is the most important factor when performing not only fuel system maintenance but any type of maintenance. Failure to conduct maintenance and repairs in a safe manner may result in serious personal injury or death. Maintenance and testing of the vehicle's fuel system components can be accomplished safely and effectively by adhering to the following rules and guidelines.

• To avoid the possibility of fire and personal injury, always disconnect the negative battery cable unless the repair or test procedure requires that battery voltage be applied.

• Always relieve the fuel system pressure prior to disconnecting any fuel system component (injector, fuel rail, pressure regulator, etc.), fitting or fuel line connection. Exercise extreme caution whenever relieving fuel system pressure to avoid exposing skin, face and eyes to fuel spray. Please be advised that fuel under pressure may penetrate the skin or any part of the body that it contacts.

• Always place a shop towel or cloth around the fitting or connection prior to loosening to absorb any excess fuel due to spillage. Ensure that all fuel spillage (should it occur) is quickly removed from engine surfaces. Ensure that all fuel soaked cloths or towels are deposited into a suitable waste container.

• Always keep a dry chemical (Class B) fire extinguisher near the work area.

• Do not allow fuel spray or fuel vapors to come into contact with a spark or open flame.

• Always use a back-up wrench when loosening and tightening fuel line connection fittings. This will prevent unnecessary stress and torsion to fuel line piping.

• Always replace worn fuel fitting O-rings with new Do not substitute fuel hose or equivalent where fuel pipe is installed.

Before servicing the vehicle, make sure to also refer to the precautions in the beginning of this section as well.

RELIEVING FUEL SYSTEM PRESSURE

✳✳ CAUTION

Fuel that flows out at high pressure can cause serious injury to the skin and eyes. ALWAYS depressurize the fuel system before removing components that are under high fuel pressure.

✳✳ CAUTION

If a scan tool is not available, WAIT at LEAST 2 hours after the engine has been run, before removing the high pressure fuel line.

1. Before servicing the vehicle, refer to the Precautions Section.

2. Remove the fuel pump module 20A fuse from the underhood electrical center.

3. Start the vehicle and allow the engine to idle until the engine stops. The engine will stop in approximately 20–30 seconds.

4. Turn the ignition OFF.

FUEL FILTER

REMOVAL & INSTALLATION

The fuel filter is located in the primary fuel tank module. It is designed to last the life of the vehicle and is not serviceable.

FUEL INJECTORS

REMOVAL & INSTALLATION

3.0L Engine

See Figures 107 through 109.

✳✳ WARNING

Remove the fuel rail assembly carefully to prevent damage to the injector electrical connector terminals and spray tips. Support the fuel rail after it is removed in order to avoid damaging the fuel rail components. Cap the fittings and plug the holes when servicing the fuel system to prevent debris from entering open ports.

1. Before servicing the vehicle, refer to the Precautions Section.

2. Properly relieve the fuel system pressure.

3. Remove the fuel pipe shield.

4. Remove the intake manifold.

5. Remove the fuel feed intermediate pipe.

6. Remove the foam insulator from the fuel rails.

7. Cut the plastic tie strap.

8. Disconnect the fuel pressure sensor electrical connector.

9. Remove the fuel pressure sensor.

10. Remove the left side fuel rail fasteners.

11. Remove the right side fuel rail fasteners for clearance purposes.

12. Using the EN-49248-4 hook, raise the fuel rail as an assembly.

13. Once the fuel rail is free, remove the EN-49248 special tool.

14. For Bank 1 fuel rail assembly, slide the fuel rail toward the front of the engine approximately 1 in. (25.4 mm), in order to clear the center injector bore.

15. For Bank 2 fuel rail assembly, slide the fuel rail toward the rear of the engine approximately 1 in. (25.4 mm), in order to clear the center injector bore.

➡**The direct fuel injectors must be rebuilt whenever the injector has been released from the fuel rail or cylinder head.**

16. Once the fuel rail is removed, remove the fuel injectors and rebuild them.

To install:

17. For Bank 1 fuel rail assembly, slide the fuel rail toward the rear of the engine approximately 1 in. (25.4 mm), in order to align the center injector bore.

18. For Bank 2 fuel rail assembly, slide the fuel rail toward the front of the engine approximately 1 in. (25.4 mm), in order to align the center injector bore.

19. Hand tighten the two outer fuel rail fasteners to seat the injectors.

20. Start and hand tighten the remaining fuel rail fasteners.

21. Tighten the fuel rail fasteners in the sequence shown:

    a. First pass 106 inch lbs. (12 Nm).

    b. Final pass 17 ft. lbs. (23 Nm).

22. Tighten the fuel pressure sensor to 25 ft. lbs. (33 Nm).

23. Connect the fuel pressure sensor electrical connector and secure it with a new plastic zip tie.

24. Install a new fuel feed intermediate pipe. Lubricate the pipes with silicon free

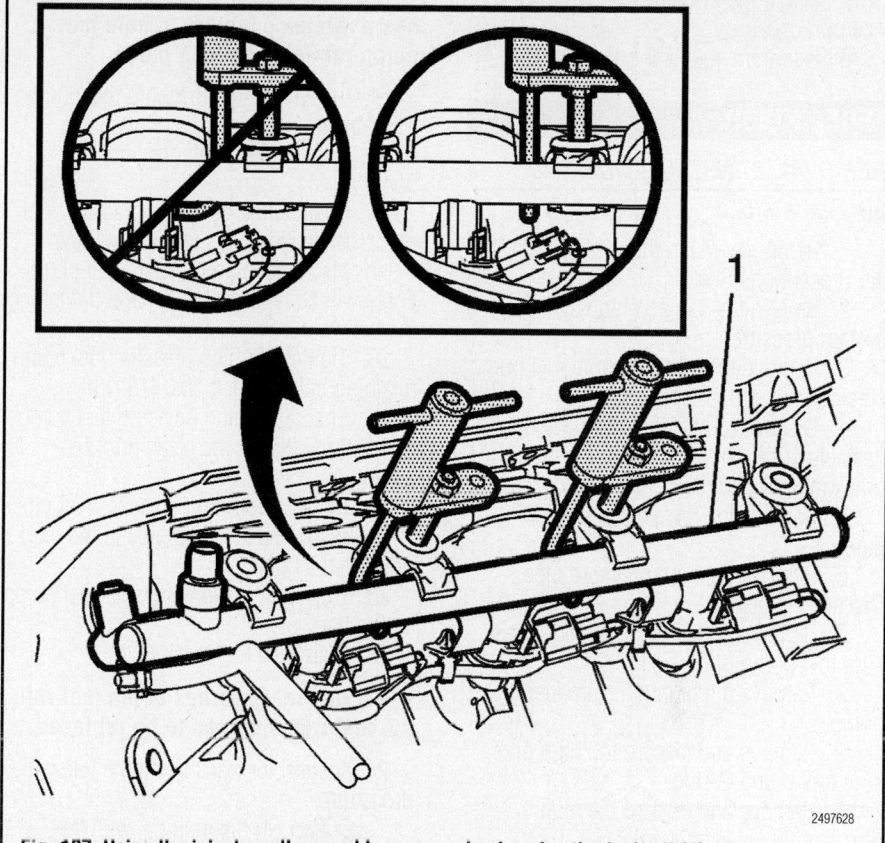

Fig. 107 Using the injector rail assembly remover hook, raise the fuel rail (1)

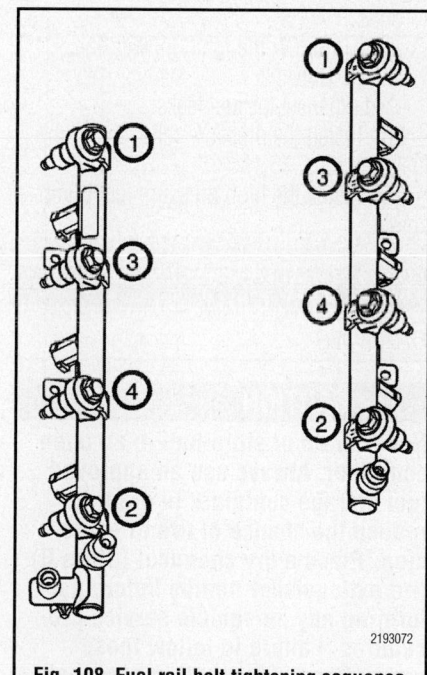

Fig. 108 Fuel rail bolt tightening sequence

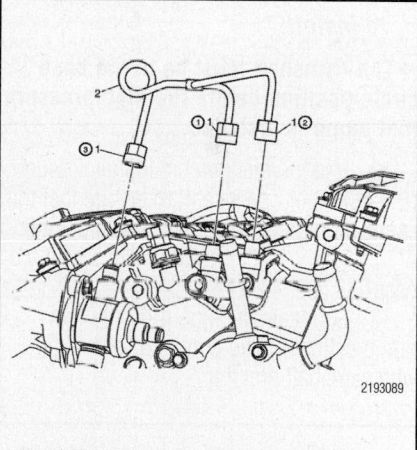

Fig. 109 Fuel feed intermediate pipe fitting tightening sequence

engine oil. Tighten the fittings in sequence as numbered (1, 2, 3):

    a. First Pass 11 ft. lbs. (15 Nm).

    b. Second Pass 22 ft. lbs. (30 Nm).

25. Inspect for fuel leaks using the following procedure:

    a. Turn ON the ignition, with the engine OFF for 2 seconds.

    b. Turn OFF the ignition, for 10 seconds.

    c. Turn ON the ignition, with the engine OFF.

    d. Inspect for fuel leaks.

26. Install the foam insulator to the fuel rails.

27. Install the intake manifold.

28. Install the fuel pipe shield and tighten the bolts to 80 inch lbs. (9 Nm).

29. Install the low side fuel pressure service port cap.

30. Install the fuel tank cap.

FUEL PUMP

REMOVAL & INSTALLATION

See Figure 110.

1. Before servicing the vehicle, refer to the Precautions Section.

2. Relieve the low and high side fuel system pressure.

3. Remove the high pressure fuel pump shield.

4. Disconnect the engine wiring harness electrical connector from the high pressure fuel pump.

5. Remove the low pressure feed pipe.

6. Remove the high pressure pipe. Discard the pipe.

7. Remove and discard the high pressure fuel pump bolts.

8. Remove the high pressure fuel pump.

9. Remove and discard the high pressure fuel pump O-ring.

10. Remove and discard the high pressure fuel pump gasket.

11. Remove the high pressure fuel pump roller lifter.

To install:

➡**The camshaft must be in the base circle position before the high pressure fuel pump is installed.**

12. Use the fuel pump alignment gauge (EN-48896 or equivalent) to ensure that the camshaft lobe is in the base circle position. At base circle the tool will be flush with the head.

13. Lubricate the high pressure fuel pump cylinder head bore and roller lifter with camshaft prelube.

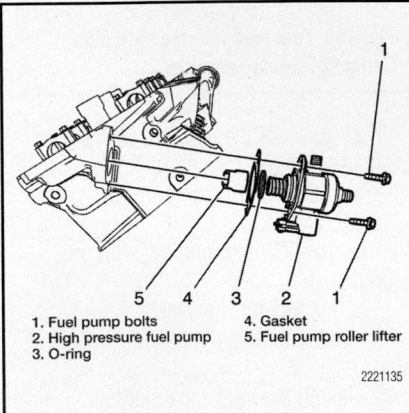

1. Fuel pump bolts
2. High pressure fuel pump
3. O-ring
4. Gasket
5. Fuel pump roller lifter

2221135

Fig. 110 Fuel pump components

➡**The high pressure fuel pump gasket has a retaining feature to hold the pump retaining bolts in place.**

14. Install the high pressure fuel pump roller lifter.

15. Install a new high pressure fuel pump O-ring.

16. Position the new high pressure fuel pump gasket and bolts to the fuel pump.

17. Install the high pressure fuel pump. Force will be required while hand tightening the bolts.

18. Tighten the high pressure fuel pump retaining bolts to 11 ft. lbs. (15 Nm).

19. Ensure the high pressure fuel pump and fuel rail fittings are clean prior to assembly.

20. Install a new high pressure fuel pipe.

21. Install the fuel feed pipe to the high pressure fuel pump.

22. Connect the high pressure fuel pump wiring harness.

23. Install the fuel tank cap.

➡**If a fuel leak accrues at the fuel rail, the fuel rail will need to be replaced.**

24. Inspect for leaks using the following procedure:

   a. Turn ON the ignition, with the engine OFF for 2 seconds.

   b. Turn OFF the ignition, for 10 seconds.

   c. Turn ON the ignition, with the engine OFF.

   d. Inspect for fuel leaks.

25. Install the pressure relief cap to the fuel feed pipe.

26. Install the high pressure fuel pump shield.

FUEL TANK

DRAINING

✳✳ CAUTION

Never drain or store fuel in an open container. Always use an approved fuel storage container in order to reduce the chance of fire or explosion. Place a dry chemical (Class B) fire extinguisher nearby before performing any on-vehicle service procedures. Failure to follow these precautions may result in personal injury.

1. Before servicing the vehicle, refer to the Precautions Section.

2. Remove the fuel fill cap.

3. Raise and suitably support the vehicle.

4. Loosen the fuel fill pipe hose clamps and slide the fill pipe hose up the filler pipe.

5. Insert the fuel tank drain hose (CH-45004 or equivalent) fuel tank drain hose into the fuel tank until the hose reaches the bottom of the fuel tank.

6. Use an hand or air operated pump device in order to drain as much fuel as possible.

REMOVAL & INSTALLATION

1. Before servicing the vehicle, refer to the Precautions Section.

2. Drain the fuel tank.

3. Relieve the fuel system pressure.

4. Remove the exhaust system.

5. Remove the rear driveshaft, if necessary.

6. Disconnect the evaporative emission line.

7. Loosen the upper fill pipe clamp and hose clamp and slide the hose up the filler pipe.

8. Disconnect the fuel tank electrical connector.

9. Disconnect the fuel line and evaporative emission line connectors.

10. Disconnect the evaporative emission line from the canister.

11. Support the fuel tank with a suitable jack.

12. Remove the fuel tank strap bolts and reposition the straps downward toward the front of the vehicle.

13. Using a suitable jack, lower the fuel tank.

14. Remove the following components if replacing just the fuel tank:

   - The primary fuel tank pump module
   - The secondary fuel tank pump module

To install:

15. Install the following components if fuel tank replacement was necessary:

   - The primary fuel tank pump module
   - The secondary fuel tank pump module

16. Raise the fuel tank to the vehicle.

17. Ensure the fuel tank straps are seated properly. Install the fuel tank straps and bolts and tighten to 33 ft. lbs. (45 Nm).

18. Connect the evaporative emission line to the canister.

19. Connect the fuel tank electrical connector.

20. Connect the fuel line and evaporative emission line connectors.

21. Connect the evaporative emission line.

22. Install the filler tube and tighten the hose both clamp to 44 inch lbs. (5 Nm).

23. Perform a leak down test.
24. Install the driveshaft, if removed.
25. Install the exhaust system.
26. Refill the fuel tank.
27. Inspect for fuel leaks.

IDLE SPEED

ADJUSTMENT

Idle speed is maintained by the Engine Control Module (ECM). No adjustment is necessary or possible.

THROTTLE BODY

REMOVAL & INSTALLATION

See Figures 111 and 112.

1. Before servicing the vehicle, refer to the Precautions Section.
2. Turn the ignition to the OFF position.
3. For 2.8L engines, remove the charge air cooler outlet duct and support bracket.
4. For 3.0L engines, remove the air cleaner outlet duct.
5. Remove the throttle body mounting bolts.
6. Disconnect the electrical connector and remove the throttle assembly and gasket. Discard the gasket.

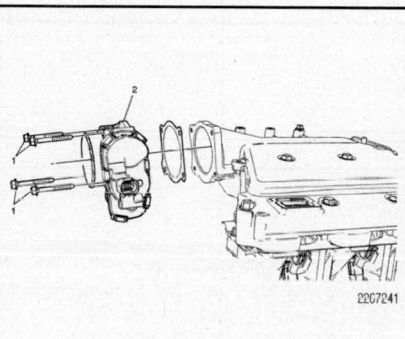

Fig. 111 Remove the mounting bolts (1) and the throttle body (2)—2.8L engine

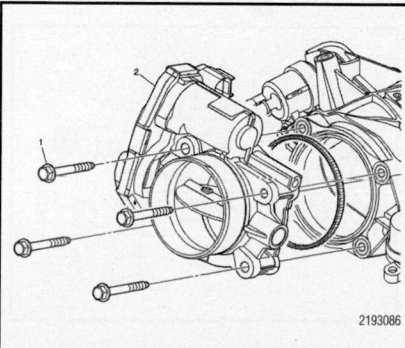

Fig. 112 Remove the mounting bolts (1) and the throttle body (2)—3.0L engine

To install:

7. Installation is the reverse order of removal. Install a new throttle body gasket. Tighten the mounting bolts to 89 inch lbs. (10 Nm).

THROTTLE LEARN/RESET PROCEDURE

2.8L Engine

1. Perform the procedure under the following conditions:
- DTCs P0121, P0122, P0123, P0221, P0222, P0223, P0638, P2100, P2101, P2105, and P2119 are not set
- The engine speed is less than 40 RPM
- The vehicle speed is 0 mph (0 km/h)
- The accelerator pedal position is less than 14.9 percent
- The ignition 1 voltage is more than 10 volts
- The engine coolant temperature is between 41–185°F (5–85°C)
- The intake air temperature is between 41–140°F (5–60°C)

✳✳ WARNING

Ensure the above conditions are met before performing with this procedure. Do not perform this procedure if a throttle position sensor or other Throttle Actuator Control (TAC) system DTCs are set other than P2176. The ECM will not perform the idle learn procedure with a DTC set.

2. Turn OFF the ignition for 30 seconds.
3. Turn ON the ignition, with the engine OFF for 60 seconds.
4. Turn OFF the ignition.
5. Turn ON the ignition, with the engine OFF.
6. Clear the DTCs with a scan tool.

3.0L Engine

1. Perform the reset procedure under the following conditions:
- DTCs P0068, P0101, P0102, P0103, P0106, P0107, P0108, P0116, P0117, P0118, P0120, P0122, P0123, P0128, P0171, P0172, P0174, P0175, P0201, P0202, P0203, P0204, P0205, P0206, P0220, P0222, P0223, P0300, P0351, P0352, P0353, P0496, P0601, P0604, P0606, P060D, P0641, P0651, P1516, P2101, P2119, P2120, P2122,

P2123, P2125, P2127, P2128, P2135, P2138, or P2176 are not set
- Ignition ON, engine OFF
- The vehicle speed is 0 mph (0 km/h)

2. Perform the reset procedure as follows (Performed after the throttle body is cleaned or replaced):
   a. Ignition ON, engine OFF, perform the Idle Learn Reset in Module Setup with a scan tool.
   b. Start the engine and monitor the TB Idle Airflow Compensation parameter. The TB Idle Airflow Compensation value should equal 0 percent and the engine should be idling at a normal idle speed.
   c. Clear the DTCs.

3. Perform the learn procedure under the following conditions:
- DTCs P0068, P0101, P0102, P0103, P0106, P0107, P0108, P0116, P0117, P0118, P0120, P0122, P0123, P0128, P0171, P0172, P0174, P0175, P0201, P0202, P0203, P0204, P0205, P0206, P0220, P0222, P0223, P0300, P0351, P0352, P0353, P0496, P0601, P0604, P0606, P060D, P0641, P0651, P1516, P2101, P2119, P2120, P2122, P2123, P2125, P2127, P2128, P2135, P2138, or P2176 are not set
- The engine speed is between 450-4,000 RPM
- The manifold absolute pressure (MAP) is greater than 5 kPa
- The Mass Air Flow (MAF) is greater than 2 g/s
- The ignition voltage is greater than 10 volts

4. Perform the learn procedure as follows (Performed after the ECM is flashed or replaced):

✳✳ WARNING

Do NOT perform this procedure if DTCs are set.

   a. Start and idle the engine for 3 minutes.
   b. With a scan tool, monitor the Desired Idle Speed and the actual Engine Speed.
   c. The ECM will start to learn the new idle cells and Desired Idle Speed should start to decrease.
   d. Ignition OFF for 60 seconds.
   e. Start and idle the engine for 3 minutes.

f. After the 3 minute run time the engine should be idling normal. If the engine idle speed has not been learned the vehicle will need to be driven at speeds above 44 mph (70 km/h) with several decelerations and extended idles.

➡ **During the drive cycle the check engine light may come on with idle speed DTCs. If idle speed codes are set, clear codes so the ECM can continue to learn.**

g. After the drive cycle, the engine should be idling normally. If the engine idle speed has not been learned, turn OFF the ignition for 60 seconds and repeat the previous step.

h. Once the engine speed has returned to normal, clear DTCs.

HEATING & AIR CONDITIONING SYSTEM

BLOWER MOTOR

REMOVAL & INSTALLATION

See Figure 113.

�֍ CAUTION

Before servicing components near or affected by the SRS (air bag) system, read and observe all SRS Service Precautions. Refer to Supplemental Restraint System (SRS), in the Chassis Electrical section. Failure to observe all precautions may result in accidental airbag deployment, personal injury, or death. Refer to Airbag Removal & Installation.

1. Disable the SIR system.
2. Remove the right instrument panel insulator panel.
3. Disconnect the blower motor electrical connector.
4. Remove the blower motor mounting bolts.
5. Remove the blower motor.

To install:

6. Installation is the reverse of removal. Tighten the mounting bolts to 15 inch lbs. (2 Nm).

HEATER CORE

REMOVAL & INSTALLATION

See Figure 114.

✷ CAUTION

Before servicing components near or affected by the SRS (air bag) system, read and observe all SRS Service Precautions. Refer to Supplemental Restraint System (SRS), in the Chassis Electrical section. Failure to observe all precautions may result in accidental airbag deployment, personal injury, or death. Refer to Airbag Removal & Installation.

1. Disable the SIR system.
2. Recover the refrigerant.
3. Drain the cooling system.

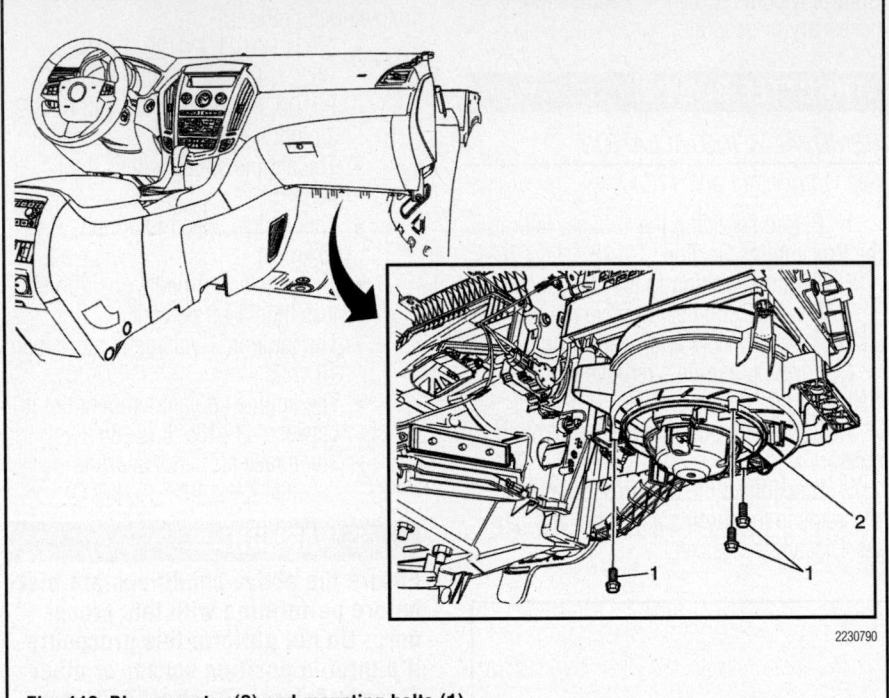

Fig. 113 Blower motor (2) and mounting bolts (1)

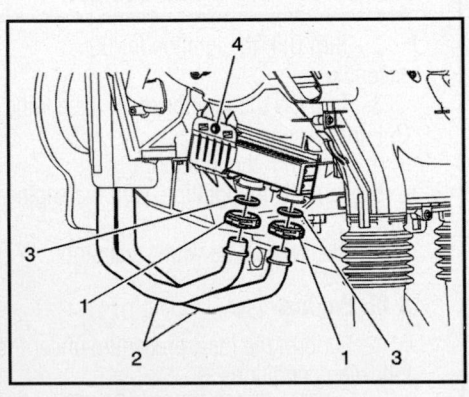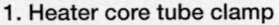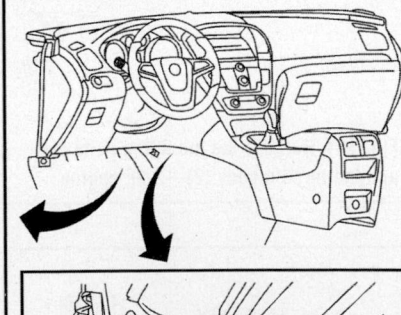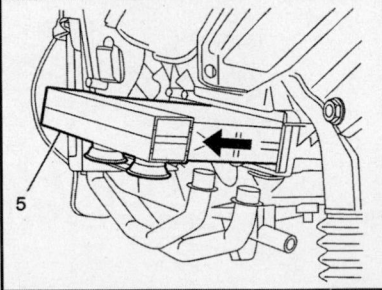

1. Heater core tube clamp
2. Heater core tube assembly
3. Heater core tube seal
4. Heater core bracket bolt
5. Heater core

Fig. 114 Heater core components

4. Remove the instrument panel insulator panel, left side.

5. Remove the instrument panel lower trim panel.

6. Disconnect the heater inlet and outlet hoses from the heater core tube.

7. Remove the heater core tube.

8. Remove the heater core bracket.

9. Remove the heater core.

To install:

10. Installation is the reverse of removal.

Tighten the heater core bracket bolt to 12 inch lbs. (1 Nm).

11. Fill the coolant.

12. Evacuate and recharge the AC system.

STEERING

POWER STEERING GEAR

REMOVAL & INSTALLATION

See Figures 115 and 116.

❄ CAUTION

Before servicing components near or affected by the SRS (air bag) system, read and observe all SRS Service Precautions. Refer to Supplemental Restraint System (SRS), in the Chassis Electrical section. Failure to observe all precautions may result in accidental airbag deployment, personal injury, or death. Refer to Airbag Removal & Installation.

1. Before servicing the vehicle, refer to the Precautions Section.

2. Disable the SIR system.

3. With wheels of the vehicle facing straight ahead, secure the steering wheel utilizing steering column anti-rotation pin, steering column lock, or a strap to prevent rotation. Locking of the steering column will prevent damage and a possible malfunction of the SIR system.

❄ WARNING

After disconnecting components, do not rotate the steering wheel or move the front tires and wheels. Failure to follow this procedure may cause the SIR coil assembly to become un-centered and cause possible damage to the SIR coil. **If you think the SIR coil has became un-centered, refer to your specific SIR coil's centering procedure to re-center SIR Coil.**

4. With the wheels of the vehicle in the straight ahead position, lock the steering column.

5. Disconnect the intermediate steering shaft from the steering gear.

6. Place drain pans under the vehicle.

7. Remove as much power steering fluid from the reservoir as possible.

8. Disconnect the front stabilizer shaft from the 2 stabilizer shaft links. Rotate the front stabilizer shaft as necessary for access.

9. Disconnect the 2 steering linkage outer tie rods from the steering knuckles.

10. Disconnect the power steering gear inlet hose from the steering gear.

11. Disconnect the power steering gear outlet hose and the outlet hose bracket from the steering gear.

12. Perform the following steps:

a. Support the front frame with a jack.

b. If equipped with all wheel drive, remove the driveshaft.

c. Remove the rear transmission mount through bolt.

d. Remove the rear frame-to-body bolts.

e. Lower the rear part of the frame a maximum of 2 inches in order to gain clearance for the steering gear.

13. If equipped with variable effort steering, disconnect the electrical connector

14. Remove the steering gear nuts and bolts.

15. Remove the steering gear from the frame.

To install:

16. Installation is the reverse of removal, noting the following:

a. Hold the steering gear bolt with a wrench and tighten the steering gear nut to 44 ft. lbs. (60 Nm), plus 120 degrees.

b. Fill and bleed the power steering system.

c. Measure and adjust the front toe.

POWER STEERING PUMP

REMOVAL & INSTALLATION

See Figure 117.

1. Before servicing the vehicle, refer to the Precautions Section.

2. Place drain pans under the vehicle.

3. Remove as much power steering fluid from the power steering fluid reservoir as possible.

4. Remove the drive belt from the power steering pump pulley only.

5. Remove the right front tire and wheel assembly.

6. Disconnect the power steering fluid reservoir outlet hose from the power steering pump.

7. Disconnect the power steering gear inlet hose from the power steering pump.

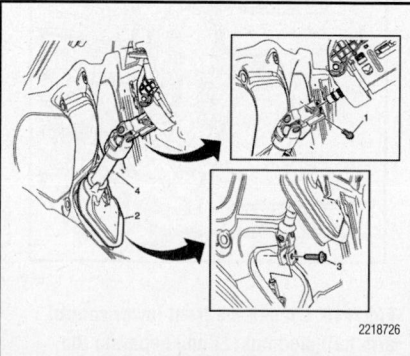

Fig. 115 Intermediate steering shaft (4), bolts (1, 3), and seal (2)

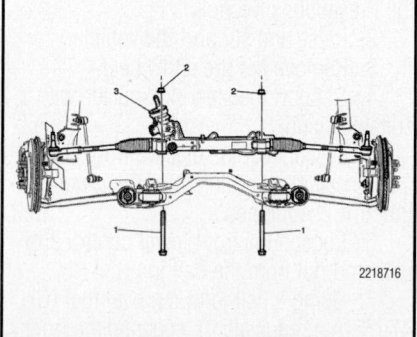

Fig. 116 Steering gear (3), bolt (1), and nut (2)

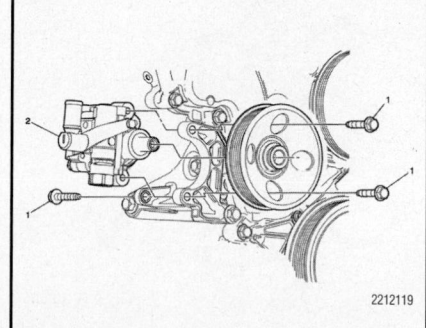

Fig. 117 Power steering pump (2) and bolts (1)

8. Remove the power steering pump bolts. Note the routing for installation.

9. Remove the power steering pump through the right front wheel well opening.

To install:

10. Installation is the reverse of removal, noting the following:

   a. Install the power steering pump bolts in the reverse order of removal and tighten to 16 ft. lbs. (22 Nm).

   b. Fill and bleed the power steering system.

   c. Clean any excess power steering fluid from the vehicle.

BLEEDING

➥**Use clean, new power steering fluid only. Hoses touching the frame, body or engine may cause system noise. Ensure the hoses do not touch any other part of the vehicle. Loose connections may not leak, but could allow air into the steering system. Ensure all connections are tight. Maintain the power steering fluid level throughout the bleeding procedure.**

1. Fill pump reservoir with fluid to minimum system level, FULL COLD level, or middle of hash mark on cap stick fluid level indicator.

2. Raise the vehicle until the front wheels are off the ground.

3. With the key in the ON position and the engine OFF, turn the steering wheel from stop to stop 12 times. Vehicles equipped with longer length power steering hoses may require turns up to 15 to 20 stop to stops.

4. Verify power steering fluid level.

5. Start the engine. Rotate steering wheel from left to right. Check for sign of cavitation or fluid aeration (pump noise/whining).

6. Lower the vehicle.

7. Verify the fluid level. Repeat the bleed procedure, if necessary.

6. Lower the vehicle.

FLUID FILL PROCEDURE

1. Run the engine until the power steering fluid reaches about 170°F (80°C).

2. Turn the engine OFF.

3. For 3.0L engines, remove the intake manifold cover.

4. Clean the power steering fluid reservoir and the reservoir cap.

5. Remove the reservoir cap.

➥**Inspect the power steering pump fluid level at regular intervals.**

6. Inspect the power steering fluid level on the cap stick. Ensure that the fluid level is at the MAX mark on the cap stick.

❊❊ WARNING

When adding fluid or making a complete fluid change, always use the proper power steering fluid. Failure to use the proper fluid will cause hose and seal damage and fluid leaks.

➥**If the power steering fluid color is red or pink, use GM DEXRON®-VI Automatic Transmission Fluid. If the power steering fluid color is amber or brown, use GM Power Steering Fluid.**

7. Add the proper fluid to the reservoir, if necessary.

8. Install the reservoir cap.

9. For 3.0L engines, install the intake manifold cover.

SUSPENSION

CONTROL LINKS

REMOVAL & INSTALLATION

See Figure 118.

1. Before servicing the vehicle, refer to the Precautions Section.

2. Raise and support the vehicle.

3. Remove the tire and wheel.

4. Remove the stabilizer shaft link nuts.

5. Remove the stabilizer shaft links.

To install:

6. Installation is the reverse of removal. Tighten the stabilizer shaft link nuts to 55 ft. lbs. (75 Nm).

LOWER BALL JOINT

REMOVAL & INSTALLATION

The lower control arm must be replaced. The ball joint is not serviced separately.

LOWER CONTROL ARM

REMOVAL AND & INSTALLATION

See Figures 119 through 122.

1. Before servicing the vehicle, refer to the Precautions Section.

2. Raise and support the vehicle.

3. Remove the tire and wheel.

4. Support the steering knuckle with a suitable stand.

5. Disconnect the electric front suspension accelerometer link from the lower control arm, if equipped.

6. Loosen the front lower control arm ball stud nut from the ball joint.

7. Using a ball joint removal tool (CH 47975-A or equivalent), separate the front lower control arm from the steering knuckle.

8. Remove the ball joint removal tool.

FRONT SUSPENSION

9. Remove the front lower control arm rear nuts and the front lower control arm rear bolts.

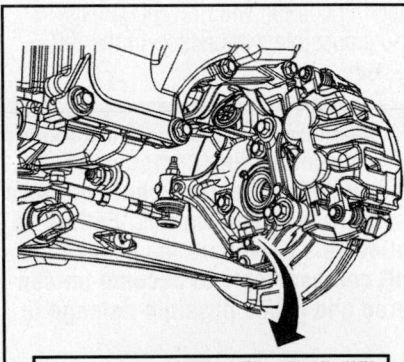
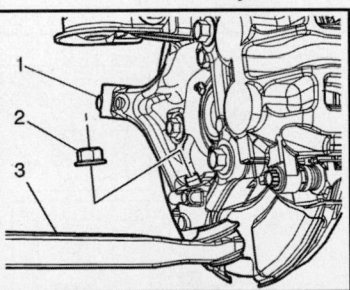

2223060

Fig. 119 Loosen the front lower control arm ball stud nut (2) and separate the front lower control arm (3) from the steering knuckle (1)

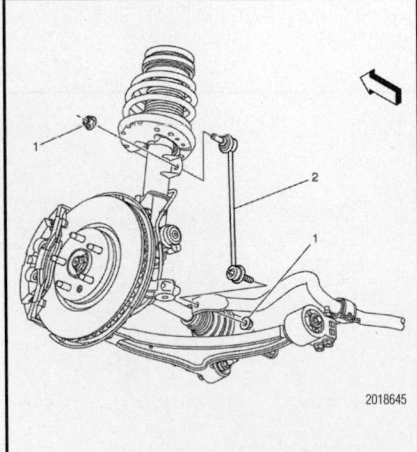

2018645

Fig. 118 Stabilizer shaft link (2) and nuts (1)

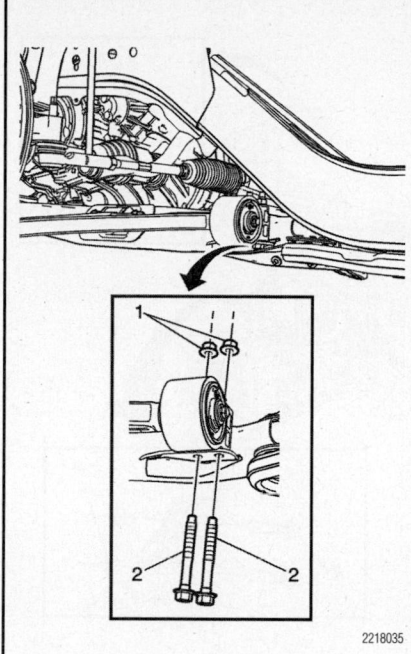

Fig. 120 Remove the front lower control arm rear nuts (1) and the front lower control arm rear bolts (2)

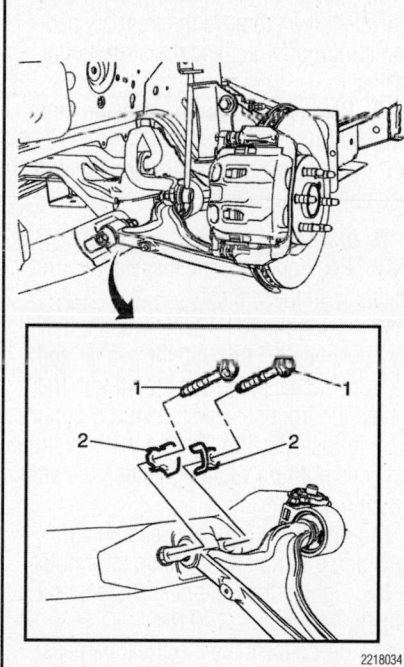

Fig. 121 Remove front lower control arm front bolts (1) and the brackets (2)

10. Remove front lower control arm front bolts and the brackets. Note the position of the brackets.

11. Remove the front lower control arm from the vehicle.

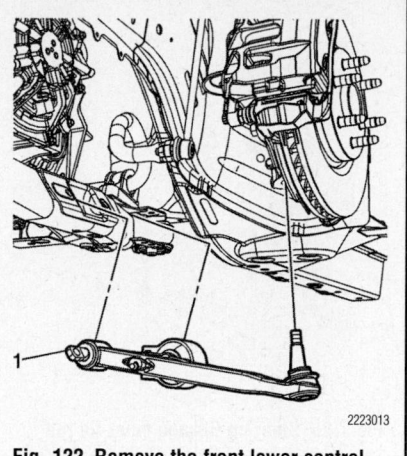

Fig. 122 Remove the front lower control arm (1)

To install:

12. Position the front lower control arm in the frame.

✶✶ WARNING

Failure to replace the front lower control brackets will cause premature wear and damage to the front lower control arm bushings.

13. Install the front lower control arm front mounting brackets bolts and tighten to 74 ft. lbs. (100 Nm) plus an additional 90 degrees.

14. Install the front lower control arm rear bolts and the front lower control arm rear nuts.

15. Tighten the front lower control arm rear bolts to 81 ft. lbs. (110 Nm).

16. Install the front lower control arm ball stud nut to the ball joint and tighten to 22 ft. lbs. (30 Nm) plus an additional 130 degrees.

17. Reconnect the electric front suspension accelerometer link to the lower control arm, if equipped.

18. Remove the support from the steering knuckle.

19. Install the tire and wheel assembly.

20. Remove the support and lower the vehicle.

STABILIZER BAR

REMOVAL & INSTALLATION

See Figures 123 and 124.

1. Before servicing the vehicle, refer to the Precautions Section.

2. Raise and support the vehicle.

3. Remove the tire and wheel.

4. Remove the stabilizer shaft links.

5. Remove the rear bolts of the front dri-

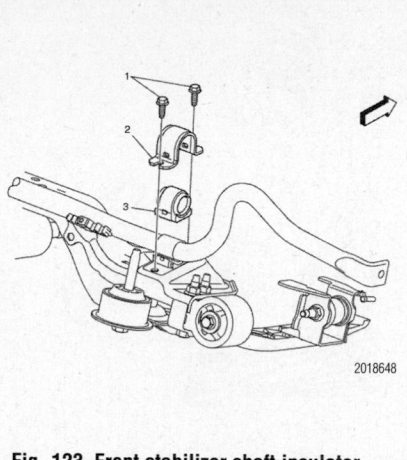

Fig. 123 Front stabilizer shaft insulator (3), bolts (1), and clamp (2)

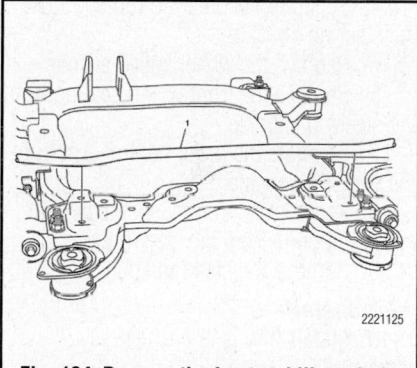

Fig. 124 Remove the front stabilizer shaft (1)

vetrain and front suspension frame and lower to gain access to the stabilizer shaft insulators.

6. Remove the stabilizer shaft insulators.

7. Remove the stabilizer shaft. It may be necessary to maneuver the stabilizer shaft in such a way as to remove it from the vehicle.

To install:

8. Installation is the reverse of removal, noting the following:

    a. Install the stabilizer bar insulator so that the chamfer edge is facing toward the outside of the vehicle. This will put the slits in the bushing facing opposite directions.

    b. Tighten stabilizer shaft insulator bolts to 33 ft. lbs. (45 Nm)

STEERING KNUCKLE

REMOVAL & INSTALLATION

See Figure 125.

1. Before servicing the vehicle, refer to the Precautions Section.

2. Raise and support the vehicle.

3. Remove the tire and wheel.

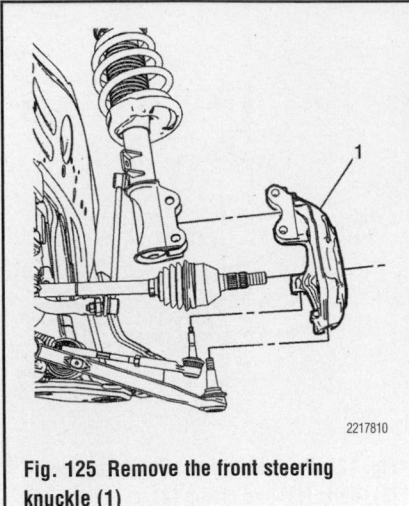

Fig. 125 Remove the front steering knuckle (1)

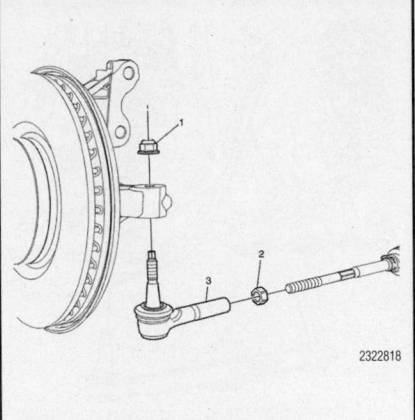

Fig. 126 Steering linkage outer tie rod (3), inner tie rod nut (2), and outer tie rod nut (1)

4. Separate the outer tie rod end from the steering knuckle.

5. Remove the wheel speed sensor.

6. Remove the front wheel bearing from the steering knuckle.

7. Separate the lower control arm from the steering knuckle.

8. Remove the front suspension strut mounting bolts from the steering knuckle

9. Remove the steering knuckle.

To install:

10. Installation is the reverse of removal.

11. Check the front end alignment.

STEERING LINKAGE OUTER TIE ROD

REMOVAL & INSTALLATION

See Figure 126.

1. Before servicing the vehicle, refer to the Precautions Section.

2. Raise and safely support the vehicle.

3. Remove the tire and wheel.

4. Remove the steering linkage outer tie rod nut.

5. Remove the steering linkage inner tie rod nut. Use paint in order to place matchmarks on the steering linkage inner tic rod nut and on the steering linkage inner tie rod. Discard the nut.

> ※※ WARNING
>
> **Do not free the ball stud by using a pickle fork or a wedge-type tool. Damage to the seal or bushing may result.**

6. Separate the steering linkage outer tie rod from the steering knuckle using a steering linkage/tie rod puller (J-24319-B or equivalent).

7. Clean the tapered surface of the steering knuckle.

To install:

8. Installation is the reverse of removal, noting the following:

　a. Align the matchmarks on the inner tie rod and inner tie rod nut.

　b. Do not tighten the inner tie rod nut during installation. Tighten the nut after adjusting the front toe.

　c. Tighten the outer tie rod nut to 18 ft. lbs. (25 Nm), plus an additional 90 degrees.

　d. After the installation is complete, measure and adjust the front toe.

STRUT & SPRING ASSEMBLY

REMOVAL & INSTALLATION

See Figure 127.

1. Before servicing the vehicle, refer to the Precautions Section.

2. Raise and safely support the vehicle.

3. Remove the tire and wheel.

4. Remove the stabilizer shaft link from the strut.

5. Disconnect the head lamp level sensor link from the lower control arm, if equipped.

6. Support the lower control arm and the steering knuckle.

> ※※ WARNING
>
> **DO NOT allow the lower control arm and the steering knuckle drop more than 2 inches when the strut assembly has been removed.**

7. Disconnect the electrical harness/sensor from the strut, if equipped.

8. Remove the front compartment side sight shields.

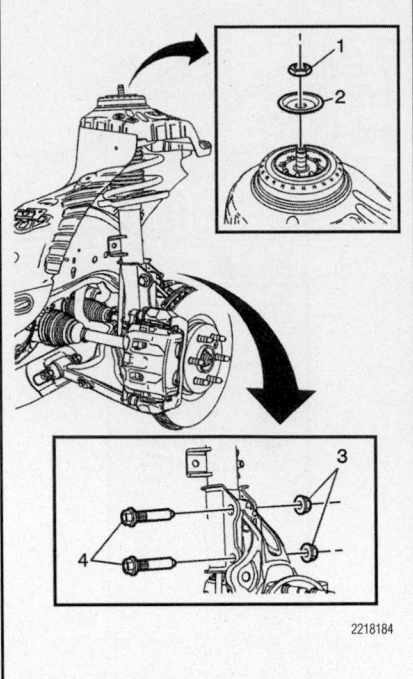

Fig. 127 Remove the front suspension strut mount nut (1) and washer (2) and the strut bolts (4) and nuts (3)

9. Using the CH 49375 wrench, or equivalent tool, remove the front suspension strut mount nut and the strut mount washer.

10. Remove the front suspension strut bolts and nuts.

11. Remove the front suspension strut assembly from the vehicle

To install:

12. Position the front suspension strut assembly in the vehicle.

13. Using the CH 49375 wrench, install front suspension strut mount washer and the front suspension strut mount nut, then tighten the front suspension strut mount nut to 52 ft. lbs. (70 Nm). Ensure that the strut rod does not turn while tightening the strut mount nut.

14. Install the front suspension strut bolts and the front suspension strut nuts.

15. Tighten the front suspension strut bolts to 140 ft. lbs. (190 Nm).

16. Re-connect the electrical harness/sensor from the strut, if equipped.

17. Reconnect the head lamp level sensor link to the lower control arm, if equipped.

18. Remove the support from the lower control arm and the steering knuckle.

19. Install the front stabilizer shaft link.

20. Install the tire and wheel assembly.

21. Install the front compartment side sight shields.

22. Remove the support and lower the vehicle.

WHEEL BEARINGS

REMOVAL & INSTALLATION

See Figure 128.

1. Before servicing the vehicle, refer to the Precautions Section.
2. Raise and safely support the vehicle.
3. Remove the tire and wheel.
4. Remove the front brake rotor.
5. Loosen the halfshaft from the wheel bearing/hub.

6. Remove the wheel bearing/hub mounting bolts. Discard the bolts.
7. Remove the wheel bearing/hub assembly.

To install:

8. Install the wheel bearing/hub assembly. Tighten the new bolts to 81 ft. lbs. (110 Nm).
9. Install the halfshaft.
10. Install the brake rotor.
11. Install the tire and wheel.
12. Lower the vehicle.

ADJUSTMENT

The wheel bearings are not adjustable.

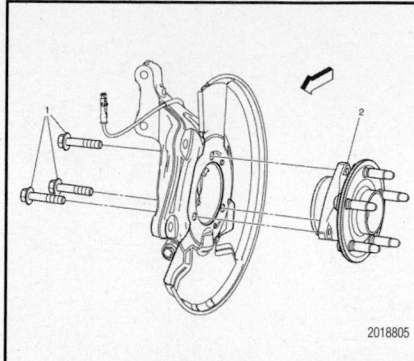

Fig. 128 Remove the front wheel bearing/hub assembly (2) and bolts (1)

SUSPENSION

COIL SPRING

REMOVAL & INSTALLATION

See Figures 129 through 131.

1. Before servicing the vehicle, refer to the Precautions Section.
2. Raise and support the vehicle.
3. Remove the tire and wheel assembly.
4. Remove the stabilizer shaft link.
5. Remove the lower control arm from the knuckle.
6. Remove the lower shock absorber bolt from the lower control arm.
7. Remove the lower bolt for the rear suspension link upper to lower control arm.
8. Remove the rear wheel speed sensor wiring harness from the lower control arm.

9. Remove the electrical suspension harness for the rear shock, if equipped.
10. Rotate the lower control arm as much as possible and remove the rear spring.

To install:

11. Installation is the reverse of removal, noting the following:
    a. Tighten the rear suspension link lower control arm bolt to 66 ft. lbs. (40 Nm) plus an additional 90 degrees.
    b. Align the rear suspension.

REAR SUSPENSION

KNUCKLE

REMOVAL & INSTALLATION

See Figures 132 and 133.

1. Before servicing the vehicle, refer to the Precautions Section.
2. Raise and support the vehicle.
3. Remove the tire and wheel.
4. Remove the rear disc brake backing plate.

Fig. 129 Stabilizer shaft link, nut (1), bolts (2), and spacers (3)

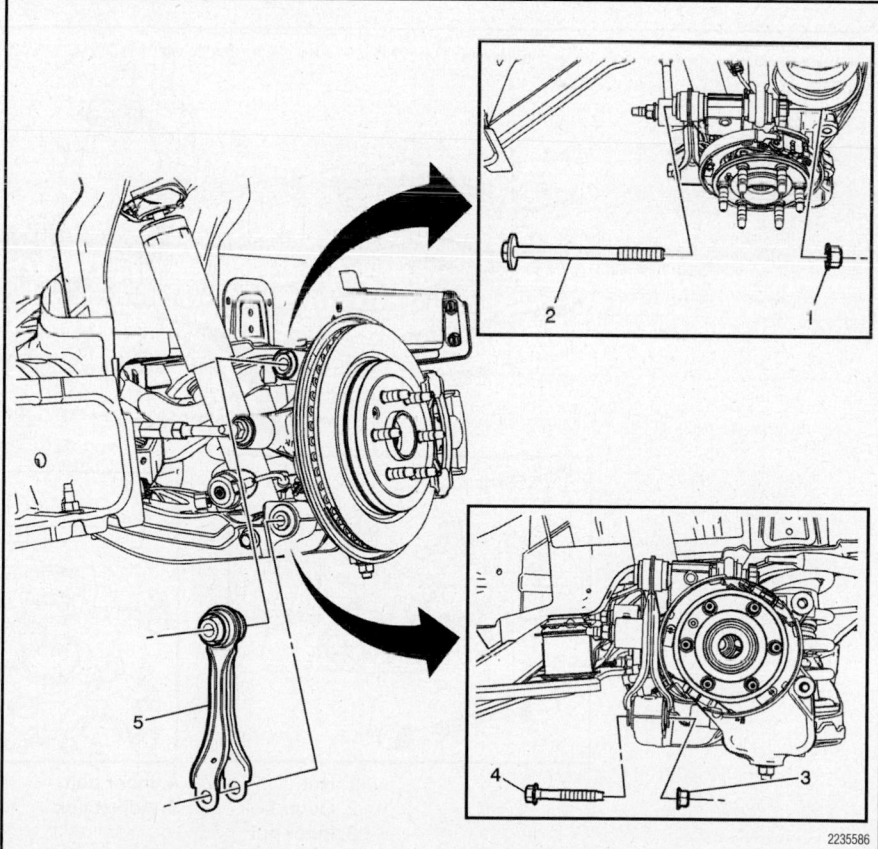

Fig. 130 Rear suspension link lower control arm bolt (4)

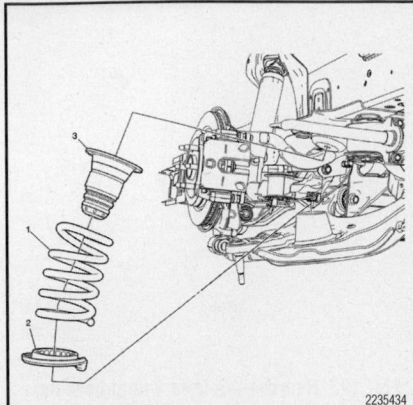

Fig. 131 Remove the coil spring (1), lower insulator (2) and the jounce bumper (3)

5. Remove the parking brake cable from the knuckle.

6. Separate the lower control arm from the knuckle.

7. Remove the upper control arm bolt.

8. Remove the adjust link nuts and bolts, and remove the adjust link from the knuckle. For AWD vehicles, remove the bolt from the upper control arm to the knuckle.

9. Remove the knuckle.

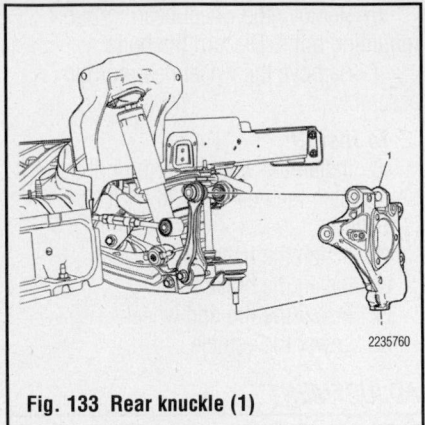

Fig. 133 Rear knuckle (1)

To install:

10. Installation is the reverse of removal.

11. After the installation is complete, adjust the toe.

LOWER CONTROL ARM

REMOVAL & INSTALLATION

See Figure 134.

1. Before servicing the vehicle, refer to the Precautions Section.

2. Raise and support the vehicle.

3. Remove the tire and wheel.

4. Remove the rear spring.

5. Remove the lower control arm ball joint nut.

6. Remove the lower control arm nuts and bolts.

7. Using a ball joint removal tool (CH 43631 or equivalent), remove the lower control arm from the knuckle.

To install:

8. Installation is the reverse of removal, noting the following:

   a. Tighten the lower control arm bolts to 74 ft. lbs. (100 Nm), plus an additional 90 degrees.

   b. Tighten the lower control arm ball joint nut to 30 ft. lbs. (40 Nm), plus an additional 125 degrees.

   c. Align the rear suspension.

SHOCK ABSORBER

REMOVAL & INSTALLATION

See Figure 135.

1. Before servicing the vehicle, refer to the Precautions Section.

2. Raise and support the vehicle.

3. Remove the tire and wheel.

4. Disconnect the electrical for the electronic suspension, if equipped.

5. Support the lower control arm with the proper jackstand.

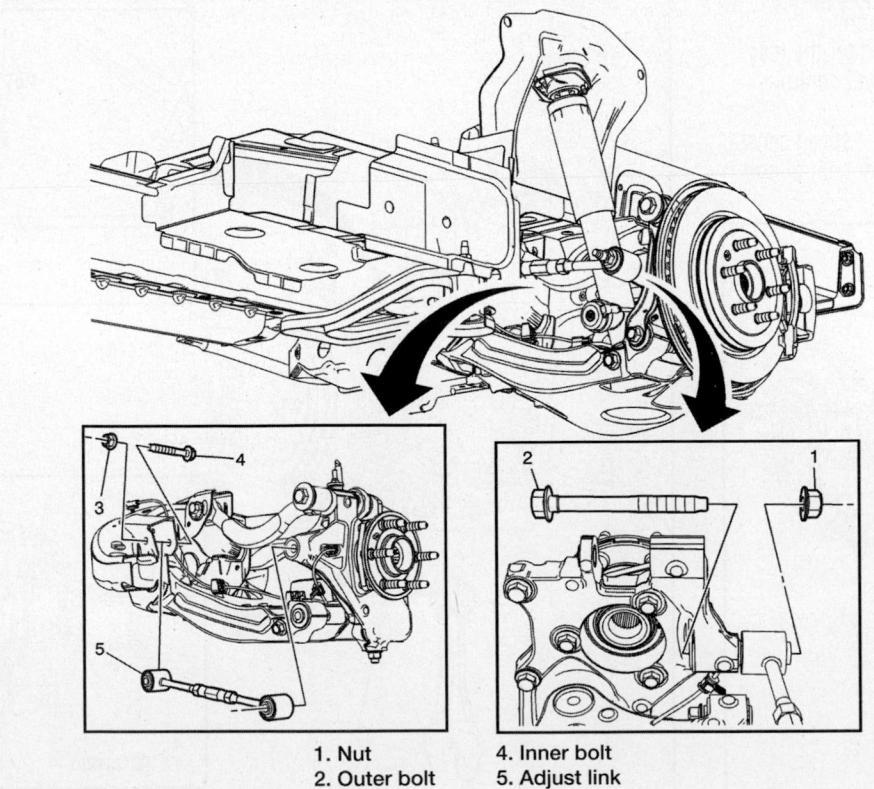

1. Nut
2. Outer bolt
3. Inner nut
4. Inner bolt
5. Adjust link

Fig. 132 Rear adjust link components

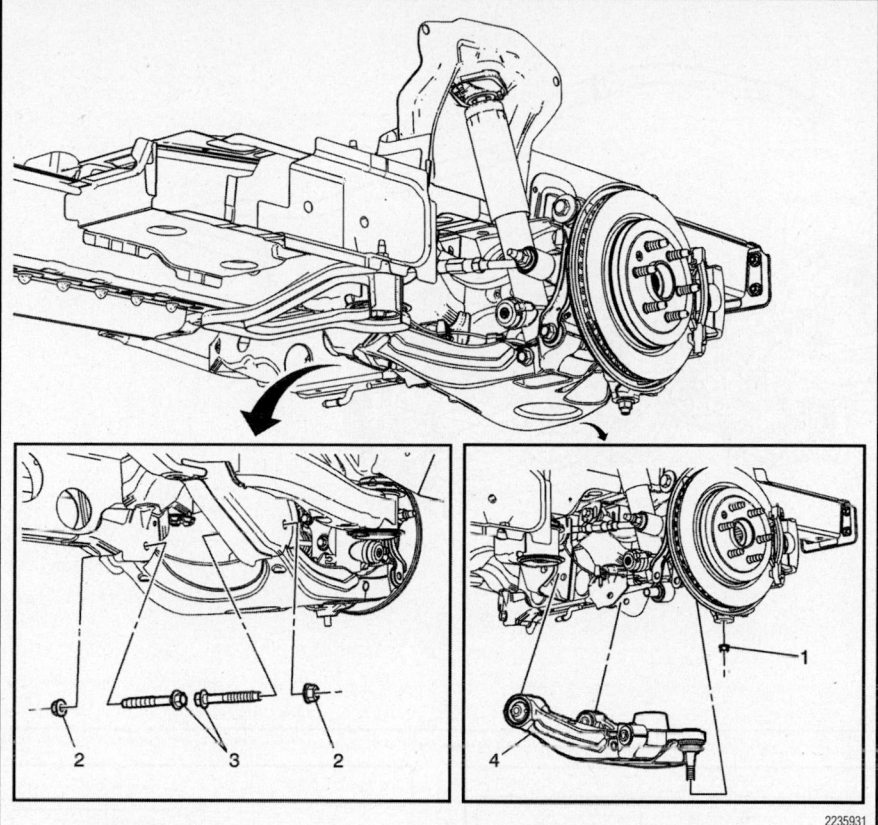

Fig. 134 Lower control arm (4), ball joint nut (1), control arm nuts (2), and bolts (3)

6. Remove the shock absorber mounting bolt and nuts.

7. Remove the shock absorber.

To install:

8. Installation is the reverse of removal, noting the following:

 a. Tighten the nuts to 13 ft. lbs. (17 Nm).

 b. Tighten the bolt to 13 ft. lbs. (17 Nm).

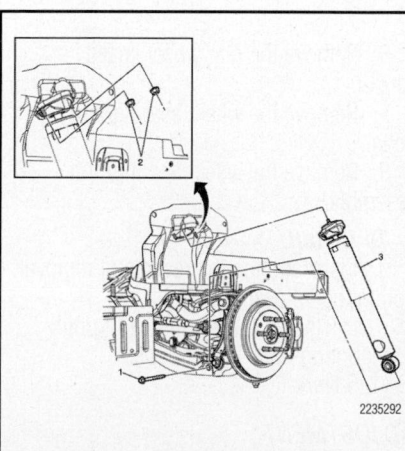

Fig. 135 Rear shock absorber (3), bolt (1), and nuts (2)

STABILIZER BAR

REMOVAL & INSTALLATION

See Figures 136 through 138.

1. Before servicing the vehicle, refer to the Precautions Section.

2. Raise and support the vehicle.

3. Remove the tire and wheel.

4. Remove the stabilizer shaft link mounting nuts and remove the stabilizer shaft link from the stabilizer shaft.

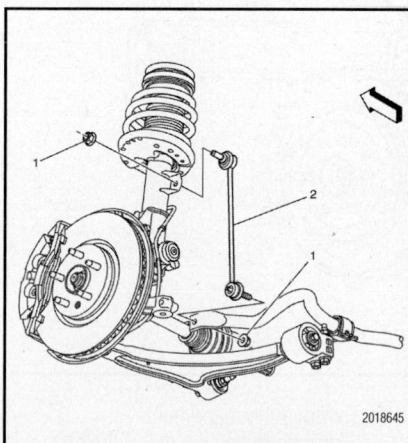

Fig. 136 Stabilizer shaft link (2) and nuts (1)

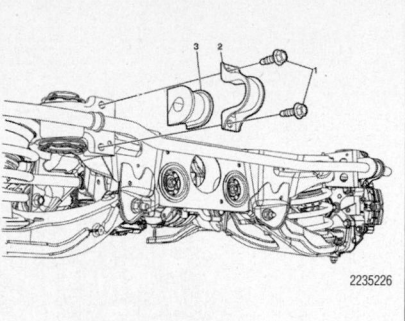

Fig. 137 Stabilizer shaft insulator (3), bracket (2), and bolts (1)

5. Remove the stabilizer shaft insulators.

6. Remove the rear stabilizer shaft insulators.

7. Remove the stabilizer shaft.

To install:

8. Installation is the reverse of removal, noting the following:

 a. Tighten the insulator bolts to 16 ft. lbs. (22 Nm), plus an additional 30 degrees. Install the insulator with the slit facing down.

 b. Tighten the stabilizer shaft link mounting nuts to 55 ft. lbs. (75 Nm).

UPPER CONTROL ARM

REMOVAL & INSTALLATION

See Figure 139.

1. Before servicing the vehicle, refer to the Precautions Section.

2. Raise and support the vehicle.

3. Remove the tire and wheel.

4. Support the rear lower control arm, if necessary.

5. Remove the upper control arm nuts and bolts.

6. Remove the upper control arm from the vehicle.

To install:

7. Installation is the reverse of removal, noting the following:

 a. Tighten the upper control arm mounting bolt to 111 ft. lbs. (150 Nm), plus an additional 90 degrees.

 b. Tighten the upper control arm adjuster bolt to 52 ft. lbs. (70 Nm), plus an additional 60 degrees.

 c. Check and adjust the rear camber.

WHEEL BEARINGS

REMOVAL & INSTALLATION

See Figure 140.

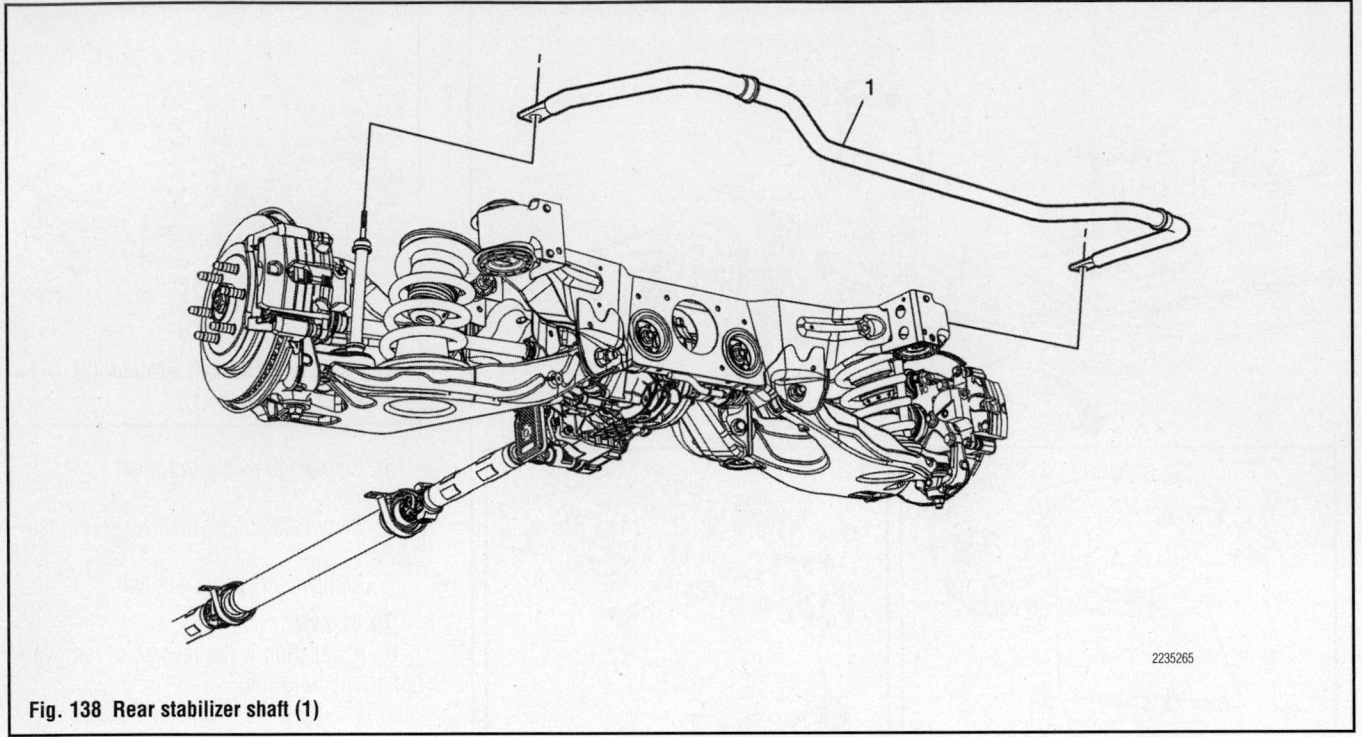

Fig. 138 Rear stabilizer shaft (1)

1. Rear upper control arm nut
2. Rear upper control arm adjuster cam
3. Rear upper control arm adjuster bolt
4. Rear upper control arm bolt
5. Rear upper control arm nut
6. Rear upper control arm

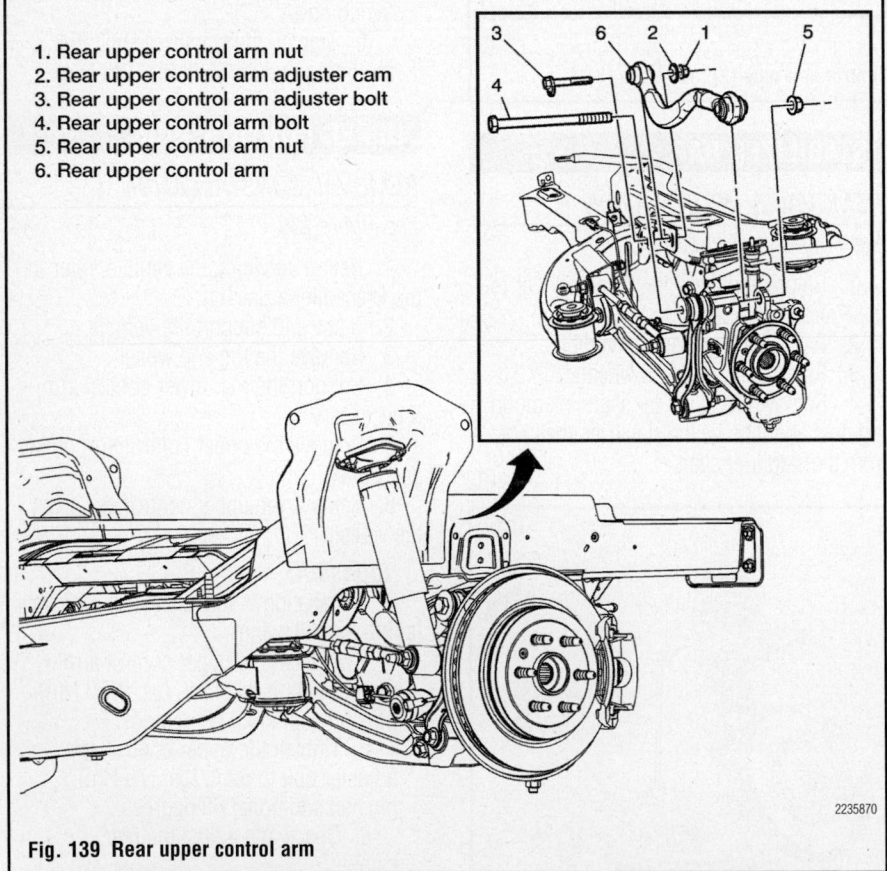

Fig. 139 Rear upper control arm

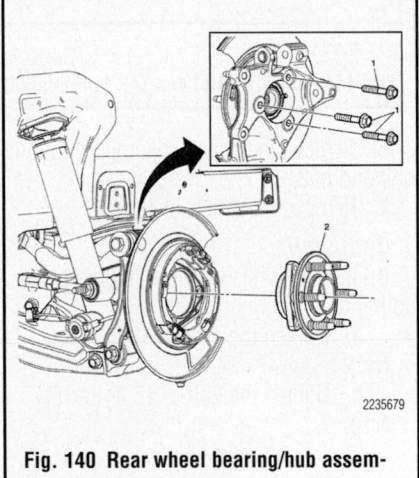

Fig. 140 Rear wheel bearing/hub assembly (2) and bolts (1)

6. Remove the rear wheel speed sensor.

7. Remove the wheel bearing/hub bolts.

8. Remove the wheel bearing/hub assembly.

To install:

9. Installation is the reverse of removal, noting the following:

  a. Tighten the wheel bearing/hub mounting bolts to 92 ft. lbs. (125 Nm).

ADJUSTMENT

The wheel bearings are not adjustable.

1. Before servicing the vehicle, refer to the Precautions Section.

2. Raise and safely support the vehicle.

3. Remove the rear wheel.

4. Separate the wheel drive shaft from the knuckle, if necessary.

5. Remove the rear brake rotor.

PONTIAC

Vibe

SPECIFICATIONS AND MAINTENANCE CHARTS

ENGINE AND VEHICLE IDENTIFICATION

			Engine				Model Year	
Code ①	Liters	Cu. In.	Cyl.	Fuel Sys. ②	Engine Type	Eng. Mfg.	Code ③	Year
8	1.8	110	4	SIDI	DOHC I4	NS	A	2010
0	2.4	146	4	SIDI	DOHC I4	NS		

① 8th position of VIN

② Spark Ignition Direct Injection

③ 10th position of VIN

NS: Not Specified.

25742_VIBE_C0001

GENERAL ENGINE SPECIFICATIONS

All measurements are given in inches.

Year	Model	Engine Displacement Liters (cc)	Engine ID/VIN	Fuel System Type	Net Horsepower @ rpm	Net Torque @ rpm (ft. lbs.)	Bore x Stroke (in.)	Com-pression Ratio	Oil Pressure @ rpm
2010	Base	1.8	8	DI	132 @ 6000	128 @ 4400	3.17 x 3.47	10.0:1	NS
		2.4	0	DI	158 @ 6000	162 @ 4000	3.48 x 3.78	9.8:1	NS
	GT	2.4	0	DI	158 @ 6000	162 @ 4000	3.48 x 3.78	9.8:1	NS
	AWD	2.4	0	DI	158 @ 6000	162 @ 4000	3.48 x 3.78	9.8:1	NS

NS: Not Specified

25742_VIBE_C0002

ENGINE TUNE-UP SPECIFICATIONS

Year	Engine Displacement Liters	Engine ID/VIN	Spark Plug Gap (in.)	Ignition Timing (deg.) MT	Ignition Timing (deg.) AT	Fuel Pump (psi)	Idle Speed (rpm) MT	Idle Speed (rpm) AT	Valve Clearance Intake	Valve Clearance Exhaust
2010	1.8	8	0.040-0.048	8 - 12 ①	8 - 12 ①	NS	600-700	600-700	NS	NS
	2.4	0	0.040-0.148	8 - 12 ①	8 - 12 ①	NS	600-700	600-700	0.0075-0.0114	0.015-0.189

① BTDC at idle.

NS: Not specified

25742_VIBE_C0003

CAPACITIES

Year	Model	Engine Displacement (Liters)	ID/VIN	Engine Oil (qts.)	Transmission/axle (pts.)		Drive Axle (pts.)		Transfer Case (pts.)	Fuel Tank (gals.)	Cooling System (qts.)
					Auto.	Manual	Front	Rear			
2010	Base	1.8	8	4.4 ①	②	4.0	N/A	N/A	N/A	13.2	5.8
		2.4	0	4.0 ①	③	5.2	N/A	N/A	N/A	13.2	6.0
	GT	2.4	0	4.0 ①	③	5.2	N/A	N/A	N/A	13.2	6.0
	AWD	2.4	0	4.0 ①	④	N/A	N/A	0.5	N/A	13.2	6.0

NOTE: All capacities are approximate. Add fluid gradually and ensure a proper fluid level is obtained.

NA: Not Applicable.

① With oil filter change.

② Drain and Refill: 5.2 Pints.
Dry Fill: 13.8 Pints.

③ Drain and Refill: 7.4 Pints.
Dry Fill: 15.8 Pints.

④ Drain and Refill: 7.4 Pints.
Dry Fill: 17.2 Pints.

25742_VIBE_C0004

FLUID SPECIFICATIONS

Year	Model	Engine Disp. Liters	Engine Oil	Manual Trans.	Auto. Trans.	Drive Axle		Transfer Case	Power Steering Fluid	Brake Master Cylinder	Cooling System
						Front	Rear				
2010	Base	1.8	5W-30	①	WS ATF	NA	NA	NA	NS	②	DEX-COOL
		2.4	5W-30	①	WS ATF	NA	NA	NA	NS	②	DEX-COOL
	GT	2.4	5W-30	①	WS ATF	NA	NA	NA	NS	②	DEX-COOL
	AWD	2.4	5W-30	①	WS ATF	NA	③	③	NS	②	DEX-COOL

① 75W-90 GL-5

NS: Not Specified

② DOT 3 Hydraulic Brake Fluid

③ 80W-90 GL-5 Hypoid

25742_VIBE_C0005

VALVE SPECIFICATIONS

Year	Engine Displacement Liters	Engine ID/VIN	Seat Angle (deg.)	Face Angle (deg.)	Spring Test Pressure (lbs. @ in.)	Spring Free-Length (in.)	Spring Installed Height (in.)	Stem-to-Guide Clearance (in.)		Stem Diameter (in.)	
								Intake	Exhaust	Intake	Exhaust
2010	1.8	8	①	45	NS	2.1008	NS	.0010-.0024	.0012-.0026	.2154-.2159	.2154-.2159
	2.4	0	①	45	NS	1.867	NS	.0010-.0035	.0012-.0037	.2154-.2159	.2152-.2157

① 3-angle seat: 30 - 45 - 90 degrees

25742_VIBE_C0006

CAMSHAFT SPECIFICATIONS

All measurements in inches unless noted

Year	Engine Displacement Liters	Engine Code/VIN	Camshaft	Journal Diameter	Brg. Oil Clearance	Shaft End-play	Runout	Journal Bore	Lobe Height
2010	1.8	8	Intake	①	②	0.0024-0.0067	0.0016	NA	1.6798-1.6896
			Exhaust	①	②	0.0024-0.0067	0.0016	NA	1.7396-1.7494
	2.4	0	Intake	③	④	0.0016-0.0043	0.0012	NA	1.8581-1.8664
			Exhaust	③	⑤	0.0035-0.0059	0.0012	NA	1.8092-1.8174

NA: Not Applicable

① #1 Journal Diameter: 1.3563 - 1.3569. All other journals: .9035 - .9041
② #1 Journal Oil Clearance: .0012 - .0033. All other journals: .0014 - .0035
③ #1 Journal Diameter: 1.4162 - 1.4167. All other journals: .9039 - .9045
④ #1 Journal Oil Clearance: ..0003 - .0015. All other journals: .0010 - .0028
⑤ #1 Journal Oil Clearance: .0016 - .0028 All other journals: .0010 - .0039

25742_VIBE_C0007

CRANKSHAFT AND CONNECTING ROD SPECIFICATIONS

All measurements are given in inches.

Year	Engine Displacement Liters	Engine ID/VIN	Crankshaft Main Brg. Journal Dia.	Main Brg. Oil Clearance	Shaft End-play	Thrust on No.	Connecting Rod Journal Diameter	Oil Clearance	Side Clearance
2010	1.8	8	1.8893-1.8898	.0006-.0020	.0016-.0071	NS	1.7320-1.7323	.0012-.0028	.0063-.0135
	2.4	0	2.1649-2.1654	.0007-.0024	.0016-.0118	NS	1.8894-1.8898	.0009-.0025	.0063-.0143

NS: Not Specified

25742_VIBE_C0008

PISTON AND RING SPECIFICATIONS

All measurements are given in inches.

Year	Engine Displacement Liters	Engine ID/VIN	Piston Clearance	Ring Gap Top Compression	Bottom Compression	Oil Control	Ring Side Clearance Top Compression	Bottom Compression	Oil Control
2010	1.8	8	0.0011-0.0035	0.0079-0.0197	0.0118-0.0276	0.0039-0.0276	0.0008-0.0028	0.0008-0.0024	0.0008-0.0026
	2.4	0	0.0008-0.0039	0.0094-0.0122	0.0130-0.0168	0.0040-0.0118	0.0008-0.0028	0.0008-0.0024	0.0008-0.0028

25742_VIBE_C0009

TORQUE SPECIFICATIONS
All readings in ft. lbs.

Year	Engine Disp. Liters	Engine ID/VIN	Cylinder Head Bolts	Main Bearing Bolts	Rod Bearing Bolts	Crankshaft Pulley Bolts	Flywheel Bolts	Manifold		Spark Plugs	Oil Pan Drain Plug
								Intake	Exhaust		
2010	1.8	8	①	②	③	140	④	21	16	18	27
	2.4	0	⑤	⑥	⑦	133	⑧	22	27	18	30

① Step 1: 36 ft. lbs.
  Step 2: Plus 90 degrees
  Step 3: Plus 45 degrees

② Step 1: 30 ft. lbs.
  Step 2: Plus 90 degrees

③ Step 1: 15 ft. lbs.
  Step 2: Plus 90 degrees

④ With automatic transmissions: 61 ft. lbs.
  With manual transmissions:
    Step 1: 36 ft. lbs.
    Step 2: Plus 90 degrees

⑤ Step 1: 52 ft. lbs.
  Step 2: Plus 90 degrees

⑥ Step 1: 15 ft. lbs.
  Step 2: 30 ft. lbs.
  Step 3: Plus 90 degrees

⑦ Step 1: 18 ft. lbs.
  Step 2: Plus 90 degrees

⑧ With automatic transmissions: 72 ft. lbs.
  With manual transmissions: 96 ft. lbs.

25742_VIBE_C0010

WHEEL ALIGNMENT

Year	Model		Caster		Camber		Toe-in (in.)
			Range (+/-Deg.)	Preferred Setting (Deg.)	Range (+/-Deg.)	Preferred Setting (Deg.)	
2010	Base	Front	0.75	+2.90	0.75	-0.55	0 +/- 0.20
		Rear	NA	NA	0.75	-1.45	+0.30 +/- 0.25
	GT	Front	0.75	+3.00	0.75	-0.60	0 +/- 0.20
		Rear	NA	NA	0.75	-1.05	+0.25 +/- 0.25
	AWD	Front	0.75	+3.00	0.75	-0.60	0 +/- 0.20
		Rear	NA	NA	0.75	-1.05	+0.25 +/- 0.25

NA: Not Applicable

25742_VIBE_C0011

TIRE, WHEEL AND BALL JOINT SPECIFICATIONS

| Year | Model | OEM Tires | | Tire Pressures (psi) | | Wheel Size | Ball Joint Inspection | Lug Nut (ft. lbs.) |
		Standard	Optional	Front	Rear			
2010	Base	P205/55HR16		①	①	16	②	③
			P215/45HR17	①	①	17	②	③
	GT	P215/45HR18	NA	①	①	18	②	③
	AWD	P205/55HR16		①	①	16	②	③
			P215/45HR17	①	①	17	②	③

OEM: Original Equipment Manufacturer

PSI: Pounds Per Square Inch

① Always refer to the owner's manual and/or vehicle label

② Replace if any measurable movement is found

③ Step 1: 38.4 ft. lbs.

   Step 2: 76 ft. lbs.

NA: Not Available

25742_VIBE_C0012

BRAKE SPECIFICATIONS
All measurements in inches unless noted

| Year | Model | | Brake Disc | | | Brake Drum Diameter | | | Minimum Pad/Lining Thickness | | Brake Caliper | |
			Original Thickness	Minimum Thickness	Max. Runout	Original Inside Diameter	Max. Wear Limit	Maximum Machine Diamter	Front	Rear	Bracket Bolts (ft. lbs.)	Mounting Bolts (ft. lbs.)
2010	Base	F	①	②	0.002	NA	NA	NA	0.039	0.039	79	25
		R	③	④	0.006	NA	NA	NA	0.039	0.039	46	26
	GT	F	1.102	0.984	0.002	NA	NA	NA	0.039	0.039	79	25
		R	0.393	0.335	0.006	NA	NA	NA	0.039	0.039	43	20
	AWD	F	1.102	0.984	0.002	NA	NA	NA	0.039	0.039	79	25
		R	0.393	0.335	0.006	NA	NA	NA	0.039	0.039	43	20

F: Front

R: Rear

NA: Not available.

① With 1.8L: 0.866

   With 2.4L: 1.102

② With 1.8L: 0.748

   With 2.4L: 0.984

③ With 1.8L: 0.354

   With 2.4L: 0.393

④ With 1.8L: 0.295

   With 2.4L: 0.335

25742_VIBE_C0013

MAINTENANCE I AND II SERVICE SCHEDULES
VIBE

When the CHANGE ENGINE OIL light appears, certain services and inspections are required.

Required services are described as Maintenance I and Maintenance II.

The first service of a vehicle should be Maintenance I, and the second service should be Maintenance II.

Alternate between the 2 services thereafter. However, in some cases, Maintenance II may be required more often.

Maintenance I: Use Maintenance I if the CHANGE ENGINE OIL light comes on within 10 months since the vehicle was purchased or, if Maintenance II was performed.

Maintenance II: Use Maintenance II if the previous service performed was Maintenance I. Always use Maintenance II whenever the CHANGE ENGINE OIL light comes on 10 months or more since the last service, or, if the CHANGE ENGINE OIL light has not come on at all for one year.

Service Item	Maintenance I	Maintenance II
Change the engine oil and filter.	✓	✓
Reset the oil life system.	✓	✓
Visually inspect the vehicle for leaks or damage. A fluid loss in the vehicle system could indicate a problem. Inspect, repair and add fluid to the system if necessary.	✓	✓
Inspect the engine air cleaner filter. If necessary, replace the filter.	—	✓
Rotate the tires. Inspect the tire inflation pressures and the tire wear.	✓	✓
Visually inspect the brake lines and hoses for proper hook-up, binding, leaks, cracks, chafing, etc. Inspect the disc brake pads for wear and the rotors for surface condition. Inspect the drum brake linings for wear or cracks. Inspect other brake parts, including drums, wheel cylinders, calipers, parking brake, etc. Inspect the parking brake adjustment.	✓	✓
Inspect the engine coolant and the windshield washer fluid levels. Add fluid as needed.	✓	✓
Inspect the suspension and steering components. Inspect the front and rear suspension and the steering system for damaged, loose or missing parts, or signs of wear. Inspect the power steering lines and the hoses for proper hook-up, binding, leaks, cracks, chafing, etc.	—	✓
Visually inspect the coolant hoses and replace the hoses if they are cracked, swollen or deteriorated. Inspect all pipes, fittings and clamps; replace with GM parts as needed. To help ensure proper operation, a pressure test of the cooling system and pressure cap and cleaning the outside of the radiator and air conditioning condenser is recommended at least once a year.	—	✓
Ensure the safety belt reminder light and all the belts, buckles, latch plates, retractors and anchorages are working properly. Look for any other loose or damaged safety belt system parts. If you see anything that might keep a safety belt system from working correctly, repair or replaced the damaged part. Replace torn or frayed safety belts, refer to Operational and Functional Checks in Seat Belts. Inspect for any opened or broken air bag coverings, and repair or replace as needed. The air bag system does require regular maintenance.	—	✓
Lubricate the body components.	✓	✓
Lubricate all key lock cylinders, hood latch assemblies, secondary latches, pivots, spring anchor and release pawl, hood and door hinges, rear folding seats and liftgate hinges. Frequent lubrication may be required when exposed to a corrosive environment, refer to Fluid and Lubricant Recommendations . Applying dielectric silicone grease GM P/N 12345579 (Canadian P/N 1974984) or equivalent on the weatherstrips with a clean cloth.	—	✓
Inspect the wiper blades and replace as necessary.	✓	✓
Inspect the throttle and fuel system.	—	✓
Replace the passenger compartment air filter.	—	✓
Inspect exhaust system and heat shields.	✓	✓

To reset the CHANGE ENGINE OIL light:

1. Turn the ignition key to the ON/RUN position with the engine OFF.
2. Press and release the stem in the lower center of the instrument cluster until the OIL LIFE message is displayed.
3. Once the alternating OIL LIFE and RESET messages appear, press and hold the stem until several beeps sound.
   This confirms that the oil life system has been reset to 100 percent.
4. Turn the ignition key to the OFF position.
   If the CHANGE ENGINE OIL message comes back on when the vehicle is started, the engine oil life system has not been reset. Repeat the procedure.

25742_VIBE_C0014

ADDITIONAL MAINTENANCE SERVICES - NORMAL
VIBE

TO BE SERVICED	TYPE OF SERVICE	VEHICLE MILEAGE INTERVAL (x1000)					
		25	50	75	100	125	150
Engine coolant	Replace						✓
Air cleaner filter	Replace		✓		✓		✓
Automatic transaxle fluid & filter	Replace				✓		
Spark plugs	Replace				✓		
Exhaust system & heat shields	Service/Inspect	✓	✓	✓	✓	✓	✓
Cooling system hoses and clamps	Service/Inspect	✓	✓	✓	✓	✓	✓
Fuel system	Inspect	✓	✓	✓	✓	✓	✓
Accessory drive belts	Replace						✓
Evaporative control system	Inspect		✓		✓		✓
Passenger compartment air filter	Replace	✓	✓	✓	✓	✓	✓

25742_VIBE_C0015

ADDITIONAL MAINTENANCE SERVICES - SEVERE
VIBE

TO BE SERVICED	TYPE OF SERVICE	VEHICLE MILEAGE INTERVAL (x1000)					
		25	50	75	100	125	150
Engine coolant	Replace						✓
Air cleaner filter	Replace	✓	✓	✓	✓	✓	✓
Automatic transaxle fluid & filter	Replace		✓		✓		✓
Spark plugs	Replace				✓		
Exhaust system & heat shields	Inspect	✓	✓	✓	✓	✓	✓
Cooling system hoses and clamps	Inspect	✓	✓	✓	✓	✓	✓
Fuel system	Inspect	✓	✓	✓	✓	✓	✓
Accessory drive belt(s)	Replace						✓
Evaporative control system	Inspect		✓		✓		✓
Passenger compartment air cleaner	Replace	✓	✓	✓	✓	✓	✓

25742_VIBE_C0016

GENERAL INFORMATION

PRECAUTIONS

• Certain components within the ABS system are not intended to be serviced or repaired individually.

• Do not use rubber hoses or other parts not specifically specified for and ABS system. When using repair kits, replace all parts included in the kit. Partial or incorrect repair may lead to functional problems and require the replacement of components.

• Lubricate rubber parts with clean, fresh brake fluid to ease assembly. Do not use shop air to clean parts; damage to rubber components may result.

• Use only DOT 3 brake fluid from an unopened container.

• If any hydraulic component or line is removed or replaced, it may be necessary to bleed the entire system.

• A clean repair area is essential. Always clean the reservoir and cap thoroughly before removing the cap. The slightest amount of dirt in the fluid may plug an orifice and impair the system function. Perform repairs after components have been thoroughly cleaned; use only denatured alcohol to clean components. Do not allow ABS components to come into contact with any substance containing mineral oil; this includes used shop rags.

• The Anti-Lock control unit is a microprocessor similar to other computer units in the vehicle. Ensure that the ignition switch is **OFF** before removing or installing controller harnesses. Avoid static electricity discharge at or near the controller.

• If any arc welding is to be done on the vehicle, the control unit should be unplugged before welding operations begin.

• Do not spill brake fluid on painted or plastic surfaces or damage to the surface may occur. If brake fluid is spilled onto a painted or plastic surface, immediately wash the surface with water.

✳✳ CAUTION

Brake fluid contains polyglycol ethers and polyglycols. Avoid contact with the eyes. Wash hands thoroughly after handling. If brake fluid contacts the eyes, flush the eyes for 15 minutes with cold running water. Get medical attention if irritation persists. If taken internally, drink water and induce vomiting. Get medical attention immediately. Failure to fol-

low these instructions may result in personal injury.

SPEED SENSORS

REMOVAL & INSTALLATION

Front Speed Sensor

See Figure 1.

1. Before servicing the vehicle, refer to the Precautions Section.
2. Remove the wheel housing.

➡ **The wheel speed sensor is serviceable only as an assembly. Do NOT attempt to service the sensor harness pigtail.**

3. Disconnect the wheel speed sensor electrical connector.
4. Remove the bolt retaining the wheel speed sensor pigtail harness.
5. Remove the bolt and separate the brake hose.
6. Remove the bolt and the sensor clamp from the strut.
7. Remove the sensor harness clamp.
8. Remove the front wheel speed sensor retaining bolt, and remove the wheel speed sensor from the steering knuckle.

To install:

9. To install, reverse the removal procedure and note the following:
   • Tighten the front wheel speed sensor bolt to 76 inch lbs. (8.5 Nm).
   • Tighten the sensor harness clamp bolt to 21 ft. lbs. (29 Nm).
   • Tighten the wheel speed sensor pigtail harness bolt to 71 inch lbs. (8 Nm).

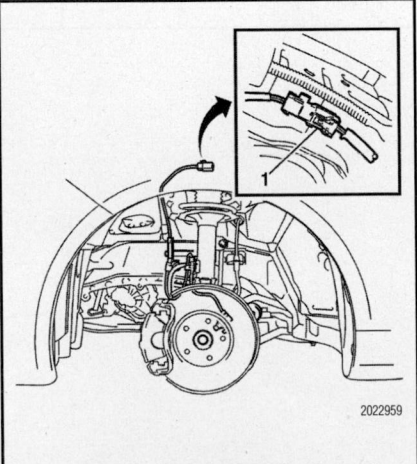

Fig. 1 Disconnect the front wheel speed sensor electrical connector

10. Perform vehicle diagnostic system check.

Rear Speed Sensor

AWD

See Figure 2.

1. Before servicing the vehicle, refer to the Precautions Section.
2. Remove the fuel tank filler pipe protector bolts and remove the fuel tank filler pipe protector.
3. Remove the rear seat bottom and seat back.

➡ **The wheel speed sensor is serviceable only as an assembly. Do NOT attempt to service the sensor harness pigtail.**

4. Disconnect the electrical connector from the wheel speed sensor.
5. Raise and suitably support the vehicle.
6. Pull the sensor harness and grommet out through the body.
7. Remove the bolt which retains the wheel speed sensor harness to the vehicle.
8. Remove the bolt and nut which retains the wheel speed sensor harness to the upper arm and suspension member.
9. Remove the wheel speed sensor retaining bolt and remove the wheel speed sensor from suspension knuckle.

To install:

10. To install, reverse the removal procedure and note the following:
   • Tighten the rear wheel speed sensor bolt to 71 inch lbs. (8 Nm).
   • Tighten the wheel speed sensor harness to the upper arm and suspension member bolt and nut bolt to 44 inch lbs. (5 Nm).

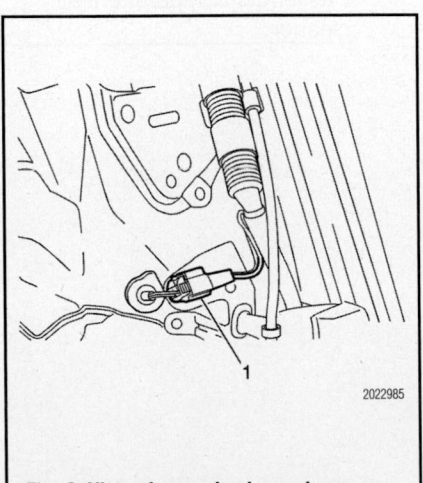

Fig. 2 View of rear wheel speed sensor—AWD

- Tighten the wheel speed sensor harness bolt and nut bolt to 44 inch lbs. (5 Nm).

11. Perform vehicle diagnostic system check.

FWD

See Figures 3 and 4.

1. Disconnect the electrical connector from the wheel speed sensor.

2. Remove the rear axle hub and bearing assembly.

3. Remove the wheel speed sensor from the rear axle hub.

To install:

4. Installation is the reverse of the removal procedure.

5. Perform vehicle diagnostic system check.

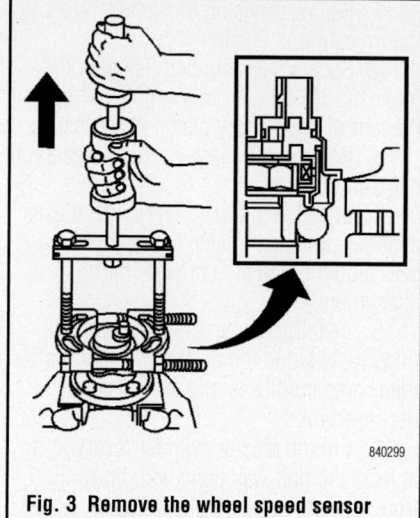

Fig. 3 Remove the wheel speed sensor from the rear axle hub—FWD

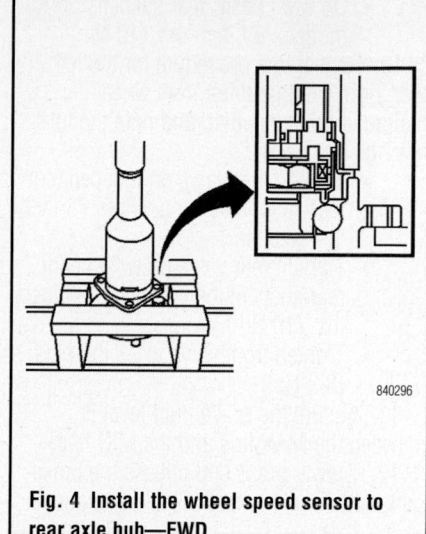

Fig. 4 Install the wheel speed sensor to rear axle hub—FWD

BRAKES   BLEEDING THE BRAKE SYSTEM

BLEEDING PROCEDURE

BLEEDING PROCEDURE

1. Before servicing the vehicle, refer to the Precautions Section.

2. With the engine OFF, press on the brake pedal several times in order to remove vacuum from the vacuum brake booster.

3. If the vehicle has an automatic transmission, shift into park.

4. Apply the park brake.

5. Place a clean shop cloth beneath the brake master cylinder in order to absorb brake fluid spills.

6. Place a drain pan below the master cylinder.

7. Remove the left side air inlet grill panel and fill the brake fluid reservoir up to the MAX line. Ensure the brake fluid level is between the MAX line and the MIN line during this bleeding procedure. Refer to Bleeding Procedure, fluid fill procedure.

❊❊ CAUTION

Remove all the air from the hydraulic brake system any time the hydraulic brake system is opened for repair. The entire bleeding procedure must be followed. Failure to remove all the air in the hydraulic brake system will result in reduced braking performance and possible personal injury.

8. If you disconnected the brake pipes from the master cylinder, perform the following steps:

a. Ensure the rear brake pipe is installed to the master cylinder.

b. Remove the front brake pipe from the front port of the brake master cylinder.

c. Allow a small amount of brake fluid to gravity bleed from the open port of the master cylinder.

d. Using a torque wrench with a fulcrum length of 9.84 inches (250 mm) and a union nut wrench, reconnect the front brake pipe to the master cylinder port and tighten to 124 inch lbs. (14 Nm).

e. Have an assistant slowly press the brake pedal fully and maintain steady pressure on the pedal.

f. Loosen the front brake pipe in order to purge air from the open front port of the master cylinder.

g. Using the torque wrench and union nut wrench, tighten the front brake pipe on the master cylinder to 124 inch lbs. (14 Nm).

h. Have the assistant slowly release the brake pedal.

i. Wait 15 seconds.

j. Ensure the brake fluid level is between the MAX line and the MIN line during this bleeding procedure.

k. Repeat this procedure until all air is purged from the front port of the master cylinder.

l. Using the torque wrench and union nut wrench, tighten the front brake pipe on the master cylinder to 124 inch lbs. (14 Nm).

m. Repeat this procedure for the rear

brake pipe until all air is purged from the rear port of the master cylinder.

9. Perform the following steps in order to bleed the right rear wheel hydraulic brake circuit:

a. Remove the valve cap from the wheel hydraulic circuit bleeder valve.

b. Use a proper wrench on the bleeder valve.

c. Install a transparent hose over the end of the bleeder valve.

d. Submerge the open end of the transparent hose into a transparent container partially filled with DOT-3 brake fluid from a clean, sealed brake fluid container.

e. Have an assistant slowly press the brake pedal fully and maintain steady pressure on the pedal.

f. Loosen the bleeder valve in order to purge air from the wheel hydraulic circuit.

g. Tighten the bleeder valve:
- On independent rear suspension models: 73 inch lbs. (8.3 Nm).
- On twist beam rear suspension models: 89 inch lbs. (10 Nm).

h. Have the assistant slowly release the brake pedal.

i. Wait 15 seconds.

j. Ensure the brake fluid level is between the MAX line and the MIN line during this bleeding procedure.

k. Repeat this procedure until all air is purged from the wheel hydraulic circuit.

l. Tighten the bleeder valve:
- On independent rear suspension models: 73 inch lbs. (8.3 Nm).

- On twist beam rear suspension models: 89 inch lbs. (10 Nm).

10. Repeat this procedure for the left rear, right front, and left front wheel hydraulic brake circuits, and note the following:

- Tighten rear valve on independent rear suspension models to 73 inch lbs. (8.3 Nm).
- Tighten rear valve on twist beam rear suspension models to 89 inch lbs. (10 Nm).
- Tighten front valve to 73 inch lbs. (8.3 Nm).

11. Ensure the brake fluid level is between the MAX line and the MIN line.

12. Slowly press and release the brake pedal. Observe the feel of the brake pedal.

※※ CAUTION

Do not move the vehicle until a firm brake pedal is obtained. Failure to obtain a firm pedal before moving vehicle may result in personal injury.

13. If the brake pedal feels spongy, repeat the bleeding procedure again. If the brake pedal still feels spongy after repeating the bleeding procedure, inspect the brake system for external leaks.

To inspect:

Turn the ignition key ON, with the engine OFF. Verify if the brake system warning lamp remains illuminated. If the brake system warning lamp remains illuminated, repair as necessary.

➡**DO NOT allow the vehicle to be driven until the symptom is diagnosed and repaired.**

MASTER CYLINDER BLEEDING

※※ WARNING

Do not use any fluid other than clean brake fluid meeting manufacturer's specification. Additionally, do not use brake fluid that has been previously drained. Following these instructions will help prevent system contamination, brake component damage, and the risk of serious personal injury.

※※ WARNING

Do not allow the brake master cylinder to run dry during the bleeding operation. The master cylinder may be damaged if operated without fluid, resulting in degraded braking performance.

1. Before servicing the vehicle, refer to the Precautions Section.

2. Secure the mounting flange of the brake master cylinder in a bench vise so that the rear of the primary piston is accessible.

3. Remove the master cylinder reservoir cap and diaphragm.

4. Install suitable fittings to the master cylinder ports that match the type of flare seat required and also provide for hose attachment.

5. Install transparent hoses to the fittings installed to the master cylinder ports, then route the hoses into the master cylinder reservoir.

6. Fill the master cylinder reservoir to at least the half-way point with brake fluid from a clean, sealed brake fluid container. Refer to Bleeding Procedure, fluid fill procedure.

7. Ensure that the ends of the transparent hoses running into the master cylinder reservoir are fully submerged in the brake fluid.

8. Using a smooth, round-ended tool, depress and release the primary piston as far as it will travel, a depth of about 1 inch (25 mm), several times. Observe the flow of fluid coming from the ports.

9. As air is bled from the primary and secondary pistons, the effort required to depress the primary piston will increase and the amount of travel will decrease.

10. Continue to depress and release the primary piston until fluid flows freely from the ports with no evidence of air bubbles.

11. Remove the transparent hoses from the master cylinder reservoir.

12. Install the master cylinder reservoir cap and diaphragm.

13. Remove the fittings with the transparent hoses from the master cylinder ports. Wrap the master cylinder with a clean shop cloth to prevent brake fluid spills.

14. Remove the master cylinder from the vise.

BRAKE LINE BLEEDING

Refer to Bleeding Procedure.

FLUID FILL PROCEDURE

Master Cylinder Reservoir Filling

※※ WARNING

When filling the master cylinder, use only DOT 3-approved brake fluid. Do not use a container which has been used for petroleum based fluids, or a container which is wet with water. Petroleum based fluids will cause

swelling and distortion of rubber parts in the hydraulic brake system, and water will mix with brake fluid, lowering the boiling point. Keep all fluid containers capped to prevent contamination.

➡The brake fluid level MUST be between the MIN line and the MAX line to provide adequate brake fluid reserve, prevent air from entering the hydraulic brake system, and to allow the brake fluid to expand due to the heat from the brakes and from the engine.

1. Before servicing the vehicle, refer to the Precautions Section.

2. Visually inspect the brake fluid reservoir and verify if the brake fluid is between the MIN line and the MAX line.

3. If the brake fluid level is between the MIN line and the MAX line, do not add brake fluid. If the brake fluid level is above the MAX line or below the MIN line, continue with this procedure.

4. If the brake fluid level is below the MIN line during a routine fluid inspection, inspect the brake system for wear and potential brake fluid leaks.

5. Slide the hood rear seal to the right and up in order to disengage the clip.

6. Disengage the 5 claws and remove the left side access panel.

7. Clean the outside of the reservoir and the reservoir cap in order to avoid dirt contamination of the brake fluid.

8. Remove the reservoir cap.

※※ CAUTION

Do not overfill the brake fluid reservoir. Overfilling the brake fluid reservoir may cause the brake fluid to overflow onto the engine exhaust components during brake system service. The brake fluid is flammable and may cause a fire and personal injury if the brake fluid contacts the engine exhaust system components.

9. If the brake fluid level is below the MIN mark, the brake pads are not worn, and there are no brake fluid leaks, add brake fluid from a clean, sealed brake fluid container, to the reservoir up to the MAX line. If the brake fluid level is above the MAX line, siphon the brake fluid level down to the MAX line.

10. Install the reservoir cap.

11. Install the left side access panel and engage the 5 claws.

12. Install the hood rear seal and engage the clip.

BRAKES

FRONT DISC BRAKES

BRAKE CALIPER

REMOVAL & INSTALLATION

See Figure 5.

1. Before servicing the vehicle, refer to the Precautions Section.
2. Use a siphon in order to remove half of the brake fluid from the reservoir.
3. Raise and support the vehicle.
4. Remove the tire and wheel assembly.
5. Place a container below the brake hose in order to catch the brake fluid.
6. Remove the front brake hose fitting and the washer from the caliper.
7. Discard the washer.
8. Use a wrench in order to hold the caliper slide pins. Remove the caliper bolts.
9. Remove the caliper from the caliper bracket.

To inspect:

10. Clean and inspect the disc brake mounting and hardware components. Repair or replace parts as necessary.
11. Clean and inspect the caliper. Repair or replace parts as necessary.

To install:

12. If the caliper piston is not compressed into the caliper bore, complete the following steps:

a. Wrap the handle of a hammer with tape.
b. Use the handle of a hammer in order to compress the caliper piston into the caliper bore.

13. Ensure the caliper slide pins are lubricated with lithium soap base glycol grease or Silicone Brake Lubricant, or equivalent. Replace if necessary.
14. Install the caliper to the caliper bracket.
15. Use a wrench in order to hold the caliper slide pins. Install the caliper bolts and tighten to 25 ft. lbs. (34 Nm).
16. Install a NEW washer to the flexible hose lock hole in the caliper.
17. Install the brake hose to the caliper. Install the hose lock securely into the lock hole in the caliper.
18. Install the brake hose fitting and tighten to 21 ft. lbs. (29 Nm).
19. Install the tire and wheel assembly.
20. Lower the vehicle.

✳✳ CAUTION

Do not move the vehicle until a firm brake pedal is obtained. Failure to obtain a firm pedal before moving vehicle may result in personal injury.

21. With the engine OFF, gradually apply and release the brake pedal several times in order to position the caliper pistons and the brake pads.
22. Fill the master cylinder reservoir. Refer to Bleeding Procedure, fluid fill procedure.
23. Bleed the brake system. Refer to Bleeding Procedure.

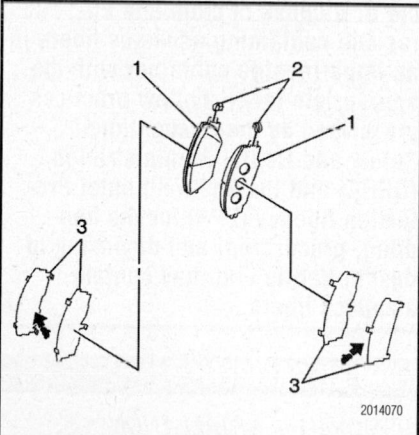

1. Caliper bolt
2. Caliper
3. Caliper slide pin
4. Grease seal
5. Caliper bracket
6. NS
7. NS
8. NS
9. NS
10. Caliper bracket bolt
11. Grease seal
12. NS
13. Caliper slide pin
14. Caliper bolt

2014053

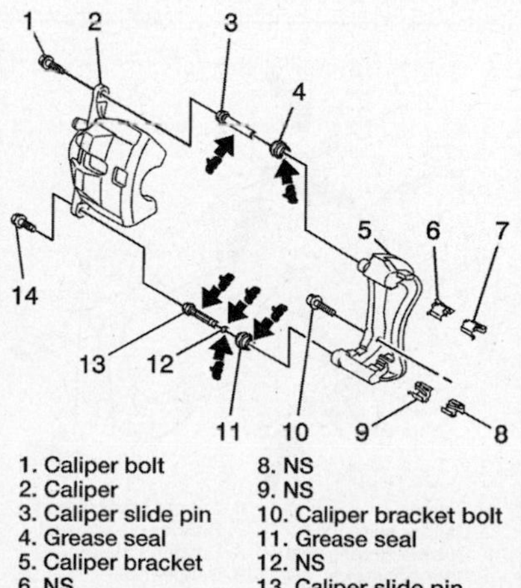

Fig. 5 View of front brake caliper

DISC BRAKE PADS

REMOVAL & INSTALLATION

See Figure 6.

1. Before servicing the vehicle, refer to the Precautions Section.
2. Use a siphon in order to remove half of the brake fluid from the master cylinder reservoir.
3. Raise and support the vehicle.
4. Remove the front tire and wheel assembly from the vehicle.
5. Install a large C-clamp over the brake caliper. Position the ends of the C-clamp against the rear of the caliper body and against the outer brake pad.
6. Tighten the C-clamp in order to compress the caliper piston into the caliper bore.
7. Remove the C-clamp from the caliper.
8. Use a wrench in order to hold the caliper slide pins. Remove the caliper bolts.

✳✳ WARNING

Support the brake caliper with heavy mechanic wire, or equivalent, whenever it is separated from its mount and the hydraulic flexible brake hose is still connected. Failure to support the caliper in this manner will cause the flexible brake hose to bear the weight of the caliper, which may cause damage to the brake hose and in turn may cause a brake fluid leak.

9. Remove the caliper housing from the caliper bracket. Support the caliper with a

2014070

Fig. 6 Remove the 4 insulators (3) from the 2 brake pads (1). On 2.4L, remove the 2 wear indicators (2) from the 2 brake pads (1)

wire in order to prevent damage to the brake hose.

10. Remove the brake pads with the insulators.

11. Remove the 4 insulators from the 2 brake pads. On 2.4L, remove the 2 wear indicators from the 2 brake pads.

➡ **Refinish or replace the rotor ONLY if the condition of the rotor requires service. DO NOT refinish the rotor if the brake pads are the only components requiring service.**

To install:

12. If the caliper piston is not compressed into the caliper bore, complete the following steps:

 a. Place an old brake pad or a block of wood against the caliper piston.

 b. Install a large C-clamp over the body of the brake caliper.

 c. Position the ends of the C-clamp against the rear of the caliper body and against the pad or the wood.

 d. Tighten the C-clamp in order to compress the caliper piston into the caliper bore.

 e. Remove the C-clamp.

13. Apply disc brake grease to both sides of the 2 inner insulators (1.8L) or outer insulators (2.4L).

14. Ensure the disc brake grease covers the area where the outer insulators contact the inner insulators.

15. Install the 2 inner insulators to the 2 brake pads.

16. Install the 2 outer insulators to the 2 inner insulators.

17. On 2.4L, install the 2 wear indicators to the 2 brake pads.

18. On all models, install the brake pads with the insulators to the caliper bracket.

19. Remove the wire and install the caliper housing to the caliper bracket.

20. Use a wrench in order to hold the caliper slide pins. Install the caliper bolts and tighten to 25 ft. lbs. (34 Nm).

21. Install the front tire and wheel assembly to the vehicle.

22. Lower the vehicle.

23. With the engine OFF, gradually apply and release the brake pedal several times in order to position the caliper pistons and the brake pads.

24. Fill the master cylinder fluid reservoir. Refer to Bleeding Procedure.

25. Burnish the pads and the rotors.

BRAKES

✳✳ CAUTION

Dust and dirt accumulating on brake parts during normal use may contain asbestos fibers from production or aftermarket brake linings. Breathing excessive concentrations of asbestos fibers can cause serious bodily harm. Exercise care when servicing brake parts. Do not sand or grind brake lining unless equipment used is designed to contain the dust residue. Do not clean brake parts with compressed air or by dry brushing. Cleaning should be done by dampening the brake components with a fine mist of water, then wiping the brake components clean with a dampened cloth. Dispose of cloth and all residue containing asbestos fibers in an impermeable container with the appropriate label. Follow practices prescribed by the Occupational Safety and Health Administration (OSHA) and the Environmental Protection Agency (EPA) for the handling, processing, and disposing of dust or debris that may contain asbestos fibers.

BRAKE CALIPER

REMOVAL & INSTALLATION

AWD & GT

See Figure 7.

1. Before servicing the vehicle, refer to the Precautions Section.

2. Use a siphon in order to remove half of the brake fluid from the reservoir.

3. Raise and support the vehicle.

4. Remove the rear tire and wheel assembly.

5. Place a container below the rear brake hose and the fitting in order to catch the brake fluid.

6. Remove the rear brake hose, the fitting, and the washer from the caliper.

7. Discard the washer.

8. Use a wrench in order to hold the slide pins. Remove the caliper bolts.

9. Remove the caliper from the vehicle.

To install:

10. If the caliper piston is not compressed into the caliper bore, complete the following steps:

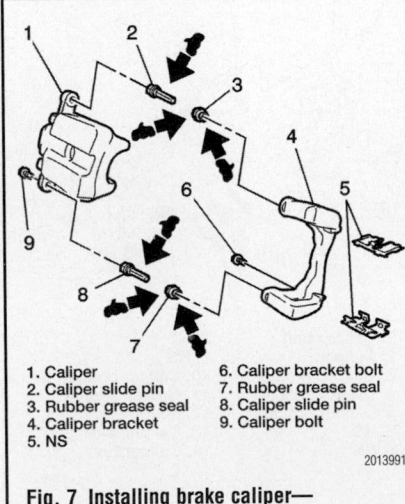

1. Caliper
2. Caliper slide pin
3. Rubber grease seal
4. Caliper bracket
5. NS
6. Caliper bracket bolt
7. Rubber grease seal
8. Caliper slide pin
9. Caliper bolt

2013991

Fig. 7 Installing brake caliper— AWD & GT

REAR DISC BRAKES

 a. Wrap the handle of a hammer with tape.

 b. Use the handle of a hammer in order to compress the caliper piston into the caliper bore.

11. Ensure the caliper slide pins are lubricated with lithium soap base glycol grease or Silicone Brake Lubricant, or equivalent. Replace if necessary.

12. Position the caliper to the vehicle.

13. Install the caliper bolts and tighten to 20 ft. lbs. (27 Nm).

14. Install a NEW washer to the flexible hose lock hole in the caliper.

15. Install the brake hose to the caliper.

16. Install the brake hose fitting and tighten to 24 ft. lbs. (33 Nm).

17. Install the rear tire and wheel assembly.

18. Lower the vehicle.

19. Fill the master cylinder reservoir. Refer to Bleeding Procedure, fluid fill procedure.

✳✳ CAUTION

Do not move the vehicle until a firm brake pedal is obtained. Failure to obtain a firm pedal before moving vehicle may result in personal injury.

20. With the engine OFF, gradually apply and release the brake pedal several times in order to position the caliper pistons and the brake pads.

21. Bleed the brake system. Refer to Bleeding Procedure.

EXCEPT AWD & GT

See Figures 8 and 9.

1. Before servicing the vehicle, refer to the Precautions Section.

2. Loosen the park brake system. Refer to Parking Brake Cables, adjustment.

3. Use a siphon in order to remove half of the brake fluid from the reservoir.

4. Raise and support the vehicle.

5. Remove the rear tire and wheel assembly.

6. Remove the park brake lever protector from the rear park brake cable.

7. Disengage the clamp from the rear park brake cable.

8. Remove the bolt.

9. Separate the rear park brake cable from the bracket on the rear brake caliper.

10. Use an offset wrench in order to disengage the clip and separate the rear park brake cable from the caliper.

11. Place a container below the rear brake hose and the fitting in order to catch the brake fluid.

12. Remove the rear brake hose, the fitting, and the washer from the caliper.

13. Discard the washer.

14. Use a wrench in order to hold the slide pins. Remove the caliper bolts.

15. Remove the caliper from the vehicle.

To install:

16. To install, reverse the removal procedure and note the following:

- If the caliper piston is not compressed enough into the bore in order to install the caliper, use a caliper piston tool in order to turn the piston in as far as possible.

- Turn the piston in order to align the piston groove 90 degrees from the line between the caliper slide pin bores.

- Align the piston groove with the protrusion in the brake pad.

- Ensure the cylinder boot is installed in the groove of the piston.

- >Ensure the caliper slide pins are lubricated with lithium soap base glycol grease or Silicone Brake Lubricant, or equivalent.

- Tighten the caliper bolts to 26 ft. lbs. (35 Nm).

- Install a NEW washer to the flexible hose lock hole in the caliper.

- Install the brake hose lock securely into the lock hole in the caliper.

- Tighten the brake hose fitting to 21 ft. lbs. (29 Nm).

- Tighten the rear park brake cable bolt to 53 inch lbs. (6 Nm).

17. Lower the vehicle.

18. Fill the master cylinder reservoir. Refer to Bleeding Procedure, fluid fill procedure.

✳✳ CAUTION

Do not move the vehicle until a firm brake pedal is obtained. Failure to obtain a firm pedal before moving vehicle may result in personal injury.

19. With the engine OFF, gradually apply and release the brake pedal several times in order to position the caliper pistons and the brake pads.

20. Bleed the brake system. Refer to Bleeding Procedure.

21. Adjust the parking brake system. Refer to Parking Brake Cables, adjustment.

DISC BRAKE PADS

REMOVAL & INSTALLATION

AWD & GT

See Figure 10.

1. Before servicing the vehicle, refer to the Precautions Section.

2. Use a siphon in order to remove half of the brake fluid from the master cylinder reservoir.

3. Raise and support the vehicle.

4. Remove the rear tire and wheel assembly.

5. Install a large C-clamp over the brake caliper. Position the ends of the C-clamp against the rear of the caliper body and against the outer brake pad.

6. Tighten the C-clamp in order to compress the caliper piston into the caliper bore.

7. Remove the C-clamp from the caliper.

8. Use a wrench in order to hold the caliper slide pins. Remove the caliper bolts.

✳✳ WARNING

Support the brake caliper with heavy mechanic wire, or equivalent, whenever it is separated from its mount and the hydraulic flexible brake hose is still connected. Failure to support the caliper in this manner will cause the flexible brake hose to bear the weight of the caliper, which may cause damage to the brake hose and in turn may cause a brake fluid leak.

9. Remove the caliper housing from the caliper bracket. Support the caliper with a wire in order to prevent damage to the brake hose.

10. Remove the brake pads with the insulators.

11. Remove the wear indicators and the insulators from the pads.

➡Refinish or replace the rotor ONLY if the condition of the rotor requires service. DO NOT refinish the rotor if the brake pads are the only components requiring service.

To install:

12. If the caliper piston is not compressed into the caliper bore, complete the following steps:

a. Place an old brake pad or a block of wood against the caliper piston.

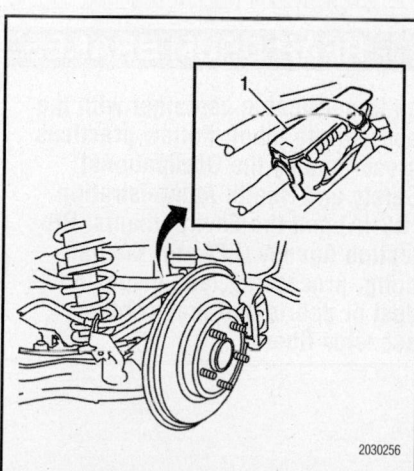

Fig. 8 Remove the park brake lever protector (1) from the rear park brake cable—Except AWD & GT

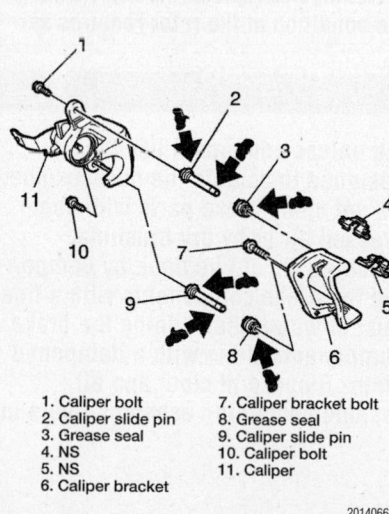

1. Caliper bolt	7. Caliper bracket bolt
2. Caliper slide pin	8. Grease seal
3. Grease seal	9. Caliper slide pin
4. NS	10. Caliper bolt
5. NS	11. Caliper
6. Caliper bracket	

Fig. 9 View of rear brake caliper—Except AWD & GT

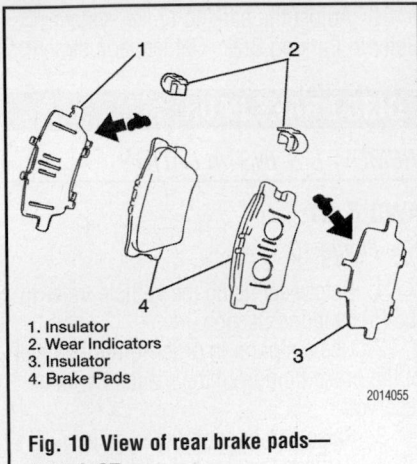

1. Insulator
2. Wear Indicators
3. Insulator
4. Brake Pads

2014055

Fig. 10 View of rear brake pads—AWD & GT

b. Install a large C-clamp over the body of the brake caliper.

c. Position the ends of the C-clamp against the rear of the caliper body and against the pad or the wood.

d. Tighten the C-clamp in order to compress the caliper piston into the caliper bore.

e. Remove the C-clamp.

f. Apply disc brake grease to the pad side of the 2 insulators. Ensure the disc brake grease covers the area where the insulators contact the pads .

13. Install the 2 insulators to the 2 brake pads.

14. Install the 2 wear indicators to the 2 brake pads.

15. Install the brake pads with the insulators and the wear indicators to the caliper bracket.

16. Remove the wire from the caliper and install the caliper to the caliper bracket.

17. Use a wrench in order to hold the caliper slide pins. Install the 2 bolts and tighten to 20 ft. lbs. (27 Nm).

18. Install the rear tire and wheel assembly to the vehicle.

19. Lower the vehicle.

20. With the engine OFF, gradually apply and release the brake pedal several times in order to position the caliper pistons and the brake pads.

21. Fill the master cylinder reservoir. Refer to Bleeding Procedure, fluid fill procedure.

22. Burnish the pads and the rotors.

EXCEPT AWD & GT

See Figure 11.

1. Before servicing the vehicle, refer to the Precautions Section.

2. Remove the brake caliper. Refer to Brake Caliper, Removal & Installation.

❋❋ WARNING

Support the brake caliper with heavy mechanic wire, or equivalent, whenever it is separated from its mount and the hydraulic flexible brake hose is still connected. Failure to support the caliper in this manner will cause the flexible brake hose to bear the weight of the caliper, which may cause damage to the brake hose and in turn may cause a brake fluid leak.

3. Remove the caliper housing from the caliper bracket. Support the caliper with a wire in order to prevent damage to the brake hose.

4. Remove the brake pads with the insulators.

5. Remove the insulators from the pads.

➡Refinish or replace the rotor ONLY if the condition of the rotor requires ser-

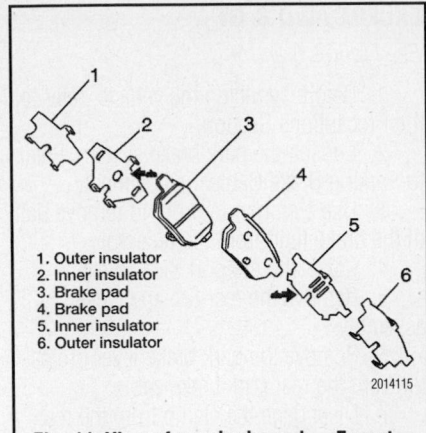

1. Outer insulator
2. Inner insulator
3. Brake pad
4. Brake pad
5. Inner insulator
6. Outer insulator

2014115

Fig. 11 View of rear brake pads—Except AWD & GT

vice. DO NOT refinish the rotor if the brake pads are the only components requiring service.

To install:

6. Apply disc brake grease to the pad side of the 2 inner insulators.

7. Ensure the disc brake grease covers the area where the inner insulators contact the brake pads.

8. Install the 2 inner insulators to the 2 brake pads.

9. Install the 2 outer insulators to the 2 inner insulators.

10. Lower the vehicle.

11. With the engine OFF, gradually apply and release the brake pedal several times in order to position the caliper pistons and the brake pads.

12. Fill the master cylinder reservoir. Refer to Bleeding Procedure, fluid fill procedure.

13. Adjust the parking brake system. Refer to Parking Brake Cables, adjustment.

14. Burnish the pads and the rotors.

BRAKES

❋❋ CAUTION

Dust and dirt accumulating on brake parts during normal use may contain asbestos fibers from production or aftermarket brake linings. Breathing excessive concentrations of asbestos fibers can cause serious bodily harm. Exercise care when servicing brake parts. Do not sand or grind brake lin-

ing unless equipment used is designed to contain the dust residue. Do not clean brake parts with compressed air or by dry brushing. Cleaning should be done by dampening the brake components with a fine mist of water, then wiping the brake components clean with a dampened cloth. Dispose of cloth and all residue containing asbestos fibers in

REAR DRUM BRAKES

an impermeable container with the appropriate label. Follow practices prescribed by the Occupational Safety and Health Administration (OSHA) and the Environmental Protection Agency (EPA) for the handling, processing, and disposing of dust or debris that may contain asbestos fibers.

BRARKES

PARKING BRAKE CABLES

INSPECTION

1. Raise and support the vehicle.
2. Pull the park brake lever with approximately 20 kg (45 lb) of force.
3. Count the number of clicks or ratchet notches.

- The minimum number of clicks is 6.
- The maximum number of clicks is 9.

4. Attempt to rotate the rear wheels. Verify the rear wheels do not rotate.
5. Turn the ignition switch to the ON position. Verify the red BRAKE warning indicator stays ON.
6. Release the park brake.
7. Attempt to rotate the rear wheels. Verify the rear wheels rotate freely.
8. Turn the ignition switch to the ON position. Verify the red BRAKE warning indicator is OFF.
9. If the park brake lever travel is correct, lower the vehicle.
10. If the park brake lever travel is not correct, refer to Adjustment.

ADJUSTMENT

AWD & GT

See Figure 12.

1. Remove the rear floor console.
2. Release the park brake.
3. Loosen the lock nut.
4. Loosen the adjusting nut in order to fully release the park brake.
5. With the engine OFF, press and release the brake pedal 5 times.

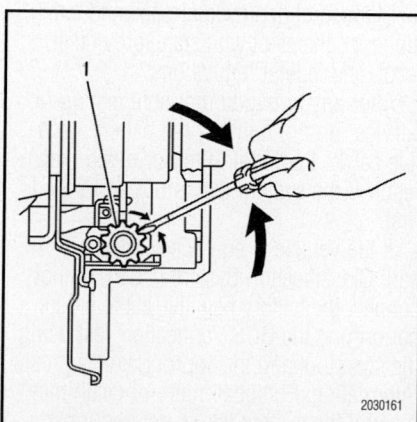

Fig. 12 Turn the shoe adjuster (1) and expand the shoes until the brake rotor locks—AWD & GT

6. Turn the adjusting nut in order to adjust the park brake lever travel. Refer to Inspection.
7. Use a wrench in order to hold the adjusting nut. Tighten the lock nut to 53 inch lbs. (6.0 Nm).
8. Apply and release the park brake 4 times.
9. Inspect the park brake lever travel. Refer to Inspection.
10. If the park brake lever travel is correct, install the rear floor console.
11. If the park brake lever travel is not correct, continue with this procedure.
12. Release the park brake.
13. Loosen the lock nut.
14. Loosen the adjusting nut in order to fully release the park brake.
15. Remove the rear tire and wheel assemblies.
16. Install conical brake rotor washers (J-45101-100) to the wheel studs.
17. Install the wheel nuts finger tight.
18. Remove the shoe adjusting hole plug.
19. Turn the shoe adjuster and expand the shoes until the brake rotor locks.
20. Turn the shoe adjuster and contract the shoes until the brake rotor rotates smoothly. The standard return is 8 notches.
21. Ensure there is no brake drag against the shoes.
22. Install the shoe adjusting hole plug.
23. Turn the adjusting nut in order to adjust the park brake lever travel. Refer to Inspection.
24. Use a wrench in order to hold the adjusting nut. Tighten the lock nut to 53 inch lbs. (6.0 Nm).
25. Apply and release the park brake 4 times.
26. Inspect the park brake lever travel. Refer to Inspection.
27. Remove the wheel nuts.
28. Remove the conical brake rotor washers.
29. Install the rear tire and wheel assemblies.
30. Install the rear floor console.
31. Lower the vehicle.

Except AWD & GT

See Figure 13.

1. Remove the rear floor console.
2. Release the park brake.
3. Loosen the lock nut.
4. Loosen the adjusting nut in order to fully release the park brake.

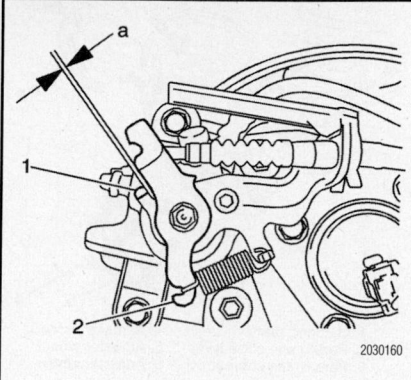

Fig. 13 Measure the clearance (a) between the rear brake cylinder operation lever (2) and the stopper (1)—Except AWD & GT

5. With the engine OFF, press and release the brake pedal 5 times.
6. Turn the adjusting nut in order to adjust the park brake lever travel. Refer to Inspection.
7. Use a wrench in order to hold the adjusting nut. Tighten the lock nut to 53 inch lbs. (6.0 Nm).
8. Apply and release the park brake 4 times.
9. Inspect the park brake lever travel. Refer to Inspection.
10. If the park brake lever travel is correct, install the rear floor console.
11. If the park brake lever travel is not correct, continue with this procedure.
12. Release the park brake.
13. Measure the clearance between the rear brake cylinder operation lever and the stopper. The clearance specification is 0.197 inch (0.5 mm) or less.
14. If the clearance is not within the specified range, replace the rear brake caliper. Refer to the appropriate Caliper, removal & installation.
15. Install the rear floor console.
16. Lower the vehicle.

PARKING BRAKE SHOES

REMOVAL & INSTALLATION

AWD & GT

See Figure 14.

1. Remove the rear brake rotor.
2. Remove the return springs.
3. Turn the front hold down pin and remove the front hold down spring from the front shoe.

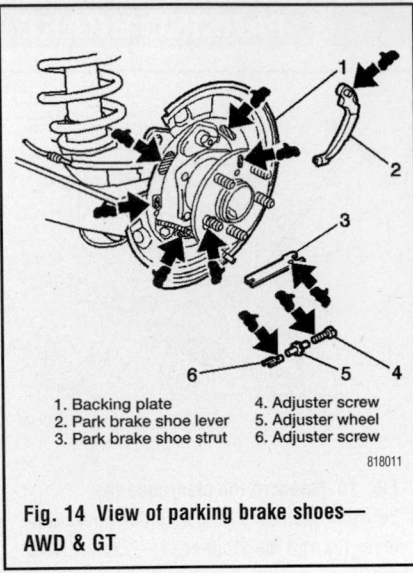

1. Backing plate
2. Park brake shoe lever
3. Park brake shoe strut
4. Adjuster screw
5. Adjuster wheel
6. Adjuster screw

818011

Fig. 14 View of parking brake shoes— AWD & GT

4. Pull the front shoe forward.
5. Remove the park brake shoe strut.
6. Turn the rear hold down pin and

remove the rear hold down spring from the rear shoe.

7. While pulling apart, remove the shoes with the adjuster and the tension spring.

8. Remove the shoes from the park brake shoe lever.

9. Remove the adjuster from the shoes.

10. Remove the tension spring from the shoes.

11. Remove the park brake shoe lever from the park brake rear cable.

12. Remove the front hold down pin.

13. Remove the rear hold down pin.

To install:

14. To install, reverse the removal procedure and note the following:

- Apply high temperature lubricant to the metal contact points on the backing plate and on the adjuster.
- Ensure there is no oil or lubricant on the friction surfaces of the shoes or on the brake rotor.

✳✳ CAUTION

Road test vehicle under safe conditions and while obeying all traffic laws. Do not attempt any maneuvers that could jeopardize vehicle control. Failure to adhere to these precautions could lead to serious personal injury and vehicle damage.

15. Perform the following procedure:
    a. Drive the vehicle at about 31 mph (50 km/h) on a safe, level, and dry road.
    b. With the vehicle in motion, pull the park brake lever with 150 N (15 kgf, 34 lbf) of force.
    c. Drive the vehicle for about 25 miles (400 m) with the park brake on.
    d. Release the park brake and drive the vehicle for 5 minutes in order to cool the park brake system.

16. Perform the above procedure two more times.

17. Adjust the parking brake system. Refer to Parking Brake Cables, adjustment.

CHASSIS ELECTRICAL   AIR BAG (SUPPLEMENTAL RESTRAINT SYSTEM)

GENERAL INFORMATION

✳✳ CAUTION

These vehicles are equipped with an air bag system. The system must be disarmed before performing service on, or around, system components, the steering column, instrument panel components, wiring and sensors. Failure to follow the safety precautions and the disarming procedure could result in accidental air bag deployment, possible injury and unnecessary system repairs.

SERVICE PRECAUTIONS

Disconnect and isolate the battery negative cable before beginning any airbag system component diagnosis, testing, removal, or installation procedures. Allow system capacitor to discharge for two minutes before beginning any component service. This will disable the airbag system. Failure to disable the airbag system may result in accidental airbag deployment, personal injury, or death.

Do not place an intact undeployed airbag face down on a solid surface. The airbag will propel into the air if accidentally deployed and may result in personal injury or death.

When carrying or handling an undeployed airbag, the trim side (face) of the

airbag should be pointing towards the body to minimize possibility of injury if accidental deployment occurs. Failure to do this may result in personal injury or death.

Replace airbag system components with OEM replacement parts. Substitute parts may appear interchangeable, but internal differences may result in inferior occupant protection. Failure to do so may result in occupant personal injury or death.

Wear safety glasses, rubber gloves, and long sleeved clothing when cleaning powder residue from vehicle after an airbag deployment. Powder residue emitted from a deployed airbag can cause skin irritation. Flush affected area with cool water if irritation is experienced. If nasal or throat irritation is experienced, exit the vehicle for fresh air until the irritation ceases. If irritation continues, see a physician.

Do not use a replacement airbag that is not in the original packaging. This may result in improper deployment, personal injury, or death.

The factory installed fasteners, screws and bolts used to fasten airbag components have a special coating and are specifically designed for the airbag system. Do not use substitute fasteners. Use only original equipment fasteners listed in the parts catalog when fastener replacement is required.

During, and following, any child restraint anchor service, due to impact event or

vehicle repair, carefully inspect all mounting hardware, tether straps, and anchors for proper installation, operation, or damage. If a child restraint anchor is found damaged in any way, the anchor must be replaced. Failure to do this may result in personal injury or death.

Deployed and non-deployed airbags may or may not have live pyrotechnic material within the airbag inflator.

Do not dispose of driver/passenger/ curtain airbags or seat belt tensioners unless you are sure of complete deployment. Refer to the Hazardous Substance Control System for proper disposal.

Dispose of deployed airbags and tensioners consistent with state, provincial, local, and federal regulations.

After any airbag component testing or service, do not connect the battery negative cable. Personal injury or death may result if the system test is not performed first.

If the vehicle is equipped with the Occupant Classification System (OCS), do not connect the battery negative cable before performing the OCS Verification Test using the scan tool and the appropriate diagnostic information. Personal injury or death may result if the system test is not performed properly.

Never replace both the Occupant Restraint Controller (ORC) and the Occupant Classification Module (OCM) at the same time. If both require replacement, replace one, then perform the Airbag System test before replacing the other.

Both the ORC and the OCM store Occupant Classification System (OCS) calibration data, which they transfer to one another when one of them is replaced. If both are replaced at the same time, an irreversible fault will be set in both modules and the OCS may malfunction and cause personal injury or death.

If equipped with OCS, the Seat Weight Sensor is a sensitive, calibrated unit and must be handled carefully. Do not drop or handle roughly. If dropped or damaged, replace with another sensor. Failure to do so may result in occupant injury or death.

If equipped with OCS, the front passenger seat must be handled carefully as well. When removing the seat, be careful when setting on floor not to drop. If dropped, the sensor may be inoperative, could

result in occupant injury, or possibly death.

If equipped with OCS, when the passenger front seat is on the floor, no one should sit in the front passenger seat. This uneven force may damage the sensing ability of the seat weight sensors. If sat on and damaged, the sensor may be inoperative, could result in occupant injury, or possibly death.

CLOCKSPRING CENTERING

See Figure 15.

✱✱ WARNING

The new SIR coil assembly will be centered. Improper alignment of the SIR coil assembly may damage the unit, causing an inflatable restraint malfunction.

1. While holding the coil outer casing, turn the coil center casing counterclockwise slowly until the coil reaches the stop.

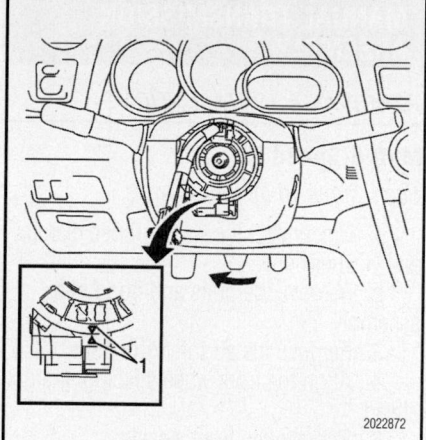

Fig. 15 Align the arrow on the center casing with the arrow on the outer casing (1)

2. Turn the coil center casing clockwise 2.5 turns.
3. Align the arrow on the center casing with the arrow on the outer casing.

DRIVE TRAIN

AUTOMATIC TRANSMISSION FLUID

FILTER REPLACEMENT

MVB 4-Speed

See Figure 16.

1. Place the transaxle onto wooden blocks.
2. Remove the bolts, and remove the oil pan and oil pan gasket.
3. Remove the 2 oil cleaner magnets from the oil pan.

4. Examine the particles in the oil pan.
5. Collect any steel chips with the removed magnets.
6. Carefully look at the foreign matter and particles in the oil pan and on the magnets to predict the type of wear which might be found in the transaxle.
   - Steel (magnetic): bearing, gear and clutch plate wear.
   - Brass (non-magnetic): bearing wear.
7. Remove the bolts and remove the transmission filter.
8. Remove the transmission filter seal from the transmission filter.

To install:

9. Installation is the reverse of the removal procedure.

MVD 5-Speed

See Figure 17.

1. Remove the drain plug and drain plug gasket from the oil pan.
2. Remove the bolts, oil pan, and gasket.
3. Remove the transmission magnets from the oil pan.
4. Remove the bolts and oil strainer.
5. Remove the O-ring from the oil strainer.

To install:

6. Coat a new O-ring with ATF WS, and install it to the oil strainer.

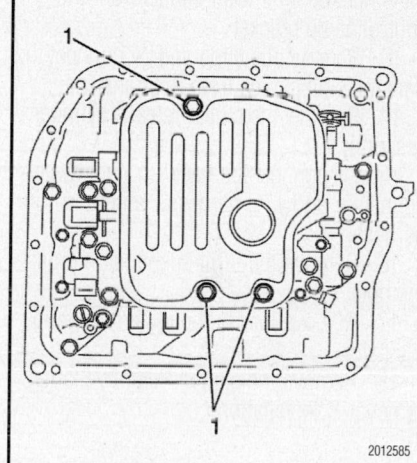

Fig. 17 Install a new oil pan gasket and the oil pan to the transaxle case with the bolts (1)—MVD 5-Speed

7. Install the oil strainer to the valve body with the bolts and tighten to 97 inch lbs. (11 Nm).
8. Install the magnets to the oil pan.
9. Apply sealant Three Bond 1281 or equivalent to the bolts.
10. Install a new oil pan gasket and the oil pan to the transaxle case with the bolts and tighten to 71 inch lbs. (8 Nm).
11. Install a new gasket to the drain plug.
12. Install the drain plug and tighten to 36 ft. lbs. (49 Nm).

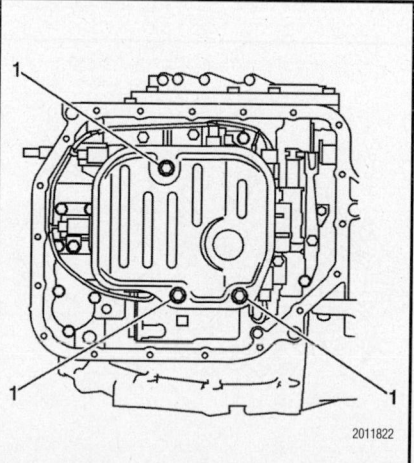

Fig. 16 Remove the bolts (1) and remove the oil pan and oil pan gasket—MVB 4-Speed

MANUAL TRANSMISSION ASSEMBLY

REMOVAL & INSTALLATION

MVC 5-Speed

See Figures 18 through 30.

1. Disconnect the washer hose clamps and washer hose.

2. Remove the bolts and hood sub-assembly.

3. Remove the air inlet grill panel.

4. Align the front wheels facing straight ahead.

5. Remove the front wheels.

6. Remove the engine splash shields.

7. Drain the manual transaxle oil.

8. Remove the engine cover assembly.

9. Remove the air cleaner assembly.

10. Remove the battery. Refer to Battery, removal & installation.

11. Remove the battery tray. Refer to Battery Tray, removal & installation.

12. Remove the clips and disconnect the transmission shift lever cables from the control cable bracket.

13. Remove the clips and disconnect the transmission cables from the transaxle.

14. Remove the clutch release cylinder assembly.

15. Disconnect the back-up light switch connector and wire harness clamp and wire harness.

16. Remove the front suspension cross-member.

17. Remove the front engine mounting insulator.

18. Remove the starter. Refer to Starter, removal & installation.

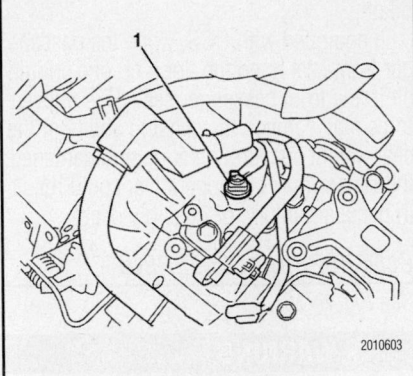

Fig. 19 Disconnect the back-up light switch connector (1) and wire harness clamp and wire harness—MVC 5-Speed

19. Remove the nut, and disconnect the wire harness clamp and wire harness.

20. Support the manual transaxle with a transmission jack.

21. Remove the bolt and wire harness clamp bracket.

22. Remove the through-bolt and nut, then separate the left engine mounting insulator sub-assembly.

➡**Take care so that the rear side of the engine assembly does not come into contact with the body.**

23. Tilt the manual transaxle downward.

24. Remove the 3 bolts and the left engine mounting bracket.

25. Remove the 6 bolts.

26. Remove the 4 bolts and the manual transaxle.

27. Remove the 2 bolts and the front engine mounting bracket.

28. Remove the rear engine mounting insulator.

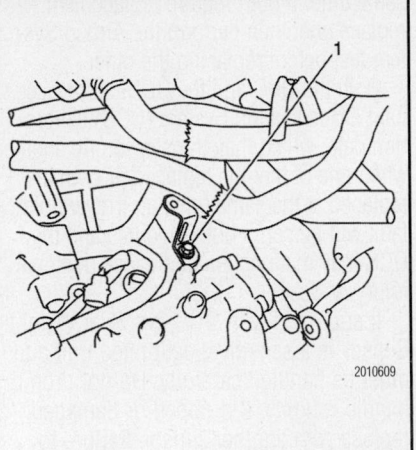

Fig. 21 Remove the bolt (1) and wire harness clamp bracket—MVC 5-Speed

29. Remove the 3 bolts and the rear engine mounting bracket.

30. Remove the 2 bolts and the manual transmission case protector.

31. Remove the bolt and wire harness clamp bracket.

To install:

32. Install the wire harness clamp bracket with the bolt and tighten to 19 ft. lbs. (26 Nm).

33. Install the manual transmission case protector with the 2 bolts and tighten to 13 ft. lbs. (18 Nm).

34. Install the rear engine mounting bracket with the bolts and tighten to 33 ft. lbs. (45 Nm).

35. Install the rear engine mounting insulator.

36. Install the front engine mounting bracket with the bolts and tighten to 47 ft. lbs. (64 Nm).

37. Align the input shaft with the clutch

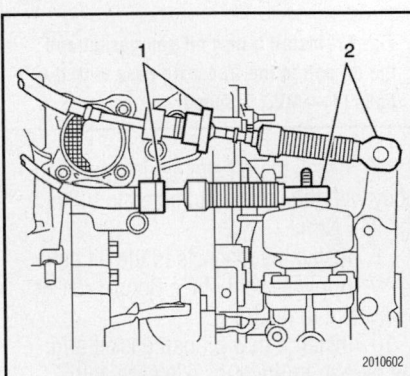

Fig. 18 Remove the clips and disconnect the transmission shift lever cables from the control cable bracket (1). Remove the clips and disconnect the transmission cables from the transaxle (2)—MVC 5-Speed

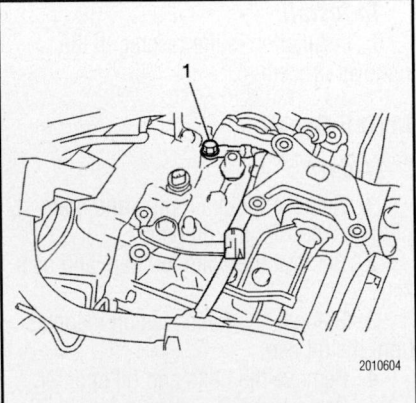

Fig. 20 Remove the nut (1), and disconnect the wire harness clamp and wire harness)—MVC 5-Speed

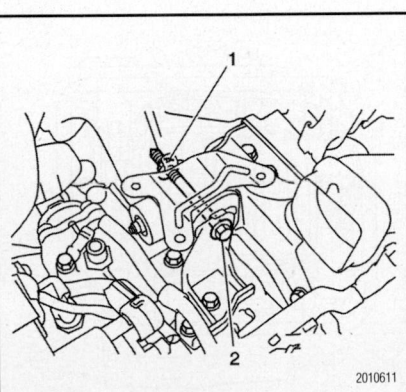

Fig. 22 Remove the through-bolt (1) and nut (2), then separate the left engine mounting insulator sub-assembly—MVC 5-Speed

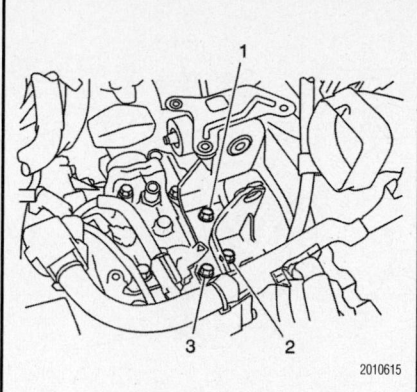

Fig. 23 Remove the bolts (1–3) and the left engine mounting bracket—MVC 5-Speed

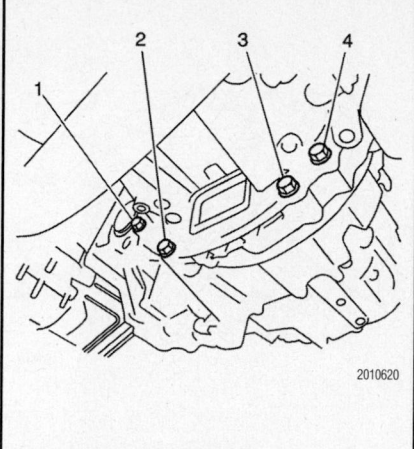

Fig. 25 Remove the bolts (1–4) and the manual transaxle—MVC 5-Speed

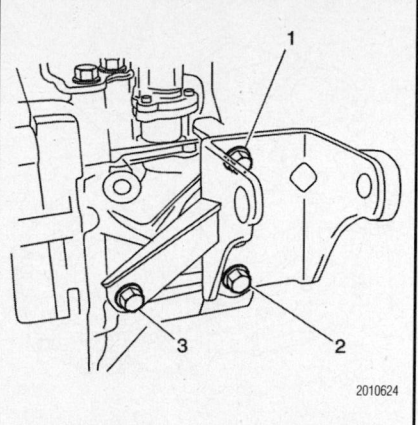

Fig. 27 Remove the bolts (1–3) and the rear engine mounting bracket—MVC 5-Speed

disc and install the manual transaxle onto the engine.

➡**Insert dowel pins into the dowel holes securely so that the end face of the transaxle assembly fits close against the engine assembly before tightening the bolts.**

38. Install the bolts (1–4) and tighten:
   • Bolt 1 to 47 ft. lbs. (64 Nm).
   • Bolt 2 to 47 ft. lbs. (64 Nm).
   • Bolt 3 to 34 ft. lbs. (46 Nm)
   • Bolt 4 to 34 ft. lbs. (46 Nm)
39. Install the 4 manual transaxle bolts and tighten to 32 ft. lbs. (44 Nm).
40. Hand tighten the left engine mounting bracket bolts.
41. Tighten the bolts to 38 ft. lbs. (52 Nm).
42. Install the left engine mounting insulator sub-assembly with the through-bolt and nut, and tighten to 41 ft. lbs. (56 Nm).

43. Install the wire harness clamp with the bolt and tighten to 115 inch lbs. (13 Nm).
44. Install the wire harness with the bolt and tighten to 115 inch lbs. (13 Nm).
45. Connect the wire harness to the wire harness clamp.
46. Install the starter. Refer to Starter, removal & installation.
47. Install the front engine mounting insulator.
48. Install the front suspension cross-member assembly.
49. Connect the wire harness to the wire harness clamp.
50. Connect the back-up light switch connector.
51. Install the clutch release cylinder assembly.
52. Install the transmission shift lever cables to the control cable bracket with new clips.
53. Install the transmission cables to the transaxle with the clips.

54. Install the battery tray. Refer to Battery Tray, removal & installation.
55. Install the battery. Refer to Battery, removal & installation.

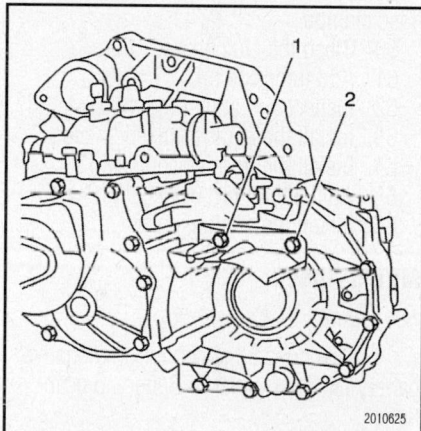

Fig. 28 Remove the bolts (1, 2) and the manual transmission case protector—MVC 5-Speed

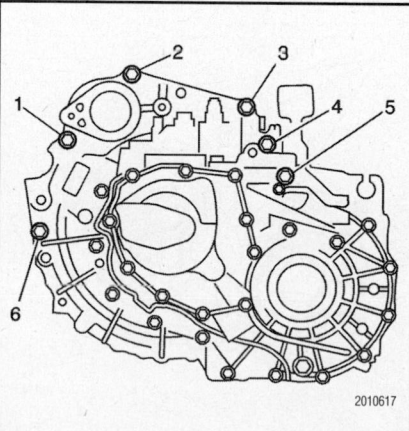

Fig. 24 Remove the bolts (1–6)—MVC 5-Speed

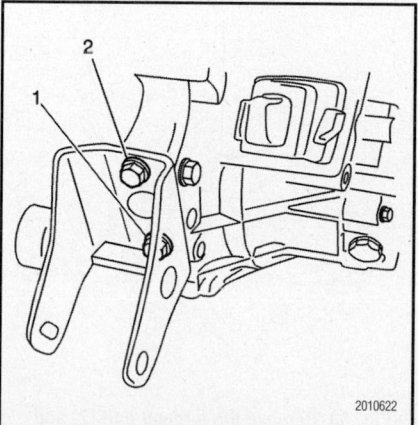

Fig. 26 Remove the bolts (1, 2) and the front engine mounting bracket—MVC 5-Speed

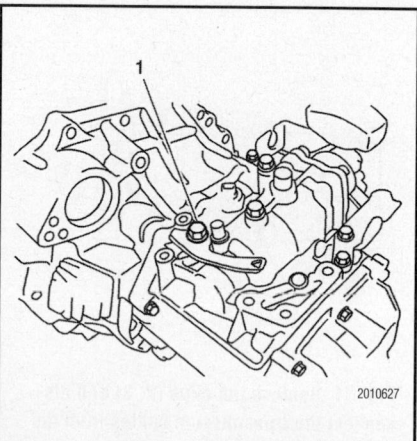

Fig. 29 Remove the bolt (1) and wire harness clamp bracket—MVC 5-Speed

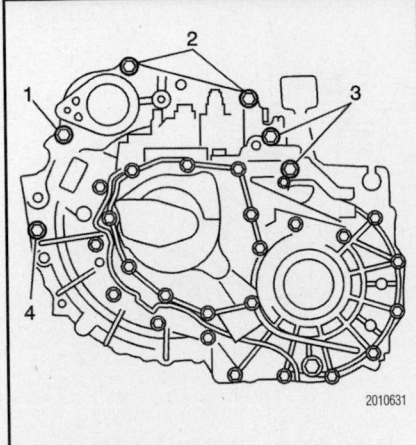

Fig. 30 Install the bolts (1–4) and tighten as specified—MVC 5-Speed

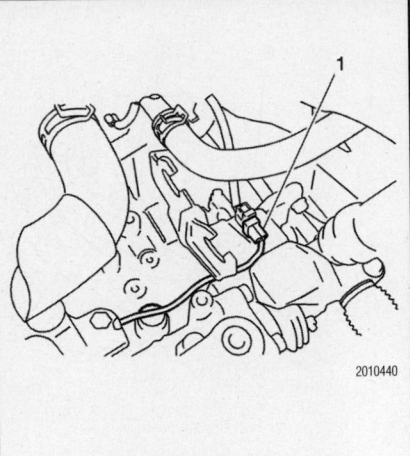

Fig. 32 Disconnect the back-up light switch connector (1)—MVE 5-Speed

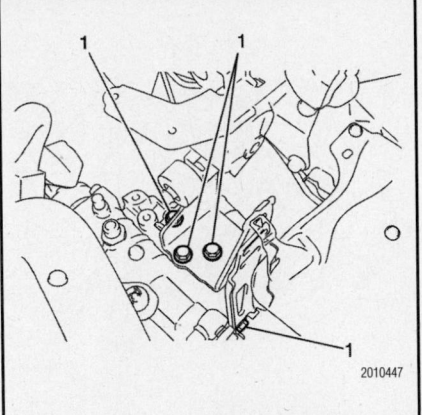

Fig. 34 Remove the bolts (1) and the engine mounting bracket, left hand side—MVE 5-Speed

56. Install the air cleaner assembly.
57. Install the air inlet grill panel.
58. Install the hood assembly with the bolts and tighten to 115 inch lbs. (13 Nm).
59. Install the washer hose and washer hose clamps.
60. Bleed the clutch line.
61. Add transaxle oil.
62. Inspect and adjust the transaxle oil.
63. Install the engine splash shields.
64. Install the front wheels.
65. Adjust the front wheel alignment.
66. Install the engine cover.

MVE 5-Speed

See Figures 31 through 38.

1. Disconnect the cable from negative battery terminal. Refer to Battery, precautions.
2. Disconnect the washer hose clamps and washer hose.
3. Remove the bolts and hood sub-assembly.

4. Remove the windshield wiper transmission assembly.
5. Remove the outer cowl top panel.
6. Align the front wheels facing straight ahead.
7. Remove the front wheels.
8. Remove the engine splash shields.
9. Drain the manual transaxle oil.
10. Remove the engine cover
11. Remove the air cleaner assembly.
12. Remove the battery. Refer to Battery, removal & installation.
13. Remove the battery tray. Refer to Battery Tray, removal & installation.
14. Remove the clips and disconnect the transmission cables from the cable bracket.
15. Remove the clips and disconnect the transmission cables from the manual transaxle.
16. Separate the clutch release cylinder assembly.
17. Disconnect the back-up light switch connector.

18. Disconnect the wire harness clamp.
19. Remove the bolt and disconnect the wire harness.
20. Secure the steering wheel.
21. Remove the column hole cover silencer sheet.
22. Separate the No. 2 steering intermediate shaft assembly.
23. Disconnect the No. 1 steering column hole cover sub-assembly.
24. Disconnect the oxygen sensor.
25. Remove the catalytic converter. Refer to Catalytic Converter, removal & installation.
26. Remove the front suspension crossmember.
27. Remove the front engine mounting insulator.
28. Remove the starter. Refer to Starter, removal & installation.
29. Support the manual transaxle with a transmission jack.
30. Remove the through-bolt and nut,

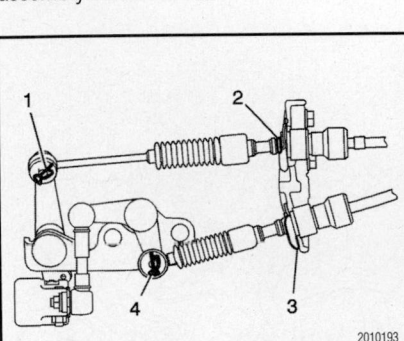

Fig. 31 Remove the clips (2, 3) and disconnect the transmission cables from the cable bracket. Remove the clips (1, 4) and disconnect the transmission cables from the manual transaxle—MVE 5-Speed

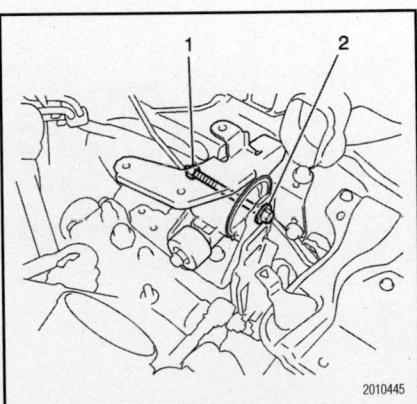

Fig. 33 Remove the through-bolt (2) and nut (1), then separate the engine mounting insulator sub-assembly, left hand side—MVE 5-Speed

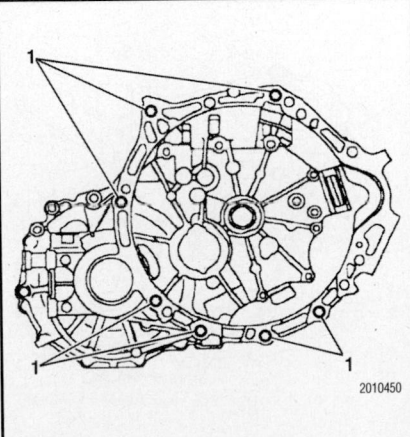

Fig. 35 Remove the bolts (1) and the manual transaxle—MVE 5-Speed

Fig. 36 Remove the bolts (1) and the shift lever cable bracket—MVE 5-Speed

then separate the engine mounting insulator sub-assembly, left hand side.

➡**Be careful that the rear side of the engine assembly does not come into contact with the body.**

31. Tilt the manual transaxle downward.
32. Remove the 3 bolts and the engine mounting bracket, left hand side.
33. Remove the 7 bolts and the manual transaxle.
34. Remove the 2 bolts and the shift lever cable bracket.
35. Remove the 3 bolts and the front engine mounting bracket.
36. Remove the rear engine mounting insulator.
37. Remove the 3 bolts and the rear engine mounting bracket.

To install:

38. Install the rear engine mounting bracket with the bolts and tighten to 33 ft. lbs. (45 Nm).

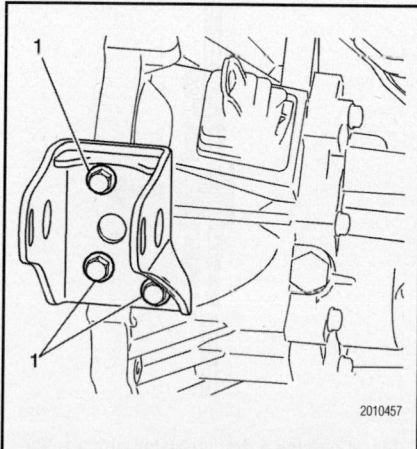

Fig. 37 Remove the bolts (1) and the front engine mounting bracket—MVE 5-Speed

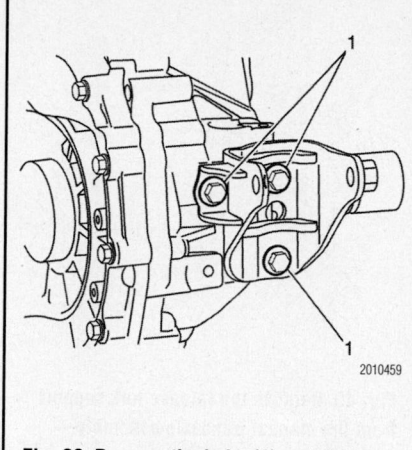

Fig. 38 Remove the bolts (1) and the rear engine mounting bracket—MVE 5-Speed

39. Install the rear engine mounting insulator.
40. Install the front engine mounting bracket with the bolts and tighten to 47 ft. lbs. (64 Nm).
41. Install the shift lever bracket with the bolts and tighten to 18 ft. lbs. (25 Nm).
42. Align the input shaft with the clutch disc and install the manual transaxle onto the engine.

➡**Insert dowel pins into the dowel holes securely so that the end face of the transaxle assembly fits close against the engine assembly before tightening the bolts.**

➡**Make sure that the dowel pins are not loose, bent, damaged, or scratched and then install the transaxle onto the engine with the contact surfaces of the engine and transaxle flat against each other.**

43. Install the bolts and tighten to 24 ft. lbs. (33 Nm).
44. Hand tighten the engine mounting bracket, left hand side, bolts.
45. Tighten the bolts to 38 ft. lbs. (52 Nm).
46. Install the engine mounting insulator sub-assembly, left hand side, with the through-bolt and nut and tighten the bolt to 41 ft. lbs. (56 Nm).
47. Install the starter. Refer to Starter, removal & installation.
48. Install the front engine mounting insulator.
49. Install the front suspension crossmember.
50. Install the catalytic converter. Refer to Catalytic Converter, removal & installation.
51. Install the oxygen sensor.
52. Install the No. 1 steering column hole cover sub-assembly.

53. Install the No. 2 steering intermediate shaft assembly.
54. Install the column hole cover silencer sheet.
55. Connect the wire harness with the bolt and tighten to 19 ft. lbs. (26 Nm).
56. Connect the wire harness clamp.
57. Connect the back-up light switch connector.
58. Install the clutch release cylinder assembly.
59. Install the transmission cables to the cable bracket with new clips.
60. Install the 2 transmission cables to the transaxle with the 2 clips.
61. Install the battery tray. Refer to Battery Tray, removal & installation.
62. Install the battery. Refer to Battery, removal & installation.
63. Install the air cleaner assembly.
64. Install the outer cowl top panel.
65. Install the windshield wiper transmission assembly.
66. Install the hood assembly with the bolts and tighten to 115 inch lbs. (13 Nm).
67. Install the washer hose and the washer hose clamps.
68. Adjust the hood sub-assembly.
69. Add transaxle fluid.
70. Inspect and adjust the transaxle oil.
71. Inspect for an oil leak.
72. Inspect for an exhaust gas leak.
73. Install the engine splash shields.
74. Install the front wheels.
75. Adjust the front wheel alignment.
76. Install the engine cover.

MANUAL TRANSMISSION FLUID

DRAIN AND REFILL

MVC 5-Speed/MVE 5-Speed

See Figure 39.

1. Remove the filler plug and the gasket.
2. Remove the drain plug and gasket, and then drain the manual transaxle oil.

To install:

3. Install a new gasket and drain plug and tighten:
   - To 36 ft. lbs. (49 Nm) on MVC models.
   - To 29 ft. lbs. (39 Nm) on MVE models.
4. Add manual transaxle oil to the proper level.
5. Install the transmission filler plug and new gasket and tighten:
   - To 36 ft. lbs. (49 Nm) on MVC models.

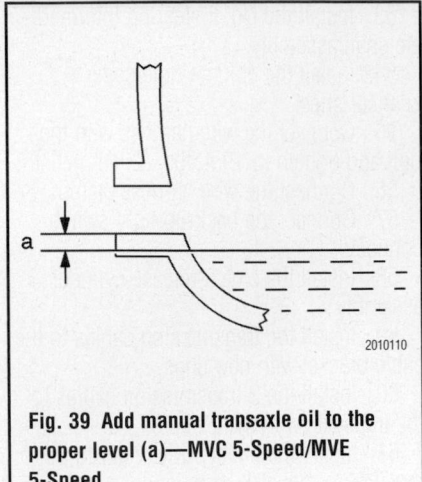

Fig. 39 Add manual transaxle oil to the proper level (a)—MVC 5-Speed/MVE 5-Speed

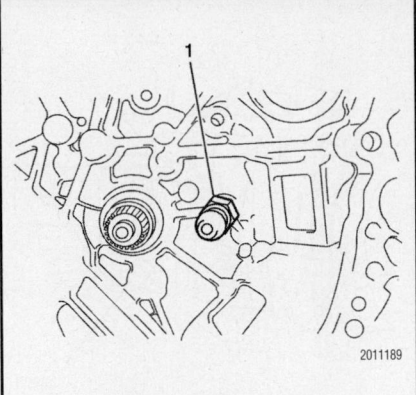

Fig. 40 Remove the release fork support from the manual transaxle assembly— MVC 5-Speed

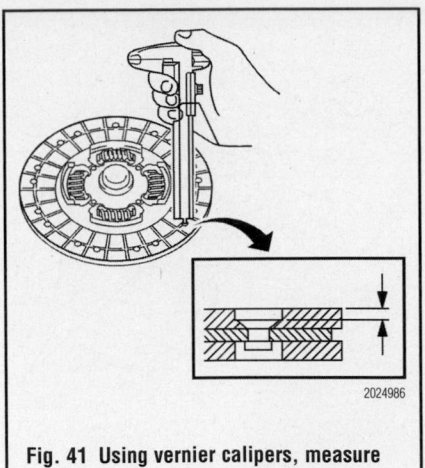

Fig. 41 Using vernier calipers, measure the rivet head depth—MVC 5-Speed

- To 29 ft. lbs. (39 Nm) on MVE models.

To inspect:

6. Inspect the manual transaxle oil.
7. Stop the vehicle in a level place.
8. Remove the transmission filler plug and gasket.
9. Check that the oil surface is within 0.20 inch (5 mm) from the lowest position of the hole for the transmission filler plug opening.

➡ **Excessively large or small amounts of oil may cause problems.**

10. After replacing the oil, drive the vehicle and check the oil level again.
11. Check for oil leakage when the oil level is low.
12. Install a new gasket and the transmission filler plug and tighten:
- To 36 ft. lbs. (49 Nm) on MVC models.
- To 29 ft. lbs. (39 Nm) on MVE models.

CLUTCH

REMOVAL & INSTALLATION

MVC 5-Speed

See Figures 40 through 47.

1. Remove the manual transaxle assembly. Refer to Manual Transaxle Assembly, removal & installation.
2. Remove the clutch release fork with the clutch release bearing from the transaxle assembly.
3. Remove the release bearing hub clip and clutch release bearing assembly from the clutch release fork.
4. Remove the release fork support from the manual transaxle assembly.
5. Remove the clutch release fork boot.

6. Put matchmarks on the clutch cover assembly and flywheel sub-assembly.
7. Loosen the bolts one turn at a time until the spring tension is released.
8. Remove the bolts and pull off the clutch cover assembly.
9. Remove the clutch disc assembly.
10. Using vernier calipers, measure the rivet head depth.
- Minimum rivet depth: 0.012 inch (0.3 mm).
11. If necessary, replace the clutch disc assembly.
12. Install the clutch disc assembly to the transaxle assembly.
13. Using a dial indicator with a roller instrument, measure the clutch disc assembly runout.
- Maximum runout: 0.031 inch (0.8 mm).
14. If necessary, replace the clutch disc assembly.
15. Using vernier calipers, inspect the diaphragm spring for depth (a) and width (b) of wear. If necessary, replace the clutch cover assembly.
- Maximum A (Depth): 0.020 inch (0.5 mm).
- Maximum B (Width): 0.236 inch (6.0 mm).
16. Using a dial indicator, measure the flywheel runout.
- Maximum runout: 0.004 inch (0.1 mm).
17. If necessary, replace the flywheel sub-assembly.
18. Check that the bearing moves smoothly without abnormal resistance by turning the sliding parts of the bearing—contact surfaces with the clutch cover—while applying force in the axial direction.
19. Inspect the bearing for damage or wear. If necessary, replace the release bearing assembly.

20. Using a dial indicator with a roller instrument, check the diaphragm spring tip alignment.
- Maximum variation: 0.020 inch (0.5 mm).
21. If the alignment is not as specified, adjust the diaphragm spring tip alignment with a clutch pilot tool.

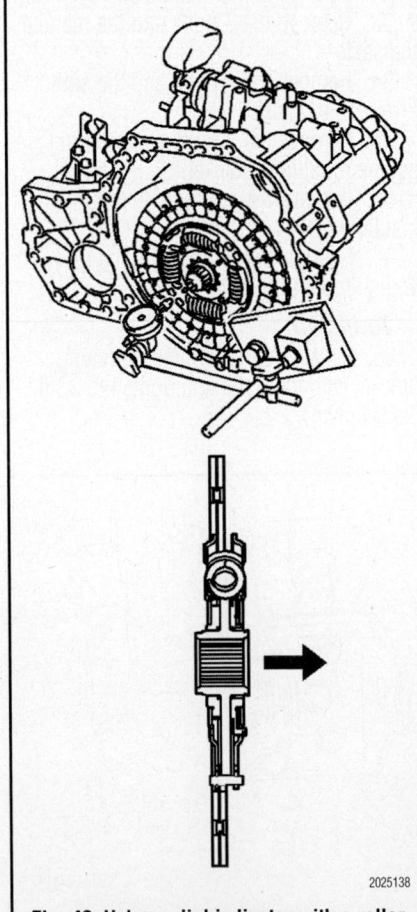

Fig. 42 Using a dial indicator with a roller instrument, measure the clutch disc assembly runout—MVC 5-Speed

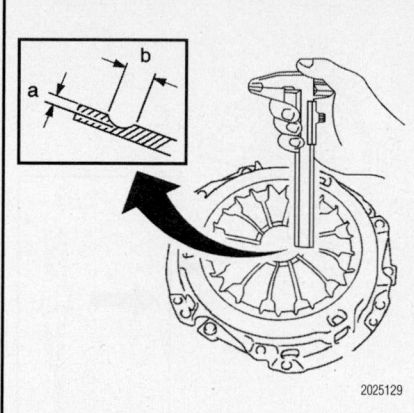

Fig. 43 Using vernier calipers, inspect the diaphragm spring for depth (a) and width (b) of wear—MVC 5-Speed

To install:

22. Insert a clutch pilot tool into the clutch disc assembly, then insert them into the flywheel assembly.

23. Align the matchmarks on the clutch cover assembly with the one on the flywheel sub-assembly.

➡**Evenly tighten the bolts one turn at a time. Lightly move the clutch pilot tool up and down, and right and left after checking that the disc is centered and tighten the bolts.**

24. Tighten the bolts in order, starting with the bolt located near the knock pin at the top to 14 ft. lbs. (19 Nm).

25. Install the release fork support to the manual transaxle assembly and tighten to 35 ft. lbs. (47 Nm).

26. Install the release bearing hub clip to the release bearing assembly.

27. Apply grease to the contact surfaces

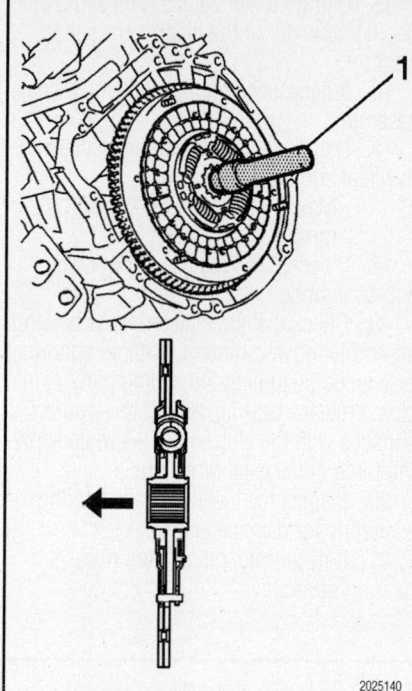

Fig. 45 Insert a clutch pilot tool (1) into the clutch disc assembly, then insert them into the flywheel assembly—MVC 5-Speed

between the release fork, release bearing, fork, push rod, and fork support.

28. Install the release fork to the release bearing assembly.

29. Apply grease to the input shaft spline.

➡**After installation, move the fork back and forth to check that the release bearing slides smoothly.**

30. Install the release fork with the release bearing assembly to the manual transaxle assembly.

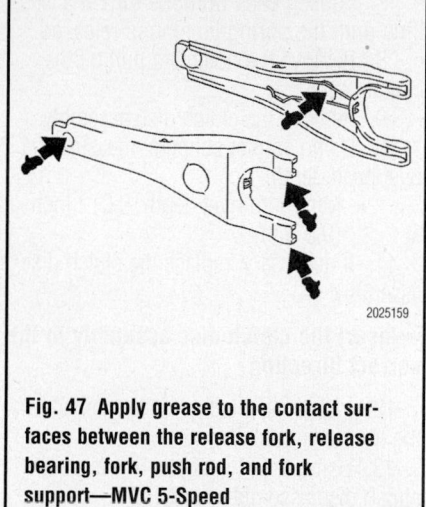

Fig. 47 Apply grease to the contact surfaces between the release fork, release bearing, fork, push rod, and fork support—MVC 5-Speed

31. Install the clutch release fork boot.

32. Install the manual transaxle assembly. Refer to Manual Transaxle Assembly, removal & installation.

MVE 5-Speed

See Figures 48 through 56.

1. Remove the manual transaxle assembly. Refer to Manual Transaxle Assembly, removal & installation.

2. Remove the clutch release fork with the clutch release bearing from the manual transaxle.

3. Remove the clutch release fork boot from the manual transaxle.

4. Remove the release bearing and clip from the clutch release fork.

5. Remove the release fork support from the manual transaxle.

6. Put matchmarks on the clutch cover assembly and the flywheel sub-assembly.

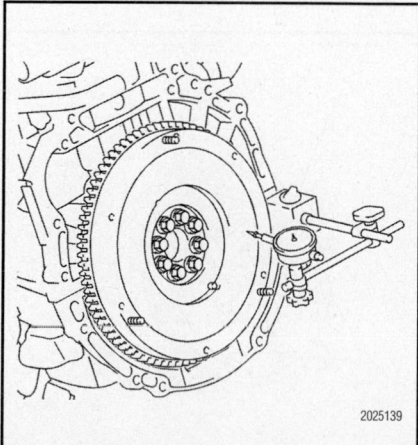

Fig. 44 Using a dial indicator, measure the flywheel runout—MVC 5-Speed

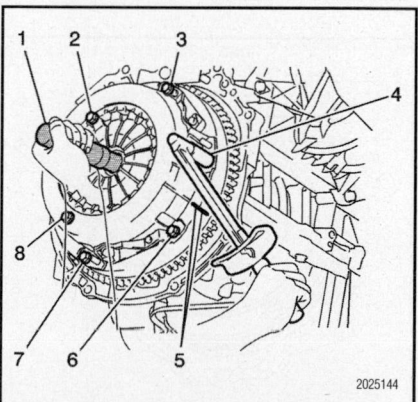

Fig. 46 Align the matchmarks (5) on the clutch cover assembly with the one on the flywheel sub-assembly. Tighten the bolts (2–4, 6–8) in order, and install the release fork support (1)—MVC 5-Speed

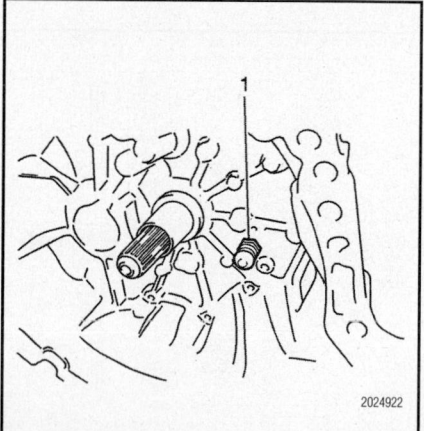

Fig. 48 Remove the release fork support (1) from the manual transaxle—MVE 5-Speed

7. Loosen each bolt one turn at a time until the spring tension is released.

8. Remove the bolts and pull off the clutch cover.

9. Remove the clutch disc assembly.

10. Using vernier calipers, measure the rivet head depth.
   - Minimum rivet depth: 0.012 inch (0.3 mm).

11. If necessary, replace the clutch disc assembly.

➡**Insert the clutch disc assembly in the correct direction.**

12. Install the clutch disc assembly onto the transaxle assembly.

13. Using a dial indicator, measure the clutch disc assembly runout.
   - Maximum runout: 0.031 inch (0.8 mm).

14. If necessary, replace the clutch disc assembly.

15. Using vernier calipers, measure the depth and width of the diaphragm spring wear.

16. If necessary, replace the clutch cover assembly.

17. Using a dial indicator, measure the flywheel sub-assembly runout.
   - Maximum runout: 0.004 inch (0.1 mm).

18. If necessary, replace the flywheel sub-assembly.

19. Check that the clutch release bearing assembly moves smoothly without abnormal resistance by turning the sliding parts of the clutch release bearing assembly—contact surfaces with the clutch cover—while applying force in the axial direction.

20. Inspect the clutch release bearing assembly for damage and wear.

21. If necessary, replace the release bearing assembly.

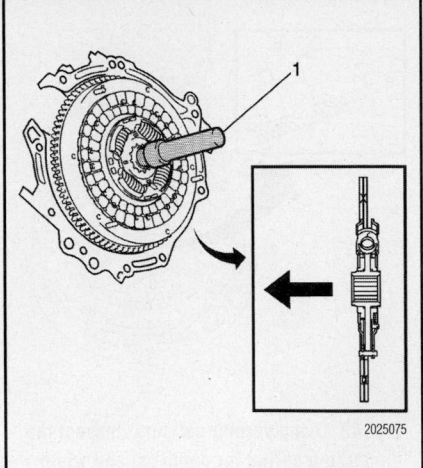

Fig. 53 Insert a clutch pilot tool (1) into the clutch disc assembly, then insert them both into the flywheel sub-assembly— MVE 5-Speed

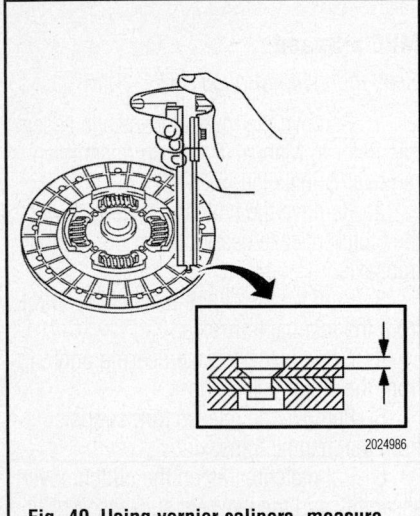

Fig. 49 Using vernier calipers, measure the rivet head depth—MVE 5-Speed

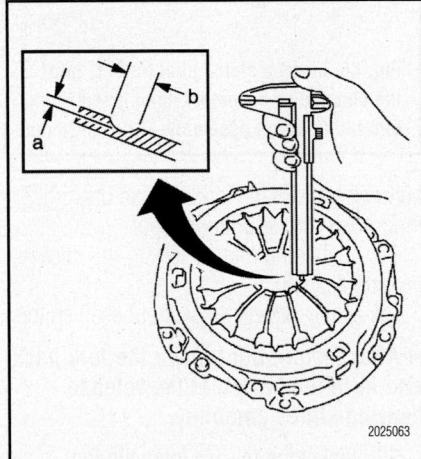

Fig. 51 Using vernier calipers, measure the depth (a) and width (b) of the diaphragm spring wear—MVE 5-Speed

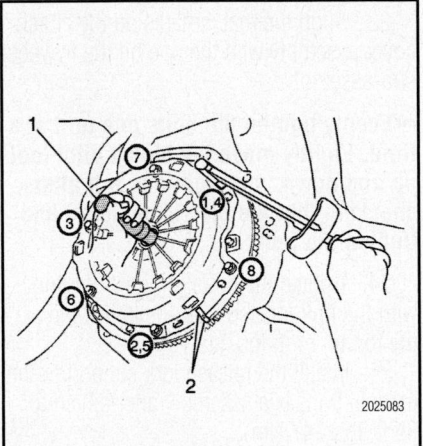

Fig. 54 Tighten the bolts in order, starting with the bolt located near the knock pin at the top—MVE 5-Speed

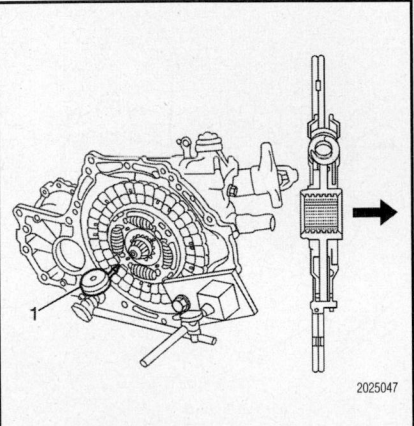

Fig. 50 Using a dial indicator (1), measure the clutch disc assembly runout— MVE 5-Speed

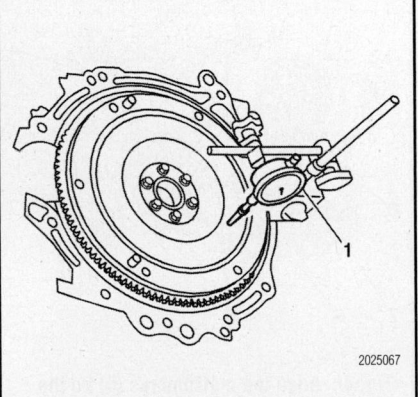

Fig. 52 Using a dial indicator (1), measure the flywheel sub-assembly runout— MVE 5-Speed

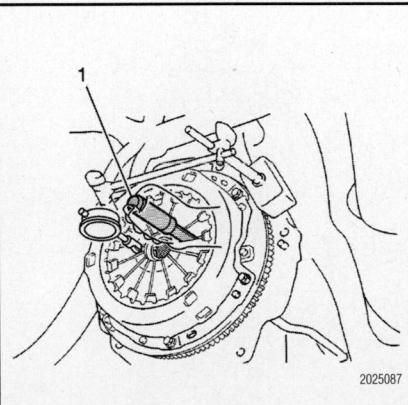

Fig. 55 Using a dial indicator with a roller instrument (1), check the diaphragm spring tip alignment—MVE 5-Speed

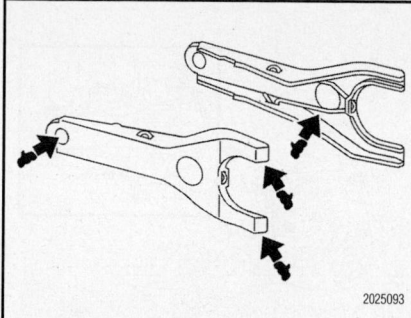

Fig. 56 Apply grease to the contact surfaces of the release fork, release bearing assembly, release fork push rod, and release fork support—MVE 5-Speed

To install:

➡**Insert the clutch disc assembly in the correct direction.**

22. Insert a clutch pilot tool into the clutch disc assembly, then insert them both into the flywheel sub-assembly.

23. Align the matchmark on the clutch cover assembly with the one on the flywheel sub-assembly.

➡**Tighten the bolts evenly one turn at a time. Move the pilot tool up and down, right and left lightly after checking that the disc is in the center, and tighten the bolts.**

24. Tighten the bolts in order, starting with the bolt located near the knock pin at the top to 14 ft. lbs. (19 Nm).

25. Using a dial indicator with a roller instrument, check the diaphragm spring tip alignment.

- Maximum non-alignment: 0.035 inch (0.9 mm).

26. If the alignment is not as specified, adjust the diaphragm spring tip alignment.

27. Install the release fork support onto the transaxle assembly and tighten to 27 ft. lbs. (37 Nm).

28. Install the clutch release fork boot to the manual transaxle.

29. Apply grease to the contact surfaces of the release fork, release bearing assembly, release fork push rod, and release fork support.

30. Install the release fork onto the release bearing assembly with the clip.

31. Apply grease to the input shaft spline.

32. Install the clutch release bearing with the release fork onto the transaxle assembly.

33. Install the manual transaxle assembly. Refer to Manual Transaxle Assembly, removal & installation.

BLEEDING

1. Fill the brake fluid reservoir.
2. Remove the bleeder plug cap.
3. Connect a vinyl tube to the bleeder plug.
4. Depress the clutch pedal several times, and then loosen the bleeder plug while the pedal is depressed.
5. When fluid no longer comes out, tighten the bleeder plug, and then release the clutch pedal.
6. Repeat the previous 2 steps until all the air in the fluid is completely bled.
7. Tighten the bleeder plug to 71 inch lbs. (8 Nm).
8. Install the bleeder plug cap.
9. Check that all the air has been bled from the clutch line.
10. Inspect the brake fluid level in reservoir.

TRANSFER CASE ASSEMBLY

REMOVAL & INSTALLATION
See Figures 57 and 58.

1. Remove the transmission. Refer to Automatic Transmission Assembly, removal & installation.
2. Remove the engine mounting bracket.
3. Remove the 4 bolts and the transfer stiffener plate.
4. Remove the bolts and nuts.

➡**Remove the transfer assembly from the transaxle assembly without tilting it. When removing the transfer assembly, do not hold the oil seal parts on both sides of the assembly.**

5. Using a plastic hammer, remove the transfer assembly from the transaxle assembly.

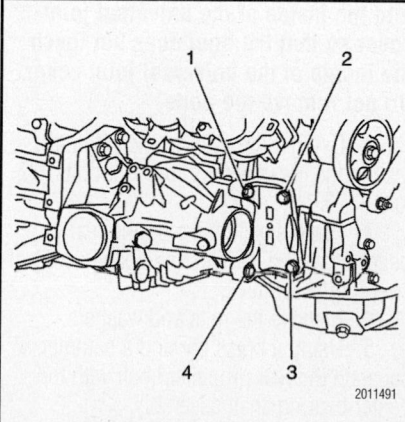

Fig. 57 Remove the bolts (1, 2, 3, 4) and the transfer stiffener plate

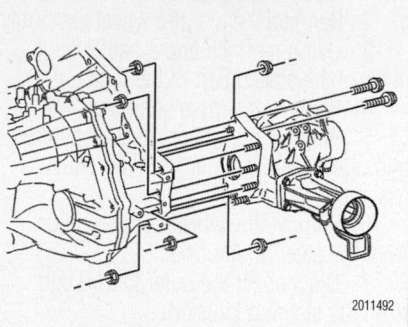

Fig. 58 Install the transfer assembly with the bolts and nuts to the transaxle assembly

To install:

6. Install the transfer assembly with the bolts and nuts to the transaxle assembly and tighten to 51 ft. lbs. (69 Nm).
7. Install the transfer assembly to the transaxle assembly horizontally.
8. Install the transfer stiffener plate with the bolts and tighten to 25 ft. lbs. (34 Nm).
9. Install the engine mounting bracket.
10. Install the transmission. Refer to Automatic Transmission Assembly, removal & installation.

FLUID FILL PROCEDURE

1. Remove the No. 1 transfer case plug and gasket.

➡**When changing oil, recheck the oil level after driving.**

2. Check that the oil level is within 0–0.197 inch (0–5 mm) from the lowest position of the hole for No. 1 transfer case plug.
3. When the oil level is too low, check for oil leakage.
4. When checking oil, make sure that the vehicle is level.
5. When adding oil, pour it slowly.
6. Add oil gradually at several intervals.
7. After leaving it alone for 5 minutes, check the oil level again.
8. Install the No. 1 transfer case plug with a new gasket.
9. Tighten the plug to 36 ft. lbs. (49 Nm).

FRONT DRIVESHAFT

REMOVAL & INSTALLATION

➡**Prevent the seals (boots) from contacting the other components in order to prevent damage to the seals (boots).**

1. Raise and support the vehicle.
2. Remove the tire and wheel assembly.
3. Using a punch and a hammer, unstake the staked part of the lock nut.
4. Remove the drive shaft lock nut.
5. Remove the wheel speed sensor wire and brake hose retainer from the strut assembly.
6. Remove the wheel speed sensor from the steering knuckle.
7. Disconnect the outer tie rod end from the steering knuckle.
8. Disconnect the lower ball joint from the steering knuckle.

CAUTION

Do not attempt to move vehicle with drive axle(s) removed from wheel bearing. Wheel(s) could fall off, dropping vehicle to the ground and causing personal injury or damage to the vehicle.

9. Using a plastic hammer, disengage the wheel drive shaft from the wheel hub and bearing and support the wheel drive shaft.
10. If removing left side shaft, use slide hammer to remove the left side axle shaft from the transaxle. If removing right side shaft, continue with procedure.

➡On AWD models, the transfer case and transaxle must be drained before removing the right hand drive shaft. If the right hand drive shaft is removed without draining the fluids, the fluids will mix and contaminate both components.

11. On AWD models, drain the transaxle and transfer case.
12. Using slide hammer, remove the right side axle shaft from the transaxle.
13. On AWD models, remove the bearing lock bolt.
14. Use pliers to remove the snap ring and drive shaft from the vehicle.
15. Remove the right hand wheel drive shaft from the vehicle.
16. Remove and discard the wheel drive shaft retaining ring.

To install:

➡Prevent the boots from contacting other components to prevent damage to the boots.

17. Install a new wheel drive shaft retaining ring.
18. On AWD models, set the snap ring on the right hand drive shaft with the opening facing downward.
19. Install the right hand wheel drive shaft to the transaxle.
20. Push the wheel drive shaft into transaxle until the retaining ring is fully seated.
21. Verify that the wheel drive shaft retaining ring is properly seated.
    a. Grasp the inner tripod housing.
    b. Pull the inner tripod housing outboard. Do not pull on the wheel drive shaft bar.
22. The wheel drive shaft will remain in place when the retaining ring is properly seated.
23. On AWD models, install the bearing lock bolt and tighten to 24 ft. lbs. (32 Nm).
24. Install the wheel drive shaft to the wheel hub and bearing.
25. Connect the ball joint to the steering knuckle and tighten to 66 ft. lbs. (89 Nm).
26. Connect the outer tie rod end assembly to the steering knuckle and tighten to 36 ft. lbs. (49 Nm).
27. Install a NEW wheel drive shaft nut and tighten to 159 ft. lbs. (216 Nm). Insert a drift or a flat-bladed tool through the caliper and into the brake rotor to prevent the rotor from turning.
28. Using a punch and hammer, stake the locknut.
29. Install the wheel speed sensor and tighten the retaining bolt to 71 inch lbs. (8 Nm).
30. Install the tire and wheel assembly.
31. On AWD models, inspect the transfer case fluid level.
32. Lower the vehicle.
33. Inspect the transaxle fluid level.

PROPELLER SHAFT

REMOVAL & INSTALLATION

See Figures 59 through 64.

1. Depress the brake pedal and hold it.

➡Put a piece of cloth or equivalent into the inside of the universal joint cover so that the boot does not touch the inside of the universal joint cover. Do not remove the bolts.

2. Using a hexagon wrench (6 mm), loosen the cross groove joint set bolts 1/2 turn.
3. Place matchmarks on the rear propeller shaft and the electromagnetic control coupling assembly.
4. Remove the nuts and washers.
5. Using a brass bar and a hammer, separate the rear propeller shaft with the center bearing shaft assembly.

➡When removing the bolts and washers, do not apply excessive force to the universal joint.

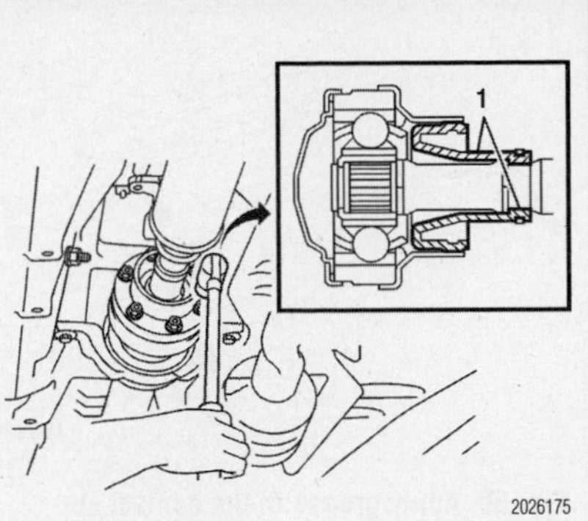

Fig. 59 Put a piece of cloth or equivalent (1) into the inside of the universal joint cover so that the boot does not touch the inside of the universal joint cover

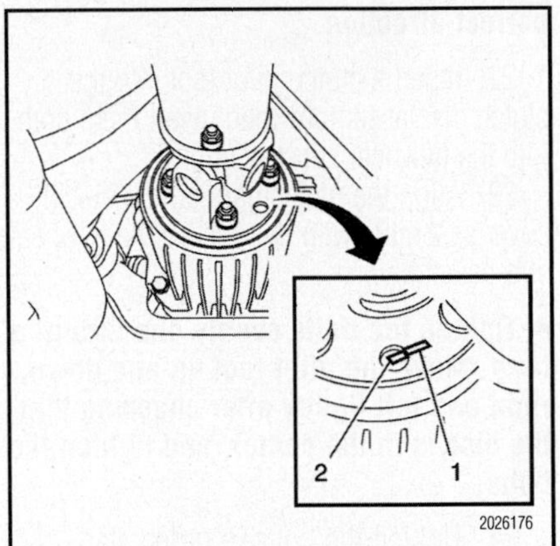

Fig. 60 Place matchmarks (1, 2) on the rear propeller shaft and the electromagnetic control coupling assembly.

6. Remove the bolts and No. 2 center support bearing washers.

➡When removing the propeller shaft, note the following:

- Do not apply a large force to the universal joint.
- During and after the removal of the propeller shaft, keep the universal joint angle straight (within 15 degrees).
- Be careful not to damage the oil seal.

7. Pull out the propeller with center bearing shaft assembly from the transfer case.
8. Insert a suitable seal installer into the transfer case to prevent oil leakage.

To install:

9. Remove the seal installer from the transfer.

➡Be careful not to damage the oil seal.

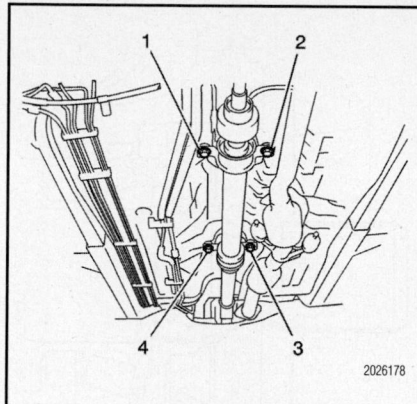

Fig. 61 Remove the bolts (1–4) and No. 2 center support bearing washers

➡**Be careful not to damage the universal joint boot when installing the propeller shaft.**

10. Install the propeller with center bearing shaft assembly.

11. Align matchmarks on the rear propeller shaft and the electromagnetic control coupling assembly and install the nuts and washers temporarily.

➡**Use the removed washers when installing.**

12. Install the 2 No. 1 center support bearing assembly with the bolts and No. 2 center support bearing washers.

13. Align the matchmarks.

14. Install the center support bearing nuts and tighten to 27 ft. lbs. (37 Nm).

15. Remove the piece of cloth from the universal joint.

16. Depress the brake pedal and hold it.

17. Using a hexagon wrench (6 mm), tighten the bolts to 19 ft. lbs. (26 Nm).

18. With the vehicle unloaded, adjust the dimension between the rear side of the cover and shaft.

- Length A : 0.579 to 2.776 inches (65.5 to 70.5 mm).

19. With the vehicle unloaded, adjust the front and rear dimensions between the edge

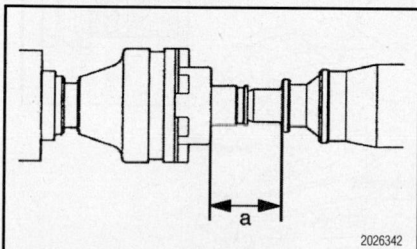

Fig. 62 With the vehicle unloaded, adjust the dimension between the rear side of the cover and shaft (a)

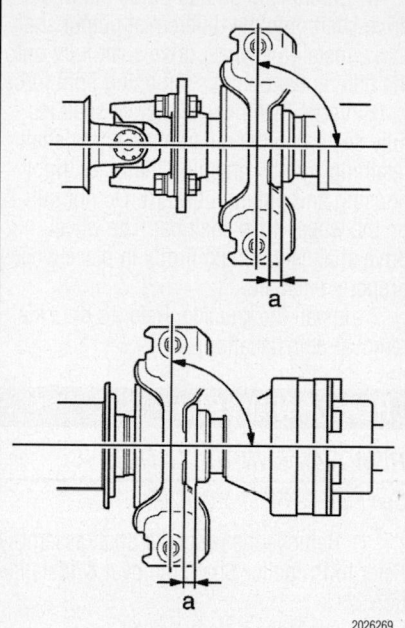

Fig. 63 With the vehicle unloaded, adjust the front and rear dimensions between the edge surface of the center support bearing and the edge surface of the cushion respectively as shown

surface of the center support bearing and the edge surface of the cushion respectively as shown, and then tighten the bolts.

- Length A: 0.453 to 0.532 inch (11.5 to 13.5 mm).

20. Check that the center line of the bracket is at a right angle to the shaft axial direction.

21. Tighten the bolts to 27 ft. lbs. (37 Nm).

22. If any vibration or noise occurs, perform joint angle check as follows and replace the No. 2 center support bearing washer with a proper one.

23. Turn the propeller shaft several times by hand to stabilize the center support bearings.

24. Using a jack, raise and lower the differential to stabilize the differential mounting cushion.

25. Remove the transfer dynamic damper.

26. Using an angle meter or equivalent, measure the propeller shaft installation angle and intermediate shaft installation angle.

- No. 1 joint angle (1) - (6) - (5) = -1.74 degrees to +0.26 degrees

➡**Make sure to use a washer of the same thickness on both right and left sides. Do not use 2 or more washers on a bolt.**

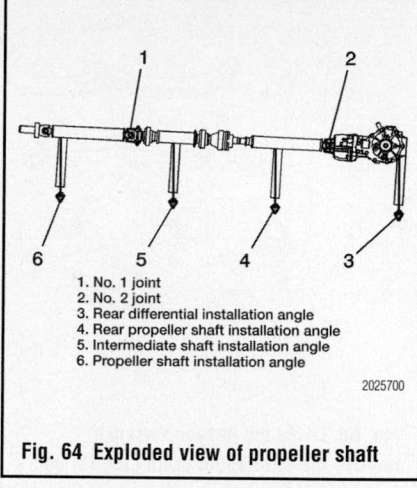

1. No. 1 joint
2. No. 2 joint
3. Rear differential installation angle
4. Rear propeller shaft installation angle
5. Intermediate shaft installation angle
6. Propeller shaft installation angle

Fig. 64 Exploded view of propeller shaft

27. Using an angle meter or equivalent, measure the rear propeller shaft installation angle and rear differential installation angle.

- No. 2 joint angle (2) - (4) - (3) = 1.20 degrees to 2.20 degrees

28. If the calculated amount is not within the specification, adjust it with the No. 2 center support bearing washer.

29. Install the transfer dynamic damper and tighten to 19 ft. lbs. (26 Nm).

REAR AXLE FLUID

DRAIN & REFILL

See Figures 65 and 66.

1. Using a hexagon wrench (10 mm), remove the differential cover plug and gasket.

2. Using the hexagon wrench, remove the differential drain plug and gasket, then drain the oil.

To install:

3. Using the hexagon wrench, install the differential drain plug with a new gasket and tighten to 29 ft. lbs. (39 Nm).

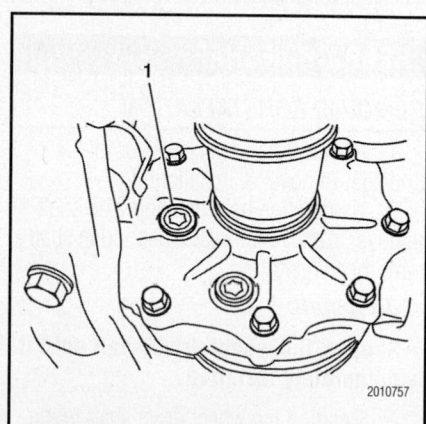

Fig. 65 Using a hexagon wrench (10 mm), remove the differential cover plug and gasket

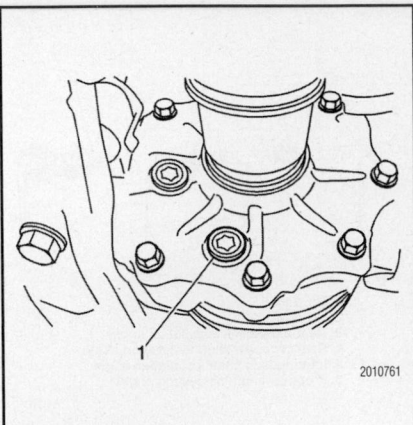

Fig. 66 Using the hexagon wrench, remove the differential drain plug (1) and gasket

4. Add oil.

5. Check the oil level.

6. Install the rear differential carrier cover plug.

➡**After replacing oil, recheck the oil level after driving.**

7. Using the hexagon wrench, install the differential carrier cover plug with a new gasket and tighten to 29 ft. lbs. (39 Nm).

8. Stop the vehicle in a level place.

➡**Excessively large or small amount of oil may cause damage.**

9. After replacing oil, recheck the oil level after driving.

10. Check that the oil surface is within 0.197 inch (5 mm) of the lowest position of the inner surface of the differential filler plug opening.

11. Check for oil leakage if the oil level is low.

12. Using the hexagon wrench, install the differential carrier cover plug and a new gasket and tighten to 29 ft. lbs. (39 Nm).

REAR DRIVESHAFT

REMOVAL & INSTALLATION

1. Remove the knuckle. Refer to Knuckle, removal & installation.

2. Using slide hammer, and axle shaft remover, remove the rear wheel drive shaft from the vehicle.

To install:

➡**Support the wheel drive shaft until it is completely installed.**

3. Position the wheel drive shaft to the differential output shaft.

➡**Do not damage the differential output shaft oil seal.**

4. Carefully align and guide the wheel drive shaft onto the differential output shaft.

5. Install the wheel drive shaft fully onto the differential output shaft using light force.

6. Verify that the wheel drive shaft is fully seated on the differential output shaft retaining ring by grasping the inner tripot housing and pulling outward. Do not pull on the wheel drive shaft bar. The wheel drive shaft will remain firmly in place when properly engaged.

7. Install the knuckle. Refer to Knuckle, removal & installation.

REAR PINION SEAL

REMOVAL & INSTALLATION

See Figures 67 through 70.

1. Remove the propeller shaft assembly. Refer to Propeller Shaft, removal & installation.

2. Drain the differential oil.

3. Disconnect the electromagnetic control coupling sub-assembly connector and tube.

4. Remove the bolts.

5. Using a brass bar and a hammer, tap the electromagnetic control coupling sub-assembly to remove the rear differential carrier cover with the electromagnetic control coupling sub-assembly from the rear differential carrier assembly.

➡**Check the direction of the washer to face.**

6. Remove the transmission coupling conical spring washer from the rear differential carrier assembly.

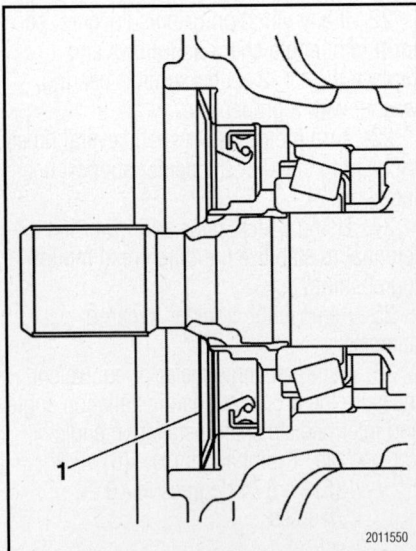

Fig. 67 Remove the transmission coupling conical spring washer (1) from the rear differential carrier assembly

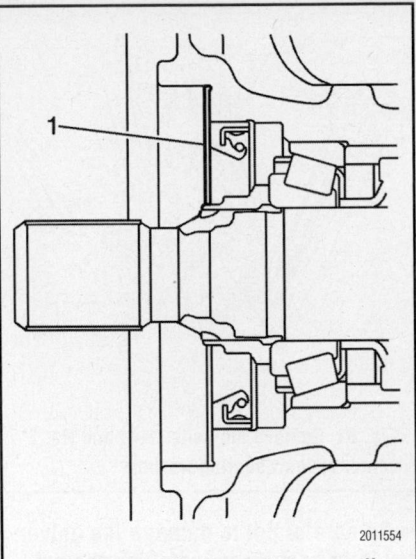

Fig. 68 Remove the transmission coupling spacer (1) from the rear differential carrier assembly.

7. Remove the transmission coupling spacer from the rear differential carrier assembly.

8. Remove the rear differential carrier oil seal.

To install:

9. Apply MP grease to the lip of a new rear differential carrier oil seal.

10. Install the rear differential carrier oil seal using a suitable tool.

- Oil seal installation depth (A): 0.0276–0.0512 inch (0.7–1.3 mm).

11. Install the transmission coupling spacer to the rear differential carrier assembly.

➡**Install the washer so that the marked surface faces the front of the vehicle.**

12. Install the transmission coupling conical spring washer to the rear differential carrier assembly.

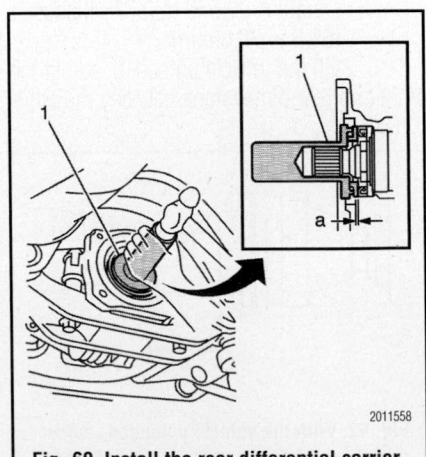

Fig. 69 Install the rear differential carrier oil seal (1) to installation depth (A)

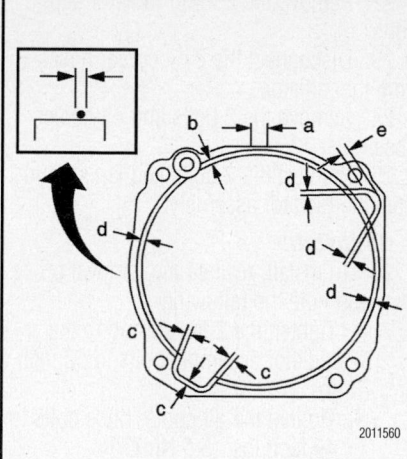

Fig. 70 Apply sealant Three Bond 1281 or equivalent, to the areas indicated in the illustration of the electromagnetic control coupling sub-assembly

13. Using a scraper and wire brush, remove the sealant from the rear differential carrier and differential side bearing retainer.

14. Using non-residue solvent, remove the grease and oil from the alignment surfaces of the rear differential carrier and the electromagnetic control coupling sub-assembly.

➡**Perform the next step, and note the following:**

- Apply sealant in a continuous bead 2–3 mm (0.0787–0.118 in) in diameter.
- Install the electromagnetic control coupling sub-assembly within 3 minutes after applying sealant.
- Stop applying sealant after allowing it to overlap with the beginning of the bead by at least 10 mm (0.394 in) within range A.

15. Apply sealant Three Bond 1281 or equivalent, to the areas indicated in the illustration of the electromagnetic control coupling sub-assembly.

- Area (B) : Apply sealant to 0.0394 inch (1.0 mm).
- Area (C) : Apply sealant 0.0787 inch (2.0 mm).
- Area (D) : Apply sealant 0.0118 inch (3.0 mm).
- Area (E) : Apply sealant to 0.1969 inch (5.0 mm).

16. Install the electromagnetic control coupling sub-assembly with the bolts and tighten to 15 ft. lbs. (20 Nm).

17. Connect the electromagnetic control coupling subassembly connector and tube.

18. Add the differential oil.

19. Install the propeller shaft assembly. Refer to Propeller Shaft, removal & installation.

ENGINE COOLING

ENGINE COOLANT

DRAIN & REFILL PROCEDURE

See Figure 71.

➡**Do not loosen the lower radiator drain cock plug while the engine and radiator are still hot. Pressurized, hot engine coolant and steam may be released and cause serious burns.**

➡**Collect the coolant in a container and dispose of it according to the regulations in your area.**

1. Loosen the lower radiator drain cock plug.

2. Remove the radiator cap.

3. Loosen the cylinder block drain cock plug.

4. Install the lower radiator drain cock plug and allow the engine and radiator to drain correctly.

5. Install the cylinder block drain cock plug.

6. Tighten the bolts to 115 inch lbs. (13 Nm).

7. Loosen the upper radiator drain cock plug.

8. Slowly fill the radiator with DEX-COOL®.

➡**Never use water as a substitute for engine coolant.**

➡**In order to avoid damage to the engine cooling system and other technical problems, only use DEX-COOL® or** similar high quality ethylene glycol based non-silicate, non-amine, non-nitrite, non-borate coolant with long-life hybrid organic acid technology (coolant with long-life hybrid organic acid technology consists of a combination of low phosphates and organic acids).

9. Squeeze the inlet and outlet radiator hoses several times by hand and then check the level of the coolant.

10. If the coolant level is low, add coolant.

11. Tighten the upper radiator drain cock plug.

12. Slowly pour coolant into the radiator reservoir tank until it reaches the FULL line.

13. Install the radiator cap sub-assembly and reservoir tank cap.

14. Start the engine and warm it up.

15. Bleed the air from the cooling system.

16. Before starting the engine, turn the A/C switch off.

17. Adjust the air conditioning temperature setting to MAX (HOT).

18. Adjust the air conditioning blower setting to LO.

➡**Wear protective gloves. Be careful as the radiator hoses are hot. Keep your hands away from the radiator fan.**

19. Warm up the engine until the thermostat opens. While the thermostat is open, allow the coolant to circulate for several minutes.

20. Thermostat opening timing can be

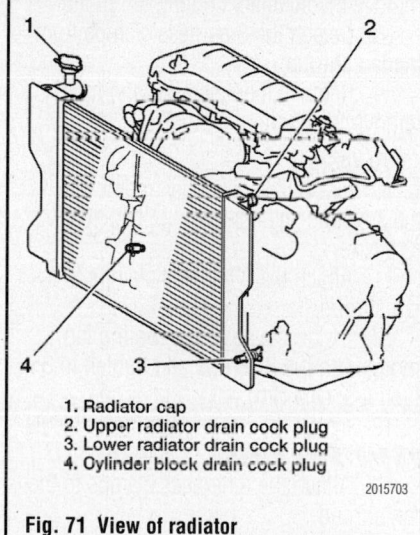

1. Radiator cap
2. Upper radiator drain cock plug
3. Lower radiator drain cock plug
4. Cylinder block drain cock plug

Fig. 71 View of radiator

determined by squeezing the inlet radiator hose and sensing vibrations when the engine coolant starts to flow inside the hose.

21. Stop the engine and wait until the engine coolant cools down.

22. Add engine coolant to the FULL line on the radiator reservoir.

23. Inspect for coolant leaks.

ENGINE FAN

REMOVAL & INSTALLATION

1.8L

1. Remove the radiator. Refer to Radiator, removal & installation.

2. Remove the center nut, then remove the fan.

3. Disconnect the connector and 2 clamps from the fan shroud.

4. Remove the 3 screws, then remove the cooling fan motor.

To install:

5. To install, reverse the removal procedure and note the following:
- Tighten the fan nut to 56 inch lbs. (6.3 Nm).

2.4L

1. Remove the radiator. Refer to Radiator, removal & installation.

2. If equipped with air conditioning system, remove the 2 nuts and 2 fans.

3. Remove the nut and fan.

4. Remove the auxiliary cooling fan motor, with air conditioning system.

5. Detach the 4 harness clamps from the fan shroud.

6. Remove the 2 screws and cooling fan motor insulator.

7. Remove the 3 screws, and then remove the auxiliary cooling fan motor.

8. Detach the 3 harness clamps from the fan shroud.

9. Remove the 3 screws, and then remove the cooling fan motor.

To install:

10. Install the cooling fan motor with the 3 screws and tighten to 35 inch lbs. (3.9 Nm).

11. Attach the 3 harness clamps to the fan shroud.

12. Install the auxiliary cooling fan motor with the 3 screws and tighten to 35 inch lbs. (3.9 Nm).

13. Install the cooling fan motor insulator with the 2 screws.

14. Attach the 4 harness clamps to the fan shroud.

15. Install auxiliary fan with air conditioning system.

16. Install the 2 fans with the 2 nuts and tighten to 56 inch lbs. (6.3 Nm).

17. Install the fan with the nut and tighten to 56 inch lbs. (6.3 Nm).

18. Install the radiator. Refer to Radiator, removal & installation.

RADIATOR

REMOVAL & INSTALLATION

1.8L

See Figure 72.

1. Remove the left engine under cover.

2. Remove the right engine under cover.

3. Remove the front bumper assembly.

4. Disconnect the cable from negative battery terminal. Refer to Battery, precautions.

5. Drain the engine coolant. Refer to Engine Coolant, Drain & Refill Procedure.

6. Remove the battery. Refer to Battery, removal & installation.

7. Remove the thermistor assembly.

8. Disconnect the radiator reservoir tank hose from the radiator assembly.

9. Disconnect the upper radiator hose from the radiator assembly.

10. Disconnect the lower radiator hose from the radiator assembly.

11. Disconnect the oil cooler hose.

12. Remove the 2 bolts and 2 upper radiator supports.

13. Remove the 2 support cushions from the 2 upper radiator supports.

14. Disconnect the hood lock assembly.

15. Disconnect the water by-pass hose from the radiator assembly.

16. Remove the 2 bolts and the hood lock support subassembly.

17. Disconnect the horn connector.

18. Remove the 4 bolts and upper radiator support subassembly.

19. Remove the 2 bolts, disengage the 2 claws, and remove the fan shroud from the radiator assembly.

20. Disconnect the cooling fan motor connector and wire harness clamp.

➡**For vehicles with the air conditioning system, do not apply any excessive force to the cooler condenser assembly or pipe when removing the radiator assembly.**

21. Remove the radiator assembly with the fan shroud.

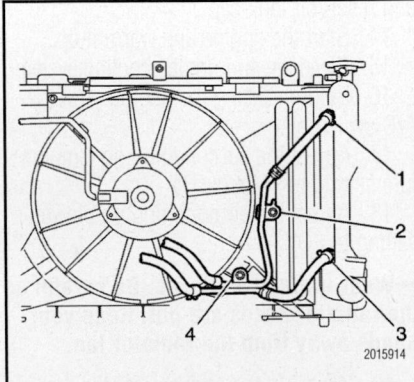

Fig. 72 Disconnect the 2 oil cooler hoses (1, 3) from the radiator. Remove the 2 bolts and oil cooler hose (2, 4)—1.8L

22. Remove the 2 lower radiator supports.

23. Disconnect the 2 oil cooler hoses from the radiator.

24. Remove the 2 bolts and oil cooler hose.

25. Remove the 2 bolts and fan shroud from the radiator assembly.

To install:

26. To install, reverse the removal procedure and note the following:
- Tighten the 2 fan shroud to the radiator assembly bolts to 62 inch lbs. (7.0 Nm).
- Tighten the oil cooler hose bolts to 49 inch lbs. (5.5 Nm).
- Tighten the 2 fan shroud to the radiator assembly bolts to 62 inch lbs. (7.0 Nm).
- Tighten the 4 upper radiator support sub-assembly bolts to 49 inch lbs. (5.5 Nm).
- Tighten the 2 lock support sub-assembly bolts to 62 inch lbs. (7.0 Nm).
- Tighten the bolts of the 2 upper radiator supports to 14 ft. lbs. (19 Nm).

➡**For vehicles with the air conditioning system, do not apply any excessive force to the cooler condenser assembly or pipe when installing the radiator assembly.**

27. Add engine coolant. Refer to Engine Coolant, Drain & Refill Procedure.

28. Inspect for coolant leaks.

29. Inspect the reservoir tank engine coolant level.

30. Install the front bumper assembly.

31. Adjust fog light alignment.

32. Install left engine under cover.

33. Install right engine under cover.

2.4L

See Figure 73.

1. Disconnect the cable from negative battery terminal. Refer to Battery, precautions.

2. Remove the left engine under cover.

3. Remove the right engine under cover.

4. Drain the engine coolant. Refer to Engine Coolant, Drain & Refill Procedure.

5. Remove the battery. Refer to Battery, removal & installation.

6. Remove the front bumper assembly.

7. Remove the thermistor assembly.

8. Disconnect the radiator reservoir tank hose from the radiator assembly.

9. Disconnect the upper radiator hose from the radiator assembly.

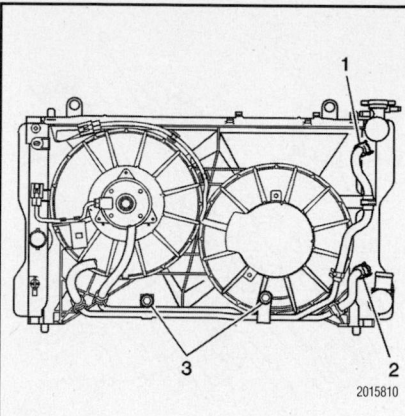

Fig. 73 Disconnect the 2 oil cooler hoses (1, 2) from the radiator. Remove the 2 bolts (3) and oil cooler hose—2.4L

10. Disconnect the lower radiator hose from the radiator assembly.

11. Disconnect the oil cooler hose.

12. Remove the 2 bolts and 2 upper radiator supports.

13. Remove the 2 support cushions from the 2 upper radiator supports.

14. Remove hood lock assembly.

15. Separate the water by-pass hose from the 2 clamps.

16. Disconnect the water by-pass hose from the radiator assembly.

17. Remove the 2 bolts and the hood lock support subassembly.

18. Disconnect the horn connector.

19. Remove the 4 bolts and the upper radiator support sub-assembly.

20. Remove the 2 bolts, disengage the 2 claws, and remove the fan shroud from the radiator assembly.

21. Disconnect the cooling fan motor connector and the wire harness clamp.

22. Disconnect the 2 cooling fan motor connectors and the wire harness clamp.

23. Remove the radiator assembly with the fan shroud.

24. Remove the 2 lower radiator supports.

25. Disconnect the 2 oil cooler hoses from the radiator.

26. Disconnect the clamp from the fan shroud.

27. Remove the 2 bolts and oil cooler hose.

28. Remove the 2 bolts and fan shroud from the radiator assembly.

To install:

29. To install, reverse the removal procedure and note the following:
- Tighten the 2 fan shroud to the radiator assembly bolts to 62 inch lbs. (7.0 Nm).

- Tighten the 2 oil cooler hose bolts to 49 inch lbs. (5.5 Nm).
- Tighten the 2 No. 2 fan shroud to the radiator assembly bolts to 62 inch lbs. (7.0 Nm).
- Tighten the 4 upper radiator support sub-assembly to 49 inch lbs. (5.5 Nm).
- Tighten the 2 hood lock support sub-assembly bolts to 62 inch lbs. (7.0 Nm).
- Tighten the bolts of the 2 upper radiator supports to 14 ft. lbs. (19 Nm).

30. Add engine coolant. Refer to Engine Coolant, Drain & Refill Procedure.

31. Inspect for coolant leaks.

32. Inspect the reservoir tank engine coolant level.

33. Install front bumper assembly.

34. Inspect the fog light alignment.

THERMOSTAT

REMOVAL & INSTALLATION

1.8L

See Figures 74 and 75.

1. Drain the engine coolant. Refer to Engine Coolant, Drain & Refill Procedure.

2. Remove the 2 nuts and water inlet.

3. Remove the thermostat and gasket.

4. Remove the gasket from the thermostat.

To inspect:

➡**The valve opening temperature is inscribed on the thermostat.**

5. Inspect thermostat.

6. Hanging from wire, immerse the thermostat in water and then gradually heat the water.

➡**If the valve opening temperature is not as specified, replace the thermostat.**

7. Inspect the standard valve opening temperature of the thermostat.
- Standard valve opening temperature: 176–183°F (80–84°C).

➡**If the valve lift is not as specified, replace the thermostat.**

8. Check the valve lift.
- Standard valve lift: 0.394 inch (10 mm) or more at 203°F (95°C).

➡**If it is not fully closed, replace the thermostat.**

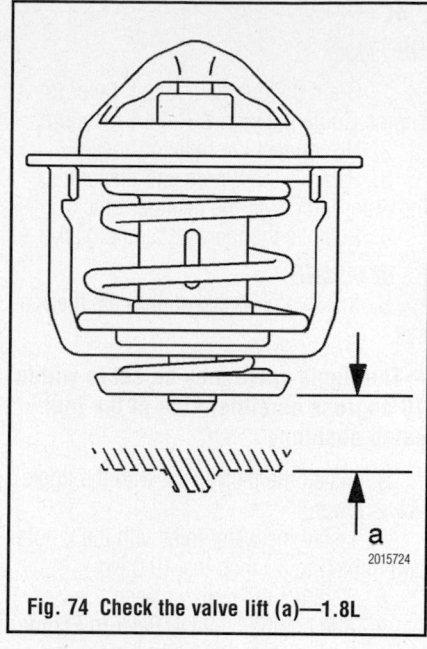

Fig. 74 Check the valve lift (a)—1.8L

9. Ensure that the valve is fully closed when the thermostat is at low temperatures, below 171°F (77°C).

To install:

10. Install the thermostat.

11. Install a new gasket on the thermostat.

➡**The jiggle valve may be set to within 10 degrees on either side of the indicated position.**

12. Install the thermostat to the water inlet with the jiggle valve upward.

13. Install the water inlet with the 2 nuts and tighten to 7 ft. lbs. (10 Nm).

14. Add engine coolant. Refer to Engine Coolant, Drain & Refill Procedure.

15. Inspect for coolant leaks.

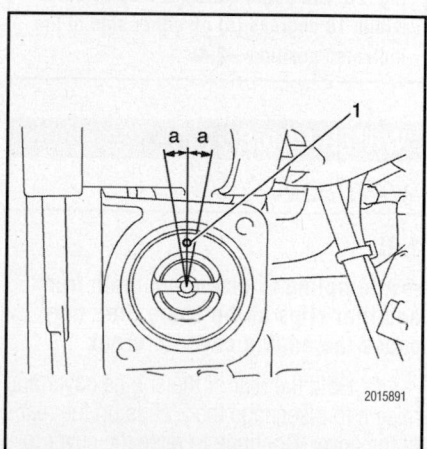

Fig. 75 The jiggle valve (1) may be set to within 10 degrees (a) on either side of the indicated position—1.8L

2.4L

See Figure 76.

1. Drain the engine coolant. Refer to Engine Coolant, Drain & Refill Procedure.
2. Disconnect the radiator hose.
3. Remove the 2 nuts and disconnect the water inlet from the cylinder block.
4. Remove the thermostat and gasket.

To install:

5. Install a new gasket onto the thermostat.

➡**The jiggle valve may be set to within 10 degrees on either side of the indicated position.**

6. Install the thermostat with the jiggle valve upward.
7. Install the water inlet with the 2 nuts and tighten to 80 inch lbs. (9.0 Nm).
8. Connect the radiator hose.
9. Add engine coolant. Refer to Engine Coolant, Drain & Refill Procedure.
10. Inspect for coolant leaks.
11. Inspect the reservoir tank engine coolant level.

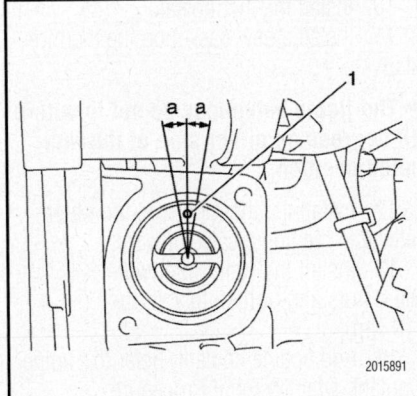

Fig. 76 The jiggle valve (1) may be set to within 10 degrees (a) on either side of the indicated position—2.4L

WATER PUMP

INSPECTION

1.8L

➡**Attempting to disengage both front and rear clips at the same time may cause the engine cover to break.**

1. Hold the rear of the engine cover and raise it to disengage the 2 clips on the rear of the cover. Continue to raise the cover to disengage the 2 clips on the front of the cover and remove the cover.
2. Remove the right engine under cover.

3. Remove the accessory drive belt. Refer to Accessory Drive Belts, removal & installation.
4. Inspect water pump assembly.
5. Turn the pulley and check that the water pump bearing moves smoothly and quietly.
6. If necessary, replace the water pump assembly.
7. Make sure that there are no drops of coolant on the water pump housing.
8. If necessary, replace the water pump assembly.
9. Install the accessory drive belt. Refer to Accessory Drive Belts, removal & installation.
10. Install the right engine under cover.
11. Position the engine cover and engage the two front fasteners. Engage the two fasteners on the rear of the cover.

2.4L

See Figure 77.

1. Remove the radiator surge tank assembly.
2. Remove the alternator. Refer to Alternator, removal & installation.
3. Disconnect the negative battery cable. Refer to Battery, precautions.
4. Raise and properly support the engine.

➡**Do not apply excessive force to the return tube when removing the right engine mounting insulator sub-assembly.**

➡**Keep clearance by lowering the engine using the engine support fixture when removing the front engine mounting insulator.**

5. Remove the 4 bolts and 2 nuts, then remove the right engine mounting insulator.
6. Remove the 3 bolts and transverse engine mounting bracket.
7. Remove water pump pulley.
8. Inspect water pump assembly.
9. Visually check the drain hole and air hole for coolant leakage.
10. If leakage is found, replace the water pump assembly.
11. Turn the pulley, and then check that the water pump bearing moves smoothly without making a "click" sound.
12. If it does not move smoothly, replace the water pump assembly.
13. Install the water pump pulley.
14. Install the engine transverse engine mounting bracket with the 3 bolts and tighten to 41 ft. lbs. (55 Nm).
15. Install the right engine mounting insulator sub-assembly with the 4 bolts and 2 nuts and tighten:

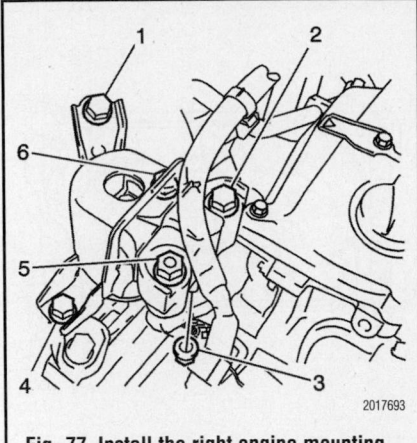

Fig. 77 Install the right engine mounting insulator sub-assembly with the 4 bolts (1, 2, 4, 6) and 2 nuts (3, 5)

- Bolts 1, 4 and 6 to 38 ft. lbs. (52 Nm).
- Bolt 2 to 70 ft. lbs. (95 Nm).
- Nut 5 to 70 ft. lbs. (95 Nm).
- Nut 3 to 38 ft. lbs. (52 Nm).

16. Install the alternator. Refer to Alternator, removal & installation.
17. Install the radiator surge tank assembly.

REMOVAL & INSTALLATION

1.8L

See Figure 78.

1. Disconnect the cable from negative battery terminal. Refer to Battery, precautions.

➡**Attempting to disengage both front and rear clips at the same time may cause the engine cover to break.**

2. Hold the rear of the engine cover and raise it to disengage the 2 clips on the rear of the cover. Continue to raise the cover to disengage the 2 clips on the front of the cover and remove the cover.
3. Remove the right engine under cover.
4. Drain the engine coolant. Refer to Engine Coolant, Drain & Refill Procedure.
5. Remove the accessory drive belt. Refer to Accessory Drive Belts, removal & installation.
6. Remove the alternator. Refer to Alternator, removal & installation.
7. Remove the 5 bolts and water pump assembly from the timing chain cover.
8. Remove the water pump gasket from the timing chain cover.

To install:

➡**Be sure to clean the contact surfaces.**

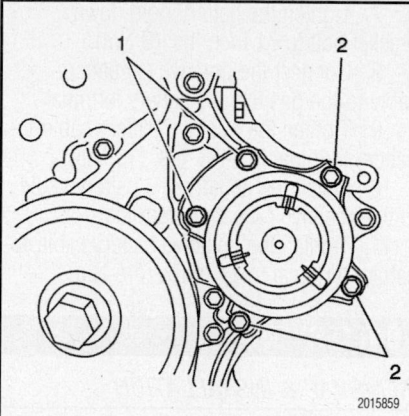

Fig. 78 Install the water pump assembly to the timing chain cover with the 5 bolts (1, 2)—1.8L

9. Align the protrusion of a new water pump gasket with the cutout in the timing chain cover and install the gasket to the groove of the timing chain cover.

10. Install the water pump assembly to the timing chain cover with the 5 bolts and tighten:
- Bolt 1 to 19 ft. lbs. (26 Nm).
- Bolt 2 to 18 ft. lbs. (24 Nm).

11. Install the alternator. Refer to Alternator, removal & installation.

12. Install the accessory drive belt. Refer to Accessory Drive Belts, removal & installation.

13. Connect the cable to negative battery terminal.

14. Add engine coolant. Refer to Engine Coolant, Drain & Refill Procedure.

15. Inspect for coolant leaks.

16. Inspect the reservoir tank engine coolant level.

17. Install the right engine under cover.

18. Position the engine cover and engage the two front fasteners. Engage the two fasteners on the rear of the cover.

2.4L

See Figure 79.

1. Disconnect the cable from negative battery terminal. Refer to Battery, precautions.

2. Remove the left engine under cover.

3. Remove the right engine under cover.

4. Drain the engine coolant. Refer to Engine Coolant, Drain & Refill Procedure.

5. Separate the radiator reserve tank assembly.

6. Remove the accessory drive belt. Refer to Accessory Drive Belts, removal & installation.

7. Remove the alternator. Refer to Alternator, removal & installation.

➡**Do not apply excessive force to the return tube when removing the right engine mounting insulator sub-assembly.**

➡**Keep clearance by lowering the engine using the engine support fixture when removing the front engine mounting insulator.**

8. Remove the 4 bolts and 2 nuts, then remove the right engine mounting insulator.

9. Remove the 3 bolts and transverse engine mounting bracket.

10. Using water pump pulley holding tool (EN-46104), remove the 4 bolts and water pump pulley.

11. Remove the clamp of the crankshaft position sensor from the water pump.

12. Disconnect the wire of the crankshaft position sensor from the clamp bracket.

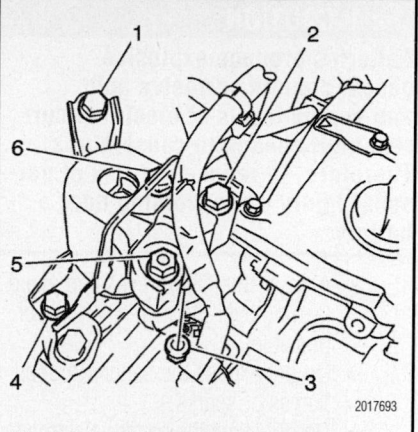

Fig. 79 Install the right engine mounting insulator sub-assembly with the 4 bolts (1, 2, 4, 6) and 2 nuts (3, 5)—2.4L

13. Remove the 4 bolts, 2 nuts and the clamp bracket.

➡**Tape the screwdriver tip before use.**

14. Using a screwdriver, pry between the water pump and cylinder block, and then remove the water pump.

To install:

15. To install, reverse the removal procedure and note the following:
- Install the engine transverse engine mounting bracket with the 3 bolts and tighten to 41 ft. lbs. (55 Nm).
- Install the right engine mounting insulator sub-assembly with the 4 bolts and 2 nuts and tighten:
- Bolts 1, 4 and 6 to 38 ft. lbs. (52 Nm).
- Bolt 2 to 70 ft. lbs. (95 Nm).
- Nut 5 to 70 ft. lbs. (95 Nm).
- Nut 3 to 38 ft. lbs. (52 Nm).

Top of Form

ENGINE ELECTRICAL

BATTERY

PRECAUTIONS

❉❉ **CAUTION**

Unless directed otherwise, the ignition and start switch must be in the OFF or LOCK position, and all electrical loads must be OFF before servicing any electrical component. Disconnect the negative battery cable to prevent an electrical spark should a tool or equipment come in contact with an exposed electrical terminal. Failure to follow these precautions may

result in personal injury and/or damage to the vehicle or its components.

❉❉ **WARNING**

For Vehicles equipped with OnStar® (UE1) with Back Up Battery: The Back Up Battery is a redundant power supply to allow limited OnStar® functionality in the event of a main vehicle battery power disruption to the VCIM (OnStar®module). Do not disconnect the main vehicle battery or remove the OnStar® fuse with the ignition key in any position other than OFF. Retained accessory

BATTERY SYSTEM

power (RAP) should be allowed to time out or be disabled (simply opening the driver door should disable RAP) before disconnecting power. Disconnecting power to the OnStar® module in any way while the ignition is On or with RAP activated may cause activation of the OnStar® Back-Up Battery (BUB) system and will discharge and permanently damage the back-up battery. Once the Back-Up Battery is activated it will stay on until it has completely discharged. The BUB is not rechargeable and once activated the BUB must be replaced.

REMOVAL & INSTALLATION

See Figure 80.

✳✳ WARNING

Refer to Battery, precautions.

1. Disconnect the negative (-) battery cable from the negative (-) battery terminal.
2. Disconnect the positive (+) battery cable from the positive (+) battery terminal.
3. Remove the bolt and the battery hold down bracket.
4. Remove the battery from the vehicle.

To install:

5. Install the battery into the vehicle. Position the battery into the battery tray.
6. Install the battery hold down bracket. Secure with the bolt.

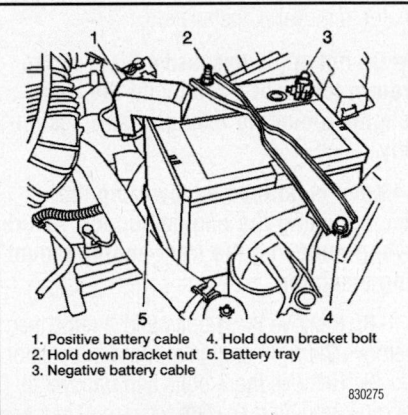

1. Positive battery cable
2. Hold down bracket nut
3. Negative battery cable
4. Hold down bracket bolt
5. Battery tray

830275

Fig. 80 View of battery

7. Tighten the battery hold down bracket bolt to 71 inch lbs. (8 Nm).
8. Connect the positive (+) battery cable to the positive (+) battery terminal.
9. Tighten the positive battery cable-to-battery terminal to 11 ft. lbs. (15 Nm).
10. Install the negative (-) battery cable to the negative (-) battery terminal.
11. Tighten the negative battery cable-to-battery terminal to 11 ft. lbs. (15 Nm).

BATTERY TRAY

REMOVAL & INSTALLATION

1. Remove the battery. Refer to Battery, removal & installation.
2. Separate the 2 wire harness clamps from the battery tray.
3. Remove the 2 bolts.
4. Separate the radiator pipe from the battery tray.
5. Remove the 4 bolts and battery tray.

To install:

6. To install, reverse the removal procedure and note the following:
- Tighten the battery tray bolts to 14 ft. lbs. (19 Nm).
- Tighten the radiator pipe bolts to 78 inch lbs. (8.8 Nm).
- Tighten the battery clamp bolts to 58 inch lbs. (6.5 Nm).
- Tighten the battery clamp nut to 31 inch lbs. (3.5 Nm).

ENGINE ELECTRICAL

ALTERNATOR

REMOVAL & INSTALLATION

See Figure 81.

➡When disconnecting the cable, some systems need to be initialized after the cable is reconnected.

1. Disconnect the negative battery terminal cable. Refer to Battery, precautions.
2. Remove the engine under cover.
3. Remove the accessory drive belt. Refer to Accessory Drive Belts, removal & installation.
4. Remove the terminal cap.
5. Remove the nut and disconnect the wire harness from terminal B.
6. Disconnect the alternator connector and 2 harness clamps.
7. Remove the 2 bolts and alternator assembly.
8. Remove the bolt and wire harness clamp bracket.

9. Remove the alternator assembly.

To install:

10. Install alternator assembly.
11. Install the wire harness clamp bracket with the bolt.

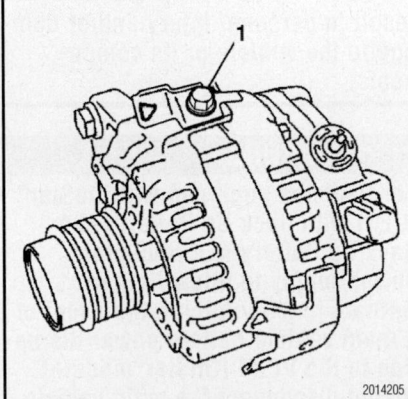

2014205

Fig. 81 Install the wire harness clamp bracket with the bolt (1)

CHARGING SYSTEM

12. Tighten to 74 inch lbs. (8.4 Nm).
13. On 1.8L Engines, temporarily install the alternator assembly with the 2 bolts.
14. On 2.4L Engines, install the alternator assembly with the 2 bolts.
- Tighten bolt 1 to 16 ft. lbs. (21 Nm).
- Tighten bolt 2 to 38 ft. lbs. (52 Nm).
15. On all models, install the alternator connector and wire 2 harness clamps.
16. Install the wire harness to terminal B with the nut and install the terminal cap.
17. Tighten to 87 inch lbs. (9.8 Nm).
18. Install the accessory drive belt. Refer to Accessory Drive Belts, removal & installation.
19. Install the engine under cover right hand side.
20. Connect cable to the negative battery terminal.

ENGINE ELECTRICAL

FIRING ORDER

1.8L (LAY) Engine firing order: 1–3–4–2
2.4L (LAX) Engine firing order: 1–3–4–2

IGNITION COIL

REMOVAL & INSTALLATION

1.8L (LAY)

➡**Attempting to disengage both front and rear clips at the same time may cause the engine cover to break.**

1. Hold the rear of the engine cover and raise it to disengage the 2 clips on the rear of the cover. Continue to raise the cover to disengage the 2 clips on the front of the cover and remove the cover.
2. Disconnect the 4 ignition coil connectors.
3. Remove the 4 bolts and 4 ignition coils.

To install:
4. Install the 4 ignition coils with the 4 bolts and tighten to 80 inch lbs. (9.0 Nm).

5. Connect the 4 ignition coil connectors.
6. Position the engine cover and engage the two front fasteners. Engage the two fasteners on the rear of the cover.

2.4L (LAX)

1. Remove the 2 engine cover fasteners and 2 plastic retainers. Remove the engine cover from the engine.
2. Disconnect the 4 ignition coil connectors.
3. Remove the 4 bolts and 4 ignition coils.

To install:
4. Install the 4 ignition coils with the 4 bolts and tighten to 80 inch lbs. (9.0 Nm).
5. Connect the 4 ignition coil connectors.
6. Position the engine cover to the engine.
7. Install the 2 engine cover fasteners and tighten to 62 inch lbs. (7 Nm).

IGNITION SYSTEM

8. Install the 2 engine cover plastic retainers.

IGNITION TIMING

ADJUSTMENT

The ignition timing is controlled by the Powertrain Control Module (PCM). No adjustment is necessary.

SPARK PLUGS

REMOVAL & INSTALLATION

1. Remove the ignition coils.
Refer to Ignition Coil, removal & installation.
2. Using a 14-mm spark plug wrench, remove the 4 spark plugs.

To install:
3. Using a 14-mm spark plug wrench, install the 4 spark plugs and tighten to 15 ft. lbs. (20 Nm).
4. Install the ignition coils.
Refer to Ignition Coil, removal & installation.

ENGINE ELECTRICAL

STARTER

REMOVAL & INSTALLATION

1.8L

See Figure 82.

1. Disconnect the cable from negative battery terminal. Refer to Battery, precautions.
2. Remove the transmission oil filler tube sub-assembly.

3. Disconnect the terminal 50 connector from the starter assembly.
4. Remove the nut and disconnect the wire harness from terminal 30.
5. Remove the 2 bolts and starter assembly.

To install:
6. To install, reverse the removal procedure and note the following:
- Tighten the starter assembly bolts to 27 ft. lbs. (37 Nm).
- Tighten the wire harness to terminal 30 nut to 87 inch lbs. (9.8 Nm).

2.4L

See Figures 83 through 85.

1. Disconnect the cable from negative battery terminal. Refer to Battery, precautions.
2. Remove the 2 engine cover fasteners and 2 plastic retainers. Remove the engine cover from the engine.
3. Remove the air cleaner cap assembly.
4. Remove the battery. Refer to Battery, removal & installation.
5. Remove the battery tray. Refer to Battery Tray, removal & installation.
6. Disconnect the terminal 50 connector from the starter assembly.

STARTING SYSTEM

7. Remove the nut and disconnect the wire harness from terminal 30.
8. Remove the 2 bolts, wire harness clamp bracket and starter assembly.

To install:
9. To install, reverse the removal procedure and note the following:
- Tighten the starter assembly, clutch accumulator bracket and

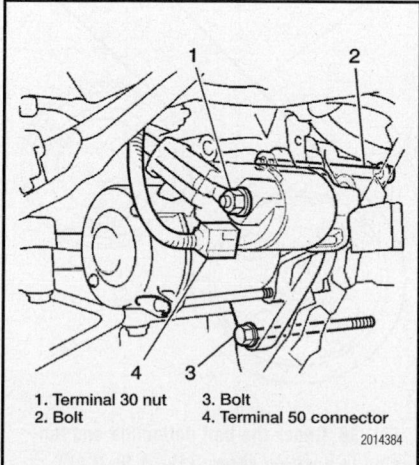

1. Terminal 30 nut
2. Bolt
3. Bolt
4. Terminal 50 connector

2014384

Fig. 82 View of the starter—1.8L

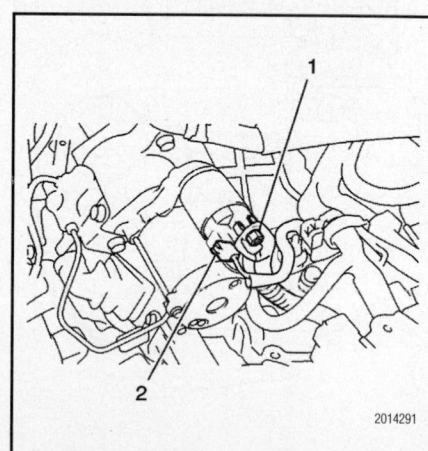
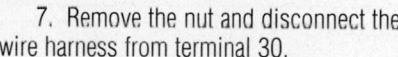

2014291

Fig. 83 View of terminal 30 nut (1) and terminal 50 connector (2)—2.4L

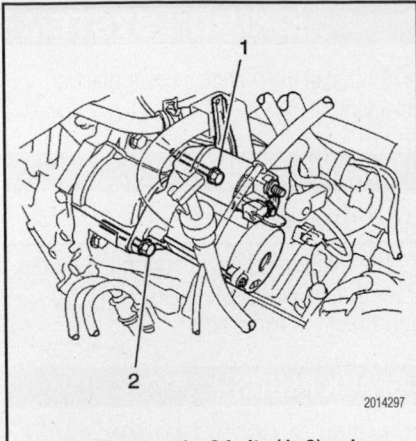

Fig. 84 Remove the 2 bolts (1, 2), wire harness clamp bracket and starter assembly

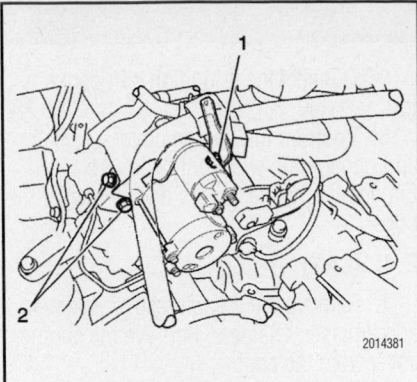

Fig. 85 Install the starter assembly, clutch accumulator bracket and wire harness clamp bracket with the 3 bolts (1, 2)—2.4L

wire harness clamp bracket with the 3 bolts: Tighten Bolt 1 to 27 ft. lbs. (37 Nm), and Bolt 2 to 9 ft. lbs. (12 Nm).

- Tighten the wire harness to terminal 30 nut to 87 inch lbs. (9.8 Nm).
- Tighten the starter assembly and wire harness clamp bracket bolts to 27 ft. lbs. (37 Nm).

10. Position the engine cover to the engine.

11. Install the 2 engine cover fasteners and tighten to 62 inch lbs. (7 Nm).

12. Install the 2 engine cover plastic retainers.

13. Connect the cable to negative battery terminal.

ENGINE MECHANICAL

➡**Disconnecting the negative battery cable may interfere with the functions of the on board computer systems and may require the computer to undergo a relearning process, once the negative battery cable is reconnected.**

ACCESSORY DRIVE BELTS

ACCESSORY BELT ROUTING

1.8L (LAY)

For accessory belt routing, refer to Inspection.

2.4L (LAX)

See Figure 86.

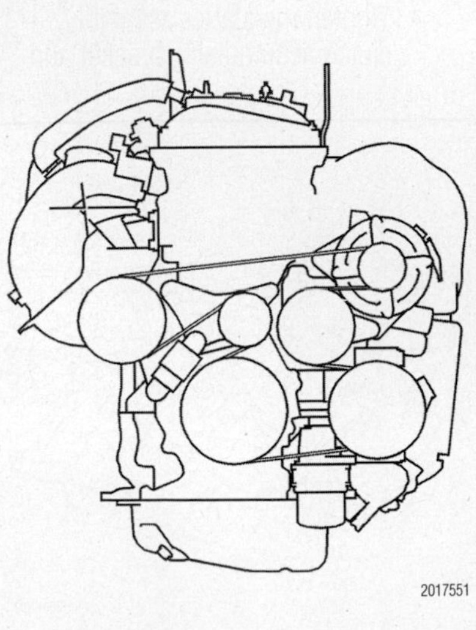

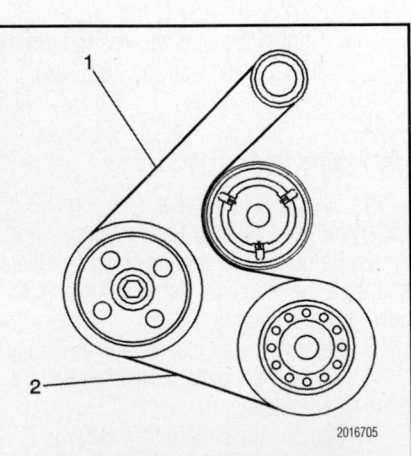

INSPECTION

1.8L (LAY)

See Figures 87 and 88.

1. Inspect the V-ribbed belt for wear, cracks or other signs of damage.

2. If any of the following defects is found, replace the V-ribbed belt:
- The belt is cracked.
- The belt is worn out to the extent that wires are exposed.
- The belt has chunks missing from the ribbed grooves.

➡**Check by hand to confirm that the belt has not slipped out of the grooves on the bottom to the pulley. If it has slipped out, replace the V-ribbed belt. Install a new V-ribbed belt correctly.**

3. Check that the belt fits properly in the ribbed grooves.

4. On vehicles equipped with air conditioning, check the belt deflection and tension in the 2 positions shown.

5. On vehicles without air conditioning, check the belt deflection and tension in the position shown.

6. If the belt deflection is not as specified, adjust it.

7. When inspecting the belt deflection, apply 98 N (10 kgf) tensile force to it.

8. After installing a new belt, run the engine for approximately 5 minutes and then re-adjust the tension to (new belt) specifications.

Fig. 86 Identifying V-ribbed belt layout—2.4L (LAX)

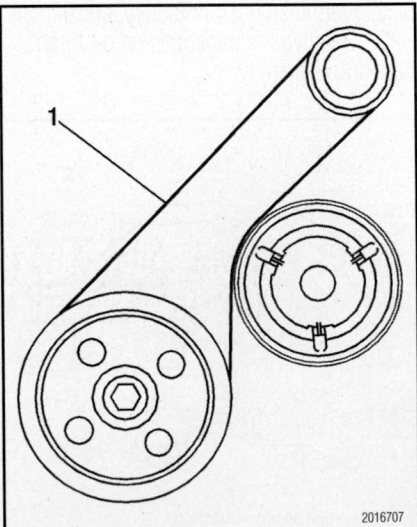

Fig. 87 Check the belt deflection and tension in positions shown (1, 2)—1.8L (LAY) With A/C

Fig. 88 Check the belt deflection and tension in position shown (1)—1.8L (LAY) Without A/C

9. Check the V-ribbed belt deflection and tension at the specified point.

10. V-ribbed belt tension and deflection should be checked after 2 revolutions of the engine.

11. V-ribbed belt tension and deflection should be checked at TDC crank angle and cold condition.

12. When adjusting a belt, adjust its deflection and tension to the intermediate values of the specification.

13. When reinstalling a belt which has been used for over 5 minutes, adjust its deflection and tension to the used belt specification.

14. When using a belt tension gauge, confirm its accuracy by using a master gauge first.

2.4L (LAX)

See Figure 89.

1. Check the V-ribbed belt for wear, cracks, or other signs of damage.

2. If any of the following defects is found, replace the V-ribbed belt:
- The belt is cracked.
- The belt is worn out to the extent that cords are exposed.
- The belt has chunks missing from the ribs.

➡**Check by hand to confirm that the belt has not slipped out of the groove on the bottom to the pulley.**

3. If it has slipped out, replace the V-ribbed belt. Install a new V-ribbed belt correctly.

4. Check that the belt fits properly in the ribbed grooves.

ADJUSTMENT

1.8L (LAY)

Refer to Removal & Installation, 1.8L (LAY).

REMOVAL & INSTALLATION

1.8L (LAY)

See Figure 90.

➡**Attempting to disengage both front and rear clips at the same time may cause the engine cover to break.**

1. Hold the rear of the engine cover and raise it to disengage the 2 clips on the rear of the cover.

2. Continue to raise the cover to disengage the 2 clips on the front of the cover and remove the cover.

3. Remove the right engine under cover.

4. Remove the V-ribbed belt:
    a. Loosen bolts 2 and 4.
    b. Loosen bolt 3, then remove the V-ribbed belt.

To install:

5. Install the V-ribbed belt.

6. Adjust the V-ribbed belt:
    a. Turn bolt 3 to adjust the tension of the belt.
    b. Install bolt 2 and tighten to 14 ft. lbs. (19 Nm).
    c. Install bolt 4 and tighten to 32 ft. lbs. (43 Nm).

7. Inspect the V-ribbed belt.

8. Install the right engine under cover.

9. Position the engine cover and engage the two front fasteners. Engage the two fasteners on the rear of the cover.

2.4L (LAX)

See Figures 86 and 91.

1. Remove right engine under cover.

2. Remove V-ribbed belt.

3. Using the serpentine belt tension unloader (J-39914), slowly turn the V-ribbed belt tensioner clockwise.

➡**Make sure that the unloader and other tools are set to the tensioner securely. When compressing the V-ribbed belt tensioner, slowly turn the tensioner. Be careful not to pinch your fingers between the parts.**

4. Remove the V-ribbed belt from each pulley and slowly return the tensioner.

To install:

➡**Note V-ribbed belt layout.**

5. Install V-ribbed belt.

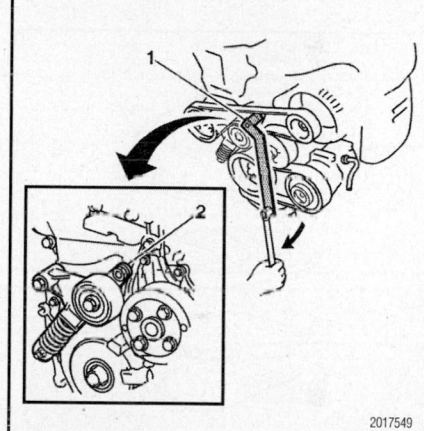

Fig. 91 Using the unloader (1), slowly turn the V-ribbed belt tensioner (2) clockwise—2.4L (LAX)

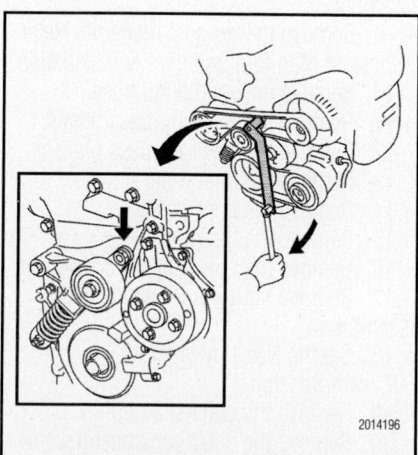

Fig. 89 Check that the belt fits properly in the ribbed grooves—2.4L (LAX)

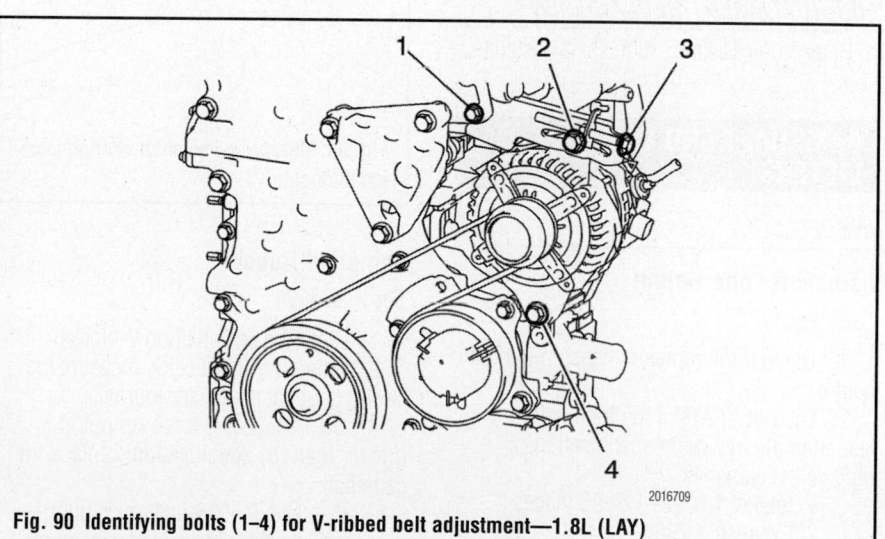

Fig. 90 Identifying bolts (1–4) for V-ribbed belt adjustment—1.8L (LAY)

6. Using the unloader, slowly turn the V-ribbed belt tensioner EM clockwise and install the V-ribbed belt.

7. Install the right engine under cover.

AIR CLEANER

REMOVAL & INSTALLATION

See Figure 92.

1. Disconnect the mass air flow (MAF) sensor.

2. Release the two retaining clips.

3. Lift the air cleaner cover up and away from the lower assembly.

4. Remove the air cleaner element.

To install:

5. Install the air cleaner element.

6. Lower the air cleaner cover onto the lower assembly.

7. Secure the air cleaner cover with the two retaining clips.

8. Connect the MAF sensor.

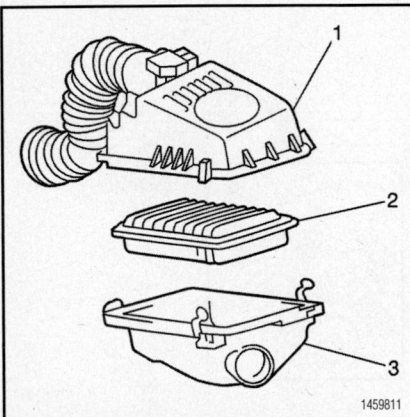

Fig. 92 Lift the air cleaner cover (1) up and away from the lower assembly (3). Remove the air cleaner element (2)

FILTER/ELEMENT REPLACEMENT

Refer to Air Cleaner, removal & installation.

CAMSHAFT AND VALVE LIFTERS

INSPECTION

Camshaft Lobe Height

See Figure 93.

1. Using a micrometer, measure the lobe height.

2. On 1.8L (LAY), if the lobe height is less than the minimum specification, replace the camshaft.
- Intake: 1.6798–1.6896 inches
- Exhaust: 1.7396–1.7494 inches

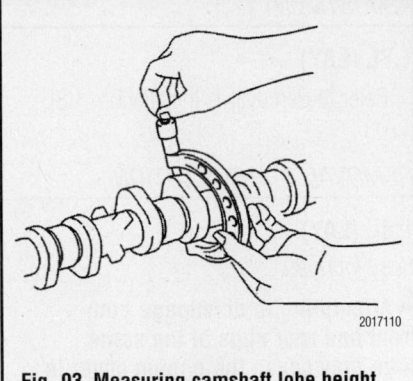

Fig. 93 Measuring camshaft lobe height

3. On 2.4L (LAX), if the lobe height is less than the minimum specification, replace the camshaft.
- Intake: 1.8581–1.8664 inches
- Exhaust: 1.8092–1.8174 inches

Camshaft Bearing Journal Diameter

See Figure 94.

1. Using a micrometer, measure each journal diameter.

2. If the journal diameter is not within specification, check the journal bearing oil clearance. Refer to Camshaft Specifications in Specifications and Maintenance Charts section.

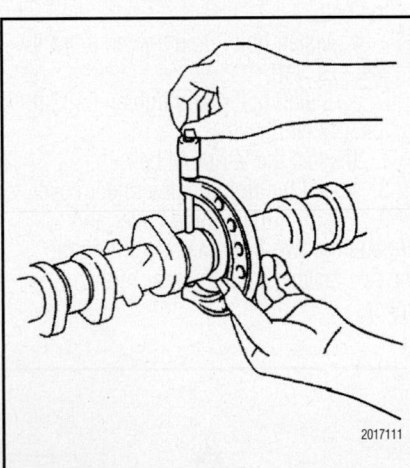

Fig. 94 Measuring camshaft bearing journal diameter

Camshaft Runout

See Figure 95.

1. Place the camshaft on v-blocks.

2. Using a dial indicator, measure the circle runout at the center journal.

3. On 1.8L (LAY), if the runout is greater than the specification, replace the camshaft.
- Intake: 0.0016 inch maximum.
- Exhaust: 0.0016 inch maximum.

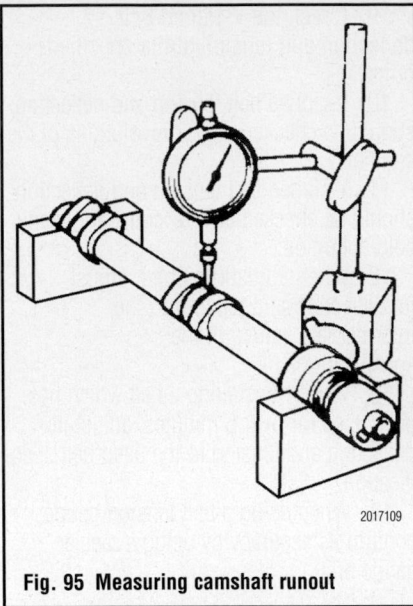

Fig. 95 Measuring camshaft runout

4. On 2.4L (LAX), if the runout is greater than the specification, replace the camshaft.
- Intake: 0.0012 inch maximum.
- Exhaust: 0.0012 inch maximum.

REMOVAL & INSTALLATION

1.8L (LAY)

See Figures 96 through 116.

1. Remove the engine assembly with transaxle. Refer to Engine Assembly, removal & installation.

2. Install the engine stand.

3. Remove the intake manifold. Refer to Intake Manifold, removal & installation.

4. Remove the fuel tube assembly.

5. Remove the fuel delivery pipe assembly.

6. Remove the fuel injector assembly.

7. Remove the ignition coil assembly.

8. Remove the oil level dipstick sub-assembly.

9. Remove the exhaust manifold. Refer to Exhaust Manifold, removal & installation.

10. Remove the ventilation hose.

11. Remove the water by-pass hoses.

12. Remove the water by-pass pipe.

13. Remove the inlet water hose.

14. Remove the inlet water.

15. Remove the thermostat.

16. Remove the radio setting condenser.

17. Remove the cylinder head cover assembly.

18. Set the No. 1 cylinder to TDC/compression.

19. Remove the crankshaft pulley.

20. Remove the chain tensioner assembly.

21. Remove the timing chain cover assembly.

22. Remove the timing chain cover oil seal.

23. Remove the chain tensioner slipper.

24. Remove the timing gear chain vibration damper.

25. Remove the chain assembly.

26. Remove the oil pump chain vibration damper.

27. Inspect the camshaft timing gear assembly.

28. Check the lock of the camshaft timing gear.

➡ **Be sure to cover the oil hole completely, because air leaks due to insufficient sealing will prevent the lock pin from being released.**

29. After cleaning and degreasing the VVT oil hole on the intake side of the camshaft bearing cap, completely seal the oil hole with adhesive tape as shown to prevent air from leaking.

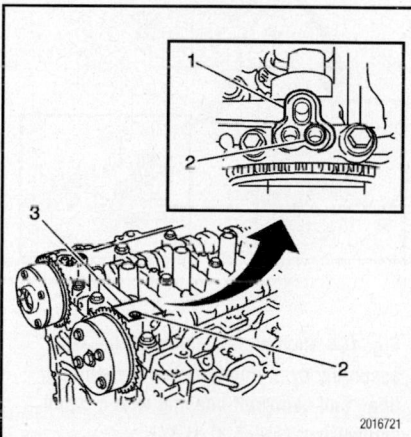

Fig. 96 After cleaning and degreasing the VVT oil hole (1) on the intake side of the camshaft bearing cap, completely seal the oil hole with adhesive tape (3) as shown. Prick a hole (2) in the tape covering the oil hole—1.8L (LAY)

Fig. 97 Apply approximately 150 kPa (22 psi) of air pressure to the hole to release the lock pin—1.8L (LAY)

30. Prick a hole in the tape covering the oil hole as shown.

➡ **If air leaks out, reattach the adhesive tape.**

31. Cover the oil hole with a shop rag or piece of cloth when applying air pressure to prevent oil from spraying.

32. Apply approximately 150 kPa (22 psi) of air pressure to the hole to release the lock pin.

➡ **Depending on the air pressure applied, the camshaft timing gear assembly may turn in the advanced direction without assistance by hand.**

33. Forcibly turn the camshaft timing gear assembly in the advanced dirrection (counterclockwise).

34. Turn the camshaft timing gear assembly within its movable range (26.5-28.5 degrees) 2 or 3 times without turning it to the most retarded position. Make sure that the camshaft timing gear assembly turns smoothly.

35. Remove the adhesive tape from the camshaft bearing cap.

36. Inspect the camshaft timing exhaust gear assembly.

37. Check the lock of the camshaft timing exhaust gear.

➡ **Be sure to cover the oil hole completely, because air leaks due to insufficient sealing will prevent the lock pin from being released.**

38. After cleaning and degreasing the VVT oil hole on the exhaust side of the

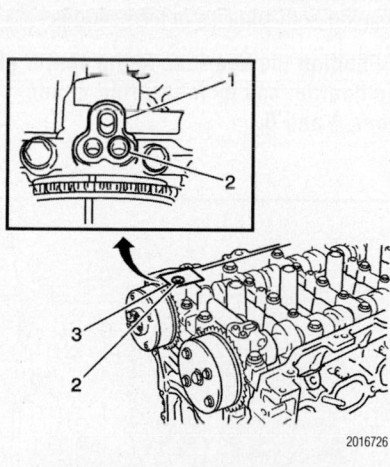

Fig. 98 After cleaning and degreasing the VVT oil hole (1) on the exhaust side of the camshaft bearing cap, completely seal the oil hole with adhesive tape (3). Prick a hole (2) in the tape covering the oil hole—1.8L (LAY)

Fig. 99 Apply approximately 200 kPa (28 psi) of air pressure to the hole to release the lock pin—1.8L (LAY)

camshaft bearing cap, completely seal the oil hole with adhesive tape as shown to prevent air from leaking.

39. Prick a hole in the tape covering the oil hole as shown.

➡ **If air leaks out, reattach the adhesive tape. Cover the oil hole with a shop rag or piece of cloth when applying air pressure to prevent oil from spraying.**

40. Apply approximately 200 kPa (28 psi) of air pressure to the hole to release the lock pin.

➡ **Be sure to keep the camshaft timing exhaust gear in the retard direction using a screwdriver. If the gear is released, it will return to the most advanced position automatically due to force from the spring.**

41. Using a screwdriver with its tip wrapped with tape, forcibly turn the camshaft timing exhaust gear in the retard direction (clockwise).

42. Using the taped screwdriver, turn the camshaft timing exhaust gear within its movable range (19 to 21 degrees) 2 or 3 times without turning it to the most advanced position. Make sure that the camshaft timing exhaust gear turns smoothly.

43. Remove the adhesive tape from the camshaft bearing cap.

44. Remove the flange bolt while holding the hexagonal portion of the camshaft, and then remove the camshaft timing gear assembly.

➡ **Before removing the camshaft timing gear, make sure that the lock pin has been released. Be sure not to remove the other 4 bolts. Keep the camshaft timing gear assembly horizontal while removing it from the camshaft.**

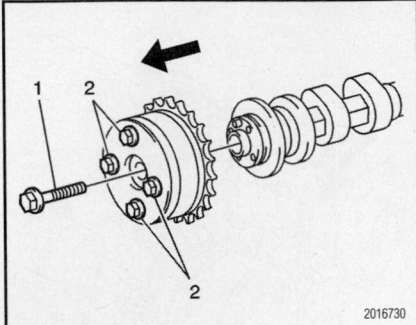

Fig. 100 Remove the flange bolt (1) while holding the hexagonal portion of the camshaft, and then remove the camshaft timing gear assembly. Be sure not to remove the other 4 bolts (2)—1.8L (LAY)

45. Remove the flange bolt while holding the hexagonal portion of the camshaft, and then remove the camshaft timing exhaust gear assembly.

➡**Be sure not to remove the other 4 bolts. Keep the camshaft timing exhaust gear assembly horizontal while removing it from the camshaft.**

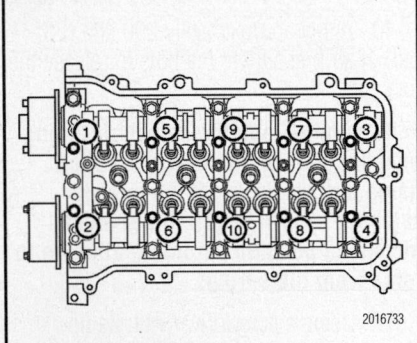

Fig. 101 Uniformly loosen and remove the 10 bearing cap bolts in the sequence shown—1.8L (LAY)

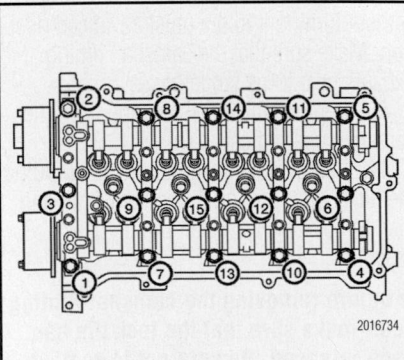

Fig. 102 Uniformly loosen and remove the 15 bearing cap bolts in the sequence shown—1.8L (LAY)

46. Remove camshaft bearing cap. Uniformly loosen and remove the 10 bearing cap bolts in the sequence shown.

➡**Uniformly loosen the bolts while keeping the camshaft level.**

47. Uniformly loosen and remove the 15 bearing cap bolts in the sequence shown.

➡**Arrange the removed parts in the correct order.**

48. Remove the 5 bearing caps.
49. Remove the intake camshaft.
50. Remove the exhaust camshaft.
51. Remove the valve rocker arm subassembly.
52. Remove the valve lash adjuster assembly.
53. Remove the 2 camshaft bearings from the cylinder head.
54. Remove the 2 bolts.
55. Remove the camshaft housing assembly by prying between the cylinder head and camshaft housing with a screwdriver.

➡**Tape the screwdriver tip before use.**

56. Inspect the valve rocker arm assembly.
57. Inspect the valve lash adjuster assembly.
58. Clean the camshaft housing and cylinder head.

To install:

59. Install the valve lash adjuster assembly.
60. Install the valve rocker arm assembly.
61. Install the 2 camshaft bearings after cleaning both surfaces of the bearings.

➡**Position the bearings to the center of the bearing cap by measuring dimensions A and B.**

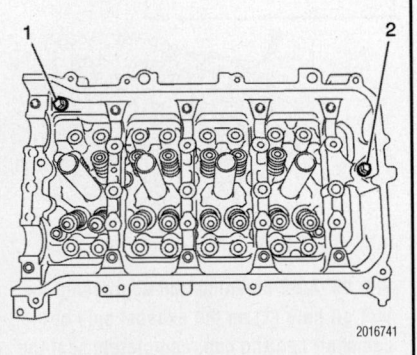

Fig. 103 Remove the 2 bolts (1, 2)—1.8L (LAY)

62. Using vernier calipers, measure the distance between the bearing cap edge and the camshaft bearing edge. Ensure the dimension (A-B) is 0.0276 inch (0.7 mm) or less.
63. Clean both surfaces of the bearings.
64. Install the 2 camshaft bearings.

➡**Position the bearings to the center of the bearing cap by measuring dimension A.**

65. Using vernier calipers, measure the distance between the bearing cap edge and the camshaft bearing edge. Ensure the dimension (A) is 0.0413-0.0689 inch (1.05-1.75 mm).
66. Clean the camshaft journals.
67. Apply a light coat of engine oil to the

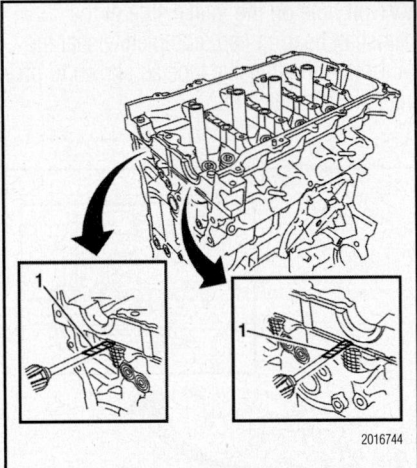

Fig. 104 Remove the camshaft housing assembly by prying between the cylinder head and camshaft housing with a taped screwdriver (1)—1.8L (LAY)

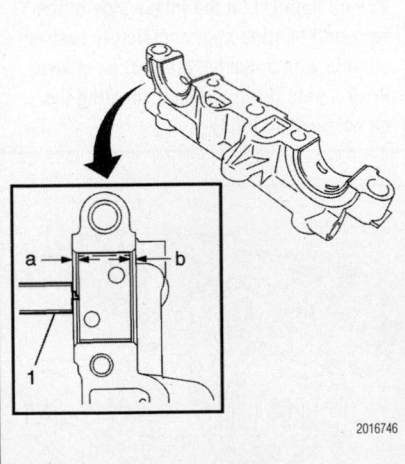

Fig. 105 Using vernier calipers (1), measure the distance between the bearing cap edge and the camshaft bearing edge to obtain the dimension of (A-B)—1.8L (LAY)

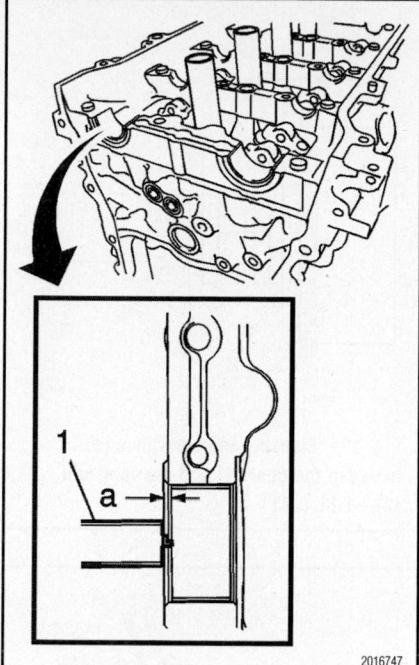

Fig. 106 Using vernier calipers (1), measure the distance (A) between the bearing cap edge and the camshaft bearing edge—1.8L (LAY)

camshaft journals, camshaft housings and bearing caps.

68. Install the exhaust camshaft to the camshaft housing.

69. Clean the camshaft journals.

70. Apply engine oil to the camshaft journals, camshaft housings and bearing caps.

71. Install the intake camshaft to the camshaft housing.

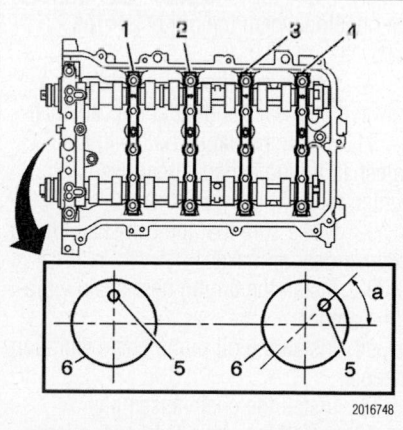

Fig. 107 Using the marks and numbers on the camshaft bearing caps (1–4), place them in the proper position and direction. Make sure that the knock pin (5) of the camshafts (6) are positioned as shown—1.8L (LAY)

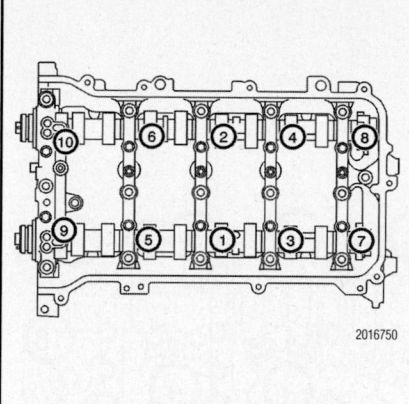

Fig. 108 Install the 10 bolts in the order shown—1.8L (LAY)

➡ **Make sure that the knock pin of the camshafts are positioned as shown.**

72. Using the marks and numbers on the camshaft bearing caps, place them in the proper position and direction.

73. Install the 10 bolts in the order shown and tighten to 12 ft. lbs. (16 Nm).

74. Install the camshaft housing sub-assembly.

75. Make sure that the valve rocker arm is installed as shown.

➡ **Before installing camshaft housing assembly, note the following:**

- Remove any oil from the contact surface.
- Install the camshaft housing assembly within 3 minutes and tighten the bolts within 15 minutes after applying seal packing.
- Do not start the engine for at least 2 hours after installing.

76. Apply a continuous bead of sealant (Three Bond 1217B, or equivalent), diame-

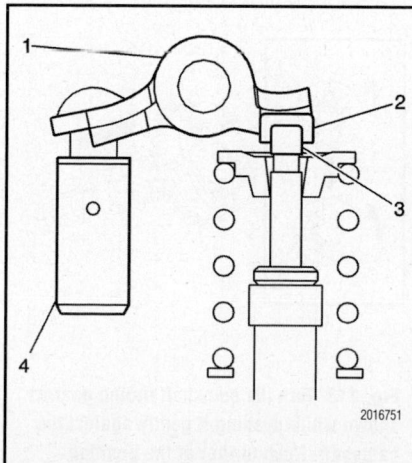

Fig. 109 Make sure that the valve rocker arm (1) is installed as shown—1.8L (LAY)

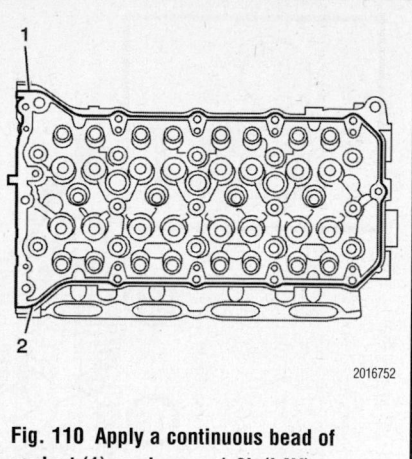

Fig. 110 Apply a continuous bead of sealant (1) as shown—1.8L (LAY)

ter: 0.138–0.158 inch (3.5–4.0 mm), as shown.

77. Set the intake camshaft and the exhaust camshaft:

- After installing the camshaft housing, make sure that the cam lobes are positioned as shown.
- If any of the bolts are loosened during installation, remove the camshaft housing, clean the installation surfaces, and reapply seal packing.
- If the camshaft housing is removed because any of the bolts are loosened during installation, make sure that the previously applied seal packing does not enter any oil passages.
- After installing the camshaft housing, wipe off any seal packing that seeped out from between the housing and the cylinder head.

78. Install the camshaft housing and tighten the 17 bolts in the order shown to 20 ft. lbs. (27 Nm).

79. Install the camshaft timing gear assembly.

80. Check that the knock pin is installed on the camshaft.

➡ **Do not forcefully push in the camshaft timing gear assembly. This may cause the camshaft knock pin tip to damage the installation surface of the camshaft timing gear assembly.**

81. Put the camshaft timing gear and camshaft together with the straight pin and key groove misaligned, as shown.

➡ **Do not turn the camshaft timing gear in the retard direction (clockwise).**

82. Turn the camshaft timing gear as shown while pushing it gently against the camshaft. Push further at the position where the pin fits into the groove.

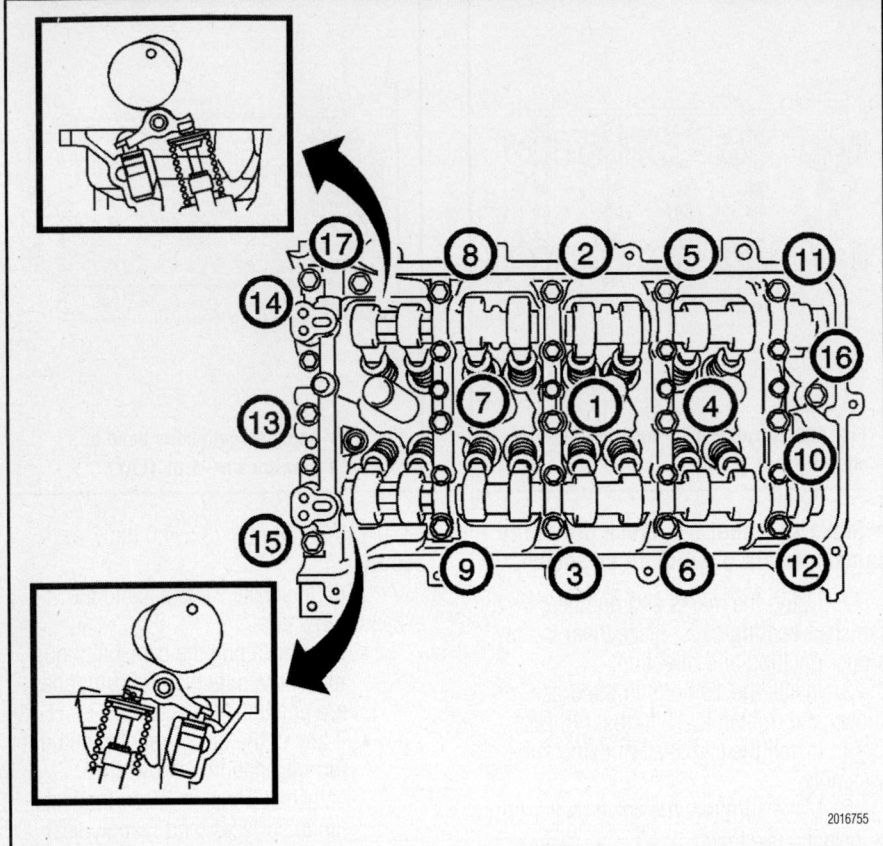

Fig. 111 Install the camshaft housing and tighten the 17 bolts in the order shown—1.8L (LAY)

83. Measure the clearance between the gear and the camshaft. Ensure clearance is 0.004-0.016 inch (0.1-0.4 mm).

84. Install the flange bolt with the camshaft timing gear fixed in place and tighten to 40 ft. lbs. (54 Nm).

85. Check that the camshaft timing gear can move in the retard direction (clockwise) and is locked in the most retarded position.

86. Install the camshaft timing exhaust gear assembly.

87. Check that the knock pin is installed on the camshaft.

88. Put the camshaft timing exhaust gear and camshaft together by aligning the key groove and straight pin.

➡ Be sure not to turn the camshaft timing exhaust gear in the retard direction (clockwise).

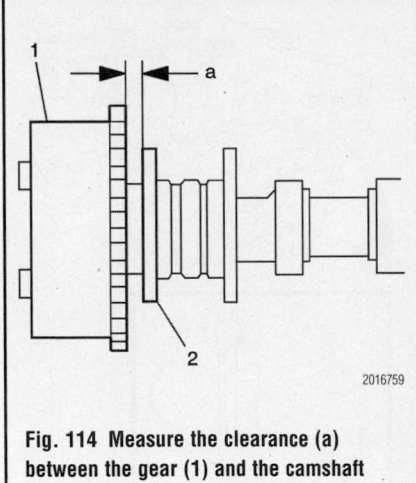

Fig. 114 Measure the clearance (a) between the gear (1) and the camshaft (2)—1.8L (LAY)

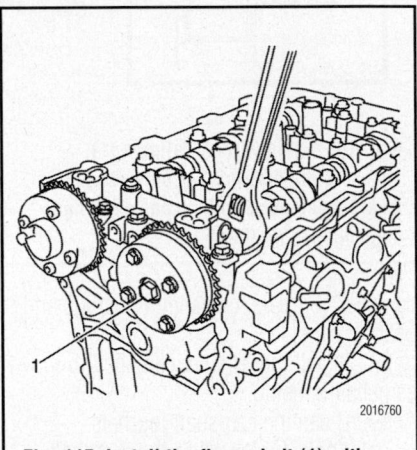

Fig. 115 Install the flange bolt (1) with the camshaft timing gear fixed in place—1.8L (LAY)

89. Lightly press the gear against the camshaft, and turn the gear. Push further at the position where the pin enters the groove.

90. Check that there is no clearance between the gear flange and the camshaft.

91. Install the flange bolt with the camshaft timing exhaust gear fixed and tighten to 40 ft. lbs. (54 Nm).

92. Make sure that the camshaft timing exhaust gear is locked.

93. Install the timing gear chain vibration damper.

94. Install the oil pump chain vibration damper.

95. Install the chain assembly.

96. Install the chain tensioner slipper.

97. Install the timing chain cover oil seal.

98. Install the timing chain cover assembly.

99. Install the crankshaft pulley.

100. Install the chain tensioner assembly.

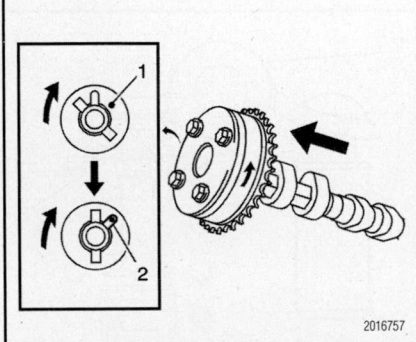

Fig. 112 Check that the knock pin (1) is installed on the camshaft. Put the camshaft timing gear and camshaft together with the straight pin and key groove (2) misaligned as shown—1.8L (LAY)

Fig. 113 Turn the camshaft timing gear as shown while pushing it gently against the camshaft. Push further at the position where the pin (1) fits into the groove (2)—1.8L (LAY)

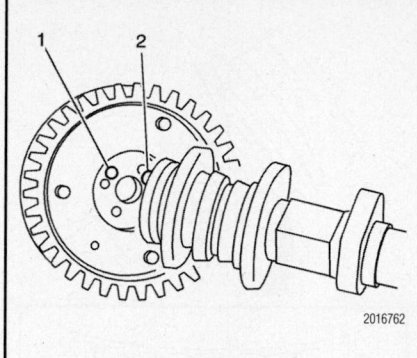

Fig. 116 Put the camshaft timing exhaust gear and camshaft together by aligning the key groove (1) and straight pin (2)— 1.8L (LAY)

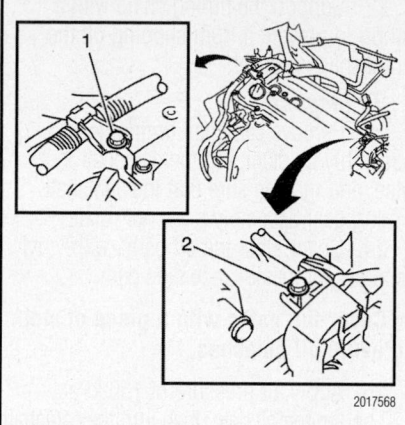

Fig. 117 Remove the 2 bolts (1, 2) and separate the 2 wire harness brackets— 2.4L (LAX)

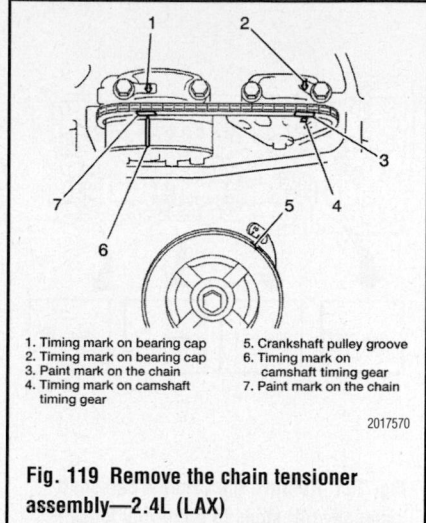

1. Timing mark on bearing cap
2. Timing mark on bearing cap
3. Paint mark on the chain
4. Timing mark on camshaft timing gear
5. Crankshaft pulley groove
6. Timing mark on camshaft timing gear
7. Paint mark on the chain

Fig. 119 Remove the chain tensioner assembly—2.4L (LAX)

101. Install the cylinder head cover assembly.

102. Install the radio setting condenser.

103. Install the thermostat.

104. Install the inlet water.

105. Install the inlet water hose.

106. Install the water by-pass hoses.

107. Install the water by-pass pipe.

108. Install the ventilation hose.

109. Install the exhaust manifold. Refer to Exhaust Manifold, removal & installation.

110. Install the oil level dipstick sub-assembly.

111. Install the ignition coil assembly.

112. Install the fuel injector assembly.

113. Install the delivery pipe spacer.

114. Install the fuel delivery pipe assembly.

115. Install the fuel tube assembly.

116. Install the intake manifold. Refer to Intake Manifold, removal & installation.

117. Remove the engine stand.

118. Install the engine. Refer to Engine Assembly, removal & installation.

2.4L (LAX)

See Figures 117 through 142.

1. Remove the right engine under cover.

2. Remove the 2 engine cover fasteners and 2 plastic retainers. Remove the engine cover from the engine.

3. Remove the ignition coil assembly. Refer to Ignition Coil, removal & installation.

4. Remove the spark plug. Refer to Spark Plugs, removal & installation.

5. Remove the 2 ventilation hoses from the cylinder head cover sub-assembly.

6. Remove the 2 bolts and separate the 2 wire harness brackets.

7. Remove the 8 bolts and 2 nuts, then remove the cylinder head cover sub-assembly and gasket.

8. Set No. 1 cylinder to TDC/compression by turning the crankshaft pulley until the groove and the timing mark "" on the timing chain cover are aligned.

9. Check that each timing mark on the camshaft timing gear and sprocket is aligned with each timing mark located on the bearing caps, as shown.

10. If not, turn the crankshaft pulley by 1 revolution (360°) to align the timing marks as illustrated.

11. Place paint marks on the chain in alignment with the timing marks on the camshaft timing gear and camshaft timing sprocket.

12. Remove the chain tensioner assembly.

13. Loosen the camshaft timing gear or sprocket. While holding the exhaust camshaft with a wrench, loosen the No. 2 camshaft timing set bolt.

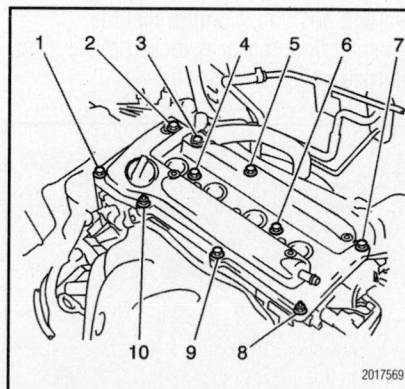

Fig. 118 Remove the 8 bolts (1–7, 9) and 2 nuts (8, 10), then remove the cylinder head cover sub-assembly and gasket— 2.4L (LAX)

14. Remove the exhaust camshaft using several steps to uniformly loosen and remove the 10 bearing cap bolts in the sequence shown.

15. Remove the 5 bearing caps.

16. While holding the exhaust camshaft by hand, remove the camshaft timing sprocket set bolt.

17. Remove the camshaft timing sprocket from the exhaust camshaft with the timing chain wrapped on the sprocket.

18. Remove the camshaft timing sprocket from the timing chain.

19. Remove the intake camshaft using several steps to uniformly loosen and remove the 10 bearing caps bolts in the sequence shown.

20. Remove the 5 bearing caps.

21. Remove the camshaft and camshaft timing gear assembly while holding the timing chain by hand.

➡ **Be careful not to drop anything inside the timing chain cover.**

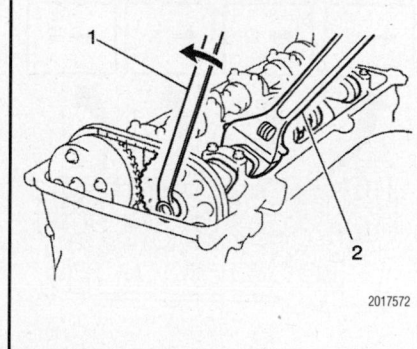

Fig. 120 Loosen the camshaft timing gear or sprocket (1). While holding the exhaust camshaft with a wrench (2), loosen the No. 2 camshaft timing set bolt—2.4L (LAX)

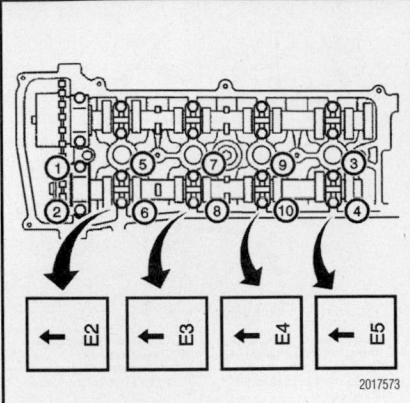

Fig. 121 Remove the exhaust camshaft using several steps to uniformly loosen and remove the 10 bearing cap bolts in the sequence shown—2.4L (LAX)

Fig. 122 While holding the exhaust camshaft by hand, remove the camshaft timing sprocket set bolt (1)—2.4L (LAX)

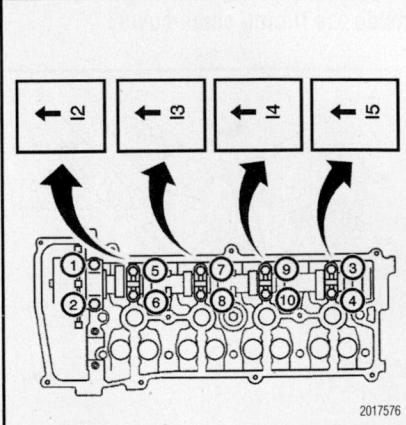

Fig. 123 Remove the intake camshaft using several steps to uniformly loosen and remove the 10 bearing caps bolts in the sequence shown—2.4L (LAX)

22. Support the timing chain with a string to prevent it from slipping off the crankshaft sprocket.

To inspect:

23. Remove camshaft timing gear assembly by clamping the camshaft in a vise, and making sure that the camshaft timing gear assembly does not rotate.

24. Cover all of the oil paths with vinyl tape except the advance side path.

➡**Cover the paths with a piece of cloth to avoid oil splashes.**

25. Apply air pressure of 150 kPa (22 psi) to the oil path, then turn the camshaft timing gear assembly to the advance direction (counterclockwise) by hand.

➡**Be sure not to remove the other 4 bolts. When reusing the camshaft timing gear, release the straight pin lock first, then install the gear.**

➡**Depending on the air pressure, the camshaft timing gear assembly may turn to the advance side without applying force by hand. Also, if the pressure is difficult to apply because of air leakage from the port, the lock pin may be difficult to release.**

26. Remove the flange bolt of the camshaft timing gear.

27. Check that the camshaft timing gear revolves in the advance direction (counterclockwise) by hand.

➡**Do not use air pressure to perform the smooth rotation check.**

28. Check for smooth rotation. Turn the camshaft timing gear within its movable range (21°) 2 or 3 times, but do not turn it to the most retarded position. Make sure that the gear turns smoothly.

29. Check the lock in the most retarded position. Confirm that the camshaft timing gear is locked at the most retarded position.

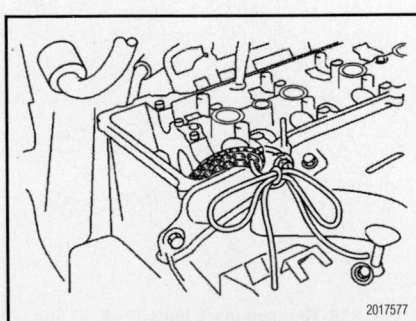

Fig. 124 Support the timing chain with a string to prevent it from slipping off the crankshaft sprocket—2.4L (LAX)

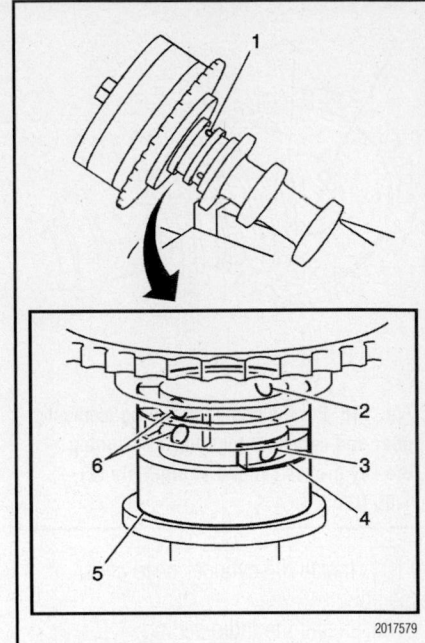

Fig. 125 Cover all of the oil paths (2–6) with vinyl tape except the advance side path (1)—2.4L (LAX)

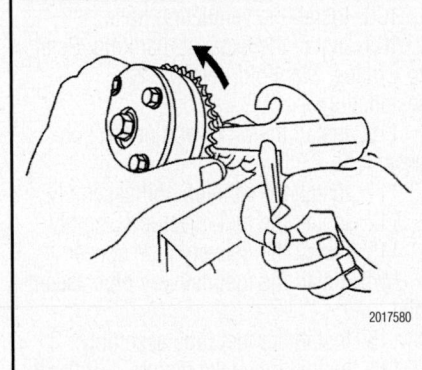

Fig. 126 Apply air pressure of 150 kPa (22 psi) to the oil path, then turn the camshaft timing gear assembly to the advance direction (counterclockwise) by hand— 2.4L (LAX)

Fig. 127 Remove the flange bolt of the camshaft timing gear—2.4L (LAX)

30. Remove the camshaft timing gear assembly.

To install:

31. Install camshaft timing gear assembly by putting the camshaft timing gear and camshaft together with the straight pin and key groove misaligned as shown.

➡**Be sure not to turn the camshaft timing gear to the retard direction (clockwise).**

32. Turn the camshaft timing gear as shown while pushing it gently against the camshaft. Push further at the position where the pin fits into the groove.

33. Check that there is no clearance between the gear flange and camshaft.

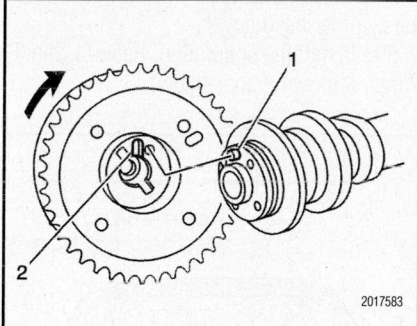

Fig. 128 Install camshaft timing gear assembly by putting the camshaft timing gear and camshaft together with the straight pin (1) and key groove (2) misaligned as shown—2.4L (LAX)

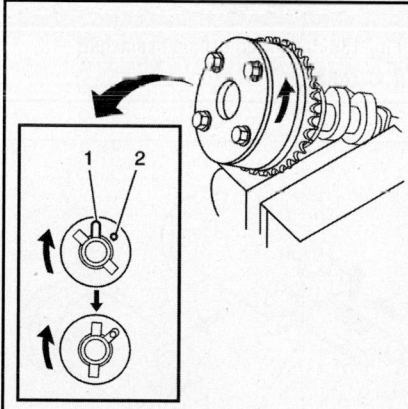

Fig. 129 Be sure not to turn the camshaft timing gear to the retard direction (clockwise). Turn the camshaft timing gear as shown while pushing it gently against the camshaft. Push further at the position where the pin (2) fits into the groove (1)—2.4L (LAX)

34. Check that there is no clearance between the gear flange and camshaft.

35. Install the flange bolt with the camshaft timing gear assembly fixed in place and tighten to 40 ft. lbs. (54 Nm).

36. Check that the camshaft timing gear assembly can move to the retard direction (clockwise) and is locked in the most retarded position.

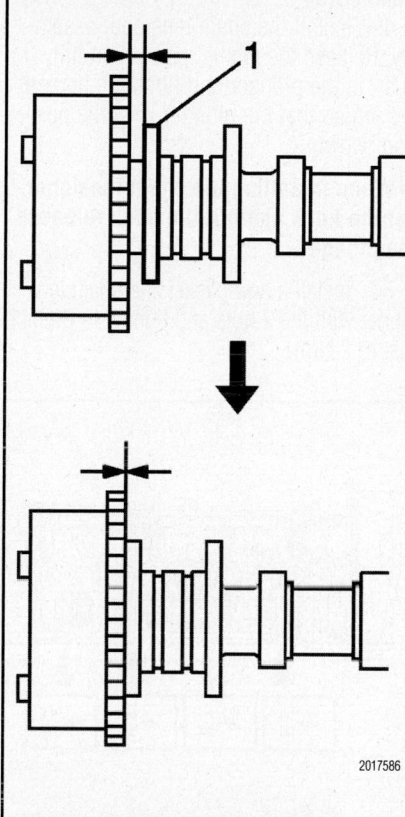

Fig. 130 Check that there is no clearance (1) between the gear flange and camshaft—2.4L (LAX)

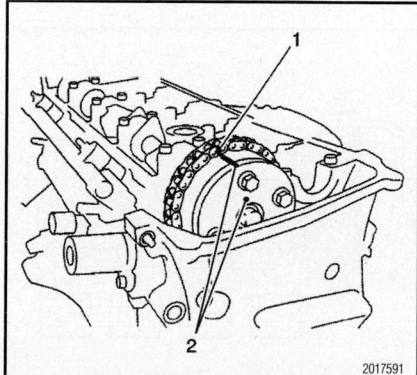

Fig. 131 Install the timing chain onto the camshaft timing gear with the paint mark (1) aligned with the timing mark on the camshaft timing gear as shown—2.4L (LAX)

37. Apply a light coat of engine oil to the journal portion of the intake camshaft.

38. Install the timing chain onto the camshaft timing gear with the paint mark aligned with the timing mark on the camshaft timing gear as shown.

39. Examine the front marks and numbers, and check that the order is as shown. Then install the bearing caps into the cylinder head.

40. Apply a light coat of engine oil on the threads and under the heads of the bearing cap bolts.

41. Using several steps, uniformly install the 10 bearing cap bolts in the sequence shown and tighten:

- The thrust bearing bolts to 22 ft. lbs. (30 Nm).
- The remaining bearing bolts to 80 inch lbs. (9.0 Nm).

42. Install the exhaust camshaft:

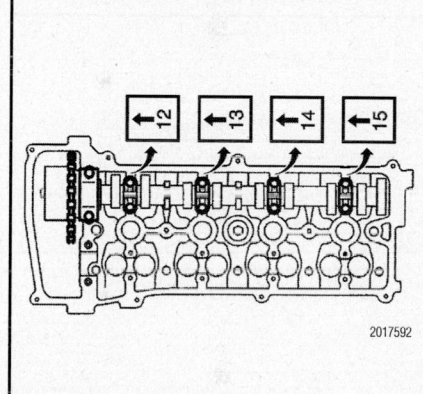

Fig. 132 Examine the front marks and numbers, and check that the order is as shown—2.4L (LAX)

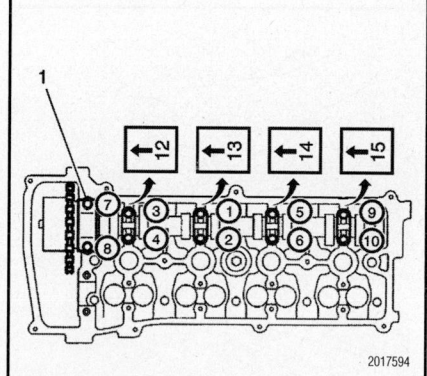

Fig. 133 Using several steps, uniformly install the 10 bearing cap bolts (1) in the sequence shown—2.4L (LAX)

a. Apply a light coat of engine oil to the journal portion of the exhaust camshaft.

b. Put the exhaust camshaft on the cylinder head with the paint mark on the chain aligned with the timing mark on the camshaft timing sprocket.

43. While holding the exhaust camshaft by hand, temporarily tighten the camshaft timing sprocket set bolt.

44. Examine the front marks and numbers, and check that the order is as shown. Then install the bearing caps onto the cylinder head.

45. Apply a light coat of engine oil to the threads and under the heads of the bearing cap bolts.

46. Using several steps, uniformly install the 10 bearing cap bolts in the sequence shown and tighten:
- The thrust bearing bolts to 22 ft. lbs. (30 Nm).
- The remaining bearing bolts to 80 inch lbs. (9.0 Nm).

47. While holding the exhaust camshaft with a wrench, tighten the camshaft timing sprocket set bolt to 40 ft. lbs. (54 Nm).

48. Check that the paint marks on the chain are aligned with the timing marks on the camshaft timing gear and camshaft timing sprocket. Also, check that the crankshaft pulley groove is aligned with the timing mark 0 on the timing mark chain cover.

49. Install the chain tensioner assembly. Release the ratchet pawl, then fully push in the plunger and hook the hook to the pin so that the plunger is in the position shown.

➡ **When installing the chain tensioner, set the hook again if the hook releases the plunger.**

50. Install a new gasket and chain tensioner with the 2 nuts and tighten to 80 inch lbs. (9.0 Nm).

51. Turn the crankshaft counterclockwise, then disconnect the plunger knock pin from the hook.

52. Turn the crankshaft clockwise, then check that the plunger is extended.

53. Set the No. 1 cylinder to TDC/compression.

54. Check the valve clearance. Refer to Valve Lash, Adjustment.

55. Remove any old packing material from the contact surface.

56. Install the cylinder head cover gasket with the 8 bolts and 2 nuts and tighten:
- Bolts 1 to 8 ft. lbs. (11 Nm).
- Bolts 2 to 10 ft. lbs. (14 Nm).
- Nuts to 8 ft. lbs. (11 Nm).

57. Install the 2 engine wire harness brackets with the 2 bolts and tighten to 74 inch lbs. (8.4 Nm).

58. Connect the 2 ventilation hoses to the cylinder head cover.

59. Install the spark plug. Refer to Spark Plugs, removal & installation.

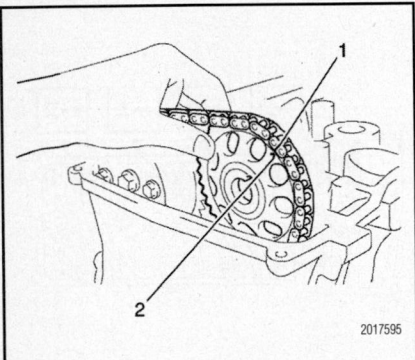

Fig. 134 Put the exhaust camshaft on the cylinder head with the paint mark (1) on the chain aligned with the timing mark (2) on the camshaft timing sprocket—2.4L (LAX)

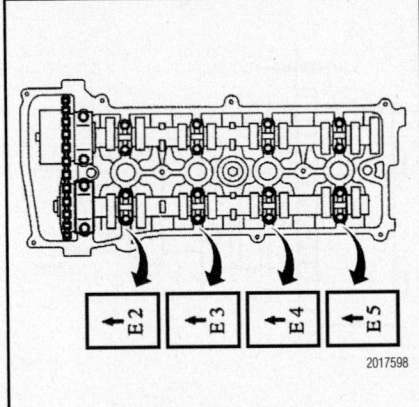

Fig. 136 Examine the front marks and numbers, and check that the order is as shown—2.4L (LAX)

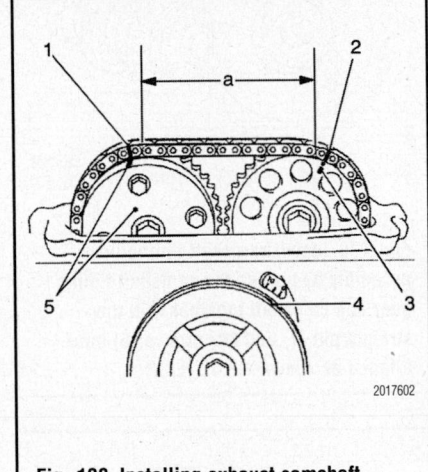

Fig. 138 Installing exhaust camshaft—2.4L (LAX)

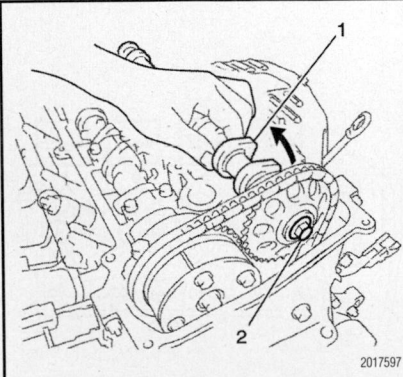

Fig. 135 While holding the exhaust camshaft (1) by hand, temporarily tighten the camshaft timing sprocket set bolt (2)—2.4L (LAX)

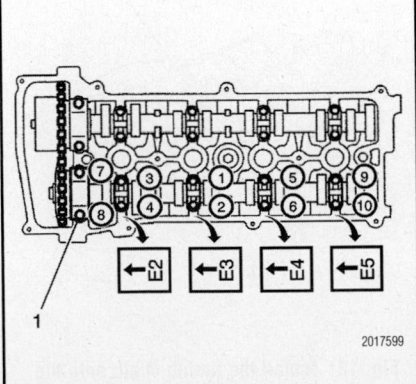

Fig. 137 Using several steps, uniformly install the 10 bearing cap bolts (1) in the sequence shown—2.4L (LAX)

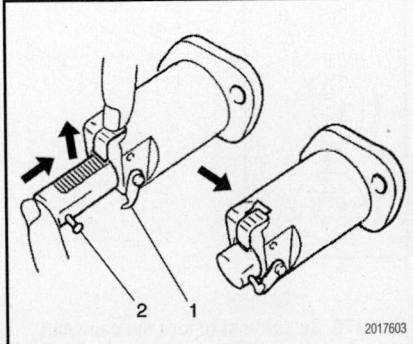

Fig. 139 Install the chain tensioner assembly. Release the ratchet pawl, then fully push in the plunger and hook the hook (1) to the pin (2) so that the plunger is in the position shown—2.4L (LAX)

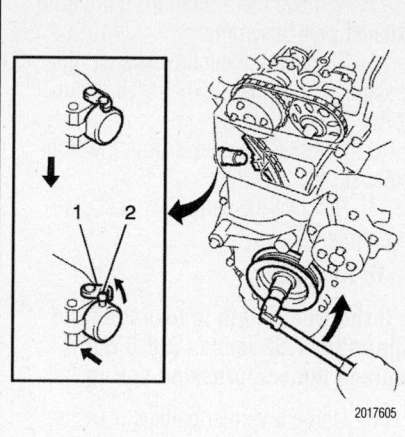

Fig. 140 Turn the crankshaft counterclockwise, then disconnect the plunger knock pin (2) from the hook (1)—2.4L (LAX)

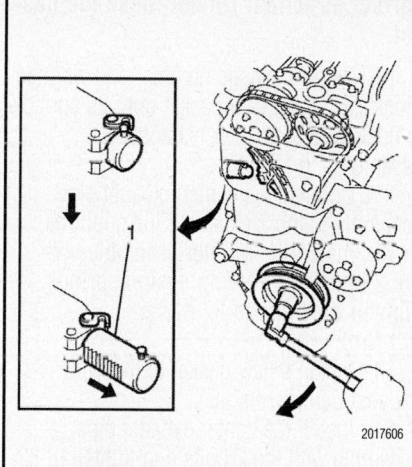

Fig. 141 Turn the crankshaft clockwise, then check that the plunger (1) is extended—2.4L (LAX)

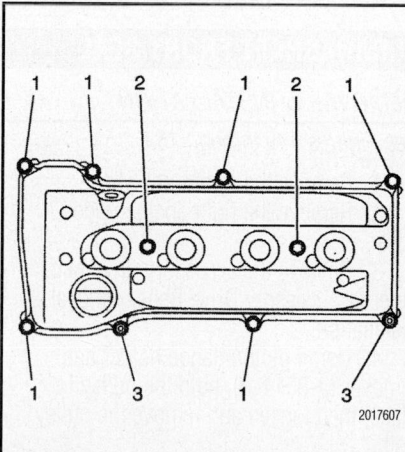

Fig. 142 Install the cylinder head cover gasket with the 8 bolts (1) and 2 nuts (3)—2.4L (LAX)

60. Install the ignition coil assembly. Refer to Ignition Coil, removal & installation.

61. Inspect for oil leak.

62. Inspect the ignition timing.

63. Position the engine cover to the engine.

64. Install the 2 engine cover fasteners and tighten to 62 inch lbs. (7 Nm).

65. Install the 2 engine cover plastic retainers.

66. Install the engine under right cover.

CATALYTIC CONVERTER

REMOVAL & INSTALLATION

1.8L

See Figures 143 and 144.

1. Remove heated oxygen sensor 2. Refer to Heated Oxygen (HO2S) Sensor, removal & installation.

2. Remove the 2 bolts and 2 compression springs from the front pipe assembly.

3. Remove the 2 bolts and 2 compression springs from the rear muffler assembly.

4. Remove the pipe assembly from the 2 exhaust pipe supports.

To install:

➡**If the free length is less than the minimum 1.63 inches (41.5 mm), replace the compression spring.**

5. Using a vernier caliper, measure the free length of the compression springs.

6. Fully insert a new gasket to the exhaust manifold.

➡**Be sure to install the gasket in the correct direction. Do not reuse the gasket.**

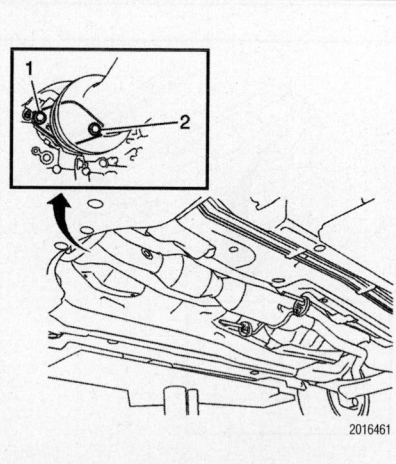

Fig. 143 Remove the 2 bolts (1, 2) and 2 compression springs from the front pipe assembly—1.8L

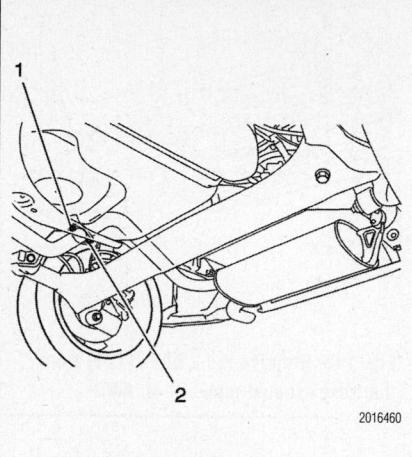

Fig. 144 Remove the 2 bolts (1) and 2 compression springs (2) from the rear muffler assembly—1.8L

7. Using a plastic hammer and wooden block, tap in the new gasket until its surface is flush with the exhaust manifold.

8. Connect the front exhaust pipe assembly to the 2 exhaust pipe supports.

➡**If the free length is less than the minimum 1.52 inches (38.5 mm), replace the compression spring.**

9. Install the front exhaust pipe assembly with the 2 bolts and 2 compression springs. Tighten the bolts to 32 ft. lbs. (43 Nm).

10. Install heated oxygen sensor. Refer to Heated Oxygen (HO2S) Sensor, removal & installation.

11. Using a vernier caliper, measure the free length of the compression springs.

12. Fully insert a new gasket to the front exhaust pipe assembly.

➡**Be sure to install the gasket in the correct direction.**

13. Using a plastic hammer and wooden block, tap in the new gasket until its surface is flush with the front exhaust pipe assembly.

14. Install the tail exhaust pipe assembly with the 2 bolts and 2 compression springs. Tighten the bolts to 32 ft. lbs. (43 Nm).

15. Inspect for exhaust gas leak.

2.4L AWD

See Figures 145 and 146.

1. Remove the heated oxygen sensor 2. Refer to Heated Oxygen (HO2S) Sensor, removal & installation.

2. Remove the 2 bolts from the front exhaust pipe.

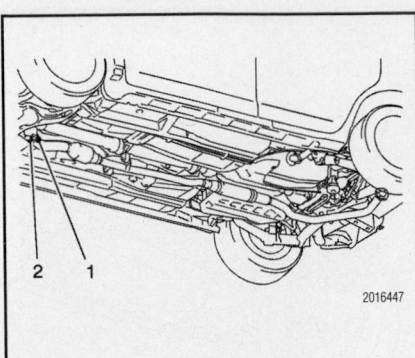

Fig. 145 Remove the 2 bolts (1, 2) from the front exhaust pipe—2.4L AWD

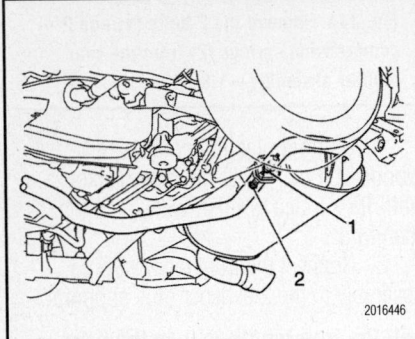

Fig. 146 Remove the two bolts (1) and springs (2) from the muffler assembly—2.4L AWD

3. Remove the two bolts and springs from the muffler assembly.

4. Remove the center exhaust pipe assembly from the 3 exhaust pipe supports.

5. Remove the gasket from the front exhaust pipe assembly.

To install:

6. Install a new gasket to the front exhaust pipe assembly.

7. Connect the center exhaust pipe assembly to the 3 exhaust pipe supports.

8. Install the center exhaust pipe assembly with the 2 bolts.

9. Tighten the center exhaust pipe bolts to 32 ft. lbs. (43 Nm).

➡ **If the free length is less than the minimum 1.52 inches (38.5 mm), replace the compression spring.**

10. Using a vernier caliper, measure the free length of the compression springs.

11. Fully insert a new gasket to the center exhaust pipe assembly.

➡ **Be sure to install the gasket in the correct direction. Do not reuse the gasket.**

12. Using a plastic hammer and wooden block, tap in the new gasket until its surface is flush with the center exhaust pipe assembly.

13. Install the muffler assembly with the 2 bolts and 2 compression springs.

14. Tighten the tail exhaust pipe bolts to 32 ft. lbs. (43 Nm).

15. Install the heated oxygen sensor 2. Refer to Heated Oxygen (HO2S) Sensor, removal & installation.

16. Inspect for exhaust gas leaks.

2.4L FWD

See Figures 147 and 148.

1. Remove the 2 bolts and 2 compression springs from the muffler assembly.

2. Remove the gasket from the center exhaust pipe assembly.

3. Remove heated oxygen sensor 2. Refer to Heated Oxygen (HO2S) Sensor, removal & installation.

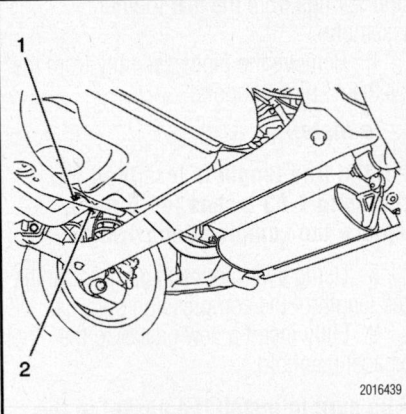

Fig. 147 Remove the 2 bolts (1) and 2 compression springs (2) from the muffler assembly—2.4L FWD

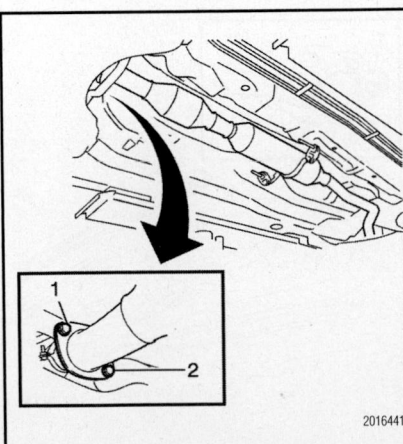

Fig. 148 Remove the 2 bolts (1) from the front exhaust pipe assembly—2.4L FWD

4. Remove the 2 bolts from the front exhaust pipe assembly.

5. Remove the center exhaust pipe assembly from the 2 exhaust pipe supports.

6. Remove the gasket from the front exhaust pipe assembly.

7. Remove the center exhaust pipe assembly.

To install:

➡ **If the free length is less than the minimum 1.52 inches (38.5 mm), replace the compression spring.**

8. Using a vernier caliper, measure the free length of the compression springs.

9. Fully insert a new gasket to the center exhaust pipe assembly.

➡ **Be sure to install the gasket in the correct direction. Do not reuse the gasket.**

10. Using a plastic hammer and wooden block, tap in the new gasket until its surface is flush with the center exhaust pipe assembly.

11. Connect the center exhaust pipe assembly to the 2 exhaust pipe supports.

12. Install the muffler assembly with the 2 bolts and 2 compression springs. Tighten the bolts to 32 ft. lbs. (43 Nm).

13. Install a new gasket to the front exhaust pipe assembly.

14. Install the center exhaust pipe assembly with the 2 bolts and tighten to 32 ft. lbs. (43 Nm).

15. Install the heated oxygen sensor 2. Refer to Heated Oxygen (HO2S) Sensor, removal & installation.

16. Inspect for exhaust gas leaks.

CRANKSHAFT FRONT SEAL

REMOVAL & INSTALLATION

See Figures 149 through 153.

1. Remove the right front wheel.

2. Remove the right engine under cover.

3. Remove the accessory drive belt. Refer to Accessory Drive Belts, removal & installation.

4. Using pinion flange holder and remover (J-8614-A), hold the pulley in place, then loosen and remove the pulley bolt.

5. Place the crankshaft end protector (J-21052-4) on the end of the crankshaft.

6. Using the holder and remover, remove the crankshaft pulley.

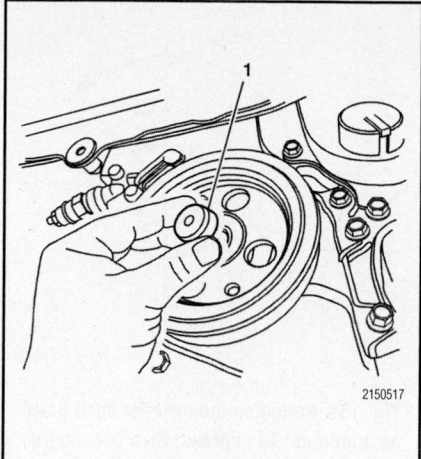

Fig. 149 Place the crankshaft end protector (1) on the end of the crankshaft—

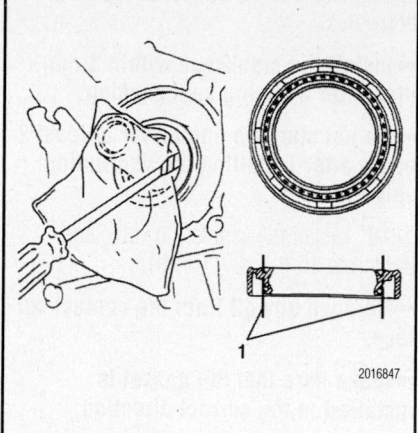

Fig. 151 Using a knife, cut off the lip (1) of the oil seal

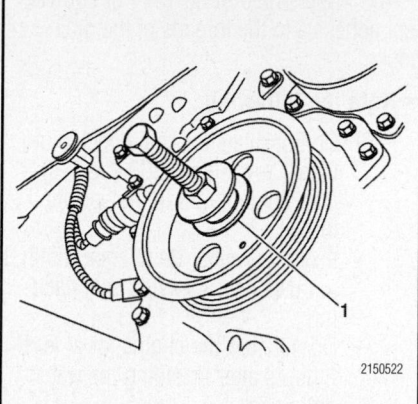

Fig. 153 Using crankshaft balancer and sprocket installer (1), push the pulley onto the crankshaft

7. Remove the timing chain cover oil seal.

➡**After removing, check the crankshaft for nicks or burrs. Smooth the surface with 400-grit sandpaper.**

8. Using a knife, cut off the lip of the oil seal.

9. Using a screwdriver with its tip wrapped with tape, pry out the oil seal.

To install:

10. Install the timing chain cover oil seal.

11. Apply MP grease to the lip of a new oil seal.

➡**Wipe off extra grease from the crankshaft.**

12. Using crankshaft balancer installer (J-41998-A) and a hammer, tap in the oil seal until its surface is flush with the rear oil seal retainer edge.

13. Align the pulley set key with the key groove of the pulley.

14. Using crankshaft balancer and sprocket installer (J-41665-A), push the pulley onto the crankshaft.

15. Using the J-8614-A holder and remover, hold the pulley in place and tighten the bolt to 140 ft. lbs. (190 Nm).

16. Install the accessory drive belt. Refer to Accessory Drive Belts, removal & installation.

17. Add the engine oil.

18. Inspect for engine oil leaks.

19. Position the engine cover and engage the two front fasteners. Engage the two fasteners on the rear of the cover.

20. Install the right engine under cover.

21. Install the right front wheel.

CYLINDER HEAD

REMOVAL & INSTALLATION

1.8L (LAY)

See Figures 154 through 159.

➡**Head warpage or cracking could result from removing the bolts in the wrong order.**

1. Using several steps, uniformly loosen and remove the 10 cylinder head bolts and 10 plate washers with a 10 mm bi-hexagon wrench in the sequence shown.

2. Using a screwdriver with its tip wrapped with tape, pry between the cylinder head and cylinder block, and remove the cylinder head.

3. Remove the cylinder head gasket.

To install:

4. Install cylinder block water drain cock sub-assembly.

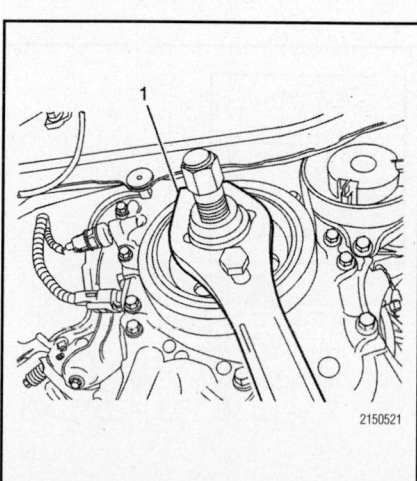

Fig. 150 Using the holder and remover (1), remove the crankshaft pulley

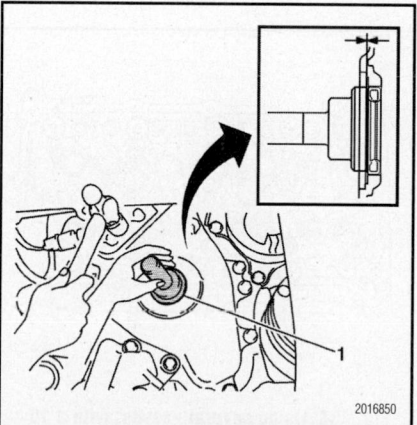

Fig. 152 Using crankshaft balancer installer (1) and a hammer, tap in the oil seal until its surface flush with the rear oil seal retainer edge

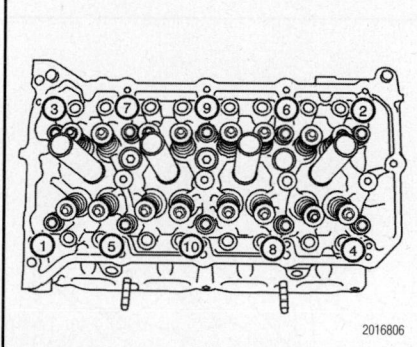

Fig. 154 Using several steps, uniformly loosen and remove the 10 cylinder head bolts and 10 plate washers with a 10 mm bi-hexagon wrench in the sequence shown—1.8L (LAY)

5. Apply Three Bond 1344 or equivalent adhesive to the threads of the drain cock.

→**Note the following:**

- Do not rotate the drain cock more than 1 revolution (360 degrees) after tightening it to the specified torque.
- Install the water drain cock within 3 minutes after applying seal packing.
- Do not start the engine for at least 2 hours after installing the water drain cock.

6. Install the water drain cock and tighten to 15 ft. lbs. (20 Nm).

7. Install the water drain cock plug to the engine block and tighten to 115 inch lbs. (13 Nm).

8. Install the ventilation valve sub-assembly.

9. Apply Three Bond 1324 or equiva-

lent adhesive to the threads of the ventilation valve.

→**Install the crankcase within 3 minutes after applying seal packing.**

→**Do not start the engine for at least 2 hours after installing the ventilation valve.**

10. Install the ventilation valve and tighten to 15 ft. lbs. (20 Nm).

→**Remove any oil from the contact surface.**

→**Make sure that the gasket is installed in the correct direction.**

11. Install cylinder head gasket:
- Place a new gasket on the cylinder block surface with the Lot No. stamp facing upward.

→**The cylinder head bolts are tightened in 2 progressive steps.**

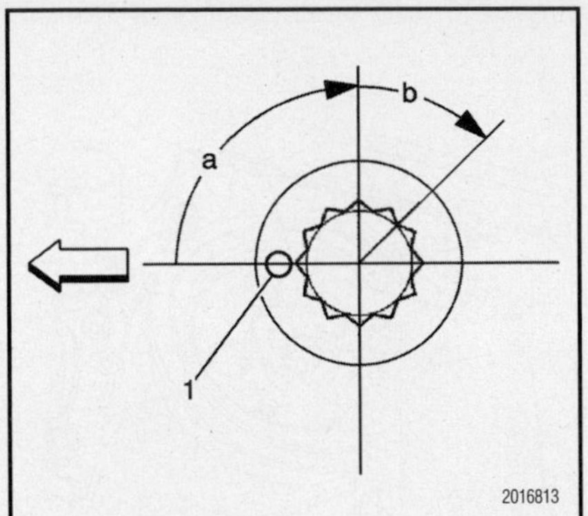

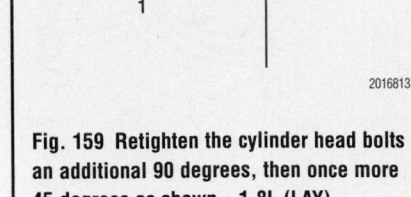

Fig. 159 Retighten the cylinder head bolts an additional 90 degrees, then once more 45 degrees as shown—1.8L (LAY)

12. Install the cylinder head assembly:
- Apply a light coat of engine oil to the bolt threads and the area beneath the bolt heads that come in contact with the washers.
- Install the bolts and plate washers to the cylinder head.

13. Using several passes, with a 10 mm bi-hexagon wrench, uniformly install and tighten the 10 cylinder head set bolts and plate washers in the order shown and tighten to 36 ft. lbs. (49 Nm).

14. Mark the front side of the cylinder head bolts with paint.

15. Retighten the cylinder head bolts an additional 90 degrees, then once more 45 degrees as shown.

16. Check that the paint mark is now at a 135 degrees angle to the front.

2.4L (LAX)

See Figures 160 through 163.

1. Remove cylinder head sub-assembly.
2. Remove cylinder head gasket.

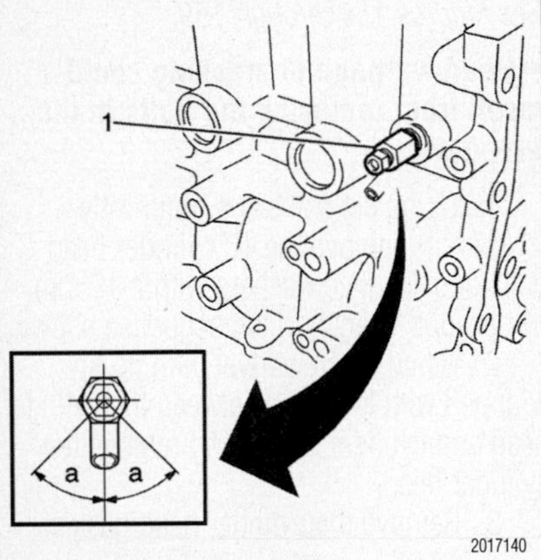

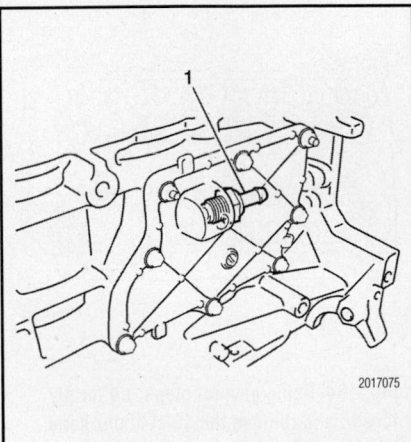

Fig. 155 Install the water drain cock plug (1) to the engine block—1.8L (LAY)

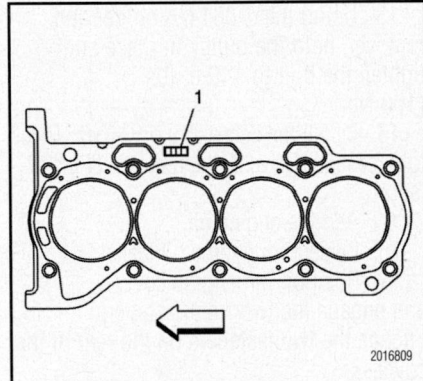

Fig. 157 Place a new gasket on the cylinder block surface with the Lot No. stamp (1) facing upward—1.8L (LAY)

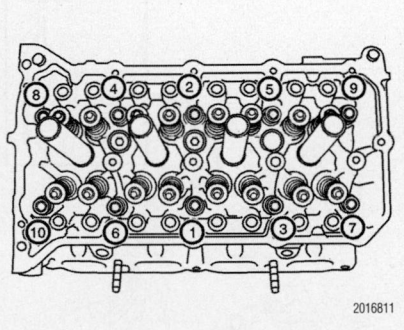

Fig. 156 Install the ventilation valve (1)—1.8L (LAY)

Fig. 158 Using several passes, with a 10 mm bi-hexagon wrench, uniformly install and tighten the 10 cylinder head set bolts and plate washers in the order shown—1.8L (LAY)

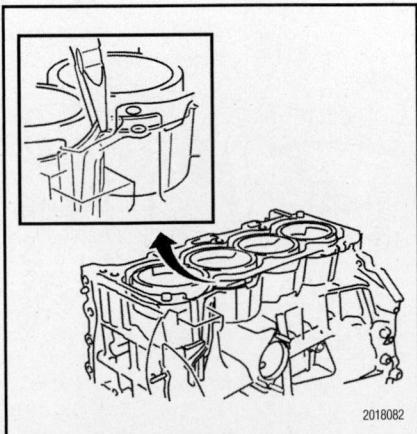

Fig. 160 Using needle nose pliers, remove the cylinder block water jacket spacer from the water jacket—2.4L (LAX)

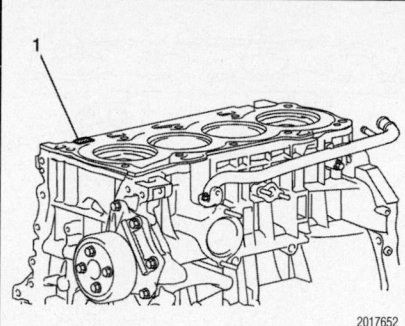

Fig. 161 Place a new cylinder head gasket on the cylinder block surface with the Lot No. stamp (1) facing upward—2.4L (LAX)

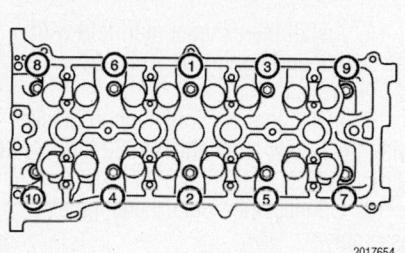

Fig. 162 Using several passes, with a 10 mm bi-hexagon wrench, uniformly install and tighten the 10 cylinder head set bolts and plate washers in the order shown—2.4L (LAX)

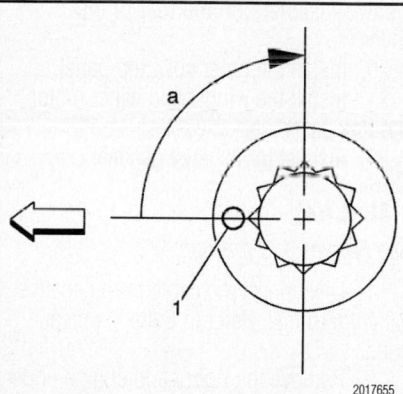

Fig. 163 Mark the front of the cylinder head bolts with paint (1). Further tighten the cylinder head bolts by 90 degrees (a) as shown. Ensure the paint mark is now at a 90-degree angle to the front—2.4L (LAX)

➡Before turning the cylinder block upside down, make sure that the water jacket spacer is removed, as it will fall out.

3. Using needle nose pliers, remove the cylinder block water jacket spacer from the water jacket.

To install:

➡Remove any oil from the contact surface. Be careful of the installation direction.

4. Place a new cylinder head gasket on the cylinder block surface with the Lot No. stamp facing upward.

➡Place the cylinder head gently in order to avoid damaging the cylinder head gasket.

5. Place the cylinder head on the cylinder head gasket.

➡The cylinder head bolts are tightened in 2 successive steps. Apply a light coat of engine oil to the threads and under the heads of the cylinder head set bolts.

6. Using several passes, with a 10 mm bi-hexagon wrench, uniformly install and tighten the 10 cylinder head set bolts and plate washers in the order shown and tighten to 52 ft. lbs. (70 Nm).

7. Mark the front of the cylinder head bolts with paint.

8. Further tighten the cylinder head bolts by 90 degrees.

9. Ensure the paint mark is now at a 90-degree angle to the front.

ENGINE OIL & FILTER

REPLACEMENT

1.8L (LAY)

See Figures 164 and 165.

➡For environmental protection, used oil and used oil filters must be disposed of at designated disposal sites.

1. Remove the oil filler cap.

2. Remove the oil drain plug and drain the oil into a container.

3. Clean and install the oil drain plug with a new gasket and tighten to 27 ft. lbs. (37 Nm).

4. Using a strap type wrench, loosen the oil filter cap 4 revolutions, align the cap ribs vertically, and drain the remaining engine oil in the oil filter and cap.

➡Set a container below the oil filter cap assembly before loosening the oil filter cap.

5. Remove the oil filter cap assembly.

➡Be sure to remove the O-ring (for the cap) by hand, without using any tools,

to prevent damage to the groove for the O-ring on the cap.

6. Remove oil filter element and O-ring from the oil filter cap.

7. Clean the oil filter cap threads and O-ring groove.

8. Apply a small amount of engine oil to a new O-ring and install it to the oil filter cap.

9. Set a new oil filter element in the oil filter cap.

10. Remove any dirt or foreign matter from the installation surfaces.

➡Make sure that the O-ring does not get caught between the parts.

11. Apply a small amount of engine oil to the O-ring of the oil filter cap assembly. Align the cutout in the oil filter cap threads 90 degrees to the grooves in the oil filter bracket and temporarily tighten the cap.

➡After tightening the oil filter cap assembly, check for gaps between the installation surfaces. Do not remove

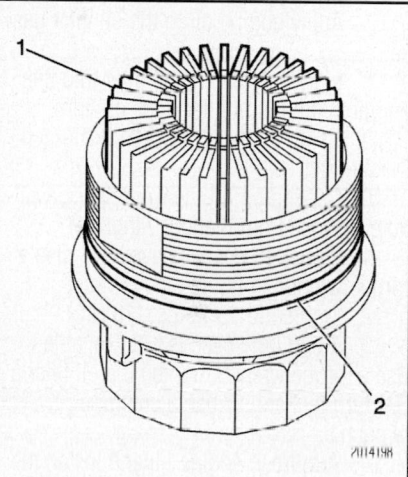

Fig. 164 Remove oil filter element (1) and O-ring (2) from the oil filter cap—1.8L (LAY)

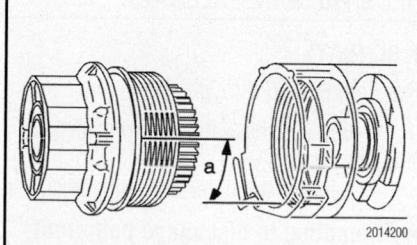

Fig. 165 Align the cutout in the oil filter cap threads 90 degrees to the grooves in the oil filter bracket and temporarily tighten the cap—1.8L (LAY)

the oil filter bracket clip when installing the oil filter cap assembly. Do not cross thread the oil filter cap assembly.

12. Using a strap type wrench, tighten the oil filter cap assembly to 18 ft. lbs. (25 Nm).

13. Add fresh engine oil and install the oil filler cap.

14. Inspect for oil leaks.

2.4L (LAX)

➡For environmental protection, used oil and used oil filters must be disposed of at designated disposal sites.

1. Remove the oil filler cap.

2. Remove the oil drain plug and drain the oil into a container.

3. Clean and install the oil drain plug with a new gasket.

4. Tighten to 29 ft. lbs. (40 Nm).

5. Using a strap type wrench, remove the oil filter.

6. Clean the oil filter installation surface.

7. Apply engine oil to the oil filter gasket.

8. Lightly screw the oil filter into the engine until the oil filter does not turn.

9. Using a strap type wrench, tighten the oil filter.

10. Depending on the work space available, choose from the following:

11. If enough space is available, use a torque wrench to tighten the oil filter.

12. Tighten to 13 ft. lbs. (18 Nm).

13. If enough space is not available to use a torque wrench, tighten the oil filter a 3/4 turn by hand or use a common wrench.

14. Add fresh engine oil and install the oil filler cap.

15. Inspect for oil leaks.

EXHAUST MANIFOLD

REMOVAL & INSTALLATION

1.8L (LAY)

See Figures 166 through 168.

1. Remove the windshield wiper motor and link assembly.

2. Remove the outer cowl top panel.

➡Attempting to disengage both front and rear clips at the same time may cause the engine cover to break.

3. Hold the rear of the engine cover and raise it to disengage the 2 clips on the rear of the cover.

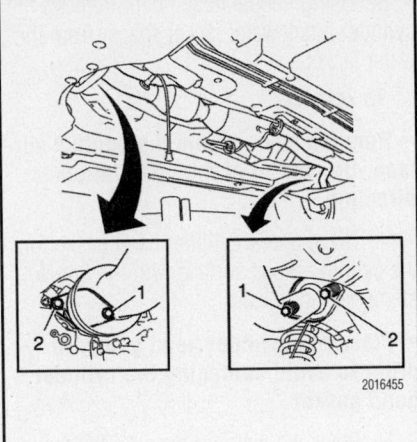

Fig. 166 Disconnect the front exhaust pipe assembly (1, 2)—1.8L (LAY)

4. Continue to raise the cover to disengage the 2 clips on the front of the cover and remove the engine cover.

5. Remove the heated oxygen sensor 1. Refer to Heated Oxygen (HO2S) Sensor, removal & installation.

6. Remove the 4 bolts and the exhaust manifold heat insulator.

7. Disconnect the front exhaust pipe assembly.

8. Remove the 3 bolts and the manifold support bracket.

9. Remove the 5 nuts and the exhaust manifold.

10. Remove the exhaust manifold gasket.

11. Remove the 3 bolts and the exhaust manifold heat insulator.

To install:

12. Install the exhaust manifold heat insulator with the 3 bolts and tighten to 110 inch lbs. (12 Nm).

13. Install a new exhaust manifold gasket.

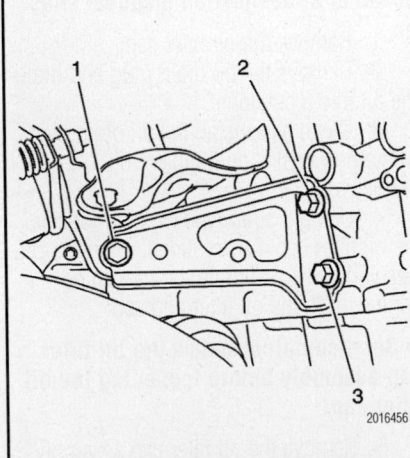

Fig. 167 Remove the bolts (1–3) and the manifold support bracket—1.8L (LAY)

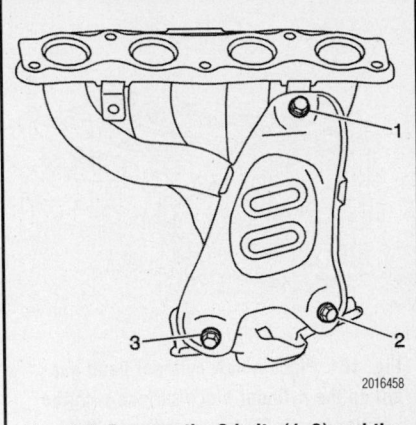

Fig. 168 Remove the 3 bolts (1–3) and the exhaust manifold heat insulator—1.8L (LAY)

14. Install the exhaust manifold with the 5 nuts and tighten to 16 ft. lbs. (21 Nm).

15. Install the manifold support bracket with the 3 bolts and tighten to 32 ft. lbs. (43 Nm).

16. Connect the front exhaust pipe assembly.

17. Install the exhaust manifold heat insulator with the 4 bolts and tighten to 110 inch lbs. (12 Nm).

18. Install the heated oxygen sensor 1. Refer to Heated Oxygen (HO2S) Sensor, removal & installation.

19. Position the engine cover and engage the two front fasteners. Engage the two fasteners on the rear of the cover.

20. Install the outer cowl top panel.

21. Install the windshield wiper motor and link assembly.

22. Inspect for exhaust gas leak.

2.4L (LAX)

See Figures 169 through 173.

1. Disconnect the cable from negative battery terminal. Refer to Battery, precautions.

2. Remove the right hand engine under cover.

3. Disconnect the front exhaust pipe assembly.

4. Disconnect the heated oxygen sensor connector.

5. Remove the 2 bolts, compression springs and the front exhaust pipe assembly.

6. Remove the gasket from the exhaust manifold.

7. Remove the 4 bolts and the exhaust manifold heat insulator.

8. Remove the air fuel ratio sensor.

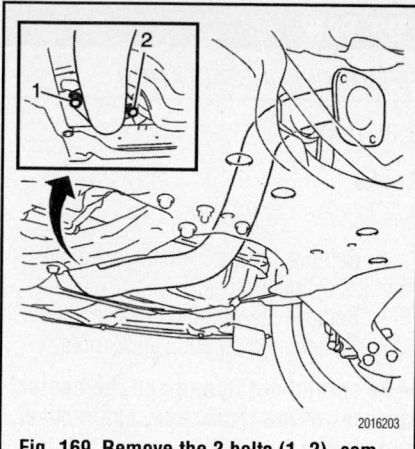

Fig. 169 Remove the 2 bolts (1, 2), compression springs and the front exhaust pipe assembly—2.4L (LAX)

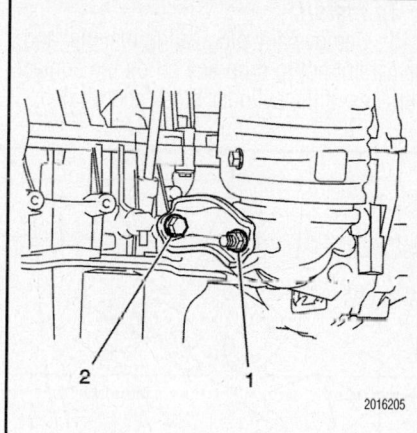

Fig. 170 Remove the bolt (2), nut (1) and manifold support bracket—2.4L (LAX)

9. Remove the bolt, nut and manifold support bracket.

10. Remove the bolt, nut and the manifold support bracket.

11. Remove the 5 nuts and the exhaust manifold converter sub-assembly.

12. Remove the gasket.

13. Remove the 2 bolts and the exhaust manifold heat insulator.

14. Remove the 4 bolts and the manifold converter heat insulator.

To install:

15. Install the manifold converter heat insulator with the 4 bolts and tighten to 110 inch lbs. (12 Nm).

16. Install the exhaust manifold heat insulator with the 2 bolts and tighten to 110 inch lbs. (12 Nm).

17. Install a new gasket.

18. Install the exhaust manifold converter sub-assembly with the 5 nuts in the order shown and tighten to 27 ft. lbs. (37 Nm).

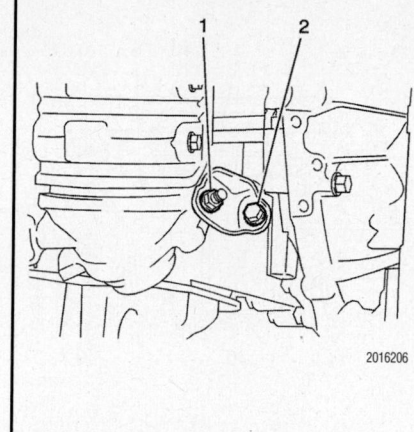

Fig. 171 Remove the bolt (2), nut (1) and the manifold support bracket—2.4L (LAX)

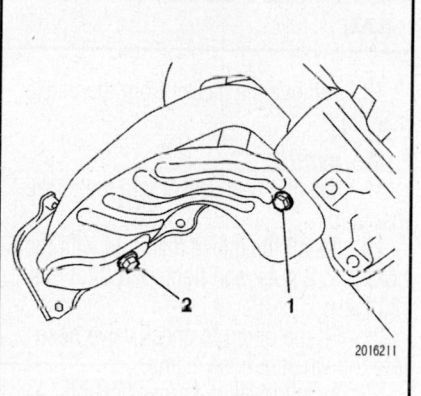

Fig. 172 Remove the 2 bolts (1, 2) and the exhaust manifold heat insulator—2.4L (LAX)

19. Install the 2 manifold support brackets with the bolt and nut, and tighten to 33 ft. lbs. (44 Nm).

20. Install air fuel ratio sensor.

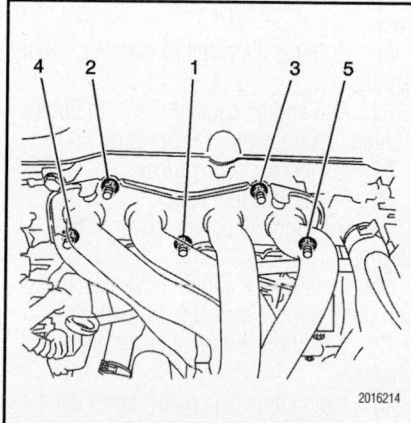

Fig. 173 Install the exhaust manifold converter sub-assembly with the 5 nuts in the order shown—2.4L (LAX)

21. Install the exhaust manifold heat insulator with the 4 bolts and tighten to 110 inch lbs. (12 Nm).

22. Connect the front exhaust pipe assembly.

23. Using a plastic hammer and wooden block, tap in the new gasket until its surface is flush with the exhaust manifold.

24. Install right hand engine under cover.

25. Connect cable to negative battery terminal.

26. Inspect for exhaust gas leaks.

INTAKE MANIFOLD

REMOVAL & INSTALLATION

1.8L (LAY)

See Figure 174.

1. Drain the engine coolant. Refer to Engine Coolant, Drain & Refill Procedure.

➡ **Attempting to disengage both front and rear clips at the same time may cause the engine cover to break.**

2. Hold the rear of the engine cover and raise it to disengage the 2 clips on the rear of the cover. Continue to raise the cover to disengage the 2 clips on the front of the cover and remove the cover.

3. Remove the air cleaner assembly with hose.

4. Remove the throttle body. Refer to Throttle Body, removal & installation.

5. Remove the bolt and wire harness bracket.

6. Disconnect the 3 hoses.

7. Remove the 4 bolts, 2 nuts, intake manifold support and intake manifold.

8. Remove the gasket from the intake manifold.

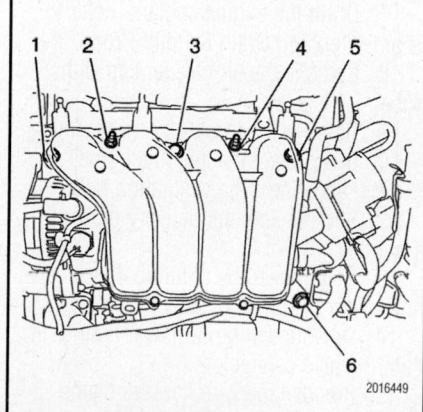

Fig. 174 Remove the 4 bolts (1, 3, 5, 6), 2 nuts (2, 4), intake manifold support and intake manifold—1.8L (LAY)

9. Using a TORX® socket E6, remove the 2 stud bolts from the intake manifold.

To install:

10. Using a TORX® socket E6, install the 2 stud bolts to the intake manifold and tighten to 44 inch lbs. (5.0 Nm).

11. Connect the bracket with the bolt and tighten to 8 ft. lbs. (10 Nm).

12. Install a new gasket into the intake manifold.

13. Install the intake manifold and intake manifold support with the 4 bolts and 2 nuts, and tighten to 21 ft. lbs. (28 Nm).

14. Connect the 3 hoses.

15. Connect the wire harness bracket with the bolt and tighten to 8 ft. lbs. (10 Nm).

16. Install the throttle body. Refer to Throttle Body, removal & installation.

17. Install the air cleaner assembly with hose.

18. Position the engine cover and engage the two front fasteners. Engage the two fasteners on the rear of the cover.

19. Add engine coolant. Refer to Engine Coolant, Drain & Refill Procedure.

20. Inspect for coolant leak.

2.4L (LAX)

See Figure 175.

1. Release the fuel system pressure. Refer to Relieving Fuel System Pressure.

2. Disconnect the cable from negative battery terminal. Refer to Battery, precautions.

3. Remove the windshield wiper motor and link assembly.

4. Remove the outer cowl top panel.

5. Remove the suspension tower damper assembly (with front strut bar).

6. Remove the 2 engine cover fasteners and 2 plastic retainers. Remove the engine cover from the engine.

7. Drain the engine coolant. Refer to Engine Coolant, Drain & Refill Procedure.

8. Remove the air cleaner cap with hose.

9. Remove the throttle body assembly.

10. Disconnect the fuel main tube.

11. Disconnect the ventilation hose.

12. Remove the fuel delivery pipe sub-assembly.

13. Disconnect the union to check valve hose from the brake booster.

14. Disconnect the camshaft timing oil control valve connector.

15. Remove the wire harness clamp.

16. Remove the union to check valve hose from the vacuum hose clamp.

17. Remove the 5 bolts, 2 nuts and intake manifold.

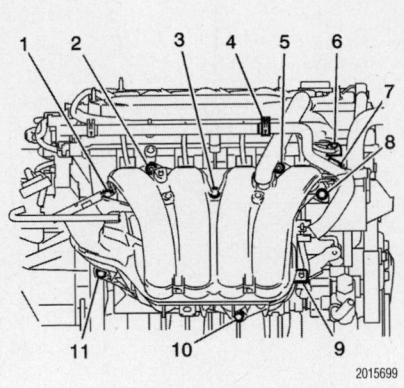

Fig. 175 Disconnect the union to check valve hose (4) from the brake booster. Remove the 5 bolts (1, 3, 8, 10, 11), 2 nuts (2, 5) and intake manifold—2.4L (LAX)

18. Remove the gasket from the intake manifold.

To install:

19. Install a new gasket into the intake manifold.

20. Install the intake manifold with the 5 bolts and 2 nuts, and tighten to 22 ft. lbs. (30 Nm).

21. Fit the union to check valve hose into the vacuum hose clamp.

22. Install the wire harness clamp.

23. Connect the camshaft timing oil control valve connector.

24. Connect the union to check valve hose to the brake booster.

25. Install fuel delivery pipe sub-assembly.

26. Connect the ventilation hose.

27. Connect the fuel main tube.

28. Install the throttle body assembly.

29. Install the air cleaner cap with hose.

30. Connect the cable to negative battery terminal.

31. Add engine coolant. Refer to Engine Coolant, Drain & Refill Procedure.

32. Inspect for coolant leak.

33. Inspect for fuel leak.

34. Position the engine cover to the engine.

35. Install the 2 engine cover fasteners and tighten to 62 inch lbs. (7 Nm).

36. Install the 2 engine cover plastic retainers.

37. Install the suspension tower damper assembly (with front strut bar).

38. Install the outer cowl top panel.

39. Install the windshield wiper motor and link assembly.

OIL PAN

REMOVAL & INSTALLATION

1.8L (LAY)

Lower

See Figures 176 through 179.

1. Remove the water drain cock plug from the cylinder block.

2. Remove the ventilation valve.

3. Remove the 10 bolts and 2 nuts.

➡ **Be careful not to damage the contact surfaces of the crankcase, chain cover, and oil pan.**

4. Insert the blade of oil pan seal cutter between the crankcase and oil pan. Cut through the sealer and remove the oil pan.

To install:

5. Remove any old sealing material and be careful not to drop any oil on the contact surfaces of the cylinder block and oil pan.

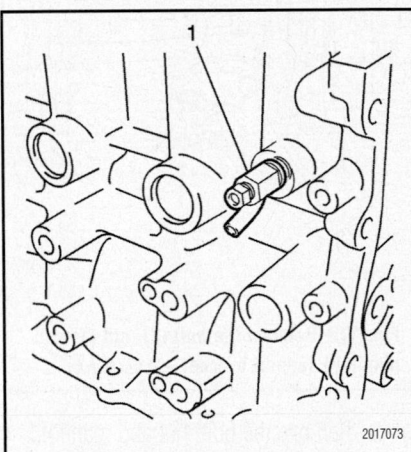

Fig. 176 Remove the water drain cock plug (1) from the cylinder block—1.8L (LAY)

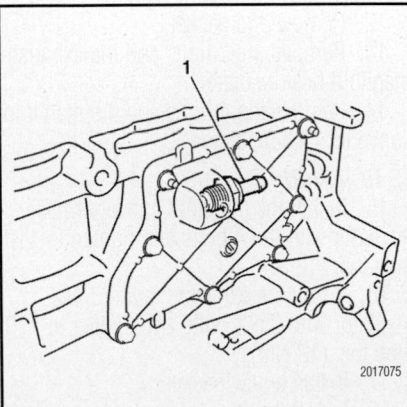

Fig. 177 Remove the ventilation valve (1)—1.8L (LAY)

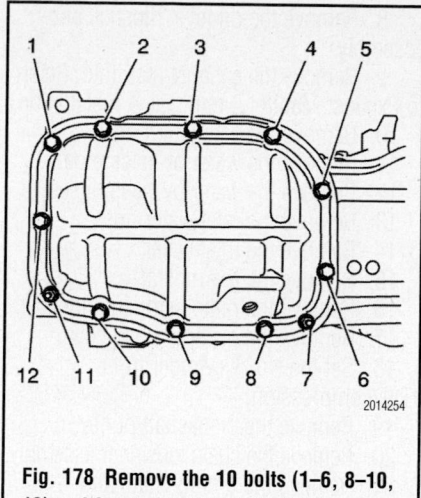

Fig. 178 Remove the 10 bolts (1–6, 8–10, 12) and 2 nuts (7, 11)—1.8L (LAY)

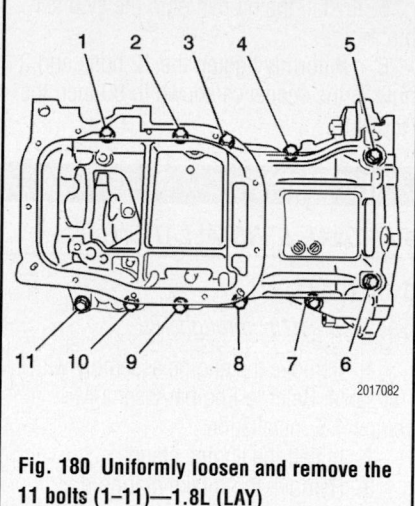

Fig. 180 Uniformly loosen and remove the 11 bolts (1–11)—1.8L (LAY)

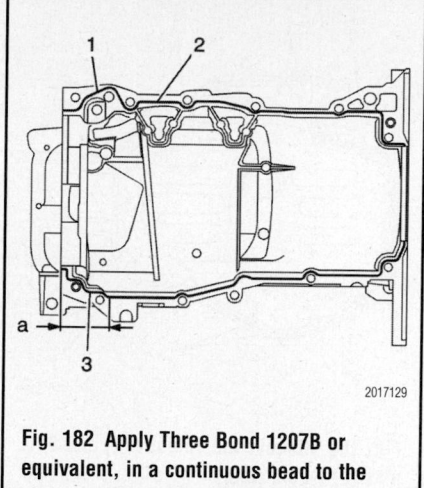

Fig. 182 Apply Three Bond 1207B or equivalent, in a continuous bead to the places shown (1–3)—1.8L (LAY)

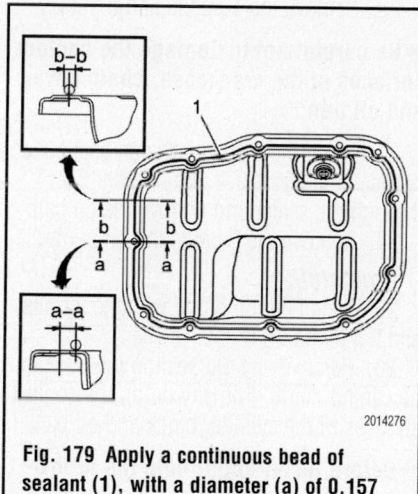

Fig. 179 Apply a continuous bead of sealant (1), with a diameter (a) of 0.157 inch (4.0 mm)—1.8L (LAY)

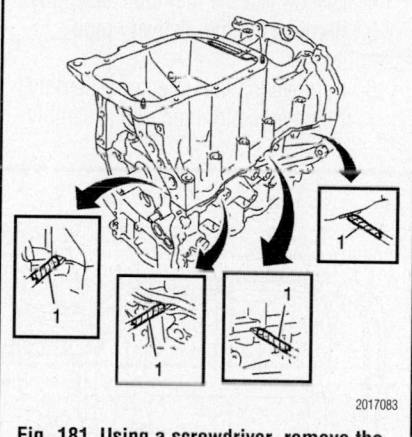

Fig. 181 Using a screwdriver, remove the stiffening crankcase by prying between the crankcase and cylinder block—1.8L (LAY)

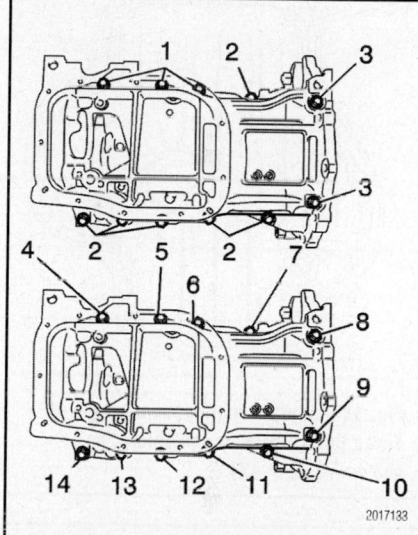

Fig. 183 Install the stiffening crankcase with the 11 bolts (4–14). Check the torque for bolts 1 and 2—1.8L (LAY)

➡**Before installation, note the following:**

- Remove any oil from the contact surfaces.
- Install the oil pan within 3 minutes after applying sealant.
- Do not start the engine for at least 2 hours after installing the oil pan.

6. Apply a continuous bead of sealant (Three Bond 1217B, or equivalent) (1), with a diameter (a) of 0.157 inch (4.0 mm).

7. Install the oil pan with the 10 bolts and 2 nuts, and tighten to 7 ft. lbs. (10 Nm).

8. Install a new gasket and the oil pan drain plug and tighten to 27 ft. lbs. (37 Nm).

Upper

See Figures 180 through 183.

1. Uniformly loosen and remove the 11 bolts.

2. Using a screwdriver, remove the stiff-

ening crankcase by prying between the crankcase and cylinder block.

To Install:

➡**Before installation, note the following:**

- Remove any oil from the contact surface.
- Install the crankcase within 3 minutes after applying seal packing.
- Do not start the engine for at least 2 hours after installing the stiffening crankcase.

3. Apply Three Bond 1207B or equivalent, in a continuous bead (diameter: 0.098 inch (2.5 mm)) to the places shown.

4. Install the stiffening crankcase with the 11 bolts and tighten to 16 ft. lbs. (21 Nm).

5. Check the torque for bolts 1 and 2 and tighten to 16 ft. lbs. (21 Nm).

6. Wipe off any excess seal packing with a clean piece of cloth.

2.4L (LAX)

See Figures 184 through 186.

1. Remove the oil pan drain plug from the oil pan.

2. Remove the 12 bolts and 2 nuts.

➡**Be careful not to damage the contact surfaces of the crankcase, chain cover and oil pan.**

3. Insert the blade of oil pan seal cutter between the crankcase, chain cover and oil pan, then cut through the applied sealer and remove the oil pan.

To install:

➡**Remove any oil from the contact surfaces. Install the oil pan within 3 minutes of applying sealant. Do not add engine oil for at**

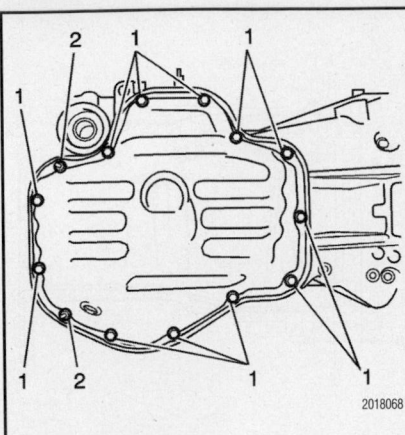

Fig. 184 Remove the 12 bolts (1) and 2 nuts (2)—2.4L (LAX)

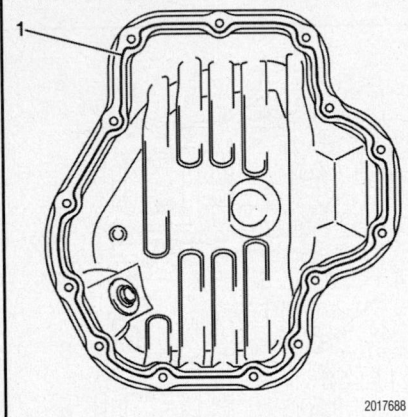

Fig. 185 Apply a continuous bead (1) of Three Bond 1207B or equivalent, as shown—2.4L (LAX)

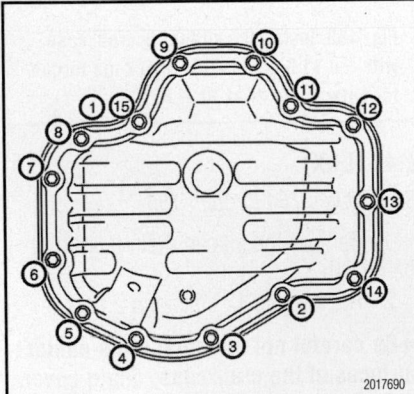

Fig. 186 Uniformly tighten the 12 bolts and 2 nuts in the sequence shown—2.4L (LAX)

least 2 hours after installing the oil pan.

4. Apply a continuous bead of Three Bond 1207B or equivalent, diameter 0.158-0.177 inch (4.0-4.5 mm), as shown.

5. Install the oil pan onto the cylinder block.

6. Uniformly tighten the 12 bolts and 2 nuts in the sequence shown to 80 inch lbs. (9.0 Nm).

OIL PUMP

REMOVAL & INSTALLATION

1.8L (LAY)

See Figures 187 through 189.

1. Remove the engine assembly with transaxle. Refer to Engine Assembly, removal & installation.
2. Install the engine stand.
3. Remove the intake manifold. Refer to Intake Manifold, removal & installation.
4. Disconnect the fuel tube assembly.
5. Remove the fuel delivery pipe assembly.
6. Remove the fuel injector assembly.
7. Remove the ignition coil assembly.

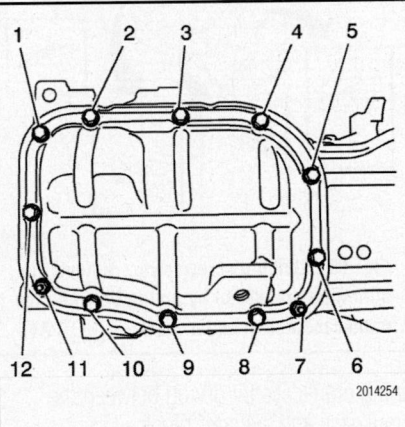

Fig. 187 Remove the 10 bolts (1–6, 8–10, 12) and 2 nuts (7, 11)—1.8L (LAY)

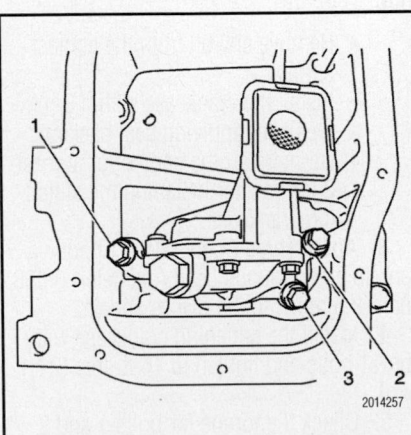

Fig. 188 Remove the bolts (1–3) and oil pump—1.8L (LAY)

8. Remove the oil level dipstick sub-assembly.
9. Remove the exhaust manifold. Refer to Exhaust Manifold, removal & installation.
10. Remove the ventilation hose.
11. Remove the water by-pass pipe.
12. Remove the water by-pass hoses.
13. Remove the inlet water hose.
14. Remove the inlet water.
15. Remove the thermostat.
16. Remove the radio setting condenser.
17. Remove the cylinder head cover.
18. Set the No. 1 cylinder to TDC/compression.
19. Remove the crankshaft pulley.
20. Remove the chain tensioner assembly.
21. Remove the timing chain and sprockets. Refer to Timing Chain & Sprockets, removal & installation.
22. Remove the 10 bolts and 2 nuts.

➡**Be careful not to damage the contact surfaces of the crankcase, chain cover, and oil pan.**

23. Insert the blade of oil pan seal cutter between the crankcase and oil pan. Cut through the sealer and remove the oil pan.
24. Remove the 3 bolts and oil pump.

To install:

25. Install the oil pump with the 3 bolts and tighten to 16 ft. lbs. (21 Nm).
26. Remove any old sealing material and be careful not to drop any oil on the contact surfaces of the cylinder block and oil pan.

➡**Before installation, note the following:**

- Remove any oil from the contact surfaces.
- Install the oil pan within 3 minutes after applying seal packing.
- Do not start the engine for at least 2 hours after installing the oil pan.

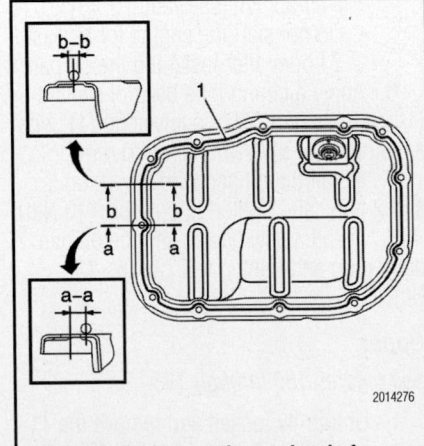

Fig. 189 Apply a continuous bead of sealant (1) as shown—1.8L (LAY)

27. Apply a continuous bead of sealant (Three Bond 1217B, or equivalent), with a diameter of 0.157 inch (4.0 mm), as shown.

28. Install the No. 2 oil pan with the 10 bolts and 2 nuts and tighten to 7 ft. lbs. (10 Nm).

29. Install the crankshaft position sensor plate.

30. Install timing chain and sprockets. Refer to Timing Chain & Sprockets, removal & installation.

31. Install the chain tensioner assembly.

32. Install the cylinder head cover.

33. Install the radio setting condenser.

34. Install the thermostat.

35. Install the inlet water.

36. Install the inlet water hose.

37. Install the water by-pass hoses.

38. Install the water by-pass pipe.

39. Install the ventilation hose.

40. Install the exhaust manifold. Refer to Exhaust Manifold, removal & installation.

41. Install the oil level dipstick assembly.

42. Install the ignition coil assembly.

43. Install the fuel injector assembly.

44. Install the delivery pipe spacer.

45. Install the fuel delivery pipe assembly.

46. Install the fuel tube assembly.

47. Install the intake manifold. Refer to Intake Manifold, removal & installation.

48. Remove the engine stand.

49. Install the engine. Refer to Engine Assembly, removal & installation.

2.4L (LAX)

See Figures 190 through 195.

1. Release the fuel system pressure. Refer to Relieving Fuel System Pressure.

2. Disconnect the cable from negative battery terminal. Refer to Battery, precautions.

3. Remove the windshield wiper motor and link assembly.

4. Remove the outer cowl top panel.

5. Remove the suspension tower damper assembly, with front strut bar.

6. Remove the right front wheel.

7. Remove the left engine under cover.

8. Remove the right engine under cover.

9. Remove the 2 engine cover fasteners and 2 plastic retainers. Remove the engine cover from the engine.

10. Drain the engine coolant. Refer to Engine Coolant, Drain & Refill Procedure.

11. Drain the engine oil. Refer to Engine Oil and Filter, replacement.

12. Remove the catalytic converter. Refer to Catalytic Converter, removal & installation.

13. Remove the front exhaust pipe assembly.

14. Remove the accessory drive belt. Refer to Accessory Drive Belts, removal & installation.

15. Remove the alternator. Refer to Alternator, removal & installation.

16. Disconnect the radiator hose.

17. Disconnect the outlet heater water hose.

18. Disconnect the inlet heater water hose.

19. Separate the radiator reserve tank assembly.

20. Remove the air cleaner cap with hose.

21. Remove the throttle body assembly.

22. Remove the ignition coil assembly. Refer to Ignition Coil, removal & installation.

23. Remove the spark plug. Refer to Spark Plugs, removal & installation.

24. Remove the cylinder head cover.

25. Remove the engine oil level dipstick.

26. Remove the engine oil level dipstick guide.

27. Remove the fuel main tube.

28. Remove the fuel delivery pipe sub-assembly.

29. Remove the camshaft timing oil control valve assembly.

30. Remove the intake manifold. Refer to Intake Manifold, removal & installation.

31. Remove the intake manifold insulator.

32. Remove the exhaust manifold converter. Refer to Exhaust Manifold, removal & installation.

33. Remove the right engine mount.

34. Remove the idler pulley.

35. Remove the oil pan.

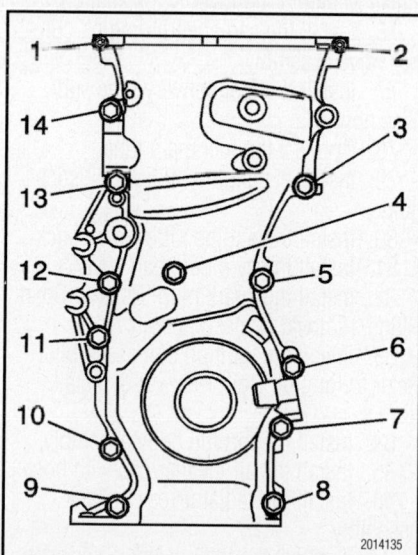

Fig. 190 Remove the 12 bolts (3–14) and 2 nuts (1, 2)—2.4L (LAX)

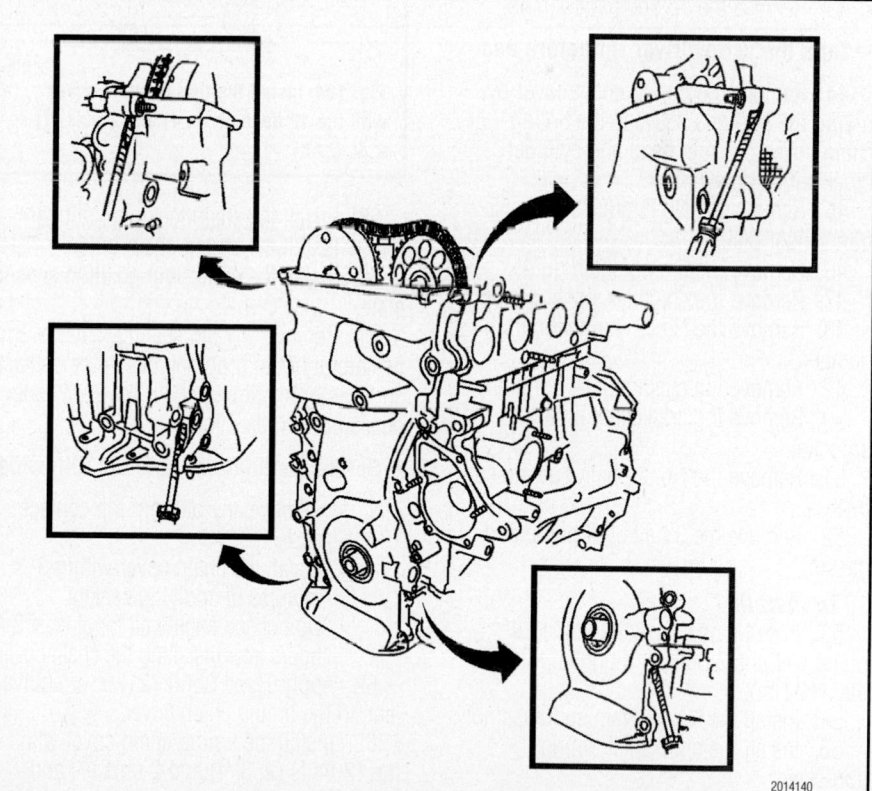

Fig. 191 Remove the timing chain cover by prying the portions between the timing chain cover, cylinder head and cylinder block with a screwdriver—2.4L (LAX)

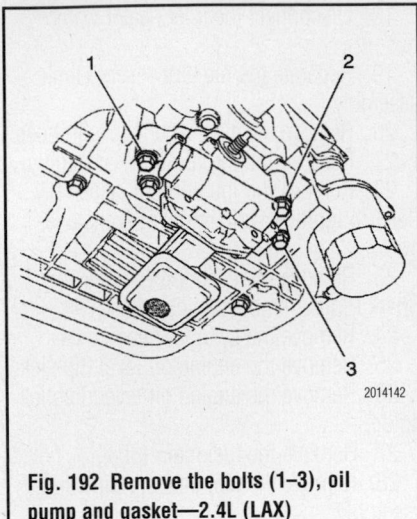

Fig. 192 Remove the bolts (1–3), oil pump and gasket—2.4L (LAX)

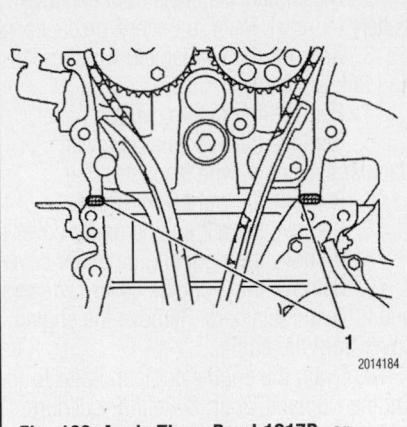

Fig. 193 Apply Three Bond 1217B, or equivalent, to the timing chain cover (1)—2.4L (LAX)

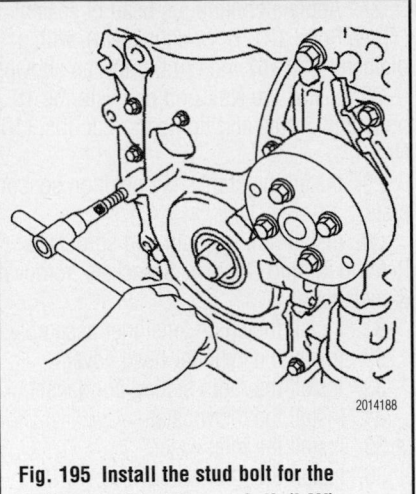

Fig. 195 Install the stud bolt for the V-ribbed belt tensioner—2.4L (LAX)

36. Set the cylinder to TDC/compression.

37. Remove the crankshaft pulley.

38. Remove the chain tensioner assembly.

39. Remove the transverse engine mounting bracket.

40. Remove the v-ribbed belt tensioner assembly.

41. Remove the crankshaft position sensor.

42. Using an E10 TORX® socket, remove the stud bolt for the V-ribbed belt tensioner.

43. Remove the 12 bolts and 2 nuts.

➡Tape the screwdriver tip before use.

44. Remove the timing chain cover by prying the portions between the timing chain cover, cylinder head and cylinder block with a screwdriver.

45. Remove the No. 1 crankshaft position sensor plate.

46. Remove the timing chain guide.

47. Remove the chain tensioner slipper.

48. Remove the No. 1 chain vibration damper.

49. Remove the chain sub-assembly.

50. Remove the crankshaft timing sprocket.

51. Remove the No. 2 chain sub-assembly.

52. Remove the 3 bolts, oil pump and gasket.

To install:

53. Install a new gasket and the oil pump with the 3 bolts and tighten to 14 ft. lbs. (19 Nm).

54. Install the No. 2 chain sub-assembly.

55. Install the crankshaft timing sprocket.

56. Install the No. 1 chain vibration damper.

57. Install the chain sub-assembly.

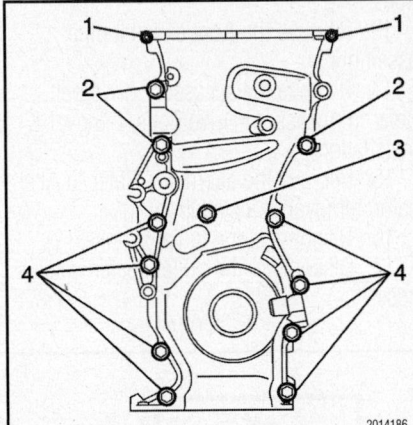

Fig. 194 Install the timing chain cover with the 12 bolts (2, 3, 4) and 2 nuts (1)—2.4L (LAX)

58. Install the chain tensioner slipper.

59. Install the timing chain guide.

60. Install the crankshaft position sensor plate.

61. Remove any old sealing material and be careful not to drop any oil on the contact surfaces of the timing chain cover, cylinder head and cylinder block.

➡Before installation, note the following:

• Remove any oil from the contact surfaces.
• Install the chain cover within 3 minutes of applying sealant.
• Do not add engine oil for at least 2 hours after installing the chain cover.

62. Apply Three Bond 1217B, or equivalent, to the timing chain cover.

63. Install the timing chain cover with the 12 bolts (2, 3, 4) and 2 nuts (1) and tighten:

• Bolt 3 to 80 inch lbs. (9.0 Nm).
• Bolts 4 to 18 ft. lbs. (25 Nm).

• Bolts 2 to 41 ft. lbs. (55 Nm).
• Nuts 1 to 8 ft. lbs. (11 Nm).

64. Using an E10 TORX® socket, install the stud bolt for the V-ribbed belt tensioner and tighten to 16 ft. lbs. (22 Nm).

65. Install the chain tensioner assembly.

66. Install the v-ribbed belt tensioner assembly.

67. Install the transverse engine mounting bracket.

68. Install the crankshaft pulley.

69. Install the oil pan.

70. Install the crankshaft position sensor.

71. Install the idler pulley.

72. Install the right engine mount.

73. Install the exhaust manifold converter. Refer to Exhaust Manifold, removal & installation.

74. Install the intake manifold insulator.

75. Install the intake manifold. Refer to Intake Manifold, removal & installation.

76. Install the camshaft timing oil control valve assembly.

77. Install the fuel delivery pipe sub-assembly.

78. Connect the fuel main tube.

79. Install the engine oil level dipstick guide.

80. Install the engine oil level dipstick.

81. Install the cylinder head cover.

82. Install the spark plug. Refer to Spark Plugs, removal & installation.

83. Install the ignition coil assembly. Refer to Ignition Coil, removal & installation.

84. Install the throttle body assembly.

85. Install the air cleaner cap with hose.

86. Install the radiator reserve tank assembly.

87. Connect the inlet heater water hose.

88. Connect the outlet heater water hose.

89. Install the radiator hose.
90. Install the alternator. Refer to Alternator, removal & installation.
91. Install the accessory drive belt. Refer to Accessory Drive Belts, removal & installation.
92. Install the front exhaust pipe assembly.
93. Install the catalytic converter. Refer to Catalytic Converter, removal & installation.
94. Connect the cable to negative battery terminal.
95. Add the engine oil. Refer to Engine Oil and Filter, replacement.
96. Add engine coolant. Refer to Engine Coolant, Drain & Refill Procedure.
97. Inspect the fuel leak.
98. Inspect the coolant leak.
99. Inspect the oil leak.
100. Inspect the exhaust gas leak.
101. Inspect the ignition timing.
102. Inspect the engine idle speed.
103. Install the suspension tower damper assembly (with front strut bar).
104. Install the outer cowl top panel.
105. Install the windshield wiper motor and link assembly.
106. Position the engine cover (1) to the engine.
107. Install the 2 engine cover fasteners and tighten to 62 inch lbs. (7 Nm).
100. Install the 2 engine cover plastic retainers.
109. Install the left engine under cover.
110. Install the right engine under cover.
111. Install the right front wheel.

DISASSEMBLY & REASSEMBLY

1.8L (LAY)

See Figures 196 and 197.

1. Using a 27 mm socket wrench, remove the plug.
2. Remove the valve spring and relief valve.

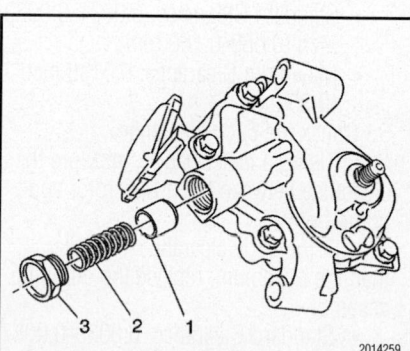

Fig. 196 Remove the plug (3). Remove the valve spring (2) and relief valve (1)— 1.8L (LAY)

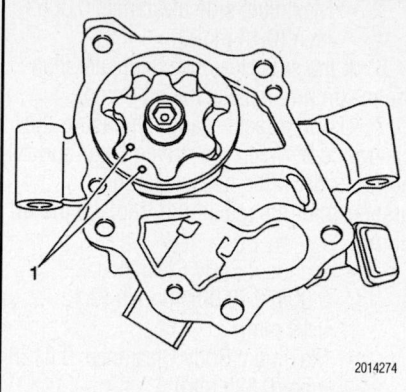

Fig. 197 Coat the oil pump drive and driven rotors with engine oil, and place them into the oil pump with the marks (1) facing the oil pump cover side—1.8L (LAY)

3. Remove the 5 bolts and oil pump cover.
4. Remove the oil pump drive and driven rotors from the oil pump.

To reassemble:

5. Coat the oil pump drive and driven rotors with engine oil, and place them into the oil pump with the marks facing the oil pump cover side.
6. Install the oil pump cover with the 5 bolts and tighten to 78 inch lbs. (8.8 Nm).
7. Coat the relief valve with engine oil.
8. Insert the relief valve and spring into the pump body hole.
9. Using a 27 mm socket wrench, install the plug and tighten to 36 ft. lbs. (49 Nm).

2.4L (LAX)

See Figures 198 and 199.

1. Remove the 2 nuts, oil pump strainer and gasket.
2. Using a 27 mm socket wrench, remove the plug.
3. Remove the valve spring and relief valve.

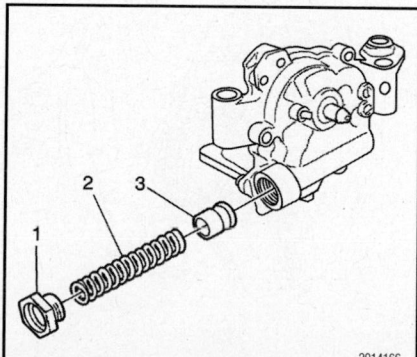

Fig. 198 Remove the plug (1). Remove the valve spring (2) and relief valve (3)—2.4L (LAX)

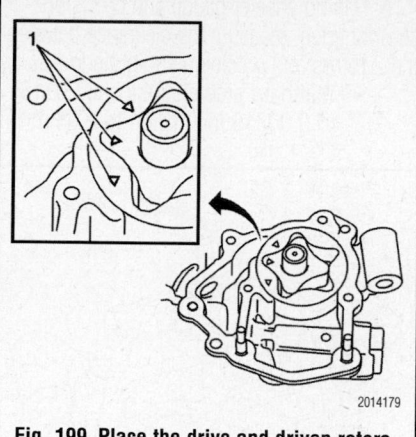

Fig. 199 Place the drive and driven rotors into the oil pump with the marks (1) facing the pump cover side—2.4L (LAX)

4. Remove the 5 bolts and oil pump cover.
5. Remove the oil pump drive and driven rotors from the oil pump.

To reassemble:

6. Coat the drive rotor and driven rotor with engine oil.
7. Place the drive and driven rotors into the oil pump with the marks facing the pump cover side.
8. Install the oil pump cover with the 5 bolts and tighten to 78 inch lbs. (8.8 Nm).
9. Coat the relief valve with engine oil.
10. Insert the relief valve and spring into the pump body hole.
11. Using a 27 mm socket wrench, install the plug and tighten to 36 ft. lbs. (49 Nm).
12. Install a new gasket and the oil strainer with the 2 nuts and tighten to 78 inch lbs. (8.8 Nm).

INSPECTION

1.8L (LAY)

See Figures 200 through 202.

1. Coat the oil pump relief valve with engine oil, then check that it falls smoothly into the valve hole by its own weight.
2. If this does not occur, replace the oil pump.
3. Using a feeler gauge, measure the clearance between the drive and driven rotor tips:

- Standard tip clearance: 0.00315 to 0.00630 inch (0.08 to 0.160 mm).
- Maximum tip clearance: 0.0138 inch (0.35 mm).

4. If the tip clearance is greater than the maximum, replace the oil pump.

5. Using a feeler gauge and precision straight edge, measure the clearance between the 2 rotors and precision straight edge:
- Standard side clearance: 0.00118 to 0.00315 inch (0.03 to 0.08 mm).

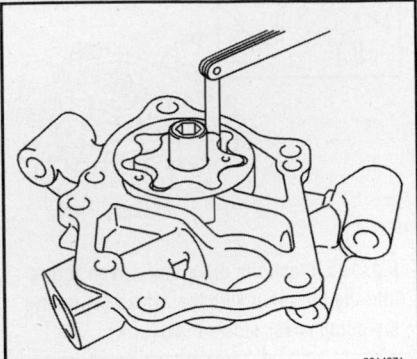

Fig. 200 Using a feeler gauge, measure the clearance between the drive and driven rotor tips—1.8L (LAY)

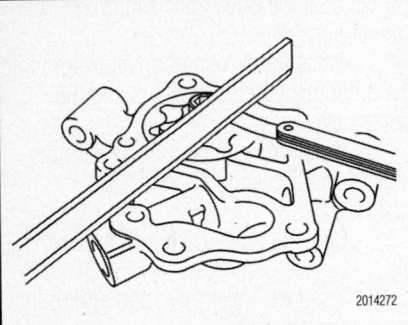

Fig. 201 Using a feeler gauge and precision straight edge, measure the clearance between the 2 rotors and precision straight edge—1.8L (LAY)

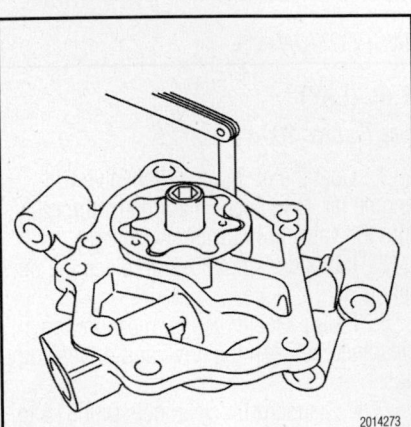

Fig. 202 Using a feeler gauge, measure the clearance between the driven rotor and oil pump body—1.8L (LAY)

- Maximum side clearance: 0.0063 inch (0.16 mm).
6. If the side clearance is greater than the maximum, replace the oil pump.
7. Using a feeler gauge, measure the clearance between the driven rotor and oil pump body. If the body clearance is greater than the maximum, replace the oil pump:
- Standard Body Clearance: 0.00472 -0.00748 inch (0.12-0.19 mm).
- Maximum Body Clearance: 0.0128 inch (0.325 mm).

2.4L (LAX)

See Figures 203 through 207.

1. Check the oil jet for damage or clogging. If necessary, repair the cylinder block.
2. Check the relief valve:
a. Coat the valve with engine oil, and then check that the valve falls smoothly into the valve hole by its own weight.
b. If it does not, replace the relief valve. If necessary, replace the oil pump assembly.
3. Check the side clearance:
a. Using a feeler gauge and precision straightedge, measure the clearance between the rotors and precision straightedge.
b. If the side clearance is greater than the maximum, replace the oil pump assembly.
- Standard Clearance: 0.0012 to 0.0034 inch (0.030 to 0.085 mm).
- Maximum Clearance: 0.0063 inch (0.160 mm).

Fig. 203 Check the oil jet (1) for damage or clogging. If necessary, repair the cylinder block—2.4L (LAX)

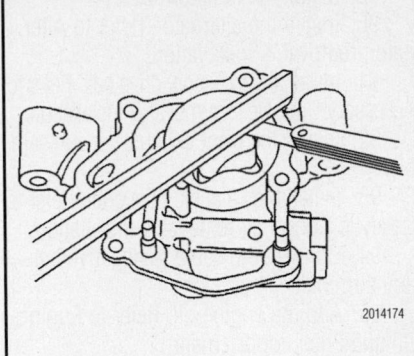

Fig. 204 Using a feeler gauge and precision straightedge, measure the clearance between the rotors and precision straightedge—2.4L (LAX)

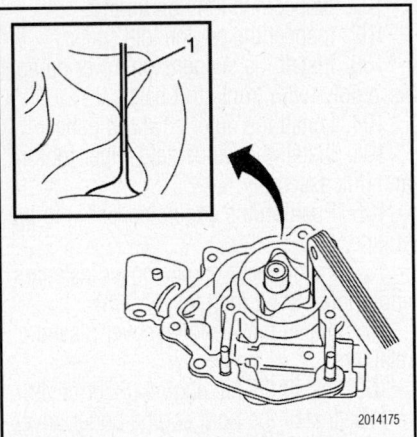

Fig. 205 Using a feeler gauge (1), measure the clearance between the drive and driven rotor tips—2.4L (LAX)

4. Check the tip clearance:
a. Using a feeler gauge (1), measure the clearance between the drive and driven rotor tips.
b. If the tip clearance is greater than the maximum, replace the oil pump assembly.
- Standard Clearance: 0.0031-0.0063 inch (0.080-0.160 mm).
- Maximum Clearance: 0.0138 inch (0.35 mm).
5. Check the body clearance:
a. Using a feeler gauge, measure the clearance between the driven rotor and pump body.
b. If the body clearance is greater than the maximum, replace the oil pump assembly.
- Standard Clearance: 0.0039-0.0067 inch (0.100-0 0.170 mm).
- Maximum Clearance: 0.0128 inch (0.325 mm).
6. Inspect No. 2 chain sub-assembly.

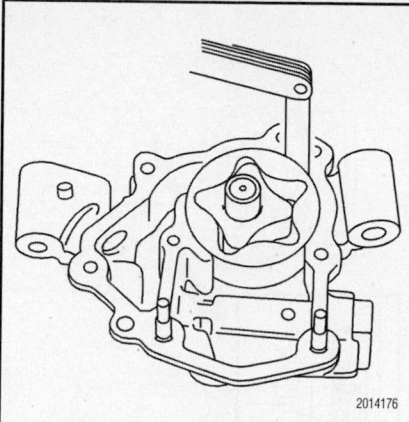

Fig. 206 Using a feeler gauge, measure the clearance between the driven rotor and pump body—2.4L (LAX)

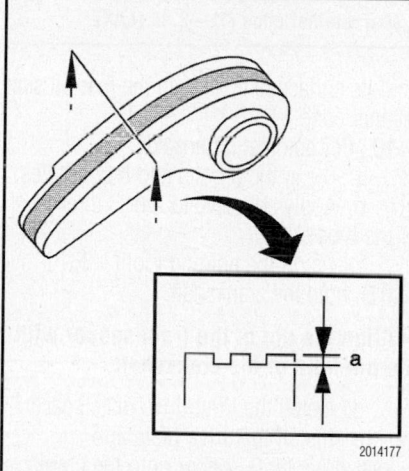

Fig. 207 Measure the chain tensioner plate wear (a)—2.4L (LAX)

7. Inspect chain tensioner plate.

8. Measure the chain tensioner plate wear. If the wear (a) is greater than the maximum, replace the chain tensioner plate. Maximum wear is 0.5 mm (0.020 in.).

PISTON AND RING

POSITIONING

1.8L (LAY)

See Figure 208.

➡**Do not align the ring ends.**

1. Position the piston rings so that the ring ends are as shown.

2.4L (LAX)

See Figure 209.

Check the position of the piston ring ends.

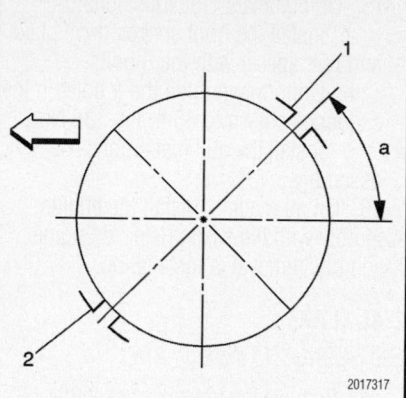

Fig. 208 Position the piston rings so that the ring ends (1,2) are as shown—1.8L (LAY)

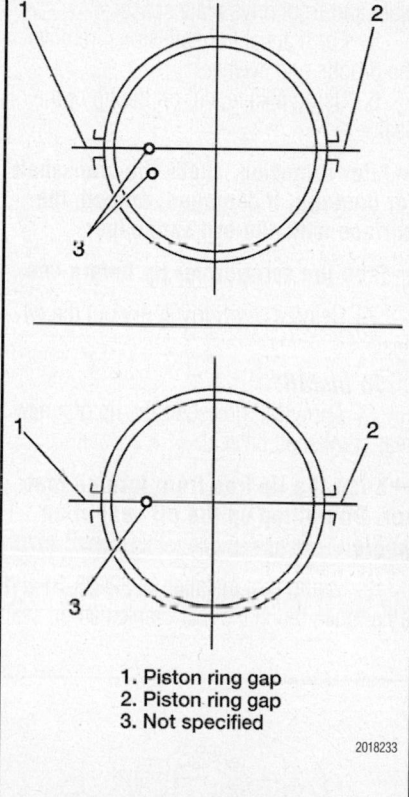

1. Piston ring gap
2. Piston ring gap
3. Not specified

Fig. 209 Check the position of the piston ring ends (1, 2)—2.4L (LAX)

REAR MAIN SEAL

REMOVAL & INSTALLATION

1.8L (LAY)

See Figures 210 through 212.

1. Remove the engine assembly with transaxle. Refer to Engine Assembly, removal & installation.

2. Remove the transaxle assembly.

3. Remove the clutch cover assembly and disc for the manual transaxle.

4. Using pinion flange holder and remover (J-8614-A), hold the crankshaft.

5. Remove the 8 bolts and the flywheel for manual transmissions.

6. Remove the 8 bolts, rear spacer, drive plate and front spacer for automatic transmissions.

7. Using a knife, cut off the lip of the oil seal.

➡**After removing, check the crankshaft for nicks or burrs. Smooth the surface with 400-grit sandpaper.**

8. Using a screwdriver with its tip wrapped with tape, pry out the oil seal.

To install:

➡**Keep the lip free from foreign matter.**

9. Apply MP grease to the lip of a new oil seal.

➡**Wipe any extra grease off the crankshaft. Do not tap the oil seal at an angle.**

10. Using seal installer (J-22928-B) and a hammer, tap in the oil seal until its surface is flush with the rear oil seal retainer edge.

11. Using the pinion flange holder and remover, hold the crankshaft.

12. Clean the bolts and bolt holes.

13. Apply adhesive Three Bond 1324 or equivalent to 2 or 3 end threads of the new bolts.

14. On manual transmissions:

a. Use several steps to uniformly install and tighten the 8 bolts in the sequence shown to 36 ft. lbs. (49 Nm).

b. Mark the front of the bolts with paint.

Fig. 210 Using seal installer (1) and a hammer, tap in the oil seal (2) until its surface is flush with the rear oil seal retainer edge—1.8L (LAY)

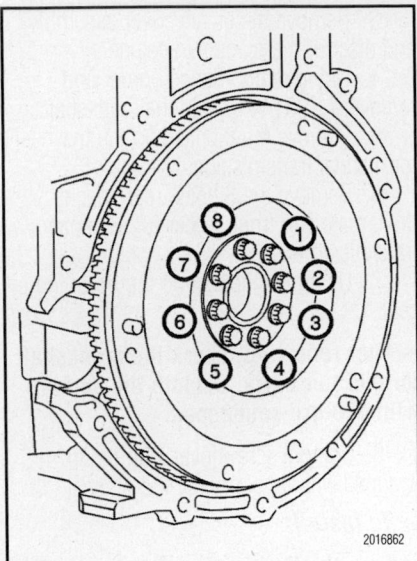

Fig. 211 On manual transmissions, use several steps to uniformly install and tighten the 8 bolts in the sequence shown—1.8L (LAY)

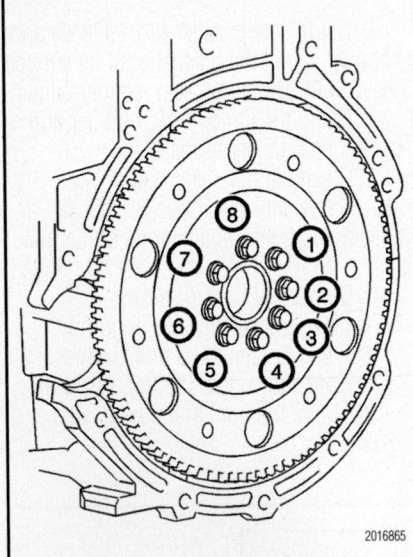

Fig. 212 On automatic transmissions, uniformly tighten the 8 bolts in the sequence shown—1.8L (LAY)

c. Retighten the 8 bolts an additional 90 degrees in the same sequence.

d. Check that the paint marks are now at a 90 degree angle to the front.

e. Check that the crankshaft turns smoothly.

f. Install the clutch disc assembly and clutch cover.

g. Inspect and adjust the clutch cover assembly.

h. Install the manual transaxle assembly.

15. On automatic transmissions:
   a. Install the front spacer, drive plate and rear spacer with the 8 bolts.
   b. Uniformly tighten the 8 bolts in the sequence shown to 65 ft. lbs. (88 Nm).
   c. Install the automatic transaxle assembly.

16. On all models, install the engine assembly with transaxle. Refer to Engine Assembly, removal & installation.

2.4L (LAX)

See Figures 213 through 218.

1. Remove the transaxle assembly.
2. Remove the clutch cover and disc assembly (manual transaxle).
3. Using flange and pulley holding tool (J-8614-01), hold the crankshaft.
4. For automatic transmissions, remove the 8 bolts, rear drive plate spacer, drive plate and front drive plate spacer.
5. For manual transmissions, remove the 8 bolts and flywheel.
6. Using a knife, cut off the lip of the oil seal.

➡**After removing, check the crankshaft for damage. If damaged, smooth the surface with 400-grit sandpaper.**

➡**Tape the screwdriver tip before use.**

7. Using a screwdriver, pry out the oil seal.

To install:

8. Apply MP grease to the lip of a new rear crankshaft oil seal.

➡**Keep the lip free from foreign matter. Do not tap on the oil seal at an angle.**

9. Using seal installer (J-22928-B) and a hammer, tap in the rear crankshaft oil seal

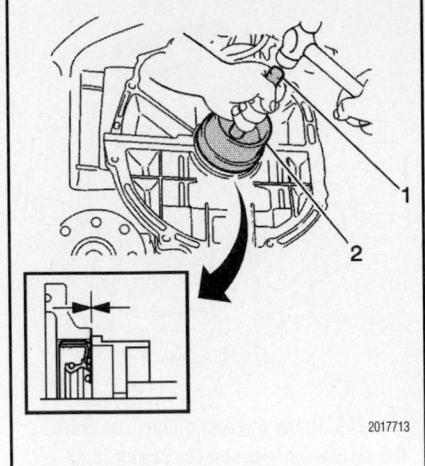

Fig. 214 Using seal installer (2) and a hammer, tap in the rear crankshaft oil seal until its surface is flush with the rear oil seal retainer edge (1)—2.4L (LAX)

until its surface is flush with the rear oil seal retainer edge.

10. For automatic transaxle:
   a. Clean the 8 bolts and 8 bolt holes.
   b. Apply adhesive to 2 or 3 threads of the 8 bolts.
   c. Using the holding tool (J-8614-01), hold the crankshaft.

➡**Align the pin of the front spacer with the pin hole of the crankshaft.**

   d. Install the front drive plate spacer.
   e. Install the drive plate and rear drive plate spacer onto the crankshaft.
   f. In several steps, uniformly install and tighten the 8 bolts in the sequence shown to 72 ft. lbs. (98 Nm).

11. For manual transaxle:
   a. Clean the 8 bolts and 8 bolt holes.

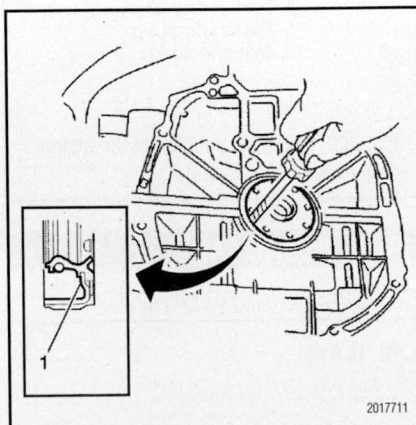

Fig. 213 Using a knife, cut off the lip of the oil seal (1). Using a screwdriver, pry out the oil seal—2.4L (LAX)

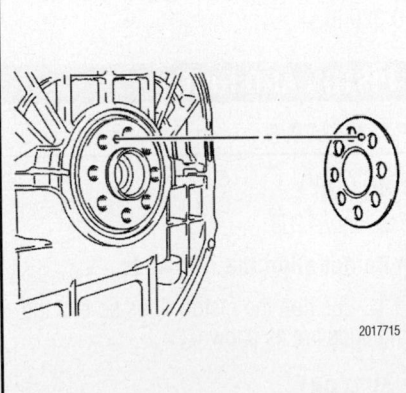

Fig. 215 On automatic transaxle, align the pin of the front spacer with the pin hole of the crankshaft—2.4L (LAX)

b. Apply adhesive to the end 2 or 3 threads of the 8 bolts.

c. In several steps, uniformly install and tighten the 8 bolts in the sequence shown to 96 ft. lbs. (130 Nm).

d. Install the clutch disc assembly.

e. Install the clutch cover assembly.

f. Install the transaxle assembly.

TIMING CHAIN FRONT COVER

REMOVAL & INSTALLATION

1.8L (LAY)

See Figures 219 through 233.

1. Remove the 3 bolts and engine mounting bracket.
2. Remove the 4 bolts and oil filter bracket.
3. Remove the 2 O-rings.
4. Remove the 19 bolts.

➡**Tape the screwdriver tip before use.**

5. Remove the timing chain cover by prying between the timing chain cover and cylinder head or cylinder block with a screwdriver.

To install:

6. Apply MP grease to the lip of the oil seal.

7. Remove any old sealant material and be careful not to drop any oil on the contact surfaces of the timing chain cover assembly, cylinder head, and cylinder block.

8. Install the 3 new O-rings.

➡**Note the following:**

- Remove any oil from the contact surfaces.
- Install the chain cover within 3 minutes after applying sealant.
- Do not start the engine for at least 2 hours after installing the timing chain cover sub-assembly.

9. Apply Three Bond 1217B, or equivalent, to the parting lines of the camshaft

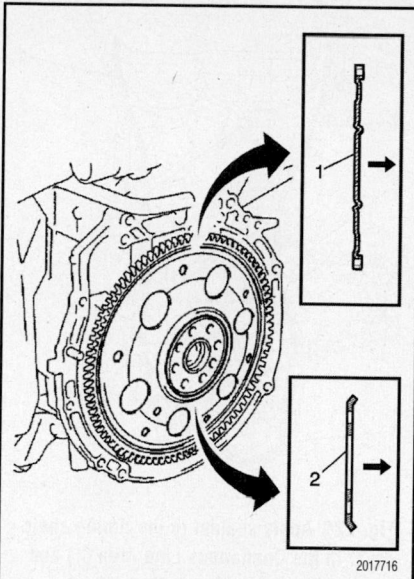

Fig. 216 Install the drive plate (1) and rear drive plate spacer (2) onto the crankshaft on automatic transaxle—2.4L (LAX)

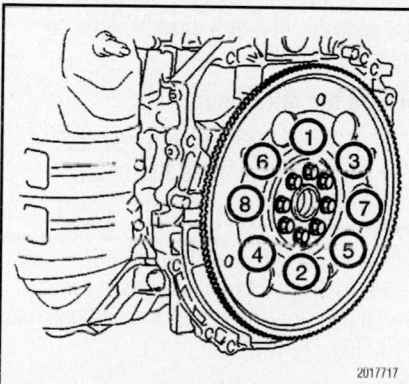

Fig. 217 In several steps, uniformly install and tighten the 8 bolts in the sequence shown on automatic transaxle—2.4L (LAX)

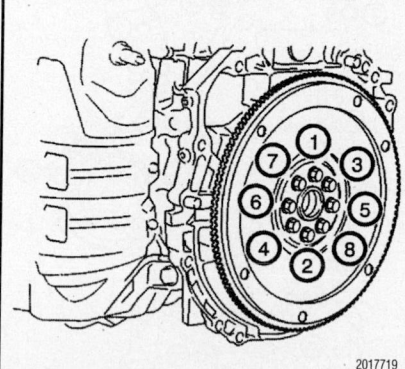

Fig. 218 In several steps, uniformly install and tighten the 8 bolts in the sequence shown for manual transaxle—2.4L (LAX)

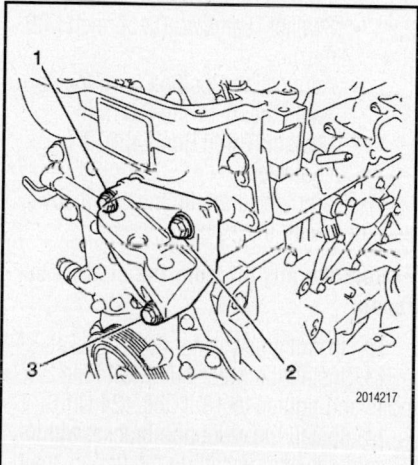

Fig. 219 Remove the bolts (1–3) and engine mounting bracket—1.8L (LAY)

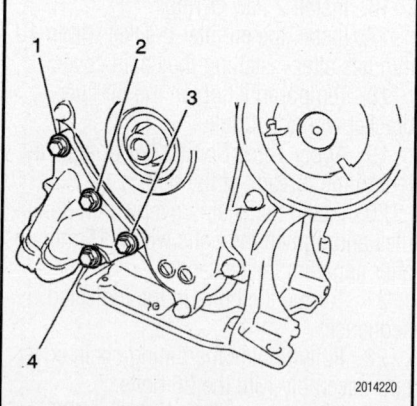

Fig. 220 Remove the bolts (1–4) and oil filter bracket—1.8L (LAY)

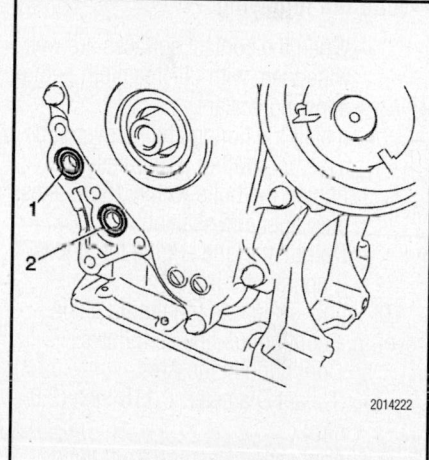

Fig. 221 Remove the O-rings (1, 2)—1.8L (LAY)

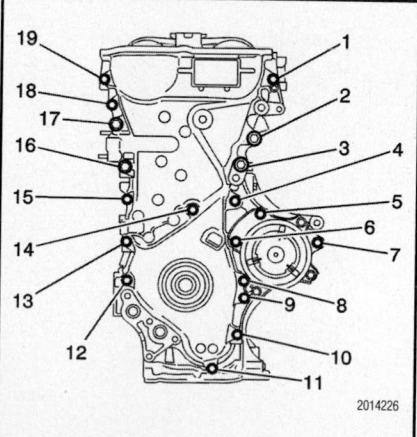

Fig. 222 Remove the bolts (1–19)—1.8L (LAY)

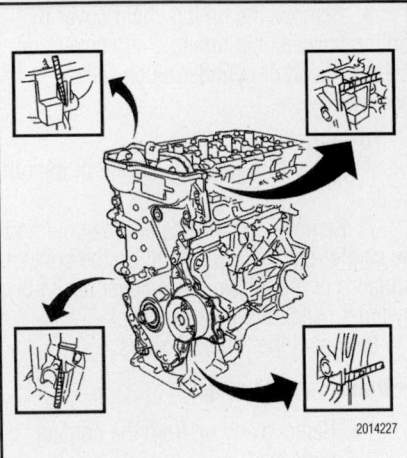

Fig. 223 Remove the timing chain cover by prying between the timing chain cover and cylinder head or cylinder block with a screwdriver—1.8L (LAY)

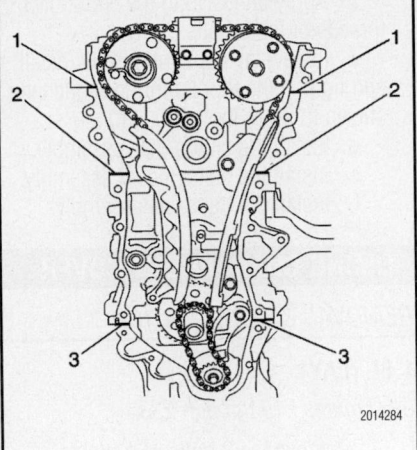

Fig. 225 Apply Three Bond 1217B, or equivalent, to the parting lines of the camshaft housing (1), cylinder head (2) and lower crankcase (3)—1.8L (LAY)

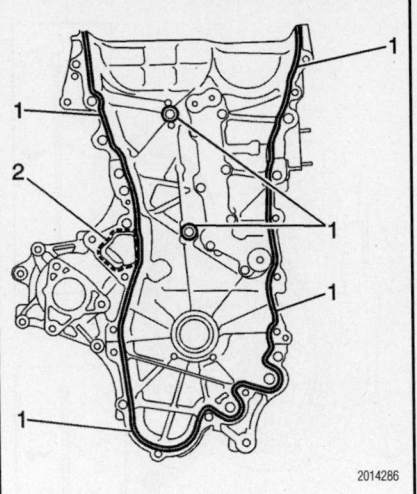

Fig. 226 Apply sealant to the timing chain cover in the Continuous Line Area (1) and Dashed Line Area (2)—1.8L (LAY)

housing, cylinder head and lower crankcase.

➡Note the following:

- When the contact surfaces are wet, wipe them with oil-free cloth before applying sealant.
- Install the timing chain cover sub-assembly within 3 minutes and tighten the bolts within 15 minutes after applying sealant.
- Do not start the engine for at least 2 hours after installing.

10. Apply sealant to the timing chain cover in a continuous line as follows:
  a. Continuous Line Area:
  - Sealant Diameter: 0.118 inch (3.0 mm).
  - Application Position from Inside Seal Line: 0.098 inch (2.5 mm).

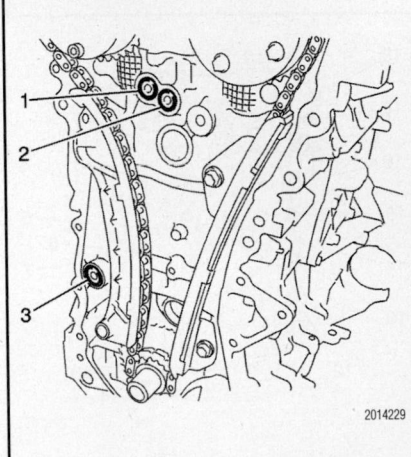

Fig. 224 Install new O-rings (1–3)—1.8L (LAY)

- Sealant: Three Bond 1207B or equivalent
  b. Dashed Line Area:
  - Sealant Diameter: 0.156 inch (4.0 mm).
  - Application Position form Inside Seal Line: 0.118 in (3.0 mm).
  - Sealant: Three Bond 1207B or equivalent

11. Hand install the timing chain cover assembly with the 19 bolts.

➡Remove any oil from the contact surfaces.

12. Install a new water pump gasket.
13. Install the water pump with the 3 bolts and tighten to 18 ft. lbs. (24 Nm).
14. Install the mounting bracket within 10 minutes after installing the timing chain cover assembly.
15. Hand tighten the engine mounting bracket with the 3 bolts.
16. Install 2 new O-rings.
17. Install the oil filter bracket within 10 minutes after installing the chain cover.
18. Temporarily tighten the oil filter bracket with the 4 bolts.
19. Apply Three Bond 1324 or equivalent to the threads of the bolt 5.
20. Install the chain cover within 3 minutes and tighten the bolts within 15 minutes after applying the sealant.
21. Torque the bolts in the indicated sequence.
22. Fully tighten the timing chain cover sub-assembly with the 26 bolts:
  - Bolts 1 and 5 to 19 ft. lbs. (26 Nm).
  - Bolts 2 and 3 to 37 ft. lbs. (51 Nm).
  - Bolt 4 to 7 ft. lbs. (10 Nm).
23. Install the crankshaft pulley.

24. Install the engine oil pressure switch assembly.
25. Apply Three Bond 1344 or equivalent adhesive to 2 or 3 threads of the oil pressure switch.

➡Note the following:

- Install the oil pressure switch within 3 minutes after applying adhesive.
- Do not start the engine within 1 hour after installation.

26. Using a 24 mm deep socket wrench, install the oil pressure switch and tighten to 11 ft. lbs. (15 Nm).

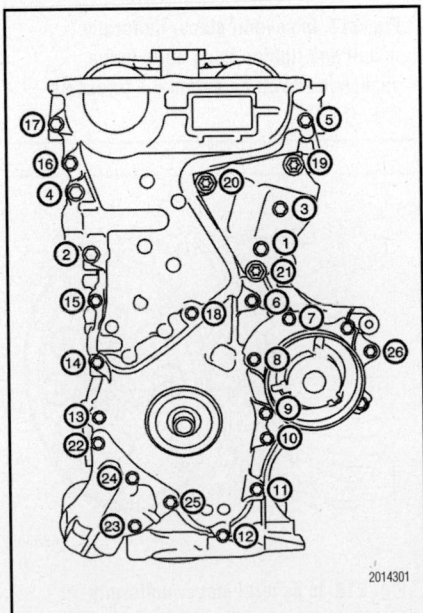

Fig. 227 Torque the bolts in the indicated sequence—1.8L (LAY)

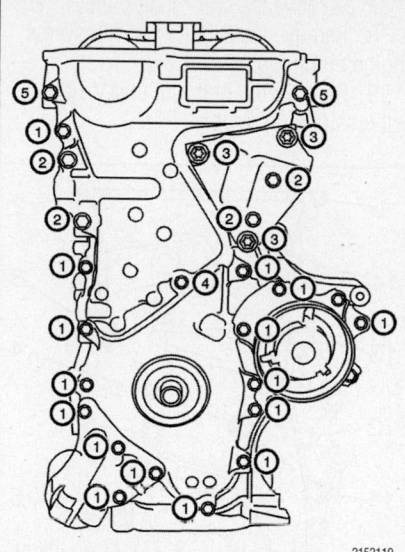

Fig. 228 Fully tighten the timing chain cover sub-assembly bolts (1–5)—1.8L (LAY)

Fig. 229 Install the oil pressure switch (1)—1.8L (LAY)

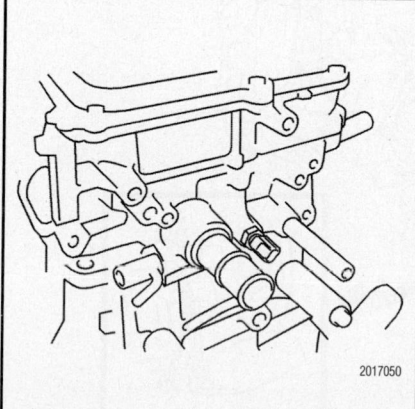

Fig. 230 Install the temperature sensor— 1.8L (LAY)

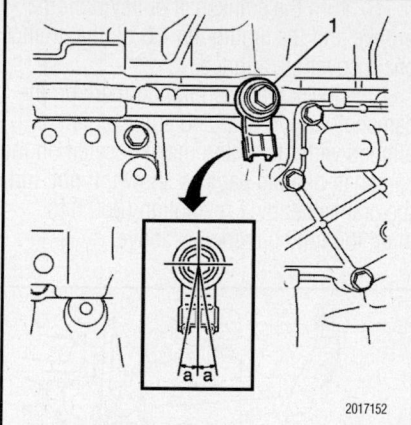

Fig. 232 Make sure that the knock control sensor (1) is in the correct position—1.8L (LAY)

27. Install the engine coolant temperature sensor.

28. Install a new gasket to the engine coolant temperature sensor.

29. Using a 19 mm deep socket wrench, install the temperature sensor and tighten to 15 ft. lbs. (20 Nm).

➡**Make sure that the knock control sensor is in the correct position.**

30. Install the knock control sensor with the bolt and tighten to 16 ft lbs. (21 Nm).

➡**Install the plug within 3 minutes after applying adhesive. Do not start the engine within 1 hour after installation.**

31. Install the taper screw plug.
   - Apply Three Bond 1324 or equivalent adhesive to 2 or 3 threads of the plug, install the plug and tighten to 32 ft. lbs. (43 Nm).
32. Install the crankshaft position sensor.

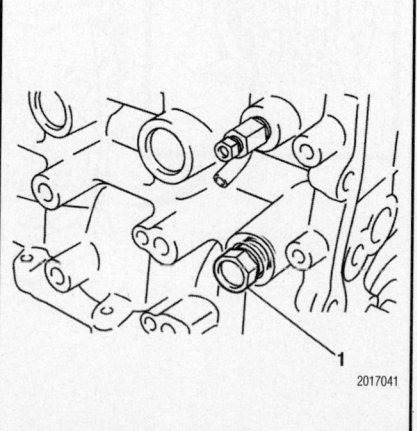

Fig. 232 Install the taper screw plug (1)— 1.8L (LAY)

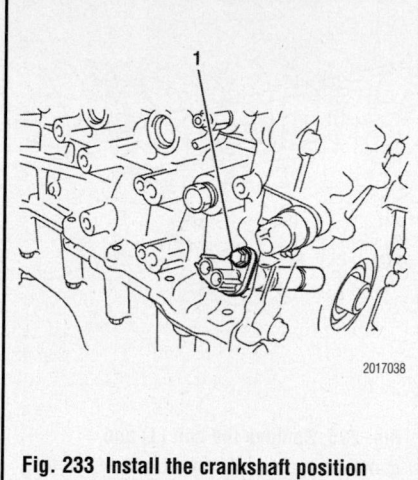

Fig. 233 Install the crankshaft position sensor (1) with the bolt—1.8L (LAY)

   - Apply a light coat of engine oil to the O-ring of the sensor.
   - Install the crankshaft position sensor with the bolt and tighten to 7 ft. lbs. (10 Nm).
33. Install the oil filter cap assembly.

2.4L (LAX)

See Figures 234 through 242.

1. Remove the bolt and camshaft position sensor.

➡**The camshaft timing oil control valve may be damaged when loosening the cylinder head bolt if the camshaft timing oil control valve is not removed.**

2. Remove the bolt and camshaft timing oil control valve from the cylinder head.

3. Loosen the 2 bolts and remove the idler pulley.

4. Set No. 1 cylinder to TDC/compression.

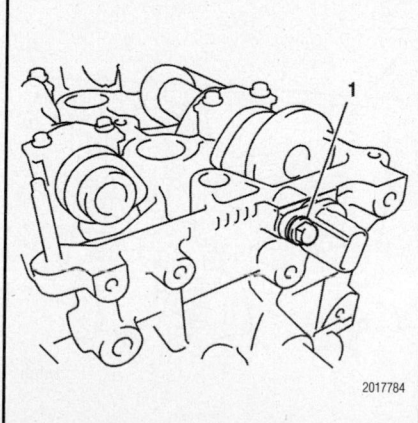

Fig. 234 Remove the bolt (1) and camshaft position sensor—2.4L (LAX)

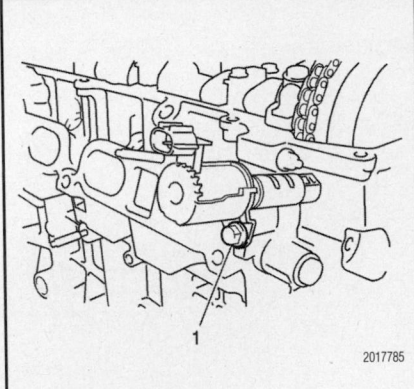

Fig. 235 Remove the bolt (1) and camshaft timing oil control valve from the cylinder head—2.4L (LAX)

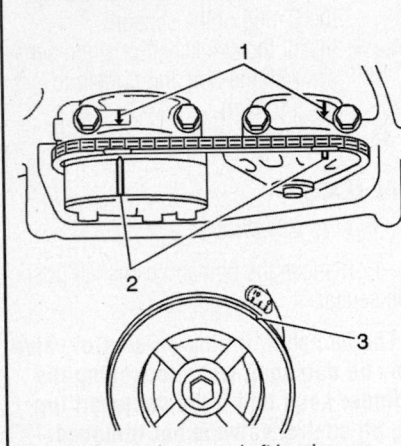

1. Timing mark on camshaft bearing cap
2. Timing mark on camshaft timing gear
3. Crankshaft pulley groove

Fig. 236 Remove the crankshaft pulley—2.4L (LAX)

Fig. 237 Remove the bolts (1–3) and transverse engine mounting bracket—2.4L (LAX)

5. Turn the crankshaft pulley until the groove and the timing mark 0 on the timing chain cover are aligned.

6. Check that each timing mark on the camshaft timing gear and sprocket is aligned with the timing marks located on the camshaft bearing caps as shown. If not, turn the crankshaft by 1 revolution (360°) to align the timing marks as above.

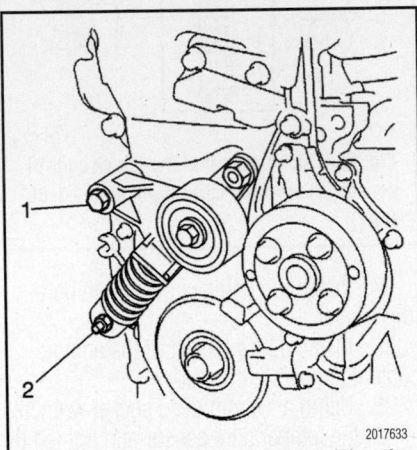

Fig. 238 Remove the bolt (1), nut (2) and V-ribbed belt tensioner assembly—2.4L (LAX)

7. Remove the crankshaft pulley.
8. Remove the 3 bolts and transverse engine mounting bracket.
9. Remove the bolt, nut and V-ribbed belt tensioner assembly.

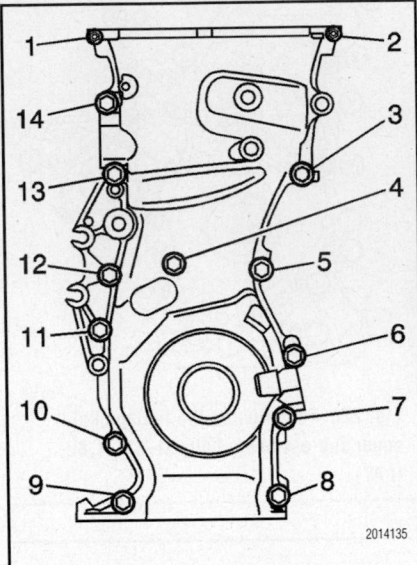

Fig. 239 Remove the 12 bolts (3–14) and 2 nuts (1, 2)—2.4L (LAX)

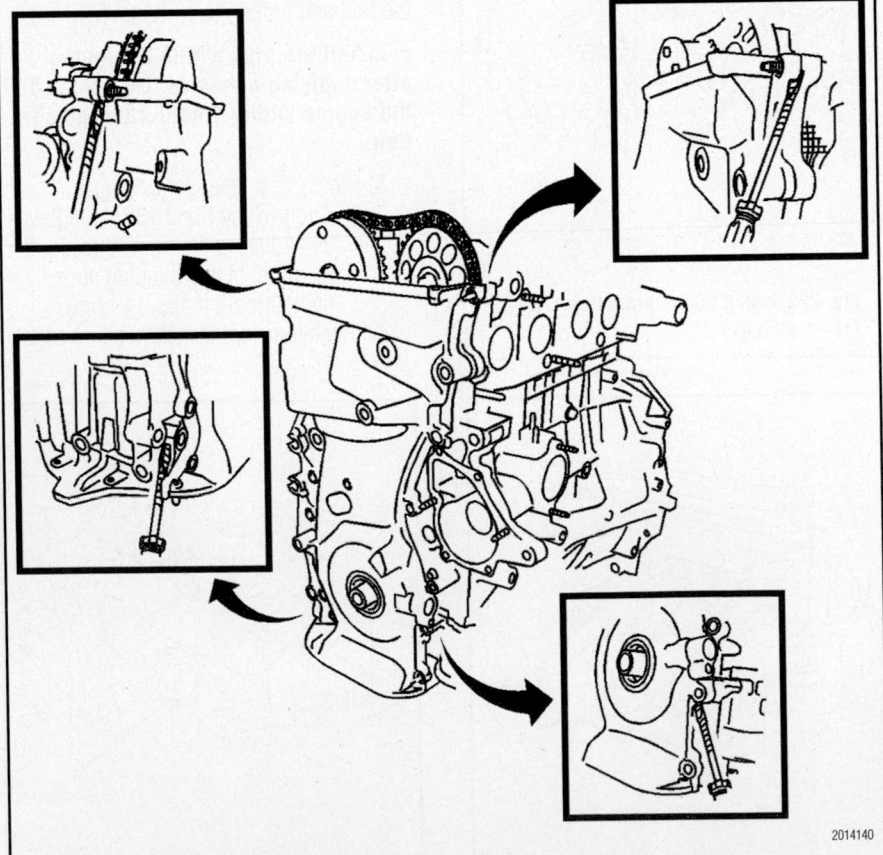

Fig. 240 Remove the timing chain cover by prying the portions between the timing chain cover, cylinder head and cylinder block with a screwdriver—2.4L (LAX)

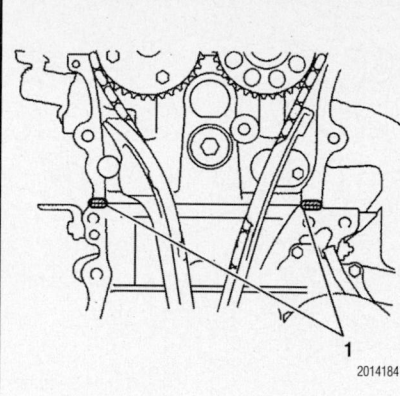

Fig. 241 Apply Three Bond 1207B or equivalent to the indicated areas (1)—2.4L (LAX)

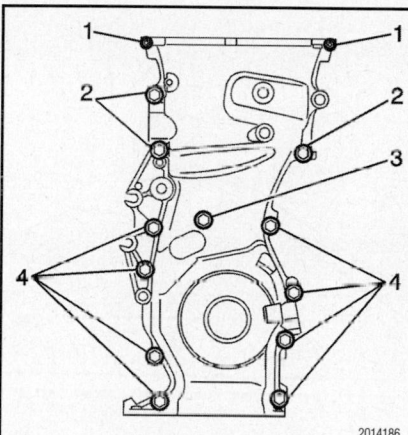

Fig. 242 Install the timing chain cover with the 12 bolts (2–4) and 2 nuts (1)—2.4L (LAX)

10. Remove the crankshaft position sensor.

11. Using an E10 TORX® socket, remove the stud bolt for the V-ribbed belt tensioner.

12. Remove the 12 bolts and 2 nuts.

➡**Tape the screwdriver tip before use.**

13. Remove the timing chain cover by prying the portions between the timing chain cover, cylinder head and cylinder block with a screwdriver.

To install:

➡**Note the following:**

• Remove any oil from the contact surfaces.
• Install the chain cover within 3 minutes of applying seal packing.
• Do not add engine oil for at least 2 hours after installing the chain cover.

14. Apply Three Bond 1207B or equivalent to the indicated areas (Diameter: 0.157–0.177 inch (4.0–4.5 mm).

15. Apply Three Bond 1207B or equivalent to the timing chain cover.

16. Install the timing chain cover with the 12 bolts and 2 nuts.

   a. Tighten bolt 1 to 80 inch lbs. (9.0 Nm).

   b. Tighten bolt 2 to 18 ft. lbs. (25 Nm).

   c. Tighten bolt 3 to 41 ft. lbs. (55 Nm).

   d. Tighten bolt 4 to 8 ft. lbs. (11 Nm).

TIMING CHAIN & SPROCKETS

REMOVAL & INSTALLATION

1.8L (LAY)

See Figures 243 through 255.

1. Before servicing the vehicle, refer to the Precautions Section.

2. Remove the front cover. Refer to Timing Chain Front Cover, removal & installation.

3. Remove the 3 O-rings.

4. Remove the 3 bolts and water pump.

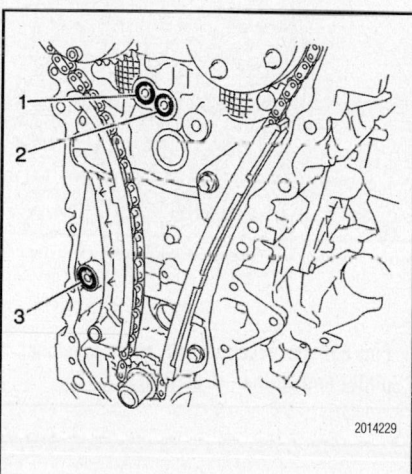

Fig. 243 Remove the 3 O-rings (1–3)—1.8L (LAY)

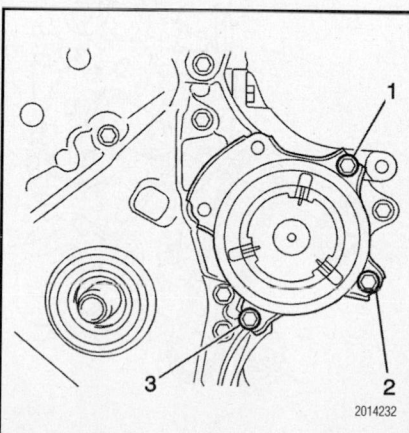

Fig. 244 Remove the bolts (1–3) and water pump—1.8L (LAY)

5. Remove the water pump gasket.

➡**Tape the screwdriver tip before use.**

6. Using a screwdriver and hammer, remove the timing chain cover oil seal.

7. Remove the 3 bolts, gasket and inlet water housing.

8. Remove the 4 bolts and generator bracket.

9. Remove the chain tensioner slipper.

10. Remove the chain vibration damper.

11. Remove the chain assembly.

12. Remove the 2 bolts and chain vibration damper.

13. Hand tighten the crank pulley bolt.

➡**Do not rotate the crankshaft more than 90 degrees.**

14. Turn the crankshaft 90 degrees clockwise to align the adjusting hole of the oil pump drive shaft sprocket with the groove of the oil pump.

15. Remove the crank pulley bolt.

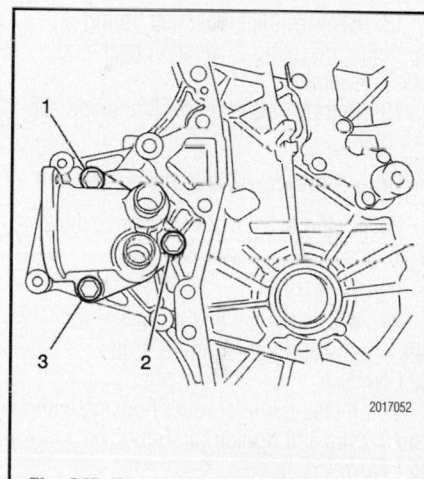

Fig. 245 Remove the bolts (1–3), gasket and inlet water housing—1.8L (LAY)

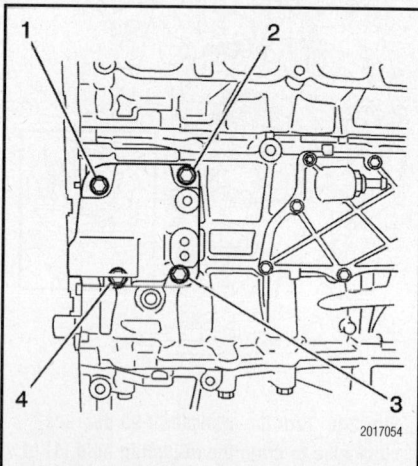

Fig. 246 Remove the bolts (1–4) and generator bracket—1.8L (LAY)

Fig. 247 Remove the 2 bolts (1) and chain vibration damper—1.8L (LAY)

16. Insert a pin punch (3 mm) into the adjusting hole of the oil pump drive shaft sprocket to lock the gear in position, and then remove the nut.

17. Remove the bolt, chain tensioner plate, and spring.

18. Remove the crankshaft timing sprocket, oil pump drive shaft gear, and chain assembly.

19. Remove the crankshaft position sensor plate.

➡ **Tape the screwdriver tip before use.**

20. Using a screwdriver, remove the 2 crankshaft timing gear keys.

To install:

21. Install the generator bracket with the 4 bolts and tighten to 16 ft. lbs. (21 Nm).

22. Install the inlet water housing with the 3 bolts and tighten to 16 ft. lbs. (21 Nm).

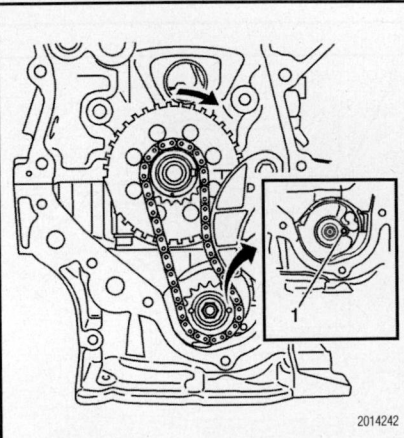

Fig. 248 Turn the crankshaft 90 degrees clockwise to align the adjusting hole (1) of the oil pump drive shaft sprocket with the groove of the oil pump—1.8L (LAY)

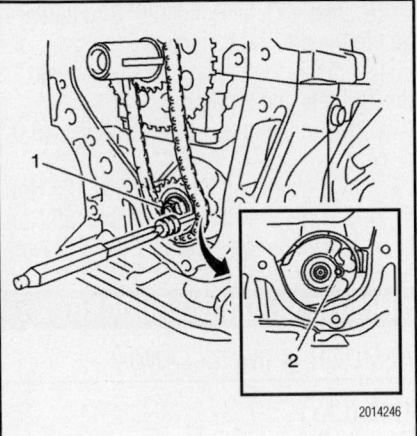

Fig. 249 Insert a pin punch (3 mm) into the adjusting hole (2) of the oil pump drive shaft sprocket (1) to lock the gear in position—1.8L (LAY)

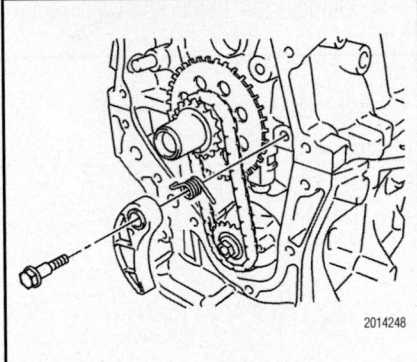

Fig. 250 Remove the bolt, chain tensioner plate, and spring—1.8L (LAY)

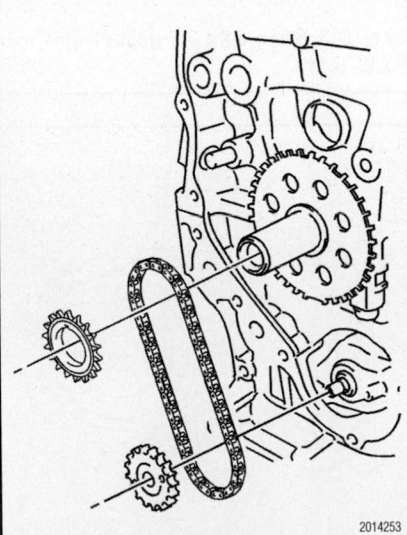

Fig. 251 Remove the crankshaft timing sprocket, oil pump drive shaft gear, and chain assembly—1.8L (LAY)

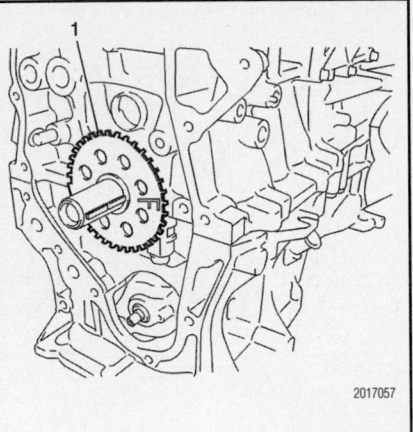

Fig. 252 Remove the crankshaft position sensor plate (1)—1.8L (LAY)

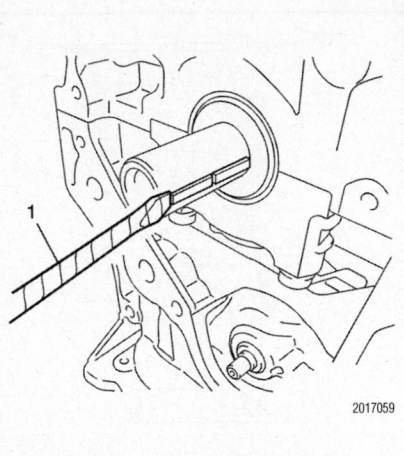

Fig. 253 Using a taped screwdriver (1), remove the 2 crankshaft timing gear keys—1.8L (LAY)

23. Set the crankshaft key.

24. Turn the drive shaft so that the cutout faces right horizontal position.

25. Align the yellow mark links with the timing marks of each gear.

26. Install the sprockets onto the crankshaft and oil pump shaft with the chain on the gears.

27. Insert the damper spring into the adjusting hole, and then install the chain tensioner plate with the bolt and tighten to 7 ft. lbs. (10 Nm).

28. Align the adjusting hole of the oil pump drive shaft sprocket with the groove of the oil pump.

29. Insert a pin punch (3 mm) into the adjusting hole of the oil pump drive shaft gear to lock the gear in position, and then tighten the nut to 21 ft. lbs. (28 Nm).

30. Install the chain vibration damper with the 2 bolts and tighten to 7 ft. lbs. (10 Nm).

31. Install the chain assembly.

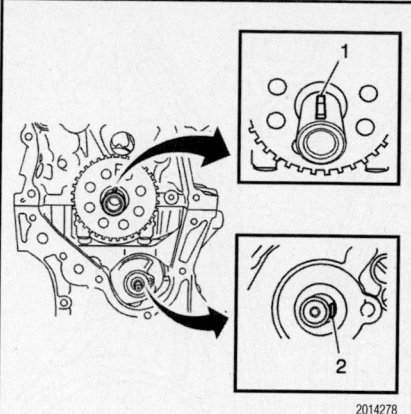

Fig. 254 Set the crankshaft key (1). Turn the drive shaft (2) so that the cutout faces right horizontal position—1.8L (LAY)

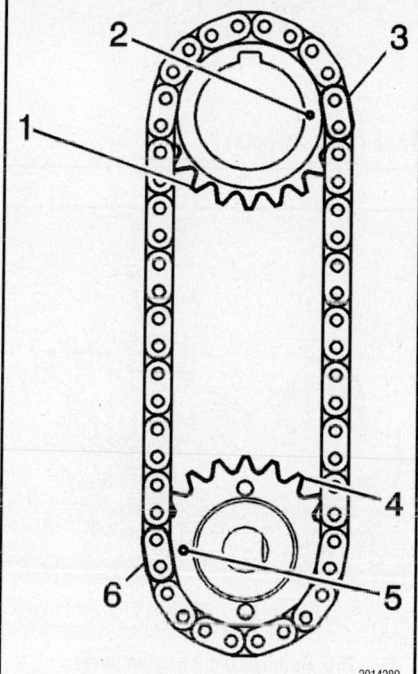

Fig. 255 Align the yellow mark links (3, 6) with the timing marks (2, 5) of each gear (1, 4)—1.8L (LAY)

32. Install the chain tensioner slipper.
33. Install the front cover. Refer to Timing Chain Front Cover, removal & installation.

2.4L (LAX)

See Figures 256 through 264.

1. Remove crankshaft position sensor plate.
2. Remove timing chain guide.
3. Remove chain tensioner slipper.
4. Remove No. 1 chain vibration damper.
5. Remove chain sub-assembly.

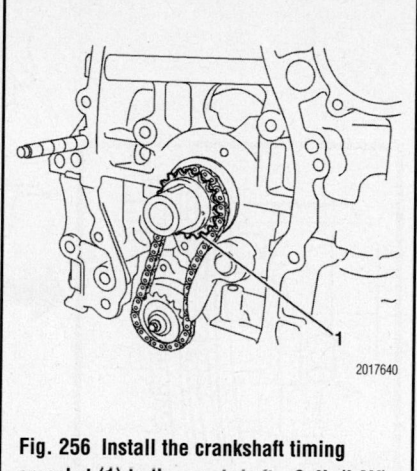

Fig. 256 Install the crankshaft timing sprocket (1) to the crankshaft—2.4L (LAX)

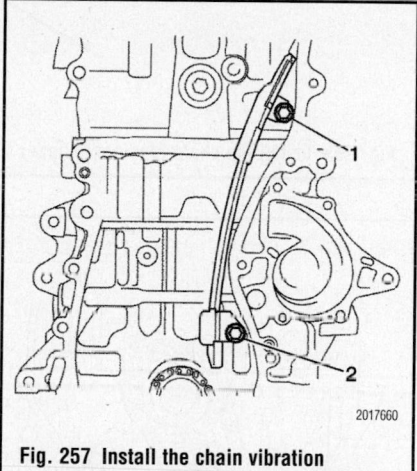

Fig. 257 Install the chain vibration damper with the 2 bolts (1)—2.4L (LAX)

6. Remove crankshaft timing gear or sprocket.

To install:

7. Install the crankshaft timing sprocket to the crankshaft.
8. Install the chain vibration damper with the 2 bolts.
9. Tighten the bolts to 80 inch lbs. (9.0 Nm).
10. Install chain sub-assembly.
11. Set the No. 1 cylinder to TDC/compression.

➡ **The exhaust camshaft gear timing mark corresponds to the exhaust camshaft dowel.**

12. Turn the camshafts with a wrench (using the hexagonal lobe) to align the timing marks on the camshaft timing gear with the timing marks located on the No. 1 and No. 2 bearing caps as shown.
13. Using the crankshaft pulley bolt, turn the crankshaft to position the key on the crankshaft upward.

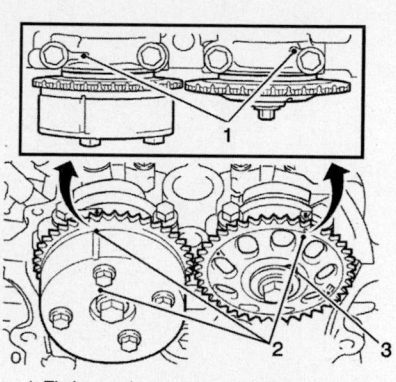

1. Timing marks on the camshaft bearing cap
2. Timing marks on the camshaft timing gear
3. Exhaust camshaft dowel

Fig. 258 Aligning camshaft timing gear—2.4L (LAX)

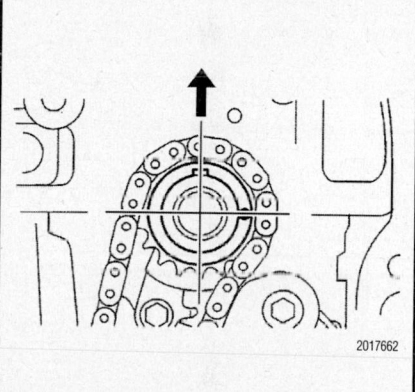

Fig. 259 Using the crankshaft pulley bolt, turn the crankshaft to position the key on the crankshaft upward—2.4L (LAX)

14. Install the chain onto the crankshaft timing sprocket with the gold orange mark link aligned with the timing mark on the crankshaft.
15. Using a suitable tool and a hammer, tap in the crankshaft timing sprocket.
16. Align the gold or yellow links with the timing marks located on the camshaft timing gear and sprocket, then install the chain.
17. Install the chain tensioner slipper with the bolt.
18. Tighten the bolt to 14 ft. lbs. (19 Nm).
19. Install the timing chain guide with the bolt.
20. Tighten the bolt to 80 inch lbs. (9.0 Nm).

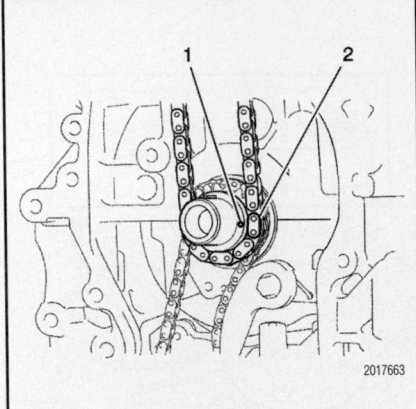

Fig. 260 Install the chain onto the crankshaft timing sprocket with the gold orange mark link (2) aligned with the timing mark (1) on the crankshaft—2.4L (LAX)

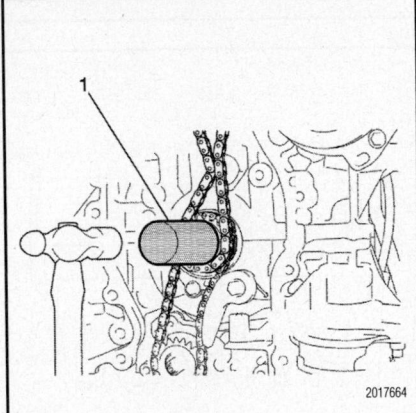

Fig. 261 Using a suitable tool (1) and a hammer, tap in the crankshaft timing sprocket—2.4L (LAX)

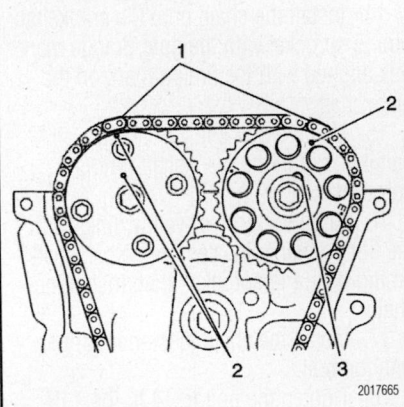

Fig. 262 Align the gold or yellow links (1) with the timing marks (2, 3) located on the camshaft timing gear and sprocket, then install the chain—2.4L (LAX)

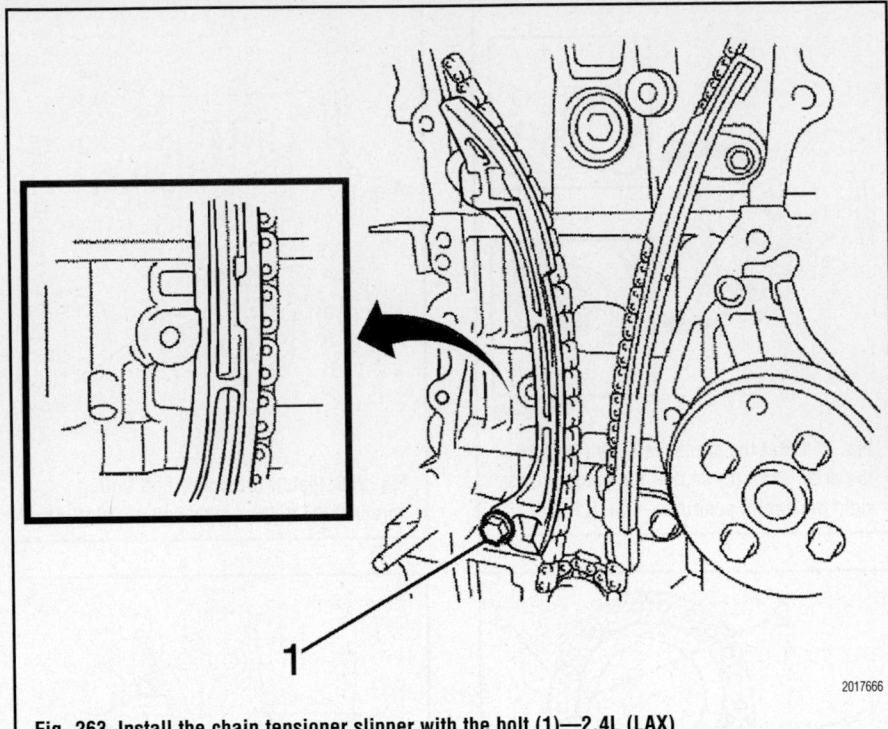

Fig. 263 Install the chain tensioner slipper with the bolt (1)—2.4L (LAX)

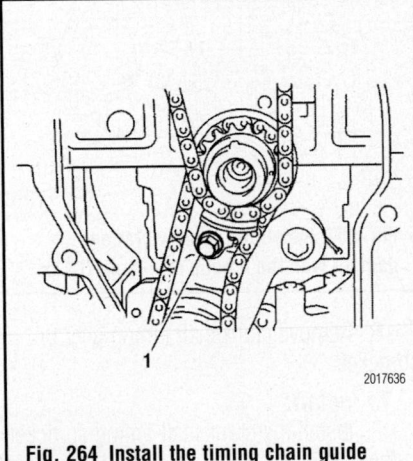

Fig. 264 Install the timing chain guide with the bolt (1)—2.4L (LAX)

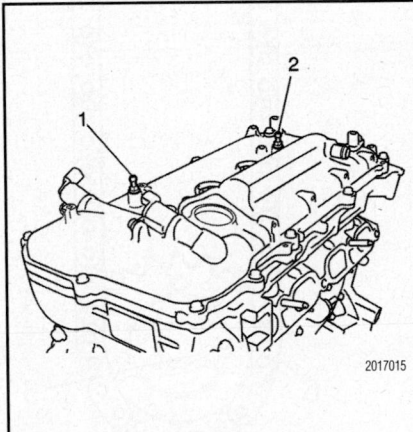

Fig. 265 Remove the 2 engine cover joints (1, 2)—1.8L (LAY)

VALVE COVERS

REMOVAL & INSTALLATION

1.8L (LAY)

See Figures 265 through 268.

➡ Attempting to disengage both front and rear clips at the same time may cause the engine cover to break.

1. Hold the rear of the engine cover and raise it to disengage the 2 clips on the rear of the cover. Continue to raise the cover to disengage the 2 clips on the front of the cover and remove the cover.
2. Remove the oil filler cap.

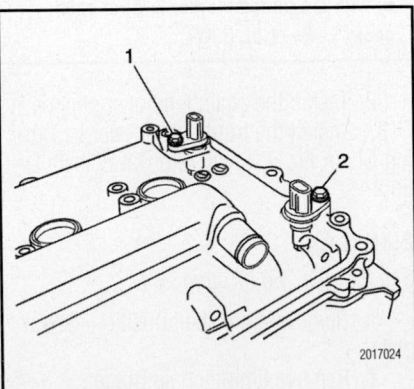

Fig. 266 Remove the bolts (1, 2) and 2 camshaft position sensors—1.8L (LAY)

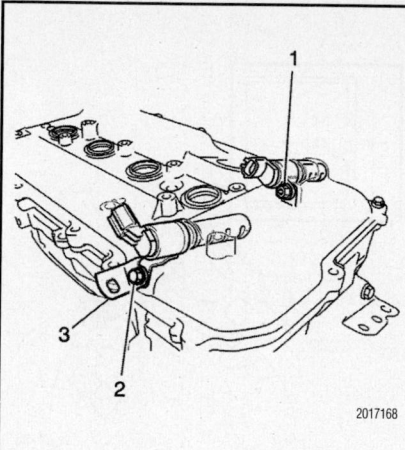

Fig. 267 Remove the bolts (1, 2), O-rings, bracket and 2 oil camshaft timing control valves—1.8L (LAY)

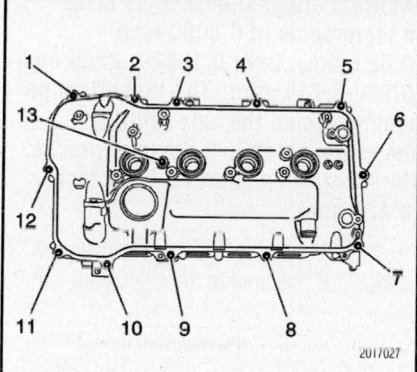

Fig. 268 Remove the bolts (1–13), seal washer and cylinder head cover—1.8L (LAY)

3. Remove the oil filler cap gasket.

4. Remove the 2 engine cover joints.

5. Remove the ignition coils.

6. Using a 14 mm spark plug wrench, remove the 4 spark plugs.

7. Remove the 2 bolts and 2 camshaft position sensors.

8. Remove the 2 bolts, O-rings, bracket and 2 oil camshaft timing control valves.

9. Remove the 13 bolts, seal washer and cylinder head cover.

10. Install a new gasket to the cylinder head cover.

➡**Note the following:**

- Remove any oil from the contact surfaces.
- Install the cylinder head cover within 3 minutes and tighten the bolts within 15 minutes after applying seal packing.
- Do not start the engine for at least 2 hours after the installation.

11. Apply Three Bond 1217B, or equivalent.

12. Install the cylinder head cover with a new seal washer and the bolts and tighten to 7 ft. lbs. (10 Nm).

13. Apply a light coat of engine oil to a new O-ring, then install it onto the camshaft timing oil control valve.

14. Install the 2 camshaft timing oil control valves and bracket with the 2 bolts and tighten to 7 ft. lbs. (10 Nm).

15. Install the camshaft position sensor:

a. Apply a light coat of engine oil to the O-ring of the sensor.

b. Install the 2 sensors with the 2 bolts and tighten to 7 ft. lbs. (10 Nm).

16. Using a 14 mm spark plug wrench, install the 4 spark plugs and tighten to 15 ft. lbs. (20 Nm).

17. Install the ignition coils.

18. Install the 2 engine cover joints and tighten to 7 ft. lbs. (10 Nm).

19. Install the oil filler cap gasket.

20. Install the oil filler cap.

21. Position the engine cover and engage the two front fasteners. Engage the two fasteners on the rear of the cover.

2.4L (LAX)

See Figures 269 through 271.

1. Remove the 2 engine cover fasteners and 2 plastic retainers. Remove the engine cover.

2. Remove ignition coil assembly. Refer to Ignition Coil, removal & installation.

3. Remove the 2 ventilation hoses from the cylinder head cover.

4. Remove the 2 bolts and separate the 2 wire harness brackets.

5. Remove the 8 bolts and 2 nuts, then remove the cylinder head cover and gasket.

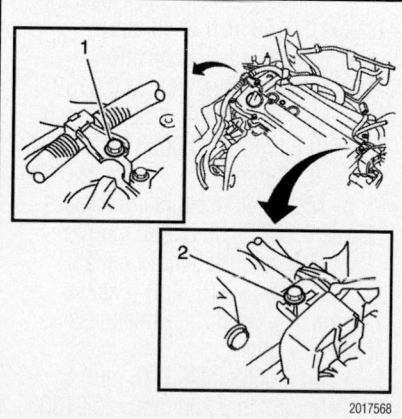

Fig. 269 Remove the bolts (1, 2) and separate the 2 wire harness brackets—2.4L (LAX)

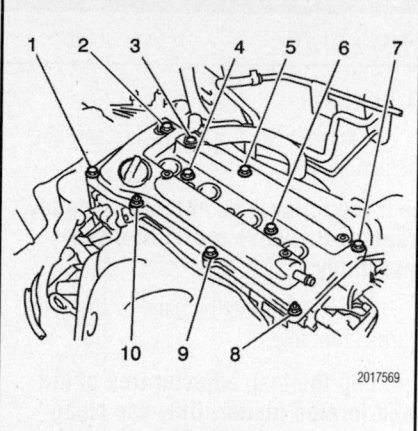

Fig. 270 Remove the 8 bolts (1–7, 9) and 2 nuts (8, 10), then remove the cylinder head cover and gasket—2.4L (LAX)

To install:

6. Remove any old sealing material from the contact surface.

7. Install the cylinder head cover gasket and cover with the 8 bolts and 2 nuts, then tighten:

- Bolt 1 to 8 ft. lbs. (11 Nm).
- Bolt 2 to 10 ft. lbs. (14 Nm).
- Nut 3 to 8 ft. lbs. (11 Nm).

8. Install the 2 engine wire harness brackets with the 2 bolts and tighten to 74 inch lbs. (8.4 Nm).

9. Connect the 2 ventilation hoses to the cylinder head cover.

10. Install the ignition coil assembly. Refer to Ignition Coil, removal & installation.

11. Inspect for oil leak.

12. Install engine cover and tighten fasteners to 62 inch lbs. (7 Nm).

13. Install the 2 engine cover plastic retainers.

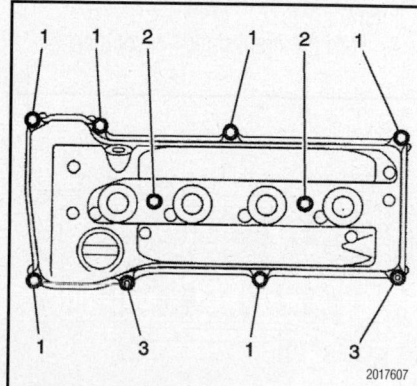

Fig. 271 Install the cylinder head cover gasket and cover with the 8 bolts (1, 2) and 2 nuts (3), then tighten as specified—2.4L (LAX)

VALVE LASH

INSPECTION

1.8L (LAY)

1. Inspect No. 1 valve rocker arm sub-assembly.

➡**If the roller does not turn smoothly, replace the valve rocker arm sub-assembly.**

2. Turn the roller by hand to check that it turns smoothly.

➡**Keep the lash adjuster free of dirt and foreign matter. Only use clean engine oil.**

3. Inspect valve lash adjuster assembly.

2.4L (LAX)

See Figures 272 and 273.

1. Remove the engine under right cover.
2. Remove the 2 engine cover fasteners and 2 plastic retainers. Remove the engine cover.
3. Remove ignition coil assembly. Refer to Ignition Coil, removal & installation.
4. Remove the spark plug. Refer to Spark Plugs, removal & installation.
5. Remove the cylinder head cover.
6. Set No. 1 cylinder to TDC/compression.
7. Check only the valves indicated:
    a. Using a feeler gage, measure the clearance between the valve lifter and camshaft.
    b. Record any out-of-specification valve clearance measurements. They will be used later to determine the required replacement valve clearance lifters.
8. Turn the crankshaft 1 revolution

Fig. 272 Set No. 1 cylinder to TDC/compression. Check only the valves indicated—2.4L (LAX)

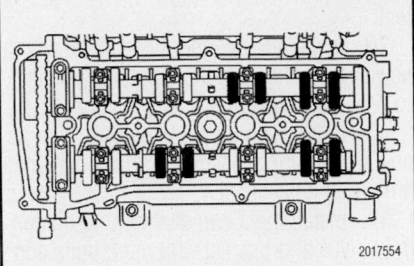

Fig. 273 Turn the crankshaft 1 revolution (360°) and set the No. 4 cylinder to TDC/compression. Check only the valves indicated—2.4L (LAX)

(360°) and set the No. 4 cylinder to TDC/compression.

9. Check only the valves indicated:
    a. Using a feeler gage, measure the clearance between the valve lifter and camshaft.
    b. Record any out-of-specification valve clearance measurements. They will be used later to determine the required replacement valve lifters.

ADJUSTMENT

2.4L (LAX)

See Figures 274 and 275.

1. Remove the exhaust camshaft. Refer to Camshaft and Valve Lifters, removal & installation.
2. Remove the intake camshaft. Refer to Camshaft and Valve Lifters, removal & installation.
3. Using a micrometer, measure the thickness of the removed valve lifters.
4. Calculate the thickness of a new lifter so that the valve clearance comes within the specified values.
    • Calculation Example (intake):
    a. Measured intake valve clearance equals 0.0158 inch (0.40 mm).
    • (Measured-Specification = Excess clearance) (a) 0.0158 inch (0.40 mm) - 0.0094 inch (0.24 mm) = 0.0063 inch (0.16 mm)
    b. Measured used lifter thickness equals 0.2067 inch (5.250 mm).
    c. New lifter thickness equals 0.2130 inch (5.410 mm) (Excess clearance + Used lifter thickness = Ideal new lifter).
    • (a) 0.0063 inch (0.16 mm) + 0.2067 in 5.250 mm) = 0.2130 inch (5.410 mm)
    d. Closest new lifter equals 5.420 mm (0.2134 in.) - Select No. 42 lifter.

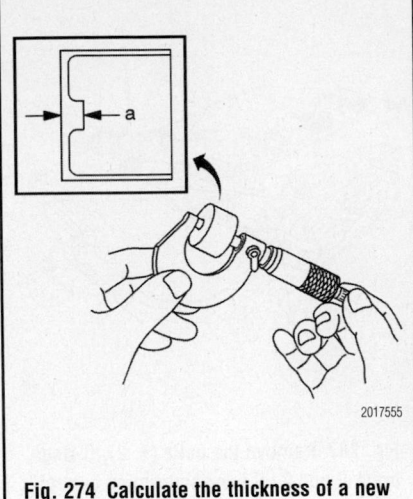

Fig. 274 Calculate the thickness of a new lifter—2.4L (LAX)

➡**Lifters are available in 35 sizes in increments of 0.0008 inch (0.020 mm), from 0.1992-0.2260 inch (5.060-5.740 mm). The identification number inside the valve lifters shows the value to 2 decimal places. The illustration shows 0.2134 inch (5.420 mm).**

5. Select a new lifter with a thickness as close as possible to the calculated values.
    a. Standard intake valve clearance (cold): 0.007-0.011 inch (0.19-0.29 mm).
    • EXAMPLE: The 0.2067 inch (5.250 mm) lifter is installed, and the measured clearance is 0.0157 inch (0.400 mm). Replace the 0.2067 inch (5.250 mm) lifter with a new No. 42 lifter.

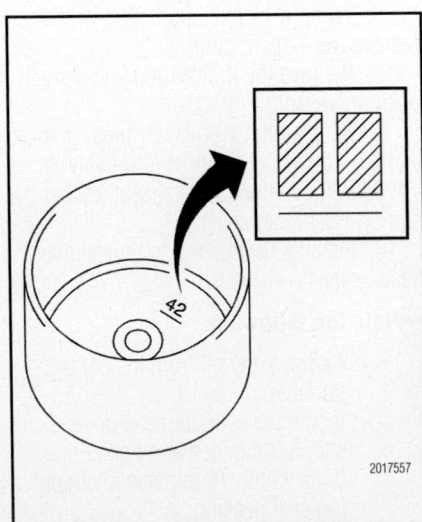

Fig. 275 View of 0.2134 inch (5.420 mm) valve lifter—2.4L (LAX)

b. Standard exhaust valve clearance (cold): 0.38-0.48 mm (0.015-0.019 in).

- EXAMPLE: The 0.2102 inch (5.340 mm) lifter is installed, and the measured clearance is 0.020 inch (0.510 mm). Replace the 0.2102 inch (5.340 mm) lifter with a new No. 42 lifter.

6. Install the selected valve lifter.
7. Install the intake camshaft. Refer to Camshaft and Valve Lifters, removal & installation.

8. Install the exhaust camshaft. Refer to Camshaft and Valve Lifters, removal & installation.
9. Install the No. 1 chain tensioner.
10. Install the cylinder head cover.
11. Install the spark plug. Refer to Spark Plugs, removal & installation.
12. Install the ignition coil assembly.

Refer to Ignition Coil, removal & installation.
13. Inspect for oil leak.
14. Inspect the ignition timing.
15. Install engine cover and tighten fasteners to 62 inch lbs. (7 Nm).
16. Install the 2 engine cover plastic retainers.
17. Install the engine under right cover.

ENGINE PERFORMANCE & EMISSION CONTROLS

CAMSHAFT POSITION (CMP) SENSOR

LOCATION

See Figures 276 and 277.

REMOVAL & INSTALLATION

1.8L (LAY)

See Figures 278 through 280.

➡Attempting to disengage both front and rear clips at the same time may cause the engine cover to break.

1. Hold the rear of the engine cover and raise it to disengage the 2 clips on the rear of the cover.
2. Continue to raise the cover to disengage the 2 clips on the front of the cover and remove the cover.
3. If removing the exhaust sensor, disconnect the duty vacuum switching valve

connector and the 3 engine wire harness clamps.
4. Disconnect the camshaft position sensor connector.
5. Remove the bolt and the camshaft position sensor.

To install:
6. Apply a light coat of engine oil to the O-ring on the camshaft position sensor.
7. Install the camshaft position sensor with the bolt and tighten to 7 ft. lbs. (10 Nm).
8. Connect the camshaft position sensor.
9. For exhaust sensor, connect the 3 engine wire harness clamps and duty vacuum switching connector (3).
10. Inspect for oil leaks.
11. Position the engine cover and engage the two front fasteners. Engage the two fasteners on the rear of the cover.

2.4L (LAX)

See Figure 281.

1. Remove the 2 engine cover fasteners and 2 plastic retainers. Remove the engine cover from the engine.
2. Remove the air cleaner cap with hose.
3. Disconnect the camshaft position sensor connector.
4. Remove the bolt and the camshaft position sensor.

To install:
5. Apply a light coat of engine oil to the O-ring of the sensor.
6. Install the camshaft position sensor with the bolt and tighten to 80 inch lbs. (9.0 Nm).
7. Connect the camshaft position sensor connector.
8. Install the air cleaner cap with hose.
9. Inspect for engine oil leak.
10. Install engine cover and tighten fasteners to 62 inch lbs. (7 Nm).
11. Install the 2 engine cover plastic retainers.

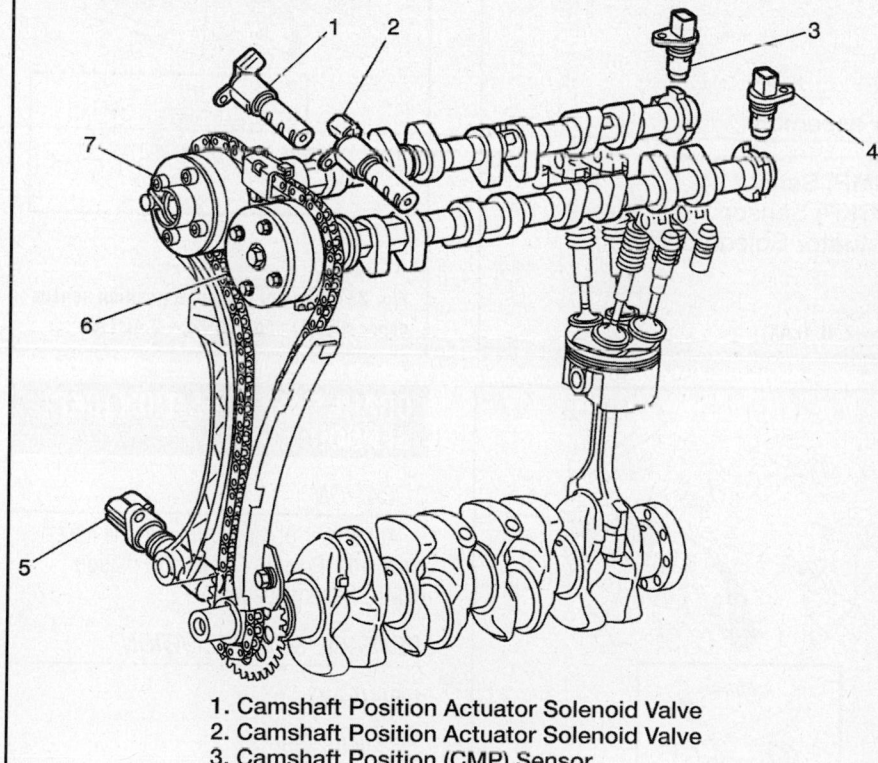

1. Camshaft Position Actuator Solenoid Valve
2. Camshaft Position Actuator Solenoid Valve
3. Camshaft Position (CMP) Sensor
4. Camshaft Position (CMP) Sensor
5. Crankshaft Position (CKP) Sensor
6. Camshaft timing gear assembly
7. Camshaft timing gear assembly

2034347

Fig. 276 Camshaft Position (CMP) and Crankshaft Position (CKP) Sensor Locations—1.8L (LAY)

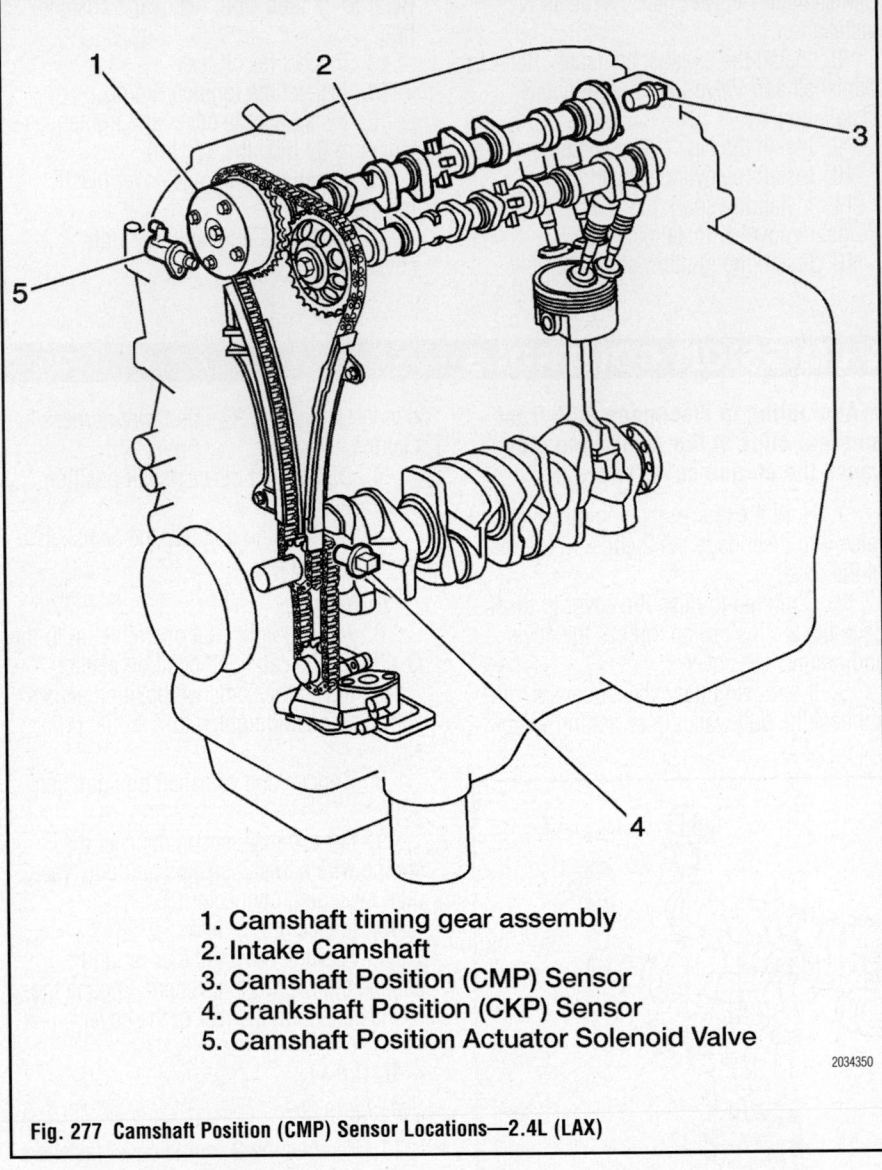

1. Camshaft timing gear assembly
2. Intake Camshaft
3. Camshaft Position (CMP) Sensor
4. Crankshaft Position (CKP) Sensor
5. Camshaft Position Actuator Solenoid Valve

Fig. 277 Camshaft Position (CMP) Sensor Locations—2.4L (LAX)

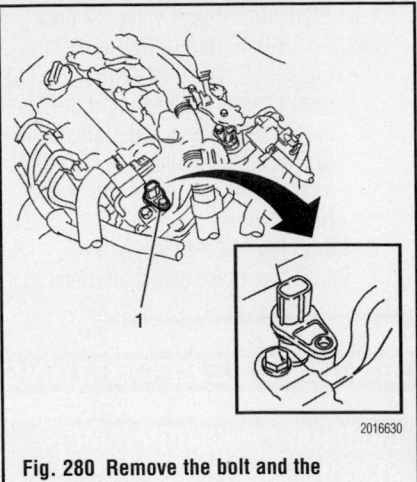

Fig. 280 Remove the bolt and the camshaft position sensor (1)—Intake—1.8L (LAY)

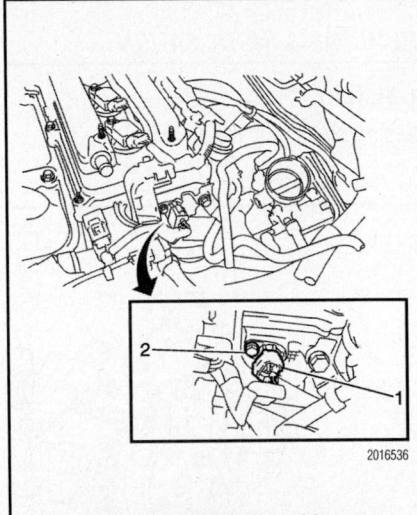

Fig. 281 View of camshaft position sensor connector (1) and bolt (2)—2.4L LAX

CRANKSHAFT POSITION (CKP) SENSOR

LOCATION

At the rear of the engine, on the lower back side. Refer to Camshaft Position (CMP) Sensor, location.

REMOVAL & INSTALLATION

1.8L (LAY)

See Figure 282.

1. Remove the right engine under cover.
2. Disconnect the crankshaft position sensor connector.
3. Remove the bolt and crankshaft position sensor.

To install:

4. Apply a light coat of engine oil to the O-ring on the crankshaft position sensor.

Fig. 278 If removing the exhaust sensor, disconnect the duty vacuum switching valve connector (3) and the 3 engine wire harness clamps (1, 2, 4)—1.8L (LAY)

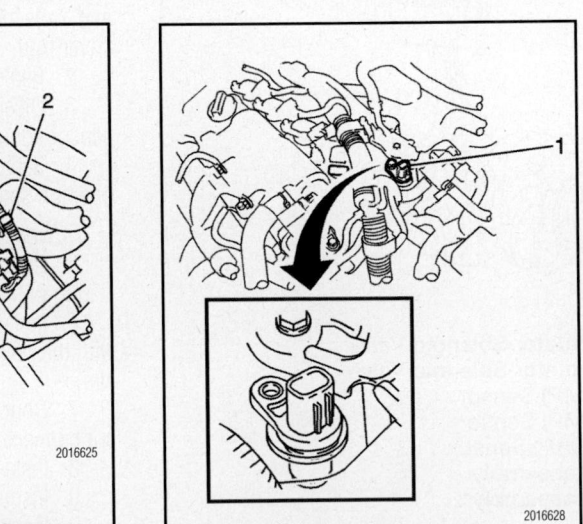

Fig. 279 Remove the bolt and the camshaft position sensor (1)—Exhaust—1.8L (LAY)

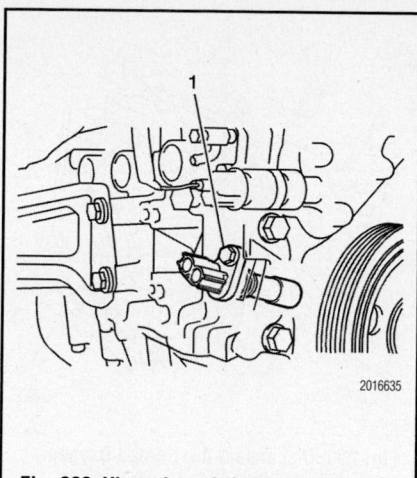

Fig. 282 View of crankshaft position sensor with the bolt (1)—1.8L LAY

5. Install the crankshaft position sensor with the bolt and tighten to 80 inch lbs. (9.0 Nm).

6. Connect the crankshaft position sensor connector.

7. Inspect for an oil leak.

8. Install the right engine under cover.

2.4L (LAX)

See Figure 283

1. Disconnect the cable from the negative battery terminal. Refer to Battery, precautions.

2. Remove the right engine under cover.

3. Remove the alternator. Refer to Alternator, removal & installation.

4. Disconnect the crankshaft position sensor connector.

5. Separate the crankshaft position sensor connector clamp and wire harness.

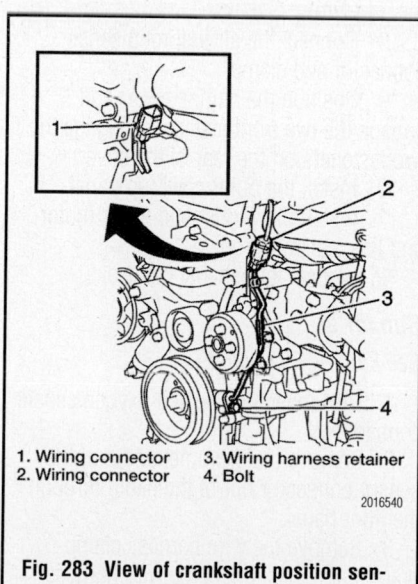

1. Wiring connector   3. Wiring harness retainer
2. Wiring connector   4. Bolt

Fig. 283 View of crankshaft position sensor and wiring harness—2.4L LAX

6. Remove the bolt and crankshaft position sensor.

To install:

7. Apply a light coat of engine oil to the O-ring on the crankshaft position sensor.

8. Install the crankshaft position sensor with the bolt and tighten to 80 inch lbs. (9.0 Nm).

→**Do not twist the O-ring.**

9. Install the wire harness and crankshaft position sensor connector clamp.

10. Connect the crankshaft position sensor connector.

11. Install the alternator. Refer to Alternator, removal & installation.

12. Install the right engine under cover.

13. Connect the cable to the negative battery terminal.

14. Inspect for oil leak.

ENGINE COOLANT TEMPERATURE (ECT) SENSOR

LOCATION

See Figures 284 and 285.

At the rear of the engine cylinder head, below the brake master cylinder

REMOVAL & INSTALLATION

1.8L (LAY)

See Figure 284.

1. Drain the engine coolant. Refer to Engine Coolant, Drain & Refill Procedure.

→**Attempting to disengage both front and rear clips at the same time may cause the engine cover to break.**

2. Hold the rear of the engine cover and raise it to disengage the 2 clips on the rear of the cover.

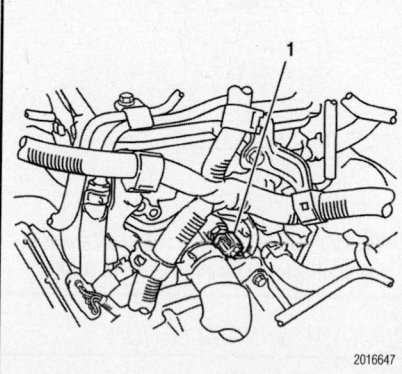

Fig. 284 Engine coolant temperature sensor and electrical connector (1) location—1.8L (LAY)

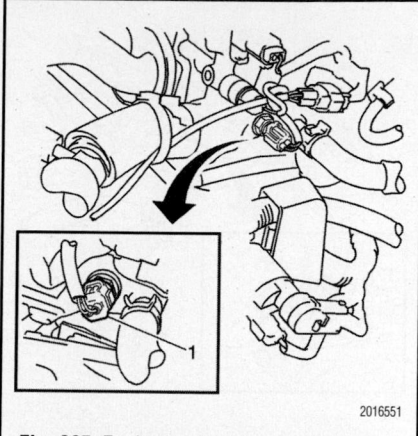

Fig. 285 Engine coolant temperature sensor and electrical connector (1) location—2.4L (LAX)

3. Continue to raise the cover to disengage the 2 clips on the front of the cover and remove the cover.

4. Remove the air cleaner cap sub-assembly with hose.

5. Disconnect the engine coolant temperature sensor connector.

6. Remove the engine coolant temperature sensor.

To install:

7. Install the engine coolant temperature sensor through a new gasket and tighten to 14 ft. lbs. (20 Nm).

8. Connect the engine coolant temperature sensor connector.

9. Add engine coolant. Refer to Engine Coolant, Drain & Refill Procedure.

10. Inspect for a coolant leak.

11. Install the air cleaner cap sub-assembly with hose.

12. Position the engine cover and engage the two front fasteners. Engage the two fasteners on the rear of the cover.

2.4L (LAX)

See Figure 286.

1. Remove the 2 engine cover fasteners and 2 plastic retainers. Remove the engine cover from the engine.

2. Drain the engine coolant. Refer to Engine Coolant, Drain & Refill Procedure.

3. Remove the air cleaner cap with hose.

4. Remove the air cleaner case.

5. Disconnect the engine coolant temperature sensor connector.

6. Remove the engine coolant temperature sensor and gasket.

To install:

7. Install the engine coolant temperature sensor through a new gasket and tighten to 14 ft. lbs. (20 Nm).

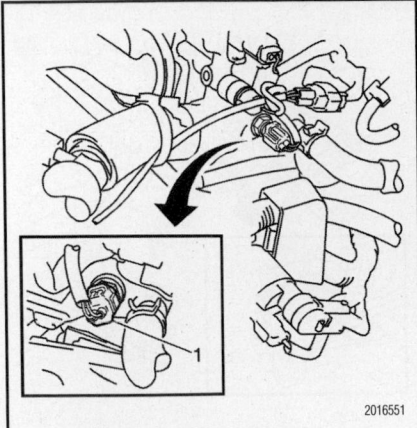

Fig. 286 Engine coolant temperature sensor and electrical connector (1) location—2.4L (LAX)

8. Connect the engine coolant temperature sensor connector.

9. Install the air cleaner case.

10. Install the air cleaner cap with hose.

11. Add engine coolant. Refer to Engine Coolant, Drain & Refill Procedure.

12. Inspect for coolant leak.

13. Install engine cover and tighten fasteners to 62 inch lbs. (7 Nm).

14. Install the 2 engine cover plastic retainers.

HEATED OXYGEN (HO2S) SENSOR

LOCATION

See Figures 287 through 290.

The Heated Oxygen Sensor (HO2S) is located as noted:

- Bank 1 Sensor 1—On the rear exhaust bank, above the catalytic converter
- Bank 1 Sensor 2—On the rear exhaust bank, below the catalytic converter

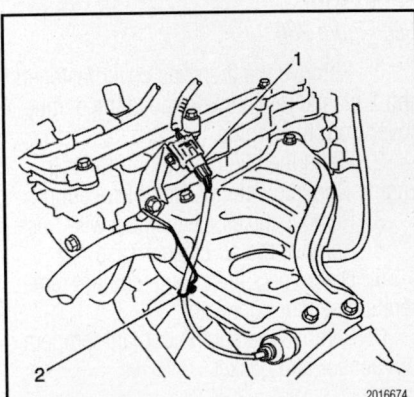

Fig. 287 Heated Oxygen (HO2S) Sensor 1, connector (1), and wire retainer (2)—1.8L (LAY)

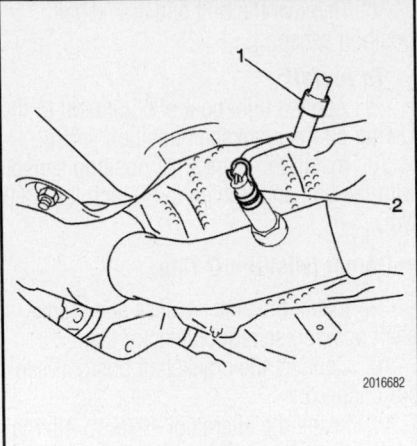

Fig. 288 Heated Oxygen (HO2S) Sensor 2 (2) and connector (1)—1.8L (LAY)

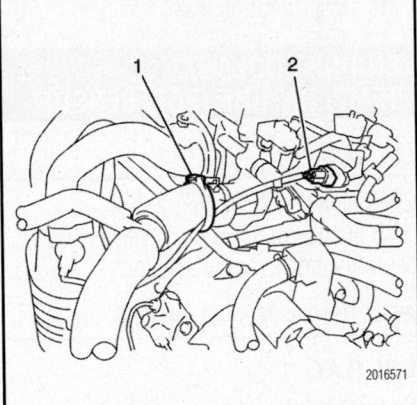

Fig. 289 Heated Oxygen (HO2S) Sensor 1, connector (2), and wiring harness clamp (1) location—2.4L (LAX)

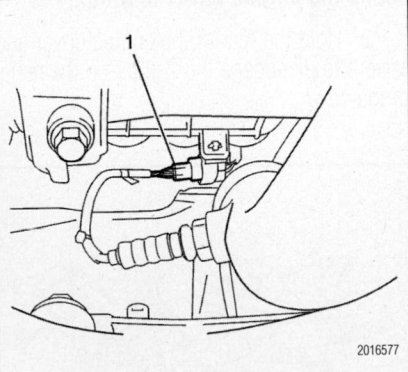

Fig. 290 Heated Oxygen (HO2S) Sensor 2 and connector (1) location—2.4L (LAX)

REMOVAL & INSTALLATION

1.8L (LAY)

Sensor 1

See Figure 291.

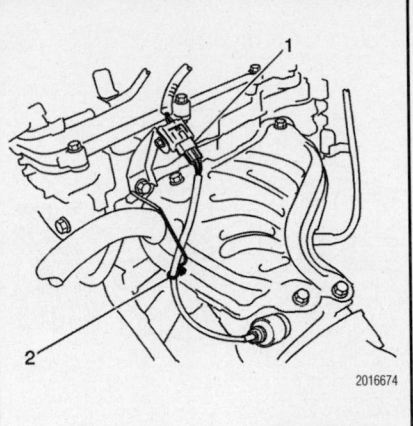

Fig. 291 Disconnect the Heated Oxygen (HO2S) Sensor 1 connector (1) and clamp (2)—1.8L (LAY)

1. Remove the windshield wiper motor and link assembly.

2. Remove the outer cowl top panel.

➡**Attempting to disengage both front and rear clips at the same time may cause the engine cover to break.**

3. Hold the rear of the engine cover and raise it to disengage the 2 clips on the rear of the cover.

4. Continue to raise the cover to disengage the 2 clips on the front of the cover and remove the cover.

5. Disconnect the Heated Oxygen (HO2S) Sensor 1 and clamp.

6. Using the oxygen sensor remover/installer (EN-46577), remove the air fuel ratio sensor.

To install:

7. Using the remover/installer, install the air fuel ratio sensor and tighten to 32 ft. lbs. (44 Nm).

8. Connect the air fuel ratio sensor connector and clamp.

9. Position the engine cover and engage the two front fasteners. Engage the two fasteners on the rear of the cover.

10. Install the outer cowl top panel.

11. Install the windshield wiper motor and link assembly.

12. Inspect for exhaust gas leaks.

Sensor 2

See Figures 292 and 293.

1. Disconnect the heated oxygen sensor connector.

2. Remove the grommet and pull the sensor connector out of the cabin through the floor panel.

3. Remove the wire harness clamp bracket and disconnect the wire harness clamp.

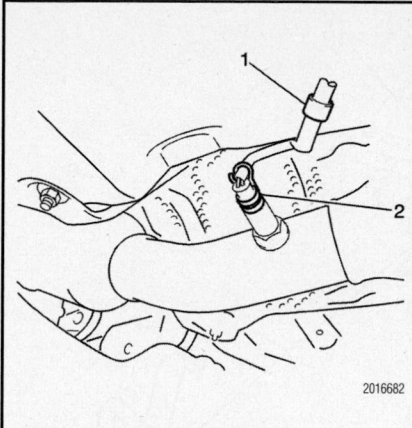

Fig. 292 Disconnect the Heated Oxygen (HO2S) Sensor 1 connector (2) and clamp (1)

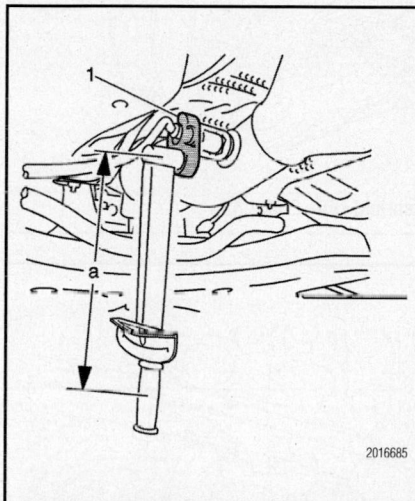

Fig. 293 Installing Heated Oxygen (HO2S) Sensor 2—1.8L (LAY)

4. Using an oxygen sensor wrench (J-39194-C), remove the heated oxygen sensor.

To install:

➡ This torque value can be obtained by using a torque wrench with a fulcrum length (a) of 11.81 inches (300 mm) and J-39194-C wrench of 1.18 inches (30 mm). This torque value is effective when the J-39194-C wrench is parallel to the torque wrench.

5. Using the oxygen sensor wrench, install the heated oxygen sensor onto the front exhaust pipe and tighten:
- Tighten without the wrench to 32 ft. lbs. (44 Nm).
- Tighten with the wrench to 30 ft. lbs. (40 Nm).

6. Install the wire harness clamp bracket and connect the wire harness clamp.

7. Pass the sensor connector through the floor panel and install the grommet.

8. Connect the heated oxygen sensor connector.

9. Inspect for exhaust gas leaks.

2.4L (LAX)

Sensor 1

See Figures 294 and 295.

1. Disconnect the air fuel ratio sensor connector and wire harness clamp.

2. Using oxygen sensor wrench (J-39194-C), remove the air fuel ratio sensor.

To install:

➡ This torque value can be obtained by using a torque wrench with a fulcrum length (a) of 11.81 inches (300 mm) and J-39194-C wrench of 1.18 inches (30 mm). This torque value is effective when the J-39194-C wrench is parallel to the torque wrench.

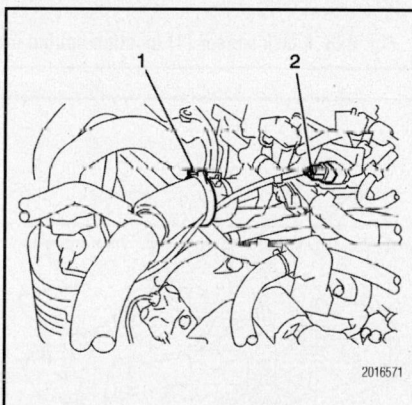

Fig. 294 Disconnect the Heated Oxygen (HO2S) Sensor 1 connector (2) and clamp (1)—2.4L (LAX)

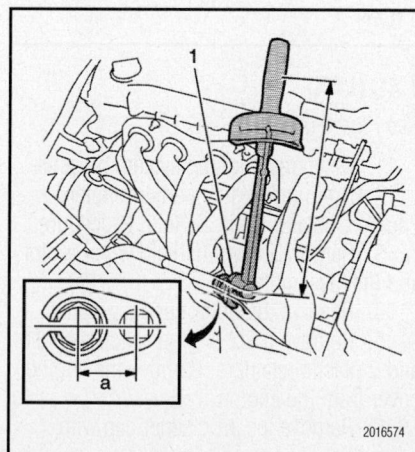

Fig. 295 Installing Heated Oxygen (HO2S) Sensor 1—2.4L (LAX)

3. Using the oxygen sensor wrench, install the heated oxygen sensor and tighten:
- Tighten without the wrench to 32 ft. lbs. (44 Nm).
- Tighten with the wrench to 30 ft. lbs. (40 Nm).

4. Connect the heated oxygen sensor connector and wire harness clamp.

5. Install the exhaust manifold heat insulator with the 4 bolts and tighten to 9 ft. lbs. (12 Nm).

6. Inspect for exhaust leaks.

Sensor 2

See Figure 296.

1. Disconnect the heated oxygen sensor connector.

2. Separate the wire harness grommet.

3. Disconnect the heated oxygen sensor connector.

4. Using the oxygen sensor wrench (J-39194-C), remove the heated oxygen sensor.

To install:

➡ This torque value can be obtained by using a torque wrench with a fulcrum length (a) of 11.81 inches (300 mm) and J-39194-C wrench of 1.18 inches (30 mm). This torque value is effective when the J-39194-C wrench is parallel to the torque wrench.

5. Install the heated oxygen sensor and tighten:
- Tighten without the wrench to 32 ft. lbs. (44 Nm).
- Tighten with the wrench to 30 ft. lbs. (40 Nm).

6. Connect the wire harness grommet.

7. Connect the heated oxygen sensor connector.

8. Inspect for exhaust leaks.

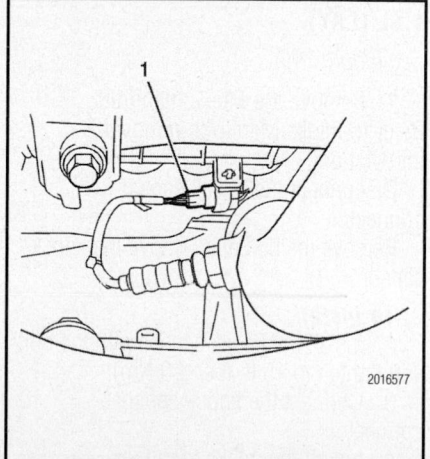

Fig. 296 Heated Oxygen (HO2S) Sensor 2 location (1)—2.4L (LAX)

INTAKE AIR TEMPERATURE (IAT) SENSOR

LOCATION

The Intake Air Temperature (IAT) sensor is an integral part of the Mass Air Flow (MAF) sensor that is mounted in the air cleaner assembly.

REMOVAL & INSTALLATION

Refer to Mass Air Flow (MAF) Sensor, removal & installation.

KNOCK SENSOR (KS)

LOCATION

1.8L (LAY)

See Figure 297.

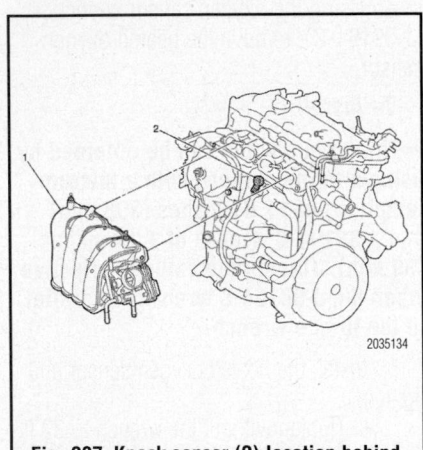

Fig. 297 Knock sensor (2) location behind intake manifold (1)—1.8L (LAY)

2.4L (LAX)

See Figure 298.

REMOVAL & INSTALLATION

1.8L (LAY)

See Figure 299.

1. Remove the intake manifold. Refer to Intake Manifold, removal & installation.

Disconnect the knock sensor connector.

Remove the bolt and remove the knock sensor.

To install:

2. Install the knock sensor with the bolt and tighten to 15 ft. lbs. (20 Nm).
3. Connect the knock sensor connector.
4. Install the intake manifold. Refer to Intake Manifold, removal & installation.

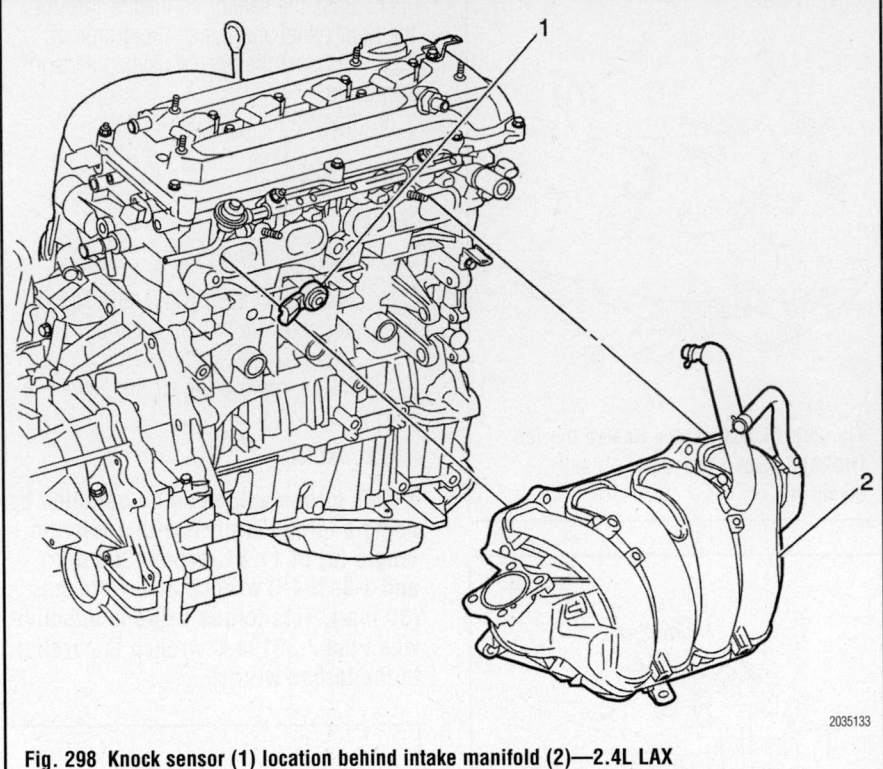

Fig. 298 Knock sensor (1) location behind intake manifold (2)—2.4L LAX

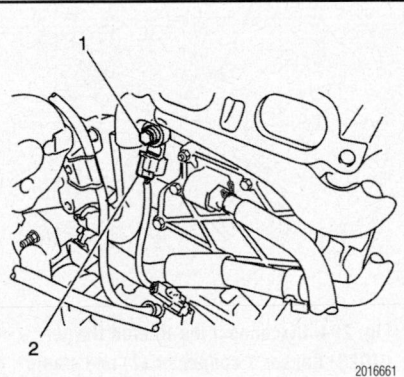

Fig. 299 Disconnect the knock sensor connector (2). Remove the bolt (1)—1.8L (LAY)

2.4L (LAX)

See Figure 300.

1. Discharge the fuel system pressure.
2. Drain the engine coolant. Refer to Engine Coolant, Drain & Refill Procedure.
3. Remove the windshield wiper motor and link assembly.
4. Remove the outer cowl top panel.
5. Remove the 2 engine cover fasteners and 2 plastic retainers. Remove the engine cover from the engine.
6. Remove the air cleaner cap with hose.
7. Remove the throttle body. Refer to Throttle Body, removal & installation.

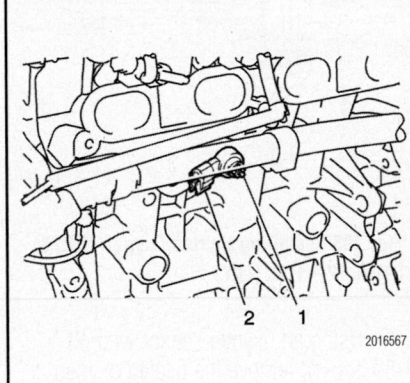

Fig. 300 Remove the nut (1) and knock sensor (2)—2.4L LAX

8. Remove the fuel delivery pipe with fuel tube.
9. Remove the intake manifold. Refer to Intake Manifold, removal & installation.
10. Disconnect the ventilation hose.
11. Disconnect the union to check valve hose.
12. Separate the wire harness clamp from the intake manifold.
13. Disconnect the knock sensor connector.
14. Remove the nut and knock sensor.

To install:

15. To install, reverse the removal procedure and note the following:

- Tighten the knock sensor nut to 15 ft. lbs. (20 Nm).

16. Add engine coolant. Refer to Engine Coolant, Drain & Refill Procedure.

17. Inspect for coolant leak.

18. Inspect for fuel leak.

19. Install engine cover and tighten fasteners to 62 inch lbs. (7 Nm).

20. Install the 2 engine cover plastic retainers.

MASS AIR FLOW (MAF) SENSOR

LOCATION

See Figure 301.

The Mass Air Flow (MAF)/Intake Air Temperature (IAT) Sensor—On the right side of the engine compartment, to the right side of the throttle body, in the cold air duct. The intake air temperature (IAT) sensor is an integral part of the mass air flow (MAF) sensor that is mounted in the air cleaner assembly.

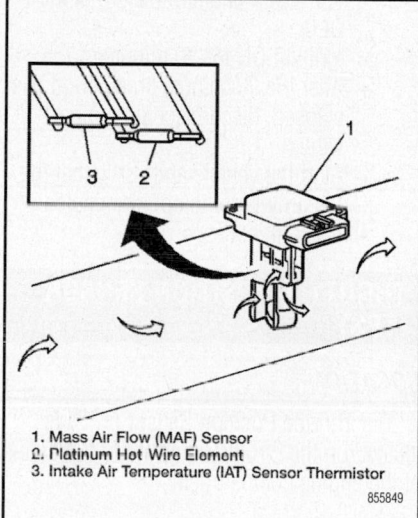

1. Mass Air Flow (MAF) Sensor
2. Platinum Hot Wire Element
3. Intake Air Temperature (IAT) Sensor Thermistor

855849

Fig. 301 Mass Air Flow (MAF)/Intake Air Temperature (IAT) Sensor location

REMOVAL & INSTALLATION

See Figure 302.

1. Disconnect the mass air flow sensor connector.

2. Remove the 2 screws and the mass air flow sensor.

To install:

3. Install the mass air flow sensor with the 2 screws, and tighten to 9 inch lbs. (1.0 Nm).

4. Connect the mass air flow sensor connector.

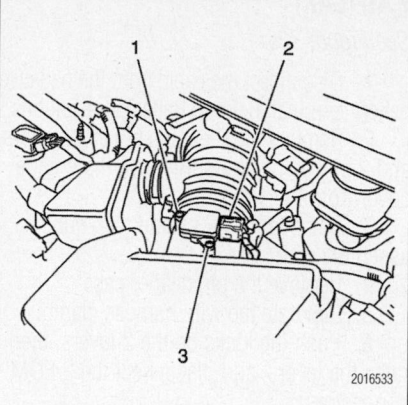

2016533

Fig. 302 Locating mass air sensor connector (2) and 2 screws (1, 3)—2.4L (LAX) Shown

POWERTRAIN CONTROL MODULE (PCM)

PRECAUTIONS

※※ WARNING

Turn the ignition OFF when installing or removing the control module connectors and disconnecting or reconnecting the power to the control module (battery cable, powertrain control module (PCM)/engine control module (ECM)/transaxle control module (TCM) pigtail, control module fuse, jumper cables, etc.) in order to prevent internal control module damage.

※※ WARNING

Control module damage may result when the metal case contacts battery voltage. DO NOT contact the control module metal case with battery voltage when servicing a control module, using battery booster cables, or when charging the vehicle battery.

※※ WARNING

In order to prevent any possible electrostatic discharge damage to the control module, do no touch the connector pins or the soldered components on the circuit board.

※※ WARNING

Remove any debris from around the control module connector surfaces before servicing the control

module. Inspect the control module connector gaskets when diagnosing or replacing the control module. Ensure that the gaskets are installed correctly. The gaskets prevent contaminant intrusion into the control module.

➡The replacement control module must be programmed.

➡It is necessary to record the remaining engine oil life. If the replacement module is not programmed with the remaining engine oil life, the engine oil life will default to 100 percent. If the replacement module is not programmed with the remaining engine oil life, the engine oil will need to be changed at 5 000 km (3,000 mi) from the last engine oil change.

LOCATION

See Figures 303 and 304.

At the left front corner of the engine compartment, mounted on top of the battery cover.

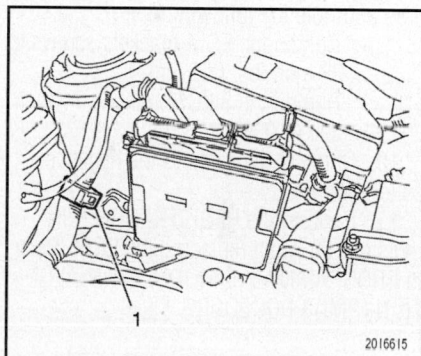

2016615

Fig. 303 Powertrain Control Module (PCM) and wire harness clamp (1) location—1.8L (LAY)

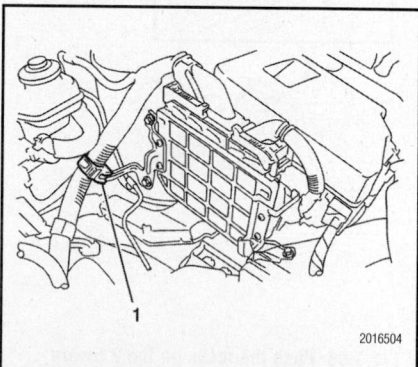

2016504

Fig. 304 Powertrain Control Module (PCM) and wire harness clamp (1) location—2.4L (LAX)

REMOVAL & INSTALLATION

1.8L (LAY)

See Figure 305.

1. Before servicing the vehicle, refer to Precautions at beginning of this section.

2. Disconnect the cable from the negative battery terminal. Refer to Battery, precautions.

3. Remove air cleaner assembly with hose. Refer to Air Cleaner, removal & installation.

4. Separate the wire harness clamp.

➡**After disconnecting the connectors, make sure that dirt, water or other foreign matter does not contact the connecting parts of the connectors.**

5. Disconnect the 2 ECM connectors.

6. Push the locks on the 2 levers, then raise the levers, and disconnect the 2 ECM connectors.

7. Remove the 3 bolts and the ECM.

8. Remove the 4 screws and 2 ECM brackets.

To install:

9. To install, reverse the removal procedure and note the following:

- Tighten the ECM brackets screws to 28 inch lbs. (3.2 Nm).
- Tighten the 3 ECM bolts to 71 inch lbs. (8.0 Nm).

10. Connect the cable to the negative battery terminal.

11. Perform the REGISTRATION (VIN registration) when replacing the ECM. Refer to PROGRAMMABLE MODULE INSTALLATION (PMI) PROCEDURE.

2.4L (LAX)

See Figure 306.

1. Disconnect the cable from the negative battery terminal. Refer to Battery, precautions.

2. Remove the 2 engine cover fasteners and 2 plastic retainers. Remove the engine cover from the engine.

3. Remove the air cleaner cap sub-assembly with hose.

4. Remove the air cleaner case.

5. Separate the wire harness clamp.

6. Push the locks on the 2 levers, then raise the levers, and disconnect the 2 ECM connectors.

7. Remove the 3 bolts and the ECM.

8. Remove the 4 screws and the 2 ECM brackets.

To install:

9. To install, reverse the removal procedure and note the following:

- Tighten the ECM brackets screws to 28 inch lbs. (3.2 Nm).
- Tighten the 3 ECM bolts to 71 inch lbs. (8.0 Nm).

10. Install engine cover and tighten fasteners to 62 inch lbs. (7 Nm).

11. Install the 2 engine cover plastic retainers.

12. Connect the cable to the negative battery terminal.

13. Perform the REGISTRATION (VIN registration) when replacing the ECM. Refer to PROGRAMMABLE MODULE INSTALLATION (PMI) PROCEDURE.

PROGRAMMABLE MODULE INSTALLATION (PMI) PROCEDURE

➡**The powertrain control module (PCM) cannot be programmed with** updated software. The correct replacement PCM is already programmed. The following setup procedure below must be performed to write the vehicle identification number (VIN) to the new PCM and to register the ECU communication ID to the theft deterrent key transponder to complete the PCM replacement.

1. If the PCM requires replacement, perform the following:

- Ignition ON with a currently learned master key
- Access Service Programming System (SPS). On the Select Diagnostic Tool and Programming Process screen, select J2534 Tech 2. Follow all on-screen instructions.
- On the SPS Supported Controllers screen, select VIN-Write VIN to PCM (J2534). Follow the on-screen instructions.
- Clear all codes and cycle the ignition OFF for at least 30 seconds.
- Remove the scan tool and install a 3-amp fused jumper wire between terminal 4 and terminal 13 at the DLC.
- Ignition ON for 30 minutes.
- After the 30-minute time period has elapsed, disconnect the jumper wire.
- Start the vehicle and verify that the Security Light is not illuminated.
- Clear all codes.

THROTTLE POSITION SENSOR (TPS)

LOCATION

The Throttle Position Sensor (TPS) is located on the throttle body, at the right side of the engine compartment.

REMOVAL & INSTALLATION

The Throttle Position Sensor (TPS) is integral to the electronic throttle body. Refer to Throttle Body, removal & installation.

VEHICLE SPEED SENSOR (VSS)

LOCATION

See Figures 307 and 308.

REMOVAL & INSTALLATION

MVA 4-Speed/ MVB 4-Speed

See Figure 309.

➡**Attempting to disengage both front and rear clips at the same time may cause the engine cover to break.**

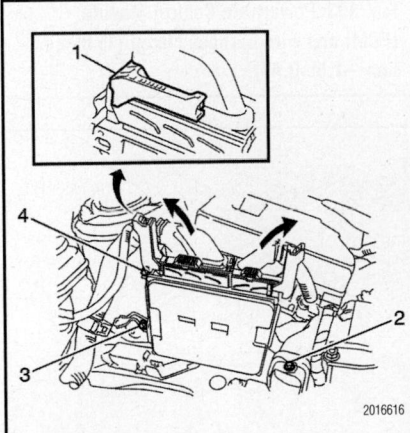

Fig. 305 Push the locks on the 2 levers (1), then raise the levers, and disconnect the 2 ECM connectors. Remove the 3 bolts (2–4) and the ECM—1.8L (LAY)

2016616

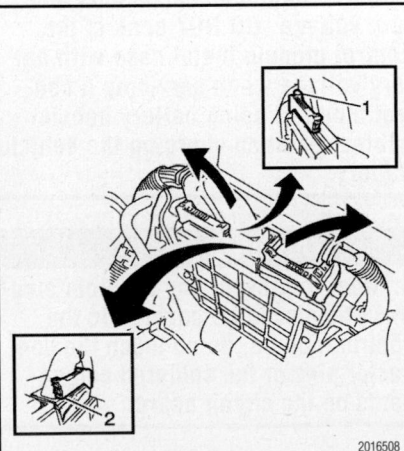

Fig. 306 Push the locks on the 2 levers (1, 2), then raise the levers, and disconnect the 2 ECM connectors—2.4L LAX

2016508

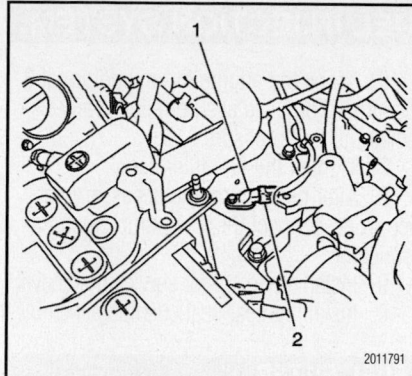

Fig. 307 Vehicle Speed Sensor (VSS) (1) and sensor connector (2) location—MVA 4-Speed/ MVB 4-Speed

Fig. 309 Vehicle Speed Sensor (VSS) (1) and sensor connector (2) location

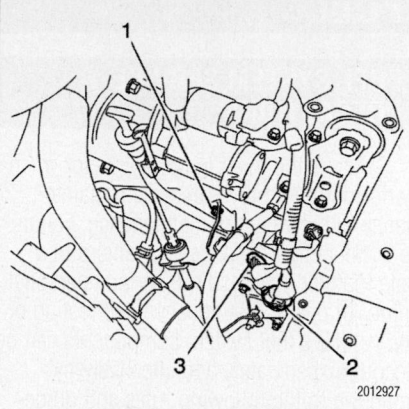

Fig. 310 Connect the transmission wire connector (3), park/neutral position switch connector (2) and wire harness clamps (1)—MVD 5-Speed

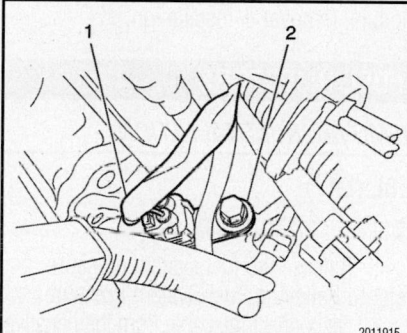

Fig. 308 Vehicle Speed Sensor (2) and electrical connector (1) location—MVD 5-Speed

1. On 1.8L, hold the rear of the engine cover and raise it to disengage the 2 clips on the rear of the cover. Continue to raise the cover to disengage the 2 clips on the front of the cover and remove the cover.

2. On 2.4L, remove the 2 engine cover fasteners and 2 plastic retainers. Remove the engine cover.

3. On all models, remove the air cleaner cap sub-assembly.

4. Remove the air cleaner case.

5. Disconnect the speed sensor connector.

6. Remove the bolt and speed sensor.

7. Remove the O-ring from the speed sensor.

To inspect:

8. Measure the resistance according to the value(s):
- Standard Resistance
- Tester Connection: 1-2
- Condition: 20°C (68°F)
- Specified Condition: 560 to 680 Ω

9. If the resistance value is not as specified, replace the speed sensor.

To install:

10. Coat a new O-ring with ATF WS and install it to the speed sensor.

11. Install the speed sensor with the bolt and tighten to 44 inch lbs. (5 Nm).

12. Install the air cleaner case.

13. Install the air cleaner cover.

14. On 1.8L, position the engine cover and engage the two front fasteners. Engage the two fasteners on the rear of the cover.

15. On 2.4L, install engine cover and tighten fasteners to 62 inch lbs. (7 Nm).

16. Install the 2 engine cover plastic retainers.

MVD 5-Speed

See Figures 308 and 310.

1. Remove the battery. Refer to Battery, removal & installation.

2. Remove the battery tray. Refer to Battery Tray, removal & installation.

3. Remove the 2 engine cover fasteners and 2 plastic retainers. Remove the engine cover.

4. Remove the air cleaner assembly.

5. Disconnect the transmission wire connector, park/neutral position switch connector and wire harness clamps.

6. Remove the bolt and transmission oil level indicator tube sub-assembly.

7. Remove the O-ring from the transmission oil level indicator tube sub-assembly.

8. Disconnect the speed sensor connector.

9. Remove the bolt and speed sensor.

10. Remove the O-ring from the speed sensor.

To install:

11. To install, reverse the removal procedure and note the following:

12. Coat a new O-ring with ATF WS and install it to the speed sensor.
- Tighten the speed sensor bolt to 80 inch lbs. (9.0 Nm).

13. Apply ATF WS to a new O-ring, and install it to the transmission oil level indicator tube assembly.

14. Tighten transmission oil level indicator tube sub-assembly to the automatic transaxle bolt to 53 inch lbs. (6 Nm).

15. Tighten engine cover fasteners to 62 inch lbs. (7 Nm).

FUEL SYSTEM SERVICE PRECAUTIONS

Safety is the most important factor when performing not only fuel system maintenance but any type of maintenance. Failure to conduct maintenance and repairs in a safe manner may result in serious personal injury or death. Maintenance and testing of the vehicle's fuel system components can be accomplished safely and effectively by adhering to the following rules and guidelines.

• To avoid the possibility of fire and personal injury, always disconnect the negative battery cable unless the repair or test procedure requires that battery voltage be applied.

• Always relieve the fuel system pressure prior to disconnecting any fuel system component (injector, fuel rail, pressure regulator, etc.), fitting or fuel line connection. Exercise extreme caution whenever relieving fuel system pressure to avoid exposing skin, face and eyes to fuel spray. Please be advised that fuel under pressure may penetrate the skin or any part of the body that it contacts.

• Always place a shop towel or cloth around the fitting or connection prior to loosening to absorb any excess fuel due to spillage. Ensure that all fuel spillage (should it occur) is quickly removed from engine surfaces. Ensure that all fuel soaked cloths or towels are deposited into a suitable waste container.

• Always keep a dry chemical (Class B) fire extinguisher near the work area.

• Do not allow fuel spray or fuel vapors to come into contact with a spark or open flame.

• Always use a back-up wrench when loosening and tightening fuel line connection fittings. This will prevent unnecessary stress and torsion to fuel line piping.

• Always replace worn fuel fitting O-rings with new Do not substitute fuel hose or equivalent where fuel pipe is installed.

Before servicing the vehicle, make sure to also refer to the precautions in the beginning of this section as well.

RELIEVING FUEL SYSTEM PRESSURE

✷✷ CAUTION

Remove the fuel tank cap and relieve the fuel system pressure before ser-

vicing the fuel system in order to reduce the risk of personal injury. After you relieve the fuel system pressure, a small amount of fuel may be released when servicing the fuel lines, the fuel injection pump, or the connections. In order to reduce the risk of personal injury, cover the fuel system components with a shop towel before disconnection. This will catch any fuel that may leak out. Place the towel in an approved container when the disconnection is complete.

✷✷ WARNING

Do not perform this procedure if the engine is hot. Unburned fuel entering the catalytic converter could damage the converter catalyst.

1. Loosen the fuel filler cap in order to relieve the fuel tank pressure.
2. Remove the rear seat cushion assembly.
3. Remove the rear floor service hole cover.
4. Disconnect the fuel pump electrical connector.
5. Start the engine and allow the engine to stall.

6. Crank the engine for an additional 3 seconds in order to assure relief of any remaining fuel pressure.
7. Tighten the fuel filler cap.
8. After performing the necessary service work, connect the fuel pump electrical connector.
9. Install the rear floor service hole cover.
10. Install the rear seat cushion assembly.

FUEL FILTER

REMOVAL & INSTALLATION

The fuel filter is serviced as part of the fuel pump module. Refer to Fuel Pump Module, removal & installation.

FUEL INJECTORS

REMOVAL & INSTALLATION

1.8L (LAY)

See Figures 311 through 319.

1. Release the fuel system pressure. Refer to Relieving Fuel System Pressure.
2. Disconnect the cable from the negative battery terminal. Refer to Battery, precautions.

➡**Attempting to disengage both front and rear clips at the same time may cause the engine cover to break.**

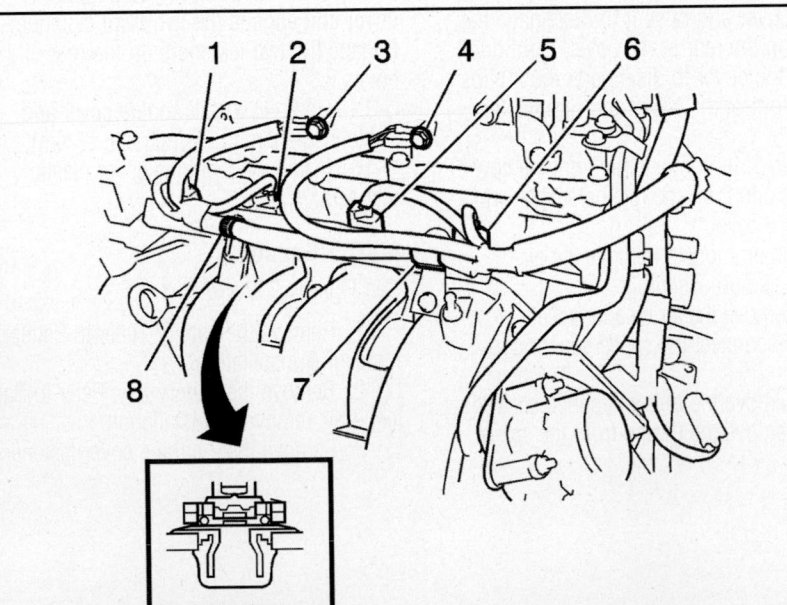

1. Fuel injector assembly connector
2. Fuel injector assembly connector
3. Ground wire
4. Ground wire
5. Fuel injector assembly connector
6. Fuel injector assembly connector
7. Wire harness clamp
8. Wire harness clamp

2016594

Fig. 311 View of fuel injector assembly—1.8L (LAY)

3. Hold the rear of the engine cover and raise it to disengage the 2 clips on the rear of the cover. Continue to raise the cover to disengage the 2 clips on the front of the cover and remove the cover.

4. Disconnect the ventilation hose.

5. Remove the air cleaner assembly with hose.

6. Remove the engine wire.

7. Remove the 2 bolts and disconnect the ground wire.

8. Disconnect the 4 fuel injector assembly connectors.

9. Disconnect the 2 wire harness clamps.

10. Disconnect the 4 wire harness clamps.

11. Remove the 2 bolts and 2 wire harness brackets.

12. Remove the fuel pipe clamps.

13. Using the fuel line disconnect tool (J-43178), disconnect the fuel tube.

14. Remove the fuel delivery pipe.

15. Remove the bolt and remove the wire harness bracket.

16. Remove the 2 bolts.

17. Remove the bolt and the fuel delivery pipe.

18. Remove the 2 delivery pipe spacers.

19. Pull the 4 fuel injector assemblies out of the fuel delivery pipe.

➡**Prevent entry of foreign objects by covering the fuel injector with a plastic bag.**

20. For reinstallation, attach a tag or label to the injector shaft.

21. Remove the 4 injector vibration insulators.

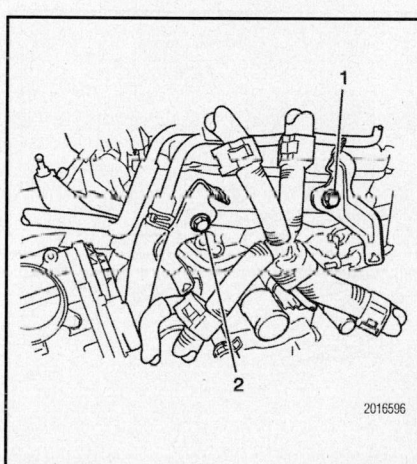

Fig. 312 Remove the 2 bolts (1, 2) and 2 wire harness brackets—1.8L (LAY)

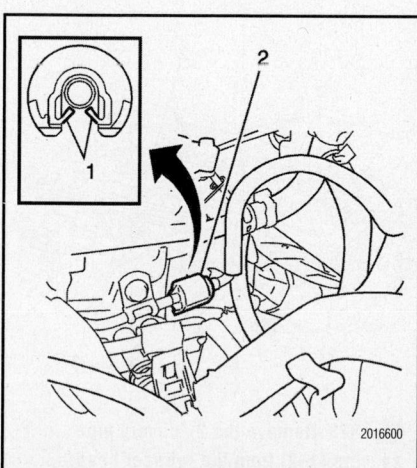

Fig. 313 Remove the fuel pipe clamps (1–2)—1.8L (LAY)

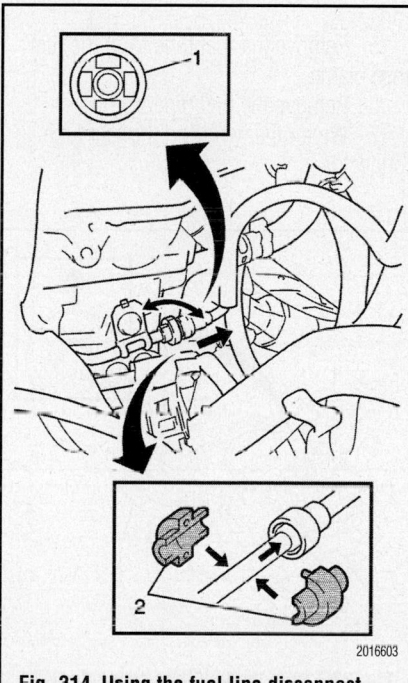

Fig. 314 Using the fuel line disconnect tool, disconnect the fuel tube (1)—1.8L (LAY)

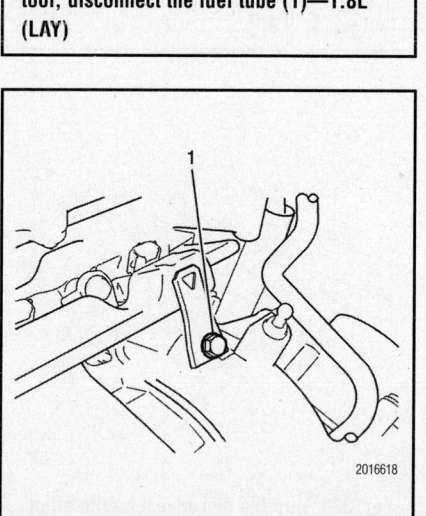

Fig. 315 Remove the bolt (1) and remove the wire harness bracket—1.8L (LAY)

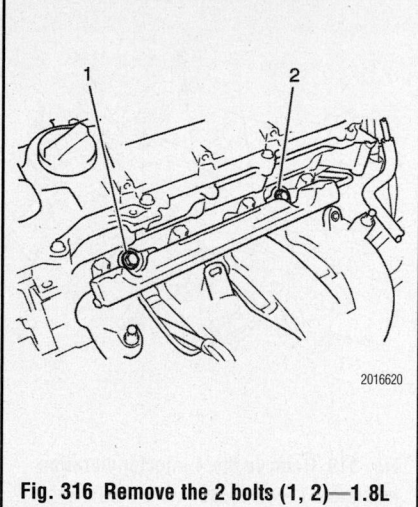

Fig. 316 Remove the 2 bolts (1, 2)—1.8L (LAY)

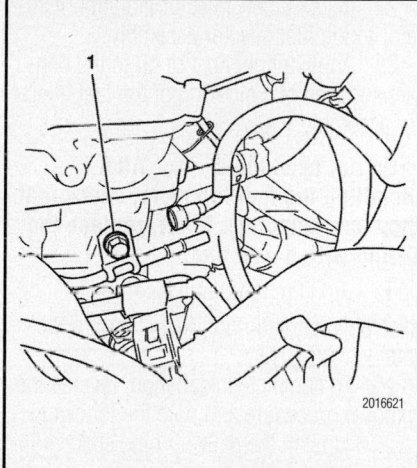

Fig. 317 Remove the bolt (1) and the fuel delivery pipe—1.8L (LAY)

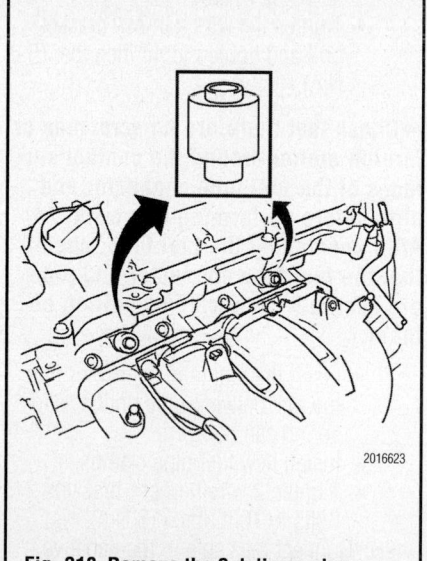

Fig. 318 Remove the 2 delivery pipe spacers—1.8L (LAY)

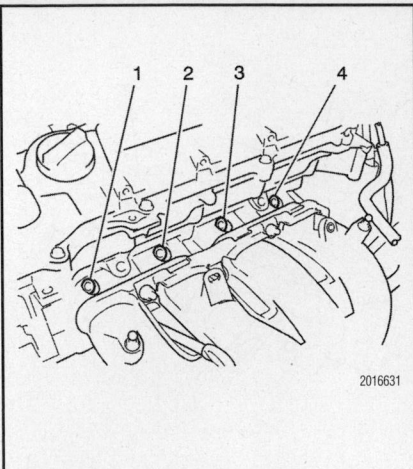

Fig. 319 Remove the 4 injector vibration insulators (1–4)—1.8L (LAY)

To install:

22. Install a new injector vibration insulator to the fuel injector assembly.

23. Apply a light coat of oil to the contact surfaces of the O-ring of the fuel injector assembly.

➡ **Do not twist the O-ring. After installing the fuel injectors, check that they turn smoothly. If not, replace the O-ring with a new one.**

24. While turning the fuel injector assembly left and right, install it onto the fuel delivery pipe.

25. To complete installation, reverse the removal procedure and note the following:
  • Install the delivery pipe spacers in the correct direction.
  • Tighten the delivery pipe spacer bolts to 15 ft. lbs. (21 Nm).
  • Tighten the delivery pipe bolt to 15 ft. lbs. (21 Nm).
  • Tighten the wire harness bracket bolt and tighten to 44 inch lbs. (5.0 Nm).

➡ **Check that there are no scratches or foreign matter around the contact surfaces of the fuel tube connector and pipe before performing this work. After connecting the fuel tube, check that the fuel tube connector and pipe are securely connected by pulling on them.**

  • Insert the fuel tube connector into the fuel delivery pipe until a "click" sound can be heard.
  • Install new fuel pipe clamps.
  • Tighten 2 wire harness brackets 2 bolts to 10 ft. lbs. (13 Nm).

26. Connect the cable to the negative battery terminal.

27. Inspect for a fuel leak.

28. Position the engine cover and engage the two front fasteners. Engage the two fasteners on the rear of the cover.

2.4L (LAX)

See Figures 320 through 325.

1. Release the fuel system pressure. Refer to Relieving Fuel System Pressure.

2. Disconnect the cable from the negative battery terminal. Refer to Battery, precautions.

3. Remove the 2 engine cover fasteners and 2 plastic retainers. Remove the engine cover.

4. Remove the air cleaner assembly. Refer to Air Cleaner, removal & installation.

5. Remove the fuel tube from the fuel hose clamp.

6. Remove the fuel pipe clamp.

7. Wipe off any dirt on the fuel tube connector.

8. Hold the fuel tube connector, and then install the fuel line disconnect tool (J-43178).

9. Turn the disconnect tool to align the retainer inside the fuel tube connector with the chamfered part of the disconnect tool.

10. Insert the disconnect tool into the fuel tube and hold it. Then push the fuel tube connector toward the disconnect tool.

11. Mount the retainer of the fuel tube connector onto the chamfered part of the disconnect tool.

12. Slide the disconnect tool and fuel tube connector together towards the fuel tube until they make a "click" sound, and then disconnect the fuel tube.

13. Drain the fuel remaining inside the fuel tube.

14. Cover the fuel tube and fuel pipe with a plastic bag to protect the disconnected part.

15. Disconnect the ventilation hose from the ventilation valve.

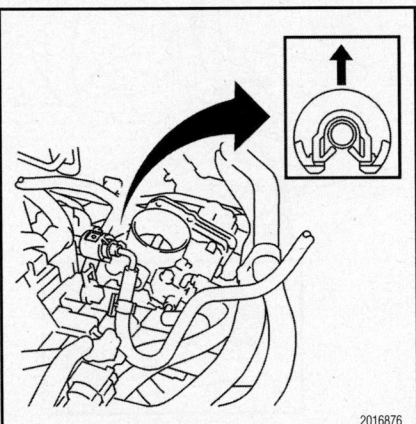

Fig. 320 Hold the fuel tube connector (1), and then install the fuel line disconnect tool—2.4L (LAX)

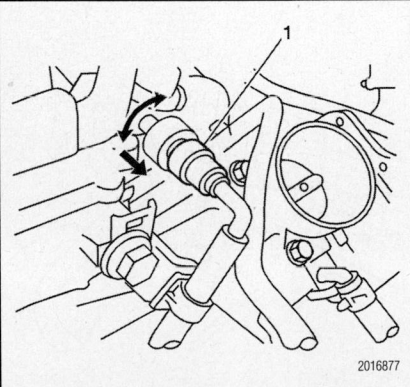

Fig. 321 Turn the disconnect tool to align the retainer inside the fuel tube connector with the chamfered part of the disconnect tool—2.4L (LAX)

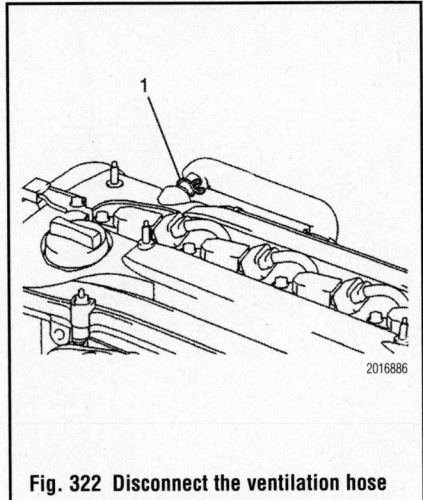

Fig. 322 Disconnect the ventilation hose (1) from the ventilation valve—2.4L (LAX)

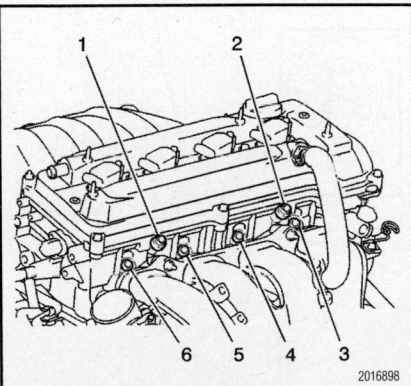

Fig. 323 Remove the 2 delivery pipe spacers (1–2) from the cylinder head. Remove the 4 insulators (3–6) from the cylinder head—2.4L (LAX)

16. Remove the 2 wire harness clamps.

17. Disconnect the 4 fuel injector connectors.

18. Remove the 2 bolts, then remove the fuel delivery pipe together with the 4 fuel injectors.

19. Remove the 2 delivery pipe spacers from the cylinder head.

20. Remove the 4 insulators from the cylinder head.

21. Remove fuel injector assembly.

22. Pull the 4 fuel injectors out of the fuel delivery pipe.

To install:

23. Apply a light coat of oil to new O-rings, then install one onto each fuel injector.

24. Apply a light coat of oil to the part of the fuel delivery pipe which comes into contact with the O-ring of the fuel injector.

25. Apply a light coat of oil to the O-ring again, then install the right and left fuel injectors onto the fuel delivery pipe.

26. Check that the fuel injector rotates smoothly. If the fuel injector does not rotate, replace the O-ring.

27. Install 4 new insulators to the cylinder head.

28. Install the 2 delivery pipe spacers onto the cylinder head.

29. Install the fuel delivery pipe together with the 4 fuel injectors, then hand tighten the 2 bolts.

30. Check that the fuel injector rotates smoothly. If the fuel injector does not rotate, replace the O-ring.

31. Install the 2 bolts and tighten to 15 ft. lbs. (20 Nm).

32. Connect the 4 fuel injector connectors.

33. Install the 2 wire harness clamps.

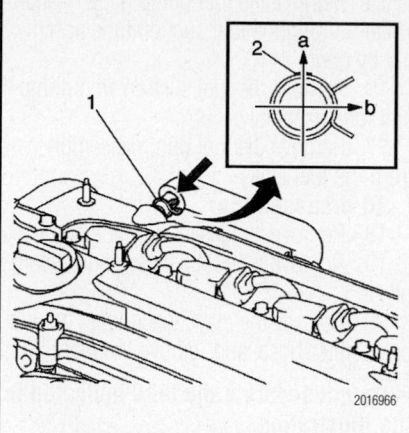

Fig. 325 Make sure that the paint mark and hose clamp are at the correct angle (2) when installing the ventilation hose (1)—2.4L (LAX)

➡**Make sure that the paint mark and hose clamp are at the correct angle when installing the hose.**

34. Connect the ventilation hose to the ventilation valve.

35. Connect the fuel main tube.

36. Push the fuel tube connector until it makes a "click" sound.

37. Install the fuel pipe clamp.

38. Install the fuel tube to the fuel hose clamp.

39. Install the air cleaner assembly. Refer to Air Cleaner, removal & installation.

40. Install engine cover and tighten fasteners to 62 inch lbs. (7 Nm).

41. Install the 2 engine cover plastic retainers.

42. Connect the cable to the negative battery terminal.

43. Inspect for a fuel leak.

FUEL PUMP

REMOVAL & INSTALLATION

1.8L (LAY)

See Figures 326 through 335.

1. Remove the rear seat cushion assembly.

2. Remove the rear floor service hole cover.

3. Disconnect the connector from the fuel suction tube assembly.

4. Release the fuel system pressure. Refer to Relieving Fuel System Pressure.

5. Start the engine. After the engine stops naturally, turn the ignition switch off.

6. Crank the engine again and make sure that the engine does not start.

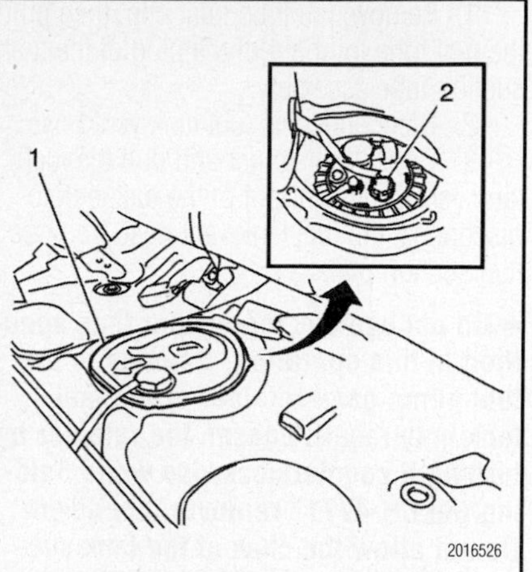

Fig. 326 Remove the rear floor service hole cover (1). Disconnect the connector (2) from the fuel suction tube assembly

7. Remove the fuel tank cap to relieve any pressure from the fuel tank.

8. Disconnect the cable from the negative battery terminal. Refer to Battery, precautions.

9. Disconnect the fuel tank main tube sub-assembly.

10. Disconnect the fuel tank main tube.

➡**Check that there is no dirt or other foreign objects around the fuel tube joint before disconnecting it. Clean the joint if necessary. It is necessary to prevent mud or dirt from entering the joint. If mud or dirt gets in the joint, the O-rings may not seal properly. Only disconnect the joint by hand. Do not bend, kink or twist the nylon tubes. Protect the contact surfaces by covering it with a plastic bag.**

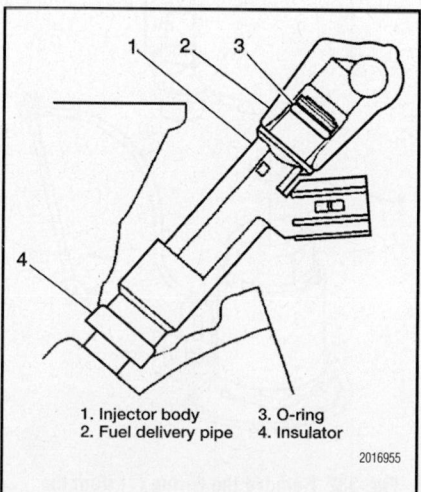

1. Injector body   3. O-ring
2. Fuel delivery pipe   4. Insulator

Fig. 324 View of fuel injector—2.4L (LAX)

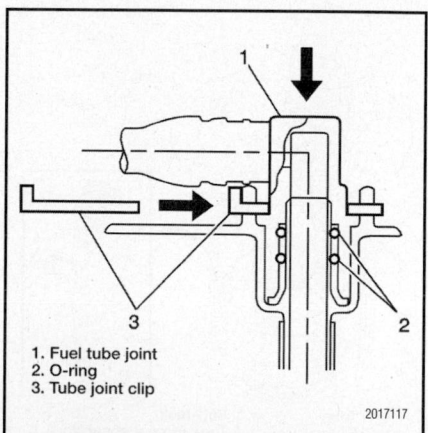

1. Fuel tube joint
2. O-ring
3. Tube joint clip

Fig. 327 Remove the tube joint clip, then pull the fuel tube joint out of the plug of the fuel suction tube assembly

11. Remove the tube joint clip, then pull the fuel tube joint out of the plug of the fuel suction tube assembly.

12. Disconnect the fuel tank vent hose.

13. Pinch the retainer and pull the fuel tank vent connector out of the fuel tank to disconnect the fuel tank vent hose from the fuel suction plate.

➡ Do not use any tools other than specified in this operation. Damage to the fuel pump gage retainer or the fuel tank may result. Loosen the retainer by turning it counterclockwise while holding the CH-47717 remover tool down. Do not allow the claw of the tank suction tube support to slip out of its groove on the fuel tank.

➡ The ribs on the fuel pump gage retainer can be fitted into the tips of the remover tool.

14. Using the fuel lock ring remover tool (CH-47717), loosen the fuel pump gage retainer.

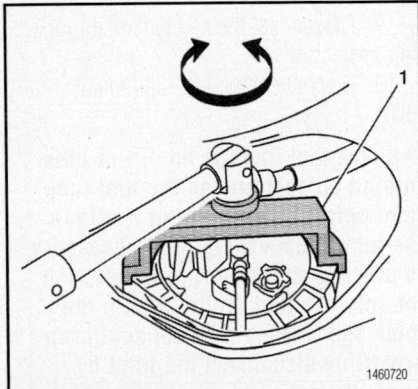

Fig. 328 The ribs on the fuel pump gage retainer can be fitted into the tips of the remover tool (1)

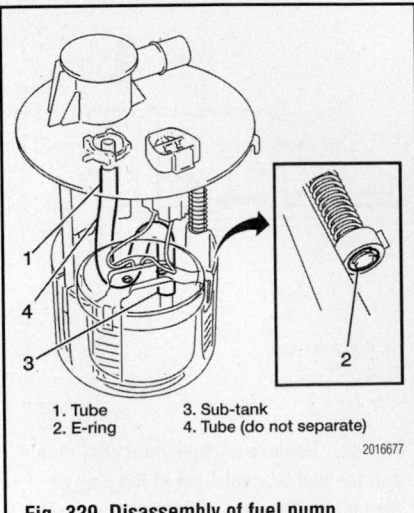

1. Tube
2. E-ring
3. Sub-tank
4. Tube (do not separate)

Fig. 329 Disassembly of fuel pump

15. Remove the fuel pump gage retainer while holding the fuel suction tube assembly by hand.

16. Remove the fuel suction with pump and tube assembly.

17. Remove the fuel pump assembly from the fuel tank.

To disassemble:

18. Remove the gasket from the fuel tank.

19. Remove the fuel sender gage assembly.

20. Release the claw, disconnect the fuel pump filter hose, and remove the fuel pump.

➡ Do not separate the tube indicated in the illustration.

21. Remove the E-ring and separate the 2 claws, then remove the fuel pump subtank.

22. Disconnect the fuel pump harness connector.

23. Using a screwdriver with its tip wrapped in protective tape, disengage the 2 claws and remove the No. 1 fuel suction support.

➡ Do not remove the suction filter. Do not use either the fuel pump or the suction filter if the suction filter is removed from the fuel pump.

24. Using a screwdriver with its tip wrapped in protective tape, disengage the 5 claws, and remove the fuel pump filter and fuel pump from the fuel filter.

25. Disconnect the fuel pump harness connector.

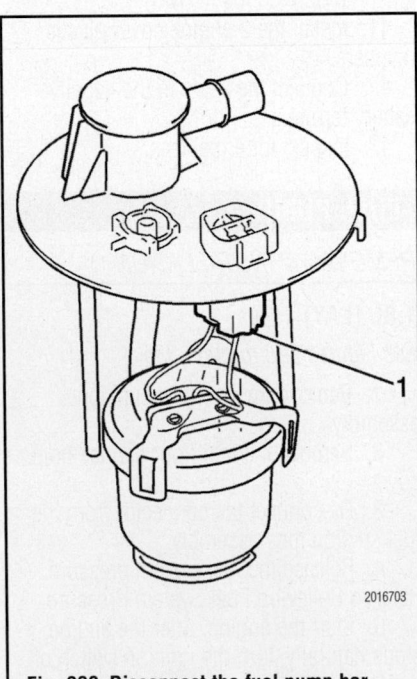

Fig. 330 Disconnect the fuel pump harness connector (1)

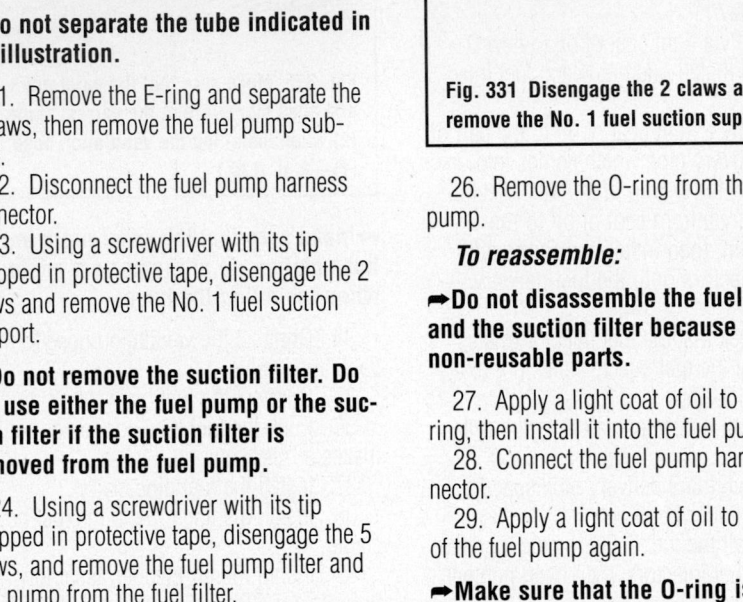

Fig. 331 Disengage the 2 claws and remove the No. 1 fuel suction support

26. Remove the O-ring from the fuel pump.

To reassemble:

➡ Do not disassemble the fuel pump and the suction filter because they are non-reusable parts.

27. Apply a light coat of oil to a new O-ring, then install it into the fuel pump.

28. Connect the fuel pump harness connector.

29. Apply a light coat of oil to the O-ring of the fuel pump again.

➡ Make sure that the O-ring is not cracked or jammed when installing.

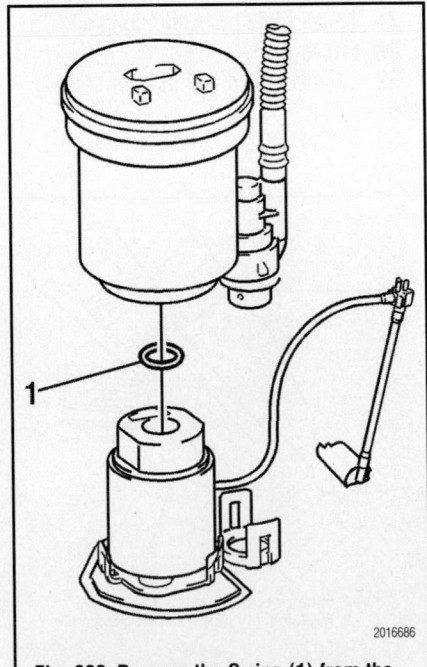

Fig. 332 Remove the O-ring (1) from the fuel pump

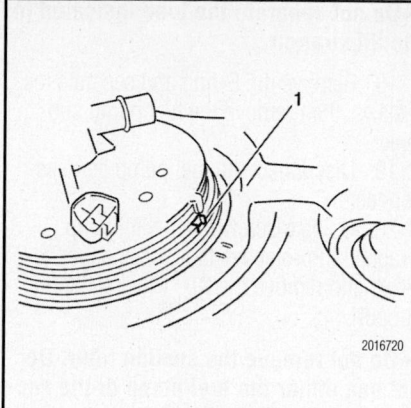

Fig. 333 Align the protrusion (1) of the fuel suction tube with the notch of the fuel tank

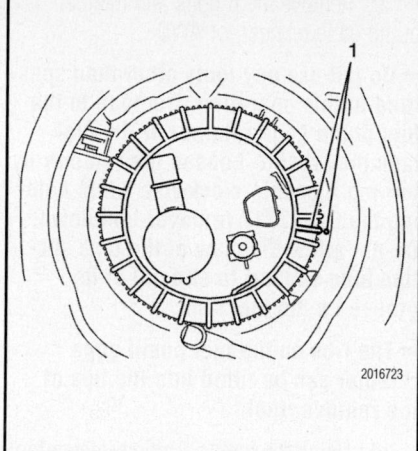

Fig. 334 Align the starting marks (1) on the fuel pump gage retainer and fuel tank

30. Engage the 5 claws, and install the fuel pump filter onto the fuel filter.
31. Engage the 2 claws of the No. 1 fuel suction support.
32. Connect the fuel pump harness connector.
33. Engage the 2 claws and install the E-ring and fuel pump sub-tank.

➡ **Do not apply excessive force to the fuel tube or the suction support.**

34. Align the groove of the fuel pump filler hose with the cutout of the fuel sub-tank and install the hose.
35. Connect the connector of the fuel pump harness.
36. Install the fuel sender gage assembly.

To install:
37. Install the fuel suction tube assembly.
38. Install a new gasket onto the fuel tank.

➡ **Make sure that the fuel sender gauge arm does not bend.**

39. Set the fuel suction tube to the fuel tank.
40. Install the fuel pump gage retainer.
41. Align the protrusion of the fuel suction tube with the notch of the fuel tank.
42. While holding the fuel suction tube assembly by hand to prevent it from tilting, align the starting marks on the fuel pump gage retainer and fuel tank, and tighten the fuel pump gage retainer.

➡ **Use CH-47717 remover tool only. Do not use any other tools, such as a screwdriver.**

43. Insert the notch of remover tool into the rib of the fuel pump gage retainer.

44. Using remover tool and your hand, tighten the fuel pump gage retainer 2 revolutions so that the mark of the retainer comes within the range shown.
45. Connect the fuel tank vent hose.

➡ **Check that there are no scratches or foreign objects around the connecting surfaces of the fuel tank vent connector and pipe before performing this work. After connecting the fuel tank vent hose, check that the fuel tank vent hose is securely connected by pulling on the quick connector.**

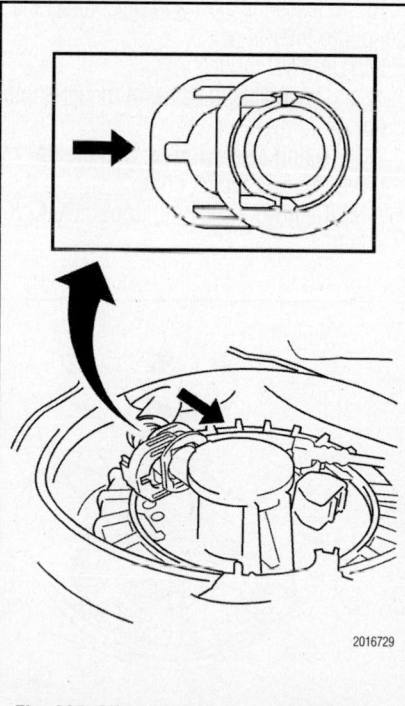

Fig. 335 Align the fuel tank vent connector with the pipe, then push in the fuel tank vent connector until the retainer makes a "click" sound

46. Align the fuel tank vent connector with the pipe, then push in the fuel tank vent connector until the retainer makes a "click" sound to connect the fuel tank vent hose to the fuel suction plate.
47. Connect the fuel tank main tube.
48. Push the fuel tube joint in the plug of the fuel suction plate, then install the tube joint clip.
49. Connect the cable to the negative battery terminal.
50. Inspect for a fuel leak.
51. Connect the fuel pump connector.
52. Install the rear floor service hole cover.
53. Install the rear seat cushion assembly.

2.4L (LAX)
See Figures 336 through 347.

1. Remove the rear seat cushion assembly.
2. Remove the rear floor service hole cover.
3. Disconnect the connector from the fuel suction tube assembly.

✴✴ WARNING
Refer to Battery, precautions.

4. Release the fuel system pressure. Refer to Relieving Fuel System Pressure.
5. Disconnect the fuel tank main tube sub-assembly.
6. Disconnect the fuel tank main tube.

➡ **Check that there is no dirt or other foreign objects around the fuel tube joint before disconnecting it. Clean the joint if necessary. It is necessary to prevent mud or dirt from entering the joint. If mud or dirt gets in the joint,**

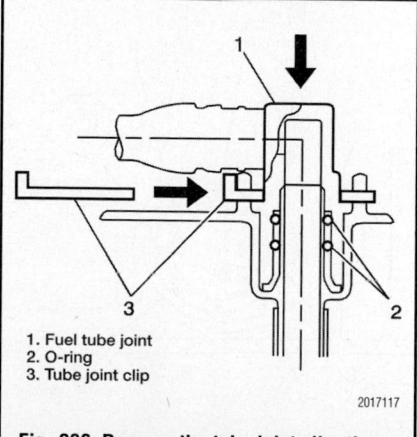

1. Fuel tube joint
2. O-ring
3. Tube joint clip

Fig. 336 Remove the tube joint clip, then pull the fuel tube joint out of the plug of the fuel suction tube assembly

the O-rings may not seal properly. Only disconnect the joint by hand. Do not bend, kink or twist the nylon tubes. Protect the contact surfaces by covering it with a plastic bag.

7. Remove the tube joint clip, then pull the fuel tube joint out of the plug of the fuel suction tube assembly.

8. Disconnect the fuel tank vent hose for FWD.

• Pinch the retainer and pull the fuel tank vent connector out of the fuel tank to disconnect the fuel tank vent hose from the fuel suction plate.

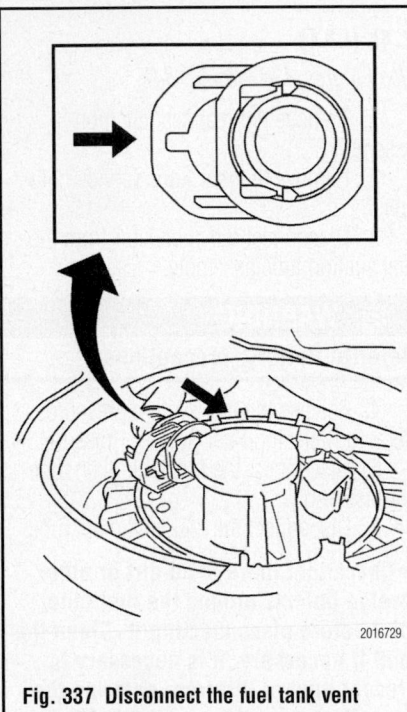

Fig. 337 Disconnect the fuel tank vent hose for FWD

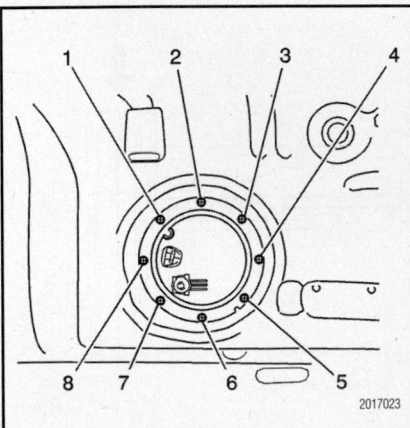

Fig. 338 Remove the bolts (1–8) and the fuel pump gage retainer for AWD

9. Remove the 8 bolts and the fuel pump gage retainer for AWD.

➡Do not use any tools other than specified in this operation. Damage to the fuel pump gage retainer or the fuel tank may result. Loosen the retainer by turning it counterclockwise while holding the CH-47717 remover tool down. Do not allow the claw of the tank suction tube support to slip out of its groove on the fuel tank.

➡The ribs on the fuel pump gage retainer can be fitted into the tips of the remover tool.

10. Using the fuel lock ring remover tool (CH-47717), loosen the fuel pump gage retainer.

11. Remove the fuel pump gage retainer while holding the fuel suction tube assembly by hand.

12. Remove the fuel suction tube assembly.

13. Disconnect the hose and remove the fuel suction tube assembly.

➡Make sure that the fuel sender gage arm does not bend.

14. Remove the gasket from the fuel suction tube assembly.

15. Remove the gasket from the fuel tank.

To disassemble:

16. Release the claw and disconnect the fuel pump filter hose.

17. On AWD models:

a. Disengage the claw of the jet pump nozzle.

b. Using a screwdriver with the tip taped, remove the jet pump.

c. Remove the O-ring from the jet pump.

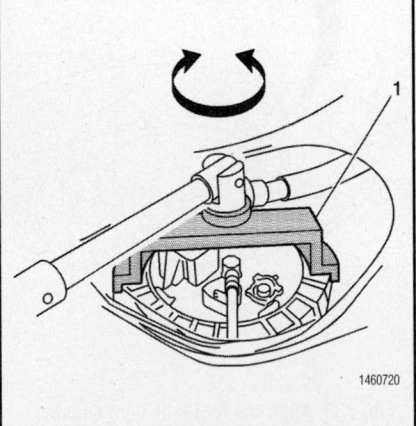

Fig. 339 The ribs on the fuel pump gage retainer can be fitted into the tips of the remover tool (1)

➡Do not separate the tube indicated in the illustration.

18. Remove the E-ring and separate the 2 claws, then remove the fuel pump sub-tank.

19. Disconnect the fuel pump harness connector.

20. Using a screwdriver with its tip wrapped in protective tape, disengage the 2 claws and remove the No. 1 fuel suction support.

➡Do not remove the suction filter. Do not use either the fuel pump or the suction filter if the suction filter is removed from the fuel pump.

21. Using a screwdriver with its tip wrapped in protective tape, disengage the 5 claws, and remove the fuel pump filter and fuel pump from the fuel filter.

22. Disconnect the fuel pump harness connector.

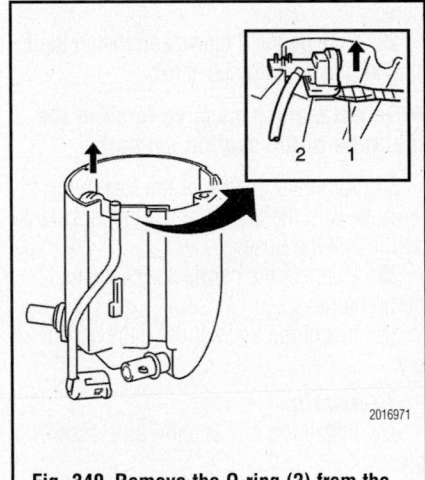

Fig. 340 Remove the O-ring (2) from the jet pump (1)—AWD

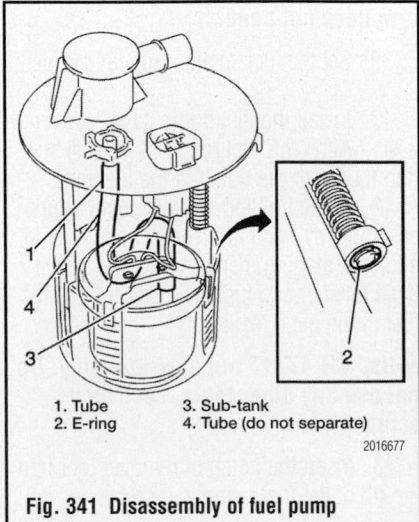

1. Tube   3. Sub-tank
2. E-ring   4. Tube (do not separate)

Fig. 341 Disassembly of fuel pump

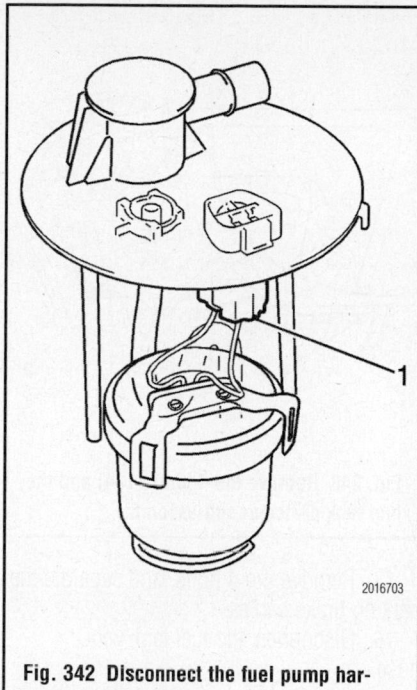

Fig. 342 Disconnect the fuel pump harness connector (1)

23. Remove the O-ring from the fuel pump.

To reassemble:

➡**Do not disassemble the fuel pump and the suction filter because they are non-reusable parts.**

24. Apply a light coat of oil to a new O-ring, then install it into the fuel pump.

25. Connect the fuel pump harness connector.

26. Apply a light coat of oil to the O-ring of the fuel pump again.

➡**Make sure that the O-ring is not cracked or jammed when installing.**

27. Engage the 5 claws, and install the fuel pump filter onto the fuel filter.

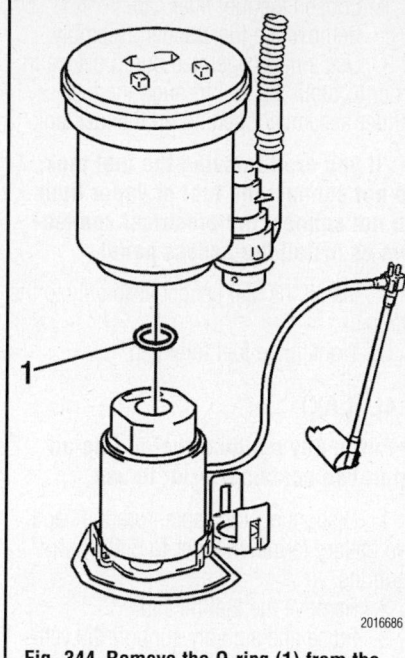

Fig. 344 Remove the O-ring (1) from the fuel pump

28. Engage the 2 claws of the No. 1 fuel suction support.

29. Connect the fuel pump harness connector.

30. Engage the 2 claws and install the E-ring and fuel pump sub-tank.

31. On AWD models:

   a. Apply gasoline to a new O-ring and install it to the jet pump.

   b. Install the jet pump to the tank.

   c. Align the groove of the fuel pump filter hose with the cutout of the fuel sub-tank and install the hose.

To install:

32. Install the fuel suction tube assembly for AWD.

33. Install a new gasket to the fuel suction tube assembly.

➡**Make sure that the fuel sender gage arm does not bend.**

34. Connect the fuel hose with the clip.

35. Set the fuel suction tube to the fuel tank.

36. Install the fuel suction tube assembly.

37. Connect the hose and set the fuel suction tube assembly to the fuel tank.

38. On AWD models, while holding the fuel suction tube by hand, install the fuel tank vent tube to the fuel tank with the 8 bolts, and tighten to 53 inch lbs. (6.0 Nm).

39. Align the protrusion of the fuel suction tube with the notch of the fuel tank for AWD.

40. While holding the fuel suction tube assembly by hand to prevent it from tilting, align the starting marks on the fuel pump gage retainer and fuel tank, and tighten the fuel pump gage retainer.

➡**Use CH-47717 remover tool only. Do not use any other tools, such as a screwdriver.**

41. Insert the notch of remover tool into the rib of the fuel pump gage retainer.

42. Using remover tool and your hand, tighten the fuel pump gage retainer 2 revolutions so that the mark of the retainer comes within the range shown.

43. Connect the fuel tank vent hose.

➡**Check that there are no scratches or foreign objects around the connecting surfaces of the fuel tank vent connector and pipe before performing this work. After connecting the fuel tank vent hose, check that the fuel tank vent hose is securely connected by pulling on the quick connector.**

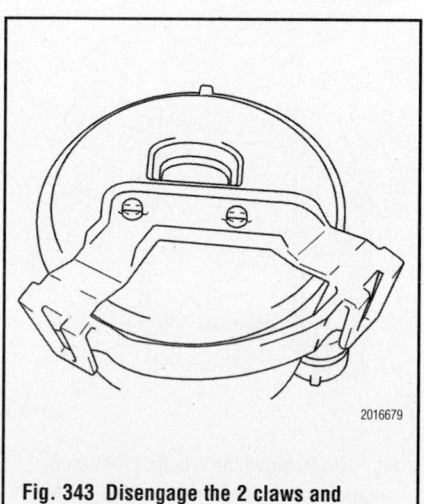

Fig. 343 Disengage the 2 claws and remove the No. 1 fuel suction support

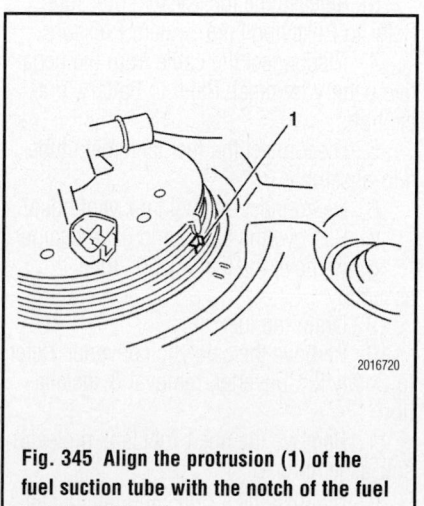

Fig. 345 Align the protrusion (1) of the fuel suction tube with the notch of the fuel tank for AWD

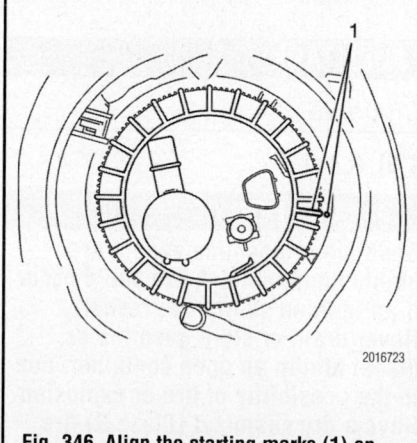

Fig. 346 Align the starting marks (1) on the fuel pump gage retainer and fuel tank

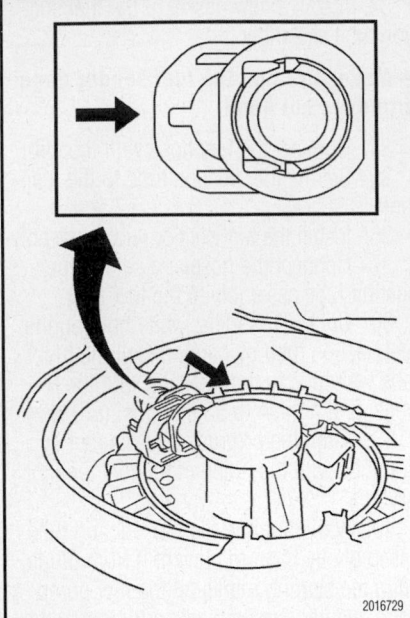

Fig. 347 Align the fuel tank vent connector with the pipe, then push in the fuel tank vent connector until the retainer makes a "click" sound

44. Align the fuel tank vent connector with the pipe, then push in the fuel tank vent connector until the retainer makes a "click" sound to connect the fuel tank vent hose to the fuel suction plate.

45. Install the fuel tank main tube sub-assembly.

46. Connect the fuel tank main tube.

47. Push the fuel tube joint in the plug of the fuel suction plate, then install the tube joint clip.

48. Connect the cable to the negative battery terminal.

49. Inspect for a fuel leak.

50. Connect the fuel pump connector.

51. Install the rear floor service hole cover.

52. Install the rear seat cushion assembly.

FUEL TANK

DRAINING

1.8L (LAY)

> ✳✳ **CAUTION**
>
> **Gasoline or gasoline vapors are highly flammable. A fire could occur if an ignition source is present. Never drain or store gasoline or diesel fuel in an open container, due to the possibility of fire or explosion. Have a dry chemical (Class B) fire extinguisher nearby.**

1. Loosen the fuel filler cap.

2. Remove the fuel sender assembly.

3. Use a hand operated pump device in order to drain the fuel through the fuel sender assembly opening on the fuel tank.

➡: **If you are removing the fuel tank, do not connect the fuel or vapor lines. Do not connect the electrical connectors or install the access panel.**

4. Install the fuel sender assembly to the fuel tank.

5. Tighten the fuel filler cap.

2.4L (LAX)

➡**Purge any residual fuel in into an approved container prior to use.**

1. Disconnect the cable from the negative battery terminal. Refer to Battery, precautions.

2. Remove the fuel fill cap.

3. Raise and suitably support the vehicle.

4. Loosen the fuel fill pipe clamp.

5. Remove the fuel fill pipe from the fuel tank.

6. Insert fuel tank drain hose (J-45004) into the tank.

7. Attach the hose to the hose used with the hand or air operated pump devise.

8. Using a hand or air operated pump, drain as much fuel from the tank as possible.

REMOVAL & INSTALLATION

1.8L (LAY)

See Figures 347 through 356.

1. Remove the rear seat cushion assembly.

2. Remove the rear floor service hole cover.

3. Release the fuel system pressure. Refer to Relieving Fuel System Pressure.

4. Disconnect the cable from the negative battery terminal. Refer to Battery, precautions.

5. Disconnect the fuel tank main tube sub-assembly.

6. Disconnect the fuel tank vent hose.

7. Remove the fuel pump gage retainer.

8. Remove the fuel suction tube assembly.

9. Drain the fuel.

10. Remove the catalytic converter. Refer to Catalytic Converter, removal & installation.

11. Remove the no. 1 fuel tank protector sub-assembly.

12. Remove the 4 bolts and the fuel tank protector sub-assembly.

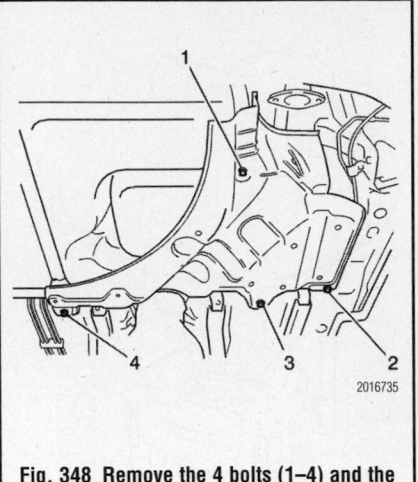

Fig. 348 Remove the 4 bolts (1–4) and the fuel tank protector sub-assembly

13. Remove the 4 bolts, and separate the parking brake cables.

14. Disconnect the fuel tank vent hose.

➡**Check that there is no dirt or other foreign objects around the connector before disconnecting it. Clean the connector if necessary. It is necessary to prevent mud or dirt from entering the connector. If mud or dirt gets in the connector, the O-rings may not seal properly. Only disconnect the quick connector by hand. Do not bend, kink or twist the nylon tubes. Protect the connector by covering it with a plastic bag.**

15. Pull the fuel tank vent hose out of the pipe.

16. Disconnect the breather tube fuel hose.

17. Remove the checker of the fuel tube connector from the pipe.

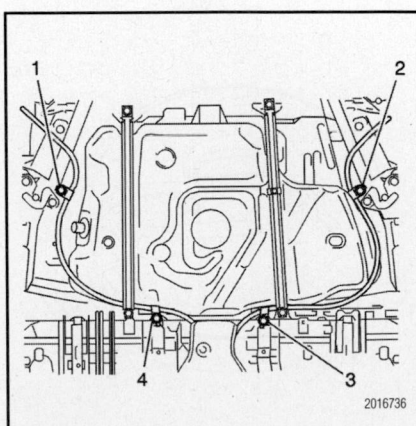

Fig. 349 Remove the 4 bolts (1–4), and separate the parking brake cables—1.8L (LAY)

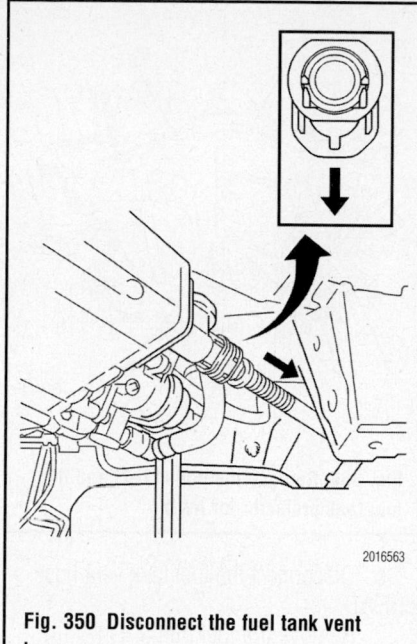

Fig. 350 Disconnect the fuel tank vent hose

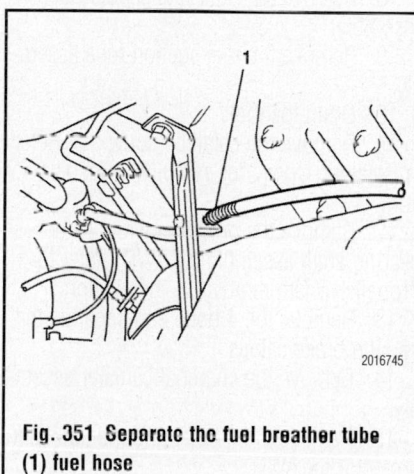

Fig. 351 Separate the fuel breather tube (1) fuel hose

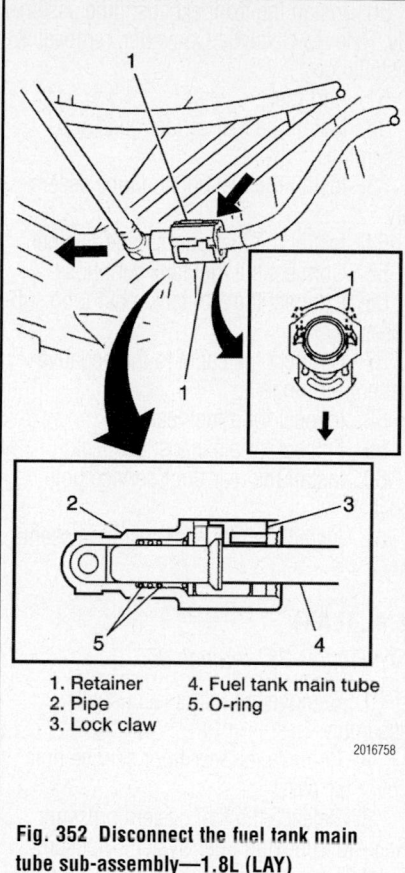

1. Retainer   4. Fuel tank main tube
2. Pipe   5. O-ring
3. Lock claw

Fig. 352 Disconnect the fuel tank main tube sub-assembly—1.8L (LAY)

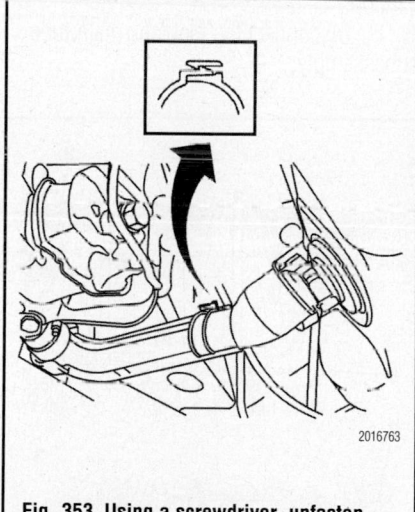

Fig. 353 Using a screwdriver, unfasten the claw—1.8L (LAY)

18. Pinch the retainer of the fuel tube connector, then pull the fuel tube connector out of the pipe.

19. Separate the fuel breather tube fuel hose.

20. Disconnect the fuel tank main tube sub-assembly.

21. Pinch the tabs of the retainer of the fuel tube connector to remove the lock claws and push it down.

22. Pull the fuel tank main tube out of the pipe.

23. Using a screwdriver, unfasten the claw. Then remove the fuel tank filler pipe cover from the fuel tank filler pipe.

24. Loosen the hose clamp bolt, then disconnect the fuel tank filler pipe hose from the fuel tank.

25. Hold the fuel tank using a transmission jack.

26. Remove the 4 bolts, and remove the 2 fuel tank bands.

27. Operate the transmission jack, then remove the fuel tank.

28. Remove the fuel tank main tube from the fuel tank.

29. Remove the fuel tank vent hose from the fuel tank clamp.

30. Remove the fuel tank cushions from the fuel tank.

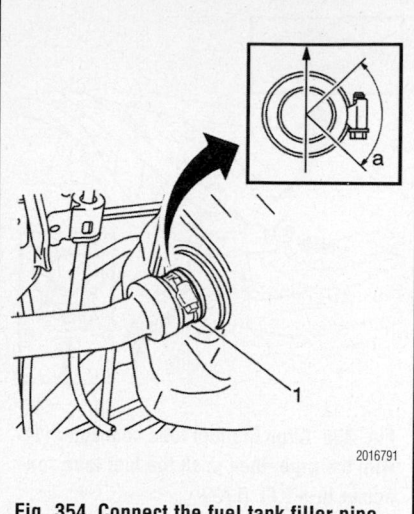

Fig. 354 Connect the fuel tank filler pipe (1) to the fuel tank with hose clamp facing in the correct direction

To install:

31. Install the new fuel tank cushions onto the fuel tank.

32. Install the fuel tank vent hose onto the fuel tube clamp.

33. Install the fuel tank main tube onto the fuel tank.

34. Set the fuel tank on a transmission jack.

35. Operate the transmission jack, then install the fuel tank into the vehicle.

36. Install the 2 fuel tank bands with the 4 bolts and tighten to 29 ft. lbs. (39 Nm).

➡ **Make sure that the hose clamp is facing in the correct direction when installing.**

37. Connect the fuel tank filler pipe to the fuel tank.

38. Engage the claw, then install the fuel tank filler pipe cover onto the fuel tank filler pipe.

➡ **Check that there are no scratches or foreign objects around the connecting surfaces of the fuel tube connector and pipe before performing this work. After connecting the fuel tank main tube, check that the fuel tank main tube is securely connected by pulling on the fuel tube connector and pipe.**

39. Connect the fuel tank main tube.

40. Align the fuel tube connector with the pipe, then push the fuel tube connector in until it comes into contact with the seat to connect the fuel tank main tube to the pipe, then push the retainer up until the claws lock.

41. Connect the breather tube fuel hose.

42. Align the fuel tube connector with the pipe, then push the fuel tube connector

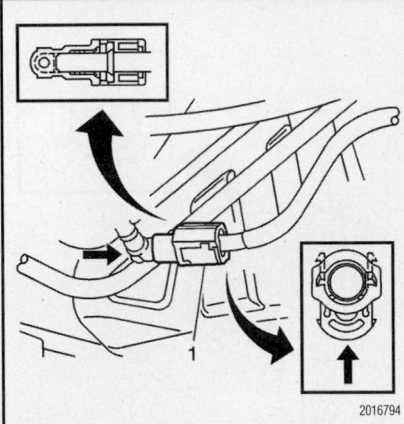

Fig. 355 Align the fuel tube connector (1) with the pipe, then push the fuel tube connector in—1.8L (LAY)

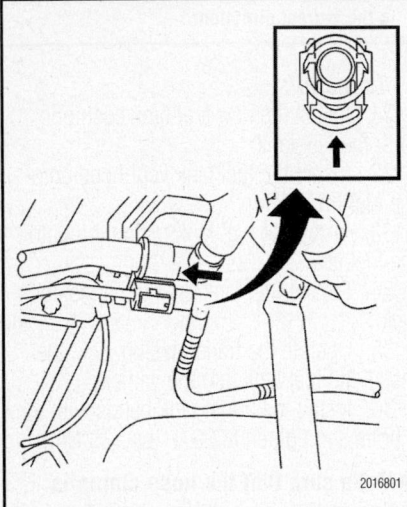

Fig. 356 Align the fuel tube connector with the pipe, then push the fuel tube connector in until the retainer makes a "click" sound to connect the fuel tank breather tube to the pipe

in until the retainer makes a "click" sound to connect the fuel tank breather tube to the pipe.

43. Install the checker onto the pipe.

44. Connect the fuel tank vent hose.

45. Align the fuel tube connector with the pipe, then push the fuel tube connector in until it comes into contact with the seat to connect the fuel tank vent hose to the pipe.

46. Slide the retainer of the fuel tube connector in to lock the claws.

47. Install the charcoal canister assembly.

48. Install the fuel tank protector subassembly with the 4 bolts, and tighten to 49 inch lbs. (5.5 Nm).

49. Install the parking cables with the 4 bolts.

50. Install the front exhaust pipe assembly. Refer to Catalytic Converter, removal & installation.

51. Add fuel.

52. Install the fuel sender gage subassembly.

53. Install the fuel suction tube assembly.

54. Install the fuel pump gage retainer.

55. Connect the fuel tank vent hose.

56. Connect the fuel tank main tube subassembly.

57. Connect the cable to the negative battery terminal.

58. Inspect for a fuel leak.

59. Inspect for a exhaust gas leak.

60. Install the rear floor service hole cover.

61. Install the rear seat cushion assembly.

2.4L (LAX)

See Figures 357 through 366.

1. Remove the rear seat cushion assembly.

2. Remove the rear floor service hole cover for AWD.

3. Release the fuel system pressure. Refer to Relieving Fuel System Pressure.

4. Disconnect the cable from the negative battery terminal. Refer to Battery, precautions.

5. Disconnect the fuel tank main tube subassembly.

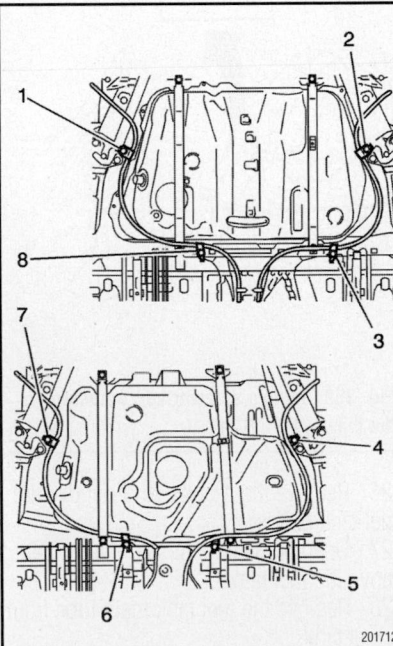

Fig. 357 Remove the 4 bolts (1, 2, 3, 8) or (4, 5, 6, 7), and separate the parking brake cables—2.4L (LAX)

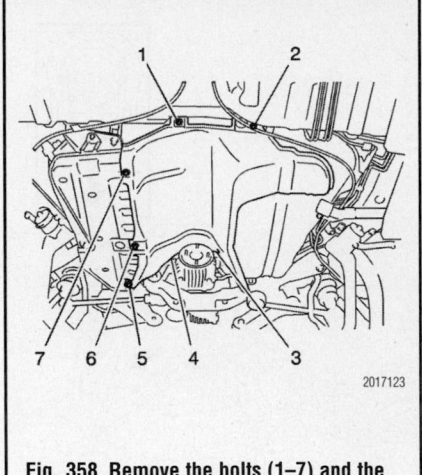

Fig. 358 Remove the bolts (1–7) and the fuel tank protector for AWD

6. Disconnect the fuel tank vent hose for FWD.

7. Remove the fuel pump gage retainer.

8. Remove the right fuel sender gage assembly.

9. Remove the fuel suction tube assembly.

10. Drain the fuel.

11. Remove the catalytic converter. Refer to Catalytic Converter, removal & installation.

12. Remove the propeller with center bearing shaft assembly for AWD. Refer to Propeller Shaft, removal & installation.

13. Remove the 4 bolts and separate the parking brake cables.

14. Remove the charcoal canister assembly.

15. Remove the 7 bolts and the fuel tank protector for AWD.

16. Remove the 4 bolts and the fuel tank protector sub-assembly for FWD.

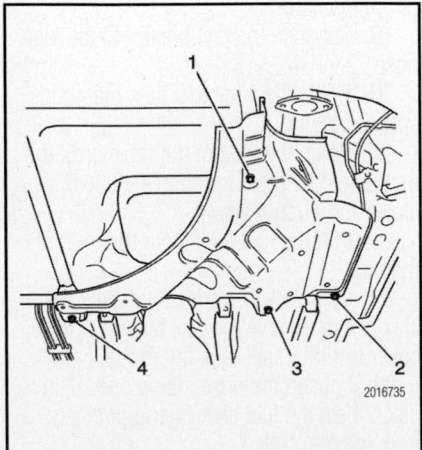

Fig. 359 Remove the bolts (1–4) and the fuel tank protector sub-assembly for FWD

17. Remove the rear suspension member subassembly for AWD.

➡Check that there is no dirt or other foreign objects around the connector before disconnecting it. Clean the connector if necessary. It is necessary to prevent mud or dirt from entering the connector. If mud or dirt gets in the connector, the O-rings may not seal properly. Only disconnect the quick connector by hand. Do not bend, kink or twist the nylon tubes. Protect the connector by covering it with a plastic bag.

18. Disconnect the fuel tank vent hose for Torsion Beam Type Suspension.

19. Pinch the tabs of the retainer of the fuel tube connector to remove the lock claws.

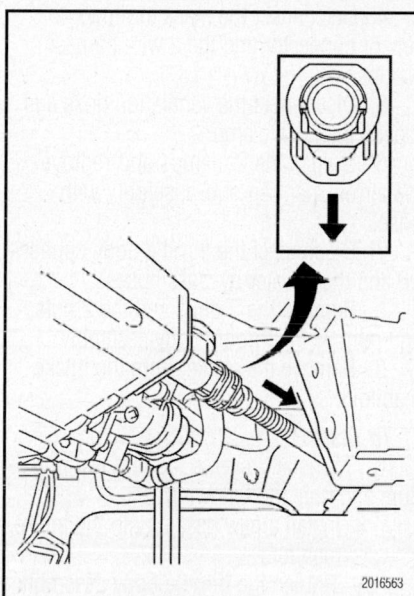

Fig. 360 Pinch the retainer of the fuel tube connector, then pull the fuel tube connector out of the pipe

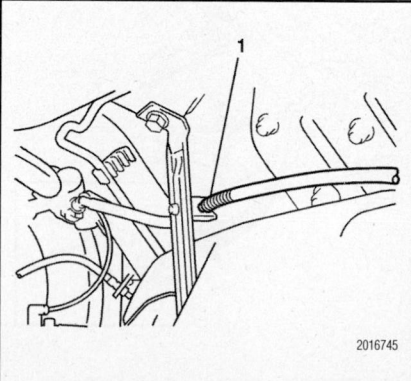

Fig. 361 Separate the breather tube fuel hose (1)

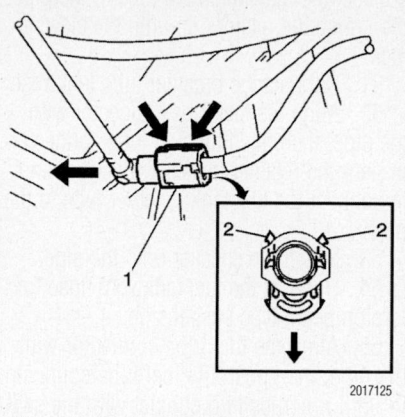

Fig. 362 Pinch the tabs of the retainer (1) of the fuel tube connector to remove the lock claws (2)—2.4L (LAX)

20. Pull the fuel tank vent hose out of the pipe.

21. Disconnect the breather tube fuel hose.

22. Remove the checker of the fuel tube connector from the pipe.

23. Pinch the retainer of the fuel tube connector, then pull the fuel tube connector out of the pipe.

24. Separate the breather tube fuel hose.

25. Pinch the tabs of the retainer of the fuel tube connector to remove the lock claws and push it down.

26. Pull the fuel tank main tube out of the pipe.

27. Using a screwdriver, unfasten the claw. Then remove the fuel tank filler pipe cover from the fuel tank filler pipe.

28. Loosen the hose clamp bolt, then disconnect the fuel tank filler pipe hose from the fuel tank.

29. Hold the fuel tank using a transmission jack.

30. Remove the 4 bolts, then remove the 2 fuel tank bands.

31. Operate the transmission jack, then remove the fuel tank.

32. Remove the fuel tank main tube from the fuel tank.

33. Remove the fuel tank vent hose for AWD.

34. Remove the fuel tank vent hose from the fuel tank clamp for FWD.

35. Remove the fuel tank cushions from the fuel tank.

To install:

36. Install the new fuel tank cushions onto the fuel tank.

37. Install the fuel tank vent hose for AWD.

38. Install the fuel tank vent hose onto the fuel tube clamp for FWD.

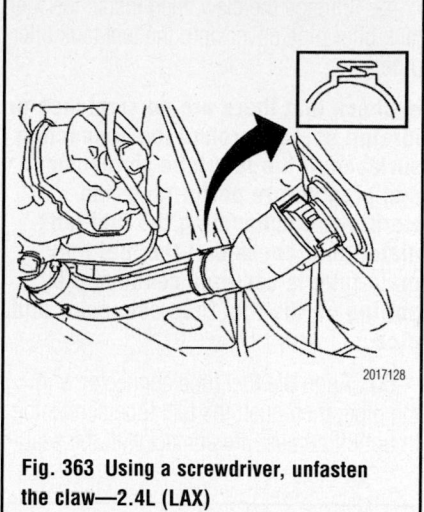

Fig. 363 Using a screwdriver, unfasten the claw—2.4L (LAX)

39. Install the fuel tank main tube onto the fuel tank.

40. Install the fuel tank assembly for AWD.

41. Set the fuel tank on a transmission jack.

42. Operate the transmission jack, then install the fuel tank into the vehicle.

43. Install the 2 fuel tank bands with the 4 bolts and tighten to 29 ft lbs. (39 Nm).

44. Install the fuel tank assembly for FWD.

45. Set the fuel tank on a transmission jack.

46. Operate the transmission jack, then install the fuel tank into the vehicle.

47. Install the 2 fuel tank bands with the 4 bolts and tighten to 29 ft lbs. (39 Nm).

➡Make sure that the hose clamp is facing in the correct direction when installing.

48. Connect the fuel tank to filler pipe hose to the fuel tank.

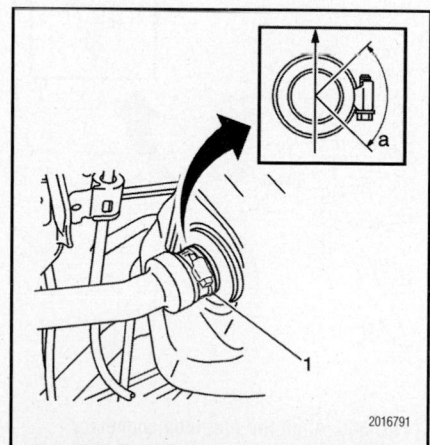

Fig. 364 Connect the fuel tank filler pipe (1) to the fuel tank with hose clamp facing in the correct direction

49. Engage the claw, then install the fuel tank filler pipe cover onto the fuel tank filler pipe.

➡ Check that there are no scratches or foreign objects around the connecting surfaces of the fuel tube connector and pipe before performing this work. After connecting the fuel tank main tube, check that the fuel tank main tube is securely connected by pulling on the fuel tube connector and pipe.

50. Align the fuel tube connector with the pipe, then push the fuel tube connector in until it comes into contact with the seat to

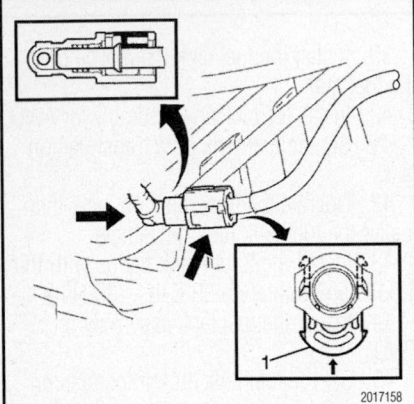

Fig. 365 Align the fuel tube connector with the pipe, then push the fuel tube connector in until it comes into contact with the seat to connect the fuel tank main tube to the pipe, then push the retainer (1) up until the claws lock—2.4L (LAX)

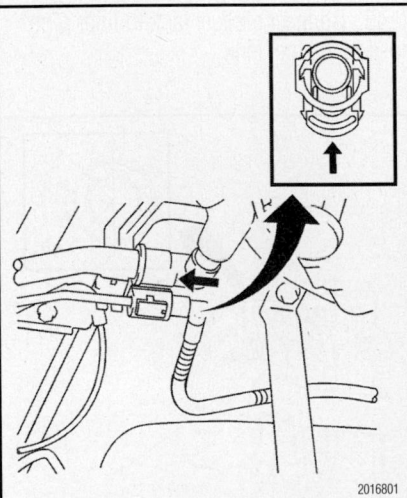

Fig. 366 Align the fuel tube connector with the pipe, then push the fuel tube connector in until the retainer makes a "click" sound

connect the fuel tank main tube to the pipe, then push the retainer up until the claws lock.

51. Connect the breather tube fuel hose.

52. Align the fuel tube connector with the pipe, then push the fuel tube connector in until the retainer makes a "click" sound to connect the fuel tank breather tube to the pipe.

53. Install the checker onto the pipe.

54. Connect the fuel tank vent hose for torsion beam type suspension.

55. Align the fuel tube connector with the pipe, then push the fuel tube connector in until it comes into contact with the seat to connect the fuel tank vent hose to the pipe.

56. Slide the retainer of the fuel tube connector in to lock the claws.

57. Install the rear suspension member sub-assembly for Double Wishbone Type Suspension.

58. Install the charcoal canister assembly.

59. Install the fuel tank protector with the 7 bolts for AWD and tighten to 49 inch lbs. (5.5 Nm).

60. Install the fuel tank protector sub-assembly with the 4 bolts for FWD and tighten to 49 inch lbs. (5.5 Nm).

61. Install the parking cables with the 4 bolts and tighten to 48 inch lbs. (5.4 Nm).

62. Install the propeller with center bearing shaft assembly for AWD. Refer to Propeller Shaft, removal & installation.

63. Install the catalytic converter

64. Add fuel.

65. Install the right fuel sender gage assembly for AWD.

66. Install the fuel suction tube assembly.

67. Install the fuel pump gage retainer.

68. Connect the fuel tank vent hose for FWD.

69. Connect the fuel tank main tube sub-assembly.

70. Connect the cable to the negative battery terminal.

71. Inspect for a fuel leak.

72. Inspect for an exhaust gas leak.

73. Install the rear floor service hole cover.

74. Install the rear seat cushion assembly.

IDLE SPEED

ADJUSTMENT

The idle speed is controlled by the Powertrain Control Module (PCM).

THROTTLE BODY

REMOVAL & INSTALLATION

1.8L (LAY)

See Figure 367.

1. Drain the engine coolant. Refer to Engine Coolant, Drain & Refill Procedure.

➡ Attempting to disengage both front and rear clips at the same time may cause the engine cover to break.

2. Hold the rear of the engine cover and raise it to disengage the 2 clips on the rear of the cover. Continue to raise the cover to disengage the 2 clips on the front of the cover and remove the cover.

3. Remove the air cleaner cap sub-assembly with hose.

4. Disconnect the mass air flow sensor connector and the 2 wire harness clamps.

5. Disconnect the ventilation hose and loosen the hose clamp.

6. Unlock the 2 clamps and remove the air cleaner cap sub-assembly with hose.

7. Disconnect the throttle body connector and the 2 water by-pass hoses.

8. Remove the 2 bolts and the 2 nuts, and remove the throttle body assembly.

9. Remove the gasket from the intake manifold.

To install:

10. To install, reverse the removal procedure and note the following:
- Install a new gasket onto the intake manifold.
- Tighten the throttle body assembly with the 2 bolts and 2 nuts and tighten to 7 ft. lbs. (10 Nm).

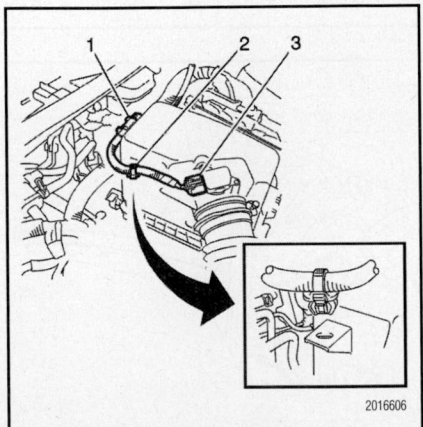

Fig. 367 Disconnect the mass air flow sensor connector (3) and the 2 wire harness clamps (1, 2)—1.8L (LAY)

- Tighten the air cleaner cap sub-assembly hose clamp to 18 inch lbs. (2.0 Nm).
11. Add engine coolant. Refer to Engine Coolant, Drain & Refill Procedure.
12. Inspect for a coolant leak.
13. Position the engine cover and engage the two front fasteners. Engage the two fasteners on the rear of the cover.

2.4L (LAX)

See Figures 368 through 371.

1. Drain the engine coolant. Refer to Engine Coolant, Drain & Refill Procedure.
2. Remove the 2 engine cover fasteners and 2 plastic retainers. Remove the engine cover.
3. Remove the air cleaner cap with hose.
4. Disconnect the mass air flow meter connector.
5. Separate the 2 wire harness clamps.
6. Disconnect the vacuum switching valve connector and the 2 vacuum hoses.
7. Disconnect the ventilation hose.
8. Loosen the air cleaner hose clamp, unlock the 3 air cleaner assembly clamps and remove the air cleaner cap sub-assembly with hose.
9. Remove the throttle body assembly.
10. Disconnect the 2 water by-pass hoses.
11. Disconnect the throttle body assembly connector.
12. Disconnect the throttle body hose.
13. Remove the 4 bolts and the throttle body assembly.
14. Remove the gasket from the intake manifold.

To install:

15. To install, reverse the removal procedure and note the following:

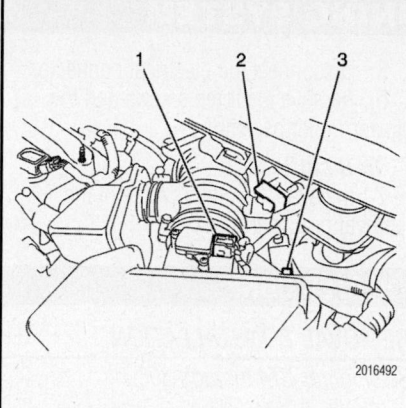

Fig. 368 Disconnect the mass air flow meter connector (1). Separate the 2 wire harness clamps (2, 3)—2.4L (LAX)

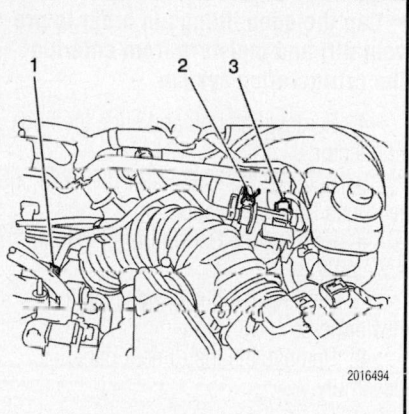

Fig. 369 Disconnect the vacuum switching valve connector (2) and the 2 vacuum hoses (1, 3)—2.4L (LAX)

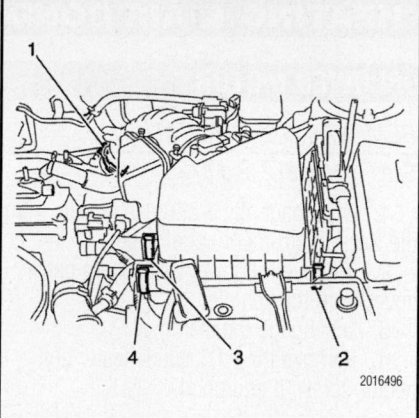

Fig. 370 Loosen the air cleaner hose clamp (1), and unlock the 3 air cleaner assembly clamps (2–4)—2.4L (LAX)

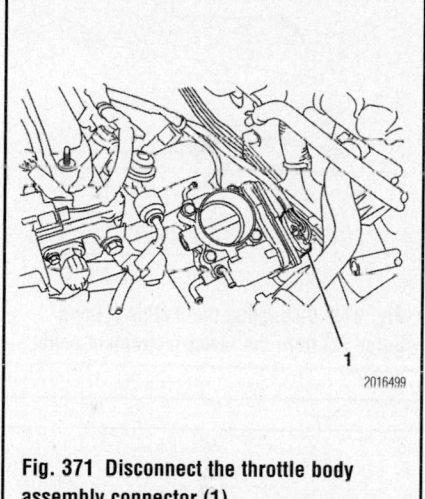

Fig. 371 Disconnect the throttle body assembly connector (1)

- Install a new gasket onto the intake manifold.
- Tighten the 4 throttle body assembly bolts to 22 ft. lbs. (30 Nm).
16. Add engine coolant. Refer to Engine Coolant, Drain & Refill Procedure.

17. Inspect for coolant leak.
18. Install engine cover and tighten fasteners to 62 inch lbs. (7 Nm).
19. Install the 2 engine cover plastic retainers.

HEATING & AIR CONDITIONING SYSTEM

BLOWER MOTOR

REMOVAL & INSTALLATION

See Figures 372 and 373.

1. Disengage the 3 clips and guide from the lower instrument panel cover.
2. Remove the lower instrument panel cover from the vehicle.
3. Disengage the clamp.
4. Remove the PTC quick heater connector screw, if equipped.

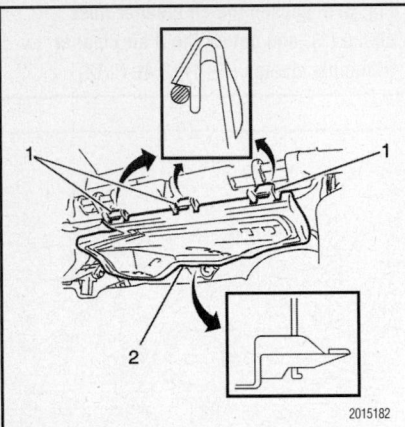

Fig. 372 Disengage the 3 clips (1) and guide (2) from the lower instrument panel cover

5. Disconnect the electrical connector.
6. Remove the three screws and the blower motor assembly.

To install:

7. Installation is the reverse of the removal procedure.

HEATER CORE

REMOVAL & INSTALLATION

See Figures 374 through 395.

1. Disconnect the negative battery cable. Refer to Battery, precautions.
2. Discharge and recover the refrigerant.
3. Drain the engine coolant. Refer to Engine Coolant, Drain & Refill Procedure.

➡ Cap the open fittings in order to prevent dirt and moisture from entering the refrigeration system.

4. Remove the bolt and slide the hook connector.
5. Remove the evaporator inlet and outlet tubes from the evaporator.
6. Remove the O-ring from the tube assembly.
7. Remove the heater hoses at the heater core.
8. Remove the instrument panel assembly.

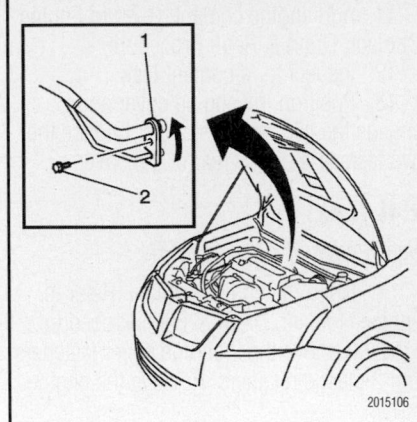

Fig. 374 Remove the bolt (2), then remove evaporator inlet and outlet tubes (1)

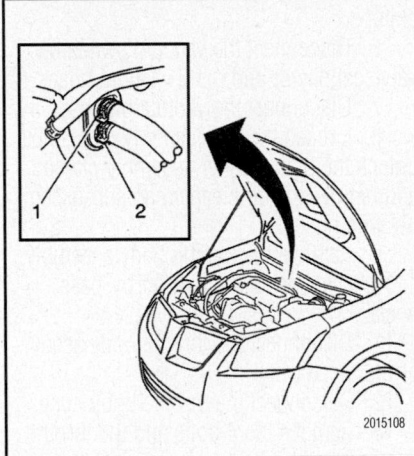

Fig. 375 Remove the heater hoses (1, 2) at the heater core

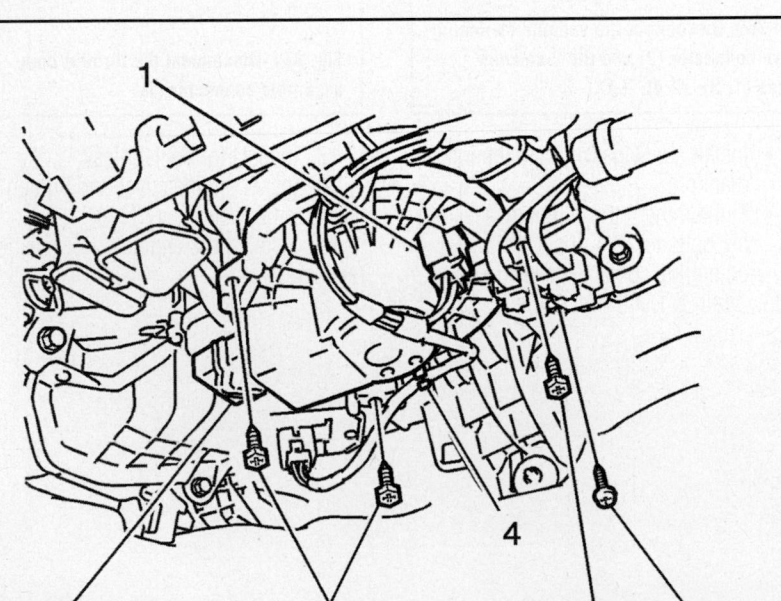

1. Electrical connector
2. PTC quick heater connector screw
3. Screw
4. Harness retainer
5. Blower motor assembly

Fig. 373 Remove the blower motor assembly

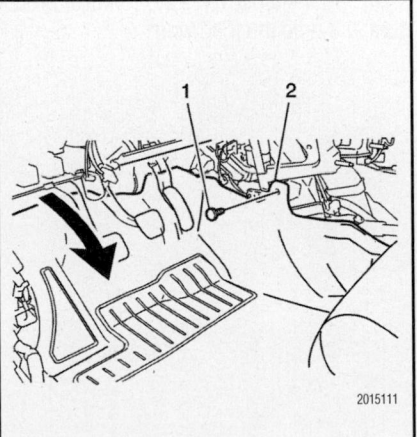

Fig. 376 Remove the clip (1). Turn back the driver side floor carpet (2)

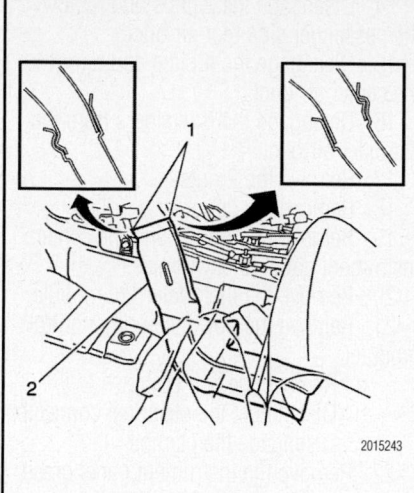

Fig. 377 Disengage the two clips (1) and remove the driver side rear air duct (2)

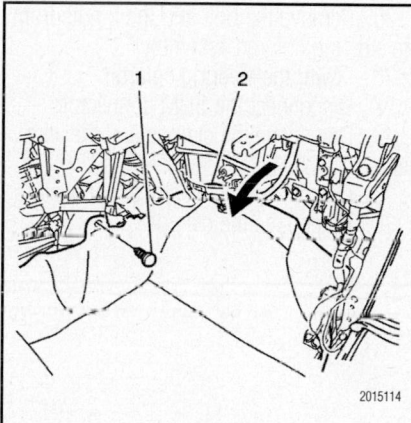

Fig. 378 Remove the clip (1). Turn back the passenger side floor carpet (2)

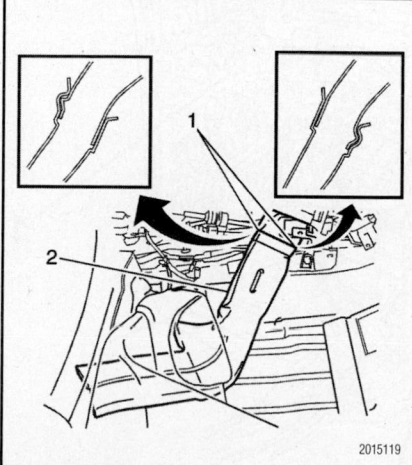

Fig. 379 Disengage the 2 clips (1) and remove the passenger side rear air duct (2)

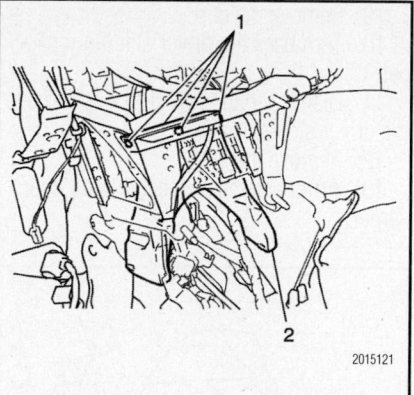

Fig. 380 Disengage the 4 clips (1) and remove the center air duct (2)

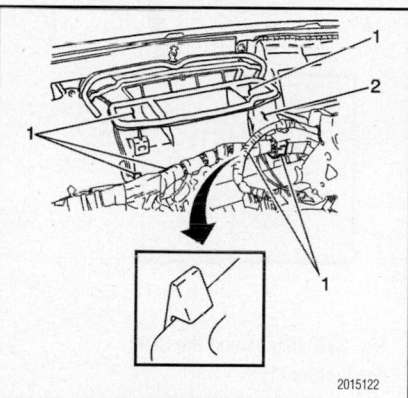

Fig. 381 Disengage the 6 retainers (1) from the defroster air duct (2)

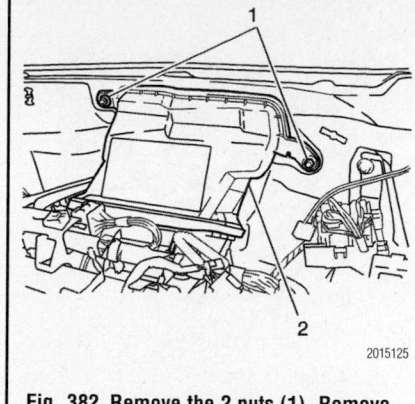

Fig. 382 Remove the 2 nuts (1). Remove the defroster air duct (2)

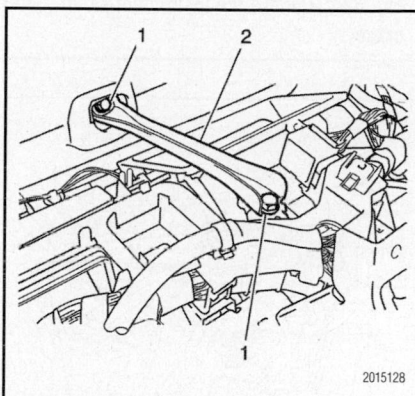

Fig. 383 Remove the 2 bolts (1) and the center instrument panel to cowl brace (2)

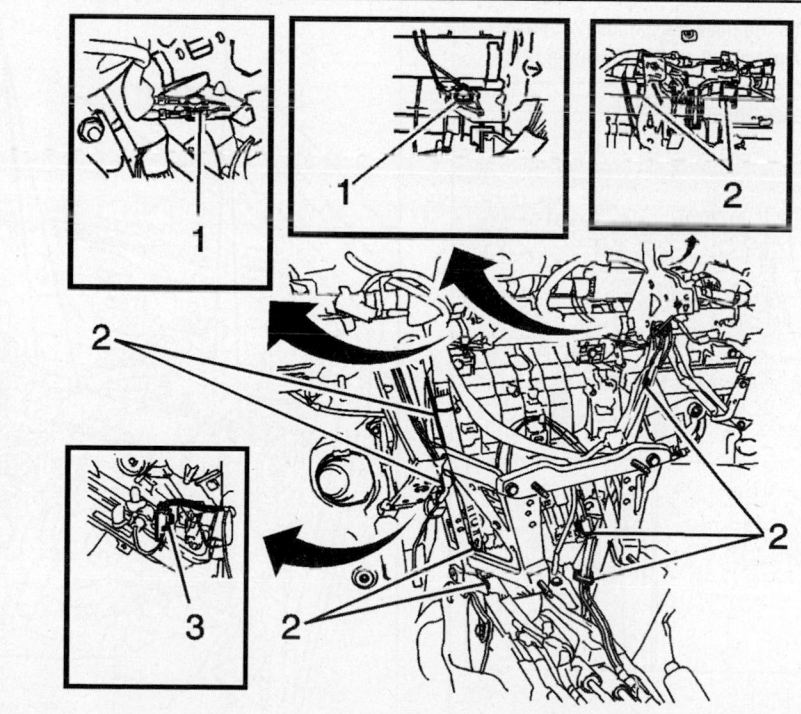

Fig. 384 Remove the 2 power steering control module bolts (1). Disconnect the electrical connector (3). Disengage the clamps (2)

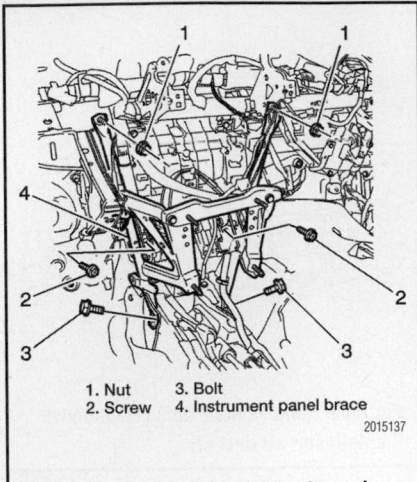

1. Nut
2. Screw
3. Bolt
4. Instrument panel brace

2015137

Fig. 385 Remove the instrument panel brace

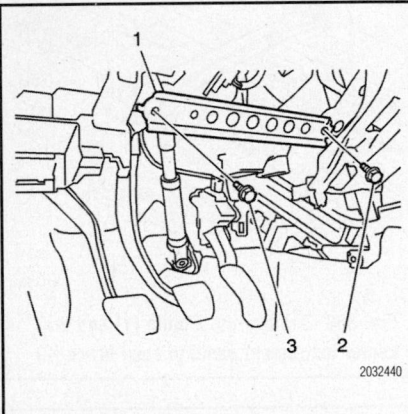

2032440

Fig. 386 Remove the 2 bolts (2, 3) and instrument panel sub reinforcement (1)

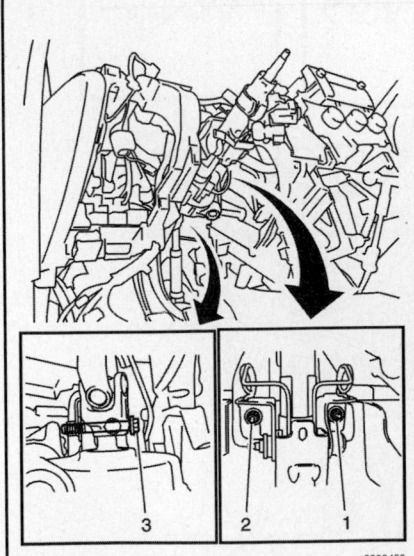

2032455

Fig. 387 Remove the bolt (3) and the 2 nuts (1, 2) from the steering column assembly

9. Remove the clip.
10. Turn back the driver side floor carpet.
11. Disengage the two clips and remove the driver side rear air duct.
12. Remove the clip.
13. Turn back the passenger side floor carpet.

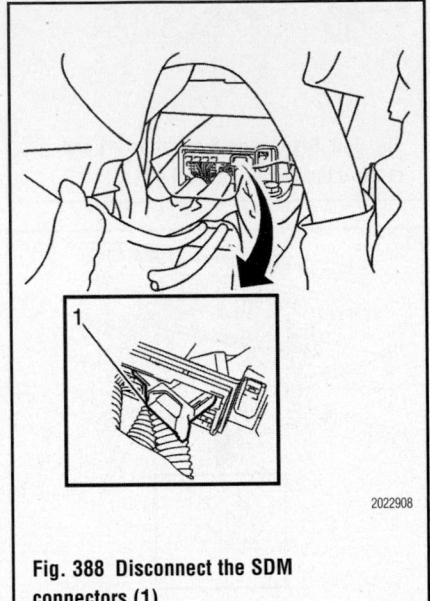

2022908

Fig. 388 Disconnect the SDM connectors (1)

14. Disengage the 2 clips and remove the passenger side rear air duct.
15. Disengage the 4 clips and remove the center air duct.
16. Disengage the 6 retainers from the defroster air duct.
17. Remove the 2 nuts.
18. Remove the defroster air duct.
19. Remove the 2 bolts and the center instrument panel to cowl brace.
20. Remove the theft deterrent module.
21. Remove the power steering control module:
    a. Remove the two bolts.
    b. Disconnect the electrical connector.
    c. Disengage the clamps.
22. Remove the instrument panel brace by removing 2 screws, 2 bolts and 2 nuts.
23. Remove the 2 bolts and instrument panel sub reinforcement.
24. Separate the wire harness clamps from the steering column.
25. Remove the bolt and the 2 nuts from the steering column assembly.
26. Lower the steering column.
27. Disconnect the SDM connectors.
28. Disengage the clamps and the wire harness.
29. Disconnect the electrical connectors.
30. Disengage the clamps.

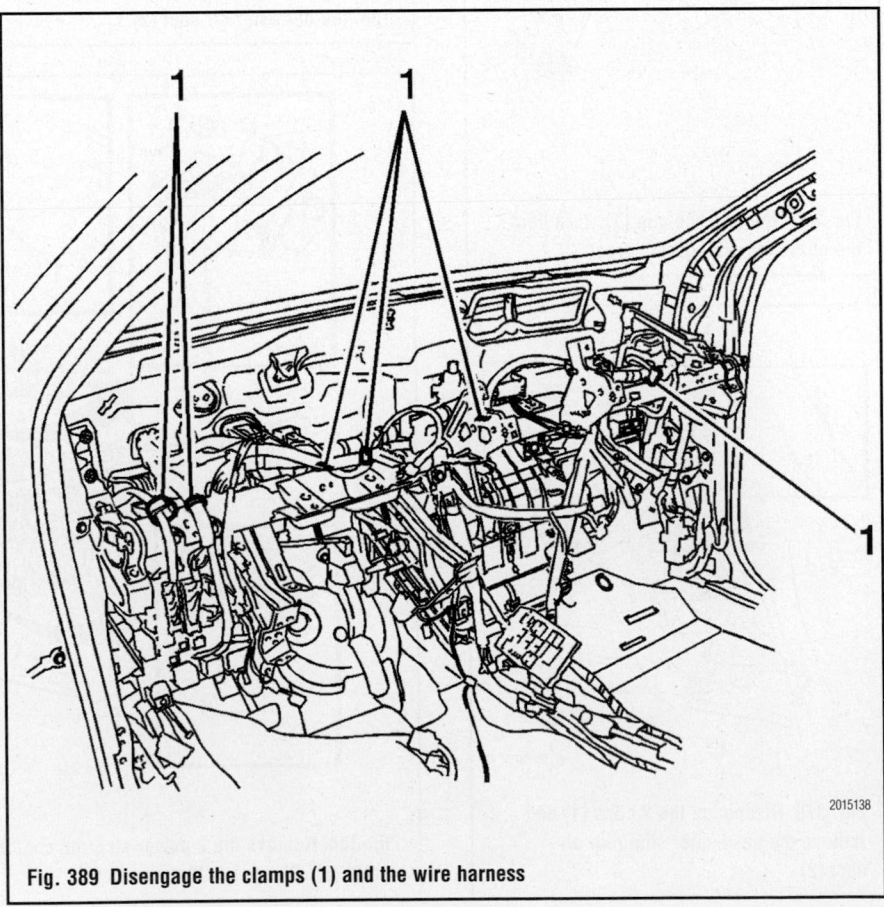

2015138

Fig. 389 Disengage the clamps (1) and the wire harness

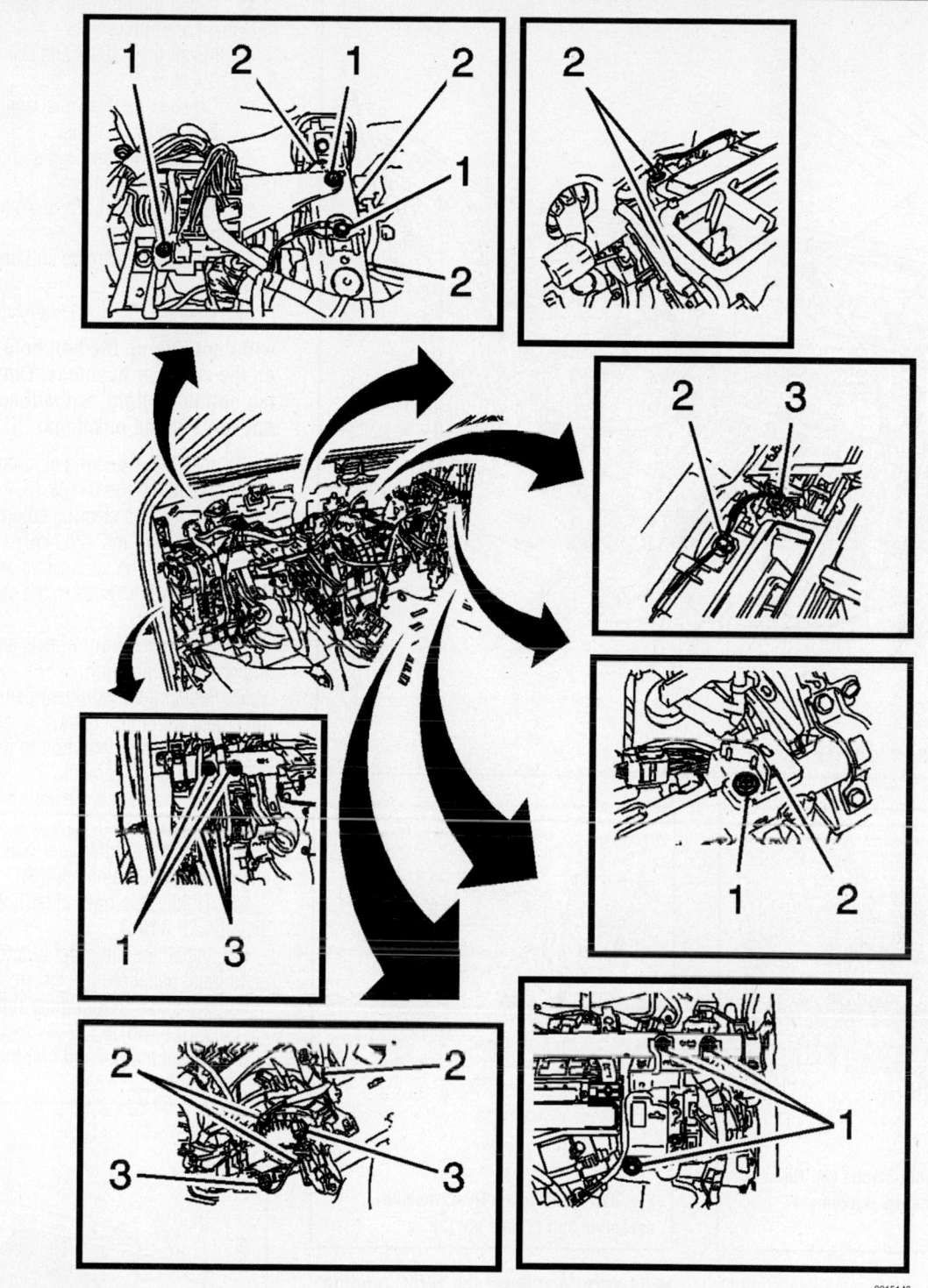

Fig. 390 Disconnect the electrical connectors (3). Disengage the clamps (2). Remove the 9 bolts (1) and disengage wire harness and junction block

31. Remove the 9 bolts and disengage wire harness and junction block.

32. Remove the 7 bolts.

33. Remove the 3 bolts.

34. Remove the instrument panel reinforcement assembly.

35. Disengage the drain cooler hose.

36. Remove the bolt.

37. Remove the nut.

➡Be sure to support the HVAC module assembly when removing it because failure to do so may cause the bracket of the HVAC module assembly to break.

➡When disassembling the HVAC module assembly, eliminate static electricity by touching the vehicle body to prevent the components from being damaged.

38. Remove the HVAC module assembly from the vehicle.

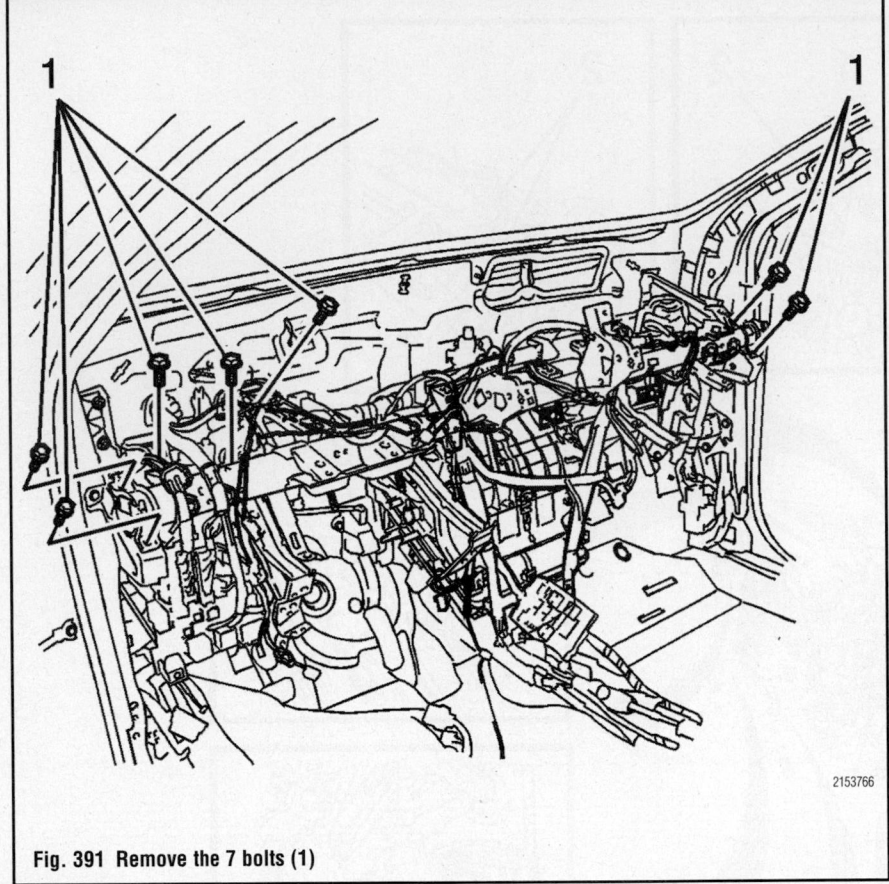

Fig. 391 Remove the 7 bolts (1)

Fig. 392 Remove the 3 bolts (2). Remove the instrument panel reinforcement assembly (1)

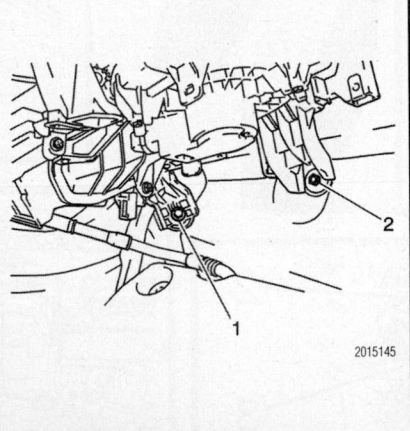

Fig. 393 Remove the HVAC module assembly bolt (1) and nut (2)

39. Remove the HVAC module assembly from the vehicle.

40. Remove the heater core clamp retainer screw, clamp and heater core from the HVAC module assembly.

To install:

41. Install the heater core to the HVAC module assembly and secure with the clamp and screw.

42. Install the HVAC module assembly to the vehicle.

43. Engage the drain cooler hose.

➡**Be sure to support the HVAC module assembly when removing it, as failure to do so may cause the bracket of the HVAC module assembly to break.**

➡**When disassembling the HVAC module assembly, eliminate static electricity by touching the vehicle body to prevent the components from being damaged.**

44. Install the HVAC module nut and bolt, do not tighten at this time.

45. Install the instrument panel reinforcement assembly.

46. Install the 7 bolts and tighten to 18 ft. lbs. (24 Nm).

47. Connect the electrical connectors.

48. Engage the clamps.

49. Engage wire harness and junction block with the nine bolts.

50. Tighten the 9 bolts to 74 inch lbs. (8.4 Nm).

51. Engage the clamps and the wire harness.

52. Connect the SDM connectors.

➡**Do not line-up the bolt hole by prying on the collar or bushings. Only install the bolt in straight, without applying any force to the bushings.**

53. Install the steering column assembly with the bolt and the 2 nuts.

54. Tighten the steering column bolts and nuts to 18 ft. lbs. (25 Nm).

55. Connect the connectors and engage the wire harness clamps to the steering column assembly.

56. Ensure the front wheels are in the straight ahead position.

57. Install the instrument panel sub reinforcement with the 2 bolts.

58. Install the center bolt to the instrument panel reinforcement.

59. Tighten the center bolt to 87 inch lbs. (9.8 Nm).

60. Install the right outer bolt to the instrument panel reinforcement.

61. Tighten the right outer bolt to 87 inch lbs. (9.8 Nm).

62. Install the left outer bolt to the instrument panel reinforcement.

63. Tighten the right outer bolt to 87 inch lbs. (9.8 Nm).

64. Install the nut and bolt for HVAC

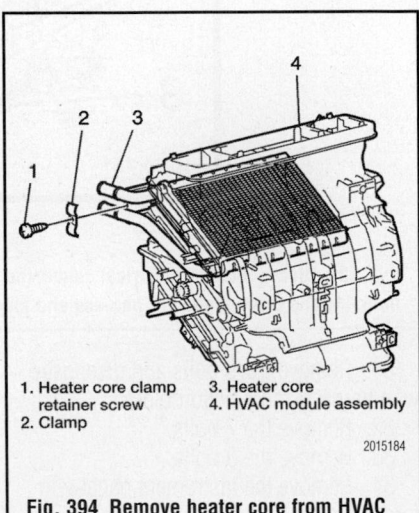

1. Heater core clamp retainer screw
2. Clamp
3. Heater core
4. HVAC module assembly

Fig. 394 Remove heater core from HVAC module assembly

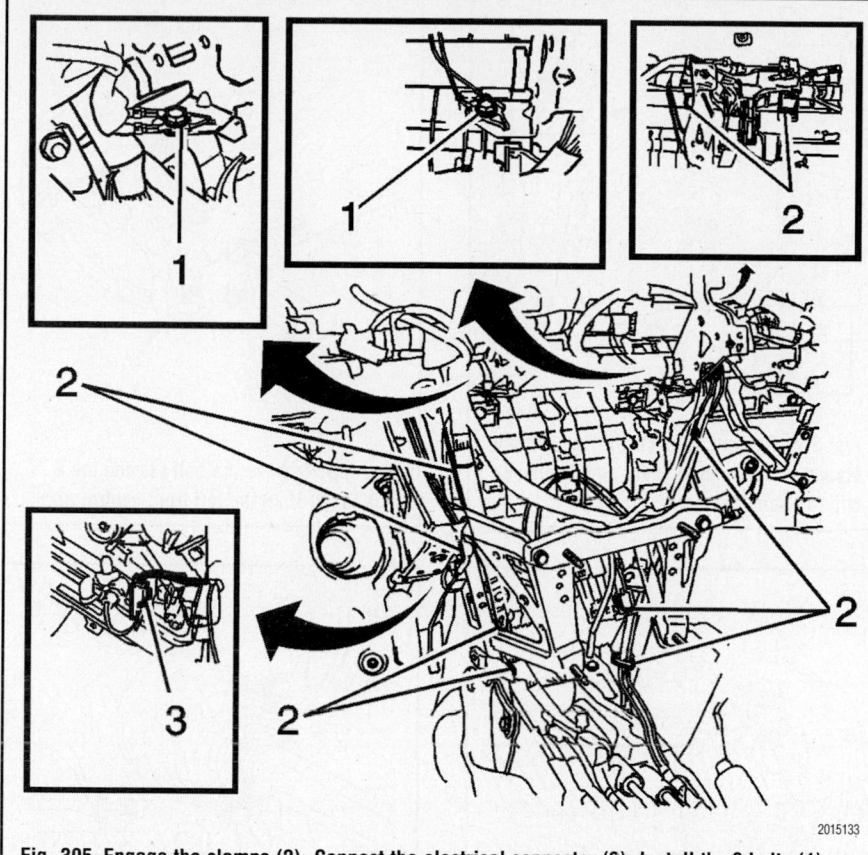

Fig. 395 Engage the clamps (2). Connect the electrical connector (3). Install the 2 bolts (1)

71. Install the defroster air duct.

72. Install the 2 nuts.

73. Tighten the nuts to 87 inch lbs. (9.8 Nm).

74. Install the power steering control module.

75. Engage the 6 retainers to the defroster air duct.

76. Engage the 4 clips and install the center air duct.

77. Engage the 2 clips and install the passenger side rear air duct.

78. Install the passenger side carpet and install the clip.

79. Engage the 2 clips and install the driver side rear air duct.

80. Install the passenger side carpet and install the clip.

81. Install the instrument panel assembly.

82. Install the heater hoses at the heater core.

83. Install new O-rings lubricated with mineral base 525 viscosity refrigerant oil.

84. Install the evaporator inlet and outlet tubes to the evaporator.

85. Install the bolt and slide the hook connector.

86. Tighten the bolt to 87 inch lbs. (9.8 Nm).

87. Add engine coolant. Refer to Engine Coolant, Drain & Refill Procedure.

88. Evacuate and recharge the A/C system.

89. Connect the cable to the negative battery terminal.

90. Operate the A/C system and test for refrigerant leaks.

module assembly and tighten to 87 inch lbs. (9.8 Nm).

65. Install the 2 nuts, 2 bolts and 2 screws for instrument panel brace, and tighten to 87 inch lbs. (9.8 Nm).

66. Engage the clamps.

67. Connect the electrical connector.

68. Install the 2 bolts and tighten to 74 inch lbs. (8.4 Nm).

69. Install the theft deterrent module.

70. Install the 2 bolts and the center instrument panel to cowl brace.

STEERING

POWER STEERING GEAR

REMOVAL & INSTALLATION

AWD

See Figures 396 through 407.

✸✸ WARNING

With wheels of the vehicle facing straight ahead, secure the steering wheel utilizing steering column anti-rotation pin, steering column lock, or a strap to prevent rotation. Locking of the steering column will prevent damage and a possible malfunction of the SIR system. After disconnecting steering column components, do not rotate the steering wheel or move the front tires and wheels. Failure to follow this procedure may cause the

SIR coil assembly to become un-centered and cause possible damage to the SIR coil. If you think the SIR coil has became un-centered, refer to Clockspring Centering.

1. LOCK the steering column with the front wheels in the straight ahead position.

2. Turn back the floor carpet and remove the 2 clips.

3. Remove the column hole cover silencer sheet.

4. Place matchmarks on the intermediate shaft assembly and on the steering gear pinion shaft.

5. Remove the bolt from the intermediate shaft.

6. Separate the intermediate shaft assembly from the steering gear pinion shaft.

7. Remove the 3 clips.

8. Remove the steering column hole cover and disengage the fourth clip from the body.

9. Raise and support the vehicle.

10. Remove the front tire and wheel assemblies.

11. Remove the left side engine splash shield.

12. Remove the right side engine splash shield.

13. Remove the cotter pin and the nut from the left side tie rod end.

14. Use tie rod puller (J-6627-A), or equivalent, to separate the left side tie rod end from the knuckle.

15. Install, but do not tighten, the nut in order to loosely hold the left tie rod end to the knuckle.

16. Remove the cotter pin and the nut from the right side tie rod end.

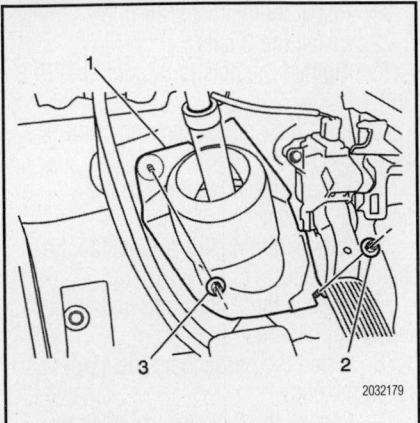

Fig. 396 Turn back the floor carpet and remove the clips (2, 3) and the column hole cover silencer sheet (1)

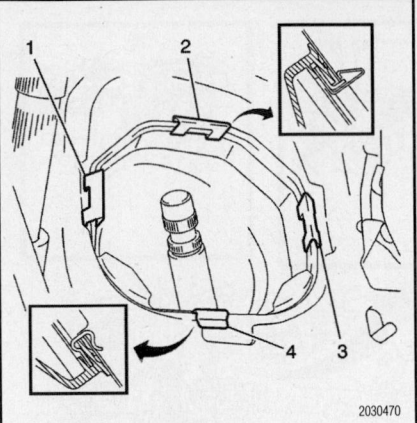

Fig. 398 Remove clips (1–3). Remove the steering column hole cover and disengage clip (4) from the body

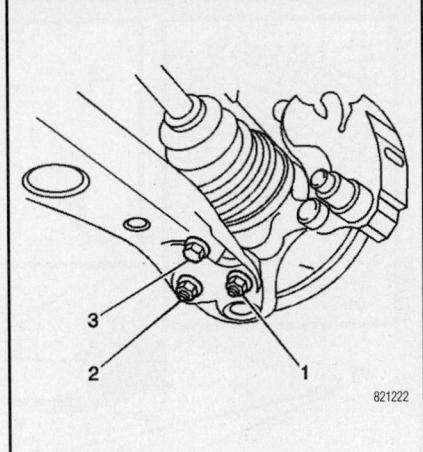

Fig. 400 Remove the bolt (3) and the 2 nuts (1, 2) from the left front control arm

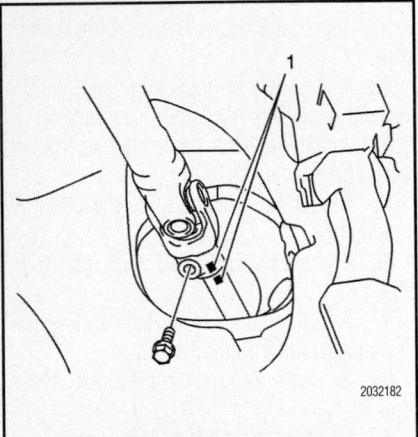

Fig. 397 Place matchmarks (1) on the intermediate shaft assembly and steering gear pinion shaft

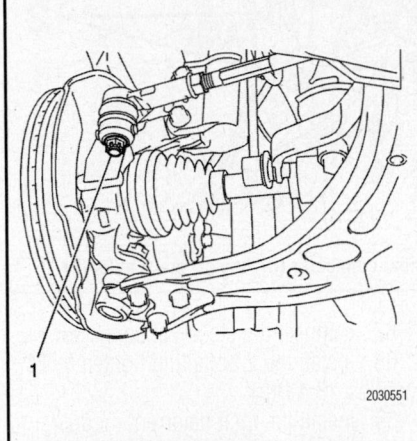

Fig. 399 Remove the cotter pin and nut (1) from the left side tie rod end—AWD

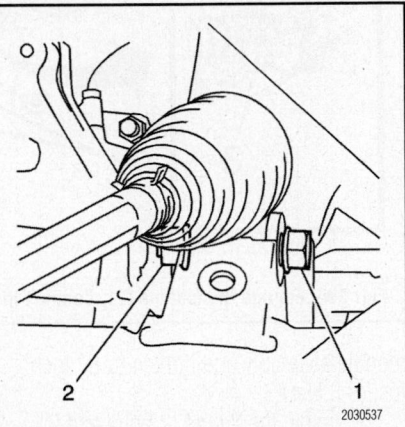

Fig. 401 On the left side, hold the nut (2) and remove the bolt (1) from the steering gear—AWD

17. Using tie rod puller, separate the right side tie rod end from the knuckle.

18. Install, but do not tighten, the nut in order to loosely hold the right tie rod end to the knuckle.

19. Remove the bolt and 2 nuts from the left front control arm.

20. Remove the bolt and the 2 nuts from the right front control arm.

21. Use wire to secure the steering gear to the transfer case.

22. Lower the front suspension crossmember as necessary to allow access to the steering gear.

23. On the left side, hold the nut and remove the bolt from the steering gear.

24. On the right side, hold the nut and remove the bolt from the steering gear.

25. Remove the 4 bolts from the stabilizer shaft insulator clamps.

26. Remove the 2 nuts from the 2 outer tie rod ends.

27. Remove the wire and the steering gear from the crossmember.

28. Remove the steering column hole cover from the steering gear.

29. Inspect the steering column hole cover for damage. If the cover is damaged, replace the cover.

30. Wrap tape around the Steering Gear Support (CH-49200).

31. Use the CH-49200 support and a vise to hold the steering gear securely.

32. Paint matchmarks on the tie rod ends and on the inner tie rods.

33. Loosen the locknuts.

34. Remove the tie rod ends and the lock nuts.

To inspect:

35. Using a torque wrench and a socket, inspect the total preload around the steering rack center position. If the total preload is not within the specified range, replace the steering gear. The standard preload is 7-9 inch lbs. (0.7-1.1 Nm).

36. Inspect the ball joint seal on each of the tie rod ends. If the seal is damaged or not holding the lubricant, replace the damaged tie rod end.

37. Clamp each of the tie rod ends in a soft-jawed vise.

38. Install a nut to the stud.

39. Move the ball joint back and forth 5 times.

40. Use a beam type torque wrench and a socket on the nut in order to turn the ball joint continuously at a rate of 2–4 seconds per turn.

41. Measure the turning torque on the 5th turn. If the turning torque is not within the specified range, replace the tie rod end. The standard turning torque is 3-17 inch lbs. (0.3-1.9 Nm).

42. Inspect the steering column hole cover for damage. If the cover is damaged, replace the cover.

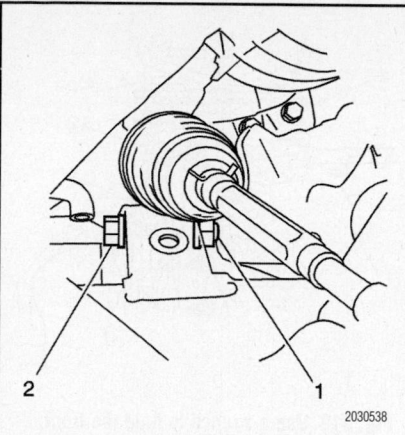

Fig. 402 On the right side, hold the nut (1) and remove the bolt (2) from the steering gear—AWD

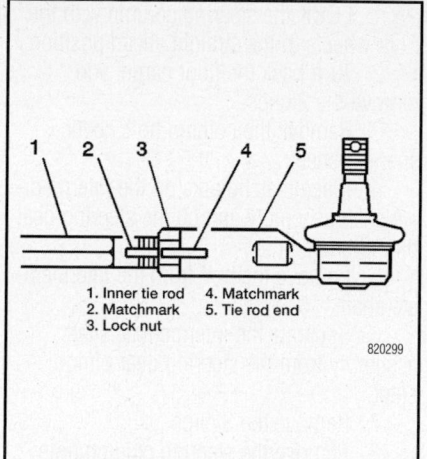

1. Inner tie rod   4. Matchmark
2. Matchmark   5. Tie rod end
3. Lock nut

Fig. 404 Remove the tie rod ends and the lock nuts

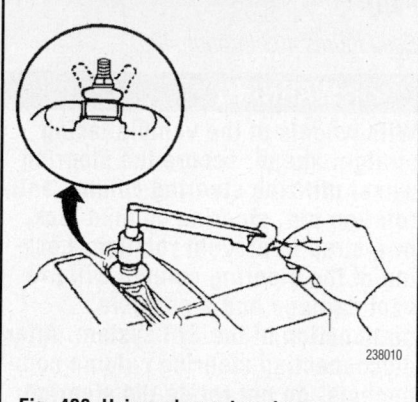

Fig. 406 Using a beam type torque wrench and a socket on the nut, turn the ball joint continuously at a rate of 2–4 seconds per turn

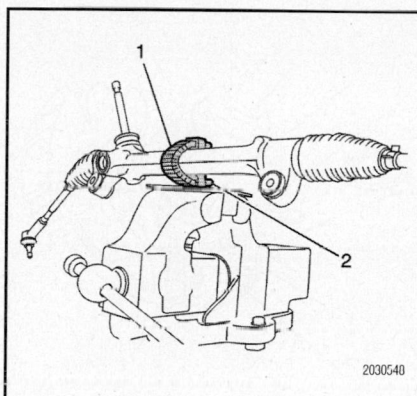

Fig. 403 Wrap tape (1) around the Steering Gear Support (CH-49200) (2). Use the CH-49200 support and a vise to hold the steering gear securely—AWD

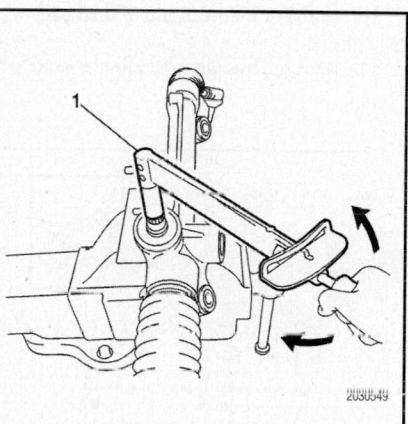

Fig. 405 Using a torque wrench (1) and a socket, inspect the total preload around the steering rack center position

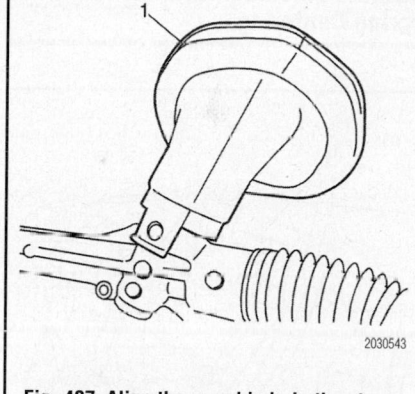

Fig. 407 Align the round hole in the steering column hole cover (1) with the protrusion on the steering gear—AWD

To install:

43. Install, but do not tighten, the lock nuts and the tie rod ends to the inner tie rods. Align the matchmarks.

44. Align the round hole in the steering column hole cover with the protrusion on the steering gear. Install the cover.

45. Position the steering gear near the transfer case. Use wire to secure the steering gear to the transfer case.

46. Position the tie rod ends on the knuckles. Install, but do not tighten, the nuts in order to loosely hold the tie rod ends to the knuckles.

47. Raise and support the front suspension crossmember close to the steering gear.

48. Install the stabilizer shaft insulator brackets.

49. Install the 4 bolts to the brackets and tighten to 18 ft. lbs. (24 Nm).

50. On the left side, install the bolt and the nut to retain the steering gear to the crossmember. Hold the nut and tighten the bolt to 60 ft. lbs. (82 Nm).

51. On the right side, install the bolt and the nut to retain the steering gear to the crossmember. Hold the nut and tighten the bolt to 60 ft. lbs. (82 Nm).

52. Install the front suspension crossmember.

53. Remove the wire supporting the steering gear.

54. Install the 2 nuts and the bolt to the left front control arm and tighten to 66 ft. lbs. (89 Nm).

55. Install the 2 nuts and the bolt to the right front control arm and tighten to 66 ft. lbs. (89 Nm).

56. Tighten the 2 tie rod end nuts to 36 ft. lbs. (49 Nm).

57. If the nut does not align with the hole for the cotter pin, tighten the nut up to an additional 60 degrees.

58. Install 2 NEW cotter pins.

59. Engage the steering column hole cover clip onto the body and install the steering column hole cover onto the body.

60. Install the 3 remaining the steering column hole cover clips.

61. Align the matchmarks and install the intermediate shaft to the steering gear pinion shaft.

62. Install the bolt and tighten to 26 ft. lbs. (35 Nm).

63. Ensure the front wheels are in the straight ahead position.

64. Install the column hole cover silencer sheet with the 2 clips.

65. Install the floor carpet.

66. Install the right side engine splash shield.

67. Install the left side engine splash shield.

68. Install the front tire and wheel assemblies.

69. Measure the wheel alignment.

70. Adjust the front toe and tighten the tie rod end lock nuts.

71. Lower the vehicle.

FWD

See Figures 408 through 420.

✳✳ WARNING

With wheels of the vehicle facing straight ahead, secure the steering wheel utilizing steering column anti-rotation pin, steering column lock, or a strap to prevent rotation. Locking of the steering column will prevent damage and a possible malfunction of the SIR system. After disconnecting steering column components, do not rotate the steering wheel or move the front tires and wheels. Failure to follow this procedure may cause the SIR coil assembly to become un-centered and cause possible damage to the SIR coil. If you think the SIR coil has became un-centered, refer to Clockspring Centering.

1. LOCK the steering column with the front wheels in the straight ahead position.
2. Turn back the floor carpet and remove the 2 clips.
3. Remove the column hole cover silencer sheet.
4. Place matchmarks on the intermediate shaft assembly and on the steering gear pinion shaft.
5. Remove the bolt from the intermediate shaft.
6. Separate the intermediate shaft assembly from the steering gear pinion shaft.
7. Remove the 3 clips.
8. Remove the steering column hole cover and disengage the fourth clip from the body.
9. Raise and support the vehicle.
10. Remove the front tire and wheel assemblies.
11. Remove the left side engine splash shield.

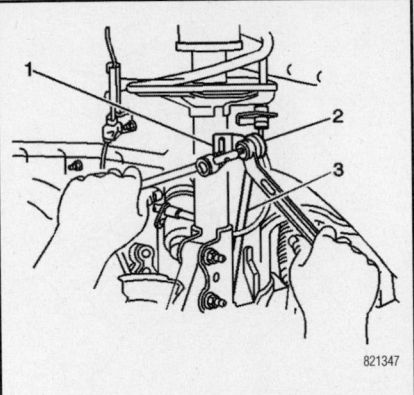

Fig. 412 Use a wrench to hold the front stabilizer shaft link stud (2). Remove the nut from the stud and separate the link (3) from the front strut bracket (1)—FWD

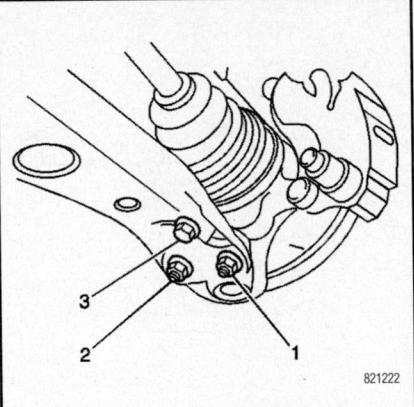

Fig. 413 Remove the bolt (3) and the 2 nuts (1, 2) from the left front control arm

12. Remove the right side engine splash shield.
13. Using paint, place matchmarks on the tie rod ends and on the inner tie rods.
14. Remove the cotter pin from the left side tie rod end ball stud.
15. Loosen the left side tie rod end nut.
16. Use the puller (J-6627-A), or equivalent, to separate the left side tie rod end from the knuckle.
17. Remove the left side tie rod nut.
18. Remove the cotter pin from the right side tie rod end ball stud.
19. Loosen the right side tie rod nut.
20. Use the puller in order to separate the right side tie rod end from the knuckle.
21. Remove the right side tie rod nut.
22. Use a wrench to hold the left front stabilizer shaft link stud. Remove the nut from the stud and separate the link from the left front strut bracket.
23. Use a wrench to hold the right front stabilizer shaft link stud. Remove the nut from the stud and separate the link from the right front strut bracket.

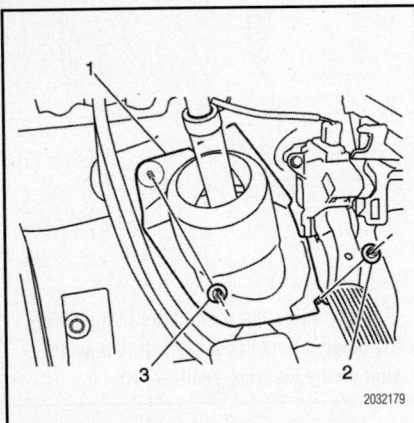

Fig. 408 Turn back the floor carpet and remove the clips (2, 3) and the column hole cover silencer sheet (1)

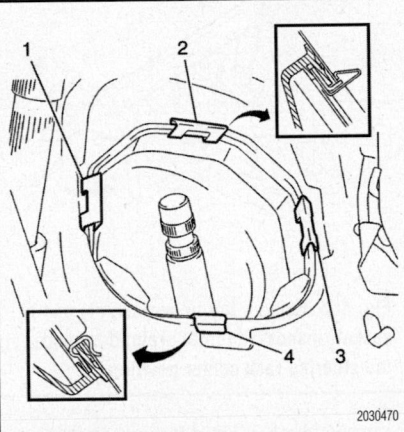

Fig. 410 Remove clips (1–3). Remove the steering column hole cover and disengage clip (4) from the body

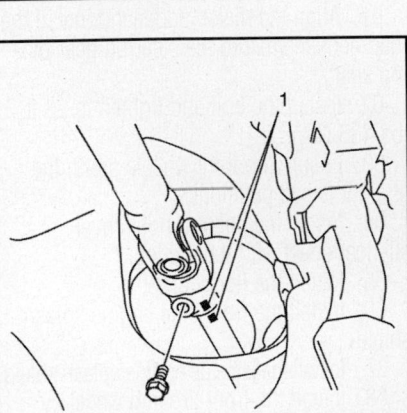

Fig. 409 Place matchmarks (1) on the intermediate shaft assembly and steering gear pinion shaft

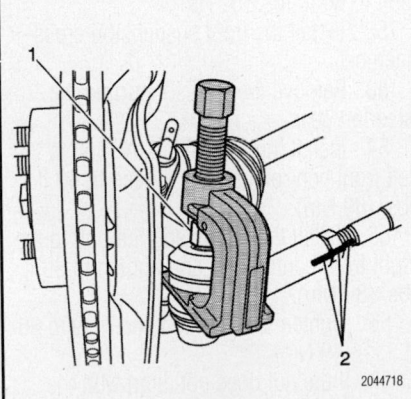

Fig. 411 Place matchmarks (2) on the tie rod ends and on the inner tie rods. Loosen the left side tie rod end nut (1)—FWD

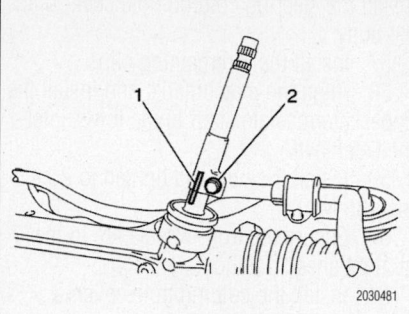

Fig. 414 Place matchmarks (1) on the lower intermediate shaft and on the steering gear pinion shaft. Remove the bolt (2) and the lower intermediate shaft from the steering gear—FWD

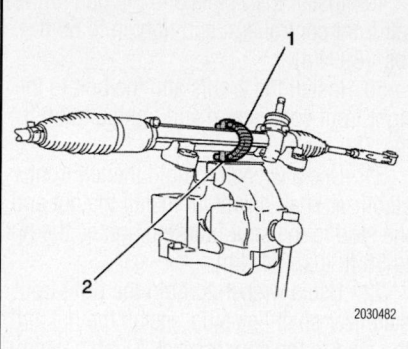

Fig. 416 Wrap tape (1) around the steering gear support (2). Use the support and a vise to hold the steering gear securely—FWD

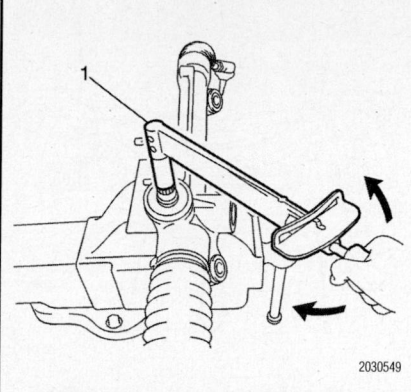

Fig. 418 Using a torque wrench (1) and a socket, inspect the total preload around the steering rack center position

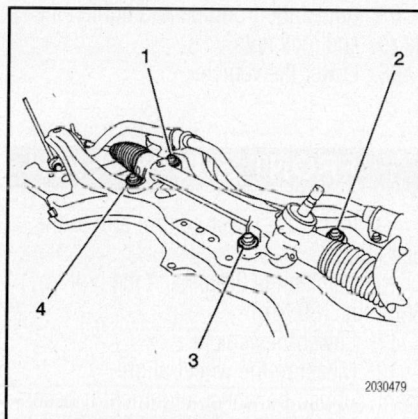

Fig. 415 Remove bolts (1–4) and the steering gear from the front suspension crossmember—FWD

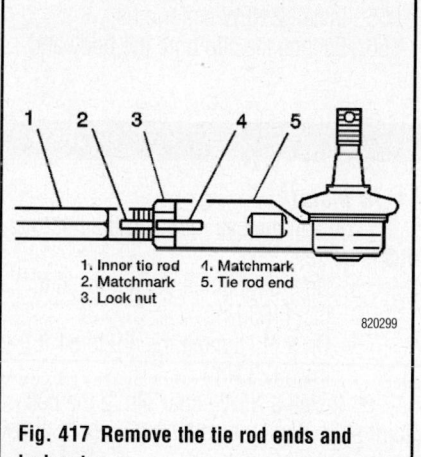

1. Inner tie rod
2. Matchmark
3. Lock nut
4. Matchmark
5. Tie rod end

Fig. 417 Remove the tie rod ends and lock nuts

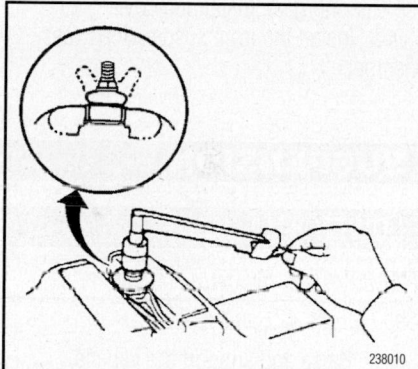

Fig. 419 Using a beam type torque wrench and a socket on the nut, turn the ball joint continuously at a rate of 2–4 seconds per turn

24. Remove the bolt and 2 nuts from the left front control arm.

25. Remove the bolt and the 2 nuts from the right front control arm

26. Lower the front suspension crossmember as necessary to allow access to the steering gear.

27. Remove the steering column hole cover from the steering gear.

28. Using paint, place matchmarks on the lower intermediate shaft and on the steering gear pinion shaft.

29. Remove the bolt and the lower intermediate shaft from the steering gear.

30. Remove the 4 bolts and the steering gear from the front suspension crossmember.

31. Wrap tape around the Steering Gear Support (CH-49200).

32. Use the steering gear support and a vise to hold the steering gear securely.

33. Loosen the lock nuts.

34. Remove the tie rod ends.

35. Remove the lock nuts.

To inspect:

36. Using a torque wrench and a socket, inspect the total preload around the steering rack center position. If the total preload is not within the specified range, replace the steering gear. The standard preload is 7-9 inch lbs. (0.7-1.1 Nm).

37. Inspect the ball joint seal on each of the tie rod ends. If the seal is damaged or not holding the lubricant, replace the damaged tie rod end.

38. Clamp each of the tie rod ends in a soft-jawed vise.

39. Install a nut to the stud.

40. Move the ball joint back and forth 5 times.

41. Use a beam type torque wrench and a socket on the nut in order to turn the ball joint continuously at a rate of 2–4 seconds per turn.

42. Measure the turning torque on the 5th turn. If the turning torque is not within the specified range, replace the tie rod end. The standard turning torque is 3–17 inch lbs. (0.3–1.9 Nm).

43. Inspect the steering column hole cover for damage. If the cover is damaged, replace the cover.

To install:

44. Install, but do not tighten, the lock nuts and the tie rod ends to the inner tie rods. Align the matchmarks.

   a. Install the steering gear to the front suspension crossmember sub-assembly with the 4 bolts:

   b. Tighten the right front bolt 4 to 43 ft. lbs. (58 Nm).

   c. Tighten the left front bolt 3 to 43 ft. lbs. (58 Nm).

   d. Tighten the left rear bolt 2 to 43 ft. lbs. (58 Nm).

   e. Tighten the right rear bolt 1 to 43 ft. lbs. (58 Nm).

45. Align the matchmarks and install the lower intermediate shaft to the steering gear pinion shaft.

46. Install the bolt and tighten to 26 ft. lbs. (35 Nm).

47. Align the round hole in the steering

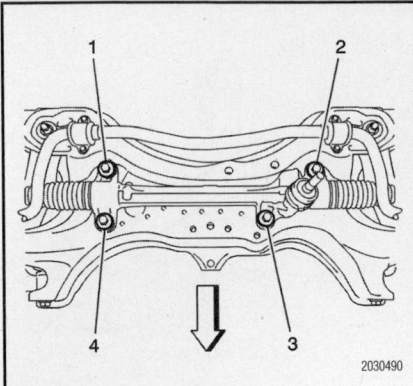

Fig. 420 Install the steering gear to the front suspension crossmember subassembly with the bolts (1–4)—FWD

column hole cover with the protrusion on the steering gear. Install the cover.

48. Install the front suspension crossmember.

49. Install the 2 nuts and the bolt to the left front control arm and tighten to 66 ft. lbs. (89 Nm).

50. Install the 2 nuts and the bolt to the right front control arm and tighten to 66 ft. lbs. (89 Nm).

51. Use a wrench to hold the left front stabilizer shaft link stud. Install the nut and the stud to the strut bracket. Tighten the nut to 55 ft. lbs. (74 Nm).

52. Use a wrench to hold the right front stabilizer shaft link stud. Install the nut and the stud to the strut bracket. Tighten the nut to 55 ft. lbs. (74 Nm).

53. Connect the tie rod ends to the steering knuckles with the nuts. Tighten the nuts to 36 ft. lbs. (49 Nm).

54. If the nut does not align with the hole for the cotter pin, tighten the nut up to an additional 60 degrees.

55. Install 2 NEW cotter pins.

56. Engage the clip onto the body and install the steering column hole cover onto the body.

57. Install the 3 remaining clips.

58. Align the matchmarks and install the upper intermediate shaft to the lower intermediate shaft.

59. Install the bolt and tighten to 26 ft. lbs. (35 Nm).

60. Ensure the front wheels are in the straight ahead position.

61. Install the column hole cover silencer sheet with the 2 clips.

62. Install the floor carpet.

63. Install the right side engine splash shield.

64. Install the left side engine splash shield.

65. Install the front tire and wheel assemblies.

66. Measure the wheel alignment.

67. Adjust the front toe and tighten the tie rod end lock nuts.

68. Lower the vehicle.

SUSPENSION

LOWER BALL JOINT

REMOVAL & INSTALLATION

See Figures 421 and 422.

1. Raise and support the vehicle.

2. Remove the bolt and the 2 nuts from the control arm.

3. Remove the lower control arm from the ball joint.

4. Remove the cotter pin from the ball joint stud.

5. Remove the nut from the ball joint stud.

6. Use the appropriate ball joint remover to remove the ball joint from the knuckle.

To install:

7. Install the ball joint and the nut to the knuckle.

- On 1.8L, tighten the nut to 76 ft. lbs. (103 Nm).
- On 2.4L, tighten the nut to 91 ft. lbs. (123 Nm).

8. Install a NEW cotter pin to the ball joint stud. Bend the cotter pin ends in order to retain the nut.

➡**Do not loosen the nut in order to insert the cotter pin. Instead, tighten the nut up to 1/6 additional turn in order to insert the cotter pin.**

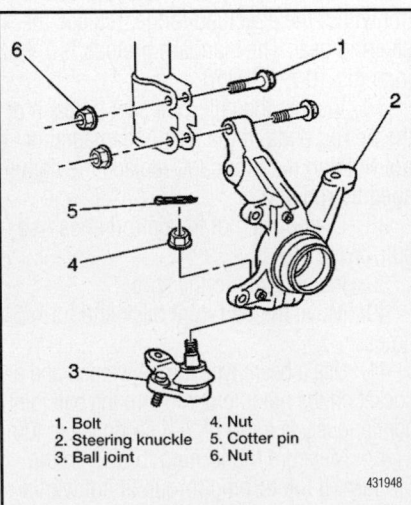

1. Bolt
2. Steering knuckle
3. Ball joint
4. Nut
5. Cotter pin
6. Nut

Fig. 422 Remove the ball joint from the knuckle

FRONT SUSPENSION

9. Install the lower control arm to the ball joint.

10. Tighten the 2 nuts and the bolt to 66 ft. lbs. (89 Nm).

11. Lower the vehicle.

12. Measure the wheel alignment. Adjust the wheel alignment if necessary.

LOWER CONTROL ARM

REMOVAL & INSTALLATION

See Figures 421 and 423.

1. Remove the bolt and the 2 nuts from the control arm.

2. Lower the front suspension crossmember as far as necessary to remove the control arm fasteners.

3. Remove the upper bolt holding the control arm to the crossmember.

4. Hold the nut and remove the lower bolt holding the control arm to the crossmember.

➡**DO NOT turn the nut.**

5. Remove the control arm from the crossmember.

To install:

➡**DO NOT completely tighten the nut and bolts holding the control arm to the crossmember. The weight of the vehicle must be on the tire and wheel assemblies before tightening the nut and the bolts.**

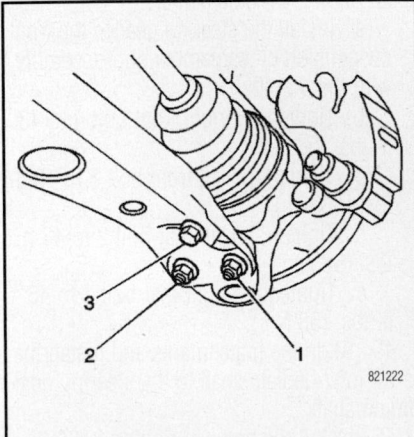

Fig. 421 Remove the bolt (3) and the 2 nuts (1, 2) from the control arm

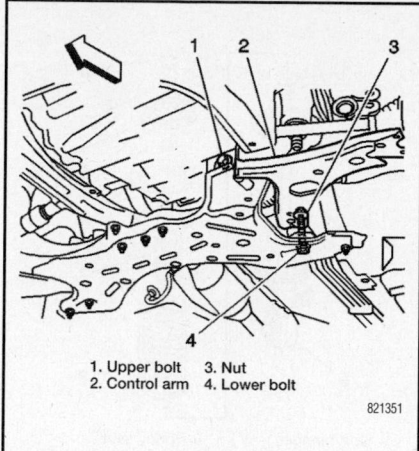

1. Upper bolt 3. Nut
2. Control arm 4. Lower bolt

821351

Fig. 423 Remove the bolts and the control arm

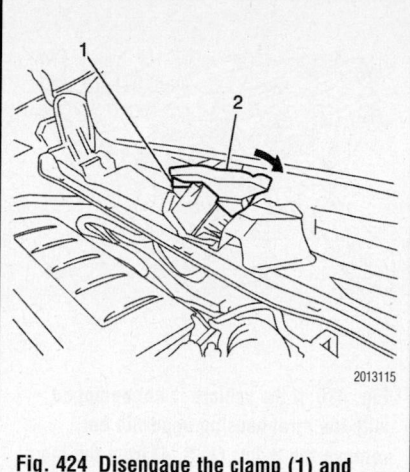

2013115

Fig. 424 Disengage the clamp (1) and bend the right side water guard plate (2)

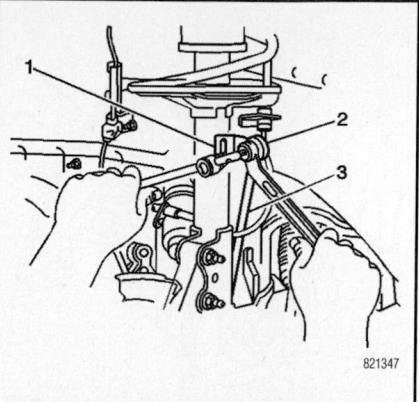

821347

Fig. 426 Use a wrench to hold the front stabilizer shaft link stud (2). Remove the nut and the stud from the bracket (1). Separate the link (3) from the strut

6. Install the lower control arm and the upper bolt to the crossmember.

7. Hold the nut and install the lower bolt.

8. Raise and install the lower control arms and the crossmember to the vehicle.

9. Install the 2 nuts and the bolt to the control arm and tighten to 66 ft. lbs. (89 Nm).

10. With the weight of the vehicle on the tire and wheel assemblies, push down on the front bumper 3 times in order to bounce the vehicle and stabilize the suspension.

11. Hold the nut and tighten the lower bolt holding the control arm to the crossmember to 101 ft. lbs. (137 Nm).

12. Tighten the upper bolt holding the control arm to the crossmember to 101 ft. lbs. (137 Nm).

13. Measure the wheel alignment. Adjust the wheel alignment if necessary.

MACPHERSON STRUT

REMOVAL & INSTALLATION

See Figures 424 through 430.

1. Remove the windshield wiper motor.

2. Disengage the clamp and bend the right side water guard plate.

3. Disengage the clamp on the left side of the dash upper extension panel.

4. Remove the 4 bolts from the right side of the panel.

5. Remove the 5 bolts from the left side of the panel

6. Remove the 3 bolts from the center of the panel.

7. Remove the dash upper extension panel.

8. Raise and support the vehicle.

9. Remove the front tire and wheel assembly.

10. Use a wrench to hold the front stabilizer shaft link stud.

11. Remove the nut and the stud from the bracket.

12. Separate the link from the strut.

13. Remove the ABS wheel speed sensor from the steering knuckle. Position the sensor to the side. Refer to Speed Sensors, removal & installation.

14. Remove the front brake hose bolt and the hose from the bracket on the strut. Position the hose and the bolt to the side.

15. Position the speed sensor wire away from the strut.

16. Loosen the 2 nuts on the lower side of the strut assembly. Do not remove the nuts or the bolts yet.

17. Partially lower the vehicle.

18. If equipped with the strut housing upper tie bar, remove the 3 nuts and the tie bar bracket.

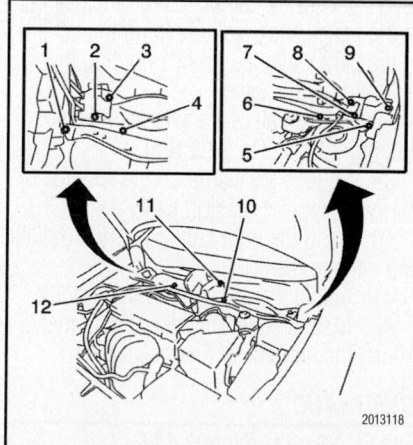

2013118

Fig. 425 Remove the 4 bolts (1–4) from the right side of the panel, the 5 bolts (5–9) from the left side of the panel, and the 3 bolts (10–12) from the center of the panel

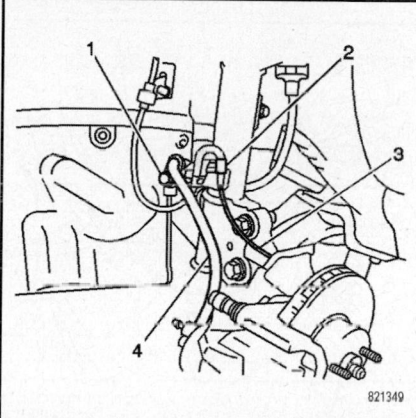

821349

Fig. 427 Remove the front brake hose bolt (1) and the hose (4) from the bracket (2) on the strut. Position the hose and the bolt to the side. Position the speed sensor wire (3) away from the strut

19. If the vehicle is not equipped with the strut housing upper tie bar, remove the 3 nuts from the top of the strut.

20. Remove the strut cover from the top of the strut mount.

21. Remove the 2 nuts and the 2 bolts from the lower side of the strut.

22. Remove the strut assembly from the vehicle. For strut, strut component or spring replacement, refer to Overhaul.

To install:

✳✳ WARNING

Care should be taken to avoid scratching or cracking the spring coating when handling the front suspension coil spring. Damage can cause premature failure.

23. Install the 2 bolts and the 2 nuts to the lower side of the strut assembly:

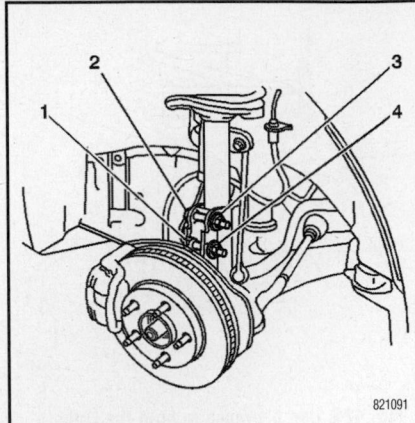

Fig. 428 Loosen the 2 nuts (3, 4) on the lower side of the strut assembly. Do not remove the nuts or the bolts (1, 2) yet

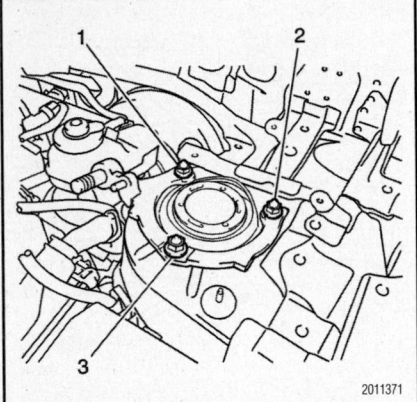

Fig. 429 If equipped with the strut housing upper tie bar, remove the nuts (1–3) and the tie bar bracket

➡**Do not tighten the nuts or the bolts yet.**

24. If the vehicle is not equipped with the strut housing upper tie bar, install the top of the strut assembly and the 3 nuts to the strut tower.

25. Tighten the nuts to 37 ft. lbs. (50 Nm).

26. If equipped with the strut housing upper tie bar, install the tie bar bracket and the 3 nuts to the studs on the top of the strut.

➡**Do not tighten the tie bar bracket nuts yet.**

    a. Install the strut housing upper tie bar.

    b. Tighten the 3 nuts on the tie bar bracket to 37 ft. lbs. (50 Nm).

    c. Install the strut cover to the top of the strut mount.

27. Hold the bolts with a wrench and tighten the nuts on the lower side of the strut assembly to 177 ft. lbs. (240 Nm).

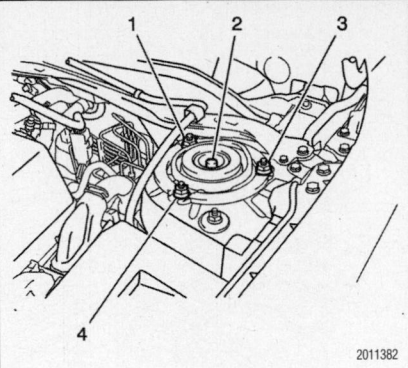

Fig. 430 If the vehicle is not equipped with the strut housing upper tie bar, remove the 3 nuts (1, 3, 4) from the top of the strut, and remove the strut cover (2) from the top of the strut mount

28. Install the ABS wheel speed sensor to the knuckle. Refer to Speed Sensors, removal & installation.

29. Install the speed sensor wire and the bracket to the strut. Ensure the wire is not twisted.

30. Install the front brake hose to the bracket on the strut. Ensure the hose is not twisted.

31. Install the brake hose bracket bolt to the bracket and tighten to 21 ft. lbs. (29 Nm).

32. Install the nut and the stud to the bracket in order to connect the link to the strut.

33. Use a wrench to hold the front stabilizer shaft link stud. Tighten the nut to 55 ft. lbs. (74 Nm).

34. Install the tire and wheel assembly.

35. Lower the vehicle.

36. Install the dash upper extension panel.

37. Install the 3 bolts holding the center of the panel, the 5 bolts holding the left side of the panel, and the 4 bolts holding the right side of the panel.

38. Tighten all of the extension panel bolts to 78 inch lbs. (8.8 Nm).

39. Engage the clamp on the left side of the dash upper extension panel.

40. Bend the right side water guard plate and engage the clamp.

41. Install the windshield wiper motor.

42. Measure the front wheel alignment. Adjust the alignment if necessary.

OVERHAUL

See Figures 431 through 436.

1. Remove the strut assembly from the vehicle.

2. Using strut spring compressor (J-45400), compress the spring.

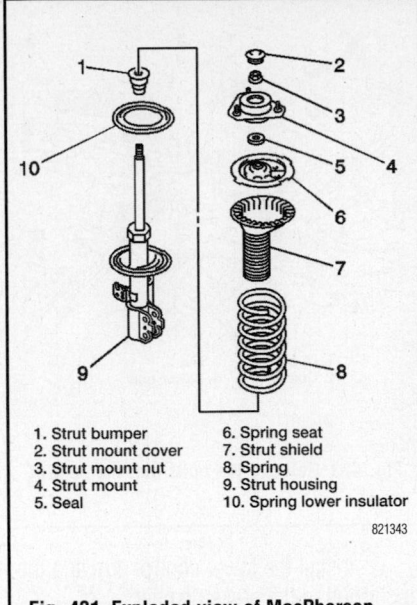

1. Strut bumper
2. Strut mount cover
3. Strut mount nut
4. Strut mount
5. Seal
6. Spring seat
7. Strut shield
8. Spring
9. Strut housing
10. Spring lower insulator

Fig. 431 Exploded view of MacPherson strut assembly

3. Remove the following components:
- The strut mount cover.
- The strut mount nut.
- The strut mount.
- The seal.
- The spring seat.
- The strut shield.
- The spring.
- The strut bumper.
- The spring lower insulator.
- The strut housing.

To install:

4. Install the spring lower insulator to the strut housing. Ensure the insulator fits properly in the depression of the lower spring seat.

5. Install the strut bumper.

6. Using strut spring compressor, compress the spring.

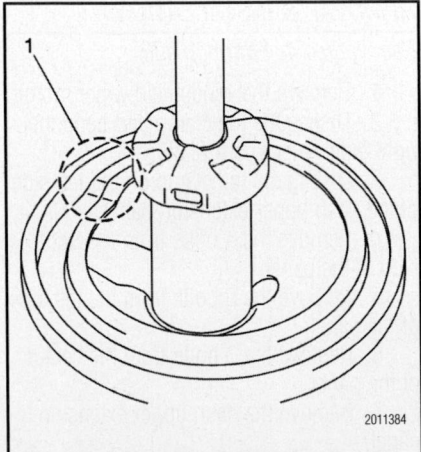

Fig. 432 Ensure the insulator fits properly in the depression of the lower spring seat (1)

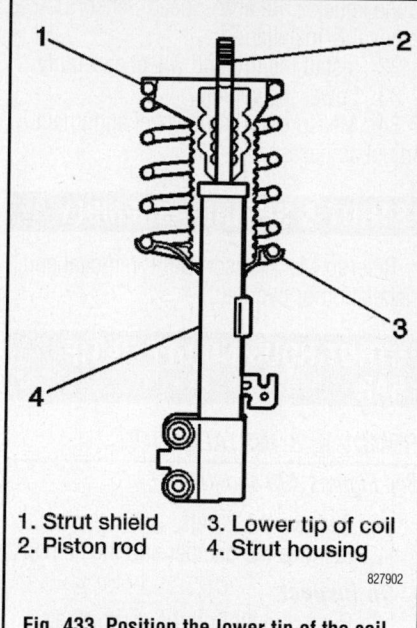

1. Strut shield   **3.** Lower tip of coil
2. Piston rod   **4.** Strut housing

827902

Fig. 433 Position the lower tip of the coil on the gap in the lower insulator (3)

7. Install the spring. Position the lower tip of the coil on the gap in the lower insulator.

8. Install the strut shield. Position the protrusion on the strut shield toward the outer side of the vehicle.

9. Install the spring seat.

  a. Position the cutout on the spring seat toward the outer side of the vehicle.

  b. Align the cutout on the spring seat with the protrusion on the strut shield.

  c. Align the slot on the piston rod with the spring seat.

10. Install the seal.

11. Install the strut mount.

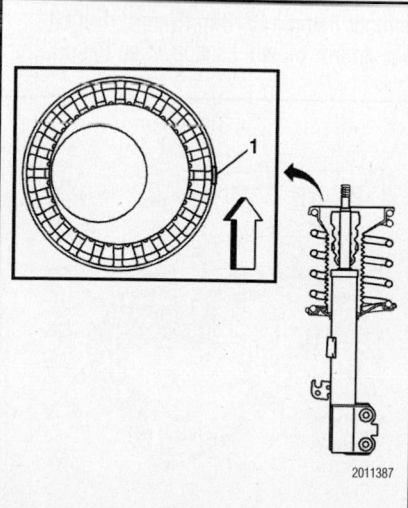

Fig. 434 Position the protrusion (1) on the strut shield toward the outer side of the vehicle

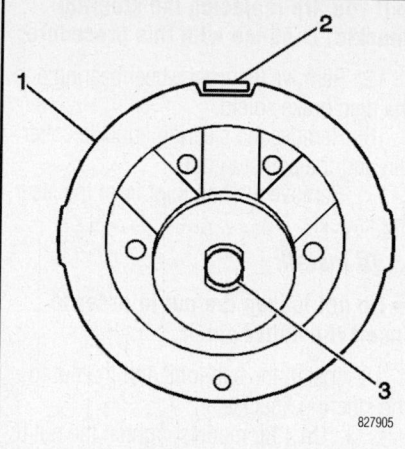

827905

Fig. 435 Install the spring seat (1). Align the cutout on the spring seat with the protrusion (2) on the strut shield. Align the slot on the piston rod (3) with the spring seat

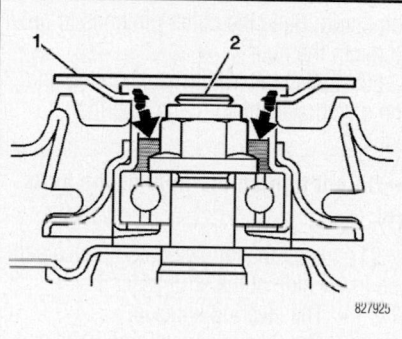

827925

Fig. 436 Apply multi-purpose lubricant to the crevice around the nut

➡**Do not tighten the strut mount nut yet.**

12. Install, but do not tighten, the strut mount nut.

13. Remove the strut from the spring compressor.

14. Install the strut assembly to the vehicle.

15. Tighten the strut mount nut to 35 ft. lbs. (47 Nm).

16. Apply multi-purpose lubricant to the crevice around the nut. Ensure the lubricant does not contact the rubber part of the upper strut mount.

17. Install the strut mount cover.

STABILIZER BAR

REMOVAL & INSTALLATION

See Figure 437.

1. Lower the following components as an assembly as far as necessary in order to access the stabilizer shaft.

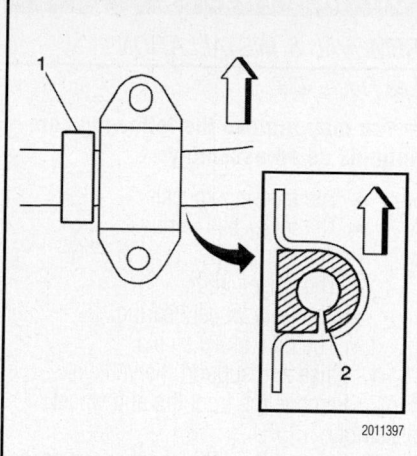

2011397

Fig. 437 Install the 2 stabilizer shaft insulators to the outer side of the rings (1) on the stabilizer shaft. Position the cutout (2) in the insulator toward the rear of the vehicle.

The front suspension crossmember
- The trans support
- The front control arms
- The stabilizer shaft
- The stabilizer shaft links
- The stabilizer shaft clamps
- The stabilizer shaft insulators

2. Use a 6-mm wrench to hold each stabilizer shaft lower link stud. Remove the 2 nuts and the 2 stabilizer shaft links from the stabilizer shaft.

3. Remove the 4 bolts from the stabilizer shaft clamps.

4. Remove the 2 stabilizer shaft clamps.

5. Remove the 2 stabilizer shaft insulators.

6. Remove the stabilizer shaft from the crossmember.

To install:

7. Position the stabilizer shaft on the crossmember.

8. Install the 2 stabilizer shaft insulators to the outer side of the rings on the stabilizer shaft. Position the cutout in the insulator toward the rear of the vehicle.

9. Install the 2 clamps to the insulators.

10. Install the 4 bolts to the clamps. Tighten the bolts to 18 ft. lbs. (24 Nm).

11. Use a 6-mm wrench in order to hold each stabilizer shaft link lower stud. Install the 2 stabilizer shaft links and the 2 nuts to the stabilizer shaft. Tighten the nuts to 55 ft. lbs. (74 Nm).

12. Install the stabilizer shaft and the crossmember to the vehicle.

STEERING KNUCKLE

REMOVAL & INSTALLATION

See Figure 438.

➡**You may remove the following components as an assembly:**

- The steering knuckle.
- The lower ball joint.
- The front hub.
- The wheel studs.
- The front wheel bearing.
- The disc brake shield.

1. Raise and support the vehicle.
2. Remove the front tire and wheel assembly.
3. Remove the ABS wheel speed sensor from the steering knuckle. Position the sensor to the side. Refer to Speed Sensors, removal & installation.
4. Support the front wheel drive shaft with wire.
5. Unstake the front wheel drive shaft nut.
6. Remove the drive shaft nut from the drive axle while an assistant presses the brake pedal.
7. Remove the 2 nuts and the bolt from the lower control arm.
8. Remove the brake rotor.
9. Loosen the nuts on the lower side of the strut assembly. Do not remove the bolts.
10. Remove the cotter pin.
11. Remove the outer tie rod end nut.
12. Use the J 6627-A puller, or equivalent, to separate the outer tie rod end from the knuckle.
13. Remove the 2 nuts and the 2 bolts from lower side of the strut assembly.
14. Remove the steering knuckle assembly from the strut.

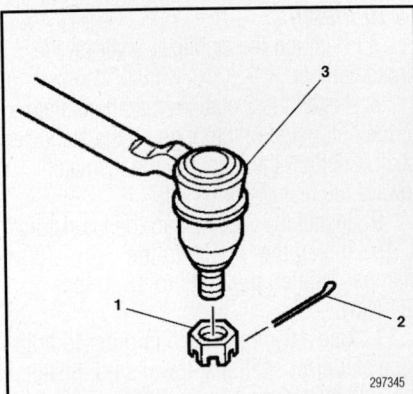

Fig. 438 Remove the cotter pin (2) from the lower control arm (3). Remove the outer tie rod end nut (1)

➡**If you are replacing the steering knuckle, continue with this procedure.**

15. Remove the front wheel bearing and the disc brake shield.
16. Remove the steering knuckle cotter pin and the ball stud nut.
17. Remove the ball joint from the steering knuckle.

To install:

➡**Do not loosen the nut in order to insert the cotter pin.**

18. Install the ball joint and the nut to the steering knuckle.
- On 1.8L models, tighten the nut to 76 ft. lbs. (103 Nm).
- On 2.4L models, tighten the nut to 91 ft. lbs. (123 Nm).
- On all models, tighten the nut up to 1/6 additional turn in order to insert the cotter pin.

19. Install a NEW cotter pin to the ball joint stud. Bend the cotter pin ends in order to retain the nut.
20. Install the front wheel bearing and the disc brake shield to the steering knuckle.

➡**Do not tighten the nuts or the bolts yet.**

21. Install the following components to the lower side of the strut assembly:
- The steering knuckle.
- The 2 knuckle retaining bolts and nuts.

22. Install the outer tie rod end and the nut to the steering knuckle. Tighten the nut to 36 ft. lbs. (49 Nm).
23. Tighten the nut up to 1/6 additional turn in order to insert the cotter pin.
24. Install a NEW cotter pin to the outer tie rod end ball joint stud. Bend the cotter pin ends in order to retain the nut.

➡**Do not loosen the nut in order to insert the cotter pin.**

25. Install the front brake rotor.
26. Install a NEW drive shaft nut while an assistant applies the brakes. Tighten the nut to 159 ft. lbs. (216 Nm).
27. Stake the drive shaft nut into the slot on the wheel drive shaft.
28. Remove the wire supporting the front wheel drive shaft.
29. Install the bolt and the 2 nuts to the control arm. Tighten the bolt and the 2 nuts to 66 ft. lbs. (89 Nm).
30. Tighten the nuts and the bolts that retain the knuckle to the strut assembly to 177 ft. lbs. (240 Nm).
31. Install the ABS wheel speed sensor

to the knuckle. Refer to Speed Sensors, removal & installation.

32. Install the tire and wheel assembly.
33. Lower the vehicle.
34. Measure the front wheel alignment. Adjust as necessary.

STRUT & SPRING ASSEMBLY

Refer to MacPherson Strut, removal and installation or overhaul.

STRUT HOUSING UPPER TIE BAR

REMOVAL & INSTALLATION

See Figures 439 and 440.

1. Remove the 2 nuts.
2. Remove the damper and the tie bar.

To inspect:

3. Push and pull on the damper rod 4 times. Test the damper for a lack of resistance or a noise.
4. Inspect the damper for oil leaks.
5. Inspect the tie bar assembly for bent or scratched components.
6. If the damper is damaged, dispose the damper.

Disposal Procedure:

✳✳ CAUTION

Use the proper eye protection when drilling to prevent metal chips from causing physical injury.

7. Clamp the damper in a vise horizontally with the rod completely extended.
8. Make an indentation on the end of the damper with a center punch.
9. Drill a hole in the indentation on the damper using a 3/16 in (5 mm) drill bit. Gas and/or oil will escape when the drill bit

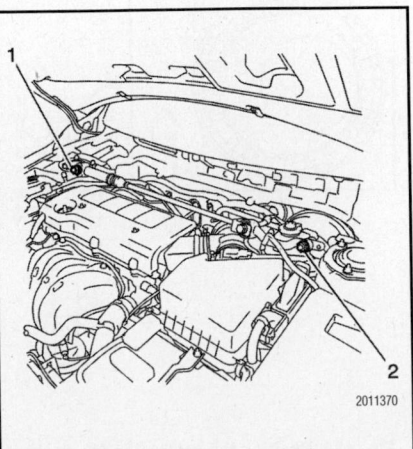

Fig. 439 Remove the nuts (1, 2). Remove the damper and the tie bar

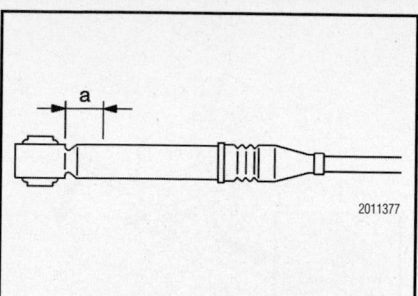

Fig. 440 Make an indentation on the end of the damper (a) with a center punch

penetrates the damper. Use shop towels in order to contain the escaping oil.

10. Remove the damper from the vise.

11. Hold the damper over a drain pan with the hole down. Move the rod in and out of the damper in order to drain the oil from the damper.

To install:

12. Install the damper and the tie bar to the brackets.

13. Install the 2 nuts that retain the tie bar to the brackets.

14. Tighten the 2 nuts to 38 ft. lbs. (52 Nm).

WHEEL BEARINGS

REMOVAL & INSTALLATION

See Figures 441 through 444.

1. Remove the knuckle. Refer to Knuckle, removal & installation.

2. If the vehicle has a front wheel bearing inner seal shield, use a hammer and a flat blade tool to remove the shield.

3. Discard the shield.

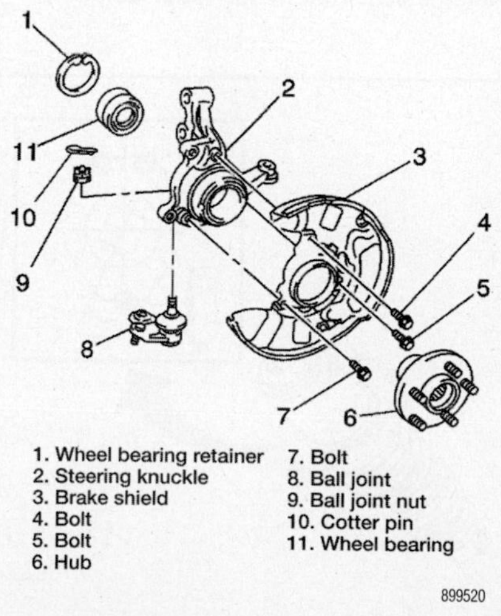

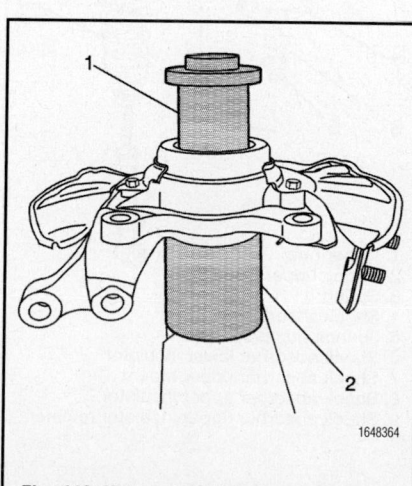

1. Wheel bearing retainer
2. Steering knuckle
3. Brake shield
4. Bolt
5. Bolt
6. Hub
7. Bolt
8. Ball joint
9. Ball joint nut
10. Cotter pin
11. Wheel bearing

899520

Fig. 441 View of front wheel hub, bearing, and seal

4. Use snap ring pliers in order to remove the wheel bearing retainer.

5. Place the outboard side of the knuckle assembly on a press split plate.

6. Place a bearing driver collar on the inboard end of the hub.

7. Use a press in order to remove the hub from the wheel bearing.

8. Press from the inboard side of the hub toward the outboard side of the hub.

9. Remove the 3 bolts and the brake shield from the knuckle.

10. On 1.8L models, using wheel bearing remover and installer kit (CH-48023), perform the following steps:

   a. Place the CH-48023-2 (2) on a press support plate.

   b. Place the inboard side of the knuckle on the CH-48023-2.

   c. Place the CH-48023-1 (1) on the outside outer race of the bearing.

11. On 2.4L models, using wheel bearing remover and installer kit (CH-49684), perform the following steps:

   a. Place the CH-49684-2 (2) on a press support plate.

   b. Place the inboard side of the knuckle on the CH-49684-2.

   c. Place the CH-49684-1 (1) on the outside outer race of the bearing.

12. On all models, use a press to remove the bearing from the knuckle.

13. Press from the outboard side of the bearing toward the inboard side of the knuckle.

To install:

14. Place the outboard side of the knuckle on a press support plate.

15. Place the wheel bearing on the inboard side of the knuckle.

16. Place the appropriate CH-XXXXX-1 (1) on the bearing.

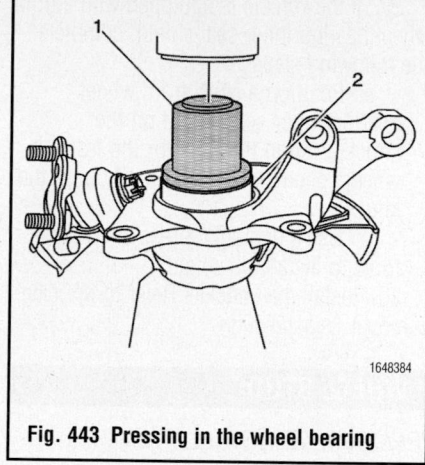

Fig. 443 Pressing in the wheel bearing

17. Use a press to install the bearing into the knuckle.

18. Press from the inboard side of bearing toward the outboard side of the knuckle.

19. Install the brake shield to the knuckle.

20. Install the 3 bolts that retain the brake shield to the knuckle.

21. Tighten the bolts to 73.46 inch lbs. (8.3 Nm).

22. Place the appropriate CH-XXXXX-2 (3) on a press support plate.

23. Place the hub (2) on the appropriate CH-XXXXX-2.

24. Place the knuckle and bearing assembly on the hub.

25. Place the appropriate CH-XXXXX-1 (1) on the bearing.

26. Use a press to install the hub to the bearing.

27. Press from the inboard side of bearing toward the outboard side of the hub.

28. Use snap ring pliers to install the wheel bearing retainer.

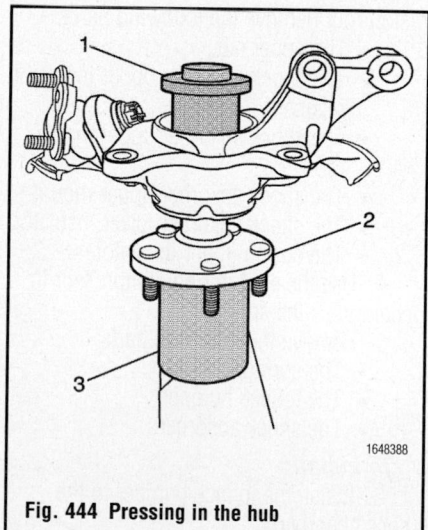

Fig. 442 Using wheel bearing remover and installer kit (1, 2)

Fig. 444 Pressing in the hub

29. If the vehicle is equipped with a front wheel bearing inner seal shield, complete the following steps:

    a. Position a NEW front wheel bearing inner seal shield on the knuckle. Align the hole for the front wheel speed sensor with the hole in the knuckle.

    b. Use a hydraulic press and press tools to install the shield.

30. Install the knuckle. Refer to Knuckle, removal & installation.

WHEEL STUD

REMOVAL & INSTALLATION

See Figure 445.

1. Raise and support the vehicle.
2. Remove the front tire and wheel assembly.
3. Remove the front brake rotor.
4. Remove the front brake shield.
5. Install 2 wheel nuts onto 2 wheel studs.
6. Use a pry bar on the 2 nuts in order to prevent the hub from turning.

7. Using ball joint remover (J-43631), press out the wheel stud from the hub.

To install:

✳✳ CAUTION

If one stud is damaged, replace all the studs. A loose-running wheel may cause only one stud to break, but the other studs could have internal fatigue. Replacing only the broken stud and remounting the wheel may cause further damage and personal injury. If the stud holes in the wheels have become enlarged or distorted, replace the wheel.

8. Install the wheel stud to the stud hole in the hub flange from the bearing side of the hub flange.
9. Place a flat washer over the wheel stud being installed.
10. Install the wheel nut or a hex head nut to the wheel stud. The thread diameter is 0.472 inch (12.0 mm). The thread pitch is 0.0591 inch (1.5 mm).
11. Use a pry bar on the 2 nuts in order to prevent the hub from turning.

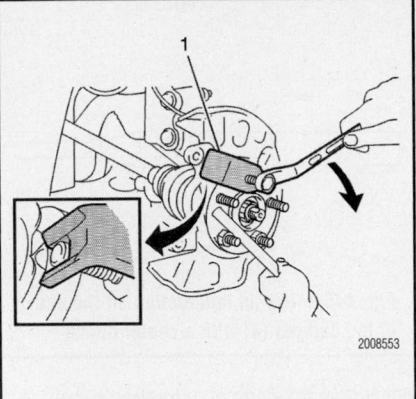

Fig. 445 Using ball joint remover (1), press out the wheel stud from the hub

12. Gradually tighten the nut in order to draw the stud into the hub flange until the head of the wheel stud is fully seated against the hub flange.
13. Remove the nuts and the flat washer.
14. Install the front brake shield.
15. Install the front brake rotor.
16. Install the front tire and wheel assembly.
17. Lower the vehicle.

SUSPENSION

COIL SPRING

REMOVAL & INSTALLATION

AWD & GT

See Figures 446 through 448.

1. Remove the spring and shock absorber assembly. Refer to MacPherson Strut, removal & installation.
2. Using strut spring compressor, compress the spring.
3. Use a wrench in order to hold the piston rod. Remove the following parts:
- The upper nut.
- The shock absorber upper insulator retainer.
- The shock absorber upper insulator.
- The shock absorber upper mount.
- The shock absorber lower insulator.
- The spring upper insulator.
4. Use the strut spring compressor to decompress the spring.
5. Remove the following parts:
- The spring.
- The jounce bumper.
- The shock absorber.

To install:

6. Install the jounce bumper to the shock absorber.

7. Install the spring to the shock absorber. Position the lower tip of the spring on the depression in the lower spring seat.

8. Use the strut spring compressor to compress the spring.

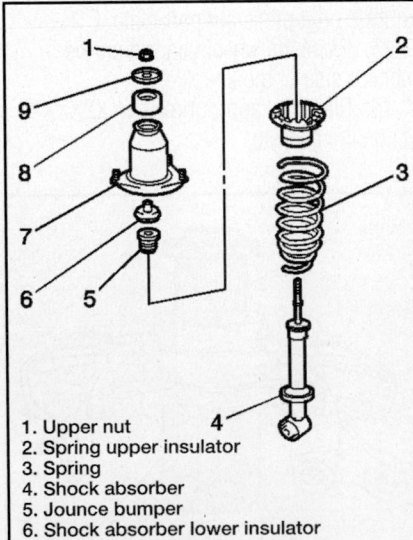

1. Upper nut
2. Spring upper insulator
3. Spring
4. Shock absorber
5. Jounce bumper
6. Shock absorber lower insulator
7. Shock absorber upper mount
8. Shock absorber upper insulator
9. Shock absorber upper insulator retainer

Fig. 446 Exploded view of shock absorber assembly—AWD & GT

REAR SUSPENSION

9. Install the spring upper insulator.
10. Install the shock absorber lower insulator.

➡**The right rear shock mount is the mirror image of the left rear shock mount.**

11. Install the shock absorber upper mount.

12. Position the front stud 23.3 degrees from the centerline of the lower bolt hole.

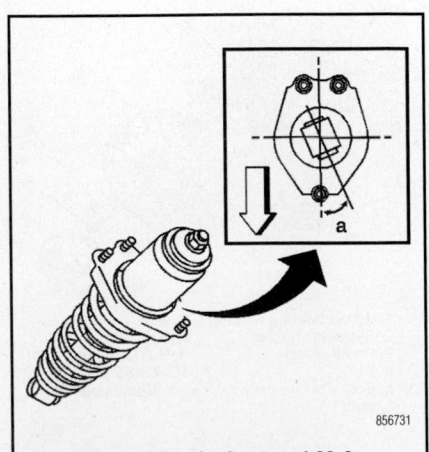

Fig. 447 Position the front stud 23.3 degrees (a) from the centerline of the lower bolt hole—AWD & GT

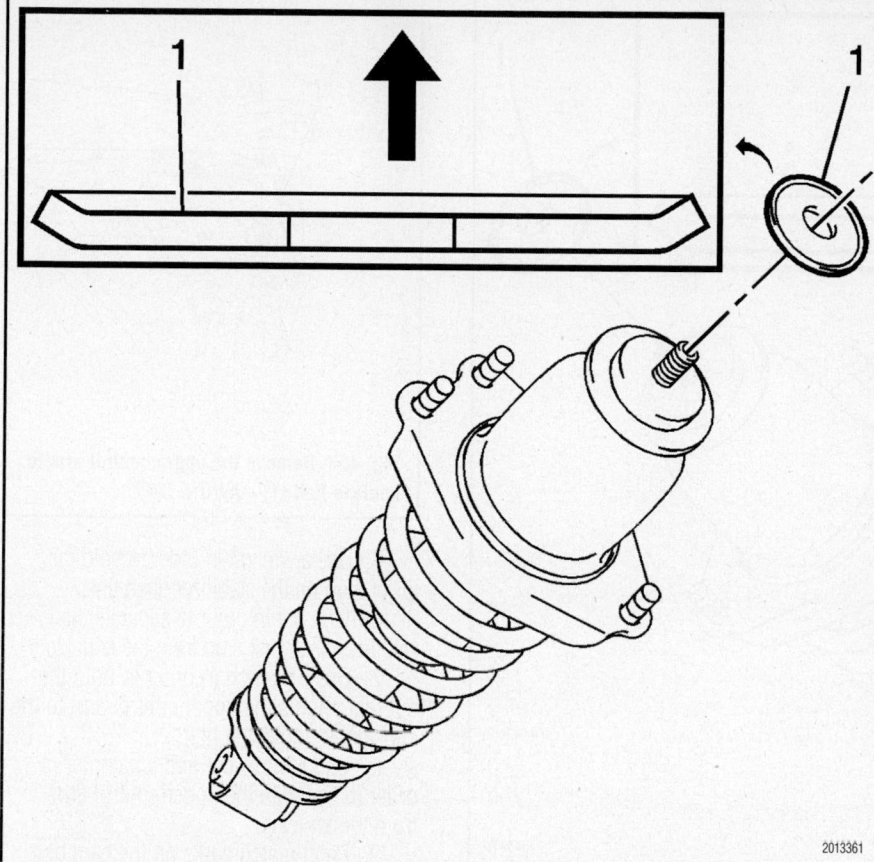

Fig. 448 Install the shock absorber upper insulator retainer (1). Ensure the retainer is in the correct position

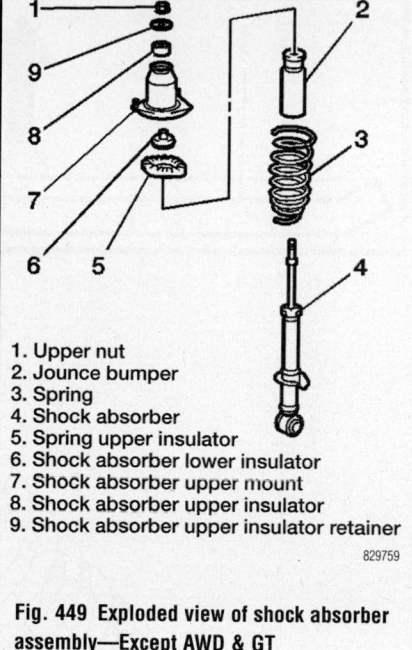

1. Upper nut
2. Jounce bumper
3. Spring
4. Shock absorber
5. Spring upper insulator
6. Shock absorber lower insulator
7. Shock absorber upper mount
8. Shock absorber upper insulator
9. Shock absorber upper insulator retainer

Fig. 449 Exploded view of shock absorber assembly—Except AWD & GT

13. Install the shock absorber upper insulator.

14. Install the shock absorber upper insulator retainer. Ensure the retainer is in the correct position.

➡The right rear shock mount is the mirror image of the left rear shock mount.

➡Do not tighten the nut. Verify the position of the shock absorber upper mount is correct before tightening the nut.

15. Install the upper nut.

16. Verify the position of the shock absorber upper mount is correct.

17. Remove the spring and shock absorber assembly from the strut compressor.

18. Use a wrench in order to hold the piston rod. Tighten the nut to 29 ft. lbs. (39 Nm).

19. Install the spring and shock absorber assembly. Refer to MacPherson Strut, removal & installation.

EXCEPT AWD & GT

See Figures 449 through 451.

1. Remove the spring and shock absorber assembly. Refer to MacPherson Strut, removal & installation.

2. Use strut spring compressor to compress the spring.

3. Use a wrench in order to hold the piston rod. Remove the following parts:
- The upper nut.
- The shock absorber upper insulator retainer.
- The shock absorber upper insulator.
- The shock absorber upper mount.
- The shock absorber lower insulator.
- The spring upper insulator.

4. Use strut spring compressor to decompress the spring. Remove the following parts:
- The spring.
- The jounce bumper.
- The shock absorber.

To install:

5. Install the jounce bumper to the shock absorber.

6. Install the spring to the shock absorber. Position the lower tip of the spring on the depression in the lower spring seat.

7. Use the strut spring compressor to compress the spring.

8. Install the spring upper insulator.

9. Install the shock absorber lower insulator.

➡The right rear shock mount is the mirror image of the left rear shock mount.

10. Install the shock absorber upper mount.

11. Position the front stud 80.6 degrees from the centerline of the lower bolt hole.

12. Install the shock absorber upper insulator.

13. Install the shock absorber upper insulator retainer. Ensure the retainer is in the correct position.

➡Do not tighten the nut. Verify the position of the shock absorber upper

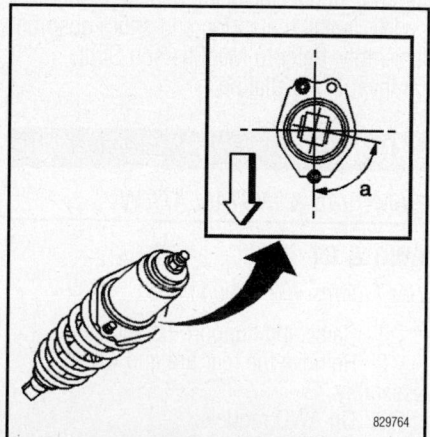

Fig. 450 Position the front stud 80.6 degrees (a) from the centerline of the lower bolt hole—Except AWD & GT

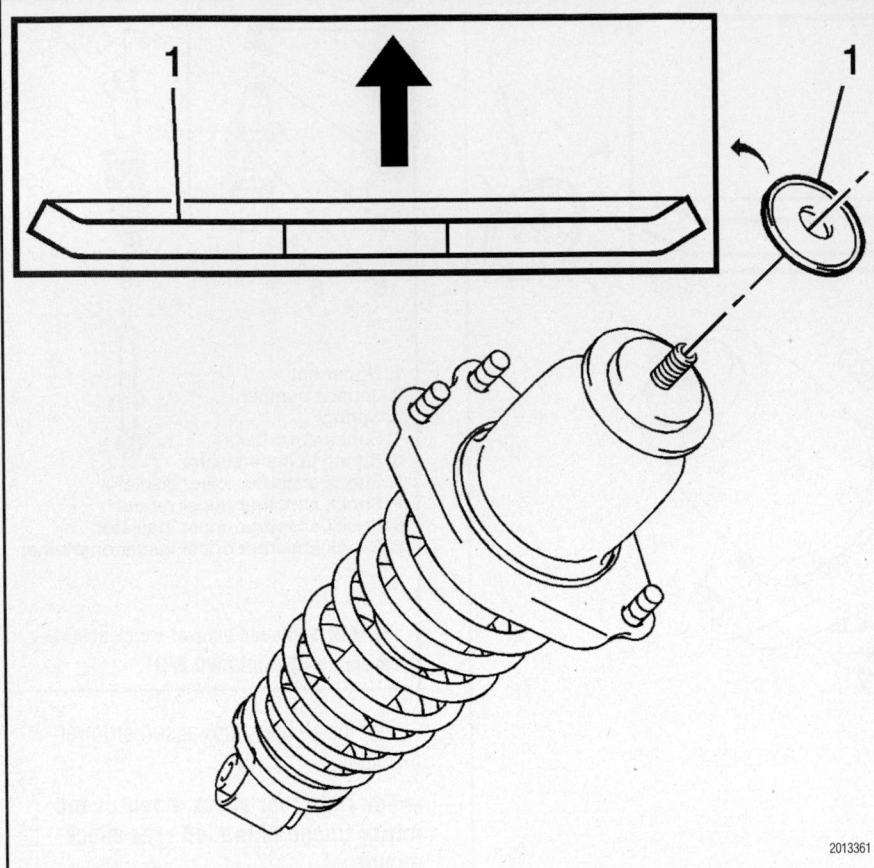

Fig. 451 Install the shock absorber upper insulator retainer (1). Ensure the retainer is in the correct position

mount is correct before tightening the nut.

14. Install the upper nut.
15. Verify the position of the shock absorber upper mount is correct.
16. Remove the spring and shock absorber assembly from the strut spring compressor.
17. Use a wrench in order to hold the piston rod. Tighten the nut to 29 ft. lbs. (39 Nm).
18. Install the spring and shock absorber assembly. Refer to MacPherson Strut, removal & installation.

KNUCKLE

REMOVAL & INSTALLATION

AWD & GT

See Figures 452 through 458.

1. Raise and support the vehicle.
2. Remove the rear tire and wheel assembly.
3. On AWD models:
    a. Use a drift and a hammer in order to unstake the rear wheel drive shaft nut.
    b. Have an assistant apply the brakes.
    c. Remove the rear wheel drive shaft nut.
    d. Release the brakes.
4. On all models, remove the brake rotor and the park brake hardware.
5. Remove the rear wheel speed sensor and the pigtail wire. Refer to Speed Sensors, removal & installation.

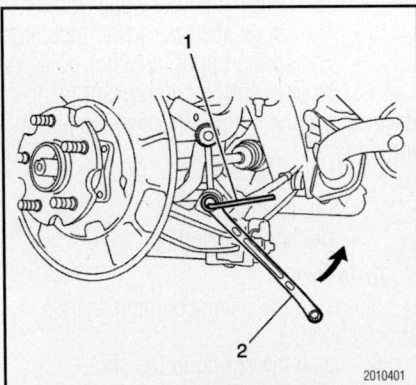

Fig. 452 Use a wrench (1) in order to hold the lower stud on the stabilizer shaft link. Remove the nut (2) in order to separate the lower stabilizer shaft link stud from the knuckle—AWD & GT

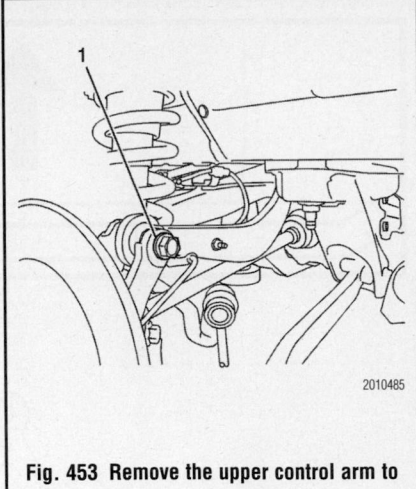

Fig. 453 Remove the upper control arm to knuckle bolt (1)—AWD & GT

6. Use a wrench in order to hold the lower stud on the stabilizer shaft link. Remove the nut in order to separate the lower stabilizer shaft link stud from the knuckle.
7. Use a wrench in order to hold the nut that retains the upper control arm to the knuckle. Remove the bolt.
8. Use a brass bar and a hammer in order to separate the upper control arm from the knuckle.
9. Paint matchmarks on the cam bolt and on the lower control arm.
10. Paint matchmarks on the adjust cam and on the lower control arm.
11. Remove the nut from the adjust cam and from the cam bolt.
12. Remove the adjust cam.
13. Remove the cam bolt.
14. Remove the nut and the bolt in order to separate the lower control arm from the knuckle.
15. Use mechanics wire or the equivalent in order to support the wheel drive shaft.

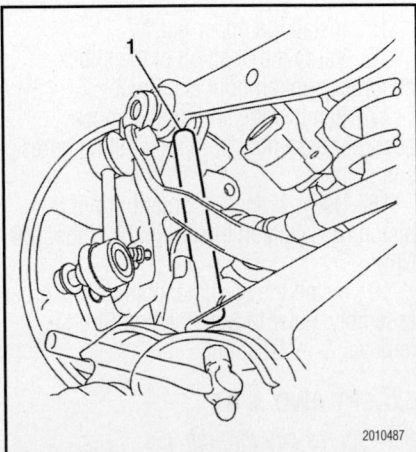

Fig. 454 Use a brass bar (1) and a hammer in order to separate the upper control arm from the knuckle—AWD & GT

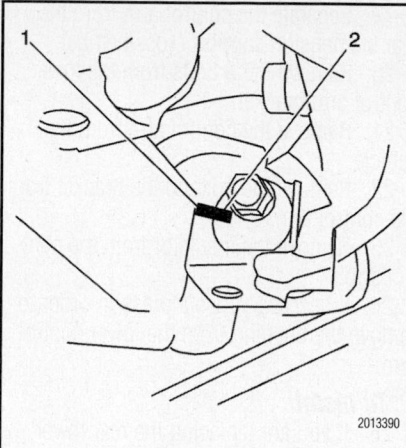

Fig. 455 Paint matchmarks on the cam bolt (2) and on the lower control arm (1)

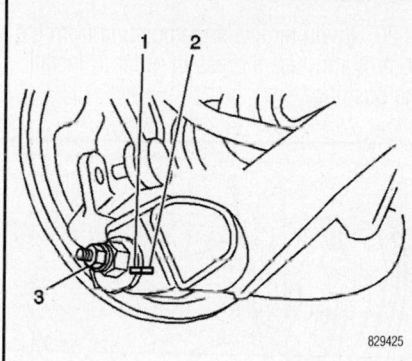

Fig. 456 Paint matchmarks on the adjust cam (1) and on the lower control arm (2). Remove the nut (3) from the adjust cam and from the cam bolt

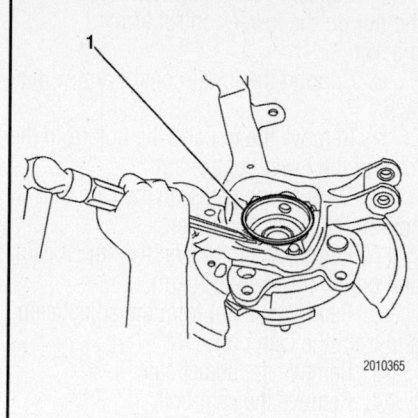

Fig. 457 On AWD, remove the wheel bearing dust deflector (1)

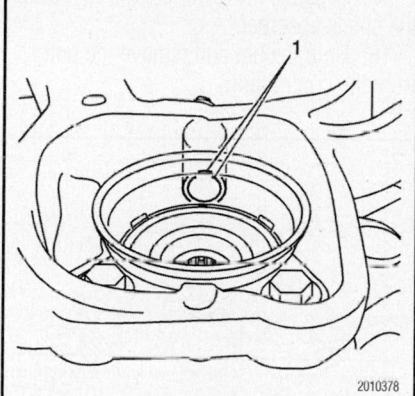

Fig. 458 On AWD models, align the hole (1) for rear wheel speed sensor in a NEW dust deflector with the hole in the knuckle

16. Remove the knuckle.
17. On AWD, remove the wheel bearing dust deflector.
18. On all models, remove the 4 wheel hub and bearing bolts.
19. Remove the wheel hub and bearing.
20. Remove the brake shield.

To install:
21. Install the brake shield to the knuckle.
22. Install the wheel hub and bearing to the knuckle.
23. Install the 4 bolts to the knuckle and tighten to 41 ft. lbs. (56 Nm).
24. On AWD models:
    a. Align the hole for rear wheel speed sensor in a NEW dust deflector with the hole in the knuckle.
    b. Use a hydraulic press and press tools, or use a hammer and a piece of flat steel stock, in order to install the NEW dust deflector.
    c. Install the knuckle to the wheel drive shaft.

➡ **Do not tighten the nuts or the bolts on the control arms yet. The weight of the vehicle must be on the tire and wheel assemblies before tightening the nuts and the bolts.**

25. On all models, install, but do not tighten, the bolt and the nut in order to retain the knuckle to the upper control arm.
26. Remove the mechanics wire or the equivalent from the wheel drive shaft.
27. Install, but do not tighten, the bolt and the nut to the front of the lower control arm.
28. Align the matchmarks and install the cam bolt to the rear of the lower control arm.
29. Align the matchmarks and install the adjust cam to the cam bolt.
30. Install, but do not tighten, the nut.
31. Install the nut in order to retain the stabilizer shaft link stud to the knuckle. Use a wrench in order to hold the link stud. Tighten the nut to 32 ft. lbs. (44 Nm).

32. Install the rear wheel speed sensor and the pigtail wire. Refer to Speed Sensors, removal & installation.
33. Install the brake rotor and the park brake hardware.
34. On AWD models:
    a. Clean the threaded portion of the rear wheel drive shaft.
    b. Clean the threads on the rear wheel drive shaft nut.
    c. Use 3 wheel nuts in order to hold the brake rotor on the hub.
    d. Apply the park brake.
    e. Have an assistant apply the brakes.
    f. Install a NEW rear wheel drive shaft nut and tighten to 159 ft. lbs. (216 Nm).
    g. Release the brakes and the park brake.
35. On AWD, remove the wheel nuts and the brake rotor.
36. On all models, inspect the rear wheel bearing for looseness and runout.
37. On AWD, install the brake rotor and the caliper.
38. On GT, install the brake rotor and the park brake hardware.
39. On all models, adjust the parking brake system. Refer to Parking Brake Cables, adjustment.
40. On AWD, use a chisel and a hammer in order to stake the rear wheel drive shaft nut.
41. On all models, install the rear tire and wheel assembly.
42. Lower the vehicle.
43. Raise and support the vehicle on an alignment rack.
44. With the weight of the vehicle on the tires, push down on the rear bumper 3 times in order to stabilize the suspension.
45. Use a wrench in order to hold the nut. Tighten the bolt that retains the upper control arm to the knuckle to 55 ft. lbs. (74 Nm).
46. Use a wrench in order to hold the nut. Tighten the bolt that retains the front of the lower control arm to the knuckle to 103 ft. lbs. (140 Nm).
47. Align the matchmarks on the cam bolt and on the control arm.
48. Align the matchmarks on the adjust cam and on the control arm.
49. Tighten the nut that retains the rear of the lower control arm to the knuckle to 55 ft. lbs. (74 Nm).
50. Measure the wheel alignment and perform the zero point calibrations. Adjust the wheel alignment if necessary.
51. Lower the vehicle.

LOWER CONTROL ARM

REMOVAL & INSTALLATION

AWD & GT

See Figures 459 through 465.

1. Raise and support the vehicle.
2. Remove the rear tire and wheel assembly.
3. If you are removing the left rear lower control arm, remove the 2 bolts and the rear floor side member brace.
4. Remove the 2 bolts in order to separate the park brake cable from the lower control arm.
5. Use a wrench in order to hold the lower stud on the stabilizer shaft link. Remove the nut in order to separate the lower stabilizer shaft link stud from the knuckle.
6. Loosen, but do not remove, the nut and the bolt at the bottom of the shock absorber.

7. Loosen, but do not remove, the nut on the lower control arm bracket.
8. Support the lower control arm with a jack.
9. Remove the nut and the bolt from the front of the lower control arm.
10. Paint matchmarks on the cam bolt and on the lower control arm.
11. Paint matchmarks on the adjust cam and on the lower control arm.
12. Remove the nut from the adjust cam and from the cam bolt.
13. Remove the adjust cam.
14. Remove the cam bolt.
15. Separate the control arm from the knuckle.
16. Remove the nut and the bolt from the shock absorber.
17. Separate the lower control arm from the shock absorber.
18. Hold the nut and remove the bolt from the control arm.

19. Separate the control arm from the rear suspension support crossmember.
20. Remove the 3 bolts from the lower control arm bracket.
21. Remove the control arm from the vehicle.
22. Remove the nut and the bracket from the control arm.
23. Remove the insulator from the control arm.
24. If necessary, use a press in order to remove the bushing from the lower control arm.

To install:

25. If you are replacing the rear lower control arm, copy the matchmarks from the old components to the new components.

➡**Install the bushing in the correct position.**

26. If you removed the bushing from the control arm, use a press in order to install the bushing.

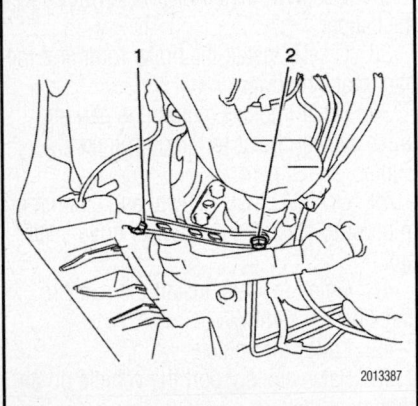

Fig. 459 If you are removing the left rear lower control arm, remove the bolts (1, 2) and the rear floor side member brace

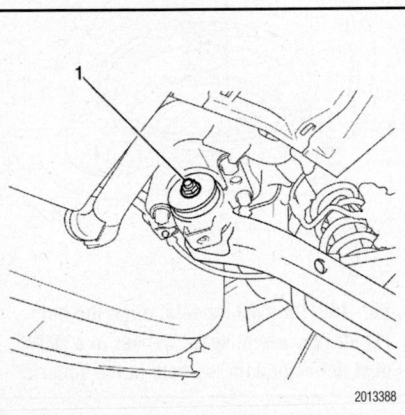

Fig. 461 Loosen, but do not remove, the nut (1) on the lower control arm bracket—AWD & GT

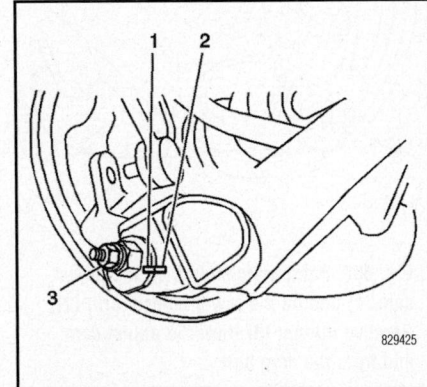

Fig. 463 Paint matchmarks on the adjust cam (1) and on the lower control arm (2). Remove the nut (3) from the adjust cam and from the cam bolt

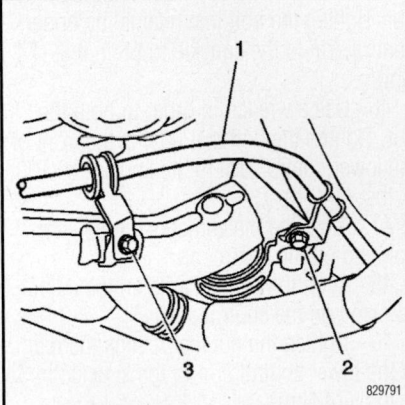

Fig. 460 Remove the 2 bolts (2, 3) in order to separate the park brake cable (1) from the lower control arm—AWD & GT

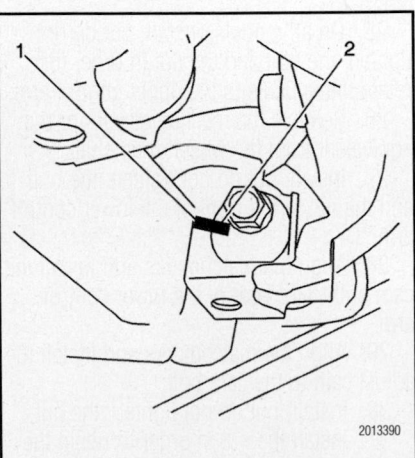

Fig. 462 Paint matchmarks on the cam bolt (2) and on the lower control arm (1)

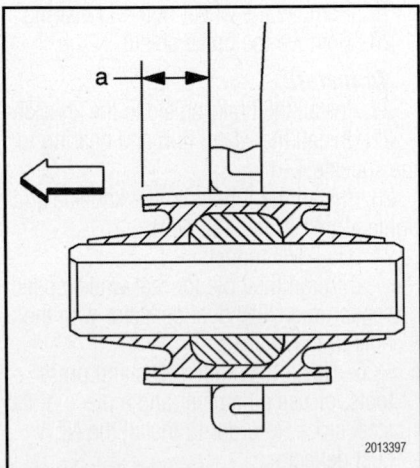

Fig. 464 Use a press in order to install the bushing to distance (a)—AWD & GT

The distance (a) is 15 ± 0.5 mm (0.59 ± 0.02 in).

➡**Install the insulator in the correct position.**

27. Install the insulator to the control arm.

28. Install the bracket to the control arm.

➡**Do not tighten the nuts or the bolts. The weight of the vehicle must be on the tire and wheel assemblies before tightening the nuts and the bolts.**

29. Install, but do not tighten, the nut to the control arm.

30. Raise and support the lower control arm with a jack.

31. Install the control arm to the shock absorber.

32. Install, but do not tighten, the nut and the bolt to the shock absorber.

33. Install the control arm to the rear suspension support crossmember.

34. Install, but do not tighten, the nut and the bolt.

35. Install the 3 bolts and the lower control arm bracket to the body. Tighten the bolts to 48 ft. lbs. (65 Nm).

36. Install the control arm to the knuckle.

37. Install, but do not tighten, the bolt and the nut to the front of the lower control arm.

38. Align the matchmarks and install the cam bolt to the rear of the lower control arm.

39. Align the matchmarks and install the adjust cam to the cam bolt.

40. Install, but do not tighten, the nut.

41. Install the nut in order to retain the stabilizer shaft link stud to the knuckle. Use a wrench in order to hold the stud. Tighten the nut to 32 ft. lbs. (44 Nm).

42. Install the 2 bolts in order to retain the park brake cable to the lower control arm. Tighten the bolts to 53 inch lbs. (6.0 Nm).

43. If you installed the left rear lower control arm, install the rear floor side member brace with the 2 bolts. Tighten the bolts to 22 ft. lbs. (30 Nm).

44. Lower the vehicle.

45. Raise and support the vehicle on a wheel alignment rack.

46. With the weight of the vehicle on the tires, push down on the rear bumper 3 times in order to stabilize the suspension.

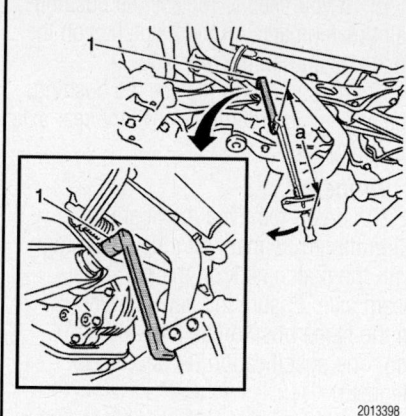

Fig. 465 Select a torque wrench with the fulcrum length (a) of 16.73 inches (425 mm). Use the torque wrench adapter (1) and the torque wrench—AWD & GT

47. Select a torque wrench with the fulcrum length (a) of 16.73 inches (425 mm).

➡**Ensure the torque wrench is parallel to the torque wrench adapter (EN-49191).**

48. Use a wrench in order to hold the nut that retains the lower control arm to the rear suspension support crossmember. Use the torque wrench adapter and the torque wrench in order to tighten the bolt to 47 ft. lbs. (64 Nm).

49. Use a wrench in order to hold the nut that retains the front of the lower control arm to the knuckle.

50. Tighten the bolt to 103 ft. lbs. (140 Nm).

51. Align the matchmarks on the cam bolt and on the control arm.

52. Align the matchmarks on the adjust cam and on the control arm.

53. Tighten the nut that retains the rear of the lower control arm to the knuckle to 55 ft. lbs. (74 Nm).

54. Select a torque wrench with the fulcrum length of 16.73 inches (425 mm).

➡**Ensure the torque wrench is parallel to the torque wrench adapter.**

55. Use the torque wrench adapter and the torque wrench in order to tighten the nut on the control arm bracket to 60 ft. lbs. (81 Nm).

56. Tighten the nut and the bolt on the shock absorber to 155 ft. lbs. (210 Nm).

57. Measure the wheel alignment. Adjust the wheel alignment if necessary.

58. Remove the jacks.

59. Lower the vehicle.

REAR AXLE

REMOVAL & INSTALLATION

EXCEPT AWD & GT

See Figures 466 through 469.

1. Disconnect the cable from the negative battery terminal. Refer to Battery, precautions.

2. Raise and support the vehicle.

3. Disconnect the 2 rear park brake cables from the rear brakes.

4. Disconnect the 2 connectors from the 2 rear wheel speed sensors.

5. Remove the bolt from the left rear speed sensor wire clamp.

6. Disengage the clamps and separate the left rear speed sensor wire from the rear twist beam axle.

7. Remove the bolt from the right rear speed sensor wire clamp.

8. Disengage the clamps and separate the right rear speed sensor wire from the rear axle.

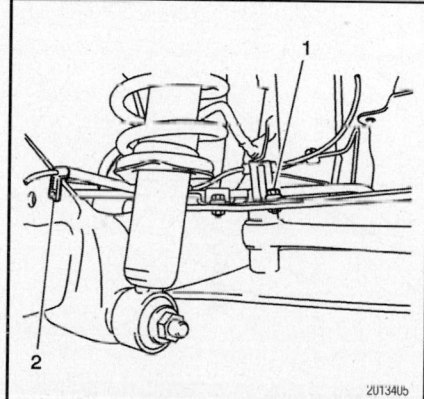

Fig. 466 Remove the bolt (1) from the left rear speed sensor wire clamp (2)—Except AWD & GT

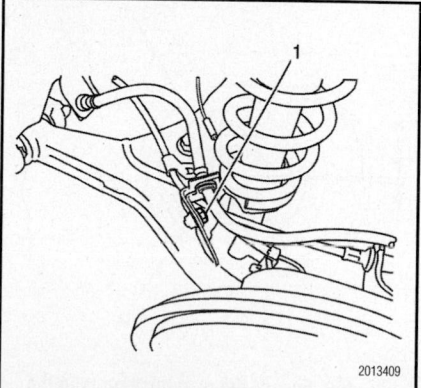

Fig. 467 Remove the bolt (1) and separate the left rear brake hose from the rear axle—Except AWD & GT

9. Remove the bolt and separate the left rear brake hose from the rear axle.

10. Remove the bolt and separate the right rear brake hose from the rear axle.

11. Remove the rear brakes and the brake shields.

12. Remove the stabilizer shaft and the bushing. Refer to Stabilizer Bar, removal & installation.

13. Support the rear axle with blocks of wood and jacks.

14. Remove the following components in order to separate the 2 shock absorbers from the rear axle:
- The 2 bolts.
- The 2 nuts.
- The 2 retainers.

15. Hold the nut and remove the bolt from the left rear axle bracket.

16. Hold the nut and remove the bolt from the right rear axle bracket.

17. Remove the rear axle from the vehicle.

Fig. 468 Hold the nut and remove the bolt (1) from the right rear axle bracket— Except AWD & GT

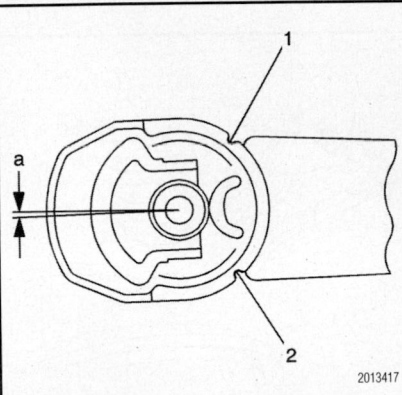

Fig. 469 Ensure the new bushing is in the same position as the old bushing. The specification (a) is 0.88 ±3 degrees— Except AWD & GT

18. If you need to replace the bushings, paint matchmarks on the 2 notches on the bushings and on the rear axle.

19. If you need to replace the bushings, use a press in order to remove the rear axle bushings.

To install:

20. If you removed the bushings, align the arrow mark on a new bushing with the matchmark on the rear twist beam axle. Ensure the new bushing is in the same position as the old bushing. The specification (a) is 0.88 ±3 degrees.

21. If you removed the bushings, use a press in order to install the bushings.

22. Raise and support the rear axle with blocks of wood and jacks.

➡**Do not tighten the nuts or the bolts yet. The weight of the vehicle must be on the tire and wheel assemblies before tightening the nuts and the bolts.**

23. Install, but do not tighten, the bolt and the nut in order to retain the left side of the rear axle to the body.

24. Install, but do not tighten, the bolt and the nut in order to retain the right side of the rear axle to the body.

25. Install, but do not tighten, the following components in order to retain the 2 shock absorbers to the rear axle:
- The 2 bolts.
- The 2 retainers.
- The 2 nuts.

26. Install the stabilizer shaft and the bushing. Refer to Stabilizer Bar, removal & installation.

27. Install the rear brakes and the brake shields.

28. Install the bolt in order to retain the left rear brake hose to the rear axle. Tighten the bolt to 21 ft. lbs. (29 Nm).

29. Install the bolt in order to retain the right rear brake hose to the rear axle. Tighten the bolt to 21 ft. lbs. (29 Nm).

30. Install the 2 rear park brake cables to the rear brakes.

31. Adjust the parking brake system. Refer to Parking Brake Cables, adjustment.

32. Engage the clamps on the left rear speed sensor wire.

33. Install the bolt in order to retain the left rear speed sensor wire to the rear axle. Tighten the bolt to 71 inch lbs. (8 Nm).

34. Connect the left rear speed sensor connector.

35. Engage the clamps on the right rear speed sensor wire.

36. Install the bolt in order to retain the

right rear speed sensor wire to the rear axle. Tighten the bolt to 71 inch lbs. (8 Nm).

37. Connect the right rear speed sensor connector.

38. Remove the jacks and lower the vehicle.

39. Raise and support the vehicle on an alignment rack or a lift that places the weight of the vehicle on the tires.

40. With the weight of the vehicle on the tires, push down on the rear bumper 3 times.

41. Hold the nut and tighten the bolt that retains the left side of the rear axle to the body. Tighten the bolt to 63 ft. lbs. (85 Nm).

42. Hold the nut and tighten the bolt that retains the right side of the rear axle to the body. Tighten the bolt to 63 ft. lbs. (85 Nm).

43. Ensure the shock absorbers and the coil springs are compressed to the distance (a) is 8.11 inch (206 mm). If necessary, use blocks of wood and jacks in order to raise the rear axle. If necessary, add weight, or even add an assistant to the rear seat.

44. Tighten the 2 nuts that retain the shock absorbers to the rear axle. Tighten the nuts to 59 ft. lbs. (80 Nm).

45. Connect the negative battery cable.

46. Perform the vehicle system check.

47. Measure the rear wheel alignment and perform the zero point calibrations.

48. Lower the vehicle.

SHOCK ABSORBER

REMOVAL & INSTALLATION

AWD & GT

See Figures 470 through 473.

1. Remove the rear quarter lower trim panel.

2. Raise and support the vehicle.

3. Remove the rear tire and wheel assembly.

4. If you are removing the left rear shock absorber, remove the 2 bolts and the rear floor side member brace.

5. Use a wrench in order to hold the lower stud on the stabilizer shaft link.

6. Remove the nut from the lower stud on the link.

7. Separate the link from the control arm.

8. Use a block of wood and a jack in order to support the lower control arm.

9. Remove the nut and the bolt from the shock absorber.

10. Separate the shock absorber from the lower control arm.

11. Remove the 3 nuts from the top mount.

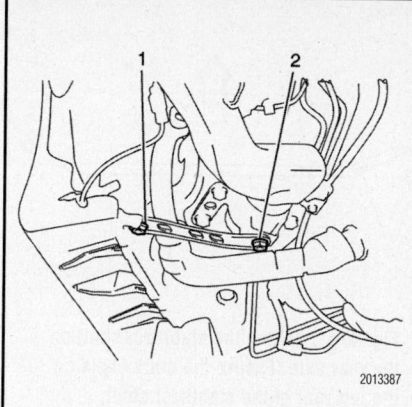

Fig. 470 If you are removing the left rear shock absorber, remove the bolts (1, 2) and the rear floor side member brace

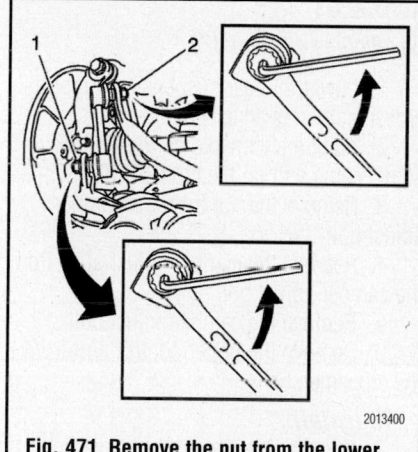

Fig. 471 Remove the nut from the lower stud on the link. Separate the link from the control arm (2)—AWD & GT

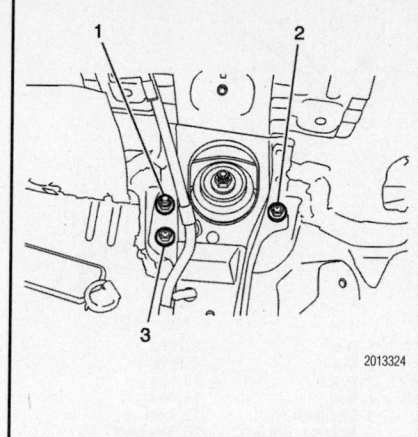

Fig. 472 Remove the nuts (1–3) from the top mount—AWD & GT

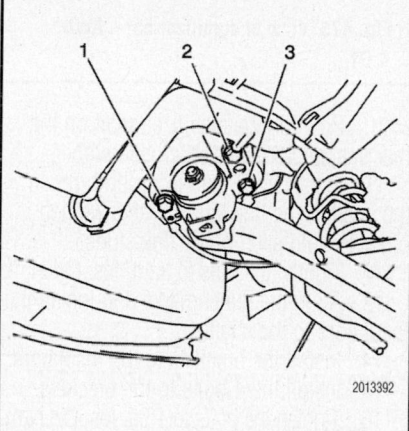

Fig. 473 Remove the bolts (1–3) from the lower control arm—AWD & GT

12. Remove the 3 bolts from the lower control arm.

13. Move the front of the lower control arm down and toward the outside of the vehicle.

14. Remove the shock absorber with the coil spring.

15. Remove the coil spring, if necessary. Refer to Coil Spring, removal & installation.

To install:

16. If you removed the coil spring, install the coil spring. Refer to Coil Spring, removal & installation.

17. Install the shock absorber with the 3 nuts and tighten to 59 ft. lbs. (80 Nm).

18. Install the shock absorber to the control arm.

➡**Do not tighten the lower shock absorber fasteners. The weight of the vehicle must be on the tire and wheel assemblies before tightening the lower shock absorber fasteners.**

19. Install, but do not tighten, the bolt and the nut to the shock absorber.

20. Install the 3 bolts in order to retain the lower control arm to the body and tighten to 48 ft. lbs. (65 Nm).

21. Install the rear floor side member brace with the 2 bolts and tighten to 22 ft. lbs. (30 Nm).

22. Install the lower stabilizer shaft link stud to the lower control arm.

23. Install the nut to the stud. Use a wrench in order to hold the stud. Tighten the nut to 32 ft. lbs. (44 Nm).

24. Remove the jack and the block of wood.

25. Install the rear tire and wheel assembly.

26. Lower the vehicle.

27. Install the rear quarter lower trim panel.

28. Raise and support the vehicle on an alignment rack or a lift that places the weight of the vehicle on the tires.

29. With the weight of the vehicle on the tires, push down on the rear bumper 3 times.

30. Tighten the lower shock absorber nut and the bolt to 155 ft. lbs. (210 Nm).

31. Measure the wheel alignment. Adjust the wheel alignment if necessary.

32. Lower the vehicle.

EXCEPT AWD & GT

See Figure 474.

1. Remove the rear quarter lower trim panel.

2. Raise and support the vehicle.

3. Remove the rear tire and wheel assembly.

4. Use a block of wood and a jack in order to support the rear torsion beam axle.

5. Remove the nut and the washer from the shock absorber.

6. Remove the 2 nuts from the upper portion of the shock absorber.

7. Remove the bolt from the lower portion of the shock absorber.

8. Slowly lower the jack and remove the shock absorber with the coil spring.

9. Remove the coil spring, if necessary. Refer to Coil Spring, removal & installation.

To install:

10. If you removed the coil spring, install the coil spring. Refer to Coil Spring, removal & installation.

11. Install the bolt to the lower portion of the shock absorber.

12. Tighten the bolt to 59 ft. lbs. (80 Nm).

13. Install the 2 nuts to the upper portion of the shock absorber.

14. Tighten the nuts to 59 ft. lbs. (80 Nm).

15. Use a block of wood and a jack in order to support the rear torsion beam axle.

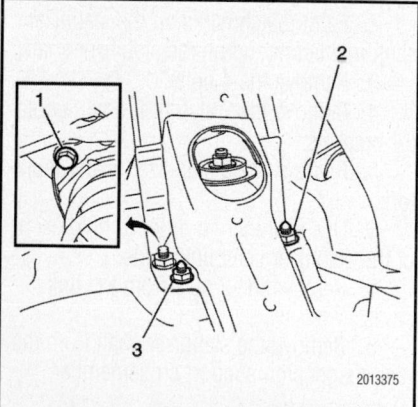

Fig. 474 Remove the 2 nuts (2, 3) from the upper portion of the shock absorber. Remove the bolt (1) from the lower portion of the shock absorber—Except AWD & GT

16. Install the washer to the lower portion of the shock absorber.

➡**Do not tighten the lower shock absorber fasteners yet. The weight of the vehicle must be on the tire and wheel assemblies before tightening the lower shock absorber fasteners.**

17. Install, but do not tighten, the nut to the lower portion of the shock absorber.

18. Remove the jack and the block of wood.

19. Install the rear tire and wheel assembly.

20. Lower the vehicle.

21. Install the rear quarter lower trim panel.

22. With the weight of the vehicle on the tires, push down on the rear bumper 3 times.

23. Ensure the shock absorbers and the coil springs are compressed to the distance (a) of 8.11 inches (206 mm). If necessary, use a block of wood and a jack in order to raise the axle. If necessary, add weight, or even an assistant, to the rear seat.

24. Tighten the lower shock absorber nut to 59 ft. lbs. (80 Nm).

25. Lower the jack.

26. Measure the wheel alignment and perform the zero point calibrations.

27. Lower the vehicle.

STABILIZER BAR

REMOVAL & INSTALLATION

AWD & GT

See Figure 475.

1. Remove the rear suspension support crossmember in order to access the stabilizer shaft.

2. Paint matchmarks on the stabilizer shaft insulators and on the stabilizer shaft.

3. Remove the 4 bolts.

4. Remove the 2 stabilizer shaft insulator brackets.

5. Remove the 2 stabilizer shaft insulators.

6. Use a wrench in order to hold each of the stabilizer shaft link studs.

7. Remove the 2 nuts from the link studs.

8. Remove the stabilizer shaft from the rear suspension support crossmember.

To install:

9. If you are replacing the stabilizer shaft or the insulators, copy the matchmarks from the old components to the new components.

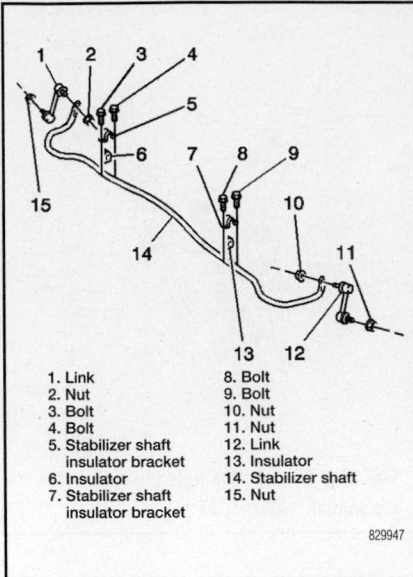

1. Link
2. Nut
3. Bolt
4. Bolt
5. Stabilizer shaft insulator bracket
6. Insulator
7. Stabilizer shaft insulator bracket
8. Bolt
9. Bolt
10. Nut
11. Nut
12. Link
13. Insulator
14. Stabilizer shaft
15. Nut

829947

Fig. 475 View of stabilizer bar—AWD & GT

10. Position the stabilizer shaft on the rear suspension support crossmember.

11. Install the 2 nuts in order to retain the shaft to the link studs. Use a wrench in order to hold each of the link studs.

12. Tighten the nuts to 32 ft. lbs. (44 Nm).

13. Align the matchmarks and install the insulators to the shaft.

14. Install the brackets to the insulators.

15. Install the 4 bolts to the brackets.

16. Tighten the bolts to 13 ft. lbs. (18 Nm).

17. Install the rear suspension support crossmember.

EXCEPT AWD & GT

See Figure 476.

1. Raise and support the vehicle.

2. Remove the insulator from the stabilizer shaft.

3. Remove the 2 nuts.

4. Remove the 2 bolts.

5. Remove the stabilizer shaft from the twist beam rear axle.

To install:

6. Position the stabilizer shaft on the rear axle. Ensure the mark is on the left rear of the stabilizer shaft.

7. Install the 2 bolts and the 2 nuts in order to retain the stabilizer shaft to the rear axle.

8. Hold the bolts with a wrench and tighten the nuts.

9. Tighten the nuts to 184 ft. lbs. (250 Nm).

10. Install the insulator to the center of the stabilizer shaft.

11. Lower the vehicle.

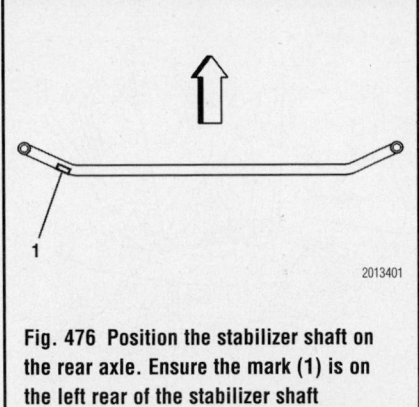

2013401

Fig. 476 Position the stabilizer shaft on the rear axle. Ensure the mark (1) is on the left rear of the stabilizer shaft

UPPER CONTROL ARM

REMOVAL & INSTALLATION

AWD & GT

See Figures 477 and 478.

1. Lower the rear suspension support crossmember as an assembly.

2. Paint matchmarks on the camber adjust cams and on the crossmember.

3. Remove the nut from the camber adjust bolt.

4. Remove the camber adjust plate from the camber adjust bolt.

5. Remove the camber adjust bolt.

6. Remove the upper control arm from the crossmember.

To install:

7. If you are replacing the upper control arm, copy the matchmarks from the old components to the new components.

➡**Do not tighten the nuts or the bolts yet. The weight of the vehicle must be on the tire and wheel assemblies before tightening the nuts and the bolts.**

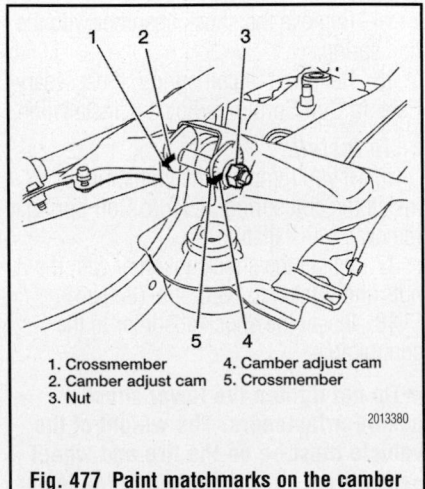

1. Crossmember
2. Camber adjust cam
3. Nut
4. Camber adjust cam
5. Crossmember

2013380

Fig. 477 Paint matchmarks on the camber adjust cams—AWD & GT

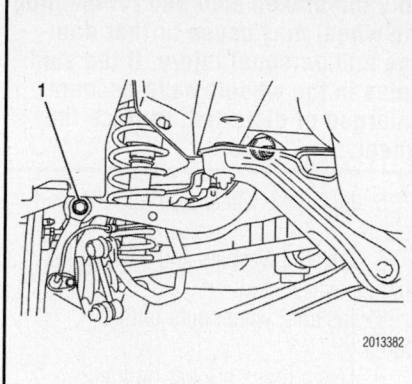

Fig. 478 Tighten the bolt (1) that retains the upper control arm to the knuckle—AWD & GT

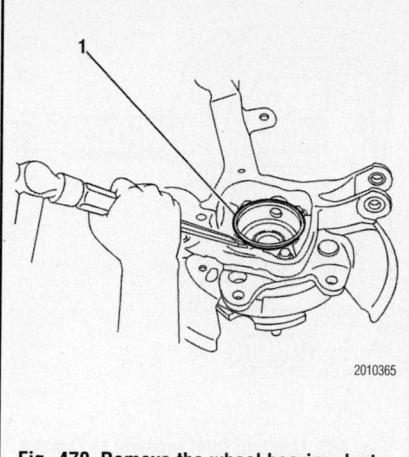

Fig. 479 Remove the wheel bearing dust deflector—AWD

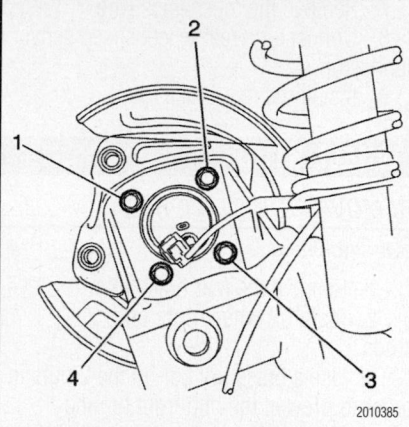

Fig. 481 Identifying the rear wheel bearing and hub assembly with the bolts (1–4)—Except AWD & GT

8. Align the matchmarks and install the upper control arm and the camber adjust bolt to the rear suspension crossmember. Install the bolt from the front toward the rear of the vehicle.

9. Align the matchmarks and install the camber adjust plate and the nut to the camber adjust bolt.

10. Install the rear suspension support crossmember as an assembly.

11. Lower the vehicle.

12. Raise and support the vehicle on an alignment rack or a lift that places the weight of the vehicle on the tires.

13. With the weight of the vehicle on the tires, push down on the rear bumper 3 times.

14. Align the matchmarks on the camber adjust bolt and the plate.

15. Hold the camber adjust bolt with a wrench and tighten the nut that retains the upper control arm to the crossmember.

16. Tighten the nut to 55 ft. lbs. (74 Nm).

17. Hold the nut with a wrench and tighten the bolt that retains the upper control arm to the knuckle.

18. Tighten the bolt to 55 ft. lbs. (74 Nm).

19. Measure the wheel alignment. Adjust the wheel alignment if necessary.

20. Lower the vehicle.

WHEEL BEARINGS

REMOVAL & INSTALLATION

AWD

See Figures 479 and 480.

1. Remove the rear knuckle. Refer to Knuckle, removal & installation.

2. Remove the wheel bearing dust deflector.

3. Remove the 4 bolts.

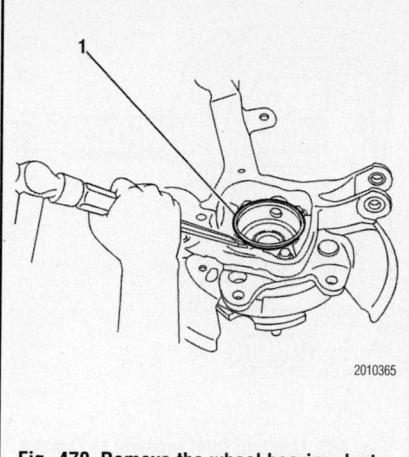

Fig. 480 Align the hole (1) for the rear wheel speed sensor in a NEW dust deflector with the hole in the knuckle—AWD

4. Remove the wheel bearing and hub assembly from the knuckle.

To install:

5. Ensure the brake shield is on the knuckle.

6. Install the wheel bearing and hub assembly to the knuckle.

7. Install the 4 bolts to the knuckle and tighten to 41 ft. lbs. (56 Nm).

8. Align the hole for the rear wheel speed sensor in a NEW dust deflector with the hole in the knuckle.

9. Use a hydraulic press and press tools, or use a hammer and a piece of flat steel stock, in order to install a NEW dust deflector.

EXCEPT AWD & GT

See Figure 481.

1. Remove the rear brake rotor.

2. Disconnect the rear wheel speed sensor electrical connector from the sensor.

3. Position the sensor harness to the side.

4. Remove the 4 bolts and the rear wheel bearing and hub assembly.

To install:

5. Install the rear wheel bearing and hub assembly with the 4 bolts. Tighten the bolts to 74 ft. lbs. (100 Nm).

6. Connect the rear wheel speed sensor connector.

7. Install the rear brake rotor.

GT

See Figure 482.

1. Remove the rear brake rotor.

2. Disconnect the rear wheel speed sensor connector from the sensor.

3. Position the sensor harness to the side.

4. Use mechanics wire in order to support the park brake assembly.

5. Remove the 4 bolts and the rear wheel bearing and hub assembly.

To install:

6. Install the rear wheel bearing and hub assembly with the 4 bolts and tighten to 41 ft. lbs. (56 Nm).

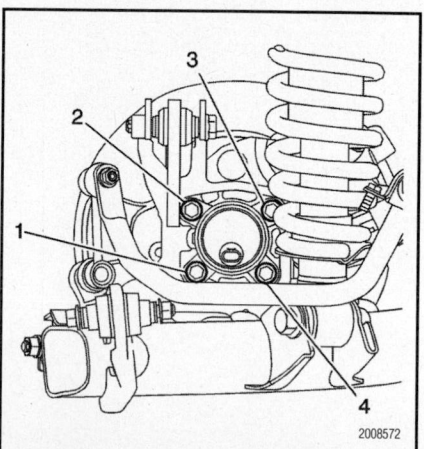

Fig. 482 Identifying the rear wheel bearing and hub assembly with the bolts (1–4)—GT

7. Remove the mechanics wire.
8. Connect the rear wheel speed sensor connector.
9. Install the rear brake rotor.

WHEEL STUD

REMOVAL & INSTALLATION

See Figure 483.

1. Remove the rear brake rotor.
2. Install 2 wheel nuts onto 2 studs.
3. Use a brass pry bar on the 2 nuts in order to prevent the hub from turning.
4. Use ball joint remover (J-43631) to remove the wheel stud.

To install:

✳✳ CAUTION

If one stud is damaged, replace all the studs. A loose-running

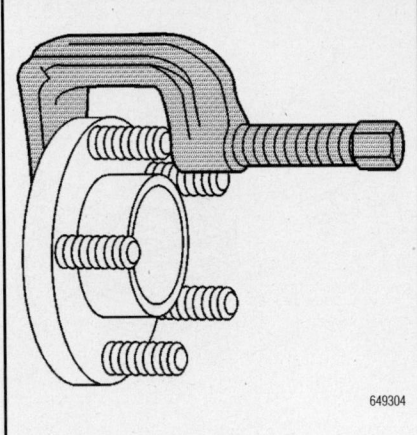

Fig. 483 Use ball joint remover to remove the wheel stud

wheel may cause only one stud to break, but the other studs could have internal fatigue. Replacing only the broken stud and remounting the wheel may cause further damage and personal injury. If the stud holes in the wheels have become enlarged or distorted, replace the wheel.

5. Install the wheel stud into the stud hole.
6. Install 3 washers and a wheel nut onto the wheel stud.
7. Install 2 wheel nuts onto 2 studs.
8. Use a brass pry bar on the 2 nuts in order to prevent the hub from turning.
9. Tighten the wheel nut in order to seat the wheel stud.
10. Remove the 3 wheel nuts and the 3 washers.
11. Install the rear brake rotor.

CHEVROLET

Volt

24

SPECIFICATIONS AND MAINTENANCE CHARTS

ENGINE AND VEHICLE IDENTIFICATION

			Engine					Model Year	
Code ①	Liters	Cu. In.	Cyl.	Fuel Sys.	Engine Type	Eng. Mfg.		Code ②	Year
4	1.4	85.0	4	MFI	DOHC	GM		B	2011

MFI: Multiport Fuel Injection

DOHC: Double Overhead Camshafts

① 8th position of VIN

② 10th position of VIN

25742_VOLT_C0001

GENERAL ENGINE SPECIFICATIONS

All measurements are given in inches.

Year	Model	Engine Displacement Liters	Engine ID/VIN	Fuel System Type	Net Horsepower @ rpm	Net Torque @ rpm (ft. lbs.)	Bore x Stroke (in.)	Compression Ratio	Oil Pressure @ rpm
2011	Volt	1.4	4	MFI	74@4,200	91@4,000	2.85 x 3.30	10.5:1	55-94 psi @3,000-3,500

25742_VOLT_C0002

ENGINE TUNE-UP SPECIFICATIONS

				Ignition Timing (deg.)			Idle Speed (rpm)		Valve Clearance	
Year	Engine Displacement Liters	Engine ID/VIN	Spark Plug Gap (in.)	MT	AT	Fuel Pump (psi)	MT	AT	Intake	Exhaust
2011	1.4	4	0.027	N/A	①	55-62	N/A	②	HYD	HYD

NOTE: The Vehicle Emission Control Information label often reflects specification changes made during production.

The label figures must be used if they differ from those in this chart.

HYD: Hydraulic

N/A: Not Applicable

① Ignition timing is controlled by the ECM and is not adjustable

② Idle speed is controlled by the ECM and is not adjustable

25742_VOLT_C0003

CAPACITIES

Year	Model	Engine Displacement Liters	Engine ID/VIN	Engine Oil with Filter (qts.)	Transaxle (pts.) Auto.	Transaxle (pts.) Manual	Fuel Tank (gal.)	Cooling System (qts.)
2011	Volt	1.4	4	3.7	①	N/A	9.3	6.7

NOTE: All capacities are approximate. Add fluid gradually and ensure a proper fluid level is obtained.

N/A: Not Applicable

① Drain and refill capacity: 14-14.8 pints. Total capacity: 18.8 pints.

25742_VOLT_C0004

FLUID SPECIFICATIONS

Year	Model	Engine Disp. Liters	Engine Oil	Manual Trans.	Auto. Trans.	Drive Axle Front	Drive Axle Rear	Power Steering Fluid	Brake Master Cylinder	Cooling System
2011	Volt	1.4	5W-30	N/A	DEXRON®-VI ATF	N/A	N/A	N/A	DOT 3	DEX-COOL® Coolant

DOT: Department Of Transportation

N/A: Not Applicable

25742_VOLT_C0005

VALVE SPECIFICATIONS

Year	Engine Displacement Liters	Engine ID/VIN	Seat Angle (deg.)	Face Angle (deg.)	Spring Test Pressure (lbs. @ in.)	Spring Free-Length (in.)	Spring Installed Height (in.)	Stem-to-Guide Clearance (in.) Intake	Stem-to-Guide Clearance (in.) Exhaust	Stem Diameter (in.) Intake	Stem Diameter (in.) Exhaust
2011	1.4	4	①	NS	NS	1.575	1.181	0.0010-0.0022	0.0018-0.0030	0.1949-0.1955	0.1941-0.1947

NS: Not Specified

① Cylinder head valve seat angle: 90° 30`

25742_VOLT_C0006

CAMSHAFT SPECIFICATIONS

All measurements in inches unless noted

Year	Engine Displacement Liters	Engine Code/VIN	Journal Diameter	Brg. Oil Clearance	Shaft End-play	Runout	Journal Bore	Lobe Height	
								Intake	Exhaust
2011	1.4	4	NS	NS	NS	NS	NS	NS	NS

NS: Not Specified

25742_VOLT_C0007

CRANKSHAFT AND CONNECTING ROD SPECIFICATIONS

All measurements are given in inches.

Year	Engine Displacement Liters	Engine ID/VIN	Crankshaft				Connecting Rod		
			Main Brg. Journal Dia.	Main Brg. Oil Clearance	Shaft End-play	Thrust on No.	Journal Diameter	Oil Clearance	Side Clearance
2011	1.4	4	1.9687-1.9692	0.0003-0.0012	0.0039-0.0080	3	1.6918-1.6924	0.0005-0.0024	NS

NS: Not Specified

25742_VOLT_C0008

PISTON AND RING SPECIFICATIONS

All measurements are given in inches.

Year	Engine Displacement Liters	Engine ID/VIN	Piston Clearance	Ring Gap			Ring Side Clearance		
				Top Compression	Bottom Compression	Oil Control	Top Compression	Bottom Compression	Oil Control
2011	1.4	4	0.0010-0.0022	0.0098-0.0157	0.0157-0.0236	0.0098-0.0295	0.0010-0.0028	0.0010-0.0028	0.0016-0.0047

25742_VOLT_C0009

TORQUE SPECIFICATIONS
All readings in ft. lbs.

Year	Engine Disp. Liters	Engine ID/VIN	Cylinder Head Bolts	Main Bearing Bolts	Rod Bearing Bolts	Crankshaft Damper Bolts	Flywheel Bolts	Manifold		Spark Plugs	Oil Pan Drain Plug
								Intake	Exhaust		
2011	1.4	4	①	②	③	④	⑤	15	16	18	10

① Step 1: 26 ft. lbs.
   Step 2: Plus 180 degrees
② M6 bolts Step 1: 89 inch lbs.
   M6 bolts Step 2: Plus 60 degrees
   M6 bolts Step 3: Plus 15 degrees
   M8 bolts Step 1: 18 ft. lbs.
   M8 bolts Step 2: Plus 60 degrees
   M8 bolts Step 3: Plus 15 degrees

③ Step 1: 18 ft. lbs.
   Step 2: Plus 45 degrees
④ Step 1: 111 ft. lbs.
   Step 2: Plus 45 degrees
   Step 3: Plus 15 degrees
⑤ Step 1: 26 ft. lbs.
   Step 2: Plus 30 degrees
   Step 3: Plus 15 degrees

25742_VOLT_C0010

WHEEL ALIGNMENT

Year	Model		Caster		Camber		Toe-in (in.)
			Range (+/-Deg.)	Preferred Setting (Deg.)	Range (+/-Deg.)	Preferred Setting (Deg.)	
2011	Volt	F	0.75	0.00	0.75	0.00	0.20 +/- 0.20
		R	N/A	N/A	0.75	0.00	0.00 +/- 0.40

N/A: Not Applicable

25742_VOLT_C0011

TIRE, WHEEL AND BALL JOINT SPECIFICATIONS

Year	Model	OEM Tires Standard	OEM Tires Optional	Tire Pressures (psi) Front	Tire Pressures (psi) Rear	Wheel Size	Ball Joint Inspection	Lug Nut (ft. lbs.)
2011	Volt	P215/55R17	NA	①	①	17 x 7 inch	②	103

OEM: Original Equipment Manufacturer

PSI: Pounds Per Square Inch

NA: Information not available

① Always refer to the owner's manual and/or vehicle label

② Check for smooth rotation of the ball stud and for any damage to the ball stud or dust cover. If damage is found, replace the lower control arm.

25742_VOLT_C0012

BRAKE SPECIFICATIONS

All measurements in inches unless noted

Year	Model		Brake Disc Original Thickness	Brake Disc Minimum Thickness	Brake Disc Max. Runout	Brake Drum Diameter Original Inside Diameter	Brake Drum Diameter Max. Wear Limit	Brake Drum Diameter Maximum Machine Diameter	Minimum Pad/Lining Thickness Front	Minimum Pad/Lining Thickness Rear	Brake Caliper Bracket Bolts (ft. lbs.)	Brake Caliper Guide Pin Bolts (ft. lbs.)
2011	Volt	F	1.023	0.905	0.002	N/A	N/A	N/A	0.078	0.078	111	21
		R	0.472	0.393	0.002	N/A	N/A	N/A	0.078	0.078	74	21

F: Front

R: Rear

N/A: Not Applicable

25742_VOLT_C0013

MAINTENANCE I AND II SERVICE SCHEDULES
VOLT

When the CHANGE ENGINE OIL light appears, certain services and inspections are required.

Required services are described as Maintenance I and Maintenance II.

The first service of a vehicle should be Maintenance I, and the second service should be Maintenance II.

Alternate between the 2 services thereafter. However, in some cases, Maintenance II may be required more often.

Maintenance I: Use Maintenance I if the CHANGE ENGINE OIL light comes on within 10 months since the vehicle was purchased or, if Maintenance II was performed.

Maintenance II: Use Maintenance II if the previous service performed was Maintenance I. Always use Maintenance II whenever the CHANGE ENGINE OIL light comes on 10 months or more since the last service, or, if the CHANGE ENGINE OIL light has not come on at all for one year.

Service Item	Maintenance I	Maintenance II
Change the engine oil and filter.	✓	✓
Reset the oil life system.	✓	✓
Visually inspect the vehicle for leaks or damage. A fluid loss in the vehicle system could indicate a problem. Inspect, repair and add fluid to the system if necessary.	✓	✓
Inspect the engine air cleaner filter. If necessary, replace the filter.	✓	✓
Visually inspect the brake lines and hoses for proper hook-up, binding, leaks, cracks, chafing, etc. Inspect the disc brake pads for wear and the rotors for surface condition. Inspect the brake calipers.	✓	✓
Inspect engine coolant and windshield washer fluid levels. Add fluid as needed.	✓	✓
Inspect the suspension and steering components. Inspect the front and rear suspension and the steering system for damaged, loose or missing parts, or signs of wear. Inspect the power steering lines and the hoses for proper hook-up, binding, leaks, cracks,	—	✓
Visually inspect the coolant hoses and replace the hoses if they are cracked, swollen or deteriorated. Inspect all pipes, fittings and clamps; replace parts as needed. To help ensure proper operation, a pressure test of the cooling system and pressure cap and cleaning the outside of the radiator and air conditioning condenser is recommended at least once a year.	—	✓
Body hinges and latches, key lock cylinders, folding seat hardware, and rear compartment hinges lubrication. Applying silicone grease on weatherstrips with a clean cloth makes them last longer, seal better, and not stick or squeak.	✓	✓
Inspect the throttle system for interference or binding and for damaged or missing parts. Replace the parts as needed. Replace any components that have high effort or excessive wear. Do not lubricate the accelerator or the cruise control cables.	—	✓
Inspect exhaust system and heat shields for loose or damaged components.	✓	✓
Inspect restraint system.	✓	✓
Check the sealant expiration date printed on the instruction label of the tire sealant and compressor kit.	✓	✓
Chech high voltage battery coolant.	—	✓
Perform the propulsion system start check.	—	✓
Perform the electrical drive shift lock control function check.	—	✓
Perform the park brake and park mechanism check.	—	✓
Check fuel system for leaks, check the accelerator pedal for high effort or binding.	✓	✓
Rotate tires every 7,500 miles, check for wear and inflation pressure.	✓	✓

To reset the CHANGE ENGINE OIL light:

1. Turn the ignition key to the ON/RUN position with the engine OFF.
2. Press and release the stem in the lower center of the instrument cluster until the OIL LIFE message is displayed.
3. Once the alternating OIL LIFE and RESET messages appear, press and hold the stem until several beeps sound.
   This confirms that the oil life system has been reset to 100 percent.
4. Turn the ignition key to the OFF position.
   If the CHANGE ENGINE OIL message comes back on when the vehicle is started, the engine oil life system has not been reset. Repeat the procedure.

ADDITIONAL MAINTENANCE SERVICES
VOLT

TO BE SERVICED	TYPE OF SERVICE	VEHICLE MILEAGE INTERVAL (x1000)					
		25	50	75	100	125	150
Spark plugs	Replace				✓		
Air cleaner filter	Replace		✓		✓		✓
Engine coolant	Replace						✓
Exhaust system & heat shields	Service/ Inspect	✓	✓	✓	✓	✓	✓
Cooling system hoses and clamps	Service/ Inspect	✓	✓	✓	✓	✓	✓
Fuel system	Inspect	✓	✓	✓	✓	✓	✓
Evaporative control system	Inspect		✓		✓		✓
Accessory drive belts	Replace						✓
Accessory drive belts	Inspect	✓	✓	✓	✓	✓	✓

25742_VOLT_C0015

PRECAUTIONS

Before servicing any vehicle, please be sure to read all of the following precautions, which deal with personal safety, prevention of component damage, and important points to take into consideration when servicing a motor vehicle:

- Never open, service or drain the radiator or cooling system when the engine is hot; serious burns can occur from the steam and hot coolant.

- Observe all applicable safety precautions when working around fuel. Whenever servicing the fuel system, always work in a well-ventilated area. Do not allow fuel spray or vapors to come in contact with a spark, open flame, or excessive heat (a hot drop light, for example). Keep a dry chemical fire extinguisher near the work area. Always keep fuel in a container specifically designed for fuel storage; also, always properly seal fuel containers to avoid the possibility of fire or explosion. Refer to the additional fuel system precautions later in this section.

- Fuel injection systems often remain pressurized, even after the engine has been turned **OFF**. The fuel system pressure must be relieved before disconnecting any fuel lines. Failure to do so may result in fire and/or personal injury.

- Brake fluid often contains polyglycol ethers and polyglycols. Avoid contact with the eyes and wash your hands thoroughly after handling brake fluid. If you do get brake fluid in your eyes, flush your eyes with clean, running water for 15 minutes. If eye irritation persists, or if you have taken brake fluid internally, IMMEDIATELY seek medical assistance.

- The EPA warns that prolonged contact with used engine oil may cause a number of skin disorders, including cancer. You should make every effort to minimize your exposure to used engine oil. Protective gloves should be worn when changing oil. Wash your hands and any other exposed skin areas as soon as possible after exposure to used engine oil. Soap and water, or waterless hand cleaner should be used.

- All new vehicles are now equipped with an air bag system, often referred to as a Supplemental Restraint System (SRS) or Supplemental Inflatable Restraint (SIR) system. The system must be disabled before performing service on or around system components, steering column, instrument panel components, wiring and sensors. Failure to follow safety and disabling procedures could result in accidental air bag deployment, possible personal injury and unnecessary system repairs.

- Always wear safety goggles when working with, or around, the air bag system. When carrying a non-deployed air bag, be sure the bag and trim cover are pointed away from your body. When placing a non-deployed air bag on a work surface, always face the bag and trim cover upward, away from the surface. This will reduce the motion of the module if it is accidentally deployed. Refer to the additional air bag system precautions later in this section.

- Clean, high quality brake fluid from a sealed container is essential to the safe and proper operation of the brake system. You should always buy the correct type of brake fluid for your vehicle. If the brake fluid becomes contaminated, completely flush the system with new fluid. Never reuse any brake fluid. Any brake fluid that is removed from the system should be discarded. Also, do not allow any brake fluid to come in contact with a painted surface; it will damage the paint.

- Never operate the engine without the proper amount and type of engine oil; doing so WILL result in severe engine damage.

- Timing belt maintenance is extremely important. Many models utilize an interference-type, non-freewheeling engine. If the timing belt breaks, the valves in the cylinder head may strike the pistons, causing potentially serious (also time-consuming and expensive) engine damage. Refer to the maintenance interval charts for the recommended replacement interval for the timing belt, and to the timing belt section for belt replacement and inspection.

- Disconnecting the negative battery cable on some vehicles may interfere with the functions of the on-board computer system(s) and may require the computer to undergo a relearning process once the negative battery cable is reconnected.

- When servicing drum brakes, only disassemble and assemble one side at a time, leaving the remaining side intact for reference.

- Only an MVAC-trained, EPA-certified automotive technician should service the air conditioning system or its components.

BRAKES

GENERAL INFORMATION

PRECAUTIONS

- Certain components within the ABS system are not intended to be serviced or repaired individually.

- Do not use rubber hoses or other parts not specifically specified for and ABS system. When using repair kits, replace all parts included in the kit. Partial or incorrect repair may lead to functional problems and require the replacement of components.

- Lubricate rubber parts with clean, fresh brake fluid to ease assembly. Do not use shop air to clean parts; damage to rubber components may result.

- Use only DOT 3 brake fluid from an unopened container.

- If any hydraulic component or line is removed or replaced, it may be necessary to bleed the entire system.

- A clean repair area is essential. Always clean the reservoir and cap thoroughly before removing the cap. The slightest amount of dirt in the fluid may plug an orifice and impair the system function. Perform repairs after components have been thoroughly cleaned; use only denatured alcohol to clean components. Do not allow ABS components to come into contact with any substance containing mineral oil; this includes used shop rags.

- The Anti-Lock control unit is a microprocessor similar to other computer units in the vehicle. Ensure that the ignition switch is **OFF** before removing or installing controller harnesses. Avoid static electricity discharge at or near the controller.

ANTI-LOCK BRAKE SYSTEM (ABS)

- If any arc welding is to be done on the vehicle, the control unit should be unplugged before welding operations begin.

SPEED SENSORS

REMOVAL & INSTALLATION

Front Speed Sensor
See Figure 1.

✳✳ CAUTION

Do not use a service jack in locations other than those specified to lift this vehicle. Lifting the vehicle with a jack in those other locations could cause the vehicle to slip off the jack and roll; this could cause injury or death.

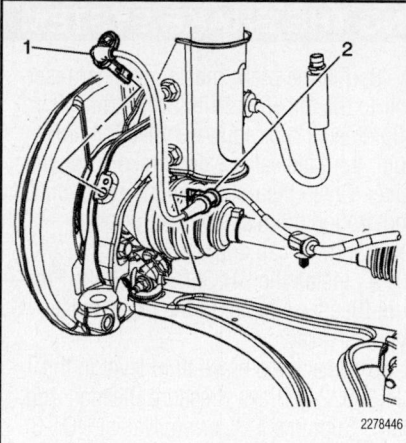

Fig. 1 View of front wheel speed sensor (1) and harness clip (2)

1. Before servicing the vehicle, refer to the Precautions Section.
2. Raise and safely support the vehicle.
3. Remove the tire and wheel assembly.
4. Remove the lower fasteners securing the front wheelhouse liner front liner to the frame.
5. Pull the front wheelhouse liner away from the frame to access the wheel speed sensor electrical connector.
6. Disconnect the wheel speed sensor electrical connector and release the connector from the frame.
7. Release the harness clip from the frame.
8. Release the harness clips from the lower control arm.
9. Clean the wheel speed sensor mounting area on the steering knuckle of any accumulated dirt and debris.
10. Remove the wheel speed sensor bolt.
11. Remove the wheel speed sensor from the steering knuckle.
12. Release the harness clip from the steering knuckle and remove the wheel speed sensor.

To install:
13. Install the wheel speed sensor to the steering knuckle.
14. Install the harness clip to the steering knuckle.
15. Install the wheel speed sensor bolt and tighten to 89 inch lbs. (10 Nm).
16. Connect the wheel speed sensor electrical connector and secure the connector to the frame.
17. Install the harness clip to the frame.
18. Install the harness clips to the lower control arm.
19. Install the lower fasteners securing the front wheelhouse liner front liner to the

frame. Tighten the screws to 27 inch lbs. (3 Nm).

✳✳ WARNING
Improperly tightened wheel bolts or nuts can lead to brake pulsation and rotor damage. In order to avoid expensive brake repairs, evenly tighten the wheel bolts or nuts to the proper torque specification.

20. Install the tire and wheel assembly and tighten the wheel nuts in a crisscross pattern to 103 ft. lbs. (140 Nm).
21. Ensure the proper function of electronic components.

Rear Speed Sensor
See Figures 2 and 3.

1. Before servicing the vehicle, refer to the Precautions Section.
2. Raise and safely support the vehicle.

✳✳ CAUTION
Do not use a service jack in locations other than those specified to lift this vehicle. Lifting the vehicle with a jack in those other locations could cause the vehicle to slip off the jack and roll; this could cause injury or death.

3. Raise and support the vehicle.
4. Remove the tire and wheel assembly.
5. Clean the wheel speed sensor mounting area on the suspension knuckle of any accumulated dirt and debris.
6. Remove the wheel speed sensor bolt.
7. Remove the wheel speed sensor from the suspension knuckle.

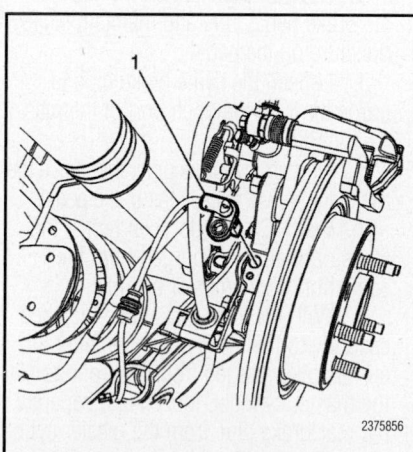

Fig. 2 Remove the rear wheel speed sensor (1) from the suspension knuckle

8. Release the wheel speed sensor harness from the rear brake hose retainers and the brake hose bracket.
9. Remove the lower forward wheelhouse liner pushpin, lift the wheelhouse liner away from the body slightly and disconnect the wheel speed sensor electrical connector.
10. Release the wheel speed sensor harness retainer from the frame rail and remove the wheel speed sensor.

To install:
11. Install the wheel speed sensor to the suspension knuckle.
12. Install the wheel speed sensor bolt and tighten to 80 inch lbs. (9 Nm).
13. Install the wheel speed sensor harness to the rear brake hose retainers and the brake hose bracket.
14. Lift the wheelhouse liner away from the body slightly and connect the wheel speed sensor electrical connector.
15. Install the forward lower wheelhouse liner pushpin.
16. Install the wheel speed sensor harness retainer to the frame rail.

✳✳ WARNING
Improperly tightened wheel bolts or nuts can lead to brake pulsation and rotor damage. In order to avoid expensive brake repairs, evenly tighten the wheel bolts or nuts to the proper torque specification.

17. Install the tire and wheel assembly and tighten the wheel nuts in a crisscross pattern to 103 ft. lbs. (140 Nm).
18. Ensure the proper function of electronic components.

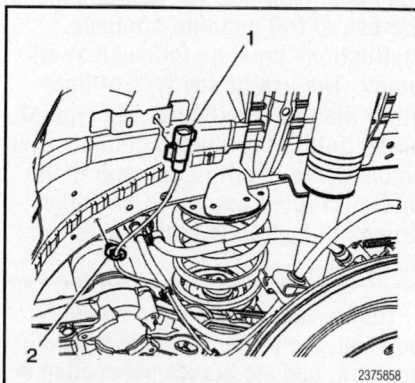

Fig. 3 Disconnect the rear wheel speed sensor electrical connector (1) and release the wheel speed sensor harness retainer (2) from the frame rail

BLEEDING PROCEDURE

HYDRAULIC BRAKE SYSTEM BLEEDING

Special Tools
- CH-29532-A Brake Pressure Bleeder, or equivalent
- CH-35589-A Brake Pressure Bleeder Adapter

✳✳ CAUTION

Brake fluid may irritate eyes and skin. In case of contact, take the following actions:

- Eye contact—rinse thoroughly with water
- Skin contact—wash with soap and water
- If ingested—consult a physician immediately

✳✳ WARNING

Avoid spilling brake fluid onto painted surfaces, electrical connections, wiring, or cables. Brake fluid will damage painted surfaces and cause corrosion to electrical components. If any brake fluid comes in contact with painted surfaces, immediately flush the area with water. If any brake fluid comes in contact with electrical connections, wiring, or cables, use a clean shop cloth to wipe away the fluid.

✳✳ WARNING

Only use products that comply with GM specifications. We recommend the use of GM genuine products. Instructions must be followed at all times. The use of any type of fluid other than the recommended type of brake fluid, may cause contamination which could result in damage to the internal rubber seals and/or rubber linings of hydraulic brake system components.

➡**The transaxle must be in the PARK position, the power button in the OFF position, and the brakes not applied to ensure the brake modulator and High Pressure Accumulator (HPA) pressure relief occurs. This process will take approximately 1–3 minutes.**

1. Before servicing the vehicle, refer to the Precautions Section.

2. Place the transaxle in PARK.

3. Place the power button in the OFF position.

4. Remove the Remote Keyless Entry (RKE) transmitter and close all of the vehicle doors.

5. Place a clean shop cloth beneath the brake master cylinder to prevent brake fluid spills.

6. With the power button OFF and the brakes cool, apply the brakes 3–5 times, or until the brake pedal effort increases significantly, in order to deplete the brake booster power reserve.

7. If you have performed a brake master cylinder bench bleeding on this vehicle, or if you disconnected the brake pipes from the master cylinder, you must perform the following steps:

    a. Ensure that the brake master cylinder reservoir is full to the maximum-fill level. If necessary add Delco Supreme 11®, or equivalent DOT-3 brake fluid, from a clean, sealed brake fluid container.

➡**If removal of the reservoir cap and diaphragm is necessary, clean the outside of the reservoir on and around the cap prior to removal.**

    b. With the rear brake pipe installed securely to the master cylinder, loosen and separate the front brake pipe from the front port of the brake master cylinder.

    c. Allow a small amount of brake fluid to gravity bleed from the open port of the master cylinder.

    d. Reconnect the brake pipe to the master cylinder port and tighten securely.

    e. Have an assistant slowly depress the brake pedal fully and maintain steady pressure on the pedal.

    f. Loosen the same brake pipe to purge air from the open port of the master cylinder.

    g. Tighten the brake pipe, then have the assistant slowly release the brake pedal.

    h. Wait 15 seconds, then repeat the steps until all air is purged from the same port of the master cylinder.

    i. With the front brake pipe installed securely to the master cylinder, after all air has been purged from the front port of the master cylinder, loosen and separate the rear brake pipe from the master cylinder, then repeat the above steps.

    j. After completing the final master cylinder port bleeding procedure, ensure that both of the brake pipe-to-master cylinder fittings are properly tightened.

8. Fill the brake master cylinder reservoir to the maximum-fill level with Delco Supreme 11®, or equivalent DOT-3 brake fluid, from a clean, sealed brake fluid container. Clean the outside of the reservoir on and around the reservoir cap prior to removing the cap and diaphragm.

9. Install the CH-35589-A Brake Pressure Bleeder Adapter to the brake master cylinder reservoir.

10. Check the brake fluid level in the CH-29532-A Brake Pressure Bleeder. Add Delco Supreme 11®, or equivalent DOT-3 brake fluid, from a clean, sealed brake fluid container as necessary to bring the level to approximately the half-full point.

11. Connect the CH-29532-A Brake Pressure Bleeder, to the CH-35589-A Brake Pressure Bleeder Adapter.

12. Charge the CH-29532-A Brake Pressure Bleeder air tank to 25–30 psi (175–205 kPa).

13. Open the CH-29532-A Brake Pressure Bleeder fluid tank valve to allow pressurized brake fluid to enter the brake system.

14. Wait approximately 30 seconds, then inspect the entire hydraulic brake system in order to ensure that there are no existing external brake fluid leaks. Any brake fluid leaks identified require repair prior to completing this procedure.

15. Install a proper box-end wrench onto the RIGHT REAR wheel hydraulic circuit bleeder valve.

16. Install a transparent hose over the end of the bleeder valve.

17. Submerge the open end of the transparent hose into a transparent container partially filled with DOT-3 brake fluid from a clean, sealed brake fluid container.

18. Loosen the bleeder valve to purge air from the wheel hydraulic circuit. Allow fluid to flow until air bubbles stop flowing from the bleeder, then tighten the bleeder valve.

19. With the right rear wheel hydraulic circuit bleeder valve tightened securely, after all air has been purged from the right rear hydraulic circuit, install a proper box-end wrench onto the LEFT REAR wheel hydraulic circuit bleeder valve.

20. Install a transparent hose over the end of the bleeder valve, then repeat the bleeding steps.

21. With the left rear wheel hydraulic circuit bleeder valve tightened securely, after all air has been purged from the left rear hydraulic circuit, install a proper box-end wrench onto the RIGHT FRONT wheel hydraulic circuit bleeder valve.

22. Install a transparent hose over the end of the bleeder valve, then repeat the bleeding steps.

23. With the right front wheel hydraulic circuit bleeder valve tightened securely, after all air has been purged from the right front hydraulic circuit, install a proper box-end wrench onto the LEFT FRONT wheel hydraulic circuit bleeder valve.

24. Install a transparent hose over the end of the bleeder valve, then repeat the bleeding steps.

25. After completing the final wheel hydraulic circuit bleeding procedure, ensure that each of the 4 wheel hydraulic circuit bleeder valves are properly tightened.

26. Close the CH-29532-A Brake Pressure Bleeder fluid tank valve, then disconnect the CH-29532-A Brake Pressure Bleeder from the CH-35589-A Brake Pressure Bleeder Adapter.

27. Remove the CH-35589-A Brake Pressure Bleeder Adapter from the brake master cylinder reservoir.

28. Fill the brake master cylinder reservoir to the maximum-fill level with Delco Supreme 11®, or equivalent DOT-3 brake fluid, from a clean, sealed brake fluid container.

29. Slowly depress and release the brake pedal. Observe the feel of the brake pedal.

30. If the brake pedal feels spongy perform the following steps:

   a. Inspect the brake system for external leaks.

   b. Using a scan tool, perform the antilock brake system automated bleeding procedure to remove any air that may have been trapped in the Brake Pressure Modulator Valve (BPMV). Refer to Bleeding the ABS System, ABS Automated Bleed.

31. Turn the power button ON, with the engine OFF. Check to see if the brake system warning lamp remains illuminated.

✳✳ CAUTION

If the brake system warning lamp remains illuminated, DO NOT allow the vehicle to be driven until it is diagnosed and repaired.

32. If the brake system warning lamp remains illuminated, determine the cause and repair as needed.

MASTER CYLINDER BLEEDING

Bench Bleeding Procedure

✳✳ CAUTION

Brake fluid may irritate eyes and skin. In case of contact, take the following actions:

• Eye contact—rinse thoroughly with water

• Skin contact—wash with soap and water

• If ingested—consult a physician immediately

✳✳ WARNING

Avoid spilling brake fluid onto painted surfaces, electrical connections, wiring, or cables. Brake fluid will damage painted surfaces and cause corrosion to electrical components. If any brake fluid comes in contact with painted surfaces, immediately flush the area with water. If any brake fluid comes in contact with electrical connections, wiring, or cables, use a clean shop cloth to wipe away the fluid.

✳✳ WARNING

Only use products that comply with GM specifications and check manufacturer information respectively. We recommend the use of GM genuine products. Instructions must be followed at all times. The use of any type of fluid other than the recommended type of brake fluid, may cause contamination which could result in damage to the internal rubber seals and/or rubber linings of hydraulic brake system components.

1. Before servicing the vehicle, refer to the Precautions Section.

2. Secure the mounting flange of the brake master cylinder in a bench vise so that the rear of the primary piston is accessible.

3. Remove the master cylinder reservoir cap and diaphragm.

4. Install suitable fittings to the master cylinder ports that match the type of flare seat required and also provide for hose attachment.

5. Install transparent hoses to the fittings installed to the master cylinder ports, then route the hoses into the master cylinder reservoir.

6. Fill the master cylinder reservoir to at least the half-way point with GM approved brake fluid from a clean, sealed brake fluid container.

7. Ensure that the ends of the transparent hoses running into the master cylinder reservoir are fully submerged in the brake fluid.

8. Using a smooth, round-ended tool, depress and release the primary piston as far as it will travel, a depth of about 1 inch

(25mm), several times. Observe the flow of fluid coming from the ports. As air is bled from the primary and secondary pistons, the effort required to depress the primary piston will increase and the amount of travel will decrease.

9. Continue to depress and release the primary piston until fluid flows freely from the ports with no evidence of air bubbles.

10. Remove the transparent hoses from the master cylinder reservoir.

11. Install the master cylinder reservoir cap and diaphragm.

12. Remove the fittings with the transparent hoses from the master cylinder ports. Wrap the master cylinder with a clean shop cloth to prevent brake fluid spills.

13. Remove the master cylinder from the vise.

BRAKE LINE BLEEDING

Refer to Hydraulic Brake System Bleeding and/or Bleeding The ABS System procedure.

BLEEDING THE ABS SYSTEM

ABS Automated Bleed

  Special Tools
  • CH-29532-A Brake Pressure Bleeder
  • CH-35589-A Brake Bleeder Adapter

✳✳ CAUTION

At times during this brake bleed procedure brake fluid will be under higher pressures than during typical brake bleed procedures. Ensure the bleeder hose attached to the bleeder valve is securely maintained in position whenever the bleeder valve is opened. Failure to maintain the bleeder hose securely to the valve when opened, may allow the hose to blow off and brake fluid to spray out of the bleeder valve, possibly resulting in personal injury.

✳✳ WARNING

Only use products that comply with GM specifications and check manufacturer information respectively. We recommend the use of GM genuine products. Instructions must be followed at all times. The use of any type of fluid other than the recommended type of brake fluid, may cause contamination which could result in damage to the internal rubber seals and/or rubber linings of hydraulic brake system components.

✳✳ WARNING

Avoid spilling brake fluid onto painted surfaces, electrical connections, wiring, or cables. Brake fluid will damage painted surfaces and cause corrosion to electrical components. If any brake fluid comes in contact with painted surfaces, immediately flush the area with water. If any brake fluid comes in contact with electrical connections, wiring, or cables, use a clean shop cloth to wipe away the fluid.

➡Do not pressurize the CH-29532-A Brake Pressure Bleeder and thereby the master cylinder reservoir until instructed to do so by the scan tool. Portions of the automated bleed process require the master cylinder reservoir not be pressurized through the CH-29532-A Brake Pressure Bleeder.

➡Do not apply the brake pedal until instructed to do so by the scan tool. Applying the brake pedal before instructed by the scan tool may result in setting a DTC and may require the sensor and boost valve calibration and Electronic Brake Control Module (EBCM) learn procedures to be repeated manually.

➡The transaxle must be in the PARK position, the power button in the OFF position, and the brakes not applied to ensure the brake modulator and High Pressure Accumulator (HPA) pressure relief occurs. This process will take approximately 1–3 minutes.

1. Before servicing the vehicle, refer to the Precautions Section.
2. Place the transaxle in PARK.
3. Place the power button in the OFF position.
4. Wait approximately 3 minutes for the HPA pressure relief to occur.

✳✳ CAUTION

Do not use a service jack in locations other than those specified to lift this vehicle. Lifting the vehicle with a jack in those other locations could cause the vehicle to slip off the jack and roll; this could cause injury or death.

5. Raise and safely support the vehicle.
6. Remove the tire and wheel assemblies.
7. Inspect the brake system for leaks

and visual damage. Repair or replace components as necessary.

8. Lower the vehicle to allow for entry and exit while bleeding the brake corners and other components.
9. Connect a battery charger with a 20 AMP output to the 12 volt battery. The battery charger must remain connected for the entire automated bleed procedure.
10. Install a scan tool to the vehicle.

➡The power button must remain ON during this entire procedure.

11. Place the power button in the ON position.
12. Using the scan tool, perform the following steps:
   - Select Diagnostics
   - Select the appropriate vehicle information
   - Select Chassis
   - Select Electronic Brake Control Module (EBCM)
   - Select Special Functions
   - Select Automated Bleed
13. Press Start to begin the automated bleed procedure. Ensure the CH-29532-A Brake Pressure Bleeder has not yet been installed to the vehicle. The travel and pressure sensors are being calibrated and learned by the EBCM during this step.
14. Press Start to continue.

➡Approximately 2.6–3.2 quarts (2.5–3.0L) of brake fluid will be used throughout this procedure. Ensure there is an adequate supply of brake fluid in the CH-29532-A Brake Pressure Bleeder.

15. Inspect the fluid level in the CH-29532-A Brake Pressure Bleeder. Clean the outside of the CH-29532-A Brake Pressure Bleeder and add GM approved or equivalent DOT-3 brake fluid from a clean, sealed brake fluid container, as necessary.
16. Clean the outside of the master cylinder reservoir on and around the reservoir cap prior to removing the cap and diaphragm.

➡Do not pressurize the CH-29532-A Brake Pressure Bleeder and thereby the master cylinder reservoir until instructed to do so by the scan tool.

17. Install the CH-35589-A Brake Bleeder Adapter and the CH-29532-A Brake Pressure Bleeder to the vehicle.

➡Ensure a MINIMUM of 30 psi (200 kPa) of pressure is MAINTAINED in the CH-29532-A Brake Pressure Bleeder throughout this procedure, except as instructed.

18. Set the pressure regulator of the CH-29532-A Brake Pressure Bleeder to 30–60 psi (207–414 kPa).
19. Open the CH-29532-A Brake Pressure Bleeder fluid tank valve to allow pressurized brake fluid to enter the brake system.
20. Wait approximately 30 seconds, then inspect the entire hydraulic brake system to ensure there are no existing external brake fluid leaks.
21. Secure bleeder hoses to all 4 brake caliper bleeder valves.
22. Bleed each of the 4 brake corners using the CH-29532-A Brake Pressure Bleeder in the following sequence. Ensure the brake fluid is clear and free of air bubbles at each corner.
   - Left front
   - Right front
   - Left rear
   - Right rear
23. Ensure each of the 4 brake caliper bleeder valves are tightened securely.
24. Press Start to begin the system automated bleed steps.
25. Follow all instructions on the scan tool. Only apply the brake pedal when instructed to do so by the scan tool.
26. When instructed, firmly apply and release the brake pedal using smooth, consistent full brake pedal strokes. The brake pedal will go fully to the floor with some pedal feedback felt. The master cylinder reservoir supply circuit is being flushed through these steps.
27. Continue the brake applications until instructed by the scan tool. The scan tool will instruct to perform 10 brake applications.
28. When instructed by the scan tool, stop performing the brake applications and press Enter.
29. When instructed by the scan tool, press Start to continue.

✳✳ CAUTION

The hydraulic brake system will be under high pressure during the next bleed sequence. Ensure the bleeder hose is maintained securely to the bleeder valve, and open the bleeder valve slowly.

30. Following the instructions on the scan tool, open the Right Rear (RR) brake caliper bleeder valve.
31. With the bleeder valve open and the bleeder hose maintained firmly in place, press Start to begin the bleeding process. This process will run in a 30-second cycle. The pump and HPA circuits are being flushed during these steps.

32. Press Enter when instructed to repeat the bleeding process 3 more times on the scan tool.

33. Press Enter when instructed at the end of the 4th bleeding process.

34. Ensure the RR brake caliper bleeder valve is tightened securely.

35. Following the instructions on the scan tool, open the Left Rear (LR) brake caliper bleeder valve.

36. With the bleeder valve open and the bleeder hose maintained firmly in place, press Start to begin the bleeding process.

37. Press Enter when instructed to repeat the bleeding process 3 more times on the scan tool.

38. Press Enter when instructed at the end of the 4th bleeding process.

39. Ensure the LR brake caliper bleeder valve is tightened securely.

40. Reduce the charge in the air tank of the CH-29532-A Brake Pressure Bleeder to 0 psi (0 kPa).

41. Press Start to continue. This sequence will run in a 20-second cycle. The brake pedal simulator circuit is being flushed through this step.

42. Press Enter when instructed to repeat the bleeding process 5 more times on the scan tool.

43. Set the pressure regulator of the CH-29532-A Brake Pressure Bleeder to 30 60 psi (207 414 kPa).

44. Press Enter to continue. This sequence will run in a 120-second cycle. The boost side of the secondary master cylinder is being flushed through this step.

45. Open the Right Rear (RR) brake caliper bleeder valve.

46. Press Enter when instructed to repeat the bleeding process 1 more time on the scan tool.

47. Press Enter to continue.

48. Following the instructions on the scan tool, press Start to begin the next bleed sequence.

49. Open the Right Rear (RR) brake caliper bleeder valve. Ensure the RR bleeder valve is fully bled and securely tightened before the 60-second cycle is completed. Do not leave the bleeder valve open for longer than 60-seconds.

50. If the RR bleeder valve was not fully bled within the 60-second cycle time, press Start to repeat until the brake fluid is clear of any air.

51. Press Enter to continue.

52. Following the instructions on the scan tool, press Start to begin the next bleed sequence.

53. Open the Left Rear (LR) brake caliper bleeder valve. Ensure the LR bleeder valve

is fully bled and securely tightened before the 60-second cycle is completed. Do not leave the bleeder valve open for longer than 60-seconds.

54. If the RR bleeder valve was not fully bled within the 60-second cycle time, press Start to repeat until the brake fluid is clear of any air.

55. Press Enter to continue.

56. Secure bleeder hoses to all 4 brake caliper bleeder valves.

57. Bleed each of the 4 brake corners using the CH-29532-A Brake Pressure Bleeder, in the following sequence. Ensure the brake fluid is clear and free of air bubbles at each corner.
- Left front
- Right front
- Left rear
- Right rear

58. Ensure each of the 4 brake caliper bleeder valves are tightened securely.

59. Press Enter to continue.

60. Remove the CH-35589-A Brake Bleeder Adapter and the CH-29532-A Brake Pressure Bleeder from the vehicle.

➡**The system is active and pressurized, therefore the brake fluid level in the master cylinder reservoir cannot be allowed to be higher than the MAX mark of the operating range.**

61. Ensure the master cylinder reservoir is filled no higher than the MAX operating range line. Add or remove brake fluid as necessary.

62. Start the engine.

63. Press Start to continue the final sequence. The pump and the HPA circuits are being flushed, and the boost valve is being calibrated and learned by the EBCM through this step.

64. Continue to follow the instructions on the scan tool.

65. Allow the engine to idle for 1 minute to allow the system to recalibrate.

66. Place the power button in the OFF position, then place the power button in the ON position.

67. Clear any DTCs from the EBCM.

68. The brake control modulator is an OBDII compliant module. As such, brake related DTCs may be stored in the powertrain control modules. After addressing any other stored DTCs, clear any brake related DTCs stored in the powertrain control modules.

69. Place the power button in the OFF position, without applying the brake pedal.

70. Allow the vehicle to remain OFF for at least 1 minute before applying the brake pedal or performing a test drive. This waiting period is essential to complete the sensor and boost valve calibration and EBCM

learn processes, and to allow the HPA to depressurize to allow for a deactivated system pedal feel check.

71. Remove the scan tool from the vehicle.

72. Before activating the power button, firmly apply the brake pedal several times. Observe the brake pedal feel.

73. If the brake pedal feels spongy, perform the following:

a. Repeat the base hydraulic brake system bleeding procedure. Refer to Hydraulic Brake System Bleeding.

b. If the brake pedal feel is now firm, repeat the automated bleeding procedure.

c. If the brake pedal stills feels spongy after repeating the base hydraulic brake system bleeding procedure, inspect the brake system for external leaks.

74. If the brake pedal stills feels spongy, and if no external brake fluid leaks are found, inspect the brake system for internal leaks and inspect the brake pedal travel.

75. If internal leaks are found, replace the master cylinder.

76. If the brake pedal travel exceeds specification and there is no damage to the pedal system or pushrod, replace the master cylinder.

➡**Brake pedal travel specifications: Maximum Brake Master Cylinder (BMC) primary piston travel, (measured with the ignition ON, engine OFF and the brakes cool), at a brake pedal apply force of 725 psi (5000 kPa): 0.71 inch (18mm).**

77. Place the power button in the ON position. Observe if the brake system warning lamp remains illuminated.

78. If the brake system warning lamp remains illuminated, DO NOT allow the vehicle to be driven until the brake system is diagnosed and repaired.

79. Firmly apply the brake pedal several times. Observe the brake pedal feel.

80. If the brake pedal feels spongy, repeat the automated bleeding procedure until a firm brake pedal is obtained.

81. Drive the vehicle to a speed above 8 MPH (13 km/h) to allow ABS initialization to occur. Observe the brake pedal feel.

82. If the brake pedal feels spongy, repeat the automated bleeding procedure until a firm brake pedal is obtained.

FLUID FILL PROCEDURE

❊❊❊ CAUTION

Brake fluid may irritate eyes and skin. In case of contact, take the following actions:

- Eye contact—rinse thoroughly with water
- Skin contact—wash with soap and water
- If ingested—consult a physician immediately

✳ WARNING

Avoid spilling brake fluid onto painted surfaces, electrical connections, wiring, or cables. Brake fluid will damage painted surfaces and cause corrosion to electrical components. If any brake fluid comes in contact with painted surfaces, immediately flush the area with water. If any brake fluid comes in contact with electrical connections, wiring, or cables, use a clean shop cloth to wipe away the fluid.

✳ WARNING

Only use products that comply with GM specifications and check manufacturer information respectively. We recommend the use of GM genuine products. Instructions must be followed at all times. The use of any type of fluid other than the recommended type of brake fluid, may cause contamination which could result in damage to the internal rubber seals and/or rubber linings of hydraulic brake system components.

1. Before servicing the vehicle, refer to the Precautions Section.
2. Visually inspect the brake fluid level through the brake master cylinder reservoir.
3. If the brake fluid level is at or below the half-full point during routine fluid checks,

the brake system should be inspected for wear and possible brake fluid leaks.

4. If the brake fluid level is at or below the half-full point during routine fluid checks, and an inspection of the brake system did not reveal wear or brake fluid leaks, the brake fluid may be topped-off up to the maximum-fill level.

5. If brake system service was just completed, the brake fluid may be topped-off up to the maximum-fill level.

6. If the brake fluid level is above the half-full point, adding brake fluid is not recommended under normal conditions.

7. If brake fluid is to be added to the master cylinder reservoir, clean the outside of the reservoir on and around the reservoir cap prior to removing the cap and diaphragm. Use only Delco Supreme 11®, or equivalent DOT-3 brake fluid, from a clean, sealed brake fluid container.

BRAKES

✳ CAUTION

Dust and dirt accumulating on brake parts during normal use may contain asbestos fibers from production or aftermarket brake linings. Breathing excessive concentrations of asbestos fibers can cause serious bodily harm. Exercise care when servicing brake parts. Do not sand or grind brake lining unless equipment used is designed to contain the dust residue. Do not clean brake parts with compressed air or by dry brushing. Cleaning should be done by dampening the brake components with a fine mist of water, then wiping the brake components clean with a dampened cloth. Dispose of cloth and all residue containing asbestos fibers in an impermeable container with the appropriate label. Follow practices prescribed by the Occupational Safety and Health Administration (OSHA) and the Environmental Protection Agency (EPA) for the handling, processing, and disposing of dust or debris that may contain asbestos fibers.

BRAKE CALIPER

REMOVAL & INSTALLATION
See Figures 4 and 5.

✳ CAUTION

Brake fluid may irritate eyes and skin. In case of contact, take the following actions:

- Eye contact—rinse thoroughly with water
- Skin contact—wash with soap and water
- If ingested—consult a physician immediately

✳ WARNING

Avoid spilling brake fluid onto painted surfaces, electrical connections, wiring, or cables. Brake fluid will damage painted surfaces and cause corrosion to electrical components. If any brake fluid comes in contact with painted surfaces, immediately flush the area with water. If any brake fluid comes in contact with electrical connections, wiring, or cables, use a clean shop cloth to wipe away the fluid.

✳ WARNING

Only use products that comply with GM specifications and check manufacturer information respectively. We recommend the use of GM genuine products. Instructions must be followed at all times. The use of any type of fluid other than the recommended type of brake fluid, may cause contamination which could result in damage to the internal rubber seals and/or rubber linings of hydraulic brake system components.

FRONT DISC BRAKES

✳ CAUTION

Do not use a service jack in locations other than those specified to lift this vehicle. Lifting the vehicle with a jack in those other locations could cause the vehicle to slip off the jack and roll; this could cause injury or death.

1. Before servicing the vehicle, refer to the Precautions Section.
2. Raise and safely support the vehicle.
3. Remove the tire and wheel assembly.
4. Remove the brake hose fitting bolt.

➡Do not reuse the brake hose fitting gaskets.

5. Remove and discard the brake hose fitting gaskets from the brake hose fitting.

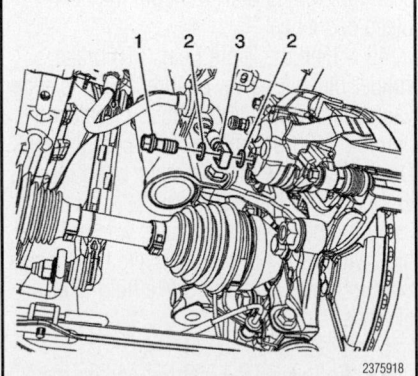

2375918

Fig. 4 Remove the brake hose fitting bolt (1) and discard the brake hose fitting gaskets (2) from the brake hose fitting (3)

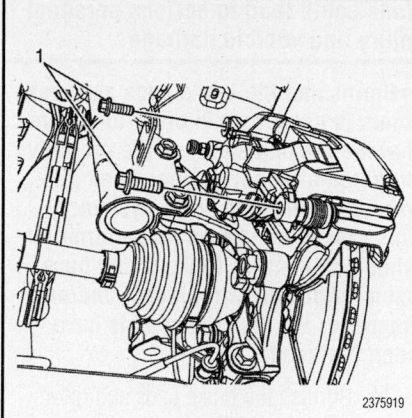

**Fig. 5 Removing the front brake caliper
and caliper guide pin bolts (1)**

6. Cap the brake hose fitting to prevent brake fluid loss and contamination.

➡**DO NOT use any air tools to remove or install the guide pin bolts. Use hand tools ONLY. Install an open end wrench to hold the caliper guide pin in line with the brake caliper while removing or installing the caliper guide pin bolt. DO NOT allow the open end wrench to come in contact with the brake caliper. Allowing the open end wrench to come in contact with the brake caliper may cause a pulsation when the brakes are applied.**

7. Using a backup wrench to hold the brake caliper guide pin stationary, remove the brake caliper guide pin bolts.

8. Remove the brake caliper.

To install:

9. Position the brake caliper over the brake pads and to the caliper bracket.

10. Using a backup wrench to hold the brake caliper guide pin stationary, install the brake caliper guide pin bolts and tighten to 21 ft. lbs. (28 Nm).

➡**Install new brake hose fitting gaskets.**

11. Assemble the brake hose fitting bolt and the 2 new brake hose fitting gaskets to the brake hose fitting.

12. Install the brake hose assembly and tighten the brake hose fitting bolt to 30 ft. lbs. (40 Nm).

13. Bleed the hydraulic brake system. Refer to Hydraulic Brake System Bleeding.

❊❊ WARNING

Improperly tightened wheel bolts or nuts can lead to brake pulsation and rotor damage. In order to avoid expensive brake repairs, evenly

tighten the wheel bolts or nuts to the proper torque specification.

14. Install the tire and wheel assembly and tighten the wheel nuts in a crisscross pattern to 103 ft. lbs. (140 Nm).

DISC BRAKE PADS

REMOVAL & INSTALLATION

See Figures 6 through 8.

1. Before servicing the vehicle, refer to the Precautions Section.

2. Inspect the fluid level in the brake master cylinder reservoir.

a. If the brake fluid level is midway between the maximum-full point and the minimum allowable level, no brake fluid needs to be removed before proceeding.

b. If the brake fluid level is higher than midway between the maximum-full point and the minimum allowable level, remove brake fluid to the midway point before proceeding.

❊❊ CAUTION

Do not use a service jack in locations other than those specified to lift this vehicle. Lifting the vehicle with a jack in those other locations could cause the vehicle to slip off the jack and roll; this could cause injury or death.

3. Raise and safely support the vehicle.

4. Remove the tire and wheel assembly.

5. Place a large C-clamp over the brake caliper body and against the outer brake pad.

6. Using the C-clamp, compress the brake caliper piston fully into the brake caliper bore.

➡**DO NOT use any air tools to remove or install the guide pin bolts. Use hand tools ONLY. Install an open end wrench to hold the caliper guide pin in line with the brake caliper while removing or installing the caliper guide pin bolt. DO NOT allow the open end wrench to come in contact with the brake caliper. Allowing the open end wrench to come in contact with the brake caliper may cause a pulsation when the brakes are applied.**

7. Using a backup wrench to hold the brake caliper guide pin stationary, remove the lower brake caliper guide pin bolt.

**Fig. 6 Lower brake caliper guide pin bolt
(1) location—front disc brake**

❊❊ WARNING

Support the brake caliper with heavy mechanic wire, or equivalent, whenever it is separated from its mount and the hydraulic flexible brake hose is still connected. Failure to support the caliper in this manner will cause the flexible brake hose to bear the weight of the caliper, which may cause damage to the brake hose and in turn may cause a brake fluid leak.

8. Rotate the brake caliper upward and support with heavy mechanics wire or equivalent.

➡**Note the location of the brake pad wear sensor for correct installation.**

9. Remove the inner brake pad.

10. Remove the outer brake pad.

11. Remove the upper and lower brake pad springs.

12. If installing new brake pads, discard the brake pad springs.

To Install:

13. Thoroughly clean the contact surfaces

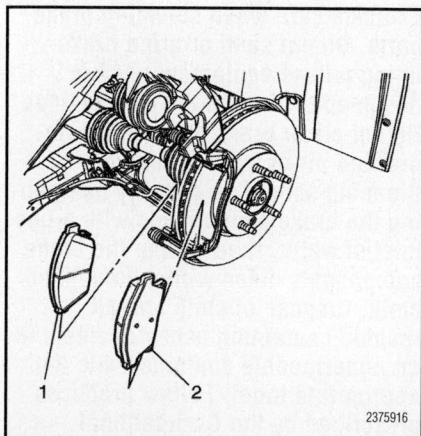

Fig. 7 Removing the inner (1) and outer brake pads (2)

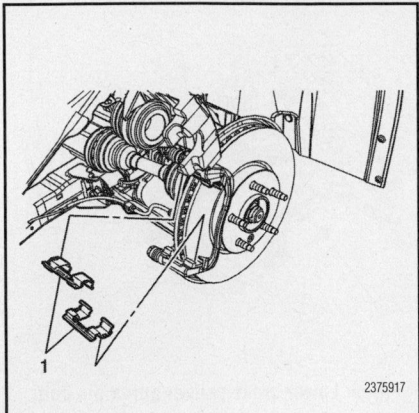

Fig. 8 Removing the upper and lower brake pad springs (1)

of the brake caliper bracket of any corrosion or debris.

➡**If installing new brake pads, install new brake pad springs.**

14. Install the upper and lower brake pad springs.

➡**Note the location of the brake pad wear sensor for correct installation.**

15. Install the inner brake pad.
16. Install the outer brake pad.
17. Position the brake caliper over the brake pads and to the caliper bracket.

18. Using a backup wrench to hold the brake caliper guide pin stationary, install the lower brake caliper guide pin bolt and tighten to 21 ft. lbs. (28 Nm).

✺✺ WARNING

Improperly tightened wheel bolts or nuts can lead to brake pulsation and rotor damage. In order to avoid expensive brake repairs, evenly tighten the wheel bolts or nuts to the proper torque specification.

19. Install the tire and wheel assembly and tighten the wheel nuts in a crisscross pattern to 103 ft. lbs. (140 Nm).
20. With the engine OFF, gradually apply the brake pedal to approximately ⅔ of its travel distance.
21. Slowly release the brake pedal.
22. Wait 15 seconds, repeat until a firm brake pedal is obtained. This will properly seat the brake caliper piston and brake pads.
23. Fill the master cylinder reservoir. Refer to Fluid Fill Procedure.

✺✺ CAUTION

Road test a vehicle under safe conditions and while obeying all traffic laws. Do not attempt any maneuvers that could jeopardize vehicle control. Failure to adhere to these precau-

tions could lead to serious personal injury and vehicle damage.

➡**Burnishing the brake pads and brake rotors is necessary in order to ensure that the braking surfaces are properly prepared after service has been performed on the disc brake system. This procedure should be performed whenever the disc brake rotors have been refinished or replaced, and/or whenever the disc brake pads have been replaced.**

24. Burnish the brake pads and rotors.
   a. Select a smooth road with little or no traffic.
   b. Accelerate the vehicle to 30 MPH (48 km/h).

✺✺ WARNING

Use care to avoid overheating the brakes while performing this step.

   c. Using moderate to firm pressure, apply the brakes to bring the vehicle to a stop. Do not allow the brakes to lock.
   d. Repeat the above steps until approximately 20 stops have been completed. Allow sufficient cooling periods between stops in order to properly burnish the brake pads and rotors.

BRAKES

✺✺ CAUTION

Dust and dirt accumulating on brake parts during normal use may contain asbestos fibers from production or aftermarket brake linings. Breathing excessive concentrations of asbestos fibers can cause serious bodily harm. Exercise care when servicing brake parts. Do not sand or grind brake lining unless equipment used is designed to contain the dust residue. Do not clean brake parts with compressed air or by dry brushing. Cleaning should be done by dampening the brake components with a fine mist of water, then wiping the brake components clean with a dampened cloth. Dispose of cloth and all residue containing asbestos fibers in an impermeable container with the appropriate label. Follow practices prescribed by the Occupational Safety and Health Administration (OSHA) and the Environmental Protection Agency (EPA) for the han-

dling, processing, and disposing of dust or debris that may contain asbestos fibers.

BRAKE CALIPER

REMOVAL & INSTALLATION
See Figures 9 through 11.

✺✺ CAUTION

Brake fluid may irritate eyes and skin. In case of contact, take the following actions:

• Eye contact—rinse thoroughly with water
• Skin contact—wash with soap and water
• If ingested—consult a physician immediately

✺✺ WARNING

Avoid spilling brake fluid onto painted surfaces, electrical connections, wiring, or cables. Brake fluid

REAR DISC BRAKES

will damage painted surfaces and cause corrosion to electrical components. If any brake fluid comes in contact with painted surfaces, immediately flush the area with water. If any brake fluid comes in contact with electrical connections, wiring, or cables, use a clean shop cloth to wipe away the fluid.

✺✺ WARNING

Only use products that comply with GM specifications and check manufacturer information respectively. We recommend the use of GM genuine products. Instructions must be followed at all times. The use of any type of fluid other than the recommended type of brake fluid, may cause contamination which could result in damage to the internal rubber seals and/or rubber linings of hydraulic brake system components.

☀☀ CAUTION

Do not use a service jack in locations other than those specified to lift this vehicle. Lifting the vehicle with a jack in those other locations could cause the vehicle to slip off the jack and roll; this could cause injury or death.

1. Before servicing the vehicle, refer to the Precautions Section.
2. Raise and safely support the vehicle.
3. Remove the tire and wheel assembly.
4. Disable the parking brake cable adjuster using a scan tool.
5. Disconnect the parking brake cable from the actuator lever.
6. Compress the parking brake cable conduit retainers.
7. Remove the parking brake cable from the cable bracket and position the parking brake cable aside.
8. Remove the brake hose fitting bolt.

➡**Do not reuse the brake hose fitting gaskets.**

9. Remove and discard the brake hose fitting gaskets from the brake hose.
10. Plug the brake hose fitting to prevent brake fluid loss and contamination.

☀☀ WARNING

DO NOT use any air tools to remove or install the guide pin bolts. Use hand tools ONLY. Install an open end wrench to hold the caliper guide pin in line with the brake caliper while removing or installing the caliper

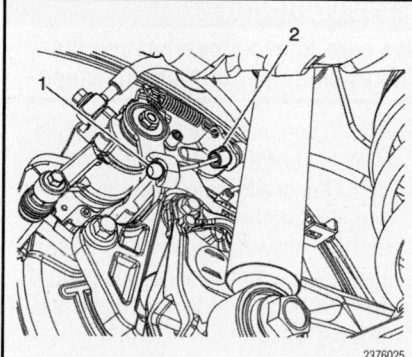

Fig. 9 Disconnect the parking brake cable (1) from the actuator lever and compress the parking brake cable conduit retainers (2)

Fig. 10 Remove the brake hose fitting bolt (1) and the brake hose fitting gaskets (2) from the brake hose (3)

guide pin bolt. DO NOT allow the open end wrench to come in contact with the brake caliper. Allowing the open end wrench to come in contact with the brake caliper may cause a pulsation when the brakes are applied.

11. Using a backup wrench to hold the brake caliper guide pin stationary, remove the brake caliper guide pin bolts.
12. Remove the brake caliper.

To install:

13. Position the brake caliper over the brake pads and to the caliper bracket.
14. Using a backup wrench to hold the brake caliper guide pin stationary, install the brake caliper guide pin bolts and tighten to 21 ft. lbs. (28 Nm).
15. Assemble the brake hose fitting bolt and the 2 new brake hose fitting gaskets to the brake hose.

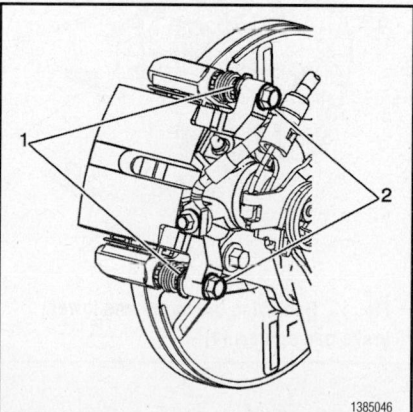

Fig. 11 Removing the brake caliper guide pin (1) and brake caliper guide pin bolts (2)

16. Install the brake hose assembly to the brake caliper and tighten the fitting bolt to 30 ft. lbs. (40 Nm).
17. Insert the parking brake cable through the parking brake cable bracket on the brake caliper.
18. Connect the parking brake cable to the actuator lever and engage the parking brake cable conduit retainers to the cable bracket.
19. Enable the parking brake cable adjuster using a scan tool.
20. Bleed the hydraulic brake system. Refer to Hydraulic Brake System Bleeding.

☀☀ WARNING

Improperly tightened wheel bolts or nuts can lead to brake pulsation and rotor damage. In order to avoid expensive brake repairs, evenly tighten the wheel bolts or nuts to the proper torque specification.

21. Install the tire and wheel assembly and tighten the wheel nuts in a crisscross pattern to 103 ft. lbs. (140 Nm).

DISC BRAKE PADS

REMOVAL & INSTALLATION
See Figures 12 and 13.

1. Before servicing the vehicle, refer to the Precautions Section.
2. Inspect the fluid level in the brake master cylinder reservoir.
   a. If the brake fluid level is midway between the maximum-full point and the minimum allowable level, no brake fluid needs to be removed before proceeding.
   b. If the brake fluid level is higher than midway between the maximum-full point and the minimum allowable level, remove brake fluid to the midway point before proceeding.

☀☀ CAUTION

Do not use a service jack in locations other than those specified to lift this vehicle. Lifting the vehicle with a jack in those other locations could cause the vehicle to slip off the jack and roll; this could cause injury or death.

3. Raise and safely support the vehicle.
4. Remove the tire and wheel assembly.

5. Using a backup wrench to hold the brake caliper guide pin stationary, remove the lower brake caliper guide pin bolt.

6. Unclip the parking brake cable from the body allowing the brake caliper to pivot unrestricted.

7. Rotate the brake caliper upward and support with heavy mechanics wire or equivalent.

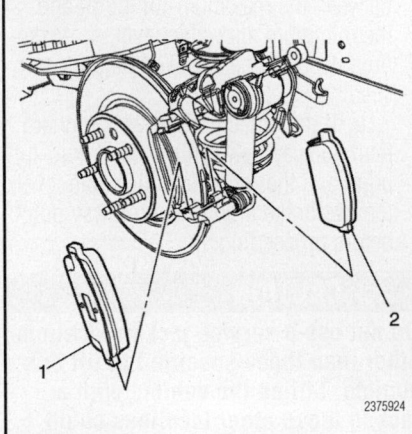

Fig. 12 Removing the outer (1) and inner brake pads (2)

➥Note the location of the brake pad wear sensor for correct installation.

8. Remove the outer brake pad.

9. Remove the inner brake pad.

10. Remove the upper and lower brake pad springs.

11. If installing new brake pads, discard the brake pad springs.

To install:

12. Using a brake caliper piston spanner tool, rotate the brake caliper piston clockwise while applying pressure to the face of the caliper piston to compress the piston into the caliper bore.

13. Thoroughly clean the contact surfaces of the brake caliper bracket of any corrosion or debris.

➥**If installing new brake pads, install new brake pad springs.**

14. Install the upper and lower brake pad springs.

➥Note the location of the brake pad wear sensor for correct installation.

15. Install the outer brake pad.

16. Install the inner brake pad.

17. Position the brake caliper over the brake pads and to the caliper bracket.

18. Secure the parking brake cable to the body.

19. Using a backup wrench to hold the brake caliper guide pin stationary, install the lower brake caliper guide pin bolt and tighten to 21 ft. lbs. (28 Nm).

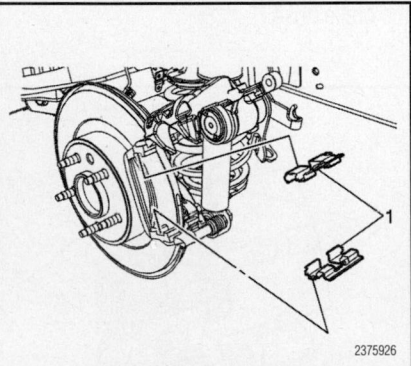

Fig. 13 Removing the upper and lower brake pad springs (1)

20. Install the tire and wheel assembly and tighten the wheel nuts in a crisscross pattern to 103 ft. lbs. (140 Nm).

21. With the engine OFF, gradually apply the brake pedal to approximately ⅔ of its travel distance.

22. Slowly release the brake pedal.

23. Wait 15 seconds, then repeat the steps until a firm brake pedal is obtained. This will properly seat the brake caliper piston and brake pads.

24. Fill the master cylinder reservoir. Refer to Fluid Fill Procedure.

➥Burnishing the brake pads and brake rotors is necessary in order to ensure that the braking surfaces are properly prepared after service has been performed on the disc brake system. This procedure should be performed whenever the disc brake rotors have been refinished or replaced, and/or whenever the disc brake pads have been replaced.

25. Burnish the brake pads and rotors.
   a. Select a smooth road with little or no traffic.
   b. Accelerate the vehicle to 30 MPH (48 km/h).

   c. Using moderate to firm pressure, apply the brakes to bring the vehicle to a stop. Do not allow the brakes to lock.
   d. Repeat the above steps until approximately 20 stops have been completed. Allow sufficient cooling periods between stops in order to properly burnish the brake pads and rotors.

BRReakES

PARKING BRAKE CABLES

ADJUSTMENT

Electronic Parking Brake Cable Tensioning

The park brake cable tension is controlled by the Electronic Park Brake (EPB) module. Cable tension needs to be set and the EPB module needs to be calibrated following the cable tension disabling procedure. Perform one of the following two methods to fully restore cable tension.

With Scan Tool—Preferred Method

1. Before servicing the vehicle, refer to the Precautions Section.

2. Block the drive wheels.
3. Install a scan tool to the vehicle.
4. Turn the ignition switch to the ON/RUN position with the engine OFF.
5. Select Configuration/Reset Functions from the electronic parking brake control module menu.
6. Follow the instructions on the scan tool.

Without Scan Tool—Optional Method

1. Before servicing the vehicle, refer to the Precautions Section.
2. Block the drive wheels.
3. Turn the ignition switch to the ON/RUN position with the engine OFF.
4. Apply the brake pedal.
5. Place the transaxle in PARK.

PARKING BRAKE

6. Momentarily lift then release the EPB switch to apply the EPB.
7. Momentarily press down then release the EPB switch to release the EPB.
8. Repeat steps 6–7 to cycle the EPB on then off an additional 4 times.
9. The EPB module will be calibrated and proper tension will be applied to the parking brake cables.

PARKING BRAKE SHOES

REMOVAL & INSTALLATION

On vehicles equipped with rear disc brakes, the parking brakes utilize the regular service brake pads. Refer to Rear Disc Brakes, Disc Brake Pads, removal & installation.

CHASSIS ELECTRICAL

GENERAL INFORMATION

✳✳ CAUTION

These vehicles are equipped with an air bag system. The system must be disarmed before performing service on, or around, system components, the steering column, instrument panel components, wiring and sensors. Failure to follow the safety precautions and the disarming procedure could result in accidental air bag deployment, possible injury and unnecessary system repairs.

SERVICE PRECAUTIONS

Disconnect and isolate the battery negative cable before beginning any airbag system component diagnosis, testing, removal, or installation procedures. Allow system capacitor to discharge for two minutes before beginning any component service. This will disable the airbag system. Failure to disable the airbag system may result in accidental airbag deployment, personal injury, or death.

Do not place an intact undeployed airbag face down on a solid surface. The airbag will propel into the air if accidentally deployed and may result in personal injury or death.

When carrying or handling an undeployed airbag, the trim side (face) of the airbag should be pointing towards the body to minimize possibility of injury if accidental deployment occurs. Failure to do this may result in personal injury or death.

AIR BAG (SUPPLEMENTAL RESTRAINT SYSTEM)

Replace airbag system components with OEM replacement parts. Substitute parts may appear interchangeable, but internal differences may result in inferior occupant protection. Failure to do so may result in occupant personal injury or death.

Wear safety glasses, rubber gloves, and long sleeved clothing when cleaning powder residue from vehicle after an airbag deployment. Powder residue emitted from a deployed airbag can cause skin irritation. Flush affected area with cool water if irritation is experienced. If nasal or throat irritation is experienced, exit the vehicle for fresh air until the irritation ceases. If irritation continues, see a physician.

Do not use a replacement airbag that is not in the original packaging. This may result in improper deployment, personal injury, or death.

The factory installed fasteners, screws and bolts used to fasten airbag components have a special coating and are specifically designed for the airbag system. Do not use substitute fasteners. Use only original equipment fasteners listed in the parts catalog when fastener replacement is required.

During, and following, any child restraint anchor service, due to impact event or vehicle repair, carefully inspect all mounting hardware, tether straps, and anchors for proper installation, operation, or damage. If a child restraint anchor is found damaged in any way, the anchor must be replaced. Failure to do this may result in personal injury or death.

Deployed and non-deployed airbags may or may not have live pyrotechnic material within the airbag inflator.

Do not dispose of driver/passenger/curtain airbags or seat belt tensioners unless you are sure of complete deployment. Refer to the Hazardous Substance Control System for proper disposal.

Dispose of deployed airbags and tensioners consistent with state, provincial, local, and federal regulations.

After any airbag component testing or service, do not connect the battery negative cable. Personal injury or death may result if the system test is not performed first.

If the vehicle is equipped with the Occupant Classification System (OCS), do not connect the battery negative cable before performing the OCS Verification Test using the scan tool and the appropriate diagnostic information. Personal injury or death may result if the system test is not performed properly.

Never replace both the Occupant Restraint Controller (ORC) and the Occupant Classification Module (OCM) at the same time. If both require replacement, replace one, then perform the Airbag System test before replacing the other.

Both the ORC and the OCM store Occupant Classification System (OCS) calibration data, which they transfer to one another when one of them is replaced. If both are replaced at the same time, an irreversible fault will be set in both modules and the OCS may malfunction and cause personal injury or death.

If equipped with OCS, the Seat Weight Sensor is a sensitive, calibrated unit and must be handled carefully. Do not drop or handle roughly. If dropped or damaged, replace with another sensor. Failure to do so may result in occupant injury or death.

If equipped with OCS, the front passenger seat must be handled carefully as well. When removing the seat, be careful when setting on floor not to drop. If dropped, the sensor may be inoperative, could result in occupant injury, or possibly death.

If equipped with OCS, when the passenger front seat is on the floor, no one should sit in the front passenger seat. This uneven force may damage the sensing ability of the seat weight sensors. If sat on and damaged, the sensor may be inoperative, could result in occupant injury, or possibly death.

DISARMING THE SYSTEM

> **❋❋ CAUTION**
>
> **When performing service on or near the SIR components or the SIR wiring, the SIR system must be disabled. Failure to observe the correct procedure could cause deployment of the SIR components. Serious injury can occur. Failure to observe the correct procedure could also result in unnecessary SIR system repairs.**

> **❋❋ CAUTION**
>
> **The inflatable restraint Sensing and Diagnostic Module (SDM) maintains a reserved energy supply. The reserved energy supply provides deployment power for the air bags if the SDM loses battery power during a collision. Deployment power is available for as much as 1 minute after disconnecting the vehicle power. Waiting 1 minute before working on the system after disabling the SIR system prevents deployment of the air bags from the reserved energy supply.**

Disarming Procedure—Air Bag Fuse

1. Before servicing the vehicle, refer to the Precautions Section.
2. Turn the steering wheel so that the vehicle wheels are pointing straight ahead.
3. Place the ignition in the OFF position.

> **❋❋ CAUTION**
>
> **The inflatable restraint Sensing and Diagnostic Module (SDM) may have more than one fused power input. To ensure there is no unwanted SIR deployment, personal injury, or unnecessary SIR system repairs, remove all fuses supplying power to**

the SDM. **With all SDM fuses removed and the ignition switch in the ON position, the AIR BAG warning indicator illuminates. This is a normal operation, and does not indicate a SIR system malfunction.**

4. Locate and remove the fuse(s) supplying power to the SDM.
5. Wait 1 minute before working on the system.

Disarming Procedure—Negative Battery Cable

1. Before servicing the vehicle, refer to the Precautions Section.
2. Turn the steering wheel so that the vehicles wheels are pointing straight ahead.
3. Place the ignition in the OFF position.
4. Disconnect the negative battery cable from the battery.
5. Wait 1 minute before working on system.

ARMING THE SYSTEM

> **❋❋ CAUTION**
>
> **When performing service on or near the SIR components or the SIR wiring, the SIR system must be disabled. Failure to observe the correct procedure could cause deployment of the SIR components. Serious injury can occur. Failure to observe the correct procedure could also result in unnecessary SIR system repairs.**

> **❋❋ CAUTION**
>
> **The inflatable restraint Sensing and Diagnostic Module (SDM) maintains a reserved energy supply. The reserved energy supply provides deployment power for the air bags if the SDM loses battery power during a collision. Deployment power is available for as much as 1 minute after disconnecting the vehicle power. Waiting 1 minute before working on the system after disabling the SIR system prevents deployment of the air bags from the reserved energy supply.**

Arming Procedure—Air Bag Fuse

1. Before servicing the vehicle, refer to the Precautions Section.
2. Place the ignition in the OFF position.
3. Install the fuse(s) supplying power to the inflatable restraint Sensing and Diagnostic Module (SDM).

4. Turn the ignition switch to the ON position. The AIR BAG indicator will flash then turn OFF.

Arming Procedure—Negative Battery Cable

1. Before servicing the vehicle, refer to the Precautions Section.
2. Place the ignition in the OFF position.
3. Connect the negative battery cable to the battery. Refer to Battery, removal & installation.
4. Turn the ignition switch to the ON position. The AIR BAG indicator will flash then turn OFF.

CLOCKSPRING CENTERING

See Figures 14 and 15.

> **❋❋ WARNING**
>
> **The new SIR coil assembly will be centered. Improper alignment of the SIR coil assembly may damage the**

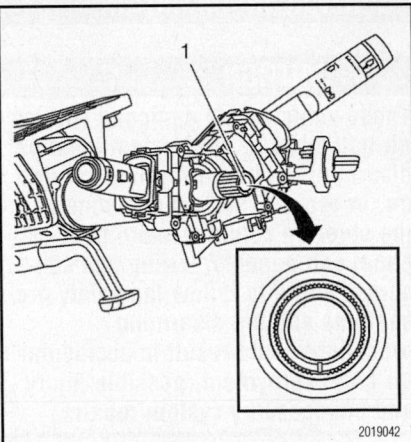

Fig. 14 The centering mark (1) of the steering shaft must be in the 6 o'clock position

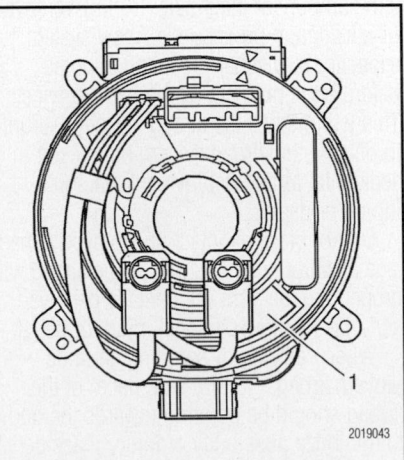

Fig. 15 Align until the centering window turns yellow (1)

unit, causing an inflatable restraint malfunction.

1. Before servicing the vehicle, refer to the Precautions Section.

2. Verify the following conditions before centering the Supplemental Inflatable Restraint (SIR) steering wheel module coil:

a. The wheels on the vehicle are straight ahead.

b. The centering mark of the steering shaft is in the 6 o'clock position.

3. Turn the lobe of the clock spring clockwise until the coil ribbon stops. Do not force.

4. Turn the lobe of the clock spring counterclockwise approximately 3 turns to the Neutral position.

5. Properly align until the centering window turns yellow. This indicates the CENTER position.

DRIVE TRAIN

AUTOMATIC TRANSAXLE FLUID

DRAIN AND REFILL

See Figure 16.

❋❋ CAUTION

Do not use a service jack in locations other than those specified to lift this vehicle. Lifting the vehicle with a jack in those other locations could cause the vehicle to slip off the jack and roll; this could cause injury or death.

1. Before servicing the vehicle, refer to the Precautions Section.

2. Clean any debris surrounding the transaxle fluid fill plug and remove the fluid fill plug.

3. Raise and safely support the vehicle.

4. Place a drain pan capable of containing more than 5 quarts of fluid under the transaxle before removing the plug to drain the fluid.

5. Remove the fluid drain plug and drain the transaxle fluid.

To install:

6. Install the fluid drain plug and tighten to 106 inch lbs. (12 Nm).

7. Fill the transaxle with the proper type and amount of fluid. Refer to Transaxle Fluid Level and Condition Check.

➡ **The transaxle will require approximately 7–7.4 quarts (6.5–7L) of fluid.**

8. Install and tighten the fluid fill plug to 15 ft. lbs. (20 Nm).

TRANSAXLE FLUID LEVEL AND CONDITION CHECK

Transaxle Fluid Level

1. Before servicing the vehicle, refer to the Precautions Section.

2. Ensure vehicle is OFF.

3. Remove the transaxle fluid fill cap on top of the transaxle.

➡ **The vehicle hood must be open or engine will NOT start.**

4. Start the vehicle.

5. Idle the engine in Park (P) for 5 minutes (to ensure the dampener is full).

6. Move the PRND to Park (P) and wait for the transaxle to heat up to 104–140°F (40–60°C).

7. Move the PRND through Neutral (N), Drive (D), Park (P), and Reverse (R) 2 times.

8. Move the PRND to Park (P).

9. Remove the transaxle oil setting plug.

10. Allow the oil to drain until it becomes a slow drip. If no oil drains, add 0.52 quarts (0.5L) until oil drips slowly from the plug.

11. Reinstall the oil setting plug.

12. Turn the vehicle OFF.

13. Install the oil fill cap.

➡ **Total transaxle fluid fill is approximately 9.4 quarts (8.9L).**

Transaxle Fluid Condition Inspection

1. Before servicing the vehicle, refer to the Precautions Section.

2. Inspect the fluid color. The fluid should be red in color. The fluid may also turn brown form normal use, and does not always indicate contamination.

➡ **Fluid that is very dark or black and has a burnt odor usually indicates contamination or overheating.**

3. If the fluid color is very dark or black and has a burnt odor, inspect the fluid for excessive metal particles or other debris which may indicate transaxle damage. Change the transaxle fluid if no other conditions are found.

4. Fluid that is cloudy or milky or appears to be contaminated with water indicates engine coolant or water contamination. Determine the cause and repair as needed.

FRONT HALFSHAFT

REMOVAL & INSTALLATION

Intermediate Shaft

See Figure 17.

Special Tools

• DT 44394-A Seal Protector

1. Before servicing the vehicle, refer to the Precautions Section.

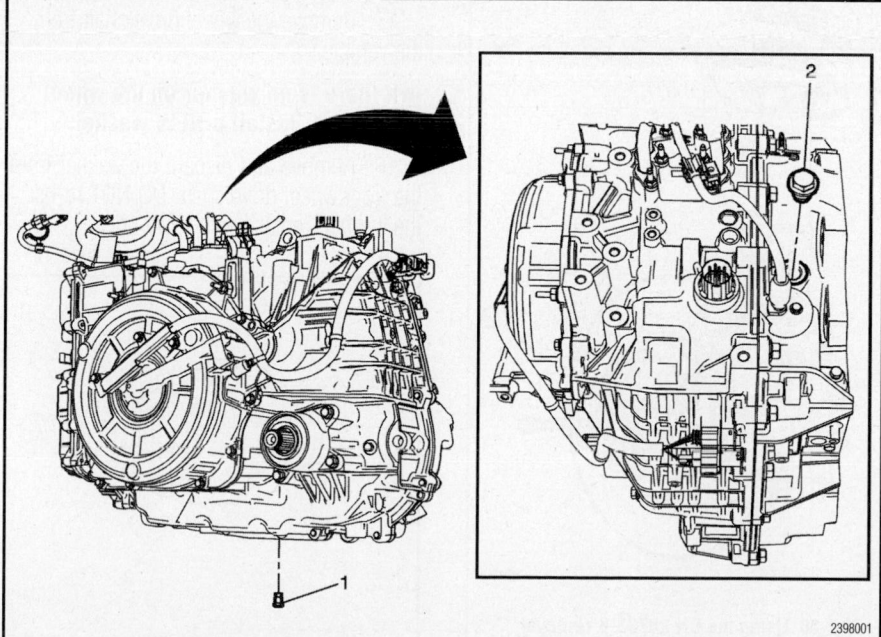

2398001

Fig. 16 Location of transaxle fluid drain (1) and fill plugs (2)

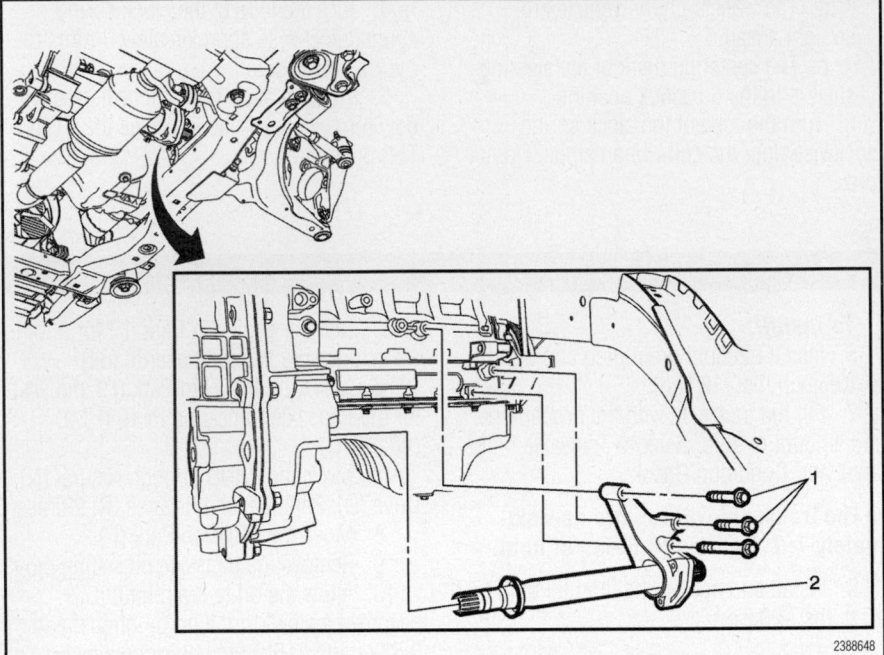

Fig. 17 View of front wheel drive intermediate shaft with bracket (2) and attaching bolts (1)

2. Raise and support the vehicle.

3. Remove the tire and wheel assembly.

4. Remove the front wheel drive shaft. Refer to Left or Right Side Halfshaft, removal & installation.

5. Remove the intermediate shaft bracket bolts.

6. Remove the intermediate shaft and bracket from the vehicle.

7. Remove and discard the O-ring. DO NOT re-use, replace with NEW only.

To install:

8. Use the DT 44394-A protector to install the front wheel drive intermediate shaft.

9. Install the intermediate shaft bracket and tighten the bolts to 43 ft. lbs. (58 Nm).

10. Install the front wheel drive shaft. Refer to Left or Right Side Halfshaft, removal & installation.

> ✳✳ WARNING
>
> **Improperly tightened wheel bolts or nuts can lead to brake pulsation and rotor damage. In order to avoid expensive brake repairs, evenly tighten the wheel bolts or nuts to the proper torque specification.**

11. Install the tire and wheel assembly and tighten the wheel nuts in a crisscross pattern to 103 ft. lbs. (140 Nm).

Left or Right Side Halfshaft

See Figures 18 and 19.

Special Tools
• CH 28733-B Wheel Hub and Drive-shaft Remover

1. Before servicing the vehicle, refer to the Precautions Section.

2. Raise and safely support the vehicle.

3. Remove the tire and wheel assembly.

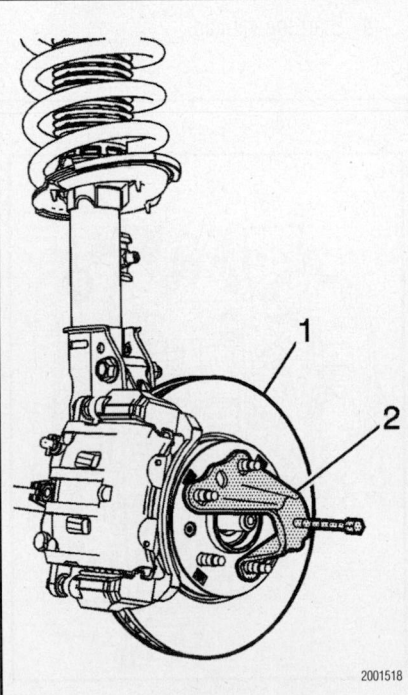

Fig. 18 Using the CH 28733-B remover (2), separate the wheel drive shaft from the front wheel hub (1)

4. Remove the front wheel house panel splash shield.

5. Disconnect the electrical connector for the front wheel speed sensor at the frame.

6. Remove the front wheel speed sensor wiring harness from the front lower control arm.

7. Remove the stabilizer shaft link. Refer to Front Suspension, Control Links, removal & installation.

8. Insert a drift or a punch in the brake rotor cooling fins.

9. Rotate the brake rotor until the drift or punch is resting against the brake caliper mounting bracket.

10. Using a breaker bar and the proper size socket, loosen the wheel drive shaft nut.

11. Remove and discard the wheel drive shaft nut.

12. Using the CH 28733-B remover, separate the wheel drive shaft from the front wheel hub.

13. Remove the outer tie rod end from the knuckle.

14. Remove the lower control arm ball joint bolt from the knuckle. Refer to Steering Knuckle, removal & installation.

➡**Position a drain pan under the transaxle when servicing the left wheel drive shaft.**

15. With the aid of an assistant, move the front knuckle assembly to the side.

16. Using a large flat bladed screwdriver or pry bar, remove the wheel drive shaft from the differential or intermediate shaft.

17. Remove the wheel drive shaft from the vehicle.

➡**If there is no washer on the wheel drive shaft, install a NEW washer.**

18. Remove and discard the washer from the front wheel drive shaft. DO NOT re-use the washer, replace with NEW only.

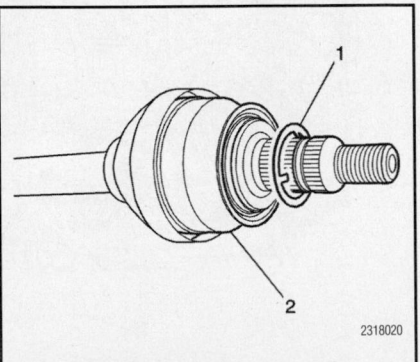

Fig. 19 Remove and discard the washer (1) from the front wheel drive shaft (2)

To install:

19. With the NEW washers installed, position the wheel drive shaft in the vehicle.

20. With the aid of an assistant, move the front knuckle assembly into the proper position.

21. Install the wheel drive shaft in the front wheel hub.

22. Install the lower control arm ball joint bolt.

23. Install the outer tie rod end.

24. Install the stabilizer shaft link. Refer to Front Suspension, Control Links, removal & installation.

25. Install wheel drive shaft nut and hand-tighten.

26. Insert a drift or a punch in the brake cooling fin.

27. Rotate the brake rotor until the drift or the punch rests against the brake caliper mounting bracket.

28. Using a torque wrench tighten the wheel drive shaft nut:

    a. First Pass: tighten to 111 ft. lbs. (150 Nm).

    b. Second Pass: Loosen the nut 45°.

    c. Final Pass: Tighten to 185 ft. lbs. (250 Nm).

29. Reconnect the electrical connector for the front wheel speed sensor.

30. Install the front wheel speed sensor wiring harness.

31. Install the front wheel house panel splash shield.

✳✳ WARNING

Improperly tightened wheel bolts or nuts can lead to brake pulsation and rotor damage. In order to avoid expensive brake repairs, evenly tighten the wheel bolts or nuts to the proper torque specification.

32. Install the tire and wheel assembly and tighten the wheel nuts in a crisscross pattern to 103 ft. lbs. (140 Nm).

33. Lower the vehicle.

34. Check the fluid level of the transaxle. Refer to Transaxle Fluid Level and Condition Check.

ENGINE COOLING

ENGINE COOLANT

DRAIN & REFILL PROCEDURE
See Figures 20 through 22.

✳✳ CAUTION

Always allow the engine to cool before opening the cooling system. Do not unscrew the coolant pressure relief cap when the engine is operating or the cooling system is hot. The cooling system is under pressure; steam and hot liquid can come out forcefully when the cap is loosened slightly. Failure to follow these instructions may result in serious personal injury.

➡The coolant must be recovered in a suitable, clean container for reuse. If the coolant is contaminated, it must be recycled or disposed of correctly. Using contaminated coolant may result in damage to the engine or cooling system components.

➡The addition of stop leak pellets may darken engine coolant.

➡Engine coolant provides boil protection, corrosion protection, freeze protection, and cooling efficiency to the engine and cooling components. In order to obtain these protections, maintain the engine coolant at the correct concentration and fluid level in the surge tank.

Special Tools
- GE-26568 Coolant and Battery Tester
- GE-47716 Vac-N-Fill Coolant Refill Tool

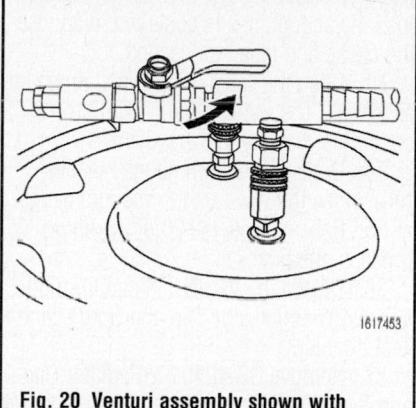

Fig. 20 Venturi assembly shown with valve opened to start a vacuum draw

- GE-42401-A Radiator Cap and Surge Tank Test Adapter

1. Before servicing the vehicle, refer to the Precautions Section.

2. To drain the engine radiator, remove the engine coolant temperature sensor from the radiator. Refer to Engine Coolant Temperature (ECT) Sensor, removal & installation.

3. Attach the venturi assembly to the vacuum tank.

4. Attach a shop air hose to the venturi assembly. Ensure the valve on the venturi assembly is closed.

5. Attach the vacuum hose to the vacuum tank.

6. Attach the extraction hose to the vacuum hose.

7. Insert the extraction hose into the radiator outlet front hose until the extraction hose contacts the bottom of the radiator outlet hose.

8. Open the valve on the venturi assembly to start a vacuum draw.

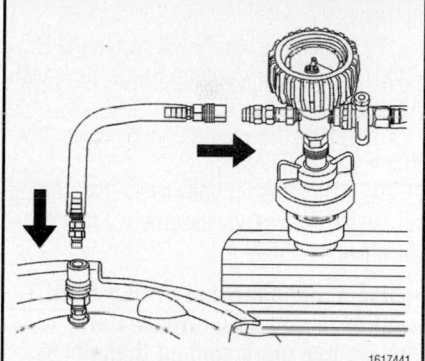

Fig. 21 Attach the vacuum hose to the vacuum gauge assembly and the vacuum tank

9. Use the extraction hose to draw out coolant until the radiator is empty.

10. The vacuum tank has a drain valve on the bottom of the tank. Open the valve to drain coolant from the vacuum tank into a suitable container for disposal.

11. If a complete engine block drain is required, remove the engine block drain plug.

12. To drain the heater cooling loop, remove the hose from the inlet of the heater water auxiliary pump.

13. Inspect the coolant.

14. Follow the appropriate procedure based on the condition of the coolant.

    a. Normal in appearance: Continue with the following fill procedure.

    b. Discolored: Follow the flush procedure. Refer to Flushing.

To fill:

➡To prevent boiling of the coolant/water mixture in the vehicle cooling system, do not apply vacuum to a cooling system above 120°F (49°C). The

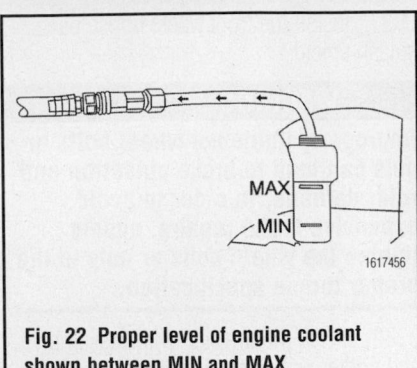

Fig. 22 Proper level of engine coolant shown between MIN and MAX

tool will not operate properly when the coolant is boiling.

15. Install GE-42401-2 Radiator Cap and Surge Tank Test Adapter into the surge tank fill neck.

16. Install GE-42401-3 Radiator Cap and Surge Tank Test Adapter to the surge tank fill neck.

17. Attach the Vac-N-Fill cap to the GE-42401-3 Radiator Cap and Surge Tank Test Adapter.

18. Attach the vacuum gauge assembly to the Vac-N-Fill cap.

19. Attach the fill hose to the barb fitting on the vacuum gauge assembly. Ensure that the valve is closed.

➡**Use a 50/50 mixture of DEX-COOL® antifreeze and de-ionized water. Always use more coolant than necessary. This will eliminate air from being drawn into the cooling system.**

20. Pour the coolant mixture into the graduated reservoir.

21. Place the fill hose in the graduated reservoir.

➡**Prior to installing the vacuum tank onto the graduated reservoir, ensure that the drain valve located on the bottom of the tank is closed.**

22. Install the vacuum tank on the graduated reservoir with the fill hose routed through the cut-out area in the vacuum tank.

23. Attach the venturi assembly to the vacuum tank.

24. Attach a shop air hose to the venturi assembly. Ensure the valve on the venturi assembly is closed.

25. Attach the vacuum hose to the vacuum gauge assembly and the vacuum tank.

26. Position the passenger compartment heater coolant control solenoid valve to normal using GDS. The hybrid powertrain control module 2 controls the passenger compartment heater coolant control solenoid valve.

27. Open the valve on the venturi assembly. The vacuum gauge will begin to rise and a hissing noise will be present.

28. Continue to draw vacuum until the needle stops rising. This should be 24–26 inches HG (610–660mm Hg). Cooling hoses may start to collapse. This is normal due to vacuum draw.

29. To aid in the fill process, position the graduated reservoir above the coolant fill port.

30. Slowly open the valve on the vacuum gauge assembly. When the coolant reaches the top of the fill hose, close the valve. This will eliminate air from the fill hose.

31. Close the valve on the venturi assembly.

32. If there is a suspected leak in the cooling system, allow the system to stabilize under vacuum and monitor for vacuum loss. If vacuum loss is observed, diagnose the cause and repair as needed.

33. Open the valve on the vacuum gauge assembly. The vacuum gauge will drop as coolant is drawn into the system.

34. Once the vacuum gauge reaches zero, close the valve on the vacuum gauge.

35. Repeat steps 14–20 of the filling process one time.

36. Detach the Vac-N-Fill cap from the GE-42401-3 Radiator Cap and Surge Tank Test Adapter.

37. Remove GE-42401-2 Radiator Cap and Surge Tank Test Adapter from the surge tank fill neck.

38. Add coolant to the system as necessary.

39. Turn on the auxiliary coolant pump for 2 minutes using the GDS. The remote HVAC module controls the auxiliary coolant pump.

40. Start the engine.

41. Using GDS, increase the speed to 2,000 RPM until the thermostat opens at approximately 212°F (100°C).

➡**Do not allow the engine coolant temperature to exceed 230°F (110°C) or damage to the Coolant Heater Control Module could occur.**

42. Turn the engine OFF.

43. Turn on the auxiliary coolant pump for 1 minute using GDS.

44. Turn off the auxiliary coolant pump and wait 5 minutes.

45. Repeat steps 24–30 of the refill procedure, three times.

46. Inspect the concentration of the coolant mixture using GE-26568 Coolant and Battery Tester.

➡**After filling the cooling system, the extraction hose can be used to remove excess coolant to achieve the proper coolant level.**

47. Detach the vacuum hose from the vacuum gauge assembly.

48. Attach the extraction hose to the vacuum hose.

49. Open the valve on the venturi assembly to start a vacuum draw.

50. Use the extraction hose to draw out coolant to the proper level.

51. The vacuum tank has a drain valve on the bottom of the tank. Open the valve to drain coolant from the vacuum tank into a suitable container for disposal.

BLEEDING

Refer to Drain & Refill Procedure.

FLUSHING

See Figure 23.

This procedure is intended for the engine cooling system only. Never use this procedure to flush the hybrid cooling system.

❈❈ CAUTION

Store used coolant in the proper manner, such as in a used engine coolant holding tank. Do not pour used coolant down a drain. Ethylene glycol antifreeze is a very toxic chemical. Do not dispose of coolant into the sewer system or ground water.

❈❈ WARNING

Do not use a chemical flush.

➡**Various methods and equipment can be used to flush the cooling system. If special equipment is used, such as a back flusher, follow the manufacturer's instruction. Always remove the thermostat before flushing the cooling system.**

❈❈ WARNING

When the cooling system becomes contaminated, the cooling system should be flushed thoroughly to remove the contaminants before the engine is seriously damaged.

1. Before servicing the vehicle, refer to the Precautions Section.

2. Drain the cooling system. Refer to Drain & Refill Procedure.

3. Remove the coolant recovery reservoir.

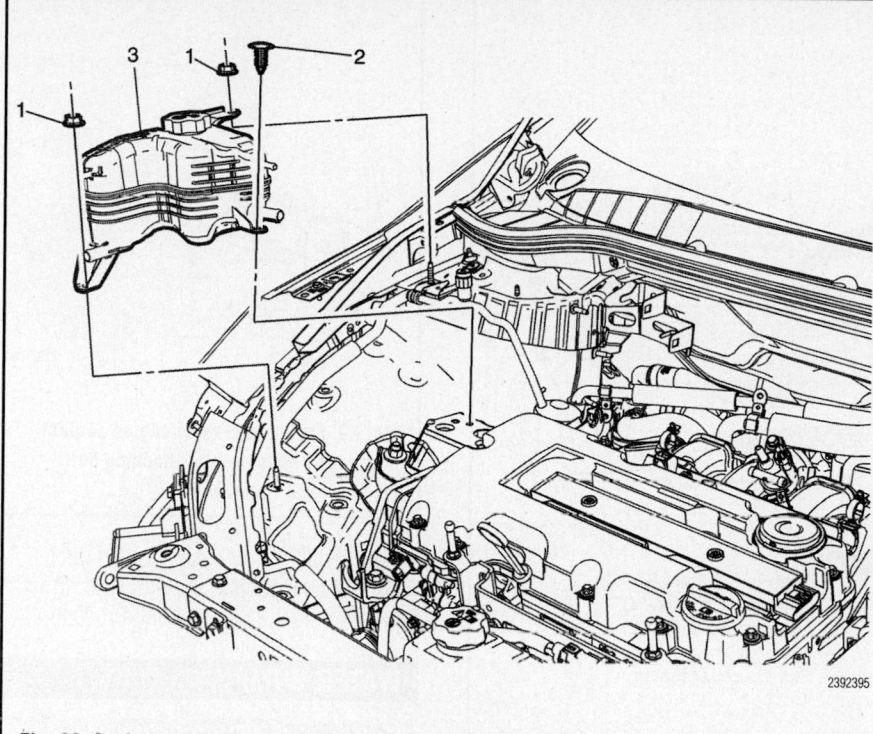

Fig. 23 Coolant recovery reservoir (3) shown with attaching nuts (1) and retainer (2)

4. Clean and flush the coolant recovery reservoir with clean, drinkable water.

5. Install the coolant recovery reservoir and tighten the nuts to 80 inch lbs. (9 Nm).

6. Follow the drain and fill procedure using only clean, drinkable water. Refer to Drain & Refill Procedure.

7. Run the engine for 20 minutes.

8. Stop the engine.

9. Drain the cooling system. Refer to Drain & Refill Procedure.

10. Repeat the procedure if necessary, until the fluid is nearly colorless.

11. Fill the cooling system. Refer to Drain & Refill Procedure.

ENGINE FAN

REMOVAL & INSTALLATION

See Figure 24.

1. Before servicing the vehicle, refer to the Precautions Section.

2. Remove the drive motor battery radiator surge tank. Refer to Drive Motor Battery Radiator Surge Tank, removal & installation.

3. Remove the drive motor battery coolant pump. Refer to Drive Motor Battery Coolant Pump, removal & installation.

4. Disconnect the electrical connector from the coolant fans.

5. Disconnect all wire retainers from the shroud.

6. Remove the engine cooling fan and shroud from the vehicle.

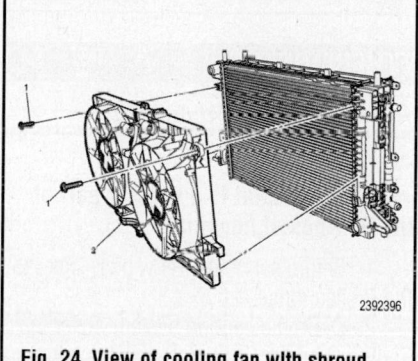

Fig. 24 View of cooling fan with shroud (2) and bolt (1) location

To install:

7. Installation is the reverse of the removal procedure.

8. Tighten the cooling fan and shroud bolts to 44 inch lbs. (5 Nm).

RADIATOR

REMOVAL & INSTALLATION

See Figures 25 through 28.

1. Before servicing the vehicle, refer to the Precautions Section.

2. Drain the coolant. Refer to Engine Coolant, Drain & Refill Procedure.

3. Remove the cooling fan and shroud. Refer to Engine Fan, removal & installation.

4. Remove the transaxle fluid auxiliary cooler.

5. Drain the coolant from the drive motor generator power inverter module cooling system.

6. Remove the front end panel outer deflector.

7. Remove the front compartment front sight shield.

8. Remove the windshield washer solvent container filler tube.

9. Remove the side four front screws from the front wheelhouse liners.

10. Carefully push a small nylon wedge between the fascia and the front fascia retainers. Insert a small flat-bladed tool into the fascia slot and depress the snaps one at a time and pull on the fascia at the same time to gradually remove the fascia from the front fascia retainers of the fender.

11. Disconnect any electrical connectors.

12. Remove the front bumper fascia from the vehicle.

13. Remove the drive motor generator control module coolant pump hose.

14. Remove the drive motor generator control module radiator outlet hose.

15. Remove the generator control module coolant tank hose.

16. Disconnect the drive motor battery coolant/air separator from the radiator.

17. Disconnect the heater vent hose from the radiator.

18. Remove the radiator inlet hose.

19. Remove radiator outlet front hose.

20. Disconnect the electrical connector from the engine coolant temperature sensor.

21. Remove the radiator from the vehicle

22. Installation is the reverse of the removal procedure.

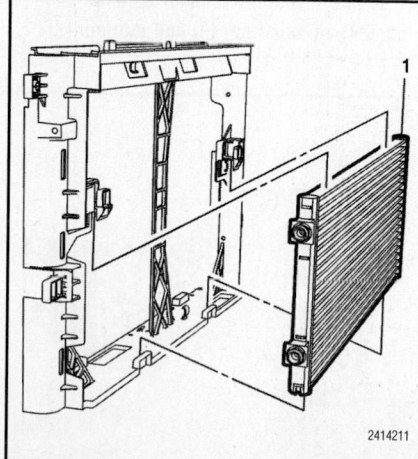

Fig. 25 Remove the transaxle fluid auxiliary cooler (1)

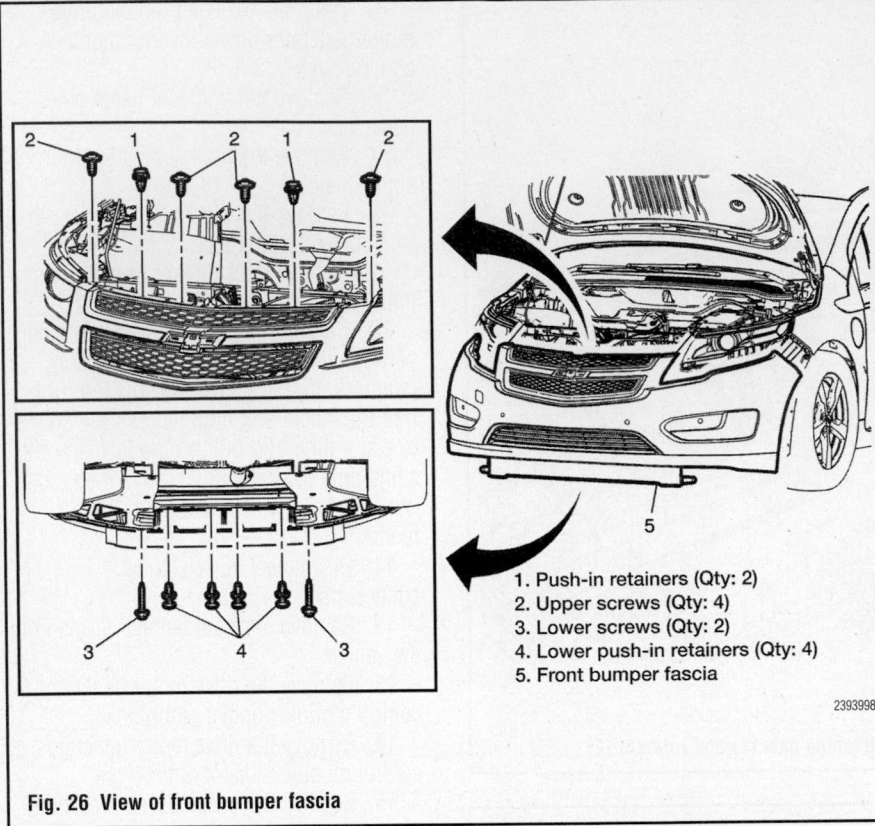

1. Push-in retainers (Qty: 2)
2. Upper screws (Qty: 4)
3. Lower screws (Qty: 2)
4. Lower push-in retainers (Qty: 4)
5. Front bumper fascia

Fig. 26 View of front bumper fascia

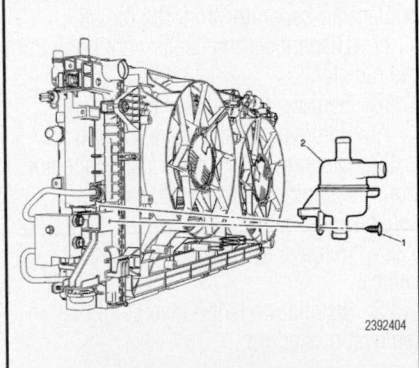

Fig. 27 View of drive motor battery coolant air separator (2) and retainer (1)

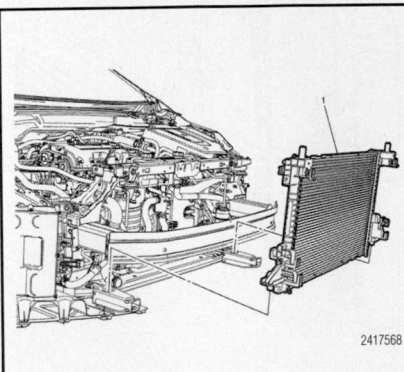

Fig. 28 Radiator (1) removal shown

THERMOSTAT

REMOVAL & INSTALLATION

See Figure 29.

➤ **The thermostat is a regular part of the thermostat housing.**

1. Before servicing the vehicle, refer to the Precautions Section.
2. Drain the cooling system. Refer to Engine Coolant, Drain & Refill Procedure.
3. Remove the air cleaner outlet duct.
4. Remove the radiator outlet hose from the engine coolant thermostat housing.
5. Disconnect the engine coolant temperature sensor wiring harness connector.
6. Remove the 3 engine coolant thermostat housing bolts.
7. Remove the engine coolant thermostat housing and the engine coolant thermostat housing seal ring.

To install:

8. Clean the sealing surfaces.
9. Install the engine coolant thermostat housing along with a NEW seal ring.
10. Install the 3 engine coolant thermostat housing bolts and tighten to 71 inch lbs. (8 Nm).
11. Connect the engine coolant temperature sensor wiring harness connector.
12. Install the radiator outlet hose to the engine coolant thermostat housing.

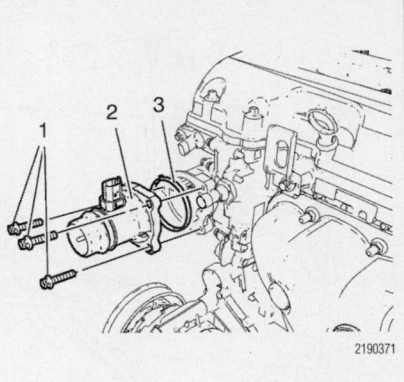

Fig. 29 Exploded view of engine coolant thermostat housing (2), attaching bolts (1), and seal ring (3)

13. Install the air cleaner outlet duct.
14. Fill the cooling system. Refer to Engine Coolant, Drain & Refill Procedure.

WATER PUMP

REMOVAL & INSTALLATION

See Figures 30 through 32.

1. Before servicing the vehicle, refer to the Precautions Section.
2. Drain the coolant. Refer to Engine Coolant, Drain & Refill Procedure.
3. Remove the water pump belt. Refer to Accessory Drive Belts, removal & installation.
4. Loosen the 3 water pump pulley bolts while holding the water pump pulley hub with a spanner.
5. Remove the 3 water pump pulley bolts and the water pump pulley.
6. Remove the radiator inlet hose and the engine coolant temperature sensor connector, from the water inlet pipe.

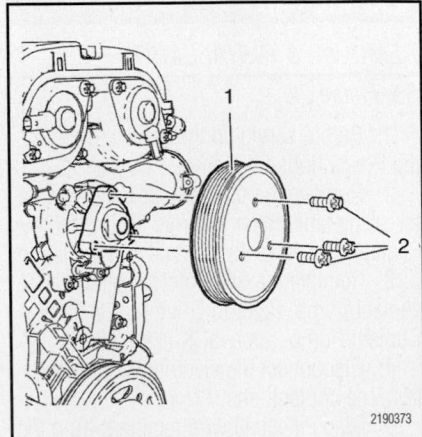

Fig. 30 Removing the water pump pulley (1) and bolts (2)

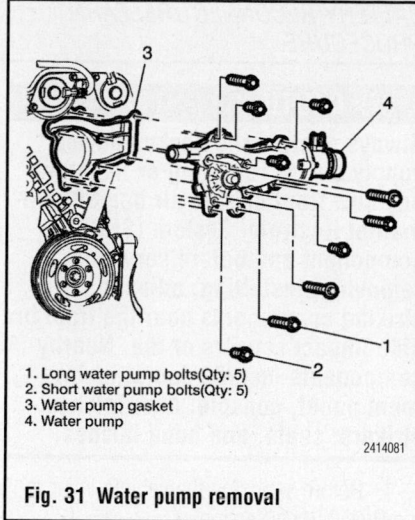

1. Long water pump bolts(Qty: 5)
2. Short water pump bolts(Qty: 5)
3. Water pump gasket
4. Water pump

2414081

Fig. 31 Water pump removal

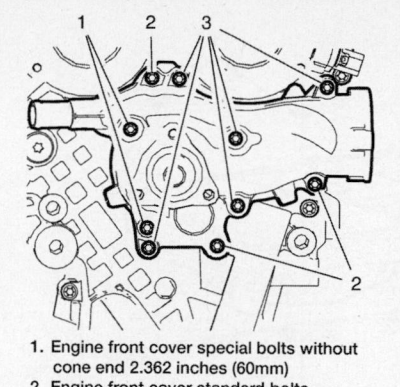

1. Engine front cover special bolts without cone end 2.362 inches (60mm)
2. Engine front cover standard bolts with cone end 2.047 inches (52mm)
3. Water pump bolts 0.984 inch (25mm)

2631338

Fig. 32 Water pump bolt identification

7. Remove the heater water shutoff hose.

8. Remove the 5 short water pump bolts and the 5 long water pump bolts.

9. Remove the water pump.

10. Remove the water pump gasket.

11. If replacing the water pump, transfer the water inlet pipe and the thermostat to the new water pump.

To install:

12. Clean the sealing surfaces.

13. Ensure the correct location of the water pump and engine front cover bolts.

14. Install the water pump and a NEW water pump gasket.

15. Install the 5 water pump bolts and the 5 engine front cover and tighten in a cross sequence to 71 inch lbs. (8 Nm).

16. Install the water pump pulley and the 3 bolts. Tighten to 89 inch lbs. (10 Nm) while holding the water pump pulley hub with a spanner.

17. Install the water pump belt. Refer to Accessory Drive Belts, removal & installation.

18. Install the heater water shutoff hose.

19. Install the radiator inlet hose and the engine coolant temperature sensor connector, to the water inlet pipe.

20. Fill the engine coolant with the proper type and amount of fluid. Refer to Engine Coolant, Drain & Refill Procedure.

21. Start the engine and check for coolant leaks.

ENGINE ELECTRICAL

BATTERY

REMOVAL & INSTALLATION

See Figures 33 through 36.

※※ CAUTION

Unless directed otherwise, the ignition and start switch must be in the OFF or LOCK position, and all electrical loads must be OFF before servicing any electrical component. Disconnect the negative battery cable to prevent an electrical spark should a tool or equipment come in contact with an exposed electrical terminal. Failure to follow these precautions may result in personal injury and/or damage to the vehicle or its components.

※※ WARNING

For Vehicles equipped with OnStar® (UE1) with Back Up Battery—The Back Up Battery is a redundant power supply to allow limited OnStar® functionality in the event of a main vehicle battery power disruption to the VCIM (OnStar®module). Do not disconnect the main vehicle battery or remove the OnStar® fuse with the ignition key in any position other than OFF. Retained Accessory Power (RAP) should be allowed to time out

or be disabled (simply opening the driver door should disable RAP) before disconnecting power. Disconnecting power to the OnStar® module in any way while the ignition is On or with RAP activated may cause activation of the OnStar® Back-Up Battery (BUB) system and will discharge and permanently damage the back-up battery. Once the BUB is activated, it will stay on until it has completely discharged. The BUB is not rechargeable and once activated the BUB must be replaced.

1. Before servicing the vehicle, refer to the Precautions Section.

2. Turn off all the lamps and accessories.

3. Turn the ignition OFF.

4. Lift the floor trim panel up to unsnap the clips, then slide the floor panel out to release the retainers.

5. The carpet flaps on the forward side of the floor panel trim are installed with the rear seats in the folded down position.

6. Please note the location of the 2 integral retainers and hooks.

7. Remove the rear compartment floor panel trim assembly.

8. Remove the rear compartment floor stowage trim compartment assembly.

9. Loosen the negative cable nut.

10. Remove the negative battery cable from the battery terminal.

BATTERY SYSTEM

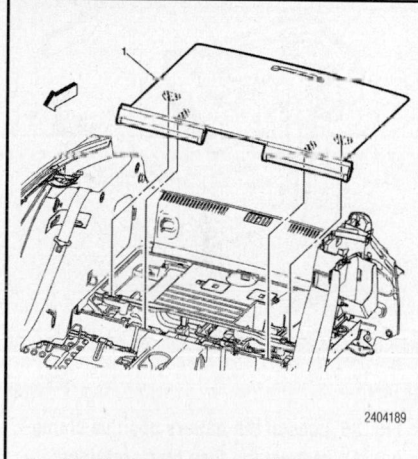

2404189

Fig. 33 Rear compartment floor panel trim assembly shown (1)

11. Reposition the negative battery cable away from the battery.

12. Remove the battery vent hose.

13. Remove the battery positive cable to fuse block nut.

14. Reposition the positive battery cable away from the battery.

15. Loosen the battery positive clamp nut.

16. Remove the fuse block retainer clips and reposition the fuse block.

17. Remove the battery retainer bolt.

18. Remove the battery hold down strap and the hold down retainer.

19. Remove the battery from the rear compartment area.

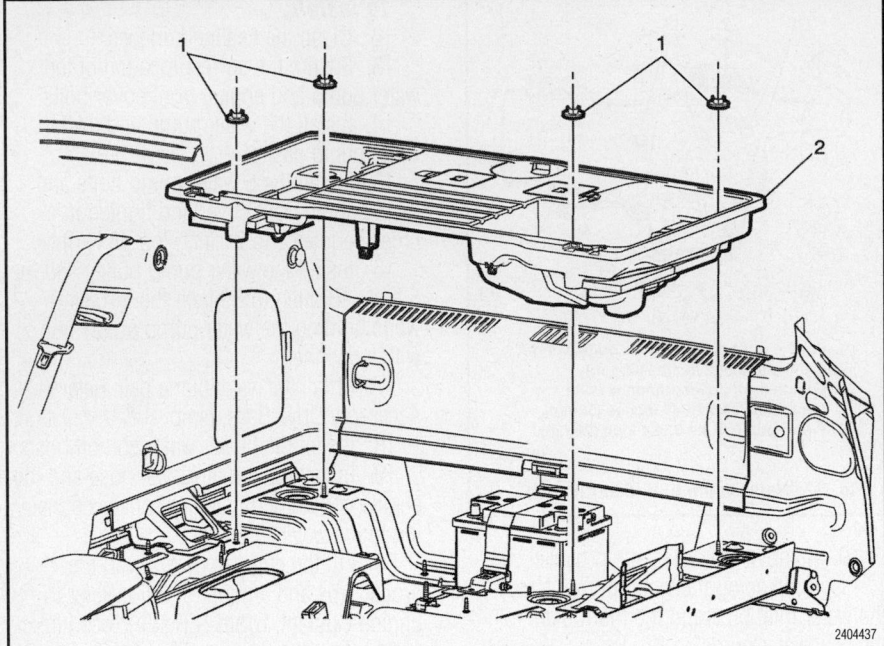

Fig. 34 Rear compartment floor stowage trim compartment assembly shown (2) with panel fasteners (1)

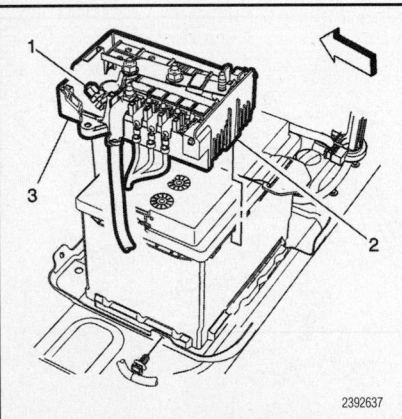

Fig. 35 Loosen the battery positive clamp nut (1), remove the fuse block retainer clips (2), and reposition the fuse block (3)

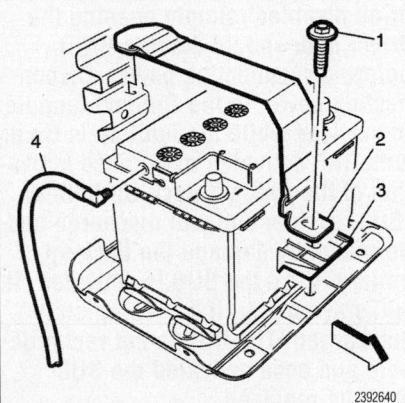

Fig. 36 Remove the battery retainer bolt (1), the battery hold down strap (2), and the hold down retainer (3)

To install:

20. Clean any existing corrosion from the battery terminal and the battery cable end.

21. Position the battery onto the tray with the posts towards the rear of the vehicle.

22. Install the battery hold down retainer and hold down strap.

23. Tighten the battery retainer bolt to 80 inch lbs. (9 Nm).

24. Install the fuse block to the top of the battery with the tabs.

25. Slide the battery clamp onto the battery post and tighten the nut to 80 inch lbs. (9 Nm).

26. Install the battery positive terminal to the fuse block and tighten nut to 106 inch lbs. (12 Nm).

➡**Clean any existing corrosion from the negative battery terminal and the battery cable end.**

27. Position the negative battery cable to the battery.

28. Install the negative battery cable onto the battery terminal and tighten cable nut to 80 inch lbs. (9 Nm).

29. Install the rear compartment floor stowage trim compartment. Tighten the fasteners to 53 inch lbs. (6 Nm).

30. Install the rear compartment floor panel trim into position.

BATTERY RECONNECT/RELEARN PROCEDURE

✳✳ CAUTION

Always deplete the backup power supply before repairing or installing any new front or side air bag Supplemental Restraint System (SRS) component and before servicing, removing, installing, adjusting, or striking components near the front or side impact sensors or the. Nearby components include doors, instrument panel, console, door latches, strikers, seats, and hood latches.

1. Before servicing the vehicle, refer to the Precautions Section.

2. To deplete the backup power supply energy, disconnect the battery ground cable and wait at least 1 minute. Be sure to disconnect auxiliary batteries and power supplies (if equipped).

✳✳ CAUTION

Battery posts, terminals and related accessories contain lead and lead components. Wash hands after handling. Failure to follow these instructions may result in serious personal injury.

3. When the battery (or ECM) is disconnected and connected, some abnormal drive symptoms may occur while the vehicle relearns its adaptive strategy. The charging system set point may also vary. The vehicle may need to be driven to relearn its strategy.

Electric Window Lifters

1. Before servicing the vehicle, refer to the Precautions Section.

2. Move all the windows to the topmost position and hold the switch pressed down for 2 seconds.

Sliding Sunroof

1. Before servicing the vehicle, refer to the Precautions Section.

2. Move the sliding roof to the respective end stops to recalibrate the sensors.

Initialize Steering Angle Sensor (Vehicles without ESP and with Electric Power Steering)

✳✳ CAUTION

For vehicles with Electric Power Steering (EPS) and without a vehicle stability enhancement program, the steering angle sensor MUST always

be initialized after the battery has been disconnected. **Failure to initialize the steering angle sensor could limit the operation of the EPS system and result in personal injury.**

1. Before servicing the vehicle, refer to the Precautions Section.
2. To ensure proper initialization of the EPS system, do the following:
   a. The engine should be on with the vehicle stationary.

b. Turn the steering wheel counter-clockwise until it stops.
c. Turn the steering wheel clockwise until it stops.

ENGINE ELECTRICAL

ALTERNATOR

REMOVAL & INSTALLATION

The drive motor/generators are components located within the Hybrid transaxle housing. When the rotors are spun, an Alternating Current (AC) is induced into the stator windings. This AC voltage is then sent to the drive motor generator Power Inverter Module (PIM) where it is converted to high voltage Direct Current (DC) power.

CHARGING SYSTEM

The output of the PIM is converted into low voltage electrical power by the Accessory DC Power Converter Module (APM) for use by the vehicle's electrical system to maintain electrical loads and battery charge.

ENGINE ELECTRICAL

PRECAUTIONS

See Figure 37.

Before working on any part of the Hybrid high voltage system, observe the following precautions:

❊ CAUTION

Always perform the High Voltage Disabling procedure prior to servicing any High Voltage component or connection. Refer to Disarming the High Voltage System. Failure to follow these instructions may result in severe personal injury or death.

❊ CAUTION

Personal Protection Equipment (PPE) and proper procedures must be followed. Failure to follow these instructions may result in severe personal injury or death.

❊ CAUTION

Before working on any high voltage system, be sure to wear the following PPE:

- Safety glasses with appropriate side shields when within 50 ft. (15m) of the vehicle, either indoors or outdoors.
- Certified and up-to-date Class "0" Insulation gloves rated at 1,000 volts with leather protectors.
- Visually and functionally inspect the gloves before use.
- Wear the Insulation gloves with leather protectors at all times when working with the high voltage

battery assembly, whether the system is energized or not.
- Failure to follow the procedures exactly as written may result in serious injury or death.

❊ CAUTION

High voltage circuits should only be tested using a Digital Multimeter (DMM) and test leads with at least a CAT III rating, such as the J 39200-A Digital Multimeter. Failure to follow the procedures exactly as written may result in serious injury or death.

❊ CAUTION

This vehicle is equipped with a high voltage battery that is completely isolated from the chassis ground. Never utilize AC powered test equipment to probe the high voltage system. Serious injury, death and component damage could occur if the high voltage system is grounded through the electric utility. Failure to follow the procedure exactly as written may result in serious injury or death.

❊ CAUTION

Precautions when Performing Service or Inspections

- Always verify that the high voltage has been disabled before working on or around high voltage components, wires, cables, or harnesses.
- Remove all metal objects such as rings and watches.
- The EL-48900 HEV safety kit contains safety cones. Place the safety cones around the vehicle to alert

other technicians that you are working on the high voltage system.
- Remove all keyless entry transmitters and the manual service disconnect from the vehicle and secure in a place outside the vehicle.
- Always wear certified and tested high voltage insulation gloves when inspecting or testing any high voltage wires and components.
- Use the "One Hand" rule: Work with only one hand whenever possible, keep the other hand behind your back.
- DO NOT carry any metal objects such as a mechanical pencil or a measuring tape that could fall and cause a short circuit.
- After removing any high voltage wires, protect and insulate the terminal ends immediately with the EL-50209 high voltage terminal cover and UL® Listed or equivalent insulation tape rated at a minimum of 600 volts.
- Always tighten the high voltage terminal fasteners to the specified torque. Insufficient or excessive torque will cause malfunctions or damage.
- After finishing work on the high voltage systems and before reinstalling the high voltage manual disconnect, inspect for the following: Verify high voltage system integrity and that all connectors are installed; Verify that all tools or loose components have been removed.

Labels for Components, Wire Harness, and Connectors

The wire harnesses and cables for high voltage circuits are encased in an orange

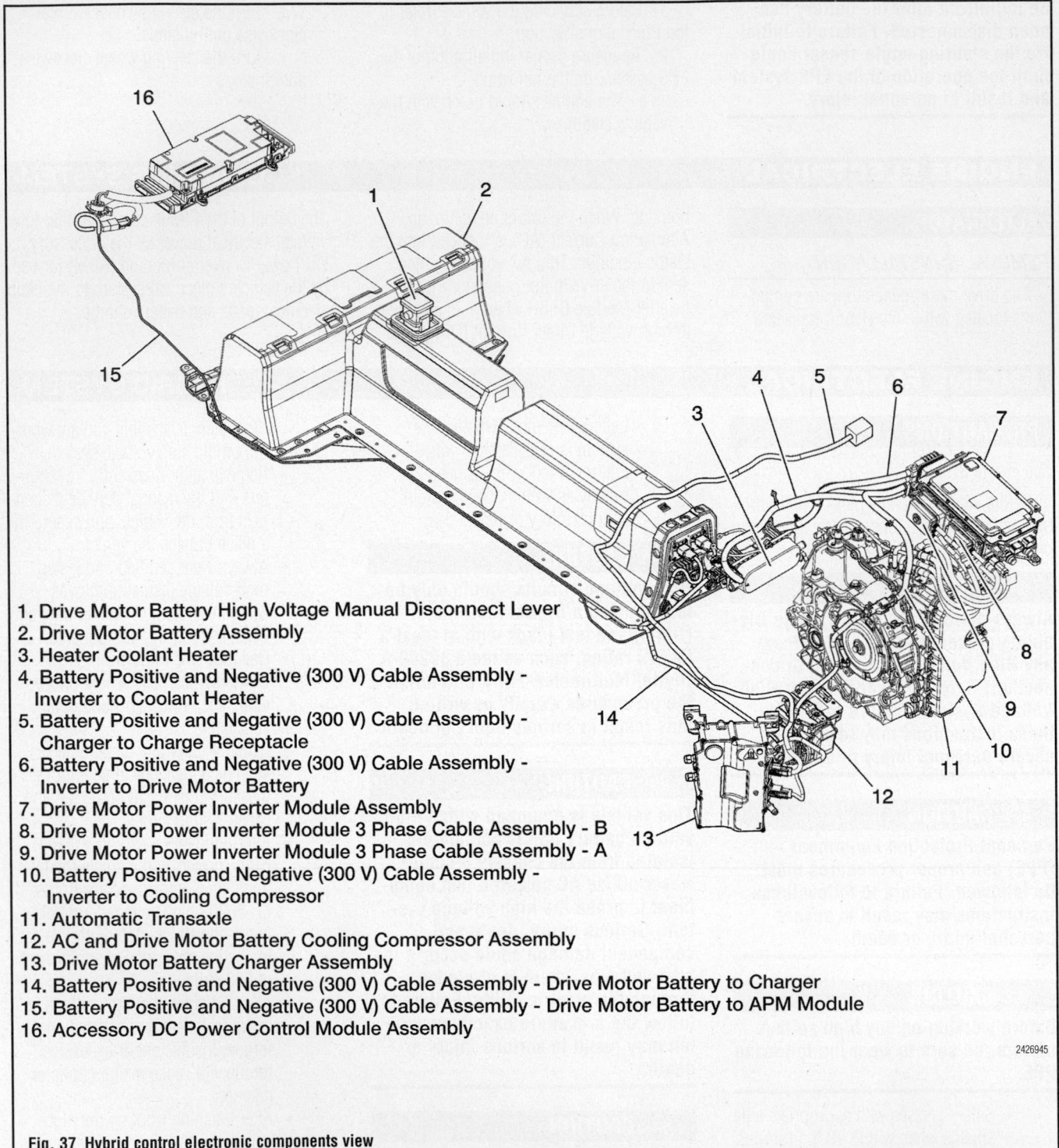

1. Drive Motor Battery High Voltage Manual Disconnect Lever
2. Drive Motor Battery Assembly
3. Heater Coolant Heater
4. Battery Positive and Negative (300 V) Cable Assembly - Inverter to Coolant Heater
5. Battery Positive and Negative (300 V) Cable Assembly - Charger to Charge Receptacle
6. Battery Positive and Negative (300 V) Cable Assembly - Inverter to Drive Motor Battery
7. Drive Motor Power Inverter Module Assembly
8. Drive Motor Power Inverter Module 3 Phase Cable Assembly - B
9. Drive Motor Power Inverter Module 3 Phase Cable Assembly - A
10. Battery Positive and Negative (300 V) Cable Assembly - Inverter to Cooling Compressor
11. Automatic Transaxle
12. AC and Drive Motor Battery Cooling Compressor Assembly
13. Drive Motor Battery Charger Assembly
14. Battery Positive and Negative (300 V) Cable Assembly - Drive Motor Battery to Charger
15. Battery Positive and Negative (300 V) Cable Assembly - Drive Motor Battery to APM Module
16. Accessory DC Power Control Module Assembly

2426945

Fig. 37 Hybrid control electronic components view

colored covering. In addition, high voltage components such as the Energy Storage System and high voltage cables are affixed with "High Voltage" red danger and orange warning labels.

High Voltage Insulation Glove Inspection Procedure

The following procedure visually and functionally inspects the insulation gloves to be used while performing service on high voltage systems. This inspection procedure should be performed prior to any procedure that requires the use of class "0" insulation gloves rated at 1,000 volts.

1. Remove the glove from the leather protector.
2. Inflate the glove and seal the opening. Pinch the opening closed tightly to prevent any air loss.

3. Press the glove to increase the pressure.
4. Inspect for the following conditions:
   - Pin holes
   - Air leaks
   - Wear, tears, or abrasions
   - Damp or wet material
   - Certification NOT up-to-date
5. If any of the above conditions are found, DO NOT use the gloves.

ARMING THE HIGH VOLTAGE SYSTEM

See Figure 38.

Ensure all High Voltage safety procedures are followed. Failure to follow the procedure exactly as written may result in serious injury or death. For additional information, refer to Hybrid System, Precautions.

➡After finishing work on the high voltage systems and before reinstalling the high voltage manual disconnect lever, inspect for the following:

- Verify that all tools or loose components have been removed
- Verify high voltage system integrity and that all connectors are installed
- Verify that all high voltage interlock circuit connectors and covers are installed
- Install any components or connectors that have been removed or replaced during diagnosis

❄❄ **WARNING**

Always tighten the high voltage fasteners to the specified torque. Insufficient or excessive torque may cause malfunction or damage.

1. Before servicing the vehicle, refer to the Precautions Section.
2. Ensure that the 12 volt battery is disconnected. Refer to Battery, removal & installation.
3. Install the S15 hybrid/EV battery pack high voltage manual disconnect lever.

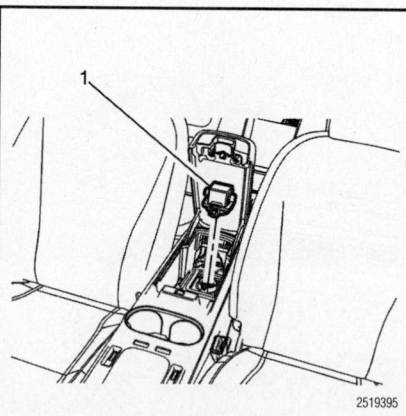

1

Fig. 38 View of S15 hybrid/EV battery pack high voltage manual disconnect lever

2519395

4. Connect the 12 volt battery. Refer to Battery, removal & installation.
5. Vehicle in Service Mode, if the A4 hybrid/EV battery pack, K16 battery energy control module, or any of the hybrid/EV battery interface control modules have been replaced, program the K16 battery energy control module and the hybrid/EV battery interface control modules. Refer to Battery Energy Control Module Programming and Setup.
6. With the hood open, start the engine, then turn the vehicle OFF.
7. With the vehicle in Service Mode, perform the driver window express learn and clear all DTC Information with a scan tool.
8. With the vehicle OFF and all vehicle systems OFF, it may take up to 2 minutes for all vehicle systems to power down.
9. With the vehicle in Service Mode, verify with a scan tool that no DTCs are set.

- If DTCs are set, go to appropriate DTC information and make any needed repairs.

10. Start and idle the engine for 2 minutes.
11. Turn the vehicle OFF and wait 5 minutes.
12. With the vehicle in Service Mode, verify with the scan tool that the T6 traction power inverter module and K114B hybrid/EV powertrain control module 2 DTC Information that the following DTCs have Run Since Code Clear and have not set:

   a. Motor position sensor learn DTCs P0C17 and P0C18.
   b. Contactor DTCs P0AD9, P0ADD, P0D0A, P0D11, P0AE4, and P1EBC.
   c. Discharge and Pre-charge DTCs P0C76, P0C77, P0C78 and P0AFB.
   d. High voltage loss of isolation DTCs P0AA6, P1AE6 and P1F0E.

- If the DTCs have Run and Passed, test drive the vehicle and verify no DTCs are set.
- If the DTCs are set, go to the appropriate DTC information and make repairs as needed.
- If the DTCs have Not Run Since Code Clear, review and operate the vehicle according to the applicable DTC Conditions for Running and ensure the DTCs run and pass.

BATTERY ENERGY CONTROL MODULE PROGRAMMING AND SETUP

❄❄ **WARNING**

DO NOT program a control module unless directed to by a service procedure or a service bulletin. If the ECU is not properly configured with the correct calibration software, the ECU will not control all of the vehicle features properly.

❄❄ **WARNING**

Ensure the programming tool is equipped with the latest software and is securely connected to the data link connector. If there is an interruption during programming, programming failure or ECU damage may occur.

➡Stable battery voltage is critical during programming. Any fluctuation, spiking, over voltage or loss of voltage will interrupt programming. Install the EL-49642 SPS Programming Support Tool to maintain system voltage. If not available, connect a fully charged 12 volt jumper or booster pack disconnected from the AC voltage supply. DO NOT connect a battery charger.

➡Turn OFF or disable systems that may put a load on the vehicles battery such as; interior lights, exterior lights (including daytime running lights), HVAC, radio, etc.

➡During the programming procedure, follow the SPS prompts for the correct ignition switch position.

➡Clear DTCs after programming is complete. Clearing powertrain DTCs will set the Inspection/Maintenance (I/M) system status indicators to NO.

1. Before servicing the vehicle, refer to the Precautions Section.
2. To program a replacement or an existing LCU, perform the following procedure.

   a. Install EL-49642 SPS programming support tool.
   b. Access the Service Programming System (SPS) and follow the on-screen instructions.
   c. On the SPS Supported Controllers screen, select Battery Energy Control Module-Programming and follow the on-screen instructions.
   d. At the end of programming, choose the "Clear All DTCs" function on the SPS screen.

3. In the event of an interrupted or unsuccessful programming event, perform the following steps:

   a. DO NOT turn the Vehicle OFF. Ensure that all ECU, DLC and programming tool connections are secure and the TIS terminal operating software is up-to-date.

b. Attempt to reprogram the ECU.

c. If the ECU can still not be programmed, turn the Vehicle OFF for at least one minute.

d. Turn the Vehicle in Service Mode and attempt to reprogram the ECU. The ECU should program.

- If the ECU still cannot be programmed, replace the ECU.

BUFFER ZONE

✳✳ CAUTION

Before proceeding, read and observe all of the Hybrid System, Precautions.

1. Before servicing the vehicle, refer to the Precautions Section.

2. Establish a buffer zone around the vehicle:

a. Position the vehicle in the repair bay.

b. Position 4 orange cones at the corners of the vehicle to mark off a 3 ft. (1m) perimeter around the vehicle.

c. Do not allow any unauthorized personnel into the buffer zone during repairs involving the high voltage system. Only personnel trained for repair on the high voltage system are to be permitted in the buffer zone.

DISARMING THE HIGH VOLTAGE SYSTEM

See Figures 39 through 42.

Special Tools
- EL-48900 HEV Safety Kit
- EL-50554-1 14 V Power Inverter Assurance Harness
- EL-50554-2 Charger Assurance Harness

✳✳ CAUTION

Ensure all High Voltage safety procedures are followed. Failure to follow the procedure exactly as written may result in serious injury or death. Read and observe all of the Hybrid System, Precautions.

1. Before servicing the vehicle, refer to the Precautions Section.

2. Disconnect and remove all 12 volt battery chargers and the AC Charge Cable from the X98 Hybrid Battery Charger Receptacle.

3. Remove all keyless entry transmitters from the vehicle and secure in a place outside the vehicle.

4. Attempt to start the vehicle with the Ignition Mode Switch.

- If the vehicle enters Propulsion System Active mode or the engine starts, locate and remove all keyless entry transmitters from within the vehicle and return to step 4.

➡ **The 12 volt battery must be disconnected to ensure proper test results.**

5. Disconnect the 12 volt battery. Refer to Battery, removal & installation.

6. Remove the S15 manual service disconnect. Place the manual service disconnect in a secure place outside the vehicle.

7. Cover the exposed high voltage opening with UL® listed, or equivalent, insulation tape rated at a minimum of 600 volts.

8. Wait 5 minutes before continuing, to allow the high voltage capacitors to discharge.

9. Verify the EL-50554 voltage disable assurance test harness using an approved Digital Multimeter (DMM). Verify the EL-50554-1 and EL-50554-2 cables measure less than 1 ohm at the following points:

a. High voltage DC (-360 V) negative terminal B to the High voltage DC (-360 V) negative terminal.

b. High voltage DC (+360 V) positive terminal A to the High voltage DC (+360 V) positive terminal.

- If the test result was greater than the specified range, repair or replace the EL-50554-1 or EL-50554-2 and repeat all measurements

10. Using the DMM, verify the EL-50554-1 and EL-50554-2 have infinite resistance between the High voltage DC (+360 V) positive terminal A to High voltage DC (-360 V) negative terminal B.

- If the test result was less than the specified range, repair or replace the EL-50554-1 or EL-50554-2 and repeat all measurements

11. Verify the EL-50554-1 and EL-50554-2 High voltage DC (-360 V) negative terminal B and the High voltage DC (+360 V) positive terminal A have the proper terminal tension.

- If a poor connection is found, repair or replace the EL-50554-1 or EL-50554-2 and repeat all measurements

12. Remove the T6 power inverter module cover.

✳✳ CAUTION

Wear High Voltage Insulation gloves until determining that a high voltage exposure risk is no longer present.

13. Disconnect the X3 harness connector at the T6 power inverter module.

➡ **A 9 volt DC battery can be used to test the DMM.**

14. Test the DMM by measuring a 12 volt battery.

- If the DMM does not properly measure a 12 volt battery, repair or replace the DMM and repeat all voltage measurements.

➡ **5 minutes must elapse since removing the manual service disconnect. The high voltage capacitors must discharge to ensure proper test results.**

15. Verify that the voltage has been disabled at the T6 power inverter module. Using the DMM, verify the voltage measures less than 3 volts at the following points:

a. High voltage DC (-360 V) negative terminal B to vehicle chassis ground.

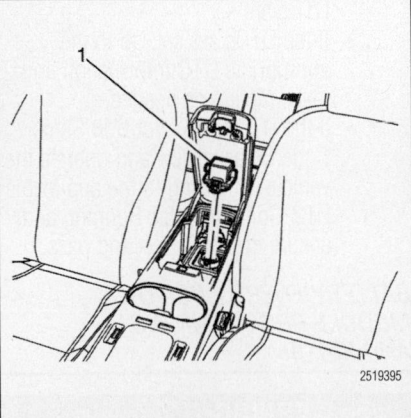

Fig. 39 View of S15 hybrid/EV battery pack high voltage manual disconnect lever

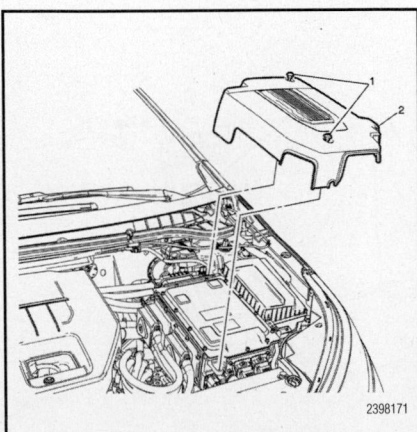

Fig. 40 Removing the T6 power inverter module cover (2) and fasteners (1)

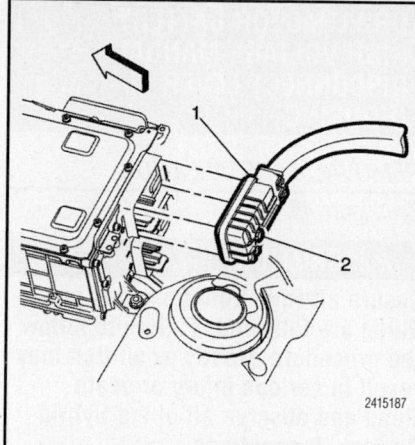

Fig. 41 Disconnect the X3 (1) harness connector at the T6 power inverter module

b. High voltage DC (+360 V) positive terminal A to vehicle chassis ground.

c. High voltage DC (+360 V) positive terminal A and high voltage DC (-360 V) negative terminal B.

• If the test result was greater than 3 volts, leave the DMM connected to the terminals until the voltage drops below 3 volts to allow the high voltage capacitors to discharge. Continue to the next step once the voltage is below 3 volts.

16. Verify that the voltage has been disabled at the X3 harness connector at the T6 power inverter module. Using the DMM, verify the voltage measures less than 3 volts at the following points:

a. High voltage DC (-360 V) negative terminal B to vehicle chassis ground.

b. High voltage DC (+360 V) positive terminal A to vehicle chassis ground.

c. High voltage DC (+360 V) positive terminal A and high voltage DC (-360 V) negative terminal B.

• If the test result was greater than 3 volts, there is a stuck closed contactor and a loss of isolation within the A4 battery pack assembly.

17. Remove the 3 catalytic converter nuts. Disconnect catalytic converter from the exhaust manifold. Move and secure the exhaust to one side.

18. Remove the front exhaust pipe heat shield.

19. Disconnect the X1 and X2 harness connectors at the A28 hybrid battery contactor assembly.

20. Disconnect the high voltage interlock harness connector listed below at the A28 hybrid battery contactor assembly.

• F118 hybrid battery pack connector jumper connector

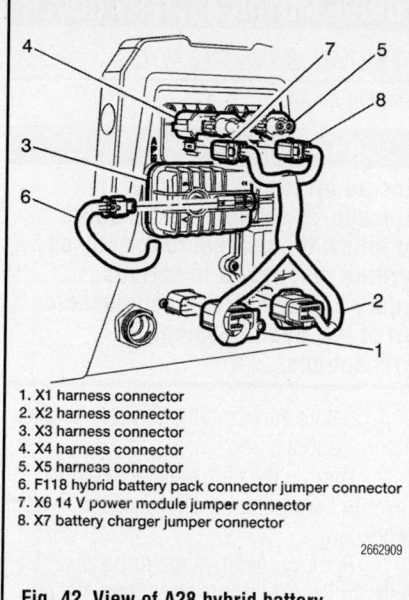

1. X1 harness connector
2. X2 harness connector
3. X3 harness connector
4. X4 harness connector
5. X5 harness connector
6. F118 hybrid battery pack connector jumper connector
7. X6 14 V power module jumper connector
8. X7 battery charger jumper connector

Fig. 42 View of A28 hybrid battery contactor assembly

• X6 14 V power module jumper connector
• X7 battery charger jumper connector

21. Disconnect the X4 harness connector at the A28 hybrid battery contactor assembly.

22. Connect the EL-50554-1 to the A28 hybrid battery contactor assembly. Using the DMM, verify the voltage measures less than 3 volts at the following points:

a. High voltage DC (-360 V) negative terminal B to vehicle chassis ground.

b. High voltage DC (+360 V) positive terminal A to vehicle chassis ground.

c. High voltage DC (+360 V) positive terminal A and high voltage DC (-360 V) negative terminal B.

• If the test result was greater than 3 volts, there is a stuck closed contactor and a loss of isolation within the A4 battery pack assembly.

23. Verify that the voltage has been disabled at the X4 harness connector at the A28 hybrid battery contactor assembly. Using the DMM, verify the voltage measures less than 3 volts at the following points:

a. High voltage DC (-360 V) negative terminal B to vehicle chassis ground.

b. High voltage DC (+360 V) positive terminal A to vehicle chassis ground.

c. High voltage DC (+360 V) positive terminal A and high voltage DC (-360 V) negative terminal B.

• If the test result was greater than 3 volts, leave the DMM connected to the terminals until the voltage

drops below 3 volts to allow the high voltage capacitors to discharge. Continue to the next step once the voltage is below 3 volts.

24. Disconnect the X5 harness connector at the A28 hybrid battery contactor assembly.

25. Connect the EL-50554-2 to the A28 hybrid battery contactor assembly. Using the DMM, verify the voltage measures less than 3 volts at the following points:

a. High voltage DC (-360 V) negative terminal B to vehicle chassis ground.

b. High voltage DC (+360 V) positive terminal A to vehicle chassis ground.

c. High voltage DC (+360 V) positive terminal A and high voltage DC (-360 V) negative terminal B.

• If the test result was greater than 3 volts, there is a stuck closed contactor and a loss of isolation within the A4 battery pack assembly.

26. Verify that the voltage has been disabled at the X5 harness connector at the A28 hybrid battery contactor assembly harness. Using the DMM, verify the voltage measures less than 3 volts at the following points:

a. High voltage DC (-360 V) negative terminal B to vehicle chassis ground.

27. High voltage DC (+360 V) positive terminal A to vehicle chassis ground.

28. High voltage DC (+360 V) positive terminal A and high voltage DC (-360 V) negative terminal B.

• If the test result was greater than 3 volts, leave the DMM connected to the terminals until the voltage drops below 3 volts to allow the high voltage capacitors to discharge. Continue to the next step once the voltage is below 3 volts.

29. Disconnect the X3 harness connector at the A28 hybrid battery contactor assembly.

30. Verify that the voltage has been disabled at the A28 hybrid battery contactor assembly. Using the DMM, verify the voltage measures less than 3 volts at the following points:

a. High voltage DC (-360 V) negative terminal B to vehicle chassis ground.

b. High voltage DC (+360 V) positive terminal A to vehicle chassis ground.

c. High voltage DC (+360 V) positive terminal A and high voltage DC (-360 V) negative terminal B.

• If the test result was greater than 3 volts, there is a stuck closed contactor and a loss of isolation within the A4 battery pack assembly.

31. Test the DMM by measuring a 12 volt battery.
- If the DMM does not properly measure a 12 volt battery, repair or replace the DMM and repeat all voltage measurements.

32. If all the test results were less than 3 volts, the A4 battery pack assembly, 360 V DC power inverter cables or general vehicle can now be serviced.

DRIVE MOTOR BATTERY COOLANT PUMP

REMOVAL & INSTALLATION

See Figure 43.

✳✳ CAUTION

Do not use a service jack in locations other than those specified to lift this vehicle. Lifting the vehicle with a jack in those other locations could cause the vehicle to slip off the jack and roll; this could cause injury or death.

1. Before servicing the vehicle, refer to the Precautions Section.
2. Drain the coolant.
3. Raise and support the vehicle.
4. Remove the drive motor battery coolant pump inlet hose from the pump.
5. Remove the drive motor battery coolant inlet hose from pump.
6. Disconnect the electrical connector and remove the drive motor battery coolant pump from the vehicle.

To install:

7. Installation is the reverse of the removal procedure.
8. Tighten the drive motor battery coolant pump bolts to 80 inch lb. (9 Nm).

DRIVE MOTOR BATTERY COVER

REMOVAL & INSTALLATION

See Figure 44.

✳✳ CAUTION

Ensure all High Voltage safety procedures are followed. Failure to follow the procedure exactly as written may result in serious injury or death. Read and observe all of the Hybrid System, Precautions.

1. Before servicing the vehicle, refer to the Precautions Section.
2. Disable the high voltage system. Refer to Disarming the High Voltage System procedure.
3. Remove the drive motor battery. Refer to Drive Motor High Voltage Battery, removal & installation.
4. Remove the battery cover fasteners.

✳✳ CAUTION

Use insulated tools when servicing components beneath the drive motor generator cover.

5. Remove the battery cover.

To install:

6. Install the battery cover.
7. Clean all cover fasteners and apply a medium strength thread-locker to the threads. Tighten to 80 inch lbs. (9 Nm).
8. Install the drive motor battery. Refer to Drive Motor High Voltage Battery, removal & installation.
9. Enable the high voltage system. Refer to Arming the High Voltage System.

DRIVE MOTOR BATTERY HIGH VOLTAGE MANUAL DISCONNECT LEVER (HOUSING)

REMOVAL & INSTALLATION

See Figure 45.

✳✳ CAUTION

Ensure all High Voltage safety procedures are followed. Failure to follow the procedure exactly as written may result in serious injury or death. Read and observe all of the Hybrid System, Precautions.

1. Before servicing the vehicle, refer to the Precautions Section.
2. Disable the high voltage system. Refer to Disarming the High Voltage System.
3. Remove the battery cover. Refer to Drive Motor Battery Cover, removal & installation.
4. Disconnect the electrical connector on the disconnect lever.
5. Remove the drive motor battery high voltage manual disconnect lever housing.

To install:

6. Installation is the reverse of the removal procedure.
7. Tighten the disconnect housing fasteners to 80 inch lbs. (9 Nm).
8. Enable the high voltage system. Refer to Arming the High Voltage System.

DRIVE MOTOR BATTERY RADIATOR SURGE TANK

REMOVAL & INSTALLATION

See Figures 46 and 47.

✳✳ CAUTION

Ensure all High Voltage safety procedures are followed. Failure to follow the procedure exactly as written may result in serious injury or death. Read and observe all of the Hybrid System, Precautions.

1. Before servicing the vehicle, refer to the Precautions Section.
2. Remove the drive motor generator control module coolant pump hose from the pump. Drain the coolant.
3. Remove the drive motor battery coolant pump inlet hose.
4. Remove drive motor battery coolant cooler outlet hose.
5. Remove drive motor battery radiator outlet hose.

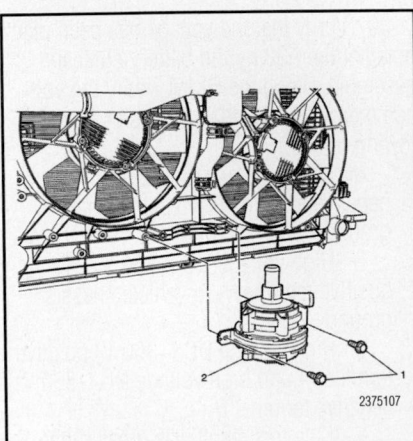

Fig. 43 Removing the drive motor battery coolant pump (2) and bolts (1)

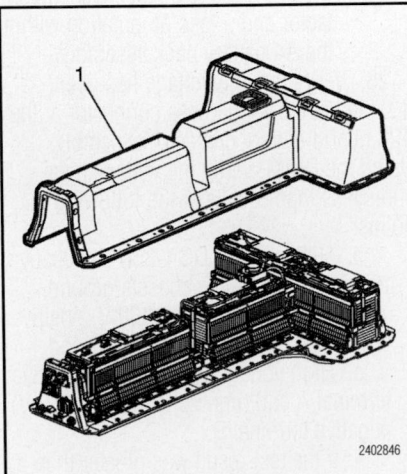

Fig. 44 Battery cover (1) removal

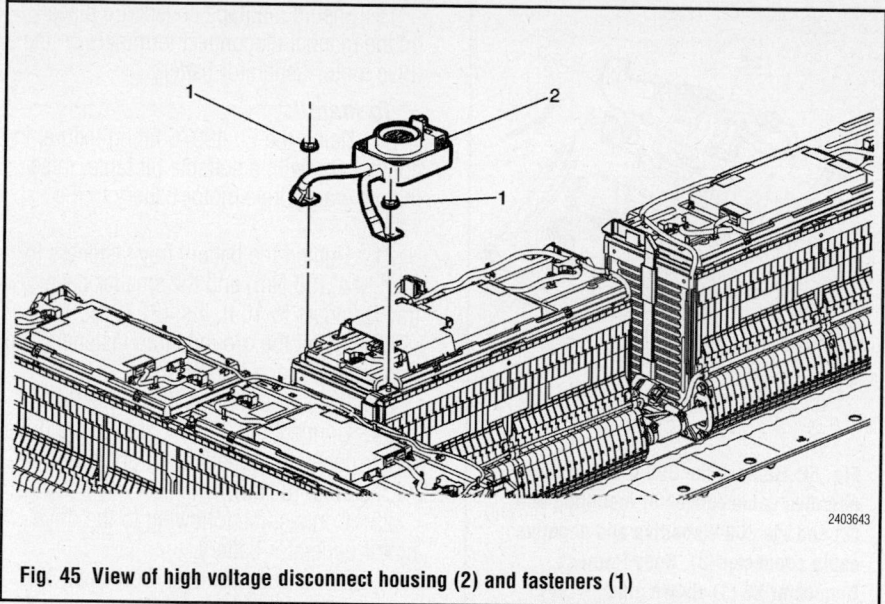

Fig. 45 View of high voltage disconnect housing (2) and fasteners (1)

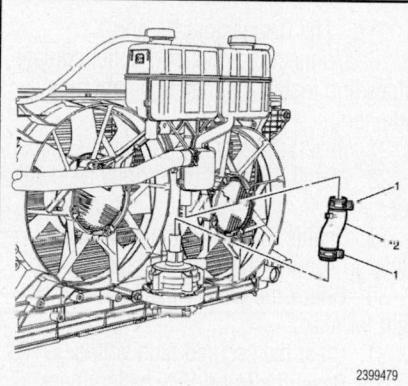

Fig. 46 Loosen the clamps (1) and remove the drive motor battery coolant pump inlet hose

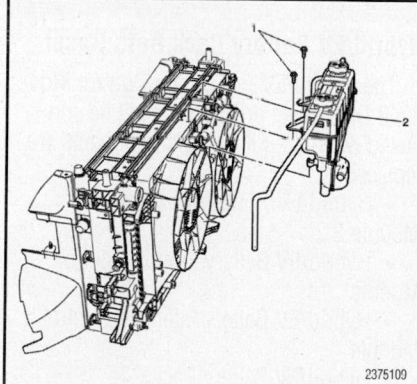

Fig. 47 View of drive motor battery radiator surge tank (2) and attaching bolts (2)

6. Remove the generator control module coolant tank hose.

7. Remove radiator upper brackets and reposition the radiator rearward to allow access to the bolts.

To install:

8. Installation is the reverse of the removal procedure.

9. Fill the cooling system with the proper type and amount of fluid.

DRIVE MOTOR HIGH VOLTAGE BATTERY

REMOVAL AND INSTALLATION

See Figures 48 through 53.

Drive Motor Battery System Description

The hybrid battery contains 288 cells. Groups of three cells are welded together in parallel called cell groups. There are a total of 96 cell groups in the hybrid battery assembly. These cell groups are electrically connected in series. Each individual cell group is rated at 3.7 V, for a nominal system voltage of 355 volts direct current. The battery cell groups are joined to form 3 distinct sections. The first 30 battery cell groups make up battery section 1. This section is adjacent to the cowl and contains battery cell groups 67 through 96. The next 24 battery cell groups make up battery section 2. This section is located behind section 1 and contains battery cell groups 43 through 66. The transverse battery section is section number 3 and it contains the remaining battery cell groups 1 through 42. The 3 battery sections are individually serviceable components.

The hybrid battery is located beneath the vehicle. The battery energy control module, hybrid battery interface control modules 1–4, current sensor, and high voltage contactors are located within the hybrid battery assembly.

Special Tools
- EL 49976 Battery Pack Lifting Fixture
- EL 50209 Battery Terminal Covers

❋❋ CAUTION

Ensure all High Voltage safety procedures are followed. Failure to follow the procedure exactly as written may result in serious injury or death. Read and observe all of the Hybrid System, Precautions.

1. Before servicing the vehicle, refer to the Precautions Section.

2. Disable the high voltage system. Refer to Disarming the High Voltage System.

3. Remove the rear exhaust pipe heat shields.

➡**It is not necessary to remove the underbody battery shield.**

4. Remove the right underbody air deflectors.

5. Remove the drive motor generator radiator surge tank cap.

➡**Document the color of the fluid and the quantity of fluid drained. Replace the drain plug with a NEW drain plug.**

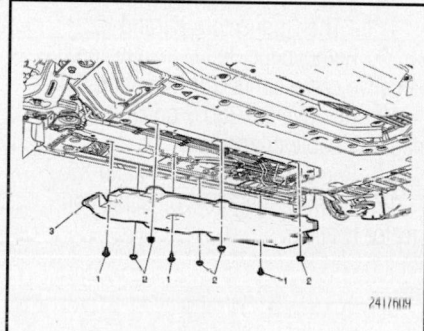

Fig. 48 Removing the right underbody air deflector (3) and fasteners (1, 2)

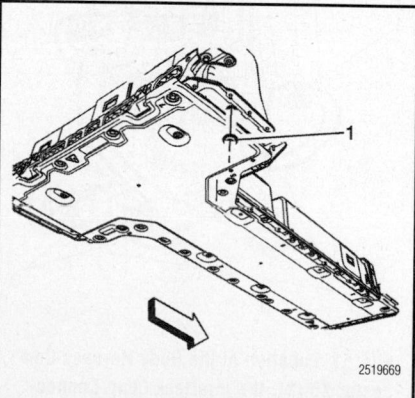

Fig. 49 Remove the drain plug (1) and drain the drive motor battery of fluid

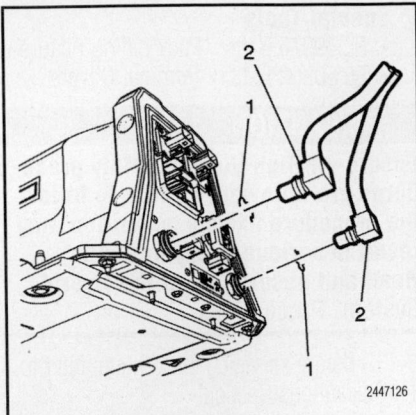

Fig. 50 Remove the metal coolant pipe retainers (1) and disconnect the inlet and outlet coolant pipes (2)

6. Using a drain pan to collect any fluid, remove the drain plug and drain the drive motor battery of fluid.

7. Using a drain pan to collect any coolant, remove the metal coolant pipe retainers and disconnect the inlet and outlet coolant pipes.

8. Disconnect the following from the drive motor battery:

   a. The Body Harness Connector X5.

   b. The Interlock Loop Connectors X3, X4.

   c. The Connectors X1 and X2.

9. Remove the 300 V positive and negative cable connector mounting bolt.

10. Remove the 300 V positive and negative cable connector.

11. Remove connectors X4 and X5.

12. Remove the 300-Volt cable connector fastener.

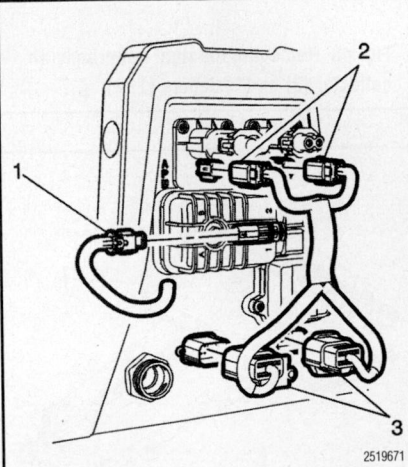

Fig. 51 Location of the Body Harness Connector X5 (1), the Interlock Loop Connectors X3, X4 (2), and the Connectors X1 and X2 (3)

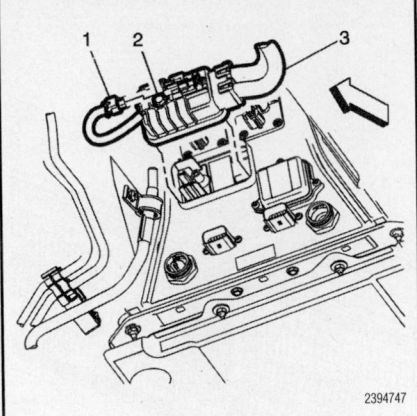

Fig. 52 Remove the 300 V positive and negative cable connector mounting bolt (2) and the 300 V positive and negative cable connector (3). Body Harness Connector X5 (1) shown also

13. Remove the ground strap fasteners, from the body side.

14. Support the battery using the EL 49976 lifting fixture, in conjunction with a suitable lift table. The battery mass is approximately 450 lbs. (204 kg).

15. Remove the battery tray fasteners.

16. Remove the drive motor generator battery and the EL-49976 battery lifting fixture from the lift table and set aside.

17. Remove the replacement drive motor generator battery and the replacement EL-49976 battery lifting fixture from the container and mount to the lift table.

18. If the drive motor generator battery is to be out of the vehicle for an extended period of time, place the drive motor generator battery in a safe location with the appropriate safety cones and protocols. Install EL50209 protective terminal covers on connection points.

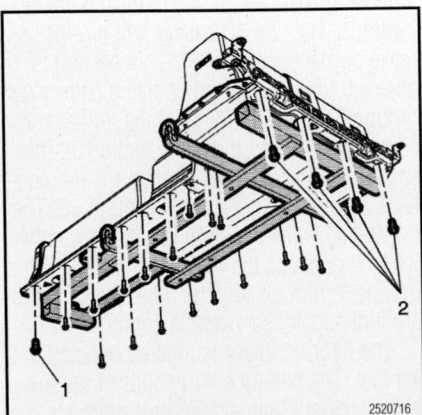

Fig. 53 EL 49976 lifting fixture shown supporting the battery, while removing the tray fasteners (1, 2)

19. Ensure that tape covers are placed on the manual disconnect terminals on the drive motor generator battery.

To install:

20. Using the EL 49976 lifting fixture, in conjunction with a suitable lift table, raise the generator drive motor battery to the vehicle.

21. Tighten the battery tray fasteners to 43 ft. lbs. (58 Nm) and the smaller battery tray fasteners to 16 ft. lbs. (22 Nm).

22. Install the ground strap fasteners and tighten to 80 inch lbs. (9 Nm).

23. Install the X4 and X5 connectors.

24. Connect the 300 V Cable to the drive motor generator battery and tighten bolt to 71 inch lbs. (8 Nm).

25. Connect the following to the drive motor generator battery:

   a. The Body Harness Connector X5.

   b. The Interlock Loop Connectors X3, X4.

   c. The Connectors X1 and X2.

26. Connect the inlet and outlet coolant pipes and install the metal coolant pipe retainers.

27. Install the rear exhaust heat shields.

28. Install the right underbody air deflector.

29. Enable the high voltage system. Refer to Arming the High Voltage System.

30. Check the battery pack cooling system for leaks.

31. Clear the secured high voltage DTCs.

32. Reset the Hybrid/EV battery pack data. Refer to Hybrid/EV Battery Pack Data Reset.

33. Perform the Hybrid/EV battery pack capacity learn procedure. Refer to Hybrid/EV Battery Pack Capacity Learn.

Hybrid/EV Battery Pack Data Reset

The Hybrid/EV Powertrain Control Module 2 Data Reset procedure must be completed when the following components are replaced:

• Hybrid/EV Powertrain Control Module 2

• Hybrid/EV Battery Energy Control Module

• Hybrid/EV Battery Interface Control Module

• Hybrid/EV Battery Pack

1. Before servicing the vehicle, refer to the Precautions Section.

2. The Hybrid/EV Powertrain Control Module 2 Data Reset procedure can be completed with a scan tool using the following steps:

   a. Install the scan tool to the data link connector.

b. Vehicle in Service Mode, engine OFF.

c. Select Hybrid/EV Battery Pack Data Reset in the Hybrid/EV Powertrain Control Module 2 Control Functions list

d. Follow the scan tool directions to complete the procedure.

e. Clear any DTCs that may be set.

Hybrid/EV Battery Pack Capacity Learn

The Hybrid/EV Battery Pack Capacity Learn procedure must be completed when the following components are replaced:

- Hybrid/EV Powertrain Control Module 2
- Hybrid/EV Battery Energy Control Module
- Hybrid/EV Battery Interface Control Module
- Hybrid/EV Battery Pack

1. Before servicing the vehicle, refer to the Precautions Section.

2. The Hybrid/EV Powertrain Control Module 2 Capacity Learn procedure can be completed with a scan tool using the following steps:

a. Install the scan tool to the data link connector.

b. Vehicle in Service Mode, engine OFF.

c. Select Hybrid/EV Battery Pack Capacity Reset in the Hybrid/EV Powertrain Control Module 2 Control Functions list

d. Follow the scan tool directions to complete the procedure.

e. Select Hybrid/EV Battery Pack Capacity Learn in the Hybrid/EV Powertrain Control Module 2 Control Functions list

f. Follow the scan tool directions to complete the procedure.

g. Clear any DTCs that may be set.

ENGINE ELECTRICAL

IGNITION SYSTEM

FIRING ORDER

Engine firing order: 1–3–4–2

IGNITION COIL

REMOVAL & INSTALLATION

See Figures 54 and 55.

Special Tools

- EN-6009 Remover and Installer Ignition Module

1. Before servicing the vehicle, refer to the Precautions Section.

2. Disconnect the ignition coil wiring harness plug from the ignition coil.

3. Remove the 2 ignition coil bolts.

4. Install EN-6009 remover/installer to the ignition coil.

5. Remove the ignition coil.

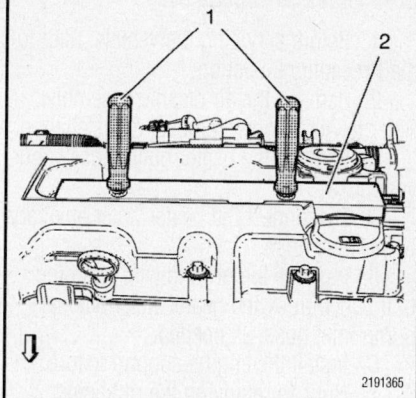

Fig. 55 Using Special Tool, EN-6009 remover/installer (1), to remove the ignition coil (2)

To install:

6. Install the ignition coil.

7. Remove EN-6009 remover from the ignition coil.

8. Install the 2 ignition coil bolts and tighten to 71 inch lbs. (8 Nm).

9. Connect the ignition coil wiring harness plug to the ignition coil.

IGNITION TIMING

ADJUSTMENT

The ignition timing is controlled by the Engine Control Module (ECM). No adjustment is necessary.

SPARK PLUGS

REMOVAL & INSTALLATION

See Figure 56.

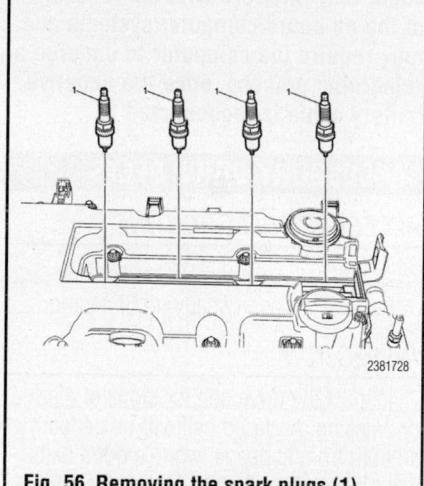

Fig. 56 Removing the spark plugs (1)

1. Before servicing the vehicle, refer to the Precautions Section.

2. Remove the ignition coil. Refer to Ignition Coil, removal & installation.

※※ WARNING

Only use hand tools when removing or installing the spark plugs, or damage can occur to the cylinder head or spark plug.

3. Use compressed air to remove any foreign material in the spark plug wells prior to removing the spark plugs.

4. Remove the spark plugs.

To install:

5. Installation is the reverse of the removal procedure.

6. Tighten the spark plugs to 18 ft. lbs. (25 Nm).

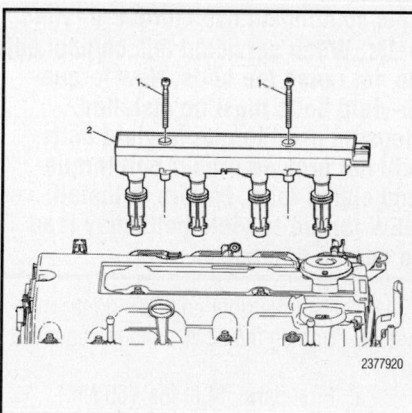

Fig. 54 Remove the 2 ignition coil bolts (1) and the ignition coil (2)

ENGINE ELECTRICAL

STARTER

REMOVAL & INSTALLATION

This vehicle does not use a 12 volt starter motor to crank the Internal Combustion Engine (ICE). A much more powerful 300 volt motor/generator located within the transaxle is utilized to crank the ICE. The 300 volt drive motor generator can rotate the ICE to operating speed (800 RPM)

within just a few hundred milliseconds. The 300 volt drive motor generator allows near-instant starting of the ICE.

The vehicles on-board computers determine when the ICE needs to run. Some of the normal vehicle conditions that force the ICE to run are:

- The high voltage battery has a low state of charge
- The hood is open or not completely latched

STARTING SYSTEM

- The ICE is needed to maintain the high voltage battery temperature
- The ICE needs to run for maintenance
- Extremely low ambient temperatures

When the hood is open, the ICE will run without turning off. The high voltage battery is neither charged nor discharged when this occurs.

Some high voltage battery faults will cause the ICE to run without turning off.

ENGINE MECHANICAL

➡**Disconnecting the negative battery cable may interfere with the functions of the on board computer systems and may require the computer to undergo a relearning process, once the negative battery cable is reconnected.**

ACCESSORY DRIVE BELTS

ACCESSORY BELT ROUTING

See Figure 57.

Refer to the accompanying illustration.

INSPECTION

Inspect the drive belt for signs of glazing or cracking. A glazed belt will be perfectly smooth from slippage, while a good belt will have a slight texture of fabric visible. Cracks will usually start at the inner edge of the belt and run outward. All worn or damaged drive belts should be replaced immediately.

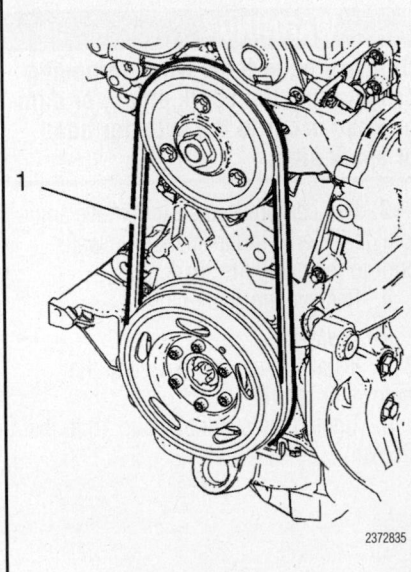

Fig. 57 Water pump belt (1) routing

2372835

REMOVAL & INSTALLATION

See Figures 58 through 61.

1. Before servicing the vehicle, refer to the Precautions Section.
2. Remove the air cleaner assembly. Refer to Air Cleaner, removal & installation.
3. Remove the heater outlet hose vapor vent hose.
4. Disconnect the heater water auxiliary pump inlet hose.
5. Remove the ground wire retaining bolt and wire by the heater water auxiliary pump inlet hose, as needed.
6. Install the engine support fixture.
7. Prior to removing the right side engine mount, mark the mount location using spray paint or a marker for correct positioning during installation.
8. Remove the right side engine mount.
9. Remove the front wheelhouse front liner.

❊❊ **CAUTION**

Ensure all High Voltage safety procedures are followed. Failure to follow the procedures may result in serious injury or death.

10. Remove the nuts retaining the drive motor battery to charge cable to the frame rail and reposition.
11. Raise and lower the engine as needed to access the right side engine mount bracket bolts.
12. Remove the right side engine mount bolts and bracket.
13. Cut the water pump belt with an appropriate cutting tool.
14. Remove and discard the water pump belt.

To install:

15. Position the water pump pulley with 1 of the 3 pulley bolts located at the 12 o'clock position. The position of the pulley

bolts will help prevent the belt from catching on the bolts and provide ease of installation.

16. Position a NEW water pump belt on the crankshaft pulley and water pump pulley.

➡**Using the thumb of your free hand, hold the water pump belt on the water pump pulley. Push the belt onto the pulley with your thumb while rotating the crankshaft pulley.**

17. Using a socket and ratchet on the crankshaft pulley bolt, rotate the crankshaft in the direction of the arrow until the belt is fully installed on the water pump pulley.
18. After the belt is on the water pump pulley, rotate the crankshaft an additional complete revolution and ensure the water pump belt is fully seated on the crankshaft and water pump pulleys.

❊❊ **WARNING**

This component uses torque-to-yield bolts. When servicing this component do not reuse the bolts, New torque-to-yield bolts must be installed. Reusing used torque-to-yield bolts will not provide proper bolt torque and clamp load. Failure to install NEW torque-to-yield bolts may lead to engine damage.

19. Install the right engine mount bracket. Tighten the NEW bolts in sequence to:
   a. First pass: 44 ft. lbs. (60 Nm).
   b. Final pass: An additional 45–60°.
20. Install the right engine mount.
   a. Tighten the engine mount nut to 37 ft. lbs. (50 Nm).
   b. Tighten the engine mount bolts to 43 ft. lbs. (58 Nm).

➡**Ensure the washers are in place where appropriate.**

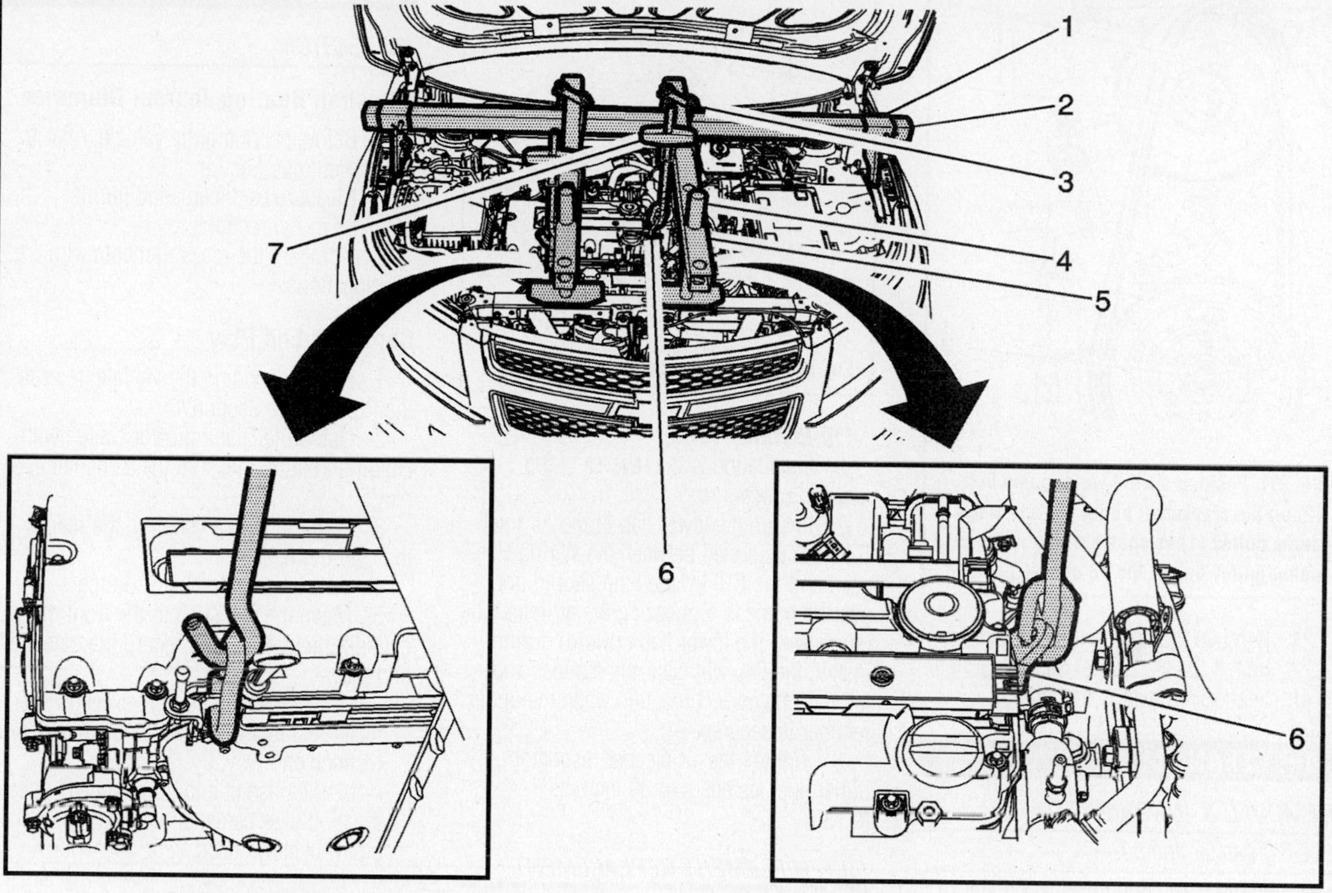

1. Engine support fixture adapter leg (Qty: 2)
2. Main support beam
3. Cross bracket (Qty: 2)
4. Strut tower support assembly (Qty: 2)
5. Radiator tube shelf assembly (Qty: 2)
6. Engine lift bracket
7. Hook assembly (Qty: 2)

2446055

Fig. 58 Engine support fixture shown installed

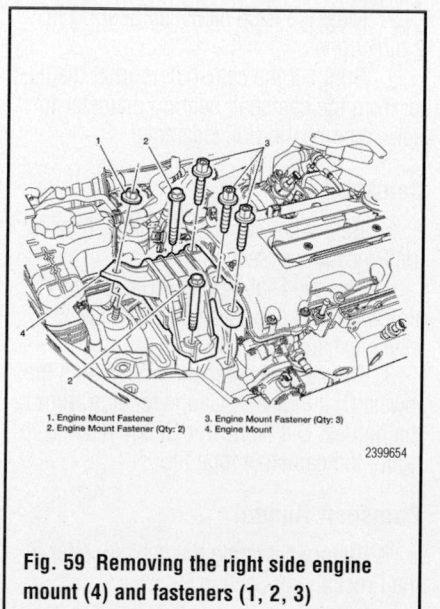

1. Engine Mount Fastener
2. Engine Mount Fastener (Qty: 2)
3. Engine Mount Fastener (Qty: 3)
4. Engine Mount

2399654

**Fig. 59 Removing the right side engine
mount (4) and fasteners (1, 2, 3)**

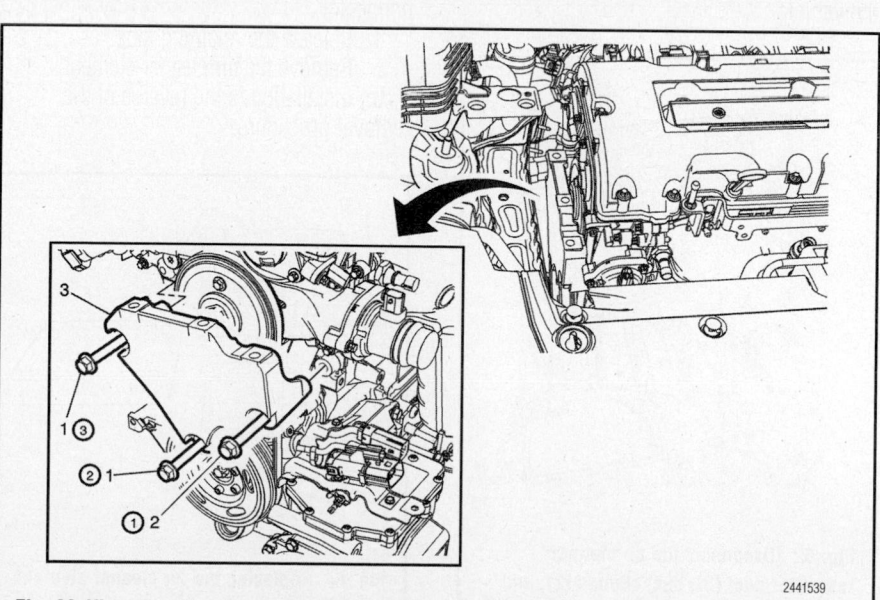

2441539

Fig. 60 View of right side engine mount bracket (3) and bolts (1, 2) and bolt torque sequence

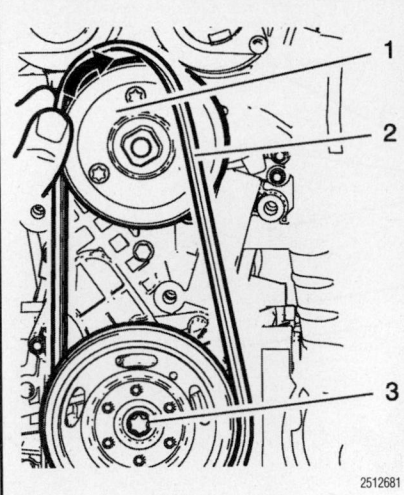

Fig. 61 Position a NEW water pump belt (2) on the crankshaft pulley (3) and water pump pulley (1) as shown with a water pump pulley bolt at the 12 o'clock position

21. Remove the engine support fixture.
22. Install the air cleaner assembly. Refer to Air Cleaner, removal & installation.

AIR CLEANER

REMOVAL & INSTALLATION

See Figures 62 and 63.

1. Before servicing the vehicle, refer to the Precautions Section.
2. Remove the oil level indicator.
3. Disconnect the air cleaner resonator duct from the air cleaner assembly.
4. Disconnect the electrical connectors from the air cleaner assembly.
5. Remove the air cleaner assembly from the vehicle.

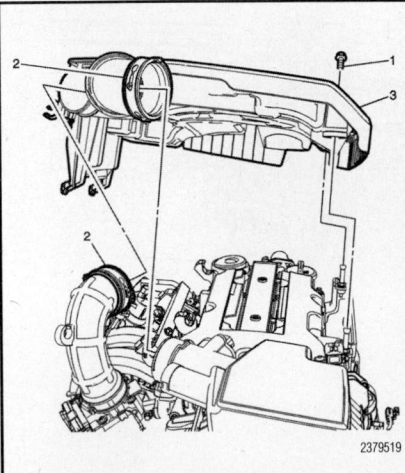

Fig. 62 Disconnect the air cleaner resonator duct (3), duct clamps (2), and fasteners (1)

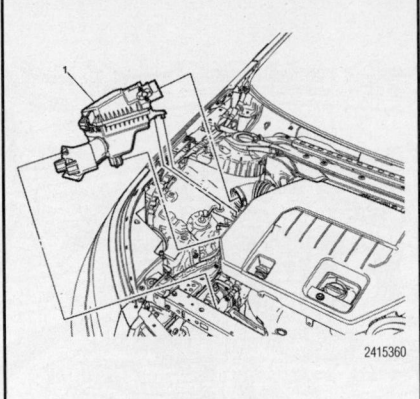

Fig. 63 Air cleaner assembly (1) removal

To install:

6. Installation is the reverse of the removal procedure.
7. Ensure the lower flap of the Air Inlet Tube is positioned between the Wiring Harness and the CRFM; the Flap should not overlap harness. Squeezing the air inlet tube (squeezing the lower flap upward) during install, the flap will clear the harness and fall into the correct location when the upper retainer is secured.
8. Tighten the air cleaner resonator outlet duct fasteners to 80 inch lbs. (9 Nm).

FILTER/ELEMENT REPLACEMENT

See Figure 64.

1. Before servicing the vehicle, refer to the Precautions Section.
2. Disconnect the air cleaner resonator duct from the air cleaner. Refer to Air Cleaner, removal & installation.
3. Disconnect the mass airflow electrical connector.
4. Release the retaining tabs.
5. Remove the air cleaner element.
6. Installation is the reverse of the removal procedure.

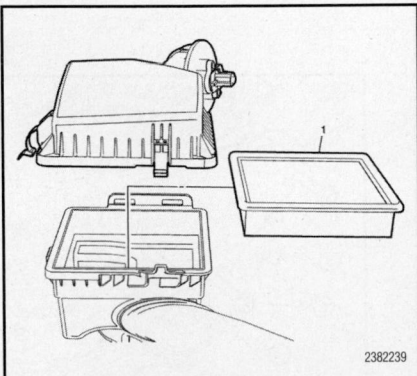

Fig. 64 Replacing the Air cleaner element (1)

CAMSHAFT AND VALVE LIFTERS

INSPECTION

Camshaft Bearing Journal Diameter

1. Before servicing the vehicle, refer to the Precautions Section.
2. Measure each camshaft journal diameter in 2 directions.
3. Compare the measurements with specifications.

Camshaft End Play

1. Before servicing the vehicle, refer to the Precautions Section.
2. Using the Dial Indicator Gauge with Holding Fixture, measure the camshaft end play.
3. Position the camshaft to the rear of the cylinder head.
4. Zero the Dial Indicator Gauge.
5. Move the camshaft to the front of the cylinder head. Note and record the camshaft end play.
   a. If camshaft end play exceeds specifications, install a new camshaft and recheck end play.
   b. If camshaft end play exceeds specification after camshaft installation, install a new cylinder head.

Camshaft Journal To Bearing Clearance

1. Before servicing the vehicle, refer to the Precautions Section.

➡ **The camshaft journals must meet specifications before checking camshaft journal clearance.**

2. Measure each camshaft bearing in 2 directions.
3. Subtract the camshaft journal diameter from the camshaft bearing diameter to determine bearing oil clearance.

Camshaft Lobe Lift

1. Before servicing the vehicle, refer to the Precautions Section.
2. Use the Dial Indicator Gauge with Holding Fixture to measure camshaft intake/exhaust lobe lift.
3. Rotate the camshaft and subtract the lowest Dial Indicator Gauge reading from the highest Dial Indicator Gauge reading to figure the camshaft lobe lift.

Camshaft Runout

1. Before servicing the vehicle, refer to the Precautions Section.

➥**Camshaft journals must be within specifications before checking runout.**

2. Using the Dial Indicator Gauge with Holding Fixture, measure the camshaft runout.

3. Rotate the camshaft and subtract the lowest Dial Indicator Gauge reading from the highest Dial Indicator Gauge reading.

Camshaft Surface

1. Before servicing the vehicle, refer to the Precautions Section.

2. Inspect camshaft lobes for pitting or damage in the contact area. Minor pitting is acceptable outside the contact area.

REMOVAL & INSTALLATION

Intake Camshaft

See Figures 65 through 67.

1. Before servicing the vehicle, refer to the Precautions Section.

2. Remove the camshaft intake sprocket. Refer to Timing Chain & Sprockets, removal & installation.

3. Remove the camshaft bearing cap bolts in a spiral sequence one turn at a time until there is no spring tension pushing on the camshaft.

➥**Mind the markings on the camshaft bearing caps to ensure they will be installed in the same position.**

4. Remove the 10 camshaft bearing cap bolts.

5. Remove the 5 camshaft bearing caps.

6. Remove the intake camshaft.

To install:

➥**The camshaft bearing caps should be installed in their original position.**

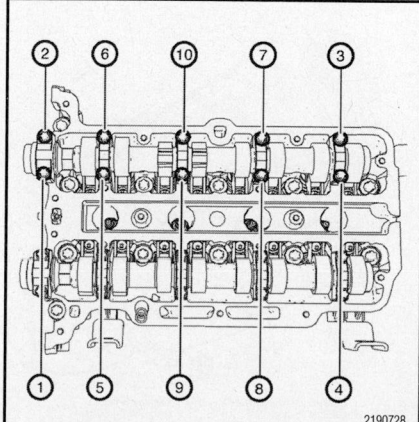

Fig. 65 Intake camshaft bearing cap bolt removal sequence

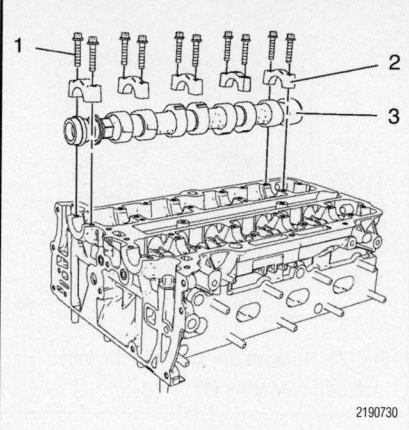

Fig. 66 Removing the intake camshaft (3), bearing caps (2), and bolts (1)

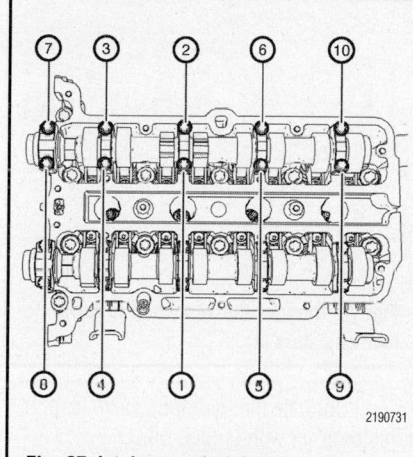

Fig. 67 Intake camshaft bearing cap bolt tightening sequence

7. Lubricate the camshaft and camshaft bearing caps with engine oil.

8. Install the intake camshaft.

9. Install the 5 camshaft bearing caps.

10. Install the 10 camshaft bearing cap bolts and hand tighten.

✳✳ WARNING

Tighten the camshaft bearing cap bolts one turn a time to avoid shape distortion of the camshaft.

11. Tighten the camshaft bearing cap bolts one turn at a time in a spiral sequence to 71 inch lbs. (8 Nm).

12. Install the camshaft intake sprocket. Refer to Timing Chain & Sprockets, removal & installation.

Exhaust Camshaft

See Figures 68 through 70.

1. Before servicing the vehicle, refer to the Precautions Section.

2. Remove the camshaft exhaust sprocket. Refer to Timing Chain & Sprockets, removal & installation.

3. Remove the camshaft bearing cap bolts in a spiral sequence one turn at a time until there is no spring tension pushing on the camshaft.

➥**Mind the markings on the camshaft bearing caps to ensure they will be installed in the same position.**

4. Remove the 10 camshaft bearing cap bolts.

5. Remove the 5 camshaft bearing caps.

6. Remove the exhaust camshaft.

To install:

➥**The camshaft bearing caps should be installed in their original position.**

7. Lubricate the camshaft and camshaft bearing caps with engine oil.

8. Install the exhaust camshaft.

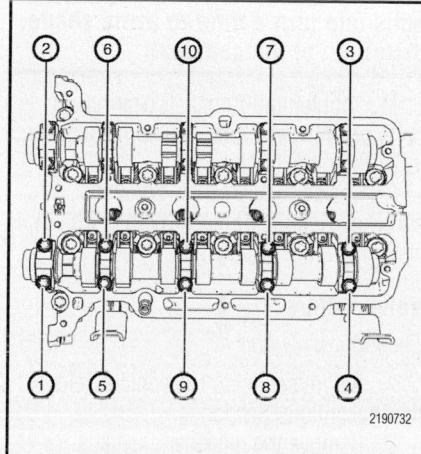

Fig. 68 Intake camshaft bearing cap bolt removal sequence

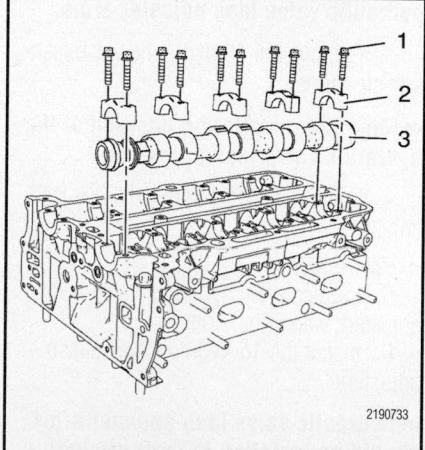

Fig. 69 Removing the exhaust camshaft (3), bearing caps (2), and bolts (1)

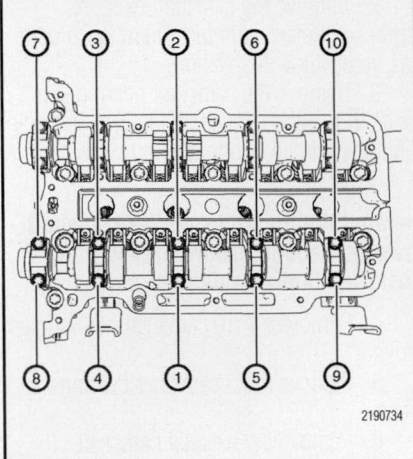

Fig. 70 Exhaust camshaft bearing cap bolt tightening sequence

9. Install the 5 camshaft bearing caps.
10. Install the 10 camshaft bearing cap bolts and hand tighten.

✳✳ WARNING

Tighten the camshaft bearing cap bolts one turn a time to avoid shape distortion of the camshaft.

11. Tighten the camshaft bearing cap bolts one turn at a time in a spiral sequence to 71 inch lbs. (8 Nm).
12. Install the camshaft exhaust sprocket. Refer to Timing Chain & Sprockets, removal & installation.

Valve Lifters

See Figures 71 and 72.

1. Before servicing the vehicle, refer to the Precautions Section.
2. Remove the intake and exhaust camshafts. Refer to Camshaft and Valve Lifters, removal & installation.

➥**Mind the installation position of the hydraulic valve lash adjuster arms.**

3. Remove the 16 hydraulic valve lash adjuster arms.

➥**Mind the installation position of the hydraulic valve lash adjusters.**

4. Remove the 16 hydraulic valve lash adjusters.

> *To install:*

5. Lubricate the hydraulic valve lash adjusters with engine oil.
6. Install the 16 hydraulic valve lash adjusters.

➥**Hydraulic valve lash adjuster arms should be installed in their original position**

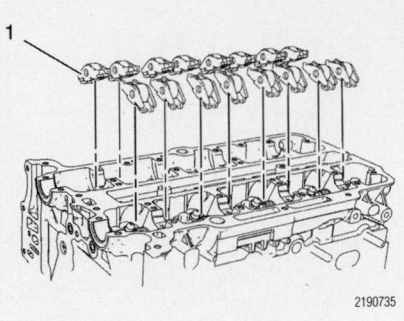

Fig. 71 Remove the 16 hydraulic valve lash adjuster arms (1)

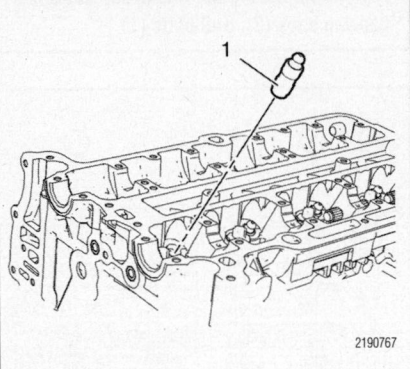

Fig. 72 Remove the 16 hydraulic valve lash adjusters (1)

7. Lubricate the hydraulic valve lash adjuster arms with engine oil.
8. Install the 16 hydraulic valve lash adjuster arms.
9. Install the intake and exhaust camshafts. Refer to Camshaft and Valve Lifters, removal & installation.

CATALYTIC CONVERTER

REMOVAL & INSTALLATION

Exhaust Manifold with Catalytic Converter

Refer to Exhaust Manifold, removal & installation.

Catalytic Converter (Rear)

See Figure 73.

✳✳ CAUTION

Do not use a service jack in locations other than those specified to lift this vehicle. Lifting the vehicle with a jack in those other locations could cause the vehicle to slip off the jack and roll; this could cause injury or death.

✳✳ CAUTION

While the engine is operating, the exhaust system will become extremely hot. To prevent burns, avoid contacting a hot exhaust system.

1. Before servicing the vehicle, refer to the Precautions Section.
2. Raise and safely support the vehicle.
3. Disconnect the heated oxygen sensor. Refer to Heated Oxygen (HO2S) Sensor, removal & installation.
4. Remove the exhaust muffler clamp.
5. If reinstalling the original intermediate pipe, the tail pipe/muffler band clamp should be replaced. Mark the position of the band clamp on the intermediate exhaust pipe. Remove the band clamp by grinding the welds.
6. Remove the catalytic converter nuts.
7. Remove the catalytic converter from the exhaust isolator and from the vehicle.
8. Remove and discard the exhaust the exhaust gasket.

> *To install:*

9. Installation is the reverse of the removal procedure.
10. Install a NEW exhaust gasket.
11. Install the NEW band clamp on the intermediate pipe. Position the NEW band clamp using the alignment mark created previously. Ensure that the clamp is rotated such that the band portion covers the slot on the intermediate pipe.
12. Tighten the catalytic converter nuts to 16 ft. lbs. (22 Nm).
13. Tighten the exhaust clamp to 41 ft. lbs. (55 Nm).

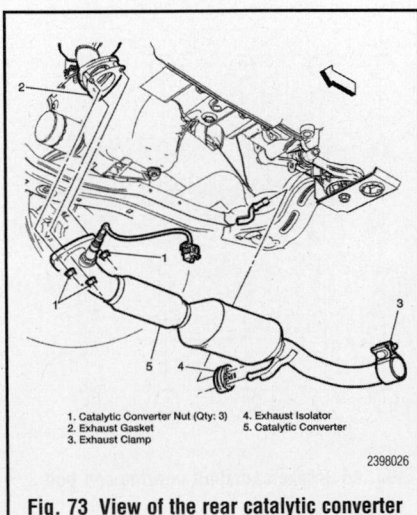

1. Catalytic Converter Nut (Qty: 3)   4. Exhaust Isolator
2. Exhaust Gasket   5. Catalytic Converter
3. Exhaust Clamp

Fig. 73 View of the rear catalytic converter

➡**If replacing the catalytic converter, transfer the heated oxygen sensor over to the new catalytic converter.**

CRANKSHAFT DAMPER (BALANCER)

REMOVAL & INSTALLATION

See Figures 74 through 76.

Special Tools
• EN-470-B Angular Torque Wrench
• EN-956-1 Extension
• EN-49979 Crankshaft Shock Mount Retainer

1. Before servicing the vehicle, refer to the Precautions Section.
2. Raise and safely support the vehicle.
3. Drain the coolant. Refer to Engine Coolant, Drain & Refill Procedure.
4. Remove the front wheelhouse front liner on the passenger side.
5. Mark the crankshaft damper (balancer)-to-cover relationship or Set to Top Dead Center (TDC).
6. Remove the water pump belt. Refer to Accessory Drive Belts, removal & installation.
7. Remove the heater coolant heater heat shield.
8. Remove the healer inlet and outlet pipe.
9. Disconnect the electrical connector from the heater water auxiliary pump.
10. Remove the heater water auxiliary pump.
11. Remove the drive motor battery coolant cooler Inlet hose assembly.
12. Use EN-49979 retainer and EN-956-1 extension to remove the crankshaft damper pulley.

Fig. 74 Remove the clamps (1) and the heater inlet and outlet pipe (2)

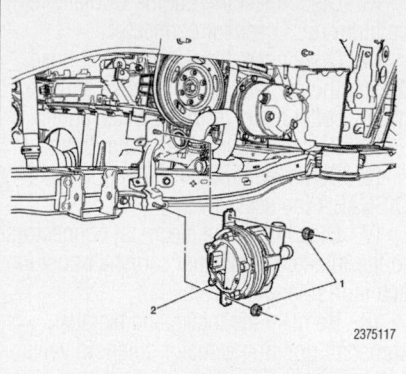

Fig. 75 Remove the nuts (1) and heater water auxiliary pump (2)

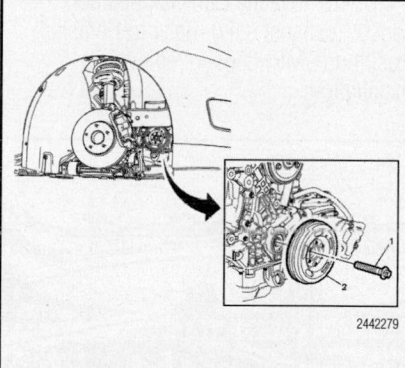

Fig. 76 View of crankshaft damper (balancer) pulley (2) and bolt (1)

To install:
13. Installation is the reverse of the removal procedure.
14. Install the crankshaft damper (balancer) pulley into position according to markings made during removal.
15. Tighten the crankshaft pulley bolt:
   a. Step 1: Tighten to 111 ft. lbs. (150 Nm).
   b. Step 2: Tighten 60°.
16. To ensure correct installation of the crankshaft pulley, measure the distance between the pulley and the front cover. Specification should be 0.18 inch (4.5mm) from the pulley to the mark on the front cover.
17. Tighten the heater water auxiliary pump nuts to 80 inch lbs. (9 Nm).

CRANKSHAFT FRONT SEAL

REMOVAL & INSTALLATION
See Figure 77.

Special Tools
• EN-960 Crankshaft Front Oil Seal Installer
1. Before servicing the vehicle, refer to the Precautions Section.

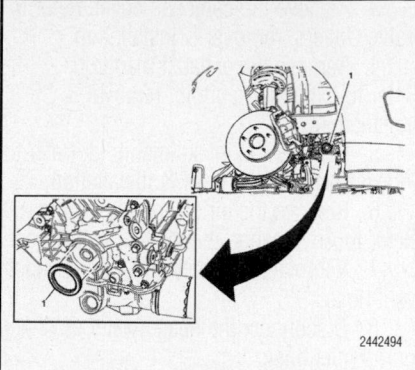

Fig. 77 Crankshaft front oil seal (1) location

2. Remove the crankshaft balancer. Refer to Crankshaft Damper (Balancer), removal & installation.
3. Using a flat-bladed tool, remove the crankshaft front oil seal.

To install:
4. Use the EN-960 installer to install the new crankshaft front oil seal.
5. Install the crankshaft balancer. Refer to Crankshaft Damper (Balancer), removal & installation.

CYLINDER HEAD

REMOVAL & INSTALLATION
See Figures 78 through 93.

Special Tools
• EN-470-B Angular Torque Wrench
• EN-955 Fixing Pin
• EN-43405 Engine Support Fixture Adapter
• EN-28467-1A Cross Bracket
• EN-28467-5A Strut Tower Support Assembly
• EN-28467-8A Hook Assembly
• EN-28467-2A Radiator Tube Shelf Assembly
• EN-36857 Engine Lift Bracket

❋❋ CAUTION

Always perform the High Voltage Disabling procedure prior to servicing any High Voltage component or connection. Personal Protection Equipment (PPE) and proper procedures must be followed. Failure to follow the procedures exactly as written may result in serious injury or death.

1. Before servicing the vehicle, refer to the Precautions Section.
2. Disable the high voltage system. Refer to Disarming the High Voltage System procedure.

3. Remove the camshaft cover. Refer to Valve Covers, removal & installation.

4. Remove the exhaust manifold. Refer to Exhaust Manifold, removal & installation.

5. Remove the intake manifold. Refer to Intake Manifold, removal & installation.

6. Remove the air cleaner assembly. Refer to Air Cleaner, removal & installation.

7. Remove the heater outlet hose vapor vent hose.

8. Disconnect the heater water auxiliary pump inlet hose.

9. Remove the ground wire retaining bolt and wire by the heater water auxiliary pump inlet hose, as needed.

10. Install the engine support fixture.

11. Remove the water pump. Refer to Water Pump, removal & installation.

12. Drain the cooling system. Refer to Engine Coolant, Drain & Refill Procedure.

13. Disconnect the Engine Coolant Temperature (ECT) sensor connector.

14. Disconnect the radiator inlet hose, the engine coolant air bleed hose and the heater outlet hose, from the water outlet.

15. Remove the 4 water outlet bolts.

16. Remove the water outlet and DISCARD the seal.

17. Disconnect the electrical connectors to the intake and exhaust camshaft position actuator solenoid valves.

18. Remove the intake and exhaust camshaft position actuator solenoid valve fasteners.

19. Remove the intake and exhaust camshaft position actuator solenoid valves.

20. Remove the camshaft position sensor (exhaust only). Refer to Camshaft Position (CMP) Sensor, removal & installation.

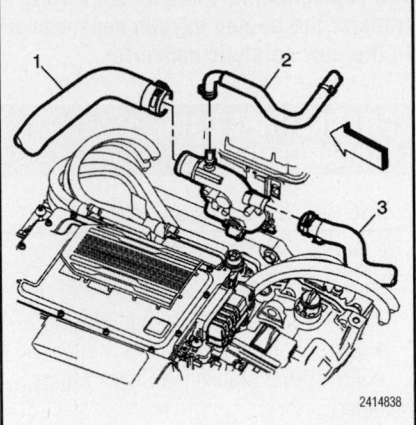

2414838

Fig. 79 Disconnect the radiator inlet hose (1), the engine coolant air bleed hose (2), and the heater outlet hose (3) from the water outlet

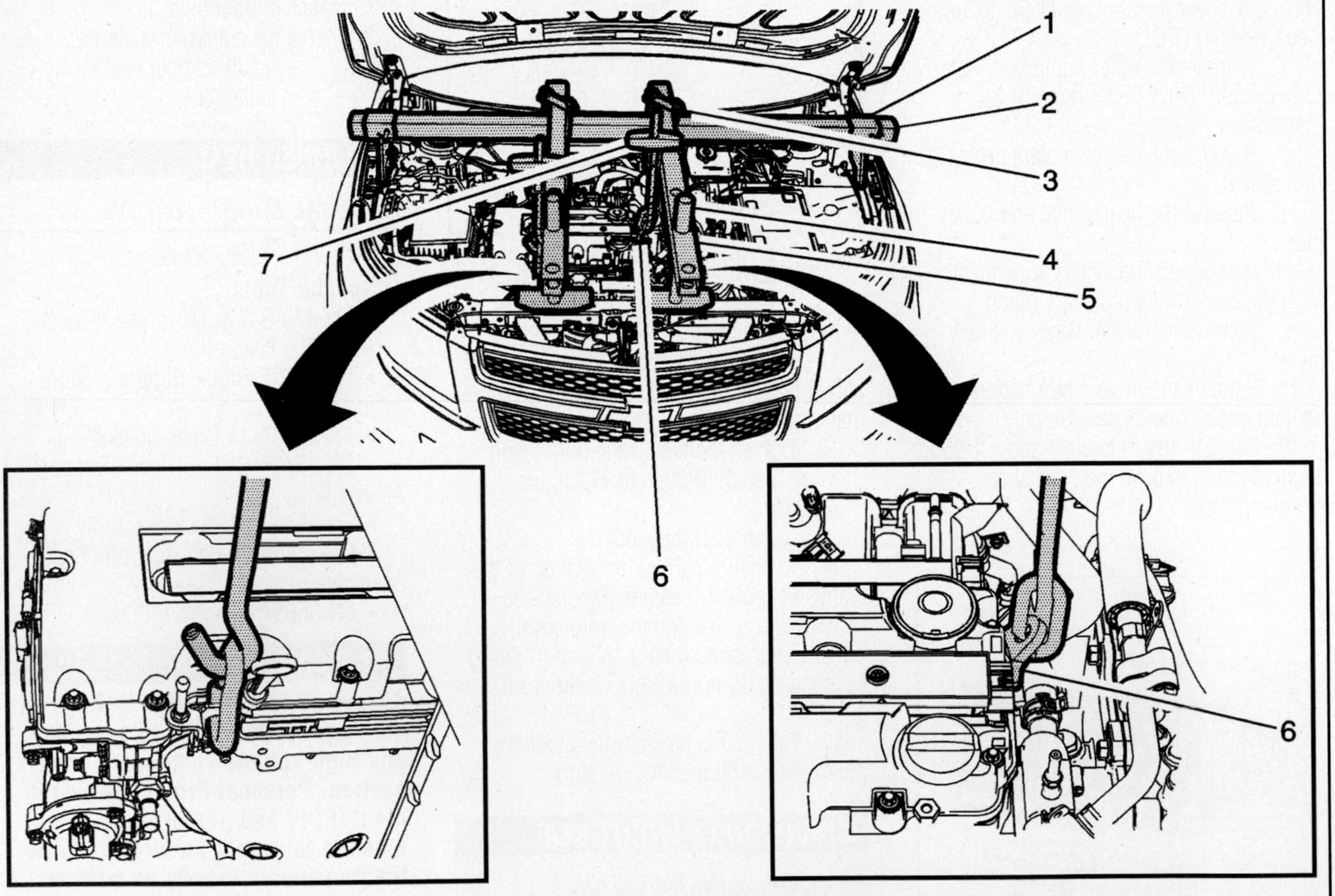

1. Engine support fixture adapter leg (Qty: 2)
2. Main support beam
3. Cross bracket (Qty: 2)
4. Strut tower support assembly (Qty: 2)
5. Radiator tube shelf assembly (Qty: 2)
6. Engine lift bracket
7. Hook assembly (Qty: 2)

2446055

Fig. 78 Engine support fixture shown installed

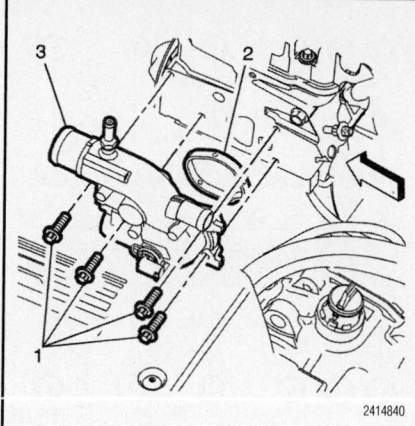

Fig. 80 Remove the water outlet bolts (1), the water outlet (3), and seal (2)

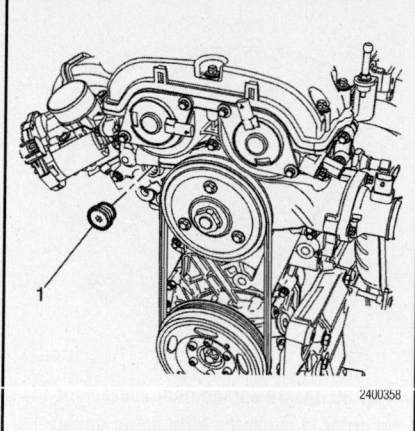

Fig. 83 Remove the timing chain tensioner plug (1) from the engine front cover

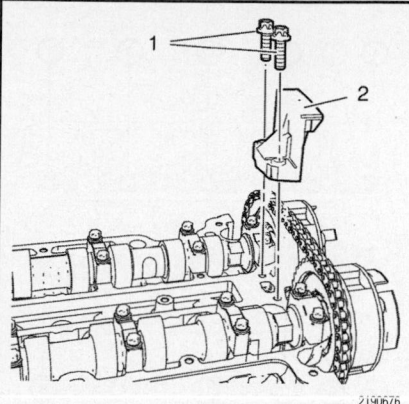

Fig. 85 Remove the 2 upper timing chain guide bolts (1) and the upper timing chain guide (2)

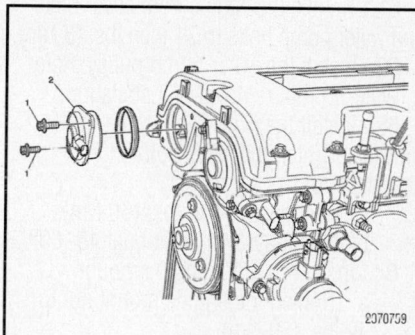

Fig. 81 Intake camshaft position actuator solenoid valve (2) and fasteners (1) shown

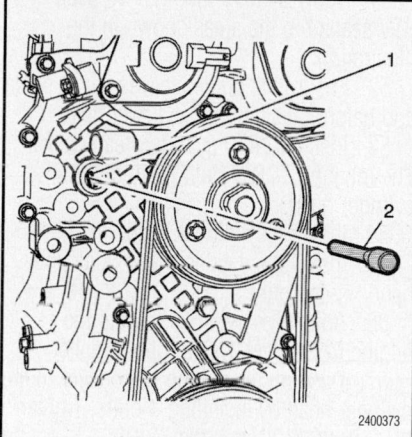

Fig. 84 Install EN-955 Locking Pin (2) to the timing chain tensioner bore (1)

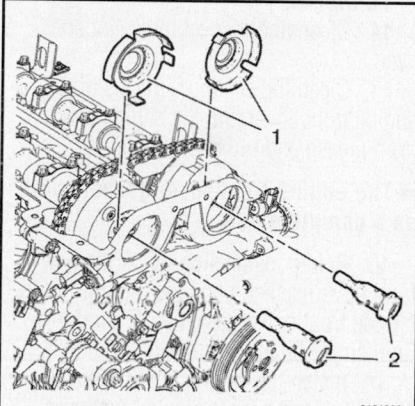

Fig. 86 Remove the camshaft sprocket bolts (2) and the camshaft position exciter wheels (1)

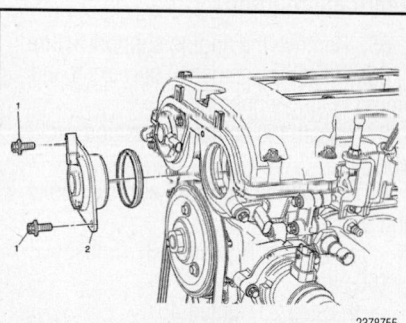

Fig. 82 Exhaust camshaft position actuator solenoid valve (2) and fasteners (1) shown

21. Adjust the engine to TDC. Refer to Timing Chain & Sprockets, Camshaft Timing Chain Inspection procedure.

22. Remove the timing chain tensioner plug from the engine front cover.

23. Install a wrench on the cast hexagonal portion of the intake camshaft and rotate the intake camshaft toward the exhaust camshaft in order to apply tension.

24. Install EN-955 Locking Pin to the timing chain tensioner bore.

25. Remove the wrench from intake camshaft.

26. Remove the 2 upper timing chain guide bolts.

27. Remove the upper timing chain guide.

28. Loosen the intake camshaft sprocket bolt while holding up the hexagon of the intake camshaft with a wrench.

29. Loosen the exhaust camshaft sprocket bolt while holding up the hexagon of the exhaust camshaft with a wrench.

30. Remove the camshaft sprocket bolts and the camshaft position exciter wheels.

31. Remove the camshaft sprockets and timing chain as one unit.

32. Disconnect electrical connectors as necessary.

33. Reposition electrical harness aside.

34. Allow the camshaft sprockets and timing chain rest on the front cover Do NOT remove sprockets or chain.

35. Place a floor jack with block of wood under the oil pan.

36. Remove engine support fixture.

37. Loosen the 12 cylinder head bolts in the sequence:

   a. First pass: Loosen the cylinder head bolts 90°.

   b. Final pass: Loosen the cylinder head bolts 180°.

✳✳ WARNING

Do not damage the guide sleeves during removal of the cylinder head.

38. Remove the cylinder head bolts.

39. With the aid of helper, lift the timing chain side of the cylinder head assembly slightly in the direction of the transaxle.

40. Remove the cylinder head.

41. Remove the cylinder head gasket and discard the gasket.

42. With the cylinder head out of the vehicle bend the top third of the engine front cover gasket back and forth until it snaps off at the breaking point.

43. Transfer any parts as necessary.

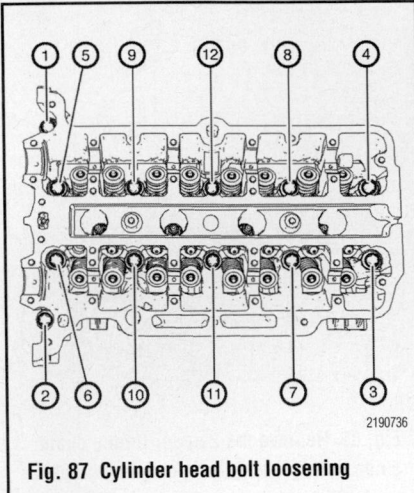

Fig. 87 Cylinder head bolt loosening sequence

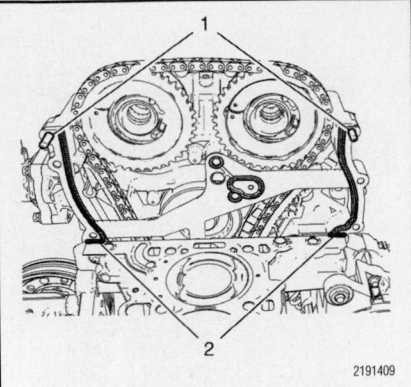

Fig. 89 Install engine front cover bolts (1) in order to guide the NEW upper engine front cover gasket. Apply RTV sealant to the areas shown (2)

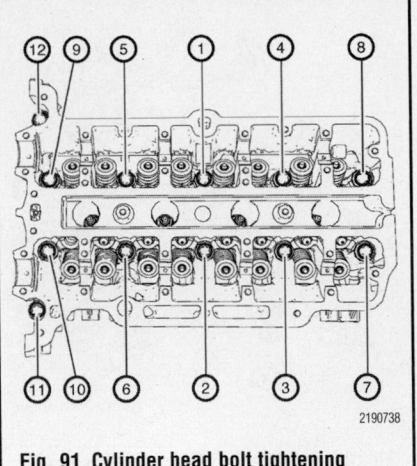

Fig. 91 Cylinder head bolt tightening sequence

To install:

44. Clean and inspect the cylinder head.

45. Clean the sealing surfaces of the engine front cover and the engine block from grease and old gasket material.

➡ **The engine front cover gasket comes as a complete unit.**

46. Before installation the of the new front cover gasket, bend the top third of the engine front cover gasket back and forth until snaps off at the breaking point.

47. Install the engine front cover gasket to ensure for a proper fit and alignment.

48. Clean the surface of the cylinder head and engine front cover.

49. Install the cylinder head gasket to the engine block.

50. Install engine front cover bolts in order to guide the NEW upper engine front cover gasket.

51. Apply a 0.079 inch (2mm) bead of RTV sealant to the areas shown in the illustration.

52. Ensure the guide sleeves are in place and before installing the cylinder head.

53. Install a NEW cylinder head gasket. The marking TOP should point to the cylinder head.

54. Install the cylinder head.

55. Install the cylinder head bolts and hand tighten only.

56. Adjust the cylinder head to the engine front cover. Use a rubber mallet.

57. Position the engine front cover to the cylinder head by installing 3 bolts. Tighten the 3 bolts to 71 inch lbs. (8 Nm).

58. Using the EN-470-B angular torque wench, or equivalent, tighten the cylinder head bolts in sequence to 18 ft. lbs. (25 Nm), plus 180°.

59. Loosen the bolts from the engine front cover.

60. Install the remaining bolts to the engine front cover and water pump.

61. Tighten the engine front cover bolts and water pump bolts to 71 inch lbs. (8 Nm).

62. Install the water pump pulley. Refer to Water Pump, removal & installation.

63. Install the right engine mount bracket. Tighten the NEW bolts in sequence to:

   a. First pass: 44 ft. lbs. (60 Nm).

   b. Final pass: An additional 45–60°.

64. Install the right engine mount.

   a. Tighten the engine mount nut to 37 ft. lbs. (50 Nm).

   b. Tighten the engine mount bolts to 43 ft. lbs. (58 Nm).

➡ **Ensure the washers are in place where appropriate.**

65. Remove the engine support fixture.

66. Install the camshaft sprockets and timing chain as one unit.

67. Install the camshaft position exciter wheels.

68. Install the camshaft sprocket bolts and tighten:

   a. Step 1: Tighten to 37 ft. lbs. (50 Nm).

   b. Step 2: Tighten 45°.

   c. Step 3: Tighten an additional 15°.

69. Remove the EN-955 locking pin.

70. Adjust the camshaft timing chain. Refer to Timing Chain & Sprockets, Camshaft Timing Chain Inspection.

71. Install the upper timing chain guide.

72. Install the upper timing chain guide bolts and tighten to 71 inch lbs. (8 Nm).

73. Install the timing chain tensioner plug and tighten to 37 ft. lbs. (50 Nm).

74. Install the intake and exhaust camshaft position actuator solenoid valves. Tighten the fasteners to 71 inch lbs. (8 Nm).

75. Install the camshaft position sensor (exhaust only). Refer to Camshaft Position (CMP) Sensor, removal & installation.

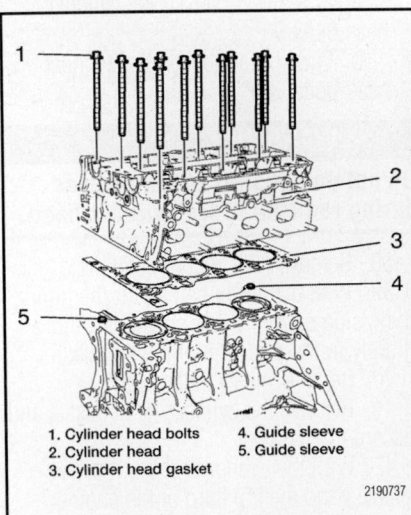

1. Cylinder head bolts   4. Guide sleeve
2. Cylinder head   5. Guide sleeve
3. Cylinder head gasket

Fig. 88 Exploded view of cylinder head removal

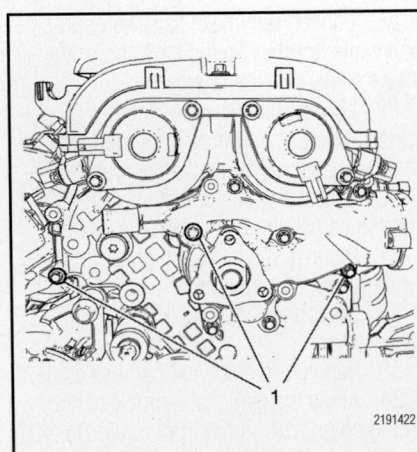

Fig. 90 Position the engine front cover to the cylinder head by installing 3 bolts (1)

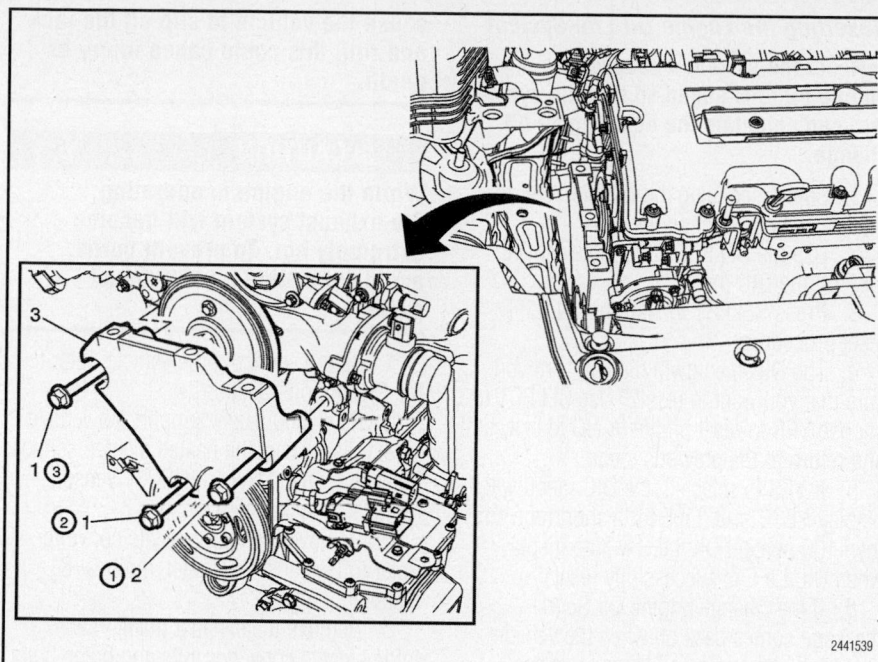

Fig. 92 View of right side engine mount bracket (3) and bolts (1, 2) and bolt torque sequence

76. Install the camshaft cover. Refer to Valve Covers, removal & installation.

77. Install the exhaust manifold. Refer to Exhaust Manifold, removal & installation.

78. Install intake manifold. Refer to Intake Manifold, removal & installation.

79. Position the water outlet and a NEW seal, to the cylinder head.

80. Install the 4 water outlet bolts and tighten to 71 inch lbs. (8 Nm).

81. Connect the radiator inlet hose, the engine coolant air bleed hose and the heater outlet hose, to the water outlet.

82. Install the engine coolant temperature sensor and the battery positive cable, to the A/C compressor hose.

83. Fill the cooling system. Refer to Engine Coolant, Drain & Refill Procedure.

84. Enable the high voltage system. Refer to Arming the High Voltage System.

85. Test the vehicle using the following procedure:

a. Crank the engine several times. Listen for any unusual noises or evidence that parts are binding.

b. Start the engine and listen for unusual noises.

c. Check the vehicle oil pressure gauge or light and confirm that the engine has acceptable oil pressure.

d. Run the engine speed at about 1,000 RPM until the engine has reached normal operating temperature.

e. Listen for a possible sticking lifter or other unusual noises.

f. Inspect for fuel, oil and/or coolant leaks while the engine is running.

86. Road test the vehicle for normal operation.

87. Inspect for coolant, oil, gas, or exhaust leaks.

ENGINE OIL & FILTER

REPLACEMENT

See Figures 94 and 95.

✳✳ CAUTION

Do not use a service jack in locations other than those specified to lift this vehicle. Lifting the vehicle with a jack in those other locations could cause the vehicle to slip off the jack and roll; this could cause injury or death.

1. Before servicing the vehicle, refer to the Precautions Section.

2. Raise and safely support the vehicle.

3. Place a drain pan under the oil pan drain plug.

4. Remove the oil pan drain plug and allow the oil to drain completely.

5. Install the oil pan drain plug and tighten to 10 ft. lbs. (14 Nm).

✳✳ CAUTION

While the engine is operating, the exhaust system will become extremely hot. To prevent burns, avoid contacting a hot exhaust system.

6. Place the drain pan under the oil filter.

7. Remove the oil filter. Allow the oil to drain completely.

To install:

8. Lubricate the NEW oil filter gasket with clean engine oil.

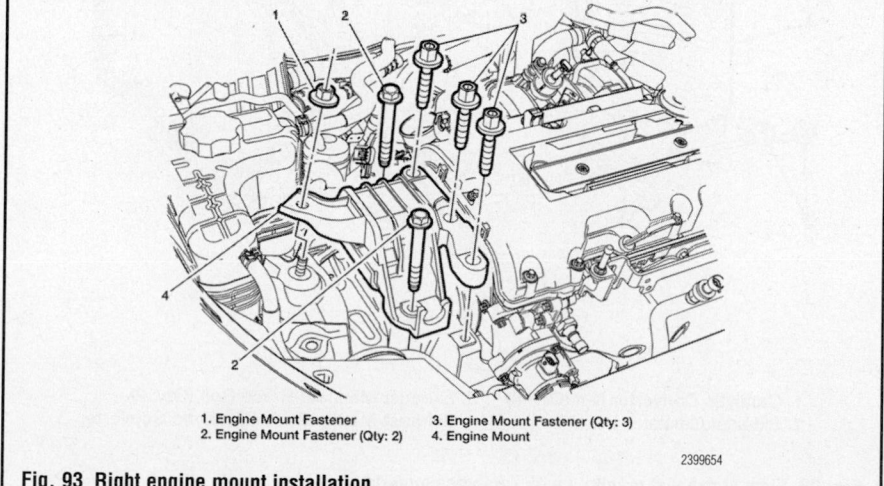

1. Engine Mount Fastener
2. Engine Mount Fastener (Qty: 2)
3. Engine Mount Fastener (Qty: 3)
4. Engine Mount

Fig. 93 Right engine mount installation

Fig. 94 Remove the oil pan drain plug (1) and allow the oil to drain completely

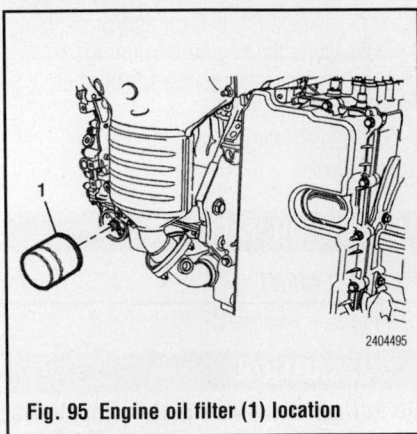

Fig. 95 Engine oil filter (1) location

9. Tighten the oil filter to 18 ft. lbs. (25 Nm).

10. Lower the vehicle.

11. Fill the engine oil with the proper type and amount of oil.

➡**Engine oil capacity with filter is approximately 3.7 quarts. 5W-30 is recommended.**

12. Start the engine and inspect for leaks.

13. Reset the oil life monitor. Refer to GM Oil Life System Resetting.

GM Oil Life System Resetting

Description

This vehicle has a computer system that indicates when to change the engine oil and filter. This is based on a combination of factors which includes engine revolutions and engine temperature, and miles driven. Based on driving conditions, the mileage at which an oil change is indicated can vary considerably. For the oil life system to work properly, the system must be reset every time the oil is changed.

When the system has calculated that oil life has been diminished, it indicates that an oil change is necessary. A CHANGE ENGINE OIL SOON message comes on. Change the oil as soon as possible within the next 600 miles (1,000 km).

It is possible that, if driving under the best conditions, the oil life system might indicate that an oil change is not necessary for up to two years. The engine oil and filter must be changed at least once every two years and, at this time, the system must be reset. It is also important to check the oil regularly over the course of an oil drain interval and keep it at the proper level.

If the system is ever reset accidentally, the oil must be changed at 3,000 miles (5,000 km) since the last oil change. Remember to reset the oil life system whenever the oil is changed.

Resetting the Engine Oil Life System

➡Reset the system whenever the engine oil is changed so that the system can calculate the next engine oil change.

1. Before servicing the vehicle, refer to the Precautions Section.

2. Use the SELECT knob to select OIL LIFE on the DIC menu.

3. Press SELECT to start the OIL LIFE reset procedure.

4. The DIC menu will display "Are you sure that you want to reset?" Use SELECT to choose YES to reset oil life or NO to exit and return to the previous menu.

5. If YES is selected, the DIC menu will display RESET OIL LIFE for a short time and then 100 percent OIL LIFE will be display when OIL LIFE is successfully reset.

6. If the Change Engine Oil Soon message comes back on when the vehicle is started, the engine oil life system has not reset. Repeat the procedure.

EXHAUST MANIFOLD

REMOVAL & INSTALLATION

See Figure 96.

✳✳ CAUTION

Do not use a service jack in locations other than those specified to lift this vehicle. Lifting the vehicle with a jack in those other locations could cause the vehicle to slip off the jack and roll; this could cause injury or death.

✳✳ CAUTION

While the engine is operating, the exhaust system will become extremely hot. To prevent burns, avoid contacting a hot exhaust system.

1. Before servicing the vehicle, refer to the Precautions Section.

2. Raise and safely support the vehicle.

3. Disconnect the heated oxygen sensor. Refer to Heated Oxygen (HO2S) Sensor, removal & installation.

4. Remove the rear catalytic converter. Refer to Catalytic Converter, removal & installation.

5. Remove the exhaust manifold/catalytic converter nuts and brace bolts.

6. Remove the exhaust manifold/catalytic converter from the vehicle.

To install:

7. Installation is the reverse of the removal procedure.

➡**Replace the exhaust gasket with a NEW one. If replacing the catalytic converter, transfer the heated oxygen sensor over to the new catalytic converter.**

8. Tighten the catalytic convert nuts and the brace bolts to 16 ft. lbs. (22 Nm).

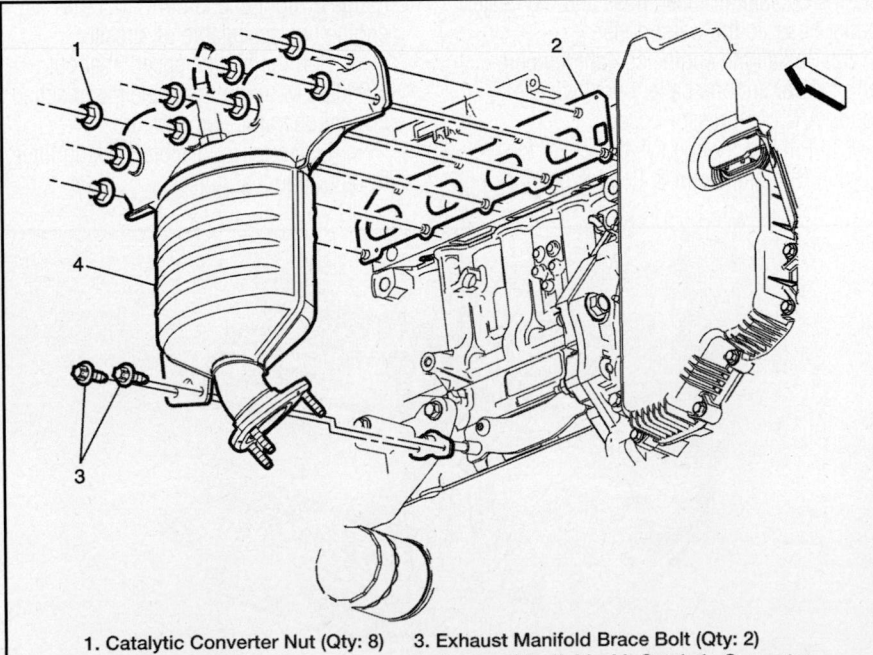

1. Catalytic Converter Nut (Qty: 8)
2. Exhaust Gasket
3. Exhaust Manifold Brace Bolt (Qty: 2)
4. Exhaust Manifold with Catalytic Converter

Fig. 96 View of exhaust manifold with catalytic converter removal

FLEXPLATE

REMOVAL & INSTALLATION

See Figure 97.

Special Tools
- EN-470-B Angular Torque Wrench
- EN-956-1 Extension
- EN-49979 Crankshaft Shock Mount Retainer

1. Before servicing the vehicle, refer to the Precautions Section.
2. Remove the transaxle.
3. Inspect the engine flexplate for the following:

   a. Stress cracks around the engine flexplate.

   b. Cracks at welded areas that retain the ring gear onto the engine flexplate.

   c. Damaged or missing ring gear teeth.

   d. Do not attempt to repair the welded areas that retain the ring gear to the engine flexplate plate. If damaged, install a new engine flexplate.

4. Remove the flexplate bolts and the flexplate.

To install:

5. Installation is the reverse of the removal procedure.
6. Install the flexplate bolts:

   a. Step 1: Tighten to 26 ft. lbs. (35 Nm).

   b. Step 2: Tighten 30°.

   c. Step 3: Tighten an additional 15°.

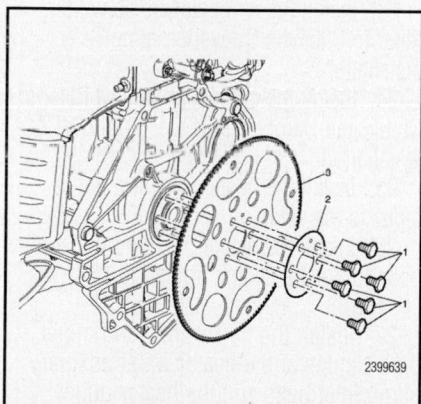

Fig. 97 View of automatic transaxle flexplate (3), flexplate (2), and bolts (1)

INTAKE MANIFOLD

REMOVAL & INSTALLATION

See Figures 98 and 99.

✳✳ CAUTION

Always perform the High Voltage Disabling procedure prior to servic-ing any High Voltage component or connection. Personal Protection Equipment (PPE) and proper procedures must be followed. Failure to follow the procedures exactly as written may result in serious injury or death.

1. Before servicing the vehicle, refer to the Precautions Section.
2. Disable the high voltage system. Refer to Disarming the High Voltage System.
3. Remove the air cleaner outlet duct. Refer to Air Cleaner, removal & installation.
4. Remove the fuel injection fuel rail assembly only. Refer to Fuel Injectors, removal & installation.
5. Remove the evaporative emission canister purge solenoid valve hose.
6. Unclip and reposition the engine coolant air bleed hose without draining coolant.
7. Remove the 6 intake manifold bolts.
8. Remove the intake manifold from the vehicle.
9. Disconnect the electrical connectors as necessary.
10. Transfer the components as necessary.

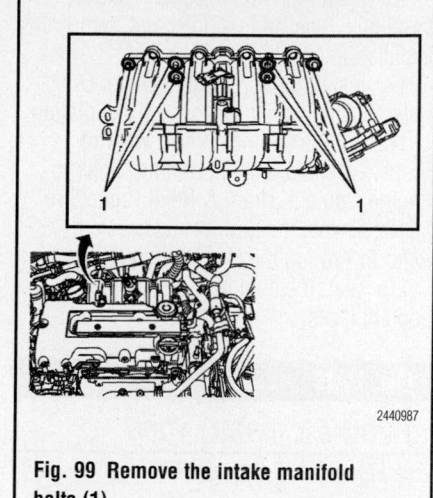

Fig. 99 Remove the intake manifold bolts (1)

To install:

11. Ensure the surface of the intake manifold is clean before installing the NEW gasket.
12. Install the intake manifold gasket.
13. Install the intake manifold in the vehicle.
14. Install the intake manifold bolts and tighten to 15 ft. lbs. (20 Nm).
15. Install the evaporative emission canister purge solenoid valve hose.

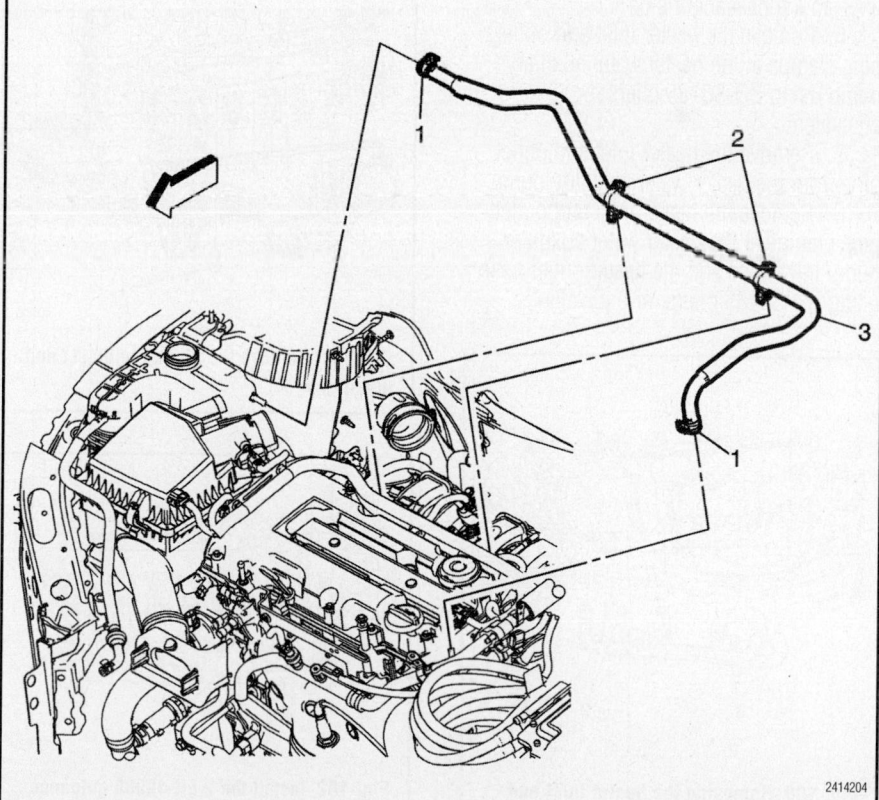

Fig. 98 View of engine coolant air bleed hose (3), retainer clips (2), and hose clamps (3)

16. Install the fuel injection fuel rail assembly. Refer to Fuel Injectors, removal & installation.

17. Install the Air Cleaner Outlet Duct. Refer to Air Cleaner, removal & installation.

18. Fill the engine coolant with the proper type and amount of fluid. Refer to Engine Coolant, Drain & Refill Procedure.

19. Enable the high voltage system. Refer to Arming the High Voltage System.

20. Start the engine and check for coolant leaks.

OIL PAN

REMOVAL & INSTALLATION

See Figures 100 through 103.

Special Tools
- EN-49980 Guidance Pins
- BO-38185 Hose Clamp Pliers

1. Before servicing the vehicle, refer to the Precautions Section.

2. Remove the oil filter and drain the engine oil. Refer to Engine Oil & Filter, Replacement.

3. Remove the rear catalytic converter. Refer to Catalytic Converter, removal & installation.

4. Drain the cooling system. Refer to Drain & Refill Procedure.

5. Remove the front wheelhouse front liner on the passenger side.

6. Remove the heater inlet and outlet pipe clamps at the heater water auxiliary pump using BO-38185 pliers, or equivalent.

7. Remove the heater inlet and outlet pipe from the heater water auxiliary pump.

8. Remove the heater inlet and outlet pipe clamps at the heater water auxiliary pump inlet hose and the heater outlet hose using BO-38185 pliers, or equivalent.

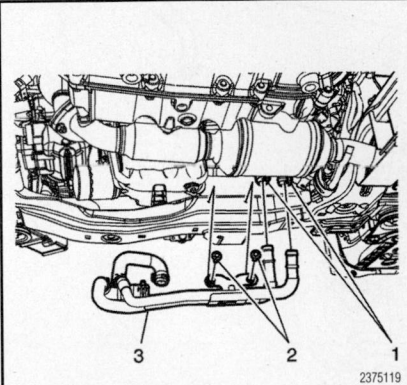

Fig. 100 Removing the heater inlet and outlet pipes (3), pipe bolts (2), and clamps (1)

9. Remove the heater inlet and outlet pipe bolts from the cradle.

10. Remove the heater inlet and outlet pipes from the vehicle.

11. Remove the crankshaft pulley. Refer to Crankshaft Damper (Balancer), removal & installation.

12. Remove the oil pan-to-transaxle bolts.

13. Remove the oil pan bolts and the oil pan.

To install:

14. Clean the sealing surface of crankshaft bearing cap tie plate and the groove in the engine front cover from old gasket material, oil, dirt, and grease.

15. Install the 2 EN-49980 guidance pins to the oil pan screw bores.

➡**The sealing bead should be applied close to the inner edge of the oil pan. Take care that the oil suction gallery does not get contaminated with sealing compound or dirt.**

16. Apply 0.079 inch (2mm) thickness of sealing compound to the appropriate areas of the oil pan and engine block.

➡**The complete installation procedure of the oil pan should be done within 10 minutes.**

Fig. 101 Remove the oil pan bolts (1) and the oil pan

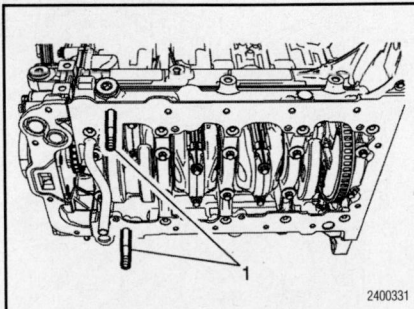

Fig. 102 Install the 2 EN-49980 guidance pins (1) to the oil pan screw bores as illustrated

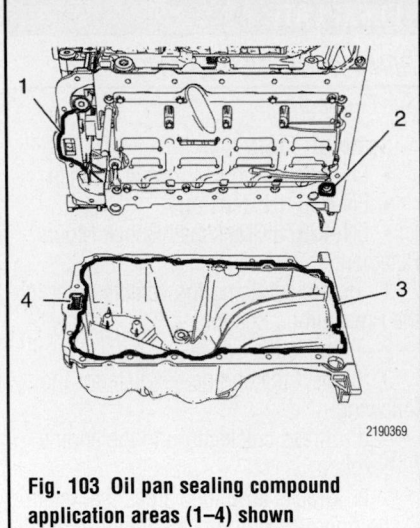

Fig. 103 Oil pan sealing compound application areas (1–4) shown

17. Loosely install the oil pan bolts in all but the guidance pin locations.

18. Remove the EN-49980 guidance pins and install the remaining oil pan bolts.

19. Tighten the oil pan bolts to 89 inch lbs. (10 Nm).

20. Position the transaxle converter cover and hand tighten the cover-to-transaxle bolts.

21. Install the oil pan-to-transaxle bolts, and tighten to 30 ft. lbs. (40 Nm).

22. Install a NEW oil filter and fill the engine with the proper type and amount of oil. Refer to Engine Oil & Filter, Replacement.

23. Install the rear catalytic converter. Refer to Catalytic Converter, removal & installation.

24. Install the crankshaft pulley. Refer to Crankshaft Damper (Balancer), removal & installation.

25. Install the heater inlet and outlet pipes to the vehicle.

26. Install the heater inlet and outlet pipe bolts to the cradle and tighten to 13 ft. lbs. (17 Nm).

27. Install the heater inlet and outlet pipe clamps at the heater water auxiliary pump inlet hose and the heater outlet hose using BO-38185 pliers, or equivalent.

28. Install the heater inlet and outlet pipes to the heater water auxiliary pump.

29. Install the heater inlet and outlet pipe clamps at the heater water auxiliary pump using BO-38185 pliers, or equivalent.

30. Install the front wheelhouse front liner on passenger side.

31. Fill the cooling system. Refer to Drain & Refill Procedure.

OIL PUMP

REMOVAL & INSTALLATION

See Figures 104 through 110.

1. Before servicing the vehicle, refer to the Precautions Section.
2. Measure the oil pressure and compare with the specified values.
3. Remove the engine front cover. Refer to Timing Chain Front Cover, removal & installation.
4. Remove the 8 oil pump cover bolts.
5. Remove the oil pump cover.

✳✳ CAUTION

Before removing the spring, cover the spring with a towel to prevent the spring from flying and possibly causing damage or personal injury.

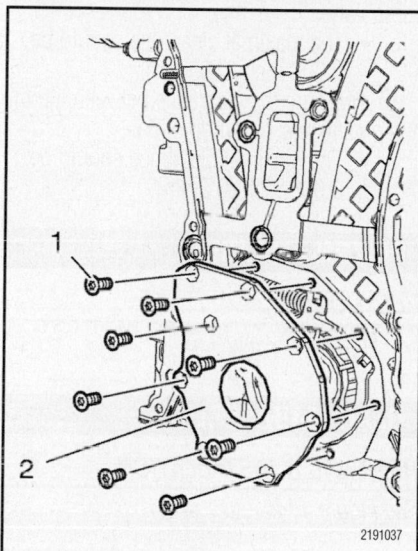

Fig. 104 Oil pump cover bolts (1) and the oil pump cover (2) removal

➡️**Use a screwdriver between the oil pump slide spring windings, but protect the engine front cover edge with a suitable piece of plastic.**

6. Compress the oil pump slide spring with a screw driver and remove the oil pump slide spring in compound with the oil pump slide spring pin.

➡️**Mind the installation position of the oil pump components.**

7. Remove the oil pump components in the following order:
   a. Outer oil pump vane ring.
   b. Oil pump vane rotor and the 7 oil pump vanes.
   c. Inner oil pump vane ring.
   d. Oil pump slide and the 2 oil pump slide seals with the 2 oil pump slide seal springs.

To install:

8. Clean and inspect the oil pump. Refer to Inspection in this section.

➡️**Oil pump slide spring pin and oil pump slide spring, as well as slide seal and slide seal spring can be ordered as single parts. All other oil pump components can only be ordered as a replacement kit.**

9. Install the oil pan components in the following order:

➡️**The bore in the oil pump slide must fit smooth-running and without clearance to the oil pump slide pivot pin.**

   a. Install the oil pump slide.
   b. Install the inner oil pump vane ring.

➡️**Mind the installation position of the oil pump vane rotor. The mark must point to direction of the oil pump cover.**

c. Install the oil pump vane rotor.

➡️**Mind the localized flattening on the oil pump vanes caused by the oil pump vane rings. The localized flattening must point to the oil pump vane rotor.**

   d. Install the 7 oil pump vanes.
   e. Install the outer oil pump vane ring.
10. Install the 2 oil pump slide seals and the 2 oil pump slide seal springs to the 2 grooves of the oil pump slide.
11. Protect the engine front cover edge with a suitable piece of plastic.

➡️**The length of the removed oil pump slide spring should be 3.012 inches (76.5mm) for suction engines.**

12. Install the oil pump slide spring pin in compound with the oil pump slide spring. Use a screwdriver to compress the oil pump slide spring. The flat side of oil pump slide spring pin must face upwards.
13. Lubricate the oil pump vanes, the oil pump vane rotor, the oil pump slide spring, and the chambers with engine oil.
14. Inspect the oil pump slide spring mechanism for proper function.
15. Measure the oil pump axial and radial clearances and compare with the specified values. Refer to Inspection in this section.
16. Install the oil pump cover and the 8 oil pump cover bolts.
17. Tighten the oil pump cover bolts in a sequence to 71 inch lbs. (8 Nm).
18. Install the crankshaft balancer and rotate in the specified direction in order to inspect the function of the oil pump mechanism. The crankshaft balancer should rotate easily.
19. Remove the timing chain and replace the engine front cover gasket. Refer to Tim-

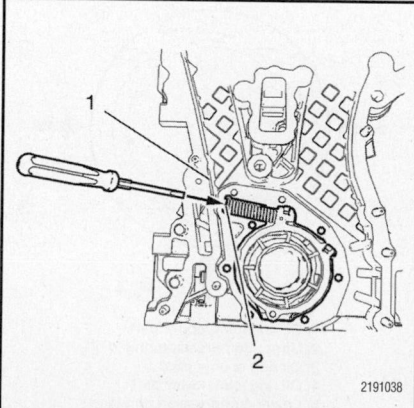

Fig. 105 Use a screwdriver between the oil pump slide spring windings (2) but protect the engine front cover edge (1)

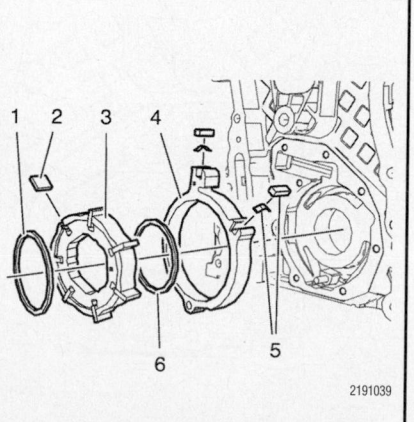

Fig. 106 Exploded view of oil pump component removal

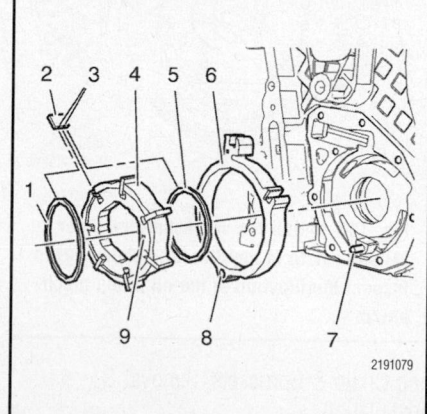

Fig. 107 Exploded view of oil pump component installation

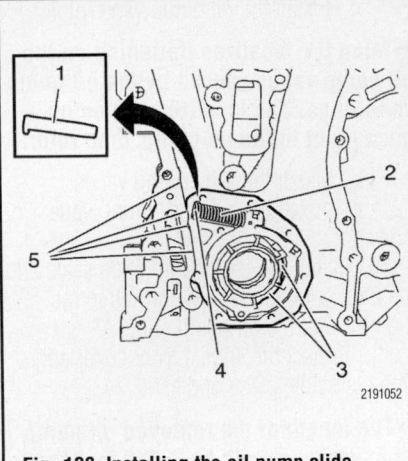

Fig. 108 Installing the oil pump slide spring mechanism

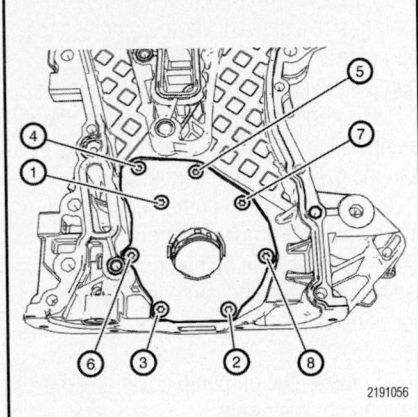

Fig. 109 Oil pump cover bolt tightening sequence shown

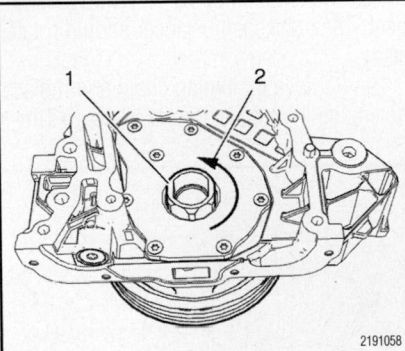

Fig. 110 Install the crankshaft balancer (1) and rotate in the direction shown (2) to inspect the function of the oil pump mechanism

ing Chain & Sprockets, removal & installation.

20. Install the timing chain. Refer to Timing Chain & Sprockets, removal & installation.

21. Install the engine front cover. Refer to Timing Chain Front Cover, removal & installation.

22. Measure the oil pressure and compare with the specified values.

INSPECTION

See Figure 111.

1. Before servicing the vehicle, refer to the Precautions Section.

2. Inspect the engine front cover for cracks, scratches, and damage.

3. Inspect the oil pump cover and the engine front cover for flatness.

4. Inspect the oil pump vanes, the oil pump vane rotor, the oil pump vane rings, and the oil pump slide for localized flatting.

5. Inspect the oil pump slide pivot pin for firm seat.

> ❋❋ **CAUTION**
>
> **Wear safety glasses when using compressed air in order to prevent eye injury.**

> ❋❋ **WARNING**
>
> **To ensure proper engine lubrication, clean clogged or contaminated oil galleries in an approved solvent and with compressed air. Failure to clean oil galleries may cause engine damage.**

6. Clean the oil galleries with solvent and compressed air.

7. With the oil pump components installed, measure the oil pump axial clearances. Use a straight edge and a feeler gauge.

   a. The maximal axial clearance between the engine front cover and oil

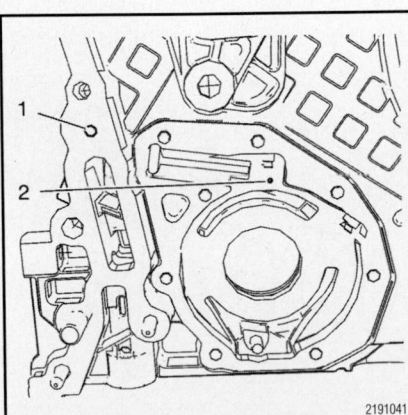

Fig. 111 Clean the oil galleries with solvent and compressed air. Blow compressed air from bore (2) to bore (1)

pump vane rotor should be 0.004 inch (0.1mm).

   b. The maximal axial clearance between the engine front cover and oil pump vane should be 0.0035 inch (0.09mm).

   c. The maximal axial clearance between the engine front cover and oil pump vane ring should be 0.016 inch (0.4mm).

   d. The maximal axial clearance between the engine front cover and oil pump slide should be 0.0031 inch (0.08mm).

   e. The maximal axial clearance between the engine front cover and oil pump slide seal should be 0.0035 inch (0.09mm).

8. Using a feeler gauge, measure the oil pump radial clearance. Measure the clearance between oil pump vane rotor and oil pump vane.

   • The maximal clearance should be 0.002 inch (0.05mm)

9. Measure the clearance between the oil pump vane and oil pump slide.

   • The maximal clearance should be 0.008 inch (0.2mm)

PISTON AND RING

POSITIONING

See Figures 112 and 113.

REAR MAIN SEAL

REMOVAL & INSTALLATION

See Figure 114.

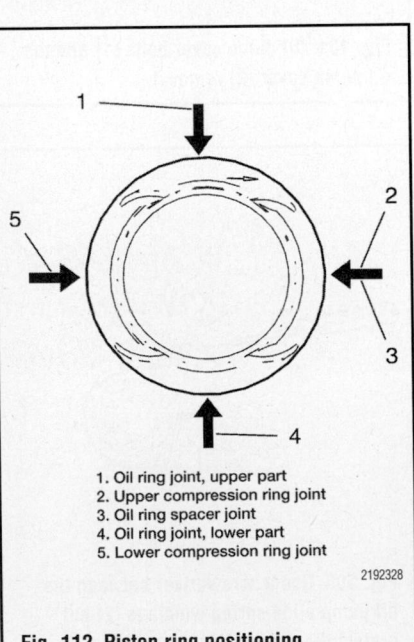

1. Oil ring joint, upper part
2. Upper compression ring joint
3. Oil ring spacer joint
4. Oil ring joint, lower part
5. Lower compression ring joint

Fig. 112 Piston ring positioning

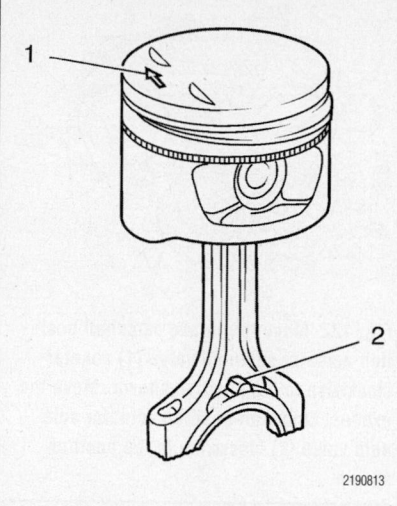

Fig. 113 Arrow (1) on the piston head must point to the timing side. Markings on the connecting rods (2) must point to the transaxle side

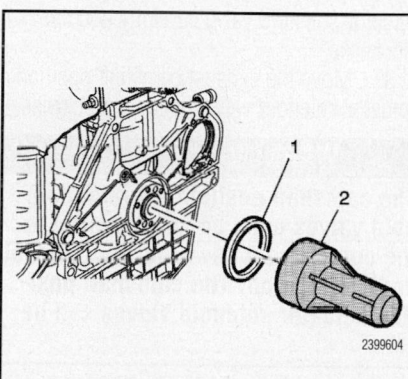

Fig. 114 Using the EN-658 installer (2) to install a NEW crankshaft real oil seal (1)

Special Tools

• EN-658 Rear Main Seal Installer

1. Before servicing the vehicle, refer to the Precautions Section.

2. Remove the automatic transaxle flexplate. Refer to Flexplate, removal & installation.

❊❊ WARNING

Do not damage the outside diameter of the crankshaft or chamber with any tool.

3. Using a flat-bladed tool, remove the rear crankshaft oil seal.

To install:

4. Using the EN-658 installer, install a NEW crankshaft real oil seal.

5. Install the automatic transaxle flexplate. Refer to Flexplate, removal & installation.

TIMING CHAIN FRONT COVER

REMOVAL & INSTALLATION

See Figures 115 through 126.

Special Tools

• EN-952 Fixing Pin
• EN-953-A Fixing Tool
• EN-49977-100 Transmitter Disc Fixation

1. Before servicing the vehicle, refer to the Precautions Section.

2. Disconnect the battery negative cable. Refer to Battery, removal & installation.

3. Remove the ignition coil. Refer to Ignition Coil, removal & installation.

4. Remove the camshaft cover. Refer to Valve Covers, removal & installation.

5. Remove the front wheelhouse liner.

6. Remove the front compartment insulator as needed.

7. Rotate the engine clockwise until the bore in the crankshaft balancer aligns with the mark on the engine front cover.

8. Examine that the camshaft grooves are visible. If the camshaft grooves are not visible, rotate the crankshaft 360°.

9. Remove the crankshaft bearing cap tie plate hole plug and the seal ring.

❊❊ WARNING

To ensure proper crankshaft TDC alignment, the retention pin should fit easily through the bore in the crankshaft tie plate and into the crankshaft. Binding of the retention pin could affect proper engine timing.

10. Install EN-952 fixing pin to hold the crankshaft in TDC position.

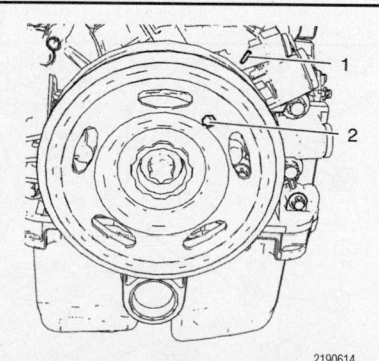

Fig. 115 Rotate the engine clockwise until the bore (2) in the crankshaft balancer aligns with the mark (1) on the engine front cover

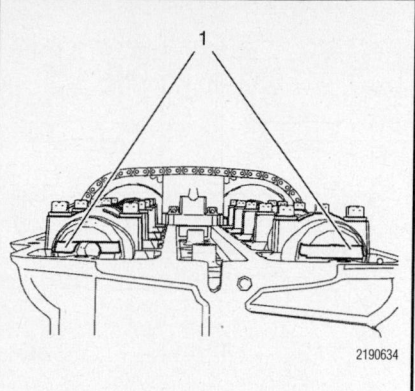

Fig. 116 The camshaft grooves (1) should be as shown to be at TDC

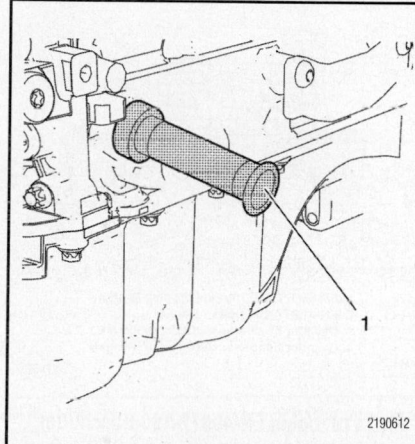

Fig. 117 EN-952 fixing pin (1) installed to hold the crankshaft in TDC position

➡The fixing tool should be installed completely to the camshaft grooves without high effort.

11. Install EN-953-A fixing tool to the camshafts.

➡A wrong installation position is possible in the next procedure. Make sure that the fixation tool is installed without clearance to the cylinder head in areas and.

12. Install EN-49977-100 transmitter disc fixation to inspect the correct position of the camshaft position exciter wheels.

13. Tighten the bolts of EN-49977-100 transmitter disc fixation.

14. Remove EN-49977-100 transmitter disc fixation.

15. Remove EN-953-A fixing tool.

16. Remove EN-952 fixing pin.

17. Install the crankshaft bearing cap tie plate hole plug and seal ring and tighten to 30 ft. lbs. (40 Nm).

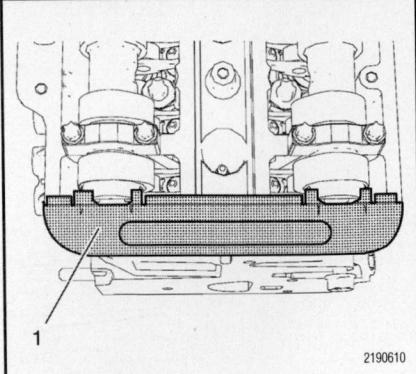

Fig. 118 EN-953-A fixing tool (1) installed to the camshafts

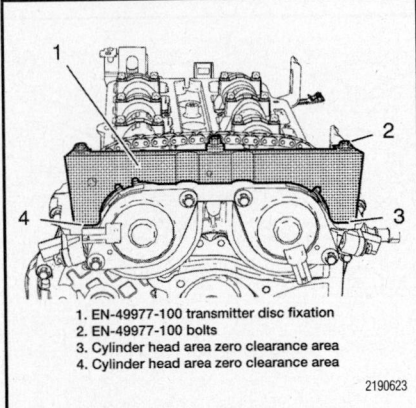

1. EN-49977-100 transmitter disc fixation
2. EN-49977-100 bolts
3. Cylinder head area zero clearance area
4. Cylinder head area zero clearance area

Fig. 119 Using EN-49977-100 transmitter disc fixation to inspect the correct position of the camshaft position exciter wheels

18. Raise and safely support the vehicle.

19. Remove the drive belt from crankshaft balancer and water pump. Refer to Accessory Drive Belts, removal & installation.

20. Disconnect the air conditioning compressor wiring harness plug.

21. Unclip the air conditioning compressor wiring harness from the 2 retainer clips.

➡ Do not remove the air conditioning compressor and condenser hose from air conditioning compressor.

22. Remove the air conditioning compressor from the air conditioning compressor bracket and hang aside.

23. Remove the 3 air conditioning compressor bracket bolts.

24. Remove the air conditioning compressor bracket.

25. Place a collecting basin underneath the vehicle.

26. Remove the crankshaft balancer. Refer to Crankshaft Damper (Balancer), removal & installation.

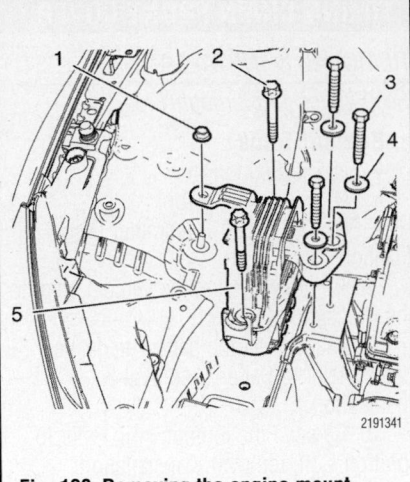

Fig. 120 Removing the engine mount

27. Remove the oil pan. Refer to Oil Pan, removal & installation.

28. Lower the vehicle.

29. Install an engine lifter to the right engine lift bracket and apply tension to the engine lifter chain in order to support the engine.

30. Remove and DISCARD the 3 engine mount-to-engine mount bracket bolts and the 3 washers.

31. Remove the 2 engine mount-to-body bolts and the engine mount nut.

32. Remove the engine mount.

33. Remove the right side engine mount bracket.

34. Remove the water pump pulley and

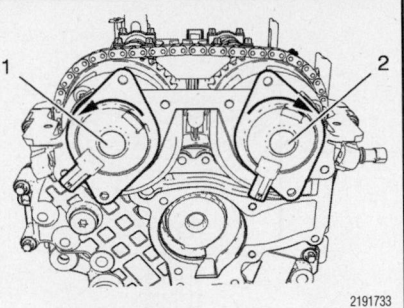

Fig. 122 Move the intake camshaft position actuator solenoid valve (1) counter-clockwise to the position shown. Move the exhaust camshaft position actuator solenoid valve (2) clockwise to the position shown

the water pump. Refer to Water Pump, removal & installation.

35. Remove the 4 camshaft position actuator solenoid valve bolts.

36. Move the intake camshaft position actuator solenoid valve carefully counter-clockwise.

37. Move the exhaust camshaft position actuator solenoid valve carefully clockwise.

❊❊ WARNING

The camshaft position actuator solenoid valves must be kept parallel to the engine front cover during removal and installation. The camshaft position actuator solenoid valves can be

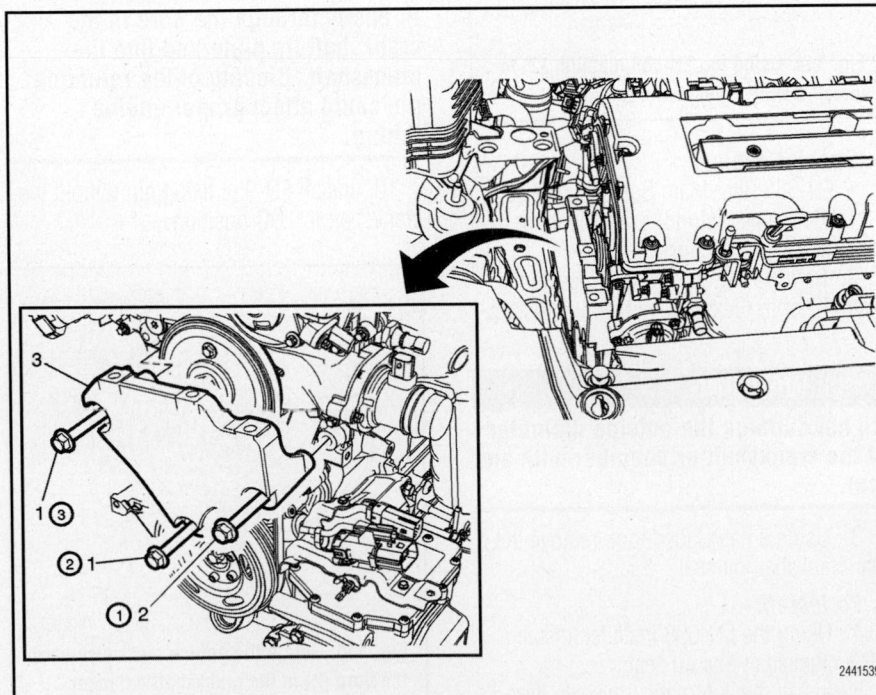

Fig. 121 View of right side engine mount bracket (3) and bolts (1, 2) and bolt torque sequence

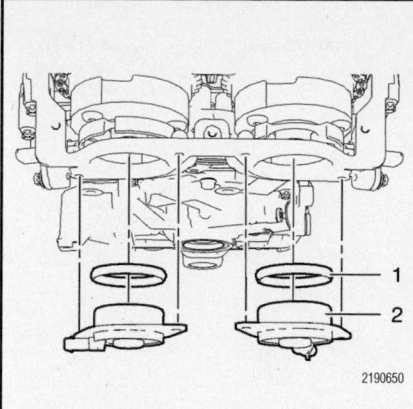

Fig. 123 Removing the 2 camshaft position actuator solenoid valves (2) and the seal rings (1)

damaged if they become wedged or stuck during this process.

38. Carefully remove the 2 camshaft position actuator solenoid valves and the seal rings.

39. Remove the camshaft position sensors. Refer to Camshaft Position (CMP) Sensor, removal & installation.

40. Loosen the camshaft sprocket bolts until the camshaft position exciter wheels freely rotate.

41. Remove the 13 M6 engine front cover bolts.

42. Remove the 2 M10 engine front cover bolts.

43. Remove the engine front cover.

➡**Removal of the timing chain is necessary to get access to the engine front cover gasket.**

44. Remove the camshaft timing chain. Refer to Timing Chain & Sprockets, removal & installation.

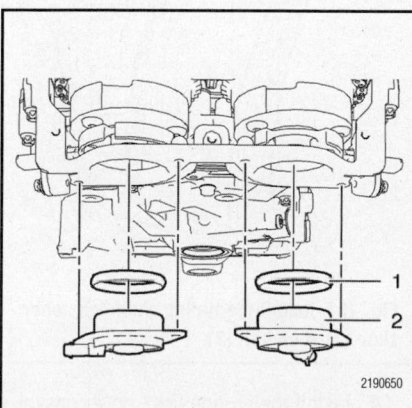

Fig. 124 Remove the M6 engine front cover bolts (1), the M10 engine front cover bolts (2), and the engine front cover (3)

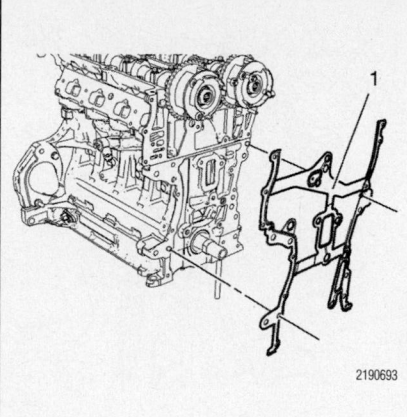

Fig. 125 Engine front cover gasket (1) removal

45. Remove the engine front cover gasket.

To install:

46. Install the crankshaft front oil seal, if necessary.

47. Install the oil pressure relief valve, if necessary. Tighten to 37 ft. lbs. (50 Nm).

48. Install the exhaust camshaft position sensor and the seal ring. Tighten the bolt to 53 ft. lbs. (6 Nm).

49. Install the intake camshaft position sensor and the seal ring. Tighten the bolt to 53 ft. lbs. (6 Nm).

50. Clean the engine front cover sealing surfaces on engine block and cylinder head.

➡**The thickness of the sealing bead should be 0.079 inch (2mm).**

51. Apply sealing compound to the appropriate areas and.

52. Install a NEW engine front cover gasket.

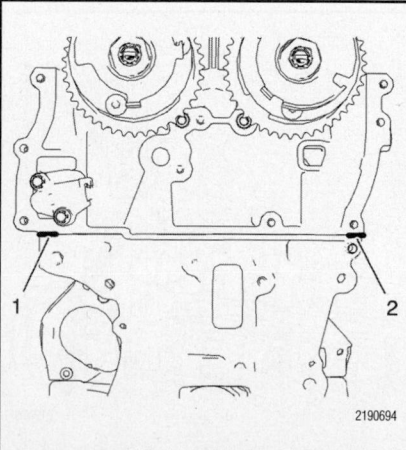

Fig. 126 Apply sealing compound to the areas shown (1) and (2)

53. Install the timing chain. Refer to Timing Chain & Sprockets, removal & installation.

➡**Mind the guide sleeves when installing the engine front cover. The complete installation procedure of the engine front cover should not take longer than 10 minutes.**

54. Install the engine front cover.

55. Install the 13 M6 engine front cover bolts.

56. Install the 2 M10 engine front cover bolts.

57. Tighten the 13 M6 engine front cover bolts to 71 inch lbs. (8 Nm).

58. Tighten the 2 M10 engine front cover bolts to 26 ft. lbs. (35 Nm).

➡**The engine should be adjusted and fixed in TDC position.**

59. Tighten the camshaft sprockets, install the upper timing chain guide and remove all special tools. Refer to Timing Chain & Sprockets, removal & installation.

60. Install the camshaft position sensors. Refer to Camshaft Position (CMP) Sensor, removal & installation.

✳✳ WARNING

The camshaft position actuator solenoid valves must be kept parallel to the engine front cover during removal and installation. The camshaft position actuator solenoid valves can be damaged if they become wedged or stuck during this process.

61. Install the 2 camshaft position actuator solenoid valves and the 2 seal rings by carefully and evenly pressing.

62. Install the 4 camshaft position actuator solenoid valve bolts and tighten to 71 inch lbs. (8 Nm).

63. The 2 camshaft position actuator solenoid valves should be installed in the correct positions.

64. Install the water pump and the water pump pulley. Refer to Water Pump, removal & installation.

65. Install the engine mount bracket.

66. Install the 3 NEW engine mount bracket bolts and tighten to 45 ft. lbs. (60 Nm), plus 45–60°.

67. Remove the engine lifter from the right engine lift bracket.

68. Install the engine mount.

69. Install the 2 engine mount-to-body bolts.

70. Install the engine mount nut.

71. Install the 3 NEW engine mount-to-engine mount bracket bolts and the 3 washers.

72. Tighten the 2 engine mount-to-body bolts and the engine mount nut to 46 ft. lbs. (62 Nm).

73. Tighten the 3 engine mount-to-engine mount bracket bolts to 37 ft. lbs. (50 Nm), plus 60–70°.

74. Remove the engine lifter from the engine lift bracket.

75. Install the camshaft cover. Refer to Valve Covers, removal & installation.

76. Install the air cleaner assembly. Refer to Air Cleaner, removal & installation.

77. Raise the vehicle.

78. Install the crankshaft balancer. Refer to Crankshaft Damper (Balancer), removal & installation.

79. Install the oil pan. Refer to Oil Pan, removal & installation.

80. Install the air conditioning compressor and power steering pump bracket.

81. Install the 3 air conditioning compressor bracket bolts and tighten to 16 ft. lbs. (22 Nm).

82. Install the air conditioning compressor-to-air conditioning compressor bracket.

83. Install the drive belt to crankshaft balancer and water pump pulley. Refer to Accessory Drive Belts, removal & installation.

84. Install the front wheelhouse liner.

85. Lower the vehicle.

86. Connect all electrical connectors.

87. Lower the vehicle

88. Connect the battery negative cable. Refer to Battery, removal & installation.

89. Fill the engine with the proper type and amount of engine oil.

TIMING CHAIN & SPROCKETS

REMOVAL & INSTALLATION

See Figures 127 through 132.

Special Tools
• EN-955-1 Fixing Pin from EN-955 Kit

1. Before servicing the vehicle, refer to the Precautions Section.

2. Remove the engine front cover with oil pump. Refer to Timing Chain Front Cover, removal & installation.

➡**If EN-955-1 fixing pin cannot be inserted, compress the timing chain tensioner further with the aid of a flat-bladed tool to allow complete insertion of the pin.**

3. Push the timing chain in direction to the timing chain tensioner and secure the tensioner with EN-955-1 fixing pin.

4. Remove the 2 upper timing chain guide bolts.

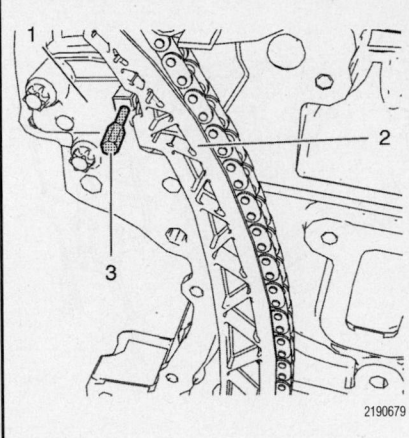

Fig. 127 Push the timing chain (2) in the direction of the timing chain tensioner (1) and secure the tensioner with EN-955-1 fixing pin (3)

5. Remove the upper timing chain guide.

6. Remove the 2 timing chain guide right side bolts.

7. Remove the timing chain guide right side.

8. Remove the timing chain tensioner shoe bolt.

9. Remove the timing chain tensioner shoe.

10. Remove the timing chain along with the crankshaft sprocket.

11. Remove the engine front cover gasket.

To install:

12. Clean the engine front cover sealing surfaces on the engine block and the cylinder head.

➡**The thickness of the sealing bead should be 0.079 inch (2mm).**

13. Apply sealing compound to the appropriate areas.

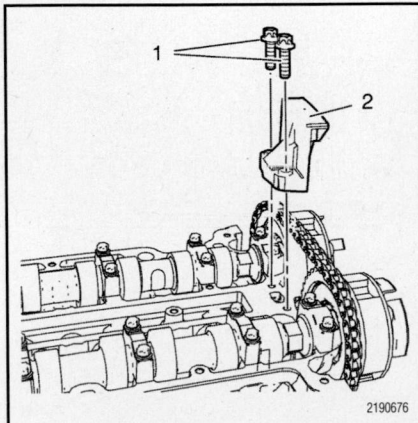

Fig. 128 Remove the upper timing chain guide (2) and bolts (1)

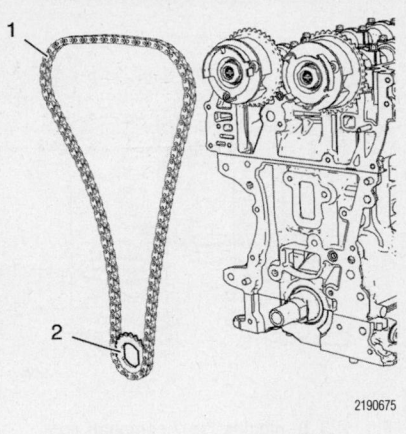

Fig. 129 Remove the timing chain (1) along with the crankshaft sprocket (2)

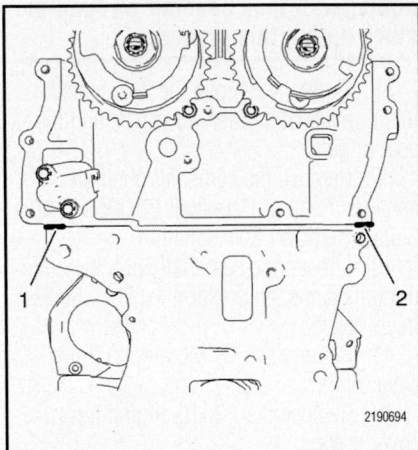

Fig. 130 Apply sealing compound to the areas shown (1) and (2)

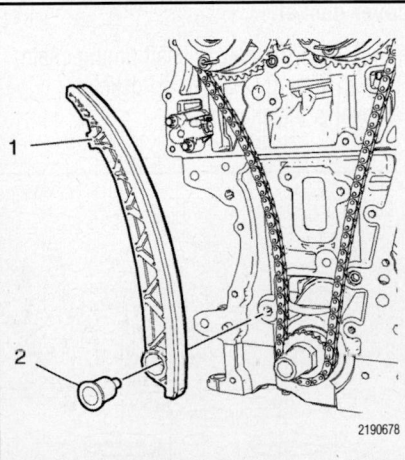

Fig. 131 Install the timing chain tensioner shoe (1) shoe bolt (2)

14. Install the engine front cover gasket.

15. Install the timing chain along with the crankshaft sprocket.

16. Install the timing chain tensioner shoe.

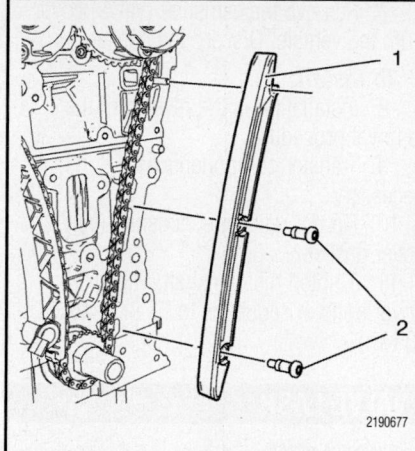

Fig. 132 Install the timing chain guide right side (1) and bolts (2)

17. Install the timing chain tensioner shoe bolt and tighten to 15 ft. lbs. (20 Nm).

18. Install the timing chain guide right side.

19. Install the 2 timing chain guide right side bolts and tighten to 71 inch lbs. (8 Nm).

20. Push the timing chain in the direction of the timing chain tensioner and remove EN-955-1 fixing pin.

21. Install the engine front cover with the oil pump. Refer to Timing Chain Front Cover, removal & installation.

Camshaft Timing Chain Inspection

See Figures 133 through 139.

Special Tools
- EN-952 Fixing Pin
- EN-953-A Fixing Tool
- EN-49977-100 Transmitter Disc Fixation

1. Before servicing the vehicle, refer to the Precautions Section.

2. Remove the ignition coil. Refer to Ignition Coil, removal & installation.

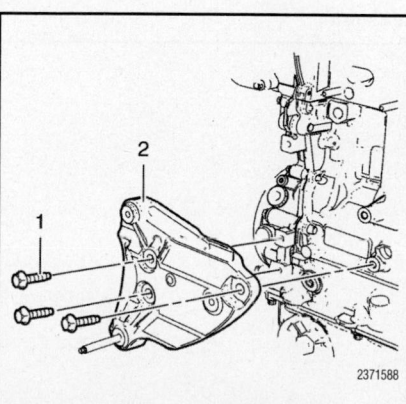

Fig. 133 Remove the air conditioning compressor bracket bolts (1) and the air conditioning compressor bracket (2)

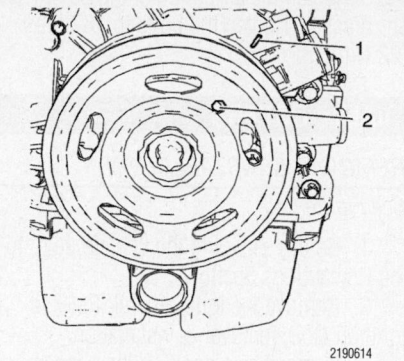

Fig. 134 Rotate the engine clockwise until the bore (2) in the crankshaft balancer aligns with the mark (1) on the engine front cover

3. Remove the camshaft cover. Refer to Valve Covers, removal & installation.

4. Remove the 3 air conditioning compressor bracket bolts.

5. Remove the air conditioning compressor bracket.

6. Rotate the engine clockwise until the bore in the crankshaft balancer aligns with the mark on the engine front cover.

7. Ensure that the camshaft grooves are visible. If the camshaft grooves are not visible, rotate the crankshaft 360°.

8. Remove the crankshaft bearing cap tie plate hole plug and the seal ring.

✳✳ WARNING

To ensure proper crankshaft Top Dead Center (TDC) alignment, the retention pin should fit easily through the bore in the crankshaft tie plate and into the crankshaft. Binding of the retention pin could affect proper engine timing.

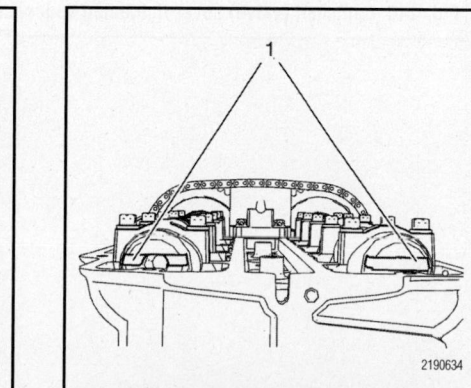

Fig. 135 Ensure that the camshaft grooves (1) are visible as shown. If the camshaft grooves are not visible, rotate the crankshaft 360°

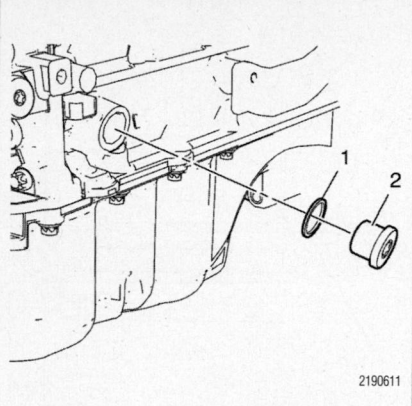

Fig. 136 Remove the crankshaft bearing cap tie plate hole plug (2) and the seal ring (1)

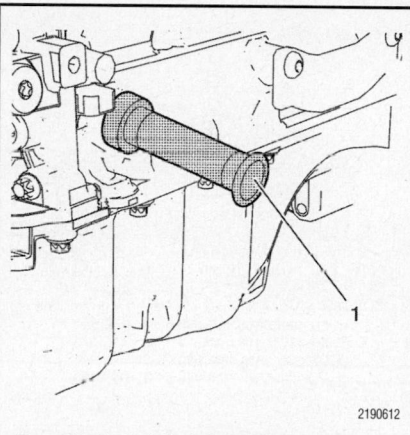

Fig. 137 Install the EN-952 fixing pin (1) in order to fix the crankshaft in the TDC position

9. Install the EN-952 fixing pin in order to fix the crankshaft in the TDC position.

➡The fixing tool should be installed completely to both camshaft grooves without high effort.

10. Install the EN-953-A fixing tool to the camshafts.

11. Install EN-49977-100 fixation in order to inspect the correct position of the camshaft position exciter wheels.

➡A wrong installation position is possible. Make sure that the fixation tool is installed without clearance to the cylinder head in the areas shown.

12. Tighten the bolts of EN-49977-100 fixation.

13. If EN-953-A fixing tool or EN-49977-100 fixation cannot be installed, the camshaft timing chain may be out of adjustment.

14. Remove the EN-49977-100 fixation.

15. Remove the EN-953-A fixing tool.

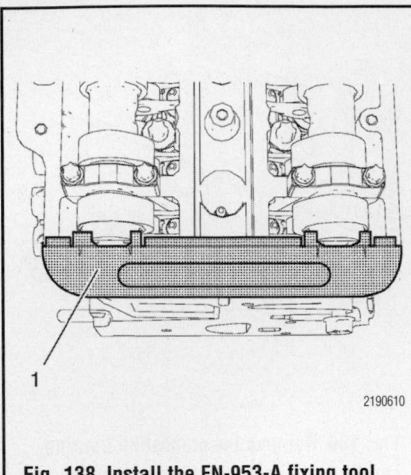

Fig. 138 Install the EN-953-A fixing tool (1) to the camshafts

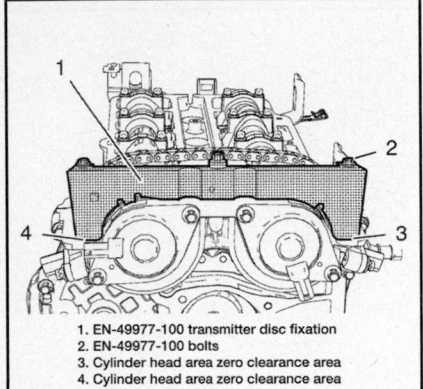

1. EN-49977-100 transmitter disc fixation
2. EN-49977-100 bolts
3. Cylinder head area zero clearance area
4. Cylinder head area zero clearance area

2190623

Fig. 139 EN-49977-100 fixation tool shown installed

16. Remove the EN-952 fixing pin.

17. Install the crankshaft bearing cap tie plate hole plug and seal ring and tighten to 30 ft. lbs. (40 Nm).

18. Install the camshaft cover. Refer to Valve Covers, removal & installation.

19. Install the ignition coil. Refer to Ignition Coil, removal & installation.

20. Install the air conditioning compressor bracket. Tighten the bolts to 16 ft. lbs. (22 Nm).

VALVE COVERS

REMOVAL & INSTALLATION

See Figure 140.

1. Before servicing the vehicle, refer to the Precautions Section.

2. Remove the ignition coil. Refer to Ignition Coil, removal & installation.

3. Remove or reposition the clips as necessary.

4. Disconnect electrical connectors as necessary.

5. Remove the oil level indicator.

6. Remove the camshaft (valve) cover bolts.

7. Remove the camshaft (valve) cover from the vehicle. Discard the gasket.

To install:

8. Installation is the reverse of the removal procedure.

9. Transfer components as necessary.

10. Do not reuse the camshaft (valve) cover gasket.

11. Tighten the camshaft (valve) cover bolts in sequence to 71 inch lbs. (8 Nm).

VALVE LASH

ADJUSTMENT

These engines utilize hydraulic lash adjusters; no adjustment is necessary.

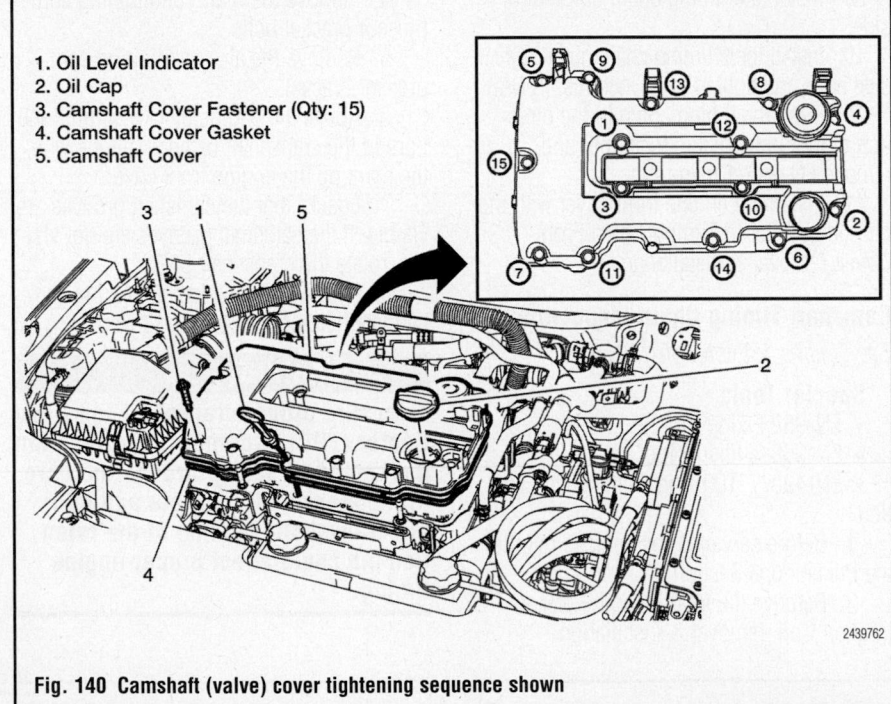

1. Oil Level Indicator
2. Oil Cap
3. Camshaft Cover Fastener (Qty: 15)
4. Camshaft Cover Gasket
5. Camshaft Cover

2439762

Fig. 140 Camshaft (valve) cover tightening sequence shown

ENGINE PERFORMANCE & EMISSION CONTROLS

COMPONENT LOCATIONS

See Figures 141 through 145.

Refer to the accompanying illustrations.

CAMSHAFT POSITION (CMP) SENSOR

LOCATION

See Figures 146 and 147.

Refer to the accompanying illustrations.

REMOVAL & INSTALLATION

See Figures 146 and 147.

1. Before servicing the vehicle, refer to the Precautions Section.
2. Remove the air cleaner assembly. Refer to Air Cleaner, removal & installation.
3. Disconnect the camshaft position sensor wiring harness plug.
4. Remove the camshaft position sensor bolt.
5. Remove the camshaft position sensor and the seal ring.

To install:

6. Install the camshaft position sensor and the seal ring.
7. Install the camshaft position sensor bolt and tighten to 71 inch lbs. (8 Nm).
8. Connect the camshaft position sensor wiring harness plug.

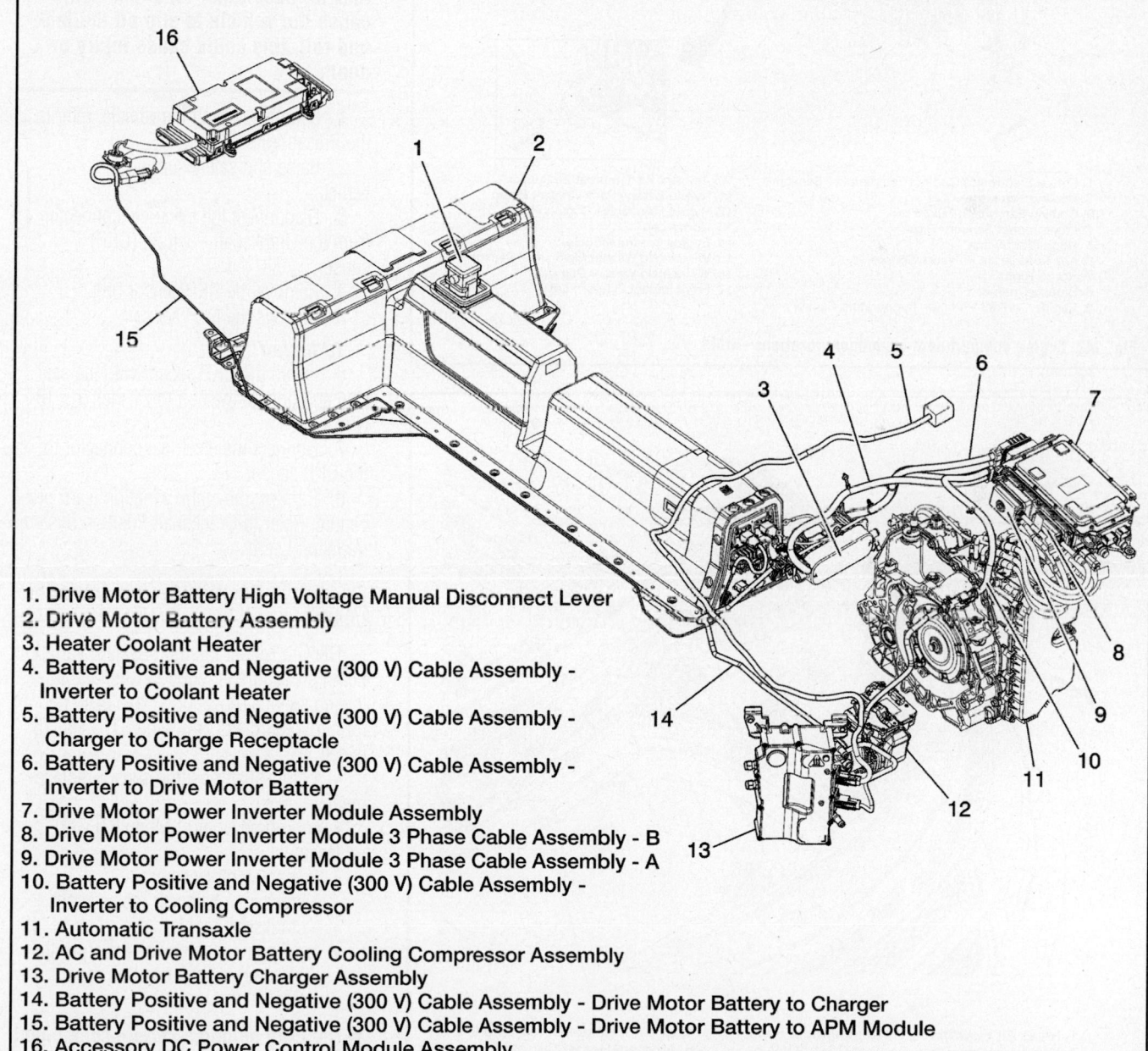

1. Drive Motor Battery High Voltage Manual Disconnect Lever
2. Drive Motor Battery Assembly
3. Heater Coolant Heater
4. Battery Positive and Negative (300 V) Cable Assembly - Inverter to Coolant Heater
5. Battery Positive and Negative (300 V) Cable Assembly - Charger to Charge Receptacle
6. Battery Positive and Negative (300 V) Cable Assembly - Inverter to Drive Motor Battery
7. Drive Motor Power Inverter Module Assembly
8. Drive Motor Power Inverter Module 3 Phase Cable Assembly - B
9. Drive Motor Power Inverter Module 3 Phase Cable Assembly - A
10. Battery Positive and Negative (300 V) Cable Assembly - Inverter to Cooling Compressor
11. Automatic Transaxle
12. AC and Drive Motor Battery Cooling Compressor Assembly
13. Drive Motor Battery Charger Assembly
14. Battery Positive and Negative (300 V) Cable Assembly - Drive Motor Battery to Charger
15. Battery Positive and Negative (300 V) Cable Assembly - Drive Motor Battery to APM Module
16. Accessory DC Power Control Module Assembly

2426945

Fig. 141 Hybrid control electronic component locations

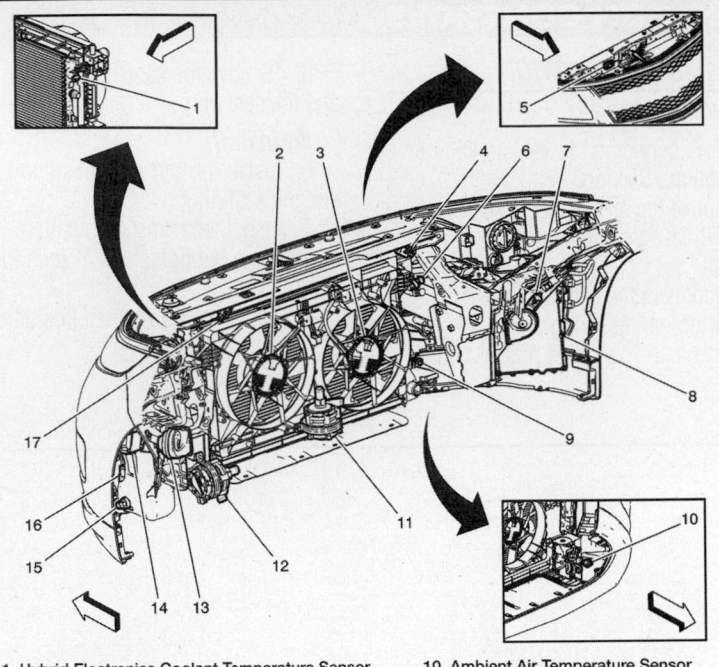

Fig. 142 Engine compartment component locations—front

1. Hybrid Electronics Coolant Temperature Sensor
2. Cooling Fan Motor - Left
3. Cooling Fan Motor - Right
4. Front Impact Sensor - Right
5. Hood Ajar Switch
6. A/C Refrigerant Pressure Sensor
7. Horn - Right
8. Battery Charger
9. Engine Coolant Radiator Temperature Sensor
10. Ambient Air Temperature Sensor
11. Hybrid Battery Pack Coolant Pump
12. Hybrid Electronics Coolant Pump
13. Horn - Left
14. Engine Control Module
15. Windshield Washer Fluid Level Sensor
16. Windshield Washer Pump
17. Front Impact Sensor - Left

2477058

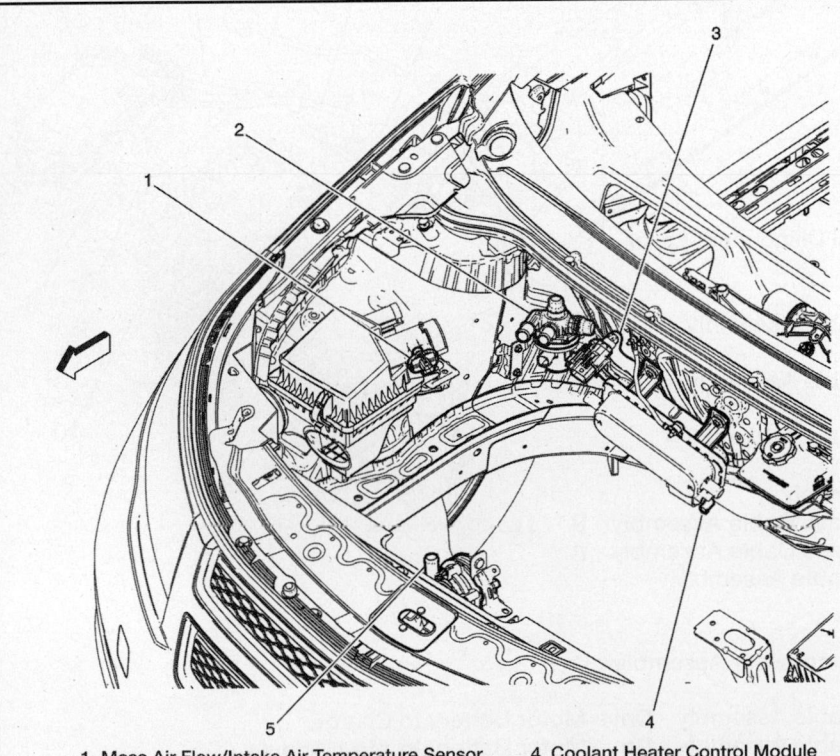

1. Mass Air Flow/Intake Air Temperature Sensor
2. Hybrid Battery Pack Coolant Control Valve
3. Coolant Heater Temperature Sensor
4. Coolant Heater Control Module
5. Auxiliary Heater Coolant Pump

2477049

Fig. 143 Engine compartment component locations—right side

CRANKSHAFT POSITION (CKP) SENSOR

LOCATION

See Figure 148.

Refer to the accompanying illustrations.

REMOVAL & INSTALLATION

See Figure 148.

✳✳ CAUTION

Do not use a service jack in locations other than those specified to lift this vehicle. Lifting the vehicle with a jack in those other locations could cause the vehicle to slip off the jack and roll; this could cause injury or death.

1. Before servicing the vehicle, refer to the Precautions Section.
2. Raise and safely support the vehicle.
3. Disconnect the electrical connector from the Crankshaft Position (CKP) sensor.
4. Remove the CKP sensor bolt.
5. Remove the CKP sensor.

To install:

6. Install the CKP sensor with the seal ring and tighten the bolt to 71 inch lbs. (8 Nm).
7. Connect the electrical connector to the CKP sensor.
8. Perform the crank variation learn procedure. Refer to Crankshaft Position System Variation Learn.

Crankshaft Position System Variation Learn

The Crankshaft Position System Variation Learn procedure is required when the following service procedures have been performed, regardless of whether DTC P0315 is set:

- A crankshaft position sensor replacement
- An Engine Control Module (ECM) replacement
- An engine replacement
- A crankshaft balancer replacement
- A crankshaft replacement
- Any engine repairs which disturb the crankshaft to crankshaft position sensor relationship.

➥The ECM monitors certain component signals to determine if all the conditions are met to continue with the Crankshaft System Position Variation Learn procedure.

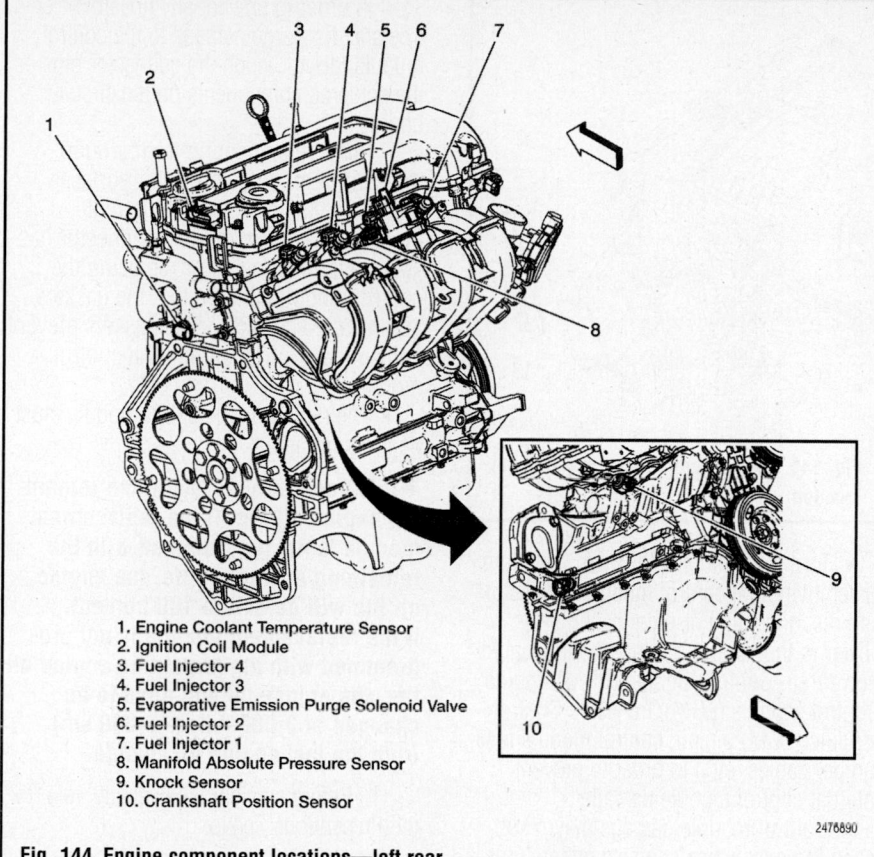

1. Engine Coolant Temperature Sensor
2. Ignition Coil Module
3. Fuel Injector 4
4. Fuel Injector 3
5. Evaporative Emission Purge Solenoid Valve
6. Fuel Injector 2
7. Fuel Injector 1
8. Manifold Absolute Pressure Sensor
9. Knock Sensor
10. Crankshaft Position Sensor

Fig. 144 Engine component locations—left rear

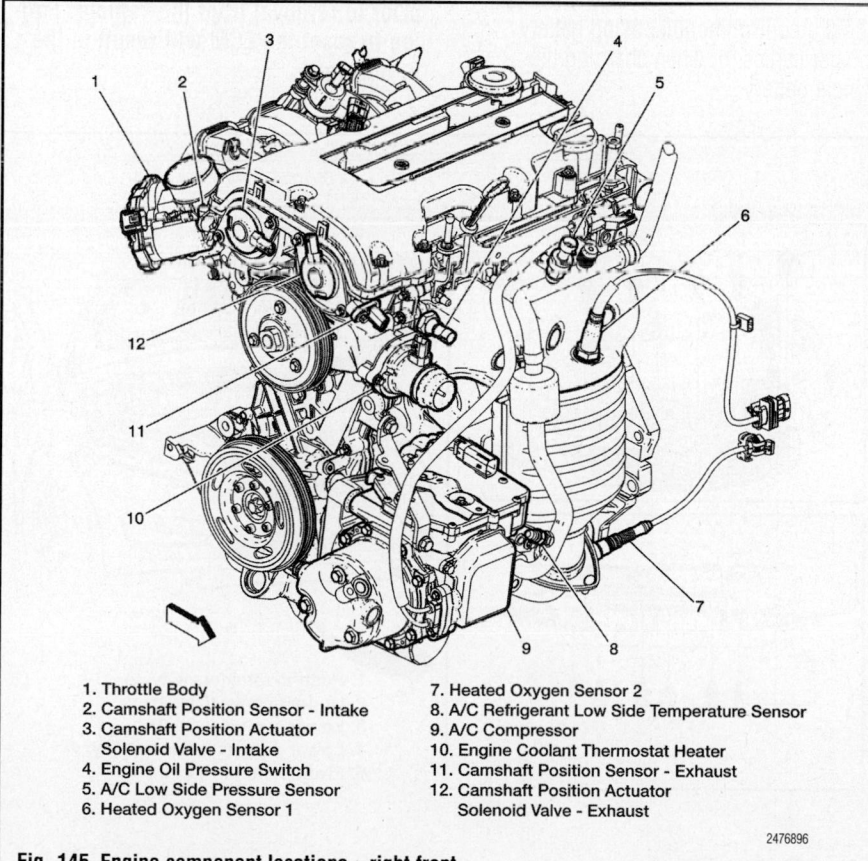

1. Throttle Body
2. Camshaft Position Sensor - Intake
3. Camshaft Position Actuator
   Solenoid Valve - Intake
4. Engine Oil Pressure Switch
5. A/C Low Side Pressure Sensor
6. Heated Oxygen Sensor 1
7. Heated Oxygen Sensor 2
8. A/C Refrigerant Low Side Temperature Sensor
9. A/C Compressor
10. Engine Coolant Thermostat Heater
11. Camshaft Position Sensor - Exhaust
12. Camshaft Position Actuator
    Solenoid Valve - Exhaust

Fig. 145 Engine component locations—right front

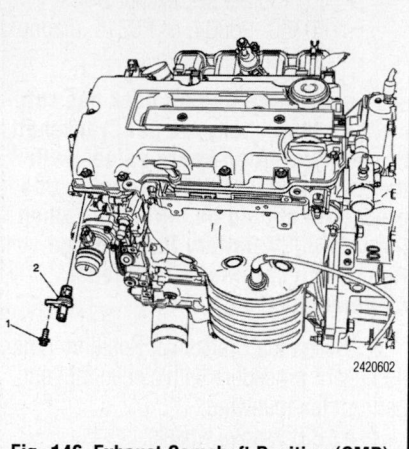

Fig. 146 Exhaust Camshaft Position (CMP) sensor (2) and bolt (1) location

Fig. 147 Intake Camshaft Position (CMP) sensor (2) and bolt (1) location

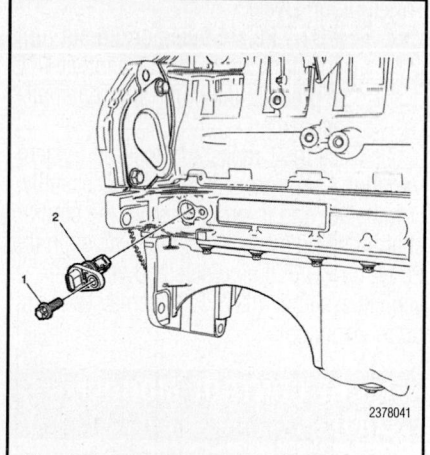

Fig. 148 Crankshaft Position (CKP) sensor (2) and bolt (1) location

1. Before servicing the vehicle, refer to the Precautions Section.

2. With the vehicle in Service Mode, observe the DTC information with a scan tool. Verify no other DTCs are set, except DTCs P0300–P0304, or P0315.

- If DTCs are set, except DTCs P0300–P0304, or P0315, diagnose and repair as needed.

➡To ensure the battery pack has sufficient state of charge to get Crankshaft Position Variation Learn values with the lowest engine noise present, this procedure should be performed when the Hybrid/EV Battery Pack Charge Remaining parameter is at least 40 percent.

3. Select the Crankshaft Position Variation Learn procedure with a scan tool and perform the following:
   a. Block drive wheels.
   b. Set parking brake.
   c. DO NOT apply brake pedal.
   d. Turn the air conditioning (A/C) OFF.
   e. When directed, apply and hold brake pedal for the duration of the procedure.
   f. Vehicle ON, engine running at operating temperature.
   g. The vehicle must remain in Park or Neutral.

➡The ECM controls the engine speed during the Crankshaft Position System Variation Learn procedure.

   h. Tap and release the accelerator pedal to start the Crankshaft Position Variation Learn procedure.

4. The scan tool displays Learn In Progress.

5. The scan tool displays Learn Successful.

6. Verify DTC P0315 ran and passed This Ignition Cycle.
   - If DTC P0315 failed or did not run This Ignition Cycle, or another DTC is present, diagnose and repair as needed.

7. Once the Crankshaft Position System Variation Learn procedure has successfully completed, and in order to store the crankshaft position system variation values in the ECM, turn OFF the vehicle and verify all vehicle systems are OFF. This may take up to 2 minutes.

ENGINE CONTROL MODULE (ECM)

LOCATION

See Figure 149.

Refer to the accompanying illustration.

REMOVAL & INSTALLATION

See Figures 149 and 150.

Note the following precautions before starting this procedure:

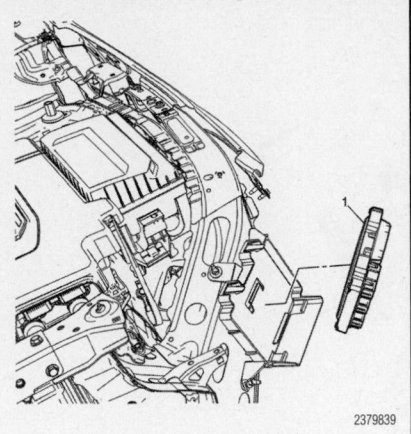

Fig. 149 Engine Control Module (ECM) (1) location

2379839

- Turn the ignition OFF when installing or removing the control module connectors and disconnecting or reconnecting the power to the control module (battery cable, Powertrain Control Module (PCM)/Engine Control Module (ECM)/Transaxle Control Module (TCM) pigtail, control module fuse, jumper cables, etc.) in order to prevent internal control module damage.

- Control module damage may result when the metal case contacts battery voltage. DO NOT contact the control module metal case with battery voltage when servicing a control module, using battery booster cables, or when charging the vehicle battery.

- In order to prevent any possible electrostatic discharge damage to the control module, do not touch the connector pins or the soldered components on the circuit board.

- Remove any debris from around the control module connector surfaces before servicing the control module. Inspect the control module connector gaskets when diagnosing or replacing the control module. Ensure that the gaskets are installed correctly. The gaskets prevent contaminant intrusion into the control module.

- The replacement control module must be programmed.

➡It is necessary to record the remaining engine oil life. If the replacement module is not programmed with the remaining engine oil life, the engine oil life will default to 100 percent. If the replacement module is not programmed with the remaining engine oil life, the engine oil will need to be changed at 3,000 miles (5,000 km) from the last engine oil change.

1. Before servicing the vehicle, refer to the Precautions Section.

➡If the ECM is to be replaced, the ECM must be RESET (prepared for removal) prior to removal from the vehicle. Failing to reset the ECM will result in the following:

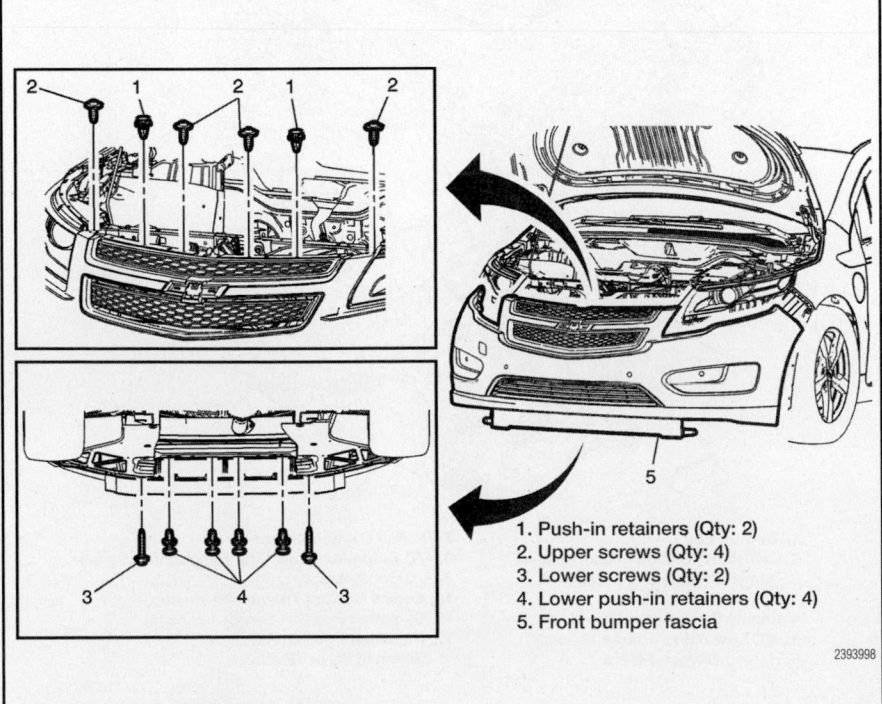

1. Push-in retainers (Qty: 2)
2. Upper screws (Qty: 4)
3. Lower screws (Qty: 2)
4. Lower push-in retainers (Qty: 4)
5. Front bumper fascia

2393998

Fig. 150 View of front bumper fascia

- Inability to test the ECM for warranty purposes
- Inability to use the ECM in other vehicles

2. Before servicing the vehicle, refer to the Precautions Section.

3. Prepare the ECM for replacement.

4. If the ECM is to be replaced, the following procedures must be performed:

a. Connect a scan tool to the vehicle and access the Service Programming System (SPS).

➡ **The Prepare Control Module for Removal function can only be performed when communication with the old control module is still possible.**

b. Before removing the old control module, perform the SPS function Prepare Control Module for Removal.

5. Using a scan tool, retrieve the percentage of remaining engine oil. Record the remaining engine oil life.

6. Disconnect the battery negative cable. Refer to Battery, removal & installation.

7. Remove the front bumper fascia.

8. Disconnect the 2 wiring harness plugs from the Engine Control Module (ECM).

9. Unclip the ECM bracket from the battery tray.

10. Remove the attaching nuts.

11. Remove the ECM from the ECM bracket.

To install:

12. Install the ECM to the ECM bracket.

13. Install the 4 nuts and tighten to 80 inch lbs. (9 Nm).

14. Clip the ECM bracket to the battery tray.

15. Connect the 2 wiring harness plug to the ECM.

16. Connect the battery negative cable. Refer to Battery, removal & installation.

17. Program the ECM.

18. Using a scan tool, perform the SPS function Engine Control Module Programming and follow the on-screen instructions.

19. Perform the SPS Function Immobilizer Learn.

20. Perform the SPS function Engine Control Module Configuration and Setup and follow the on-screen instructions. On the screen Control Module Configuration and Setup Function(s), select both control module Configuration/Reconfiguration and the appropriate control module Setup.

21. Clear any DTCs after completing the programming procedure.

22. Start and idle the engine.

ENGINE COOLANT TEMPERATURE (ECT) SENSOR

LOCATION

See Figure 151.

Refer to the accompanying illustration.

REMOVAL & INSTALLATION

See Figure 151.

✳✳ CAUTION

Allow sufficient time for the engine to cool before removing the ECT sensor. A hot engine may cause an excessive coolant loss or a personal injury.

1. Before servicing the vehicle, refer to the Precautions Section.

2. Partially drain the cooling system. Refer to Engine Coolant, Drain & Refill Procedure.

3. Disconnect the ECT sensor electrical connector.

4. Remove the retainer clip.

5. Remove the ECT sensor from the water outlet.

6. Installation is the reverse of the removal procedure.

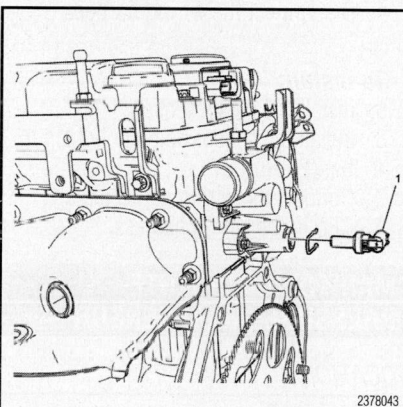

Fig. 151 Engine Coolant Temperature (ECT) sensor (1) and retainer clip (1) location (in water outlet)

HEATED OXYGEN (HO2S) SENSOR

LOCATION

See Figures 152 and 153.

Refer to the accompanying illustrations.

REMOVAL & INSTALLATION

See Figures 152 and 153.

Special Tools

- EN-6179 Heated Oxygen Sensor Remover/Installer

✳✳ CAUTION

In order to avoid being burned, do not service the exhaust system while it is still hot. Service the system when it is cool.

✳✳ CAUTION

Do not use a service jack in locations other than those specified to lift this vehicle. Lifting the vehicle with a jack in those other locations could cause the vehicle to slip off the jack and roll; this could cause injury or death.

1. Before servicing the vehicle, refer to the Precautions Section.

2. Disconnect the battery negative cable. Refer to Battery, removal & installation.

3. Disconnect the heated oxygen sensor wiring harness connector.

4. Remove the heated oxygen sensor using EN-6179 tool, or equivalent.

To install:

5. Installation is the reverse of the removal procedure.

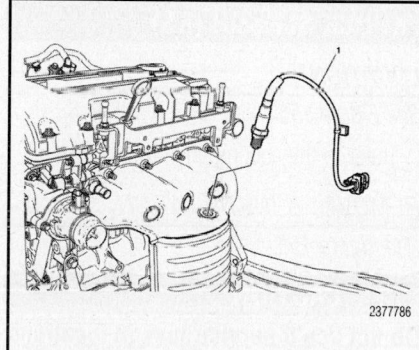

Fig. 152 Heated Oxygen (HO2S) sensor-1 location (1)

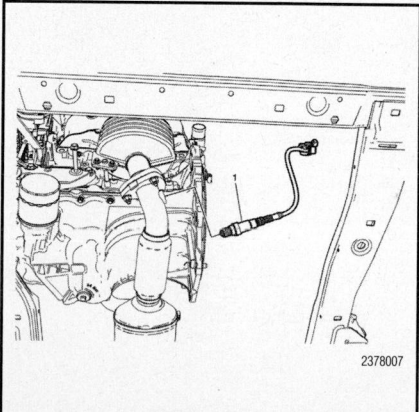

Fig. 153 Heated Oxygen (HO2S) sensor-2 location (1)

6. If reusing the heated oxygen sensor, coat the threads with anti-seize compound.

7. Tighten the heated oxygen sensor to 31 ft. lbs. (42 Nm).

8. After replacement of the heated oxygen sensor, use a scan tool to speed up learn functions.

INTAKE AIR TEMPERATURE (IAT) SENSOR

LOCATION

See Figure 154.

Refer to the accompanying illustration.

REMOVAL & INSTALLATION

See Figure 154.

1. Before servicing the vehicle, refer to the Precautions Section.

2. Disconnect the electrical connector from the Intake Air Temperature (IAT) sensor and pressure sensor.

3. Remove the IAT attaching bolt and the IAT sensor.

4. Installation is the reverse of the removal procedure.

KNOCK SENSOR (KS)

LOCATION

See Figure 155.

Refer to the accompanying illustration.

REMOVAL & INSTALLATION

See Figure 155.

✻✻ CAUTION

Do not use a service jack in locations other than those specified to lift this vehicle. Lifting the vehicle with a

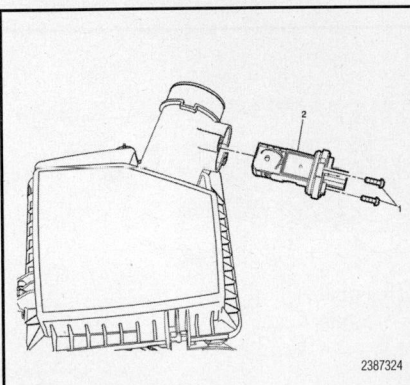

Fig. 154 Mass Airflow (MAF) and Intake Air Temperature (IAT) sensor (2) and bolt (1) locations

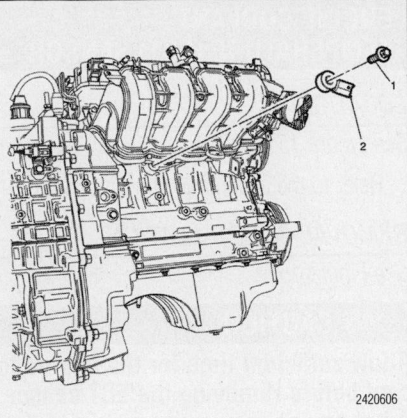

Fig. 155 Knock Sensor (KS) (2) and bolt (1) location

jack in those other locations could cause the vehicle to slip off the jack and roll; this could cause injury or death.

1. Before servicing the vehicle, refer to the Precautions Section.

2. Raise and safely support the vehicle.

3. Remove the sensor bolt.

4. Disconnect the wiring harness plug.

To install:

5. Install the knock sensor.

6. Install the sensor bolt and tighten to 15 ft. lbs. (20 Nm).

7. Connect the wiring harness plug.

8. Clip in the wiring harness.

MANIFOLD ABSOLUTE PRESSURE (MAP) SENSOR

LOCATION

See Figure 156.

Refer to the accompanying illustration.

REMOVAL & INSTALLATION

See Figure 156.

1. Before servicing the vehicle, refer to the Precautions Section.

2. Remove the fuel injection fuel rail. Refer to Fuel Injectors, removal & installation.

3. Disconnect the electrical connector from the Manifold Absolute Pressure (MAP) sensor.

4. Remove the MAP sensor bolt and the MAP sensor.

To install:

5. Installation is the reverse of the removal procedure.

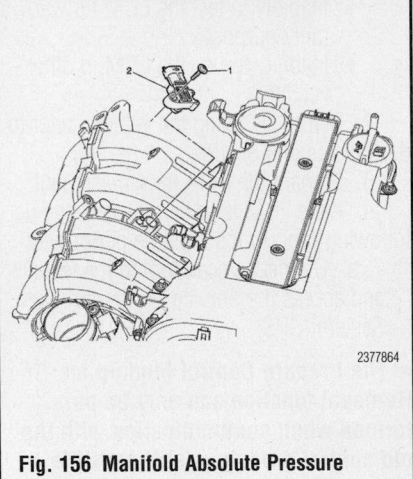

Fig. 156 Manifold Absolute Pressure (MAP) sensor (2) and bolt (1) location

6. Tighten the MAP sensor bolt to 44 inch lbs. (5 Nm).

MASS AIR FLOW (MAF) SENSOR

LOCATION

See Figure 154.

Refer to the accompanying illustration.

REMOVAL & INSTALLATION

See Figure 154.

1. Before servicing the vehicle, refer to the Precautions Section.

2. Disconnect the electrical connector from the Intake Air Temperature (IAT) sensor and pressure sensor.

3. Remove the IAT attaching bolt and the IAT sensor.

4. Installation is the reverse of the removal procedure.

OUTPUT SHAFT SPEED (OSS) SENSOR

LOCATION

See Figure 157.

Refer to the accompanying illustration.

REMOVAL & INSTALLATION

See Figure 157.

1. Before servicing the vehicle, refer to the Precautions Section.

2. Disconnect the sensor electrical connection.

3. Remove the sensor bolt.

➡**Compress the locking tabs on the plug to release it from the case and to avoid damaging the retainers.**

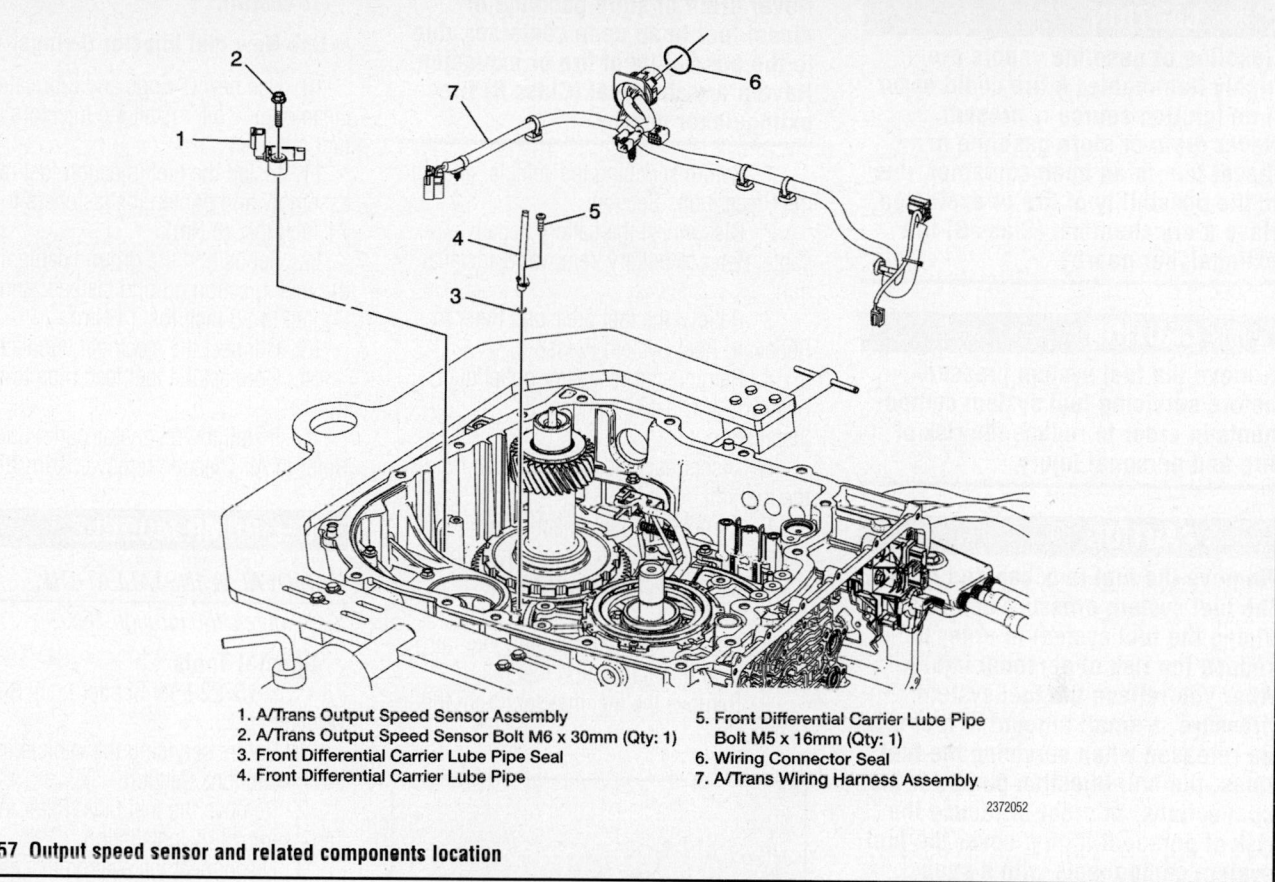

1. A/Trans Output Speed Sensor Assembly
2. A/Trans Output Speed Sensor Bolt M6 x 30mm (Qty: 1)
3. Front Differential Carrier Lube Pipe Seal
4. Front Differential Carrier Lube Pipe
5. Front Differential Carrier Lube Pipe
   Bolt M5 x 16mm (Qty: 1)
6. Wiring Connector Seal
7. A/Trans Wiring Harness Assembly

2372052

Fig. 157 Output speed sensor and related components location

4. Remove the sensor.
5. Discard the seals. They are not reusable.
6. Installation is the reverse of the removal procedure.
7. Tighten the sensor bolts to 80 inch lbs. (9 Nm).

THROTTLE POSITION SENSOR (TPS)

LOCATION

The Throttle Position (TP) sensor is located on the throttle body.

REMOVAL & INSTALLATION

The Throttle Position Sensor (TPS) is integral to the electronic throttle body. Refer to Throttle Body, removal & installation.

FUEL   GASOLINE FUEL INJECTION SYSTEM

FUEL SYSTEM SERVICE PRECAUTIONS

Safety is the most important factor when performing not only fuel system maintenance but any type of maintenance. Failure to conduct maintenance and repairs in a safe manner may result in serious personal injury or death. Maintenance and testing of the vehicle's fuel system components can be accomplished safely and effectively by adhering to the following rules and guidelines.

• To avoid the possibility of fire and personal injury, always disconnect the negative battery cable unless the repair or test procedure requires that battery voltage be applied.

• Always relieve the fuel system pressure prior to disconnecting any fuel system

component (injector, fuel rail, pressure regulator, etc.), fitting or fuel line connection. Exercise extreme caution whenever relieving fuel system pressure to avoid exposing skin, face and eyes to fuel spray. Please be advised that fuel under pressure may penetrate the skin or any part of the body that it contacts.

• Always place a shop towel or cloth around the fitting or connection prior to loosening to absorb any excess fuel due to spillage. Ensure that all fuel spillage (should it occur) is quickly removed from engine surfaces. Ensure that all fuel soaked cloths or towels are deposited into a suitable waste container.

• Always keep a dry chemical (Class B) fire extinguisher near the work area.

• Do not allow fuel spray or fuel vapors

to come into contact with a spark or open flame.

• Always use a back-up wrench when loosening and tightening fuel line connection fittings. This will prevent unnecessary stress and torsion to fuel line piping.

• Always replace worn fuel fitting O-rings with new Do not substitute fuel hose or equivalent where fuel pipe is installed.

Before servicing the vehicle, make sure to also refer to the precautions in the beginning of this section as well.

RELIEVING FUEL SYSTEM PRESSURE

Special Tools
• EN-34730-91 Pressure Tester

✳✳ CAUTION

Gasoline or gasoline vapors are highly flammable. A fire could occur if an ignition source is present. Never drain or store gasoline or diesel fuel in an open container, due to the possibility of fire or explosion. Have a dry chemical (Class B) fire extinguisher nearby.

✳✳ CAUTION

Relieve the fuel system pressure before servicing fuel system components in order to reduce the risk of fire and personal injury.

✳✳ CAUTION

Remove the fuel tank cap and relieve the fuel system pressure before servicing the fuel system in order to reduce the risk of personal injury. After you relieve the fuel system pressure, a small amount of fuel may be released when servicing the fuel lines, the fuel injection pump, or the connections. In order to reduce the risk of personal injury, cover the fuel system components with a shop towel before disconnection. This will catch any fuel that may leak out. Place the towel in an approved container when the disconnection is complete.

1. Before servicing the vehicle, refer to the Precautions Section.
2. Disconnect the battery. Refer to Battery, removal & installation.
3. Remove the protective cap from the test connection or fuel injector rail cap.
4. Relieve the fuel pressure, using the EN-34730-91 Pressure Tester.

FUEL FILTER

REMOVAL & INSTALLATION

A lifetime fuel filter is serviced as part of the fuel pump module. Refer to Fuel Pump Module, removal & installation.

FUEL INJECTORS

REMOVAL & INSTALLATION

See Figures 158 and 159.

✳✳ CAUTION

Gasoline or gasoline vapors are highly flammable. A fire could occur if an ignition source is present.

Never drain or store gasoline or diesel fuel in an open container, due to the possibility of fire or explosion. Have a dry chemical (Class B) fire extinguisher nearby.

1. Before servicing the vehicle, refer to the Precautions Section.
2. Disconnect the battery negative cable. Refer to Battery, removal & installation.
3. Relieve the fuel pressure. Refer to Relieving Fuel System Pressure.
4. Remove the resonator outlet duct. Refer to Air Cleaner, removal & installation.
5. Disconnect the fuel feed pipe from the fuel rail.
6. Remove the fuel injection ground fastener and reposition the ground cable.
7. Disconnect the electrical connectors.
8. Remove the fuel injection fuel rail fasteners and fuel injection fuel rail.
9. Remove the fuel injectors from the fuel rail.

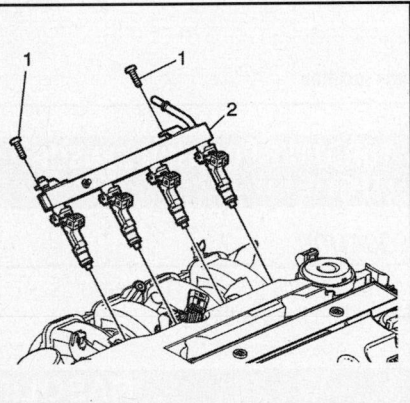

Fig. 158 Remove the fuel injection fuel rail fasteners (1) and fuel injection fuel rail (2)

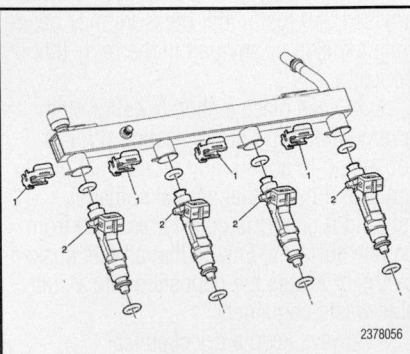

Fig. 159 Exploded view of fuel injector (2) and fuel injector clip (1) removal

To install:

➡ Use New fuel injector O-rings.

10. Use new O-rings and lubricate with clean engine oil. Install the injectors to the fuel rail.
11. Install the fuel injection fuel rail assembly and tighten the fasteners to 71 inch lbs. (8 Nm).
12. Reposition the ground cable, install the fuel injection ground fastener and tighten to 35 inch lbs. (4 Nm).
13. Connect the electrical connectors.
14. Connect the fuel feed pipe to the fuel rail.
15. Install the resonator outlet duct. Refer to Air Cleaner, removal & installation.

FUEL PUMP MODULE

REMOVAL & INSTALLATION

See Figures 160 through 163.

Special Tools
- CH 45722 Fuel Sender Lock Ring Wrench

1. Before servicing the vehicle, refer to the Precautions Section.
2. Remove the fuel tank. Refer to Fuel Tank, removal & installation.
3. Disconnect the evaporative emission and fuel lines.
4. Disconnect the electrical connector.
5. Using the CH 45722 wrench, remove the lock ring by turning counterclockwise.
6. Partially raise the fuel pump module and disconnect the vent valve connector.
7. Remove the fuel pump module and O-ring from the fuel tank.

To install:

8. Install a NEW O-ring and the fuel pump module.

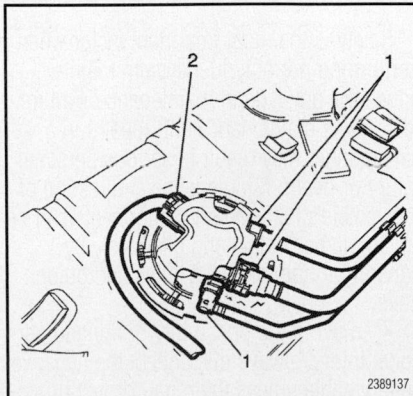

Fig. 160 Disconnect the evaporative emission and fuel lines (1) and the electrical connector (2) from the fuel pump module

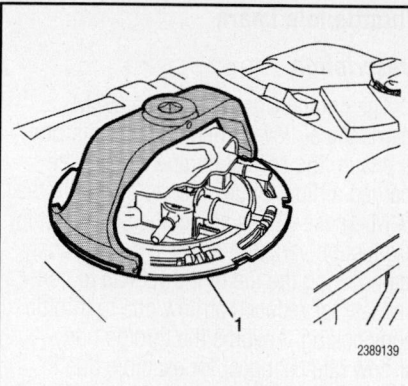

Fig. 161 Using the CH 45722 wrench to remove the fuel pump module lock ring (1)

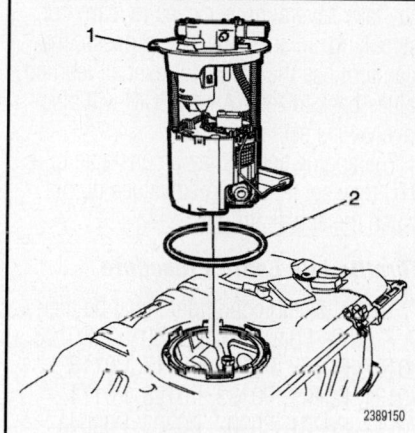

Fig. 162 Remove the fuel pump module (1) and O-ring (2)

9. Connect the vent valve connector.
10. Using the CH 45722 wrench, install the lock ring by turning clockwise.
11. Connect the electrical connector.
12. Connect the evaporative emission and fuel lines.
13. Install the fuel tank. Refer to Fuel Tank, removal & installation.

FUEL TANK

DRAINING

Special Tools
• CH-45004 Fuel Tank Drain Hose

> ✴✴ **CAUTION**
>
> Never drain or store fuel in an open container. Always use an approved fuel storage container in order to reduce the chance of fire or explosion.

> ✴✴ **CAUTION**
>
> Gasoline or gasoline vapors are highly flammable. A fire could occur

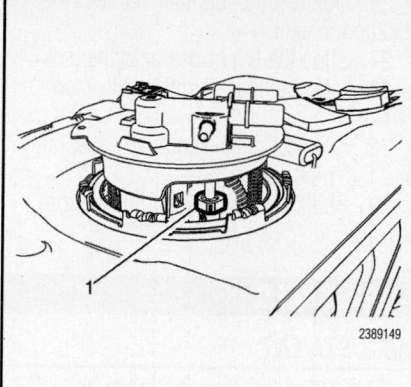

Fig. 163 Vent valve connector (1) location

if an ignition source is present. Never drain or store gasoline or diesel fuel in an open container, due to the possibility of fire or explosion. Have a dry chemical (Class B) fire extinguisher nearby. Failure to follow these precautions may result in personal injury.

> ✴✴ **CAUTION**
>
> Always wear safety goggles when working with fuel in order to protect the eyes from fuel splash.

> ✴✴ **CAUTION**
>
> Do not use a service jack in locations other than those specified to lift this vehicle. Lifting the vehicle with a jack in those other locations could cause the vehicle to slip off the jack and roll; this could cause injury or death.

1. Before servicing the vehicle, refer to the Precautions Section.
2. Disconnect the battery negative cable. Refer to Battery, removal & installation.
3. Remove the fuel fill cap.
4. Raise and safely support the vehicle.
5. Loosen the fuel fill pipe hose clamp at the fuel tank.
6. Separate the fuel fill pipe hose from the fuel tank.
7. Insert the CH-45004 drain hose into the fuel tank until the hose reaches the bottom of the fuel tank.
8. Use a hand or air-operated pump device in order to drain as much fuel as possible.
9. When fuel tank draining is complete, install the removed components in the reverse order of the removal procedure.

REMOVAL & INSTALLATION
See Figures 164 and 165.

> ✴✴ **CAUTION**
>
> Gasoline or gasoline vapors are highly flammable. A fire could occur if an ignition source is present. Never drain or store gasoline or diesel fuel in an open container, due to the possibility of fire or explosion. Have a dry chemical (Class B) fire extinguisher nearby. Failure to follow these precautions may result in personal injury.

> ✴✴ **CAUTION**
>
> Always wear safety goggles when working with fuel in order to protect the eyes from fuel splash.

> ✴✴ **CAUTION**
>
> Do not use a service jack in locations other than those specified to lift this vehicle. Lifting the vehicle with a jack in those other locations could cause the vehicle to slip off the jack and roll; this could cause injury or death.

1. Before servicing the vehicle, refer to the Precautions Section.
2. Disconnect the battery negative cable. Refer to Battery, removal & installation.
3. Drain the fuel tank. Refer to Fuel Tank, Draining.
4. Disconnect the evaporative emission and fuel pipe connectors.
5. Loosen the hose clamps and slide the filler tube away from the fuel tank.
6. Disconnect the fuel tank harness electrical connector.

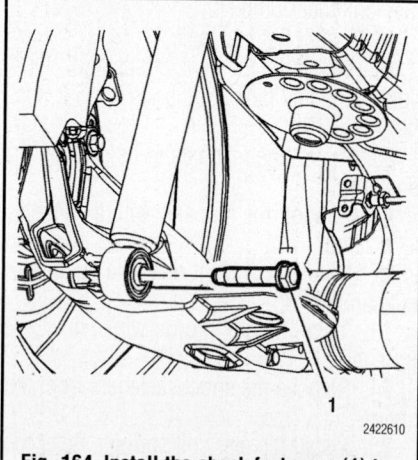

Fig. 164 Install the shock fasteners (1) to the shock without the rear coil spring

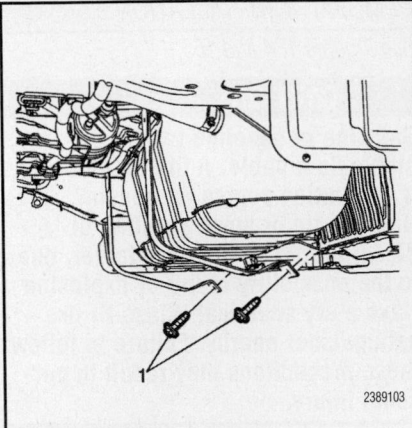

Fig. 165 Remove the fuel tank strap bolts (1) and reposition the fuel tank straps toward the back of the vehicle

7. Remove the rear coil springs. Refer to Rear Suspension, Coil Spring, removal & installation.

8. Reinstall the shock fasteners to the shock without the coil spring.

9. Support the rear axle with a suitable jack stand.

10. Remove the right lower wheel liner fasteners.

11. Remove and discard the right rear axle bushing nuts and bolts.

12. Reposition the rear axle rearward and up.

13. Support the fuel tank with a suitable jack.

14. Remove the fuel tank strap bolts and reposition the fuel tank straps toward the back of the vehicle.

15. Remove the fuel tank.

16. If replacing the tank, remove the fuel tank fuel pump. Refer to Fuel Pump Module, removal & installation.

To install:

17. If the tank was replaced, install the fuel tank fuel pump.

18. Install the fuel tank.

19. Install the fuel tank straps and tighten the fuel tank strap bolts to 15 ft. lbs. (20 Nm).

20. Return the rear axle to its original position.

21. Support the rear axle with a suitable jack stand.

22. Install NEW right rear axle bushing nuts and bolts.

23. Install the right lower wheel liner fasteners.

24. Remove the shock fasteners from the shock.

25. Install the rear coil springs. Refer to Rear Suspension, Coil Spring, removal & installation.

26. Connect the fuel tank harness electrical connector.

27. Slide the filler hose onto the tank and tighten the hose clamps to 35 inch lbs. (4 Nm).

28. Connect the evaporative emission and fuel pipe connectors.

29. Refill the fuel tank and check for leakage.

IDLE SPEED

ADJUSTMENT

The idle speed is controlled by the Engine Control Module (ECM). No adjustment is necessary.

THROTTLE BODY

REMOVAL & INSTALLATION

See Figure 166.

1. Before servicing the vehicle, refer to the Precautions Section.

2. Remove the air cleaner outlet duct. Refer to Air Cleaner, removal & installation.

3. Disconnect the throttle body wiring harness plug.

4. Remove the 4 throttle body bolts.

5. Remove the throttle body along with the throttle body seal ring.

To install:

6. Install the throttle body along with a NEW throttle body seal ring.

7. Install the 4 throttle body bolts and tighten to 71 inch lbs. (8 Nm).

8. Connect the throttle body wiring harness plug.

9. Install the air cleaner outlet duct. Refer to Air Cleaner, removal & installation.

10. Perform the throttle learn procedure. Refer to Throttle Idle Learn.

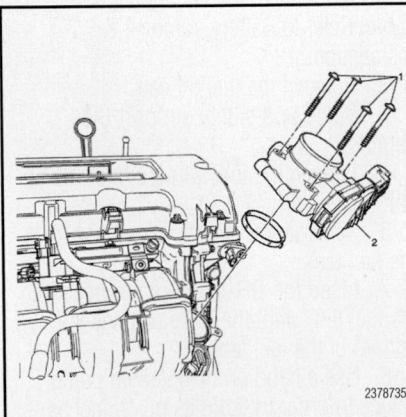

Fig. 166 View of throttle body (2), seal ring, and throttle body bolts (1)

Throttle Idle Learn

Description

The Engine Control Module (ECM) learns the airflow through the throttle body to ensure the correct engine speed. The learned airflow values are stored within the ECM. These values are learned to adjust for production variation and will continuously learn during the life of the vehicle to compensate for reduced airflow due to throttle body coking. Anytime the throttle body airflow rate changes, for example due to cleaning or replacing, the values must be relearned.

An engine that had a heavily coked throttle body that has been cleaned or replaced may take several drive cycles to learn out the coking. To accelerate the process, the scan tool has the ability to reset all learned values back to zero. A new ECM will also have values set to zero.

The engine speed may be unstable or a DTC may set if the learned values do not match the actual airflow.

Throttle Idle Learn Procedure

The following conditions must be met:
• DTCs P0101, P0102, P0103, P0106, P0107, P0108, P0116, P0117, P0118, P0121, P0122, P0123, P0128, P0171, P0172, P0201, P0202, P0203, P0204, P0222, P0223, P0300, P0351, P0352, P0353, P0354, P0601, P0604, P0606, P060D, P0641, P0651, P0697, P06A3, P1101, P1516, P2101, P2119, P2122, P2123, P2127, P2128, P2135, P2138, or P2176 are not set
• The engine speed is between 1,400–4,000 RPM
• The Manifold Absolute Pressure (MAP) is greater than 5 kPa
• The Mass Air Flow (MAF) is greater than 2 g/s
• The ignition voltage is greater than 10 volts

Reset Procedure—Performed after the throttle body is cleaned or replaced

1. Before servicing the vehicle, refer to the Precautions Section.

2. With the vehicle in Service Mode, perform the Idle Learn Reset with a scan tool.

3. With the engine running, monitor the TB Idle Airflow Compensation parameter with a scan tool. The TB Idle Airflow Compensation value should equal 0 percent.

4. Clear any DTCs.

Learn Procedure—Performed after the ECM is programmed or replaced

➡**Do NOT perform this procedure if DTCs are set.**

5. Run the engine for 3 minutes.

6. Monitor the Engine Speed with a scan tool.

7. The ECM will start to learn the new idle cells and the Engine Speed should start to decrease.

8. Turn the vehicle OFF for 60 seconds.

9. Start and run the engine for 3 minutes.

10. After the 3 minute run time, the engine speed should be normal.

11. Once the engine speed has returned to normal, clear any DTCs that were set.

HEATING & AIR CONDITIONING SYSTEM

BLOWER MOTOR

REMOVAL & INSTALLATION

See Figures 167 through 170.

1. Before servicing the vehicle, refer to the Precautions Section.

2. Disable the SIR system. Refer to Chassis Electrical, Air Bag (Supplemental Restraint System), Disarming the System.

3. Remove the instrument panel insulator panel.

4. Remove the inflatable restraint instrument panel lower module, if equipped.

5. Remove the instrument panel outer trim cover on the right side.

6. Remove the right floor air outlet duct.

7. Remove the blower motor wire harness connector.

8. Remove the blower motor cup bolts.

9. Remove the blower motor cup from the blower motor.

10. Remove the blower motor bolts.

11. Remove the blower motor from the heater case.

To install:

12. Install the blower motor to the heater case.

13. Install the blower motor bolts and tighten to 40 inch lbs. (5 Nm).

14. Install the motor blower cup to the blower motor.

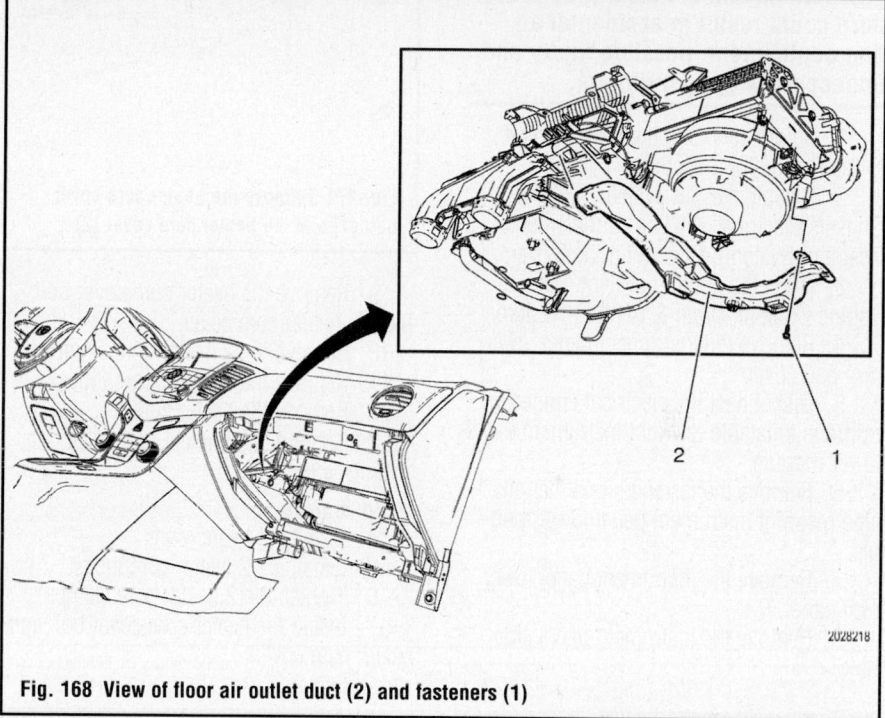

Fig. 168 View of floor air outlet duct (2) and fasteners (1)

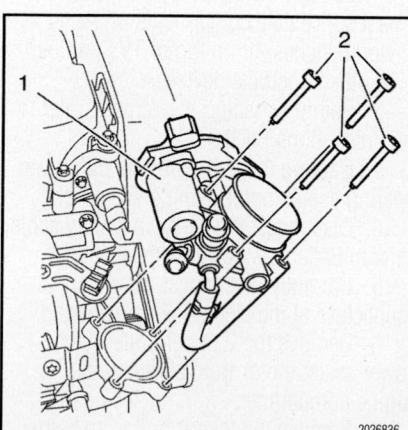

Fig. 167 View of instrument panel compartment (2) and fastening screws (1)

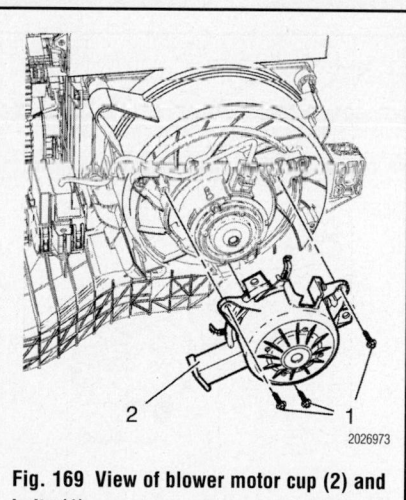

Fig. 169 View of blower motor cup (2) and bolts (1)

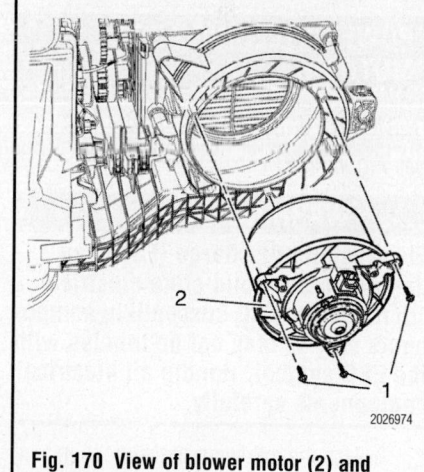

Fig. 170 View of blower motor (2) and mounting bolts (1)

15. Install the blower motor cup bolts and tighten to 23 inch lbs. (3 Nm).

16. Install the blower motor wire harness connector.

17. Install the right floor air outlet duct and tighten the bolt to 22 inch lbs. (3 Nm).

18. Install the instrument compartment. Tighten the screws to 22 inch lbs. (3 Nm).

HEATER CORE

REMOVAL & INSTALLATION

See Figures 171 and 172.

☀☀ CAUTION

These vehicles are equipped with an air bag system. The system must be disarmed before performing service on, or around, system components, the steering column, instrument panel components, wiring and sensors. Failure to follow the safety precautions and the disarming procedure could result in accidental air bag deployment, possible injury and unnecessary system repairs.

1. Before servicing the vehicle, refer to the Precautions Section.

2. Disable the SIR system. Refer to Chassis Electrical, Air Bag (Supplemental Restraint System), Disarming the System.

3. Drain the cooling system. Refer to Engine Coolant, Drain & Refill Procedure.

4. Remove the instrument panel lower trim pad cover.

5. Disconnect the electrical connector from the inflatable restraint instrument panel lower module.

6. Remove the fasteners and the inflatable restraint instrument panel lower module.

7. Remove the instrument panel lower trim panel.

8. Remove the instrument panel side bolt.

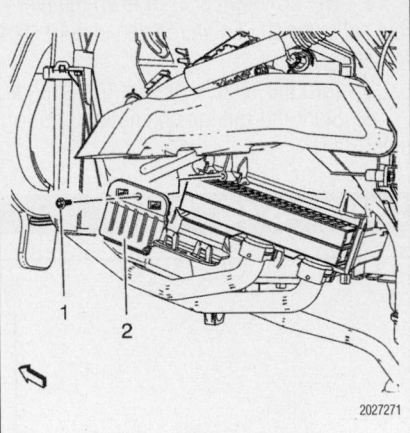

Fig. 171 Remove the heater core cover bolt (1) and the heater core cover (2)

9. Remove the heater core cover bolt and the heater core cover.

10. Remove the 2 heater core clamps.

11. Remove the 2 heater core tubes.

12. Remove the heater core.

13. Change the 2 heater core tube sealing rings.

To install:

14. Install the heater core.

15. Install the 2 heater core tubes.

16. Tighten the 2 heater core clamps.

17. Install the heater core cover bolt and heater core cover.

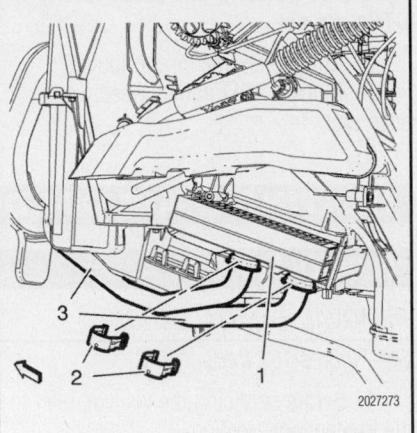

Fig. 172 View of heater core (1), heater core clamps (2), and heater core tubes (3)

18. Install instrument panel side bolt.

19. Install the instrument panel lower trim panel.

20. Install the inflatable restraint instrument panel lower module on the driver's side. Tighten the module fasteners to 89 inch lbs. (10 Nm).

21. Fill the cooling system. Refer to Engine Coolant, Drain & Refill Procedure.

22. Enable the SIR system. Refer to Chassis Electrical, Air Bag (Supplemental Restraint System), Arming the System.

STEERING

POWER STEERING ASSIST MOTOR

REMOVAL & INSTALLATION

See Figure 173.

☀☀ WARNING

Electrostatic Discharge (ESD) can damage many solid-state electrical components. ESD susceptible components may or may not be labeled with the ESD symbol. Handle all electrical components carefully.

1. Use the following precautions in order to avoid ESD damage:

   a. Touch a metal ground point in order to remove your body's static charge before servicing any electronic component; especially after sliding across the vehicle seat.

   b. Do not touch exposed terminals. Terminals may connect to circuits susceptible the ESD damage.

   c. Do not allow tools to contact

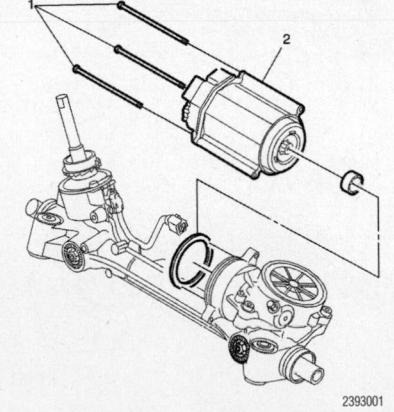

Fig. 173 Exploded view of power steering assist motor (2) and attaching bolts (1)

exposed terminals when servicing connectors.

   d. Do not remove components from their protective packaging until required to do so.

   e. Avoid the following actions unless required by the diagnostic procedure:

• Jumpering or grounding of the components or connectors

• Connecting test equipment probes to components or connectors. Connect the ground lead first when using test probes

   f. Ground the protective packaging of any component before opening. Do not rest solid-state components on metal workbenches, or on top of TVs, radios, or other electrical devices.

2. Before servicing the vehicle, refer to the Precautions Section.

3. Capture the data from the old power steering assist motor using a scan tool.

4. Disconnect the negative battery cable. Refer to Battery, removal & installation.

5. Carefully disconnect the electrical connectors of the electric power steering.

6. Remove the 2 upper bolts of the power assist motor from above in the engine compartment.

7. Remove the lowest bolt from below the vehicle.

8. Remove the power steering assist motor from the vehicle.

To install:

9. DISCARD the drive boot and use NEW ONLY.

10. Install the drive boot to the assist motor armature.

11. Align the drive boot on the assist motor armature to the steering gear.

12. DISCARD the O-ring and use NEW ONLY.

13. Lubricate the O-ring. Place the O-ring correctly in the groove on the motor housing.

> ☀☀ **WARNING**
>
> **This component is equipped with torque-to-yield fasteners. Install a NEW torque-to-yield fastener when installing this component. Failure to replace the torque-to-yield fastener could cause damage to the vehicle or component.**

14. Install the power steering assist motor with NEW bolts and tighten to 71 inch lbs. (8 Nm).

15. Attach all electrical connections.

16. Connect the battery negative cable. Refer to Battery, removal & installation.

17. Transfer the data from the old assist motor to the new power steering assist motor. Refer to Power Steering Control Module Programming and Setup.

18. Calibrate the steering angle sensor and learn the softend stops. Refer to Power Steering Control Module Calibration.

POWER STEERING GEAR

REMOVAL & INSTALLATION

See Figures 174 through 177.

Special Tools
- EN-45059 Angle Meter

> ☀☀ **WARNING**
>
> **With the wheels of the vehicle facing straight ahead, secure the steering wheel utilizing a steering column anti-rotation pin, steering column lock, or a strap to prevent rotation. Locking of the steering column will prevent damage and a possible malfunction of the SIR system. The steering wheel must be secured in position before disconnecting the following components:**

- The steering column
- The intermediate shaft(s)
- The steering gear

> ☀☀ **WARNING**
>
> **After disconnecting steering components, do not rotate the steering wheel or move the front tires and wheels. Failure to follow this procedure may cause the SIR coil assembly to become un-centered and cause possible damage to the SIR coil.**

1. Before servicing the vehicle, refer to the Precautions Section.

2. Disable the SIR system. Refer to Chassis Electrical, Air Bag (Supplemental Restraint System), Disarming the System.

3. Disconnect the battery. Refer to Battery, removal & installation.

4. Turn the front wheels to the straight forward position and secure the steering wheel from moving.

5. Remove the upper intermediate steering shaft bolt.

6. Remove and DISCARD the lower intermediate steering shaft bolts.

7. Remove the intermediate steering shaft.

8. Raise and safely support the vehicle.

9. Perform the following steps in order to gain access to the steering gear.

  a. Remove the front tire and wheel assemblies.

  b. Remove the exhaust front pipe.

  c. Remove the front compartment splash shield.

  d. Remove the engine shield, if equipped.

  e. Remove the front compartment insulator, if equipped.

  f. Disconnect the 2 steering linkage outer tie rods from the 2 steering knuckles.

  g. Disconnect the 2 stabilizer shaft links.

  h. Remove the transaxle mount bracket bolts.

  i. Support the drivetrain and front suspension frame.

  j. Remove the rear frame bolts.

  k. Remove the frame reinforcement bolts and the frame reinforcements.

  l. Lower the drivetrain and front suspension frame 2 inches (55mm).

> ☀☀ **WARNING**
>
> **Electrostatic Discharge (ESD) can damage many solid-state electrical components. ESD susceptible components may or may not be labeled with the ESD symbol. Handle all electrical components carefully.**

10. Use the following precautions in order to avoid ESD damage:

  a. Touch a metal ground point in order to remove your body's static charge before servicing any electronic component; especially after sliding across the vehicle seat.

  b. Do not touch exposed terminals. Terminals may connect to circuits susceptible the ESD damage.

  c. Do not allow tools to contact exposed terminals when servicing connectors.

  d. Do not remove components from their protective packaging until required to do so.

  e. Avoid the following actions unless required by the diagnostic procedure:

- Jumpering or grounding of the components or connectors
- Connecting test equipment probes to components or connectors. Connect the ground lead first when using test probes

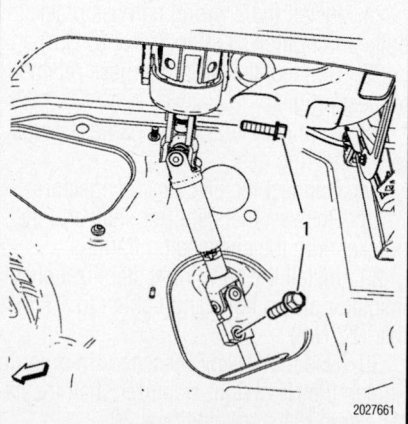

Fig. 174 Removing the upper and lower intermediate steering shaft bolts (1)

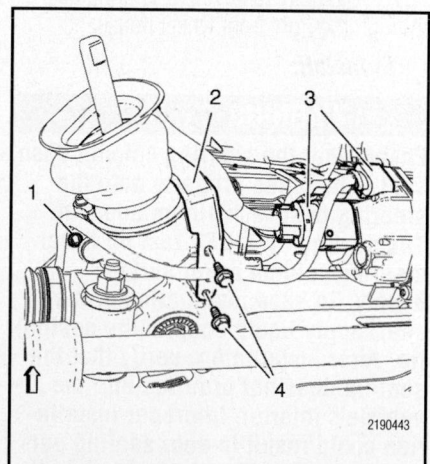

Fig. 175 Steering gear electrical connector locations

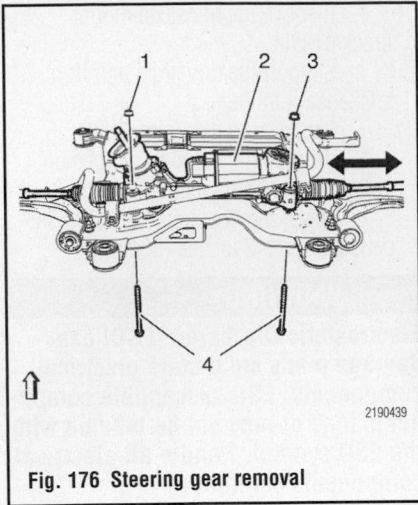

Fig. 176 Steering gear removal

f. Ground the protective packaging of any component before opening. Do not rest solid-state components on metal workbenches, or on top of TVs, radios, or other electrical devices.

➡ **Connector latches may be difficult to access.**

11. Disconnect the electrical connectors.

12. Use a suitable tool in order to carefully disconnect the 2 wiring harness plugs from the steering gear.

13. Remove the 2 wiring harness bracket bolts.

14. Remove the bracket.

15. Disconnect the wiring harness retainer from the steering gear.

16. Remove and DISCARD the 2 right stabilizer shaft insulator clamp bolts.

17. Reposition the stabilizer shaft in order to gain clearance for the steering gear.

18. Remove and DISCARD the 2 steering gear bolts and the nuts from front suspension frame.

19. Carefully remove the steering gear through the right front wheel house.

To install:

✳✳ WARNING

Ensure that the steering column dash seal is installed properly onto the steering gear rack pinion housing. The sealing lip MUST rest on lower steering column cover surface evenly. To ease installation of the seal, apply liquid soap to the sealing lip. After installation, verify that the seal lip does not protrude into the vehicle's interior. Improper installation could result in poor sealing performance and water intrusion into the vehicle.

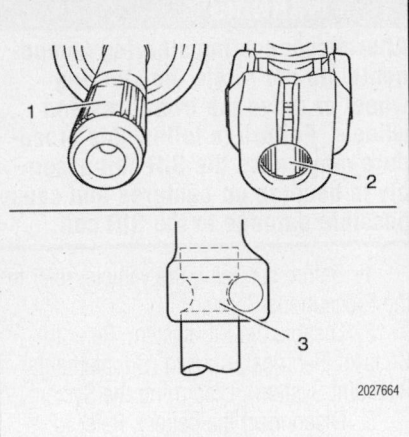

Fig. 177 The recess (2) of the splines in the universal joint must align precisely with the recess (1) of the splines on the steering pinion. The bore in the universal joint must align with the groove on the steering pinion (3)

➡ **Ensure the wiring routing is correct.**

20. Carefully install the steering gear through the right front wheel house and position the steering gear on the frame.

✳✳ WARNING

This component is equipped with torque-to-yield fasteners. Install a NEW torque-to-yield fastener when installing this component. Failure to replace the torque-to-yield fastener could cause damage to the vehicle or component.

21. Install the 2 NEW steering gear bolts and the 2 NEW nuts and tighten to 81 ft. lbs. (110 Nm).

22. Use the EN-45059 sensor in order to tighten the steering gear bolts and nuts an additional 150–160°.

23. Install the wiring harness bracket.

24. Install the 2 wiring harness bracket bolts and tighten to 80 inch lbs. (9 Nm).

25. Connect the wiring harness retainer to steering gear.

26. Connect the 2 wiring harness plugs to the steering gear.

27. Connect the electrical connectors.

28. Position the stabilizer shaft and the bracket onto the suspension frame.

29. Install the NEW right stabilizer shaft insulator clamp bolts and tighten to 16 ft. lbs. (22 Nm).

30. Use the EN-45059 sensor in order to tighten the NEW right stabilizer shaft insulator clamp bolts an additional 30°.

31. Perform the following steps.

a. Position the drivetrain and front suspension frame in the vehicle.

b. Install the frame reinforcements and the frame reinforcement bolts.

c. Install the rear frame bolts.

d. Install the transaxle mount bracket bolts.

e. Connect the 2 stabilizer shaft links.

f. Connect the 2 steering linkage outer tie rods to the 2 steering knuckles.

g. Install the front compartment insulator, if equipped.

h. Install the engine shield, if equipped.

i. Install the front compartment splash shield.

j. Install the exhaust front pipe.

k. Install the front tire and wheel assemblies.

32. Lower the vehicle.

33. Install the intermediate steering shaft.

34. Push the upper universal joint onto the steering column carefully.

35. Push down the lower universal joint onto the steering gear pinion.

36. Insert the lower bolt with thread lock compound.

➡ **The recess of the splines in the universal joint must align precisely with the recess of the splines on the steering pinion. The bore in the universal joint must align with the groove on the steering pinion.**

37. Push the universal joint onto the steering pinion carefully.

38. Apply thread lock adhesive to the upper shaft bolt.

39. Install the upper intermediate steering shaft bolt. Tighten the bolt to 25 ft. lbs. (34 Nm).

✳✳ WARNING

This component is equipped with torque-to-yield fasteners. Install a NEW torque-to-yield fastener when installing this component. Failure to replace the torque-to-yield fastener could cause damage to the vehicle or component.

40. Install the NEW lower intermediate steering shaft bolt. Tighten the bolt to 18 ft. lbs. (25 Nm), plus 180°.

41. Center the steering angle sensor using a scan tool.

42. Connect the battery. Refer to Battery, removal & installation.

43. Measure and adjust the front toe alignment.

44. Program the power steering control module. Refer to Power Steering Control Module Programming and Setup.

45. Center the steering angle sensor and learn the software end stops. Refer to Power Steering Control Module Calibration.

Power Steering Control Module Programming and Setup

Do not program or reprogram the electronic power steering control module unless directed by a service procedure or a service bulletin.

➡**This procedure applies to reprogramming of the existing steering gear or the initial programming if the complete steering gear assembly including the assist motor was replaced.**

1. Before servicing the vehicle, refer to the Precautions Section.

2. Connect a scan tool to the vehicle and access Service Programming System (SPS).

3. Perform the SPS function Electronic Power Steering—Programming and follow the on-screen instructions.

4. Perform the SPS function Electronic Power Steering—Setup and follow the on-screen instructions.

5. Perform the Steering Angle Sensor Centering and Software Endstop Learning procedure. Refer to Power Steering Control Module Calibration.

6. Clear DTCs after completing the programming and setup procedures.

Power Steering Control Module Replacement

During the procedures below, critical data is retrieved from vehicle components and stored in the scan tool computer's hard drive. This data is needed during the programming and setup sequences. Ensure the same scan tool is used and capable of reading, storing, and writing the vehicle's system data.

1. Before servicing the vehicle, refer to the Precautions Section.

2. Connect a scan tool to the vehicle and access Service Programming System (SPS).

➡**The next step copies the worm gear wear counter data from the power steering control module PRIOR to the module's removal and stores it on the scan tool computer's hard drive. AFTER completing the step, the power steering control module can be removed and replaced.**

3. Perform the SPS function Electronic Power Steering—Prepare Control Module for Removal and follow the on-screen instructions.

4. Replace the Power Steering Assist Motor containing the Power Steering Control Module.

➡**The next two steps will transfer the vehicle's critical data, including the worm gear wear counter data saved earlier, back to the vehicle components.**

5. With the Power Steering Assist Motor replaced and reconnected, using the same scan tool, perform the SPS function Electronic Power Steering—Programming and follow the on-screen instructions.

6. Perform the SPS function Electronic Power Steering—Setup and follow the on-screen instructions.

7. Perform the Steering Angle Sensor Centering and Software Endstop Learning procedure. Refer to Power Steering Control Module Calibration.

8. Clear DTCs after completing the programming and setup procedures.

Power Steering Control Module Calibration

☀ CAUTION

An inaccurate or not centered steering angle sensor could limit the operation of the Electric Power Steering (EPS) and result in personal injury.

Centering of the steering angle sensor and software endstop learning might be required after certain service procedures are performed. Some of these procedures are as follows:

- Steering angle sensor replacement
- Steering gear replacement
- Power steering assist motor replacement
- Steering column replacement
- Steering linkage inner tie rod replacement
- Steering linkage outer tie rod replacement

➡**It is necessary to perform the steering angle sensor centering BEFORE the software endstop learning.**

Steering Angle Sensor Centering

The following conditions should be met: Front axle measured and set, engine running, vehicle speed 0 MPH (0 km/h), and the internal steering angle sensor is activated.

1. Before servicing the vehicle, refer to the Precautions Section.

2. Using the steering wheel, align the front wheels in the center forward position.

3. Using a scan tool, perform the Configuration/Reset Functions, Steering Wheel Angle Sensor Centering procedure.

4. Steer from the center position slowly 90° to the left.

5. Steer slowly back to the center position and then slowly 90° to the right.

6. Steer slowly back to the center position.

7. Perform the steering movements again.

8. The centering procedure is completed.

Software Endstop Learning

The following conditions should be met: Front axle measured and set, vehicle speed 0 MPH (0 km/h), internal steering angle sensor is calibrated or external steering angle sensor sends a valid CAN signal.

1. Before servicing the vehicle, refer to the Precautions Section.

2. Using a scan tool, perform the Configuration/Reset Functions, Power Steering Softstops Reset procedure and follow the on-screen instructions.

3. Using a scan tool, perform the Configuration/Reset Functions, Power Steering Softstops Learn procedure and follow the on-screen instructions.

4. The software endstop learning procedure is completed.

CONTROL LINKS

REMOVAL & INSTALLATION

See Figure 178.

1. Before servicing the vehicle, refer to the Precautions Section.
2. Raise and safely support the vehicle.
3. Remove the tire and wheel assembly.
4. Using the proper size Allen® wrench, hold the stabilizer shaft link ball stud while removing the stabilizer shaft nut.
5. Remove and discard the nut. DO NOT re-use the nut, replace with NEW only.
6. Remove the stabilizer shaft control link.

To install:

✳✳ WARNING

This component is equipped with torque-to-yield fasteners. Install a NEW torque-to-yield fastener when installing this component. Failure to replace the torque-to-yield fastener could cause damage to the vehicle or component.

7. Installation is the reverse of the removal procedure.
8. Tighten the stabilizer shaft link nuts to 48 ft. lbs. (65 Nm).

LOWER BALL JOINT

REMOVAL & INSTALLATION

Clean and inspect the ball joint seal for cuts or tears. If the ball joint seal is damaged, replace the lower control arm. Refer to Lower Control Arm, removal & installation.

LOWER CONTROL ARM

REMOVAL AND & INSTALLATION

See Figures 179 and 180.

Special Tools
- EN-45059 Torque Angle Sensor Kit

1. Before servicing the vehicle, refer to the Precautions Section.
2. Raise and safely support the vehicle.
3. Remove the tire and wheel.
4. If equipped, remove the front compartment insulator.
5. Remove the wheel speed sensor wiring harness from the control arm and steering knuckle.
6. If servicing the right lower control arm, reposition the heater water auxiliary pump and bracket to the side. DO NOT drain the cooling system.

✳✳ WARNING

Do not pry in such a way that the ball joint seal is contacted. Damage to the seal may result.

7. Separate the lower control arm from the knuckle.
8. Remove the front lower control arm nut and bolt. DISCARD the bolt.
9. Remove the rear lower control arm bushing nuts and bolts. DISCARD the bolts.
10. Remove the lower control arm from the front frame.

To install:

11. Position the lower control arm in the cradle.
12. Install and hand tighten the rear lower control arm bushing nuts and NEW bolts.
13. Install and hand tighten the front lower control arm nut and NEW bolt.

✳✳ WARNING

This component is equipped with torque-to-yield fasteners. Install NEW torque-to-yield fasteners when installing this component. Failure to replace the torque-to-yield fasteners could cause damage to the vehicle or component.

14. Support the lower control arm with a hydraulic jack and lift the control arm to the proper trim height inspection. Use the EN-45059 Torque Angle Sensor Kit, or equivalent, to tighten the bolts and nuts.
15. Tighten the front lower control arm bolt to 52 ft. lbs. (70 Nm), plus 85°.
16. Tighten the rear bushing-to-frame bolts to 52 ft. lbs. (70 Nm), plus 85°.
17. Remove the hydraulic jack.
18. Install the NEW ball joint to knuckle bolt and nut and tighten to 22 ft. lbs. (30 Nm), plus 60–75°.
19. Ensure that the ball joint boot is properly seated between the lower control arm and the knuckle.
20. Install the front compartment insulator.
21. Install the tire and wheel assembly. Tighten the wheel nuts in a star pattern to 103 ft. lbs. (140 Nm).
22. Lower the vehicle.
23. Check and adjust the front camber and front end alignment, as needed.

CONTROL ARM BUSHING REPLACEMENT

See Figure 181.

Special Tools
- EN-45059 Torque Angle Sensor Kit

1. Before servicing the vehicle, refer to the Precautions Section.

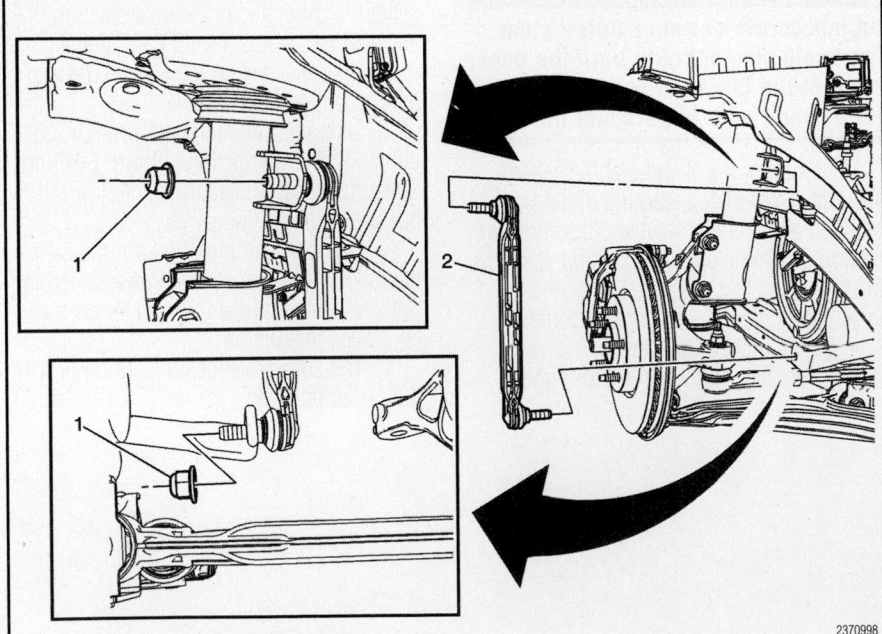

2370998

Fig. 178 View of stabilizer shaft control link (2) and nuts (1)

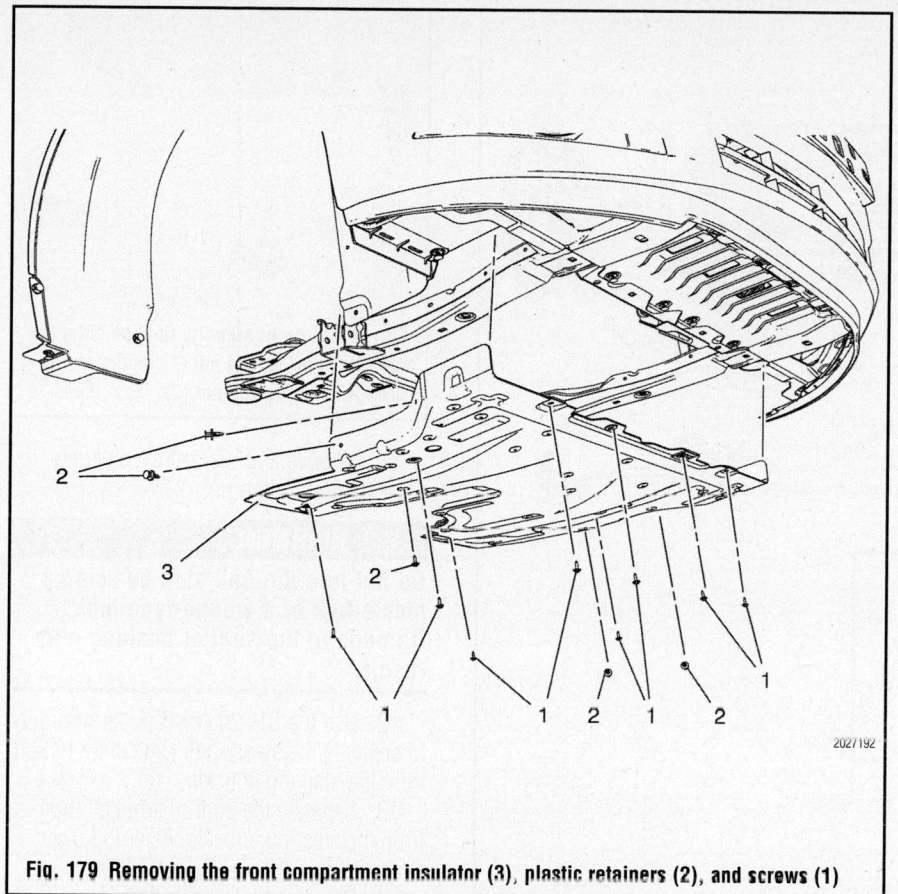

Fig. 179 Removing the front compartment insulator (3), plastic retainers (2), and screws (1)

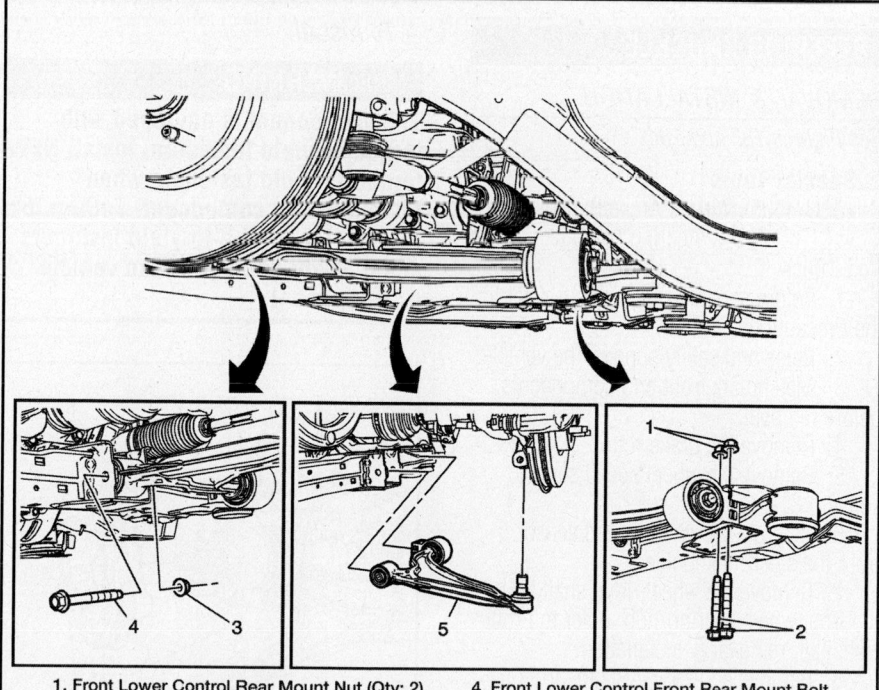

1. Front Lower Control Rear Mount Nut (Qty: 2)
2. Front Lower Control Rear Mount Bolt (Qty: 2)
3. Front Lower Control Front Mount Nut
4. Front Lower Control Front Rear Mount Bolt
5. Front Lower Control Arm

Fig. 180 Exploded view of lower control arm—front suspension

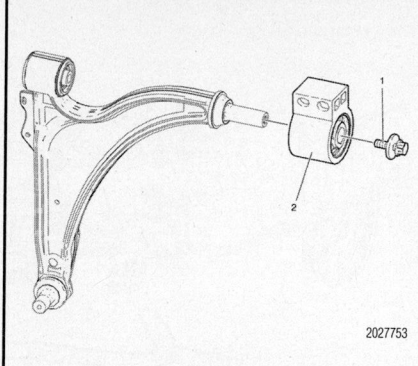

Fig. 181 Lower control arm rear bushing (2) and bushing bolt (1)

2. Raise and support the vehicle.
3. Remove the tire and wheel.
4. Remove the front compartment insulator.
5. Remove the lower control arm. Refer to Lower Control Arm, removal & installation.
6. Remove the bushing bolt and the lower control arm bushing.

To install:

> ❉❉❉ **WARNING**
>
> **This component is equipped with torque-to-yield fasteners. Install NEW torque-to-yield fasteners when installing this component. Failure to replace the torque-to-yield fasteners could cause damage to the vehicle or component.**

7. Install and hand tighten the NEW bushing bolt. Do NOT reuse an old bolt.
8. Install the lower control arm to the vehicle. Refer to Lower Control Arm, removal & installation.
9. Support the lower control arm with a hydraulic jack and lift the control arm into the neutral position.
10. Tighten the lower control arm bushing bolt to 41 ft. lbs. (55 Nm), plus 100°.

STABILIZER BAR

REMOVAL & INSTALLATION

See Figure 182.

1. Before servicing the vehicle, refer to the Precautions Section.
2. Raise and safely support the vehicle.
3. Remove the stabilizer shaft (bar) link from the stabilizer shaft. Refer to Control Links, removal & installation.
4. Lower the drivetrain and front suspension frame assembly.

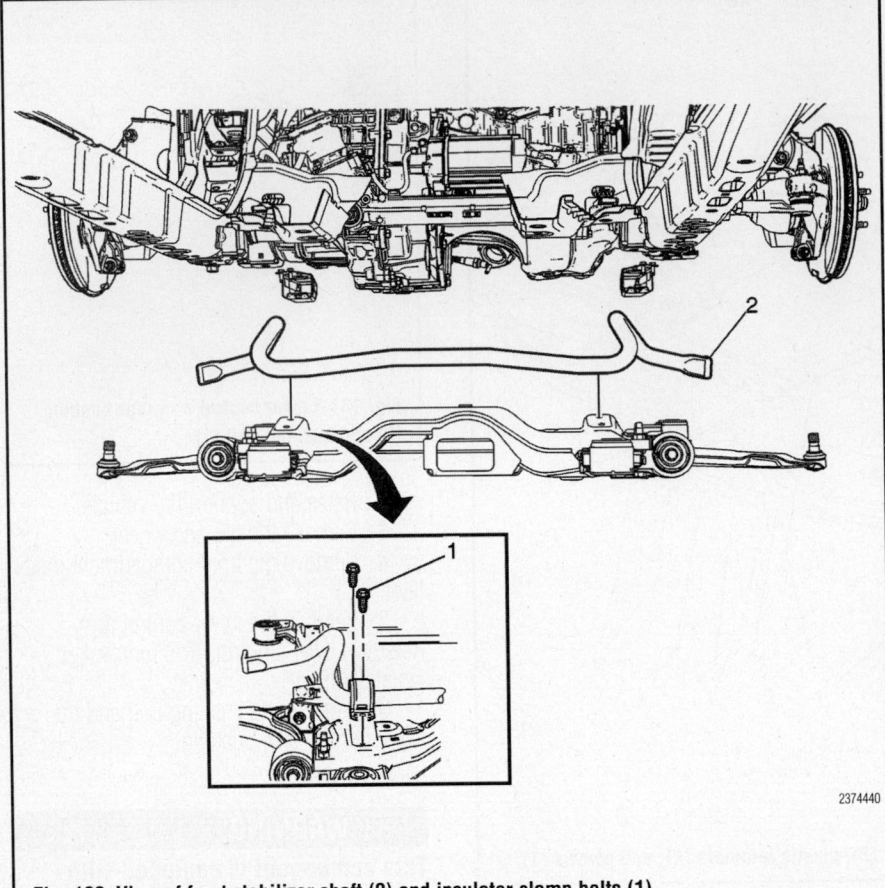

Fig. 182 View of front stabilizer shaft (2) and insulator clamp bolts (1)

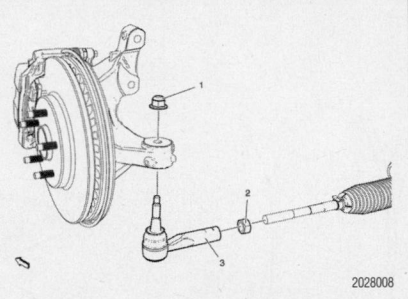

Fig. 183 View of steering linkage outer tie rod (3), outer tie rod nut (1), and steering linkage inner tie rod nut (2)

5. Lower the front suspension frame assembly enough to gain access to the stabilizer shaft insulator bolts.

6. Remove the stabilizer shaft insulator clamp bolts.

7. Remove the stabilizer shaft from the vehicle.

To install:

✷✷ WARNING

This component is equipped with torque-to-yield fasteners. Install NEW torque-to-yield fasteners when installing this component. Failure to replace the torque-to-yield fasteners could cause damage to the vehicle or component.

➡The stabilizer shaft insulator and the clamps are serviced with the stabilizer shaft. They are not serviced separately.

8. Install the stabilizer shaft and tighten the insulator bolts:

   a. Step 1: Tighten to 16 ft. lbs. (22 Nm).

   b. Step 2: Tighten an additional 40°.

STEERING KNUCKLE

REMOVAL & INSTALLATION

See Figures 183 and 184.

Special Tools
• EN-45059 Torque Angle Sensor Kit
• CH-24319-B Steering Linkage and Tie Rod Puller

1. Before servicing the vehicle, refer to the Precautions Section.

2. Raise and safely support the vehicle.

3. Matchmark front end components before removal.

4. Remove the brake rotor.

5. Remove the wheel speed sensor screw.

6. Remove the wheel speed sensor from the steering knuckle.

7. Remove the wheel drive shaft from the front wheel bearing/hub. Refer to Front Halfshaft, removal & installation.

8. Remove and DISCARD the front wheel bearing/hub bolts.

9. Remove the front wheel bearing/hub and front brake shield from the steering knuckle.

10. Use paint in order to place match marks on the steering linkage inner tie rod nut and on the steering linkage inner tie rod.

11. Remove and discard the steering linkage outer tie rod nut.

✷✷ WARNING

Do not free the ball stud by using a pickle fork or a wedge-type tool. Damage to the seal or bushing may result.

12. Use the CH-24319-B puller in order to separate the steering linkage outer tie rod from the steering knuckle.

13. Separate the control arm ball joint from the steering knuckle. Refer to Lower Control Arm, removal & installation.

14. Remove the steering knuckle bolts and nuts and the steering knuckle.

To install:

✷✷ WARNING

This component is equipped with torque-to-yield fasteners. Install NEW torque-to-yield fasteners when installing this component. Failure to replace the torque-to-yield fasteners could cause damage to the vehicle or component.

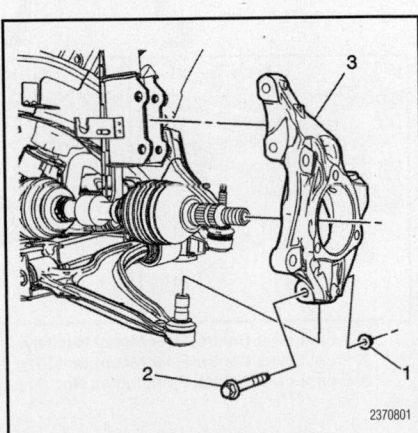

Fig. 184 Exploded view of steering knuckle (3), ball joint nut (1), and ball joint bolt (2)

15. Installation is the reverse of the removal procedure.

16. Install the steering knuckle using NEW bolts and nuts.

   a. Front strut nuts at the knuckle: Tighten to 63 ft. lbs. (85 Nm), plus 65°.

   b. Lower control arm ball joint:
- Step 1: Tighten to 37 ft. lbs. (50 Nm).
- Step 2: Loosen 120°.
- Step 3: Tighten 37 ft. lbs. (50 Nm), plus 35°.

17. Install the steering linkage outer tie rod.

18. During the installation, align the match marks.

19. Do not tighten the nut during the installation. Tighten the nut after adjusting the front toe.

20. Install a NEW steering linkage outer tie rod nut. Do NOT reuse old nut. Tighten to 26 ft. lbs. (35 Nm).

21. Inspect the steering linkage inner tie rod for bent or damaged threads.

22. Clean the tapered surface of the steering knuckle.

23. After the installation, measure and adjust the front toe.

24. Position the front brake shield and front wheel bearing/hub assembly in the steering knuckle.

✳✳ WARNING

This component is equipped with torque-to-yield fasteners. Install NEW torque-to-yield fasteners when installing this component. Failure to replace the torque-to-yield fasteners could cause damage to the vehicle or component.

25. Install the NEW front wheel bearing/hub bolts.

26. Tighten the bearing/hub bolts. Use the EN-45059 angle meter.

   a. Step 1: Tighten to 74 ft. lbs. (100 Nm).

   b. Step 2: Tighten 60°.

27. Install the wheel drive shaft at the front wheel bearing/hub. Refer to Front Halfshaft, removal & installation.

28. Install the wheel speed sensor to the steering knuckle.

29. Install the wheel speed sensor screw and tighten to 53 ft. lbs. (6 Nm).

30. Install the brake rotor.

31. Lower the vehicle.

STRUT & SPRING ASSEMBLY

REMOVAL & INSTALLATION

See Figures 185 and 186.

Special Tools
- CH-35669 Wrench

1. Before servicing the vehicle, refer to the Precautions Section.

2. Raise and safely support the vehicle.

3. Remove the tire and wheel assembly.

4. Separate the brake hose from the shock absorber.

5. Remove the steering knuckle nuts and bolts. DISCARD the bolts.

6. Remove and DISCARD the stabilizer shaft link nut from the front strut.

7. Lower the vehicle.

8. Open the hood.

9. Remove the upper strut mount nut, using the CH-35669 wrench.

10. Remove the strut mounting plate.

11. Separate the front strut from the knuckle.

12. Remove the front strut assembly from the vehicle.

To install:

13. Install the front strut assembly.

14. Install the strut mounting plate.

15. Install the upper strut mount nut, using the CH-35669 wrench and tighten to 34 ft. lbs. (45 Nm).

16. Insert the front strut in the knuckle.

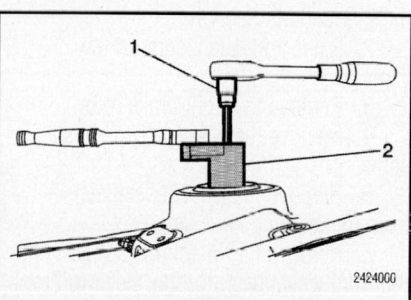

Fig. 185 Using the CH-35669 wrench (2) and Torx® tool (1) to remove the strut mounting plate

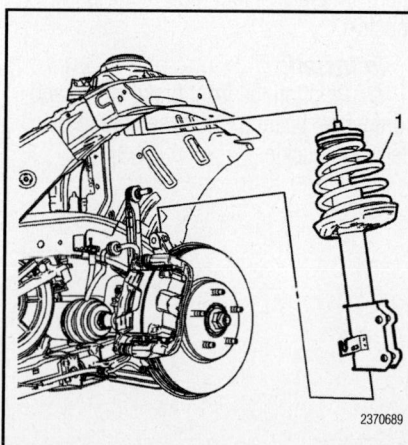

Fig. 186 Removing the front strut assembly (1)

✳✳ WARNING

This component is equipped with torque-to-yield fasteners. Install NEW torque-to-yield fasteners when installing this component. Failure to replace the torque-to-yield fasteners could cause damage to the vehicle or component.

17. Tighten the steering knuckle nuts and NEW bolts:

   a. Step 1: Tighten to 63 ft. lbs. (85 Nm).

   b. Step 2: Tighten 65°.

18. Install a NEW stabilizer shaft link nut and tighten to 48 ft. lbs. (65 Nm).

19. Install the brake hose to the strut.

20. Install the tire and wheel assembly. Tighten the wheel nuts in a star pattern to 103 ft. lbs. (140 Nm).

21. Lower the vehicle.

22. Check the front camber alignment specifications.

OVERHAUL

See Figures 187 through 189.

Special Tools
- CH 6066 Strut Spring Compressor
- CH 35669 Wrench

1. Before servicing the vehicle, refer to the Precautions Section.

2. Remove the front suspension strut from the vehicle. Refer to Strut & Spring Assembly, removal & installation.

3. Install the front suspension strut in the CH 6066 compressor.

➡ **The spring is compressed when the strut moves freely.**

4. Using the CH 6066 compressor, compress the front spring.

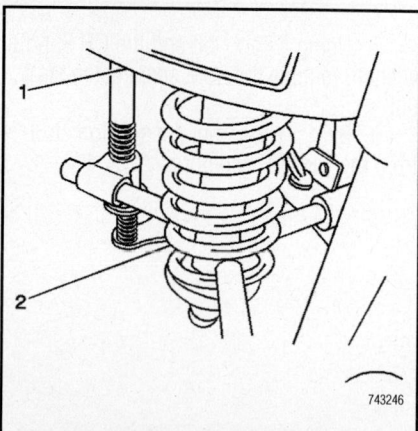

Fig. 187 CH 6066 Strut Spring Compressor (1) installed to the front suspension strut (2)

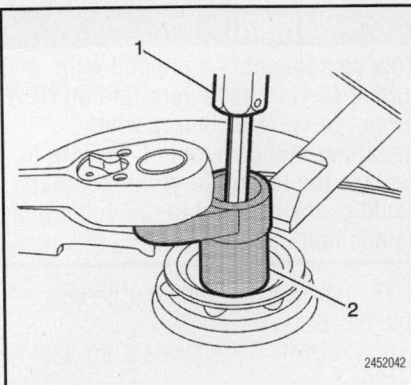

Fig. 188 Using a Torx® bit (1) and the CH 35669 wrench (2) to remove the front suspension strut nut

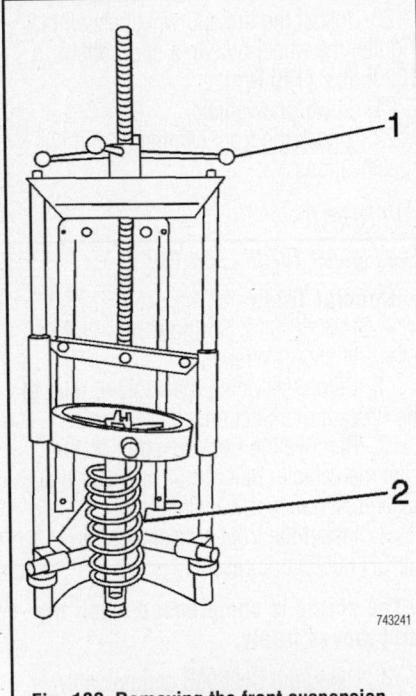

Fig. 189 Removing the front suspension strut (2) from the CH 6066 compressor (1)

5. Using a Torx® bit and the CH 35669 wrench, remove the front suspension strut nut.

6. Remove the front suspension strut from the CH 6066 compressor.

7. Remove the front suspension strut mount and the front spring from the CH 6066 compressor.

To assemble:

8. Install the front spring and front suspension strut mount to the CH 6066 compressor.

9. Using the CH 6066 compressor, compress the front spring.

10. Hand tighten the front suspension strut nut.

11. Using the CH 35669 wrench and the Torx® bit, tighten the front suspension strut nut to 52 ft. lbs. (70 Nm).

12. Remove the front suspension strut from the CH 6066 compressor.

13. Install the front suspension strut to the vehicle. Refer to Strut & Spring Assembly, removal & installation.

WHEEL BEARINGS

REMOVAL & INSTALLATION

See Figure 190.

Special Tools
• EN-45059 Torque Angle Sensor Kit

1. Before servicing the vehicle, refer to the Precautions Section.

2. Raise and safely support the vehicle.

3. Remove the front brake rotor.

4. Remove the wheel speed sensor screw.

5. Remove the wheel speed sensor from the steering knuckle.

6. Remove the wheel drive shaft from the front wheel bearing/hub. Refer to Front Halfshaft, removal & installation.

7. Remove and DISCARD the front wheel bearing/hub bolts.

8. Remove the front wheel bearing/hub and front brake shield from the steering knuckle.

To install:

9. Position the front brake shield and front wheel bearing/hub assembly in the steering knuckle.

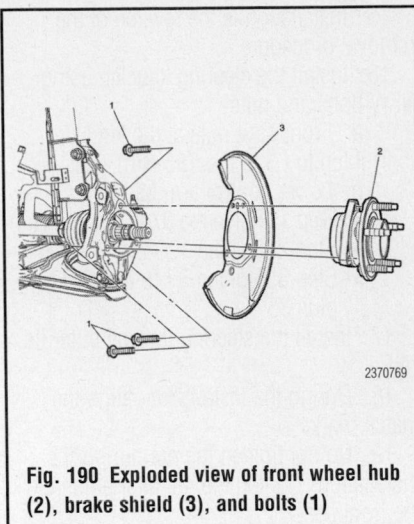

Fig. 190 Exploded view of front wheel hub (2), brake shield (3), and bolts (1)

✴✴ WARNING

This component is equipped with torque-to-yield fasteners. Install NEW torque-to-yield fasteners when installing this component. Failure to replace the torque-to-yield fasteners could cause damage to the vehicle or component.

10. Install the NEW front wheel bearing/hub bolts.

11. Tighten the bearing/hub bolts. Use the EN-45059 angle meter, or equivalent.

 a. Step 1: Tighten to 74 ft. lbs. (100 Nm).

 b. Step 2: Tighten 60°.

12. Install the wheel drive shaft at the front wheel bearing/hub. Refer to Front Halfshaft, removal & installation.

13. Install the wheel speed sensor to the steering knuckle.

14. Install the wheel speed sensor screw and tighten to 53 inch lbs. (6 Nm).

15. Install the brake rotor.

16. Lower the vehicle.

ADJUSTMENT

The wheel bearings are sealed at the factory and do not require any adjustment or maintenance.

SUSPENSION

COIL SPRING

REMOVAL & INSTALLATION

See Figure 191.

1. Before servicing the vehicle, refer to the Precautions Section.

2. Raise and safely support the vehicle.

3. Support the rear axle with a tall jack stand near the shock absorber.

4. If the springs are being removed to service other components and the spring tags are missing, mark the position of the rear spring to ensure proper installation.

5. Remove the lower shock absorber bolts. Refer to Shock Absorber, removal & installation.

6. Using the tall jack stands, slowly lower the rear axle in order to remove tension from the rear springs.

7. Remove the spring.

8. Remove the upper spring seat/jounce bumper from the spring, while leaving the lower spring seat on the axle.

To Install:

9. Install the upper spring seat/jounce bumper on the spring.

➡**If the spring is equipped with tags, ensure that the tags are at the upper rear portion of the spring. If marks were made during removal, ensure the marks are properly aligned.**

10. Install the spring making sure the lower coil is seated into the lower spring seat.

---

11. Using the jack stands, raise the rear axle in order to compress the rear springs.

12. Install the lower shock absorber bolts. Refer to Shock Absorber, removal & installation.

13. Lower the vehicle.

SHOCK ABSORBER

REMOVAL & INSTALLATION

See Figure 192.

Special Tools
- EN-45059 Torque Angle Sensor Kit

1. Before servicing the vehicle, refer to the Precautions Section.

2. Raise and safely support the vehicle.

3. Remove the tire and wheel assembly.

4. Support the rear axle with a suitable jack stand.

5. Remove the rear shock absorber upper and lower bolts and DISCARD.

6. Remove the rear shock absorber from the vehicle.

To install:

❊❊ WARNING

This component is equipped with torque-to-yield fasteners. Install NEW torque-to-yield fasteners when installing this component. Failure to replace the torque-to-yield fasteners could cause damage to the vehicle or component.

---

7. Install the shock absorber to the vehicle.

8. Install NEW bolts. Do NOT reuse old bolts.

9. Support the front of the vehicle and raise the rear axle to the proper trim height specifications.

10. Tighten the lower rear shock absorber bolt:

   a. Step 1: Tighten to 111 ft. lbs. (150 Nm).

   b. Step 2: Tighten 65°.

11. Tighten the upper rear shock absorber bolts to 74 ft. lbs. (100 Nm).

12. Tighten the rear shock absorber nut to 15 ft. lbs. (20 Nm).

13. Install the tire and wheel assembly. Tighten the wheel nuts in a star pattern to 103 ft. lbs. (140 Nm).

WHEEL BEARINGS

REMOVAL & INSTALLATION

See Figure 193.

Special Tools
- EN 45059 Torque Angle Sensor Kit

1. Before servicing the vehicle, refer to the Precautions Section.

2. Raise and safely support the vehicle.

3. Remove the tire and wheel assembly.

4. Without disconnecting the hydraulic brake flex hose, remove and support the rear brake caliper and bracket as an assembly.

5. Remove the rear brake rotor.

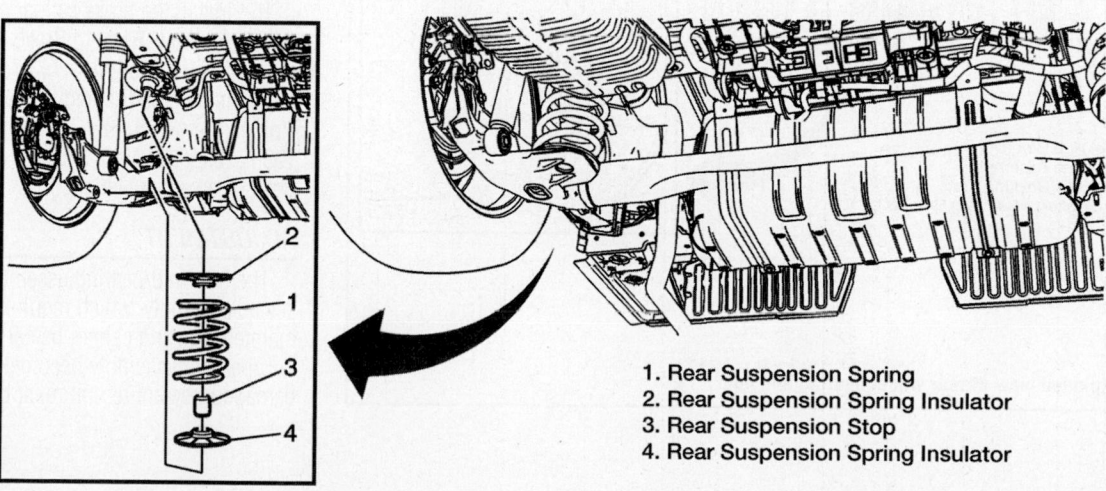

1. Rear Suspension Spring
2. Rear Suspension Spring Insulator
3. Rear Suspension Stop
4. Rear Suspension Spring Insulator

2370716

Fig. 191 Exploded view of rear spring assembly

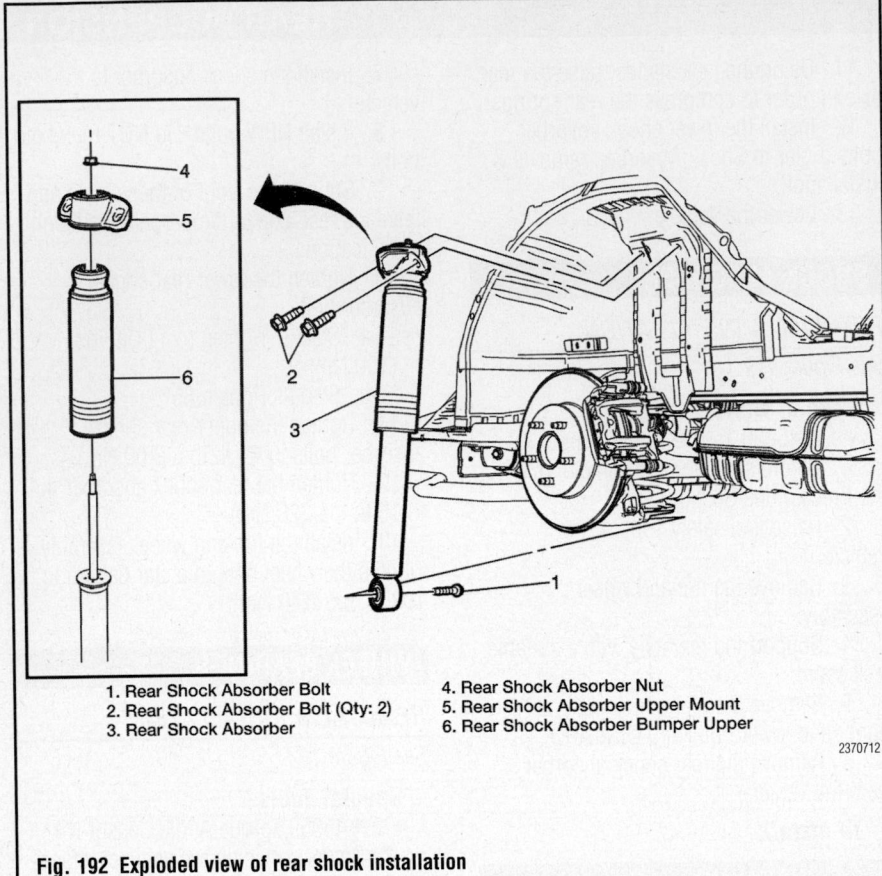

1. Rear Shock Absorber Bolt
2. Rear Shock Absorber Bolt (Qty: 2)
3. Rear Shock Absorber
4. Rear Shock Absorber Nut
5. Rear Shock Absorber Upper Mount
6. Rear Shock Absorber Bumper Upper

2370712

Fig. 192 Exploded view of rear shock installation

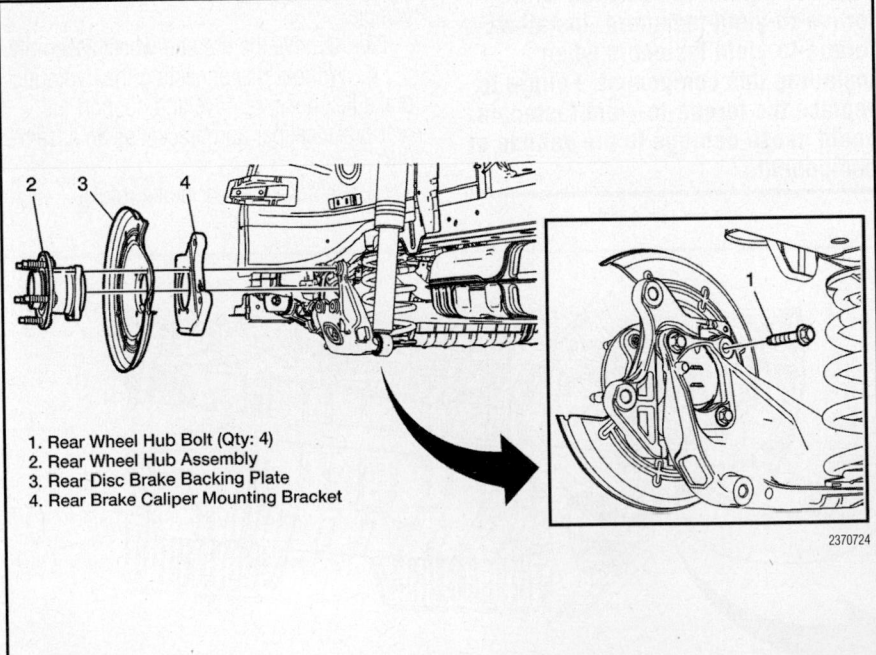

1. Rear Wheel Hub Bolt (Qty: 4)
2. Rear Wheel Hub Assembly
3. Rear Disc Brake Backing Plate
4. Rear Brake Caliper Mounting Bracket

2370724

Fig. 193 Exploded view of rear wheel bearing and hub

✳✳ WARNING

Support the brake caliper with heavy mechanics wire, or equivalent, whenever it is separated from its mount and the hydraulic flexible brake hose is still connected. Failure to support the caliper in this manner will cause the flexible brake hose to bear the weight of the caliper, which may cause damage to the brake hose and in turn may cause a brake fluid leak.

6. Remove the wheel speed sensor bolt.
7. Remove the wheel speed sensor.
8. Remove and DISCARD the 4 wheel bearing/hub mounting bolts.
9. Remove the wheel bearing/hub assembly and rear brake shield from the rear axle.

To install:

10. Position the rear brake shield and wheel bearing/hub assembly in the rear axle.

✳✳ WARNING

This component is equipped with torque-to-yield fasteners. Install NEW torque-to-yield fasteners when installing this component. Failure to replace the torque-to-yield fasteners could cause damage to the vehicle or component.

11. Install the 4 NEW wheel bearing/hub mounting bolts, applying thread locker, and tighten to 37 ft. lbs. (50 Nm), plus 40°, using the EN 45059 angle meter, or equivalent. Tighten the bolts evenly, in a cross-pattern.
12. Install the wheel speed sensor.
13. Install the wheel speed sensor bolt and tighten to 53 inch lbs. (6 Nm).
14. Install the brake rotor.
15. Install the brake caliper and bracket as an assembly. Refer to Brake Caliper, removal & installation.
16. Install the tire and wheel assembly. Tighten the wheel nuts in a star pattern to 103 ft. lbs. (140 Nm).
17. Lower the vehicle.

ADJUSTMENT

The rear hub/bearing assembly is a sealed assembly, which requires no periodic maintenance and cannot be serviced. If the hub/bearing assembly becomes worn or damaged, the entire unit must be replaced.

SPECIFICATIONS AND MAINTENANCE CHARTS

ENGINE AND VEHICLE IDENTIFICATION

Code ①	Liters (cc)	Cu. In.	Cyl.	Fuel Sys.	Engine Type	Eng. Mfg.	Code ②	Year
			Engine				Model Year	
B/P	2.4 (2393)	146	4	MFI	DOHC	Saturn	A	2010
7	3.6 (3556)	217	6	SFI	DOHC	Saturn		
5/Z	2.4 (2393)	146	4	MFI/Hybrid	DOHC	Saturn		

MFI: Multi-point Fuel Injection

SFI: Sequential Fuel Injection

DOHC: Double Overhead Camshafts

① 8th digit of VIN

② 10th digit of VIN

25742_SVUE_C0001

GENERAL ENGINE SPECIFICATIONS

Year	Model	Engine Displacement Liters (VIN)	Net Horsepower @ rpm	Net Torque @ rpm (ft. lbs.)	Bore x Stroke (in.)	Com- pression Ratio	Oil Pressure @ rpm
2010	VUE	2.4 (P)	169@6200	161@5100	①	10.0:1	50-80@1000
		2.4 (Z)	169@6200	161@5100	①	10.0:1	50-80@1000
		3.5 (7)	222@5900	219@3200	3.90x2.99	9.8:1	30-45@1850
		3.6 (N)	257@6500	248@2100	3.70x3.37	10.2:1	20@2000

① 3.4668-3.44675x3.861 inches

25742_SVUE_C0002

ENGINE TUNE-UP SPECIFICATIONS

Year	Engine Displacement Liters (VIN)	Spark Plug Gap (in.)	Ignition Timing (deg.) MT	Ignition Timing (deg.) AT	Fuel Pump (psi)	Idle Speed (rpm) MT	Idle Speed (rpm) AT	Valve Clearance In.	Valve Clearance Ex.
2010	2.4 (P)	0.043	NA	①	50-60	NA	②	HYD	HYD
	2.4 (Z)	0.043	NA	①	50-60	NA	②	HYD	HYD
	3.5 (7)	0.043	NA	①	48-56	NA	②	HYD	HYD
	3.6 (N)	0.043	NA	①	48-56	NA	②	HYD	HYD

NOTE: The Vehicle Emission Control Information label often reflects specification changes made during production. The label figures must be used if they differ from those in this chart.

HYD: Hydraulic

NA: Not Available

① Engines equipped with Distributorless Ignition System (DIS). Ignition timing is not adjustable

② Idle speed is set by the Powertrain Control Module.

25742_SVUE_C0003

CAPACITIES

Year	Model	Engine Displacement Liters (VIN)	Engine Oil with Filter (qts.)	Transaxle (qts.) Manual	Auto.	Fuel Tank (gal.)	Cooling System (qts.)
2010	VUE	2.4 (P)	5.0	NA	①	19.0	6.3
		2.4 (Z)	5.0	NA	7.0	19.0	6.3
		3.5 (7)	4.5	NA	①	17.0	11.6
		3.6 (N)	4.5	NA	①	17.0	11.6

NOTE: All capacities are approximate. Add fluid gradually and ensure a proper fluid level is obtained.

NA: Not Available

① 4T45-E Automatic - 7.0 qts.

   6T70/6T75 Automatic - 9.5 qts.

25742_SVUE_C0004

FLUID SPECIFICATIONS

Year	Model	Engine Displacement Liters	Engine ID/VIN	Engine Oil	Auto. Trans.	Manual Trans.	Power Steering Fluid	Brake Master Cylinder
2010	VUE	2.4	P	5W-30	Dexron VI	NA	GM Part No. 89021184	①
		2.4	Z	5W-30	Dexron VI	NA	GM Part No. 89021184	①
		3.5	7	5W-30	Dexron VI	NA	GM Part No. 89021184	①
		3.6	N	5W-30	Dexron VI	NA	GM Part No. 89021184	①

NA: Not Available

① Delco® Supreme 11 brake fluid or equivalent DOT-3 brake fluid.

25742_SVUE_C0005

VALVE SPECIFICATIONS

Year	Engine Displacement Liters (VIN)	Seat Angle (deg.)	Face Angle (deg.)	Spring Test Pressure (lbs. @ in.)	Spring Free-Length (in.)	Stem-to-Guide Clearance (in.) Intake	Exhaust	Stem Diameter (in.) Intake	Exhaust
2010	2.4 (P)	44.5-45.4	45-45.5	①	1.6100	0.0012-0.0022	0.0020-0.0026	0.2344-0.2355	0.2337-0.2343
	2.4 (Z)	44.5-45.4	45-45.5	①	1.6100	0.0012-0.0022	0.0020-0.0026	0.2344-0.2355	0.2337-0.2343
	3.5 (7)	46	45	②	2.08	0.0009-0.0025	0.0009-0.0025	NA	NA
	3.6 (N)	45	44.25	③	1.6555-1.766	0.0010-0.0026	0.0014-0.0030	0.2344-0.2352	0.2341-0.2348

NA: Not available

① Valve spring load closed: 55-61 lbs.

   Valve spring load open: 118-129 lbs.

② Valve spring load closed: 76.4 lbs. @ 1.701 inches

   Valve spring load open: 230 lbs. @ 1.260 inches

③ Valve spring load closed: 56-61 lbs.

   Valve spring load open: 134-149 lbs.

25742_SVUE_C0006

CAMSHAFT AND BEARING SPECIFICATIONS CHART

All measurements are given in inches.

Year	Engine Displ. Liters	Engine ID/VIN	Journal Dia.	Brg. Oil Clearance	Shaft End-play	Runout	Journal Bore	Lobe Height Intake	Exhaust
2010	2.4	P	1.0604-1.0614	NA	0.0016-0.0057	NA	NA	NA	NA
	2.4	Z	1.0604-1.0614	NA	0.0016-0.0057	NA	NA	NA	NA
	3.5	7	1.6900-1.6910	NA	NA	NA	NA	NA	NA
	3.6	N	①	NA	0.0018-0.0085	NA	②	1.6687-1.6805	1.6703-1.6821

NA: Not Available

① Journal No. 1: 1.3754-1.3764 inches
　Journal No. 2-4: 1.0605-1.0614 inches

② Journal No. 1: 1.3770-1.3797 inches
　Journal No. 2-4: 1.0621-1.0647 inches

25742_SVUE_C0007

CRANKSHAFT AND CONNECTING ROD SPECIFICATIONS

All measurements are given in inches.

Year	Engine Displacement Liters (VIN)	Crankshaft Main Brg. Journal Dia.	Main Brg. Oil Clearance	Shaft End-play	Thrust on No.	Connecting Rod Journal Diameter	Oil Clearance	Side Clearance
2010	2.4 (P)	2.2045-2.2050	0.0012-0.0026	0.0012-0.0150	2	1.9291-1.9297	0.0011-0.0029	0.0028-0.0146
	2.4 (Z)	2.2045-2.2050	0.0012-0.0026	0.0012-0.0150	2	1.9291-1.9297	0.0011-0.0029	0.0028-0.0146
	3.5 (7)	2.6473-2.6483	①	0.0024-0.0083	3	2.2489-2.2495	0.0007-0.0017	0.0080-0.0090
	3.6 (N)	2.6768-2.6775	0.0004-0.0024	0.0039-0.0130	3	2.2044-2.2050	0.0004-0.0028	0.0074-0.0140

NA: Not available

① All main bearings except No. 3: 0.0008-0.0025 inches
　Main bearing No. 3: 0.0012-0.0030 inches

25742_SVUE_C0008

PISTON AND RING SPECIFICATIONS
All measurements are given in inches.

Year	Engine Displacement Liters (VIN)	Piston Clearance	Ring Gap			Ring Side Clearance		
			Top Compression	Bottom Compression	Oil Control	Top Compression	Bottom Compression	Oil Control
2010	2.4 (P)	0.0004-0.0016	0.008-0.016	0.0014 0.0022	0.0010 0.0030	0.0028-0.0146	0.0005-0.0024	SNUG
	2.4 (Z)	0.0004-0.0016	0.008-0.016	0.0014 0.0022	0.0010 0.0030	0.0028-0.0146	0.0005-0.0024	SNUG
	3.5 (7)	0.0011-0.0110	0.007-0.0150	0.0190-0.0290	0.0100-0.0290	0.0010-0.0030	0.0020-0.0030	0.004
	3.6 (N)	0.0010-0.0021	0.0059-0.0118	0.0110-0.0189	0.0059-0.0236	0.0012-0.0026	0.0006-0.0024	0.0012-0.0067

25742_SVUE_C0009

TORQUE SPECIFICATIONS
All readings in ft. lbs.

Year	Engine Displacement Liters (VIN)	Cylinder Head Bolts	Main Bearing Bolts	Rod Bearing Bolts	Crankshaft Damper Bolts	Flywheel Bolts	Manifold		Spark Plugs	Oil Pan Drain Plug
							Intake	Exhaust		
2010	2.4 (P)	①	②	③	④	⑤	⑥	⑦	15	18
	2.4 (Z)	①	②	③	④	⑤	⑥	10	15	18
	3.5 (7)	⑧	⑨	⑩	⑪	52	⑫	15	11	18
	3.6 (N)	⑬	⑭	⑮	⑯	⑰	17	15	13	18

① Step 1: 22 ft. lbs.
   Step 2: Additional 155 degrees
② Step 1: 15 ft. lbs.
   Step 2: Additional 70 degrees
③ Step 1: 18 ft. lbs.
   Step 2: Additional 100 degrees
④ Step 1: 74 ft. lbs.
   Step 2: Additional 125 degrees
⑤ Step 1: 39 ft. lbs.
   Step 2: Additional 25 degrees
⑥ 89 inch lbs.
⑦ 124 inch lbs.
⑧ Step 1: 44 ft. lbs.
   Step 2: Additional 95 degrees
⑨ Step 1: 37 ft. lbs
   Step 2: Additional 77 degrees
⑩ Step 1: 18 ft. lbs.
   Step 2: Additional 110 degrees

⑪ Step 1: 92 ft. lbs.
   Step 2: Additional 130 degrees
⑫ Center Bolt Step 1: 62 inch lbs.
   Step 2: 115 inch lbs.
   Corner Bolt Step 1: 62 inch lbs
   Step 2: 18 ft. lbs.
⑬ M8 Bolts Step 1: 11 ft. lbs.
   Step 2: Additional 75 degrees
   M11 Bolts Step 1: 22 ft. lbs
   Step 2: Additional 150 degrees
⑭ Inner Step 1: 15 ft. lbs.
   Step 2: Additional 80 degrees
   Outer Step 1: 10 ft. lbs.
   Step 2: Additional 110 degrees
   Side Step 1: 220 ft. lbs.
   Step 2: Additional 60 degrees

⑮ Step 1: 22 ft. lbs.
   Step 2: Counterclockwise - back off to 0
   Step 3: 18 ft. lbs.
   Step 4: Additional 110 degrees
⑯ Step 1: 74 ft. lbs.
   Step 2: Additional 150 degrees
⑰ Step 1: 22 ft. lbs.
   Step 2: Additional 45 degrees

25742_SVUE_C0010

WHEEL ALIGNMENT

Year	Model		Caster Range (+/-Deg.)	Caster Preferred Setting (Deg.)	Camber Range (+/-Deg.)	Camber Preferred Setting (Deg.)	Toe-in (in.)
2010	VUE	F	0.75	3.00	0.75	-.040	+0.20 +/- 0.20
	2.4L/3.5L	R	—	—	0.75	-0.45	+0.20 +/- 0.20
	VUE	F	0.75	2.90	0.75	-0.60	+0.20 +/- 0.20
	3.6L	R	—	—	0.75	-0.45	+0.20 +/- 0.20

25742_SVUE_C0011

TIRE, WHEEL AND BALL JOINT SPECIFICATIONS

Year	Model		OEM Tires Standard	OEM Tires Optional	Tire Pressures (psi) Front	Tire Pressures (psi) Rear	Wheel Size	Ball Joint Inspection	Lug Nuts (ft. lbs.)
2010	VUE	F	P235/65R16	P235/60R17	①	①	16x6.5	②	125
		R	P235/65R16	P235/60R17	①	①	16x6.5	②	125

OEM: Original Equipment Manufacturer

PSI: Pounds Per Square Inch

① Check the placard on the drivers side sill

② Remove tension from the ball joint.

Horizontal and vertical looseness no greater than 0.125 in. reading on a dial indicator.

25742_SVUE_C0012

BRAKE SPECIFICATIONS

All measurements in inches unless noted

Year	Model		Brake Disc Original Thickness	Brake Disc Minimum Thickness	Brake Disc Maximum Runout	Brake Drum Diameter Original Inside Diameter	Brake Drum Diameter Max. Wear Limit	Brake Drum Diameter Maximum Machine Diameter	Minimum Lining Thickness	Brake Caliper Bracket Bolt (ft. lbs.)	Brake Caliper Mounting Bolt (ft. lbs.)
2010	VUE	F	NA	1.079	0.002	—	—	—	0.080	136	20
		R	NA	0.724	0.002	—	—	—	0.080	89	20

NA: Not Available

F: Front

R: Rear

25742_SVUE_C0013

MAINTENANCE I AND II SERVICE SCHEDULES
VUE & VUE HYBRID

When the CHANGE ENGINE OIL light appears, certain services and inspections are required.

Required services are described as Maintenance I and Maintenance II.

The first service of a vehicle should be Maintenance I, and the second service should be Maintenance II.

Alternate between the 2 services thereafter. However, in some cases, Maintenance II may be required more often.

Maintenance I: Use Maintenance I if the CHANGE ENGINE OIL light comes on within 10 months since the vehicle was purchased or, if Maintenance II was performed.

Maintenance II: Use Maintenance II if the previous service performed was Maintenance I. Always use Maintenance II whenever the CHANGE ENGINE OIL light comes on 10 months or more since the last service, or, if the CHANGE ENGINE OIL light has not come on at all for one year.

Service Item	Maintenance I	Maintenance II
Change the engine oil and filter.	✓	✓
Reset the oil life system.	✓	✓
Visually inspect the vehicle for leaks or damage. A fluid loss in the vehicle system could indicate a problem. Inspect, repair and add fluid to the system if necessary.	✓	✓
Inspect the engine air cleaner filter. If necessary, replace the filter.	✓	✓
Rotate the tires. Inspect the tire inflation pressures and the tire wear.	✓	✓
Visually inspect the brake lines and hoses for proper hook-up, binding, leaks, cracks, chafing, etc. Inspect the disc brake pads for wear and the rotors for surface condition. Inspect the drum brake linings for wear or cracks. Inspect other brake parts, including drums, wheel cylinders, calipers, parking brake, etc. Inspect the parking brake adjustment.	✓	✓
Inspect engine coolant and windshield washer fluid levels. Add fluid as needed.	✓	✓
Inspect the suspension and steering components. Inspect the front and rear suspension and the steering system for damaged, loose or missing parts, or signs of wear. Inspect the power steering lines and the hoses for proper hook-up, binding, leaks, cracks, chafing, etc.	—	✓
Visually inspect the coolant hoses and replace the hoses if they are cracked, swollen or deteriorated. Inspect all pipes, fittings and clamps; replace with GM parts as needed. To help ensure proper operation, a pressure test of the cooling system and pressure cap and cleaning the outside of the radiator and air conditioning condenser is recommended at least once a year.	—	✓
Ensure the safety belt reminder light and all the belts, buckles, latch plates, retractors and anchorages are working properly. Look for any other loose or damaged safety belt system parts. If you see anything that might keep a safety belt system from working correctly, repair or replaced the damaged part. Replace torn or frayed safety belts, refer to Operational and Functional Checks in Seat Belts. Inspect for any opened or broken air bag coverings, and repair or replace as needed. The air bag system does require regular maintenance.	—	✓
Lubricate the body components.	—	✓
Lubricate all key lock cylinders, hood latch assemblies, secondary latches, pivots, spring anchor and release pawl, hood and door hinges, rear folding seats and liftgate hinges. Frequent lubrication may be required when exposed to a corrosive environment, refer to Fluid and Lubricant Recommendations . Applying dielectric silicone grease GM P/N 12345579 (Canadian P/N 1974984) or equivalent on the weatherstrips with a clean cloth.	—	✓
Inspect the transaxle fluid level and add fluid as needed.	—	✓
Inspect the wiper blades and replace as necessary	✓	✓
Inspect the throttle system.	—	✓
Replace the passenger compartment air filter.	—	✓
Inspect vehicle restraint system components.	—	✓

To reset the CHANGE ENGINE OIL light:

1. Turn the ignition key to the ON/RUN position with the engine OFF.
2. Press and release the stem in the lower center of the instrument cluster until the OIL LIFE message is displayed.
3. Once the alternating OIL LIFE and RESET messages appear, press and hold the stem until several beeps sound.
   This confirms that the oil life system has been reset to 100 percent.
4. Turn the ignition key to the OFF position.
   If the CHANGE ENGINE OIL message comes back on when the vehicle is started, the engine oil life system has not been reset. Repeat the procedure.

ADDITIONAL MAINTENANCE SERVICES - NORMAL
VUE & VUE HYBRID

TO BE SERVICED	TYPE OF SERVICE	VEHICLE MILEAGE INTERVAL (x1000)					
		25	50	75	100	125	150
Engine coolant	Replace						✓
Air cleaner filter	Replace		✓		✓		✓
Automatic Transmission Fluid (and filter if applicable)	Replace				✓		
Spark plugs	Replace				✓		
Transfer case fluid	Replace				✓		
Exhaust system & heat shields	Inspect	✓	✓	✓	✓	✓	✓
Cooling system hoses and clamps	Inspect						✓
Fuel system	Inspect	✓	✓	✓	✓	✓	✓
Accessory drive belt	Replace						✓
Evaporative control system	Inspect		✓		✓		✓

25742_SVUE_C0015

ADDITIONAL MAINTENANCE SERVICES - SEVERE
VUE & VUE HYBRID

TO BE SERVICED	TYPE OF SERVICE	VEHICLE MILEAGE INTERVAL (x1000)					
		25	50	75	100	125	150
Engine coolant	Replace						✓
Air cleaner filter	Replace	✓	✓	✓	✓	✓	✓
Automatic Transmission Fluid (and filter if applicable)	Replace		✓		✓		✓
Spark plugs	Replace				✓		
Transfer case fluid	Replace		✓		✓		✓
Exhaust system & heat shields	Service/Inspect	✓	✓	✓	✓	✓	✓
Cooling system hoses and clamps	Service/Inspect	✓	✓	✓	✓	✓	✓
Fuel system	Inspect	✓	✓	✓	✓	✓	✓
Accessory drive belt	Inspect						✓
Evaporative control system	Inspect		✓		✓		✓

25742_SVUE_C0016

PRECAUTIONS

Before servicing any vehicle, please be sure to read all of the following precautions, which deal with personal safety, prevention of component damage, and important points to take into consideration when servicing a motor vehicle:

• Never open, service or drain the radiator or cooling system when the engine is hot; serious burns can occur from the steam and hot coolant.

• Observe all applicable safety precautions when working around fuel. Whenever servicing the fuel system, always work in a well-ventilated area. Do not allow fuel spray or vapors to come in contact with a spark, open flame, or excessive heat (a hot drop light, for example). Keep a dry chemical fire extinguisher near the work area. Always keep fuel in a container specifically designed for fuel storage; also, always properly seal fuel containers to avoid the possibility of fire or explosion. Refer to the additional fuel system precautions later in this section.

• Fuel injection systems often remain pressurized, even after the engine has been turned **OFF**. The fuel system pressure must be relieved before disconnecting any fuel lines. Failure to do so may result in fire and/or personal injury.

• Brake fluid often contains polyglycol ethers and polyglycols. Avoid contact with the eyes and wash your hands thoroughly after handling brake fluid. If you do get brake fluid in your eyes, flush your eyes with clean, running water for 15 minutes. If eye irritation persists, or if you have taken brake fluid internally, IMMEDIATELY seek medical assistance.

• The EPA warns that prolonged contact with used engine oil may cause a number of skin disorders, including cancer. You should make every effort to minimize your exposure to used engine oil. Protective gloves should be worn when changing oil. Wash your hands and any other exposed skin areas as soon as possible after exposure to used engine oil. Soap and water, or waterless hand cleaner should be used.

• All new vehicles are now equipped with an air bag system, often referred to as a Supplemental Restraint System (SRS) or Supplemental Inflatable Restraint (SIR) system. The system must be disabled before performing service on or around system components, steering column, instrument panel components, wiring and sensors. Failure to follow safety and disabling procedures could result in accidental air bag deployment, possible personal injury and unnecessary system repairs.

• Always wear safety goggles when working with, or around, the air bag system. When carrying a non-deployed air bag, be sure the bag and trim cover are pointed away from your body. When placing a non-deployed air bag on a work surface, always face the bag and trim cover upward, away from the surface. This will reduce the motion of the module if it is accidentally deployed. Refer to the additional air bag system precautions later in this section.

• Clean, high quality brake fluid from a sealed container is essential to the safe and proper operation of the brake system. You should always buy the correct type of brake fluid for your vehicle. If the brake fluid becomes contaminated, completely flush the system with new fluid. Never reuse any brake fluid. Any brake fluid that is removed from the system should be discarded. Also, do not allow any brake fluid to come in contact with a painted surface; it will damage the paint.

• Never operate the engine without the proper amount and type of engine oil; doing so WILL result in severe engine damage.

• Timing belt maintenance is extremely important. Many models utilize an interference-type, non-freewheeling engine. If the timing belt breaks, the valves in the cylinder head may strike the pistons, causing potentially serious (also time-consuming and expensive) engine damage. Refer to the maintenance interval charts for the recommended replacement interval for the timing belt, and to the timing belt section for belt replacement and inspection.

• Disconnecting the negative battery cable on some vehicles may interfere with the functions of the on-board computer system(s) and may require the computer to undergo a relearning process once the negative battery cable is reconnected.

• When servicing drum brakes, only disassemble and assemble one side at a time, leaving the remaining side intact for reference.

• Only an MVAC-trained, EPA-certified automotive technician should service the air conditioning system or its components.

BRAKES

GENERAL INFORMATION

PRECAUTIONS

• Certain components within the ABS system are not intended to be serviced or repaired individually.

• Do not use rubber hoses or other parts not specifically specified for and ABS system. When using repair kits, replace all parts included in the kit. Partial or incorrect repair may lead to functional problems and require the replacement of components.

• Lubricate rubber parts with clean, fresh brake fluid to ease assembly. Do not use shop air to clean parts; damage to rubber components may result.

• Use only DOT 3 brake fluid from an unopened container.

• If any hydraulic component or line is removed or replaced, it may be necessary to bleed the entire system.

• A clean repair area is essential. Always clean the reservoir and cap thoroughly before removing the cap. The slightest amount of dirt in the fluid may plug an orifice and impair the system function. Perform repairs after components have been thoroughly cleaned; use only denatured alcohol to clean components. Do not allow ABS components to come into contact with any substance containing mineral oil; this includes used shop rags.

• The Anti-Lock control unit is a microprocessor similar to other computer units in the vehicle. Ensure that the ignition switch is **OFF** before removing or installing controller harnesses. Avoid static electricity discharge at or near the controller.

ANTI-LOCK BRAKE SYSTEM (ABS)

• If any arc welding is to be done on the vehicle, the control unit should be unplugged before welding operations begin.

WHEEL SPEED SENSORS

REMOVAL & INSTALLATION

Front

See Figure 1.

1. Raise and safely support the vehicle.
2. Remove the tire and wheel.
3. Remove the brake rotor.
4. Disconnect the wheel speed sensor connector (1).
5. Remove the wheel speed sensor bolt (2).
6. Remove the wheel speed senor (3).
7. Installation is the reverse of removal.

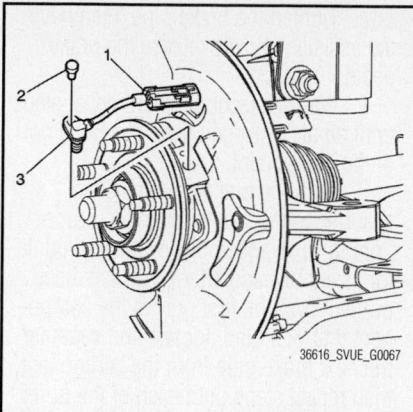

Fig. 1 Disconnect the wheel speed sensor connector (1)

Rear

See Figure 2.

1. Raise and safely support the vehicle.
2. Remove the tire and wheel.
3. Remove the parking brake shoes.
4. Disconnect the wheel speed sensor connector (1).
5. Remove the wheel speed sensor bolt (2).
6. Remove the wheel speed sensor (3).
   a. Release the wheel speed sensor electrical harness grommet from the backing plate.
   b. Route the wheel speed sensor electrical harness through the backing plate.
7. Installation is the reverse of removal.

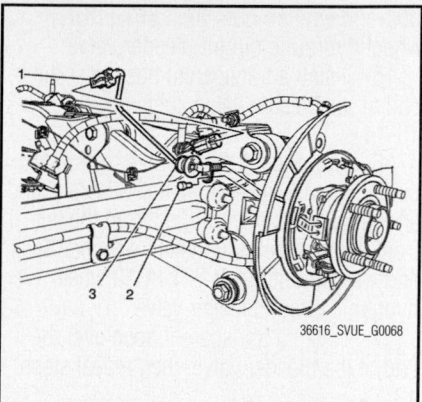

Fig. 2 Disconnect the wheel speed sensor connector (1)

BRAKES

BLEEDING THE BRAKE SYSTEM

BLEEDING PROCEDURE

BLEEDING PROCEDURE

Pressure Bleeding

➡When adding fluid to the brake master cylinder reservoir, use only GM approved or equivalent DOT-3 brake fluid from a clean, sealed brake fluid container. The use of any type of fluid other than the recommended type of brake fluid may cause contamination which could result in damage to the internal rubber seals and/or rubber linings of hydraulic brake system components.

➡Avoid spilling brake fluid onto painted surfaces, electrical connections, wiring, or cables. Brake fluid will damage painted surfaces and cause corrosion to electrical components. If any brake fluid comes in contact with painted surfaces, immediately flush the area with water. If any brake fluid comes in contact with electrical connections, wiring, or cables, use a clean shop cloth to wipe away the fluid.

1. Place a clean shop cloth beneath the brake master cylinder to catch brake fluid spills.
2. With the ignition OFF and the brakes cool, apply the brakes 3-5 times, or until the brake pedal becomes firm, in order to deplete the brake booster power reserve.
3. If you have performed a brake master cylinder bench bleeding on this vehicle, or if you disconnected the brake pipes from the master cylinder, or if you have disconnected the brake pipes from the proportioning valve assembly or the brake modulator assembly, you must perform the following steps to bleed air at the ports of the hydraulic component:

   a. If removal of the reservoir cap and diaphragm is necessary, clean the outside of the reservoir on and around the cap prior to removal.

   b. With the brake pipes installed securely to the master cylinder, proportioning valve assembly, or brake modulator assembly, loosen and separate one of the brake pipes from the port of the component.

4. For the proportioning valve assembly or the brake modulator assembly, perform these steps in the sequence of system flow; begin with the fluid feed pipes from the master cylinder.

   a. Allow a small amount of brake fluid to gravity bleed from the open port of the component.

   b. Reconnect the brake pipe to the component and tighten securely.

   c. Have an assistant slowly depress the brake pedal fully and maintain steady pressure on the pedal.

   d. Loosen the same brake pipe to purge air from the open port of the component.

   e. Tighten the brake pipe, then have the assistant slowly release the brake pedal.

   f. Wait 15 seconds, then repeat steps until all air is purged from the same port of the component.

   g. With the brake pipe installed securely to the master cylinder, proportioning valve assembly, or brake modulator assembly, and after all air has been purged from the first port of the component that was bled, loosen and separate the next brake pipe from the component, then repeat steps until each of the ports on the component has been bled.

   h. After completing the final component port bleeding procedure, ensure that each of the brake pipe-to-component fittings is properly tightened.

5. Clean the outside of the reservoir on and around the reservoir cap prior to removing the cap and diaphragm.

6. Install the J 44894-A to the brake master cylinder reservoir.

7. Connect the J 29532, or equivalent, to the J 44894-A.

8. Charge the J 29532, or equivalent, air tank to 25-30 psi (175-205 kPa).

9. Open the J 29532, or equivalent, fluid tank valve to allow pressurized brake fluid to enter the brake system.

10. Wait approximately 30 seconds, then inspect the entire hydraulic brake system in order to ensure that there are no existing external brake fluid leaks.

➡Any brake fluid leaks identified require repair prior to completing this procedure.

11. Install a proper box-end wrench onto the RIGHT REAR wheel hydraulic circuit bleeder valve.

12. Install a transparent hose over the end of the bleeder valve.

13. Loosen the bleeder valve to purge air from the wheel hydraulic circuit. Allow fluid to flow until air bubbles stop flowing from the bleeder, then tighten the bleeder valve.

14. With the right rear wheel hydraulic circuit bleeder valve tightened securely, and after all air has been purged from the right rear hydraulic circuit, install a proper

box-end wrench onto the LEFT FRONT wheel hydraulic circuit bleeder valve.

15. Install a transparent hose over the end of the bleeder valve, then repeat steps 13-14.

16. With the left front wheel hydraulic circuit bleeder valve tightened securely, and after all air has been purged from the left front hydraulic circuit, install a proper box-end wrench onto the LEFT REAR wheel hydraulic circuit bleeder valve.

17. Install a transparent hose over the end of the bleeder valve, then repeat steps 13-14.

With the left rear wheel hydraulic circuit bleeder valve tightened securely, and after all air has been purged from the left rear hydraulic circuit, install a proper box-end wrench onto the RIGHT FRONT wheel hydraulic circuit bleeder valve.

18. Install a transparent hose over the end of the bleeder valve, then repeat steps 13-14.

19. After completing the final wheel hydraulic circuit bleeding procedure, ensure that each of the 4 wheel hydraulic circuit bleeder valves is properly tightened.

20. Close the J 29532, or equivalent, fluid tank valve, then disconnect the J 29532, or equivalent, from the J 44894-A.

21. Remove the J 44894-A from the brake master cylinder reservoir.

22. Slowly depress and release the brake pedal. Observe the feel of the brake pedal.

23. If the brake pedal feels spongy perform the following steps:

a. Inspect the brake system for external leaks.

b. If equipped with antilock brakes, using a scan tool, perform the antilock brake system automated bleeding procedure to remove any air that may have been trapped in the brake pressure modulator valve (BPMV).

24. Turn the ignition key ON, with the engine OFF. Check to see if the brake system warning lamp remains illuminated.

❊❊ CAUTION

DO NOT allow the vehicle to be driven until it is diagnosed and repaired.

25. If the brake system warning lamp remains illuminated.

Manual Bleeding

➡**When adding fluid to the brake master cylinder reservoir, use only GM approved or equivalent DOT-3 brake fluid from a clean, sealed brake fluid container. The use of any type of fluid** other than the recommended type of brake fluid may cause contamination which could result in damage to the internal rubber seals and/or rubber linings of hydraulic brake system components.

➡**Avoid spilling brake fluid onto painted surfaces, electrical connections, wiring, or cables. Brake fluid will damage painted surfaces and cause corrosion to electrical components. If any brake fluid comes in contact with painted surfaces, immediately flush the area with water. If any brake fluid comes in contact with electrical connections, wiring, or cables, use a clean shop cloth to wipe away the fluid.**

1. Place a clean shop cloth beneath the brake master cylinder to catch brake fluid spills.

2. With the ignition OFF and the brakes cool, apply the brakes 3-5 times, or until the brake pedal effort increases significantly, in order to deplete the brake booster power reserve.

3. If you have performed a brake master cylinder bench bleeding on this vehicle, or if you disconnected the brake pipes from the master cylinder, or if you have disconnected the brake pipes from the proportioning valve assembly or the brake modulator assembly, you must perform the following steps to bleed air at the ports of the hydraulic component:

a. If removal of the reservoir cap and diaphragm is necessary, clean the outside of the reservoir on and around the cap prior to removal.

b. With the brake pipes installed securely to the master cylinder, proportioning valve assembly, or brake modulator assembly, loosen and separate one of the brake pipes from the port of the component.

4. For the proportioning valve assembly or the brake modulator assembly, perform these steps in the sequence of system flow; begin with the fluid feed pipes from the master cylinder.

a. Allow a small amount of brake fluid to gravity bleed from the open port of the component.

b. Reconnect the brake pipe to the component and tighten securely.

c. Have an assistant slowly depress the brake pedal fully and maintain steady pressure on the pedal.

d. Loosen the same brake pipe to purge air from the open port of the component.

e. Tighten the brake pipe, then have the assistant slowly release the brake pedal.

f. Wait 15 seconds, then repeat steps until all air is purged from the same port of the component.

g. With the brake pipe installed securely to the master cylinder, proportioning valve assembly, or brake modulator assembly, and after all air has been purged from the first port of the component that was bled, loosen and separate the next brake pipe from the component, then repeat steps until each of the ports on the component has been bled.

h. After completing the final component port bleeding procedure, ensure that each of the brake pipe-to-component fittings is properly tightened.

5. Ensure the brake master cylinder reservoir remains at least half-full during this bleeding procedure. Add fluid as needed to maintain the proper level.

➡**Clean the outside of the reservoir on and around the reservoir cap prior to removing the cap and diaphragm.**

6. Install a proper box-end wrench onto the RIGHT REAR wheel hydraulic circuit bleeder valve.

7. Install a transparent hose over the end of the bleeder valve.

8. Have an assistant slowly depress the brake pedal fully and maintain steady pressure on the pedal.

9. Loosen the bleeder valve to purge air from the wheel hydraulic circuit.

10. Tighten the bleeder valve, then have the assistant slowly release the brake pedal.

11. Wait 15 seconds, then repeat steps 8-10 until all air is purged from the same wheel hydraulic circuit.

12. With the right rear wheel hydraulic circuit bleeder valve tightened securely, and after all air has been purged from the right rear hydraulic circuit, install a proper box-end wrench onto the LEFT FRONT wheel hydraulic circuit bleeder valve.

13. Install a transparent hose over the end of the bleeder valve, then repeat steps 7-11.

14. With the left front wheel hydraulic circuit bleeder valve tightened securely, and after all air has been purged from the left front hydraulic circuit, install a proper box-end wrench onto the LEFT REAR wheel hydraulic circuit bleeder valve.

15. Install a transparent hose over the end of the bleeder valve, then repeat steps 7-11.

16. With the left rear wheel hydraulic circuit bleeder valve tightened securely, and after all air has been purged from the left

rear hydraulic circuit, install a proper box-end wrench onto the RIGHT FRONT wheel hydraulic circuit bleeder valve.

17. Install a transparent hose over the end of the bleeder valve, then repeat steps 7-11.

18. After completing the final wheel hydraulic circuit bleeding procedure, ensure that each of the 4 wheel hydraulic circuit bleeder valves is properly tightened.

19. Slowly depress and release the brake pedal. Observe the feel of the brake pedal.

20. If the brake pedal feels spongy, repeat the bleeding procedure again. If the brake pedal still feels spongy after repeating the bleeding procedure, perform the following steps:

a. Inspect the brake system for external leaks.

b. Pressure bleed the hydraulic brake system in order to purge any air that may still be trapped in the system.

21. Turn the ignition key ON, with the engine OFF. Check to see if the brake system warning lamp remains illuminated.

✳✳ CAUTION

DO NOT allow the vehicle to be driven until it is diagnosed and repaired.

22. If the brake system warning lamp remains illuminated

BLEEDING THE ABS SYSTEM

➡**Before performing the Antilock Brake System (ABS) Automated Bleed Procedure, first perform a manual or pressure bleed of the base brake system. The automated bleed proce-**dure is recommended when one of the following conditions exist:

- Base brake system bleeding does not achieve the desired pedal height or feel
- Extreme loss of brake fluid has occurred
- Air ingestion is suspected in the secondary circuits of the brake modulator assembly

The ABS Automated Bleed Procedure uses a scan tool to cycle the system solenoid valves and run the pump in order to purge any air from the secondary circuits. These circuits are normally closed off, and are only opened during system initialization at vehicle start up and during ABS operation. The automated bleed procedure opens these secondary circuits and allows any air trapped in these circuits to flow out toward the brake corners.

Automated Bleed Procedure

➡**The Auto Bleed Procedure may be terminated at any time during the process by pressing the EXIT button. No further Scan Tool prompts pertaining to the Auto Bleed procedure will be given. After exiting the bleed procedure, relieve bleed pressure and disconnect bleed equipment per manufacturer's instructions. Failure to properly relieve pressure may result in spilled brake fluid causing damage to components and painted surfaces.**

1. Raise and support the vehicle.
2. Remove all 4 tire and wheel assemblies.

3. Inspect the brake system for leaks and visual damage. Repair or replace components as needed.

4. Lower the vehicle.
5. Inspect the battery state of charge.
6. Install a scan tool.
7. Turn the ignition ON, with the engine OFF.

8. With the scan tool, establish communications with the ABS system. Select Special Functions. Select Automated Bleed from the Special Functions menu.

9. Raise and support the vehicle.

10. Following the directions given on the scan tool, pressure bleed the base brake system.

11. Follow the scan tool directions until the desired brake pedal height is achieved.

12. If the bleed procedure is aborted, a malfunction exists. Perform the following steps before resuming the bleed procedure:

a. If a DTC is detected, refer to Diagnostic Trouble Code (DTC) List and diagnose the appropriate DTC.

b. If the brake pedal feels spongy, perform the conventional brake bleed procedure again.

13. When the desired pedal height is achieved, press the brake pedal to inspect for firmness.

14. Lower the vehicle.
15. Remove the scan tool.
16. Install the tire and wheel assemblies.
17. Inspect the brake fluid level.
18. Road test the vehicle while inspecting that the pedal remains high and firm.

BRAKES   **FRONT DISC BRAKES**

BRAKE CALIPER

REMOVAL & INSTALLATION

See Figures 3 and 4.

1. Raise and support the vehicle.
2. Remove the tire and wheel assembly.
3. Remove the brake hose fitting bolt (1).
4. Remove the brake hose fitting (2) from the brake caliper.

➡**Do not reuse the brake hose fitting gaskets.**

5. Remove and discard the brake hose fitting gaskets (3).
6. Cap the brake hose fitting to prevent brake fluid loss and contamination.

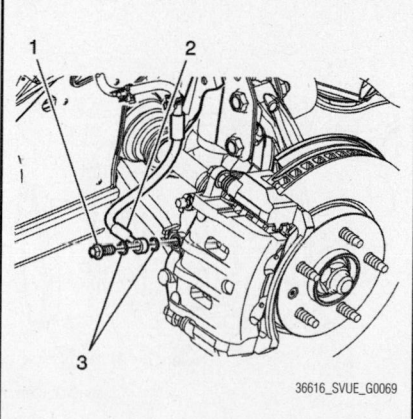

36616_SVUE_G0069

Fig. 3 Remove the brake hose fitting bolt (1)

➡**DO NOT use any air tools to remove or install the guide pin bolts. Use hand tools ONLY. Install an open end wrench to hold the caliper guide pin in line with the brake caliper while removing or installing the caliper guide pin bolt. DO NOT allow the open end wrench to come in contact with the brake caliper. Allowing the open end wrench to come in contact with the brake caliper will cause a pulsation when the brakes are applied.**

7. Remove the brake caliper guide pin bolts (1).

➡**Hold the brake caliper guide pins stationary when removing the guide pin bolts.**

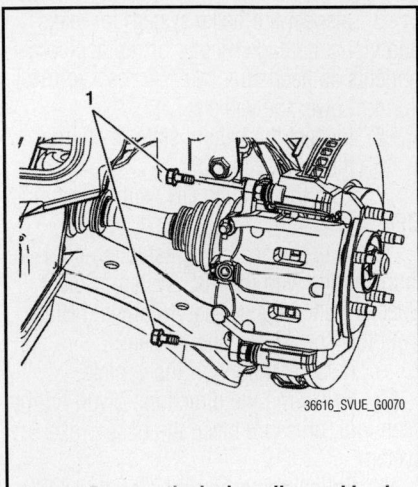

Fig. 4 Remove the brake caliper guide pin bolts (1)

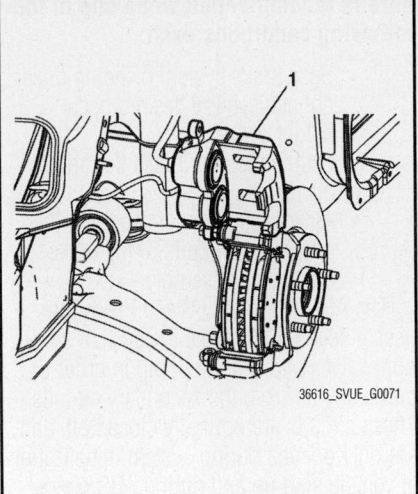

Fig. 5 Pivot the brake caliper (1) upward

8. Remove the brake caliper.

To install:

9. Install the brake caliper.

10. Install the brake caliper guide pin bolts. Tighten the bolts to 20 ft. lbs. (27 Nm).

➡ **Hold the brake caliper guide pins stationary when installing the guide pin bolts.**

➡ **Install new brake hose fitting gaskets.**

11. Install new brake hose fitting gaskets to the brake hose fitting.

12. Install the brake hose fitting to the brake caliper.

13. Install the brake hose fitting bolt. Tighten the bolt to 38 ft. lbs. (52 Nm).

14. Bleed the hydraulic brake system.

15. Install the tire and wheel assembly.

16. Lower the vehicle.

DISC BRAKE PADS

REMOVAL AND INSTALLATION

See Figures 4 through 7.

➡ **Support the brake caliper with heavy mechanic wire, or equivalent, whenever it is separated from its mount and the hydraulic flexible brake hose is still connected. Failure to support the caliper in this manner will cause the flexible brake hose to bear the weight of the caliper, which may cause damage to the brake hose and in turn may cause a brake fluid leak.**

1. Inspect the fluid level in the brake master cylinder reservoir.

2. If the brake fluid level is midway between the maximum-full point and the minimum allowable level, no brake fluid needs to be removed before proceeding.

3. If the brake fluid level is higher than midway between the maximum-full point and the minimum allowable level, remove brake fluid to the midway point before proceeding.

4. Raise and support the vehicle.

5. Remove the tire and wheel assembly.

➡ **DO NOT use any air tools to remove or install the guide pin bolts. Use hand tools ONLY. Install an open end wrench to hold the caliper guide pin in line with the brake caliper while removing or installing the caliper guide pin bolt. DO NOT allow the open end wrench to come in contact with the brake caliper. Allowing the open end wrench to come in contact with the brake caliper will**

cause a pulsation when the brakes are applied.

6. Remove the lower brake caliper guide pin bolt (1).

➡ **Hold the brake caliper guide pin stationary when removing the guide pin bolt.**

7. Pivot the brake caliper (1) upward and support with heavy mechanics wire or equivalent.

8. Place a block of wood or an old brake pad against the brake caliper pistons.

9. Using a brake pad spreader tool or equivalent, fully seat the caliper pistons in the caliper bores.

10. Remove the inner brake pad (1) and the outer brake pad (2).

➡ **Note the location of the brake pad wear sensor for correct installation.**

11. Remove the upper and lower brake pad shims (1).

➡ **If installing new brake pads, discard the shims.**

To install:

12. Install the upper and lower brake pad shims.

➡ **If installing new brake pads, install new shims.**

13. Install the inner brake pad and the outer brake pad.

➡ **Note the location of the brake pad wear sensor for correct installation.**

14. Pivot the brake caliper into position and install the lower brake caliper guide pin bolt (1). Tighten the bolt to 20 ft. lbs. (27 Nm).

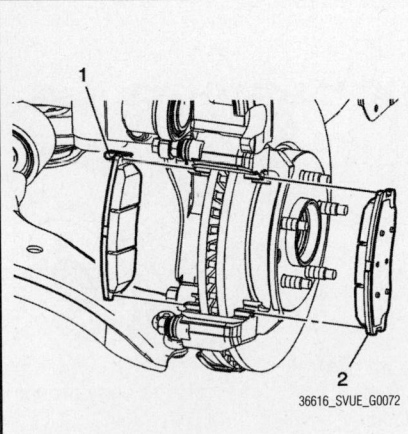

Fig. 6 Remove the inner brake pad (1) and the outer brake pad (2)

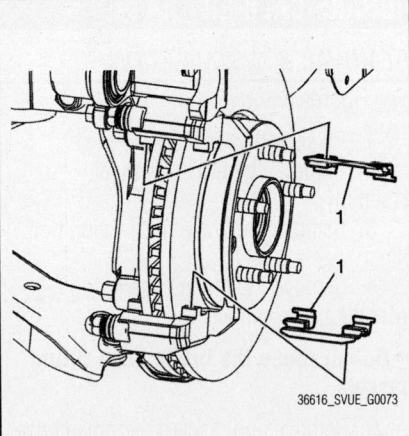

Fig. 7 Remove the upper and lower brake pad shims (1)

➥Hold the brake caliper guide pin stationary when installing the guide pin bolt.

15. Install the tire and wheel assembly.
16. Lower the vehicle.
17. With the engine OFF, gradually apply the brake pedal to approximately ⅔ of its travel distance.
18. Slowly release the brake pedal.
19. Wait 15 seconds, then repeat steps until a firm brake pedal is obtained. This will properly seat the brake caliper pistons and brake pads.
20. Fill the master cylinder reservoir to the proper level.
21. Burnish the pads and rotors.

BRAKES

REAR DISC BRAKES

BRAKE CALIPER

REMOVAL & INSTALLATION

See Figures 8 and 9.

1. Raise and support the vehicle.
2. Remove the tire and wheel assembly.
3. Remove the brake hose fitting bolt (1).
4. Remove the brake hose fitting (2) from the brake caliper.

➥Do not reuse the brake hose fitting gaskets.

5. Remove and discard the brake hose fitting gaskets (3).
6. Cap the brake hose fitting to prevent brake fluid loss and contamination.

➥DO NOT use any air tools to remove or install the guide pin bolts. Use hand tools ONLY. Install an open end wrench to hold the caliper guide pin in line with the brake caliper while removing or installing the caliper guide pin bolt. DO NOT allow the open end wrench to come in contact with the brake caliper. Allowing the open end wrench to come in contact with the brake caliper will cause a pulsation when the brakes are applied.

7. Remove the brake caliper guide pin bolts (1).

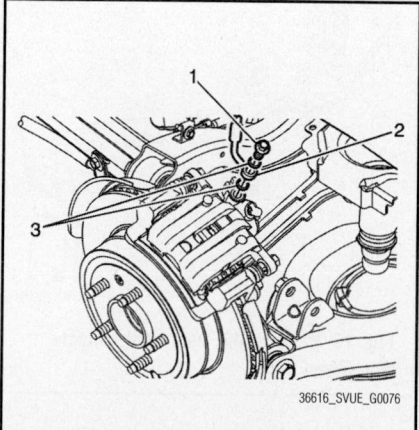

Fig. 8 Remove the brake hose fitting bolt (1)

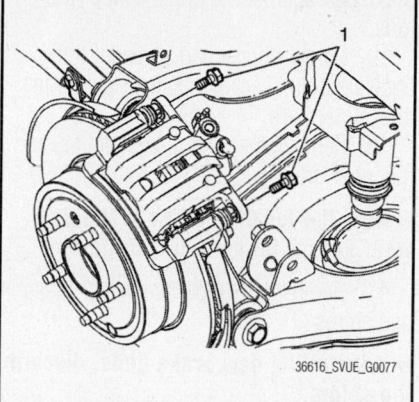

Fig. 9 Remove the brake caliper guide pin bolts (1)

➥Hold the brake caliper guide pins stationary when removing the guide pin bolts.

8. Remove the brake caliper.

To install:

9. Install the brake caliper.
10. Install the brake caliper guide pin bolts. Tighten the bolts to 20 ft. lbs. (27 Nm).

➥Hold the brake caliper guide pins stationary when installing the guide pin bolts.

➥Install new brake hose fitting gaskets.

11. Install new brake hose fitting gaskets to the brake hose fitting.
12. Install the brake hose fitting to the brake caliper.
13. Install the brake hose fitting bolt. Tighten the bolt to 38 ft. lbs. (52 Nm).
14. Bleed the hydraulic brake system.
15. Install the tire and wheel assembly.
16. Lower the vehicle.

DISC BRAKE PADS

REMOVAL AND INSTALLATION

See Figures 10 through 13.

➥Support the brake caliper with heavy mechanic wire, or equivalent, whenever it is separated from its mount and the hydraulic flexible brake hose is still connected. Failure to support the caliper in this manner will cause the flexible brake hose to bear the weight of the caliper, which may cause damage to the brake hose and in turn may cause a brake fluid leak.

1. Inspect the fluid level in the brake master cylinder reservoir.
2. If the brake fluid level is midway between the maximum-full point and the minimum allowable level, no brake fluid needs to be removed before proceeding.
3. If the brake fluid level is higher than midway between the maximum-full point and the minimum allowable level, remove brake fluid to the midway point before proceeding.
4. Raise and support the vehicle.
5. Remove the tire and wheel assembly.

➥DO NOT use any air tools to remove or install the guide pin bolts. Use hand tools ONLY. Install an open end wrench to hold the caliper guide pin in line with the brake caliper while removing or installing the caliper guide pin bolt. DO NOT allow the open end wrench to come in contact with the brake caliper. Allowing the open end wrench to come in contact with the brake caliper will cause a pulsation when the brakes are applied.

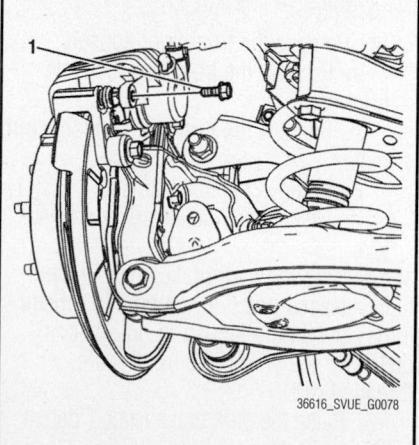

Fig. 10 Remove the lower brake caliper guide pin bolt (1)

Fig. 11 Pivot the brake caliper (1) upward

Fig. 12 Remove the outer brake pad (1) and the inner brake pad (2)

6. Remove the lower brake caliper guide pin bolt (1).

➡**Hold the brake caliper guide pin stationary when removing the guide pin bolt.**

7. Pivot the brake caliper (1) upward and support with heavy mechanics wire or equivalent.

8. Place a block of wood or an old brake pad against the brake caliper pistons.

9. Using a brake pad spreader tool or equivalent, fully seat the caliper piston in the caliper bore.

10. Remove the outer brake pad (1) and the inner brake pad (2).

➡**Note the location of the brake pad wear sensor for correct installation.**

11. Remove the upper and lower brake pad shims (1).

➡**If installing new brake pads, discard the shims.**

To install:

12. Install the upper and lower brake pad shims.

➡**If installing new brake pads, install new shims.**

13. Install the outer brake pad and the inner brake pad.

➡**Note the location of the brake pad wear sensor for correct installation.**

14. Pivot the brake caliper into position

Fig. 13 Remove the upper and lower brake pad shims (1)

and install the lower brake caliper guide pin bolt. Tighten the bolt to 20 ft. lbs. (27 Nm).

➡**Hold the brake caliper guide pin stationary when installing the guide pin bolt.**

15. Install the tire and wheel assembly.

16. Lower the vehicle.

17. With the engine OFF, gradually apply the brake pedal to approximately ⅔ of its travel distance.

18. Slowly release the brake pedal.

19. Wait 15 seconds, then repeat steps until a firm brake pedal is obtained. This will properly seat the brake caliper pistons and brake pads.

20. Fill the master cylinder reservoir to the proper level.

21. Burnish the pads and rotors.

BRAKES

PARKING BRAKE CABLES

ADJUSTMENT

See Figures 14 through 17.

1. Remove the front floor console.

   a. Remove the front floor console front cover.

   b. Remove the front floor console trim plate.

   c. Remove the floor console bolts (1).

   d. Disconnect the electrical connectors

2. With the park brake lever in the fully released position, using ONLY hand tools, loosen the adjusting nut (1) completely to the end of the front cable threaded rod.

3. Raise the park brake lever 1 detent position.

4. Using ONLY hand tools, tighten the park brake cable adjusting nut until light to

PARKING BRAKE

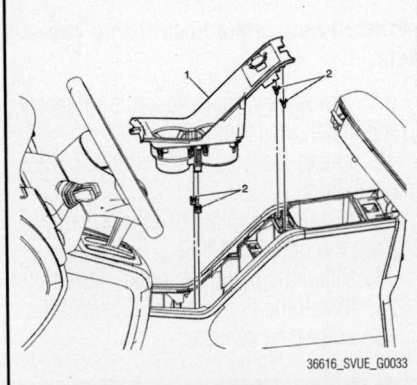

Fig. 14 Remove the front floor console front cover

moderate drag is exhibited while rotating the rear wheels.

5. Attempt to rotate the rear wheels. There should be no rotation forward or rearward.

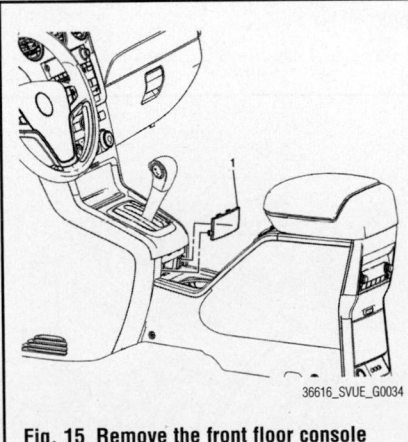

Fig. 15 Remove the front floor console trim plate

6. Fully release the park brake lever.

7. Verify the park brake is released by rotating the rear wheels. The wheels should

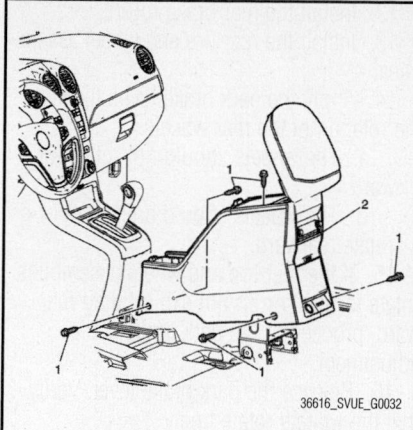

Fig. 16 Remove the front floor console bolts (1)

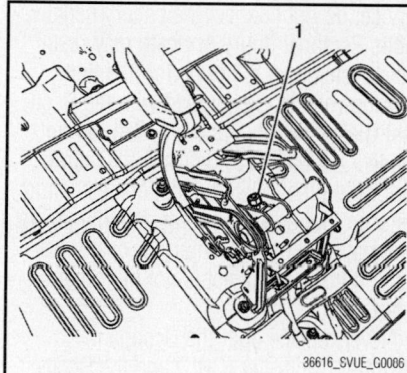

Fig. 17 Loosen the adjusting nut (1) completely

rotate freely and exhibit no park brake shoe drag.

8. If the wheels do not rotate freely, repeat the park brake cable adjustment procedure.

9. Raise the park brake lever 3 detent positions and attempt to rotate the rear wheels.

a. One of the wheels should not rotate forward or rearward.

b. The other wheel should not rotate forward or rearward, or should require substantial effort to rotate.

10. Install the front floor console.

11. Release the park brake lever.

PARKING BRAKE SHOES

REMOVAL & INSTALLATION

See Figure 18.

1. Raise and safely support the vehicle.

2. Remove the tire and wheel.

3. Remove the brake rotor.

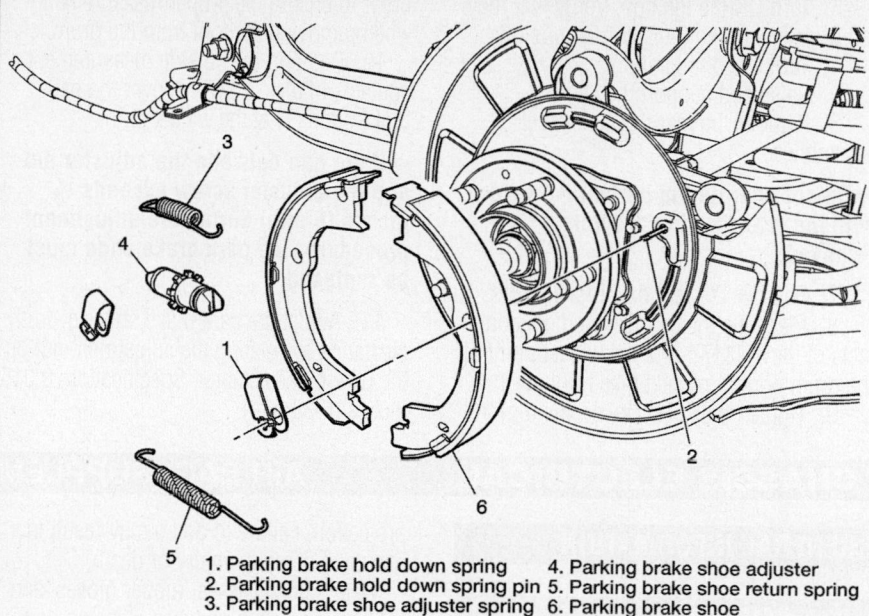

1. Parking brake hold down spring
2. Parking brake hold down spring pin
3. Parking brake shoe adjuster spring
4. Parking brake shoe adjuster
5. Parking brake shoe return spring
6. Parking brake shoe

Fig. 18 Exploded view or parking brake assembly

4. Remove the two parking brake hold down springs (1).

a. Compress the spring and rotate ¼ turn to release.

5. Remove the two parking brake hold down spring pins (2).

6. Using the J 38400, remove the adjuster spring (3).

7. Remove the parking brake adjuster screw (4).

➡**Clean the threads and apply high temperature grease to the adjuster screw.**

8. Remove the parking brake return spring (5) using the J 30400.

9. Remove the two parking brake shoes (6).

10. Installation is the reverse of removal.

a. Use denatured alcohol to clean brake dust or grease from the park brake shoes and hardware.

b. If reinstalling the park brake shoes, note the location of the park brake shoes for installation.

c. Apply a small amount of high temperature silicone grease to the brake shoe and backing plate contact points.

d. Adjust the park brake.

ADJUSTMENT

See Figures 19 and 20.

1. Apply and fully release the park brake lever.

2. Verify that the park brake lever releases completely.

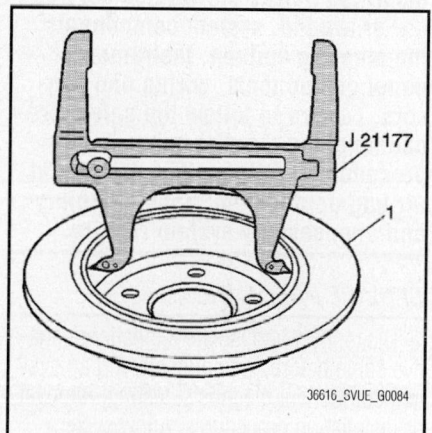

Fig. 19 Widest point of the drum portion of the brake rotor (1)

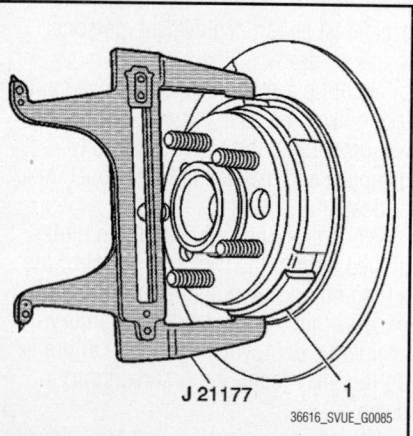

Fig. 20 Park brake shoe (1) at the widest point

3. Turn ON the ignition. Verify that the red BRAKE warning indicator lamp is off.

4. Turn OFF the ignition.

5. Raise and support the vehicle.

6. Remove the rear tire and wheel assemblies.

➡**Do not operate the park brake lever with the rear disc brake rotors removed.**

7. Remove the rear disc brake rotors.

8. Place the inside measurement contacts of the J 21177-A at the widest point of the drum portion of the brake rotor (1).

9. Tighten the set screw on the tool in order to ensure the proper measurement when removing the tool from the drum.

10. Position the outside measurement contacts of the J 21177-A over the park brake shoe (1) at the widest point.

➡**If the gap between the adjuster nut and the adjuster screw exceeds ¼ inches (5 mm) during the adjustment procedure, the park brake shoe must be replaced.**

11. Adjust the park brake shoe-to-drum clearance by rotating the adjustment nut on the park brake actuator. Specification: 0.015 inches (0.38 mm).

12. Install the rear brake rotors.

13. Install the rear tire and wheel assemblies.

14. Apply the park brake lever. Inspect the rotation of the rear wheels.

   a. The wheels should not rotate forward.

   b. The wheels should drag or not rotate rearward.

15. If the rear tire and wheel assemblies rotate forward or do not exhibit drag rearward, proceed to the park brake cable adjustment.

16. Release the park brake lever. Verify that the wheels rotate freely.

CHASSIS ELECTRICAL

AIR BAG (SUPPLEMENTAL RESTRAINT SYSTEM)

GENERAL INFORMATION

❋❋ CAUTION

These vehicles are equipped with an air bag system. The system must be disarmed before performing service on, or around, system components, the steering column, instrument panel components, wiring and sensors. Failure to follow the safety precautions and the disarming procedure could result in accidental air bag deployment, possible injury and unnecessary system repairs.

SERVICE PRECAUTIONS

Disconnect and isolate the battery negative cable before beginning any airbag system component diagnosis, testing, removal, or installation procedures. Allow system capacitor to discharge for two minutes before beginning any component service. This will disable the airbag system. Failure to disable the airbag system may result in accidental airbag deployment, personal injury, or death.

Do not place an intact undeployed airbag face down on a solid surface. The airbag will propel into the air if accidentally deployed and may result in personal injury or death.

When carrying or handling an undeployed airbag, the trim side (face) of the airbag should be pointing towards the body to minimize possibility of injury if accidental deployment occurs. Failure to do this may result in personal injury or death.

Replace airbag system components with OEM replacement parts. Substitute parts may appear interchangeable, but internal differences may result in inferior occupant protection. Failure to do so may result in occupant personal injury or death.

Wear safety glasses, rubber gloves, and long sleeved clothing when cleaning powder residue from vehicle after an airbag deployment. Powder residue emitted from a deployed airbag can cause skin irritation. Flush affected area with cool water if irritation is experienced. If nasal or throat irritation is experienced, exit the vehicle for fresh air until the irritation ceases. If irritation continues, see a physician.

Do not use a replacement airbag that is not in the original packaging. This may result in improper deployment, personal injury, or death.

The factory installed fasteners, screws and bolts used to fasten airbag components have a special coating and are specifically designed for the airbag system. Do not use substitute fasteners. Use only original equipment fasteners listed in the parts catalog when fastener replacement is required.

During, and following, any child restraint anchor service, due to impact event or vehicle repair, carefully inspect all mounting hardware, tether straps, and anchors for proper installation, operation, or damage. If a child restraint anchor is found damaged in any way, the anchor must be replaced. Failure to do this may result in personal injury or death.

Deployed and non-deployed airbags may or may not have live pyrotechnic material within the airbag inflator.

Do not dispose of driver/passenger/curtain airbags or seat belt tensioners unless you are sure of complete deployment. Refer to the Hazardous Substance Control System for proper disposal.

Dispose of deployed airbags and tensioners consistent with state, provincial, local, and federal regulations.

After any airbag component testing or service, do not connect the battery negative cable. Personal injury or death may result if the system test is not performed first.

If the vehicle is equipped with the Occupant Classification System (OCS), do not connect the battery negative cable before performing the OCS Verification Test using the scan tool and the appropriate diagnostic information. Personal injury or death may result if the system test is not performed properly.

Never replace both the Occupant Restraint Controller (ORC) and the Occupant Classification Module (OCM) at the same time. If both require replacement, replace one, then perform the Airbag System test before replacing the other.

Both the ORC and the OCM store Occupant Classification System (OCS) calibration data, which they transfer to one another when one of them is replaced. If both are replaced at the same time, an irreversible fault will be set in both modules and the OCS may malfunction and cause personal injury or death.

If equipped with OCS, the Seat Weight Sensor is a sensitive, calibrated unit and must be handled carefully. Do not drop or handle roughly. If dropped or damaged, replace with another sensor. Failure to do so may result in occupant injury or death.

If equipped with OCS, the front passenger seat must be handled carefully as well. When removing the seat, be careful when setting on floor not to drop. If dropped, the sensor may be inoperative, could result in occupant injury, or possibly death.

If equipped with OCS, when the passenger front seat is on the floor, no one should sit in the front passenger seat. This uneven force may damage the sensing ability of the seat weight sensors. If sat on and damaged, the sensor may be inoperative, could result in occupant injury, or possibly death.

DISARMING THE SYSTEM

Disabling Procedure - Air Bag Fuse

1. Turn the steering wheel so that the vehicles wheels are pointing straight ahead.
2. Place the ignition in the OFF position.

➡️ **The SDM may have more than one fused power input. To ensure there is no unwanted SIR deployment, personal injury, or unnecessary SIR system repairs, remove all fuses supplying power to the SDM. With all SDM fuses removed and the ignition switch in the ON position, the AIR BAG warning indicator illuminates. This is normal operation, and does not indicate a SIR system malfunction.**

3. Locate and remove the fuse(s) supplying power to the SDM.
4. Wait 1 minute before working on the system.

Disabling Procedure - Negative Battery Cable

1. Turn the steering wheel so that the vehicles wheels are pointing straight ahead.
2. Place the ignition in the OFF position.
3. Disconnect the negative battery cable from the battery.
4. Wait 1 minute before working on system.

ARMING THE SYSTEM

Enabling Procedure - Air Bag Fuse

1. Place the ignition in the OFF position.
2. Install the fuse(s) supplying power to the SDM.
3. Turn the ignition switch to the ON position. The AIR BAG indicator will flash then turn OFF.
4. Perform the Diagnostic System Check - Vehicle if the AIR BAG warning indicator does not operate as described.

Enabling Procedure - Negative Battery Cable

1. Place the ignition in the OFF position.
2. Connect the negative battery cable to the battery.
3. Turn the ignition switch to the ON position. The AIR BAG indicator will flash then turn OFF.
4. Perform the Diagnostic System Check - Vehicle if the AIR BAG warning indicator does not operate as described.

CLOCKSPRING CENTERING

See Figure 21.

➡️ **The new SIR coil assembly will be centered. Improper alignment of the SIR coil assembly may damage the unit, causing an inflatable restraint malfunction.**

1. If available, remove the yellow tab (2) and save for reassembly.

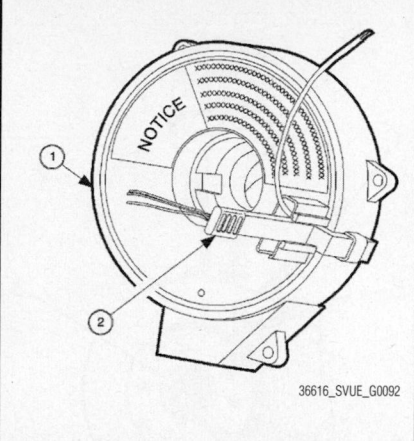

Fig. 21 Remove the yellow tab (2) and save for reassembly

2. Gently rotate the coil hub (1) clockwise until a slight tension is present.
3. Count the number of revolutions, while gently rotating the coil hub (1) counter clockwise until a slight tension is present.
4. Gently rotate the coil hub (1) clockwise one half of the previously counted revolutions.
5. Rotate the coil hub as required to align the yellow tab (2)
6. Install the yellow tab (2) into the coil hub. Use tape if the tab is unavailable.

DRIVE TRAIN

FRONT HALFSHAFTS

REMOVAL & INSTALLATION

See Figures 22 through 32.

1. Raise and support the vehicle.
2. Remove the tire and wheel assembly.

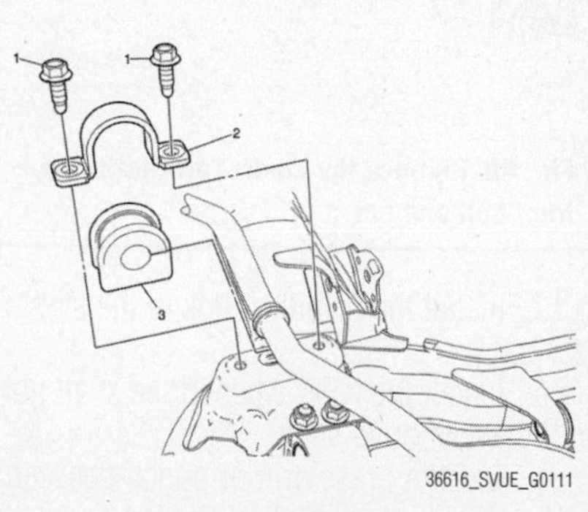

Fig. 22 Remove the engine splash shield

3. Remove the engine splash shield.
4. Insert a brass drift or punch (1) between the brake rotor cooling fins (2) and the brake caliper mounting bracket (4).
5. Using the appropriate size socket and a breaker bar (4), remove the wheel drive shaft nut (3).

➡️ **Once the wheel drive shaft nut has been removed, discard and replace with NEW. DO NOT re-use the nut.**

6. Remove the wheel drive shaft nut (2) from the wheel drive shaft (1).
7. Using the J 42129 (2), separate the wheel drive shaft from the brake rotor and wheel bearing/hub assembly (1).
8. Remove the outer tie rod end from the steering knuckle.
9. Remove the stabilizer bar link from the stabilizer shaft.
10. Remove the lower control arm from the steering knuckle.

a. Remove the lower ball joint stud cotter pin. Discard the cotter pin.
b. Loosen the ball stud nut until the nut is level with the top of the ball stud.
c. Using J-42188-B, separate the lower control arm from the steering knuckle.
d. Remove the lower ball joint stud nut.
e. Remove the control arm-to-frame front bolt and nut. Discard the bolt and nut.
f. Remove the control arm-to-frame rear bolts and nuts. Discard the bolts and nuts.
g. Remove the control arm.
11. Install the J 2619-01, J 29794, and the J 45341 on the wheel drive shaft inner joint groove.
12. Using the J 2619-01, J 29794, and the J 45341, remove the wheel drive shaft.
13. Remove the wheel drive shaft from the knuckle.

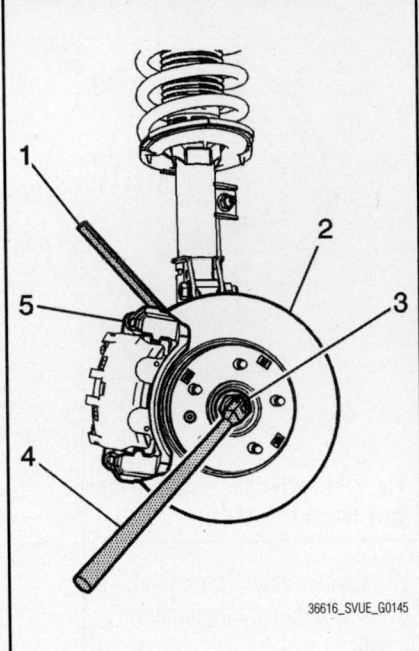

Fig. 23 Insert a brass drift or punch (1) between the brake rotor cooling fins (2) and the brake caliper mounting bracket (4)

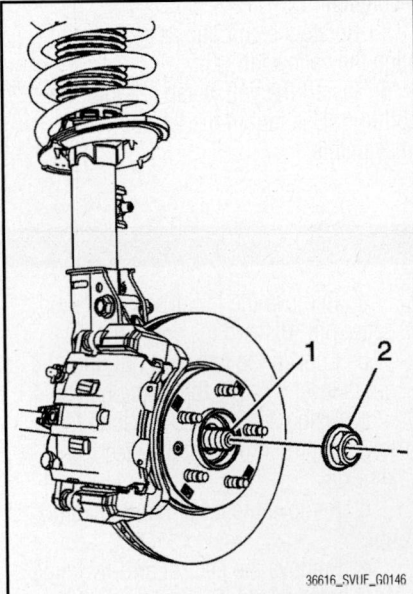

Fig. 24 Remove the wheel drive shaft nut (2) from the wheel drive shaft (1)

To install:

14. Install the SA91112T seal protector.
15. Install the wheel drive shaft in the vehicle.
16. Remove the SA91112T seal protector.
17. Install the lower control arm to the knuckle.
18. Install the outer tie rod end for the steering gear to the knuckle.

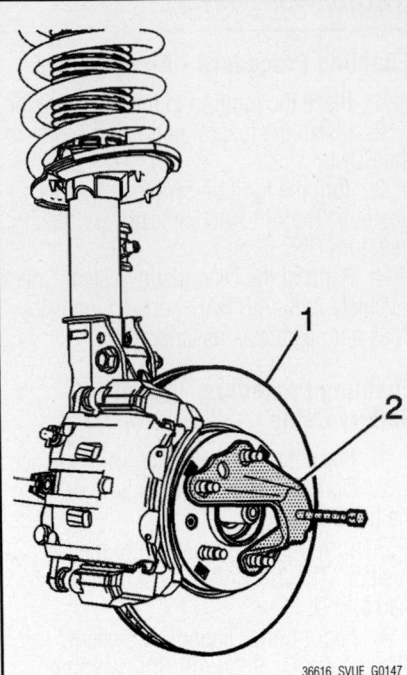

Fig. 25 Separate the wheel drive shaft from the brake rotor and wheel bearing/hub assembly (1)

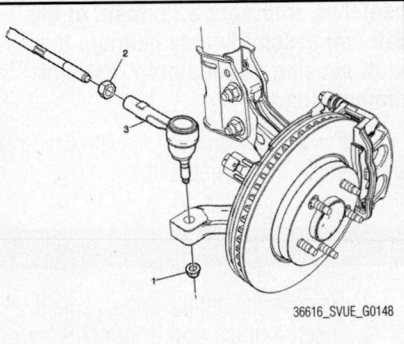

Fig. 26 Remove the outer tie rod end from the steering knuckle

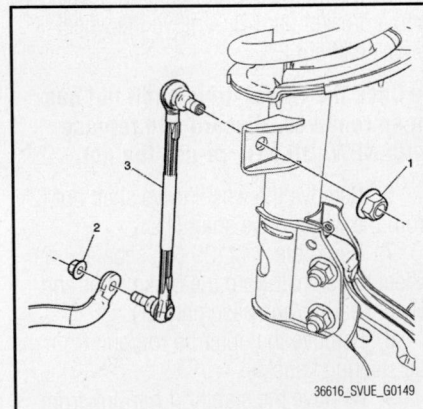

Fig. 27 Remove the stabilizer bar link from the stabilizer shaft

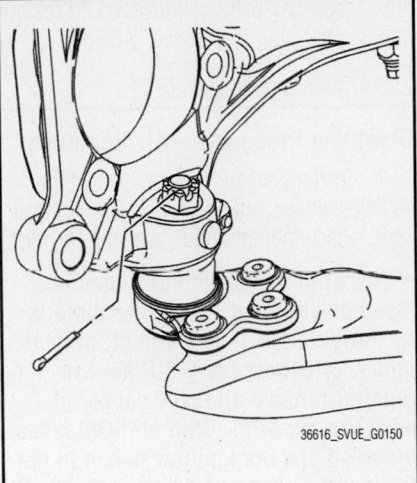

Fig. 28 Remove the lower ball joint stud cotter pin

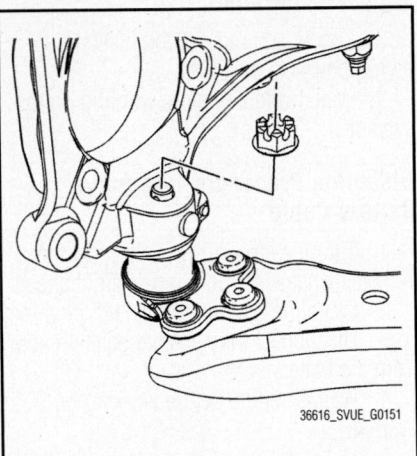

Fig. 29 Remove the lower ball joint stud nut

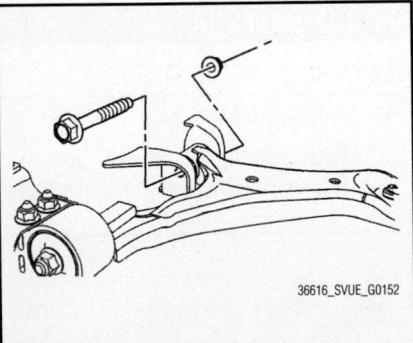

Fig. 30 Remove the control arm-to-frame front bolt and nut

19. Install the stabilizer link to the stabilizer bar.
20. Install the NEW wheel drive shaft nut on the wheel drive shaft.
21. Insert a brass drift or punch between the brake rotor cooling fins and the brake caliper mounting bracket.
22. Using a torque wrench, tighten the

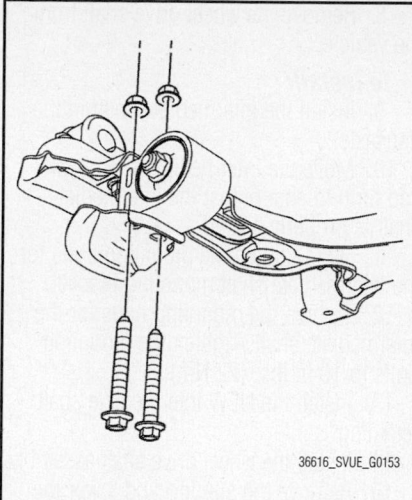

Fig. 31 Remove the control arm-to-frame rear bolts and nuts

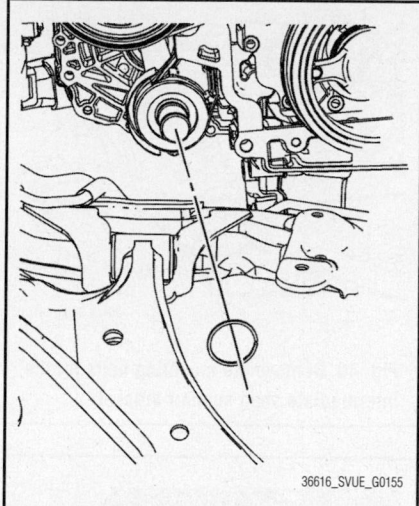

Fig. 33 Remove and discard the wheel drive shaft retaining ring

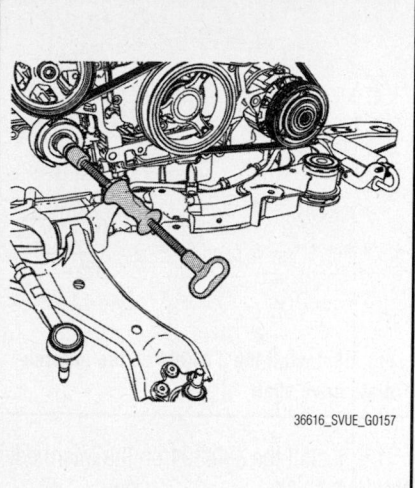

Fig. 35 Remove the intermediate shaft from the transaxle

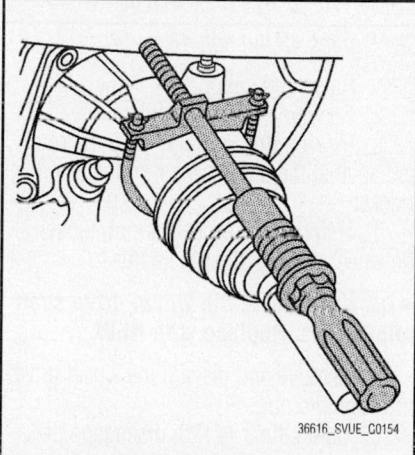

Fig. 32 Install the J 2619-01, J 29794, and the J 45341 on the wheel drive shaft inner joint groove

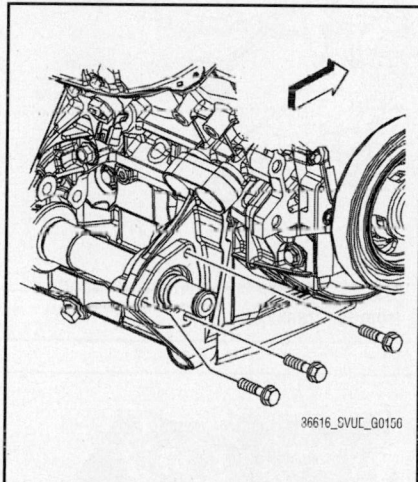

Fig. 34 Remove the intermediate drive shaft mounting bolts

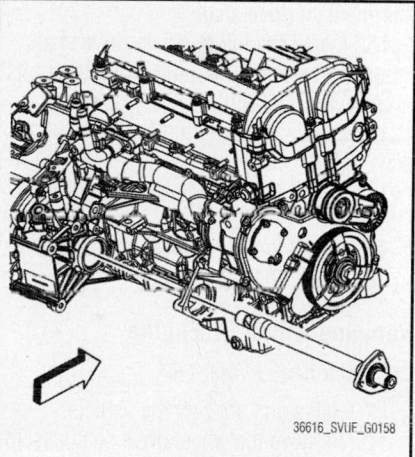

Fig. 36 Remove the intermediate drive shaft from the mounting bracket

wheel drive shaft nut. Tighten the wheel drive shaft nut to 151 ft. lbs. (205 Nm).

23. Inspect the transmission fluid level and add fluid if necessary.
24. Install the engine splash shield.
25. Install the tire and wheels.
26. Lower the vehicle.

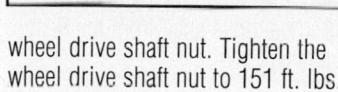
INTERMEDIATE SHAFT

REMOVAL & INSTALLATION

Vehicles with 2.4L Engine

See Figures 33 through 38.

1. Raise and support the vehicle.
2. Remove the right front wheel drive shaft.
3. Remove and discard the wheel drive shaft retaining ring.

4. Remove the O-ring seal from the intermediate drive shaft.
5. Remove the intermediate drive shaft mounting bolts.
6. Using the J 2619-01 and the J 44467, remove the intermediate shaft from the transaxle.
7. Remove the J 2619-01 and the J 44467 from the intermediate shaft.
8. Remove the intermediate drive shaft from the mounting bracket.
9. Remove the intermediate drive shaft bracket mounting bolts and bracket, if needed.

To install:

10. Position the intermediate drive shaft mounting bracket on the engine block.
11. Install the intermediate drive shaft mounting bracket bolts. Tighten the mounting bolts to 16 ft. lbs. (22 Nm).

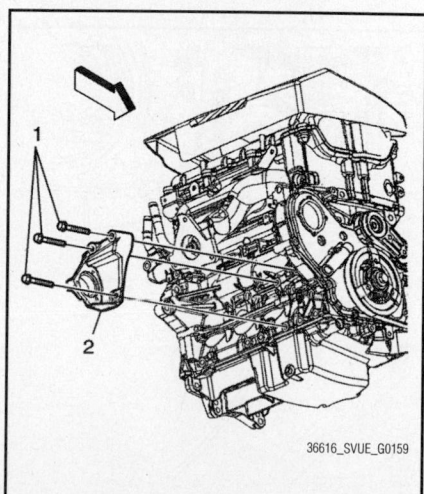

Fig. 37 Remove the intermediate drive shaft bracket mounting bolts and bracket

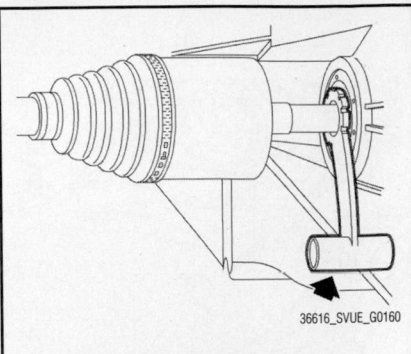

36616_SVUE_G0160

Fig. 38 Install the J 44394 on the interme-diate drive shaft

12. Install the J 44394 on the intermedi-ate drive shaft.

13. Install the intermediate drive shaft.

14. Remove the J 44394 from the inter-mediate drive shaft.

15. Install the mounting bolts for the intermediate drive shaft.

16. Install the intermediate drive shaft mounting bolts. Tighten the mounting bolts to 22 ft. lbs. (30 Nm).

17. Install a new O-ring for the interme-diate drive shaft.

18. Install a new retaining ring for the intermediate drive shaft.

19. Install the right wheel drive shaft.

20. Lower the vehicle.

Vehicles with 3.6L Engine

See Figures 39 through 42.

1. Raise and support the vehicle.

2. Remove the wheel drive shaft assem-bly.

➡**Remove the retaining ring. DO NOT re-use the retaining ring discard. Use NEW only.**

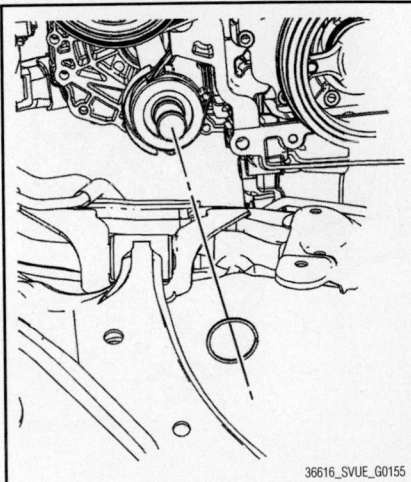

36616_SVUE_G0155

Fig. 39 Remove the retaining clip for the wheel drive shaft

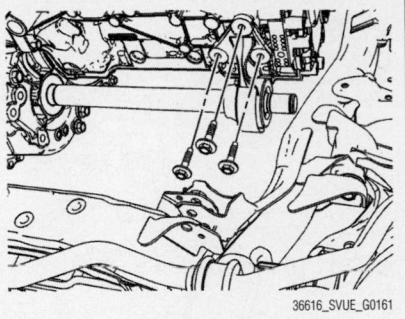

36616_SVUE_G0161

Fig. 40 Remove the mounting bolts for the intermediate shaft support bracket

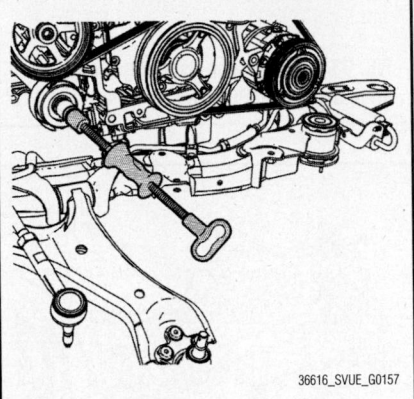

36616_SVUE_G0157

Fig. 41 Remove the intermediate shaft from the transaxle

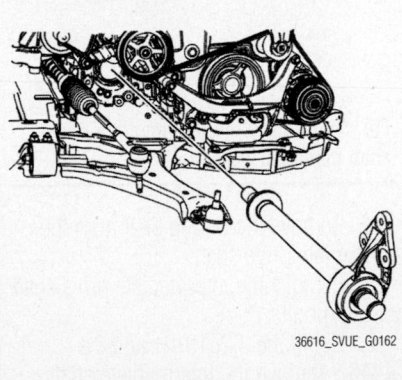

36616_SVUE_G0162

Fig. 42 Remove the wheel drive shaft from the vehicle

3. Remove the retaining clip for the wheel drive shaft.

4. Remove the mounting bolts for the intermediate shaft support bracket.

5. Support the wheel drive shaft.

6. Install the J 44467 and the J 2619-01 in the retaining ring groove on the wheel drive shaft.

7. Using the J 44467 and the J 2619-01, remove the wheel drive shaft from the transaxle.

8. Remove the wheel drive shaft from the vehicle.

To install:

9. Install the intermediate shaft in the transaxle.

10. Move the intermediate shaft back and forth to ensure that the intermediate shaft is properly seated.

11. Hand tighten the mounting bolts for the intermediate shaft mounting bracket.

12. Tighten the mounting bolts for the intermediate shaft. Tighten the mounting bolts to 16 ft. lbs. (22 Nm).

13. Install the NEW intermediate shaft retaining.

14. Install the wheel drive shaft assembly.

15. Remove the support and lower the vehicle.

REAR HALFSHAFTS

REMOVAL & INSTALLATION

See Figures 43 through 48.

1. Raise and support the vehicle.

2. Remove the tire and wheel.

3. Insert a drift or punch into the rotor and against the brake caliper mounting bracket.

4. Using the appropriate tool, loosen the wheel drive shaft spindle nut.

➡**DO NOT re-use the wheel drive shaft spindle nut. Replace with NEW.**

5. Remove and discard the wheel drive shaft spindle nut.

6. Using the J 42129, disengage the wheel drive shaft from the wheel hub/bearing.

7. Remove the rear suspension knuckle.

8. Using a suitable tool, carefully release the wheel drive shaft from the Rear Drive Module (RDM).

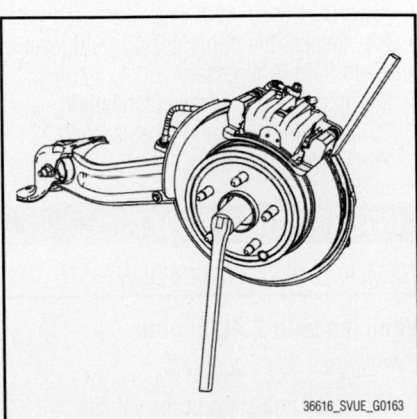

36616_SVUE_G0163

Fig. 43 Insert a drift or punch into the rotor and against the brake caliper mount-ing bracket

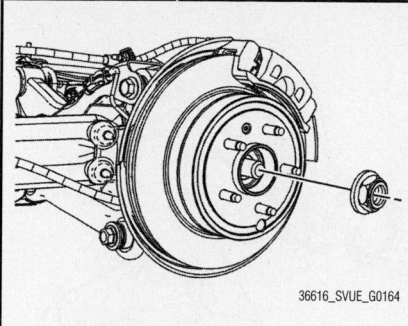

Fig. 44 Remove and discard the wheel drive shaft spindle nut

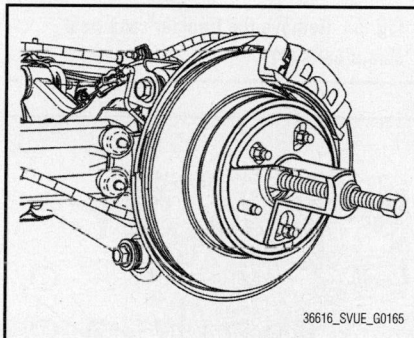

Fig. 45 Disengage the wheel drive shaft from the wheel hub/bearing

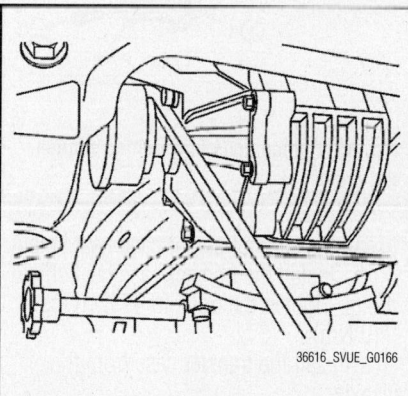

Fig. 46 Release the wheel drive shaft from the Rear Drive Module (RDM)

➡️**Because of the design of the inner seal wheel drive shaft seal, the seal will be removed at the same time the as wheel drive shaft. Replace the seal, DO NOT re-use the seal.**

9. Remove the wheel drive shaft from the vehicle.
10. Remove the wheel drive seal.

➡️**DO NOT re-use the retaining clip, replace with new.**

11. Remove the retaining ring from the tripod.

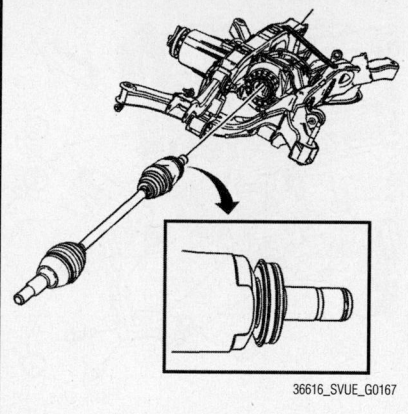

Fig. 47 The seal will be removed at the same time the as wheel drive shaft

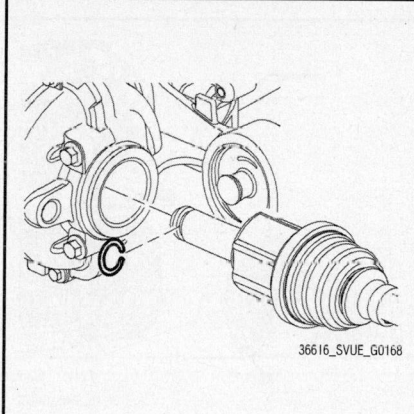

Fig. 48 Remove the retaining ring from the tripod

To install:

12. Install the new retaining clip on the tripod.
13. Install the new wheel drive shaft seal.

➡️**While installing the wheel drive shaft, you will notice a slight resistance. This is the wheel drive shaft seal. A snap or click should be heard when the wheel drive shaft is fully seated.**

14. Install the wheel drive shaft.
15. Install the rear suspension knuckle.
16. Install a new wheel drive shaft spindle nut. Hand tighten only.
17. Insert a drift or punch into the rotor and against the brake caliper mounting bracket.
18. Tighten the wheel drive shaft spindle nut. Tighten the nut to 151 ft. lbs. (205 Nm).
19. Install the tire and wheel assembly.
20. Remove the support and lower the vehicle.

REAR PINION SEAL

REMOVAL & INSTALLATION
See Figures 49 and 50

1. Raise and support the vehicle.
2. Remove the propeller shaft from the differential clutch drum assembly.
3. Disconnect the electrical clutch control connector (1).
4. Remove the two retaining clips (2) for the connector harness.

1. Electrical clutch control connector
2. Retaining Clip
3. Differential clutch drum bolts
4. Differential clutch drum
5. Differential clutch drum gasket

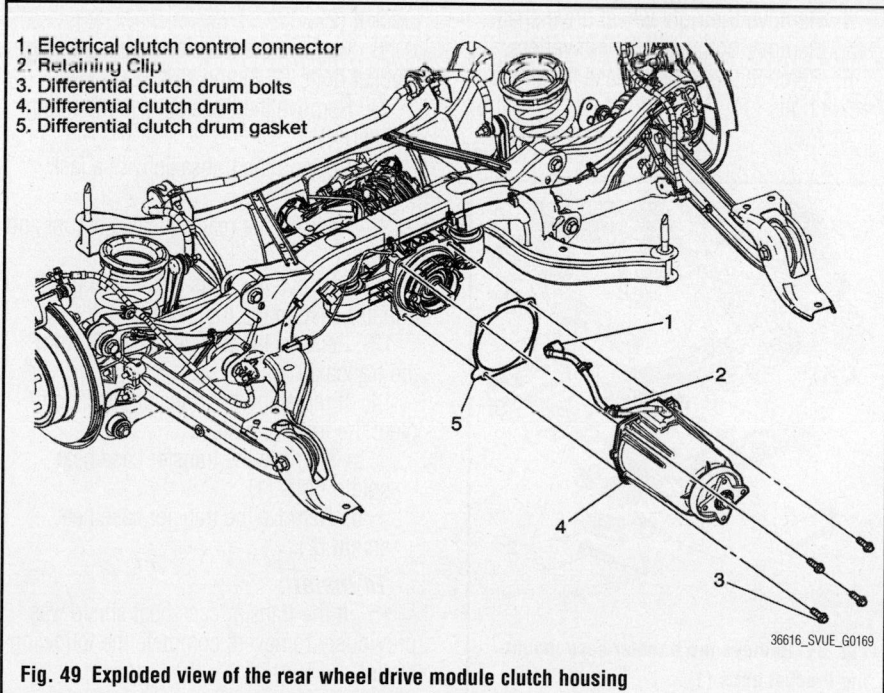

Fig. 49 Exploded view of the rear wheel drive module clutch housing

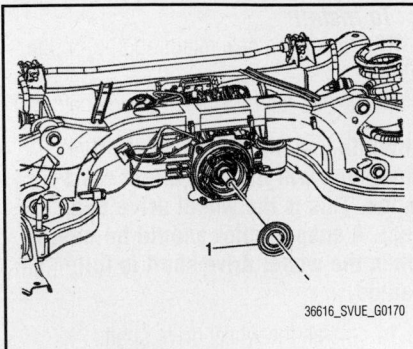

Fig. 50 Remove the differential pinion seal (1)

5. Remove the four differential clutch drum bolts (3).

6. Remove the differential clutch drum and gasket.

7. Remove the differential pinion seal (1).

 a. Install a sheet metal screw into the seal.

 b. Attach a pair of pliers or a slider hammer to the screw and remove the seal.

8. Installation is the reverse of removal.

TRANSFER CASE ASSEMBLY

REMOVAL & INSTALLATION

Vehicles with 3.5L Engines

See Figures 51 through 55.

1. Raise and support the vehicle.
2. Drain the transfer case fluid.
3. Remove the propeller shaft.
4. Remove the right wheel drive shaft.
5. Remove both catalytic converters.
6. Remove the transfer case mounting bracket bolts (1).

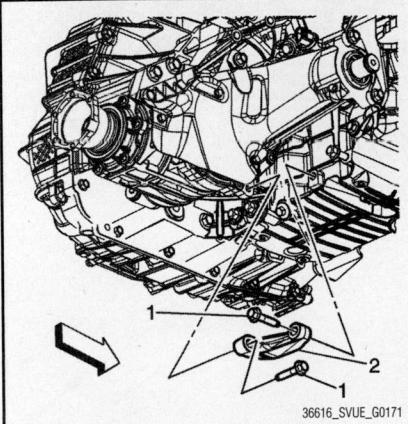

Fig. 51 Remove the transfer case mounting bracket bolts (1)

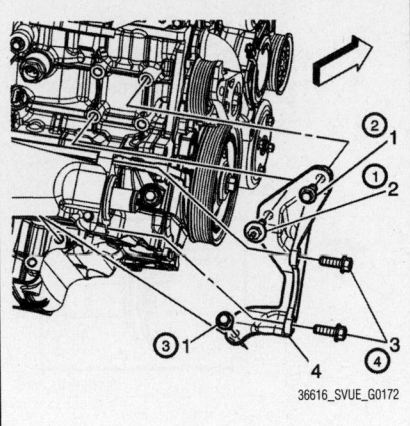

Fig. 52 Remove the transfer case mounting bracket bolts (1, 3) and stud (2)

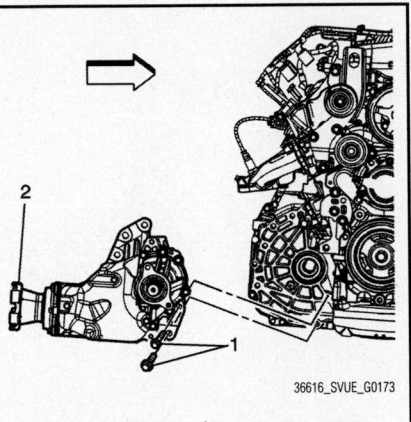

Fig. 53 Remove the bolts (1) securing the transfer case to the transaxle

7. Remove the transfer case mounting bracket (2).

8. Remove the transfer case mounting bracket bolts (1, 3) and stud (2).

9. Remove the transfer case mounting bracket (4).

10. Support the transaxle with a jack stand.

11. Remove the rear transaxle mount and bracket.

12. Remove the bolts (1) securing the transfer case to the transaxle.

13. Remove the transfer case (2) from the transaxle.

14. If replacing the transfer case, complete the following steps:

 a. Remove the transfer case heat shield bolts (1).

 b. Remove the transfer case heat shield (2).

To install:

15. If the transfer case heat shield was previously removed, complete the following steps:

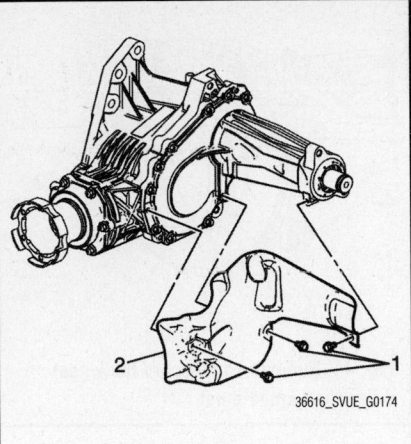

Fig. 54 Remove the transfer case heat shield bolts (1)

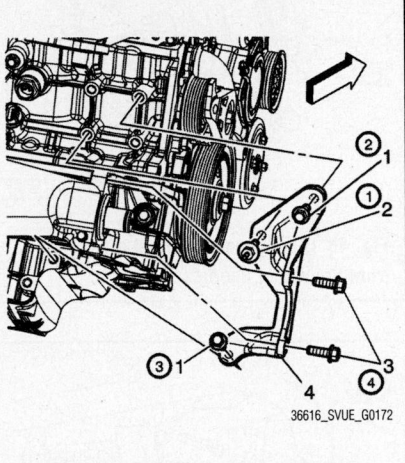

Fig. 55 Tighten bolts in specified sequential order

 a. Install the transfer case heat shield.

 b. Install the transfer case heat shield bolts. Tighten the bolts to 89 inch lbs. (10 Nm).

16. Install the transfer case from the transaxle.

17. Install the bolts securing the transfer case to the transaxle. Tighten the bolts to 37 ft. lbs. (50 Nm).

18. Install the rear transaxle mount and bracket.

19. Remove the jack stand supporting the transaxle.

➡Tighten bolts in specified sequential order.

20. Install the transfer case mounting bracket.

21. Install the transfer case mounting bracket bolts and stud. Tighten the bolts and stud in specified sequential order to 37 ft. lbs. (50 Nm).

22. Install the transfer case mounting bracket bolt. Tighten the bolts in specified sequential order to 17 ft. lbs. (23 Nm).

23. Install the transfer case mounting bracket.

24. Install the transfer case mounting bracket bolts. Tighten the bolts to 37 ft. lbs. (50 Nm).

25. Install both catalytic converters.

26. Install the right wheel drive shaft.

27. Install the propeller shaft.

28. Fill the transfer case with fluid.

29. Lower the vehicle.

Vehicles with 3.6L Engines

See Figures 54, 56 through 58.

1. Raise and support the vehicle.

2. Drain the transfer case fluid.

3. Remove the propeller shaft.

4. Remove the right wheel drive shaft.

5. Remove both catalytic converters.

6. Remove the transfer case mounting bracket bolts (1, 2, 4).

7. Remove the transfer case mounting bracket (3).

8. Support the transaxle with a jack stand.

9. Remove the rear transaxle mount and bracket.

10. Remove the bolts (1) securing the transfer case to the transaxle.

11. Remove the transfer case (2) from the transaxle.

12. If replacing the transfer case, complete the following steps:

    a. Remove the transfer case heat shield bolts (1).

    b. Remove the transfer case heat shield (2).

To Install:

13. If the transfer case heat shield was previously removed, complete the following steps:

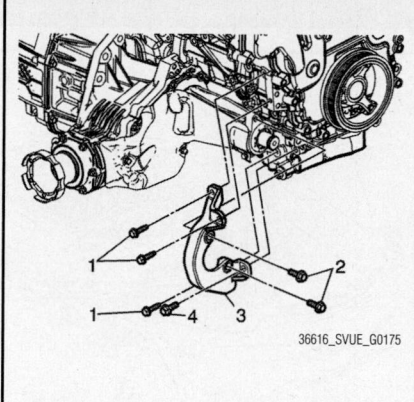

Fig. 56 Remove the transfer case mounting bracket bolts (1, 2, 4)

36616_SVUE_G0175

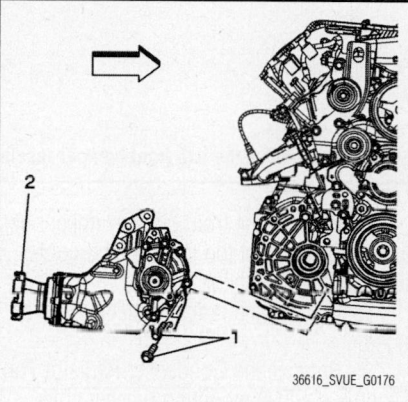

Fig. 57 Remove the bolts (1) securing the transfer case to the transaxle

36616_SVUE_G0176

    a. Install the transfer case heat shield.

    b. Install the transfer case heat shield bolts. Tighten the bolts to 89 inch lbs. (10 Nm).

14. Install the transfer case from the transaxle.

15. Install the bolts securing the transfer

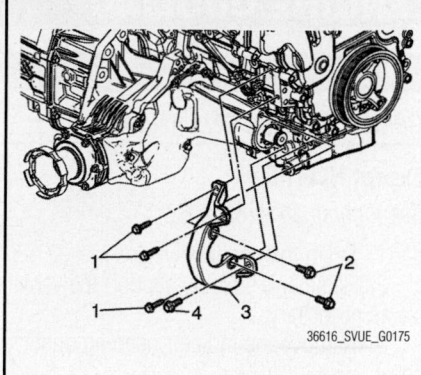

Fig. 58 Tighten bolts in specified sequential order

36616_SVUE_G0175

case to the transaxle. Tighten the bolts to 37 ft. lbs. (50 Nm).

16. Install the rear transaxle mount and bracket.

17. Remove the jack stand supporting the transaxle.

➡**Tighten bolts in specified sequential order.**

18. Install the transfer case mounting bracket.

19. Install the transfer case mounting bracket bolts. Tighten the bolts to 17 ft. lbs. (23 Nm).

20. Install the transfer case mounting bracket bolt. Tighten the bolts to 37 ft. lbs. (50 Nm).

21. Install the transfer case mounting bracket bolt. Tighten the bolts to 37 ft. lbs. (50 Nm).

22. Install both catalytic converters.

23. Install the right wheel drive shaft.

24. Install the propeller shaft.

25. Fill the transfer case with fluid.

26. Lower the vehicle.

ENGINE COOLING

ENGINE FAN

REMOVAL & INSTALLATION

Except Hybrid

See Figures 59 through 62.

1. Drain the cooling system.
2. Raise and suitably support the vehicle as necessary.
3. Remove the radiator opening upper cover.
4. Disconnect the electrical connector from the fan motor.
5. Remove the front fascia.
   a. Remove the front wheelhouse liner to fascia screw only.
   b. Remove front bumper fascia air deflector.
   c. Remove the two front bumper fascia bolts (1).
   d. Remove the front bumper fascia by pulling forward.

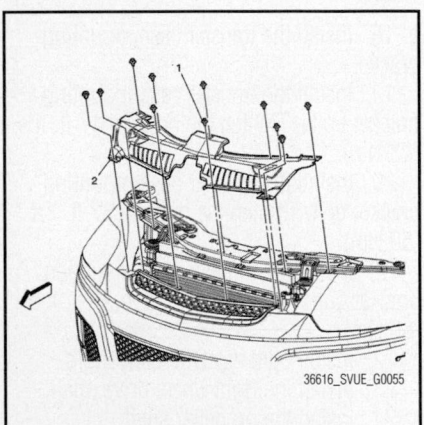

Fig. 59 Remove the radiator opening upper cover

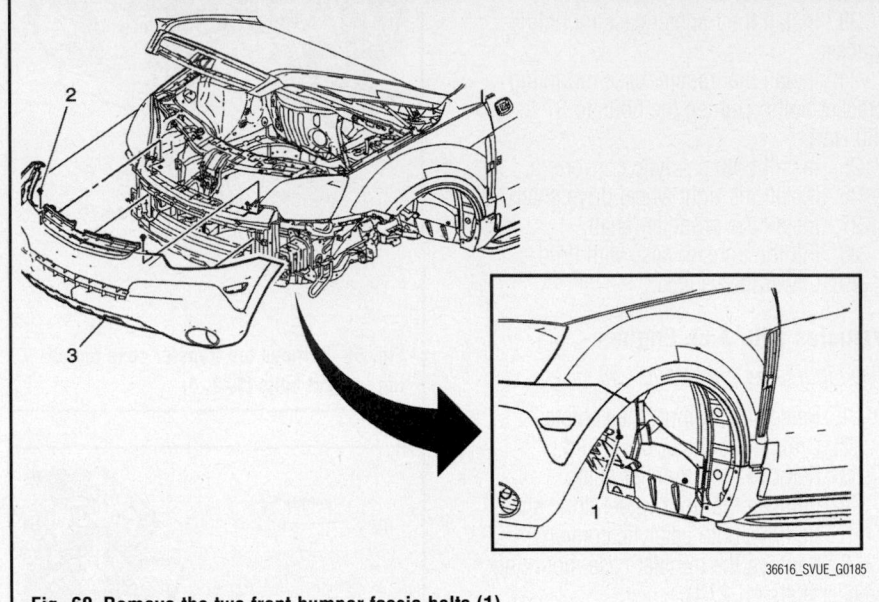

Fig. 60 Remove the two front bumper fascia bolts (1)

6. Remove the front bumper impact bar.
7. Disconnect the transaxle oil cooler lines from the radiator.
8. Remove the radiator inlet and outlet hose.
9. Remove the Condenser Radiator Fan Module (CRFM) mounting bracket bolts from the radiator support.
10. Remove the CRFM mounting brackets from the radiator support.
11. Lift the CRFM assembly from the lower mounts and carefully move the bottom of the assembly rearward while tilting the top forward.
12. Remove the fan assembly bolts (1) from the radiator.
13. Remove the fan and shroud assembly (2).

14. Installation is the reverse of removal.

Hybrid

See Figures 59 through 61 and 63 through 65.

1. Drain the cooling system.
2. Disconnect the hybrid system.
3. Raise and suitably support the vehicle as necessary.
4. Remove the radiator opening upper cover.
5. Disconnect the electrical connector from the fan motor.
6. Remove the front fascia.
   a. Remove the front wheelhouse liner to fascia screw only.
   b. Remove front bumper fascia air deflector.

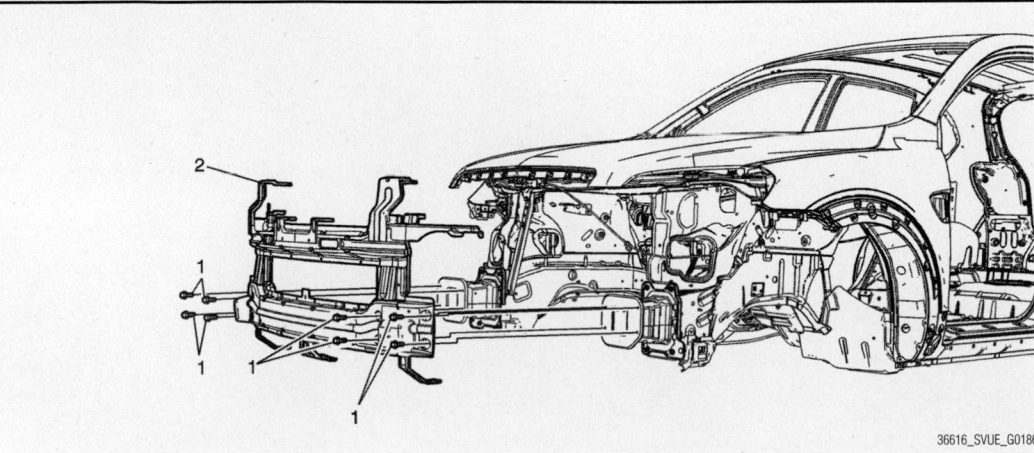

Fig. 61 Remove the front bumper impact bar

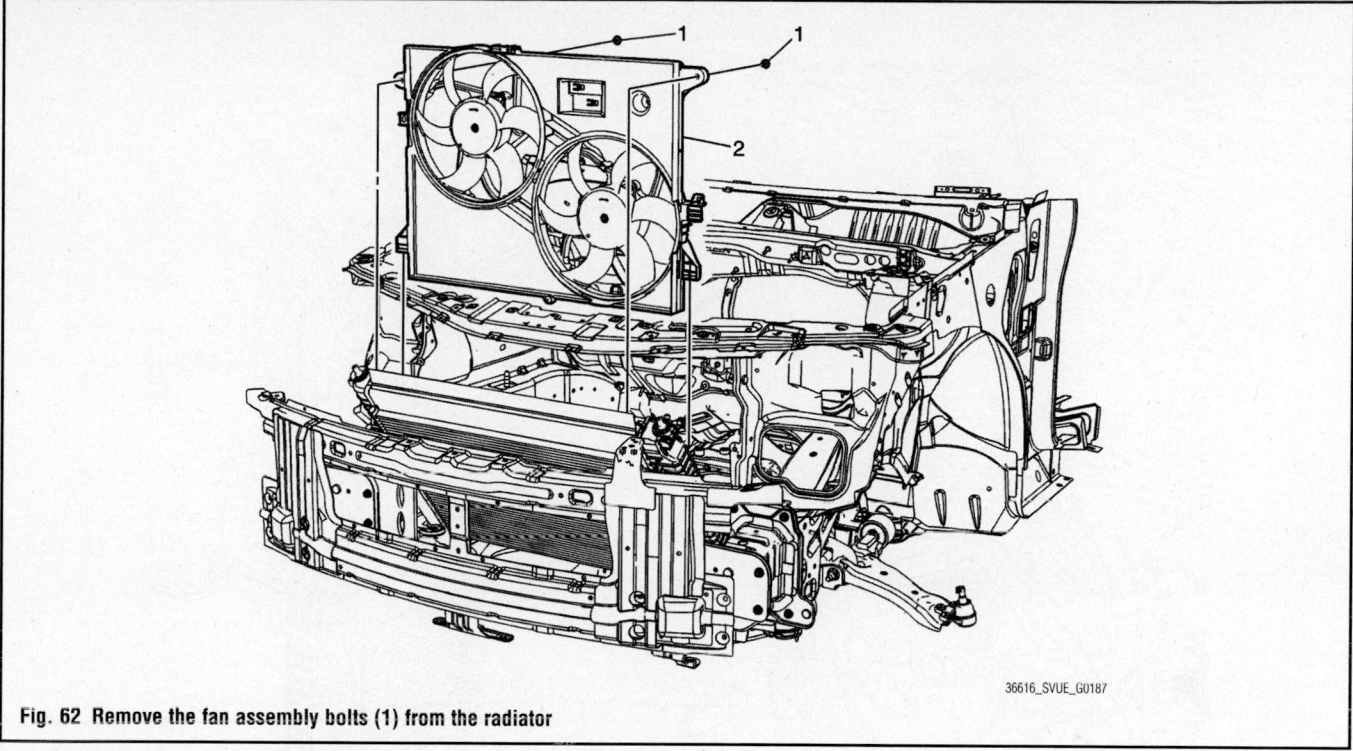

Fig. 62 Remove the fan assembly bolts (1) from the radiator

36616_SVUE_G0187

c. Remove the two front bumper fascia bolts (1).

d. Remove the front bumper fascia by pulling forward.

7. Remove the front bumper impact bar.

8. Disconnect the transaxle oil cooler lines from the radiator.

9. Remove the radiator inlet and outlet hoses.

a. Disconnect the compressor hose from the condenser.

b. Disconnect the liquid line from the condenser.

10. Remove the Condenser Radiator Fan Module (CRFM) mounting bracket bolts from the radiator support.

11. Remove the CRFM mounting brackets from the radiator support.

12. Lift the CRFM assembly from the lower mounts and carefully move the bottom of the assembly rearward while tilting the top forward.

13. Remove the fan assembly bolts (1) from the radiator.

14. Remove the fan and shroud assembly (2).

15. Installation is the reverse of removal.

RADIATOR

REMOVAL & INSTALLATION

See Figures 66 through 69.

1. Drain the cooling system.

2. Raise and suitably support the vehicle as necessary.

3. Remove radiator opening upper cover.

4. Remove front fascia.

a. Remove the front wheelhouse liner to fascia screw only.

b. Remove front bumper fascia air deflector.

c. Remove the two front bumper fascia bolts (1).

d. Remove the front bumper fascia by pulling forward.

5. Remove the front bumper impact bar.

6. Remove the compressor hose/pipe bolt from the bracket at the top radiator support.

7. Remove the mounting bolts from the condenser. Reposition and support the condenser.

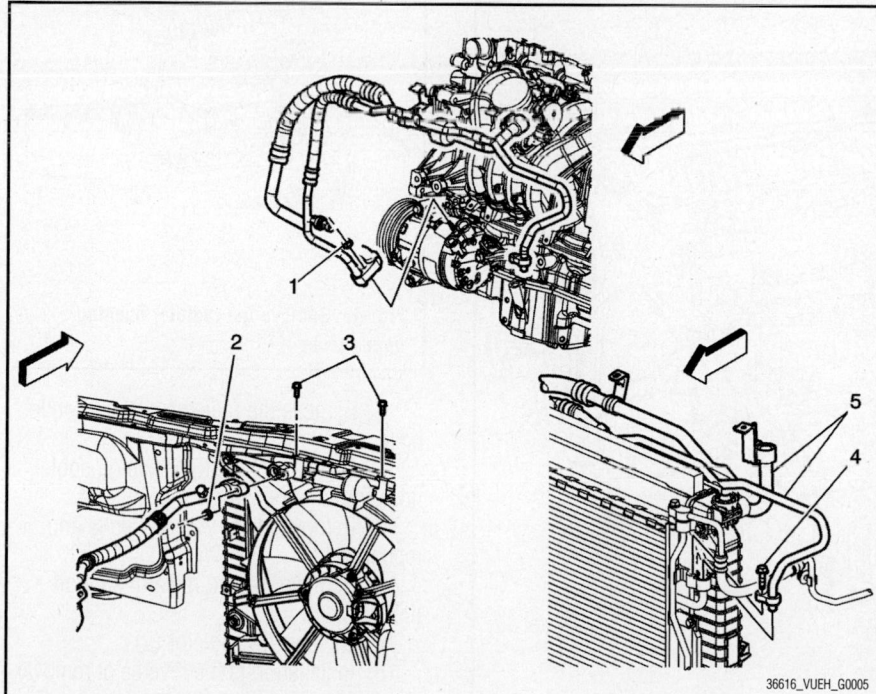

Fig. 63 Disconnect the compressor hose from the condenser

36616_VUEH_G0005

5
2
3
4
5
2
5
5
1
36616_VUEH_G0004

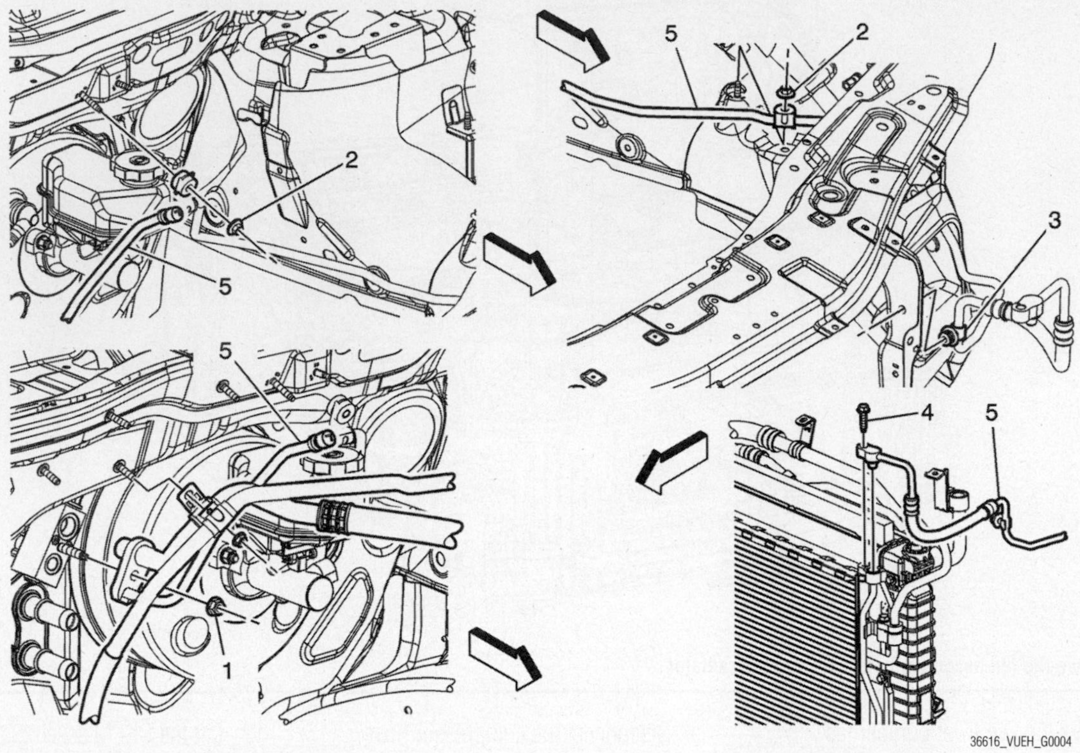

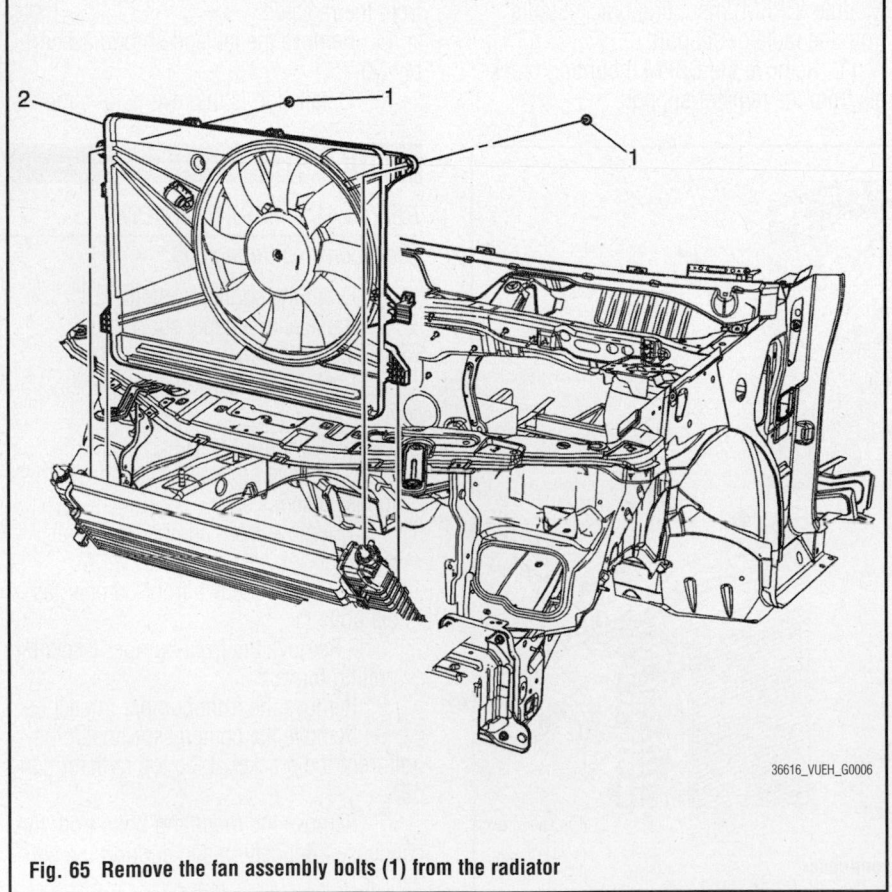

Fig. 64 Disconnect the liquid line from the condenser

2
1
1
36616_VUEH_G0006

Fig. 65 Remove the fan assembly bolts (1) from the radiator

1
2
36616_SVUE_G0055

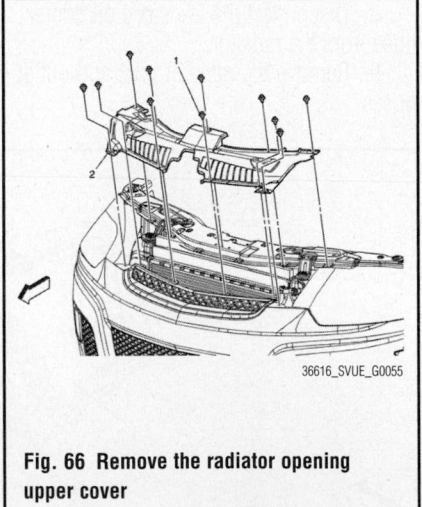

Fig. 66 Remove the radiator opening upper cover

8. Remove the radiator inlet and outlet hoses.
9. Disconnect the transaxle oil cooler lines from the radiator.
10. Remove the fan shroud bolts and reposition.
11. Remove the two radiator support bolts (1).
12. Remove the radiator (2).
13. Installation is the reverse of removal.
   a. Tighten the radiator support bolts to 16 ft. lbs. (22 Nm).

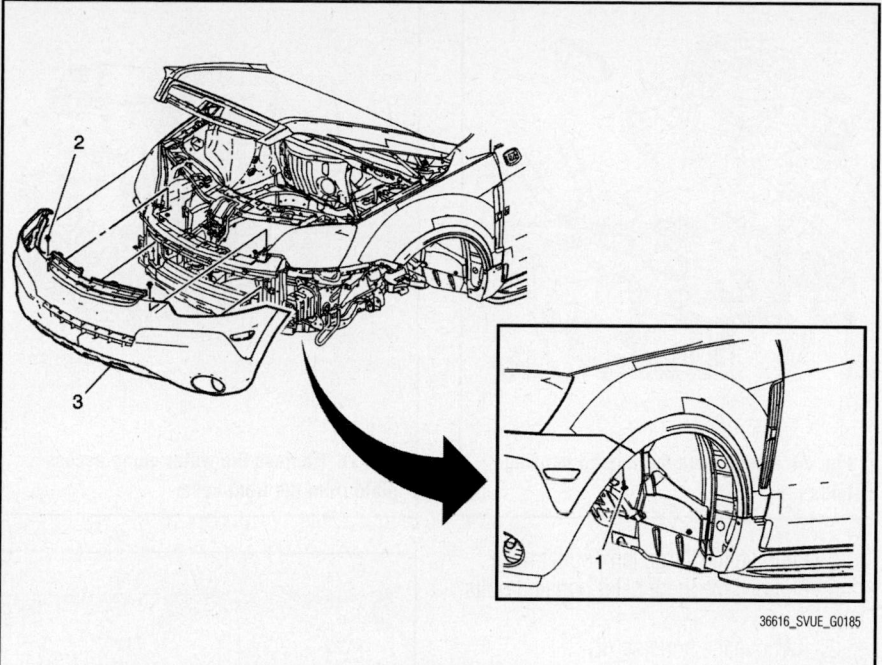

Fig. 67 Remove the two front bumper fascia bolts (1)

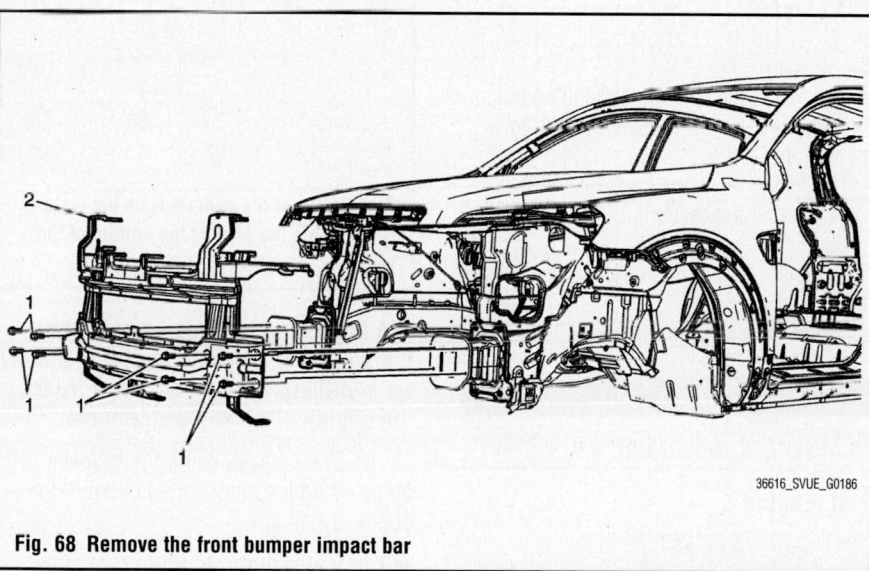

Fig. 68 Remove the front bumper impact bar

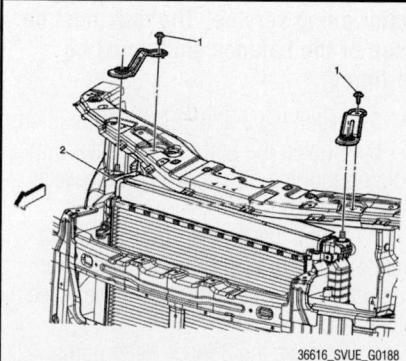

Fig. 69 Remove the two radiator support bolts (1)

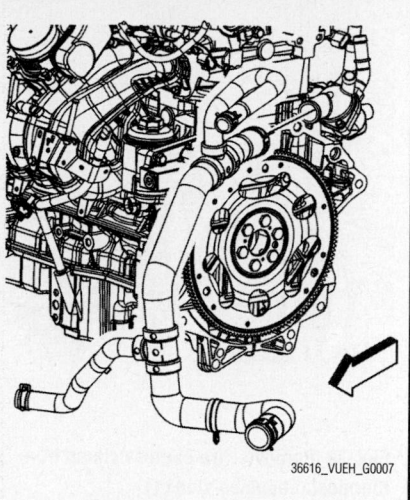

Fig. 70 Remove the radiator outlet hose from the thermostat cover

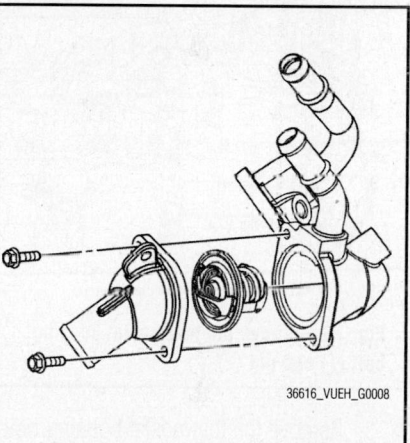

Fig. 71 Remove the thermostat cover bolts and cover

THERMOSTAT

REMOVAL & INSTALLATION

2.4L Engine

See Figures 70 and 71.

1. Drain the cooling system.
2. Reposition the radiator outlet hose clamp at the thermostat cover.
3. Remove the radiator outlet hose from the thermostat cover.
4. Remove the battery tray.
5. Remove the thermostat cover bolts and cover.
6. Remove the thermostat.
7. Remove and discard the thermostat cover O-ring seal.

To install:

8. Install a NEW thermostat cover O-ring seal.
9. Install the thermostat.
10. Install the thermostat cover bolts. Tighten the bolts to 89 inch lbs. (10 Nm).
11. Install the battery tray.
12. Install the radiator outlet hose to the thermostat cover.
13. Position the radiator outlet hose clamp at the thermostat cover.
14. Fill the cooling system.

3.5L Engine

See Figures 72 and 73.

1. Remove the radiator outlet hose.
2. Remove wire harness clamp from thermostat housing stud (1).

Fig. 72 Remove wire harness clamp from thermostat housing stud (1)

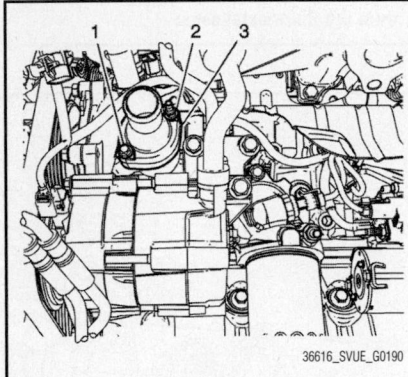

Fig. 73 Remove the thermostat housing bolt (1) and nut (2)

3. Remove the thermostat housing bolt (1) and nut (2).

4. Remove the thermostat housing (3).

5. Remove the thermostat.

To install:

6. Install the thermostat with housing.

  a. Install a new gasket.

  b. Position the thermostat with the housing.

  c. Apply thread sealant PST 565® to the bolt threads.

  d. Install the housing bolt and nut. Tighten the thermostat housing nut and bolt to 89 inch lbs. (10 Nm).

7. Install the wire harness clamp to the thermostat housing stud.

8. Install the radiator outlet hose.

3.6L Engine

See Figure 74.

1. Partially drain the cooling system.

2. Remove the radiator outlet hose from the thermostat housing.

3. Remove the heater inlet and outlet hoses.

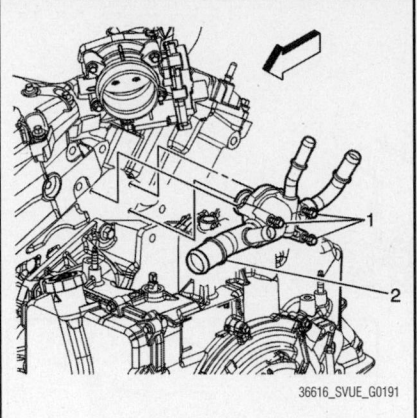

Fig. 74 Remove the thermostat housing bolts (1)

4. Remove the surge tank outlet hose.

5. Remove the thermostat housing bolts (1).

6. Remove the housing (2).

7. Remove the thermostat and discard the thermostat gasket.

To install:

8. Install the thermostat with a NEW thermostat gasket.

9. Install the thermostat housing bolts. Tighten the thermostat housing bolts to 89 inch lbs. (10 Nm).

10. Install the surge tank outlet hose.

11. Install the heater inlet and outlet hoses.

12. Install the radiator outlet hose to the thermostat housing.

13. Fill the cooling system.

WATER PUMP

REMOVAL & INSTALLATION

2.4L Engine

See Figures 75 through 81.

1. Remove the thermostat housing.

2. Remove the engine splash shield.

3. Remove the water pump access plate from the front cover.

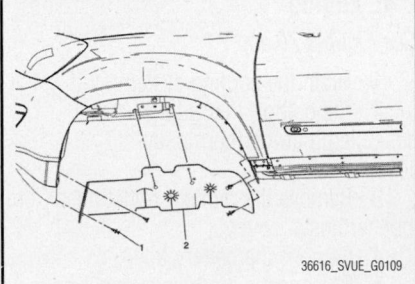

Fig. 75 Remove the engine splash shield

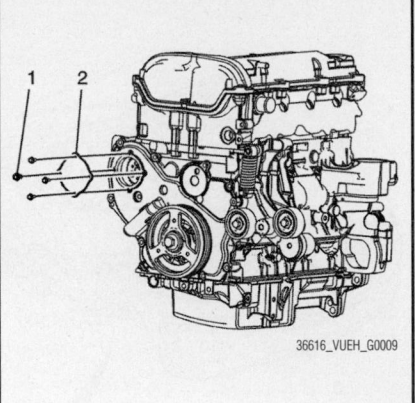

Fig. 76 Remove the water pump access plate from the front cover

Fig. 77 Drain the coolant from the water pump using the plug at the bottom of the pump

➡**A drain plug has been provided at the bottom of the water pump assembly for additional coolant drainage from the engine block and water pump.**

4. Drain the coolant from the water pump using the plug at the bottom of the pump.

➡**The water pump holding tool supports the sprocket and chain during water pump service. The tool must be used or the balance shaft must be re-timed.**

5. Install the J 43651 (1) into position.

6. Tighten the bolts on the water pump holding tool into the threads on the water pump sprocket.

7. Install the access cover bolts that were removed earlier to secure the water pump holding tool to the front cover assembly.

8. Remove the 3 inner water pump sprocket to water pump blots.

➡**Be sure to remove both water pump bolts from the front of the engine block.**

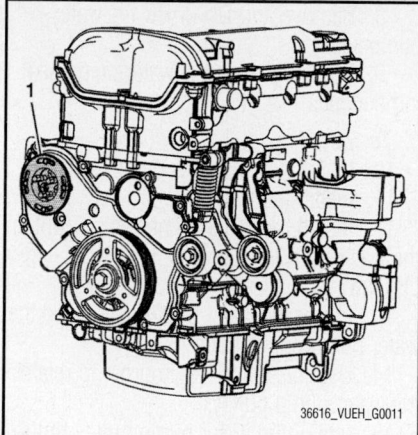

Fig. 78 Install the J 43651 (1) into position

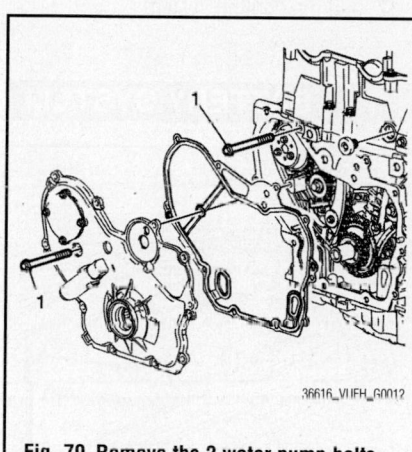

Fig. 79 Remove the 2 water pump bolts

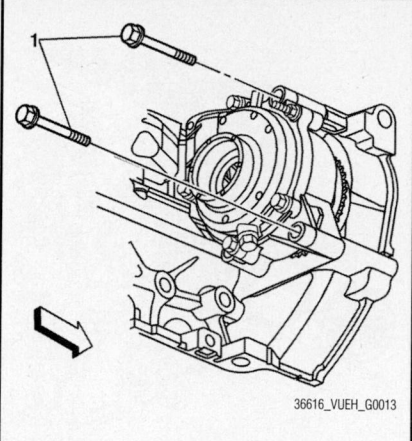

Fig. 80 Remove the rear 2 water pump bolts

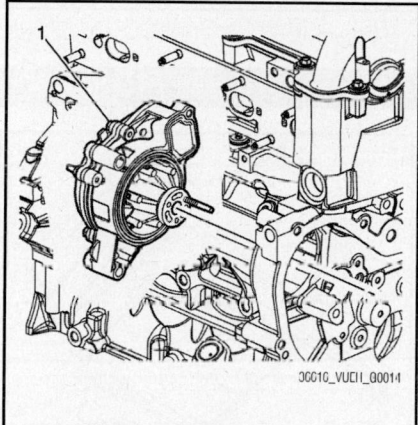

Fig. 81 Remove the water pump

Fig. 82 Remove the water pump pulley bolts (1)

9. Remove the 2 water pump bolts.
10. Remove the rear 2 water pump bolts.
11. Remove the water pump.
12. Remove and discard the water pump O-ring seal.

To install:

➡ Prior to installing the water pump, read the entire procedure. This will help avoid balance shaft chain re-timing and ensure proper sealing.

13. Install a NEW water pump O-ring seal.

➡ A guide pin can be created to aid in water pump alignment. Use a M6 m x 6 mm stud. Thread the pin into the water pump sprocket.

14. Using the guide pin, align the pin with the water pump holding tool.
15. Position the water pump against the engine block and hand tighten the water pump bolts.
16. Install the inner water pump sprocket bolts. After 2 are snug, remove the guide pin and install the 3rd bolt. Tighten the water pump bolts to 18 ft. lbs. (25 Nm).

17. Tighten the water pump sprocket bolts last. Tighten the water pump sprocket bolts to 89 inch lbs. (10 Nm).
18. Remove the J 43651 (1).
19. Install the water pump access plate and bolts. Tighten the bolts to 89 inch lbs. (10 Nm).
20. Install the engine splash shield.
21. Install the thermostat housing.

3.5L Engine

See Figure 82.

1. Remove the radiator outlet hose.
2. Remove the front wheelhouse liner.
3. Remove the drive belt.
4. Remove the water pump pulley bolts (1).
5. Remove the water pump assembly bolts (2).
6. Remove the water pump and O-ring.

To install:

7. Clean the engine block at the water pump mating surface.

8. Install a new water pump O-seal to the water pump.
9. Install the water pump assembly.
10. Install the water pump bolts. Tighten the water pump bolts to 18 ft. lbs. (25 Nm).
11. Install the water pump pulley bolts. Tighten the water pump bolts to 18 ft. lbs. (25 Nm).
12. Install the drive belt.
13. Install the front wheelhouse liner.
14. Install the radiator outlet hose.

3.6L Engine

See Figures 83 through 85.

1. Drain the cooling system.
2. Remove the drive belt.
3. Use the EN 46104 in order to retain the water pump pulley.
4. Remove the water pump pulley bolts.
5. Remove the water pump pulley.
6. Remove the water pump bolts.
7. Remove the water pump.

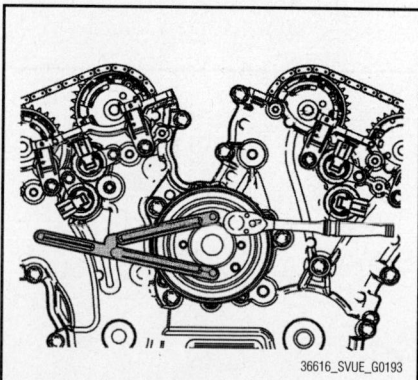

Fig. 83 Use the EN 46104 in order to retain the water pump pulley

Fig. 84 Remove the water pump pulley bolts

Fig. 85 Remove the water pump bolts.

8. Remove and DISCARD the water pump seal.

9. Carefully clean the water pump sealing surfaces.

To install:

10. Install a NEW water pump seal.

11. Install the water pump.

12. Install the water pump bolts. Tighten the water pump bolts to 89 inch lbs. (10 Nm).

13. Install the water pump pulley and the water pump pulley bolts.

14. Use the EN 46104 in order to retain the water pump pulley.

15. Install the water pump pulley bolts. Tighten the water pump pulley bolts to 89 inch lbs. (10 Nm).

16. Install the drive belt.

17. Fill the cooling system.

ENGINE ELECTRICAL   BATTERY SYSTEM

BATTERY

REMOVAL & INSTALLTION

Except Hybrid

See Figures 86 through 90.

1. Disconnect the negative battery cable.

   a. Turn on the radio and record all of the radio station presets.

   b. Ensure all lamps and accessories are turned off.

   c. Ensure the ignition switch is in the OFF position, and remove the ignition key.

2. Depress the tab (1) retaining the engine control Module (2).

3. Slide the engine control module (2) in order to disengage the engine control module bracket from the battery upper cover (3).

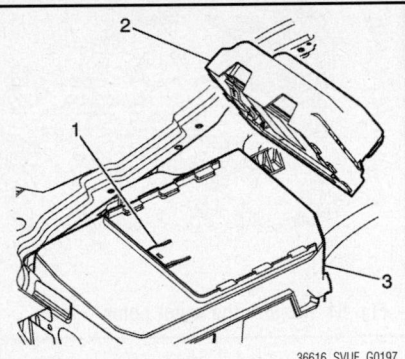

Fig. 87 Depress the tab (1) retaining the engine control Module (2)

4. Position the engine control module assembly (2) to the side. Do not disconnect the wiring harness.

5. Release the two tabs (2).

6. Remove the battery upper (1) cover from the battery lower cover (3).

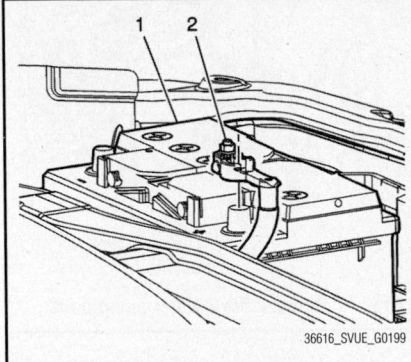

Fig. 89 Loosen the positive battery cable retaining nut (2)

7. Loosen the positive battery cable retaining nut (2).

8. Remove the positive battery cable from the battery (1).

9. Remove the battery retaining bolt (2) and retainer block (3).

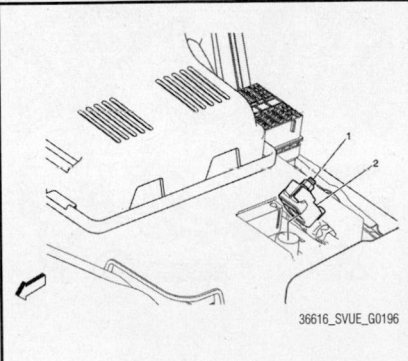

Fig. 86 Disconnect the negative battery cable

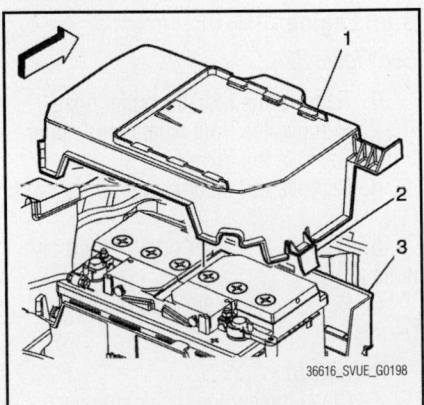

Fig. 88 Release the two tabs (2)

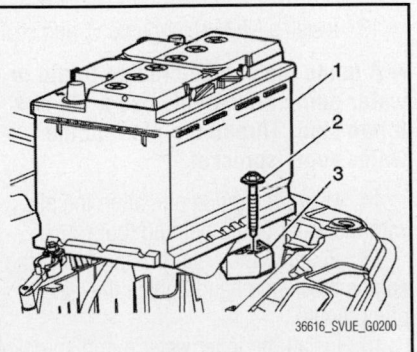

Fig. 90 Remove the battery retaining bolt (2) and retainer block (3)

10. Remove the battery (1) from the vehicle.

To install:

11. Position the battery into the vehicle.
12. Install the battery retaining bolt and retainer block. Tighten the bolt to 89 inch lbs. (10 Nm).
13. Install the positive battery cable to the battery.
14. Tighten the positive battery cable retaining nut.
15. Install the battery upper cover to the battery lower cover.
16. Ensure that the two retaining tabs are securely latched.
17. Slide the engine control module assembly onto the battery upper cover.
18. Ensure that the tab retaining the engine control Module is securely latched.
19. Connect the negative battery cable.

Hybrid

Starter Battery

See Figures 91 through 95.

※※ CAUTION

Do not tip the battery over a 45 degree angle or acid could spill causing serious personal injury.

1. Remove the generator battery control module cover.
2. Disconnect the negative battery cable.
   a. Turn on the radio and record all of the radio station presets.
   b. Ensure all lamps and accessories are turned off.

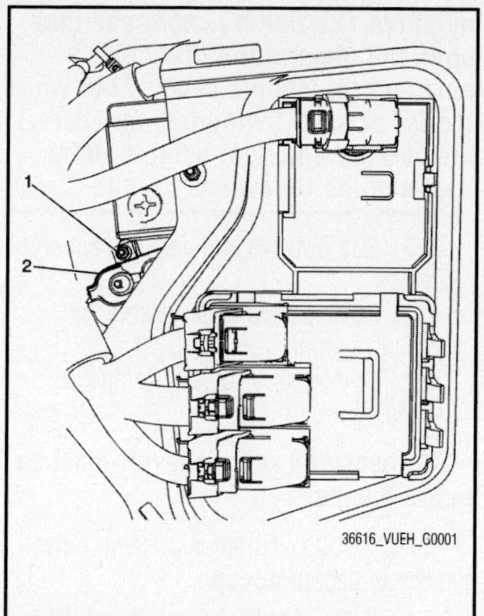

Fig. 92 Remove the negative battery cable terminal nut (1)

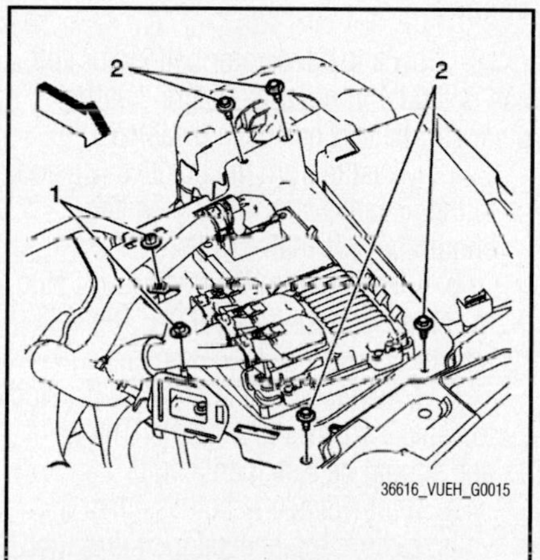

Fig. 93 Remove the ECM bracket bolts (2), nuts (1) and ECM bracket

   c. Ensure the ignition switch is in the OFF position, and remove the ignition key.
   d. Remove the negative battery cable terminal nut (1).
   e. Disconnect the negative battery cable (2).
3. Remove the ECM bracket bolts (2), nuts (1) and ECM bracket.
4. Set the ECM assembly aside.
5. Loosen the positive battery cable terminal nut (1) and secure the battery positive cable (2) out of the way.
6. Remove the battery hold down nuts (1) and the battery hold down retainer bracket (2).
7. Remove the battery from the vehicle.

To install:

※※ CAUTION

Do not tip the battery over a 45 degree angle or acid could spill causing serious personal injury.

8. Install the battery to the vehicle.
9. Install the battery hold down nuts and the battery hold down retainer bracket. Tighten the nut to 89 inch lbs. (10 Nm).

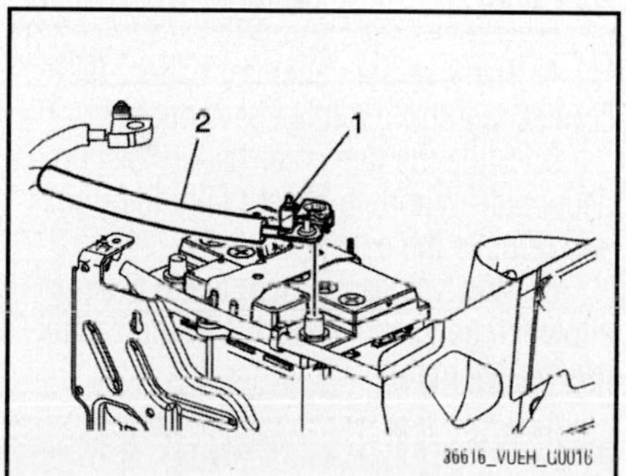

Fig. 94 Loosen the positive battery cable terminal nut (1) and secure the battery positive cable (2)

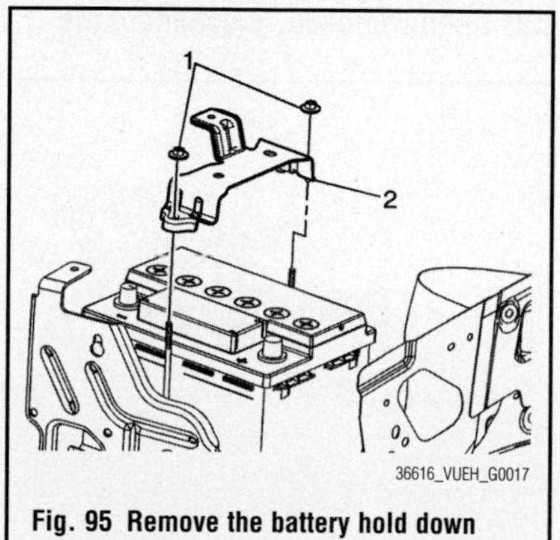

Fig. 95 Remove the battery hold down nuts (1) and the battery hold down retainer bracket (2)

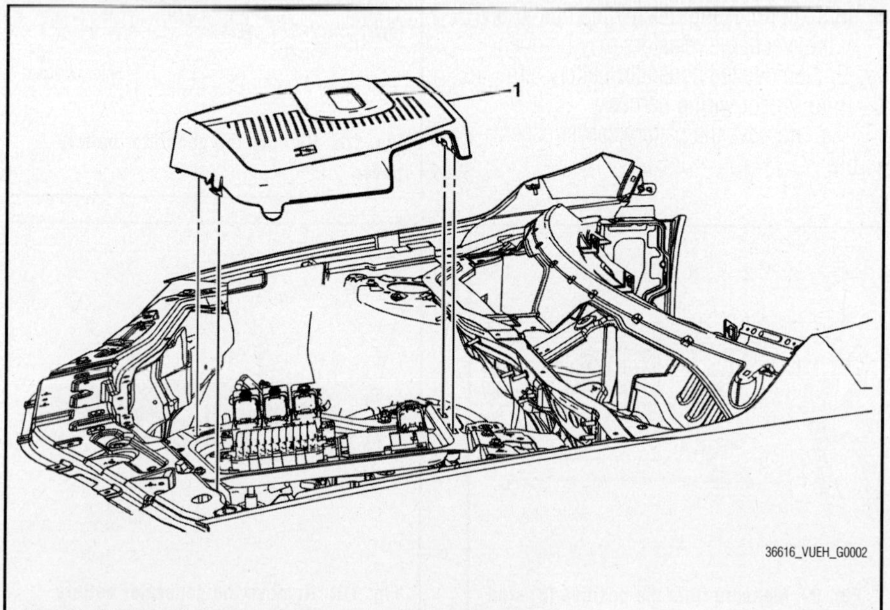

Fig. 91 Remove the generator battery control module cover

10. Install the positive battery cable terminal nut.

11. Install the ECM bracket, bolts and nuts. Tighten the nuts and bolts to 89 inch lbs. (10 Nm).

12. Connect the negative battery cable.

13. Install the generator battery control module cover.

Hybrid Battery

See Figures 96 through 106.

1. Remove the ignition key from the ignition switch. Secure the ignition key in order to ensure that the key CANNOT be re-installed without your knowledge.

2. Disconnect the 12 volt negative battery cable.

3. Tilt the rear seats forward by releasing the latches on the inside of the rear seat riser.

> **※ CAUTION**
>
> **To help avoid personal injury, be careful when working in the vicinity of the generator battery disconnect control module. Internal components will still be live, 36V potential, even when the cover has been opened or removed.**

4. Remove the generator battery disconnect control module cover nut (2).

5. Slide the generator battery disconnect control module cover (1) to the right and remove the cover.

6. WAIT at least 5 minutes in order to allow the generator control module capacitors to discharge.

> **※ CAUTION**
>
> **To help avoid personal injury, always ensure the ignition switch is in the OFF position and the ignition key has been removed prior to working on any 36V components. After the key has been removed, disconnect the**

negative 12V battery cable and then open the generator battery disconnect control module cover. After waiting for at least 5 minutes, measure the voltage potential using a DMM between the following:

   a. 36V positive and negative battery cables

   b. 36V positive battery cable and vehicle ground

   c. 36V negative battery cable and vehicle ground

➡**All measured voltage levels must be below 3 volts.**

7. If 3 volts or more is present, repeat the disconnect procedure.

➡**Never assume the battery pack is disabled when the generator battery disconnect control module cover is opened.**

8. Check the generator battery for voltage potential in order to ensure that the generator battery has been disabled.

   a. Measure from the positive (3) stud to the negative stud (2). The voltage should be less than 3 volts.

   b. Measure from the positive (3) stud to vehicle chassis ground (1). The voltage should be less than 3 volts.

   c. Measure from the negative (2) stud to vehicle chassis ground (1). The voltage should be less than 3 volts.

   d. If the voltage is not less than 3 volts, remove the generator control module cover to discharge the generator control module capacitors. Removal of both covers is only necessary when the capacitors are not being discharged due to one of the discharge resistors may be open.

9. Remove the generator battery temperature sensor wiring harness.

   a. Remove the battery carrier assembly.

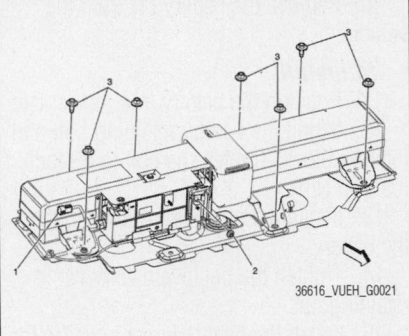

Fig. 98 Remove the battery carrier assembly

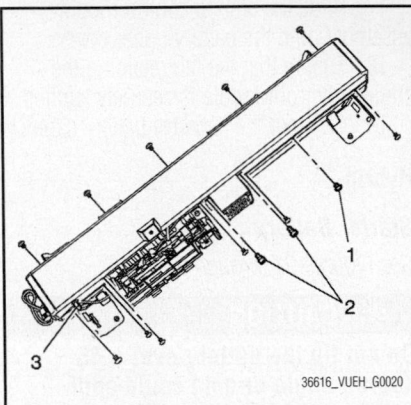

Fig. 99 Remove the 2 generator battery fan bolts (2)

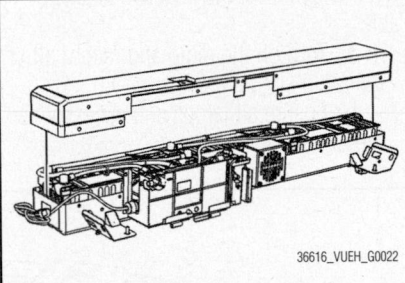

Fig. 100 Remove the generator battery cover

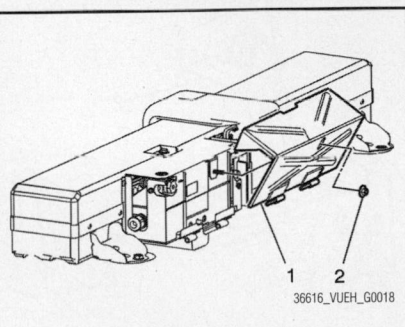

Fig. 96 Remove the generator battery disconnect control module cover nut (2)

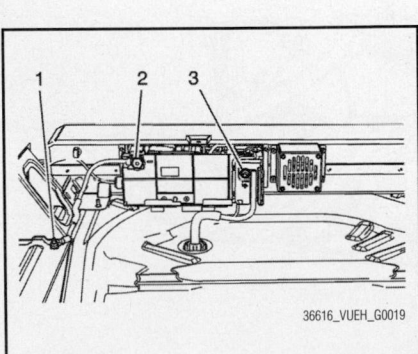

Fig. 97 Measure from the positive (3) stud to the negative stud (2)

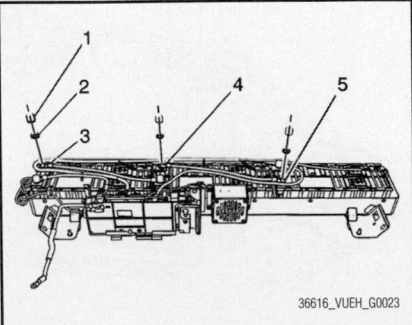

Fig. 101 Remove the generator battery terminal covers (1)

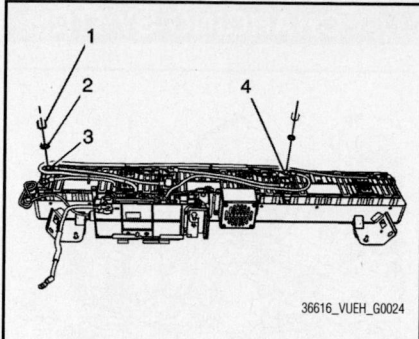

Fig. 102 Remove the generator battery terminal covers (1)

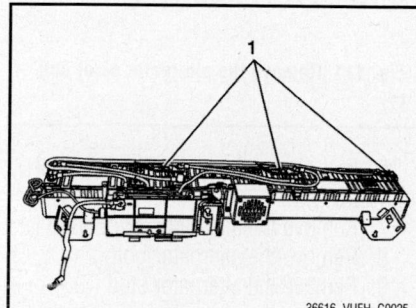

Fig. 103 Disconnect the generator battery temperature sensor wiring harness electrical connectors (1)

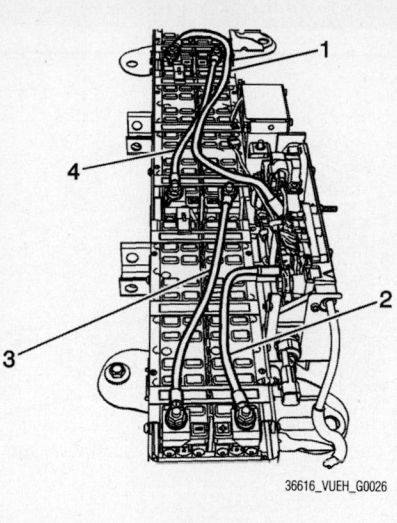

Fig. 104 Remove the generator battery nuts (1-4) from the battery cables

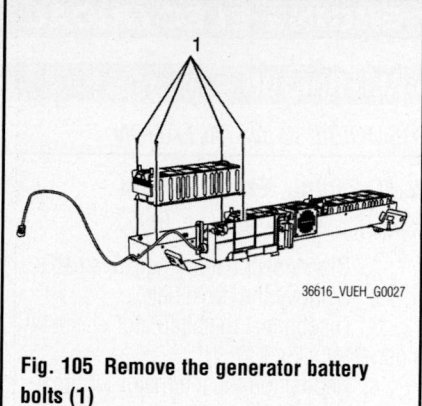

Fig. 105 Remove the generator battery bolts (1)

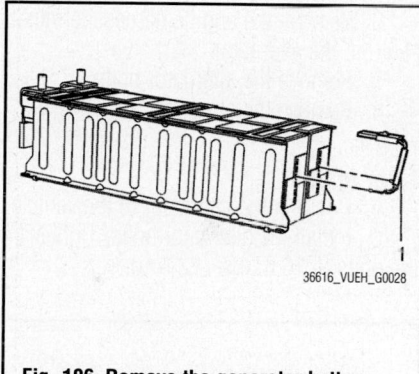

Fig. 106 Remove the generator battery temperature sensor (1) from the battery

b. Remove the 2 generator battery fan bolts (2).

c. Remove the 12 generator battery cover bolts (1).

d. Remove the generator battery wiring harness from the clip (3) on the generator battery cover.

e. Remove the generator battery cover.

→**Removing the interconnect cables will disable the 36 volts within the generator battery control module.**

f. Remove the generator battery terminal covers (1).

g. Remove the generator battery cable nuts (2).

h. Remove and reposition the generator battery cable leads (3, 4, 5) from the batteries.

i. Remove the generator battery terminal covers (1).

j. Remove the generator battery cable nuts (2) from the batteries.

k. Remove and reposition the generator battery cable leads (3, 4) from the battery terminals.

l. Disconnect the generator battery temperature sensor wiring harness electrical connectors (1) from the battery temperature sensors.

m. Cut the tie straps securing the battery cables to the generator battery temperature sensor wiring harness.

n. Remove the generator battery temperature sensor wiring harness.

10. Remove the generator battery nuts (1-4) from the battery cables.

→**Note original routing of battery cables to ensure proper installation.**

11. Remove the generator battery cables (1-4) from the batteries.

12. Remove the generator battery bolts (1).

13. Remove the generator battery.

14. If required, remove the generator battery temperature sensor (1) from the battery.

To install:

15. Before installing the NEW batteries, perform a voltage check. Voltage should be between 11 Volts and 14 Volts. There should not be more than a 0.7 Volt difference between each cassette.

16. If required, install the generator battery temperature sensor to the battery.

17. Install the generator battery.

18. Install the generator battery bolts. Tighten the bolts to 89 inch lbs. (10 Nm).

19. Install the generator battery cables to the batteries.

20. Install the generator battery nuts to the battery cables.

21. Install the generator battery temperature sensor wiring harness.

22. Install and close the generator battery disconnect control module cover and nut.

23. Install the generator battery cover bolt. Tighten the bolt to 89 inch lbs. (10 Nm).

24. Connect the 12 volt negative battery cable.

ALTERNATOR

REMOVAL & INSTALLATION

2.4L Engine, Except Hybrid

See Figures 107 through 109.

1. Disconnect battery negative cable.
2. Remove the drive belt.
3. Disconnect the alternator electrical connector (3).
4. Reposition the alternator terminal protective boot (3).
5. Remove the alternator terminal nut (2).
6. Remove the engine harness terminal (1) from the alternator.
7. Remove the alternator bolts.
8. Remove the alternator from the vehicle.

To install:

9. Position the alternator to the vehicle.
10. Install the alternator bolts. Tighten the bolts to 16 ft. lbs. (22 Nm).

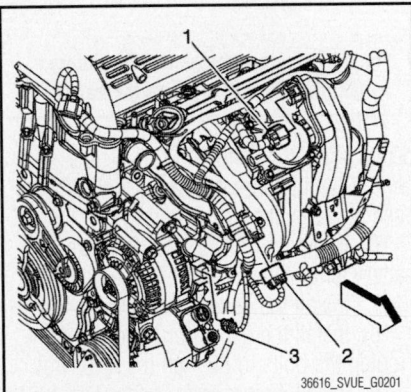

Fig. 107 Disconnect the alternator electrical connector (3)

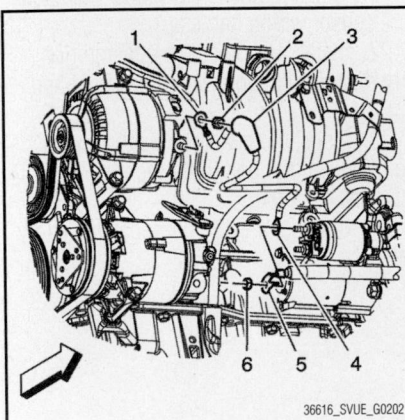

Fig. 108 Reposition the alternator terminal protective boot (3)

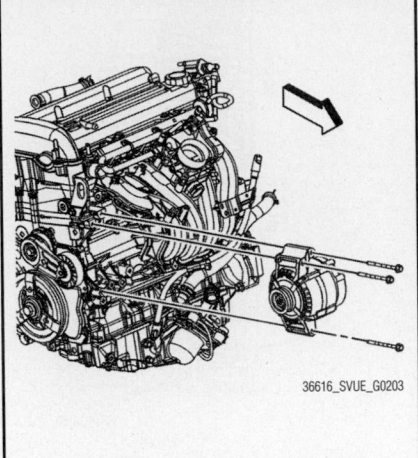

Fig. 109 Remove the alternator bolts

11. Install the engine harness terminal to the alternator.
12. Install the alternator terminal nut. Tighten the nut to 11 ft. lbs. (15 Nm).
13. Position the alternator terminal protective boot.
14. Connect the alternator electrical connector.
15. Install the drive belt.
16. Connect the battery negative cable.

3.5L Engine

See Figures 110 and 114.

1. Disconnect the battery negative cable.
2. Remove the drive belt.
3. Reposition the alternator terminal protective boot (1).
4. Remove the alternator terminal nut (4).
5. Remove the engine harness terminal (3) from the alternator.

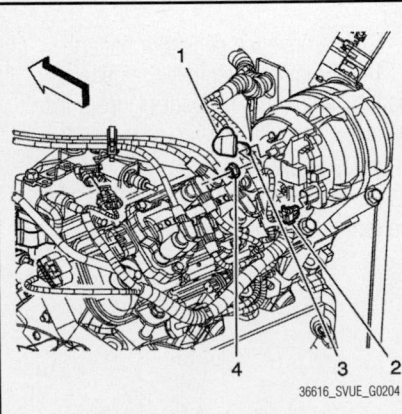

Fig. 110 Reposition the alternator terminal protective boot (1)

Fig. 111 Remove the alternator pivot bolt (1)

6. Disconnect the alternator electrical connector (2).
7. Remove the alternator pivot bolt (1).
8. Remove the alternator bolt (2).
9. Remove the alternator stud (3).
10. Remove the alternator (4) from the vehicle.

To install:

11. Install the alternator to the vehicle.

➡ **Hand start all bolts before finalizing any torques.**

12. Install the alternator stud. Tighten the stud to 37 ft. lbs. (50 Nm).
13. Install the alternator bolt. Tighten the bolt to 37 ft. lbs. (50 Nm).
14. Install the alternator pivot bolt. Tighten the bolt to 37 ft. lbs. (50 Nm).
15. Connect the alternator electrical connector.
16. Install the engine harness terminal to the alternator.
17. Install the alternator terminal nut. Tighten the nut to 11 ft. lbs. (15 Nm).
18. Position the alternator terminal protective boot.
19. Install the drive belt.
20. Connect the battery negative cable.

3.6L Engine

See Figures 112 and 113.

1. Disconnect the battery negative cable.
2. Remove the drive belt.
3. Disconnect the engine wiring harness electrical connector (5) from the alternator.
4. Reposition the engine wiring harness boot (6).
5. Remove the alternator terminal nut (4).

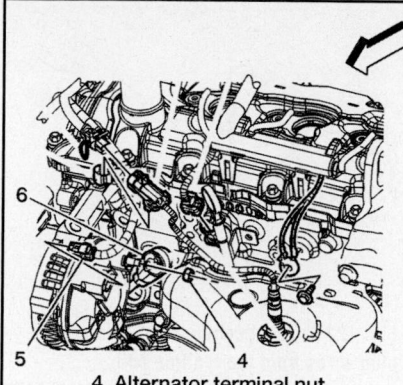

4. Alternator terminal nut
5. Electrical connector
6. Wiring harness boot

36616_SVUE_G0206

Fig. 112 Disconnect the engine wiring harness electrical connector (5) from the alternator

6. Remove the engine harness terminal from the alternator.
7. Loosen the idler pulley bolt (4).
8. Remove the alternator bolts (1).
9. Separate the alternator from the engine block.

10. Remove the idler pulley (3) from the vehicle.

➡It may be necessary to maneuver the alternator around in the engine compartment to in order to install it to the vehicle.

11. Remove the alternator (2) from the vehicle.

To install:

➡It may be necessary to maneuver the alternator around in the engine compartment to in order to install it to the vehicle.

12. Install the alternator to the vehicle.
13. Install the idler pulley to the vehicle.
14. Position the alternator and idler pulley to the engine block.
15. Install the idler pulley bolt and alternator bolts finger tight.
16. Tighten the idler pulley bolt first, then the alternator bolts. Tighten the bolts to 37 ft. lbs. (50 Nm).
17. Install the engine harness terminal to the alternator.
18. Install the alternator terminal nut. Tighten the nut to 89 inch lbs. (10 Nm).

36616_SVUE_G0207

Fig. 113 Loosen the idler pulley bolt (4)

19. Position the engine wiring harness boot over the terminal.
20. Connect the engine wiring harness electrical connector to the alternator.
21. Install the drive belt.
22. Connect the battery negative cable.

ENGINE ELECTRICAL
IGNITION SYSTEM

FIRING ORDER

Firing order for the 2.4L 4 cylinder engine is 1–3–4–2.
Firing order for 3.5L and 3.6L V6 engine is 1–2–3–4–5–6.

IGNITION COIL

REMOVAL & INSTALLATION

2.4L Engine

See Figures 114 through 117.

1. Remove the air cleaner outlet duct.
2. Remove the intake manifold cover.
   a. Remove the engine oil fill cap (1).
   b. Pull up on the cover (2) in order to disengage the cover from the studs (3).
3. Disconnect the engine wiring harness electrical connector(s) (1) from the ignition coil(s).
4. Remove the ignition coil bolt(s).
5. Remove the ignition coil(s).

To install:

6. Install the ignition coil(s).
7. Install the ignition coil bolt(s). Tighten the bolt(s) to 89 inch lbs. (10 Nm).
8. Connect the engine wiring harness electrical connector(s) to the ignition coil(s).

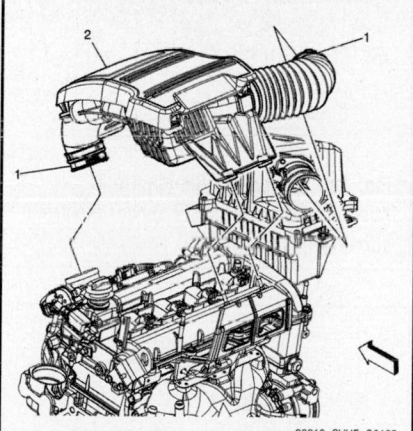

36616_SVUE_G0105

Fig. 114 Remove the air cleaner outlet duct

9. Install the intake manifold cover.
10. Install the air cleaner outlet duct.

3.5L Engine

See Figures 118 through 123.

1. Remove the air cleaner outlet duct, if required.
   a. Remove the intake manifold cover.
   b. Remove the two air cleaner outlet duct clamps (1).

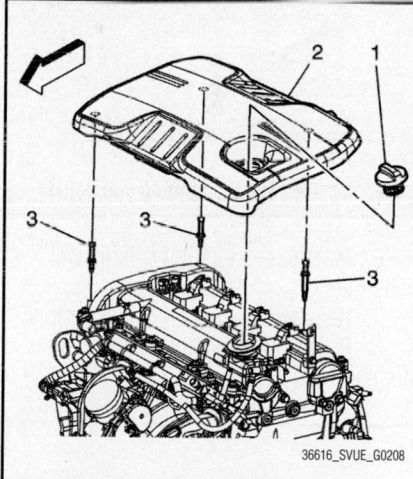

36616_SVUE_G0208

Fig. 115 Remove the intake manifold cover

   c. Remove the positive crankcase valve tube. (2).
2. Disconnect the Manifold Absolute Pressure (MAP) sensor electrical connector (1).
3. Disconnect the ignition coil electrical connector (6).
4. Disconnect the left side spark plug wires from the ignition coil.
5. Disconnect the right side spark plug wires from the ignition coil.

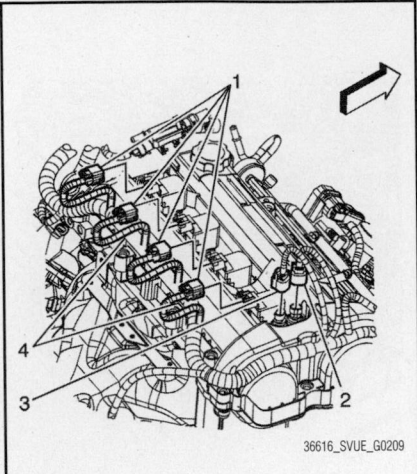

Fig. 116 Disconnect the engine wiring harness electrical connector(s) (1) from the ignition coil(s)

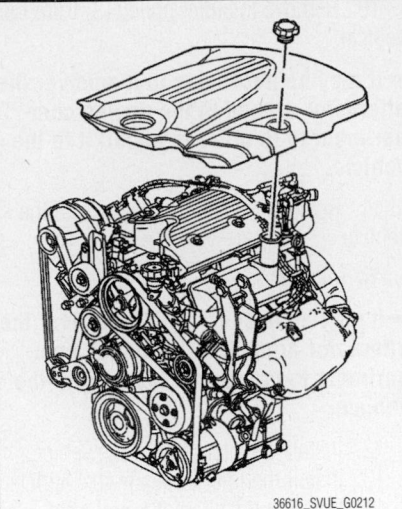

Fig. 119 Remove the intake manifold cover

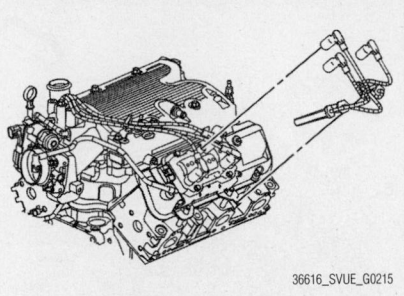

Fig. 122 Disconnect the right side spark plug wires from the ignition coil

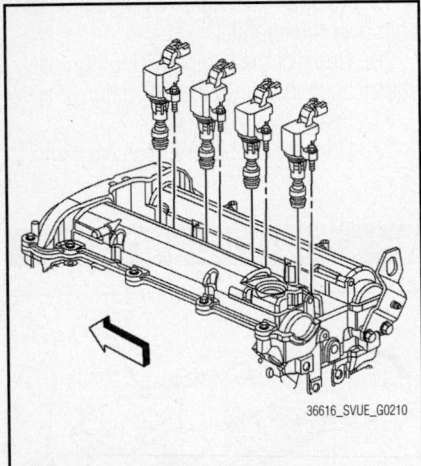

Fig. 117 Remove the ignition coil bolt(s)

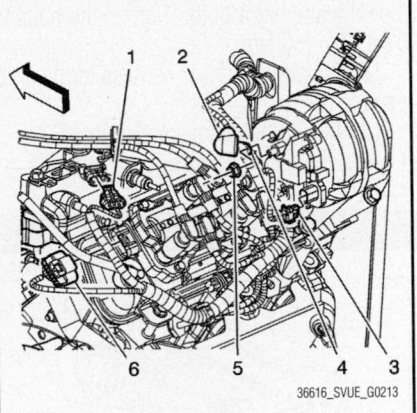

Fig. 120 Disconnect the Manifold Absolute Pressure (MAP) sensor electrical connector (1)

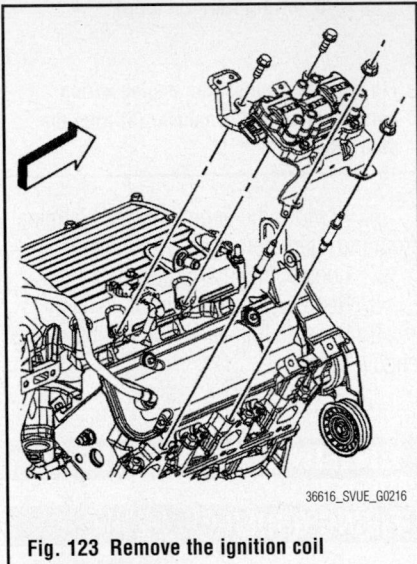

Fig. 123 Remove the ignition coil bracket bolts/nuts

6. Remove the ignition coil bracket bolts/nuts.

7. Remove the ignition coil assembly.

8. Remove the ignition coil bracket studs, if necessary.

To install:

9. Install the ignition coil bracket studs, if necessary. Tighten the studs to 15 ft. lbs. (25 Nm).

10. Install the ignition coil assembly.

11. Install the ignition coil bracket bolts/nuts. Tighten the bolts/nuts to 15 ft. lbs. (25 Nm).

12. Connect the right side spark plug wires to the ignition coil.

13. Connect the left side spark plug wires to the ignition coil.

14. Connect the ignition coil electrical connector.

15. Connect the MAP sensor electrical connector.

16. Install the air cleaner outlet duct, if required.

3.6L Engine—Bank 1

See Figures 124 through 126.

1. Remove the injector sight shield.

2. Disconnect the engine wiring harness electrical connectors (1) from the ignition coils.

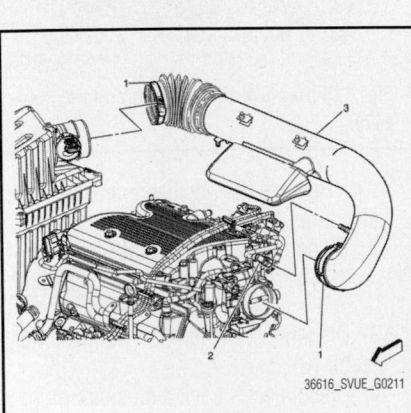

Fig. 118 Remove the air cleaner outlet duct

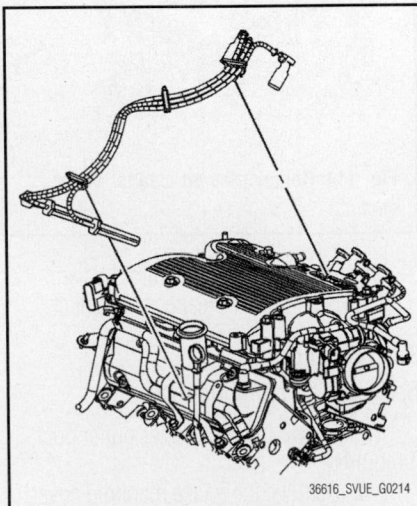

Fig. 121 Disconnect the left side spark plug wires from the ignition coil

3. Remove the ignition coil bolts.
4. Remove the ignition coils.

To install:
5. Install the ignition coils.

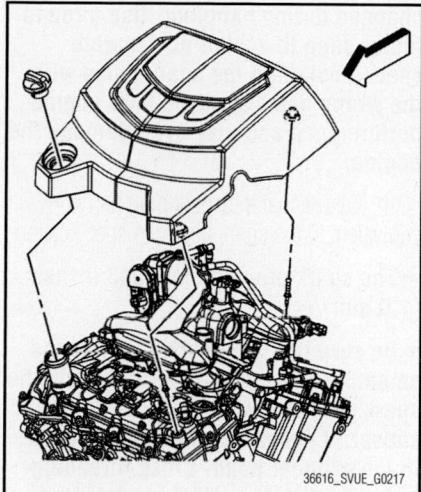

Fig. 124 Remove the injector sight shield

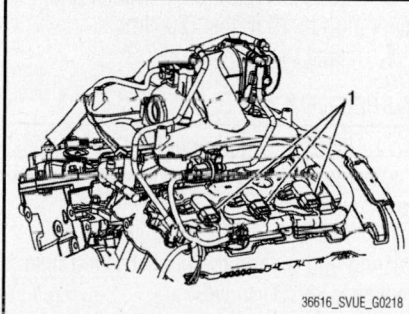

Fig. 126 Disconnect the engine wiring harness electrical connectors (1) from the ignition coils

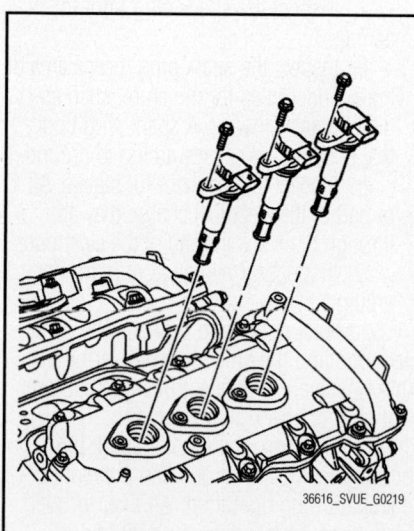

Fig. 126 Remove the ignition coil bolts

6. Install the ignition coil bolts. Tighten the bolts to 89 inch lbs. (10 Nm).
7. Connect the engine wiring harness electrical connectors to the ignition coils.
8. Install the injector sight shield.

3.6L Engine—Bank 2
See Figures 127 through 129.

1. Remove the air fuel injector sight shield.
2. Disconnect the engine wiring harness electrical connectors (1) from the ignition coils.
3. If removing the No. 6 ignition coil (1), disconnect the Positive Crankcase Ventilation (PCV) fresh air line (2) from the camshaft cover.
4. Remove the ignition coil bolts.
5. Remove the ignition coils.

To install:
6. Install the ignition coils.
7. Install the ignition coil bolts. Tighten the bolts to 89 inch lbs. (10 Nm).
8. If the No. 6 ignition coil was

Fig. 127 Disconnect the engine wiring harness electrical connectors (1) from the ignition coils

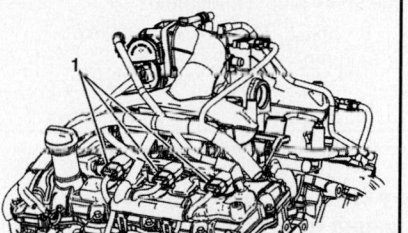

Fig. 128 Disconnect the Positive Crankcase Ventilation (PCV) fresh air line (2) from the camshaft cover

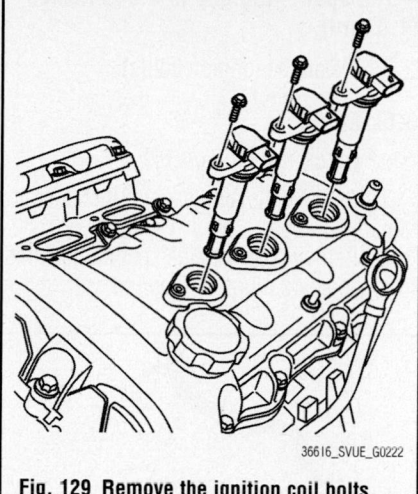

Fig. 129 Remove the ignition coil bolts

removed, connect the PCV fresh air line to the camshaft cover.
9. Connect the engine wiring harness electrical connectors to the ignition coils.
10. Install the air fuel injector sight shield.

IGNITION TIMING

ADJUSTMENT

Timing is controlled by the Electronic Control Module (ECM). The timing cannot be adjusted.

SPARK PLUGS

REMOVAL & INSTALLATION

2.4L Engine

➡This engine has aluminum cylinder heads. Do not remove the spark plugs from a hot engine, allow it to cool first. Removing the spark plugs from a hot engine may cause spark plug thread damage or cylinder head damage.

1. Remove the ignition coil(s).

➡Make sure that any water and/or debris are blown out of the spark plug holes prior to removing the spark plugs.

2. Remove the spark plugs using a ⅝ inch spark plug socket.

To install:

➡Do not coat spark plug threads with anti-seize compound. If anti-seize compound is used and spark plugs are over-torqued, damage to the cylinder head threads may result.

3. Install the spark plugs. Tighten the plugs to 15 ft. lbs. (20 Nm).

➡The spark plug gap is 0.043 inches
(1.0 mm).

4. Install the ignition coil(s).

3.5L Engine

See Figures 130 through 132.

1. Remove the air cleaner outlet duct, if
required.

2. Remove the left side spark plug wires
from the spark plugs, if required.

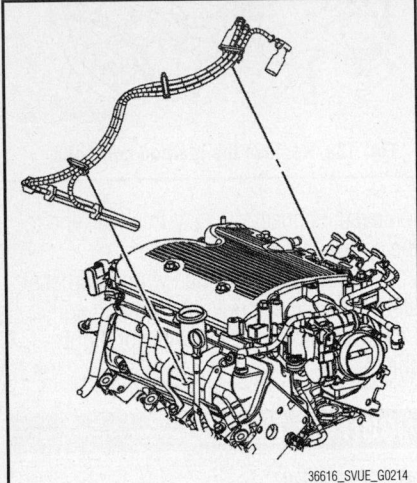

**Fig. 130 Remove the left side spark plug
wires from the spark plugs**

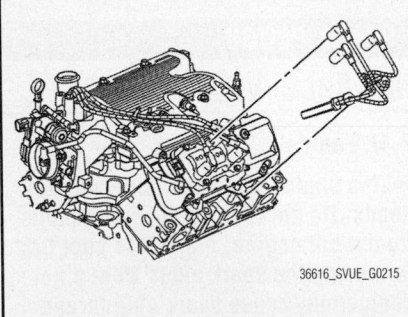

**Fig. 131 Remove the right side spark plug
wires from the spark plugs**

Fig. 132 Remove the spark plugs

3. Remove the right side spark plug
wires from the spark plugs, if required.

4. Remove the spark plugs as
needed.

To install:

➡It is important to check the gap of
all new and reconditioned spark plugs
before installation. Pre-set gaps may
have changed during handling. Use a
round wire feeler gauge to be sure of
an accurate check, particularly on used
plugs. Installing plugs with the wrong
gap can cause poor engine performance and may even damage the
engine.

5. Gap the NEW spark plugs, if replacing.

➡The spark plug gap is 0.043 inches
(1.0 mm).

6. Install the spark plugs as needed.
Tighten the plugs to 11 ft. lbs. (15 Nm).

7. Install the right side spark plug wires
to the spark plugs, if required.

8. Install the left side spark plug wires to
the spark plugs, if required.

9. Install the air cleaner outlet duct,
if required.

3.6L Engine

1. Remove the ignition coil(s)

➡Clean the spark plug recess area
before removing the spark plug. Failure
to do so could result in engine damage
because of dirt or foreign material
entering the cylinder head, or by the
contamination of the cylinder head
threads. The contaminated threads may
prevent the proper seating of the new
plug. Use a thread chaser to clean the
threads of any contamination.

2. Use compressed air in order to
remove debris from the spark plug cavity.

✳✳ WARNING

**Allow the engine to cool before
removing the spark plugs. Attempting
to remove the spark plugs from a hot
engine may cause the plug threads to
seize, causing damage to cylinder
head threads.**

3. Remove the spark plug.

To install:

➡Use only the spark plugs specified
for use in the vehicle. Do not install
spark plugs that are either hotter or
colder than those specified for the
vehicle. Installing spark plugs of

another type can severely damage the
engine.

➡Check the gap of all new and reconditioned spark plugs before installation. The pre-set gaps may have
changed during handling. Use a round
feeler gage to ensure an accurate
check. Installing the spark plugs with
the wrong gap can cause poor engine
performance and may even damage the
engine.

4. Ensure that the spark plug gap is
equivalent to the spark plug gap specification.

➡The spark plug gap is 0.043 inches
(1.0 mm).

➡Be sure that the spark plug threads
smoothly into the cylinder head and the
spark plug is fully seated. Use a thread
chaser, if necessary, to clean threads
in the cylinder head. Cross-threading
or failing to fully seat the spark plug
can cause overheating of the plug,
exhaust blow-by, or thread damage.

5. Install the spark plug. Tighten the
spark plug to 15 ft. lbs. (20 Nm).

6. Install the ignition coil(s).

INSPECTION

1. Inspect the terminal post for damage.

2. Inspect for a bent or broken terminal
post.

3. Test for a loose terminal post by
twisting and pulling the post. The terminal
post should NOT move.

4. Inspect the insulator for flashover or
carbon tracking, soot. This is caused by the
electrical charge traveling across the insulator between the terminal post and ground.
Inspect for the following conditions:

a. Inspect the spark plug boot for
damage.

b. Inspect the spark plug recess area of
the cylinder head for moisture, such as
oil, coolant, or water. A spark plug boot
that is saturated causes arcing to ground.

c. Inspect the insulator for cracks. All
or part of the electrical charge may arc
through the crack instead of the electrodes.

d. Inspect for evidence of improper
arcing.

5. Measure the gap between the center
electrode and the side electrode terminals.
An excessively wide electrode gap can prevent correct spark plug operation.

6. Inspect for the correct spark plug
torque. Insufficient torque can prevent correct spark plug operation. An over torqued
spark plug, causes the insulator to crack.

7. Inspect for signs of tracking that

occurred near the insulator tip instead of the center electrode.

8. Inspect for a broken or worn side electrode.

9. Inspect for a broken, worn, or loose center electrode by shaking the spark plug.

10. A rattling sound indicates internal damage.

11. A loose center electrode reduces the spark intensity.

12. Inspect for bridged electrodes. Deposits on the electrodes reduce or eliminates the gap.

13. Inspect for worn or missing platinum pads on the electrodes, if equipped.

14. Inspect for excessive fouling.

15. Inspect the spark plug recess area of the cylinder head for debris. Dirty or damaged threads can cause the spark plug not to seat correctly during installation.

Spark Plug Visual Inspection

1. Normal operation—Brown to grayish-tan with small amounts of white powdery deposits are normal combustion by-products from fuels with additives.

2. Carbon fouled—Dry, fluffy, black carbon or soot caused by the following conditions:

- Rich fuel mixtures
- Leaking fuel injectors
- Excessive fuel pressure
- Restricted air filter element
- Incorrect combustion
- Reduced ignition system voltage output
- Weak coils
- Worn ignition wires
- Incorrect spark plug gap

3. Excessive idling or slow speeds under light loads can keep spark plug temperatures so low that normal combustion deposits may not burn off.

4. Deposit fouling—Oil, coolant, or additives that include substances such as silicone, very white coating, reduces the spark intensity. Most powdery deposits will not affect spark intensity unless they form into a glazing over the electrode.

SPARK PLUG WIRES

REMOVAL & INSTALLATION

3.5L Engine

See Figures 133 and 134.

➡**Twist the spark plug boot one-half turn in order to release the boot. Pull on the spark plug boot only. Do not pull on the spark plug wire or the wire could be damaged.**

1. Remove the air cleaner outlet duct, if required.

2. Disconnect the left side spark plug wires from the spark plugs.

3. Disconnect the left side spark plug wires from the ignition coil.

4. If replacing only one plug wire, open the retaining clips and remove the spark plug wire.

5. Remove the left side spark plug wire clips from the intake manifold bracket and heater inlet and outlet pipe.

6. Remove the spark plug wire assembly.

7. Disconnect the right side spark plug wires from the right side spark plugs.

8. Disconnect the left side spark plug wires from the ignition coil.

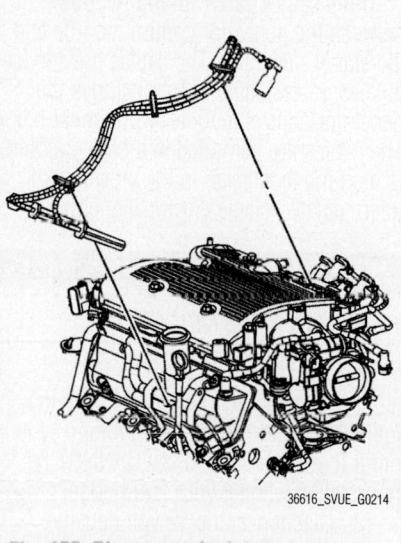

Fig. 133 Disconnect the left side spark plug wires from the spark plugs

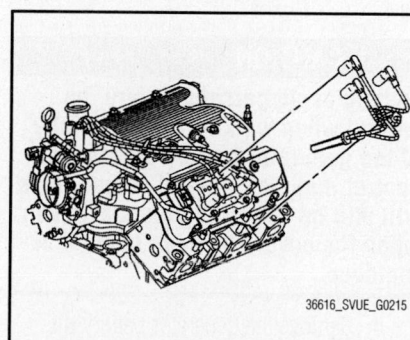

Fig. 134 Disconnect the right side spark plug wires from the spark plugs

9. If replacing only one plug wire, open the retaining clips and remove the spark plug wire.

10. Remove the right side spark plug wire clip from the ignition coil bracket.

11. Remove the spark plug wire assembly.

To install:

12. Install the spark plug wire assembly.

13. Install the right side spark plug wire clip at the ignition coil bracket.

14. If only one plug wire was replaced, install the plug wire and close the retaining clip.

15. Connect the right side spark plug wires to the ignition coil.

16. Connect the right side spark plug wires to the right side spark plugs.

17. Install the spark plug wire assembly.

18. Install the left side spark plug wire clips at the intake manifold bracket and heater inlet and outlet pipe.

19. If only one plug wire was replaced, install the plug wire and close the retaining clips.

20. Connect the left side spark plug wires to the ignition coil.

21. Connect the left side spark plug wires to the spark plugs.

22. Install the air cleaner outlet duct, if required.

INSPECTION

Spark plug wire integrity is vital for proper engine operation. A thorough inspection will be necessary to accurately identify conditions that may affect engine operation. Refer to the list below for items to be inspected.

1. Inspect for correct routing of the spark plug wires. Improper routing may cause cross-firing.

2. Inspect each wire for any signs of cracks or splits in the wire.

3. Inspect each boot for the following conditions:

- Tearing
- Piercing
- Arcing
- Carbon Tracking
- Corroded terminal

If corrosion, carbon tracking or arcing are indicated on a spark plug wire boot or terminal both the wire and the component connected to the wire should be replaced.

GENERAL INFORMATION

The generator control module, also referred to as the starter generator control module, is a serviceable GMLAN device located under the hood, toward the front of the vehicle on the driver's side. It is connected to the vehicles 12 and 36-volt DC power circuits, and it is also joined to the starter-generator by 3-phase AC cables. The generator control module is cooled by engine coolant, which is circulated through a cold plate. A separate, electrically driven pump is used to ensure adequate coolant flow, and individual coolant inlet and outlet hoses connect the cold plate to the cooling system. The generator control module performs three main functions:

1. As the power inverter for the starter-generator, the generator control module converts 36-volt DC power into 3-phase AC power to drive the starter-generator as a motor. The power inverter also rectifies 36-volt AC output power from the starter-generator into the 36-volt DC power used to charge the 36-volt generator battery.

2. An auxiliary power module contained within the generator control module converts 36-volt DC power into the 12-volt DC power which is used for 12-volt vehicle loads and to charge the underhood 12-volt battery. A serviceable 175 Amp Fuse (GM P/N 15305191) located beneath the generator control module DC cable terminal box cover protects the vehicles 12-volt electrical system from excessive current.

3. The generator control module contains a Renesas M32 processor, and it directly controls the starter-generator, transmission auxiliary oil pump, hill-hold solenoids, auxiliary coolant pump and the generator control module coolant pump. The pumps and solenoids are driven by 12-volt Pulse Width Modulated (PWM) power through vehicle wiring harnesses.

The starter generator, also referred to as the Motor Generator Unit (MGU), is a serviceable 16 pole, permanent magnet, enhanced Lundell AC machine. This device not only serves as a 36-volt AC generator, it is also used to provide engine power assist and to start the engine following hybrid "autostops". 36-volt AC power flows between the starter generator and the generator control module through a three phase cable assembly.

As a generator, the starter-generator provides up to 3 KW of AC power to the generator control module power inverter. Field current is provided by the generator control module through a seven pin connector, and starter generator RPM feedback is transmitted back to the controller through the same connector. Starter generator temperature data is provided to the generator control module through a separate three pin connector.

As a motor, the machine provides up to 48 ft. lbs. (65 Nm) of torque for power assist and engine starting. The motor receives three phase AC power from the power inverter within the generator control module.

The generator control module coolant pump is a serviceable component which is connected to the vehicle cooling system and the module cold plate using separate, serviceable hoses. The pump augments the engine driven water pump to ensure adequate coolant flow to the cold plate.

Three cables carry 36-volt AC power between the generator control module and the starter generator. The cables are serviceable as an assembly which includes the generator control module AC terminal box. The cables are shrouded in a blue conduit to alert the technician to the presence of intermediate voltage electrical energy.

HYBRID BATTERY

REMOVAL & INSTALLATION

See Figures 135 through 145.

1. Remove the ignition key from the ignition switch. Secure the ignition key in order to ensure that the key CANNOT be re-installed without your knowledge.
2. Disconnect the 12 volt negative battery cable.
3. Tilt the rear seats forward by releasing the latches on the inside of the rear seat riser.

✳✳ CAUTION

To help avoid personal injury, be careful when working in the vicinity of the generator battery disconnect control module. Internal components will still be live, 36V potential, even when the cover has been opened or removed.

4. Remove the generator battery disconnect control module cover nut (2).
5. Slide the generator battery disconnect control module cover (1) to the right and remove the cover.
6. WAIT at least 5 minutes in order to allow the generator control module capacitors to discharge.

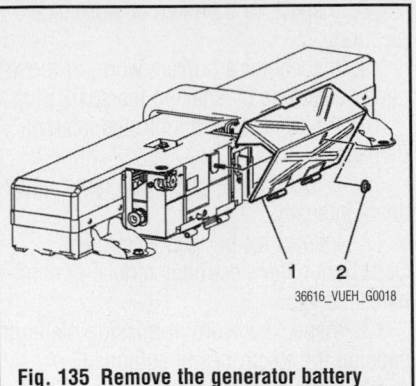

Fig. 135 Remove the generator battery disconnect control module cover nut (2)

✳✳ CAUTION

To help avoid personal injury, always ensure the ignition switch is in the OFF position and the ignition key has been removed prior to working on any 36V components. After the key has been removed, disconnect the negative 12V battery cable and then open the generator battery disconnect control module cover. After waiting for at least 5 minutes, measure the voltage potential using a DMM between the following:

   a. 36V positive and negative battery cables
   b. 36V positive battery cable and vehicle ground
   c. 36V negative battery cable and vehicle ground

➡**All measured voltage levels must be below 3 volts.**

7. If 3 volts or more is present, repeat the disconnect procedure.

➡**Never assume the battery pack is disabled when the generator battery**

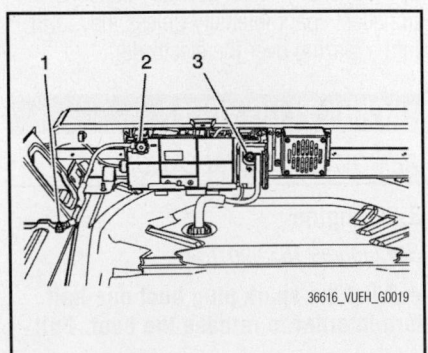

Fig. 136 Measure from the positive (3) stud to the negative stud (2)

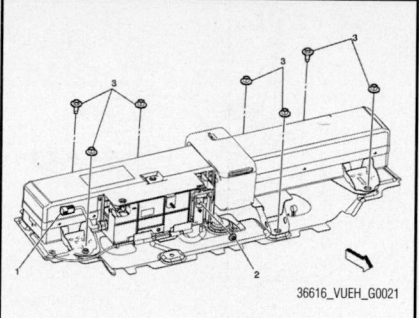

Fig. 137 Remove the battery carrier assembly

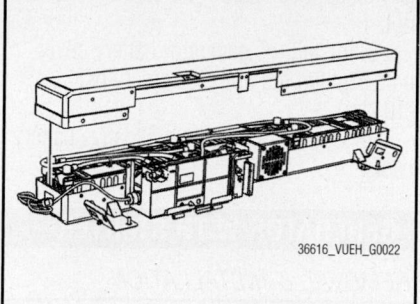

Fig. 139 Remove the generator battery cover

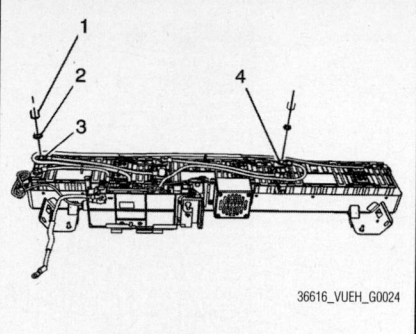

Fig. 141 Remove the generator battery terminal covers (1)

disconnect control module cover is opened.

8. Check the generator battery for voltage potential in order to ensure that the generator battery has been disabled.

    a. Measure from the positive (3) stud to the negative stud (2). The voltage should be less than 3 volts.

    b. Measure from the positive (3) stud to vehicle chassis ground (1). The voltage should be less than 3 volts.

    c. Measure from the negative (2) stud to vehicle chassis ground (1). The voltage should be less than 3 volts.

    d. If the voltage is not less than 3 volts, remove the generator control module cover to discharge the generator control module capacitors. Removal of both covers is only necessary when the capacitors are not being discharged due to one of the discharge resistors may be open.

9. Remove the generator battery temperature sensor wiring harness.

    a. Remove the battery carrier assembly.

    b. Remove the 2 generator battery fan bolts (2).

    c. Remove the 12 generator battery cover bolts (1).

    d. Remove the generator battery wiring harness from the clip (3) on the generator battery cover.

    e. Remove the generator battery cover.

➡**Removing the interconnect cables will disable the 36 volts within the generator battery control module.**

    f. Remove the generator battery terminal covers (1).

    g. Remove the generator battery cable nuts (2).

    h. Remove and reposition the generator battery cable leads (3, 4, 5) from the batteries.

    i. Remove the generator battery terminal covers (1).

    j. Remove the generator battery cable nuts (2) from the batteries.

    k. Remove and reposition the generator battery cable leads (3, 4) from the battery terminals.

    l. Disconnect the generator battery temperature sensor wiring harness electrical connectors (1) from the battery temperature sensors.

    m. Cut the tie straps securing the battery cables to the generator battery temperature sensor wiring harness.

    n. Remove the generator battery temperature sensor wiring harness.

10. Remove the generator battery nuts (1-4) from the battery cables.

➡**Note original routing of battery cables to ensure proper installation.**

11. Remove the generator battery cables (1-4) from the batteries.

12. Remove the generator battery bolts (1).

13. Remove the generator battery.

14. If required, remove the generator battery temperature sensor (1) from the battery.

To install:

15. Before installing the NEW batteries, perform a voltage check. Voltage should be between 11 Volts and 14 Volts. There should not be more than a 0.7 Volt difference between each cassette.

16. If required, install the generator battery temperature sensor to the battery.

17. Install the generator battery.

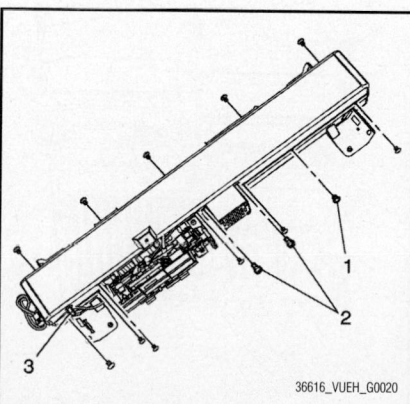

Fig. 138 Remove the 2 generator battery fan bolts (2)

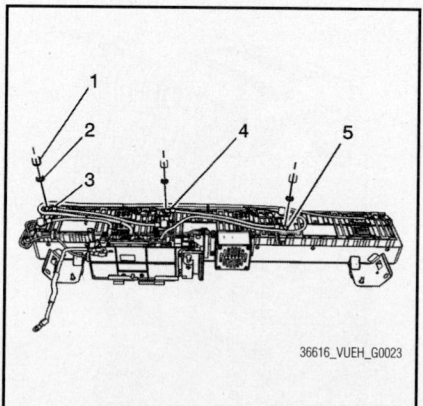

Fig. 140 Remove the generator battery terminal covers (1)

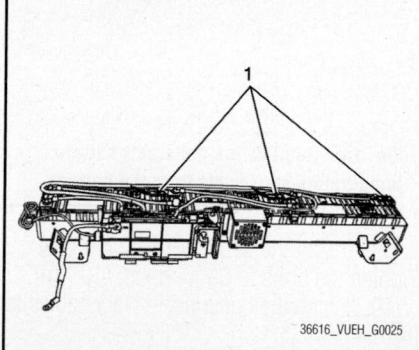

Fig. 142 Disconnect the generator battery temperature sensor wiring harness electrical connectors (1)

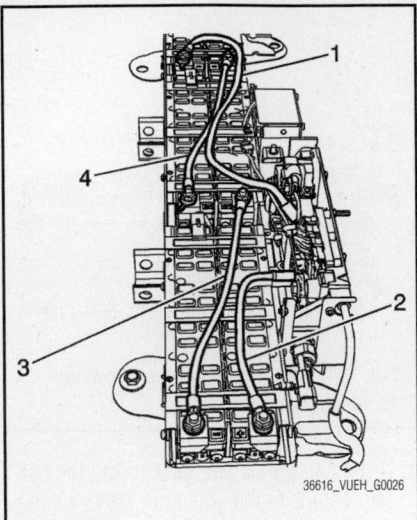

Fig. 143 Remove the generator battery nuts (1-4) from the battery cables

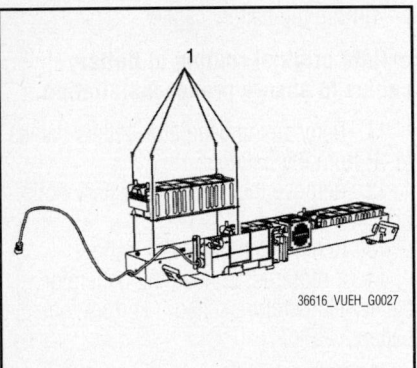

Fig. 144 Remove the generator battery bolts (1)

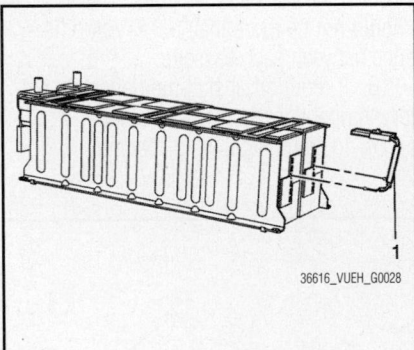

Fig. 145 Remove the generator battery temperature sensor (1) from the battery

18. Install the generator battery bolts. Tighten the bolts to 89 inch lbs. (10 Nm).

19. Install the generator battery cables to the batteries.

20. Install the generator battery nuts to the battery cables.

21. Install the generator battery temperature sensor wiring harness.

22. Install and close the generator bat-

tery disconnect control module cover and nut.

23. Install the generator battery cover bolt. Tighten the bolt to 89 inch lbs. (10 Nm).

24. Connect the 12 volt negative battery cable.

GENERATOR WITH STARTER

REMOVAL & INSTALLATION

See Figures 146 through 156.

1. Disconnect the hybrid battery.
2. Remove the air cleaner outlet duct.
3. Remove the drive belt.
4. Drain the cooling system.
5. Recover the refrigerant.
6. Unclip the battery positive cable jumper block (1) from the engine control module (ECM) bracket (4).
7. Disconnect the ECM electrical connectors (2) and the transmission control module (TCM) electrical connector (3).
8. Remove the ECM bracket bolts (1), nuts (2) and ECM bracket.
9. Remove the generator control module cover bolts (1) and cover (2).

✷✷ CAUTION

To help avoid personal injury, additional precautions must be taken prior to working on the generator control module or the generator starter. After removing the 36V battery cables from the generator battery, remove both engine wiring harness connectors from the generator control module. Wait at least 5 minutes and then remove the generator control module cover. Verify voltage levels at all 36V, 12V, and 3-phase connections, are less

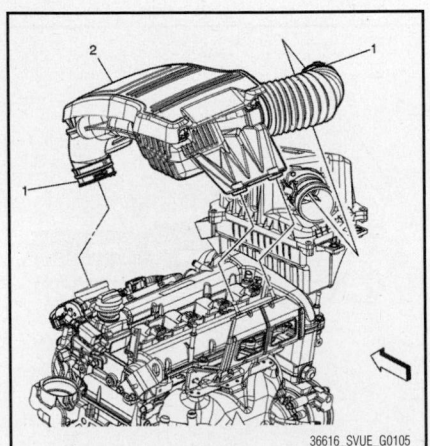

Fig. 146 Remove the air cleaner outlet duct

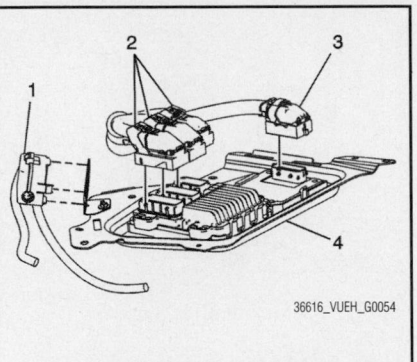

Fig. 147 Unclip the battery positive cable jumper block (1)

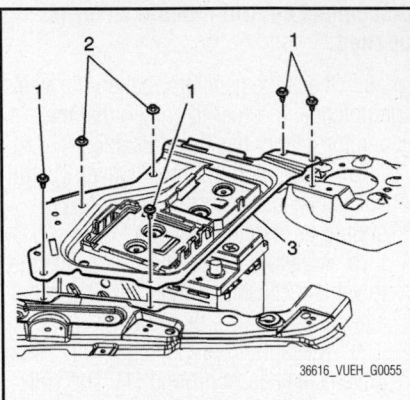

Fig. 148 Remove the ECM bracket bolts (1), nuts (2) and ECM bracket

than 3 volts using a DMM before proceeding.

10. Check the generator control module for voltage potential, in order to ensure that the module has been disabled.

a. Measure from the 36-volt positive terminal (3) to a known good chassis ground. The voltage should be less than 3 volts.

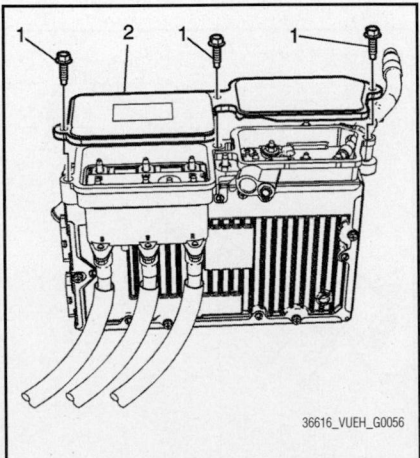

Fig. 149 Remove the generator control module cover bolts (1) and cover (2)

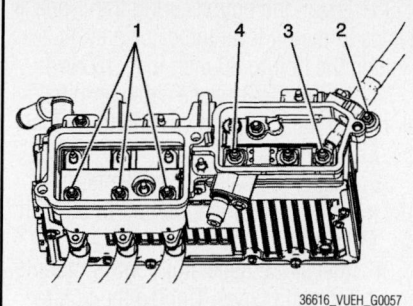

Fig. 150 Measure from the 36-volt positive terminal (3) to a known good chassis ground

b. Measure from the 12-volt positive terminal (4) to a known good chassis ground. The voltage should be less than 3 volts.

c. Measure from the ground terminal (2) to a known good chassis ground, checking for continuity.

✷✷ CAUTION

To help avoid personal injury, always treat the 3-phase cable and connectors as if voltage is present and as if the surface of all parts of the cable is hot.

11. Verify that the generator control module 3-phase cables are disabled.

a. Measure from each phase 1, 2 and 3 connection (1) to a known good chassis ground. The voltage should be less than 3 volts.

b. After verifying that there is no voltage present, the generator control module 3-phase cables can now be removed from the generator control module.

c. If 3 volts or more is present, repeat the disconnect procedure.

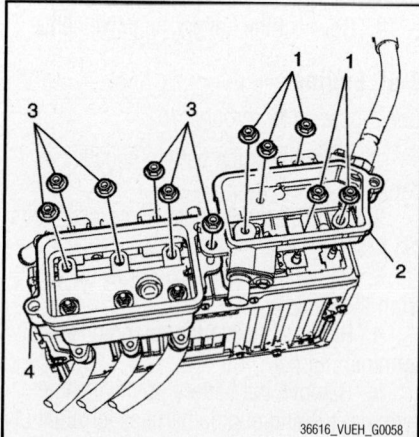

Fig. 151 Remove the battery positive terminal block nuts (1)

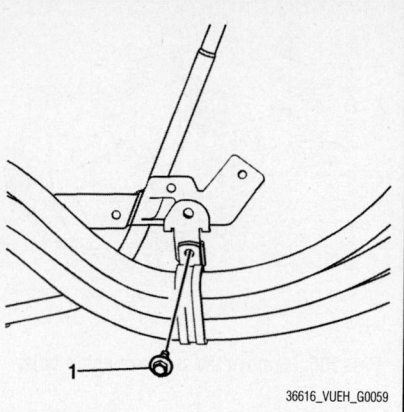

Fig. 152 Remove the bolt securing the 3-phase cables to the oil level indicator bracket

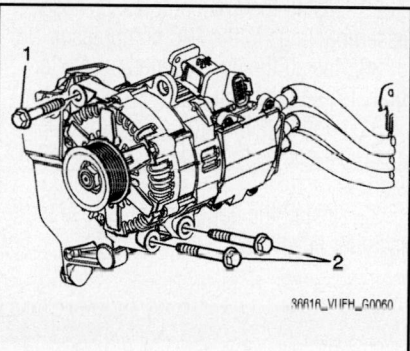

Fig. 153 Remove the upper generator starter bolt (1)

12. Remove the battery positive terminal block nuts (1) and reposition the battery positive terminal block (2).

13. Remove the 3-phase cable terminal block nuts (3) and reposition the 3-phase cable terminal block (4).

14. Remove the bolt securing the 3-phase cables to the oil level indicator bracket.

15. Disconnect the radiator inlet hose from the cylinder head water outlet and secure it out of the way.

16. Disconnect the engine wiring harness electrical connectors next to the generator starter and secure them out of the way.

17. Remove the upper generator starter bolt (1).

18. Raise the vehicle and disconnect the Air Conditioning (A/C) compressor hose assembly lines from the A/C compressor.

19. Remove the lower generator starter bolts (2).

20. Remove the generator starter from the vehicle with the 3-phase cables.

21. Remove the generator starter cover bolts (1) and the 3-phase cable bracket bolts (2).

22. Remove the 3-phase cable nuts underneath the cover.

23. Remove the 3-phase cable bolts (1).

To install:

24. Install the 3-phase cable bolts to the generator starter.

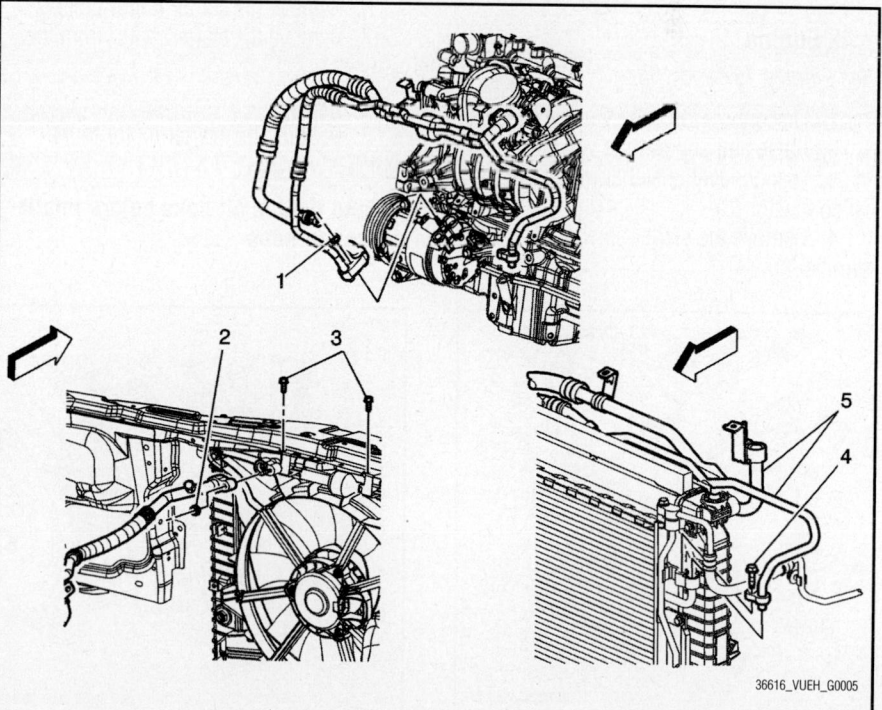

Fig. 154 Disconnect the Air Conditioning (A/C) compressor hose assembly lines from the A/C compressor

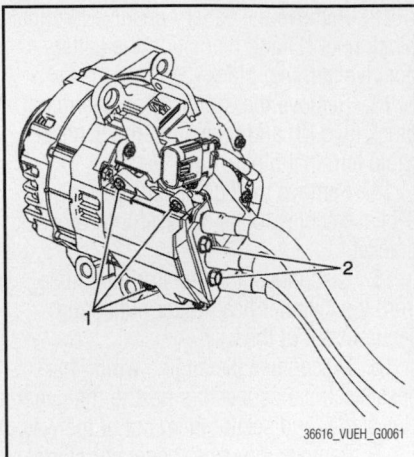

Fig. 155 Remove the generator starter cover bolts (1) and the 3-phase cable bracket bolts (2)

25. Install the 3-phase cable nuts underneath the generator starter cover.

26. Install the generator starter cover bolts and the 3-phase cable bracket bolts.

27. Install the generator starter to the vehicle with the 3-phase cables.

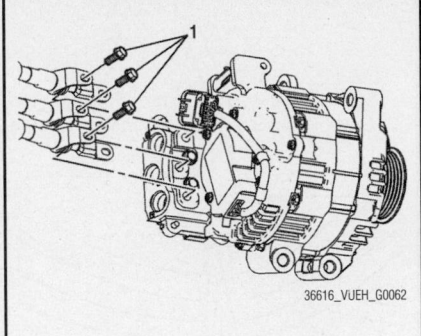

Fig. 156 Remove the 3-phase cable bolts (1)

28. Install the lower generator starter bolts. Tighten the bolts to 43 ft. lbs. (58 Nm).

29. Install the A/C compressor hose assembly lines to the A/C compressor.

30. Install the upper generator starter bolt. Tighten the bolt to 43 ft. lbs. (58 Nm).

31. Connect the engine wiring harness electrical connectors next to the generator starter.

32. Install the upper radiator hose to the cylinder head.

33. Install the bolt securing the 3-phase cables to the oil level indicator bracket. Tighten the bolt to 89 inch lbs. (10 Nm).

34. Install the 3-phase cable terminal block and nuts. Tighten the bolt to 89 inch lbs. (10 Nm).

35. Install the battery positive terminal block and nuts. Tighten the bolt to 89 inch lbs. (10 Nm).

36. Install the generator control module cover bolts and cover. Tighten the bolt to 89 inch lbs. (10 Nm).

37. Install the ECM bracket, bolts and nuts. Tighten the bolt to 89 inch lbs. (10 Nm).

38. Connect the ECM electrical connectors and the TCM electrical connectors.

39. Clip in the battery positive cable jumper block to the ECM bracket.

40. Recharge the A/C system.

41. Fill the cooling system.

42. Install the drive belt.

43. Install the air cleaner outlet duct.

44. Connect the hybrid battery.

45. Using a Tech 2, command an autostart in order to verify that the system is working properly.

ENGINE ELECTRICAL

STARTER

REMOVAL & INSTALLATION

2.4L Engine

See Figures 157 and 158.

1. Disconnect the battery negative cable.
2. Raise and support the vehicle.
3. Disconnect the starter motor electrical connector (3).
4. Remove the starter solenoid BAT terminal nut (4).

5. Remove the battery positive cable terminal (1) and engine harness terminal (2) from the starter motor.

6. Remove the starter motor bolts.

7. Remove the starter motor from the vehicle.

To install:

8. Position the starter motor to the vehicle.

➡ **Hand tighten all bolts before finalizing any torques.**

STARTING SYSTEM

9. Install the starter motor bolts. Tighten the bolts to 32 ft. lbs. (43 Nm).

10. Install the engine harness terminal and the battery positive cable terminal to the starter motor. Ensure that the battery positive cable terminal anti-rotation feature is aligned correctly.

11. Install the starter solenoid BAT terminal nut. Tighten the nut to 11 ft. lbs. (15 Nm).

12. Connect the starter motor electrical connector.

13. Connect the battery negative cable.

3.5L Engine

See Figures 159 through 162.

1. Disconnect the battery negative cable.

2. Remove the 3 transaxle bracket bolts (1).

3. Remove the transaxle bracket (2) from the vehicle.

4. Remove the starter solenoid BAT terminal nut (3).

5. Remove the battery positive cable terminal (2) and engine harness terminal (1) from the starter motor.

6. Disconnect the starter motor electrical connector (1).

7. Remove the starter motor bolts.

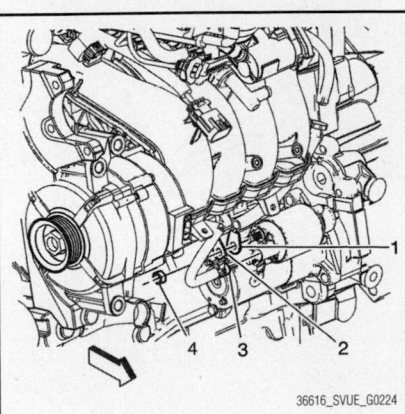

Fig. 157 Disconnect the starter motor electrical connector (3)

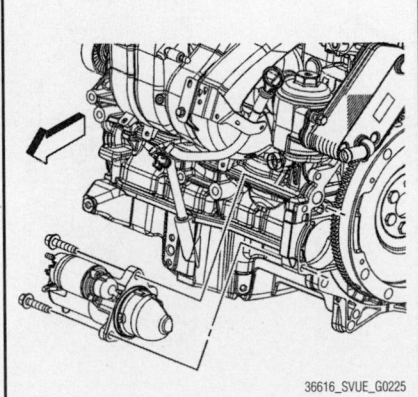

Fig. 158 Remove the starter motor bolts

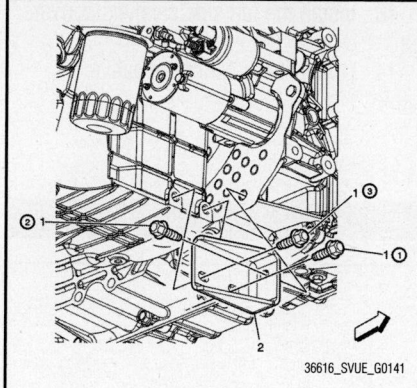

Fig. 159 Remove the 3 transaxle bracket bolts (1)

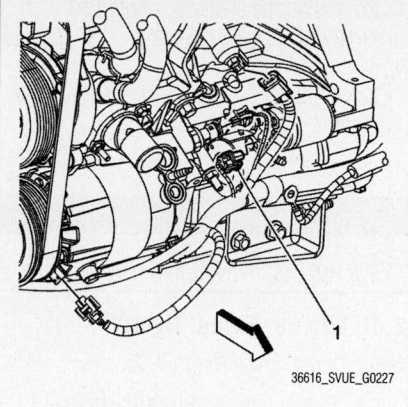

Fig. 161 Disconnect the starter motor electrical connector (1)

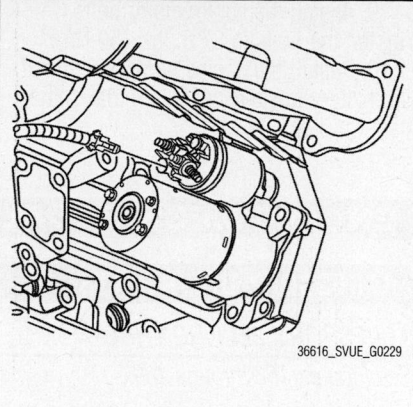

Fig. 163 Disconnect the starter motor electrical connector

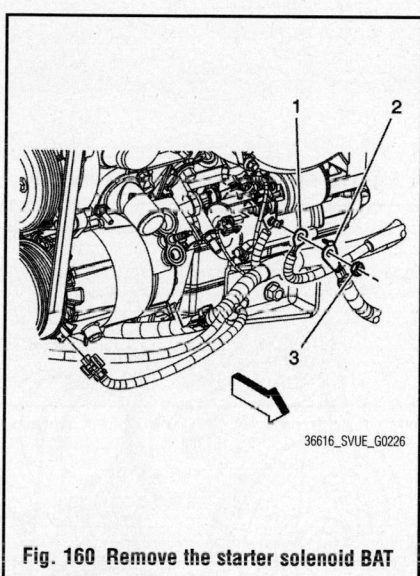

Fig. 160 Remove the starter solenoid BAT terminal nut (3)

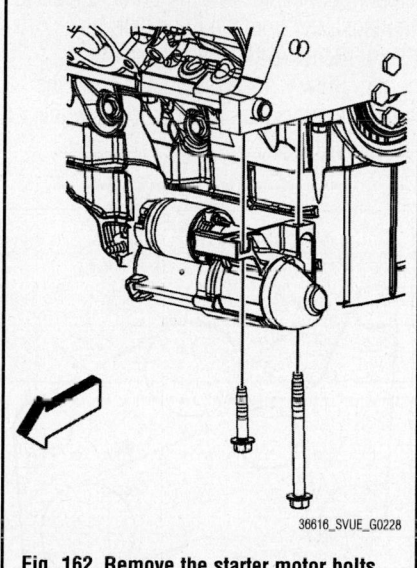

Fig. 162 Remove the starter motor bolts

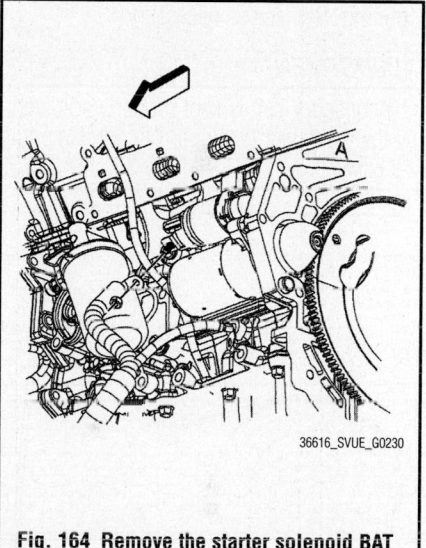

Fig. 164 Remove the starter solenoid BAT terminal nut

8. Remove the starter motor from the vehicle.

To install:

9. Position the starter motor to the vehicle.

➡**Hand tighten all bolts before finalizing any torques.**

10. Install the starter bolts. Tighten the bolts to 32 ft. lbs. (43 Nm).

11. Connect the starter motor electrical connector.

12. Install the engine harness terminal and battery positive cable terminal to the starter. Ensure that the battery positive cable terminal anti-rotation feature is aligned correctly.

13. Install the starter solenoid BAT terminal nut. Tighten the nut to 11 ft. lbs. (15 Nm).

14. Position the transaxle bracket to the vehicle.

15. Install the 3 transaxle bracket bolts.
Tighten the bolts to 37 ft. lbs. (50 Nm).

16. Connect the battery negative cable.

3.6L Engine

See Figures 163 through 165.

1. Disconnect the battery negative cable.

2. Remove the left side catalytic convertor.

3. Disconnect the starter motor electrical connector.

4. Remove the starter solenoid BAT terminal nut.

5. Remove the battery positive cable terminal and engine harness terminal from the starter motor.

6. Remove the starter motor bolts.

7. Remove the starter motor from the vehicle.

To install:

8. Install the starter motor to the vehicle.

➡**Hand tighten all bolts before finalizing any torques.**

Fig. 165 Remove the starter motor bolts

9. Install the starter motor bolts. Tighten the bolts to 37 ft. lbs. (50 Nm).

10. Install the engine harness terminal and battery positive cable terminal to the starter motor.

11. Install the starter solenoid BAT terminal nut. Tighten the nut to 11 ft. lbs. (15 Nm).

12. Connect the starter motor electrical connector.

13. Install the left side catalytic converter.

14. Connect the battery negative cable.

ENGINE MECHANICAL

ACCESSORY DRIVE BELTS

ACCESSORY BELT ROUTING

See Figures 166 through 169.

Refer to the accompanying illustrations.

INSPECTION

Inspect belts for cracking, fraying or splitting. Replace as necessary.

ADJUSTMENT

Accessory belt is kept properly adjusted by the drive belt tensioner. No adjustment is necessary.

REMOVAL & INSTALLATION

2.4L Engine, Except Hybrid

See Figures 170 through 172.

1. Remove the engine splash shield.
2. Install the J 44811 to the drive belt tensioner.
3. Using the J 44811, rotate the tensioner counterclockwise in order to release the tensioner from the drive belt.
4. Remove the drive belt.
5. Slowly rotate the J 44811 and the tensioner clockwise in order to allow the tensioner to rest.

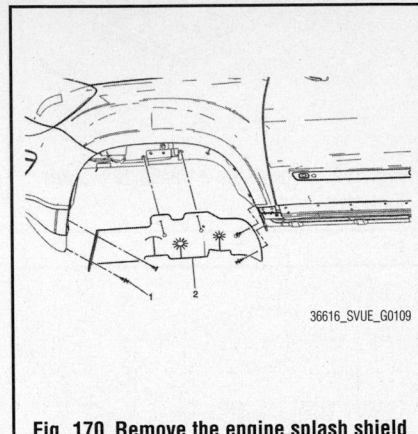

36616_SVUE_G0109

Fig. 170 Remove the engine splash shield

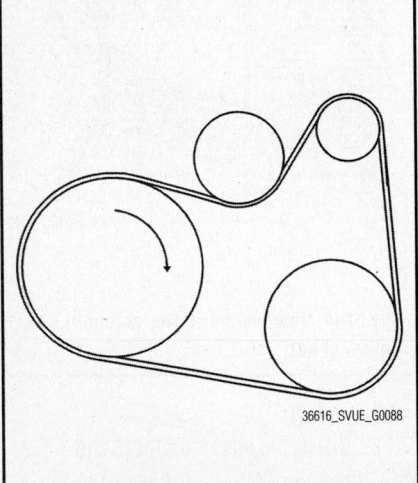

36616_SVUE_G0088

Fig. 166 Drive belt routing—2.4L engine, except Hybrid

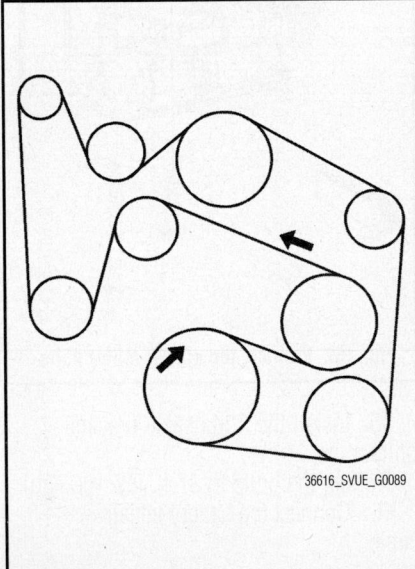

36616_SVUE_G0089

Fig. 168 Drive belt routing—3.5L engine

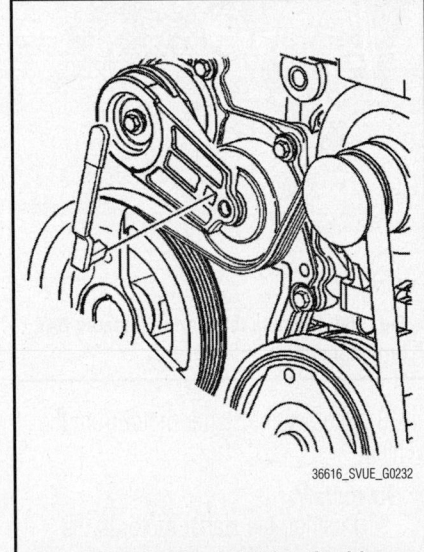

36616_SVUE_G0232

Fig. 171 Install the J 44811 to the drive belt tensioner

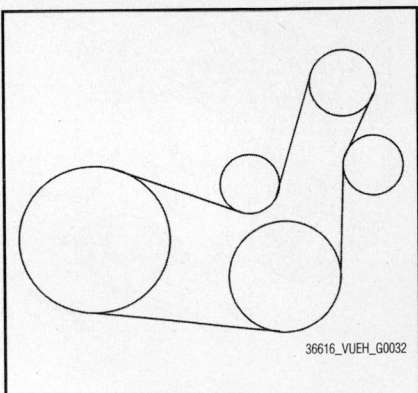

36616_VUEH_G0032

Fig. 167 Drive belt routing—2.4L Hybrid

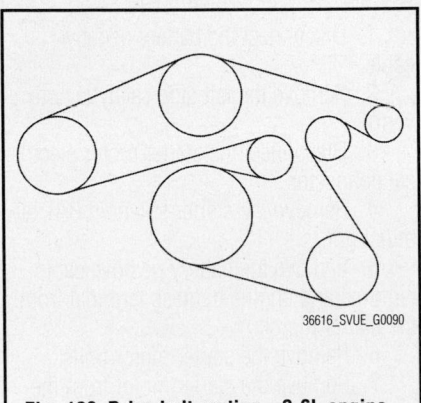

36616_SVUE_G0090

Fig. 169 Drive belt routing—3.6L engine

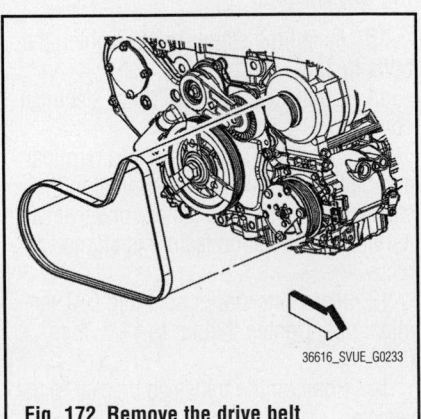

36616_SVUE_G0233

Fig. 172 Remove the drive belt

6. Remove the J 44811 from the drive belt tensioner.

To install:

7. Install and position the drive belt around all of the pulleys except for the drive belt tensioner.

8. Install the J 44811 to the drive belt tensioner.

9. Using the J 44811, rotate the tensioner counterclockwise.

10. Position the drive belt under the tensioner pulley.

11. Using the J 44811, rotate the tensioner clockwise in order to seat the tensioner pulley onto the drive belt.

12. Install the engine splash shield.

2.4L Hybrid Engine

See Figures 173 through 175.

➡ **The engine drive belt on this hybrid vehicle is under a higher tension than the engine drive belt on a non-hybrid vehicle and requires the use of a special tool (EN-48932) to service.**

1. Remove the air cleaner assembly.

2. Install the EN-48932 (1) to the drive belt tensioner spring.

3. Compress the drive belt tensioner spring fully using the EN-48932 (1).

4. Remove the tensioner spring bolts (1) from the tensioner.

5. Remove the tensioner spring from the tensioner.

6. Rotate the tensioner, then remove the drive belt from under the middle idler pulley.

7. Remove the drive belt from the vehicle.

To install:

8. Install and position the drive belt around all of the pulleys except for the middle idler pulley.

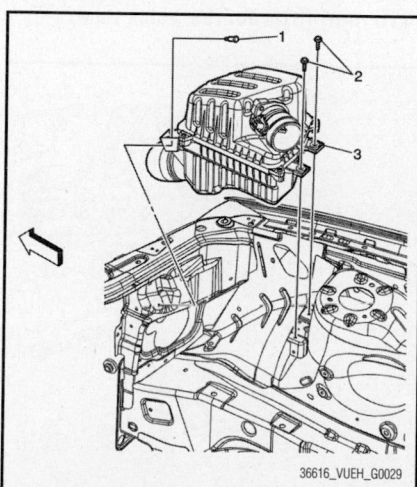

Fig. 173 Remove the air cleaner assembly

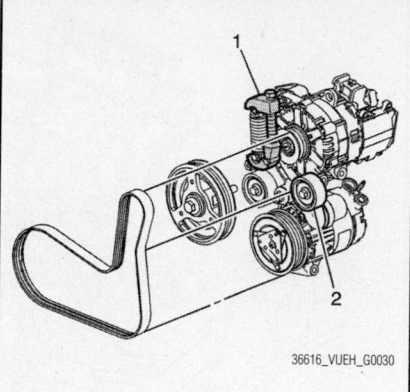

36616_VUEH_G0030

Fig. 174 Install the EN-48932 (1) to the drive belt tensioner spring

36616_VUEH_G0031

Fig. 175 Remove the tensioner spring bolts (1) from the tensioner

9. Install the tensioner spring on the tensioner.

10. Install the tensioner spring bolts to the tensioner. Tighten the bolts to 16 ft. lbs. (22 Nm).

11. Install the drive belt under the middle idler pulley.

12. Loosen the forcing bolt on the EN-48932 and remove from the drive belt tensioner spring.

13. Install and position the drive belt around all of the pulleys except for the middle idler pulley.

14. Ensure that the drive belt tensioner idler is fully seated against the drive belt.

15. Install the air cleaner assembly.

3.5L Engine

See Figures 176 through 179.

1. Remove the intake manifold cover.

2. Remove the air cleaner assembly.

3. Remove the engine mount bracket.

4. Rotate the drive belt tensioner clockwise in order to release the spring tension.

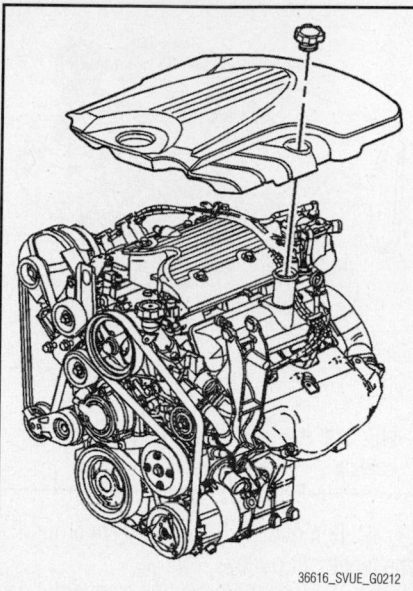

36616_SVUE_G0212

Fig. 176 Remove the intake manifold cover

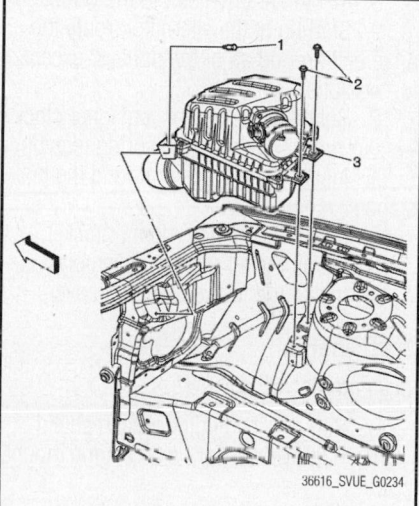

36616_SVUE_G0234

Fig. 177 Remove the air cleaner assembly

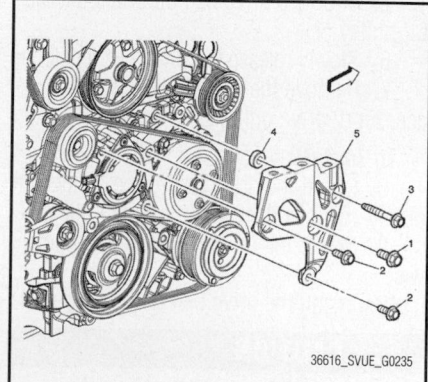

36616_SVUE_G0235

Fig. 178 Remove the engine mount bracket

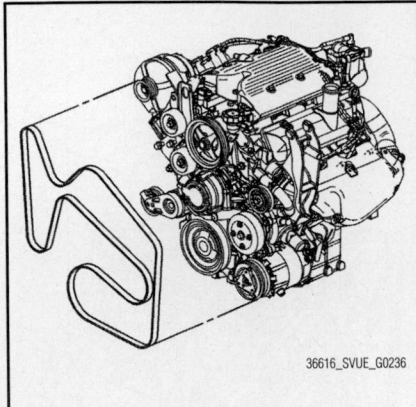

36616_SVUE_G0236

Fig. 179 Remove the drive belt from the vehicle

5. Remove the drive belt from around the tensioner pulley.

6. Remove the drive belt from around all the other pulleys.

7. Remove the drive belt from the vehicle.

To install:

8. Install the drive belt to the vehicle.

9. Starting at the alternator, route the drive belt around all of the pulleys, except for tensioner.

10. Rotate the drive belt tensioner clockwise in order to release the spring tension.

11. Install the drive belt around the tensioner.

12. Install the engine mount bracket.

13. Install the air cleaner assembly.

14. Install the intake manifold cover.

3.6L Engine

See Figures 180 and 181.

1. Remove the engine splash shield.

2. Remove the right side engine mount bracket.

3. Completely remove the lower engine mount bracket bolt.

4. Rotate the drive belt tensioner clockwise to release the drive belt tension.

5. Slide the drive belt off of the alternator pulley (1).

6. Slowly release the drive belt tensioner.

7. Remove the drive belt from the accessory drive pulleys.

To install:

8. Install the drive belt to the crankshaft pulley, the tensioner and the idler pulley.

9. Rotate the drive belt tensioner clockwise.

10. Install the drive belt to the alternator.

✳✳ CAUTION

Ensure the drive belt is properly aligned and seated into the grooves of the accessory drive pulleys.

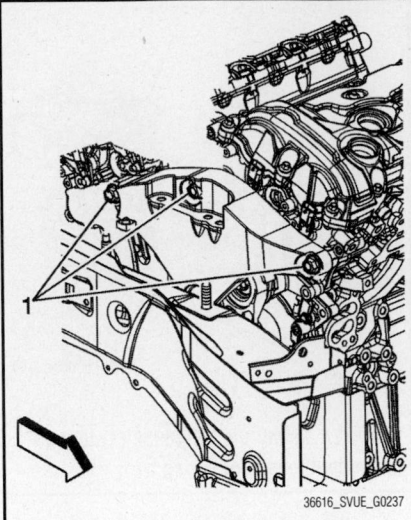

36616_SVUE_G0237

Fig. 180 Remove the right side engine mount bracket

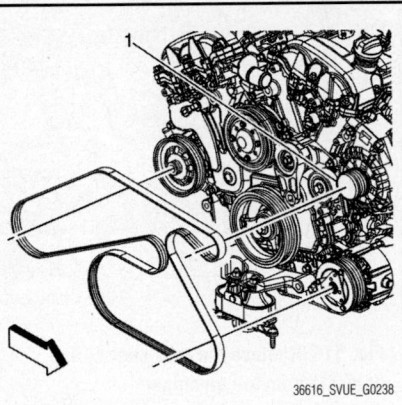

36616_SVUE_G0238

Fig. 181 Slide the drive belt off of the alternator pulley (1)

11. Slowly release the drive belt tensioner.

12. Raise the vehicle.

13. Partially thread the lower right side engine mount bracket bolt in place.

14. Install the right side engine mount bracket.

15. Install the engine splash shield.

BALANCE SHAFT

REMOVAL & INSTALLATION

2.4L Engine

See Figures 182 through 187

1. Remove the balance shaft bearing carrier bolts.

➡**It is possible to install the intake side balance shaft into the exhaust side and vice versa. Please use care not to install the balance shafts into the wrong bores. Engine vibration will result.**

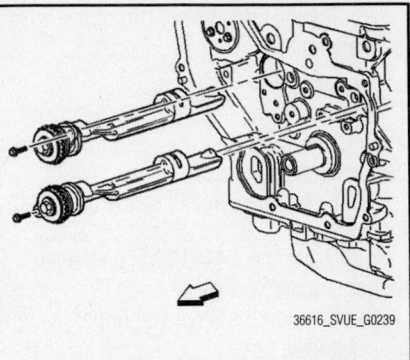

36616_SVUE_G0239

Fig. 182 Remove the balance shaft bearing carrier bolts

➡**Do not remove the bolt holding the sprocket.**

2. Remove the balance shaft assemblies.

➡**Proper centering of the tool is required on the balance shaft bushing. If the tool is not properly centered then damage to the bearing bore and block will occur.**

3. Install the J 43650 into the balance shaft hole. Insert the tool with the foot parallel to the shaft.

4. When the J 43650 is inserted in the block turn the J 43650 so that the foot becomes perpendicular to the shaft.

5. Center the foot of the J 43650 on the balance shaft bushing.

6. Once the J 43650 is centered on the balance shaft bushing, then insert the centering guide into the front balance shaft bore and tighten the nut with an appropriate wrench.

➡**When the J 43650 is properly installed, before removing the bushing, the end of the tool should be 4.6 inches (116 mm) (a) from the block face.**

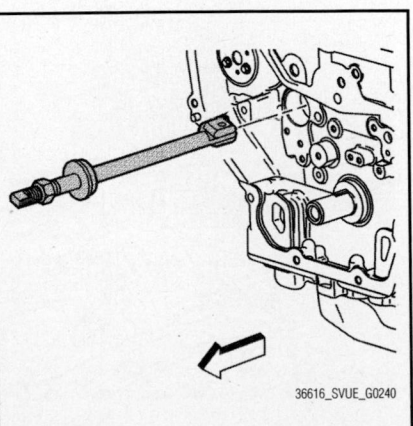

36616_SVUE_G0240

Fig. 183 Install the J 43650 into the balance shaft hole

Fig. 184 Turn the J 43650 so that the foot becomes perpendicular to the shaft

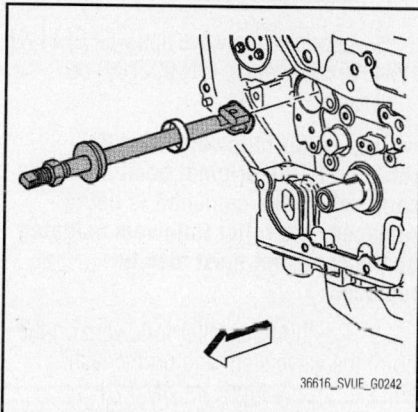

Fig. 185 Remove the J 43650 and the balance shaft bushing

➡**If the J 43650 is less than approximately 4.5 inches (114 mm) (a), recheck the tool alignment.**

7. Tighten the nut on the J 43650 until the tension releases. When the tension releases, remove the J 43650 and the balance shaft bushing.

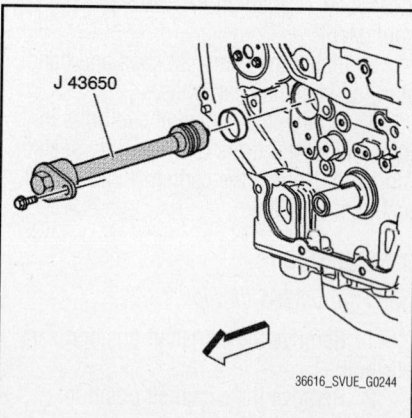

Fig. 186 Install the balance shaft bushing using the J 43650

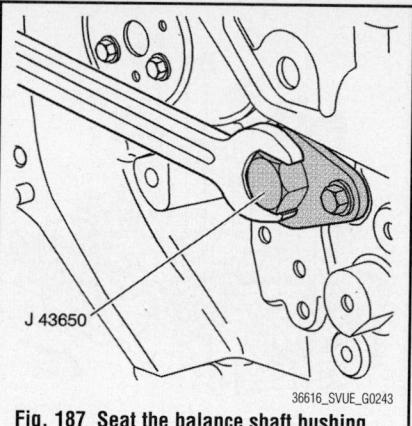

Fig. 187 Seat the balance shaft bushing into the bore using the J 43650 and a wrench

To install:

8. Install the balance shaft bushing using the J 43650.

9. Seat the balance shaft bushing into the bore using the J 43650 and a wrench.

10. When the J 43650 is fully seated in the engine block, remove it with a wrench.

➡**If the balance shafts are not properly timed to the engine, the engine may vibrate or make noise.**

11. Place the number one piston at Top Dead Center (TDC).

12. Lubricate the balance shaft lobes with engine oil.

13. Install the balance shafts into their bores.

14. Install the balance shaft retaining bolts. Tighten the balance shaft retaining bolts to 89 inch lbs. (10 Nm).

CAMSHAFT AND VALVE LIFTERS

REMOVAL & INSTALLATION

2.4L Engine—Intake Camshaft

See Figures 188 through 191.

➡**Remove each bolt on each cap one turn at a time until there is no spring tension pushing on the camshaft.**

1. Mark camshaft caps to ensure they are installed in the same position.
2. Remove the intake camshaft cap bolts.
3. Remove the camshaft caps.
4. Remove the intake camshaft.

➡**Keep all of the roller finger followers and hydraulic lash adjusters in order so that they can be reinstalled in their respective locations.**

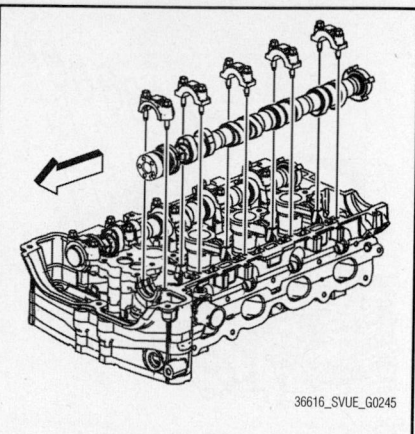

Fig. 188 Remove the intake camshaft cap bolts

Fig. 189 Remove the intake camshaft roller finger followers

5. Remove the intake camshaft roller finger followers.
6. Remove the hydraulic lash adjusters.

To Install:

7. Install the hydraulic lash adjusters into their bores in the cylinder head.
8. Lubricate the hydraulic lash adjusters with GM P/N 12345501 (Canadian P/N 992704) or equivalent.
9. Lubricate the valve tips.

➡**Used roller followers must be returned to the original position on the camshaft. If the camshaft is being replaced, the roller followers actuated by the camshaft must also be replaced.**

10. Position the roller followers on the tip of the valve stem and on the lash adjuster. Lubricate roller followers with GM P/N 12345501 (Canadian P/N 992704) or equivalent.

11. When installing the camshafts, ensure the intake camshaft notch is in the 5 o'clock position (2) and the exhaust camshaft notch

Fig. 190 Remove the hydraulic lash adjusters

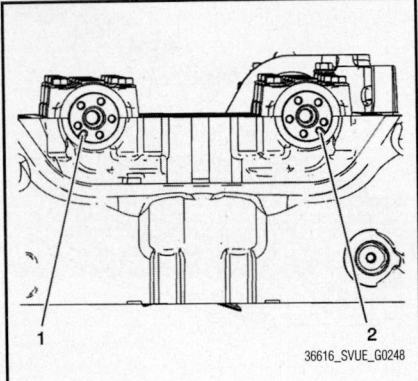

Fig. 191 When installing the camshafts, ensure the intake camshaft notch is in the 5 o'clock position (2) and the exhaust camshaft notch is in the 7 o'clock position (1)

is in the 7 o'clock position (1). The number 1 piston should be at Top Dead Center (TDC), crankshaft key at 12 o'clock.

12. Set the intake camshaft on top of the roller followers in the camshaft bearing journals. Lubricate with GM P/N 12345501 (Canadian P/N 992704) or equivalent.

13. Install the camshaft caps and hand start the camshaft cap bolts.

14. Tighten the camshaft cap bolts in increments of 3 turns until they are seated. Tighten the camshaft caps to 89 inch lbs. (10 Nm).

2.4L Engine—Exhaust Camshaft
See Figures 191 through 194.

➡**Remove each bolt on each cap one turn at a time until there is no spring tension pushing on the camshaft.**

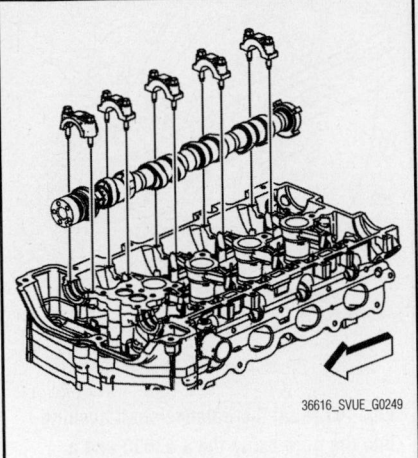

Fig. 192 Remove the exhaust camshaft cap bolts

1. Mark camshaft caps to ensure they are installed in the same position.

2. Remove the exhaust camshaft cap bolts.

3. Remove the camshaft caps ensuring they are marked and refitted in same position on assembly.

4. Remove the exhaust camshaft.

➡**Keep all of the roller finger followers and hydraulic lash adjusters in order so that they can be reinstalled in their respective locations.**

5. Remove the exhaust camshaft roller finger followers.

6. Remove the hydraulic lash adjusters.

To install:

7. Install the hydraulic lash adjusters into their bores in the cylinder head. Apply lubricant GM P/N 12345501 (Canadian P/N 992704) or equivalent.

Fig. 193 Remove the exhaust camshaft roller finger followers

8. Lubricate the valve tips with GM P/N 12345501 (Canadian P/N 992704) or equivalent.

➡**Used roller followers must be returned to the original position on the camshaft. If the camshaft is being replaced, the roller followers actuated by the camshaft must also be replaced.**

9. Position the roller followers on the tip of the valve stem and on the lash adjuster. Apply lubricant GM P/N 12345501 (Canadian P/N 992704) or equivalent.

10. When installing the camshafts, ensure the intake camshaft notch is in the 5 o'clock position (2) and the exhaust camshaft notch is in the 7 o'clock position (1). The number 1 piston should be at top dead center (TDC), crankshaft key at 12 o'clock.

11. Set the exhaust camshaft on top of the roller followers in the camshaft bearing journals. Lubricate with GM P/N 12345501 (Canadian P/N 992704) or equivalent.

12. Install the camshaft caps and hand start the camshaft cap bolts.

13. Tighten the camshaft cap bolts in increments of 3 turns until they are seated, lubricate. Tighten the camshaft caps to 89 inch lbs. (10 Nm).

3.5L Engine
See Figures 195 through 197.

1. Remove the camshaft position sensor bolt.

2. Remove the camshaft position sensor.

3. Remove the camshaft thrust plate screws.

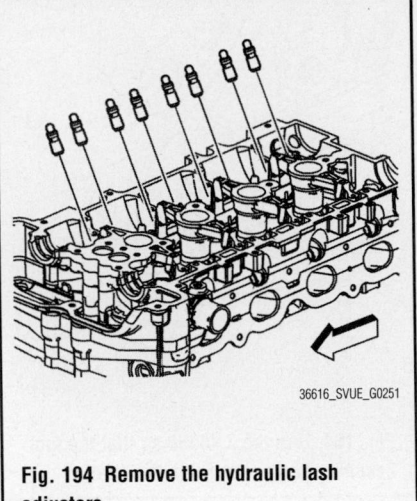

Fig. 194 Remove the hydraulic lash adjusters

4. Remove the camshaft thrust plate.

All camshaft journals are the same diameter, so care must be used in removing or installing the camshaft to avoid damage to the camshaft bearings.

5. Install a camshaft sprocket bolt into the camshaft. Tighten finger tight only.

6. Carefully rotate and remove the camshaft from the engine block.

To install:

7. Coat the camshaft journals with clean engine oil.

8. Coat the camshaft lobes with pre-lube GM P/N 12345501 (Canadian P/N 992704) or the equivalent.

9. Install the camshaft using the following procedure:

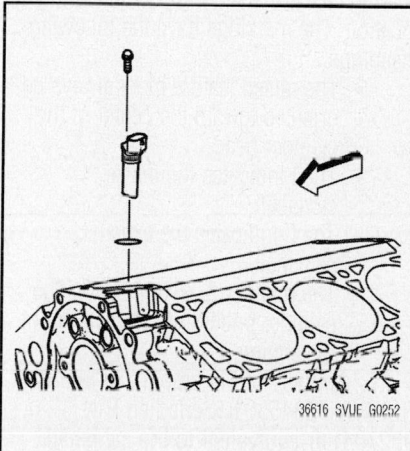

Fig. 195 Remove the camshaft position sensor bolt

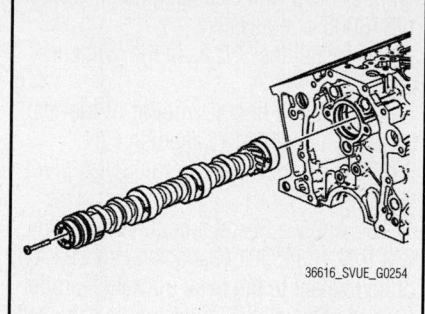

Fig. 197 Remove the camshaft from the engine block

a. Install a camshaft sprocket bolt into the camshaft. Tighten finger tight only.

b. Carefully rotate the camshaft while installing the camshaft into the camshaft bearings.

10. Install the camshaft thrust plate.

11. Install the camshaft thrust plate screws. Tighten the camshaft thrust plate screws to 89 inch lbs. (10 Nm).

12. Install the camshaft position sensor.

13. Install the camshaft position sensor bolt. Tighten the camshaft position sensor bolt to 89 inch lbs. (10 Nm).

3.6L Engine—Left Side

See Figures 198 through 205.

1. Observe the markings on the bearing caps. Each bearing cap is marked in order to identify its location. The markings have the following meanings:

- The raised feature must always be oriented toward the center of the cylinder head.

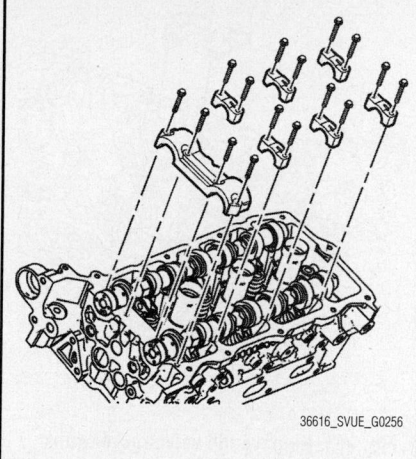

Fig. 199 Remove the camshaft bearing cap bolts

- The I indicates the intake camshaft.
- The E indicates the exhaust camshaft.
- The number indicates the journal position from the front of the engine.

2. Remove the camshaft bearing cap bolts.

3. Remove the camshaft bearing caps.

➡ Mark the camshafts upon removal to ensure installation is in the correct position.

4. Remove the camshafts.

5. Replace the camshaft bearing caps and bolts.

6. Remove the valve rocker arms from the cylinder head. If the rocker arms are to be reused, keep in order so they can be reinstalled in the same position.

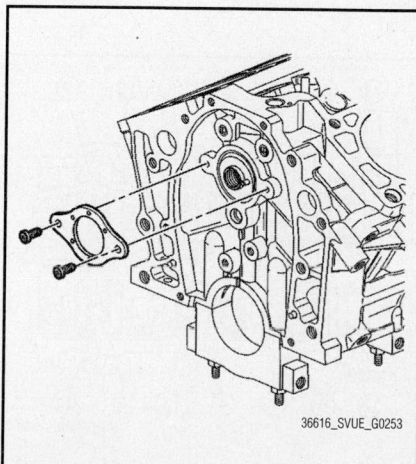

Fig. 196 Remove the camshaft thrust plate screws

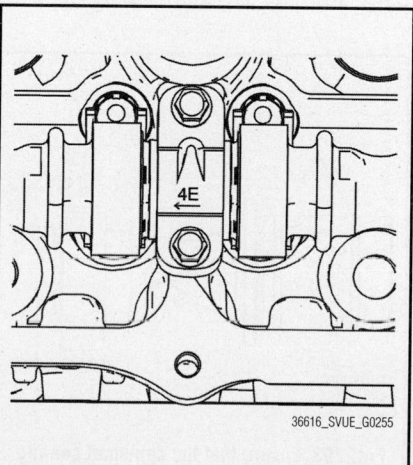

Fig. 198 Observe the markings on the bearing caps

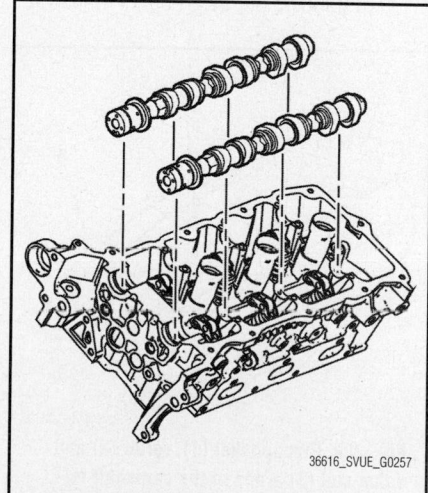

Fig. 200 Remove the camshafts

Fig. 201 Remove the valve rocker arms from the cylinder head

➡**Do not stroke/cycle the stationary hydraulic lash adjuster plunger without oil in the lower pressure chamber. Do not allow the stationary hydraulic lash adjuster to tip over, plunger down, after the oil fill.**

7. Remove the valve lifters (SHLAs) from the cylinder head. If the lifters are to be reused, keep in order so they can be reinstalled in the same position.

To install:

➡**Do not stroke/cycle the stationary hydraulic lash adjuster plunger without oil in the lower pressure chamber. Do not allow the stationary hydraulic lash adjuster to tip over, plunger down, after the oil fill.**

8. Fill the Stationary Hydraulic Lash Adjuster (SHLA) with clean engine oil GM P/N 12378006 or equivalent. Take precautions to prevent scratching the pivot sphere area of the SHLA.
9. Lubricate the SHLA bores in the

cylinder head with clean engine oil GM P/N 12378006 or equivalent.
10. Install the SHLAs in the cylinder head.
11. Apply a liberal amount of lubricant GM P/N 12345501 (Canadian P/N 992704) or equivalent to the SHLA pivot spheres.
12. Apply a liberal amount of lubricant GM P/N 12345501 (Canadian P/N 992704) or equivalent to the pivot pocket (1), roller (2) and valve slot (3) areas of the camshaft followers.

➡**The follower must be positioned squarely on the valve tip so that the full width of the roller will completely contact the camshaft lobe. If the followers are being reused you must put them back in their original location.**

13. Place the camshaft followers in position on the valve tip and Stationary Hydraulic Lash Adjuster (SHLA).
14. The rounded head end of the follower goes on the SHLA while the flat end goes on the valve tip.
15. Clean the camshaft journals and carriers with a clean, lint-free cloth.
16. Ensure that the camshaft sealing rings (1) are in place in the camshaft grooves. Camshaft sealing rings must be in place below the surface of the camshaft journal in order to avoid being pinched between the cylinder head and the camshaft caps.
17. Apply a liberal amount of lubricant GM P/N 12345501 (Canadian P/N 992704) or equivalent to the camshaft journals and the left cylinder head camshaft carriers.
18. Place the left intake and left exhaust camshafts in position in the left cylinder head.
19. Position the camshaft lobes in a

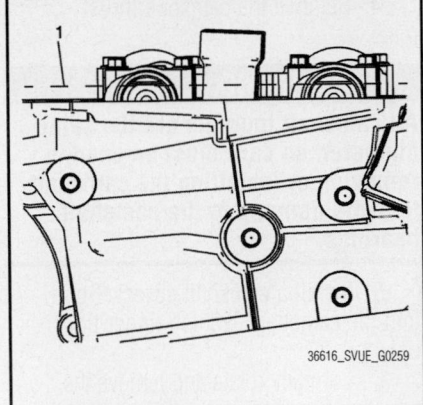

Fig. 204 Position the camshaft lobes in a neutral position

neutral position with the flats on the back of the camshafts up and parallel (1) with the left cylinder head camshaft cover rail.
20. Observe the markings on the left cylinder head camshaft bearing caps. Each bearing cap is marked in order to identify its location. The markings have the following meanings:
- The raised feature must always be oriented toward the center of the cylinder head.
- The I indicates the intake camshaft.
- The E indicates the exhaust camshaft.
- The number 2, 4, 6 indicates the cylinder position from the front of the engine.
21. Apply a liberal amount of lubricant GM P/N 12345501 (Canadian P/N 992704) or equivalent to the camshaft bearing caps.
22. Install the camshaft bearing thrust cap in the first journal of the left cylinder head.

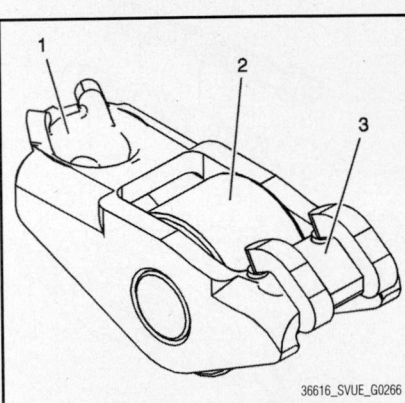

Fig. 202 Pivot pocket (1), roller (2) and valve slot (3) areas of the camshaft followers

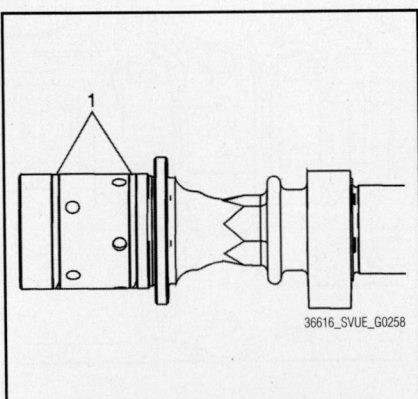

Fig. 203 Ensure that the camshaft sealing rings (1) are in place in the camshaft grooves

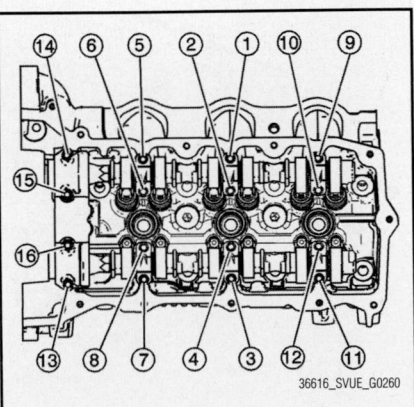

Fig. 205 Tighten the camshaft bearing cap bolts in the sequence shown

23. Install the remaining bearing caps with their orientation mark toward the center of the cylinder head.

24. Hand start all the camshaft bearing cap bolts.

25. Tighten the camshaft bearing cap bolts in the sequence shown. Tighten the camshaft bearing cap bolts in sequence to 89 inch lbs. (10 Nm).

26. Loosen the center intake camshaft bearing cap bolts (1, 2) and the center exhaust camshaft bearing cap bolts (3, 4).

27. Retighten the center camshaft bearing cap bolts (1, 2, 3, 4). Retighten the camshaft bearing cap bolts to 89 inch lbs. (10 Nm).

3.6L Engine—Right Side

See Figures 202, 206 through 211.

1. Observe the markings on the bearing caps. Each bearing cap is marked in order to identify its location. The markings have the following meanings:

- The raised feature must always be oriented toward the center of the cylinder head.
- The I indicates the intake camshaft.
- The E indicates the exhaust camshaft.
- The number indicates the journal position from the front of the engine.

2. Remove the camshaft bearing cap bolts.

3. Remove the camshaft bearing caps.

➡**Mark the camshafts upon removal to ensure installation is in the correct position.**

Fig. 206 Observe the markings on the bearing caps

36616_SVUE_G0261

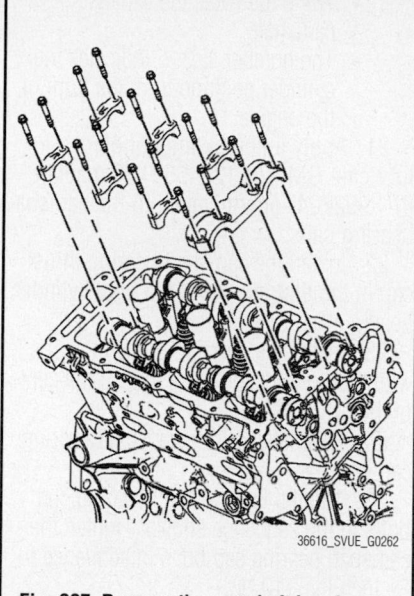

Fig. 207 Remove the camshaft bearing cap bolts

36616_SVUE_G0262

4. Remove the camshafts.

5. Replace the camshaft bearing caps and bolts.

6. Remove the valve rocker arms from the cylinder head. If the rocker arms are to be reused, keep in order so they can be reinstalled in the same position.

➡**Do not stroke/cycle the stationary hydraulic lash adjuster plunger without oil in the lower pressure chamber. Do not allow the stationary hydraulic lash adjuster to tip over, plunger down, after the oil fill.**

7. Remove the valve lifters (SHLAs) from the cylinder head. If the lifters are to be reused, keep in order so they can be reinstalled in the same position.

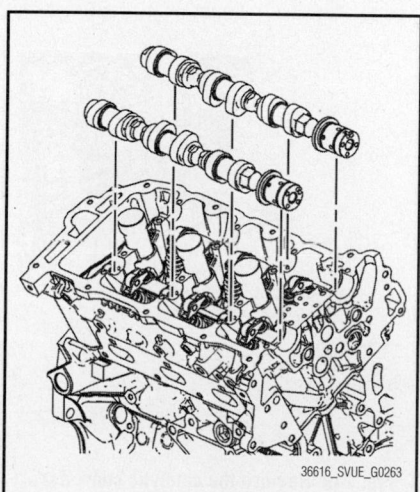

Fig. 208 Remove the camshafts

36616_SVUE_G0263

To install:

➡**Do not stroke/cycle the stationary hydraulic lash adjuster plunger without oil in the lower pressure chamber. Do not allow the stationary hydraulic lash adjuster to tip over, plunger down, after the oil fill.**

8. Fill the Stationary Hydraulic Lash Adjuster (SHLA) with clean engine oil GM P/N 12378006 or equivalent. Take precautions to prevent scratching the pivot sphere area of the SHLA.

9. Lubricate the SHLA bores in the cylinder head with clean engine oil GM P/N 12378006 or equivalent.

10. Install the SHLAs in the cylinder head.

11. Apply a liberal amount of lubricant GM P/N 12345501 (Canadian P/N 992704) or equivalent to the SHLA pivot spheres.

12. Apply a liberal amount of lubricant GM P/N 12345501 (Canadian P/N 992704) or equivalent to the pivot pocket (1), roller (2) and valve slot (3) areas of the camshaft followers.

➡**The follower must be positioned squarely on the valve tip so that the full width of the roller will completely contact the camshaft lobe. If the followers are being reused you must put them back in their original location.**

13. Place the camshaft followers in position on the valve tip and Stationary Hydraulic Lash Adjuster (SHLA).

14. The rounded head end of the follower goes on the SHLA while the flat end goes on the valve tip.

15. Clean the camshaft journals and carriers with a clean, lint-free cloth.

16. Ensure that the camshaft sealing rings (1) are in place in the camshaft grooves. Camshaft sealing rings must be in place below the surface of the camshaft journal in order to avoid being pinched between the cylinder head and the camshaft caps.

17. Apply a liberal amount of lubricant GM P/N 12345501 (Canadian P/N 992704) or equivalent to the camshaft journals and the right cylinder head camshaft carriers.

18. Place the right intake and right exhaust camshafts in position in the right cylinder head.

19. Position the camshaft lobes in a neutral position with the flats on the back of the camshafts up and parallel (1) with the right cylinder head camshaft cover rail.

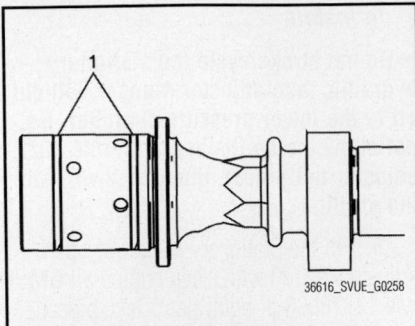

Fig. 209 Ensure that the camshaft sealing rings (1) are in place in the camshaft grooves

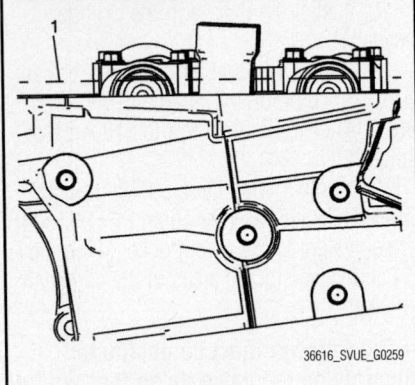

Fig. 210 Position the camshaft lobes in a neutral position

20. Observe the markings on the right cylinder head camshaft bearing caps. Each bearing cap is marked in order to identify its location. The markings have the following meanings:

- The raised feature must always be oriented toward the center of the cylinder head.
- The I indicates the intake camshaft.

- The E indicates the exhaust camshaft.
- The number 1, 3, 5 indicates the cylinder position from the front of the engine.

21. Apply a liberal amount of lubricant GM P/N 12345501 (Canadian P/N 992704) or equivalent to the camshaft bearing caps.

22. Install the camshaft bearing thrust cap in the first journal of the right cylinder head.

23. Install the remaining bearing caps with their orientation mark toward the center of the cylinder head.

24. Hand start all the camshaft bearing cap bolts.

25. Tighten the camshaft bearing cap bolts in the sequence shown. Tighten the camshaft bearing cap bolts in sequence to 89 inch lbs. (10 Nm).

26. Loosen the center intake camshaft bearing cap bolts (1, 2) and the center exhaust camshaft bearing cap bolts (3, 4).

27. Retighten the center camshaft bearing cap bolts (1, 2, 3, 4). Retighten the camshaft bearing cap bolts to 89 inch lbs. (10 Nm).

CATALYTIC CONVERTER

REMOVAL & INSTALLATION

2.4L Engine

See Figures 212 and 213.

1. Remove the heated oxygen sensor.
2. Remove the catalytic converter to exhaust manifold nuts (1).
3. Remove the catalytic converter to muffler nuts (1).
4. Separate the exhaust pipe from the catalytic converter studs.

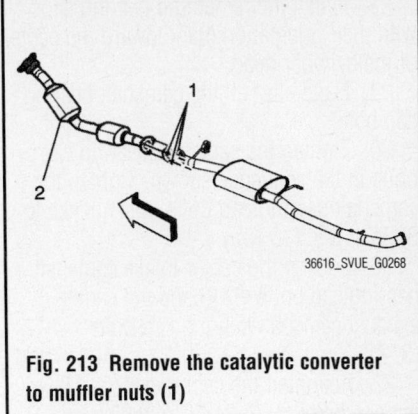

Fig. 213 Remove the catalytic converter to muffler nuts (1)

5. Position and support the exhaust pipe out of the way.
6. Remove the catalytic converter (2) and gasket.

To install:

7. Install the catalytic converter along with a NEW gasket to the exhaust manifold.

8. Position and join the exhaust pipe to the catalytic converter studs.

9. Install the catalytic converter to muffler nuts. Tighten the catalytic converter to muffler nuts to 13 ft. lbs. (17 Nm).

10. Install the catalytic converter to exhaust manifold nuts. Tighten the nuts to 37 ft. lbs. (50 Nm).

11. Install the heated oxygen sensor.

3.5L Engine—Left Side

See Figures 214 through 216.

➡The catalytic converter is serviced by replacing the entire assembly. Always replace the gaskets at the front and rear flanges when servicing the catalytic converter. Never install the original gasket.

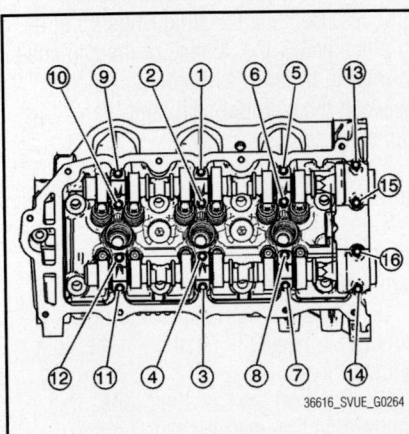

Fig. 211 Tighten the camshaft bearing cap bolts in the sequence shown

Fig. 212 Remove the catalytic converter to exhaust manifold nuts (1)

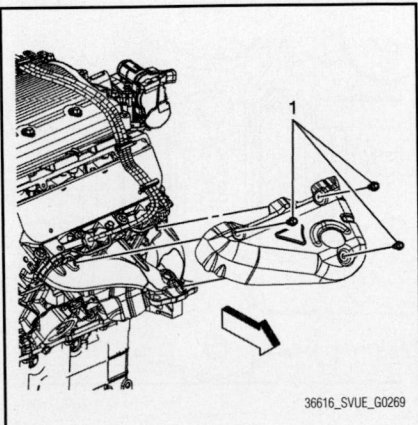

Fig. 214 Remove the left side exhaust manifold heat shield bolts (1)

1. Remove the Heated Oxygen Sensors (HO2S).

2. Lower the vehicle.

3. Remove the left side exhaust manifold heat shield bolts (1).

4. Remove the left side exhaust manifold heat shield.

5. Remove the left side catalytic converter to exhaust manifold nuts (1).

6. Raise and support the vehicle.

7. Support the exhaust system.

8. Remove the catalytic converter to muffler nuts (1).

9. Reposition the muffler assembly rearward until the catalytic converter can be removed.

10. Remove the catalytic converter.

11. Remove the catalytic converter gaskets.

12. Clean and inspect the exhaust manifold and the exhaust pipe gasket mating surfaces.

To install:

13. Install the catalytic converter gasket onto the catalytic converter.

14. Reposition the muffler assembly rearward until the catalytic converter can be installed.

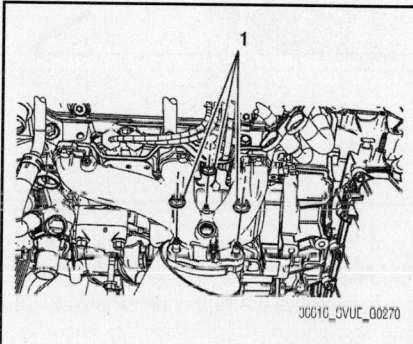

Fig. 215 Remove the left side catalytic converter to exhaust manifold nuts (1)

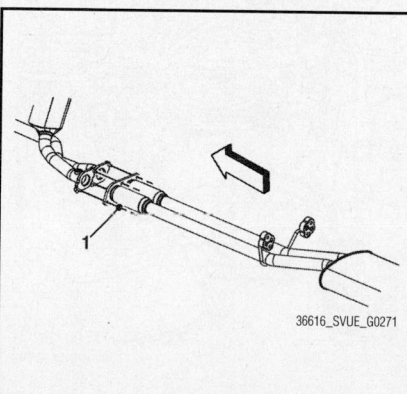

Fig. 216 Remove the catalytic converter to muffler nuts (1)

15. Install the catalytic converter.

16. Install the catalytic converter nuts. Tighten the nuts to 44 ft. lbs. (60 Nm).

17. Remove the support from the exhaust system.

18. Lower the vehicle.

19. Install the left side catalytic converter to exhaust manifold nuts. Tighten the nuts to 26 ft. lbs. (35 Nm).

20. Install the exhaust manifold heat shield.

21. Install the left side exhaust manifold heat shield bolts. Tighten the nuts to 89 inch lbs. (10 Nm).

22. Install the HO2S sensor.

3.5L Engine—Right Side

See Figures 216 through 218.

➡**The catalytic converter is serviced by replacing the entire assembly. Always replace the gaskets at the front and rear flanges when servicing the catalytic converter. Never install the original gasket.**

1. Remove the Heated Oxygen Sensor (HO2S).

2. Lower the vehicle.

3. Remove the right side exhaust manifold heat shield bolts (1).

4. Remove the right side exhaust manifold heat shield.

5. Remove the right side catalytic converter to exhaust manifold nuts (1).

6. Raise and support the vehicle.

7. Support the exhaust system.

8. Remove the catalytic converter to muffler nuts (1).

9. Reposition the muffler assembly rearward until the catalytic converter can be removed.

10. Remove the catalytic converter.

11. Remove the catalytic converter gaskets.

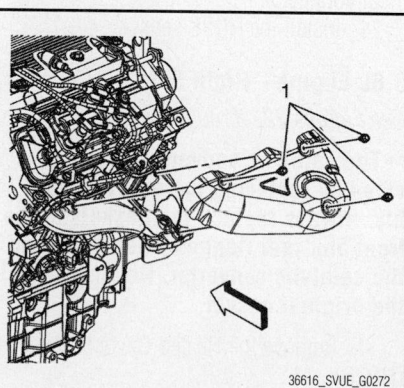

Fig. 217 Remove the right side exhaust manifold heat shield bolts (1)

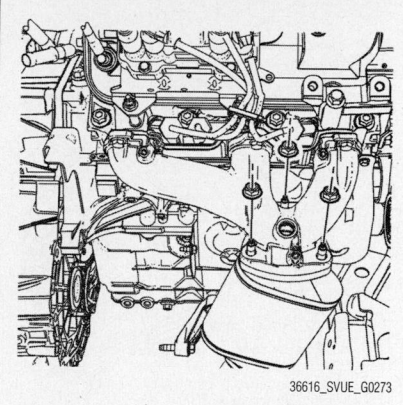

Fig. 218 Remove the right side catalytic converter to exhaust manifold nuts (1)

12. Clean and inspect the exhaust manifold and the exhaust pipe gasket mating surfaces.

To install:

13. Install the catalytic converter gasket onto the catalytic converter.

14. Reposition the muffler assembly rearward until the catalytic converter can be installed.

15. Install the catalytic converter.

16. Install the catalytic converter nuts. Tighten the nuts to 44 ft. lbs. (60 Nm).

17. Remove the support from the exhaust system.

18. Install the right side catalytic converter to exhaust manifold nuts. Tighten the nuts to 26 ft. lbs. (35 Nm).

19. Install the right side exhaust manifold heat shield.

20. Install the right side exhaust manifold heat shield bolts. Tighten the nuts to 89 inch lbs. (10 Nm).

21. Install the HO2S sensor.

3.6L Engine—Left Side

See Figures 219 through 222.

➡**The catalytic converter is serviced by replacing the entire assembly. Always replace the gaskets at the front and rear flanges when servicing the catalytic converter. Never install the original gasket.**

1. Remove the Heated Oxygen Sensor (HO2S).

2. Lower the vehicle.

3. Disconnect the oxygen sensor electrical connector (1).

4. Remove the left side exhaust manifold heat shield bolts (1).

5. Remove the left side exhaust manifold heat shield.

6. Remove the left side catalytic converter to exhaust manifold nuts (1).

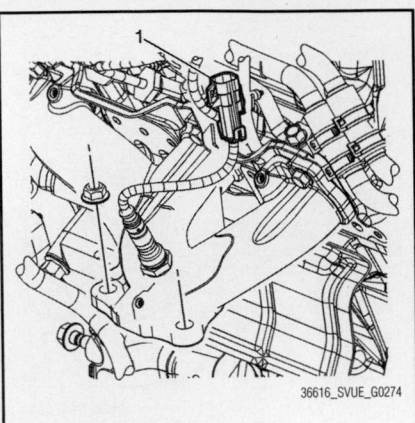

Fig. 219 Disconnect the oxygen sensor
electrical connector (1)

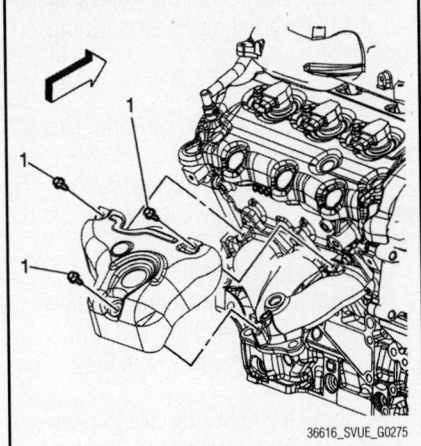

Fig. 220 Remove the left side exhaust
manifold heat shield bolts (1)

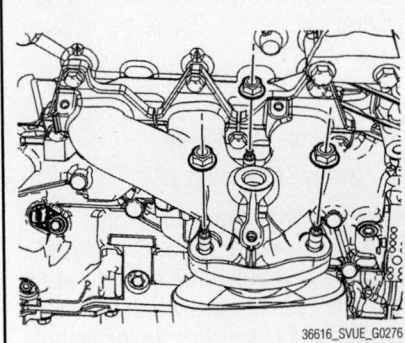

Fig. 221 Remove the left side catalytic
converter to exhaust manifold nuts (1)

7. Raise and support the vehicle.
8. Support the exhaust system.
9. Remove the catalytic converter to
muffler nuts (1).
10. Reposition the muffler assembly
rearward until the catalytic converter can be
removed.
11. Remove the catalytic converter.

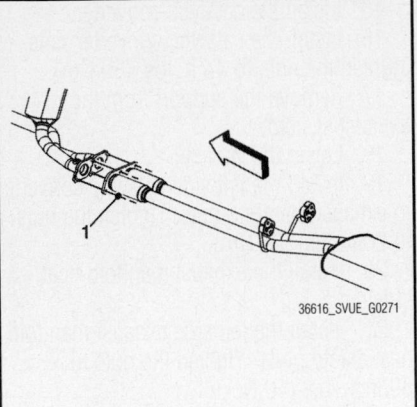

Fig. 222 Remove the catalytic converter
to muffler nuts (1)

12. Remove the catalytic converter
gaskets.
13. Clean and inspect the exhaust manifold and the exhaust pipe gasket mating
surfaces.

To install:

14. Install the catalytic converter gasket
onto the catalytic converter.
15. Reposition the muffler assembly
rearward until the catalytic converter can be
installed.
16. Install the catalytic converter.
17. Install the catalytic converter nuts.
Tighten the nuts to 44 ft. lbs. (60 Nm).
18. Remove the support from the
exhaust system.
19. Lower the vehicle.
20. Install the left side catalytic converter
to exhaust manifold nuts. Tighten the nuts
to 26 ft. lbs. (35 Nm).
21. Install the exhaust manifold heat
shield.
22. Install the left side exhaust manifold
heat shield bolts. Tighten the nuts to 89
inch lbs. (10 Nm).
23. Disconnect the oxygen sensor electrical connector.
24. Install the HO2S sensor.

3.6L Engine—Right Side

See Figures 222 through 225.

➡The catalytic converter is serviced by replacing the entire assembly. Always replace the gaskets at the
front and rear flanges when servicing
the catalytic converter. Never install
the original gasket.

1. Remove the Heated Oxygen Sensor
(HO2S).
2. Lower the vehicle.
3. Disconnect the engine wiring harness electrical connector from the HO2S
electrical connector (1).

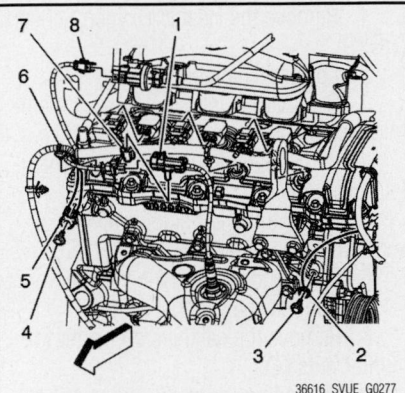

Fig. 223 Disconnect the engine wiring
harness electrical connector from the
HO2S electrical connector (1)

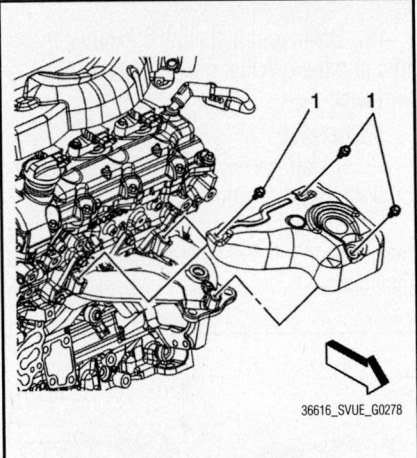

Fig. 224 Remove the right side exhaust
manifold heat shield bolts (1)

4. Remove the right side exhaust manifold heat shield bolts (1).
5. Remove the right side exhaust manifold heat shield.

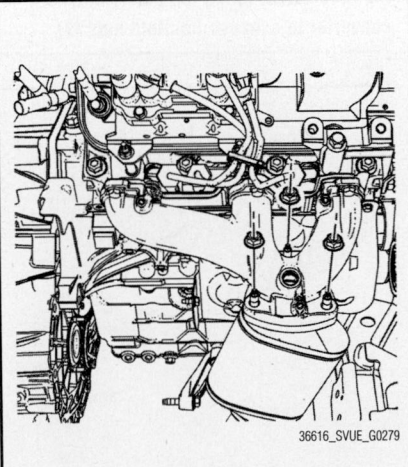

Fig. 225 Remove the right side catalytic
converter to exhaust manifold nuts (1)

6. Remove the right side catalytic converter to exhaust manifold nuts (1).

7. Raise and support the vehicle.

8. Support the exhaust system.

9. Remove the catalytic converter to intermediate muffler nuts (1).

10. Reposition the muffler assembly rearward until the catalytic converter can be removed.

11. Remove the catalytic converter.

12. Remove the catalytic converter gaskets.

13. Clean and inspect the exhaust manifold and the exhaust pipe gasket mating surfaces.

To install:

14. Install the catalytic converter gasket onto the catalytic converter.

15. Reposition the muffler assembly rearward until the catalytic converter can be installed.

16. Install the catalytic converter.

17. Install the catalytic converter to intermediate muffler nuts. Tighten the nuts to 44 ft. lbs. (60 Nm).

18. Remove the support from the exhaust system.

19. Install the right side catalytic converter to exhaust manifold nuts. Tighten the nuts to 26 ft. lbs. (35 Nm).

20. Install the right side exhaust manifold heat shield.

21. Install the right side exhaust manifold heat shield bolts. Tighten the nuts to 89 inch lbs. (10 Nm).

22. Connect the engine wiring harness electrical connector to the HO2S electrical connector

23. Install the HO2S sensor.

CRANKSHAFT BALANCER

REMOVAL & INSTALLATION

2.4L Engine, Except Hybrid

See Figure 226.

1. Remove the drive belt.

2. Use J 38122-A to prevent the crankshaft from rotating while loosening the crankshaft balancer bolt.

3. Remove and discard the crankshaft balancer bolt.

4. Remove the crankshaft balancer.

To install:

5. Position the crankshaft balancer.

6. Install a NEW crankshaft balancer bolt.

7. Use the J 38122-A to hold the crankshaft balancer in order to prevent the balancer from rotating while tightening the bolt.

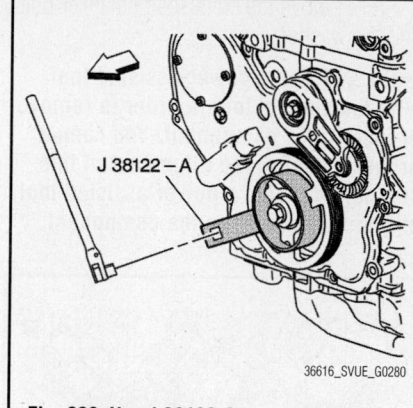

Fig. 226 Use J 38122-A to prevent the crankshaft from rotating while loosening the crankshaft balancer bolt

8. Tighten the crankshaft balancer bolt. Tighten the bolt to 74 ft. lbs. (100 Nm) plus an additional 125 degrees using the J 45059.

9. Install the drive belt.

2.4L Hybrid Engine

See Figures 227 and 228.

1. Remove the drive belt.

2. Remove the engine splash shield.

3. Install the J 38122-A (1), and a breaker bar to the balancer in order to prevent the balancer from rotating when loosening the balancer bolt.

4. Remove the J 38122-A (1) and breaker bar.

5. Remove and discard the crankshaft balancer bolt.

6. Remove the crankshaft balancer.

To install:

7. Position the crankshaft balancer.

8. Install a NEW crankshaft balancer bolt.

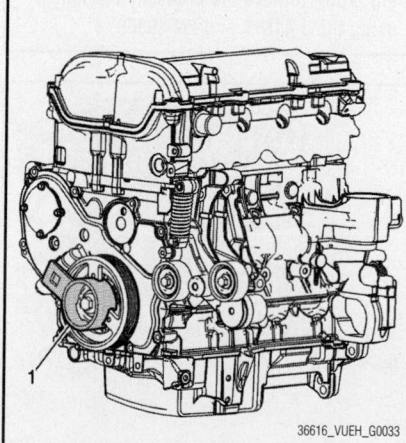

Fig. 227 Install the J 38122-A (1)

Fig. 228 Remove and discard the crankshaft balancer bolt

9. Install the J 38122-A, and a breaker bar to the balancer in order to prevent the balancer from rotating while tightening the bolt.

10. Tighten the crankshaft balancer bolt. Tighten the bolt to 74 ft. lbs. (100 Nm) plus an additional 125 degrees using the J 45059.

11. Install the engine splash shield.

12. Install the drive belt.

3.5L Engine

See Figures 229 through 234.

➡The inertial weight section of the crankshaft balancer is assembled to the hub with a rubber type material. The correct installation procedures (with the proper tool) must be followed or movement of the inertial weight section of the hub will destroy the tuning of the crankshaft balancer.

1. Install the Engine Support Fixture, supporting the right hand lift hook only.

2. Remove the engine mount.

   a. Remove the air cleaner assembly.

   b. Remove the engine mount bolts (1).

   c. Remove the engine mount nuts (1).

   d. Remove the engine mount (2).

3. Lower the engine using the engine support fixture

4. Remove the right front tire and wheel.

5. Remove the right engine splash shield.

6. Remove the torque converter covers.

7. Install the J 37096 to the flywheel in order to prevent flywheel rotation.

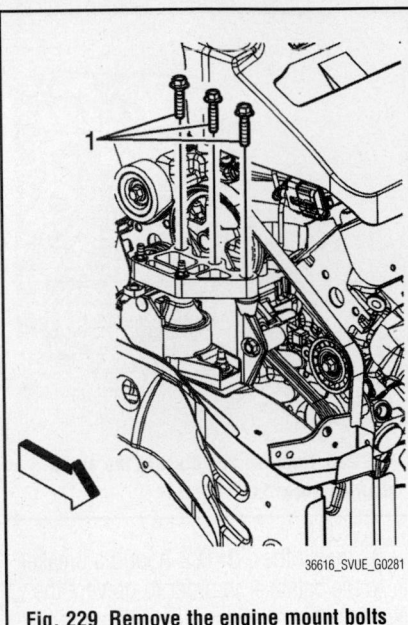

Fig. 229 Remove the engine mount bolts (1)

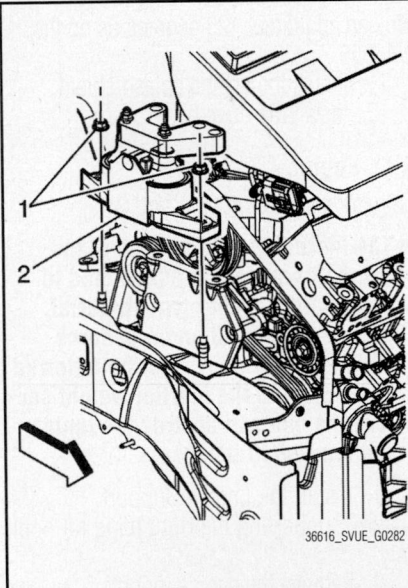

Fig. 230 Remove the engine mount nuts (1)

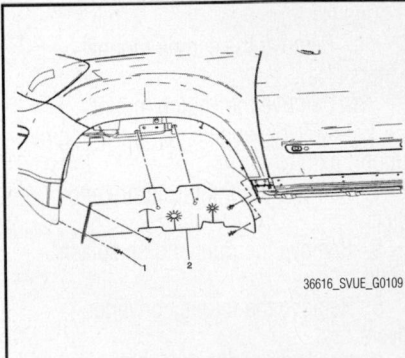

Fig. 231 Remove the right engine splash shield

8. Remove the crankshaft balancer bolt and the washer.

➡**Do NOT use a power-assisted tool with the special tool in order to remove or install this component. You cannot properly control the alignment of this component using a power-assisted tool, and this can damage the component.**

Fig. 232 Remove the crankshaft balancer bolt and the washer

Fig. 233 Remove the crankshaft balancer using the J 41816 and EN 46359

Fig. 234 Thread the J 29113 into the crankshaft

9. Remove the crankshaft balancer using the J 41816 and EN 46359.

To install:

10. Apply sealer to the keyway of the crankshaft balancer.

11. Place the crankshaft balancer into position over the key in the crankshaft.

➡**Do NOT use a power-assisted tool with the special tool in order to remove or install this component. You cannot properly control the alignment of this component using a power-assisted tool, and this can damage the component.**

12. Thread the J 29113 into the crankshaft.

13. Rotate the hex nut on the J 29113 in order to install the crankshaft balancer onto the crankshaft.

14. Remove the J 29113 from the crankshaft.

15. Install the crankshaft balancer washer and the bolt.

16. Install the used crankshaft balancer bolt. Tighten the used crankshaft balancer bolt to 92 ft. lbs. (125 Nm).

17. Remove the used crankshaft balancer bolt.

18. Install the NEW crankshaft balancer bolt.

 a. Tighten the crankshaft balancer bolt a first pass to 92 ft. lbs. (125 Nm).

 b. Tighten the crankshaft balancer bolt a final pass to 130 degrees using the J 45059.

19. Remove the J 37096 from the flywheel.

20. Install the torque converter covers.

21. Install the right engine splash shield.

22. Install the right front tire and wheel.

23. Lower the vehicle.

24. Raise the engine using the engine support fixture.

25. Install the drive belt.

26. Install the engine mount.

27. Remove the Engine Support Fixture

CRANKSHAFT FRONT SEAL

REMOVAL & INSTALLATION

2.4L Engine

See Figures 235 and 236.

1. Remove the crankshaft balancer.

2. Use a flat-bladed tool to remove the seal from the front cover.

To install:

3. Use the J 35268-A in order to install

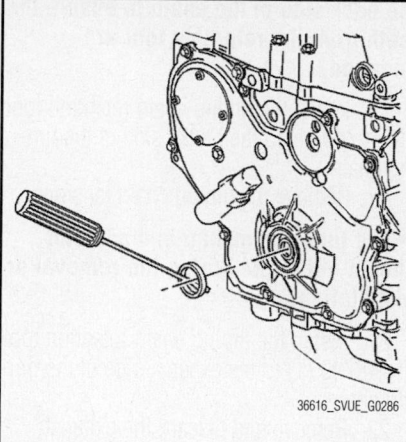

Fig. 235 Use a flat-bladed tool to remove the seal from the front cover

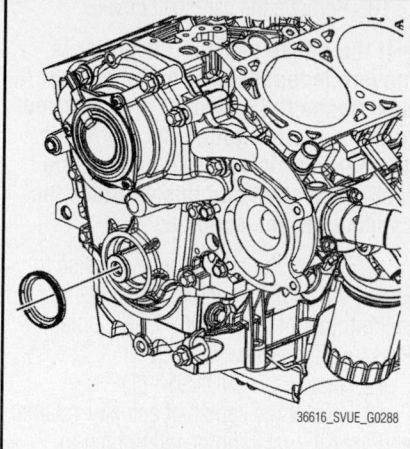

Fig. 237 Pry out the crankshaft front oil seal using a suitable tool

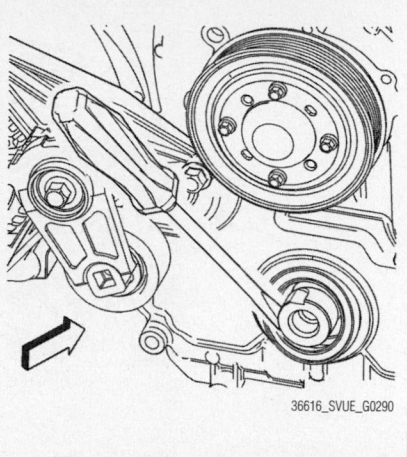

Fig. 239 Use a flat-bladed tool in order to remove the crankshaft oil seal

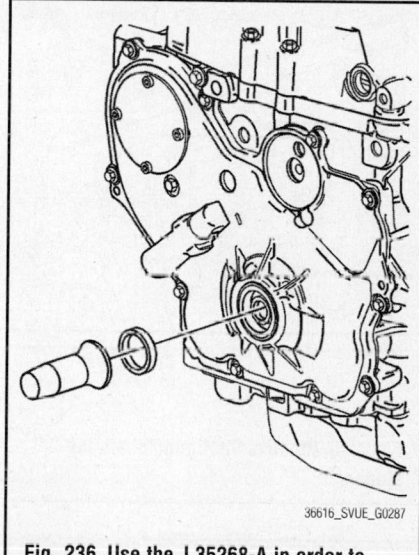

Fig. 236 Use the J 35268-A in order to install the crankshaft front oil seal

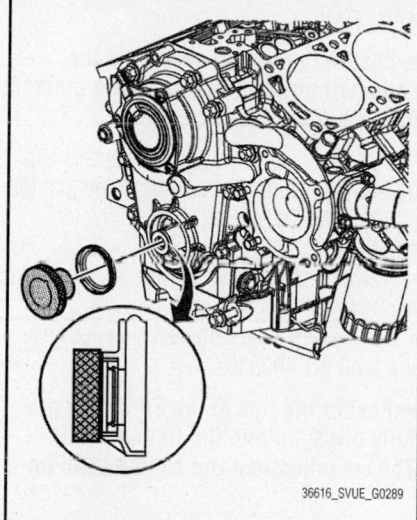

Fig. 238 Align the EN-48869 and the crankshaft front oil seal

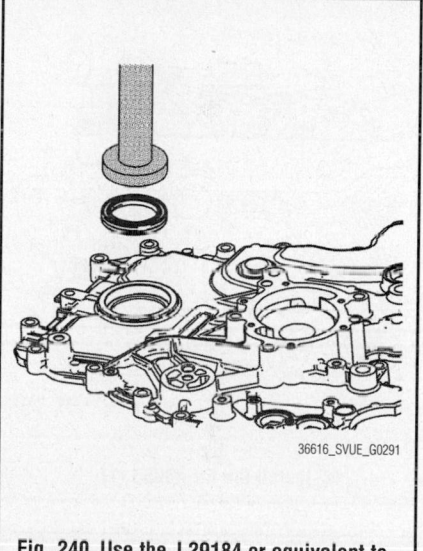

Fig. 240 Use the J 29184 or equivalent to install the crankshaft front oil seal

the crankshaft front oil seal to the engine front cover.

4. Install the crankshaft balancer.

3.5L Engine

See Figures 237 and 238.

1. Remove the crankshaft balancer.
2. Remove the crankshaft key from the keyway.
3. Pry out the crankshaft front oil seal using a suitable tool. Use care not to damage the engine front cover or the crankshaft.

To install:

4. Lubricate the NEW oil seal with clean engine oil.
5. Align the EN-48869 and the crankshaft front oil seal with the engine front cover and crankshaft.
6. Install the crankshaft front oil

seal using EN-48869 and a suitable tool.

7. Install the crankshaft key into the keyway.
8. Install the crankshaft balancer.

3.6L Engine

See Figures 239 and 240.

1. Remove the crankshaft balancer.
2. Use a flat-bladed tool in order to remove the crankshaft oil seal. Use care not to damage the engine front cover or the crankshaft.

To install:

3. Use the J 29184 or equivalent to install the crankshaft front oil seal.
4. Install the crankshaft balancer.

CYLINDER HEAD

REMOVAL & INSTALLATION

2.4L Engine

See Figures 241 through 255.

1. Drain the cooling system.
2. Remove the exhaust manifold.
3. Remove the intake manifold.
4. Reposition the radiator surge tank air bleed hose clamp.
5. Remove the radiator surge tank air bleed hose from the cylinder head.
6. Reposition the radiator inlet hose clamp using the J 38185.
7. Remove the radiator inlet hose from the cylinder head.
8. Disconnect all electrical connectors as necessary.
9. Remove the vue spark plugs.

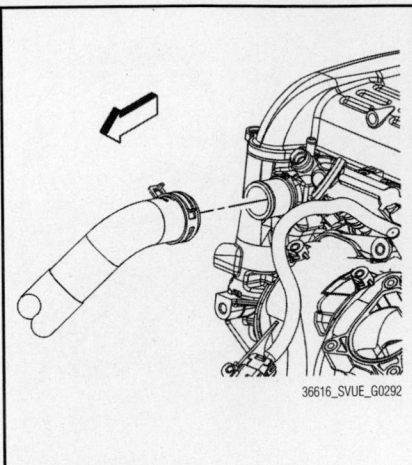

Fig. 241 Remove the radiator inlet hose from the cylinder head

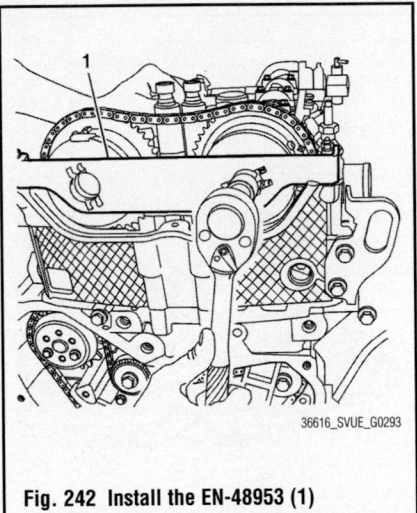

Fig. 242 Install the EN-48953 (1)

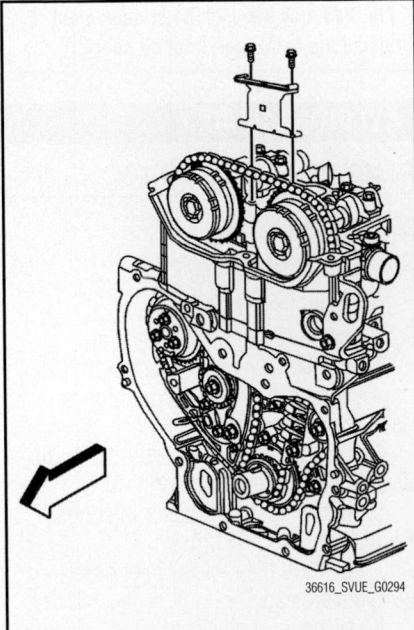

Fig. 243 Remove the upper timing chain guide bolts and guide

10. Remove the camshaft cover.

➡If the intake camshaft actuator is moving independently of the camshaft, this means the camshaft is not locked to the actuator. Rotate the camshaft counter-clockwise while the holding tool is installed and this will lock the camshaft to the actuator.

11. Rotate the crankshaft clockwise to install the camshaft actuator retainer by locking the tool EN-48953 EGR Cooler Pressure Tester Adapter Set.

12. Install the EN-48953 (1).

13. Install the camshaft actuator retainer and lock it. Install bolts and tighten to 89 inch lbs. (10 Nm).

14. Remove the upper timing chain guide bolts and guide.

15. Clean the timing chain and gears with solvent.

➡Ensure the timing chain and the camshaft position actuators are marked for proper assembly.

16. Mark the timing gear sprockets and the timing chain. It is recommended that the paint marks are located in the 12 o'clock position.

17. Loosen, but do not remove the intake and exhaust camshaft actuator bolts.

18. Remove the camshaft actuator locking tool, EN-48953.

➡Ensure the tips of the EN-48749 are fully engaged into the timing chain. The retention tool rod can be used on

the back side of the chain to ensure the teeth from the retention tool are engaged.

19. Install the timing chain retention tool EN-48749 (1) to the intake side of the timing chain.

20. Remove the timing chain tensioner.

➡The Intake camshaft and actuator should not rotate during the removal or installation.

21. Install the timing chain retention tool EN-48749 (1) to the exhaust side of the timing chain.

22. Remove and discard the exhaust camshaft actuator bolt (2).

23. Remove the exhaust cam actuator (3)

Fig. 245 Remove the timing chain tensioner

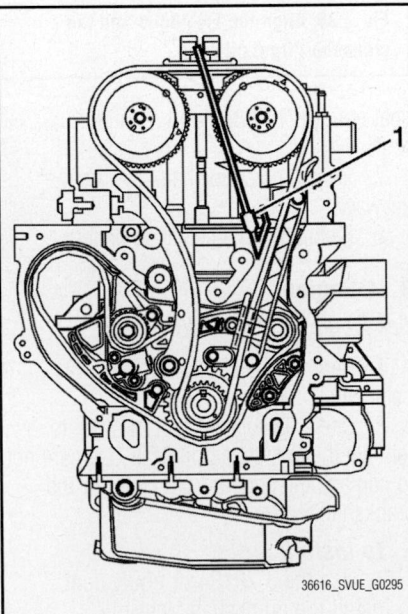

Fig. 244 Install the timing chain retention tool EN-48749 (1)

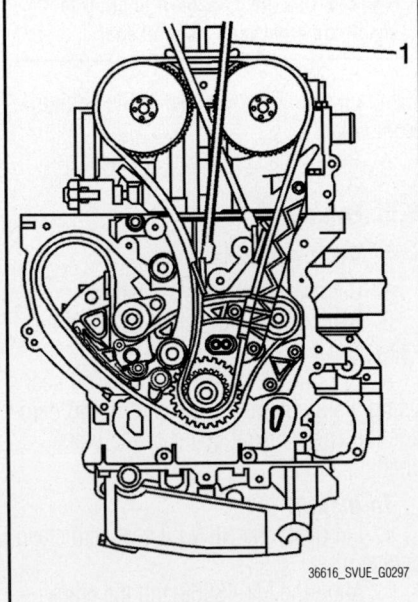

Fig. 246 Install the timing chain retention tool EN-48749 (1)

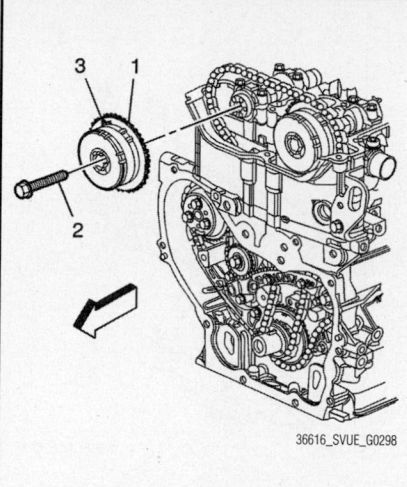

Fig. 247 Remove and discard the exhaust camshaft actuator bolt (2)

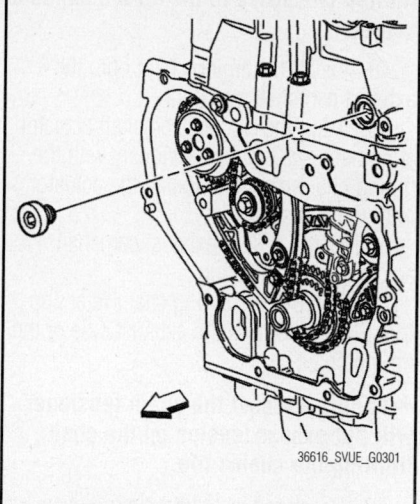

Fig. 250 Remove the fixed timing chain guide access plug

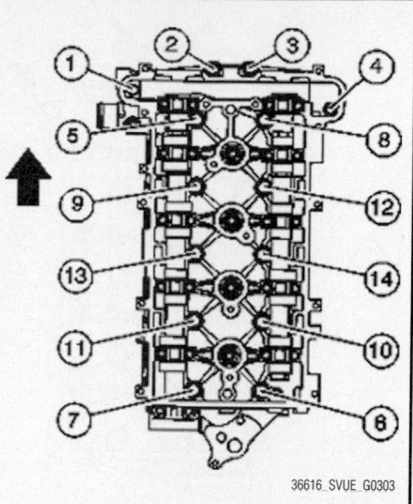

Fig. 252 Remove the cylinder head bolts in the sequence shown

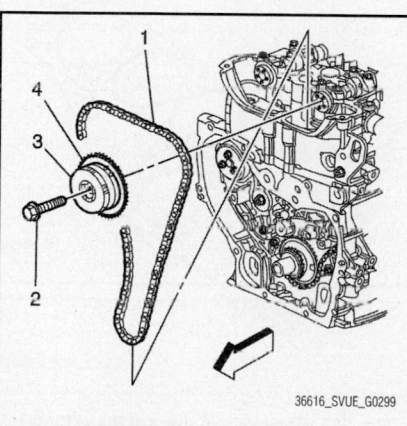

Fig. 248 Remove and discard the intake camshaft actuator bolt (2)

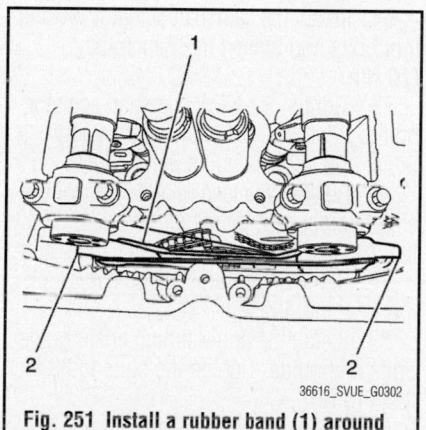
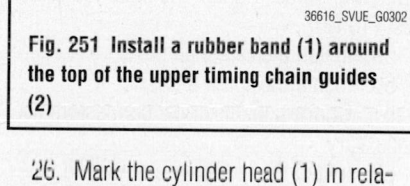

Fig. 251 Install a rubber band (1) around the top of the upper timing chain guides (2)

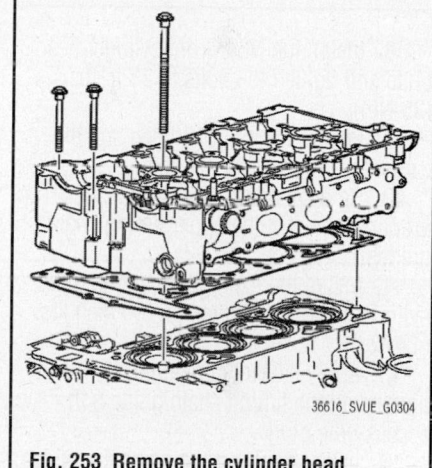
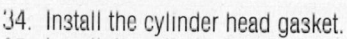

Fig. 253 Remove the cylinder head

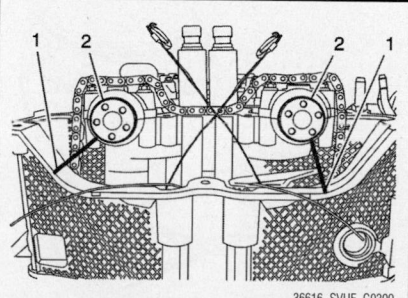

Fig. 249 Mark the cylinder head (1) in relationship to the camshaft actuator notch is on the camshaft (2)

from the exhaust camshaft while also removing the actuator from the chain.

24. Remove and discard the intake camshaft actuator bolt (2).

25. Remove the intake camshaft actuator (3) from the camshaft while also removing the actuator from the timing chain.

26. Mark the cylinder head (1) in relationship to the camshaft actuator notch is on the camshaft (2).

27. Remove the fixed timing chain guide access plug.

28. Remove the upper fixed timing chain guide bolt.

➡ **The threaded rod from the timing chain retention tool can be used to help feed the rubber band around the chain guides.**

29. Install a rubber band (1) around the top of the upper timing chain guides (2) in order to pull the guides together.

30. Remove the cylinder head bolts in the sequence shown. Discard the bolts.

31. Remove the cylinder head.

32. Remove the cylinder head gasket.

33. Clean all of the gasket surfaces.

To install:

➡ **DO NOT use any sealing material.**

34. Install the cylinder head gasket.

35. Install the cylinder head.

36. Install NEW cylinder head bolts.

37. Install and tighten the cylinder head bolts in the sequence shown to 22 ft. lbs. (30 Nm) plus an additional 155 degrees using the J 45059.

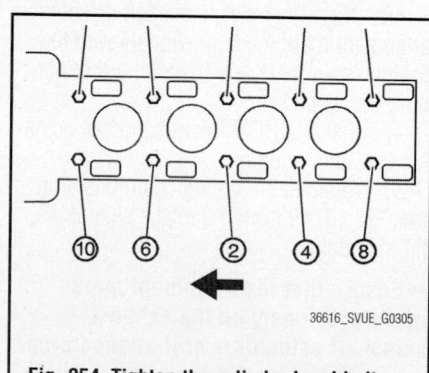

Fig. 254 Tighten the cylinder head bolts in the sequence shown

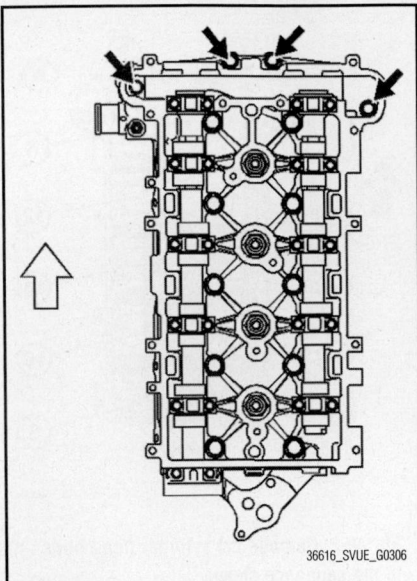

Fig. 255 Install the NEW front cylinder head bolts

38. Install the NEW front cylinder head bolts and tighten the bolts to 26 ft. lbs. (35 Nm).

39. Ensure the cylinder head and the camshaft are correctly aligned.

40. Remove the rubber band from around the top of the upper timing chain guides.

41. Install the fixed guide bolt into the cylinder head and tighten to 106 inch lbs. (12 Nm).

42. Apply sealant compound to thread and install the timing chain guide bolt access hole plug.

43. Install the fixed timing chain guide access plug and tighten the plug to 59 ft. lbs. (90 Nm).

→Ensure that the alignment mark made previously on the intake camshaft actuator is still aligned properly with the mark on the timing chain.

44. Install the timing chain onto the intake camshaft actuator.

45. Align the intake camshaft actuator alignment mark made previously with the timing chain mark and install the actuator onto the camshaft.

46. Install a NEW intake camshaft actuator bolt until snug.

47. Remove the timing chain retention tool EN-48749 from the intake side of the timing chain.

→Ensure that the alignment mark made previously on the exhaust camshaft actuator is still aligned properly with the mark on the timing chain. The exhaust cam may have to be

rotated clockwise to install the exhaust actuator.

48. Install the timing chain onto the exhaust camshaft actuator.

49. Align the exhaust camshaft actuator alignment mark made previously with the timing chain mark and install the actuator onto the camshaft.

50. Install a NEW exhaust camshaft actuator bolt until snug.

51. Remove the timing chain retention tool EN-48749 from the exhaust side of the timing chain.

→Failure to reset the chain tensioner will put excess tension on the chain, limiting the chains life.

52. Reset and install the timing chain tensioner.

53. Install the EN-48953 to the actuators.

54. Install the camshaft actuator locking tool bolts and tighten to 89 inch lbs. (10 Nm).

55. Tighten the NEW camshaft actuator bolt to 22 ft. lbs. (30 Nm), plus an additional 100 degrees using the J 45059.

56. Release the tensioner by applying a counterclockwise rotational torque of 33 ft. lbs. (45 Nm) to the harmonic balancer bolt.

57. Remove the camshaft actuator locking tool, EN-48953.

58. Install the upper timing chain guide bolts and guide. Tighten the bolts to 89 inch lbs. (10 Nm).

59. Install the camshaft cover.

60. Install the spark plugs.

61. Connect all electrical connectors as necessary.

62. Install the radiator inlet hose to the cylinder head.

63. Position the radiator inlet hose clamp using the J 38185.

64. Install the radiator surge tank air bleed hose to the cylinder head.

65. Position the radiator surge tank air bleed hose clamp.

66. Install the exhaust manifold.

67. Install the intake manifold.

68. Fill the cooling system.

3.5L Engine—Left Side

See Figures 256 through 259.

1. Drain the cooling system.
2. Drain the engine oil.
3. Lower the vehicle.
4. Remove the lower intake manifold.
5. Remove the valve rocker arms and the pushrods.
6. Remove the exhaust manifold.
7. Remove the oil level indicator tube.

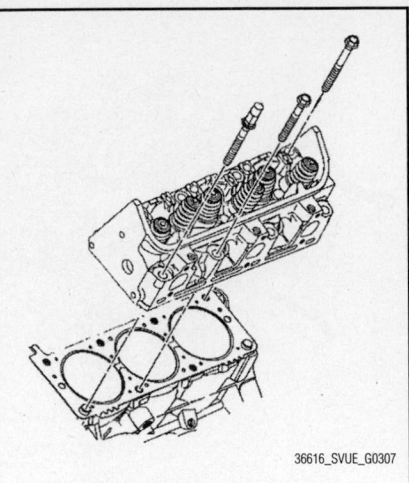

Fig. 256 Remove and discard the cylinder head bolts

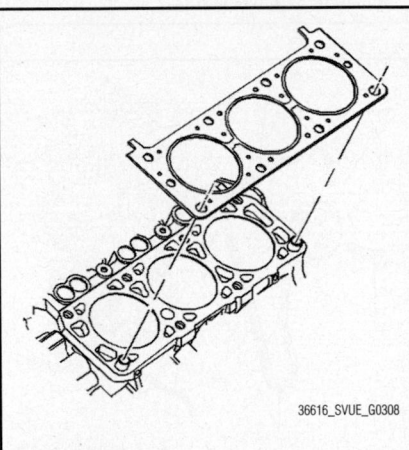

Fig. 257 Remove and discard the cylinder head gasket

8. Disconnect the left spark plug wires from the spark plugs.

9. Remove the spark plug wire clips from the brackets.

10. Disconnect and remove the left spark plug wires from the ignition coil.

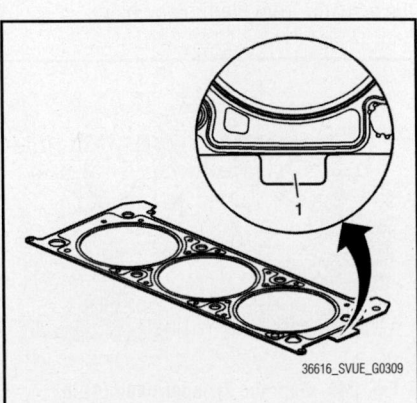

Fig. 258 Note the markings (1) on the head gaskets for proper installation

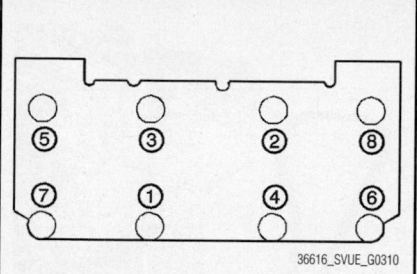

Fig. 259 Tighten the cylinder head bolts in sequence

11. Remove the left spark plugs.
12. Remove and discard the cylinder head bolts.
13. Remove the cylinder head.
14. Remove and discard the cylinder head gasket.
15. Remove the cylinder head locator dowel pins, if necessary.

To install:

➡Head gaskets are specific for right hand and left hand applications, and also must be installed with the correct side facing up. Note the markings (1) on the head gaskets for proper installation. Failure to do so may lead to engine damage.

16. Install the cylinder head locator dowel pins, if necessary.
17. Inspect the cylinder head locator dowel pins for proper installation.
18. Install a NEW cylinder head gasket.
19. Install the cylinder head onto the locator pins and the engine.

➡This component uses torque-to-yield bolts. When servicing this component do not reuse the bolts, New torque-to-yield bolts must be installed. Reusing used torque-to-yield bolts will not provide proper bolt torque and clamp load. Failure to install NEW torque-to-yield bolts may lead to engine damage.

20. Install NEW cylinder head bolts finger tight.
21. Tighten the cylinder head bolts. Tighten the bolts in sequence to 44 ft. lbs. (60 Nm) plus an additional 95 degrees using the J 45059.
22. Install the left spark plugs.
23. Install and connect the left spark plug wires to the ignition coil.
24. Install the spark plug wire clips to the brackets.
25. Connect the left spark plug wires to the spark plugs.

26. Install the oil level indicator tube.
27. Install the exhaust manifold.
28. Install the valve rocker arms and the pushrods.
29. Install the lower intake manifold.
30. Fill the engine with oil.
31. Fill the cooling system.
32. Inspect for leaks.

3.5L Engine—Right Side

See Figures 260 through 263.

1. Drain the cooling system.
2. Remove the spark plug wires from the right side of the vehicle.
3. Remove the lower intake manifold.
4. Remove the valve rocker arms and pushrods from the right cylinder head.
5. Remove the right side exhaust manifold.
6. Remove the spark plugs from the right side cylinder head.

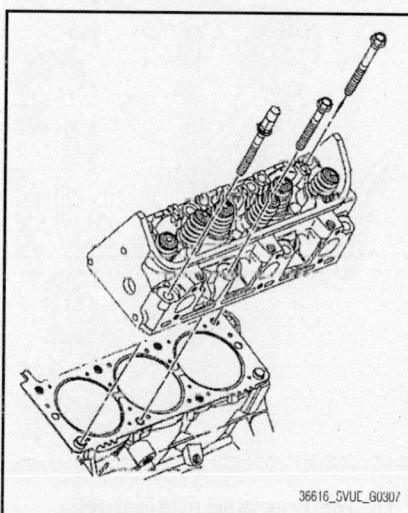

Fig. 260 Remove and discard the right side cylinder head bolts

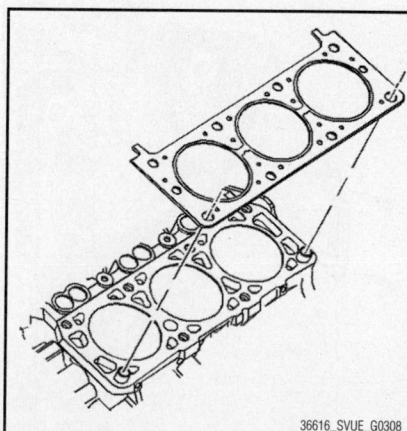

Fig. 261 Remove and discard the right side cylinder head gasket

7. Remove and discard the right side cylinder head bolts.
8. Remove the right side cylinder head.
9. Remove and discard the right side cylinder head gasket.
10. Remove the right side cylinder head locator dowel pins, if necessary.
11. Clean and transfer any parts as needed.

To install:

➡Head gaskets are specific for right hand and left hand applications, and also must be installed with the correct side facing up. Note the markings (1) on the head gaskets for proper installation. Failure to do so may lead to engine damage.

12. Install the right side cylinder head locator dowel pins and ensure proper installation before proceeding.
13. Install the NEW right side cylinder head gasket.

➡This component uses torque-to-yield bolts. When servicing this component do not reuse the bolts, New torque-to-yield bolts must be installed. Reusing used torque-to-yield bolts will not pro-

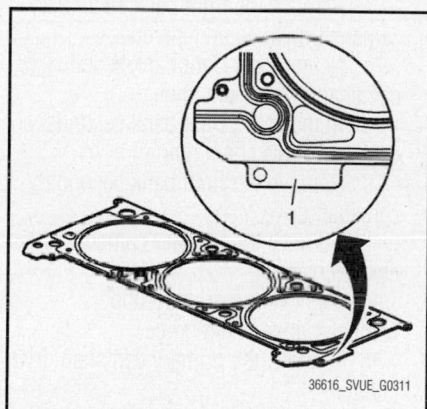

Fig. 262 Note the markings (1) on the head gaskets for proper installation

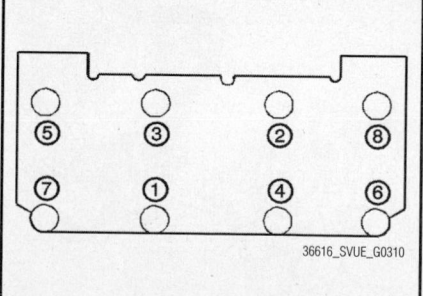

Fig. 263 Tighten the right side cylinder head bolts in sequence

vide proper bolt torque and clamp load. **Failure to install NEW torque-to-yield bolts may lead to engine damage.**

14. Install the right side cylinder head onto the locator dowel pins and the engine block.

15. Install the NEW right side cylinder head bolts finger tight.

16. Tighten the right side cylinder head bolts. Tighten the bolts in sequence to 44 ft. lbs. (60 Nm) plus an additional 95 degrees using angle meter J 45059.

17. Install the spark plugs to the right side cylinder head.

18. Install the right side exhaust manifold.

19. Install the valve rocker arms and pushrods to the right cylinder head.

20. Install the lower intake manifold.

21. Install the spark plug wires to the right side of the vehicle.

22. Change the engine oil.

23. Fill the cooling system.

24. Inspect for any leaks.

3.6L Engine—Left Side

See Figures 264 through 282.

1. Remove the left bank secondary timing chain.

   a. Remove the engine front cover.

   b. Remove the right bank secondary camshaft drive chain tensioner.

   c. Remove the right bank secondary camshaft drive chain shoe.

   d. Remove the right bank secondary camshaft drive chain guide.

   e. Remove the right bank secondary camshaft drive chain.

   f. Remove the primary camshaft drive chain tensioner.

   g. Remove the primary upper camshaft drive chain guide.

   h. Remove the primary camshaft drive chain.

   i. Remove the right bank camshaft intermediate drive chain idler.

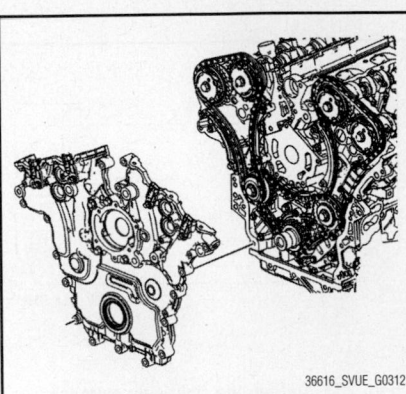

Fig. 264 Remove the engine front cover

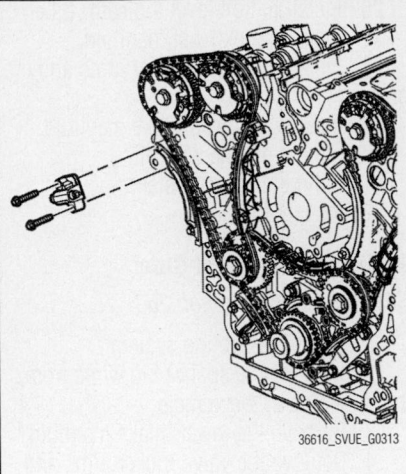

36616_SVUE_G0313

Fig. 265 Remove the right bank secondary camshaft drive chain tensioner

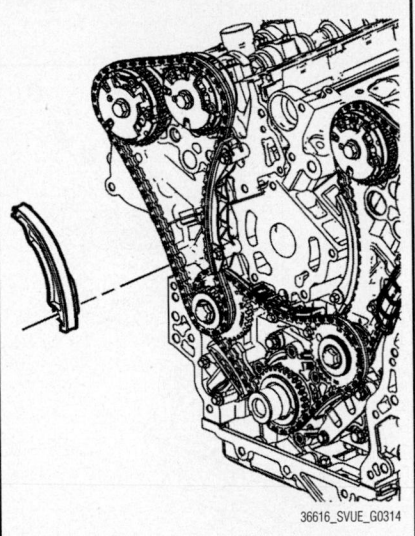

36616_SVUE_G0314

Fig. 266 Remove the right bank secondary camshaft drive chain shoe

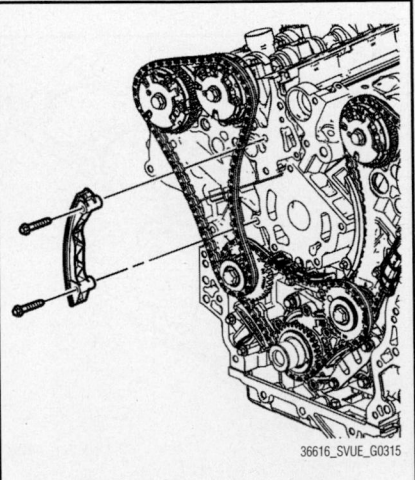

36616_SVUE_G0315

Fig. 267 Remove the right bank secondary camshaft drive chain guide

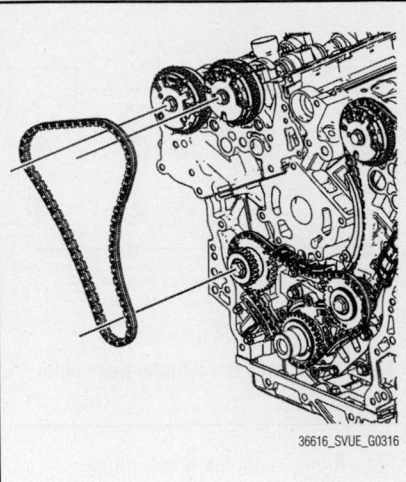

36616_SVUE_G0316

Fig. 268 Remove the right bank secondary camshaft drive chain

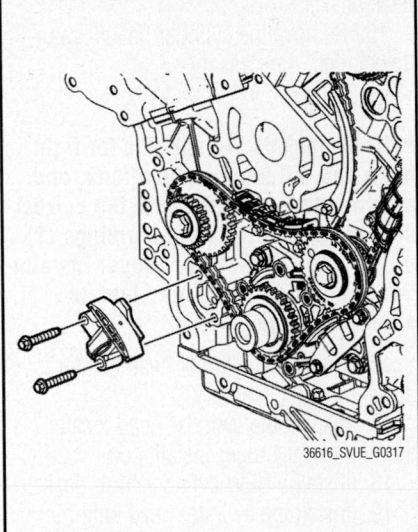

36616_SVUE_G0317

Fig. 269 Remove the primary camshaft drive chain tensioner

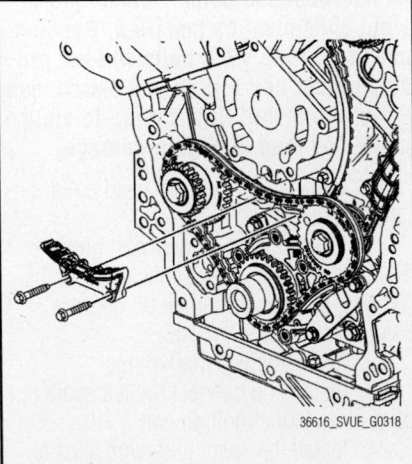

36616_SVUE_G0318

Fig. 270 Remove the primary upper camshaft drive chain guide

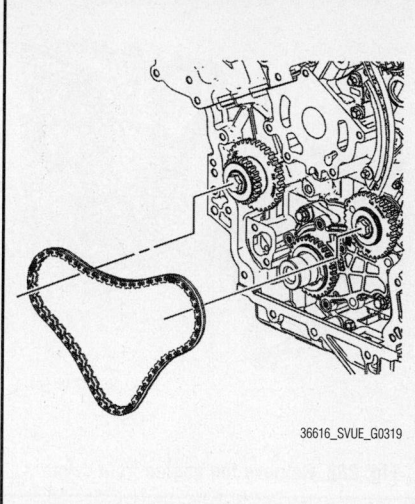

Fig. 271 Remove the primary camshaft drive chain

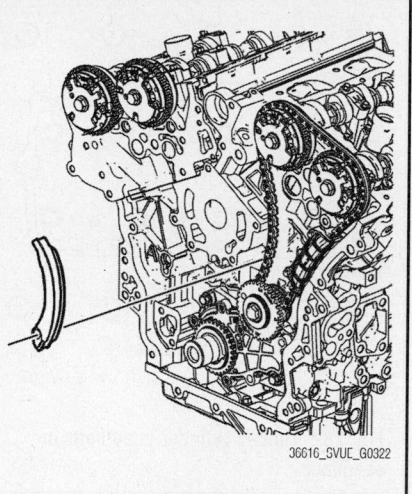

Fig. 274 Remove the left bank secondary camshaft drive chain shoe

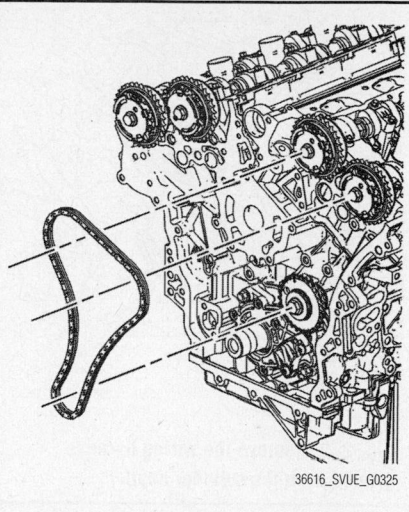

Fig. 277 Remove the left bank secondary camshaft drive chain

Fig. 272 Remove the right bank camshaft Intermediate drive chain idler

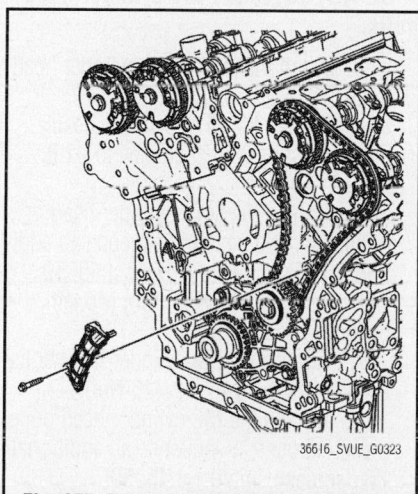

Fig. 275 Remove the left bank secondary camshaft drive chain guide

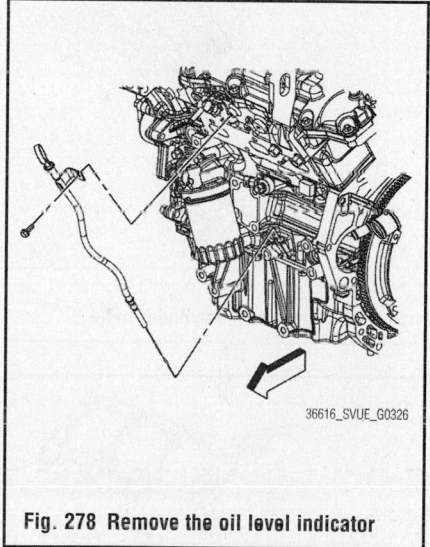

Fig. 278 Remove the oil level indicator

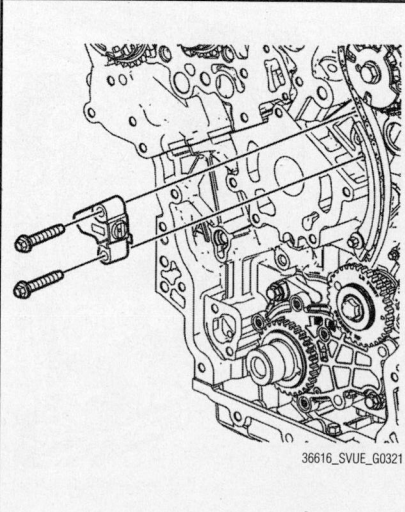

Fig. 273 Remove the left bank secondary camshaft drive chain tensioner

Fig. 276 Remove the left bank camshaft intermediate drive chain idler

  j. Remove the left bank secondary camshaft drive chain tensioner.

  k. Remove the left bank secondary camshaft drive chain shoe.

  l. Remove the left bank secondary camshaft drive chain guide.

  m. Remove the left bank camshaft intermediate drive chain idler.

  n. Remove the left bank secondary camshaft drive chain.

  2. Remove the oil level indicator.

  3. Disconnect the coolant temperature sensor electrical connector.

  4. Remove the wiring harness ground from the cylinder head.

  5. Remove the catalytic converter.

  6. Remove the cylinder head with the exhaust manifold.

  7. Remove and discard the cylinder head gasket.

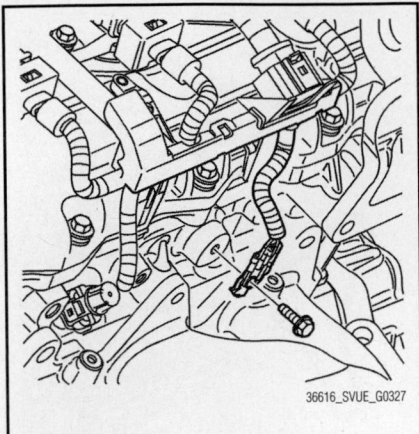

Fig. 279 Remove the wiring harness ground from the cylinder head

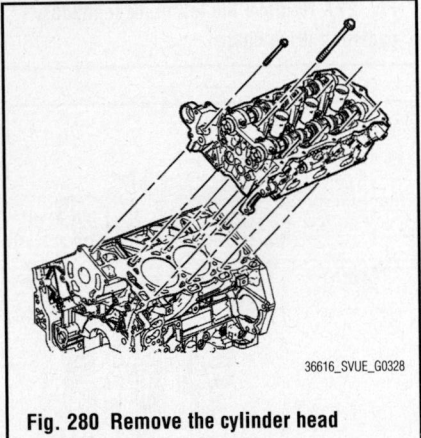

Fig. 280 Remove the cylinder head

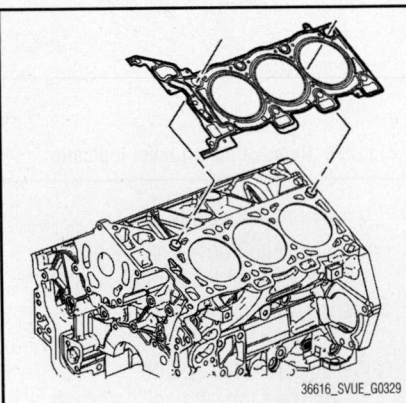

Fig. 281 Remove and discard the cylinder head gasket

8. Clean and inspect the cylinder head and the engine block sealing surfaces.

To install:

9. Install a NEW cylinder head gasket.
10. Carefully install the cylinder head with the exhaust manifold to the engine.

    a. Align the left cylinder head with the deck face locating pins.

    b. Place the left cylinder head in position on the deck face.

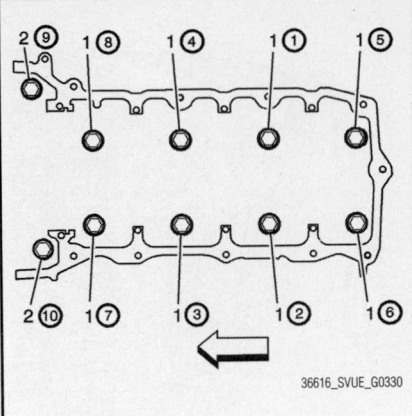
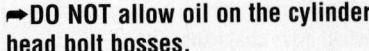

Fig. 282 Tighten cylinder head bolts in sequence

➡ **DO NOT allow oil on the cylinder head bolt bosses.**

➡ **DO NOT reuse the old cylinder head bolts.**

    c. Install the NEW M11 cylinder head bolts (1).

    d. Tighten the M11 cylinder head bolts a first pass in sequence to 22 ft. lbs. (30 Nm).

    e. Tighten the M11 cylinder head bolts a second pass in sequence an additional 150 degrees using the J 45059.

    f. Install the 2 NEW front M8 left cylinder head bolts (2).

    g. Tighten the M8 cylinder head bolts a first pass to 11 ft. lbs. (15 Nm).

    h. Tighten the M8 cylinder head bolts a second pass in sequence an additional 75 degrees using the J 45059.

11. Install the catalytic converter to the exhaust manifold.

12. Connect the wiring harness electrical connector located at the side of the cylinder head.

13. Install the wiring harness ground to the cylinder head. Tighten the wiring harness ground bolt to 89 inch lbs. (10 Nm).

14. Install the coolant temperature sensor electrical connector.

15. Install the oil level indicator.

16. Install the left bank secondary timing chain.

3.6L Engine—Right Side

See Figures 283 through 290.

1. Remove the engine.
2. Remove the right bank secondary timing chain.

    a. Remove the spark plugs in order to ease crankshaft/engine rotation.

    b. Remove the engine front cover.

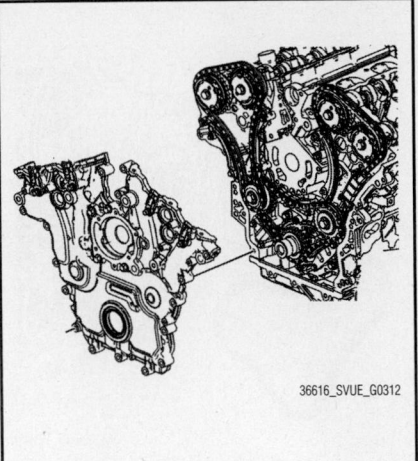

Fig. 283 Remove the engine front cover

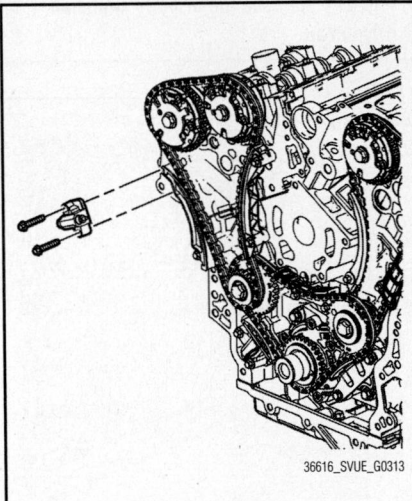

Fig. 284 Remove the right bank secondary camshaft drive chain tensioner

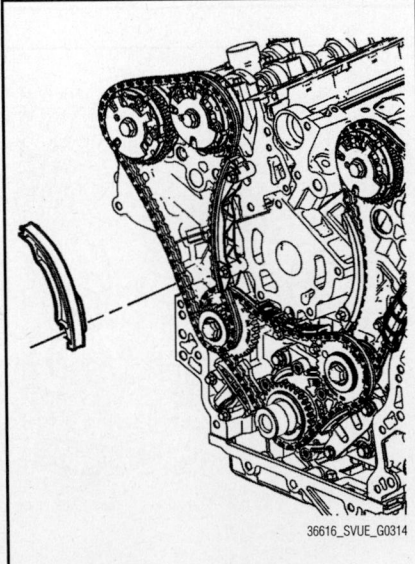

Fig. 285 Remove the right bank secondary camshaft drive chain shoe

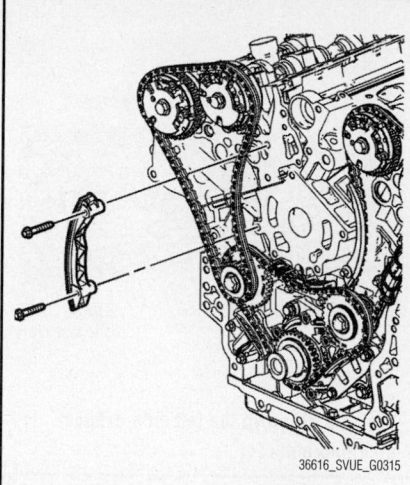

Fig. 286 Remove the right bank secondary camshaft drive chain guide

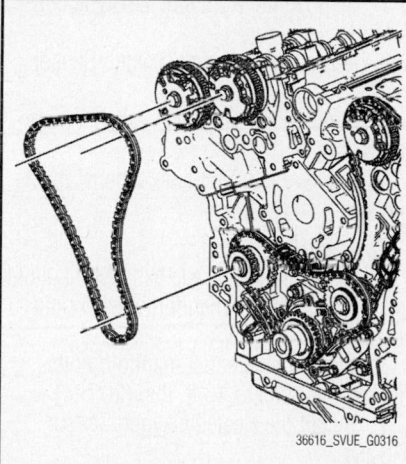

Fig. 287 Remove the right bank secondary camshaft drive chain

c. Remove the right bank secondary camshaft drive chain tensioner.
d. Remove the right bank secondary camshaft drive chain shoe.
e. Remove the right bank secondary camshaft drive chain guide.

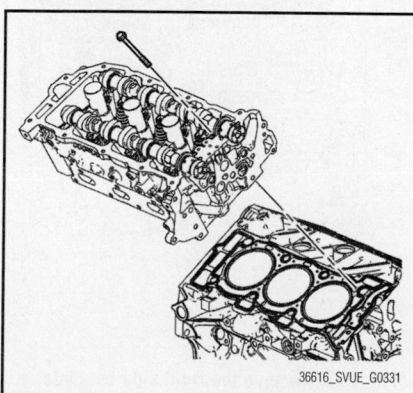

Fig. 288 Remove the cylinder head

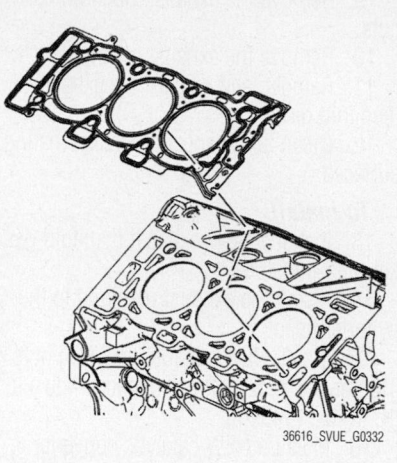

Fig. 289 Remove and discard the cylinder head gasket

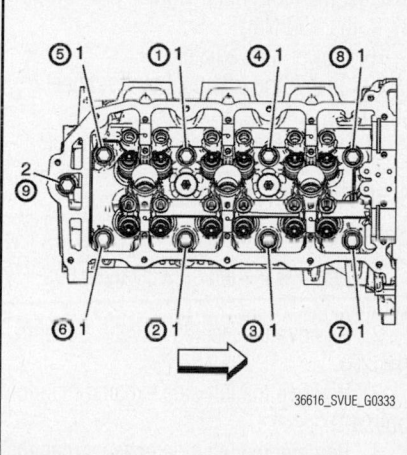

Fig. 290 Tighten the cylinder head bolts in sequence

f. Remove the right bank secondary camshaft drive chain.
3. If equipped with LCS, remove the right side fuel injector.
4. Remove the cylinder head with the exhaust manifold.
5. Remove the Right side Catalytic Converter.
6. Remove and discard the cylinder head gasket.
7. Clean and inspect the cylinder head and the engine block sealing surfaces.

To install:
8. Install a NEW cylinder head gasket.
9. Carefully install the cylinder head with the exhaust manifold to the engine.
    a. Align the right cylinder head with the deck face locating pins.
    b. Place the right cylinder head in position on the deck face.

➡ **DO NOT allow oil on the cylinder head bolt bosses.**

➡ **DO NOT reuse the old cylinder head bolts.**

c. Install the NEW M11 cylinder head bolts (1).
d. Tighten the M11 cylinder head bolts a first pass in sequence to 22 ft. lbs. (30 Nm).
e. Tighten the M11 cylinder head bolts a second pass in sequence an additional 150 degrees using the J 45059.
f. Install the NEW M8 cylinder head bolt (2).
g. Tighten the M8 cylinder head bolt a first pass to 11 ft. lbs. (15 Nm).
h. Tighten the M8 cylinder head bolt a second pass an additional 75 degrees using the J 45059.
10. Install the right bank secondary timing chain.
11. Install the engine.

EXHAUST MANIFOLD

REMOVAL & INSTALLATION

2.4L Engine

See Figures 291 through 294.

1. Raise and support the vehicle.

➡ **Do not bend the exhaust flex decoupler more than 3 degrees in any direction. Movement of more than 3 degrees will damage the exhaust flex decoupler.**

2. Remove the catalytic converter to exhaust manifold nuts.
3. Pull down and back on the exhaust

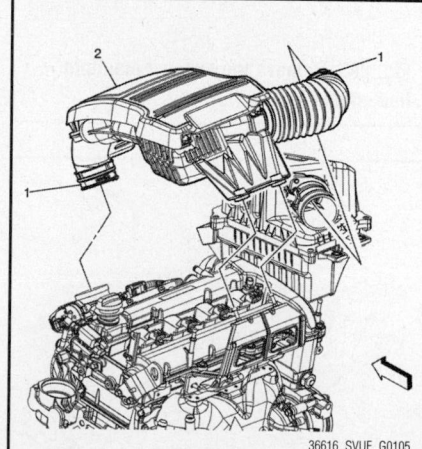

Fig. 291 Remove the air cleaner outlet duct

pipe in order to separate the catalytic converter from the exhaust manifold.

4. Remove and discard the catalytic converter gasket.

5. Remove the air cleaner outlet duct.

6. Remove the outlet duct retaining bracket.

7. Remove the exhaust manifold heat shield.

8. Remove the HO2S.

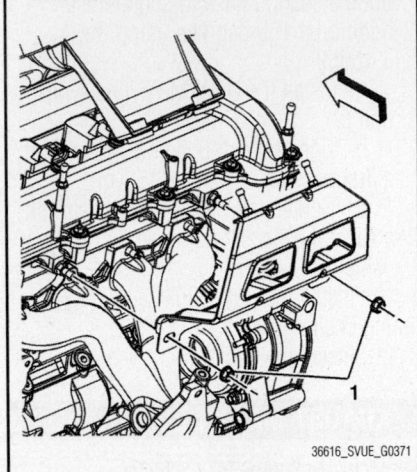

Fig. 292 Remove the outlet duct retaining bracket

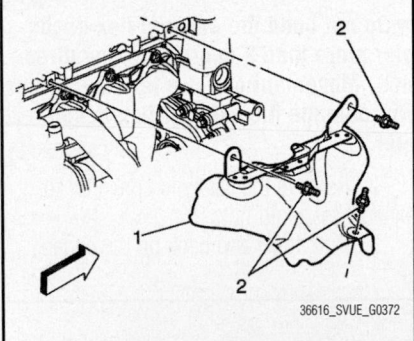

Fig. 293 Remove the exhaust manifold heat shield

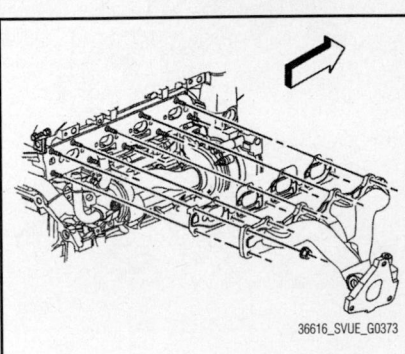

Fig. 294 Remove the exhaust manifold

9. Remove the exhaust manifold nuts.

10. Remove the exhaust manifold.

11. Remove and discard the exhaust manifold gasket.

12. Clean and inspect all gasket mating surfaces.

To install:

13. Install a NEW exhaust manifold gasket onto the studs.

14. Install the exhaust manifold to the cylinder head.

15. Install NEW exhaust manifold nuts. Tighten the nuts in the sequence shown to 10 ft. lbs. (14 Nm).

16. Install a NEW catalytic converter gasket .

17. Install the catalytic converter to the exhaust manifold studs.

18. Install the catalytic converter to exhaust manifold nuts. Tighten the nuts to 37 ft. lbs. (50 Nm).

19. Lower the vehicle.

20. Install the exhaust manifold heat shield.

21. Install the air cleaner outlet duct.

3.5L Engine—Left Side

See Figures 295 and 296.

1. Remove the left side catalytic converter.

2. Remove the Heated Oxygen Sensors (HO2S).

3. Remove the left side exhaust manifold bolts (1).

4. Remove the left side exhaust manifold and gasket.

To install:

5. Install the left side exhaust manifold and a NEW exhaust manifold gasket onto the cylinder.

6. Install the exhaust manifold bolts. Tighten the bolts to 15 ft. lbs. (20 Nm).

7. Install the HO2S.

8. Install the left side catalytic converter.

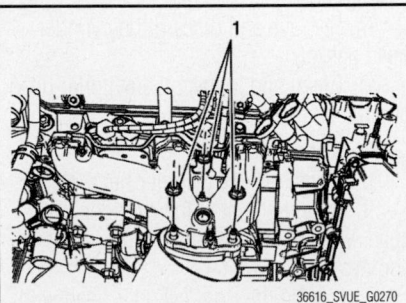

Fig. 295 Remove the left side catalytic converter

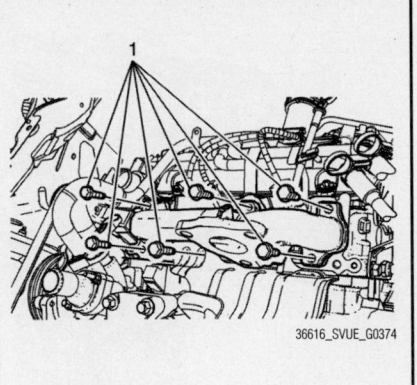

Fig. 296 Remove the left side exhaust manifold bolts (1)

3.5L Engine—Right Side

See Figures 297 and 298.

1. Remove the right side catalytic converter.

2. Remove the Heated Oxygen Sensor (HO2S).

3. Remove the right side exhaust manifold bolts (1).

4. Remove the right side exhaust manifold and gasket.

To install:

5. Install the right side exhaust manifold and a NEW exhaust manifold gasket onto the cylinder.

6. Install the exhaust manifold bolts. Tighten the bolts to 15 ft. lbs. (20 Nm).

7. Install the Heated Oxygen Sensor (HO2S).

8. Install the right side catalytic converter.

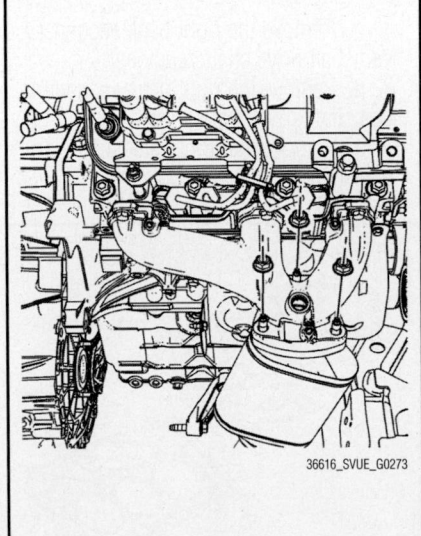

Fig. 297 Remove the right side catalytic converter

Fig. 298 Remove the right side exhaust manifold bolts (1)

3.6L Engine—Left Side

See Figures 299 through 302.

1. Remove the oil level indicator and tube.

2. Remove the Heated Oxygen Sensors (HO2S).

3. Remove the exhaust manifold heat shield.

4. Remove the left side catalytic converter.

5. Remove the left side exhaust manifold bolts (1).

6. Remove the left side exhaust manifold and gasket.

To install:

7. Install the left side exhaust manifold and a NEW exhaust manifold gasket onto the cylinder.

8. Install the exhaust manifold bolts. Tighten the bolts to 15 ft. lbs. (20 Nm).

9. Install the left side catalytic converter.

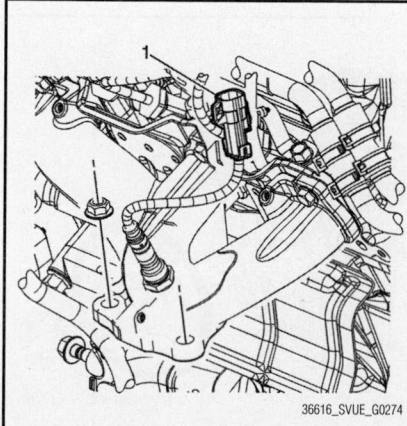

Fig. 299 Remove the Heated Oxygen Sensors (HO2S)

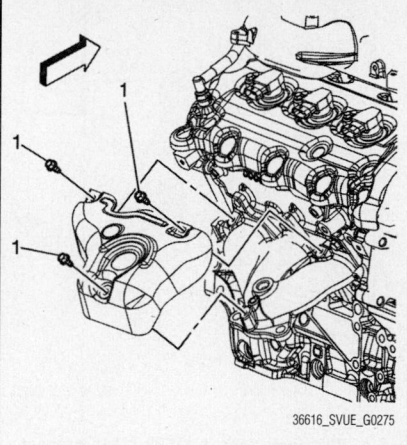

Fig. 300 Remove the exhaust manifold heat shield

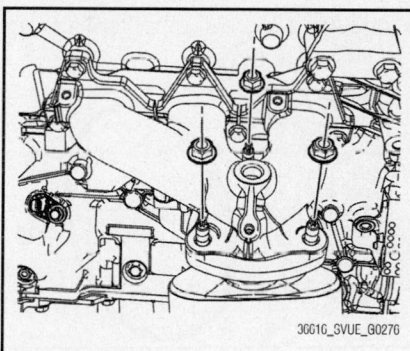

Fig. 301 Remove the left side catalytic converter

Fig. 302 Remove the left side exhaust manifold bolts (1)

10. Remove the exhaust manifold heat shield.

11. Install the HO2S.

12. Install the oil level indicator and tube.

3.6L Engine—Right Side

See Figures 303 through 306.

1. Remove the Heated Oxygen Sensor(HO2S).

2. Remove the exhaust manifold heat shield.

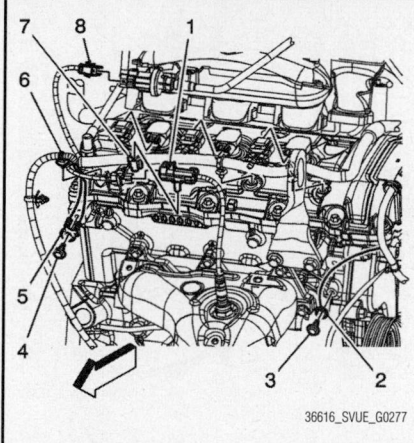

Fig. 303 Remove the Heated Oxygen Sensor(HO2S)

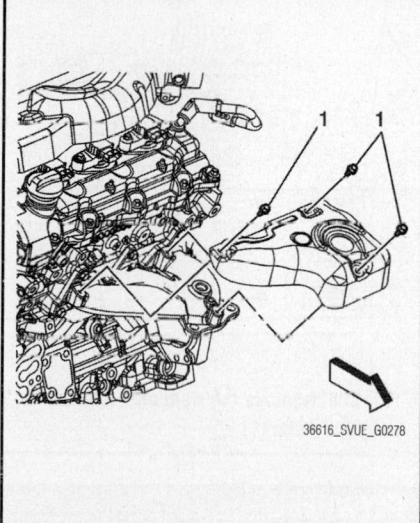

Fig. 304 Remove the exhaust manifold heat shield

3. Remove the right side catalytic converter.

4. Remove the right side exhaust manifold bolts (1).

5. Remove the right side exhaust manifold and gasket.

To install:

6. Install the right side exhaust manifold and a NEW exhaust manifold gasket onto the cylinder.

7. Install the exhaust manifold bolts. Tighten the bolts to 15 ft. lbs. (20 Nm).

8. Install the right side catalytic converter.

9. Install the exhaust manifold heat shield.

10. Install the Heated Oxygen Sensor (HO2S).

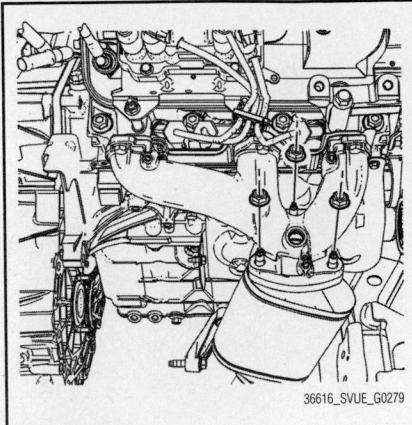

Fig. 305 Remove the right side catalytic converter

Fig. 306 Remove the right side exhaust manifold bolts (1)

FLYWHEEL

REMOVAL & INSTALLATION

2.4L Engine

See Figures 307 and 308.

1. Install the J 43653 (1) to prevent crankshaft rotation.
2. Remove the flywheel attaching bolts.
3. Remove the flywheel retainer.
4. Remove the flywheel.
5. Clean the thread adhesive from the flywheel bolt holes. Use a nylon bristle brush to clean the holes in the crankshaft.
6. Remove J 43653.

To install:

7. Install the flywheel.
8. Install the NEW bolts.
9. Holding the crankshaft balancer with J 38122-A, tighten the bolts evenly. Tighten the bolts to 39 ft. lbs. (53 Nm, plus 25 degrees using the J 45059.

Fig. 307 Install the J 43653 (1) to prevent crankshaft rotation

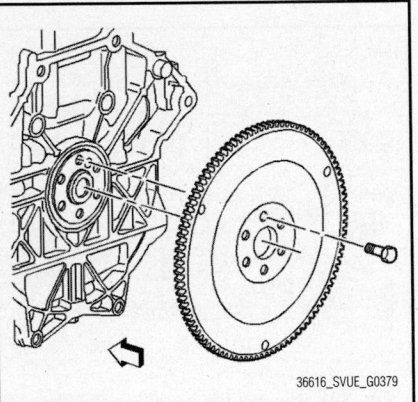

Fig. 308 Remove the flywheel attaching bolts

3.5L Engine

See Figure 309.

1. Remove the flywheel bolts.
2. Remove the flywheel.

To install:

3. Install the flywheel.
4. Install the flywheel bolts. Tighten the flywheel bolts to 52 ft. lbs. (70 Nm).

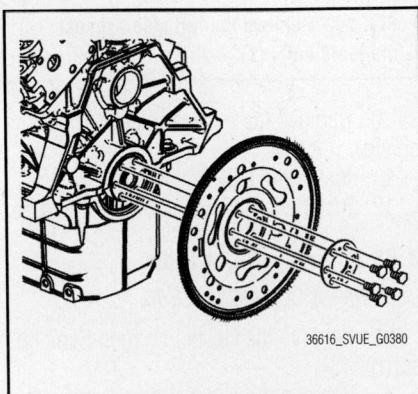

Fig. 309 Remove the flywheel bolts

3.6L Engine

See Figures 310 and 311.

1. Install the EN 46106, flywheel holding tool, through the starter mounting hole.
2. Remove the engine flywheel bolts and discard.
3. Remove the engine flywheel from the crankshaft.
4. Remove the EN 46106.

To install:

5. Place the engine flywheel in position on the crankshaft.
6. Install 2 NEW bolts in location at the top and bottom of the engine flywheel bolt pattern allowing the engine flywheel to hang in position.
7. Install the EN 46106.
8. Install the remaining NEW engine flywheel bolts. Tighten the NEW engine flywheel bolts to 22 ft. lbs. (30 Nm). Tighten the NEW engine flywheel bolts an additional 45 degrees using the J 45059.
9. Remove the EN 46106.

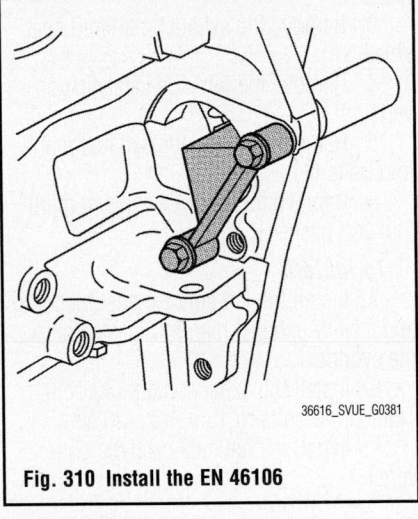

Fig. 310 Install the EN 46106

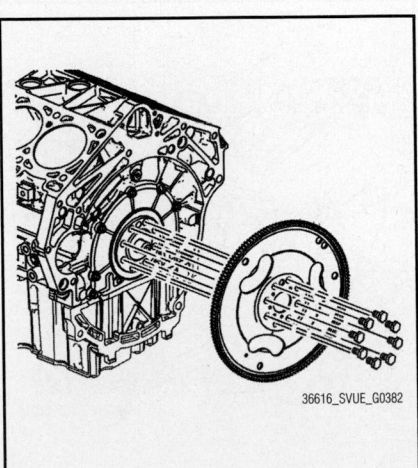

Fig. 311 Remove the engine flywheel bolts

INTAKE MANIFOLD

REMOVAL & INSTALLATION

2.4L Engine, Except Hybrid

See Figures 312 through 322.

1. Remove the intake manifold cover.
2. Remove the air cleaner outlet duct.
3. Disconnect the engine harness electrical connector (1) from the Throttle Actuator Control (TAC).
4. Disconnect the engine harness electrical connector (2) from the fuel injector harness.
5. Disconnect the engine harness electrical connector from the Manifold Absolute Pressure (MAP) sensor.
6. Disconnect the engine harness clips (1, 3) from the intake manifold.
7. Disconnect the engine harness clip (2) from the oil level indicator tube.

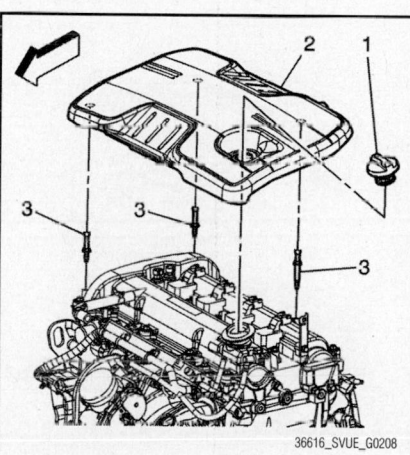

36616_SVUE_G0208

Fig. 312 Remove the intake manifold cover

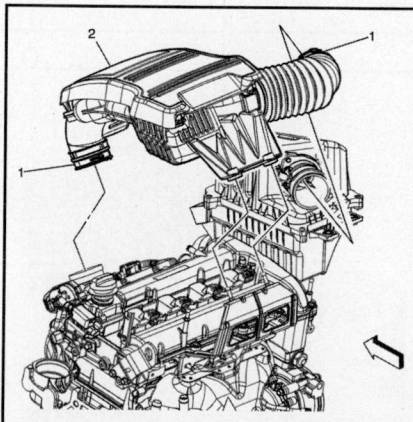

36616_SVUE_G0105

Fig. 313 Remove the air cleaner outlet duct

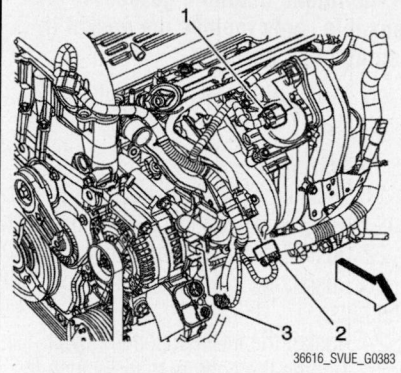

36616_SVUE_G0383

Fig. 314 Disconnect the engine harness electrical connector (1) from the Throttle Actuator Control (TAC)

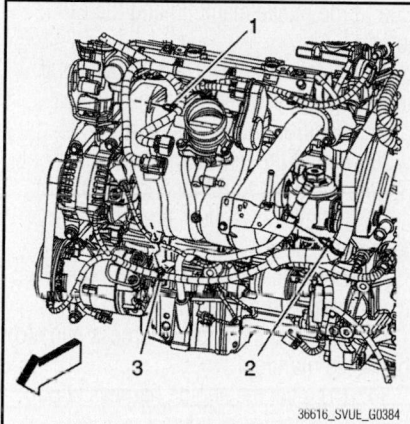

36616_SVUE_G0384

Fig. 315 Disconnect the engine harness clips (1, 3) from the intake manifold

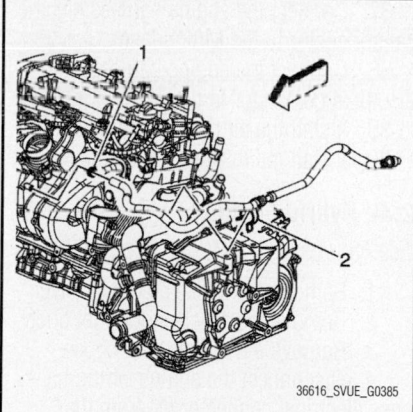

36616_SVUE_G0385

Fig. 316 Reposition the vacuum brake booster hose clamp (1) at the intake manifold

8. Disconnect the fuel injector electrical connector clip from the intake manifold.
9. Reposition the vacuum brake booster hose clamp (1) at the intake manifold.
10. Remove the vacuum brake booster hose from the intake manifold.

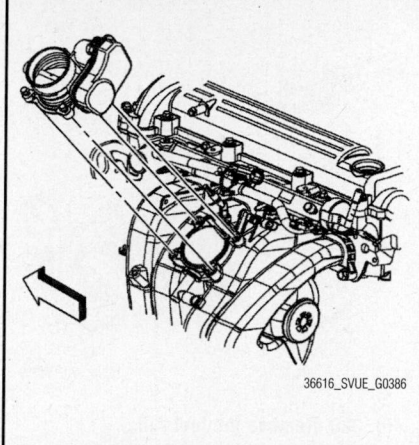

36616_SVUE_G0386

Fig. 317 Remove the throttle body bolts

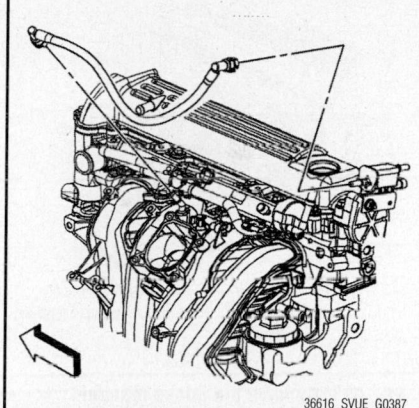

36616_SVUE_G0387

Fig. 318 Disconnect the Evaporative Emission (EVAP) canister purge tube from the intake manifold and the EVAP solenoid

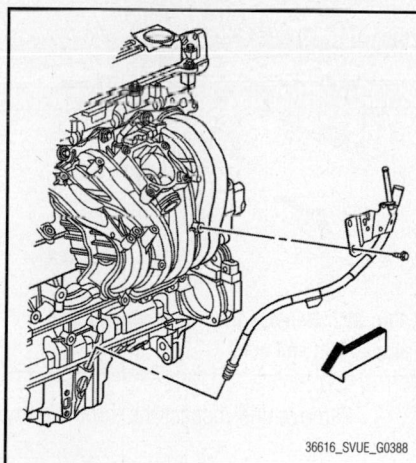

36616_SVUE_G0388

Fig. 319 Remove the oil level indicator tube

11. Remove the throttle body bolts.

➡ **The throttle body seal is reusable, only replace the seal if damaged.**

12. Remove the throttle body and seal.

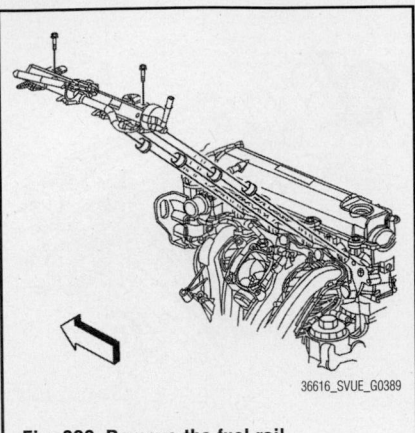

Fig. 320 Remove the fuel rail

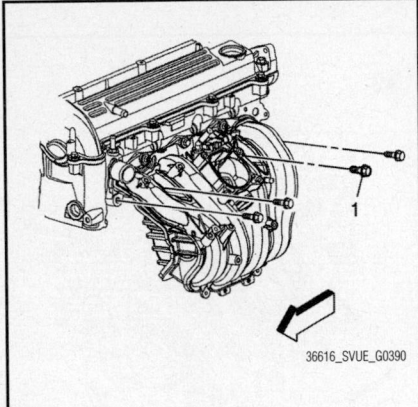

Fig. 321 Remove the intake manifold lower bolts

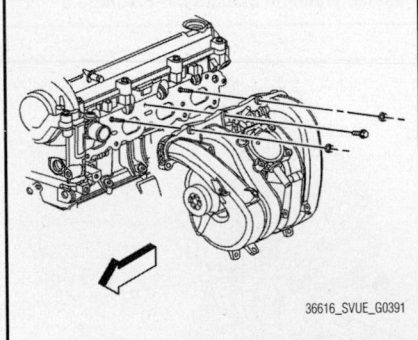

Fig. 322 Remove the intake manifold upper bolt and nuts

13. Remove and inspect the throttle body seal.

14. Disconnect the Evaporative Emission (EVAP) canister purge tube from the intake manifold and the EVAP solenoid.

15. Remove the oil level indicator tube.

16. Remove the fuel rail.

17. Remove the intake manifold lower bolts.

18. Remove the intake manifold upper bolt and nuts.

19. Remove the intake manifold.

➡The intake manifold gasket is reusable, only replace the gasket if damage has occurred.

20. Remove and inspect the intake manifold gasket.

To install:

21. Install a NEW intake manifold gasket if necessary, otherwise install the old gasket.

22. Install the intake manifold.

23. Install the intake manifold upper bolt and nuts.

24. Install the intake manifold lower bolts. Tighten the bolts/nuts to 89 inch lbs. (10 Nm).

25. Install the fuel rail.

26. Install the oil level indicator tube.

27. Connect the EVAP canister purge tube to the intake manifold and the EVAP solenoid.

28. Install a NEW throttle body seal if necessary, otherwise install the old seal.

29. Position the throttle body.

30. Install the throttle body bolts. Tighten the bolts to 89 inch lbs. (10 Nm).

31. Install the vacuum brake booster hose to the intake manifold.

32. Position the vacuum brake booster hose clamp at the intake manifold.

33. Connect the engine harness clips to the intake manifold.

34. Connect the engine harness clip to the oil level indicator tube.

35. Connect the fuel injector electrical connector clip to the intake manifold.

36. Connect the engine harness electrical connector to the fuel injector harness.

37. Connect the engine harness electrical connector to the MAP sensor.

38. Connect the engine harness electrical connector to the TAC.

39. Install the air cleaner outlet duct.

40. Install the intake manifold cover.

2.4L Hybrid Engine

See Figures 320, 321, 323 through 332.

1. Remove the intake manifold cover.

2. Remove the air cleaner outlet duct.

3. Remove the radiator inlet hose.

4. Disconnect the engine wiring harness electrical connector (1) from the Throttle Actuator Control (TAC).

5. Disconnect the engine wiring harness electrical connector (2) from the generator starter.

6. Disconnect the engine wiring harness electrical connector (4) from the generator starter.

7. Remove the fuel injector wiring harness electrical connector retainer (6) from the generator starter.

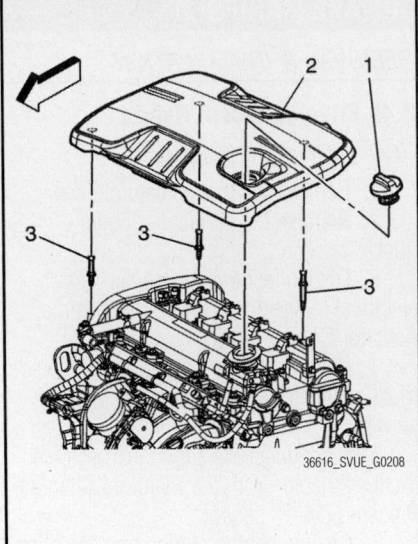

Fig. 323 Remove the intake manifold cover

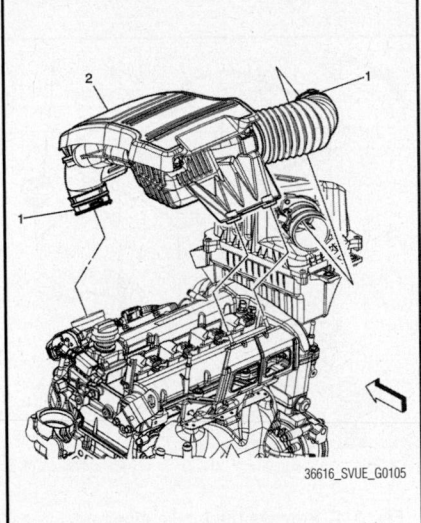

Fig. 324 Remove the air cleaner outlet duct

Fig. 325 Remove the radiator inlet hose

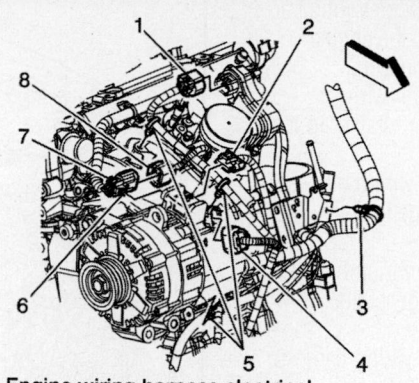

1. Engine wiring harness electrical connector from throttle actuator control
2. Engine wiring harness electrical connector from generator starter
3. Engine wiring harness retainer
4. Engine wiring harness electrical connector from generator starter
5. Engine wiring harness clips
6. Fuel injector wiring harness electrical connector retainer
7. Fuel injector wiring harness electrical connector
8. Engine wiring harness electrical connector

36616_VUEH_G0042

Fig. 326 Disconnect the engine wiring harness electrical connectors

8. Disconnect the fuel injector wiring harness electrical connector (7) from the engine wiring harness electrical connector (8).

9. Remove the engine wiring harness clips (5) from the intake manifold.

10. Reposition the vacuum brake booster hose clamp (1) at the intake manifold.

11. Remove the vacuum brake booster hose (2) from the intake manifold.

12. Remove the throttle body bolts.

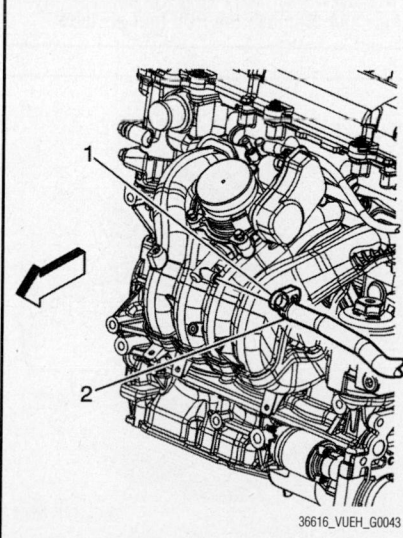

Fig. 327 Reposition the vacuum brake booster hose clamp (1)

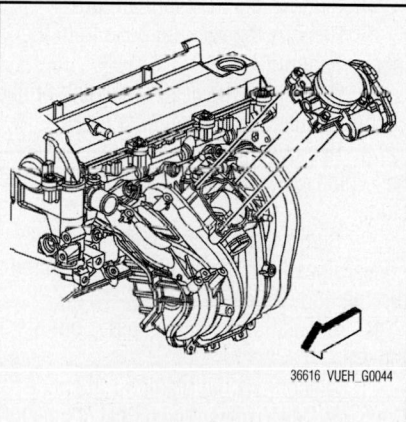

36616_VUEH_G0044

Fig. 328 Remove the throttle body bolts

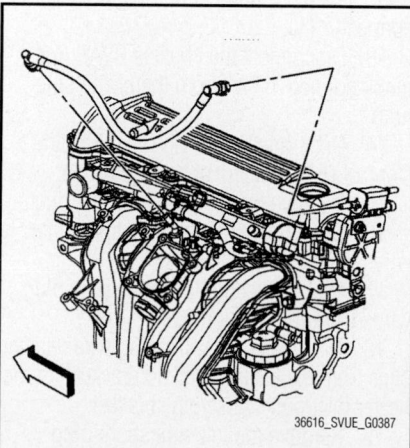

36616_SVUE_G0387

Fig. 329 Disconnect the Evaporative Emission (EVAP) canister purge tube

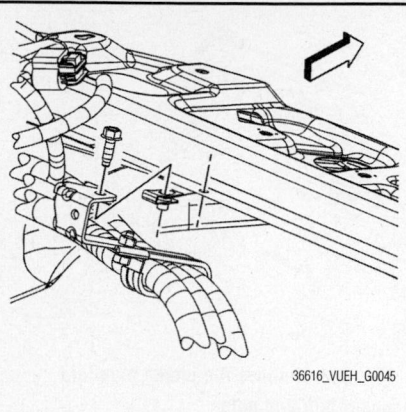

36616_VUEH_G0045

Fig. 330 Remove the 3-phase voltage cable bracket bolt at the tie bar

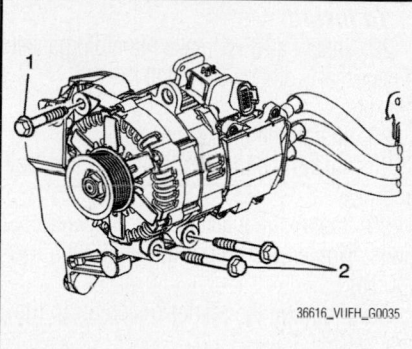

36616_VUFH_G0035

Fig. 331 Remove the generator starter bolts

➡**The throttle body seal is reusable. Only replace the seal if damaged.**

13. Remove the throttle body and seal.

14. Remove and inspect the throttle body seal.

15. Disconnect the engine wiring harness electrical connector from the Manifold Absolute Pressure (MAP) sensor.

16. Disconnect the Evaporative Emission (EVAP) canister purge tube from the intake manifold and the EVAP solenoid.

17. Remove the oil level indicator tube.

18. Remove the fuel rail.

19. Remove the 3-phase voltage cable bracket bolt at the tie bar.

20. Remove the generator starter bolts.

21. Reposition and secure the generator starter out of the way.

22. Remove the intake manifold lower bolts.

23. Remove the intake manifold upper bolt and nuts.

24. Remove the intake manifold.

➡**The intake manifold gasket is reusable. Only replace the gasket if damage has occurred.**

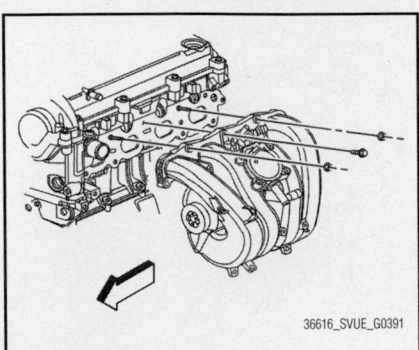

Fig. 332 Remove the intake manifold upper bolt and nuts

25. Remove and inspect the intake manifold gasket.

To install:

26. Install a NEW intake manifold gasket if necessary, otherwise install the old gasket.

27. Install the intake manifold.

28. Install the intake manifold upper bolt and nuts.

29. Install the intake manifold lower bolts. Tighten the bolts/nuts to 89 inch lbs. (10 Nm).

30. Position the starter/generator to the bracket.

31. Install the starter/generator bolts until snug.

32. Tighten the starter generator bolts in the following sequence:
   a. Front
   b. Bottom

33. Tighten the bolts to 43 ft. lbs. (58 Nm).

34. Install the 3-phase voltage cable bracket to the tie bar.

35. Install the 3-phase voltage cable bracket bolt at the tie bar. Tighten the bolt to 89 inch lbs. (10 Nm).

36. Install the fuel rail.

37. Install the oil level indicator tube.

38. Connect the EVAP canister purge tube to the intake manifold and the EVAP solenoid.

39. Connect the engine wiring harness electrical connector to the MAP sensor.

40. Install a NEW throttle body seal if necessary, otherwise install the old seal.

41. Position the throttle body.

42. Install the throttle body bolts. Tighten the bolts to 89 inch lbs. (10 Nm).

43. Install the vacuum brake booster hose to the intake manifold.

44. Position the vacuum brake booster hose clamp at the intake manifold.

45. Install the engine wiring harness clips to the intake manifold.

46. Connect the fuel injector wiring harness electrical connector to the engine wiring harness electrical connector.

47. Install the fuel injector wiring harness electrical connector retainer to the generator starter.

48. Connect the engine wiring harness electrical connector to the generator starter.

49. Connect the engine wiring harness electrical connector to the generator starter.

50. Connect the engine wiring harness electrical connector to the TAC.

51. Install the radiator inlet hose.

52. Install the air cleaner outlet duct.

3.5L Engine—Upper Intake Manifold

See Figures 333 through 343.

1. Disconnect the negative battery cable.

2. Remove the intake manifold cover.

3. Drain the cooling system.

4. Remove the Positive Crankcase Ventilation (PCV) fresh air tube.

5. Remove the PCV foul air tube.

6. Remove the vacuum hose from the intake manifold.

7. Reposition the heater inlet and outlet hose/pipe clamps at the engine pipes.

8. Remove the heater inlet and outlet hose/pipe clamp nuts from the throttle body studs.

9. Remove the heater inlet and outlet hoses/pipes from the engine pipes and the throttle body studs.

10. Reposition the hoses/pipes out of the way.

11. Disconnect the Manifold Absolute Pressure (MAP) sensor electrical connector (1).

12. Disconnect the Evaporative Emission (EVAP) canister purge solenoid electrical connector (1).

13. Disconnect the chassis EVAP line quick connect fitting from the purge solenoid.

14. Disconnect the Electronic Throttle Control (ETC) electrical connector (2).

15. Remove the air cleaner outlet duct.

16. Disconnect the left side spark plug wires from the spark plugs.

17. Disconnect the left side spark plug wires from the ignition coil.

18. Disengage the spark plug wire retainer clips from the intake manifold bracket and the heater inlet/outlet hose/pipe bracket.

19. Remove the left side spark plug wires.

20. Remove the throttle body bolts and nuts.

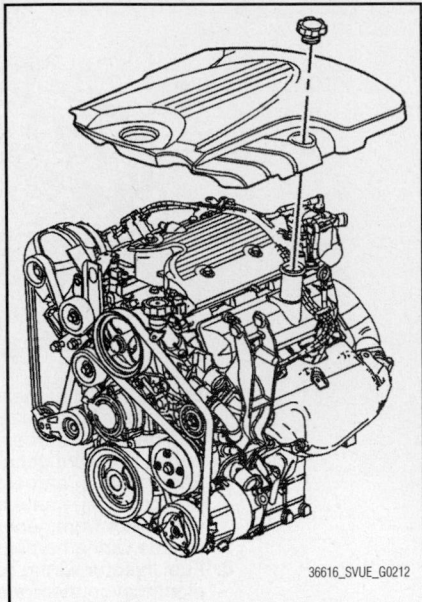

Fig. 333 Remove the intake manifold cover

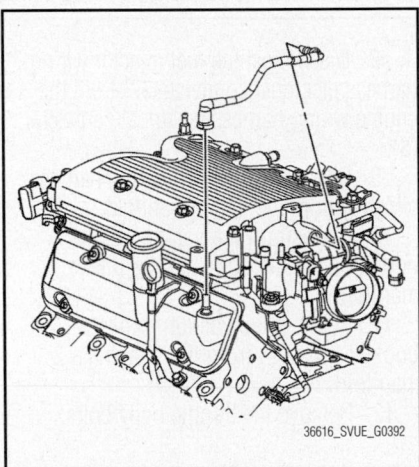

Fig. 334 Remove the PCV foul air tube

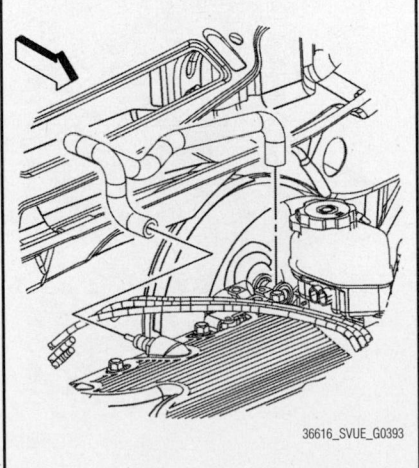

Fig. 335 Remove the vacuum hose from the intake manifold

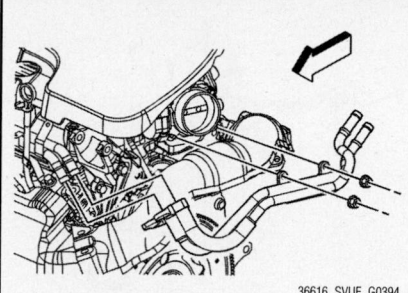

Fig. 336 Remove the heater inlet and outlet hose/pipe clamp nuts from the throttle body studs

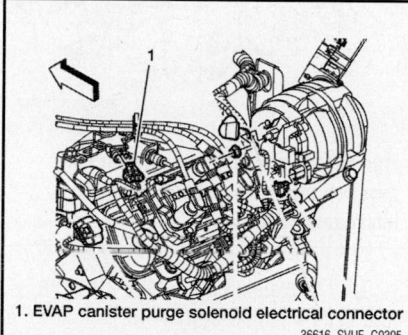

1. EVAP canister purge solenoid electrical connector
36616_SVUE_G0395

Fig. 337 Disconnect the Manifold Absolute Pressure (MAP) sensor electrical connector (1)

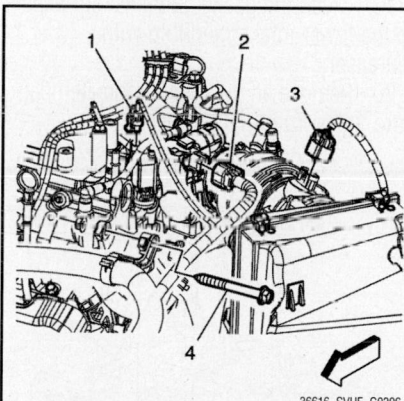

Fig. 338 Disconnect the Evaporative Emission (EVAP) canister purge solenoid electrical connector (1)

21. Remove the throttle body and gasket.
22. Remove the EVAP canister purge solenoid valve bolt.
23. Remove the EVAP canister purge solenoid valve.
24. Remove the MAP sensor bracket bolts.
25. Remove the MAP sensor bracket and sensor.
26. Remove the ignition coil bracket (to intake manifold) bolts.

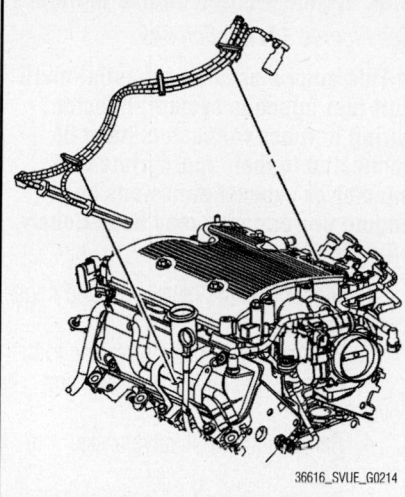

Fig. 339 Disconnect the left side spark plug wires from the spark plugs

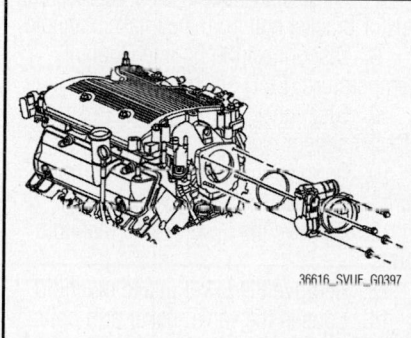

Fig. 340 Remove the throttle body bolts and nuts

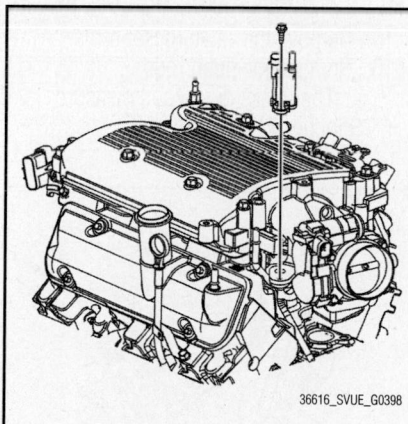

Fig. 341 Remove the EVAP canister purge solenoid valve bolt

27. Remove the intake manifold cover ball stud nut from the intake manifold stud.
28. Remove the upper intake manifold bolts and stud.
29. Separate and remove the upper intake manifold from the lower intake manifold.

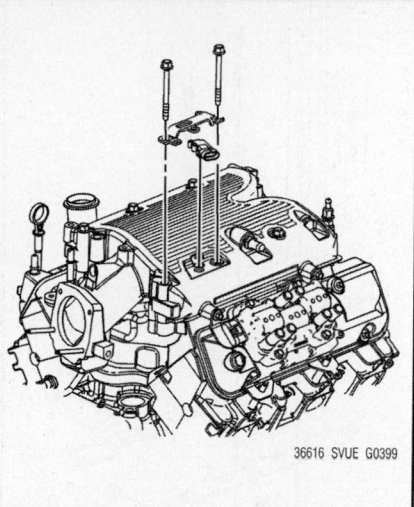

Fig. 342 Remove the MAP sensor bracket bolts

30. Remove the upper to lower intake manifold gaskets.
31. Clean the upper intake to lower intake gasket mating surfaces.

To install:
32. Install NEW upper to lower intake manifold gaskets.
33. Install the upper intake manifold onto the lower intake manifold.
34. Apply thread-lock to the upper intake manifold bolts/stud threads.
35. Install the upper intake manifold bolts and stud. Tighten the bolts and stud to 18 ft. lbs. (25 Nm).
36. Install the intake manifold cover ball stud nut to the intake manifold stud.
37. Install the ignition coil bracket (to intake manifold) bolts. Tighten the bolts to 18 ft. lbs. (25 Nm).
38. Install the MAP sensor and bracket.
39. Install the MAP sensor bracket bolts. Tighten the bolts to 18 ft. lbs. (25 Nm).
40. Install the EVAP canister purge solenoid valve.
41. Install the EVAP canister purge solenoid valve bolt. Tighten the bolts to 12 ft. lbs. (16 Nm).
42. Inspect the throttle body seal for damage, replace as necessary.
43. Apply thread-lock to the throttle body bolts/studs threads.
44. Position the throttle body gasket and throttle body to the intake.
45. Install the throttle body bolts and nuts. Tighten the bolts/studs to 89 inch lbs. (10 Nm).
46. Install the left side spark plug wires.
47. Engage the spark plug wire retainer clips to the intake manifold bracket and the heater inlet/outlet hose/pipe bracket.

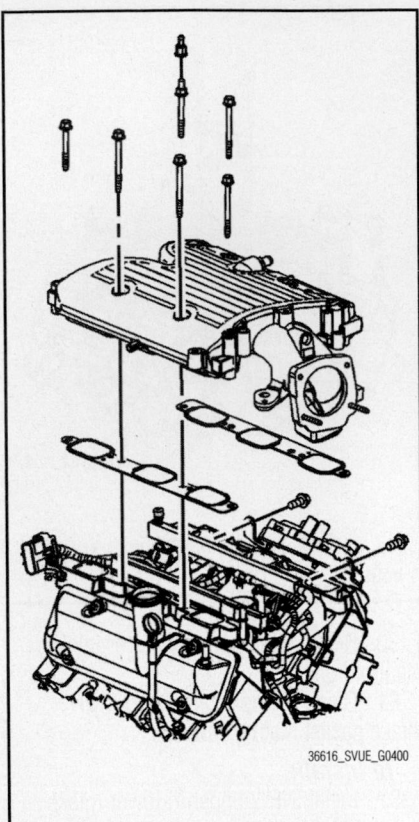

Fig. 343 Remove the upper intake manifold bolts and stud

48. Connect the left side spark plug wires to the ignition coil.

49. Connect the left side spark plug wires to the spark plugs.

50. Install the air cleaner outlet duct.

51. Connect the EVAP canister purge solenoid electrical connector.

52. Connect the chassis EVAP line quick connect fitting to the purge solenoid.

53. Connect the ETC electrical connector.

54. Connect the MAP sensor electrical connector.

55. Position the hoses/pipes.

56. Install the heater inlet and outlet hoses/pipes to the engine pipes and the throttle body studs.

57. Install the heater inlet and outlet hose/pipe clamp nuts to the throttle body studs. Tighten the nuts to 89 inch lbs. (10 Nm).

58. Position the heater inlet and outlet hose/pipe clamps at the engine pipes.

59. Install the vacuum hose to the intake manifold.

60. Install the PCV foul air tube.

61. Install the PCV fresh air tube.

62. Fill the cooling system.

63. Connect the negative battery cable.

64. Install the intake manifold cover.

3.5L Engine—Lower Intake Manifold

See Figures 344 through 349.

➡**This engine uses a sequential multiport fuel injection system. Injector wiring harness connectors must be connected to their appropriate fuel injector or exhaust emissions and engine performance may be seriously affected.**

1. Disconnect the battery ground negative cable.

2. Remove the upper intake manifold.

3. Remove the left valve rocker arm cover.

4. Remove the right valve rocker arm cover.

5. Disconnect the fuel feed line from the fuel rail.

6. Disconnect fuel injector inline connector.

7. Remove the fuel injector harness connector bracket bolt from the intake manifold.

8. Disconnect the Engine Coolant Temperature (ECT) electrical connector.

9. Disconnect the Camshaft Position (CMP) sensor electrical connector.

10. Remove the fuel injector rail bolts.

11. Remove the fuel rail.

12. Remove the lower intake manifold bolts.

13. Remove the lower intake manifold.

14. Loosen the valve rocker arm bolts.

➡**Place the valve train components in a rack in order to ensure that the components are installed in the same location from which they were removed.**

15. Remove the valve rocker arms.

16. Remove the push rods.

  a. The intake push rods measure 5.75 inches (146.0 mm).

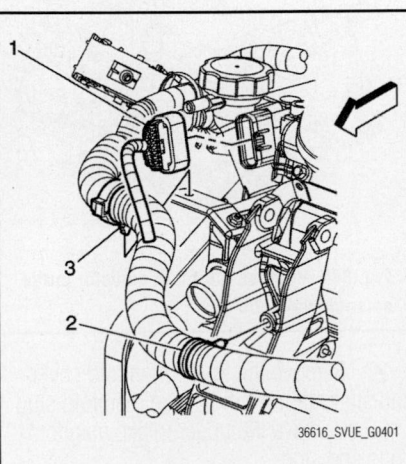

Fig. 344 Disconnect fuel injector inline connector

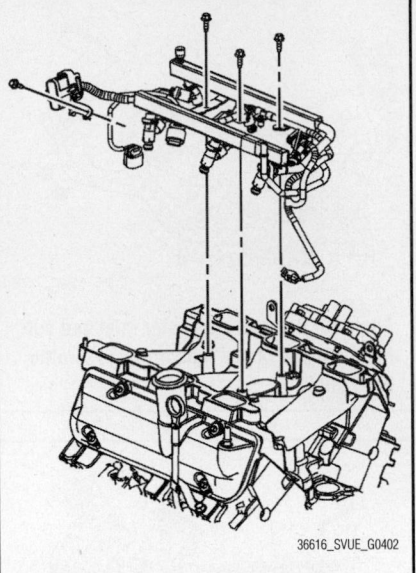

Fig. 345 Remove the fuel injector harness connector bracket bolt from the intake manifold

  b. The exhaust push rods measure 6.0 inches (152.5 mm).

17. Remove the lower intake manifold gaskets and seals.

18. Clean the lower intake manifold gasket and seal surfaces on the cylinder heads and the engine block.

19. Clean the gasket and seal surfaces on the lower intake manifold with degreaser.

20. Remove all the loose Room Temperature Vulcanizing (RTV) sealer.

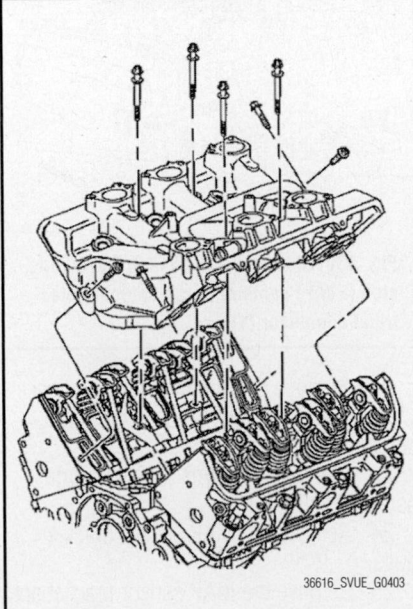

Fig. 346 Remove the lower intake manifold bolts

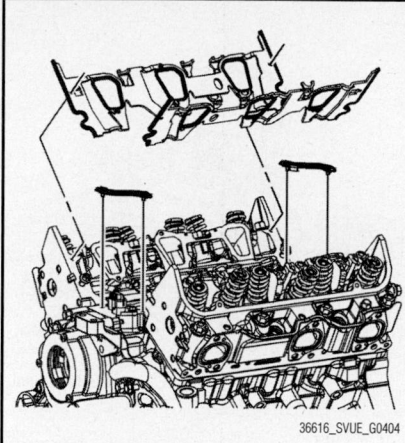

Fig. 347 Remove the lower intake manifold gaskets and seals

To install:

→All gasket mating surfaces need to be free of oil and foreign material. Use cleaner to clean the surfaces.

→RTV sealer is NOT to be placed under the lower intake manifold gaskets.

21. Install the lower intake manifold gaskets and seals.

22. Coat the ends of the push rods using prelube.

→The intake valve push rods measure 5.75 inches (146.0 mm) and the exhaust valve push rods measure 6.0 inches (152.5 mm).

23. Install the push rods in their original location.

24. Coat the rocker arm friction surfaces using prelube.

→Shims (P/N 88894006) may be required under the valve rocker arm

pedestals if reconditioning has been performed on the cylinder head or its components.

25. Install the valve rocker arms in their original positions.

26. Install the valve rocker arm bolts. Tighten the bolts to 25 ft. lbs. (34 Nm).

27. With the NEW gaskets and seals in place, apply a small drop of RTV sealer to the 4 corners of the intake manifold to engine block joints (1).

28. Install the lower intake manifold.

→Maximum gasket performance is achieved when using new fasteners, which contain a thread-locking patch. If the fasteners are not replaced, a thread locking chemical must be applied to the fastener threads. Failure to replace the fasteners or apply a thread-locking chemical MAY reduce gasket sealing capability.

→Failure to tighten vertical bolts before the diagonal bolts may cause an oil leak.

29. Apply sealer to the lower intake manifold bolt threads.

30. Install the lower intake manifold bolts.

31. Tighten the lower intake manifold bolts in the sequence shown.

   a. Tighten the bolts (1, 2, 3, 4) in sequence to 12 ft. lbs. (16 Nm).

   b. Tighten the bolts (5, 6, 7, 8) in sequence to 18 ft. lbs. (25 Nm).

32. Inspect the fuel rail, fuel injectors and fuel injector O-rings for damage and replace, as necessary.

33. Lubricate the fuel injector O-rings using engine oil.

34. Install the injector nozzles into the lower intake manifold injector bores.

35. Press on the injector rail using the palms of both hands until the injector are fully seated.

36. Install the fuel injector rail bolts. Tighten the bolts to 89 inch lbs. (10 Nm).

37. Connect the CMP sensor electrical connector.

38. Connect the ECT electrical connector.

39. Position the fuel injector harness connector bracket to the intake manifold.

40. Install the fuel injector harness connector bracket bolt. Tighten the bolt to 71 inch lbs. (8 Nm).

41. Connect fuel injector inline connector.

42. Connect the fuel feed line to the fuel rail.

43. Install the right valve rocker arm cover.

44. Install the left valve rocker arm cover.

45. Install the upper intake manifold.

46. Connect the battery ground negative cable.

3.6L Engine—Upper Intake Manifold

See Figures 350 through 358.

1. Remove the air cleaner outlet duct.

2. Disconnect the wiring harness electrical connector (3) from the throttle body (4).

3. Disconnect the PCV line (1) from the top of the intake manifold and reposition aside.

4. Disconnect the Evaporative Emissions (EVAP) canister purge line (1) and reposition aside.

5. Disconnect the coolant hose bleed pipe.

6. Remove the engine harness retaining clips (1) from the bleed pipe.

7. Remove the bleed pipe bolts (2).

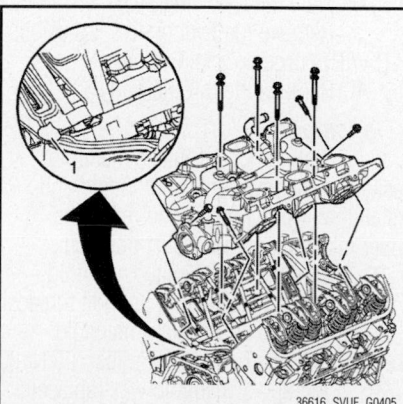

Fig. 348 Apply a small drop of RTV sealer to the 4 corners of the intake manifold to engine block joints (1)

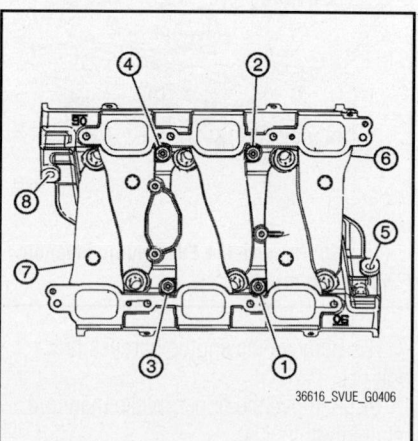

Fig. 349 Tighten the lower intake manifold bolts in the sequence shown

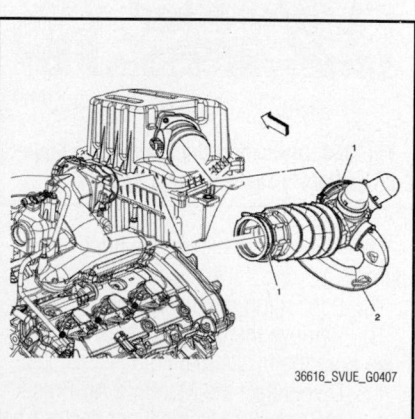

Fig. 350 Remove the air cleaner outlet duct

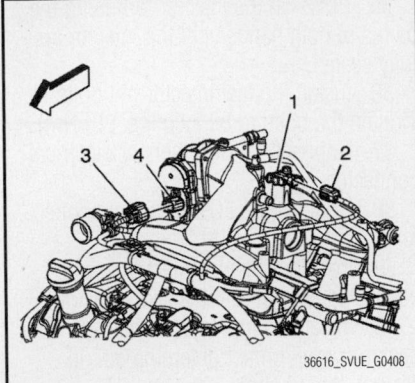

Fig. 351 Disconnect the wiring harness electrical connector (3) from the throttle body (4)

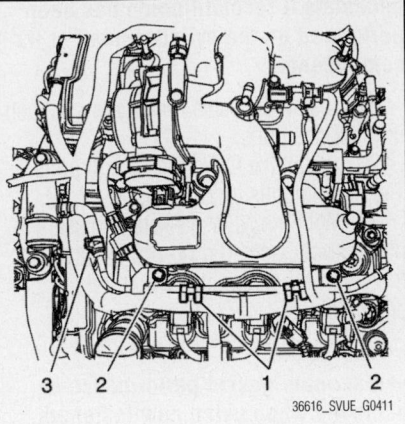

Fig. 354 Remove the engine harness retaining clips (1) from the bleed pipe

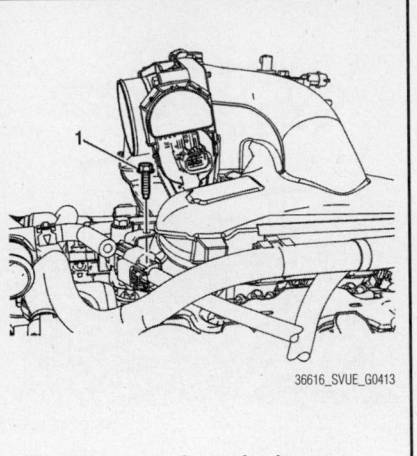

Fig. 357 Remove the engine harness bracket bolt (1)

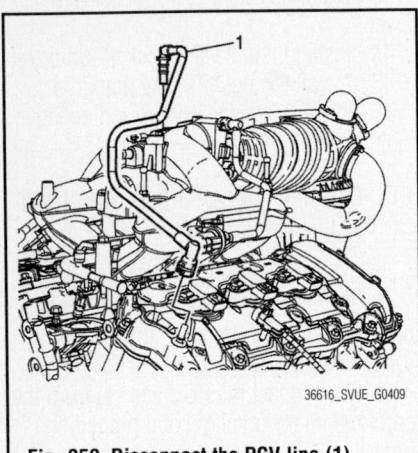

Fig. 352 Disconnect the PCV line (1)

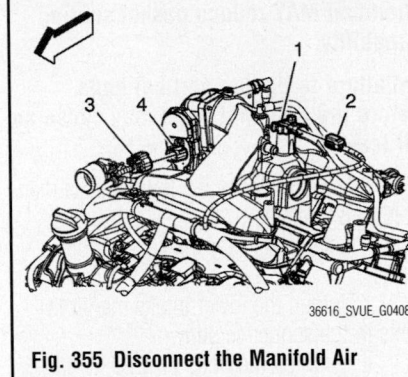

Fig. 355 Disconnect the Manifold Air Pressure (MAP) sensor electrical connector from the MAP sensor (1)

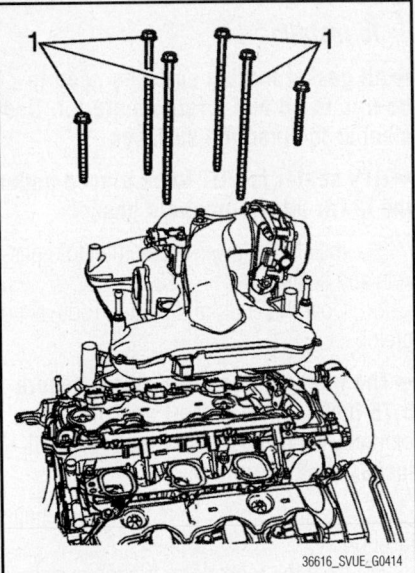

Fig. 358 Remove the upper intake manifold retaining bolts (1)

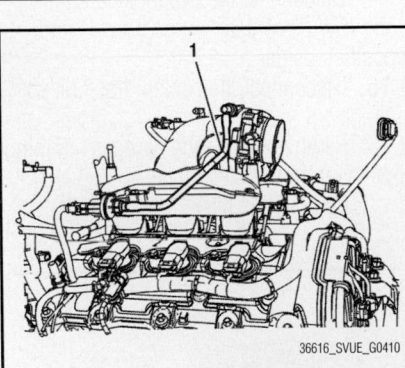

Fig. 353 Disconnect the Evaporative Emissions (EVAP) canister purge line (1)

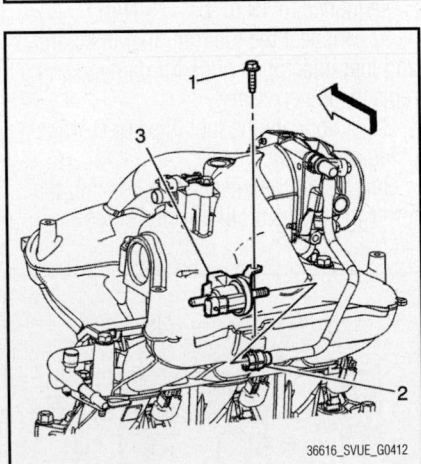

Fig. 356 Remove the EVAP purge solenoid valve bolt (1)

8. Remove the bleed pipe hose clamp (3).

9. Reposition the bleed pipe.

10. Remove the brake booster vacuum hose from the intake manifold.

11. Disconnect the Manifold Air Pressure (MAP) sensor electrical connector from the MAP sensor (1).

12. Remove the EVAP purge solenoid valve bolt (1).

13. Remove the engine harness bracket bolt (1).

14. Remove the upper intake manifold retaining bolts (1).

15. Remove the upper intake manifold and gasket. Discard the gasket.

16. If replacing the upper intake manifold complete the following steps:

a. Remove the Evaporative Emissions (EVAP) purge solenoid valve.

b. Remove the throttle body.

To install:

17. Install the upper intake manifold gaskets to the lower intake manifold and install the fir tree retainers to retain the upper intake manifold gasket position.

18. Install the upper intake manifold.

19. Apply thread-lock to the bolt threads.

20. Install the upper intake manifold bolts. Tighten the bolts to 18 ft. lbs. (25 Nm).

21. If the upper manifold was replaced, complete the following steps:

a. Install the throttle body.

b. Install the EVAP purge solenoid valve.

22. Install the engine harness bracket bolt.

23. Install the EVAP purge solenoid valve bolt. Tighten the bolt to 89 inch lbs. (10 Nm).

24. Connect the Manifold Air Pressure (MAP) sensor electrical connector to the map sensor.

25. Install the brake booster vacuum hose to the intake manifold.

26. Position the bleed pipe.

27. Install the bleed pipe hose clamp.

28. Install the bleed pipe bolts. Tighten the nut to 89 inch lbs. (10 Nm).

29. Install the engine harness retaining clips to the fuel feed pipe.

30. Connect the coolant hose bleed pipe.

31. Connect the EVAP canister purge line.

32. Connect the PCV line to the top of the intake manifold.

33. Connect the wiring harness electrical connector to the throttle body.

34. Install the air cleaner outlet duct.

3.6L Engine—Lower Intake Manifold

See Figure 359.

1. Remove the fuel injectors and fuel rail.

2. Remove the lower intake manifold bolts (1).

3. Remove the lower intake manifold and gasket from engine. Discard the gasket.

4. Clean and inspect the intake manifold and the sealing surfaces.

To install:

5. Install the lower intake manifold gasket.

6. Install the lower intake manifold bolts.

7. Install the fuel injectors and fuel rail. Tighten the bolts to 17 ft. lbs. (23 Nm).

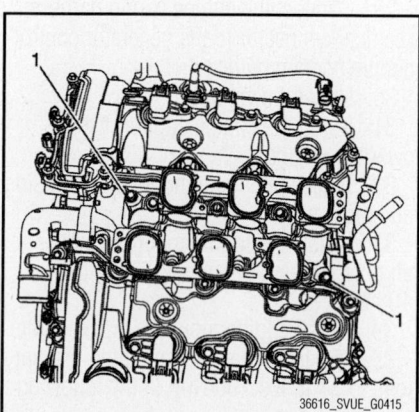

Fig. 359 Remove the lower intake manifold bolts (1)

OIL PAN

REMOVAL & INSTALLATION

2.4L Engine, Except Hybrid

See Figures 360 through 362.

1. Raise and support the vehicle.

2. Place a drain pan under the oil pan drain plug.

3. Remove the oil pan drain plug.

4. Drain the engine oil.

5. Remove the engine drive belt.

6. Remove the lower AC compressor bolt.

7. Remove the 4 oil pan to transaxle bolts (1).

8. Remove the oil pan to engine bolts.

9. Remove the oil pan.

10. Remove any old oil pan sealant (1).

To install:

11. Ensure that the oil pan and the sealing surface on the lower crankcase are free of all oil and debris.

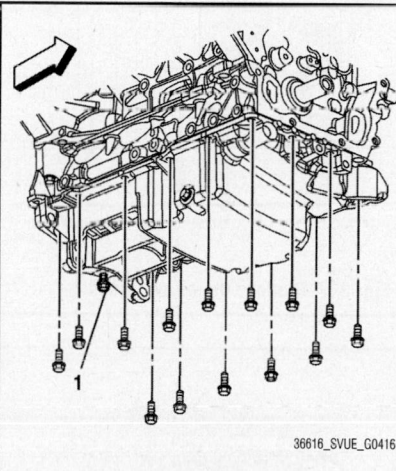

Fig. 360 Remove the 4 oil pan to transaxle bolts (1)

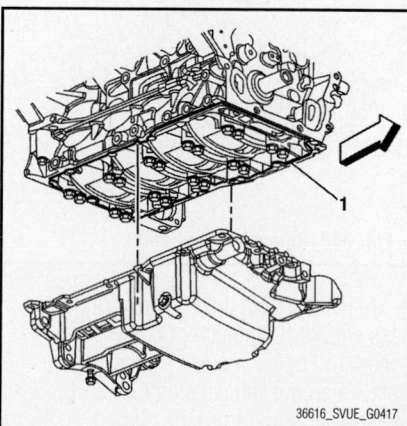

Fig. 361 Remove any old oil pan sealant (1)

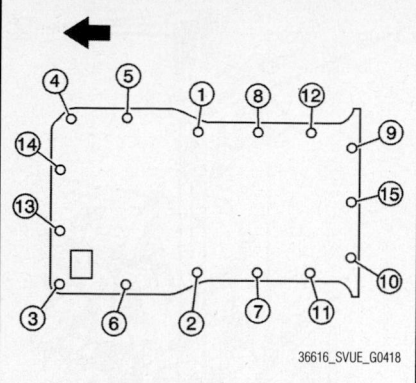

Fig. 362 Tighten the oil pan to engine bolts in the sequence shown

12. Apply a 2 mm bead of sealant around the perimeter of the oil pan and the oil suction port opening. DO NOT over apply the sealant.

13. Install the oil pan.

14. Install the oil pan bolts.

15. Install the 4 oil pan to transaxle bolts and tighten to 55 ft. lbs. (75 Nm).

16. Tighten the oil pan to engine bolts in the sequence shown to 18 ft. lbs. (25 Nm).

17. Install the lower AC compressor bolt.

18. Install the engine drive belt.

19. Lower the vehicle.

20. Fill the engine oil to the proper level.

2.4L Hybrid Engine

See Figures 363 through 369.

1. Remove the drive belt.

2. Remove the oil level indicator tube.

➡**The support fixture bar must be installed to provide enough access to remove and properly tighten the oil pan bolts.**

3. Install the engine support fixture.

4. Remove engine mount to bracket bolts (2).

5. Remove the engine mount to side rail nuts (1).

6. Remove the engine mount from the engine compartment.

7. Using the engine support fixture, raise the engine approximately 3 inches.

8. Raise and support the vehicle.

9. Loosen the upper Air Conditioning (A/C) compressor bolts.

10. Remove the lower A/C compressor bolt.

11. Place a suitable drain pan under the oil pan drain plug.

12. Remove the oil pan drain plug.

13. Drain the engine oil.

14. Reinstall the oil pan drain plug until snug.

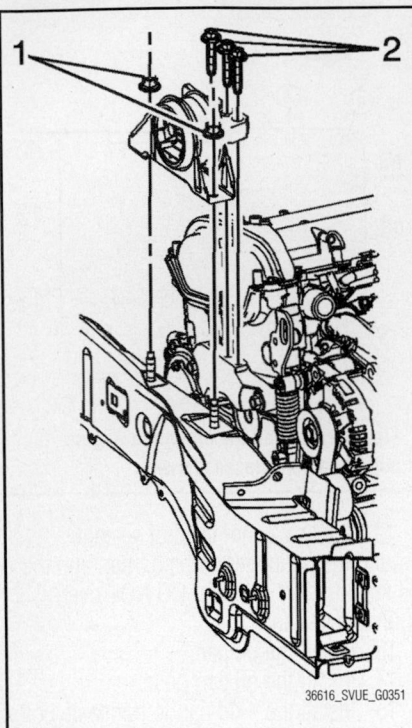

Fig. 363 Remove engine mount to bracket bolts (2)

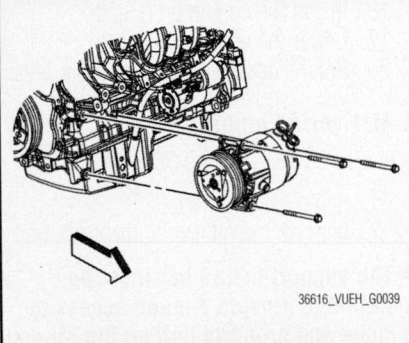

Fig. 364 Loosen the upper Air Conditioning (A/C) compressor bolts

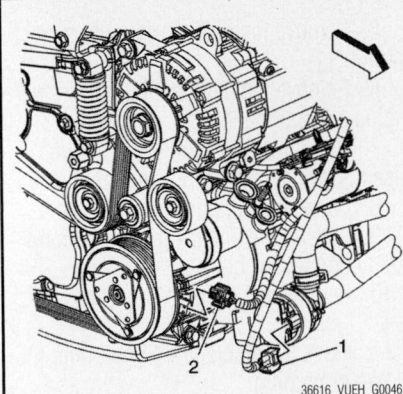

Fig. 365 Disconnect the electrical connector (1) from the generator control module coolant pump

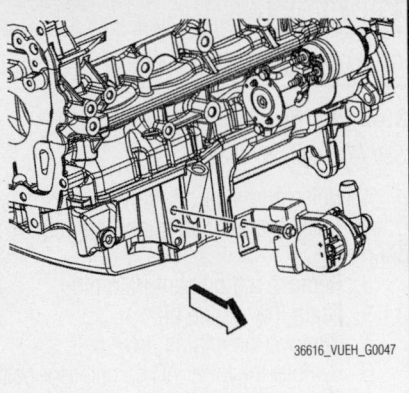

Fig. 366 Remove the generator control module coolant pump from the oil pan

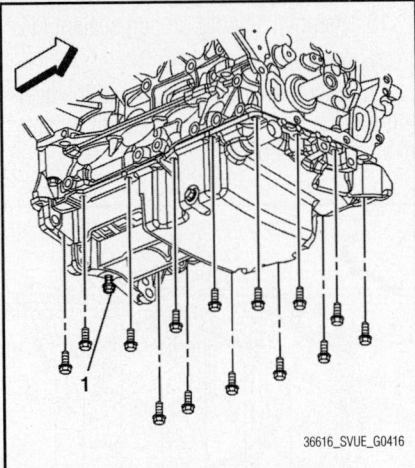

Fig. 367 Remove the oil pan bolts

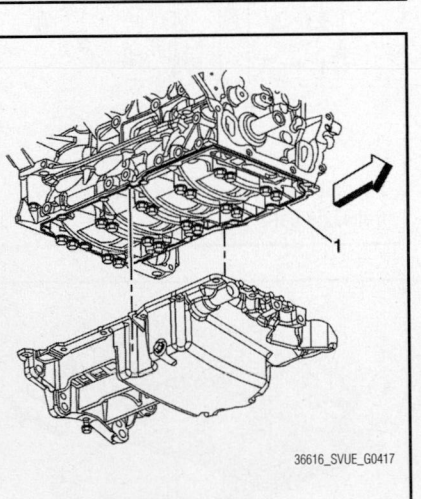

Fig. 368 Remove the oil pan

15. Disconnect the engine wiring harness electrical connector (1) from the generator control module coolant pump.

16. Remove the generator control module coolant pump from the oil pan.

17. Remove the 4 oil pan to transaxle bolts.

18. Remove the oil pan bolts.

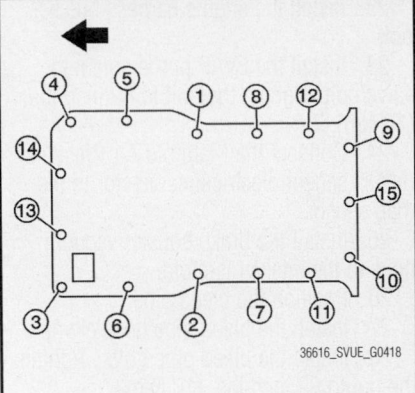

Fig. 369 Tighten the oil pan bolts in the sequence shown

19. Remove the oil pan.

20. Remove any old oil pan sealant (1).

To install:

21. Ensure that the oil pan and the sealing surface on the lower crankcase are free of all oil and debris.

22. Apply a bead of sealant around the perimeter of the oil pan and the oil suction port opening. DO NOT over apply the sealant. More than a 2 mm bead is not required.

23. Install the oil pan.

24. Install the oil pan bolts.

25. Install the 4 oil pan to transaxle bolts. Tighten the bolts to 55 ft. lbs. (75 Nm).

26. Tighten the oil pan bolts in the sequence shown. Tighten the bolts to 18 ft. lbs. (25 Nm).

27. Install the generator control module coolant pump to the oil pan. Ensure that the anti-rotation tab is inserted into the hole in the oil pan.

28. Install the generator control module coolant pump bolt. Tighten the bolt to 18 ft. lbs. (25 Nm).

29. Connect the engine wiring harness electrical connector to the generator control module coolant pump.

30. Lower the vehicle.

31. Using the engine support fixture, lower the engine.

32. Place the engine mount onto the side rail studs.

33. Install the engine mount to side rail nuts. Tighten the nuts to 74 ft. lbs. (100 Nm).

34. Install engine mount to bracket bolts.

35. Tighten the engine mount to bracket bolts to 37 ft. lbs. (50 Nm) in the following sequence:

- Middle
- Rear
- Front

36. Remove the engine support fixture.

37. Install the oil level indicator tube.

38. Install the drive belt.

39. Fill the engine oil to the proper level.

3.5L Engine

See Figures 370 through 372.

1. Disconnect the negative battery cable.

2. Drain the engine oil.

3. Remove the oil filter adapter and bypass valve assembly.

4. Remove the starter motor.

5. Remove the left side catalytic converter.

6. Remove the transfer case.

7. Remove the Air Conditioning (A/C) compressor nut and bolt.

8. Remove the A/C compressor rear bolt and position the A/C compressor aside.

Fig. 370 Remove the Air Conditioning (A/C) compressor nut and bolt

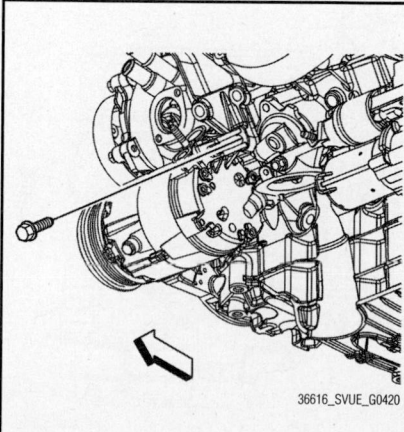

Fig. 371 Remove the A/C compressor rear bolt

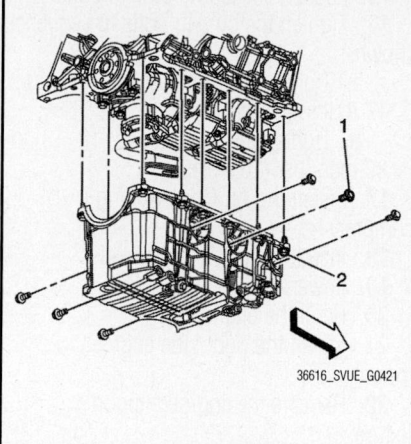

Fig. 372 Remove the horizontal oil pan bolts (1)

9. Remove the horizontal oil pan bolts (1).

10. Remove the vertical oil pan bolts (2).

11. Remove the oil pan.

12. Remove the oil pan gasket.

13. Clean the following items:
   - The oil pan flanges
   - The oil pan rail
   - The engine front cover
   - All threaded holes

To install:

14. Install a NEW oil pan gasket.

15. Position the oil pan to the engine and hand start all the oil pan bolts.

16. Torque the vertical oil pan bolts to 18 ft. lbs. (25 Nm).

17. Torque the horizontal oil pan bolts to 37 ft. lbs. (50 Nm) plus 50 degrees.

➡**Hand start all the A/C compressor bolts before finalizing any torques.**

18. Install the A/C compressor, and hand start the A/C compressor nut and bolt. Tighten the bolt/nut to 37 ft. lbs. (50 Nm).

19. Tighten the A/C compressor rear bolt to 37 ft. lbs. (50 Nm).

20. Install the transfer case.

21. Install the left side catalytic converter.

22. Install the starter motor.

23. Install the oil filter adapter and bypass valve assembly.

24. Fill the engine oil.

25. Connect the negative battery cable.

3.6L Engine

See Figures 373 through 377.

➡**Graphics depict the engine upside down for clarity.**

1. Disconnect the battery negative cable.

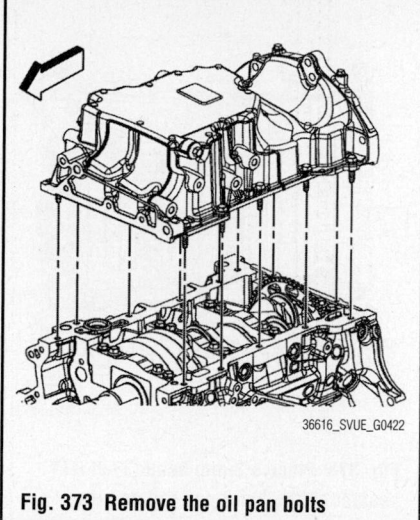

Fig. 373 Remove the oil pan bolts

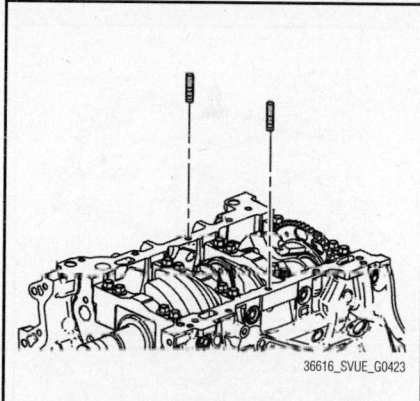

Fig. 374 Install the guide pin set into the center oil pan rail bolt hole

2. Install the engine support fixture.

3. Remove the right side engine mount.

4. Raise and support the vehicle.

5. Drain the engine oil and remove the oil filter.

6. Remove the catalytic converter.

7. Remove the Air Conditioning (A/C) compressor.

8. Remove the oil pan bolts.

9. Remove the oil pan.

10. Clean the oil pan and the engine block gasket surface.

To install:

11. Install the guide pin set (EN 46109) into the center oil pan rail bolt hole on each side of the engine block.

12. Place a 3 mm bead (1) of RTV sealant, GM P/N 12378521 (Canadian P/N 88901148) or equivalent, on the block pan rail and the crankshaft rear oil seal housing.

13. Position the oil pan onto the block.

14. Remove the guide pin set from the engine block.

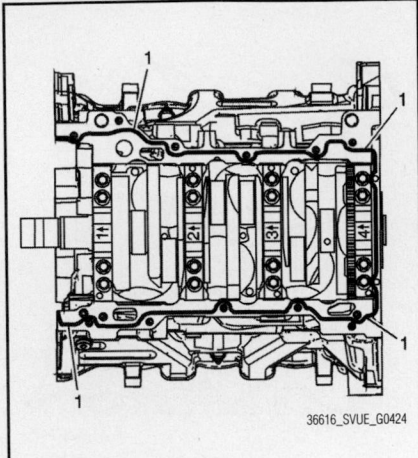

Fig. 375 Place a 3 mm bead (1) of RTV sealant on the block pan rail and the crankshaft rear oil seal housing

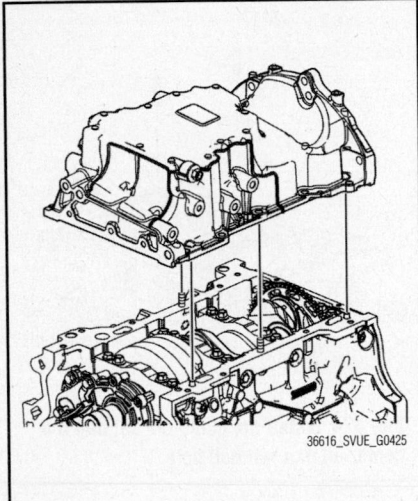

Fig. 376 Position the oil pan onto the block

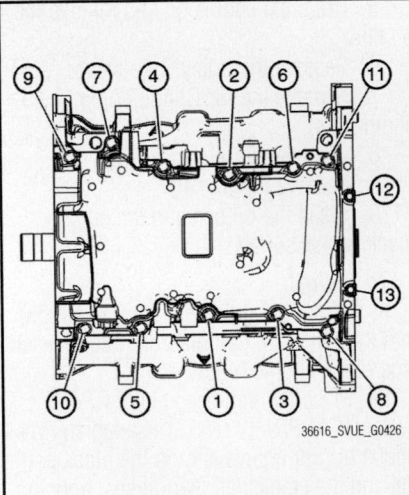

Fig. 377 Tighten the oil pan bolts in sequence shown

15. Loosely install the oil pan bolts.
16. Tighten the oil pan bolts in sequence shown.
    a. Tighten the 8 mm bolts (1-11) to 17 ft. lbs. (23 Nm).
    b. Tighten the 6 mm bolts (12, 13) to 89 inch lbs. (10 Nm).
17. Install the Air Conditioning (A/C) compressor.
18. Install the catalytic converter.
19. Lower the vehicle.
20. Refill the engine oil.
21. Install the right side engine mount.
22. Remove the engine support fixture.
23. Connect the battery negative cable.

OIL PRESSURE SENSOR/SWITCH

REMOVAL & INSTALLATION

2.4L Engine

See Figures 378 and 379.

1. Remove the starter.
2. Disconnect the engine wiring harness electrical connector (2) from the oil pressure switch.
3. Remove the engine oil pressure switch.

To install:

4. Install the engine oil pressure switch. Tighten the switch to 16 ft. lbs. (22 Nm).
5. Connect the engine wiring harness electrical connector to the oil pressure switch.
6. Install the starter.

Fig. 378 Disconnect the engine wiring harness electrical connector (2) from the oil pressure switch

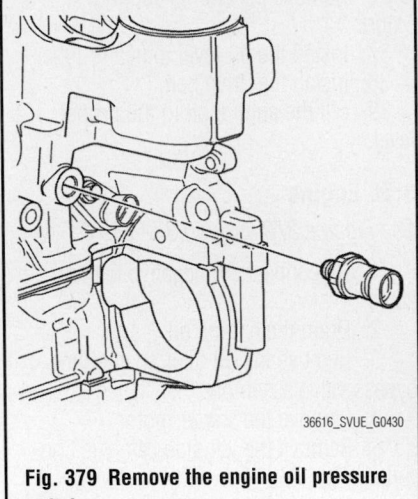

Fig. 379 Remove the engine oil pressure switch

3.5L Engine

See Figure 380.

1. Raise and suitably support the vehicle.
2. Disconnect the engine oil pressure sensor/switch electrical connector.
3. Remove the engine oil pressure sensor/switch.

To install:

4. Install the engine oil pressure sensor/switch and tighten to 12 ft. lbs. (16 Nm).
5. Connect the engine oil pressure sensor/switch electrical connector.

3.6L Engine

See Figure 381.

1. Turn the ignition OFF.
2. Disconnect the oil pressure sensor electrical connector.

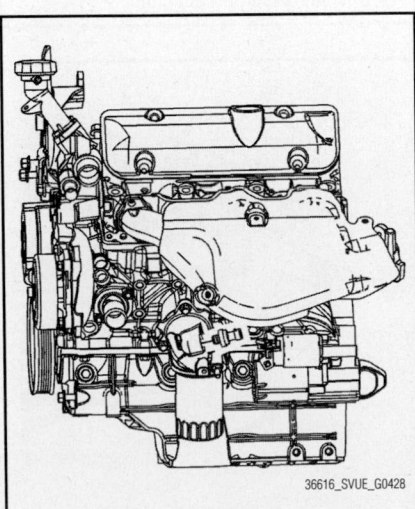

Fig. 380 Remove the engine oil pressure sensor/switch

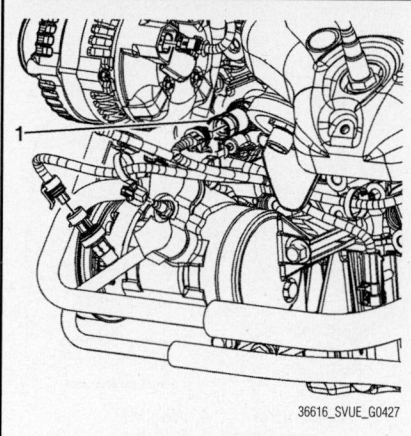

Fig. 381 Remove the oil pressure sensor (1)

3. Remove the oil pressure sensor (1).

To install:

4. Install the oil pressure sensor and tighten to 15 ft. lbs. (20 Nm).
5. Connect the oil pressure sensor electrical connector.

OIL PUMP

REMOVAL & INSTALLATION

3.5L Engine

See Figure 382.

1. Remove the oil pan.
2. Remove the oil pump bolt.
3. Remove the oil pump and the oil pump drive shaft.

To install:

➡ Rotate the oil pump drive shaft as necessary in order to obtain the

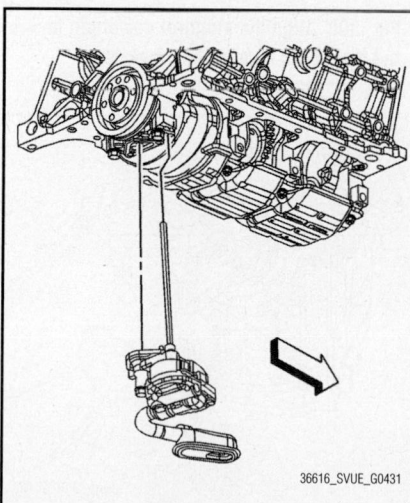

Fig. 382 Remove the oil pump and the oil pump drive shaft

engagement with the oil pump drive unit.

4. Install the oil pump drive shaft and the oil pump.
5. Install the oil pump bolt and tighten to 30 ft. lbs. (41 Nm).
6. Install the oil pan.

3.6L Engine

See Figure 383.

1. Remove the oil pump bolts.
2. Remove the oil pump.

To install:

3. Align the oil pump drive gear with the crankshaft flats and install the oil pump to the engine block.
4. Align the pump body with the mounting holes in the cylinder block.
5. Install the oil pump bolts. Tighten the oil pump bolts to 17 ft. lbs. (23 Nm).

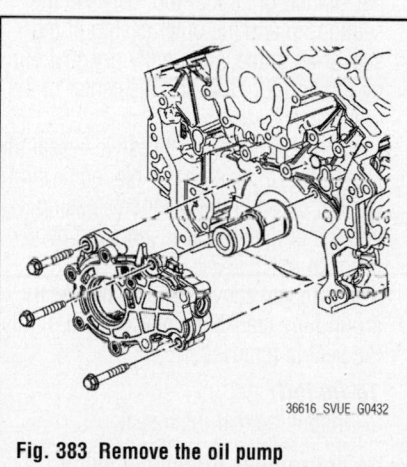

Fig. 383 Remove the oil pump

INSPECTION

➡ There are no serviceable components within the oil pump. Disassemble the pump only to diagnose an oiling concern. A disassembled oil pump must not be reused. A disassembled oil pump must be replaced.

PISTON AND RING

POSITIONING
See Figure 384.

➡ Use a piston ring expander to install the piston rings. The rings may be damaged if expanded more than necessary.

1. Install the following components of the oil control ring assembly (bottom ring):
    a. The expander
    b. The lower oil control ring
    c. The upper control ring

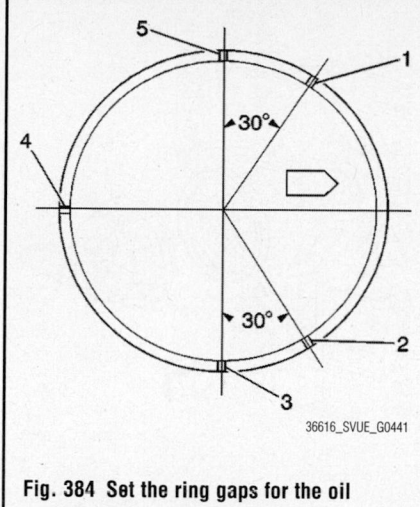

Fig. 384 Set the ring gaps for the oil control, second and top ring

2. Install the lower compression ring (second ring). Place the manufacturer's mark facing up.
3. Install the upper compression ring (top ring).
4. Once the rings are installed, set the ring gaps for the oil control, second and top ring as follows. Use the piston location arrow for reference.
    a. Lower oil control ring—position 1
    b. Upper oil control ring—position 2
    c. Top Ring—position 3
    d. Oil control ring expander—position 4
    e. Second ring—position 5

REAR MAIN SEAL

REMOVAL & INSTALLATION

2.4L Engine

See Figures 385 and 386.

1. Remove the flywheel.

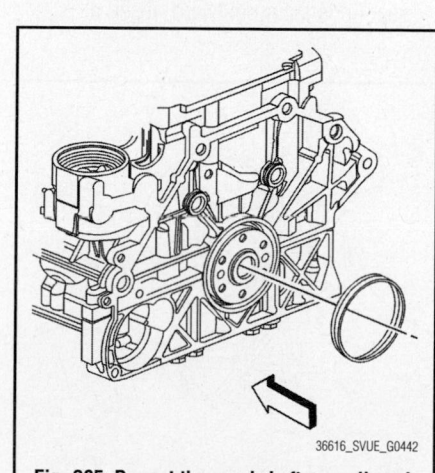

Fig. 385 Pry out the crankshaft rear oil seal

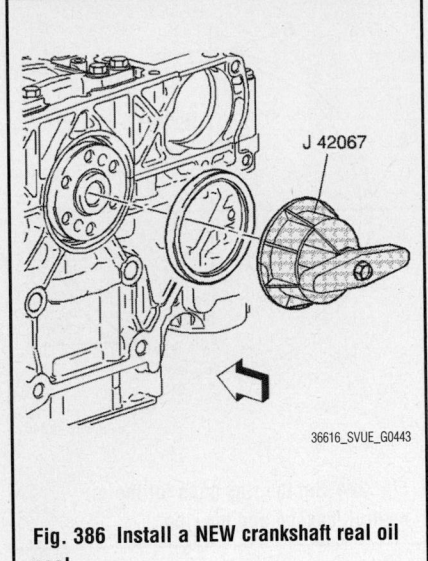

Fig. 386 Install a NEW crankshaft real oil seal

➡️ **Do not damage the outside diameter of the crankshaft or chamber with any tool.**

2. Pry out the crankshaft rear oil seal using a flat-bladed tool.

To install:

3. Using the J 42067, install a NEW crankshaft real oil seal.
4. Install the flywheel.

3.5L Engine

See Figures 387 through 394.

1. Remove the engine flywheel.
2. Remove the crankshaft rear main oil seal.

➡️ **Do not nick the crankshaft sealing surface when removing the seal.**

a. Remove crankshaft rear main oil seal using one of the following techniques:

b. If removing a NEW style seal— seal lip is facing outward, insert a

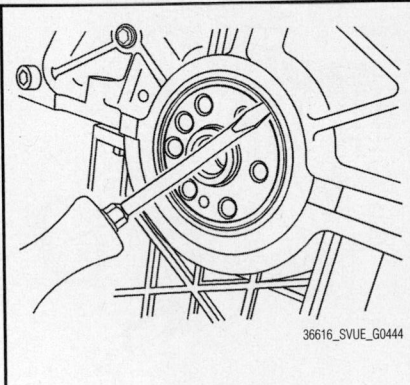

Fig. 387 NEW style seal removal

flat-bladed or similar tool between the sealing lip and the outer casing of the seal at an angle, and gently pry seal out by moving tool towards the center of the crankshaft.

c. If removing an OLD style—seal lip faces inward, insert a flat-bladed or similar tool between the outer seal casing and the engine block casting and gently pry seal out.

d. Repeat above steps as necessary around the crankshaft rear oil seal, until the seal is removed.

To install:

3. Install the rear main seal.

➡️ **Do not remove protective nylon sleeve prior to installation. The rear main oil seal installation tool is designed to install the rear main seal with the protective sleeve in place. Never apply or use any oil, lubricants or sealing compounds on the crankshaft rear main oil seal.**

➡️ **Clean the crankshaft sealing surface with a clean, lint free towel. Inspect lead-in edge of crankshaft for burrs/sharp edges that could damage the rear main oil seal. Remove burrs/sharp edges with crocus cloth before proceeding.**

a. The rear main oil seal installer (EN-48108) tool has a unique design to allow the technician to easily install the rear main seal squarely to the correct depth and direction. Before proceeding with installation, review the illustration to become familiar with the following components:

- Mandrel (1)
- Drive Drum (2)

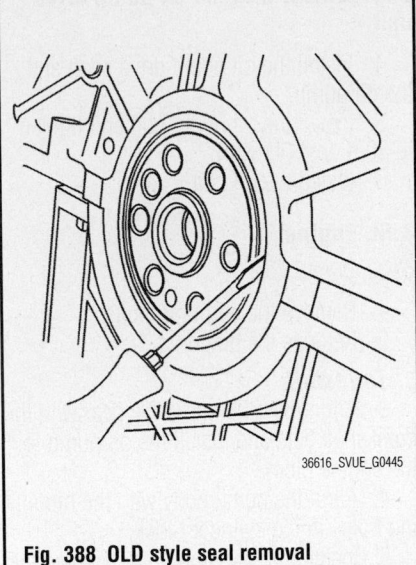

Fig. 388 OLD style seal removal

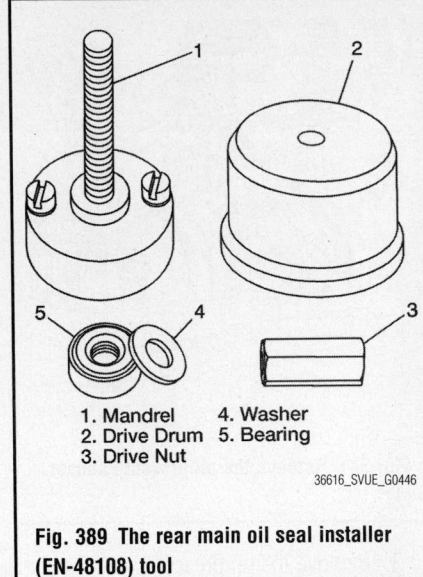

1. Mandrel   4. Washer
2. Drive Drum   5. Bearing
3. Drive Nut

Fig. 389 The rear main oil seal installer (EN-48108) tool

- Drive Nut (3)
- Washer (4)
- Bearing (5)

b. Align the mandrel dowel pin to the dowel pin hole in the crankshaft.

c. Using a large flat blade screwdriver, tighten the two mandrel screws to

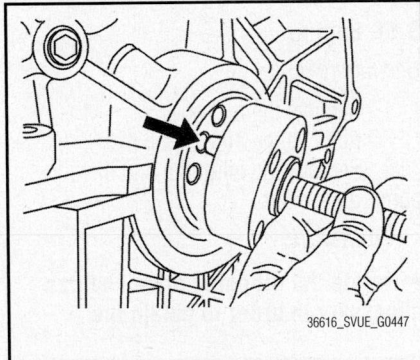

Fig. 390 Align the mandrel dowel pin to the dowel pin hole in the crankshaft

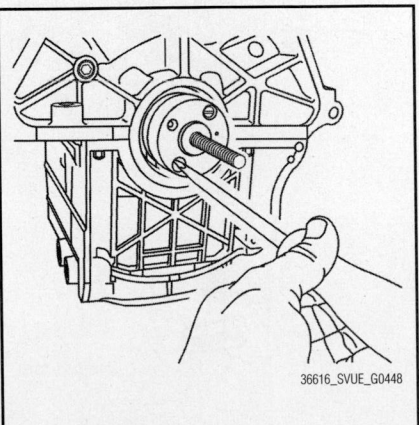

Fig. 391 Tighten the two mandrel screws to the crankshaft

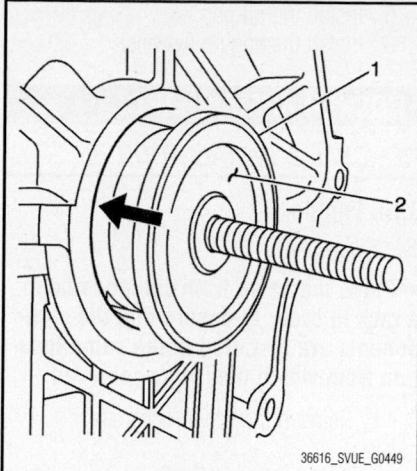

Fig. 392 Install the rear main seal (1), with the protective nylon sleeve attached (2)

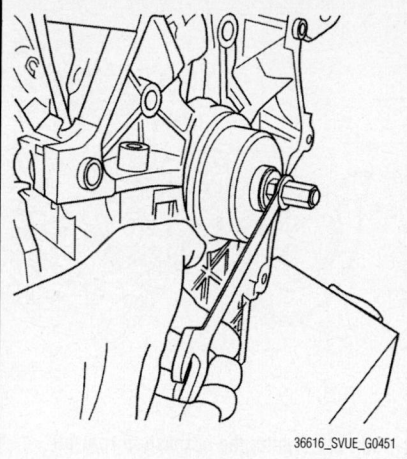

Fig. 394 Turn the drive nut on the mandrel, which will push the seal into the engine block bore

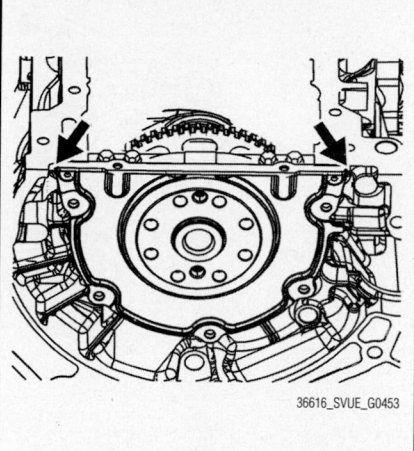

Fig. 396 Use the pry points located at the edge of the crankshaft rear oil seal housing to separate the RTV sealant

the crankshaft, ensuring the mandrel is snug to the crankshaft hub.

➡ **The seal will only fit one way onto the mandrel, and if properly installed, will center on a step that protrudes from the center of the mandrel.**

d. Install the rear main seal (1), with the protective nylon sleeve attached (2), onto the mandrel.

e. Install the outer drive drum onto the mandrel.

f. Install the bearing, washer, and the drive nut onto the threaded shaft.

g. Using a wrench, turn the drive nut on the mandrel, which will push the seal into the engine block bore.

h. Turn the wrench until the drive drum is snug and flush against the engine block.

i. Loosen and remove the drive nut,

washer, bearing and drive drum. Discard the nylon plastic seal protector.

j. Verify that the seal has seated properly.

k. Use a flat blade screwdriver to remove the two attachment screws from the mandrel and remove the mandrel from the crankshaft hub.

4. Install the engine flywheel.

3.6L Engine

See Figures 395 through 403.

1. Remove the engine flywheel.
2. Remove the oil pan.
3. Remove the crankshaft rear oil seal and housing.

a. Remove the crankshaft rear oil seal housing bolts.

b. Use the pry points located at the edge of the crankshaft rear oil seal housing to separate the RTV sealant.

c. Remove and discard the crankshaft rear oil seal housing.

To install:

4. Install the crankshaft rear oil seal and housing.

a. Install the guide pins from the EN 46109 into the 2 crankshaft rear oil seal housing corner bolt holes of the engine block.

b. Install the EN-47839 Crankshaft Rear Oil Seal Installation Tool with the J 42183 Handle (1, 2) onto the rear of the crankshaft flange.

c. Place a bead of RTV sealant, GM P/N 12378521 (Canadian P/N 88901148) or equivalent, to the NEW crankshaft rear oil seal housing as shown (1).

➡ **DO NOT allow any engine oil on the area where the crankshaft rear oil seal housing is to be installed.**

Fig. 393 Install the outer drive drum onto the mandrel

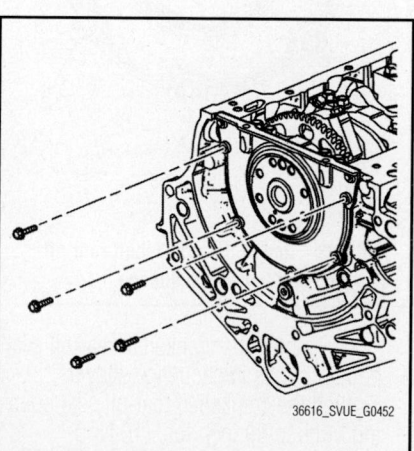

Fig. 395 Remove the crankshaft rear oil seal housing bolts

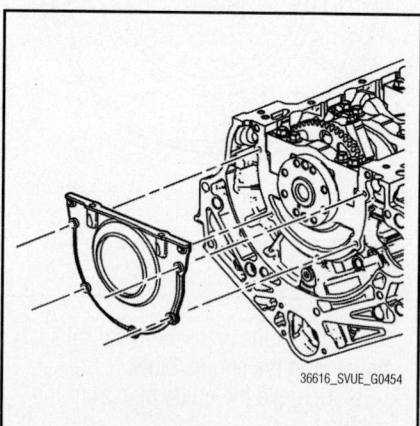

Fig. 397 Remove and discard the crankshaft rear oil seal housing

Fig. 398 Install the guide pins

Fig. 399 Install crankshaft rear oil seal installation tool and handle

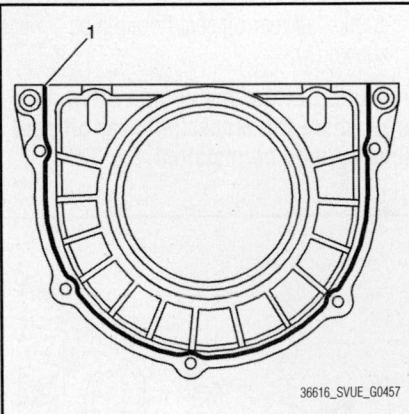

Fig. 400 Place a bead of RTV sealant as shown (1)

d. Install the crankshaft rear oil seal housing to the engine block.

e. Remove the guide pins from the engine block.

f. Install the crankshaft rear oil seal housing bolts.

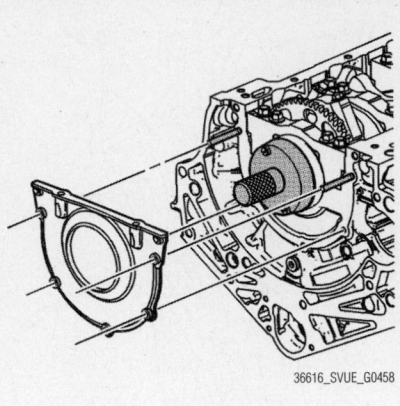

Fig. 401 Install the crankshaft rear oil seal housing to the engine block

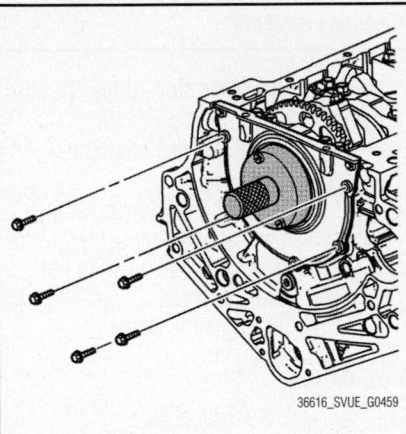

Fig. 402 Install the crankshaft rear oil seal housing bolts

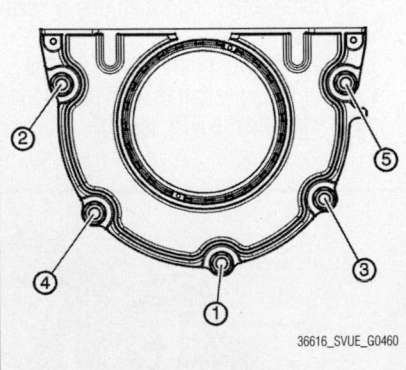

Fig. 403 Tighten the crankshaft rear oil seal housing bolts in sequence

g. Tighten the crankshaft rear oil seal housing bolts in sequence shown. Tighten the crankshaft rear oil seal housing bolts to 89 inch lbs. (10 Nm).

h. Remove the EN-47839 and J 42183 (1, 2) from the crankshaft flange.

5. Install the oil pan.
6. Install the engine flywheel.

ROCKER ARMS/SHAFTS

REMOVAL & INSTALLATION

3.5L Engine

See Figure 404.

➡Place the valve train components in a rack in order to ensure that the components are installed in the same location from which they were removed.

1. Remove the valve rocker arm cover(s).
2. Loosen the valve rocker arm bolts.
3. Remove the rocker arms.
4. Remove the pushrods.
   a. The intake push rods measure 5.75 inches (146.0 mm).
   b. The exhaust push rods measure 6.0 inches (152.5 mm).

To install:

5. Coat the ends of the pushrods using prelube.
6. Install the pushrods.
   a. The intake pushrods are identified with yellow stripes.
   b. The exhaust pushrods are identified with blue stripes.
7. Ensure that the pushrods seat in the lifter bore.
8. Coat the rocker arm friction surfaces using prelube.

➡Shims (88894006) may be required under the valve rocker arm pedestals if reconditioning has been performed on the cylinder head or its components.

9. Install the rocker arms.
10. Install the rocker arm bolts.
11. Install the valve rocker arm cover(s).

Fig. 404 Remove the rocker arms

3.6L Engine

See Figures 405 and 406.

1. Remove the applicable camshaft(s).
2. Remove the rocker arms.

➡**If the rocker arms are to be reused, keep in order so they can be reinstalled in the same position.**

3. Remove the valve lifters (SHLAs) from the cylinder head.

➡**If the lifters are to be reused, keep in order so they can be reinstalled in the same position.**

4. Clean and inspect the camshaft(s) lifter(s) and the rocker arm(s). Repair or replace as necessary.

To install:

➡**Do not stroke/cycle the stationary hydraulic lash adjuster plunger without oil in the lower pressure chamber. Do not allow the stationary hydraulic lash adjuster to tip over, plunger down, after the oil fill.**

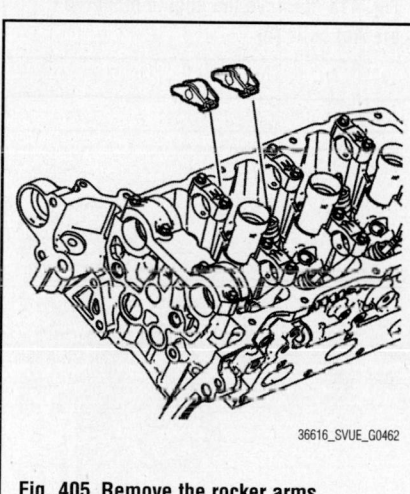

Fig. 405 Remove the rocker arms

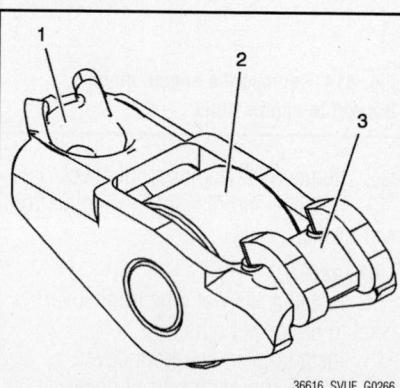

Fig. 406 Pivot pocket (1), roller (2) and valve slot (3) areas of the camshaft followers

5. Fill the Stationary Hydraulic Lash Adjuster (SHLA) with clean engine oil GM P/N 12378006 or equivalent. Take precautions to prevent scratching the pivot sphere area of the SHLA.
6. Lubricate the SHLA bores in the cylinder head with clean engine oil GM P/N 12378006 or equivalent.
7. Install the SHLAs in the cylinder head.
8. Apply a liberal amount of lubricant GM P/N 12345501 (Canadian P/N 992704) or equivalent to the SHLA pivot spheres.
9. Install the rocker arms.
10. Apply a liberal amount of lubricant GM P/N 12345501 (Canadian P/N 992704) or equivalent to the pivot pocket (1), roller (2) and valve slot (3) areas of the camshaft followers.
11. Install the applicable camshaft(s).

TIMING CHAIN COVER AND SEAL

REMOVAL & INSTALLATION

2.4L Engine, Except Hybrid

See Figures 407 through 412.

1. Remove the drive belt tensioner.
2. Remove the crankshaft balancer.
3. Remove the air cleaner assembly.
4. Install the engine support fixture.
5. Remove the engine mount to bracket bolts.
6. Remove the engine mount to side rail nuts.

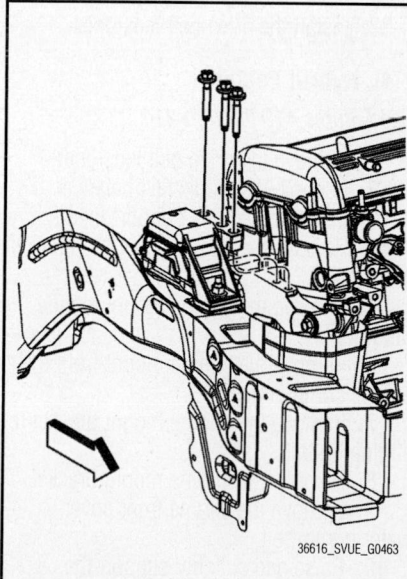

Fig. 407 Remove the engine mount to bracket bolts

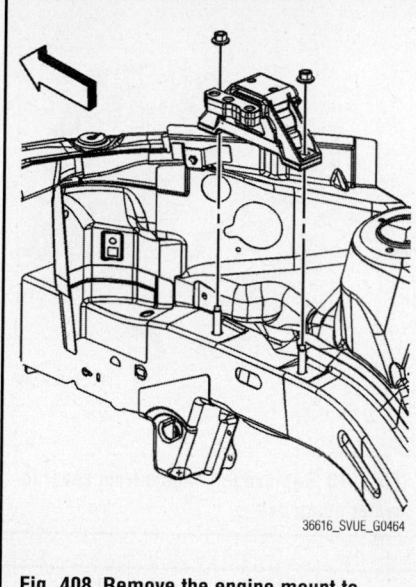

Fig. 408 Remove the engine mount to side rail nuts

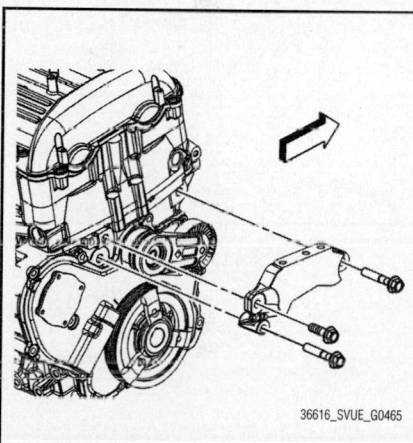

Fig. 409 Remove the engine mount bracket to engine bolts

7. Remove the engine mount from the engine compartment.
8. Remove the engine mount bracket to engine bolts.
9. Remove the engine mount bracket.
10. Remove the engine front cover to water pump bolt.
11. Raise and suitably support the vehicle.
12. Remove the engine front cover bolts.
13. Remove the engine front cover.
14. Remove and discard the engine front cover gasket.

To install:

15. Install a NEW engine front cover gasket to the dowel pins.
16. Install the engine front cover.

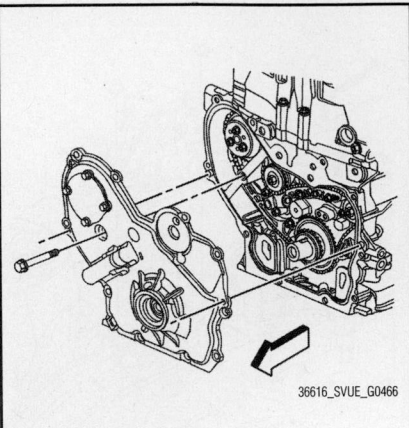

Fig. 410 Remove the engine front cover to water pump bolt

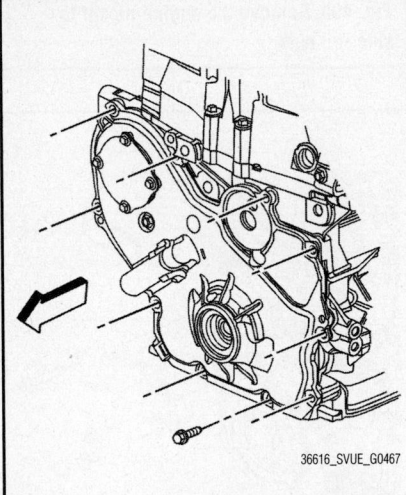

Fig. 411 Remove the engine front cover bolts

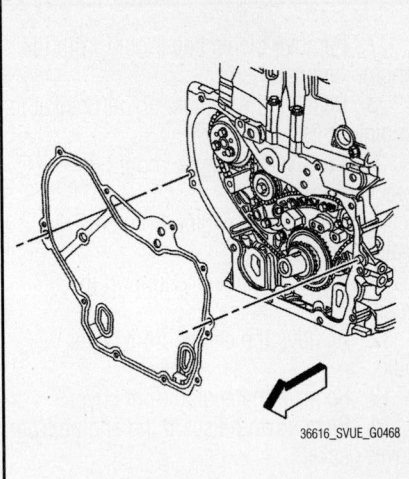

Fig. 412 Remove and discard the engine front cover gasket

17. Install the engine front cover bolts. Tighten the bolts to 18 ft. lbs. (25 Nm).

18. Lower the vehicle.

19. Install the engine front cover to water pump bolt. Tighten the bolt to 18 ft. lbs. (25 Nm).

20. Position the engine mount bracket to the engine.

21. Install the engine mount bracket bolts in the following locations:
- The long bolts in the forward and lower rear holes
- The short bolt in the upper rear hole

22. Tighten the engine mount bracket bolts in the following sequence:
   a. Upper rear
   b. Lower rear
   c. Forward

23. Tighten the bolts to 37 ft. lbs. (50 Nm).

24. Install the engine mount to the engine compartment.

25. Install the engine mount to side rail nuts. Tighten the nuts to 74 ft. lbs. (100 Nm).

26. Install the engine mount to bracket bolts.

27. Tighten the engine mount to bracket bolts in the following sequence:
   a. Middle
   b. Rear
   c. Front

28. Tighten the bolts to 37 ft. lbs. (50 Nm).

29. Remove the engine support fixture.

30. Install the air cleaner assembly.

31. Install the crankshaft balancer.

32. Install the drive belt tensioner.

2.4L Hybrid Engine

See Figures 410 through 414.

1. Remove the drive belt tensioner.

2. Remove the crankshaft balancer.

3. Install the engine support fixture.

4. Remove the engine mount to bracket bolts (2).

5. Remove the engine mount to side rail nuts (1).

6. Remove the engine mount from the engine compartment.

7. Remove the engine mount bracket to engine bolts.

8. Remove the engine mount bracket.

9. Remove the engine front cover to water pump bolt.

10. Raise and suitably support the vehicle.

11. Remove the engine front cover bolts.

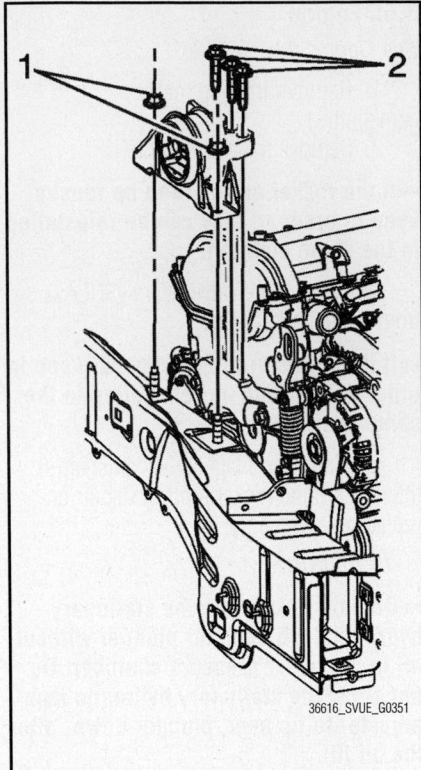

Fig. 413 Remove the engine mount to bracket bolts (2)

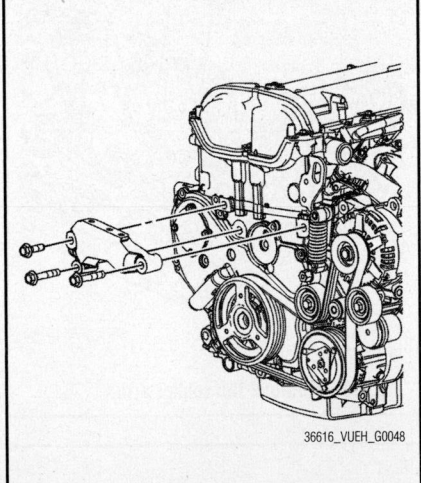

Fig. 414 Remove the engine mount bracket to engine bolts

12. Remove the engine front cover.

13. Remove and discard the engine front cover gasket.

To install:

14. Install a NEW engine front cover gasket to the dowel pins.

15. Install the engine front cover.

16. Install the engine front cover bolts. Tighten the bolts to 18 ft. lbs. (25 Nm).

17. Lower the vehicle.

18. Install the engine front cover to water pump bolt. Tighten the bolt to 18 ft. lbs. (25 Nm).

19. Position the engine mount bracket to the engine.

20. Install the engine mount bracket bolts in the following locations:

- The long bolts in the forward and lower rear holes
- The short bolt in the upper rear hole

21. Tighten the engine mount bracket bolts to 74 ft. lbs. (100 Nm) in the following sequence:

- Upper left
- Lower left
- Right

22. Install the engine mount to the engine compartment.

23. Install the engine mount to side rail nuts. Tighten the nuts to 74 ft. lbs. (100 Nm).

24. Install the engine mount to bracket bolts.

25. Tighten the engine mount to bracket bolts to 37 ft. lbs. (50 Nm) in the following sequence:

- Middle
- Rear
- Front

26. Remove the engine support fixture.

27. Install the crankshaft balancer.

28. Install the drive belt tensioner.

3.5L Engine

See Figures 415 and 416.

1. Drain the cooling system.
2. Remove the drive belt tensioner.
3. Remove the crankshaft balancer.
4. Remove the crankshaft position actuator magnet.
5. Remove the thermostat housing.

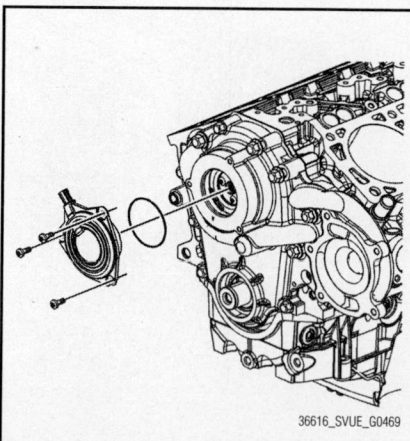

Fig. 415 Remove the crankshaft position actuator magnet

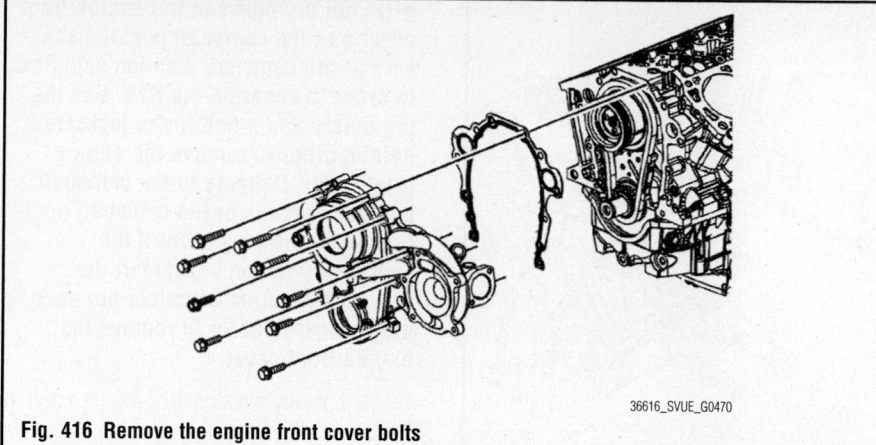

36616_SVUE_G0470

Fig. 416 Remove the engine front cover bolts

6. Remove the water pump.
7. Drain the engine oil.
8. Remove the oil pan.
9. Remove the engine front cover bolts.
10. Remove the engine front cover.
11. Remove the engine front cover gasket.
12. Clean and transfer any parts as needed.

To install:

13. Install the engine front cover gasket.
14. Install the engine front cover.
15. Install the engine front cover bolts. Tighten the bolts to 18 ft. lbs. (25 Nm).
16. Install the oil pan.
17. Install the water pump.
18. Install the thermostat housing.
19. Install the crankshaft position actuator magnet.
20. Install the crankshaft balancer.
21. Install the drive belt tensioner.
22. Fill the cooling system.
23. Fill the engine with oil.

3.6L Engine

See Figures 417 through 427.

1. Remove the camshaft position sensor bolts.
2. Remove the camshaft position sensors.
3. Remove the camshaft position actuator valve bolts.

➡The camshaft position actuator valves must be removed from the front cover prior to front cover removal or damage to the valves may occur.

4. Remove the camshaft position actuator valves from the front cover.

➡The front cover and deadener may vary in appearance depending on application but are retained by the same number of bolts.

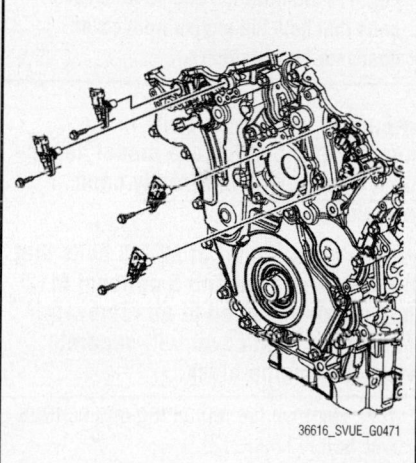

36616_SVUE_G0471

Fig. 417 Remove the camshaft position sensor bolts

5. Remove the engine front cover bolts that hold the engine front cover deadener into position.

6. Remove the engine front cover deadener.

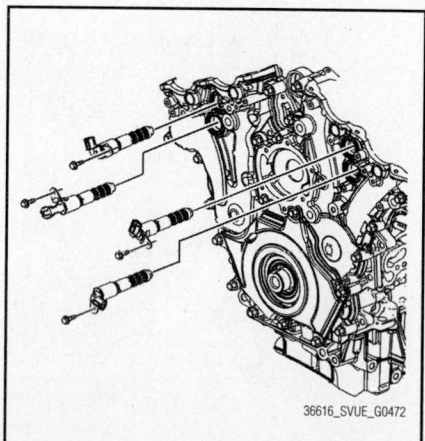

36616_SVUE_G0472

Fig. 418 Remove the camshaft position actuator valve bolts

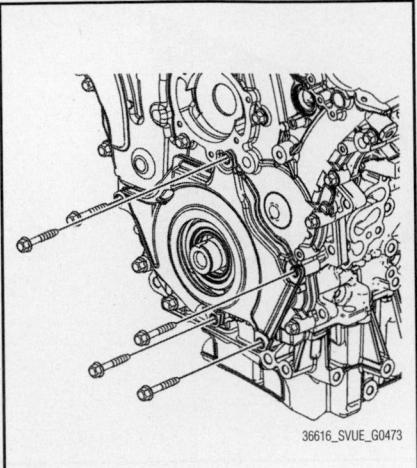

Fig. 419 Remove the engine front cover bolts that hold the engine front cover deadener into position

➡Engine front cover bolts in the number (2) location are model dependent and may have already been removed.

➡There are a total of 22 M8 bolts that must be removed and 3 optional M12 bolts that may need to be removed before the front cover will separate from the engine block.

7. Remove the remaining engine front cover bolts (1) and (2).

➡Do not use the jackscrew hole without first removing all engine front cover bolts. Failure to remove all engine front cover bolts before using the jackscrew hole could result in damage to components.

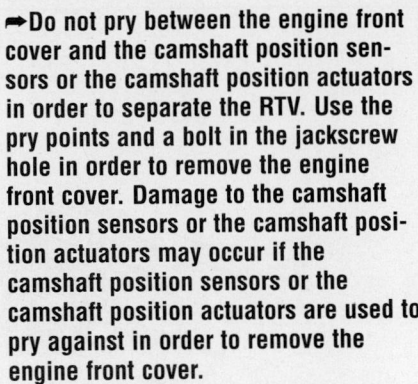

➡Do not pry between the engine front cover and the camshaft position sensors or the camshaft position actuators in order to separate the RTV. Use the pry points and a bolt in the jackscrew hole in order to remove the engine front cover. Damage to the camshaft position sensors or the camshaft position actuators may occur if the camshaft position sensors or the camshaft position actuators are used to pry against in order to remove the engine front cover.

8. Loosely install a 10 x 1.5 mm bolt in the jackscrew hole (1).

9. Using the pry points (2) located at the edge of the front cover and the jackscrew, separate the Room Temperature Vulcanizing (RTV) sealant.

10. Remove the engine front cover.

To install:

11. Install the guide pins from the EN 46109 into the cylinder block positions as shown.

12. Install the NEW engine front cover to cylinder block seal.

13. Place a bead of RTV sealant, GM P/N 12378521 (Canadian P/N 88901148) or equivalent, on the engine front cover as shown (1).

14. Place the engine front cover onto the guide pins and slide into position.

15. Remove the guide pins from the cylinder block.

16. Install the engine front cover deadener.

➡The front cover and deadener may vary in appearance depending on application but are retained by the same number of bolts.

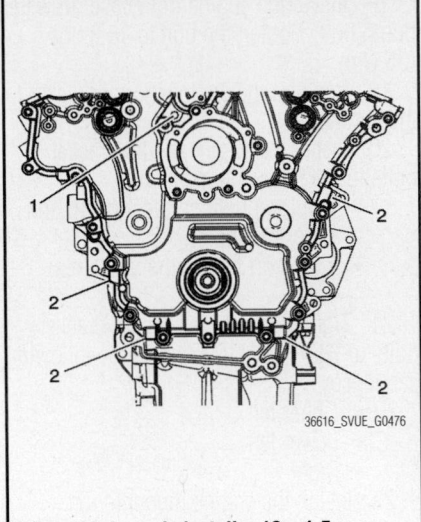

Fig. 422 Loosely install a 10 x 1.5 mm bolt in the jackscrew hole (1)

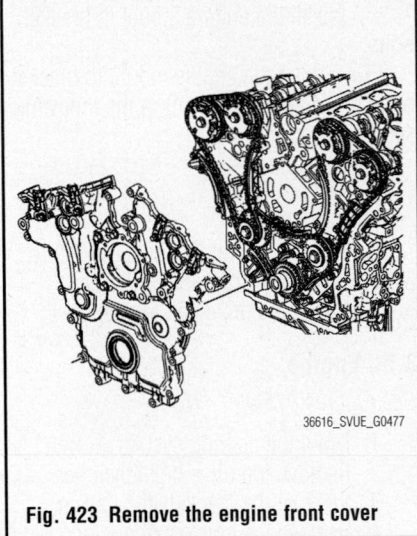

Fig. 423 Remove the engine front cover

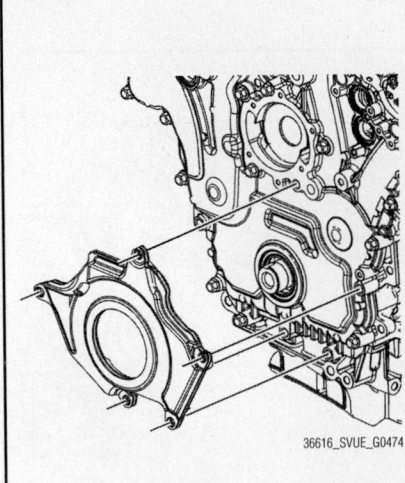

Fig. 420 Remove the engine front cover deadener

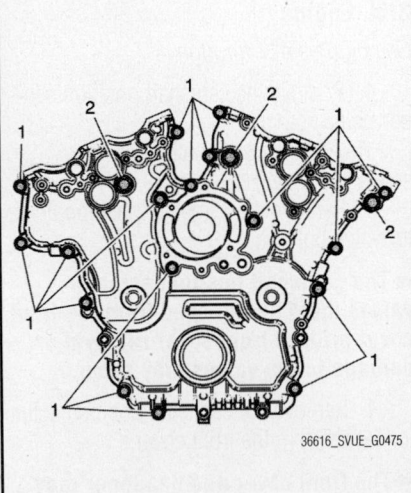

Fig. 421 Remove the remaining engine front cover bolts (1) and (2)

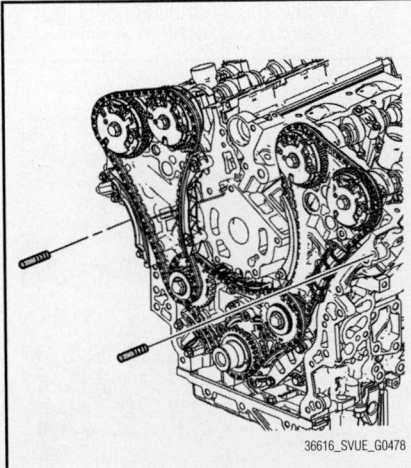

Fig. 424 Install the guide pins from the EN 46109 into the cylinder block positions as shown

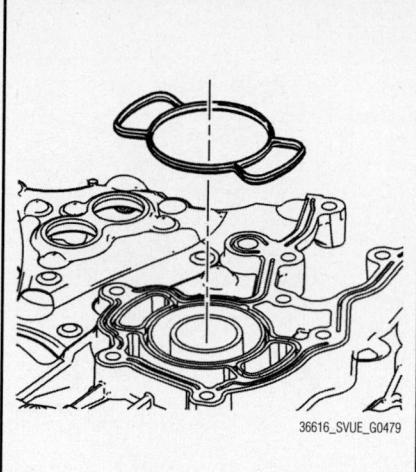

Fig. 425 Install the NEW engine front cover to cylinder block seal

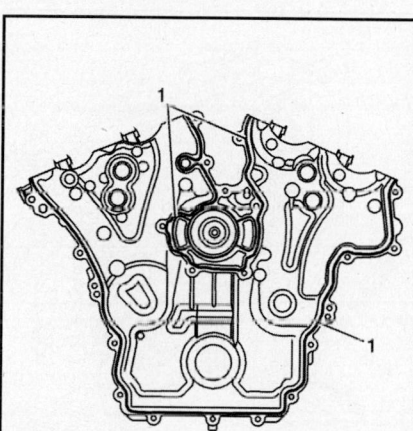

Fig. 426 Place a bead of RTV sealant on the engine front cover as shown (1)

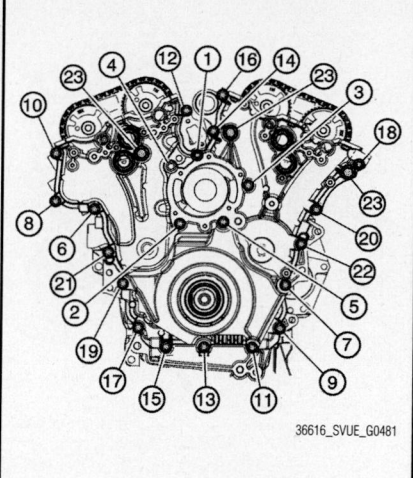

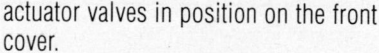

Fig. 427 Tighten the engine front cover bolts (1–22) in the sequence shown

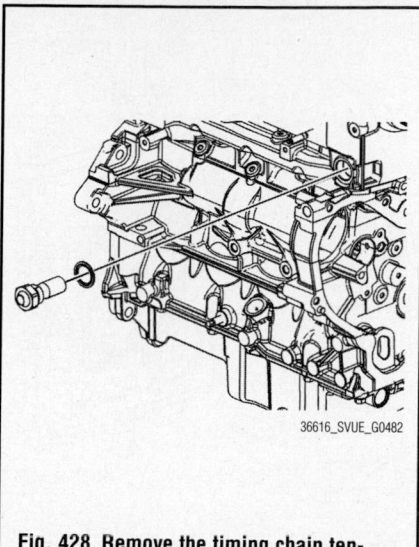

Fig. 428 Remove the timing chain tensioner

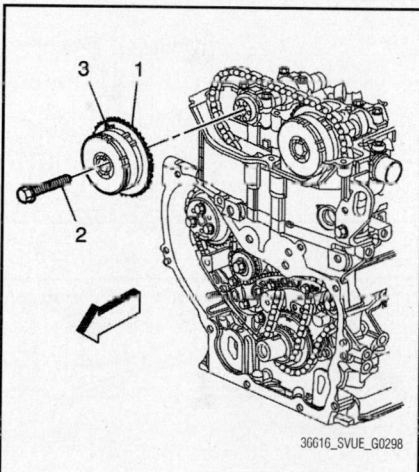

Fig. 429 Remove and discard the exhaust camshaft actuator bolt (2)

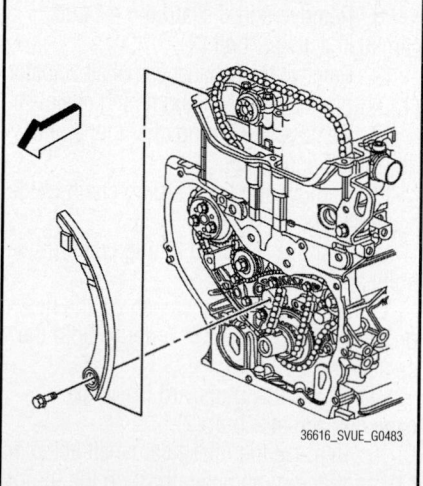

Fig. 430 Remove the timing chain tensioner guide bolt and guide

17. Loosely install the engine front cover bolts to hold the engine front cover deadener into position.

18. Loosely install the remaining engine front cover bolts.

➡ **Engine front cover bolts in the number (23) location are model dependent and may not apply.**

19. Tighten the engine front cover bolts (1–22) in the sequence shown.

   a. Tighten the engine front cover bolts (1–22) in sequence shown to 14 ft. lbs. (20 Nm).

   b. Tighten the engine front cover bolts (1–22) a second pass in sequence an additional 60 degrees.

20. Tighten the engine front cover bolts (23). Tighten the engine front cover bolts (23) to 48 ft. lbs. (65 Nm).

21. Place the camshaft position actuator valves in position on the front cover.

22. Install the camshaft position actuator valve bolts. Tighten the camshaft position actuator valve bolts to 89 inch lbs. (10 Nm).

23. Install NEW O-rings on the camshaft position sensor.

24. Place the camshaft position sensors in position on the front cover.

25. Install the camshaft position sensor bolts. Tighten the camshaft position sensor bolts to 89 inch lbs. (10 Nm).

TIMING CHAIN AND SPROCKETS

REMOVAL & INSTALLATION

2.4L Engine

See Figures 428 through 447.

1. Remove the No. 1 cylinder spark plug.

2. Rotate the crankshaft in the engine rotational direction clockwise, until the number 1 piston is at Top Dead Center (TDC) on the exhaust stroke.

3. Remove the camshaft cover.

4. Remove the engine front cover.

5. Remove the upper timing chain guide bolts and guide.

➡ **The timing chain tensioner must be removed to unload chain tension before the timing chain is removed. If it is not, the timing chain will become cocked and it will be difficult to remove.**

6. Remove the timing chain tensioner.

7. Install a 23 mm wrench on the hex on the exhaust camshaft in order to hold the camshaft.

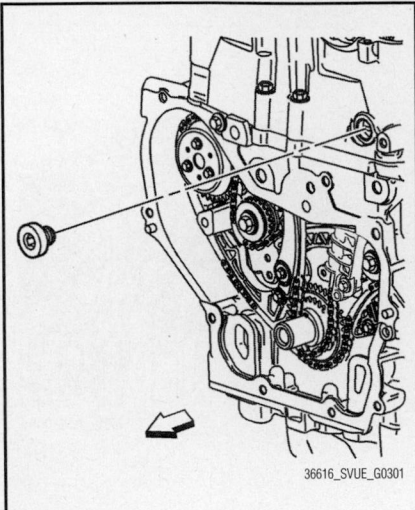

Fig. 431 Remove the fixed timing chain guide access plug

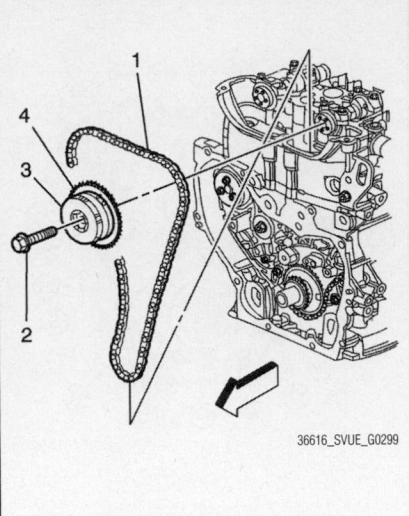

Fig. 433 Remove and discard the intake camshaft actuator bolt (2)

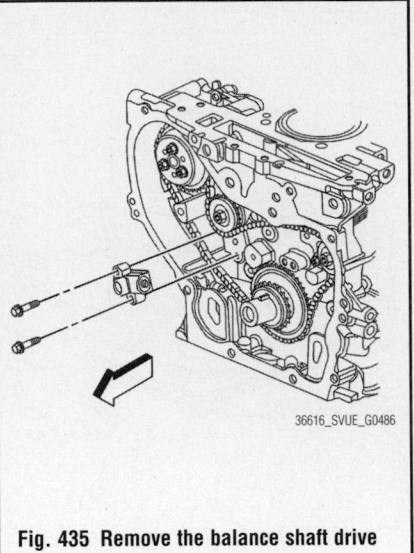

Fig. 435 Remove the balance shaft drive chain tensioner bolts and tensioner

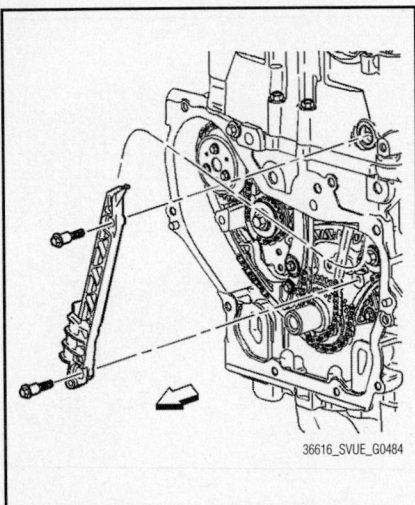

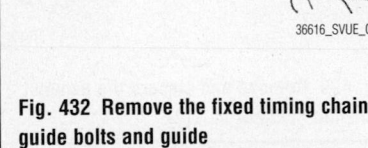

Fig. 432 Remove the fixed timing chain guide bolts and guide

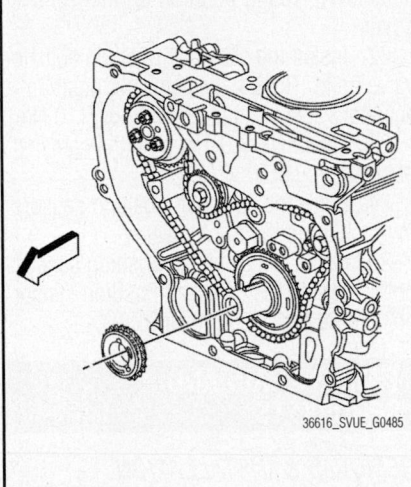

Fig. 434 Remove the timing chain crankshaft sprocket

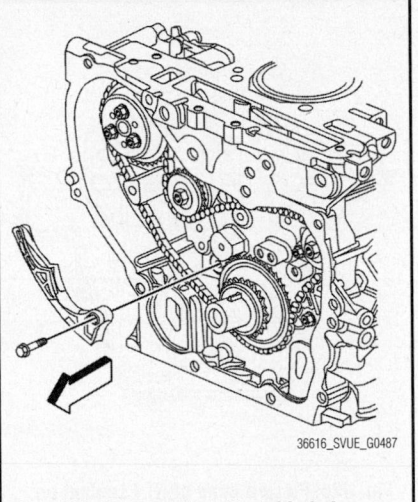

Fig. 436 Remove the adjustable balance shaft chain guide bolt and guide

8. Remove and discard the exhaust camshaft actuator bolt (2).

9. Remove the exhaust camshaft actuator (1, 3) from the camshaft and timing chain.

10. Remove the timing chain tensioner guide bolt and guide.

11. Remove the fixed timing chain guide access plug.

12. Remove the fixed timing chain guide bolts and guide.

13. Install a 23 mm wrench on the hex on the intake camshaft in order to hold the camshaft.

14. Remove and discard the intake camshaft actuator bolt (2).

15. Remove the intake camshaft actuator (3), and the timing chain through the top of the cylinder head.

16. Remove the timing chain crankshaft sprocket.

17. If replacing the balance shaft timing chain and sprocket, perform the following steps, if not proceed to step 34 in the installation procedure.

18. Remove the balance shaft drive chain tensioner bolts and tensioner.

19. Remove the adjustable balance shaft chain guide bolt and guide.

20. Remove the small balance shaft drive chain guide bolts and guide.

21. Remove the upper balance shaft drive chain guide bolts and guide.

➡**It may ease removal of the balance shaft drive chain to get all the slack in the chain between the crankshaft and water pump sprockets.**

22. Remove the balance shaft drive chain (7).

23. Remove the balance shaft drive sprocket.

To install:

24. If replacing the balance shaft timing chain, perform the following steps, if not proceed to step 34.

25. Install the balance shaft drive sprocket.

➡**If the balance shafts are not properly timed to the engine, the engine may vibrate or make noise.**

26. Install the balance shaft drive chain with the colored link lined up with the marks on the balance shaft sprockets and the balance shaft drive sprocket.

27. There are three colored links on the chain. Two are chrome and one is copper. Use the following steps in order to line up the links with the sprockets.

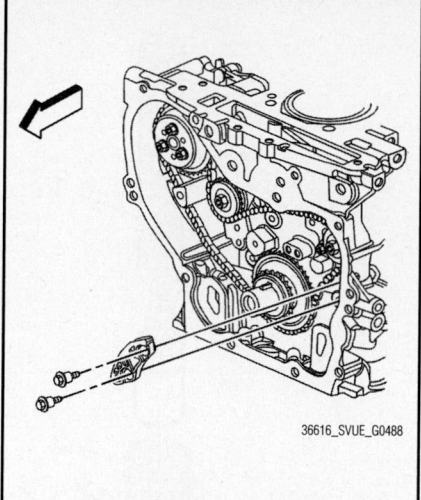

Fig. 437 Remove the small balance shaft drive chain guide bolts and guide

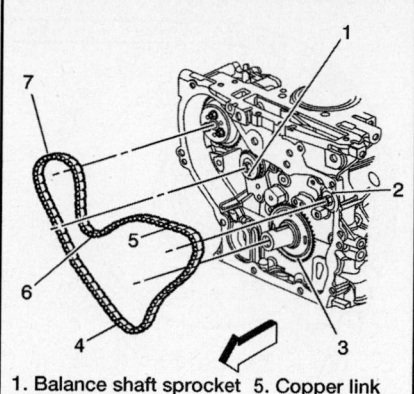

1. Balance shaft sprocket
2. Timing mark
3. Timing mark
4. Chrome link
5. Copper link
6. Chrome link
7. Chain

Fig. 439 Remove the balance shaft drive chain (7)

Fig. 441 Timing chain drive sprocket timing mark location

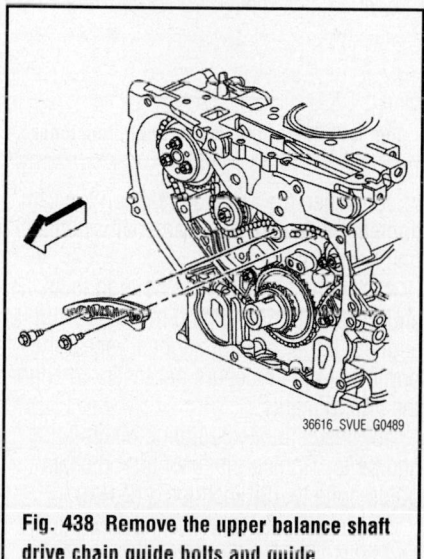

Fig. 438 Remove the upper balance shaft drive chain guide bolts and guide

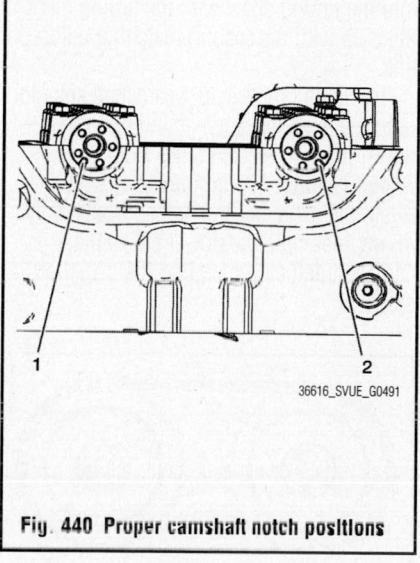

Fig. 440 Proper camshaft notch positions

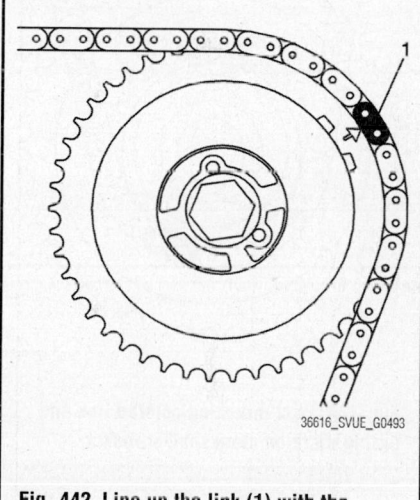

Fig. 442 Line up the link (1) with the actuators

a. Place the copper link so that it lines up with the timing mark on the intake side balance shaft sprocket.

b. Working clockwise around the chain, place the chrome link in line with the timing mark on the balance shaft drive sprocket. (Approximately 6 o'clock position on the sprocket).

c. Place the chain on the water pump drive sprocket. The alignment is not critical.

d. Align the last chrome link with the timing mark on the exhaust side balance shaft drive sprocket.

28. Install the upper balance shaft drive chain guide and bolts. Tighten the bolts to 11 ft. lbs. (15 Nm).

29. Install the small balance shaft drive chain guide and bolts. Tighten the bolts to 11 ft. lbs. (15 Nm).

30. Install the adjustable balance shaft chain guide and bolt. Tighten the bolt to 89 inch lbs. (10 Nm).

31. Reset the timing chain tensioner by performing the following steps:

a. Rotate the tensioner plunger 90 degrees in its bore and compress the plunger.

b. Rotate the tensioner back to the original 12 o'clock position and insert a paper clip through the hole in the plunger body and into the hose in the tensioner plunger.

32. Install the balance shaft drive chain tensioner and bolts. Tighten the bolts to 89 inch lbs. (10 Nm).

33. Remove the paper clip from the balance shaft drive chain tensioner.

34. Ensure the intake camshaft notch is in the 5 o'clock position (2) and the exhaust

camshaft notch is in the 7 o'clock position (1). The number 1 piston should be at Top Dead Center (TDC), crankshaft key at 12 o'clock.

35. Install the timing chain drive sprocket to the crankshaft with the timing mark in the 5 o'clock position and the front of the sprocket facing out.

➡There are 3 colored links on the timing chain. 2 links are of matching color, and 1 link is of a unique color. Use the following procedure to line up the links with the actuators. Orient the chain so that the colored links are visible.

➡Always use new actuator bolts.

36. Assemble the intake camshaft actuator into the timing chain with the timing mark lined up with the uniquely colored link (1).

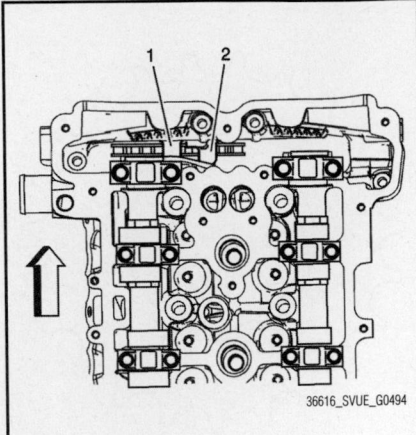

Fig. 443 Ensure that the chain goes around both sides of the cylinder block bosses (1, 2)

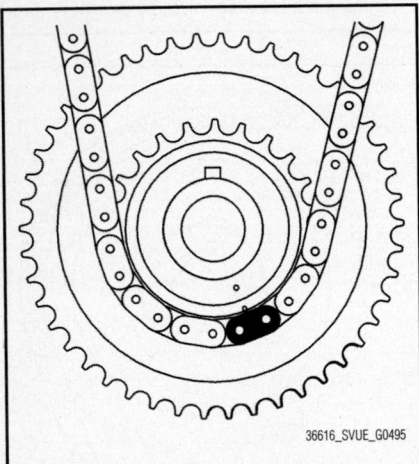

Fig. 444 First matching colored link and timing mark on crankshaft sprocket

37. Lower the timing chain through the opening in the cylinder head. Use care to ensure that the chain goes around both sides of the cylinder block bosses (1, 2).

38. Install the intake camshaft actuator onto the intake camshaft while aligning the dowel pin into the camshaft slot.

39. Hand tighten the new intake camshaft actuator bolt.

40. Route the timing chain around the crankshaft sprocket and line up the first matching colored link with the timing mark on the crankshaft sprocket, in approximately the 5 o'clock position.

41. Rotate the crankshaft clockwise to remove all chain slack. Do not rotate the intake camshaft.

42. Install the adjustable timing chain guide down through the opening in the cylinder head and install the adjustable timing chain bolt. Tighten the adjustable timing chain guide bolt to 89 inch lbs. (10 Nm).

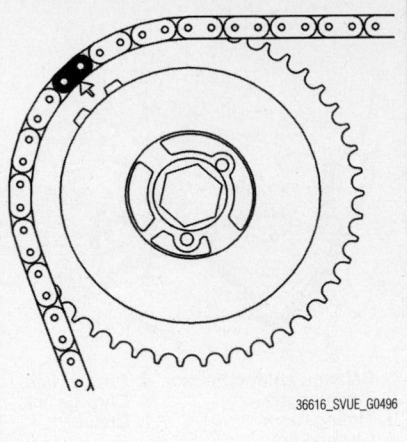

Fig. 445 Exhaust camshaft actuator and second matching colored link

➡ Always install NEW actuator bolts.

43. Install the exhaust camshaft actuator into the timing chain with the timing mark lined up with the second matching colored link.

44. Install the exhaust camshaft actuator onto the exhaust camshaft, aligning the dowel pin into the camshaft slot.

45. Using a 23 mm open end wrench, rotate the exhaust camshaft approximately 45 degrees until the dowel pin in the camshaft actuator goes into the camshaft slot.

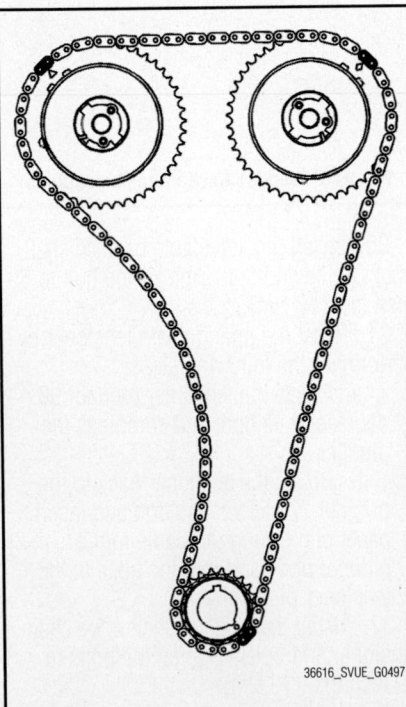

Fig. 446 Verify that all of the colored links and the appropriate timing marks are still aligned

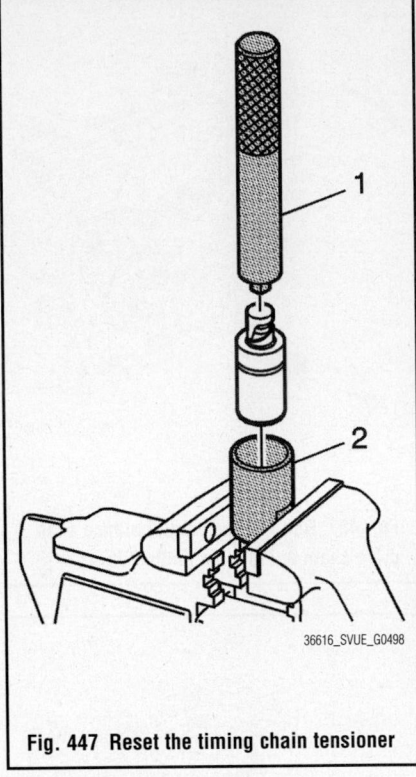

Fig. 447 Reset the timing chain tensioner

46. When the actuator seats on the cam, tighten the new exhaust camshaft actuator bolt hand tight.

47. Verify that all of the colored links and the appropriate timing marks are still aligned. If they are not aligned, repeat the portion of the procedure necessary to align the timing marks.

48. Install the fixed timing chain guide and bolts. Tighten the fixed timing chain guide bolts to 106 inch lbs. (12 Nm).

49. Install the upper timing chain guide and bolts. Tighten the upper timing chain guide bolts to 89 inch lbs. (10 Nm).

50. Reset the timing chain tensioner by performing the following steps:

    a. Remove the snap ring.

    b. Remove the piston assembly from the body of the timing chain tensioner.

    c. Install the J 45027-2 (2) into a vise.

    d. Install the notch end of the piston assembly into the J 45027-2 (2).

    e. Using the J 45027-1 (1), turn the ratchet cylinder into the piston.

    f. Reinstall the piston assembly into the body of the tensioner.

    g. Install the snap ring.

51. Inspect the timing chain tensioner seal for damage. If damaged, replace the seal.

52. Inspect to ensure all dirt and debris is removed from the timing chain tensioner threaded hole in the cylinder head.

➡Ensure the timing chain tensioner seal is centered throughout the torque procedure to eliminate the possibility of an oil leak.

53. Install the timing chain tensioner assembly. Tighten the timing chain tensioner to 55 ft. lbs. (75 Nm).

54. The timing chain tensioner is released by compressing it ¾ inch, which will release the locking mechanism in the ratchet. To release the timing chain tensioner, use a suitable tool with a rubber tip on the end. Feed the tool down through the cam drive chest to rest on the cam chain. Then give a sharp jolt diagonally downwards to release the tensioner.

55. Using a 23 mm wrench, engage the hex on the intake camshaft, and using a torque wrench, tighten the camshaft actuator bolt. Tighten the intake camshaft position actuator bolt to 22 ft. lbs. (30 Nm), plus 100 degrees using the J 45059.

56. Using a 23 mm wrench, engage the hex on the exhaust camshaft, and using a torque wrench, tighten the camshaft actuator bolt. Tighten the exhaust camshaft position actuator bolt to 22 ft. lbs. (30 Nm), plus 100 degrees using the J 45059.

57. Install the timing chain oiling nozzle. Tighten the timing chain oiling nozzle bolt to 89 inch lbs. (10 Nm).

58. Apply sealant compound GM P/N 12345382 (Canadian P/N 10953489) to the thread of the timing chain guide bolt access hole plug.

59. Install the timing chain guide bolt access hole plug. Tighten the access hole plug to 66 ft. lbs. (90 Nm).

60. Install the engine front cover.
61. Install the camshaft cover.
62. Install the No. 1 cylinder spark plug.

3.5L Engine

See Figures 448 through 454.

1. Remove the engine front cover.
2. Align the crankshaft timing mark (1) to the timing mark on the bottom of the timing chain tensioner (2).
3. Align the timing mark on the camshaft position actuator gear (4) with the timing mark on top of the timing chain tensioner (3).
4. Remove the camshaft position actuator bolts.
5. Remove the timing chain, camshaft position actuator, and crankshaft sprockets.
6. Remove the timing chain tensioner bolts.
7. Remove the timing chain tensioner.
8. Remove the crankshaft sprocket.

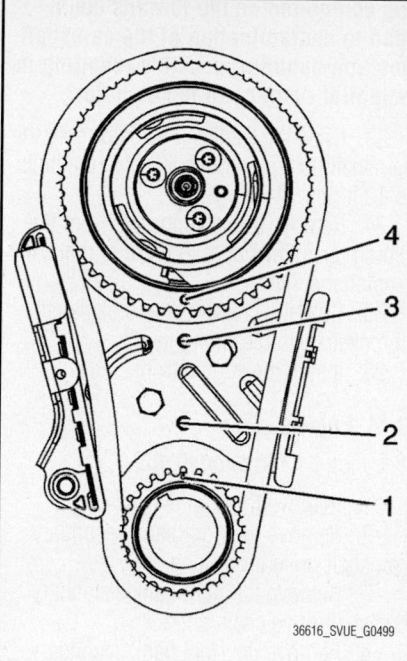

Fig. 448 Align the crankshaft timing mark (1) to the timing mark on the bottom of the timing chain tensioner (2)

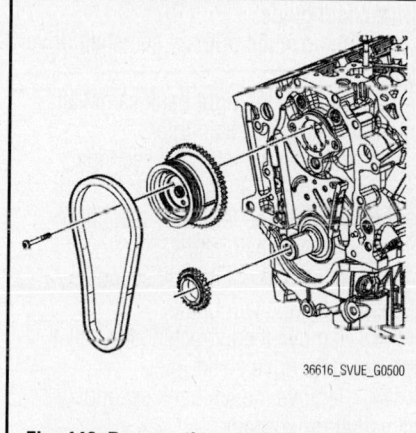

Fig. 449 Remove the camshaft position actuator bolts

9. Remove the timing chain dampener bolts.
10. Remove the timing chain dampener.
11. Remove and discard the camshaft position actuator filter (1) from the end of the camshaft.

To install:

➡Always install a NEW camshaft position actuator filter anytime the camshaft actuator is removed.

12. Install a NEW the camshaft position actuator filter to the end of the camshaft.
13. Install the crankshaft sprocket.

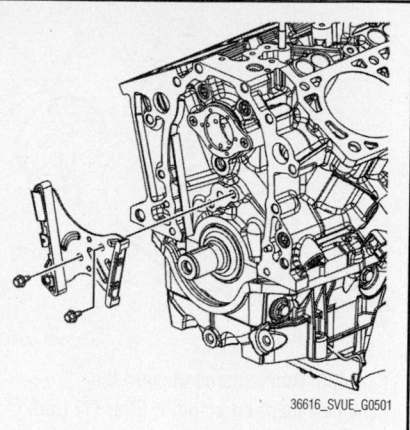

Fig. 450 Remove the timing chain tensioner bolts

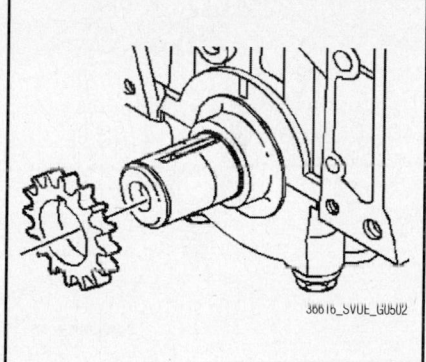

Fig. 451 Remove the crankshaft sprocket

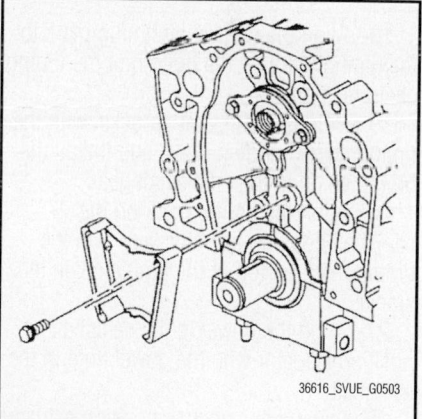

Fig. 452 Remove the timing chain dampener bolts

14. Apply prelube to the crankshaft sprocket thrust surface.
15. Install the timing chain tensioner.
16. Install the timing chain tensioner bolts. Tighten the bolts to 15 ft. lbs. (21 Nm).
17. Using the EN-47719, fully collapse the tensioner, and place he tensioner retaining pin into the retaining hole (1).

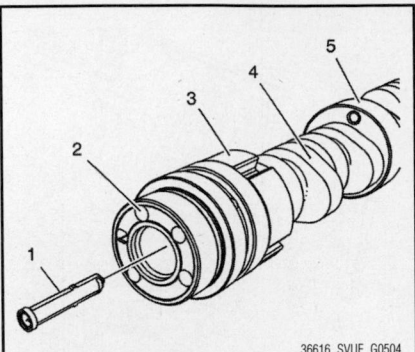

Fig. 453 Remove and discard the camshaft position actuator filter (1) from the end of the camshaft

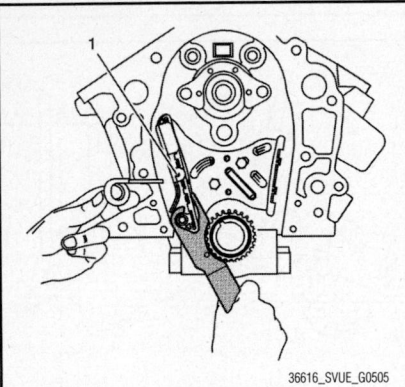

Fig. 454 Fully collapse the tensioner, and place he tensioner retaining pin into the retaining hole (1)

18. Align the crankshaft timing mark to the timing mark on the bottom of the timing chain tensioner.

19. Hold the camshaft sprocket with the timing chain hanging down and install the timing chain to the crankshaft gear.

20. Align the timing mark on the camshaft position actuator gear with the timing mark on top of the timing chain tensioner.

21. Align the dowel in the camshaft position actuator with the dowel hole in the camshaft.

22. Install the camshaft position actuator bolts.

➡Use only a Torx Plus® Bit when removing or installing the camshaft position actuator fasteners (1). The Torx Plus® design differs from typical Torx® fastener. Use of a standard Torx® bit on Torx Plus® fasteners may result in a rounded out fastener head or incorrect faster torque.

➡DO NOT use any type of thread locking compound on the camshaft position actuator bolts. Usage of a thread lock-ing compound on the threads could lead to contamination of the camshaft position actuator, possibly resulting in potential damage to the actuator.

23. Draw the camshaft actuator onto the camshaft using the bolts. Tighten the bolts to 12 ft. lbs. (16 Nm).

24. Remove the retaining pin from the timing chain tensioner in order to make the tensioner active.

25. Coat the crankshaft and camshaft sprockets with clean engine oil.

26. Install the engine front cover.

3.6L Engine

See Figures 455 through 469.

1. Remove the engine front cover.

2. Remove the right bank secondary camshaft drive chain tensioner.

3. Remove the right bank secondary camshaft drive chain shoe.

4. Remove the right bank secondary camshaft drive chain guide.

5. Remove the right bank secondary camshaft drive chain.

6. Remove the primary camshaft drive chain tensioner.

7. Remove the primary upper camshaft drive chain guide.

8. Remove the primary camshaft drive chain.

9. Remove the right bank camshaft intermediate drive chain idler.

10. Remove the left bank secondary camshaft drive chain tensioner.

11. Remove the left bank secondary camshaft drive chain shoe.

12. Remove the left bank secondary camshaft drive chain guide.

13. Remove the left bank camshaft intermediate drive chain idler.

14. Remove the left bank secondary camshaft drive chain.

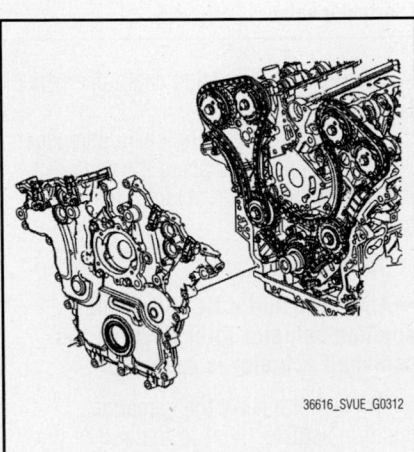

Fig. 455 Remove the engine front cover

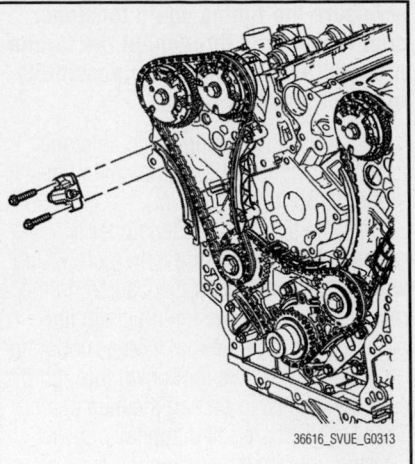

Fig. 456 Remove the right bank secondary camshaft drive chain tensioner

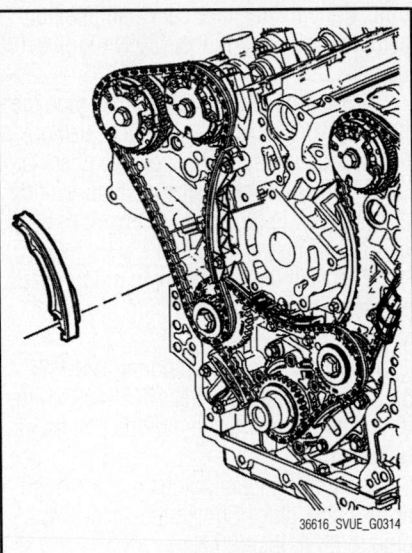

Fig. 457 Remove the right bank secondary camshaft drive chain shoe

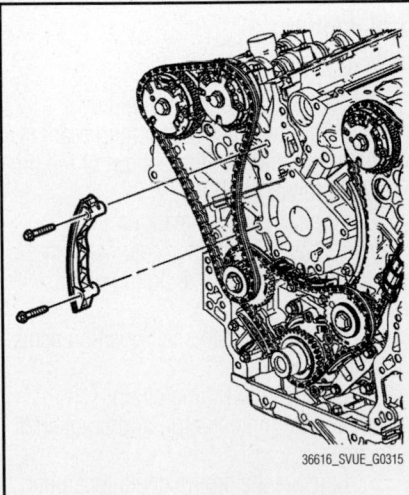

Fig. 458 Remove the right bank secondary camshaft drive chain guide

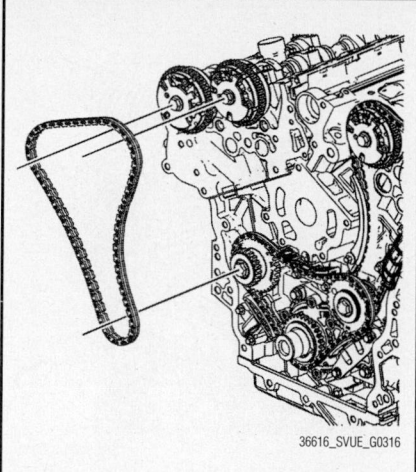

Fig. 459 Remove the right bank secondary camshaft drive chain

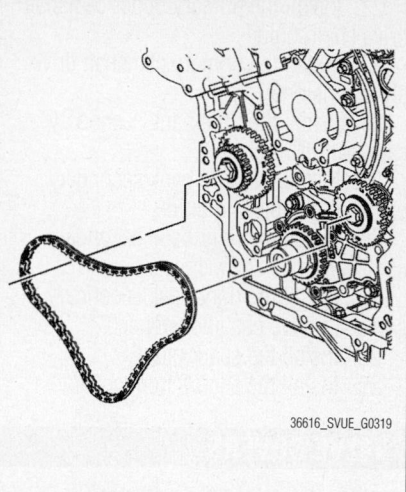

Fig. 462 Remove the primary camshaft drive chain

Fig. 465 Remove the left bank secondary camshaft drive chain shoe

Fig. 460 Remove the primary camshaft drive chain tensioner

Fig. 463 Remove the right bank camshaft intermediate drive chain idler

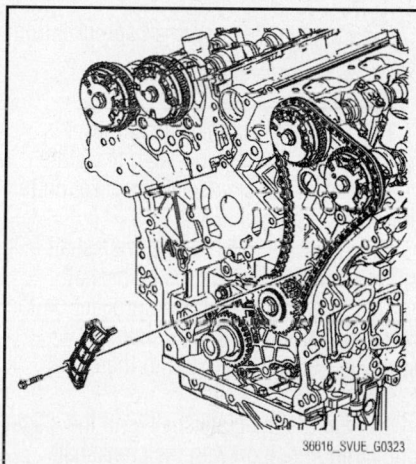

Fig. 466 Remove the left bank secondary camshaft drive chain guide

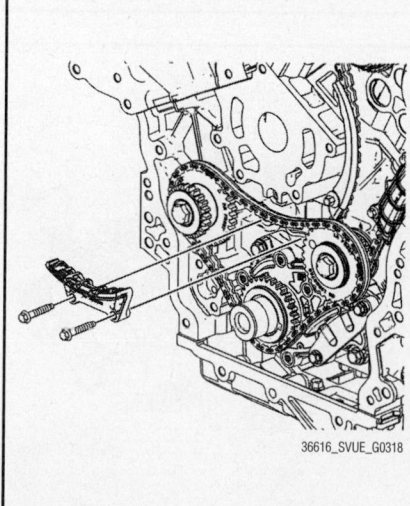

Fig. 461 Remove the primary upper camshaft drive chain guide

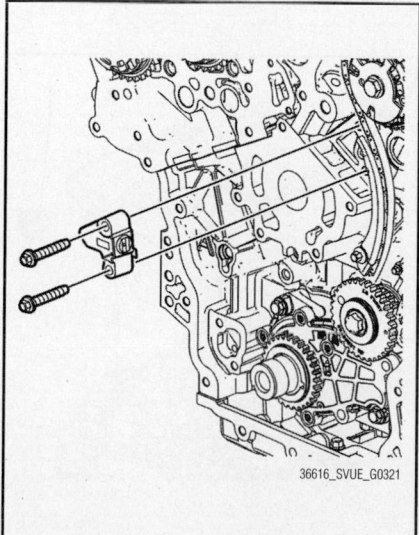

Fig. 464 Remove the left bank secondary camshaft drive chain tensioner

Fig. 467 Remove the left bank camshaft intermediate drive chain idler

Fig. 468 Remove the left bank secondary camshaft drive chain

15. Remove the crankshaft sprocket from the nose of the crankshaft.

To install:

16. Ensure the crankshaft sprocket is installed with the timing mark (1) visible.

17. Install the crankshaft sprocket on to the nose of the crankshaft.

18. Align the notch in the crankshaft sprocket with the pin in the crankshaft.

19. Slide the crankshaft sprocket on the crankshaft nose until the crankshaft sprocket contacts the step in the crankshaft.

20. Ensure the crankshaft is in the stage one timing position with the crankshaft sprocket timing mark (1) aligned to the stage one timing mark on the oil pump cover (2) using the EN 46111.

21. Install the primary camshaft timing chain.

22. Install the primary upper camshaft drive chain guide.

23. Install the primary camshaft drive chain tensioner.

24. Install the right bank secondary camshaft drive chain.

25. Install the right bank secondary camshaft drive chain guide.

26. Install the right bank secondary camshaft drive chain shoe.

27. Install the right bank secondary camshaft drive chain tensioner.

28. Install the spark plugs.

29. Install the engine front cover.

VALVE COVERS

REMOVAL & INSTALLATION

2.4L Engine, Except Hybrid

See Figures 470 through 475.

1. Remove the intake manifold cover.

2. Remove the air cleaner outlet duct.

3. Disconnect the intake (3) and exhaust (2) camshaft position actuator solenoid valve electrical connectors.

4. Remove the ignition coils.

5. Remove the engine harness clips (1, 2) from the cover.

6. Remove the fuel feed line retainers (1, 2) from the engine brackets.

7. Remove the camshaft cover bolts.

8. Remove the camshaft cover.

To install:

9. Install the camshaft cover and bolts. Tighten the bolts to 89 inch lbs. (10 Nm).

10. Install the ignition coils.

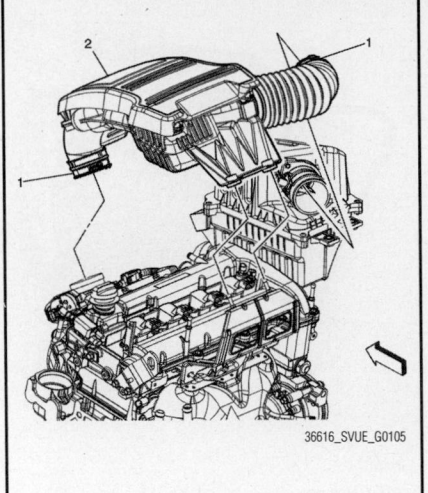

Fig. 471 Remove the air cleaner outlet duct

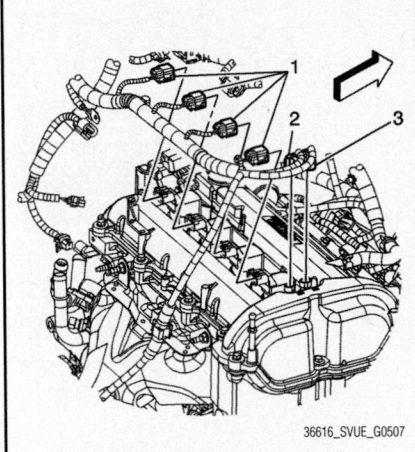

Fig. 472 Disconnect the intake (3) and exhaust (2) camshaft position actuator solenoid valve electrical connectors

Fig. 469 Crankshaft sprocket timing mark (1) aligned to the stage one timing mark on the oil pump cover (2)

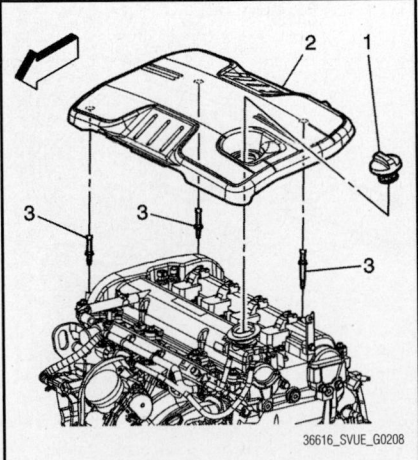

Fig. 470 Remove the intake manifold cover

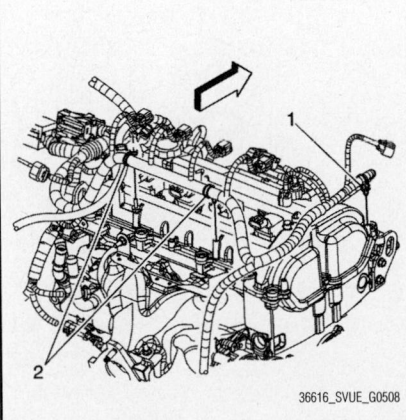

Fig. 473 Remove the engine harness clips (1, 2) from the cover

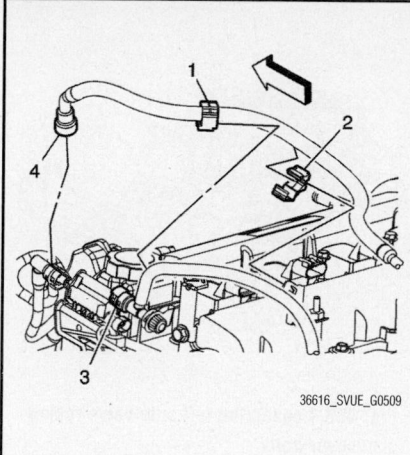

Fig. 474 Remove the fuel feed line retainers (1, 2)

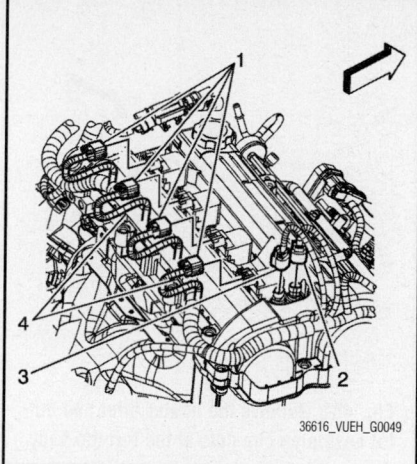

Fig. 476 Disconnect the engine wiring harness electrical connectors (2, 3)

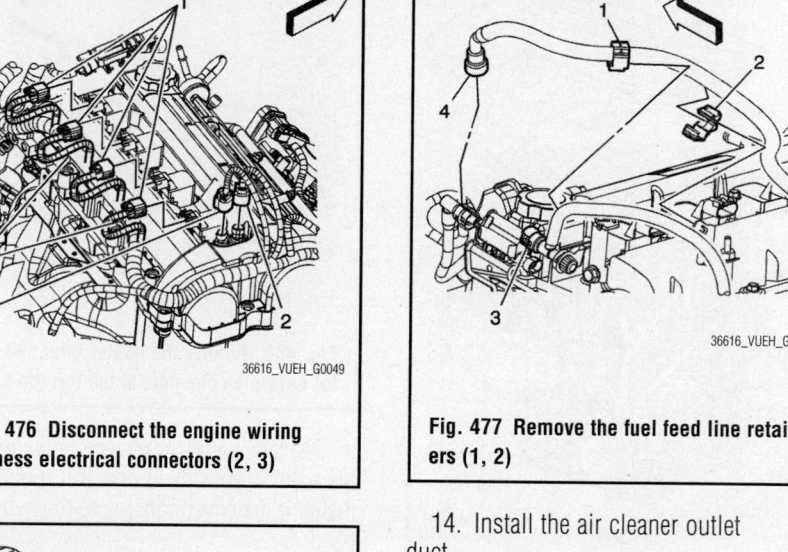

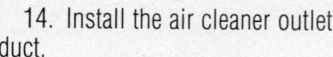

Fig. 477 Remove the fuel feed line retainers (1, 2)

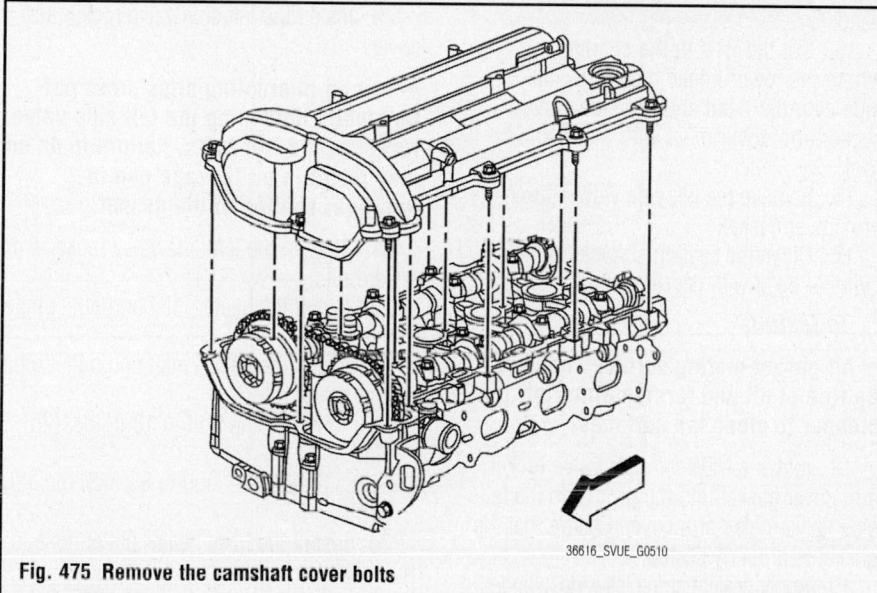

Fig. 475 Remove the camshaft cover bolts

11. Install the engine harness clips to the cover.

12. Install the feed line retainers to the engine brackets.

13. Connect the intake and exhaust camshaft position actuator solenoid valve electrical connectors.

14. Install the air cleaner outlet duct.

15. Install the intake manifold cover.

2.4L Hybrid Engine

See Figures 471, 475 through 477.

1. Remove the air cleaner outlet duct.

2. Disconnect the engine wiring harness electrical connectors (2, 3) from the intake and exhaust camshaft position actuator solenoid valves.

3. Remove the ignition coils.

4. Remove the engine harness clips (4) from the cover.

5. Reposition the engine wiring harness out of the way.

6. Remove the fuel feed line retainers (1, 2) from the engine brackets.

7. Remove the camshaft cover bolts.

8. Remove the camshaft cover.

To install:

9. Install the camshaft cover and bolts. Tighten the bolts to 89 inch lbs. (10 Nm).

10. Install the feed line retainers to the engine brackets.

11. Install the ignition coils.

12. Position the engine wiring harness and install the clips to the cover.

13. Connect the engine wiring harness electrical connectors to the intake and exhaust camshaft position actuator solenoid valves.

14. Install the air cleaner outlet duct.

3.5L Engine—Left Side

See Figures 478 through 484.

1. Partially drain the cooling system.

2. Remove the intake manifold cover.

3. Remove the oil level indicator and tube.

4. Remove the left side spark plug wires from the vehicle.

5. Remove the Positive Crankcase Ventilation (PCV) foul air tube.

6. Reposition the heater inlet and outlet hose/pipe clamps at the engine inlet and outer pipes.

7. Remove the heater inlet and outlet hose/pipe clip nuts at the throttle body.

8. Remove the heater inlet and outer hoses/pipes from the engine inlet and outlet pipes.

9. Remove the clips from the throttle body studs. Reposition the hose/pipe assembly.

10. Remove the front heater outlet hose from the outlet heater pipe.

11. Remove the heater inlet and outlet pipe bolt and stud.

12. Remove the heater inlet and outlet pipe from the vehicle.

13. Loosen the left side valve rocker arm cover bolts.

➡**When removing the left side valve rocker arm cover, ensure the left side valve rocker arm cover gasket stays in place attached to the left side cylinder head.**

14. Remove the left side valve rocker arm cover. If necessary, bump the end of

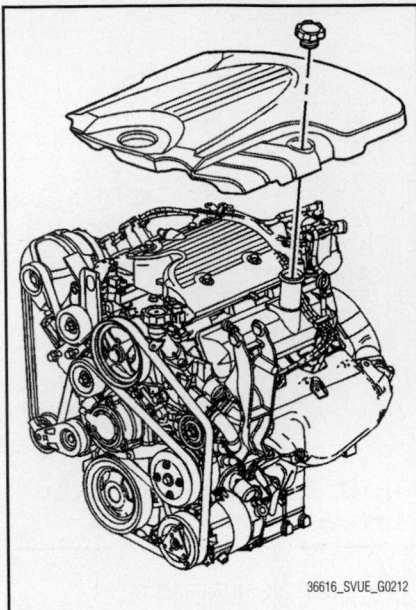

Fig. 478 Remove the intake manifold cover

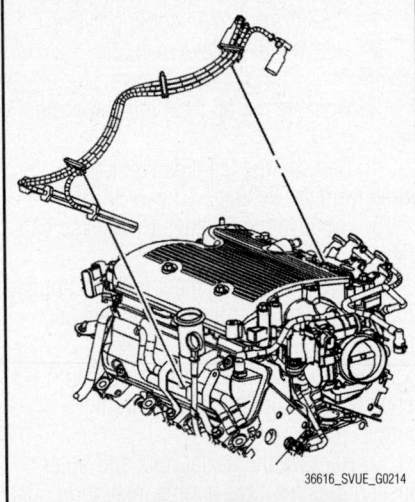

Fig. 479 Remove the left side spark plug wires from the vehicle

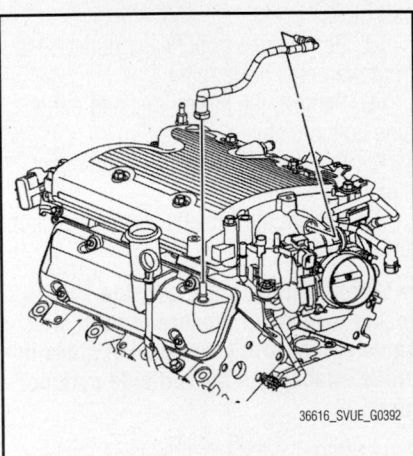

Fig. 480 Remove the PCV foul air tube

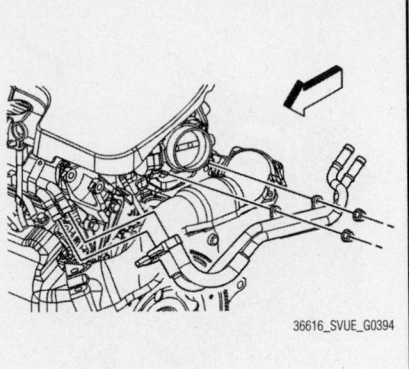

Fig. 481 Remove the heater inlet and outlet hose/pipe clip nuts at the throttle body

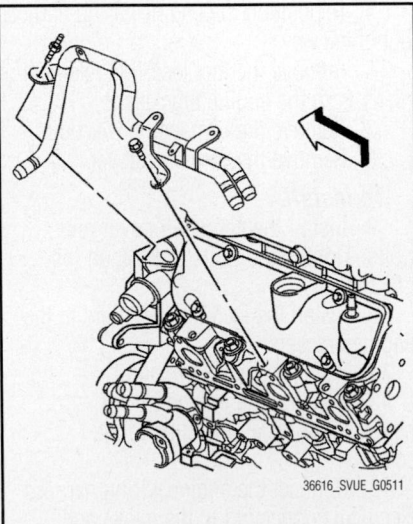

Fig. 482 Remove the front heater outlet hose from the outlet heater pipe

the left side valve rocker arm cover with the palm of your hand or a soft rubber mallet if the cover adheres to the cylinder head.

15. Cut the RTV in the channel where the lower intake manifold, left side cylinder head and left side valve rocker arm cover meet with a suitable tool.

16. Remove the left side valve rocker arm cover gasket.

17. Clean the sealing surface on the cylinder head with degreaser.

To install:

➡**All gasket mating surfaces need to be free of oil and foreign material. Use cleaner to clean the surfaces.**

18. Install a NEW left side valve rocker arm cover gasket into the groove in the left side valve rocker arm cover. Ensure that the gasket is properly seated.

19. Apply sealant at the left side cylinder

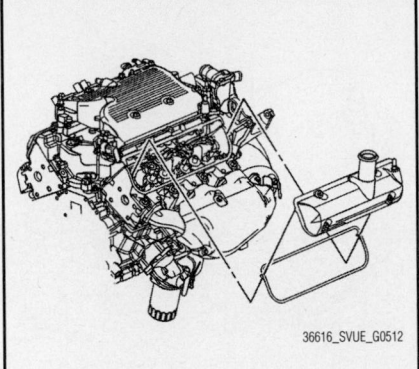

Fig. 483 Loosen the left side valve rocker arm cover bolts

head to the surfaces where the left side cylinder head and lower intake manifold meet (1).

20. Install the left side valve rocker arm cover.

➡**Use an alternating criss-cross pattern when tightening the left side valve rocker arm cover bolts. Failure to do so may result in oil leakage due to improper seating of the gasket.**

21. Tighten the left side valve rocker arm cover bolts.

22. Install the heater inlet and outlet pipe to the vehicle.

23. Install the heater inlet and outlet pipe bolt and stud.

   a. Tighten the bolt to 18 ft. lbs. (25 Nm).

   b. Tighten the stud to 89 inch lbs. (10 Nm).

24. Install the front heater outlet hose to the outlet heater pipe.

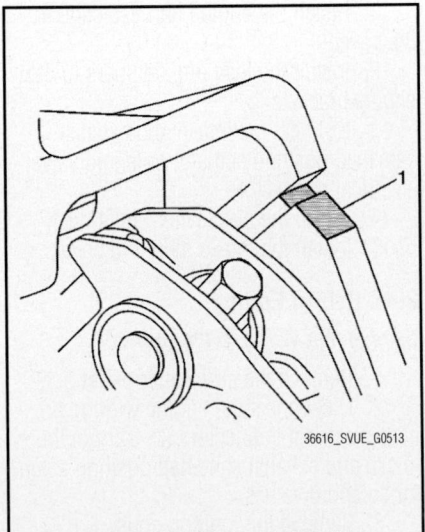

Fig. 484 Apply sealant at the left side cylinder head

25. Position the hose/pipe assembly. Install the clips to the throttle body studs.

26. Install the heater inlet and outer hoses/pipes to the engine inlet and outlet pipes.

27. Install the heater inlet and outlet hose/pipe clip nuts at the throttle body. Tighten the nuts to 89 inch lbs. (10 Nm).

28. Position the heater inlet and outlet hose/pipe clamps at the engine inlet and outer pipes.

29. Install the PCV foul air tube.

30. Install the left side spark plug wires.

31. Install the oil level indicator and tube.

32. Install the intake manifold cover.

33. Fill the cooling system.

3.5L Engine—Right Side

See Figures 485 through 492.

1. Remove the alternator.

2. Disconnect the Positive Crankcase Ventilation (PCV) fresh air tube from the air cleaner outlet duct.

3. Remove the PCV fresh air tube from the right side valve rocker arm cover.

4. Disconnect the right side spark plug wires from the spark plugs.

5. Disconnect the right side spark plug wires from the ignition coil.

6. Remove the right side spark plug harness clip from the ignition coil bracket.

7. Remove the spark plug harness.

8. Disconnect the Manifold Absolute Pressure (MAP) sensor electrical connector.

9. Disconnect the ignition coil electrical connector.

10. Remove the engine harness clip from the ignition coil bracket.

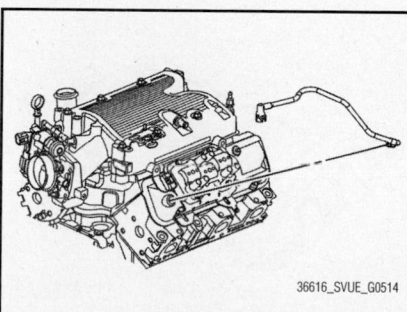

Fig. 485 Remove the PCV fresh air tube from the right side valve rocker arm cover

Fig. 486 Disconnect the right side spark plug wires from the spark plugs

11. Remove the Healed Oxygen Sensor (HO2S) electrical connector clip from the ignition coil bracket.

12. Remove the ignition coil bracket nuts.

13. Remove the ignition coil bracket bolts.

14. Remove the ignition coil.

15. Remove the coolant crossover pipe.

a. Drain the engine coolant.

b. Disconnect the Engine Coolant Temperature (ECT) sensor electrical connector.

c. Remove the ECT sensor.

d. Remove the radiator inlet and outlet hoses from the crossover pipe.

e. Disconnect the wiring harness ground terminal from the crossover pipe.

f. Remove the thermostat housing and thermostat from the crossover pipe.

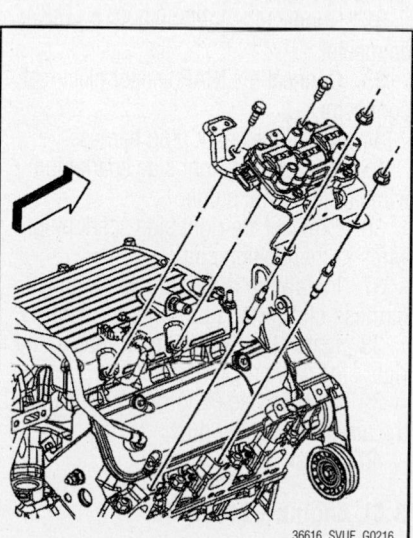

Fig. 487 Remove the ignition coil bracket nuts

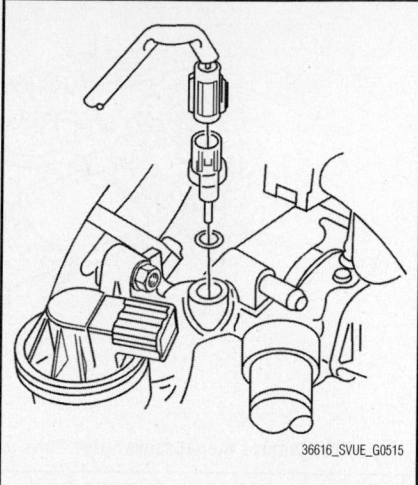

Fig. 488 Disconnect the Engine Coolant Temperature (ECT) sensor electrical connector

g. Remove the crossover pipe bolts and crossover pipe.

16. Loosen the valve rocker arm cover bolts.

➡**When removing the valve rocker arm cover, ensure the gasket stays in place attached to the cylinder head.**

17. Remove the valve rocker arm cover. Bump the end of the cover with the palm of your hand or a soft rubber mallet if the cover adheres to the cylinder head.

18. Cut the Room Temperature Vulcanizing (RTV) sealer in the channel where the intake, cylinder head and valve rocker arm cover meet with a suitable tool.

19. Remove the valve cover gasket.

20. Clean the sealing surface on the cylinder head with degreaser.

To install:

➡**All gasket mating surfaces need to be free of oil and foreign material. Use cleaner to clean the surfaces.**

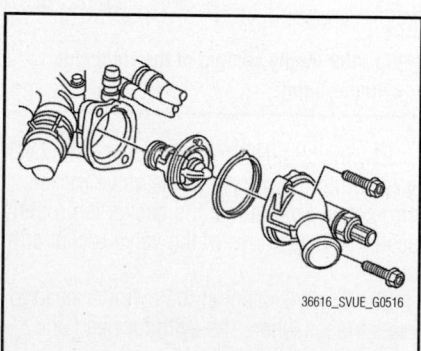

Fig. 489 Remove the thermostat housing and thermostat from the crossover pipe

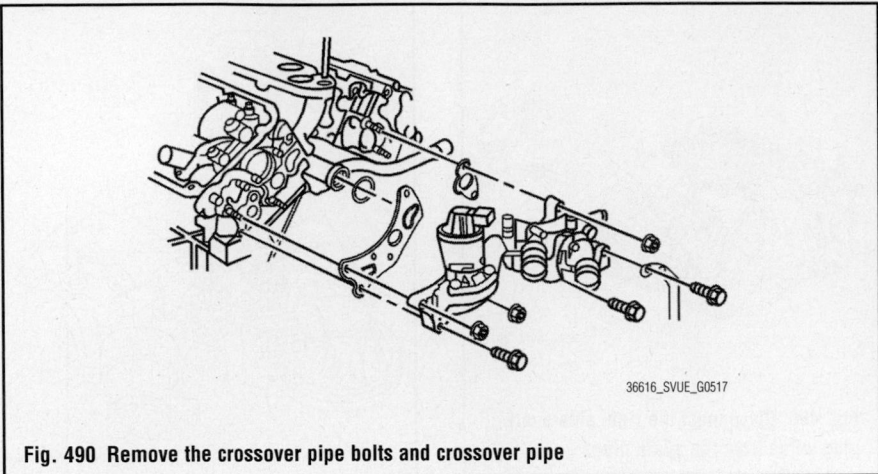

Fig. 490 Remove the crossover pipe bolts and crossover pipe

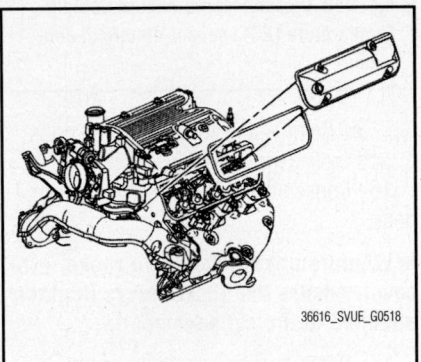

Fig. 491 Loosen the valve rocker arm cover bolts

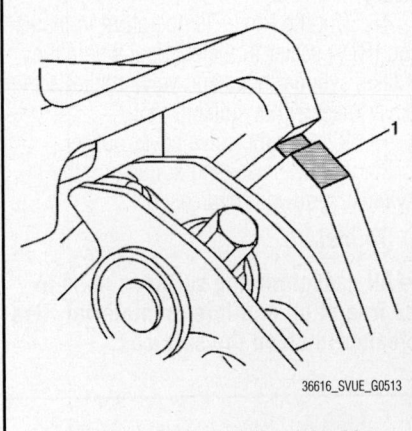

Fig. 492 Apply sealant at the right side cylinder head

21. Install a NEW valve rocker arm cover gasket into the groove in the valve rocker arm cover. Ensure that the gasket is properly seated in the groove of the valve rocker arm cover.

22. Apply sealant at the cylinder head to the surfaces where the cylinder head and intake manifold meet.

23. Install a new gasket to the valve rocker arm cover. Ensure that the gasket is properly seated in the groove of the valve rocker arm cover.

24. Install the right valve rocker arm cover.

➡**Use an alternating criss-cross pattern when tightening the valve rocker cover bolts. Failure to do so may result in oil leakage from the valve cover due to improper seating of the gasket.**

25. Install the valve rocker arm cover bolts.

26. Install the coolant crossover pipe.

27. Install the ignition coil.

28. Install the ignition coil bracket bolts.

29. Install the ignition coil bracket nuts. Tighten the bolts/nuts to 18 ft. lbs. (25 Nm).

30. Install the HO2S electrical connector clip to the ignition coil bracket.

31. Install the engine harness clip to the ignition coil bracket.

32. Connect the ignition coil electrical connector.

33. Connect the MAP sensor electrical connector.

34. Install the spark plug harness.

35. Connect the right side spark plug wires to the spark plugs.

36. Connect the right side spark plug wires to the ignition coil.

37. Install the right side spark plug harness clip to the ignition coil bracket.

38. Install the PCV fresh air tube to the right side valve rocker arm cover.

39. Connect the PCV fresh air tube to the air cleaner outlet duct.

40. Install the alternator.

3.6L Engine—Left Side

See Figures 494 through 497.

1. Remove the left bank spark plugs.

2. Remove the left camshaft cover bolts.

3. Remove the left camshaft cover from the left cylinder head.

4. Clean the mating surfaces of the cylinder head and the camshaft cover.

5. Install the EN 46101 onto the spark plug tubes of the left cylinder head.

To install:

6. Install new camshaft cover bolt grommets prior to installing the camshaft cover bolts.

7. Place a bead of RTV sealant, GM P/N 12378521 (Canadian P/N 88901148) or equivalent, on the engine front cover split lines (1).

8. Place the left camshaft cover into position onto the left cylinder head.

9. Loosely install the left camshaft cover bolts.

10. Tighten the left camshaft cover bolts in the sequence shown. Tighten the left camshaft cover bolts in the sequence to 89 inch lbs. (10 Nm).

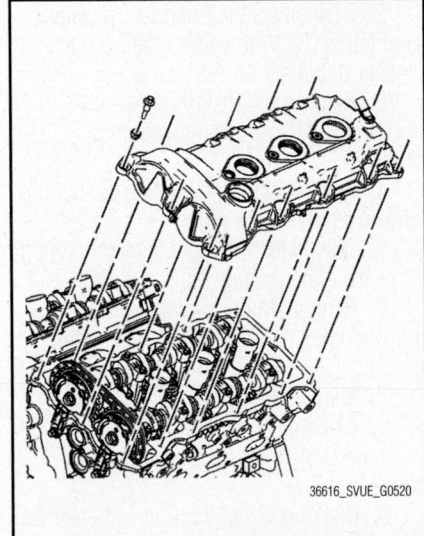

Fig. 494 Install the EN 46101 onto the spark plug tubes of the left cylinder1 head

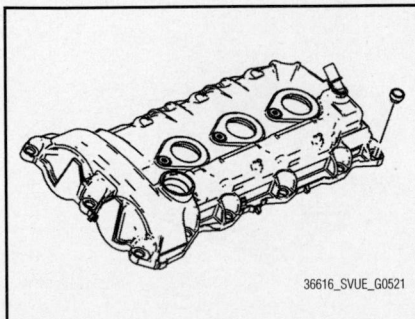

Fig. 495 Install new camshaft cover bolt grommets

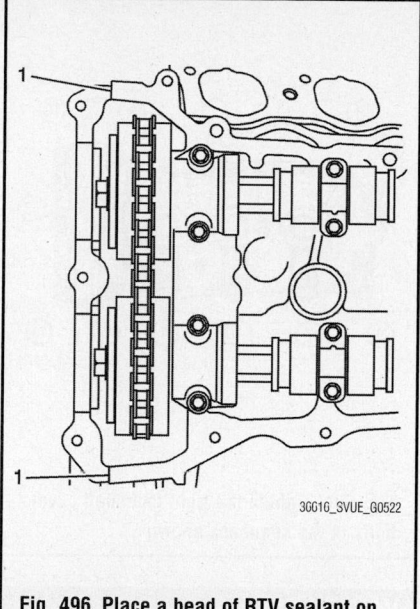

Fig. 496 Place a bead of RTV sealant on the engine front cover split lines (1)

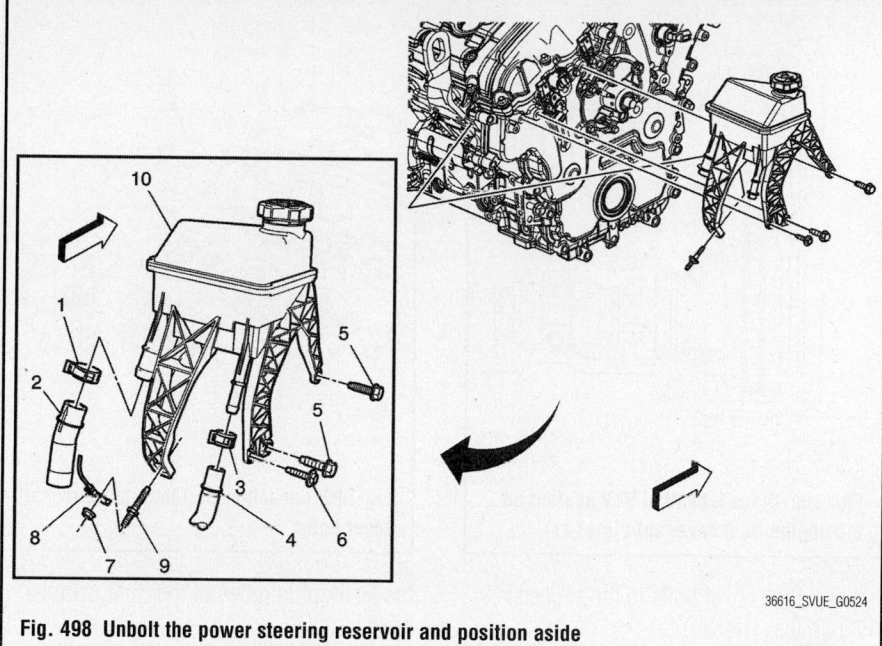

Fig. 498 Unbolt the power steering reservoir and position aside

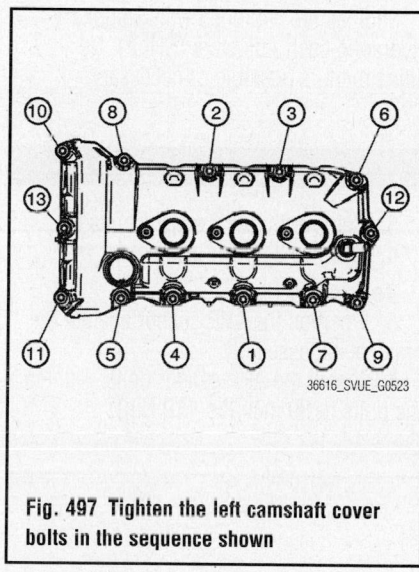

Fig. 497 Tighten the left camshaft cover bolts in the sequence shown

Fig. 499 Remove the right camshaft cover bolts

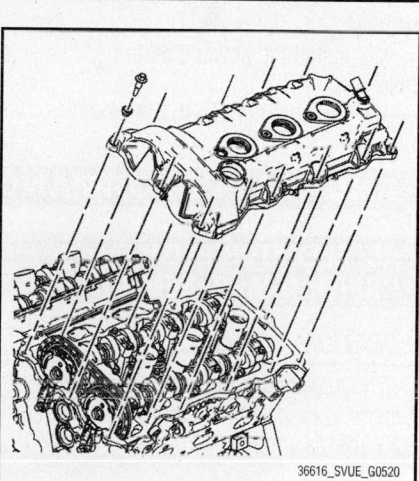

Fig. 500 Install the EN 46101 onto the spark plug tubes of the right cylinder1 head

11. Remove the EN 46101 from the spark plug tubes of the left cylinder head.

12. Install NEW spark plugs into the left cylinder head.

3.6L Engine—Right Side

See Figures 498 through 504.

1. Remove the upper intake manifold.

2. Remove the right bank spark plugs.

3. Unbolt the power steering reservoir and position aside.

4. Reposition engine wiring harness aside.

5. Remove the right camshaft cover bolts.

6. Remove the right camshaft cover from the right cylinder head.

7. Clean the mating surfaces of the cylinder head and the camshaft cover.

8. Install the EN 46101 onto the spark plug tubes of the right cylinder head.

To install:

9. Install new camshaft cover bolt grommets prior to installing the camshaft cover bolts.

10. Place a bead of RTV sealant, GM P/N 12378521 (Canadian P/N 88901148) or equivalent, on the engine front cover split lines (1).

11. Place the right camshaft cover into position onto the right cylinder head.

12. Loosely install the right camshaft cover bolts.

13. Tighten the right camshaft cover bolts in the sequence shown. Tighten the

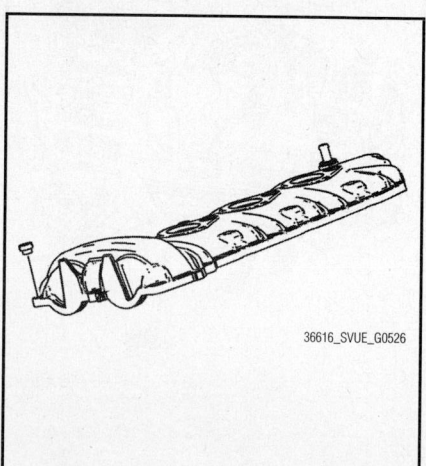

Fig. 501 Install new camshaft cover bolt grommets

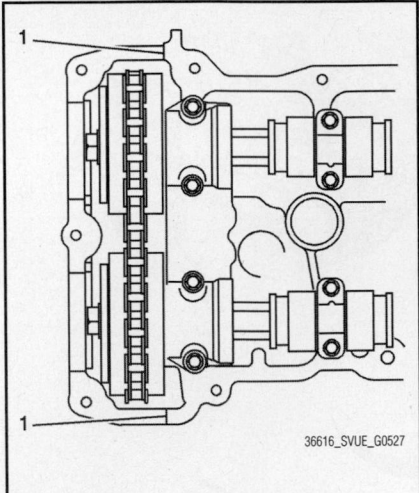

Fig. 502 Place a bead of RTV sealant on the engine front cover split lines (1)

Fig. 503 Loosely install the right camshaft cover bolts

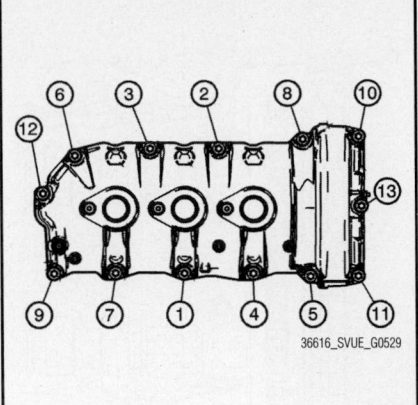

Fig. 504 Tighten the right camshaft cover bolts in the sequence shown

left camshaft cover bolts in the sequence to 89 inch lbs. (10 Nm).

14. Reposition engine wiring hearses.

15. Install the power steering reservoir.

16. Remove the EN 46101 from

the spark plug tubes of the right cylinder head.

17. Install NEW spark plugs into the right cylinder head.

18. Install the upper intake manifold.

VALVE LASH

ADJUSTMENT

Engines are equipped with Stationary Hydraulic Lash Adjusters (SHLA). No adjustment is possible or necessary.

ENGINE PERFORMANCE & EMISSION CONTROLS

ACCELERATOR PEDAL POSITION (APP) SENSOR

LOCATION

The Accelerator Pedal Position (APP) Sensor is located at the top of the accelerator pedal assembly.

REMOVAL & INSTALLATION

See Figures 505 through 507.

1. Remove the driver knee bolster reinforcement.

2. Disconnect the instrument panel wiring harness electrical connector (2) from the Accelerator Pedal Position (APP) sensor (1).

3. Remove the APP sensor bolts (1).

4. Remove the APP sensor (2).

To install:

5. Position the APP sensor against the brake pedal assembly.

6. Install the APP sensor bolts. Tighten the bolts to 89 inch lbs. (10 Nm).

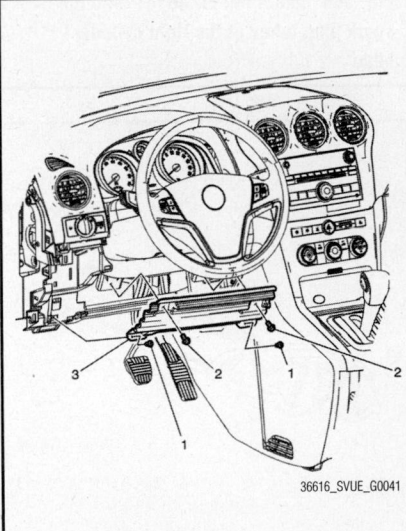

Fig. 505 Remove the driver knee bolster reinforcement

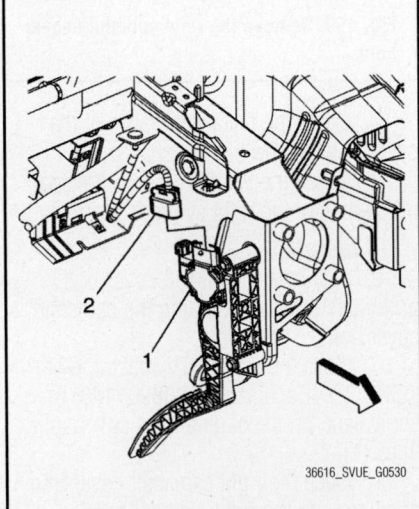

Fig. 506 Disconnect the instrument panel wiring harness electrical connector (2) from the APP sensor (1)

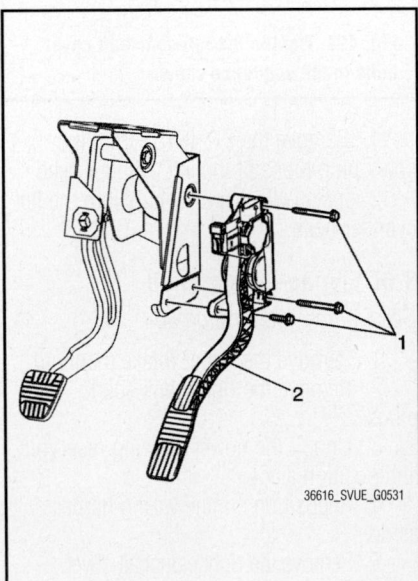

Fig. 507 Remove the APP sensor bolts (1)

7. Connect the instrument panel wiring harness electrical connector to the APP sensor.

8. Install the driver knee bolster reinforcement.

CAMSHAFT POSITION (CMP) SENSOR

REMOVAL & INSTALLATION

2.4L Engine—Intake

See Figures 508 through 511.

1. Remove the air cleaner outlet duct.
2. Remove the intake manifold cover.
3. Disconnect the engine wiring harness electrical connector (1) from the intake Camshaft Position (CMP) sensor.

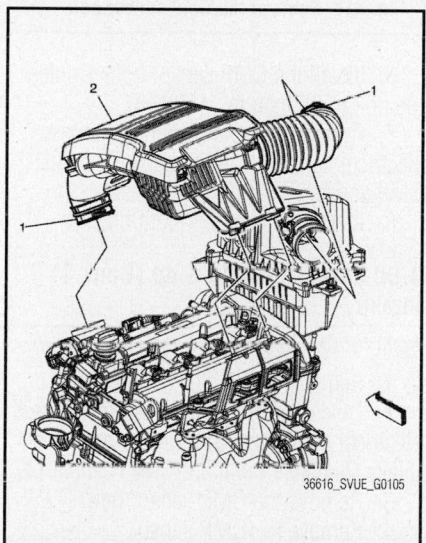

Fig. 508 Remove the air cleaner outlet duct

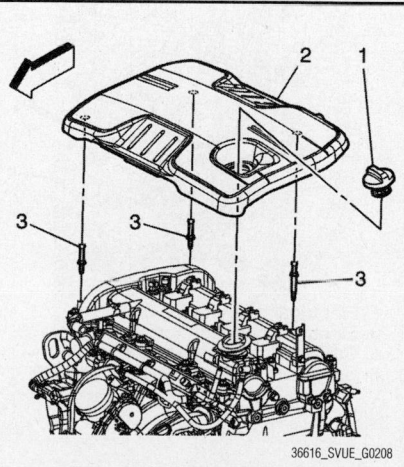

Fig. 509 Remove the intake manifold cover

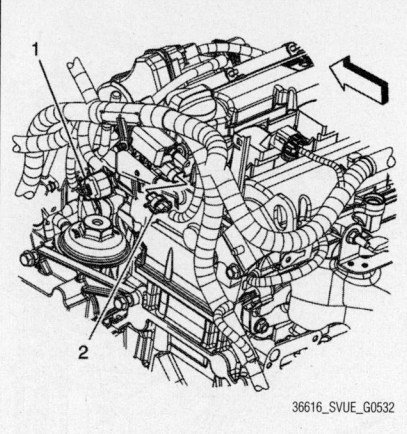

Fig. 510 Disconnect the engine wiring harness electrical connector (1) from the intake CMP sensor

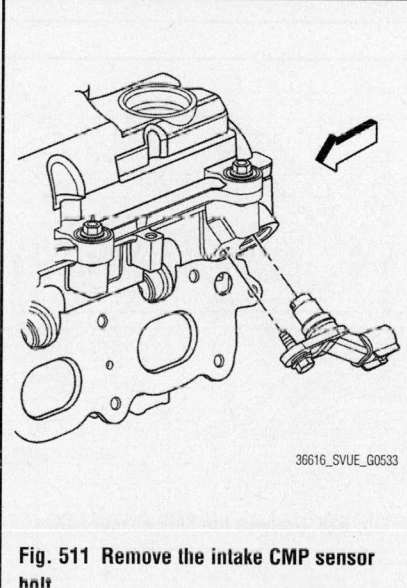

Fig. 511 Remove the intake CMP sensor bolt

4. Remove the intake CMP sensor bolt.
5. Remove the intake CMP sensor.

To install:

➡**Inspect the intake CMP sensor for damage, replace as necessary.**

6. Lubricate the intake CMP sensor O-ring seal with clean engine oil.
7. Install the intake CMP sensor.
8. Install the intake CMP sensor bolt. Tighten the bolt to 89 inch lbs. (10 Nm).
9. Connect the engine wiring harness electrical connector to the intake CMP sensor.
10. Install the intake manifold cover.
11. Install the air cleaner outlet duct.

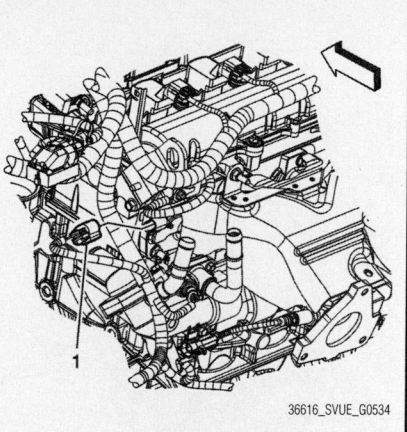

Fig. 512 Disconnect the engine wiring harness electrical connector (1) from the exhaust CMP sensor

2.4L Engine—Exhaust

See Figures 508, 509, 511 and 512.

1. Remove the air cleaner outlet duct.
2. Remove the intake manifold cover.
3. Disconnect the engine wiring harness electrical connector (1) from the exhaust Camshaft Position (CMP) sensor.
4. Remove the exhaust CMP sensor bolt. (Intake CMP shown, exhaust CMP similar).
5. Remove the exhaust CMP sensor.

To install:

➡**Inspect the exhaust CMP sensor for damage, replace as necessary.**

6. Lubricate the exhaust CMP sensor O-ring seal with clean engine oil.
7. Install the exhaust CMP sensor.
8. Install the exhaust CMP sensor bolt. Tighten the bolt to 89 inch lbs. (10 Nm).
9. Connect engine wiring harness electrical connector to the exhaust CMP sensor.
10. Install the intake manifold cover.
11. Install the air cleaner outlet duct.

3.5L Engine

See Figures 513 and 514.

1. Remove the power steering pump.
2. Disconnect the Camshaft Position (CMP) sensor electrical connector.
3. Remove the CMP sensor bolt.
4. Remove the CMP sensor.
5. Inspect the sensor O-ring for wear, cracks, or leakage if the sensor is not being replaced.

Fig. 513 Remove the power steering pump

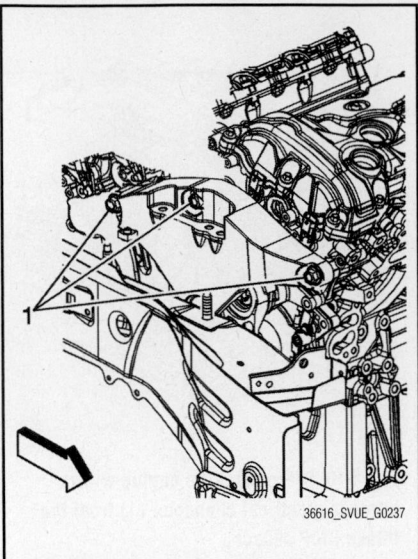

Fig. 515 Remove the engine mount bracket

Fig. 514 Remove the CMP sensor bolt

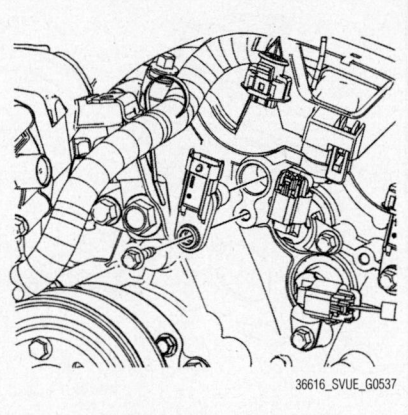

Fig. 516 Remove the CMP sensor bolt

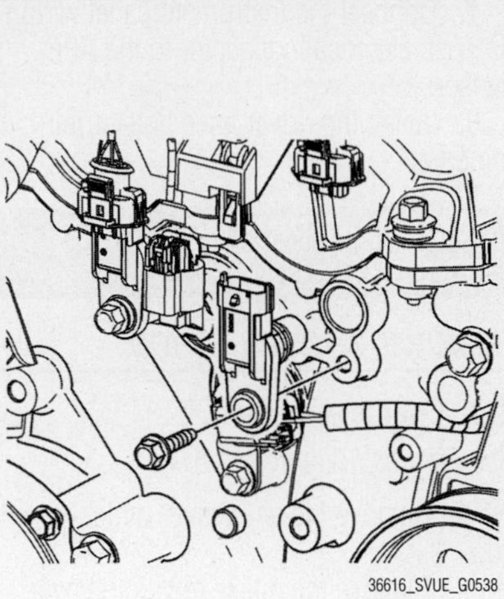

Fig. 517 Remove the CMP sensor bolt

To install:

6. Replace the O-ring if damaged, lubricate the NEW O-ring with clean engine oil.

7. Install the CMP sensor.

8. Install the CMP sensor bolt. Tighten the bolt to 89 inch lbs. (10 Nm).

9. Connect the CMP sensor electrical connector.

10. Install the power steering pump.

3.6L Engine—Left Side (Bank 2) Intake

See Figures 515 and 516.

1. Remove the engine mount bracket.

2. Disconnect the engine wiring harness electrical connector from the bank 2 intake Camshaft Position (CMP) sensor.

3. Remove the CMP sensor bolt.

4. Remove the CMP sensor.

To install:

5. Install the CMP sensor.

6. Install the CMP sensor bolt. Tighten the bolt to 89 inch lbs. (10 Nm).

7. Connect the engine wiring harness electrical connector to the bank 2 intake CMP sensor.

8. Install the engine mount bracket.

3.6L Engine—Left Side (Bank 2) Exhaust

See Figures 515 and 517.

1. Remove the engine mount bracket.

2. Disconnect the engine wiring harness electrical connector from the bank 2 exhaust Camshaft Position (CMP) sensor.

3. Remove the CMP sensor bolt.

4. Remove the CMP sensor.

To install:

5. Install the CMP sensor.

6. Install the CMP sensor bolt. Tighten the bolt to 89 inch lbs. (10 Nm).

7. Connect the engine wiring harness electrical connector to the bank 2 exhaust CMP sensor.

8. Install the engine mount bracket.

3.6L Engine—Right Side (Bank 1) Intake

See Figure 518.

1. Remove the air cleaner assembly.

2. Disconnect the engine wiring harness electrical connector (3) from the bank 1 intake Camshaft Position (CMP) sensor (4).

3. Remove the CMP sensor bolt.

4. Remove the CMP sensor.

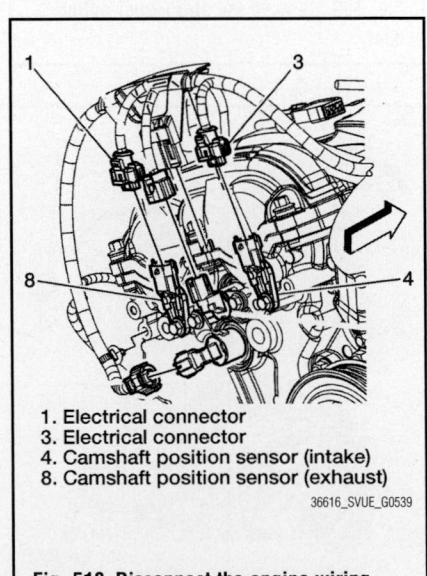

1. Electrical connector
3. Electrical connector
4. Camshaft position sensor (intake)
8. Camshaft position sensor (exhaust)

Fig. 518 Disconnect the engine wiring harness electrical connector (3) from the CMP sensor (4)

To install:

5. Install the CMP sensor bolt. Tighten the bolt to 89 inch lbs. (10 Nm).

6. Connect the engine wiring harness electrical connector to the bank 1 intake CMP sensor.

7. Install the air cleaner assembly.

3.6L Engine—Right Side (Bank 1) Exhaust

See Figures 518 and 519.

1. Remove the air cleaner assembly.

2. Disconnect the engine wiring harness electrical connector (1) from the bank 1 exhaust Camshaft Position (CMP) sensor (8).

3. Remove the CMP sensor bolt.

4. Remove the CMP sensor.

To install:

5. Install the CMP sensor.

6. Install the CMP sensor bolt. Tighten the bolt to 89 inch lbs (10 Nm).

7. Connect the engine wiring harness electrical connector to the bank 1 exhaust CMP sensor.

8. Install the air cleaner assembly.

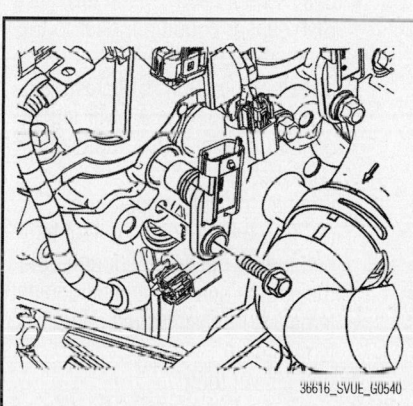

Fig. 519 Remove the CMP sensor bolt

CRANKSHAFT POSITION (CKP) SENSOR

REMOVAL & INSTALLATION

2.4L Engine

See Figures 520 through 522.

1. Remove the starter motor.

2. Disconnect the engine wiring harness electrical connector (1) from the Crankshaft Position (CKP) sensor.

3. Remove the CKP sensor bolt.

4. Remove the CKP sensor.

To install:

5. Lubricate the CKP sensor O-ring seal with clean engine oil.

6. Install the CKP sensor.

7. Install the CKP sensor bolt. Tighten the bolt to 89 inch lbs. (10 Nm).

8. Connect the engine wiring harness electrical connector to the CKP sensor.

9. Install the starter motor.

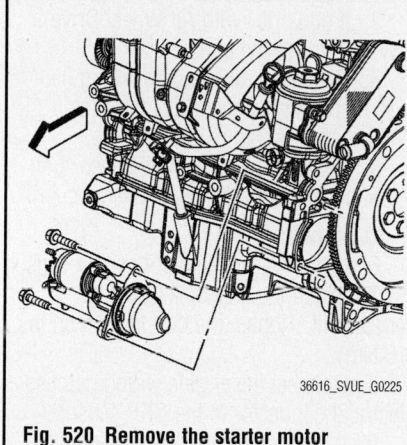

Fig. 520 Remove the starter motor

Fig. 521 Disconnect the engine wiring harness electrical connector (1) from the CKP sensor

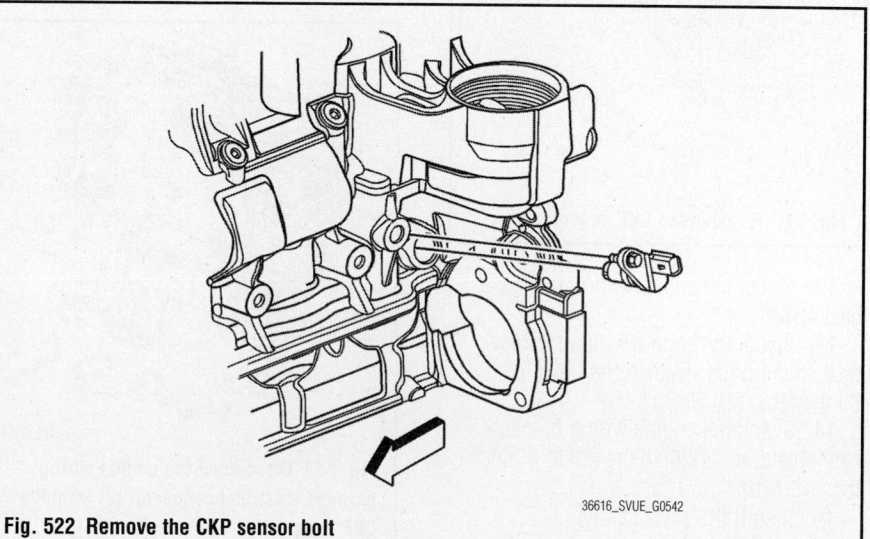

Fig. 522 Remove the CKP sensor bolt

3.5L Engine

See Figures 523 through 526.

1. Remove the right catalytic converter.

2. Remove the engine wiring harness heat shield nut (3).

3. Remove the engine wiring harness heat shield bolts (1 and 4).

4. Remove the engine wiring harness heat shield (2).

5. Disconnect the engine wiring harness electrical connector (4) from the Crankshaft Position (CKP) sensor (3).

6. Remove the CKP sensor stud.

7. Remove the CKP sensor.

To install:

8. Lubricate the CKP sensor O-ring with clean engine oil.

9. Remove the CKP sensor.

10. Remove the CKP sensor stud. Tighten the stud to 89 inch lbs. (10 Nm).

11. Connect the engine wiring harness electrical connector to the CKP sensor.

Fig. 523 Remove the right catalytic converter

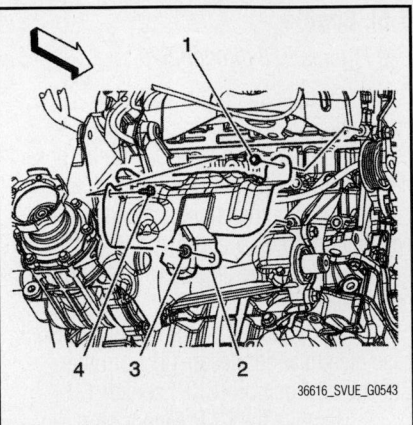

Fig. 524 Remove the engine wiring harness heat shield nut (3)

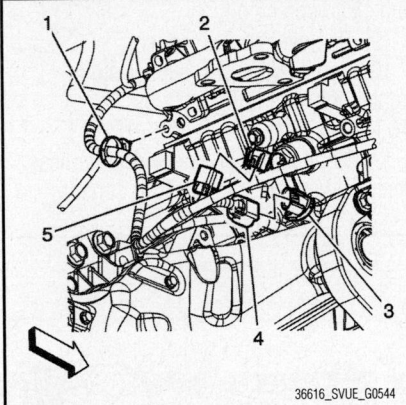

Fig. 525 Disconnect the engine wiring harness electrical connector (4) from the CKP sensor (3)

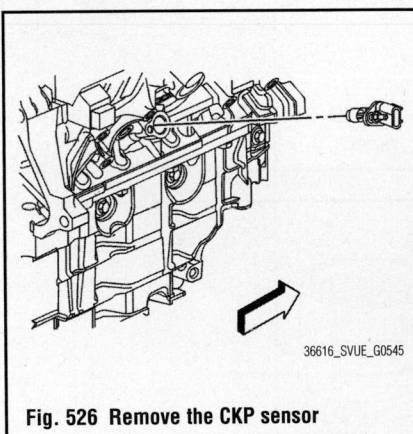

Fig. 526 Remove the CKP sensor

12. Install the engine wiring harness heat shield.

13. Install the engine wiring harness heat shield bolts. Tighten the bolts to 89 inch lbs. (10 Nm).

14. Install the engine wiring harness heat shield nut. Tighten the nut to 89 inch lbs. (10 Nm).

15. Install the right catalytic converter.

16. Perform the CKP system variation learn procedure.

3.6L Engine

See Figures 527 and 528.

1. Raise and support the vehicle.

2. If equipped with All Wheel Drive (AWD), remove the transfer case.

3. Disconnect the engine wiring harness electrical connector (2) from the Crankshaft Position (CKP) sensor.

4. Remove the crankshaft sensor bolt.

5. Remove the crankshaft sensor.

To install:

6. Install the crankshaft position sensor.

7. Install the crankshaft position sensor bolt. Tighten the bolt to 89 inch lbs. (10 Nm).

8. Connect the engine wiring harness electrical connector to the CKP sensor.

9. If equipped with AWD, install the transfer case.

10. Lower the vehicle.

11. Perform the Crankshaft Position System Variation Learn procedure.

LEARN PROCEDURE

➡**The Crankshaft Position (CKP) system variation learn procedure is also required when the following service procedures have been performed, regardless of whether DTC P0315 is set:**

- An engine replacement
- A Engine Control Module (ECM) replacement
- A crankshaft balancer replacement
- A crankshaft replacement
- A CKP sensor replacement
- Any engine repairs which disturb the crankshaft to CKP sensor relationship.

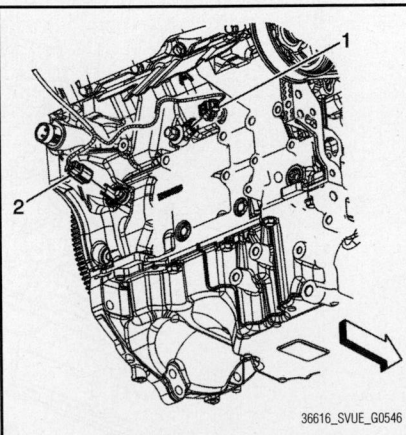

Fig. 527 Disconnect the engine wiring harness electrical connector (2) from the CKP sensor

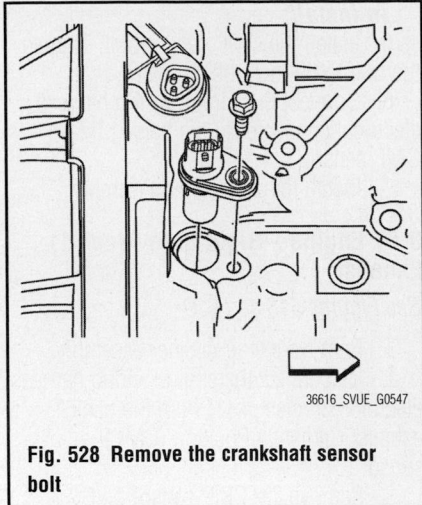

Fig. 528 Remove the crankshaft sensor bolt

➡**The ECM monitors certain component signals to determine if all the conditions are met to continue with the CKP System Variation Learn Procedure. The scan tool only displays the condition that inhibits the procedure. The scan tool displays the signals of the following components:**

- CKP sensors activity—If there is a CKP sensor condition, refer to the applicable DTC that set.
- Camshaft position (CMP) signal activity—If there is a CMP signal condition, refer to the applicable DTC that set.
- Engine Coolant Temperature (ECT)—If the engine coolant temperature is not warm enough, idle the engine until the engine coolant temperature reaches the correct temperature.

1. Install a scan tool.

2. Monitor the ECM for DTCs with a scan tool. If other DTCs are set, except DTC P0315, refer to Diagnostic Trouble Code (DTC) List for the applicable DTC that set.

3. With a scan tool, select the CKP System Variation Learn Procedure and perform the following:

   a. Block the drive wheels.

   b. Set the parking brake.

   c. DO NOT apply the brake pedal.

   d. Cycle the ignition from OFF to ON.

   e. Apply and hold the brake pedal for the duration of the procedure.

   f. Start and idle the engine.

   g. Turn the Air Conditioning (A/C) OFF.

   h. The vehicle must remain in Park or Neutral.

➡**While the learn procedure is in progress, release the throttle immedi-**

ately when the engine starts to decelerate. The engine control is returned to the operator and the engine responds to throttle position after the learn procedure is complete.

   i. Accelerate to Wide Open Throttle (WOT) and release when the fuel cut-off occurs.

4. The scan tool displays Learn Status: Learned this Ignition. If the scan tool indicates that DTC P0315 ran and passed, the CKP variation learn procedure is complete. If the scan tool indicates DTC P0315 failed or did not run, or another DTC is present, refer to Diagnostic Trouble Code (DTC) List and perform the appropriate diagnostic procedure.

5. Turn OFF the ignition for 30 seconds after the learn procedure is completed successfully in order to store the CKP system variation values in the ECM memory.

ENGINE CONTROL MODULE (ECM)

REMOVAL & INSTALLATION

See Figures 529 and 530.

➡ **Ensure the following:**

- Turn the ignition OFF when installing or removing the control module connectors and disconnecting or reconnecting the power to the control module (battery cable, Powertrain Control Module (PCM)/Engine Control Module (ECM)/Transaxle Control Module (TCM) pigtail, control module fuse, jumper cables, etc.) in order to prevent internal control module damage.
- Control module damage may result when the metal case contacts battery voltage. DO NOT contact the control module metal case with battery voltage when servicing a control module, using battery booster cables, or when charging the vehicle battery.
- In order to prevent any possible electrostatic discharge damage to the control module, do not touch the connector pins or the soldered components on the circuit board.
- Remove any debris from around the control module connector surfaces before servicing the control module. Inspect the control module connector gaskets when diagnosing or replacing the control module. Ensure that the gaskets are

installed correctly. The gaskets prevent contaminant intrusion into the control module.
- The replacement control module must be programmed.

➡ It is necessary to record the remaining engine oil life. If the replacement module is not programmed with the remaining engine oil life, the engine oil life will default to 100 percent. If the replacement module is not programmed with the remaining engine oil life, the engine oil will need to be changed at 3,000 miles (5000 km) from the last engine oil change.

➡ It is necessary to record the remaining automatic transmission fluid life. If the replacement module is not programmed with the remaining automatic transmission fluid life, the automatic transmission fluid life will default to 100 percent. If the replacement module is not programmed with the remaining automatic transmission fluid life, the automatic transmission fluid will need to be changed at 50,000 miles (83000 km) from the last automatic transmission fluid change.

1. Using a scan tool, retrieve the percentage of remaining engine oil and the remaining automatic transmission fluid life. Record the remaining engine oil and the remaining automatic transmission fluid life.

2. Release the Engine Control Module (ECM) bracket (1) from the battery cover (2).

3. Release the retaining tabs on the ECM bracket and slide the ECM out of it.

4. Disconnect the engine wiring harness electrical connectors (1) from the ECM (5).

To install:

5. Connect the engine wiring harness electrical connectors to the ECM.

6. Slide the ECM into the ECM bracket until it locks into place.

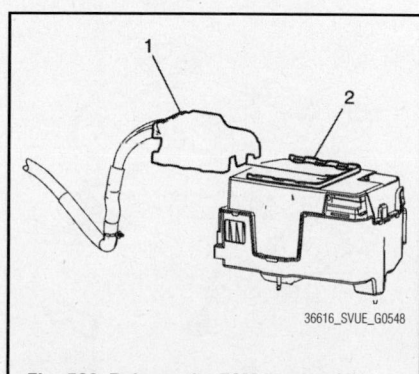

Fig. 529 Release the ECM bracket (1) from the battery cover (2)

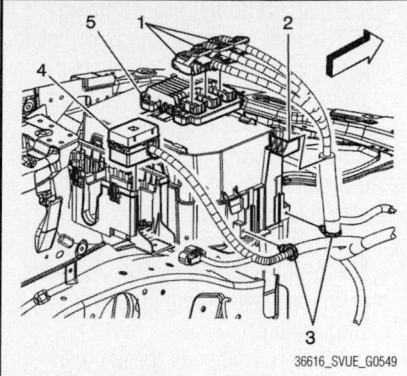

36616_SVUE_G0549

Fig. 530 Disconnect the engine wiring harness electrical connectors (1) from the ECM (5)

7. Install the ECM bracket onto the air cleaner assembly cover until it locks in place.

8. If replacing the ECM, program the ECM.

RESET

For step-by-step programming instructions, please refer to the Techline Information System (TIS) terminal.

Review the information below to ensure proper programming protocol.

DO NOT program a control module unless you are directed by a service procedure or you are directed by a General Motors Corporation service bulletin. Programming a control module at any other time will not permanently correct a customer's concern.

It is essential that the Tech 2, MDI and the TIS terminal are all equipped with the latest software before performing service programming.

Due to the time requirements of programming a controller, it is recommended that an external power source be used to maintain system voltage. Stable battery voltage is critical during programming. Any fluctuation, spiking, over voltage or loss of voltage will interrupt programming. To ensure trouble-free programming, GM recommends using one of the following external power sources:
- A Midtronics PSC charger
- A fully charged 12V jumper or booster pack disconnected from the AC voltage supply

Some modules will require additional programming/setup events performed before or after programming.

Some vehicles may require the use of a CANDi or MDI module for programming. Review the appropriate service information for these procedures.

DTCs may set during programming. Clear DTCs after programming is complete.

Clearing powertrain DTCs will set the Inspection/Maintenance (I/M) system status indicators to NO.

Ensure the following conditions are met before programming a control module:

1. Vehicle system voltage:

a. There is not a charging system concern. All charging system concerns must be repaired before programming a control module.

b. Battery voltage is greater than 12 volts but less than 16 volts. The battery must be fully charged before programming the control module.

c. Turn OFF or disable any system that may put a load on the vehicles battery, such as the following components:

- Twilight sentinel
- Interior lights
- Daytime Running Lights (DRL)— Applying the parking brake, on most vehicles, disables the DRL system
- Heating, Ventilation, And Air Conditioning (HVAC) systems
- Engine cooling fans, radio, etc.

2. The ignition switch must be in the proper position. SPS prompts you to turn ON the ignition, with the engine OFF. DO NOT change the position of the ignition switch during the programming procedure, unless instructed to do so.

3. Make certain all tool connections are secure, including the following components and circuits:

a. Tech 2:

- The RS-232 communication cable port
- The connection at the Data Link Connector (DLC)
- The voltage supply circuits

b. MDI:

- The USB, Ethernet or Wireless communication port
- The connection at the Data Link Connector (DLC)

4. DO NOT disturb the tool harnesses while programming. If an interruption occurs during the programming procedure, programming failure or control module damage may occur.

5. DO NOT turn OFF the ignition if the programming procedure is interrupted or unsuccessful. Ensure that all control module and DLC connections are secure and the TIS terminal operating software is up to date. Attempt to reprogram the control module. If the control module cannot be programmed, replace the control module.

ENGINE COOLANT TEMPERATURE (ECT) SENSOR

REMOVAL & INSTALLATION

2.4L Engine

See Figures 531 and 532.

➡**Use care when handling the coolant sensor. Damage to the coolant sensor will affect the operation of the fuel control system.**

1. Partially drain the cooling system.
2. Disconnect the engine wiring harness electrical connector (1) from the Engine Coolant Temperature (ECT) sensor.
3. Remove the ECT sensor.

To install:

4. If reinstalling the original ECT sensor, or if installing a NEW ECT sensor without a sealer, coat the threads with sealant.
5. Install the ECT sensor. Tighten the sensor to 15 ft. lbs. (20 Nm).
6. Connect the engine wiring harness electrical connector to the ECT sensor.
7. Fill the cooling system.

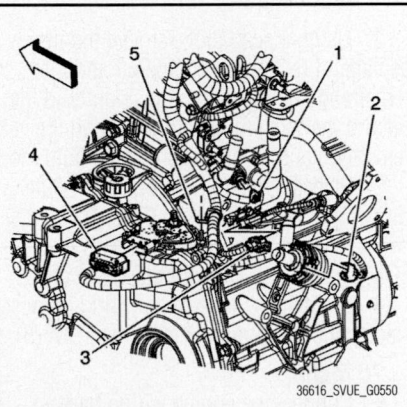

Fig. 531 Disconnect the engine wiring harness electrical connector (1) from the ECT sensor

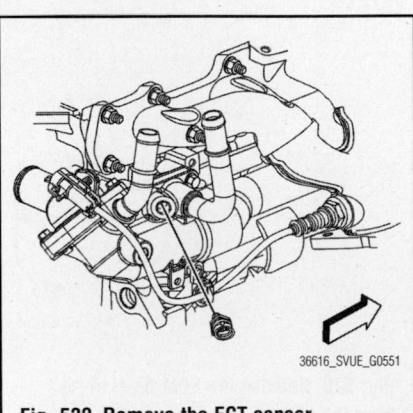

Fig. 532 Remove the ECT sensor

3.5L Engine

See Figure 533.

➡**Use care when handling the coolant sensor. Damage to the coolant sensor will affect the operation of the fuel control system.**

1. Partially drain the cooling system.
2. Remove the intake manifold cover, if required.
3. Disconnect the Engine Coolant Temperature (ECT) sensor electrical connector.
4. Remove the ECT sensor.

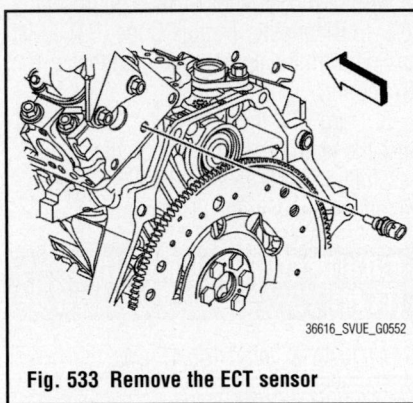

Fig. 533 Remove the ECT sensor

To install:

5. Coat the threads of the ECT sensor with sealer GM P/N 13246004 (Canadian P/N 10953480) or equivalent.
6. Install the ECT sensor. Tighten the ECT sensor to 15 ft. lbs. (20 Nm).
7. Connect the ECT electrical connector.
8. Install the intake manifold cover, if required.
9. Fill the cooling system.

3.6L Engine

See Figure 534.

1. Partially drain the cooling system.
2. Disconnect the engine wiring harness electrical connector from the Engine Coolant Temperature (ECT) sensor.

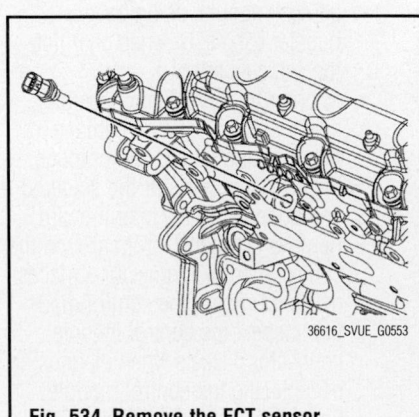

Fig. 534 Remove the ECT sensor

3. Remove the ECT sensor.

To install:

4. Install the ECT sensor. Tighten the sensor to 16 ft. lbs. (22 Nm).

5. Connect the engine wiring harness electrical connector to the ECT sensor.

6. Fill the cooling system.

EVAPORATIVE EMISSIONS (EVAP) CANISTER

LOCATION

The Evaporative Emission (EVAP) canister is located on the underbody inside the frame rail.

REMOVAL & INSTALLATION

See Figures 535 through 537.

1. Raise and suitably support the vehicle.

2. Disconnect the fuel tank wiring harness electrical connector (1) from the Evaporative Emission (EVAP) canister vent solenoid valve.

3. Disconnect the fuel tank vapor line quick connect fitting (4) from the EVAP canister.

4. Disconnect the chassis EVAP line quick connect fitting (1) from the EVAP canister.

5. Disconnect the EVAP canister line quick connect fitting (2) from the fuel tank fresh air line (3).

6. Remove the EVAP canisters nuts.

7. Remove the canister from the vehicle underbody.

To install:

8. Position the EVAP canister to the underbody studs.

9. Install the EVAP canister nuts. Tighten the nuts to 71 inch lbs. (8 Nm).

10. Connect the EVAP canister line quick connect fitting to the fuel tank fresh air line.

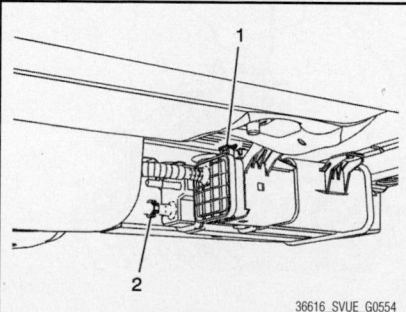

Fig. 535 Disconnect the fuel tank wiring harness electrical connector (1) from the EVAP canister vent solenoid valve

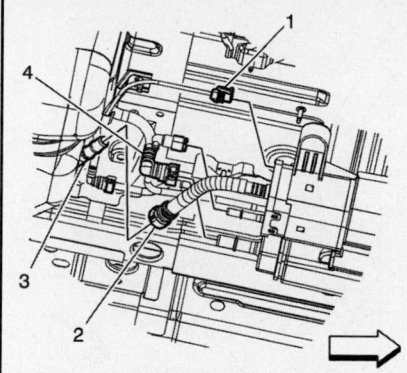

1. Chassis EVAP line quick connect fitting
2. EVAP canister line quick fitting
3. Fuel tank fresh air line
4. Fuel tank vapor line quick connect fitting

36616_SVUE_G0555

Fig. 536 Disconnect the fuel tank vapor line quick connect fitting (4) from the EVAP canister

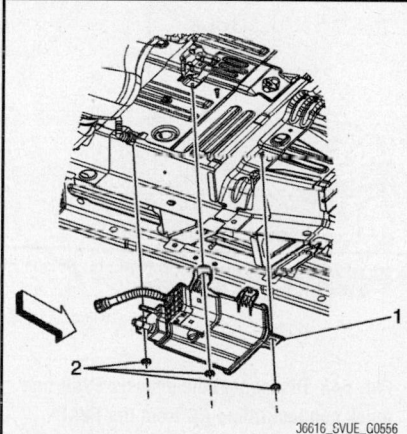

36616_SVUE_G0556

Fig. 537 Disconnect the fuel tank vapor line quick connect fitting (4) from the EVAP canister

11. Connect the fuel tank vapor line quick connect fitting to the EVAP canister.

12. Connect the chassis EVAP line quick connect fitting to the EVAP canister.

13. Connect the fuel tank wiring harness electrical connector to the EVAP canister vent solenoid valve.

14. Lower the vehicle.

EVAPORATIVE EMISSIONS (EVAP) PURGE CONTROL SOLENOID

REMOVAL & INSTALLATION

2.4L Engine

See Figures 538 through 540.

1. Remove the intake manifold cover.

2. Disconnect the engine wiring harness electrical connector from the Evaporative Emission (EVAP) canister purge valve.

3. Disconnect the EVAP canister purge valve tube.

4. Disconnect the chassis EVAP vapor line from the EVAP canister purge valve.

5. Remove the EVAP canister purge valve bracket bolt.

6. Remove the EVAP canister purge valve with bracket.

7. Remove the EVAP canister purge valve from the bracket.

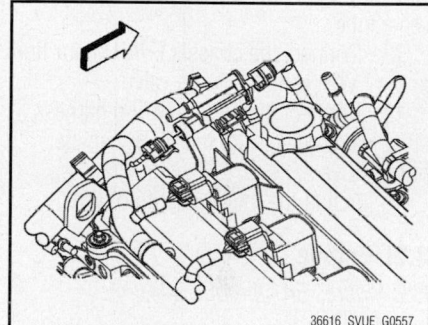

36616_SVUE_G0557

Fig. 538 Disconnect the engine wiring harness electrical connector from the EVAP canister purge valve

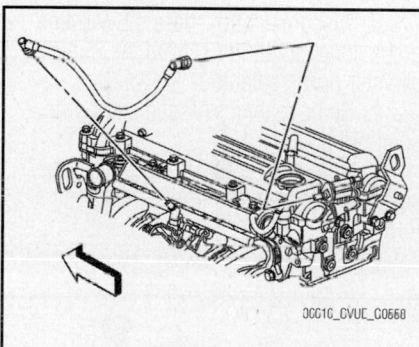

36616_SVUE_G0558

Fig. 539 Disconnect the EVAP canister purge valve tube

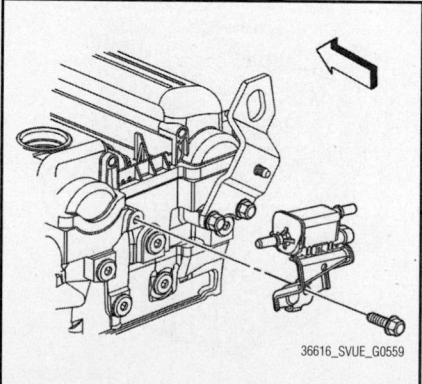

36616_SVUE_G0559

Fig. 540 Remove the EVAP canister purge valve bracket bolt

8. Inspect for carbon release in the EVAP canister purge valve ports. If there is any loose carbon, replace the EVAP canister and any components necessary to remove the carbon particles.

To install:

9. Install the EVAP canister purge valve to the bracket.

10. Position the EVAP canister purge valve with bracket to the cylinder head.

11. Install the EVAP canister purge valve bracket bolt. Tighten the bolt to 18 ft. lbs. (25 Nm).

12. Connect the EVAP canister purge valve tube.

13. Connect the chassis EVAP vapor line to the EVAP canister purge valve.

14. Connect the engine wiring harness electrical connector to the EVAP canister purge valve.

15. Install the intake manifold cover.

3.5L Engine

See Figures 541 through 544.

1. Remove the intake manifold cover.

2. Disconnect the engine wiring harness electrical connector (1) from the Evaporative Emission (EVAP) canister purge solenoid (4).

3. Disconnect the chassis EVAP line quick connect fitting (3) from the EVAP canister purge solenoid.

4. Remove the EVAP canister purge solenoid bolt (1).

5. Remove the EVAP canister purge solenoid (2) from the upper intake manifold.

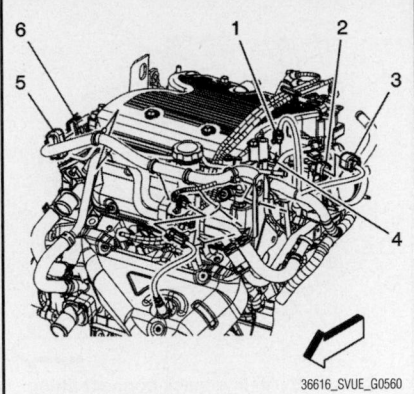

Fig. 542 Disconnect the engine wiring harness electrical connector (1) from the EVAP canister purge solenoid (4)

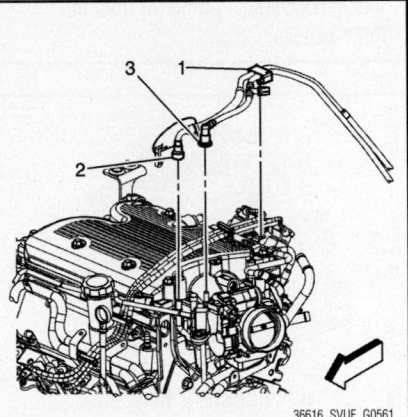

Fig. 543 Disconnect the chassis EVAP line quick connect fitting (3) from the EVAP canister purge solenoid

6. Remove and discard the EVAP canister purge solenoid O-ring seal (3).

To install:

7. Install a NEW EVAP canister purge solenoid O-ring seal to the upper intake manifold.

8. Install the EVAP canister purge solenoid to the upper intake manifold.

9. Install the EVAP canister purge solenoid bolt. Tighten the bolt to 12 ft. lbs. (16 Nm).

10. Connect the chassis EVAP line quick connect fitting to the EVAP canister purge solenoid.

11. Connect the engine wiring harness electrical connector to the EVAP canister purge solenoid.

12. Install the intake manifold cover.

3.6L Engine

See Figures 545 through 547.

1. Remove the fuel injector sight shield.

2. Disconnect the engine wiring harness electrical connector from the Evaporative Emission (EVAP) purge solenoid.

3. Disconnect the chassis EVAP line quick connect fitting (1) from the EVAP canister purge solenoid valve.

4. Disconnect the EVAP line quick connect fitting (1) from the EVAP canister purge solenoid valve.

5. Remove the EVAP purge solenoid bracket bolt (1).

6. Remove the EVAP purge solenoid (3).

To install:

7. Position the EVAP purge solenoid to the upper intake manifold.

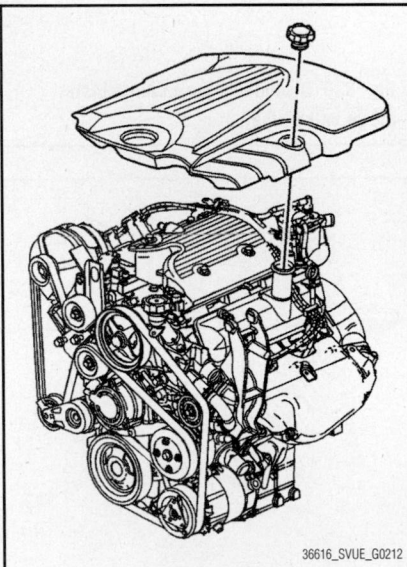

Fig. 541 Remove the intake manifold cover

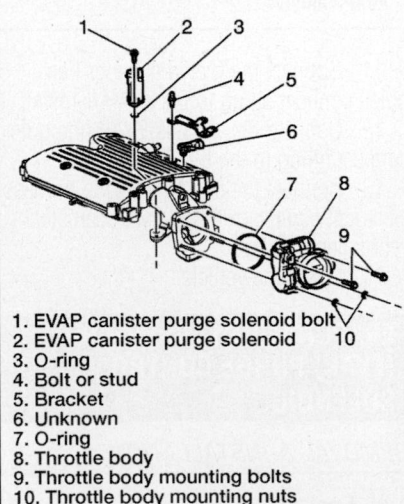

1. EVAP canister purge solenoid bolt
2. EVAP canister purge solenoid
3. O-ring
4. Bolt or stud
5. Bracket
6. Unknown
7. O-ring
8. Throttle body
9. Throttle body mounting bolts
10. Throttle body mounting nuts

Fig. 544 Remove the EVAP canister purge solenoid bolt (1)

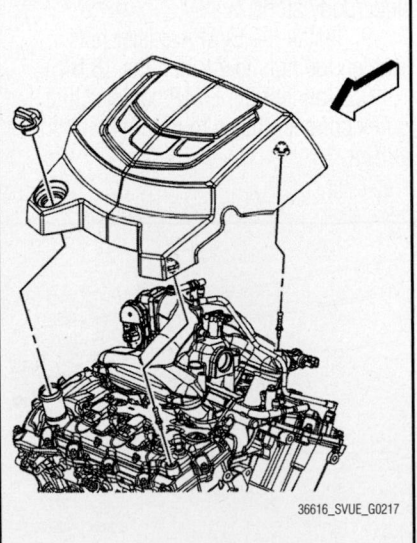

Fig. 545 Remove the fuel injector sight shield

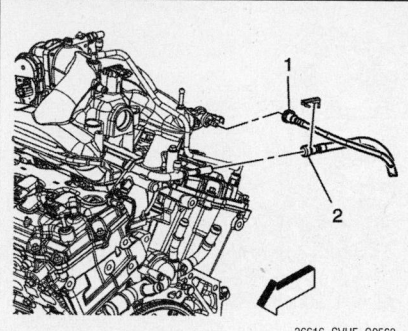

Fig. 546 Disconnect the chassis EVAP line quick connect fitting (1) from the EVAP canister purge solenoid valve

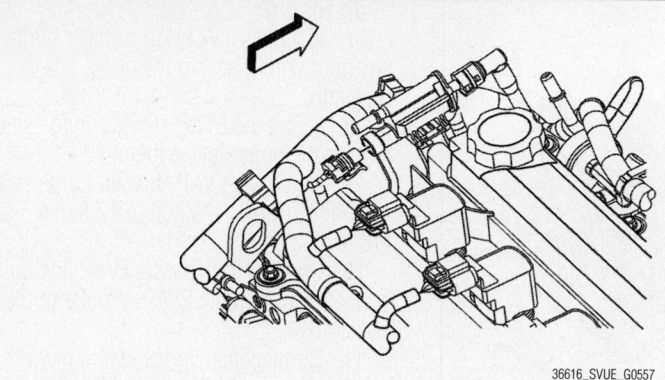

Fig. 548 Disconnect the engine wiring harness electrical connector from the EVAP canister purge valve

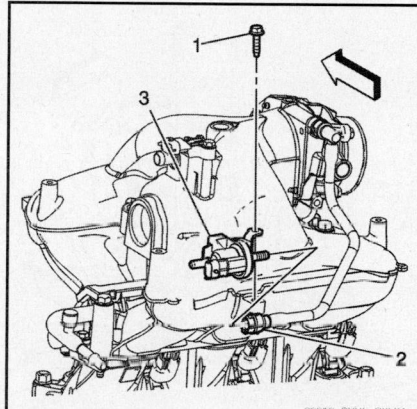

Fig. 547 Disconnect the EVAP line quick connect fitting (1) from the EVAP canister purge solenoid valve

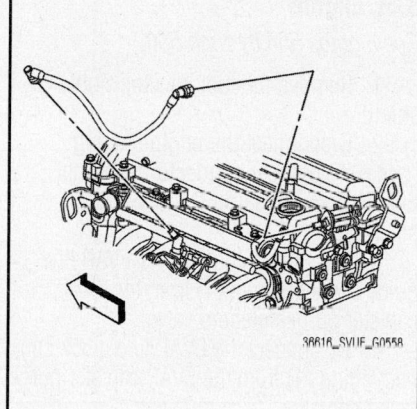

Fig. 549 Disconnect the EVAP canister purge valve tube

8. Install the EVAP purge solenoid bracket bolt. Tighten the bolt to 89 inch lbs. (10 Nm).

9. Connect the EVAP line quick connect fitting to the EVAP canister purge solenoid valve.

10. Connect the chassis EVAP line quick connect fitting to the EVAP canister purge solenoid valve.

11. Connect the engine wiring harness electrical connector to the EVAP purge solenoid.

12. Install the fuel injector sight shield.

EVAPORATIVE EMISSIONS (EVAP) PURGE CONTROL VALVE

REMOVAL & INSTALLATION

2.4L Engine

See Figures 548 through 550.

1. Remove the intake manifold cover.
2. Disconnect the engine wiring harness electrical connector from the Evapo-

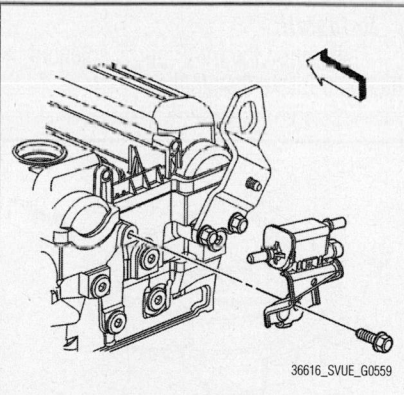

Fig. 550 Remove the EVAP canister purge valve bracket bolt

rative Emission (EVAP) canister purge valve.

3. Disconnect the EVAP canister purge valve tube.

4. Disconnect the chassis EVAP vapor line from the EVAP canister purge valve.

5. Remove the EVAP canister purge valve bracket bolt.

6. Remove the EVAP canister purge valve with bracket.

7. Remove the EVAP canister purge valve from the bracket.

8. Inspect for carbon release in the EVAP canister purge valve ports. If there is any loose carbon, replace the EVAP canister and any components necessary to remove the carbon particles.

To install:

9. Install the EVAP canister purge valve to the bracket.

10. Position the EVAP canister purge valve with bracket to the cylinder head.

11. Install the EVAP canister purge valve bracket bolt. Tighten the bolt to 18 ft. lbs. (25 Nm).

12. Connect the EVAP canister purge valve tube.

13. Connect the chassis EVAP vapor line to the EVAP canister purge valve.

14. Connect the engine wiring harness electrical connector to the EVAP canister purge valve.

15. Install the intake manifold cover.

3.5L Engine

See Figures 541, 551 through 553.

1. Remove the intake manifold cover.

2. Disconnect the engine wiring harness electrical connector (1) from the Evaporative Emission (EVAP) canister purge solenoid (4).

3. Disconnect the chassis EVAP line quick connect fitting (3) from the EVAP canister purge solenoid.

4. Remove the EVAP canister purge solenoid bolt (1).

5. Remove the EVAP canister purge solenoid (2) from the upper intake manifold.

6. Remove and discard the EVAP canister purge solenoid O-ring seal (3).

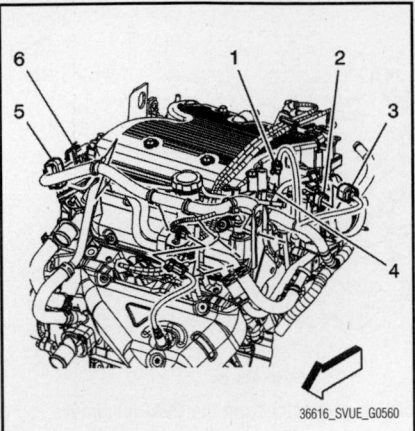

Fig. 551 Disconnect the engine wiring harness electrical connector (1) from the EVAP canister purge solenoid (4)

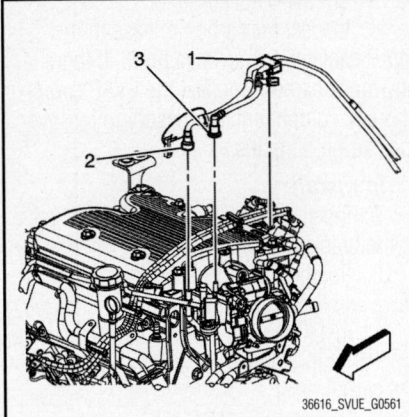

Fig. 552 Disconnect the chassis EVAP line quick connect fitting (3) from the EVAP canister purge solenoid

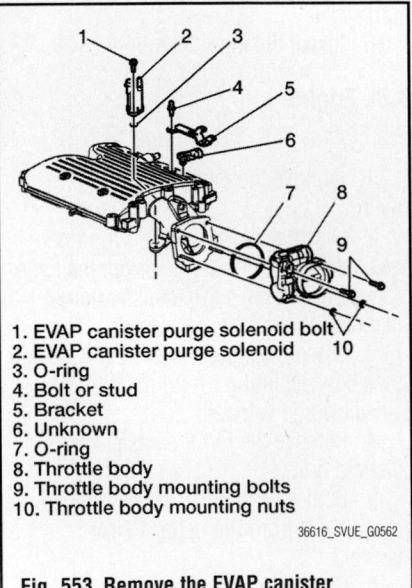

1. EVAP canister purge solenoid bolt
2. EVAP canister purge solenoid
3. O-ring
4. Bolt or stud
5. Bracket
6. Unknown
7. O-ring
8. Throttle body
9. Throttle body mounting bolts
10. Throttle body mounting nuts

Fig. 553 Remove the EVAP canister purge solenoid bolt (1)

To install:

7. Install a NEW EVAP canister purge solenoid O-ring seal to the upper intake manifold.

8. Install the EVAP canister purge solenoid to the upper intake manifold.

9. Install the EVAP canister purge solenoid bolt. Tighten the bolt to 12 ft. lbs. (16 Nm).

10. Connect the chassis EVAP line quick connect fitting to the EVAP canister purge solenoid.

11. Connect the engine wiring harness electrical connector to the EVAP canister purge solenoid.

12. Install the intake manifold cover.

3.6L Engine

See Figures 554 through 556.

1. Remove the fuel injector sight shield.

2. Disconnect the engine wiring harness electrical connector from the Evaporative Emission (EVAP) purge solenoid.

3. Disconnect the chassis EVAP line quick connect fitting (1) from the EVAP canister purge solenoid valve.

4. Disconnect the EVAP line quick connect fitting (1) from the EVAP canister purge solenoid valve.

5. Remove the EVAP purge solenoid bracket bolt (1).

6. Remove the EVAP purge solenoid (3).

To install:

7. Position the EVAP purge solenoid to the upper intake manifold.

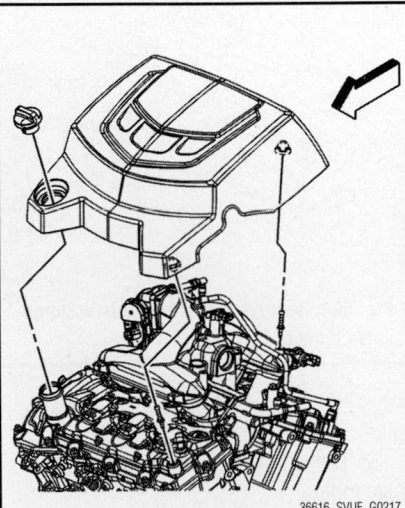

Fig. 554 Remove the fuel injector sight shield

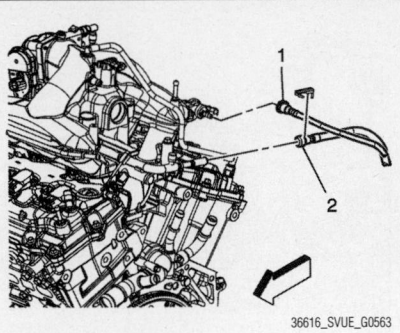

Fig. 555 Disconnect the chassis EVAP line quick connect fitting (1) from the EVAP canister purge solenoid valve

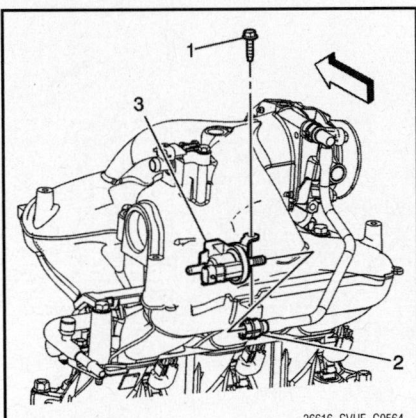

Fig. 556 Disconnect the EVAP line quick connect fitting (1) from the EVAP canister purge solenoid valve

8. Install the EVAP purge solenoid bracket bolt. Tighten the bolt to 89 inch lbs. (10 Nm).

9. Connect the EVAP line quick connect fitting to the EVAP canister purge solenoid valve.

10. Connect the chassis EVAP line quick connect fitting to the EVAP canister purge solenoid valve.

11. Connect the engine wiring harness electrical connector to the EVAP purge solenoid.

12. Install the fuel injector sight shield.

FUEL TANK (EVAP) VAPOR PRESSURE SENSOR

LOCATION

The fuel tank pressure sensor is located on the top of the fuel tank.

REMOVAL & INSTALLATION

See Figures 557 and 558.

1. Remove the fuel tank.
2. Disconnect the fuel tank wiring harness

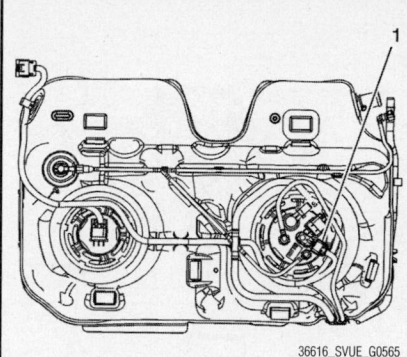

Fig. 557 Disconnect the fuel tank wiring harness electrical connector (1) from the fuel tank pressure sensor

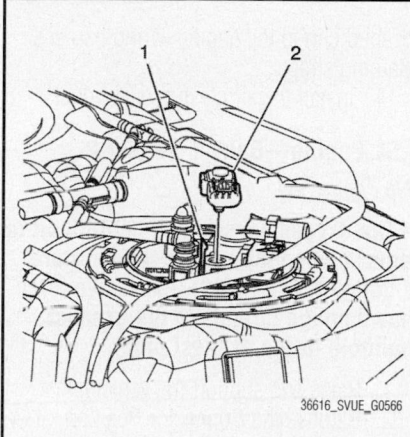

Fig. 558 Disengage the retaining tab (1) securing the fuel tank pressure sensor

electrical connector (1) from the fuel tank pressure sensor.

3. Disengage the retaining tab (1) securing the fuel tank pressure sensor.

4. Carefully lift and remove the fuel tank pressure sensor (2) from the fuel pump module.

To install:

5. Install the fuel tank pressure sensor to the fuel pump module assembly until the sensor engages the retaining tab.

6. Connect the fuel tank wiring harness electrical connector to the fuel tank pressure sensor.

7. Install the fuel tank.

HEATED OXYGEN SENSOR (HO2S)

LOCATION

Heated Oxygen Sensors (HO2S) are located at the exhaust manifold and on the exhaust system near the catalytic converter.

REMOVAL & INSTALLATION

2.4L Engine—Sensor 1

See Figure 559.

➡The oxygen sensor uses a permanently attached pigtail and connector. Do not remove the pigtail from the oxygen sensor. Damage to or removal of the pigtail connector could affect proper operation of the oxygen sensor.

➡The use of excessive force may damage the threads in the exhaust manifold/pipe.

➡The in-line connector and louvered end must be kept clear of grease, dirt or other contaminants. Avoid using cleaning solvents of any type. DO NOT drop or roughly handle the Heated Oxygen Sensor (HO2S).

➡The HO2S may be difficult to remove when the engine temperature is less than 120°F (48°C).

1. Remove the Connector Position Assurance (CPA) tab from the HO2S electrical connection.

2. Disconnect the engine wiring harness electrical connector from the HO2S electrical connector.

3. Remove the HO2S electrical connector from the thermostat housing.

4. Remove the HO2S using wrench J 39194-C.

To install:

➡A special anti-seize compound is used on the heated oxygen sensor threads. The compound consists of a liquid graphite and glass beads. The graphite will burn away, but the glass beads will remain, making the heated oxygen sensor easier to remove. New or service replacement heated oxygen sensors will have the compound applied to the threads. If a heated

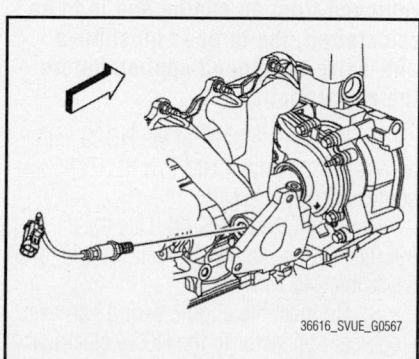

Fig. 559 Remove the HO2S using wrench J 39194-C

oxygen sensor is removed and is to be reinstalled without replacement then the threads must have an appropriate anti-seize compound applied prior to installation.

5. If necessary, coat the threads of the HO2S with anti-seize compound Saturn P/N 21485279 or equivalent.

6. Install the HO2S using wrench J 39194-C. Tighten the sensor to 31 ft. lbs. (42 Nm).

7. Install the HO2S electrical connector to the thermostat housing.

8. Connect the engine wiring harness electrical connector to the HO2S electrical connector.

9. Install the CPA tab to the HO2S electrical connection.

2.4L Engine—Sensor 2

See Figure 560.

➡The oxygen sensor uses a permanently attached pigtail and connector. Do not remove the pigtail from the oxygen sensor. Damage to or removal of the pigtail connector could affect proper operation of the oxygen sensor.

➡The use of excessive force may damage the threads in the exhaust manifold/pipe.

➡The in-line connector and louvered end must be kept clear of grease, dirt or other contaminants. Avoid using cleaning solvents of any type. DO NOT drop or roughly handle the Heated Oxygen Sensor (HO2S).

➡The HO2S may be difficult to remove when the engine temperature is less than 120°F (48°C).

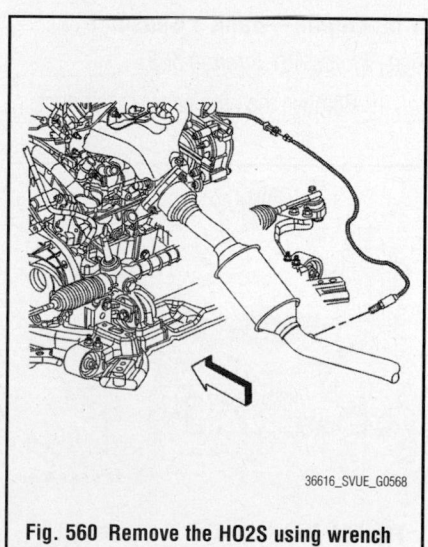

Fig. 560 Remove the HO2S using wrench J 39194

1. Raise the vehicle.
2. Remove the Connector Position Assurance (CPA) tab from the HO2S electrical connection.
3. Disconnect the engine wiring harness electrical connector from the HO2S electrical connector.
4. Remove the HO2S wiring from the exhaust heat shield.
5. Remove the HO2S using wrench J 39194.

To install:

➡A special anti-seize compound is used on the heated oxygen sensor threads. The compound consists of a liquid graphite and glass beads. The graphite will burn away, but the glass beads will remain, making the heated oxygen sensor easier to remove. New or service replacement heated oxygen sensors will have the compound applied to the threads. If a heated oxygen sensor is removed and is to be reinstalled without replacement then the threads must have an appropriate anti-seize compound applied prior to installation.

6. If necessary, coat the threads of the HO2S with anti-seize compound Saturn P/N 21485279 or equivalent.
7. Install the HO2S using wrench J 39194-C. Tighten the sensor to 31 ft. lbs. (42 Nm).
8. Install the HO2S wiring in the exhaust heat shield.
9. Connect the engine wiring harness electrical connector to the HO2S electrical connector.
10. Install the CPA tab to the HO2S electrical connection.

3.5L Engine—Bank 1 Sensor 1

See Figures 561 through 563.

1. Remove the air cleaner outlet duct.

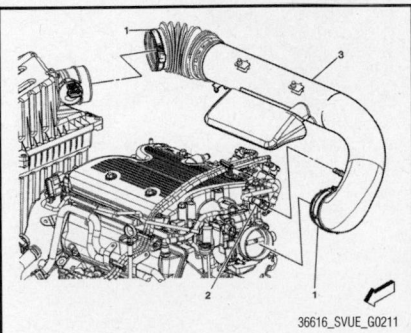

Fig. 561 Remove the air cleaner outlet duct

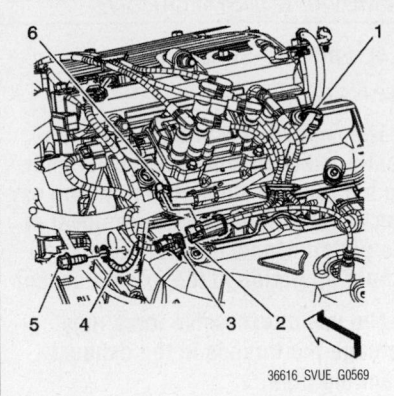

Fig. 562 Disconnect the engine wiring harness electrical connector (3) from the HO2S electrical connector (2)

2. Remove the Connector Position Assurance (CPA) retainer.
3. Disconnect the engine wiring harness electrical connector (3) from the Heated Oxygen Sensor (HO2S) electrical connector (2).
4. Remove the HO2S electrical connector rosebud clip from the engine wiring harness retaining strap (6).

➡The oxygen sensor may be difficult to remove when the engine temperature is below 120°F (48°C). Excessive force may damage threads in the exhaust manifold or the exhaust pipe.

5. Remove the HO2S (4). Use the J 39194-B, if necessary.

To install:

➡A special anti-seize compound is used on the HO2S threads. The compound consists of graphite suspended in fluid and glass beads. The graphite will burn away, but the glass beads will remain, making the sensor easier to remove. New or service sensors will already have the compound applied to the threads. If a sensor is removed from an engine and is to be reinstalled, the threads must have anti-seize compound applied before the reinstallation.

6. Coat the threads of the HO2S with anti-seize compound GM P/N 12377953 or equivalent, if necessary.
7. Install the HO2S (4). Use the J 39194-B, if necessary. Tighten the sensor to 31 ft. lbs. (42 Nm).
8. Connect the engine wiring harness electrical connector to the HO2S electrical connector.
9. Install the CPA retainer.
10. Install the HO2S electrical connector

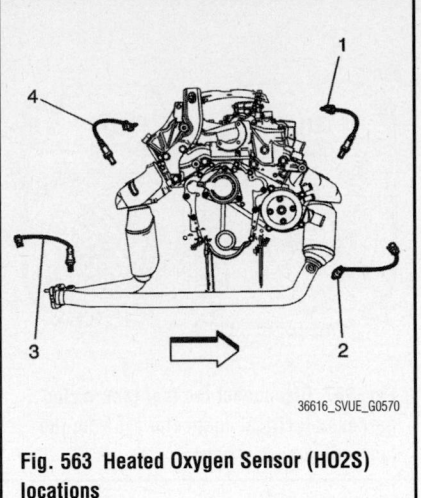

Fig. 563 Heated Oxygen Sensor (HO2S) locations

rosebud clip to the engine wiring harness retaining strap.
11. Install the air cleaner outlet duct.

3.5L Engine—Bank 1 Sensor 2

See Figure 564.

➡The oxygen sensor may be difficult to remove when the engine temperature is below 120°F (48°C). Excessive force may damage threads in the exhaust manifold or the exhaust pipe.

1. Raise and support the vehicle.
2. Remove the Connector Position Assurance (CPA) retainer.
3. Disconnect the Heated Oxygen Sensor (HO2S) electrical connector from the engine wiring harness electrical connector.
4. Remove the HO2S (3). Use the J 39194-B, if necessary.

To install:

➡A special anti-seize compound is used on the HO2S 2 threads. The compound consists of graphite suspended in fluid and glass beads. The graphite will burn away, but the glass beads

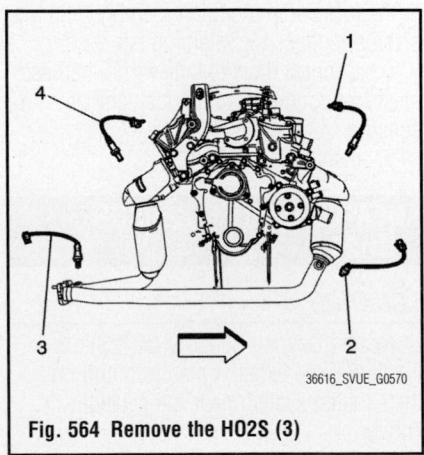

Fig. 564 Remove the HO2S (3)

will remain, making the sensor easier to remove. New or service sensors will already have the compound applied to the threads. If a sensor is removed from an engine and is to be reinstalled, the threads must have anti-seize compound applied before reinstallation.

5. Coat the threads of the HO2S with anti-seize compound GM P/N 12377953 or equivalent, if necessary.

6. Install the HO2S (3). Use the J 39194-B, if necessary.

Tighten the sensor to 31 ft. lbs. (42 Nm).

7. Connect the HO2S electrical connector to the engine wiring harness electrical connector.

8. Install the CPA retainer.

9. Lower the vehicle.

3.5L Engine—Bank 2 Sensor 1

See Figures 565 and 566.

1. Remove the intake manifold cover, if necessary.

2. Remove the Connector Position Assurance (CPA) retainer.

3. Disconnect the engine wiring harness electrical connector (3) from the Heated Oxygen Sensor (HO2S) electrical connector (2).

4. Remove the HO2S rosebud clip from the oil level indicator tube tab (1).

➡ **The oxygen sensor may be difficult to remove when the engine temperature is below 120°F (48°C). Excessive force may damage threads in the exhaust manifold or the exhaust pipe.**

5. Remove the HO2S (1). Use the J 39194-B, if necessary.

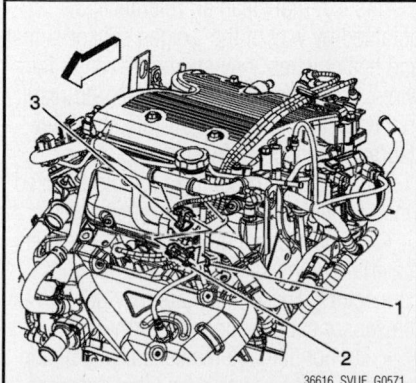

Fig. 565 Disconnect the engine wiring harness electrical connector (3) from the HO2S electrical connector (2)

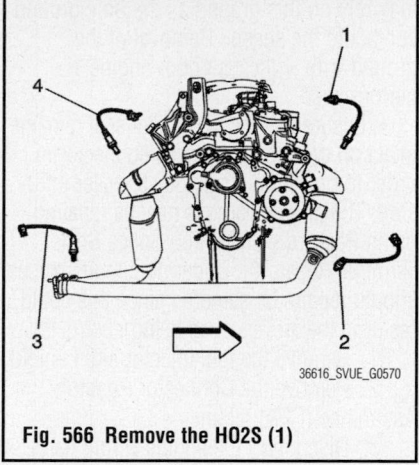

Fig. 566 Remove the HO2S (1)

To install:

➡ **A special anti-seize compound is used on the HO2S 1 threads. The compound consists of graphite suspended in fluid and glass beads. The graphite will burn away, but the glass beads will remain, making the sensor easier to remove. New or service sensors will already have the compound applied to the threads. If a sensor is removed from an engine and is to be reinstalled, the threads must have anti-seize compound applied before the reinstallation.**

6. Coat the threads of the HO2S with anti-seize compound GM P/N 12377953 or equivalent, if necessary.

7. Install the HO2S (1). Use the J 39194-B, if necessary. Tighten the sensor to 31 ft. lbs. (42 Nm).

8. Connect the engine wiring harness electrical connector to the HO2S electrical connector.

9. Install the CPA retainer.

10. Install the HO2S rosebud clip to the oil level indicator tube tab.

3.5L Engine—Bank 2 Sensor 2

See Figures 567 and 568.

1. Raise and support the vehicle.

2. Remove the Connector Position Assurance (CPA) retainer.

3. Disconnect the Heated Oxygen Sensor (HO2S) electrical connector (2) from the engine wiring harness electrical connector (3).

➡ **The oxygen sensor may be difficult to remove when the engine temperature is below 120°F (48°C). Excessive force may damage threads in the exhaust manifold or the exhaust pipe.**

4. Remove the HO2S (2). Use the J 39194-B, if necessary.

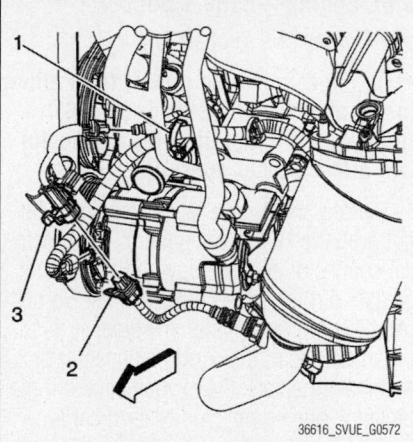

Fig. 567 Disconnect the HO2S electrical connector (2) from the engine wiring harness electrical connector (3)

To install:

➡ **A special anti-seize compound is used on the HO2S 2 threads. The compound consists of graphite suspended in fluid and glass beads. The graphite will burn away, but the glass beads will remain, making the sensor easier to remove. New or service sensors will already have the compound applied to the threads. If a sensor is removed from an engine and is to be reinstalled, the threads must have anti-seize compound applied before reinstallation.**

5. Coat the threads of the HO2S with anti-seize compound GM P/N 12377953 or equivalent, if necessary.

6. Install the HO2S (2). Use the J 39194-B, if necessary. Tighten the sensor to 31 ft. lbs. (42 Nm).

7. Connect the HO2S electrical connector to the engine wiring harness electrical connector.

8. Install the CPA retainer.

9. Lower the vehicle.

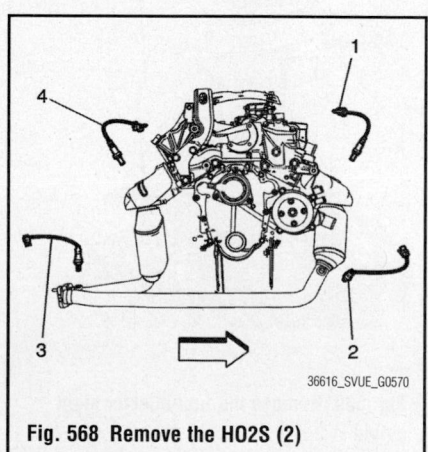

Fig. 568 Remove the HO2S (2)

3.6L Engine—Bank 1 Sensor 1

See Figures 569 through 571.

➡**Do not remove the pigtail from either the Heated Oxygen Sensor (HO2S). Removing the pigtail or the connector will affect sensor operation.**

Handle the oxygen sensor carefully. Do not drop the HO2S. Keep the in-line electrical connector and the louvered end free of grease, dirt, or other contaminants. Do not use cleaning solvents of any type.

Do not repair the wiring, connector or terminals. Replace the oxygen sensor if the pigtail wiring, connector, or terminal is damaged.

This external clean air reference is obtained by way of the oxygen sensor signal and heater wires. Any attempt to repair the wires, connectors, or terminals could result in the obstruction of the air reference and degraded sensor performance.

The following guidelines should be used when servicing the heated oxygen sensor:

• Do not apply contact cleaner or other materials to the sensor or vehicle harness connectors. These materials may get into the sensor causing poor performance.

• Do not damage the sensor pigtail and harness wires in such a way that the wires inside are exposed. This could provide a path for foreign materials to enter the sensor and cause performance problems.

• Ensure the sensor or vehicle lead wires are not bent sharply or kinked. Sharp bends or kinks could block the reference air path through the lead wire.

• Do not remove or defeat the oxygen sensor ground wire, where applicable. Vehicles that utilize the ground wired sensor may rely on this ground as the only ground contact to the sensor. Removal of the ground wire will cause poor engine performance.

• Ensure that the peripheral seal remains intact on the vehicle harness connector in order to prevent damage due to water intrusion. The engine harness may be repaired using Packard's Crimp and Splice Seals Terminal Repair Kit. Under no circumstances should repairs be soldered since this could result in the air reference being obstructed.

1. Remove the fuel injector sight shield.
2. Remove the Connector Position Assurance (CPA) retainer.
3. Disconnect the engine wiring harness electrical connector from the Heated Oxygen Sensor (HO2S) electrical connector (1).
4. Remove the HO2S electrical connector retainer from the harness clip (7).
5. Remove the HO2S (1) from the exhaust manifold.

To install:

➡**A special anti-seize compound is used in the HO2S threads. The compound consists of liquid graphite and glass beads. The graphite tends to burn away, but the glass beads remain, making the sensor easier to remove. New, or service replacement sensors already have the compound applied to the threads. If the sensor is removed from an exhaust component and if for any reason the sensor is to reinstalled, the threads must have anti-seize compound applied before the reinstallation.**

6. If reinstalling the old sensor, coat the threads with anti-seize compound GM P/N 12377953, or equivalent.

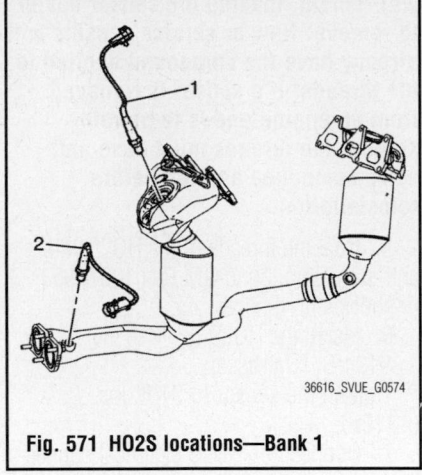

Fig. 571 HO2S locations—Bank 1

7. Install the HO2S to the exhaust manifold. Tighten the sensor to 31 ft. lbs. (42 Nm).
8. Connect the engine wiring harness electrical connector to the HO2S electrical connector.
9. Install the HO2S electrical connector retainer to the harness clip.
10. Install the CPA retainer.
11. Install the fuel injector sight shield.

3.6L Engine—Bank 1 Sensor 2

See Figures 571 and 572.

➡**Do not remove the pigtail from either the Heated Oxygen Sensor (HO2S). Removing the pigtail or the connector will affect sensor operation.**

Handle the oxygen sensor carefully. Do not drop the HO2S. Keep the in-line electrical connector and the louvered end free of grease, dirt, or other contaminants. Do not use cleaning solvents of any type.

Do not repair the wiring, connector or terminals. Replace the oxygen sensor if the pigtail wiring, connector, or terminal is damaged.

This external clean air reference is obtained by way of the oxygen sensor signal and heater wires. Any attempt to repair the wires, connectors, or terminals could result in the obstruction of the air reference and degraded sensor performance.

The following guidelines should be used when servicing the heated oxygen sensor:

• Do not apply contact cleaner or other materials to the sensor or vehicle harness connectors. These materials may get into the sensor causing poor performance.

• Do not damage the sensor pigtail and harness wires in such a way that the wires inside are exposed. This could provide a path for foreign materials to enter the sensor and cause performance problems.

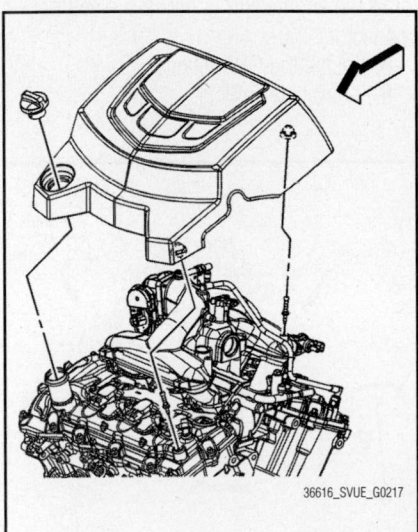

Fig. 569 Remove the fuel injector sight shield

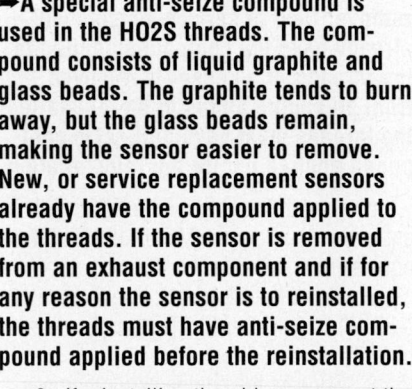

Fig. 570 Disconnect the engine wiring harness electrical connector from the HO2S electrical connector (1)

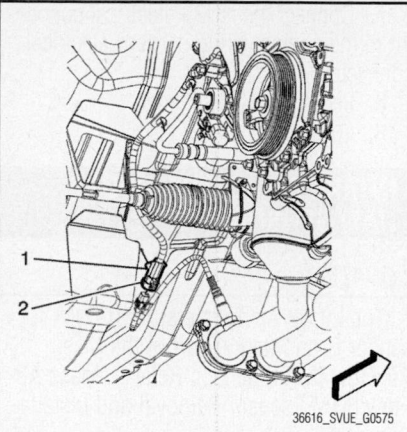

Fig. 572 Disconnect the HO2S electrical connector (2) from the engine wiring harness electrical connector

• Ensure the sensor or vehicle lead wires are not bent sharply or kinked. Sharp bends or kinks could block the reference air path through the lead wire.

• Do not remove or defeat the oxygen sensor ground wire, where applicable. Vehicles that utilize the ground wired sensor may rely on this ground as the only ground contact to the sensor. Removal of the ground wire will cause poor engine performance.

• Ensure that the peripheral seal remains intact on the vehicle harness connector in order to prevent damage due to water intrusion. The engine harness may be repaired using Packard's Crimp and Splice Seals Terminal Repair Kit. Under no circumstances should repairs be soldered since this could result in the air reference being obstructed.

1. Raise and support the vehicle.
2. Remove the Connector Position Assurance (CPA) retainer.
3. Disconnect the Heated Oxygen Sensor (HO2S) electrical connector (2) from the engine wiring harness electrical connector.
4. Remove the HO2S (2) from the catalytic converter.

To install:

➡ **A special anti-seize compound is used in the HO2S threads. The compound consists of liquid graphite and glass beads. The graphite tends to burn away, but the glass beads remain, making the sensor easier to remove. New, or service replacement sensors already have the compound applied to the threads. If the sensor is removed from an exhaust component and if for any reason the sensor is to reinstalled, the threads must have anti-seize compound applied before the reinstallation.**

5. If reinstalling the old sensor, coat the threads with anti-seize compound GM P/N 12377953, or equivalent.
6. Install the HO2S to the catalytic converter. Tighten the sensor to 31 ft. lbs. (42 Nm).
7. Connect the HO2S electrical connector to the engine wiring harness electrical connector.
8. Install the CPA retainer.
9. Lower the vehicle.

3.6L Engine—Bank 2 Sensor 1

See Figures 569 and 573.

➡ **Do not remove the pigtail from either the Heated Oxygen Sensor (HO2S). Removing the pigtail or the connector will affect sensor operation.**

Handle the oxygen sensor carefully. Do not drop the HO2S. Keep the in-line electrical connector and the louvered end free of grease, dirt, or other contaminants. Do not use cleaning solvents of any type.

Do not repair the wiring, connector or terminals. Replace the oxygen sensor if the pigtail wiring, connector, or terminal is damaged.

This external clean air reference is obtained by way of the oxygen sensor signal and heater wires. Any attempt to repair the wires, connectors, or terminals could result in the obstruction of the air reference and degraded sensor performance.

The following guidelines should be used when servicing the heated oxygen sensor:

• Do not apply contact cleaner or other materials to the sensor or vehicle harness connectors. These materials may get into the sensor causing poor performance.

• Do not damage the sensor pigtail and harness wires in such a way that the wires inside are exposed. This could provide a path for foreign materials to enter the sensor and cause performance problems.

• Ensure the sensor or vehicle lead wires are not bent sharply or kinked. Sharp bends or kinks could block the reference air path through the lead wire.

• Do not remove or defeat the oxygen sensor ground wire, where applicable. Vehicles that utilize the ground wired sensor may rely on this ground as the only ground contact to the sensor. Removal of the ground wire will cause poor engine performance.

• Ensure that the peripheral seal remains intact on the vehicle harness connector in order to prevent damage due to water intrusion. The engine harness may be repaired using Packard's Crimp and Splice Seals Terminal Repair Kit. Under no circum-

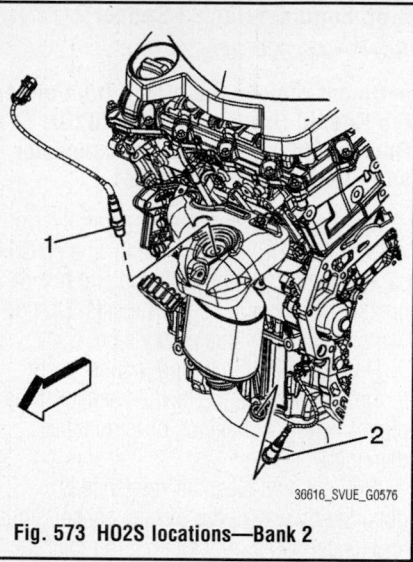

Fig. 573 HO2S locations—Bank 2

stances should repairs be soldered since this could result in the air reference being obstructed.

1. Remove the fuel injector sight shield.
2. Remove the Connector Position Assurance (CPA) retainer.
3. Disconnect the engine wiring harness electrical connector from the Heated Oxygen Sensor (HO2S) electrical connector.
4. Remove the HO2S electrical connector retainer from the harness clip.
5. Remove the HO2S (1) from the exhaust manifold.

To install:

➡ **A special anti-seize compound is used in the HO2S threads. The compound consists of liquid graphite and glass beads. The graphite tends to burn away, but the glass beads remain, making the sensor easier to remove. New, or service replacement sensors already have the compound applied to the threads. If the sensor is removed from an exhaust component and if for any reason the sensor is to reinstalled, the threads must have anti-seize compound applied before the reinstallation.**

6. If reinstalling the old sensor, coat the threads with anti-seize compound GM P/N 12377953, or equivalent.
7. Install the HO2S to the exhaust manifold. Tighten the sensor to 31 ft. lbs. (42 Nm).
8. Connect the engine wiring harness electrical connector to the HO2S electrical connector.
9. Install the HO2S electrical connector retainer to the harness clip.
10. Install the CPA retainer.
11. Install the fuel injector sight shield.

3.6L Engine—Bank 2 Sensor 2

See Figures 574 and 575.

➡ **Do not remove the pigtail from either the Heated Oxygen Sensor (HO2S). Removing the pigtail or the connector will affect sensor operation.**

Handle the oxygen sensor carefully. Do not drop the HO2S. Keep the in-line electrical connector and the louvered end free of grease, dirt, or other contaminants. Do not use cleaning solvents of any type.

Do not repair the wiring, connector or terminals. Replace the oxygen sensor if the pigtail wiring, connector, or terminal is damaged.

This external clean air reference is obtained by way of the oxygen sensor signal and heater wires. Any attempt to repair the wires, connectors, or terminals could result in the obstruction of the air reference and degraded sensor performance.

The following guidelines should be used when servicing the heated oxygen sensor:

• Do not apply contact cleaner or other materials to the sensor or vehicle harness connectors. These materials may get into the sensor causing poor performance.

• Do not damage the sensor pigtail and harness wires in such a way that the wires inside are exposed. This could provide a path for foreign materials to enter the sensor and cause performance problems.

• Ensure the sensor or vehicle lead wires are not bent sharply or kinked. Sharp bends or kinks could block the reference air path through the lead wire.

• Do not remove or defeat the oxygen sensor ground wire, where applicable. Vehicles that utilize the ground wired sensor may rely on this ground as the only ground

contact to the sensor. Removal of the ground wire will cause poor engine performance.

• Ensure that the peripheral seal remains intact on the vehicle harness connector in order to prevent damage due to water intrusion. The engine harness may be repaired using Packard's Crimp and Splice Seals Terminal Repair Kit. Under no circumstances should repairs be soldered since this could result in the air reference being obstructed.

1. Raise and support the vehicle.
2. Remove the Connector Position Assurance (CPA) retainer.
3. Disconnect the Heated Oxygen Sensor (HO2S) electrical connector (1) from the engine wiring harness electrical connector (2).
4. Remove the HO2S (2) from the catalytic converter.

To install:

➡ **A special anti-seize compound is used in the HO2S threads. The compound consists of liquid graphite and glass beads. The graphite tends to burn away, but the glass beads remain, making the sensor easier to remove. New, or service replacement sensors already have the compound applied to the threads. If the sensor is removed from an exhaust component and if for any reason the sensor is to reinstalled, the threads must have anti-seize compound applied before the reinstallation.**

5. If reinstalling the old sensor, coat the threads with anti-seize compound GM P/N 12377953, or equivalent.
6. Install the HO2S (2) to the catalytic converter. Tighten the sensor to 31 ft. lbs. (42 Nm).

7. Connect the HO2S electrical connector to the engine wiring harness electrical connector.
8. Install the CPA retainer.
9. Lower the vehicle.

INTAKE AIR TEMPERATURE (IAT) SENSOR

LOCATION

The Intake Air Temperature (IAT) sensor is an integral part of the Mass Air Flow (MAF) sensor. Refer to Mass Air Flow (MAF) sensor Removal and Installation.

REMOVAL & INSTALLATION

Refer to Mass Air Flow (MAF) sensor Removal and Installation.

KNOCK SENSOR (KS)

LOCATION

See Removal and Installation for each engine to determine the location.

REMOVAL & INSTALLATION

2.4L Engine

See Figures 576 and 577.

1. Raise the vehicle.
2. Disconnect the engine wiring harness electrical connector (3) from the knock sensor electrical connector (4).
3. Remove the knock sensor electrical connector (4) from the oil level indicator tube bracket.
4. Remove the knock sensor bolt.
5. Remove the knock sensor.

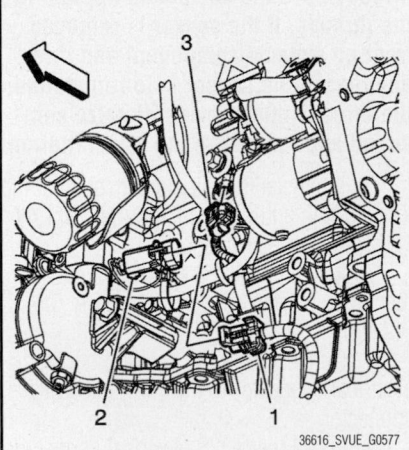

36616_SVUE_G0577

Fig. 574 Disconnect the HO2S electrical connector (1) from the engine wiring harness electrical connector (2)

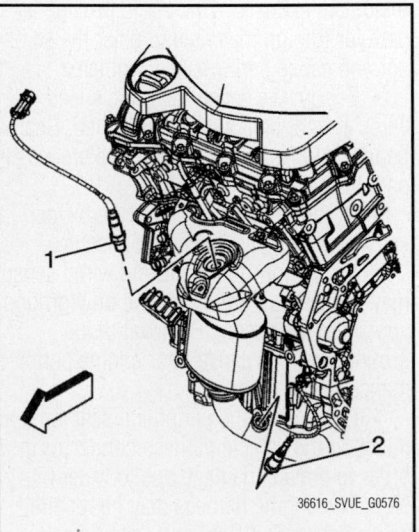

36616_SVUE_G0576

Fig. 575 HO2S locations—Bank 2

36616_SVUE_G0578

Fig. 576 Disconnect the engine wiring harness electrical connector (3) from the knock sensor electrical connector (4)

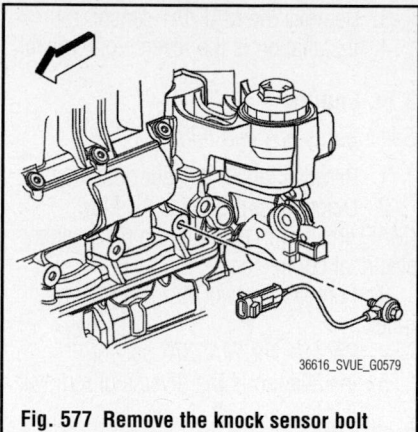

Fig. 577 Remove the knock sensor bolt

To install:

6. Install the knock sensor.
7. Install the knock sensor bolt. Tighten the bolt to 18 ft. lbs. (25 Nm).

➡️**Rotate the knock sensor electrical connector 90 degrees from vertical before securing the fastener.**

8. Install the knock sensor electrical connector to the oil level indicator tube bracket.
9. Connect the engine wiring harness electrical connector to the knock sensor electrical connector.

3.5L Engine—Bank 1

See Figures 578 through 580.

1. Remove the right catalytic converter.
2. Remove the engine wiring harness heat shield nut (3).
3. Remove the engine wiring harness heat shield bolts (1, 4).
4. Remove the engine wiring harness heat shield (2).
5. Disconnect the engine wiring harness electrical connector (5) from the knock sensor (2).

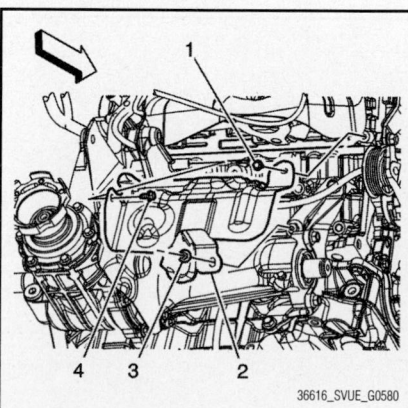

Fig. 578 Remove the engine wiring harness heat shield nut (3)

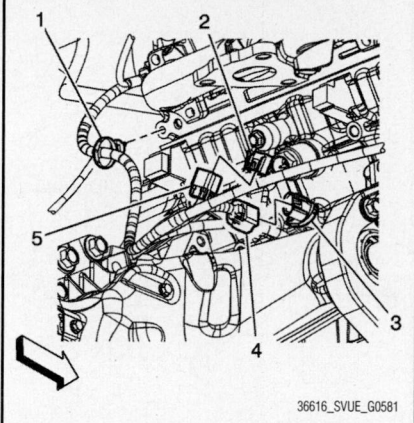

Fig. 579 Disconnect the engine wiring harness electrical connector (5) from the knock sensor (2)

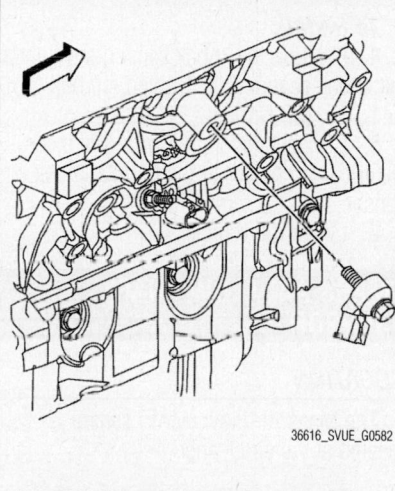

Fig. 580 Remove the knock sensor bolt and sensor

6. Remove the knock sensor bolt and sensor.

To install:

7. Position the knock sensor to the engine block and install the knock sensor bolt. Tighten the bolt to 18 ft. lbs. (25 Nm).
8. Connect the engine wiring harness electrical connector to the knock sensor.
9. Install the engine wiring harness heat shield.
10. Install the engine wiring harness heat shield bolts. Tighten the bolts to 89 inch lbs. (10 Nm).
11. Install the engine wiring harness heat shield nut. Tighten the nut to 89 inch lbs. (10 Nm).
12. Install the right catalytic converter.

3.5L Engine—Bank 2

See Figure 581.

1. Raise and support the vehicle.

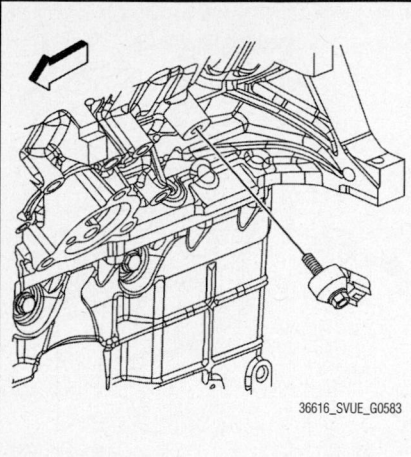

Fig. 581 Remove the knock sensor bolt and sensor

2. Disconnect the engine wiring harness electrical connector from the knock sensor.
3. Remove the knock sensor bolt and sensor.

To install:

4. Position the knock sensor to the engine block and install the knock sensor bolt. Tighten the bolt to 18 ft. lbs. (25 Nm).
5. Connect the engine wiring harness electrical connector to the knock sensor.
6. Lower the vehicle.

3.6L Engine—Bank 1

See Figures 582 and 583.

1. Remove the right catalytic converter.
2. Remove the exhaust manifold heat shield.
3. Disconnect the engine wiring harness electrical connector (1) from the Bank 1 knock sensor.
4. Remove the knock sensor bolt and the knock sensor.

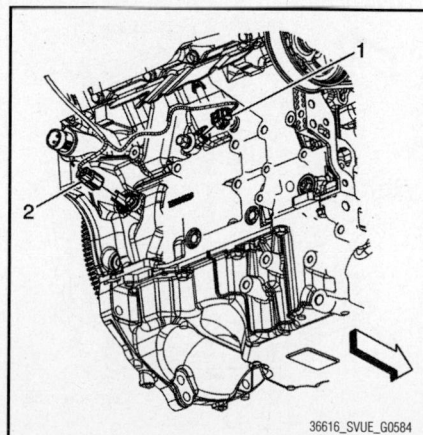

Fig. 582 Disconnect the engine wiring harness electrical connector (1) from the Bank 1 knock sensor

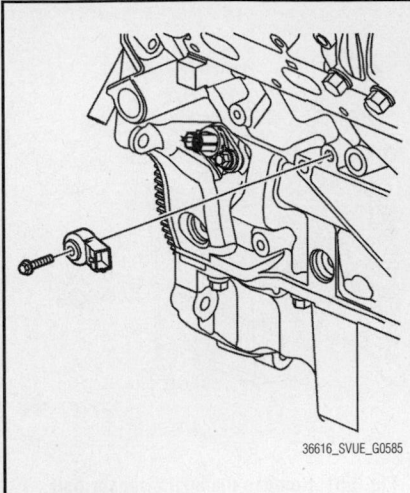

Fig. 583 Remove the knock sensor bolt and the knock sensor

To install:

5. Position the knock sensor and tighten the knock sensor bolt. Tighten the bolt to 17 ft. lbs. (23 Nm).

6. Connect the engine wiring harness electrical connector to the Bank 1 knock sensor.

7. Install the exhaust manifold heat shield.

8. Install the right catalytic converter.

3.6L Engine—Bank 2

See Figures 584 and 585.

1. Raise and suitably support the vehicle.

2. Disconnect the engine wiring harness electrical connector (2) from the Bank 2 knock sensor.

3. Remove the knock sensor bolt and the knock sensor.

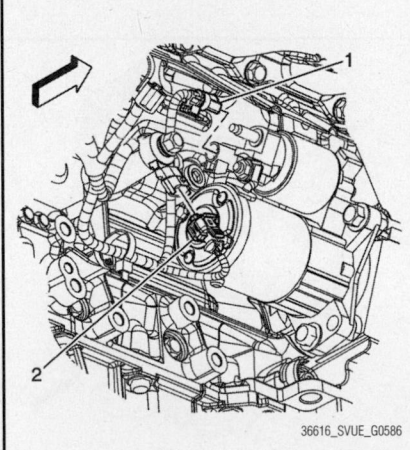

Fig. 584 Disconnect the engine wiring harness electrical connector (2) from the Bank 2 knock sensor

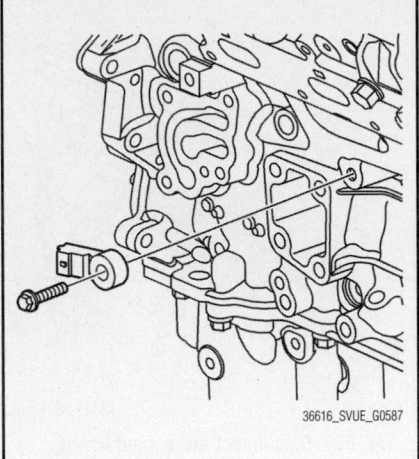

Fig. 585 Remove the knock sensor bolt and the knock sensor

To install:

4. Position the knock sensor and tighten the knock sensor bolt. Tighten the bolt to 17 ft. lbs. (23 Nm).

5. Connect the engine wiring harness electrical connector to the Bank 2 knock sensor.

6. Lower the vehicle.

MASS AIR FLOW (MAF) SENSOR

LOCATION

The Mass Air Flow (MAF) sensor is located at the air cleaner.

REMOVAL & INSTALLATION

2.4L Engine

See Figure 586.

1. Disconnect the Mass Air Flow (MAF)/Intake Air Temperature (IAT) sensor electrical connector.

2. Remove the two MAF/IAT sensor bolts.

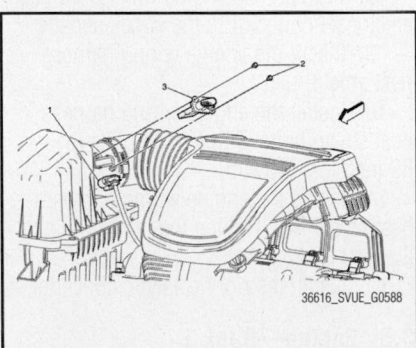

Fig. 586 Mass Air Flow (MAF) sensor location

3. Remove the MAF/IAT sensor.

4. Installation is the reverse of removal.

3.5L Engine

See Figures 587 and 588.

1. Remove the air cleaner outlet duct.

2. Disconnect the Mass Air Flow (MAF)/Intake Air Temperature (IAT) sensor electrical connector.

3. Remove the two MAF/IAT sensor bolts.

4. Remove the MAF/IAT sensor.

5. Installation is the reverse of removal.

3.6L Engine

See Figure 589.

1. Remove the air cleaner outlet duct.

2. Disconnect the Mass Air Flow (MAF)/Intake Air Temperature (IAT) sensor electrical connector.

3. Remove the two MAF/IAT sensor bolts.

4. Remove the MAF/IAT sensor.

5. Installation is the reverse of removal.

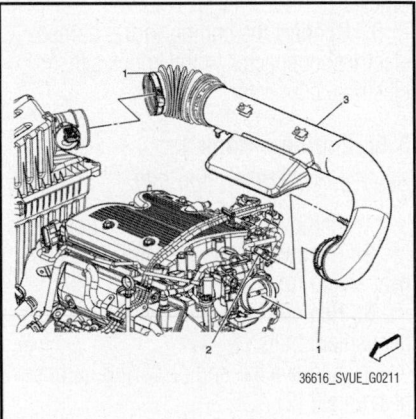

Fig. 587 Remove the air cleaner outlet duct

Fig. 588 Mass Air Flow (MAF) sensor location

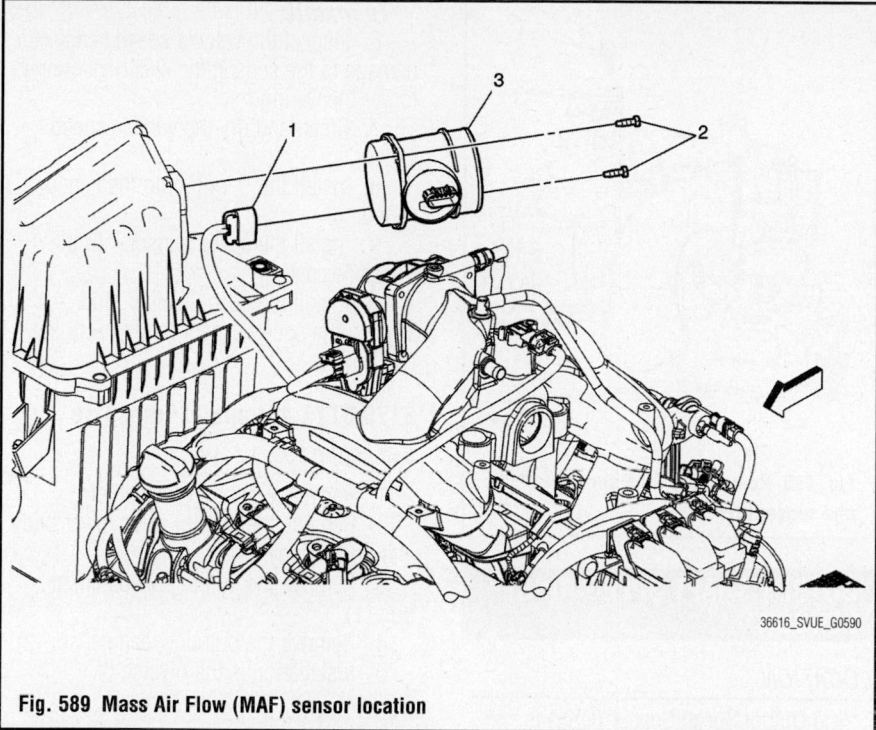

Fig. 589 Mass Air Flow (MAF) sensor location

MANIFOLD ABSOLUTE PRESSURE (MAP) SENSOR

LOCATION

The Manifold Absolute Pressure (MAP) sensor is located on the intake manifold.

REMOVAL & INSTALLATION

2.4L Engine

See Figures 590 and 591.

1. Remove the air cleaner outlet duct.
2. Remove the Evaporative Emission

(EVAP) canister purge tube from the intake manifold.

3. Reposition the EVAP canister purge tube out of the way.
4. Disconnect and reposition the fuel injector wiring harness out of the way.
5. Disconnect the engine harness electrical connector from the Manifold Absolute Pressure (MAP) sensor.
6. Remove the MAP sensor and seal.

To install:

7. Lubricate the NEW MAP sensor seal with clean engine oil.

8. Install the MAP sensor into the intake manifold.
9. Connect the engine harness electrical connector to the MAP sensor.
10. Position and connect the fuel injector wiring harness.
11. Position the EVAP canister purge tube to the intake manifold.
12. Connect the EVAP canister purge tube to the intake manifold.
13. Install the air cleaner outlet duct.

3.5L Engine

See Figures 587 and 592.

1. Remove the air cleaner outlet duct.
2. Disconnect the Manifold Absolute Pressure (MAP) sensor electrical connector.
3. Remove the spark plug wire clip from the intake manifold bracket.
4. Remove the upper intake manifold bolts.
5. Remove the MAP sensor and bracket.
6. Remove the MAP sensor seal from the upper intake manifold.

To install:

7. Install the MAP sensor seal into the upper intake manifold.
8. Install the MAP sensor and bracket.
9. Install the upper intake manifold bolts. Tighten the bolts to 18 ft. lbs. (25 Nm).
10. Install the spark plug wire clip to the intake manifold bracket.
11. Connect the MAP sensor electrical connector.
12. Install the air cleaner outlet duct.

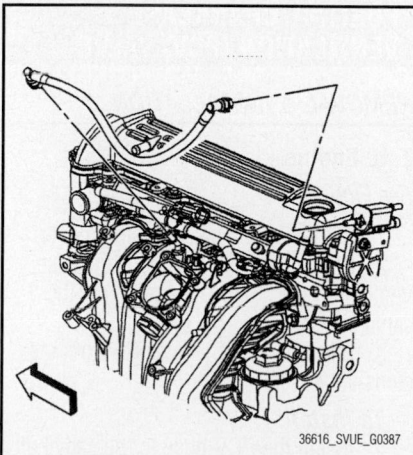

Fig. 590 Remove the Evaporative Emission (EVAP) canister purge tube from the intake manifold

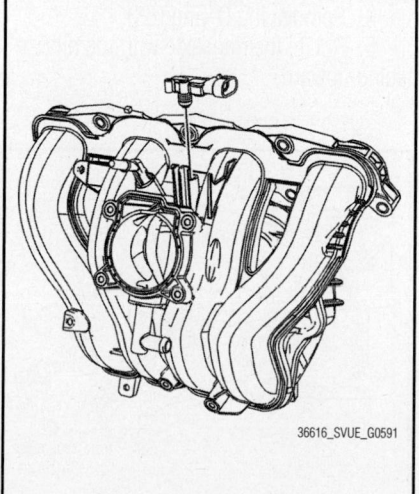

Fig. 591 Remove the MAP sensor and seal

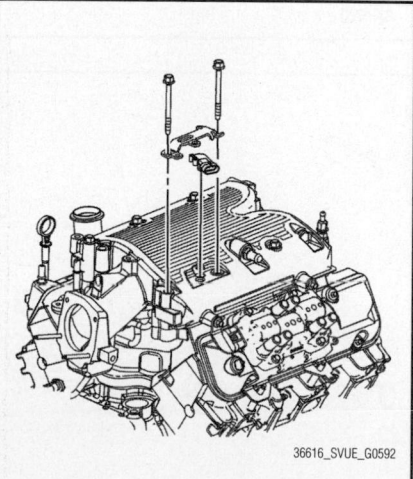

Fig. 592 Remove the MAP sensor and bracket

3.6L Engine

See Figures 593 through 595.

1. Remove the fuel injector sight shield.

2. Disconnect the engine wiring harness electrical connector (2) from the Manifold Absolute Pressure (MAP) sensor (1).

3. Remove the MAP sensor bolt (1) and sensor (2).

To install:

4. Lubricate the MAP sensor O-ring seal with clean engine oil.

5. Install the MAP sensor and bolt. Tighten the bolt to 89 inch lbs. (10 Nm).

6. Connect the engine wiring harness electrical connector to the MAP sensor.

7. Install the fuel injector sight shield.

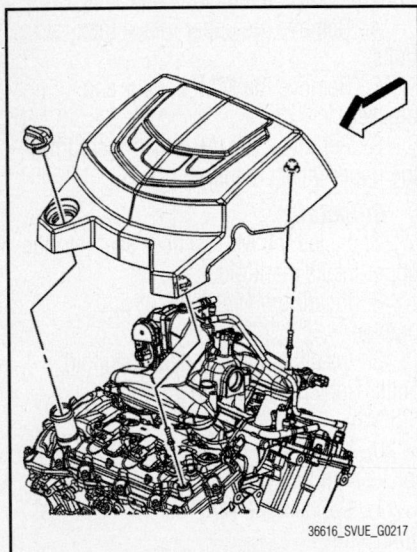

Fig. 593 Remove the fuel injector sight shield

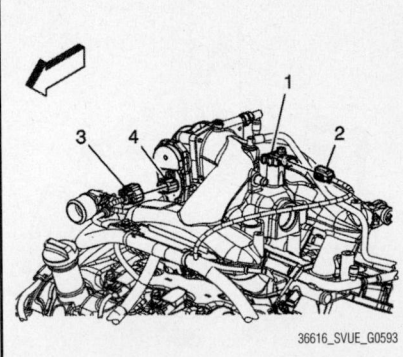

Fig. 594 Disconnect the engine wiring harness electrical connector (2) from the MAP sensor (1)

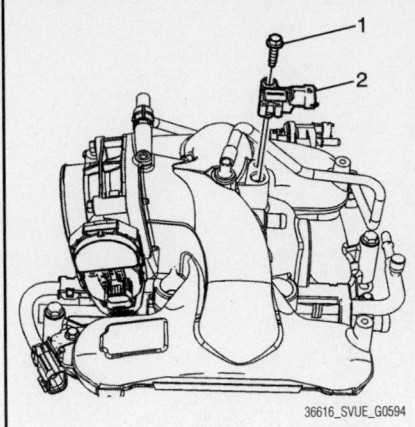

Fig. 595 Remove the MAP sensor bolt (1) and sensor (2)

OUTPUT SHAFT SPEED (OSS) SENSOR

LOCATION

The Output Speed Sensor (OSS) is located on the transaxle case.

REMOVAL & INSTALLATION

4T45-E Automatic Transaxle

See Figure 596.

1. Rotate the transaxle so that the case side cover is facing upward in order to drain the transmission fluid through the stub shaft end of the transaxle.

2. Remove the speed sensor stud (61).

3. Remove the speed sensor assembly (62). Pull the speed sensor assembly straight out from the transaxle case in order to prevent damage to the case bore.

4. Remove the O-ring (63).

5. Rotate the transaxle with the oil pan facing upward.

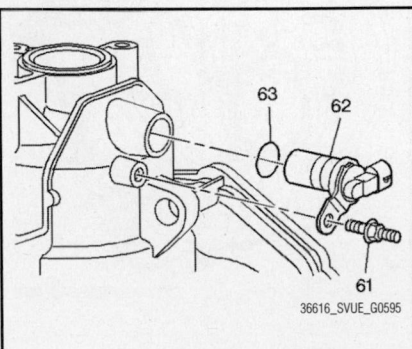

Fig. 596 Remove the speed sensor stud (61)

To install:

6. Inspect the vehicle speed sensor for damage to the sensor, the electrical connector, or the O-ring.

7. Clean and dry the vehicle speed sensor.

8. Install the O-ring onto the speed sensor.

9. Install the speed sensor into the transaxle case.

10. Install the speed sensor stud. Tighten the speed sensor stud to 9 ft. lbs. (12 Nm).

6T70/6T75 Automatic Transaxle

See Figure 597.

1. Raise and support the vehicle.

2. Remove the control valve lower body and upper body.

3. Remove the output speed sensor bolt (1).

4. Remove the output speed sensor (2).

5. Installation is the reverse of removal.

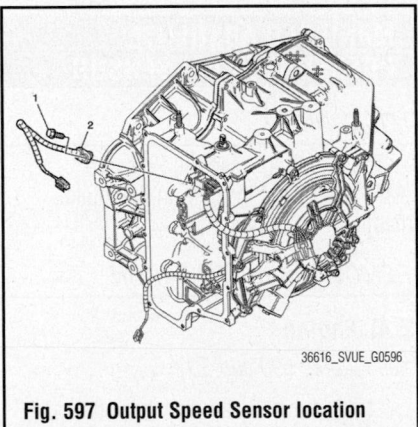

Fig. 597 Output Speed Sensor location

POSITIVE CRANKCASE VENTILATION (PCV) VALVE

REMOVAL & INSTALLATION

2.4L Engine

See Figure 598.

1. Remove the intake manifold cover.

2. Reposition the Positive Crankcase Ventilation (PCV) hose clamp (1) at the camshaft cover.

3. Remove the PCV hose (2) from the camshaft cover.

To install:

4. Install the PCV hose to the camshaft cover.

5. Position the PCV hose clamp at the camshaft cover.

6. Install the intake manifold cover.

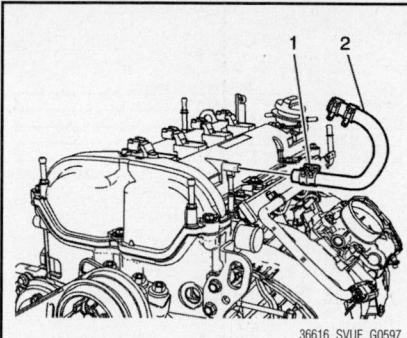

Fig. 598 Reposition the Positive Crankcase Ventilation (PCV) hose clamp (1) at the camshaft cover

3.5L Engine

See Figures 599 through 601.

1. Remove the intake manifold cover.
2. Disconnect the Positive Crankcase Ventilation (PCV) fresh air tube from the air cleaner outlet duct.
3. Remove the PCV fresh air tube from the rocker arm cover.
4. Remove the PCV fresh air tube from the vehicle.
5. Disconnect the PCV foul air tube from the PCV valve.
6. Remove the PCV foul air tube from the intake manifold.
7. Remove the PCV foul air tube from the vehicle.

To install:

8. Install the PCV foul air tube to the vehicle.

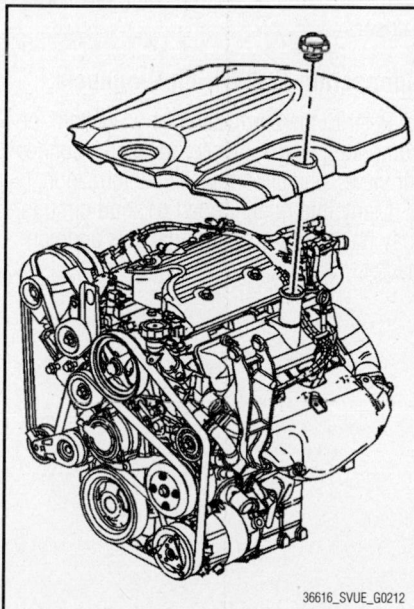

Fig. 599 Remove the intake manifold cover

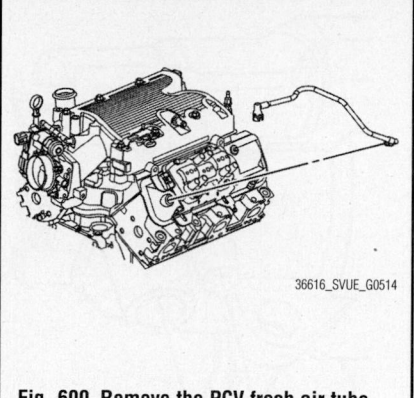

Fig. 600 Remove the PCV fresh air tube from the vehicle

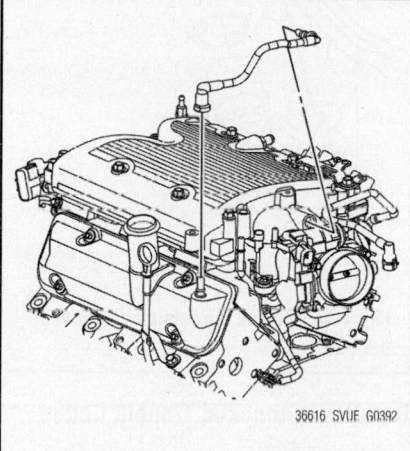

Fig. 601 Disconnect the PCV foul air tube from the PCV valve

9. Install the PCV foul air tube to the intake manifold.
10. Connect the PCV foul air tube to the PCV valve.
11. Install the PCV fresh air tube to the vehicle.
12. Install the PCV fresh air tube to the rocker arm cover.
13. Connect the PCV fresh air tube to the air cleaner outlet duct.
14. Install the intake manifold cover.

3.6L Engine

See Figures 602 and 603.

1. Remove the engine cover.
2. Disconnect the Positive Crankcase Ventilation (PVC) fresh air pipe (1) from the upper intake manifold.
3. Disconnect the PVC foul air pipe from the PVC valve.

To install:

4. Connect the PVC foul air pipe to the PVC valve.
5. Connect the PVC fresh air pipe to the upper intake manifold.

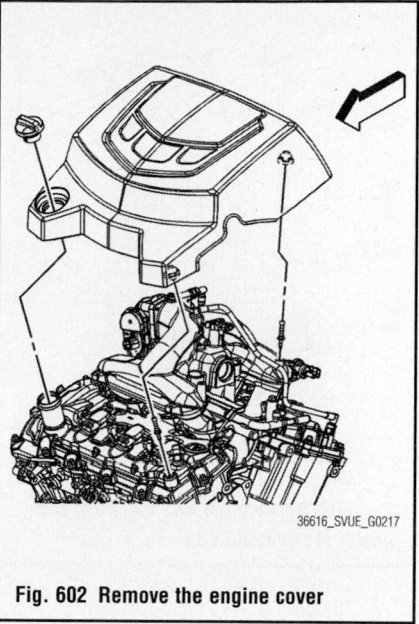

Fig. 602 Remove the engine cover

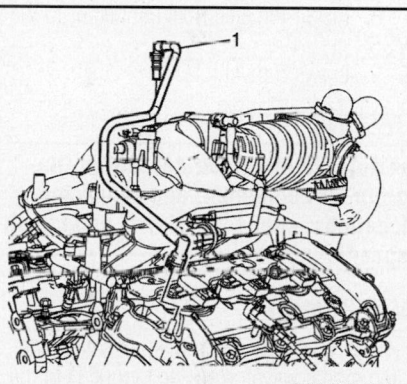

Fig. 603 Disconnect the Positive Crankcase Ventilation (PVC) fresh air pipe (1) from the upper intake manifold

6. Install the engine cover.

VEHICLE SPEED SENSOR (VSS)

REMOVAL & INSTALLATION

4T45-E Automatic Transaxle

See Figures 604 and 605.

1. Raise and support the vehicle.
2. Remove the Vehicle Speed Sensor (VSS) electrical connector (1) from the VSS.
3. Remove the VSS electrical harness retainer (2) from the VSS.
4. Remove the retaining stud and the VSS. Pull straight out in order to avoid damage to the case.

To install:

5. Clean and dry the VSS.
6. Install the VSS and the retaining stud. Tighten the stud to 97 inch lbs. (12 Nm).

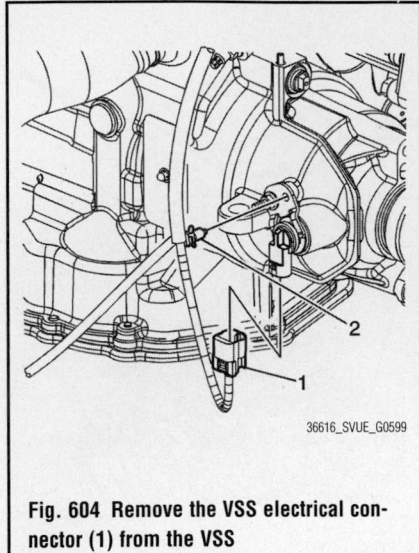

Fig. 604 Remove the VSS electrical connector (1) from the VSS

7. Install the VSS electrical harness retainer to the VSS.

8. Install the electrical connector to the VSS.

9. Lower the vehicle.

TESTING

➡️**Refer to the Electrical Wiring Diagram for component and connector locations, connector views, and circuit-specific information.**

VSS Strategy

The VSS provides a magnetically generated signal waveform (See Figure 1) to the Powertrain Control Module (PCM) for a number of engine control, drive train, and information display system calculations. The VSS signal frequency varies according to vehicle speed, and is compared with the Crankshaft Position (CKP) Sensor and Camshaft Position (CMP) Sensor signals for measured operating conditions. The magnetic waveform pattern is used by the Powertrain Control Module (PCM) to calculate engine and vehicle load, ignition timing, fuel injector timing and pulse width, and the speedometer display.

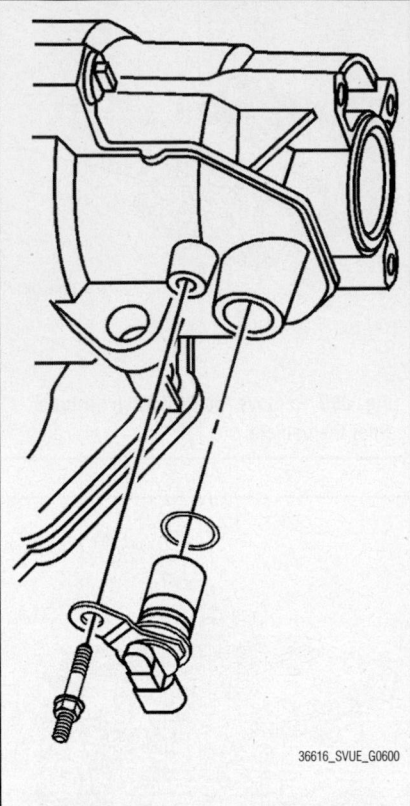

Fig. 605 Remove the retaining stud and the VSS

Related Diagnostic Trouble Codes

See Figure 606.

VSS Circuit Testing

See Figure 607.

Use a suitable scan tool or a Graphing Multi–Meter (GMM in order to view the VSS data.

VSS logic is based on alternating lines of magnetic flux which generate an analog signal to the PCM, and are based on the vehicle speed.

Verify that the engine that there is no foreign material obstructing the path between the reluctor and the VSS. If any engine mechanical faults are evident, locate and repair as required before continuing.

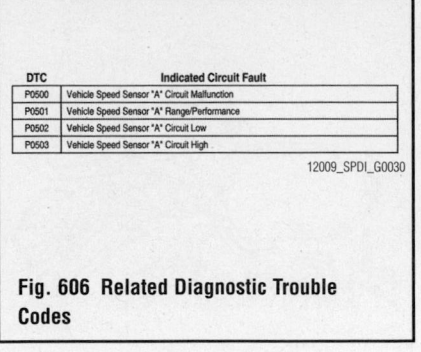

DTC	Indicated Circuit Fault
P0500	Vehicle Speed Sensor "A" Circuit Malfunction
P0501	Vehicle Speed Sensor "A" Range/Performance
P0502	Vehicle Speed Sensor "A" Circuit Low
P0503	Vehicle Speed Sensor "A" Circuit High

Fig. 606 Related Diagnostic Trouble Codes

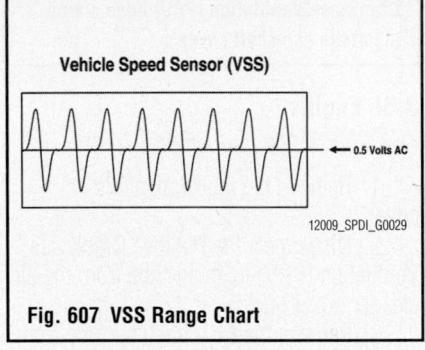

Fig. 607 VSS Range Chart

A Digital Volt–Ohm Meter (DVOM) may be used to verify the condition of the wiring: additional information may be acquired by taking measurements at the sensor connector as well as the PCM connector. If significant resistance is measured (greater than 5 ohms), check the wiring harness and connections for corrosion, poor pin connections, or damaged wires.

If all engine wiring and pin connections are confirmed, disconnect the VSS to verify the signal with a GMM, and verify PCM communication before replacing the VSS Sensor.

Connection and Wiring Diagnosis

Refer to the Electrical Wiring Diagram for component and connector locations, connector views, and circuit-specific information.

Many intermittent open or short circuits may be caused by wiring harness and connector.

FUEL SYSTEM SERVICE PRECAUTIONS

Safety is the most important factor when performing not only fuel system maintenance but any type of maintenance. Failure to conduct maintenance and repairs in a safe manner may result in serious personal injury or death. Maintenance and testing of the vehicle's fuel system components can be accomplished safely and effectively by adhering to the following rules and guidelines.

- To avoid the possibility of fire and personal injury, always disconnect the negative battery cable unless the repair or test procedure requires that battery voltage be applied.
- Always relieve the fuel system pressure prior to disconnecting any fuel system component (injector, fuel rail, pressure regulator, etc.), fitting or fuel line connection. Exercise extreme caution whenever relieving fuel system pressure to avoid exposing skin, face and eyes to fuel spray. Please be advised that fuel under pressure may penetrate the skin or any part of the body that it contacts.
- Always place a shop towel or cloth around the fitting or connection prior to loosening to absorb any excess fuel due to spillage. Ensure that all fuel spillage (should it occur) is quickly removed from engine surfaces. Ensure that all fuel soaked cloths or towels are deposited into a suitable waste container.
- Always keep a dry chemical (Class B) fire extinguisher near the work area.
- Do not allow fuel spray or fuel vapors to come into contact with a spark or open flame.
- Always use a back-up wrench when loosening and tightening fuel line connection fittings. This will prevent unnecessary stress and torsion to fuel line piping.
- Always replace worn fuel fitting O-rings with new Do not substitute fuel hose or equivalent where fuel pipe is installed.

Before servicing the vehicle, make sure to also refer to the precautions in the beginning of this section as well.

RELIEVING FUEL SYSTEM PRESSURE

Using A Digital Pressure Gage
See Figure 608.

1. Remove the engine cover, if required.
2. Loosen the fuel fill cap in order to relieve the fuel tank vapor pressure.
3. Remove the fuel rail service port cap.

Wrap a shop towel around the fuel pressure connection in order to reduce the risk of fire and personal injury. The towel will absorb any fuel leakage that occurs during the connection of the fuel pressure gage. Place the towel in an approved container when the connection of the fuel pressure gage is complete.

4. Wrap a shop towel around the fuel rail service port.
5. Connect the CH-48027-3 (3) to the fuel rail service port.
6. Connect the CH-48027-2 (2) to the CH-48027-3 (3).
7. Place the hose on the CH-48027-2 (2) into an approved gasoline container.
8. Open the valve on the CH-48027-2 (2) in order to bleed any fuel from the fuel rail.
9. Close the valve on the CH-48027-2 (2).
10. Remove the hose on the CH-48027-2 (2) from the approved gasoline container.

➡**Clean all of the following areas before performing any disconnections in order to avoid possible contamination in the system:**

- The fuel pipe connections
- The hose connections
- The areas surrounding the connections

➡**If relieving the fuel pressure for the fuel pressure gage installation and removal, it is NOT necessary to proceed with the following steps.**

11. Disconnect the CH-48027-2 (2) from the CH-48027-3 (3).

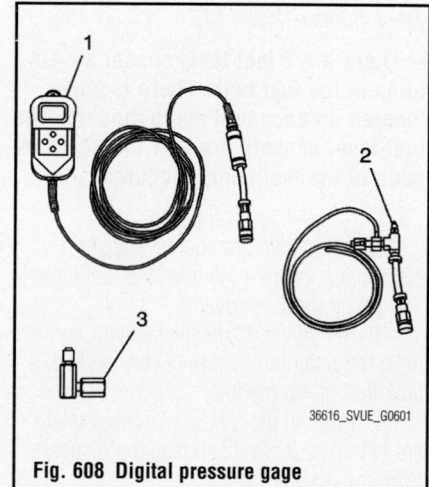

Fig. 608 Digital pressure gage

12. Disconnect the CH-48027-3 (3) from the fuel rail service port.
13. Remove the shop towel from around the fuel rail service port, and place in an approved gasoline container.
14. Install the fuel rail service port cap.
15. Install the engine cover, if required.
16. Tighten the fuel fill cap.

Without Digital Pressure Gage

1. Loosen the fuel fill cap in order to relieve the fuel tank vapor pressure.
2. Remove the engine cover, if required.
3. Remove the fuel rail service port cap.
4. Wrap a shop towel around the fuel rail service port and using a small flat bladed tool, depress (open) the fuel rail test port valve.
5. Remove the shop towel from around the fuel rail service port, and place in an approved gasoline container.
6. Install the fuel rail service port cap.
7. Install the engine cover, if required.
8. Tighten the fuel fill cap.

FUEL FILTER

REMOVAL & INSTALLATION

The fuel filter is located in the primary fuel tank module.

FUEL LEVEL SENSOR

LOCATION

The Fuel Level Sensor is a component of the Fuel Tank Module.

OPERATION

The Fuel Level Sensor consists of a float, a wire float arm, and a ceramic resistor card. The position of the float arm indicates the fuel level. The fuel level sensor contains a variable resistor which changes resistance in correspondence with the position of the float arm. The Engine Control Module (ECM) monitors the signal circuits of the primary fuel level sensor and the secondary fuel level sensor in order to determine the fuel level. When the fuel tank is full, the resistance of both fuel level sensors are low and the ECM senses a low signal voltage on both the signal circuits of the primary fuel level sensor and the secondary fuel level sensor. When the fuel tanks are empty, the resistances of the fuel level sensors are high and the ECM senses a high signal voltage. The ECM uses the signal circuits of the primary fuel level sensor and the secondary fuel level sensor in order to calculate the percentage of remaining fuel in the tank. The ECM sends the fuel level percentage via serial data circuit to the instrument cluster in order to control the fuel gage.

REMOVAL & INSTALLATION

Primary Fuel Level Sensor

See Figures 609 through 611.

➡There are 2 fuel level sensor assemblies in the fuel tank. There is one located on each fuel pump module. The fuel level sensors are NOT the same for each of the fuel pump modules.

1. Remove the fuel pump module.
2. Disconnect the fuel level sensor electrical connector (1) from the fuel tank fuel pump module cover.
3. Remove the fuel level sensor wiring from behind the retaining features (1) molded into the fuel tank fuel pump module reservoir.

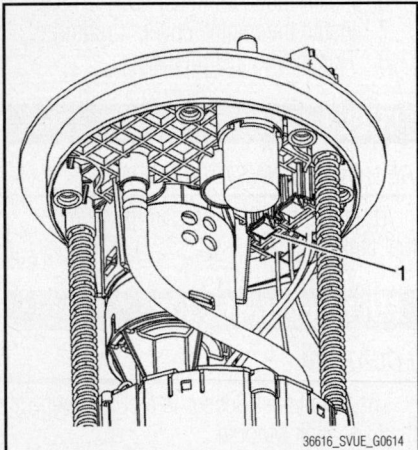

Fig. 609 Disconnect the fuel level sensor electrical connector (1) from the fuel tank fuel pump module cover

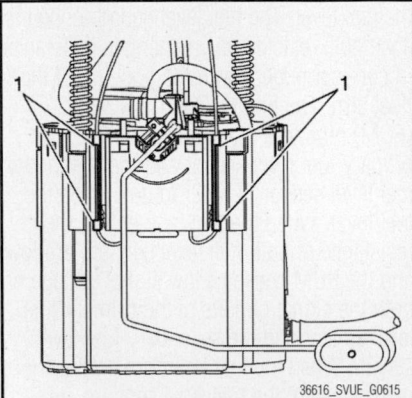

Fig. 610 Remove the fuel level sensor wiring from behind the retaining features (1)

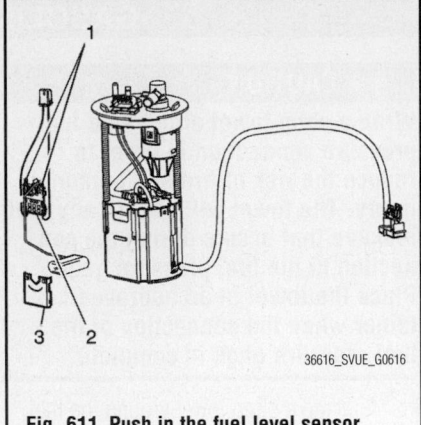

Fig. 611 Push in the fuel level sensor retainers (1)

4. Slide the fuel level sensor up and remove the sensor from the fuel tank fuel pump module.
5. Place the fuel level sensor on a clean work surface.
6. Push in the fuel level sensor retainers (1), in order to remove the sensor from the cover.
7. Remove the fuel level sensor (2) from the cover (3).

To install:

8. Install the fuel level sensor cover to the fuel level sensor.
9. Ensure that the fuel level sensor retainers are fully engaged to the cover.
10. Position the fuel level sensor to the fuel tank fuel pump module and slide the sensor down into position.
11. Connect the fuel level sensor electrical connector to the fuel tank fuel pump module cover.
12. Install the fuel level sensor wiring behind the retaining features molded into the fuel tank fuel pump module reservoir.
13. Install the fuel pump module.

Secondary Fuel Level Sensor

See Figures 612 and 613.

➡There are 2 fuel level sensor assemblies in the fuel tank. There is one located on each fuel pump module. The fuel level sensors are NOT the same for each of the fuel pump modules.

1. Remove the fuel pump module.
2. Disconnect the fuel level sender electrical connector (1) from the fuel tank fuel pump module cover.
3. Remove the fuel level sensor wiring from the retaining feature (2) on the fuel tank fuel pump module.
4. Push in the fuel level sensor retainers (1), in order to disengage the retainers from the module.

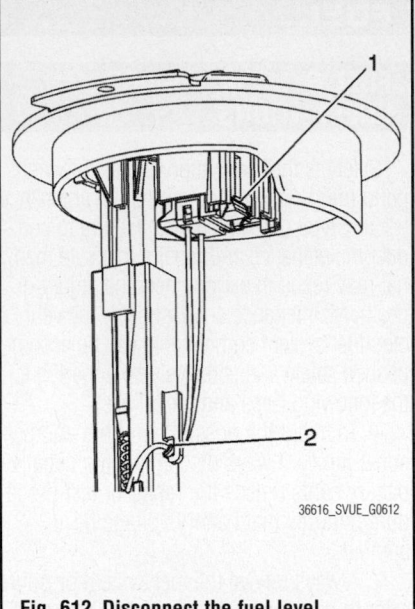

Fig. 612 Disconnect the fuel level sender electrical connector (1) from the fuel tank fuel pump module cover

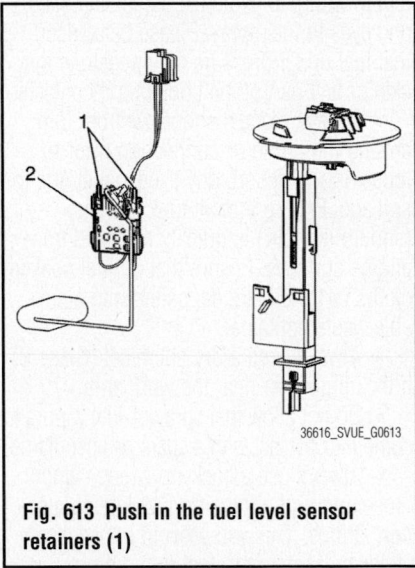

Fig. 613 Push in the fuel level sensor retainers (1)

5. Slide the fuel level sensor (2) up, out of the fuel tank fuel pump module.

To install:

6. Position the fuel level sensor to the fuel tank fuel pump module.
7. Push the fuel level sensor down until the retainers engage the fuel tank fuel pump module.
8. Connect the fuel level sender electrical connector to the fuel tank fuel pump module cover.
9. Install the fuel level sensor wiring to the retaining feature on the fuel tank fuel pump module.
10. Install the fuel pump module.

FUEL TANK MODULE

REMOVAL & INSTALLATION

Primary Fuel Tank Module

See Figures 614 through 618.

1. Remove the fuel tank.
2. Remove the secondary fuel tank fuel pump module.
3. Disconnect the fuel feed line quick connect fitting (1) from the fuel tank fuel pump module.
4. Open the retaining clip (3) on the fuel tank and remove the fuel feed line (2).
5. Disconnect the engine wiring harness electrical connectors (2) from the fuel tank fuel pump primary module and the fuel tank pressure sensor.
6. Disconnect the vapor line quick connect fittings (1) from the fuel tank fuel pump module.
7. Install the J 45722 (1) to the fuel tank fuel pump module lock ring.

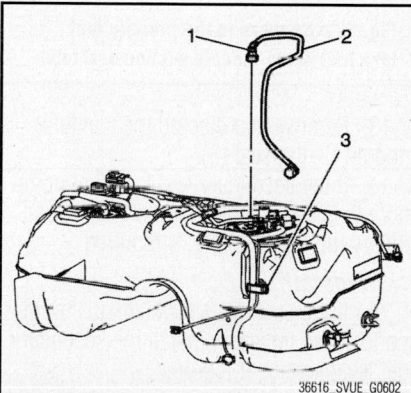

Fig. 614 Disconnect the fuel feed line quick connect fitting (1) from the fuel tank fuel pump module

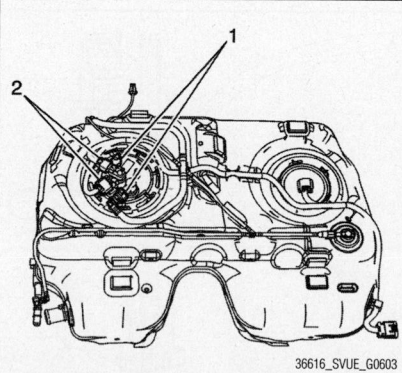

Fig. 615 Disconnect the engine wiring harness electrical connectors (2) from the fuel tank fuel pump primary module and the fuel tank pressure sensor

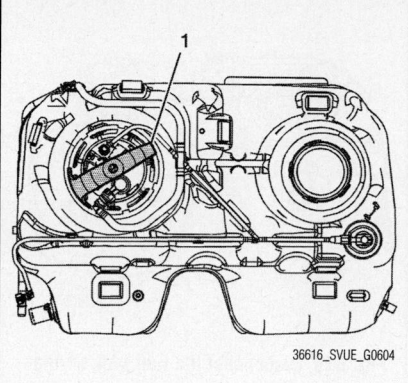

Fig. 616 Install the J 45722 (1) to the fuel tank fuel pump module lock ring

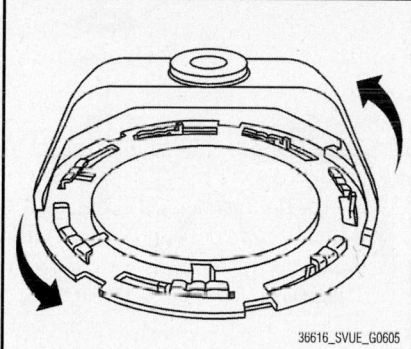

Fig. 617 Rotate the lock ring counterclockwise unlocking the fuel tank fuel pump module lock ring

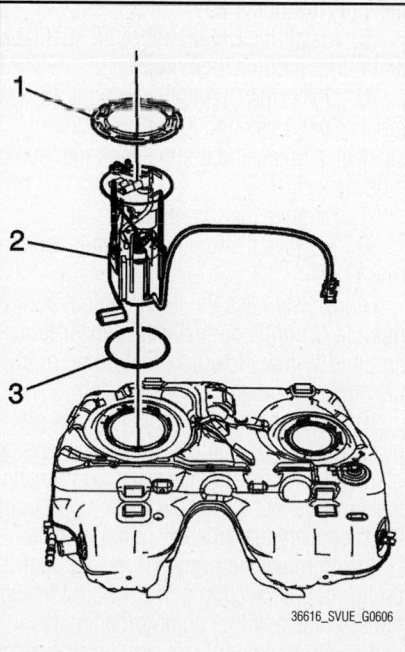

Fig. 618 Remove the fuel tank fuel pump module lock ring (1)

✳✳ CAUTION

Avoid damaging the lock ring. Use only J-45722 to prevent damage to the lock ring.

➡Do NOT use impact tools. Significant force will be required to release the lock ring. The use of a hammer and screwdriver is not recommended. Secure the fuel tank in order to prevent fuel tank rotation.

8. Using the J 45722 and a long breaker bar, rotate the lock ring counterclockwise unlocking the fuel tank fuel pump module lock ring.
9. Remove the J 45722.
10. Remove the fuel tank fuel pump module lock ring (1).

✳✳ CAUTION

Not handle the fuel sender assembly by the fuel pipes. The amount of leverage generated by handling the fuel pipes could damage the joints.

11. Slowly raise the module (2) until the fuel level sensor float arm is just visible.

➡When removing the module from the fuel tank, be aware that the module reservoir bucket is full of fuel. The module must be tipped slightly during removal to avoid bending the fuel level sensor float arm.

12. Tilt the module toward the rear of the fuel tank to allow the level sensor float arm to clear the tank opening. Remove the module from the tank.
13. Carefully discard the fuel in the module reservoir bucket into an approved fuel container.

➡DO NOT reuse the old fuel tank module O-ring seal.

14. Remove and discard the fuel tank fuel pump module O-ring seal (3).
15. If replacing the fuel tank fuel pump module, remove the fuel level sensor, if required.

➡Some lock rings were manufactured with "DO NOT REUSE" stamped into them. These lock rings may be reused if they are not damaged or warped. Inspect the lock ring for damage due to improper removal or installation procedures. If damage is found, install a NEW lock ring. Check the lock ring for flatness.

16. Place the lock ring on a flat surface. Measure the clearance between the lock ring

and the flat surface using a feeler gage at 7 points.

17. If warpage is less than 0.0016 inches (0.41 mm), the lock ring does not require replacement.

18. If warpage is greater than 0.0016 inches (0.41 mm), the lock ring must be replaced.

To install:

19. If the fuel tank fuel pump module was replaced, install the fuel level sensor, if required.

20. Install a NEW fuel tank module O-ring seal onto the fuel tank.

21. Tilt the module toward the rear of the fuel tank to allow the fuel level sensor float arm to clear the tank opening. Install the module into the fuel tank.

22. Lower the module assembly into the tank.

23. Position and install the fuel tank module lock ring.

24. Install the J 45722 to the fuel tank fuel pump module lock ring.

➡ **Always replace the fuel tank module seal when installing the fuel tank module. Replace the lock ring if necessary. DO NOT apply any type of lubrication in the seal groove. Ensure the lock ring is installed with the correct side facing upward. A correctly installed lock ring will only turn in a clockwise direction.**

25. Use the J 45722 and a long breaker bar, rotate the lock ring clockwise locking the fuel tank module lock ring.

26. Remove the J 45722 from the fuel tank fuel pump module lock ring.

27. Connect the vapor line quick connect fittings to the fuel tank fuel pump module.

28. Connect the engine wiring harness electrical connectors to the fuel tank fuel pump primary module and the fuel tank pressure sensor.

29. Lay the fuel feed line into position and connect the fuel feed line quick connect fitting to the fuel tank fuel pump module.

30. Close the retaining clip on the fuel tank.

31. Install the secondary fuel tank fuel pump module.

32. Install the fuel tank.

Secondary Fuel Tank Module

See Figures 619 through 623.

1. Remove the fuel tank.

2. Disconnect the fuel tank wiring harness electrical connector (2) from the secondary fuel tank fuel pump module.

3. Remove the fuel tank wiring harness from the retaining clip (3).

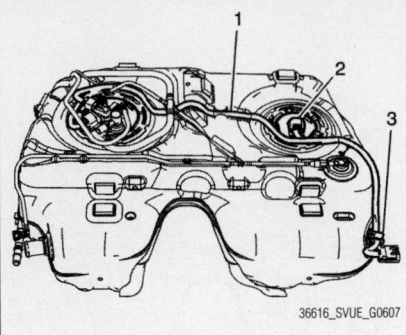

Fig. 619 Disconnect the fuel tank wiring harness electrical connector (2) from the secondary fuel tank fuel pump module

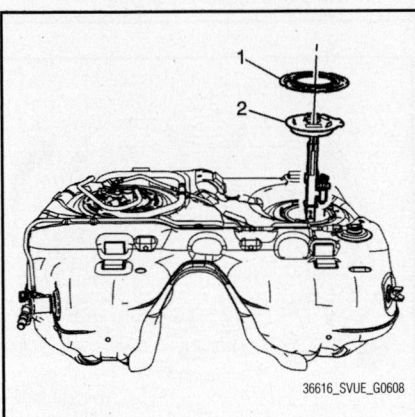

Fig. 620 Remove the fuel tank module lock ring (1)

4. Reposition the fuel tank wiring harness (1) out of the way.

5. Install the CH-48482 to the fuel tank fuel pump module lock ring.

6. Using the CH-48482 and a long breaker bar, rotate the lock ring counterclockwise unlocking the fuel tank fuel pump module lock ring.

7. Remove the CH-48482.

8. Remove the fuel tank module lock ring (1).

9. Slowly raise the fuel tank fuel pump module (2) until the fuel level sensor float arm and primary fuel tank fuel pump module suction port are just visible.

10. Squeeze in the primary fuel tank fuel pump module suction port tabs on either side of the port in order to disengage the primary fuel tank fuel pump module suction port from the secondary fuel tank fuel pump module.

11. Remove the primary fuel tank fuel pump module suction port (2) from the secondary fuel tank fuel pump module (1).

12. Tilt the module toward the rear of the fuel tank to allow the level sensor float arm to clear the tank opening. Remove the module (1) from the tank.

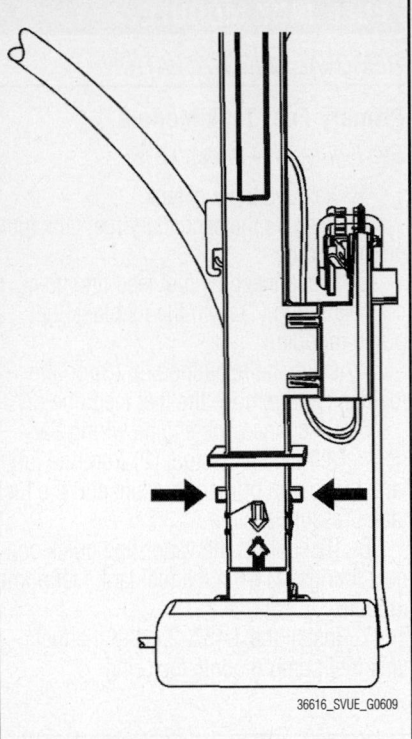

Fig. 621 Squeeze in the primary fuel tank fuel pump module suction port tabs

13. Remove and discard the fuel tank module O-ring seal (2).

14. If the secondary fuel tank fuel pump module is being replaced, remove the secondary fuel level sensor, if required.

To install:

15. If the secondary fuel tank fuel pump module was replaced, install the secondary fuel level sensor, if required.

16. Install a NEW fuel tank module O-ring seal onto the fuel tank.

17. Tilt the module toward the rear of the fuel tank to allow the fuel level sensor float

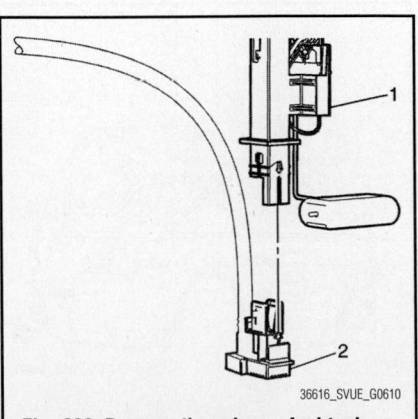

Fig. 622 Remove the primary fuel tank fuel pump module suction port (2) from the secondary fuel tank fuel pump module (1)

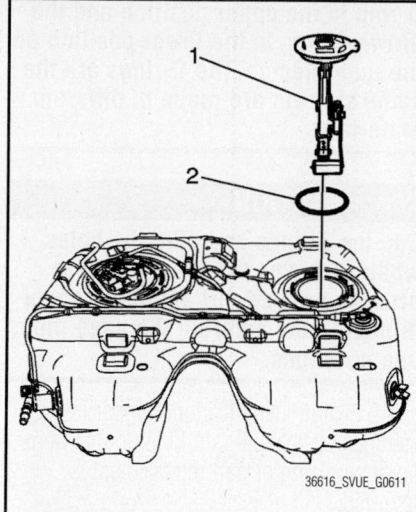

Fig. 623 Remove the module (1) from the tank

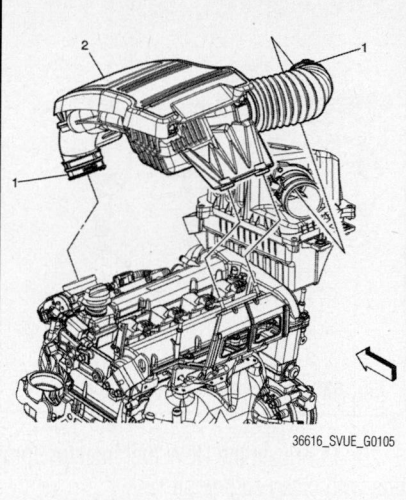

Fig. 624 Remove the air cleaner outlet duct

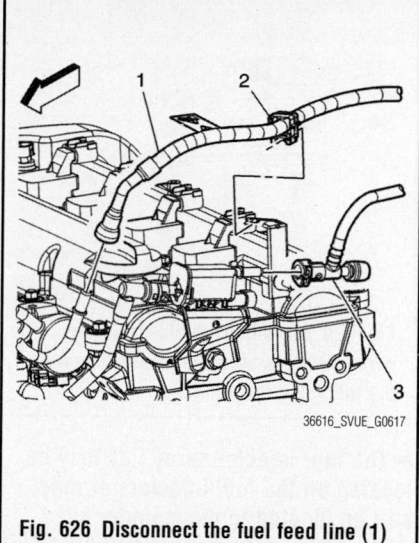

Fig. 626 Disconnect the fuel feed line (1) quick connect fitting from the fuel rail

arm to clear the tank opening. Install the module into the fuel tank.

18. Align the arrow on the primary fuel tank fuel pump module suction port to the arrow on the secondary fuel tank fuel pump module. Install the primary fuel tank fuel pump module suction port to the secondary fuel tank fuel pump module.

19. Lower the fuel tank fuel pump module into the fuel tank.

20. Install the fuel tank module lock ring.

21. Install the CH-48482 to the fuel tank fuel pump module lock ring.

22. Using the CH-48482 and a long breaker bar, rotate the lock ring clockwise locking the fuel tank fuel pump module lock ring.

23. Remove the CH-48482 from the fuel tank fuel pump module lock ring.

24. Position the fuel tank wiring harness to the module.

25. Connect the fuel tank wiring harness electrical connector to the secondary fuel tank fuel pump module.

26. Install the fuel tank wiring harness to the retaining clip.

27. Install the fuel tank.

FUEL RAIL & INJECTORS

REMOVAL & INSTALLATION

2.4L Engine

See Figures 624 through 630.

1. Relieve the fuel system pressure.
2. Disconnect the negative battery cable.
3. Remove the air cleaner outlet duct.
4. Remove the intake manifold cover.

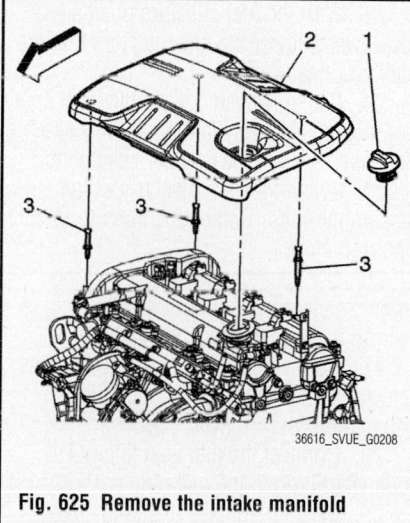

Fig. 625 Remove the intake manifold cover

5. Disconnect the fuel feed line (1) quick connect fitting from the fuel rail.

6. Disconnect the engine wiring harness electrical connector from the Manifold Absolute Pressure (MAP) sensor.

7. Disconnect the fuel injector wiring harness electrical connector from the engine wiring harness electrical connector.

8. Remove the fuel injection fuel rail assembly bolts.

➡**Use care when removing the fuel injection fuel rail assembly in order to prevent damage to the fuel injector spray tips.**

9. Pull the fuel injector fuel rail assembly back and upward in order to release the fuel injectors from the cylinder head ports.

10. Remove the fuel injection fuel rail assembly.

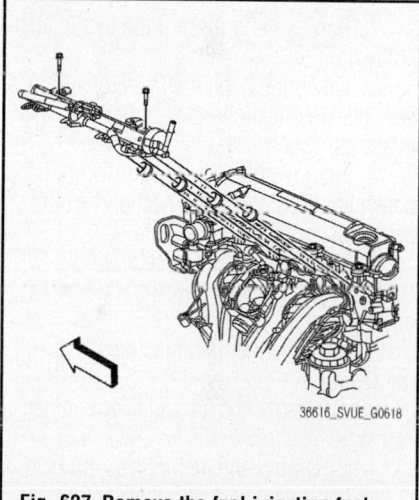

Fig. 627 Remove the fuel injection fuel rail assembly bolts

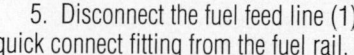

Fig. 628 Remove and discard the fuel injector spray tips

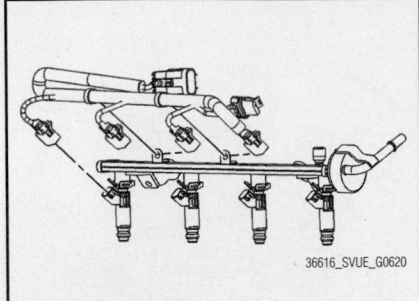

Fig. 629 Disconnect the fuel injector wiring harness electrical connectors from the fuel injectors

➡The fuel injector spray tips may be located on the fuel injectors or may still be located in the cylinder head ports. Either way, ensure that all 4 fuel injector spray tips are removed and discarded.

11. Remove and discard the fuel injector spray tips.

12. Disconnect the fuel injector wiring harness electrical connectors from the fuel injectors.

13. Remove the fuel injector wiring harness clips from the fuel injection fuel rail assembly.

14. Remove the fuel injector wiring harness from the fuel injection fuel rail assembly.

15. Remove the fuel injectors, if necessary.

    a. Remove the fuel injector retainer (1).

    b. Remove the fuel injector (3) from the fuel injection fuel rail assembly.

    c. Remove the fuel injector upper O-ring (2).

    d. Remove the fuel injector lower O-ring (4).

To install:

➡If the fuel injection fuel rail assembly and fuel injectors were removed and re-installed without separating them then install NEW lower O-rings only. If the fuel injection fuel rail assembly was replaced then install NEW upper and lower O-rings.

16. Install the fuel injectors, if necessary.

17. Install the fuel injector wiring harness to the fuel injection fuel rail assembly.

18. Install the fuel injector wiring harness clips to the fuel injection fuel rail assembly.

19. Connect the fuel injector wiring harness electrical connectors to the fuel injectors.

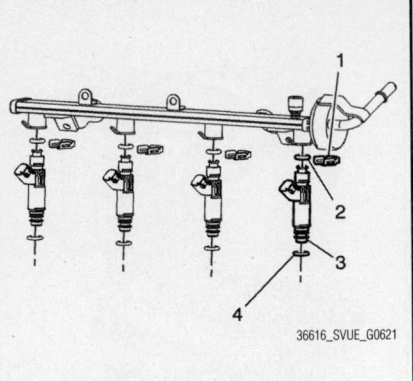

Fig. 630 Remove the fuel injectors

20. Lubricate the NEW fuel injector spray tips with clean engine oil.

21. Install the NEW fuel injector spray tips to the cylinder head ports.

22. Lubricate the fuel injector O-rings with clean engine oil.

23. With the fuel injectors positioned downward, lower the fuel injectors into the cylinder head ports.

24. Carefully push down on the fuel injector-fuel rail assembly in order to fully seat the fuel injectors into the cylinder head ports.

25. Install the fuel injector fuel rail assembly bolts. Tighten the bolts to 89 inch lbs. (10 Nm).

26. Connect the fuel injector wiring harness electrical connector to the engine wiring harness electrical connector.

27. Connect the engine wiring harness electrical connector to the Manifold Absolute Pressure (MAP) sensor.

28. Connect the fuel feed line quick connect fitting to the fuel rail.

29. Install the intake manifold cover.

30. Install the air cleaner outlet duct.

31. Connect the negative battery cable.

32. Inspect for fuel leaks using the following procedure:

    a. Turn ON the ignition, with the engine OFF for 2 seconds.

    b. Turn OFF the ignition for 10 seconds.

    c. Turn ON the ignition.

    d. Inspect for fuel leaks.

3.5L Engine

See Figures 631 through 637.

❊❊ WARNING

In order to reduce the risk of fire and personal injury that may result from a fuel leak, always install the fuel injector O-rings in the proper position. If the upper and lower O-rings are different colors (black and brown), be sure to install the black

O-ring in the upper position and the brown O-ring in the lower position on the fuel injector. The O-rings are the same size but are made of different materials.

❊❊ CAUTION

Cap the fittings and plug the holes when servicing the fuel system in order to prevent dirt and other contaminants from entering the open pipes and passages.

An 8-digit identification number is stamped on the fuel rail. Refer to this number if servicing or part replacement is required.

1. Disconnect the chassis fuel feed line quick connect fitting (2) from the fuel rail.

2. Remove the upper intake manifold.

3. Disconnect the fuel injector wiring harness electrical connector from the Engine Coolant Temperature (ECT) sensor.

4. Disconnect the fuel injector wiring harness electrical connector from the Camshaft Position (CMP) sensor.

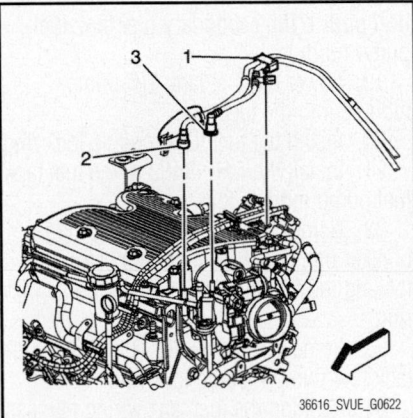

Fig. 631 Disconnect the chassis fuel feed line quick connect fitting (2) from the fuel rail

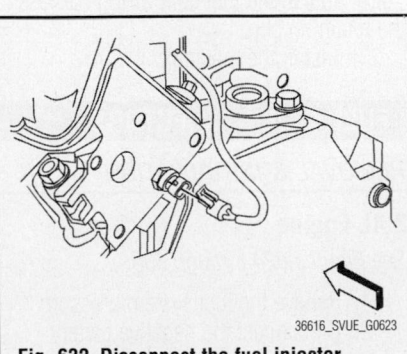

Fig. 632 Disconnect the fuel injector wiring harness electrical connector from the ECT sensor

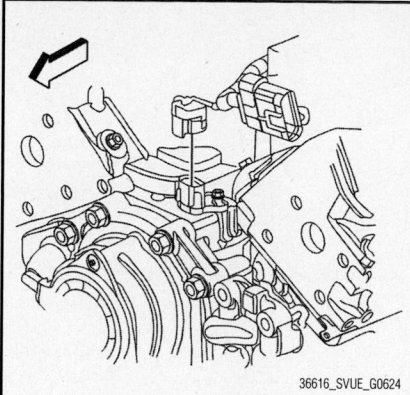

Fig. 633 Disconnect the fuel injector wiring harness electrical connector from the Camshaft Position (CMP) sensor

5. Remove the fuel injector wiring harness electrical connector bracket bolt from the intake manifold.

6. Remove the fuel rail bolts.

7. Remove the fuel rail (1).

8. Remove the fuel injector O-ring seal from the spray tip end of each injector, if the fuel rail was removed for other purposes.

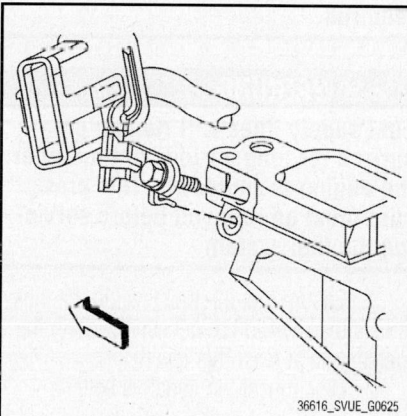

Fig. 634 Remove the fuel injector wiring harness electrical connector bracket bolt from the intake manifold

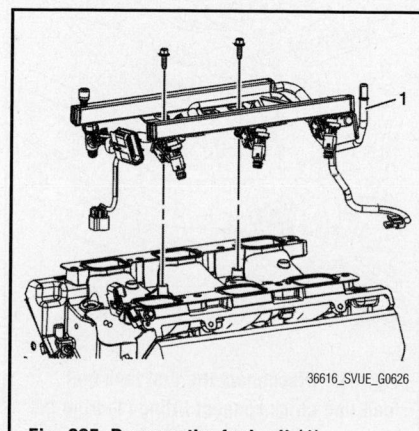

Fig. 635 Remove the fuel rail (1)

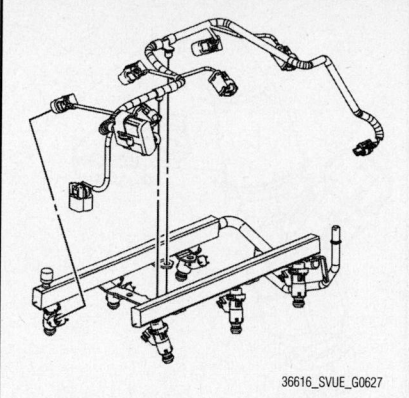

Fig. 636 Disconnect the fuel injector wiring harness electrical connectors from the fuel injectors

9. If replacing the fuel rail proceed to the disassembly procedure, otherwise proceed to the Installation Procedure.

10. Disconnect the fuel injector wiring harness electrical connectors from the fuel injectors.

11. Remove the fuel injector wiring harness retainers from the fuel rail.

12. Remove the fuel injector wiring harness.

13. Remove the fuel injector retainers (1).

14. Remove the fuel injectors (3).

15. Remove the fuel injector upper (2) and lower (4) O-ring seals.

To install:

16. Lubricate the NEW injector O-ring seals with clean engine oil.

17. Install the NEW fuel injector upper and lower O-ring seals.

18. Install the fuel injectors.

19. Install the fuel injector retainers.

20. Position the fuel injector wiring harness.

21. Install the fuel injector wiring harness retainers to the fuel rail.

22. Connect the fuel injector wiring harness electrical connectors to the fuel injectors.

❋❋ CAUTION

Use care when servicing the fuel system components, especially the fuel injector electrical connectors, the fuel injector tips, and the injector O-rings. Plug the inlet and the outlet ports of the fuel rail in order to prevent contamination. Do not use compressed air to clean the fuel rail assembly as this may damage the fuel rail components. Do not immerse the fuel rail assembly in a solvent bath in order to prevent damage to the fuel rail assembly.

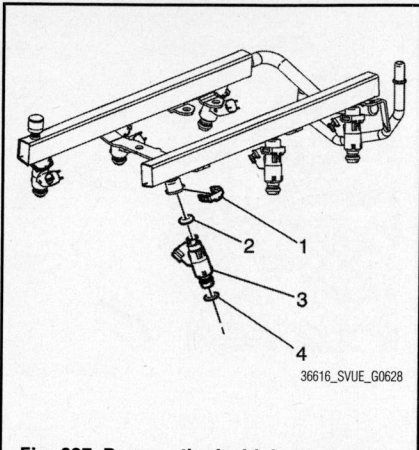

Fig. 637 Remove the fuel injector retainers (1)

23. Install NEW fuel injector O-ring seals onto the spray tip end of each injector, if the fuel rail was removed for other purposes.

24. Install the fuel rail.

25. Install the fuel rail bolts. Tighten the bolts to 89 inch lbs. (10 Nm).

26. Align the bracket pin to the hole in the lower intake manifold.

27. Install the fuel injector wiring harness electrical connector bracket bolt to the intake manifold. Tighten the bolt to 10 ft. lbs. (14 Nm).

28. Connect the fuel injector wiring harness electrical connector to the CMP sensor.

29. Connect the fuel injector wiring harness electrical connector to the ECT sensor.

30. Install the upper intake manifold.

31. Connect the chassis fuel feed line quick connect fitting to the fuel rail.

32. Connect the negative battery cable.

33. Inspect for leaks.

   a. Turn ON the ignition, with the engine OFF for 10 seconds.

   b. Turn OFF the ignition for 10 seconds.

   c. Turn ON the ignition for 10 seconds.

   d. Inspect for fuel leaks.

3.6L Engine

See Figures 638 through 640.

1. Remove the upper intake manifold.

2. Disconnect the fuel feed line quick connect fitting (2) from the fuel rail.

3. Use compressed air in order to remove any debris from the around the area where the fuel injectors enter the lower intake manifold.

4. Remove the fuel rail bolts.

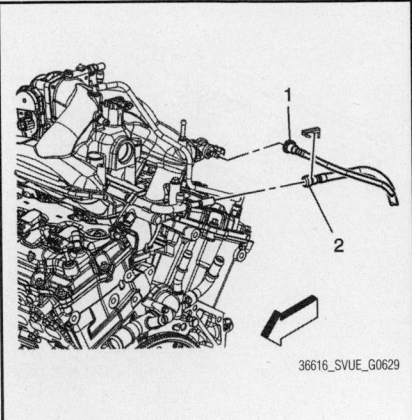

Fig. 638 Disconnect the fuel feed line quick connect fitting (2) from the fuel rail

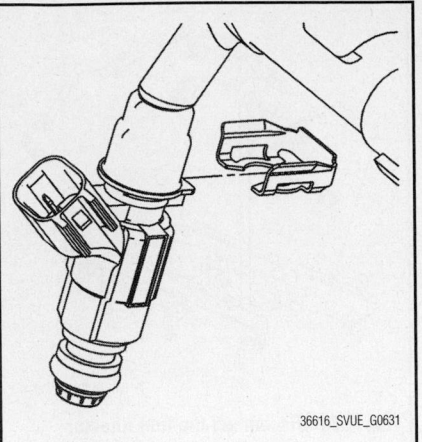

Fig. 640 Remove the fuel injector retainer clip

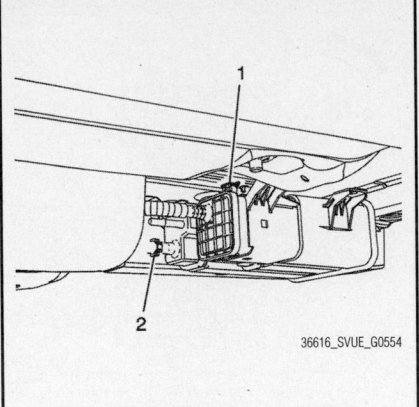

Fig. 641 Disconnect the fuel tank wiring harness electrical connector (1) from the EVAP canister vent solenoid valve

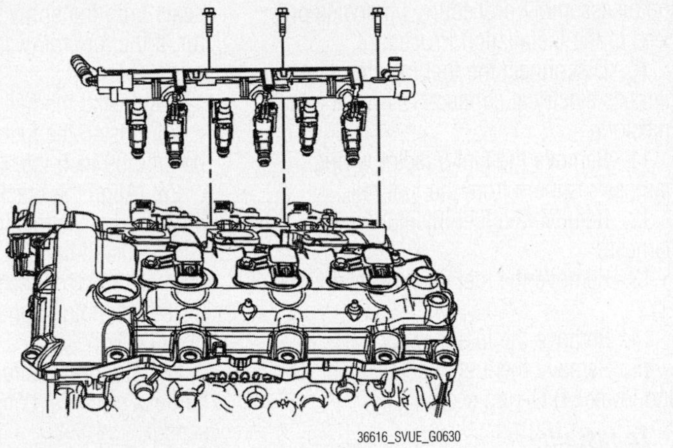

Fig. 639 Remove the fuel rail bolts

✳✳ CAUTION

Remove the fuel rail assembly carefully in order to prevent damage to the injector electrical connector terminals and the injector spray tips. Support the fuel rail after the fuel rail is removed in order to avoid damaging the fuel rail components. Cap the fittings and plug the holes when servicing the fuel system in order to prevent dirt and other contaminants from entering open pipes and passages.

5. Remove the fuel rail with fuel injectors from the lower intake manifold.

6. Disengage the fuel injector electrical connector lock.

7. Disconnect the fuel injector electrical connector.

8. Remove the fuel injector retainer clip.

9. Remove the fuel injector.

10. Remove and discard the fuel injector seals.

To install:

11. Install NEW fuel injector seals.

12. Install the fuel injector.

13. Install the fuel injector retainer clip.

14. Install the fuel injector electrical connector.

15. Engage the fuel injector electrical connector lock.

16. Install the fuel rail with fuel injectors to the lower intake manifold.

17. Install the fuel rail bolts. Tighten the bolts to 89 inch lbs. (10 Nm).

18. Connect the fuel feed line quick connect fitting to the fuel rail.

19. Install the upper intake manifold.

FUEL TANK

REMOVAL & INSTALLATION

Front Wheel Drive

See Figures 641 through 644.

✳✳ WARNING

Do not allow smoking or the use of open flames in the area where work on the fuel or EVAP system is taking place. Anytime work is being done on the fuel system, disconnect the negative battery cable, except for those tests where battery voltage is required.

✳✳ WARNING

Fuel supply lines will remain pressurized for long periods of time after the engine is shutdown. This pressure must be relieved before servicing the fuel system.

1. Ensure that the fuel level in the tank is less than 1/4 full. If necessary, drain the fuel tank to at least this level.

2. Disconnect the negative battery cable.

3. Raise and suitably support the vehicle.

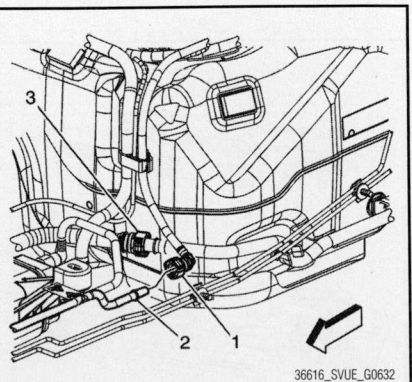

Fig. 642 Disconnect the fuel tank fuel feed line quick connect fitting (1) from the chassis fuel feed line (2)

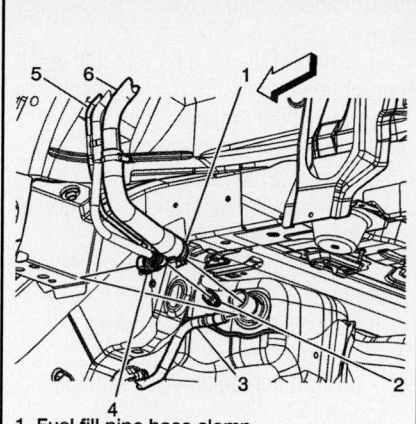

1. Fuel fill pipe hose clamp
2. Fuel tank vapor line quick connect fitting
3. Fuel tank fresh air line
4. Fill pipe vent line quick connect fitting
5. Fill pipe recirculation line
6. Fuel fill pipe

36616_SVUE_G0633

Fig. 643 Disconnect the fill pipe vent line quick connect fitting (4) from the fuel tank fresh air line (3)

4. Remove the exhaust system.
5. Disconnect the fuel tank wiring harness electrical connector (1) from the EVAP canister vent solenoid valve.
6. Disconnect the fresh air tube quick disconnect (2).

※ **WARNING**

Whenever fuel lines are removed, catch fuel in an approved container. Container opening must be a minimum of 12 inches (300 mm) diameter to adequately catch the fluid.

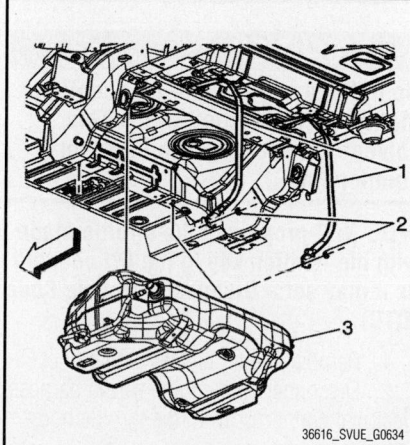

36616_SVUE_G0634

Fig. 644 Remove the fuel tank strap nuts (2) and straps (1)

※ **CAUTION**

Clean all fuel pipe connections and surrounding areas before disconnecting the fuel pipes to avoid contamination of the fuel system.

7. Disconnect the fuel tank fuel feed line quick connect fitting (1) from the chassis fuel feed line (2), if necessary.
8. Disconnect the fresh air tube quick disconnect (3).
9. Disconnect the fill pipe vent line quick connect fitting (4) from the fuel tank fresh air line (3).
10. Disconnect the fuel tank vapor line quick connect fitting (2) from the fill pipe recirculation line (5).
11. Loosen the fuel fill pipe hose clamp (1) at the fuel tank.
12. Remove the fuel fill pipe (6) hose from the fuel tank.
13. Using a suitable adjustable jack, support the fuel tank.

※ **CAUTION**

Do not bend the fuel tank straps. Bending the fuel tank straps may cause damage to the straps.

14. Remove the fuel tank strap nuts (2) and straps (1).
15. Using the adjustable jack, slowly lower and reposition the fuel tank (3) in order to remove the tank from the vehicle.

To install:

16. Using the adjustable jack, slowly raise and reposition the fuel tank in order to install the tank to the vehicle.

※ **CAUTION**

Do not bend the fuel tank straps. Bending the fuel tank straps may cause damage to the straps.

17. Install the fuel tank straps and nuts. Tighten the nuts to 15 ft. lbs. (20 Nm).
18. Remove the adjustable jack from under the fuel tank.

➡ **Ensure that the notch in the fuel fill pipe hose aligns with the locating tab on the fuel tank.**

19. Install the fuel fill pipe hose to the fuel tank.
20. Tighten the fuel fill pipe hose clamp at the fuel tank.
21. Connect the fuel tank vapor line quick connect fitting to the fill pipe recirculation line.
22. Connect the fill pipe vent line quick connect fitting to the fuel tank fresh air line.

23. Connect the fuel tank fuel feed line quick connect fitting to the chassis fuel feed line.
24. Connect the fresh air tube quick disconnect.
25. Connect the fuel tank wiring harness electrical connector to the EVAP canister vent solenoid valve.
26. Connect the fresh air tube quick disconnect.
27. Connect the EVAP canister fresh air line quick connect fitting to the fuel tank fresh air line.
28. Connect the fuel tank vapor line quick connect fitting to the EVAP canister.
29. Install the exhaust system.
30. Connect the negative battery cable.
31. Perform the following procedure in order to inspect for leaks:
   a. Turn the ignition ON, with the engine OFF, for 2 seconds.
   b. Turn the ignition OFF for 10 seconds.
   c. Turn the ignition ON, with the engine OFF.
   d. Inspect for fuel leaks.

All Wheel Drive

See Figures 642, 645 and 646.

※ **WARNING**

Do not allow smoking or the use of open flames in the area where work on the fuel or EVAP system is taking place. Anytime work is being done on the fuel system, disconnect the negative battery cable, except for those tests where battery voltage is required.

※ **WARNING**

Fuel supply lines will remain pressurized for long periods of time after the engine is shutdown. This pressure must be relieved before servicing the fuel system.

1. Ensure that the fuel level in the tank is less than 1/4 full. If necessary, drain the fuel tank to at least this level.
2. Disconnect the negative battery cable.
3. Raise and suitably support the vehicle.
4. Remove the exhaust system.
5. Remove the propeller shaft.

※ **WARNING**

Whenever fuel lines are removed, catch fuel in an approved container. Container opening must be a minimum of 12 inches (300 mm) diameter to adequately catch the fluid.

⁂ CAUTION

Clean all fuel pipe connections and surrounding areas before disconnecting the fuel pipes to avoid contamination of the fuel system.

6. Remove the evaporative emission canister.

7. Disconnect the fuel tank fuel feed line quick connect fitting (1) from the chassis fuel feed line (2), if necessary.

8. Disconnect the fresh air tube quick disconnect (3).

9. Disconnect the fill pipe vent line quick connect fitting (4) from the fuel tank fresh air line (3).

10. Disconnect the fuel tank vapor line quick connect fitting (2) from the fill pipe recirculation line (5).

11. Loosen the fuel fill pipe hose clamp (1) at the fuel tank.

12. Remove the fuel fill pipe (6) hose from the fuel tank.

13. Remove the rear parking brake cable to frame rail bolts. Unclip parking brake cables from fuel tank straps, and reposition parking brake cables to provide clearance for fuel tank removal.

14. Using a suitable adjustable jack, support the fuel tank.

⁂ CAUTION

Do not bend the fuel tank straps. Bending the fuel tank straps may cause damage to the straps.

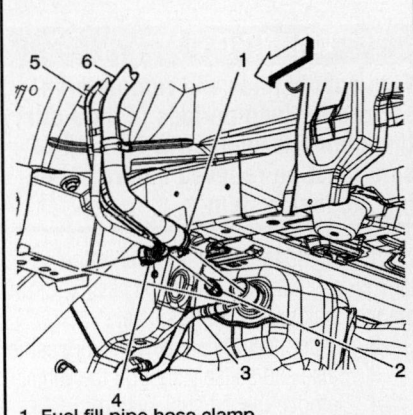

1. Fuel fill pipe hose clamp
2. Fuel tank vapor line quick connect fitting
3. Fuel tank fresh air line
4. Fill pipe vent line quick connect fitting
5. Fill pipe recirculation line
6. Fuel fill pipe

36616_SVUE_G0633

Fig. 645 Disconnect the fill pipe vent line quick connect fitting (4) from the fuel tank fresh air line (3)

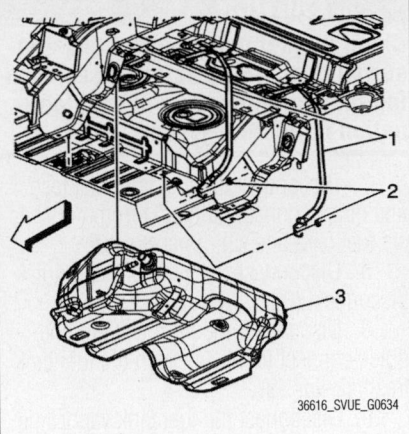

36616_SVUE_G0634

Fig. 646 Remove the fuel tank strap nuts (2) and straps (1)

15. Remove the fuel tank strap nuts (2) and straps (1).

➡**It is not necessary to remove the Rear Drive Module (RDM) in order to remove the fuel tank.**

16. Using the adjustable jack, slowly lower and reposition the fuel tank (3) in order to remove the tank from the vehicle. Using the adjustable jack, slowly lower the front of the fuel tank. Pull the fuel tank forward to clear the Rear Drive Module (RDM) and remove the fuel tank assembly with shield from the vehicle.

To install:

17. Using the adjustable jack, slowly raise and reposition the fuel tank in order to install the tank to the vehicle.

⁂ CAUTION

Do not bend the fuel tank straps. Bending the fuel tank straps may cause damage to the straps.

18. Install the fuel tank straps and nuts. Tighten the nuts to 15 ft. lbs. (20 Nm).

19. Remove the adjustable jack from under the fuel tank.

➡**Ensure that the notch in the fuel fill pipe hose aligns with the locating tab on the fuel tank.**

20. Clip the parking brake cables to the fuel tank straps. Install the rear parking brake cable to frame rail bolts.

21. Install the evaporative emission canister.

22. Install the fuel fill pipe hose to the fuel tank.

23. Tighten the fuel fill pipe hose clamp at the fuel tank.

24. Connect the fuel tank vapor line

quick connect fitting to the fill pipe recirculation line.

25. Connect the fill pipe vent line quick connect fitting to the fuel tank fresh air line.

26. Install the propeller shaft.

27. Install the exhaust system.

28. Connect the negative battery cable.

29. Perform the following procedure in order to inspect for leaks:

a. Turn the ignition ON, with the engine OFF, for 2 seconds.

b. Turn the ignition OFF for 10 seconds.

c. Turn the ignition ON, with the engine OFF.

d. Inspect for fuel leaks.

IDLE SPEED

ADJUSTMENT

Idle speed is controlled by the Engine Control Module (ECM). No adjustment is necessary or possible.

THROTTLE BODY

REMOVAL & INSTALLATION

2.4L Engine

See Figures 647 and 648.

⁂ CAUTION

Do not use solvent of any type when cleaning the gasket surfaces on the intake manifold and the throttle body assembly, as damage to the gasket surfaces and throttle body assembly may result. Use care in cleaning the gasket surfaces on the intake manifold and the throttle body assembly, as sharp tools may damage the gasket surfaces.

⁂ CAUTION

Do not use any solvent that contains Methyl Ethyl Ketone (MEK). This solvent may damage fuel system components.

➡**DO NOT prop open the throttle blade with the ignition key in the ON position as it may set a Diagnostic Trouble Code (DTC).**

1. Remove the air cleaner outlet duct.

2. Disconnect the engine wiring harness electrical connector from the throttle body assembly.

3. Remove the throttle body assembly bolts.

4. Remove the throttle body assembly.

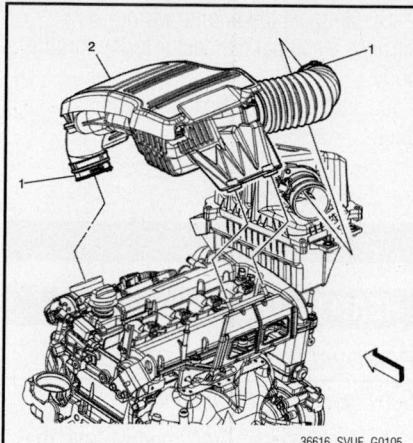

Fig. 647 Remove the air cleaner outlet duct

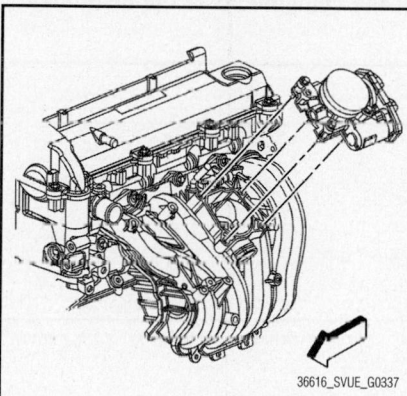

Fig. 648 Remove the throttle body assembly

5. Inspect the throttle body assembly gasket, and replace it if necessary.

To install:

6. Install the throttle body assembly to the vehicle.

7. Install the throttle body assembly bolts. Tighten the bolts to 89 inch lbs. (10 Nm).

8. Connect the engine wiring harness electrical connector to the throttle body assembly.

9. Install the air cleaner outlet duct.

3.5L Engine

See Figures 649 and 650.

✳✲ CAUTION

Do not use solvent of any type when cleaning the gasket surfaces on the intake manifold and the throttle body assembly, as damage to the gasket surfaces and throttle body assembly may result. Use care in cleaning the

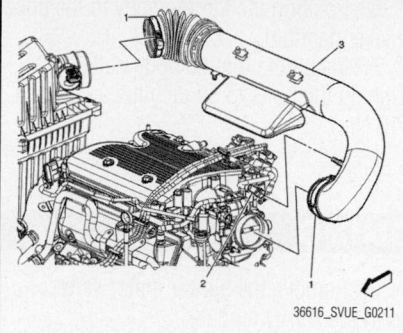

Fig. 649 Remove the air cleaner outlet duct

gasket surfaces on the intake manifold and the throttle body assembly, as sharp tools may damage the gasket surfaces.

1. Remove the air cleaner outlet duct.

2. Disconnect the engine wiring harness electrical connector from the Electronic Throttle Control (ETC).

3. Remove the throttle body bolts (9) and nuts (10).

4. Remove the throttle body (8).

5. Remove and discard the throttle body gasket (7).

To install:

6. Install a NEW throttle body gasket.

7. Install the throttle body.

8. Install the throttle body bolts and nuts. Tighten the bolts/nuts to 89 inch lbs. (10 Nm).

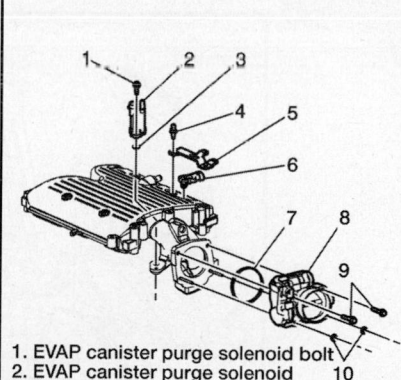

1. EVAP canister purge solenoid bolt
2. EVAP canister purge solenoid
3. O-ring
4. Bolt or stud
5. Bracket
6. Unknown
7. O-ring
8. Throttle body
9. Throttle body mounting bolts
10. Throttle body mounting nuts

Fig. 650 Remove the throttle body bolts (9) and nuts (10)

9. Connect the engine wiring harness electrical connector to the ETC.

10. Install the air cleaner outlet duct.

11. Perform the throttle learn procedure.

3.6L Engine

See Figures 651 through 653.

1. Remove the air cleaner outlet duct.

2. Disconnect the engine wiring harness electrical connector (3) from the throttle body (4).

3. Remove the throttle body bolts (2).

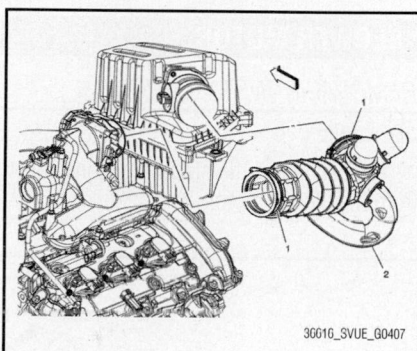

Fig. 651 Remove the air cleaner outlet duct

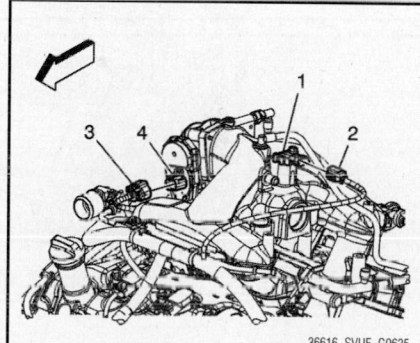

Fig. 652 Disconnect the engine wiring harness electrical connector (3) from the throttle body (4)

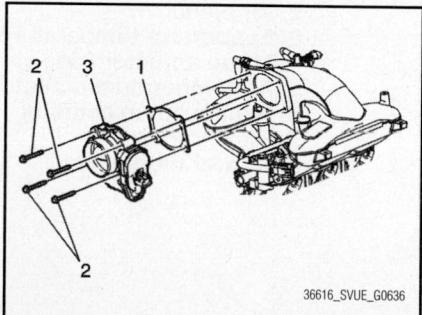

Fig. 653 Remove the throttle body bolts (2)

4. Remove the throttle body (3) and gasket (1). Discard the gasket.

To install:

5. Position a NEW throttle body gasket to the upper intake manifold.

6. Position the throttle body to the upper intake manifold.

7. Install the throttle body bolts. Tighten the bolts to 89 inch lbs. (10 Nm).

8. Connect the engine wiring harness electrical connector to the throttle body.

9. Install the air cleaner outlet duct.

HEATING & AIR CONDITIONING

COMPONENT LOCATIONS

See Figures 654 and 655.

BLOWER MOTOR

REMOVAL & INSTALLATION

See Figure 656.

1. Disconnect the electrical connector from the blower motor.

2. Remove the blower motor screws from the HVAC module.

3. Remove the blower motor from the HVAC module.

To install:

4. Install the blower motor to the HVAC module.

5. Install the blower motor screws to the HVAC module.

6. Connect the electrical connector to the blower motor.

HEATER CORE

REMOVAL & INSTALLATION

See Figures 657 through 659.

1. Remove the HVAC module from the vehicle.

❋❖❋ CAUTION

To avoid damage to the vehicle and/ or the components of the instrument

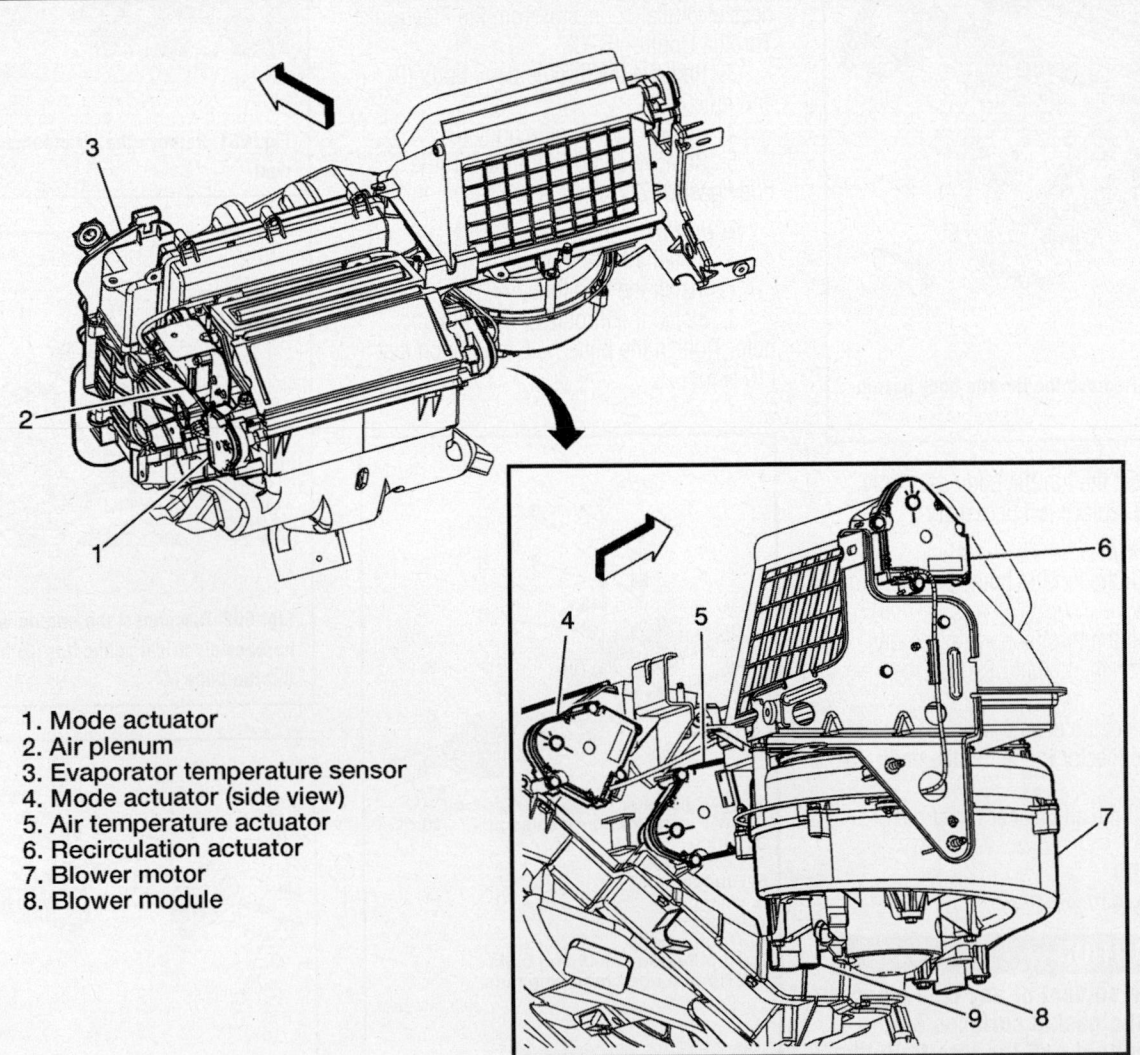

1. Mode actuator
2. Air plenum
3. Evaporator temperature sensor
4. Mode actuator (side view)
5. Air temperature actuator
6. Recirculation actuator
7. Blower motor
8. Blower module

36616_SVUE_G0020

Fig. 654 HVAC module components without C68

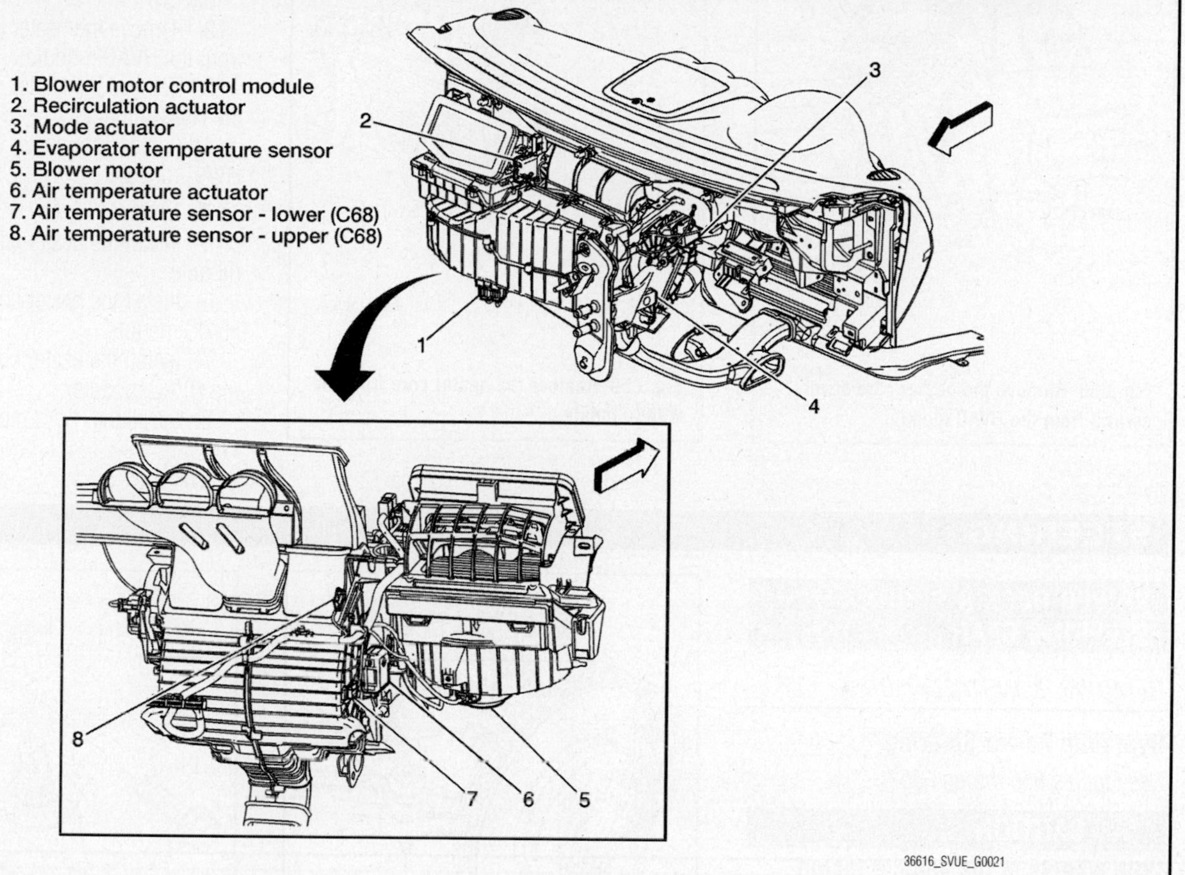

1. Blower motor control module
2. Recirculation actuator
3. Mode actuator
4. Evaporator temperature sensor
5. Blower motor
6. Air temperature actuator
7. Air temperature sensor - lower (C68)
8. Air temperature sensor - upper (C68)

36616_SVUE_G0021

Fig. 655 HVAC module components with C68

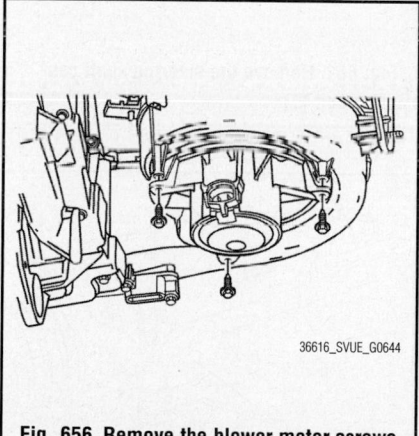

36616_SVUE_G0644

Fig. 656 Remove the blower motor screws from the HVAC module

panel because of hidden fasteners and retainers the instrument panel must be removed from the vehicle as an assembly.

   a. Remove the instrument panel.
   b. Remove the three HVAC module nuts (1).
   c. Remove the two HVAC module bolts (2).

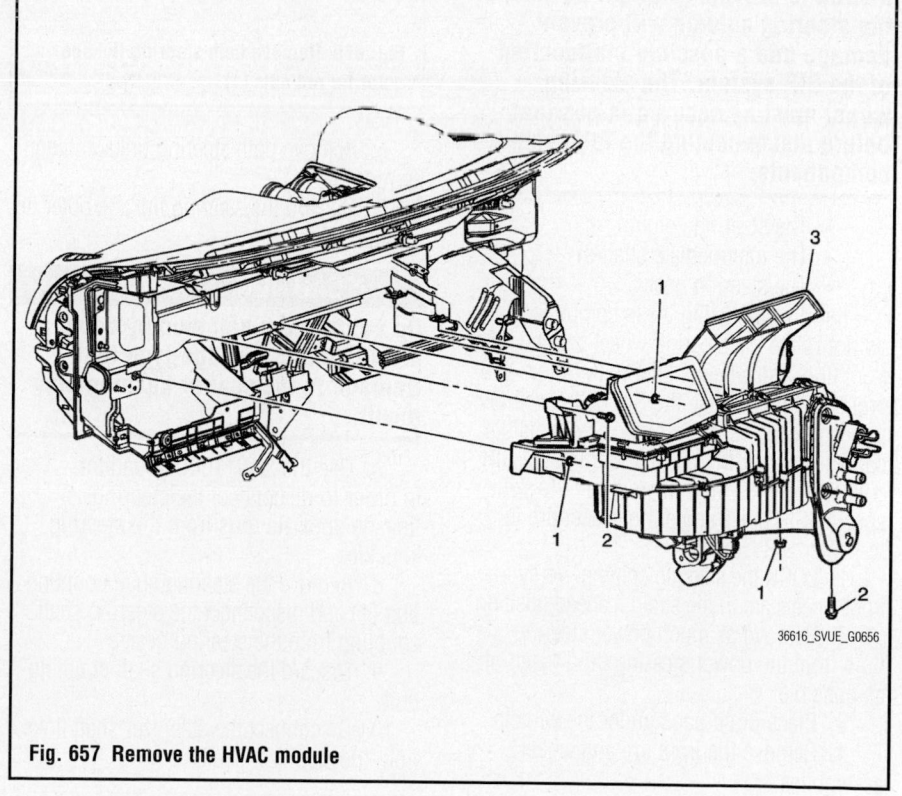

36616_SVUE_G0656

Fig. 657 Remove the HVAC module

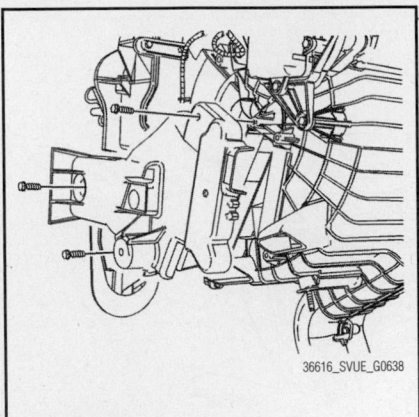

Fig. 658 Remove the heater core cover screws from the HVAC module

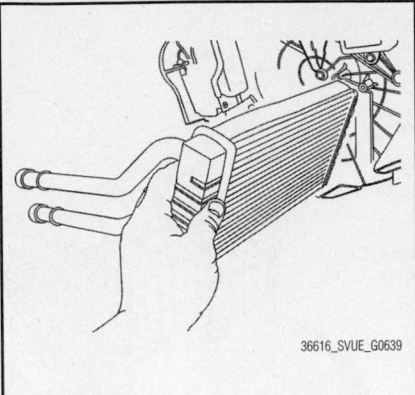

Fig. 659 Remove the heater core from the HVAC module

d. Remove the HVAC module assembly (3).

2. Remove the heater core cover screws from the HVAC module.

3. Remove the heater core cover from the HVAC module.

4. Remove the heater core from the HVAC module.

To install:

5. Install the heater core to the HVAC module.

6. Install the heater core cover to the HVAC module.

7. Install the heater core cover screws to the HVAC module.

8. Install the HVAC module to the vehicle.

STEERING

POWER RACK & PINION STEERING GEAR

REMOVAL & INSTALLATION

Hydraulic Power Steering

See Figures 666 through 667.

❋ CAUTION

With wheels of the vehicle facing straight ahead, secure the steering wheel utilizing steering column anti-rotation pin, steering column lock, or a strap to prevent rotation. Locking of the steering column will prevent damage and a possible malfunction of the SIR system. The steering wheel must be secured in position before disconnecting the following components:

- The steering column
- The intermediate shaft(s)
- The steering gear

After disconnecting these components, do not rotate the steering wheel or move the front tires and wheels. Failure to follow this procedure may cause the SIR coil assembly to become un-centered and cause possible damage to the SIR coil. If you think the SIR coil has became un-centered, refer to your specific SIR coil's centering procedure to re-center SIR Coil.

1. LOCK the steering column. Verify the front wheels are in the straight ahead position.

2. Remove as much power steering fluid from the power steering fluid reservoir as possible.

3. Place drain pans under the vehicle.

4. Remove the front tire and wheel assemblies.

Fig. 660 Remove both steering linkage outer tie rod nuts (1)

5. Remove both steering linkage outer tie rod nuts (1).

6. Discard the steering linkage outer tie rod nuts.

❋ CAUTION

Do not free the ball stud by using a pickle fork or a wedge-type tool. Damage to the seal or bushing may result.

7. Use the SA91100C separator in order to disconnect the steering linkage outer tie rods from the steering knuckles.

8. Remove the steering shaft coupling bolt (1) and disconnect the steering shaft coupling from the steering gear.

9. Discard the steering shaft coupling bolt.

10. Disconnect the stabilizer shaft links from the stabilizer shaft.

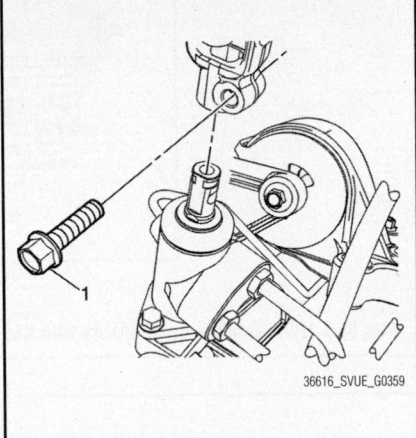

Fig. 661 Remove the steering shaft coupling bolt (1)

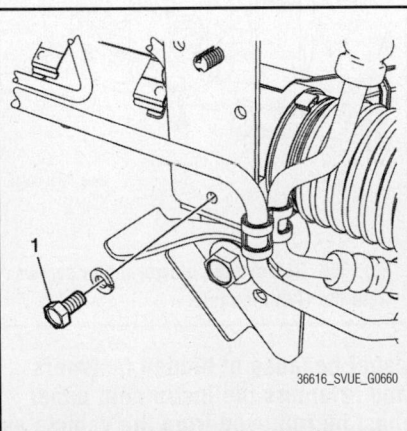

Fig. 662 Remove the power steering gear inlet hose bracket bolt (1)

11. Rotate the stabilizer shaft in order to provide clearance for the steering gear.

12. Remove the power steering gear inlet hose bracket bolt (1).

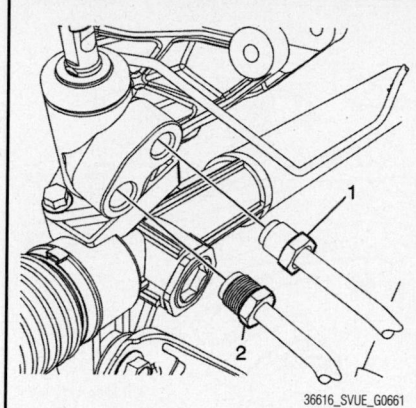

Fig. 663 Disconnect the power steering gear inlet hose (2) and the power steering cooler hose (1)

13. Disconnect the power steering gear inlet hose (2) and the power steering cooler hose (1) from the steering gear.

14. Discard the O-ring seals.

15. Remove the rear transaxle mount through bolt (1).

16. Remove the 3 rear transaxle mount bolts (1).

17. Position the rear transaxle mount to the side.

18. Remove the steering gear bolts (1).

19. Maneuver and remove the steering gear through the left wheelhouse opening.

To install:

20. Position the steering gear in the vehicle through the left wheelhouse opening. Ensure the steering gear bushings are centered in the frame.

➡**Hand start the steering gear bolts before finalizing any torques.**

21. Install the steering gear bolts and tighten to 81 ft. lbs. (110 Nm).

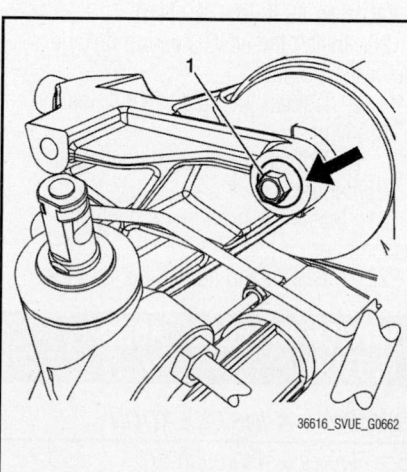

Fig. 664 Remove the rear transaxle mount through bolt (1)

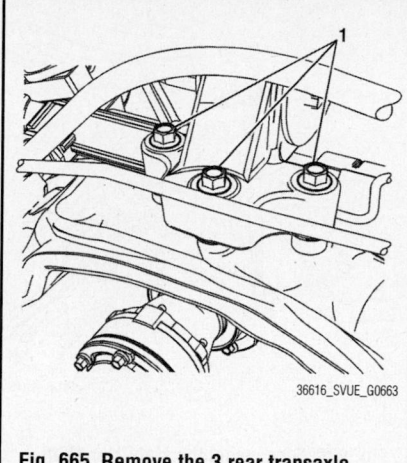

Fig. 665 Remove the 3 rear transaxle mount bolts (1)

22. Connect the steering shaft coupling to the steering gear.

23. Install a NEW steering shaft coupling bolt and tighten to 24 ft. lbs. (33 Nm).

24. Install a NEW O-ring seal and connect the power steering gear inlet hose to the steering gear. Tighten the power steering gear inlet hose fitting to 18 ft. lbs. (25 Nm).

25. Install a NEW O-ring seal and connect the power steering cooler hose to the steering gear. Tighten the power steering cooler hose fitting to 18 ft. lbs. (25 Nm).

26. Install the power steering gear inlet hose bracket bolt and tighten to 80 inch lbs. (9 Nm).

27. Install the rear transaxle mount.

28. Install the 3 rear transaxle mount bolts and tighten to 37 ft. lbs. (50 Nm).

29. Install the rear transaxle mount through bolt and tighten to 81 ft. lbs. (110 Nm).

30. Connect the stabilizer shaft links to the stabilizer shaft.

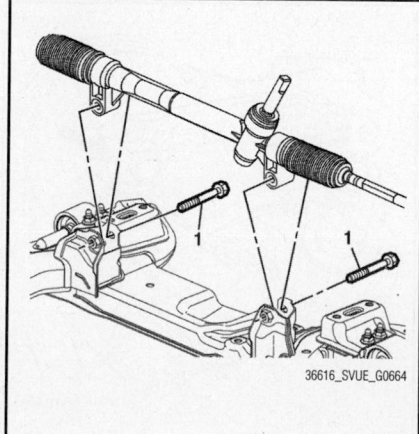

Fig. 666 Remove the steering gear bolts (1)

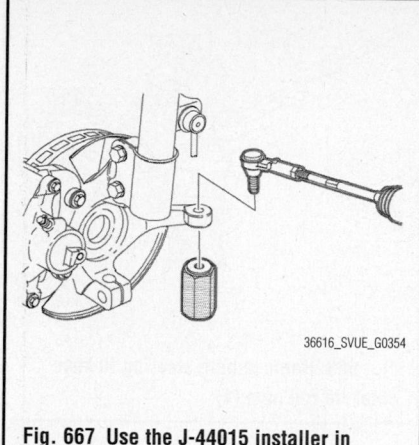

Fig. 667 Use the J-44015 installer in order to seat the steering linkage outer tie rods

31. Use the J-44015 installer in order to seat the steering linkage outer tie rods. Tighten the J-44015 installer to 30 ft. lbs. (40 Nm).

32. Install new steering linkage outer tie rod nuts and tighten to 18 ft. lbs. (25 Nm).

33. Tighten the steering linkage outer tie rod nuts an additional 90 degrees.

34. Clean any excess fluid from the vehicle.

35. Remove the drain pans.

36. Fill and bleed the power steering system.

37. Install the front tire and wheel assemblies.

38. Measure and adjust the front toe.

Electronic Power Steering

See Figures 668 through 673.

➡**With wheels of the vehicle facing straight ahead, secure the steering wheel utilizing steering column anti-rotation pin, steering column lock, or a strap to prevent rotation. Locking of the steering column will prevent damage and a possible malfunction of the SIR system. The steering wheel must be secured in position before disconnecting the following components:**

- The steering column
- The intermediate shaft(s)
- The steering gear

After disconnecting these components, do not rotate the steering wheel or move the front tires and wheels. Failure to follow this procedure may cause the SIR coil assembly to become un-centered and cause possible damage to the SIR coil. If you think the SIR coil has became un-centered, refer to your specific SIR coil's centering procedure to re-center SIR Coil.

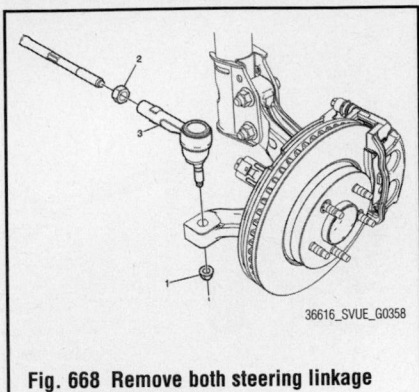

Fig. 668 Remove both steering linkage outer tie rod nuts (1)

1. LOCK the steering column. Verify the front wheels are in the straight ahead position.

2. Remove the front tire and wheel assemblies.

3. Remove both steering linkage outer tie rod nuts (1). Discard the steering linkage outer tie rod nuts.

➡**Do not free the ball stud by using a pickle fork or a wedge-type tool. Damage to the seal or bushing may result.**

4. Use the SA91100C in order to disconnect the steering linkage outer tie rods from the steering knuckles.

5. Remove the steering shaft coupling bolt (1) and disconnect the steering shaft coupling from the steering gear. Discard the steering shaft coupling bolt.

6. Disconnect the stabilizer shaft links from the stabilizer shaft.

7. Rotate the stabilizer shaft in order to provide clearance for the steering gear.

8. Remove the rear transaxle mount through bolt (1).

9. Remove the 3 rear transmission mount bolts (1).

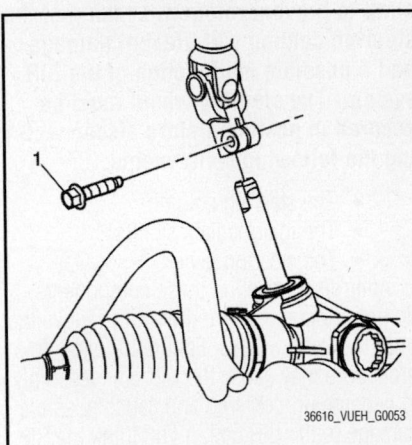

Fig. 669 Remove the steering shaft coupling bolt (1)

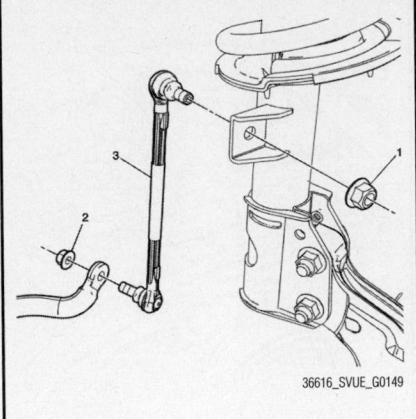

Fig. 670 Disconnect the stabilizer shaft links from the stabilizer shaft

10. Position the rear transmission mount to the side.

11. Remove the steering gear bolts (1).

12. Maneuver and remove the steering gear through the left wheelhouse opening.

To install:

13. Position the steering gear in the vehicle through the left wheelhouse opening. Ensure the steering gear bushings are centered in the frame.

➡**Hand start the steering gear bolts before finalizing any torques.**

14. Install the steering gear bolts. Tighten the bolts to 81 ft. lbs. (110 Nm).

15. Connect the steering shaft coupling to the steering gear and install a NEW steering shaft coupling bolt. Tighten the bolt to 25 ft. lbs. (34 Nm).

16. Install the rear transmission mount and the 3 rear transmission mount bolts. Tighten the bolts to 37 ft. lbs. (50 Nm).

17. Install the rear transmission mount

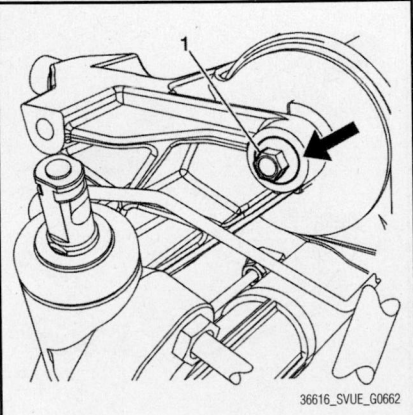

Fig. 671 Remove the rear transaxle mount through bolt (1)

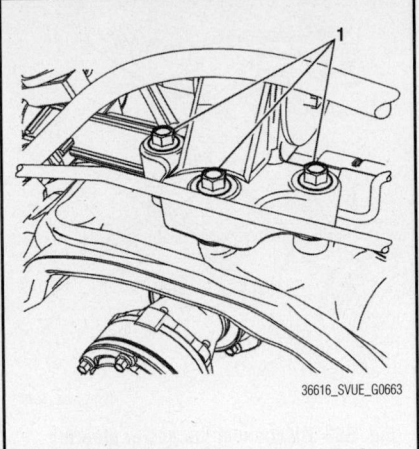

Fig. 672 Remove the 3 rear transmission mount bolts (1)

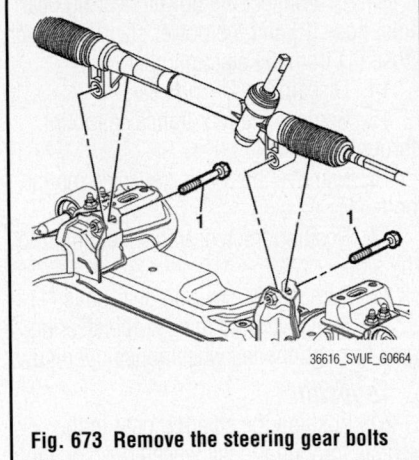

Fig. 673 Remove the steering gear bolts (1)

through bolt. Tighten the bolt to 81 ft. lbs. (110 Nm).

18. Connect the stabilizer shaft links to the stabilizer shaft.

19. Use the J 44015 in order to seat the steering linkage outer tie rods. Tighten the J 44015 to 30 ft. lbs. (40 Nm).

20. Install the NEW steering linkage outer tie rod nuts.

   a. Tighten the nuts to 18 ft. lbs. (25 Nm).

   b. Tighten the nuts an additional 90 degrees.

21. Install the front tire and wheel assemblies..

22. Measure and adjust the front toe.

POWER STEERING ASSIST MOTOR

REMOVAL & INSTALLATION

See Figures 674 through 676.

1. Remove the left instrument panel side trim panel.

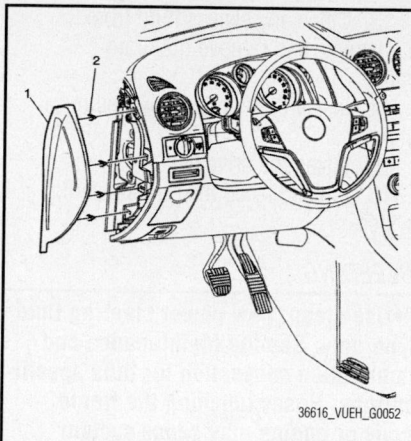

Fig. 674 Remove the left instrument panel side trim panel

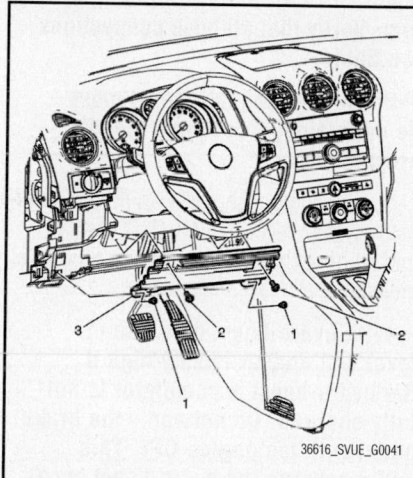

Fig. 675 Remove the driver knee bolster reinforcement

2. Remove the driver knee bolster reinforcement.

3. Remove the two power steering assist motor mounting bolts (1).

4. Remove the power steering assist motor (2).

5. Disconnect any electrical connectors as needed.

6. Installation is the reverse of removal.

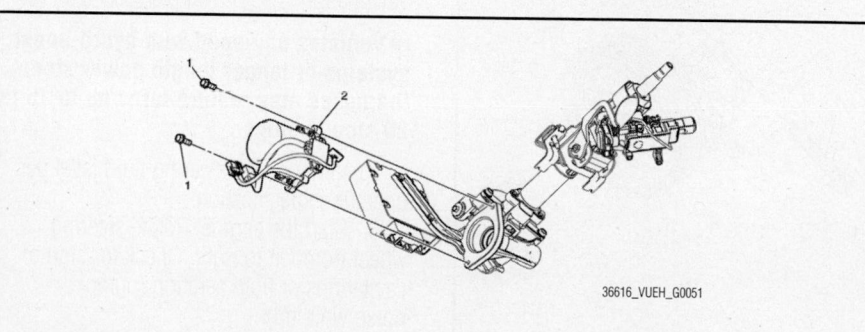

Fig. 676 Remove the two power steering assist motor mounting bolts (1)

a. Tighten the power steering assist motor mounting bolts to 13 ft. lbs. (18 Nm).

POWER STEERING PUMP

REMOVAL & INSTALLATION

2.4L Engine

See Figures 677 and 678.

1. Place drain pans under the vehicle as needed.

2. Remove as much fluid from the remote power steering fluid reservoir as possible.

3. Compress the power steering reservoir outlet hose clamp and disconnect the power steering reservoir outlet hose (2) from the power steering pump.

4. Disconnect the power steering gear inlet hose fitting (1) from the power steering pump.

5. Remove the power steering pump bolts (2).

6. Remove the power steering pump (1) from the vehicle.

7. Remove the power steering pump pulley using puller J 25034-C.

To install:

8. Install the power steering pump pulley using installer J 25033-C.

9. Position the power steering pump to the vehicle.

10. Install the power steering pump bolts and tighten to 16 ft. lbs. (22 Nm).

11. Connect the power steering gear inlet hose fitting to the power steering pump. Tighten the fitting to 18 ft. lbs. (25 Nm).

12. Compress the power steering reservoir outlet hose clamp and connect the power steering reservoir outlet hose to the power steering pump.

13. Clean any excess fluid from the vehicle and remove the drain pans.

14. Fill and bleed the power steering system.

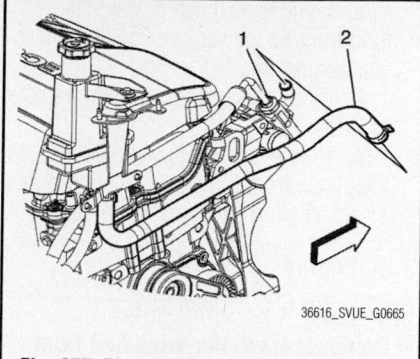

Fig. 677 Disconnect the power steering reservoir outlet hose (2)

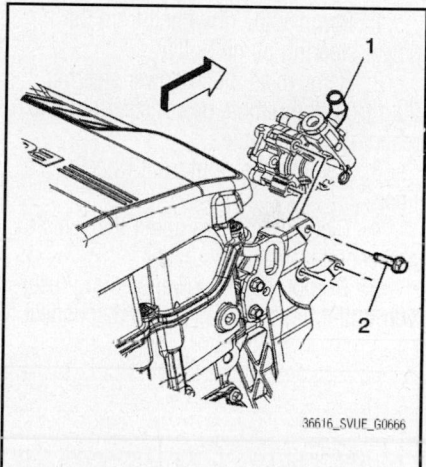

Fig. 678 Remove the power steering pump bolts (2)

3.5L Engine

See Figure 679.

1. Remove the power steering pump pulley.

2. Remove the three power steering pump bolts.

3. Remove the power steering pump.

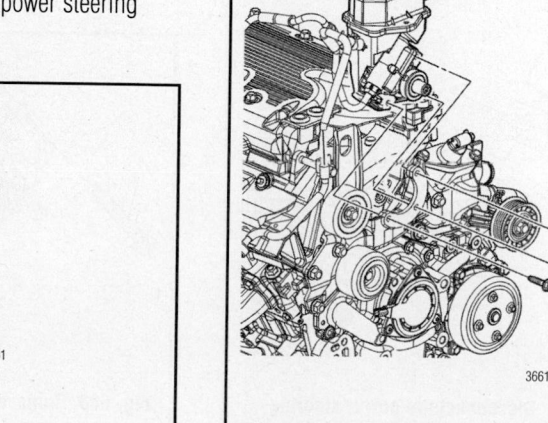

Fig. 679 Power steering pump removal

a. Remove as much power steering fluid from the power steering fluid reservoir as possible.

b. Place drain pans under the vehicle as needed.

c. Disconnect the power steering gear inlet hose from the power steering pump.

4. Installation is the reverse of removal.

3.6L Engine

See Figures 680 through 683.

➡ **Do not remove the drive belt from the vehicle entirely. Only slip it off the power steering pump pulley and set it aside in the engine compartment.**

1. Remove the drive belt from the power steering pump pulley.

2. Remove as much power steering fluid from the remote power steering fluid reservoir as possible.

3. Remove the right front wheelhouse liner.

4. Place drain pans under the vehicle as needed.

5. Compress the power steering reservoir outlet hose clamp (1) and disconnect

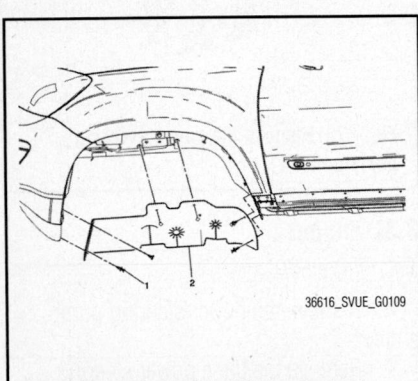

Fig. 680 Remove the right front wheelhouse liner

Fig. 681 Disconnect the power steering reservoir outlet hose (2)

Fig. 682 Disconnect the power steering gear inlet hose (1)

the power steering reservoir outlet hose (2) from the power steering pump.

6. Disconnect the power steering gear inlet hose (1) from the power steering pump.

7. Remove the power steering pump bolts (1).

8. Remove the power steering pump through the right wheelhouse area.

To install:

9. Position the power steering pump to the vehicle through the right wheelhouse area.

➡ **Hand start both bolts before finalizing any torques.**

10. Install the power steering pump bolts and tighten to 37 ft. lbs. (50 Nm).

11. Connect the power steering gear inlet hose to the power steering pump. Tighten the fitting to 18 ft. lbs. (25 Nm).

12. Compress the power steering reservoir outlet hose clamp and connect the power steering reservoir outlet hose to the power steering pump.

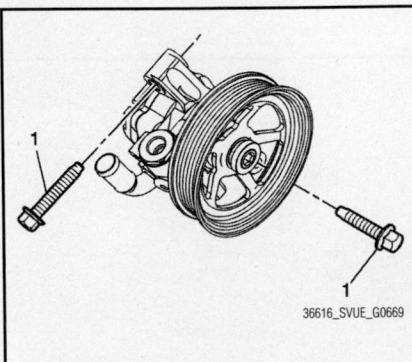

Fig. 683 Remove the power steering pump bolts (1)

13. Clean any excess fluid from the vehicle and remove the drain pans.

14. Install the right front wheelhouse liner.

15. Install the drive belt.

16. Fill and bleed the power steering system.

BLEEDING

➡ **Use clean, new power steering fluid type only. See the Maintenance and Lubrication subsection for fluid specifications. Hoses touching the frame, body or engine may cause system noise. Verify that the hoses do not touch any other part of the vehicle. Loose connections may not leak, but could allow air into the steering system. Verify that all hose connections are tight.**

➡ **Power steering fluid level must be maintained throughout bleed procedure.**

1. Fill pump reservoir with fluid to minimum system level, FULL COLD level, or middle of hash mark on cap stick fluid level indicator.

➡ **With hydro-boost only, the oil level will appear falsely high if the hydro-boost accumulator is not fully charged. Do not apply the brake pedal with the engine OFF. This will discharge the hydro-boost accumulator.**

2. If equipped with hydro-boost, fully charge the hydro-boost accumulator using the following procedure:

a. Start the engine.

b. Firmly apply the brake pedal 10-15 times.

c. Turn the engine OFF.

3. Raise the vehicle until the front wheels are off the ground.

4. Key on engine OFF, turn the steering wheel from stop to stop 12 times.

➡ **Vehicles equipped with hydro-boost systems or longer length power steering hoses may require turns up to 15 to 20 stop to stops.**

5. Verify power steering fluid level per operating specification.

6. Start the engine. Rotate steering wheel from left to right. Check for sign of cavitations or fluid aeration (pump noise/whining).

7. Verify the fluid level. Repeat the bleed procedure, if necessary.

STEERING LINKAGE

REMOVAL & INSTALLATION

Inner Tie Rod

See Figure 684.

1. Remove the steering gear and place it in a vise.
2. Remove the steering gear boot.

✳✳ CAUTION

Do not change the steering gear pre-load adjustment before moving the inner tie rod from the steering gear. Changing the steering gear preload adjustment before moving the inner tie rod could result in damage to the pinion and the steering gear.

3. Bend the tabs to release the steering linkage inner tie rod retaining washer (1).

✳✳ CAUTION

The pipe wrench must be placed at the valve end of the steering gear and positioned up against the inner tie rod housing. Placing the pipe

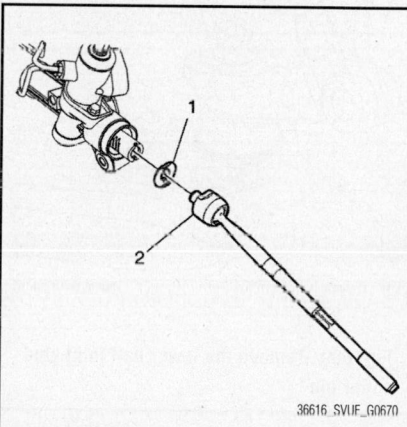

Fig. 684 Bend the tabs to release the steering linkage inner tie rod retaining washer (1)

wrench in any other location will cause damage to the steering gear.

4. Place a pipe wrench on the steering gear rack next to the steering linkage inner tie rod housing.
5. Place a wrench on the flats of the steering linkage inner tie rod housing (2).
6. Rotate the steering linkage inner tie rod housing counterclockwise while holding the steering gear rack stationary until the steering linkage inner tie rod separates from the steering gear rack.
7. Remove and discard the steering linkage inner tie rod retaining washer (1).

To install:

8. Position the NEW steering linkage inner tie rod retaining washer.
9. Attach the steering linkage inner tie rod onto the steering gear rack.
10. Place a pipe wrench on the steering gear rack next to the steering linkage inner tie rod housing.

✳✳ CAUTION

The pipe wrench must be placed at the valve end of the steering gear and positioned up against the inner tie rod housing. Placing the pipe wrench in any other location will cause damage to the steering gear.

11. Place a torque wrench and OTC 09922-10010-01 Inner Tie Rod Wrench on the flats of the steering linkage inner tie rod housing and tighten to 58 ft. lbs. (78 Nm).
12. Bend the tabs over on the steering linkage inner tie rod retaining washer to secure it.
13. Install the steering gear boot.
14. Install the steering gear

Tie Rod End

See Figure 685.

1. Remove the front tire and wheel assembly.
2. Remove the steering linkage outer tie rod nut (1).

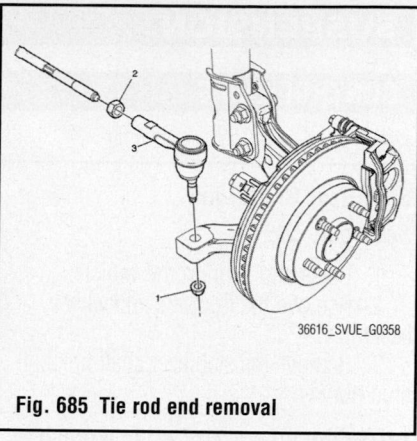

Fig. 685 Tie rod end removal

3. Mark the location of the steering linkage inner tie rod nut (2) and loosen it.
4. Use the separator SA91100C to separate the steering linkage outer tie rod from the steering knuckle.

✳✳ CAUTION

Do not free the steering linkage outer tie rod from the steering knuckle by use of a pickle fork or a wedge type tool. Damage to the steering linkage outer tie rod seal may result.

To Install:

5. Inspect the steering linkage inner tie rod for bent or damaged threads.
6. Clean the tapered surface of the steering knuckle.
7. Lubricate the tie rod threads with chassis lubricant.
8. Tighten the steering linkage inner tie rod nut. Tighten nut to 44 ft. lbs. (60 Nm).
9. Prior to re-installing the steering linkage outer tie rod nut use installer J 44015 to seat the steering linkage outer tie rod in the steering knuckle.
10. Tighten installer J 44015 to 30 ft. lbs. (40 Nm) and then remove.
11. Install the steering linkage outer tie rod nut. Tighten the nut to 18 ft. lbs. (25 Nm) plus an additional 90 degrees.
12. Adjust the front toe.

CONTROL LINKS

REMOVAL & INSTALLATION

Stabilizer Shaft Link

See Figure 686.

1. Raise and support the vehicle.
2. Remove the front tire and wheel assembly.
3. Remove the stabilizer shaft link ball stud nut (1).

➡ **Use the proper size Allen wrench to keep the stabilizer link ball stud from rotate while removing or installing the nut.**

4. Remove the stabilizer shaft link ball stud nut (2).
5. Remove the stabilizer shaft link.
6. Installation is the reverse of removal.

    a. Tighten the stabilizer shaft link ball stud nut (2) to 55 ft. lbs. (75 Nm).

    b. Tighten the stabilizer shaft link ball stud nut (1) to 63 ft. lbs. (85 Nm).

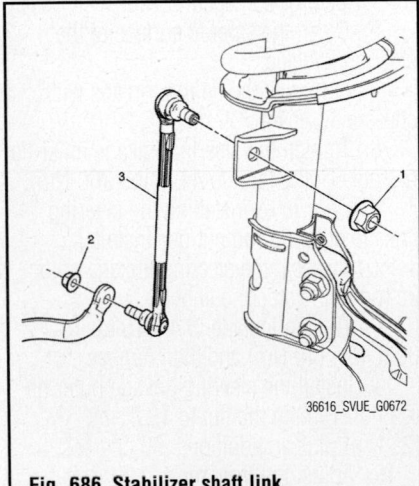

Fig. 686 Stabilizer shaft link

LOWER BALL JOINT

REMOVAL & INSTALLATION

See Figures 687 and 688.

1. Remove the lower control arm.
2. Place the control arm in a vise or suitable holding device.
3. Remove the ball joint rivets using the following procedure:

    a. Drill through the rivets using a ⁵⁄₁₆ inches (8 mm) drill bit.

Fig. 687 Remove the ball joint rivets

    b. Enlarge the hole using a ³¹⁄₆₄ inches (12 mm) drill bit.
    c. Remove any remaining burs from the control arm.
4. Remove the ball joint from the control arm.
5. Note the position of the ball joint for reassembly.

To install:

➡ **The control arm must be clean and free of debris.**

6. Install the ball joint to the control arm.

➡ **Only use hardware provided with the new ball joint. The bolts must be installed with the bolt head on top of the ball joint.**

7. Install the ball joint to control arm bolts and tighten the bolts/nuts to 50 ft. lbs. (68 Nm).
8. Install the lower control arm.

Fig. 688 Install the ball joint to the control arm

LOWER CONTROL ARM

REMOVAL & INSTALLATION

See Figures 689 through 692.

1. Raise and support the vehicle.
2. Remove the wheel and tire assembly.
3. Remove the lower ball joint stud cotter pin. Discard the cotter pin.
4. Loosen the ball stud nut until the nut is level with the top of the ball stud.
5. Using J-42188-B, separate the lower control arm from the steering knuckle.
6. Remove the lower ball joint stud nut.
7. Remove the control arm-to-frame front bolt and nut. Discard the bolt and nut.
8. Remove the control arm-to-frame rear bolts and nuts. Discard the bolts and nuts.
9. Remove the control arm.

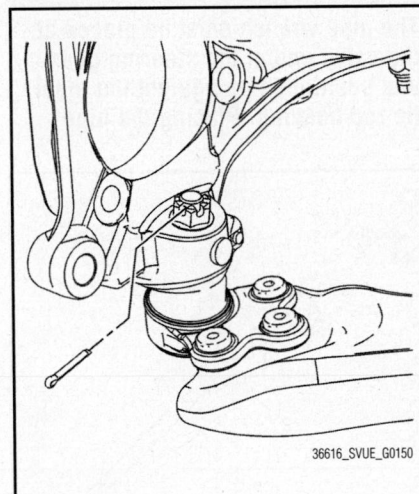

Fig. 689 Remove the lower ball joint stud cotter pin

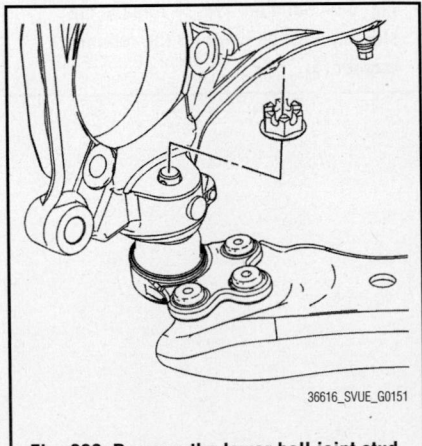

Fig. 690 Remove the lower ball joint stud nut

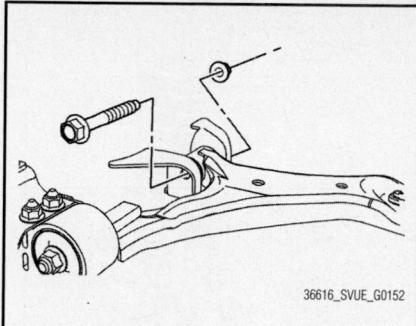

Fig. 691 Remove the control arm-to-frame front bolt and nut

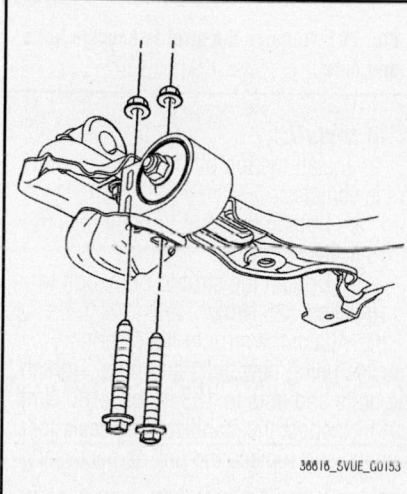

Fig. 692 Remove the control arm-to-frame rear bolts and nuts

To install:

10. Position the control arm to the cradle/frame.

11. Install new control arm-to-frame rear bolts and nuts and tighten to 52 ft. lbs. (70 Nm).

12. Install a new arm-to-frame front bolt and nut. Tighten the control arm front bolt and nut to 85 ft. lbs. (115 Nm) plus 90 degrees.

13. Position the control arm ball stud into the steering knuckle and install the nut. Tighten the nut to 30 ft. lbs. (40 Nm).

➡**Do not loosen the castle nut, only tighten to align the ball stud slot. Ensure that the cotter pin ends do not contact the Antilock Brake System (ABS) sensor harness or drive axle.**

14. Continue to tighten the nut only enough to align the castle nut slots with the ball stud.

15. Install a new cotter pin.
16. Install the wheel and tire assembly.
17. Verify front end alignment.
18. Lower the vehicle.

STEERING KNUCKLE

REMOVAL & INSTALLATION

See Figures 693 through 696.

1. Raise and support the vehicle.
2. Remove the tire and wheel.
3. Remove the wheel bearing/hub assembly.

➡**Do not allow the stabilizer link ball stud to rotate while removing the link nut.**

4. Remove the nut (1) and separate the stabilizer link from the strut assembly.

5. Loosen the steering knuckle to strut bolts and nuts.

6. Remove and discard the lower ball joint cotter pin.

7. Loosen the ball stud nut, until level with the top of the ball stud.

8. Using the J-42188-B, separate the lower ball joint from the steering knuckle.

9. Remove the lower control arm and nut.

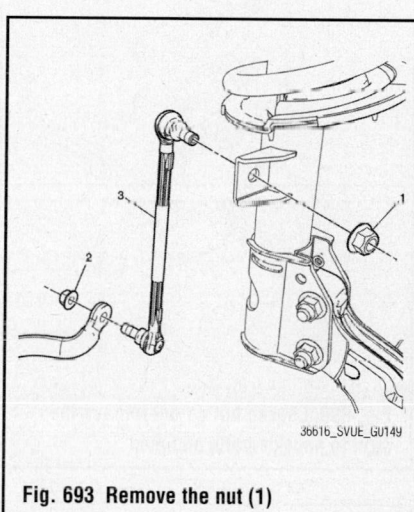

Fig. 693 Remove the nut (1)

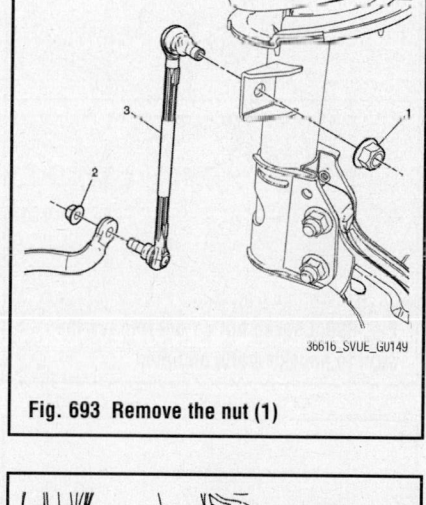

Fig. 694 Remove and discard the lower ball joint cotter pin

➡**Do not free the ball stud from the steering knuckle by use of a pickle fork or a wedge type tool. Damage to the seal or bushing may result.**

10. Remove the tie rod.

11. Remove the steering knuckle to strut bolts and nuts.

12. Remove the steering knuckle from the vehicle.

To install:

13. Position the steering knuckle to strut assembly.

14. Loosely install the strut to steering knuckle bolts and nuts.

15. Position the lower ball joint stud into the steering knuckle.

16. Using the SA9140E, install the ball stud nut and tighten to 30 ft. lbs. (40 Nm).

17. Tighten the strut to steering knuckle bolts and nuts to 133 ft. lbs. (180 Nm).

➡**Do not loosen the castle nut for cotter pin installation.**

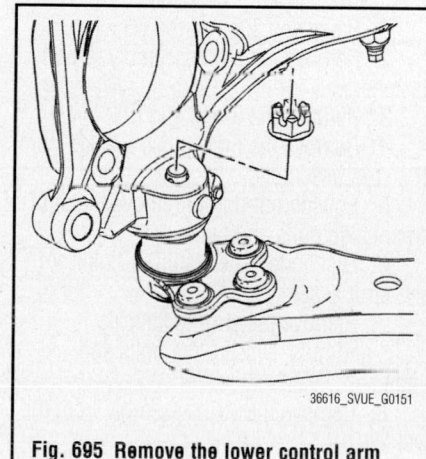

Fig. 695 Remove the lower control arm and nut

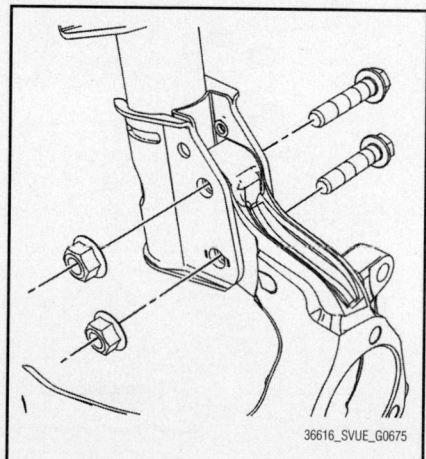

Fig. 696 Remove the steering knuckle to strut bolts and nuts

18. Tighten the castle nut enough to allow for cotter pin installation.

➥**The cotter pin must not contact the wheel speed sensor or drive axle.**

19. Install a new cotter pin.
20. Install the tie rod.

➥**Do not allow the stabilizer link ball stud to rotate while installing the link nut.**

21. Position the stabilizer shaft link to the strut assembly and install the nut. Tighten the nut to 48 ft. lbs. (65 Nm).
22. Install the wheel bearing/hub assembly.
23. Install the tire and wheel.
24. Lower the vehicle.
25. Perform a wheel alignment.

STRUT

REMOVAL & INSTALLATION

See Figures 697 through 701.

1. Raise and support the vehicle.
2. Remove the strut assembly to body fasteners.
3. Remove the wheel and tire.
4. Remove the brake hose bracket from the strut assembly.
5. Loosen but do not remove the strut to knuckle bolts and nuts.
6. Disconnect the stabilizer link from the strut assembly.
7. Remove the strut to knuckle bolts and nuts. Discard the bolts and nuts.
8. Remove the strut assembly from the vehicle.

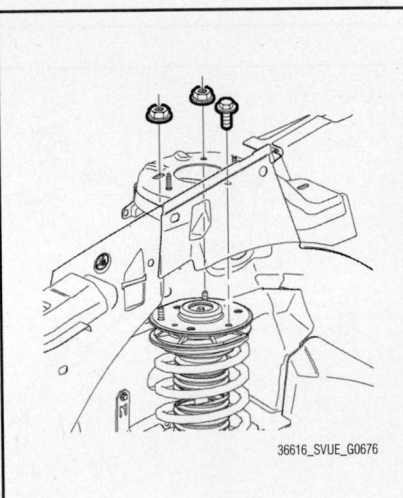

Fig. 697 Remove the strut assembly to body fasteners

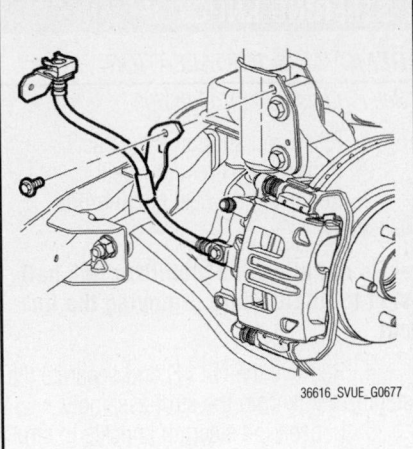

Fig. 698 Remove the brake hose bracket from the strut assembly

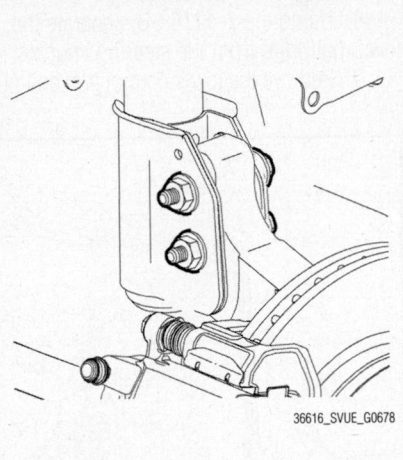

Fig. 699 Loosen but do not remove the strut to knuckle bolts and nuts

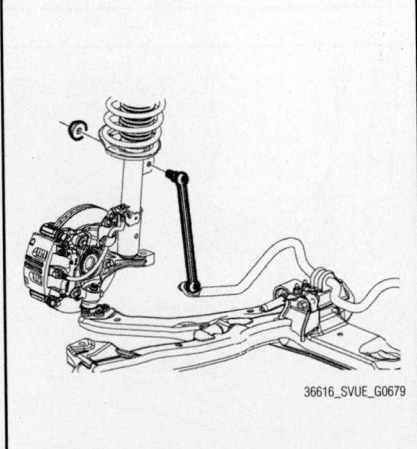

Fig. 700 Disconnect the stabilizer link from the strut assembly

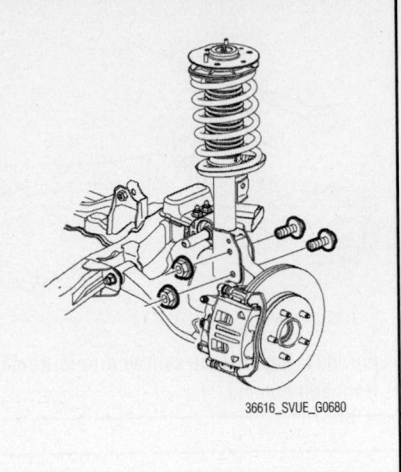

Fig. 701 Remove the strut to knuckle bolts and nuts

To install:

9. Install the top of the strut assembly to the vehicle.
   a. Tighten the strut to body nuts to 18 ft. lbs. (25 Nm).
   b. Tighten the strut to body bolt to 18 ft. lbs. (25 Nm).
10. Attach the strut to the steering knuckle using new bolts and nuts. Tighten the bolts and nuts to 133 ft. lbs. (180 Nm).
11. Inspect the stabilizer link seals for damage and replace the link as necessary.

➥**Do not allow the stabilizer link ball stud to rotate while installing the link nut.**

12. Connect the stabilizer link to the strut and tighten the nut to.
13. Install the brake hose bracket to the strut assembly. Tighten the brake bracket bolt to 11 ft. lbs. (15 Nm).
14. Install the wheel and tire.
15. Lower the vehicle.
16. Perform a wheel alignment.

STABILIZER BAR

REMOVAL & INSTALLATION

See Figures 702 through 705.

1. Turn the front wheels to the full right position.
2. Raise and support the vehicle.
3. Remove the front tire and wheels.
4. Disconnect the stabilizer link from the stabilizer bar.
5. Remove the left outer tie rod to steering knuckle nut. Discard the nut.
6. Using the SA91100C, separate the outer tie rod from the steering knuckle.
7. Remove the stabilizer bar clamp to cradle bolts.

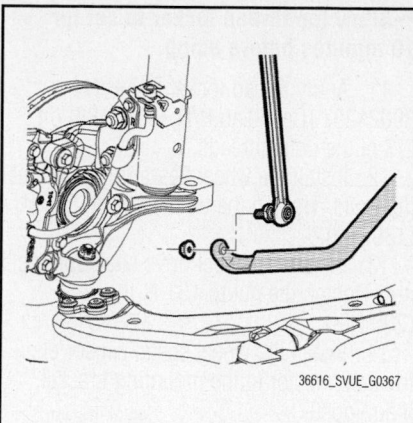

Fig. 702 Disconnect the stabilizer link from the stabilizer bar

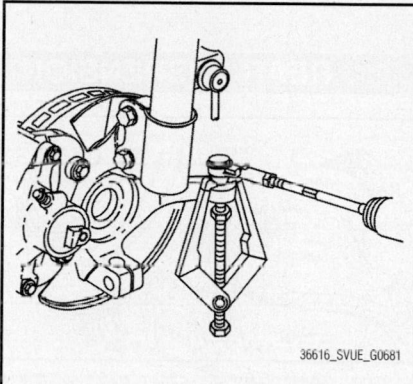

Fig. 703 Separate the outer tie rod from the steering knuckle

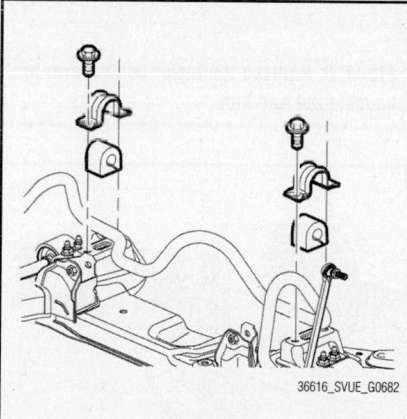

Fig. 704 Remove the stabilizer bar clamp to cradle bolts

8. Remove the stabilizer bar clamps and bushings from the stabilizer bar.

➡**Take care not to catch the transaxle shift cable or left wheel house plastic trim when removing the stabilizer bar.**

9. Remove the stabilizer bar from the vehicle through the left wheel opening.

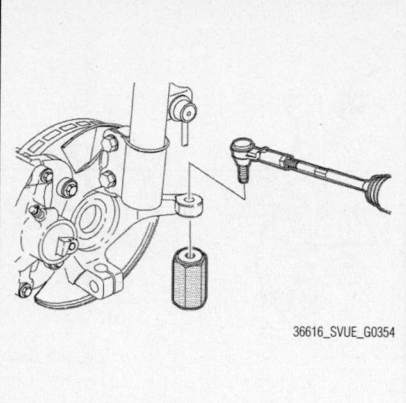

Fig. 705 Use the J 44015 in order to seat the ball stud taper

To install:

➡**Take care not to catch the transaxle shift cable or left wheel house plastic trim when installing the stabilizer bar.**

10. Install the stabilizer bar to the vehicle through the left wheel opening.

11. Install the stabilizer bar clamps and bushings to the stabilizer bar.

12. Install the stabilizer bar clamp bolts. Tighten the bolts to 37 ft. lbs. (50 Nm).

13. Inspect the stabilizer link boots for damage and replace the stabilizer link if needed.

➡**Hold the ball stud when tightening the nut.**

14. Connect the stabilizer links to the stabilizer bar. Do not allow the boot to twist. Tighten the bar to link nut to 48 ft. lbs. (65 Nm).

15. Connect the left outer tie rod to the steering knuckle.

16. Use the J 44015 to seat the ball stud taper to 30 ft. lbs. (40 Nm).

17. Remove the J 44015.

18. install a new tie rod retention nut. Tighten the nut to 37 ft. lbs. (50 Nm).

19. Install the front tire and wheels.

20. Lower the vehicle.

WHEEL HUB & BEARING

REMOVAL & INSTALLATION
See Figures 706 through 710.

1. Remove the front brake rotor.

2. Disconnect the wheel speed sensor electrical connector, if equipped.

3. Remove the wheel speed sensor electrical connector from the connector bracket.

4. Remove the front wheel drive shaft spindle nut.

5. Remove the speed sensor.

6. Support the wheel drive shaft with heavy mechanic's wire or equivalent.

7. Remove and discard the wheel bearing/hub mounting bolts.

8. Remove the wheel bearing/hub assembly from the steering knuckle.

To install:

9. Install the wheel bearing/hub assembly to the steering knuckle.

10. Clean the threads of the bolts with the proper cleaner.

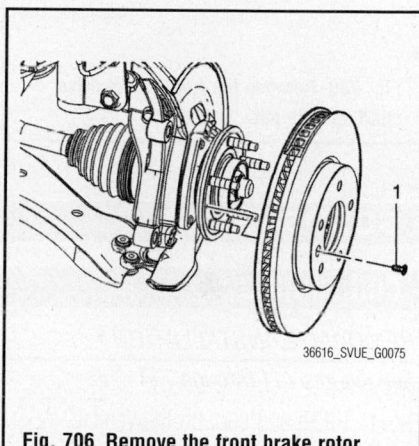

Fig. 706 Remove the front brake rotor

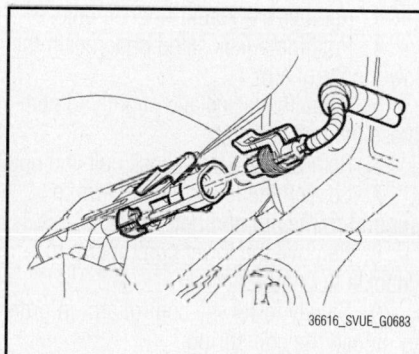

Fig. 707 Disconnect the wheel speed sensor electrical connector

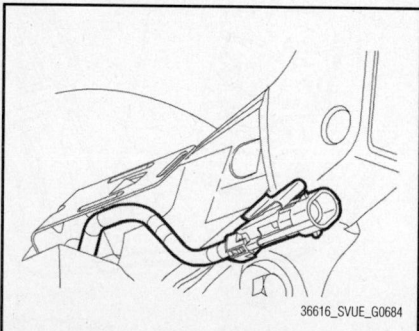

Fig. 708 Remove the wheel speed sensor electrical connector from the connector bracket

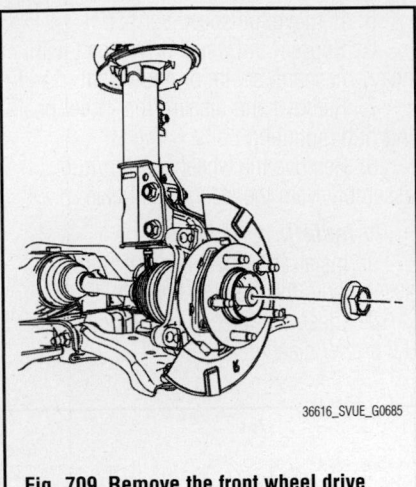

Fig. 709 Remove the front wheel drive shaft spindle nut

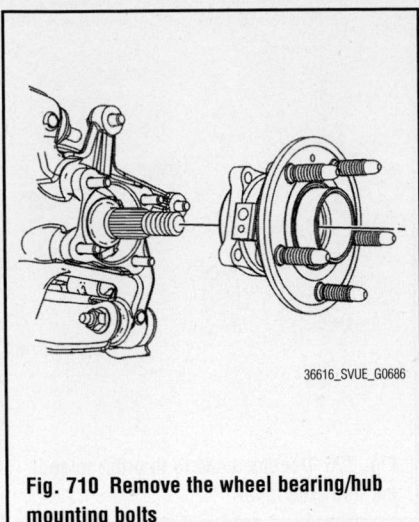

Fig. 710 Remove the wheel bearing/hub mounting bolts

➡ **Allow the thread locker to set for 10 minutes before using.**

11. Apply thread locker GM P/N 89021297 (Canadian P/N 10953488) on 2/3 of the bolts threads.

12. Install the wheel bearing/hub mounting bolts. Tighten the bolts to 96 ft. lbs. (130 Nm).

13. Install the wheel drive shaft spindle nut. Tighten the nut to 151 ft. lbs. (205 Nm).

14. Install the wheel speed sensor electrical connector to the mounting bracket, if equipped.

15. Connect the wheel speed sensor electrical connector.

16. Install the speed sensor.

17. Install the front brake rotor.

SUSPENSION

REAR SUSPENSION

COIL SPRING

REMOVAL & INSTALLATION

See Figures 711 through 714.

1. Raise and support the vehicle.
2. Remove the rear tire and wheel assembly.
3. Remove the stabilizer shaft link.
4. Position a jack stand underneath the lower control arm.
5. Raise the jack stand slightly to compress the coil spring.
6. Remove the lower shock bolt and nut.
7. Loosen the lower control arm to support frame nut and bolt.
8. Remove the lower control arm to knuckle nut and bolt.
9. Slowly lower the control arm in order to unload the coil spring.
10. Remove the coil spring and insulators.

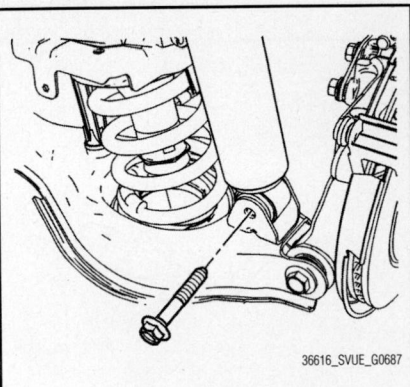

Fig. 711 Remove the lower shock bolt and nut

Fig. 712 Loosen the lower control arm to support frame nut and bolt

To install:

11. Inspect the coil spring upper and lower insulators, if damage exists replace the insulators.

12. Position the spring with the rubber insulators into the vehicle.

13. Raise the jack stand to compress the spring.

14. Position the lower control arm to the knuckle and install the nut and bolt and tighten the bolt/nut to 118 ft. lbs. (160 Nm).

15. Tighten the lower control arm to support nut and bolt to 81 ft. lbs. (110 Nm).

16. Install the shock to the lower control arm nut and bolt and tighten to 81 ft. lbs. (110 Nm).

17. Remove the jack stand from under the vehicle.

18. Install the stabilizer shaft link.

19. Install the rear tire and wheel assembly.

20. Lower the vehicle.

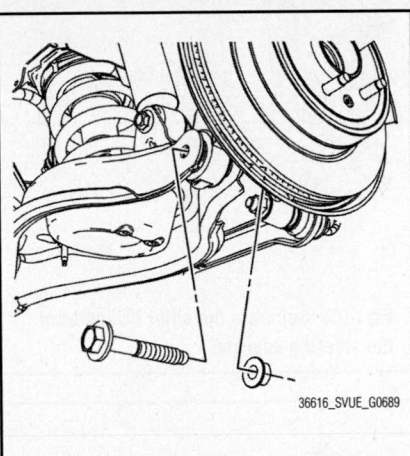

Fig. 713 Remove the lower control arm to knuckle nut and bolt

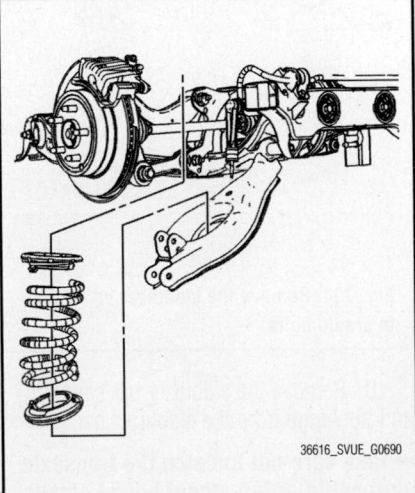

Fig. 714 Remove the coil spring and insulators

CONTROL ARMS/LINKS

REMOVAL & INSTALLATION

Upper Control Arm

See Figures 715 and 716.

1. Raise and support the vehicle.
2. Remove the rear tire and wheel assembly.
3. Disconnect the Antilock Brake System (ABS) wiring harness from the upper control arm.
4. Remove the rear brake hose routing nut and bolt.
5. Remove the upper control arm to knuckle nut and bolt.
6. Remove the upper control to support cam nut and bolt.
7. Remove the upper control arm.

To install:

8. Install the upper control arm to the knuckle.
9. Loosely install the upper control arm to knuckle nut and bolt.

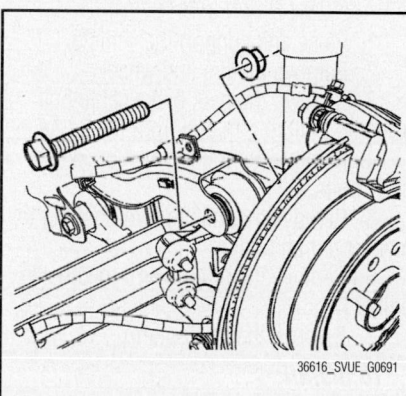

Fig. 715 Remove the upper control arm to knuckle nut and bolt

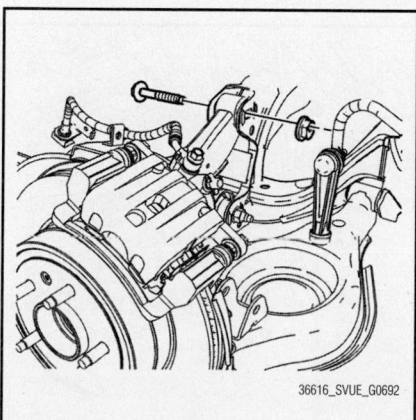

Fig. 716 Remove the upper control to support cam nut and bolt

10. Install the upper control to support bolt and cam nut.
11. Tighten the upper control arm to knuckle nut and bolt to 118 ft. lbs. (160 Nm).
12. Tighten the upper control arm to support bolt to 121 ft. lbs. (164 Nm).
13. Install the rear brake hose routing nut and bolt and tighten to 9 ft. lbs. (12 Nm).
14. Connect the ABS brake wiring harness to the upper control arm.
15. Install the rear tire and wheel assembly.
16. Lower the vehicle.
17. Check the rear alignment.

Lower Control Arm

See Figures 711 through 713 and 717.

1. Raise and support the vehicle.
2. Remove the rear tire and wheel assembly.
3. Remove the stabilizer shaft link.
4. Position a jackstand underneath the lower control arm.
5. Raise the jackstand slightly to compress the coil spring.
6. Remove the lower shock bolt and nut.
7. Loosen the lower control arm to support frame nut and bolt.
8. Remove the lower control arm to knuckle nut and bolt.
9. Slowly lower the control arm in order to unload the coil spring.
10. Remove the coil spring.
11. Remove the jackstand.
12. Remove the lower control arm to support frame nut and bolt.
13. Remove the lower control arm.

To install:

14. Inspect the coil spring upper and

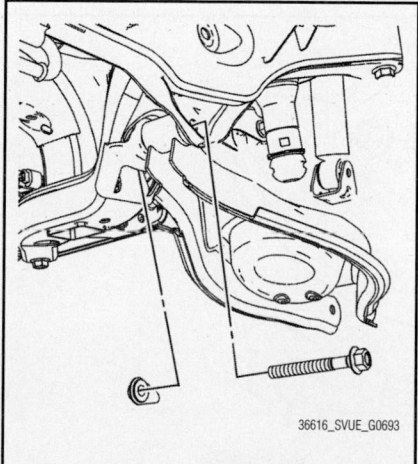

Fig. 717 Remove the lower control arm to support frame nut and bolt

lower insulators, if damage exists replace the insulators.
15. Position the lower control arm to the support frame and loosely install the nut and bolt.
16. Position the jack stand under the lower control arm.
17. Position the spring with the rubber insulators into the vehicle.
18. Raise the jack stand to compress the spring.
19. Position the lower control arm to the knuckle and install the nut and bolt. Tighten the nut/bolt to 118 ft. lbs. (160 Nm).
20. Tighten the lower control arm to support nut and bolt to 81 ft. lbs. (110 Nm).
21. Install the shock to the lower control arm nut and bolt and tighten to 81 ft. lbs. (110 Nm).
22. Remove the jack stand from under the vehicle.
23. Install the stabilizer shaft link.
24. Install the rear tire and wheel assembly.
25. Lower the vehicle.
26. Check the rear alignment.

Adjust Link

See Figure 718.

1. Raise and support the vehicle.
2. Remove the rear wheel and tire assembly.
3. Remove the adjust link to knuckle nut and bolt (1).
4. Remove the adjust link to support nut and bolt (2).
5. Remove the adjust link (3).

To install:

6. Install the adjust link.

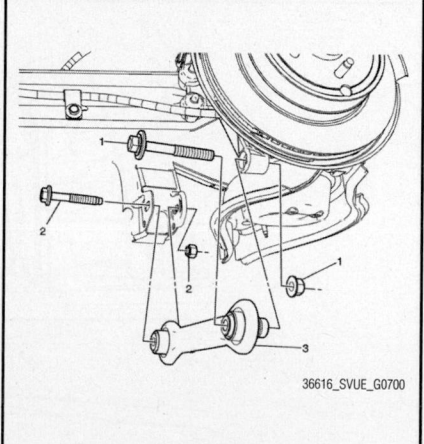

Fig. 718 Remove the adjust link to knuckle nut and bolt (1)

7. Install the adjust link to support bolt and nut. Tighten to 118 ft. lbs. (160 Nm).

8. Install the adjust link to knuckle bolt and nut. Tighten to 118 ft. lbs. (160 Nm).

9. Install the rear wheel and tire assembly.

10. Lower the vehicle.

Stabilizer Shaft Link

See Figures 719 through 721.

1. Raise and support the vehicle.

2. Remove the rear tire and wheel assembly.

3. Loosen the stabilizer shaft clamp bolts.

➡**Use a 90 degree bend TORX® bit to hold the ball stud when tightening the nut.**

4. Remove the stabilizer link to stabilizer shaft nut.

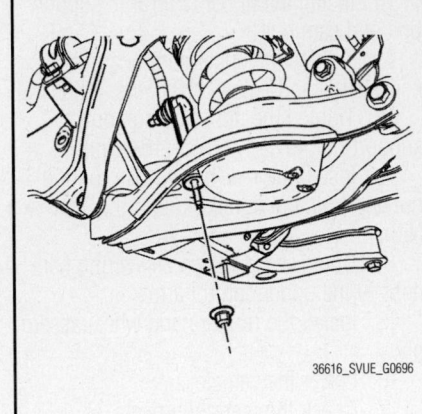

Fig. 721 Remove the stabilizer link to lower control arm nut

➡**When connecting the stabilizer link, hold the link with a wrench to prevent turning.**

5. Remove the stabilizer link to lower control arm nut.

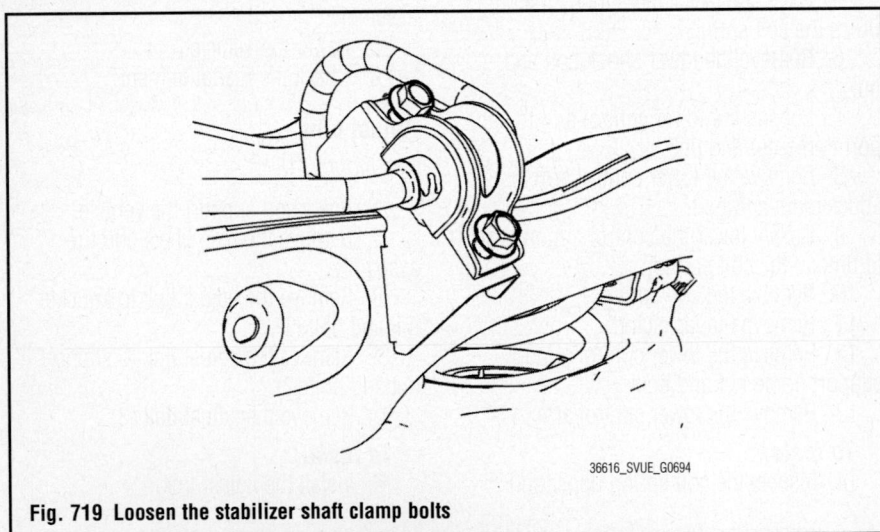

Fig. 719 Loosen the stabilizer shaft clamp bolts

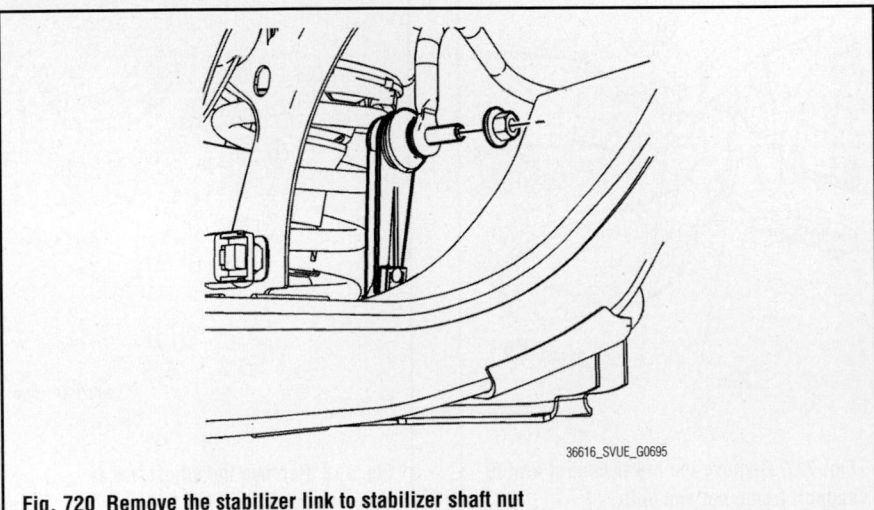
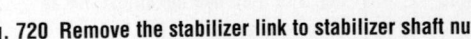

Fig. 720 Remove the stabilizer link to stabilizer shaft nut

6. Remove the stabilizer link from the vehicle.

To install:

7. Position the stabilizer link through the lower control arm.

➡**When connecting the stabilizer link, hold the link with a wrench to prevent turning.**

8. Install the stabilizer link to lower control arm nut and tighten to 11 ft. lbs. (15 Nm).

➡**Use a 90 degree bend TORX® bit to hold the ball stud when tightening the nut.**

9. Install the stabilizer link to stabilizer shaft nut and tighten to 37 ft. lbs. (50 Nm).

10. Tighten the loose stabilizer shaft clamp bolts to 52 ft. lbs. (70 Nm).

11. Install the rear tire and wheel assembly.

12. Lower the vehicle.

Trailing Arm

See Figures 722 through 724.

1. Raise and support the vehicle.

2. Remove the tire and wheel.

3. Remove the park brake cable bolt from the trailing arm and from the frame.

4. Remove the trailing arm bracket to body bolts.

5. Remove the trailing arm bushing to bracket nut and bolt.

6. Remove the trailing arm to knuckle bolts (1).

7. Remove the trailing arm.

To install:

8. Position the trailing arm to the vehicle.

9. Install the trailing arm to knuckle bolts and tighten to 81 ft. lbs. (110 Nm).

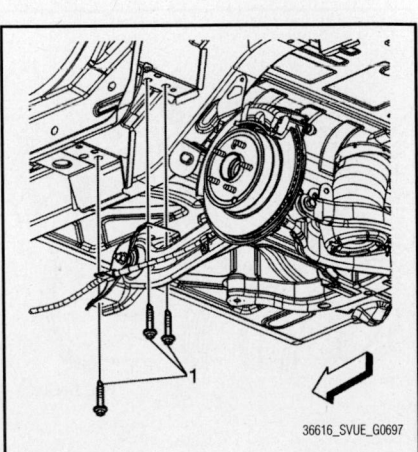

Fig. 722 Remove the trailing arm bracket to body bolts

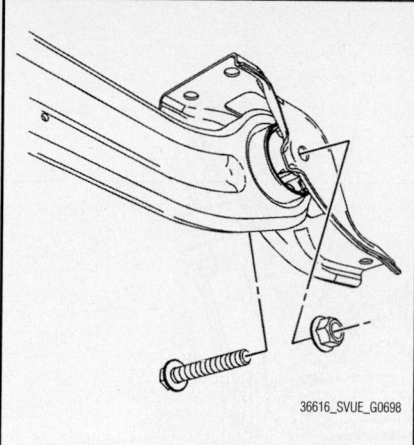

Fig. 723 Remove the trailing arm bushing to bracket nut and bolt

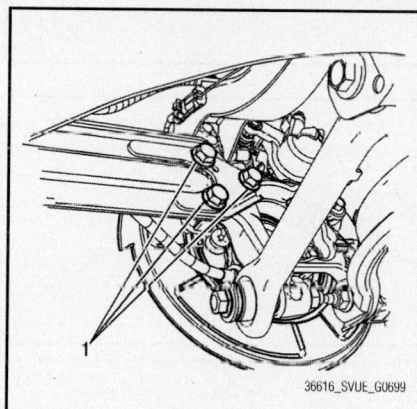

Fig. 724 Remove the trailing arm to knuckle bolts (1)

10. Position the trailing arm bracket to the trailing arm.

11. Loosely install the trailing arm bushing to bracket nut and bolt.

12. Install the trail arm bracket.

13. Tighten the trailing arm bushing to bracket nut and bolt to 118 ft. lbs. (160 Nm).

14. Install the park brake cable bolt to trailing arm and to the frame.

15. Install the tire and wheel.

16. Lower the vehicle.

KNUCKLE

REMOVAL & INSTALLATION

See Figures 725 through 729.

1. Raise and support the vehicle.
2. Remove the tire and wheel.
3. Disconnect the rear park brake cable from the park brake actuator.
4. Using the J 37043, remove the park brake cable from the mounting bracket

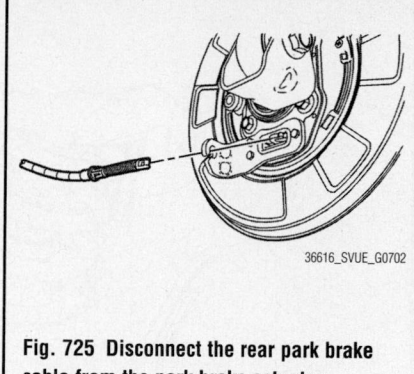

Fig. 725 Disconnect the rear park brake cable from the park brake actuator

Fig. 726 Remove the upper control arm to knuckle bolt and nut

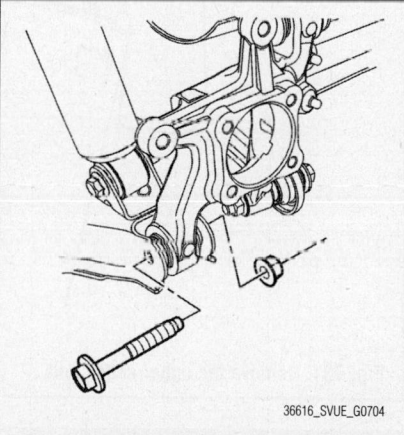

Fig. 727 Remove the lower control arm to knuckle bolt and nut

✳✳ CAUTION

Support the brake caliper with heavy mechanic wire, or equivalent, whenever it is separated from its mount and the hydraulic flexible brake hose is still connected. Failure to support the caliper in this manner will cause the flexible brake hose to bear the weight of the caliper, which may cause damage to the brake hose and in turn may cause a brake fluid leak.

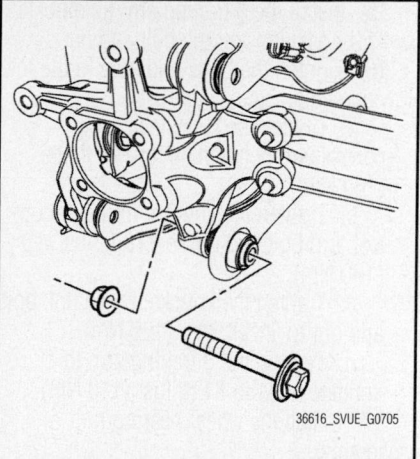

Fig. 728 Remove the toe link to knuckle bolt and nut

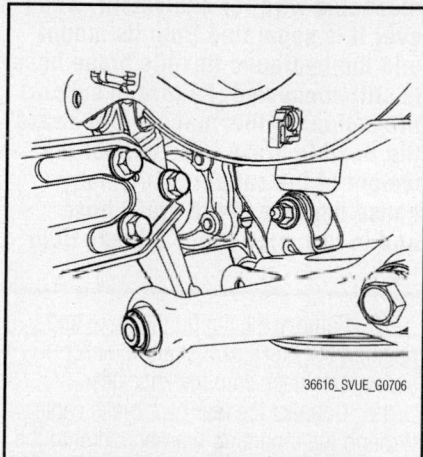

Fig. 729 Remove the 3 trailing arm to knuckle bolts

5. Remove the brake caliper and bracket as an assembly and support it with heavy mechanics wire or equivalent.

6. Remove the wheel bearing/hub assembly.

7. Remove the upper control arm to knuckle bolt and nut.

8. Remove the lower control arm to knuckle bolt and nut.

9. Remove the toe link to knuckle bolt and nut.

10. Remove the 3 trailing arm to knuckle bolts.

11. Remove the knuckle from the vehicle.

To install:

12. Install the knuckle to the lower control arm. Loosely install the bolt and nut.

13. Install the knuckle to the upper control arm. Loosely install the bolt and nut.

14. Install the knuckle to the toe link. Loosely install the bolt and nut.

15. Install the 3 trailing arm to knuckle bolts. Loosely install the bolt and nut.

16. Tighten the bolts and nuts in the following sequence:

    a. Tighten the knuckle to lower control arm bolt and nut to 118 ft. lbs. (160 Nm).

    b. Tighten the knuckle to upper control arm bolt and nut to 118 ft. lbs. (160 Nm).

    c. Tighten the knuckle to toe link bolt and nut to 118 ft. lbs. (160 Nm).

    d. Tighten the 3 trailing arm to knuckle bolts to 81 ft. lbs. (110 Nm).

17. Install the wheel bearing/hub assembly.

✳✳ CAUTION

Support the brake caliper with heavy mechanic wire, or equivalent, whenever it is separated from its mount and the hydraulic flexible brake hose is still connected. Failure to support the caliper in this manner will cause the flexible brake hose to bear the weight of the caliper, which may cause damage to the brake hose and in turn may cause a brake fluid leak.

18. Remove the supporting wire and position the brake caliper and bracket assemblies back onto the knuckles.

19. Connect the rear park brake cable through the mounting bracket and onto the park brake actuator.

20. Install the tire and wheel.

21. Lower the vehicle.

22. Perform a vehicle wheel alignment.

SHOCK ABSORBER

REMOVAL & INSTALLATION

See Figures 730 and 731.

1. Raise and support the vehicle.
2. Remove the rear tire and wheel assembly.
3. Remove the lower shock bolt.
4. Remove the upper shock bolt.
5. Remove the shock from the vehicle.

To install:

6. Position the shock to the vehicle.
7. Install the upper shock bolt and tighten to 81 ft. lbs. (110 Nm).
8. Install the lower shock bolt and nut and tighten to 81 ft. lbs. (110 Nm).
9. Install the rear tire and wheel assembly.
10. Lower the vehicle.

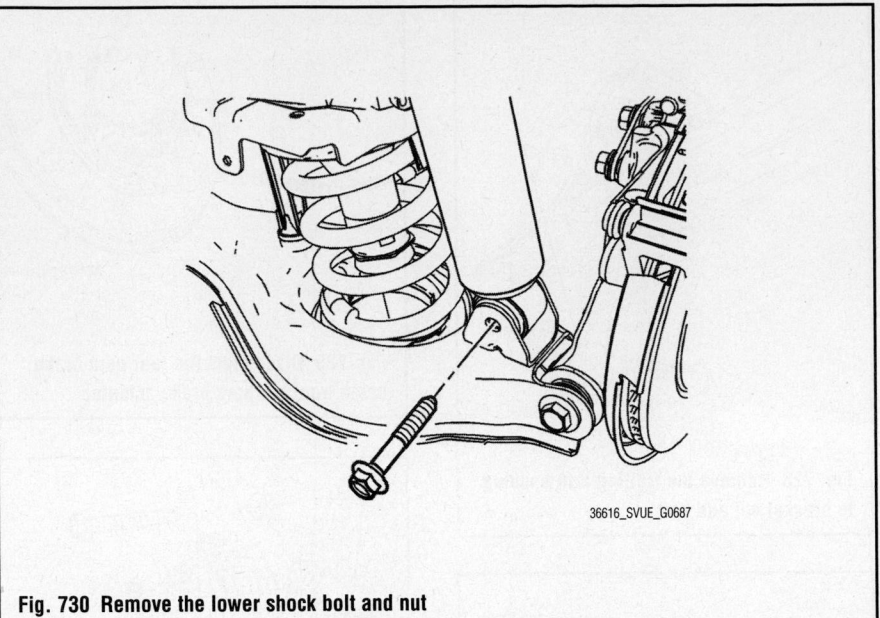

Fig. 730 Remove the lower shock bolt and nut

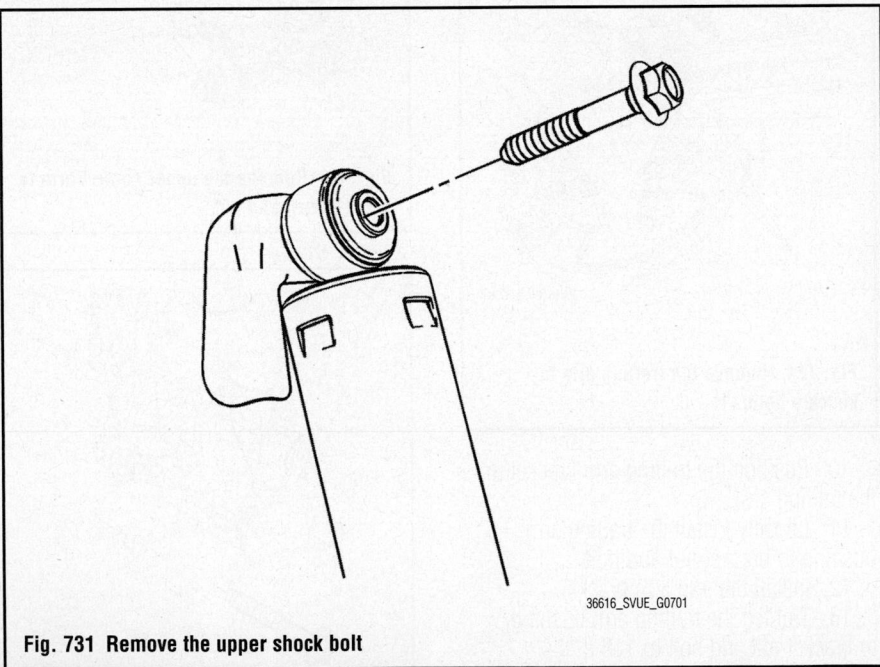

Fig. 731 Remove the upper shock bolt

STABILIZER SHAFT

REMOVAL & INSTALLATION

See Figures 732 through 734.

1. Raise and support the vehicle.

➡**In the following service procedure, it is not necessary to remove the rear suspension support. Lower the support enough to remove the stabilizer bar.**

2. Lower the rear suspension support.

➡**Hold the ball shaft secure with a 90° bend style TORX® bit, when removing the nut.**

3. Remove the stabilizer link to stabilizer shaft nut.

4. Remove the stabilizer shaft clamp bolts.

5. Remove the stabilizer shaft clamps and bushings from the stabilizer shaft.

6. Disengage the stabilizer shaft from the stabilizer link ball studs, while removing the stabilizer shaft from the vehicle.

To install:

7. Position the stabilizer shaft in the vehicle, while positioning the links to the stabilizer bar.

8. Install the stabilizer shaft clamps and bushings to the stabilizer shaft.

9. Install the stabilizer shaft clamp bolts and tighten to 52 ft. lbs. (70 Nm).

➡**Hold the ball shaft secure with a TORX® bit, when installing the nut.**

10. Install the stabilizer link to stabilizer shaft nut and tighten to 37 ft. lbs. (50 Nm).

11. Install the rear suspension support.

12. Lower the vehicle.

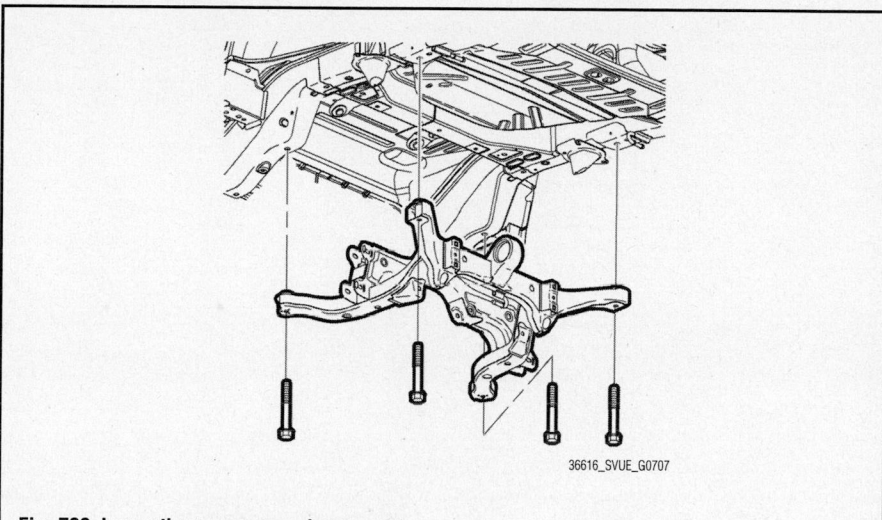

Fig. 732 Lower the rear suspension support

Fig. 733 Remove the stabilizer link to stabilizer shaft nut

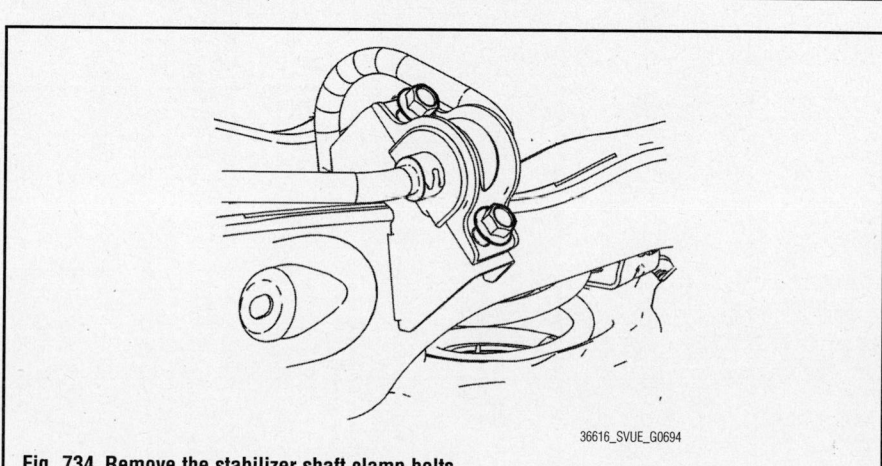

Fig. 734 Remove the stabilizer shaft clamp bolts

WHEEL HUB & BEARING

REMOVAL & INSTALLATION

See Figures 735 through 737.

1. Raise and support the vehicle.
2. Remove the rear tire and wheel assembly.
3. Remove the brake rotor.
4. Remove the wheel speed sensor.
5. If equipped with All Wheel Drive (AWD), remove the rear wheel driveshaft nut.

➡**The splash shield and park brake assembly are supported to the knuckle**

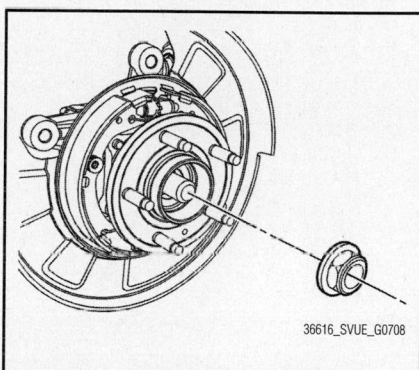

Fig. 735 Remove the rear wheel drive-shaft nut

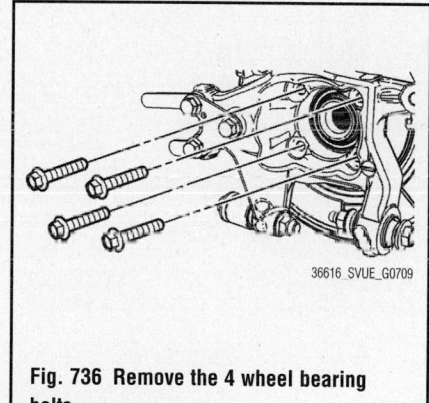

Fig. 736 Remove the 4 wheel bearing bolts

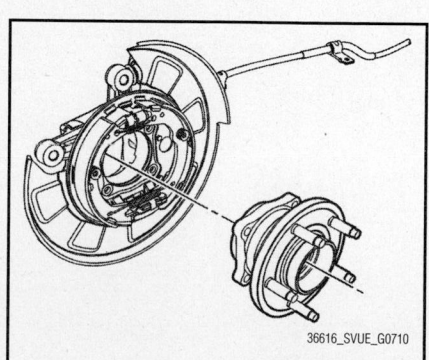

Fig. 737 Remove the wheel bearing from the knuckle

between the wheel bearing mounting bolts and the wheel bearing. Care should be taken to support these items while the wheel bearing is being replaced.

6. Remove the 4 wheel bearing bolts.

7. Remove the wheel bearing from the knuckle.

To install:

8. Position the wheel bearing to the knuckle.

9. Install the 4 wheel bearing bolts and tighten to 55 ft. lbs. (75 Nm).

10. If equipped with AWD, install the rear wheel driveshaft nut and tighten to 151 ft. lbs. (205 Nm).

11. Install the wheel speed sensor.

12. Install the brake rotor.

13. Install the rear tire and wheel assembly.

14. Lower the vehicle.

GENERAL MOTORS

Diagnostic Trouble Codes

DIAGNOSTIC TROUBLE CODES

OBD II VEHICLE APPLICATIONS

GENERAL MOTORS

Malibu
2010–2011
- 2.4L . . . . VIN 5
- 2.4L . . . . VIN B
- 3.6L . . . . VIN 7

Regal
2011
- 2.0L . . . . VIN V
- 2.4L . . . . VIN C

Sierra
2010–2011
- 4.3L . . . . VIN X
- 4.8L . . . . VIN A
- 5.3L . . . . VIN 3
- 5.3L . . . . VIN M
- 5.3L . . . . VIN O
- 6.0L . . . . VIN K
- 6.0L . . . . VIN G
- 6.0L . . . . VIN J
- 6.2L . . . . VIN 2
- 6.6L . . . . VIN 6
- 6.6L . . . . VIN 8
- 6.6L . . . . VIN L

Silverado
- 4.3L . . . . VIN X
- 4.8L . . . . VIN A
- 5.3L . . . . VIN 3

- 5.3L . . . . VIN M
- 5.3L . . . . VIN O
- 6.0L . . . . VIN K
- 6.0L . . . . VIN G
- 6.0L . . . . VIN J
- 6.2L . . . . VIN 2
- 6.6L . . . . VIN 6
- 6.6L . . . . VIN 8
- 6.6L . . . . VIN L

Sky
2010
- 2.0L Turbo . . . . VIN M
- 2.4L . . . . VIN B

Solstice
2010
- 2.0L Turbo . . . . VIN M
- 2.4L . . . . VIN B

SRX
2010–2011
- 2.8L . . . . VIN 6
- 3.0L . . . . VIN Y

Vibe
2010–2011
- 1.8L . . . . VIN 8
- 2.4L . . . . VIN 0

Vue
2010
- 2.4L . . . . VIN B
- 2.4L . . . . VIN P
- 2.4L . . . . VIN 5

- 2.4L . . . . VIN Z
- 3.6L . . . . VIN 7

Volt
2011
- 1.4L . . . . VIN 4

GM REFERENCE INFORMATION

OBD II TROUBLE CODE LIST

To use this information, first read and record All codes in memory along with Freeze Frame data. *If a ECM Reset function is done prior to recording this data,* All codes and freeze frame data are lost!

Look up the appropriate trouble code in the list on the following pages. The left hand column includes the code number, the number of trips to set the code (e.g., **1T or 2T**), the year, model description and type of OBD II Monitor that failed (e.g., **CCM or O2S**). This data can be used to determine how to drive a vehicle after a repair in order to validate the repair has been completed.

The **(N/MIL)** designator in the left hand column indicates the trouble code does not turn on the Malfunction Indicator Lamp or MIL. The **(STS Lamp)** indicator in the left column indicates a code that turns on the Service Transmission Soon lamp. This code may or may not turn "on" the MIL.

OBD II Trouble Code List (xxxx Codes)

DTC	Trouble Code Title, Conditions, Possible Causes
DTC: 1380	**Misfire Detected - Rough Road Data Not Available:** The vehicle speed is greater than 8 km/h (5 mph). The engine speed is less than 8,192 RPM. The engine load is less than 60 percent. Engine misfire is detected and DTC P0300 sets with the MIL illuminated. DTCs P1380 and P1381 run continuously when the above conditions are met.
DTC: 1381	**Misfire Detected - No Communication with Brake Control Module:** The vehicle speed is greater than 8 km/h (5 mph). The engine speed is less than 8,192 RPM. The engine load is less than 60 percent. Engine misfire is detected and DTC P0300 sets with the MIL illuminated. DTCs P1380 and P1381 run continuously when the above conditions are met.

OBD II Trouble Code List (P0xxx Codes)

DTC	Trouble Code Title, Conditions, Possible Causes
DTC: P0002 00	**Fuel Pressure Regulator 1 Circuit Resistance Too High:** The ignition is ON, or the engine is running. The ignition voltage is less than 16 V. These DTCs runs continuously once the above conditions are met.
DTC: P0003 00	**Fuel Pressure Regulator 1 Control Circuit Low Current:** The ignition is ON, or the engine is running. The ignition voltage is less than 16 V. These DTCs runs continuously once the above conditions are met.
DTC: P0004 00	**Fuel Pressure Regulator 1 Control Circuit High Current:** The ignition is ON, or the engine is running. The ignition voltage is less than 16 V. These DTCs runs continuously once the above conditions are met.
DTC: P0008	**Engine Position System Performance Bank 1:** DTC P0010, P0011, P0013, P0014, P0020, P0021, P0023, P0024, P0341, P0342, P0343, P0346, P0347, P0348, P0366, P0367, P0368, P0391, P0392, P0393, P2088, P2089, P2090, P2091, P2092, P2093, P2094, or P2095 is not set. The engine is operating for greater than 50 seconds. The engine coolant temperature is between 0-95°C (32-203°F). The calculated engine oil temperature is colder than 120°C (248°F). The engine must accelerate such that the CMP actuator system is commanded from the park position to the phased position. This is considered a cam control cycle. There must be a minimum of 2 cam control cycles for at least 2.5 seconds each, in the phased position. DTC P0008 and P0009 run continuously once the above conditions are met, approximately 600 seconds.
DTC: P0009	**Engine Position System Performance Bank 2:** DTC P0010, P0011, P0013, P0014, P0020, P0021, P0023, P0024, P0341, P0342, P0343, P0346, P0347, P0348, P0366, P0367, P0368, P0391, P0392, P0393, P2088, P2089, P2090, P2091, P2092, P2093, P2094, or P2095 is not set. The engine is operating for greater than 50 seconds. The engine coolant temperature is between 0-95°C (32-203°F). The calculated engine oil temperature is colder than 120°C (248°F). The engine must accelerate such that the CMP actuator system is commanded from the park position to the phased position. This is considered a cam control cycle. There must be a minimum of 2 cam control cycles for at least 2.5 seconds each, in the phased position. DTC P0008 and P0009 run continuously once the above conditions are met, approximately 600 seconds.
DTC: P000A	**Intake Camshaft Position System Slow Response Bank 1:** Before the ECM can report DTC P000A, P000B, P000C, P000D, P0011, P0014, P0021, or P0024 failed, DTCs P0010, P0013, P0020, P0023, P0341, P0342, P0343, P0346, P0347, P0348, P0366, P0367, P0368, P0391, P0392, P0393, P2088, P2089, P2090, P2091, P2092, P2093, P2094, and P2095 must run and pass. DTC P0016, P0017, P0018, P0019, P0335, P0336, or P0338 is not set. The engine is operating for greater than 1 seconds. The engine speed is greater than 520 RPM. The engine must accelerate such that the CMP actuator system is commanded from the park position to the phased position. This is considered a cam control cycle. There must be a minimum of 2 cam control cycles for at least 2.5 seconds each in the phased position. DTCs P000A, P000B, P000C, P000D, P0011, P0014, P0021, and P0024 run continuously once the above conditions are met for greater than 600 seconds.
DTC: P000A 00	**Intake Camshaft Position System Slow Response:** The engine speed is between 736-6016 RPM. The engine oil temperature is between -10 to +130°C (14-266°F). The commanded camshaft position is stable. The battery voltage is between 10-16 VDTCs P000A 00, P000B 00, P0010 00, P0013 00, P0014 00, P0016 00, P0017 00, P0335 00, P0336 00, P0340 00, P0341 00, P0365 00, P0366 00, P2088 00, P2089 00, P2090 00, P2091 00 are not set.
DTC: P000B	**Exhaust Camshaft Position System Slow Response Bank 1:** Before the ECM can report DTC P000A, P000B, P000C, P000D, P0011, P0014, P0021, or P0024 failed, DTCs P0010, P0013, P0020, P0023, P0341, P0342, P0343, P0346, P0347, P0348, P0366, P0367, P0368, P0391, P0392, P0393, P2088, P2089, P2090, P2091, P2092, P2093, P2094, and P2095 must run and pass. DTC P0016, P0017, P0018, P0019, P0335, P0336, or P0338 is not set. The engine is operating for greater than 1 seconds. The engine speed is greater than 520 RPM. The engine must accelerate such that the CMP actuator system is commanded from the park position to the phased position. This is considered a cam control cycle. There must be a minimum of 2 cam control cycles for at least 2.5 seconds each in the phased position. DTCs P000A, P000B, P000C, P000D, P0011, P0014, P0021, and P0024 run continuously once the above conditions are met for greater than 600 seconds.

DTC	Trouble Code Title, Conditions, Possible Causes
DTC: P000B 00	**Exhaust Camshaft Position System Slow Response:** The engine speed is between 736-6016 RPM. The engine oil temperature is between -10 to +130°C (14-266°F). The commanded camshaft position is stable. The battery voltage is between 10-16 VDTCs P000A 00, P000B 00, P0010 00, P0013 00, P0014 00, P0016 00, P0017 00, P0335 00, P0336 00, P0340 00, P0341 00, P0365 00, P0366 00, P2088 00, P2089 00, P2090 00, P2091 00 are not set.
DTC: P000C	**Intake Camshaft Position System Slow Response Bank 2:** Before the ECM can report DTC P000A, P000B, P000C, P000D, P0011, P0014, P0021, or P0024 failed, DTCs P0010, P0013, P0020, P0023, P0341, P0342, P0343, P0346, P0347, P0348, P0366, P0367, P0368, P0391, P0392, P0393, P2088, P2089, P2090, P2091, P2092, P2093, P2094, and P2095 must run and pass. DTC P0016, P0017, P0018, P0019, P0335, P0336, or P0338 is not set. The engine is operating for greater than 1 seconds. The engine speed is greater than 520 RPM. The engine must accelerate such that the CMP actuator system is commanded from the park position to the phased position. This is considered a cam control cycle. There must be a minimum of 2 cam control cycles for at least 2. 5 seconds each in the phased position. DTCs P000A, P000B, P000C, P000D, P0011, P0014, P0021, and P0024 run continuously once the above conditions are met for greater than 600 seconds.
DTC: P000D	**Exhaust Camshaft Position System Slow Response Bank 2:** Before the ECM can report DTC P000A, P000B, P000C, P000D, P0011, P0014, P0021, or P0024 failed, DTCs P0010, P0013, P0020, P0023, P0341, P0342, P0343, P0346, P0347, P0348, P0366, P0367, P0368, P0391, P0392, P0393, P2088, P2089, P2090, P2091, P2092, P2093, P2094, and P2095 must run and pass. DTC P0016, P0017, P0018, P0019, P0335, P0336, or P0338 is not set. The engine is operating for greater than 1 seconds. The engine speed is greater than 520 RPM. The engine must accelerate such that the CMP actuator system is commanded from the park position to the phased position. This is considered a cam control cycle. There must be a minimum of 2 cam control cycles for at least 2. 5 seconds each in the phased position. DTCs P000A, P000B, P000C, P000D, P0011, P0014, P0021, and P0024 run continuously once the above conditions are met for greater than 600 seconds.
DTC: P0010	**Intake Camshaft Position Actuator Solenoid Valve Control Circuit Bank 1:** The ignition voltage is between 11-32 V. The ignition switch is in the Crank or Run position. The ECM commanded the Camshaft Position Actuator Solenoid Valve ON. DTCs P0010, P0013, P0020, and P0023 run continuously when the above conditions are met.
DTC: P0010	**Camshaft Position (CMP) Actuator Solenoid Control Circuit:** The ignition is in Crank or Run. The system voltage is between 11 18 volts. DTC P0010 runs continuously when the above conditions are met.
DTC: P0010	**Intake Camshaft Position Actuator Solenoid Control Circuit:** The engine speed is greater than 80 RPM. The ignition voltage is between 10-18 volts. The ECM has commanded the CMP actuator solenoid ON and OFF at least once during the ignition cycle. DTCs P0010, P0013, P2088, P2089, P2090, and P2091 run continuously once the above conditions are met.
DTC: P0010 00	**Intake Camshaft Position Actuator Solenoid Valve Control Circuit:** The engine speed is greater than 80 RPM. DTC P0606 00 is not set. The ignition voltage is between 10-18 V. The ECM has commanded the camshaft position actuator intake or camshaft position actuator exhaust solenoid ON and OFF at least once during the ignition cycle. DTCs P0010 00, P0013 00, P2088 00, P0289 00, P2090 00, and P2091 00 run continuously once the above conditions are met for greater than 1 s.
DTC: P0010 00	**Intake Camshaft Position Actuator Solenoid Valve Control Circuit:** The engine is running. The ignition voltage is between 11-18 V. The camshaft position actuator is commanded on. The DTCs run continuously when the above conditions are met.
DTC: P0011	**Intake Camshaft Position (CMP) System Performance:** Before the ECM can report DTC P000A, P000B, P0011, or P0014 failed, DTCs P0010, P0013, P0341, P0342, P0343, P0366, P0367, P0368, P2088, P2089, P2090, and P2091 must run and pass. DTC P0016, P0017, P0335, P0336, or P0338 is not set. The engine is operating for greater than 2 seconds. The engine speed is greater than 480 RPM. The engine must accelerate such that the CMP actuator system is commanded from the park position to the phased position. This is considered a cam control cycle. There must be a minimum of 2 cam control cycles for at least 2. 5 seconds each in the phased position. DTC P000A, P000B, P0011, and P0014 run continuously once the above conditions are met for greater than 20 seconds.
DTC: P0011	**Intake Camshaft Position System Performance:** DTC P0010, P0013, P0016, P0017, P0335, P0336, P0340, P0341, P0365, or P0366 is not set. The ignition voltage is greater than 11 V. The engine is operating. The desire camshaft position is not changing greater than 4. 5 degrees for at least 1 s. Both of the desired and actual camshaft position actuator values cannot be greater than 25 degrees or less than 5 degrees. DTCs P0011 and P0014 run continuously once the above conditions are met.
DTC: P0011 00	**Camshaft Position System Performance:** The ignition is ON, or the engine is running. The ignition voltage is less than 16 V. DTCs P0336 00, P0339 00, or P0344 00 are not set. This DTC runs continuously once the above conditions are met.
DTC: P0013	**Exhaust Camshaft Position Actuator Solenoid Valve Control Circuit Bank 1:** The ignition voltage is between 11-32 V. The ignition switch is in the Crank or Run position. The ECM commanded the Camshaft Position Actuator Solenoid Valve ON. DTCs P0010, P0013, P0020, and P0023 run continuously when the above conditions are met.

DTC	Trouble Code Title, Conditions, Possible Causes
DTC: P0013	**Exhaust Camshaft Position Actuator Solenoid Control Circuit:** The engine speed is greater than 80 RPM. The ignition voltage is between 10-18 volts. The ECM has commanded the CMP actuator solenoid ON and OFF at least once during the ignition cycle. DTCs P0010, P0013, P2088, P2089, P2090, and P2091 run continuously once the above conditions are met.
DTC: P0013 00	**Exhaust Camshaft Position Actuator Solenoid Valve Control Circuit:** The engine is running. The ignition voltage is between 11-18 V. The camshaft position actuator is commanded on. The DTCs run continuously when the above conditions are met.
DTC: P0013 00	**Exhaust Camshaft Position Actuator Solenoid Valve Control Circuit:** The engine speed is greater than 80 RPM. DTC P0606 00 is not set. The ignition voltage is between 10-18 V. The ECM has commanded the camshaft position actuator intake or camshaft position actuator exhaust solenoid ON and OFF at least once during the ignition cycle. DTCs P0010 00, P0013 00, P2088 00, P0289 00, P2090 00, and P2091 00 run continuously once the above conditions are met for greater than 1 s.
DTC: P0014	**Exhaust Camshaft Position System Performance Bank 1:** Before the ECM can report DTC P000A, P000B, P000C, P000D, P0011, P0014, P0021, or P0024 failed, DTCs P0010, P0013, P0020, P0023, P0341, P0342, P0343, P0346, P0347, P0348, P0366, P0367, P0368, P0391, P0392, P0393, P2088, P2089, P2090, P2091, P2092, P2093, P2094, and P2095 must run and pass. DTC P0016, P0017, P0018, P0019, P0335, P0336, or P0338 is not set. The engine is operating for greater than 1 seconds. The engine speed is greater than 520 RPM. The engine must accelerate such that the CMP actuator system is commanded from the park position to the phased position. This is considered a cam control cycle. There must be a minimum of 2 cam control cycles for at least 2. 5 seconds each in the phased position. DTCs P000A, P000B, P000C, P000D, P0011, P0014, P0021, and P0024 run continuously once the above conditions are met for greater than 600 seconds.
DTC: P0014 00	**Exhaust Camshaft Position System Performance:** DTC P0010 00, P0013 00, P0016 00, P0017 00, P0335 00, P0336 00, P0340 00, P0341 00, P0365 00, or P0366 00 is not set. The engine is running. The ignition voltage is between 11-18 V. The camshaft position actuator is enabled. The rate of change in the camshaft position is less than 5° for 4 s.
DTC: P0014 00	**Exhaust Camshaft Position System Performance:** The engine speed is between 736-6016 RPM. The engine oil temperature is between -10 to +130°C (14-266°F). The commanded camshaft position is stable. The battery voltage is between 10-16 VDTCs P000A 00, P000B 00, P0010 00, P0013 00, P0014 00, P0016 00, P0017 00, P0335 00, P0336 00, P0340 00, P0341 00, P0365 00, P0366 00, P2088 00, P2089 00, P2090 00, P2091 00 are not set.
DTC: P0016	**Crankshaft Position - Intake Camshaft Position Not Plausible Bank 1:** P0016 DTC P0040, P0041, P0335, P0336, P0641, and P0651 are not set. The engine is cranking or running. The crankshaft and camshaft position signals are synchronized. The camshaft position actuator is in the parked position. DTC P0016, P0017, P0018, and P0019 run continuously when the above conditions are met.
DTC: P0016	**Crankshaft Position (CKP) Camshaft Position (CMP) Correlation:** DTCs P0191 and P0315 are not set. The engine speed is greater than 600 RPM. DTC P0016 runs continuously when the above conditions are met.
DTC: P0016	**Crankshaft Position (CKP) Camshaft Position (CMP) Correlation:** DTC P0335, P0336, P0340, P0341, P0641, or P0651 is not set. The engine is running. The engine speed is less than 2,000 RPM. The CMP actuator is commanded to the parked position - if equipped. DTC P0016 runs continuously when the above conditions are met.
DTC: P0016	**Crankshaft Position - Intake Camshaft Position Not Plausible Bank 1:** Before the ECM can report DTC P0016, P0017, P0018, or P0019 failed, DTCs P0010, P0011, P0013, P0014, P0020, P0021, P0023, P0024, P0335, P0336, P0338, P0341, P0342, P0343, P0346, P0347, P0348, P0366, P0367, P0368, P0391, P0392, P0393, P2088, P2089, P2090, P2091, P2092, P2093, P2094, and P2095 must run and pass. The engine is operating for greater than 50 s. The engine coolant temperature is between 0-95°C (32-203°F). The calculated engine oil temperature is less than 120°C (248°F). DTC P0016, P0017, P0018, and P0019 run continuously once the above conditions are met for approximately 10 minutes.
DTC: P0016 00	**Crankshaft Position - Intake Camshaft Position Not Plausible:** DTCs P000A 00, P000B 00, P0010 00, P0013 00, P0014 00, P0335 00, P0336 00, P0340 00, P0341 00, P0365 00, P0366 00, P2088 00, P2089 00, P2090 00, or P2091 00 are not set. The ignition is ON. The engine is running. The engine speed is between 672-4 000 RPM. The battery voltage is between 10-16 V. The engine oil temperature is more than -10°C (14°F). The engine coolant temperature (ECT) is more than -9. 8°C (14. 4°F). These DTCs run continuously when the above conditions are met.
DTC: P0016 00	**Crankshaft Position - Intake Camshaft Position Not Plausible:** DTC P0335 00, P0336 00, P0340 00, P0341 00, P0365 00, P0366 00, P0641 00, or P0651 00 is not set. The engine is cranking or running. The camshaft position actuator solenoid valves are in the parked position. The DTCs run continuously when the above conditions are met.

DTC	Trouble Code Title, Conditions, Possible Causes
DTC: P0016 5A	**Crankshaft Position-Camshaft Position Not Plausible:** DTCs P0335 and P0336 are not set. The engine is running. The engine speed is greater than 50 RPM. The DTC runs continuously once the above conditions are met.
DTC: P0017	**Crankshaft Position - Exhaust Camshaft Position Not Plausible Bank 1:** Before the ECM can report DTC P0016, P0017, P0018, or P0019 failed, DTCs P0010, P0011, P0013, P0014, P0020, P0021, P0023, P0024, P0335, P0336, P0338, P0341, P0342, P0343, P0346, P0347, P0348, P0366, P0367, P0368, P0391, P0392, P0393, P2088, P2089, P2090, P2091, P2092, P2093, P2094, and P2095 must run and pass. The engine is operating for greater than 50 s. The engine coolant temperature is between 0-95°C (32-203°F). The calculated engine oil temperature is less than 120°C (248°F). DTC P0016, P0017, P0018, and P0019 run continuously once the above conditions are met for approximately 10 minutes.
DTC: P0017	**Crankshaft Position - Exhaust Camshaft Position Not Plausible Bank 1:** P0017 DTC P0335, P0336, P0365, P0366, P0641, and P0651 are not set. The engine is cranking or running. The crankshaft and camshaft position signals are synchronized. The camshaft position actuator is in the parked position. DTC P0016, P0017, P0018, and P0019 run continuously when the above conditions are met.
DTC: P0017	**Crankshaft Position (CKP) - Exhaust Camshaft Position (CMP) Correlation Bank 1:** DTC P0335, P0336, P0340, P0341, P0345, P0346, P0365, P0366, P0390, P0391, P0641, or P0651 is not set. The engine speed is less than 1,200 RPM and the CMP actuator is commanded to the home or parked position. The engine is running. DTC P0016, P0017, P0018, and P0019 run continuously once the above conditions are met.
DTC: P0017 00	**Crankshaft Position - Exhaust Camshaft Position Not Plausible:** DTCs P000A 00, P000B 00, P0010 00, P0013 00, P0014 00, P0335 00, P0336 00, P0340 00, P0341 00, P0365 00, P0366 00, P2088 00, P2089 00, P2090 00, or P2091 00 are not set. The ignition is ON. The engine is running. The engine speed is between 672-4 000 RPM. The battery voltage is between 10-16 V. The engine oil temperature is more than -10°C (14°F). The engine coolant temperature (ECT) is more than -9. 8°C (14. 4°F). These DTCs run continuously when the above conditions are met.
DTC: P0018	**Crankshaft Position - Intake Camshaft Position Not Plausible Bank 2:** P0018 or P0019 DTC P0018, P0019, P0335, P0336, P0345, P0346, P0390, P0391, P0641, and P0651 are not set. The engine is cranking or running. The crankshaft and camshaft position signals are synchronized. The camshaft position actuator is in the parked position. DTC P0016, P0017, P0018, and P0019 run continuously when the above conditions are met.
DTC: P0018	**Crankshaft Position - Intake Camshaft Position Not Plausible Bank 2:** Before the ECM can report DTC P0016, P0017, P0018, or P0019 failed, DTCs P0010, P0011, P0013, P0014, P0020, P0021, P0023, P0024, P0335, P0336, P0338, P0341, P0342, P0343, P0346, P0347, P0348, P0366, P0367, P0368, P0391, P0392, P0393, P2088, P2089, P2090, P2091, P2092, P2093, P2094, and P2095 must run and pass. The engine is operating for greater than 50 s. The engine coolant temperature is between 0-95°C (32-203°F). The calculated engine oil temperature is less than 120°C (248°F). DTC P0016, P0017, P0018, and P0019 run continuously once the above conditions are met for approximately 10 minutes.
DTC: P0019	**Crankshaft Position - Exhaust Camshaft Position Not Plausible Bank 2:** Before the ECM can report DTC P0016, P0017, P0018, or P0019 failed, DTCs P0010, P0011, P0013, P0014, P0020, P0021, P0023, P0024, P0335, P0336, P0338, P0341, P0342, P0343, P0346, P0347, P0348, P0366, P0367, P0368, P0391, P0392, P0393, P2088, P2089, P2090, P2091, P2092, P2093, P2094, and P2095 must run and pass. The engine is operating for greater than 50 s. The engine coolant temperature is between 0-95°C (32-203°F). The calculated engine oil temperature is less than 120°C (248°F). DTC P0016, P0017, P0018, and P0019 run continuously once the above conditions are met for approximately 10 minutes.
DTC: P0019	**Crankshaft Position - Exhaust Camshaft Position Not Plausible Bank 2:** P0018 or P0019 DTC P0018, P0019, P0335, P0336, P0345, P0346, P0390, P0391, P0641, and P0651 are not set. The engine is cranking or running. The crankshaft and camshaft position signals are synchronized. The camshaft position actuator is in the parked position. DTC P0016, P0017, P0018, and P0019 run continuously when the above conditions are met.
DTC: P0020	**Intake Camshaft Position (CMP) Actuator Solenoid Control Circuit Bank 2:** The ignition is in the Crank or Run position. The ECM has commanded the Camshaft Position Actuator Solenoid Valve ON. The ignition voltage is between 11-18 volts. DTCs P0010, P0013, P0020, and P0023 run continuously once the above conditions are met.
DTC: P0021	**Intake Camshaft Position System Performance Bank 2:** Before the ECM can report DTC P000A, P000B, P000C, P000D, P0011, P0014, P0021, or P0024 failed, DTCs P0010, P0013, P0020, P0023, P0341, P0342, P0343, P0346, P0347, P0348, P0366, P0367, P0368, P0391, P0392, P0393, P2088, P2089, P2090, P2091, P2092, P2093, P2094, and P2095 must run and pass. DTC P0016, P0017, P0018, P0019, P0335, P0336, or P0338 is not set. The engine is operating for greater than 1 seconds. The engine speed is greater than 520 RPM. The engine must accelerate such that the CMP actuator system is commanded from the park position to the phased position. This is considered a cam control cycle. There must be a minimum of 2 cam control cycles for at least 2. 5 seconds each in the phased position. DTCs P000A, P000B, P000C, P000D, P0011, P0014, P0021, and P0024 run continuously once the above conditions are met for greater than 600 seconds.

DTC	Trouble Code Title, Conditions, Possible Causes
DTC: P0021	**Intake Camshaft Position System Performance Bank 2:** DTC P0010, P0013, P0020, P0023, P0016, P0017, P0018, P0019, P0335, P0336, P0340, P0341, P0345, P0346, P0365, P0366, P0390, and P0391 is not set. The ignition voltage is between 11-32 V. The engine is running. The desired camshaft position is not changing greater than 4. 5° for at least 1 s. Both of the desired and actual camshaft position actuator values cannot be greater than 20° or less than 5°. DTCs P0011, P0014, P0021, and P0024 run continuously when the above conditions are met.
DTC: P0023	**Exhaust Camshaft Position Actuator Solenoid Valve Control Circuit Bank 2:** The ignition voltage is between 11-32 V. The ignition switch is in the Crank or Run position. The ECM commanded the Camshaft Position Actuator Solenoid Valve ON. DTCs P0010, P0013, P0020, and P0023 run continuously when the above conditions are met.
DTC: P0023	**Exhaust Camshaft Position (CMP) Actuator Solenoid Control Circuit Bank 2:** The ignition is in the Crank or Run position. The ECM has commanded the Camshaft Position Actuator Solenoid Valve ON. The ignition voltage is between 11-18 volts. DTCs P0010, P0013, P0020, and P0023 run continuously once the above conditions are met.
DTC: P0024	**Exhaust Camshaft Position System Performance Bank 2:** DTC P0010, P0013, P0020, P0023, P0016, P0017, P0018, P0019, P0335, P0336, P0340, P0341, P0345, P0346, P0365, P0366, P0390, and P0391 is not set. The ignition voltage is between 11-32 V. The engine is running. The desired camshaft position is not changing greater than 4. 5° for at least 1 s. Both of the desired and actual camshaft position actuator values cannot be greater than 20° or less than 5°. DTCs P0011, P0014, P0021, and P0024 run continuously when the above conditions are met.
DTC: P0024	**Exhaust Camshaft Position System Performance Bank 2:** Before the ECM can report DTC P000A, P000B, P000C, P000D, P0011, P0014, P0021, or P0024 failed, DTCs P0010, P0013, P0020, P0023, P0341, P0342, P0343, P0346, P0347, P0348, P0366, P0367, P0368, P0391, P0392, P0393, P2088, P2089, P2090, P2091, P2092, P2093, P2094, and P2095 must run and pass. DTC P0016, P0017, P0018, P0019, P0335, P0336, or P0338 is not set. The engine is operating for greater than 1 seconds. The engine speed is greater than 520 RPM. The engine must accelerate such that the CMP actuator system is commanded from the park position to the phased position. This is considered a cam control cycle. There must be a minimum of 2 cam control cycles for at least 2. 5 seconds each in the phased position. DTCs P000A, P000B, P000C, P000D, P0011, P0014, P0021, and P0024 run continuously once the above conditions are met for greater than 600 seconds.
DTC: P0030	**HO2S Heater Control Circuit Sensor 1:** P0030 or P0036The ignition voltage is between 11-32 V. The engine speed is greater than 400 RPM. The DTCs run continuously once the above conditions are met for 10 s.
DTC: P0030	**HO2S Heater Control Circuit Bank 1 Sensor 1:** P0030, P0036, P0050, or P0056The ignition 1 voltage is between 11-18 V. The engine speed is greater than 400 RPM. The DTCs run continuously when the above conditions are met.
DTC: P0030 00	**HO2S Heater Control Circuit Sensor 1:** P0030 00, P0031 00, and P0030 02The ignition is ON. The ignition signal parameter is more than 9 V. DTC P0030 00, P0031 00, and P0032 00 run continuously when the above conditions are met for 1 s. P0135 00 DTCs P0030 00, P0031 00, P0032 00, are not set. The ignition is ON. The ignition signal parameter is more than 9 V. DTC P0135 00 runs continuously.
DTC: P0031	**HO2S Heater Control Circuit Low Voltage Sensor 1:** P0030, P0031, P0032The engine is running The Ignition 1 Signal parameter is 10. 5-18. 1 volts.
DTC: P0031	**HO2S Heater Control Circuit Low Voltage Bank 1 Sensor 1:** P0030, P0031, P0032, P0050, P0051, P0052The ignition voltage is between 10-18 volts. The engine speed is greater than 240 RPM. The HO2S heater is commanded ON. The DTCs run continuously once the above conditions are met for 5 seconds.
DTC: P0031 00	**HO2S Heater Control Circuit Low Voltage Sensor 1:** P0030 00, P0031 00, and P0030 02The ignition is ON. The ignition signal parameter is more than 9 V. DTC P0030 00, P0031 00, and P0032 00 run continuously when the above conditions are met for 1 s. P0135 00 DTCs P0030 00, P0031 00, P0032 00, are not set. The ignition is ON. The ignition signal parameter is more than 9 V. DTC P0135 00 runs continuously.
DTC: P0032	**HO2S Heater Control Circuit High Voltage Bank 1 Sensor 1:** P0030, P0031, P0032, P0050, P0051, P0052The ignition voltage is between 10-18 volts. The engine speed is greater than 240 RPM. The HO2S heater is commanded ON. The DTCs run continuously once the above conditions are met for 5 seconds.
DTC: P0032	**HO2S Heater Control Circuit High Voltage Sensor 1:** P0030, P0031, P0032The engine is running. The Ignition 1 Signal parameter is 10. 5-18. 1 volts.
DTC: P0032 00	**HO2S Heater Control Circuit High Voltage Sensor 1:** P0030 00, P0031 00, and P0030 02The ignition is ON. The ignition signal parameter is more than 9 V. DTC P0030 00, P0031 00, and P0032 00 run continuously when the above conditions are met for 1 s. P0135 00 DTCs P0030 00, P0031 00, P0032 00, are not set. The ignition is ON. The ignition signal parameter is more than 9 V. DTC P0135 00 runs continuously.
DTC: P0033	**Turbocharger Bypass Valve Solenoid Control Circuit:** The engine speed is greater than 80 RPM. The battery voltage is between 10-18 V. The bypass valve must be activated in order to set the open and short to ground faults. This DTC runs continuously within the enabling conditions.

DTC	Trouble Code Title, Conditions, Possible Causes
DTC: P0033 00	**Turbocharger Bypass Solenoid Valve Control Circuit:** The engine speed is greater than 40 RPM. The ignition voltage is between 8-16 V. The bypass valve must be activated in order to set the open and short to ground faults. These DTCs runs continuously within the enabling conditions.
DTC: P0034	**Turbocharger Bypass Valve Solenoid Control Circuit Low Voltage:** The engine speed is greater than 80 RPM. The battery voltage is between 10-18 V. The bypass valve must be activated in order to set the open and short to ground faults. This DTC runs continuously within the enabling conditions.
DTC: P0034 00	**Turbocharger Bypass Solenoid Valve Control Circuit Low Voltage:** The engine speed is greater than 40 RPM. The ignition voltage is between 8-16 V. The bypass valve must be activated in order to set the open and short to ground faults. These DTCs runs continuously within the enabling conditions.
DTC: P0035	**Turbocharger Bypass Valve Solenoid Control Circuit High Voltage:** The engine speed is greater than 80 RPM. The battery voltage is between 10-18 V. The bypass valve must be activated in order to set the open and short to ground faults. This DTC runs continuously within the enabling conditions.
DTC: P0035 00	**Turbocharger Bypass Solenoid Valve Control Circuit High Voltage:** The engine speed is greater than 40 RPM. The ignition voltage is between 8-16 V. The bypass valve must be activated in order to set the open and short to ground faults. These DTCs runs continuously within the enabling conditions.
DTC: P0036	**HO2S Heater Control Circuit Sensor 2:** P0036, P0037, and P0038The Ignition 1 Signal parameter is between 10-18 volts. The engine speed is more than 80 RPM. DTC P0036, P0037, and P0038 run continuously when the above conditions are met for 1 second.
DTC: P0036	**HO2S Heater Control Circuit Sensor 2:** P0030 and P0036The engine is cranking or running. The system voltage is between 11-18V.
DTC: P0036	**HO2S Heater Control Circuit Sensor 2:** P0030 or P0036The ignition voltage is between 11-32 V. The engine speed is greater than 400 RPM. The DTCs run continuously once the above conditions are met for 10 s.
DTC: P0036 00	**HO2S Heater Control Circuit Sensor 2:** P0036 00, P0037 00, and P0038 00The ignition is ON. The Ignition Signal parameter is more than 9 V. DTC P0036 00, P0037 00, and P0038 00 run continuously when the above conditions are met for 1 s.
DTC: P0037	**HO2S Heater Control Circuit Low Voltage Bank 1 Sensor 2:** P0036, P0037, P0038, P0056, P0057, P0058The ignition voltage is between 10-18 volts. The engine speed is greater than 80 RPM. The HO2S heater is commanded ON and OFF at least once during the ignition cycle. The HO2S 2 is at operating temperature. The DTCs run continuously once the above conditions are met.
DTC: P0037	**HO2S Heater Control Circuit Low Voltage Sensor 2:** P0036, P0037, and P0038The Ignition 1 Signal parameter is between 10-18 volts. The engine speed is more than 80 RPM. DTC P0036, P0037, and P0038 run continuously when the above conditions are met for 1 second.
DTC: P0037 00	**HO2S Heater Control Circuit Low Voltage Sensor 2:** P0037 00, and P0038 00The engine is running. The ignition voltage is between 11-16 V. DTC P0037 00, and P0038 00 run continuously when the above conditions are met for 1 s.
DTC: P0037 00	**HO2S Heater Control Circuit Low Voltage Sensor 2:** P0036 00, P0037 00, and P0038 00The ignition is ON. The Ignition Signal parameter is more than 9 V. DTC P0036 00, P0037 00, and P0038 00 run continuously when the above conditions are met for 1 s.
DTC: P0038	**HO2S Heater Control Circuit High Voltage Sensor 2:** P0036, P0037, and P0038The Ignition 1 Signal parameter is between 10-18 volts. The engine speed is more than 80 RPM. DTC P0036, P0037, and P0038 run continuously when the above conditions are met for 1 second.
DTC: P0038	**HO2S Heater Control Circuit High Voltage Bank 1 Sensor 2:** P0036, P0037, P0038, P0056, P0057, P0058The ignition voltage is between 10-18 volts. The engine speed is greater than 80 RPM. The HO2S heater is commanded ON and OFF at least once during the ignition cycle. The HO2S 2 is at operating temperature. The DTCs run continuously once the above conditions are met.
DTC: P0038 00	**HO2S Heater Control Circuit High Voltage Sensor 2:** P0036 00, P0037 00, and P0038 00The ignition is ON. The Ignition Signal parameter is more than 9 V. DTC P0036 00, P0037 00, and P0038 00 run continuously when the above conditions are met for 1 s.
DTC: P0038 00	**HO2S Heater Control Circuit High Voltage Sensor 2:** P0037 00, and P0038 00The engine is running. The ignition voltage is between 11-16 V. DTC P0037 00, and P0038 00 run continuously when the above conditions are met for 1 s.

DTC	Trouble Code Title, Conditions, Possible Causes
DTC: P003A	**Turbocharger Vane Position Not Learned:** The ECM is commanding the turbocharger vanes open or closed during a position learn procedure. The engine speed is between 640-850 RPM. DTC P003A runs once per key cycle when the above conditions are met.
DTC: P003A	**Turbocharger Boost Control Position Not Learned:** DTCs P0107, P0108, P0117, P0118, P2563, P2564, P2565, P2228, P2229 are not set. The battery voltage is equal to or greater than 11 V. The ECM is commanding the turbocharger vanes open or closed during a position learn process. The engine speed is between 600-750 RPM. The engine coolant temp (ECT) is between 73-96°C (163-205°F). The calculated fuel rate is less than 30 mm ;. DTC P003A runs once per key cycle when the above conditions are met.
DTC: P003A 00	**Turbocharger Vane Position Not Learned:** The battery voltage is equal to or greater than 11 V. The ECM is commanding the turbocharger vanes open or closed during a position learn process. The engine speed is between 750-850 RPM. The engine coolant temperature (ECT) is between 73-96°C (163-205°F). DTC P003A 00 runs once per key cycle when the above conditions are met.
DTC: P0045	**Turbocharger Boost Control Solenoid Control Circuit:** P0045, P0047, P0048 and P006EThe battery voltage is greater than 11 V. The engine is running. DTCs P0045, P0047, P0048 and P006E run continuously when the above conditions are met.
DTC: P0045 00	**Turbocharger Boost Control Solenoid Control Circuit Malfunction:** The ignition is ON or the engine is running. The ignition voltage is greater than 16. 5 V. The ECM has commanded the turbocharger boost control solenoid ON and OFF at least once during the ignition cycle. The DTCs run continuously once the above conditions are met.
DTC: P0045 01	**Turbocharger Boost Control Solenoid Control Circuit Short to Battery:** The ignition is ON or the engine is running. The ignition voltage is greater than 11 V. The ECM has commanded the turbocharger boost control solenoid ON and OFF at least once during the ignition cycle. The DTCs run continuously once the above conditions are met.
DTC: P0045 02	**Turbocharger Boost Control Solenoid Control Circuit Short to Ground:** The ignition is ON or the engine is running. The ignition voltage is greater than 11 V. The ECM has commanded the turbocharger boost control solenoid ON and OFF at least once during the ignition cycle. The DTCs run continuously once the above conditions are met.
DTC: P0045 04	**Turbocharger Boost Control Solenoid Control Circuit Open:** The ignition is ON or the engine is running. The ignition voltage is greater than 11 V. The ECM has commanded the turbocharger boost control solenoid ON and OFF at least once during the ignition cycle. The DTCs run continuously once the above conditions are met.
DTC: P0045 54	**Turbocharger Boost Control Solenoid Control Circuit High Temperature:** The ignition is ON or the engine is running. The ignition voltage is greater than 11 V. The ECM has commanded the turbocharger boost control solenoid ON and OFF at least once during the ignition cycle. The DTCs run continuously once the above conditions are met.
DTC: P0047	**Turbocharger Boost Control Solenoid Control Circuit Low Voltage:** The engine run time is greater than 60 seconds. DTCs P0047 and P0048 run continuously when the above condition is met.
DTC: P0047	**Turbocharger Boost Control Solenoid Control Circuit Low Voltage:** P0045, P0047, P0048 and P006EThe battery voltage is greater than 11 V. The engine is running. DTCs P0045, P0047, P0048 and P006E run continuously when the above conditions are met.
DTC: P0047 00	**Turbocharger Boost Control Solenoid Control Circuit Low Voltage:** The ignition is ON or the engine is running. The ignition voltage is greater than 16. 5 V. The ECM has commanded the turbocharger boost control solenoid ON and OFF at least once during the ignition cycle. The DTCs run continuously once the above conditions are met.
DTC: P0048	**Turbocharger Boost Control Solenoid Control Circuit High Voltage:** P0045, P0047, P0048 and P006EThe battery voltage is greater than 11 V. The engine is running. DTCs P0045, P0047, P0048 and P006E run continuously when the above conditions are met.
DTC: P0048	**Turbocharger Boost Control Solenoid Control Circuit High Voltage:** The engine run time is greater than 60 seconds. DTCs P0047 and P0048 run continuously when the above condition is met.
DTC: P0048 00	**Turbocharger Boost Control Solenoid Control Circuit High Voltage:** The ignition is ON or the engine is running. The ignition voltage is greater than 16. 5 V. The ECM has commanded the turbocharger boost control solenoid ON and OFF at least once during the ignition cycle. The DTCs run continuously once the above conditions are met.
DTC: P0050	**HO2S Heater Control Circuit Bank 2 Sensor 1:** P0030, P0031, P0032, P0050, P0051, P0052The ignition voltage is between 10-18 volts. The engine speed is greater than 240 RPM. The HO2S heater is commanded ON. The DTCs run continuously once the above conditions are met for 5 seconds.

DTC	Trouble Code Title, Conditions, Possible Causes
DTC: P0051	**HO2S Heater Control Circuit Low Voltage Bank 2 Sensor 1:** P0030, P0031, P0032, P0050, P0051, P0052The ignition voltage is between 10-18 volts. The engine speed is greater than 240 RPM. The HO2S heater is commanded ON. The DTCs run continuously once the above conditions are met for 5 seconds.
DTC: P0052	**HO2S Heater Control Circuit High Voltage Bank 2 Sensor 1:** P0030, P0031, P0032, P0050, P0051, P0052The ignition voltage is between 10-18 volts. The engine speed is greater than 240 RPM. The HO2S heater is commanded ON. The DTCs run continuously once the above conditions are met for 5 seconds.
DTC: P0053	**HO2S Heater Resistance Sensor 1:** P0053 or P0054 DTCs P0112, P0113, P0116, P0117, P0118, P2610 are not set. The engine is started. The ignition is OFF for more than 8 hours. The ECT Sensor parameter is between -30 to +45°C (-22 to +113°F) at engine start-up. The ECT Sensor parameter minus the IAT Sensor parameter is less than 8°C (14°F) at engine start-up. The Ignition Voltage parameter is less than 18 volts. DTCs P0053 and P0054 run once per drive cycle when the above conditions are met.
DTC: P0053	**HO2S Heater Resistance Bank 1 Sensor 1:** P0053, P0054, or P0059 DTCs P0112, P0113, P0117, P0118, or P2610 are not set. The engine run time is greater than 3 seconds. The ignition voltage is less than 18 volts. The ignition is OFF for greater than 8 hours. The engine coolant temperature (ECT) is between -30 to +45°C (-22 to +113°F) at engine start-up. The ECT and the intake air temperature (IAT) are within 8°C (14°F) at engine start-up. The DTCs run once per drive cycle when the above conditions are met.
DTC: P0053	**HO2S Heater Resistance Sensor 1:** P0053The engine is started. The Ignition 1 Signal parameter is 10. 5-18. 1 volts. DTC P0053 runs once per drive cycle when the above conditions are met.
DTC: P0054	**HO2S Heater Resistance Bank 1 Sensor 2:** P0053, P0054, or P0059 DTCs P0112, P0113, P0117, P0118, or P2610 are not set. The engine run time is greater than 3 seconds. The ignition voltage is less than 18 volts. The ignition is OFF for greater than 8 hours. The engine coolant temperature (ECT) is between -30 to +45°C (-22 to +113°F) at engine start-up. The ECT and the intake air temperature (IAT) are within 8°C (14°F) at engine start-up. The DTCs run once per drive cycle when the above conditions are met.
DTC: P0054	**HO2S Heater Resistance Sensor 2:** P0053 and P0054 DTC P2610 has run and passed. The ignition is OFF for more than 10 hours. The ECT Sensor parameter is between -30 and +45°C (-22 and +113°F) at engine start-up. The system voltage is less than 18V. This diagnostic runs one time per valid cold start when the above conditions are met.
DTC: P0056	**HO2S Heater Control Circuit Bank 2 Sensor 2:** P0036, P0037, P0038, P0056, P0057, P0058The ignition voltage is between 10-18 volts. The engine speed is greater than 80 RPM. The HO2S heater is commanded ON and OFF at least once during the ignition cycle. The HO2S 2 is at operating temperature. The DTCs run continuously once the above conditions are met.
DTC: P0057	**HO2S Heater Control Circuit Low Voltage Bank 2 Sensor 2:** P0036, P0037, P0038, P0056, P0057, P0058The ignition voltage is between 10-18 volts. The engine speed is greater than 80 RPM. The HO2S heater is commanded ON and OFF at least once during the ignition cycle. The HO2S 2 is at operating temperature. The DTCs run continuously once the above conditions are met.
DTC: P0058	**HO2S Heater Control Circuit High Voltage Bank 2 Sensor 2:** P0036, P0037, P0038, P0056, P0057, P0058The ignition voltage is between 10-18 volts. The engine speed is greater than 80 RPM. The HO2S heater is commanded ON and OFF at least once during the ignition cycle. The HO2S 2 is at operating temperature. The DTCs run continuously once the above conditions are met.
DTC: P0059	**HO2S Heater Resistance Bank 2 Sensor 1:** P0053, P0054, or P0059 DTCs P0112, P0113, P0117, P0118, or P2610 are not set. The engine run time is greater than 3 seconds. The ignition voltage is less than 18 volts. The ignition is OFF for greater than 8 hours. The engine coolant temperature (ECT) is between -30 to +45°C (-22 to +113°F) at engine start-up. The ECT and the intake air temperature (IAT) are within 8°C (14°F) at engine start-up. The DTCs run once per drive cycle when the above conditions are met.
DTC: P0060	**HO2S Heater Resistance Bank 2 Sensor 2:** P0053, P0054, P0059, or P0060 DTCs P0112, P0113, P0117, P0118, or P2610 are not set. The engine run time is greater than 20 s. The ignition voltage is less than 18 V. The ignition is OFF for greater than 8 h. The engine coolant temperature (ECT) is between -30 to +45°C (-22 to +113°F) at engine start-up. The ECT and the intake air temperature (IAT) are within 8°C (14°F) at engine start-up. The DTCs run once per drive cycle when the above conditions are met.
DTC: P0068	**Throttle Body Airflow Performance:** P0068 DTCs P0122, P0123, P0220, P0221, P0222, P0223, P0601, P0602, P0603, P0604, P060D, P062F, P0606, P0652, P0653, P1516, P2101, P2119, P2135, P2176 are not set. The engine is running. DTC P0068 runs continuously when the above conditions are met.
DTC: P0068 00	**Throttle Body Air Flow Performance:** DTCs P0106 00, P0107 00, P0108 00, and P0112 00 are not set. The engine is running. The DTC runs continuously when the above conditions are met.

DTC	Trouble Code Title, Conditions, Possible Causes
DTC: P0068 00	**Throttle Body Air Flow Performance:** DTCs P000A 00, P000B 00, P0016 00, P0017 00, P0111 00, P0112 00, P0113 00, P0114 00, P0116 00, P0117 00, P0118 00, P0119 00, P0122 00, P0123 00, P0222 00, P0223 00, P0121 00, P0221 00, P0340 00, P0341 00, P0365 00, P0366 00, P0458 00, P0459 00, P0642 00, P0643 00, P0652 00, P0653 00, P065B 00 are not set. The engine is running. DTCs P0068 00, P0642 00, P0643 00 are not set.
DTC: P0069 00	**Manifold Absolute Pressure (MAP) - Barometric Pressure (BARO) Not Plausible:** DTCs P010 007, or P0108 00 are not set. The ignition is ON. The DTC runs continuously when the above conditions are met.
DTC: P0069 5A	**Manifold Absolute Pressure (MAP) - Barometric Pressure (BARO) Not Plausible:** DTCs P0105, P0107, or P0108 are not set. The ignition is ON. The DTC runs continuously when the above conditions are met.
DTC: P006E	**Turbocharger Boost Control Solenoid High Control Circuit Low Voltage:** P0045, P0047, P0048 and P006EThe battery voltage is greater than 11 V. The engine is running. DTCs P0045, P0047, P0048 and P006E run continuously when the above conditions are met.
DTC: P006F	**Turbocharger Boost Control Solenoid High Control Circuit High Voltage:** P006FThe battery voltage is greater than 11 V. The ignition is OFF. The engine is in after-run. DTC P006F runs continuously when the above conditions are met.
DTC: P007C	**Charge Air Cooler (CAC) Temperature Sensor Circuit Low Voltage:** P007C or P007DThe engine is running for longer than 10 s. The DTCs run continuously when the enabling condition is met.
DTC: P007D	**Charge Air Cooler (CAC) Temperature Sensor Circuit High Voltage:** P007C or P007DThe engine is running for longer than 10 s. The DTCs run continuously when the enabling condition is met.
DTC: P0087	**Fuel Rail Low Pressure:** DTCs P0090, P0091, P0092, P0191, P0192, P0193 are not set. The ignition 1 signal parameter is less than 18. 1 V. The relative injected fuel mass is between 5. 016-500 %. The deceleration fuel cut-off is inactive. The engine speed is greater than 25 RPM. The engine start temperature is greater than -48°C (-54. 4°F). The DTCs run continuously when the above conditions are met for 2 s.
DTC: P0087	**Fuel Rail Pressure (FRP) Too Low:** Fuel tank level is greater than 15 %. Engine is in crank or run mode. Ambient air temperature is greater than -7°C (+19°F). Ambient pressure is greater than 74. 8 kPa.
DTC: P0087 00	**Fuel Rail Low Pressure:** The engine is running. The DTCs runs continuously once the above conditions are met.
DTC: P0088	**Fuel Rail High Pressure:** DTCs P0090, P0091, P0092, P0191, P0192, P0193 are not set. The ignition 1 signal parameter is less than 18. 1 V. The relative injected fuel mass is between 5. 016-500 %. The deceleration fuel cut-off is inactive. The engine speed is greater than 25 RPM. The engine start temperature is greater than -48°C (-54. 4°F). The DTCs run continuously when the above conditions are met for 2 s.
DTC: P0088	**Fuel Rail Pressure (FRP) Too High:** Fuel tank level is greater than 15 %. Engine is in crank or run mode. Ambient air temperature is greater than -7°C (+19°F). Ambient pressure is greater than 74. 8 kPa.
DTC: P0088 00	**Fuel Rail High Pressure:** The engine is running. The DTCs runs continuously once the above conditions are met.
DTC: P0089	**Fuel Pressure Regulator Performance:** P0089, P228C, or P228DDTC P0016, P0017, P0018, P0019, P0090, P0091, P0092, P00C8, P00C9, P00CA, P0111, P0112, P0113, P0116, P0117, P0118, P0128, P0192, P0193, P0335, P0336, P0340, P0341, P0345, P0346, P0365, P0366, P0390, P0391, P0627, P0628, or P0629 is not set. The ignition voltage is greater than 8 V. The low side fuel pressure is greater than 275 kPa (40 psi). The engine is running. The DTCs run continuously when the above conditions are met for 10 s.
DTC: P0089 00	**Fuel Pressure Regulator Performance Malfunction:** The engine is running. The DTCs runs continuously once the above conditions are met.
DTC: P0089 11	**Fuel Pressure Regulator Performance High Input:** The engine is running. The DTCs runs continuously once the above conditions are met.
DTC: P0089 12	**Fuel Pressure Regulator Performance Low Input:** The engine is running. The DTCs runs continuously once the above conditions are met.
DTC: P0089 18	**Fuel Pressure Regulator Performance Low Signal Amplitude:** The engine is running. The DTCs runs continuously once the above conditions are met.
DTC: P0089 19	**Fuel Pressure Regulator Performance High Signal Amplitude:** The engine is running. The DTCs runs continuously once the above conditions are met.

DTC	Trouble Code Title, Conditions, Possible Causes
DTC: P008F	**Engine Coolant Temperature (ECT) Fuel Temperature Not Plausible:** DTC P0016, P0112, P0113, P0117, P0118, P0182, P0183, P0335, P0336, P0340 or P0341 is not set. Condition 1Ignition has been OFF for 8 hours or more. The ambient temperature is greater than -60°C (-76°F). The engine is running. OR Condition 2Ignition has been OFF for 8 hours or more. The ambient temperature is greater than -60°C (-76°F). The engine is running. In the first 60 s of engine run time, the ECM determines the block heater is OFF. DTC P008F will only run once per ignition cycle until a Pass, Fail or Disable condition exists.
DTC: P0090	**Fuel Pressure Regulator 1 Control Circuit:** The ignition 1 signal parameter is between 6-18. 1 V. The DTCs run continuously within the enabling condition.
DTC: P0090	**Fuel Pressure Regulator Solenoid 1 Control Circuit:** Engine speed is greater than 600 RPM. Battery voltage is greater than 11 V.
DTC: P0090 00	**Fuel Pressure Regulator Control Circuit:** The ignition is ON, or the engine is running. The ignition voltage is less than 16 V. These DTCs runs continuously once the above conditions are met.
DTC: P0090 01	**Fuel Pressure Regulator Control Circuit Short to Battery:** The ignition is ON, or the engine is running. The Ignition voltage is less than 16 V. The DTCs runs continuously once the above conditions are met.
DTC: P0090 02	**Fuel Pressure Regulator Control Circuit Short to Ground:** The ignition is ON, or the engine is running. The ignition voltage is less than 16 V. The DTCs runs continuously once the above conditions are met.
DTC: P0090 04	**Fuel Pressure Regulator Control Circuit Open:** The ignition is ON, or the engine is running. The ignition voltage is less than 16 V. The DTCs runs continuously once the above conditions are met.
DTC: P0090 54	**Fuel Pressure Regulator Control Circuit High Temperature:** The ignition is ON, or the engine is running. The ignition voltage Is less than 16 V. The DTCs runs continuously once the above conditions are met.
DTC: P0091	**Fuel Pressure Regulator Solenoid 1 Control Circuit Low Voltage:** Engine speed is greater than 600 RPM. Battery voltage is greater than 11 V.
DTC: P0091	**Fuel Pressure Regulator Control Circuit Low Voltage:** The ignition voltage is between 11-18 V. The DTCs run continuously within the enabling conditions.
DTC: P0091 00	**Fuel Pressure Regulator Control Circuit Low Voltage:** The ignition is ON, or the engine is running. The ignition voltage is less than 16 V. These DTCs runs continuously once the above conditions are met.
DTC: P0092	**Fuel Pressure Regulator Solenoid 1 Control Circuit High Voltage:** Engine speed is greater than 600 RPM. Battery voltage is greater than 11 V.
DTC: P0092	**Fuel Pressure Regulator 1 Control Circuit High Voltage:** The ignition 1 signal parameter is between 6-18. 1 V. The DTCs run continuously within the enabling condition.
DTC: P0092	**Fuel Pressure Regulator Control Circuit High Voltage:** The ignition voltage is between 11-18 V. The DTCs run continuously within the enabling conditions.
DTC: P0092 00	**Fuel Pressure Regulator Control Circuit High Voltage:** The ignition is ON, or the engine is running. The ignition voltage is less than 16 V. These DTCs runs continuously once the above conditions are met.
DTC: P0093 00	**Fuel System Large Leak Detected:** The engine is running. The DTCs runs continuously once the above conditions are met.
DTC: P0095 03	**Intake Air Temperature (IAT) Sensor 2 Circuit Low Voltage:** The ignition is ON, or the engine is running. The DTCs run continuously once the above conditions are met.
DTC: P0095 07	**Intake Air Temperature (IAT) Sensor 2 Circuit High Voltage:** The ignition is ON, or the engine is running. The DTCs run continuously once the above conditions are met.
DTC: P0096	**Intake Air Temperature (IAT) Sensor 2 Performance:** DTC P0097, P0098, or P0099 is not set. The engine coolant temperature (ECT) at start-up is colder than 88°C (190°F). The ECT reaches a target temperature that is warmer than 60°C (140°F). The engine is idling. The mass air flow (MAF) is less than 8 g/s. The vehicle speed is less than 16 km/h (10 mph). Drive period. DTC P0097, P0098, or P0099 is not set. The mass air flow (MAF) is between 6-111 g/s. The vehicle speed is greater than 35 km/h (22 mph). This DTC runs continuously within the enabling conditions.

DTC	Trouble Code Title, Conditions, Possible Causes
DTC: P0096 00	**Intake Air Temperature (IAT) Sensor 2 Performance:** The ignition is ON or the engine is running. The ignition voltage is greater than 8.5 V. The DTCs run continuously once the above conditions are met.
DTC: P0097	**Intake Air Temperature (IAT) Sensor 2 Circuit Low Voltage:** The ignition is ON or the engine is running. The DTCs run continuously when the enabling conditions are met.
DTC: P0097 00	**Intake Air Temperature (IAT) Sensor 2 Circuit Low Voltage:** The ignition is ON or the engine is running. The ignition voltage is greater than 8.5 V. The DTCs run continuously once the above conditions are met.
DTC: P0098	**Intake Air Temperature (IAT) Sensor 2 Circuit High Voltage:** P0097 or P0098The engine is running for longer than 10 s. The DTCs run continuously when the enabling condition is met.
DTC: P0098	**Intake Air Temperature (IAT) Sensor 2 Circuit High Voltage:** The ignition is ON or the engine is running. The DTCs run continuously when the enabling conditions are met.
DTC: P0098	**Intake Air Temperature (IAT) Sensor 2 Circuit High Voltage:** P0098The engine is running. This DTC runs continuously within the enabling conditions.
DTC: P0098 00	**Intake Air Temperature (IAT) Sensor 2 Circuit High Voltage:** The ignition is ON or the engine is running. The ignition voltage is greater than 8.5 V. The DTCs run continuously once the above conditions are met.
DTC: P0099	**Intake Air Temperature (IAT) Sensor 2 Circuit Intermittent:** P0099The ignition is ON or the engine is running. This DTC runs continuously within the enabling conditions.
DTC: P0099 00	**Intake Air Temperature (IAT) Sensor 2 Circuit Intermittent:** The ignition is ON or the engine is running. The ignition voltage is greater than 8.5 V. The DTCs run continuously once the above conditions are met.
DTC: P00B3	**Radiator Coolant Temperature (RCT) Sensor Circuit Low Voltage:** The ignition is ON, or the engine is running. The battery voltage is greater than 9 V. The intake air temperature (IAT) is warmer than -30°C (-22°F) or the IAT is colder than -30°C (-22°F) and the engine run time is greater than 120 s. This DTC runs continuously within the enabling conditions.
DTC: P00B3 00	**Radiator Coolant Temperature (RCT) Sensor Circuit Low Voltage:** The ignition is ON, or the engine is running. The battery voltage is greater than 9 V. The intake air temperature (IAT) is warmer than -30°C (-22°F) or the IAT is colder than -30°C (-22°F) and the engine run time is greater than 120 s. This DTC runs continuously within the enabling conditions.
DTC: P00B4	**Radiator Coolant Temperature (RCT) Sensor Circuit High Voltage:** The ignition is ON, or the engine is running. The battery voltage is greater than 9 V. The intake air temperature (IAT) is warmer than -30°C (-22°F) or the IAT is colder than -30°C (-22°F) and the engine run time is greater than 120 s. This DTC runs continuously within the enabling conditions.
DTC: P00B4 00	**Radiator Coolant Temperature (RCT) Sensor Circuit High Voltage:** The ignition is ON, or the engine is running. The battery voltage is greater than 9 V. The intake air temperature (IAT) is warmer than -30°C (-22°F) or the IAT is colder than -30°C (-22°F) and the engine run time is greater than 120 s. This DTC runs continuously within the enabling conditions.
DTC: P00B6	**Radiator Coolant Temperature (RCT) - Engine Coolant Temperature (ECT) Correlation:** DTCs P00B3, P00B4, P0112, P0113, P0117, P0118 or P2610 are not set. The ignition has been off for greater than 8 h before vehicle is started. The ignition is ON, or the engine is running. The intake air temperature (IAT) is greater than -7°C (19°F). The fuel level is greater than 10%. The DTC runs once per ignition cycle when the above conditions are met.
DTC: P00B6 00	**Radiator Coolant Temperature (RCT) - Engine Coolant Temperature (ECT) Not Plausible:** DTCs P00B3 00, P00B4 00, P0112 00, P0113 00, P0117 00, or P0118 00 are not set. The ignition has been off for greater than 8 h before vehicle is started. The ignition is ON, or the engine is running. The intake air temperature (IAT) is greater than -7°C (19°F). The fuel level is greater than 10%. The DTC runs once per ignition cycle when the above conditions are met.
DTC: P00C6	**Fuel Rail Pressure Low During Engine Cranking:** P00C6 DTC P0016, P0017, P0090, P0091, P0092, P00C8, P00C9, P00CA, P0112, P0113, P0116, P0117, P0118, P0128, P0192, P0193, P0335, P0336, P0340, P0341, P0365, P0366, P0627, P0628, P0629 or P1682 is not set. The ignition voltage is more than 8 V. The engine coolant temperature is between -100 and +80°C (-148 and +176°F). The low side fuel pressure is more than 300 kPa (43.5 psi). The engine is not running. The DTC runs once for each engine start.
DTC: P00C7 00	**Intake Air Pressure Measurement System - Multiple Sensors Not Plausible:** The engine is running. This DTC runs continuously within the enabling conditions.

DTC	Trouble Code Title, Conditions, Possible Causes
DTC: P00C8	**Fuel Pressure Regulator High Control Circuit:** The ignition voltage is between 11-18 V. The DTCs run continuously within the enabling conditions.
DTC: P00C9	**Fuel Pressure Regulator High Control Circuit Low Voltage:** The ignition voltage is between 11-18 V. The DTCs run continuously within the enabling conditions.
DTC: P00C9	**Fuel Pressure Regulator 1 High Control Circuit Low Voltage:** Engine speed is greater than 600 RPM. Battery voltage is greater than 11 V.
DTC: P00CA	**Fuel Pressure Regulator 1 High Control Circuit High Voltage:** Engine speed is greater than 600 RPM. Battery voltage is greater than 11 V.
DTC: P00CA	**Fuel Pressure Regulator High Control Circuit High Voltage:** The ignition voltage is between 11-18 V. The DTCs run continuously within the enabling conditions.
DTC: P0100	**Mass Air Flow (MAF) Sensor Circuit:** The engine is running. The engine speed is greater than 300 RPM. The ignition 1 voltage signal is greater than 10 V. The above conditions are met for greater than 1 s. This DTC runs continuously within the enabling conditions.
DTC: P0100	**Mass Air Flow (MAF) Sensor Circuit:** The ignition is ON, or the engine is operating. The ignition voltage is greater than 10. 5 V. DTC P0100, P0102 and P0103 run continuously once the above conditions are met for 200 mS.
DTC: P0100 00	**Mass Air Flow (MAF) Sensor Circuit Malfunction:** The ignition is ON. The battery voltage is greater than 8. 5 V. The engine speed is between 1 000-4 000 RPM.
DTC: P0101	**Mass Air Flow (MAF) Sensor Performance:** DTCs P0102, P0103, P0107, P0108, P0112, P0113, P0116, P0117, P0118, P0128, P0335 or P0336 are not set. The engine is running. The engine coolant is between 69-127°C (156-261°F). The intake air temperature is between -20 and +125°C (-4 and +257°F). The DTC runs continuously when the above conditions are met.
DTC: P0101	**Mass Air Flow (MAF) Sensor Circuit Performance:** Before the ECM can report DTC P0101 failed, DTCs P0010, P0011, P0013, P0014, P0020, P0021, P0023, P0024, P0100, P0102, P0103, P0111, P0112, P0113, P0121, P0122, P0123, P0221, P0222, P0223, P0335, P0336, P0338, P2088, P2089, P2090, P2091, P2092, P2093, P2094, P2095, P2227, P2228, or P2229 must run and pass. DTC P2176 is not set. The engine is operating for greater than 1 s. The MAF signal is greater than 0. 00g/s and steady. The ignition voltage is greater than 10. 5 V. The engine coolant temperature (ECT) is greater than 10°C (50°F). The long term fuel trim is enabled. The throttle angle is steady +/-2 %. The ECM detects greater than 150 revolutions of the crankshaft. DTC P0101 runs continuously once the above conditions are met for greater than 2 s.
DTC: P0101 00	**Mass Air Flow (MAF) Sensor Performance:** The ignition is ON. The battery voltage is greater than 8. 5 V. The engine speed is between 1 000-4 000 RPM.
DTC: P0101 00	**Mass Air Flow (MAF) Sensor Performance:** DTCs P0102 00, P0103 00, P0106 00, P0107 00, P0108 00, P0112 00, P0113 00, P0117 00, P0118 00, P0335 00, P0336 00 are not set. The engine speed is between 400-6 500 RPM. The IAT sensor is between -20 to +125°C (-4 to +257°F). The engine coolant temperature (ECT) sensor is between 70-125°C (158-257°F). The DTC runs continuously when the above conditions are met.
DTC: P0101 11	**Mass Air Flow (MAF) Sensor Performance High Input:** The ignition is ON. The battery voltage is greater than 8. 5 V. The engine speed is between 1 000-4 000 RPM.
DTC: P0101 12	**Mass Air Flow (MAF) Sensor Performance Low Input:** The ignition is ON. The battery voltage is greater than 8. 5 V. The engine speed is between 1 000-4 000 RPM.
DTC: P0102	**Mass Air Flow (MAF) Sensor Circuit Low Frequency:** The engine is running for greater than 1 s. The ignition 1 signal is greater than 8 V. The above conditions are met for greater than 0. 5 s. The DTC runs continuously when the above conditions are met.
DTC: P0102 00	**Mass Air Flow (MAF) Sensor Circuit Low Frequency:** The ignition is ON. The battery voltage is greater than 8. 5 V. The engine speed is between 1 000-4 000 RPM.
DTC: P0102 00	**Mass Air Flow (MAF) Sensor Circuit Low Frequency:** The engine is running for greater than 1 s. The engine speed is greater than 300 RPM. The ignition voltage is greater than 10 V. The DTCs run continuously when the above conditions are met for greater than 1 s.
DTC: P0103	**Mass Air Flow (MAF) Sensor Circuit High Frequency:** The ignition is ON, or the engine is operating. The ignition voltage is greater than 10. 5 V. DTC P0100, P0102 and P0103 run continuously once the above conditions are met for 200 mS.
DTC: P0103 00	**Mass Air Flow (MAF) Sensor Circuit High Frequency:** The ignition is ON. The battery voltage is greater than 8. 5 V. The engine speed is between 1 000-4 000 RPM.

DTC	Trouble Code Title, Conditions, Possible Causes
DTC: P0103 00	**Mass Air Flow (MAF) Sensor Circuit High Frequency:** The engine is running for greater than 1 s. The engine speed is greater than 300 RPM. The ignition voltage is greater than 10 V. The DTCs run continuously when the above conditions are met for greater than 1 s.
DTC: P0105 03	**Manifold Absolute Pressure (MAP) Sensor Circuit Low Voltage:** DTCs P0069, P0652, P2226, P2228, and P2229 are not set. The ignition is ON.
DTC: P0105 07	**Manifold Absolute Pressure (MAP) Sensor Circuit High Voltage:** DTCs P0069, P0652, P2226, P2228, and P2229 are not set. The ignition is ON.
DTC: P0105 5A	**Manifold Absolute Pressure (MAP) Sensor Circuit Not Plausible:** DTCs P0069, P0652, P2226, P2228, and P2229 are not set. The ignition is ON.
DTC: P0106	**Manifold Absolute Pressure (MAP) Sensor Performance:** DTCs P0102, P0103, P0107, P0108, P0112, P0113, P0116, P0117, P0118, P0128, P0335, P0336 are not set. The engine is running. The IAT Sensor parameter is between -20 and +125°C (-4 and 257°F). The ECT Sensor parameter is between -20 and +125°C (-4 and 257°F). This DTC runs continuously when the above conditions are met.
DTC: P0106	**Manifold Absolute Pressure (MAP) Sensor Performance:** DTCs P0016, P0102, P0103, P0107, P0108, P0112, P0113, P0116, P0117, P0118, P0128, P0335, or P0336 are not set. The engine is running. The engine coolant is between 70-125°C (158-257°F). The intake air temperature is between -7 and +125°C (+19.4 and +257°F). This DTC runs continuously when the above conditions are met.
DTC: P0106	**Manifold Absolute Pressure (MAP) Sensor Performance:** P0106 - Engine Cranking DTCs P0096, P0097, P0098, P0099, P0107, P0108, P0121, P0122, P0123, P0221, P0222, P0223, P0236, P0237, P0238, P0455, P0496, P2176, P2227, P2228, P2229 are not set. The engine OFF timer is greater than 4 seconds before cranking begins. The engine is cranking at less than 400 RPM for at least 200 ms. This DTC runs once per key cycle within the enabling conditions. P0106 - Engine Running DTCs P0010, P0011, P0013, P0014, P0107, P0108, P0121, P0122, P0123, P0221, P0222, P0223, P0236, P0237, P0238, P0341, P0342, P0343, P0366, P0367, P0368, P2088, P2089, P2090, P2091, P2227, P2228, P2229 are not set. The engine is running and the ECM has counted greater than 200 RPM. The engine speed is greater than 1,500 RPM once during the drive cycle. If start-up ECT is colder than -8°C (+18°F), then the diagnostic is disabled until the ECT reaches 30°C (86°F). The change in the MAP Sensor parameter is greater than 10 kPa once during the drive cycle. The TP Sensor parameter is less than 25 percent once during the drive cycle. This DTC runs continuously within the enabling conditions.
DTC: P0106 00	**Manifold Absolute Pressure (MAP) Sensor Performance:** P0106 00 DTCs P0107 00, P0108 00, P0111 00, P0112 00, P0113 00, P0114 00, P0116 00, P0117 00, P0118 00, P0119 00, P0128 00, P0335 00, P0336 00 are not set. The engine speed is between 400-6 500 RPM. The engine coolant temperature (ECT) sensor is between 70-125°C (158-257°F). The intake air temperature (IAT) sensor is between -20 to +125°C (-4 to +257°F). This DTC runs continuously when the above conditions are met.
DTC: P0106 00	**Manifold Absolute Pressure (MAP) Sensor Performance:** P0106 00 DTCs P0107 00, P0108 00, P0112 00, P0113 00, P0117 00, P0118 00, P0335 00, P0336 00 are not set. The engine is running greater than or equal to 400 RPM. The intake air temperature (IAT) Sensor parameter is between -7 to +125°C (19-257°F). The engine coolant temperature (ECT) Sensor parameter is between 70-125°C (158-257°F). This DTC runs continuously when the above conditions are met.
DTC: P0106 00	**Manifold Absolute Pressure (MAP) Sensor Performance:** DTCs P0102 00, P0103 00, P0107 00, P0108 00, P0112 00, P0113 00, P0117 00, P0118 00, P0335 31, or P0335 31 are not set. The engine speed is between 400-6 500 RPM. The engine coolant temperature (ECT) sensor is between 70-125°C (158-257°F). The intake air temperature (IAT) sensor is between -20 to +125°C (-4 to +257°F). The DTC runs continuously when the above conditions are met.
DTC: P0106 00	**Manifold Absolute Pressure (MAP) Sensor Performance:** P0106 00 DTCs P0107 00, P0108 00, P0111 00, P0112 00, P0113 00, P0114 00, P0116 00, P0117 00, P0118 00, P0119 00, P0128 00, P0335 00, P0336 00 are not set. The engine is running greater than or equal to 400 RPM. The intake air temperature (IAT) Sensor parameter is between -7 to +125°C (19-257°F). The engine coolant temperature (ECT) Sensor parameter is between 70-125°C (158-257°F). This DTC runs continuously when the above conditions are met.
DTC: P0107	**Manifold Absolute Pressure (MAP) Sensor Circuit Low Voltage:** P0107 DTCs P0120, P0121, P0122, P0123, P0220, P0221, P0222, P0223, P0641, or P0651 are not set. The throttle angle is greater than 0 percent when the engine speed is less than 800 RPM. OR The throttle angle is greater than 12 percent when the engine speed is more than 800 RPM. This DTC runs continuously when the above enabling conditions are met.
DTC: P0107 00	**Manifold Absolute Pressure (MAP) Sensor Circuit Low Voltage:** P0107 00 DTCs P0120 00, P0121 00, P0122 00, P0123 00, P0220 00, P0221 00, P0222 00, P0223 00 or P0641 00 are not set. The engine speed is between 400-6 500 RPM. The throttle position is greater than or equal to 0% when the engine speed is less than or equal to 1 000 RPM or The throttle position is greater than or equal to 12.5% when the engine speed is greater than 1 000 RPM. This DTC runs continuously when the above conditions are met.

DTC	Trouble Code Title, Conditions, Possible Causes
DTC: P0108	**Manifold Absolute Pressure (MAP) Sensor Circuit High Voltage:** P0108The engine has been running for a length of time that is determined by the start-up coolant temperature. The length of time ranges from 5. 5 minutes at colder than -30°C (-22°F) to 10 seconds at greater than +30°C (+86°F). DTCs P0120, P0121, P0122, P0123, P0220, P0222, P0223, or P2135 are not set. The throttle position is less than or equal to one percent when the engine speed is less than or equal to 1,200 RPM. OR The throttle position is less than or equal to 20 percent when the engine speed is greater than 1,200 RPM. The DTC runs continuously when the above conditions are met.
DTC: P0108 00	**Manifold Absolute Pressure (MAP) Sensor Circuit High Voltage:** P0108 00The engine has been running for a length of time that is determined by the start-up coolant temperature. The length of time ranges from 5. 5 min at colder than -30°C (-22°F) to 10s at greater than 30°C (+86°F). DTCs P0120 00, P0121 00, P0122 00, P0123 00, P0220 00, P0221 00, P0222 00, P0223 00 or P0641 00 are not set. The throttle position is less than or equal to 1% when the engine speed is less than or equal to 1 200 RPM. OR The throttle position is less than or equal to 20% when the engine speed is greater than 1 200 RPM. The DTC runs continuously when the above conditions are met.
DTC: P0110 00	**Intake Air Temperature (IAT) Sensor 1 Circuit Malfunction:** The ignition is ON or the engine is running. The ignition voltage is greater than 8. 5 V. The DTCs run continuously once the above conditions are met.
DTC: P0110 03	**Intake Air Temperature (IAT) Sensor 1 Circuit Low Voltage:** The ignition is ON or the engine is running. The ignition voltage is greater than 8. 5 V. The DTCs run continuously once the above conditions are met.
DTC: P0110 07	**Intake Air Temperature (IAT) Sensor 1 Circuit High Voltage:** The ignition is ON or the engine is running. The ignition voltage is greater than 8. 5 V. The DTCs run continuously once the above conditions are met.
DTC: P0110 09	**Intake Air Temperature (IAT) Sensor 1 Circuit Too Fast Transitions:** The ignition is ON or the engine is running. The ignition voltage is greater than 8. 5 V. The DTCs run continuously once the above conditions are met.
DTC: P0110 0A	**Intake Air Temperature (IAT) Sensor 1 Circuit Too Slow Transitions:** The ignition is ON or the engine is running. The ignition voltage is greater than 8. 5 V. The DTCs run continuously once the above conditions are met.
DTC: P0110 11	**Intake Air Temperature (IAT) Sensor 1 Circuit High Input:** The ignition is ON or the engine is running. The ignition voltage is greater than 8. 5 V. The DTCs run continuously once the above conditions are met.
DTC: P0110 12	**Intake Air Temperature (IAT) Sensor 1 Circuit Low Input:** The ignition is ON or the engine is running. The ignition voltage is greater than 8. 5 V. The DTCs run continuously once the above conditions are met.
DTC: P0111	**Intake Air Temperature (IAT) Sensor Circuit Performance:** P0111 Idle Test Before the ECM can report DTC P0111 failed, DTC P0101 must run and pass. DTC P0112, P0113, P0116, P0117, P0118, P0119, P0125, or P0128 is not set. The engine coolant temperature (ECT) at engine start is less than 110°C (230°F). The ECT is warmer than 66°C (151°F). The vehicle speed is less than 5 km/h (3 mph). The MAF is less than 8 g/s. DTC P0111 runs continuously when the above conditions are met for greater than 300 s. P0111 Cruise Test Before the ECM can report DTC P0111 failed, DTC P0101 must run and pass. DTC P0112, P0113, P0116, P0117, P0118, P0119, or P0128 is not set. The ECT at engine start is less than 110°C (230°F). The vehicle speed is greater than 29 km/h (18 mph). The MAF is between 7-67 g/s. Decel fuel cut-off is not active. DTC P0111 runs continuously when the above conditions are met for greater than 300 s.
DTC: P0111	**Intake Air Temperature (IAT) Sensor Performance:** DTCs P0112, P0113, P0117, P0118 are not set. The ignition has been OFF at least 8 hours. The ignition is ON. This DTC runs once per ignition cycle when the enabling conditions are met.
DTC: P0111 00	**Intake Air Temperature (IAT) Sensor Performance:** P0111 00 DTCs P0501 00, P0116 00, P0117 00, P0118 00, P0119 00, P0112 00, P0113 00, P0114 00, P0107 00 or P0108 00 are not set. The engine run time is greater than 10 min.
DTC: P0111 00	**Intake Air Temperature (IAT) Sensor 1 Performance:** The ignition is ON or the engine is running. The ignition voltage is greater than 8. 5 V. The DTCs run continuously once the above conditions are met.
DTC: P0112	**Intake Air Temperature (IAT) Sensor Circuit Low Voltage:** P0112 DTC P0116, P0117, P0118, or P0128 are not set. The engine is running for greater than 10 s. The engine coolant temperature (ECT) is colder than 150°C (302°F). This DTC runs continuously within the enabling conditions.

DTC	Trouble Code Title, Conditions, Possible Causes
DTC: P0112 00	**Intake Air Temperature (IAT) Sensor Circuit Low Voltage:** P0112 00 DTCs P0117 00, P0118 00 or P0501 00 are not set. The engine run time is greater than 10 s. The engine coolant temperature (ECT) sensor is less than 150°C (302°F). The vehicle speed is greater than 80 km/h (50 MPH). The DTC runs continuously once the above conditions are met.
DTC: P0112 00	**Intake Air Temperature (IAT) Sensor 1 Circuit Low Voltage:** The ignition is ON or the engine is running. The ignition voltage is greater than 8.5 V. The DTCs run continuously once the above conditions are met.
DTC: P0113	**Intake Air Temperature (IAT) Sensor Circuit High Voltage:** P0113 DTC P0101, P0102, P0103, P0116, P0117, P0118, P0128, P0502 or P0503 is not set. The engine is running for greater than 10 s. The ECT is warmer than -40°C (-40°F). This DTC runs continuously within the enabling conditions.
DTC: P0113 00	**Intake Air Temperature (IAT) Sensor Circuit High Voltage:** P0113 00 DTCs P0107 00, P0108 00, P0117 00, P0118 00 or P0501 00 are not set. The engine run time is greater than 10 s. The airflow into the engine is less than 512 g/s. The engine coolant temperature (ECT) sensor is greater than -40°C (-40°F). The vehicle speed is less than 25 km/h (40 MPH). The DTC runs continuously once the above conditions are met.
DTC: P0114	**Intake Air Temperature (IAT) Sensor Circuit Intermittent:** P0114The ignition is ON or the engine is running. This DTC runs continuously within the enabling conditions.
DTC: P0114 00	**Intake Air Temperature (IAT) Sensor Circuit Intermittent:** P0114 00 DTC P0112 00, or P0113 00 is not set. The ignition is ON, or the engine is running. The battery voltage is greater than 9 V.
DTC: P0115 03	**Engine Coolant Temperature (ECT) Sensor Circuit Low Voltage:** The ignition is ON.
DTC: P0115 07	**Engine Coolant Temperature (ECT) Sensor Circuit High Voltage:** The ignition is ON.
DTC: P0116	**Engine Coolant Temperature (ECT) Sensor Performance:** Condition 1Before the ECM can report DTC P0116 failed, DTC P0101 must run and pass. DTC P0112, P0113, P0117, P0118 or P2610 is not set. The engine run time of the previous ignition cycle was greater than 10 min. The calculated engine cool down of the previous test was greater than 50°C (120°F). The ignition was OFF for greater than 330 min after the previous engine shut down. The accumulated air mass of the previous ignition cycle was greater than 6,000 grams. The DTC runs once an ignition cycle when the above conditions are met for greater than 35 s. Condition 2Before the ECM can report DTC P0116 failed, DTC P0101 must run and pass. DTCs P0112, P0113, P0117, P0118 are not set. The ECT at the previous engine shut down is warmer than 82°C (180°F). The block heater is not detected. The ignition was OFF for greater than 330 min after the previous engine shut down. DTC runs once an ignition cycle when the above conditions are met.
DTC: P0116 00	**Engine Coolant Temperature (ECT) Sensor Performance:** DTCs P0112 00, P0113 00, P0117 00, P0118 00, and P2610 00 are not set. The ignition has been off for greater than 8 h before the engine is started. The engine is running. This DTC runs once per ignition cycle when the above conditions are met.
DTC: P0117	**Engine Coolant Temperature (ECT) Sensor Circuit Low Voltage:** P0117 DTCs P0106, P0191, P0234, P0263, P0266, P0269, P0272, P0275, P0278, P0281, P0284, P0299, P0300, P0301, P0302, P0303, P0304, P0305, P0306, P0307, P0308, P0401, P0402, P0506, P0507, P2080, P2084, P242B or P246F are not set. The ignition is ON. DTC P0117 runs continuously within the enabling condition.
DTC: P0117 00	**Engine Coolant Temperature (ECT) Sensor Circuit Low Voltage:** P0117 00 and P0118 00The ignition is ON, or the engine is running. The battery voltage is greater than 9 V. The intake air temperature (IAT) is warmer than -30°C (-22°F) or the IAT is colder than -30°C (-22°F) and the engine run time is greater than 120 s. This DTC runs continuously within the enabling conditions.
DTC: P0118	**Engine Coolant Temperature (ECT) Sensor Circuit High Voltage:** P0118 DTCs P0106, P0191, P0234, P0263, P0266, P0269, P0272, P0275, P0278, P0281, P0284, P0299, P0300, P0301, P0302, P0303, P0304, P0305, P0306, P0307, P0308, P0401, P0402, P0506, P0507, P2080, P2084, P242B or P246F are not set. The ignition is ON. DTC P0118 runs continuously within the enabling condition.
DTC: P0118 00	**Engine Coolant Temperature (ECT) Sensor Circuit High Voltage:** P0117 00 and P0118 00The ignition is ON, or the engine is running. The battery voltage is greater than 9 V. The intake air temperature (IAT) is warmer than -30°C (-22°F) or the IAT is colder than -30°C (-22°F) and the engine run time is greater than 120 s. This DTC runs continuously within the enabling conditions.
DTC: P0119	**Engine Coolant Temperature (ECT) Sensor Circuit Intermittent:** The ignition is ON. The engine speed is greater than 1 000 RPM. These DTCs run continuously once the above conditions are met.
DTC: P0119 00	**Engine Coolant Temperature (ECT) Sensor Circuit Intermittent:** P0119 00The ignition is ON, or the engine is running. The battery voltage is greater than 9 V. DTC P0117 00 or P0118 00 are not set

DTC	Trouble Code Title, Conditions, Possible Causes
DTC: P0120	**Throttle Position (TP) Sensor 1 Circuit:** P0120, P0122, P0123, P0220, P0222, and P0223 DTC P0601, P0602, P0603, P0604, P0606, P0607, P0641, or P0651 is not set. The system voltage is greater than 5. 23 V. The ignition is in the Unlock/Accessory or Run position. The DTCs run continuously when the above conditions are met.
DTC: P0121	**Throttle Position (TP) Sensor Performance:** P0121 DTCs P0102, P0103, P0107, P0108, P0112, P0113, P0117, P0118, P0116, P0128, P0122, P0123, P0220, P0221, P0222, P0223, P0335, P0336, P0401, P0405, P0601, P0602, P0603, P0604, P060D, P062F, P0606, P0652, P0653, P1404, P1516, P2101, P2119, P2135, P2176 are not set. The engine coolant temperature (ECT) is between 70-125°C (158-257°F). The engine IAT is between -7 and +100°C (+19 and +212°F). The engine speed is between 550-5,000 RPM. DTC P0121 runs continuously when the above conditions are met.
DTC: P0121 00	**Throttle Position Sensor 1 Performance:** P0121 00 DTCs P0102 00, P0103 00, P0107 00, P0108 00, P0112 00, P0113 00, P0117 00, P0118 00, P0335 00, or P0336 00 are not set. The engine speed is between 400-6 500 RPM. The engine coolant temperature (ECT) is between 70-125°C (158-257°F). The intake air temperature (IAT) is between -20 to +125°C (-4 to +257°F). The DTC runs continuously when the above conditions are met.
DTC: P0121 00	**Throttle Position Sensor 1 Performance:** DTCs P000A 00, P000B 00, P0016 00, P0017 00, P0111 00, P0112 00, P0113 00, P0114 00, P0116 00, P0117 00, P0118 00, P0119 00, P0122 00, P0123 00, P0222 00, P0223 00, P0121 00, P0221 00, P0340 00, P0341 00, P0365 00, P0366 00, P0458 00, P0459 00, P0642 00, P0643 00, P0652 00, P0653 00, P065B 00 are not set. The engine is running. DTCs P0068 00, P0642 00, P0643 00 are not set.
DTC: P0121 00	**Throttle Position Sensor Performance:** DTC P0641 00 or P0651 00 are not set. The run/crank or powertrain relay voltage is greater than 6 V and reduced power is not active. The ignition is ON or the engine is operating. DTC P0122 00, P0123 00, P0222 00, P0223 00, and P2135 00 run continuously when the above conditions are met.
DTC: P0122	**Throttle Position (TP) Sensor 1 Circuit Low Voltage:** P0120, P0122, P0123, P0220, P0222, or P0223 DTCs P0601, P0602, P0603, P0604, P0606, P060D, P062F, P0641, P0651 are not set. The system voltage is greater than 5. 23 V. The ignition is in the Unlock/Accessory or Run position. The DTCs run continuously when the above conditions are met.
DTC: P0122 00	**Throttle Position Sensor 1 Circuit Low Voltage:** DTC P0641 00 or P0651 00 are not set. The run/crank or powertrain relay voltage is greater than 6 V and reduced power is not active. The ignition is ON or the engine is operating. DTC P0122 00, P0123 00, P0222 00, P0223 00, and P2135 00 run continuously when the above conditions are met.
DTC: P0122 00	**Throttle Position Sensor 1 Circuit Low Voltage:** P0122 00, P0123 00, P0222 00, P0223 00The system voltage is more than 6 V. The ignition is in the unlock/accessory or run position. DTC P0641 00 or P06A3 00 are not set. DTCs P0122 00, P0123 00, P0222 00, P0223 00 run continuously when the above conditions are met.
DTC: P0123	**Throttle Position (TP) Sensor 1 Circuit High Voltage:** P0120, P0122, P0123, P0220, P0222, and P0223 DTC P0641 or P0651 are not set. The run/crank or powertrain relay voltage is greater than 6 V and reduced power is not active. The ignition is ON or the engine is running. DTC P0120, P0122, P0123, P0220, P0222, P0223 run continuously when the above conditions are met.
DTC: P0123 00	**Throttle Position Sensor 1 Circuit High Voltage:** P0122 00, P0123 00, P0222 00, P0223 00The system voltage is more than 6 V. The ignition is in the unlock/accessory or run position. DTC P0641 00 or P06A3 00 are not set. DTCs P0122 00, P0123 00, P0222 00, P0223 00 run continuously when the above conditions are met.
DTC: P0128	**Engine Coolant Temperature (ECT) Below Thermostat Regulating Temperature:** DTCs P0068, P0101, P0102, P0103, P0106, P0107, P0108, P0111, P0112, P0113, P0116, P0117, P0118, P0121, P0122, P0123, P0223, P0502, P0503, P1516, P2101, P2135 are not set. The start-up IAT is warmer than -7°C (+19°F). The start-up ECT is colder than 70°C (158°F), when the IAT is above 10°C (50°F). OR The start-up ECT is colder than 50°C (122°F), when the IAT is below 10°C (50°F). The engine run time is between 90 s and 22 min. The vehicle has traveled greater than 2. 4 kilometers (1. 5 miles) at greater than 8 km/h (5 mph). The accumulated airflow is between 20-75 g/s, with the minimum average airflow greater than 10 g/s. The fuel ethanol percentage is less than 87 %. This DTC runs once per ignition cycle when the above conditions are met.
DTC: P0128 00	**Engine Coolant Temperature (ECT) Below Thermostat Regulating Temperature:** DTC P0102 00, P0103 00, P0111 00, P0112 00, P0113 00, P0114 00, P0116 00, P0117 00, P0118 00, P0119 00, P0121 00, P0122 00, P0123 00, P0221 00, P0222 00, P0223 00, P0335 00, P0336 00, or P0501 00 are not set. The ignition voltage is greater than 10 V. The startup ECT is between -10 to +75°C (+14 to +167°F). The startup IAT is warmer than -10°C (+14°F). The engine run time at minimum load is less than 50%. The engine run time at maximum load is less than 90%. The engine idle time is less than 40%.

DTC	Trouble Code Title, Conditions, Possible Causes
DTC: P0130	**HO2S Circuit Closed Loop (CL) Performance Sensor 1:** P0130The engine is running. The Ignition 1 Signal parameter is between 11-18 volts. DTC P0130 runs continuously when the above conditions are met.
DTC: P0131	**HO2S Circuit Low Voltage Sensor 1:** P0131 and P0137 DTCs P0068, P0101, P0102, P0103, P0107, P0108, P0112, P0113, P0116, P0117, P0118, P0120, P0121, P0122, P0123, P0128, P0201, P0202, P0203, P0204, P0205, P0206, P0220, P0222, P0223, P0442, P0443, P0446, P0449, P0451, P0452, P0453, P0454, P0455, P0496, P1516, P2101, P2119, P2135, P2176 are not set. The system voltage is between 10-18V. The scan tool special functions are not active. The Air Fuel Ratio parameter is between 0. 9-1. 1. The TP Indicated Angle parameter is between 3-45 percent. The Loop Status parameter is closed. The ECT parameter is less than 131°C (268°F). All fuel injectors are ON. The traction control is not active.
DTC: P0131 00	**HO2S Circuit Low Voltage Sensor 1:** DTCs P0031 00, P0032 00, P0037 00, P0038 00, P0106 00, P0107 00, P0108 00, P0112 00, P0113 00, P0117 00, P0118 00, P0122 00, P0123 00, P0135 00, P0141 00, P0171 00, P0172 00, P0261 00, P0262 00, P0264 00, P0265 00, P0267 00, P0268 00, P0260 00, P0271 00, P0300 00, P0335 00, P0336 00, P0351 00, P0352 00, P0401 00, P0402 00, P0404 00, P0405 00, P0406 00, P0458 00, P0459 00, P0502 00,P0506 00, P0507 00, P0562 00, P0563 00, or P2110 00 are not set. The engine has been operating for greater than 60 s. The calculated airflow into the engine is greater than 9 g/s. The engine coolant temperature is greater than 60°C (140°F). The ignition voltage is between 11-18 V. The fuel system is in closed loop. The vehicle is not decelerating. These DTCs run continuously when the above conditions are met for 3 s.
DTC: P0132	**HO2S Circuit High Voltage Sensor 1:** P0132 DTCs P0068, P0101, P0102, P0103, P0106, P0107, P0108, P0120, P0121, P0122, P0123, P0201, P0202, P0203, P0204, P0220, P0222, P0223, P0442, P0443, P0446, P0449, P0451, P0452, P0453, P0454, P0455, P0496, P1516, P2101, P2119, P2135, P2176 are not set. The Loop Status parameter is Closed. The Ignition 1 Signal parameter is between 10-18V. The Fuel Level Sensor parameter is more than 10 percent. The Throttle Position (TP) Sensor parameter is between 0-50 percent. DTC P0132 runs continuously when the above conditions are met for 5 seconds.
DTC: P0132 00	**HO2S Circuit High Voltage Sensor 1:** DTCs P0031 00, P0032 00, P0037 00, P0038 00, P0106 00, P0107 00, P0108 00, P0112 00, P0113 00, P0117 00, P0118 00, P0122 00, P0123 00, P0135 00, P0141 00, P0171 00, P0172 00, P0261 00, P0262 00, P0264 00, P0265 00, P0267 00, P0268 00, P0260 00, P0271 00, P0300 00, P0335 00, P0336 00, P0351 00, P0352 00, P0401 00, P0402 00, P0404 00, P0405 00, P0406 00, P0458 00, P0459 00, P0502 00,P0506 00, P0507 00, P0562 00, P0563 00, or P2110 00 are not set. The engine has been operating for greater than 60 s. The calculated airflow into the engine is greater than 9 g/s. The engine coolant temperature is greater than 60°C (140°F). The ignition voltage is between 11-18 V. The fuel system is in closed loop. The vehicle is not decelerating. These DTCs run continuously when the above conditions are met for 3 s.
DTC: P0133	**HO2S Slow Response Sensor 1:** P0133 DTCs P0068, P0101, P0102, P0103, P0106, P0107, P0108, P0112, P0113, P0116, P0117, P0118, P0120, P0121, P0122, P0123, P0128, P0131, P0132, P0134, P0201, P0202, P0203, P0204, P0220, P0222, P0223, P0300, P0442, P0443, P0446, P0449, P0451, P0452, P0453, P0454, P0455, P0496, P1516, P2101, P2119, P2135, P2176 are not set. The Engine Coolant Temperature (ECT) Sensor parameter is more than 70°C (158°F). The Ignition 1 Signal parameter is between 10-18 volts. The Fuel Level Sensor parameter is more than 10 percent. The Engine Run Time parameter is more than 120 seconds. The Engine Speed parameter is between 1,000-3,500 RPM. The barometric pressure (BARO) is more than 70 kPa. The Mass Airflow (MAF) Sensor parameter is between 13-40 g/s. The intake air temperature is more than -40°C (-40°F). The Loop Status parameter is Closed. The Throttle Position (TP) Indicated Angle parameter is more than 4 percent. DTC P0133 runs once per drive cycle when the above conditions are met for 3 seconds.
DTC: P0133 00	**HO2S Slow Response Sensor 1:** DTCs P0106 00, P0107 00, P0108 00, P0112 00, P0113 00, P0116 00, P0117 00, P0118 00, P0121 00, P0122 00, P0123 00, P0131 00, P0132 00, P0134 00, P0201 00, P0202 00, P0203 00, P0204 00, P0300 00, P0315 00, P0335 00, P0336 00, P044 00, P0443 00, P0446 00, P0449 00, P0451 00, P0452 00, P0453 00, and P0496 00 are not set. The calculated airflow into the engine is between 10-45 g/s. The engine speed is between 1 100-3 500 RPM. The engine coolant temperature is greater than 60°C (140°F). The Barometric Pressure (BARO) is greater than 70 kPa (10 PSI). The ignition voltage is between 10-18 V. The fuel system is in closed loop. The evaporative emissions (EVAP) purge is less than 20%. The EVAP purge is not changing states. The engine run time is greater than 3 min. The fuel level is greater than 10%. The long term fuel trim is enabled. The HO2S heater is enabled for greater than 40 s. The vehicle is not decelerating. The vehicle is not operating in power enrichment. The DTCs run once per ignition cycle when the above conditions are met for greater than 1 s.
DTC: P0134	**HO2S Circuit Insufficient Activity Sensor 1:** P0134 DTCs P0030, P0053, P0068, P0101, P0102, P0103, P0107, P0108, P0112, P0113, P0116, P0117, P0118, P0120, P0121, P0122, P0123, P0128, P0201, P0202, P0203, P0204, P0205, P0206, P0220, P0222, P0223, P0442, P0443, P0446, P0449, P0451, P0452, P0453, P0454, P0455, P0496, P1516, P2101, P2119, P2135, P2176 are not set. The system voltage is between 10-18 volts. The scan tool special functions are not active. The HO2S Sensor 1 Heater command parameter is ON. The Fuel Alcohol Content parameter is less than 87 percent for 3. 9L (RPO LGD), VIN code M, E85 compatible engines only. The Engine Run Time parameter is more than 2 minutes.

DTC	Trouble Code Title, Conditions, Possible Causes
DTC: P0134 00	**HO2S Circuit Insufficient Activity Sensor 1:** DTCs P0031 00, P0032 00, P0037 00, P0038 00, P0106 00, P0107 00, P0108 00, P0112 00, P0113 00, P0117 00, P0118 00, P0122 00, P0123 00, P0135 00, P0141 00, P0171 00, P0172 00, P0261 00, P0262 00, P0264 00, P0265 00, P0267 00, P0268 00, P0260 00, P0271 00, P0300 00, P0335 00, P0336 00, P0351 00, P0352 00, P0401 00, P0402 00, P0404 00, P0405 00, P0406 00, P0458 00, P0459 00, P0502 00, P0506 00, P0507 00, P0562 00, P0563 00, or P2110 00 are not set. The engine has been operating for greater than 60 s. The calculated airflow into the engine is greater than 9 g/s. The engine coolant temperature is greater than 60°C (140°F). The ignition voltage is between 11-18 V. The fuel system is in closed loop. The vehicle is not decelerating. These DTCs run continuously when the above conditions are met for 3 s.
DTC: P0135	**HO2S Heater Performance Sensor 1:** P0135 DTCs P0030, P0053, P0068, P0101, P0102, P0103, P0106, P0107, P0108, P0112, P0113, P0116, P0117, P0118, P0120, P0121, P0122, P0123, P0128, P0135, P0141, P0201, P0202, P0203, P0204, P0205, P0206, P0220, P0222, P0223, P0442, P0443, P0446, P0449, P0451, P0452, P0453, P0454, P0455, P0496, P1516, P2101, P2135, P2176 are not set. The system voltage is between 10-18V. The scan tool special functions are not active. The Engine Run Time parameter is more than 180 seconds. The ECT Sensor parameter is at least 65°C (149°F). The MAF Sensor parameter is between 5-30 g/s. The Engine Speed parameter is between 500-3,000 RPM. The above conditions have been met for more than 6 seconds.
DTC: P0135 00	**HO2S Heater Performance Sensor 1:** P0030 00, P0031 00, and P0030 02 The ignition is ON. The ignition signal parameter is more than 9 V. DTC P0030 00, P0031 00, and P0032 00 run continuously when the above conditions are met for 1 s. P0135 00 DTCs P0030 00, P0031 00, P0032 00, are not set. The ignition is ON. The ignition signal parameter is more than 9 V. DTC P0135 00 runs continuously.
DTC: P0136 00	**HO2S Circuit Sensor 2:** P0136 00 DTC P0031 00, P0032 00, P0037 00, P0038 00, P0112 00, P0113 00, P0117 00, P0118 00, P0121 00, P0122 00, P0123 00, P0125 00, P0171 00, P0172 00, P0300 00 - P0304 00, P0335 00, P0340 00, P0341 00, P0455 00, P0456 00, P0500 00, P2A00 00 are not set. The battery voltage is greater than 11 V. The engine coolant temperature (ECT) is greater than or equal to 75°C (167°F). The engine speed is between 1600-4000 RPM. The engine is operating in closed loop fuel control. DTC P0136 00 runs once per drive cycle when the above conditions are met for 2 s.
DTC: P0137	**HO2S Circuit Low Voltage Sensor 2:** P0131 and P0137 DTCs P0068, P0101, P0102, P0103, P0107, P0108, P0112, P0113, P0116, P0117, P0118, P0120, P0121, P0122, P0123, P0128, P0201, P0202, P0203, P0204, P0205, P0206, P0220, P0222, P0223, P0442, P0443, P0446, P0449, P0451, P0452, P0453, P0454, P0455, P0496, P1516, P2101, P2119, P2135, P2176 are not set. The system voltage is between 10-18V. The scan tool special functions are not active. The Air Fuel Ratio parameter is between 0. 9-1. 1. The TP Indicated Angle parameter is between 3-45 percent. The Loop Status parameter is closed. The ECT parameter is less than 131°C (268°F). All fuel injectors are ON. The traction control is not active.
DTC: P0137 00	**HO2S Circuit Low Voltage Sensor 2:** DTCs P0031 00, P0032 00, P0037 00, P0038 00, P0106 00, P0107 00, P0108 00, P0112 00, P0113 00, P0117 00, P0118 00, P0122 00, P0123 00, P0135 00, P0141 00, P0171 00, P0172 00, P0261 00, P0262 00, P0264 00, P0265 00, P0267 00, P0268 00, P0260 00, P0271 00, P0300 00, P0335 00, P0336 00, P0351 00, P0352 00, P0401 00, P0402 00, P0404 00, P0405 00, P0406 00, P0458 00, P0459 00, P0502 00, P0506 00, P0507 00, P0562 00, P0563 00, or P2110 00 are not set. The engine has been operating for greater than 60 s. The calculated airflow into the engine is greater than 2 g/s. The engine coolant temperature is greater than 60°C (140°F). The ignition voltage is between 11-18 V. The fuel system is in closed loop. The vehicle is not decelerating. These DTCs run continuously when the above conditions are met for 3 s.
DTC: P0138	**HO2S Circuit High Voltage Bank 1 Sensor 2:** P0132, P0138, P0152, or P0158 DTCs P0068, P0101, P0102, P0103, P0106, P0107, P0108, P0112, P0113, P0116, P0117, P0118, P0120, P0121, P0122, P0123, P0128, P0201, P0202, P0203, P0204, P0205, P0206, P0207, P0208, P0220, P0222, P0223, P0442, P0443, P0446, P0449, P0455, P0496, P1516, P2101, P2119, P2135, P2176 are not set. The engine is operating in Closed Loop. The Ignition 1 voltage is between 10-32 V. The fuel level is greater than 10 %. The throttle position (TP) is between 0-70 %. The DTCs run continuously when the above conditions are met for 3 s.
DTC: P0138 00	**HO2S Circuit High Voltage Sensor 2:** DTCs P0031 00, P0032 00, P0037 00, P0038 00, P0106 00, P0107 00, P0108 00, P0112 00, P0113 00, P0117 00, P0118 00, P0122 00, P0123 00, P0135 00, P0141 00, P0171 00, P0172 00, P0261 00, P0262 00, P0264 00, P0265 00, P0267 00, P0268 00, P0260 00, P0271 00, P0300 00, P0335 00, P0336 00, P0351 00, P0352 00, P0401 00, P0402 00, P0404 00, P0405 00, P0406 00, P0458 00, P0459 00, P0502 00, P0506 00, P0507 00, P0562 00, P0563 00, or P2110 00 are not set. The engine has been operating for greater than 60 s. The calculated airflow into the engine is greater than 2 g/s. The engine coolant temperature is greater than 60°C (140°F). The ignition voltage is between 11-18 V. The fuel system is in closed loop. The vehicle is not decelerating. These DTCs run continuously when the above conditions are met for 3 s.

DTC	Trouble Code Title, Conditions, Possible Causes
DTC: P0139 00	**HO2S Slow Response Sensor 2:** P0139 00 DTCs P000A 00, P000B 00, P0010 00, P0011 00, P0013 00, P0014 00, P0016 00, P0017 00, P0107 00, P0108 00, P0117 00, P0118 00, P0119 00, P0121 00, P0122 00, P0123 00, P0136 00, P0137 00, P0138 00, P0141 00, P0171 00, P0172 00, P0201 00, P0202 00, P0203 00, P0204 00, P0221 00, P0222 00, P0223 00, P0261 00, P0262 00, P0264 00, P0265 00, P0267 00, P0268 00, P0270 00, P0271 00, P0300 00, P030 001, P0302 00, P0303 00, P0304 00, P0313 00, P0335 00, P0336 00, P0340 00, P0341 00, P0365 00, P0366 00, P0443 00, P0458 00, P0459 00, P0496 00, P0501 00, P2088 00, P2089 00, P2090 00, P2091 00, P2100 00, P2101 00, P2176 00, P2270 00, P2271 00, P2A01 00 are not set. The ignition is ON. The engine coolant is hotter than 60°C (140°F). The heated oxygen sensor (HO2S) 2 signal voltage is more than 552 mV. The vehicle speed is between 19-31 km/h (12-93 MPH). DTC P0140 00 runs continuously when the above conditions are met for 60 min.
DTC: P013A	**HO2S Slow Response Rich to Lean Bank 1 Sensor 2:** P013A P013C, P013E, or P014ABefore the ECM can report DTC P013A, or P013C failed, DTCs P013E, P014A, P2270, and P2272 must run and pass. Before the ECM can report DTC P013E, or P014A failed, DTCs P2270 and P2272 must run and pass. DTCs P0030, P0036, P0053, P0054, P0101, P0102, P0103, P0106, P0107, P0108, P0120, P0121, P0122, P0123, P0131, P0132, P0133, P0134, P0135, P0137, P0138, P013A, P013B, P013E, P013F, P0140, P0141, P0171, P0172, P0201, P0202, P0203, P0204, P0220, P0222, P0223, P0300, P0442, P0443, P0446, P0449, P0455, P0496, P1133, P1174, P1516, P2101, P2119, P2135, P2176, P2270, P2271, P2A00 are not set. The ignition 1 voltage is between 10-32 V. The learned heater resistance is valid. The fuel level is greater than 10%. The engine run time is equal to or greater than 5 minutes. The accelerator pedal (APP) is steady. The torque converter clutch (TCC) is applied. The DTCs run once per ignition cycle, during decel fuel cut-off (DFCO), when the above conditions are met.
DTC: P013A 00	**HO2S Slow Response Rich to Lean Sensor 2:** P013A 00 DTCs P0030 00, P0036 00, P0053 00, P0054 00, P0101 00, P0102 00, P0103 00, P0106 00, P0107 00, P0108 00, P0120 00, P0121 00, P0122 00, P0123 00, P0131 00, P0132 00, P0133 00, P0134 00, P0135 00, P0137 00, P0138 00, P013A 00, P013B 00, P013E 00, P013F 00, P0140 00, P0141 00, P0171 00, P0172 00, P0201 00, P0202 00, P0203 00, P0204 00, P0220 00, P0222 00, P0223 00, P0300 00, P0443 00, P1133 00, P1516 00, P2101 00, P2119 00, P2135 00, P2176 00, P2270 00, P2271 00, P2A00 00 are not set. The system voltage is between 10-18 V. The fuel level is more than 10%. Engine run time is equal to or more than 40 s. The engine coolant is hotter than 50. 25°C (122. 45°F). The Deceleration fuel cut-off is active. The accelerator pedal position (APP) is stable. The torque converter clutch (TCC) is locked. DTC P013E 00 and P2270 00 have run and passed. DTC P013A 00 runs once per trip.
DTC: P013B	**HO2S Slow Response Lean to Rich Bank 1 Sensor 2:** P013B P013D, P013F, or P014BBefore the ECM can report DTC P013B, or P013D failed, DTCs P013A, P013C, P013E, P013F, P014A, P014B, P2270, P2271, P2272, and P2273 must run and pass. Before the ECM can report DTC P013F, or P014B failed, DTCs P013A, P013C, P013E, P014A, P2270, P2271, P2272, and P2273 must run and pass. DTCs P0030, P0036, P0053, P0054, P0101, P0102, P0103, P0106, P0107, P0108, P0120, P0121, P0122, P0123, P0131, P0132, P0133, P0134, P0135, P0137, P0138, P013A, P013B, P013E, P013F, P0140, P0141, P0171, P0172, P0201, P0202, P0203, P0204, P0220, P0222, P0223, P0300, P0442, P0443, P0446, P0449, P0455, P0496, P1133, P1174, P1516, P2101, P2119, P2135, P2176, P2270, P2271, P2A00 are not set. The ignition 1 voltage is between 10-32 V. The learned heater resistance is valid. The fuel level is greater than 10 %. The engine run time is equal to or greater than 5 min. The DTCs run once per ignition cycle when the above conditions are met.
DTC: P013B 00	**HO2S Slow Response Lean to Rich Sensor 2:** P013B 00 and P013F 00 DTCs P0068 00, P0101 00, P0102 00, P0103 00, P0106 00, P0107 00, P0108 00, P0112 00, P0113 00, P0116 00, P0117 00, P0118 00, P0121 00, P0122 00, P0123 00, P0128 00, P013B 00, P013E 00, P013F 00, P0171 00, P0172 00, P0201 00, P0202 00, P0203 00, P0204 00, P0222 00, P0223 00, P0300 00, P1516 00, P2101 00, P2119 00, P2135 00, P2176 00, P2270 00, P2271 00 are not set. The system voltage is between 10-32 V. The fuel level is more than 10%. Engine run time is equal to or more than 40 s. DTCs P013A 00, P013E 00, P013F 00, P2270 00, and P2271 00 have run and passed. DTCs P013B 00 and P013F 00 run once per trip.
DTC: P013C	**HO2S Slow Response Rich to Lean Bank 2 Sensor 2:** P013A P013C, P013E, or P014ABefore the ECM can report DTC P013A, or P013C failed, DTCs P013E, P014A, P2270, and P2272 must run and pass. Before the ECM can report DTC P013E, or P014A failed, DTCs P2270 and P2272 must run and pass. DTCs P0030, P0036, P0053, P0054, P0101, P0102, P0103, P0106, P0107, P0108, P0120, P0121, P0122, P0123, P0131, P0132, P0133, P0134, P0135, P0137, P0138, P013A, P013B, P013E, P013F, P0140, P0141, P0171, P0172, P0201, P0202, P0203, P0204, P0220, P0222, P0223, P0300, P0442, P0443, P0446, P0449, P0455, P0496, P1133, P1174, P1516, P2101, P2119, P2135, P2176, P2270, P2271, P2A00 are not set. The ignition 1 voltage is between 10-32 V. The learned heater resistance is valid. The fuel level is greater than 10%. The engine run time is equal to or greater than 5 minutes. The accelerator pedal (APP) is steady. The torque converter clutch (TCC) is applied. The DTCs run once per ignition cycle, during decel fuel cut-off (DFCO), when the above conditions are met.
DTC: P013D	**HO2S Slow Response Lean to Rich Bank 2 Sensor 2:** P013B P013D, P013F, or P014BBefore the ECM can report DTC P013B, or P013D failed, DTCs P013A, P013C, P013E, P013F, P014A, P014B, P2270, P2271, P2272, and P2273 must run and pass. Before the ECM can report DTC P013F, or P014B failed, DTCs P013A, P013C, P013E, P014A, P2270, P2271, P2272, and P2273 must run and pass. DTCs P0030, P0036, P0053, P0054, P0101, P0102, P0103, P0106, P0107, P0108, P0120, P0121, P0122, P0123, P0131, P0132, P0133, P0134, P0135, P0137, P0138, P013A, P013B, P013E, P013F, P0140, P0141, P0171, P0172, P0201, P0202, P0203, P0204, P0220, P0222, P0223, P0300, P0442, P0443, P0446, P0449, P0455, P0496, P1133, P1174, P1516, P2101, P2119, P2135, P2176, P2270, P2271, P2A00 are not set. The ignition 1 voltage is between 10-32 V. The learned heater resistance is valid. The fuel level is greater than 10%. The engine run time is equal to or greater than 5 minutes. The DTCs run once per ignition cycle when the above conditions are met.

DTC	Trouble Code Title, Conditions, Possible Causes
DTC: P013E	**HO2S Delayed Response Rich to Lean Bank 1 Sensor 2:** P013A P013C, P013E, or P014ABefore the ECM can report DTC P013A, or P013C failed, DTCs P013E, P014A, P2270, and P2272 must run and pass. Before the ECM can report DTC P013E, or P014A failed, DTCs P2270 and P2272 must run and pass. DTCs P0030, P0036, P0053, P0054, P0101, P0102, P0103, P0106, P0107, P0108, P0120, P0121, P0122, P0123, P0131, P0132, P0133, P0134, P0135, P0137, P0138, P013A, P013B, P013E, P013F, P0140, P0141, P0171, P0172, P0201, P0202, P0203, P0204, P0220, P0222, P0223, P0300, P0442, P0443, P0446, P0449, P0455, P0496, P1133, P1174, P1516, P2101, P2119, P2135, P2176, P2270, P2271, P2A00 are not set. The ignition 1 voltage is between 10-32 V. The learned heater resistance is valid. The fuel level is greater than 10 %. The engine run time is equal to or greater than 5 min. The accelerator pedal (APP) is steady. The torque converter clutch (TCC) is applied. The DTCs run once per ignition cycle, during decel fuel cut-off (DFCO), when the above conditions are met.
DTC: P013E 00	**HO2S Delayed Response Rich to Lean Sensor 2:** P013E 00 DTCs P0030 00, P0036 00, P0053 00, P0054 00, P0101 00, P0102 00, P0103 00, P0106 00, P0107 00, P0108 00, P0120 00, P0121 00, P0122 00, P0123 00, P0131 00, P0132 00, P0133 00, P0134 00, P0135 00, P0137 00, P0138 00, P013A 00, P013B 00, P013E 00, P013F 00, P0140 00, P0141 00, P0171 00, P0172 00, P0201 00, P0202 00, P0203 00, P0204 00, P0220 00, P0222 00, P0223 00, P0300 00, P0443 00, P1133 00, P1516 00, P2101 00, P2119 00, P2135 00, P2176 00, P2270 00, P2271 00, P2A00 00 are not set. The system voltage is between 10-18 V. The fuel level is more than 10%. Engine run time is equal to or more than 40 s. The engine coolant is hotter than 50. 25°C (122. 45°F). The Deceleration fuel cut-off is active. The accelerator pedal position (APP) is stable. The torque converter clutch (TCC) is locked. DTCs P2270 00 has run and passed. DTC P013E 00 runs once per trip.
DTC: P013F	**HO2S Delayed Response Lean to Rich Bank 1 Sensor 2:** P013B P013D, P013F, or P014BBefore the ECM can report DTC P013B, or P013D failed, DTCs P013A, P013C, P013E, P013F, P014A, P014B, P2270, P2271, P2272, and P2273 must run and pass. Before the ECM can report DTC P013F, or P014B failed, DTCs P013A, P013C, P013E, P014A, P2270, P2271, P2272, and P2273 must run and pass. DTCs P0030, P0036, P0053, P0054, P0101, P0102, P0103, P0106, P0107, P0108, P0120, P0121, P0122, P0123, P0131, P0132, P0133, P0134, P0135, P0137, P0138, P013A, P013B, P013E, P013F, P0140, P0141, P0171, P0172, P0201, P0202, P0203, P0204, P0220, P0222, P0223, P0300, P0442, P0443, P0446, P0449, P0455, P0496, P1133, P1174, P1516, P2101, P2119, P2135, P2176, P2270, P2271, P2A00 are not set. The ignition 1 voltage is between 10-32 V. The learned heater resistance is valid. The fuel level is greater than 10 %. The engine run time is equal to or greater than 5 min. The DTCs run once per ignition cycle when the above conditions are met.
DTC: P013F 00	**HO2S Delayed Response Lean to Rich Sensor 2:** P013F 00 DTCs P0030 00, P0036 00, P0053 00, P0054 00, P0101 00, P0102 00, P0103 00, P0106 00, P0107 00, P0108 00, P0120 00, P0121 00, P0122 00, P0123 00, P0131 00, P0132 00, P0133 00, P0134 00, P0135 00, P0137 00, P0138 00, P013A 00, P013B 00, P013E 00, P013F 00, P0140 00, P0141 00, P0171 00, P0172 00, P0201 00, P0202 00, P0203 00, P0204 00, P0220 00, P0222 00, P0223 00, P0300 00, P0443 00, P1133 00, P1516 00, P2101 00, P2119 00, P2135 00, P2176 00, P2270 00, P2271 00, P2A00 00 are not set. The system voltage is between 10-18 V. The fuel level is more than 10%. Engine run time is equal to or more than 40 s. The DTCs P013A 00, P013E 00, P2270 00, and P2271 00 have run and passed. DTC P013F 00 runs once per trip.
DTC: P0140	**HO2S Circuit Insufficient Activity Bank 1 Sensor 2:** DTCs P0068, P0101, P0102, P0103, P0106, P0107, P0108, P0112, P0113, P0116, P0117, P0118, P0120, P0121, P0122, P0123, P0128, P0201, P0202, P0203, P0204, P0205, P0206, P0207, P0208, P0220, P0222, P0223, P0442, P0443, P0446, P0449, P0455, P0496, P1516, P2101, P2119, P2135, P2176 are not set. The ignition 1 voltage is between 10-32 V. The engine run time is greater than 300 s. The fuel system is in Closed Loop. The DTCs run continuously when the above conditions are met.
DTC: P0140	**HO2S Circuit Insufficient Activity Sensor 2:** P0140 DTCs P0068, P0101, P0102, P0103, P0120, P0121, P0122, P0123, P0220, P0222, P0223, P1516, P2101, P2119, P2135, P2176 are not set. The ECT Sensor parameter is more than 70°C (158°F). The Ignition 1 Signal parameter is between 10-18 volts. The Engine Run Time parameter is more than 200 seconds. The Loop Status parameter is closed. DTC P0140 runs once per drive cycle when the above conditions are met.
DTC: P0140	**HO2S Circuit Insufficient Activity Sensor 2:** P0140 - Regular Test DTCs P0036, P0054, P0068, P0101, P0102, P0103, P0107, P0108, P0112, P0113, P0116, P0117, P0118, P0120, P0121, P0122, P0123, P0128, P0201, P0202, P0203, P0204, P0205, P0206, P0220, P0222, P0223, P0442, P0443, P0446, P0449, P0451, P0452, P0453, P0454, P0455, P0496, P1516, P2101, P2119, P2135, P2176 are not set. The system voltage is between 10-18 volts. The scan tool special functions are not active. The Engine Run Time parameter is more than 2 minutes. The TP Indicated Angle parameter has changed more than 3 percent at least 1 time. The Fuel Alcohol Content parameter is more than 87 percent for 3. 9L (RPO LGD), VIN code M, E85 compatible engines only. The Loop Status parameter is closed. P0140 - Fast Pass Test DTCs P0036, P0054, P0068, P0101, P0102, P0103, P0107, P0108, P0112, P0113, P0116, P0117, P0118, P0120, P0121, P0122, P0123, P0128, P0201, P0202, P0203, P0204, P0205, P0206, P0220, P0222, P0223, P0442, P0443, P0446, P0449, P0451, P0452, P0453, P0454, P0455, P0496, P1516, P2101, P2119, P2135, P2176 are not set. The system voltage is between 10-18 volts. The Fuel Alcohol Content parameter is more than 87 percent for 3. 9L (RPO LGD), VIN code M, E85 compatible engines only. The scan tool special functions are not active. The Engine Run Time parameter is less than 90 seconds.

DTC	Trouble Code Title, Conditions, Possible Causes
DTC: P0140 00	**HO2S Circuit Insufficient Activity Sensor 2:** DTCs P0031 00, P0032 00, P0037 00, P0038 00, P0106 00, P0107 00, P0108 00, P0112 00, P0113 00, P0117 00, P0118 00, P0122 00, P0123 00, P0135 00, P0141 00, P0171 00, P0172 00, P0261 00, P0262 00, P0264 00, P0265 00, P0267 00, P0268 00, P0260 00, P0271 00, P0300 00, P0335 00, P0336 00, P0351 00, P0352 00, P0401 00, P0402 00, P0404 00, P0405 00, P0406 00, P0458 00, P0459 00, P0502 00, P0506 00, P0507 00, P0562 00, P0563 00, or P2110 00 are not set. The engine has been operating for greater than 60 s. The calculated airflow into the engine is greater than 2 g/s. The engine coolant temperature is greater than 60°C (140°F). The ignition voltage is between 11-18 V. The fuel system is in closed loop. The vehicle is not decelerating. These DTCs run continuously when the above conditions are met for 3 s.
DTC: P0140 00	**HO2S Circuit Insufficient Activity Sensor 2:** P0140 00 DTCs P000A 00, P000B 00, P0010 00, P0011 00, P0013 00, P0014 00, P0016 00, P0017 00, P0030 00, P0031 00, P0032 00, P0107 00, P0108 00, P0117 00, P0118 00, P0119 00, P0121 00, P0122 00, P0123 00, P0130 00, P0131 00, P0132 00, P0133 00, P0137 00, P0138 00, P0139 00, P0141 00, P0171 00, P0172 00, P0221 00, P0222 00, P0223 00, P0300 00, P0301 00, P0302 00, P0303 00, P0304 00, P0313 00, P0335 00, P0336 00, P0340 00, P0341 00, P0365 00, P0366 00, P0443 00, P0458 00, P0459 00, P0496 00, P2088 00, P2089 00, P2090 00, P2091 00, P2176 00, P2270 00, P2271 00, P2297 00, P2A01 00 are not set. The engine has been running for more than 5 min. The engine coolant is greater than 75°C (167°F). The engine run time parameter is less than 90 s.
DTC: P0141	**HO2S Heater Performance Sensor 2:** P0141 DTCs P0036, P0054, P0068, P0101, P0102, P0103, P0107, P0108, P0112, P0113, P0116, P0117, P0118, P0120, P0121, P0122, P0123, P0128, P0201, P0202, P0203, P0204, P0205, P0206, P0220, P0222, P0223, P0442, P0443, P0446, P0449, P0451, P0452, P0453, P0454, P0455, P0496, P1516, P2101, P2135, P2176 are not set. The system voltage is between 10-18V. The scan tool special functions are not active. The Engine Run Time parameter is at least 180 seconds. The ECT parameter is at least 65°C (149°F). The MAF Sensor parameter is between 5-30 g/s. The Engine Speed parameter is between 500-3,000 RPM. The above conditions have been met for more than 6 seconds.
DTC: P0141	**HO2S Heater Performance Bank 1 Sensor 2:** P0135, P0141, or P0155 DTCs P0068, P0101, P0102, P0103, P0106, P0107, P0108, P0112, P0113, P0116, P0117, P0118, P0120, P0121, P0122, P0123, P0125, P0128, P0201, P0202, P0203, P0204, P0220, P0222, P0223, P0442, P0443, P0446, P0449, P0455, P0496, P1101, P1516, P2101, P2119, P2135, P2176 are not set. The engine coolant temperature (ECT) is greater than 60°C (140°F). The ignition 1 voltage is between 10-18 volts. The mass air flow (MAF) is between 5-45 g/s. The engine run time is greater than 180 seconds. The engine speed is between 500-3,000 RPM. The DTCs run twice per drive cycle when the above conditions are met for 2 seconds.
DTC: P0141 00	**HO2S Heater Performance Sensor 2:** P0141 00 Heater Resistance Test DTCs P0036 00, P0037 00, or P0038 00, are not set. The ignition is ON. The Ignition Signal parameter is more than 9 V. DTC P0141 00 runs continuously.
DTC: P0141 00	**HO2S Heater Performance Sensor 2:** P0141 00 DTCs P0037 00, or P0038 00, are not set. The engine is running. The ignition voltage is between 11-18 V. The engine is not in deceleration fuel cut-off. DTC P0141 00 runs continuously.
DTC: P014A	**HO2S Delayed Response Rich to Lean Bank 2 Sensor 2:** P014A DTCs P0030, P0036, P0053, P0054, P0101, P0102, P0103, P0106, P0107, P0108, P0120, P0121, P0122, P0123, P0131, P0132, P0133, P0134, P0135, P0137, P0138, P013A, P013B, P013E, P013F, P0140, P0141, P0171, P0172, P0201, P0202, P0203, P0204, P0220, P0222, P0223, P0300, P0442, P0443, P0446, P0449, P0455, P0496, P1133, P1174, P1516, P2101, P2119, P2135, P2176, P2270, P2271, P2A00, P2A03 are not set. The system voltage is between 10-18 volts. The learned heater resistance is valid. The fuel level is more than 10 percent. The engine run time is equal to or more than 5 minutes. THENDFCO is active. The accelerator pedal position (APP) is stable. The torque converter clutch (TCC) is locked. DTCs P2270 and P2272 have run and passed. This DTC runs once per trip.
DTC: P014B	**HO2S Delayed Response Lean to Rich Bank 2 Sensor 2:** P013B P013D, P013F, or P014BBefore the ECM can report DTC P013B, or P013D failed, DTCs P013A, P013C, P013E, P013F, P014A, P014B, P2270, P2271, P2272, and P2273 must run and pass. Before the ECM can report DTC P013F, or P014B failed, DTCs P013A, P013C, P013E, P014A, P2270, P2271, P2272, and P2273 must run and pass. DTCs P0030, P0036, P0053, P0054, P0101, P0102, P0103, P0106, P0107, P0108, P0120, P0121, P0122, P0123, P0131, P0132, P0133, P0134, P0135, P0137, P0138, P013A, P013B, P013E, P013F, P0140, P0141, P0171, P0172, P0201, P0202, P0203, P0204, P0220, P0222, P0223, P0300, P0442, P0443, P0446, P0449, P0455, P0496, P1133, P1174, P1516, P2101, P2119, P2135, P2176, P2270, P2271, P2A00 are not set. The ignition 1 voltage is between 10-32 V. The learned heater resistance is valid. The fuel level is greater than 10 %. The engine run time is equal to or greater than 5 min. The DTCs run once per ignition cycle when the above conditions are met.
DTC: P0151	**HO2S Circuit Low Voltage Bank 2 Sensor 1:** P0131, P0137, P0151, or P0157 DTCs P0068, P0101, P0102, P0103, P0106, P0107, P0108, P0112, P0113, P0116, P0117, P0118, P0120, P0121, P0122, P0123, P0128, P0201, P0202, P0203, P0204, P0205, P0206, P0207, P0208, P0220, P0222, P0223, P0442, P0443, P0446, P0449, P0455, P0496, P1516, P2101, P2119, P2135, P2176 are not set. The engine is operating in Closed Loop. The Ignition 1 voltage is between 10-32 V. The fuel level is greater than 10 %. The throttle position (TP) is between 3-70 %. The DTCs run continuously when the above conditions are met for 2 s.

DTC	Trouble Code Title, Conditions, Possible Causes
DTC: P0152	**HO2S Circuit High Voltage Bank 2 Sensor 1:** P0152 DTCs P0068, P0101, P0102, P0103, P0106, P0107, P0108, P0112, P0113, P0116, P0117, P0118, P0120, P0121, P0122, P0123, P0128, P0201, P0202, P0203, P0204, P0205, P0206, P0207, P0208, P0220, P0222, P0223, P0442, P0443, P0446, P0449, P0455, P0496, P1516, P2101, P2119, P2135, P2176 are not set. The Loop Status parameter is Closed. The Ignition 1 Signal parameter is between 10-18 volts. The Fuel Level Sensor parameter is more than 10 percent. The Throttle Position (TP) Sensor parameter is between 0-70 percent. DTC P0152 runs continuously when the above conditions are met.
DTC: P0153	**HO2S Slow Response Bank 2 Sensor 1:** P0133, P0153, P1133, or P1153 DTCs P0068, P0101, P0102, P0103, P0106, P0107, P0108, P0112, P0113, P0116, P0117, P0118, P0120, P0121, P0122, P0123, P0128, P0201, P0202, P0203, P0204, P0205, P0206, P0207, P0208, P0220, P0222, P0223, P0442, P0443, P0446, P0449, P0455, P0496, P1516, P2101, P2119, P2135, P2176 are not set. The engine coolant temperature (ECT) is greater than 71°C (159°F). The intake air temperature (IAT) is warmer than -40°C (-40°F)The ignition 1 voltage is between 10-32 V. The fuel level is greater than 10 %. The engine run time is greater than 60 s. The engine speed is between 1,000-3,000 RPM. The barometric (BARO) pressure is greater than 70 kPa. The mass airflow (MAF) is between 15-55 g/s. The fuel system is in Closed Loop. The throttle position (TP) is greater than 5 %. The DTCs run once per drive cycle when the above conditions are met.
DTC: P0153	**HO2S Slow Response Bank 2 Sensor 1:** P0153 DTCs P0068, P0101, P0102, P0103, P0106, P0107, P0108, P0112, P0113, P0116, P0117, P0118, P0120, P0121, P0122, P0123, P0128, P0201, P0202, P0203, P0204, P0205, P0206, P0207, P0208, P0220, P0222, P0223, P0442, P0443, P0446, P0449, P0455, P0496, P1516, P2101, P2119, P2135, P2176 are not set. The Engine Coolant Temperature (ECT) Sensor parameter is more than 60°C (140°F). The Intake Air Temperature (IAT) Sensor parameter is more than -40°C (-40°F). The Ignition 1 Signal parameter is between 10-18 volts. The Fuel Level Sensor parameter is more than 10 percent. The Engine Run Time parameter is more than 160 seconds. The Engine Speed parameter is between 1,200-3,000 RPM. The Barometric (BARO) Pressure parameter is more than 70 kPa. The Mass Airflow (MAF) Sensor parameter is between 20-55 g/s. The Loop Status parameter is Closed. The Throttle Position (TP) Indicated Angle parameter is more than 5 percent. DTC P0153 runs once per drive cycle when the above conditions are met for 1 second.
DTC: P0154	**HO2S Circuit Insufficient Activity Bank 2 Sensor 1:** DTCs P0068, P0101, P0102, P0103, P0106, P0107, P0108, P0112, P0113, P0116, P0117, P0118, P0120, P0121, P0122, P0123, P0128, P0201, P0202, P0203, P0204, P0205, P0206, P0207, P0208, P0220, P0222, P0223, P0442, P0443, P0446, P0449, P0455, P0496, P1516, P2101, P2119, P2135, or P2176 are not set. The ignition 1 voltage is between 10-18 volts. The engine run time is greater than 101 seconds. The fuel system is in Closed Loop. The DTCs run continuously when the above conditions are met.
DTC: P0155	**HO2S Heater Performance Bank 2 Sensor 1:** P0135, P0141, or P0155 DTCs P0068, P0101, P0102, P0103, P0106, P0107, P0108, P0112, P0113, P0116, P0117, P0118, P0120, P0121, P0122, P0123, P0125, P0128, P0201, P0202, P0203, P0204, P0220, P0222, P0223, P0442, P0443, P0446, P0449, P0455, P0496, P1101, P1516, P2101, P2119, P2135, P2176 are not set. The engine coolant temperature (ECT) is greater than 60°C (140°F). The ignition 1 voltage is between 10-18 volts. The mass air flow (MAF) is between 5-45 g/s. The engine run time is greater than 180 seconds. The engine speed is between 500-3,000 RPM. The DTCs run twice per drive cycle when the above conditions are met for 2 seconds.
DTC: P0157	**HO2S Circuit Low Voltage Bank 2 Sensor 2:** P0131, P0137, P0151, or P0157 DTCs P0068, P0101, P0102, P0103, P0106, P0107, P0108, P0112, P0113, P0116, P0117, P0118, P0120, P0121, P0122, P0123, P0128, P0201, P0202, P0203, P0204, P0205, P0206, P0207, P0208, P0220, P0222, P0223, P0442, P0443, P0446, P0449, P0455, P0496, P1516, P2101, P2119, P2135, P2176 are not set. The engine is operating in Closed Loop. The Ignition 1 voltage is between 10-32 V. The fuel level is greater than 10 %. The throttle position (TP) is between 3-70 %. The DTCs run continuously when the above conditions are met for 2 s.
DTC: P0158	**HO2S Circuit High Voltage Bank 2 Sensor 2:** P0132, P0138, P0152, or P0158 DTCs P0068, P0101, P0102, P0103, P0106, P0107, P0108, P0112, P0113, P0116, P0117, P0118, P0120, P0121, P0122, P0123, P0128, P0201, P0202, P0203, P0204, P0205, P0206, P0207, P0208, P0220, P0222, P0223, P0442, P0443, P0446, P0449, P0455, P0496, P1516, P2101, P2119, P2135, P2176 are not set. The engine is operating in Closed Loop. The Ignition 1 voltage is between 10-32 V. The fuel level is greater than 10 %. The throttle position (TP) is between 0-70 %. The DTCs run continuously when the above conditions are met for 3 s.
DTC: P0158	**HO2S Circuit High Voltage Bank 2 Sensor 2:** P0158 DTCs P0068, P0101, P0102, P0103, P0106, P0107, P0108, P0112, P0113, P0116, P0117, P0118, P0120, P0121, P0122, P0123, P0128, P0201, P0202, P0203, P0204, P0205, P0206, P0207, P0208, P0220, P0222, P0223, P0442, P0443, P0446, P0449, P0455, P0496, P1516, P2101, P2119, P2135, P2176 are not set. The Loop Status parameter is Closed. The Ignition 1 Signal parameter is between 10-18 volts. The Fuel Alcohol Content parameter is less than 87 percent. The Fuel Level Sensor parameter is more than 10 percent. The TP Sensor parameter is between 3-70 percent. DTC P0158 runs the rich test continuously when the above conditions are met.

DTC	Trouble Code Title, Conditions, Possible Causes
DTC: P015A 00	**HO2S Delayed Response Rich to Lean Bank 1 Sensor 1:** P015A 00 DTCs P0030 00, P0036 00, P0053 00, P0054 00, P0101 00, P0102 00, P0103 00, P0106 00, P0107 00, P0108 00, P0120 00, P0121 00, P0122 00, P0123 00, P0131 00, P0132 00, P0133 00, P0134 00, P0135 00, P0137 00, P0138 00, P013A 00, P013B 00, P013E 00, P013F 00, P0140 00, P0141 00, P0171 00, P0172 00, P0201 00, P0202 00, P0203 00, P0204 00, P0220 00, P0222 00, P0223 00, P0300 00, P0443 00, P1133 00, P1516 00, P2101 00, P2119 00, P2135 00, P2176 00, P2270 00, P2271 00, P2A00 00 are not set. The system voltage is between 10-18 V. The fuel level is more than 10%. Engine run time is equal to or more than 40 s. The engine coolant is hotter than 50. 25°C (122. 45°F). The Deceleration fuel cut-off is active. The accelerator pedal position (APP) is stable. The torque converter clutch (TCC) is locked. DTC P013E 00 and P2270 00 have run and passed. DTC P015A 00 runs once per trip.
DTC: P015B 00	**HO2S Delayed Response Lean to Rich Bank 1 Sensor 1:** P015B 00 DTCs P0030 00, P0036 00, P0053 00, P0054 00, P0101 00, P0102 00, P0103 00, P0106 00, P0107 00, P0108 00, P0120 00, P0121 00, P0122 00, P0123 00, P0131 00, P0132 00, P0133 00, P0134 00, P0135 00, P0137 00, P0138 00, P013A 00, P013B 00, P013E 00, P013F 00, P0140 00, P0141 00, P0171 00, P0172 00, P0201 00, P0202 00, P0203 00, P0204 00, P0220 00, P0222 00, P0223 00, P0300 00, P0443 00, P1133 00, P1516 00, P2101 00, P2119 00, P2135 00, P2176 00, P2270 00, P2271 00, P2A00 00 are not set. The system voltage is between 10-18 V. The fuel level is more than 10%. Engine run time is equal to or more than 40 s. The engine coolant is hotter than 50. 25°C (122. 45°F). The DTCs P013A 00, P013E 00, P013F 00, P2270 00, and P2271 00 have run and passed. DTC P015B 00 runs once per trip.
DTC: P0160	**HO2S Circuit Insufficient Activity Bank 2 Sensor 2:** P0160 DTCs P0068, P0101, P0102, P0103, P0106, P0107, P0108, P0112, P0113, P0116, P0117, P0118, P0120, P0121, P0122, P0123, P0128, P0201, P0202, P0203, P0204, P0205, P0206, P0207, P0208, P0220, P0222, P0223, P0442, P0443, P0446, P0449, P0455, P0496, P1516, P2101, P2119, P2135, P2176 are not set. The Ignition 1 Signal parameter is between 10-18 volts. The Engine Run Time parameter is more than 200 seconds. The Loop Status parameter is closed. DTC P0160 runs once per drive cycle when the above conditions are met.
DTC: P0161	**HO2S Heater Performance Bank 2 Sensor 2:** P0135, P0141, P0155, or P0161 DTCs P0116, P0117, P0118, P0125, or P0128 are not set. The ignition 1 voltage is between 10-32 V. The HO2S is at operating temperature. The HO2S is commanded ON. The DTCs run once per drive cycle when the above conditions are met for 120 s.
DTC: P0168	**Engine Fuel Over-Temperature:** The ignition is ON. DTC P0168 runs continuously within the enabling conditions.
DTC: P0171	**Fuel Trim System Lean:** DTCs P0030, P0036, P0053, P0054, P0068, P0101, P0102, P0103, P0107, P0108, P0112, P0113, P0116, P0120, P0121, P0122, P0123, P0128, P0131, P0132, P0133, P0134, P0135, P0137, P0138, P013A, P013B, P013E, P013F, P0140, P0141, P0201-P0206, P0220, P0222, P0223, P0300, P0442, P0443, P0446, P0449, P0451, P0452, P0453, P0454, P0455, P0461, P0462, P0463, P0464, P0496, P0506, P0507, P1133, P1516, P2101, P2119, P2120, P2122, P2123, P2125, P2127, P2128, P2135, P2138, P2176, P2270, P2271, P2A00 are not set. The engine is in Closed Loop status. The Fuel Trim Learn is enabled. The engine coolant temperature (ECT) is between -38 and +150°C (-36. 4 and +302°F). The intake air temperature (IAT) is between -38 and +150°C (-36. 4 and +302°F). The manifold absolute pressure (MAP) is between 10-105 kPa. OR The MAP is between 10-255 kPa for vehicles equipped with secondary air injection (AIR) reaction systems. The vehicle speed is less than 300 km/h (186 mph). The engine speed is between 400-7,000 RPM. The mass airflow (MAF) is between 1-510 g/s. The barometric pressure (BARO) is more than 70 kPa. The fuel level is more than 10 percent. DTC P0171 and P0172 run continuously when the above conditions have been met.
DTC: P0171	**Fuel Trim System Lean Bank 1:** DTCs P0030, P0036, P0050, P0053, P0054, P0056, P0059, P0060, P0068, P0101, P0102, P0103, P0107, P0108, P0112, P0113, P0116, P0120, P0121, P0122, P0123, P0128, P0131, P0132, P0133, P0134, P0135, P0137, P0138, P0140, P0141, P0151, P0152, P0153, P0154, P0155, P0157, P0158, P0160, P0161, P0201-P0206, P0220, P0222, P0223, P0300-P0306, P0442, P0443, P0446, P0449, P0451, P0452, P0453, P0454, P0455, P0461, P0462, P0463, P0464, P0496, P0506, P0507, P1133, P1153, P1516, P2101, P2119, P2120, P2122, P2123, P2125, P2127, P2128, P2135, P2138, P2176, P2A00, P2A03 are not set. Where applicable DTCs P2270, P2271, P2272, P2273, P2A01, P2A04 are not set. The Loop Status parameter indicates Closed. The Fuel Trim Learn is enabled. The engine coolant temperature (ECT) is between -38 and +150°C (-36. 4 and +302°F). The intake air temperature (IAT) is between -38 and +150°C (-36. 4 and +302°F). The manifold absolute pressure (MAP) is between 5-255 kPa. The vehicle speed is less than 134 km/h (83 mph). The engine speed is between 400-6,000 RPM. The mass air flow (MAF) is between 1-510 g/s. The barometric pressure (BARO) is more than 70 kPa. The scan tool special functions are not active. DTCs P0171, P0172, P0174, and P0175 run continuously when the above conditions have been met.

DTC	Trouble Code Title, Conditions, Possible Causes
DTC: P0171 00	**Fuel Trim System Lean:** P0171 00 DTCs P0030 00, P0031 00, P0032 00, P0107 00, P0108 00, P0112 00, P0113 00, P0121 00, P0122 00, P0123 00, P0128 00, P0131 00, P0132 00, P0133 00, P0134 00, P0135 00, P0137 00, P0138 00, P0140 00, P0141 00, P0201 00 - P0204 00, P0220 00, P0222 00, P0223 00, P0300 00 - P0304 00, P0442 00, P0443 00, P0446 00, P0451 00, P0452 00, P0453 00, P0454 00, P0455 00, P0461 00, P0462 00, P0463 00, P0496 00, P0506 00, P0507 00, P2101 00, P2119 00, P2122 00, P2123 00, P2127 00, P2128 00, P2138 00, P2176 00, P2A00 00 are not set. Where applicable DTCs P2270 00, P2271 00, P2272 00, P2A01 00 are not set. The loop status parameter indicates closed. The fuel trim learn is enabled. The engine coolant temperature (ECT) is between -38 to +150°C (-36. 4 to +302°F). The intake air temperature (IAT) is between -38 to +150°C (-36. 4 to +302°F). The manifold absolute pressure (MAP) is between 5-255 kPa (0. 73-37 PSI). The vehicle speed is less than 134 km/h (83 MPH). The engine speed is between 400-6 000 RPM. The barometric pressure (BARO) is more than 70 kPa (10 PSI). DTCs P0171 00 and P2096 00 run continuously when the above conditions have been met.
DTC: P0172	**Fuel Trim System Rich:** DTCs P0030, P0036, P0053, P0054, P0068, P0101, P0102, P0103, P0107, P0108, P0112, P0113, P0116, P0120, P0121, P0122, P0123, P0128, P0131, P0132, P0133, P0134, P0135, P0137, P0138, P0140, P0141, P0201-P0206, P0220, P0222, P0223, P0300, P0442, P0443, P0446, P0449, P0451, P0452, P0453, P0454, P0455, P0461, P0462, P0463, P0464, P0496, P0506, P0507, P1133, P1516, P2101, P2119, P2120, P2122, P2123, P2125, P2127, P2128, P2135, P2138, P2176, P2A00, P2270, P2271 are not set. The Loop Status parameter indicates Closed. The Fuel Trim Learn is enabled. The engine coolant temperature (ECT) is between -38 and +150°C (-36. 4 and +302°F). The intake air temperature (IAT) is between -38 and +150°C (-36. 4 and +302°F). The manifold absolute pressure (MAP) is between 10-255 kPa. The vehicle speed is less than 300 km/h (186 mph). The engine speed is between 400-7,000 RPM. The mass air flow (MAF) is between 1-510 g/s. The barometric pressure (BARO) is more than 70 kPa. The fuel level is more than 10 percent. DTC P0171 or P0172 runs continuously when the above conditions have been met.
DTC: P0172 00	**Fuel Trim System Rich:** P0172 00 DTCs P0030 00, P0031 00, P0032 00, P0111 00, P0112 00, P0113 00, P0114 00, P0117 00, P0118 00, P0119 00, P0122 00, P0123 00, P0130 00, P0131 00, P0132 00, P0133 00, P0134 00, P0135 00, P0201 00, P0202 00, P0203 00, P0204 00, P0222 00, P0223 00, P0261 00, P0262 00, P0264 00, P0265 00, P0267 00, P0268 00, P0270 00, P0271 00, P0301 00, P0302 00, P0303 00, P0304 00, P0335 00, P0336 00, P0340 00, P0341 00, P0365 00, P0366 00, P0443 00, P0458 00, P0459 00, P0496 00, P2227 00, P2228 00, P2229 00, P2297 00, P2A00 00 are not set. The loop status parameter indicates closed. The engine coolant temperature (ECT) is between -38 to +150°C (-36. 4 to +302°F). The intake air temperature (IAT) is between -38 to +150°C (-36. 4 to +302°F). The manifold absolute pressure (MAP) is between 5-255 kPa (0. 73-37 PSI). The engine speed is between 400-6 000 RPM. The barometric pressure (BARO) is more than 70 kPa (10 PSI). DTCs P0172 00 and P2097 00 run continuously when the above conditions have been met.
DTC: P0174	**Fuel Trim System Lean Bank 2:** DTCs P0101, P0102, P0103, P0106, P0107, P0108, P0178, P0179, P0201-P0206, P0261, P0262, P0264, P0265, P0267, P0268, P0270, P0271, P0273, P0274, P0275, P0277, P0300-P0306, P0442, P0443, P0446, P0449, P0451-P0455, P0496, P0506, P0507, P1248, P1249, P124A, P124B, P124C, P124D, P2147, P2148, P2150, P2151, P2153, P2154, P2156, P2157, P216B, P216C, P216E, P216F, P2227-P2230, P2269 are not set. The engine is in Closed Loop status. The catalyst monitor diagnostic intrusive test, post 02 diagnostic intrusive test, device control, and EVAP diagnostic Tank Pull Down test are not active. The engine coolant temperature (ECT) is between -38 and +150°C (-36 and +302°F). The intake air temperature (IAT) is between -38 and +150°C (-36 and +302°F). The manifold absolute pressure (MAP) is between 5-255 kPa (1 45.37 psi). The engine speed is between 400-6,600 RPM. The mass air flow (MAF) is between 0. 5-510 g/s. The barometric pressure (BARO) is greater than 70 kPa (10. 2 psi). The fuel level is greater than 10 %. This diagnostic runs continuously when the above conditions have been met.
DTC: P0175	**Fuel Trim System Rich Bank 2:** DTCs P0101, P0102, P0103, P0106, P0107, P0108, P0178, P0179, P0201-P0206, P0261, P0262, P0264, P0265, P0267, P0268, P0270, P0271, P0273, P0274, P0275, P0277, P0300-P0306, P0442, P0443, P0446, P0449, P0451-P0455, P0496, P0506, P0507, P1248, P1249, P124A, P124B, P124C, P124D, P2147, P2148, P2150, P2151, P2153, P2154, P2156, P2157, P216B, P216C, P216E, P216F, P2227-P2230, P2269 are not set. The engine is in Closed Loop status. The catalyst monitor diagnostic intrusive test, post 02 diagnostic intrusive test, device control, and EVAP diagnostic Tank Pull Down test are not active. The engine coolant temperature (ECT) is between -38 and +150°C (-36 and +302°F). The intake air temperature (IAT) is between -38 and +150°C (-36 and +302°F). The manifold absolute pressure (MAP) is between 5-255 kPa (1. 45-37 psi). The engine speed is between 400-6,600 RPM. The mass air flow (MAF) is between 0. 5-510 g/s. The barometric pressure (BARO) is greater than 70 kPa (10. 2 psi). The fuel level is greater than 10 %. This diagnostic runs continuously when the above conditions have been met.
DTC: P0180 03	**Fuel Temperature Sensor Circuit Low Voltage:** The ignition is ON or the engine is running. The DTCs run continuously once the above condition is met
DTC: P0180 07	**Fuel Temperature Sensor Circuit High Voltage:** The ignition is ON or the engine is running. The DTCs run continuously once the above condition is met
DTC: P0181 00	**Fuel Temperature Sensor Performance:** The ignition is ON or the engine is running. The DTCs run continuously once the above condition is met.

DTC	Trouble Code Title, Conditions, Possible Causes
DTC: P0182	**Fuel Temperature Sensor 1 Circuit Low:** P0182 or P0187Engine speed is greater than 600 RPM. Engine has been running for greater than 10 seconds. DTCs P0182 and P0187 run continuously within the enabling conditions.
DTC: P0183	**Fuel Temperature Sensor 1 Circuit High:** P0183 or P0188Engine speed is greater than 600 RPM. Engine has been running for greater than 10 seconds. DTCs P0183 and P0188 run continuously within the above enabling conditions.
DTC: P0187	**Fuel Temperature Sensor 2 Circuit Low:** P0182 or P0187Engine speed is greater than 600 RPM. Engine has been running for greater than 10 seconds. DTCs P0182 and P0187 run continuously within the enabling conditions.
DTC: P0188	**Fuel Temperature Sensor 2 Circuit High:** P0183 or P0188Engine speed is greater than 600 RPM. Engine has been running for greater than 10 seconds. DTCs P0183 and P0188 run continuously within the above enabling conditions.
DTC: P018B	**Fuel Pressure Sensor Performance:** The engine is running. DTC P018C, P018D, P0231, P0232, P023F, P064A, P1255 or P06A6 are not active. DTC P0641 has not failed this ignition cycle. Fuel pump control is enabled and the fuel pump control state is normal. The engine has been running for at least 5 seconds.
DTC: P018C	**Fuel Pressure Sensor Circuit Low Voltage:** The engine is running. DTC P018C, P018D, P0231, P0232, P023F, P064A, P1255 or P06A6 are not active. DTC P0641 has not failed this ignition cycle. Fuel pump control is enabled and the fuel pump control state is normal. The engine has been running for at least 5 seconds.
DTC: P018D	**Fuel Pressure Sensor Circuit High Voltage:** The engine is running. DTC P018C, P018D, P0231, P0232, P023F, P064A, P1255 or P06A6 are not active. DTC P0641 has not failed this ignition cycle. Fuel pump control is enabled and the fuel pump control state is normal. The engine has been running for at least 5 seconds.
DTC: P0190 00	**Fuel Rail Pressure Sensor Performance:** The engine is running. DTC P0651 00 is not set. The DTCs run continuously when the above conditions are met.
DTC: P0190 03	**Fuel Rail Pressure Sensor Circuit Low Voltage:** The ignition is ON or the engine is running. The DTCs run continuously once the above condition is met.
DTC: P0190 07	**Fuel Rail Pressure Sensor Circuit High Voltage:** The ignition is ON or the engine is running. The DTCs run continuously once the above condition is met.
DTC: P0191	**Fuel Rail Pressure Sensor Performance:** Condition 1 DTC P0016, P0017, P0068, P0090, P0091, P0092, P00C8, P00C9, P00CA, P0101, P0102, P0103, P0106, P0107, P0108, P0112, P0113, P0117, P0118, P0121, P0122, P0123, P0128, P0192, P0193, P0201, P0202, P0203, P0204, P0222, P0223, P0261, P0262, P0264, P0265, P0267, P0268, P0270, P0271, P0300, P0301, P0302, P0303, P0304, P0335, P0336, P0340, P0341, P0351-P0354, P0365, P0366, P0506, P0507, P0627, P0628, P0629, P0722, P0723, P1248, P1249, P124A, P124B, P1682, P16F3, P2101, P2122, P2123, P2127, P2128, P2135, P2147, P2148, P2150, P2151, P2153, P2154, P2156, P2157 is not set. The engine is not cranking. The ignition voltage is greater than 11 V. The vehicle speed is less than or equal to 1 km/h (0. 62 mph). The low side fuel pressure is greater than or equal to 275 kPa (40 psi). The Accelerator Pedal Position is 0 percent for 12. 5 s. DTC P0191 runs continuously when the above conditions have been met. Condition 2 and 3 DTC P0016, P0017, P0068, P0090, P0091, P0092, P00C8, P00C9, P00CA, P0101, P0102, P0103, P0106, P0107, P0108, P0112, P0113, P0117, P0118, P0121, P0122, P0123, P0128, P0192, P0193, P0201, P0202, P0203, P0204, P0222, P0223, P0261, P0262, P0264, P0265, P0267, P0268, P0270, P0271, P0300, P0301, P0302, P0303, P0304, P0335, P0336, P0340, P0341, P0351-P0354, P0365, P0366, P0506, P0507, P0627, P0628, P0629, P0722, P0723, P1248, P1249, P124A, P124B, P1682, P16F3, P2101, P2122, P2123, P2127, P2128, P2135, P2147, P2148, P2150, P2151, P2153, P2154, P2156, P2157 is not set. The engine is not cranking. The ignition voltage is greater than 11 V. The engine speed is between 1,000-2,200 RPM. The vehicle speed is greater than or equal to 45 km/h (27. 96 mph). The low side fuel pressure is greater than or equal to 275 kPa (40 psi). The Desired Fuel Rail Pressure is between 7-8 MPa (1,015-1,160 psi). DTC P0191 runs continuously when the above conditions have been met. Condition 4 DTC P0016, P0017, P0068, P0090, P0091, P0092, P00C8, P00C9, P00CA, P0101, P0102, P0103, P0106, P0107, P0108, P0112, P0113, P0117, P0118, P0121, P0122, P0123, P0128, P0192, P0193, P0201, P0202, P0203, P0204, P0222, P0223, P0261, P0262, P0264, P0265, P0267, P0268, P0270, P0271, P0300, P0301, P0302, P0303, P0304, P0335, P0336, P0340, P0341, P0351-P0354, P0365, P0366, P0506, P0507, P0627, P0628, P0629, P0722, P0723, P1248, P1249, P124A, P124B, P1682, P16F3, P2101, P2122, P2123, P2127, P2128, P2135, P2147, P2148, P2150, P2151, P2153, P2154, P2156, P2157 is not set. The engine is not cranking. The vehicle speed is greater than or equal to 30 km/h (18. 64 mph). The engine speed is greater than or equal to 2,000 RPM. DTC P0191 runs continuously when the above conditions have been met.
DTC: P0191 00	**Fuel Rail Pressure Sensor Performance:** The engine is running. DTC P0651 00 is not set. The DTCs run continuously when the above conditions are met.

DTC	Trouble Code Title, Conditions, Possible Causes
DTC: P0191 11	**Fuel Rail Pressure Sensor Performance High Input:** The ignition is ON or the engine is running. The DTCs run continuously once the above condition is met.
DTC: P0191 12	**Fuel Rail Pressure Sensor Performance Low Input:** The ignition is ON or the engine is running. The DTCs run continuously once the above condition is met.
DTC: P0192	**Fuel Rail Pressure Sensor Circuit Low Voltage:** The engine is running. The ignition voltage is between 11-18 V. The DTCs run continuously within the enabling conditions.
DTC: P0192 00	**Fuel Rail Pressure Sensor Circuit Low Voltage:** The engine is running. DTC P0651 00 is not set. The DTCs run continuously when the above conditions are met.
DTC: P0193	**Fuel Rail Pressure Sensor Circuit High Voltage:** The engine is running. The ignition voltage is between 11-18 V. The DTCs run continuously within the enabling conditions.
DTC: P0193 00	**Fuel Rail Pressure Sensor Circuit High Voltage:** The engine is running. DTC P0651 00 is not set. The DTCs run continuously when the above conditions are met.
DTC: P0201	**Cylinder 1 Injector Control Circuit:** The engine speed is greater than 80 RPM. The ignition 1 signal parameter is between 10-18 V. The injector has been commanded ON and OFF at least once. The DTCs run continuously once the above conditions are met.
DTC: P0201 00	**Cylinder 1 Injector Control Circuit:** DTCs P0607 00, P0628 00, P0629 00 are not set. The battery voltage is greater than 9 V. The engine is running. The engine speed is between 320-6016 RPM. All fuel injectors are active. These DTCs run continuously when the above conditions are met
DTC: P0202	**Cylinder 2 Injector Control Circuit:** The engine is running. The ignition voltage is between 11-18 V. The DTCs run continuously once the above conditions are met.
DTC: P0202 00	**Cylinder 2 Injector Control Circuit:** DTCs P0607 00, P0628 00, P0629 00 are not set. The battery voltage is greater than 9 V. The engine is running. The engine speed is between 320-6016 RPM. All fuel injectors are active. These DTCs run continuously when the above conditions are met
DTC: P0203	**Injector 3 Control Circuit:** The engine is running. The ignition voltage is more than 11 volts. DTCs P0201-P0208 runs continuously when the above conditions are met.
DTC: P0203 00	**Cylinder 3 Injector Control Circuit:** DTCs P0607 00, P0628 00, P0629 00 are not set. The battery voltage is greater than 9 V. The engine is running. The engine speed is between 320-6016 RPM. All fuel injectors are active. These DTCs run continuously when the above conditions are met
DTC: P0204	**Cylinder 4 Injector Control Circuit:** The engine speed is greater than 80 RPM. The ignition 1 signal parameter is between 8-18. 1 V. The DTCs run continuously within the enabling conditions.
DTC: P0204 00	**Cylinder 4 Injector Control Circuit:** DTCs P0607 00, P0628 00, P0629 00 are not set. The battery voltage is greater than 9 V. The engine is running. The engine speed is between 320-6016 RPM. All fuel injectors are active. These DTCs run continuously when the above conditions are met
DTC: P0205	**Injector 5 Control Circuit:** The engine is running. The ignition voltage is more than 11 V for 5 seconds. DTCs P0201-P0206 run continuously when the above conditions are met.
DTC: P0205	**Cylinder 5 Injector Control Circuit:** The engine speed is greater than 80 RPM. The ignition 1 signal parameter is between 10-18 V. The injector has been commanded ON and OFF at least once. The DTCs run continuously once the above conditions are met.
DTC: P0206	**Injector 6 Control Circuit:** The engine is running. The ignition voltage is more than 11 volts. DTCs P0201-P0208 runs continuously when the above conditions are met.
DTC: P0206	**Cylinder 6 Injector Control Circuit:** The engine speed is greater than 80 RPM. The ignition 1 signal parameter is between 10-18 V. The injector has been commanded ON and OFF at least once. The DTCs run continuously once the above conditions are met.
DTC: P0207	**Injector 7 Control Circuit:** The engine is running. The ignition voltage is greater than 11 V. DTC P0201-P0208 runs continuously when the above conditions are met.
DTC: P0208	**Fuel Injector 8 Control Circuit:** The engine is running. The charging system voltage is between 10-18 V.

DTC	Trouble Code Title, Conditions, Possible Causes
DTC: P0208	**Injector 8 Control Circuit:** The engine is running. The ignition voltage is greater than 11 V. DTC P0201-P0208 runs continuously when the above conditions are met.
DTC: P0218	**Transmission Fluid Over temperature:** Ignition voltage is 8. 6 volts or greater. The TFT is -39 to +149°C (-38 to +300°F) for 5 seconds.
DTC: P0219	**Engine Overspeed Condition:** The engine is running.
DTC: P0219 00	**Engine Overspeed:** The engine is running. The DTC runs continuously once the above condition is met.
DTC: P0220	**Throttle Position (TP) Sensor 2 Circuit:** P0120, P0122, P0123, P0220, P0222, or P0223 DTCs P0601, P0602, P0603, P0604, P0606, P060D, P062F, P0641, P0651 are not set. The system voltage is greater than 5. 23 V. The ignition is in the Unlock/Accessory or Run position. The DTCs run continuously when the above conditions are met.
DTC: P0221	**Throttle Position Sensor 2 Performance:** The ignition voltage is greater than 7 V. The ignition is ON, with the engine OFF, or the engine is operating. DTC P0121 runs continuously once the above conditions are met.
DTC: P0221	**Throttle Position Sensor 2 Performance:** The ignition is ON, with the engine OFF, or the engine is operating. The ignition voltage is greater than 7 volts. DTCs run continuously once the above conditions are met.
DTC: P0221 00	**Throttle Position Sensor 2 Performance:** DTCs P000A 00, P000B 00, P0016 00, P0017 00, P0111 00, P0112 00, P0113 00, P0114 00, P0116 00, P0117 00, P0118 00, P0119 00, P0122 00, P0123 00, P0222 00, P0223 00, P0121 00, P0221 00, P0340 00, P0341 00, P0365 00, P0366 00, P0458 00, P0459 00, P0642 00, P0643 00, P0652 00, P0653 00, P065B 00 are not set. The engine is running. DTCs P0068 00, P0642 00, P0643 00 are not set.
DTC: P0222	**Throttle Position (TP) Sensor 2 Circuit Low Voltage:** P0120, P0122, P0123, P0220, P0222, and P0223 DTC P0641 or P0651 are not set. The run/crank or powertrain relay voltage is greater than 6 V and reduced power is not active. The ignition is ON or the engine is running. DTC P0120, P0122, P0123, P0220, P0222, P0223 run continuously when the above conditions are met.
DTC: P0222 00	**Throttle Position Sensor 2 Circuit Low Voltage:** P0122 00, P0123 00, P0222 00, P0223 00The ignition is ON, or the engine is running. The engine is not operating in reduced power mode. The ignition voltage is greater than 6 V. The DTCs runs continuously when the above condition is met.
DTC: P0223	**Throttle Position (TP) Sensor 2 Circuit High Voltage:** P0120, P0122, P0123, P0220, P0222, and P0223 DTC P0601, P0602, P0603, P0604, P0606, P0607, P0641, or P0651 is not set. The system voltage is greater than 5. 23 V. The ignition is in the Unlock/Accessory or Run position. The DTCs run continuously when the above conditions are met.
DTC: P0223 00	**Throttle Position Sensor 2 Circuit High Voltage:** DTC P0641 00 or P0651 00 are not set. The run/crank or powertrain relay voltage is greater than 6 V and reduced power is not active. The ignition is ON or the engine is operating. DTC P0122 00, P0123 00, P0222 00, P0223 00, and P2135 00 run continuously when the above conditions are met.
DTC: P0230	**Fuel Pump Relay Control Circuit:** The ignition voltage is between 9-18 V. DTC P0230 runs continuously once the above conditions are met.
DTC: P0230	**Fuel Pump Relay Control Circuit:** The ignition voltage is between 11-32 volts. Engine speed is greater than 0 RPM. DTC P0230 runs continuously when the above conditions are met.
DTC: P0230 00	**Fuel Pump Relay Control Circuit:** The ignition is ON. The ignition voltage is between 11-18 V. The DTCs run continuously once the above conditions are met.
DTC: P0231	**Fuel Pump Control Circuit Low Voltage:** P0231, P023FThe ignition voltage is between 9-18 V.
DTC: P0232	**Fuel Pump Control Circuit High Voltage:** P0232The control enable voltage signal supplied for the ECM to fuel pump control module is inactive for 4 seconds after engine has been shut off.
DTC: P0234	**Turbocharger Engine Overboost:** DTCs P0106, P0563, P2564 or P2565 are not set. The engine speed is between 800-3,600 RPM. DTC P0234 runs continuously when the above conditions are met.

DTC	Trouble Code Title, Conditions, Possible Causes
DTC: P0234	**Turbocharger Engine Overboost:** DTC P0045, P0047, P0048, P006E, P006F, P007C, P007D, P0102, P0103, P0106, P0107, P0108, P0117, P0118, P0200, P02E0, P02E3, P02E8, P02E9, P02EB, P0403, P046C, P0489, P0490, P122B, P122C, P122F, P1407, P140B, P140D, P140E, P140F, P2228, P2229, P2263, P2453, P2494, P2495, P2564, or P2565 is not set. The engine speed is stable between 1,600-3,000 RPM. Fuel injector delivery rate is greater than 45 mm ; and stable. Ambient air temperature is greater than -7°C (19. 4°F). BARO is greater than 75 kPa (11 psi). Turbocharger actuator position sensor offset learning is not active. Turbocharger vane cleaning, wiping, procedure is not active. DTC P0234 runs continuously when the above conditions are met.
DTC: P0234 00	**Engine Overboost:** P0234 00 DTCs P0237 00, or P0238 00 are not set. The driver requested boost pressure level exceeds the level of the base boost pressure. This DTC runs continuously within the enabling conditions.
DTC: P0234 00	**Engine Overboost Malfunction:** The engine is running. The DTCs run continuously when the above conditions are met.
DTC: P0236	**Turbocharger Boost System Performance:** P0236 - Engine Cranking DTCs P0107, P0108, P0121, P0122, P0123, P0221, P0222, P0223, P0237, P0238, P2227, P2228, or P2229 are not set. The engine OFF timer is greater than 4 s. The engine is cranking at less than 400 RPM for at least 200 ms. This DTC runs during engine cranking only. P0236 - Engine Idling. DTCs P0121, P0122, P0123, P0221, P0222, P0223, P0237, P0238, P2227, P2228, or P2229 are not set. The engine is running and the ECM has counted greater than three revolutions. The engine speed is less than 1000 RPM. The Throttle Position Sensor parameter is less than 24 %. The ECM is not in limp home mode. This DTC runs continuously within the enabling conditions.
DTC: P0236 00	**Turbocharger Boost Sensor Performance:** The ignition is ON or the engine is running. These DTCs runs continuously within the enabling conditions.
DTC: P0237	**Turbocharger Boost Sensor Circuit Low Voltage:** P0237 The ignition is ON or the engine is running. This DTC runs continuously within the enabling conditions.
DTC: P0237 00	**Turbocharger Boost Sensor Circuit Low Voltage:** The ignition is ON or the engine is running. These DTCs runs continuously within the enabling conditions.
DTC: P0238	**Turbocharger Boost Sensor Circuit High Voltage:** P0238 The ignition is ON or the engine is running. This DTC runs continuously within the enabling conditions.
DTC: P0238 00	**Turbocharger Boost Sensor Circuit High Voltage:** The ignition is ON or the engine is running. These DTCs runs continuously within the enabling conditions.
DTC: P023F	**Fuel Pump Control Circuit:** P0231, P023F The ignition voltage is between 9-18 V.
DTC: P023F	**Fuel Pump Control Circuit:** P0231, P023F The ignition voltage is between 9-18 V.
DTC: P0243	**Turbocharger Wastegate Solenoid Control Circuit:** The engine speed is greater than 80 RPM. The battery voltage is between 10-18 V. This DTC runs continuously within the enabling conditions.
DTC: P0243 00	**Turbocharger Wastegate Solenoid Valve Control Circuit:** The engine speed is greater than 40 RPM. The battery voltage is between 10-18 V. This DTC runs continuously within the enabling conditions.
DTC: P0245	**Turbocharger Wastegate Solenoid Control Circuit Low Voltage:** The engine speed is greater than 80 RPM. The battery voltage is between 10-18 V. This DTC runs continuously within the enabling conditions.
DTC: P0245 00	**Turbocharger Wastegate Solenoid Valve Control Circuit Low Voltage:** The engine speed is greater than 40 RPM. The battery voltage is between 10-18 V. This DTC runs continuously within the enabling conditions.
DTC: P0246	**Turbocharger Wastegate Solenoid Control Circuit High Voltage:** The engine speed is greater than 80 RPM. The battery voltage is between 10-18 V. This DTC runs continuously within the enabling conditions.
DTC: P0246 00	**Turbocharger Wastegate Solenoid Valve Control Circuit High Voltage:** The engine speed is greater than 40 RPM. The battery voltage is between 10-18 V. This DTC runs continuously within the enabling conditions.
DTC: P0253 00	**Fuel Pressure Regulator Control Circuit Low Voltage:** The ignition is ON, or the engine is running. The ignition voltage is less than 16 V. The DTCs runs continuously once the above conditions are met.

DTC	Trouble Code Title, Conditions, Possible Causes
DTC: P0254 00	**Fuel Pressure Regulator Control Circuit High Voltage:** The ignition is ON, or the engine is running. The ignition voltage is less than 16 V. The DTCs runs continuously once the above conditions are met.
DTC: P025A	**Fuel Pump Control Module Enable Circuit:** The ignition is ON.
DTC: P0261	**Cylinder 1 Injector Control Circuit Low Voltage:** The engine speed is greater than 80 RPM. The ignition 1 signal parameter is between 10-18 V. The injector has been commanded ON and OFF at least once. The DTCs run continuously once the above conditions are met.
DTC: P0261 00	**Cylinder 1 Injector Control Circuit Low Voltage:** The battery voltage is greater than 9 V. The engine speed is greater than 40 RPM. All fuel injectors are active. These DTCs run continuously when the above conditions are met.
DTC: P0262	**Cylinder 1 Injector Control Circuit High Voltage:** The engine speed is greater than 80 RPM. The ignition 1 signal parameter is between 10-18 V. The injector has been commanded ON and OFF at least once. The DTCs run continuously once the above conditions are met.
DTC: P0262	**Cylinder 1 Injector Control Circuit High Voltage:** The engine speed is greater than 80 RPM. The ignition 1 signal parameter is between 8-18. 1 V. The DTCs run continuously within the enabling conditions.
DTC: P0262 00	**Cylinder 1 Injector Control Circuit High Voltage:** The battery voltage is greater than 9 V. The engine speed is greater than 40 RPM. All fuel injectors are active. These DTCs run continuously when the above conditions are met.
DTC: P0263	**Cylinder 1 Balance System:** DTCs P0117, P0118, P0335, P0336, P2146, P2149, P2152, P2155 and P062C are not set. The ECT is more than 40°C (104°F). The engine is running at idle for more than 10 s. The engine RPM is between 600-1,500 RPM. The calculated fuel rate is between 15 mm; and 50 mm;. DTC will run once per ignition cycle when the above conditions are met.
DTC: P0263 00	**Cylinder 1 Injector Control Performance:** The engine is running. The DTCs run continuously when the above conditions are met.
DTC: P0264	**Cylinder 2 Injector Control Circuit Low Voltage:** The engine speed is greater than 80 RPM. The ignition 1 signal parameter is between 10-18 V. The injector has been commanded ON and OFF at least once. The DTCs run continuously once the above conditions are met.
DTC: P0264 00	**Cylinder 2 Injector Control Circuit Low Voltage:** The battery voltage is greater than 9 V. The engine speed is greater than 40 RPM. All fuel injectors are active. These DTCs run continuously when the above conditions are met.
DTC: P0265	**Cylinder 2 Injector Control Circuit High Voltage:** The engine speed is greater than 80 RPM. The ignition 1 signal parameter is between 10-18 V. The injector has been commanded ON and OFF at least once. The DTCs run continuously once the above conditions are met.
DTC: P0265 00	**Cylinder 2 Injector Control Circuit High Voltage:** The battery voltage is greater than 9 V. The engine speed is greater than 40 RPM. All fuel injectors are active. These DTCs run continuously when the above conditions are met.
DTC: P0266	**Cylinder 2 Balance System:** DTCs P0117, P0118, P0335, P0336, P2146, P2149, P2152, P2155 and P062C are not set. The ECT is more than 40°C (104°F). The engine is running at idle for more than 10 s. The engine RPM is between 600-1,500 RPM. The calculated fuel rate is between 15 mm ; and 50 mm ;. DTC will run once per ignition cycle when the above conditions are met.
DTC: P0266 00	**Cylinder 2 Injector Control Performance:** The engine is running. The DTCs run continuously when the above conditions are met.
DTC: P0267	**Cylinder 3 Injector Control Circuit Low Voltage:** The engine speed is greater than 80 RPM. The ignition 1 signal parameter is between 10-18 V. The injector has been commanded ON and OFF at least once. The DTCs run continuously once the above conditions are met.
DTC: P0267 00	**Cylinder 3 Injector Control Circuit Low Voltage:** The battery voltage is greater than 9 V. The engine speed is greater than 40 RPM. All fuel injectors are active. These DTCs run continuously when the above conditions are met.
DTC: P0268	**Cylinder 3 Injector Control Circuit High Voltage:** The engine speed is greater than 80 RPM. The ignition 1 signal parameter is between 10-18 V. The injector has been commanded ON and OFF at least once. The DTCs run continuously once the above conditions are met.

DTC	Trouble Code Title, Conditions, Possible Causes
DTC: P0268 00	**Cylinder 3 Injector Control Circuit High Voltage:** The battery voltage is greater than 9 V. The engine speed is greater than 40 RPM. All fuel injectors are active. These DTCs run continuously when the above conditions are met.
DTC: P0269	**Cylinder 3 Balance System:** DTCs P0117, P0118, P0335, P0336, P2146, P2149, P2152, P2155 and P062C are not set. The ECT is more than 40°C (104°F). The engine is running at idle for more than 10 s. The engine RPM is between 600-1,500 RPM. The calculated fuel rate is between 15 mm ; and 50 mm ;. DTC will run once per ignition cycle when the above conditions are met.
DTC: P0269 00	**Cylinder 3 Injector Control Performance:** The engine is running. The DTCs run continuously when the above conditions are met.
DTC: P026A	**Charge Air Cooler (CAC) Low Efficiency:** Engine speed is greater than 600 to 850 RPM, depending on engine coolant temperature (ECT) and BARO, for at least 10 s. The ECT is between 70-123°C (158-253°F). The Ambient Air Temperature is warmer than -7°C (+19. 4°F). The difference between the CAC Inlet Temperature and the Ambient Air Temperature is at least 40°C (72°F). The Intake Air Flow (IAF) Valve Position is 5 % or less. The MAF signal is between 83. 33-152. 77 g/s. The vehicle speed is at least 60 Km/h (37 mph). The BARO is greater than 75 kPa. The calculated fuel rate is between 20 mm ; and 50 mm ;. This DTC runs once per key cycle when the above conditions exist.
DTC: P0270	**Cylinder 4 Injector Control Circuit Low Voltage:** The engine is running. The ignition voltage is between 11-18 V. The DTCs run continuously once the above conditions are met.
DTC: P0270	**Cylinder 4 Injector Control Circuit Low Voltage:** The engine speed is greater than 80 RPM. The ignition 1 signal parameter is between 10-18 V. The injector has been commanded ON and OFF at least once. The DTCs run continuously once the above conditions are met.
DTC: P0270 00	**Cylinder 4 Injector Control Circuit Low Voltage:** The battery voltage is greater than 9 V. The engine speed is greater than 40 RPM. All fuel injectors are active. These DTCs run continuously when the above conditions are met.
DTC: P0271	**Cylinder 4 Injector Control Circuit High Voltage:** The engine speed is greater than 80 RPM. The ignition 1 signal parameter is between 10-18 V. The injector has been commanded ON and OFF at least once. The DTCs run continuously once the above conditions are met.
DTC: P0271	**Cylinder 4 Injector Control Circuit High Voltage:** The engine is running. The ignition voltage is between 11-18 V. The DTCs run continuously once the above conditions are met.
DTC: P0271	**Cylinder 4 Injector Control Circuit High Voltage:** The engine speed is greater than 80 RPM. The ignition 1 signal parameter is between 8-18. 1 V. The DTCs run continuously within the enabling conditions.
DTC: P0271 00	**Cylinder 4 Injector Control Circuit High Voltage:** DTCs P0607 00, P0628 00, P0629 00 are not set. The battery voltage is greater than 9 V. The engine is running. The engine speed is between 320-6016 RPM. All fuel injectors are active. These DTCs run continuously when the above conditions are met
DTC: P0271 00	**Cylinder 4 Injector Control Circuit High Voltage:** The battery voltage is greater than 9 V. The engine speed is greater than 40 RPM. All fuel injectors are active. These DTCs run continuously when the above conditions are met.
DTC: P0272	**Cylinder 4 Balance System:** DTCs P0117, P0118, P0335, P0336, P2146, P2149, P2152, P2155 and P062C are not set. The ECT is more than 40°C (104°F). The engine is running at idle for more than 10 s. The engine RPM is between 600-1,500 RPM. The calculated fuel rate is between 15 mm ; and 50 mm ;. DTC will run once per ignition cycle when the above conditions are met.
DTC: P0272 00	**Cylinder 4 Injector Control Performance:** The engine is running. The DTCs run continuously when the above conditions are met.
DTC: P0273	**Cylinder 5 Injector Control Circuit Low Voltage:** The engine speed is greater than 80 RPM. The ignition 1 signal parameter is between 10-18 V. The injector has been commanded ON and OFF at least once. The DTCs run continuously once the above conditions are met.
DTC: P0274	**Cylinder 5 Injector Control Circuit High Voltage:** The engine speed is greater than 80 RPM. The ignition 1 signal parameter is between 10-18 V. The injector has been commanded ON and OFF at least once. The DTCs run continuously once the above conditions are met.
DTC: P0275	**Cylinder 5 Balance System:** DTCs P0117, P0118, P0335, P0336, P2146, P2149, P2152, P2155 and P062C are not set. The ECT is more than 40°C (104°F). The engine is running at idle for more than 10 s. The engine RPM is between 600-1,500 RPM. The calculated fuel rate is between 15 mm ; and 50 mm ;. DTC will run once per ignition cycle when the above conditions are met.

DTC	Trouble Code Title, Conditions, Possible Causes
DTC: P0276	**Cylinder 6 Injector Control Circuit Low Voltage:** The engine speed is greater than 80 RPM. The ignition 1 signal parameter is between 10-18 V. The injector has been commanded ON and OFF at least once. The DTCs run continuously once the above conditions are met.
DTC: P0277	**Cylinder 6 Injector Control Circuit High Voltage:** The engine speed is greater than 80 RPM. The ignition 1 signal parameter is between 10-18 V. The injector has been commanded ON and OFF at least once. The DTCs run continuously once the above conditions are met.
DTC: P0278	**Cylinder 6 Balance System:** DTCs P0117, P0118, P0335, P0336, P2146, P2149, P2152, P2155 and P062C are not set. The ECT is more than 40°C (104°F). The engine is running at idle for more than 10 s. The engine RPM is between 600-1,500 RPM. The calculated fuel rate is between 15 mm ; and 50 mm ;. DTC will run once per ignition cycle when the above conditions are met.
DTC: P0281	**Cylinder 7 Balance System:** DTCs P0117, P0118, P0335, P0336, P2146, P2149, P2152, P2155 and P062C are not set. The ECT is more than 40°C (104°F). The engine is running at idle for more than 10 s. The engine RPM is between 600-1,500 RPM. The calculated fuel rate is between 15 mm ; and 50 mm ;. DTC will run once per ignition cycle when the above conditions are met.
DTC: P0284	**Cylinder 8 Balance System:** DTCs P0117, P0118, P0335, P0336, P2146, P2149, P2152, P2155 and P062C are not set. The ECT is more than 40°C (104°F). The engine is running at idle for more than 10 s. The engine RPM is between 600-1,500 RPM. The calculated fuel rate is between 15 mm ; and 50 mm ;. DTC will run once per ignition cycle when the above conditions are met.
DTC: P0299	**Turbocharger Engine Underboost:** DTC P0045, P0047, P0048, P006E, P006F, P007C, P007D, P0102, P0103, P0107, P0108, P0117, P0118, P02E0, P02E8, P02E9, P02EB, P0403, P122D, P140F, P2228, P2229, P2453, P2494, P2495, P2564, P2565, or P268A is not set. The engine speed is stable between 1400-3000 RPM. Fuel injector delivery rate is stable. Ambient air temperature is greater than -7°C (19. 4°F). BARO is greater than 75 kPa (11 psi). Turbocharger actuator position sensor offset learning is not active. Turbocharger vane cleaning, wiping, procedure is not active. DTC P0299 runs continuously when the above conditions are met.
DTC: P0299 00	**Engine Underboost Malfunction:** The engine is running. The DTCs run continuously when the above conditions are met.
DTC: P029C	**Cylinder 1 Injector Stuck Closed:** The engine is running. The ECM monitors for a condition once per camshaft revolution.
DTC: P029D	**Injector 1 Leak:** Engine has been running for more than 10 seconds. Engine coolant is more than 45°C (113°F). DTCs P0201-P0208, P1224, P1227, P122A, P1233, P1236, P1239, P1242, P1247, P2146, P2149, P2152 or P2155 are not set. The vehicle speed is in Park or Neutral. Engine speed is between 600-850 RPM. This diagnostic runs once per ignition cycle once the above criteria has been met.
DTC: P02A0	**Cylinder 2 Injector Stuck Closed:** The engine is running. The ECM monitors for a condition once per camshaft revolution.
DTC: P02A1	**Injector 2 Leak:** Engine has been running for more than 10 seconds. Engine coolant is more than 45°C (113°F). DTCs P0201-P0208, P1224, P1227, P122A, P1233, P1236, P1239, P1242, P1247, P2146, P2149, P2152 or P2155 are not set. The vehicle speed is in Park or Neutral. Engine speed is between 600-850 RPM. This diagnostic runs once per ignition cycle once the above criteria has been met.
DTC: P02A4	**Cylinder 3 Injector Stuck Closed:** The engine is running. The ECM monitors for a condition once per camshaft revolution.
DTC: P02A5	**Injector 3 Leak:** Engine has been running for more than 10 seconds. Engine coolant is more than 45°C (113°F). DTCs P0201-P0208, P1224, P1227, P122A, P1233, P1236, P1239, P1242, P1247, P2146, P2149, P2152 or P2155 are not set. The vehicle speed is in Park or Neutral. Engine speed is between 600-850 RPM. This diagnostic runs once per ignition cycle once the above criteria has been met.
DTC: P02A8	**Cylinder 4 Injector Stuck Closed:** The engine is running. The ECM monitors for a condition once per camshaft revolution.
DTC: P02A9	**Injector 4 Leak:** Engine has been running for more than 10 seconds. Engine coolant is more than 45°C (113°F). DTCs P0201-P0208, P1224, P1227, P122A, P1233, P1236, P1239, P1242, P1247, P2146, P2149, P2152 or P2155 are not set. The vehicle speed is in Park or Neutral. Engine speed is between 600-850 RPM. This diagnostic runs once per ignition cycle once the above criteria has been met.
DTC: P02AD	**Injector 5 Leak:** Engine has been running for more than 10 seconds. Engine coolant is more than 45°C (113°F). DTCs P0201-P0208, P1224, P1227, P122A, P1233, P1236, P1239, P1242, P1247, P2146, P2149, P2152 or P2155 are not set. The vehicle speed is in Park or Neutral. Engine speed is between 600-850 RPM. This diagnostic runs once per ignition cycle once the above criteria has been met.

DTC	Trouble Code Title, Conditions, Possible Causes
DTC: P02B1	**Injector 6 Leak:** Engine has been running for more than 10 seconds. Engine coolant is more than 45°C (113°F). DTCs P0201-P0208, P1224, P1227, P122A, P1233, P1236, P1239, P1242, P1247, P2146, P2149, P2152 or P2155 are not set. The vehicle speed is in Park or Neutral. Engine speed is between 600-850 RPM. This diagnostic runs once per ignition cycle once the above criteria has been met.
DTC: P02B5	**Injector 7 Leak:** Engine has been running for more than 10 seconds. Engine coolant is more than 45°C (113°F). DTCs P0201-P0208, P1224, P1227, P122A, P1233, P1236, P1239, P1242, P1247, P2146, P2149, P2152 or P2155 are not set. The vehicle speed is in Park or Neutral. Engine speed is between 600-850 RPM. This diagnostic runs once per ignition cycle once the above criteria has been met.
DTC: P02B9	**Injector 8 Leak:** Engine has been running for more than 10 seconds. Engine coolant is more than 45°C (113°F). DTCs P0201-P0208, P1224, P1227, P122A, P1233, P1236, P1239, P1242, P1247, P2146, P2149, P2152 or P2155 are not set. The vehicle speed is in Park or Neutral. Engine speed is between 600-850 RPM. This diagnostic runs once per ignition cycle once the above criteria has been met.
DTC: P02CC	**Cylinder 1 Injector Exceeded Minimum Learning Limit:** The engine is running. The ECM monitors for a condition once per camshaft revolution.
DTC: P02CD	**Cylinder 1 Injector Exceeded Maximum Learning Limit:** The engine is running. The ECM monitors for a condition once per camshaft revolution.
DTC: P02CE	**Cylinder 2 Injector Exceeded Minimum Learning Limit:** The engine is running. The ECM monitors for a condition once per camshaft revolution.
DTC: P02CF	**Cylinder 2 Injector Exceeded Maximum Learning Limit:** The engine is running. The ECM monitors for a condition once per camshaft revolution.
DTC: P02D0	**Cylinder 3 Injector Exceeded Minimum Learning Limit:** The engine is running. The ECM monitors for a condition once per camshaft revolution.
DTC: P02D1	**Cylinder 3 Injector Exceeded Maximum Learning Limit:** The engine is running. The ECM monitors for a condition once per camshaft revolution.
DTC: P02D2	**Cylinder 4 Injector Exceeded Minimum Learning Limit:** The engine is running. The ECM monitors for a condition once per camshaft revolution.
DTC: P02D3	**Cylinder 4 Injector Exceeded Maximum Learning Limit:** The engine is running. The ECM monitors for a condition once per camshaft revolution.
DTC: P02E0	**Diesel Intake Air (IA) Flow Control Circuit:** The ECM is powered up for more than 0. 5 second. The IA valve duty cycle is greater than 10 percent. DTC P02E0 runs continuously.
DTC: P02E0	**Intake Air (IA) Flow Valve Control Circuit:** P02E0The ignition is OFF. The engine is in after-run. The battery voltage is greater than 11 V. The throttle valve motor control circuit is active. The DTC runs continuously whenever the above conditions are met.
DTC: P02E0 00	**Intake Air Flow Valve Control Circuit:** The ignition is ON, or the engine is running. The throttle actuator motor is commanded ON or OFF. The ignition voltage is less than 16 V. The DTCs run continuously when the above conditions are met.
DTC: P02E0 01	**Intake Air Flow Valve Control Circuit Short to Battery:** The ignition is ON, or the engine is running. The throttle actuator motor is commanded ON or OFF. The ignition voltage is less than 16 V. The DTCs run continuously when the above conditions are met.
DTC: P02E0 02	**Intake Air Flow Valve Control Circuit Short to Ground:** The ignition is ON, or the engine is running. The throttle actuator motor is commanded ON or OFF. The ignition voltage is less than 16 V. The DTCs run continuously when the above conditions are met.
DTC: P02E0 04	**Intake Air Flow Valve Control Circuit Open:** The ignition is ON, or the engine is running. The throttle actuator motor is commanded ON or OFF. The ignition voltage is less than 16 V. The DTCs run continuously when the above conditions are met.
DTC: P02E0 54	**Intake Air Flow Valve Control Circuit High Temperature:** The ignition is ON, or the engine is running. The throttle actuator motor is commanded ON or OFF. The ignition voltage is less than 16 V. The DTCs run continuously when the above conditions are met.
DTC: P02E1 00	**Intake Air Flow Valve Control Performance:** The ignition is ON, or the engine is running. The throttle actuator motor is commanded ON or OFF. The ignition voltage is less than 16 V. The DTCs run continuously when the above conditions are met.

DTC	Trouble Code Title, Conditions, Possible Causes
DTC: P02E2	**Intake Air (IA) Flow Valve Control Circuit Low Voltage:** P02E2, P02E3, P02EB, P122C, P122E and P122FThe battery voltage is greater than 11 V. The Engine is running. The throttle valve motor control circuit is active. The DTCs run continuously whenever the above conditions are met.
DTC: P02E2 00	**Intake Air Flow Valve Control Circuit Low Voltage:** The ignition is ON, or the engine is running. The throttle actuator motor is commanded ON or OFF. The ignition voltage is less than 16 V. The DTCs run continuously when the above conditions are met.
DTC: P02E3	**Intake Air (IA) Flow Valve Control Circuit High Voltage:** P02E2, P02E3, P02EB, P122C, P122E and P122FThe battery voltage is greater than 11 V. The Engine is running. The throttle valve motor control circuit is active. The DTCs run continuously whenever the above conditions are met.
DTC: P02E3 00	**Intake Air Flow Valve Control Circuit High Voltage:** The ignition is ON, or the engine is running. The throttle actuator motor is commanded ON or OFF. The ignition voltage is less than 16 V. The DTCs run continuously when the above conditions are met.
DTC: P02E7	**Intake Air (IA) Flow Valve Position Sensor Performance:** P02E7The engine speed is greater than 600 RPM for greater than 10 s. The engine is not in afterrun mode. The charge air cooler temperature is less than 199°C (390°F). DTC P02E7 runs continuously when the above conditions are met.
DTC: P02E7	**Diesel Intake Air (IA) Flow Position Sensor Performance:** DTCs P02E0, P02E8, P02E9, P0642 or P0643 are not set. DTC P02E7 runs continuously while the IA valve is actively being controlled.
DTC: P02E8	**Diesel Intake Air (IA) Flow Position Sensor Circuit Low Voltage:** P02E8 and P02E9 DTCs P0698 or P0699 are not set. The ignition is ON. DTCs P02E8 and P02E9 run continuously.
DTC: P02E8	**Intake Air (IA) Flow Valve Position Sensor Circuit Low Voltage:** P02E8 and P02E9The engine speed is greater than 600 RPM for greater than 10 s. The engine is not in afterrun mode. DTC P02E8 and P02E9 run continuously when the above conditions are met.
DTC: P02E8 00	**Intake Air Flow Valve Position Sensor Circuit Low Voltage:** The ignition is ON, or the engine is running. The throttle actuator motor is commanded ON or OFF. The ignition voltage is less than 16 V. The DTCs run continuously when the above conditions are met.
DTC: P02E9	**Diesel Intake Air (IA) Flow Position Sensor Circuit High Voltage:** P02E8 and P02E9 DTCs P0698 or P0699 are not set. The ignition is ON. DTCs P02E8 and P02E9 run continuously.
DTC: P02E9	**Intake Air (IA) Flow Valve Position Sensor Circuit High Voltage:** P02E8 and P02E9The engine speed is greater than 600 RPM for greater than 10 s. The engine is not in afterrun mode. DTC P02E8 and P02E9 run continuously when the above conditions are met.
DTC: P02E9 00	**Intake Air Flow Valve Position Sensor Circuit High Voltage:** The ignition is ON, or the engine is running. The throttle actuator motor is commanded ON or OFF. The ignition voltage is less than 16 V. The DTCs run continuously when the above conditions are met.
DTC: P02EB	**Intake Air (IA) Flow Valve Control Motor Current Performance:** P02E2, P02E3, P02EB, P122C, P122E and P122FThe battery voltage is greater than 11 V. The Engine is running. The throttle valve motor control circuit is active. The DTCs run continuously whenever the above conditions are met.
DTC: P02EB 00	**Intake Air Flow Valve Control Motor Current Performance:** The ignition is ON, or the engine is running. The throttle actuator motor is commanded ON or OFF. The ignition voltage is less than 16 V. The DTCs run continuously when the above conditions are met.
DTC: P0300	**Engine Misfire Detected:** DTC P0010, P0011, P0013, P0014, P0016, P0017, P0018, P0019, P0020, P0021, P0023, P0024, P0068, P0101, P0102, P0103, P0106, P0107, P0108, P0112, P0113, P0117, P0118, P0120, P0121, P0122, P0123, P0220, P0222, P0223, P0335, P0336, P0606, P0641, P0651, P1516, P2101, P2122, P2123, P2127, P2128 or P2176 is not set. The engine speed is between 450-6,600 RPM. The evaporative emissions (EVAP) leak detection is not active. The delivered torque signal is greater than 5 % at idle. The delivered torque signal is between 6-29 % with the transmission in drive. The engine coolant temperature (ECT) is between -7 and +127°C (+19 and +261°F). The ECM is not receiving a rough road signal. The fuel level is greater than 11 %. The antilock brake system (ABS) and the traction control system (TCS) are not active or detecting rough road. Torque Converter Clutch (TCC) is not applied/active. The ECM is not in fuel cut-off or decel fuel cut-off mode. DTCs P0300 through P0306 run continuously when the above conditions exist for greater than 1,000 engine revolutions. 200 revolutions after the first failure.

DTC	Trouble Code Title, Conditions, Possible Causes
DTC: P0300 00	**Engine Misfire Detected:** DTCs P0016 00, P0121 00, P0122 00, P0123 00, P0222 00, P0223 00, P0335 00, P0336 00 or P0502 00 are not set. The engine speed is between 520-6 200 RPM. The ignition voltage is between 11-18 V. The engine coolant temperature (ECT) is between -7 to +120°C (+19 to +248°F). The A/C compressor clutch is not changing states. The fuel tank level is more than 15%. The ECM is not in fuel cut-off or deceleration fuel cut-off mode. The ECM is not receiving a rough road signal. The throttle angle is steady within 10%. The throttle angle is less than 4% when the vehicle speed is more than 10 km/h (6 MPH). The transmission is not changing gears. DTCs P0300 00 - P0304 00 run continuously when the above conditions are met.
DTC: P0301	**Cylinder 1 Misfire Detected:** DTCs P0016, P0101, P0102, P0103, P0107, P0108, P0116, P0117, P0118, P0120, P0121, P0122, P0123, P0125, P0128, P0220, P0222, P0223, P0335, P0336, P0608, P1516, P2101, P2119, P2120, P2122, P2123, P2125, P2135, or P2138 are not set. DTC P0315 is not set and the engine speed is between 525-6,000 RPM. ORDTC P0315 is set and the engine speed is less than 1,000 RPM. The ignition voltage is between 9-18 V. The engine coolant temperature (ECT) parameter is between -7 and +126°C (+19 and +259°F). If the ECT is less than -7°C (+19°F) at engine start-up, this diagnostic is disabled until the ECT is more than +21°C (+69°F). The fuel level is more than 10 %. The antilock brake system (ABS) and the traction control system (TCS) are not active or detecting rough road. The ECM is not in fuel shut-off or decel fuel cut-off mode. The power management is not active. Excessive drive wheel slip is not detected. DTC P0300 runs continuously when the above conditions are met.
DTC: P0301 00	**Cylinder 1 Misfire Detected:** DTCs P0016 00, P0121 00, P0122 00, P0123 00, P0222 00, P0223 00, P0335 00, P0336 00 or P0502 00 are not set. The engine speed is between 520-6 200 RPM. The ignition voltage is between 11-18 V. The engine coolant temperature (ECT) is between -7 to +120°C (+19 to +248°F). The A/C compressor clutch is not changing states. The fuel tank level is more than 15%. The ECM is not in fuel cut-off or deceleration fuel cut-off mode. The ECM is not receiving a rough road signal. The throttle angle is steady within 10%. The throttle angle is less than 4% when the vehicle speed is more than 10 km/h (6 MPH). The transmission is not changing gears. DTCs P0300 00 - P0304 00 run continuously when the above conditions are met.
DTC: P0302	**Cylinder 2 Misfire Detected:** DTC P0010, P0011, P0016, P0068, P0101, P0102, P0103, P0106, P0107, P0108, P0112, P0113, P0116, P0117, P0118, P0120, P0122, P0123, P0128, P0220, P0222, P0223, P0335, P0336, P0606, P0641, P0651, P1516, P2101, P2119, P2120, P2122, P2123, P2125, P2127, P2128, P2135, P2138, P2176, P3401, P3425, P3441, and P3449 are not set. The engine speed is between 375-5,800 RPM and DTC P0315 is not set. OR The engine speed is greater than 1,000 rpm and DTC P0315 is set. The Ignition voltage is between 9-18 volts. The engine coolant temperature (ECT) is between -7 and +130°C (+19 and +266°F). If the ECT is less than -7°C (+19°F) at startup this diagnostic will not run until the ECT is more than +21°C (+69°F). The fuel level is more than 10 percent. The antilock brake system (ABS) and the traction control system (TCS) are not active or detecting rough road. Torque Converter Clutch (TCC) is not applied/active. The power management is not active. The ECM is not in fuel shut-off, or decel fuel cut-off mode. Excessive drive wheel slip is not detected. The power take-off (PTO) is disabled; where applicable. The cylinder deactivation is not in progress; where applicable. A manual transmission with a throttle position less than 95 percent. DTCs P0300-P0308 run continuously when the above conditions are met.
DTC: P0302 00	**Cylinder 2 Misfire Detected:** DTCs P0010 00, P0011 00, P0013 00, P0014 00, P0016 00, P0017 00, P0101 00, P0102 00, P0103 00, P0112 00, P0113 00, P0117 00, P0118 00, P0121 00, P0122 00, P0123 00, P0222 00, P0223 00, P0315 00, P0335 00, P0336 00, P0502 00, P0651 00, and P2135 00 are not set. The engine speed is between 600-6 528 RPM. The ignition voltage is between 11-18 V. The engine coolant temperature (ECT) sensor is between -7 to +125°C (+19 to +257°F). The A/C compressor clutch is not changing states. The fuel tank level is greater than 15%. The ECM is not in fuel cut-off or deceleration fuel cut-off mode. The ECM is not receiving a rough road signal. The throttle angle is steady within 5%. The throttle angle is greater than 3% when the vehicle speed is greater than 5 km/h (3 MPH). The transmission is not changing gears. The antilock brake system (ABS) and the traction control system , if equipped, is not active. DTCs P0300 00, P0301 00, P0302 00, P0303 00, and P0304 00 run continuously when the above conditions are met.
DTC: P0303	**Cylinder 3 Misfire Detected:** DTC P0010, P0011, P0016, P0068, P0101, P0102, P0103, P0106, P0107, P0108, P0112, P0113, P0116, P0117, P0118, P0120, P0122, P0123, P0128, P0220, P0222, P0223, P0335, P0336, P0606, P0641, P0651, P1516, P2101, P2119, P2120, P2122, P2123, P2125, P2127, P2128, P2135, P2138, P2176, P3401, P3425, P3441, and P3449 are not set. The engine speed is between 375-5,800 RPM and DTC P0315 is not set. OR The engine speed is greater than 1,000 rpm and DTC P0315 is set. The ignition voltage is between 9-18 volts. The engine coolant temperature (ECT) is between -7 and +130°C (+19 and +266°F). If the ECT is less than -7°C (+19°F) at startup this diagnostic will not run until the ECT is more than +21°C (+69°F). The fuel level is more than 10 percent. The antilock brake system (ABS) and the traction control system (TCS) are not active or detecting rough road. The power management is not active. The ECM is not in fuel shut-off, or decel fuel cut-off mode. Excessive drive wheel slip is not detected. Power Take Off (PTO) is disabled. Cylinder Deactivation is not in progress. A manual transmission with a throttle position less than 95 percent. DTC P0300-P0306 runs continuously when the above conditions are met.

DTC	Trouble Code Title, Conditions, Possible Causes
DTC: P0303 00	**Cylinder 3 Misfire Detected:** DTCs P0010 00, P0011 00, P0013 00, P0014 00, P0016 00, P0017 00, P0101 00, P0102 00, P0103 00, P0112 00, P0113 00, P0117 00, P0118 00, P0121 00, P0122 00, P0123 00, P0222 00, P0223 00, P0315 00, P0335 00, P0336 00, P0502 00, P0651 00, and P2135 00 are not set. The engine speed is between 600-6 528 RPM. The ignition voltage is between 11-18 V. The engine coolant temperature (ECT) sensor is between -7 to +125°C (+19 to +257°F). The A/C compressor clutch is not changing states. The fuel tank level is greater than 15%. The ECM is not in fuel cut-off or deceleration fuel cut-off mode. The ECM is not receiving a rough road signal. The throttle angle is steady within 5%. The throttle angle is greater than 3% when the vehicle speed is greater than 5 km/h (3 MPH). The transmission is not changing gears. The antilock brake system (ABS) and the traction control system , if equipped, is not active. DTCs P0300 00, P0301 00, P0302 00, P0303 00, and P0304 00 run continuously when the above conditions are met.
DTC: P0304	**Cylinder 4 Misfire Detected:** DTCs P0016, P0068, P0101, P0102, P0103, P0106, P0107, P0108, P0111, P0112, P0113, P0117, P0118, P0119, P0120, P0122, P0123, P0220, P0222, P0223, P0335, P0336, P0606, P0641, P0651, P1516, P2101, P2120, P2122, P2123, P2125, P2127, P2128, P2135, P2138, and P2176 are not set. DTCs P0010 and P0011 are not set – without LU3. When DTC P0315 is set, the engine speed must be greater than 1,000 RPM. Engine run time is greater than 2 crankshaft revolutions. The engine speed is between 375-5,600 RPM. The ignition voltage is between 9-32 volts. The engine coolant temperature (ECT) is between -7 and +130°C (+19 and +266°F). When the startup ECT is colder than -7°C (+19°F), this diagnostic will be delayed until the ECT is warmer than +21°C (+69°F). The fuel level is greater than 10 percent. The ECM is not in fuel shut-off, or decel fuel cut-off mode. The electronic brake control module (EBCM) and the traction control system (TCS) are not active or detecting rough road. An automatic transmission shift with a throttle position greater than 95 percent is not occurring. The power management is not active. Excessive drive wheel slip is not detected. The power take-off (PTO) is disabled, where applicable. The cylinder deactivation is not in progress, where applicable. DTCs P0300-P0308 run continuously when the above conditions are met.
DTC: P0304 00	**Cylinder 4 Misfire Detected:** DTCs P0010 00, P0011 00, P0013 00, P0014 00, P0016 00, P0017 00, P0101 00, P0102 00, P0103 00, P0112 00, P0113 00, P0117 00, P0118 00, P0121 00, P0122 00, P0123 00, P0222 00, P0223 00, P0315 00, P0335 00, P0336 00, P0502 00, P0651 00, and P2135 00 are not set. The engine speed is between 600-6 528 RPM. The ignition voltage is between 11-18 V. The engine coolant temperature (ECT) sensor is between -7 to +125°C (+19 to +257°F). The A/C compressor clutch is not changing states. The fuel tank level is greater than 15%. The ECM is not in fuel cut-off or deceleration fuel cut-off mode. The ECM is not receiving a rough road signal. The throttle angle is steady within 5%. The throttle angle is greater than 3% when the vehicle speed is greater than 5 km/h (3 MPH). The transmission is not changing gears. The antilock brake system (ABS) and the traction control system , if equipped, is not active. DTCs P0300 00, P0301 00, P0302 00, P0303 00, and P0304 00 run continuously when the above conditions are met.
DTC: P0305	**Cylinder 5 Misfire Detected:** DTC P0010, P0011, P0016, P0068, P0101, P0102, P0103, P0106, P0107, P0108, P0112, P0113, P0116, P0117, P0118, P0120, P0122, P0123, P0128, P0220, P0222, P0223, P0335, P0336, P0606, P0641, P0651, P1516, P2101, P2119, P2120, P2122, P2123, P2125, P2127, P2128, P2135, P2138, P2176, P3401, P3425, P3441, and P3449 are not set. The engine speed is between 375-5,800 RPM and DTC P0315 is not set. OR The engine speed is greater than 1,000 rpm and DTC P0315 is set. The ignition voltage is between 9-18 volts. The engine coolant temperature (ECT) is between -7 and +130°C (+19 and +266°F). If the ECT is less than -7°C (+19°F) at startup this diagnostic will not run until the ECT is more than +21°C (+69°F). The fuel level is more than 10 percent. The antilock brake system (ABS) and the traction control system (TCS) are not active or detecting rough road. The power management is not active. The ECM is not in fuel shut-off, or decel fuel cut-off mode. Excessive drive wheel slip is not detected. Power Take Off (PTO) is disabled. Cylinder Deactivation is not in progress. A manual transmission with a throttle position less than 95 percent. DTC P0300-P0306 runs continuously when the above conditions are met.
DTC: P0306	**Cylinder 6 Misfire Detected:** DTC P0010, P0011, P0013, P0014, P0016, P0017, P0018, P0019, P0020, P0021, P0023, P0024, P0068, P0101, P0102, P0103, P0106, P0107, P0108, P0112, P0113, P0117, P0118, P0120, P0121, P0122, P0123, P0220, P0222, P0223, P0335, P0336, P0606, P0641, P0651, P1516, P2101, P2122, P2123, P2127, P2128 or P2176 is not set. The engine speed is between 450-6,600 RPM. The evaporative emissions (EVAP) leak detection is not active. The delivered torque signal is greater than 5 % at idle. The delivered torque signal is between 6-29 % with the transmission in drive. The engine coolant temperature (ECT) is between -7 and +127°C (+19 and +261°F). The ECM is not receiving a rough road signal. The fuel level is greater than 11 %. The antilock brake system (ABS) and the traction control system (TCS) are not active or detecting rough road. Torque Converter Clutch (TCC) is not applied/ active. The ECM is not in fuel cut-off or decel fuel cut-off mode. DTCs P0300 through P0306 run continuously when the above conditions exist for greater than 1,000 engine revolutions. 200 revolutions after the first failure.

DTC	Trouble Code Title, Conditions, Possible Causes
DTC: P0307	**Cylinder 7 Misfire Detected:** DTC P0010, P0011, P0016, P0068, P0101, P0102, P0103, P0106, P0107, P0108, P0112, P0113, P0116, P0117, P0118, P0120, P0122, P0123, P0128, P0220, P0222, P0223, P0335, P0336, P0606, P0641, P0651, P1516, P2101, P2119, P2120, P2122, P2123, P2125, P2127, P2128, P2135, P2138, P2176, P3401, P3425, P3441, and P3449 are not set. The engine speed is between 375-5,800 RPM and DTC P0315 is not set. OR The engine speed is greater than 1,000 rpm and DTC P0315 is set. The ignition voltage is between 9-18 volts. The engine coolant temperature (ECT) is between -7 and +130°C (+19 and +266°F). If the ECT is less than -7°C (+19°F) at startup this diagnostic will not run until the ECT is more than +21°C (+69°F). The fuel level is more than 10 percent. The antilock brake system (ABS) and the traction control system (TCS) are not active or detecting rough road. Torque Converter Clutch (TCC) is not applied/active. The power management is not active. The ECM is not in fuel shut-off, or decel fuel cut-off mode. Excessive drive wheel slip is not detected. The power take-off (PTO) is disabled; where applicable. The cylinder deactivation is not in progress; where applicable. A manual transmission with a throttle position less than 95 percent. DTCs P0300-P0308 run continuously when the above conditions are met.
DTC: P0308	**Cylinder 8 Misfire Detected:** DTCs P0016, P0068, P0101, P0102, P0103, P0106, P0107, P0108, P0111, P0112, P0113, P0117, P0118, P0119, P0120, P0122, P0123, P0220, P0222, P0223, P0335, P0336, P0606, P0641, P0651, P1516, P2101, P2120, P2122, P2123, P2125, P2127, P2128, P2135, P2138, and P2176 are not set. DTCs P0010 and P0011 are not set – without LU3. When DTC P0315 is set, the engine speed must be greater than 1,000 RPM. Engine run time is greater than 2 crankshaft revolutions. The engine speed is between 375-5,600 RPM. The ignition voltage is between 9-32 volts. The engine coolant temperature (ECT) is between -7 and +130°C (+19 and +266°F). When the startup ECT is colder than -7°C (+19°F), this diagnostic will be delayed until the ECT is warmer than +21°C (+69°F). The fuel level is greater than 10 percent. The ECM is not in fuel shut-off, or decel fuel cut-off mode. The electronic brake control module (EBCM) and the traction control system (TCS) are not active or detecting rough road. An automatic transmission shift with a throttle position greater than 95 percent is not occurring. The power management is not active. Excessive drive wheel slip is not detected. The power take-off (PTO) is disabled, where applicable. The cylinder deactivation is not in progress, where applicable. DTCs P0300-P0308 run continuously when the above conditions are met.
DTC: P0313 00	**Misfire Detected With Low Fuel Level:** DTCs P0016 00, P0121 00, P0122 00, P0123 00, P0221 00, P0222 00, P0223 00, P0335 00 or P0336 00 are not set. The engine speed is between 600-6528 RPM. The ECM is not in fuel cut-off mode. DTCs P0300 00, P0304 00, and P0313 00 run continuously when the above conditions are met.
DTC: P0315	**Crankshaft Position System Variation Not Learned:** DTCs P0016, P0335, P0336, P0340, and P0341 are not set. The engine speed is between 900-1,900 RPM. The ECM is in fuel shut-off, or decel fuel cut-off mode. The Crankshaft Position Reluctor Wheel Learn has not learned successfully. The diagnostic runs continuously when the above conditions are met.
DTC: P0315	**Crankshaft Position System Variation Not Learned:** The engine is running. The DTC runs continuously.
DTC: P0315 00	**Crankshaft Position System Variation Not Learned:** The engine is running. DTC P0315 00 runs continuously once the above conditions are met.
DTC: P0318 00	**Rough Road Sensor Circuit:** The ignition is ON or the engine is operating. DTC P0318 00 runs continuously once the above conditions are met.
DTC: P0324	**Knock Sensor System Performance:** P0324 and P0326–Excessive Knock Detection Mode. Engine speed is between 400-8,500 RPM. The engine coolant temperature (ECT) is warmer than -40°C (-40°F). The intake air temperature (IAT) is warmer than -40°C (-40°F). The DTCs run continuously when the above conditions are met. P0324 and P0326–Abnormal Noise Detection Mode–Improperly Bolted Knock Sensor. Engine speed is between 2,200-8,500 RPM. The ECT is greater than -40°C (-40°F). The IAT is greater than -40°C (-40°F). The DTCs run continuously when the above conditions are met.
DTC: P0324 00	**Knock Sensor System Performance:** P0324 00, and P0326 00 Excessive Knock Detection Mode. Engine speed is between 400-8 500 RPM. The ECT is greater than -40°C (-40°F). The IAT is greater than -40°C (-40°F). The DTCs run continuously when the above conditions are met. P0324 00 and P0326 00 Abnormal Noise Detection Mode, Improperly Bolted Knock Sensor. Engine speed is between 2 200-8 500 RPM. The ECT is greater than -40°C (-40°F). The IAT is greater than -40°C (-40°F). The DTCs run continuously when the above conditions are met.
DTC: P0325	**Knock Sensor (KS) Circuit Bank 1:** DTC P0324 runs continuously when the engine speed is greater than 2,000 RPM and the engine load is greater than a calibrated amount. DTC P0326 runs continuously when: The engine speed is greater than or equal to 800 RPM. The MAP is greater than 42 kPa. DTCs P0120, P0121, P0122, or P0123 are not set. DTC P0325, P0330, P0327, P0328, P0332, P0333 run continuously when: The engine coolant temperature (ECT) is greater than 75°C (167°F). The engine run time is greater than 90 s.
DTC: P0325 00	**Knock Sensor Circuit:** DTCs P0106 00, P0107 00, and P0108 00 are not set. The engine speed is greater than 1 600 RPM. The engine coolant temperature (ECT) is more than 50°C (122°F). The manifold absolute pressure (MAP) is between 10-50 kPa (1. 4-7. 2 PSI) which depends on engine speed. This DTC runs continuously within the enabling conditions.

DTC	Trouble Code Title, Conditions, Possible Causes
DTC: P0326	**Knock Sensor Performance:** P0324 and P0326–Excessive Knock Detection Mode. Engine speed is between 400-8,500 RPM. The engine coolant temperature (ECT) is warmer than -40°C (-40°F). The intake air temperature (IAT) is warmer than -40°C (-40°F). The DTCs run continuously when the above conditions are met. P0324 and P0326–Abnormal Noise Detection Mode–Improperly Bolted Knock Sensor. Engine speed is between 2,200-8,500 RPM. The ECT is greater than -40°C (-40°F). The IAT is greater than -40°C (-40°F). The DTCs run continuously when the above conditions are met.
DTC: P0326 00	**Knock Sensor Performance:** The engine speed is greater than 700 RPM. The engine speed is between 700-2 500 RPM for DTC P06B6 00. The airflow into the engine is between 40-2 000 mg/cylinder. This DTC runs continuously within the enabling conditions. DTCs P0324 00, P0326 00 and P06B6 00 run continuously once the above conditions are met.
DTC: P0326 00	**Knock Sensor 1 Performance:** The engine is running. The ignition voltage is less than 16 V. These DTC runs continuously once the above conditions are met.
DTC: P0327	**Knock Sensor (KS) Circuit Low Frequency Bank 1:** P0327, P0328, P0332, and P0333 DTC P0112, P0113, P0116, P0117, P0118, or P0128 is not set. The engine coolant temperature (ECT) is greater than -40°C (-40°F). The engine oil temperature is less than 256°C (492. 8°F). The engine run time is greater than 2 minutes. DTCs P0327, P0328, P0332, and P0333 run continuously when the above conditions are met.
DTC: P0327 00	**Knock Sensor Circuit Low Voltage:** P0325 00, P0327 00, and P0328 00Engine speed is between 400-8 500 RPM. The engine coolant temperature (ECT) is greater than -40°C (-40°F). The intake air temperature (IAT) is greater than -40°C (-40°F). The DTCs run continuously when the above conditions are met.
DTC: P0328	**Knock Sensor (KS) Circuit High Frequency Bank 1:** P0327, P0328, P0332, and P0333 DTC P0112, P0113, P0116, P0117, P0118, or P0128 is not set. The engine coolant temperature (ECT) is greater than -40°C (-40°F). The engine oil temperature is less than 256°C (492. 8°F). The engine run time is greater than 2 minutes. DTCs P0327, P0328, P0332, and P0333 run continuously when the above conditions are met.
DTC: P0328	**Knock Sensor (KS) Circuit High Bank 1:** P0325, P0326, and P0330The engine is idling. The manifold absolute pressure (MAP) is greater than 19 kPa. The DTCs run continuously when the above conditions are met. P0324, P0327, P0328, and P0333The ignition is ON. The DTCs run continuously when the above condition is met.
DTC: P0328 00	**Knock Sensor Circuit High Voltage:** The engine speed is greater than 700 RPM. The engine speed is between 700-2 500 RPM for DTC P06B6 00. The airflow into the engine is between 40-2 000 mg/cylinder. This DTC runs continuously within the enabling conditions. DTCs P0324 00, P0326 00 and P06B6 00 run continuously once the above conditions are met.
DTC: P0330	**Knock Sensor (KS) Circuit Bank 2:** DTC P0324 runs continuously when the engine speed is greater than 2,000 RPM and the engine load is greater than a calibrated amount. DTC P0326 runs continuously when: The engine speed is greater than or equal to 800 RPM. The MAP is greater than 42 kPa. DTCs P0120, P0121, P0122, or P0123 are not set. DTC P0325, P0330, P0327, P0328, P0332, P0333 run continuously when: The engine coolant temperature (ECT) is greater than 75°C (167°F). The engine run time is greater than 90 s.
DTC: P0330	**Knock Sensor (KS) Circuit Bank 2:** P0325 and P0330 DTC P0324, P0325, P0326, P0327, P0328, P0330, P0332, or P0333 is not set. The engine speed is greater than 400 RPM. The engine coolant temperature (ECT) is greater than -40°C (-40°F). The engine run time is greater than 2 minutes. The power take-off (PTO) is not active. DTCs P0325 and P0330 run continuously when the above conditions are met.
DTC: P0331	**Knock Sensor Performance Bank 2:** P0324, P0326 and P0331–Excessive Knock Detection Mode. Engine speed is between 400-8,500 RPM. The engine coolant temperature (ECT) is warmer than -40°C (-40°F). The intake air temperature (IAT) is warmer than -40°C (-40°F). The DTCs run continuously when the above conditions are met. P0324, P0326 and P0331–Abnormal Noise Detection Mode–Improperly Bolted Knock Sensor. Engine speed is between 2,200-8,500 RPM. The ECT is warmer than -40°C (-40°F). The IAT is warmer than -40°C (-40°F). The DTCs run continuously when the above conditions are met.
DTC: P0331 00	**Knock Sensor 2 Performance:** The engine is running. The ignition voltage is less than 16 V. These DTC runs continuously once the above conditions are met.
DTC: P0332	**Knock Sensor Circuit Low Bank 2:** P0324, P0327, P0328, P0332, and P0333The ignition is ON. The DTCs run continuously when the above condition is met.
DTC: P0332	**Knock Sensor (KS) Circuit Low Bank 2:** P0325, P0326, and P0330The engine is idling. The manifold absolute pressure (MAP) is greater than 19 kPa. The DTCs run continuously when the above conditions are met. P0324, P0327, P0328, and P0333The ignition is ON. The DTCs run continuously when the above condition is met.

DTC	Trouble Code Title, Conditions, Possible Causes
DTC: P0332	**Knock Sensor (KS) Circuit Low Voltage Bank 2:** DTC P0324 runs continuously when the engine speed is greater than 2,000 RPM and the engine load is greater than a calibrated amount. DTC P0326 runs continuously when: The engine speed is greater than or equal to 800 RPM. The MAP is greater than 42 kPa. DTCs P0120, P0121, P0122, or P0123 are not set. DTC P0325, P0330, P0327, P0328, P0332, P0333 run continuously when: The engine coolant temperature (ECT) is greater than 75°C (167°F). The engine run time is greater than 90 s.
DTC: P0332	**Knock Sensor (KS) Circuit Low Frequency Bank 2:** P0327, P0328, P0332, and P0333 DTC P0112, P0113, P0116, P0117, P0118, or P0128 is not set. The engine coolant temperature (ECT) is greater than -40°C (-40°F). The engine oil temperature is less than 256°C (492. 8°F). The engine run time is greater than 2 minutes. DTCs P0327, P0328, P0332, and P0333 run continuously when the above conditions are met.
DTC: P0333	**Knock Sensor Circuit High Bank 2:** P0327, P0328, P0332, and P0333The ignition is ON. The DTCs run continuously when the above condition is met.
DTC: P0333	**Knock Sensor (KS) Circuit High Frequency Bank 2:** P0327, P0328, P0332, and P0333 DTC P0112, P0113, P0116, P0117, P0118, or P0128 is not set. The engine coolant temperature (ECT) is greater than -40°C (-40°F). The engine oil temperature is less than 256°C (492. 8°F). The engine run time is greater than 2 minutes. DTCs P0327, P0328, P0332, and P0333 run continuously when the above conditions are met.
DTC: P0333	**Knock Sensor (KS) Circuit High Voltage Bank 2:** DTC P0324 runs continuously when the engine speed is greater than 2,000 RPM and the engine load is greater than a calibrated amount. DTC P0326 runs continuously when: The engine speed is greater than or equal to 800 RPM. The MAP is greater than 42 kPa. DTCs P0120, P0121, P0122, or P0123 are not set. DTC P0325, P0330, P0327, P0328, P0332, P0333 run continuously when: The engine coolant temperature (ECT) is greater than 75°C (167°F). The engine run time is greater than 90 s.
DTC: P0335	**Crankshaft Position Sensor Circuit:** The engine is cranking or running. The camshaft position sensor signal is present. DTC P0335 runs continuously when the above conditions are met.
DTC: P0335	**Crankshaft Position Sensor Circuit:** P0335 Condition 1The engine cranking starter is engaged. DTC P0101, P0102 and P0103, are not set. Engine Air Flow is greater than 3. 0 grams/second. Condition 2Engine is running and starter is not engaged. DTC P0651 not active. Condition 3The engine is running or starter is engaged. DTCs P0365, P0366, P0641, or P0651 are not set. P0336 Condition 1Engine Air Flow is greater than 3. 0 grams/second. Engine speed is greater than 450 RPM. DTC P0335 or P0651 is not set. Condition 2Engine is running, starter is not engaged P0651 is not set. Condition 3Starter is engaged. DTC P0101, P0102, or P0103 are not set. Engine Air Flow is greater than 3. 0 grams/second. Condition 4Engine is running or starter is engaged. DTC P0365, P0366, P0641, or P0651 is not set.
DTC: P0335 00	**Crankshaft Position Sensor Circuit:** DTC P0016 00, P0201 00, P0202 00, P0203 00, P0204 00, P0261 00, P0262 00, P0264 00, P0265 00, P0267 00, P0268 00, P0270 00, P0271 00, P0340 00, P0341 00, P0365 00, P0366 00, P0443 00, P0453 00, P0458 00 are not set. The engine is running. The DTC runs continuously.
DTC: P0335 00	**Crankshaft Position Sensor Circuit Malfunction:** The engine is cranking or running. The DTCs run continuously once the above condition is met for greater than 5 s.
DTC: P0335 00	**Crankshaft Position Sensor Circuit:** DTCs P0101 00, P0102 00, P0103 00, P0365 00, P0366 00, P0641 00, and P0651 00 are not set. The engine is cranking or running. The airflow into the engine is greater than 3 g/s. The DTCs run continuously once the above conditions are met.
DTC: P0335 28	**Crankshaft Position Sensor Circuit Incorrect Frequency:** The engine is cranking or running. The DTCs run continuously once the above condition is met for greater than 5 s.
DTC: P0335 29	**Crankshaft Position Sensor Circuit Too Few Pulses:** The engine is cranking or running. The DTCs run continuously once the above condition is met for greater than 5 s.
DTC: P0336	**Crankshaft Position (CKP) Sensor Performance:** The engine is cranking or running. DTC P0336 runs continuously when the above condition is met. DTCs P0642 or P0643 are not set.
DTC: P0336	**Crankshaft Position Sensor Performance:** DTC P0101, P0102, P0103, P0641, or P0651 is not set. The engine is cranking or running. The airflow into the engine is greater than 3 g/s. The DTCs run continuously when the above conditions are met.
DTC: P0336	**Crankshaft Position Sensor Performance:** DTCs P0340, P0341, P0345, P0346, P0365, P0366, P0380, P0381, P0641 or P0651 are not set. The engine is cranking or running. The DTC runs continuously when the above conditions are met.

DTC	Trouble Code Title, Conditions, Possible Causes
DTC: P0336	**Crankshaft Position Sensor Performance:** P0335 Condition 1The engine cranking starter is engaged. DTC P0101, P0102 and P0103, are not set. Engine Air Flow is greater than 3. 0 grams/second. Condition 2Engine is running and starter is not engaged. DTC P0651 not active. Condition 3The engine is running or starter is engaged. DTCs P0365, P0366, P0641, or P0651 are not set. P0336 Condition 1Engine Air Flow is greater than 3. 0 grams/second. Engine speed is greater than 450 RPM. DTC P0335 or P0651 is not set. Condition 2Engine is running, starter is not engaged P0651 is not set. Condition 3Starter is engaged. DTC P0101, P0102, or P0103 are not set. Engine Air Flow is greater than 3. 0 grams/second. Condition 4Engine is running or starter is engaged. DTC P0365, P0366, P0641, or P0651 is not set.
DTC: P0336 00	**Crankshaft Position Sensor Performance:** The engine is cranking or operating. The engine control module detects no or wrong signal. The DTC runs continuously once the above conditions are met.
DTC: P0336 00	**Crankshaft Position Sensor Performance:** DTC P0016 00 and P0340 00 are not set. The engine is cranking or running. These DTCs runs continuously once the above conditions are met.
DTC: P0336 00	**Crankshaft Position Sensor Performance:** DTC P0016 00, P0201 00, P0202 00, P0203 00, P0204 00, P0261 00, P0262 00, P0264 00, P0265 00, P0267 00, P0268 00, P0270 00, P0271 00, P0340 00, P0341 00, P0365 00, P0366 00, P0443 00, P0453 00, P0458 00 are not set. The engine is running. The DTC runs continuously.
DTC: P0336 00	**Crankshaft Position Sensor Performance:** DTCs P0101 00, P0102 00, P0103 00, P0365 00, P0366 00, P0641 00, and P0651 00 are not set. The engine is cranking or running. The airflow into the engine is greater than 3 g/s. The DTCs run continuously once the above conditions are met.
DTC: P0338	**Crankshaft Position Sensor Circuit High Duty Cycle:** P0335 Condition 1The engine cranking starter is engaged. DTC P0101, P0102 and P0103, are not set. Engine Air Flow is greater than 3. 0 grams/second. Condition 2Engine is running and starter is not engaged. DTC P0651 not active. Condition 3The engine is running or starter is engaged. DTCs P0365, P0366, P0641, or P0651 are not set. P0336 Condition 1Engine Air Flow is greater than 3. 0 grams/second. Engine speed is greater than 450 RPM. DTC P0335 or P0651 is not set. Condition 2Engine is running, starter is not engaged P0651 is not set. Condition 3Starter is engaged. DTC P0101, P0102, or P0103 are not set. Engine Air Flow is greater than 3. 0 grams/second. Condition 4Engine is running or starter is engaged. DTC P0365, P0366, P0641, or P0651 is not set.
DTC: P0338	**Crankshaft Position Sensor Circuit High Duty Cycle:** The engine is cranking or operating. The ECM has detected greater than 12 camshaft revolutions. The DTCs run continuously once the above conditions are met for greater than 5 s.
DTC: P0339 00	**Crankshaft Position Sensor Performance:** The engine is cranking or operating. The engine control module detects no or wrong signal. The DTC runs continuously once the above conditions are met.
DTC: P0340	**Camshaft Position Sensor Circuit:** The ignition is ON. The engine is turning faster than 50 RPM. DTC P0340 runs continuously when the above conditions are met. DTCs P0335, P0336 are not set.
DTC: P0340	**Camshaft Position Sensor Circuit:** The mass air flow (MAF) is greater than 3 grams per second. DTC P0101, P0102, P0103, P0641, or P0651 is not set. The engine is cranking or running. DTC P0340 runs continuously when the above conditions are met.
DTC: P0340	**Intake Camshaft Position Sensor Circuit Bank 1:** DTC P0335, P0336, P0641 or P0651 is not set. The engine is cranking or running. The DTCs run continuously when the above conditions are met.
DTC: P0340	**Intake Camshaft Position Sensor Circuit Bank 1:** **NOTE: The ECM detects engine movement by sensing the airflow through the MAF sensor when airflow is greater than 3 g/s, or by sensing crankshaft position sensor pulses.** DTC P0102, P0103, P0335, P0336, P0641, P0651, or P0697 is not set. The engine is cranking or running. The DTC runs continuously when the above conditions are met.
DTC: P0340 00	**Intake Camshaft Position Sensor Circuit:** DTC P0101 00, P0102 00, P0103 00, P0335 00, P0336 00, P0641 00, or P0651 00 are not set. The engine is cranking or running. The mass air flow (MAF) is greater than 3 g/s. The DTCs run continuously when the above conditions are met.
DTC: P0340 00	**Camshaft Position Sensor Circuit Malfunction:** DTCs P0016, P0335 and P0336 are not set. The engine is running. The engine speed is greater than 50 RPM. The DTCs run continuously once the above conditions are met.
DTC: P0340 00	**Camshaft Position Sensor Circuit:** DTCs P0335 00 and P0336 00 are not set. The engine is running. This DTC run continuously when the above conditions are met.

DTC	Trouble Code Title, Conditions, Possible Causes
DTC: P0340 28	**Camshaft Position Sensor Circuit Incorrect Frequency:** DTCs P0016, P0335 and P0336 are not set. The engine is running. The engine speed is greater than 50 RPM. The DTCs run continuously once the above conditions are met.
DTC: P0340 29	**Camshaft Position Sensor Circuit Too Few Pulses:** DTCs P0016, P0335 and P0336 are not set. The engine is running. The engine speed is greater than 50 RPM. The DTCs run continuously once the above conditions are met.
DTC: P0341	**Intake Camshaft Position Sensor Performance Bank 1:** DTCs P0335, P0336, P0641, P0651, or P0697 are not set. The engine is cranking or running. The DTC runs continuously when the above conditions are met.
DTC: P0341	**Camshaft Position Sensor Performance:** DTC P0641, or P0651 is not set. The engine is cranking or running. DTCs run continuously when the above conditions are met.
DTC: P0341	**Intake Camshaft Position Sensor Performance:** The engine is running. DTCs P0341, P0342 and P0343 run continuously when the above condition is met.
DTC: P0341	**Intake Camshaft Position Sensor Performance:** P0341 - Near Engine Start, Camshaft Position Fast Event Based Test. The engine is cranking. The medium resolution is less than or equal to 10 counts. P0341 - After Engine Start, Camshaft Position Slow Event Based Test. The engine is running. DTCs P0335, P0336, and P0340 are not set. DTC P0341 runs continuously when the above conditions are met.
DTC: P0341 00	**Intake Camshaft Position Sensor Performance:** The engine is cranking or running. The DTC runs continuously.
DTC: P0341 00	**Intake Camshaft Position Sensor Performance:** DTC P0335 00, P0336 00, P0641 00, or P0651 00 are not set. The engine is cranking or running. The mass air flow (MAF) is greater than 3 g/s. The DTCs run continuously when the above conditions are met.
DTC: P0341 00	**Camshaft Position Sensor Performance Malfunction:** DTCs P0016, P0335 and P0336 are not set. The engine is running. The engine speed is greater than 50 RPM. The DTCs run continuously once the above conditions are met.
DTC: P0342	**Intake Camshaft Position Sensor Circuit Low Voltage:** The engine is running. DTCs P0341, P0342 and P0343 run continuously when the above condition is met.
DTC: P0343	**Intake Camshaft Position Sensor Circuit High Voltage:** The engine is running. DTCs P0341, P0342 and P0343 run continuously when the above condition is met.
DTC: P0344 00	**Camshaft Position Sensor Performance:** DTC P0016 00, P0336 00 or P0339 00 are not set. The engine is running. The engine speed is greater than 50 RPM. The DTC run continuously once the above conditions are met.
DTC: P0345	**Intake Camshaft Position Sensor Circuit Bank 2:** DTC P0335, P0336, P0641 or P0651 is not set. The engine is cranking or running. The DTCs run continuously when the above conditions are met.
DTC: P0345	**Intake Camshaft Position Sensor Circuit Bank 2:** **NOTE: The ECM detects engine movement by sensing the airflow through the MAF sensor when airflow is greater than 3 g/s, or by sensing crankshaft position sensor pulses.** DTC P0102, P0103, P0335, P0336, P0641, P0651, or P0697 is not set. The engine is cranking or running. The DTC runs continuously when the above conditions are met.
DTC: P0346	**Intake Camshaft Position Sensor Performance Bank 2:** DTCs P0335, P0336, P0641, P0651, or P0697 are not set. The engine is cranking or running. The DTC runs continuously when the above conditions are met.
DTC: P0351	**Ignition Coil 1 Control Circuit:** The engine speed is less than 6,000 RPM. The ignition 1 voltage signal is between 9-18 volts. DTCs P0351, P0352, P0353, P0354 run continuously when the above conditions are met.
DTC: P0351 00	**Ignition Coil 1 Control Circuit:** The engine is running. The ignition voltage is greater than 6 V. The DTC runs continuously once the above condition is met.
DTC: P0352	**Ignition Coil 2 Control Circuit:** Engine running. Ignition voltage greater than 6V. DTC P0351-P0358 runs continuously when the above condition is met.
DTC: P0352	**Ignition Coil 2 Control Circuit:** The engine speed is less than 6,000 RPM. The ignition 1 voltage signal is between 9-18 volts. DTCs P0351, P0352, P0353, P0354 run continuously when the above conditions are met.

DTC	Trouble Code Title, Conditions, Possible Causes
DTC: P0352 00	**Ignition Coil 2 Control Circuit:** The engine is running. The ignition voltage is greater than 6 V. The DTC runs continuously once the above condition is met.
DTC: P0353	**Ignition Coil 3 Control Circuit:** The engine speed is less than 6,000 RPM. The ignition 1 voltage signal is between 9-18 volts. DTCs P0351, P0352, P0353, P0354 run continuously when the above conditions are met.
DTC: P0353	**Ignition Coil 3 Control Circuit:** The engine is running. DTCs P0351-P0354 run continuously when the above condition is met.
DTC: P0353 00	**Ignition Coil 3 Control Circuit:** The engine is running. The ignition voltage is greater than 6 V. The DTC runs continuously once the above condition is met.
DTC: P0354	**Ignition Coil 4 Control Circuit:** The engine speed is less than 6,000 RPM. The ignition 1 voltage signal is between 9-18 volts. DTCs P0351, P0352, P0353, P0354 run continuously when the above conditions are met.
DTC: P0354	**Ignition Coil 4 Control Circuit:** The engine is running. The ignition voltage is greater than 6 V. DTC P0351-P0356 runs continuously when the above conditions are met.
DTC: P0354 00	**Ignition Coil 4 Control Circuit:** The engine is running. The ignition voltage is greater than 6 V. The DTC runs continuously once the above condition is met.
DTC: P0355	**Ignition Coil 5 Control Circuit:** Engine running. Ignition voltage greater than 6V. DTC P0351-P0358 runs continuously when the above condition is met.
DTC: P0355	**Ignition Coil 5 Control Circuit:** The engine is cranking or running. The DTCs run continuously when the above condition is met.
DTC: P0356	**Ignition Coil 6 Control Circuit:** The engine is running. The ignition voltage is greater than 6 V. DTC P0351-P0356 runs continuously when the above conditions are met.
DTC: P0357	**Ignition Coil 7 Control Circuit:** Engine running. Ignition voltage greater than 6V. DTC P0351-P0358 runs continuously when the above condition is met.
DTC: P0358	**Ignition Coil 8 Control Circuit:** Engine running. Ignition voltage greater than 6V. DTC P0351-P0358 runs continuously when the above condition is met.
DTC: P0365	**Exhaust Camshaft Position Sensor Circuit Bank 1:** **NOTE: The ECM detects engine movement by sensing the airflow through the MAF sensor when airflow is greater than 3 g/s, or by sensing crankshaft position sensor pulses.** DTC P0102, P0103, P0335, P0336, P0641, P0651, or P0697 is not set. The engine is cranking or running. The DTC runs continuously when the above conditions are met.
DTC: P0365	**Exhaust Camshaft Position Sensor Circuit:** DTCs P0101, P0102, P0103, P0340 and P0365 are not set. The engine is cranking or running. The mass air flow (MAF) is greater than 3 grams per s. The DTCs run continuously when the above condition is met.
DTC: P0365	**Exhaust Camshaft Position Sensor Circuit Bank 1:** DTC P0335, P0336, P0641 or P0651 is not set. The engine is cranking or running. The DTCs run continuously when the above conditions are met.
DTC: P0365 00	**Exhaust Camshaft Position Sensor Circuit:** The engine is cranking or running. The DTC runs continuously.
DTC: P0366	**Exhaust Camshaft Position Sensor Performance Bank 1:** DTC P0335, P0336, P0641 or P0651 is not set. The engine is cranking or running. The DTCs run continuously when the above conditions are met.
DTC: P0366	**Exhaust Camshaft Position Sensor Performance:** P0366 - Near Engine Start, Camshaft Position Fast Event Based Test. The engine is cranking. The medium resolution is less than or equal to 10 counts. P0366 - After Engine Start, Camshaft Position Slow Event Based Test. The engine is running. DTCs P0335, P0336, and P0365 are not set. DTC P0366 runs continuously when the above conditions are met.
DTC: P0366 00	**Exhaust Camshaft Position Sensor Performance:** The engine is cranking or running. The DTC runs continuously.
DTC: P0367	**Exhaust Camshaft Position Sensor Circuit Low Voltage:** The engine is running. DTCs P0366, P0367 and P0368 run continuously when the above condition is met.

DTC	Trouble Code Title, Conditions, Possible Causes
DTC: P0368	**Exhaust Camshaft Position Sensor Circuit High Voltage:** The engine is running. DTCs P0366, P0367 and P0368 run continuously when the above condition is met.
DTC: P037E 00	**Glow Plug Control Module Feedback Circuit Low Voltage:** The ignition is ON. The ignition voltage is between 9-16 V. The DTCs run once per ignition cycle when the above conditions are met.
DTC: P037F 00	**Glow Plug Control Module Feedback Circuit High Voltage:** The ignition is ON. The ignition voltage is between 9-16 V. The DTCs run once per ignition cycle when the above conditions are met.
DTC: P0381	**Wait to Start Lamp Control Circuit:** Battery voltage is greater than 11 V. DTC P0381 runs continuously when the ignition is ON.
DTC: P0383 00	**Glow Plug Control Module Control Circuit Low Voltage:** The ignition is ON. The ignition voltage is between 9-16 V. The DTCs run once per ignition cycle when the above conditions are met.
DTC: P0384 00	**Glow Plug Control Module Control Circuit High Voltage:** The ignition is ON. The ignition voltage is between 9-16 V. The DTCs run once per ignition cycle when the above conditions are met.
DTC: P0390	**Exhaust Camshaft Position Sensor Circuit Bank 2:** **NOTE: The ECM detects engine movement by sensing the airflow through the MAF sensor when airflow is greater than 3 g/s, or by sensing crankshaft position sensor pulses.** DTC P0102, P0103, P0335, P0336, P0641, P0651, or P0697 is not set. The engine is cranking or running. The DTC runs continuously when the above conditions are met.
DTC: P0390	**Exhaust Camshaft Position Sensor Circuit Bank 2:** DTC P0335, P0336, P0641 or P0651 is not set. The engine is cranking or running. The DTCs run continuously when the above conditions are met.
DTC: P0391	**Exhaust Camshaft Position Sensor Performance Bank 2:** DTCs P0335, P0336, P0641, P0651, or P0697 are not set. The engine is cranking or running. The DTC runs continuously when the above conditions are met.
DTC: P0391	**Exhaust Camshaft Position Sensor Performance Bank 2:** DTC P0335, P0336, P0641 or P0651 is not set. The engine is cranking or running. The DTCs run continuously when the above conditions are met.
DTC: P0400	**Exhaust Gas Recirculation (EGR) Flow Incorrect:** DTC P0045, P0047, P0048, P006E, P006F, P007C, P007D, P0101, P0102, P0103, P0106, P0107, P0108, P0112, P0113, P0117, P0118, P02E0, P02E7, P02E8, P02E9, P02EB, P0403, P0405, P0406, P0489, P0490, P122C, P122E, P122F, P1407, P140D, P140E, P140F, P1411, P1412, P1413, P1414, P16A0, P16A1, P16A2, P2228, P2229, P2263, P2453, P245A, P245C, P245D, P2493, P2494, P2495, P2564, P2565, P2598, or P2599 is not set. The engine is running. The DTC runs continuously when the above conditions are met.
DTC: P0400 00	**Exhaust Gas Recirculation (EGR) Current Performance:** The ignition is ON, or the engine is running. The DTCs run continuously when the above conditions are met.
DTC: P0401	**Exhaust Gas Recirculation (EGR) Flow Insufficient:** DTCs P0101, P0102, P0103, P0403, P0405, P0406, P046C are not set. The engine is running. The engine coolant temperature (ECT) is greater than 60°C (140°F). The EGR valve is active. DTCs P0401 and P0402 run continuously when the above conditions are met.
DTC: P0401	**Exhaust Gas Recirculation (EGR) Flow Insufficient:** P0401 DTC P0045, P0047, P0048, P006E, P006F, P007C, P007D, P0101, P0102, P0103, P0106, P0107, P0108, P0112, P0113, P0117, P0118, P02E0, P02E7, P02E8, P02E9, P02EB, P0403, P0405, P0406, P0489, P0490, P122C, P122E, P122F, P1407, P140D, P140E, P140F, P1411, P1412, P1413, P1414, P16A0, P16A1, P16A2, P2228, P2229, P2263, P2453, P245A, P245C, P245D, P2493, P2494, P2495, P2564, P2565, P2598, or P2599 is not set. The engine speed is between 500-950 RPM. The calculated fuel rate is between 1-15 mm ;The ambient air temperature is greater than -7°C (19. 4°F). The engine coolant temperature is greater than 70°C (158°F). The Barometric Pressure is greater than 74. 8 kPa (10. 9 psi). The system is not in Diesel Particulate Filter (DPF) regeneration. The EGR valve position is greater than 5 %. The throttle valve position is less than 5 %. The DTC runs continuously when the above conditions are met.
DTC: P0401 00	**Exhaust Gas Recirculation (EGR) Flow Insufficient:** P0401 00 DTCs P0106 00, P0107 00, P0108 00, P0112 00, P0113 00, P0117 00, P0118 00, P0122 00, P0123 00, P0351 00, P0352 00, P0402 00, P0404 00, P0405 00, P0406 00, P0502 00, P0506 00, and P0507 00 are not set. The EGR flow test is ran in deceleration fuel cut-off mode with the following conditions present before deceleration occurs: The A/C compressor clutch does not change state during deceleration. The intake air temperature (IAT) sensor is between -3 to +120°C (+27 to +248°F). The barometric pressure (BARO) is greater than 82 kPa (11. 89 PSI). The vehicle speed is greater than 30 km/h (19 MPH) before deceleration. The throttle position is less than 1. 5%. The EGR flow test is ran when the following conditions are met during deceleration fuel cut-off mode: The EGR position is less than 1%. The MAP is between 11-55 kPa (1. 5-7. 9 PSI). The engine speed is between 1 600-3 200 RPM. The MAP does not vary greater than 3 kPa (0. 4 PSI). The EGR flow test is performed once per ignition cycle. This DTC runs multiple times on the first ignition cycle after the DTC is cleared from the ECM memory.

DTC	Trouble Code Title, Conditions, Possible Causes
DTC: P0402	**Exhaust Gas Recirculation (EGR) Flow Excessive:** DTCs P0101, P0102, P0103, P0403, P0405, P0406, P046C are not set. The engine is running. The engine coolant temperature (ECT) is greater than 60°C (140°F). The EGR valve is active. DTCs P0401 and P0402 run continuously when the above conditions are met.
DTC: P0402	**Exhaust Gas Recirculation (EGR) Flow Excessive:** P0402 DTC P0045, P0047, P0048, P006E, P006F, P007C, P007D, P0101, P0102, P0103, P0106, P0107, P0108, P0112, P0113, P0117, P0118, P02E0, P02E7, P02E8, P02E9, P02EB, P0403, P0405, P0406, P0489, P0490, P122C, P122E, P122F, P1407, P140D, P140E, P140F, P1411, P1412, P1413, P1414, P16A0, P16A1, P16A2, P2228, P2229, P2263, P2453, P245A, P245C, P245D, P2493, P2494, P2495, P2564, P2565, P2598, or P2599 is not set. The engine speed is between 1,200-1,400 RPM. The calculated fuel rate is greater than 40 mm ;. The ambient air temperature is greater than -7°C (19. 4°F). The Barometric Pressure is greater than 74. 8 kPa (10. 9 psi). The system is not in Diesel Particulate Filter (DPF) regeneration. The EGR valve is active. The DTC runs continuously when the above conditions are met.
DTC: P0402 00	**Exhaust Gas Recirculation (EGR) Flow Excessive:** The ignition is ON, or the engine is running. The DTCs run continuously when the above conditions are met.
DTC: P0403	**Exhaust Gas Recirculation (EGR) Motor Control Circuit:** P0403The Ignition is OFF. The engine is in after-run. The battery voltage is greater than 11 V. The EGR valve offset learning procedure is active. The starter is not cranking. The DTC runs continuously when the above conditions are met. OR The Ignition is ON. The battery voltage is greater than 11 V. The EGR control circuit is active. The starter is not cranking. The DTC runs continuously when the above conditions are met.
DTC: P0403	**Exhaust Gas Recirculation (EGR) Solenoid Control Circuit:** P0403The engine is running for more than 0. 5 second. The EGR duty cycle is more than 10 percent. DTC P0403 runs continuously when the above conditions are met.
DTC: P0403 00	**Exhaust Gas Recirculation (EGR) Control Circuit:** P0403 00, P0404 00, and P042EDTCs P0112 00, P0113 00, P0405 00, P0406 00, P0502 00, P0562 00, and P0563 00 are not set. The engine is running. The intake air temperature (IAT) is between 3-80°C (37-176°F). The ignition voltage is between 11-16 V. The Desired EGR position is greater than 0% and does not change more than 3%. These DTCs run continuously when the above conditions are met. P0405 00 and P0406 00The engine is running. The ignition voltage is between 11-16 V. This DTC runs continuously when the above conditions are met.
DTC: P0403 01	**Exhaust Gas Recirculation (EGR) Control Circuit Short to Battery:** The engine is running. The ignition voltage is less than 16. 5 v. The EGR is commanded ON. The DTCs run continuously when the above conditions are met.
DTC: P0403 02	**Exhaust Gas Recirculation (EGR) Control Circuit Short to Ground:** The engine is running. The ignition voltage is less than 16. 5 v. The EGR is commanded ON. The DTCs run continuously when the above conditions are met.
DTC: P0403 04	**Exhaust Gas Recirculation (EGR) Control Circuit Open:** The engine is running. The ignition voltage is less than 16. 5 v. The EGR is commanded ON. The DTCs run continuously when the above conditions are met.
DTC: P0403 54	**Exhaust Gas Recirculation (EGR) Control Circuit High Temperature:** The engine is running. The ignition voltage is less than 16. 5 v. The EGR is commanded ON. The DTCs run continuously when the above conditions are met.
DTC: P0404 00	**Exhaust Gas Recirculation (EGR) Open Position Performance:** P0403 00, P0404 00, and P042EDTCs P0112 00, P0113 00, P0405 00, P0406 00, P0502 00, P0562 00, and P0563 00 are not set. The engine is running. The intake air temperature (IAT) is between 3-80°C (37-176°F). The ignition voltage is between 11-16 V. The Desired EGR position is greater than 0% and does not change more than 3%. These DTCs run continuously when the above conditions are met. P0405 00 and P0406 00The engine is running. The ignition voltage is between 11-16 V. This DTC runs continuously when the above conditions are met.
DTC: P0404 00	**Exhaust Gas Recirculation (EGR) Open Position Performance:** The ignition is ON, or the engine is running. The DTCs run continuously when the above conditions are met.
DTC: P0405	**Exhaust Gas Recirculation (EGR) Position Sensor Circuit Low Voltage:** Engine speed is greater than 600 RPM for 10 s. The DTCs run continuously when the above conditions are met.
DTC: P0405 00	**Exhaust Gas Recirculation (EGR) Position Sensor Circuit Low Voltage:** The ignition is ON, or the engine is running. The DTCs run continuously when the above conditions are met.

DTC	Trouble Code Title, Conditions, Possible Causes
DTC: P0405 00	**Exhaust Gas Recirculation (EGR) Position Sensor Circuit Low Voltage:** P0403 00, P0404 00, and P042EDTCs P0112 00, P0113 00, P0405 00, P0406 00, P0502 00, P0562 00, and P0563 00 are not set. The engine is running. The intake air temperature (IAT) is between 3-80°C (37-176°F). The ignition voltage is between 11-16 V. The Desired EGR position is greater than 0% and does not change more than 3%. These DTCs run continuously when the above conditions are met. P0405 00 and P0406 00The engine is running. The ignition voltage is between 11-16 V. This DTC runs continuously when the above conditions are met.
DTC: P0406	**Exhaust Gas Recirculation (EGR) Position Sensor Circuit High Voltage:** Engine speed is greater than 600 RPM for 10s. The DTCs run continuously when the above conditions are met.
DTC: P0406 00	**Exhaust Gas Recirculation (EGR) Position Sensor Circuit High Voltage:** P0403 00, P0404 00, and P042EDTCs P0112 00, P0113 00, P0405 00, P0406 00, P0502 00, P0562 00, and P0563 00 are not set. The engine is running. The intake air temperature (IAT) is between 3-80°C (37-176°F). The ignition voltage is between 11-16 V. The Desired EGR position is greater than 0% and does not change more than 3%. These DTCs run continuously when the above conditions are met. P0405 00 and P0406 00The engine is running. The ignition voltage is between 11-16 V. This DTC runs continuously when thc above conditions are met.
DTC: P0406 00	**Exhaust Gas Recirculation (EGR) Position Sensor Circuit High Voltage:** The ignition is ON, or the engine is running. The DTCs run continuously when the above conditions are met.
DTC: P040C	**Exhaust Gas Recirculation (EGR) Temperature Sensor 1 Circuit Low Voltage:** P040CThe engine is running for 30 seconds or longer. The engine coolant temperature is 60°C (140°F) or warmer. The engine is not in diesel particulate filter (DPF) regeneration. This DTC runs continuously when the above conditions are met. The EGR valve is open more than 4 percent.
DTC: P040C	**Exhaust Gas Recirculation (EGR) Temperature Sensor 2 Circuit Low Voltage:** The engine speed is greater than 600 RPM for 10s. The DTCs run continuously when the above conditions are met.
DTC: P040D	**Exhaust Gas Recirculation (EGR) Temperature Sensor 2 Circuit High Voltage:** The engine speed is greater than 600 RPM for 10s. The DTCs run continuously when the above conditions are met.
DTC: P040F	**Exhaust Gas Recirculation (EGR) Temperature Sensor 1-2 Correlation:** The engine has been OFF for more than 5 hours. The ambient temperature is warmer than -7°C (+20°F). DTC P040F runs once per key cycle within the above enabling conditions.
DTC: P040F	**Exhaust Gas Recirculation (EGR) Temperature Sensor 1-2 Correlation:** Condition 1 DTC P0016, P0112, P0113, P0335, P0336, P0340, P0341, P040C, P040D, P041C, or P041D is not set. The ignition has been OFF for greater than 8 hours. The engine is running. The ambient air temperature is greater than -60°C (-76°F). OR Condition 2 DTC P0016, P0112, P0113, P0335, P0336, P0340, P0341, P040C, P040D, P041C, or P041D is not set. The ignition has been OFF for greater than 8 hours. The engine is running. The ambient air temperature is greater than -60°C (-76°F). In the first 60s of engine run time, the ECM determines the block heater is OFF. AND In the first 10 minutes of engine run time, the vehicle speed as been at least 24 km/h (15 mph) for at least 5 minutes and the ECM determines there is no Sunload. DTC P040F runs once per key cycle when Condition 1 or Condition 2 above is met.
DTC: P0411	**Secondary Air Injection (AIR) System Incorrect Air Flow Detcotod:** DTC P0101, P0102, P0103, P0107, P0108, P0112, P0113, P0116, P0117, P0118, P0201, P0202, P0203, P0204, P0205, P0206, P0300, P0301, P0302, P0303, P0304, P0305, P0306, P0412, P0418, P0420, P0606, P2430, P2431, P2432, or P2433 is not set. Greater than 120 minutes has elapsed since the last cold start. The ignition voltage is between 9-18 V. The start-up intake air temperature (IAT) is between 5-60°C (41-140°F). The barometric pressure (BARO) is greater than 60 kPa (8. 7 psi). The mass air flow (MAF) is between 3-24 g/s. The engine coolant temperature (ECT) is between 5-60°C (41-140°F). The secondary air injection system is commanded ON. DTC P0411 runs once per trip start up when the above conditions are met for greater than 5s.
DTC: P0411	**Secondary Air Injection System Incorrect Air Flow Detected:** DTCs P0101, P0102, P0103, P0106, P0107, P0108, P0112, P0113, P0114, P0116, P0117, P0118, P0121, P0122, P0123, P0128, P0201, P0202, P0203, P0204, P0222, P0223, P0261, P0262, P0264, P0265, P0267, P0268, P0270, P0271, P0300, P0301, P0302, P0303, P0304, P0351, P0352, P0353, P0354, P0412, P0418, P0420, P0606, P0641, P0651, P1248, P1249, P124A, P124B, P2147, P2148, P2150, P2151, P2153, P2154, P2156, P2157, P2430, P2431, P2432 or P2433 are not set. The ignition voltage is between 10-32 V. The intake air temperature (IAT) is greater than -11°C (+12°F). The barometric pressure (BARO) is greater than 60 kPa (8. 7 psi). The engine coolant temperature (ECT) is between -11 to +60°C (12-140°F). The manifold absolute pressure (MAP) sensor is greater than 20 kPa (2. 9 psi). The engine speed is less than 5,000 RPM. The mass air flow (MAF) is less than 50 g/s. Greater than 60 min has elapsed since the last cold start. The Secondary Air Injection system is commanded ON. DTC P0411 runs once per trip at start up when the above conditions are met.
DTC: P0412	**Secondary Air Injection (AIR) Solenoid Control Circuit:** The ignition is ON, or the engine is operating. The ignition voltage is between 9-18 V. The ECM has commanded the air system ON and OFF at least once during the ignition cycle. The DTCs run continuously once the above conditions are met.
DTC: P0412	**Secondary Air Injection Valve Control Circuit:** The ignition voltage is between 10-32 V. The DTCs run continuously once the above conditions are met.

DTC	Trouble Code Title, Conditions, Possible Causes
DTC: P0418	**Secondary Air Injection (AIR) Pump Control Circuit:** The ignition is ON, or the engine is operating. The ignition voltage is between 9-18 V. The ECM has commanded the air system ON and OFF at least once during the ignition cycle. The DTCs run continuously once the above conditions are met.
DTC: P0418	**Secondary Air Injection Pump Relay Control Circuit:** The ignition voltage is between 10-32 V. The DTCs run continuously once the above conditions are met.
DTC: P0418	**Secondary Air Injection (AIR) Pump Control Circuit:** The engine speed is greater than 80 RPM. The ignition voltage is between 10-18 V. The ECM has commanded the air system ON and OFF at least once during the ignition cycle. The DTCs run continuously once the above conditions are met.
DTC: P041C	**Exhaust Gas Recirculation (EGR) Temperature Sensor 2 Circuit Low Voltage:** P041CThe engine is running for 30 seconds or longer. The engine coolant temperature is 60°C (140°F) or warmer. The engine is not in regeneration. This DTC runs continuously when the above conditions are met. The EGR valve is open more than 4 percent.
DTC: P041C	**Exhaust Gas Recirculation (EGR) Temperature Sensor 1 Circuit Low Voltage:** The engine speed is greater than 600 RPM for 10 s. The DTCs run continuously when the above conditions are met.
DTC: P041D	**Exhaust Gas Recirculation (EGR) Temperature Sensor 1 Circuit High Voltage:** The engine speed is greater than 600 RPM for 10 s. The DTCs run continuously when the above conditions are met.
DTC: P041D	**Exhaust Gas Recirculation (EGR) Temperature Sensor 2 Circuit High Voltage:** P041DThe engine is running for 30 seconds or longer. The engine coolant temperature is 60°C (140°F) or warmer. This DTC runs continuously when the above conditions are met. The EGR valve is open more than 4 percent.
DTC: P0420	**Catalyst System Low Efficiency Bank 1:** DTCs P0030, P0036, P0050, P0053, P0054, P0056, P0059, P0060, P0068, P0101, P0012, P0103, P0107, P0108, P0112, P0113, P0116, P0117, P0118, P0120, P0121, P0122, P0128, P0131, P0132, P0133, P0134, P0135, P0137, P0138, P0140, P0141, P0151, P0152, P0153, P0154, P0155, P0156, P0157, P0158, P0160, P0161, P0171, P0172, P0174, P0175, P0201, P0202, P0203, P0204, P0205, P0206, P0220, P0222, P0223, P0300-P0306, P0325, P0327, P0332, P0335, P0336, P0340, P0341, P0442, P0443, P0446, P0449, P0455, P0496, P0506, P0507, P1133, P1153, P1258, P1516, P2101, P2119, P2120, P2122, P2123, P2125, P2127, P2128, P2135, P2138, P2176, P2270, P2271, P2272, P2273, P2A00, or P2A03 are not set. Before the ECM performs the idle test, the vehicle must be driven under the following conditions: The engine speed is greater than 1,000 RPM. The condition exists for greater than 1 minute. The engine run time is greater than 10 minutes. The engine is operating in Closed Loop. The engine coolant temperature (ECT) is between 70-125°C (156-257°F). The barometric pressure (BARO) is greater than 70 kPa. The catalytic converter (TWC) calculated temperature is greater than 450°C (842°F). The intake air temperature (IAT) is between -20 to +85°C (-4 to +185°F). The ignition voltage is greater than 11 volts. The vehicle speed is less than 2 km/h (1 mph). The throttle position is in the rest position. The short term fuel trim (FT) is between -10 and +10 percent. The transmission is not in P/N (automatic transmission only). This diagnostic attempts one test during each valid idle period once the above conditions have been met. This diagnostic attempts up to 6 tests during each drive cycle.
DTC: P0420	**Catalyst System Low Efficiency:** The hydrocarbon converted in the diesel oxidation catalyst is greater than 115 g and the hydrocarbon mass flow is greater than 0. 0009 g/s. The ECM is commanding a regeneration. The exhaust gas temperature sensor 1 is greater than 250°C (482°F). The engine speed is between 700-3,400 RPM. The barometric pressure (BARO) is greater than 74. 8 kPa (10. 8 psi). The ambient air temperature is greater than -7°C (19. 4°F). DTC P0420 runs once per driving cycle when the above conditions are met.
DTC: P0420 00	**Catalyst System Low Efficiency:** DTCs P000A 00, P000B 00, P0010 00, P0013 00, P0016 00, P0017 00, P0030 00, P0031 00, P0032 00, P0036 00, P0038 00, P0117 00, P0118 00, P0119 00, P0121 00, P0122 00, P0123 00, P0131 00, P0132 00, P0133 00, P0134 00, P0135 00, P0136 00, P0137 00, P0138 00, P0139 00, P0140 00, P0141 00, P0171 00, P0201 00, P0202 00, P0203 00, P0204 00, P0221 00, P0222 00, P0223 00, P0261 00, P0262 00, P0264 00, P0265 00, P0267 00, P0268 00, P0270 00, P0271 00, P0301 00, P0302 00, P0303 00, P0304 00, P0335 00, P0336 00, P0340 00, P0365 00, P0366 00, P0443 00, P0446 00, P0458 00, P0459 00, P0496 00, P0562 00, P0563 00, P0642 00, P0643 00, P0652 00, P0653 00, P0661 00, P0662 00, P2088 00, P2089 00, P2090 00, P2091 00, P2096 00, P2097 00, P2100 00, P2101 00, P2122 00, P2123 00, P2127 00, P2128 00, P2176 00, P2297 00, P2301 00, P2303 00, P2304 00, P2306 00, P2307 00, P2309 00, P2310 00, P2A00 00, P2A0 001 are not set. The engine speed is between 1 040-2 760 RPM. The engine load is between 15-50%. The vehicle is in closed loop. The calculated exhaust mass gas flow is between 5-55. 56 g/s, and stable. The calculated catalyst temperature is between 400-850°C (852-1 562°F), and stable. The rear heated oxygen sensor (HO2S) has exceeded the dew point for more than 60 s. This diagnostic attempts one test during each period when the above conditions have been met. This diagnostic attempts up to 4 tests during each drive cycle.
DTC: P042E 00	**Exhaust Gas Recirculation (EGR) Closed Position Performance:** P0403 00, P0404 00, and P042EDTCs P0112 00, P0113 00, P0405 00, P0406 00, P0502 00, P0562 00, and P0563 00 are not set. The engine is running. The intake air temperature (IAT) is between 3-80°C (37-176°F). The ignition voltage is between 11-16 V. The Desired EGR position is greater than 0% and does not change more than 3%. These DTCs run continuously when the above conditions are met. P0405 00 and P0406 00The engine is running. The ignition voltage is between 11-16 V. This DTC runs continuously when the above conditions are met.

DTC	Trouble Code Title, Conditions, Possible Causes
DTC: P0430	**Catalyst System Low Efficiency Bank 2:** LF1 DTCs P000A, P000B, P000C, P000D, P0010, P0011, P0013, P0014, P0020, P0021, P0023, P0024, P0030, P0031, P0032, P0050, P0051, P0052, P0100, P0101, P0102, P0103, P0116, P0117, P0118, P0119, P0121, P0122, P0123, P0128, P0130, P0131, P0132, P0133, P0135, P0137, P0138, P013A, P013C, P013E, P0140, P0141, P014A, P0150, P0151, P0152, P0153, P0155, P0157, P0158, P0160, P0161, P0221, P0222, P0223, P0300, P0301-P0306, P0443, P0455, P0458, P0459, P0496, P2088, P2089, P2090, P2091, P2092, P2093, P2094, P2095, P2096, P2097, P2098, P2099, P2100, P2101, P2107, P2119, P2122, P2123, P2127, P2128, P2138, P2176, P2177, P2178, P2179, P2180, P2187, P2188, P2189, P2190, P2232, P2235, P2270, P2271, P2272, or P2273 is not set. Before the ECM performs the idle test, the vehicle must be driven under the following conditions: The engine speed is greater than 915 RPM. The engine run time is greater than a calibrated value. Both conditions exist for greater than 15 seconds. The throttle is in the rest position. The intake air temperature (IAT) is between -20 to +250°C (-4 to +482°F). The ignition voltage is greater than 11 volts. The engine coolant temperature (ECT) is between 40-127°C (104-261°F). The barometric pressure (BARO) is greater than 70 kPa. The engine has been idling less than 50 seconds. The vehicle speed is less than 2 km/h (1 mph). The short term fuel trim is learned. The air flow into the engine is between 3-13 g/s. The EVAP purge concentration is learned. The catalytic converter (TWC) calculated temperature is between 450-250°C (842-1,742°F). The engine is operating in Closed Loop. The transmission is not in P/N (automatic transmission only). This diagnostic attempts one test during each valid idle period once the above conditions have been met. This diagnostic attempts up to 8 tests during each drive cycle. Before the ECM can report DTC P0420 or P0430 failed, DTCs P0030, P0031, P0032, P0036, P0037, P0038, P0050, P0051, P0052, P0056, P0057, P0058, P0100, P0101, P0102, P0103, P0121, P0122, P0123, P0131, P0132, P0133, P0135, P0137, P0138, P0140, P0141, P0151, P0152, P0153, P0155, P0157, P0158, P0160, P0161, P0221, P0222, P0223, P0335, P0336, P0338, P2096, P2097, P2098, P2099, P2195, P2196, P2197, P2198, P2232, P2235, P2237, P2240, P2243, P2247, P2251, P2254, P2270, P2271, P2272, P2273, P2297, P2298, P2626, and P2629 must run and pass. DTC P0010, P0011, P0013, P0014, P0020, P0021, P0023, P0024, P0030, P0031, P0032, P0050, P0051, P0052, P0100, P0101, P0102, P0103, P0116, P0117, P0118, P0119, P0121, P0122, P0123, P0128, P013A, P013C, P013E, P0130, P0131, P0132, P0133, P0135, P0137, P0138, P014A P0140, P0141, P0150, P0151, P0152, P0153, P0155, P0157, P0158, P0160, P0161, P0221, P0222, P0223, P0300, P0301-P0306, P0443, P0455, P0458, P0459, P0496, P0497, P2088, P2089, P2090, P2091, P2092, P2093, P2094, P2095, P2096, P2097, P2098, P2099, P2100, P2101, P2107, P2119, P2122, P2123, P2127, P2128, P2138, P2176, P2177, P2178, P2179, P2180, P2187, P2188, P2189, P2190, P2232, P2235, P2270, P2271, P2272, or P2273 is not set. The engine speed is between 1,160-2,440 RPM. The engine load is between 13-80 percent. The air flow into the engine is between 3-28 g/s and steady. The ambient air temperature is warmer than -30°C (-22°F). The HO2S 2 is at operating temperature for greater than a range of 140-210 seconds. The engine is operating in Closed Loop. The calculated TWC temperature is between 500-900°C (932-1,652°F) and steady. The above conditions exist for approximately 17 minutes. This diagnostic attempts one test during each period when the above conditions have been met. This diagnostic attempts up to 3 tests during each drive cycle.
DTC: P0430	**Catalyst System Low Efficiency Bank 2:** DTC P0016, P0017, P0018, P0019, P0053, P0054, P0059, P0060, P0068, P0090, P0091, P0092, P00C8, P00C9, P00CA, P0101, P0102, P0103, P0112, P0113, P0116, P0117, P0118, P0119, P0121, P0122, P0123, P0128, P0131, P0132, P0133, P0135, P0137, P0138, P013A, P013B, P013C, P013D, P013E, P013F, P0140, P0141, P014A, P014B, P0151, P0152, P0153, P0155, P0157, P0158, P0160, P0161, P0171, P0172, P0174, P0175, P0191, P0192, P0193, P0222, P0223, P0300, P0301, P0302, P0303, P0304, P0305, P0306, P0335, P0336, P0341, P0345, P0346, P0365, P0366, P0390, P0391, P0443, P0506, P0507, P0606, P1153, P16F3, P2101, P2122, P2123, P2127, P2128, P2135, P2138, P2227, P2228, P2229, P2230, P2270, P2271, P2272, or P2273 is not set. Before the ECM performs the idle test, the vehicle must be driven under the following conditions: The engine speed is greater than 965 RPM. The engine run time is greater than a calibrated value. Both conditions exist for greater than 15s. The throttle is in the rest position. The Intake Air Temperature (IAT) is between -20 to +250°C (-4 to +482°F). The ignition voltage is greater than 11 V. The Engine Coolant Temperature (ECT) is between 40-127°C (104-261°F). The Barometric Pressure (BARO) is greater than 70 kPa. The engine has been idling less than 50s. The vehicle speed is less than 2 km/h (1 mph). The short term fuel trim is learned. The air flow into the engine is between 3-13 g/s. The Evaporative Emission (EVAP) purge concentration is learned. The catalytic converter calculated temperature is between 450-850°C (842-1,562°F). The engine is operating in Closed Loop. The transmission is not in P/N (automatic transmission only). This diagnostic attempts one test during each valid idle period once the above conditions have been met. This diagnostic attempts up to 8 tests during each drive cycle.
DTC: P0442	**Evaporative Emission (EVAP) System Small Leak Detected:** Important: The following conditions must be met prior to ignition OFF. DTCs P0106, P0107, P0108, P0112, P0113, P0117, P0118, P0122, P0128, P0446, P0452, P0453, P0455, P0496, P0502, P0562, P0563, P0601, P0602, P0606, P2610 are not set. The diagnostic runs once after a cold start drive cycle. The start-up intake air temperature (IAT) is between 2-32°C (36-90°F). The start-up engine coolant temperature (ECT) is colder than 42°C (108°F). The start-up IAT and ECT are within 9°C (16°F). The barometric pressure (BARO) is more than 68 kPa. The ambient air temperature is between 2-32°C (36-90°F). The engine run time minimum is 10 minutes. The vehicle has traveled more than 8 km (5 mi) this trip. The shut-down ECT is warmer than 74°C (165°F). The fuel level is between 12-88 percent. The ignition is OFF. A refueling event is not detected. DTC P0442 runs once per drive cycle when the above conditions are met. One test occurs at ignition OFF after a drive cycle and may require up to 45 minutes to complete. No more than 2 tests per day are allowed.

DTC	Trouble Code Title, Conditions, Possible Causes
DTC: P0442 00	**Evaporative Emission (EVAP) System Small Leak Detected:** DTCs P000A 00, P000B 00, P0010 00, P0013 00, P0016 00, P0017 00, P0030 00, P0031 00, P0032 00, P0111 00, P0112 00, P0113 00, P0114 00, P0117 00, P0118 00, P0119 00, P0121 00, P0122 00, P0123 00, P0131 00, P0132 00, P0133 00, P0134 00, P0135 00, P0171 00, P0172 00, P0201 00, P0202 00, P0203 00, P0204 00, P0221 00, P0222 00, P0223 00, P0261 00, P0262 00, P0264 00, P0265 00, P0267 00, P0268 00, P0270 00, P0271 00, P0300 00, P0301 00, P0302 00, P0303 00, P0304 00, P0335 00, P0336 00, P0340 00, P0341 00, P0365 00, P0366 00, P0442 00, P0443 00, P0446 00, P0451 00, P0452 00, P0453 00, P0454 00, P0455 00, P0456 00, P0458 00, P0459 00, P0496 00, P0498 00, P0499 00, P0501 00, P0506 00, P0507 00, P0562 00, P0563 00, P0601 00, P0602 00, P0604 00, P0606 00, P0607 00, P061A 00, P0642 00, P0643 00, P2088 00, P2089 00, P2090 00, P2091 00, P2100 00, P2101 00, P2119 00, P2176 00, P2297 00, P2301 00, P2304 00, P2307 00, P2310 00, P2610 00, and P2A00 00 are not set. The barometric pressure (BARO) is more than 75 kPa (11 PSI). The engine has been running between 1-10 min. The engine is idling. The fuel level is between 6-40 L (2-10 gal). The fuel tank pressure is between -3 to +1 kPa (-0. 4 to +0. 1 PSI). The vehicle speed is 0 km/h (0 MPH). The intake air temperature (IAT) is between -8 to +70°C (+17 to +158°F). The battery voltage is more than 10 V. The engine is operating in closed loop fuel control. DTC P0442 00 runs once per drive cycle when the above conditions have been met.
DTC: P0443	**Evaporative Emission (EVAP) Purge Solenoid Control Circuit:** The engine RPM is greater than 80. The system voltage is between 10-18 volts. DTCs P0443, P0449, P0458, P0459, P0498, or P0499 run continuously when the above conditions are met.
DTC: P0443	**Evaporative Emission (EVAP) Purge Solenoid Control Circuit:** The ignition is ON. The system voltage is greater than 11 V. DTCs P0443 and P0449 run continuously when the above conditions are met.
DTC: P0443 00	**Evaporative Emission (EVAP) Purge Solenoid Valve Control Circuit:** Engine is running. DTCs P0606 00, P0628 00, or P0629 00 are not set. The battery voltage is greater than 9 V.
DTC: P0446	**Evaporative Emissions (EVAP) Vent System Performance:** Before the ECM can report DTC P0446 failed, DTCs P0450, P0451, P0452, and P0453 must run and pass. DTC P0100, P0101, P0102, P0103, P0111, P0112, P0113, P0116, P0117, P0118, P0119, P0121, P0122, P0123, P0128, P0221, P0222, P0223, P0443, P0449, P0451, P0452, P0453, P0458, P0459, P0496, P0497, P0498, P0499, P0560, P0562, P0563, P0700, P2122, P2123, P2127, P2128 or P2138 is not set. The ignition voltage is 10-18 volts. The Closed Loop fuel control is enabled. The engine run time is greater than 10 minutes or the fuel trim is stable. The engine is idling. The Fuel Tank Pressure is between -18. 7 and +9. 8 mm Hg (-10. 0 and +5. 2 in. H2O). The ambient air temperature (AAT) is between 2-32°C (35-90°F). The ECT and the IAT are within 10°C (18°F) of each other at engine start-up. The barometric pressure (BARO) is greater than 68 kPa. The long term fuel trim remains steady, less than 3 percent change in 200 ms over a period of 8 seconds. The fuel level is between 11-88 percent. The vehicle speed sensor (VSS) is less than 3 km/h (2 mph). The above conditions exist for greater than 5 seconds. DTC P0446 will attempt to run up to 10 times or until the test completes successfully once per ignition cycle.
DTC: P0446	**Evaporative Emissions (EVAP) Vent System Performance:** DTCs P0107, P0108, P0112, P0113, P0116, P0117, P0118, P0125, P0128, P0502, P1106, P1107, P1111, P1112, P1114, P1115, P1125, P1516, P2101, P2108, P2119, P2120, P2125, P2138 are not set. The ignition voltage is between 10-18 volts. The barometric pressure (BARO) is more than 75 kPa. The fuel level is between 15-85 percent. The start-up engine coolant temperature (ECT) is between 4-30°C (39-86°F). The start-up intake air temperature (IAT) is between 4-30°C (39-86°F). The start-up ECT and IAT are within 9°C (16°F) of each other. The vehicle speed sensor (VSS) is less than 129 km/h (80 mph). DTC P0446 runs once per trip when the above conditions have been met.
DTC: P0446 00	**Evaporative Emission (EVAP) Vent System Performance:** DTCs P0449 00, P0451 00, P0452 00, P0453 00, P0454 00, P0498 00, P0499 00, P0562 00, P0563 00, P0642 00, P0643 00 are not set. The ignition voltage is between 10-18 V. The EVAP system is purging. DTC P0446 00 runs once per trip when the above conditions have been met.
DTC: P0446 00	**Evaporative Emission (EVAP) Vent System Performance:** **NOTE: The following conditions must be met prior to ignition OFF:** DTCs P0106 00, P0107 00, P0108 00, P0112 00, P0113 00, P0114 00, P0116 00, P0117 00, P0118 00, P0122 00, P0123 00, P0222 00, P0223 00, P0443 00, P0449 00, P0451 00, P0452 00, P0453 00, P0454 00, P0502 00, and P2135 00 are not set. The ignition voltage is greater than 11 V. The barometric pressure (BARO) is greater than 70 kPa (10. 15 PSI). The startup Engine Coolant Temperature (ECT) is less than 35°C (95°F). The startup Intake Air Temperature (IAT) is between 4-30°C (40-86°F). The purge enable time is less than predetermined value based on startup ECT. The fuel level is between 10-90%. The engine run time is between 1-360 s plus purge enable time. The DTC run once an ignition cycle when the above conditions are met.
DTC: P0449	**Evaporative Emission (EVAP) Vent Solenoid Control Circuit:** The engine RPM is greater than 80. The system voltage is between 10-18 volts. DTCs P0443, P0449, P0458, P0459, P0498, or P0499 run continuously when the above conditions are met.
DTC: P0449	**Evaporative Emission (EVAP) Vent Solenoid Control Circuit:** The ignition is ON. The system voltage is greater than 11 V. DTCs P0443 and P0449 run continuously when the above conditions are met.

DTC	Trouble Code Title, Conditions, Possible Causes
DTC: P0449 00	**Evaporative Emission (EVAP) Vent Solenoid Valve Control Circuit:** The ignition is ON. The system voltage is between 9-18 V. DTCs P0443 and P0449 run continuously when the above conditions are met.
DTC: P0450	**Fuel Tank Pressure (FTP) Sensor Circuit:** P0450The engine is running. The estimated ambient air temperature is warmer than -7°C (+19. 4°F). The EVAP canister vent valve has been open for more than 3 seconds. The vehicle speed is less than 29 km/h (18 mph). DTC P0450 runs continuously when the above conditions have been met.
DTC: P0451	**Fuel Tank Pressure Sensor Performance:** P0451 Condition 1 DTC P0100, P0101, P0102, P0103, P0116, P0117, P0118, P0119, P0443, P0449, P0458, P0459, P0498, P0499, P050A, P0506, P0507, P0700, P2227, P2228, or P2229 is not set. The engine is operating for greater than 1 second. The engine is idling. The ambient air temperature is warmer than -7°C (+19°F). The vehicle speed is less than 10 km/h (6 mph) for greater than 30 seconds. The BARO is greater than 68 kPa. The fuel level is between 11-88 percent. The ECM has commanded the EVAP canister purge solenoid ON. The ECM has commanded the EVAP canister vent valve closed for greater than 4 seconds. DTC P0451 runs continuously once the above conditions are met for approximately 25 seconds. P0451 Condition 2 DTC P0100, P0101, P0102, P0103, P0116, P0117, P0118, P0119, P0443, P0449, P0458, P0459, P0498, P0499, P050A, P0506, P0507, P0700, P2227, P2228, or P2229 is not set. The engine is operating. The BARO is greater than 68 kPa. The ECM has commanded the EVAP canister purge solenoid OFF. The ECM has commanded the EVAP canister vent valve open. OR The vehicle speed is between 10-76 km/h (6-47 mph) for greater than 30 seconds. The fuel level is between 11-73 percent. The EVAP purge solenoid is commanded ON. OR The calculated ambient air temperature is 4-35°C (39-95°F) for greater than 3 seconds. DTC P0451 runs continuously once the above conditions are met for approximately 7 seconds.
DTC: P0451	**Fuel Tank Pressure (FTP) Sensor Performance:** P0451 DTC P0451 runs only when the engine-off natural vacuum small leak test, P0442, executes. The number of times this test runs can range from 0-2 per engine-off period. The length of the test can be up to 10 minutes.
DTC: P0451	**Fuel Tank Pressure (FTP) Sensor Performance:** P0451 - Part 1The engine is running. The vehicle speed is greater than 0 km/h (0 mph). The ambient pressure is greater than 68 kPa. The estimated ambient air temperature is warmer than -7°C (+19. 4°F). The fuel level is between 12-88 percent. DTC P0451 runs continuously when the above conditions have been met. P0451 - Part 2The EVAP canister purge solenoid valve is closed and the EVAP canister vent solenoid valve is open. The vehicle speed is between 10-75 km/h (6-46 mph). The time since engine start is greater than 450 seconds. DTC P0451 runs whenever the above conditions have been met.
DTC: P0451 00	**Fuel Tank Pressure Sensor Performance:** P0451 00This diagnostic runs when the engine off natural vacuum small leak test, DTC P0442 00, is in progress. This diagnostic can be tested 2 times during the engine off period.
DTC: P0451 00	**Fuel Tank Pressure Sensor Performance:** P0451 00 DTCs P0452 00, P0453 00, P0642 00, P0643 00 are not set. The engine has been running for more than 10 s. The fuel tank pressure sensor signal is between 0. 2-4. 9 V. The vehicle speed reached once during drive cycle of 20 km/h (14. 2 MPH). The evaporative emission (EVAP) system has reached full purge and no purge once during drive cycle. The EVAP system is purging. DTC P0451 00 runs continuously when the above conditions have been met.
DTC: P0452	**Fuel Tank Pressure (FTP) Sensor Circuit Low Voltage:** P0452 and P0453 DTC P0452 and P0453 run continuously when the ignition is ON.
DTC: P0452 00	**Fuel Tank Pressure Sensor Circuit Low Voltage:** P0452 00 and P0453 00 DTCs P0642 00 and P0643 00 are not set. The average fuel level is between 6-40 L (0-10 gal). DTCs P0452 00 and P0453 00 run continuously when the ignition is ON.
DTC: P0452 00	**Fuel Tank Pressure Sensor Circuit Low Voltage:** The ignition is ON or the engine is running. The DTCs run continuously once the above condition is met.
DTC: P0453	**Fuel Tank Pressure Sensor Circuit High Voltage:** P0452 and P0453 DTC P0452 and P0453 run continuously when the ignition is ON.
DTC: P0453 00	**Fuel Tank Pressure Sensor Circuit High Voltage:** P0452 00 and P0453 00 DTCs P0642 00 and P0643 00 are not set. The average fuel level is between 6-40 L (0-10 gal). DTCs P0452 00 and P0453 00 run continuously when the ignition is ON.
DTC: P0453 00	**Fuel Tank Pressure Sensor Circuit High Voltage:** The ignition is ON or the engine is running. The DTCs run continuously once the above condition is met.
DTC: P0454 00	**Fuel Tank Pressure Sensor Circuit Intermittent:** P0454 00This diagnostic runs when the engine off natural vacuum small leak test, DTC P0442 00, is in progress. This diagnostic can be tested 1 time during the engine off period. The ECM does not detect a refueling event.

DTC	Trouble Code Title, Conditions, Possible Causes
DTC: P0454 00	**Fuel Tank Pressure Sensor Circuit Intermittent:** P0454 00 DTCs P000A 00, P000B 00, P0010 00, P0013 00, P0016 00, P0017 00, P0030 00, P0031 00, P0032 00, P011 001, P0112 00, P0113 00, P0114 00, P0117 00, P0118 00, P0119 00, P0121 00, P0122 00, P0123 00, P0131 00, P0132 00, P0133 00, P0134 00, P0135 00, P0171 00, P0172 00, P0201 00, P0202 00, P0203 00, P0204 00, P0221 00, P0222 00, P0223 00, P0261 00, P0262 00, P0264 00, P0265 00, P0267 00, P0268 00, P0270 00, P0271 00, P0300 00, P0301 00, P0302 00, P0303 00, P0304 00, P0335 00, P0336 00, P0340 00, P0341 00, P0365 00, P0366 00, P0442 00, P0443 00, P0446 00, P0451 00, P0452 00, P0453 00, P0454 00, P0455 00, P0456 00, P0458 00, P0459 00, P0496 00, P0498 00, P0499 00, P0500 00, P0501 00, P0506 00, P0507 00, P0562 00, P0563 00, P0601 00, P0602 00, P0603 00, P0604 00, P0605 00, P0606 00, P0607 00, P061A 00, P0642 00, P0643 00, P2088 00, P2089 00, P2090 00, P2091 00, P2100 00, P2101 00, P2119 00, P2176 00, P2297 00, P2301 00, P2304 00, P2307 00, P2310 00, and P2A00 00 are not set. The ignition is ON. The barometric pressure (BARO) is more than 75 kPa (11 PSI). The engine coolant temperature (ECT) sensor is less than 110°C (230°F). The engine is idling. The vehicle speed is 0 km/h (0 MPH). The fuel level is between 6-40 L (2-10 gal). The fuel tank pressure sensor is between -3 to +1 kPa (-0. 4 to +0. 1 PSI). The intake air temperature (IAT) is between -8. 25 to +70°C (+17 to +158°F). The battery voltage is more than 10 V. The engine is operating in closed loop fuel control. DTC P045 004 runs once per drive cycle when the above conditions have been met.
DTC: P0455	**Evaporative Emission System Large Leak Detected:** DTCs P00C8, P00C9, P16F3, P0068, P0101, P0102, P0103, P010C, P010D, P0106, P0107, P0108, P0111, P0112, P0113, P0114, P0116, P0117, P0118, P0120, P0121, P0122, P0123, P0125, P0128, P160E, P160D, P0191, P0192, P0193, P0220, P0222, P0223, P0442, P0443, P0449, P0451, P0452, P0453, P0454, P0464, P0496, P0502, P0503, P0606, P0608, P0609, P0641, P0651, P0722, P0723, P1104, P1516, P2100, P2101, P2102, P2103, P2119, P2120, P2122, P2123, P2125, P2127, P2128, P2135, P2138, P2227, P2228, P2229, P2230 is not set. The ignition voltage is greater than 11 V. The barometric pressure (BARO) is more than 70 kPa. The fuel level is between 10-90 percent. The engine coolant temperature (ECT) at start-up is less than 35°C (95°F). The intake air temperature (IAT) is between 4-30°C (39-86°F). DTC P0455 runs once per cold start when the above conditions are met.
DTC: P0455	**Evaporative Emission (EVAP) System Large Leak:** DTCs P0106, P0107, P0108, P0112, P0113, P0116, P0117, P0118, P0121, P0122, P0123, P0222, P0223, P0128, P0443, P0449, P0452, P0453, P0454, P0502, P0503 are not set. The engine is running. The ignition voltage is between 10-18 volts. The barometric pressure (BARO) is more than 74 kPa. The fuel level is between 15-85 percent. The start-up intake air temperature (IAT) is between 4-30°C (39-86°F). The start-up engine coolant temperature (ECT) is less than 30°C (86°F). The start-up ECT and IAT are within 8°C (14. 4°F) of each other. DTC P0455 runs once per cold start within 17 minutes of start-up.
DTC: P0455 00	**Evaporative Emission (EVAP) System Large Leak Detected:** DTCs P0106 00, P0107 00, P0108 00, P0112 00, P0113 00, P0116 00, P0117 00, P0118 00, P0442 00, P0443 00, P0446 00, P0449 00, P0452 00, P0453 00, P0454 00, and P0502 00 are not set. One of the following conditions is met: The ignition is off for greater than 12 h. or The start-up intake air temperature (IAT) and the start-up engine coolant temperature (ECT) are within 8°C (14°F). The ignition voltage is between 11-18 V. The barometric pressure (BARO) is more than 75 kPa (10. 87 PSI). The fuel level is between 15-85%. The startup engine coolant temperature (ECT) is between 4-30°C (39-86°F). The startup intake air temperature (IAT) is between 4-30°C (39-86°F). The EVAP purge is greater than 2%. The fuel level is between 10-90%. The engine run time is less than 17 min. The DTC run once an ignition cycle when the above conditions are met.
DTC: P0455 00	**Evaporative Emission (EVAP) System Large Leak Detected:** DTCs P000A 00, P000B 00, P0010 00, P0013 00, P0016 00, P0017 00, P0030 00, P0031 00, P0032 00, P0111 00, P0112 00, P0113 00, P0114 00, P0117 00, P0118 00, P0119 00, P0121 00, P0122 00, P0123 00, P0130 00, P013 001, P0132 00, P0133 00, P0134 00, P0135 00, P0171 00, P0172 00, P0201 00, P0202 00, P0203 00, P0204 00, P0221 00, P0222 00, P0223 00, P0261 00, P0262 00, P0264 00, P0265 00, P0267 00, P0268 00, P0270 00, P0271 00, P0300 00, P0301 00, P0302 00, P0303 00, P0304 00, P0335 00, P0336 00, P0340 00, P0341 00, P0365 00, P0366 00, P0436 00, P0442 00, P0443 00, P0446 00, P0449 00, P0451 00, P0452 00, P0453 00, P0454 00, P0456 00, P0458 00, P0459 00, P0496 00, P0498 00, P0499 00, P0500 00, P0506 00, P050 007, P0562 00, P0563 00, P0601 00, P0602 00, P0604 00, P0606 00, P0607 00, P061A 00, P0642 00, P0643 00, P2088 00, P2089 00, P2090 00, P2091 00, P2100 00, P2101 00, P2119 00, P2176 00, P2297 00, P2301 00, P2304 00, P2307 00, P2310 00, P2610 00, and P2A00 00 are not set. The engine is running. The ignition voltage is between 10-18 V. The barometric pressure (BARO) is more than 75 kPa (11 PSI). The engine coolant temperature (ECT) sensor is less than 110°C (230°F). The fuel level is between 6-40 L (2-10 gal). The vehicle speed is 0 km/h (0 MPH). The intake air temperature (IAT) sensor is between -8 to +70°C (+17 to +158°F). The engine is operating in closed loop fuel control. DTC P0455 00 runs once per cold start within 10 min of start-up.
DTC: P0458	**Evaporative Emission (EVAP) Purge Solenoid Control Circuit Low Voltage:** The engine RPM is greater than 80. The system voltage is between 10-18 volts. DTCs P0443, P0449, P0458, P0459, P0498, or P0499 run continuously when the above conditions are met.
DTC: P0458 00	**Evaporative Emission (EVAP) Purge Solenoid Valve Control Circuit Low Voltage:** The engine is running. The ignition voltage is between 1-16 V. These DTCs runs continuously once the above conditions are met.
DTC: P0458 00	**Evaporative Emission (EVAP) Purge Solenoid Valve Control Circuit Low Voltage:** Engine is running. DTCs P0606 00, P0628 00, or P0629 00 are not set. The battery voltage is greater than 9 V.
DTC: P0459	**Evaporative Emission (EVAP) Purge Solenoid Control Circuit High Voltage:** The engine RPM is greater than 80. The system voltage is between 10-18 volts. DTCs P0443, P0449, P0458, P0459, P0498, or P0499 run continuously when the above conditions are met.

DTC	Trouble Code Title, Conditions, Possible Causes
DTC: P0459 00	**Evaporative Emission (EVAP) Purge Solenoid Valve Control Circuit High Voltage:** The engine is running. The ignition voltage is between 1-16 V. These DTCs runs continuously once the above conditions are met.
DTC: P0459 00	**Evaporative Emission (EVAP) Purge Solenoid Valve Control Circuit High Voltage:** Engine is running. DTCs P0606 00, P0628 00, or P0629 00 are not set. The battery voltage is greater than 9 V.
DTC: P0460	**Fuel Level Sensor Circuit:** The engine is running. The system voltage is between 11-16 V.
DTC: P0461	**Fuel Level Sensor 1 Performance:** The engine is running. The system voltage is between 11-16 V.
DTC: P0462	**Fuel Level Sensor 1 Circuit Low Voltage:** The engine is running. The system voltage is between 11-16 V.
DTC: P0463	**Fuel Level Sensor Circuit High Voltage:** The engine is running. The system voltage is between 11-16 V
DTC: P0464	**Fuel Level Sensor Circuit Intermittent:** The engine is running. The system voltage is between 11-16 V.
DTC: P046C	**Exhaust Gas Recirculation (EGR) Position Sensor Performance:** Engine speed is greater than 600 RPM. The Battery voltage is greater than 11 V. The Air Intake Heater duty cycle is less than 5 %. The EGR Valve is active. The EGR Valve offset learning from the previous drive cycle is complete. EGR offset learning is not active. DTC P046C runs continuously when the above conditions are met.
DTC: P046C	**Exhaust Gas Recirculation (EGR) Position Sensor Performance:** P046CDTCs P0401, P0402, P0403, P0642, or P0643 are not set. The EGR valve is actively being controlled. DTC P046C runs continuously when the above conditions have been met.
DTC: P0480	**Cooling Fan Relay 1 Control Circuit:** The ignition voltage is between 10-26 volts. The engine speed is greater than 80 RPM. The ECM driver transitions from ON to OFF or from OFF to ON. DTC P0480, P0481, P0691, P0692, P0693, and P0694 run continuously when the conditions above are met.
DTC: P0480	**Cooling Fan Speed Output Circuit:** The ignition voltage is greater than 11 volts. The engine is operating. The engine speed is greater than 600 RPM. DTC P0480 runs continuously when the conditions above exist for greater than 3 seconds.
DTC: P0480	**Cooling Fan Relay 1 Control Circuit:** The engine speed is greater than 400 RPM. The ignition voltage is between 11-18 volts. The relay control circuit is commanded from OFF to ON, or ON to OFF. DTC P0480 and P0481 run continuously when the conditions above are met.
DTC: P0480	**Cooling Fan Relay 1 Control Circuit:** The ignition voltage is between 10-18 volts. The engine speed is greater than 80 RPM. The ECM driver transitions from ON to OFF or from OFF to ON. DTC P0480, P0481, P0691, P0692, P0693, and P0694 run continuously when the conditions above are met.
DTC: P0480 00	**Cooling Fan Relay 1 Control Circuit:** The engine is running. The ignition voltage is between 11-16 V. The ECM driver transitions from ON to OFF or from OFF to ON.
DTC: P0480 01	**Cooling Fan Relay 1 Control Circuit Short to Battery:** The ignition is ON, or the engine is running. The ignition voltage is greater than 10 V. The DTCs run continuously once the above conditions are met.
DTC: P0480 02	**Cooling Fan Relay 1 Control Circuit Short to Ground:** The ignition is ON, or the engine is running. The ignition voltage is greater than 10 V. The DTCs run continuously once the above conditions are met.
DTC: P0480 04	**Cooling Fan Relay 1 Control Circuit Open:** The ignition is ON, or the engine is running. The ignition voltage is greater than 10 V. The DTCs run continuously once the above conditions are met.
DTC: P0480 54	**Cooling Fan Relay 1 Control Circuit High Temperature:** The ignition is ON, or the engine is running. The ignition voltage is greater than 10 V. The DTCs run continuously once the above conditions are met.
DTC: P0481	**Cooling Fan Relay 2 and 3 Control Circuit:** The engine speed is greater than 400 RPM. The ignition voltage is between 11-18 volts. The relay control circuit is commanded from OFF to ON, or ON to OFF. DTC P0480 and P0481 run continuously when the conditions above are met.
DTC: P0481 00	**Cooling Fan Relay 2 Control Circuit:** The engine is running. The ignition voltage is between 11-16 V. The ECM driver transitions from ON to OFF or from OFF to ON.

DTC	Trouble Code Title, Conditions, Possible Causes
DTC: P0481 01	**Cooling Fan Relay 2 Control Circuit Short to Battery:** The ignition is ON, or the engine is running. The ignition voltage is greater than 10 V. The DTCs run continuously once the above conditions are met.
DTC: P0481 02	**Cooling Fan Relay 2 Control Circuit Short to Ground:** The ignition is ON, or the engine is running. The ignition voltage is greater than 10 V. The DTCs run continuously once the above conditions are met.
DTC: P0481 04	**Cooling Fan Relay 2 Control Circuit Open:** The ignition is ON, or the engine is running. The ignition voltage is greater than 10 V. The DTCs run continuously once the above conditions are met.
DTC: P0481 54	**Cooling Fan Relay 2 Control Circuit High Temperature:** The ignition is ON, or the engine is running. The ignition voltage is greater than 10 V. The DTCs run continuously once the above conditions are met.
DTC: P0482 01	**Cooling Fan Relay 3 Control Circuit Short to Battery:** The ignition is ON, or the engine is running. The ignition voltage is greater than 10 V. The DTCs run continuously once the above conditions are met.
DTC: P0482 02	**Cooling Fan Relay 3 Control Circuit Short to Ground:** The ignition is ON, or the engine is running. The ignition voltage is greater than 10 V. The DTCs run continuously once the above conditions are met.
DTC: P0482 04	**Cooling Fan Relay 3 Control Circuit Open:** The ignition is ON, or the engine is running. The ignition voltage is greater than 10 V. The DTCs run continuously once the above conditions are met.
DTC: P0482 54	**Cooling Fan Relay 3 Control Circuit High Temperature:** The ignition is ON, or the engine is running. The ignition voltage is greater than 10 V. The DTCs run continuously once the above conditions are met.
DTC: P0483	**Cooling Fan System Performance:** DTC P0016, P007C, P007D, P0112, P0113, P0117, P0118, P0335, P0336, P0340, P0341, P0480, P0495, or P0526 is not set. The engine is operating for greater than 10 seconds. The engine speed is between 1,200-3,429 RPM. The BARO is greater than 75 kPa. The engine coolant temperature is warmer than 70°C (158°F). The ECM commanded fan clutch solenoid duty cycle is greater than 36 percent. The cooling fan input shaft speed is steady. DTC P0483 runs continuously every 100 mS when the conditions above exist.
DTC: P0483	**Cooling Fan System Performance:** The engine coolant temperature is warmer than 70°C (158°F). The engine RPM is greater than 1,200 RPM. The fan duty cycle is greater than 36 percent. The engine speed variation is less than 250 RPM.
DTC: P0489	**Exhaust Gas Recirculation (EGR) Motor Control Circuit 1 Low Voltage:** P0489, P0490, P1407, P140D, P140E and P140FThe Ignition is ON. The battery voltage is greater than 11 V. The EGR control circuit is active. The starter is not cranking. The DTCs run continuously when the above conditions are met.
DTC: P0490	**Exhaust Gas Recirculation (EGR) Motor Control Circuit 1 High Voltage:** P0489, P0490, P1407, P140D, P140E and P140FThe Ignition is ON. The battery voltage is greater than 11 V. The EGR control circuit is active. The starter is not cranking. The DTCs run continuously when the above conditions are met.
DTC: P0495	**Cooling Fan Speed High:** The engine is running.
DTC: P0495	**Cooling Fan Speed High:** DTC P0016, P0112, P0113, P0117, P0118, P0335, P0336, P0340, P0341, P0480, P0483, P0526, P2228, or P2229 is not set. The engine is operating for greater than 10 seconds. The engine speed is greater than 1,071 RPM. The engine OFF time after the previous ignition cycle was greater than 0 seconds. The ambient air temperature (AAT) is warmer than -40°C (-40°F). The BARO is greater than 55 kPa. The ECM commanded fan clutch solenoid duty cycle is less than 36 percent. DTC P0495 runs continuously when the conditions above exist.
DTC: P0496	**Evaporative Emission System Flow During Non-Purge:** DTCs P0107, P0108, P0112, P0113, P0117, P0118, P0125, P0128, P0442, P0443, P0446, P0449, P0452, P0453, P0445, P1106, P1107, P1111, P1112, P1114, P1115, P1516 are not set. The ignition voltage is between 10-18 volts. The barometric pressure (BARO) is more than 74 kPa. The fuel level is between 15-85 percent. The engine coolant temperature (ECT) is between 4-30°C (39-86°F). The intake air temperature (IAT) is between 4-30°C (39-86°F). DTC P0496 runs once per cold start for 96 seconds.

DTC	Trouble Code Title, Conditions, Possible Causes
DTC: P0496	**Evaporative Emissions (EVAP) System Flow During Non-Purge:** Before the engine control module (ECM) can report DTC P0496 failed, DTCs P0450, P0451, P0452, and P0453 must run and pass. DTC P0100, P0101, P0102, P0103, P0111, P0112, P0113, P0116, P0117, P0118, P0119, P0443, P0446, P0449, P0450, P0451, P0452, P0453, P0458, P0459, P0498, P0499, P0560, P0562, P0563, P0700, P2122, P2123, P2127, P2128, P2138, P2227, P2228, or P2229 is not set. The fuel system is in closed loop. The engine run time is greater than 10 minutes, or the long term fuel trim is stable. The vehicle speed sensor (VSS) is less than 3 km/h (2 mph). The engine is idling. The ignition voltage is between 10-18 volts. The Closed Loop fuel control is enabled. The fuel tank pressure (FTP) is between -10. 0 and +5. 0 in. H2O (-18. 7 and +9. 8mm Hg). The ambient air temperature is between 2-32°C (36-90°F). The start-up engine coolant temperature (ECT) is within 10°C (18°F) of ambient air temperature. The fuel tank level is between 11-88 percent. The barometric pressure (BARO) is greater than 68 kPa. The above conditions are met for greater than 30 seconds. DTC P0496 will attempt to run up to 10 times or the test completes successfully once per ignition cycle.
DTC: P0496 00	**Evaporative Emission (EVAP) System Flow During Non-Purge:** DTCs P0106 00, P0107 00, P0108 00, P0112 00, P0113 00, P0116 00, P0117 00, P0118 00, P0442 00, P0443 00, P0446 00, P0449 00, P0452 00, P0453 00, P0454 00, and P0502 00 are not set. The ECM is not commanding reduced engine power. The ignition voltage is between 11-18 V. The barometric pressure (BARO) is more than 75 kPa (10. 87 PSI). The fuel level is between 15-85%. The startup engine coolant temperature (ECT) is between 4-30°C (39-86°F). The startup intake air temperature (IAT) is between 4-30°C (39-86°F). The ignition is OFF for greater than 8 h. The fuel level is between 10-90%. The EVAP canister purge and EVAP vent valves are closed. The DTC run once an ignition cycle when the above conditions are met.
DTC: P0496 00	**Evaporative Emission (EVAP) System Flow During Non-Purge:** DTCs P000A 00, P000B 00, P0010 00, P001 003, P0016 00, P0017 00, P0030 00, P003 001, P0032 00, P0111 00, P0112 00, P0113 00, P0114 00, P0116 00, P0117 00, P0118 00, P0119 00, P0121 00, P0122 00, P0123 00, P0131 00, P0132 00, P0133 00, P0134 00, P0135 00, P0171 00, P0172 00, P0201 00, P0202 00, P0203 00, P0204 00, P0261 00, P0262 00, P0264 00, P0265 00, P0267 00, P0268 00, P0270 00, P0271 00, P0301 00, P0302 00, P0303 00, P0304 00, P0335 00, P0336 00, P0340 00, P0341 00, P0365 00, P0366 00, P0442 00, P0443 00, P0446 00, P0451 00, P0452 00, P0453 00, P0454 00, P0455 00, P0456 00, P0458 00, P0459 00, P0496 00, P0498 00, P0499 00, P0501 00, P0506 00, P0507 00, P0562 00, P0563 00, P061A 00, P0642 00, P0643 00, P2088 00, P2089 00, P2090 00, P2091 00, P2100 00, P2101 00, P2119 00, P2176 00, P2297 00, P2301 00, P2304 00, P2307 00, P2310 00, P2610 00, and U0073 00 are not set. The ignition voltage is between 10-18 V. The barometric pressure (BARO) is more than 75 kPa (11 PSI). The fuel level is between 15-85%. The engine coolant temperature (ECT) is less than 110°C (230°F). The intake air temperature (IAT) is between 4-30°C (39-86°F). The start-up ECT and IAT are within 9°C (16°F) of each other. The vehicle speed sensor (VSS) is less than 121 km/h (75 MPH). The fuel tank pressure sensor is less than -0. 6 kPa (-4. 3 PSI) at ignition ON. DTC P0496 00 runs once per cold start for 96 s.
DTC: P0497	**Evaporative Emission System Low Purge Flow:** DTCs P0030, P0031, P0032, P0053, P0100, P0101, P0102, P0103, P0106, P0107, P0108, P0112, P0113, P0114, P0117, P0118, P0119, P0122, P0123, P0128, P0130, P0131, P0132, P0133, P0135, P0221, P0222, P0223, P0443, P0449, P0450, P0451, P0452, P0453, P0458, P0459, P0498, P0499, P0501, P0502, P2122, P2123, P2127, P2128, P2138, P2177, P2178, P2187, P2188, P2195, P2196, P2199, P2227, P2228, P2229, P2243, P2251, P2297, P2626 are not set. The ignition voltage is between 11-18 volts. The barometric pressure (BARO) is more than 68 kPa. The fuel level is between 15-85 percent. The fuel tank pressure is between -2. 5 and +1. 3 kPa (-10 and +5 in H2O). The engine coolant temperature (ECT) is between 4-30°C (39-86°F). The intake air temperature is between 2-32°C (35. 6-90°F). The start-up ECT and IAT are within 9°C (14. 4°F) of each other. The vehicle speed sensor (VSS) is less than 1. 7 km/h (2 mph). DTC P0497 will attempt to run up to 10 times until it successfully completes. DTC P0497 completes one test per cold start within 10 minutes of start-up.
DTC: P0497	**Evaporative Emission (EVAP) System No Flow During Purge:** Before the engine control module (ECM) can report DTC P0455 or DTC P0497 failed, DTCs P0446 and P0496 must run and pass. DTC P0100, P0101, P0102, P0103, P0111, P0112, P0113, P0116, P0117, P0118, P0119, P0443, P0446, P0449, P0450, P0451, P0452, P0453, P0458, P0459, P0496, P0498, P0499, P0560, P0562, P0563, P0700, P2122, P2123, P2127, P2128, P2138, P2227, P2228, or P2229 is not set. The ignition voltage is between 10-18 volts. The engine run time is greater than 10 minutes or the fuel trim is stable. The FTP is between -18. 7 and +9. 8mm Hg (-10. 0 and +5. 2 in. H2O). The Closed Loop fuel control is enabled. The engine is idling. The barometric pressure (BARO) is greater than 68 kPa. The fuel level is between 11-88 percent. The ambient air temperature (IAT) is between 2-32°C (36-90°F). The engine coolant temperature (ECT) is within 10°C (18°F) of the ambient air temperature at engine start. The vehicle speed sensor (VSS) is less than 3 km/h (2 mph). The above conditions are met for greater than 30 seconds. DTC P0455 or DTC P0497 will attempt to run up to 10 times or until the test completes successfully once per ignition cycle.
DTC: P0498	**Evaporative Emission (EVAP) Vent Solenoid Control Circuit Low Voltage:** The engine RPM is greater than 80. The system voltage is between 10-18 volts. DTCs P0443, P0449, P0458, P0459, P0498, or P0499 run continuously when the above conditions are met.
DTC: P0499	**Evaporative Emission (EVAP) Vent Solenoid Control Circuit High Voltage:** The engine RPM is greater than 80. The system voltage is between 10-18 volts. DTCs P0443, P0449, P0458, P0459, P0498, or P0499 run continuously when the above conditions are met.

DTC	Trouble Code Title, Conditions, Possible Causes
DTC: P049D	**Exhaust Gas Recirculation (EGR) Position Not Learned:** DTC P0403, P0405, P0406, or P140F is not set. The ignition is OFF and the engine is in after-run/post drive. The EGR Valve offset learning procedure is active or complete for current drive cycle. The Engine Coolant Temperature (ECT) is between 5-123°C (41-253°F). Battery voltage is greater than 10 V. The DTC runs continuously when the above conditions are met.
DTC: P049D 00	**Exhaust Gas Recirculation (EGR) Position Not Learned:** DTC P0404 00, P0405 00, P0406 00, or P1407 00 are not set. The ignition is OFF and the engine is in after run/post drive. The EGR Valve offset learning procedure is active or complete for current drive cycle. The engine coolant temperature (ECT) is between 5-123°C (41-253°F). Battery voltage is greater than 10 V. This DTCs run continuously when the above conditions are met.
DTC: P0500 08	**Vehicle Speed Sensor (VSS) Circuit Signal Invalid:** The engine is running. The DTCs run continuously once the above condition is met.
DTC: P0500 11	**Vehicle Speed Sensor (VSS) Circuit Above Maximum Threshold:** The engine is running. The DTCs run continuously once the above condition is met.
DTC: P0502	**Vehicle Speed Sensor (VSS) Circuit Low Voltage:** P0502 DTCs P0117, P0118, P0119, P0128, P0335, P0336, P0338 or P0501 are not set. The diesel fuel cut-off (DFCO) is active. The engine coolant temperature is more than 40°C (104°F). The engine speed is 1,440-3,520 RPM.
DTC: P0506	**Idle Speed Low:** The engine is operating for greater than 180 s. The engine speed is greater than 300 RPM. The engine coolant temperature (ECT) is between -7 to +123°C (19-253°F). The vehicle speed is less than 3 km/h (2 mph). DTC P0506 and P0507 run continuously when the above conditions are met.
DTC: P0506	**Idle Speed Low:** DTCs P0068, P0101, P0102, P0103, P0106, P0107, P0108, P0116, P0117, P0118, P0120, P0122, P0123, P0128, P0171, P0172, P0174, P0175, P0201, P0202, P0203, P0204, P0205, P0206, P0220, P0222, P0223, P0300, P0351, P0352, P0353, P0496, P0601, P0604, P0606, P060D, P0641, P0651, P1516, P2101, P2119, P2120, P2122, P2123, P2125, P2127, P2128, P2135, P2138, or P2176 are not set. The engine has been running for greater than 60 seconds. The engine is idling for greater than 10 seconds. The intake air temperature (IAT) is more than -40°C (-40°F). The AC mode state has not changed. The barometric pressure (BARO) is greater than 72 kPa. The power steering load state has not changed. The transmission gear selector state has not changed. The engine coolant temperature (ECT) is greater than -40°C (-40°F). The system voltage is between 9-18 volts. The vehicle speed is less than 4.8 km/h (3 mph). The DTCs run continuously when the above conditions are met.
DTC: P0506	**Idle Speed Low:** DTCs P0068, P0101, P0102, P0103, P0106, P0107, P0108, P0112, P0113, P0116, P0117, P0118, P0120, P0121, P0122, P0123, P0128, P0171, P0172, P0174, P0175, P0201-P0208, P0220, P0222, P0223, P0300- P0308, P0336, P0462, P0463, P0496, P0606, P0722, P0723, P1516, P2101, P2120, P2122, P2123, P2125, P2127, P2128, P2135, P2176 are not set. The engine is operating for at least 60 s. The engine is idling for greater than 10 s. The barometric pressure (BARO) is greater than 70 kPa (11 psi). The engine coolant temperature (ECT) is between 60-125°C (140-257°F). The intake air temperature (IAT) is warmer than -20°C (-4°F). The system voltage is between 11-32 V. The vehicle speed is less than 1. 9 km/h (1. 2 mph). The fuel level is greater than 10 percent. The commanded engine speed is steady within 25 RPM. The transmission is not changing gears. The torque converter clutch (TCC) is not changing states. The transfer case is not in 4WD Low - If equipped. The power take-off (PTO) is not active - If equipped. The manual transmission clutch pedal position top of travel is greater than 5 percent - If equipped. The manual transmission clutch pedal position bottom of travel is less than 5 percent - If equipped. The manual transmission clutch is not depressed - If equipped. A scan tool output control is not active. DTC P0506 and P0507 run continuously once the above conditions are met.
DTC: P0506 00	**Idle Speed Low:** DTCs P0016 00, P0068 00, P0106 00, P0107 00, P0108 00, P0117 00, P0118 00, P0122 00, P0123 00, P0171 00, P0172 00, P0222 00, P0223 00, P0261 00, P0262 00, P0264 00, P0265 00, P0267 00, P0268 00, P0270 00, P0271 00, P0335 00, P0336 00, P0340 00, P0341 00, P0458 00, P0459 00, P0502 00, P2101 00, P2122 00, P2123 00, P2127 00, P2128 00 or P2138 00 are not set. The engine has been running for more than 60 s. The long term fuel trim is learned. The vehicle speed is less than 3 km/h (2 MPH). The engine coolant temperature (ECT) is between 70-109°C (160-228°F). The intake air temperature (IAT) is between -7 to +105°C (+19 to +221°F). The barometric pressure (BARO) is more than 72 kPa (10. 4 PSI). The ignition voltage is between 11-18 V. DTC P0506 00 and P0507 00 run continuously when the above conditions are met.
DTC: P0506 00	**Idle Speed Low:** DTCs P0107 00, P0108 00, P0117 00, P0118 00, P0120 00, P0122 00, P0123 00, P0128 00, P0171 00, P0172 00, P0201 00, P0202 00, P0203 00, P0204 00, P0222 00, P0223 00, P0300 00, P0496 00, P0601 00, P0604 00, P0606 00, P061A 00, P0641 00, P2101 00, P2119 00, P2122 00, P2123 00, P2127 00, P2128 00, P2138 00, or P2176 00 are not set. The engine has been running for greater than 60 s. The engine is idling for greater than 10 s. The intake air temperature (IAT) is greater than -40°C (-40°F). The transmission gear selector state has not changed. The engine coolant temperature (ECT) is greater than 50°C (122°F). The system voltage is between 9-18 V. The vehicle speed is less than 4. 8 km/h (3 MPH). DTCs P0506 00 or P0507 00 run continuously when the above conditions are met.

DTC	Trouble Code Title, Conditions, Possible Causes
DTC: P0507	**Idle Speed High:** DTCs P0068, P0101, P0102, P0103, P0106, P0107, P0108, P0112, P0113, P0116, P0117, P0118, P0120, P0121, P0122, P0123, P0128, P0171, P0172, P0174, P0175, P0201-P0208, P0220, P0222, P0223, P0300- P0308, P0336, P0462, P0463, P0496, P0606, P0722, P0723, P1516, P2101, P2120, P2122, P2123, P2125, P2127, P2128, P2135, P2176 are not set. The engine is operating for at least 60 s. The engine is idling for greater than 10 s. The barometric pressure (BARO) is greater than 70 kPa (11 psi). The engine coolant temperature (ECT) is between 60-125°C (140-257°F). The intake air temperature (IAT) is warmer than -20°C (-4°F). The system voltage is between 11-32 V. The vehicle speed is less than 1. 9 km/h (1. 2 mph). The fuel level is greater than 10 percent. The commanded engine speed is steady within 25 RPM. The transmission is not changing gears. The torque converter clutch (TCC) is not changing states. The transfer case is not in 4WD Low - If equipped. The power take-off (PTO) is not active - If equipped. The manual transmission clutch pedal position top of travel is greater than 5 percent - If equipped. The manual transmission clutch pedal position bottom of travel is less than 5 percent - If equipped. The manual transmission clutch is not depressed - If equipped. A scan tool output control is not active. DTC P0506 and P0507 run continuously once the above conditions are met.
DTC: P0507 00	**Idle Speed High:** DTCs P0107 00, P0108 00, P0117 00, P0118 00, P0120 00, P0122 00, P0123 00, P0128 00, P0171 00, P0172 00, P0201 00, P0202 00, P0203 00, P0204 00, P0222 00, P0223 00, P0300 00, P0496 00, P0601 00, P0604 00, P0606 00, P061A 00, P0641 00, P2101 00, P2119 00, P2122 00, P2123 00, P2127 00, P2128 00, P2138 00, or P2176 00 are not set. The engine has been running for greater than 60 s. The engine is idling for greater than 10 s. The intake air temperature (IAT) is greater than -40°C (-40°F). The transmission gear selector state has not changed. The engine coolant temperature (ECT) is greater than 50°C (122°F). The system voltage is between 9-18 V. The vehicle speed is less than 4. 8 km/h (3 MPH). DTCs P0506 00 or P0507 00 run continuously when the above conditions are met.
DTC: P0507 00	**Idle Speed High:** DTCs P0016 00, P0068 00, P0106 00, P0107 00, P0108 00, P0117 00, P0118 00, P0122 00, P0123 00, P0171 00, P0172 00, P0222 00, P0223 00, P0261 00, P0262 00, P0264 00, P0265 00, P0267 00, P0268 00, P0270 00, P0271 00, P0335 00, P0336 00, P0340 00, P0341 00, P0458 00, P0459 00, P0502 00, P2101 00, P2122 00, P2123 00, P2127 00, P2128 00 or P2138 00 are not set. The engine has been running for more than 60 s. The long term fuel trim is learned. The vehicle speed is less than 3 km/h (2 MPH). The engine coolant temperature (ECT) is between 70-109°C (160-228°F). The intake air temperature (IAT) is between -7 to +105°C (+19 to +221°F). The barometric pressure (BARO) is more than 72 kPa (10. 4 PSI). The ignition voltage is between 11-18 V. DTC P0506 00 and P0507 00 run continuously when the above conditions are met.
DTC: P050A	**Cold Start Idle Air Control System Performance:** P050ADTC P0111, P0112, P0113, P0116, P0117, P0118, P0119, P0121, P0122, P0123, P0221, P0222, P0223, P0442, P0443, P0446, P0455, P0458, P0459, P0496, or P0700 is not set. The engine load is between 70-90 percent, for under speed or manual transmission only. The vehicle speed is 0 km/h (0 mph) and accelerator pedal position (APP) input is at 0 percent. The engine coolant temperature (ECT) is colder than 65°C (149°F). The catalyst cold start heating strategy is active. DTC P050A runs once an ignition cycle when the conditions above have been met for 7 s.
DTC: P050A	**Cold Start Idle Air Control System Performance:** DTCs P0096, P0097, P0098, P0099, P0117, P0118, P0121, P0122, P0123, P0300, P0336, P0446, P0455, P0496, P2101, P2176 are not set. The startup engine coolant temperature (ECT) is between -10 and +40°C (+14 and +104°F). The barometric pressure (BARO) is more than 65 kPa. The engine is running. DTC P050A runs continuously when the above conditions are met.
DTC: P050A 00	**Cold Start Idle Air Control System Performance:** DTCs P000A 00, P0010 00, P0016 00, P0068 00, P0106 00, P0107 00, P0108 00, P0116 00, P0117 00, P0118 00, P0119 00, P0121 00, P0123 00, P0171 00, P0172 00, P0201 00, P0202 00, P0203 00, P0204 00, P0222 00, P0261 00, P0262 00, P0264 00, P0265 00, P0267 00, P0268 00, P0270 00, P0271 00, P0335 00, P0336 00, P0340 00, P0341 00, P0365 00, P0366 00, P0443 00, P0459 00, P0496 00, P2088 00, P2089 00, P2100 00, P2101 00, P2122 00, P2123 00, P2127 00, P2128 00, P2138 00 are not set. The battery voltage is greater than 10 V. The engine speed is at idle. The engine coolant temperature (ECT) is greater than -9. 75°C (14. 45°F). DTC P050A 00 runs continuously when the above conditions are met.
DTC: P050B 00	**Cold Start Ignition Timing Performance:** DTCs P0010 00, P0016 00, P0068 00, P0106 00, P0107 00, P0108 00, P0116 00, P0117 00, P0118 00, P0119 00, P0121 00, P0123 00, P0171 00, P0172 00, P0201 00, P0202 00, P0203 00, P0204 00, P0222 00, P0261 00, P0262 00, P0264 00, P0265 00, P0267 00, P0268 00, P0270 00, P0271 00, P0335 00, P0336 00, P0340 00, P0341 00, P0365 00, P0366 00, P0443 00, P0459 00, P0496 00, P2088 00, P2089 00, P2100 00, P2101 00, P2122 00, P2123 00, P2127 00, P2128 00, P2138 00 are not set. The battery voltage is greater than 10 V. The engine speed is at idle. The engine coolant temperature (ECT) is greater than -9. 75°C (14. 45°F). DTC P050B 00 runs continuously when the above conditions are met.

DTC	Trouble Code Title, Conditions, Possible Causes
DTC: P050D	**Cold Start Rough Idle:** DTCs P0010, P0011, P0013, P0014, P0016, P0017, P0018, P0019, P0020, P0021, P0023, P0024, P0089, P0090-P0092, P00C6, P00C8, P00C9, P00CA, P0101-P0103, P0106-P0108, P0112-P0114, P0116-P0118, P0121-P0123, P0128, P0192, P0193, P0201-P0206, P0222, P0223, P0261, P0262, P0264, P0265, P0267, P0268, P0270, P0271, P0273, P0274, P0276, P0277, P0315, P0335, P0336, P0351-P0356, P0627-P0629, P069E, P0716, P0717, P0722, P0723, P0850-P0852, P1248, P1249, P124A, P124B, P124C, P124D, P1258, P135A, P135B, P150C, P163A, P1762, P1763, P1915, P2122, P2123, P2127, P2128, P2135, P2138, P2147, P2148, P2150, P2151, P2153, P2154, P2156, P2157, P216B, P216C, P216E, P216F, P228C, P228D, U0109 are not set. The catalyst temperature is less than 100°C (212°F). The engine coolant temperature is warmer than 10°C (14°F). The barometric pressure is greater than 70 kPa. The engine speed is between 450-1800 RPM. The engine is running and a cold start has been detected. DTC P050D runs once per cold start.
DTC: P050D	**Cold Start Rough Idle:** DTCs P0101, P0102, P0103, P0106, P0107, P0108, P0112, P0113, P0116, P0117, P0118, P0121, P0122, P0123, P0128, P0171, P0172, P0191, P0192, P0193, P0201, P0202, P0203, P0204, P0205, P0206, P0220, P0223, P0231, P0232, P0315, P0335, P0336, P0340, P0341, P0345, P0346, P1682 are not set. The engine is running and a cold start has been detected. DTC P050D runs once per cold start.
DTC: P050E 00	**Cold Start Exhaust Low Temperature:** DTCs P0010 00, P0016 00, P0068 00, P0106 00, P0107 00, P0108 00, P0116 00, P0117 00, P0118 00, P0119 00, P0121 00, P0123 00, P0171 00, P0172 00, P0201 00, P0202 00, P0203 00, P0204 00, P0222 00, P0261 00, P0262 00, P0264 00, P0265 00, P0267 00, P0268 00, P0270 00, P0271 00, P0335 00, P0336 00, P0340 00, P0341 00, P0365 00, P0366 00, P0443 00, P0459 00, P0496 00, P2088 00, P2089 00, P2100 00, P2101 00, P2122 00, P2123 00, P2127 00, P2128 00, P2138 00 are not set. The battery voltage is greater than 10 V. The engine speed is at idle. The engine coolant temperature (ECT) is between 2-37°C (35-100°F) at start. The catalyst temperature is between 2-52°C (35-125°F) at start. The fuel level is greater than 15%.
DTC: P0513	**Immobilizer Key Incorrect:** Ignition is in the ACCESSORY or RUN position.
DTC: P0520	**Engine Oil Pressure Switch Circuit Malfunction:** The engine is running.
DTC: P0521	**Engine Oil Pressure Sensor Performance Malfunction:** The engine is running.
DTC: P0521	**Engine Oil Pressure (EOP) Sensor Performance:** The engine is running.
DTC: P0524 00	**Engine Oil Pressure Too Low:** The engine is running.
DTC: P0526	**Cooling Fan Speed Sensor Circuit:** The engine is operating for greater than 10 S. The engine speed is greater than 550 RPM. The ECM commanded fan clutch solenoid duty cycle is greater than 45 percent. DTC P0526 runs continuously when the conditions above exist for greater than 30 S.
DTC: P0526	**Cooling Fan Speed Sensor Circuit:** The engine is running at a minimum of 550 RPM.
DTC: P0530 03	**Air Conditioning (A/C) Refrigerant Pressure Sensor Circuit Low Voltage:** Engine is running.
DTC: P0530 07	**Air Conditioning (A/C) Refrigerant Pressure Sensor Circuit High Voltage:** Engine is running.
DTC: P0531 00	**Air Conditioning (A/C) Refrigerant Pressure Sensor Performance:** Engine is running.
DTC: P0532	**Air Conditioning A/C Refrigerant Pressure Sensor Circuit Low Voltage:** The engine is running. The battery voltage is between 11-18 volts.
DTC: P0532 00	**Air Conditioning (A/C) Refrigerant Pressure Sensor Circuit Low Voltage:** Engine is running.
DTC: P0532 00	**Air Conditioning (A/C) Refrigerant Pressure Sensor Circuit Low Voltage:** Engine is running.
DTC: P0533	**Air Conditioning A/C Refrigerant Pressure Sensor Circuit High Voltage:** The engine is running. The battery voltage is between 11-18 volts.
DTC: P0533 00	**Air Conditioning (A/C) Refrigerant Pressure Sensor Circuit High Voltage:** Engine is running.

DTC	Trouble Code Title, Conditions, Possible Causes
DTC: P0544 03	**Exhaust Gas Temperature Sensor 1 Circuit Low Voltage:** The ignition is ON. The DTCs run continuously when the above condition is met.
DTC: P0544 07	**Exhaust Gas Temperature Sensor 1 Circuit High Voltage:** The ignition is ON. The DTCs run continuously when the above condition is met.
DTC: P0545	**Exhaust Gas Temperature Sensor 1 Circuit Low Voltage:** The ignition is ON or the engine is running. The DTCs run continuously when the above conditions are met.
DTC: P0545	**Exhaust Temperature Sensor 1 (EGT-1) Circuit Low Voltage:** The ignition is ON. This DTC runs continuously when the above condition is met.
DTC: P0545 00	**Exhaust Gas Temperature Sensor 1 Circuit Low Voltage:** The ignition is ON. The DTCs run continuously when the above condition is met.
DTC: P0546	**Exhaust Gas Temperature Sensor 1 Circuit High Voltage:** The ignition is ON or the engine is running. The DTCs run continuously when the above conditions are met.
DTC: P0546	**Exhaust Temperature Sensor 1 (EGT-1) Circuit High Voltage:** The ignition is ON. This DTC runs continuously when the above condition is met.
DTC: P0546 00	**Exhaust Gas Temperature Sensor 1 Circuit High Voltage:** The ignition is ON. The DTCs run continuously when the above condition is met.
DTC: P0560	**System Voltage Low:** The engine is running.
DTC: P0560 00	**System Voltage - ECM:** The ignition is ON.
DTC: P0562	**System Voltage Low:** P0562 The engine speed is 1,200 RPM or greater for 5 seconds.
DTC: P0562	**System Voltage Low:** The system voltage is between 9. 5-18 V.
DTC: P0562	**System Voltage Low:** Engine Control Module. The engine is running. The system voltage is between 9. 5-18 V. Fuel Pump Control Module. The engine is running. Transmission Control Module. Engine speed is 1200 RPM or greater. The system voltage is between 8. 6-18 V.
DTC: P0562	**System Voltage Low - ECM:** The vehicle speed is greater than 8 km/h (5 mph). Engine speed is above 600 RPM
DTC: P0563	**System Voltage High:** The vehicle speed is above 8 km/h (5 mph). The system voltage is between 9. 5-18. 0 V.
DTC: P0563	**System Voltage High:** Engine Control Module. The vehicle speed is above 8 km/h (5 mph). The system voltage is between 9. 5-18 V. Fuel Pump Control Module. The ignition is ON. Transmission Control Module. The system voltage is between 8. 6-18. 0 V.
DTC: P0564	**Cruise Control Multifunction Switch Circuit:** The engine is running. The cruise switch is ON.
DTC: P0565 00	**Cruise Control Switch Circuit Malfunction:** The ignition is ON. The cruise switch is ON.
DTC: P0567	**Cruise Control Resume Switch Circuit:** The cruise switch is ON. The ignition is ON.
DTC: P0567 00	**Cruise Control Resume Switch Circuit Malfunction:** The cruise switch is ON. The ignition is ON.
DTC: P0568	**Cruise Control Set Switch Circuit:** The cruise switch is ON. The ignition is ON.
DTC: P0568 00	**Cruise Control Set Switch Circuit Malfunction:** The cruise switch is ON. The ignition is ON.
DTC: P056C 00	**Cruise Control Cancel Switch Circuit Malfunction:** The cruise switch is ON. The ignition is ON.

DTC	Trouble Code Title, Conditions, Possible Causes
DTC: P0571	**Cruise Control Brake Switch Circuit:** The engine speed is greater than 700 RPM. The traction control system or the antilock brake system are not active and have not failed. The vehicle speed is greater than 48 km/h (30 mph). The diagnostic will disable when the wheel speed is less than 16 km/h (10 mph).
DTC: P0571	**Cruise Control Brake Switch Circuit:** The engine is running. Battery voltage is greater than 11. 5 volts.
DTC: P0572	**Brake Switch Circuit 1 Low Voltage:** The engine is running. Battery voltage is greater than 11. 5 volts.
DTC: P0573	**Brake Switch Circuit 1 High Voltage:** The engine is ON. Battery voltage is greater than 11. 5 volts.
DTC: P0575	**Cruise Control Switch Signal Circuit:** The ignition is ON. The cruise switch is ON.
DTC: P057B 00	**Brake Pedal Position Sensor Performance:** Battery voltage must be between 9-16 V. Brakes APPLIED.
DTC: P057B 00	**Brake Pedal Position Sensor Performance:** The engine is ON.
DTC: P057C	**Brake Pedal Position Sensor Circuit Low Voltage:** P057C and P057DIgnition voltage is greater than 10 Volts.
DTC: P057C 00	**Brake Pedal Position Sensor Circuit Low Voltage:** The engine is ON.
DTC: P057C 00	**Brake Pedal Position Sensor Circuit Low Voltage:** Battery voltage must be between 9-16 V. Brakes APPLIED.
DTC: P057D	**Brake Pedal Position Sensor Circuit High Voltage:** P057C and P057DIgnition voltage is greater than 10 Volts.
DTC: P057D 00	**Brake Pedal Position Sensor Circuit High Voltage:** Battery voltage must be between 9-16 V. Brakes APPLIED.
DTC: P057E 00	**Brake Pedal Position Sensor Circuit Erratic:** The engine is ON.
DTC: P057E 00	**Brake Pedal Position Sensor Circuit Erratic:** Battery voltage must be between 9-16 V. Brakes APPLIED.
DTC: P0580 00	**Cruise Control Multifunction Switch Circuit Low Voltage:** The cruise switch is ON. The ignition is ON.
DTC: P0581 00	**Cruise Control Multifunction Switch Circuit High Voltage:** The cruise switch is ON. The ignition is ON.
DTC: P0597 00	**Engine Coolant Thermostat Heater Control Circuit:** The ignition is ON, or the engine is running. The ignition voltage is greater than 9 V. DTC P0597 00, P0598 00, and P0599 00 run continuously once the above conditions are met.
DTC: P0598 00	**Engine Coolant Thermostat Heater Control Circuit Low Voltage:** The ignition is ON, or the engine is running. The ignition voltage is greater than 9 V. DTC P0597 00, P0598 00, and P0599 00 run continuously once the above conditions are met.
DTC: P0599 00	**Engine Coolant Thermostat Heater Control Circuit High Voltage:** The ignition is ON, or the engine is running. The ignition voltage is greater than 9 V. DTC P0597 00, P0598 00, and P0599 00 run continuously once the above conditions are met.
DTC: P059F 00	**Active Grille Air Shutter Performance:** Engine running. The ignition voltage is greater than 10 V. The DTC runs continuously when the above conditions are met. If the ambient temperature is below 2. 5°C (36°F) when the vehicle is first started, this DTC will be disabled.
DTC: P059F 00	**Active Grille Air Shutter Performance:** Engine running. The ignition voltage is greater than 10 V. The DTC runs continuously when the above conditions are met.
DTC: P0601	**Transmission Control Module (TCM) Read Only Memory (ROM):** The TCM runs the program to detect an internal fault when the engine is running. The only requirements are voltage and ground. This program runs even if the voltage is out of the valid operating range.

DTC	Trouble Code Title, Conditions, Possible Causes
DTC: P0601 00	**Control Module Read Only Memory Performance:** P0601 00, P0605 00The ignition switch is in run or crank. The system voltage is more than 5. 23 V. The check sum calculation at power down in the last drive cycle had completely finished. DTC P0601 00 and DTC P0605 run once per ignition cycle when the above condition is met. P0602 00The ignition switch is in run or crank. DTC P0602 00 runs once per ignition cycle. P0604 00The ignition switch is in run or crank. The read/write test at power down in the last drive cycle had completely finished. DTC P0604 00 runs once per ignition cycle when the above condition is met. P0606 00The ignition switch is in the unlock, accessory, run, or crank positions. DTC P0606 00 runs continuously when the above conditions are met. P0607 00The engine is running or cranking. DTC P0607 00 runs continuously when the above condition is met. . P061B 00The ignition is ON or the engine is running. The system voltage is more than 5. 23 V. DTC P061B 00 runs continuously when the above conditions are met. P061C 00The ignition is ON or the engine is running. The system voltage is more than 5. 23 V. DTC P061C 00 runs continuously when the above conditions are met. P2610 00The ECM is powered down. DTC P2610 00 runs once per ignition cycle. or The ECM is powered up with the ignition switch in the run or crank position. The engine OFF timer value is less than or greater than an internal reference counter during an 2s interval. DTC P2610 00 runs continuously when the above conditions are met.
DTC: P0602	**Transmission Control Module (TCM) Not Programmed:** The TCM runs the program to detect an internal fault when the engine is running. The only requirements are voltage and ground. This program runs even if the voltage is out of the valid operating range.
DTC: P0602 00	**Control Module Not Programmed:** P0601 00, P0605 00The ignition switch is in run or crank. The system voltage is more than 5. 23 V. The check sum calculation at power down in the last drive cycle had completely finished. DTC P0601 00 and DTC P0605 run once per ignition cycle when the above condition is met. P0602 00The ignition switch is in run or crank. DTC P0602 00 runs once per ignition cycle. P0604 00The ignition switch is in run or crank. The read/write test at power down in the last drive cycle had completely finished. DTC P0604 00 runs once per ignition cycle when the above condition is met. P0606 00The ignition switch is in the unlock, accessory, run, or crank positions. DTC P0606 00 runs continuously when the above conditions are met. P0607 00The engine is running or cranking. DTC P0607 00 runs continuously when the above condition is met. . P061B 00The ignition is ON or the engine is running. The system voltage is more than 5. 23 V. DTC P061B 00 runs continuously when the above conditions are met. P061C 00The ignition is ON or the engine is running. The system voltage is more than 5. 23 V. DTC P061C 00 runs continuously when the above conditions are met. P2610 00The ECM is powered down. DTC P2610 00 runs once per ignition cycle. or The ECM is powered up with the ignition switch in the run or crank position. The engine OFF timer value is less than or greater than an internal reference counter during an 2s interval. DTC P2610 00 runs continuously when the above conditions are met.
DTC: P0602 46	**Control Module Not Programmed Configuration Not Programmed:** P0602, P0606, P0607, P060A, P060B, P061C, and P062FThe ignition is ON. The DTCs run continuously once the above condition is met. P062BThe engine is running. The DTC runs continuously once the above condition is met.
DTC: P0603	**Control Module Long Term Memory Reset:** Ignition voltage is between 9. 0 and 18. 0 volts.
DTC: P0603	**Control Module Long Term Memory Reset:** P0601, P0602, P0603, P0604The ignition switch is in Run or Crank. These DTCs run once per ignition cycle.
DTC: P0603	**Transmission Control Module (TCM) Long Term Memory Reset:** The TCM runs the program to detect an internal condition at key ON. The only requirements are voltage and ground. This program runs even if the voltage is out of the valid operating range. Ignition voltage is between 8. 0 and 18. 0 volts - DTC P062F only.
DTC: P0604	**Transmission Control Module (TCM) Random Access Memory (RAM):** The TCM runs the program to detect an internal condition at Ignition ON. The only requirements are voltage and ground. This program runs even if the voltage is out of the valid operating range. Ignition voltage is between 8. 0 and 18. 0 volts – DTC P062F only.
DTC: P0604	**Control Module Random Access Memory Performance:** P0601, P0604, P0606The ignition switch is in Run or Crank. These DTCs run continuously when the above condition is met.
DTC: P0604 00	**Control Module Random Access Memory Performance:** P0601 00, P0602 00, P0604 00The ignition is ON, or the engine is operating. . The check sum calculation at power-down in the last drive cycle had completely finished. DTCs P0601 00, P0602 00, P0604 00 runs once per ignition cycle when the above condition is met.
DTC: P0604 00	**Control Module Random Access Memory Performance:** The ignition is ON. This DTCs run continuously once the above condition is met.

DTC	Trouble Code Title, Conditions, Possible Causes
DTC: P0604 00	**Control Module Random Access Memory Performance:** P0601 00, P0605 00The ignition switch is in run or crank. The system voltage is more than 5. 23 V. The check sum calculation at power down in the last drive cycle had completely finished. DTC P0601 00 and DTC P0605 run once per ignition cycle when the above condition is met. P0602 00The ignition switch is in run or crank. DTC P0602 00 runs once per ignition cycle. P0604 00The ignition switch is in run or crank. The read/write test at power down in the last drive cycle had completely finished. DTC P0604 00 runs once per ignition cycle when the above condition is met. P0606 00The ignition switch is in the unlock, accessory, run, or crank positions. DTC P0606 00 runs continuously when the above conditions are met. P0607 00The engine is running or cranking. DTC P0607 00 runs continuously when the above condition is met. . P061B 00The ignition is ON or the engine is running. The system voltage is more than 5. 23 V. DTC P061B 00 runs continuously when the above conditions are met. P061C 00The ignition is ON or the engine is running. The system voltage is more than 5. 23 V. DTC P061C 00 runs continuously when the above conditions are met. P2610 00The ECM is powered down. DTC P2610 00 runs once per ignition cycle. or The ECM is powered up with the ignition switch in the run or crank position. The engine OFF timer value is less than or greater than an internal reference counter during an 2 s interval. DTC P2610 00 runs continuously when the above conditions are met.
DTC: P0605 00	**Control Module Programming Read Only Memory Performance:** P0601 00, P0605 00The ignition switch is in run or crank. The system voltage is more than 5. 23 V. The check sum calculation at power down in the last drive cycle had completely finished. DTC P0601 00 and DTC P0605 run once per ignition cycle when the above condition is met. P0602 00The ignition switch is in run or crank. DTC P0602 00 runs once per ignition cycle. P0604 00The ignition switch is in run or crank. The read/write test at power down in the last drive cycle had completely finished. DTC P0604 00 runs once per ignition cycle when the above condition is met. P0606 00The ignition switch is in the unlock, accessory, run, or crank positions. DTC P0606 00 runs continuously when the above conditions are met. P0607 00The engine is running or cranking. DTC P0607 00 runs continuously when the above condition is met. . P061B 00The ignition is ON or the engine is running. The system voltage is more than 5. 23 V. DTC P061B 00 runs continuously when the above conditions are met. P061C 00The ignition is ON or the engine is running. The system voltage is more than 5. 23 V. DTC P061C 00 runs continuously when the above conditions are met. P2610 00The ECM is powered down. DTC P2610 00 runs once per ignition cycle. or The ECM is powered up with the ignition switch in the run or crank position. The engine OFF timer value is less than or greater than an internal reference counter during an 2 s interval. DTC P2610 00 runs continuously when the above conditions are met.
DTC: P0606	**Control Module Processor Performance:** P0601, P0604, P0606The ignition switch is in Run or Crank. These DTCs run continuously when the above condition is met.
DTC: P0606	**Control Module Internal Performance:** P0606The ignition switch is in the Unlock/Accessory, Run, or Crank positions. DTC P0606 runs continuously.
DTC: P0606	**Control Module Internal Performance:** P0606 DTCs P1224, P1227, P122A, P1233, P1236, P1239, P1242, P1244, P1247, P2146, P2149, P2152, P2155 are not set. The engine speed is greater than 1,200 RPM. The engine run time is greater than 10 s. The battery voltage is greater than 8 V. DTC P0606 runs continuously when the above conditions are met.
DTC: P0606 00	**Control Module Processor Performance Malfunction:** P0602, P0606, P0607, P060A, P060B, P061C, and P062FThe ignition is ON. The DTCs run continuously once the above condition is met. P062BThe engine is running. The DTC runs continuously once the above condition is met.
DTC: P0606 00	**Control Module Processor Performance:** P0601 00, P0605 00The ignition switch is in run or crank. The system voltage is more than 5. 23 V. The check sum calculation at power down in the last drive cycle had completely finished. DTC P0601 00 and DTC P0605 run once per ignition cycle when the above condition is met. P0602 00The ignition switch is in run or crank. DTC P0602 00 runs once per ignition cycle. P0604 00The ignition switch is in run or crank. The read/write test at power down in the last drive cycle had completely finished. DTC P0604 00 runs once per ignition cycle when the above condition is met. P0606 00The ignition switch is in the unlock, accessory, run, or crank positions. DTC P0606 00 runs continuously when the above conditions are met. P0607 00The engine is running or cranking. DTC P0607 00 runs continuously when the above condition is met. . P061B 00The ignition is ON or the engine is running. The system voltage is more than 5. 23 V. DTC P061B 00 runs continuously when the above conditions are met. P061C 00The ignition is ON or the engine is running The system voltage is more than 5. 23 V. DTC P061C 00 runs continuously when the above conditions are met. P2610 00The ECM is powered down. DTC P2610 00 runs once per ignition cycle. or The ECM is powered up with the ignition switch in the run or crank position. The engine OFF timer value is less than or greater than an internal reference counter during an 2 s interval. DTC P2610 00 runs continuously when the above conditions are met.
DTC: P0606 11	**Control Module Processor Performance High Input:** P0602, P0606, P0607, P060A, P060B, P061C, and P062FThe ignition is ON. The DTCs run continuously once the above condition is met. P062BThe engine is running. The DTC runs continuously once the above condition is met.
DTC: P0606 12	**Control Module Processor Performance Low Input:** P0602, P0606, P0607, P060A, P060B, P061C, and P062FThe ignition is ON. The DTCs run continuously once the above condition is met. P062BThe engine is running. The DTC runs continuously once the above condition is met.
DTC: P0606 31	**Control Module Processor Performance Internal Checksum Error:** P0602, P0606, P0607, P060A, P060B, P061C, and P062FThe ignition is ON. The DTCs run continuously once the above condition is met. P062BThe engine is running. The DTC runs continuously once the above condition is met.

DTC	Trouble Code Title, Conditions, Possible Causes
DTC: P0606 33	**Control Module Processor Performance Special Memory Malfunction:** P0602, P0606, P0607, P060A, P060B, P061C, and P062FThe ignition is ON. The DTCs run continuously once the above condition is met. P062BThe engine is running. The DTC runs continuously once the above condition is met.
DTC: P0606 37	**Control Module Processor Performance Software Malfunction:** P0602, P0606, P0607, P060A, P060B, P061C, and P062FThe ignition is ON. The DTCs run continuously once the above condition is met. P062BThe engine is running. The DTC runs continuously once the above condition is met.
DTC: P0606 3C	**Control Module Processor Performance Internal Communication Malfunction:** P0602, P0606, P0607, P060A, P060B, P061C, and P062FThe ignition is ON. The DTCs run continuously once the above condition is met. P062BThe engine is running. The DTC runs continuously once the above condition is met.
DTC: P0606 5A	**Control Module Processor Performance Not Plausible:** P0602, P0606, P0607, P060A, P060B, P061C, and P062FThe ignition is ON. The DTCs run continuously once the above condition is met. P062BThe engine is running. The DTC runs continuously once the above condition is met.
DTC: P0607	**Control Module Performance:** P0606, P0607, P060DThe ignition switch is in Run or Crank. Reduced engine power is not active. The system voltage is more than 6 V. These DTCs run continuously when the above conditions are met.
DTC: P0607 00	**Control Module Performance:** P0601 00, P0605 00The ignition switch is in run or crank. The system voltage is more than 5. 23 V. The check sum calculation at power down in the last drive cycle had completely finished. DTC P0601 00 and DTC P0605 run once per ignition cycle when the above condition is met. P0602 00The ignition switch is in run or crank. DTC P0602 00 runs once per ignition cycle. P0604 00The ignition switch is in run or crank. The read/write test at power down in the last drive cycle had completely finished. DTC P0604 00 runs once per ignition cycle when the above condition is met. P0606 00The ignition switch is in the unlock, accessory, run, or crank positions. DTC P0606 00 runs continuously when the above conditions are met. P0607 00The engine is running or cranking. DTC P0607 00 runs continuously when the above condition is met. . P061B 00The ignition is ON or the engine is running. The system voltage is more than 5. 23 V. DTC P061B 00 runs continuously when the above conditions are met. P061C 00The ignition is ON or the engine is running. The system voltage is more than 5. 23 V. DTC P061C 00 runs continuously when the above conditions are met. P2610 00The ECM is powered down. DTC P2610 00 runs once per ignition cycle. or The ECM is powered up with the ignition switch in the run or crank position. The engine OFF timer value is less than or greater than an internal reference counter during an 2 s interval. DTC P2610 00 runs continuously when the above conditions are met.
DTC: P0607 39	**Control Module Performance Internal Malfunction:** P0602, P0606, P0607, P060A, P060B, P061C, and P062FThe ignition is ON. The DTCs run continuously once the above condition is met. P062BThe engine is running. The DTC runs continuously once the above condition is met.
DTC: P0609	**Vehicle Speed Output Circuit:** Ignition ON. Ignition voltage is greater than 10 volts.
DTC: P060A 07	**Control Module Monitoring Processor Performance High Voltage:** P0602, P0606, P0607, P060A, P060B, P061C, and P062FThe ignition is ON. The DTCs run continuously once the above condition is met. P062BThe engine is running. The DTC runs continuously once the above condition is met.
DTC: P060B	**Control Module Analog to Digital Performance:** P060B, P062FThese DTCs run continuously when the ignition is ON.
DTC: P060B	**Control Module Analog to Digital Performance:** P060BThe engine speed is more than 650 RPM. The ECM is powered up. DTC P060B runs continuously when the above conditions are met.
DTC: P060B 03	**Control Module Analog to Digital Converter Performance Low Voltage:** P0602, P0606, P0607, P060A, P060B, P061C, and P062FThe ignition is ON. The DTCs run continuously once the above condition is met. P062BThe engine is running. The DTC runs continuously once the above condition is met.
DTC: P060B 07	**Control Module Analog to Digital Converter Performance High Voltage:** P0602, P0606, P0607, P060A, P060B, P061C, and P062FThe ignition is ON. The DTCs run continuously once the above condition is met. P062BThe engine is running. The DTC runs continuously once the above condition is met.
DTC: P060B 08	**Control Module Analog to Digital Converter Performance - Signal Invalid:** P0602, P0606, P0607, P060A, P060B, P061C, and P062FThe ignition is ON. The DTCs run continuously once the above condition is met. P062BThe engine is running. The DTC runs continuously once the above condition is met.
DTC: P060B 11	**Control Module Analog to Digital Converter Performance High Input:** P0602, P0606, P0607, P060A, P060B, P061C, and P062FThe ignition is ON. The DTCs run continuously once the above condition is met. P062BThe engine is running. The DTC runs continuously once the above condition is met.

DTC	Trouble Code Title, Conditions, Possible Causes
DTC: P060D	**Control Module Accelerator Pedal (APP) Position System Circuitry Performance:** P0606, P0607, P060DThe ignition voltage is more than 6. 0 V. Reduced Engine Power is not active. These DTCs run continuously when the above conditions are met.
DTC: P060D	**Control Module Accelerator Pedal (APP) Position System Circuitry Performance:** P060DDTC P0606 is not set. The ignition switch is in the Unlock, Accessory, Run, or Crank position. The system voltage is more than 5. 23 V. DTC P060D runs continuously when the above conditions are met.
DTC: P0615	**Starter Relay Control Circuit:** The ignition is ON. The system voltage is between 9. 5-18 volts.
DTC: P0615 01	**Starter Relay Control Circuit Short to Battery:** The Ignition is in the START position. The system voltage is between 9. 5-18 V.
DTC: P061A 00	**Control Module Torque System Circuitry Performance:** P0601 00, P0605 00The ignition switch is in run or crank. The system voltage is more than 5. 23 V. The check sum calculation at power down in the last drive cycle had completely finished. DTC P0601 00 and DTC P0605 run once per ignition cycle when the above condition is met. P0602 00The ignition switch is in run or crank. DTC P0602 00 runs once per ignition cycle. P0604 00The ignition switch is in run or crank. The read/write test at power down in the last drive cycle had completely finished. DTC P0604 00 runs once per ignition cycle when the above condition is met. P0606 00The ignition switch is in the unlock, accessory, run, or crank positions. DTC P0606 00 runs continuously when the above conditions are met. P0607 00The engine is running or cranking. DTC P0607 00 runs continuously when the above condition is met. . P061B 00The ignition is ON or the engine is running. The system voltage is more than 5. 23 V. DTC P061B 00 runs continuously when the above conditions are met. P061C 00The ignition is ON or the engine is running. The system voltage is more than 5. 23 V. DTC P061C 00 runs continuously when the above conditions are met. P2610 00The ECM is powered down. DTC P2610 00 runs once per ignition cycle. or The ECM is powered up with the ignition switch in the run or crank position. The engine OFF timer value is less than or greater than an internal reference counter during an 2 s interval. DTC P2610 00 runs continuously when the above conditions are met.
DTC: P061A 00	**Control Module Torque System Circuitry Performance:** P061A 00The ignition voltage is between 11-18 V. The ignition is in the unlock, accessory, run, or crank position. DTC P0601 00, P0602 00, P0604 00, P0606 00, P0641 00, P2610 00 are not set.
DTC: P061B 00	**Control Module Torque Calculation Performance:** P0601 00, P0605 00The ignition switch is in run or crank. The system voltage is more than 5. 23 V. The check sum calculation at power down in the last drive cycle had completely finished. DTC P0601 00 and DTC P0605 run once per ignition cycle when the above condition is met. P0602 00The ignition switch is in run or crank. DTC P0602 00 runs once per ignition cycle. P0604 00The ignition switch is in run or crank. The read/write test at power down in the last drive cycle had completely finished. DTC P0604 00 runs once per ignition cycle when the above condition is met. P0606 00The ignition switch is in the unlock, accessory, run, or crank positions. DTC P0606 00 runs continuously when the above conditions are met. P0607 00The engine is running or cranking. DTC P0607 00 runs continuously when the above condition is met. . P061B 00The ignition is ON or the engine is running. The system voltage is more than 5. 23 V. DTC P061B 00 runs continuously when the above conditions are met. P061C 00The ignition is ON or the engine is running. The system voltage is more than 5. 23 V. DTC P061C 00 runs continuously when the above conditions are met. P2610 00The ECM is powered down. DTC P2610 00 runs once per ignition cycle. or The ECM is powered up with the ignition switch in the run or crank position. The engine OFF timer value is less than or greater than an internal reference counter during an 2 s interval. DTC P2610 00 runs continuously when the above conditions are met.
DTC: P061C	**Control Module Engine Speed Performance:** P061CThe ignition is ON. The engine speed is less than 1,300 RPM. DTC P061C runs continuously when the above conditions are met.
DTC: P061C 00	**Control Module Engine Speed System Circuitry Performance:** P0601 00, P0605 00The ignition switch is in run or crank. The system voltage is more than 5. 23 V. The check sum calculation at power down in the last drive cycle had completely finished. DTC P0601 00 and DTC P0605 run once per ignition cycle when the above condition is met. P0602 00The ignition switch is in run or crank. DTC P0602 00 runs once per ignition cycle. P0604 00The ignition switch is in run or crank. The read/write test at power down in the last drive cycle had completely finished. DTC P0604 00 runs once per ignition cycle when the above condition is met. P0606 00The ignition switch is in the unlock, accessory, run, or crank positions. DTC P0606 00 runs continuously when the above conditions are met. P0607 00The engine is running or cranking. DTC P0607 00 runs continuously when the above condition is met. . P061B 00The ignition is ON or the engine is running. The system voltage is more than 5. 23 V. DTC P061B 00 runs continuously when the above conditions are met. P061C 00The ignition is ON or the engine is running. The system voltage is more than 5. 23 V. DTC P061C 00 runs continuously when the above conditions are met. P2610 00The ECM is powered down. DTC P2610 00 runs once per ignition cycle. or The ECM is powered up with the ignition switch in the run or crank position. The engine OFF timer value is less than or greater than an internal reference counter during an 2 s interval. DTC P2610 00 runs continuously when the above conditions are met.
DTC: P061C 00	**Control Module Engine Speed System Circuitry Performance Malfunction:** P0602, P0606, P0607, P060A, P060B, P061C, and P062FThe ignition is ON. The DTCs run continuously once the above condition is met. P062BThe engine is running. The DTC runs continuously once the above condition is met.

DTC	Trouble Code Title, Conditions, Possible Causes
DTC: P0621 00	**Generator L-Terminal Circuit:** The ignition ON, engine OFF for ignition on test. The engine is running for the run test.
DTC: P0621 58	**Generator L-Terminal Circuit Performance:** The ignition ON, engine OFF for ignition on test. The engine is running for the run test.
DTC: P0621 59	**Generator L-Terminal Circuit Protection Time Out:** The ignition ON, engine OFF for ignition on test. The engine is running for the run test.
DTC: P0622	**Generator F-Terminal Circuit:** No generator, crankshaft position (CKP) sensor, or camshaft (CMP) sensor DTCs are set. Ignition ON engine OFF, for the Ignition ON test. Engine running, engine speed less than 3,000 RPM for the RUN test.
DTC: P0622 00	**Generator F-Terminal Circuit:** Ignition ON engine OFF, for the Ignition ON test. Engine running, engine speed less than 3 000 RPM for the RUN test.
DTC: P0622 11	**Generator F-Terminal Circuit High Input:** Ignition ON engine OFF, for the Ignition ON test. Engine running, engine speed less than 3 000 RPM for the RUN test.
DTC: P0622 12	**Generator F-Terminal Circuit Low Input:** Ignition ON engine OFF, for the Ignition ON test. Engine running, engine speed less than 3 000 RPM for the RUN test.
DTC: P0625	**Generator F-Terminal Circuit Low Voltage:** P0625The engine is running. The engine speed is less than 3 000 RPM.
DTC: P0626	**Generator F-Terminal Circuit High Voltage:** P0626The engine is not running. The ignition is in the ON position.
DTC: P0627	**Fuel Pump Enable Circuit:** The engine speed is greater than 80 RPM. The ignition 1 signal parameter is 10-18 V. The ECM has commanded the fuel pump enable circuit ON and OFF at least once during the ignition cycle. The DTCs run continuously when the conditions above are met.
DTC: P0627	**Fuel Pump Enable Circuit:** The engine speed is greater than 0 RPM. The ignition voltage is between 11-18 V. The DTCs run continuously when the conditions above are met.
DTC: P0627 00	**Fuel Pump Relay Control Circuit Open:** P0627 00 and P0629 00The ignition voltage is between 10-18 V. The ECM has commanded the fuel pump OFF. The above conditions are met for greater than 1 s. The DTCs run continuously when the above conditions are met.
DTC: P0627 01	**Fuel Pump Relay Control Circuit Short to Battery:** P0627 01 and P0627 54The ignition is ON, or the engine is running. The power stage is active. The DTCs run continuously once the above conditions are met
DTC: P0627 02	**Fuel Pump Relay Control Circuit Short to Ground:** P0627 02 and P0627 04The ignition is ON. The power stage is not active. The DTCs run continuously once the above conditions are met
DTC: P0627 04	**Fuel Pump Relay Control Circuit Open:** P0627 02 and P0627 04The ignition is ON. The power stage is not active. The DTCs run continuously once the above conditions are met
DTC: P0627 54	**Fuel Pump Relay Control Circuit High Temperature:** P0627 01 and P0627 54The ignition is ON, or the engine is running. The power stage is active. The DTCs run continuously once the above conditions are met
DTC: P0628	**Fuel Pump Enable Circuit Low Voltage:** The engine speed is greater than 80 RPM. The ignition 1 signal parameter is 10-18 V. The ECM has commanded the fuel pump enable circuit ON and OFF at least once during the ignition cycle. The DTCs run continuously when the conditions above are met.
DTC: P0628	**Fuel Pump Relay Control Circuit Low Voltage:** P0628The engine speed is greater than 80 RPM. The ignition voltage is between 10-18. 1 V. The ECM has commanded the fuel pump relay ON. The above conditions are met for greater than 1 second. The DTC runs continuously once the above conditions are met.
DTC: P0628 00	**Fuel Pump Relay Control Circuit Low Voltage:** P0628 00The ignition voltage is between 10-18 V. The ECM has commanded the fuel pump ON. The above conditions are met for greater than 1 s. The DTC runs continuously when the above conditions are met.
DTC: P0628 00	**Fuel Pump Relay Control Circuit Low Voltage:** The engine speed is greater than 80 RPM. The ignition voltage is 10-18 V. The ECM has commanded the fuel pump relay ON and OFF at least once during the ignition cycle. The above conditions are met for less than 1 s. DTCs P0628 00 or P0629 00 runs continuously once the above conditions are met.

DTC	Trouble Code Title, Conditions, Possible Causes
DTC: P0629	**Fuel Pump Relay Control Circuit High Voltage:** P0627 and P0629The engine speed is greater than 80 RPM. The ignition voltage is between 10-18. 1 V. The ECM has commanded the fuel pump relay OFF. The above conditions are met for greater than 1 second. The DTCs run continuously once the above conditions are met.
DTC: P0629 00	**Fuel Pump Relay Control Circuit High Voltage:** P0627 00 and P0629 00The ignition voltage is between 10-18 V. The ECM has commanded the fuel pump OFF. The above conditions are met for greater than 1 s. The DTCs run continuously when the above conditions are met.
DTC: P0629 00	**Fuel Pump Relay Control Circuit High Voltage:** The engine speed is greater than 80 RPM. The ignition voltage is 10-18 V. The ECM has commanded the fuel pump relay ON and OFF at least once during the ignition cycle. The above conditions are met for less than 1 s. DTCs P0628 00 or P0629 00 runs continuously once the above conditions are met.
DTC: P062B	**Control Module Fuel Injector Control Performance:** The engine is running or cranking. The system voltage is between 8-18. 1 V. DTC P062B runs continuously when the above conditions are met.
DTC: P062B 00	**Control Module Fuel Injector Control Performance Malfunction:** P0602, P0606, P0607, P060A, P060B, P061C, and P062FThe ignition is ON. The DTCs run continuously once the above condition is met. P062BThe engine is running. The DTC runs continuously once the above condition is met.
DTC: P062B 00	**Control Module Fuel Injector Control Performance:** The ignition is ON. This DTCs run continuously once the above condition is met.
DTC: P062B 03	**Control Module Fuel Injector Control Performance Low Voltage:** P0602, P0606, P0607, P060A, P060B, P061C, and P062FThe ignition is ON. The DTCs run continuously once the above condition is met. P062BThe engine is running. The DTC runs continuously once the above condition is met.
DTC: P062B 32	**Control Module Fuel Injector Control Performance General Memory Malfunction:** P0602, P0606, P0607, P060A, P060B, P061C, and P062FThe ignition is ON. The DTCs run continuously once the above condition is met. P062BThe engine is running. The DTC runs continuously once the above condition is met.
DTC: P062B 39	**Control Module Fuel Injector Control Performance Internal Malfunction:** P0602, P0606, P0607, P060A, P060B, P061C, and P062FThe ignition is ON. The DTCs run continuously once the above condition is met. P062BThe engine is running. The DTC runs continuously once the above condition is met.
DTC: P062B 3B	**Control Module Fuel Injector Control Performance Self-Test Malfunction:** P0602, P0606, P0607, P060A, P060B, P061C, and P062FThe ignition is ON. The DTCs run continuously once the above condition is met. P062BThe engine is running. The DTC runs continuously once the above condition is met.
DTC: P062B 3C	**Control Module Fuel Injector Control Performance Internal Communication Malfunction:** P0602, P0606, P0607, P060A, P060B, P061C, and P062FThe ignition is ON. The DTCs run continuously once the above condition is met. P062BThe engine is running. The DTC runs continuously once the above condition is met.
DTC: P062B 59	**Control Module Fuel Injector Control Performance Protection Time-Out:** P0602, P0606, P0607, P060A, P060B, P061C, and P062FThe ignition is ON. The DTCs run continuously once the above condition is met. P062BThe engine is running. The DTC runs continuously once the above condition is met.
DTC: P062B 73	**Control Module Fuel Injector Control Performance Parity Error:** P0602, P0606, P0607, P060A, P060B, P061C, and P062FThe ignition is ON. The DTCs run continuously once the above condition is met. P062BThe engine is running. The DTC runs continuously once the above condition is met.
DTC: P062C	**Control Module Vehicle Speed Performance:** P062C, P2610These DTCs run continuously when the ignition is ON.
DTC: P062F	**Transmission Control Module (TCM) Long Term Memory Performance:** The TCM runs the program to detect an internal fault when the engine is running. The only requirements are voltage and ground. This program runs even if the voltage is out of the valid operating range.
DTC: P062F	**Control Module Long Term Memory Performance:** P0602, P0603, P062FThe ignition switch is in ON. These DTCs run once per ignition cycle.
DTC: P062F 00	**Control Module Long Term Memory Performance Malfunction:** P0602, P0606, P0607, P060A, P060B, P061C, and P062FThe ignition is ON. The DTCs run continuously once the above condition is met. P062BThe engine is running. The DTC runs continuously once the above condition is met.
DTC: P062F 36	**Control Module Long Term Memory Performance EEPROM Performance/Malfunction:** P0602, P0606, P0607, P060A, P060B, P061C, and P062FThe ignition is ON. The DTCs run continuously once the above condition is met. P062BThe engine is running. The DTC runs continuously once the above condition is met.

DTC	Trouble Code Title, Conditions, Possible Causes
DTC: P062F 41	**Control Module Long Term Memory Performance Not Programmed:** P0602, P0606, P0607, P060A, P060B, P061C, and P062FThe ignition is ON. The DTCs run continuously once the above condition is met. P062BThe engine is running. The DTC runs continuously once the above condition is met.
DTC: P0630	**VIN Not Programmed or Mismatched – Engine Control Module (ECM):** P0601, P0606, P062B, P0630, P16F3These DTCs run continuously when the ignition is ON.
DTC: P0634	**Transmission Control Module (TCM) Over temperature:** The ignition voltage is greater than 8. 6 volts. The TCM temperature is between 0-170°C (32-338°F) for 0. 25 second or greater. DTC P0634 has not set this ignition cycle.
DTC: P0638	**Throttle Actuator Control (TAC) Command Performance:** P0638 and P2101The engine is operating. The ignition voltage is greater than 7 V. DTCs P0638 and P2101 run continuously once the above conditions are met for greater than 5 s.
DTC: P0640	**Intake Air (IA) Heater Control Circuit:** The intake air heater is commanded OFF. DTC P0640 runs continuously when the above condition is met.
DTC: P0641	**5 V Reference 1 Circuit:** Reduced engine power is not active. The ignition voltage is more than 6 V. DTCs P0641 and P0651 run continuously when the above conditions are met.
DTC: P0641 00	**5 V Reference 1 Circuit:** The ignition is ON. The ECM is not commanding reduced engine power. The ignition voltage is greater than 6 V. These DTCs run continuously when the above conditions are met.
DTC: P0641 03	**5V Reference 1 Circuit Low Voltage:** The ignition is ON. The DTCs run continuously when the above condition is met.
DTC: P0641 07	**5V Reference 1 Circuit High Voltage:** The ignition is UN. The DTCs run continuously when the above condition is met.
DTC: P0642	**5-Volt Reference 1 Circuit Low Voltage:** The ignition is ON. The diagnostics run continuously.
DTC: P0642 00	**5V Reference 1 Circuit Low Voltage:** DTCs P0601 00, P0602 00, P0604 00, P0606 00, P0607 00, and P2610 00 are not set. The ignition is in unlock, accessory, run, or crank. DTCs P0642 00, P0643 00, P0652 00 and P0653 00 run continuously when the above conditions are met.
DTC: P0643	**5-Volt Reference 1 Circuit High Voltage:** The ignition is ON. The diagnostics run continuously.
DTC: P0643 00	**5V Reference 1 Circuit High Voltage:** DTCs P0601 00, P0602 00, P0604 00, P0606 00, P0607 00, and P2610 00 are not set. The ignition is in unlock, accessory, run, or crank. DTCs P0642 00, P0643 00, P0652 00 and P0653 00 run continuously when the above conditions are met.
DTC: P0645	**Air Conditioning (A/C) Clutch Relay Control Circuit:** The ignition voltage is between 9 and 18 volts. The engine speed is more than 800 RPM. The ECM/PCM A/C compressor clutch relay control transitions between ON to OFF or from OFF to ON.
DTC: P0646	**Air Conditioning (A/C) Clutch Relay Control Circuit Low Voltage:** The ignition voltage is between 9 and 18 volts. The engine speed is more than 800 RPM. The ECM/PCM A/C compressor clutch relay control transitions between ON to OFF or from OFF to ON.
DTC: P0647	**Air Conditioning (A/C) Clutch Relay Control Circuit High Voltage:** The ignition voltage is between 9 and 18 volts. The engine speed is more than 800 RPM. The ECM/PCM A/C compressor clutch relay control transitions between ON to OFF or from OFF to ON.
DTC: P0649 01	**Cruise Engaged Indicator Control Circuit Short to Battery:** The engine is operating. The ignition 1 voltage is between 7. 5-16 V. The DTCs run continuously once the above conditions are met.
DTC: P0649 02	**Cruise Engaged Indicator Control Circuit Short to Ground:** The engine is operating. The ignition 1 voltage is between 7. 5-16 V. The DTCs run continuously once the above conditions are met.
DTC: P0649 04	**Cruise Engaged Indicator Control Circuit Open:** The engine is operating. The ignition 1 voltage is between 7. 5-16 V. The DTCs run continuously once the above conditions are met.
DTC: P0649 54	**Cruise Engaged Indicator Control Circuit High Temperature:** The engine is operating. The ignition 1 voltage is between 7. 5-16 V. The DTCs run continuously once the above conditions are met.
DTC: P064A	**Fuel Pump Control Module Performance:** The engine is running.

DTC	Trouble Code Title, Conditions, Possible Causes
DTC: P064C	**Glow Plug Module Control Performance:** The ignition is ON. DTC P064C runs continuously.
DTC: P064C	**Glow Plug Module Control Performance:** The ignition is ON. DTC P064C runs continuously.
DTC: P064C 00	**Glow Plug Control Module Performance Malfunction:** The ignition is ON. The battery voltage is between 9-16 V. The DTC runs once per ignition cycle when the above condition is met.
DTC: P064D	**Control Module HO2S 1 System Performance:** P064DThe ignition switch is in Run or Crank. The system voltage is between 10. 7-18. 1 V. DTC P064D runs continuously when the above conditions are met.
DTC: P064D 00	**Control Module HO2S 1 System Circuitry Performance:** The ignition voltage is between 10-18 V. The engine speed is greater than 80 RPM. The HO2S heater is commanded ON and OFF at least once during the ignition cycle. The DTCs run continuously once the above conditions are met for 2 s.
DTC: P0650	**Malfunction Indicator Lamp (MIL) Control Circuit:** The ignition is in the Run or Crank position. The ignition voltage is between 11-32 V. The ECM has commanded the MIL ON and OFF at least once during the ignition cycle. The DTC runs continuously when the above conditions are met.
DTC: P0650	**Malfunction Indicator Lamp (MIL) Control Circuit:** DTC P0650 runs continuously when the ignition is ON and the ignition voltage is between 9-18 volts.
DTC: P0650 00	**Malfunction Indicator Lamp (MIL) Control Circuit:** DTCs P0601 00, P0604 00, P0605 00, P0606 00, P0607 00, and P2610 00 are not set. DTC P0650 00 runs continuously when the ignition is ON.
DTC: P0650 01	**Malfunction Indicator Lamp (MIL) Control Circuit Short to Battery:** DTCs P0601 00, P0604 00, P0605 00, P0606 00, P0607 00, and P2610 00 are not set. DTC P0650 runs continuously when the ignition is ON.
DTC: P0650 02	**Malfunction Indicator Lamp (MIL) Control Circuit Short to Ground:** DTCs P0601 00, P0604 00, P0605 00, P0606 00, P0607 00, and P2610 00 are not set. DTC P0650 runs continuously when the ignition is ON.
DTC: P0650 04	**Malfunction Indicator Lamp (MIL) Control Circuit Open:** DTCs P0601 00, P0604 00, P0605 00, P0606 00, P0607 00, and P2610 00 are not set. DTC P0650 runs continuously when the ignition is ON.
DTC: P0650 54	**Malfunction Indicator Lamp (MIL) Control Circuit High Temperature:** DTCs P0601 00, P0604 00, P0605 00, P0606 00, P0607 00, and P2610 00 are not set. DTC P0650 runs continuously when the ignition is ON.
DTC: P0651	**5 V Reference 2 Circuit:** Reduced engine power is not active. The ignition voltage is more than 6 V. DTCs P0641 and P0651 run continuously when the above conditions are met.
DTC: P0651	**5 V Reference 2 Circuit:** The ignition is in Unlock, Accessory, Run, or Crank. The ignition voltage is more than 5. 23 V. DTCs P0641 and P0651 run continuously when the above conditions are met.
DTC: P0651	**5 V Reference 2 Circuit:** DTCs P0601, P0602, P0603, P0604, P0605, P0606, P0607, P060D, P062F and P2610 are not set. The ignition is ON. The ignition voltage is greater than 5. 23 V. The DTCs run continuously when the above conditions are met.
DTC: P0651 00	**5 V Reference 2 Circuit:** The ignition is ON. The ECM is not commanding reduced engine power. The ignition voltage is greater than 6 V. These DTCs run continuously when the above conditions are met.
DTC: P0651 03	**5V Reference 2 Circuit Low Voltage:** The ignition is ON. The DTCs run continuously when the above condition is met.
DTC: P0651 07	**5V Reference 2 Circuit High Voltage:** The ignition is ON. The DTCs run continuously when the above condition is met.
DTC: P0652	**5 Volt Reference 2 Circuit Low Voltage:** The ignition is ON. The diagnostics run continuously.
DTC: P0652 00	**5V Reference 2 Circuit Low Voltage:** DTCs P0601 00, P0602 00, P0604 00, P0606 00, P0607 00, and P2610 00 are not set. The ignition is in unlock, accessory, run, or crank. DTCs P0642 00, P0643 00, P0652 00 and P0653 00 run continuously when the above conditions are met.

DTC	Trouble Code Title, Conditions, Possible Causes
DTC: P0653	**5 Volt Reference 2 Circuit High Voltage:** The ignition is ON. The diagnostics run continuously.
DTC: P0653 00	**5V Reference 2 Circuit High Voltage:** DTCs P0601 00, P0602 00, P0604 00, P0606 00, P0607 00, and P2610 00 are not set. The ignition is in unlock, accessory, run, or crank. DTCs P0642 00, P0643 00, P0652 00 and P0653 00 run continuously when the above conditions are met.
DTC: P0658	**Actuator High Control Circuit Group 1 Low Voltage:** P0658 High side driver 1 is enabled. DTC P0658 is not set.
DTC: P0658	**Solenoid High Control Circuit Group 1 Low Voltage:** P0658 High side driver 1 is enabled. DTC P0658 has not set this ignition cycle.
DTC: P0658	**Solenoid High Control Circuit Group 1 Low Voltage:** P0658 The engine speed is greater than 500 RPM for 5 seconds. Ignition voltage is 8. 6 volts or greater. High side driver 1 is enabled. DTC P0658 has not set this ignition.
DTC: P0659	**Solenoid High Control Circuit Group 1 High Voltage:** P0659 DTC P0659 is not set. The ignition transitions from OFF to ON.
DTC: P0659	**Solenoid High Control Circuit Group 1 High Voltage:** P0659 DTC P0659 has not set this ignition. Ignition voltage is 8. 6 volts or greater. Ignition switch transitions from OFF to run position.
DTC: P0659	**Actuator High Control Circuit Group 1 High Voltage:** P0659 DTC P0659 is not set. Ignition transitions from OFF to ON.
DTC: P0661 00	**Intake Manifold Tuning Control Valve Control Circuit Low Voltage:** DTC P0606 00 is not set. The ignition is ON, or the engine is running. The battery voltage is greater than 9 V. DTCs P0661 00 and P0662 00 run continuously when the above conditions are met.
DTC: P0662 00	**Intake Manifold Tuning Control Valve Control Circuit High Voltage:** DTC P0606 00 is not set. The ignition is ON, or the engine is running. The battery voltage is greater than 9 V. DTCs P0661 00 and P0662 00 run continuously when the above conditions are met.
DTC: P0667	**Control Module Temperature Sensor Performance:** P0667 DTC P0101, P0102, P0103, P0106, P0107, P0108, P0171, P0172, P0174, P0175, P0201, P0202, P0203, P0204, P0205, P0206, P0207, P0208, P0300, P0301, P0302, P0303, P0304, P0305, P0306, P0307, P0308, P0401, P042F, P0658, P0667, P0668, P0669, P06AD, P06AE, P0712, P0713, P0716, P0717, P0722, P0723, P0962, P0963, P0966, P0967, P0970, P0971, P215C, P2720, P2721, P2729, or P2730 is not set. Brake torque is not active. The engine speed is 400 RPM or greater for 5 seconds. The ignition voltage is 8. 6 volts or greater. The engine torque signal is valid. The throttle position signal is valid.
DTC: P0667	**Transmission Control Module (TCM) Temperature Sensor Performance:** P0667 No DTCs P0101, P0102, P0103, P0106, P0107, P0108, P0171, P0172, P0174, P0175, P0201, P0202, P0203, P0204, P0205, P0206, P0207, P0208, P0300, P0301, P0302, P0303, P0304, P0305, P0306, P0307, P0308, P0401, P042E, P0658, P0668, P0669, P06AD, P06AE, P0712, P0713, P0716, P0717, P0722, P0723, P0962, P0963, P0966, P0967, P0970, P0971, P215C, P2720, P2721, P2729, or P2730. Brake torque is not active. The engine speed is greater than 400 RPM for 5 seconds or greater. The ignition voltage is 8. 6 volts or greater.
DTC: P0668	**Transmission Control Module (TCM) Temperature Sensor Circuit Low Voltage:** DTC P0667, P0668, or P0669 DTCs P0667, P0716, P0717, P0722, or P0723 are not set. The TCM internal temperature is between -55°C and +150°C (-67°F and +302°F). The engine speed is 500 RPM or more for 5 seconds. The ignition voltage is 8. 6V or greater.
DTC: P0668	**Transmission Control Module (TCM) Temperature Sensor Circuit Low Voltage:** P0668 The ignition voltage is 9. 0 volts or greater. The engine speed is greater than 500 RPM for 5 seconds or greater. DTC P0668 has not set.
DTC: P0669	**Transmission Control Module (TCM) Temperature Sensor Circuit High Voltage:** P0669 No ISS DTCs P0716 or P0717. No OSS DTCs P0722 or P0723. The ignition voltage is 9. 0 volts or greater. The engine speed is greater than 500 RPM for 5 seconds or greater. DTC P0669 has not set.
DTC: P0669	**Control Module Temperature Sensor Circuit High Voltage:** P0669 DTC P0669, P0716, P0717, P0722, or P0723 is not set. The ignition voltage is 9. 0 volts or greater. The engine speed is greater than 400 RPM for 5 seconds or greater.
DTC: P0669	**Transmission Control Module (TCM) Temperature Sensor Circuit High Voltage:** P0669 No ISS DTCs P0716 or P0717. No OSS DTCs P0722 or P0723. The transmission output shaft speed is 200 RPM or greater for 200 seconds or more. The engine speed is greater than 400 RPM for 5 seconds. The ignition voltage is 8. 6 volts or greater.

DTC	Trouble Code Title, Conditions, Possible Causes
DTC: P0670 00	**Glow Plug Control Module Control Circuit:** The ignition is ON, or the engine is running. The ignition voltage is between 9-16 V. The DTCs run once per ignition cycle when the above conditions are met.
DTC: P0670 01	**Glow Plug Control Module Control Circuit Short to Battery:** P0670 01 or P0670 54The ignition is ON, or the engine is running. The ignition voltage is between 9-16 V. The DTCs run once per ignition cycle when the above conditions are met. P0670 02 or P0670 44The ignition is ON. The ignition voltage is between 9-16 V. The DTCs run once per ignition cycle when the above conditions are met.
DTC: P0670 02	**Glow Plug Control Module Control Circuit Short to Ground:** P0670 01 or P0670 54The ignition is ON, or the engine is running. The ignition voltage is between 9-16 V. The DTCs run once per ignition cycle when the above conditions are met. P0670 02 or P0670 44The ignition is ON. The ignition voltage is between 9-16 V. The DTCs run once per ignition cycle when the above conditions are met.
DTC: P0670 04	**Glow Plug Control Module Control Circuit Open:** P0670 01 or P0670 54The ignition is ON, or the engine is running. The ignition voltage is between 9-16 V. The DTCs run once per ignition cycle when the above conditions are met. P0670 02 or P0670 44The ignition is ON. The ignition voltage is between 9-16 V. The DTCs run once per ignition cycle when the above conditions are met.
DTC: P0670 54	**Glow Plug Control Module Control Circuit High Temperature:** P0670 01 or P0670 54The ignition is ON, or the engine is running. The ignition voltage is between 9-16 V. The DTCs run once per ignition cycle when the above conditions are met. P0670 02 or P0670 44The ignition is ON. The ignition voltage is between 9-16 V. The DTCs run once per ignition cycle when the above conditions are met.
DTC: P0671	**Cylinder #1 Glow Plug Control Circuit:** The ignition is ON. DTCs P0671-P0678 run continuously.
DTC: P0671 00	**Cylinder 1 Glow Plug Control Circuit:** The ignition is ON, or the engine is running. The ignition voltage is less than 16 V. These DTCs run once per ignition cycle when the above conditions are met.
DTC: P0671 02	**Cylinder 1 Glow Plug Control Circuit Short to Ground:** The ignition is ON, or the engine is running. The ignition voltage is less than 16 V. The DTCs run once per ignition cycle when the above conditions are met.
DTC: P0671 04	**Cylinder 1 Glow Plug Control Circuit Open:** The ignition is ON, or the engine is running. The ignition voltage is less than 16 V. The DTCs run once per ignition cycle when the above conditions are met.
DTC: P0672	**Cylinder #2 Glow Plug Control Circuit:** The ignition is ON. DTCs P0671-P0678 run continuously.
DTC: P0672 00	**Cylinder 2 Glow Plug Control Circuit:** The ignition is ON, or the engine is running. The ignition voltage is less than 16 V. These DTCs run once per ignition cycle when the above conditions are met.
DTC: P0672 02	**Cylinder 2 Glow Plug Control Circuit Short to Ground:** The ignition is ON, or the engine is running. The ignition voltage is less than 16 V. The DTCs run once per ignition cycle when the above conditions are met.
DTC: P0672 04	**Cylinder 2 Glow Plug Control Circuit Open:** The ignition is ON, or the engine is running. The ignition voltage is less than 16 V. The DTCs run once per ignition cycle when the above conditions are met.
DTC: P0673	**Cylinder #3 Glow Plug Control Circuit:** The ignition is ON. DTCs P0671-P0678 run continuously.
DTC: P0673 00	**Cylinder 3 Glow Plug Control Circuit:** The ignition is ON, or the engine is running. The ignition voltage is less than 16 V. These DTCs run once per ignition cycle when the above conditions are met.
DTC: P0673 02	**Cylinder 3 Glow Plug Control Circuit Short to Ground:** The ignition is ON, or the engine is running. The ignition voltage is less than 16 V. The DTCs run once per ignition cycle when the above conditions are met.
DTC: P0673 04	**Cylinder 3 Glow Plug Control Circuit Open:** The ignition is ON, or the engine is running. The ignition voltage is less than 16 V. The DTCs run once per ignition cycle when the above conditions are met.
DTC: P0674	**Cylinder #4 Glow Plug Control Circuit:** The ignition is ON. DTCs P0671-P0678 run continuously.

DTC	Trouble Code Title, Conditions, Possible Causes
DTC: P0674 00	**Cylinder 4 Glow Plug Control Circuit:** The ignition is ON, or the engine is running. The ignition voltage is less than 16 V. These DTCs run once per ignition cycle when the above conditions are met.
DTC: P0674 02	**Cylinder 4 Glow Plug Control Circuit Short to Ground:** The ignition is ON, or the engine is running. The ignition voltage is less than 16 V. The DTCs run once per ignition cycle when the above conditions are met.
DTC: P0674 04	**Cylinder 4 Glow Plug Control Circuit Open:** The ignition is ON, or the engine is running. The ignition voltage is less than 16 V. The DTCs run once per ignition cycle when the above conditions are met.
DTC: P0675	**Cylinder #5 Glow Plug Control Circuit:** The ignition is ON. DTCs P0671-P0678 run continuously.
DTC: P0676	**Cylinder #6 Glow Plug Control Circuit:** The ignition is ON. DTCs P0671-P0678 run continuously.
DTC: P0677	**Cylinder #7 Glow Plug Control Circuit:** The ignition is ON. DTCs P0671-P0678 run continuously.
DTC: P0678	**Cylinder #8 Glow Plug Control Circuit:** The ignition is ON. DTCs P0671-P0678 run continuously.
DTC: P0683 00	**Glow Plug Control Module Communication Circuit Malfunction:** The ignition is ON, or the engine is running. The ignition voltage is greater than 9 V. The DTCs run continuously once the above conditions are met.
DTC: P0683 3A	**Glow Plug Control Module Communication Circuit Incorrect Component Installed:** The ignition is ON, or the engine is running. The ignition voltage is greater than 9 V. The DTCs run continuously once the above conditions are met.
DTC: P0683 71	**Glow Plug Control Module Communication Circuit Invalid Data:** The ignition is ON, or the engine is running. The ignition voltage is greater than 9 V. The DTCs run continuously once the above conditions are met.
DTC: P0685	**Engine Controls Ignition Relay Control Circuit:** P0685, P0686, and P0687The ignition voltage is between 10-18 V. The engine speed is greater than 80 RPM. The engine control module relay has been commanded ON and OFF. The DTCs run continuously when the above conditions are met.
DTC: P0685 00	**Engine Controls Ignition Relay Control Circuit:** The ignition is ON, or the engine is running. The ignition voltage is between 11-18 V. This DTCs run continuously once the above conditions arc met.
DTC: P0686	**Engine Controls Ignition Relay Control Circuit Low Voltage:** P0685 and P0686The battery voltage is between 10. 5-18 V. The ignition is ON. The relay has been commanded ON. These DTCs run continuously when the above conditions have been met.
DTC: P0686 00	**Engine Controls Ignition Relay Control Circuit Low Voltage:** P0686 00 and P0687 00The ignition is ON, or the engine is running. DTC P0606 00 is not set. P0688 00 and P0689 00The ignition is ON. DTC P0686 00 or P0687 00 is not set. P068BThe ignition is switched OFF. The DTC runs continuously until the ECM powers down.
DTC: P0687	**Engine Controls Ignition Relay Control Circuit High Voltage:** P0687, P0689, and P0690The battery voltage is between 10. 5-18 V. The ignition is OFF. The powertrain relay has been commanded OFF. These DTCs run continuously when the above conditions have been met.
DTC: P0687	**Engine Controls Ignition Relay Control Circuit High Voltage:** P0685, P0686, and P0687The ignition voltage is between 10-18 V. The engine speed is greater than 80 RPM. The engine control module relay has been commanded ON and OFF. The DTCs run continuously when the above conditions are met.
DTC: P0687 00	**Engine Controls Ignition Relay Control Circuit High Voltage:** P0686 00 and P0687 00The ignition is ON, or the engine is running. DTC P0606 00 is not set. P0688 00 and P0689 00The ignition is ON. DTC P0686 00 or P0687 00 is not set. P068BThe ignition is switched OFF. The DTC runs continuously until the ECM powers down.
DTC: P0688 00	**Engine Controls Ignition Relay Feedback Circuit:** P0686 00 and P0687 00The ignition is ON, or the engine is running. DTC P0606 00 is not set. P0688 00 and P0689 00The ignition is ON. DTC P0686 00 or P0687 00 is not set. P068BThe ignition is switched OFF. The DTC runs continuously until the ECM powers down.
DTC: P0688 00	**Engine Controls Ignition Relay Feedback Circuit:** P0688 00 and P0689 00The ignition is ON. DTC P0686 00 or P0687 00 is not set.

DTC	Trouble Code Title, Conditions, Possible Causes
DTC: P0689	**Engine Controls Ignition Relay Feedback Circuit Low Voltage:** The ignition is ON. The ignition voltage is between 11-18 V. The DTCs run continuously when the above conditions are met.
DTC: P0689 00	**Engine Controls Ignition Relay Feedback Circuit Low Voltage:** The ignition is ON, or the engine is running. The ignition voltage is between 11-18 V. These DTCs run continuously once the above conditions are met.
DTC: P0689 00	**Engine Controls Ignition Relay Feedback Circuit Low Voltage:** P0686 00 and P0687 00The ignition is ON, or the engine is running. DTC P0606 00 is not set. P0688 00 and P0689 00The ignition is ON. DTC P0686 00 or P0687 00 is not set. P068BThe ignition is switched OFF. The DTC runs continuously until the ECM powers down.
DTC: P068A 00	**Engine Controls Ignition Relay De-Energized Too Early:** The ignition is ON, or the engine is running. The ignition voltage is between 11-18 V. These DTCs run continuously once the above conditions are met.
DTC: P068B 00	**Engine Controls Ignition Relay De-Energized Too Late:** The ignition is ON, or the engine is running. The ignition voltage is between 11-18 V. These DTCs run continuously once the above conditions are met.
DTC: P0690	**Engine Controls Ignition Relay Feedback Circuit High Voltage:** P0689 and P0690The ignition voltage is between 10-18 V. The ignition is ON. The DTCs runs continuously when the above conditions are met.
DTC: P0690	**Engine Controls Ignition Relay Feedback Circuit High Voltage:** P0689, P0690The ignition voltage is greater than 11 V. The engine control module relay is commanded ON. DTC P0685 is not set. These DTCs run continuously when the above conditions are met.
DTC: P0690	**Engine Controls Relay Feedback Circuit High Voltage:** P0690This DTC will run with the ignition ON or OFF. This DTC will run when the powertrain relay is commanded ON or OFF. DTC P0685 is not set.
DTC: P0690 00	**Engine Controls Ignition Relay Feedback Circuit High Voltage:** The ignition is ON, or the engine is running. The ignition voltage is between 11-18 V. These DTCs run continuously once the above conditions are met.
DTC: P0691	**Cooling Fan Relay 1 Control Circuit Low Voltage:** The ignition voltage is between 10-26 volts. The engine speed is greater than 80 RPM. The ECM driver transitions from ON to OFF or from OFF to ON. DTC P0480, P0481, P0691, P0692, P0693, and P0694 run continuously when the conditions above are met.
DTC: P0691 00	**Cooling Fan Relay 1 Control Circuit Low Voltage:** The ignition voltage is between 8-18 V. The engine is running greater than or equal to 400 RPM.
DTC: P0692	**Cooling Fan Relay 1 Control Circuit High Voltage:** The ignition voltage is between 10-26 volts. The engine speed is greater than 80 RPM. The ECM driver transitions from ON to OFF or from OFF to ON. DTC P0480, P0481, P0691, P0692, P0693, and P0694 run continuously when the conditions above are met.
DTC: P0692 00	**Cooling Fan Relay 1 Control Circuit High Voltage:** The ignition voltage is between 8-18 V. The engine is running greater than or equal to 400 RPM.
DTC: P0693	**Cooling Fan Relays 2 and 3 Control Circuit Low Voltage:** The ignition voltage is between 10-18 volts. The engine speed is greater than 80 RPM. The ECM driver transitions from ON to OFF or from OFF to ON. DTC P0480, P0481, P0691, P0692, P0693, and P0694 run continuously when the conditions above are met.
DTC: P0693	**Cooling Fan Relays 2 and 3 Control Circuit Low Voltage:** The ignition voltage is between 10-26 volts. The engine speed is greater than 80 RPM. The ECM driver transitions from ON to OFF or from OFF to ON. DTC P0480, P0481, P0691, P0692, P0693, and P0694 run continuously when the conditions above are met.
DTC: P0693 00	**Cooling Fan Relay 2 Control Circuit Low Voltage:** The ignition voltage is between 8-18 V. The engine is running greater than or equal to 400 RPM.
DTC: P0694	**Cooling Fan Relays 2 and 3 Control Circuit High Voltage:** The ignition voltage is between 10-26 volts. The engine speed is greater than 80 RPM. The ECM driver transitions from ON to OFF or from OFF to ON. DTC P0480, P0481, P0691, P0692, P0693, and P0694 run continuously when the conditions above are met.
DTC: P0694 00	**Cooling Fan Relay 2 Control Circuit High Voltage:** The ignition voltage is between 8-18 V. The engine is running greater than or equal to 400 RPM.
DTC: P0697	**5 V Reference 3 Circuit:** DTCs P0641, P0651, P0697, P06A3 run continuously when the ignition is ON.

DTC	Trouble Code Title, Conditions, Possible Causes
DTC: P0697	**5 V Reference 3 Circuit:** Ignition voltage is greater than 6. 4 V. Reduced engine power is not active. DTCs P0641, P0651, P0697, P06A3 run continuously when the above conditions are met.
DTC: P0697 00	**5V Reference 3 Circuit:** The ignition is ON, or the engine is running. The ignition voltage is between 9-16 V. The DTCs run continuously when the above condition is met.
DTC: P0697 03	**5V Reference 3 Circuit Low Voltage:** The ignition is ON. The DTCs run continuously when the above condition is met.
DTC: P0697 07	**5V Reference 3 Circuit High Voltage:** The ignition is ON. The DTCs run continuously when the above condition is met.
DTC: P069E	**Fuel Pump Control Module Requested MIL Illumination:** The ignition is ON, or the engine is running for greater than 3 s.
DTC: P069E	**Fuel Pump Control Module Requested MIL Illumination:** The ignition is ON, or the engine is running.
DTC: P069E 00	**Fuel Pump Control Module Requested MIL Illumination:** The ignition is ON, or the engine is running. The ignition voltage is between 11-18 V. DTC P069E 00 runs continuously once the above condition is met.
DTC: P06A3	**5 V Reference 4 Circuit:** DTCs P0641, P0651, P0697, P06A3 run continuously when the ignition is ON.
DTC: P06A6	**5 V Reference Performance:** The ignition is ON.
DTC: P06AC	**Control Module Power Up Temperature Sensor Performance:** P06ACDTC P0101, P0102, P0103, P0106, P0107, P0108, P0171, P0172, P0174, P0175, P0201, P0202, P0203, P0204, P0205, P0206, P0207, P0208, P0300, P0301, P0302, P0303, P0304, P0305, P0306, P0307, P0308, P0401, P042E, P0658, P0668, P0669, P06AC, P06AD, P06AE, P0712, P0713, P0716, P0717, P0722, P0723, P0962, P0963, P0966, P0967, P0970, P0971, P215C, P2720, P2721, P2729, or P2730 is not set. The engine speed is 400 RPM or greater for 5 seconds. The ignition voltage is 8. 6 volts or greater. Brake torque is not active. The engine torque signal is valid. The throttle position signal is valid.
DTC: P06AD	**Transmission Control Module (TCM) Power Up Temperature Sensor Circuit Low Voltage:** P06ADDTCs P06AD, P0716, P0717, P0722, or P0723 are not set. The transmission output shaft speed is 200 RPM or greater for 4 minutes. The torque converter clutch (TCC) slip speed is 120 RPM or greater for 4 minutes. The engine speed is 500 RPM or greater for 5 seconds. The ignition voltage is 8. 6 volts or greater.
DTC: P06AE	**Transmission Control Module (TCM) Power Up Temperature Sensor Circuit High Voltage:** P06AFThe engine speed is 500 RPM or greater for 5 seconds. The ignition voltage is 8. 6 volts or greater. DTC P06AE has not failed set this ignition
DTC: P06B6	**Control Module Knock Sensor Processor 1 Performance:** P06B6Engine speed is between 400-4,000 RPM. The engine coolant temperature (ECT) is warmer than -40°C (-40°F). The intake air temperature (IAT) is warmer than -40°C (-40°F). The DTC runs continuously when the above conditions are met.
DTC: P06B6 00	**Control Module Knock Sensor Processor 1 Performance:** P06B6 00Engine speed is between 400-4 000 RPM. The ECT is greater than -40°C (-40°F). The IAT is greater than -40°C (-40°F). The DTC runs continuously when the above conditions are met.
DTC: P06B6 00	**Control Module Knock Sensor Processor 1 Performance:** The engine speed is greater than 700 RPM. The engine speed is between 700-2 500 RPM for DTC P06B6 00. The airflow into the engine is between 40-2 000 mg/cylinder. This DTC runs continuously within the enabling conditions. DTCs P0324 00, P0326 00 and P06B6 00 run continuously once the above conditions are met.
DTC: P06B7	**Control Module Knock Sensor Processor 2 Performance:** P06B6 and P06B7Engine speed is between 400-4,000 RPM. The ECT is warmer than -40°C (-40°F). The IAT is warmer than -40°C (-40°F). The DTCs run continuously when the above conditions are met.
DTC: P06B8 00	**Control Module Random Access Memory Performance:** The ignition is ON. This DTCs run continuously once the above condition is met.
DTC: P0700	**Transmission Control Module (TCM) Requested MIL Illumination:** The ignition is ON or the engine is operating. DTC P0700 runs continuously.

DTC	Trouble Code Title, Conditions, Possible Causes
DTC: P0700 00	**Transmission Control Module Requested MIL Illumination:** The ignition is ON, or the engine is running. The ignition voltage is between 11-18 V. This DTCs run continuously once the above conditions are met.
DTC: P0703	**Brake Switch Circuit 2:** The engine is ON.
DTC: P0705	**Transmission Range (TR) Switch Circuit:** The engine is running for 5 seconds.
DTC: P0711	**Transmission Fluid Temperature Sensor Performance:** P0711 DTC P0101, P0102, P0103, P0106, P0107, P0108, P0171, P0172, P0174, P0175, P0201, P0202, P0203, P0204, P0205, P0206, P0207, P0208, P0300, P0301, P0302, P0303, P0304, P0305, P0306, P0307, P0308, P0401, P042E, P0658, P0668, P0669, P06AD, P06AE, P0711, P0712, P0713, P0716, P0717, P0722, P0723, P0962, P0963, P0966, P0967, P0970, P0971, P215C, P2720, P2721, P2729, or P2730 is not set. The engine speed is 400 RPM or greater for 5 seconds. The ignition voltage is 8. 6 volts or greater. Brake torque is not active. The engine torque signal is valid. The throttle position signal is valid.
DTC: P0711	**Transmission Fluid Temperature (TFT) Sensor Performance:** No ECT DTC P0117 or P0118. No input speed sensor (ISS) DTCs P0716 or P0717. No output speed sensor (OSS) DTCs P0722 or P0723. DTC P0711 has not passed in the current ignition cycle. The transmission fluid temperature is -40 to +150°C (-40 to +302°F). Condition 1The engine coolant temperature (ECT) is at least 70°C (158°F) and has changed by 55°C (131°F) since start up. The vehicle speed is 8 km/h (5 mph) or more for at least 5 minutes cumulative. The torque converter clutch (TCC) slip is 120 RPM or more for at least 5 minutes cumulative. Condition 2The engine coolant temperature is at least 70°C (158°F) and has changed by 55°C (131°F) since start up. The vehicle speed is 8 km/h (5 mph) or more for at least 5 minutes cumulative. Condition 3The calc. throttle position is between 8 and 90 percent. The engine torque is 37 ft. lbs. (50 Nm) or more. The vehicle speed is 8 km/h (5 mph) or more. The engine speed is greater than 500 RPM.
DTC: P0711	**Transmission Fluid Temperature (TFT) Sensor Performance:** P0711No DTCs P0101, P0102, P0103, P0106, P0107, P0108, P0171, P0172, P0174, P0175, P0201, P0202, P0203, P0204, P0205, P0206, P0207, P0208, P0300, P0301, P0302, P0303, P0304, P0305, P0306, P0307, P0308, P0401, P042E, P0658, P0668, P0669, P06AD, P06AE, P0711, P0712, P0713, P0716, P0717, P0722, P0723, P0962, P0963, P0966, P0967, P0970, P0971, P215C, P2720, P2721, P2729, or P2730. The engine speed is greater than 400 RPM for 5 seconds. The ignition voltage is 8. 6 volts or greater. Brake torque is not active. The engine torque signal is valid. The throttle position signal is valid.
DTC: P0712	**Transmission Fluid Temperature (TFT) Sensor Circuit Low Voltage:** P0712The engine speed is greater than 500 RPM for 5 seconds. The ignition voltage is greater than 9. 0 volts. DTC P0712 has not set this ignition cycle. No DTCs P0716, P0717, P0722, or P0723.
DTC: P0713	**Transmission Fluid Temperature (TFT) Sensor Circuit High Voltage:** P0713No input speed sensor (ISS) DTCs P0716 or P0717. No output speed sensor (OSS) DTCs P0722 or P0723. The output shaft speed is greater than 200 RPM for 200 seconds (3 minutes and 20 seconds) cumulative. The TCC slip speed is greater than 120 RPM for 200 seconds (3 minutes and 20 seconds) cumulative.
DTC: P0713	**Transmission Fluid Temperature (TFT) Sensor Circuit High Voltage:** P0713 DTCs P0716, P0717, P0722 or P0723. The ignition voltage is between 8-18 volts. The engine speed is between 500-6,500 RPMs for 5 seconds. The transmission output shaft speed is 64 RPM or greater for 200 seconds cumulatively. The TCC slip speed is 120 RPM or greater for 200 seconds cumulatively.
DTC: P0716	**Input Speed Sensor Performance:** P0716 DTC P0101, P0102, P0103, P0121, P0122, P0123, P0716, P0717, P0752, P0973, or P0974 is not set. Vehicle speed is 10 km/h (6 mph) or greater. The engine speed is greater than 400 RPM for 5 seconds. The ignition voltage is 9. 0 volts or greater. The engine torque signal is valid. Throttle position signal is valid. P0717 DTC P0717 is not set. The engine speed is greater than 400 RPM for 5 seconds. The ignition voltage is 9. 0 volts or greater. The vehicle speed is 16 km/h (10 mph) or greater. The engine torque is 37 ft. lbs. (50 Nm) or greater. P07BF or P070CThe ignition voltage is 9. 0 volts or greater.
DTC: P0717	**Input Speed Sensor Circuit No Signal:** P0716 DTC P0101, P0102, P0103, P0121, P0122, P0123, P0716, P0717, P0752, P0973, or P0974 is not set. Vehicle speed is 10 km/h (6 mph) or greater. The engine speed is greater than 400 RPM for 5 seconds. The ignition voltage is 9. 0 volts or greater. The engine torque signal is valid. Throttle position signal is valid. P0717 DTC P0717 is not set. The engine speed is greater than 400 RPM for 5 seconds. The ignition voltage is 9. 0 volts or greater. The vehicle speed is 16 km/h (10 mph) or greater. The engine torque is 37 ft. lbs. (50 Nm) or greater. P07BF or P070CThe ignition voltage is 9. 0 volts or greater.
DTC: P071A	**Transmission Tow Mode Switch Circuit:** DTC P1762 is not set. The engine speed is greater than 400 RPM for 5 seconds. The ignition voltage is 8. 6 volts or greater.
DTC: P071D	**Transmission Sport Mode Switch circuit:** The engine speed is greater than 500 RPM for 5 seconds. Ignition voltage is between 9. 0 volts and 19. 0 volts.

DTC	Trouble Code Title, Conditions, Possible Causes
DTC: P0722	**Output Speed Sensor (OSS/VSS) Circuit Low Voltage:** P0722No ISS DTC P0716 or P0717. No OSS/VSS DTC P0723. No TPS DTC P0120, P0121, P0122, P0123, P0220, P0221, P0222, P0223, P0225, P0226, P0227, P0228, P1120, P1121, P1122, P1125, P1280, P1281, P1282, P1283, P1285, P1286, P1287 or P1288. Ignition voltage is 8. 0-18. 0 V. The transmission is not in PARK or NEUTRAL. The engine speed is greater than 500 RPM for 5 seconds. The engine torque is greater than 37 ft. lbs. (50 Nm). The calc. throttle position is 8 percent or greater. The input shaft speed is greater than 1,500 RPM. The torque converter clutch (TCC) slip speed is -20 RPM or greater. The transmission fluid temperature (TFT) is -40°C (-40°F) or greater.
DTC: P0723	**Output Speed Sensor (OSS) Intermittent:** P0723 DTCs P0101, P0102, P0103, P0121, P0122, P0123, P0716, P0717, P0722, P0723, P0973, P0974, P0976, or P0977 are not set. Ignition voltage is 8. 6 volts or greater. The engine speed is 3200 RPM or greater for 5 seconds. Greater than 5 seconds since last range change. The TCM must receive a valid torque signal from the ECM. Accelerator pedal position signal is valid.
DTC: P0741	**Torque Converter Clutch (TCC) - Stuck Off:** P0741 DTCs P0101, P0102, P0103, P0121, P0122, P0123, P0716, P0717, P0722, P0723, P0742, P2762, P2763, or P2764 are not set. Ignition voltage is 8. 6 volts or greater. The engine run time is greater than 5 seconds. The transmission fluid temperature (TFT) is 20-130°C (68-266°F). The accelerator pedal position signal is valid. The throttle position is greater than 8 percent. The TCM must receive a valid torque signal from the ECM. The engine torque is greater than 37 ft. lbs. (50 Nm). The TCC is commanded ON and PWM duty cycle is greater than 60 percent for 5 seconds. The following 6L80/6L90 gear ratios are achieved in the specified gear range while the TCC is commanded On: The 2nd gear ratio is between 2. 19-2. 52. The 3rd gear ratio is between 1. 42-1. 63. The 4th gear ratio is between 1. 07-1. 23. The 5th gear is between 0. 79-0. 91. The 6th gear is between 0. 62-0. 71. The following 6L50 gear ratios are achieved in the specified gear range while the TCC is commanded On: The 2nd gear ratio is between 2. 20-2. 53. The 3rd gear ratio is between 1. 44-1. 65. The 4th gear ratio is between 1. 07-1. 23. The 5th gear is between 0. 79-0. 91. The 6th gear is between 0. 62-0. 72.
DTC: P0742	**Torque Converter Clutch (TCC) System Stuck On:** P0742 DTC P0101, P0102, P0103, P0106, P0107, P0108, P0171, P0172, P0174, P0175, P0201, P0202, P0203, P0204, P0205, P0206, P0207, P0208, P0300, P0301, P0302, P0303, P0304, P0305, P0306, P0307, P0308, P0401, P042E, P0716, P0717, P0722, P0723, P0741, P0742, P2763, or P2764 is not set. The engine speed is greater than 400 RPM for 5 seconds. The ignition voltage is 9. 0 volts or greater. The TFT is 20-130°C (68-266°F). The calculated throttle position is greater than 8 percent. The engine torque is greater than 59 ft. lbs. (80 Nm). The vehicle speed greater than 16 km/h (10 mph). Commanded gear is 2nd or greater. The gear ratio is between 0. 69-1. 97. Solenoid A is enabled.
DTC: P0751	**1-2 Shift solenoid (SS) Valve Performance - No First or Fourth Gear:** P0751 and P0756 DTCs P0120, P0121, P0122, P0123, P0220, P0221, P0222, P0223, P0225, P0226, P0227, P0228, P0716, P0717, P0722, P0723, P0742, P0842, P0843, P0973, P0974, P0976, P0977, P1120, P1121, P1122, P1125, P1280, P1281, P1282, P1283, P1285, P1286, P1287, or P1288 are not set. The ignition voltage is between 8 and 18 volts. The engine speed is between 500 and 6,500 RPM for 5 seconds. The transmission fluid temperature (TFT) is between 20-130°C (68-266°F). The engine torque is between 37-1,100 ft. lbs. (50-1,492 Nm). The calc. throttle position is 8 percent or greater. The transmission input speed sensor (ISS) is between 150-6,500 RPM. The transmission output speed sensor (OSS) is 64 RPM or greater. The time since the last gear change is 1 second.
DTC: P0752	**1-2 Shift Solenoid (SS) Valve Performance - No Second or Third Gear:** P0752No TP sensor DTC P0120 or P0220. No ISS DTC P0716 or P0717. No OSS DTC P0722 or P0723. No TCC system stuck ON DTC P0742. The engine speed is greater than 500 RPM for 5 seconds. The TFT is between 20-130°C (68-266°F). No TCC system stuck ON DTC P0742. No 1-2 SS valve electrical DTC P0973 or P0974. No 2-3 SS valve electrical DTC P0976 or P0977. The calc. throttle position is 8 percent or greater. The transmission ISS is 150 RPM or greater. The transmission OSS is 160 RPM or greater. The engine torque is greater than 37 ft. lbs. (50 Nm). The time since the last gear change is 1. 5 seconds.
DTC: P0752	**1-2 Shift solenoid (SS) Valve Performance - No Second or Third Gear:** P0752 and P0757 DTCs P0120, P0121, P0122, P0123, P0220, P0221, P0222, P0223, P0225, P0226, P0227, P0228, P0716, P0717, P0722, P0723, P0742, P0842, P0843, P0973, P0974, P0976, P0977, P1120, P1121, P1122, P1125, P1280, P1281, P1282, P1283, P1285, P1286, P1287, or P1288 are not set. The ignition voltage is between 8 and 18 volts. The engine speed is between 500 and 6,500 RPM for 5 seconds. The transmission fluid temperature (TFT) is between 20-130°C (68-266°F). The engine torque is between 37-1,100 ft. lbs. (50-1,492 Nm). The calc. throttle position is 8 percent or greater. The transmission input speed sensor (ISS) is between 150-6,500 RPM. The transmission output speed sensor (OSS) is 64 RPM or greater. The time since the last gear change is 1 second.
DTC: P0752	**1-2 Shift solenoid (SS) Valve Performance - No Second or Third Gear:** P0752No TP sensor DTCs P0121, P0122, or P0123. No ISS DTCs P0716 or P0717. No OSS DTCs P0722 or P0723. No TCC system stuck ON DTC P0742. No 1-2 SS valve electrical DTCs P0973 or P0974. No 2-3 SS valve electrical DTCs P0976 or P0977. The calc. throttle position is 8 percent or more. The transmission ISS is 150 RPM or more. The transmission OSS is 200 RPM or more. The engine torque is greater than 50 N·m (37 lb ft). The time since the last gear change is 1 second. The engine speed is greater than 500 RPM for 5 seconds. The transmission fluid temperature is between 20-130°C (68-266°F).
DTC: P0756	**Shift Solenoid Valve 2 Performance - Stuck Off:** No DTCs P0101, P0102, P0103, P0106, P0107, P0108, P0171, P0172, P0174, P0175, P0201, P0202, P0203, P0204, P0205, P0206, P0207, P0208, P0300, P0301, P0302, P0303, P0304, P0305, P0306, P0307, P0308, P0401, P042E, P0716, P0717, P0722, P0723, or P182E. The engine speed is 400 RPM or greater for 5 seconds. The high side driver (HSD) is enabled. The ignition voltage is 8. 6 volts or greater. Throttle position signal is valid. Transmission fluid temperature (TFT) is 0°C (32°F) or greater.

DTC	Trouble Code Title, Conditions, Possible Causes
DTC: P0756	**2-3 Shift Solenoid (SS) Valve Performance - No First or Second Gear:** No input speed sensor (ISS) DTCs P0716 or P0717. No output speed sensor (OSS) DTCs P0722 or P0723. No torque converter clutch (TCC) performance DTCs P0741 or P0742. No shift solenoid electrical DTCs P0973, P0974, P0976, or P0977. No internal mode switch (IMS) DTCs P1820, P1822, P1823, P1825, P1826 or P1915. No torque converter clutch pulse width module (TCC PWM) DTCs P2763 or P2764. No torque converter clutch enable DTCs P2769 or P2770. The engine torque is greater than 50 N·m (37 lb ft). The engine run time is greater than 5 seconds. The engine is not in fuel cutoff. The gear range is D4. The throttle position is 8 percent or greater. The input shaft speed is 50 RPM or greater. The output shaft speed is 50 RPM or greater. The transmission fluid temperature is 20-130°C (68-266°F).
DTC: P0757	**2-3 Shift Solenoid (SS) Valve Performance - No Third, Fourth or Fifth Gear:** No input speed sensor (ISS) DTCs P0716 or P0717. No output speed sensor (OSS) DTCs P0722 or P0723. No torque converter clutch (TCC) performance DTCs P0741 or P0742. No shift solenoid electrical DTCs P0973, P0974, P0976, or P0977. No internal mode switch (IMS) DTCs P1820, P1822, P1823, P1825, P1826 or P1915. No torque converter clutch pulse width module (TCC PWM) DTCs P2763 or P2764. No torque converter clutch enable DTCs P2769 or P2770. The engine torque is greater than 50 N·m (37 lb ft). The engine run time is greater than 5 seconds. The engine is not in fuel cutoff. The gear range is D4. The throttle position is 8 percent or greater. The input shaft speed is 50 RPM or greater. The output shaft speed is 50 RPM or greater. The transmission fluid temperature is 20-130°C (68-266°F).
DTC: P0776	**Clutch Pressure Control (PC) Solenoid 2 - Stuck Off:** P0776No ISS DTCs P0101, P0102, P0103, P0106, P0107, P0108, P0171, P0172, P0174, P0175, P0201, P0202, P0203, P0204, P0205, P0206, P0207, P0208, P0300, P0301, P0302, P0303, P0304, P0305, P0306, P0307, P0308, P0401, P042E, P0716, P0717, P0722, P0723, or P182E. The engine speed is greater than 500 RPM for 5 seconds. The ignition voltage is 9. 0 volts or greater. The transmission fluid temperature is 0°C (32°F) or greater. The transmission output speed is 650 RPM or greater or the throttle position is 0. 5 percent or greater. The throttle position signal is valid. The high side driver (HSD) is enabled.
DTC: P0777	**Clutch Pressure Control (PC) Solenoid 2 - Stuck On:** P0777No DTCs P0101, P0102, P0103, P0106, P0107, P0108, P0171, P0172, P0174, P0175, P0201, P0202, P0203, P0204, P0205, P0206, P0207, P0208, P0300, P0301, P0302, P0303, P0304, P0305, P0306, P0307, P0308, P0401, P042E, P0716, P0717, P0722, P0723, or P182E. The transmission fluid temperature is 0°C (32°F) or greater. The transmission output shaft speed is 350 RPM or greater. The transmission input speed is 200 RPM or greater. The commanded gear is not 1st range. The HSD is enabled.
DTC: P077C	**Output Speed Sensor Circuit Low Voltage:** P077CDTC P077D is not set. The ignition voltage is 9. 0 volts or greater.
DTC: P077D	**Output Speed Sensor Circuit High Voltage:** P077DDTC P077C is not set. The ignition voltage is 9. 0 volts or greater.
DTC: P0796	**Clutch Pressure Control Solenoid 3 - Stuck Off:** P0796 DTC P0101, P0102, P0103, P0106, P0107, P0108, P0171, P0172, P0174, P0175, P0201, P0202, P0203, P0204, P0205, P0206, P0207, P0208, P0300, P0301, P0302, P0303, P0304, P0305, P0306, P0307, P0308, P0401, P042E, P0716, P0717, P0722, P0723, or P182E is not set. The engine speed is greater than 500 RPM for 5 seconds. The transmission output speed is 650 RPM or greater or the throttle position is 0. 5 percent or greater. The ignition voltage is 9. 0 volts or greater. The transmission fluid temperature is 0°C (32°F) or greater. The high side driver (HSD) is enabled. The throttle position signal is valid.
DTC: P0797	**Clutch Pressure Control (PC) Solenoid 3 - Stuck On:** P0796 or P0797No ISS DTCs P0101, P0102, P0103, P0106, P0107, P0108, P0171, P0172, P0174, P0175, P0201, P0202, P0203, P0204, P0205, P0206, P0207, P0208, P0300, P0301, P0302, P0303, P0304, P0305, P0306, P0307, P0308, P0401, P042E, P0716, P0717, P0722, P0723, or P182E. The ignition voltage is greater than 8. 6 volts. The engine speed is greater than 400 RPM for 5 seconds. The output speed is 16 RPM or greater, or the throttle position is 0. 4 percent or greater. The throttle position signal is valid. The high side driver is commanded on. The transmission fluid temperature is 0°C (32°F) or greater.
DTC: P07BF	**Input Speed Sensor Circuit Low Voltage:** P0716 DTC P0101, P0102, P0103, P0121, P0122, P0123, P0716, P0717, P0752, P0973, or P0974 is not set. Vehicle speed is 10 km/h (6 mph) or greater. The engine speed is greater than 400 RPM for 5 seconds. The ignition voltage is 9. 0 volts or greater. The engine torque signal is valid. Throttle position signal is valid. P0717 DTC P0717 is not set. The engine speed is greater than 400 RPM for 5 seconds. The ignition voltage is 9. 0 volts or greater. The vehicle speed is 16 km/h (10 mph) or greater. The engine torque is 50 N·m (37 lb ft) or greater. P07BF or P070CThe ignition voltage is 9. 0 volts or greater.
DTC: P07C0	**Input Speed Sensor Circuit High Voltage:** P0716 DTC P0101, P0102, P0103, P0121, P0122, P0123, P0716, P0717, P0752, P0973, or P0974 is not set. Vehicle speed is 10 km/h (6 mph) or greater. The engine speed is greater than 400 RPM for 5 seconds. The ignition voltage is 9. 0 volts or greater. The engine torque signal is valid. Throttle position signal is valid. P0717 DTC P0717 is not set. The engine speed is greater than 400 RPM for 5 seconds. The ignition voltage is 9. 0 volts or greater. The vehicle speed is 16 km/h (10 mph) or greater. The engine torque is 50 N·m (37 lb ft) or greater. P07BF or P070CThe ignition voltage is 9. 0 volts or greater.
DTC: P0806	**Clutch Pedal Position (CPP) Sensor Performance:** P0806, P0807 and P0808 DTCs P0641 or P0651 are not set. The system voltage is more than 9 V. The ignition is in the RUN position.

DTC	Trouble Code Title, Conditions, Possible Causes
DTC: P0807	**Clutch Pedal Position (CPP) Sensor Circuit Low Voltage:** P0806, P0807 and P0808 DTCs P0641 or P0651 are not set. The system voltage is more than 9 V. The ignition is in the RUN position.
DTC: P0808	**Clutch Pedal Position (CPP) Sensor Circuit High Voltage:** P0806, P0807 and P0808 DTCs P0642, P0643, P0335, P0336, P0607 or P080A are not set. The system voltage is more than 9 V. The ignition is in the RUN position.
DTC: P0815	**Upshift Switch Circuit:** P0815 or P0816The engine speed is greater than 500 RPM for at least 5 seconds. The ignition voltage is between 9. 0 volts and 19. 0 volts. No TAP system DTC P0826. No IMS DTCs P1825 or P1915. The time since the last gear selector range change is greater than 6 seconds.
DTC: P0816	**Downshift Switch Circuit:** P0815 or P0816The engine speed is greater than 400 RPM for at least 5 seconds. The ignition voltage is 9. 0 volts or greater. DTC P0815, P0816, P0826, P182E, P1761, P1876, P1877, or P1915 is not set. The time since the last gear range change is greater than 1 second.
DTC: P0826	**Up and Down Shift Switch Circuit:** P0826The engine speed is 400 RPM or greater for 5 seconds. The ignition voltage is 8. 6 volts or greater. DTC P0826 or P1761 is not set.
DTC: P0833 03	**Clutch Pedal Position (CPP) Sensor Circuit Low Voltage:** P0833 DTCs P0641 is not set. The system voltage is more than 9 V. The ignition is in the RUN position.
DTC: P0833 07	**Clutch Pedal Position (CPP) Sensor Circuit High Voltage:** P0833 DTCs P0641 is not set. The system voltage is more than 9 V. The ignition is in the RUN position.
DTC: P0833 08	**Clutch Pedal Position (CPP) Sensor Circuit Performance - Signal Invalid:** P0833 DTC P0641 is not set. The system voltage is more than 9 V. The ignition is in the RUN position.
DTC: P0833 58	**Clutch Pedal Position (CPP) Sensor Circuit Performance:** P0833 DTC P0641 is not set. The system voltage is more than 9 V. The ignition is in the RUN position.
DTC: P0842	**Transmission Fluid Pressure (TFP) Sensor Circuit Low Voltage:** P0842No ISS DTC P0716 or P0717. No TCC performance DTC P0741 or P0742. No TCC PWM solenoid valve electrical DTC P2763 or P2764. The engine speed is greater than 500 RPM for 5 seconds. The transmission fluid temperature (TFT) is between 20-130°C (68-266°F). The engine torque is 50 N·m (37 lb ft) or greater. The TCC is commanded OFF. the TCC slip speed is greater than 80 RPM. The vehicle speed is 16 km/h (10 mph) or greater.
DTC: P0843	**Transmission Fluid Pressure (TFP) Switch 1 Circuit High Voltage:** P0842 or P0843 DTCs P0751, P0752, P0756, P0757, P0973, P0974, P0977, P1825 or P1915 are not set. Ignition voltage is 8. 6 volts or greater. The transmission fluid temperature (TFT) is 0-120°C (32-248°F). Engine speed is 500 RPM or greater for 5 seconds.
DTC: P0843	**Transmission Fluid Pressure (TFP) Switch Circuit High Voltage:** P0843No ISS DTCs P0716 or P0717. No TCC performance DTCs P0741 or P0742. No TCC PWM solenoid valve electrical DTCs P2763 or P2764. The TCC is commanded ON. The TCC slip speed is -20 to +60 RPM. The engine speed is greater than 500 RPM for 5 seconds. The transmission fluid temperature is between 20-130°C (68-266°F). The engine torque is 50 N·m (37 lb ft) or more.
DTC: P0850	**Park/Neutral Position (PNP) Switch Circuit:** Ignition voltage is between 8-18 volts. Engine speed is greater than 1,000 RPM.
DTC: P0851	**Park/Neutral Position (PNP) Switch Circuit Low Voltage:** P0851Ignition voltage is between 9-18 volts. No TCM DTC P0601, P0602, P0603, or P0604. No IMS DTC P1825 or P1915. No Communication DTC U0073, U0100, U0121, or U0140.
DTC: P0852	**Park/Neutral Position (PNP) Switch Circuit High Voltage:** P0852Ignition voltage is between 9-18 volts. No TCM DTC P0601, P0602, P0603, or P0604. No IMS DTC P1825 or P1915. No Communication DTC U0073, U0100, U0121, or U0140. No TP DTC P0121, P0122, or P0123. No OSS DTC P0722 or P0723. No MAF DTC P0101, P0102, or P0103. No MAP DTC P0106, P0107, or P0108. Engine speed is greater than 400 RPM.
DTC: P0856	**Traction Control Torque Request Circuit:** The ignition is ON. The DTCs run continuously once the above condition is met.
DTC: P0856	**Engine Control Module (ECM) Traction Control Torque Request Circuit:** Engine Running.
DTC: P0856	**Traction Control Torque Request Circuit Malfunction:** Engine running.
DTC: P0856 00	**Traction Control Torque Request Circuit:** The ignition is ON. Ignition voltage is greater than 8 volts.

DTC	Trouble Code Title, Conditions, Possible Causes
DTC: P0864	**Invalid Data Received From Transmission Control Module:** Battery voltage is between 9-16 V and data link communications operate normally.
DTC: P0872	**Transmission Fluid Pressure Switch 3 Circuit Low Voltage:** No DTCs P0711, P0712, P0713, P0716, P0717, P0722, P0723, P0742, P0751, P0756, P0757, P0973, P0974, P0976, P0977, P182E, or P1915. The engine speed is 500 RPM or greater for 5 seconds. Ignition voltage is 9. 0 volts or greater. The transmission fluid temperature (TFT) is 0-110°C (32-230°F). The High Side Driver is ON. The engine speed is 550 RPM or greater.
DTC: P0873	**Transmission Fluid Pressure Switch 3 Circuit High Voltage:** No DTCs P0711, P0712, P0713, P0716, P0717, P0722, P0723, P0742, P0751, P0756, P0757, P0973, P0974, P0976, P0977, P182E, or P1915. The engine speed is 500 RPM or greater for 5 seconds. Ignition voltage is 9. 0 volts or greater. The transmission fluid temperature (TFT) is 0-110°C (32-230°F). The High Side Driver is ON. The engine speed is 550 RPM or greater.
DTC: P0877	**Transmission Fluid Pressure Switch 4 Circuit Low Voltage:** P0877 or P0878 DTC P0711, P0712, P0713, P0716, P0717, P0722, P0723, P0742, P0751, P0756, P0757, P0973, P0974, P0976, P0977, P1915, P182E is not set. The engine speed is 400 RPM or greater for 5 seconds. The engine speed is 550 RPM or greater. Ignition voltage is 8. 6 volts or greater. The transmission fluid temperature (TFT) is 0-120°C (32-248°F).
DTC: P0878	**Transmission Fluid Pressure Switch 4 Circuit High Voltage:** P0877 or P0878 DTC P0711, P0712, P0713, P0716, P0717, P0722, P0723, P0742, P0751, P0756, P0757, P0973, P0974, P0976, P0977, P1915, or P182E is not set. The high side driver is enabled. The engine speed is 400 RPM or greater for 5. 0 seconds. The engine speed is 550 RPM or greater. The ignition voltage is 8. 6 volts or greater. The transmission fluid temperature (TFT) is -7 to +120°C (19-248°F).
DTC: P0878	**Transmission Fluid Pressure (TFP) Switch 4 Circuit High Voltage:** No DTCs P0711, P0712, P0713, P0973, P0974, P0976, P0977, P182E or P1915. The engine speed is 500 RPM or greater for 5 seconds. Ignition voltage is between 9. 0 volts and 18. 0 volts. The transmission fluid temperature (TFT) is 0-120°C (32-248°F).
DTC: P0897	**Transmission Fluid Life:** DTCs P0711, P0712, or P0713 are not set. The ignition voltage is between 8 and 18 volts.
DTC: P0961	**Line Pressure Control (PC) Solenoid System Performance:** The engine speed is greater than 400 RPM for 5 seconds. The ignition voltage is 8. 6 volts or greater.
DTC: P0962	**Line Pressure Control Solenoid Valve Control Circuit Low Voltage:** P0961, P0962, or P0963The engine speed is 500 RPM or greater for 5 seconds. The ignition voltage is 9. 0 volts or greater.
DTC: P0963	**Line Pressure Control Solenoid Valve Control Circuit High Voltage:** P0961, P0962, or P0963The engine speed is 400 RPM or greater for 5 seconds. The ignition voltage is 9. 0 volts or greater.
DTC: P0965	**Clutch Pressure Control (PC) Solenoid 2 System Performance:** P0965, P0966, or P0967 DTCs P0965, P0966, or P0967 have not set this ignition. The ignition voltage is 8. 6 volts or greater. The engine run time is greater than 5 seconds. The clutch PC solenoid 2 is commanded ON.
DTC: P0966	**Clutch Pressure Control (PC) Solenoid 2 Control Circuit Low Voltage:** P0965, P0966, or P0967 DTCs P0965, P0966, or P0967 have not set this ignition. The ignition voltage is 8. 6 volts or greater. The clutch PC solenoid 2 is commanded ON. The engine speed is greater than 400 RPM for 5 seconds.
DTC: P0967	**Clutch Pressure Control (PC) Solenoid 2 Control Circuit High Voltage:** P0965, P0966, or P0967 DTCs P0965, P0966, or P0967 have not set this ignition. The ignition voltage is 8. 6 volts or greater. The clutch PC solenoid 2 is commanded ON. The engine speed is greater than 400 RPM for 5 seconds.
DTC: P0969	**Clutch Pressure Control (PC) Solenoid 3 System Performance:** P0969, P0970, or P0971 DTCs P0969, P0970, or P0971 have not set this ignition. The ignition voltage is 8. 6 volts or greater. The engine speed is 500 RPM or greater for 5 seconds. The clutch PC solenoid 3 is commanded ON.
DTC: P0970	**Clutch Pressure Control (PC) Solenoid 3 Control Circuit Low Voltage:** P0969, P0970, or P0971 DTCs P0969, P0970, or P0971 have not set this ignition. The ignition voltage is 8. 6 volts or greater. The engine speed is 500 RPM or greater for 5 seconds. The clutch PC solenoid 3 is commanded ON.
DTC: P0971	**Clutch Pressure Control (PC) Solenoid 3 Control Circuit High Voltage:** P0969, P0970, or P0971 DTCs P0969, P0970, or P0971 have not set this ignition. The ignition voltage is 8. 6 volts or greater. The engine speed is 500 RPM or greater for 5 seconds. The clutch PC solenoid 3 is commanded ON.
DTC: P0973	**Shift Solenoid Valve 1 Control Circuit Low Voltage:** P0973The engine speed is 400 RPM or greater for 5 seconds. The ignition voltage is 8. 6 volts or greater. DTC P0973 is not set.
DTC: P0973	**1-2 Shift Solenoid (SS) Control Circuit Low Voltage:** No DTC P0335, P0336, P0340, P0345, P0346, P0365, P0366, P0390 or P0391. The engine speed is greater than 500 RPM for 5 seconds. The ignition voltage is greater than 8. 0V.

DTC	Trouble Code Title, Conditions, Possible Causes
DTC: P0974	**Shift Solenoid (SS) 1 Control Circuit High Voltage:** P0973 or P0974 The engine speed is 500 RPM or greater for 5 seconds. The ignition voltage is between 9. 0 volts and 18. 0 volts.
DTC: P0974	**1-2 Shift Solenoid (SS) Control Circuit High Voltage:** No DTC P0335, P0336, P0340, P0345, P0346, P0365, P0366, P0390 or P0391. The engine speed is greater than 500 RPM for 5 seconds. The ignition voltage is greater than 8. 0 V.
DTC: P0976	**2-3 Shift Solenoid (SS) Control Circuit Low Voltage:** No DTC P0335, P0336, P0340, P0345, P0346, P0365, P0366, P0390 or P0391. The engine speed is greater than 500 RPM for 5 seconds. The ignition voltage is greater than 8. 0 V.
DTC: P0976	**Shift Solenoid (SS) 2 Control Circuit Low Voltage:** P0976 or P0977 DTCs P0976 or P0977 have not set this ignition. The ignition voltage is 8. 6 volts or greater. The engine speed is 500 RPM or greater for 5 seconds. The SS 2 is commanded ON or OFF.
DTC: P0977	**2-3 Shift Solenoid (SS) Control Circuit High Voltage:** No DTC P0335, P0336, P0340, P0345, P0346, P0365, P0366, P0390 or P0391. The engine speed is greater than 500 RPM for 5 seconds. The ignition voltage is greater than 8. 0 V.
DTC: P0977	**2-3 Shift Solenoid (SS) Control Circuit High Voltage:** The engine speed is 500 RPM for 5 seconds. The 2-3 SS is commanded ON.
DTC: P0990	**Transmission Fluid Pressure Switch 5 Circuit High Voltage:** DTC P0989 or P0990 DTC P0711, P0712, P0713, P0716, P0717, P0722, P0723, P0742, P0751, P0756, P0757, P0973, P0974, P0976, P0977, P1915, or P182E is not set. The engine speed is 400 RPM or greater for 5 seconds. The engine speed is 550 RPM or greater. Ignition voltage is 8. 6 volts or greater. The transmission fluid temperature (TFT) is 0-120°C (32-248°F).

OBD II Trouble Code List (P1xxx Codes)

DTC	Trouble Code Title, Conditions, Possible Causes
DTC: Pw1043	**Reductant Pump High Control Circuit Low Voltage:** DTCs P204F, P20A1, or P2510 are not set. The battery voltage is greater than 11 V. The engine speed is greater than 600 RPM. The engine run time is greater than 10 s. The DTCs run continuously once the above conditions are met.
DTC: P1044	**Reductant Pump High Control Circuit High Voltage:** DTCs P204F, P20A1, or P2510 are not set. The battery voltage is greater than 11 V. The engine speed is greater than 600 RPM. The engine run time is greater than 10 s. The DTCs run continuously once the above conditions are met.
DTC: P1045	**Reductant Purge Valve High Control Circuit Low Voltage:** The battery voltage is greater than 11 V. The engine speed is greater than 600 RPM. The engine run time is greater than 10 s. The DTCs run continuously when the above conditions are met.
DTC: P1048	**Reductant Injector High Control Circuit Low Voltage:** The engine is running. The battery voltage is greater than 11 V. The ECM is commanding the reductant injector duty cycle greater than 0 %. The Reductant Injection Inhibit Reason displays None. The DTCs run continuously once the above conditions are met.
DTC: P1049	**Reductant Injector High Control Circuit High Voltage:** The engine is running. The battery voltage is greater than 11 V. The ECM is commanding the reductant injector duty cycle greater than 0 %. The Reductant Injection Inhibit Reason displays None. The DTCs run continuously once the above conditions are met.
DTC: P1082	**Fuel Filter Pressure Switch Performance:** ECM monitors the circuit 30 s into the after-run mode.
DTC: P10CC	**Exhaust Aftertreatment Fuel Injector Control Circuit Shorted:** Battery Voltage is greater than 11 V. Engine speed is greater than 600 RPM.
DTC: P10CD	**Exhaust Aftertreatment Fuel Injector High Control Circuit Low Voltage:** Battery Voltage is greater than 11 V. Engine speed is greater than 600 RPM.
DTC: P10CE	**Exhaust Aftertreatment Fuel Injector High Control Circuit High Voltage:** Battery Voltage is greater than 11 V. Engine speed is greater than 600 RPM.
DTC: P1101	**Intake Air Flow System Performance:** DTC P0102, P0103, P0107, P0108, P0112, P0113, P0116, P0117, P0118, P0128, P0335, or P0336 are not set. The engine speed is between 400-7,192 RPM. The IAT Sensor parameter is between -7 to +125°C (+19 to +257°F). The Engine Coolant Temperature (ECT) Sensor parameter is between 70-125°C (158-257°F). This DTC runs continuously within the enabling conditions.

DTC	Trouble Code Title, Conditions, Possible Causes
DTC: P1101 00	**Intake Air Flow System Performance:** P1101 00 DTCs P0102 00, P0103 00, P0106 00, P0107 00, P0108 00, P0112 00, P0113 00, P0117 00, P0118 00, P0335 00, P0336 00 are not set. The engine speed is between 400-6 500 RPM. The engine coolant temperature (ECT) Sensor is between 70-125°C (158-257°F). The intake air temperature (IAT) Sensor is between -20 to +125°C (-4 to +257°F). DTC P1101 00 run continuously when the above conditions are met.
DTC: P1104 00	**Throttle Actuator Control (TAC) Motor Control Circuit Shorted:** P1104 00The ignition is ON or the engine is operating. The ignition voltage is greater than 7 V. The system is not in battery safe mode. DTC P0068 00 is not set. DTCs P1516 00 and P2101 00 run continuously once the above conditions are met for greater than 5 s.
DTC: P111C	**Charge Air Cooler (CAC) Temperature - Intake Air Temperature (IAT) Sensor 2 Correlation:** Condition 1 DTCs P0016, P007C, P0097, P0098, P0112, P0113, P0335, P0336, P0340, or P0341 are not set. Ignition has been OFF for 8 hours or more. The engine is running. OR Condition 2 DTCs P0016, P007C, P0097, P0098, P0112, P0113, P0335, P0336, P0340, or P0341 are not set. . Ignition has been OFF for 8 hours or more. The engine is running. In the first 60 s of engine run time, the ECM determines the block heater is OFF. AND In the first 60 s of engine run time, the ECM determines the block heater is OFF. AND In the first 10 minutes of engine run time, the vehicle speed as been at least 24 km/h (15 mph) for at least 5 minutes and the ECM determines there is no Sunload. This DTC runs once per key cycle when the conditions in 1 or 2 are met.
DTC: P111D	**Intake Air Temperature (IAT) Sensor 1-Fuel Temperature Sensor 2 Correlation:** Condition 1 DTCs P0016, P0112, P0113, P0187, P0188, P0335, P0336, P0340, or P0341 are not set. Ignition has been OFF for 8 hours or more. The ambient temperature is warmer than -60°C (-76°F). The engine is running. OR Condition 2 DTCs P0016, P0112, P0113, P0187, P0188, P0335, P0336, P0340, or P0341 are not set. Ignition has been OFF for 8 hours or more. The ambient temperature is warmer than -60°C (-76°F). The engine is running. In the first 60 s of engine run time, the ECM determines the block heater is OFF. AND In the first 10 minutes of engine run time, the vehicle speed as been at least 24 km/h (15 mph) for at least 5 minutes and the ECM determines there is no Sunload. This DTC runs once per key cycle when the conditions in 1 or 2 are met.
DTC: P1125 00	**Accelerator Pedal Position (APP) System:** DTCs P0641 00, P0651 00, or P0697 00 are not set. The ignition is ON or the engine is operating. The DTCs run continuously once the above conditions are met.
DTC: P1133	**HO2S Insufficient Switching Sensor 1:** P0133 and P1133 DTCs P0101, P0102, P0103, P0106, P0107, P0108, P0116, P0117, P0118, P0128, P0131, P0132, P0134, P0201, P0202, P0203, P0204, P0300, P0411, P0412, P0418, P0442, P0443, P0446, P0449, P0451, P0452, P0453, P0454, P0455, P0496 are not set. The Engine Coolant Temperature (ECT) Sensor parameter is more than 70°C (158°F). The Ignition 1 Signal parameter is between 10-32 V. The Fuel Level Sensor parameter is more than 10 percent. The Engine Run Time parameter is more than 120 s. The Engine Speed parameter is between 1,000-3,500 RPM. The EGR device control is not active. The idle speed device control is not active. the fuel device control is not active. The AIR device control is not active. The HO2S heaters have been ON for more than 40 s. The learned HO2S heater resistance is valid. The IAT parameter is more than -40°C (-40°F). The fuel composition is less than 87 percent ethanol. The BARO parameter is more than 70 kPa. The fuel control is not in power enrichment. DFCO is not active. The Mass Airflow (MAF) Sensor parameter is between 14-40 g/s. The Loop Status parameter is Closed. DTCs P0133 and P1133 run once per drive cycle when the above conditions are met for 3 s.
DTC: P1133	**HO2S Insufficient Switching Bank 1 Sensor 1:** P0133, P0153, P1133, or P1153 DTCs P0068, P0101, P0102, P0103, P0106, P0107, P0108, P0112, P0113, P0116, P0117, P0118, P0120, P0121, P0122, P0123, P0128, P0201, P0202, P0203, P0204, P0205, P0206, P0207, P0208, P0220, P0222, P0223, P0442, P0443, P0446, P0449, P0455, P0496, P1516, P2101, P2119, P2135, P2176 are not set. The engine coolant temperature (ECT) is greater than 71°C (159°F). The intake air temperature (IAT) is warmer than -40°C (-40°F)The ignition 1 voltage is between 10-32 V. The fuel level is greater than 10 %. The engine run time is greater than 60 s. The engine speed is between 1,000-3,000 RPM. The barometric (BARO) pressure is greater than 70 kPa. The mass airflow (MAF) is between 15-55 g/s. The fuel system is in Closed Loop. The throttle position (TP) is greater than 5 %. The DTCs run once per drive cycle when the above conditions are met.
DTC: P1133 00	**HO2S Insufficient Switching Sensor 1:** DTCs P0106 00, P0107 00, P0108 00, P0112 00, P0113 00, P0116 00, P0117 00, P0118 00, P0121 00, P0122 00, P0123 00, P0131 00, P0132 00, P0134 00, P0201 00, P0202 00, P0203 00, P0204 00, P0300 00, P0315 00, P0335 00, P0336 00, P044 00, P0443 00, P0446 00, P0449 00, P0451 00, P0452 00, P0453 00, and P0496 00 are not set. The calculated airflow into the engine is between 10-45 g/s. The engine speed is between 1 100-3 500 RPM. The engine coolant temperature is greater than 60°C (140°F). The Barometric Pressure (BARO) is greater than 70 kPa (10 PSI). The ignition voltage is between 10-18 V. The fuel system is in closed loop. The evaporative emissions (EVAP) purge is less than 20%. The EVAP purge is not changing states. The engine run time is greater than 3 min. The fuel level is greater than 10%. The long term fuel trim is enabled. The HO2S heater is enabled for greater than 40 s. The vehicle is not decelerating. The vehicle is not operating in power enrichment. The DTCs run once per ignition cycle when the above conditions are met for greater than 1 s.
DTC: P113A	**Exhaust Gas Temperature Sensors 3-4 Not Plausible:** P113ADTC P0112, P0113, P242C, P242D, P2470, or P2471 is not set. The ignition has been OFF for greater than 8 hours. The engine is running. The ambient air temperature is greater than -60°C (-76°F). DTC P113A runs once per key cycle when the above conditions are met.

DTC	Trouble Code Title, Conditions, Possible Causes
DTC: P1153	**HO2S Insufficient Switching Bank 2 Sensor 1:** P0133, P0153, P1133, or P1153 DTCs P0068, P0101, P0102, P0103, P0106, P0107, P0108, P0112, P0113, P0116, P0117, P0118, P0120, P0121, P0122, P0123, P0128, P0201, P0202, P0203, P0204, P0205, P0206, P0207, P0208, P0220, P0222, P0223, P0442, P0443, P0446, P0449, P0455, P0496, P1516, P2101, P2119, P2135, or P2176 are not set. The engine coolant temperature (ECT) is greater than 70°C (158°F). The intake air temperature (IAT) is warmer than -40°C (-40°F)The ignition 1 voltage is between 10-18 volts. The fuel level is greater than 10 percent. The engine run time is greater than 202 seconds. The engine speed is between 1,100-2,500 RPM. The barometric (BARO) pressure is greater than 70 kPa. The mass airflow (MAF) is between 20-40 g/s. The fuel system is in Closed Loop. The throttle position (TP) is greater than 3 percent. The DTCs run once per drive cycle when the above conditions are met.
DTC: P1159 00	**Exhaust Gas Recirculation (EGR) Control Circuit:** The ignition is ON, or the engine is running. The DTCs run continuously when the above conditions are met.
DTC: P1161 00	**Exhaust Gas Recirculation (EGR) Control Circuit Low Voltage:** The ignition is ON, or the engine is running. The DTCs run continuously when the above conditions are met.
DTC: P1166 00	**HO2S Circuit Low Voltage During Power Enrichment Sensor 1:** The startup engine coolant temperature is greater than 60°C (140°F). The ignition voltage is greater than 10 V. The engine has been operating greater than 60 s. The engine is in power enrichment mode. The DTCs run continuously when the above conditions are met for 2 s.
DTC: P1168 00	**Exhaust Gas Recirculation (EGR) Control Circuit High Voltage:** The ignition is ON, or the engine is running. The DTCs run continuously when the above conditions are met.
DTC: P1174	**Air Fuel Imbalance Bank 1:** DTCs P0053, P0059, P0068, P0101, P0102, P0103, P0106, P0107, P0108, P0117, P0118, P0120, P0122, P0123, P0128, P0131, P0132, P0133, P0134, P0135, P0151, P0152, P0153, P0154, P0155, P0201-P0206, P0220, P0222, P0223, P0300, P0301-P0306, P0442, P0443, P0446, P0449, P0452, P0453, P0455, P0496, P0606, P0641, P0651, P1133, P1516, P2101, P2120, P2122, P2123, P2125, P2127, P2128, P2135, P2176, P2A00 are not set. The device control is not active. The intrusive diagnostics are not active. The engine overspeed protection is not active. Reduced engine power is not active. The traction control is not active. The engine is in Closed Loop status. The system voltage is between 10-32 V for greater than 4 s. The engine run time is greater than 50 seconds. The engine coolant temperature (ECT) is warmer than -20°C (-4°F). The engine speed is between 500-4,000 RPM. The mass air flow is between 5-600 g/s.
DTC: P1174	**Fuel Trim Cylinder Balance:** DTCs P0030, P0053, P0068, P0101, P0102, P0103, P0106, P0107, P0108, P0116, P0117, P0118, P0120, P0121, P0122, P0123, P0128, P0131, P0132, P0133, P0134, P0135, P0201-P0204, P0220, P0222, P0223, P0300, P0442, P0443, P0446, P0449, P0451, P0452, P0453, P0454, P0455, P0496, P060D, P1133, P1516, P2101, P2119, P2120, P2122, P2123, P2125, P2127, P2128, P2135, P2138, P2176, P2A00 are not set. The device control is not active. The intrusive diagnostics are not active. The engine overspeed protection is not active. The traction control is not active. The fuel control is in air-fuel Closed Loop. The system voltage is greater than 10 volts, or less than 18 volts. The engine run time is greater than 50 seconds. The engine coolant temperature (ECT) is greater than 10°C (50°F). The engine speed is greater than 1,000 RPM, but less than 4,000 RPM. The mass air flow is greater than 7 g/s, but less than 400 g/s. This DTC runs continuously when the above conditions are met.
DTC: P1175	**Fuel Trim Cylinder Balance Bank 2:** DTCs P0030, P0036, P0050, P0053, P0059, P0101, P0102, P0103, P0106, P0107, P0108, P0117, P0118, P0128, P0131, P0132, P0133, P0134, P0135, P0151, P0152, P0153, P0154, P0155, P0201-P0206, P0300, P0301-P0306, P0411, P0412, P0418, P0442, P0443, P0446, P0449, P0452, P0453, P0454, P0455, P0496, P1133, P1153, P1516, P2101, P2119, P2120, P2125, P2135, P2138, P2176, P2431, P2432, P2433, P2440, P2A00, P2A03 are not set. The device control is not active. The intrusive diagnostics are not active. The engine overspeed protection is not active. The power take-off (PTO) is not active. The traction control is not active. The fuel control is in air-fuel Closed Loop. The system voltage is more than 10 volts, or less than 18 volts. The engine run time is greater than 100 seconds. The engine coolant temperature (ECT) is greater than -20°C (-4°F). The engine speed is greater than 425 RPM, but less than 6,000 RPM. The mass air flow is greater than 25 g/s, but less than 510 g/s.
DTC: P11AF	**HO2S Performance - Signal High During Moderate Load Sensor 2:** P11AF or P11B2The engine run time is greater than 10 s. The engine speed is between 1,300 and 2,600 RPM. The intake air temperature is between -43 to +123°C (-45 to +253°F). The BARO pressure is between 75-110 kPa (11-16 psi). The battery voltage is greater than 11 V. The EGR is commanded ON and the exhaust gas temperature sensor 2 is between 100-1,000°C (212-1,832° F). The DPF regeneration is not active. The fuel level is greater than 15 percent. The DTCs run continuously once the above conditions are met.
DTC: P11B2	**HO2S Performance - Signal Low During Moderate Load Sensor 2:** P11AF or P11B2The engine run time is greater than 10 s. The engine speed is between 1,300 and 2,600 RPM. The intake air temperature is between -43 to +123°C (-45 to +253°F). The BARO pressure is between 75-110 kPa (11-16 psi). The battery voltage is greater than 11 V. The EGR is commanded ON and the exhaust gas temperature sensor 2 is between 100-1,000°C (212-1,832° F). The DPF regeneration is not active. The fuel level is greater than 15 percent. The DTCs run continuously once the above conditions are met.

DTC	Trouble Code Title, Conditions, Possible Causes
DTC: P11B5	**HO2S Current Performance Sensor 2:** P11B5The engine speed is greater than 600 RPM. The battery voltage is greater than 11 V. The engine run time is greater than 10 s. The NOx sensor is at operating temperature. The DTC runs continuously once the above conditions are met.
DTC: P11CB	**NOx Sensor 1 Performance - Signal High:** P11CB or P11CCDTCs P0101, P0234, P0299, P0401, P0402, P140B, P140C, P2228, or P2229 are not set. The DPF Regeneration is not active. The BARO is between 75-106 kPa (11-15 psi). The ambient air temperature is between -7 to +38°C (19-100°F). The engine run time is greater than 30 s. The engine coolant temperature is between -7 to +123°C (19-253°F). The engine speed is greater than 600 RPM. The battery voltage is greater than 11 V. The NOx sensor is at operating temperature. The DTCs run once per drive cycle when the above conditions are met.
DTC: P11CC	**NOx Sensor 1 Performance - Signal Low:** P11CB or P11CCDTCs P0101, P0234, P0299, P0401, P0402, P140B, P140C, P2228, or P2229 are not set. The DPF Regeneration is not active. The BARO is between 75-106 kPa (11-15 psi). The ambient air temperature is between -7 to +38°C (19-100°F). The engine run time is greater than 30 s. The engine coolant temperature is between -7 to +123°C (19-253°F). The engine speed is greater than 600 RPM. The battery voltage is greater than 11 V. The NOx sensor is at operating temperature. The DTCs run once per drive cycle when the above conditions are met.
DTC: P11DB	**NOx Sensor 1 Current Performance:** P11DBDTCs P064C, P163C, P2200, P2205, P220A, P220B, U029D and U029E are not set. The exhaust temperature sensor 2 is greater than 95°C (203° F). The engine speed is greater than 600 RPM. The battery voltage is greater than 11 V. The DPF regeneration is not active. The DTCs run continuously when the above conditions are met.
DTC: P11DC	**NOx Sensor 2 Current Performance:** P11DCThe exhaust temperature sensor 4 is greater than 95°C (203°F). The engine speed is greater than 600 RPM. The battery voltage is greater than 11 V. The DPF regeneration is not active. The DTC runs continuously when the above conditions are met.
DTC: P1224	**Fuel Injector 1 Control Circuit Shorted:** The engine is running. The charging system voltage is between 10-18 volts.
DTC: P1224 00	**Cylinder 1 Injector Control Circuit Malfunction:** The engine is running. The ECM monitors for a condition once per camshaft revolution.
DTC: P1227	**Fuel Injector 2 Control Circuit Shorted:** Engine speed is greater than 600 RPM. The charging system voltage is between 10-18 V.
DTC: P1227 00	**Cylinder 2 Injector Control Circuit Malfunction:** The engine is running. The ECM monitors for a condition once per camshaft revolution.
DTC: P122A	**Fuel Injector 3 Control Circuit Shorted:** Engine speed is greater than 600 RPM. The charging system voltage is between 10-18 V.
DTC: P122A 00	**Cylinder 3 Injector Control Circuit Malfunction:** The engine is running. The ECM monitors for a condition once per camshaft revolution.
DTC: P122B 00	**Intake Air Flow Valve Control Circuit Low Voltage:** The ignition is ON, or the engine is running. The throttle actuator motor is commanded ON or OFF. The ignition voltage is less than 16 V. The DTCs run continuously when the above conditions are met.
DTC: P122C	**Intake Air (IA) Flow Valve Control Circuit Shorted:** P02E2, P02E3, P02EB, P122C, P122E and P122FThe battery voltage is greater than 11 V. The Engine is running. The throttle valve motor control circuit is active. The DTCs run continuously whenever the above conditions are met.
DTC: P122C 00	**Intake Air Flow Valve Control Circuit Shorted:** P122C 00The ignition is ON, or the engine is running. The throttle valve motor control circuit is active. The ignition voltage is less than 16 V. This DTCs run continuously when the above conditions are met.
DTC: P122D	**Intake Air (IA) Flow Position Sensor Exceeded Learning Limit:** DTC P02E0 or P02EB is not set. The ignition is ON. Offset learning for the throttle valve was successful in the previous driving cycle. The battery voltage is greater than 8 V. DTC P122D runs continuously when the above conditions are met.
DTC: P122D 00	**Intake Air Flow Position Sensor Exceeded Learning Limit:** P122D 00The ignition is ON, or the engine is running. DTC P02E0 00 or P02EB 00 is not set. Offset learning for the throttle valve was successful in the previous driving cycle. The ignition voltage is less than 16 V. This DTCs run continuously when the above conditions are met.
DTC: P122E	**Intake Air (IA) Flow Valve Control Circuit 2 Low Voltage:** P02E2, P02E3, P02EB, P122C, P122E and P122FThe battery voltage is greater than 11 V. The Engine is running. The throttle valve motor control circuit is active. The DTCs run continuously whenever the above conditions are met.

DTC	Trouble Code Title, Conditions, Possible Causes
DTC: P122F	**Intake Air (IA) Flow Valve Control Circuit 2 High Voltage:** P02E2, P02E3, P02EB, P122C, P122E and P122FThe battery voltage is greater than 11 V. The Engine is running. The throttle valve motor control circuit is active. The DTCs run continuously whenever the above conditions are met.
DTC: P1233	**Fuel Injector 4 Control Circuit Shorted:** The engine is running. The charging system voltage is between 10-18 volts.
DTC: P1233 00	**Cylinder 4 Injector Control Circuit Malfunction:** The engine is running. The ECM monitors for a condition once per camshaft revolution.
DTC: P1236	**Fuel Injector 5 Control Circuit Shorted:** The engine is running. The charging system voltage is between 10-18 volts.
DTC: P1239	**Fuel Injector 6 Control Circuit Shorted:** Engine speed is greater than 600 RPM. The charging system voltage is between 10-18 V.
DTC: P1242	**Fuel Injector 7 Control Circuit Shorted:** Engine speed is greater than 600 RPM. The charging system voltage is between 10-18 V.
DTC: P1247	**Fuel Injector 8 Control Circuit Shorted:** The engine is running. The charging system voltage is between 10-18 volts.
DTC: P1248	**Cylinder 1 Injector High Control Circuit Shorted to Control Circuit:** The engine is running. The ignition voltage is between 11-18 V. The DTCs run continuously when the above conditions are met.
DTC: P1248 00	**Cylinder 1 Injector High Control Circuit Shorted to Control Circuit:** The engine is running. The ECM monitors for a condition once per camshaft revolution.
DTC: P1249	**Cylinder 2 Injector High Control Circuit Shorted to Control Circuit:** The engine is running. The ignition voltage is between 11-18 V. The DTCs run continuously when the above conditions are met.
DTC: P1249 00	**Cylinder 2 Injector High Control Circuit Shorted to Control Circuit:** The engine is running. The ECM monitors for a condition once per camshaft revolution.
DTC: P124A	**Cylinder 3 Injector High Control Circuit Shorted to Control Circuit:** The engine is running. The ignition voltage is between 11-18 V. The DTCs run continuously when the above conditions are met.
DTC: P124A 00	**Cylinder 3 Injector High Control Circuit Shorted to Control Circuit:** The engine is running. The ECM monitors for a condition once per camshaft revolution.
DTC: P124B	**Cylinder 4 Injector High Control Circuit Shorted to Control Circuit:** The engine is running. The ignition voltage is between 11-18 V. The DTCs run continuously when the above conditions are met.
DTC: P124B 00	**Cylinder 4 Injector High Control Circuit Shorted to Control Circuit:** The engine is running. The ECM monitors for a condition once per camshaft revolution.
DTC: P124C	**Cylinder 5 Injector High Control Circuit Shorted to Control Circuit:** The engine is running. The ignition voltage is between 11-18 V. The DTCs run continuously when the above conditions are met.
DTC: P124D	**Cylinder 6 Injector High Control Circuit Shorted to Control Circuit:** The engine is running. The ignition voltage is between 11-18 V. The DTCs run continuously when the above conditions are met.
DTC: P1255	**Fuel Pump Control Module Driver Over-temperature:** The engine is running.
DTC: P1258	**Engine Coolant Over temperature - Protection Mode Active:** The engine is operating for greater than 30 seconds. DTC P1258 runs continuously when the condition above is met.
DTC: P1258	**Engine Coolant Over temperature - Protection Mode Active:** The engine is operating.
DTC: P125A	**Fuel Pressure Regulator 2 High Control Circuit Low Voltage:** Engine speed is greater than 600 RPM. Battery voltage is greater than 11 V.
DTC: P125B	**Fuel Pressure Regulator 2 High Control Circuit High Voltage:** Engine speed is greater than 600 RPM. Battery voltage is greater than 11 V.
DTC: P128E	**Fuel Rail Pressure Performance:** Fuel tank level is greater than 15 %Engine is in crank or run mode

DTC	Trouble Code Title, Conditions, Possible Causes
DTC: P12B3	**Cylinder 1 Injection Timing Retarded:** Ambient air temperature is above -5° C (23° F). Fuel temperature is between 0-80° C (32-176° F). Engine temperature is greater the 50° C (122° F). Battery voltages is greater than 10 V. Time since last combustion event is between 10-30 s. Vehicle is in decel fuel shut off mode. Engine speed is between 950-1850 RPM. The difference between the Desired Fuel Rail Pressure and the Actual Fuel Rail Pressure is less than 2. 2 MPa (320 psi). No gear change has occurred. Lambda sensors are adapted. Vehicle is not in 4WD (if equipped). Exhaust brake is not ON (if equipped). No other DTCs are present. The DTC runs when the above conditions exists.
DTC: P12B4	**Cylinder 1 Injection Timing Advanced:** Ambient air temperature is above -5° C (23° F)Fuel temperature is between 0-80° C (32-176° F)Engine temperature is greater the 50° C (122° F)Battery voltages is greater than 10 V. Time since last combustion event is between 10-30 s. Vehicle is in decel fuel shut off mode. Engine speed is between 950-1850 RPM. The difference between the Desired Fuel Rail Pressure and the Actual Fuel Rail Pressure is less than 2. 2 MPa (320 psi)No gear change has occurred. Lambda sensors are adapted. Vehicle is not in 4WD (if equipped). Exhaust brake is not ON (if equipped). No other DTCs are present. The DTC runs when the above conditions exists
DTC: P12B5	**Cylinder 2 Injection Timing Retarded:** Ambient air temperature is above -5° C (23° F). Fuel temperature is between 0-80° C (32-176° F). Engine temperature is greater the 50° C (122° F). Battery voltages is greater than 10 V. Time since last combustion event is between 10-30 s. Vehicle is in decel fuel shut off mode. Engine speed is between 950-1850 RPM. The difference between the Desired Fuel Rail Pressure and the Actual Fuel Rail Pressure is less than 2. 2 MPa (320 psi). No gear change has occurred. Lambda sensors are adapted. Vehicle is not in 4WD (if equipped). Exhaust brake is not ON (if equipped). No other DTCs are present. The DTC runs when the above conditions exists.
DTC: P12B6	**Cylinder 2 Injection Timing Advanced:** Ambient air temperature is above -5° C (23° F)Fuel temperature is between 0-80° C (32-176° F)Engine temperature is greater the 50° C (122° F)Battery voltages is greater than 10 V. Time since last combustion event is between 10-30 s. Vehicle is in decel fuel shut off mode. Engine speed is between 950-1850 RPM. The difference between the Desired Fuel Rail Pressure and the Actual Fuel Rail Pressure is less than 2. 2 MPa (320 psi)No gear change has occurred. Lambda sensors are adapted. Vehicle is not in 4WD (if equipped)Exhaust brake is not ON (if equipped)No other DTCs are present. The DTC runs when the above conditions exists
DTC: P12B7	**Cylinder 3 Injection Timing Retarded:** Ambient air temperature is above -5° C (23° F). Fuel temperature is between 0-80° C (32-176° F). Engine temperature is greater the 50° C (122° F). Battery voltages is greater than 10 V. Time since last combustion event is between 10-30 s. Vehicle is in decel fuel shut off mode. Engine speed is between 950-1850 RPM. The difference between the Desired Fuel Rail Pressure and the Actual Fuel Rail Pressure is less than 2. 2 MPa (320 psi). No gear change has occurred. Lambda sensors are adapted. Vehicle is not in 4WD (if equipped). Exhaust brake is not ON (if equipped). No other DTCs are present. The DTC runs when the above conditions exists.
DTC: P12B8	**Cylinder 3 Injection Timing Advanced:** Ambient air temperature is above -5° C (23° F)Fuel temperature is between 0-80° C (32-176° F)Engine temperature is greater the 50° C (122° F)Battery voltages is greater than 10 V. Time since last combustion event is between 10-30 s. Vehicle is in decel fuel shut off mode. Engine speed is between 950-1850 RPM. The difference between the Desired Fuel Rail Pressure and the Actual Fuel Rail Pressure is less than 2. 2 MPa (320 psi)No gear change has occurred. Lambda sensors are adapted. Vehicle is not in 4WD (if equipped)Exhaust brake is not ON (if equipped)No other DTCs are present. The DTC runs when the above conditions exists
DTC: P12B9	**Cylinder 4 Injection Timing Retarded:** Ambient air temperature is above -5° C (23° F). Fuel temperature is between 0-80° C (32-176° F). Engine temperature is greater the 50° C (122° F). Battery voltages is greater than 10 V. Time since last combustion event is between 10-30 s. Vehicle is in decel fuel shut off mode. Engine speed is between 950-1850 RPM. The difference between the Desired Fuel Rail Pressure and the Actual Fuel Rail Pressure is less than 2. 2 MPa (320 psi). No gear change has occurred. Lambda sensors are adapted. Vehicle is not in 4WD (if equipped). Exhaust brake is not ON (if equipped). No other DTCs are present. The DTC runs when the above conditions exists.
DTC: P12BA	**Cylinder 4 Injection Timing Advanced:** Ambient air temperature is above -5° C (23° F)Fuel temperature is between 0-80° C (32-176° F)Engine temperature is greater the 50° C (122° F)Battery voltages is greater than 10 V. Time since last combustion event is between 10-30 s. Vehicle is in decel fuel shut off mode. Engine speed is between 950-1850 RPM. The difference between the Desired Fuel Rail Pressure and the Actual Fuel Rail Pressure is less than 2. 2 MPa (320 psi)No gear change has occurred. Lambda sensors are adapted. Vehicle is not in 4WD (if equipped)Exhaust brake is not ON (if equipped)No other DTCs are present. The DTC runs when the above conditions exists
DTC: P12BB	**Cylinder 5 Injection Timing Retarded:** Ambient air temperature is above -5° C (23° F). Fuel temperature is between 0-80° C (32-176° F). Engine temperature is greater the 50° C (122° F). Battery voltages is greater than 10 V. Time since last combustion event is between 10-30 s. Vehicle is in decel fuel shut off mode. Engine speed is between 950-1850 RPM. The difference between the Desired Fuel Rail Pressure and the Actual Fuel Rail Pressure is less than 2. 2 MPa (320 psi). No gear change has occurred. Lambda sensors are adapted. Vehicle is not in 4WD (if equipped). Exhaust brake is not ON (if equipped). No other DTCs are present. The DTC runs when the above conditions exists.

DTC	Trouble Code Title, Conditions, Possible Causes
DTC: P12BC	**Cylinder 5 Injection Timing Advanced:** Ambient air temperature is above -5° C (23° F)Fuel temperature is between 0-80° C (32-176° F)Engine temperature is greater the 50° C (122° F)Battery voltages is greater than 10 V. Time since last combustion event is between 10-30 s. Vehicle is in decel fuel shut off mode. Engine speed is between 950-1850 RPM. The difference between the Desired Fuel Rail Pressure and the Actual Fuel Rail Pressure is less than 2. 2 MPa (320 psi)No gear change has occurred. Lambda sensors are adapted. Vehicle is not in 4WD (if equipped)Exhaust brake is not ON (if equipped)No other DTCs are present. The DTC runs when the above conditions exists
DTC: P12BD	**Cylinder 6 Injection Timing Retarded:** Ambient air temperature is above -5° C (23° F). Fuel temperature is between 0-80° C (32-176° F). Engine temperature is greater the 50° C (122° F). Battery voltages is greater than 10 V. Time since last combustion event is between 10-30 s. Vehicle is in decel fuel shut off mode. Engine speed is between 950-1850 RPM. The difference between the Desired Fuel Rail Pressure and the Actual Fuel Rail Pressure is less than 2. 2 MPa (320 psi). No gear change has occurred. Lambda sensors are adapted. Vehicle is not in 4WD (if equipped). Exhaust brake is not ON (if equipped). No other DTCs are present. The DTC runs when the above conditions exists.
DTC: P12BE	**Cylinder 6 Injection Timing Advanced:** Ambient air temperature is above -5° C (23° F)Fuel temperature is between 0-80° C (32-176° F)Engine temperature is greater the 50° C (122° F)Battery voltages is greater than 10 V. Time since last combustion event is between 10-30 s. Vehicle is in decel fuel shut off mode. Engine speed is between 950-1850 RPM. The difference between the Desired Fuel Rail Pressure and the Actual Fuel Rail Pressure is less than 2. 2 MPa (320 psi)No gear change has occurred. Lambda sensors are adapted. Vehicle is not in 4WD (if equipped)Exhaust brake is not ON (if equipped)No other DTCs are present. The DTC runs when the above conditions exists
DTC: P12BF	**Cylinder 7 Injection Timing Retarded:** Ambient air temperature is above -5° C (23° F). Fuel temperature is between 0-80° C (32-176° F). Engine temperature is greater the 50° C (122° F). Battery voltages is greater than 10 V. Time since last combustion event is between 10-30 s. Vehicle is in decel fuel shut off mode. Engine speed is between 950-1850 RPM. The difference between the Desired Fuel Rail Pressure and the Actual Fuel Rail Pressure is less than 2. 2 MPa (320 psi). No gear change has occurred. Lambda sensors are adapted. Vehicle is not in 4WD (if equipped). Exhaust brake is not ON (if equipped). No other DTCs are present. The DTC runs when the above conditions exists.
DTC: P12C0	**Cylinder 7 Injection Timing Advanced:** Ambient air temperature is above -5° C (23° F)Fuel temperature is between 0-80° C (32-176° F)Engine temperature is greater the 50° C (122° F)Battery voltages is greater than 10 V. Time since last combustion event is between 10-30 s. Vehicle is in decel fuel shut off mode. Engine speed is between 950-1850 RPM. The difference between the Desired Fuel Rail Pressure and the Actual Fuel Rail Pressure is less than 2. 2 MPa (320 psi)No gear change has occurred. Lambda sensors are adapted. Vehicle is not in 4WD (if equipped)Exhaust brake is not ON (if equipped)No other DTCs are present. The DTC runs when the above conditions exists
DTC: P12C1	**Cylinder 8 Injection Timing Retarded:** Ambient air temperature is above -5° C (23° F). Fuel temperature is between 0-80° C (32-176° F). Engine temperature is greater the 50° C (122° F). Battery voltages is greater than 10 V. Time since last combustion event is between 10-30 s. Vehicle is in decel fuel shut off mode. Engine speed is between 950-1850 RPM. The difference between the Desired Fuel Rail Pressure and the Actual Fuel Rail Pressure is less than 2. 2 MPa (320 psi). No gear change has occurred. Lambda sensors are adapted. Vehicle is not in 4WD (if equipped). Exhaust brake is not ON (if equipped). No other DTCs are present. The DTC runs when the above conditions exists.
DTC: P12C2	**Cylinder 8 Injection Timing Advanced:** Ambient air temperature is above -5° C (23° F)Fuel temperature is between 0-80° C (32-176° F)Engine temperature is greater the 50° C (122° F)Battery voltages is greater than 10 V. Time since last combustion event is between 10-30 s. Vehicle is in decel fuel shut off mode. Engine speed is between 950-1850 RPM. The difference between the Desired Fuel Rail Pressure and the Actual Fuel Rail Pressure is less than 2. 2 MPa (320 psi)No gear change has occurred. Lambda sensors are adapted. Vehicle is not in 4WD (if equipped)Exhaust brake is not ON (if equipped)No other DTCs are present. The DTC runs when the above conditions exists
DTC: P135B	**Ignition Coil Supply Voltage Circuit Bank 2:** The ignition is ON. The ignition module supply voltage is less than 2. 5 V. The DTCs run continuously when the above condition is met.
DTC: P1392 00	**Left Rough Road Sensor Circuit Low Voltage:** DTC P0502 00 is not set. The vehicle speed is more than 5 km/h (3 MPH). The engine coolant temperature (ECT) is between 70-109°C (160-228°F). The ignition voltage is between 11-18 V. These DTCs run continuously when the above conditions are met.
DTC: P1393 00	**Left Rough Road Sensor Circuit High Voltage:** DTC P0502 00 is not set. The vehicle speed is more than 5 km/h (3 MPH). The engine coolant temperature (ECT) is between 70-109°C (160-228°F). The ignition voltage is between 11-18 V. These DTCs run continuously when the above conditions are met.

DTC	Trouble Code Title, Conditions, Possible Causes
DTC: P1400	**Cold Start Emission Reduction Control System:** The engine is running, and a cold start has been detected. The vehicle speed is less than 2 km/h (1 mph). The catalyst temperature is greater than 1,000°C (1,832°F). The coolant temperature is greater than 56°C (133°F). The engine run time is greater than 18 s. The engine is at idle with no input from the accelerator pedal for greater than 5 s. DTCs P0101, P0102, P0103, P0106, P0107, P0108, P0112, P0113, P0116, P0117, P0118, P0120, P0121, P0122, P0123, P0220, P0222, P0223, P0201, P0202, P0203, P0204, P0300, P0335, P0336, P0351, P0352, P0353, P0506, P0507, P0601, P0602, P0603, P0604, P0606, P0607, P062F, P0641, P0651, P1516, P1682, P2101, P2119, P2120, P2122, P2123, P2125, P2127, P2128, P2135, P2138, P2176, P2610 are not set. This DTC runs within 15 seconds within the first 2 minutes of start-up. This diagnostic runs once per trip when a cold start has been determined.
DTC: P1400	**Cold Start Injection Monitoring:** Engine is in Exhaust Warm-up mode. DTC runs continuously when the above condition exists.
DTC: P1400 00	**Cold Start Emission Reduction Control System:** DTCs P0101 00, P0102 00, P0103 00, P0106 00, P0107 00, P0108 00, P0112 00, P0113 00, P0114 00, P0116 00, P0117 00, P0118 00, P0121 00, P0122 00, P0123 00, P0222 00, P0223 00, P0201 00, P0202 00, P0203 00, P0204 00, P0300 00, P0301 00, P0302 00, P0303 00, P0304 00, P0335 00, P0336 00, P0351 00, P0352 00, P0353 00, P0354 00, P0502 00, P0503 00, P0506 00, P0507 00, P0641 00, P0651 00, P0697 00, P06A3 00, P0806 00, P0807 00, P080A 00, P2122 00, P2123 00, P2125 00, P2127 00, P2128 00, P2135 00, and P2138 00 are not set. The engine is idling less than 30 s. The Engine Coolant Temperature (ECT) sensor is greater than -10°C (14°F). The calculated three way catalyst temperature is less than 350°C (662°F). The ECM will exit the diagnostic if the calculated three way catalyst temperature is greater than 420°C (788°F) when the engine run time is greater than 30 s. The ECM will exit the diagnostic if the engine run time is greater than 90 s. The vehicle speed is less than 2 km/h (1 MPH). The engine is at idle with no input from the accelerator pedal. The clutch pedal position switch is less than 10% or greater than 80%, manual transmissions only. This DTC runs within the first 90 s of start up. This diagnostic runs once per trip when a cold start has been determined.
DTC: P1402 00	**Exhaust Gas Recirculation (EGR) Control Circuit Low Voltage:** The ignition is ON, or the engine is running. The DTCs run continuously when the above conditions are met.
DTC: P1407	**Exhaust Gas Recirculation (EGR) Motor Control Circuit Shorted:** P0489, P0490, P1407, P140D, P140E and P140FThe Ignition is ON. The battery voltage is greater than 11 V. The EGR control circuit is active. The starter is not cranking. The DTCs run continuously when the above conditions are met.
DTC: P1407 00	**Exhaust Gas Recirculation (EGR) Control Circuit Shorted:** The ignition is ON, or the engine is running. The DTCs run continuously when the above conditions are met.
DTC: P140B	**Exhaust Gas Recirculation (EGR) Flow Insufficient:** DTC P0045, P0047, P0048, P006E, P006F, P007C, P007D, P008F, P0101, P0102, P0103, P0106, P0107, P0108, P0112, P0113, P0117, P0118, P0128, P0200, P02E0, P02E7, P02E8, P02E9, P02EB, P0400, P0403, P0405, P0406, P0489, P0490, P122C, P122E, P122F, P140D, P140E, P140F, P1407, P1411, P1412, P1413, P1414, P168C, P168D, P16A0, P16A1, P16A2, P2228, P2229, P2263, P2453, P245A, P245C, P245D, P2493, P2494, P2495, P2564, P2565, P2598, or P2599, is not set. The engine speed is between 1,300-2,000 RPM. The calculated fuel rate is between 28-55 mm 3The ambient air temperature is greater than -7°C (19. 4°F). The engine coolant temperature is greater than 70°C (158°F)The Barometric Pressure is greater than 74. 8 kPa (10. 9 psi). The MAF rate is not in a steady state condition. The EGR valve is in closed loop and active. The DTCs run continuously when the above conditions are met.
DTC: P140C	**Exhaust Gas Recirculation (EGR) Flow Excessive:** DTC P0045, P0047, P0048, P006E, P006F, P007C, P007D, P008F, P0101, P0102, P0103, P0106, P0107, P0108, P0112, P0113, P0117, P0118, P0128, P0200, P02E0, P02E7, P02E8, P02E9, P02EB, P0400, P0403, P0405, P0406, P0489, P0490, P122C, P122E, P122F, P140D, P140E, P140F, P1407, P1411, P1412, P1413, P1414, P168C, P168D, P16A0, P16A1, P16A2, P2228, P2229, P2263, P2453, P245A, P245C, P245D, P2493, P2494, P2495, P2564, P2565, P2598, or P2599, is not set. The engine speed is between 1,300-2,000 RPM. The calculated fuel rate is between 28-55 mm 3The ambient air temperature is greater than -7°C (19. 4°F). The engine coolant temperature is greater than 70°C (158°F)The Barometric Pressure is greater than 74. 8 kPa (10. 9 psi). The MAF rate is not in a steady state condition. The EGR valve is in closed loop and active. The DTCs run continuously when the above conditions are met.
DTC: P140D	**Exhaust Gas Recirculation (EGR) Motor Control Circuit 2 Low Voltage:** P0489, P0490, P1407, P140D, P140E and P140FThe Ignition is ON. The battery voltage is greater than 11 V. The EGR control circuit is active. The starter is not cranking. The DTCs run continuously when the above conditions are met.
DTC: P140E	**Exhaust Gas Recirculation (EGR) Motor Control Circuit 2 High Voltage:** P0489, P0490, P1407, P140D, P140E and P140FThe Ignition is ON. The battery voltage is greater than 11 V. The EGR control circuit is active. The starter is not cranking. The DTCs run continuously when the above conditions are met.
DTC: P140F	**Exhaust Gas Recirculation (EGR) Motor Current Performance:** P0489, P0490, P1407, P140D, P140E and P140FThe Ignition is ON. The battery voltage is greater than 11 V. The EGR control circuit is active. The starter is not cranking. The DTCs run continuously when the above conditions are met.
DTC: P1446 00	**Pre-Catalyst Low Temperature During Regeneration Malfunction:** The DTC runs during the DPF regeneration process.

DTC	Trouble Code Title, Conditions, Possible Causes
DTC: P1447 00	**Pre-Catalyst High Temperature During Regeneration Malfunction:** The DTC runs during the DPF regeneration process.
DTC: P1448	**Diesel Particulate Filter Regeneration Frequency Too Low:** The engine is running. DTC P1448 runs continuously when the above condition is met.
DTC: P144B	**Closed Loop Diesel Particulate Filter (DPF) Regeneration Control At Limit - Stage 1 Temperature Too Low:** P144B or P144CThe engine run time is greater than 10 s. The engine speed is greater than 600 RPM. The ignition voltage is greater than 11 V. The ECM is commanding a DPF regeneration. The vehicle speed is between 0-200 km/h (0-124 mph). The exhaust temperature sensor 1 is between 100-650°C (212-1,200°F). The exhaust temperature sensor 1 and 4 is less than 650°C (1,200°F). The DTCs run continuously once the above conditions are met for 10 minutes.
DTC: P144C	**Closed Loop Diesel Particulate Filter (DPF) Regeneration Control At Limit - Stage 1 Temperature Too High:** P144B or P144CThe engine run time is greater than 10 s. The engine speed is greater than 600 RPM. The ignition voltage is greater than 11 V. The ECM is commanding a DPF regeneration. The vehicle speed is between 0-200 km/h (0-124 mph). The exhaust temperature sensor 1 is between 100-650°C (212-1,200°F). The exhaust temperature sensor 1 and 4 is less than 650°C (1,200°F). The DTCs run continuously once the above conditions are met for 10 minutes.
DTC: P144E	**Closed Loop Diesel Particulate Filter (DPF) Regeneration Control At Limit - Stage 2 Temperature Too Low:** P144E or P144FThe engine run time is greater than 10 s. The engine speed is greater than 600 RPM. The ignition voltage is greater than 11 V. The ECM is commanding a DPF regeneration. The vehicle speed is between 24-200 km/h (15-124 mph). The exhaust temperature sensor 1 and 4 is greater than 230°C (446°F). The exhaust temperature sensor 1 and 4 is less than 750°C (1,382°F). The DTCs run continuously once the above conditions are met for 10 minutes.
DTC: P144F	**Closed Loop Diesel Particulate Filter (DPF) Regeneration Control At Limit - Stage 2 Temperature Too High:** P144E or P144FThe engine run time is greater than 10 s. The engine speed is greater than 600 RPM. The ignition voltage is greater than 11 V. The ECM is commanding a DPF regeneration. The vehicle speed is between 24-200 km/h (15-124 mph). The exhaust temperature sensor 1 and 4 is greater than 230°C (446°F). The exhaust temperature sensor 1 and 4 is less than 750°C (1,382°F). The DTCs run continuously once the above conditions are met for 10 minutes.
DTC: P150A	**Transmission Output Speed Signal Circuit:** P150AThe TCM indicates the transmission output speed signal is valid. Transmission output speed is 1,200 RPM or greater.
DTC: P150B	**Transmission Output Speed Sensor Circuit Intermittent:** P150BThe ignition voltage is greater than 18 volts. The engine speed is greater than 500 RPM. The transmission output speed is greater than 1200 RPM.
DTC: P150C	**Transmission Control Module Engine Speed Request Signal Message Counter Incorrect:** The engine run time is greater than 5 seconds. No other CAN errors are present.
DTC: P150C	**Transmission Control Module Engine Speed Request Signal Message Counter Incorrect:** The ignition switch is in Unlock, Accessory, Run or Crank. The system voltage is more than 5. 23 V. DTCs P0601, P0602, P0603, P0604, P0606, P0607, P062F, P0641, P0651, P2610 and U0101 are not set.
DTC: P150C	**Transmission Control Module Engine Speed Request Signal Message Counter Incorrect:** The engine is running. No other CAN errors are present.
DTC: P1516	**Throttle Actuator Control (TAC) Module Throttle Actuator Position Performance:** P1516 and P2101 DTC P0606 and P1682 is not set. The run/crank or powertrain relay voltage is greater than 6 V and reduced power is not active. The engine is running or the following conditions are met: The engine is not running. The ignition voltage is greater than 11 V. The TAC system is not in the Battery Saver mode. The ECM is commanding the throttle. The ECM has learned the minimum throttle position. DTC P1516 and P2101 run continuously when the above conditions are met.
DTC: P1516 00	**Throttle Actuator Control (TAC) Module Throttle Actuator Position Performance:** P1516 00 or P2101 00The ignition is ON or the engine is operating. The ignition voltage is greater than 7 V. The system is not in battery safe mode. DTC P0068 00 is not set. DTCs P1516 00 and P2101 00 run continuously once the above conditions are met for greater than 5 s.
DTC: P1516 00	**Throttle Actuator Control (TAC) Module Throttle Actuator Position Performance:** P1516 00The engine is running. The throttle angle does not change greater than 2%. DTC P1516 00 runs continuously when the above conditions are met.
DTC: P1516 00	**Throttle Actuator Control (TAC) Module Throttle Actuator Position Performance:** P1516 00 or P2101 00 DTC P1682 00 is not set. The engine is running. The ECM has learned the minimum throttle position. The ignition voltage is greater than 6 volts and reduced power is not active. DTCs P1516 00 and P2101 00 run continuously when the above conditions are met.
DTC: P154A	**Intake Air (IA) Heater Feedback Circuit:** Engine speed is greater than 600 RPM. The intake air heater is commanded ON. The battery voltage is more than 8. 6 V. DTCs P154A runs continuously when the above conditions exists.

DTC	Trouble Code Title, Conditions, Possible Causes
DTC: P154B	**Intake Air (IA) Heater Voltage Signal Circuit:** The intake air heater is commanded ON. The glow plug control module battery voltage is between 9. 5-15 V. DTC P154B runs continuously when the above condition is met.
DTC: P154C	**Intake Air (IA) Heater Current Signal Circuit:** The intake air heater is commanded ON. The intake air heater battery voltage is more than 6. 9 V. Glow plug control module ignition voltage is more than 6. 9 V. DTC P154C runs continuously when the above conditions are met.
DTC: P154D	**Intake Air (IA) Heater Temperature Signal Circuit:** The intake air heater is commanded ON. The intake air heater battery voltage is between 6. 9-16 V. DTC P154D runs continuously when the above conditions are met.
DTC: P1551	**Throttle Valve Rest Position Not Reached During Learn:** The vehicle speed is 0 km/h (0 mph). The engine speed is 0 RPM. The engine coolant temperature (ECT) is between 5-100°C (41-212°F). The intake air temperature (IAT) is between 5-144°C (41-291°F). The ignition voltage is greater than 10 volts. The accelerator pedal position (APP) is less than 15 percent. DTC P1551 runs when the conditions above have been met for greater than 5 seconds.
DTC: P159F	**Fuel Economy Mode Switch Circuit Low Voltage:** Ignition key must be turned to ON. DTCs P159F and P15A0 run continuously when the above condition is met.
DTC: P15A0	**Fuel Economy Mode Switch Circuit High Voltage:** Ignition key must be turned to ON. DTCs P159F and P15A0 run continuously when the above condition is met.
DTC: P15A1	**Fuel Economy Mode Switch Performance:** The ignition key is turned to ON. DTC P15A1 runs continuously when the above condition is met.
DTC: P160C	**Engine Calibration Information Not Programmed - GPCM:** The ignition is ON.
DTC: P161A	**Glow Plug Control Module Not Programmed:** DTC P161A runs continuously when the ignition is ON.
DTC: P161C 00	**Tire Size Not Programmed Malfunction:** The ignition is ON. The DTC runs continuously once the above condition is met.
DTC: P161E 00	**Glow Plug Control Module Control Circuit Malfunction:** The ignition is ON, or the engine is running. The ignition voltage is between 9-16 V. The DTC runs once per ignition cycle when the above conditions are met.
DTC: P161F 32	**Assembly Plant Mode Counter Not Programmed General Memory Malfunction:** The ignition is ON. The DTC runs continuously once the above condition is met.
DTC: P161F 36	**Assembly Plant Mode Counter Not Programmed EEPROM Performance/Malfunction:** The ignition is ON. The DTC runs continuously once the above condition is met.
DTC: P161F 44	**Assembly Plant Mode Counter Not Programmed Security Access Not Activated:** The ignition is ON. The DTC runs continuously once the above condition is met.
DTC: P1629	**Immobilizer Fuel Enable Signal Not Received:** Ignition is in the ACCESSORY or RUN position.
DTC: P162B	**Remote Vehicle Speed Limiting Signal Message Counter Incorrect:** The engine run time is greater than 5 seconds. A remote slow-down request is sent from OnStar
DTC: P1630 00	**Immobilizer Learn Mode Active Malfunction:** The ECM is in immobilizer learn mode.
DTC: P1631	**Immobilizer Fuel Enable Signal Not Correct:** Ignition is in the ACCESSORY or RUN position.
DTC: P1631	**Theft Deterrent Fuel Enable Signal Not Correct:** Ignition is in the ACCESSORY or RUN position.
DTC: P1632	**Immobilizer Fuel Disable Signal Received:** Ignition is in the RUN position.
DTC: P163A	**Control Module Fuel Pressure Regulator 1 Control System Circuitry Performance:** DTCs P0016, P0017, P0090, P0091, P0092, P00C8, P00C9, P00CA, P0112, P0113, P0116, P0117, P0118, P0128, P0192, P0193, P0335, P0336, P0340, P0341, P0365, P0366, P0627-P0629, P1682 are not set. The engine is running. The ignition voltage is greater than 11 V. The low side fuel pressure is greater than 275 kPa (40 psi). DTC P163A runs continuously when the conditions are met for greater than 500 mS.

DTC	Trouble Code Title, Conditions, Possible Causes
DTC: P163A	**Control Module Fuel Pressure Regulator 1 Control System Circuitry Performance:** The engine is running or cranking. The ignition voltage is between 8-18 V. DTC P163A runs continuously when the conditions are met for greater than 500 mS.
DTC: P163C	**Glow Plug Module Primary Circuit:** The ignition is ON. DTC P163C runs continuously.
DTC: P163D	**Glow Plug Control Module Secondary Circuit:** The ignition is ON. DTC P163D runs continuously.
DTC: P163E	**Glow Plug Control Module Over temperature:** The ignition is ON. DTC P163E runs continuously.
DTC: P1649	**Immobilizer Security Code Not Programmed:** The ECM is in learn mode.
DTC: P1668	**Generator L-Terminal Control Circuit:** The engine is running.
DTC: P166B	**Intake Air (IA) Heater Over Temperature:** The IAH is commanded ON. The engine is running for more than 40 seconds.
DTC: P166B	**Intake Air (IA) Heater Over Temperature:** The intake air heater is commanded ON. The engine is running for more than 40 seconds. Engine coolant temperature is less than 60°C (140°F).
DTC: P166C	**Intake Air (IA) Heater Resistance:** The IAH is commanded ON.
DTC: P1678	**Immobilizer System - Incorrect Engine Control Module (ECM) Identification:** Ignition is in the ACCESSORY or RUN position.
DTC: P167D	**Control Module Ignition Coil Internal Circuit:** P167DThe engine is operating. The ignition voltage is between 10-18 V. The engine speed is less than 6,000 RPM. DTC P167D runs continuously when the above conditions are met.
DTC: P1682	**Ignition 1 Switch Circuit 2:** P1682The powertrain relay is commanded on. Ignition 1 Signal voltage is greater than 5. 5 V. The DTC runs continuously when the above conditions are met.
DTC: P1682	**Ignition 1 Switch Circuit 2:** P1682The ignition is ON. The system voltage is greater than 6 V. The engine control module relay is commanded ON. DTC P1682 runs continuously when the above conditions are met.
DTC: P1682 00	**Ignition 1 Switch Circuit 2:** The ignition is ON. System voltage is more than 6 V. Powertrain relay is commanded ON. DTC P1682 00 runs continuously when the above conditions are met.
DTC: P1684	**Transmission Control Module (TCM) Power Up Temperature Sensor Performance:** P1684 - Fail Case 1 and 2No TFT DTCs P0711, P0712, or P0713. No ISS DTCs P0716 or P0717. No OSS DTCs P0722 or P0723. DTC P1684 has not passed this key ON. The engine speed is 500 RPM or greater for 5 seconds. The ignition voltage is between 8. 6 volts and 19. 0 volts. The TCM power up temperature is between -39 and +149°C (-38 and +300°F). P1684 - Fail Case 3The engine speed is 500 RPM or greater for 5 seconds. The ignition voltage is between 8. 6 volts and 19. 0 volts.
DTC: P1685	**Transmission Control Module (TCM) Power Up Temperature Sensor Circuit Low Voltage:** P1685No ISS DTCs P0716 or P0717. No OSS DTCs P0722 or P0723. The transmission output shaft speed is 200 RPM or greater for 200 seconds or more. The torque converter clutch (TCC) slip speed is 120 RPM or greater for 200 seconds or more. DTC P1686 has not failed this ignition cycle. The engine speed is 500 RPM or greater for 5 seconds. The ignition voltage is between 8. 6 volts and 19. 0 volts.
DTC: P1686	**Transmission Control Module (TCM) Power Up Temperature Sensor Circuit High Voltage:** P1686The engine speed is 500 RPM or greater for 5 seconds. The ignition voltage is between 8. 6 volts and 19. 0 volts. DTC P1686 has not failed this ignition cycle.
DTC: P168C	**Turbocharger Boost Control Position Slow Response - Increasing Position:** DTC P0045, P0047, P0048, P006E, P007C, P007D, P008F, P0117, P0118, P02E8, P02E9, P0401, P0402, P128E, P140B, P140C, P16A0, P16A1, P16A2, P2228, or P2229 is not set. The coolant temperature is greater than 70°C (158°F). The engine speed is between 1,000-1,800 RPM. The barometric pressure (BARO) is greater than 74. 8 kPa (10. 85 psi). The ambient air temperature is greater than -7°C (19. 4°F). The throttle position is less than 5 %. The turbocharger actuator position sensor offset learning is not active. The turbocharger vane cleaning/ wiping, procedure is not active. DTC P168C and P168D run continuously whenever the above conditions are met.

DTC	Trouble Code Title, Conditions, Possible Causes
DTC: P168D	**Turbocharger Boost Control Position Slow Response - Decreasing Position:** DTC P0045, P0047, P0048, P006E, P007C, P007D, P008F, P0117, P0118, P02E8, P02E9, P0401, P0402, P128E, P140B, P140C, P16A0, P16A1, P16A2, P2228, or P2229 is not set. The coolant temperature is greater than 70°C (158°F). The engine speed is between 1,000-1,800 RPM. The barometric pressure (BARO) is greater than 74. 8 kPa (10. 85 psi). The ambient air temperature is greater than -7°C (19. 4°F). The throttle position is less than 5 %. The turbocharger actuator position sensor offset learning is not active. The turbocharger vane cleaning/ wiping, procedure is not active. DTC P168C and P168D run continuously whenever the above conditions are met.
DTC: P16F3	**Control Module Redundant Memory Performance:** P0601, P0606, P062B, P0630, P16F3These DTCs run continuously when the ignition is ON.
DTC: P16F3	**Control Module Redundant Memory Performance:** P16F3 DTCs P0101, P0102, P0103, P0106, P0107, P0108 are not set. Engine speed is greater than 750 RPM. DTC P16F3 runs continuously when the above conditions have been met.
DTC: P16F3 00	**Control Module Redundant Memory Performance:** The ignition is in the unlock, accessory, run, or crank position. The system voltage is more than 5. 23 VDTCs P16F3 00 runs continuously when the above conditions are met.
DTC: P1750	**1-2 Shift Valve Performance:** No ISS DTCs P0716 or P0717. No OSS DTCs P0722 or P0723. The engine is running for 5 seconds or more. The vehicle speed is greater than 24 km/h (15 mph). The calc. throttle position is greater than 8 percent. The transmission fluid temperature (TFT) is 20°C (68°F) or more. The engine torque is greater than 50 N·m (37 lb ft). The time since the last gear change is 2 seconds.
DTC: P1751	**Shift Valve 1 Performance:** DTCs P0716, P0717, P0722, P0723, P0741, P0742, P1751, P2762, P2763, or P2764 are not set. The engine speed is 500 RPM or greater for 5 seconds or greater. The transmission fluid temperature (TFT) is 20-130°C (68-266°F). The calculated throttle position is between 8-90 percent. The engine torque is greater than 50 N·m (36 lb ft). No upshift or downshift in process. The attained gear slip is 70 RPM or greater.
DTC: P1751	**Shift Valve 1 Performance:** No ISS DTCs P0716 or P0717. No OSS DTCs P0722 or P0723. No TCC Performance DTCs P0741 or P0742. No TCC Electrical DTCs P2763, P2763, or P2764. DTC 1751 has not failed this ignition cycle. The engine run time is greater than 5 seconds. The ignition voltage is between 8. 6 volts and 19. 0 volts. The transmission fluid temperature (TFT) is 20-130°C (68-266°F). The calc. throttle position is 8 percent or greater. The engine torque is greater than 59 ft. lbs. (80 Nm). No upshift or downshift in process. The attained gear slip is equal to or greater than 100 RPM. The TCC is commanded OFF. Vehicle speed is greater than 16 km/h (20 mph). The TISS is equal to or greater than 1,100 RPM. Commanded gear is 2nd or greater. The gear ratio is between 0. 69-1. 97. Solenoid A is enabled.
DTC: P1761	**Up and Down Shift Switch Signal Circuit:** The engine speed is 400 RPM or greater for 5 seconds.
DTC: P1761	**Up and Down Shift Switch Signal Message Counter:** The TCM rolling counter diagnostic is enabled. The Tap Up and Tap Down message health is received from the BCM. The engine speed is 400 RPM or greater for 5 seconds.
DTC: P1762	**Transmission Mode Switch Signal Message:** The engine run time is greater than 5 seconds. No other CAN errors are present.
DTC: P1762	**Trans Mode Switch Signal Circuit:** The engine speed is greater than 500 RPM for 5 seconds. Ignition voltage is between 9. 0 volts and 19. 0 volts.
DTC: P1763	**Trans Mode Switch C circuit:** The engine speed is greater than 500 RPM for 5 seconds. Ignition voltage is between 9. 0 volts and 19. 0 volts.
DTC: P1793 71	**Vehicle Speed Sensor Performance Invalid Data:** The ignition is ON.
DTC: P1811	**Maximum Adapt and Long Shift:** The shift is adaptable. The 1-2, 2-3, or 3-4 shift adapt cell has reached the limit.
DTC: P1820	**Internal Mode Switch A Circuit Low Voltage:** P1820, P1822, P1823, P1825The engine is running for 5 seconds. The IMS indicates PARK for 1 second or greater. The engine torque is 50 N·m (37 lb ft) or greater. No engine torque malfunction.
DTC: P1822	**Internal Mode Switch B Circuit High Voltage:** P1820, P1822, P1823, P1825The engine is running for 5 seconds. The IMS indicates PARK for 1 second or greater. The engine torque is 50 N·m (37 lb ft) or greater. No engine torque malfunction.

DTC	Trouble Code Title, Conditions, Possible Causes
DTC: P1823	**Internal Mode Switch P Circuit Low Voltage:** P1820, P1822, P1823, P1825The engine is running for 5 seconds. The IMS indicates PARK for 1 second or greater. The engine torque is 50 N·m (37 lb ft) or greater. No engine torque malfunction.
DTC: P1825	**Internal Mode Switch - Invalid Range:** P1825 or P182EThe engine speed is 500 RPM or greater for 5 seconds. The ignition voltage is between 9. 0 volts and 18. 0 volts. Either the C1234 or CB26 pressure switch is pressurized. DTC P0101, P0102, P0103, P0121, P0122, P0123, P0722, P0723, or P182E is not set.
DTC: P1826	**Internal Mode Switch C Circuit High Voltage:** P1826No OSS DTC P0722 or P0723. DTC P1826 has not passed this key cycle. The engine is running for 5 seconds. The IMS indicates PARK for 1 second or greater. The engine torque is 50 N·m (37 lb ft) or greater. Vehicle speed is 16 km/h (10 mph) or greater. No engine torque malfunction.
DTC: P182A	**Internal Mode Switch A Circuit Low Voltage:** P182A, P182C or P182DThe ignition voltage is between 8 and 18 volts. The engine speed is between 500 and 6,500 RPMs for 5 seconds. The IMS indicates PARK for at least 1 second. No engine torque malfunction. The engine torque is between 37-1,100 ft. lbs. (50-1,492 Nm).
DTC: P182C	**Internal Mode Switch B Circuit High Voltage:** P182A, P182C or P182DThe ignition voltage is between 8 and 18 volts. The engine speed is between 500 and 6,500 RPMs for 5 seconds. The IMS indicates PARK for at least 1 second. No engine torque malfunction. The engine torque is between 37-1,100 ft. lbs. (50-1,492 Nm).
DTC: P182D	**Internal Mode Switch P Circuit Low Voltage:** P182A, P182C or P182DThe ignition voltage is between 8 and 18 volts. The engine speed is between 500 and 6,500 RPMs for 5 seconds. The IMS indicates PARK for at least 1 second. No engine torque malfunction. The engine torque is between 37-1,100 ft. lbs. (50-1,492 Nm).
DTC: P182E	**Internal Mode Switch - Invalid Range:** P182EDTC P0101, P0102, P0103, P0106, P0107, P0108, P0171, P0172, P0174, P0175, P0201, P0202, P0203, P0204, P0205, P0206, P0207, P0208, P0300, P0301, P0302, P0303, P0304, P0305, P0306, P0307, P0308, P0401, P042E, P0722, or P0723 is not set. The engine speed is 400 RPM or greater for 5 seconds. The ignition voltage is 8. 6 volts or greater. The engine torque signal is valid.
DTC: P182F	**Internal Mode Switch C Circuit High Voltage:** P182FNo output speed sensor (OSS) DTCs P0722 or P0723. No engine torque signal DTC P2637. Vehicle speed is greater than 16 km/h (10 mph). The engine torque is greater than 50 N·m (37 lb ft). The IMS indicates Park/Neutral for at least 1 second. DTC P1826 has not passed during the current ignition cycle. The gear ratio is within one of the following ranges:3. 33:1 to 3. 50:1 for first gear2. 16:1 to 2. 27:1 for second gear1. 56:1 to 1. 64:1 for third gear0. 98:1 to 1. 03:1 for fourth gear
DTC: P1831	**Pressure Control (PC)/Shift Lock Solenoid Control Circuit Low Voltage:** P1831The engine speed is greater than 500 RPM for 5 seconds. Ignition voltage is between 8. 6-19. 0 volts. High side driver 1 is enabled. DTC P1831 has not failed this ignition cycle
DTC: P1832	**Pressure Control (PC)/Shift Lock Solenoid Control Circuit High Voltage:** P1832 DTC P1832 has not failed this ignition cycle.
DTC: P1876	**Up and Down Shift Enable Switch Circuit Low Voltage:** The engine speed is 400 RPM or greater for 5 seconds. The ignition voltage is 9. 0 volts or greater. No DTCs P0815, P0816, P0826, P1761, P1825, P1876, P1877, P1915, or U0100.
DTC: P1876	**Up and Down Shift Enable Switch Circuit Low Voltage:** P1876To TR switch DTC P0705. No TAP system DTCs P0815, P0816, or P0826. No TFP DTCs P1810, P1816, or P1818. No DTC P1877. No Communication DTC U0100. The engine speed is greater than 500 RPM for 5 seconds. The ignition is ON.
DTC: P1877	**Up and Down Shift Enable Switch Circuit High Voltage:** P1877To TR switch DTC P0705. No TAP system DTCs P0815, P0816, or P0826. No TFP DTCs P1810, P1816, or P1818. No DTC P1876. No Communication DTC U0100. The engine speed is greater than 500 RPM for 5 seconds. The ignition is ON.
DTC: P1915	**Internal Mode Switch Does Not Indicate Park/Neutral (P/N) During Start:** P1915The engine is cranking for more than 2. 5 seconds. The engine speed is greater than 500 RPM. 1st gear request for 7 minutes.
DTC: P1915	**Internal Mode Switch Does Not Indicate Park/Neutral During Start:** P1915 DTC P0722, P0723, or P1915 is not set. The transmission output shaft speed is 90 RPM or less. The ignition voltage is 6. 0 volts or greater.
DTC: P1915	**Internal Mode Switch Does Not Indicate Park/Neutral (P/N) During Start:** P1915 DTC P0722, P0723, or P1915 is not set. The transmission output shaft speed is less than 90 RPM or less. The ignition voltage is between 9. 0 volts and 18. 0 volts. The IMS does not indicate park or neutral.

OBD II Trouble Code List (P2xxx Codes)

DTC	Trouble Code Title, Conditions, Possible Causes
DTC: P2002	**Diesel Particulate Filter Efficiency:** DTCs P0101, P2228, P2229, P2453, P2454, and P2455 are not set. The engine speed is greater than 600 RPM. The ambient air temperature is greater than -7°C (19°F). The BARO is greater than 75 kPa (11 psi). The engine run time is greater than 10 s. A regeneration event must be complete. The DPF inlet and outlet temperatures are between 100-400°C (212-752°F). The time since last DPF regeneration is less than 20 minutes. The distance since last DPF regeneration is less than 48 km (30 mi). The Soot Mass is less than 44 grams. DTC P2002 runs once when the above conditions are met.
DTC: P2002 00	**Diesel Particulate Filter (DPF) Low Efficiency Malfunction:** The engine is running. The DTC runs continuously when the above condition is met.
DTC: P2008	**Intake Manifold Runner Control Valve Control Circuit:** Engine is running
DTC: P2008 00	**Intake Manifold Runner Control Valve Control Circuit:** The engine is operating. The ignition voltage is between 11-16 V. The DTCs run continuously once the above condition is met.
DTC: P2009	**Intake Manifold Runner Control Valve Control Circuit Low Voltage:** Engine is running
DTC: P200A	**Intake Manifold Runner Control Valve Control Circuit Performance:** Engine is running
DTC: P2010	**Intake Manifold Runner Control Valve Control Circuit High Voltage:** Engine is running
DTC: P2016	**Intake Manifold Runner Control Valve Feedback Circuit Low Voltage:** Engine is running
DTC: P2017	**Intake Manifold Runner Control Valve Feedback Circuit High Voltage:** Engine is running
DTC: P202E	**Reductant Injector Performance:** P202EDTCs P1048, P1049, P2047, P2048, or P2049 are not set. SCR reductant level not in restriction or empty level state. The engine speed is greater than 600 RPM. The battery voltage is greater than 11 V. The ambient air and emission reduction fluid tank temperatures are warmer than -7°C (19°F). The engine run time is greater than 10 s. The calculated reductant injector temperature is between -7 to +100°C (19-212°F). The reductant pressure is between 350-650 kPa (51-94 psi). The BARO pressure is between 75-130 kPa (11-19 psi). The DTC runs continuously once the above conditions are met.
DTC: P2031 03	**Exhaust Gas Temperature Sensor 2 Circuit Low Voltage:** The ignition is ON. The DTCs run continuously when the above condition is met.
DTC: P2031 07	**Exhaust Gas Temperature Sensor 2 Circuit High Voltage:** The ignition is ON. The DTCs run continuously when the above condition is met.
DTC: P2032	**Exhaust Gas Temperature Sensor 2 Circuit Low Voltage:** The ignition is ON or the engine is running. The DTCs run continuously when the above conditions are met.
DTC: P2032 00	**Exhaust Gas Temperature Sensor 2 Circuit Low Voltage:** The ignition is ON. The DTCs run continuously when the above condition is met.
DTC: P2033	**Exhaust Gas Temperature Sensor 2 Circuit High Voltage:** The ignition is ON or the engine is running. The DTCs run continuously when the above conditions are met.
DTC: P2033 00	**Exhaust Gas Temperature Sensor 2 Circuit High Voltage:** The ignition is ON. The DTCs run continuously when the above condition is met.
DTC: P203B	**Reductant Level Sensor Performance:** The engine speed is greater than 600 RPM. The battery voltage is greater than 11 V. The ambient air and emission reduction fluid tank temperatures are warmer than -7°C (19°F) - DTC P203B only. The engine run time is greater than 10 s. The DTCs run continuously once the above conditions are met.
DTC: P203C	**Reductant Level Sensor 1 Circuit Low Voltage:** The engine speed is greater than 600 RPM. The battery voltage is greater than 11 V. The ambient air and emission reduction fluid tank temperatures are warmer than -7°C (19°F) - DTC P203B only. The engine run time is greater than 10 s. The DTCs run continuously once the above conditions are met.
DTC: P203D	**Reductant Level Sensor 1 Circuit High Voltage:** The engine speed is greater than 600 RPM. The battery voltage is greater than 11 V. The ambient air and emission reduction fluid tank temperatures are warmer than -7°C (19°F) - DTC P203B only. The engine run time is greater than 10 s. The DTCs run continuously once the above conditions are met.

DTC	Trouble Code Title, Conditions, Possible Causes
DTC: P2047	**Reductant Injector Control Circuit:** The engine is running. The battery voltage is greater than 11 V. The ECM is commanding the reductant injector duty cycle greater than 0 %. The Reductant Injection Inhibit Reason displays None. The DTCs run continuously once the above conditions are met.
DTC: P2048	**Reductant Injector Control Circuit Low Voltage:** The engine is running. The battery voltage is greater than 11 V. The ECM is commanding the reductant injector duty cycle greater than 0 %. The Reductant Injection Inhibit Reason displays None. The DTCs run continuously once the above conditions are met.
DTC: P2049	**Reductant Injector Control Circuit High Voltage:** The engine is running. The battery voltage is greater than 11 V. The ECM is commanding the reductant injector duty cycle greater than 0 %. The Reductant Injection Inhibit Reason displays None. The DTCs run continuously once the above conditions are met.
DTC: P204B	**Reductant Pressure Sensor Performance:** DTCs P204C or P204D are not set. The ignition is ON. The BARO pressure is greater than 75 kPa (11 psi). The ambient air temperatures is warmer than -7°C (+19°F). The exhaust temperature sensor 2 is less than 170°C (338° F). The DTC runs continuously when the above conditions are met.
DTC: P204C	**Reductant Pressure Sensor Circuit Low Voltage:** The engine speed is greater than 600 RPM. The battery voltage is greater than 11 V. The DTCs run continuously when the above condition is met.
DTC: P204D	**Reductant Pressure Sensor Circuit High Voltage:** The engine speed is greater than 600 RPM. The battery voltage is greater than 11 V. The DTCs run continuously when the above condition is met.
DTC: P204F	**Reductant System Performance:** DTCs P204B, P204C, P204D, P208A, P208D, P20A0, P20A2, or P20A3, are not set. The engine speed is greater than 600 RPM. The battery voltage is greater than 11 V. The engine run time is greater than 10 s. The DTC runs continuously once the above conditions are met.
DTC: P205D	**Reductant Tank Temperature Sensor Performance:** DTC P205D is not set. - for P205B only. The ignition is OFF for 8 hours. The ECM monitors the ECT, EGT 2, and EGT 4 for the coldest and warmest of the three sensors. The difference between the coldest and warmest should be less than 7°C (45°F). The engine speed is greater than 600 RPM. The battery voltage is greater than 11 V. The DTCs run once per drive cycle when the above conditions are met for greater than 20 s.
DTC: P205C	**Reductant Tank Temperature Sensor Circuit Low Voltage:** DTC P205D is not set. - for P205B only. The ignition is OFF for 8 hours. The ECM monitors the ECT, EGT 2, and EGT 4 for the coldest and warmest of the three sensors. The difference between the coldest and warmest should be less than 7°C (45°F). The engine speed is greater than 600 RPM. The battery voltage is greater than 11 V. The DTCs run once per drive cycle when the above conditions are met for greater than 20 s.
DTC: P205D	**Reductant Tank Temperature Sensor Circuit High Voltage:** DTC P205D is not set. - for P205B only. The ignition is OFF for 8 hours. The ECM monitors the ECT, EGT 2, and EGT 4 for the coldest and warmest of the three sensors. The difference between the coldest and warmest should be less than 7°C (45°F). The engine speed is greater than 600 RPM. The battery voltage is greater than 11 V. The DTCs run once per drive cycle when the above conditions are met for greater than 20 s.
DTC: P2066	**Fuel Level Sensor 2 Performance:** The engine is running. The system voltage is between 11-16 V.
DTC: P2067	**Fuel Level Sensor 2 Circuit Low Voltage:** The engine is running. The system voltage is between 11-16 V.
DTC: P2068	**Fuel Level Sensor 2 Circuit High Voltage:** The engine is running. The system voltage is between 11-16 V.
DTC: P2070 00	**Intake Manifold Tuning Control Valve Stuck Open:** The ignition is ON or the engine is operating. The intake manifold tuning valve solenoid has been commanded ON and OFF at least once during the ignition cycle. These DTCs run continuously once the above condition is met.
DTC: P2071 00	**Intake Manifold Tuning Control Valve Stuck Closed:** The ignition is ON or the engine is operating. The intake manifold tuning valve solenoid has been commanded ON and OFF at least once during the ignition cycle. These DTCs run continuously once the above condition is met.
DTC: P2076 00	**Intake Manifold Tuning Control Valve Position Sensor Performance:** The ignition is ON or the engine is operating. The intake manifold tuning valve solenoid has been commanded ON and OFF at least once during the ignition cycle. These DTCs run continuously once the above condition is met.

DTC	Trouble Code Title, Conditions, Possible Causes
DTC: P2077 00	**Intake Manifold Tuning Control Valve Position Sensor Circuit Low Voltage:** The ignition is ON or the engine is operating. The intake manifold tuning valve solenoid has been commanded ON and OFF at least once during the ignition cycle. These DTCs run continuously once the above condition is met.
DTC: P2078 00	**Intake Manifold Tuning Control Valve Position Sensor Circuit High Voltage:** The ignition is ON or the engine is operating. The intake manifold tuning valve solenoid has been commanded ON and OFF at least once during the ignition cycle. These DTCs run continuously once the above condition is met.
DTC: P207F	**Incorrect Reductant Composition:** The BARO pressure is greater than 75 kPa (11 psi). The ambient air and reductant temperatures are warmer than -7°C (19°F). The engine speed is between 1,000-3,000 RPM. The average SCR temperature is between 240-290°C (464-554°F). The emission reduction fluid tank level is not empty. The battery voltage is greater than 11 V. The engine run time is greater than 10 s. The DTCs run once per drive cycle when the above conditions are met.
DTC: P2080	**Exhaust Gas Temperature Sensor 1 Performance:** P2080 DTC P007C, P007D, P0097, P0098, P0101, P0102, P0103, P0107, P0108, P0112, P0113, P0401, P0402, P0403, P0405, P0406, P046C, P0545, P0546, P111C, P111D, P20E2, P2032, P2033, P2228 or P2229 is not set. The engine is running for at least 327 s. The engine speed is between 700-3000 RPM for 60 s. The calculated fuel rate is between 5-80mm ; for 60 s. DPF regeneration or exhaust gas temperature monitoring has not been active in the last 25 minutes. Exhaust gas temperature sensor 1 has changed less than 7°C (12. 6°F) in 5 s. The DTC runs continuously when the above conditions are met.
DTC: P2080 08	**Exhaust Gas Temperature Sensor 1 Performance Signal Invalid:** The ignition is ON, or the engine is running. The DTCs run continuously when the above conditions are met.
DTC: P2080 13	**Exhaust Gas Temperature Sensor 1 Performance Low Voltage/High Temperature:** The ignition is ON, or the engine is running. The DTCs run continuously when the above conditions are met.
DTC: P2080 14	**Exhaust Gas Temperature Sensor 1 Performance High Voltage/Low Temperature:** The ignition is ON, or the engine is running. The DTCs run continuously when the above conditions are met.
DTC: P2081 00	**Exhaust Gas Temperature Sensor 1 Circuit Intermittent:** The ignition is ON. The DTCs run continuously when the above condition is met.
DTC: P2084	**Exhaust Gas Temperature Sensor 2 Performance:** P2084 DTC P007C, P007D, P0097, P0098, P0101, P0102, P0103, P0107, P0108, P0112, P0113, P0401, P0402, P0403, P0405, P0406, P046C, P0545, P0546, P111C, P111D, P20E2, P2032, P2033, P2228 or P2229 is not set. The engine is running for at least 327 s. The engine speed is between 700-3000 RPM for 60 s. The calculated fuel rate is between 5-80mm ; for 60 s. DPF regeneration or exhaust gas temperature monitoring has not been active in the last 25 minutes. Exhaust gas temperature sensor 2 has changed less than 7°C (12. 6°F) in 5 s. The DTC runs continuously when the above conditions are met.
DTC: P2084 08	**Exhaust Gas Temperature Sensor 2 Performance Signal Invalid:** The ignition is ON, or the engine is running. The DTCs run continuously when the above conditions are met.
DTC: P2084 13	**Exhaust Gas Temperature Sensor 2 Performance Low Voltage/High Temperature:** The ignition is ON, or the engine is running. The DTCs run continuously when the above conditions are met.
DTC: P2084 14	**Exhaust Gas Temperature Sensor 2 Performance High Voltage/Low Temperature:** The ignition is ON, or the engine is running. The DTCs run continuously when the above conditions are met.
DTC: P2085 00	**Exhaust Gas Temperature Sensor 2 Circuit Intermittent:** The ignition is ON. The DTCs run continuously when the above condition is met.
DTC: P2088	**Intake Camshaft Position Actuator Solenoid Control Circuit Low Voltage:** The engine speed is greater than 80 RPM. The ignition voltage is between 10-18 volts. The ECM has commanded the CMP actuator solenoid ON and OFF at least once during the ignition cycle. DTCs P0010, P0013, P2088, P2089, P2090, and P2091 run continuously once the above conditions are met.
DTC: P2088 00	**Intake Camshaft Position Actuator Solenoid Valve Control Circuit Low Voltage:** The engine speed is greater than 80 RPM. DTC P0606 00 is not set. The ignition voltage is between 10-18 V. The ECM has commanded the camshaft position actuator intake or camshaft position actuator exhaust solenoid ON and OFF at least once during the ignition cycle. DTCs P0010 00, P0013 00, P2088 00, P0289 00, P2090 00, and P2091 00 run continuously once the above conditions are met for greater than 1 s.
DTC: P2089	**Intake Camshaft Position Actuator Solenoid Control Circuit High Voltage:** The engine speed is greater than 80 RPM. The ignition voltage is between 10-18 volts. The ECM has commanded the CMP actuator solenoid ON and OFF at least once during the ignition cycle. DTCs P0010, P0013, P2088, P2089, P2090, and P2091 run continuously once the above conditions are met.

DTC	Trouble Code Title, Conditions, Possible Causes
DTC: P2089 00	**Intake Camshaft Position Actuator Solenoid Valve Control Circuit High Voltage:** The engine speed is greater than 80 RPM. DTC P0606 00 is not set. The ignition voltage is between 10-18 V. The ECM has commanded the camshaft position actuator intake or camshaft position actuator exhaust solenoid ON and OFF at least once during the ignition cycle. DTCs P0010 00, P0013 00, P2088 00, P0289 00, P2090 00, and P2091 00 run continuously once the above conditions are met for greater than 1 s.
DTC: P208A	**Reductant Pump Control Circuit:** DTCs P204F, P20A1, or P2510 are not set. The battery voltage is greater than 11 V. The engine speed is greater than 600 RPM. The engine run time is greater than 10 s. The DTCs run continuously once the above conditions are met.
DTC: P208B	**Reductant Pump Performance:** The engine speed is greater than 600 RPM. The engine run time is greater than 10 s. The reductant remaining defrost time is less than 120 s. The reductant motor operating for greater than 2 s. The BARO is greater than 75 kPa (11 psi). The emission reduction fluid tank is not empty. The ambient air and the emission reduction fluid tank is warmer than -7°C (19°F). The DTC runs continuously once the above conditions are met.
DTC: P208D	**Reductant Pump Control Circuit High Voltage:** DTCs P204F, P20A1, or P2510 are not set. The battery voltage is greater than 11 V. The engine speed is greater than 600 RPM. The engine run time is greater than 10 s. The DTCs run continuously once the above conditions are met.
DTC: P2090	**Exhaust Camshaft Position Actuator Solenoid Control Circuit Low Voltage:** The engine speed is greater than 80 RPM. The ignition voltage is between 10-18 volts. The ECM has commanded the CMP actuator solenoid ON and OFF at least once during the ignition cycle. DTCs P0010, P0013, P2088, P2089, P2090, and P2091 run continuously once the above conditions are met.
DTC: P2090 00	**Exhaust Camshaft Position Actuator Solenoid Valve Control Circuit Low Voltage:** The engine speed is greater than 80 RPM. DTC P0606 00 is not set. The ignition voltage is between 10-18 V. The ECM has commanded the camshaft position actuator intake or camshaft position actuator exhaust solenoid ON and OFF at least once during the ignition cycle. DTCs P0010 00, P0013 00, P2088 00, P0289 00, P2090 00, and P2091 00 run continuously once the above conditions are met for greater than 1 s.
DTC: P2091	**Exhaust Camshaft Position Actuator Solenoid Control Circuit High Voltage:** The engine speed is greater than 80 RPM. The ignition voltage is between 10-18 volts. The ECM has commanded the CMP actuator solenoid ON and OFF at least once during the ignition cycle. DTCs P0010, P0013, P2088, P2089, P2090, and P2091 run continuously once the above conditions are met.
DTC: P2091 00	**Exhaust Camshaft Position Actuator Solenoid Valve Control Circuit High Voltage:** The engine speed is greater than 80 RPM. DTC P0606 00 is not set. The ignition voltage is between 10-18 V. The ECM has commanded the camshaft position actuator intake or camshaft position actuator exhaust solenoid ON and OFF at least once during the ignition cycle. DTCs P0010 00, P0013 00, P2088 00, P0289 00, P2090 00, and P2091 00 run continuously once the above conditions are met for greater than 1 s.
DTC: P2096	**Post Catalyst Fuel Trim System Low Limit Bank 1:** Before the ECM can report DTC P2096 or P2098 failed, DTCs P0030, P0031, P0032, P0036, P0037, P0038, P0050, P0051, P0052, P0056, P0057, P0058, P013A, P013C, P013E, P0130, P0131, P0132, P0133, P0135, P0137, P0138, P014A, P014U, P0141, P0150, P0151, P0152, P0153, P0155, P0157, P0158, P0160, P0161, P2232, P2235, P2270, P2271, P2272, and P2273 must run and pass. DTC P0100, P0101, P0102, P0103, P0420, P0430, P0442, P0443, P0455, P0458, P0459, P2177, P2178, P2179, P2180, P2187, P2188, P2189 or P2190 is not set. The engine speed is 1,280-3,480 RPM. The engine load is 17-65 percent and steady. The closed loop fuel control is active for greater than 1 second. The calculated exhaust gas temperature is greater than 250°C (482°F). DTC P2096 and P2098 run continuously when the conditions above have been met for greater than 130 seconds.
DTC: P2096 00	**Post Catalyst Fuel Trim System Low Limit Bank 1:** The engine is running. The ignition voltage is greater than 10 V. The barometric pressure is greater than 72 kPa (10.44 PSI). The intake air temperature (IAT) sensor parameter is less than -40°C (-40°F).
DTC: P2096 00	**Post Catalyst Fuel Trim System Low Limit:** P2096 00 DTCs P000A 00, P000B 00, P0010 00, P0011 00, P0013 00, P0016 00, P0017 00, P0030 00, P0031 00, P0032 00, P0106 00, P0107 00, P0108 00, P0117 00, P0118 00, P0119 00, P0121 00, P0122 00, P0123 00, P0131 00, P0132 00, P0133 00, P0137 00, P0138 00, P0139 00, P0140 00, P0141 00, P0171 00, P0172 00, P0201 00, P0202 00, P0203 00, P0204 00, P0221 00, P0222 00, P0223 00, P0261 00, P0262 00, P0264 00, P0265 00, P0267 00, P0268 00, P0270 00, P0271 00, P0300 00, P0301 00, P0302 00, P0303 00, P0304 00, P0313 00, P0335 00, P0336 00, P0340 00, P0341 00, P0365 00, P0366 00, P0420 00, P0443 00, P0458 00, P0459 00, P1106 00, P2088 00, P2089 00, P2090 00, P2091 00, P2100 00, P2101 00, P2176 00, P2270 00, P2271 00, P2297 00, P2300 00, P2301 00, P2303 00, P2304 00, P2306 00, P2307 00, P2309 00, P2310 00, P2A00 00, P2A01 00 are not set. The ignition is ON. The evaporative emission (EVAP) system is not purging. The post catalyst fuel trim is enabled. These DTCs run continuously when the above conditions have been met.

DTC	Trouble Code Title, Conditions, Possible Causes
DTC: P2097	**Post Catalyst Fuel Trim System High Limit Bank 1:** Before the ECM can report DTC P2097 or P2099 failed, DTCs P0030, P0031, P0032, P0036, P0037, P0038, P0050, P0051, P0052, P0056, P0057, P0058, P013A, P013C, P013E, P0130, P0131, P0132, P0133, P0135, P0137, P0138, P014A, P0140, P0141, P0150, P0151, P0152, P0153, P0155, P0157, P0158, P0160, P0161, P2232, P2235, P2270, P2271, P2272, and P2273 must run and pass. DTC P0100, P0101, P0102, P0103, P0420, P0430, P0442, P0443, P0455, P0458, P0459, P2177, P2178, P2179, P2180, P2187, P2188, P2189 or P2190 is not set. The engine speed is 1,280-3,480 RPM. The engine load is 17-65 percent and steady. The closed loop fuel control is active for greater than 1 second. The calculated exhaust gas temperature is greater than 250°C (482°F). DTC P2097 and P2099 run continuously when the conditions above have been met for greater than 130 seconds.
DTC: P2097	**Post Catalyst Fuel Trim System High Limit Bank 1:** P2097 DTCs P0030, P0031, P0032, P0053, P0130, P0131, P0132, P0133, P0135, P0137, P0138, P0140, P2231, P2232, P2243, P2251, P2270, P2271, P2297, P2626 are not set. The engine speed is between 1,200-2,900 RPM. The engine load is between 16-21 percent. The engine is in Closed Loop for 3 seconds. The DTC runs continuously when the above conditions have been met for 1 second.
DTC: P2097 00	**Post Catalyst Fuel Trim System High Limit Bank 1:** The engine is running. The ignition voltage is greater than 10 V. The barometric pressure is greater than 72 kPa (10. 44 PSI). The intake air temperature (IAT) sensor parameter is less than -40°C (-40°F).
DTC: P2097 00	**Post Catalyst Fuel Trim System High Limit:** P2097 00 DTCs P000A 00, P000B 00, P0010 00, P0011 00, P0013 00, P0016 00, P0017 00, P0030 00, P0031 00, P0032 00, P0117 00, P0118 00, P0119 00, P0121 00, P0122 00, P0123 00, P0131 00, P0132 00, P0133 00, P0137 00, P0138 00, P0139 00, P0140 00, P0141 00, P0171 00, P0172 00, P0201 00, P0202 00, P0203 00, P0204 00, P0221 00, P0222 00, P0223 00, P0261 00, P0262 00, P0264 00, P0265 00, P0267 00, P0268 00, P0270 00, P0271 00, P0300 00, P0301 00, P0302 00, P0303 00, P0304 00, P0313 00, P0335 00, P0336 00, P0340 00, P0341 00, P0365 00, P0366 00, P0420 00, P0443 00, P0458 00, P0459 00, P2088 00, P2089 00, P2090 00, P2091 00, P2100 00, P2101 00, P2176 00, P2270 00, P2271 00, P2297 00, P2300 00, P2301 00, P2303 00, P2304 00, P2306 00, P2307 00, P2309 00, P2310 00, P2A00 00, P2A01 00 are not set. The ignition is ON. The evaporative emission (EVAP) system is not purging. The post catalyst fuel trim is enabled. This DTC P2097 00 runs continuously when the above conditions have been met.
DTC: P2098	**Post Catalyst Fuel Trim System Low Limit Bank 2:** Before the ECM can report DTC P2096 or P2098 failed, DTCs P0030, P0031, P0032, P0036, P0037, P0038, P0050, P0051, P0052, P0056, P0057, P0058, P013A, P013C, P013E, P0130, P0131, P0132, P0133, P0135, P0137, P0138, P014A, P0140, P0141, P0150, P0151, P0152, P0153, P0155, P0157, P0158, P0160, P0161, P2232, P2235, P2270, P2271, P2272, and P2273 must run and pass. DTC P0100, P0101, P0102, P0103, P0420, P0430, P0442, P0443, P0455, P0458, P0459, P2177, P2178, P2179, P2180, P2187, P2188, P2189 or P2190 is not set. The engine speed is 1,280-3,480 RPM. The engine load is 17-65 percent and steady. The closed loop fuel control is active for greater than 1 second. The calculated exhaust gas temperature is greater than 250°C (482°F). DTC P2096 and P2098 run continuously when the conditions above have been met for greater than 130 seconds.
DTC: P2099	**Post Catalyst Fuel Trim System High Limit Bank 2:** Before the ECM can report DTC P2097 or P2099 failed, DTCs P0030, P0031, P0032, P0036, P0037, P0038, P0050, P0051, P0052, P0056, P0057, P0058, P013A, P013C, P013E, P0130, P0131, P0132, P0133, P0135, P0137, P0138, P014A, P0140, P0141, P0150, P0151, P0152, P0153, P0155, P0157, P0158, P0160, P0161, P2232, P2235, P2270, P2271, P2272, and P2273 must run and pass. DTC P0100, P0101, P0102, P0103, P0420, P0430, P0442, P0443, P0455, P0458, P0459, P2177, P2178, P2179, P2180, P2187, P2188, P2189 or P2190 is not set. The engine speed is 1,280-3,480 RPM. The engine load is 17-65 percent and steady. The closed loop fuel control is active for greater than 1 second. The calculated exhaust gas temperature is greater than 250°C (482°F). DTC P2097 and P2099 run continuously when the conditions above have been met for greater than 130 seconds.
DTC: P20A0	**Reductant Purge Valve Control Circuit:** The battery voltage is greater than 11 V. The engine speed is greater than 600 RPM. The engine run time is greater than 10 s. The DTCs run continuously when the above conditions are met.
DTC: P20A1	**Reductant Purge Valve Performance:** DTCs P1045, P204C, P204D, P208A, P208D, P20A0, P20A2, or P20A3 are not set. The battery voltage is greater than 11 V. The engine speed is greater than 600 RPM. The engine run time is greater than 10 s. The initial reductant system pressure is greater than 350 kPa (51 psi). The ambient and DEF temperature is warmer than -7°C (19°F). The DTCs run continuously when the above conditions are met.
DTC: P20A2	**Reductant Purge Valve Control Circuit Low Voltage:** The battery voltage is greater than 11 V. The engine speed is greater than 600 RPM. The engine run time is greater than 10 s. The DTCs run continuously when the above conditions are met.
DTC: P20A3	**Reductant Purge Valve Control Circuit High Voltage:** The battery voltage is greater than 11 V. The engine speed is greater than 600 RPM. The engine run time is greater than 10 s. The DTCs run continuously when the above conditions are met.

DTC	Trouble Code Title, Conditions, Possible Causes
DTC: P20B9	**Reductant Heater 1 Control Circuit:** P20B9, P20BD, or P20C1 DTC P220B is not set. The DEF heater is commanded ON. The glow plug control module temperature is less than 123°C (254°F). The glow plug control module battery voltage is between 7-16 V. The DTCs run continuously once the above conditions are met.
DTC: P20BA	**Reductant Heater 1 Performance:** P20BADTC P205B, P205C, and P205D are not set. The emission reduction fluid tank heaters are active for 1,000-3,000 s. The emission reduction fluid tank level is greater than 20 %. The emission reduction fluid tank temperature is colder than -16°C (3°F) or hotter than 3003°C (5437°F). The vehicle speed is greater than 5 km/h (3 mph). The battery voltage is greater than 11 V. The engine speed is greater than 600 RPM.
DTC: P20BB	**Reductant Heater 1 Control Circuit Low Voltage:** P20BB, P20BF, or P20C3 DTC P220B is not set. The DEF heater is commanded ON. The glow plug control module temperature is less than 123°C (254°F). The glow plug control module battery voltage is between 7-16. 5 V. The DTCs run continuously once the above conditions are met.
DTC: P20BC	**Reductant Heater 1 Control Circuit High Voltage:** P20BC, P20C0, or P20C4The DEF heater is commanded OFF.
DTC: P20BD	**Reductant Heater 2 Control Circuit:** P20B9, P20BD, or P20C1 DTC P220B is not set. The DEF heater is commanded ON. The glow plug control module temperature is less than 123°C (254°F). The glow plug control module battery voltage is between 7-16 V. The DTCs run continuously once the above conditions are met.
DTC: P20BF	**Reductant Heater 2 Control Circuit Low Voltage:** P20BB, P20BF, or P20C3 DTC P220B is not set. The DEF heater is commanded ON. The glow plug control module temperature is less than 123°C (254°F). The glow plug control module battery voltage is between 7-16. 5 V. The DTCs run continuously once the above conditions are met.
DTC: P20C0	**Reductant Heater 2 Control Circuit High Voltage:** P20BC, P20C0, or P20C4The DEF heater is commanded OFF.
DTC: P20C1	**Reductant Heater 3 Control Circuit:** P20B9, P20BD, or P20C1 DTC P220B is not set. The DEF heater is commanded ON. The glow plug control module temperature is less than 123°C (254°F). The glow plug control module battery voltage is between 7-16 V. The DTCs run continuously once the above conditions are met.
DTC: P20C3	**Reductant Heater 3 Control Circuit Low Voltage:** P20BB, P20BF, or P20C3 DTC P220B is not set. The DEF heater is commanded ON. The glow plug control module temperature is less than 123°C (254°F). The glow plug control module battery voltage is between 7-16. 5 V. The DTCs run continuously once the above conditions are met.
DTC: P20C4	**Reductant Heater 3 Control Circuit High Voltage:** P20BC, P20C0, or P20C4The DEF heater is commanded OFF.
DTC: P20CB	**Exhaust Aftertreatment Fuel Injector Control Circuit:** Battery Voltage is greater than 11 V. Engine speed is greater than 600 RPM.
DTC: P20CC	**Exhaust Aftertreatment Fuel Injector Performance:** Engine speed is greater than 600 RPM. Exhaust temperature is greater than 300° C (572° F). Time since last completed regeneration is greater than 15 minutes. Time since last indirect fuel injector nozzle cleaning request is greater than 5 minutes.
DTC: P20CD	**Exhaust Aftertreatment Fuel Injector Control Circuit Low Voltage:** Battery Voltage is greater than 11 V. Engine speed is greater than 600 RPM.
DTC: P20CE	**Exhaust Aftertreatment Fuel Injector Control Circuit High Voltage:** Battery Voltage is greater than 11 V. Engine speed is greater than 600 RPM.
DTC: P20E2	**Exhaust Temperature Sensor 1-2 Correlation:** DTCs P0545, P0546, P2032, P2033 are not set. The engine has been OFF for greater than 5 hours. The engine is running. The ambient temperature is greater than 10°C (50°F). DTC P20E2 runs once per key cycle within the above enabling conditions.
DTC: P20E2	**Exhaust Gas Temperature Sensors 1-2 Not Plausible:** P20E2Condition 1 DTC P0016, P0112, P0113, P0335, P0336, P0340, P0341, P0545, P0546, P2032, or P2033 is not set. The ignition has been OFF for greater than 8 hours. The engine is running. The ambient air temperature is greater than -60°C (-76°F). OR Condition 2 DTC P0016, P0112, P0113, P0335, P0336, P0340, P0341, P0545, P0546, P2032, or P2033 is not set. The ignition has been OFF for greater than 8 hours. The engine is running. The ambient air temperature is greater than -60°C (-76°F). In the first 60 s of engine run time, the ECM determines that the engine block heater is OFF. DTC P02E0 runs once per key cycle when condition 1 or condition 2 above is met.

DTC	Trouble Code Title, Conditions, Possible Causes
DTC: P20EE	**NOx Catalyst Efficiency Below Threshold:** The BARO pressure is greater than 75 kPa (11 psi). The ambient air and reductant temperatures are warmer than -7°C (19°F). The engine speed is between 1,000-3,000 RPM. The average SCR temperature is between 240-290°C (464-554°F). The emission reduction fluid tank level is not empty. The battery voltage is greater than 11 V. The engine run time is greater than 10 s. The DTCs run once per drive cycle when the above conditions are met.
DTC: P2100	**Throttle Actuator Control (TAC) Motor Control Circuit:** P2100The ECM is active. DTC P2100 runs continuously once the above conditions are met.
DTC: P2100 00	**Throttle Actuator Control (TAC) Motor Control Circuit:** P2100 00The ignition is ON or the engine is operating. The ignition voltage is greater than 7 V. DTCs P210 001 run continuously once the above conditions are met for greater than 5 s.
DTC: P2101	**Throttle Actuator Position Performance:** P1516 and P2101 DTC P0606 and P1682 is not set. The run/crank or powertrain relay voltage is greater than 6 V and reduced power is not active. The engine is running or the following conditions are met: The engine is not running. The ignition voltage is greater than 11 V. The TAC system is not in the Battery Saver mode. The ECM is commanding the throttle. The ECM has learned the minimum throttle position. DTC P1516 and P2101 run continuously when the above conditions are met.
DTC: P2101 00	**Throttle Actuator Position Performance:** P1516 00 or P2101 00The ignition is ON or the engine is operating. The ignition voltage is greater than 7 V. The system is not in battery safe mode. DTC P0068 00 is not set. DTCs P1516 00 and P2101 00 run continuously once the above conditions are met for greater than 5 s.
DTC: P2101 00	**Throttle Actuator Position Performance:** P1516 00 or P2101 00 DTC P1682 00 is not set. The engine is running. The ECM has learned the minimum throttle position. The ignition voltage is greater than 6 volts and reduced power is not active. DTCs P1516 00 and P2101 00 run continuously when the above conditions are met.
DTC: P2101 00	**Throttle Actuator Position Performance:** P2101 00The engine is running. The ignition voltage is between 11-18 V. DTC P2101 00 runs continuously when the above conditions are met.
DTC: P2101 00	**Throttle Actuator Position Performance:** P2101 00, P2119 00, P2176 00The ignition is ON or the engine is operating. DTC P2101 00, P2119 00, and P2176 00 runs continuously once the above conditions are met.
DTC: P2104 00	**Throttle Actuator Control (TAC) System - Forced Engine Idle Speed:** The ignition is ON or the engine is running.
DTC: P2105	**Throttle Actuator Control (TAC) System - Forced Engine Shutdown:** The ECM power down process in the last drive cycle was completely finished. DTC P2105 runs continuously once the above condition is met.
DTC: P2105 00	**Throttle Actuator Control (TAC) System - Forced Engine Shutdown:** The ignition is ON or the engine is running.
DTC: P2106 00	**Throttle Actuator Control System - Throttle Limitation Active:** The ignition is ON or the engine is running.
DTC: P2108 00	**Throttle Actuator Position Performance:** P2108 00 DTCs P0111 00, P0112 00, P0113 00, P0117 00, P0118 00, P0119 00, P0700 00, P2122 00, P2123 00, P2127 00, P2128 00, or P2138 00 is not set. DTCs P0121 00, P0122 00, P0123 00, P0221 00, P0222 00, P0223 00, P2176 00 are not set. DTC P2176 00 run continuously when the above conditions are met.
DTC: P2110 00	**Throttle Actuator Control (TAC) System - Forced Limited Engine Speed:** The ignition is ON or the engine is running.
DTC: P2119	**Throttle Closed Position Performance:** P2119 DTC P0111, P0112, P0113, P0116, P0117, P0118, P0119, P0700, P2122, P2123, P2127, P2128, or P2138 is not set. The ignition is ON. The vehicle speed is 0 km/h (0 mph). The engine speed is less than 40 RPM. The engine coolant temperature (ECT) is 5-100°C (41-212°F). The intake air temperature (IAT) is 5-143°C (41-290°F). The ignition voltage is greater than 10 volts. The accelerator pedal position (APP) is less than 15 percent. DTC P2119 runs once per ignition cycle when the above conditions are met for less than 1 second.
DTC: P2119 00	**Throttle Closed Position Performance:** P2119 00 DTCs P0121 00, P0122 00, P0123 00, P0222 00, P0223 00, P0641 00, P0651 00, P0697 00, P06A3 00, or P2135 00 are not set. The ignition voltage is greater than 8 V. DTC P2119 00 runs when the ignition is turned to the OFF position, when the above conditions are met.

DTC	Trouble Code Title, Conditions, Possible Causes
DTC: P2120	**Accelerator Pedal Position (APP) Sensor 1 Circuit:** P2120, P2122, P2123, P2125, P2127, P2128 DTC P0641 and P0651 are not set. The ignition is ON or the engine is running. The run/crank or powertrain relay voltage is greater than 6. 0 V and reduced power is not active. DTC 2120, P2122, P2123, P2125, P2127, P2128 run continuously when the above conditions are met.
DTC: P2120 03	**Accelerator Pedal Position (APP) Sensor 1 Circuit Low Voltage:** The ignition is ON or the engine is operating. The DTCs run continuously once the above conditions are met.
DTC: P2120 07	**Accelerator Pedal Position (APP) Sensor 1 Circuit High Voltage:** The ignition is ON or the engine is operating. The DTCs run continuously once the above conditions are met.
DTC: P2122	**Accelerator Pedal Position (APP) Sensor 1 Circuit Low Voltage:** P2120, P2122, P2123, P2125, P2127, P2128 DTC P0641 and P0651 are not set. The ignition is ON or the engine is running. The run/crank or powertrain relay voltage is greater than 6. 0 V and reduced power is not active. DTC 2120, P2122, P2123, P2125, P2127, P2128 run continuously when the above conditions are met.
DTC: P2122 00	**Accelerator Pedal Position (APP) Sensor 1 Circuit Low Voltage:** P2122 00, P2123 00, P2127 00, P2128 00 DTC P06A3 00 or P0697 00 are not set. The ignition is ON or the engine is operating. The ignition voltage is greater than 6 V. The ECM is not commanding reduced power. The DTCs run continuously when the above conditions are met.
DTC: P2123	**Accelerator Pedal Position (APP) Sensor 1 Circuit High Voltage:** P2120, P2122, P2123, P2125, P2127, P2128 DTC P0641 and P0651 are not set. The ignition is ON or the engine is running. The run/crank or powertrain relay voltage is greater than 6. 0 V and reduced power is not active. DTC 2120, P2122, P2123, P2125, P2127, P2128 run continuously when the above conditions are met.
DTC: P2123 00	**Accelerator Pedal Position (APP) Sensor 1 Circuit High Voltage:** P2122 00, P2123 00, P2127 00, P2128 00 DTC P06A3 00 or P0697 00 are not set. The ignition is ON or the engine is operating. The ignition voltage is greater than 6 V. The ECM is not commanding reduced power. The DTCs run continuously when the above conditions are met.
DTC: P2125	**Accelerator Pedal Position (APP) Sensor 2 Circuit:** P2120, P2122, P2123, P2125, P2127, P2128 DTC P0641 and P0651 are not set. The ignition is ON or the engine is running. The run/crank or powertrain relay voltage is greater than 6. 0 V and reduced power is not active. DTC 2120, P2122, P2123, P2125, P2127, P2128 run continuously when the above conditions are met.
DTC: P2125 03	**Accelerator Pedal Position (APP) Sensor 2 Circuit Low Voltage:** The ignition is ON or the engine is operating. The DTCs run continuously once the above conditions are met.
DTC: P2125 07	**Accelerator Pedal Position (APP) Sensor 2 Circuit High Voltage:** The ignition is ON or the engine is operating. The DTCs run continuously once the above conditions are met.
DTC: P2127	**Accelerator Pedal Position (APP) Sensor 2 Circuit Low Voltage:** P2120, P2122, P2123, P2125, P2127, P2128 DTC P0641 and P0651 are not set. The ignition is ON or the engine is running. The run/crank or powertrain relay voltage is greater than 6. 0 V and reduced power is not active. DTC 2120, P2122, P2123, P2125, P2127, P2128 run continuously when the above conditions are met.
DTC: P2127 00	**Accelerator Pedal Position (APP) Sensor 2 Circuit Low Voltage:** P2122 00, P2123 00, P2127 00, P2128 00 DTC P06A3 00 or P0697 00 are not set. The ignition is ON or the engine is operating. The ignition voltage is greater than 6 V. The ECM is not commanding reduced power. The DTCs run continuously when the above conditions are met.
DTC: P2128	**Accelerator Pedal Position (APP) Sensor 2 Circuit High Voltage:** P2120, P2122, P2123, P2125, P2127, P2128 DTC P0641 and P0651 are not set. The ignition is ON or the engine is running. The run/crank or powertrain relay voltage is greater than 6. 0 V and reduced power is not active. DTC 2120, P2122, P2123, P2125, P2127, P2128 run continuously when the above conditions are met.
DTC: P2128 00	**Accelerator Pedal Position (APP) Sensor 2 Circuit High Voltage:** P2122 00, P2123 00, P2127 00, P2128 00 DTC P06A3 00 or P0697 00 are not set. The ignition is ON or the engine is operating. The ignition voltage is greater than 6 V. The ECM is not commanding reduced power. The DTCs run continuously when the above conditions are met.
DTC: P2135	**Throttle Position (TP) Sensor 1-2 Correlation:** P2135 DTC P0120, P0122, P0123, P0220, P0222, P0223, P0641, or P0651 are not set. The ignition is ON or the engine is running. The run/crank or powertrain relay voltage is greater than 6. 0 V and reduced power is not active. DTC P2135 runs continuously when the above conditions are met.

DTC	Trouble Code Title, Conditions, Possible Causes
DTC: P2135 00	**Throttle Position Sensors 1-2 Not Plausible:** DTC P0641 00 or P0651 00 are not set. The run/crank or powertrain relay voltage is greater than 6 V and reduced power is not active. The ignition is ON or the engine is operating. DTC P0122 00, P0123 00, P0222 00, P0223 00, and P2135 00 run continuously when the above conditions are met.
DTC: P2135 00	**Throttle Position Sensors 1-2 Not Plausible:** P2135 00 DTCs P0122 00, P0123 00, P0222 00, or P0223 00 are not set. The ignition is ON, or the engine is running. The engine is not operating in reduced power mode. The ignition voltage is greater than 6 V. The DTCs runs continuously when the above condition is met.
DTC: P2138	**Accelerator Pedal Position (APP) Sensor 1-2 Correlation:** P2138 DTC P0641, P0651, P2120, P2122, P2123, P2125, P2127, and P2128 are not set. The ignition is ON or the engine is running. The run/crank or powertrain relay voltage is greater than 6. 0 V and reduced power is not active. DTC P2138 runs continuously when the above conditions are met.
DTC: P2138	**Accelerator Pedal Position (APP) Sensor 1-2 Correlation:** P2138 DTC P0641, P0651, P2120, P2122, P2123, P2125, P2127, and P2128 are not set. The ignition is ON or the engine is running. The run/crank or powertrain relay voltage is greater than 6. 0 V and reduced power is not active. DTC P2138 runs continuously when the above conditions are met.
DTC: P2138 00	**Accelerator Pedal Position (APP) Sensors 1-2 Not Plausible:** P2138 00 DTCs P06A3 00, P0697 00, P2122 00, P2123 00, P2127 00, or P2128 00 are not set. The ignition is ON or the engine is operating. The ignition voltage is greater than 6 V. The ECM is not commanding reduced power. The DTC runs continuously when the above conditions are met.
DTC: P2138 5A	**Accelerator Pedal Position (APP) Sensor 1-2 Not Plausible:** The ignition is ON or the engine is operating. The DTCs run continuously once the above conditions are met.
DTC: P2146	**Cylinder 1 Injector High Control Circuit:** The engine speed is greater than 80 RPM. The ignition 1 signal parameter is between 10-18 V. The injector has been commanded ON and OFF at least once. The DTCs run continuously once the above conditions are met.
DTC: P2146	**Cylinder 1 Injector High Control Circuit:** The engine speed is greater than 80 RPM. The ignition 1 signal parameter is between 8-18. 1 V. The DTCs run continuously within the enabling conditions.
DTC: P2146 00	**Injector High Control Circuit Group 1 Malfunction:** The engine is running. The ECM monitors for a condition once per camshaft revolution.
DTC: P2147	**Cylinder 1 Injector High Control Circuit Low Voltage:** The engine is running. The ignition voltage is between 11-18 V. The DTCs run continuously when the above conditions are met.
DTC: P2147 00	**Injector High Control Circuit Group 1 Low Voltage:** The engine is running. The ECM monitors for a condition once per camshaft revolution.
DTC: P2148	**Cylinder 1 Injector High Control Circuit High Voltage:** The engine is running. The ignition voltage is between 11-18 V. The DTCs run continuously when the above conditions are met.
DTC: P2148 00	**Injector High Control Circuit Group 1 High Voltage:** The engine is running. The ECM monitors for a condition once per camshaft revolution.
DTC: P2149	**Cylinder 2 Injector High Control Circuit:** The engine speed is greater than 80 RPM. The ignition 1 signal parameter is between 10-18 V. The injector has been commanded ON and OFF at least once. The DTCs run continuously once the above conditions are met.
DTC: P2149 F0	**Injector High Control Circuit Group 2 Malfunction:** The engine is running. The ECM monitors for a condition once per camshaft revolution.
DTC: P2150	**Cylinder 2 Injector High Control Circuit Low Voltage:** The engine is running. The ignition voltage is between 11-18 V. The DTCs run continuously when the above conditions are met.
DTC: P2150 00	**Injector High Control Circuit Group 2 Low Voltage:** The engine is running. The ECM monitors for a condition once per camshaft revolution.
DTC: P2151	**Cylinder 2 Injector High Control Circuit High Voltage:** The engine is running. The ignition voltage is between 11-18 V. The DTCs run continuously when the above conditions are met.
DTC: P2151 00	**Injector High Control Circuit Group 2 High Voltage:** The engine is running. The ECM monitors for a condition once per camshaft revolution.

DTC	Trouble Code Title, Conditions, Possible Causes
DTC: P2152	**Cylinder 3 Injector High Control Circuit:** The engine speed is greater than 80 RPM. The ignition 1 signal parameter is between 10-18 V. The injector has been commanded ON and OFF at least once. The DTCs run continuously once the above conditions are met.
DTC: P2153	**Cylinder 3 Injector High Control Circuit Low Voltage:** The engine is running. The ignition voltage is between 11-18 V. The DTCs run continuously when the above conditions are met.
DTC: P2154	**Cylinder 3 Injector High Control Circuit High Voltage:** The engine is running. The ignition voltage is between 11-18 V. The DTCs run continuously when the above conditions are met.
DTC: P2155	**Cylinder 4 Injector High Control Circuit:** The engine speed is greater than 80 RPM. The ignition 1 signal parameter is between 10-18 V. The injector has been commanded ON and OFF at least once. The DTCs run continuously once the above conditions are met.
DTC: P2156	**Cylinder 4 Injector High Control Circuit Low Voltage:** The engine is running. The ignition voltage is between 11-18 V. The DTCs run continuously when the above conditions are met.
DTC: P2157	**Cylinder 4 Injector High Control Circuit High Voltage:** The engine is running. The ignition voltage is between 11-18 V. The DTCs run continuously when the above conditions are met.
DTC: P216A	**Cylinder 5 Injector High Control Circuit:** The engine speed is greater than 80 RPM. The ignition 1 signal parameter is between 10-18 V. The injector has been commanded ON and OFF at least once. The DTCs run continuously once the above conditions are met.
DTC: P216B	**Cylinder 5 Injector High Control Circuit Low Voltage:** The engine is running. The ignition voltage is between 11-18 V. The DTCs run continuously when the above conditions are met.
DTC: P216C	**Cylinder 5 Injector High Control Circuit High Voltage:** The engine is running. The ignition voltage is between 11-18 V. The DTCs run continuously when the above conditions are met.
DTC: P216D	**Cylinder 6 Injector High Control Circuit:** The engine speed is greater than 80 RPM. The ignition 1 signal parameter is between 10-18 V. The injector has been commanded ON and OFF at least once. The DTCs run continuously once the above conditions are met.
DTC: P216E	**Cylinder 6 Injector High Control Circuit Low Voltage:** The engine is running. The ignition voltage is between 11-18 V. The DTCs run continuously when the above conditions are met.
DTC: P216F	**Cylinder 6 Injector High Control Circuit High Voltage:** The engine is running. The ignition voltage is between 11-18 V. The DTCs run continuously when the above conditions are met.
DTC: P2176	**Minimum Throttle Position Not Learned:** The engine speed is less than 40 RPM. The vehicle speed is 0 km/h (0 mph). The engine coolant temperature (ECT) is between 5-101°C (41-214°F). The intake air temperature (IAT) is between 5-144°C (41-291°F). The accelerator pedal position (APP) sensor angle is less than 15 percent. The ignition voltage is greater than 10 volts. DTC P2176 runs once per ignition cycle, when the ignition is ON and the above conditions are met for greater than 1 second.
DTC: P2176 00	**Minimum Throttle Position Not Learned:** P2101 00, P2119 00, P2176 00The ignition is ON or the engine is operating. DTC P2101 00, P2119 00, and P2176 00 runs continuously once the above conditions are met.
DTC: P2176 00	**Minimum Throttle Position Not Learned:** P2176 00The ignition voltage is greater than 8 V. DTC P2176 00 runs once per ignition cycle when the above conditions are met.
DTC: P2177	**Fuel Trim System Lean at Cruise or Acceleration Bank 1:** P2177 or P2179Before the ECM can report DTC P2177 or P2179, failed, DTCs P000A, P000B, P000C, P000D, P0008, P0009, P0010, P0011, P0013, P0014, P0016, P0017, P0018, P0019, P0020, P0021, P0023, P0024, P0201, P0202, P0203, P0204, P0205, P0206, P0261, P0262, P0264, P0265, P0267, P0268, P0270, P0271, P0273, P0274, P0276, P0277, P0300, P0301, P0302, P0303, P0304, P0305, P0306, P0461, P0462, P0463, P2068 P2088, P2089, P2090, P2091, P2092, P2093, P2094, P2095 P2146, P2149, P2152, P2155, P216A, and P216D must run and pass. The engine speed is between 1,200-3,400 RPM. The engine load is between 13-50 %. The throttle angle is less than 100 %. The cold start fuel control is not active. The Closed Loop fuel control is enabled. The engine is not in decel fuel cut-off. The engine coolant temperature is warmer than 60°C (140°F). The intake air temperature (IAT) is colder than 60°C (140°F). DTC P2177 and P2179 run continuously once the above conditions are met for approximately 300 s, after Closed Loop fuel control is enabled.

DTC	Trouble Code Title, Conditions, Possible Causes
DTC: P2178	**Fuel Trim System Rich at Cruise or Acceleration Bank 1:** P2178 or P2180Before the ECM can report DTC P2178 or P2180, failed, DTCs P000A, P000B, P000C, P000D, P0008, P0009, P0010, P0011, P0013, P0014, P0016, P0017, P0018, P0019, P0020, P0021, P0023, P0024, P0201, P0202, P0203, P0204, P0205, P0206, P0221, P0222, P0223, P0261, P0262, P0264, P0265, P0267, P0268, P0270, P0271, P0273, P0274, P0276, P0277, P0300, P0301, P0302, P0303, P0304, P0305, P0306, P0461, P0462, P0463, P2068 P2088, P2089, P2090, P2091, P2092, P2093, P2094, P2095 P2146, P2149, P2152, P2155, P216A, and P216D must run and pass. The engine speed is between 1,200-3,400 RPM. The engine load is between 13-50 %. The throttle angle is less than 100 %. The cold start fuel control is not active. The Closed Loop fuel control is enabled. The engine is not in decel fuel cut-off. The engine coolant temperature is warmer than 60°C (140°F). The intake air temperature (IAT) is colder than 60°C (140°F). DTCs P2178 and P2180 run continuously when the above conditions are met for approximately 300 s, after Closed Loop fuel control is enabled.
DTC: P2179	**Fuel Trim System Lean at Cruise or Acceleration Bank 2:** P2177 or P2179Before the ECM can report DTC P2177 or P2179, failed, DTCs P000A, P000B, P000C, P000D, P0008, P0009, P0010, P0011, P0013, P0014, P0016, P0017, P0018, P0019, P0020, P0021, P0023, P0024, P0201, P0202, P0203, P0204, P0205, P0206, P0261, P0262, P0264, P0265, P0267, P0268, P0270, P0271, P0273, P0274, P0276, P0277, P0300, P0301, P0302, P0303, P0304, P0305, P0306, P0461, P0462, P0463, P2068 P2088, P2089, P2090, P2091, P2092, P2093, P2094, P2095 P2146, P2149, P2152, P2155, P216A, and P216D must run and pass. The engine speed is between 1,200-3,400 RPM. The engine load is between 13-50 %. The throttle angle is less than 100 %. The cold start fuel control is not active. The Closed Loop fuel control is enabled. The engine is not in decel fuel cut-off. The engine coolant temperature is warmer than 60°C (140°F). The intake air temperature (IAT) is colder than 60°C (140°F). DTC P2177 and P2179 run continuously once the above conditions are met for approximately 300 s, after Closed Loop fuel control is enabled.
DTC: P2180	**Fuel Trim System Rich at Cruise or Acceleration Bank 2:** P2178 or P2180Before the ECM can report DTC P2178 or P2180, failed, DTCs P000A, P000B, P000C, P000D, P0008, P0009, P0010, P0011, P0013, P0014, P0016, P0017, P0018, P0019, P0020, P0021, P0023, P0024, P0201, P0202, P0203, P0204, P0205, P0206, P0221, P0222, P0223, P0261, P0262, P0264, P0265, P0267, P0268, P0270, P0271, P0273, P0274, P0276, P0277, P0300, P0301, P0302, P0303, P0304, P0305, P0306, P0461, P0462, P0463, P2068 P2088, P2089, P2090, P2091, P2092, P2093, P2094, P2095 P2146, P2149, P2152, P2155, P216A, and P216D must run and pass. The engine speed is between 1,200-3,400 RPM. The engine load is between 13-50 %. The throttle angle is less than 100 %. The cold start fuel control is not active. The Closed Loop fuel control is enabled. The engine is not in decel fuel cut-off. The engine coolant temperature is warmer than 60°C (140°F). The intake air temperature (IAT) is colder than 60°C (140°F). DTCs P2178 and P2180 run continuously when the above conditions are met for approximately 300 s, after Closed Loop fuel control is enabled.
DTC: P2181	**Engine Cooling System Performance:** DTCs P00B3, P00B4, P0101, P0102, P0103, P0112, P0113, or P0114 are not set. The engine run time is between 70 s and 22 m. The engine coolant temperature (ECT) sensor at start-up is between -20°C to +75°C (19 to 140°F). The intake air temperature (IAT) sensor is between -7°C to +75°C (-4°F to +167°F). The airflow into the engine is between 11 to 100 g/s. The DTC runs once per ignition cycle when the above conditions are met.
DTC: P2181 00	**Engine Cooling System Performance:** DTCs P00B3 00, P00B4 00, P0101 00, P0102 00, P0103 00, P0112 00, P0113 00, or P0114 00 are not set. The engine run time is between 70 s and 22 min. The engine coolant temperature (ECT) sensor at start-up is between -20 to +75°C (19-140°F). The intake air temperature (IAT) sensor is between -7 to +75°C (-4 to +167°F). The engine coolant thermostat heater command is greater than 50%. The airflow into the engine is between 11-100 g/s. The DTC runs once per ignition cycle when the above conditions are met.
DTC: P2186 00	**Engine Coolant Temperature (ECT) Sensor 2 Circuit Erratic:** DTCs P00B3 00, P00B4 00, P0101 00, P0102 00, P0103 00, P0112 00, P0113 00, or P0114 00 are not set. The engine run time is between 70 s and 22 m. The engine coolant temperature (ECT) sensor at start up is between -20 to +75°C (19-140°F). The intake air temperature (IAT) sensor is between -7 to +75°C (-4 to +167°F). The engine coolant thermostat heater command is greater than 50%. The airflow into the engine is between 11-100 g/s. The DTC runs once per ignition cycle when the above conditions are met.
DTC: P2187	**Fuel Trim System Lean at Idle Bank 1:** P2187 or P2189Before the ECM can report DTC P2187 or P2189, failed, DTCs P000A, P000B, P000C, P000D, P0008, P0009, P0010, P0011, P0013, P0014, P0016, P0017, P0018, P0019, P0020, P0021, P0023, P0024, P0201, P0202, P0203, P0204, P0205, P0206, P0261, P0262, P0264, P0265, P0267, P0268, P0270, P0271, P0273, P0274, P0276, P0277, P0300, P0301, P0302, P0303, P0304, P0305, P0306, P0461, P0462, P0463, P2068 P2088, P2089, P2090, P2091, P2092, P2093, P2094, P2095 P2146, P2149, P2152, P2155, P216A, and P216D must run and pass. The engine speed is between 520-1,000 RPM. The engine load is between 0-23 %. The throttle angle is less than 100 %. The cold start fuel control is not active. The Closed Loop fuel control is enabled. The engine is not in decel fuel cut-off. The engine coolant temperature (ECT) is warmer than 60°C (140°F). The intake air temperature (IAT) is colder than 60°C (140°F). DTC P2187 and P2189 run continuously once the above conditions are met for approximately 600 s, after Closed Loop fuel control is enabled.

DTC	Trouble Code Title, Conditions, Possible Causes
DTC: P2187 00	**Fuel Trim System Lean at Idle:** DTCs P0031 00, P0032 00, P0112 00, P0113 00, P0117 00, P0118 00, P0122 00, P0123 00, P0131 00, P0132 00, P0133 00, P0134 00, P0135 00, P0261 00, P0262 00, P0264 00, P0265 00, P0267 00, P0268 00, P0270 00, P0271 00, P0300 00, P0335 00, P0336 00, P0458 00, P0459 00, P0562 00, and P0563 00 are not set. The fuel system is in closed loop. The engine speed is between 700-6 000 RPM. The engine coolant temperature (ECT) is between 70-115°C (158-239°F). The intake air temperature (IAT) sensor is between -40 to +120°C (-40 to +248°F). The throttle position is between 0-95%. The manifold absolute pressure (MAP) is between 25-99. 7 kPa (3. 6-14. 46 PSI). The barometric pressure (BARO) is greater than 72 kPa (10. 44 PSI). The engine airflow is between 1. 5-45 g/s. The vehicle speed is less than 140 km/h (87 MPH). The ignition voltage is greater than 11 V. The DTCs run continuously when the above conditions are met.
DTC: P2188	**Fuel Trim System Rich at Idle Bank 1:** P2188 or P2190Before the ECM can report DTC P2188 or P2190, failed, DTCs P000A, P000B, P000C, P000D, P0008, P0009, P0010, P0011, P0013, P0014, P0016, P0017, P0018, P0019, P0020, P0021, P0023, P0024, P0201, P0202, P0203, P0204, P0205, P0206, P0261, P0262, P0264, P0265, P0267, P0268, P0270, P0271, P0273, P0274, P0276, P0277, P0300, P0301, P0302, P0303, P0304, P0305, P0306, P0461, P0462, P0463, P2068 P2088, P2089, P2090, P2091, P2092, P2093, P2094, P2095 P2146, P2149, P2152, P2155, P216A, and P216D must run and pass. The engine speed is between 520-1,000 RPM. The engine load is between 0-23 %. The throttle angle is less than 100 %. The cold start fuel control is not active. The Closed Loop fuel control is enabled. The engine is not in decel fuel cut-off. The engine coolant temperature (ECT) is warmer than 60°C (140°F). The intake air temperature (IAT) is colder than 60°C (140°F). DTCs P2188 and P2190 run continuously when the above conditions are met for approximately 600 s, after Closed Loop fuel control is enabled.
DTC: P2188 00	**Fuel Trim System Rich at Idle:** DTCs P0031 00, P0032 00, P0112 00, P0113 00, P0117 00, P0118 00, P0122 00, P0123 00, P0131 00, P0132 00, P0133 00, P0134 00, P0135 00, P0261 00, P0262 00, P0264 00, P0265 00, P0267 00, P0268 00, P0270 00, P0271 00, P0300 00, P0335 00, P0336 00, P0458 00, P0459 00, P0562 00, and P0563 00 are not set. The fuel system is in closed loop. The engine speed is between 700-6 000 RPM. The engine coolant temperature (ECT) is between 70-115°C (158-239°F). The intake air temperature (IAT) sensor is between -40 to +120°C (-40 to +248°F). The throttle position is between 0-95%. The manifold absolute pressure (MAP) is between 25-99. 7 kPa (3. 6-14. 46 PSI). The barometric pressure (BARO) is greater than 72 kPa (10. 44 PSI). The engine airflow is between 1. 5-45 g/s. The vehicle speed is less than 140 km/h (87 MPH). The ignition voltage is greater than 11 V. The DTCs run continuously when the above conditions are met.
DTC: P2189	**Fuel Trim System Lean at Idle Bank 2:** P2187 or P2189Before the ECM can report DTC P2187 or P2189, failed, DTCs P000A, P000B, P000C, P000D, P0008, P0009, P0010, P0011, P0013, P0014, P0016, P0017, P0018, P0019, P0020, P0021, P0023, P0024, P0201, P0202, P0203, P0204, P0205, P0206, P0261, P0262, P0264, P0265, P0267, P0268, P0270, P0271, P0273, P0274, P0276, P0277, P0300, P0301, P0302, P0303, P0304, P0305, P0306, P0461, P0462, P0463, P2068 P2088, P2089, P2090, P2091, P2092, P2093, P2094, P2095 P2146, P2149, P2152, P2155, P216A, and P216D must run and pass. The engine speed is between 520-1,000 RPM. The engine load is between 0-23 %. The throttle angle is less than 100 %. The cold start fuel control is not active. The Closed Loop fuel control is enabled. The engine is not in decel fuel cut-off. The engine coolant temperature (ECT) is warmer than 60°C (140°F). The intake air temperature (IAT) is colder than 60°C (140°F). DTC P2187 and P2189 run continuously once the above conditions are met for approximately 600 s, after Closed Loop fuel control is enabled.
DTC: P2190	**Fuel Trim System Rich at Idle Bank 2:** P2188 or P2190Before the ECM can report DTC P2188 or P2190, failed, DTCs P000A, P000B, P000C, P000D, P0008, P0009, P0010, P0011, P0013, P0014, P0016, P0017, P0018, P0019, P0020, P0021, P0023, P0024, P0201, P0202, P0203, P0204, P0205, P0206, P0261, P0262, P0264, P0265, P0267, P0268, P0270, P0271, P0273, P0274, P0276, P0277, P0300, P0301, P0302, P0303, P0304, P0305, P0306, P0461, P0462, P0463, P2068 P2088, P2089, P2090, P2091, P2092, P2093, P2094, P2095 P2146, P2149, P2152, P2155, P216A, and P216D must run and pass. The engine speed is between 520-1,000 RPM. The engine load is between 0-23 %. The throttle angle is less than 100 %. The cold start fuel control is not active. The Closed Loop fuel control is enabled. The engine is not in decel fuel cut-off. The engine coolant temperature (ECT) is warmer than 60°C (140°F). The intake air temperature (IAT) is colder than 60°C (140°F). DTCs P2188 and P2190 run continuously when the above conditions are met for approximately 600 s, after Closed Loop fuel control is enabled.
DTC: P2195	**HO2S Signal Biased Lean Sensor 1:** P2195 DTCs P0030, P0031, P0032, P0036, P0037, P0038, P0053, P0130, P0131, P0132, P0133, P0135, P0137, P0138, P0140, P0141, P2232, P2237, P2243, P2251, P2297, P2626 are not set. The engine is running. The Loop Status parameter is Closed. DTC P2195 runs continuously when the above conditions are met.
DTC: P2195 00	**HO2S Signal Biased Lean Sensor 1:** The engine coolant temperature (ECT) is greater than 60°C (140°F). The ignition 1 voltage is greater than 10 V. The DTC runs continuously once the above conditions are met for 2 s.
DTC: P2196	**HO2S Signal Biased Rich Sensor 1:** P2196 DTCs P0030, P0031, P0032, P0036, P0037, P0038, P0053, P0130, P0131, P0132, P0133, P0135, P0137, P0138, P0140, P0141, P2232, P2237, P2243, P2251, P2297, P2626 are not set. The engine is running. The Loop Status parameter is Closed. DTC P2196 runs continuously when the above conditions are met.

DTC	Trouble Code Title, Conditions, Possible Causes
DTC: P219A	**Fuel Trim Cylinder Balance Bank 1:** DTCs P0030, P0036, P0050, P0053, P0059, P0101, P0102, P0103, P0106, P0107, P0108, P0117, P0118, P0128, P0131, P0132, P0133, P0134, P0135, P0151, P0152, P0153, P0154, P0155, P0201-P0206, P0300, P0301-P0306, P0411, P0412, P0418, P0442, P0443, P0446, P0449, P0452, P0453, P0454, P0455, P0496, P1133, P1153, P1516, P2101, P2119, P2120, P2125, P2135, P2138, P2176, P2431, P2432, P2433, P2440, P2A00, P2A03 are not set. The device control is not active. The intrusive diagnostics are not active. The engine overspeed protection is not active. The power take-off (PTO) is not active. The traction control is not active. The fuel control is in air-fuel Closed Loop. The system voltage is more than 10 V, or less than 18 V. The engine run time is greater than 100 s. The engine coolant temperature (ECT) is greater than -20°C (-4°F). The engine speed is greater than 425 RPM, but less than 6,000 RPM. The mass air flow is greater than 25 g/s, but less than 510 g/s.
DTC: P219A	**Air Fuel Imbalance:** DTCs P0068, P0101, P0102, P0103, P0106, P0107, P0108, P0116, P0117, P0118, P0121, P0122, P0123, P0128, P0131, P0132, P0133, P0134, P0135, P0137, P0138, P013A-P013B, P013E-P013F, P0140, P0141, P0201-P0204, P0261-P0262, P0264-P0265, P0267-P0268, P0270-P0271, P0300, P0301-P0304 P0442, P0443, P0446, P0449, P0451, P0452, P0453, P0454, P0455, P0496, P1101, P1133, P1248, P1249, P124A, P124B, P1516, P2101, P2119, P2122, P2123, P2127-P2128, P2135, P2138, P2147-P2148, P2150-P2151, P2153-P2154, P2156-P2157, P2176, P219A, P2270, P2271, P2A00 are not set. The device control is not active. The intrusive diagnostics are not active. The engine overspeed protection is not active. Reduced power mode, ETC DTC, is not active. The traction control is not active. The fuel control is in air-fuel Closed Loop. The system voltage is more than 10 V, or less than 32 V for more than 4 s. The engine coolant temperature (ECT) is greater than -20°C (-4°F). The engine speed is greater than 1,100 RPM, but less than 4,000 RPM. The mass air flow is greater than 13 g/s, but less than 600 g/s.
DTC: P219B	**Fuel Trim Cylinder Balance Bank 2:** DTCs P0030, P0036, P0050, P0053, P0059, P0101, P0102, P0103, P0106, P0107, P0108, P0117, P0118, P0128, P0131, P0132, P0133, P0134, P0135, P0151, P0152, P0153, P0154, P0155, P0201-P0206, P0300, P0301-P0306, P0411, P0412, P0418, P0442, P0443, P0446, P0449, P0452, P0453, P0454, P0455, P0496, P1133, P1153, P1516, P2101, P2119, P2120, P2125, P2135, P2138, P2176, P2431, P2432, P2433, P2440, P2A00, P2A03 are not set. The device control is not active. The intrusive diagnostics are not active. The engine overspeed protection is not active. The power take-off (PTO) is not active. The traction control is not active. The fuel control is in air-fuel Closed Loop. The system voltage is more than 10 V, or less than 18 V. The engine run time is greater than 100 s. The engine coolant temperature (ECT) is greater than -20°C (-4°F). The engine speed is greater than 425 RPM, but less than 6,000 RPM. The mass air flow is greater than 25 g/s, but less than 510 g/s.
DTC: P219B	**Air Fuel Imbalance Bank 2:** DTCs P0053, P0059, P0068, P0090, P0091, P0092, P00C8, P00C9, P00CA, P0101, P0102, P0103, P0106, P0107, P0108, P0116, P0117, P0118, P0122, P0123, P0128, P0131, P0132, P0133, P0134, P0135, P0151, P0152, P0153, P0154, P0155, P0191, P0192, P0193, P0201-P0206, P0222, P0223, P0261, P0262, P0264, P0265, P0267, P0268, P0270, P0271, P0273, P0274, P0276, P0277, P0300, P0301-P0306, P0442, P0443, P0446, P0449, P0452, P0453, P0455, P0496, P0606, P1133, P1153, P1248, P1249, P124A, P124B, P124C, P124D, P16F3, P2101, P2122, P2123, P2127, P2128, P2135, P2147, P2148, P2150, P2151, P2153, P2154, P2156, P2157, P216B, P216C, P216E, P216F, P228C, P228D, P2A00, P2A03 are not set. Device controls are not active. The intrusive diagnostics are not active. The engine overspeed protection is not active. Reduced power mode is not active. The traction control is not active. The engine is in Closed Loop status. The system voltage is between 10-32 V for greater than 4 s. The engine coolant temperature (ECT) is warmer than -20°C (-4°F). The engine speed is between 950-2750 RPM. The mass air flow is between 1-600 g/s.
DTC: P21AA	**Reductant Level Sensor 2 Circuit Low Voltage:** The engine speed is greater than 600 RPM. The battery voltage is greater than 11 V. The ambient air and emission reduction fluid tank temperatures are warmer than -7°C (19°F) - DTC P203B only. The engine run time is greater than 10 s. The DTCs run continuously once the above conditions are met.
DTC: P21AB	**Reductant Level Sensor 2 Circuit High Voltage:** The engine speed is greater than 600 RPM. The battery voltage is greater than 11 V. The ambient air and emission reduction fluid tank temperatures are warmer than -7°C (19°F) - DTC P203B only. The engine run time is greater than 10 s. The DTCs run continuously once the above conditions are met.
DTC: P21AF	**Reductant Level Sensor 3 Circuit Low Voltage:** The engine speed is greater than 600 RPM. The battery voltage is greater than 11 V. The ambient air and emission reduction fluid tank temperatures are warmer than -7°C (19°F) - DTC P203B only. The engine run time is greater than 10 s. The DTCs run continuously once the above conditions are met.
DTC: P21B0	**Reductant Level Sensor 3 Circuit High Voltage:** The engine speed is greater than 600 RPM. The battery voltage is greater than 11 V. The ambient air and emission reduction fluid tank temperatures are warmer than -7°C (19°F) - DTC P203B only. The engine run time is greater than 10 s. The DTCs run continuously once the above conditions are met.

DTC	Trouble Code Title, Conditions, Possible Causes
DTC: P2200	**NOx Sensor 1 Circuit:** P2200, P2202, P2203, P22A0, and P22A1 DTCs P2205, P2209, P22A3, or P22A7 are not set. The battery voltage is greater than 11 V for greater than 3 s. The engine speed is greater than 600 RPM. The engine run time is greater than 20 s. The exhaust gas temperature Sensor 2 is between 95-3,004°C (203-5,439°F). The NOx sensor is at operating temperature. The DTCs run continuously once the above conditions are met.
DTC: P2201	**NOx Sensor 1 Performance:** P2201The engine run time is greater than 10 s. The engine speed is greater than 600 RPM. The battery voltage is greater than 11 V. The DPF regeneration is not active. The DTC runs continuously when the above conditions are met.
DTC: P2202	**NOx Sensor 1 Circuit Low Voltage:** P2200, P2202, P2203, P22A0, and P22A1 DTCs P2205, P2209, P22A3, or P22A7 are not set. The battery voltage is greater than 11 V for greater than 3 s. The engine speed is greater than 600 RPM. The engine run time is greater than 20 s. The exhaust gas temperature Sensor 2 is between 95-3,004°C (203-5,439°F). The NOx sensor is at operating temperature. The DTCs run continuously once the above conditions are met.
DTC: P2203	**NOx Sensor 1 Circuit High Voltage:** P2200, P2202, P2203, P22A0, and P22A1 DTCs P2205, P2209, P22A3, or P22A7 are not set. The battery voltage is greater than 11 V for greater than 3 s. The engine speed is greater than 600 RPM. The engine run time is greater than 20 s. The exhaust gas temperature Sensor 2 is between 95-3,004°C (203-5,439°F). The NOx sensor is at operating temperature. The DTCs run continuously once the above conditions are met.
DTC: P2205	**NOx Sensor 1 Heater Control Circuit:** DTC P2205 or P22A3The battery voltage is greater than 11 V. The engine speed is greater than 600 RPM for greater than 10 s. The Exhaust Gas Temperature Sensor 1 is greater than 95°C (203°F). The DTCs run continuously once the above conditions are met.
DTC: P2209	**NOx Sensor 1 Heater Feedback Performance:** DTC P2209 or P22A7 DTC P064C, P163C, P220A, or P220B are not set. The battery voltage is greater than 11 V. The engine speed is between 600-5,000 RPM. The Exhaust Gas Temperature Sensor 1 is greater than 95°C (203°F). The DTCs run continuously once the above conditions are met.
DTC: P220A	**NOx Sensor 1 Supply Voltage Circuit:** The ignition is ON. The DTCs run continuously once the above conditions are met.
DTC: P220B	**NOx Sensor 2 Supply Voltage Circuit:** The ignition is ON. The DTCs run continuously once the above conditions are met.
DTC: P2226 03	**Barometric Pressure (BARO) Sensor Circuit Low Voltage:** The ignition is ON or the engine is running.
DTC: P2226 07	**Barometric Pressure (BARO) Sensor Circuit High Voltage:** The ignition is ON or the engine is running.
DTC: P2227	**Barometric Pressure (BARO) Sensor Performance:** P2227 - Engine Cranking DTCs P0121, P0122, P0123, P0221, P0222, P0223, P0335, P0336, P2176, P2228, or P2229 is not set. The engine is cranking. The engine OFF timer is greater than 4 s before cranking begins. This DTC runs once per ignition cycle within the enabling conditions. P2227 - Engine Running Rationality Test DTCs P0121, P0122, P0123, P0221, P0222, P0223, P0335, P0336, P2176, P2228, or P2229 is not set. The engine speed is less than 1000 RPM. The Throttle Position Sensor parameter is less than 24 %. The engine has been running for greater than 5 s. This DTC runs continuously within the enabling conditions. P2227 - Engine Running Range Test DTCs P0121, P0122, P0123, P0221, P0222, P0223, P0335, P0336, P2176, P2228, or P2229 is not set. The engine has been running for greater than 5 s. This DTC runs continuously within the enabling conditions.
DTC: P2228	**Barometric Pressure (BARO) Sensor Circuit Low Voltage:** P2228 or P2229The engine is operating. The DTCs run continuously once the above conditions are met for 2 s.
DTC: P2229	**Barometric Pressure (BARO) Sensor Circuit High Voltage:** P2228 or P2229The engine is running. The DTCs run continuously when the above condition is met.
DTC: P2230	**Barometric Pressure (BARO) Sensor Circuit Erratic:** P2230The engine is running. DTCs P0068, P0101, P0102, P0103, P0106, P0107, P0108, P0112, P0113, P0117, P0118, P0121, P0122, P0123, P0222, P0223, P1516, P2135, P2228 and P2229 are not set. DTC P2230 runs continuously when the above conditions are met.
DTC: P2232	**HO2S Signal Circuit Shorted to Heater Circuit Sensor 2:** P2232The engine is running. The HO2S 2 heater is stable, and the estimated exhaust temperature was more than 250°C (482°F) for more than 90 seconds. The ignition voltage is more than 10. 5 volts. The estimated exhaust temperature is less than 800°C (1,472°F). DTC P2232 runs continuously when the above conditions are met.

DTC	Trouble Code Title, Conditions, Possible Causes
DTC: P2237	**HO2S Pumping Current Control Circuit Sensor 1:** P2237 DTCs P0121, P0122, P0123, P0221, P0222, P0223, P0335, P0336, P0338 are not set. The ignition voltage is between 10. 7-18. 1 V. The engine is running. HO2S 1 voltage is between 1. 48-1. 52 V. HO2S 1 heater is at operating temperature. HO2S 1 Closed Loop is active. The catalyst temperature is stable. DTC P2237 runs continuously when the above conditions are met for 2 s.
DTC: P2237 00	**HO2S Pump Current Control Circuit Sensor 1:** P2237 00The ignition voltage is between 10. 7-18. 1 V. The engine is running. HO2S 1 voltage is between 1. 48-1. 52 V. HO2S 1 heater is at operating temperature. HO2S 1 Closed Loop is active. The catalyst temperature is stable. DTC P2237 runs continuously when the above conditions are met for 2 s.
DTC: P2238	**HO2S Pump Current Control Circuit Low Voltage Sensor 1:** P2238 and P2239The ignition voltage is between 10. 7-18. 1 V. The engine is running. DTCs P2238 and P2239 run continuously when the above conditions have been met for 1. 5 s.
DTC: P2238 00	**HO2S Pump Current Control Circuit Low Voltage Sensor 1:** P2238 00The ignition voltage is between 10. 7-18. 1 V. The engine is running. DTCs P2238 runs continuously when the above conditions have been met for 1. 5 s.
DTC: P2239	**HO2S Pump Current Control Circuit High Voltage Sensor 1:** P2238 and P2239The ignition voltage is between 10. 7-18. 1 V. The engine is running. DTCs P2238 and P2239 run continuously when the above conditions have been met for 1. 5 s.
DTC: P2243	**HO2S Reference Voltage Circuit Sensor 1:** P2243 DTCs P0030, P0031, P0032 are not set. The ignition voltage is between 10. 7-18. 1 V. The engine is running. HO2S 1 heater is at operating temperature for at least 20 s. HO2S 1 internal resistance is more than 570 Ω. DTC P2243 runs continuously when the above conditions are met for 2 s.
DTC: P2245 00	**HO2S Reference Voltage Circuit Low Voltage Sensor 1:** P2245 00 or P2246 00 DTCs P0030, P0031, P0032 are not set. The ignition voltage is between 10-18 V. The engine speed is greater than 80 RPM. The HO2S 1 heater is at operating temperature. DTC P2243 runs continuously when the above conditions are met for 2 s.
DTC: P2246 00	**HO2S Reference Voltage Circuit High Voltage Sensor 1:** P2245 00 or P2246 00 DTCs P0030, P0031, P0032 are not set. The ignition voltage is between 10-18 V. The engine speed is greater than 80 RPM. The HO2S 1 heater is at operating temperature. DTC P2243 runs continuously when the above conditions are met for 2 s.
DTC: P2251	**HO2S Low Reference Circuit Sensor 1:** P2251 DTCs P0030, P0031, P0032 are not set. The ignition voltage is between 10. 7-18. 1 V. The engine is running. The estimated exhaust temperature is less than 900°C (1,652°F). The HO2S 1 voltage is between 1. 47-1. 53 V. The HO2S 1 heater temperature has been within the normal range for more than 20 s. HO2S 1 internal resistance is more than 570 Ω. The following are true for more than 30 s. The HO2S 1 heater is ready. The engine is running. The ignition voltage is more than 11 V. DTC P2251 runs continuously when the above conditions are met for 10 minutes.
DTC: P2251 00	**HO2S Low Reference Circuit Sensor 1:** P2251 00 DTCs P0030, P0031, P0032 are not set. The ignition voltage is between 10. 7-18. 1 V. The engine is running. The estimated exhaust temperature is less than 900°C (1 652°F). The HO2S 1 voltage is between 1. 47-1. 53 V. The HO2S 1 heater temperature has been within the normal range for more than 20 s. HO2S 1 internal resistance is more than 570 Ω. The following are true for more than 30 s. The HO2S 1 heater is ready. The engine is running. The ignition voltage is more than 11 V. DTC P2251 runs continuously when the above conditions are met for 10 min.
DTC: P2261	**Turbocharger Bypass Valve Stuck Closed:** DTCs P0033, P0034, P0035, P0096, P0097, P0098, P0099, P0100, P0101, P0102, P0103, P0106, P0107, P0108, P0121, P0122, P0123, P0221, P0222, P0223, P0234, P0236, P0237, P0238, P0299, P2227, P2228, or P2229, is not set. The boost pressure versus the BARO pressure ratio is between 1. 1-3. 3. The charge air bypass valve has been commanded ON for greater than 1 s immediately after an abrupt closed throttle has occurred and the resulting pressure ratio across the compressor exceeds the calibrated pressure ratio limit. The battery voltage is between 10-18 V. This DTC runs continuously within the enabling conditions.
DTC: P2261 00	**Turbocharger Bypass Valve Stuck:** DTCs P0033 00, P0034 00, P0035 00, P0097 00, P0098 00, P0100 00, P0101 00, P0102 00, P0103 00, P0121 00, P0122 00, P0123 00, P0221 00, P0222 00, P0223 00, P0234 00, P0237 00, P0238 00, P0299 00, P2228 00, or P2229 00, are not set. The boost pressure versus the Barometric Pressure (BARO) ratio is between 1. 1-3. 3. The charge air bypass valve has been commanded ON for greater than 1 s immediately after an abrupt closed throttle has occurred and the resulting pressure ratio across the compressor exceeds the calibrated pressure ratio limit. The battery voltage is between 10-18 V. The engine coolant temperature is above 39°C (102°F). The intake air temperature is above 4. 5°C (40°F). This DTC runs continuously within the enabling conditions.
DTC: P2263	**Turbocharger Boost System Performance:** DTC P0107 or P0108 is not set. The engine is running. DTC P2263 runs continuously when the above conditions are met.

DTC	Trouble Code Title, Conditions, Possible Causes
DTC: P2264	**Water in Fuel Sensor Circuit:** The ignition is ON. The DTC runs continuously once the above condition is met.
DTC: P2264 00	**Water In Fuel Sensor Circuit Malfunction:** The ignition is ON. The DTC runs continuously once the above condition is met.
DTC: P2266	**Water in Fuel Sensor Circuit Low Voltage:** The engine is running. This diagnostic runs continuously.
DTC: P2269	**Water in Fuel:** The engine is running. The diagnostic runs continuously.
DTC: P2269 00	**Water in Fuel Malfunction:** The ignition is ON. The DTC runs continuously once the above condition is met.
DTC: P2270	**HO2S Signal Stuck Lean Sensor 2:** P2270 DTCs P0068, P0101, P0102, P0103, P0106, P0107, P0108, P0112, P0113, P0116, P0117, P0118, P0120, P0121, P0122, P0123, P0128, P013A, P013B, P013E, P013F, P0171, P0172, P0201, P0202, P0203, P0204, P0220, P0222, P0223, P0300, P1174, P1516, P2101, P2119, P2135, P2176, P2270, P2271 are not set. The system voltage is between 10-18 V. The fuel level is more than 10 percent. Engine run time is equal to or more than 40 seconds. The engine speed is between 1,250-1,950 RPM. Airflow is equal to or more than 3 g/s and equal to or less than 12 g/s. The vehicle speed is equal to or more than 55 km/h (34. 2 mph) and equal to or less than 120 km/h (74. 6 mph). The short term fuel trim is equal to or more than 0. 9 and equal to or less than 1. 065. The fuel state is in closed loop. The EVAP diagnostics are not in control of purge. The Ethanol Estimate is not in progress. The Post Cell Enabled. The Power Take-Off is not active. The EGR diagnostic is not intrusive. The Heater Warm-up Delay is more than 120 seconds. The catalytic converter temperature is equal to or more than 650°C (1,202°F), and equal to less than 900°C (1,652°F). This DTC runs once per trip when all of the above conditions have been met for 1 second.
DTC: P2270 00	**HO2S Signal Stuck Lean Sensor 2:** P2270 00 DTCs P0030 00, P0036 00, P0053 00, P0054 00, P0101 00, P0102 00, P0103 00, P0106 00, P0107 00, P0108 00, P0120 00, P0121 00, P0122 00, P0123 00, P0131 00, P0132 00, P0133 00, P0134 00, P0135 00, P0137 00, P0138 00, P013A 00, P013B 00, P013E 00, P013F 00, P0140 00, P0141 00, P0171 00, P0172 00, P0201 00, P0202 00, P0203 00, P0204 00, P0220 00, P0222 00, P0223 00, P0300 00, P0443 00, P1133 00, P1516 00, P2101 00, P2119 00, P2135 00, P2176 00, P2270 00, P2271 00, P2A00 00 are not set. The system voltage is between 10-18 V. The fuel level is more than 10%. Engine run time is equal to or more than 255 s. Then The engine speed is between 1 100-3 200 RPM. The airflow is equal to or more than 0 g/s and equal to or less than 25 g/s. The vehicle speed is equal to or more than 45 km/h (28 MPH) and equal to or less than 129 km/h (80 MPH). The short term fuel trim is equal to or more than 0. 9, and equal to or less than 1 065. The loop status parameter is closed. The evaporative emission (EVAP) diagnostics are not in control of purge. The heater warm-up delay is more than 120 s. The catalyst temperature is equal to or more than 650°C (1 202°F), and equal to less than 900°C (1 652°F). DTC P2270 00 runs once per trip when all of the above conditions have been met for 2 s.
DTC: P2271	**HO2S Signal Stuck Rich Bank 1 Sensor 2:** Before the ECM can report DTC P2271 or P2273 failed, DTCs P0036, P0037, P0038, P0056, P0057, P0058, P013A, P013C, P013E, P0137, P0138, P014A, P0140, P0141, P0157, P0158, P0160, P0161, P0443, P0458, P0459, P2097, P2099, P2178, P2180, P2188, and P2190 must run and pass. DTC P0461, P0462, P0463, P2066, P2067, or P2068 is not set. The engine is operating. The ignition voltage is greater than 10 volts. The HO2S 2 is at operating temperature for greater than 10 seconds. The long term fuel control is enabled. The engine is not in decel fuel cut-off (DEFCO). The mass air flow (MAF) sensor is greater than 10 g/s. The MAF sensor is between 6-33 g/s for greater than 3 seconds during the intrusive test. DTC P2271 and P2273 run continuously once the above conditions are met for approximately 10 minutes, or 20 minutes if the fuel level is less than 12 percent.
DTC: P2271 00	**HO2S Signal Stuck Rich Sensor 2:** P2271 00 DTCs P000A 00, P000B 00, P0010 00, P0011 00, P0013 00, P0014 00, P0016 00, P0017 00, P0030 00, P0031 00, P0032 00, P0107 00, P0108 00, P0117 00, P0118 00, P0119 00, P0121 00, P0122 00, P0123 00, P0130 00, P0131 00, P0132 00, P0133 00, P0137 00, P0138 00, P0139 00, P0141 00, P0171 00, P0172 00, P0221 00, P0222 00, P0223 00, P0300 00, P0301 00, P0302 00, P0303 00, P0304 00, P0313 00, P0335 00, P0336 00, P0340 00, P0341 00, P0365 00, P0366 00, P0443 00, P0458 00, P0459 00, P0496 00, P2088 00, P2089 00, P2090 00, P2091 00, P2176 00, P2270 00, P2271 00, P2297 00, P2A01 00 are not set. The engine has been running for more than 5 min. The engine coolant is hotter than 75°C (167°F). DTC P2271 00 runs continuously when the above conditions are met for 10 min.
DTC: P2271 00	**HO2S Signal Stuck Rich Sensor 2:** P2271 00 DTCs P0030 00, P0036 00, P0053 00, P0054 00, P0101 00, P0102 00, P0103 00, P0106 00, P0107 00, P0108 00, P0120 00, P0121 00, P0122 00, P0123 00, P0131 00, P0132 00, P0133 00, P0134 00, P0135 00, P0137 00, P0138 00, P013A 00, P013B 00, P013E 00, P013F 00, P0140 00, P0141 00, P0171 00, P0172 00, P0201 00, P0202 00, P0203 00, P0204 00, P0220 00, P0222 00, P0223 00, P0300 00, P0443 00, P1133 00, P1516 00, P2101 00, P2119 00, P2135 00, P2176 00, P2270 00, P2271 00, P2A00 00 are not set. The system voltage is between 10-18 V. The fuel level is more than 10%. Engine run time is equal to or more than 255 s. The Deceleration fuel cut-off is active. The accelerator pedal position (APP) is stable. The torque converter clutch (TCC) is locked. DTCs P013A 00, P013E 00, and P2270 00 have run and passed. DTC P2271 00 runs once per trip.

DTC	Trouble Code Title, Conditions, Possible Causes
DTC: P2272	**HO2S Signal Stuck Lean Bank 2 Sensor 2:** P2272 DTCs P0050, P0059, P0068, P0101, P0102, P0103, P0107, P0108, P0112, P0113, P0117, P0118, P0120, P0121, P0122, P0123, P0128, P0151, P0152, P0153, P0154, P0155, P0171, P0172, P0174, P0175, P0201, P0202, P0203, P0204, P0205, P0206, P0220, P0222, P0223, P0442, P0443, P0446, P0449, P0451, P0452, P0453, P0454, P0455, P0496, P1153, P1516, P2101, P2119, P2135, P2176, P2A03 are not set. The system voltage is between 10-18V. The learned heater resistance is valid. The fuel level is more than 10 percent or the fuel level data fault is active. Engine run time is equal to or more than 40 seconds. THEN The engine speed is between 1,100-2,100 RPM. Airflow is equal to or more than 3 g/s and equal to or less than 12 g/s. The vehicle speed is equal to or more than 73 km/h (45. 4 mph) and equal to or less than 120 km/h (74. 6 mph). The short term fuel trim is equal to or more than 0. 9 and equal to or less than 1. 065. The fuel state is in closed loop. The EVAP diagnostics are not in control of purge. The Post Cell Enabled. The EGR diagnostic is not intrusive. The Heater Warm-up Delay is more than 120 seconds. The catalytic converter temperature is equal to or more that 650°C (1,202°F), and equal to less than 900°C (1,652°F). This DTC runs once per trip when all of the above conditions have been met for 2 seconds.
DTC: P2273	**HO2S Signal Stuck Rich Bank 2 Sensor 2:** Before the ECM can report DTC P2271 or P2273 failed, DTCs P0036, P0037, P0038, P0056, P0057, P0058, P013A, P013C, P013E, P0137, P0138, P014A, P0140, P0141, P0157, P0158, P0160, P0161, P0443, P0458, P0459, P2097, P2099, P2178, P2180, P2188, and P2190 must run and pass. DTC P0461, P0462, P0463, P2066, P2067, or P2068 is not set. The engine is operating. The ignition voltage is greater than 10 volts. The HO2S 2 is at operating temperature for greater than 10 seconds. The long term fuel control is enabled. The engine is not in decel fuel cut-off (DEFCO). The mass air flow (MAF) sensor is greater than 10 g/s. The MAF sensor is between 6-33 g/s for greater than 3 seconds during the intrusive test. DTC P2271 and P2273 run continuously once the above conditions are met for approximately 10 minutes, or 20 minutes if the fuel level is less than 12 percent.
DTC: P228C	**Fuel Pressure Regulator 1 Control Performance - Low Pressure:** P0089, P228C, or P228DDTC P0016, P0017, P0090, P0091, P0092, P00C8, P00C9, P00CA, P0112, P0113, P0116, P0117, P0118, P0128, P0192, P0193, P0335, P0336, P0340, P0341, P0365, P0366, P0627, P0628, P0629 or P1682 is not set. The ignition voltage is more than 11 V. The engine is running. The low side fuel pressure is more than 275 kPa (40 psi). The DTC runs continuously when the above conditions are met for 60 s.
DTC: P228C 00	**Fuel Pressure Regulator 1 Control Performance - Low Pressure:** The ignition is ON, or the engine is running. The ignition voltage is less than 16 V. These DTCs runs continuously once the above conditions are met.
DTC: P228D	**Fuel Pressure Regulator 1 Control Performance – High Pressure:** P0089, P228C, or P228DDTC P0016, P0017, P0018, P0019, P0090, P0091, P0092, P00C8, P00C9, P00CA, P0111, P0112, P0113, P0116, P0117, P0118, P0128, P0192, P0193, P0335, P0336, P0340, P0341, P0345, P0346, P0365, P0366, P0390, P0391, P0627, P0628, or P0629 is not set. The ignition voltage is greater than 8 V. The low side fuel pressure is greater than 275 kPa (40 psi). The engine is running. The DTCs run continuously when the above conditions are met for 10 s.
DTC: P228D 00	**Fuel Pressure Regulator 1 Control Performance - High Pressure:** The ignition is ON, or the engine is running. The ignition voltage is less than 16 V. These DTCs runs continuously once the above conditions are met.
DTC: P2294	**Fuel Pressure Regulator 2 Control Circuit:** Engine speed is greater than 600 RPM. Battery voltage is greater than 11 V.
DTC: P2295	**Fuel Pressure Regulator Solenoid 2 Control Circuit Low Voltage:** Engine speed is greater than 600 RPM. Battery voltage is greater than 11 V.
DTC: P2296	**Fuel Pressure Regulator Solenoid 2 Control Circuit High Voltage:** Engine speed is greater than 600 RPM. Battery voltage is greater than 11 V.
DTC: P2297	**HO2S Performance During Decel Fuel Cut-Off (DFCO) Sensor 1:** P2297The engine is running. The HO2S 1 heater is at operating temperature. Lambda is less than 1. 6. All fuel injectors are active. DTC P2297 runs continuously when the above conditions are met.
DTC: P2297 00	**HO2S Performance During Deceleration Fuel Cut-Off Sensor 1:** DTCs P0106 00, P0107 00, P0108 00, P0117 00, P0118 00, P0122 00, P0123 00, P0171 00, P0172 00, P0300 00, P0336 00, P0337 00, P0351 00, P0352 00, P0401 00, P0402 00, P0404 00, P0405 00, P0406 00, P042E 00, P0502 00, P0506 00, P0507 00, and P1404 00 are not set. The engine has been running for greater than 60 s. The engine is in deceleration fuel cut off mode. The startup engine coolant temperature is greater than 60°C (140°F). The ignition voltage is between 10-16 V. The DTCs run continuously when the above conditions are met for 2 s.
DTC: P2299 00	**Brake Pedal Position - Accelerator Pedal Position Not Plausible:** The ignition is ON or the engine is running. The DTC runs continues once the above conditions are met.
DTC: P229E	**NOx Sensor 2 Circuit:** P229EThe battery voltage is greater than 11 V for greater than 3 s. The engine speed is greater than 600 RPM. The engine run time is greater than 20 s. The exhaust gas temperature sensor 4 is between 95-3,004°C (203-5,439°F). The NOx sensor is at operating temperature. The DTCs run continuously once the above conditions are met.

DTC	Trouble Code Title, Conditions, Possible Causes
DTC: P229F	**NOx Sensor 2 Performance:** P229FThe ambient air temperature is greater than -7°C (19°F)The BARO pressure is greater than 75 kPa (11 psi). The average SCR temperature is greater than 200°C (392°F). The DPF regeneration is not active. The DTC runs once per drive cycle after the above conditions are met.
DTC: P22A0	**NOx Sensor 2 Circuit Low Voltage:** P2200, P2202, P2203, P22A0, and P22A1 DTCs P2205, P2209, P22A3, or P22A7 are not set. The battery voltage is greater than 11 V for greater than 3 s. The engine speed is greater than 600 RPM. The engine run time is greater than 20 s. The exhaust gas temperature Sensor 2 is between 95-3,004°C (203-5,439°F). The NOx sensor is at operating temperature. The DTCs run continuously once the above conditions are met.
DTC: P22A1	**NOx Sensor 2 Circuit High Voltage:** P2200, P2202, P2203, P22A0, and P22A1 DTCs P2205, P2209, P22A3, or P22A7 are not set. The battery voltage is greater than 11 V for greater than 3 s. The engine speed is greater than 600 RPM. The engine run time is greater than 20 s. The exhaust gas temperature Sensor 2 is between 95-3,004°C (203-5,439°F). The NOx sensor is at operating temperature. The DTCs run continuously once the above conditions are met.
DTC: P22A3	**NOx Sensor 2 Heater Control Circuit:** DTC P2205 or P22A3The battery voltage is greater than 11 V. The engine speed is greater than 600 RPM for greater than 10 s. The Exhaust Gas Temperature Sensor 1 is greater than 95°C (203°F). The DTCs run continuously once the above conditions are met.
DTC: P22A7	**NOx Sensor 2 Heater Feedback Performance:** DTC P2209 or P22A7 DTC P064C, P163C, P220A, or P220B are not set. The battery voltage is greater than 11 V. The engine speed is between 600-5,000 RPM. The Exhaust Gas Temperature Sensor 1 is greater than 95°C (203°F). The DTCs run continuously once the above conditions are met.
DTC: P2300 00	**Ignition Coil 1 Control Circuit Low Voltage:** The engine speed is less than 6000 RPM. The ignition voltage is between 9-18 V. DTCs P2300 00, P2301 00, P2303, P2304 00, P2306 00, P2307 00, P2309 00, P2310 00 run continuously when the above conditions are met.
DTC: P2301 00	**Ignition Coil 1 Control Circuit High Voltage:** The engine speed is less than 6000 RPM. The ignition voltage is between 9-18 V. DTCs P2300 00, P2301 00, P2303, P2304 00, P2306 00, P2307 00, P2309 00, P2310 00 run continuously when the above conditions are met.
DTC: P2303 00	**Ignition Coil 2 Control Circuit Low Voltage:** The engine speed is less than 6000 RPM. The ignition voltage is between 9-18 V. DTCs P2300 00, P2301 00, P2303, P2304 00, P2306 00, P2307 00, P2309 00, P2310 00 run continuously when the above conditions are met.
DTC: P2304 00	**Ignition Coil 2 Control Circuit High Voltage:** The engine speed is less than 6000 RPM. The ignition voltage is between 9-18 V. DTCs P2300 00, P2301 00, P2303, P2304 00, P2306 00, P2307 00, P2309 00, P2310 00 run continuously when the above conditions are met.
DTC: P2306 00	**Ignition Coil 3 Control Circuit Low Voltage:** The engine speed is less than 6000 RPM. The ignition voltage is between 9-18 V. DTCs P2300 00, P2301 00, P2303, P2304 00, P2306 00, P2307 00, P2309 00, P2310 00 run continuously when the above conditions are met
DTC: P2307 00	**Ignition Coil 3 Control Circuit High Voltage:** The engine speed is less than 6000 RPM. The ignition voltage is between 9-18 V. DTCs P2300 00, P2301 00, P2303, P2304 00, P2306 00, P2307 00, P2309 00, P2310 00 run continuously when the above conditions are met.
DTC: P2309 00	**Ignition Coil 4 Control Circuit Low Voltage:** The engine speed is less than 6000 RPM. The ignition voltage is between 9-18 V. DTCs P2300 00, P2301 00, P2303, P2304 00, P2306 00, P2307 00, P2309 00, P2310 00 run continuously when the above conditions are met.
DTC: P2310 00	**Ignition Coil 4 Control Circuit High Voltage:** The engine speed is less than 6000 RPM. The ignition voltage is between 9-18 V. DTCs P2300 00, P2301 00, P2303, P2304 00, P2306 00, P2307 00, P2309 00, P2310 00 run continuously when the above conditions are met.
DTC: P2413	**Exhaust Gas Recirculation (EGR) System Performance:** DTC P0045, P0047, P0048, P006E, P006F, P007C, P007D, P0101, P0102, P0103, P0106, P0107, P0108, P0112, P0113, P0117, P0118, P0200, P02E0, P02E7, P02E8, P02E9, P02EB, P0403, P0405, P0406, P0489, P0490, P122C, P122E, P122F, P1407, P140D, P140E, P140F, P1411, P1412, ,P1413, P1414, P16A0, P16A1, P16A2, P2228, P2229, P2263, P2453, P245A, P245C, P245D, P2493, P2494, P2495, P2564, P2565, P2598, or P2599 is not set. The engine is running at idle. The DTC runs continuously when the above conditions are met.

DTC	Trouble Code Title, Conditions, Possible Causes
DTC: P242B	**Exhaust Gas Temperature Sensor 3 Performance:** P242BDTC P007C, P007D, P0097, P0098, P0101, P0102, P0103, P0107, P0108, P0112, P0113, P0401, P0402, P0403, P0405, P0406, P046C, P111C, P111D, P113A, P20E2, P2032, P2033, P2228, P2229, P242C, or P242D is not set. The engine is running for at least 327 s. The engine speed is between 700-3000 RPM for 60 s. The calculated fuel rate is between 5-80mm ; for 60 s. DPF regeneration or exhaust gas temperature monitoring has not been active in the last 25 minutes. Exhaust gas temperature sensor 3 has changed less than 7°C (12. 6°F) in 5 s. The DTC runs continuously when the above conditions are met.
DTC: P242B 00	**Exhaust Gas Temperature Sensor 3 Performance:** The ignition is ON. The DTCs run continuously when the above condition is met.
DTC: P242C	**Exhaust Gas Temperature Sensor 3 Circuit Low Voltage:** The ignition is ON or the engine is running. The DTCs run continuously when the above conditions are met.
DTC: P242C 00	**Exhaust Gas Temperature Sensor 3 Circuit Low Voltage:** The ignition is ON. The DTCs run continuously when the above condition is met.
DTC: P242D	**Exhaust Gas Temperature Sensor 3 Circuit High Voltage:** The ignition is ON or the engine is running. The DTCs run continuously when the above conditions are met.
DTC: P242D 00	**Exhaust Gas Temperature Sensor 3 Circuit High Voltage:** The ignition is ON. The DTCs run continuously when the above condition is met.
DTC: P242E 00	**Exhaust Gas Temperature Sensor 3 Circuit Intermittent:** The ignition is ON. The DTCs run continuously when the above condition is met.
DTC: P2430	**Secondary Air Injection (AIR) System Pressure Sensor Stuck in Range Bank 1:** DTC P2430 DTCs P0412, P0418, P0606, P2432, P2433, P2437, or P2438 are not set. Greater than 120 min has elapsed since the last cold start. The start-up intake air temperature (IAT) is between 5-60°C (41-140°F). The start-up engine coolant temperature (ECT) is between 5-50°C (41-122°F). DTC P2430 runs continuously when the above conditions are met.
DTC: P2430	**Secondary Air Injection (AIR) System Pressure Sensor Circuit:** DTC P2430 DTC P0411, P0412, P0418, P0601, P0602, P0603, P0604, P0606, P0607, P062F, P0641, or P0651 is not set. Greater than 60 min has elapsed since the last cold start. The Barometric Pressure (BARO) is greater than 60 kPa (8. 7 psi). The Intake Air Temperature (IAT) is warmer than -11°C (12°F). The Engine Coolant Temperature (ECT) is between -11 to +60°C (12-140°F). The ignition voltage is between 10-18 V. The Manifold Absolute Pressure (MAP) sensor is greater than 20 kPa (2. 9 psi). The engine speed is less than 5,000 RPM. The Mass Air Flow (MAF) is less than 50 g/s. The secondary air injection pump is commanded ON. DTC P2430 runs continuously when the above conditions are met.
DTC: P2431	**Secondary Air Injection System Pressure Sensor Performance:** DTC P2431 DTCs P0101, P0102, P0103, P0300, P0301, P0302, P0304, P0412, P0418, P0606, P0641 or P0651 are not set. The barometric pressure (BARO) is greater than 60 kPa (8. 7 psi). The intake air temperature (IAT) is warmer than -11°C (12°F). The engine coolant temperature (ECT) is between -11 to +60°C (12-140°F). The ignition voltage is between 10-32 V. The manifold absolute pressure (MAP) sensor is greater than 20 kPa (2. 9 psi). Run/Crank is not active. The engine speed is less than 5,000 RPM. The mass air flow (MAF) is less than 50 g/s. Greater than 60 minutes has elapsed since the last cold start. DTC P2431 runs continuously when the above conditions are met.
DTC: P2432	**Secondary Air Injection System Pressure Sensor Circuit Low Voltage:** P2432 and P2433 DTCs P0606, P0641, or P0651 are not set. The ignition is ON or the engine is running. DTC P2432 and P2433 run continuously when the above conditions are met.
DTC: P2433	**Secondary Air Injection (AIR) System Pressure Sensor Circuit High Voltage:** P2432 and P2433 DTC P0601, P0602, P0603, P0604, P0606, P0607, P062F, P0641, or P0651 is not set. The ignition is ON or the engine is running. DTC P2432 and P2433 run continuously when the above conditions are met.
DTC: P2435	**Secondary Air Injection (AIR) System Pressure Sensor Stuck in Range Bank 2:** DTC P2435 DTCs P0412, P0418, P0606, P2432, P2433, P2437, or P2438 are not set. Greater than 120 min has elapsed since the last cold start. The start-up intake air temperature (IAT) is between 5-60°C (41-140°F). The start-up engine coolant temperature (ECT) is between 5-50°C (41-122°F). DTC P2435 runs continuously when the above conditions are met.
DTC: P2436	**Secondary Air Injection (AIR) System Pressure Sensor Performance Bank 2:** DTC P2436 DTCs P0107, P0108, P0412, P0418, P0606, P0641, P0651, P2432, P2433, P2437, or P2438 are not set. The ignition is ON. DTC P2436 runs continuously when the above conditions are met.
DTC: P2437	**Secondary Air Injection (AIR) System Pressure Sensor Circuit Low Voltage Bank 2:** P2437 and P2438 DTCs P0606, P0641, or P0651 are not set. The ignition is ON, or the engine is operating. DTC P2432 and P2433 run continuously when the above conditions are met.
DTC: P2438	**Secondary Air Injection (AIR) System Pressure Sensor Circuit High Voltage Bank 2:** P2437 and P2438 DTCs P0606, P0641, or P0651 are not set. The ignition is ON, or the engine is operating. DTC P2432 and P2433 run continuously when the above conditions are met.

DTC	Trouble Code Title, Conditions, Possible Causes
DTC: P2440	**Secondary Air Injection System Shut-Off Valve Stuck Open:** DTCs P0101, P0102, P0103, P0106, P0107, P0108, P0112, P0113, P0114, P0116, P0117, P0118, P0121, P0122, P0123, P0128, P0201, P0202, P0203, P0204, P0222, P0223, P0261, P0262, P0264, P0265, P0267, P0268, P0270, P0271, P0300, P0301, P0302, P0303, P0304, P0351, P0352, P0353, P0354, P0411, P0412, P0418, P0420, P0606, P0641, P0651, P1248, P1249, P124A, P124B, P2147, P2148, P2150, P2151, P2153, P2154, P2156, P2157, P2430, P2431, P2432 or P2433 are not set. Greater than 60 min has elapsed since the last cold start. The ignition voltage is between 10-32 V. The barometric pressure (BARO) is greater than 60 kPa (8. 7 psi). The engine coolant temperature (ECT) is between -11 to +60°C (12-140°F). The intake air temperature (IAT) is warmer than -11°C (+12°F). The manifold absolute pressure (MAP) sensor is greater than 20 kPa (2. 9 psi). The mass air flow (MAF) is less than 50 g/s. The engine speed is less than 5,000 RPM. The AIR system is commanded ON. The DTC runs continuously once the above conditions are met for greater than 3 s.
DTC: P2444	**Secondary Air Injection System Pump Stuck ON:** DTCs P0101, P0102, P0103, P0106, P0107, P0108, P0112, P0113, P0114, P0116, P0117, P0118, P0121, P0122, P0123, P0128, P0201, P0202, P0203, P0204, P0222, P0223, P0261, P0262, P0264, P0265, P0267, P0268, P0270, P0271, P0300, P0301, P0302, P0303, P0304, P0351, P0352, P0353, P0354, P0411, P0412, P0418, P0420, P0606, P0641, P0651, P1248, P1249, P124A, P124B, P2147, P2148, P2150, P2151, P2153, P2154, P2156, P2157, P2430, P2431, P2432 or P2433 are not set. Greater than 60 min has elapsed since the last cold start. The ignition voltage is between 10-32 V. The barometric pressure (BARO) is greater than 60 kPa (8. 7 psi). The engine coolant temperature (ECT) is between -11 to +60°C (12-140°F). The intake air temperature (IAT) is warmer than -11°C (+12°F). The manifold absolute pressure (MAP) sensor is greater than 20 kPa (2. 9 psi). The engine speed is less than 5,000 RPM. The mass air flow (MAF) is less than 50 g/s. The AIR system is commanded ON. The DTC runs continuously once the above conditions are met for greater than 4 s.
DTC: P244B 11	**Diesel Particulate Filter (DPF) High Differential Pressure High Input:** The ignition is ON. The DTC run continuously when the above condition is met. OR The ignition is switched from ON to OFF. The DTC runs after a 2 s delay when the above condition is met.
DTC: P244C	**Catalyst Temperature Too Low During Regeneration:** The engine control system is in an active regeneration. DTC P244C runs continuously when the above condition is met.
DTC: P244C 00	**Catalyst Low Temperature During Regeneration Malfunction:** The DTC runs during the DPF regeneration process.
DTC: P244D	**Catalyst High Temperature During Regeneration:** DTC P0545, P0546, P2032, P2033, P2080, P2084, P242B, P242C, P242D, P246F, P2470 and P2471 are not set. The engine speed is greater than 600 RPM. The DTCs run continuously once the above conditions are met.
DTC: P2452 03	**Diesel Particulate Filter (DPF) Differential Pressure Sensor Circuit Low Voltage:** The ignition is ON, or the engine is running. The DTCs run continuously when the above condition is met.
DTC: P2452 07	**Diesel Particulate Filter Differential (DPF) Pressure Sensor Circuit High Voltage:** The ignition is ON, or the engine is running. The DTCs run continuously when the above condition is met.
DTC: P2453	**Diesel Particulate Filter (DPF) Differential Pressure Sensor Performance:** DTC P0101, P2454, or P2455 are not set. The engine run time is greater than 10 s. The engine speed is greater than 600 RPM. The battery voltage is greater than 11 V. The exhaust gas flow is stable. The DTC runs continuously when the above conditions are met.
DTC: P2453	**Particulate Matter Trap Differential Pressure Sensor Signal Performance:** The engine has been running and then turned off for at least 60 seconds. ORDTC P2453 runs continuously when the engine is running. ANDDTC P2453 runs once after the ignition has been turned OFF.
DTC: P2453 00	**Diesel Particulate Filter (DPF) Differential Pressure Sensor Performance:** P2453 DTC P0101, P2454, or P2455 are not set. The engine has been running and then turned off for at least 60 s. The engine speed is greater than 600 RPM. The battery voltage is greater than 11 V. The exhaust gas flow is stable. The DTC runs continue when the above conditions are met. and DTC P2453 runs once after the ignition has been turned OFF. P2454 DTC P2454 is not set. Engine run time is greater than 10 s. The engine speed is greater than 600 RPM. The DTC runs continuously when the above conditions are met. P2455 DTC P2455 is not set. Engine run time is greater than 10 s. The engine speed is greater than 600 RPM. The DTC runs continuously when the above conditions are met.
DTC: P2453 08	**Diesel Particulate Filter (DPF) Differential Pressure Sensor Performance - Signal Invalid:** P244B, P2453 08, P2453 11, P2453 12, P2453 55, P2453 58, or P2453 09The ignition is ON. The DTCs run continuously when the above condition is met. P244B, P2453 08, P2453 11, P2453 12, P2453 55The ignition is switched from ON to OFF. The DTCs run after a 2 s delay when the above condition is met. P2453 58The ignition is ON. The intake air temperature sensor is less than 0°C (32°F). The DTC runs continuously when the above condition is met.
DTC: P2453 11	**Diesel Particulate Filter (DPF) Differential Pressure Sensor Performance High Input:** P244B, P2453 08, P2453 11, P2453 12, P2453 55, P2453 58, or P2453 09The ignition is ON. The DTCs run continuously when the above condition is met. P244B, P2453 08, P2453 11, P2453 12, P2453 55The ignition is switched from ON to OFF. The DTCs run after a 2 s delay when the above condition is met. P2453 58The ignition is ON. The intake air temperature sensor is less than 0°C (32°F). The DTC runs continuously when the above condition is met.

DTC	Trouble Code Title, Conditions, Possible Causes
DTC: P2453 12	**Diesel Particulate Filter (DPF) Differential Pressure Sensor Performance Low Input:** P244B, P2453 08, P2453 11, P2453 12, P2453 55, P2453 58, or P2453 09The ignition is ON. The DTCs run continuously when the above condition is met. P244B, P2453 08, P2453 11, P2453 12, P2453 55The ignition is switched from ON to OFF. The DTCs run after a 2 s delay when the above condition is met. P2453 58The ignition is ON. The intake air temperature sensor is less than 0°C (32°F). The DTC runs continuously when the above condition is met.
DTC: P2453 18	**Diesel Particulate Filter (DPF) Differential Pressure Sensor Performance Low Signal Amplitude:** P244B, P2453 08, P2453 11, P2453 12, P2453 55, P2453 58, or P2453 09The ignition is ON. The DTCs run continuously when the above condition is met. P244B, P2453 08, P2453 11, P2453 12, P2453 55The ignition is switched from ON to OFF. The DTCs run after a 2 s delay when the above condition is met. P2453 58The ignition is ON. The intake air temperature sensor is less than 0°C (32°F). The DTC runs continuously when the above condition is met.
DTC: P2453 55	**Diesel Particulate Filter (DPF) Differential Pressure Sensor Performance Too Few Transitions:** P244B, P2453 08, P2453 11, P2453 12, P2453 55, P2453 58, or P2453 09The ignition is ON. The DTCs run continuously when the above condition is met. P244B, P2453 08, P2453 11, P2453 12, P2453 55The ignition is switched from ON to OFF. The DTCs run after a 2 s delay when the above condition is met. P2453 58The ignition is ON. The intake air temperature sensor is less than 0°C (32°F). The DTC runs continuously when the above condition is met.
DTC: P2453 58	**Diesel Particulate Filter (DPF) Differential Pressure Sensor Performance:** P244B, P2453 08, P2453 11, P2453 12, P2453 55, P2453 58, or P2453 09The ignition is ON. The DTCs run continuously when the above condition is met. P244B, P2453 08, P2453 11, P2453 12, P2453 55The ignition is switched from ON to OFF. The DTCs run after a 2 s delay when the above condition is met. P2453 58The ignition is ON. The intake air temperature sensor is less than 0°C (32°F). The DTC runs continuously when the above condition is met.
DTC: P2453 59	**Diesel Particulate Filter (DPF) Differential Pressure Sensor Performance Protection Time-Out:** P244B, P2453 08, P2453 11, P2453 12, P2453 55, P2453 58, or P2453 09The ignition is ON. The DTCs run continuously when the above condition is met. P244B, P2453 08, P2453 11, P2453 12, P2453 55The ignition is switched from ON to OFF. The DTCs run after a 2 s delay when the above condition is met. P2453 58The ignition is ON. The intake air temperature sensor is less than 0°C (32°F). The DTC runs continuously when the above condition is met.
DTC: P2454	**Diesel Particulate Filter Differential Pressure Sensor Circuit Low Voltage:** P2454 DTC P2455 is not set. The engine run time is greater than 10 s. The engine speed is greater than 600 RPM. The DTC runs continuously when the above conditions are met.
DTC: P2454	**Diesel Particulate Filter Differential Pressure Sensor Circuit Low Voltage:** The engine is running for greater than 4 seconds. The ignition 1 voltage is greater than 11V. The above conditions are met for greater than 2 seconds. DTCs P2454 and P2455 run continuously within the above enabling conditions.
DTC: P2454 00	**Diesel Particulate Filter (DPF) Differential Pressure Sensor Circuit Low Voltage:** P2453 DTC P0101, P2454, or P2455 are not set. The engine has been running and then turned off for at least 60 s. The engine speed is greater than 600 RPM. The battery voltage is greater than 11 V. The exhaust gas flow is stable. The DTC runs continue when the above conditions are met. and DTC P2453 runs once after the ignition has been turned OFF. P2454 DTC P2454 is not set. Engine run time is greater than 10 s. The engine speed is greater than 600 RPM. The DTC runs continuously when the above conditions are met. P2455 DTC P2455 is not set. Engine run time is greater than 10 s. The engine speed is greater than 600 RPM. The DTC runs continuously when the above conditions are met.
DTC: P2455	**Diesel Particulate Filter Differential Pressure Sensor Circuit High Voltage:** P2455 DTC P2454 is not set. The engine run time is greater than 10 s. The engine speed is greater than 600 RPM. The DTC runs continuously when the above conditions are met.
DTC: P2455	**Diesel Particulate Filter Differential Pressure Sensor Circuit High Voltage:** The engine is running for greater than 4 seconds. The ignition 1 voltage is greater than 11V. The above conditions are met for greater than 2 seconds. DTCs P2454 and P2455 run continuously within the above enabling conditions.
DTC: P2455 00	**Diesel Particulate Filter (DPF) Differential Pressure Sensor Circuit High Voltage:** P2453 DTC P0101, P2454, or P2455 are not set. The engine has been running and then turned off for at least 60 s. The engine speed is greater than 600 RPM. The battery voltage is greater than 11 V. The exhaust gas flow is stable. The DTC runs continue when the above conditions are met. and DTC P2453 runs once after the ignition has been turned OFF. P2454 DTC P2454 is not set. Engine run time is greater than 10 s. The engine speed is greater than 600 RPM. The DTC runs continuously when the above conditions are met. P2455 DTC P2455 is not set. Engine run time is greater than 10 s. The engine speed is greater than 600 RPM. The DTC runs continuously when the above conditions are met.
DTC: P2457	**Exhaust Gas Recirculation (EGR) Cooler Low Efficiency:** Engine speed is between 1,000-2,200 RPM. The engine is not in Diesel Particulate Filter (DPF) regeneration. The calculated fuel rate is greater than 20 mm ;. The engine coolant temperature is less than 123°C (253°F). The difference between the upstream EGR cooler temperature and the Engine Coolant Temperature (ECT) is greater than 40°C (72°F). The ambient air temperature is greater than -7°C (19°F). The EGR valve position is greater than 10 %. The Barometric Pressure (BARO) is greater than 74. 8 kPa (10. 9 psi). DTC P2457 runs once per driving cycle when the above conditions are met.

DTC	Trouble Code Title, Conditions, Possible Causes
DTC: P2458 59	**Diesel Particulate Filter (DPF) Regeneration Time Protection Time-Out:** The DTC runs during the DPF regeneration process.
DTC: P2459	**Diesel Particulate Filter Regeneration Too Often:** The engine is running. One active regeneration event has completed. DTC P2459 runs continuously when the above condition is met.
DTC: P2459	**Diesel Particulate Filter Regeneration Too Often:** DTC P0101, P0401, P0402, P2002, P2229, P2453, P2454, or P2455, are not set. The engine is running. The Intake Air Temperature is warmer than -7°C (19°F)The BARO pressure is greater than 75 kPa (11 psi). One active regeneration event has completed. DTC P2459 runs continuously when the above condition are met.
DTC: P245C 00	**Exhaust Gas Recirculation (EGR) Cooler Bypass Solenoid Valve Control Circuit Low Voltage:** Ignition is on.
DTC: P245D 00	**Exhaust Gas Recirculation (EGR) Cooler Bypass Solenoid Valve Control Circuit High Voltage:** Ignition is on.
DTC: P2463	**Diesel Particulate Filter Soot Level Accumulation:** The ignition is ON. DTC P2463 runs continuously when the above condition is met.
DTC: P2463 00	**Diesel Particulate Filter (DPF) Soot Accumulation:** The engine is running. The DTC runs continuously when the above condition is met.
DTC: P2463 00	**Diesel Particulate Filter (DPF) Soot Accumulation Malfunction:** The engine is running. The DTC runs continuously when the above condition is met.
DTC: P2463 11	**Diesel Particulate Filter (DPF) Soot Accumulation High Input:** The engine is running. The DTC runs continuously when the above condition is met.
DTC: P246C 00	**Diesel Particulate Filter (DPF) Restriction - Not Regenerable:** The engine is running. The DTC runs continuously when the above condition is met.
DTC: P246F	**Exhaust Gas Temperature Sensor 4 Performance:** P246FDTC P007C, P007D, P0097, P0098, P0101, P0102, P0103, P0107, P0108, P0112, P0113, P0401, P0402, P0403, P0405, P0406, P046C, P111C, P111D, P113A, P20E2, P2228, P2229, P242C, P242D, P2470 or P2471 is not set. The engine is running for at least 327 s. The engine speed is between 700-3000 RPM for 60 s. The calculated fuel rate is between 5-80mm ; for 60 s. DPF regeneration or exhaust gas temperature monitoring has not been active in the last 25 minutes. Exhaust gas temperature sensor 4 has changed less than 7°C (12. 6°F) in 5 s. The DTC runs continuously when the above conditions are met.
DTC: P2470	**Exhaust Gas Temperature Sensor 4 Circuit Low Voltage:** The ignition is ON or the engine is running. The DTCs run continuously when the above conditions are met.
DTC: P2471	**Exhaust Gas Temperature Sensor 4 Circuit High Voltage:** The ignition is ON or the engine is running. The DTCs run continuously when the above conditions are met.
DTC: P249D	**Closed Loop Reductant Injection Control At Limit - Flow Too Low:** DTCs P0101, P0401, P0402, P0420, P11DB, P11DC, P140B, P140C, P207F, P2200, P2202, P2203, P2205, P2209, P229E, P229F, P22A3, P22A7, or U029D, or U029E are not set. SCR reductant level not in restriction or empty level state. The engine speed is greater than 600 RPM. The battery voltage is greater than 11 V. The ambient air and emission reduction fluid tank temperatures are warmer than -7°C (19°F). The engine run time is greater than 10 s. The DTCs run continuously once the above conditions are met.
DTC: P249E	**Closed Loop Reductant Injection Control At Limit - Flow Too High:** DTCs P0101, P0401, P0402, P0420, P11DB, P11DC, P140B, P140C, P207F, P2200, P2202, P2203, P2205, P2209, P229E, P229F, P22A3, P22A7, or U029D, or U029E are not set. SCR reductant level not in restriction or empty level state. The engine speed is greater than 600 RPM. The battery voltage is greater than 11 V. The ambient air and emission reduction fluid tank temperatures are warmer than -7°C (19°F). The engine run time is greater than 10 s. The DTCs run continuously once the above conditions are met.
DTC: P24A0	**Closed Loop Diesel Particulate Filter (DPF) Regeneration Control At Limit - Temperature Too Low:** P24A0 or P24A1The engine run time is greater than 10 s. The engine speed is greater than 600 RPM. The ECM is commanding a DPF regeneration. The vehicle speed is between 24-200 km/h (15-124 mph). The exhaust temperature sensor 1 and 4 is greater than 230°C (446°F). The exhaust temperature sensor 1 and 4 is less than 750°C (1,382°F). The DTCs run continuously once the above conditions are met for 10 minutes.
DTC: P24A1	**Closed Loop Diesel Particulate Filter (DPF) Regeneration Control At Limit - Temperature Too High:** P24A0 or P24A1The engine run time is greater than 10 s. The engine speed is greater than 600 RPM. The ECM is commanding a DPF regeneration. The vehicle speed is between 24-200 km/h (15-124 mph). The exhaust temperature sensor 1 and 4 is greater than 230°C (446°F). The exhaust temperature sensor 1 and 4 is less than 750°C (1,382°F). The DTCs run continuously once the above conditions are met for 10 minutes.
DTC: P2500	**Generator L-Terminal Circuit Low:** The engine is running.

DTC	Trouble Code Title, Conditions, Possible Causes
DTC: P2501	**Generator L-Terminal Circuit High:** The ignition is ON. The engine is OFF.
DTC: P2510	**Engine Control Module Relay Circuit:** DTCs P006F, P02E0, P0403, P1049, P2049, P208D, P20A3, P245A are not set. DTC P2510 runs once per ignition cycle.
DTC: P2510 58	**Engine Controls Ignition Relay Feedback Circuit Performance:** P2510 58The ignition is ON, or the engine is running. The DTCs run continuously once the above condition is met.
DTC: P2510 59	**Engine Controls Ignition Relay Feedback Circuit Protection Time-Out:** P2510 59The ignition is switched OFF. The DTC runs continuously until the ECM powers down.
DTC: P2534	**Ignition 1 Switch Circuit Low Voltage:** The engine speed is greater than 500 RPM for 5 seconds. Ignition voltage is between 9. 0 volts and 19. 0 volts.
DTC: P2534	**Ignition On/Start Switch Circuit Low Voltage:** The engine control module (ECM) communicates that the engine is running through the controller area network (CAN).
DTC: P2544	**Transmission Torque Request Signal Message Counter Incorrect:** The ignition is ON. The DTCs run continuously once the above condition is met.
DTC: P2544	**Transmission Torque Request Circuit:** The engine run time is greater than 0. 5 s. No other CAN errors are present.
DTC: P2544 72	**Transmission Torque Request Circuit Message Counter Incorrect:** The ignition is ON. The DTCs run continuously once the above condition is met.
DTC: P2544 74	**Transmission Torque Request Circuit Bus Signal Checksum Error:** The ignition is ON. The DTCs run continuously once the above condition is met.
DTC: P2563	**Turbocharger Boost Control Position Sensor Performance:** DTCs P0047, P0048, P2564, or P2565 are not set. The engine has been running for greater than 30 seconds. DTC P2563 runs continuously when the above conditions are met.
DTC: P2564	**Turbocharger Boost Control Position Sensor Circuit Low Voltage:** The engine has been running for more than 10 s. DTC P2564 and P2565 run continuously when the above conditions are met.
DTC: P2564 00	**Turbocharger Vane Position Sensor Circuit Low Voltage:** The ignition is ON or engine is running.
DTC: P2565	**Turbocharger Boost Control Position Sensor Circuit High Voltage:** The engine has been running for more than 10 s. DTC P2564 and P2565 run continuously when the above conditions are met.
DTC: P2565 00	**Turbocharger Vane Position Sensor Circuit High Voltage:** The ignition is ON or engine is running.
DTC: P2598	**Turbocharger Boost Control Position Performance - Low Position:** DTC P003A, P006E, P006F, P0045, P0047, P0048, P2564, or P2565 is not set. The engine coolant temperature is between 70-123°C (158-253°F). The engine is running for greater than 30-210 s, depending on the engine coolant temperature at start. The turbocharger vane position learn procedure is not active and has completed and passed since the last clearing of fault code memory. The ambient air temperature is greater than -15°C (5°F). DTC P2598 and P2599 run continuously whenever the above conditions are met.
DTC: P2599	**Turbocharger Boost Control Position Performance - High Position:** DTC P003A, P006E, P006F, P0045, P0047, P0048, P2564, or P2565 is not set. The engine coolant temperature is between 70-123°C (158-253°F). The engine is running for greater than 30-210 s, depending on the engine coolant temperature at start. The turbocharger vane position learn procedure is not active and has completed and passed since the last clearing of fault code memory. The ambient air temperature is greater than -15°C (5°F). DTC P2598 and P2599 run continuously whenever the above conditions are met.
DTC: P2610	**Control Module Ignition Off Timer Performance:** P2610The engine speed is greater than 240 RPM. DTC P2610 runs continuously when the engine is operating and the real time clock is active.
DTC: P2610	**Control Module Ignition Off Timer Performance:** P062C, P2610These DTCs run continuously when the ignition is ON.
DTC: P2610 00	**Control Module Ignition Off Timer Performance:** P2610 00The engine is running for at least 10 s. The ignition voltage is between 11-18 V. DTC P2610 00 runs once per ignition cycle.

DTC	Trouble Code Title, Conditions, Possible Causes
DTC: P2610 00	**Control Module Ignition Off Timer Performance:** P0601 00, P0605 00The ignition switch is in run or crank. The system voltage is more than 5. 23 V. The check sum calculation at power down in the last drive cycle had completely finished. DTC P0601 00 and DTC P0605 run once per ignition cycle when the above condition is met. P0602 00The ignition switch is in run or crank. DTC P0602 00 runs once per ignition cycle. P0604 00The ignition switch is in run or crank. The read/write test at power down in the last drive cycle had completely finished. DTC P0604 00 runs once per ignition cycle when the above condition is met. P0606 00The ignition switch is in the unlock, accessory, run, or crank positions. DTC P0606 00 runs continuously when the above conditions are met. P0607 00The engine is running or cranking. DTC P0607 00 runs continuously when the above condition is met. . P061B 00The ignition is ON or the engine is running. The system voltage is more than 5. 23 V. DTC P061B 00 runs continuously when the above conditions are met. P061C 00The ignition is ON or the engine is running. The system voltage is more than 5. 23 V. DTC P061C 00 runs continuously when the above conditions are met. P2610 00The ECM is powered down. DTC P2610 00 runs once per ignition cycle. or The ECM is powered up with the ignition switch in the run or crank position. The engine OFF timer value is less than or greater than an internal reference counter during an 2 s interval. DTC P2610 00 runs continuously when the above conditions are met.
DTC: P2615	**Camshaft Position Signal Output Circuit Low:** The ignition is ON, engine running.
DTC: P2616	**Camshaft Position Signal Output Circuit High:** The ignition is ON, engine running.
DTC: P2626	**HO2S Pumping Current Trim Circuit Sensor 1:** P2626 DTCs P0121, P0122, P0123, P0221, P0222, P0223, P0335, P0336, P0338 are not set. The ignition voltage is between 10. 7-8. 1 V. The engine is running. Fuel cut-off is true. The estimated exhaust temperature is less than 750°C (1,382°F). The HO2S 1 heater is at operating temperature. DTC P2626 runs continuously when the above conditions are met for 4 s, or when the above conditions are met for 10 minutes if the fuel level is low.
DTC: P2635	**Fuel Pump Flow Performance:** DTC P018B, P018C, P018D, P0231, P0232, P023F, P064A, P1255 or P06A6 are not active. DTC P0641 has not failed this ignition cycle. Fuel pump control is enabled and the fuel pump control state is normal. The system voltage is greater than 11 V. The engine has been running for more than 30 s. Low fuel level warning not present.
DTC: P2687 01	**Fuel Heater Relay Control Circuit Short to Battery:** The ignition is ON. The ignition voltage is less than 16. 5 V. The DTC runs continuously once the above conditions are met
DTC: P2687 02	**Fuel Heater Relay Control Circuit Short to Ground:** The ignition is ON. The ignition voltage is less than 16. 5 V. The DTC runs continuously once the above conditions are met
DTC: P2687 04	**Fuel Heater Relay Control Circuit Open:** The ignition is ON. The ignition voltage is less than 16. 5 V. The DTC runs continuously once the above conditions are met
DTC: P2687 54	**Fuel Heater Relay Control Circuit High Temperature:** The ignition is ON. The ignition voltage is less than 16. 5 V. The DTC runs continuously once the above conditions are met
DTC: P268A	**Fuel Injector Calibration Data Not Programmed:** The ignition is ON.
DTC: P268A 00	**Fuel Injector Calibration Not Programmed Malfunction:** The ignition is ON.
DTC: P268C	**Injector 1 Calibration Incorrect:** The ignition is ON.
DTC: P268C 00	**Cylinder 1 Injector Calibration Incorrect:** The ignition is ON.
DTC: P268D	**Injector 2 Calibration Incorrect:** The ignition is ON.
DTC: P268D 00	**Cylinder 2 Injector Calibration Incorrect:** The ignition is ON.
DTC: P268E	**Injector 3 Calibration Incorrect:** The ignition is ON.
DTC: P268E 00	**Cylinder 3 Injector Calibration Incorrect:** The ignition is ON.
DTC: P268F	**Injector 4 Calibration Incorrect:** The ignition is ON.

DTC	Trouble Code Title, Conditions, Possible Causes
DTC: P268F 00	**Cylinder 4 Injector Calibration Incorrect:** The ignition is ON.
DTC: P2690	**Injector 5 Calibration Incorrect:** The ignition is ON.
DTC: P2691	**Injector 6 Calibration Incorrect:** The ignition is ON.
DTC: P2692	**Injector 7 Calibration Incorrect:** The ignition is ON.
DTC: P2693	**Injector 8 Calibration Incorrect:** The ignition is ON.
DTC: P2714	**Pressure Control Solenoid Valve 4 Stuck Off:** P2714 DTC P0101, P0102, P0103, P0106, P0107, P0108, P0171, P0172, P0174, P0175, P0201, P0202, P0203, P0204, P0205, P0206, P0207, P0208, P0300, P0301, P0302, P0303, P0304, P0305, P0306, P0307, P0308, P0401, P042E, P0716, P0717, P0722, P0723, or P182E is not set. The ignition voltage is 8. 6 volts or greater. The output speed is 16 RPM or greater, or the throttle position is 0. 5 percent or greater. The throttle position signal is valid. The engine speed is 400 RPM or greater for 5 seconds. The transmission fluid temperature is -7°C (19°F) or greater. The 2-6 clutch is commanded ON. The high side driver (HSD) is enabled.
DTC: P2714	**Clutch Pressure Control (PC) Solenoid 4 - Stuck Off:** P2714No ISS DTCs P0716 or P0717. No OSS DTCs P0722 or P0723. No IMS DTCs P1825 or P1915. The ignition voltage is between 9. 0 volts and 19. 0 volts. The transmission fluid temperature is 0°C (32°F) or greater. The transmission input shaft speed is 80 RPM or greater. The 2-6 clutch is commanded ON.
DTC: P2715	**Clutch Pressure Control Solenoid Valve 4 Stuck On:** P2715 DTC P0101, P0102, P0103, P0106, P0107, P0108, P0171, P0172, P0174, P0175, P0201, P0202, P0203, P0204, P0205, P0206, P0207, P0208, P0300, P0301, P0302, P0303, P0304, P0305, P0306, P0307, P0308, P0401, P042E, P0716, P0717, P0722, P0723, or P182E is not set. The ignition voltage is 8. 6 volts or greater. The HSD is enabled. The transmission fluid temperature is 0°C (32°F) or greater. The transmission output shaft speed is 350 RPM or greater. The transmission input shaft speed is 200 RPM or greater. The 2-6 clutch is commanded OFF. The commanded and attained gear is not 1st.
DTC: P2715	**Pressure Control Solenoid Valve 4 Stuck On:** P2715 DTC P0101, P0102, P0103, P0106, P0107, P0108, P0171, P0172, P0174, P0175, P0201, P0202, P0203, P0204, P0205, P0206, P0207, P0208, P0300, P0301, P0302, P0303, P0304, P0305, P0306, P0307, P0308, P0401, P042E, P0716, P0717, P0722, P0723, or P182E is not set. The ignition voltage is 9. 0 volts or greater. The transmission output shaft speed is 200 RPM or greater. The 2-6 clutch is commanded OFF. The TFT is 0°C (32°F) or greater. The attained range is not 1st gear. The HSD is enabled. The transmission input speed is 200 RPM or greater.
DTC: P2719	**Clutch Pressure Control (PC) Solenoid 4 System Performance:** P2719, P2720, or P2721 DTCs P2719, P2720, or P2721 have not set this ignition. The ignition voltage is 8. 6 volts or greater. The engine speed is 500 RPM or greater, for 5 seconds. The clutch PC solenoid 4 is commanded ON.
DTC: P2720	**Pressure Control Solenoid Valve 4 Control Circuit Low Voltage:** P2720The engine speed is 400 RPM or greater for 5 seconds. The ignition voltage is 8. 6 volts or greater. DTC P2720 is not set.
DTC: P2720	**Clutch Pressure Control (PC) Solenoid 4 Control Circuit Low Voltage:** P2719, P2720, or P2721 DTCs P2719, P2720, or P2721 have not set this ignition. The ignition voltage is 8. 6 volts or greater. The engine speed is 500 RPM or greater, for 5 seconds. The clutch PC solenoid 4 is commanded ON.
DTC: P2721	**Clutch Pressure Control (PC) Solenoid 4 Control Circuit High Voltage:** P2719, P2720, or P2721 DTCs P2719, P2720, or P2721 have not set this ignition. The ignition voltage is 8. 6 volts or greater. The engine speed is 500 RPM or greater, for 5 seconds. The clutch PC solenoid 4 is commanded ON.
DTC: P2721	**Pressure Control Solenoid Valve 4 Control Circuit High Voltage:** P2721The engine speed is 400 RPM or greater for 5 seconds. The ignition voltage is 8. 6 volts or greater. DTC P2721 is not set.
DTC: P2723	**Pressure Control Solenoid Valve 5 Stuck Off:** P2723 DTC P0101, P0102, P0103, P0106, P0107, P0108, P0171, P0172, P0174, P0175, P0201, P0202, P0203, P0204, P0205, P0206, P0207, P0208, P0300, P0301, P0302, P0303, P0304, P0305, P0306, P0307, P0308, P0401, P042E, P0716, P0717, P0722, P0723, or P182E is not set. The ignition voltage is 8. 6 volts or greater. The high side driver (HSD) is enabled. The output speed is 16 RPM or greater, or the throttle position is 0. 4 percent or greater. The throttle position signal is valid. The engine speed is greater than 400 RPM for 5 seconds. The transmission fluid temperature (TFT) is 0°C (32°F) or greater.
DTC: P2723	**Clutch Pressure Control (PC) Solenoid 5 - Stuck Off:** P2723No ISS DTCs P0716 or P0717. No OSS DTCs P0722 or P0723. No IMS DTCs P1825 or P1915. The transmission input shaft speed is 60 RPM or greater. 1-2-3-4 clutch is commanded ON.

DTC	Trouble Code Title, Conditions, Possible Causes
DTC: P2724	**Pressure Control Solenoid Valve 5 - Stuck On:** P2724 DTC P0101, P0102, P0103, P0106, P0107, P0108, P0171, P0172, P0174, P0175, P0201, P0202, P0203, P0204, P0205, P0206, P0207, P0208, P0300, P0301, P0302, P0303, P0304, P0305, P0306, P0307, P0308, P0401, P042E, P0716, P0717, P0722, P0723, or P182E is not set. The transmission fluid temperature is 0°C (32°F) or greater. The high HSD is ON. The transmission output shaft speed is 200 RPM or greater. The transmission input shaft speed is 200 RPM or greater. The commanded range is not 1st gear.
DTC: P2724	**Clutch Pressure Control (PC) Solenoid 5 - Stuck On:** P2724No DTCs P0101, P0102, P0103, P0106, P0107, P0108, P0171, P0172, P0174, P0175, P0201, P0202, P0203, P0204, P0205, P0206, P0207, P0208, P0300, P0301, P0302, P0303, P0304, P0305, P0306, P0307, P0308, P0401, P042E, P0716, P0717, P0722, P0723, or P182E. The ignition voltage is 8. 6 volts or greater. The high side driver is enabled. The TFT is 0°C (32°F) or greater. The transmission output shaft speed is 350 RPM or greater. The transmission input speed is 200 RPM or greater. 1-2-3-4 clutch is commanded OFF.
DTC: P2728	**Pressure Control Solenoid Valve 5 System Performance:** P2728, P2729, or P2730The engine speed is 400 RPM or greater for 5 seconds. The ignition voltage is 9. 0 volts or greater.
DTC: P2728	**Clutch Pressure Control (PC) Solenoid 5 System Performance:** P2728 DTC P2728 has not set this ignition cycle. The engine speed is 400 RPM or greater for 5 seconds. The ignition voltage is 8. 6 volts or greater.
DTC: P2729	**Pressure Control Solenoid Valve 5 Control Circuit Low Voltage:** P2729 DTC P2729 is not set. The engine speed is 400 RPM or greater for 5 seconds. The ignition voltage is 8. 6 volts or greater.
DTC: P2729	**Clutch Pressure Control (PC) Solenoid 5 Control Circuit Low Voltage:** P2728, P2729, or P2730 DTCs P2728, P2729, or P2730 have not set this ignition. The ignition voltage is 8. 6 volts or greater. The engine speed is 400 RPM or greater for 5 seconds. The clutch PC solenoid 5 is commanded ON.
DTC: P2730	**Pressure Control Solenoid Valve 5 Control Circuit High Voltage:** P2730 DTC P2730 is not set. The engine speed is 400 RPM or greater for 5 seconds. The ignition voltage is 8. 6 volts or greater.
DTC: P2730	**Clutch Pressure Control (PC) Solenoid 5 Control Circuit High Voltage:** P2728, P2729, or P2730 DTCs P2728, P2729, or P2730 have not set this ignition. The ignition voltage is 8. 6 volts or greater. The engine speed is 400 RPM or greater for 5 seconds. The clutch PC solenoid 5 is commanded ON.
DTC: P2762	**Torque Converter Clutch (TCC) Pressure Control Solenoid System Performance:** P2762 DTC P2762 has not set this ignition cycle. The engine speed is 400 RPM or greater for 5 seconds. The ignition voltage is 8. 6 volts or greater. Transmission fluid temperature is 140°C (284°F) or greater.
DTC: P2763	**Torque Converter Clutch (TCC) Pressure Control Solenoid Valve Control Circuit High Voltage:** P2763 or P2764The engine speed is 500 RPM or greater for 5 seconds. The ignition voltage is 9. 0 volts or greater. No DTCs P0658 or P0659. The high side driver is enabled.
DTC: P2764	**Torque Converter Clutch (TCC) Pressure Control (PC) Solenoid Control Circuit Low Voltage:** P2764No DTC P0335, P0336, P0340, P0345, P0346, P0365, P0366, P0390 or P0391. The engine speed is greater than 500 RPM for 5 seconds. The ignition voltage is greater than 8. 0 V.
DTC: P2769	**Torque Converter Clutch (TCC) Enable Solenoid Control Circuit Low Voltage:** P2769The system voltage is 8-18 volts. The engine speed is greater than 475 RPM for 5 seconds. Vehicle speed is less than 200 km/h (124 mph).
DTC: P2770	**Torque Converter Clutch (TCC) Enable Solenoid Control Circuit High Voltage:** P2770The system voltage is 8-18 volts. The engine speed is greater than 475 RPM for 5 seconds. Vehicle speed is less than 200 km/h (124 mph).
DTC: P2A00	**HO2S Circuit Closed Loop Performance Bank 1 Sensor 1:** P2A00 or P2A03 DTCs P0030, P0036, P0053, P0054, P0068, P0101, P0102, P0103, P0106, P0107, P0108, P0112, P0113, P0116, P0117, P0118, P0120, P0121, P0122, P0123, P0128, P0131, P0132, P0133, P0134, P0135, P0137, P0138, P0140, P0141, P0171, P0172, P0174, P0175, P0201, P0202, P0203, P0204, P0205, P0206, P0207, P0208, P0220, P0222, P0223, P0300, P0301, P0302, P0303, P0304, P0305, P0306, P0307, P0308, P0442, P0443, P0446, P0449, P0455, P0496, P1133, P1516, P2101, P2119, P2135, P2176 are not set. The engine is running. The system voltage is between 10-32 V. The ECT Sensor parameter is more than 0°C (32°F). DTCs P2A00 and P2A03 run continuously when the above conditions are met.
DTC: P2A00	**HO2S Circuit Closed Loop (CL) Performance Sensor 1:** P2A00 DTCs P0068, P0106, P0107, P0108, P0116, P0117, P0118, P0120, P0121, P0122, P0123, P0128, P0131, P0201, P0202, P0203, P0204, P0220, P0222, P0223, P1516, P2101, P2119, P2135, P2176 are not set. The Engine Run Time parameter is more than 100 s. The Engine speed parameter is between 500-3,400 RPM. The Ignition 1 Signal parameter is between 10-32 V. The Mass Airflow (MAF) Sensor parameter is between 3. 2-30 g/s. The ECT Sensor parameter is more than 70°C (158°F). DTC P2A00 runs continuously when the above conditions are met for 5 s.

DTC	Trouble Code Title, Conditions, Possible Causes
DTC: P2A00 00	**HO2S Circuit Closed Loop Performance Sensor 1:** Ignition voltage is between 10-18 V. Engine speed is between 1 000-3 400 RPM. Airflow into the engine is between 4-30 g/s. Engine coolant temperature (ECT) is greater than 70°C (158°F). Engine run time is greater than 100 s. DTC P2A00 runs continuously when the above conditions are met for greater than 5 s.
DTC: P2A01	**HO2S Performance Bank 1 Sensor 2:** DTC P2A01 DTC P2A01 runs a passive test and intrusive test when the following conditions are met. DTCs P0030, P0036, P0053, P0054, P0068, P0101, P0102, P0103, P0106, P0107, P0108, P0112, P0113, P0116, P0117, P0118, P0120, P0121, P0122, P0123, P0125, P0128, P0131, P0132, P0133, P0134, P0135, P0137, P0138, P0140, P0141, P0201, P0202, P0203, P0204, P0205, P0206, P0207, P0208, P0220, P0222, P0223, P0442, P0443, P0446, P0449, P0455, P0496, P1133, P1516, P2101, P2119, P2135, P2176, or P2A00 are not set.
DTC: P2A01 00	**HO2S Performance Sensor 2:** P2A01 00 DTCs P0107 00, P0108 00, P0136 00, P0137 00, P0138 00, P0139 00, P0140 00, P0141 00, P0171 00, P0172 00, P0201 00, P0202 00, P0203 00, P0204 00, P0261 00, P0262 00, P0264 00, P0265 00, P0267 00, P0268 00, P0270 00, P0271 00, P0300 00, P0301 00, P0302 00, P0303 00, P0304 00, P0313 00, P0443 00, P0458 00, P0459 00, P0496 00, P2270 00, P2271 00 are not set. The ignition is ON. The deceleration fuel cut-off is active. DTC P2A01 00 runs continuously when the above conditions are met.
DTC: P2A03	**HO2S Circuit Closed Loop Performance Bank 2 Sensor 1:** P2A00 or P2A03 DTCs P0030, P0036, P0053, P0054, P0068, P0101, P0102, P0103, P0106, P0107, P0108, P0112, P0113, P0116, P0117, P0118, P0120, P0121, P0122, P0123, P0128, P0131, P0132, P0133, P0134, P0135, P0137, P0138, P0140, P0141, P0171, P0172, P0174, P0175, P0201, P0202, P0203, P0204, P0205, P0206, P0207, P0208, P0220, P0222, P0223, P0300, P0301, P0302, P0303, P0304, P0305, P0306, P0307, P0308, P0442, P0443, P0446, P0449, P0455, P0496, P1133, P1516, P2101, P2119, P2135, P2176 are not set. The engine is running. The system voltage is between 10-32 V. The ECT Sensor parameter is more than 0°C (32°F). DTCs P2A00 and P2A03 run continuously when the above conditions are met.
DTC: P2A03	**HO2S Performance Bank 2 Sensor 1:** DTCs P2A00 or P2A03 DTCs P0068, P0101, P0102, P0103, P0106, P0107, P0108, P0112, P0113, P0116, P0117, P0118, P0120, P0121, P0122, P0123, P0125, P0128, P0201, P0202, P0203, P0204, P0205, P0206, P0207, P0208, P0220, P0222, P0223, P0442, P0443, P0446, P0449, P0455, P0496, P1516, P2101, P2119, P2135, or P2176 are not set. The engine run time is greater than 100 seconds. The engine speed is between 500-5,000 RPM. The Ignition 1 voltage is between 10-18 volts. The mass air flow (MAF) sensor is between 3-50 g/s. The engine coolant temperature (ECT) is greater than 70°C (158°F). The DTCs run continuously when the above conditions are met for 5 seconds.

ENGLISH TO METRIC CONVERSION: TORQUE

To convert foot-pounds (ft. lbs.) to Newton-meters (Nm), multiply the number of ft. lbs. by 1.36

To convert Newton-meters (Nm) to foot-pounds (ft. lbs.), multiply the number of Nm by 0.7376

ft. lbs.	Nm	ft. lbs.	Nm	ft. lbs.	Nm	ft. lbs.	Nm
0.1	0.1	34	46.2	76	103.4	118	160.5
0.2	0.3	35	47.6	77	104.7	119	161.8
0.3	0.4	36	49.0	78	106.1	120	163.2
0.4	0.5	37	50.3	79	107.4	121	164.6
0.5	0.7	38	51.7	80	108.8	122	165.9
0.6	0.8	39	53.0	81	110.2	123	167.3
0.7	1.0	40	54.4	82	111.5	124	168.6
0.8	1.1	41	55.8	83	112.9	125	170.0
0.9	1.2	42	57.1	84	114.2	126	171.4
1	1.4	43	58.5	85	115.6	127	172.7
2	2.7	44	59.8	86	117.0	128	174.1
3	4.1	45	61.2	87	118.3	129	175.4
4	5.4	46	62.6	88	119.7	130	176.8
5	6.8	47	63.9	89	121.0	131	178.2
6	8.2	48	65.3	90	122.4	132	179.5
7	9.5	49	66.6	91	123.8	133	180.9
8	10.9	50	68.0	92	125.1	134	182.2
9	12.2	51	69.4	93	126.5	135	183.6
10	13.6	52	70.7	94	127.8	136	185.0
11	15.0	53	72.1	95	129.2	137	186.3
12	16.3	54	73.4	96	130.6	138	187.7
13	17.7	55	74.8	97	131.9	139	189.0
14	19.0	56	76.2	98	133.3	140	190.4
15	20.4	57	77.5	99	134.6	141	191.8
16	21.8	58	78.9	100	136.0	142	193.1
17	23.1	59	80.2	101	137.4	143	194.5
18	24.5	60	81.6	102	138.7	144	195.8
19	25.8	61	83.0	103	140.1	145	197.2
20	27.2	62	84.3	104	141.4	146	198.6
21	28.6	63	85.7	105	142.8	147	199.9
22	29.9	64	87.0	106	144.2	148	201.3
23	31.3	65	88.4	107	145.5	149	202.6
24	32.6	66	89.8	108	146.9	150	204.0
25	34.0	67	91.1	109	148.2	151	205.4
26	35.4	68	92.5	110	149.6	152	206.7
27	36.7	69	93.8	111	151.0	153	208.1
28	38.1	70	95.2	112	152.3	154	209.4
29	39.4	71	96.6	113	153.7	155	210.8
30	40.8	72	97.9	114	155.0	156	212.2
31	42.2	73	99.3	115	156.4	157	213.5
32	43.5	74	100.6	116	157.8	158	214.9
33	44.9	75	102.0	117	159.1	159	216.2

METRIC TO ENGLISH CONVERSION: TORQUE

To convert foot-pounds (ft. lbs.) to Newton-meters (Nm), multiply the number of ft. lbs. by 1.36

To convert Newton-meters (Nm) to foot-pounds (ft. lbs.), multiply the number of Nm by 0.7376

Nm	ft. lbs.	Nm	ft. lbs.	Nm	ft. lbs.	Nm	ft. lbs.	Nm	ft. lbs.
0.1	0.1	34	25.0	76	55.9	118	86.8	160	117.6
0.2	0.1	35	25.7	77	56.6	119	87.5	161	118.4
0.3	0.2	36	26.5	78	57.4	120	88.2	162	119.1
0.4	0.3	37	27.2	79	58.1	121	89.0	163	119.9
0.5	0.4	38	27.9	80	58.8	122	89.7	164	120.6
0.6	0.4	39	28.7	81	59.6	123	90.4	165	121.3
0.7	0.5	40	29.4	82	60.3	124	91.2	166	122.1
0.8	0.6	41	30.1	83	61.0	125	91.9	167	122.8
0.9	0.7	42	30.9	84	61.8	126	92.6	168	123.5
1	0.7	43	31.6	85	62.5	127	93.4	169	124.3
2	1.5	44	32.4	86	63.2	128	94.1	170	125.0
3	2.2	45	33.1	87	64.0	129	94.9	171	125.7
4	2.9	46	33.8	88	64.7	130	95.6	172	126.5
5	3.7	47	34.6	89	65.4	131	96.3	173	127.2
6	4.4	48	35.3	90	66.2	132	97.1	174	127.9
7	5.1	49	36.0	91	66.9	133	97.8	175	128.7
8	5.9	50	36.8	92	67.6	134	98.5	176	129.4
9	6.6	51	37.5	93	68.4	135	99.3	177	130.1
10	7.4	52	38.2	94	69.1	136	100.0	178	130.9
11	8.1	53	39.0	95	69.9	137	100.7	179	131.6
12	8.8	54	39.7	96	70.6	138	101.5	180	132.4
13	9.6	55	40.4	97	71.3	139	102.2	181	133.1
14	10.3	56	41.2	98	72.1	140	102.9	182	133.8
15	11.0	57	41.9	99	72.8	141	103.7	183	134.6
16	11.8	58	42.6	100	73.5	142	104.4	184	135.3
17	12.5	59	43.4	101	74.3	143	105.1	185	136.0
18	13.2	60	44.1	102	75.0	144	105.9	186	136.8
19	14.0	61	44.9	103	75.7	145	106.6	187	137.5
20	14.7	62	45.6	104	76.5	146	107.4	188	138.2
21	15.4	63	46.3	105	77.2	147	108.1	189	139.0
22	16.2	64	47.1	106	77.9	148	108.8	190	139.7
23	16.9	65	47.8	107	78.7	149	109.6	191	140.4
24	17.6	66	48.5	108	79.4	150	110.3	192	141.2
25	18.4	67	49.3	109	80.1	151	111.0	193	141.9
26	19.1	68	50.0	110	80.9	152	111.8	194	142.6
27	19.9	69	50.7	111	81.6	153	112.5	195	143.4
28	20.6	70	51.5	112	82.4	154	113.2	196	144.1
29	21.3	71	52.2	113	83.1	155	114.0	197	144.9
30	22.1	72	52.9	114	83.8	156	114.7	198	145.6
31	22.8	73	53.7	115	84.6	157	115.4	199	146.3
32	23.5	74	54.4	116	85.3	158	116.2	200	147.1
33	24.3	75	55.1	117	86.0	159	116.9	201	147.8

ENGLISH/METRIC CONVERSION: TEMPERATURE

To convert Fahrenheit (F°) to Celsius (C°), take F° temperature and subtract 32, multiply the result by 5 and divide the result by 9
To convert Celsius (C°) to Fahrenheit (F°), take C° temperature and multiply it by 9, divide the result by 5 and add 32

F°	C°	F°	C°	C°	F°	C°	F°
-40	-40.0	150	65.6	-38	-36.4	46	114.8
-35	-37.2	155	68.3	-36	-32.8	48	118.4
-30	-34.4	160	71.1	-34	-29.2	50	122
-25	-31.7	165	73.9	-32	-25.6	52	125.6
-20	-28.9	170	76.7	-30	-22	54	129.2
-15	-26.1	175	79.4	-28	-18.4	56	132.8
-10	-23.3	180	82.2	-26	-14.8	58	136.4
-5	-20.6	185	85.0	-24	-11.2	60	140
0	-17.8	190	87.8	-22	-7.6	62	143.6
1	-17.2	195	90.6	-20	-4	64	147.2
2	-16.7	200	93.3	-18	-0.4	66	150.8
3	-16.1	205	96.1	-16	3.2	68	154.4
4	-15.6	210	98.9	-14	6.8	70	158
5	-15.0	212	100.0	-12	10.4	72	161.6
10	-12.2	215	101.7	-10	14	74	165.2
15	-9.4	220	104.4	-8	17.6	76	168.8
20	-6.7	225	107.2	-6	21.2	78	172.4
25	-3.9	230	110.0	-4	24.8	80	176
30	-1.1	235	112.8	-2	28.4	82	179.6
35	1.7	240	115.6	0	32	84	183.2
40	4.4	245	118.3	2	35.6	86	186.8
45	7.2	250	121.1	4	39.2	88	190.4
50	10.0	255	123.9	6	42.8	90	194
55	12.8	260	126.7	8	46.4	92	197.6
60	15.6	265	129.4	10	50	94	201.2
65	18.3	270	132.2	12	53.6	96	204.8
70	21.1	275	135.0	14	57.2	98	208.4
75	23.9	280	137.8	16	60.8	100	212
80	26.7	285	140.6	18	64.4	102	215.6
85	29.4	290	143.3	20	68	104	219.2
90	32.2	295	146.1	22	71.6	106	222.8
95	35.0	300	148.9	24	75.2	108	226.4
100	37.8	305	151.7	26	78.8	110	230
105	40.6	310	154.4	28	82.4	112	233.6
110	43.3	315	157.2	30	86	114	237.2
115	46.1	320	160.0	32	89.6	116	240.8
120	48.9	325	162.8	34	93.2	118	244.4
125	51.7	330	165.6	36	96.8	120	248
130	54.4	335	168.3	38	100.4	122	251.6
135	57.2	340	171.1	40	104	124	255.2
140	60.0	345	173.9	42	107.6	126	258.8
145	62.8	350	176.7	44	111.2	128	262.4

LENGTH CONVERSION

To convert inches (in.) to millimeters (mm), multiply the number of inches by 25.4

To convert millimeters (mm) to inches (in.), multiply the number of millimeters by 0.04

Inches	Millimeters	Inches	Millimeters	Inches	Millimeters	Inches	Millimeters
0.0001	0.00254	0.005	0.1270	0.09	2.286	4	101.6
0.0002	0.00508	0.006	0.1524	0.1	2.54	5	127.0
0.0003	0.00762	0.007	0.1778	0.2	5.08	6	152.4
0.0004	0.01016	0.008	0.2032	0.3	7.62	7	177.8
0.0005	0.01270	0.009	0.2286	0.4	10.16	8	203.2
0.0006	0.01524	0.01	0.254	0.5	12.70	9	228.6
0.0007	0.01778	0.02	0.508	0.6	15.24	10	254.0
0.0008	0.02032	0.03	0.762	0.7	17.78	11	279.4
0.0009	0.02286	0.04	1.016	0.8	20.32	12	304.8
0.001	0.0254	0.05	1.270	0.9	22.86	13	330.2
0.002	0.0508	0.06	1.524	1	25.4	14	355.6
0.003	0.0762	0.07	1.778	2	50.8	15	381.0
0.004	0.1016	0.08	2.032	3	76.2	16	406.4

ENGLISH/METRIC CONVERSION: LENGTH

To convert inches (in.) to millimeters (mm), multiply the number of inches by 25.4

To convert millimeters (mm) to inches (in.), multiply the number of millimeters by 0.04

| Inches | | Millimeters | Inches | | Millimeters | Inches | | Millimeters |
Fraction	Decimal	Decimal	Fraction	Decimal	Decimal	Fraction	Decimal	Decimal
1/64	0.016	0.397	11/32	0.344	8.731	11/16	0.688	17.463
1/32	0.031	0.794	23/64	0.359	9.128	45/64	0.703	17.859
3/64	0.047	1.191	3/8	0.375	9.525	23/32	0.719	18.256
1/16	0.063	1.588	25/64	0.391	9.922	47/64	0.734	18.653
5/64	0.078	1.984	13/32	0.406	10.319	3/4	0.750	19.050
3/32	0.094	2.381	27/64	0.422	10.716	49/64	0.766	19.447
7/64	0.109	2.778	7/16	0.438	11.113	25/32	0.781	19.844
1/8	0.125	3.175	29/64	0.453	11.509	51/64	0.797	20.241
9/64	0.141	3.572	15/32	0.469	11.906	13/16	0.813	20.638
5/32	0.156	3.969	31/64	0.484	12.303	53/64	0.828	21.034
11/64	0.172	4.366	1/2	0.500	12.700	27/32	0.844	21.431
3/16	0.188	4.763	33/64	0.516	13.097	55/64	0.859	21.828
13/64	0.203	5.159	17/32	0.531	13.494	7/8	0.875	22.225
7/32	0.219	5.556	35/64	0.547	13.891	57/64	0.891	22.622
15/64	0.234	5.953	9/16	0.563	14.288	29/32	0.906	23.019
1/4	0.250	6.350	37/64	0.578	14.684	59/64	0.922	23.416
17/64	0.266	6.747	19/32	0.594	15.081	15/16	0.938	23.813
9/32	0.281	7.144	39/64	0.609	15.478	61/64	0.953	24.209
19/64	0.297	7.541	5/8	0.625	15.875	31/32	0.969	24.606
5/16	0.313	7.938	41/64	0.641	16.272	63/64	0.984	25.003
21/64	0.328	8.334	21/32	0.656	16.669	1/1	1.000	25.400
			43/64	0.672	17.066			

CHILTON® LABOR GUIDE

Chilton's labor times are so trusted, even a competing publisher uses them!

The *Chilton 2012 Labor Guide* features new models and new labor operations in order to stay current with new technologies. Labor times have also been refined for normal and severe maintenance schedules, if applicable. The 2012 edition provides repair times for 1981-current import and domestic vehicles. Chilton's editors consider warranty times, component locations, component type, the environment in which technicians work, the training they receive, and the tools they use when calculating a labor time. To allow for vehicle age, operating conditions, and type of service, the *Chilton 2012 Labor Guide* provides standard and severe service times, plus OEM warranty times. Vehicle makes and models conform to current Automotive Aftermarket Industry Association (AAIA) standards.

978-1-4354-6155-0 Chilton 2012 Labor Guide Manual Set (Domestic & Import)

978-1-4354-6154-3 Chilton 2012 Labor Guide CD-ROM (Domestic & Import)

CD-ROM FEATURES

- access labor times for 1981-current models import and domestic vehicle models
- save time with automatically calculated labor charges, taxes, & parts as total job is estimated
- create professional estimates for your customer and worksheets for your technicians, printing them whenever needed
- keep track of customers, prior estimates, and your own parts or package jobs with less paper
- choose part names for estimates from an industry standard database to reduce typing
- estimate and track your work status with improved forms
- communicate easily with customers using re-designed printouts which show all labor and parts in an easy-to-read format.
- simplify adding parts to your estimate or work order with a helpful parts list
- locate information quick with a keyword search engine
- quickly locate work requests by day, week and month using the calendar feature

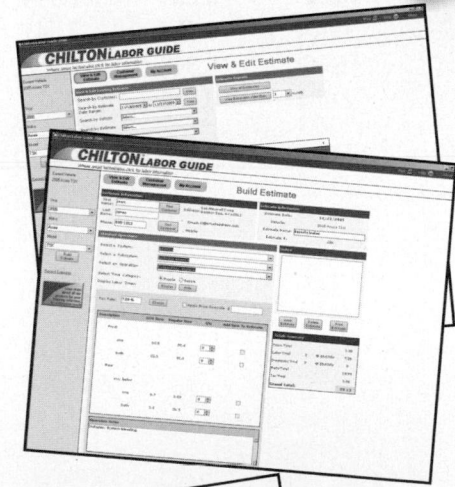

Manual FEATURES

- more than 2,500 pages of updated Chilton labor times split into two volumes includes vehicle information from 1981 to current models
- trusted by more service professionals than any other labor guide
- less flipping though pages with separate domestic and imported vehicle manuals and more specific vehicle groups
- convenient tabs display contents by manufacturer and model
- easy-to-find manufacturers are arranged alphabetically within each volume
- search using two-indexes - labor operations and systems - in each model group
- page numbers include manufacturer code so you know where you are in the book

CHILTONPRO.COM

**WHERE SMART TECHNICIANS
FOR SERVICE INFORMATION**

ChiltonPRO is the alternative for professional technicians who want a cost-effective electronic automotive repair system. It combines Chilton's famous automotive repair information into one solution covering more than 60 years of domestic and imported vehicles. The information is delivered online and is updated regularly throughout the year.

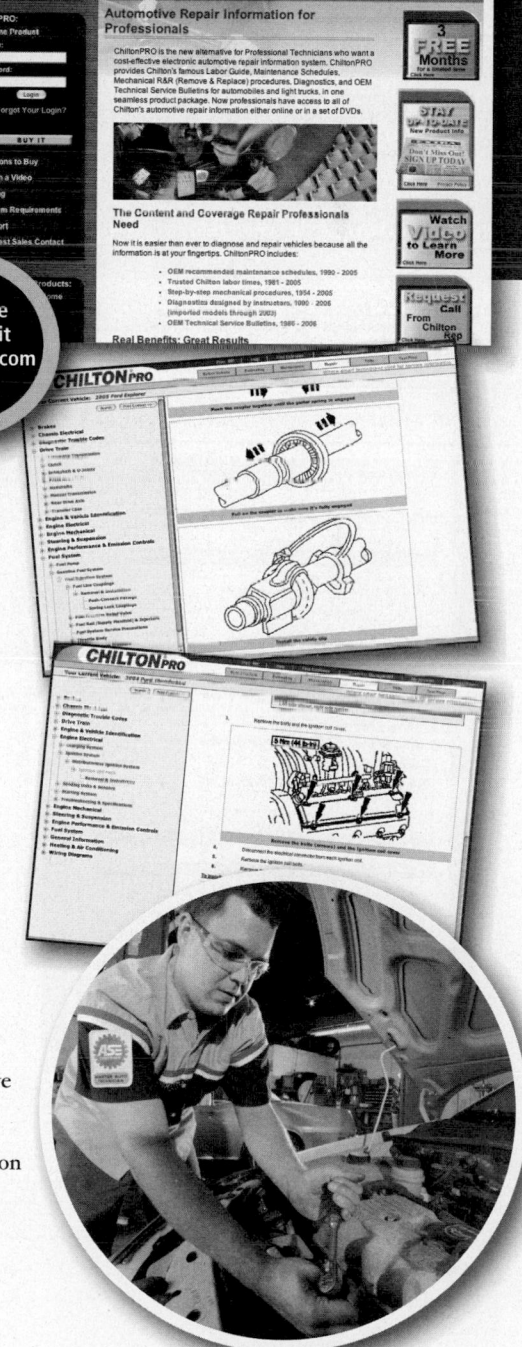

Online Monthly Payment
ISBN: 978-14180-3002-5

Online Annual Payment
ISBN: 978-14180-2876-3

For a free demo visit ChiltonPRO.com

ChiltonPRO FEATURES

- make repairs even easier with videos & animations which explain system operations & contribute to technician knowledge
- create better estimates using labor times developed with real-world factors
- save money by accurately identifying and solving engine performance problems
- save time with expert guidance through OBDII diagnostics
- increase efficiency by understanding system operation through detailed explanations and theory
- increase profits using Technical Service Bulletins (TSBs) to ensure that work is not going unperformed
- execute effective repairs by viewing cutaway diagrams and actual photos
- make better use of your time with information that can be found quicker using AAIA standards for year, make, and model
- increase confidence levels by always being able to print what you need
- eliminate guesswork with quick reference to critical specifications in helpful tables

Coverage Includes:

- OEM recommended maintenance schedules, 1990–current
- trusted Chilton labor times, 1981–current
- step-by-step mechanical procedures, 1940s–current
- diagnostics designed by instructors, 1990–current
- More than 75,000 OEM Technical Service Bulletins issued during the past 20 years

System Requirements:
Web browser
- Internet Explorer 7.0 or above (recommended)
- Firefox 3.6 or 4 or Safari
- High-speed internet connection
- Adobe Flash Player
- Adobe Reader
- Windows XP or above

CHILTON®ESTIMATING

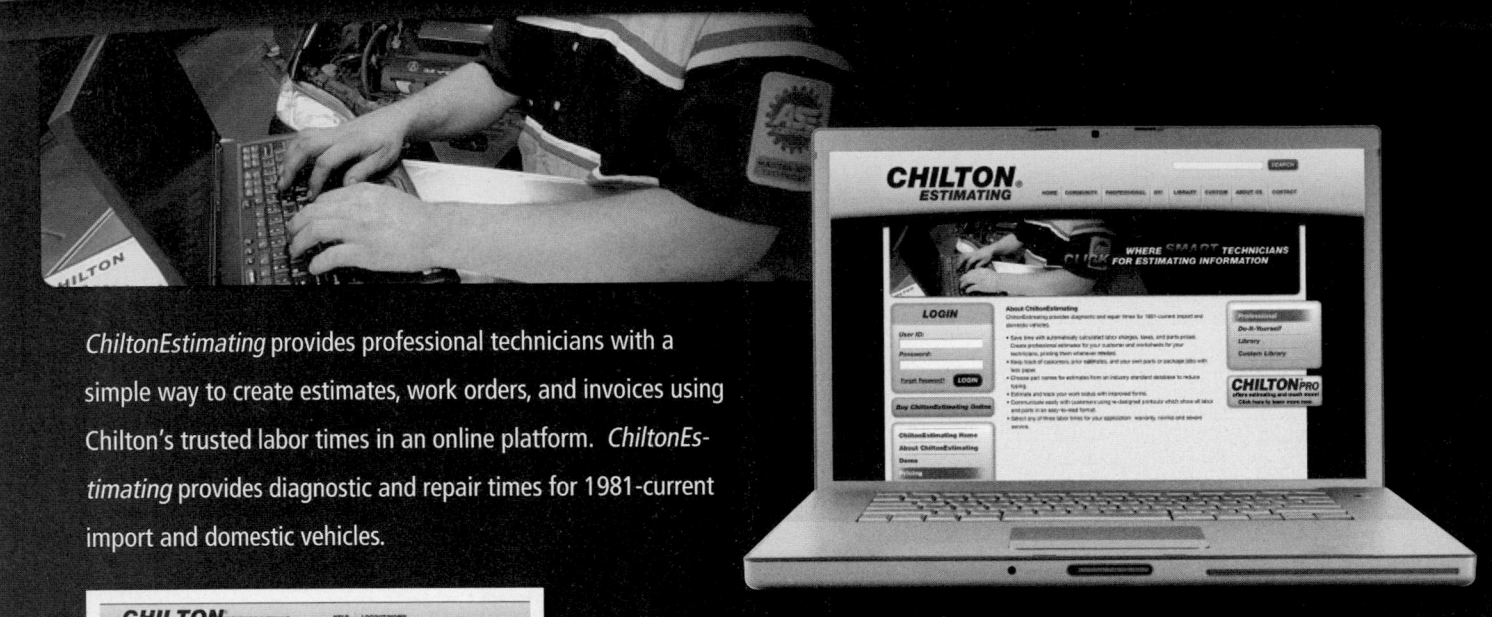

ChiltonEstimating provides professional technicians with a simple way to create estimates, work orders, and invoices using Chilton's trusted labor times in an online platform. *ChiltonEstimating* provides diagnostic and repair times for 1981-current import and domestic vehicles.

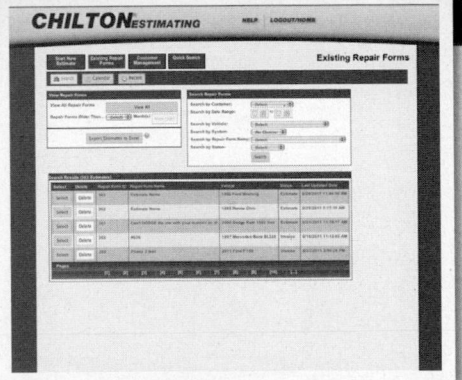

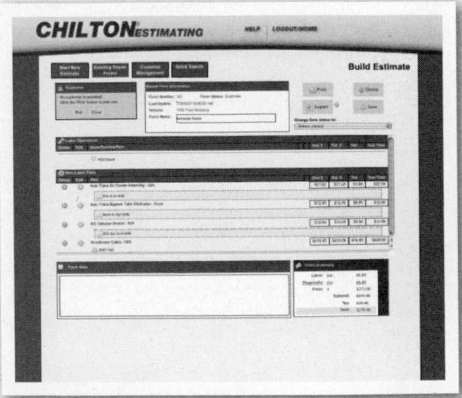

○ Access up-to-date information immediately. *ChiltonEstimating* is continuously updated!

○ Enjoy a hassle-free product with nothing to download and nothing to install.

○ Never fret over lost or damaged software or books again.

○ Secure your valuable customer data on our server, which won't be lost if your computer crashes.

○ Easily access the program from any web-enabled computer.

○ Work on more than one job at a time using *ChiltonEstimating's* two shop-user accounts.

○ Download all customer contact information easily for marketing purposes.

○ Cancel your subscription at any time by going to the "My Account" tab. No contract or obligation required. Customer data will be available to download for up to six months after a subscription has expired.

○ Save time with automatically calculated labor charges, taxes, and parts prices. Create professional estimates for your customer and worksheets for your technicians, printing them whenever needed.

○ Keep track of customers, prior estimates, and your own parts or package jobs with less paper.

○ Choose part names for estimates from an industry standard database to reduce typing.

○ Estimate and track your work status with improved forms.

○ Communicate easily with customers using re-designed printouts which show all labor and parts in an easy-to-read format.

○ Select any of three labor times for your application: warranty, normal and severe service.

System Requirements:
Web browser
- Internet Explorer 7.0 or above (recommended)
- Firefox 3.6 or 4 or Safari
- High-speed internet connection
- Adobe Flash Player
- Adobe Reader
- Windows XP or above

CHILTON SERVICE MANUALS

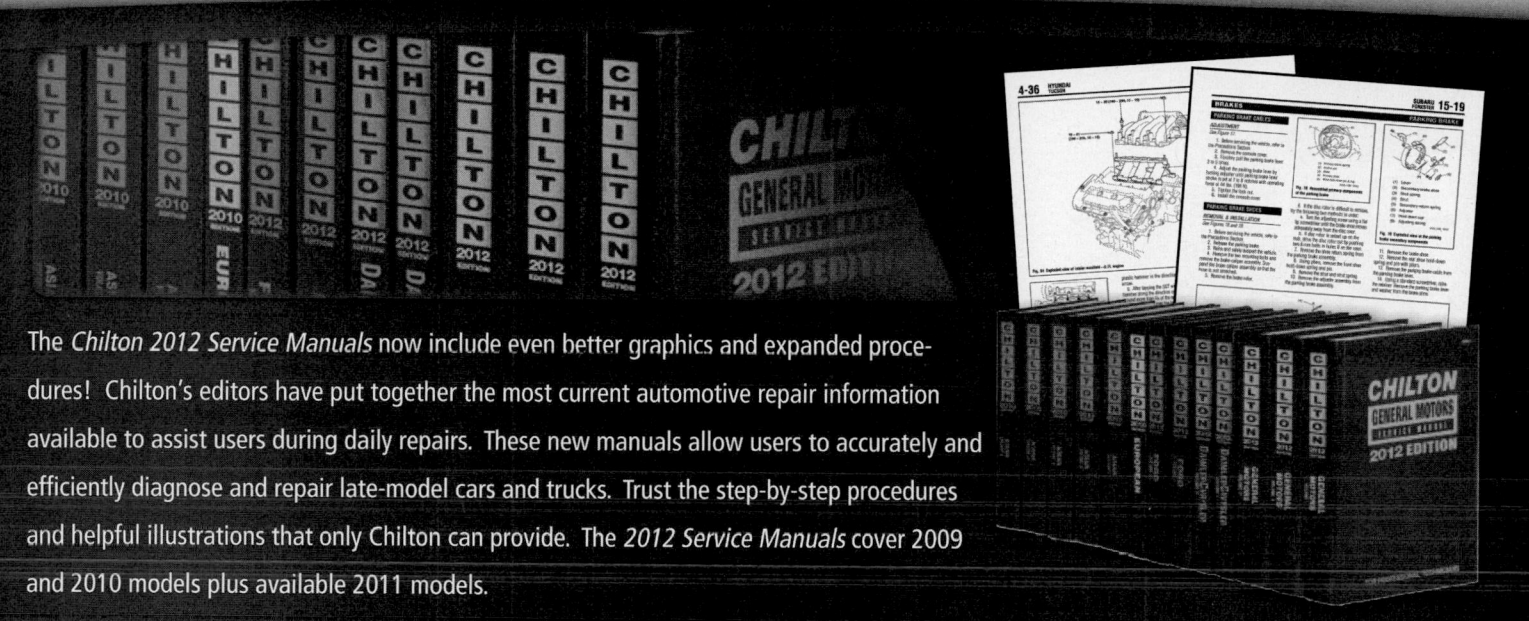

The *Chilton 2012 Service Manuals* now include even better graphics and expanded procedures! Chilton's editors have put together the most current automotive repair information available to assist users during daily repairs. These new manuals allow users to accurately and efficiently diagnose and repair late-model cars and trucks. Trust the step-by-step procedures and helpful illustrations that only Chilton can provide. The *2012 Service Manuals* cover 2009 and 2010 models plus available 2011 models.

KEY FEATURES

- organized by vehicle manufacturer
- provides thousands of pages of expertly written content
- access new year, make, and model information without repeating previous edition's content
- comprehensive, technically detailed content, including exploded view illustrations, diagnostics and specification charts, arranged alphabetically by model group for quick, easy

2012 EDITIONS

Chilton 2012 Chrysler
Service Manuals
ISBN: 978-1-1336-2576-6
Part No. 222576

Chilton 2012 Ford Service Manuals
ISBN: 978-1-1336-2575-9
Part No. 222575

Chilton 2012 General
Motor Service Manuals
ISBN: 978-1-1336-2574-2
Part No. 222574

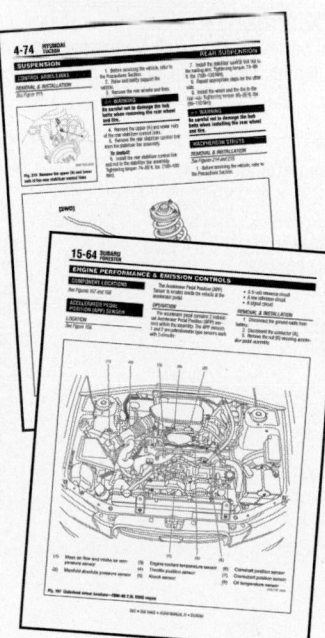

2010 EDITIONS

2010 Asian Service Manual Vol. 1
ISBN 978-1-1110-3764-2
Part No. 163764

2010 Asian Service Manual Vol. 2
ISBN 978-1-1110-3765-9
Part No. 163765

2010 Asian Service Manual Vol. 3
ISBN 978-1-1110-3766-6
Part No. 163766

2010 Asian Service Manual Vol. 4
ISBN 978-1-1110-3767-3
Part No. 163767

2010 Asian Service Manual Vol. 5
ISBN 978-1-1110-3768-0
Part No. 163768

2010 European Service Manual
ISBN 978-1-1110-3769-7
Part No. 163769

2010 Chrysler Service Manual,
Volumes 1 & 2
ISBN 978-1-1110-3654-6
Part No. 163654

2010 Ford Service Manual,
Vols. 1 & 2
ISBN 978-1-1110-3657-7
Part No. 163657

2010 General Motors Service
Manuals, Vols. 1, 2, & 3
ISBN 978-1-111-03661-4
Part No. 163661

2008 EDITIONS

2008 Chrysler Service Manual,
Vols. 1 & 2
ISBN 978-1-4283-2204-2
Part No. 142204

2008 Ford Service Manuals,
Vols. 1 & 2
ISBN 978-1-4283-2208-0
Part No. 142208

2008 Edition General Motors
Service Manuals, Vols. 1 & 2
ISBN 978-1-4283-2211-0
Part No. 142211

2008 Asian Service Manuals,
Vols. 1-4
ISBN 978-1-4283-2214-1
Part No. 142214

2008 Asian Service Manual, Vol. 1
ISBN 978-1-4283-2215-8
Part No. 142215

2008 Asian Service Manual, Vol. 2
ISBN 978-1-4283-2216-5
Part No. 142216

2008 Asian Service Manual, Vol. 3
ISBN 978-1-4283-2217-2
Part No. 142217

2008 Asian Service Manual, Vol. 4
ISBN 978-1-4283-2218-9
Part No. 142218

2008 European Service Manual
ISBN 978-1-4283-2220-2
Part No. 142220

Order Today– Quantities are Limited

Chilton® Mechanical Service Manuals–Perennial Editions

These manuals contain repair and maintenance information for all major systems. Included are repair and overhaul procedures using thousands of illustrations.

CHILTON AUTO REPAIR MANUALS

1998-2002
ISBN 978-0-8019-9362-6/Part No. 9362
Covers all popular American and Canadian cars. An added feature includes scheduled maintenance interval charts.

1993-97
ISBN 978-0-8019-7919-4/Part No. 7919
Covers all popular American and Canadian cars.

1980-87
ISBN 978-0-8019-7670-4/Part No. 7670
Covers all popular American and Canadian cars.

CHILTON IMPORT AUTO REPAIR MANUALS

1998-2002
ISBN 978-0-8019-9363-3/Part No. 9363
Covers all popular Import cars. An added feature includes scheduled maintenance intervals charts.

1993-97
ISBN 978-0-8019-7920-0/Part No. 7920
Covers all popular Import cars.

1988-92
ISBN 978-0-8019-7907-1/Part No. 7907
Covers all popular Import cars.

1980-87
ISBN 978-0-8019-7672-8/Part No. 7672
Covers all popular Import cars.

CHILTON TRUCK AND VAN REPAIR MANUALS

1998-2002
ISBN 978-0-8019-9364-0/Part No. 9364
Covers popular U.S., Canadian, and Import Pick-Ups, Vans, and 4WDs. An added feature includes scheduled maintenance interval charts.

1993-97
ISBN 978-0-8019-7921-7/Part No. 7921
Covers popular U.S., Canadian, and Import Pick-Ups, Sport-Utilities, Vans, RVs and 4 wheel drives.

1991-95
ISBN 978-0-8019-7911-8/Part No. 7911
Covers popular U.S., Canadian, and Import Pick-Ups, Vans, RVs and 4 wheel drives.

1986-90
ISBN 978-08019-7902-6/Part No. 7902
Covers popular U.S., Canadian, and Import Pick-Us, Vans, RVs and 4 wheel drives.

1979-86
ISBN 978-08019-7655-1/Part No. 7655
Covers popular U.S., Canadian, and Import Pick-Ups, Vans, RVs and 4 wheel drives.

CHILTON SUV REPAIR MANUAL

1998-2002
ISBN 978-08019-9365-7/Part No. 9365
Covers popular U.S., Canadian, and import SUVs. An added feature includes scheduled maintenance intervals charts.

COLLECTOR'S SERIES

CHILTON AUTO REPAIR MANUAL 1964-1971
ISBN 978-08019-5974-5/Part No. 5974
1971-1978
ISBN 978-08019-7012-2/Part No. 7012

Chilton Timing Belts, 1985-2005

Timing belt procedures can represent increased profits for automotive repair shops and service stations, and this manual contains all the information automotive technicians need to properly service timing belts on domestic and imported cars, vans, and light trucks through 2005 models. Clear, straightforward procedures, illustrations, and specifications help to communicate 20 years of vehicle applications for fast, accurate inspection, replacement, and tensioning of timing belts. Users will learn how to perform key procedures quickly and safely, while learning the correct labor time to charge for the service.

ISBN 978-1-4018-9880-9
Part No. 129880
544 pp, 8" x 11", SC, ©2006

ALSO AVAILABLE:
Quick-Reference Manuals
The Chilton Professional Series offers *Quick-Reference Manuals* for the automotive professional, providing complete coverage on repair and maintenance, adjustments, and diagnostic procedures for specific systems and components.

KEY FEATURES
- step-by-step procedures
- detailed illustrations and exploded views
- easy-to-use manufacturer and model indexing
- handy specifications or data charts

Heater Core Service 1990-2000,
ISBN 978-0-8019-9311-4
Part No. 9311

Brake Specifications and Service 1990-2000
ISBN 978-0-8019-9312-1
Part No. 9312

Electric Cooling Fans, Accessory Drive Belts & Water Pumps, 1995-1999,
ISBN 978-0-8019-9126-4
Part No. 9126

Powertrain Codes & Oxygen Sensors, 1990-1999,
ISBN 978-0-8019-9127-1
Part No. 9127

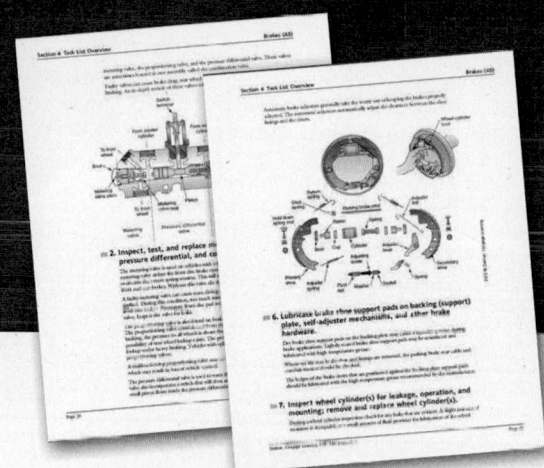

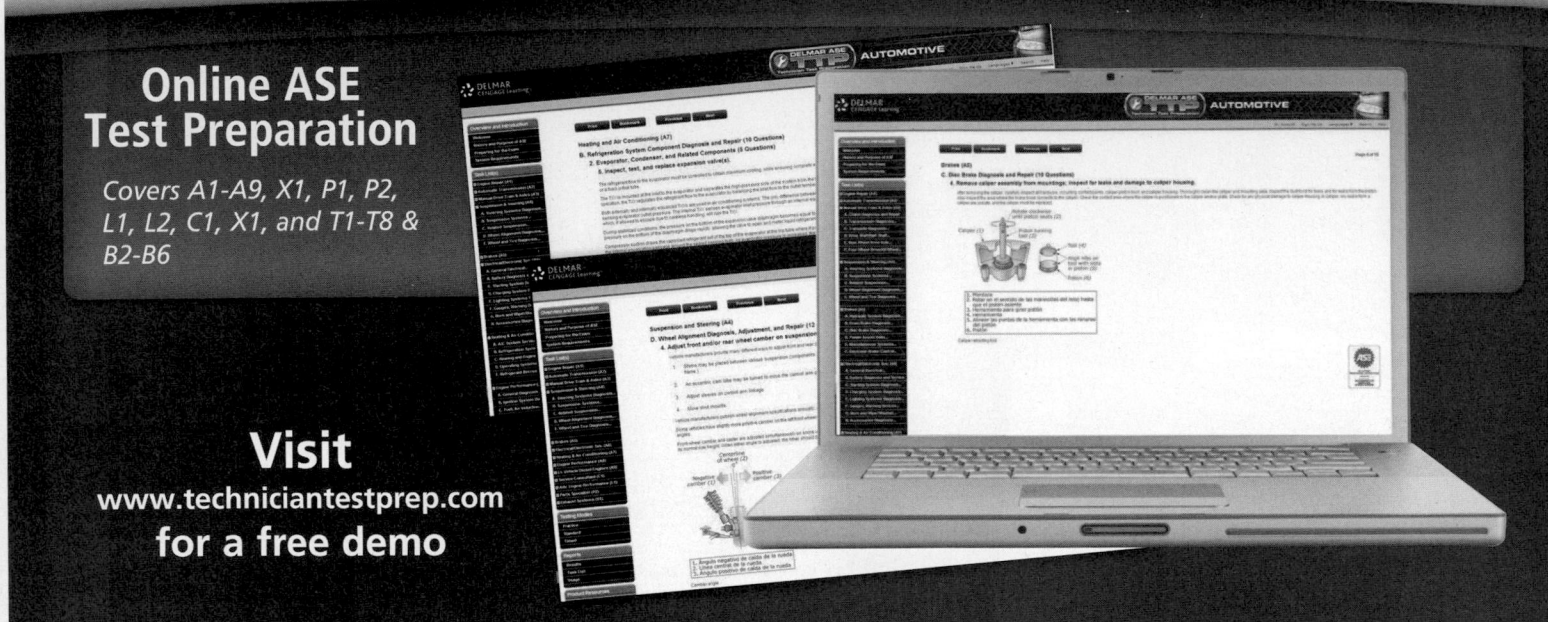

Comprehensive Skill Assessment Tool

CSAT-Automotive Series

The online *Comprehensive Skill Assessment Tool-Automotive Series* helps instructors and trainers implement the necessary training programs for individual areas needing improvement over various key automotive topics. As a true skill gap analysis tool, within each key topic, strategic learning areas are measured for knowledge of theory, hands-on application, and diagnostic skill. Areas of strength and areas needing improvement are identified. The combined phases of education and training, and post-assessment allow instructors to track skill level growth and target specific areas needing development.

Courses Available in the CSAT Automotive Series

Parts Specialist
ISBN 978-1-4180-3225-8

Service Consultant
ISBN 978-1-4180-3223-4

Advanced Engine Performance
ISBN 978-1-4180-0073-8

Brakes
ISBN 978-1-4180-0069-1

Electrical/Electronic Systems
ISBN 978-1-4180-0070-7

Engine Performance
ISBN 978-1-4180-0072-1

Engine Repair
ISBN 978-1-4180-0065-3

Exhaust Systems
ISBN 978-1-4180-0074-5

Heating and Air Conditioning
ISBN 978-1-4180-0071-4

Manual Drive Train & Axles
ISBN 978-1-4180-0067-7

Suspension & Steering
ISBN 978-1-4180-0068-4

Transmissions & Transaxles
ISBN 978-1-4180-0066-0

All-in-One (contains questions from all eight core automotive areas in one product)
ISBN 978-1-4354-2825-6

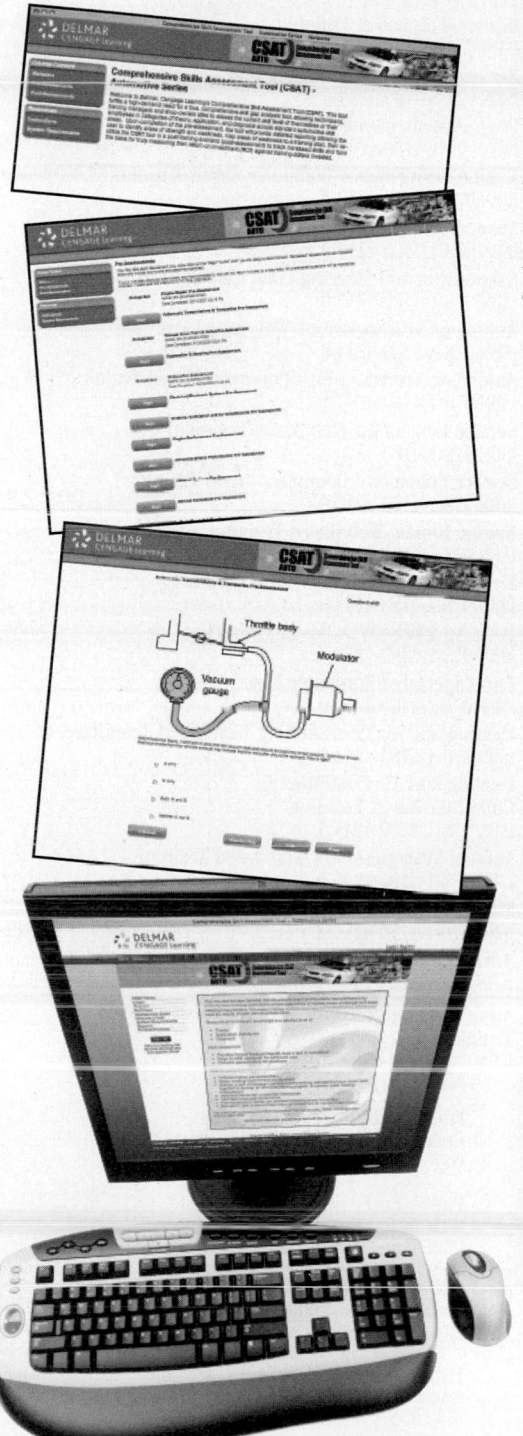

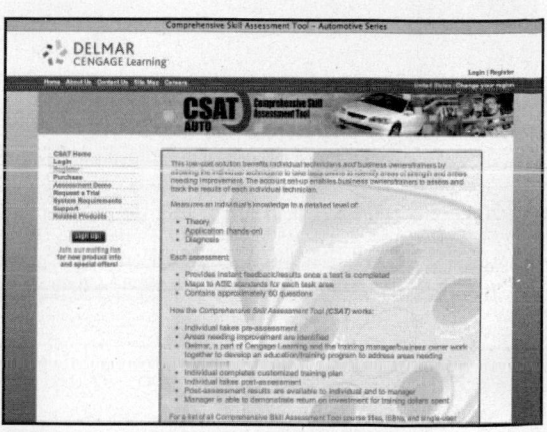

FEATURES

■ available tests include Engine Repair, Transmissions and Transaxles, Manual Drive Train and Axles, Suspension and Steering, Brakes, Electrical/Electronic Systems, Heating and Air Conditioning, Engine Performance, Advanced Engine Performance, and Exhaust Systems

■ can be utilized by companies to measure the technical skill level of individuals against an "ideal" to identify areas of strength and creates a skill gap analysis to help users address areas needing improvement

■ questions are written and reviewed by experts in the industry and offer users the opportunity to receive instant feedback

■ account set up that enables instructors and trainers to assess and track the results of individual students

■ acts as a true return on investment (ROI) tool for companies to ensure they invest their training dollars in the most appropriate areas

Visit www.skillanalysis.com
for a free demo!

Professional Automotive Technician Training Series: PATTS

Delmar

Delmar, the leader in providing first-rate educational materials for automotive technicians, now offers this exciting self-paced learning series. Choose the delivery method that best suits your needs— CD-ROM or Web-based product – and receive more than 8.5 hours worth of quality instruction. Combining theory, diagnosis, and repair information into one easy-to-use training tool, this highly interactive product helps technicians receive the most applicable delivery method for their needs, regardless of technical infrastructure.

KEY FEATURES

- attention-grabbing animations and learner interactions keep users interested and engaged throughout the course of the program
- bookmarking technology enables users to track their progress from beginning to end
- periodic progress checks and end-of-section reviews are integrated throughout to ensure the highest level of retention
- a certificate of completion can be printed by users achieving a score of 80% or higher on the final review of the course
- all material is completely AICC and SCORM compliant
- all material follows the latest ASE and NATEF standards

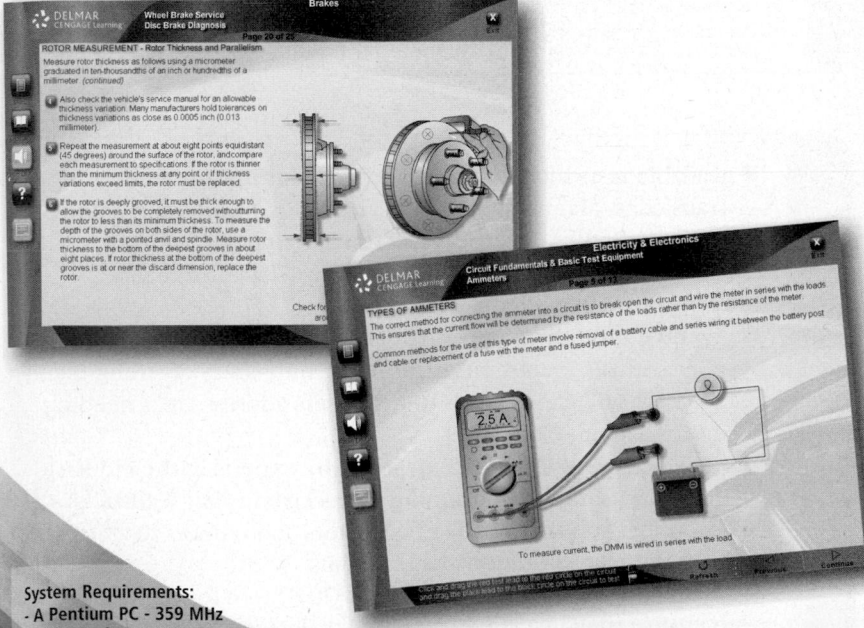

System Requirements:
- A Pentium PC - 359 MHz
- 128MB of RAM
- Windows 2000, Windows XP, Windows Vista
- Graphics adapter with Minimum 1024 x 768 display resolution, 32 bit depth
- Minimum Display Resolution 1024 x 768
- High Speed Internet Connection
- Internet Explorer 6, 7, or Firefox 2
- Not Mac Compatible

Basic Automotive Service and Maintenance Web Based Training
ISBN 978-1-4180-4101-4

Basic Automotive Service and Maintenance Computer Based Training
ISBN 978-1-4180-4100-7

Electricity and Electronics Web Based Training
ISBN 978-1-4180-4242-4

Electricity and Electronics Computer Based Training
ISBN 978-1-4180-4241-7

Brakes Web Based Training
ISBN 978-1-4180-4236-3

Brakes Computer Based Training
ISBN 978-1-4180-4235-6

Engine Performance Web Based Training
ISBN 978-1-4180-4240-0

Engine Performance Computer Based Training
ISBN 978-1-4180-4239-4

Suspension and Steering Web Based Training
ISBN 978-1-4180-4238-7

Suspension and Steering Computer Based Training
ISBN 978-1-4180-4237-0

Automatic Transmissions Web Based Training
ISBN 978-1-4180-4244-8

Automatic Transmissions Computer Based Training
ISBN 978-1-4180-4243-1

Service Consultant Web Based Training
ISBN 978-1-4180-4249-3

Service Consultant Computer Based Training
ISBN 978-1-4180-4247-9

Engine Repair Web Based Training
ISBN 978-1-4180-4254-7

Engine Repair Computer Based Training
ISBN 978-1-4180-4253-0

Parts Specialist Web Based Training
ISBN 978-1-4180-4252-3

Parts Specialist Computer Based Training
ISBN 978-1-4180-4250-9

Heating and Air Conditioning Web Based Training
ISBN 978-1-4180-4246-2

Heating and Air Conditioning Computer Based Training
ISBN 978-1-4180-4245-5

Manual Transmissions Web Based Training
ISBN 978-1-4180-4256-1

Manual Transmissions Computer Based Training
ISBN 978-1-4180-4255-4

Advanced Engine Performance Web Based Training
ISBN 978-1-4283-2098-7

Advanced Engine Performance Computer Based Training
ISBN 978-1-4283-2097-0

New Courses!

Fuels, Emissions, and Exhaust Computer Based Training
ISBN 978-1-4354-4148-4

Fuels, Emissions, and Exhaust Web Based Training
ISBN 978-1-4354-4147-7

Hybrid, Electric, and Fuel-Cell Vehicles Web Based Training
ISBN 978-1-4354-4144-6

Hybrid, Electric, and Fuel-Cell Vehicles Computer Based Training
ISBN 978-1-4354-4143-9

Visit www.techniciantraining.com for a free demo!